Do you understand Newton's laws of motion?

Review these basic laws of physics that all students must learn.
Pages 236-237

Have you forgotten how to calculate the area of a rectangle?

Use this table to review the most commonly needed formulas in arithmetic.
Pages 262-263

Are you having trouble with advanced math?

Work sample problems from algebra, geometry, and trigonometry.
Check their solutions to make sure you are right.
Pages 264-311

Are you afraid to write research papers?

Learn how to attack the assignment step by step,
from research through outline to final draft.
Pages 318-333

Are you bored with the books you are reading now?

Make exciting selections from a list of some of the greatest works ever written.
Pages 384-395

Do you know how to prepare a book report?

Here is useful information on how to write a book report and
how to present an oral report.
Pages 396-420

a young Union volunteer during a single, unnamed
battle of the Civil War.
It could be any battle, of any war, for
Crane's real focus is on another battle, the hidden
one raging inside Henry Fleming as his
romantic notions of war are crushed by the realities of fear,
suffering, and death. Through
Fleming's thoughts and actions, we see that the outer

Gallery of OFFICIAL PORTRAITS of the PRESIDENTS of the UNITED STATES

GEORGE WASHINGTON
1789–1797

JOHN ADAMS
1797–1801

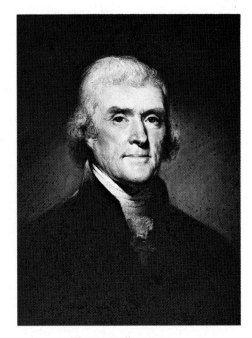

THOMAS JEFFERSON
1801–1809

JAMES MADISON
1809–1817

JAMES MONROE
1817–1825

JOHN QUINCY ADAMS
1825–1829

ANDREW JACKSON
1829–1837

MARTIN VAN BUREN
1837–1841

WILLIAM HENRY HARRISON
1841

JOHN TYLER
1841–1845

JAMES K. POLK
1845–1849

ZACHARY TAYLOR
1849–1850

MILLARD FILLMORE
1850–1853

FRANKLIN PIERCE
1853–1857

JAMES BUCHANAN
1857–1861

ABRAHAM LINCOLN
1861–1865

ANDREW JOHNSON
1865–1869

ULYSSES S. GRANT
1869–1877

RUTHERFORD B. HAYES
1877–1881

JAMES A. GARFIELD
1881

CHESTER A. ARTHUR
1881–1885

GROVER CLEVELAND
1885–1889, 1893–1897

BENJAMIN HARRISON
1889–1893

WILLIAM MCKINLEY
1897–1901

THEODORE ROOSEVELT
1901–1909

WILLIAM H. TAFT
1909–1913

WOODROW WILSON
1913–1921

WARREN G. HARDING
1921–1923

CALVIN COOLIDGE
1923–1929

HERBERT C. HOOVER
1929–1933

FRANKLIN D. ROOSEVELT
1933–1945

HARRY S. TRUMAN
1945–1953

DWIGHT D. EISENHOWER
1953–1961

JOHN F. KENNEDY
1961–1963

LYNDON B. JOHNSON
1963–1969

RICHARD M. NIXON
1969–1974

GERALD R. FORD
1974–1977

JAMES E. CARTER
1977–1981

RONALD W. REAGAN
1981–1989

GEORGE H. BUSH
1989–1993

WILLIAM J. CLINTON
1993–

Student Handbook

Including

The Young Reader's Companion

Volume **2**

Student Handbook

Including

The Young Reader's Companion

Volume 2

THE SOUTHWESTERN COMPANY
Nashville, Tennessee

Published by R. R. Bowker,
A Reed Reference Publishing Company
Copyright © 1993 by Carruth and Ehrlich Books, Inc.
All rights reserved
Printed and bound in the United States of America

Library of Congress Cataloging-in-Publication Data

Carruth, Gorton.
The young reader's companion/Gorton Carruth.
p.   cm.
"A Hudson Group Book."
Includes index.
Summary: A one-volume short-entry encyclopedia containing
information about the characters, plots, authors, and other topics
found in classic and contemporary books for young readers.
ISBN 0-8352-2765-0
1. Children's literature — Encyclopedias. 2. Young adult
literature — Encyclopedias. [1. Children's literature —
Encyclopedias. 2. Young adult literature — Encyclopedias.]
I. Title

PN1008.5.C373 1993   93-6662
809'.89282'03 — dc20   CIP
                                             AC

All copyright notices can be found beginning on page 657.

Designed by Pam Forde Graphics

Preface

This new edition of the *Student Handbook* is among the most practical and appealing student aids ever published. Consisting of 850 pages (402 in Volume One and 448 in Volume Two), it brings together information on the major subjects taught in every elementary, junior high, and high school.

For this new edition, the most important information on each subject has been distilled and presented in a visually interesting and easy-to-use way. Both volumes are filled with tables, informative line drawings, brief "dictionaries" of terms used in special fields, chronologies showing major national or world events year by year, time lines showing the life spans of important men and women in history, and many other features. All information is up to date.

The *Student Handbook* has been organized to present material usually taught in the fourth to eighth grades in Volume One and material taught in ninth grade or above in Volume Two. Useful information for all ages will be found in both volumes, however. Each *Student Handbook* is organized in two major parts. PART ONE includes material designed to help students do better in school. PART TWO features a complete reference work that readers of all ages will find useful and enjoyable.

The major headings in PART ONE of Volume One are:

Study Guide (with special emphasis on grammar and writing)
Social Studies (U.S. history and U.S. geography)
Mathematics and Science (basic arithmetic and science)
Sports and Entertainment (sports, music, film, and television)

PART TWO of Volume One is the internationally recognized *Macmillan Dictionary for Children*, which provides clear, concise, easy-to-understand definitions along with informative color photographs and illustrations and special boxed features on word histories and word usage.

The major headings in PART ONE of Volume Two are:

Social Studies (world history and geography, U.S. government, including the Constitution and the Presidents, and a color atlas of the world)
Science and Mathematics (laboratory sciences and algebra, geometry, etc.)
English and Literature (writing research papers and book reports and understanding poetry, drama, and fiction)

PART TWO of Volume Two is *The Young Reader's Companion*, an illustrated A-to-Z guide to books, authors, and subjects of special interest to young people. Its more than 2000 concise, lively entries are as entertaining as they are informative. The entries are carefully crafted to help young people find the books they will enjoy reading, provide them with useful information that will increase their enjoyment of the books they choose, and encourage them to broaden and deepen their reading experiences.

The two volumes are designed to complement each other. For example, a reader using the algebra section in Volume Two may find it helpful to review parts of arithmetic in Volume One. Similarly, a reader who has found basic material in "Physical Sciences" in Volume One will find additional, more advanced material in "Physics" in Volume Two. The Index at the end of both volumes helps locate all major information on a given topic.

In summary, the *Student Handbook* offers students and those out of school essential information on basic skills (reading, writing, mathematics) and a vast collection of easy-to-use data on all major school subjects. We are certain that this set of books will contribute to increased success in school and to the enjoyment of learning.

The Editors

Table of Contents

Social Studies 2-177 ˙

Science and Mathematics 178-315

Physics 232

Mathematics 248

English and Literature 316-420

Editorial development of the Student Handbook was directed by
The Hudson Group, Inc., Pleasantville, New York 10570

Administrative editors:	Gorton Carruth and Eugene Ehrlich
Editors-in-chief:	Lawrence T. Lorimer and Bryan Bunch
Managing editor:	Hayden Carruth
Administrative assistant:	Nicole Grandjean
Copy-editing and indexing:	Felice Levy and Chris Carruth/AEIOU, Inc.
Contributors:	Frances Barth, Nance J. Davidson, Marcia Golub, Raymond V. Hand, John Harrington, Mary Hicks, Seymour Levine, Howard Liss, Don Lorimer, Janet McHugh, Sam Plummer, Bertram Siegel, Bruce Wetterau, Richard Worth
Design and art direction:	Pam Forde Graphics
Production:	Rachelle Engelman
Illustrations and maps:	David Lindroth, H. Peter Loewer, Jean Loewer/Graphos Studio, Ric Del Rossi/Mulvey Associates, Phillip Jones/Mulvey Associates, Leslie Dunlap/Publishers' Graphics, Inc., Lloyd Birmingham, Betty Whelan, Joel Snyder/Publishers' Graphics, Inc., Kathie Kelleher/Publishers' Graphics, Inc.
Photo researchers:	Pat Vestal, Carousel Research

Student Handbook

Including

The Young Reader's Companion

Volume **2**

Social Studies

United States Government

The study of government is an important one for every citizen. In the United States, the will of the people is the final governmental authority through the votes cast for elected officials on the local, state, and national levels. The health of the government depends on an informed and concerned electorate. This section outlines the governmental system of the United States, considering the local, state, and federal governments in turn. In addition, there are features on the electoral system and on the importance of foreign affairs. The two concluding sections are the full text of the Constitution and its amendments, and profiles of each American President.

Federal system

At the time of the American Revolution, each of the 13 original states was a separate colony of Great Britain. When colonial representatives assembled to form an independent government, they favored a decentralized plan in which each state would maintain its sovereignty. The resulting Articles of Confederation were in force from 1780 to 1788, but experience proved that they gave too little power to the central government.

In 1787, representatives of the states met again to work out a new Constitution. The resulting document, which was ratified by all but one state by 1788, has been the basis of U.S. government ever since. It set up a *federal* system, apportioning responsibilities and authority between the new federal government and the individual states. Compared with other forms of government, the system was still decentralized, allowing considerable independence to the states.

The Constitution further divided authority in the central government among three branches—the legislative, the executive, and the judicial—providing that each of these branches serve as a check on the others.

The framers were fearful of two extremes: an executive so powerful that it might claim tyrannical power, and a legislature so driven by the majority that the rights of minorities and dissenters might be overlooked.

In practice, the Constitution left the assignment of responsibility between state and central government vague enough so that power might shift between them—and among the branches of the federal government. In the 200 years since the Constitution was written, the country has grown from a small coastal enclave with fewer than 4 million people to a giant superstate covering nearly half a continent and comprising more than 250 million people. During the 1900's, governmental power shifted to the federal government at the expense of the states. Within the federal establishment, the executive branch, headed by the President, has grown in importance at the expense of the legislative branch. Even under these changed conditions, however, the Constitution provides firm limits, and individual administrations may begin to shift power back to the states or back to the legislative branch.

Local government

Local governments include towns, counties, and a wide variety of single-function organizations such as sewer districts and consolidated school districts. These local governments all exist at the pleasure of the state government, but they operate with great independence, raising funds through local taxation and providing many essential services for local citizens. The table below summarizes some of the most important activities of local governments and their most significant powers of taxation.

Local government

Local responsibilities

Police protection	provide for safety of local citizens; local official may act as judge for minor offenses.
Fire protection	require building and fire safety standards; organize paid or volunteer fire departments; acquire equipment.
Public safety	create and enforce sanitation and other public health and safety laws.
Public works	build and maintain roads, sewer systems, public buildings, libraries, schools, parks, etc.
Education	maintain public school system through high school (small towns often cooperate in operation of higher schools; large cities may run full universities).
Social services	provide—in association with state and federal government and private organizations—assistance for the sick, the aged, the unemployed, and other needy persons.
Recreation	provide municipal parks, golf courses, and other recreation areas.
Regulation	pass and enforce zoning codes, consumer protection codes, and other laws to protect citizens.
Representation	represent local interests and needs to private and other governmental organizations through elected and appointed officials.

Local taxing powers

Property taxes	imposed as a rate or percentage of *assessed valuation* on all real property (land, buildings, homes, etc.).
User fees	paid by businesses and individuals for services received (water, registration of deeds, park fees, etc.).
Fines and penalties	for parking, overdue library books, etc.
Sales taxes	taxes on retail transactions, often excluding food and other essentials.
Income taxes	some cities and towns impose income taxes on residents and sometimes on commuters.

Local organization

Cities and towns usually have one of these two systems:

Mayor-council	mayor and council members are elected; mayor is executive, council is legislative; mayor may have many powers or few.
City manager	a nonpartisan manager is appointed as the administrative director of the city, serving at the pleasure of the mayor or council.

Larger towns and cities also have important independent organizations including the following:

School board	often separately elected, the board appoints a professional superintendent of schools and oversees educational policy.
Zoning board	usually made up of or including elected officials, the board decides on land use patterns in the town; it may control the economic development of the town.

State government

State governments are specifically recognized in the U.S. Constitution, and their existence is independent of the federal government. The Constitution specifically provides that powers not given to the federal government belong to the states. Each state has its own constitution, establishing that state's basic laws and administrative organization.

All states have provided for a governor as chief officer of the government (he or she usually serves a four-year term), and for a legislative branch with two houses resembling the Congress of the United States (only Nebraska has a one-house legislature). In addition, states have full judicial systems—trial courts, appeals courts, and supreme courts. The following table summarizes the responsibilities, taxing powers, and organization of state governments.

State government

State responsibilities

Police protection	provide state police to patrol unincorporated areas, state highways, etc.
Court system	maintain a system of courts to hear both civil cases (those between individuals, corporations, and the like) and criminal cases originating within state boundaries. State courts hear the vast majority of court cases in the United States. Parties to a case may appeal to federal courts only when federal laws or guarantees are at issue (see Federal government, Judicial branch, below).
Public safety	establish laws and regulations governing certain areas of public safety; maintain state penal institutions for those sentenced to imprisonment for serious crimes.
Public works	build and maintain state highways, buildings, universities, hospitals, parks, etc.
Education	set minimum standards for local elementary and high schools; maintain state colleges and universities.
Social services	provide assistance for needy citizens (states usually maintain public mental hospitals, set standards for other hospitals, and administer workmen's compensation, unemployment, and welfare benefits, receiving partial funding from the federal government).
Recreation	provide state parks and recreation areas.
Regulation	license corporations, drivers of motor vehicles, and practitioners of certain professions and occupations (doctors, lawyers, accountants, beauticians, etc.); regulate local tax rates and set minimum standards for certain local government services.
Representation	represent state interests to private and other governmental organizations through elected and appointed state officials.

State taxing powers

Income taxes	nearly all states levy taxes on the incomes of individual state residents, and most tax profits of corporations; tax rates vary considerably.
Sales taxes	most states levy broad sales taxes in addition to special taxes on such items as alcohol, tobacco, and gasoline.
Gambling	many states license gambling on horse races, and many have state lotteries, often to raise funds for particular activities.
User fees	these include those for drivers' and other licenses, and for the use of recreation facilities; resident students at state universities pay tuition that partly covers the cost of their education.
Fines and penalties	these include those for late payment of taxes.

Federal government

The official structure of the federal government is stated in the Constitution. The Constitution also prescribes the main responsibilities of the federal establishment. At the same time, a large body of tradition helps determine how government institutions work.

The Constitution provides that the federal government is responsible for four principal activities:

1. Regulation of affairs with other countries,
2. Defense of the country from foreign enemies and from civil disturbance,
3. Establishment of the monetary system, and
4. Regulation of relations among the states.

From these four activities have emerged an increasing number of other responsibilities. For example, only the federal government can declare war on another nation (in several instances it has fought "police actions" without declaring an official state of war). It can raise armed forces—by draft if necessary—and develop elaborate weapons systems. The largest employer in the federal government is the Department of Defense.

Similarly, the federal establishment has taken responsibility for regulating business by broad interpretation of its power to regulate commerce among the states.

The responsibilities of the government are carefully divided among the three branches: the legislative, the executive, and the judicial.

Apportionment in House of Representatives, 1992
Total: 435

	Number	Change from 1982		Number	Change from 1982
Alabama	7	—	Montana	1	−1
Alaska	1	—	Nebraska	3	—
Arizona	6	+1	Nevada	2	+1
Arkansas	4	—	New Hampshire	2	—
California	52	+7	New Jersey	13	−1
Colorado	6	+1	New Mexico	3	+1
Connecticut	6	—	New York	31	−3
Delaware	1	—	North Carolina	12	+1
Florida	23	+4	North Dakota	1	—
Georgia	11	+1	Ohio	19	−2
Hawaii	2	—	Oklahoma	6	—
Idaho	2	—	Oregon	5	+1
Illinois	20	−2	Pennsylvania	21	−2
Indiana	10	−1	Rhode Island	2	—
Iowa	5	−1	South Carolina	6	—
Kansas	4	−1	South Dakota	1	−1
Kentucky	6	−1	Tennessee	9	+1
Louisiana	7	−1	Texas	30	+3
Maine	2	—	Utah	3	+1
Maryland	8	—	Vermont	1	—
Massachusetts	10	−1	Virginia	11	+1
Michigan	16	−2	Washington	9	+1
Minnesota	8	—	West Virginia	3	−1
Mississippi	5	—	Wisconsin	9	—
Missouri	9	−1	Wyoming	1	—

Legislative branch.
The legislative or law-making branch consists of two elected bodies collectively called the Congress. Together, the Congress is responsible for considering and passing all laws and acts necessary to the operation of the government.

The House of Representatives. The larger of the two bodies is the House of Representatives, which consists of 435 voting members apportioned to the states by population. Every ten years, in years ending in "0," a national census determines the population of each state; states are entitled to representatives in proportion to their population. Apportionment for the period 1982 to 1992 is shown in the box above. At the beginning of this period, each congressman represented about 520,000 people.

Members of the House are called either representatives or congressmen. They are elected for two-year terms, standing for election in November of even-numbered years and taking office in January.

In general, proposed laws or acts—called *bills*—may be first introduced in either House of Congress. Two kinds of bills *must* originate in the House, however; those calling for the raising or appropriating of government funds and those impeaching (bringing charges against) a President or other high government official.

The Senate. The Senate is the smaller of the two Houses of Congress. Its members are not apportioned according to population; instead, two senators are elected from each state, regardless of population. In 1980, the senators from Alaska represented a state with fewer than 500,000 people, while the senators from California represented a state with more than 24 million. Senators represent a state as a whole rather than a particular district or region.

The framers of the Constitution provided senators with terms even longer than that of the President—six years—and arranged that only a third of them would stand for election in any election year. They hoped that longer terms and a staggered election system would make the Senate more leisurely in its deliberations and less subject to sudden enthusiasms among the electorate. The framers also provided that the senators be elected by state legislatures rather than directly by voters. This provision was changed by the 17th Amendment, ratified in 1913. Since then, all senators are elected by the full electorate of their states.

The Constitution provides the Senate with a few specific duties not shared with the House. It must ratify treaties with other nations negotiated by the President or his appointees, and it must approve Presidential appointments to major Cabinet posts, diplomatic posts, and federal judgeships. If a President or other high official is impeached by the House, the Senate sits as a jury in the impeachment trial.

How a bill is passed. The Houses of Congress are organized into committees, each of which considers legislation in a particular area, such as agriculture or defense. When a bill is introduced by a congressman (or senator), it is first referred to a committee for consideration. The committee may *table* the bill, killing it for that session of Congress; *report it out* to the full body for a vote of the whole; or report it out with amendments. If the full House votes in favor of the bill, it is sent to the Senate for consideration (and vice versa). If the vote goes against the bill, it is killed and must be reintroduced.

The presiding officer of the House is the Speaker, who is elected by the majority party and has considerable power in referring bills to committees and controlling debate once a bill reaches the floor of the House. The majority leader and majority whips often work with the Speaker on bills favored by their party. The minority leader and minority whip often organize the opposition to a bill favored by the majority party.

The Senate has no officer with the power of the Speaker of the House. The Vice President of the United States normally presides, but he has no vote unless the Senate is tied. The president pro tempore of the Senate is a senior member of the majority party who presides in the absence of the Vice President, but

this post is largely honorary. Majority and minority leaders and whips play roles similar to those of their counterparts in the House.

A bill passed in one House goes through the same process—introduction, committee consideration, floor debate—in the other House. If both Houses pass the bill in the same form, it has been passed by Congress and goes to the President for his signature. More often, the bills passed in the two Houses have differences. When this happens, they are referred to a *conference committee* comprised of senators and representatives who negotiate until they agree on a single form for the bill. This revised bill is then considered by both Houses for passage without further amendment. If both Houses pass the bill, it goes to the President for his signature.

The President acts as a check on the Congress. He signs routine bills and they become law. But if he opposes a bill, he may refuse to sign it. This is called a *veto.* The bill is then returned to both Houses. If they both pass the bill by two-thirds majorities, the Congress has *overridden* the President's veto and the bill becomes law without his signature. If the bill fails to pass both Houses by two-thirds, it dies and can only be resurrected by carrying it through the legislative process once again.

In practice, the President and his advisers often prepare legislation for consideration by Congress and help see it through the legislative process. But the Congress can also act as a check on the President by tabling, delaying, or voting down bills he has helped to frame. In most cases, both the President and the Congress make an effort to work together so that important legislation may be passed.

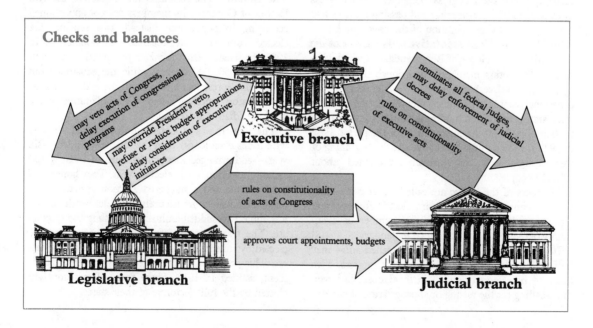

Checks and balances

may veto acts of Congress, delay execution of congressional programs

may override President's veto, refuse or reduce budget appropriations, delay consideration of executive initiatives

Executive branch

nominates all federal judges, may delay enforcement of judicial decrees

rules on constitutionality of executive acts

rules on constitutionality of acts of Congress

approves court appointments, budgets

Legislative branch

Judicial branch

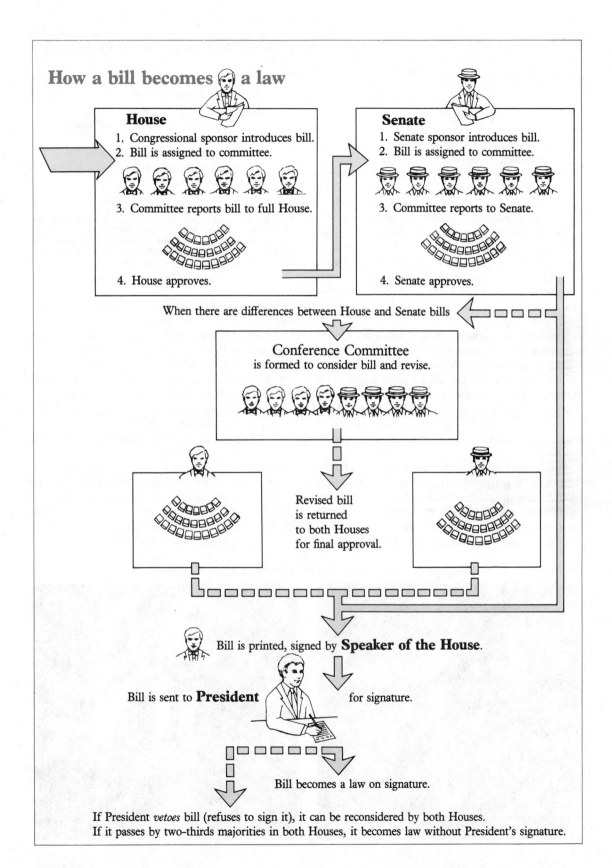

How a bill becomes a law

House
1. Congressional sponsor introduces bill.
2. Bill is assigned to committee.
3. Committee reports bill to full House.
4. House approves.

Senate
1. Senate sponsor introduces bill.
2. Bill is assigned to committee.
3. Committee reports to Senate.
4. Senate approves.

When there are differences between House and Senate bills

Conference Committee
is formed to consider bill and revise.

Revised bill
is returned
to both Houses
for final approval.

Bill is printed, signed by **Speaker of the House**.

Bill is sent to **President** for signature.

Bill becomes a law on signature.

If President *vetoes* bill (refuses to sign it), it can be reconsidered by both Houses.
If it passes by two-thirds majorities in both Houses, it becomes law without President's signature.

Executive branch.

The Constitution provides that the President be the head of the executive branch. He and his Vice President are the only two government officeholders elected by the whole electorate of the United States. The President and the Vice President run on the same ticket and serve a four-year term, being elected in November of years divisible by four and taking office the following January.

The President serves in four important capacities. First, he is Head of State, serving as a symbol of national unity and directing the foreign relations of the United States. As Head of State, he is equivalent to other nations' monarchs, emperors, or presidents.

Second, the President is Commander in Chief of the U.S. armed forces. In this capacity, he is superior even to the most senior general or admiral in the forces. Only Congress can officially declare war and appropriate money to fight a war; but in practice, the President has broad powers to direct the armed forces both in peace and in war.

Third, the President is the chief political leader of the country. In this capacity, he is equivalent to other nations' prime ministers or presidents (many of whom do not serve as head of state). He is the leader of his political party, and as the chief officeholder elected by the whole country, he has broad powers to frame legislation and make policy. He may use both persuasion and political force to encourage Congress to approve his programs.

Finally, the President is the director of the executive branch of the government, appointing the secretaries of each department and the members of many independent agencies. The executive departments employ some 3 million civilian workers in a wide variety of jobs, from protecting wildlife to collecting taxes. The Cabinet-level

Order of Succession to the Presidency*

(in case of death or disability)

1. Vice President*
2. Speaker of the House
3. President Pro Tempore of the Senate
4. Secretary of State
5. Secretary of the Treasury
6. Secretary of Defense
7. Attorney General
8–16. Other Cabinet secretaries

* The 25th Amendment to the Constitution provides a means by which a Vice President who has succeeded to the Presidency may nominate a new Vice President with the advice and consent of the Senate. The order of succession above would take effect only if the Vice President died at the same time as or soon after the President.

departments and the more important independent agencies are listed in the box on page 11.

Among the largest of the executive departments are Defense and Health and Human Services. The Defense Department is in charge of the development and deployment of weapons both in the United States and in other parts of the world. It employs a large civilian staff engaged in defense-related work and all uniformed members of the armed forces.

The Department of Health and Human Services is in charge of administering a wide variety of social service programs, including the giant Social Secutiry program. Most civilian workers in the United States are required to pay into this system and are entitled to benefits if they are widowed, disabled, or retired. More than 30 percent of the federal budget consists of payments made to and from this insurance fund.

The President is head of state and has the principal responsibility for foreign affairs (left) *and is the chief political leader of the country* (right).

Structure of the U.S. federal government

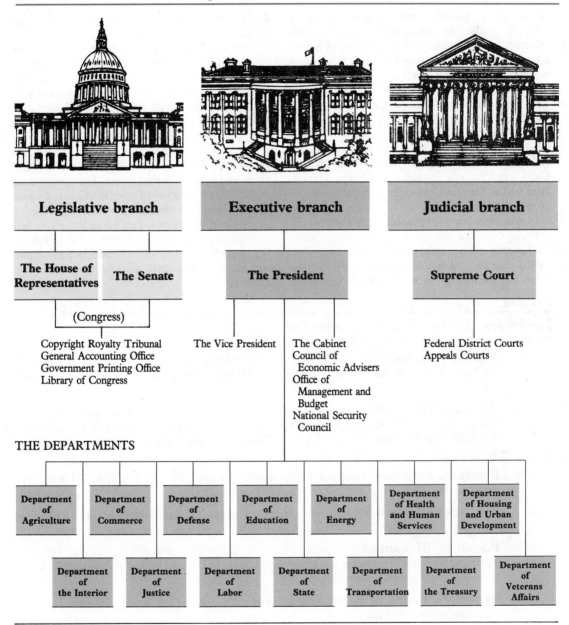

Legislative branch

The House of Representatives — **The Senate**

(Congress)

Copyright Royalty Tribunal
General Accounting Office
Government Printing Office
Library of Congress

Executive branch

The President

The Vice President

The Cabinet
Council of
    Economic Advisers
Office of
    Management and
    Budget
National Security
    Council

Judicial branch

Supreme Court

Federal District Courts
Appeals Courts

THE DEPARTMENTS

Department of Agriculture
Department of Commerce
Department of Defense
Department of Education
Department of Energy
Department of Health and Human Services
Department of Housing and Urban Development

Department of the Interior
Department of Justice
Department of Labor
Department of State
Department of Transportation
Department of the Treasury
Department of Veterans Affairs

INDEPENDENT ESTABLISHMENTS

Central Intelligence Agency
Consumer Product Safety Commission
Environmental Protection Agency
Equal Employment Opportunity Commission
Federal Communications Commission
Federal Deposit Insurance Corporation
Federal Election Commission
Federal Emergency Management Agency
Federal Home Loan Bank Board
Federal Mediation and Conciliation Service

Federal Reserve System
Federal Trade Commission
General Services Administration
Interstate Commerce Commission
National Aeronautics and Space Administration
National Foundation on the Arts and
    the Humanities
National Labor Relations Board
National Mediation Board
National Science Foundation

National Transportation Safety Board
Nuclear Regulatory Commission
Peace Corps
Securities and Exchange Commission
Selective Services System
Small Business Administration
Smithsonian Institution
Tennessee Valley Authority
United States Information Agency
United States Postal Service

Judicial branch. The Constitution provides for a federal judiciary and gives it specific responsibility for hearing cases between states or residents of different states; cases involving other countries; and cases involving the breaking of federal laws. The only court mentioned by name in the Constitution is the Supreme Court.

Today the court system consists of federal district courts, operating in every state in the Union; nine federal circuit courts, each hearing appeals from lower courts in a region of the country; several special courts for specialized cases; and the Supreme Court, the final authority in the U.S. system of law. The Supreme Court consists of nine justices, one of whom serves as chief justice. They decide cases by vote, and a majority of justices present is required.

In addition to its constitutional responsibilities, the Supreme Court has two other important jobs. One is the function called *judicial review*. Justice John Marshall declared in *Marbury* v. *Madison* (1803) that the Court had the right to decide the constitutionality of any act of Congress. Similarly, the Court may declare the act of a President unconstitutional. This power is seldom used, but it acts as a powerful check on the Congress and the President.

The Court's second extra-constitutional job is to review cases in which individuals or groups claim that their constitutionally guaranteed rights have been violated. These *civil liberties*, as they are called, are guaranteed by the first ten amendments of the Constitution, called the *Bill of Rights*. These guarantees have been extended by later amendments to the Constitution.

The Supreme Court is asked to decide thousands of cases each year, most of which come to it *on appeal* from state or lower federal courts. The Court refuses to hear the vast majority of cases; in this circumstance, the decision of the lower court stands. When the Supreme Court does agree to hear a case, lawyers for both sides present written briefs for review. Then a time for oral arguments is set, and the lawyers present brief summaries of their cases to the justices and answer questions.

Landmark decisions of the Supreme Court

1803   **Marbury vs. Madison.** Chief Justice Marshall asserted the Court's right to judicial review—to overturn a law as unconstitutional. This decision became a central part of American governmental practice.

1857   **Dred Scott vs. Sandford.** Court ruled 6–3 that black slaves were to be considered property; that they had no rights of citizenship; and that Congress could not abolish slavery in a U.S. territory. The decision sharpened divisions that led to the Civil War in 1861. It was nullified by the 13th and 14th Amendments.

1896   **Plessy vs. Ferguson.** Court ruled that "separate but equal" facilities for blacks and whites were constitutional. The decision was reversed in 1954 (see below).

1919   **Schenck vs. United States.** Free speech is protected unless authorities can prove it presents a "clear and present danger" of violence or harm to others.

1932   **Powell vs. Alabama.** A person on trial for a capital crime is entitled to legal counsel even if the state must provide it. This ruling was broadened in 1963 and 1972 to include persons on trial for any crime that could involve a jail term.

1954   **Brown vs. Board of Education of Topeka.** Separate but equal schools for blacks and whites are unconstitutional.

1962   **Engel vs. Vitale.** Public schools cannot constitutionally require students to recite prayers.

1964   **Reynolds vs. Sims.** The U.S. House of Representatives and both houses of state legislatures must create election districts of roughly equal population. This decision forced most state legislatures to redistrict.

1973   **Doe vs. Bolton and Roe vs. Wade.** Broad state prohibitions of abortion during a woman's first six months of pregnancy are unconstitutional.

1974   **Nixon vs. United States.** The President cannot withhold information required in a criminal trial; his right to keep executive matters confidential—called "executive privilege"—is limited.

Foreign relations. The federal government has exclusive power over the conduct of foreign relations. This responsibility is shared by the three branches. No state or individual may make a treaty or agreement with a foreign government without approval of the federal government.

Various agencies of the executive branch deal with such foreign relations concerns as immigration, customs, foreign travel by American nationals, tariffs, and trade relations. Direct relations with foreign governments are carried on by the State Department, which maintains U.S. embassies in most countries of the world and helps negotiate treaties, alliances, and other international agreements. Major foreign policy decisions are made by the President in consultation with the secretary of state and other advisers. In the case of treaties, the Senate must approve them before they take effect. Congress also has considerable influence in foreign affairs through its power to appropriate money for aid to other countries. The federal courts hear cases that involve foreign nationals and foreign governments.

The United States also participates in foreign affairs through its membership in international organizations. Some of these were established for joint defense, particularly the North Atlantic Treaty Organization (NATO). Others, such as the Organization of American States (OAS), are regional organizations seeking political and economic cooperation. Perhaps the most important among international organizations is the United Nations (the UN), whose headquarters are in New York and whose membership includes nearly every country in the world.

United Nations. The United Nations was organized in 1945 by the victorious nations in World War II. Today it has 184 members and pursues a wide variety of cooperative and consultive ventures. It provides a forum for the discussion of international disputes and an administrative center for cooperation among nations in economic development, agricultural improvement, and many other matters.

The main deliberative bodies in the UN are the General Assembly, in which each member nation has a voice and a vote; and the Security Council, which is made up of five permanent members (the United States, Russia, China, Great Britain, and France), and ten rotating members who serve two-year terms. In Security Council votes on important matters, any permanent member may cast a *veto*, killing a measure even if all other members are in favor.

The United Nations has no military force of its own, but it may send peacekeeping forces from consenting member nations to supervise truces and otherwise discourage bloodshed.

The Secretariat of the UN is its executive branch, directed by the secretary-general, who is elected by member nations for a term of five years. The Secretariat coordinates the work of UN organizations in many fields (see chart). The Office of the UN High Commissioner for Refugees received the Nobel Prize for Peace in 1954 and 1981.

The United Nations is supported by assessments on member nations, apportioned by population and economic strength. The largest contributor is the United States. For a list of member nations, see *Countries of the World* in Volume 1.

Organization of the United Nations

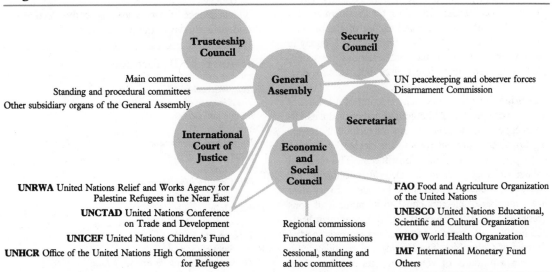

Main committees
Standing and procedural committees
Other subsidiary organs of the General Assembly

Trusteeship Council

Security Council

General Assembly

UN peacekeeping and observer forces
Disarmament Commission

Secretariat

International Court of Justice

Economic and Social Council

UNRWA United Nations Relief and Works Agency for Palestine Refugees in the Near East
UNCTAD United Nations Conference on Trade and Development
UNICEF United Nations Children's Fund
UNHCR Office of the United Nations High Commissioner for Refugees

Regional commissions
Functional commissions
Sessional, standing and ad hoc committees

FAO Food and Agriculture Organization of the United Nations
UNESCO United Nations Educational, Scientific and Cultural Organization
WHO World Health Organization
IMF International Monetary Fund
Others

Elections

All elections for federal and state officials are held by secret ballot. The elections are preceded by a complex nomination process by which each political party chooses its nominee for office.

Nominations. Those seeking a major party nomination to state or federal office often begin campaigning a year or more before the election. In some jurisdictions, a nominee is chosen by a series of party caucuses or by the vote of delegates to a party convention on the local, state, or national level. In recent years, however, primary elections have played an increasing role in choosing nominees. In most states, voters registered in a given party choose between two or more candidates for their party's nomination two to six months before the general election. Between the primary and the general election, the nominees of the various parties campaign against each other.

Presidential candidates gain their party's nomination through a combination of state caucuses, state primary elections, and party conventions. A series of state caucuses and primaries runs from January to June of an election year. These caucuses and elections select delegates to the national convention who are committed to one candidate or another. The final vote on the nominee takes place at the convention, which is held in the summer. Often the result of this nomination vote is already determined before the convention begins.

General elections. In elections for most federal and state offices, the candidate who receives a *plurality* of the votes—one more than his nearest competitor—is elected. In some cases state laws provide that if no candidate receives a certain percentage of the vote (often 40 percent), a runoff election must be held between the two top contenders. Elections for President and for all members of the Senate and House of Representatives are held on the Tuesday after the first Monday in November. Many state and local elections are scheduled for the same day. Voters often must vote for dozens of offices on the same ballot.

Presidential elections. The election of a President is more complicated. Although the names of the candidates appear on the ballot, voters are technically selecting unnamed representatives to the electoral college, a body provided for in the Constitution. The electoral college casts its votes in the December following the election and officially selects the President. Every state has a number of electors equal to its number of congressmen plus its senators (the 23rd Amendment, ratified in 1961, also provided for electors representing the District of Columbia). The Presidential candidate who receives a plurality of votes in a state receives *all* of that state's electoral votes.

Presidential elections: a schedule

Popular election
First Tuesday after first Monday in November
Candidate with plurality in each state wins that state's electoral votes.

Electoral college meetings
First Monday after second Wednesday in December
Electors meet in state capitals to cast their votes. States certify the votes and send them to Congress.

Counting the electoral vote
Results of the electoral college vote are tallied by the President of the Senate (usually the U.S. Vice President) at a joint session of Congress. If there is a tie in the electoral vote, the House of Representatives must elect the President, each state receiving *one* vote.

Inauguration
January 20
The President-elect is sworn in at noon and takes office.

To be elected President, a candidate must receive a majority of electoral votes—at least 270 of a total of 538. If no candidate receives a majority, the election is thrown into the House of Representatives. There, each state delegation receives one vote. This has happened only once, in 1824, when John Quincy Adams was elected by the House over Andrew Jackson and Henry Clay. Twice, however, a candidate who received a plurality of all popular votes cast was defeated in the electoral college.

The sequence of events leading to the election of a President is shown in the box above.

For Further Reference

Barone, Michael and Ujifusa, Grant
  The Almanac of American Politics
  Barone and Co.
Deutsch, Karl W.
  Politics and Government
  Houghton-Mifflin
Freidel, Frank
  Our Country's Presidents
  National Geographic
Hersey, John
  Aspects of the Presidency
  Ticknor and Fields
Kling, Samuel G.
  The Complete Guide to Everyday Law
  Follett

Constitution of the United States

Preamble

We the people of the United States, in order to form a more perfect union, establish justice, insure domestic tranquility, provide for the common defense, promote the general welfare, and secure the blessings of liberty to ourselves and our posterity, do ordain and establish this Constitution for the United States of America.

Article I

The Legislative Branch

Section 1. All legislative powers herein granted shall be vested in a Congress of the United States, which shall consist of a Senate and House of Representatives.

Section 2. The House of Representatives shall be composed of members chosen every second year by the people of the several States, and the electors in each State shall have the qualifications requisite for electors of the most numerous branch of the State legislature.

House of Representatives

No person shall be a Representative who shall not have attained to the age of twenty-five years, and been seven years a citizen of the United States, and who shall not, when elected, be an inhabitant of that State in which he shall be chosen.

Representatives and direct taxes shall be apportioned among the several States which may be included within this Union, according to their respective numbers, which shall be determined by adding to the whole number of free persons, including those bound to service for a term of years, and excluding Indians not taxed, three-fifths of all other persons. The actual enumeration shall be made within three years after the first meeting of the Congress of the United States, and within every subsequent term of ten years, in such manner as they shall by law direct. The number of Representatives shall not exceed one for every thirty thousand, but each State shall have at least one Representative; and until such enumeration shall be made, the State of New Hampshire shall be entitled to choose three; Massachusetts, eight; Rhode Island and Providence Plantations, one; Connecticut, five; New York, six; New Jersey, four; Pennsylvania, eight; Delaware, one; Maryland, six; Virginia, ten; North Carolina, five; South Carolina, five; and Georgia, three.

This section set up the national census to determine how many representatives in Congress each state would have. Originally, slaves and Indians were not counted "whole persons" in the census, but the 14th Amendment gave former slaves the full rights of citizenship. The number of congressmen from each state is still determined by the number of people in the state, but the total membership of the House is limited to 435.

When vacancies happen in the representation from any State, the executive authority thereof shall issue writs of election to fill such vacancies.

The House of Representatives shall choose their Speaker and other officers, and shall have the sole power of impeachment.

"Impeachment" means accusing an official of wrong conduct in office. The House of Representatives makes these charges, and the Senate acts as the court where they are tried (see Section 3).

Section 3. The Senate of the United States shall be composed of two Senators from each State, chosen by the legislature thereof for six years; and each Senator shall have one vote.

Senate
Since the 17th Amendment was passed in 1913, senators have been chosen by direct popular vote, not by the legislatures.

Immediately after they shall be assembled in consequence of the first election, they shall be divided as equally as may be into three classes. The seats of the Senators of the first class shall be vacated at the expiration of the second year, of the second class at the expiration of the fourth year, and of the third class at the expiration of the sixth year, so that one-third may be chosen every second year; and if vacancies happen by resignation, or otherwise, during the recess of the legislature of any State, the executive thereof

This clause set up a system of staggered elections to the Senate. All senators now have six-year terms, but the terms expire at different times.

In one election year, only one-third of the senators are up for election; the others still have two or four more years to serve. This gives the Senate more continuity than the House, where all members are up for election every two years. Since there is always an even number of senators, tie votes are possible, and so the Vice President was given the power to break ties.

may make temporary appointments until the next meeting of the legislature, which shall then fill such vacancies.

No person shall be a Senator who shall not have attained the age of thirty years, and been nine years a citizen of the United States, and who shall not, when elected, be an inhabitant of that State for which he shall be chosen.

The Vice-President of the United States shall be President of the Senate, but shall have no vote, unless they be equally divided.

The Senate shall choose their other officers and also a President pro tempore, in the absence of the Vice-President, or when he shall exercise the office of President of the United States.

The Senate shall have the sole power to try all impeachments. When sitting for that purpose, they shall be on oath or affirmation. When the President of the United States is tried, the Chief Justice shall preside; and no person shall be convicted without the concurrence of two-thirds of the members present.

Judgment in cases of impeachment shall not extend further than to removal from office, and disqualification to hold and enjoy any office of honor, trust, or profit under the United States; but the party convicted shall nevertheless be liable and subject to indictment, trial, judgment and punishment, according to law.

Congressional Elections

Section 4. The times, places, and manner of holding elections for Senators and Representatives shall be prescribed in each State by the legislature thereof; but the Congress may at any time by law make or alter such regulations, except as to the places of choosing Senators.

The 20th Amendment changed this meeting time to noon, January 3.

The Congress shall assemble at least once in every year, and such meeting shall be on the first Monday in December, unless they shall by law appoint a different day.

Procedures

Section 5. Each House shall be the judge of the elections, returns, and qualifications of its own members, and a majority of each shall constitute a quorum to do business; but a smaller number may adjourn from day to day, and may be authorized to compel the attendance of absent members, in such manner, and under such penalties, as each House may provide.

Each House may determine the rules of its proceedings, punish its members for disorderly behavior, and with the concurrence of two-thirds, expel a member.

In addition to the Congressional Record, which is published every day, both Houses of Congress keep a record of their proceedings.

Each House shall keep a journal of its proceedings, and from time to time publish the same, excepting such parts as may in their judgment require secrecy, and the yeas and nays of the members of either House on any question shall, at the desire of one-fifth of those present, be entered on the journal.

Neither House, during the session of Congress, shall, without the consent of the other adjourn for more than three days, nor to any other place than that in which the two Houses shall be sitting.

Payment and Privileges
These privileges are called "congressional immunity."

Section 6. The Senators and Representatives shall receive a compensation for their services, to be ascertained by law and paid out of the Treasury of the United States. They shall, in all cases except treason, felony, and breach of the peace, be privileged from arrest during their attendance at the session of their respective Houses, and in going to and returning from the same; and for any speech or debate in either House they shall not be questioned in any other place.

No Senator or Representative shall, during the time for which he was elected, be appointed to any civil office under the authority of the United

States, which shall have been created, or the emoluments whereof shall have been increased during such time; and no person holding any office under the United States shall be a member of either House during his continuance in office.

"Emoluments" are salaries. This section prevents federal officials from being members of Congress at the same time.

Section 7. All bills for raising revenue shall originate in the House of Representatives; but the Senate may propose or concur with amendments as on other bills.

Relation to Executive

Every bill which shall have passed the House of Representatives and the Senate shall, before it become a law, be presented to the President of the United States; if he approve he shall sign it, but if not he shall return it, with his objections, to that House in which it shall have originated, who shall enter the objections at large on their journal and proceed to reconsider it. If after such reconsideration two-thirds of that House shall agree to pass the bill, it shall be sent, together with the objections, to the other House, by which it shall likewise be reconsidered, and if approved by two-thirds of that House, it shall become a law. But in all such cases the vote of both Houses shall be determined by yeas and nays, and the names of the persons voting for and against the bill shall be entered on the journal of each House respectively. If any bill shall not be returned by the President within ten days (Sundays excepted) after it shall have been presented to him, the same shall be a law, in like manner as if he had signed it, unless the Congress by their adjournment prevent its return, in which case it shall not be a law.

This section describes the President's veto power. Even if a bill has been passed by both the Senate and the House, the President can veto it, or turn it down, instead of signing it and making it a law. However, a two-thirds vote by both Houses can pass the bill over his veto. Simply holding the bill when Congress is about to adjourn is a "pocket veto."

Every order, resolution or vote to which the concurrence of the Senate and House of Representatives may be necessary (except on a question of adjournment) shall be presented to the President of the United States; and before the same shall take effect shall be approved by him, or being disapproved by him, shall be repassed by two-thirds of the Senate and the House of Representatives, according to the rules and limitations prescribed in the case of a bill.

Section 8. The Congress shall have power to lay and collect taxes, duties, imposts and excises, to pay the debts and provide for the common defense and general welfare of the United States; but all duties, imposts and excises shall be uniform throughout the United States;

Specific Powers

To borrow money on the credit of the United States;

To regulate commerce with foreign nations, and among the several States, and with the Indian tribes;

To establish an uniform rule of naturalization, and uniform laws on the subject of bankruptcies throughout the United States;

To coin money, regulate the value thereof, and of foreign coin, and fix the standard of weights and measures;

To provide for the punishment of counterfeiting the securities and current coin of the United States;

To establish post offices and post roads;

To promote the progress of science and useful arts by securing for limited times to authors and inventors the exclusive right to their respective writings and discoveries;

This section allows Congress to pass laws about patents and copyrights.

To constitute tribunals inferior to the Supreme Court;

To define and punish piracies and felonies committed on the high seas, and offenses against the law of nations;

To declare war, grant letters of marque and reprisal, and make rules concerning captures on land and water;

Only Congress can declare war, but the President, as Commander in Chief, can order the armed forces to act.

To raise and support armies, but no appropriation of money to that use shall be for a longer term than two years;

To provide and maintain a navy;

To make rules for the government and regulation of the land and naval forces;

To provide for calling forth the militia to execute the laws of the Union, suppress insurrections, and repel invasions;

To provide for organizing, arming and disciplining the militia, and for governing such part of them as may be employed in the service of the United States, reserving to the States respectively the appointment of the officers, and the authority of training the militia according to the discipline prescribed by Congress;

This gave Congress the authority to establish and govern the District of Columbia.

To exercise exclusive legislation in all cases whatsoever over such district (not exceeding ten miles square) as may, by cession of particular States and the acceptance of Congress, become the seat of government of the United States, and to exercise like authority over all places purchased by the consent of the legislature of the State in which the same shall be, for the erection of forts, magazines, arsenals, dockyards, and other needful buildings;

This is sometimes called the "elastic clause" because it can be interpreted to give many powers not actually mentioned in the Constitution.

To make all laws which shall be necessary and proper for carrying into execution the foregoing powers, and all other powers vested by this Constitution in the Government of the United States, or in any department or officer thereof.

Limitations on Congress
This paragraph set up a waiting period for action on the slave trade; Congress did abolish it in 1808.

Section 9. The migration or importation of such persons as any of the States now existing shall think proper to admit shall not be prohibited by the Congress prior to the year one thousand eight hundred and eight, but a tax or duty may be imposed on such importation, not exceeding ten dollars for each person.

Habeas corpus *guards against un-just imprisonment by requiring a judge or court to decide whether a person may be held. An* ex post facto *law applies to acts committed before the law was passed. The 16th Amendment allowed the in-come tax, which is not related to the census.*

The privilege of the writ of habeas corpus shall not be suspended, unless when in cases of rebellion or invasion the public safety may require it.

No bill of attainder or ex post facto law shall be passed.

No capitation or other direct tax shall be laid, unless in proportion to the census or enumeration hereinbefore directed to be taken.

No tax or duty shall be laid on articles exported from any State.

No preference shall be given by any regulation of commerce or revenue to the ports of one State over those of another; nor shall vessels bound to or from one State be obliged to enter, clear or pay duties in another.

No money shall be drawn from the Treasury but in consequence of appropriations made by law; and a regular statement and account of the receipts and expenditures of all public money shall be published from time to time.

In fact, Presidents often exchange gifts with important foreign visitors, but the gifts are considered as gifts to the country.

No title of nobility shall be granted by the United States; and no person holding any office of profit or trust under them shall, without the consent of the Congress, accept of any present, emolument, office, or title of any kind whatever from any king, prince, or foreign state.

Limitations on States

Section 10. No State shall enter into any treaty, alliance, or confederation; grant letters of marque and reprisal; coin money; emit bills of credit; make anything but gold and silver coin a tender in payment of debts; pass any bill of attainder, ex post facto law or law impairing the obligation of contracts, or grant any title of nobility.

No State shall, without the consent of the Congress, lay any imposts or duties on imports or exports, except what may be absolutely necessary for executing its inspection laws; and the net produce of all duties and imposts, laid by any State on imports or exports, shall be for the use of the Treasury of the United States; and all such laws shall be subject to the revision and control of the Congress.

No State shall, without the consent of Congress, lay any duty of tonnage, keep troops or ships of war in time of peace, enter into any agreement or compact with another State or with a foreign power, or engage in war, unless actually invaded or in such imminent danger as will not admit of delay.

Article II

Section 1. The executive power shall be vested in a President of the United States of America. He shall hold his office during the term of four years, and together with the Vice-President, chosen for the same term, be elected as follows:

Each State shall appoint, in such manner as the legislature thereof may direct, a number of Electors, equal to the whole number of Senators and Representatives to which the State may be entitled in the Congress; but no Senator or Representative, or person holding an office of trust or profit under the United States, shall be appointed an Elector.

The Electors shall meet in their respective States and vote by ballot for two persons, of whom one at least shall not be an inhabitant of the same State with themselves. And they shall make a list of all the persons voted for, and of the number of votes for each; which list they shall sign and certify, and transmit sealed to the seat of the government of the United States, directed to the President of the Senate. The President of the Senate shall, in the presence of the Senate and House of Representatives, open all the certificates, and the votes shall then be counted. The person having the greatest number of votes shall be the President, if such number be a majority of the whole number of Electors appointed; and if there be more than one who have such majority, and have an equal number of votes, then the House of Representatives shall immediately choose by ballot one of them for President; and if no person have a majority, then from the five highest on the list the said House shall in like manner choose the President. But in choosing the President the votes shall be taken by States, the representation from each State having one vote; a quorum for this purpose shall consist of a member or members from two-thirds of the States, and a majority of all the States shall be necessary to a choice. In every case, after the choice of the President, the person having the greatest number of votes of the Electors shall be the Vice-President. But if there should remain two or more who have equal votes, the Senate shall choose from them by ballot the Vice-President.

The Congress may determine the time of choosing the Electors and the day on which they shall give their votes, which day shall be the same throughout the United States.

No person except a natural-born citizen, or citizen of the United States at the time of the adoption of this Constitution, shall be eligible to the office of President; neither shall any person be eligible to that office who shall not have attained to the age of thirty-five years, and been fourteen years a resident within the United States.

In case of the removal of the President from office, or of his death, resignation, or inability to discharge the powers and duties of the said office, the same shall devolve on the Vice-President, and the Congress may by law provide for the case of removal, death, resignation, or inability, both of the President and Vice-President, declaring what officer shall then act as President, and such officer shall act accordingly until the disability be removed or a President shall be elected.

The President shall, at stated times, receive for his services a compensation, which shall neither be increased nor diminished during the period for

The Executive Branch
The President

The system for electing the President has been changed a great deal since the Constitution was written, primarily because of the rise of political parties. The so-called "electoral college" still meets, though under the 12th Amendment electors vote separately for the President and Vice President. Originally, the candidate who came in second in the Presidential race became Vice President. Since electors now are pledged to support a party's candidates, election results are actually known before the electors meet.

The 25th Amendment (1967) makes further provisions for succession to the Presidency and for cases when the President is ill.

which he shall have been elected, and he shall not receive within that period any other emolument from the United States or any of them.

Before he enter on the execution of his office he shall take the following oath or affirmation:

"I do solemnly swear (or affirm) that I will faithfully execute the office of President of the United States, and will to the best of my ability preserve, protect, and defend the Constitution of the United States."

Presidential Powers
This is the only mention of the Cabinet made in the Constitution; the first three Cabinet secretaries—state, treasury, and war—were named in 1789.
The Senate must approve Presidential appointments to important posts, such as Cabinet members, ambassadors, and Supreme Court justices.

Section 2. The President shall be Commander-in-Chief of the Army and Navy of the United States, and of the militia of the several States when called into the actual service of the United States; he may require the opinion, in writing, of the principal officer in each of the executive departments, upon any subject relating to the duties of their respective offices, and he shall have power to grant reprieves and pardons for offenses against the United States, except in cases of impeachment.

He shall have power, by and with the advice and consent of the Senate, to make treaties, provided two-thirds of the Senators present concur; and he shall nominate, and, by and with the advice and consent of the Senate, shall appoint ambassadors, other public ministers and consuls, judges of the Supreme Court, and all other officers of the United States whose appointments are not herein otherwise provided for, and which shall be established by law; but the Congress may by law vest the appointment of such inferior officers, as they think proper, in the President alone, in the courts of law, or in the heads of departments.

The President shall have power to fill up all vacancies that may happen during the recess of the Senate, by granting commissions which shall expire at the end of their next session.

Relation to Congress
The President traditionally delivers his "State of the Union" message at the start of each session of Congress. He can suggest legislation at any time.

Section 3. He shall from time to time give to the Congress information of the state of the Union, and recommend to their consideration such measures as he shall judge necessary and expedient; he may, on extraordinary occasions, convene both Houses, or either of them, and in case of disagreement between them with respect to the time of adjournment, he may adjourn them to such time as he shall think proper; he shall receive ambassadors and other public ministers; he shall take care that the laws be faithfully executed, and shall commission all the officers of the United States.

Impeachment
All federal judges are appointed for life and can be removed only by impeachment and conviction.

Section 4. The President, Vice-President and all civil officers of the United States shall be removed from office on impeachment for and conviction of treason, bribery, or other high crimes and misdemeanors.

The Judicial Branch
Courts

Article III
Section 1. The judicial power of the United States shall be vested in one Supreme Court, and in such inferior courts as the Congress may from time to time ordain and establish. The judges, both of the Supreme and inferior courts, shall hold their offices during good behavior, and shall, at stated times, receive for their services a compensation, which shall not be diminished during their continuance in office.

Jurisdiction

Section 2. The judicial power shall extend to all cases, in law and equity, arising under this Constitution, the laws of the United States, and treaties made, or which shall be made, under their authority; to all cases affecting ambassadors, other public ministers, and consuls; to all cases of admiralty and maritime jurisdiction; to controversies to which the United States shall be a party; to controversies between two or more States; between a State and citizens of another State; between citizens of different States; between citizens of the same State claiming lands under grants of different States, and between a State, or the citizens thereof, and foreign states, citizens, or subjects.

In all cases affecting ambassadors, other public ministers and consuls, and those in which a State shall be party, the Supreme Court shall have original jurisdiction. In all the other cases before mentioned the Supreme Court shall have appellate jurisdiction, both as to law and fact, with such exceptions and under such regulations as the Congress shall make.

Certain kinds of cases are taken directly to the Supreme Court. The Court can also review cases that have been tried in other federal or state courts.

The trial of all crimes, except in cases of impeachment, shall be by jury; and such trial shall be held in the State where the said crimes shall have been committed; but when not committed within any State, the trial shall be at such place or places as the Congress may by law have directed.

Section 3. Treason against the United States shall consist only in levying war against them, or in adhering to their enemies, giving them aid and comfort. No person shall be convicted of treason unless on the testimony of two witnesses to the same overt act, or on confession in open court.

Treason

The Congress shall have power to declare the punishment of treason, but no attainder of treason shall work corruption of blood or forfeiture except during the life of the person attainted.

Article IV

Relations Between the States

Section 1. Full faith and credit shall be given in each State to the public acts, records, and judicial proceedings of every other State. And the Congress may by general laws prescribe the manner in which such acts, records, and proceedings shall be proved, and the effect thereof.

Full Faith and Credit
Contracts and other legal documents written in one state are valid in all other states.

Section 2. The citizens of each State shall be entitled to all privileges and immunities of citizens in the several States.

Other Obligations

A person charged in any State with treason, felony, or other crime, who shall flee from justice, and be found in another State, shall, on demand of the executive authority of the State from which he fled, be delivered up, to be removed to the State having jurisdiction of the crime.

Extradition is the process by which a fugitive from justice in one state is handed over to the state in which the crime was committed.

No person held to service or labor in one State, under the laws thereof, escaping into another, shall, in consequence of any law or regulation therein, be discharged from such service or labor, but shall be delivered up on claim to the party to whom such service or labor may be due.

This paragraph provided that runaway slaves should be returned; the 13th Amendment abolished slavery.

Section 3. New States may be admitted by the Congress into this Union; but no new State shall be formed or erected within the jurisdiction of any other State; nor any State be formed by the junction of two or more States or parts of States, without the consent of the legislatures of the States concerned as well as of the Congress.

New States

The Congress shall have power to dispose of and make all needful rules and regulations respecting the territory or other property belonging to the United States; and nothing in this Constitution shall be so construed as to prejudice any claims of the United States or of any particular State.

Section 4. The United States shall guarantee to every State in this Union a republican form of government, and shall protect each of them against invasion, and on application of the legislature, or of the executive (when the legislature cannot be convened) against domestic violence.

Federal Guarantees

Article V

The Congress, whenever two-thirds of both Houses shall deem it necessary, shall propose amendments to this Constitution, or, on the application of the legislatures of two-thirds of the several States, shall call a convention for proposing amendments, which, in either case shall be valid to all intents and purposes as part of this Constitution, when ratified by the legislatures of three-fourths of the several States, or by conventions in three-fourths thereof, as the one or the other mode of ratification may be proposed by the Congress; provided that no amendment which may be made prior to the year one thousand eight hundred and eight shall in any manner affect the first and fourth clauses in the Ninth Section of the First Article; and that no State, without its consent shall be deprived of its equal suffrage in the Senate.

Federal Supremacy
John Marshall, the first chief justice, gave broad interpretations to many sections of the Constitution during his tenure from 1801 to 1835. This clause was interpreted by Marshall to mean that the Supreme Court had the power to review the constitutionality of acts of Congress, since, as stated here, the Constitution is the "supreme law of the land."

Article VI

All debts contracted and engagements entered into, before the adoption of this Constitution, shall be as valid against the United States under this Constitution as under the Confederation.

This Constitution, and the laws of the United States which shall be made in pursuance thereof, and all treaties made, or which shall be made, under the authority of the United States, shall be the supreme law of the land; and the judges in every State shall be bound thereby, anything in the constitution or laws of any State to the contrary notwithstanding.

The Senators and Representatives before mentioned and the members of the several State legislatures, and all executive and judicial officers both of the United States and of the several States, shall be bound by oath or affirmation to support this Constitution; but no religious test shall ever be required as a qualification to any office or public trust under the United States.

Ratification
The Constitution was signed by 39 delegates to the Constitutional Convention, representing 12 of the 13 colonies—all except Rhode Island.

Article VII

The ratification of the conventions of nine States shall be sufficient for the establishment of this Constitution between the States so ratifying the same.

Done in convention by the unanimous consent of the States present, the seventeenth day of September in the year of our Lord one thousand seven hundred and eighty-seven, and of the independence of the United States of America the twelfth. In witness whereof we have hereunto subscribed our names.

Amendments to the Constitution

The Bill of Rights (1791)
The first ten amendments to the Constitution were proposed—and adopted—together at the request of the states. This Bill of Rights has become an integral part of the Constitution, and its guarantees to individuals are still significant today.

The conventions of a number of the States having, at the time of their adopting the Constitution, expressed a desire, in order to prevent misconstruction or abuse of its powers, that further declaratory and restrictive clauses should be added, and as extending the ground of public confidence in the Government will best insure the beneficent ends of its institution;

Resolved, by the Senate and House of Representatives of the United States of America, in Congress assembled, two-thirds of both Houses concurring, that the following articles be proposed to the Legislatures of the several States, as amendments to the Constitution of the United States; all or any of which articles, when ratified by three-fourths of the said Legislatures, to be valid to all intents and purposes as part of the said Constitution, namely:

Amendment 1. Congress shall make no law respecting an establishment of religion, or prohibiting the free exercise thereof; or abridging the freedom of speech or of the press; or the right of the people peaceably to assemble, and to petition the government for a redress of grievances.

Freedom of Religion, Speech, Press, Assembly, and Petition

Amendment 2. A well-regulated militia, being necessary to the security of a free State, the right of the people to keep and bear arms shall not be infringed.

Right to Bear Arms
This amendment is often cited by those opposed to gun-control laws.

Amendment 3. No soldier shall, in time of peace, be quartered in any house without the consent of the owner, nor in time of war, but in a manner to be prescribed by law.

Quartering Soldiers

Amendment 4. The right of the people to be secure in their persons, houses, papers, and effects, against unreasonable searches and seizures, shall not be violated, and no warrants shall issue but upon probable cause, supported by oath or affirmation, and particularly describing the place to be searched, and the persons or things to be seized.

Searches and Seizures
Police and other officials must have specific search warrants when they make investigations of people, homes, or private property.

Amendment 5. No person shall be held to answer for a capital, or otherwise infamous crime, unless on a presentment or indictment of a grand jury, except in cases arising in the land or naval forces, or in the militia, when in actual service in time of war or public danger; nor shall any person be subject for the same offense to be twice put in jeopardy of life or limb; nor shall be compelled in any criminal case to be a witness against himself, nor be deprived of life, liberty or property, without due process of law; nor shall private property be taken for public use without just compensation.

Rights of Defendants
Several legal protections are included here—the need for a grand jury hearing; protection against "double jeopardy"; and the right not to testify against oneself in a trial or hearing.

Amendment 6. In all criminal prosecutions, the accused shall enjoy the right to a speedy and public trial, by an impartial jury of the State and district wherein the crime shall have been committed, which district shall have been previously ascertained by law, and to be informed of the nature and cause of the accusation; to be confronted with the witnesses against him; to have compulsory process for obtaining witnesses in his favor, and to have the assistance of counsel for his defense.

Jury in Criminal Cases
A 1963 Supreme Court decision ruled that the right to legal counsel in felony cases applies whether or not the accused person can afford a lawyer. If the accused cannot, the court must appoint a lawyer.

Amendment 7. In suits at common law, where the value in controversy shall exceed twenty dollars, the right of trial by jury shall be preserved, and no fact tried by a jury shall be otherwise re-examined in any court of the United States, than according to the rules of the common law.

Jury in Civil Cases

Amendment 8. Excessive bail shall not be required, nor excessive fines imposed, nor cruel and unusual punishments inflicted.

Excessive Penalties

Amendment 9. The enumeration in the Constitution of certain rights shall not be construed to deny or disparage others retained by the people.

Other Rights
These amendments protect against a too-powerful federal government.

Amendment 10. The powers not delegated to the United States by the Constitution, nor prohibited by it to the States, are reserved to the States respectively, or to the people.

Additional Amendments

Suits Against States (1798)

Amendment 11. The judicial power of the United States shall not be construed to extend to any suit in law or equity, commenced or prosecuted against one of the United States by citizens of another State, or by citizens or subjects of any foreign state.

Presidential Elections (1804)
This amendment changed the election process so that electors voted separately for President and Vice President.

Amendment 12. The Electors shall meet in their respective States and vote by ballot for President and Vice-President, one of whom, at least, shall not be an inhabitant of the same state with themselves; they shall name in their ballots the person voted for as President, and in distinct ballots the person voted for as Vice-President, and they shall make distinct lists of all persons voted for as President and of all persons voted for as Vice-President, and of the number of votes for each; which lists they shall sign and certify, and transmit sealed to the seat of the government of the United States, directed to the President of the Senate. The President of the Senate shall, in the presence of the Senate and House of Representatives, open all the certificates and the votes shall then be counted. The person having the greatest number of votes for President shall be the President, if such a number be a majority of the whole number of Electors appointed; and if no person have such majority, then from the persons having the highest numbers not exceeding three on the list of those voted for as President, the House of Representatives shall choose immediately, by ballot, the President. But in choosing the President the votes shall be taken by States, the representation from each State having one vote; a quorum for this purpose shall consist of a member or members from two-thirds of the States, and a majority of all the States shall be necessary to a choice. And if the House of Representatives shall not choose a President whenever the right of choice shall devolve upon them, before the fourth day of March next following, then the Vice-President shall act as President, as in the case of the death or other constitutional disability of the President.

The person having the greatest number of votes as Vice-President shall be the Vice-President, if such number be a majority of the whole number of Electors appointed; and if no person have a majority, then from the two highest numbers on the list the Senate shall choose the Vice-President; a quorum for the purpose shall consist of two-thirds of the whole number of Senators, and a majority of the whole number shall be necessary to a choice. But no person constitutionally ineligible to the office of President shall be eligible to that of Vice-President of the United States.

Amendment 13

Abolition of Slavery (1865)
The 13th and 14th Amendments were added after the Civil War. The 13th abolished slavery in the United States. The 14th gave the rights of citizenship to former slaves.

Section 1. Neither slavery nor involuntary servitude, except as a punishment for crime whereof the party shall have been duly convicted, shall exist within the United States, or any place subject to their jurisdiction.

Section 2. Congress shall have power to enforce this article by appropriate legislation.

Amendment 14

Rights of Citizens (1868)
This section extends Bill of Rights protection to matters under state jurisdiction. It is the basis for important court decisions and legislation protecting civil rights of minorities.

Section 1. All persons born or naturalized in the United States, and subject to the jurisdiction thereof, are citizens of the United States and of the State wherein they reside. No State shall make or enforce any law which shall abridge the privileges or immunities of citizens of the United States; nor shall any State deprive any person of life, liberty or property, without due process of law; nor deny to any person within its jurisdiction the equal protection of the laws.

Section 2. Representatives shall be apportioned among the several States according to their respective numbers, counting the whole number of persons in each State, excluding Indians not taxed. But when the right to vote at any election for the choice of Electors for President and Vice-President of the United States, Representatives in Congress, the executive and judicial officers of a State, or the members of the legislature thereof, is denied to any of the male inhabitants of such State, being twenty-one years of age, and citizens of the United States, or in any way abridged except for participation in rebellion or other crime, the basis of representation therein shall be reduced in the proportion which the number of such male citizens shall bear to the whole number of male citizens twenty-one years of age in such State.

This section gave the right to vote to black men; the 19th Amendment allowed women to vote; the 26th lowered the voting age to 18.

Section 3. No person shall be a Senator or Representative in Congress, or elector of President and Vice-President, or hold any office, civil or military, under the United States or under any State, who, having previously taken an oath as a member of Congress, or as an officer of the United States, or as a member of any State legislature, or as an executive or judicial officer of any State, to support the Constitution of the United States, shall have engaged in insurrection or rebellion against the same, or given aid or comfort to the enemies thereof. But Congress may, by a vote of two-thirds of each House, remove such disability.

The idea of this clause was to keep former Confederate officials out of the federal government. Special acts of Congress later allowed some to serve.

Section 4. The validity of the public debt of the United States, authorized by law, including debts incurred for payment of pensions and bounties for services in suppressing insurrection or rebellion, shall not be questioned. But neither the United States nor any State shall assume or pay any debt or obligation incurred in aid of insurrection or rebellion against the United States, or any claim for the loss or emancipation of any slave; but all such debts, obligations, and claims shall be held illegal and void.

This clause forbade both the federal government and the states to pay any debt the Confederacy owed.

Section 5. The Congress shall have power to enforce, by appropriate legislation, the provisions of this article.

Amendment 15
Section 1. The right of citizens of the United States to vote shall not be denied or abridged by the United States or by any State on account of race, color, or previous condition of servitude.

Black Voting Rights (1870)
This amendment was added to strengthen the 14th Amendment.

Section 2. The Congress shall have power to enforce this article by appropriate legislation.

Amendment 16. The Congress shall have power to lay and collect taxes on incomes, from whatever source derived, without apportionment among the several States, and without regard to any census or enumeration.

Income Taxes (1913)
An amendment to allow an income tax was needed because the Constitution did not allow any direct tax.

Amendment 17
Section 1. The Senate of the United States shall be composed of two Senators from each State, elected by the people thereof, for six years; and each Senator shall have one vote. The electors in each State shall have the qualifications requisite for electors of the most numerous branch of the State legislatures.

Senatorial Elections (1913)

Section 2. When vacancies happen in the representation of any State in the Senate, the executive authority of such State shall issue writs of election to fill such vacancies: Provided, that the legislature of any State may empower the executive thereof to make temporary appointments until the people fill the vacancies by election as the legislature may direct.

Section 3. This amendment shall not be so construed as to affect the election or term of any Senator chosen before it becomes valid as part of the Constitution.

Amendment 18

Section 1. After one year from the ratification of this article the manufacture, sale or transportation of intoxicating liquors within, the importation thereof into, or the exportation thereof from the United States and all territory subject to the jurisdiction thereof, for beverage purposes, is hereby prohibited.

Section 2. The Congress and the several States shall have concurrent power to enforce this article by appropriate legislation.

Section 3. This article shall be inoperative unless it shall have been ratified as an amendment to the Constitution by the legislatures of the several States, as provided in the Constitution, within seven years from the date of the submission hereof to the States by the Congress.

Amendment 19

Section 1. The right of citizens of the United States to vote shall not be denied or abridged by the United States or by any State on account of sex.

Section 2. Congress shall have power to enforce this article by appropriate legislation.

Amendment 20

Section 1. The terms of the President and Vice-President shall end at noon on the 20th day of January, and the terms of Senators and Representatives at noon on the 3d day of January, of the years in which such terms would have ended if this article had not been ratified; and the terms of their successors shall then begin.

Section 2. The Congress shall assemble at least once in every year, and such meetings shall begin at noon on the 3d day of January, unless they shall by law appoint a different day.

Section 3. If, at the time fixed for the beginning of the term of the President, the President-elect shall have died, the Vice-President-elect shall become President. If a President shall not have been chosen before the time fixed for the beginning of his term or if the President-elect shall have failed to qualify, then the Vice-President-elect shall act as President until a President shall have qualified; and the Congress may by law provide for the case wherein neither a President-elect nor a Vice-President-elect shall have qualified, declaring who shall then act as President, or the manner in which one who is to act shall be selected, and such person shall act accordingly until a President or Vice-President shall have qualified.

Section 4. The Congress may by law provide for the case of the death of any of the persons from whom the House of Representatives may choose a President whenever the right of choice shall have devolved upon them, and for the case of the death of any of the persons from whom the Senate may choose a Vice-President whenever the right of choice shall have devolved upon them.

Prohibition (1919)
The Prohibition amendment was ineffective and so was repealed in 1933 by the 21st Amendment.

Women's Suffrage (1920)

Terms of Office (1933)
This is known as the "lame duck" amendment because it shortened the time between congressmen's elections and the date they took office. "Lame ducks" were defeated members who, under the old system, remained in Congress long after being defeated in an election.

26   **United States Government**

Section 5. Sections 1 and 2 shall take effect on the 15th day of October following the ratification of this article.

Section 6. This article shall be inoperative unless it shall have been ratified as an amendment to the Constitution by the legislatures of three-fourths of the several States within seven years from the date of its submission.

Amendment 21

Repeal of Prohibition (1933)

Section 1. The eighteenth article of amendment to the Constitution of the United States is hereby repealed.

Section 2. The transportation or importation into any State, territory, or possession of the United States for delivery or use therein of intoxicating liquors, in violation of the laws thereof, is hereby prohibited.

Section 3. This article shall be inoperative unless it shall have been ratified as an amendment to the Constitution by conventions in the several States, as provided in the Constitution, within seven years from the date of the submission hereof to the States by the Congress.

Amendment 22

Presidential Terms (1951)
This amendment was passed after the death of Franklin D. Roosevelt, who had been elected four times. Its purpose was to prevent subsequent Presidents from serving more than two terms.

Section 1. No person shall be elected to the office of President more than twice, and no person who has held the office of President, or acted as President, for more than two years of a term to which some other person was elected President shall be elected to the office of President more than once. But this Article shall not apply to any person holding the office of President when this Article was proposed by the Congress, and shall not prevent any person who may be holding the office of President, or acting as President, during the term within which this Article becomes operative from holding the office of President or acting as President during the remainder of such term.

Section 2. This article shall be inoperative unless it shall have been ratified as an amendment to the Constitution by the legislatures of three-fourths of the several States within seven years from the date of its submission to the States by the Congress.

Amendment 23

District of Columbia Voting Rights (1961)
Before this amendment, residents of the District of Columbia could not vote.

Section 1. The District constituting the seat of Government of the United States shall appoint in such manner as the Congress may direct:

A number of electors of President and Vice-President equal to the whole number of Senators and Representatives in Congress to which the District would be entitled if it were a State, but in no event more than the least populous State; they shall be in addition to those appointed by the States, but they shall be considered, for the purposes of the election of President and Vice-President, to be electors appointed by a State; and they shall meet in the District and perform such duties as provided by the twelfth article of amendment.

Section 2. The Congress shall have power to enforce this article by appropriate legislation.

Amendment 24

Poll Tax Prohibited (1964)
Poll taxes had been used to prevent or discourage black voters from registering or voting.

Section 1. The right of citizens of the United States to vote in any primary or other election for President or Vice-President, for electors for President or Vice-President, or for Senator or Representative in Congress, shall not be denied or abridged by the United States or any State by reason of failure to pay any poll tax or other tax.

Section 2. The Congress shall have power to enforce this article by appropriate legislation.

Presidential Succession (1967)

Amendment 25

Section 1. In case of the removal of the President from office or of his death or resignation, the Vice-President shall become President.

Section 2. Whenever there is a vacancy in the office of the Vice-President, the President shall nominate a Vice-President who shall take office upon confirmation by a majority vote of both Houses of Congress.

Section 3. Whenever the President transmits to the President pro tempore of the Senate and the Speaker of the House of Representatives his written declaration that he is unable to discharge the powers and duties of his office, and until he transmits to them a written declaration to the contrary, such powers and duties shall be discharged by the Vice-President as Acting President.

Section 4. Whenever the Vice-President and a majority of either the principal officers of the executive departments or of such other body as Congress may by law provide, transmit to the President pro tempore of the Senate and the Speaker of the House of Representatives their written declaration that the President is unable to discharge the powers and duties of his office, the Vice-President shall immediately assume the powers and duties of the office as Acting President.

Thereafter, when the President transmits to the President pro tempore of the Senate and the Speaker of the House of Representatives his written declaration that no inability exists, he shall resume the powers and duties of his office unless the Vice-President and a majority of either the principal officers of the executive department or of such other body as Congress may by law provide, transmit within four days to the President pro tempore of the Senate and the Speaker of the House of Representatives their written declaration that the President is unable to discharge the powers and duties of his office. Thereupon Congress shall decide the issue, assembling within forty-eight hours for that purpose if not in session. If the Congress, within twenty-one days after receipt of the latter written declaration, or, if Congress is not in session, within twenty-one days after Congress is required to assemble, determines by two-thirds vote of both Houses that the President is unable to discharge the powers and duties of his office, the Vice-President shall continue to discharge the same as Acting President; otherwise, the President shall resume the powers and duties of his office.

Voting Age (1971)

Amendment 26

Section 1. The right of citizens of the United States, who are eighteen years of age or older, to vote shall not be denied or abridged by the United States or by any State on account of age.

Section 2. The Congress shall have power to enforce this article by appropriate legislation.

Congressional Salaries (1992)

Amendment 27

No law varying the compensation for the services of the Senators and Representatives shall take effect, until an election of representatives shall have intervened.

Presidents of the United States

The Presidents of the United States are the only officials elected by all the people of the country. From the beginning, they have had considerable prestige and power, especially in times of national crises. In recent times, as the United States has become a world power, the office has become one of the most influential—and difficult to manage—in the world.

What kind of men were those who served as President? Thirty-nine served between 1789 and 1982, for an average of about five years each. The following pages provide thumbnail sketches of each of them, from George Washington through Ronald Reagan. For each, there is information on personal life, education and occupation, political career, and years in office. On this page, there are some interesting facts about the Presidents as a group. (For portraits of the Presidents, see the color plates in the front of this volume. For more information on U.S. history, see Volume 1.)

Which Presidents served the longest and shortest times in office?

Longest: Franklin D. Roosevelt served from March, 1933, to April, 1945, a total of 12 years, 1 month. He had been elected for a fourth term and would have served 16 years had he not died in office. The 22nd Amendment (1951) limits Presidents to two terms.

Shortest: William Henry Harrison served from March 4 to April 4, 1841. He caught a cold at his inauguration and died of pneumonia just one month after taking office. One other President, James Garfield, died of an assassin's wounds in September, 1881, after serving six months.

How many Presidents died in office?

Eight. They are: William Henry Harrison, 1841, illness; Zachary Taylor, 1850, illness; Abraham Lincoln, 1865, assassination; James Garfield, 1881, assassination; William McKinley, 1901, assassination; Warren Harding, 1923, illness; Franklin D. Roosevelt, 1945, illness; and John F. Kennedy, 1963, assassination.

Which states have been the birthplace of the most Presidents?

Virginia and Ohio. Virginia, sometimes called "the cradle of Presidents," has been the birthplace of eight Presidents, including four of the first five. They are: Washington, Jefferson, Madison, Monroe, William Henry Harrison, Tyler, Taylor, and Wilson.

Ohio follows close behind with seven, all of whom served between 1869 and 1923. They are: Grant, Hayes, Garfield, Benjamin Harrison, McKinley, Taft, and Harding.

Were any Presidents related to each other?

Yes. John Adams and John Quincy Adams, the second and sixth Presidents, were father and son. William Henry Harrison and Benjamin Harrison, the ninth and 23rd Presidents, were grandfather and grandson. Theodore and Franklin Roosevelt, the 25th and 31st Presidents, were distant cousins.

Were all the Presidents married?

All except one were married at some time in their lives. The exception is James Buchanan. Several Presidents have been married more than once, usually after the death of their first wives. The only President who has received a divorce is Ronald Reagan.

Did all Presidents retire after serving as President?

Most, but not all. John Quincy Adams returned to the House of Representatives and served there for 17 years after his Presidency. William Howard Taft became a law professor and later served nine years as chief justice of the Supreme Court.

Have any Presidents been removed from office?

No. But in two cases, impeachment proceedings were begun. Andrew Johnson was impeached (accused) by the House of Representatives in 1868 and tried before the Senate. The Senate vote was one short of the two-thirds majority required for conviction. Johnson remained in office, but did not run for reelection.

Richard Nixon was the subject of committee impeachment hearings in the House in 1974. Before the full House could vote, Nixon resigned from office, on August 9, 1974. He was the first President ever to resign.

General Washington (center)   John Adams   The Capitol Building c 1800

Name/Dates in office	Personal	Education/Occupation
1st **George Washington** April 30, 1789–March 4, 1797	Born Feb. 22, 1732, Westmoreland County, Va.; died Dec. 14, 1799, Mount Vernon, Va. Raised in part by half brother Lawrence, from whom he inherited the plantation at Mount Vernon. In 1759 married Martha Dandridge Custis (1732–1802), a widow with two children.	Schooled at home, trained as a surveyor, Washington operated and expanded the farmland of Mount Vernon. Began military career in French and Indian War in 1753. Named commander in chief of Continental Army in 1775, and led troops in most major battles of American Revolution.
2nd **John Adams** March 4, 1797–March 4, 1801	Born Oct. 30, 1735, Braintree (now Quincy), Mass.; died July 4, 1826, Quincy, Mass. Member of prominent family that arrived in Massachusetts in 1636. In 1764 married Abigail Smith (1744–1818); their five children included the sixth President, John Quincy Adams.	Graduated from Harvard, 1755; studied law, and began practice in Boston. Important writer of tracts against British taxation of colonies and in support of British military action in Boston Massacre of 1770.
3rd **Thomas Jefferson** March 4, 1801–March 4, 1809	Born April 13, 1743, Goochland (now Albemarle County), Va.; died July 4, 1826, Charlottesville, Va. Son of a tobacco farmer, he was left the family estate at age 14 and later pursued literary and musical interests. In 1772 married Martha Wayles Skelton (1748–1782); they had six children, but only two daughters survived infancy.	Attended William and Mary College, 1760–1762. A lawyer, he became an important writer on a variety of topics, especially political philosophy and education. He designed buildings for the University of Virginia at Charlottesville, which he founded, as well as his own home there, Monticello.
4th **James Madison** March 4, 1809–March 4, 1817	Born March 16, 1751, Port Conway, Va.; died June 28, 1836, Montpelier, Virginia. In 1794 married Dolley Paine Todd (1768–1849), who became popular First Lady Dolley Madison and rescued important White House art works when the British burned Washington in 1814.	Graduated from College of New Jersey (now Princeton), 1771. Lawyer and public servant in Virginia prior to political career.

United States Government

Lewis and Clark expedition

Jefferson's Monticello

Political career	*Highlights in office*
Member of Virginia House of Burgesses, 1758. Delegate to Continental Congresses 1774–1775. Chairman of Constitutional Convention, 1787.	Elected first President by unanimous vote of electoral college and inaugurated on balcony of Federal Hall in New York City. Established strong U.S. currency, Bank of the United States, and U.S. Military Academy at West Point. Ended the first American domestic crisis, the 1791 Whiskey Rebellion in Pennsylvania. Reelected in 1792 but declined a third term in 1796, setting a precedent followed by all Presidents until Franklin D. Roosevelt.
Organized opposition to Stamp Act in Boston. Delegate to First Continental Congress, 1774, and signer of Declaration of Independence, 1776. Commissioner to France with Benjamin Franklin, 1778; diplomat to Holland, 1780–1782; helped negotiate Treaty of Paris, ending the American Revolution, 1782–1783; first U.S. minister to England, 1785–1788. Elected Vice President, 1788, and reelected, 1792.	Elected President over Thomas Jefferson, who became Vice President. Prevented war with France in 1798 after relations were disrupted by XYZ Affair, in which French tried to bribe American officials. Permitted passage of Alien and Sedition Acts, 1798. Defeated for reelection by Jefferson, 1800.
Elected to Virginia House of Burgesses, 1769. Member of Continental Congress and author of Declaration of Independence, 1776. Governor of Virginia 1779–1781. Minister to France 1785–1789. Secretary of state to President Washington 1789–1793. Second to John Adams in 1796 Presidential election, he became Vice President.	Voted President by House of Representatives after electoral tie with Aaron Burr. Authorized and concluded Louisiana Purchase of 1803, and commissioned Lewis and Clark expedition. Negotiated Embargo Act to protect American interests while England and France were at war. Reelected by overwhelming majority in 1804 over C. C. Pinckney of South Carolina. Noted for ridding Presidency of royal trappings and Federal power-sharing with state government.
Member of Virginia Constitutional Convention, 1776, and Continental Congress, 1780. Chief recorder and influential organizer at U.S. Constitutional Convention in 1787. Author of *The Federalist* with Alexander Hamilton and John Jay. Congressman from Virginia, 1787–1797. Appointed secretary of state by President Thomas Jefferson in 1801.	Elected as opponent of free interpretation of U.S. Constitution and preserver of Jeffersonian policies, including unpopular trade embargo on English goods. Reelected in 1812 with firm support from new Western states. Trade embargo brought about War of 1812, declared by Madison on June 18 of that year and ended without victory for either side in 1815.

Early steamboat

Monroe expounds foreign policy

Name/Dates in office	Personal	Education/Occupation
5th **James Monroe** March 4, 1817–March 4, 1825	Born April 28, 1758, Westmoreland County, Va.; died July 4, 1831, New York City. Married Elizabeth Kortwright (1768–1830) of New York City in 1786; they had two daughters and a son who died in infancy.	Attended the College of William and Mary, where he studied law under Thomas Jefferson and became an adherent of his philosophy. Fought in Continental Army, being wounded at Trenton, New Jersey. Sacrificed personal wealth to political career, and died in relative poverty.
6th **John Quincy Adams** March 4, 1825–March 4, 1829	Born July 11, 1767, Braintree (now Quincy), Mass.; died Feb. 23, 1848, Washington, D.C. Son of John Adams, second President. In 1797 married Louise Catherine Johnson (1775–1852), daugher of U.S. consul in London; they had three sons and one daughter.	Attended schools in France and Holland; graduated from Harvard, 1787. Practiced law in Boston beginning in 1790 and wrote a series of pamphlets on political topics.
7th **Andrew Jackson** March 4, 1829–March 4, 1837	Born March 15, 1767, Waxhaw, S.C.; died June 8, 1845, at "The Hermitage," near Nashville, Tenn. The son of Irish immigrants, he joined the local militia at the age of 13. Married Rachel Donelson Robards (1767–1828) in 1791 and remarried her in 1793 when her divorce from a previous husband became final; they had one adopted son, Andrew Jackson, Jr., and raised several foster children.	No formal education, although he privately studied law. In Indian wars, defeated Creeks at Horseshoe Bend, Ala., 1814. Defeated British at New Orleans in 1815, not knowing War of 1812 had already ended. Defeated Seminole Indians, 1818, and became military governor of Florida, 1821.
8th **Martin Van Buren** March 4, 1837–March 4, 1841	Born Dec. 5, 1782, Kinderhook, N.Y.; died July 24, 1862, Kinderhook, N.Y. In 1807 married Hannah Hoes (1783–1819); they had four sons. As President, Van Buren was a widower, and a daughter-in-law served as White House hostess.	Privately studied law and was admitted to the bar in 1803 without attending college. Practiced law in his hometown.

United States Government

Battle for the Alamo

Indians and soldier

Political career	*Highlights in office*
Congressman from Virginia 1783–1786; senator from Virginia 1790–1794. Minister to France 1794–1796. Governor of Virginia 1799–1802. Member of diplomatic missions, including negotiation of Louisiana Purchase in 1803. Secretary of state to James Madison 1811–1817.	Elected by overwhelming majority in 1816, and reelected with all but one electoral vote in 1820. His administration, called the "Era of Good Feeling," included the acquisition of Florida from Spain, the improvement of relations with Canada, and the Missouri Compromise on the slavery issue in 1820. The Monroe Doctrine announced that North and South American countries would unite against European interference.
Minister to Holland, 1794, and later minister to Portugal and Prussia. Senator from Massachusetts 1803–1808. Negotiated treaty to end War of 1812. Secretary of state to James Monroe 1817–1825. After Presidency returned to Congress, 1831–1848.	Elected President by House of Representatives after Andrew Jackson received more electoral and popular votes but not a majority. Expanded executive powers and passed tariff regulations that favored New England manufacturers over plantation farmers of the South. Soundly defeated by Jackson in 1828 reelection bid.
Congressman from Tennessee, 1796, and senator, 1797–1798. After military career returned to Senate, 1823–1825. Received more electoral and popular votes than John Quincy Adams in 1824 election for President, but lacked a majority and saw the House of Representatives award the office to Adams. Resigned from Senate 1825 to prepare for new Presidential campaign.	Elected by a landslide over John Quincy Adams in second attempt to gain Presidency. Instituted the "spoils system" to reward party members and oust lifelong Washington politicians. Opposed Bank of the United States and undermined its credibility by redistributing funds. Declared a policy of "let the people rule." Renominated at the first party convention and subsequently reelected,1832.
Columbia County, N.Y., surrogate 1808–1813; state senator 1812–1820; state attorney general 1815–1819. U.S. senator 1821–1828. Elected governor of New York, 1828, but resigned soon after taking office to become secretary of state to Andrew Jackson, 1829–1831. Vice President during Jackson's second administration, 1833–1837. Campaigned unsuccessfully for the Presidency twice after his single term in office.	Took office as the Panic of 1837 launched a severe economic depression. His policies to relieve the depression were ineffective, and this led to his defeat in 1840 by William Henry Harrison.

Name/Dates in office	Personal	Education/Occupation
9th **William Henry Harrison** March 4, 1841–April 4, 1841	Born Feb. 9, 1773, Berkeley, Va.; died April 4, 1841, Washington, D.C., first President to die in office. In 1795 married Anna Symmes (1775–1864); they had six sons, and grandson Benjamin Harrison became the 23rd President.	Graduated from Hampden-Sydney College in Virginia, 1790. Joined military, 1791. Defeated Indians under Tecumseh at the Tippecanoe River in Indiana, 1811, and the British at the Battle of the Thames in Indiana in 1813.
10th **John Tyler** April 6, 1841–March 4, 1845	Born March 29, 1790, Greenway, Va.; died Jan. 18, 1862, Richmond, Va. In 1813 married Letitia Christian (1790–1842); they had seven children. After her death, married Julia Gardiner (1820–1889) in an 1844 White House ceremony; they also had seven children.	Graduated from the College of William and Mary, 1807. Studied law before commencing active political career. Returned to legal practice in Richmond following Presidency.
11th **James Knox Polk** March 4, 1845–March 4, 1849	Born Nov. 2, 1795, Mecklenburg County, N.C.; died June 15, 1849, Nashville, Tenn. In 1824 married Sarah Childress (1803–1891), who served as official secretary to him in the White House.	Graduated from University of North Carolina in 1818, studied law, and moved to Nashville to begin practice there. Gained prominence as a political speaker.
12th **Zachary Taylor** March 4, 1849–July 9, 1850	Born Nov. 24, 1784, Orange County, Va.; died July 9, 1850, Washington, D.C., while in office. In 1810 married Margaret Mackall Smith (1788–1852); they had six children.	With little formal education, rose through the military ranks as a career soldier. Veteran of War of 1812 and Black Hawk and Seminole Indian wars; commander of forces in 1845 Mexican War.
13th **Millard Fillmore** July 10, 1850–March 4, 1853	Born Jan. 7, 1800, Locke (now Summerhill), N.Y.; died March 8, 1874, Buffalo, N.Y. In 1826 married Abigail Powers (1798–1853); they had two children. After her death he married Caroline McIntosh (1814–1881) in 1858.	Educated at country schools where he later taught. Privately studied law; was admitted to bar in 1823, beginning his practice in Buffalo, N.Y. Returned to Buffalo after Presidency as chancellor of University of Buffalo.
14th **Franklin Pierce** March 4, 1853–March 4, 1857	Born Nov. 23, 1804, Hillsboro, N.H.; died Oct. 8, 1869, Concord, N.H. In 1834 married Jane Means Appleton (1806–1863); their three sons all died in childhood.	Graduated from Bowdoin College in Maine, 1824, then studied law. Interrupted political career to serve in Mexican War under General Winfield Scott.
15th **James Buchanan** March 4, 1857–March 4, 1861	Born April 23, 1791, Mercersburg, Pa.; died June 1, 1868, Lancaster, Pa. Was the only President who never married.	Graduated from Dickinson College in Pennsylvania, 1809. Served as a volunteer in War of 1812, and afterward practiced law.

Political career	*Highlights in office*
Secretary of the Northwest Territory, 1798, and its delegate to Congress, 1799. First governor of the Indian Territory, 1800, and superintendent of Indian affairs, 1801–1813. Represented Ohio in Congress, 1816–1819, and in the Senate, 1825–1828. Defeated by Martin Van Buren in 1836 Presidential election.	Elected as war hero on a ticket with John Tyler for Vice President; famous for slogan "Tippecanoe and Tyler Too." Contracted pneumonia during inauguration and died one month after taking office.
Elected to Virginia House of Delegates in 1811 at the age of 21. Congressman 1816–1821; state legislator 1823–1825; governor of Virginia 1825–1827; senator from Virginia 1827–1836. Shifted from Democratic to Whig Party and elected Vice President for William Henry Harrison. After serving as President, elected to Confederate Congress, 1861.	Assumed office when William Henry Harrison died only one month into his term. Vetoed bills for a national bank, and entire Cabinet, with the exception of Daniel Webster, resigned in protest. Refused to continue spoils system of Andrew Jackson; signed bill admitting Texas to the Union; reorganized the Navy; signed trade treaty with China. Nominated for a second term, but declined.
Tennessee state legislator 1823–1825. Member of Congress 1825–1839 and Speaker of the House 1835–1839. Governor of Tennessee 1839–1841. A protégé of Andrew Jackson, he was nominated in 1844 to resolve party differences and to launch a "dark horse" candidacy based on support for the annexation of Texas.	Sent troops under Zachary Taylor to the Mexican border, precipitating war with that country that ended with U.S. annexation of California and New Mexico. Ended Oregon Territory border dispute with Canada by retreating from "54-40 or fight" demand and settling for present border at 49th parallel.
Without political experience, he was nominated for President by the Whigs on the basis of the war career that earned him the nickname "Old Rough and Ready."	Although a Southerner, he supported the Compromise of 1850 that admitted California as a free state while toughening fugitive slave laws. Did not endorse abolition of slavery, but opposed extension of it to territories and new states. Died in office of natural causes.
Member New York state legislature 1829–1832. Congressman from New York 1833–1835 and 1837–1843. Ran unsuccessfully for governor of New York, 1844. Elected Vice President for Zachary Taylor, 1848, becoming President when Taylor died in office. Unsuccessful candidate in 1856 Presidential election.	Supported Compromise of 1850 that admitted California as a free state while strengthening fugitive slave laws. His compromise policies on territorial expansion and slavery pleased few, and he was not renominated in 1852.
New Hampshire state legislator 1829–1833. Congressman 1833–1837 and senator 1837–1842. At 1852 Democratic convention, was nominated on 49th ballot as "dark horse" alternative to a three-candidate deadlock.	Elected in landslide over General Winfield Scott, formerly Pierce's commanding officer. Signed Kansas-Nebraska Act, 1854, which made slavery subject to local rather than national legislation. Approved Gadsden Purchase of southwestern lands from Mexico, 1853. Was not renominated.
Member of Pennsylvania state legislature 1814–1816. Elected to Congress in 1820, he was an important supporter of Andrew Jackson and became minister to Russia in 1831. Returned to Washington as senator from Pennsylvania, 1834–1845. Secretary of state to Polk 1845–1849. Minister to Britain 1853–1856.	Elected as Democrat against John C. Fremont of young and growing Republican Party. Supported proslavery Dred Scott Decision of 1857 and states' choice on slavery issue, but failed to act decisively against secessionist movement.

Civil War troops, 1864

Lincoln's assassination, 1865

Name/Dates in office	Personal	Education/Occupation
16th **Abraham Lincoln** March 4, 1861–April 15, 1865	Born Feb. 12, 1809, Hardin County (now Larue), Ky.; died April 15, 1865, Washington, D.C., one day after being shot by John Wilkes Booth at Ford's Theatre. In 1842 married Mary Todd (1818–1882); they had four sons.	No formal education, but studied law privately while working as a farmer, store clerk, and riverboat pilot. Admitted to the bar in 1837; began his practice in Springfield, Ill. Became a prominent lawyer in Illinois between terms of political office, representing corporations as well as individuals.
17th **Andrew Johnson** April 15, 1865–March 4, 1869	Born Dec. 29, 1808, Raleigh, N.C.; died July 31, 1875, Carter's Station, Tenn. In 1827 married Eliza McCardle (1810–1876); they had five children.	Apprenticed as a tailor, but ran away and settled in Greenville, Tenn., where his future wife taught him to read at age 17. Supported himself with a variety of jobs while broadening his education and being drawn into politics.
18th **Ulysses Simpson Grant** March 4, 1869–March 4, 1877	Born April 27, 1822, Point Pleasant, Ohio; died July 23, 1885, Mt. McGregor, N.Y. Named at birth Hiram Ulysses Grant. In 1848 married Julia Dent (1826–1902); they had four children.	Career soldier who graduated from U.S. Military Academy at West Point in 1843. Served in Mexican War, resigned commission in 1854, and returned to Army after unsuccessful business ventures in 1861. Because of his brilliant leadership in early battles, he was made commander of Union forces late in the Civil War.
19th **Rutherford Birchard Hayes** March 4, 1877–March 4, 1881	Born Oct. 4, 1822, Delaware, Ohio; died Jan. 17, 1893, Fremont, Ohio. In 1852 married Lucy Webb (1831–1889); they had eight children.	Graduated from Kenyon College in Ohio, 1842, and from Harvard School of Law, 1845. Began practice of law in Lower Sandusky, Ohio, and became solicitor of city of Cincinnati. Served in Civil War and was wounded.

United States Government

A carpetbagger

Completing the transcontinental railroad, 1869

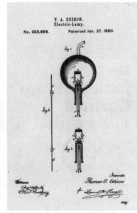

Edison's electric light, 1880

Political career	*Highlights in office*
After one unsuccessful attempt, elected to the Illinois state legislature as a Whig. Served as congressman from Illinois 1847–1849. Shifted to Republican Party established in 1854. Defeated in Senate race by Democrat Stephen A. Douglas, but his brilliance in the Lincoln-Douglas debates placed him in the front rank of antislavery Republicans and led to Republican nomination for President in 1860.	Southern states began to secede immediately following Lincoln's election to the Presidency. Lincoln began the Civil War to protect the Union, 1861. Issued Emancipation Proclamation that freed slaves in Southern states in 1863, and prepared 13th Amendment, which abolished slavery. Lincoln's many famous public addresses kept the North unified during the Civil War. Reelected in 1864, he was assassinated 43 days into his second term and five days after the Confederate surrender ended the war.
In Greenville, Tenn., elected alderman in 1828, mayor in 1830, and state representative in 1835. Served in Congress 1843–1853. Governor of Tennessee 1853–1857. Served in Senate 1857–1862. Opposed Lincoln in 1860, but was true to the Union and was named governor of occupied Tennessee in 1862. Chosen as Lincoln's running mate in 1864 to encourage return of Southern states to Union, and became President on Lincoln's assassination.	Stirred hostility by granting amnesty to Southern states and ratifying 13th Amendment abolishing slavery. Dismissed Secretary of War Edwin M. Stanton without required notification of Senate. For this the House voted to impeach him, but the Senate failed to convict by a single vote.
Appointed secretary of war by Andrew Johnson in 1867, but never confirmed by Congress. In 1868 was nominated for President by the Republicans as the hero of the Civil War, and he was elected in a close popular vote over Horatio Seymour (1810–1886), Democrat of New York.	Amnesty act for Confederate veterans and 15th Amendment to protect voting rights of all races passed during his administration. Was reelected in 1872. Grant's second administration was marred by mismanagement that permitted widespread corruption.
Congressman from Ohio 1864-1867. Governor of Ohio 1868–1872 and 1876–1877. Ran unsuccessfully for Congress, 1872.	Elected as Republican over Democrat Samuel J. Tilden in a disputed election finally decided by a special electoral commission appointed by Congress. Removed last occupation forces from the South and ended Reconstruction policies. Reformed the civil service to end evils permitted by Jackson's spoils system.

Name/Dates in office	Personal	Education/Occupation
20th **James Abram Garfield** March 4, 1881–Sept. 19, 1881	Born Nov. 19, 1831, Cuyahoga County, Ohio; died Sept. 19, 1881, Elberon, N.J.; assassinated by Charles J. Guiteau, who had been denied a government job. In 1858 married Lucretia Rudolph (1832–1918); they had seven children.	Graduated from Williams College in Massachusetts, 1856. Taught literature at Hiram College in Ohio and was its president from 1857 to 1861. Served in Civil War, distinguishing himself at Shiloh and Chickamauga.
21st **Chester Alan Arthur** Sept. 20, 1881–March 4, 1885	Born Oct. 5, 1830, Fairfield, Vt.; died Nov. 18, 1886, New York City. Son of a clergyman from Ireland. In 1859 married Ellen Herndon (1837–1880); they had three children.	Graduated from Union College in New York, 1848, and taught school at Pownall, Vermont. Studied law in New York City. Famous as an opponent of fugitive slave laws and of discrimination laws. Served in Civil War with New York militia.
22nd and 24th **Grover Cleveland** March 4, 1885–March 4, 1889 and March 4, 1893–March 4, 1897	Born March 18, 1837, Caldwell, N.J.; died June 24, 1908, Princeton, N.J. Married Frances Folsom (1864–1947) in an 1886 White House ceremony; they had five children, including two daughters born in the White House.	Never attended college. Taught at New York City Institution for the Blind and worked as a clerk in New York law offices. Admitted to the bar in 1859, and became a district attorney in Buffalo, New York, 1863.
23rd **Benjamin Harrison** March 4, 1889–March 4, 1893	Born Aug. 20, 1833, North Bend, Ohio; died March 13, 1901, Indianapolis, Ind. Grandson of ninth President, William Henry Harrison. In 1853 married Caroline Scott (1831–1892); they had two children. Married Mary Scott Dimmick (1859–1948) in 1896; they had a daughter.	Graduated from Miami University of Ohio, 1852. Was admitted to the bar in 1853 and began to practice law in Indianapolis. Served in the Civil War.
25th **William McKinley** March 4, 1897–Sept. 14, 1901	Born Jan. 29, 1843, Niles, Ohio; died Sept. 14, 1901, Buffalo, N.Y., one week after being shot by anarchist Leon Czolgosz. In 1871 married Ida Saxton (1847–1907); their two daughters both died in infancy.	Attended Allegheny College in Pennsylvania without graduating because his education was interrupted by service in the Civil War, 1861–1865. Studied law in Albany, N.Y., and in 1867 began practice in Canton, Ohio.
26th **Theodore Roosevelt** Sept. 14, 1901–March 4, 1909	Born Oct. 27, 1858, New York City; died Jan. 6, 1919, Oyster Bay, N.Y. A distant cousin of 32nd President Franklin D. Roosevelt. In 1880 married Alice Hathaway Lee (1861–1884); they had a daughter. After his wife's death, married Edith Kermit Carow (1861–1948) in 1886; they had five children.	Graduated from Harvard University, 1880; attended Columbia University Law School. Rancher and writer of travel and political books. Organized the cavalry troop known as the Rough Riders, fighting in Cuba in Spanish-American War. After leaving Presidency, pursued outdoor adventures, advocated conservation policies.

Political career	Highlights in office
Republican congressman from Ohio 1863–1880. Elected to the Senate in 1880, but never took his seat because he was elected to the Presidency that same year.	Began reform of postal system and efforts to establish better Latin-American relations, but was assassinated after only six months in office.
Collector of the Port of New York, 1871, but forced out by civil service reforms of President Hayes. Led a Republican faction called the "Stalwart Republicans" against Hayes. When Garfield was nominated by the Republicans in 1880, Arthur was given the Vice Presidential position to placate the Stalwarts.	Assumed Presidency upon assassination of Garfield in 1881. Continued the debate over civil service appointments, and signed into law the Civil Service Reform Act of 1883. Was not renominated for a second term by the Republicans.
Elected mayor of Buffalo, New York, in 1881, and governor of New York in 1882 as a Democrat who opposed the corruption of Tammany Hall Democrats in New York City. Elected President in 1884; defeated by Republican Benjamin Harrison in 1888; elected a second time (against Harrison) in 1892.	Labeled by the State Department the 22nd and 24th President because his terms were not consecutive. In first administration, he enlarged the civil service. In second administration, he introduced monetary reforms to counter economic depression caused by the Panic of 1893. Ended Pullman strike of 1894, a protracted railroad labor struggle. Desired a third term, but was not renominated in 1896.
Launched unsuccessful campaign for governor of Indiana in 1876. Served in Senate 1881–1887, and fought for government pension increases never granted by Grover Cleveland. Nominated by Republicans; defeated incumbent Cleveland in 1888. As an incumbent himself, was defeated by Cleveland in 1892.	Assisted in passage of Sherman Antitrust Act and expanded government pension system. Presided over era of territorial expansion that included admission to the Union of Idaho and Wyoming, homestead settlement of Oklahoma Territory, and acquisition of Samoa.
Congressman from Ohio 1877–1883 and 1885–1891. Defeated in reelection campaign for Congress in 1890, but elected governor of Ohio in 1892. Sought Presidential nomination in 1892; won it in 1896 and was elected over Democrat William Jennings Bryan (1860–1925) as a proponent of the gold standard monetary policy.	Opened the Spanish-American War after the battleship *Maine* was sunk in Havana harbor, Cuba, in 1898; the war ended in the same year when Spain ceded Puerto Rico, the Philippines, and Guam to the United States and granted independence to Cuba. Reelected in 1900, but was assassinated early in his second term.
Member of New York State Assembly 1882–1884, but left politics after death of first wife. Returned as member of U.S. Civil Service Commission, 1889–1895, and president of N.Y. Police Board, 1895–1897. Assistant secretary of Navy 1897–1898. As a war hero, elected governor of New York, 1898. Elected Vice President for McKinley's second term, 1900, he became President on McKinley's death. Reelected in 1904; deferred to fellow Republican Taft in 1908; defeated by Wilson in 1912.	Advocated "speak quietly but carry a big stick" foreign policy. Recognized Republic of Panama and planned canal there. Regulated big business and enforced antitrust laws. In 1905 negotiated peace between Russia and Japan and was awarded the Nobel Peace Prize.

An immigrant c 1900

The sinking of the Titanic, *1912*

John D. Rockefeller

Name/Dates in office	Personal	Education/Occupation
27th **William Howard Taft** March 4, 1909–March 4, 1913	Born Sept. 15, 1857, Cincinnati, Ohio; died March 8, 1930, Washington, D.C. In 1886 married Helen Herron (1861–1943); they had two sons.	Graduated from Yale University, 1878, and Cincinnati Law School, 1880. Was a law journalist in Cincinnati, and later a district attorney. After Presidency became professor of law at Yale, 1913–1931, and chief justice of the Supreme Court, 1921–1930.
28th **Woodrow Wilson** March 4, 1913–March 4, 1921	Born Dec. 28, 1856, Staunton, Va.; died Feb. 3, 1924, Washington, D.C. In 1885 married Ellen Axson (1860–1914); they had three daughters. After her death married Edith Bolling Galt (1872–1961), a widow who assisted Wilson during illness in second term.	Graduated from Princeton University, 1879; attended University of Virginia Law School; earned Ph.D. in political science at Johns Hopkins in 1886. Taught at Princeton, 1890–1910, and served as president of the university, 1902–1910.
29th **Warren Gamaliel Harding** March 4, 1921–Aug. 2, 1923	Born Nov. 2, 1865, Corsica (now Blooming Grove), Ohio; died Aug. 2, 1923, San Francisco, Calif., of natural causes while in office. In 1391 married Florence Kling DeWolfe (1860–1924).	Attended Ohio Central College. In 1884 brought the Marion (Ohio) *Star,* an increasingly influential newspaper under his ownership and the source of his early political power.
30th **Calvin Coolidge** Aug. 2, 1923–March 4, 1929	Born July 4, 1872, Plymouth, Vt.; died Jan. 5, 1933, Northampton, Mass. In 1905 married Grace Anna Goodhue (1879–1957); they had two sons.	Graduated from Amherst College in Massachusetts in 1895. Studied law and began practice in Northampton, Massachusetts.
31st **Herbert Hoover** March 4, 1929–March 4, 1933	Born Aug. 10, 1874, West Branch, Iowa; died Oct. 20, 1964, New York City. Raised on the Indian Territory (now Oklahoma). In 1899 married Lou Henry (1874–1944); they had two sons.	Graduated from Stanford University in 1891 as an engineer and worked for U.S. Geological Survey. As a mining engineer he worked in Asia, Australia, and Europe as well as the United States.

United States Government

Babe Ruth

Dust storm c 1930

Political career	*Highlights in office*
U.S. solicitor general, 1890. Appointed first civil governor of the Philippines, 1901. Secretary of war to Theodore Roosevelt, 1904, and provisional governor of Cuba, 1906. Adviser and protégé of Roosevelt, who supported him for Presidency in 1908. The two later disagreed; both campaigned for President in 1912, helping Democrat Woodrow Wilson win.	Continued antitrust policies of Roosevelt, dissolving Standard Oil and other monopolies. Founded the Department of Labor. Aided ratification of 16th Amendment, which authorized income taxes.
Governor of New Jersey 1911–1913. Received Democratic nomination for President in 1912 as a reform candidate supported by William Jennings Bryan to block the party's Tammany Hall political machine. Elected in 1912 when Taft and Theodore Roosevelt, as third-party candidate, split Republican vote. Reelected in 1916 on the slogan "he kept us out of war."	In first term, created Federal Reserve System and passed Clayton Antitrust Act. In second term, oversaw American involvement in World War I. Drafted Fourteen Points for world peace, which were accepted at Treaty of Versailles conference in 1919 and earned him the Nobel Peace Prize. The points included a League of Nations. The U.S. Senate refused to enter the league despite efforts by Wilson that ultimately ruined his health.
Member of Ohio state assembly 1900–1904, and lieutenant governor of Ohio 1904–1906. After an unsuccessful campaign for the governorship in 1910, was elected to the Senate in 1915. Elected President as a Republican in 1920 with a platform that included opposition to incumbent President Wilson's plans for a League of Nations.	Convened International Conference on Limitations of Armaments in 1921, which resulted in a treaty. The end of his two-year administration was marred by the Teapot Dome scandal, in which Secretary of the Interior Albert B. Fall (1861–1944) and Attorney General Harry Daugherty (1860–1941) were charged with corruption.
Member of Massachusetts state legislature 1912–1915. Lieutenant governor of Massachusetts 1916–1919, and governor 1919–1920. Became famous for ending Boston police strike of 1919. Nominated as Vice President in 1920 by the Republicans and succeeded when Harding died of natural causes.	Presided over era of economic prosperity. Reduced national debt, provided relief for farmers, and passed legislation beneficial to industry with the slogan "the business of America is business." Reelected in a landslide in 1924 but declined a further term in 1928.
Became famous as director of relief committees supplying food to countries devastated by World War I. Secretary of commerce to Presidents Harding and Coolidge, 1921–1928. Elected President as a Republican, 1928. Following Presidency headed "Hoover commissions" on government reform and founded Hoover Institute for political study.	Election followed by stock market crash of 1929 and general collapse of American economy. During subsequent Great Depression, Hoover opposed federal aid to unemployed and other welfare measures. Was defeated in 1932 by a landslide vote for Democrat Franklin D. Roosevelt.

Franklin Roosevelt

Victory in World War II, 1945

Growth of suburbia, 1950's

Name/Dates in office	Personal	Education/Occupation
32nd **Franklin Delano Roosevelt** March 4, 1933–April 12, 1945	Born Jan. 30, 1882, Hyde Park, N.Y.; died April 12, 1945, Warm Springs, Ga., while in office. In 1905 married Eleanor Roosevelt (1884–1962); they had six children, one dying in infancy. Paralyzed by polio in 1921, Roosevelt could stand or walk only with assistance.	Graduated from Harvard University, 1904, and attended Columbia University Law School. Practiced law in New York City.
33rd **Harry S. Truman** April 12, 1945–Jan. 20, 1953	Born May 8, 1884, Lamar, Mo.; died Dec. 26, 1972, Independence, Mo. In 1919 married Bess Wallace (1885–1982); they had one daughter.	After high school education in Independence, Missouri, worked a series of jobs and ran family farm. Served in World War I. Opened a clothing store and studied at Kansas City Law School.
34th **Dwight David Eisenhower** Jan. 20, 1953–Jan. 20, 1961	Born Oct. 14, 1890, Denison, Texas; died March 28, 1969, Washington, D.C. Raised in Abilene, Kansas. In 1916 married Mamie Geneva Doud (1896–1979); they had two sons, one of whom died in childhood.	Graduated from West Point, 1915. Rose in rank to Supreme Allied Commander in 1943, during World War II. Launched D-Day invasion in 1944 and accepted German surrender in 1945.
35th **John Fitzgerald Kennedy** Jan. 20, 1961–Nov. 22, 1963	Born May 29, 1917, Brookline, Mass.; died Nov. 22, 1963, Dallas Texas, assassinated while riding in a motorcade. In 1953 married Jacqueline Lee Bouvier (1929-1994); they had three children. One child died in infancy.	Graduated from Harvard University, 1940. Served in World War II as PT boat commander in Solomon Islands. Authored books, including *Profiles in Courage* (1953).
36th **Lyndon Baines Johnson** Nov. 22, 1963–Jan. 20, 1969	Born Aug. 27, 1908, near Stonewall, Texas; died Jan. 22, 1973, Johnson City, Texas. In 1934 married Claudia Alta (Lady Bird) Taylor (1912–); they had two daughters.	Graduated from Southwest Texas State Teachers College, 1930, and attended Georgetown University Law School in Washington, D.C., 1935. Taught public speaking in Houston, Texas, 1930–1932.

Khrushchev and Kennedy, 1963

Civil rights march, Selma, Alabama, 1965

Political career	*Highlights in office*
New York state senator 1910–1913. Assistant secretary of Navy 1913–1920. Unsuccessful candidate for Vice President 1920. Following recovery from polio attack, governor of New York, 1929–1933. Elected President by a landslide in 1932 and reelected three times, more than any other President.	Took office during Great Depression of 1930's. Obtained emergency powers for dispensing economic relief and proclaimed New Deal for the country. Fought with the Supreme Court over executive powers. Oversaw American involvement in World War II and pledged himself to protection of Four Freedoms (of speech, worship, want, and fear). Conferred with heads of allied countries several times during war, helping shape postwar world.
Served in a series of public offices and judgeships in Missouri until election to U.S. Senate in 1934. Served in Senate until 1945. Elected Vice President for Franklin D. Roosevelt's fourth term, and became President when Roosevelt died. Elected to full term in 1948 upset victory over Thomas E. Dewey.	Ordered atomic bombs dropped on Japanese cities of Hiroshima and Nagasaki to end Pacific combat in World War II. Created NATO and the Marshall Plan to protect and assist Europe after the war. Established the Truman Doctrine to protect countries from Russian interference. With U.N. approval, sent U.S. troops to protect South Korea.
After resignation from the Army, was considered as a Presidential candidate by both parties. Accepted Republican nomination in 1952 and was elected as a war hero over Democrat Adlai E. Stevenson. Reelected in 1956, again over Stevenson. Advised three subsequent Presidents.	Ended the Korean War, but supported American involvement in Southeast Asia, including Vietnam. Sent troops to enforce desegregation of schools in Little Rock, Arkansas, in 1957. Favored strong Cold War stance against Russia, but resisted military action and warned against power of the "military-industrial complex."
As representative from Massachusetts, served in the House 1947–1953, and the Senate 1953–1961. Nominated for President by Democrats in 1960, and defeated Republican candidate Richard Nixon, later 37th President, in part because of charm and intelligence in nationally televised Presidential debates.	Unsuccessfully attempted invasion of Cuba at Bay of Pigs; successfully blockaded Cuba until Russian missile bases there were removed. Blocked proposed increases in prices by steel industry. Preserved Western European and American presence in West Berlin despite Berlin wall isolating city. Began American program of manned space flights and promised a landing on the moon by 1970, which was accomplished after his death.
Appointed to Congress to fill a vacancy in 1937 and served until 1948. Elected to Senate in 1948 and 1954, and became Democratic leader. He was elected Vice President with President John F. Kennedy. Became President when Kennedy was assassinated, and was elected to a full term in 1964.	Launched Great Society programs to increase aid for education, housing, and medical care. Signed laws to protect civil rights and to reduce taxes. Johnson's second term was marred by the unpopular war in Vietnam. Although eligible, he did not seek reelection in 1968.

Footprint on the moon, 1969

John Dean, Watergate testimony, 1973

Bicentennial celebration, 1976

Name/Dates in office	Personal	Education/Occupation
37th **Richard Milhous Nixon** Jan. 20, 1969–Aug. 9, 1974	Born Jan. 9, 1913, Yorba Linda, Calif.; died Apr. 22, 1994, New York City. In 1940 married Thelma (Patricia) Ryan (1913-1993); they had two daughters.	Graduated from Whittier College, California, in 1934, and Duke University Law School in 1937. Practiced law in Whittier, Calif., and served in Navy during World War II.
38th **Gerald R. Ford** Aug. 9, 1974–Jan. 20, 1977	Born July 14, 1913, Omaha, Neb., named Leslie King; renamed after his stepfather. In 1948 married Elizabeth Bloomer Warren (1918–); they had four children.	Graduated from University of Michigan in 1935 and Yale Law School in 1941. Practiced law in Grand Rapids, Mich., before enlisting in Navy in 1942.
39th **Jimmy Carter** Jan. 20, 1977–Jan. 20, 1981	Born Oct. 1, 1924, Plains, Ga. Named James Earl Carter at birth, but was officially known as "Jimmy." In 1946 married Rosalynn Smith (1927–); they had four children.	Attended Georgia Tech and graduated from U.S. Naval Academy at Annapolis in 1946. Served in nuclear submarine program. After father's death in 1953 ran family peanut farm.
40th **Ronald Reagan** Jan. 20, 1981–Jan. 20, 1989	Born Feb. 6, 1911, Tampico, Ill. In 1940 married actress Jane Wyman (1914–); they had one child and adopted another. After a 1948 divorce, married Nancy Davis (1922–) in 1952; they also had two children.	Graduated from Eureka College in Illinois in 1932. Worked as a sports announcer and served in World War II. Became a major movie star, president of the Screen Actors Guild, and television spokesman.
41st **George H. Bush** Jan. 20, 1989–Jan. 20, 1993	Born June 12, 1924, Milton, Mass. In 1945 married Barbara Pierce (1925–); they had six children. One child died at a young age.	Served in the Navy from 1942 to 1945. Earned an economics degree at Yale University. Founded an oil company.
42nd **William J. Clinton** Jan. 20, 1993–	Born Aug. 19, 1946, Hope, Ark., named William Jefferson Blythe; renamed after his stepfather. In 1975 married Hillary Rodham (1948–). They had one child.	Graduated from Georgetown University in 1968 and Yale Law School in 1973. Rhodes scholar. Taught at University of Arkansas from 1973 to 1976.

Israeli-Egyptian peace accord

Burning oil wells in Kuwait following the Iraqi withdrawal

Political career	*Highlights in office*
U.S. congressman from California 1947–1951. Elected to Senate, 1950. Served as Vice President during both Eisenhower administrations. Republican candidate for President, 1960, defeated by John Kennedy. Elected President in 1968 and reelected in 1972.	Gradually ended American involvement in Vietnam. Visited China, recognized Communist regime there. Promoted cautious detente with Soviet Union. Second term disrupted by Watergate scandal. After House committee voted to impeach him, Nixon resigned August 9, 1974.
Served 25 years as Republican representative from Michigan, becoming Republican leader in the House. Appointed Vice President in 1973 following resignation of Spiro Agnew. Became President following resignation of Richard Nixon.	Granted Richard Nixon a pardon. Visited China in 1976. Vetoed numerous spending bills in pursuit of policy of fiscal austerity. Was defeated by Democrat Jimmy Carter in campaign for a full term in 1976.
Unsuccessful candidate for governor of Georgia in 1966, but elected governor as a Democrat in 1970. Limited by law to a single term, he then launched a marathon grass roots campaign for the Presidency. Elected President in 1976 over Republican incumbent Gerald R. Ford.	Initiated human rights programs and the Camp David peace talks between Israel and Egypt. His administration was marred by the Muslim takeover of the U.S. embassy in Teheran, Iran, and the holding of American hostages. He secured their release, but was defeated for reelection by Ronald Reagan.
Originally a Democrat, he became a Republican during Barry Goldwater's unsuccessful campaign for the Presidency in 1964. Served as governor of California 1967–1974. He was nominated for the Presidency in 1980 and defeated incumbent Jimmy Carter. He was reelected in 1984.	Administration launched sweeping tax cuts to fight economic recession. Nominated the first woman, Sandra Day O'Connor, to the Supreme Court. Initiated friendlier relations and an intermediate-range nuclear missile treaty with the Soviet Union. His second term was disrupted by the furor caused by the Iran Contra affair.
Elected to Congress as a Republican representative from Texas in 1966. Appointed U.S. delegate to the United Nations in 1970. In 1973 became Republican National chairman. Director of the CIA under President Ford. Elected Vice President under Reagan. Elected President in 1988.	Sent troops to Panama in December, 1989, to apprehend dictator Manuel Noriega. Nominated David Souter to replace William Brennan on the Supreme Court. Deployed American troops in the Persian Gulf as part of an international coalition that drove Iraqi invaders out of Kuwait in 1991.
Elected Arkansas state attorney general in 1976. Elected governor of Arkansas as a Democrat in 1978, he was defeated in 1980 but was returned to office in 1982. In 1992 he defeated incumbent George Bush for the Presidency.	Introduced sweeping and controversial economic program to control government spending and reduce the deficit. Initiated effort to reform national health care system.

People of the United States

The population of the United States consists of many different groups of people, called ethnic groups. Individual members of ethnic groups may not live together in the same city, or even the same state, but they share a common background or characteristic, such as race, national origin, or culture.

This section describes the biggest ethnic groups in the United States. For each group, we learn how they came here, what special problems they faced, and what they have contributed to the society and culture. The section begins with Native Americans, the first people to arrive in America, and then covers the other major groups: European-Americans, African-Americans, Asian-Americans, and Hispanic-Americans. For more information about the American people, see the United States History and United States Today sections in Volume 1.

Native Americans

About a million Native Americans already occupied territories of the United States when European settlers arrived in the late 1500's and early 1600's. These first Americans had evolved a primitive but stable culture long before the Europeans appeared. They had farmed and hunted for thousands of years and adapted their life-styles to living with the land.

Native Americans made many important contributions to the development of colonial America. Colonists generally depended on the Native Americans for food and help during the first difficult years in America. Native American agriculture, especially the growing of corn, helped colonists survive and prosper. But the Native Americans' land became their most important contribution. White settlers pushing westward slowly forced the Native Americans off nearly all their lands from the Atlantic to the Pacific coasts.

Today the most obvious reminder of our Native American heritage can be found in place-names dotting the map of the United States. Rivers like the Mississippi (Chippewa for "big river") and the Susquehanna ("muddy river"), the Shenandoah valley ("daughter of the skies"), and the Mojave Desert ("three mountains") all come to us from Native American words. So do city names such as Chicago ("place of the bad smell"), Spokane ("sun warrior"), Waukegan ("trading post"), Miami ("the peninsula people"), and Poughkeepsie ("at the little rock water"). Twenty-six states have names derived from Native American words.

Many Native American contributions are taken for granted today. Corn and tobacco became important cash crops in colonial America and remain valued commodities. Canoes, kayaks, toboggans, pipes for smoking tobacco, hammocks, moccasins, and parkas all come to us from Native American cultures as well. Native American fighting techniques influenced military tactics and figured in some successful battles against the British during the American Revolution. Even the game of lacrosse, the oldest sport on the North American continent, comes from the Ojibwa game baggataway.

History of Native Americans

Earliest period. The first Native Americans arrived in North America some 10,000 to 20,000 years ago. These first Americans were probably big game hunters and fishermen who migrated from Siberia to Alaska by way of a land bridge that disappeared about 8000 B.C. From Alaska, they moved southward and spread out over much of the continental United States, as well as into Central and South America.

The first peoples in what is now the United States hunted mammoths and other large animals. After about 7000 B.C., hunting of smaller game, fishing, and gathering of food from wild plants became more important. Finally, about 2500 B.C., the so-called Desert People in the Southwest learned how to cultivate corn from tribes farther south in modern-day Mexico. By about 1000 B.C. they had also learned to grow squash and kidney beans from the same people. Knowledge of plant cultivation then spread across the continent. Native Americans as far away as the Northeast developed primitive farming cultures by the first century A.D.

Farming encouraged a more stable way of life among the Native Americans, promoted greater social organization, and fostered development of crafts and

Siberian natives, like the one shown here, migrated to Alaska and thus became the first Native Americans.

art forms. The Pueblos of the Southwest, for example, developed a thriving village culture based on farming. They constructed large multistory housing complexes of sun-dried bricks (adobe), and had a well-organized local government and religion.

States with Native American names

State	Meaning	Native American Word
Alabama	I open the thicket	Choctaw *alba ayamule*
Alaska	great land	Inuit *Alakshak*
Arizona	place of the small spring	Papago *Arizonac*
Arkansas	land of south wind people	Arkansas tribal name
Connecticut	at the long tidal river	Mohican *quinnitukqut*
Idaho	light on the mountains	Shoshone term
Illinois	warriors	Algonquian *iliniwek*
Iowa	the sleepy one	Dakota *Ayuba*
Kansas	south wind people	Sioux term
Kentucky	meadow land	Iroquois *Kentake*
Massachusetts	at the big hill	Algonquian term
Michigan	big water	Chippewa *mica gama*
Minnesota	sky blue water	Dakota Sioux term
Mississippi	big river	Chippewa *mici sibi*
Missouri	muddy water	Algonquian term
Nebraska	river in the flatness	Omaha *ni-bthaska*
North/South Dakota	friend or ally	Sioux term
Ohio	beautiful water	Iroquois *Oheo*
Oklahoma	the red people	Choctaw term
Oregon	beautiful water	possibly Algonquian *Wauregan*
Tennessee	unknown	Cherokee village name
Texas	friend or ally	local Indian term
Utah	the upper land	Navajo term
Wisconsin	grassy place	Algonquian name of river
Wyoming	at the big flats	Algonquian *mache-weaming*

In the Southeast, the Five Civilized Tribes also built towns, complete with streets, a center square, and up to 2000 residents. To the north, around the Great Lakes, the Iroquois created the most advanced political organization of their time--the Iroquois Confederacy. This body promoted peace between member tribes and provided for common defense from enemies. None of the North American tribes developed a true writing system, however, until after the Europeans came.

Meanwhile, the Plains tribes learned to use horses from the Spanish in the 1600's. Horse-mounted warriors became fierce and proficient fighters, especially against the U.S. Army during the Indian war of the late 1800's.

European colonists. When the European colonists began arriving in the late 1500's and early 1600's, most of the million or so Native Americans in the United States lived east of the Mississippi. The 200 or more tribes had distinct cultures and spoke many different languages. Most of the tribes based their cultures on farming. Though some tribes were more warlike than others, Indians generally coexisted peacefully.

Native Americans and colonists had fairly good relations at first. At the Jamestown Colony in Virginia and Plymouth Colony in Massachusetts, Native Americans provided colonists with food when supplies ran short. They even taught the colonists how to plant

Instead of relying on hunting and fishing, many Native American tribes planted crops. Here two farmers are scaring away crows.

Geronimo (1829-1909). One of the great chiefs of the 19th century, Geronimo was a leader of the Chiricahua Apaches. This tribe lived along the U.S.-Mexican border and frequently raided settlements in the 1870's and 1880's. Geronimo surrendered for the last time in September of 1886, and was imprisoned in Florida. In 1894 the government allowed him to move to Indian Territory at Fort Sill, Oklahoma. Later, he made personal appearances, including one in Theodore Roosevelt's inaugural parade. Geronimo dictated his memoirs, *Geronimo: His Own Story*, to S. S. Barrett.

---

corn and other New World crops. At first, the colonists respected the Native Americans' sovereignty over their tribal land.

What no one realized, however, was that European explorers and colonists brought with them diseases that the indigenous peoples had never before been exposed to. As a result, contagious diseases like smallpox devastated whole tribes. These outbreaks of plague during the 1600's began reducing the total Native American population; this depopulation was later continued as a result of the Indian Wars and poor nutrition. The decline lasted to about 1900, when there were only about 250,000 Native Americans. After that the Native American population began growing again.

The first wars between Native Americans and colonists started in the 1600's. At Jamestown, colonists' demands for more land on which to grow tobacco sparked the bloody Powhatan War, which lasted from 1622 to 1644. Most of the Native Americans in the area were killed and the settlers took over nearly all their land. Similarly, the Pequot War in Connecticut in 1637 broke out over pressure for land. The war ended with the slaughter of nearly all Pequot Indians.

Other Indian Wars during colonial times were fought over demands for Native American land. At times, Native Americans also became involved in fighting between the British and French. Among these later colonial wars were King Philip's War (1675-1676), the French and Indian Wars (1689-1763), Pontiac's War (1763), and Lord Dunmore's War (1774). During the American Revolution, Native American tribes fought on both the American and the British sides.

The Indian Wars. Westward expansion by white settlers became more intense after the late 1700's. The U.S. government at first tried buying Native American land and setting aside enclaves for the original Americans. But fighting between whites and Native Americans became frequent, and in 1830 the government passed the Indian Removal Act.

Chief Crazy Horse, decorated in spotted war paint, helped defeat the U.S. cavalry in the Battle of Little Big Horn.

By this law, the U.S. military forced some hundred thousand Native Americans from their homes east of the Mississippi and moved them far westward to Indian Territory. The new homeland stretched from the Missouri River to the Oregon Territory and was to belong to the Native Americans "as long as the rivers shall run." White settlers, of course, then took over the Native Americans' original land.

The strongest resistance to the law came from the Five Civilized Tribes in the Southeast, but to no avail. The 15,000 Cherokees called their tragic march westward in 1838 and 1839 the Trail of Tears. About 4000 Cherokees died from sickness and exhaustion. About one-quarter of the Native Americans from all tribes sent to the Indian Territory during the 1830's died en route.

By the 1850's, the resettled Native Americans again faced pressure from land-hungry settlers moving westward. In the 1850's alone, the U.S. government negotiated treaties, many times by unfair means, for 174 million acres of Indian land. Even so, white settlers demanded still more.

The Sioux Wars began in Wyoming in 1854. By the 1860's Cheyenne, Apache, and other tribes farther south also resisted attempts to take their land or force them onto reservations. There were bloody massacres by both sides, but the Battle of Little Bighorn in 1876 was probably the most famous. Sitting Bull's Sioux and Cheyenne warriors overwhelmed General George Custer's cavalry unit and killed all 264 men.

The capture and imprisonment of the Apache Geronimo in 1886 all but ended military resistance by the Indians. There remained only the final tragedy of Wounded Knee in 1890, in which some 200 starving Sioux were massacred after leaving their reservation.

The new way of life. From the late 1800's, the federal government actively tried to suppress the Native Americans' tribal culture. The government wanted to make Native Americans self-sufficient and to educate them for eventual assimilation into mainstream American society.

The so-called allotment system passed by Congress in 1887 became the cornerstone of this program.

The law tried to make Native Americans self-sufficient ranchers by giving each family head 160 acres of reservation land. As it worked out, the Native American landowners first rented, then sold, their land to whites. By 1934, when the system was abolished, tribal holdings had been reduced by nearly two-thirds.

The Indian Reorganization Act of 1934 became the Native Americans' "New Deal." It ended the allotment system, reversed the policy of forced assimilation, restored tribal lands, granted religious freedom, and expanded educational and social programs. Other laws tried to help raise the standard of living of Native Americans, who had been poorly educated and were living in extreme poverty.

The 1940's brought other important changes for the Native Americans. Until World War II, most Native Americans had lived on reservations. But good-paying jobs began drawing them into urban areas, a trend that continued for decades afterward. Their service in combat during the war also gained the Native Americans greater recognition.

After again flirting with forced assimilation policies in the 1950's, the federal government adopted its current policy of self-determination. This policy encourages tribal self-government and cultural renewal while trying to raise the Native Americans' standard of living. Many federal programs enacted in the 1960's and 1970's were designed to improve economic and social conditions.

Native American activism. In the 20th century, many Native Americans have resorted to legal and political action instead of violence to resist white domination. While not always successful in the early 1900's, Indians nevertheless made important strides.

The Society of American Indians, for example, was organized in 1911 to promote collective action by the tribes. The group helped win passage of a law granting Native Americans U.S. citizenship in 1924, an important early victory. Another notable group, the National Congress of American Indians, was founded in 1944 to promote Native American rights through legislative action.

On another front, the Indian Claims Commission reviewed land transactions in which tribes claimed they had been cheated. By the time the commission finished in the 1970's, it had awarded about $800 million in compensation to Native Americans for stolen lands and broken treaties.

The civil rights and counterculture movements of the 1960's brought about a new, more militant phase in Indian activism. The American Indian Movement (AIM) of 1968, led by Dennis Banks, was among the militant groups that promoted civil disobedience, as evidenced by the takeover of Alcatraz in 1969. Hoping to dramatize the plight of Native Americans, AIM

Schools have been established in which Native American children are taught in both English and their native language.

activists occupied the Wounded Knee massacre site in 1973. The highly publicized standoff with government officials lasted 71 days and claimed three lives. Political activism by Native Americans has continued since then, but with far less militancy.

Native Americans today.
About 1.96 million people of Native American descent now live in the United States, and over 544 tribes or tribal groups are officially recognized by the U.S. government. The largest tribes, according to Census Bureau figures, are the Cherokee (308,000), Navajo (219,000), and Sioux (103,000) tribes.

The great majority of Native Americans now live west of the Mississippi River. California, Oklahoma, Arizona, and New Mexico have the highest Native American populations of all states. Of Eastern states, North Carolina and New York have the biggest Native American populations with some 80,000 and 62,000 respectively.

Once concentrated on reservations, Native Americans are now almost as likely to be found living in cities. Drawn by prospects of good-paying jobs, large numbers of Native Americans have settled in Los Angeles, the San Francisco Bay area, Tulsa and Oklahoma City, New York City, Phoenix, and other major cities.

Native Americans have adapted to urban life in different ways. The more successful work in professional and other white-collar occupations and can be found living in middle-class neighborhoods. Skilled laborers, like Iroquois steel construction workers, may live in city neighborhoods dominated by Native Americans. While these two groups may show little outward sign of

People of the United States

their ethnic background, they often continue to celebrate their heritage with pride and keep up tribal contacts.

Another group of Native American urban dwellers keeps in closer contact with the reservation and tribal culture. These workers shuttle back and forth between reservations and cities, where they take advantage of seasonal jobs.

Native American reservations. Many Native Americans still prefer life on tribal reservations. Some do not want to break emotional and cultural bonds with their people. Others may lack skills needed for jobs outside the reservation. Still others may have found the demands of city life greater than the rewards. The tribe offers these Native Americans such a strong sense of community that they prefer to remain on the reservation rather than suffer the cultural isolation of the city.

Today there are about 300 federal Native American reservations covering about 52 million acres. The largest is the 14-million-acre Navajo reservation, but others are as small as a few acres. Some states also have set aside land for Native American reservations. There are 21 of these sites, located mainly in the East.

A special relationship exists between the U.S. government and the tribes based on reservations. The government takes broad responsibility for protecting Native American property, for protecting the right of self-government, and for providing social services to help tribes to survive and advance. This does not mean that Native Americans are government wards, however. Instead, the tribal government is something like a state government.

Within the limits of federal regulations, tribes govern themselves, make and enforce laws, regulate land use and development of resources, and get subsidies for social services--just the way state governments do. Most tribes are governed by a tribal council, headed by an elected chief or president.

While many Native Americans on reservations still live in poverty, prospects for future improvement are good, largely because of current policies favoring self-determination and restoration of tribal culture. Tribes now have greater control over their affairs, and being better educated and better organized, are much less likely to be exploited than in the past. Some tribes have even formed successful business enterprises based on tourism, investment of tribal funds, or development of industry and natural resources on reservations.

Most Native Americans feel a greater sense of pride than ever before. Today there is more public acceptance of, and interest in, the Native American cultural heritage. Native American craftsmen have long produced jewelry, pottery, and traditional artifacts for a steady market of tourists and collectors. But today Native American artists have also gained acceptance in the world of fine arts, literature, theater, and film.

European-Americans

European ethnic groups, and the English in particular, have had the greatest impact on American culture and society. From colonial times, the European peoples have formed the majority of America's population. They still dominate today, though the non-European population is steadily growing larger.

English immigrants, called Anglo-Americans, have made far too many cultural contributions to do more than outline them here. English people founded and governed the original 13 colonies until their independence. The English colonists gave America a language, law, literature, and numerous traditions, which together provided a firm foundation for the new American society.

Place-names like New England, New York, and New Jersey are just one reminder of the English heritage of the United States. In fact, even after independence, Americans of English descent dominated the U.S. government. George Washington, the first President, was Anglo-American, and over half the other Presidents had at least some English blood.

Anglo-Americans also became leading figures in other walks of life, from skilled trades to business and finance, from science to literature and the arts.

While the English dominated American society during its early days, other European ethnic groups made important contributions as well. Like the English, the Scots came to America in large numbers, especially in the South, New Jersey, and Pennsylvania. Scottish-Americans became noted political leaders, authors, educators, and inventors. German-Americans gave us notable scientists, engineers, and business leaders. Irish- and Italian-Americans produced powerful urban political leaders. Scandinavian-Americans became successful farmers in the Midwest. The list goes on and on.

There are many millions of unsung heroes. European-Americans labored to clear the land, plant and harvest crops; they built homes, stores, factories, and public buildings, as well as roads, bridges, and railroads that tied the nation together. And while a few rose to become captains of industry, millions inched

Only faint ruins remain of the Lost Colony of Roanoke (1587), an English settlement that vanished, its people's fate unknown.

the American economy forward by working day-in and day-out mining coal, sewing garments, assembling automobiles, or just minding the store.

History of European-Americans

Europeans arrive in America. After Columbus discovered the New World, the Spanish focused their colonizing efforts on Central and South America. By 1600, Spain's North American settlements were limited to outposts in St. Augustine in Florida and a few Spanish missions in what became the American Southwest. The English, meanwhile, actively explored the Atlantic coast of North America and in the early 1600's established permanent English colonies there.

The first, a trading post at Jamestown, Virginia, was started by 104 colonists in the spring of 1607. However, the settlers proved unprepared for the hardships of life in America, and 58 died by fall. The rest nearly starved that winter, and only food given by local tribes kept them alive. The following summer, more ships with more colonists arrived. But when winter came, colonists again perished in a terrible "starving time," which claimed some 400 lives and left only 60 colonists in Jamestown.

Still more colonists arrived, however, and with help from tribal neighbors, Jamestown eventually prospered. In 1619 Jamestown established the first representative government in North America; the colonists there also built America's first Anglican church.

Settlers at Plymouth Colony, the first English colony in New England, faced similar hardships. But some of them had an added reason for wanting to succeed in America; about three dozen were Pilgrims, Protestant separatists then being persecuted in England for their religious beliefs. Pilgrims became the first of many immigrants who came to America seeking religious freedom.

After a stormy passage from England aboard the *Mayflower*, the Pilgrims and other settlers landed on the Massachusetts coast on December 26, 1620. Low

on food and lacking adequate shelter, about half the 101 settlers died the first winter. Then pirates captured the colony's first London-bound shipment of trade goods, including beaver pelts, sassafras, and clapboard, and merchants in London balked at sending more supplies.

The Pilgrims refused to give up, however. A friendly Native American named Squanto showed them how to plant corn and new Pilgrim settlers continued arriving at Plymouth Colony. On October 21, 1621, the Pilgrims celebrated a bountiful harvest by sharing the first Thanksgiving feast with local Native Americans. Thanksgiving became a national holiday over two centuries later, by proclamation of President Abraham Lincoln in 1863.

Plymouth Colony faded in importance after 1630, when the much larger Massachusetts Bay Colony, centered on Boston, was founded by the English Puritan John Winthrop. Before the end of the year, some thousand colonists had settled there. They established a Puritan theocracy, which governed the colony along strict Puritan lines until Massachusetts became a royal colony in 1686. Colonists at Cambridge printed the first book in the colonies, the *Bay Psalm Book*.

English-dominated America. Despite the hardships, other English colonies sprang up along the Atlantic coast during the 1600's. English Catholics seeking refuge from Protestant-dominated England founded Maryland in 1634; settlers in Connecticut accepted a colonial governor in 1636; and religious dissenter Roger Williams founded Rhode Island Colony in 1636, granting complete religious tolerance.

Meanwhile, the Dutch founded New Netherland Colony in 1621 and established a thriving port city on Manhattan Island. Soon afterward Sweden set up a small colony, New Sweden, along the Delaware River. Colonists there introduced the log cabin about 1638, a type of dwelling that became common throughout early America.

Neither the Dutch nor the Swedes remained in control long, however. Soon after New Netherland seized New Sweden (1655), the English captured New Netherland (1664), renaming it New York. The English clearly dominated the Eastern seaboard at this point.

English colonists made up the bulk of immigrants who came to America between 1607 and 1680. Many came seeking economic gain as landowners, fur traders, fishermen, and merchants. Others came to escape religious persecution. But the newly established colonies desperately needed laborers, and better than half the immigrants came as indentured servants who worked for five years to repay their passage to America.

Convicts were also sent to labor in the colonies. African slaves were imported mainly between 1680 and 1810, usually to work on plantations in the South.

New England, meanwhile, suffered no shortage of workers because of the so-called Great Migration. Sparked by religious intolerance, food shortages, and a sagging economy in England, the Great Migration became the first of many immigrant waves to reach America. This one, lasting from about 1630 to 1643, brought some 20,000 English Puritans, Baptists, Presbyterians, and others to New England. These colonists fanned out to various parts of New England, clearing land for farms and establishing new settlements.

Quakers, another group of religious dissenters, flocked to Pennsylvania some years later. Quaker William Penn established the Pennsylvania Colony as a haven from English religious persecution and founded Philadelphia, "the City of Brotherly Love," in 1682. Within three years, some 7000 Quakers had settled there, and Philadelphia eventually became one of America's leading cities.

Though English settlers were by far the largest group in the American colonies, small numbers of other European nationalities also settled there. When the English captured New York from the Dutch in 1664, for example, they found the city had already become a cosmopolitan center. People from 18 different countries lived there--including Italians, Norwegians, Danes, Germans, Poles, Swedes, French, and Spaniards.

After the late 1600's and on into the 1700's, about 15,000 French Protestants, called Huguenots, fled to America to escape religious persecution in their homeland. Faneuil Hall, a famous meeting place for colonial patriots in Boston, was built and donated to the city by a Huguenot. German and Dutch settlers founded Germantown, Pennsylvania, which became an early colonial center of printing and publishing. In 1686 German Quakers at Germantown raised the first protest against slavery in America. Years later, in 1755, another German-American, a New York newspaper publisher named Peter Zenger, helped establish freedom of the press by winning a lawsuit against his paper.

A growing ethnic diversity. Germans became the first large non-English immigrant group in America. Driven from Germany by wars and religious persecutions, some 3000 migrated to New York in 1710 alone; 200,000 German Lutherans, Baptists, Mennonites, and others followed during the 1700's. Most settled in Pennsylvania, where they became known as the Pennsylvania Dutch. Others went to Virginia, Maryland, the Carolinas, and Georgia.

About 200,000 Protestant Scotch-Irish also flooded into Pennsylvania during the 1700's. From about 1730, they also moved into the western frontier territories of the Southern colonies. Scottish Highlanders migrated to North Carolina's western frontier from about the 1760's.

Many of the German and Scotch-Irish immigrants who came to America in the 1700's and 1800's were redemptioners. Like the indentured servants before them, they repaid the cost of their passage to America by working as servants for two to seven years. Here, though, redemptioners contracted directly with ship captains, who sold their contracts on arriving in America. Like slaves, redemptioners had no say in choosing their masters or the work they were to do. When one redemptioner died during the crossing, others could be forced to compensate the captain's loss by working a longer stint.

Some 2000 Spanish and Portuguese Jews fleeing persecution in their homelands also immigrated to America in the 1700's. Many settled in New York and Rhode Island. Jewish settlers at Newport, Rhode Island, built the oldest synagogue in the United States in 1763.

European-Americans and the Revolution. European-Americans played key roles in the Revolution. Colonial patriot Patrick Henry was a Scottish-American. Thomas Paine, an Anglo-American, published the famous pamphlet *Common Sense*, which favored American independence. Thomas Jefferson, a Welsh-American, drafted the Declaration of Independence, and Swedish-American John Morton cast the deciding vote for it at the Continental Congress.

Though aided by European nationals such as Lafayette, Rochambeau, Kosciusko, and Pulaski, European-Americans themselves bore the real burden of the American Revolution. Paul Revere was of

Faneuil Hall was built in 1742 by primarily English immigrants who had settled in Boston, Massachusetts.

Ancestry of U.S. presidents

The Constitution of the United States was drafted by the Federal Constitutional Convention meeting in Philadelphia.

President/Term	Ancestry
George Washington, 1789-1797	English
John Adams, 1797-1801	English, Welsh
Thomas Jefferson, 1801-1809	Welsh
James Madison, 1809-1817	English, Welsh
James Monroe, 1817-1825	Scottish
John Quincy Adams, 1825-1829	English, Welsh
Andrew Jackson, 1829-1837	Scotch-Irish
Martin Van Buren, 1837-1841	Dutch
William Henry Harrison, 1841	English, Welsh
John Tyler, 1841-1845	English, French
James Polk, 1845-1849	Scotch-Irish
Zachary Taylor, 1849-1850	English
Millard Fillmore, 1850-1853	English
Franklin Pierce, 1853-1857	English
James Buchanan, 1857-1861	Scotch-Irish
Abraham Lincoln, 1861-1865	English
Andrew Johnson, 1865-1869	English
Ulysses S. Grant, 1869-1877	English, Scottish
Rutherford Hayes, 1877-1881	Scottish
James Garfield, 1881	English, French
Chester Arthur, 1881-1885	Scotch-Irish
Grover Cleveland, 1885-1889; 1893-1897	English, Irish
Benjamin Harrison, 1889-1893	English
William McKinley, 1897-1901	Scotch-Irish
Theodore Roosevelt, 1901-1909	Dutch, French
William H. Taft, 1909-1913	English
Woodrow Wilson, 1913-1921	Scotch-Irish
Warren Harding, 1921-1923	English, Dutch
Calvin Coolidge, 1923-1929	English
Herbert Hoover, 1929-1933	Swiss, German
Franklin D. Roosevelt, 1933-1945	Dutch, French
Harry S. Truman, 1945-1953	English, Scotch-Irish
Dwight Eisenhower, 1953-1961	Swiss, German
John F. Kennedy, 1961-1963	Irish
Lyndon B. Johnson, 1963-1969	English
Richard M. Nixon, 1969-1974	English, Scotch-Irish
Gerald Ford, 1974-1977	English
Jimmy Carter, 1977-1981	English
Ronald Reagan, 1981-1989	English, Scotch-Irish
George Bush, 1989-1993	English
Bill Clinton, 1993-	English

French descent. George Washington, an Anglo-American, took command of the colonials' Continental Army, which, by one estimate, was 38 percent Irish-American. Naval hero John Paul Jones was born in Scotland, and German General Baron von Steuben, who became an American citizen, helped organize and train the colonial army. Polish-born Jewish-American patriot Haym Solomon, a banker, lost most of his fortune through loans to help finance the Revolution.

After the Revolution, Anglo-American George Washington presided over the Constitutional Convention and Anglo-American James Madison played a major role in shaping the Constitution. With the Constitution adopted, Washington became the first of many American Presidents of English ancestry (see accompanying table). During his administration, John Jay, of French Huguenot descent, became the first chief justice of the Supreme Court. Alexander Hamilton, also of French ancestry, helped set up the nation's fiscal system.

In following years, European-Americans also helped develop American commerce and industry. For example, Samuel Slater, an Anglo-American, founded the American cotton mill industry not long after the Revolution. Soap manufacturer William Colgate, another Anglo-American, got his start in 1806. During the early 1800's, German-born John Jacob Astor became a leader in the American fur trade, and the Irish-American inventor Robert Fulton built the first practical steamboat, *Clermont*. Scottish-American inventor Peter Cooper built America's first locomotive, Tom Thumb, and the famous McCormick reaper was invented by Scottish-American Cyrus McCormick in 1831. Finally, the Irish-American inventor Samuel Morse revolutionized communications in 1844 with his telegraph system.

Meanwhile, the complexion of the European-American population in the United States changed rapidly during the 1800's. The first census taken in 1790 had already revealed a trend toward ethnic diversity in America: Of the 3.9 million people counted, about 60 percent were of English ancestry; another 14 percent were Scotch-Irish or Scottish; 9 percent German; 4 percent Irish Catholic; and the rest other nationalities. But by the end of the 1800's, the population mushroomed to some 76 million people, and a far greater number were non-English European-Americans.

Give me your tired, your poor. The United States was just under two decades old when the 1800's began. Yet the new nation possessed seemingly boundless natural resources. The great westward expansion was beginning, and there was land for all who wanted it. America lacked just one thing, people.

The difficult passage to America

European immigrants land on the tip of Manhattan Island after passing through the immigration station on Ellis Island.

Poor European immigrants boarding sailing ships for America usually had little idea of what to expect on the long transatlantic voyage. In fact, the trip often proved an unwelcome test of endurance and physical stamina. Depending on the winds, the ship might take anywhere from four to fourteen weeks or more to reach America. Meanwhile, most passengers found themselves packed into overcrowded steerage compartments where they endured hunger, storms, and sickness. A significant number did not live to see America.

Steerage was the cheapest accommodation in the days of sailing ships. It was an enclosed compartment, usually with a very low ceiling, located below the main deck. The only sunlight and ventilation came by way of an overhead hatch. Into these dirty, unhealthy quarters, unscrupulous ship captains booked hundreds of unsuspecting passengers, well beyond the normal capacity.

Immigrant passengers were allowed up on the main deck for only an hour or two each day, and they slept on narrow wooden bunks set side by side on either side of the steerage compartment. In the cramped quarters below, fights sometimes broke out between passengers and sailors. Sailors also sometimes stole passengers' belongings and attacked unwary immigrant girls. At times steerage passengers even had to work during their crossing; they might do laundry, work in the galley, wash decks, or help crewmen by handling lines.

Steerage passengers usually had to bring and prepare their own food as well. Typically, immigrants ate dried herring, potatoes, barley soup, prunes, and watery coffee. Vinegar was added to drinking water to make it potable during the voyage. Even these slim rations ran short when voyages took longer than expected, which they often did.

Weakened by inadequate diet and living in cramped, unsanitary conditions aboard ship, immigrant passengers frequently became ill with diarrhea, trench mouth, scurvy, cholera, and other diseases. By the mid 1800's, an average one out of six steerage passengers died. On some of the worst ships, about a quarter died en route.

Storms turned the immigrants' misery into a hellish nightmare. With hatches covered and heavy seas crashing over the decks, immigrants remained trapped in steerage for days on end. Amid screams as the ship tossed about roughly, passengers confronted the terror of storms at sea, sometimes without so much as a lantern for light.

Literally millions of European immigrants suffered through these hardships before transatlantic steamships revolutionized ocean travel in the late 1800's. Roomier, cleaner accommodations for even the poorest passengers and shorter travel time made crossing the Atlantic relatively easy.

That changed between 1815 and the 1920's. A flood of some 35 million immigrants--most of them Europeans--arrived on American shores. The incoming tide rose steadily during the 1800's and from 1815 to 1890, 15 million people came. The crest peaked in 1882, when 800,000, mostly European, immigrants arrived in a single year. Yet the millions of immigrants who came during the early 1900's dwarfed even that figure.

The new arrivals came from all walks of life--there were paupers, laborers, farmers, craftsmen, shopkeepers, artists, and intellectuals--and their reasons for coming were as diverse as the people themselves. Circumstances like overpopulation, famine, war, changes in agriculture, and unemployment caused by the Industrial Revolution pushed many to seek a new start in America. For example, during the 1800's, successive waves of displaced English, German, and Scandinavian farmers migrated to the Midwest and West, where they built new farms.

The Irish potato famine also caused a huge surge in immigration. During the first half of the 19th century, the population of Ireland doubled and tenant farmers there came to depend on the potato as their staple crop. But a blight destroyed Ireland's potato crop between 1845 and 1849, causing a famine that killed some 500,000 people. Farmers who could not pay their rent lost their land, and between 1845 and 1855 about 1.5 million Irish refugees emigrated to America. Most of them settled in cities along the East Coast, eventually finding work as construction laborers, shopkeepers, and factory workers.

Increasingly after 1860, it was work that drew Europeans to the United States. They came in droves, responding to the demand for railroad construction workers, miners, and factory workers, as well as the promise of get-rich-quick business opportunities.

The Civil War and its aftermath. The Union army recruited heavily from the European immigrant communities in the North, and immigrant leaders put together whole regiments of volunteers from their ethnic groups. The Irish alone contributed 38 such regiments. The South also formed immigrant units, including Irish and German soldiers, but had relatively few immigrants within its borders.

The key figures in the Civil War also came from various European ethnic groups. President Abraham Lincoln was of English descent, and Jefferson Davis, president of the Confederacy, was a Scottish-American. Both the key generals during the war, Robert E. Lee and Ulysses S. Grant, were also of Scottish descent. Judah P. Benjamin, a Jewish American, was the Confederate secretary of state.

After the Civil War, industry in the United States began growing rapidly. European-American workers provided much of the labor needed to build and run the new industries, but they also became captains of the emerging corporations. One of the most successful industrialists was Scottish-born Andrew Carnegie, who organized the Carnegie Steel Company. The German-American merchant John Wanamaker founded the famous Philadelphia department store in 1875, while other notable German-Americans made their mark in the world of foods. For example, Henry J. Heinz founded the H.J. Heinz Company. The Hershey Chocolate Company was started in the late 1800's by Milton Hershey.

European-Americans were also among the foremost inventors and builders. Alexander Graham Bell, inventor of the telephone, was born in Scotland. John A. Roebling, a German-American, designed the Brooklyn Bridge, an engineering marvel. When completed in 1883, it was the world's longest suspension bridge.

Immigrants from southern and eastern Europe. The late 1800's brought a distinct shift in the origins of Europeans emigrating to America. While new arrivals continued to come from England, Scotland, Ireland, Germany, France, and other parts of northern Europe, immigrants from southern and eastern Europe now made up the larger share. Italians, Poles, Russians, and others came in huge numbers, driven by population increases and the spread of industrialization in their homelands. These immigrants tended to settle in ethnic neighborhoods in cities, rather than on farms, because much of America's farmland had already been settled.

Jews came to America from Russia and elsewhere in eastern Europe after 1880, largely to escape pogroms and other anti-Semitic persecutions. By 1914 some 2 million Jews, including intellectuals, shopkeepers, skilled and unskilled laborers, had immigrated to the United States. Most settled in large cities, and having come from urban areas, they adapted fairly quickly.

Stemming the tide. Some 20 million immigrants, most of them Europeans, came to the United States

Fiorello La Guardia (1882-1947). The son of a Jewish mother and an Italian immigrant father, La Guardia ran for mayor of New York City as a Republican promising government reforms and an end to corruption. La Guardia won the first of his three consecutive terms as New York's mayor in 1933. He attacked organized crime in the city, worked to ease a housing shortage, and won federal money for many public works projects, of which La Guardia Airport was one. He retired from politics in 1946 after serving out his third term.

People of the United States

between 1890 and 1930. Almost 1.3 million arrived in 1907 alone and during the nine years between 1905 and 1914, over a million immigrants per year entered the country.

They came seeking jobs and often willingly worked for very low pay. The huge supply of new immigrants created competition for jobs and held wages down at a time when unions in the United States wanted to increase them.

Public pressure to control unrestricted immigration finally resulted in new federal immigration laws in 1921 and 1924, setting immigration quotas by country. The quotas favored European nations until new laws were passed in the 1960's and 1970's.

European immigrants continued coming to America, though not in such record numbers. In the World War II years, the United States became a refuge for European scientists and intellectuals from Nazi Germany and the countries it conquered. Many refugees, like world-renowned physicist Albert Einstein and nuclear physicist Enrico Fermi, remained in America after the war and made important contributions to their new homeland.

Postwar immigration from Europe included hundreds of thousands of refugees, but did not even approach levels reached in the early 1900's.

European-Americans today.
European ethnic groups in America have been fairly well assimilated over the years, though urban neighborhoods with ethnic identities remain--the "Little Italys," "Polish Hills," and the like. Other reminders persist as well, such as Saint Patrick's Day celebrations and performances by Scottish bagpipers. Ethnic pride and the recent concern for ethnic awareness tend to keep the European cultural heritage from disappearing completely. But ethnic ties today are not nearly so strong as they once were for first- and second-generation immigrants.

Something else has changed too. The millions of European immigrants who came to America from the 1800's onward drastically changed the nation's ethnic makeup. Where once people of English ancestry made up fully 60 percent of the population (in 1790), today they rank third behind people of German and Irish

Many European-Americans continued to celebrate their heritage for generations after their families arrived in America.

descent. According to the 1990 census, some 58 million people claimed German or part German ancestry. The Irish were second with 39 million, and the English third with 33 million.

The next largest European ethnic groups are Italians, with 15 million descendants in America today; French, with 10 million; Poles, with 9 million; Dutch, with 6 million; Scotch-Irish and Scottish, with about 5 million each; and Swedish, with about 4.6 million. Smaller groups include Norwegians, Russians, Welsh, Slovaks, and Danes.

Though most people of German descent live in the Midwest and South, California has the highest population of any single state. Pennsylvania, the original home of the Pennsylvania Dutch, ranks second, and Ohio is third.

California also has the largest number of Irish and English descendants. New York is the second leading state for people reporting Irish descent and Texas ranks second for those listing English ancestry. New York and New Jersey are the top two states for people with Italian ancestry. New York, Illinois, and Michigan have the largest number of Polish Americans.

African-Americans

Today there are about 32 million Americans of African descent, making them America's largest single minority. They represent about 13 percent of the population, but the population makeup is changing rapidly. The Census Bureau estimates there will be 62 million Afri-

can-Americans by 2050, almost double the current number. With large increases also expected in Hispanic and Asian-American populations, this means the proportion of nonwhite Americans will increase steadily from 25 percent in 1992 to 47 percent in

2050. This could signal greater political and economic strength for African-Americans and other groups in the future.

Like all ethnic groups, African-Americans have made many important contributions to America's development and growth. In the early history of America, they labored as slaves to create and maintain the South's plantation economy. Later, after slavery was ended, African-Americans helped build railroads, worked in factories, and slowly began making their way into other walks of life. Their progress has been slower than for other ethnic groups because they have had to overcome major barriers created by racial prejudice, poor educational opportunities, and economic disadvantages.

Most, but not all, black Americans are descended from Africans brought to this country as slaves before 1808. Other African-Americans have immigrated to the United States more recently, arriving from Caribbean islands such as Jamaica or Haiti, from South America, and directly from Africa.

History of African-Americans

First black Americans. In 1619 a Dutch warship arrived at Jamestown, Virginia, and sold 20 Africans to the English colonists there. They became the first blacks permanently settled in North America, and colonists treated them as indentured servants, not slaves. By this arrangement the first blacks in America worked for a few years before being freed, as did many white European immigrants.

Slavery. By the late 1600's, however, the status of African immigrants had changed dramatically. American colonies began to pass laws establishing automatic, lifelong slavery exclusively for these people. About this time the slave trade to American colonies also began increasing to meet the demand for cheap labor. Traders did sell slaves in Northern colonies, but English and other European immigrants satisfied most of the demand for labor there.

Ultimately, the South imported the largest number of slaves, and they eventually displaced indentured European laborers on the large plantations. The peak years for slave imports came between 1740 and 1810. The colonies imported about 427,000 slaves between the 1600's and 1810.

Slaves in America came from western and central Africa, including the modern countries of Senegal, Ghana, Gambia, Sierre Leone, Togo, Benin, Nigeria, and Angola. African tribes sometimes enslaved those defeated in intertribal wars and sold their captives to European slave traders. In other cases, tribal kingdoms raided villages along their borders to obtain slaves to trade for European goods. Slave traders generally offered the Africans guns and other manufactured goods for the slaves.

Conditions aboard ships bringing slaves to America were appalling. Slavers crowded hundreds of people into compartments below decks, fed them poorly, and left them to suffer in stifling and unsanitary conditions. During the long voyage to America, which could take months, many slaves died of diseases.

A family stands on the block at an auction in Virginia. African-Americans were sold as slaves to the highest bidder.

Life of the slaves. Cheap labor provided by slaves who survived the voyage became the key to Southern plantations' economic success. Working from sunrise to sunset, slaves cleared land, tended fields of tobacco, rice, and vegetables, harvested crops, toiled as household servants, and performed other tasks that helped make plantations almost completely self-sufficient. The slaves also contributed native African skills to rice cultivation and cattle raising.

For their labors, slaves received food, clothing, and shelter, all of it usually minimal in quantity and quality. Planters sometimes supplemented the slaves' basic ration of salt pork and corn with greens, milk, wheat flour, sweet potatoes, or beans. And many allowed slaves to grow their own vegetables. Slave clothing, fashioned from coarse cloth, provided minimal protection against the elements. Houses were small, one-room huts with no windows and dirt floors.

The oppressive conditions of slavery, and the racist attitudes against African-Americans fostered by slavery, sharply limited but did not eliminate their culture. Dancing and music became especially important common cultural links between black slaves of various African tribes. Slave musicians played traditional African instruments like drums, banjos, and xylophones (bafalos), which they made themselves.

Plantation owners constantly worried about slave revolts, and some did occur, like the Cato conspiracy in 1739 and Nat Turner's rebellion in 1831. Slaves sometimes fled westward into the wilderness, where they joined Native American tribes. Most slaves reluctantly accepted their condition, however, having no way to return to their native Africa or, for those born into slavery, knowing no other way of life.

Growing opposition to slavery. As early as 1696, Quakers in Pennsylvania took the first action against slavery by banning the importation of slaves into the colony. But opposition to slavery did not attract real support until the American Revolution brought questions about liberty and justice squarely before the colonists.

Ironically, an escaped slave named Crispus Attucks became one of the first casualties of the approaching battle for independence from Great Britain. He was killed in the infamous Boston Massacre in 1770. When war finally broke out, some 5000 African-Americans, nearly all from the North, fought against the British.

Drafting the Constitution again raised the issue of abolishing slavery. However, Southern states, whose economy depended on slavery, refused to allow its demise. Northern states, meanwhile, had already begun to end slavery within their own territories, and between 1774 and 1804 all abolished it. In 1789 and 1790, Virginians voluntarily freed some 10,000 slaves. In 1808 the slave trade was outlawed throughout the

---

Harriet Tubman (c 1821-1913). Called the "Moses of her people," Tubman risked her life leading groups of escaped slaves to the North on the Underground Railroad. She financed these efforts by working as a cook in Philadelphia and New York. Despite large rewards offered for her capture, Tubman succeeded in bringing out over 300 fugitive slaves. After the Civil War began, she worked as a nurse, a scout for Union soldiers, and a spy.

United States, though smuggling continued for a few more years.

At this time, Southern plantations also fell on hard times because the British market for tobacco and indigo virtually disappeared after the Revolution. With the economic justification for slavery weakening and popular antislavery sentiment rising, an end to slavery seemed near. But in 1793, the newly invented cotton gin changed all that. The gin made seed removal from domestic cotton quick and cheap; previously, hand removal was so costly that growing cotton had been unprofitable.

Plantation owners suddenly had a new cash crop and a new reason for keeping slavery alive. As cotton plantations followed the country's westward expansion into Alabama, Mississippi, and Texas, they took slavery with them. By the mid-1800's some 835,000 slaves had been uprooted from Southeastern states and moved to the new cotton-growing states, mainly to work on the plantations.

With the antislavery North as a secure base, freed slaves and white abolitionists worked for an end to slavery. A former slave, John Russwurm, founded *Freedom's Journal*, the first African-American newspaper, while books called "slave narratives" became popular in the North. Frederick Douglass, a fugitive slave and leading abolitionist, wrote one of the best-known narratives, *The Life and Times of Frederick Douglass*. African-Americans and white sympathizers also took more direct action, such as forming the Underground Railroad to help guide fugitive slaves to safety in the North.

Civil War and its aftermath. When war between the North and South broke out, President Lincoln tried to keep border states loyal by portraying the war as a struggle to preserve the Union, not to end slavery. As a result, the Union army at first refused to accept African-American volunteers. Pressure from abolitionists to end slavery, and from Union generals who wanted to recruit African-Americans, finally forced Lincoln to make the end of slavery an aim of the war.

Lincoln's Emancipation Proclamation, issued in preliminary form September 22, 1862, and formally January 1, 1863, declared freedom for all slaves living in states in "rebellion against the United States" as of January 1, 1863. Technically, the proclamation abolished slavery only in Confederate states not yet captured by Union armies, but the message was clear. From that time, Union armies were committed to preserving the Union and ending slavery. From 1862 on, the Union army recruited African-Americans, though they served in segregated units commanded by white officers. Eventually, some 186,000 African-Americans became combat troops.

Free blacks began organizing for greater rights even before the Civil War ended. In 1864 they formed the National Equal Rights League to press for voting rights. Later, free blacks successfully boycotted segregated streetcars in Philadelphia, New Orleans, Charleston, and Richmond. They also successfully campaigned against segregated schools and for opening up public places to African-Americans in Louisiana and South Carolina.

After the war, African-Americans and white reformers built thousands of churches and schools in the South. Fisk University for blacks was founded in Tennessee in 1866 and Howard University was established in Washington, D.C., in 1867. African-Americans, many of them freed slaves, were appointed to local offices. Some were also appointed to the U.S. Senate and House of Representatives.

Efforts at redistributing farmland to former slaves largely failed, however, virtually guaranteeing African-Americans continued dependence on white landowners. By 1900, only about one in four African-American farmers in the South owned their land; the rest worked as sharecroppers (tenant farmers) on white-owned plantation lands. Sharecroppers often fared little better than slaves had.

The amendments to the Constitution passed soon after the Civil War became the foundation for African-American civil rights, however. The 13th Amendment, ratified in 1865, abolished slavery in the United States, confirming changes already made by the Union victory in the Civil War. The 14th Amendment, ratified in 1868, granted citizenship to the former slaves and forbade states from denying any person life, liberty, or property without due process of law. The 14th also guaranteed equal protection of the law for all citizens. The 15th Amendment, ratified in 1870, barred states from denying African-Americans, or anyone else, the right to vote.

Segregation. White Southerners regained control of state governments in the South during the late 1870's, however, and reversed most all the previous gains made by former slaves. Beginning in 1882, Southern states passed Jim Crow laws that enforced strict segregation between blacks and whites and otherwise limited African-American civil rights. Finally, in *Plessy* v. *Ferguson* (1896), the Supreme Court ruled in favor of "separate but equal" public facilities and thereby made segregation the law of the land.

Conservative Southern African-Americans like Booker T. Washington favored accommodating whites and living with segregation until integration could be achieved. But the spread of laws supporting segregation and the increasing violence against African-Americans by Southern whites brought demands for quicker action from black leaders like W.E.B. Du Bois. Du Bois eventually played an important role in founding the National Association for the Advancement of Colored People (NAACP) in 1909.

Great Migration. African Americans responded to worsening treatment in the South by moving to New York, Chicago, and other Northern cities. The migration began slowly at first. Between 1890 and 1910, about 200,000 African-Americans moved north. From 1910 to 1930, however, a flood of about 1.25 million African-Americans left the South and settled in segregated neighborhoods in Northern cities. The National Urban League was formed in 1910 to help these newcomers from the South.

Music. City life brought both continued poverty and a flowering of black culture. Ragtime, blues, and jazz music, all of which originated in the South, flourished among African-Americans in Northern cities during the early 1900's. These new genres contributed greatly to a uniquely American music. Ragtime king Scott

Modern gospel singers perform at a concert in California. Gospel music, rhythmic and impassioned, is usually based on hymns.

People of the United States

Joplin, "father of the blues" W. C. Handy, and Dixieland jazz trumpeter Louis Armstrong all helped develop these music forms and establish a permanent place for African-American musicians in popular music.

In New York, pianist Fletcher Henderson organized the first big band in 1923, and musician Eubie Blake produced *Shuffle Along* (1921), one of the many African-American musicals that played on Broadway during the 1920's and 1930's. Meanwhile, Thomas A. Dorsey, the "father of gospel music," wrote nearly a thousand gospel songs and popularized this type of music in the late 1920's.

Literature. The 1920s also saw an African-American literary flowering, centered in New York, called the Harlem Renaissance. Among the many notable works were *Weary Blues* (1926) by poet Langston Hughes and *The Book of American Negro Poetry* (1922) by James Weldon Johnson.

The 1930's. The Great Depression hit African-Americans hard, but their political support for President Franklin Roosevelt's second term in the 1930's helped make them an important part of the Democratic Party's political coalition. The coalition lasted for decades and ultimately helped bring about equal rights for African-Americans. At the same time, the newly formed Congress of Industrial Organizations (CIO) and the NAACP began working together to promote union membership for African-Americans. In addition, in 1934 Elijah Muhammad organized the Black Muslims, a radical group that became popular during the 1960's civil rights movement.

Sports. Two athletes in the mid-1930's demonstrated the athletic talent of African-Americans and became national heroes in the process. Track star Jesse Owens won four gold medals in the 1936 Olympics at Berlin, Germany, publicly humiliating Hitler and his theories of Aryan racial superiority. Similarly, prizefighter Joe Louis knocked out the German Max Schmeling to win the world heavyweight title in 1937. Some years later, Jackie Robinson broke the color barrier in baseball by becoming the first African-American to play in the major leagues. He started with the Brooklyn Dodgers in 1947.

Dismantling segregation. African-Americans fared better on the job front during the 1940's, thanks to the wartime demand for labor. About a million more African-Americans left the South, generally moving to cities like Los Angeles, which had many war-related factory jobs. They also contributed directly to the war effort; some million African-Americans served in the military during World War II.

The years after the war, in which Hitler's racist ideas had been defeated, saw the end of legal segregation. In 1948 President Truman desegregated the military, and

Rosa Parks, 1971. Mrs. Parks's refusal to give up her bus seat to a white man initiated a protest against racial segregation.

Democrats adopted a strong civil rights plank, acknowledging African-Americans' importance in Democratic politics. Then, in 1954, the Supreme Court reversed its earlier ruling favoring segregation. In *Brown* v. *Board of Education*, the High Court ruled against the doctrine of separate but equal, the cornerstone of segregation.

Popular protest against segregation began the next year in Montgomery, Alabama. There, police arrested Rosa Parks for refusing to move to the back of a bus. Her arrest sparked a boycott by African-Americans of city buses that forced an end to segregated seating. Dr. Martin Luther King, Jr., joined the fight, forming what became the Southern Christian Leadership Conference (SCLC).

The drive for African-American civil rights continued despite violent attacks by white segregationists. In 1957 the federal government used troops to enforce court-ordered school desegregation at Little Rock, Arkansas. Nationwide television coverage of this and other incidents only increased public sympathy for African-American civil rights.

Meanwhile, African-Americans continued making strides in the cultural life of the United States during the 1950's. Popular singers like Nat "King" Cole and Ella Fitzgerald enjoyed wide reputations, and gospel singer Mahalia Jackson appeared on network television. Perhaps the most important cultural development was the new black music called rhythm and blues, which gave birth to rock and roll in the 1950's. Rock became mainstream American music, creating an industry that made superstars of black and white performers alike.

The 1960's: activism and reaction. The 1960's began with college students protesting segregation through lunch counter sit-ins in the South. The Student Nonviolent Coordinating Committee (SNCC)

Many African-Americans, by becoming doctors, lawyers, teachers, and businesspeople, have entered America's middle class.

Johnson won passage of two landmark civil rights bills, in 1964 and 1965. The legislation desegregated public places, helped end voting rights abuses (with the 1965 Voting Rights Act), and increased voter registration in the South.

Despite these gains, African-Americans in Northern cities began a destructive and deadly cycle of riots in urban ghettos. Starting with the 1964 Harlem riots and the 1965 Watts riots, nonviolence quickly disappeared as a standard of the civil rights movement. It was replaced by intimidation and destruction of whole neighborhoods. In 1967 rioters and looters went on the rampage in eight major cities.

The next year, 1968, the spiraling violence culminated in the assassination of Martin Luther King, who had campaigned for nonviolent solutions since the 1950's. African-Americans rioted in 125 cities to protest his death, and for a few more years militants made headlines.

African-Americans today. The civil rights movement dramatically increased participation of African-American voters in both the South and the North. By the mid-1970's some 4000 African-Americans--more than ever before--had been elected to political office at all levels of government. In 1966 African-American participation helped elect Edward Brooke of Massachusetts, the first black senator since Reconstruction, and Cleveland voters put an African-American in office as mayor in 1967. Other major American cities later installed African-American mayors as well. Shirley Chisholm became the first African-American woman elected to the House of Representatives in 1969, and ten years later Birmingham, Alabama, put its first African-American mayor in office. In 1988 Reverend Jesse Jackson made a strong bid for the Democratic Party's Presidential nomination, and the next year Ronald Brown became the first African-American chairman of a major American political party.

Qualified African-Americans now have a wider range of opportunites than ever before, even though affirmative action programs were curbed during the 1980's and major job reductions have ensued in the manufacturing sector. In sports, music, and entertainment--fields open to African-Americans for many years--blacks now hold higher positions, serving as coaches, reporters, commentators, and movie directors. But African-Americans also work in greater numbers today as scholars, scientists, and researchers. Perhaps even more promising for African-Americans as a group is the clear evidence of an emerging African-American middle class. As of the late 1980's, almost 13 percent of African-Americans earned $50,000 or more.

grew out of that movement. The Congress of Racial Equality (CORE) organized "Freedom Rides" in the Deep South to desegregate buses. Other demonstrations and civil disobedience campaigns sought to increase African-American voter registration and win better jobs. The year 1963 saw the historic March on Washington, during which over 200,000 African-Americans and white civil rights supporters congregated at the Lincoln Memorial and listened to speeches given by civil rights leaders, among them Martin Luther King, Jr.

The demonstrations, all intended as nonviolent, often provoked brutal responses by local policemen in the South and terrorist acts by whites opposed to integration. The Birmingham church bombing in which four young girls were killed;, the killing of Medgar Evers, field secretary of the NAACP, the murder of three students engaged in voter registration, and other such acts increased support for integration among whites outside the South. But the bloodshed also turned many African-Americans, especially younger ones, toward organizations that advocated violence.

The Black Muslims, organized in the 1930's, advocated black separatism, self-defense, and black superiority, and openly opposed nonviolent tactics. Malcom X actively promoted the Black Muslim cause in the early 1960's. The Black Panthers, formed in the late 1960's, were even more militant.

After President Kennedy's assassination, President

The forefathers of many Chinese-Americans immigrated to California to help build the transcontinental railroads.

Asian-Americans

Asian-Americans and Pacific Islanders form America's fastest growing population group. According to the Census Bureau, this segment of the population will grow from over 9 million in 1993 to 41 million in 2050. Part of that increase stems from new immigration laws enacted during the 1960's to end restrictive quotas on Asian immigration. But greater contact with Asians and Pacific Islanders also helped stimulate immigration and break down long-standing prejudices against these groups in the United States.

Hawaiian statehood added a significant number of Asians and Pacific Islanders to the United States population in 1959. U.S. involvement in the World War II Pacific theater, the Korean War, and the Vietnam War all increased contact with various Asian peoples and brought refugees to American shores. More recently, the United States has had extensive trade and diplomatic contact with Japan, China, and other Far Eastern countries, which helped stimulate the flow of Asian immigrants to the United States.

Chinese-Americans.
The Chinese who flocked to California in the 1800's constituted the first large-scale migration of Asians to America. Among the earliest arrivals was a cook named Ah Nam, the first recorded Chinese immigrant in California. He came in 1815, when California still belonged to Mexico. But the tide of Chinese immigrants did not begin to swell until the California gold rush of the mid-1800's.

Chinese immigrants generally planned on staying for only a few years, hoping to make enough money to return to China and live comfortably. Between 1850 and 1882, for example, some 322,000 Chinese arrived in the United States, but only about 100,000 actually remained. The new arrivals generally were men who were either single or who had left their wives behind in China.

They found plenty of work in California. The gold rush had created a serious labor shortage because many able-bodied people were busy prospecting for gold. The Chinese willingly took nonmining jobs and worked long hours for low pay as cooks, laundry workers, shopkeepers, and laborers in factories and mills. Later, Chinese people came in large numbers to work on railroad construction gangs. The Central Pacific part of the transcontinental railroad became the first big railroad construction project to use Chinese labor, employing perhaps 14,000 between 1858 and 1869.

Chinatowns. San Francisco was the main port of entry for Chinese immigrants. They called the city "the Golden Mountain" (Jinshan or Gam Saan), and established the first Chinatown in America. Later, Chinatowns sprang up in New York City, Los Angeles, and elsewhere.

Life in the early Chinatowns reflected the transient nature of the Chinese immigrant community. The Chinese made no effort to adopt the American life-style; their dress, customs, and food remained traditionally

I. M. Pei (1917-). Chinese-born American architect I.M. Pei has achieved an international reputation. A banker's son, Pei came to the United States in 1935, graduated from Massachusetts Institute of Technology in 1939, and earned his Master's in Architecture from Harvard Graduate School of Design in 1946. Pei's projects include Denver's Mile High Center and Chicago's Hyde Park Redevelopment. Among his most acclaimed designs is the elegant East Building of the National Gallery of Art in Washington, D.C.

Chinese. Few women and even fewer families could be found in U.S. Chinatowns during the 1800's. Instead, gambling, prostitution, opium dens, and frequent wars between Chinese gangs, called tongs, dominated the scene.

The 1870's brought fierce competition for the once undesirable jobs held by Chinese workers: the gold rush had ended and the California economy had soured. Anti-Chinese riots and political pressure finally prompted Congress to pass the Chinese Exclusion Acts in 1882, banning further immigration of laborers.

Between 1882 and 1943 when the acts were repealed, the Chinese-American population dropped to a low of just over 60,000 in 1920. Those who remained in the United States worked in many types of jobs, and Chinese-Americans proved to be exceptional farmers. The bing cherry, for example, was named for a Chinese immigrant in Oregon named Ah Bing. Another immigrant, Lue Gim Gong, developed an improved breed of oranges in 1888.

Chinese-Americans today. Since World War II, Chinese immigrants have come mainly from Hong Kong and Taiwan, and the Chinese-American population had increased to over 1.5 million in 1990. Changes in U.S. immigration laws during the 1960's contributed to that increase.

Most Chinese-Americans today live in urban areas such as San Francisco, Los Angeles, and New York, and over half make their home in the Western states. They are Americanized in their dress and manner, but Chinese cultural influences remain strong. The Chinese have successfully marketed part of their culture here in the United States. Chinese food is a favorite with Americans, and some 10,000 Chinese restaurants do a thriving business in cities across the country.

Japanese-Americans. About 1 million
Japanese-Americans lived in the United States by 1990, over 70 percent of them on the West Coast and in Hawaii. Other areas with larger Japanese-American populations include New York and some parts of the Midwest.

In recent decades, Japanese-Americans have benefited from laws designed to provide greater opportunities for ethnic minorities. Between 1960 and 1970, for example, the number of Japanese-American men in professional and managerial positions jumped from 15 to 31 percent. Japanese-Americans can be found working as dentists, doctors, engineers, and optometrists, as well as in more traditional Japanese occupations like gardening and skilled labor.

The Japanese began immigrating in the 1890's, mainly to Hawaii and California to work as laborers. But the Japanese aroused the same prejudices as the Chinese, and by the Gentlemen's Agreement of 1907, the Japanese government agreed to limit emigration to the United States. Then, in 1924, Congress passed a law closing off all Japanese immigration.

By 1920 there were just over 111,000 Japanese immigrants living in the United States, most of them first generation (called issei). These immigrants often worked as servants or owned small retail businesses like laundries, dry cleaners, grocery stores, restaurants, and curio shops. At that time, these first-generation Japanese immigrants could not become citizens, but children born in America automatically became U.S. citizens. However, second-generation Japanese (called nisei) suffered from the same prejudices as their parents in the years before World War II.

After Japan attacked Pearl Harbor, the government moved over 110,000 Japanese-Americans living on the West Coast to internment camps in California, Arizona, Idaho, Colorado, Utah, and Arkansas.

Asian-Americans often work in high-tech and managerial jobs that require a high level of education.

People of the United States

Though some 35,000 opted to resettle in midwestern cities, most remained confined until 1945. In 1988 the U.S. government sought to make amends for this harsh treatment by formally apologizing and paying $20,000 to each of the estimated 60,000 former internees still alive. Interestingly, no such internment strategy was adopted in Hawaii, mainly because a third of the population would have been involved.

Thousands of Japanese-Americans joined the U.S. armed forces and distinguished themselves in combat during World War II. The Japanese-American 100th Battalion and 442nd Combat Team became the most decorated American units ever.

Laws discriminating against Japanese and other Orientals were dropped after World War II, and the 1952 McCarran-Walter Act gave first-generation Japanese-Americans the right to become naturalized citizens. At that time, Japanese-Americans also came to dominate the political scene in Hawaii by gaining control of the territorial legislature.

Though Japanese-Americans advanced more slowly in California, their progress overall has been marked. Nationwide, Japanese-Americans now have educational levels and household incomes that rank above the national average.

Other Asian-Americans.
As of 1990, about 835,000 Korean-Americans lived in the United States. Because Japan controlled Korea until the end of World War II, Korean immigration was minimal until the 1950's. Then the Korean War, the continued U.S. military presence in South Korea afterward, and extensive trade between the United States and Korea helped stimulate a rapid rise in Korean emigration to the United States.

The Vietnam War also produced an influx of immigrants, this time South Vietnamese and other peoples from the region. Some 170,000 refugees, about 90 percent from Vietnam, emigrated to the United States in the mid-1970's.

When Hawaii became a state in 1959, the Hawaiians, Filipinos, Japanese, and Chinese living there all became American citizens. Today there are about 256,000 people of Hawaiian descent in the United States, most of them in Hawaii or on the West Coast.

The 1.4 million Filipino-Americans in the United States are also concentrated in the West and Hawaii, but are somewhat more dispersed to other parts of the country than the Hawaiians. Filipino laborers began arriving during the late 1800's, though their numbers remained small until after the government revised U.S. immigration quotas in the 1960's. Between 1966 and 1976 alone, about 276,000 Filipinos came to the United States and settled in cities like Honolulu, Los Angeles, Chicago, and New York.

People of many other Asian nationalities have also immigrated to the United States, but in smaller numbers. Among them are Laotians, Thais, and Cambodians from Southeast Asia, and Indians and Pakistanis from South Asia.

Hispanic-Americans

Hispanic-Americans are people who have come from the Spanish-speaking countries of North, Central, and South America, plus the Caribbean. Mexican immigrants and their descendants, called Chicanos, form the biggest group of Hispanics in the United States (about half). Puerto Ricans and Cuban-Americans make up the second and third largest groups, respectively. Dominicans, Salvadorans, Colombians, Guatemalans, Ecuadorans, Nicaraguans, and other nationalities account for the rest of the 24 million Hispanic-Americans living in the United States in 1992.

Though most Hispanics came to America in the 20th century, their Spanish cultural heritage dates back to the earliest colonial times. Spanish conquistadors, for example, discovered and named Florida in the 1500's. In 1565 they founded St. Augustine, Florida, the oldest city in the United States. Hernando De Soto explored the American Southeast and probably was the first person who was not a Native Ameri-

The oldest stone fort in America, the Castillo de San Marcos, is in St. Augustine, Florida, the oldest city in America.

States with Spanish names

California	fabled earthly paradise
Colorado	red land
Florida	land of flowers
Montana	mountainous
Nevada	snowy
New Mexico	after Mexico

can to see the Mississippi River (1541). Other conquistadors pushed northward from Mexico, exploring the American Southwest and southern California, which they claimed for Spain. Eventually they discovered the Grand Canyon (1540) and traveled as far north as Kansas. Their exploration also opened the Southwest to Spanish settlement, which proceeded slowly during the next centuries.

When the United States took control of Florida, the Southwest, and California during the 1800's, it acquired vast territories and many new Spanish-speaking citizens as well. The new territories guaranteed that a strong Hispanic element would be present in American culture.

For example, thousands of Spanish names for cities and other places dot maps of Florida and the western states. Key West (from *cayo* for low island), Las Vegas, San Diego, Los Angeles, San Francisco, and Santa Fe are just a few. Over 400 cities and towns with Spanish names can be found in California, and six states have names derived from Spanish (see accompanying table).

Spanish explorers, and the settlers who followed them, also gave names to geographical features, plants, animals, and other things they saw in the New World. Canyon, arroyo, and mesa all are derived from Spanish. So, too, are alfalfa, sassafras, buffalo, alligator, cockroach, and mosquito. Junta, calaboose, loco, and pronto are obviously Spanish, but words like breeze, cafeteria, hurricane, and tornado also came to us from the Spanish. Even the cowboys who roamed the West used words of Spanish derivation, such as ranch, corral, rodeo, lasso, and stampede.

Modern-day Hispanic-Americans have made many contributions to American life. As agricultural laborers, factory workers, and railroad workers, they helped support the economies of California and the Southwest during the 20th century. Some 350,000 Chicanos served in World War II, and after the war Hispanics began moving into managerial and professional positions in larger numbers.

Famous Hispanic-Americans. Today Hispanics can be found in all walks of life. They own successful businesses such as Goya Foods in New Jersey and Bacardi Imports in Florida, as well as banks, restau-

rants, supermarket chains, and manufacturing companies. In 1981 a Cuban business executive, Roberto Goizueta, was named chairman of the board and chief executive officer of Coca-Cola. Bolivian American teacher Jaime Escalante gained national fame for his success in teaching calculus to high school students in Los Angeles, California. Other notable Hispanics are scientists, writers, artists, and religious leaders.

Hispanics have also become important in sports, entertainment, and politics. Famous athletes include baseball players Roberto Clemente, Keith Hernandez, and Fernando Valenzuela; Chicano football player and coach Thomas Flores, and quarterback Jim Plunkett; Puerto Rican boxers Carlos Ortiz and Jose Torres; Chicana golfer Nancy Lopez, Puerto Rican golfer Chi Chi Rodriquez, and Chicano golfer Lee Trevino; and Salvadoran tennis star Rosemary Casals.

Many Hispanic-Americans have also excelled in the world of music and entertainment. Some examples include singers such as Chicana Joan Baez and Cuban-American singer and songwriter Gloria Estefan; and actors and actresses such as Bolivian Raquel Welch, Chicanos Ricardo Montalban, Lynda Carter, and Anthony Quinn, Puerto Rican Rita Moreno, Mexican-American Edward James Olmos, and Spanish-American Hector Elizondo.

Representation of Hispanic-Americans in government has been rapidly increasing in recent years. Among noted Hispanic politicians are Herman Badillo, a U.S. congressman from New York and the first Puerto Rican elected to Congress (1970); Senator Joseph Montoya, an influential member of the Senate Appropriations Committee until 1976; and Puerto Rican Antonia Novello, the first woman and first Hispanic surgeon general of the United States.

Chicanos.

Immigration to America was relatively easy for people coming from Mexico. Unlike immigrants from other continents, Chicanos had no ocean to cross. And they could travel back to Mexico if life in the new land did not work out. The history of America's Chicano population was, until recently, one of sharp increases and declines tied to the availability of jobs.

The first Mexican-Americans became U.S. citizens when Texas achieved statehood in 1845. Their number was probably small, however, because many Mexicans left when Texas first won independence from Mexico. A much larger group, about 80,000 Mexicans, became American citizens when the United States acquired the Southwest and California during the Mexican War (1846-1848). Though most Chicanos lived in southern California, the majority of New Mexico's population was Chicano until about 1900.

Chicanos faced many difficulties after the United States took over former Mexican territories. In Texas, especially, the bloody war for independence against Mexico created ill feelings against Chicanos. Worse yet, many Mexican farmers in Texas and the Southwest lost their land because U.S. courts did not automatically recognize original Spanish and Mexican land grants.

The 20th century. By 1900 the Chicano population ranged only between 400,000 and 550,000. But in following years, massive immigration by Mexicans began. The new arrivals filled semiskilled and unskilled jobs as agricultural workers, miners, railroad workers, factory workers, and unskilled laborers.

About 185,000 Mexicans emigrated to America between 1910 and 1919, partly because of a revolution going on in Mexico. World War I created a surplus of jobs in America's war industries, providing another incentive for Mexicans to move north. Between 1920 and 1929, the combination of jobs and a new revolt in Mexico sent another wave of about 500,000 Mexican immigrants to America. But when jobs became scarce during the Great Depression, a repatriation program sponsored by the U.S. and Mexican governments sent 500,000 Chicanos back to Mexico.

Labor shortages during World War II (and the Korean War) brought Mexican immigrants flowing northward again in steadily increasing numbers. In the 1960's and early 1970's, over 30,000 Mexican immigrants arrived each year. But in 1976, Congress imposed a ceiling of 20,000 immigrants from any one country, even though the demand continued for workers, especially in lower paid agricultural, service, domestic, and industrial jobs. As a result, illegal Mexican immigrants increasingly made up the difference between the demand and the labor supply. As their numbers grew during the 1980's, the government set up a program to give legal status to illegal aliens. Over 2 million Mexican immigrants applied by the 1988 cutoff date.

An estimated 11.5 million persons of Mexican descent were U.S. citizens in 1990. Most live in California and the Southwest and are concentrated in urban areas, especially Los Angeles. While many still work in

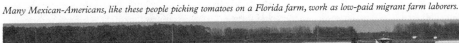

Many Mexican-Americans, like these people picking tomatoes on a Florida farm, work as low-paid migrant farm laborers.

low-paying agricultural, service, and manufacturing jobs, conditions for Chicanos have been improving steadily since the end of World War II. Civil rights legislation that increased opportunities for minorities as well as efforts by Chicano activists have contributed substantially to that improvement.

Puerto Ricans.
An estimated 1.95 million Puerto Ricans lived in the United States in 1990. The majority are in the New York City area, which has the largest Puerto Rican population of any city in the world. Chicago and cities in New Jersey, Ohio, and California also have substantial Puerto Rican populations.

Puerto Rico is a U.S. territory, and Puerto Ricans are United States citizens, so passage back and forth has always been easy. This is especially true of immigration to New York City and other places where strong Puerto Rican immigrant communities already exist.

The flow of immigrants to the United States was not large before World War II and only about 60,000 Puerto Ricans had arrived by then. Large-scale immigration began after the war, especially when cheap air travel between New York City and Puerto Rico became available. Many immigrants then traveled to the United States, worked for a few years to build up savings, and returned to Puerto Rico. Since 1976, there has been a trend toward reverse immigration back to Puerto Rico.

Cubans.
About 860,000 Cubans lived in the United States in 1990. The largest concentration of Cuban-Americans is in Miami, Florida. Other cities with smaller numbers of Cubans include New York, Jersey City, Newark, Chicago, and Los Angeles.

Many Cuban-Americans are exiles who arrived in the 1960's after Fidel Castro's Communist regime seized power. Several hundred thousand refugees came to America during the 1960's. In 1980, another 120,000 refugees arrived in the Cuban boat lift.

Because many skilled workers and professionals were among the refugees from the 1960's onward, Cuban-Americans have tended to do well. In Miami's Little Havana, especially, stores, banks, and other enterprises are owned and run by Cubans.

Hispanics, today and tomorrow.
Hispanic-Americans are fairly recent immigrants, having arrived in substantial numbers only during the 20th century. Still, about 24 million Hispanics lived in the United States by 1992, a substantial increase owing to immigration and a traditionally high birthrate among those already in the United States. The outlook for the next century is for more growth.

Taken as a group, Hispanics are now America's second-largest minority, but that is changing. According to the Census Bureau, more Hispanic-Americans will be added to the population than any other group after 1995. Between 2030 and 2050, the Census Bureau reports, the Hispanic population will contribute an estimated 57 percent of U.S. population growth. At that rate, the Hispanic population will probably reach 81 million in 2050, making Hispanic-Americans the country's largest minority group. African-Americans, currently the largest minority, are expected to rank second in 2050 with 62 million.

Los Angeles, like other cities in the United States, has attracted large numbers of immigrants from South America. Many, like this couple from Guatemala, have opened small businesses.

People of the United States

The various peoples of the United States have contributed immensely to the variety and vigor of American life. Harmony among them depends on all women and men of good will to respect and enjoy the heritage of every ethnic American.

For Further Reading

Ashe, Arthur R., Jr.
    A Hard Road to Glory: A History of the African American Athlete
    Warner
Brown, Dee
    Bury My Heart At Wounded Knee
    Holt, Rinehart & Winston
Ellison, Ralph
    The Invisible Man
    Modern Library
Geronimo
    Geronimo, His Own Story
    Dutton
Kessler, Laura
    Stubborn Twig: Three Generations in the Life of a Japanese American Family
    Random House
Levy, E.
    Cesar Chavez: Autobiography of La Causa
    Norton
Novotny, Ann
    Strangers at the Door: Ellis Island, Castle Garden, and the Great Migration to America
    Chatham Press
Portes, Alejandro and Rumbaut, Ruben G.
    Immigrant America: A Portrait
    University of California Press
Rölvaag, Ole E.
    Giants in the Earth: A Saga of the Prairie
    Harper

World History

History is an account of the important events of the past, especially of those events that somehow influence the way we live and think today. This section provides a brief *chronology*, or time line, of world history, beginning with the earliest surviving records. The history has been divided into five segments. Ancient history begins with early cultures, around 3000 B.C., and ends with the fall of the Roman Empire in 476 A.D. Medieval history includes just over a thousand years, from 476 to 1478. The section on the Renaissance and the Enlightenment takes in the next 300 years, ending on the eve of the American Revolution in 1775. The modern period runs to 1945, the end of World War II. The final section on the postwar world brings events to the present day. Following the chronology is a different kind of time line showing the birth and death dates of important leaders, discoverers, and artists.

Ancient world

The modern world owes much to the early civilizations that grew up around the Mediterranean Sea in the centuries before the birth of Christ. The Hebrews developed a religion recognizing a single God; modern Judaism and Christianity have grown from this religion. The Greeks, drawing on earlier cultures, created the poetry and art that remain a standard of perfection even today. The Romans developed methods of public administration and public works that resemble our own. The great works and wisdom of these civilizations have been rediscovered many times; their history is part of our own.

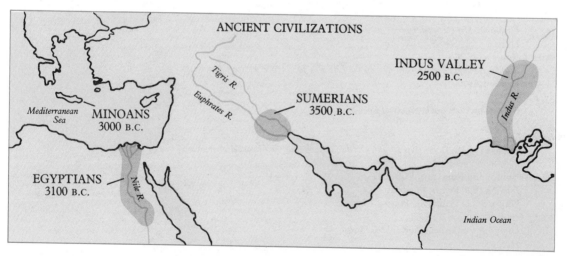

ANCIENT CIVILIZATIONS

INDUS VALLEY
2500 B.C.

Tigris R.

Euphrates R.

SUMERIANS
3500 B.C.

Indus R.

Mediterranean Sea

MINOANS
3000 B.C.

EGYPTIANS
3100 B.C.

Nile R.

Indian Ocean

Date	Event

c 3000 BC

Ancient civilizations. By the year 3000 BC, fairly advanced cultures had developed in Sumer, Crete, and Egypt. Sumer, located in Mesopotamia (modern Iraq), had an extensive village culture from about 4000 BC; at about this time Sumerians began to develop what became known as cuneiform writing. By 3000 BC, Sumerian civilization was centered on such flourishing cities as Erech, Lagash, and Ur. These cities rivaled one another for control of neighboring lands but were not unified until about 2300, when the Akkadians conquered them (see below).

Crete, lying off the coast of Greece, was the center of another early civilization, that of the Minoans. From about 3000, they had a flourishing Bronze Age culture. The Minoans became a maritime power in the Mediterranean (about 2000 BC), and their culture greatly influenced later civilizations on the Greek mainland.

In Egypt an advanced culture and a unified state developed early. In 3100 King Menes united Upper and Lower Egypt, two independent kingdoms that had arisen along the banks of the Nile River, and founded what was to become the great empire of Egypt. In the years after Menes, called the Early Dynastic Period (c 3100–c 2700), Egyptian culture developed rapidly and hieroglyphic writing became widespread. Government, administrative, technical, and artistic skills were also developed, providing the foundations for the Old Kingdom of Egypt (see below).

An Egyptian Pharaoh and his wife (below). *At* right, *the great pyramids at Giza.*

**c 2700–
c 2200 BC**

Old Kingdom of Egypt. Period in Egyptian history following Menes's unification of Upper and Lower Egypt. During a time of prosperity and cultural flowering, the Old Kingdom was known for sun worship, pyramid building, and trading expeditions as far north as the Black Sea. The capital was located at Memphis. The rise of strong provincial rulers finally broke the Pharaoh's power and ended the Old Kingdom.

**c 2600–
c 2500 BC**

Pyramids of Giza. Three great Egyptian pyramids built on the banks of the Nile River. They are one of the Seven Wonders of the World. The largest was built by the Pharaoh Khufu (or Cheops) about 2600 BC. It is 481 feet tall and its sides average 776 feet at the base.

**c 2300–
2180 BC**

Akkadian Empire. Great ancient empire in Mesopotamia, in what is now Iraq. The great Akkadian ruler Sargon ruled from 2340 to 2305 and conquered lands surrounding his capital, Akkad. Eventually he controlled an empire that included all of Mesopotamia, territories extending west to the Mediterranean, and lands as far north as the Black Sea. Destruction of the empire (c 2180) by barbarian tribes plunged Mesopotamia into a period of chaos.

c 2000– c 1786 BC
Middle Kingdom of Egypt. Period beginning when Amenemhet I seized power at the city of Thebes (c 2000). It was marked by the conquest of lower Nubia, the standardization of writing, a literary flowering, and great commercial prosperity. The Pharaohs ruled as feudal kings, not absolute monarchs, and when their power declined the Middle Kingdom came to an end.

c 1763– c 1600 BC
First Babylonian Empire. Empire in Mesopotamia created by Hammurabi (fl. 1792–1750), ruler of the city-state of Babylon. He began his conquests during the last 14 years of his reign and, by them, unified Mesopotamia under his rule. Hammurabi is best known for his Law Code, one of the earliest known written legal codes. The code was inscribed on a stone tablet in cuneiform writing; it was rediscovered in 1901. The code contained provisions for criminal, civil, commercial, and family law, and is generally thought to be based on long-established Sumerian practices. Hammurabi's empire was continued by his successors, though it was considerably reduced after his death. The empire finally fell to the Kassites in about 1600 BC.

c 1720– c 1570 BC
Hyksos rule in Egypt. After the fall of the Middle Kingdom, a Semitic people called the Hyksos made themselves masters of Egypt (c 1720). They created a powerful and prosperous empire, moved the capital from Thebes to Avaris-Tanis in the Nile delta, and introduced the horse and chariot to Egypt. Their reign was challenged by the Theban princes, however, and the Hyksos were finally defeated (c 1570) by Amasis I at the Battle of Tanis.

c 1570– c 1085 BC
New Kingdom in Egypt. Last period of greatness in ancient Egypt. The New Kingdom was marked by the centralization of power in the hands of the Pharaoh (at the expense of local rulers), the expansion of the empire into Asia, the brief religious revolution of Amenhotep IV (see below), and the building of magnificent temples. The last great ruler of this period was Ramses III (ruled 1198–c 1167); after him the priests became the real rulers of Egypt. In the centuries that followed the New Kingdom, Egypt came under the control of various peoples, including the Libyans, Nubians, Persians, Macedonian Greeks, and finally the Romans (30 BC).

c 1400 BC
Final destruction of the palace at Knossos. By the second millennium BC, the Minoans had established a flourishing Bronze Age culture on the island of Crete. It was centered on a great palace at Knossos. The final destruction (1400) of the palace by unknown causes marked the end of the Minoan culture. Thereafter the center of Aegean culture shifted to the southern part of mainland Greece, where the Mycenaean civilization flourished (c 1400–c 1200).

c 1372– c 1354 BC
Amenhotep's religious revolution. The Pharaoh Amenhotep IV (Ikhnaton) in Egypt (ruled c 1372–c 1354) attempted to convert his kingdom to the worship of one god, Aton, the sun god. Amenhotep overcame the resistance of the priesthood and attempted to eliminate all references to other gods. This monotheistic worship of Aton did not survive him, however, and a successor, Tutankhamen, was forced to restore the old gods.

c 1288 BC
Battle of Kadesh. Great battle fought by Egyptian Pharaoh Ramses II (ruled 1292–1225) against the Hittites in Syria. Ramses took up arms against the Hittites to block their advance into Egyptian domains in Syria. Though he claimed victory, the battle is thought to have been inconclusive. War between the Egyptians and Hittites continued for ten more years before a settlement was made.

c 1260? BC
Exodus from Egypt. Though dating is uncertain, the Hebrews' escape from Egypt is thought to have occurred during the reign of Ramses II (c 1292–c 1225). The Bible recounts the story of the Exodus, including Moses' efforts to win the release of the Hebrews, the escape and crossing of the Red Sea, the arduous journey to Mt. Sinai, and the giving of the Ten Commandments.

Date	Event

c 1200 BC

The Phoenicians. A Canaanite people who occupied the coastal region of what is now Lebanon as early as 3000 BC. By about 1200 they were well known as traders and navigators. Between about 1000 and 800, they established a thriving commercial empire around the Mediterranean. They established trading colonies as far west as Carthage (in North Africa) and Cadiz (in modern Spain), and may well have circumnavigated Africa. After about 600 BC, the Phoenicians submitted to the Chaldeans and then the Persians. In 332 BC Alexander the Great captured and sacked the great Phoenician city of Tyre. In ensuing centuries Phoenician civilization disappeared as a distinct entity.

In addition to being renowned traders, the Phoenicians were also skilled craftsmen. Their greatest contribution, however, was the Phoenician alphabet. The Greek alphabet is thought to have been based on the Phoenician system.

Phoenician letters:

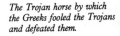

c 1200 BC

Fall of Troy. The war against the city of Troy formed the basis of two great epics of ancient Greece, the *Iliad* and the *Odyssey,* by the poet Homer. These works had an immense influence on the culture of ancient Greece, though both the city and the Trojan War were long thought to be nothing more than legend. In the late 1800's, however, an archaeologist named Heinrich Schliemann (1822–1890) used details given in Homer's epics to locate the ruins of Troy in northwest Asia Minor. There, archaeological evidence indicated the city was destroyed in about 1200 BC, apparently by the conquering Greek warriors.

The Trojan horse by which the Greeks fooled the Trojans and defeated them.

**c1012-
c 972 BC**

King David's reign in Israel. After their exodus from Egypt, the Hebrew tribes eventually reached Palestine. There they began their wars for control of the region, but conquest was not completed until David became their leader. David gave the confederated tribes a strong kingdom with Jerusalem as the capital.

**c 972–
c 932 BC**

King Solomon's reign in Israel. Under Solomon, successor to his father, King David, the ancient kingdom of Israel reached the height of its power and prosperity. Solomon brought great wealth to the kingdom by encouraging trade, built new cities throughout his domain, and constructed magnificent palaces and the first Temple at Jerusalem. He gained a legendary reputation for both his wisdom and his wealth. But the taxation required to support the luxury of his court led to unrest and, soon after Solomon's death, the kingdom split in two. The northern part became the Kingdom of Israel and the southern part became the Kingdom of Judah.

**884–
612 BC**

Assyrian Empire. The Assyrians were a warlike, Semitic people who inhabited northern Mesopotamia from about 3000 BC. Though they expanded their domain for brief periods in previous centuries, formation of their great empire did not begin until the reign of Ashurnasirpal II (ruled 884–c 860). He was followed by other conquerors, among them Tiglath-pileser III (ruled 745–728), Sargon II (ruled 722–705), and Esarhaddon (ruled 681–668). By their conquests, these rulers created a vast empire in the Near East that extended from Egypt (conquered c 670) to the Persian Gulf. The last great Assyrian ruler was Ashurbanipal (ruled 669–633), who organized a famous library of cuneiform tablets at his capital, Nineveh. The Assyrian Empire crumbled soon after his reign, when the Babylonians and their allies captured Nineveh in 612.

c 800– c 300 BC

A Greek vase, c 520 B.C.

The Greeks. The Dorian invasions (c 1100) destroyed the Bronze Age culture that had flourished on mainland Greece from about 1400 BC. Civilization on the mainland did not begin to flourish again until about 900–800. This was the time of Homer and the early development of city-states such as Athens and Sparta, which were to become the basic political units of ancient Greece.

An era of colonization in faraway lands followed from about 750 to 500 BC. It received its impetus from population growth, the relatively poor soil in Greece, and the desire for land; bands of colonizers began to form independent city-states around the Mediterranean and the Black Sea.

The period from about 500 to 300 is known as the Golden Age. It was marked by great cultural advances, as well as by strife and turmoil. From 490–479 Greek city-states turned back invasions by the Persian Empire. From 431–404 they engaged in the ruinous Peloponnesian War among themselves. Even so, this age saw great artistic and intellectual advances. The spirit of Greece, particularly in its Athenian form, was based on freedom, rationalism, individualism, and democracy. The work of Greek scientists, mathematicians, philosophers, poets, artists, dramatists, and historians surpassed that of earlier cultures and greatly influenced the development of Western civilization.

The conquests of Alexander the Great and the breakup of his great empire (from 321) marked the beginning of the decline of Greek culture on mainland Greece. But Alexander's successors helped spread Greek culture throughout the ancient world and thus brought about the Hellenistic age (see below).

776 BC

First Olympic Games. The first athletic games of what became a great tradition in ancient Greece were held at Olympia, in southern Greece, and consisted only of running events. Discontinued in the fourth century AD, the Olympic Games were revived in 1896.

753 BC

City of Rome founded. The founding of Rome is surrounded by legend, though this date is traditionally accepted. According to one legend, the brothers Romulus and Remus built the original city in 753. Soon after, the two brothers fought over the defensive wall built around it. Remus made fun of the wall by easily jumping over it. Romulus, in a rage, killed his brother and uttered the prophetic words, "Thus perish any other who leaps over my walls."

c 625– 538 BC

Second Babylonian Empire in Mesopotamia. After more than a century of Assyrian domination, Babylon reestablished its independence (c 625) under Nabopolassar (ruled c 625–c 605). Some years later Nabopolassar formed an alliance with the Medes and Persians and together they brought down the Assyrian Empire by capturing its capital, Nineveh (612). With the destruction of Assyria and the great Babylonian victory over the Egyptians at Carchemish (605), the Babylonians formed a vast Mesopotamian empire. This empire reached its zenith under Nabopolassar's son, Nebuchadnezzar (ruled c 605–562), who was both a formidable warrior and a great builder. He made Babylon into the greatest city in the ancient world and built the famous Hanging Gardens of Babylon. Following two revolts by the Jews against Babylonian rule, Nebuchadnezzar destroyed their capital of Jerusalem (586) and carried off its citizens. This began the Babylonian Captivity, which lasted until the Persians conquered the Babylonian Empire in 538.

c 621 BC — **Draco institutes his legal code in Athens.** Draco's code, which according to Aristotle was the first in Athenian history, was notoriously harsh; it prescribed the death penalty for even minor offenses. The code did establish the principle that murderers were to be punished by the state, instead of the victim's family. But the severity of the laws proved so unpopular that the entire code was reformed by Solon in 594. The word *Draconian,* used to refer to repressive laws, is derived from Draco's code.

c 616– c 509 BC — **Tarquin kings rule in Rome.** Though there is much uncertainty regarding the reign of Tarquins, they were apparently Etruscans, a powerful people of Etruria in north-central Italy. The first of the Tarquins seized power in Rome c 616; they remained in power until the Romans drove them out c 509. By this time, however, Etruscan culture had greatly influenced the development of Roman civilization. The overthrow of the Tarquin kings marked the beginning of the Roman republic.

594 BC — **Solon's reforms in Athens.** Solon (c 639–c 559), one of the great Athenian statesmen, became chief magistrate in Athens amid a grave social crisis. Under the existing system, the peasants were steadily losing their land and their freedom to the nobles. Solon canceled all debts secured with personal liberty (serfdom was the penalty for failing to pay), reformed the Athenian constitution to allow all freemen to participate in the assembly, replaced the harsh Draconian code with a new law code, and made other reforms. Solon's reforms did not go unopposed, but they did lay the foundations for Athenian democracy.

c 549– 330 BC

The Persian Empire. Beginning about 549, the Persians, under the leadership of Cyrus the Great (c 559–529), advanced from the land east of Mesopotamia (in present-day Iran) westward toward the Mediterranean, conquering Lydia and Babylonia. Within 20 years, Cyrus established the largest empire in existence before the conquests of Alexander the Great. The Greeks and Egyptians, however, held out against him. Darius the Great (521–486) was determined to conquer the Greek city-states and launched the Persian wars (see below). Following the Persian defeat in these wars, the empire sank into stagnation and collapsed before the armies of Alexander the Great.

Persian intellectual and artistic achievements were derived largely from the earlier civilizations of Mesopotamia and Egypt. The Persians did, however, spread their religion, Zoroastrianism, throughout western Asia. Zoroastrians believed that Shura Mazda, god of light, created the world and mankind to be locked in endless combat with Ahriman, the god of darkness and evil. Out of these beliefs emerged Mithraism, Manicheism, and Gnosticism, all of which had a profound influence on the Roman world and on Christianity.

Sculpture from the Persian capital of Persepolis

c 538 BC   **End of Babylonian Captivity.** Following the conquest of the Babylonian Empire by the Persians (538), the Persian ruler Cyrus the Great permitted the Hebrews of Jerusalem to return to their city. Many, but not all, left Babylon, where they had been held captive by the Babylonians since 586 as punishment for a rebellion. Their return marked the reestablishment of Jerusalem as a center of Jewish religion and the Jewish national state.

c 528 BC   **Buddhism founded in India.** Buddhism was founded by Siddhartha Gautama (c 563–c 483), who gave up a life of luxury to seek spiritual enlightenment. He found enlightenment (c 528) while meditating under a banyan tree at Buddha Gaya, in northeast India, and he devoted the rest of his life to spreading his teachings. Buddhism eventually arose as an organized religion in India, in opposition to the dominant Hindu religion. Although Buddhism later declined and nearly disappeared in India, it had spread by that time through central and eastern Asia and influenced the cultures of China, Korea, and Japan, among other countries.

Buddha

508 BC   **Constitution of Cleisthenes in Athens.** Cleisthenes rose to power amid a political crisis in Athens and used the situation to institute reforms (508) that created the Athenian democracy. His new political system was based on political districts (demes) established by region, rather than by membership in one of the four old tribes. This broke the power of the landed aristocracy, which had previously controlled Athenian government.

c 500 BC   **Confucius and the Chinese classics.** By the time of Confucius (c 551–c 479), the Chinese empire had already been in existence for a thousand years or more. In his lifetime, China was torn by wars and the tyranny of feudal nobles. Confucius sought to reform government and about 531 began teaching his principles to others. His disciples later collected these teachings into the *Analects*, which is counted among the Chinese classics, along with the writings of Lao-tze (c 604–531) and Mencius (c 371–c 288). These classics continued to influence Chinese culture for some 2000 years.

500–400 BC   **Golden Age of Greek drama.** Greek drama evolved at Athens from ceremonies honoring the god Dionysus (Bacchus); it was raised to an art form by the four acknowledged masters of this Golden Age. Three of them, Aeschylus (525–456), Sophocles (c 496–406), and Euripides (c 480–406), developed the Greek tragedy. The fourth, Aristophanes (c 448–c 388), is known for his comedies.

490–479 BC   **Persian invasions of Greece.** During this period the Greek city-states united briefly to face the common enemy, Persia. The Persians invaded Greece in 490 and 480. The first invasion was ended by the great Athenian victory at Marathon (490) and the second was turned back after the Persian fleet was destroyed at Salamis (480).

c 461–429 BC   **Age of Pericles in Athens.** Pericles was a great statesman who strengthened the Athenian democracy and who attempted to make Athens the focus of the Greek world. By his statecraft, he brought about a period of peace and prosperity for Athens. He became a great patron of the arts, glorified Athens with many splendid buildings, and built the Acropolis of Athens. Among the buildings on the Acropolis is the world-famous Parthenon, a masterpiece of Greek architecture.

c 450–c 300 BC   **Great philosophers of ancient Greece.** Among the many great Greek philosophers, three have had particularly great impact on the development of Western thought. They are Socrates (469–399), his student Plato (427?–347), and Aristotle (384–322).

431–404 BC   **Peloponnesian War.** This great war between the rival city-states of Athens and Sparta ended in the ruin of Athens and marked the beginning of the decline of ancient Greece. The first phase of the war ended in stalemate in 421. In the second phase, Spartan naval victories culminated in destruction of the Athenian navy at the Battle of Aegospotami (405). Athens, forced to surrender in 404, never again regained its former greatness.

Ruins of the Parthenon at Athens, completed in 437 B.C.

c 400 BC   **Hippocrates flourishes.** Hippocrates (c 460–c 370), a renowned Greek physician, is considered the father of medicine. The Hippocratic Oath, still taken by doctors in modern times, is said to reflect his high ethical standards.

334–323 BC   **Conquests of Alexander the Great.** One of the great conquerors of the ancient world, Alexander became ruler of Macedonia, a kingdom in northern Greece, in 336. After consolidating Macedonian control over the Greek mainland, he began a series of spectacular conquests and through them became master of a vast empire that stretched from Greece to northern India. In less than ten years he conquered Persia, Phoenicia, Egypt (where he founded the great city of Alexandria), parts of central Asia, and, finally, northern India. Alexander died in 323, soon after completing these conquests, and his empire crumbled. Nevertheless, this short-lived empire helped spread Greek culture throughout the ancient world.

300 BC–476 AD

Sculpture of an old Roman, c 80 B.C.

Rome. The Roman republic was established (509) after the overthrow of the Tarquin (Etruscan) kings. By 300 BC, the Romans had taken control of the Italian peninsula. Once they had made themselves masters of Italy, the Romans entered into conflict with Carthage in the Punic Wars (see below). The three wars (between 264 and 146 BC) ultimately resulted in Roman control over Carthage and its extensive colonial domain. Meanwhile, the Romans also conquered Macedonia, Greece, and Asia Minor. By 100 BC, Roman power extended throughout the Mediterranean.

From 133 to 31 BC, the Roman republic was torn by civil war and political unrest, which eventually led to the extinction of republican government and the establishment (27 BC) of the Roman Empire under Augustus, the first emperor. For the next 200 years, the diverse peoples of the empire enjoyed peace and prosperity. During the next three centuries, however, the western half of the empire gradually declined and was finally destroyed (476) by invading Germanic tribes.

Greco-Roman civilization continued vigorously for a thousand years in the Byzantine Empire. It profoundly influenced the Roman Catholic Church and taught Germanic invaders a civilized way of life; it also provided much of the cultural inspiration for succeeding generations.

Date	Event

c 300 BC   **Euclid flourishes.** Euclid, a Greek mathematician who taught at Alexandria, Egypt, is remembered for his texts on geometry and other branches of mathematics. His system of plane geometry remained largely unchallenged until the 1800's.

264–241 BC   **First Punic War.** The first of three wars in which Rome opposed and then conquered the great empire of Carthage, centered in northern Africa. The first war was fought over control of Sicily. After some serious reverses, the Romans finally destroyed the Carthaginian fleet in 241 and forced Carthage to give up Sicily.

218–201 BC   **Second Punic War.** One of the great wars of ancient times, it was sparked by Carthaginian conquests in Spain. Rome declared war and the Carthaginian general, Hannibal, responded by marching from Spain overland toward Rome. After his famous crossing of the Alps, Hannibal invaded the Italian peninsula and won a succession of decisive victories over Roman armies. He lacked sufficient supplies to attack Rome itself, however, and though he took control of most of southern Italy, the tide of the war turned against him after 212. In 203 he was recalled to Carthage to fight a Roman invasion force under Scipio Africanus Major (234–183), and was decisively defeated at the Battle of Zama (202). Carthage surrendered in 201 and never again regained its former greatness.

214 BC   **Great Wall of China.** One of the greatest manmade structures ever built, this defensive wall was originally constructed by the Chinese Emperor Shih Hwang-ti to check barbarian invasions from the north. Later rulers added to it, creating a 1500-mile-long, 25-foot-high barrier. The wall ultimately failed to check barbarian advances, however.

The Great Wall, more than 2000 years after completion

167 BC   **Revolt of the Maccabees in Palestine.** Persecution by the Seleucids (then in control of Palestine) caused the Jews to pursue a guerrilla war against Seleucid armies. Judas Maccabeus captured Jerusalem and rededicated the temple (164). By 142, the Maccabees had reestablished an independent kingdom of Judaea.

149–146 BC   **Third Punic War.** Final war by the Romans against Carthage. The Romans provoked the war and quickly laid siege to Carthage. The city refused surrender and was taken by the Romans only after hard fighting in the streets of the city itself. The city was destroyed, its surviving inhabitants were sold into slavery, and the Carthaginian domain was organized into the Roman province of Africa.

World History

Date	Event

60 BC

Triumvirate in Rome. From about 133 BC there was gradual breakdown of order in Rome. Rebellions and civil war plagued Rome as various factions struggled to control the empire's vast riches. The first triumvirate, an alliance between Julius Caesar (102–44), Pompey (106–48), and Crassus (115?–53), brought a brief lull in this turmoil. Though their arrangement was not a legal form of government, the three triumvirs overcame all opposition and made themselves masters of Rome. They remained in power until Crassus's death in 53 BC.

58–51 BC

Caesar's conquest of Gaul. In 58, Caesar, one of the ruling triumvirate, was given command in Gaul. By his vigorous campaigns there, Caesar conquered all of Gaul and gained great power and prestige. More important, his victories left him at the head of a strong and loyal army.

49–31 BC

Julius Caesar

Cleopatra, queen of Egypt

Roman civil wars. The death of Crassus in 53 pitted the two surviving members of the triumvirate, Caesar and Pompey, against each other. Pompey, sole consul in Rome, ordered Caesar to disband his army, but instead, Caesar marched his legions across the Rubicon, a river bounding his domains, into Italy (49). He entered Rome (from which Pompey had fled), had himself made consul, and then went in pursuit of Pompey. In 48 Caesar crushed Pompey's army at Pharsala, in Greece.

Caesar then traveled to Egypt, where he made an alliance (48) with Cleopatra, who had recently been deposed as queen of Egypt. Seeing in him an opportunity to regain her throne, she used her fabled charms to become his lover and keep him there. By 47 Caesar and his armies had restored her as queen of Egypt. In 45 she followed him to Rome.

By 44 Caesar had crushed the last remnants of Pompey's army, restored order in the provinces, and been made dictator for life. Resentment at his power had grown to dangerous proportions in Rome, however, and on March 15, Brutus, Cassius, Casca, and others stabbed him to death as a traitor to republican government. Caesar's death plunged Rome into a new and more deadly disorder.

In the turmoil following Caesar's assassination, Caesar's heir, Octavian (63 BC–14 AD), joined with Marc Antony (83–30 BC) and Lepidus (d. 13 BC) to form a second triumvirate to rule Rome. When they secured their position in Rome, Octavian and Antony pursued and defeated the armies of Brutus and Cassius (42). The triumvirate was renewed in 37, but in 36 Lepidus was ousted.

Meanwhile, Antony was given control of the eastern part of the Roman provinces. There he met Cleopatra; their love affair is among the most famous in history. From 42 to 40, they remained in Egypt. When Antony returned to Rome, he was forced to marry Octavian's sister, Octavia, in order to keep his power. But he soon returned to Cleopatra. The lovers went into opposition to Rome and prepared for war. Octavian's Roman forces finally defeated them in the great naval battle at Actium, off the western coast of Greece, in 31. Antony and Cleopatra fled to Egypt. Pursued by Octavian, they committed suicide. The story of Antony and Cleopatra is the nucleus of the famous play of that title by William Shakespeare.

27 BC–14 AD

Reign of Augustus in Rome. After defeating Antony, Octavian purged the Senate and began instituting reforms in Rome and the provinces. Octavian ruled as "first citizen" until 27 BC. Then he accepted the title of Augustus and became the first Roman emperor. This event also marked the end of the Roman republic and the beginning of the empire. Augustus's reign (27 BC–14 AD) was a Golden Age for Roman arts and literature. Among the great works completed were Vergil's epic poem on the founding of Rome, the *Aeneid*, and Ovid's great work, the *Metamorphoses*. For nearly 200 years after Augustus, the empire was relatively peaceful and a succession of emperors controlled a vast empire surrounding the Mediterranean.

Date	Event

AD

c 3 BC–30 AD

Jesus and Mary, his mother

Jesus Christ. According to the four Gospels of the Bible, Jesus was born miraculously to Mary at Bethlehem in Judea, near Jerusalem. Raised in his father's trade of carpentry, Jesus became aware of his divine calling after being baptized by John the Baptist. Following a period of solitude and meditation, Jesus chose twelve disciples and together with them he traveled through Judea. He preached that the kingdom of God had come, and his Jewish followers proclaimed him as the Messiah, a savior or new king for whom the Jews had been waiting. The Gospels tell of many miracles that Jesus accomplished, particularly in healing the sick. Jesus won a wide following but came to be regarded as a threat by Roman and Jewish authorities. He was arrested in Jerusalem (c 30 AD), turned over to Roman authorities, and crucified. But he miraculously rose from the dead. His followers soon spread his teachings through the Roman Empire, establishing churches in many cities, including Rome itself.

33–64? AD

Paul the apostle flourishes. A Jewish rabbi and a Roman citizen, Paul was converted to Christianity after experiencing a vision in 33. In following years he went on missions to Asia Minor and Greece, where he spread Christianity among non-Jews. Tradition suggests that Paul was put to death in Rome (along with Peter) about 64 during the reign of Nero. His letters to the early churches became part of the Christian Bible.

54–68 AD

Nero reigns in Rome. Perhaps the most notorious of all Roman emperors, Nero's cruelties included the murder of both his mother and his wife. Nero has also been blamed for setting the great fire that burned half of Rome in 64 AD, though this accusation has generally been discounted. Nero did blame the fire on the Christians, however, and began the first Roman persecution of Christians in 64.

At its height, the Roman Empire circled the Mediterranean; but in 476, Rome itself was conquered.

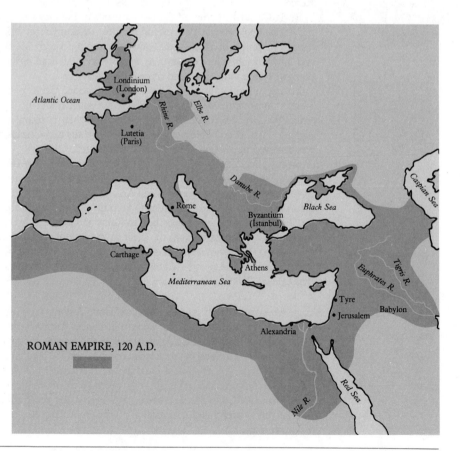

ROMAN EMPIRE, 120 A.D.

World History

Date	Event

c 100 AD   **Chinese develop use of paper.** Paper was believed to have been first made by an official at the imperial court. Knowledge of papermaking spread westward, was known in Baghdad by 793, and from there was transmitted to Europe.

132–135 AD   **Revolt of the Jews.** Led by Bar Kokba (d. 135), the Jews revolted against the rule of Palestine by the Romans. The Romans crushed the revolt, founded a Roman colony on the site of Jerusalem, and refused to allow any Jew to live within the new city.

180–192 AD   **Commodius reigns in Rome.** Ill-suited for rule, Commodius brought an end to a long period of stability in Rome. Commodius's rule was harsh, and he was finally assassinated. For nearly a hundred years afterward, Roman emperors followed in quick succession, each holding on to power for only a few years before being removed.

238 AD   **First invasions by the Goths.** The Goths were a Germanic people that seriously threatened the Roman Empire. Thought to have come originally from Sweden, they migrated southward and came into conflict with the Romans by 238. They raided Greece and gradually forced Roman legions out of Dacia (now Rumania).

284–305 AD   **Diocletian reigns in Rome.** Diocletian was a strong, effective ruler who ended nearly 100 years of instability and thus checked for a time the decline of the empire.

313 AD   **Edict of Milan.** Just before becoming emperor of the Western Roman Empire in 312, Constantine accepted Christianity. The following year, Constantine convinced Licinus, emperor of the Eastern Roman Empire, to join him in proclaiming the toleration of Christianity. The resulting Edict of Milan provided religious freedom for Christians throughout the empire and ordered the restoration of property confiscated from them.

324–337 AD   **Constantine reigns as sole Roman emperor.** Constantine united the eastern and western halves of the empire, which had been administered separately. A period of peace ensued, in which Constantine attempted to strengthen the Christian church and to restore the power of the Roman Empire. He founded the great city of Constantinople (now Istanbul, Turkey), which was the center of the Byzantine Empire for nearly 1000 years. On Constantine's death in 337, however, the empire was again divided.

325 AD   **Council of Nicaea.** The rise of Arianism, a controversial doctrine on the nature of Jesus Christ, threatened to divide the Christian church during the reign of Constantine. In attempting to resolve the dispute over Arianism, Constantine convened (325) a general council of the Christian church, at Nicaea. The council condemned Arianism and formulated the Nicene Creed, which remains the orthodox doctrine on the nature of Jesus.

434–453 AD   **Attila, leader of the Huns.** The Huns were perhaps the most savage of all the barbarian invaders and their notorious leader, Attila, was sometimes called the "Scourge of God." From 434, when he became leader of the Huns, Attila menaced the Eastern Roman Empire. In 451, he marshaled an army of about half a million Huns and barbarian peoples and swept westward into Gaul. He was defeated in a bloody battle at Chalons (in modern France), but ravaged Italy the next year. He died in 453, and his empire disintegrated.

455 AD   **Vandals sack Rome.** The Vandals, a Germanic people, had been forced westward by the Huns and finally crossed from Spain into North Africa. There they captured Carthage (439) from the Romans. Their raids on Sicily and southern Italy from this base culminated in their sack of Rome in 455, soon after the Huns had swept through Italy.

476 AD   **Fall of Rome.** Disintegration of the Western Roman Empire was nearly complete when Odoacer (c 435–493), a German chieftain in Roman service, deposed the last Roman emperor, Romulus Augustulus (ruled 475–476). This marked the end of the Roman Empire in the west and the beginning of the Middle Ages in Europe. Thereafter the Roman Empire in the east became known as the Byzantine Empire.

Medieval world

In Europe, the collapse of the Roman Empire marked the beginning of the Middle Ages, a period of more than 1000 years (476–1500). This period witnessed the rise of the Roman Catholic Church, the formation of the first European nation-states, and (near its end) the rediscovery of Greek and Roman culture during the Renaissance. But in 476, the Western Roman Empire was in the hands of the European tribes the Romans called barbarians. Italy was controlled by the Ostrogoths, Gaul was undergoing a new invasion by the Franks, Spain was ruled by the Visigoths, and Africa was held by the Vandals. Only in the eastern empire, now called the Byzantine Empire, did Roman rule continue.

Date	Event

476–1453

Emperor Justinian, c 560

The Byzantine Empire. Roman rule in the east continued under the Byzantine emperors, who proved able to withstand the barbarian attacks. Under Justinian (527–565), the empire recovered some lands from barbarians in the Latin West, but the Byzantine state was rarely free from the threat of invasion. Despite this, the empire successfully maintained the most prosperous economy in the medieval Christian world and achieved a dynamic and civilized society.

Attacks by the Seljuk Turks after 1000 seriously weakened the empire and, for a time, it was ruled (1204–1261) by the Crusaders, European warriors who had come to help the Byzantine Christians against the Muslim Turks. After Byzantine emperors regained control in 1261, the empire continued to decline until it was finally conquered by the Turks in 1453. Throughout its long history, Byzantine culture was permeated by Christianity. But the Eastern Church, which was subject to control by the Byzantine emperors, gradually split with the Western Church over doctrinal disputes, and in 1054 the division between Eastern and Western Christianity became permanent. Byzantine art and culture greatly influenced the Slavs of Eastern Europe and helped to pass on Greek and Roman culture to Western Europe.

c 500

Clovis founds the Merovingian Empire in Gaul. Clovis I (ruled 481–511) was king of the Salian Franks, a Germanic people that invaded Gaul (modern France) as Rome collapsed. By his conquests, he made himself master of Gaul and established his capital at Paris. The empire he founded was divided on his death and later was torn by internal wars, but it nevertheless provided the foundation for Charlemagne's great empire three centuries later.

527–565

Justinian reigns in the Byzantine Empire. Justinian retook Africa and Italy from the barbarians and ordered construction of the Hagia Sophia, the great masterpiece of Byzantine architecture. Justinian is also famous for his Justinian Code, a compilation of Roman law.

c 529

St. Benedict's monastery founded. Located at Monte Cassino in what is now Italy, the monastery became the symbolic center of Western monasticism. Monasteries patterned on the Benedictine model spread throughout Europe, helped Christianize the Continent, and helped preserve Latin culture during a period of great instability. The Benedictine order of monks flourished until about 1200.

590–604

Saint Gregory I is pope. Gregory promoted papal supremacy in spiritual matters and established papal authority in temporal matters as well. He also did much to promote monasticism and to reform church administration and liturgy.

618–907

T'ang dynasty in China. T'ang rulers greatly expanded the Chinese empire and by about 650 controlled regions that included China proper and parts of Korea, Manchuria, Mongolia, Tibet, and Turkistan. The T'ang period also witnessed a great flowering of the arts, especially sculpture, painting, and poetry. The rise of provincial warlords after 750 weakened and finally brought down the dynasty.

622–1258

Muslim architecture in Spain

Islam. Muhammad (570?–632), an Arab holy man, began his prophetic mission at age 40 when God appointed him as a messenger. He named his religion Islam and called on his fellow citizens at Mecca (in modern Saudi Arabia) to forsake belief in more than one God and to seek righteousness. In 622 Muhammad and his followers were forced to leave Mecca for Medina. This exodus, called the Hegira, marks the beginning of the Muslim calendar. In 630, after consolidating his hold over Medina, Muhammad took control of Mecca. By the time he died (632), much of Arabia had submitted to him.

Muhammad's successors, called caliphs, completed the conquest of Arabia and successfully attacked the Byzantines and Persians. Under the Umayyad dynasty (660–750), the empire of the caliphs reached its height and extended westward from Arabia to Spain and eastward to central Asia. In 750 the Abbasid dynasty came to power. Under Abbasid rule (750–1258), centered at Baghdad, the major cities of the Muslim empire experienced a golden age. The empire began to decline after about 900 and fell to the invading Mongols in 1258. Islam itself, however, had been established as the dominant religion from the Indian subcontinent to North Africa.

732–768

Rise of the Frankish kingdom. Frankish hero Charles Martel defeated the Muslim invaders at the battle of Tours in 732. Thus he ended the threat to Frankish domains and became ruler of the Franks. In 751, Pepin the Short became king, establishing the Carolingian line. Pepin donated his lands in central Italy to the pope in 756. These became the nucleus of the Papal States, which were controlled by the papacy until 1870.

768

Charlemagne (742?–814) succeeds Pepin as ruler of the Franks. Charlemagne embarked on series of conquests through which he created the great Carolingian Empire, defeating the Lombards in Italy, the Avars in the Danube region, and other tribes in Bavaria, Saxony, and the Spanish March (northeastern Spain). Charlemagne was crowned emperor of a reconstituted Western Roman Empire in 800. He also sought to restore education, theological studies, and art, creating a brief renaissance of learning and art.

c 800–1400

A medieval knight

Age of feudalism. Feudalism is generally believed to have been introduced in Europe during the reign of Charlemagne (768–814). It was spread across continental Europe by Frankish conquests and was introduced in England by the Normans, following their conquest in 1066. The feudal system was based on the granting of rights to lands (fiefs) in return for certain considerations. Thus, a feudal lord granted lands to his vassal (a lesser noble) in return for an oath of loyalty and the commitment to supply a number of warriors for the lord's armies. The process of subdivision (called subinfeudination) was continued by the vassals, who, in turn, divided their lands into fiefs. The vassals then became the feudal lords of the nobles who received these lands. At the bottom of the feudal hierarchy were the serfs, tenants of the feudal manor. Serfs were peasant laborers who were bound to the manor and who by farming the lands provided the economic base of the feudal system. Feudalism reached its height in the 1200's, declining thereafter until it had largely disappeared in Western Europe by about 1400.

The feudal system created petty kingdoms, encouraged wars between them, and inflicted severe hardships on the peasant serfs. But feudal society, with its brave knights and strict code of chivalry, also inspired a flourishing romantic literature in late medieval times. These romances portrayed an idealized vision of courtly life and of battle, a vision that continues to hold a special fascination even today. A great body of these romances, called the Arthurian cycle, recounted and embellished tales of King Arthur, legendary English conqueror and hero; splendid Camelot, where he held court; and the Round Table, where Arthur met with his knights.

Viking raiders

c 800–c 900   **Norse raiders flourish.** Norsemen were Scandinavian Vikings who, seeking plunder and new lands, ranged far from their homelands. Danes (Norsemen from Denmark) invaded England in 865 and many settled there permanently. In France, Norsemen conquered and settled what became Normandy by 912. The Norsemen who invaded Russia were called Varangians.

843   **Treaty of Verdun.** Charlemagne's successor, Louis I the Pious (ruled 814–840), held the Carolingian Empire together until he died in 840. Open warfare then broke out among his heirs. The Treaty of Verdun divided the empire into three parts: the western part became modern France and the eastern part eventually became Germany. The narrow middle section was largely absorbed into the eastern and western kingdoms.

871–899   **Alfred the Great rules in England.** From about 600, the Angles and Saxons, Germanic peoples who invaded England, had established a number of independent kingdoms. After 800, however, Norse invaders from Denmark (called Danes) threatened to overrun all of Anglo-Saxon England. Alfred, Anglo-Saxon king of Wessex, became a hero of early England by turning back the advancing Danes and preserving Anglo-Saxon rule in south and west England.

c 950   **First use of gunpowder.** Though it is not clear when gunpowder was invented, there is evidence that the Chinese were using it for fireworks by about this time. Knowledge of gunpowder was apparently transmitted from China, through the Arabs, to Europe by the 1400's.

960–1279   **Sung dynasty in China.** Following a period of chaos and warfare between petty kingdoms, Sung rulers reunited the Chinese empire and thus set the stage for one of the great epochs in Chinese history. Increased trade with India, Persia, and the Arabs brought commercial prosperity. There were many technological innovations (gunpowder, movable type for printing), Confucianism was revived, administrative reforms were instituted, and the arts flourished. Sung rulers lacked an effective military force, however, and finally succumbed to the invading Mongols, led by Kublai Khan (see below).

962   **Otto the Great founds the Holy Roman Empire.** After the division of the Carolingian Empire (843), the eastern part broke up into the duchies of Franconia, Saxony, Thuringia, Swabia, and Bavaria. As German king, Otto (ruled 936–973) reasserted imperial control over the rebellious German nobles; defeated the Magyars, a Slavic people threatening the empire from the east; and brought Lorraine, Burgundy, and Italy under German control. Otto also fostered ties with the church and in 962 the pope crowned him emperor. This event marked the beginning of the Holy Roman Empire, a German state that remained the most formidable kingdom in Western Europe until the 1200's.

987–996   **Hugh Capet, first Capetian king of France.** Hugh Capet was a powerful nobleman with extensive domains around Paris. He displaced the Carolingian claimant to the throne of the western (French) part of the old empire in 987 and thereupon founded the Capetian dynasty. This dynasty ruled France until 1328. The Capetian kings greatly expanded the territories of France through wars and alliances and thus laid the foundations of modern France.

c 1000   **Leif Ericsson visits North America.** Raised among Norse colonists in Greenland, Leif Ericsson is known to have visited Norway in 999. On the return voyage to Greenland, however, his ship was apparently blown off course and he landed at what he called "Vinland." Though most agree he landed in North America, the exact location is a matter of conjecture.

1016–1035   **Canute, Danish king of England.** Canute invaded England with a large force in 1015, quickly conquered the Anglo-Saxon kingdoms, and became sole ruler of England. He succeeded to the Danish throne in 1019 and added Norway to his domain in 1028, thus creating a great but short-lived northern empire.

c 1025   **Modern musical notation formulated.** In order to simplify the training required for ecclesiastical singers, a Benedictine monk named Guido of Arezzo (c 990–1050) invented a new means of musical notation in about 1025. His system introduced the use of the staff and clef and thereby provided the foundation for modern musical notation in the West.

Early musical notation

AUDE-AMUS omnes in Dó- mi- no

1054   **Schism of 1054.** Doctrinal and jurisdictional disputes between the Western Christian Church, centered at Rome, and the Eastern Christian Church, centered at Constantinople, had begun centuries before. In 1054, however, the separation became permanent and formally established the independence of the Roman Catholic Church in the West and the Eastern Orthodox Church in the East.

1066   **Normans conquer England.** The Norman invasion was launched by William the Conqueror (c 1027–1087), duke of Normandy (in modern France), to press his claim to the English throne. William won England at the Battle of Hastings (1066), though rebellions by English noblemen continued until 1072. As king of England, William replaced the English nobles with his Norman followers and distributed English lands to them according to the feudal system. Norman customs and the Norman French language became the standard in England and remained so for two centuries among nobility.

1075–1122   **Investiture controversy.** Lay investiture was a medieval church practice whereby a secular ruler became involved in the selection of bishops and other clerics. The system led to widespread corruption. Pope Gregory VII (fl. c 1020–1085) ended investiture in 1075. In 1076, the Holy Roman Emperor Henry IV (ruled 1056–1105) declared the pope deposed; but within a year he was forced to submit to Gregory in a humiliating ceremony at Canossa (1077). Henry finally attacked Rome (1081–1083), forcing Gregory to flee. The struggle outlived both of them and was finally ended in 1122 by a compromise called the Concordat of Worms.

Date	Event

1095–1291   **Crusades.** By 1095 the Muslim Turks had closed access to the Holy Land (Palestine) and threatened the Christian empire of the Byzantines. In that same year Pope Urban II encouraged European noblemen to travel to the Holy Land and protect it. This first crusade (1096–1099) was successful, resulting in the capture of Jerusalem and the founding of the Crusader States in the Holy Land.

     Muslim victories in following years sparked new crusades—eight in all—each less successful than the last. The Christians were finally driven from the Holy Land in 1291.

1138   **Guelphs and Ghibellines in the Holy Roman Empire.** The Guelphs were partisans of the papacy. The Ghibellines supported the Hohenstaufen royal house of the Holy Roman Empire. The conflict between the Guelphs and Ghibellines continued for over a hundred years and centered on attempts by the Hohenstaufens, especially Frederick I Barbarossa (1152–1190) and Frederick II (1220–1250), to strengthen imperial power through the domination of Italy. The Hohenstaufens met stubborn resistance from the popes, feudal noblemen of Germany, and the cities of northern Italy.

1170   **St. Thomas à Becket martyred in England.** From 1162, when he was elected archbishop of Canterbury, St. Thomas valiantly resisted the efforts of King Henry II (ruled 1154–1189) to curb the powers of the church in England. The conflict ended in the murder of St. Thomas by four of the king's knights.

1198–1216   **Pope Innocent reigns.** The papacy reached the height of its power during Innocent's reign. Innocent asserted papal supremacy over secular rulers, was able to enforce his will over the Holy Roman Empire and England, and acted as overlord in Spain, Hungary, and Scandinavia.

1206–1227   **Genghis Khan.** Mongol tribes were united under the rule of Genghis Khan (1167?–1227) in 1206 and in following years he and his savage bands of warriors swept across Asia. Genghis Khan first attacked China and Korea, then turned to the west. He conquered parts of Persia and Russia and raided India. His sons continued his conquests and, by 1260, they ruled a great Mongol empire that included much of Asia and eastern Europe.

1215   **Magna Charta.** One of the most famous documents in history, the Magna Charta is an early statement of the principle of subjecting even the king to a rule of law. It was drawn up by noblemen in England to halt abuses by King John (ruled 1199–1216). The nobles forced John to sign the document at Runnymede on June 19, 1215.

c 1250   **St. Thomas Aquinas flourishes.** St. Thomas (1225–1274) was the leading philosopher of the medieval church. He taught that reason and faith are compatible and systematized the doctrines of the church. St. Thomas's writings were officially adopted (1879) by the Roman Catholic Church.

1279–1290   **Kublai Khan in China.** The grandson of Genghis Khan, Kublai Khan (1215?–1294) brought the Eurasian Mongol empire to its height by conquering China in 1279. Other attempts at conquests failed, however, and the sinking of his invasion fleet off Japan (1281) by a typhoon both saved Japan from the Mongols and gave rise to the term "kamikaze" (divine wind). Kublai Khan made China the seat of the Mongol empire. At what is now Peking, he built a magnificent city as his capital. His reign was prosperous and the splendor of his court was described in the famous narratives of Marco Polo (1254?–1324?), a Venetian traveler who journeyed there in 1275.

Kublai Khan

c 1308   **Dante Alighieri (1265–1321) begins work on the *Divine Comedy*.** One of the great masterpieces of Western literature, the *Divine Comedy* was written in Italian (rather than Latin, the "official" language of diplomacy and the church). It recounts the poet's imaginary journey through Hell, Purgatory, and Paradise.

1309–1378

Babylonian Captivity of the papacy. Unsettled political conditions at Rome forced the removal of the papacy to Avignon (now in France), then under papal control. The popes during this period were French and were generally under the control of the French monarchy. Pope Gregory XI (ruled 1370–1378) ended the captivity by returning the papacy to Rome. This ushered in the Great Schism (see below).

1334–c 1354

Black Death. This terrible epidemic began in Constantinople in 1334 and quickly spread into Europe. In the next two decades an estimated 75 percent of the population of Europe and Asia was wiped out. The social and economic consequences of the plague were enormous. It contributed to the breakup of the feudal system by creating a sudden shortage of peasant labor. Because their services became more valuable, the peasants revolted in many parts of Europe and demanded more equitable treatment.

1337–1453

Hundred Years' War. This protracted war left France devastated by internal revolts and famine, as well as by fighting, and cost England its extensive domains on the European Continent. Both kingdoms were further ravaged by the outbreak of the Black Death during the war.

The war began when English King Edward III (ruled 1327–1377) claimed the French throne and invaded France. The first phase of the war ended favorably for the English in 1360, following important victories at Crecy (1346) and Poitiers (1356). Fighting resumed after 1369. In 1407, a civil war broke out over control of the French throne, and the English took advantage, conquering most of northern France by 1429. Then the great French heroine Joan of Arc (1412?–1431) rallied the French and drove the English back at Orleans. She was captured and burned at the stake by the English in 1431, but she provided the spark needed to bring about victory for France. Charles VII was crowned at Rheims in 1429, the civil war in France ended in 1435, and by 1453 the French had conquered all English domains on the Continent.

The English use bows and arrows to defeat the French at Crecy, 1346.

| Date | Event |

1368–1644   **Ming dynasty in China.** The Ming dynasty emperors ended the period of Mongol rule begun by Kublai Khan. They expanded their empire to include Korea, Vietnam, Burma, Turkistan, and Mongolia. Traditional Chinese culture was restored, and during this period European traders and missionaries began to penetrate China. Ineffective rulers and internal dissent finally ended the reign of the Ming emperors.

c 1369–1405   **Tamerlane.** Claiming to be a descendant of Genghis Khan, Tamerlane (c 1336–1405) had firmly established control around his capital, Samarkand (near the Caspian Sea), by about 1369. In following years, he ruthlessly conquered other territories in this region and created a short-lived empire that extended from the Black Sea to northern India.

1378–1417   **Great Schism of the Roman Catholic Church.** The return of the papacy to Rome in 1378 resulted in a split between the newly elected Italian pope and the cardinals. A faction of cardinals elected their own pope, sitting in Avignon, in opposition to the pope at Rome. The schism was ended after nearly 40 years by the Council of Constance, which deposed the rival popes and elected Martin V (ruled 1417–1431) as pope.

c 1387   ***The Canterbury Tales.*** A masterpiece of early English literature, this collection of tales concerning medieval English life was written by the poet Geoffrey Chaucer (c 1340–1400) in the years after 1387.

c 1438   **Gutenberg prints with movable type.** Though the use of movable type was first discovered in China sometime between 1000 and 1100, it was apparently unknown in Europe until Johann Gutenberg (c 1400–1468?) invented it there. The discovery made books far less expensive and more accessible.

1453   **Constantinople captured by Ottoman Turks.** The fall of Constantinople marked the end of the Byzantine Empire and the ascendancy of the new and powerful Ottoman Empire. Centered in northwest Asia Minor from the 1200's, the Ottoman Turks gradually extended their control into southeastern Europe and, after displacing the Byzantines there, captured Constantinople. The empire expanded rapidly thereafter and by the late 1500's it included most of the Middle East and North Africa, the Balkans in southeastern Europe, the Crimea, and parts of Hungary. After 1600, the power of the Ottomans declined, but the regime survived until 1914.

1455–1485   **Wars of the Roses in England.** This complex dynastic war was fought by the rival houses of York and Lancaster for control of the English throne. Actual fighting occurred only sporadically. The Yorkists gained the throne in 1461, but dissension among the Yorkists led to the rise of Henry Tudor, the Lancastrian claimant to the throne. He ended the wars by defeating Yorkist King Richard III (ruled 1483–1485) at the Battle of Bosworth Field (1485), and was crowned Henry VII (ruled 1485–1509).

1469   **Founding of the modern Spanish state.** The Muslim invasion of the Iberian Peninsula (711) left Christians in possession of only small kingdoms in the north, and it was not until after 1000 that Spanish Christians began to retake the peninsula. In the wake of the Christian advance, various independent kingdoms were created. Their unification into the Spanish state began with the marriage of King Ferdinand of Aragon (1452–1516) and Queen Isabella of Castile (1451–1504) in 1469. The Spanish monarchs sponsored the expeditions of Christopher Columbus (see below). His discoveries gave Spain an advantage in gaining an overseas empire. By Ferdinand's death in 1516, Spain was not only united but was becoming the richest kingdom in Europe.

Ferdinand and Isabella

1478   **Spanish Inquisition.** Instituted by King Ferdinand and Queen Isabella, the Spanish Inquisition is remembered chiefly as a symbol of barbaric cruelty and persecution. In Spain the Inquisition was concerned with cases of heresy and certain other crimes. The notorious Tomás de Torquemada (1420–1498), Grand Inquisitor from 1483, devised especially cruel procedures. Only after 1600 was the severity of the Inquisition reduced.

Renaissance and Enlightenment

The European world changed greatly in the 1500's. The Renaissance in art and learning, the Reformation in religion, and the excitement of worldwide exploration all helped bring men to a new understanding of themselves and their universe. The changes also brought terrible wars and persecutions, however. By 1700, a new world view called the Enlightenment had many of the seeds of our own modern perspective; men talked of democracy and of the new world order that the modern era would one day produce.

Date   *Event*

1490–1650

A sketch by Michelangelo

Galileo's telescope and his air thermometer

A study of proportions by Leonardo da Vinci

The Renaissance. Renaissance means literally rebirth; the term applies to the revival of classical learning and culture in Europe at the close of the Middle Ages. The reawakening began in Italy as early as 1300, and it spread gradually to other parts of Europe, mainly during the late 1400's and 1500's. The shift in viewpoint during the Renaissance was remarkable: medieval man was concerned with God, but for men in the Renaissance, man was indeed "the measure of all things."

Scholars were concerned with the secular world. Poets and philosophers were concerned with this world, not the next; with the world of nature, not that of theology; with man, not angels. Painters and sculptors sought to capture real people rather than general types, and individual personalities rather than universal human traits. Architects replaced the ornate Gothic style with a simple, classical style with straight lines and balanced proportions.

Universities concentrated heavily on secular subjects and produced large numbers of educated laymen. The "universal man"—one skilled in a variety of pursuits, from scholarship and poetry to the art of war—was the Renaissance ideal. Leonardo da Vinci (1452–1519) came closest of all to fitting this model.

The Renaissance also witnessed the consolidation of major European states under strong monarchical rule, notably in England, France, and Spain. By the early 1500's, each of these countries had achieved, approximately, its modern boundaries. Although each country developed differently, all developed a strong monarchy and centralized institutions characteristic of modern government.

Renaissance Masters

Dante, 1265–1321, *Italian poet*
Giotto, 1266–1337, *Italian painter*
Petrarch, 1304–1374, *Italian poet and humanist*
Giovanni Boccaccio, 1313–1375, *Italian writer*
Donatello, c 1386–1466, *Italian sculptor*
Leonardo da Vinci, 1452–1519, *Italian painter, sculptor, engineer, scientist*
Erasmus, 1466?–1536, *Dutch humanist scholar*
Niccolò Machiavelli, 1469–1527, *Italian writer and political philosopher*
Albrecht Dürer, 1471–1528, *German artist*
Nicolaus Copernicus, 1473–1543, *Polish astronomer*
Michelangelo, 1475–1564, *Italian painter, sculptor, architect*

Sir Thomas More, 1478–1535, *English author*
Raphael, 1483–1520, *Italian painter*
Titian, c 1490–1576, *Italian painter*
François Rabelais, 1494?–1553, *French writer*
Hans Holbein the Younger, c 1497–1543, *German artist*
Pieter Brueghel the Elder, c 1525–1569, *Flemish artist*
Michel Eyquem de Montaigne, 1533–1592, *French essayist*
Miguel de Cervantes, 1547–1616, *Spanish writer*
Francis Bacon, 1561–1626, *English philosopher*
William Shakespeare, 1564–1616, *English dramatist*
Galileo, 1564–1642, *Italian scientist*

1492–1522   **Age of Discovery.** Improvements in navigation, increased knowledge about the world beyond Europe (gained during the late Middle Ages), and successful voyages along the African coast by Portuguese explorer Henry the Navigator (1394–1460), all helped set the stage for a rapid succession of voyages of discovery. That the world was round was not a new idea in Europe, but the dangers of sailing into unknown waters were legion.

Thus, in 1492, when Christopher Columbus (1451–1506) sailed westward to find a sea route to Asia, he needed both the courage of his conviction that the world was round and more than a little good fortune. News of Columbus's discovery of land (an island in the Bahamas) on October 12, 1492, aroused great interest in Europe. It touched off an era of exploration and colonization that was to profoundly affect the history of Europe and the world. While Columbus's voyages (he made four in all) opened up the New World to the Spanish, the voyage by Portuguese navigator Vasco da Gama (c 1469–1524) in 1497–1499 resulted in the discovery of a sea route to India and the establishment of Portuguese colonies in both India and east Africa. Finally, Ferdinand Magellan (c 1480–1521), a Portuguese navigator in Spanish service, set out in 1519 to find a westward route to the Spice Islands. Magellan was killed in the Philippines, but his ships continued sailing westward, and on September 6, 1522, they completed the first circumnavigation of the world.

Vasco da Gama

MAJOR VOYAGES OF EXPLORATION, 1492–1521

GREENLAND

CABOT 1497–1498

ENGLAND

NORTH AMERICA

SPAIN   EUROPE

ASIA

Atlantic Ocean

COLUMBUS 1492

Isthmus of Panama

VESPUCCI 1497–1503

BALBOA 1513

AFRICA

ARABIA   INDIA

Indian Ocean

SOUTH AMERICA

DIAS 1498

Da GAMA 1498

MAGELLAN 1519–1521

Pacific Ocean

Cape of Good Hope

Cape Horn

1509–1547   **Henry VIII reigns in England.** A strong ruler, whose actions helped shape English history, Henry is best remembered for his many wives (he had six) and for his troubles with the Roman Catholic Church. The failure of Henry's first wife to produce a male heir led him to seek papal sanction for a divorce. This was refused but Henry married a new wife, Anne Boleyn (1507?–1536), anyway. Excommunicated by the pope, he retaliated by separating the English church from Rome (1534). Henry thus created the Church of England, which is still independent of Rome today, and made himself head of the church. He then dealt ruthlessly with all opposition to the new national church. In subsequent years, Henry became increasingly despotic, treating his wives no less harshly than his subjects.

1517–1555  *John Calvin*	**The Reformation.** The Reformation began in 1517 as a revolt against corruption in the Western Church. Within 40 years, it had established several Christian churches (which came to be called Protestant) as rivals to the chuch headed by the pope (which came to be known as Roman Catholic). Widespread abuses, such as simony (sale of church offices), violation of vows of celibacy by the clergy, and the sale of indulgences (by which the pope claimed to release souls from purgatory), had sparked calls for reform in previous centuries. But it was the matter of indulgences that finally prompted action by Martin Luther (1483-1546), a professor of theology at the University of Wittenberg, in Germany. On October 31, 1517, Luther posted his famous 95 theses, attacking church corruption, on the door of the Wittenberg church. Thus began the Reformation. Luther ultimately denied not only the doctrine of indulgences but also the infallibility of popes and church councils. Central to his emerging Protestant doctrine, however, was his assertion that salvation was achieved through faith, not sacraments and works. Luther's doctrine spread rapidly and, although he was excommunicated (1520) and put under an imperial ban by the Diet of Worms (1521), he continued to preach and teach for another 25 years. Supported by several German princes, Luther's reform movement evolved into the independent Lutheran Church. Meanwhile, other Protestant groups appeared, including the Calvinists, led by the French theologian John Calvin (1509-1564). In 1536 Calvin organized the Reformed Church in Geneva, Switzerland, and from this beginning Calvinism grew into a second major branch of Protestantism. Calvinism differed from Lutheranism chiefly in the doctrine that salvation of individuals was predestined at the time of creation. Other more radical sects also appeared. Attempts by Catholic princes to crush the Protestant movement in the Holy Roman Empire led to a series of rebellions and ruinous wars. The Religious Peace of Augsburg (see below) in 1555 brought a 50-year halt to the fighting, but religious antagonisms continued, playing a major role in the Thirty Years' War (1618-1648) (see below). Meanwhile, Protestantism spread quickly throughout Northern Europe and led to religious strife in France, England, Scotland, the Netherlands, Poland, and Hungary.

1519–1533 **Spanish conquests in South America.** After establishing themselves in the West Indies, the Spanish conquered the South American mainland. In 1519, the great Spanish conquistador Hernán Cortés (1485-1547) led a small force into what is now Mexico; by 1521 he had conquered the Mayan and Aztec empires. The Spanish extended their control into Central America in following years. In 1533 Francisco Pizarro moved against the great Inca empire, centered in Peru, and took control of it with astonishing ease. From this base, the Spanish subsequently extended their control throughout most the continent and imposed a harsh colonial regime. Native Indian cities were stripped of their fabulous wealth in gold. Indians were enslaved and forced to work in the mines to produce still more wealth for their greedy Spanish overlords.

1519–1556 **Charles V (1500-1558) reigns as Holy Roman Emperor.** One of the most powerful rulers of the famous Hapsburg family, Charles became king of Spain in 1516. On his succession as Holy Roman Emperor in 1519, he became the ruler of vast domains, including much of Europe and Spanish claims in the New World. His reign was marked by wars with the French and opposition to the Reformation within the Holy Roman Empire.

c 1530 **Copernicus revolutionizes astronomy.** Nicolaus Copernicus (1473-1543), a Polish astronomer, used his observations of heavenly bodies to disprove the traditional theory that the sun and planets rotate around Earth. Copernicus completed his book advancing a heliocentric theory (Earth and other planets rotate around the sun) in about 1530, and later came to be recognized as the founder of modern astronomy.

1545–1563   **Council of Trent and the Counter Reformation.** The rapid spread of Protestantism encouraged Catholic leaders to eliminate abuses and corruption in the Roman Catholic Church. The movement centered on the work of the Council of Trent, which was called by Pope Paul III (ruled 1534–1549) and which completed its work in 1563. The council instituted a reformulation of Catholic doctrine, measures to end abuses by the clergy, and liturgical reforms. The council's work was carried forward in subsequent years by reformminded popes, as well as by reform movements within Catholic religious orders.

1547–1584   **Ivan the Terrible reigns as first Russian czar.** Following the Mongol invasions (1200's), the Duchy of Moscow rose to power as the nucleus of the Russian state. Ivan succeeded as grand duke of Moscow in 1547, but took the title of czar; he was the first Russian ruler to do so. He greatly expanded his empire eastward by defeating the Mongol Tatars and by conquering Siberia. Ivan became ruthless and erratic in the latter part of his reign and, to consolidate his power, instituted a reign of terror in which many boyars (noblemen) were killed or exiled.

1555   **Peace of Augsburg.** This agreement ended (for about 50 years) the religious strife in the Holy Roman Empire brought about by the Protestant Reformation. Warfare between rival Protestant and Catholic nobles had threatened to tear the empire apart and the nobles readily agreed to the peace, which allowed each state to adopt either Lutheranism or Catholicism. Catholics in Lutheran states were allowed to migrate to Catholic states, and vice versa. Calvinists were not included in the settlement.

1558–1603   **Queen Elizabeth reigns in England.** One of the great English monarchs, Elizabeth presided over England's rise as a major naval power, brought about a period of commercial prosperity, and oversaw the beginnings of colonization by the English. She became a champion of the Protestant cause by restoring the Church of England in 1559, after a brief renewal of Catholicism (1555–1559), and by supporting Protestant leaders in Europe. Elizabeth's reign was also marked by a great flowering of English literature, including the works of William Shakespeare (1564–1616), Christopher Marlowe (1564–1593), and Edmund Spenser (1552?–1599).

1562–1598   **Religious wars in France.** These were a series of intermittent and bloody civil wars between Catholics and French Protestants (Huguenots). The wars were sparked by persecutions of the Protestants, and were further complicated by rivalry between Protestant and Catholic nobles for control of the French monarchy. By 1584, the conflict centered around the succession of a Protestant to the French throne. The Protestant leader, King Henry IV, took the throne in 1589, but agreed to become a Catholic (1593). In 1598, he issued the Edict of Nantes, granting full liberties to Protestants.

1582   **Gregorian calendar.** Pope Gregory XIII (ruled 1572–1585) devised this calendar to improve the accuracy of the Julian calendar, which was then in use. Gregory's calendar added eleven days (at the time of its adoption) to the Julian calendar. The modern calendar uses Gregory's system.

1588   **Spanish Armada destroyed.** Spanish King Philip II assembled his famous war fleet to invade Elizabethan England and put an end to Protestantism there. But before the armada could reach English shores, it was heavily damaged (1588) and scattered by the lighter, more maneuverable English warships. Heavy storms further damaged the fleet and only half its ships returned to Spain. Spain never regained its position as a naval power, and began a long economic decline.

1592–1611   **Shakespeare flourishes.** Regarded as the world's greatest playwright, William Shakespeare (1564–1616) began his career as a playwright in London in about 1592. He wrote nearly 40 plays; among his most famous are *Romeo and Juliet, Hamlet,* and *Macbeth* (see Literature).

1600's

> **Building empires.** During the 1500's only Spain (mainly in South America) and Portugal (mainly in Africa and the East Indies) actively sought to establish trading colonies. But in the early 1600's there began a great European movement to acquire colonial empires. The Dutch were first and they eventually dominated the East Indies. They also established footholds in India, Africa, South America, and North America (notably New Amsterdam on Manhattan Island).
>
> By 1603 the French began the settlement of New France (Canadian coastal regions); they later expanded into the Mississippi valley region of the United States. They also founded colonies in the Caribbean islands, in Africa, and in India. The British, unable to compete with the Dutch in the East Indies, focused on India. They also established themselves in West Africa, the West Indies, coastal North America, and the Hudson Bay region of Canada. British and French colonial rivalries resulted in four colonial wars between 1689 and 1763, each a part of a larger European war. By 1763 France had lost most of her colonies and Britain emerged as the leading colonial power.

1613

Romanov dynasty comes to power in Russia. Following the collapse of the old Rurik dynasty, Russia endured a chaotic period called the Time of Troubles (1598-1613). The election of Michael Romanov (ruled 1613-1645) as czar restored order and began the reign of the Romanov dynasty, which ruled Russia until the Revolution of 1917.

1618–1648

Gustavus Adolphus

Thirty Years' War. This was the last of the great European wars of religion. This complex war involved the controversy between Protestants and Catholics; the power struggle between the Holy Roman Emperor and German nobles seeking to break imperial authority; and political rivalry between the Hapsburg family (which controlled the Holy Roman Empire) and England, France, Denmark, and Sweden. The war began with a revolt against Catholicism and absolutist authority in Bohemia. Order was restored by about 1623, but in 1626 Denmark invaded the empire (with some English troops) in the name of the Protestant cause. Denmark was defeated in 1629 and in 1630 the Swedes entered the war. Sweden, under the command of King Gustavus Adolphus, brought the imperial forces to near defeat, but the Peace of Prague (1635) united Protestants and Catholics in the Holy Roman Empire against the Swedes. The French then joined the Swedes and fighting spread throughout Europe. France succeeded in dragging out the war, exhausting the Hapsburgs and the Holy Roman Empire. The Peace of Westphalia ended the war in 1648 and virtually destroyed the Holy Roman Empire by making German states practically independent of imperial control. It also gave France important territories on the German frontier; forced Spain to recognize the independence of the United Provinces (the Netherlands); and granted Calvinists religious freedoms in the Holy Roman Empire.

Delegates conclude the Treaty of Westphalia, 1648.

Date	Event

1620   **Pilgrims land at Plymouth Rock.** To escape religious persecution in England, a group of Puritans obtained the backing of a London stock company and sailed to America aboard the cargo ship *Mayflower*. After a two-month voyage, the Puritans landed at Plymouth Rock (in southeastern Massachusetts) and founded the first permanent settlement in New England.

1642–1660   **Revolution and unrest in England.** During the reign of Charles I (1625–1649), members of Parliament resisted his royal prerogatives and demanded more power for themselves. The leaders of the opposition were Puritans opposed to the Church of England and often connected to the merchant class in London and other cities. The dispute broke into open warfare, and Charles was captured and finally beheaded (1649). Until 1653 Parliament governed England. Then Oliver Cromwell (1599–1658), the leader of the victorious parliamentary forces during the civil war, dissolved Parliament and set up the Protectorate (1653–1660) under his rule. By 1660, soon after Cromwell's death, the English welcomed restoration of the monarchy. The new king was Charles II (ruled 1660–1685), son of Charles I.

1643–1715   **Louis XIV reigns in France.** One of the greatest French kings, Louis brought the absolutist powers of the monarchy to their height during his reign. He restored French finances after the Thirty Years' War, only to engage in a series of costly, expansionist wars between 1667 and 1714. In 1685 he decided to make France a Catholic state and revoked the Edict of Nantes, ending the toleration of Protestantism in France. Renewed persecution of Protestants resulted in their exodus from France by the thousands, leaving whole towns and provinces depopulated, and seriously weakening the French economy. Louis was a great spender, noted for his splendid court and his liberal patronage of the arts. His palace at Versailles is a world-famous monument to the lavish style of his reign.

Louis XIV

1644–1912   **Ch'ing dynasty in China.** During the long reign of the Ch'ing dynasty emperors, the Chinese empire reached its greatest heights, trade with Western powers began, and Western missionaries arrived in China.

1664–1666   **Newton's laws of gravity and motion.** During this pivotal two-year period, Sir Isaac Newton (1642–1727) laid the foundations for his famous laws of motion and universal gravitation. Newton's work proved to be the crowning achievement of the scientific revolution of the 1600's.

1670–1770   **The Enlightenment.** Sometimes called the Age of Reason, the Enlightenment was an intellectual movement in Europe and America that championed rationalism, natural laws, and science. The movement grew out of the great intellectual and scientific advances of the 1600's, notably the work of René Descartes (1596–1650), John Locke (1632–1704), and Sir Isaac Newton (1642–1727). Conventional social, religious, and political doctrines were challenged by the skeptical Enlightenment thinkers. Deism, or natural religion, was a product of the Enlightenment and the ideas and spirit of this age gave impetus to both the American and French revolutions. The French *Encyclopédie*, an encyclopedia of the sciences, arts, and trades by Denis Diderot (1713–1784), was a late summary of the ideas of the Enlightenment.

1700–1721   **Great Northern War.** Sweden had become the dominant power in the Baltic region. Then, in 1700, Denmark, Russia, and Poland attacked Swedish territories in the region. Swedish King Charles XII (ruled 1697–1718) was initially victorious, but his disastrous invasion of Russia (1708) turned the tide of the war against Sweden. Charles was killed in battle in 1718 and between 1719 and 1721 peace agreements were concluded. Swedish influence was broken, and Russia, which had gained considerable Baltic territories, began its rise as a major European power.

1701–1714 **War of Spanish Succession.** When French King Louis XIV's son succeeded to the Spanish throne as King Philip V, England saw a threat in the possible unification of France and Spain. England went to war against France, joined by the Holy Roman Empire and the Netherlands. The English alliance was generally successful, and the Duke of Marlborough (John Churchill) became a great war hero for his victory at Blenheim (1704). The Peace of Utrecht (1714) ended the war. The French expansionist policies of Louis XIV were successfully checked and Philip V renounced claims to the French throne. Austria gained Spanish possessions in Europe (Spanish Netherlands, Naples, and Milan), and Britain gained French colonial possessions in Canada.

1735 **Linnaeus publishes first work on plant and animal classification.** Considered the father of modern botany, Carolus Linnaeus (1707–1778) published a number of works during his lifetime. In them he set forth what has become the modern system of classifying plants and animals by genus and species.

1740–1786 **Frederick the Great reigns in Prussia.** During Frederick's reign Prussia developed from a small German state in northern Germany to a major power. Frederick used the well-organized Prussian military to greatly enlarged Prussian territories during the War of the Austrian Succession and the Seven Years' War (see below). By the time of Frederick's death, Prussia had become the major power among the German states of the Holy Roman Empire.

1752 **Benjamin Franklin's kite.** Well known in the American colonies as the publisher of the popular *Poor Richard's Almanack*, Benjamin Franklin (1706–1790) was also interested in science. Perhaps his most famous experiment, in which he flew a kite during a thunderstorm, proved his theory that electricity and lightning are identical. This led to his invention of the lightning rod and secured his reputation as an inventor and scientist. Franklin continued his scientific explorations, but late in life he became famous as a diplomat for the newly independent American colonies. He was acknowledged there as the first "great man" the North American colonies had produced.

1756–1763 **Seven Years' War.** This war was caused by the longstanding rivalry between Austria and Prussia and by the struggle between Britain and France for the possession of colonies in America and India. Prussia started the war in 1742 by attacking Saxony, an ally of Austria. In the ensuing warfare, Britain and Portugal joined Prussia. They were opposed by Austria, France, Russia, Sweden, and Spain. In the North American colonies, fighting between British and French colonists, known as the French and Indian wars, were part of the larger European struggle. By the treaties ending the war, Prussian supremacy over Austria was assured and France was virtually stripped of its colonial empire. Britain gained French possessions in the Americas and checked French power in India. This laid the basis for the great British colonial empire.

1762–1796 **Catherine the Great reigns in Russia.** A strong and ambitious ruler, Catherine made Russia an active participant in European affairs and expanded Russian territories. She conspired to overthrow (1762) and murder her erratic husband, Emperor Peter III (ruled 1762), and took power for herself. Thereafter she proved adept at playing European politics and gained control of most of Poland. She also continued the pattern of Russian expansion into territories of the Ottoman Empire by annexing the Crimea (1762), a peninsular region of the Black Sea.

1768–1779 **Voyages of James Cook.** One of the great English navigators, James Cook (1728–1779) made three voyages of discovery in which he explored the Pacific and Antarctic regions. He charted New Zealand and the eastern coast of Australia; explored the Antarctic Ocean; and unsuccessfully searched for a sea route from the northern Pacific to the Atlantic (Northwest Passage). He was killed by natives while visiting Hawaii.

Modern world

The modern world began with a series of revolutions—political ones in America and France, and an economic one called the Industrial Revolution. Improving sanitation and health care brought perhaps the greatest revolution of all—a population explosion that has continued ever since. The modern era also saw the rise and fall of huge worldwide empires and the gradual rise of two new superstates: the United States and Russia (later called the Soviet Union). By 1945 these states had become the dominant world powers. At the same time, scores of new nations became independent.

Date	Event

1775–1783

American Revolution. Many historians trace the beginnings of the modern world to the revolutions of the late 1700's. The first of these was the American Revolution (1775–1781), in which 13 British colonies in North America declared their independence from the mother country and successfully resisted British military pressures for seven years.

The American patriots based their revolution on Enlightenment ideas (see above), claiming that all men have certain God-given rights. In 1788, the new United States adopted a Constitution that offered political and civil rights to a much larger part of the population than in any European country. The new republic drew both on the political traditions of Britain and on the philosophies of French thinkers (Montesquieu, Rousseau) of the mid-1700's. In turn, the American experiment inspired a new wave of revolution in Europe. (For details of the American Revolution, see U.S. History in Volume I.)

1789–1799

French Revolution. The year after the adoption of the U.S. Constitution, the French overthrew a government dominated by an absolute monarch, hereditary nobility, and higher clergy. The middle classes and landless peasants united in their opposition to the extravagance and arbitrary policies of King Louis XVI, the aristocracy, and the powerful French church.

Pressed by the need for money, Louis was forced to call the States-General (a weak parliamentary body) in 1789. The members actually began the revolution by forming the National Assembly, which they proclaimed the true representative of the French nation. The king recognized the assembly, but rumors about his intentions and serious food shortages in Paris led a mob to storm the Bastille on July 14, 1789. They freed the prisoners there (many of whom had been sentenced for political offenses). Violence soon spread to the provinces.

The National Assembly abolished feudal privileges and enacted the famous *Declaration of the Rights of Man* (August, 1789), proclaiming individual liberties for all. The king was driven from his palace at Versailles in October, and church lands were nationalized in November. The monarchy was finally abolished in 1792.

The revolution was applauded in America and by many in Europe. But other European monarchies feared the spread of revolutionary politics, and in 1792 they began a series of wars against the new French Republic. They attempted to invade France in 1792 and 1793, both times unsuccessfully.

Meanwhile, the revolution itself was entering its most radical and bloodiest phase. In January, 1793, the king and his queen, Marie Antoinette, were beheaded. Then in September, Maximilien Robespierre (1758–1794) and his radical Jacobin faction gained control of the government. They instituted the notorious Reign of Terror (1793–1794), in which some 17,000 persons were executed. Robespierre was overthrown in July, 1794, and moderate elements again took control. By 1797, Napoleon had begun his rise to power, and in 1799, he took control of the government, ending the revolutionary period.

Marie Antoinette on her way to execution, 1793

1799–1815

Napoleon

Napoleon. Napoleon carried out a revolution of his own after taking power in 1799. He reorganized France's administrative machinery to centralize control, stabilized its currency, and arranged an agreement with the Roman Catholic Church. By 1802, he had also made peace with the countries that had taken up arms against France.

Then, in December, 1804, Napoleon proclaimed the French Empire and crowned himself emperor. The countries of Europe united once more against the new empire, and Napoleon soon faced great military challenges. But he also instituted sweeping legal reforms, codifying laws that granted all citizens legal equality and property rights. The Napoleonic Code became the basis for systems of law in much of the Western world.

In 1805, Napoleon declared himself king of Italy, and was soon at war with a new alliance that included England, Russia, Austria, and other powers. Napoleon, by his military genius, conquered most of Europe in the ensuing years. At its height, his empire included most of present-day Germany, Austria, Italy, Belgium, the Netherlands, and Spain. Then, in 1812 he invaded Russia. After initial successes, his army was forced to retreat during a severe Russian winter. The army suffered disastrous losses. In 1813, at Leipzig, in eastern Germany, Napoleon confronted an alliance of European powers and was defeated at the Battle of Nations. Napoleon abdicated on April 11, 1814, and was exiled to the island of Elba in the Mediterranean. He escaped, however, and returned to France on March 1, 1815. Beginning his famous Hundred Days, Napoleon assumed power and again began the war against the allied European powers. He met final defeat in June, 1815, at the famous Battle of Waterloo in Belgium.

c 1810– c 1825

South American independence. Longstanding resentment of harsh Spanish and Portuguese colonial policies provided ample cause for rebellion in South America. While the mother countries were embroiled in the Napoleonic wars, independence fighters succeeded in throwing off colonial rule. Simón Bolívar (1783–1830) and others drove the Spanish and Portuguese off the continent by 1825.

1814–1815

Congress of Vienna. This historic conference met to decide the future of Europe following Napoleon's abdication. The purpose was to ensure a lasting peace by establishing a balance of power between rival nations. Monarchies in France, Spain, and Austria were restored and a confederation of German states was organized. New kingdoms were set up in the Netherlands and Poland. Peace in Europe was maintained for some years following the congress, largely through the skillful diplomacy of the Austrian statesman Clemens von Metternich (1773–1859). But his repressive measures met increasing opposition.

1820–1900

An early mill for spinning thread

Industrial Revolution. The dramatic technological and social changes of the 1800's had their roots in the development of new machines and sources of power. Machinery replaced hand tools, and water, steam, or electric power replaced the muscle of man and beast. Finally, the factory system replaced ancient home or "cottage" industries. To find employment, thousands of workers left their small farms and moved to new industrial cities. Factory owners made fabulous fortunes, but men, women, and children were forced to work long hours, often in subhuman conditions.

Gradually the workers began to fight for civil rights, labor legislation, and unionization. The pattern was repeated as the Industrial Revolution spread from Britain to France (from 1830), Germany (from 1850), and the United States (from 1860). By the late 1800's, labor was a strong political force in Europe, and it inspired growing support for legislation to ensure the social welfare of workers.

1839–1860

Opium wars in China. In the first war (1839–1842), the British, who had long profited from the illicit opium trade in China, defied an attempt by the Chinese to halt the trade and easily defeated the Chinese imperial armies. China was forced to cede Hong Kong to Britain and open several ports to British trade. The British, joined by the French, sparked the second war to further extend trading rights. China was again defeated. It was forced to open still other ports to European powers and to legalize the opium trade. This marked the beginning of European political influence in China, which lasted more than 100 years.

1848

Revolutions of 1848. Conservative European monarchs kept liberal and nationalistic movements in check from 1815 to 1830, when the new monarchy in France fell. After 1830, the conservative forces took charge again, but in 1848 widespread revolts changed the politics of Europe. The rebellions began in France, where reactionary policies of the restored monarchy led to the monarchy's overthrow and to the establishment of the short-lived French Second Republic (1848–1852). Rebellions then broke out in Austria, Hungary, and Italy. Liberal elements also gained strength in the German confederation, in Britain, and elsewhere. The 1848 uprisings prepared the way for major political changes in the second half of the 1800's.

1854–1856

Crimean War. The steady deterioration of the Ottoman (Turkish) Empire led to complex rivalries among European nations seeking eventual control of Ottoman lands. In 1853 Russia occupied Ottoman territories in modern Rumania, and in 1854 the Ottoman Turks, the British, and the French declared war on Russia. Fighting centered on the Crimean peninsula on the Black Sea. Hundreds of thousands were killed and wounded. It was during this war that Florence Nightingale (1820–1910) became famous for tending to the wounded. The war ended unfavorably for Russia and, by the Treaty of Paris (1856), European powers recognized the neutrality of the Black Sea and the territorial integrity of the Ottoman Empire.

An encampment during the Crimean War

World History

1859

Darwin publishes *Origin of the Species*, advancing a theory of biological evolution. His explanations of evolutionary mechanisms and his voluminous observations provided the necessary scientific basis for his theory. Darwin's theory raised serious questions for both religious thinkers and philosophers of the 1800's, and it continues to be controversial today.

1861

Garibaldi

Unification of Italy. Sentiment for the unification of Italy (divided into petty states and often dominated by foreign powers since Rome's fall) had become especially strong by the mid-1800's. In 1859 Victor Emmanuel II, king of Sardinia, attempted unsuccessfully to drive the Austrians out of Italy. Other states rebelled and joined Sardinia in 1860. Then the Italian hero, Giuseppe Garibaldi (1807–1882), organized a small army and conquered (1860) the Kingdom of Two Sicilies. This brought southern Italy under King Victor Emmanuel's rule. In March, 1861, Victor Emmanuel proclaimed the Kingdom of Italy and thus founded the modern state. Venetia was added in 1866, while Rome (the last vestige of the Papal States) was seized in 1870.

1861–1865

Civil War in the United States. In March, 1861, the Southern states in the United States withdrew and set up the Confederate States of America, seeking to preserve slavery and to avoid the growing dominance of the industrial North. The Northern states, under the leadership of Abraham Lincoln, refused to grant the right of Southern states to secede, and in April, 1861, war began.

The war lasted four years, and more than 1 million men died. Parts of the Southern states were decimated. Finally, the North prevailed, largely as a result of its more advanced industrial and transportation systems. Slavery was abolished during the war, and soon afterward, former slaves received full legal citizenship. Within days of the South's surrender, President Lincoln was assassinated by a Southern patriot.

The Civil War was the first war in which telegraph communication, rapid transportation (by railroad), and automatic weapons played a large part. It served as a proving ground for equipment and tactics in later European wars.

1867

British North America Act. By this act, the British Parliament united the Canadian provinces and created the Dominion of Canada. Also written into the act was a constitutional framework for governing the new dominion.

1867–1895

***Das Kapital* published.** Publication of this voluminous work by Karl Marx (1818–1883) and Friedrich Engels (1820–1895) occurred over 28 years. With Marx's and Engels' earlier work, *The Communist Manifesto* (published 1848), *Das Kapital* developed Marxist socialism. Marx argued that revolution by workers in a capitalist society is historically inevitable. The socialist movement gradually split over this issue. Democratic socialists advocated gradual social change; Marxists, who came to be known as communists, advocated violent revolution to bring about social change.

1871

Bismarck

Unification of Germany. For decades Prussia in northeastern Germany sought to unify the loosely confederated German states. Austria, which controlled a large empire in southern Europe, consistently opposed unification. In 1862 Prussian King William I appointed a new premier, Otto von Bismarck (1815–1898), who ruthlessly brought about a united Germany. In 1866 Bismarck provoked the Austro-Prussian War and the Prussian military machine quickly crushed the Austrians. By the resulting peace treaty, a new confederation of north German states was created, without Austria and under Prussian domination. To bring the remaining south German states into the confederation, Bismarck precipitated the Franco-Prussian War of 1870–1871. The Prussian victory over France roused the German nationalist spirit and, as planned, brought about the union of northern and southern states. William I of Prussia was proclaimed emperor of Germany in January, 1871, and for the next 20 years Bismarck, nicknamed the "Iron Chancellor," dominated the new German government.

Date	Event

c 1875

Colonial empires. From 1820, Britain was the great colonialist country of Europe. Although it had lost the 13 colonies in North America, it gradually extended its control in India, Australia, and Canada, thus controlling large parts of three continents. In addition, Britain's smaller territories created a network of trading centers that extended around the world. By 1875, however, European powers were in a new race to acquire and control colonies. Like Britain, they were seeking new sources of raw material and new markets for manufactured goods. Germany, Belgium, France, Italy, Japan, and the United States all sought to stake out new territories. The imperialist nations carved up Africa, a large part of Asia, and the Pacific islands into colonial domains. Along with this imperialistic drive came intense rivalries among the colonial powers. These rivalries eventually led to the outbreak of World War I.

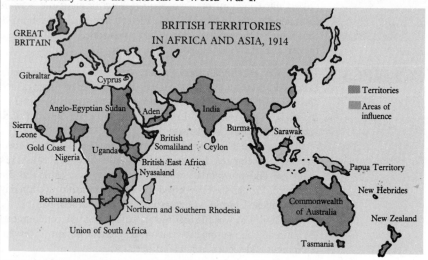

1876

Telephone invented. Alexander Graham Bell (1847–1922) was an inventor and teacher of the deaf. His experiments with telegraphic devices led to his invention of the telephone. His first working model was operational by 1876. Bell's first message over this revolutionary new device was to his assistant: "Watson, come here. I want you."

1878–1879

Practical light bulb invented. The first practical incandescent lamp, using a carbon filament inside an evacuated glass bulb, was invented in England in 1878 by Sir Joseph Swan (1828–1914). Thomas Edison (1847–1931), the famous American inventor, independently developed a similar incandescent lamp in 1879. Edison's lamp became the first widely marketed light bulb. Edison went on to create a complete electrical distribution system so that electricity could provide light and power for a whole city.

1895–1939

Freud develops psychoanalysis. Sigmund Freud (1856–1939), an Austrian doctor, began to develop his theories on the emotional life of individuals after studying patients suffering from hysteria. He asserted that much of the mind's emotional work goes on in the *unconscious*, which is not subject to the control or memory of an individual. His ideas provided the basic structure for psychoanalysis and have had a profound impact on modern society.

1898

The Curies discover radium. The French scientist Antoine H. Becquerel (1852–1891) discovered radioactivity in 1896. Soon afterward, Marie Curie (1867–1934) and Pierre Curie (1859–1906) began to investigate the mineral called pitchblende. By 1898 the Curies had isolated the previously unknown radioactive elements of radium and polonium. Their discovery was an important step toward the beginning of the atomic age.

Date	Event

1899–1900   **Boxer Rebellion in China.** The Boxers were a Chinese secret society that rebelled against foreign influence in China. They began by terrorizing Christian missionaries in 1899 and received unofficial support from the Chinese government. In Peking in June of 1900 many foreigners and Chinese Christians were massacred. A military expedition of French, Japanese, German, British, Russian, and American troops relieved the besieged section of the city. A peace treaty was signed in August of 1900.

1899–1902   **Boer War in South Africa.** In this colonial war, Britain sought to expand its rule throughout South Africa at the expense of the Boers (descendants of Dutch settlers). The British overwhelmed the Boers with thousands of British reinforcements. The fall of Pretoria (June, 1900) marked the end of organized fighting, but the Boers continued guerrilla warfare until 1902, when the Boer republics were made British Crown colonies.

English-speaking refugees in the Boer War

1903   **Age of the airplane begins.** Two American inventors, Orville Wright (1871–1948) and Wilbur Wright (1867–1912), flew the first successful powered airplane near Kitty Hawk, North Carolina, in December, 1903. The first flight lasted just 12 seconds.

Ford develops mass production. Henry Ford (1863–1947) went into partnership with several backers to form the Ford Motor Company. By 1907 he was in complete control of the company and, by his development of mass production techniques, soon made it the world's largest automobile manufacturing company. He developed the moving assembly line for production of his famous Model T (1908). By the time manufacture of the car was discontinued (1927), some 15 million had been built and sold.

1904–1905   **Russo-Japanese War.** Rivalry for control of Manchuria and Korea led Japan, which had become a modern industrial state, into war against Russia. The Japanese humiliated the Russians by capturing Port Arthur, a Russian stronghold in China, and by destroying a Russian fleet. Japan ultimately won territorial concessions in Manchuria.

1905   **Einstein's theory of relativity.** Albert Einstein (1879–1955) was earning his doctorate and working in the Swiss patent office when he formulated his theory of relativity. This theory, together with his later work on relativity, revolutionized science, introducing new concepts of space, time, and gravity, and preparing the way for an understanding of nuclear physics.

1911   **Revolution in China.** The weakening of the Ch'ing dynasty, and the domination of China helped set the stage for the outbreak of revolution in October of 1911. The boy emperor, Hsüan T'ung, was forced to abdicate in 1912, ending the long rule of the Ch'ing dynasty (1644–1912). The republic was declared, and Sun Yat-sen (1866–1925), a long-time leader of revolutionary factions, served briefly as provisional president. The Nationalist Kuomintang Party became powerful under Sun Yat-sen's leadership, but it was unable to take firm control of the country. The Chinese Communist Party was formed in 1921 and in the late 1920's and 1930's the Nationalists and Communists rivaled each other for control of China.

1914–1918

World War I. Economic and political rivalries among European powers were rapidly increasing after 1910. War was finally precipitated by the assassination of Archduke Francis Ferdinand of Austria. The Austrian government blamed Serbia (now part of Yugoslavia) and declared war. Within weeks, Serbia's allies, including Russia, France, and Britain, had declared war, as had Austria's great ally, Germany.

In slightly over four years, the conflict was played out on several widely scattered fronts. It was the most costly war ever seen. Some 10 million men were killed and 20 million wounded, and whole regions were laid waste. The Germans and Austrians took the offensive, planning to fight on two fronts, against France in the west and Russia in the east. Resistance on the western front was stronger than had been anticipated, however, and the Balkan countries offered fierce resistance. Only in Russia were the Central Powers able to win decisively. In France and Belgium, neither side seemed able to advance. Huge armies were pinned down in trenches for weeks or months, battling over a few feet of ground. Motorized tanks, poison gas, and efficient artillery made the war a nightmare for soldiers. At sea, the Germans used submarines to destroy allied shipping. The United States remained neutral through two and a half years; in April, 1917, however, Congress declared war on Germany and its allies. The arrival of American troops helped the Allies repulse a huge German offensive at the second Battle of the Marne, in early 1918, and thus turn the tide of the war against Germany. Thereafter, military defeats and economic disorder contributed to the German decision to seek an armistice in November, 1918. The Treaty of Versailles, signed in June, 1919, formally ended the war and reorganized Europe. It resulted in the dismantling of the German colonial empire and the collapse of the Austro-Hungarian and Ottoman empires. It also marked the beginning of many present-day states, including Poland, Hungary, and Yugoslavia.

Marshal Foch of France, Allied commander

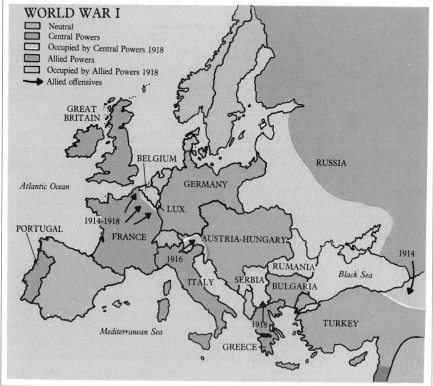

WORLD WAR I
- Neutral
- Central Powers
- Occupied by Central Powers 1918
- Allied Powers
- Occupied by Allied Powers 1918
- → Allied offensives

Date	Event

Key events in World War I

1914   Archduke Francis Ferdinand of Austria assassinated, June 28.
War declared by Austria and Germany, July 28–August 3.
Invasion of France (through Belgium and Luxembourg) begun by Germany, August 3.
Britain, soon followed by other major powers, enters the war, August 4.
Russia attacks East Prussia, opening eastern front, August 13.
Russian armies crushed at Battle of Tannenberg, August 26–29.
First Battle of the Marne (Germans halted before reaching Paris), September 5–9.
First Battle of Ypres (Germans prevented from capturing channel ports), October–November.
Trench warfare and long stalemate begins on the western front, October–November.

1915   Germans make first use of poison gas at second Battle of Ypres, April 22–May 25.
Allies' Gallipoli campaign fails to knock Ottoman Empire out of the war, April–January (1916).
Lusitania, British ocean liner, sunk by German submarine, May 7.
Italy enters war on the side of the Allies, May 23.
Allies' Salonika campaign in Greece and Balkans region begins (and is stalled soon after), October 5.

1916   Battle of Verdun in France; bloody but inconclusive German offensive, February 21–December 18.
Russian summer offensive in the east leaves both Russian and Austrian armies exhausted by tremendous losses, June 4–September 20.
Allies' Somme offensive in the west proves bloody and inconclusive, July 1–November 18.

1917   Germany begins unrestricted submarine warfare, February 1.
Russian Revolution breaks out, March; Russian army retreats in disarray.
United States enters war, April 6.
Bolsheviks seize control in Russia as Germans advance against the crumbling Russian army; Bolsheviks seek peace with Germans, November.

1918   U.S. President Wilson announces his Fourteen Points peace program, January 8.
Communist Russia concludes peace with Germany, March 3.
German Somme offensive in France is tactical success but drains German manpower, March 21–April 8.
Second Battle of Marne marks the beginning of German retreat, July 15–August 6.
Austro-Hungarian empire collapses, October.
Austria agrees to an armistice, November 4.
Germany agrees to an armistice and the war ends, November 11.

1919   Treaty of Versailles signed, formally ending the war, June 28.

1917

Lenin

Russian Revolution. The czarist regime in Russia, still an unlimited monarchy, had been weak and ineffectual for years. Agitation for a constitutional form of government had brought an unsuccessful revolution in 1905. Finally, the stresses of World War I brought the old regime down. The Russian army was badly supplied and led, and it lost disastrous battles against the Germans. The government and the economy under Czar Nicholas II (ruled 1894–1917) weakened steadily.

Workers took over St. Petersburg in February, 1917. The czar was forced to abdicate, and a moderate provisional government was set up. Various Socialist parties opposed the government and undermined it and each other. Finally, the Bolshevik faction, led by Nikolai Lenin (1870–1924), staged a coup in October, set up a Communist government with Lenin at its head, and made peace with Germany. Not all Russians went along with the Bolshevik government, and soon the Reds (Bolsheviks) and the Whites (anti-Bolsheviks) were involved in a bloody civil war. The war ended with the triumph of the Reds and the exile of the Whites in 1920. Lenin ruthlessly consolidated the rule of the Communist Party in the four years before his death.

Date	Event

1919

Gandhi and nonviolent protest in India. A national hero of India, Mohandas Gandhi (1869–1948) organized his first campaign of nonviolent civil disobedience against oppression by British colonial rulers in 1919. He eventually championed not only independence from Britain but social reforms as well. The growing success of his mass protests forced the British to grant ever greater concessions in the 1920's and 1930's and proved to be a major factor in India's fight for independence (granted in 1947).

Treaty of Versailles. The most important of the treaties ending World War I, the treaty dealt harshly with Germany. It took away most German territories, required the payment of substantial war reparations, restricted German rearmament, and demilitarized the Rhineland along Germany's western borders. The treaty established the League of Nations (see below). The U.S. Senate refused ratification of the treaty and kept the United States out of the league.

1920

First commercial radio station. Wireless telegraphy, developed by the Italian physicist Guglielmo Marconi (1874–1937) at the turn of the century, was already well established when the American David Sarnoff (1891–1971) suggested establishing stations for broadcasting speech and music to the general public. Following World War I, the first commercial radio station (KDKA) was started up in Pittsburgh; it began regular programming late in 1920 and was an immediate success. Radio stations sprang up around the world, making the radio an important medium for news reporting and entertainment.

1920–1946

League of Nations. The league was an international organization devoted to preserving world peace and promoting international cooperation. It existed from 1920 to 1946, when it was superseded by the United Nations. Important nations (especially the United States) remained outside the league, and its peace-keeping machinery was limited. The league was unable to halt aggression by Japan, Italy, and Germany in the 1930's. Yet its work in social and economic affairs was considerable.

1922

Mussolini and the rise of Fascism in Italy. Benito Mussolini (1883–1945) organized the nucleus of his Fascist Party amid the strikes and unrest that overtook Italy after World War I. By appealing to nationalistic spirit and using brutal tactics against Communists and Socialists, Mussolini quickly became a formidable power in Italy. In October, 1922, King Victor Emmanuel III (ruled 1900–1946) named him premier. Mussolini immediately set about establishing himself as dictator by ruthless means.

c 1927

Stalin takes power in the Soviet Union. Lenin's death in 1924 touched off a complex power struggle within the Communist Party for control of the Soviet Union. Joseph Stalin (1879–1953) soon ousted his rival, Leon Trotsky (1879–1940), and established himself as sole ruler of the Soviet Union. He introduced his policy of industrialization and collectivization of agriculture in 1928 and instituted harsh measures to enforce state control over Soviet society. Stalin established his absolute dictatorship by bloody purges in the 1930's and encouraged veneration of himself as supreme leader.

Lindbergh and *The Spirit of St. Louis*. A little-known American flier, Charles Lindbergh (1902–1974), became an American national hero overnight by making the first solo nonstop flight across the Atlantic Ocean. In May, 1927, Lindbergh piloted his plane, *The Spirit of St. Louis*, from an airfield on Long Island to Paris, France, in just over 33 hours. A folk hero during his lifetime, Lindbergh remains one of the best-known figures of the airplane age.

1928

Penicillin discovered. Sir Alexander Fleming (1881–1955), a Scottish biologist, first discovered penicillin and its effectiveness as an antibacterial agent. By 1941 the drug was proven to be effective in humans, and by the 1950's it was in widespread use. It was the first of a whole family of antibiotic medications.

Date	Event

1929–1939

Soup line for the hungry

Great Depression. The economic boom of the 1920's ended late in 1929 with the catastrophic stock market crash in the United States. The crash had tragic consequences: whole fortunes were wiped out; banks failed by the thousands; and millions of workers suddenly found themselves unemployed. The economic disaster quickly spread to Europe, where the other industrial nations suffered similar consequences. In the United States, Franklin D. Roosevelt's New Deal programs marked a radical departure from previous U.S. government policy. In Europe the crisis helped pave the way for the rise of totalitarian governments. Western economies did not reach their 1929 levels until after 1945.

1931

Rise of the militarists in Japan. Militarist factions began their rise to power in the late 1920's. In 1931 the militarists provoked an incident in Manchuria, then Chinese territory, as an excuse to take control there. In 1937 they marched from Manchuria into China. By 1939 Japan had become an ally of the Axis powers (Germany and Italy). With the installation of Hideki Tojo (served 1941–1944) as prime minister in October, 1941, the militarists gained complete control of the Japanese government.

1933

Hitler's rise to power in Germany. By 1921 Adolf Hitler (1889–1945) had gained control of the fledgling Nazi Party in Germany. After 1929, Hitler's frenzied appeal to German nationalism and his use of the psychology of hate gained him a mass following. In 1933 Hitler was named chancellor of Germany and soon after, his Nazi Party gained a slim majority in the German parliament. Playing on fears of a Communist uprising, Hitler arranged to have parliament give him dictatorial powers. He thus established the Third Reich in 1933 and set about ruthlessly consolidating his power. In subsequent years, he established a totalitarian state, redirected the economy to create a powerful military machine, began the persecution (and later mass killings) of the Jews, and instituted the aggressive, nationalistic foreign policy that ultimately began World War II (see below).

1934

Fermi and the beginning of the atomic age. An Italian-born physicist, Enrico Fermi (1901–1954), first used neutrons to bombard uranium atoms during experiments from 1934 to 1937. The results of his experiments puzzled the scientific world until 1938, when three German scientists discovered that Fermi's experiments had actually split the uranium atoms by the heretofore unknown process of nuclear fission. In that year Fermi went to the United States and soon became part of the secret Manhattan Project to develop an atomic bomb. Leading a team of scientists in Chicago, Fermi produced in December, 1942, the first controlled, self-sustaining chain reaction. Fermi's experiments led to the first atom bomb and to the development of nuclear reactors for peaceful uses.

1936–1939

Spanish Civil War. This war arose from conflict between the supporters of the Spanish Republic (Loyalists) and a coalition of conservative forces (Nationalists). An election victory in 1936 by the Popular Front—republicans, liberals, Socialists, and Communists—threatened conservative interests. A right-wing rebellion broke out, led by the military, and General Francisco Franco (1892–1975) emerged as the dominant Nationalist leader. Liberal sympathizers from the United States and other nations aided Loyalists. Franco's forces, however, received large-scale aid from Nazi Germany and Fascist Italy. By 1939 Franco had defeated the Loyalists. He established dictatorial control of Spain.

The swastika, the Nazis' symbol

The road to war. Hitler's aggressive nationalist policies first became apparent in 1936 when he remilitarized the Rhineland. He aided Franco's Fascist forces in the Spanish Civil War and in March 1938, annexed Austria. Meanwhile, the British and the French adopted a policy of appeasement toward the Axis powers. In September, 1938, they agreed to the Munich Pact, by which Germany was given a large part of Czechoslovakia. Hopes for appeasement ended in 1939, when Germany occupied all of Czechoslovakia and Italy took over Albania. Soon after Germany concluded the Pact of Steel (1939) with Italy and a nonaggression pact with the Soviet Union. With these alliances secured, Hitler ordered the invasion of Poland on September 1, 1939, and World War II began.

1939–1945

World War II. World War II was a global conflict fought from 1939 to 1945 on land, sea, and in the air. The world's principal nations were divided into two groups, the Axis and the Allies. The Axis was led by Germany, Italy, and Japan. The Allies were led by Britain, France, the United States, and the Soviet Union.

The early part of the conflict was marked by sweeping German victories in Europe. Poland, Denmark, Norway, Luxembourg, the Netherlands, and Belgium quickly fell to German forces. By the end of 1940, France had collapsed and the Germans had occupied Yugoslavia and Greece. Meanwhile, British forces withstood the early assault and managed to prevent a German invasion of the British Isles.

The second stage began in June, 1941, when Germany turned on its ally, the Soviet Union, and invaded that country. At first it seemed that Germany would continue its military successes, but a Soviet counteroffensive, coinciding with the early arrival of a severe winter, caused a temporary setback for the Germans. The war was also being fought in Africa, the Mediterranean, and the Atlantic, but the fighting was inconclusive.

The third stage of the war began in the Pacific in December, 1941, when Japan attacked Pearl Harbor, in Hawaii, and brought the United States into the war. The Japanese swept through the Pacific region in a rapid series of victories, but by spring of 1942, the United States had regained several key islands.

The fourth stage began in the summer of 1942, when the Allies took the offensive on almost all fronts. The Axis powers were routed successively in North Africa, Sicily, and Italy (in 1943). In the east the Soviet Union mounted another offensive during the winter months. Finally, in June, 1944, the Allied forces invaded the coast of Normandy in France. Germany, already weakened by earlier losses, was now fighting on both eastern and western fronts. Though the Germans continued to provide stiff resistance, the Allies pushed into Germany and in May, 1945, forced the Germans to surrender. The end of the war in Europe made it possible for the Allies to concentrate on defeating Japan. Naval battles in the Pacific had broken Japanese sea power and the campaign for the Pacific islands had brought the Allies to Japan's doorstep. The final blow was an atomic-bomb attack on the cities of Hiroshima and Nagasaki in August, 1945. The Japanese surrendered on September 2, and ended World War II. The Axis powers were dealt with severely in the surrender terms set by the Allies. Germany was partitioned and occupied by the United States, the Soviet Union, Britain, and France. Japan was occupied by the United States and lost all its outlying territories. Italy, which had surrendered in 1943, lost its colonial conquests in Africa.

St. Paul's Cathedral, London, during 1940 German air raid (left). *At right, Soviet soldiers at Stalingrad, 1942.*

Key events in World War II

1939   Germany invades Poland and precipitates World War II, September 1.
    Allied nations declare war on Germany.
    The Soviets (then allies of Germany) invade Poland from then east, September 17.
    Germany and the Soviet Union divide up Polish territories, September.
    The Soviets attack Finland, beginning the Russo-Finnish War (1939–1940), November 30.

1940   Germany invades (and quickly conquers) Denmark and Norway, April 9.
    Germany invades the Netherlands and Belgium, May 10.
    Winston Churchill replaces Neville Chamberlain as British prime minister, May 10.
    German victories force the famous British evacuation at Dunkirk, May 28–June 4.
    France capitulates to German troops (June 21) and a puppet government
       under Marshal Henri Pétain is set up, June.
    Germans bomb Britain, beginning the air war (the Battle of Britain), August 8.
    Italy opens fighting in the North African desert by attacking British Egypt from Libya, September.

1941   German General Erwin Rommel takes over Axis forces in North Africa and begins a rapid
       German advance there, April.
    Yugoslavia and Greece invaded by the Germans, April 6.
    German battleship *Bismarck* sunk, May 27.
    Germany invades the Soviet Union, ending German-Soviet alliance and bringing the Soviets into the
       war against Germany, June 22.
    Japanese occupy French Indochina, July 21.
    Germans' rapid eastward advance in the Soviet Union stalled by onset of heavy rains and freezing
       weather; Germans fail to capture Moscow, October–December.
    Hideki Tojo becomes Japanese prime minister, October 18.
    Japanese attack Pearl Harbor, beginning a rapid sweep through the Pacific region, December 7.
    United States enters the war, December 8.

continued on next page

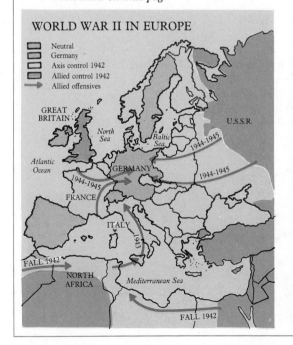

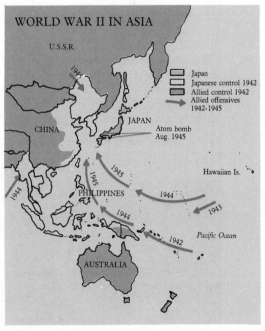

Date	Event

1942   Bataan falls, ending resistance to the Japanese in the Philippines; U.S. General Douglas MacArthur vows "I shall return," April.

U.S. planes wreck Japanese invasion fleet at the Battle of Midway, June 3–6.

General Dwight Eisenhower becomes head of United States operations in Europe, June 25.

Guadalcanal landings begin U.S. counteroffensive in the Pacific, August 7.

German eastward drive in the Soviet Union stalls at Stalingrad, August–October.

British offensive in North Africa begins at El Alamein, Egypt, October 23.

United States forces land in North Africa, November 8.

Soviet counterattack at Stalingrad drives Germans into retreat, November–March (1943).

1943   Germans defeated in North Africa, May.

Sicily invaded by Allies, June 10.

Mussolini resigns, July 25.

Soviets' final sustained advance against Germans begins, August.

Italian mainland invaded; Italy surrenders (September 3) though Germans continue resistance, September.

1944   Strategic bombing of Germany begins, February 20.

Russians enter Poland, April 2.

Rome captured by Allies, June 4.

D-Day. Massive amphibious invasion of Normandy begins, June 6.

Attempt of German officers to assassinate Hitler fails, July 20.

St.-Lô breakout in France marks the beginning of the Allied drive across Europe, July 25.

Paris liberated, August 25.

General MacArthur returns to the Philippines, October.

Battle of the Bulge in Europe marks the last major German counteroffensive, December–January (1945).

1945   Allies cross the Rhine in Germany, March 7.

U.S. forces land on Okinawa, March 26.

U.S. President Franklin Roosevelt dies in office, April 12. Harry Truman becomes President.

Soviets enter Berlin, April 20.

U.S. and Soviet troops link up at the Elbe River, April 25.

Hitler commits suicide, April 30.

Germany surrenders, May 7.

Experimental atomic bomb exploded by the United States in New Mexico test, July 16.

Potsdam Conference between Allied leaders, July 17–August 2.

Atomic bombs dropped on Hiroshima and Nagasaki, August 6, 9.

V-J Day. Japan surrenders, ending the war, September 2.

Nuremberg war crimes trials begin, November 20.

Ruins of Hiroshima after the atomic bomb

Postwar world

After World War II, the United States and the Soviet Union became competitors and were soon engaged in a great arms race, improving and producing weapons to be used in case of war. At the same time, other powers were emerging. China, the most populous nation on Earth, began developing its economic and military power after 1949. Scores of smaller nations sought ways to join together to make their needs and interests known. All peoples faced certain challenges together, including the threat of overpopulation, the diminishing of natural resources, and the hazards of manmade pollution.

Date	Event

1945

United Nations insignia

United Nations established. Plans for a new international organization to replace the League of Nations were carried forward all through World War II during meetings among leaders of the Allies. Soon after Germany surrendered, delegates at the San Francisco Conference completed work on the United Nations Charter, which was ratified on October 24, 1945. The aims of the new organization were to encourage the maintenance of international peace and security, to promote cooperation in solving international, social, and economic problems, and to develop friendly relations among all nations. In subsequent years, United Nations social and economic programs achieved considerable success. But in other areas, the advent of the Cold War (see below) brought an end to the spirit of cooperation among nations that had existed during the war years. Thus, the UN's effectiveness as an international peacekeeping organization was seriously hampered soon after it was established.

1945–1949

Mao Tse-tung

Chinese civil war. Chiang Kai-shek (1887–1975), leader of the Nationalist Kuomintang Party after Sun Yat-sen's death, purged the Communists from the party in 1927 and thus began a long and bloody rivalry for control of China. The Japanese invasion in 1937 and the outbreak of World War II forced the Nationalists and Communists, now led by Mao Tse-tung (1893–1976), to work together for a number of years. But the alliance was at best an uneasy one.

At the end of World War II, both the Nationalists and Communists scrambled to take over territories once occupied by the Japanese. Civil war broke out and though the Nationalists were at first successful, the Communists turned the tide in 1947. Peking was in Communist hands by January, 1949; in July of that year, Chiang Kai-shek withdrew his forces to the island of Taiwan, where he established his Nationalist government. The victorious Communists proclaimed (October, 1949) the People's Republic of China with Mao Tse-tung as chairman.

1945–1990

Cold War. The end of World War II marked the emergence of the Soviet Union and the United States as the two great world powers. Soon the two were in conflict over ideology, and over plans for political and economic expansion. These conflicts dominated the political climate of the postwar years and remain a source of international friction even today.

Tensions first developed when the Soviet Union set up Communist governments in the East European countries it had occupied during World War II. Between 1945 and 1948, Albania, Bulgaria, Czechoslovakia, Hungary, Poland, Rumania, and Yugoslavia came under control of the Soviet Union. The United States responded with the Truman Doctrine (1947), which offered aid to countries threatened by Communism (then Greece and Turkey). In 1948, the Marshall Plan gave the countries of Western Europe large-scale U.S. aid to rebuild their war-shattered economies and to strengthen them against Communist pressures. In 1949 the North Atlantic Treaty Organization (NATO) was established to bring the European nations together for their common defense. In addition to confrontations (Berlin blockade), and warfare (Korea), the Cold War also bred the nuclear arms race and spurred space exploration.

1946

Early TV star Milton Berle

The new electronic marvels: television and computers. Television, invented in the 1920's and perfected in the 1930's, became widely available soon after World War II. Regular broadcasting service was begun in the United States in 1946, when the government lifted wartime restrictions on the production of television receivers. By 1951 there were 10 million sets in use in the United States. During the next decades, the number continued to multiply in the United States and around the world.

The first fully electronic digital computer, ENIAC, was also completed in 1946. Advances during the next three decades (transistors, silicon chips, and miniaturization) transformed the computer from a bulky laboratory tool to a compact and versatile electronic "brain" that has found its way into businesses, offices, schools, and homes.

1948

Israel created; the first Arab-Israeli war. Zionist agitation for the creation of a Jewish state in Palestine finally resulted in the establishment of Israel by the United Nations in May, 1948. A Jewish state was thus established in Palestine for the first time since the days of the Romans. Arab nations vehemently opposed such a state, however, and invaded Israel the day it was officially founded. This first Arab-Israeli war lasted until January, 1949, and left Israel in possession of about 50 percent more territory than it had when war broke out. But no basis for a lasting peace was established.

1950–1953

Korean War. Following World War II, Korea was divided at the 38th parallel, with the Soviets occupying the north and the Americans occupying the south. Governments were established in both parts in 1948. In June, 1950, troops from Communist North Korea invaded the south. The United States requested the Security Council of the United Nations to authorize a police action in Korea. The Soviets boycotted the meeting and the resolution passed. In July, United Nations forces, made up primarily of United States contingents, landed in Korea under the command of General Douglas MacArthur (1880–1964). The Communist Chinese entered the fighting on the North Korean side in November, 1950. During the first year, the front shifted rapidly back and forth from North to South Korea. But in 1951 it stabilized at about the 38th parallel, where it remained for the rest of the war. In 1953, peace negotiations resulted in an armistice and the conflict ended. The 38th parallel was restored as the border between North and South Korea.

1953

Stalin's death and changes in Soviet leadership. On Joseph Stalin's death, his one-man rule of the Soviet Union was replaced for a time by collective leadership. There was a marked easing of the controls Stalin had imposed on Soviet society. In 1956 a "de-Stalinization" program introduced by Nikita Khrushchev (1894–1971) brought some further liberalization, as well as a denunciation of the worship of Stalin. De-Stalinization led to unrest within the Soviet sphere, marked by the short-lived Hungarian revolution in 1956. But Khrushchev nevertheless became the leading figure in the Soviet government and he held power until 1964.

1957

Sputnik

Sputnik and the space race. Sputnik, a 184-pound artificial satellite, was launched into orbit around Earth by the Soviets on October 4, 1957. The launch marked the beginning of the space age. On April 8, 1961, the Russian cosmonaut Yuri A. Gagarin became the first man to orbit Earth. U.S. astronaut John Glenn became the first American to orbit Earth, in February, 1962. But on July 20, 1969, the United States won a clear victory by landing the first men on the moon (Neil Armstrong and Edwin "Buzz" Aldrin, Jr.). Meanwhile, satellites and other space vehicles were perfected for a wide range of peaceful and military purposes by both sides.

1957

Common Market forms in Europe. Efforts to promote economic cooperation and the integration of Western European nations began after World War II. A major step was the creation of the Common Market (European Economic Community), which was designed to promote a complete customs union of Western European nations. In 1957 it included France, Belgium, Luxembourg, West Germany, Italy, and the Netherlands. Britain, Ireland, and Denmark became members in 1973. The success of the Common Market encouraged further cooperation among member nations, strengthening a movement toward a European community with political as well as economic ties.

1961–1963

Kennedy administration in the United States. John F. Kennedy (1917–1963) set the activist and idealistic tone that was to dominate U.S. government policy for much of the decade. The Kennedy years were filled with promise and with crisis. At home, Kennedy committed the federal government to civil rights for blacks during a period of mounting racial unrest, and thus began the sweeping social reform movements of the 1960's. Abroad, he actively opposed the Communists, bringing the world to the brink of nuclear war in the Cuban missile crisis (see below) and beginning the military involvement of the United States in Vietnam. The Kennedy years ended in tragedy when he was assassinated (November 22, 1963) in Dallas, Texas.

1961

Bay of Pigs invasion of Cuba. Fidel Castro (1927–) seized power in Cuba in 1959 and then joined the Soviet bloc in 1961. Soon afterward, Cuban exiles trained by the U.S. Central Intelligence Agency (CIA) staged what is called the Bay of Pigs invasion (April, 1961). The exiles hoped to spark a popular uprising against Castro but the attack was quickly crushed. The incident was a major embarrassment to the Kennedy administration.

Berlin wall erected. As Cold War tensions increased in 1961, the Communists moved in August to end the embarrassing flow of refugees from Communist East Germany into West Germany. The result was the Berlin wall, a 29-mile-long barrier separating East and West Berlin. In the West, the wall quickly became a symbol of Communist oppression. Although restrictions have been relaxed, the wall remains standing today.

1962

Cuban missile crisis. In October, 1962, the United States discovered that the Soviets were building missile sites in Cuba. President Kennedy's demand that the missile sites be dismantled and withdrawn brought the United States and the Soviet Union to the brink of nuclear war. After six days, Soviet leader Nikita Khrushchev finally backed down and agreed to withdraw the missiles. The incident was a contributing factor in Khrushchev's fall from power in 1964. However, the crisis also served to heighten public awareness of the dangerous possibility of nuclear war.

The Soviet installation of nuclear missiles in Cuba brought the United States to the brink of war.

1965–1973

Vietnam War. Fighting broke out in Vietnam soon after World War II, when followers of the Communist leader Ho Chi Minh (1890–1969) began their struggle against French rule in Indochina. The French were defeated (1954), and by the Geneva convention held that year, Vietnam was temporarily divided (at the 17th parallel) into northern and southern sectors. North Vietnam became a Communist state under Ho Chi Minh and South Vietnam became a pro-U.S. republic. South Vietnam refused to hold elections in 1956 on the reunification of Vietnam, as stipulated by the Geneva convention. In 1960 dissidents in the South were organized into the National Liberation Front (Vietcong), which had North Vietnamese backing.

The Vietcong guerrillas made significant gains against South Vietnamese government troops. The United States sent military aid to the South and brought in American military advisers in the early 1960's. By 1965 the situation had become critical. U.S. President Lyndon Baines Johnson (served 1963–1969) first ordered bombing raids on North Vietnam to halt the infiltration of North Vietnamese soldiers into the South. Soon afterward, in 1965, the first U.S. combat troops were sent to Vietnam and direct U.S. participation in the war began. Years of bloodshed followed. The United States found itself caught up in a costly and protracted war it could not win.

By 1968, over half a million U.S. troops were in Vietnam. But the Vietcong and the Soviet-backed North Vietnamese were still able to mount the demoralizing Tet offensive (February, 1968), in which cities and bases throughout the South suffered surprise attacks. The growing realization that a military victory was impossible, the pressure of world opinion, and the spread of the antiwar movement in the United States led to the opening of peace negotiations in 1968. The talks and the war dragged on until 1973, when a cease-fire agreement was reached. A complete withdrawal of U.S. forces was completed soon after, and a final offensive by the North Vietnamese brought the unconditional surrender of South Vietnam in 1975.

The Vietnam War was among the most costly and destructive ever fought. It devastated South Vietnam's economy, disrupted the social structure, decimated the population, and laid waste to the countryside. Its effect on the United States was also costly: it resulted in an unstable economy, worldwide condemnation of U.S. foreign policy, bitter internal divisions, and widespread distrust of the government's motives and credibility.

American soldiers in Vietnam, 1967

Date	Event

1966–1969   **Cultural revolution in China.** The cultural revolution was a ruthless campaign to purge Chinese society of ideas and people not friendly to the Communist government. Directed by Mao Tse-tung, brigades of young Maoists, called the Red Guard, spread the revolution throughout the country. Most schools were closed, and millions of city dwellers were shipped to remote collective farms for "reeducation." The movement eventually came to threaten the government itself. Beginning in about 1969, government leaders retreated from the cultural revolution and began to reestablish order in China.

1967   **Six Days' War in the Mideast.** Increasing tensions between the Arabs and the Israelis prompted the Israelis to launch a surprise attack on Egypt, Jordan, and Syria. After knocking out the Arab air force, the Israelis struck out on three fronts and quickly crushed Arab resistance. The war ended after six days of fighting with Israel in control of the Sinai Peninsula in Egypt, the West Bank in Jordan, and the Golan Heights in Syria.

1968   **Prague spring movement in Czechoslovakia.** Economic stagnation and resentment over the government's continuing hard-line policies brought the liberal Alexander Dubček to party leadership in January, 1968. Over the next few months, Dubček quickly adopted economic and political reforms, carrying Czechoslovakia closer to democratic government than any Communist bloc country before it. The Soviets became alarmed, however, and in August, 1968, the Warsaw Pact nations invaded Czechoslovakia. Dubček's liberal reforms were reversed and Dubček himself was ousted from the party leadership.

1970   **Detente.** The 1970's were the decade of detente, a new phase in relations between the United States and the Soviet Union. The two countries made a deliberate effort to ease Cold War tensions, to avoid direct confrontations, and to promote an era of negotiation and cooperation. The period saw the beginning of U.S.-Soviet trade, and important negotiations on the limitation of nuclear arms.

1971   **Communist China seated in the United Nations.** Since the Communist takeover of China in 1949, the Nationalist government on Taiwan had been recognized by the United Nations as the legitimate representative of the Chinese people. However, the Communist regime had firm political control of China's huge population. When the government moved to establish diplomatic relations with Western nations, including the United States in 1970, the last opposition to membership in the UN evaporated. The Taiwan government was unseated and the People's Republic was seated in its place.

1972   **Massacre at the Munich Olympics.** The 1970's witnessed the rise of terrorism in many parts of the world. Bombings, hijackings, and vicious murders, often of unarmed civilians, were committed for a variety of causes by small bands of fanatics. One of the most notorious of these incidents was the 1972 attack by Palestinian guerrillas at Olympic Village in Munich, Germany. Eleven Israeli athletes were massacred in the attack. One German policeman and five of the guerrillas were also killed.

1973   **Arab-Israeli war.** Mideast stability was again broken by warfare in October, 1973, when Egypt and Syria launched a surprise attack on Israel. Early advances by the two Arab states were soon nullified by Israeli victories on both the Egyptian and Syrian fronts, gained at the cost of many lives. By the end of the month, fighting had ceased, except for sporadic minor clashes that lasted into 1974. Although there was little change in territory, the Arabs had proved their fighting ability. Of greater importance, however, was the embargo on the sale of oil to Western nations imposed by Arab nations during the war. It marked the first effective use of oil as an economic and political weapon and signaled the rising power of the Arab oil-producing states.

1974   **Resignation of President Nixon.** Richard Nixon (served 1969–1974) resigned on August 9 under immediate threat of impeachment and conviction. The scandal that brought him down began with the attempted break-in at Democratic Party offices in the Watergate apartment complex in Washington, D.C., in June, 1972. Investigations eventually revealed a wide variety of crimes and unethical acts in the Nixon administration. Many of his aides were convicted on criminal charges, but Nixon himself was given a full pardon by his successor, Gerald Ford (served 1974–1977).

1978

Camp David accords. From the time of Israel's creation in 1948, Arab states consistently refused to recognize Israel or to enter into treaties with it. The 1973 Arab-Israeli war convinced Egyptian President Anwar el-Sadat (served 1970–1981) of the importance of seeking peace with the Israelis. Negotiations culminated in a 13-day conference (September, 1978) between Sadat, Israeli Prime Minister Menachem Begin (served 1977–1983), and U.S. President Jimmy Carter (served 1977–1981). The conference was held at the Presidential retreat at Camp David, Maryland. It ended in the signing of a "framework for peace," and called for the establishment of diplomatic relations between Israel and Egypt and the gradual withdrawal of Israel from occupied Egyptian territory.

Normalized relations between the United States and China. Normalization between the two countries began when the Chinese invited an American table tennis team to China in 1971 (beginning the so-called "Ping-Pong diplomacy"). In 1973 President Richard Nixon visited China. Cultural and diplomatic exchanges increased, and China became an important new factor in international relations.

1979

Iranian revolution. The efforts of Shah Mohammed Riza Pahlevi (ruled 1941–1979) to rapidly modernize Iran led to outbreaks of violence by conservative Muslims in 1978. Soon after, the Muslim leader Ayatollah Khomeini took control of the government. The new government imposed Muslim fundamentalist culture on Iran and pursued a violently anti-American foreign policy. In November, 1979, Iranian militants, protesting the arrival of the deposed shah in the United States, seized the American Embassy in Iran and took 52 Americans hostage. In subsequent months, the Khomeini government used the incident to humiliate the United States. As negotiations for the release of the hostages bogged down, U.S. President Jimmy Carter ordered a rescue mission, but the attempt failed and cost the lives of eight servicemen. The hostages were finally released in January, 1981, after more than a year in captivity.

Soviet invasion of Afghanistan. Attempts to establish a Marxist regime in Afghanistan following a 1978 coup sparked an armed revolt by Muslim rebels. By late 1979, a Soviet-backed puppet government had been installed and the Soviets began a massive military effort to support the regime. Nearly 100,000 Soviet troops were reported in Afghanistan but guerrillas in the rugged countryside continued to mount successful resistance. The protracted conflict seriously damaged Soviet prestige and cooled Soviet relations with the United States. The last Soviet troops withdrew from Afghanistan in 1989.

1980

The Solidarity movement in Poland. By means of strikes and other actions, workers forced the economically hard-pressed Polish government to make major concessions. For a time it seemed that the workers were ready to topple the government. By late 1981, however, the military had taken control of the government, imprisoned Solidarity leaders, and sent the movement underground.

Iran-Iraq War. After ten months of skirmishing over the Shatt-al-Arab waterway that divides the two countries, open warfare was initiated when Iraqi bombers attacked ten Iranian oilfields. Bloody fighting ensued across both borders. In 1984 Iraq began attacks on Iranian shipping in the Persian Gulf. In 1988, after over 1 million people had been killed, a cease-fire was declared. The war was generally considered a stalemate.

1981

President Anwar el-Sadat of Egypt assassinated. The assassins were directed by Muslim extremists in the Egyptian armed forces. In the same year, U.S. President Ronald Reagan and Pope John Paul II were wounded in assassination attempts.

Argentina invades British-held Falkland Islands. Britain recaptured the islands after a war lasting four weeks. The defeat was a major blow to Argentinan pride, and the country's military ruler resigned within days.

1982

Israelis launch a major attack on Beirut, Lebanon. They sought to drive out the guerrilla troops of the Palestine Liberation Army. In September, the massacre by Lebanese Christians of more than 300 Palestinians in a refugee camp prompted the sending of a peacekeeping force made up of French, Italian, and American troops to Lebanon. In October, 1983, terrorist attacks on the headquarters of the American and French forces killed over 280 people.

1983

The United States invades Grenada. The invasion came at the request of neighbors of the tiny Caribbean island, following a left-wing pro-Cuban coup, and in the belief that the lives of over a thousand American students on the island were in danger.

1984

Two tragic events in India. During a year in which religious tensions were very high, Prime Minister Indira Gandhi was assassinated by Sikh extremists. She was succeeded by her son Rajiv. Less than two months later, in the worst industrial accident in world history, over 2000 people were killed and over 150,000 injured when a cloud of toxic gas escaped from a Union Carbide chemical plant in Bhopal, India.

1986

Dictators deposed. In two stunning displays of popular will, Ferdinand Marcos of the Philippines and Francois "Baby Doc" Duvalier of Haiti fled into exile in the face of massive demonstrations of discontent by the people.

1987

Missile treaty. Ronald Reagan and Mikhail Gorbachev signed the first treaty ever to reduce the number of nuclear warheads. The treaty provides for the elimination of all medium- and short-range missiles by both countries, and establishes a mechanism for on-site inspection of the process.

1989

Crackdown in China. Millions of people participated in student-led demonstrations in favor of reform, provoking a political crisis. After a six-week standoff, the military brutally suppressed the movement. Hundreds of people were killed when troops opened fire on protesters in Tiananmen Square in Beijing.

Students demonstrate in Beijing's Tiananmen Square.

End of an era—Berliners anticipating the destruction of their hated wall.

1989

The iron curtain falls. Encouraged by reforms in the Soviet Union, the countries of the Soviet bloc in Eastern Europe moved swiftly toward democracy. Among the most dramatic events were the overwhelming Solidarity victory in Polish parliamentary elections, which forced the Communist Party to share power; the opening by East Germany of the Berlin Wall; and the violent overthrow of the Stalinist Ceausescu regime in Rumania. These changes altered radically the political and economic landscape of Europe. In 1990 East and West Germany were reunified into a single sovereign state.

1990–1991

Changes in South Africa. The South African government lifted a ban on the African National Congress (ANC) and freed Nelson Mandela, the leader of the ANC, from prison, where he had been detained for 28 years. Segregation in public places was outlawed and plans were made to put an end to all racial separation laws.

South African president Nelson Mandela and (left) former president F. W. de Klerk

1991

War in the Persian Gulf. In response to the August, 1990, Iraqi invasion of Kuwait, an international coalition of forces, including the U.S. military, gathered in the Persian Gulf and in Saudi Arabia. On January 16, 1991, the coalition launched air sorties designed to destroy missile launchers and lines of supply. After 46 days of continual air attacks and five days of battle on the ground, Iraqi officials agreed to a cease-fire on March 2.

1991

Secession and civil war in Yugoslavia. Croatia and Slovenia declared their independence, but violence broke out between Croats and ethnic Serbs in Croatia. The fighting escalated as Serbia contributed arms and supplies to the Serb rebels and the Yugoslav army engaged Croatian forces. Many cease-fires were declared, but none lasted.

1985-1994

Mikhail Gorbachev.

Upheaval in the Soviet Union. In 1985 Mikhail Gorbachev was appointed general secretary of the Communist Party. In 1987 Gorbachev introduced a program of economic and social reforms characterized by *glasnost* (openness) and *perestroika* (restructuring), to help reshape the Soviet system. The new openness, coupled with a failing economy, led to open displays of civil and ethnic unrest.

In 1991 a short-lived coup launched by hard-line Communists hastened the demise of the Soviet Union. Latvia, Lithuania, and Estonia asserted their independence. The Russian Republic dealt the fatal blow by declaring independence and creating the Commonwealth of Independent States (CIS) with Ukraine, Belarus, and eight other former Soviet republics. On December 25, 1991, Mikhail Gorbachev resigned.

In 1992 Russia began the transition to a market economy and was faced with runaway inflation, widespread shortages, rising crime, and growing opposition in the Russian parliament (dominated by former Communist hard-liners) to Russian President Boris N. Yeltsin's reform policies. In October, 1993, Yeltsin dissolved the parliament, sparking an armed uprising that was quelled by the Russian military. In December a new parliament was elected, and in 1994 reforms continued, but at a slower pace.

1994

Peace accord in the Middle East. In April, 1994, Israel and representatives of the Palestine Liberation Organization (PLO) signed an historic accord establishing Palestinian self-rule in Gaza and the area around the West Bank city of Jericho.

Disaster at sea. In one of the worst ferry disasters in history, the North Sea ferry *Estonia* sank en route from Tallinn, Estonia, to Stockholm, Sweden, killing some 900 passengers.

For Further Reference

Breasted, James H.
  Conquest of Civilization
  Harper & Row
Durant, Will and Ariel
  Story of Civilization. 11 volumes.
  Simon & Schuster
Garraty, John A.
  The Columbia History of the World
  Harper & Row
Grun, Bernard
  *The Timetables of History: A Historical
  Linkage of Peoples and Events*
  Simon & Schuster
Harrison, John B.
  A Short History of Western Civilization
  Knopf
Kirkler, Bernard
  A Reader's Guide to Contemporary History
  Quadrangle

McNeill, William H.
  A World History
  Oxford University Press
McNeill, William H. and Houser, Schuyler O.
  Medieval Europe
  Oxford University Press
Stavrianos, L.S.
  Lifelines from our Past
  Pantheon
Wallbank, T. Walter, et al.
  Civilization Past & Present
  Scott, Foresman
Wetterau, Bruce
  *The Macmillan Concise Dictionary of
  World History*
  Macmillan
Winks, Robin W., et al.
  A History of Civilization
  Prentice-Hall

Makers of world history
1000 BC to AD 2000

Peloponnesian War, 431 B.C.-404 B.C.

Hannibal crosses Alps, 218 B.C.

Caesar assassinated, 44 B.C.

1000 BC	800 BC	600 BC	400 BC	200 BC	AD 1

DAVID
c 1040-972, Hebrew king

SOLOMON
c 1000-932, Hebrew king

HOMER
fl. c 900, first Greek poet

SOLON
c 639-c 559, Greek lawmaker

NEBUCHADNEZZAR
c 630-562, Babylonian emperor

CYRUS THE GREAT
c 590-529, Persian conqueror

DARIUS THE GREAT
c 588-486, Persian king

PYTHAGORAS
581-497, Greek philosopher, scientist

BUDDHA, GAUTAMA
c 566-480, Indian religious leader

CONFUCIUS
c 551-479, Chinese philosopher, teacher

AESCHYLUS
c 525-456, Greek dramatist

SOPHOCLES
c 495-c 406, Greek dramatist

PERICLES
c 490-429, Athenian statesman

EURIPIDES
c 480-c 406, Greek dramatist

SOCRATES
469-399, Greek philosopher

HIPPOCRATES
c 460-c 370 "father of medicine"

THUCYDIDES
460-395, Greek historian

EUCLID
450-374, Greek geometrician

PLATO
427-347, Greek philosopher

ARISTOTLE
384-322, Greek philosopher

DEMOSTHENES
c 384-322, Athenian statesman, orator

PHILIP II
382-336, Macedonian king

PTOLEMY I
367-280, Egyptian ruler

ALEXANDER THE GREAT
356-323, Macedonian king, conqueror

CHANDRAGUPTA MAURYA
ruled 322-298, king of Northern India

ASOKA
ruled c 273-232, ruler of India

PLAUTUS
c 254-c 184, Roman dramatist

HANNIBAL
247-183, Carthaginian general

CATO THE ELDER
234-149, Roman statesman

JUDAS MACCABEUS
c 200-166, led Maccabean revolt

POMPEY
106-48, Roman general, statesman

CICERO
106-43, Roman statesman, orator

JULIUS CAESAR
100-44, Roman general, statesman

LUCRETIUS
98-55, Roman poet, philosopher

MARK ANTONY
83-30, Roman soldier, politician

HEROD THE GREAT
73-4, King of Judea

VERGIL
70-19, Roman poet

CLEOPATRA
69-30, Egyptian queen

HORACE
65-8, Roman poet

AUGUSTUS CAESAR
63-AD 14, Roman emperor

Confucius

Aristotle

Alexander the Great

■ Statesmen and politicians

■ Philosophers and religious leaders

■ Scientists and explorers

■ Artists and men of letters

118

World History

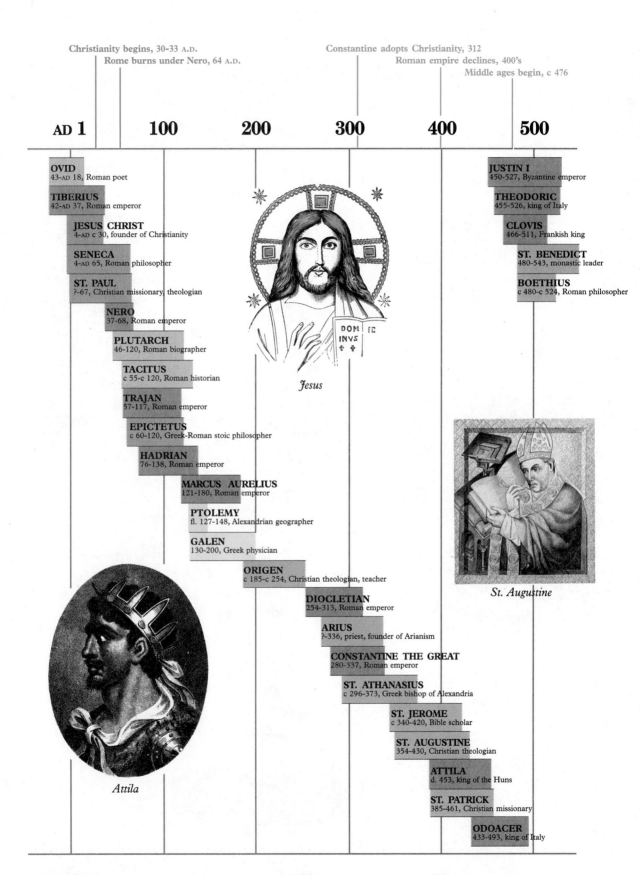

Christianity begins, 30-33 A.D.

Rome burns under Nero, 64 A.D.

Constantine adopts Christianity, 312

Roman empire declines, 400's

Middle ages begin, c 476

AD **1**   **100**   **200**   **300**   **400**   **500**

OVID
43-AD 18, Roman poet

TIBERIUS
42-AD 37, Roman emperor

JESUS CHRIST
4-AD c 30, founder of Christianity

SENECA
4-AD 65, Roman philosopher

ST. PAUL
?-67, Christian missionary, theologian

NERO
37-68, Roman emperor

PLUTARCH
46-120, Roman biographer

TACITUS
c 55-c 120, Roman historian

TRAJAN
57-117, Roman emperor

EPICTETUS
c 60-120, Greek-Roman stoic philosopher

HADRIAN
76-138, Roman emperor

MARCUS AURELIUS
121-180, Roman emperor

PTOLEMY
fl. 127-148, Alexandrian geographer

GALEN
130-200, Greek physician

ORIGEN
c 185-c 254, Christian theologian, teacher

DIOCLETIAN
254-313, Roman emperor

ARIUS
?-336, priest, founder of Arianism

CONSTANTINE THE GREAT
280-337, Roman emperor

ST. ATHANASIUS
c 296-373, Greek bishop of Alexandria

ST. JEROME
c 340-420, Bible scholar

ST. AUGUSTINE
354-430, Christian theologian

ATTILA
d. 453, king of the Huns

ST. PATRICK
385-461, Christian missionary

ODOACER
433-493, king of Italy

JUSTIN I
450-527, Byzantine emperor

THEODORIC
455-526, king of Italy

CLOVIS
466-511, Frankish king

ST. BENEDICT
480-543, monastic leader

BOETHIUS
c 480-c 524, Roman philosopher

Jesus

St. Augustine

Attila

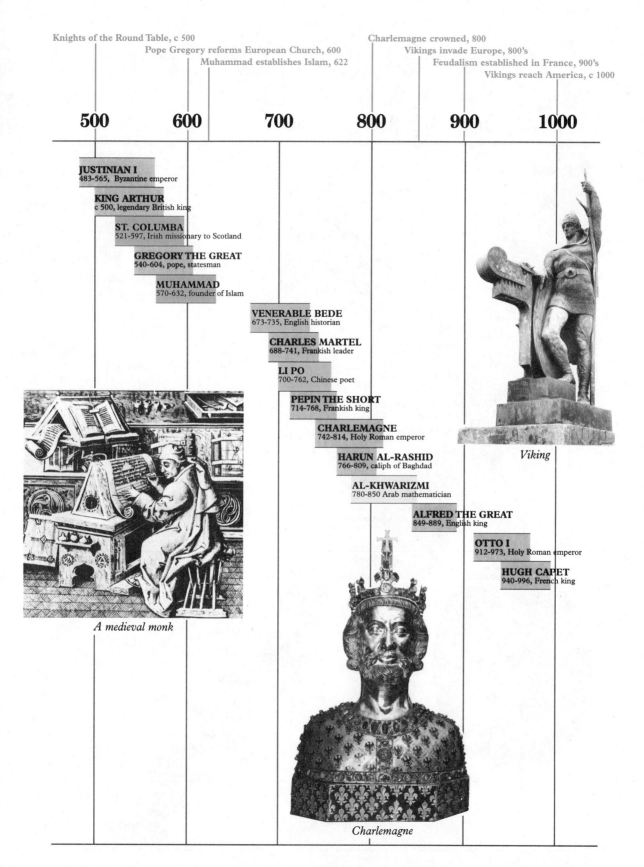

Knights of the Round Table, c 500

Pope Gregory reforms European Church, 600

Muhammad establishes Islam, 622

Charlemagne crowned, 800

Vikings invade Europe, 800's

Feudalism established in France, 900's

Vikings reach America, c 1000

500   600   700   800   900   1000

JUSTINIAN I
483-565, Byzantine emperor

KING ARTHUR
c 500, legendary British king

ST. COLUMBA
521-597, Irish missionary to Scotland

GREGORY THE GREAT
540-604, pope, statesman

MUHAMMAD
570-632, founder of Islam

VENERABLE BEDE
673-735, English historian

CHARLES MARTEL
688-741, Frankish leader

LI PO
700-762, Chinese poet

PEPIN THE SHORT
714-768, Frankish king

CHARLEMAGNE
742-814, Holy Roman emperor

HARUN AL-RASHID
766-809, caliph of Baghdad

AL-KHWARIZMI
780-850 Arab mathematician

ALFRED THE GREAT
849-889, English king

OTTO I
912-973, Holy Roman emperor

HUGH CAPET
940-996, French king

Viking

A medieval monk

Charlemagne

World History

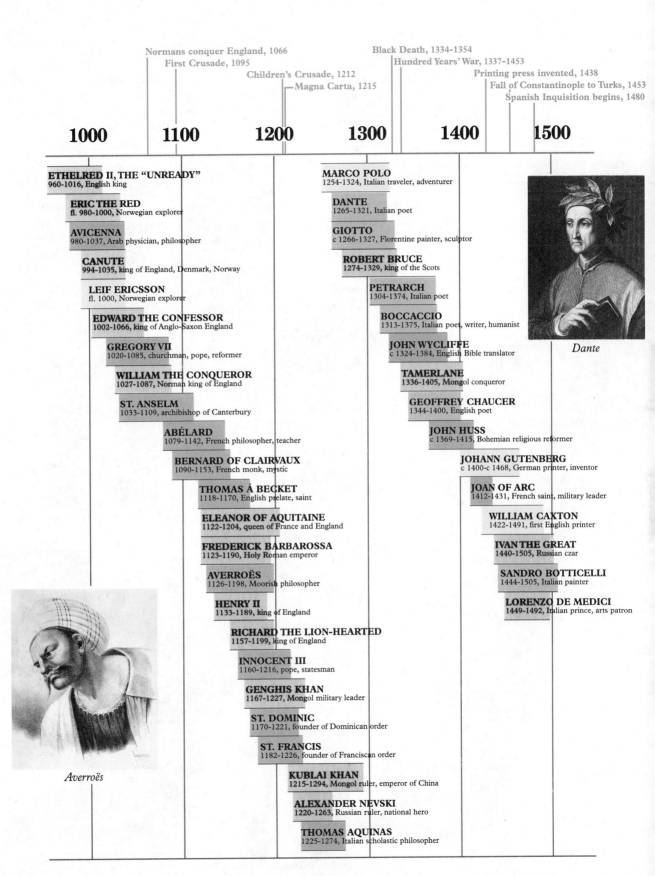

Normans conquer England, 1066
First Crusade, 1095
Children's Crusade, 1212
Magna Carta, 1215
Black Death, 1334-1354
Hundred Years' War, 1337-1453
Printing press invented, 1438
Fall of Constantinople to Turks, 1453
Spanish Inquisition begins, 1480

1000 **1100** **1200** **1300** **1400** **1500**

ETHELRED II, THE "UNREADY"
960-1016, English king

ERIC THE RED
fl. 980-1000, Norwegian explorer

AVICENNA
980-1037, Arab physician, philosopher

CANUTE
994-1035, king of England, Denmark, Norway

LEIF ERICSSON
fl. 1000, Norwegian explorer

EDWARD THE CONFESSOR
1002-1066, king of Anglo-Saxon England

GREGORY VII
1020-1085, churchman, pope, reformer

WILLIAM THE CONQUEROR
1027-1087, Norman king of England

ST. ANSELM
1033-1109, archibishop of Canterbury

ABÉLARD
1079-1142, French philosopher, teacher

BERNARD OF CLAIRVAUX
1090-1153, French monk, mystic

THOMAS Á BECKET
1118-1170, English prelate, saint

ELEANOR OF AQUITAINE
1122-1204, queen of France and England

FREDERICK BARBAROSSA
1123-1190, Holy Roman emperor

AVERROËS
1126-1198, Moorish philosopher

HENRY II
1133-1189, king of England

RICHARD THE LION-HEARTED
1157-1199, king of England

INNOCENT III
1160-1216, pope, statesman

GENGHIS KHAN
1167-1227, Mongol military leader

ST. DOMINIC
1170-1221, founder of Dominican order

ST. FRANCIS
1182-1226, founder of Franciscan order

KUBLAI KHAN
1215-1294, Mongol ruler, emperor of China

ALEXANDER NEVSKI
1220-1263, Russian ruler, national hero

THOMAS AQUINAS
1225-1274, Italian scholastic philosopher

MARCO POLO
1254-1324, Italian traveler, adventurer

DANTE
1265-1321, Italian poet

GIOTTO
c 1266-1327, Florentine painter, sculptor

ROBERT BRUCE
1274-1329, king of the Scots

PETRARCH
1304-1374, Italian poet

BOCCACCIO
1313-1375, Italian poet, writer, humanist

JOHN WYCLIFFE
c 1324-1384, English Bible translator

TAMERLANE
1336-1405, Mongol conqueror

GEOFFREY CHAUCER
1344-1400, English poet

JOHN HUSS
c 1369-1415, Bohemian religious reformer

JOHANN GUTENBERG
c 1400-c 1468, German printer, inventor

JOAN OF ARC
1412-1431, French saint, military leader

WILLIAM CAXTON
1422-1491, first English printer

IVAN THE GREAT
1440-1505, Russian czar

SANDRO BOTTICELLI
1444-1505, Italian painter

LORENZO DE MEDICI
1449-1492, Italian prince, arts patron

Dante

Averroës

Columbus' first voyage, 1492

Luther begins Protestant Reformation, 1517

Elizabeth becomes Queen of England, 1558

Spanish Armada defeated, 1588

North America colonized, 1607 on

Religious wars in Europe, England, 1618-1652

Louis XIV becomes French King, 1643

England's Glorious Revolution, 1688-1689

Peter makes Russia a European power, 1700-1725

1500　1550　1600　1650　1700　1750

CHRISTOPHER COLUMBUS
1451-1506, Italian navigator, explorer

FERDINAND
1452-1516, king of Spain

LEONARDO DA VINCI
1452-1519, Italian artist, scientist

HENRY TUDOR
1457-1509, Henry VII of England

MAXIMILIAN I
1459-1519, Holy Roman emperor

ERASMUS
1466-1536, Dutch scholar, humanist

VASCO DA GAMA
c 1469-1524, Portuguese navigator

NICCOLÓ MACHIAVELLI
1469-1527, Italian statesman, writer

MONTEZUMA
c 1470-1520, Aztec emperor of Mexico

ALBRECHT DÜRER
1471-1528, German painter, engraver

COPERNICUS
1473-1543, Polish astronomer

MICHELANGELO
1475-1564, Italian artist, architect

THOMAS MORE
1478-1535, English humanist, statesman

RAPHAEL
1483-1520, Italian painter

MARTIN LUTHER
1483-1546, German Protestant reformer

HERNÁN CORTÉS
1485-1547, Spanish explorer, conqueror

HENRY VIII
1491-1547, king of England

IGNATIUS LOYOLA
1491-1556, founder of Jesuit order

CHARLES V
1500-1558, Holy Roman emperor

JOHN CALVIN
1509-1564, French Protestant reformer

MERCATOR
1512-1594, Flemish geographer

CATHERINE DE MEDICI
1519-1589, queen of France

IVAN THE TERRIBLE
1530-1584, Russian czar

ELIZABETH I
1533-1603, queen of England

FRANCIS DRAKE
c 1540-1596, English navigator

EL GRECO
c 1545-1614, Spanish painter

MIGUEL DE CERVANTES
1547-1616, Spanish poet, novelist

WILLIAM SHAKESPEARE
1564-1616, English dramatist, poet

GALILEO
1564-1642, Italian astronomer

PETER PAUL RUBENS
1577-1640, Flemish painter

CARDINAL RICHELIEU
1585-1642, French statesman

RENÉ DESCARTES
1596-1650, French philosopher

OLIVER CROMWELL
1599-1658, English lord protector

DIEGO VELÁSQUEZ
1599-1660, Spanish painter

REMBRANDT
1606-1669, Dutch painter

JOHN MILTON
1608-1674, English epic poet

BLAISE PASCAL
1623-1662, French scientist, thinker

JAN VERMEER
1632-1675, Dutch painter

JOHN LOCKE
1632-1704, English philosopher

MOLIÈRE
1633-1673, French dramatist

LOUIS XIV
1638-1715, king of France

ISAAC NEWTON
1642-1727, English physicist

GOTTFRIED WILHELM LEIBNIZ
1646-1716, German philosopher, mathematician

PETER THE GREAT
1672-1725, Russian czar

JOHANN SEBASTIAN BACH
1685-1750, German composer

GEORGE BERKELEY
1685-1753, Irish philosopher

VOLTAIRE
1694-1778, French writer, philosopher

BENJAMIN FRANKLIN
1706-1790, American statesman, scientist

LINNAEUS
1707-1778, Swedish botanist

SAMUEL JOHNSON
1709-1784, English lexicographer, critic

DAVID HUME
1711-1776, Scottish philosopher, historian

JEAN JACQUES ROUSSEAU
1712-1778, French writer, philosopher

FREDERICK THE GREAT
1712-1786, king of Prussia

MARIA THERESA
1717-1780, Holy Roman empress

Columbus

Leonardo da Vinci

Henry VIII

Bach

World History

1750 1800 1850 1900

IMMANUEL KANT
1724-1804, German philosopher

CATHERINE THE GREAT
1729-1796, empress of Russia

GEORGE WASHINGTON
1732-1799, American general, President

THOMAS PAINE
1737-1809, American political writer

THOMAS JEFFERSON
1743-1826, American statesman, President

GOYA
1746-1828, Spanish painter

JOHANN WOLFGANG VON GOETHE
1749-1832, German poet, novelist

MARIE ANTOINETTE
1755-1793, queen of France

WOLFGANG AMADEUS MOZART
1756-1791, Austrian composer

WILLIAM BLAKE
1757-1827, English poet, artist

NAPOLEON
1769-1821, emperor of France

LUDWIG VAN BEETHOVEN
1770-1827, German composer

WILLIAM WORDSWORTH
1770-1850, English Romantic poet

CLEMENS VON METTERNICH
1773-1859, Austrian diplomat, statesman

SIMÓN BOLÍVAR
1783-1830, Venezuelan soldier, statesman

ROBERT E. LEE
1807-1870, Confederate general

ABRAHAM LINCOLN
1809-1865, American President

CHARLES DICKENS
1812-1870, English novelist

CHARLES DARWIN
1812-1870, British naturalist, writer

RICHARD WAGNER
1813-1883, German composer

OTTO VON BISMARCK
1815-1898, Prussian statesman

HENRY DAVID THOREAU
1817-1862, American writer

KARL MARX
1818-1883, German economist, philosopher

FEODOR DOSTOEVSKI
1821-1881, Russian novelist

LOUIS PASTEUR
1822-1895, French chemist

LEO TOLSTOY
1828-1910, Russian writer

MARK TWAIN
1835-1910, American writer, lecturer

PAUL CÉZANNE
1839-1906, French painter

PETER ILYICH TCHAIKOVSKY
1840-1893, Russian composer

ALEXANDER GRAHAM BELL
1847-1922, American inventor

THOMAS ALVA EDISON
1847-1931, American inventor

SIGMUND FREUD
1856-1939, Austrian psychoanalyst

THEODORE ROOSEVELT
1858-1919, American President

HENRY FORD
1863-1947, automotive industry pioneer

WILBUR WRIGHT
1867-1912, American aviation pioneer

MOHANDAS K. GANDHI
1869-1948, Indian nationalist leader

FRANK LLOYD WRIGHT
1869-1959, American architect

VLADIMIR ILYICH LENIN
1870-1924, Russian revolutionary, Soviet premier

ORVILLE WRIGHT
1871-1948, American aviation pioneer

Edison

Catherine the Great

Orville Wright

World War I, 1914-1918
Russian Revolution, 1917-1920
Great Depression, 1930's
World War II, 1939-1945

1900 | 1950

WINSTON CHURCHILL
1874-1965, English statesman

JOSEF STALIN
1879-1953, Soviet dictator

ALBERT EINSTEIN
1879-1955, German-born American physicist

POPE JOHN XXIII
1881-1963, Italian ecclesiastic, statesman

PABLO PICASSO
1881-1973, Spanish artist

FRANKLIN DELANO ROOSEVELT
1882-1945, American President

IGOR STRAVINSKY
1882-1971, Russian composer

BENITO MUSSOLINI
1883-1945, Italian dictator

DAVID BEN-GURION
1886-1973, prime minister of Israel

T.S. ELIOT
1888-1965, Anglo-American poet

ADOLF HITLER
1889-1945, German dictator

JAWAHARLAL NEHRU
1889-1964, prime minister of India

HO CHI MINH
1890-1969, Vietnamese revolutionary leader

CHARLES DE GAULLE
1890-1970, French president, general

FRANCISCO FRANCO
1892-1975, Spanish general, premier

MAO TSE-TUNG
1893-1976, Chinese Communist leader

JOMO KENYATTA
1893-1978, president of Kenya

RUFINO TAMAYO
1899-1991, Mexican artist

ISAAC BASHEVIS SINGER
1904-1991, Polish-born U.S. writer

LEONID BREZHNEV
1906-1982, Soviet leader

MOTHER TERESA OF CALCUTTA
1910- , religious leader

WERNHER VON BRAUN
1912-1977, rocket designer

JOHN CAGE
1912-1992, U.S. composer

RICHARD M. NIXON
1913-1994, American President

Churchill

Von Braun

Mother Teresa

World History

1950   **2000**

King

Havel   *Walesa*

Morita

World History   *Spielberg*

OCTAVIO PAZ
1914– , Mexican poet and essayist

JOHN F. KENNEDY
1917–1963, American President

INDIRA GANDHI
1917–1984, prime minister of India

ANWAR EL SADAT
1918–1981, president of Egypt

LEONARD BERNSTEIN
1918–1990, U.S. composer and conductor

NELSON MANDELA
1918– , president of South Africa

ISAAC ASIMOV
1920–1992, U.S. writer

AKIO MORITA
1921– , Japanese electronics executive

MARGARET THATCHER
1925– , prime minister of Great Britain

GABRIEL GARCÍA MÁRQUEZ
1928– , Colombian writer

MARTIN LUTHER KING
1929–1968, American civil rights leader

H. ROSS PEROT
1930– , U.S. businessman

MIKHAIL S. GORBACHEV
1931– , Soviet leader

BORIS YELTSIN
1931– , Russian president

F.W. de KLERK
1936– , South African statesman

VACLAV HAVEL
1936 –, Czech playright and statesman

STEPHEN HAWKING
1942– , British theoretical physicist

LECH WALESA
1943– , Polish political leader

STEPHEN SPIELBERG
1947– , U.S. film director

Countries of the World

Five hundred years ago, the peoples of the world were isolated from each other. Those in Europe did not know about the continents of North and South America. Australia and Antarctica were still undiscovered, and most of Africa was a mystery. Today, the world has shrunk. Modern transportation and communication have allowed us to explore even the most remote corners of Earth. This section provides material on the world as a whole, on each of its major regions, and on all of its countries and territories. There is much more to know about today than there was 500 years ago; even as the world has shrunk, information about it has grown and grown. At the end of the section is a color atlas with maps of all parts of the world.

World at a glance

On July 20, 1969, the United States landed the first men on the moon. One of the first things the astronauts did was to take a photograph of the planet Earth as it looked from space. Viewed from space, Earth is a sphere covered mostly by blue water, the white clouds of water vapor that create our weather, and small green patches of land.

Three-quarters of Earth's surface is covered by water. Most of this water is part of the Pacific, Atlantic, Indian, and Arctic oceans, the four major oceans of the world. The Pacific, covering Earth from the Americas west to Asia, is the largest ocean by far. The Atlantic, stretching from the Americas east toward Europe and Africa, is the second largest. The Indian Ocean covers the surface of Earth between Africa and Asia. The Arctic is the smallest of the world's oceans. It covers the North Pole, which, unlike the South Pole, is in the midst of a huge body of frozen sea.

If you could see the bottom of the world's oceans, you would see natural features very much like the ones on dry land. For example, the deepest part of the Pacific Ocean is the Mariana Trench near China. It is a region of valleys and canyons farther below sea level than any mountain on land is high. There are also mountains beneath the oceans. If they are high enough, their peaks rise above the level of the water and appear as islands. The Hawaiian Islands in the Pacific are the tops of mostly submerged mountains.

There are also extensions of the world's oceans that are surrounded by land. The largest of these are called seas. The largest seas are the Caribbean, between North and South America, and the Mediterranean, between Europe and Africa. Seas are generally more shallow than oceans.

Looking closer at Earth from space, you would see

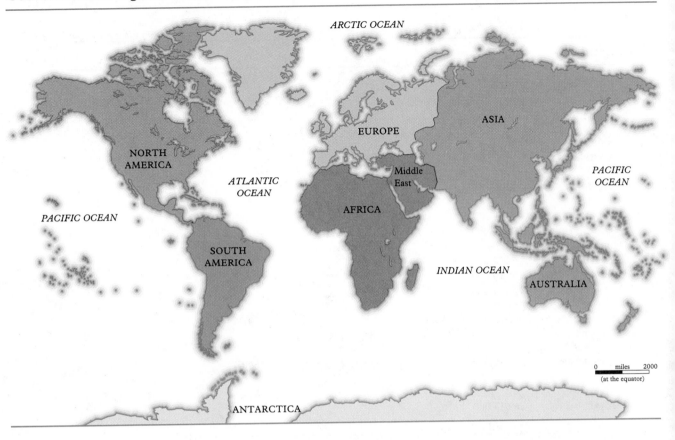

bodies of land that are green when covered by vegetation and white when covered by ice. The seven largest bodies of land are called continents. North America and South America are two continents between the Atlantic and Pacific oceans that are joined by a narrow strip of land. Europe and Asia are two joined continents between the Atlantic and Pacific on the other side of the world. Africa is the continent south of Europe between the Atlantic and Indian oceans. Australia is an "island continent" between the Indian and south Pacific oceans. Antarctica is an ice-covered continent at the South Pole. The view from space would show you that the Pacific Ocean is about four times larger than the largest continent, Asia.

Earth also has many islands, which are bodies of land too small to be continents. The largest island on Earth is Greenland, located in the north Atlantic Ocean near the North Pole. Most of the world's islands are much smaller than Greenland, and many of them are tiny atolls of rock that barely rise above sea level.

Earth's land boasts a wide variety of natural features. The highest points on Earth are the Himalaya Mountains in Asia, where Mt. Everest rises more than 29,000 feet above sea level. There are vast inland bodies of water. Water trapped on land tends to flow to the sea, thus creating rivers. The longest rivers are the Nile in Africa and the Amazon in South America. Where there is no water, inland regions of Earth become barren desert. The largest desert on Earth is the vast Sahara in north Africa; it is nearly as large as the entire United States. Asia's Gobi Desert, which is almost twice as large as the state of Texas, is cooler than the Sahara but equally dry and barren. There are also a number of active and dramatic natural features on Earth, such as smoldering volcanoes and waterfalls thousands of feet high. For more information on Earth's natural features, see Earth Sciences in Volume 1.

Earth is home to over 5 billion people. Their variety of cultures and lifestyles is as diverse as the lands around the world that are their homes. In America it is easy to forget that six out of every ten people on Earth live in Asia. Most of these people live in China, which is the most populous country on Earth by far. Asia also includes India, which alone has three times as many people as the United States.

The largest country on Earth is Russia. It stretches 5000 miles from Europe to the Pacific Ocean, and it is almost twice as large as the world's next largest country, Canada.

The population on Earth is not evenly distributed. In Asia sixty percent of the world's people live on only 30 percent of the land. The concentration of population in particular areas of our planet is caused by a variety of geographical, economic, and historical circumstances. We study the regions of the world to better understand these circumstances.

Land

Regions of the world

Name	Area (sq. mi.)	Percent of world total	High point (location)	Elevation (ft.)	Population (1993 est.)	Percent of total
Asia and Australasia	12,797,000	22.7	Everest (Nepal)	29,028	3,164,458,000	57.0
Europe	9,862,000	17.5	Elbrus (Russia)	18,510	747,143,000	13.5
Middle East and Africa	13,765,000	24.4	Kilimanjaro (Tanzania)	19,340	890,462,000	16.0
North America	8,125,000	14.4	McKinley (Alaska)	20,320	438,659,000	7.9
South America	6,770,000	12.0	Aconcagua (Argentina)	22,834	309,741,000	5.6
Antarctica	5,100,000	9.0	Vinson Massif	16,864	0	.0
Total	56,419,000	100.0			5,550,463,000	100.0

Countries: Largest

Country	Area (sq. mi.)
1. Russia	6,659,000
2. China	3,601,000
3. Canada	3,560,000
4. U.S.	3,539,000
5. Brazil	3,265,000
6. Australia	2,941,000
7. India	1,148,000
8. Kazakhstan	1,060,000
9. Argentina	1,057,000
10. Algeria	920,000
11. Sudan	917,000
12. Zaire	875,000
13. Saudi Arabia	830,000
14. Mexico	742,000
15. Indonesia	705,000
16. Libya	679,000
17. Iran	632,000
18. Mongolia	604,000
19. Peru	494,000
20 Niger	489,000

Most Populous
(1993 estimates)

Country	Population
1. China	1,177,585,000
2. India	903,159,000
3. U.S.	258,104,000
4. Indonesia	197,232,000
5. Brazil	156,664,000
6. Russia	149,300,000
7. Pakistan	125,214,000
8. Japan	124,712,000
9. Bangladesh	122,255,000
10. Nigeria	95,060,000
11. Mexico	90,420,000
12. Germany	80,768,000
13. Vietnam	71,788,000
14. Philippines	68,464,000
15. Iran	63,370,000
16. Turkey	60,898,000
17. Thailand	58,722,000
18. Italy	57,657,000
19. Egypt	58,016,000
20. U.K.	57,970,000

Cities: Most populous urban areas
(1991 estimates)

Name	Country	Population
1. Tokyo-Yokohama	Japan	27,245,000
2. Mexico City	Mexico	20,899,000
3. São Paulo	Brazil	18,701,000
4. Seoul	S. Korea	16,792,000
5. New York	U.S.	14,625,000
6. Osaka-Kyoto	Japan	13,872,000
7. Bombay	India	12,109,000
8. Calcutta	India	11,898,000
9. Rio de Janeiro	Brazil	11,688,000
10. Buenos Aires	Argentina	11,657,000
11. Moscow	Russia	10,446,000
12. Manila	Philippines	10,156,000
13. Los Angeles	U.S.	10,130,000
14. Cairo	Egypt	10,099,000
15. Jakarta	Indonesia	9,882,000
16. Teheran	Iran	9,779,000
17. London	U.K.	9,115,000
18. Delhi	India	8,778,000
19. Paris	France	8,720,000
20. Karachi	Pakistan	8,014,000

Water

Oceans

Name	Area (sq. mi.)	Percent of total ocean area	Avg. depth (ft.)	Max. depth (ft.)
Pacific	64,186,300	48.9	14,048	36,198
Atlantic	33,420,000	25.5	12,888	28,374
Indian	28,350,000	21.5	13,002	25,344
Arctic	5,427,000	4.1	5,010	17,880
Total	131,383,300	100.0		

Seas: Largest

	Name	Continent	Area (sq. mi.)	Avg. depth (ft.)
1.	Caribbean	N.-S. America	970,000	8685
2.	Mediterranean	Europe-Africa	969,100	4926
3.	South China	Asia	895,400	5400
4.	Bering	Asia-N. America	875,000	4893
5.	Gulf of Mexico	N. America	600,000	4874
6.	Okhotsk	Asia	590,000	2749
7.	East China	Asia	482,300	617
8.	Japan	Asia	391,100	5468
9.	Hudson Bay	Canada	317,500	420
10.	Andaman	Asia	308,000	2854

Waterfalls: Highest

	Name	Country	Height (ft.)
1.	Angel Falls	Venezuela	3212
2.	Tugela	South Africa	3110
3.	Mardalsfossen	Norway	2539
4.	Yosemite	U.S.	2425
5.	Cuquenan	Venezuela	2000
6.	Sutherland	New Zealand	1904
7.	Takkakan	Canada	1650
8.	Ribbon Falls	U.S.	1612
9.	Great Falls	Guyana	1600
10.	Della	Canada	1443
11.	Gavarnie	France	1385
12.	Glass	Brazil	1325
13.	Trummelbach	Switzerland	1312
14.	Krimml	Austria	1246
15.	Silver Strand	U.S.	1170

Lakes: Largest

	Name	Location	Area (sq. mi.)	Length (ft.)	Max. Depth (ft.)
1.	Caspian Sea	Asia-Europe	143,243	746	3264
2.	Superior	U.S.-Canada	31,700	383	1301
3.	Victoria	Africa	26,724	250	270
4.	Aral Sea	Asia	25,676	266	256
5.	Huron	U.S.-Canada	23,010	247	748
6.	Michigan	U.S.	22,300	321	923
7.	Tanganyika	Africa	12,650	420	4700
8.	Baikal	Asia	12,162	395	5316
9.	Great Bear	Canada	12,096	190	1316
10.	Malawi	Africa	11,555	360	2320
11.	Great Slave	Canada	11,269	300	2015
12.	Erie	U.S.-Canada	9,910	241	209

Rivers: Longest

	Name	Location	Length (miles)		Name	Location	Length (miles)
1.	Nile	Africa	4145	8.	Amur	Asia	2744
2.	Amazon	S. America	3915	9.	Lena	Russia	2734
3.	Mississippi-Missouri	U.S.	3710	10.	Mackenzie	Canada	2635
4.	Yangtze	China	3434	11.	Yenisei	Russia	2543
5.	Ob-Irtysh	Russia	3362	12.	Paraná	S. America	2450
6.	Huang	China	2903	13.	Volga	Russia	2194
7.	Congo	Africa	2900	14.	Madeira	S. America	2013
				15.	Yukon	N. America	1979

Other features

Islands: Largest

Island (country)	Location	Area (sq. mi.)
1. Greenland (Denmark)	Atlantic-Arctic	840,000
2. New Guinea	South Pacific	305,000
3. Borneo (Indonesia)	Pacific-Indian	290,000
4. Madagascar	Indian	226,400
5. Baffin (Canada)	Arctic	195,928
6. Sumatra (Indonesia)	Indian	164,000
7. Honshu (Japan)	Pacific	88,839
8. Great Britain (U.K.)	Atlantic	88,745
9. Victoria (Canada)	Arctic	83,896
10. Ellesmere (Canada)	Arctic	75,767
11. Celebes (Indonesia)	Pacific-Indian	69,000
12. South (New Zealand)	South Pacific	58,393
13. Java (Indonesia)	Pacific-Indian	48,842
14. Cuba	Caribbean Sea	44,218
15. North (New Zealand)	South Pacific	44,187

Deserts: Largest

Name	Location	Area (sq. mi.)
1. Sahara	North-Africa	3,500,000
2. Gobi	China-Mongolia	500,000
3. Great Victoria	South Australia	250,000
4. Gibson	West Australia	250,000
5. Rub al-Khali	S. Arabian Peninsula	234,000
6. Kalahari	Southern Africa	225,000
7. Taklamakam	Western China	180,000
8. Nubian	North Africa	150,000
9. Great Sandy	West Australia	150,000
10. Atacama	North Chile	140,000
11. Thar	Indian-Pakistan	137,000
12. Simpson	Central Australia	120,000
13. Sonoran	Arizona (U.S.)	120,000
14. Kara Kum	Western Asia	110,000
15. Syrian	N. Arabian Peninsula	100,000

Mountains: Highest

Continent/Name (Location)	Elevation (ft.)
Asia	
Everest (Nepal-Tibet)	29,028
Godwin-Austen (India)	28,250
Kanchenjunga (India-Nepal)	28,208
South America	
Aconcagua (Argentina)	22,834
Ojos de Salado (Arg.-Chile)	22,572
Tupungato (Arg.-Chile)	22,546
North America	
McKinley (Alaska)	20,320
Logan (Canada)	19,850
Citlaltapec (Mexico)	18,700
Africa	
Kilimanjaro (Tanzania)	19,340
Kenya (Kenya)	17,058
Margherita (Uganda-Zaire)	16,763
Europe	
El'brus (Russia)	18,510
Shkara (Russia)	17,064
Dykhtau (Russia)	17,054
Antarctica	
Vinson Massif	16,864
Australia	
Kosciusko	7,310
Other famous peaks	
Communism Peak (Tajikistan)	24,590
Ararat (Turkey)	16,804
Mont Blanc (France-Italy)	15,771
Matterhorn (Switzerland)	14,690
Whitney (California)	14,494
Elbert (Colorado)	14,433

Recent volcanic eruptions

Year	Volcano	Location	Elevation (ft.)
1991	Pinatubo	Philippines	5,770
1985	Nevado del Ruiz	Colombia	22,940
1982	El Chichon	Mexico	7,300
1981	Etna	Italy	11,053
1981	Mt. St. Helens	U.S.	9,677
1981	Santiaguito	Guatemala	12,362
1981	Semeru	Java	12,060
1980	Fuego	Guatemala	12,582
1980	Tupungatito	Chile	18,504
1979	Erebus	Antarctica	12,450
1979	Llaima	Chile	10,239

Recent earthquakes

Date	Location	Magnitude
1990, June	Iran	7.7
1989, Oct.	United States	6.9
1988, Dec.	Armenia	6.9
1988, Nov.	China/Burma	7.3
1987, Mar.	Ecuador	7.3
1985, Sept.	Mexico	8.1
1985, Mar.	Chile	7.8
1983, Oct.	Turkey	7.1
1983, May	Japan	7.7
1980, Nov.	Italy	7.2
1980, Oct.	Algeria	7.3

Countries of the world

The list below includes all the independent countries in the world. The year a country became a member of the United Nations is in parentheses. Countries without a date are not members of the United Nations. In the pages that follow, countries are organized by world region. If you want to look up a country and are not sure which region it is in, use this listing to find its page number. For additional information about the United Nations, see page 13.

Country/U.N. entry/page

Afghanistan (1946) 132
Albania (1955) 140
Algeria (1962) 148
Andorra (1993) 140
Angola (1976) 148
Antigua and Barbuda (1981) 162
Argentina (1945) 168
Armenia (1992) 140
Australia (1945) 132
Austria (1955) 141
Azerbaijan (1992) 141
Bahamas (1973) 162
Bahrain (1971) 149
Bangladesh (1974) 132
Barbados (1966) 162
Belarus (1945) 141
Belgium (1945) 142
Belize (1981) 162
Benin (1960) 149
Bhutan (1971) 133
Bolivia (1945) 168
Bosnia and Herzegovina (1992) 142
Botswana (1966) 150
Brazil (1945) 169
Brunei (1984) 133
Bulgaria (1955) 142
Burkina Faso (1960) 150
Burundi (1962) 150
Cambodia (1955) 133
Cameroon (1960) 150
Canada (1945) 162
Cape Verde (1975) 151
Central African Republic (1960) 151
Chad (1960) 151
Chile (1945) 169
China (1945) 134
Colombia (1945) 170
Comoros (1975) 151
Congo (1960) 152
Costa Rica (1945) 162
Côte d'Ivoire (1960) 154
Croatia (1992) 142
Cuba (1945) 164
Cyprus (1960) 152
Czech Republic (1993) 142
Denmark (1945) 142
Djibouti (1977) 152
Dominica (1978) 164
Dominican Republic (1945) 165
Ecuador (1945) 170
Egypt (1945) 152
El Salvador (1945) 165
Equatorial Guinea (1968) 152
Eritrea (1993) 152
Estonia (1991) 143
Ethiopia (1945) 153
Fiji (1970) 134
Finland (1955) 143
France (1945) 143
Gabon (1960) 153
Gambia (1965) 153
Georgia (1992) 143
Germany (1973) 143
Ghana (1957) 153

Country/U.N. entry/page

Greece (1945) 143
Grenada (1974) 165
Guatemala (1945) 165
Guinea (1958) 153
Guinea-Bissau (1974) 153
Guyana (1966) 170
Haiti (1945) 165
Honduras (1945) 166
Hungary (1955) 143
Iceland (1946) 143
India (1945) 134
Indonesia (1950) 134
Iran (1945) 154
Iraq (1945) 154
Ireland (1955) 144
Israel (1949) 154
Italy (1955) 144
Jamaica (1962) 166
Japan (1956) 135
Jordan (1955) 155
Kazakhstan (1992) 135
Kenya (1963) 155
Kiribati 135
Korea, North (1991) 136
Korea, South (1991) 138
Kuwait (1963) 155
Kyrgyzstan (1992) 135
Laos (1955) 135
Latvia (1991) 144
Lebanon (1945) 155
Lesotho (1966) 155
Liberia (1945) 156
Libya (1955) 156
Liechtenstein (1990) 144
Lithuania (1991) 144
Luxembourg (1945) 144
Macedonia (1993) 144
Madagascar (1960) 156
Malawi (1964) 156
Malaysia (1957) 135
Maldives (1965) 135
Mali (1960) 156
Malta (1964) 144
Marshall Islands (1991) 135
Mauritania (1961) 156
Mauritius (1968) 156
Mexico (1945) 166
Micronesia (1991) 136
Moldova (1992) 145
Monaco (1993) 145
Mongolia (1961) 136
Morocco (1956) 157
Mozambique (1975) 157
Myanmar (1948) 136
Namibia (1990) 157
Nauru 136
Nepal (1955) 136
Netherlands (1945) 145
New Zealand (1945) 136
Nicaragua (1945) 166
Niger (1960) 157
Nigeria (1960) 157
Norway (1945) 145
Oman (1971) 157

Country/U.N. entry/page

Pakistan (1947) 137
Panama (1945) 166
Papua New Guinea (1975) 137
Paraguay (1945) 170
Peru (1945) 171
Philippines (1945) 137
Poland (1945) 145
Portugal (1955) 146
Qatar (1971) 158
Romania (1955) 146
Russia (1945) 146
Rwanda (1962) 158
St. Kitts and Nevis (1983) 167
St. Lucia (1979) 167
St. Vincent and the Grenadines (1980) 167
San Marino (1992) 146
São Tomé and Príncipe (1975) 158
Saudi Arabia (1945) 158
Senegal (1960) 158
Seychelles (1976) 159
Sierra Leone (1961) 159
Singapore (1965) 137
Slovakia (1993) 146
Slovenia (1992) 146
Solomon Islands (1978) 137
Somalia (1960) 159
South Africa (1945) 159
Spain (1955) 147
Sri Lanka (1955) 138
Sudan (1956) 159
Suriname (1975) 171
Swaziland (1968) 159
Sweden (1946) 147
Switzerland 147
Syria (1945) 160
Taiwan 138
Tajikistan (1992) 138
Tanzania (1961) 160
Thailand (1946) 138
Togo (1960) 160
Tonga 138
Trinidad and Tobago (1962) 167
Tunisia (1956) 160
Turkey (1945) 160
Turkmenistan (1992) 139
Tuvalu 139
Uganda (1962) 160
Ukraine (1945) 147
United Arab Emirates (1971) 161
United Kingdom (1945) 147
United States (1945) 167
Uruguay (1945) 171
Uzbekistan (1992) 139
Vanuatu (1981) 139
Vatican City 147
Venezuela (1945) 171
Vietnam (1977) 139
Western Samoa (1976) 139
Yemen (1947) 161
Yugoslavia (1945) 147
Zaire (1960) 161
Zambia (1964) 161
Zimbabwe (1980) 161

Asia and Australasia

Asia and Australasia is the world region whose eastern shore is along the Pacific Ocean. It stretches west to Europe and the Middle East. To the south lies the Indian Ocean. To the north is the Arctic Ocean. This region is called Asia and Australasia because it includes two continents, Asia and Australia, and also the many island nations located between those two large bodies of land.

The two largest nations in area in this region are China and Australia. Together they have more than half of the land area in the region. Asia and Australasia also includes the seventh largest nation on Earth, India. India is isolated from mainland Asia by the Himalaya Mountains, the highest on Earth; for this reason it is sometimes called a subcontinent. There are also many tiny island nations that are far smaller than any state in the United States. They are separated by thousands of miles of Pacific Ocean.

Because it includes two continents and many tiny islands, Asia and Australasia is a region of great natural contrasts. Southeast Asia includes some of the rainiest tropical jungles on Earth, but northern China and central Australia are vast barren deserts. The region is divided nearly in half by the equator, where the climate is a hot tropical one with seasons of heavy rainstorms called monsoons. But the highest mountains in Asia and Australasia are covered by snow all year, and the northern reaches of Siberia are among the coldest regions on Earth.

More than half of the people in the world live in this region. Most of them live in China and India, which together have a population seven times larger than that of the United States. China alone includes three of the ten most populous cities on Earth: Shanghai, Beijing, and Tianjin. Asia and Australasia also has a greater diversity of languages and religions than any other region on Earth.

The economy of most of Asia and Australasia is based on agriculture. The great staple crop of the region is rice, but there are many other crops that are strange to us, such as copra, or coconut meat. The only important industrial countries in this region are Japan and Australia. Explorers suggest that the region may hold large mineral deposits, but much of Asia and Australasia remains a wilderness inaccessible to miners.

Country Official Name ★Capital Principal Cities	• Location • Area / Population • Languages / Religions	• Land • Economy
Afghanistan Republic of Afghanistan ★Kabul, Kandahar, Baghlan, Herat	• In central Asia, along south of Tajikistan • 250,000 sq.mi.; 16,494,000 • Pushtu and Dari (official); Sunni Muslim	• Mountainous throughout and generally arid, with arable mountain valleys. • Exports fruit products and natural gas; produces wool products, including carpets.
Australia Commonwealth of Australia ★Canberra, Sydney, Melbourne, Brisbane, Adelaide, Perth	• Island continent between Pacific and Indian oceans • 2,941,285 sq.mi.; 17,827,000 • English (official); Anglican, Roman Catholic	• Great central desert ringed by coastal ranges, arable valleys, and sandy beaches. • Iron ore, bauxite, nickel, oil, natural gas, and other mining exports; iron, steel, textiles; livestock, wool.
Bangladesh (formerly East Pakistan) People's Republic of Bangladesh ★Dacca, Chittagong, Khulna	• East of India on Bay of Bengal • 51,703 sq.mi.; 122,255,000 • Bengali (official), English; Muslim, Hindu	• Subtropical alluvial plain crossed by Ganges and other rivers. • Subsistence farming and limited textile industries.

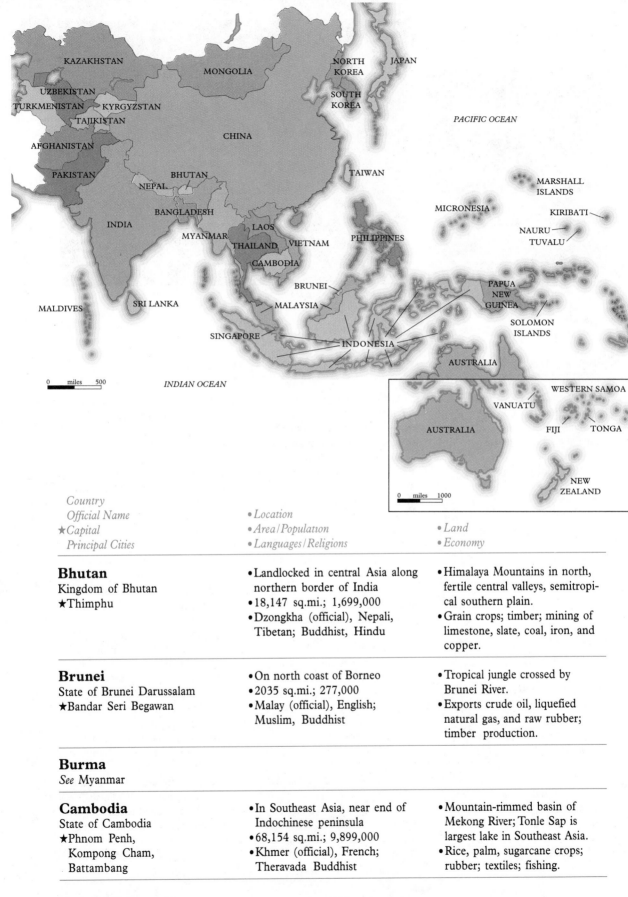

Country Official Name ★Capital Principal Cities	• Location • Area/Population • Languages/Religions	• Land • Economy
Bhutan Kingdom of Bhutan ★Thimphu	• Landlocked in central Asia along northern border of India • 18,147 sq.mi.; 1,699,000 • Dzongkha (official), Nepali, Tibetan; Buddhist, Hindu	• Himalaya Mountains in north, fertile central valleys, semitropical southern plain. • Grain crops; timber; mining of limestone, slate, coal, iron, and copper.
Brunei State of Brunei Darussalam ★Bandar Seri Begawan	• On north coast of Borneo • 2035 sq.mi.; 277,000 • Malay (official), English; Muslim, Buddhist	• Tropical jungle crossed by Brunei River. • Exports crude oil, liquefied natural gas, and raw rubber; timber production.
Burma *See* Myanmar		
Cambodia State of Cambodia ★Phnom Penh, Kompong Cham, Battambang	• In Southeast Asia, near end of Indochinese peninsula • 68,154 sq.mi.; 9,899,000 • Khmer (official), French; Theravada Buddhist	• Mountain-rimmed basin of Mekong River; Tonle Sap is largest lake in Southeast Asia. • Rice, palm, sugarcane crops; rubber; textiles; fishing.

Buddhist temple, Java, Indonesia

British influence, Bombay, India

Country Official Name ★Capital Principal Cities	• Location • Area/Population • Languages/Religions	• Land • Economy
China People's Republic of China ★Beijing, Shanghai, Tianjin, Canton, Shenyang, Wuhan, Chungking	• Occupies most of East Asian landmass • 3,600,930 sq.mi.; 1,177,585,000 • Mandarin (official), many Chinese dialects; traditionally Confucian, Buddhist, Taoist, but also Muslim, Protestant, Roman Catholic, practiced under restrictions	• Interior mountains and desert, with fertile eastern region, and climates ranging from tropical to temperate to arid. • Rice and wheat crops; sheep and hogs; textile, steel, chemical industries; trucks, agricultural implements; manufacturing; food processing; fishing.
Fiji ★Suva, Lautoka	• In south Pacific, east of Australia • 7054 sq.mi.; 757,000 • English (official), Fijian, Hindustani; Methodist, Hindu	• Over 100 inhabited islands of mountainous lands and tropical climates, with many coral islets. • Sugarcane and coconut crops; gold mining; tourism.
India Republic of India ★New Delhi, Calcutta, Bombay, Delhi, Madras, Hyderabad, Ahmedabad, Bangalore, Bhopal	• Subcontinent of south-central Asia between Arabian Sea and Bay of Bengal • 1,147,950 sq.mi.; 903,159,000 • Hindu and English (official), numerous others; Hindu, Muslim, Christian	• Himalaya Mountains in north, central Ganges River plain, southern hilly and forested Deccan peninsula. • Textile, iron and steel, aluminum, motor vehicle, food processing, chemical industries; rice, cotton, tea, wheat crops.
Indonesia Republic of Indonesia ★Djakarta, Surabaja, Semarang, Bandung, Medan, Palembang	• Southeast Asian islands along equator • 705,189 sq.mi.; 197,232,000 • Bahasa Indonesian (official), numerous Malay dialects; Muslim	• Six large, mountainous islands and more than 13,000 small volcanic and coral islets. • Rubber, rice, sugarcane, coffee, tea, nutmeg crops; timber and plywood; oil drilling; tin, nickel, bauxite mining.

Country Official Name ★Capital Principal Cities	• Location • Area/Population • Languages/Religions	• Land • Economy
Japan ★Tokyo, Osaka, Yokohama, Nagoya, Kyoto, Kobe, Sapporo	• Islands off east coast of Asia • 152,411 sq.mi.; 124,712,000 • Japanese (official); Buddhist, Shinto	• Four principal islands, mountainous in character and volcanic in origin, with 3000 small islets. • World economic power, with major automobile, steel, shipbuilding, electronic, and chemical industries.
Kazakhstan ★Alma-Ata, Karaganda, Semipalatinsk	• East of the Caspian Sea • 1,059,630 sq.mi.; 17,156,000 • Kazakh, Russian; Muslim, Russian Orthodox	• Upland plains; mountains in the southeast and northeast. • Rich deposits of coal, iron ore, copper, lead, zinc, and bauxite; grain, cotton, livestock.
Kiribati Republic of Kiribati ★Tarawa	• Islands in Pacific near equator • 277 sq.mi.; 76,000 • English and Gilbertese (official); Christian	• 33 low-lying coral islands. • Mining of phosphate rock.
Kyrgyzstan ★Bishbek, Osh	• In west Asia, bordered on east by China • 77,610 sq.mi.; 4,626,000 • Kyrghiz, Russian; Muslim	• High, glacial mountain country. • Petroleum, natural gas, mercury, and uranium; cotton.
Laos Lao People's Democratic Republic ★Vientiane, Luang Prabang, Savannakhet, Pakse	• Landlocked on Indochinese peninsula of Southeast Asia • 89,112 sq.mi.; 4,569,000 • Lao (official), French; Theravada Buddhist, animist	• Jungle-covered mountains, with Mekong River plains in north. • Rice, corn, tobacco, cotton, citrus fruit crops; tin mining; timber.
Malaysia ★Kuala Lumpur, Penang, Ipoh, Johor Baharu, Melaka	• In Southeast Asia on end of Malay peninsula and island of Borneo • 126,853 sq.mi.; 18,845,000 • Malay (official), English; Muslim, Hindu, Buddhist, Christian	• Jungle on coastal plain rising to inland mountains on both peninsular East Malaysia and island West Malaysia. • Forestry, including rubber; copper and tin mining; manufacturing, electronics; palm, rice, sugarcane crops.
Maldives Republic of Maldives ★Male	• Archipelago of Indian Ocean • 116 sq.mi.; 243,000 • Divehi (official), Arabic; Sunni Muslim	• 19 atoll groups of over 1000 coral islands. • Fishing and processing of fish goods.
Marshall Islands Republic of the Marshall Islands ★Majuro	• In Pacific Ocean, east of the Philippines • 70 sq.mi.; 52,000 • English and Marshallese (official); Protestant	• 34 coral islands. • Subsistence farming and fishing; coconuts and breadfruit.

Country Official Name ★Capital Principal Cities	• Location • Area/Population • Languages/Religions	• Land • Economy
Micronesia Federated States of Micronesia ★Kolonia	• In Pacific Ocean, north of Papua New Guinea • 271 sq.mi.; 118,000 • English (official), local languages; Roman Catholic, Protestant	• 607 coral and volcanic islands. • Subsistence farming and fishing; coconuts, cassavas, and yams.
Mongolia State of Mongolia ★Ulan Bator, Darhan, Erdenet	• In central Asia between China and Russia • 604,247 sq.mi.; 2,367,000 • Khalkha Mongol (official), Turkic; Lamaistic Buddhist, practiced under restrictions	• Central plateau of grasslands fringed by mountains; south adjoins Gobi Desert. • Livestock, primarily cattle, food processing; leather goods; textiles; coal mining, cement; coal, copper, molybdenum.
Myanmar Union of Myanmar (formerly Burma) ★Yangon (Rangoon), Mandalay, Moulmein	• In Southeast Asia, on east coast of Bay of Bengal • 253,954 sq.mi.; 43,456,000 • Burmese (official); Buddhist	• Ringed by mountains except to south, with central plains and tropical forests. • Rice, cotton, and tobacco crops; rubber; timber.
Nauru Republic of Nauru ★Yaren	• In west Pacific south of equator • 8 sq.mi.; 10,000 • Nauruan and English (official); Christian	• Barren central plateau dropping off to sandy beaches. • Mining of phosphate rock.
Nepal Kingdom of Nepal ★Katmandu, Biratnagar, Lalitpur	• In south Asia north of India • 52,819 sq.mi.; 20,535,000 • Nepali (official), Newari; Hindu, Buddhist, Shaman	• Himalayas, including Mt. Everest in north. • Grain crops and livestock; jute, sugar, cement, leather goods; tourism; timber; mining.
New Zealand ★Wellington, Christchurch, Auckland, Hamilton, Dunedin	• In south Pacific, southeast of Australia • 103,734 sq.mi.; 3,369,000 • English (official), Maori; Christian	• Two principal islands with central mountains and coastal plains, temperate in climate. • Sheep grazing and dairy farming; wool, wood and wood products; textiles; steel industries; fabricated metals, machinery, electrical equipment.
North Korea Democratic People's Republic of Korea ★Pyongyang, Chongjin, Hungnam	• In northeast Asia, on mainland peninsula, opposite Japan • 46,490 sq.mi.; 22,646,000 • Korean (official); traditionally Buddhist and Shaman, now under restrictions	• Mountainous, with narrow valleys and small plains. • Iron, steel, chemical, and textile industries; rice crops; fishing; metal ores, cement.

Fishing boats, Yangon, Myanmar

Yurts, Ulan Bator, Mongolia

Country *Official Name* ★*Capital* *Principal Cities*	• *Location* • *Area / Population* • *Languages / Religions*	• *Land* • *Economy*
Pakistan Islamic Republic of Pakistan ★Islamabad, Karachi, Lahore, Lyallpur	• Northwest of Indian subcontinent • 300,664 sq.mi.; 125,214,000 • Urdu (official), English, Bengali; Muslim, Hindu	• Himalayas in north declining to central foothills and eastern desert plain. • Wheat, cotton, barley, rice crops; textile, chemical, cement industries.
Papua New Guinea ★Port Moresby, Rabaul, Lae	• North of Australia, on eastern half of island of New Guinea • 174,405 sq.mi.; 4,101,000 • English (official), local dialects; Christian, tribal faiths	• Interior mountains and tropical forests and coastal plains; includes some small islands. • Subsistence farming, hunting, fishing; recent exploration of mineral reserves.
Philippines Republic of the Philippines ★Manila, Cebu, Davao, Zamboanga	• Island chain off southeast coast of China • 115,124 sq.mi.; 68,464,000 • English, Spanish, Filipino (all official); Roman Catholic, Muslim, Protestant	• Principally eleven mountainous islands with indented coasts; more than 7000 islets. • Rice, sugarcane, and coconut crops; food processing and textile industries; timber; growing manufacturing sector.
Singapore Republic of Singapore ★Singapore	• In Southeast Asia, at southern tip of Malay peninsula • 241 sq.mi.; 2,826,000 • Cantonese, English, Malay (all official); Muslim, Hindu, Buddhist, Christian	• Island of swamps and reclaimed sea lands joined to mainland by causeway. • International trade and banking; shipping; tourism.
Solomon Islands ★Honiara	• Island chain southeast of Papua New Guinea in west Pacific • 10,633 sq.mi.; 373,000 • English (official), local dialects; Anglican, Roman Catholic, other Christian sects	• Ten main mountainous islands, including Guadalcanal and smaller coral islands. • Fishing; coconuts, cocoa, rice; timber.

Korean man

Mountain orchard, Tajikistan

Country *Official Name* ★*Capital* *Principal Cities*	• *Location* • *Area/Population* • *Languages/Religions*	• *Land* • *Economy*
South Korea Republic of Korea ★Seoul, Pusan, Taegu, Inchon, Kwangchu, Taejon	• In northeast Asia, on mainland peninsula opposite Japan • 37,911 sq.mi.; 44,614,000 • Korean (official); Buddhist, Shaman, Christian	• Mountainous, with southern region of plains. • Textile, electronic, chemical industries; shipbuilding, automobiles; iron and steel; rice and bean crops; fishing.
Sri Lanka Democratic Socialist Republic of Sri Lanka ★Colombo, Dehiwala-Mount Lavinia, Jaffna, Kandy, Kotte	• Island off southeast coast of India • 24,996 sq.mi.; 17,838,000 • Sinhala and Tamil (official), English; Buddhist, Hindu, Muslim, Christian	• Coastal and northern plains, with hilly to mountainous south-central region. • Tea, rubber, and coconut production and processing; fishing; graphite mining.
Taiwan Republic of China ★Taipei, Kaohsiung, Taichung	• Island off the east coast of China • 12,456 sq.mi.; 21,092,000 • Mandarin Chinese; Buddhist, Taoist, Christian, folk	• Central north-south mountain range, western plain. • Textiles, clothing, chemicals, electronics; plywood, processed foods; rice, sugar, fruit.
Tajikistan ★Dushanbe, Khudzand	• Landlocked in west Asia, north of Afghanistan • 55,770 sq.mi.; 5,836,000 • Tazik, Russian; Muslim	• High mountains and plateau regions. • Farming and herding; rice, nuts, and fruits.
Thailand Kingdom of Thailand ★Bangkok, Thonburi, Chiengmai	• Indochinese peninsula of Southeast Asia • 197,595 sq.mi.; 58,722,000 • Thai (official); Theravada Buddhist	• Forested mountains in north, fertile central river valleys, tropical forest in south. • Rice, rubber, corn exports; tin, coal, and copper mining; cement, paper, and tobacco.
Tonga Kingdom of Tonga ★Nuku' Alofa	• In south Pacific, east of Fiji • 277 sq.mi.; 104,000 • Tongan (official), English; Christian	• More than 150 volcanic and coral islands, 45 inhabited. • Coconuts, bananas, taro; fishing; tourism.

Countries of the World

Buddhist monks, Thailand

Ho Chi Minh City, Vietnam

Country		
Official Name	• *Location*	
★*Capital*	• *Area/Population*	• *Land*
Principal Cities	• *Languages/Religions*	• *Economy*

Turkmenistan
★Ashkhabad,
  Chardzhou

- East of Caspian Sea, south of Kazakhstan
- 190,320 sq.mi.; 3,915,000
- Turkmen, Russian; Sunni Muslim

- Dominated by Kara Kum (black sands) Desert.
- Petroleum and natural gas; sheep and cotton.

Tuvalu
★Funafuti Island

- In southwest Pacific, north of Fiji
- 10 sq.mi.; 10,000
- English (official), Tuvaluan; Christian

- Nine low-lying coral atolls with little arable land.
- Coconut crops and processing.

Uzbekistan
★Tashkent,
  Samarkand

- Southeast of Aral Sea
- 174,330 sq.mi.; 22,128,000
- Uzbek, Russian; Sunni Muslim

- Rolling hills in southeast, flat desert in northwest.
- Coal, steel, copper and zinc; cotton farming.

Vanuatu
Republic of Vanuatu
★Vila,
  Santo,
  Farari

- In southwest Pacific, north of Australia
- 5699 sq.mi.; 166,000
- English and French (official), Bislama; Christian

- Islands of dense interior forest and arable coastal strips.
- Fishing and fish processing; cocoa and coffee crops; tourism.

Vietnam
Socialist Republic of Vietnam
★Hanoi,
  Ho Chi Minh City,
  Haiphong, Da Nang

- In Southeast Asia, along eastern side of Indochinese peninsula
- 125,622 sq.mi.; 71,788,000
- Vietnamese (official), French, Chinese, English; Buddhist, Taoist, Roman Catholic

- Northern and western mountains, eastern and southern jungle river valleys.
- Rubber and rice exports; fishing; coal, iron, chemical fertilizers, cement.

Western Samoa
Independent State of
  Western Samoa
★Apia

- In south-central Pacific
- 1100 sq.mi.; 200,000
- English and Samoan (official); Christian

- Two mountainous main islands and smaller coral islets.
- Cocoa, coconut, banana, and taro crops; fishing; tourism.

Europe

Europe is the continent across the Atlantic Ocean from the United States. Its western boundary is the Atlantic Ocean, and in the east it is separated from Asia by the Ural Mountains in Russia, the world's largest country. To the south Europe is separated from Africa by the Mediterranean Sea. At the western mouth of the Mediterranean, called the Strait of Gibraltar, Europe is separated from Africa by only eight miles of water. To the north, Europe is bordered by the vast Arctic Ocean. Great Britain and Ireland occupy the two large islands just off the Atlantic coast of western Europe.

Although Europe is smaller in area than any continent except Australia, it includes over 40 different countries and the most populated regions of Russia. Except for Russia, the largest country in Europe is France, which has an area much smaller than the state of Texas. There are also some countries in this region, such as San Marino and Monaco, that have less area than most U.S. cities.

Europe is a very densely populated continent, although some rugged and inhospitable areas such as the northern interiors of Norway and Sweden and the arctic areas of Russia are very thinly populated. Almost half of Europe's people live in four countries: Germany, Great Britain, Italy, and France. Germany is the twelfth most populous country in the world. Great Britain, or the United Kingdom, ranks twentieth, Italy eighteenth, and France twenty-first. Europe also has a higher proportion of city dwellers than the other world regions. The people live in some of the world's most famous cities: London, Paris, Rome, Vienna, Moscow, and Berlin.

Russia adjoins eastern Europe and is considered part of this region. It is the largest country on Earth. Stretching from Europe into Asia to the Pacific Ocean, it is almost 3 million square miles larger than the United States. Russia is also the sixth most populous country on Earth, and includes people with many different cultures, customs, and languages.

Europe is one of the great industrial regions of the world. Its central countries, such as France and Germany, are among the leading manufacturing nations. Other countries such as Great Britain, Poland, Hungary, and the Czech Republic are also important industrial and manufacturing nations. The southern countries of Europe, such as Spain and Greece on the Mediterranean, are warmer and more agricultural in character. Northern European countries, especially the Scandinavian nations of Sweden, Norway, and Finland, are cold forestlands of limited population and agriculture.

Country Official Name ★Capital Principal Cities	• Location • Area/Population • Languages/Religions	• Land • Economy
Albania People's Socialist Republic of Albania ★Tirana, Shkodër, Durrës, Vlonë	• West of Balkan peninsula, on Adriatic Sea • 10,579 sq.mi.; 3,334,000 • Albanian (official), Greek; Muslim, Orthodox Christian, Roman Catholic	• Mountains crossed by east-west rivers with narrow coastal plain. • Agriculture; fertilizer, chemical, and textile industries; mineral exports.
Andorra Principality of Andorra ★Andorra La Vella, Sant Juliá	• In Pyrenees Mountains between France and Spain • 174 sq.mi.; 62,000 • Catalan (official), French, Spanish; Roman Catholic	• Rugged mountain area, one of the smallest states in Europe. • Tourism; agriculture based on livestock and tobacco.
Armenia Republic of Armenia ★Yerevan, Leninakan, Kirovakan	• Landlocked in southeastern Europe, north of Iran • 11,700 sq.mi.; 3,481,000 • Armenian, Russian; Armenian Catholic	• Mountainous region with fertile soil. • Major producer of copper and zinc; agriculture relies on fruits, grains, and vegetables.

ICELAND

ATLANTIC OCEAN

NORWAY FINLAND

SWEDEN RUSSIA

ESTONIA

LATVIA

UNITED
KINGDOM LITHUANIA

IRELAND DENMARK RUSSIA

BELARUS

NETHERLANDS

BELGIUM POLAND

GERMANY

LUX. CZECH REP.

FRANCE LIECHT. SLOVAKIA UKRAINE

SWITZERLAND AUSTRIA MOLDOVA

HUNGARY

SLOVENIA

CROATIA ROMANIA

MONACO ITALY YUGOSLAVIA GEORGIA

PORTUGAL ANDORRA SAN MARINO BOSNIA- ARMENIA
HERZ.

SPAIN VATICAN BULGARIA
CITY MACEDONIA AZERBAIJAN

ALBANIA

GREECE

MALTA

0 miles 800

Country Official Name ★Capital Principal Cities	•Location •Area/Population •Languages/Religions	•Land •Economy
Austria Republic of Austria ★Vienna, Graz, Linz, Salzburg, Innsbruck	•Landlocked in central Europe northeast of Italy •31,942 sq.mi.; 7,915,000 •German (official), Slovene; Roman Catholic, Protestant	•Alpine mountains and foothills, with eastern region within Danube River basin. •Iron, steel, chemical manufac- tures; livestock and grain crops; tourism.
Azerbaijan ★Baku, Kirovabad, Sumgait	•West of Caspian Sea, east of Armenia •33,930 sq.mi.; 7,573,000 •Azerbaijani, Russian; Muslim	•Protected by mountains in west and north; low central plain. •Industry centered on produc- tion of oil and natural gas; cotton, tea, tobacco, and grain are main crops.
Belarus ★Minsk, Gomel, Vitebsk	•Landlocked in eastern Europe, north of Ukraine •33,430 sq.mi.; 10,370,000 •Belarussian, Russian; Russian Orthodox	•Gentle, rolling plains; large marshes in south. •Manufacturing of heavy trucks and farm machinery; beef and dairy cattle.

Rhine River valley, Germany

Notre Dame cathedral, Paris, France

Country Official Name ★Capital Principal Cities	• Location • Area / Population • Languages / Religions	• Land • Economy
Belgium Kingdom of Belgium ★Brussels, Antwerp, Ghent, Liège	• In northwest Europe, on the North Sea • 11,672 sq.mi.; 10,041,000 • German, French, Dutch (all official); Roman Catholic, Protestant	• Lowland plain, with hilly southeast Ardennes forest. • Iron, steel, chemical, textile manufactures; grain and potato crops; international commerce.
Bosnia and Herzegovina ★Sarajevo	• In southeastern Europe on Balkan peninsula • 19,741 sq.mi.; 4,619,000 • Serbo-Croatian; Muslim Eastern Orthodox, Roman Catholic	• Mountainous, dominated by Dinaric Alps in west. • Textiles; timber; agriculture.
Bulgaria Republic of Bulgaria ★Sofia, Plovdiv, Varna, Ruse	• East of Balkan peninsula, on Black Sea • 42,683 sq.mi.; 8,831,000 • Bulgarian (official), Turkish, Greek; restricted practice of Bulgarian Orthodox	• Danube plain in north, central Balkan Mountains, Thracian Plain in southwest. • Agriculture based on grain crops and livestock; chemicals and metallurgy; fishing.
Croatia ★Zagreb	• In southeastern Europe on Balkan peninsula • 21,829 sq.mi.; 4,694,000 • Serbo-Croatian; Roman Catholic	• Low plains in east, mountains along Adriatic coast in west. • Textiles; aluminum; chemicals; mining of coal, copper, bauxite.
Czech Republic ★Prague, Brno	• In central Europe, east of Germany • 78,864 sq.mi.; 10,389,000 • Czech; Roman Catholic, Protestant	• Elevated plateau surrounded by mountains. • Manufacture of machinery; chemicals; textile products.
Denmark Kingdom of Denmark ★Copenhagen, Aarhus, Odense	• Northern tip of European landmass • 16,359 sq.mi.; 5,176,000 • Danish (official); Evangelical Lutheran	• Lowland Jutland peninsula and rocky islands at mouth of Baltic Sea. • Exports of meat and dairy products; machinery and electrical equipment.

Country Official Name ★Capital Principal Cities	• Location • Area/Population • Languages/Religions	• Land • Economy
Estonia Republic of Estonia ★Tallinn, Tartu, Narva	• On the Baltic Sea, north of Latvia in eastern Europe • 16,464 sq.mi.; 1,608,000 • Estonian, Russian; Lutheran	• Low, rolling terrain; 800 islands and islets. • Agriculture and dairy farming; shale oil and peat; farm equipment manufacture.
Finland Republic of Finland ★Helsinki, Tampere, Turku	• North of Baltic Sea, between Scandinavia and Russia • 117,942 sq.mi.; 5,051,000 • Finnish and Swedish (official), Lappish; Evangelical Lutheran	• Predominantly low hills and lakes with northern mountains extending beyond Arctic Circle. • Forestry; agriculture based on cereal grains and livestock; manufacture of machinery.
France French Republic ★Paris, Marseilles, Lyons, Toulouse, Nice, Nantes	• In western Europe, north of Iberian peninsula • 210,668 sq.mi.; 57,566,000 • French (official); Roman Catholic, Protestant	• Predominantly rolling hills with temperate climate. • Major world exporter of foods, automobiles, aircraft, and textiles; tourism.
Georgia Republic of Georgia ★Tbilisi, Kutaisi, Rustavi	• East of Black Sea, north of Turkey • 27,300 sq.mi.; 5,634,000 • Georgian, Russian; Russian Orthodox	• Mountains in the north and south; central valley. • Tea, wine, and fruit; manganese; textiles and automobiles.
Germany Federal Republic of Germany ★Berlin, Bonn, Hamburg, Munich, Leipzig	• In north-central Europe • 135,236 sq.mi.; 80,768,000 • German (official); Protestant, Roman Catholic	• Level and temperate northern and central regions, with southern forested mountains. • Steel products, automobiles, ships, chemicals, and electrical equipment; diversified agriculture.
Greece Hellenic Republic ★Athens, Salonica, Patras	• Southern end of Balkan peninsula • 50,502 sq.mi.; 10,470,000 • Greek (official); Greek Orthdox	• Mountainous mainland with numerous sunny and rocky offshore islands. • Chemical, plastic, metallurgy industries; agriculture; shipping.
Hungary Republic of Hungary ★Budapest, Miskolc, Debrecen	• Landlocked in eastern Europe • 35,653 sq.mi.; 10,324,000 • Hungarian (official); Roman Catholic, Protestant	• Principally low hills and plains drained by Danube River. • Mining of bauxite and coal; manufacture of steel and chemical products; grain crops.
Iceland Republic of Iceland ★Reykjavik, Kópavogur	• Island in north Atlantic near Arctic Circle • 38,707 sq.mi.; 261,000 • Icelandic (official); Evangelical Lutheran	• Mountain interior of glaciers with coast warmed by gulf stream. • Fishing, sheep and dairy farming, aluminum.

Country Official Name ★Capital Principal Cities	• Location • Area/Population • Languages/Religions	• Land • Economy
Ireland Republic of Ireland ★Dublin, Cork, Limerick, Waterford, Galway	• Island in Atlantic just west of Great Britain • 26,598 sq.mi.; 3,530,000 • English and Irish Gaelic (official); Roman Catholic, Protestant	• Central lowland with hilly coasts; Northern Ireland remains part of Great Britain. • Livestock, potato and beet crops; food processing; tourism.
Italy Italian Republic ★Rome, Milan, Naples	• Peninsula into Mediterranean south of central Europe • 113,521 sq.mi.; 58,019,000 • Italian (official); Roman Catholic	• Rugged and mountainous except for northern Po River valley and coastal plains. • Automobile, textile, machine, chemical industries; livestock, grape and olive crops.
Latvia Republic of Latvia ★Riga, Daugavpils, Liepaja	• On Baltic Sea between Lithuania and Estonia • 25,194 sq.mi.; 2,736,000 • Latvian, Russian; Lutheran, Roman Catholic	• Low-lying plains and forested rolling hills. • Manufacture of railway cars, paper; oats, barley, and potatoes.
Liechtenstein Principality of Liechtenstein ★Vaduz	• In central Europe north of Italy • 62 sq.mi.; 30,000 • German (official), Alemannic; Roman Catholic	• Alpine mountains except for Rhine River valley. • Tourism; international commerce; precision instruments; dairy farming.
Lithuania Republic of Lithuania ★Vilnius, Kaunas, Klapeda	• Adjacent to Baltic Sea, north of Poland • 25,428 sq.mi.; 3,820,000 • Lithuanian, Russian; Roman Catholic, Lutheran, Jewish	• Low plains between hills in east and west. • Livestock raising and dairy farming; machinery, shipbuilding.
Luxembourg Grand Duchy of Luxembourg ★Luxembourg, Esch/Alzette	• Landlocked in western Europe north of France • 998 sq.mi.; 398,000 • French and German (official), Luxembourgish; Roman Catholic	• Hilly northern forests and southern plains. • Iron, steel, rubber, chemical industries; dairy farming; international banking; tourism.
Macedonia Republic of Macedonia ★Skopje, Bitola, Kumanovo, Tetovo	• Center of Balkan peninsula, north of Greece and south of Yugoslavia • 9928 sq. mi.; 2,039,000 • Macedonian (official), Albanian; Macedonian Orthodox, Muslim	• Rugged, landlocked country, dominated by mountainous terrain traversed by fertile river valleys. • Steel, cement, textiles; wheat, corn, cotton, tobacco, livestock.
Malta Republic of Malta ★Valletta, Sliema	• Island in Mediterranean south of Italy • 124 sq.mi.; 364,000 • Maltese and English (official), Italian; Roman Catholic	• Rocky principal island and smaller islands of Gozo and Comino. • Ship repair; textiles; tourism.

Dunluce castle, Ireland

Market, Warsaw, Poland

Country Official Name ★Capital Principal Cities	• Location • Area/Population • Languages/Religions	• Land • Economy
Moldova ★Kishinev, Tiraspol, Beltsy	• Bounded by borders of Ukraine and Romania • 13,260 sq.mi.; 4,456,000 • Romanian, Russian; Romanian Orthodox, Russian Orthodox, Jewish	• Rolling plains between Dnestr and Prut rivers. • Wine, tobacco, fruits and vegetables; light industry.
Monaco Principality of Monaco ★Monaco-Ville	• Riviera coast of southern France • 0.575 sq.mi.; 31,000 • French (official), English, Italian; Roman Catholic	• 600 acres of steep cliffs surrounding harbor. • Tourism and gambling; international commerce.
Netherlands Kingdom of the Netherlands ★Amsterdam, The Hague, Rotterdam	• In northwest Europe on North Sea • 13,104 sq.mi.; 15,275,000 • Dutch (official); Roman Catholic, Protestant	• Lowland coastal plain and reclaimed sea lands. • Chemical, steel, metallurgy, textile industries; electrical equipement; grain crops.
Norway Kingdom of Norway ★Oslo, Bergen, Trondheim	• Atlantic coast of Scandinavia • 118,865 sq.mi.; 4,297,000 • Norwegian (offical), Finnish, Lappish; Evangelical Lutheran	• Rocky coastline of islands and deep fjords, rugged mountain interior with glaciers north of Arctic Circle. • Shipping; commercial fishing; forestry; aluminum exports; metallurgy; livestock.
Poland Republic of Poland ★Warsaw, Łódź, Kraków	• In northeastern Europe, on Baltic Sea • 117,571 sq.mi.; 38,519,000 • Polish (official); Roman Catholic	• Lowland plain over most of area, with southern Carpathian Mountains. • Petrochemicals, electronics; shipbuilding; coal mining; grain, beef, pork.

Houses of Parliament, London, United Kingdom

Downtown Madrid, Spain

Country Official Name ★Capital Principal Cities	• Location • Area/Population • Languages/Religions	• Land • Economy
Portugal Republic of Portugal ★Lisbon, Oporto	• In extreme southwest of Europe, adjacent to Spain • 35,382 sq.mi.; 10,486,000 • Portuguese (official); Roman Catholic	• Cool mountainous north and warmer southern plain separated by Tagus River. • Grain, grape, olive crops; forestry, production of cork; tourism; textiles.
Romania Republic of Romania ★Bucharest, Constanta, Iași	• In southeastern Europe on Black Sea • 88,934 sq.mi.; 23,172,000 • Romanian (official), Hungarian; Romanian Orthodox	• Mountains surrounding northwest Transylvanian Plateau; east and south plains. • Steel, petrochemical, textile, machine industries; grain crop and livestock farming.
Russia ★Moscow, St. Petersburg, Novosibirsk, Nizhni Novgorod, Rostov-on-Don, Volgograd	• From Arctic Ocean to Black Sea and from Far East Asia to eastern Europe • 6,659,250 sq.mi.; 149,300,000 • Russian (official); Russian Orthodox	• Four regions: European Plain, Ural Mountains, forested west Siberian Plain, and uplands of east Siberia and Far East. • Coal, petroleum, natural gas and iron ore; automobiles and farm vehicles; wheat and cattle.
San Marino Most Serene Republic of San Marino ★San Marino	• City-state in north-central Italy • 23.6 sq.mi.; 24,000 • Italian (official); Roman Catholic	• Predominantly on slopes of Mt. Titano in Apennines. • Tourism; postage stamps; farming; light textile industries.
Slovakia Slovak Republic ★Bratislava, Kosice	• In central Europe, between Poland and Hungary • 49,035 sq.mi.; 5,376,000 • Slovak; Roman Catholic, Protestant	• Principally lowlands; Carpathian Mountains in north. • Agriculture; mining of lead and copper.
Slovenia ★Ljubljana	• In southeastern Europe on Balkan peninsula • 7819 sq.mi.; 1,968,000 • Slovenian; Roman Catholic	• Extensively forested plateau with Julian Alps in west. • Agriculture; iron and steel; timber.

Country Official Name ★Capital Principal Cities	• Location • Area/Population • Languages/Religions	• Land • Economy
Spain Spanish State ★Madrid, Barcelona, Valencia	• On Iberian peninsula of southwestern Europe • 194,896 sq.mi.; 39,207,000 • Spanish (official), with Catalan, Galician, and Basque dialects; Roman Catholic	• Central Meseta mountain plateau, with Pyrenees Mountains in the north. • Textiles; transportation, shipbuilding, and chemical industries; olive and grain crops; wines.
Sweden Kingdom of Sweden ★Stockholm, Göteborg, Malmö	• Eastern side of Scandinavia, on Baltic Sea • 192,819 sq.mi.; 8,730,000 • Swedish (official), Lappish, Finnish; Evangelical Lutheran	• Predominantly rolling hills, rising into mountains in arctic north. • Timber; mining; shipbuilding and automobile industries; grains and livestock.
Switzerland Swiss Confederation ★Berne, Zurich, Basel, Geneva	• Landlocked in central Europe north of Italy • 15,355 sq.mi.; 6,987,000 • German, French, Italian, Romansch (all official); Roman Catholic, Protestant	• Predominantly Alps and Jura Mountains surrounding small midland plateau. • Banking; precision instruments, including watches and clocks; livestock; tourism.
Ukraine ★Kiev, Kharkov, Odessa, Donets	• On northern shore of Black Sea in eastern Europe • 235,560 sq.mi.; 51,821,000 • Ukrainian, Russian; Russian Orthodox, Jewish	• Mostly plains with mountains in southwest. • Mining of coal and iron ore; steel, machinery, chemicals; beef, dairy products, grain and sugar beet.
United Kingdom United Kingdom of Great Britain and Northern Ireland ★London, Glasgow (Scotland), Belfast (N. Ireland), Cardiff (Wales)	• British Isles off northwest coast of France • 93,278 sq. mi.; 57,970,000 • English (official), Gaelic dialects; Anglican, Protestant, Roman Catholic	• Rainy region of coastal highlands and central lowlands, including Northern Ireland on separate island of Ireland. • Economic power with heavy industries, diversified agriculture, textile manufactures, international finance.
Vatican State of Vatican City	• Enclave within city of Rome • 0.17 sq.mi.; 800 • Latin (official), Italian; Roman Catholic	• 109 urban acres on west bank of Tiber River. • Tourism.
Yugoslavia Federal Republic of Yugoslavia ★Belgrade	• In southeastern Europe, on Balkan peninsula; includes Serbia and Montenegro. • 39,000 sq.mi.; 10,337,000 • Serbo-Croatian, Macedonian; Eastern Orthodox, Roman Catholic	• Fertile plain in north, hilly to mountainous in south. • Production of copper, machinery, textiles; agriculture.

Middle East and Africa

The Middle East and Africa is the world region south of Europe southeast and east of the Mediterranean Sea. Africa is the world's second largest continent after Asia, and it includes more countries than any other continent. The Middle East, which is influenced by both Europe and Asia as well as Africa, is joined to Africa by the narrow isthmus of Suez at the northern part of the Red Sea. Parts of Africa, such as Egypt in the northeast corner of the continent, resemble the Middle East in geography and culture.

The region's largest nation in area is the Sudan, a central African country that is one-quarter as large as the United States. The largest nation in the Middle East is Iran, which stretches more than 1200 miles from the Caspian Sea to the Indian Ocean. Among the numerous nations in this region are many tiny ones. Some, such as the Comoros Islands and Bahrain, are smaller in area than Rhode Island, the smallest state in the United States.

The most populous country in the region is Nigeria in west-central Africa. About one-fifth of all the people in Africa live in Nigeria. The most populous country in the Middle East is Iran.

Africa is sometimes called the "dark continent" because much of it is a deep jungle of spectacular natural features and strange wildlife isolated from the outside world by mountains and deserts. North Africa is dominated by the Sahara Desert, which is larger than the United States. Much of central Africa is a rain forest drained by the Congo River. There are also great plains in central Africa that are the homeland of the fastest animal on Earth, the cheetah, and the world's largest land animal, the elephant. The Middle East is famous for its deserts, such as the great sandy and arid plateau of the Arabian peninsula, where the most common domestic animal is the camel. The Kurdistan and Zagros mountains in the Middle East, however, are frigid and forbidding ranges crossed only by isolated and narrow mountain passes.

Although it is much larger than Europe, this region includes far fewer people. Many of the largest population centers in the Middle East and Africa are located on or near the shores of the Mediterranean Sea. A few exceptions are Teheran in Iran, Baghdad in Iraq, and Lagos in Nigeria. The inland areas, whether jungle or desert, are very sparsely populated. The people in these remote regions speak a variety of local languages and follow Islamic or tribal religions. They depend on limited agriculture for their livelihood. The only pockets of major industry in this region are the oil-producing countries of the Middle East, such as Saudi Arabia and the small but highly developed country of Israel.

Country Official Name ★Capital Principal Cities	• Location • Area/Population • Languages/Religions	• Land • Economy
Algeria Democratic and Popular Republic of Algeria ★Algiers, Oran, Constantine, Annaba, Blida	• Western North Africa, on Mediterranean Sea; between Libya on east and Morocco on northwest • 919,591 sq.mi.; 27,256,000 • Arabic (official), French, Berber; Sunni Muslim	• Temperate coastal plain isolated by Atlas Mountains in north, with interior extending into western Sahara Desert. • Steel, textile, plastic, fertilizer, oil industries; iron, zinc, lead, mercury; livestock, grain, and grape crops; commercial fishing.
Angola Republic of Angola ★Luanda, Huambo, Lobito, Benguela, Lubango	• Southwest Atlantic coast of Africa • 481,351 sq.mi.; 9,545,000 • Portuguese (official), Bantu African dialects; animist tribal religions, Roman Catholic	• Predominantly elevated plateau with narrow coastal lowland and west-central highland. • Iron, diamond, copper mining; oil production; livestock; coffee, corn, sugar crops; hardwoods, primarily mahogany; commercial fishing.

Country		
Official Name	• *Location*	
★*Capital*	• *Area/Population*	• *Land*
Principal Cities	• *Languages/Religions*	• *Economy*

Bahrain

State of Bahrain
★Manama,
  Muharraq, Jidhafs,
  Rifa'a

- Island nation in Persian Gulf east of Saudi Arabia and west of Qatar peninsula
- 239 sq.mi.; 568,000
- Arabic (official), English, Farsi; Shiite Muslim, Sunni Muslim, Christian

- Hot and humid island of sand and rock, with some 32 smaller islets.
- Oil drilling and refining; aluminum smelting; shipping; international banking.

Benin

(formerly Dahomey)
Republic of Benin
★Porto Novo,
  Cotonou, Parakou,
  Natitingou, Kandi

- West Africa, on Gulf of Guinea west of Nigeria
- 42,710 sq.mi.; 5,167,000
- French (official), tribal tongues; animist tribal religions, Christian, Muslim

- Flat and heavily vegetated in central zone; grassland in north, with hot, humid, and sandy southern coastline.
- Cotton and palm crops, peanuts, coffee, and tea; fishing; oil production; food processing industries including sugar and palm oil.

Watusi dancers, Burundi

Tribal huts, Cameroon

Country *Official Name* ★*Capital* *Principal Cities*	• *Location* • *Area/Population* • *Languages/Religions*	• *Land* • *Economy*
Botswana Republic of Botswana ★Gaborone, Mahalapye, Serowe, Tutume, Bobonong, Francistown	• Landlocked near southern end of Africa, north of South Africa and east of Namibia • 226,012 sq.mi.; 1,326,000 • English (official), Setswana; Christian, animist tribal religions, Muslim, Hindu, Bahai	• Southwest Kalahari Desert, northern swamplands, eastern fertile farmland. • Livestock, primarily beef; corn, sorghum, bean crops; diamond, copper, nickel mining; textiles.
Burkina Faso (formerly Upper Volta) ★Ouagadougou, Bobo-Dioulasso, Koudougou Ouahigouya, Banfora	• Landlocked in west Africa, south of Mali and north of Ghana and Gulf of Guinea • 105,714 sq.mi.; 9,853,000 • French (official), tribal dialects; animist tribal religions, Muslim, Christian, primarily Roman Catholic	• Arid plateau, cut by Black, White, and Red Volta river valleys. • Beef and lamb exports; cotton and peanut crops; manganese, limestone; textiles, light manufacturing.
Burundi Republic of Burundi ★Bujumbura, Gitega	• East-central Africa, between Zaire on west and Tanzania on east, at northern end of Lake Tanganyika • 9903 sq.mi.; 5,985,000 • French and Kirundi (official), Swahili; Roman Catholic, animist tribal religions	• Grassy uplands and mountains declining to Lake Tanganyika in south. • Coffee, cotton, tea, and banana crops; cobalt, copper, nickel, and platinum mining.
Cameroon Republic of Cameroon ★Yaoundé, Douala, Maroua, Garoua, Bafoussam, N'Kongsamba	• West-central Africa, southeast of Nigeria and west of Central African Republic, on Gulf of Guinea • 181,251 sq.mi.; 12,756,000 • French and English (official), local dialects; Christian, Muslim, tribal religions	• Humid coastal plain with interior plateau rising to mountains in west. • Agriculture based on coffee, cocoa, banana, cotton, sugar, and peanut crops; timber; rubber; aluminum, cement; light industry.

Young students, Chad

Weavers, Burkina Faso

Country
Official Name
★Capital
Principal Cities

• *Location*
• *Area / Population*
• *Languages / Religions*

• *Land*
• *Economy*

Cape Verde
Republic of Cape Verde
★Praia,
Mindelo, Espargos

• Atlantic island group, including ten islands and five islets, about 400 miles west of western mainland
• 1556 sq.mi.; 411,000
• Portuguese (official), Crioulo; Roman Catholic, animist tribal religions

• Two island groups (windward and leeward), mostly volcanic in origin, largely mountainous and barren except for valleys.
• Ship and aircraft refueling; fishing; corn, beans, sugarcane, and bananas; sugar refining, food processing.

Central African Republic
★Bangui,
M'baiki, Bossangoa,
Bouar, Berberati

• Landlocked at center of continental Africa
• 240,533 sq.mi.; 3,074,000
• French (official), Sangho; Roman Catholic, Protestant, tribal religions, Muslim

• Well-watered rolling plateau with Lake Chad to north and Congo River to south.
• Cotton and coffee crops; diamonds, gold; uranium deposits; food processing, textiles, footwear; hardwoods, notably mahogany.

Chad
Republic of Chad
★N'Djaména,
Sarh, Mondou
Abéché, Bongor

• Landlocked in north-central Africa south of Libya and west of Sudan
• 486,178 sq.mi.; 5,351,000
• French (official), Arabic; Muslim, Christian, animist tribal religions

• Northern mountains and Sahara Desert, with southern equatorial savanna and forest; Lake Chad on west central border.
• Cotton, sugar, subsistence farming; livestock, primarily cattle, sheep, and goats; food processing; fishing.

Comoros
Federal Islamic Republic of the Comoros
★Moroni,
Nzwani, Mwali

• Islands of southeastern Africa between Madagascar and African mainland
• 838 sq.mi.; 512,000
• French (official), Comoran, Arabic; Sunni Muslim, small Roman Catholic minority

• Three small volcanic islands: Grande Comore, Anjouan, and Moheli.
• Perfume crops and exports of processed perfumes; vanilla, copra, subsistence crops; timber production.

Country Official Name ★Capital Principal Cities	• Location • Area/Population • Languages/Religions	• Land • Economy
Congo Republic of Congo ★Brazzaville, Pointe-Noire, Loubomo, Nkayi	• West-central Africa, west of Zaire, with short Atlantic coastline • 131,853 sq.mi.; 2,389,000 • French (official), Lingala, Kikongo; Roman Catholic, animist tribal religions	• Low, coastal treeless plain rising to interior of equatorial forests and river valleys; Congo River basin dominates northeast. • Sugar, coffee, cocoa, tobacco crops; forestry; offshore oil production; gold, silver, lead, copper.
Cyprus Republic of Cyprus ★Nicosia, Limassol, Larnaca Paphos	• Island in east of Mediterranean Sea, south of Turkey and west of Syria • 3568 sq.mi.; 723,000 • Greek and Turkish (official), English; Greek Orthodox, Muslim	• Third largest island in Mediterranean; fertile central plain, with northern and southern coastal ranges. • Mining of copper, asbestos, iron; tourism; wine and textiles; grain and fruit crops; wood and wood products, textiles, light manufacturing.
Djibouti Republic of Djibouti ★Djibouti, Dikhil	• East Africa, on strait between at southern end of Red Sea and Gulf of Aden • 8486 sq.mi.; 402,000 • Arabic (official), French, Somali; Muslim, Roman Catholic	• Sandy and arid coastal plain and interior plateau. • Shipping and commerce through free port of capital city.
Egypt Arab Republic of Egypt ★Cairo, Alexandria, Giza, Shubra al Khayma, Suez, Port Said, Mahalla al Kubra	• In northeast corner of continental Africa • 384,344 sq.mi.; 58,016,000 • Arabic (official); Sunni Muslim, Coptic Christian	• Dominated by eastern Sahara Desert, crossed from south to north by Nile River valley of semiarable lands; Qattarah Depression in northwest is lowest elevation in Africa. • Cotton, wheat, rice crops; textiles and food processing; Suez Canal shipping; petroleum, phosphate, iron ore.
Equatorial Guinea Republic of Equatorial Guinea ★Malabo, Bata	• West-central coast of Africa, including offshore islands • 10,830 sq.mi.; 399,000 • Spanish (official), Bantu dialects; Roman Catholic	• Mainland coastal plain with low hills and two volcanic islands of Bioko and Annobón, as well as several smaller islets. • Timber, coffee, and cocoa exports.
Eritrea State of Eritrea ★Asmara, Massawa, Assab	• East-central Africa, on Red Sea north of Ethiopia • 36,170 sq. mi.; 3,318,000 • Several ethnic languages; Muslim, Christian	• Coastal plain on Red Sea rising to central highlands and interior mountains. • Textiles, food products; cotton, wheat, coffee, tobacco.

Country Official Name ★Capital Principal Cities	● Location ● Area/Population ● Languages/Religions	● Land ● Economy

Ethiopia
★Addis Ababa,
  Dire Dawa, Bahr Dar,
  Dire Dessie, Nazret
	● In eastern Africa, with Red Sea
	  to northeast
	● 425,097 sq. mi.; 56,746,000
	● Amharic (official), Arabic,
	  Somali, others;
	  Ethiopian Orthodox, Muslim
		● High central mountain plateau
		  divided by Rift Valley and
		  declining in elevation to eastern
		  and western plains.
		● Coffee exports and farm
		  products, primarily livestock
		  products; mining of gold,
		  copper, potash, and platinum.

Gabon
Gabonese Republic
★Libreville,
  Port-Gentil, Lambaréné,
  Masaku
	● On Atlantic coast of west-central
	  Africa south of Cameroon and
	  Equatorial Guinea
	● 99,486 sq.mi.; 1,123,000
	● French (official), Fang, Bantu;
	  Christian, primarily Roman
	  Catholic, animist tribal reli-
	  gions, small Mulsim minority
		● Lowland equatorial rain forest
		  with central and northern
		  mountains.
		● Manganese, uranium, iron ore
		  exports; oil production;
		  petroleum products; timber;
		  food processing

The Gambia
Republic of the Gambia
★Banjul,
  Serekunda
	● On Atlantic near western
	  extremity of continental Africa
	● 3861 sq.mi.; 930,000
	● English (official), tribal dialects;
	  Muslim, Christian
		● Narrow, consisting of swampy
		  Gambia River valley with small
		  Atlantic coast; bounded on all
		  other sides by Senegal.
		● Peanuts and processing of
		  peanut oil; cotton and rice; fish
		  and fish products.

Ghana
Republic of Ghana
★Accra,
  Kumasi, Tamale,
  Sekondi-Takor
	● West Africa, on northern shore
	  of Gulf of Guinea
	● 88,811 sq.mi.; 16,699,000
	● English (official), tribal tongues;
	  Christian, Muslim, animist
	  tribal religions.
		● Low hills and fertile plains
		  drained by Volta River; savanna
		  in the north; sandy coastal plain
		  in the south.
		● Cocoa, tea, palm, coffee
		  exports; aluminum and steel
		  industries; gold, diamonds,
		  bauxite, manganese; fishing.

Guinea
Republic of Guinea
★Conakry,
  Kankan, Labé,
  Kindia, N'Zérékoré
	● Along Atlantic coast of far
	  western Africa
	● 94,927 sq.mi.; 6,237,000
	● French (official), tribal dialects;
	  Muslim, animist tribal religions
		● Coastal plain, central mountain
		  and valley region, northern
		  savanna upland.
		● Bauxite, iron, gold, and
		  diamond mining; banana,
		  coffee, peanut, rice, sugarcane,
		  palm crops; fishing.

Guinea-Bissau
Republic of Guinea-Bissau
★Bissau,
  Bafata
	● On Atlantic coast of western
	  bulge of continental Africa,
	  situated between Senegal and
	  Guinea
	● 10,811 sq.mi.; 1,072,000
	● Portuguese (official), Crioulo;
	  animist tribal religions, Muslim
		● Low-lying coastal plain of
		  swamp, savanna, and rain forest;
		  includes Bijago's island group
		  offshore.
		● Agriculture based on peanuts,
		  palm, rice crops; food process-
		  ing; fish, timber.

Mosque, Baghdad, Iraq

Fruit for export, Israel

Country		
Official Name	• *Location*	
★*Capital*	• *Area / Population*	• *Land*
Principal Cities	• *Languages / Religions*	• *Economy*

Iran
Islamic Republic of Iran
★Teheran,
Isfahan, Mashhad,
Tabriz, Shiraz, Abadan, Qum,
Hamadan

- South of Caspian Sea, Georgia, and Turkmenistan, and strategically situated north of Persian Gulf
- 631,660 sq.mi.; 63,370,000
- Farsi (official), Kurdish, Turkic; Shiite Muslim

- Predominantly elevated and arid plateau ringed by mountains, with coastal lowlands on Persian Gulf and Caspian Sea.
- Drilling and refining of oil and natural gas; steel industries; iron and copper mining; coal, cement; wheat, rice, wool.

Iraq
Republic of Iraq
★Baghdad,
Mosul, Basra, Kirkuk

- Landlocked in Middle East to west of Iran, with access to Persian Gulf through Kuwait
- 167,556 sq.mi.; 19,162,000
- Arabic (official), Kurdish; Shiite Muslim, Sunni Muslim, Christian

- Central basin of Tigris and Euphrates rivers, with mountainous north, central plain, and desert to southwest and marshland to southeast.
- Oil drilling and refining; mining; date, wheat, barley, rice, cotton, and tobacco crops; wool production.

Israel
State of Israel
★Jerusalem,
Tel Aviv, Haifa

- At eastern extent of Mediterranean Sea
- 7849 sq.mi.; 4,919,000
- Hebrew and Arabic (official), English; Jewish, Muslim, small Christian and Druse minorities

- Well-watered coastal and central plains, with hills of Galilee to north and Negev Desert to south.
- Diamond, chemical, food, and textile industries; electronics, machinery, chemicals, plastics; citrus and grain crops; tourism.

Ivory Coast
Republic of Ivory Coast
★Abidjan,
Bouaké, Daloa, Yamoussoukro,
Man

- West Africa, on west-central coast of Africa, at western end of Gulf of Guinea
- 122,780 sq.mi.; 13,808,000
- French (official), tribal tongues; animist tribal religions, Muslim

- Rain forest in south and east, with savanna extending north and mountains rising to west; coastal shoals.
- Coffee, cocoa, and banana crops; timber; diamond, gold, and manganese mining; fishing, food processing, textiles.

Country Official Name ★Capital Principal Cities	• Location • Area / Population • Languages / Religions	• Land • Economy
Jordan Hashemite Kingdom of Jordan ★Amman, Zarqa', Irbid	• In Middle East between Israel on west, Saudi Arabia on east, and Syria on north • 35,344 sq.mi.; 3,824,000 • Arabic (official); Sunni Muslim	• Predominantly arid desert plateau rising from Dead Sea and Jordan River valley to west. • Fruit and vegetable crops; food processing and plastics; phosphate mining, potash production; cement, fertilizer, petroleum products.
Kenya Republic of Kenya ★Nairobi, Mombasa, Kisumu, Nakuru	• Equatorial east Africa, on Indian Ocean north of Tanzania and south of Ethiopia • 219,788 sq.mi.; 27,372,000 • Swahili and English (official); Protestant, Roman Catholic, Muslim	• Western Great Rift Valley between arid central plateau and western mountains, eastern coastal plain; forest in south and southeast. • Tourism; coffee, tea, maize, sugarcane, and wheat crops; pyrethrum, soda ash, chemical industries; textiles, food processing.
Kuwait State of Kuwait ★Kuwait City, Hawalli, Salimiya	• In Middle East at inland reach of Persian Gulf • 6880 sq.mi.; 1,698,000 • Arabic (official); Sunni Muslim, Shiite Muslim, small Christian minority.	• Almost entirely flat desert. • Drilling and refining of one of world's largest oil reserves; food processing, petroleum products; fishing; boat building.
Lebanon Republic of Lebanon ★Beirut, Tripoli, Zahlé Sidon, Tyre	• Eastern end of Mediterranean Sea, north of Israel and west of Syria • 3950 sq.mi.; 3,552,000 • Arabic (official), French; Sunni and Shiite Muslim, Christian, Druse	• Coastal plain and ranges with fertile interior mountain valleys. • International banking and commerce; tourism; oil refining and shipping; citrus fruits, grapes, livestock.
Lesotho Kingdom of Lesotho ★Maseru	• Landlocked enclave within southeastern part of Republic of South Africa • 11,718 sq.mi.; 1,896,000 • English and Sesotho (official); Christian	• Mountainous, with small western lowland. • Limited agriculture and diamond industries.
Liberia Republic of Liberia ★Monrovia, Buchanan, Harper	• West Africa, at southwestern tip of continental bulge • 37,189 sq.mi.; 2,875,000 • English (official), tribal dialects; animist tribal religions, Muslim, Christian	• Swampy coastal plain rising to heavily forested interior plateaus traversed by several rivers; northern mountains. • Iron ore, diamonds, gold rubber, timber exports; coffee and cocoa crops; rice, palm oil; timber.

Country Official Name ★Capital Principal Cities	• Location • Area/Population • Languages/Religions	• Land • Economy
Libya Socialist People's Libyan Arab Jamahiriya ★Tripoli, Benghazi, Misurata	• Northern coast of Africa, on Mediterranean Sea, between Algeria and Egypt • 679,359 sq.mi.; 4,873,000 • Arabic (official); Sunni Muslim	• Predominantly desert, with northern highlands and southern mountains. • Oil drilling and refining; barley, wheat, tomato crops; olives, dates, meat and milk; building materials, textiles, footwear; food processing.
Madagascar Democratic Republic of Madagascar ★Antananarivo, Toamasina (Tamative), Fianarantsoa, Mahajanga	• Island in Indian Ocean 250 miles off southeast coast of Africa, separated from mainland by Mozambique Channel • 224,533 sq.mi.; 13,006,000 • Malagasy (official), ethnic dialects; animist tribal religions, Christian, Muslim	• Narrow eastern and broader western coastal plains with large, fertile mountain plateau in interior. • Agriculture based on livestock and coffee crops; mining of graphite, chromite.
Malawi Republic of Malawi ★Lilongwe, Blantyre-Limbe, Zomba, Mzuzu	• Landlocked in southeast Africa south of Tanzania and north of Mozambique • 36,324 sq.mi.; 9,832,000 • English (official), Chichewa, Bantu dialects; Christian, Muslim, animist religions	• Plateaus and mountains along western and southern shores of Lake Malawi. • Tea, tobacco, peanut, sugar, and cotton crops; livestock, fishing; marble.
Mali Republic of Mali ★Bamako, Mopti, Ségou, Kayes	• Landlocked in western bulge of continental Africa • 471,042 sq.mi.; 8,869,000 • French (official), Bambara; primarily Sunni Muslim, small animist minority	• Sahara Desert in north with grassy river basins in south. • Cotton, peanut crops, livestock; Niger River fish.
Mauritania Islamic Republic of Mauritania ★Nouakchott, Nouadhibou, Kaédi, Kiffa	• Atlantic coast of western bulge of Africa • 397,838 sq.mi.; 2,125,000 • French (official), Hassaniyah Arabic; Muslim	• Narrow fertile strip in south along Senegal River valley, with most of northern section of country part of western Sahara Desert. • Iron and copper mining; livestock and date crops; fishing; fish products, dairy products.
Mauritius ★Port Louis, Beau-Bassin, Vacoas, Curepipe, Rose Belle	• Island in Indian Ocean about 500 miles east of island of Madagascar • 714 sq.mi.; 1,107,000 • English (official), French, Creole; Hindu, Roman Catholic, Muslim	• Tropical island of volcanic origin, including Rodrigues Island, some 350 miles to the east and other smaller, sparsely populated coral islands. • Sugarcane crops, processing, and exporting; tourism; clothing, jewelry, footwear.

Country
Official Name
★Capital
Principal Cities

•Location
•Area/Population
•Languages/Religions

•Land
•Economy

Morocco
Kingdom of Morocco
★Rabat,
Casablanca, Marrakesh, Fez,
Tangier Meknès, Salé,
Agadir

•Northwest coast of Africa, across from Spain at Strait of Gibraltar
•172,317 sq.mi.; 27,955,000
•Arabic (official), French, Berber; Sunni Muslim

•Fertile coastal plains rising to central mountains; western Sahara Desert along inland boundary.
•Cereal, bean, citrus fruit, and spice crops; mining of phosphate, coal, iron ore, lead, copper, manganese, and other ores and minerals.

Mozambique
Republic of Mozambique
★Maputo,
Beira, Nampula

•Southeast coast of Africa on Mozambique Channel opposite Madagascar
•302,737 sq.mi.; 16,342,000
•Portuguese (official), tribal dialects; animist tribal religions, Christian, primarily Roman Catholic, Muslim

•Coastal lowlands, central plateau traversed by numerous rivers, inland mountains.
•Sugar, cotton, nut crops; gold, bauxite, coal mining; cement, textiles, steel.

Namibia
Republic of Namibia
★Windhoek,
Swakopmund, Rehoboth,
Rundu

•In southwestern Africa, northwest of South Africa and south of Angola
•317,873 sq.mi.; 1,541,000
•Afrikaans, German, English (all official), several tribal languages; Christian

•Low coastal strip rising to high central plateau, and to semiarid, sandy Kalahari Desert in east.
•Uranium, diamonds, livestock, guano; fishing; textiles, leather goods, metal products.

Niger
Republic of Niger
★Niamey,
Zinder, Maradi,
Agadez

•Landlocked in north-central Africa north of Nigeria and south of Algeria and Libya
•489,073 sq.mi.; 8,337,000
•French (official), Hausa; Muslim, animist tribal religions, small Christian minority

•Sahara Desert in north, with semiarid central region and arable savanna in south and southwest.
•Grain crops and livestock; phosphate, and coal uranium mining; textiles, light manufacturing.

Nigeria
Federal Republic of Nigeria
★Abuja,
Lagos, Ibadan, Ogbomosho,
Kano, Oshogbo,
Abeokuta

•North coast of Gulf of Guinea south of Niger
•351,649 sq.mi.; 95,060,000
•English (official), Hausa, other tribal dialects; Muslim, Christian

•Coastal lowlands, interior rain forest, northern arid plateau.
•Oil and natural gas drilling and refining; steel industries, including automobiles; palm, peanut, cocoa, cotton crops; timber, manufactured goods.

Oman
Sultanate of Oman
★Muscat,
Salala,
Sohar,
Rustag

•In Middle East on Gulf of Oman and Arabian Sea, on southeast corner of Arabian peninsula
•82,031 sq.mi.; 1,644,000
•Arabic (official); Muslim

•Narrow, fertile coastal plain rising to hilly ranges and arid interior plateau.
•Oil drilling and refining; cereal and fruit crops; copper, cement, chemicals; food processing.

Cooking class, girls' school, Sierra Leone

Communications technician, Jidda, Saudi Arabia

Country Official Name ★Capital Principal Cities	• Location • Area/Population • Languages/Religions	• Land • Economy
Qatar State of Qatar ★Doha, Umm Said, Dukhan	• In Middle East, east of Saudi Arabia, on peninsula into center of Persian Gulf • 4247 sq.mi.; 499,000 • Arabic (official); Muslim	• Sandy and rocky lands with hot and dry climate. • Oil drilling and refining, natural gas production; grain, date, and vegetable crops; small fishing industry; iron and steel, fertilizer, cement, chemicals.
Rwanda Republic of Rwanda ★Kigali, Butare	• Landlocked southeastern part of central Africa, between Zaire and Tanzania • 9633 sq.mi.; 8,139,000 • French and Kinyarwanda (official); Christian, animist tribal religions, Muslim	• Predominantly plateau with temperate and grassy uplands and hills; marshy lands in southeast. • Coffee, tea, bananas; mining of cassiterite ore, gold, and tin; food processing.
São Tomé and Principe Democratic Republic of São Tomé and Principe ★São Tomé, Santo António	• Islands in Gulf of Guinea about 200 miles west of Gabon • 371 sq.mi.; 133,000 • Portuguese (official), Creole; Roman Catholic	• Twin islands, the larger and more populous São Tomé and smaller Principe, volcanic in origin and well forested; peripheral coral islets. • Cocoa, coffee, palm, and sugar crops exported to Portugal and The Netherlands.
Saudi Arabia Kingdom of Saudi Arabia ★Riyadh, Jidda, Mecca, Medina, Taif	• In Middle East, occupying most of Arabian peninsula • 829,996 sq.mi.; 17,615,000 • Arabic (official); Muslim	• Predominantly desert, with narrow coastal plains of rolling hills. • World's largest producer of oil; petrochemicals, fertilizer, plastics; fishing, notably shrimp.
Senegal Republic of Senegal ★Dakar, Kaolack, Thiès, Saint-Louis, Ziguinchor	• Western tip of Africa, surrounding The Gambia • 74,131 sq.mi.; 8,463,000 • French (official), Wolof, other tribal dialects; Sunni Muslim, Christian, predominantly Roman Catholic	• Predominantly grassy plains and rolling hills. • Peanut, rice, sorghum, and cotton crops; processing of peanut oil; phosphate mining; cement; commercial fishing; ship repair.

Country / Official Name / ★Capital / Principal Cities	• Location / • Area/Population / • Languages/Religions	• Land / • Economy
Seychelles Republic of Seychelles ★Victoria	• Islands northeast of Madagascar • 176 sq.mi.; 71,000 • English, French, Creole (official); Roman Catholic, small Anglican minority	• Some 86 small islands, coral or granite in composition, the main being Mahé, Praslin, Silhouette, and La Digue. • Tourism; spice and coconut exports; fishing, notably tuna; food processing.
Sierra Leone Republic of Sierra Leone ★Freetown, Bo, Kenema	• Southwestern corner of western bulge of continental Africa, next to Liberia • 27,653 sq.mi.; 4,511,000 • English (official), Krio, tribal dialects; animist tribal religions, Muslim, small Christian minority	• Relatively broad, swampy coastline rising to forested interior of plateaus and hills, with mountains in east and north. • Palm, coffee, rice, cocoa, and nut crops; diamond and iron ore mining; fishing.
Somalia Somali Democratic Republic ★Mogadishu, Kismayo, Berbera	• Easternmost tip of Africa, on Indian Ocean east of Ethiopia • 242,216 sq.mi.; 6,515,000 • Somali (official), Arabic, English; Sunni Muslim	• Predominantly desert land with northern mountains and southern plateau. • Cattle, camel, sheep, and goat raising; sugar, banana, and spice crops; sugar refining, textiles, food processing.
South Africa Republic of South Africa ★Pretoria and Cape Town, Johannesburg, Durban, Bloemfontein	• Southern tip of continental Africa • 471,444 sq.mi.; 42,793,000 • Afrikaans and English (official), Bantu dialects; numerous Christian denominations; Bantu religions, Hindu, Muslim	• Interior rolling plateau descending to hilly ranges and coastal lowlands. • Gold and diamond mining; coal, copper, manganese; iron and steel industries; textiles; livestock, fishing, food processing; chemicals, machinery, wood products, fabricated metals.
Sudan Republic of Sudan ★Khartoum, Omdurman, Port Sudan, Wadi Medani	• In east-central Africa, south of Egypt and west of Ethiopia, extending to Red Sea • 917,375 sq.mi.; 28,730,000 • Arabic (official), numerous local dialects; Sunni Muslim, animist tribal religions, substantial Christian minority	• Northern deserts, central fertile plains, southern rain forests. • Cotton, gum arabic, grains; livestock, food processing.
Swaziland Kingdom of Swaziland ★Mbabane, Manzini, Lobamba	• Southern tip of Africa, enclave within South Africa • 6641 sq.mi.; 907,000 • English, Siswati (official); Christian, animist tribal religions	• Hilly grassland velds declining in elevation from mountainous west to lowland veld in east. • Iron, asbestos, coal mining; sugarcane crops and livestock; forestry.

Country Official Name ★Capital Principal Cities	• Location • Area/Population • Languages/Religions	• Land • Economy
Syria Syrian Arab Republic ★Damascus, Aleppo, Homs, Latakia, Hamah	• In Middle East on Mediterranean Sea • 71,062 sq.mi.; 14,339,000 • Arabic (official), Kurdish, French; Muslim, Christian	• Fertile coastal plain rising to mountain ranges; central plateau and desert; eastern half domi- nated by the Euphrates River. • Grain, cotton, olive crops; dairy products; food processing and textile industries; cement, machinery, carpets; oil drilling.
Tanzania United Republic of Tanzania ★Dodoma, Dar Es Salaam, Mwanza, Zanzibar, Tanga	• In southeast Africa, on Indian Ocean, south of Uganda and Kenya and north of Mozambique • 342,100 sq.mi.; 27,286,000 • Swahili and English (official), Bantu dialects; animist tribal religions, Muslim, Christian	• Arid central plateau with western mountains and eastern coastal plain; includes coral islands of Zanzibar and Pemba; Mt. Kilimanjaro on northeast border is highest point in Africa. • Cotton, coffee, clove, coconut exports; textiles; diamond, gold, tin, and mica mining.
Togo Republic of Togo ★Lomé, Sokodé, Kpalimé, Atakpamé	• West Africa, on north coast of Gulf of Guinea • 21,000 sq.mi.; 4,105,000 • French (official), local dialects; animist tribal religions, Christian	• Plateau rising from narrow coastal lowland and divided by ranges of low hills. • Coffee and cocoa exports; phosphate mining; limestone and marble quarrying; cement, petroleum refining.
Tunisia Republic of Tunisia ★Tunis, Sfax, Sousse, Bizerte	• Northern tip of Africa on Mediterranean Sea between Algeria and Libya • 59,985 sq.mi.; 8,571,000 • Arabic (official), French; Sunni Muslim	• Northern wooded coastal ranges, central plateau sloping down to southern desert approaching the Sahara. • Tourism; chemical and steel industries; mining of phosphate and iron ore; olive, fruit, wheat crops; livestock.
Turkey Republic of Turkey ★Ankara, Istanbul, Izmir, Adana, Bursa, Konya, Gazientep	• North of Middle East, between Black and Mediterranean seas • 297,591 sq.mi.; 60,898,000 • Turkish (official), Kurdish, Arabic; Sunni Muslim, Shiite Muslim, Christian	• Semiarid eastern plateau with peripheral highlands and arable western hills. • Grain, cotton, fruit crops; cattle and sheep grazing; textile and food processing industries; iron and steel products, chemicals.
Uganda Republic of Uganda ★Kampala, Jinja, Mbale, Masaka, Entebbe	• Landlocked southeast of central Africa on Lake Victoria • 77,108 sq.mi.; 19,344,000 • English (official), Swahili, Luganda; Christian, animist tribal religions, Muslim	• Predominantly mountain plateau, dramatic peaks in southwest and numerous lakes. • Coffee, tobacco, tea, and cotton exports; forestry, fishing.

Street scene, Sadah, Yemen

Young girl, Kinshasa, Zaire

Country Official Name ★Capital Principal Cities	• Location • Area/Population • Languages/Religions	• Land • Economy
United Arab Emirates ★Abu Dhabi, Dubai, Sharjah, Ras al-Khaimah	• Southern Persian Gulf coast of Arabian peninsula • 32,278 sq.mi.; 2,657,000 • Arabic (official), Persian, English; Sunni Muslim	• Hot and dry lands of low desert plains and barren hills. • Oil drilling and refining; natural gas; aluminum, steel, cement; vegetable, date, and lime crops.
Yemen Republic of Yemen ★San'a', Ta'lz, Aden	• On southwestern tip of Arabian peninsula • 203,849 sq.mi.; 10,742,000 • Arabic; Sunni Muslim, Shiite Muslim	• Narrow southern coastal plain, mountains in the west. • Crude and refined oil, natural gas, cotton, coffee, salt; fishing.
Zaire Republic of Zaire ★Kinshasa, Kananga, Lubumbashi, Mbuji-Mayi, Kisangani	• In south-central Africa, with narrow eastern extension between Republic of Congo and Angola to Atlantic Ocean • 875,521 sq.mi.; 41,346,000 • French (official), Bantu dialects; Roman Catholic, Protestant, animist tribal religions, Muslim.	• Equatorial rain forest of Congo River basin in center, with peripheral plateaus, highlands, and mountains. • Mining of copper, zinc, tin, silver, cobalt, and other ores; diamonds; oil drilling; palm, coffee, cotton crops; timber and rubber; fishing.
Zambia Republic or Zambia ★Lusaka, Kitwe, Ndola	• Landlocked in southern Africa • 285,992 sq.mi.; 8,926,000 • English (official), Bantu dialects; animist tribal religions, Christian	• Predominantly elevated plateau, mainly savanna but heavily forested in southwest. • Mining of copper, cobalt, zinc, and other ores; emeralds and other gemstones; grain, tobacco, cotton crops.
Zimbabwe Republic of Zimbabwe (formerly Rhodesia) ★Harare, Bulawayo, Gwelo	• Landlocked in southern Africa • 149,293 sq.mi.; 10,838,000 • English (official), Shona, Ndebele; Christian animist tribal religions, Muslim	• Fertile grassland plateau broken by low ranges of hills. • Gold, nickel, coal mining; textile industries; food process- ing; diversified manufacturing, including metal and wood products; tobacco, sugarcane, cotton crops.

North America

North America is, after Asia and Africa, the third largest continent in the world. It lies between the Pacific and Atlantic oceans in the northern hemisphere. Farther north lies the Arctic Ocean and the ice cap of the North Pole. To the south, across the narrow land bridge called the Isthmus of Panama, lies South America. The North American region also includes the small countries north of the Isthmus of Panama and island nations in the Caribbean Sea southeast of the United States.

Almost 97 percent of the land area of North America is shared by three large countries: Canada, the United States, and Mexico. Of the three, Canada is the largest, the United States is slightly smaller, and Mexico is the smallest. Seventeen Central American and Caribbean countries account for just over 3 percent of the area of North America. Most of those countries are smaller in area than most states of the United States.

North America extends 5000 miles from the Arctic Circle almost to the equator, and it includes a great variety of natural features and climates. Northern Canada is a region of polar ice and some of the largest islands in the world. Central America includes dense tropical forests subject to heavy rains. The Caribbean countries are ringed by sandy beaches that attract tourists from around the world. The highest mountains in this region parallel the Pacific coast from Panama north to Alaska. This belt of mountains includes the Rockies in the United Sates and Canada. The Pacific coast of North America is subject to earthquakes and volcanic eruptions. It is part of a volcano and earthquake zone stretching in a ring around the Pacific Ocean that is sometimes called the "ring of fire." The Atlantic coast of North America is also a region of highlands, including the Appalachian Mountains in the eastern United States. The mountain ranges are not as tall as the Pacific ranges and the ground is much more stable; there are fewer and much smaller earthquakes and no active volcanoes. Between these two regions lie the Great Plains, a huge grassland that covers the central United States and much of Canada. In the United States this farmland is drained by the Mississippi River and its tributaries, one of the world's great river systems.

Six out of ten people in North America live in the United States, which is one of the largest, wealthiest, and most populous nations on Earth. Mexico has about a third as many people as the United States, and Canada has about a tenth as many. Unlike many world regions, North America is unified by a common religion. Christian faiths predominate. Islam and Judaism are also important faiths in North America, with millions of followers in each. One of two languages—English or Spanish—is the first language of most North American residents, although there are also minorities speaking French and a wide variety of Indian tongues.

North America is distinguished as a world leader in both manufacturing and agriculture. The interior plain of the continent contains the world's most productive farmland, and the Great Lakes region shared by the United States and Canada is an industrial power second in size only to Europe.

Country Official Name ★Capital Principal Cities	• Location • Area/Population • Languages/Religions	• Land • Economy
Antigua and Barbuda ★St.John's	• Caribbean Sea, 300 miles southeast of Puerto Rico • 170 sq.mi.; 64,000 • English (official); Roman Catholic	• Large island of Antigua, smaller island of Barbuda, and tiny islet of Redonda. • Tourism, manufacturing.
Bahamas Commonwealth of the Bahamas ★Nassau, Freeport	• Northern area of West Indies, east of Florida • 3888 sq.mi.; 269,000 • English (official); Protestant, Roman Catholic	• Archipelago of 700 temperate coral islands, of which 30 are inhabited. • Tourism; international banking; rum, pharmaceuticals; pineapples, bananas, citrus fruits.

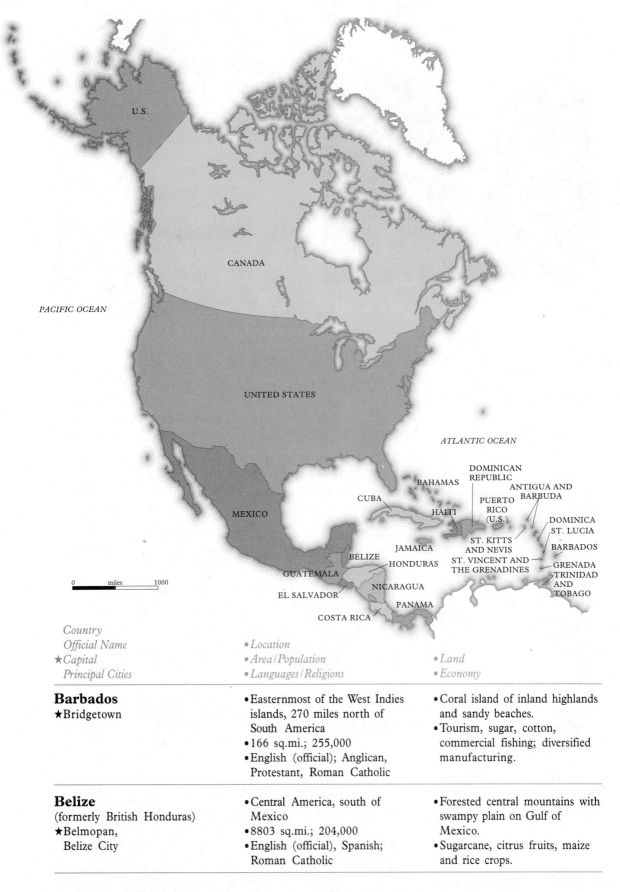

PACIFIC OCEAN

U.S.

CANADA

UNITED STATES

ATLANTIC OCEAN

MEXICO

BAHAMAS

CUBA

HAITI

DOMINICAN
REPUBLIC

PUERTO
RICO
(U.S.)

ANTIGUA AND
BARBUDA

DOMINICA

ST. LUCIA

BARBADOS

GRENADA

TRINIDAD
AND
TOBAGO

ST. KITTS
AND NEVIS

ST. VINCENT AND
THE GRENADINES

JAMAICA

BELIZE

HONDURAS

GUATEMALA

NICARAGUA

EL SALVADOR

PANAMA

COSTA RICA

0   miles   1000

Country		
Official Name	•*Location*	
★*Capital*	•*Area / Population*	•*Land*
Principal Cities	•*Languages / Religions*	•*Economy*

Barbados ★Bridgetown	•Easternmost of the West Indies islands, 270 miles north of South America •166 sq.mi.; 255,000 •English (official); Anglican, Protestant, Roman Catholic	•Coral island of inland highlands and sandy beaches. •Tourism, sugar, cotton, commercial fishing; diversified manufacturing.
Belize (formerly British Honduras) ★Belmopan, Belize City	•Central America, south of Mexico •8803 sq.mi.; 204,000 •English (official), Spanish; Roman Catholic	•Forested central mountains with swampy plain on Gulf of Mexico. •Sugarcane, citrus fruits, maize and rice crops.

Inuit couple, northern Canada

Market, Port-au-Prince, Haiti

Country Official Name ★Capital Principal Cities	• Location • Area/Population • Languages/Religions	• Land • Economy
Canada ★Ottawa, Toronto, Montreal, Vancouver, Winnipeg	• Northern half of North America, from United States to Arctic islands and Atlantic to Pacific oceans • 3,560,219 sq.mi.; 27,770,000 • English and French (official); Roman Catholic, Protestant, Jewish	• Great central landmass of level Canadian Shield, with western mountains and southeastern uplands. • Major economic power with diverse industry, agriculture, and mineral reserves, notably western oil deposits.
Costa Rica Republic of Costa Rica ★San José, Alajuela, Limón, Puntarenas	• Southern portion of Central America, from Caribbean to Pacific • 19,560 sq.mi.; 3,265,000 • Spanish (official), English; Roman Catholic	• Tropical Caribbean lowlands, temperate interior of mountains and tablelands. • Coffee, banana, sugar exports; forestry; fishing; textiles; fertilizer and petroleum industries.
Cuba Republic of Cuba ★Havana, Santiago de Cuba, Camagüey, Holguín	• Westernmost of the West Indies islands, 90 miles south of Florida • 42,803 sq.mi.; 10,957,000 • Spanish (official); restricted Roman Catholicism	• Largest Caribbean island, with rocky northern coast, marshy southern one, and interior of fertile mountain valleys. • Sugar and sugar refining; tobacco and smoking products; nickel mining; petroleum refining; food processing; textiles.
Dominica Commonwealth of Dominica ★Roseau	• Within Windward Islands in eastern Caribbean • 290 sq.mi.; 87,000 • English (official), French; Roman Catholic	• Volcanic in origin and mountainous, with thermal springs. • Banana, citrus fruit, and coconut exports; timber; tourism.

Christopher Columbus's tomb, Santo Domingo, Dominican Republic

Festival, Guatemala

Country Official Name ★Capital Principal Cities	• Location • Area/Population • Languages/Religions	• Land • Economy
Dominican Republic ★Santo Domingo, Santiago de los Caballeros	• Eastern two-thirds of the island of Hispaniola, shared with Haiti, in West Indies • 18,680 sq.mi.; 7,684,000 • Spanish (official); Roman Catholic	• Central mountains, with most fertile land to the north in Cibao valley. • Agriculture based on sugar, coffee, cocoa, and tobacco crops; rum; textiles.
El Salvador Republic of El Salvador ★San Salvador, Santa Ana, San Miguel	• Pacific coast of Central America • 8000 sq.mi.; 5,637,000 • Spanish (official), Nahuatl Indian dialects; Roman Catholic	• Hot Pacific coastal plain and subtropical interior mountain valleys. • Exports of coffee, sugar, maize; limited domestic agriculture; textiles, petroleum.
Grenada State of Grenada ★St. George's, Grenville, Gouyave	• Southern West Indies, 90 miles north of Venezuela • 131 sq.mi.; 94,000 • English (official), French; Anglican, Roman Catholic	• Volcanic main island, coral Carriacou and Petit Martinique islands. • Exports of spices, bananas, cocoa, sugar; tourism.
Guatemala Republic of Guatemala ★Guatemala City, Escuintla, Quezaltenango	• Northernmost of Central American countries • 41,865 sq.mi.; 10,446,000 • Spanish (official), Indian languages; Roman Catholic	• Mountainous, with Pacific and Caribbean coastal lowlands. • Coffee exports dominate local economy; limited agriculture and textile industries.
Haiti Republic of Haiti ★Port-au-Prince, Cap-Haitien	• Western third of island of Hispaniola, in West Indies • 10,641 sq.mi.; 6,385,000 • French (official), Creole; Roman Catholic, Protestant, folk religions	• Mountains over two-thirds of area, with arid coastal plains and valleys. • Coffee and sugarcane exports; bauxite mining; light manufactures for export.

Mural, Mexico City, Mexico

Mayan ruins, Honduras

Country Official Name ★Capital Principal Cities	• Location • Area/Population • Languages/Religions	• Land • Economy
Honduras Republic of Honduras ★Tegucigalpa, San Pedro Sula	• Central America, with long Caribbean coastline • 43,201 sq.mi.; 5,170,000 • Spanish (official), English; Roman Catholic, Protestant	• Principally mountainous, with broad and fertile Caribbean coastal plain. • Coffee, banana, and timber exports; domestic consumer goods and foods.
Jamaica ★Kingston, Montego Bay	• West Indies, 90 miles south of Cuba • 4181 sq.mi.; 2,530,000 • English (official), Creole; Protestant, Roman Catholic	• Mountainous, with western and southern coastal plains. • Sugar; bauxite mining; tourism; tobacco products; petroleum products.
Mexico United Mexican States ★Mexico City, Guadalajara, Monterrey, Ciudad Juárez, León	• Extends south from United States to Central America • 742,486 sq.mi.; 90,420,000 • Spanish (official), Indian languages; Roman Catholic	• Dry central lowland with mountains along coasts and tropical lowlands in south. • Steel, textile, and chemical industries; cotton, coffee, sugar crops; petroleum.
Nicaragua Republic of Nicaragua ★Managua, Léon, Matagalpa	• Middle country of Central America • 46,430 sq.mi.; 3,987,000 • Spanish (official), English; Roman Catholic	• Central Cordillera mountains, broad Caribbean and narrow Pacific plains. • Coffee and cotton exports; silver, gold, copper mining; forestry; commercial fishing.
Panama Republic of Panama ★Panama City, Colón, San Miguelito	• Southern end of Central American isthmus • 29,340 sq.mi.; 2,579,000 • Spanish (official), English; Roman Catholic	• Coastal tropical rain forests and interior mountains, divided by Panama Canal. • Shipping; limited agriculture, with banana, sugar, and coffee exports.

Countries of the World

Tropical beach, St. Lucia

Wheat fields, United States

Country *Official Name* ★*Capital* *Principal Cities*	• *Location* • *Area/Population* • *Languages/Religions*	• *Land* • *Economy*
St. Kitts and Nevis Federation of St. Kitts and Nevis ★Basseterre	•Eastern Caribbean, east of Puerto Rico •139 sq.mi.; 40,000 •English; Protestant	•Mountainous islands of volcanic origin. •Tourism, sugar processing; sugarcane, cotton.
St. Lucia ★Castries	•Eastern Caribbean, north of Venezuela •236 sq.mi.; 144,000 •English (official), French, local dialects; Roman Catholic	•Mountainous island of volcanic origin, with wooded slopes and streams descending to sea. •Tourism; banana, coconut, sugar, cocoa, and citrus fruit crops; timber.
St. Vincent and the Grenadines ★Kingstown	•Eastern Caribbean, north of Venezuela. •131 sq.mi.; 115,000 •English (official), local dialects; Protestant, Roman Catholic	•Volcanic and mountainous island of St. Vincent, with smaller rocky islets. •Tourism; banana and coconut crops; food processing and light manufactures.
Trinidad and Tobago Republic of Trinidad and Tobago ★Port-of-Spain, San Fernando	•Southernmost of West Indies islands, just north of Venezuela •1981 sq.mi.; 1,314,000 •English (official), Hindi; Roman Catholic, Protestant, Hindu, Muslim	•Islands 19 miles apart, chiefly mountainous, with tropical forests. •Oil drilling and refining; tourism; sugar and cocoa crops.
United States of America ★Washington, D.C., New York, Los Angeles, Chicago, Philadelphia, Detroit	•Center of North America, extending from Atlantic to Pacific oceans •3,539,227 sq.mi.; 258,104,000 •English (official); Protestant, Roman Catholic, Jewish	•Great central lowland, with western Rocky Mountains and eastern Appalachian uplands. •World's greatest economic power, with various industries, central farms, southern fuel reserves.

South America

South America is a continent located between the Atlantic and Pacific oceans, mostly south of the equator. It is linked to Central and North America by the land bridge called the Isthmus of Panama. Only 31 miles wide, this isthmus has been crossed in modern times by the Panama Canal. The equator crosses the northern part of South America. Near the equator the continent reaches its greatest width of some 3000 miles. Farther south the continent tapers toward a narrow tip called Tierra del Fuego. This most southern point of South America is only about 600 miles north of the continent of Antarctica.

There are only twelve countries in South America, fewer than in any other world region. The largest by far is Brazil, which covers most of the continent near the equator. Brazil is nearly as large as the United States, and it includes half the land area of South America. The smallest country in this region is Suriname, which is smaller than the U.S. state of Missouri.

The lands of South America fall into several different regions. The western coast of the continent is dominated by the towering Andes Mountains, which are higher than any range on Earth except the Himalayas. The central region of the continent near the equator is a dense tropical rain forest. Still largely an unexplored wilderness, this rain forest has been greatly reduced in size in recent years, but steps are being taken to preserve it. The Amazon rain forest is drained by the Amazon River, the largest on Earth except for the Nile in Africa. The southeast of the continent is an enormous grassland plain called the pampas.

South America is a sparsely populated continent. It includes 12 percent of the world's land area but only 5 percent of the world's population. Half of the people of South America live in Brazil, most of them in cities along the Atlantic coast such as São Paulo, which has a population slightly larger than that of New York City. The people of Brazil speak Portuguese, while those in the other South American countries speak mostly Spanish. Almost all of the people of South America are Roman Catholics, but Protestant faiths are growing in importance.

Because it is so sparsely populated, South America is still working to become an economic power. Some of its northern countries, such as Venezuela, are rich in oil reserves, but most of the region is economically dependent on livestock and grain crops, and on mining of ores and minerals.

Country Official Name ★Capital Principal Cities	• Location • Area/Population • Languages/Religions	• Land • Economy
Argentina Argentine Republic ★Buenos Aires, Córdoba, Rosario, La Plata, San Miguel de Tucuman	• Southern reach of South America, with Atlantic coast to east, Chilean border to west • 1,056,637 sq.mi.; 33,533,000 • Spanish (official), English; Roman Catholic	• Western Andes Mountains, central pampas plains, northeastern tropical lowlands, rainy coast of Patagonian steppes in south. • Agricultural exports of beef, corn, and wheat; chemical, textile, machine industries; mining of oil, coal, and lead.
Bolivia Republic of Bolivia ★La Paz and Sucre, Santa Cruz, Cochabamba	• Landlocked country in central South America • 418,683 sq.mi.; 7,540,000 • Spanish (official), Quechua, Aymara; Roman Catholic	• Great central plateau with Andes Mountains to the west and semitropical eastern forests. • Mining of tin; agriculture based on cotton, sugar, coffee, wheat, and barley crops.

PACIFIC OCEAN

ATLANTIC OCEAN

VENEZUELA
GUYANA
SURINAME
FRENCH GUIANA (Fr.)
COLOMBIA
ECUADOR
PERU
BRAZIL
BOLIVIA
PARAGUAY
CHILE
URUGUAY
ARGENTINA

0   miles   500

Country		
Official Name	• *Location*	
★*Capital*	• *Area / Population*	• *Land*
Principal Cities	• *Languages / Religions*	• *Economy*

Brazil		
Federative Republic of Brazil ★Brasilia, São Paulo, Rio de Janeiro, Belo Horizonte, Recife, Salvador	• Broad expanse of central and eastern South America, covering half the continent • 3,265,061 sq.mi.; 156,664,000 • Portuguese (official); Roman Catholic	• Tropical Amazon River basin in north, semiarid northeast region, fertile south-central plains, populous southern coast. • Agriculture based on coffee, cotton, sugar, and livestock; textile industries; mining of quartz, chromium, iron, tin.

Chile		
Republic of Chile ★Santiago, Valparaíso, Viña del Mar, Concepción	• Long and narrow country along southwest Pacific coast of South America • 289,112 sq.mi.; 13,740,000 • Spanish (official); Roman Catholic	• Andes Mountains along inland border sloping down to Pacific coast of desert in north and farmland in south. • Third largest copper producer in world and exporter of iron, coal, gold, and silver; limited agriculture.

Ecuadoran musician

Street scene, Acuncion, Paraguay

Country *Official Name* ★*Capital* *Principal Cities*	• *Location* • *Area/Population* • *Languages/Religions*	• *Land* • *Economy*
Colombia Republic of Colombia ★Bogotá, Medellín, Cali, Barranquilla, Cartagena, Bucaramanga	•Northwest edge of South American continent •401,042 sq.mi.; 34,943,000 •Spanish (official); Roman Catholic	•Level coastal plain, western Andes highlands, sparsely populated eastern plains. •Coffee exports; petroleum drilling; 50 percent of world's emerald yield; gold, silver, copper, platinum.
Ecuador Republic of Ecuador ★Quito, Guayaquil, Cuenca	•Northwest Pacific coast of South America, on equator •106,888 sq.mi.; 10,461,000 •Spanish (official), Quechua; Roman Catholic	•Humid coastal lowlands, temperate central Andes Mountains, tropical eastern lowlands. •Banana, coffee, rice, cocoa exports; petroleum drilling; gold, silver, copper mining; commercial fishing.
Guyana Cooperative Republic of Guyana ★Georgetown, New Amsterdam, Linden	•Northern Atlantic coast of South America •76,004 sq.mi.; 735,000 •English (official), Portuguese; Anglican, Hindu, Muslim	•Populous coastal plain and interior tropical rain forest. •Agriculture, principally sugar and rice; timber production; mining, principally bauxite, gold, and diamonds.
Paraguay Republic of Paraguay ★Asunción, Encarnación	•Landlocked country in central South America •153,398 sq.mi.; 5,071,000 •Spanish (official), Guarani Indian language; Roman Catholic	•Eastern fertile plain and drier western Chaco plain. •Cattle; corn, cotton, soy, sugarcane, and wheat crops; timber.

Machu Picchu, Peru

Oil refinery, Venezuela

Country Official Name ★Capital Principal Cities	• Location • Area/Population • Languages/Religions	• Land • Economy
Peru Republic of Peru ★Lima, Callao, Arequipa, Trujillo, Chimbote	• West-central Pacific coast of South America • 494,208 sq.mi.; 23,210,000 • Spanish and Quechua (official), Aymara; Roman Catholic	• Arid coast, central Andes Mountains, inland tropical rain forest reaching to Amazon River basin. • Lead, copper, zinc, and iron mining, with recent petroleum drilling; agriculture based on sugar, cotton, and coffee; fishing.
Suriname Republic of Suriname ★Paramaribo, Nickerie	• Northeast Atlantic coast of South America • 62,344 sq.mi.; 416,000 • Dutch (official), English, Creole; Protestant, Roman Catholic, Hindu, Muslim	• Flat Atlantic coastal plain with interior of unexplored virgin forests. • Agriculture based on rice, sugar, and coffee; bauxite mining.
Uruguay Oriental Republic of Uruguay ★Montevideo, Las Piedras, Salto	• Southeast Atlantic coast of South America • 67,035 sq.mi.; 3,175,000 • Spanish (official); Roman Catholic	• Rolling and well-watered grassland plains. • Cattle and sheep; corn, wheat, and oat crops; chemicals and textiles.
Venezuela Republic of Venezuela ★Caracas, Maracaibo, Valencia, Barquisimeto	• Northern tip of South America • 340,560 sq.mi.; 20,118,000 • Spanish (official); Roman Catholic	• Northwest Andes Mountains, Caribbean coastal plain, interior plains and southern highlands. • Drilling and refining of petroleum and exportation of iron ore; agriculture based on coffee and beef cattle.

Territories

There are numerous lands that have the governmental status of territory. These places are considered dependencies of other nations. Some are actually far larger than their mother countries: Greenland, for example, is a territory of Denmark, but this sparsely populated island is almost 50 times larger than Denmark. In most cases, however, the world's territories are tiny islands discovered by European nations and now dependent on a mother country for economic reasons. In modern times many territories have become independent nations, much as America, once a territory of Great Britain, gained its own independence. Some, however, choose to remain territories to benefit from their ties to larger, wealthier nations.

The United States has more territories than any other nation. They are listed after the states in the section on the United States. Some, such as Puerto Rico in the Caribbean, are currently debating the value of becoming a state. But most are tiny islands in the Pacific with small populations and economies.

Great Britain, France, and Australia also have many territories in the Pacific. Like the American territories, most of these are small islands that benefit from economic support from their mother countries. These dependencies are usually free to make their own decisions on matters of strictly local importance.

One special case is the great uninhabited continent of Antarctica. Many nations are exploring Antarctica in search of fuel and mineral deposits. These countries now cooperate under the terms of a special treaty. This allows them to study the mysterious continent and to support small scientific research stations in the brutal Antarctic climate.

Official Name Possession of	• Location • Area/Population	• Land • Economy
Anguilla (U.K.)	• In eastern Caribbean • 35 sq.mi.; 7000	• Main island, smaller islets. • Fishing, tourism.
Bermuda (U.K.)	• In Atlantic Ocean, 600 miles east of South Carolina • 19 sq.mi.; 61,000	• Hilly island group. • Tourism, international business.
British Indian Ocean Territory (U.K.)	• In south of Indian Ocean, opposite east coast of Africa • 22 sq.mi.; 2000	• Five atolls of coral origin.
British Virgin Islands (U.K.)	• Caribbean group 60 miles east of Puerto Rico • 58 sq.mi.; 13,000	• Mountainous tropical islands. • Tourism, fish, fruit.
Cayman Islands (U.K.)	• In Caribbean, northwest of Jamaica • 100 sq.mi.; 30,000	• Three low-lying coral islands. • Banking, tourism.
Christmas Island (Australia)	• In Indian Ocean, 200 miles south of Indonesia • 52 sq.mi.; 1700	• High central plateau. • Phosphate mining.
Cocos (Keeling) Islands (Australia)	• Twin atolls in Indian Ocean, 550 miles southwest of Indonesia • 5.5 sq.mi.; 600	• Low-lying coral islands. • Copra.
Cook Islands (New Zealand)	• In south Pacific, 1700 miles northeast of New Zealand • 93 sq.mi.; 19,000	• Two island groups of volcanic origin. • Coconuts, fruits.

Traditional dress, Guadeloupe

Street scene, Hong Kong

Stamp, St. Pierre and Miquelon

Stamp, Falkland Islands

Town in Greenland

Official Name Possession of	• Location • Area/Population	• Land • Economy
Faeroe Islands (Denmark)	• Archipelago in north Atlantic 350 miles north of Great Britain • 541 sq.mi.; 48,000	• Island chain with rugged coastlines and interior plateaus. • Fishing.
Falkland Islands, or Islas Malvinas (U.K.)	• Northeast of southern tip of South America • 4618 sq.mi.; 2100	• Two main islands and numerous islets. • Fishing, sheepherding.
French Guiana (France)	• On coast of South America north of Brazil • 34,421 sq.mi.; 133,000	• Coastal plain rising to heavily forested interior. • Fishing, lumber.
French Polynesia (France)	• 130 islands scattered in mid-south Pacific • 1413 sq.mi.; 210,000	• Five island groups of generally volcanic origin. • Copra, tourism.
Gibraltar (U.K.)	• South of Spain, on north side of entrance to Mediterranean • 2.5 sq.mi.; 32,000	• Limestone promontory at end of low isthmus. • Tourism, shipping.
Greenland (Denmark)	• Enormous and largely arctic island in north Atlantic northeast of Canada • 840,000 sq.mi.; 57,000	• Coastal mountains, ice-covered central plateau. • Fishing.
Guadeloupe (France)	• Islands in Caribbean Sea southeast of Puerto Rico • 680 sq.mi.; 422,000	• Two rugged main islands, several smaller islets. • Bananas, sugar.

Polar regions

Ice cave on Ross Ice Shelf, Antarctica

The polar regions of the world are the Arctic in the north and Antarctica in the south. These regions do not have ordinary national or territorial status.

The Arctic is a sea region bordered by the northern lands of Europe, Asia, and North America. The Arctic Ocean at its center is more than 5 million square miles, and most of it is covered by a permanent ice cap. The Norwegian explorer Roald Amundsen was the first man to sail the Northwest Passage through the Arctic from the Atlantic to the Pacific, in 1903. The American explorer Robert E. Peary was the first to reach the geographical North Pole on the ice cap in 1909. In 1926 U.S. admiral Richard E. Byrd and American aviator Floyd Bennett flew over the North Pole, and in 1958 the U.S. nuclear submarine *Nautilus* sailed completely under the polar ice cap. Eskimo people live on the lands that border the Arctic.

Antarctica is a vast ice-covered continent that is larger than Europe or Australia. The average thickness of the vast ice cap that covers most of the continent is about 8000 feet. Only the tops of a few mountain ranges and rock outcrops are ice-free. Antarctica was declared a continent in 1840 by the American explorer Charles Wilkes. In 1911 Roald Amundsen became the first man to reach the South Pole at its center. He thus won the "race to the pole" with Robert F. Scott of England, who arrived there one month later and died trying to return. Scientists now think that there are large mineral deposits on Antarctica. Twelve countries, including the United States, claim portions of the continent. Under the 1959 Antarctica Treaty, these countries all cooperate on scientific expeditions there. Antarctica has no native population, but the scientists there sometimes number in the thousands.

Official Name Possession of	•Location •Area/Population	•Land •Economy
Hong Kong (U.K.)	•On southeastern coast of China, at mouth of Canton River •382 sq.mi.; 5,553,000	•Steep-sloped terrain, numerous small islands. •Manufacturing, banking.
Macao (Portugal)	•Enclave on coast of China, at mouth of Canton River •6 sq.mi.; 478,000	•Flat, narrow peninsula and two rugged islands. •Manufacturing, textiles.
Martinique (France)	•Island in Caribbean Sea southeast of Puerto Rico •409 sq.mi.; 388,000	•Volcanic mountains in north, hilly south. •Bananas, oil, rum.

Official Name / Possession of	Location / Area/Population	Land / Economy
Montserrat (U.K.)	• Island in Caribbean east of Puerto Rico and north of Martinique • 39 sq.mi.; 13,000	• Rugged island of volcanic origin. • Agriculture, manufacturing, tourism.
Netherlands Antilles (Netherlands)	• Windward and Leeward Islands in Caribbean Sea north of Venezuela • 371 sq.mi.; 185,000	• Tropical, hilly to mountainous islands of volcanic origin. • Petroleum products, tourism.
New Caledonia (France)	• South Pacific islands 1000 miles east of Australia • 7243 sq.mi.; 178,000	• Rugged narrow main island, smaller islets, coral reefs. • Nickel, chrome, iron, and minerals.
Niue (New Zealand)	• In south Pacific 1600 miles northeast of New Zealand • 100 sq.mi.; 3000	• Uplifted coral island. • Copra, fruit, honey.
Norfolk Island (Australia)	• In south Pacific 1000 miles east of Australia • 14 sq.mi.; 1800	• Small volcanic island with steep coastal cliffs. • Tourism, customs duties, stamps.
Pitcairn Island (U.K.)	• In mid-south Pacific, between South America and Australia • 1.75 sq.mi.; 59	• Steep coastal cliffs rising to rugged interior. • Fruit, fish, vegetables.
Réunion (France)	• In Indian Ocean 600 miles east of Madagascar • 965 sq.mi.; 640,000	• Mountainous, of volcanic origin. • Sugar, rum, vanilla.
St. Helena, Ascension, and Tristan da Cunha (U.K.)	• In south Atlantic, 1200 miles west of Africa • 158 sq.mi.; 9000	• Mountainous islands of volcanic origin. • Cable communications.
St. Pierre and Miquelon (France)	• North Atlantic island groups just south of Newfoundland, Canada • 93 sq.mi.; 7000	• Eight small, rocky islands. • Fish and fish products.
Tokelau (New Zealand)	• South Pacific atoll group 300 miles north of Samoa • 4 sq.mi.; 2000	• Three small coral islands. • Copra, fishing.
Turks and Caicos Islands (U.K.)	• In Atlantic to southeast of Bahamas • 166 sq.mi.; 13,000	• Two main islands and numerous rocks and cays. • Lobsters, conch, tourism.
Wallis and Futuna Islands (France)	• In south Pacific west of Samoa • 106 sq.mi.; 14,000	• Two rugged island groups of volcanic origin. • Copra, cassava.

How to read a map

Maps have been drawn and used by man since he began to explore Earth's surface. Now, as man reaches out into space with sophisticated telescopes and photographic equipment, he has made maps of space too. The making of maps is called *cartography;* the people who draw them are called *cartographers.*

Globes and maps.

Since Earth is round, we get the truest picture of it by drawing our maps on *globes.* Globes are interesting to study because they provide a picture of the entire Earth. However, their usefulness is limited: they are cumbersome, bulky, and expensive. More important, because globes are usually quite small, they offer little room for information.

For these reasons, maps are used most of the time. Maps are flat pictures of the world or of an area of it. They are relatively inexpensive and can be folded, hung on a wall, or bound in a book, called an *atlas.* To use maps well, there are certain facts about them that you should know.

If you look at a globe of Earth, you will notice crisscross lines on it. The lines that go around the globe parallel to the equator are called *parallels,* or lines of *latitude.* Those that go up and down from the North to the South Pole are called *meridians,* or lines of *longitude.* These lines intersect to form a grid.

The grid is a system invented by navigators and scholars hundreds of years ago. With it you can locate any place on Earth accurately if you know its latitude (how many degrees it is from the equator) and longitude (how many degrees it is from the prime meridian). For example, Nashville, Tennessee, is 36.10 degrees north and 86.48 degrees west. With this information you can easily find Nashville on a map of the United States. Washington, D.C., is 38.50 degrees north and 77.00 degrees west. Find the latitude and longitude of your town.

All reliable maps and globes have parallels and meridians marked on them. They are particularly useful to navigators on ships and airplanes, who use the grid as an absolute reference when calculating their course.

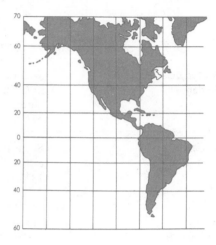

Mercator projection

Map projections.

To understand map projections, think of Earth as an orange. Imagine that you can peel off a section of Earth's crust (the skin of an orange). Then imagine that you try to flatten the section you have peeled off. You will soon find out that the section cannot be flattened without tearing it at the edges, or distorting it in some way. Cartographers must transfer the information on the globe to a flat surface with the least distortion. The solution they have developed for doing this is called *map projection.* While no single projection is better than all others, certain projections are better than others for showing specific kinds of information or specific parts of Earth.

The *Mercator projection* was devised by the great mapmaker Gerardus Mercator (1512–1594). It is a rectangle on which all parallels and meridians cross each other at right angles. Therefore, any straight line shows compass direction, which is very helpful to navigators. The drawback of the Mercator projection is that it greatly distorts land areas around the poles and in the higher latitudes, such as Greenland, making them appear much larger than they really are.

(continued on page 177)

　　　　　　　　　　　　　　Countries of the World

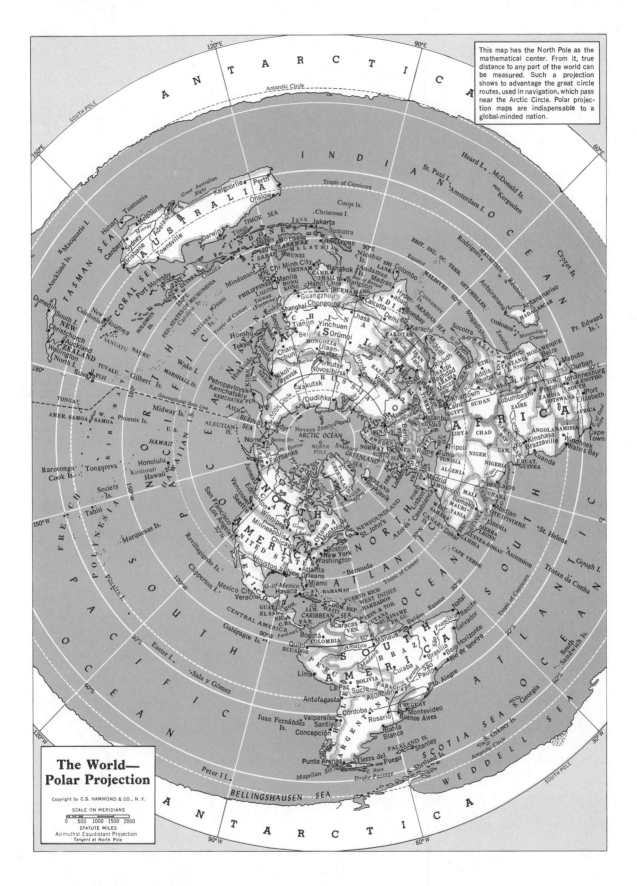

This map has the North Pole as the mathematical center. From it, true distance to any part of the world can be measured. Such a projection shows to advantage the great circle routes, used in navigation, which pass near the Arctic Circle. Polar projection maps are indispensable to a global-minded nation.

The World— Polar Projection

Copyright by C.S. Hammond & Co., N. Y.

SCALE ON MERIDIANS

0 500 1000 1500 2000
STATUTE MILES
Azimuthal Equidistant Projection
Tangent at North Pole

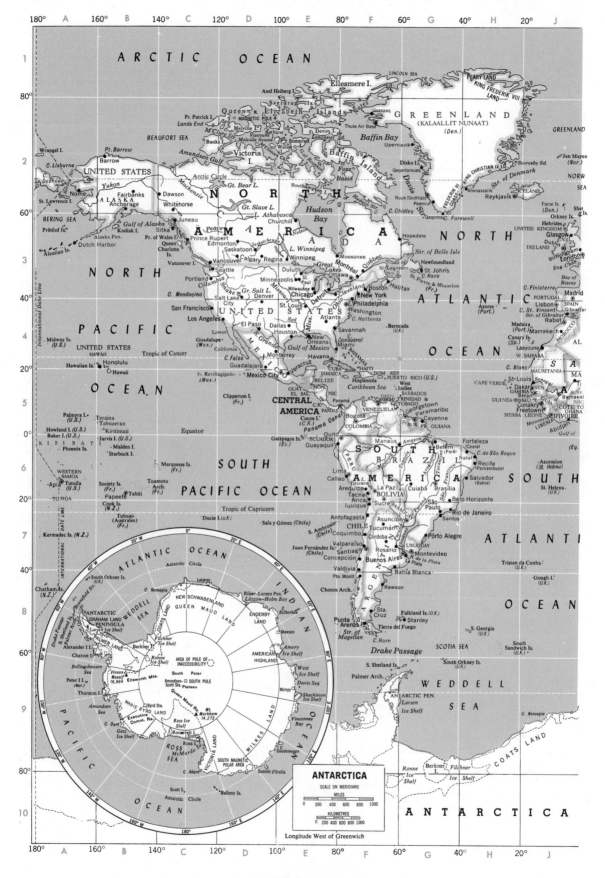

ARCTIC OCEAN

GREENLAND
(KALAALLIT NUNAAT)
(Den.)

NORTH AMERICA

UNITED STATES

NORTH ATLANTIC OCEAN

PACIFIC OCEAN

SOUTH AMERICA

SOUTH ATLANTIC OCEAN

CENTRAL AMERICA

SOUTH PACIFIC OCEAN

ANTARCTICA

SCALE ON MERIDIANS
MILES
0   200 400 600 800 1000
KILOMETRES
0 200 400 600 800 1000

Longitude West of Greenwich

Atlas 2

The World

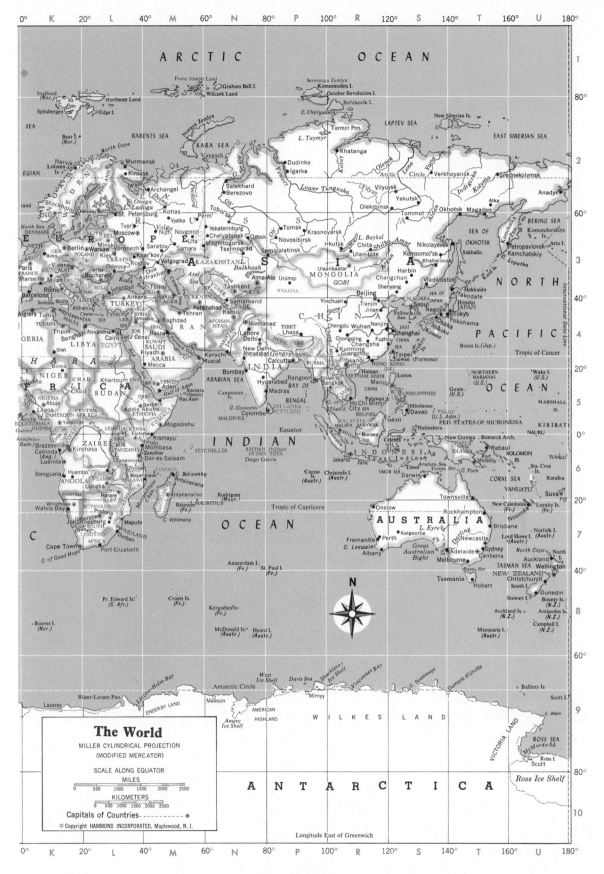

The World   Atlas 3

North America

LAMBERT AZIMUTHAL EQUAL-AREA
PROJECTION

SCALE OF MILES

0   200   400   600   800   1000

SCALE OF KILOMETERS

0 200 400 600 800 1000

Capitals of Countries .... ⊚
International Boundaries .... —·—·—
Canals .... ·········

© Copyright HAMMOND INCORPORATED, Maplewood, N.J.

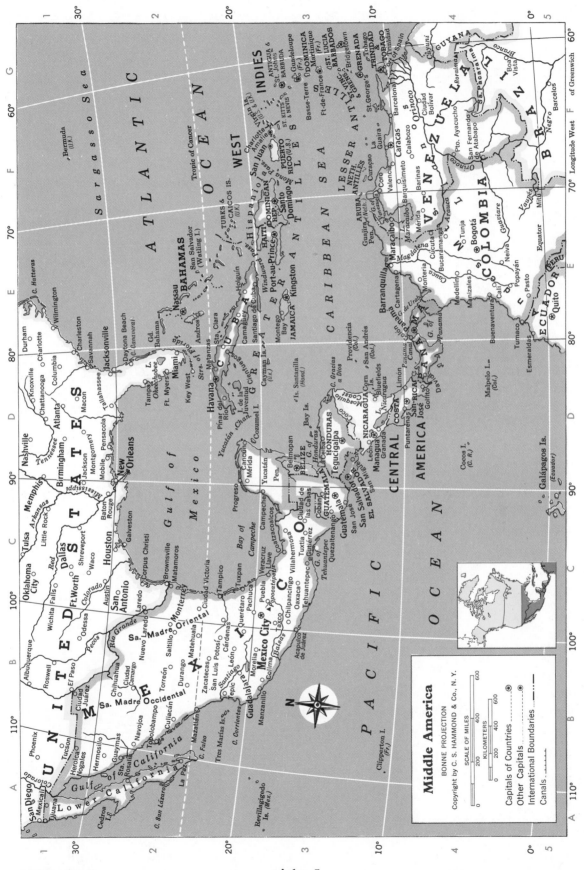

Middle America

BONNE PROJECTION

Copyright by C. S. HAMMOND & Co., N. Y.

SCALE OF MILES

0   200   400   600

KILOMETERS

0   200   400   600

Capitals of Countries .... ⊛
Other Capitals .... ⊙
International Boundaries .... ▬ ▬
Canals .... ▬ ▬ ▬

Middle America   Atlas 5

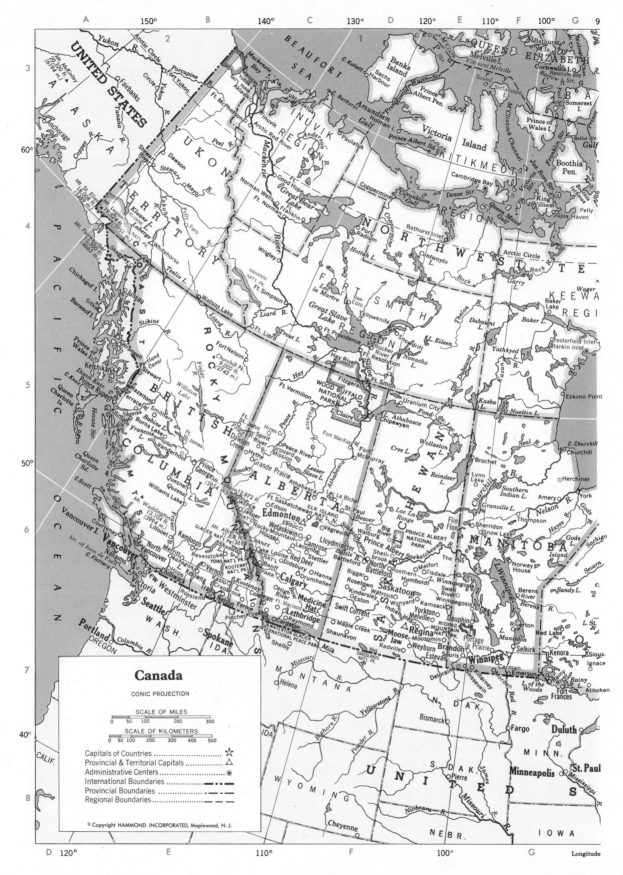

Canada

CONIC PROJECTION

SCALE OF MILES
0 50 100   200   300

SCALE OF KILOMETERS
0 50 100   200   300   400   500

Capitals of Countries	☆
Provincial & Territorial Capitals	△
Administrative Centers	◉
International Boundaries	—··—··—
Provincial Boundaries	—·—·—
Regional Boundaries	— — —

© Copyright HAMMOND INCORPORATED, Maplewood, N.J.

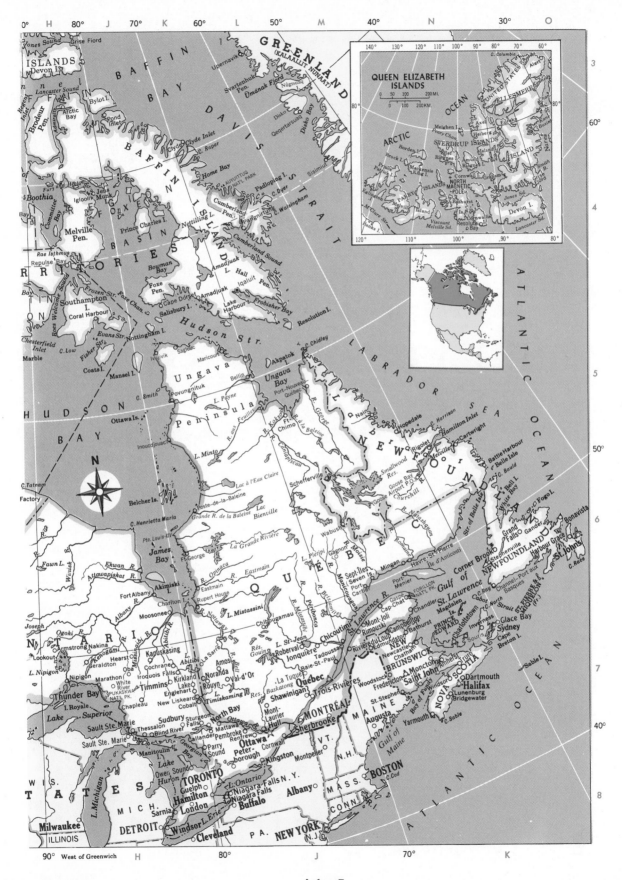

Canada

Atlas 7

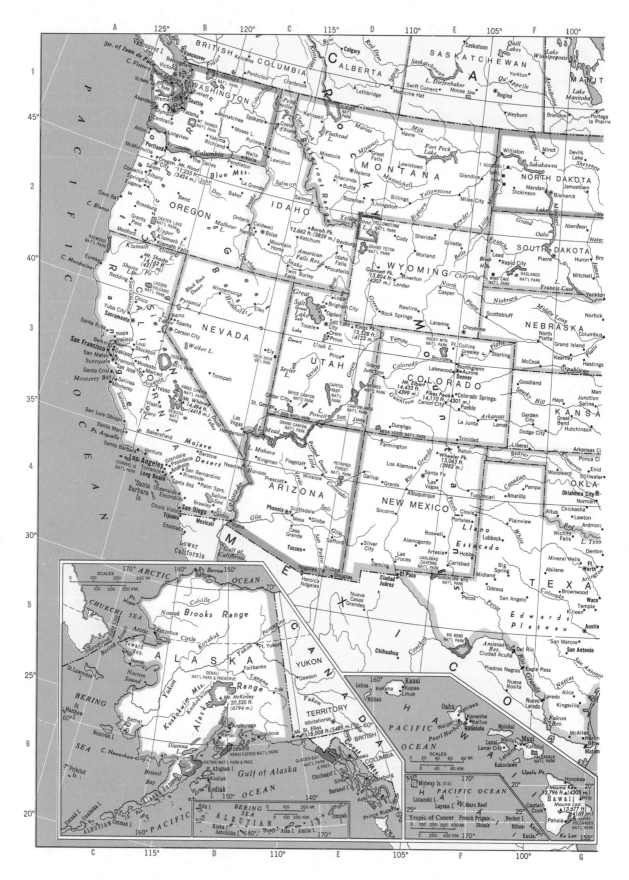

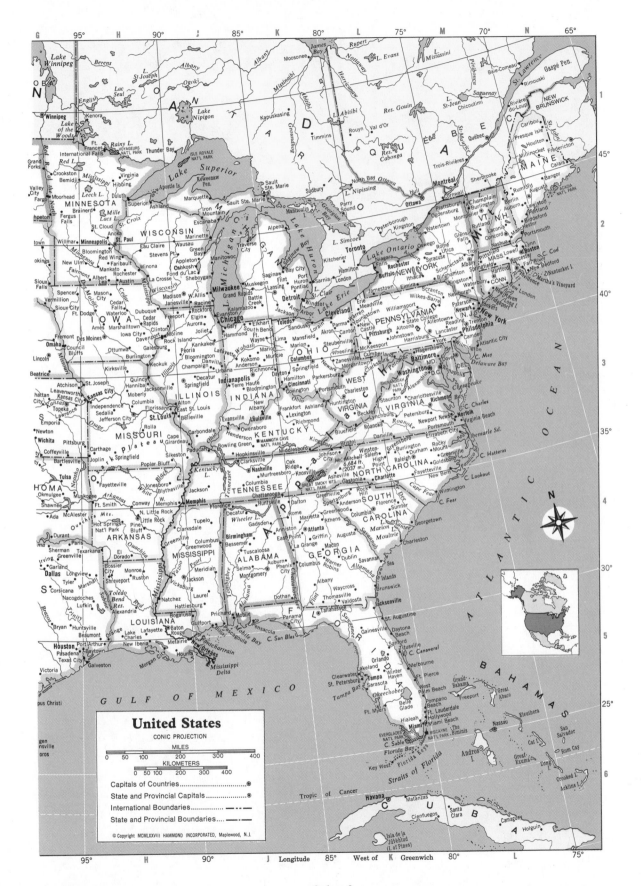

United States

CONIC PROJECTION

MILES

0 50 100   200   300   400

KILOMETERS

0 50 100 200   300   400

Capitals of Countries.....................⊛

State and Provincial Capitals..............◉

International Boundaries.............— ·· —

State and Provincial Boundaries....— · —

© Copyright MCMLXXVIII HAMMOND INCORPORATED, Maplewood, N.J.

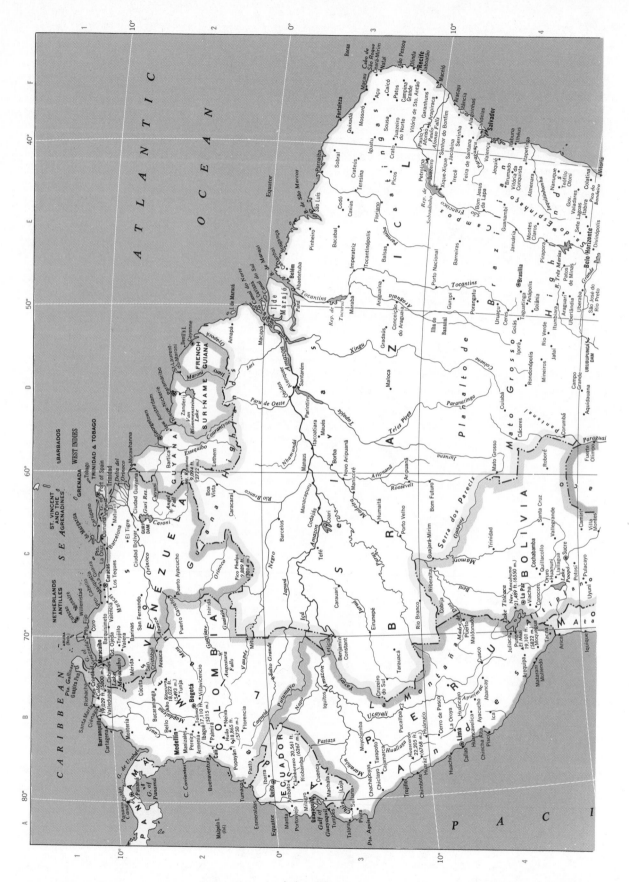

Atlas 10   **South America**

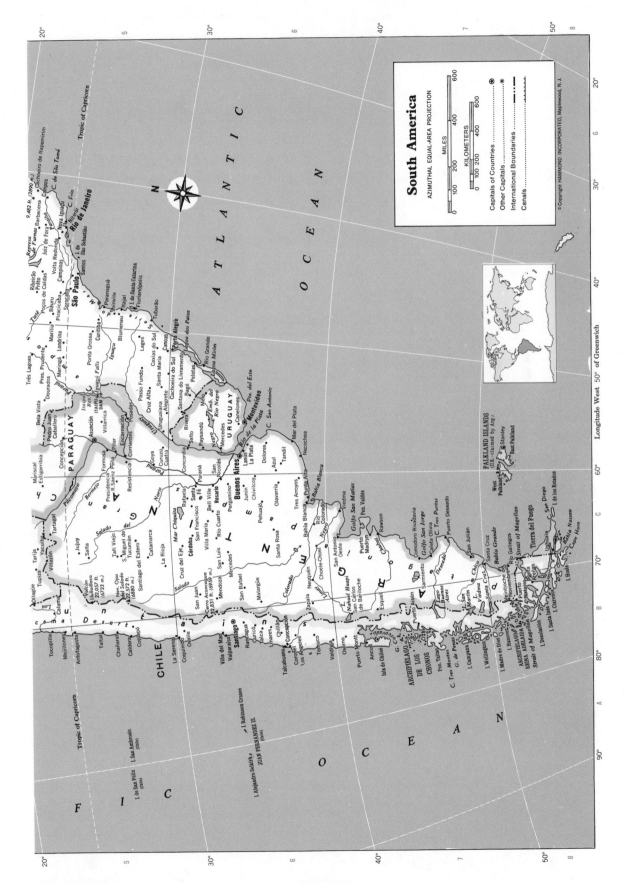

South America

AZIMUTHAL EQUAL-AREA PROJECTION

MILES
0   100   200   400   600

KILOMETERS
0   100   200   400   600

Capitals of Countries
Other Capitals
International Boundaries
Canals

©Copyright HAMMOND INCORPORATED, Maplewood, N.J.

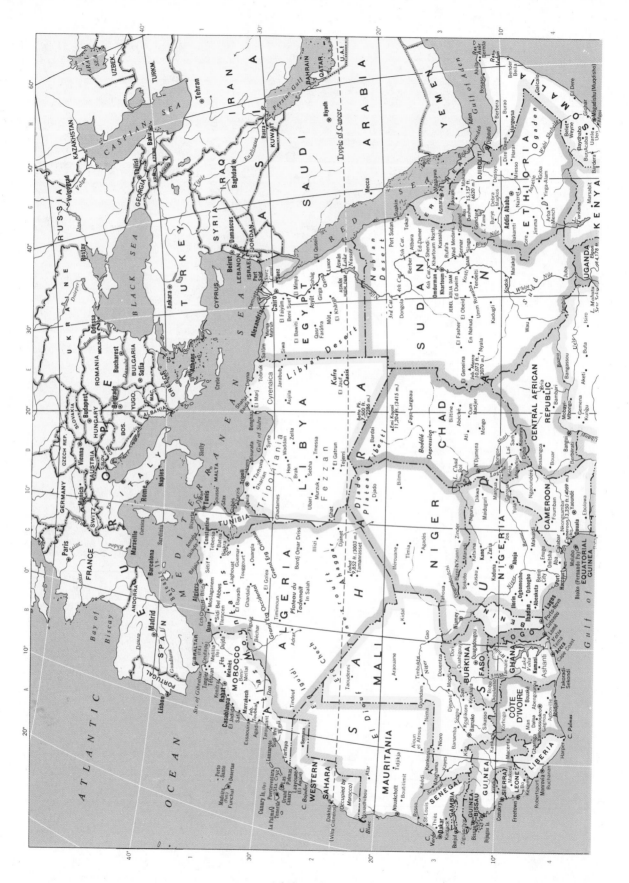

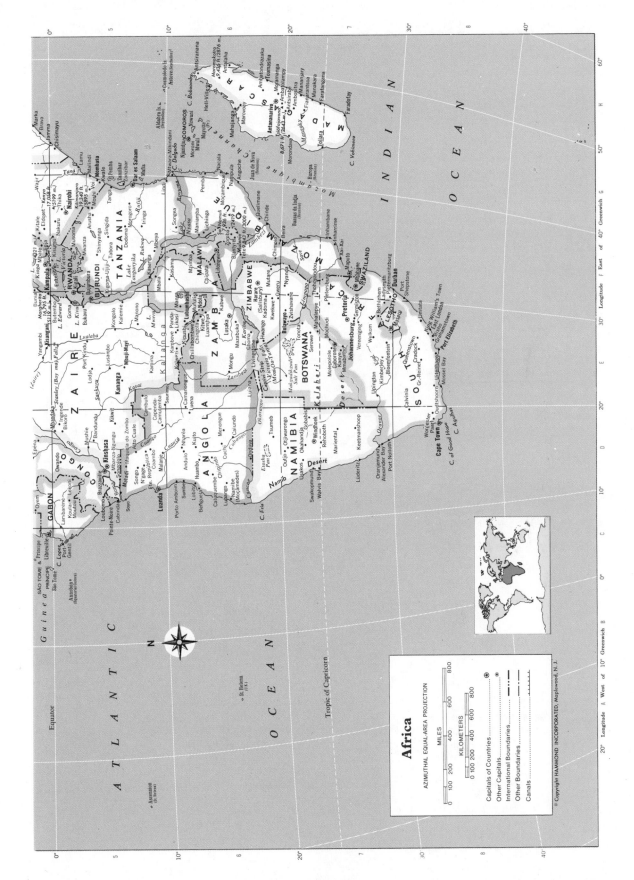

Africa

Atlas 13

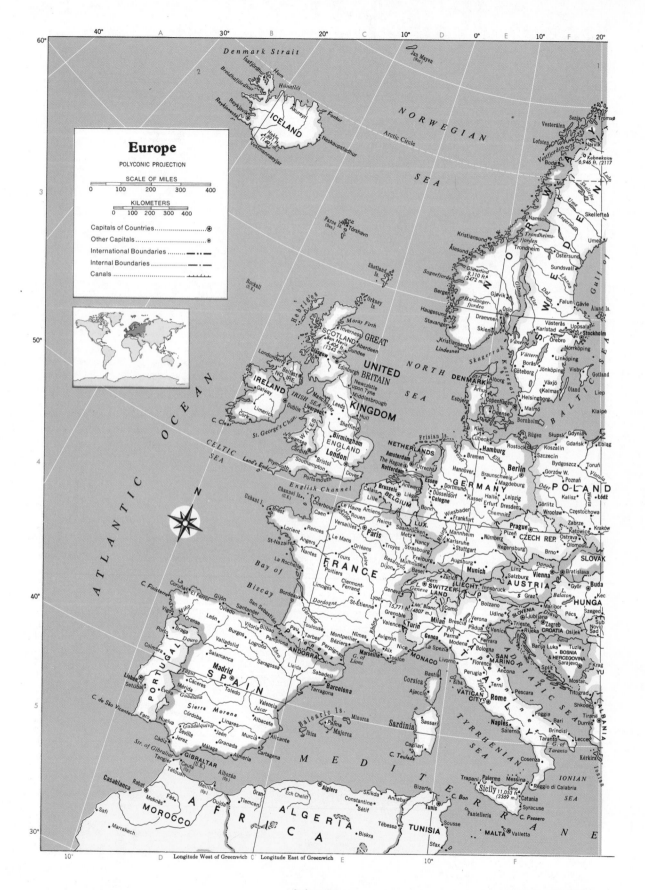

Europe

POLYCONIC PROJECTION

SCALE OF MILES

0 100 200 300 400

KILOMETERS

0 100 200 300 400

Capitals of Countries.....................⊛

Other Capitals ....⊛

International Boundaries ....—··—··—

Internal Boundaries ....—·—·—

Canals ....

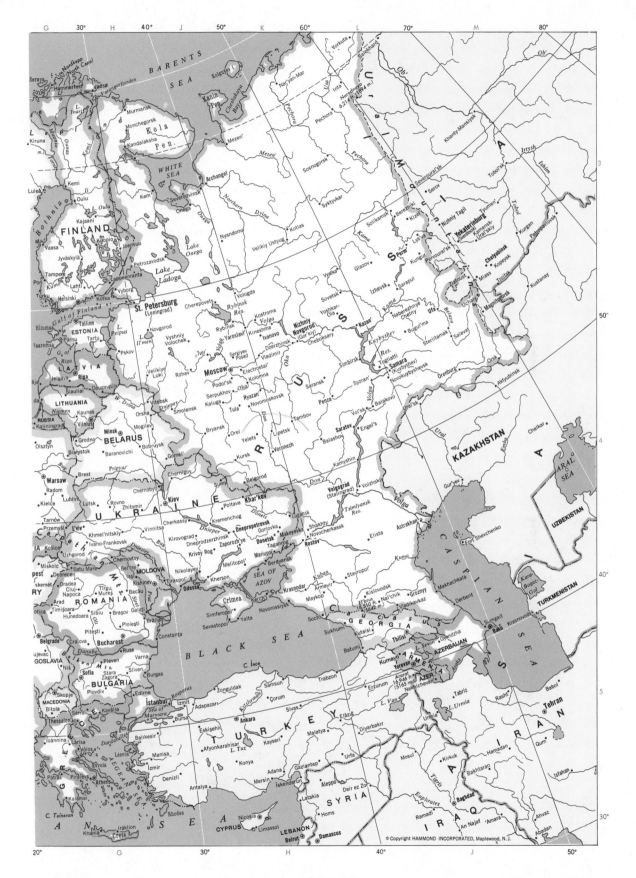

BARENTS

SEA

Nordkapp
(North Cape)
Sørøya
Hammerfest
Varangerfjorden
Vardø
Kolguyev I.
Chëshskaya
Bay
Kanin Pen.
Naryan-Mar

Inari
Murmansk
Monchegorsk
Kandalaksha
Kola
Pen.
Mezen'
Pechora
Pechora
Vorkuta
Inta
Salekhard

Kiruna
Ounas m.
Kemi
Oulu
WHITE
SEA
Archangel
Severodvinsk
Onega
Northern Dvina
Mezen'
Sosnogorsk
Pechora
U
Ob'
Khanty-Mansiysk

Luleå
Bothnia
Kemi
Kem'
Severodvinsk
Nyandoma
Syktyvkar
Solikamsk
Berezniki
Kizel
Serov
Tobol'sk
Irtysh

FINLAND
Oulu
Kajaani
Vaasa
Kuopio
Joensuu
Lake
Onega
Velikiy Ustyug
Kotlas
Kama
Kungur
Nizhniy Tagil
Tyumen'
Trobl
Ishim

Pori
Tampere
Jyväskylä
Lappeenranta
Petrozavodsk
Lake
Ladoga
Vologda
Vyatka
Glazov
Izhevsk
Sarapul
Yekaterinburg
(Sverdlovsk)
Kamensk-
Ural'skiy
Kurgan
Petropavlovsk

Turku
Kotka
Vyborg
St. Petersburg
(Leningrad)
Cherepovets
Rybinsk
Res.
Rybinsk
Volga
Kostroma
Ivanovo
Kineshma
Yoshkar-
Ola
Kazan'
Naberezhnye
Chelny
Ufa
Zlatoust
Miass
Troitsk
Chelyabinsk
Kopeysk
Magnitogorsk
Kustanay

Helsinki
Tallinn
ESTONIA
Pärnu
Tartu
L. Peipus
Novgorod
Vyshniy
Volochek
Tver'
Yaroslavl'
Nizhniy
Novgorod
(Gor'kiy)
Cheboksary
Simbirsk
Kuybyshev
Res.
Togliatti
Samara
(Kuybyshev)
Orenburg
Orsk
Aktyubinsk

Riga
L. Il'men
Pskov
Velikiye
Luki
Rzhev
Sergiyev
Posad
Vladimir
Dzerzhinsk
Saransk
Penza
Syzran'
Novokuybyshevsk
Sterlitamak
Salavat

LATVIA
Jelgava
Daugavpils
Moscow
Electrostal'
Kolomna
Oka
Vol'sk
Balakovo
Ural'sk

LITHUANIA
Šiauliai
Niemen
Vitebsk
Smolensk
Podol'sk
Serpukhov
Ryazan'
Novomoskovsk
Tambov
Saratov
Engel's
Ural

RUSSIA
Kaliningrad
Kaunas
Vilnius
Minsk
Orsha
Mogilev
Dnieper
Tula
Kaluga
Orel
Yelets
Lipetsk
Balashov
Vol'sk
Kamyshin

Olsztyn
Grodno
BELARUS
Baranovichi
Bobruysk
Gomel'
Bryansk
Kursk
Voronezh
Don
Volgograd
(Stalingrad)
Volzhskiy

Warsaw
Radom
Białystok
Brest
Pripyat'
Chernigov
Belgorod
Don
Volga
Astrakhan'
KAZAKHSTAN
Emba
Chelkar
ARAL
SEA

Kielce
Lublin
Lutsk
Rovno
Zhitomir
UKRAINE
Kiev
Chernobyl'
Poltava
Khar'kov
Tsimlyansk
Res.
Elista
Gur'yev
UZBEKISTAN

Tarnów
Przemyśl
L'viv
Khmel'nitskiy
Vinnitsa
Cherkassy
Kremenchug
Dnepropetrovsk
Gorlovka
Lugansk
Shakhty
Novocherkassk
Kuma
Fort Shevchenko

Kraków
Košice
Ivano-Frankovsk
Chernovtsy
Kirovograd
Dneprodzerzhinsk
Zaporozh'ye
Donetsk
Makeyevka
Taganrog
Rostov
Kislovodsk
Makhachkala
CASPIAN

Miskolc
Satu Mare
Uzhgorod
Bel'tsy
Nikolayev
Krivoy Rog
Melitopol'
Mariupol'
Berdyansk
Stavropol'
Armavir
Grozny
Vladikavkaz
Derbent
TURKMENISTAN

Debrecen
Oradea
Cluj-
Napoca
MOLDOVA
Kishinev
Tiraspol'
Kherson
Crimea
SEA OF
AZOV
Kerch'
Krasnodar
Maykop
El'brus
18,510 ft.
(5642 m.)
Sumqayt
Baku
Krasnovodsk
Karar
Bogaz

Arad
Timişoara
Hunedoara
Sibiu
ROMANIA
Bacău
Prut
Siret
Odessa
Simferopol'
Yalta
Sevastopol'
Novorossiysk
Sochi
Sukhumi
Kutaisi
GEORGIA
Tbilisi
Gyandzha
Sevan
AZERBAIJAN

Belgrade
Pitești
Brașov
Ploiești
Brăila
Galați
Constanța
BLACK SEA
Batumi
Kumayri
Yerevan
ARMENIA
AZER.

Craiova
Bucharest
Ruse
Danube
Erzurum
Aragats
16,945 ft.
Nakhichevan'
Tabriz
L. Urmia
Rasht
Babol

ujevac
GOSLAVIA
Niš
Pleven
Stara
Zagora
Sliven
Burgas
Zonguldak
Samsun
Trabzon
Erzurum
Ararat
16,945 ft.
(5165 m.)
Nakhichevan'
Qum
Tehran

Sofia
BULGARIA
Plovdiv
Edirne
İstanbul
İzmit
Adapazarı
L. Van
Mosul
Kirkuk
Hamadan
Bakhtaran

MACEDONIA
Skopje
Bitola
Kavála
Serrai
İzmir
Bursa
Ankara
Eskişehir
Çorum
Sivas
Malatya
Diyarbakır
Urfa
IRAQ
Baghdad
Isfahan

Thessaloníki
Ioánnina
Lárisa
Vólos
Balıkesir
Manisa
Denizli
TURKEY
Afyonkarahisar
L. Tuz
Konya
Kayseri
Gaziantep
Aleppo
Deir ez Zor
Ramadi
An Najaf
Amara
Ahvaz
Abadan

Pátrai
Piraiévs
Athens
Kalámai
İzmir
Antalya
Adana
Mersin
İskenderun
Latakia
Homs
SYRIA
Euphrates
Tigris

C. Taínaron
Iráklion
Crete
Khaniá
Rhodes
Nicosia
CYPRUS
Limassol
LEBANON
Beirut
Damascus
IRAN

AEGEAN
SEA

MEDITERRANEAN
SEA

© Copyright HAMMOND INCORPORATED, Maplewood, N.J.

Europe   **Atlas 15**

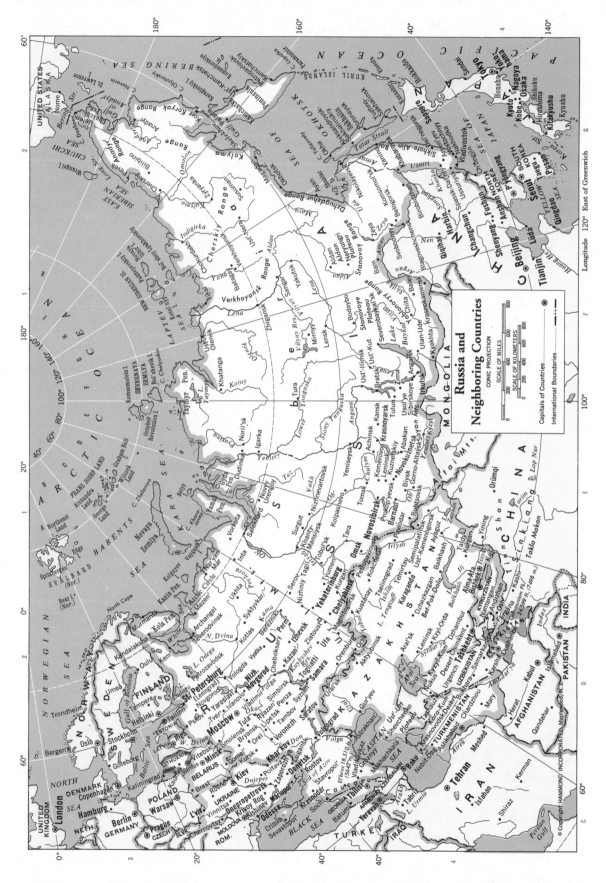

Russia and Neighboring Countries

CONIC PROJECTION

SCALE OF MILES

SCALE OF KILOMETERS

Capitals of Countries ⊛

International Boundaries ·—··—

Atlas 16   **Russia and Neighboring Countries**

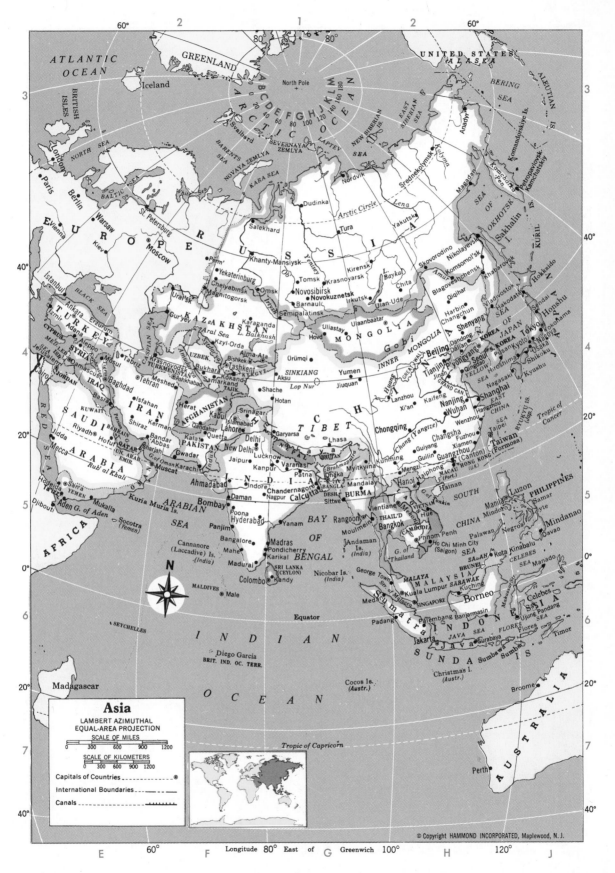

Asia

LAMBERT AZIMUTHAL
EQUAL-AREA PROJECTION

SCALE OF MILES
0   300   600   900   1200

SCALE OF KILOMETERS
0   300   600   900   1200

Capitals of Countries .... ®

International Boundaries ____ ___

Canals _____

© Copyright HAMMOND INCORPORATED, Maplewood, N.J.

Longitude 80° East of G Greenwich 100°

Asia

Atlas 17

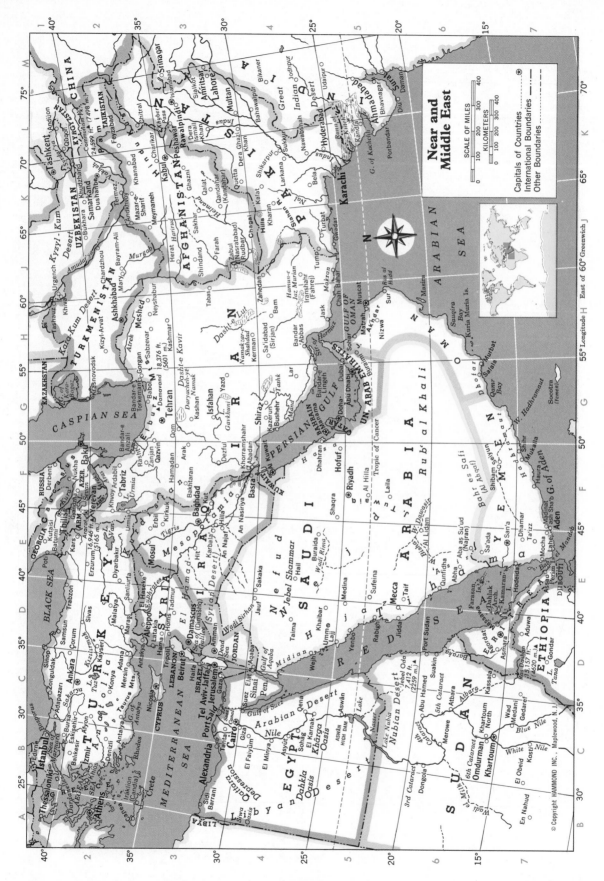

Atlas 18

Near and Middle East

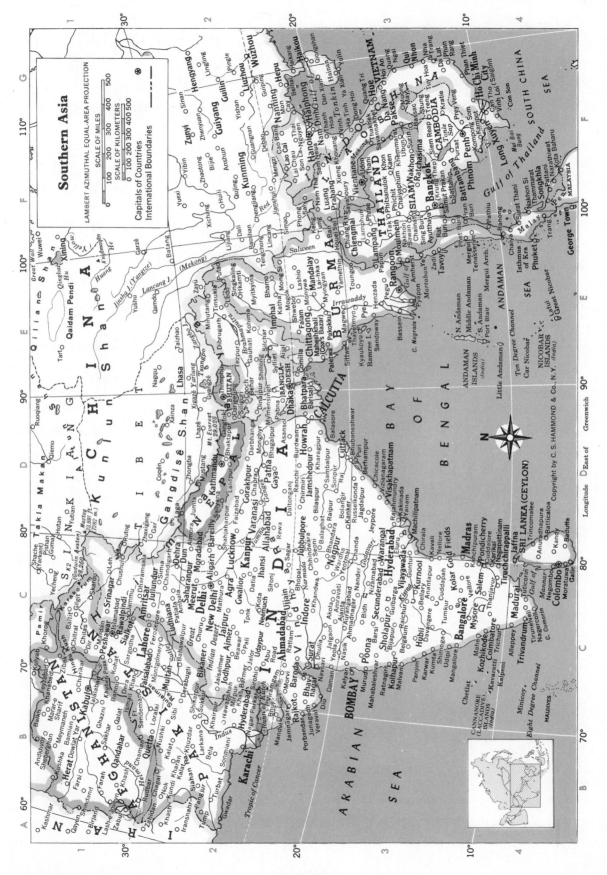

Southern Asia

LAMBERT AZIMUTHAL EQUAL-AREA PROJECTION

SCALE OF MILES
100 200 300 400 500

SCALE OF KILOMETERS
0 100 200 300 400 500

Capitals of Countries
International Boundaries

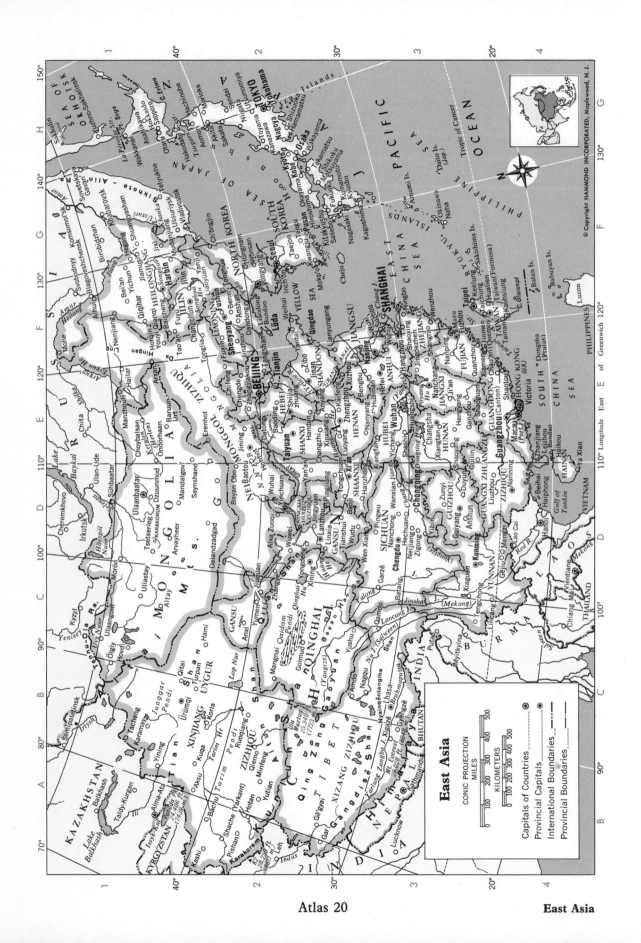

Atlas 20

East Asia

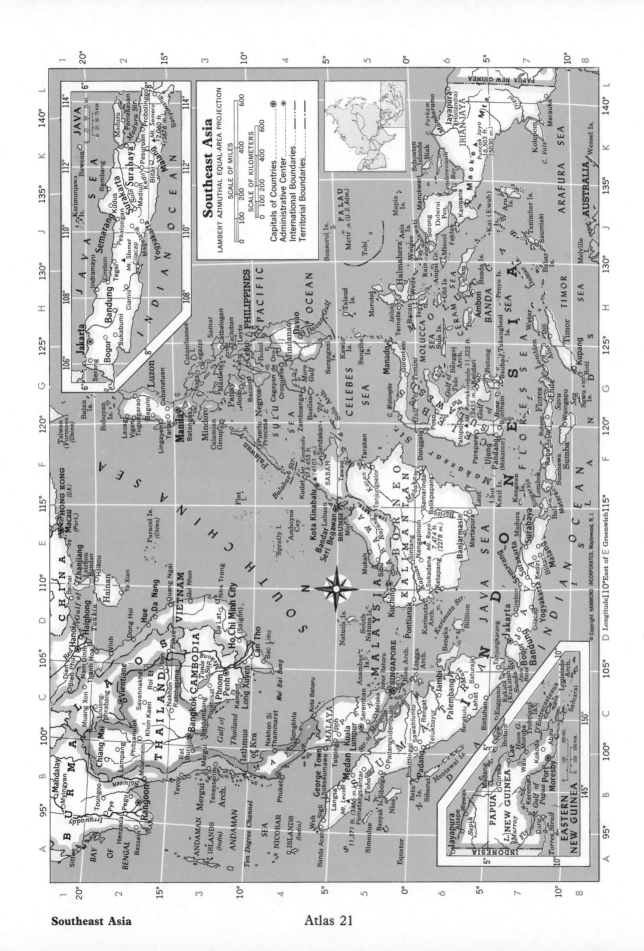

Southeast Asia   Atlas 21

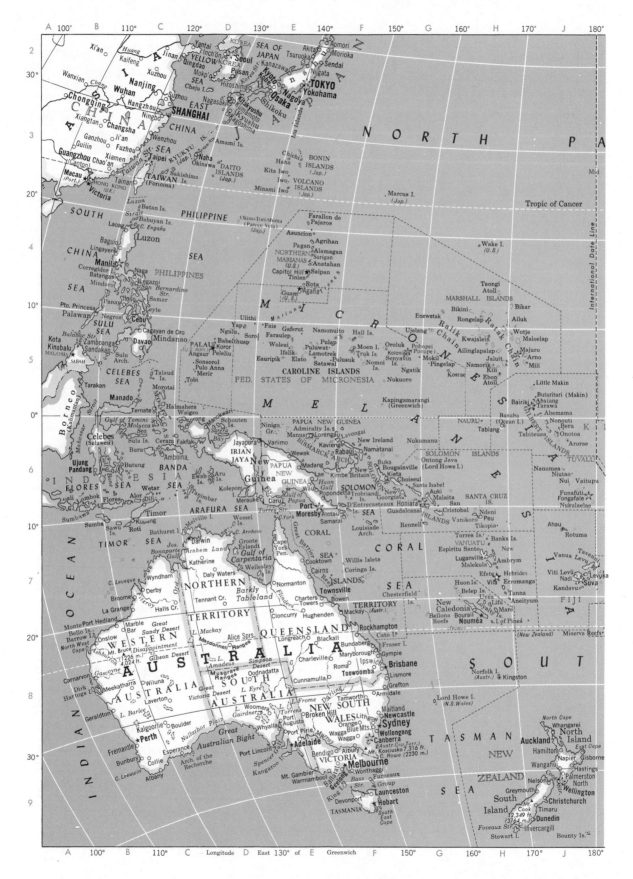

Atlas 22

Pacific Ocean

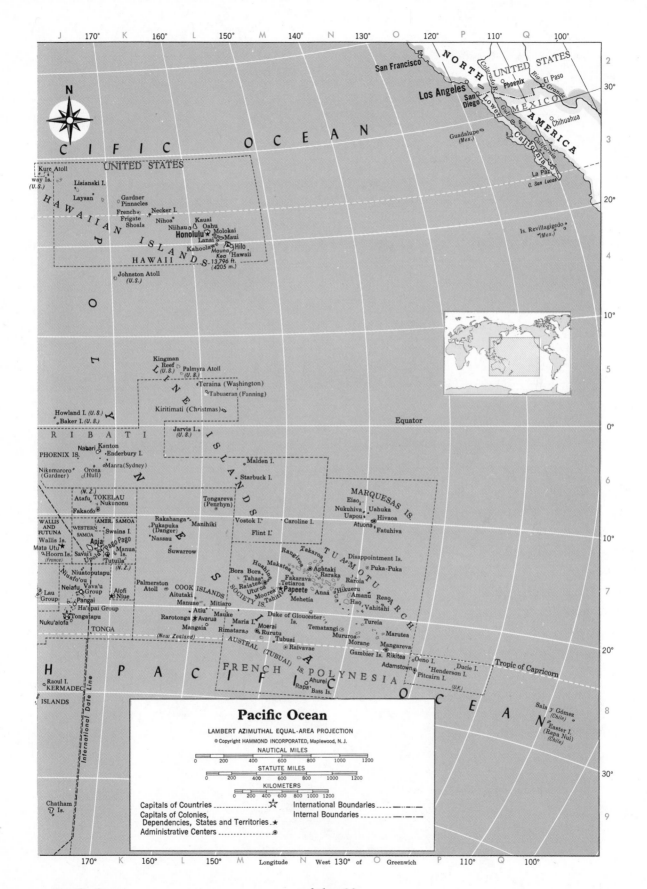

Pacific Ocean

LAMBERT AZIMUTHAL EQUAL·AREA PROJECTION

© Copyright HAMMOND INCORPORATED, Maplewood, N.J.

NAUTICAL MILES

STATUTE MILES

KILOMETERS

Capitals of Countries	☆
Capitals of Colonies, Dependencies, States and Territories	★
Administrative Centers	◉

| International Boundaries | |
| Internal Boundaries | |

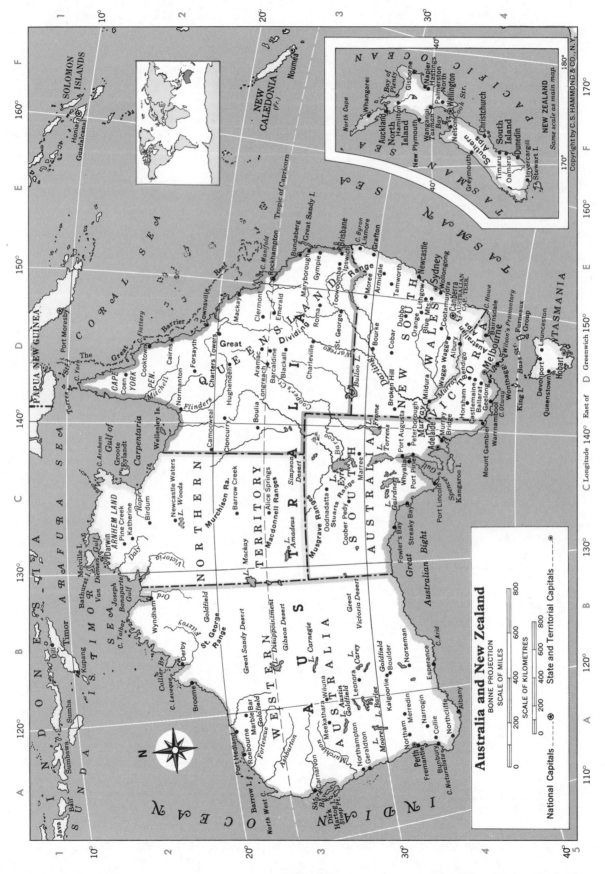

Australia and New Zealand
BONNE PROJECTION
SCALE OF MILES
SCALE OF KILOMETRES

National Capitals ----- ⊛
State and Territorial Capitals ----- •

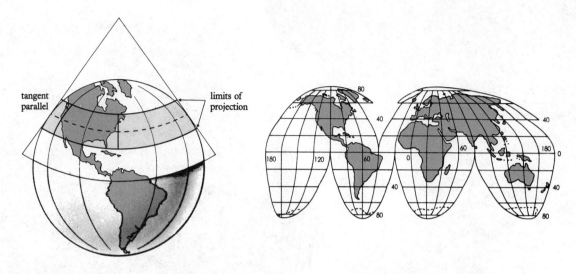

Conic projection

Goode's interrupted homolosine projection

The *conic projection* has straight or slightly curved meridians that converge at the poles (or an imaginary area beyond the poles). It has arc-shaped parallels. Shape and distances are most accurate along the straight or nearly straight meridians. Distortions increase as the meridians begin to curve. The conic projection is most often used for area or large-scale maps, especially in the United States. A popular variation is the *polyconic projection.*

In *azimuthal projections*, one point on the globe, usually the equator or one of the poles, is selected as center. All lines that radiate from the center give true direction relative to the point that is chosen. Because distortion occurs along the outer edges, azimuthal projection is a poor method for mapping the world, but useful for mapping hemispheres. The most common maps using this projection are those that show the polar regions with the pole in the center.

For the most accurate picture of the world, we use *interrupted projections*, such as Goode's projection. Although there is some distortion along the outer edges, interrupted projections are truest in size and space relationships.

Legends. Somewhere on every good map there is a legend that tells what information the cartographer intends to show. No single map can show everything, since it would be too crowded. The legend tells which of many possibilities the cartographer has chosen. It also tells the area the map covers, its projection, its scale, and the symbols used to convey information. In short, the legend tells how to use the map.

One of the most important things on the legend is the scale. It is the ratio of distances on the map to actual distances on Earth. A *verbal scale* gives the relationship in words: *1 inch equals 100 miles.* A *graphic scale* gives the ratio on a line or bar. Most of the scales on road maps are graphic scales.

The legend also identifies the *symbols* used in the map. For example, the capital of a country or a state may be distinguished from other cities by use of a star inside a dot. On road maps, highways, state roads, and country roads are marked with solid lines, which may also be of different colors or widths. One of the most important map symbols is *color.* Color is especially important on topographic maps to show elevation.

Science and

Mathematics

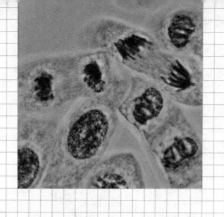

Biology

The immense variety of living things is, surprisingly, based on a few basic structures and a limited number of fundamental chemical operations. In this article, you will first encounter the most general features of life and then see how they have been combined to form the different types of living things that inhabit Earth.

Biology made a major breakthrough when scientists came to understand that all living things (except viruses, which sometimes are classed as not living) are composed of cells. Although there are many different types of cells, much of their structure and function remains the same, from microscopic bacteria to giant sequoias.

A later breakthrough has shown an even closer relationship among all living things: all life (including the viruses) is based on one of two closely related chemicals, either DNA or RNA. In fact, RNA is common to virtually all living things, although DNA is probably the more fundamental of the two giant nucleic acids.

The cell

The *cell* is a highly complex organization of matter in which the basic processes characteristic of life are performed. Monera and Protista may consist of a single cell; Plantae and Animalia, including man, may consist of billions of cells. Almost all cells are microscopic.

The cell is life's minimum unit of structure and function. Each cell must perform the processes we associate with whole organisms: taking in, storing, and releasing energy; taking in materials and metabolizing them for growth; repair; sense perception; response to stimuli; movement; and reproduction.

It is impossible to generalize about the size and shape of cells. The variety of shapes corresponds to the functions performed. Human skin cells are flat and platelike, while nerve cells are very long. A single nerve cell in a large animal may be several feet long. A bacterium may be 0.4 microns in diameter. The average diameter of a cell in man is about 10 microns (0.01 millimeters).

Organization of the cell. While there is a variety of cellular shapes and sizes, cells have certain common features. Each cell is covered by a thin *membrane* that generally allows only what the cell requires to pass through. The membrane encloses the *cytoplasm*, which itself contains many *organelles* (small organs). All cells also contain *chromosomal material* that, in many cells, is organized within a *nucleus*.

Cell membrane and cell wall. The outer boundary of a cell is a very thin, two-layered membrane. This extremely fragile and complex structure is less than 1/100,000 of a millimeter thick. This organelle controls and regulates everything that passes into and out of the cell. The membrane is made up of *protein* and *lipid* (fat) molecules. These molecules also act as adjustable pores through which molecules can selectively pass.

Multicellular organisms would collapse under their

own weight without a supporting structure of some type. Some animals have a skeletal system. Plants derive additional support from a rigid *cell wall* that lies outside the cell membrane. While there may be specialized structures that support the entire organism, each plant cell has its own wall. The function of the wall is mainly mechanical, since it is generally composed of inert cellulose. The wall does, however, play a small role in controlling the passage of material into and out of the cell.

The nucleus.

The nucleus is usually the largest and most distinct organelle within the cell. Most cells contain a single nucleus, but some cells are multinucleated. The nucleus is roughly spherical and denser than the cytoplasm that surrounds it. The nucleus is held together by a double-layered nuclear membrane. This membrane has many pores that allow material to pass in and out of the nucleus.

The nucleus contains a tangled network of material called *chromatin*. Chromatin strands come together during cell division to form a number of threadlike bodies called *chromosomes*. There is a definite number of chromosomes for each species of organism, although plants often have double, triple, or even higher multiples of their species number. Chromosomes are the carriers of the cell's heredity. They direct and guide the development of the organism and maintain its order and organization. Chromatin is made up of strands of *DNA* (*deoxyribonucleic acid*) and proteins. DNA controls the hereditary characteristics of all living things and directs the production of proteins.

A spherical body called the *nucleolus* is visible within the nucleus when the cell is not dividing. The nucleolus is composed of granules rich in *RNA* (*ribonucleic acid*). RNA is essential to the formation of proteins by the cell. Cells that contain nuclei and chromosomes are called *eukaryotes*. Bacteria are simpler in organization. While they contain DNA, they have no nuclei, nuclear membranes, or chromosomes. The hereditary material of these *prokaryotes* is within the cytoplasm.

Types of cells in the human body

Nerve cell

Muscle cells
striated (voluntary)

smooth (involuntary)

cardiac

Bone cell

Reproductive cells
ovum

sperm

Blood cells
red blood cells

white blood cells

neutrophil

monocyte

eosinophil

lymphocyte

basophil

Gland cell

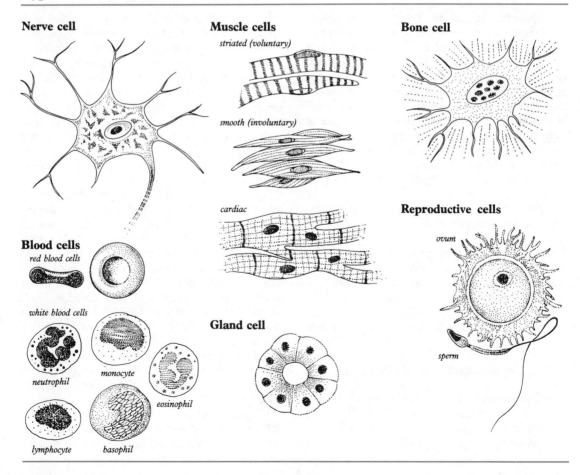

Cytoplasm. Cytoplasm is the cellular material enclosed by the cell membrane and outside the nuclear membrane. Within the cytoplasm are the several cellular organelles. The cytoplasm itself is made up mostly of water, in which are suspended carbohydrates, proteins, lipids, and other smaller molecules. Observations of living cells have shown that the viscosity of the same portion of cytoplasm varies. At one time, it will flow freely; at another, it appears to be thick and jellylike.

Cytoplasm is a *colloidal suspension*. A *colloid* is a mixture in which the motion of the particles of the solvent and the particle size of the solute (dissolved substance) are delicately balanced. The solute particles are not so large as those of a suspension, but they do not exist as individual molecules, as do the particles of a solution. The particles do not sink to the bottom of the solution unless the system itself is changed by an outside influence such as heat.

Cytoplasm is sometimes called *protoplasm*, which is the old name for all of the contents of the cell (including, of course, the cytoplasm). The word *protoplasm* reflects the incorrect idea that cell membranes were not truly living substance.

Endoplasmic reticulum. Every cell, particularly those involved in the formation of proteins, contains a network of channels bounded by membranes that run throughout the cytoplasm. This *endoplasmic reticulum* is a series of tubes that are connected to the nuclear membrane. The tubes provide a channel from the nucleus through the cytoplasm to the outside of the cell by way of the cell membrane. There are two types of endoplasmic reticulum. One is smooth; the other is rough or granular. The organelles that give the rough form its granular texture are *ribosomes*. All of the substances made within the cell must be transported to all parts of the cell for use. The main functions of the endoplasmic reticulum appear to be storage, separation, and transportation of the substances within the cell.

Ribosomes. These tiny, grainy organelles are the protein factories of the cell. Each cell contains thousands of them and in some, ribosomes may make up a quarter of the mass of the cell. Most of the cell's RNA is located in these structures. While the internal structure of ribosomes cannot be seen even under an elec-

tron microscope, two forms have been identified. One form is attached to the endoplasmic reticulum and transfers proteins to these membranes for transportation. The other form is free floating and releases proteins directly into the cytoplasm. Cells that form substances that are secreted through the cell membrane have the greatest systems of granular endoplasmic reticulum.

Golgi apparatus. Sometimes referred to as the Golgi complex, or Golgi bodies, these organelles are flat, saclike structures near the nucleus. Electron microscopy has shown that they are multilayered structures composed of smooth membranes that are probably the same as the membranes of the endoplasmic reticulum. It is thought the Golgi apparatus "packages" proteins that are secreted from the cell. While the mechanism is not known, it is thought that the molecules to be secreted are enclosed in membranous envelopes. These "packages" are sent to the surface of the cell, where they move out of the cell.

Lysosomes. These organelles seem to change their size and shape depending upon activity. They appear to be tiny drops of fluid surrounded by a membrane. The fluid consists of digestive enzymes whose function it is to break down protein, fat, and carbohydrate molecules into simpler substances. These reactions occur within the lysosome and are used in other parts of the cell. When the lysosome membrane is ruptured and the enzymes are released into the cytoplasm, the cell quickly breaks apart. The digestive enzymes also rid the cell of undigested material. The undigested material remains within the lysosome and the entire body moves to the cell surface where the waste is ejected through the membrane.

Mitochondria. *Mitochondria* are sausage-shaped structures that are the source of most body heat and energy. The mitochondria are the powerhouses of the cell and are the second largest organelles in the cell after the nucleus. Electron microscope studies have revealed their remarkably intricate structure. The outer surface of a mitochondrium is covered by a double-layered membrane. The inner surface is folded into a series of parallel ridges called *cristae*. This infolding increases the interior area of each mitochondrium. Chemical reactions take place along the cristae that produce the high energy-yielding compounds that the cells require to carry on their functions. It appears that mitochondria also control the amount of water, calcium, and other substances within the cell; break down and recycle proteins, fats, and carbohydrates; and form urea.

The mitochondria have their own genetic structure, different from that of the cell. Some scientists think they evolved separately and live in symbiosis with the cell.

Organic compounds in cells			
carbohydrates	**proteins**	**lipids**	**nucleic acids**
sugars	enzymes	fats	DNA
starches	collagen	oils	RNA
cellulose	keratin	waxes	

Some structural components of cells and their principal functions

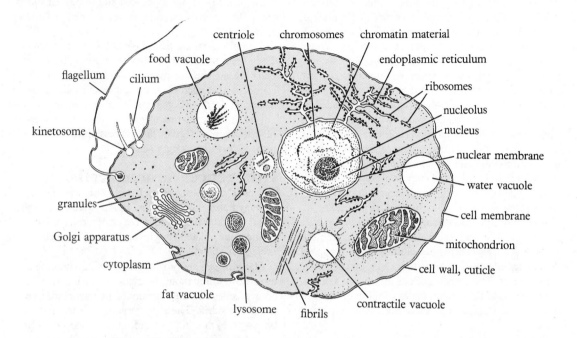

	Structure	Function
Nucleus	chromosomes	gene carriers, ultimate control of cell activities
	nucleolus	auxiliary to protein synthesis
	nuclear membrane	traffic control to and from cytoplasm
Cytoplasm	endoplasmic reticulum	secretion channels, connection between cell parts, attachment surfaces
	mitochondria	site of respiration
	ribosomes	site of protein synthesis
	Golgi bodies	site of specific secretion synthesis
	lysosomes	stores of hydrolytic enzymes
	chloroplasts	site of photosynthesis
	centrioles	auxiliary to cell division
	kinetosomes	anchor and control of flagella, cilia
	myofibrils	contraction
	neurofibrils	conduction
	granules, vacuoles	transport, storage, processing centers
Surface	plasma membrane	traffic control to and from cell
	cell wall	support, protection, cell shape
	cuticles, pellicles	support, protection, waterproofing
	cilia, flagella	locomotion, current creation, feeding
	pseudopodia	locomotion, feeding, phagocytosis

Plastids and vacuoles. *Plastids* are special organelles found in most plants and one-celled organisms. They are associated with the formation and storage of substances important in the metabolism of that cell. The green pigment chlorophyll occurs in *chloroplasts*, which are the sites of photosynthesis. *Chromoplasts* manufacture and store the pigments that give fruits, vegetables, and leaves their color. *Leucoplasts* are colorless and are the sites where fats and proteins are stored and glucose is converted to starch.

Vacuoles are cavities in the cytoplasm surrounded by membranes. They contain water with various other substances in solution. Large vacuoles are not found in most animal cells, but mature plant cells contain one or more in the cytoplasm. Small vacuoles may function to digest food, store food, and dispose of wastes. The *contractile vacuoles* of some single-celled organisms remove excess water by their rhythmic contractions.

Centrioles and kinetosomes. The *centrioles* are a pair of small, cylindrical bodies that lie near the nucleus. A centriole consists of a cluster of nine groups of delicate tubelike structures, with each group containing three tubules. The elements of one member of a centriole pair always lie at right angles to those of another. The centrioles play an important role in the division of the cell.

Some cells have organelles called *cilia*. At the base of each cilium is a *kinetosome*, the structure of which resembles a centriole. Some biologists think that both centrioles and kinetosomes function as units of locomotion within a cell, similar to the muscle cells of multicellular animals.

Microtubules and microfilaments. *Microtubules* are a series of long, thin cylinders that support, stiffen, and give shape to cells. They also assist in transporting substances in and out of the cell and in cellular movement. The cilia of certain cells are formed of bundles of microtubules.

Microfilaments are threadlike fibers made of protein. They seem to have the ability to contract like muscle. Cilia are attached to microfilaments. The contracting action of the microfilaments cause the cilia to wave back and forth. Microfilaments also seem to be involved in the formation of *pseudopodia*—the streaming of cytoplasm that gives the impression that the organism is crawling along a surface.

Differences among cells. All cells
are made up of the same basic substances: proteins, carbohydrates, nucleic acids, lipids, water, and salts. There are, however, differences among cells; these differences are related to whether certain organelles are present or absent.

Moneran cells are prokaryotic. The chromosome material floats throughout the cytoplasm. Monerans have no organelles that are surrounded by membranes, such as mitochondria. These prokaryotic cells cannot combine with each other to form multicellular organisms.

Protist cells are eukaryotic. They have a nucleus surrounded by a nuclear membrane. They also have many complex organelles that are separated from the cytoplasm by membranes. These organelles can be found in both plant and animal cells.

Fungus cells are all eukaryotic and can combine to

Differences among cells

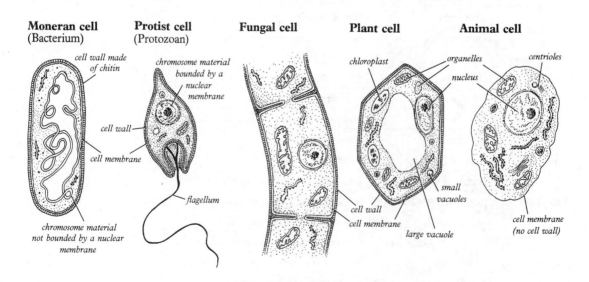

Moneran cell
(Bacterium)

Protist cell
(Protozoan)

Fungal cell

Plant cell

Animal cell

cell wall made of chitin

chromosome material bounded by a nuclear membrane

cell wall

cell membrane

flagellum

chromosome material not bounded by a nuclear membrane

chloroplast

organelles

nucleus

centrioles

small vacuoles

cell wall
cell membrane

large vacuole

cell membrane
(no cell wall)

form simple, multicellular organisms. These cells are bounded by a cell wall made of chitin. Each fungus cell is usually multinucleated. The cell walls do not completely close when the cells grow and develop. Cytoplasm can circulate freely from cell to cell.

Plant cells are eukaryotic and have rigid cell walls made of cellulose. Each cell has a nucleus and many organelles. Plastids are found only in plant cells and in some protists. Each plant cell also has a large vacuole containing salt and water to help to keep the cell wall rigid and give support to the leaves and stem.

Animal cells are also eukaryotic. They have no cell walls and no plastids. Centrioles are organelles unique to animal cells.

Microscopes

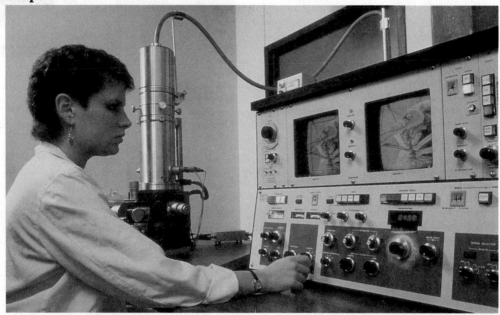

A scanning electron microscope can provide much greater detail than a light microscope. The electron microscope uses a beam of electrons to magnify an object as much as 200,000 times. The image of a scanned object is produced on the screen of a monitor.

For almost 300 years, everything that was learned about cells came from studies with the light microscope. Samples of material were cut into thin sections and stained with various dyes. The stains made certain parts of the cell show up more clearly, but they also tended to kill the cell. In the past few years, new tools and techniques have been developed that allow biologists higher magnifications, greater resolving power, and the ability to study living tissue. (The resolving power of a microscope is the limit of its useful magnification. Beyond this limit, the image is blurred.)

The Phase-Contrast Microscope is used to study living cells. This microscope is constructed in a way that causes a portion of the light passing through to slow down relative to the rest of the light. This portion of light is "out of phase." The changes in refractive power of this light show up as differences in light and shade.

Electron microscopes use electrons to form images instead of light waves. Electrons travel with a wave motion similar to that of light, but their wavelengths are over 100,000 times shorter. Therefore, their resolving power is much greater. In general, an electron microscope is an evacuated tube with an electron gun at one end. The gun accelerates a beam of electrons, which is directed onto a specimen by electromagnetic and electrostatic fields that act as lenses. The electrons interact with the atoms of the specimen, enter other lenses, and finally form an image on a viewing screen or on photographic film. The screen glows when struck by the electron beam and a camera beneath the screen records the images. Most instruments can cover a range in magnification from $50\times$ to $800,000\times$. However, standard *transmission* electron microscopes, as well as standard light microscopes, can focus only a limited depth of the specimen.

The *scanning* electron microscope is used to study the surface of a specimen. A beam of electrons moves over the surface, producing an effect similar to that of a television camera. This provides a very detailed three-dimensional picture of a living subject. Magnification can range from $10\times$ to $200,000\times$.

Cell functions

The materials needed by a cell to carry on its functions must come from outside the cell. Many of the substances produced by the cell, as well as the waste products of its activities, must pass out of the cell.

Diffusion is a process by which molecules will move from an area of higher concentration to areas of lower concentration. The cell membrane acts as a barrier to diffusion, however. The membrane is *semipermeable*. Water, carbon dioxide, oxygen, and other small molecules can pass easily through the pores in the membrane. Larger molecules, such as sugar, can pass through slowly, and still larger molecules, such as proteins and fats, cannot pass through at all.

The interior of a cell is basically made up of water. So is the environment outside the cell. The term *osmosis* describes the diffusion of water through a semipermeable membrane. The concentration of water molecules both within the cell and its environment will determine the direction of water movement. In an *isotonic* solution, the concentration of water molecules in the solution is equal to the concentration of water molecules in the cell. Osmosis will cause water to flow both in and out and the cell will not change.

In a *hypotonic* solution or environment, water concentration is higher in the solution than in the cell. Distilled water is hypotonic to red blood cells. Water will flow into the cells causing their contents to be diluted. If the difference in concentration is great enough, water will continue to move into the cells until they rupture. The cell walls of plant cells prevent them from rupturing. The excess water causes them to stiffen instead. The stiffness of plants that is caused by

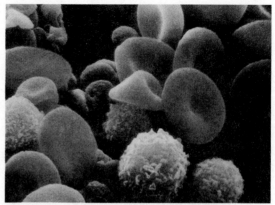

Blood cells are in balance with the pressure of the plasma around them. If the concentration of water molecules in the plasma is either higher or lower than in the cells, water will flow through the cell membranes until the cell is again in balance with the surrounding plasma.

pressure of water is called *turgor*, or *turgor pressure*.

Salt water is *hypertonic* to red blood cells. A hypertonic solution is one in which the concentration of water molecules in the solution is lower than the water concentration in the cell. Water will move by osmosis from the cell to its environment. If the difference in concentration is great enough, the cell will continue to lose water, shrivel, and die. *Plasmolysis* is the condition that results when cells shrink from a loss of water.

There are situations in which molecules pass in and out of cells against the pressure of osmosis and diffusion. The cell must use energy to pull particles from an area of lower concentration to one of higher concentration. This process, called *active transport*, allows the cell to eliminate substances that would be harmful in high concentrations and to bring in food particles in high concentrations.

Respiration

Cells perform chemical work, which includes synthesizing molecules and other chemical reactions that allow the cell to perform its activities. All cells obtain their required energy from the chemical bonds of the same molecule, ATP (adenosine triphosphate). In addition, all cells manufacture their own ATP. Energy is required to form ATP. The main source of this energy is the compound *glucose*. Certain organisms, called *autotrophs*, can transform light energy into the chemical energy of glucose, and use glucose to form the chemical bond energy of ATP. Other organisms, *heterotrophs*, cannot use light energy and must use energy in the bonds of organic molecules formed by other cells. Heterotrophic organisms digest or break down these large molecules into simpler glucose molecules.

Photosynthesis.

Autotrophic cells are found in green plants. Certain bacteria are also autotrophic. The structures within autotrophic cells that allow them to transform light energy are the *chloroplasts*. There may be as many as 50 chloroplasts in the cell of a leaf. Photosynthesis begins with the absorption of light by the *chlorophyll* in the chloroplasts.

Photosynthesis takes place in two steps or phases. The first phase requires the presence of light. During this *light reaction* phase, red wavelengths of light are absorbed by chlorophyll. This energy is used to split water molecules. The chemical energy released by this reaction is stored in two compounds called ATP and NADP. This stored energy is used in the second step of photosynthesis, which does not require light. The *dark reaction* involves synthesizing needed compounds. The energy stored in the chemical bonds of ATP and NADP is used to combine carbon dioxide with other molecules to form glucose, other carbohydrates, amino acids, fats, and proteins. Photosynthesis can be described by the following equation:

$$\text{carbon dioxide} + \text{water} \xrightarrow{\text{light } + \text{ chlorophyll}} \text{glucose} + \text{oxygen} + \text{water}$$

$$6CO_2 + 12H_2O \longrightarrow C_6H_{12}O_6 + 6O_2 + 6H_2O$$

ATP and respiration.

ATP is the energy-storing molecule of the cell. A molecule of ATP consists of an adenosine group with three phosphate groups bonded to it and forming a "tail." The bond between the second and third phosphate groups is the high energy bond. When this bond is broken, energy is released and the third phosphate group is freed. ADP (adenosine diphosphate) is formed. When energy is available, ADP will combine with a free phosphate, reforming ATP. Energy is thus stored for future use.

The sum total of all chemical reactions that take food molecules apart and transfer their energy to ATP is called *respiration*. Respiration is described in two steps or phases, *anaerobic* and *aerobic*. All cells are capable of performing the anaerobic phase; most cells can perform both phases.

Anaerobic respiration does not require oxygen. In this phase, glucose molecules undergo a series of chemical reactions. A glucose molecule containing six carbon atoms is split into two molecules of pyruvic acid ($C_3H_4O_3$), each containing three carbons. The energy from two molecules of ATP is used during these reactions. However, four molecules of ATP are formed by this process. For every molecule of glucose split

Photosynthesis and respiration

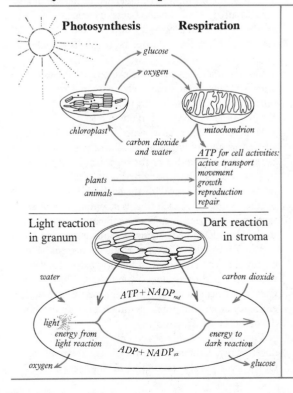

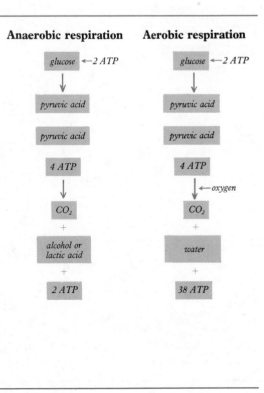

into two molecules of pyruvic acid, there is a gain of two molecules of ATP. This anaerobic phase is similar to those reactions that occur during the fermentation of yeast. The *glycolysis* reaction in muscle cells is also anaerobic. In this series of reactions, the starch glycogen is split into two glucose molecules. These are split into molecules of lactic acid.

Aerobic respiration is the second phase of cellular respiration. Oxygen is required to complete the chemical reactions involved. In this phase, the two pyruvic acid molecules formed in phase one are broken down into carbon dioxide and water. When the bonds of pyruvic acid are broken, 38 molecules of ATP have been formed from the one original glucose molecule. Sixty percent of the available energy in a glucose molecule has been made available to the cell. Carbon dioxide is given off at different stages in these reactions. Water is formed at the end, when hydrogen made available from the decomposition of the pyruvic acid combines with oxygen. Without oxygen, these reactions could not be completed and the death of cells would result, although cells live for a time using anaerobic respiration.

Enzymes and respiration. An important property of chemical reactions in the cell is

that they usually occur in sequence. Most of the chemical changes take place in steps. Often 20 or more individual reactions are involved. This "production line" saves both energy and raw materials and provides the energy to produce the next reaction. A sequence of reactions enables the cell to make full use of the compounds and energy available.

Chemical compounds called *enzymes* provide the energy to start the reaction and to control the rate of the reactions within the temperature range tolerated by the substance within the cell. Enzymes are proteins and act as *catalysts*. They cause chemical reactions to occur without being changed themselves. In addition, these organic catalysts are specific. One enzyme can only catalyze one specific reaction.

In some situations, enzymes can function only when associated with smaller molecules called *coenzymes*. Certain B vitamins are coenzymes and are essential to our diets because they cannot be synthesized by cells. Enzymes are proteins and are synthesized in the cell by the series of reactions involving DNA and RNA. All energy transformations are dependent upon the ability of DNA to implement the genetic code of the cell. The molecules that react with an enzyme attach to it, and are called the *substrate*. The enzyme-molecule combination is called the *enzyme-substrate complex*.

Enzymes, coenzymes, ATP, and vitamins function in such a way that some of the basic materials needed for respiration are available at the end of the process as well as at the beginning. In other words, although energy is used, some of the same chemicals that are needed to start the process are also a result of the process. For this reason, the set of reactions is called a *cycle*.

One common name for this cycle is the *Krebs cycle*, after Sir Hans Adolf Krebs, who first described it. Another name is the *citric-acid cycle*, since citric acid is the first product produced in the first step of the cycle.

Some other chemicals needed in the cycle are destroyed as energy is produced. These chemicals must be supplied by the diet of the organism if they cannot be produced in other specialized cells because they are destroyed at each "turn" of the cycle. The key chemical that is destroyed each time is a combination of acetic acid and a coenzyme. This combination is produced in the breakdown of proteins, carbohydrates, and fats.

The Krebs cycle liberates about 60 percent of the energy that was contained in the original molecules of the acetic acid-coenzyme combination. This is extremely efficient. It is far better, for example, than the efficiency of an automobile getting energy by breaking down molecules of gasoline.

The Krebs cycle is not the only way that cells produce energy, although it is the most important way. Other processes also produce ATP for energy.

The ADP-ATP cycle

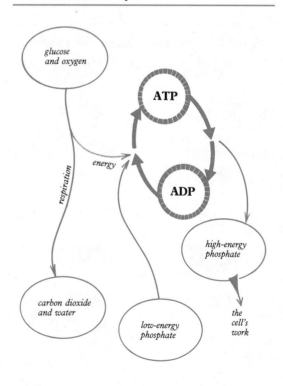

188

DNA

DNA, or deoxyribonucleic acid, is found only in the chromosomes of the cell. The amount of DNA is remarkably constant from cell to cell within an organism and within a single species. Only the egg cells and sperm cells contain a different amount: half the normal amount of DNA (and half the number of chromosomes) found in other body cells.

Proteins and ribonucleic acid (RNA), which are also found in the chromosomes, vary considerably in the amounts found in different tissues within a species. However, they are associated with DNA in carrying and transferring information.

The Watson-Crick model. DNA is
a polymer with a high molecular weight, a giant molecule formed from a few simple molecules linked repeatedly by chemical bonds. The repeating units that form the molecule are nucleotides, each built from similar components: a phosphate group, a 5-carbon sugar, deoxyribose, and a nitrogenous base. The base may be any one of four—the purines adenine (A) or guanine (G) or the pyrimidines cytosine (C) and thymine (T). The nucleotides are connected by a bond between the phosphate group of one and the adjacent sugar (deoxyribose) of the next.

Various studies, including x-ray diffraction analyses by Maurice Wilkins, led James Watson and F.H.C. Crick to propose in 1953 the *double helix* structure of the DNA molecule. A double helix is something like a twisted ladder or zipper; the sides are made of the linked sugar-phosphate backbone, and the rungs are the bases (purines or pyrimidines). The sequence of bases in one strand determines the base sequence in the complementary strand—A matches with T, C matches with G. These bases are held together by weak hydrogen bonds, making the "ladder" firm but still able to separate during mitosis.

With this model (for which Watson, Crick, and Wilkins won the Nobel Prize in 1962), it is possible to explain how genetic information is duplicated and transmitted. When the strands of the double helix "unzip," or separate, each strand becomes a mold, or *template*, that governs the replication of its new complementary strand. The result is two DNA molecules, each identical with the original because each new strand is based on a specified pattern.

DNA replication

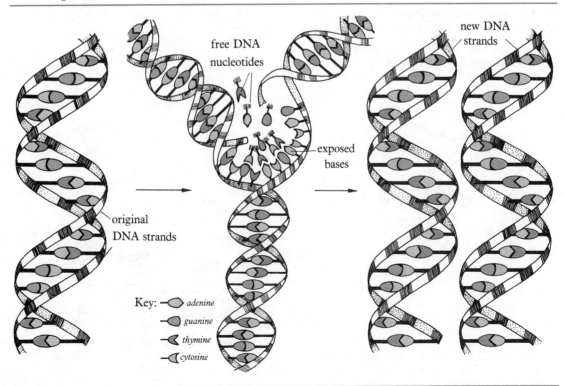

free DNA
nucleotides

new DNA
strands

exposed
bases

original
DNA strands

Key: — adenine
— guanine
— thymine
— cytosine

The genetic code.

DNA, according to the Watson-Crick model, carries genetic information in a kind of code, which depends on the varying sequence of the four bases in relation to each other—in effect, a four-letter alphabet. Since there are ten base pairs in each complete turn of the double helix (which is only a small part of the entire large molecule), the theoretical number of possible combinations in a turn is 4^{10} or 1,048,576. Thus, the storage potential for different items of genetic information is vast, even with only four bases to work with.

The information carried by DNA must be translated into the formation of proteins, for DNA itself is inactive in the metabolic processes of the cell. So the DNA "message" carrying the coded instructions is given to the RNA within the nucleus. Messenger RNA then transmits the information to the place in the cytoplasm where proteins are synthesized. These protein-producing areas, in the ribosomes, are another form of RNA; there a template is formed according to the coded instructions.

Proteins themselves are long chains of amino acids hooked together by peptide bonds in which the 20-odd basic amino acids are repeated several times and arranged in different orders. Even the smallest protein is a chain of 124 amino acids. The protein chains (polypeptides) form a helix that folds into a definite shape, determined by the sequence of amino acids in the chain.

For proteins to be synthesized on the RNA model in the ribosome, another kind of RNA (transfer-RNA or t-RNA) must pick up the right amino acid and fit it to the right place in the template. When the amino acid sequence has been established, peptide bonds are formed, and the new protein "unzips" from the template to carry out its functions in the cell.

RNA structure.

Not as much is known of the structure of RNA as of DNA, though RNA plays a vital role in carrying the information from DNA and in translating the message into protein structure. Like DNA, RNA is a long-chain giant molecule (a polymer); its components are similar except that the sugar in RNA is ribose (not deoxyribose) and one of the pyrimidine bases that form the nucleotides is uracil (U) instead of thymine.

Studies of RNA have concluded that its code is read in groups of three bases (triplets or trinucleotides), with each triplet (say, GUU or AUC) coding the formation of a given amino acid. Experiments have been done to discover which triplet combinations govern the formation of which amino acids; it has been found that several different triplets may code the same amino acid.

Evidence suggests that the genetic code is universal; that is, more or less the same code governs genetic information and protein building in all living species. Interest is building in the possibility of cloning, an asexual reproduction achieved by transplanting the nucleus of a donor's cell into a fertile egg cell, whose nucleus has been removed. The cloned offspring develops as a genetically identical copy of the individual supplying the donor cell.

RNA as messenger in protein synthesis

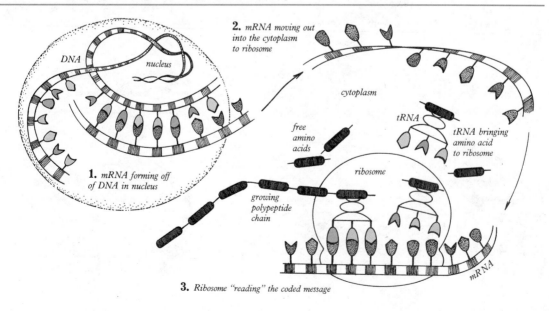

DNA

nucleus

2. *mRNA moving out into the cytoplasm to ribosome*

cytoplasm

tRNA

free amino acids

tRNA bringing amino acid to ribosome

1. *mRNA forming off of DNA in nucleus*

ribosome

growing polypeptide chain

mRNA

3. *Ribosome "reading" the coded message*

Reproduction

All cells are derived from other cells. Cells reproduce themselves by a general process called *fission*. Simple cells such as the monera seem to pinch in half to form two new cells. In eukaryotic cells, the major aspect of cell division is the duplication of the nucleus with its DNA and chromosomes in a process called *mitosis*. In addition to duplication of the nucleus, mitosis also involves duplication of the structures within the cytoplasm. Mitosis as a term refers to both nuclear and cell division. Because of mitosis, all body cells of an organism have identical molecules of DNA, and the number of chromosomes characteristic of each species remains constant.

Mitosis is a continuous process but is described in terms of five phases.

Mitosis

Interphase. This is the time between cell divisions. The amount of time a cell spends in interphase varies with the species, its age, temperature, and other factors. Most cells divide on a regular basis in order to repair or replace other cells. During interphase, each cell begins to grow to mature size, and RNA and protein synthesis occurs. DNA replication begins when the cell reaches a particular size. Each chromosome duplicates itself to form identical sister chromosomes. The DNA is duplicated, more proteins are synthesized, and the cell continues to increase in size. The cell becomes ready to divide and interphase ends.

Prophase. The chromosomes condense or coil into short, thick structures that become visible under a light microscope. The membrane around the nucleus breaks down and disappears. If centrioles are present, they begin to migrate to opposite regions of the cell, forming two poles. A football-shaped structure, the *spindle*, made of tubelike structures, forms. The spindle fibers form between the poles. The spindle forms in plant cells without centrioles. The chromosomes begin to move toward the middle of the spindle.

Metaphase. The chromosomes line up along the middle of the spindle, apparently pushed or pulled along by the spindle fibers.

Anaphase. The sister chromosomes separate from each other. Each daughter chromosome, as they are now called, migrates toward opposite poles. The chromosomes often have a V or J shape.

Telophase. The daughter chromosomes are at opposite poles of the spindle, and the spindle starts to break down. The individual chromosomes become thinner, longer, and less visible. The nuclear membrane reforms around each set of chromosomes. The centrioles replicate. A furrow or groove appears in the membrane of animal cells and a cell plate forms in plant cells. The animal cell furrow curves inward until a complete membrane separates the two daughter cells. The plant cell plate expands until a wall is formed that separates the two cells. A new interphase then begins in each daughter cell.

Mitosis

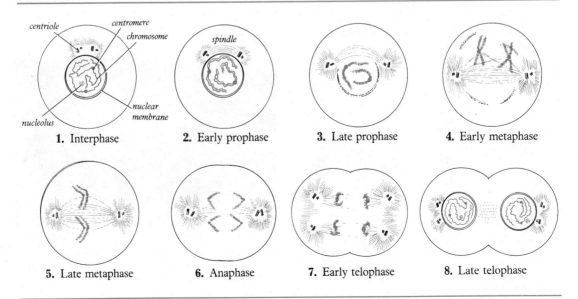

1. Interphase
2. Early prophase
3. Late prophase
4. Early metaphase
5. Late metaphase
6. Anaphase
7. Early telophase
8. Late telophase

Reproduction of organisms. Cells

reproduce through the process of mitosis. Organisms reproduce in one of two ways: through asexual reproduction or through sexual reproduction.

There are three basic types of asexual reproduction. *Vegetative* reproduction is common to many plants and some animals. In vegetative reproduction, another organism will develop from a portion of an organism that separates or has been removed from it. For example, potato tubers can be cut up and planted to produce a number of new potatoes; a branch of a willow tree can grow a new root system and develop into a new tree; the animal hydra develops buds. The buds are special collections of cells that develop into new hydra and eventually separate and become independent organisms.

Regeneration means the regrowth of missing parts. If a starfish or a planarian is cut into several pieces, each may develop into an independent organism. Some organisms can only regenerate missing parts, however.

Some organisms produce specialized cells that can grow into complete organisms. These cells are called *spores*. Bread mold and mushrooms reproduce thousands of organisms by this method. The smoky cloud emitted by fungi known as puffballs is actually a cloud of extremely tiny spores.

Organisms that have formed from asexual reproduction have the same exact DNA structure as their parent, and each daughter organism carries the exact hereditary information that is found in the parent.

Many organisms produce specialized cells that differ from spores in that they do not develop directly into a new organism. These cells, called *gametes*, will form a new individual only after they have fused or become fertilized by another gamete. Fertilization is the key event in sexual reproduction. Organisms formed by sexual reproduction are truly new and different from their parents since the organism receives DNA from each parent. To accomplish this another form of cell division, called *meiosis*, is required.

Sexual reproduction

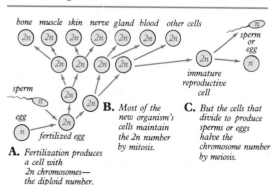

A. *Fertilization produces a cell with 2n chromosomes— the diploid number.*

B. *Most of the new organism's cells maintain the 2n number by mitosis.*

C. *But the cells that divide to produce sperms or eggs halve the chromosome number by meiosis.*

Types of asexual reproduction

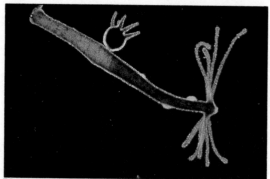

Vegetative reproduction. Both plants and animals can reproduce "vegetatively." The hydra, a tiny water animal, grows buds that break off to form "daughter" hydras.

Regeneration. Many plants can reproduce by regeneration. A few animals, such as the starfish, can also regenerate. Since starfish prey on oysters, oyster fishermen used to catch starfish and tear them into pieces. This practice was stopped when the fishermen realized that each piece regenerated into a new starfish.

Spores. Many plants reproduce by spores, which are special cells that grow into new plants when they reach a suitable environment. Ferns, for example, reproduce by releasing spores.

Meiosis.

Meiosis. The chromosomes in each cell occur in pairs. In humans there are 46 chromosomes or 23 pairs. If the gametes (usually called egg and sperm) fuse, the chromosome number would double. Meiosis is a process of cell division unique to gametes where the chromosome number is halved. In this way, the proper chromosome number is ensured after fertilization occurs.

Meiosis differs from mitosis in a number of ways. In meiosis there are two cell divisions resulting in four daughter cells; the chromosomes can exchange parts; the chromosomes duplicate only once, even though there are two cell divisions; the chromosomes line up and randomly move to either pole. In this way, each gamete is unique and has one-half the chromosome number of its species. Meiosis occurs in two stages.

First meiotic division. Each chromosome has duplicated itself. Each replicated chromosome seeks out its sister. Frequently, chromosome pairs will become entangled and exchange sections of DNA. This process is called *crossing over*. The duplicated chromosomes pair up, forming a four-stranded group called a *tetrad*. As tetrads are forming, the nuclear membrane is break-

ing down and spindle fibers are forming. The tetrads migrate toward the center and line up randomly. Complete chromosomes gather at each pole and the cytoplasm divides either by furrowing or forming a cell plate. Each new cell now has half the chromosome number of its species (in humans, 23).

Second meiotic division. This phase is very similar to mitosis. Spindle fibers form, the paired chromosomes line up at the center of the cell, and the spindle fiber begins to draw the chromosomes apart. The chromosomes group and migrate together at each pole. The cytoplasm again divides. Four daughter cells, each with half the chromosome number, have formed. Usually in male organisms the cytoplasm divides evenly and all four cells function as sperm cells. In females, the cytoplasm divides unequally with one cell receiving the majority of the cytoplasm. This cell becomes the functioning gamete.

Meiosis produces organisms that are genetically different. Crossing over and the random assortment of chromosomes ensures that each daughter cell will be different. Additional genetic mixing will occur at fertilization when the chromosome number is restored.

Meiosis

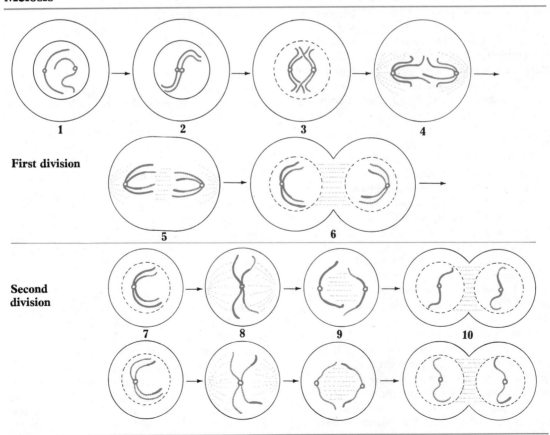

First division

Second division

Genetics

The study of the inheritance of biological characteristics in living things—characteristics that are passed from one generation to the next—is called *genetics*. What is inherited is a code message in the genetic material (genes) of egg and sperm. The code directs embryonic development and organization of cells into tissues and organs; in addition, it directs the function of each tissue and organ. This development is also influenced by the external and internal environment. Thus, an organism is the product of interaction between genetic material and environment.

Mendelian genetics.
Gregor Johann Mendel (1822–1884), an Austrian monk, analyzed the basic laws of inheritance in 1866. He proved that hereditary traits are transmitted by pairs of distinct units, later called *genes*, which reshuffle, segregate, and redistribute, rather than blend, in offspring.

Mendel used garden peas in his experiments because they hybridize easily. When a purebred tall plant was crossed with a purebred short plant, all hybrid offspring were tall, no matter which type was the mother and which the father. The hybrids self-fertilized. Mendel counted the offspring and found 787 tall plants and 277 short plants, a ratio of about three to one. When the short plants self-fertilized, they produced only short offspring, but when the tall plants self-fertilized, there were two types of offspring: one-third had only tall offspring, and two-thirds produced both tall and short in a ratio of three to one. Mendel crossed six other characters: round and wrinkled peas, colored and uncolored flowers, and yellow and green peas. He had approximately the same results.

Mendel then formulated the law of segregation. Today this principal states that hereditary traits (such as tallness or shortness) are transmitted by *zygotes* (fertilized eggs). One member of each pair of traits comes from the female parent; the other, from the male. In the mature plant, paired genes segregate during the formation of gametes (sperm and egg cells), so that just one of the pair is transmitted by a particular gamete. The gamete has only one gene from each pair and is called *haploid*. When the male and female gametes unite to form the zygote, the zygote is called double or *diploid*.

Mendel's studies showed the principle of *dominance*. For instance, in garden peas, the trait of tallness is dominant over shortness; when there is a gene for tallness and one for shortness, all peas are tall. The opposite, unexpressed factor is *recessiveness*.

To a geneticist, an individual with unlike paired genes is represented as Tt. T represents the dominant

Some traits in man that are inherited in a simple Mendelian fashion

Recessive	Dominant
red hair	not red hair
white forelock	normal
normal	premature grayness of hair
normal	no iris
normal	glaucoma
extreme myopia	normal
night blindness	normal
normal	congenital cataract
albinism	normal
polydactyl	normal
normal	split foot
normal	no incisor teeth
normal	rootless teeth
no A or B antigens	A and B antigens
normal	sickle cell
no Rh antigen	Rh antigen
attached ear lobe	free ear lobe
normal size	achondroplastic dwarf
St. Vitus' dance	normal
Friedreich's ataxia	normal
normal	Huntington's chorea
diabetes mellitus	normal

gene for tallness; t, the recessive gene for shortness. Such an individual is called a *heterozygote*.

Genetic makeup is called *genotype*; the character determined by genotype and expressed in an individual is called *phenotype*. The phenotype can be changed by the environment, but the genotype cannot. If the genotype is TT, the phenotype is tallness, but a different genotype—Tt—can also give the phenotype tallness. The alternative forms of genes are called *alleles*.

Mendel concluded that dominant and recessive genes do not affect each other; gametes are haploid and have only one of a pair of genes; each type of gamete is produced in equal numbers by a hybrid parent. Combination between gametes depends on chance—the frequency of each class of offspring depends on the frequency of the gametes produced by each parent.

Mendel next determined how two or more pairs of genes would behave in crosses. He crossed plants with round yellow seeds with those with wrinkled green seeds. He knew that a cross between round (R) and wrinkled (r) seeds produced round seeds in the F_1, or first, generation, and three round seeds to one wrinkled seed in the F_2, or second generation, plants. He also knew that crossing yellow (Y) with green (y) produced all yellow seeds in the F_1 and three yellow to one green in the F_2 generation. This showed the dominance of roundness and yellowness over their respective contrasting alleles. Thus, when Mendel crossed round yellow with wrinkled green, the first generation (F_1) produced all round yellow seeds.

In the second generation (F_2), a more complicated assortment of differing seed types resulted:

Type	Proportion
Round yellow	$\frac{9}{16}$
Round green	$\frac{3}{16}$
Wrinkled yellow	$\frac{3}{16}$
Wrinkled green	$\frac{1}{16}$

Two combinations, round green and wrinkled yellow, not present in either the parents or the first generation, have appeared. This result can be explained by Mendel's law of independent assortment, which states that members of one pair of genes segregate independently of other pairs.

Mendel also tested F_2 plants to determine whether all of a single phenotype class, such as round yellow, were alike in genotype. According to his hypothesis, there should be four different genotypes in this group: RR, YY; RR, Yy; Rr, YY; and Rr, Yy. When F_2 plants self-fertilized, he found four classes of round yellow seeded plants; the ratios fitted expectations. The breed-

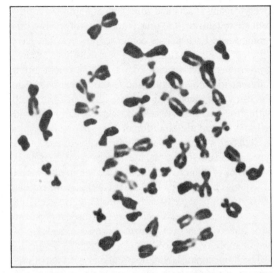

Not all traits that are thought of as hereditary are caused by the genes. Down's syndrome results from a defect in chromosomes, not from the genetic composition of the parents. Shown here are the chromosomes of a person with Down's syndrome.

ing behavior of the F_2 round green, wrinkled yellow, and wrinkled green seeded plants also fitted the hypothesis that each pair of genes segregates independently from other pairs of genes and is transmitted independently to the next generation.

Mendelian square

Phenotype parents	RRYY *round yellow*		rryy *wrinkled green*	

Genotype 1st generation: RrYy *round yellow*

	RY	Ry	rY	ry
Gametes 2nd generation ry	RrYy	Rryy	rrYy	rryy
rY	RrYY	RrYy	rrYY	rrYy
Ry	RRYy	RRyy	RrYy	Rryy
RY	RRYY	RRYy	RrYY	RrYy

Key:
R *round*
r *wrinkled*
Y *yellow*
y *green*

Sex-linked inheritance

♀ X X

A sex-linked gene is passed on in a family through "criss-cross" transmission. A woman who has the hemophilia gene will be normal when her second X chromosome has a normal gene. But she is a carrier.

♂ X Y

One of every two of her sons may be a bleeder. The bleeder is the son who receives an X from her that carries a hemophilia gene. His Y has no normal gene to block the effect of the X gene. All his sons (who receive only his Y chromosome) are normal.

♀ X X

All his daughters, though, are carriers like their grandmother. The process of transmitting the gene begins again in their families.

Multicellular organization

Every organism acts and functions as a unit. In multicellular organisms, the unit is made up of visibly different parts. Each part is composed of cells that have different forms and functions. These cells have become *differentiated* and specialized. A cell in a root tip is different in both structure and function from a cell in the surface of a leaf, and both are different from a cell within the leaf. A nerve cell, muscle cell, and red blood cell in a human are all different.

Each cell type is grouped with many others of its type and shares the same life processes. A muscle is composed of thousands of cells, similar in shape and function. The surface of a leaf is covered with similar cells. A group of cells and the material between the cells is called *tissue*. *Simple tissue* is made up of the same types of cells, while *composite tissue* is made up of two or more types of cells.

The "division of labor" does not end with the development of tissue. In complex organisms, groups of tissues are combined to form *organs*. An organ is a group of tissues that works together to perform a special function for the benefit of the organism. Organs can become interacting parts of an anatomical and physiological *system*. The human digestive system is a sequence of organs from the mouth through the esophagus, the stomach, and the small and large intestine to the anus. Each organ is different, but each interacts with the others to accomplish the process of digestion.

The bodies of more highly complex plants consist of four types of tissue and two organ systems.

Meristematic tissue is involved in plant growth; *protective* tissue covers and protects both organ systems; one type of *fundamental* tissue adds strength to a plant's organs while a second type is the site of photosynthesis; *conductive*, or vascular, tissue helps transport fluids and dissolved materials within the plant.

The organ systems are the *root system* and the *shoot system*, which includes the stem and leaves. Organization into systems is more common in animals than in plants. Humans and other more complex multicellular animals have ten systems.

1. The *integumentary system* encloses or covers the animal. Hair, skin, nails, scales, feathers, and hooves are parts of the integumentary system.

2. The *skeletal system* provides support, protection, and help in movement.

3. The *muscular system* provides for movement of the animal and its internal organs.

4. The *respiratory system* moves gases in and out of the organisms.

5. The *excretory system* eliminates liquid wastes from the body. A kidney is a key organ in this system.

6. The *nervous system* receives stimuli from the environment and causes organs to respond.

7. The *endocrine system*, through its *hormones*, regulates and controls the growth, development, and functions of the organism.

8. The *digestive system* changes food into a form that can be used by the individual cells.

9. The *circulatory system* moves food, hormones, and other materials throughout the body.

10. The *reproductive system* produces gametes to continue the species of organism.

Plant and animal functions

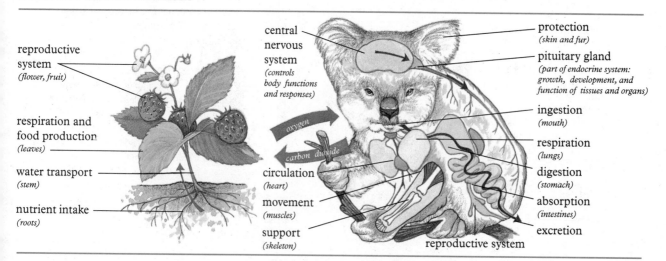

reproductive system
(flower, fruit)

respiration and food production
(leaves)

water transport
(stem)

nutrient intake
(roots)

central nervous system
(controls body functions and responses)

oxygen

carbon dioxide

circulation
(heart)

movement
(muscles)

support
(skeleton)

reproductive system

protection
(skin and fur)

pituitary gland
(part of endocrine system: growth, development, and function of tissues and organs)

ingestion
(mouth)

respiration
(lungs)

digestion
(stomach)

absorption
(intestines)

excretion

Biology

Tissues

Tissue			Location	Function
Epithelial	Simple squamous		Lungs	Exchange of gases
			Lining of blood/lymph vessels	Absorption by diffusion
			Surface layer of organs	Absorption by diffusion
	Stratified squamous		Skin, mouth, esophagus	Protection
	Simple columnar		Lining of stomach, intestines, and respiratory tract	Protection; secretion; absorption; moving of mucus
Muscle	Skeletal		Attached to bones and eyes	Movement
			Upper third of esophagus	First part of swallowing
	Visceral		Walls of digestive, respiratory, and genitourinary tracts	Movement of substances along respective tracts
			Walls of blood and lymph vessels	Change diameter of vessels
			In ducts of glands	Movement of substances
			Intrinsic eye muscles	Adjust vision
			Arrector muscles of hairs	Erection of hairs (gooseflesh)
	Cardiac		Wall of heart	Contraction of heart
Connective	Reticular tissue		Spleen, lymph nodes, bone marrow	Defense for harmful substances; synthesis of reticular fibers
	Loose, ordinary (areolar)		Between other tissues and organs	Connection
			Superficial fascia	Connection
	Fat		Under skin and padding at various points	Protection, insulation, support, and reserve food
	Dense fibrous		Tendons, ligaments, dermis, scars, capsule of kidney, etc.	Flexible but strong connection
	Bone		Skeleton	Support and protection
	Cartilage:	Hyaline	Nose, bones, larynx, rings in trachea and bronchi	Firm but flexible support
		Fibrous	Disks between vertebrae	
		Elastic	External ear, Eustachian tube	
	Hemopoietic:	Bone marrow	Marrow spaces of bones	Formation of red blood cells, granular leukocytes, platelets
		Lymphatic	Lymph nodes, spleen, tonsils and adenoids, thymus gland	Formation of lymphocytes and monocytes
Blood			In blood vessels	Transportation and protection
Nervous			Brain, spinal cord, nerves	Irritability; conduction

Variety of living things

Imagine trying to order items from a catalog that is completely disorganized! On a single page there might be clothing and toys as well as hardware and household appliances. In addition, none of the items is labeled, so it is almost impossible to refer to an item by its name or to distinguish it from another item. Fortunately, catalogs are not usually organized in this way. Every object is given a specific name, and similar objects are generally grouped together.

The same situation exists in the world of living things. Each living thing is given a specific name, and those living things with similar characteristics are classified together. This makes it much easier for scientists, as well as the rest of us, to study living things and to discuss them.

The variety of organisms is enormous. For instance, over 1 million animals have already been discovered and named; and there are many others yet to be investigated. By organizing this large number of creatures into groups based on similar characteristics, we can bring order to the animal kingdom and make sense of it. As more animals are discovered, they can be added to the existing classifications. If an animal is found for which no classification exists, a new one can be created.

A system of classifying living things was developed by the Swedish naturalist Linnaeus during the 18th century. (His actual name was Carl von Linné.) The largest divisions established by Linnaeus are the *kingdoms*. These include many organisms that share a few of the same characteristics. All members of the plant kingdom, for example, manufacture their own food and do not move around. Today scientists often speak of five kingdoms. These include Animalia (animal), Plantae (plant), Fungi, Protista, and Monera.

Five kingdom classification system

Kingdom Monera
Most organisms in this kingdom are made up of a simple, *prokaryotic* cell.
Some monerans make their own food; others take in food from an outside source.

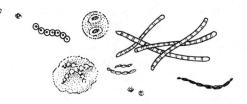

Kingdom Protista
Organisms in this kingdom are made up of a complex, *eukaryotic* cell.
Like monerans, protists either make their own food or take it in from an outside source.

Kingdom Animalia
Members of this kingdom are multicellular, but they obtain food from *outside sources*.
Animals move from place to place to obtain food, swallow the food, and digest it inside the body.

Kingdom Fungi
These organisms are made up of many cells, but lack the ability to move about.
They obtain food by *absorbing* it from dead or living organisms.

Kingdom Plantae
Members of the plant kingdom are also multicellular, but the cells are *specialized* for different tasks—such as support or transport.
Plants use chlorophyll to *make their own food*, and so lack the ability to move about.

Biology

Every kingdom is further broken down into smaller groups. These groups have fewer organisms with more characteristics in common. Each of the various groups into which a kingdom is divided is called a *phylum*. The phyla (plural of phylum) are broken into *classes*, which are subdivided into *orders*. These, in turn, are subdivided into *families*. Finally, the families are broken down into *genera* (singular genus) and *species*. The smallest grouping is generally the species. All members of a species are very similar, and they can mate to produce fertile offspring. According to this system, the classification for humans would be:

Kingdom:	**Animalia**	Family:	HOMINIDAE
Phylum:	**CHORDATA**	Genus:	*Homo*
Class:	**Mammalia**	Species:	*sapiens*
Order:	PRIMATA		

Each living thing has its own special name, which is a combination of its genus and its species. Humans are called *Homo sapiens*. This name is unique: there is no other organism that possesses it.

Latin is the language used to label living things. When Linnaeus invented his system of classification, Latin was the language used by most scientists. Using Latin avoids confusion. Instead of calling the same species by different names in different languages, one name is used universally.

At present, all scientists do not subscribe to a single system of classification. For example, some scientists classify most of the algae as protists, while others split them between the protist and the plant kingdoms. What follows is one classification system that is accepted in the scientific community. But alternatives exist that are equally valid.

A partial classification of corn plants and men

Taxonomic rank	Corn plant	Man
phylum	**TRACHEOPHYTA** plants with vascular tissues	**CHORDATA** animals with notochords
subphylum	**PTEROPSIDA** types with large leaves	**VERTEBRATA** types with vertebral columns
superclass	**Spermatophyta** seed producers	**Tetrapoda** terrestrial; four limbs; bony skeletons
class	**Angiospermae** flowering plants; seeds inside fruits	**Mammalia** types with hair and milk glands
subclass	**Monocotyledonae** parallel-veined leaves; single seed leaf; flower parts in threes or multiples	**Eutheria** offspring develop within female parent, nourished by placenta
order	GRAMINALES grasses	PRIMATA fingers; flat nails
family	GRAMINACEAE leaves in two rows on round or flattened stem	HOMINIDAE upright posture; flat face; stereoscopic vision; large brain; hands and feet
genus	*Zea* corn plants	*Homo* double-curved spine; long life span and long youth
species	*mays* cultivated, domesticated corn plants	*sapiens* well-developed chin; high forehead; thin skull bones

Viruses

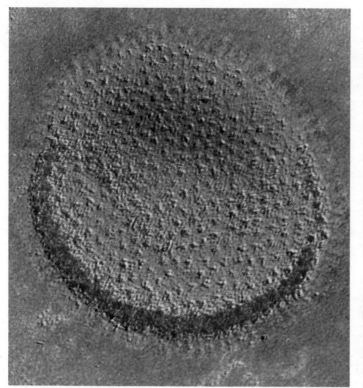

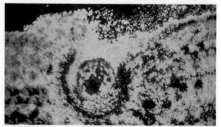

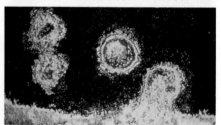

An influenza virus

The human immunodeficiency virus (HIV) is shown here invading a cell where it will reproduce and then find new cells to invade.

Virus. A virus is a piece of nucleic acid—DNA or RNA—enclosed within a protective shell of protein. A virus particle is very tiny, smaller than a bacteria cell. Under the electron microscope, some viruses have been shown to look like the bacteriaphage. Others have a rod or a helix shape.

On its own, a virus shows no signs of life; consequently, scientists cannot agree on whether it is a living thing. A virus does not move; it must be carried by air, water, or some organism. Once in contact with a cell, a virus seems to come alive. After attaching itself to the cell wall, the virus enters the cell and takes control of its reproductive mechanisms to replicate itself; in the process, it prevents the cell from operating normally.

Once a cell has been infected by a virus, it may change and become a tumor cell. While some tumors, such as warts, are benign, others are malignant, or cancerous. Viruses cause cancer in plants and animals. As the virus replicates, producing more particles, the particles may burst out of a cell, destroying it. Then the particles may be carried by the bloodstream to infect other cells. Human diseases caused by viruses include influenza, measles, mumps, polio, and the common cold.

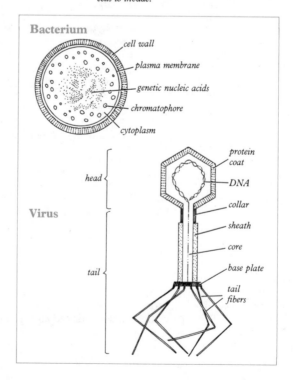

Bacterium

- cell wall
- plasma membrane
- genetic nucleic acids
- chromatophore
- cytoplasm

Virus

- head
- tail
- protein coat
- DNA
- collar
- sheath
- core
- base plate
- tail fibers

Bacteria

Staphylococcus

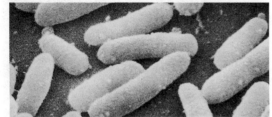
Common bacteria used in gene splicing, Escherichia coli

Streptococcus shows that cocci are often joined in chains.

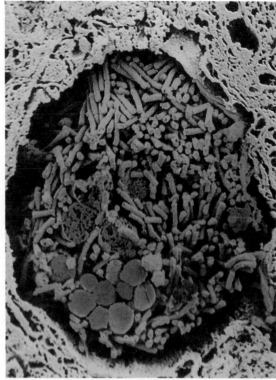
The anthrax bacterium is a typical bacillus.

Kingdom Monera.

This kingdom is comprised of all bacteria. Bacteria are thought to be the most numerous type of living thing in our environment. They are grouped into two phyla: bacteria and blue-green bacteria. Formerly, the bacteria were classified as plants because bacteria have cell walls.

Bacteria are tiny organisms that generally consist of a single cell. This is called a *prokaryotic* cell. A prokaryotic cell has a definite cell wall, but, unlike the cells in other organisms, it lacks an organized nucleus. The prokaryotic cell is also missing specialized cell structures, such as mitochondria and golgi.

Bacteria generally reproduce by a process called *fission*. In fission, one cell simply divides, producing an offspring. Monerans may also reproduce sexually.

PHYLUM SCHIZOPHYTA:

BACTERIA. Bacteria exist in three different shapes. The spherical bacteria are called **cocci**. The rod-shaped bacteria are known as **bacilli**. The spiral-shaped cells are called **spirilla**. Some bacteria possess a long hairlike structure that resembles a tail. Known as a *flagellum*, it moves very rapidly and propels the bacterium.

Bacteria play an essential role in the ecosystem as decomposers. After plants and animals have died, bacteria break them down, releasing vital substances such as oxygen, carbon, and sulfur, which are essential for life. Certain bacteria attached to plants "capture" nitrogen and transform it into a compound that plants can use. This process, called nitrogen fixation, is necessary for these plants to function.

Some bacteria cause serious illnesses. These illnesses include tuberculosis, cholera, typhoid fever, and tetanus. Disease-causing bacteria can be transmitted directly from one individual to another. They may also be carried by an animal, such as an insect. The bacteria that cause bubonic plague are carried by fleas from rodents to humans.

PHYLUM CYANOPHYTA:

BLUE-GREEN BACTERIA. These are sometimes called blue-green algae. They contain chlorophyll and carry on photosynthesis, but the chlorophyll is not contained in chloroplasts as it is in other photosynthetic organisms. Blue-green bacteria may be single-celled or multicellular. They grow mainly in a freshwater environment.

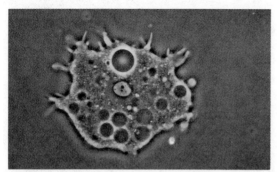

An amoeba

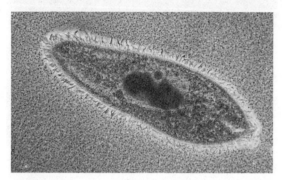

A paramecium

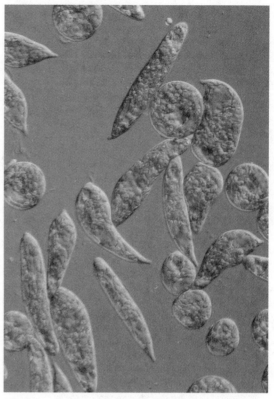

Euglena

Kingdom Protista.

The members of this kingdom range from tiny single-celled organisms to giant seaweed. Protists are comprised of *eukaryotic* cells that contain a distinct nucleus as well as other cell bodies. (The members of the remaining three kingdoms are also composed of eukaryotic cells.)

PHYLUM PROTOZOA:

Protozoa are like animals because they move and obtain their food from outside sources. They reproduce sexually and asexually. There are perhaps 30,000 species of protozoa organized into four classes.

Mastigophora. This class includes protozoa that move by means of flagella. One species causes the disease called African sleeping sickness.

Sarcodina. The best-known member of this class is the amoeba. The amoeba possesses projections, called pseudopods, used to capture food and in movement.

Ciliophora. These protozoans use hairlike projections called *cilia* to swim. The paramecium is a member of this class. Paramecia are shaped like a slipper and found in fresh water. Each cell has two nuclei. One directs reproduction and the other directs the rest of the paramecium's functions.

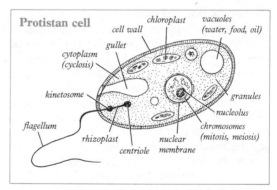

Protistan cell

chloroplast
vacuoles (water, food, oil)
cell wall
gullet
cytoplasm (cyclosis)
kinetosome
granules
nucleolus
flagellum
chromosomes (mitosis, meiosis)
rhizoplast
centriole
nuclear membrane

Sporozoa. This class includes protozoans that glide. One of them, the plasmodium, causes malaria.

The remaining phyla consist of photosynthetic organisms. There are perhaps 25,000 species of such *algae.* Most are found in water environments.

PHYLUM EUGLENOPHYTA:

EUGLENA. The euglena are protists that have characteristics of plants and animals. Euglena contain chlorophyll and can make their own food; or they can capture it. Euglena move by using flagella.

Spirogyras

Kelp

PHYLUM CHRYSOPHYTA:
GOLDEN ALGAE AND DIATOMS. In the golden algae the green chlorophyll is masked by yellow to brown pigments, giving these organisms their characteristic color. Diatoms are single-celled algae. They are among the living things that comprise *plankton*—tiny organisms that float along the water's surface. Plankton serves as food for many marine animals. Diatoms have cell walls composed of silica, which are found in a variety of shapes.

PHYLUM PYRROPHYTA:
DINOFLAGELLATES. Many of these organisms spin from the motion of their flagella. One species creates the so-called "red tide" that occurs in the Gulf of Mexico. This phenomenon is produced by a large number of dinoflagellates whose pigments create the red color. Red tides kill many types of marine life. Some species of dinoflagellates are bioluminescent; that is, they emit light.

PHYLUM CHLOROPHYTA:
GREEN ALGAE. The members of this phylum come in a variety of shapes and sizes. There are single-celled algae such as CHLAMYDOMONAS and DESMIDS. A desmid consists of two symmetrical halves connected by a bridge. The *Ulva* is a type of green algae that looks like leafy lettuce. *Spirogyra* is a long filament that makes up the scum that covers ponds. The filament consists of a series of elongated algal cells that are connected to each other. Another type of filamentous algae, *Ulothrix*, is held in place by means of a structure called a *holdfast*. It attaches to rocks and twigs. The multicellular algae have specialized cells that perform various functions.

PHYLUM PHAEOPHYTA:
BROWN ALGAE.
PHYLUM RHODOPHYTA:
RED ALGAE. These are multicelled algae known as seaweeds. The brown algae are the largest and include the giant kelp. Some of the kelps are over 40 feet in length. The kelps contain rudimentary transport systems that carry nutrients from those parts on the surface to the rest of the organism below. The giant kelps are anchored to the ocean floor by large holdfasts. Another type of brown algae, called *Fucus*, has air bladders that help its leaflike parts float on the surface.

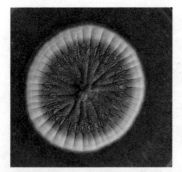

Colony of Penicillium *mold*

Fruiting part of a mushroom

Lichens can grow on bare rock.

Kingdom Fungi.

In this kingdom there are approximately 100,000 species that have been named. Fungi cannot produce their own food; they obtain it by absorbing material from other organisms. Along with bacteria and protozoa, fungi act as decomposers. They reproduce by sexual and asexual means. Some species of fungi can also cause diseases such as ringworm and athlete's foot.

Ascomycetes. These are sometimes known as "sac fungi" because of their shape. The class also includes powdery mildews and yeasts. Mildews are parasites that live on many green plants, such as lilacs and roses. Yeasts carry on a process known as *fermentation*, which is important in baking and in the production of alcoholic beverages. Truffles and morels, which are both edible fungi, are other members of this class.

Basidomycetes. This class includes mushrooms and toadstools as well as rusts and smuts. While some mushrooms are edible, others are poisonous and should be avoided. Only that part of the mushroom involved in reproduction appears above the surface; the rest remains below ground. Rusts and smuts are parasites that attack wheat, trees, and other plants. Rusts have a rusty color, while smuts are dark.

Deuteromycetes. Among these fungi are the *Penicillium* molds. Species of this mold are the source of the drug penicillin. Some species are also used in the production of cheeses such as Roquefort, blue, and Camembert. Many types of molds spoil food; for example, the *Trichothecium* grows on apples and produces rot.

LICHENS. A lichen is composed of a species of algae and a species of fungi living together. The algae manufacture food, while the fungi form a framework that protects the algae. Some lichens are crustlike; others are leaflike; still others are branchy. These are hearty organisms that can survive in even the most inhospitable environments, such as the icy conditions of Antarctica, where lichens can be found living inside the outer layers of some rock formations.

PHYLUM GYMNOMYCOTA:

SLIME MOLDS. These are not true molds. In one stage, slime molds are individual cells that move around like amoeba; they are often classified in the protist kingdom. In other stages, the slime molds gather in colonies that resemble fungi. There are almost 500 species in this phylum.

Plantae

Moss

Ferns

Kingdom Plantae. This kingdom consists of multicellular, photosynthetic organisms that range in size from tiny mosses to giant sequoia trees. Reproduction among the plants is both sexual and asexual.

PHYLUM BRYOPHYTA:
LIVERWORTS, HORNWORTS, MOSSES.
These are nonvascular plants; that is, they do not possess a system of specialized cells for carrying water and food through the plants. As a result the bryophytes are frequently found near water, and they remain small. There are over 23,000 species.

Hepaticae. These are low, flat plants numbering about 9000 species. People in the ancient world believed these liverworts would cure diseases of the liver.

Antherocerotae. This class includes about 100 species of hornworts.

Musci. Mosses are tiny plants that grow in clumps. They have leaflike parts above ground and rootlike structures, called *rhizoids*, that absorb water and nutrients. Mosses are often called "pioneer plants" because they may be among the first species to inhabit harsh environments. Mosses growing on rocky surfaces, for example, break up the rocks and create a more fertile soil where other plants can survive. A special type of moss, called *Sphagnum*, grows in heavy mats in ponds. Sphagnum eventually forms *peat*, which is burned as a fuel and used as fertilizer in gardens. There are over 14,000 species of mosses.

PHYLUM TRACHEOPHYTA:
VASCULAR PLANTS. With vascular systems, plants can grow very tall, and even the highest branches can receive the nutrients necessary to survive. Tracheophytes have roots, stems, and leaves. Roots hold the plant in the ground. They absorb water and minerals, transport them to the rest of the plant, and act as storage areas for food. Stems also serve as transport structures. Additionally, they provide sturdiness and support for the plant's leaves and branches. Leaves manufacture food through photosynthesis.

Filicinae. Ferns are seedless plants, numbering about 11,000 species. In spring the coiled leaf buds, called *fiddleheads*, uncoil into broad fern leaves known as *fronds*. These are attached to the ferns' underground stems, or *rhyzomes*. Although ferns are generally small, some giant tree ferns grow to heights of over 40 feet.

Plantae

Gingko

Cycad

A white pine

Gymnospermae. This class comprises seed-bearing plants. Seeds consist of a tough outer shell enveloping in embryo plant and nutrients to sustain it. Seeds can survive in a very harsh environment; then, under just the right conditions, they germinate and begin to sprout. Seeds can also be carried easily by wind, water, and animals. All these advantages have helped seed-bearing plants proliferate.

Gymnosperm means "naked" or "exposed" seed. In gymnosperm plants, the seed is not enclosed by a fruit. *ORDER CYCADINAE:* CYCADS. There are about 550 species of these trees, which look like palms. *ORDER GINKGOINAE:* GINKGO. Only one species exists today. *ORDER CONIFERINAE:* CONIFERS. There are over 500 species; they include pines, firs, spruces, hemlocks, and sequoias. The conifers, or "cone-bearers," develop their seeds in cones. They have sharp needle-like leaves that are shed at intervals throughout the year. This gives conifers the appearance of always being green; hence the term "evergreen." Vast forests of conifers stretch across Canada and the northern United States, forming a huge biome called the taiga. Conifers are important as sources of lumber.

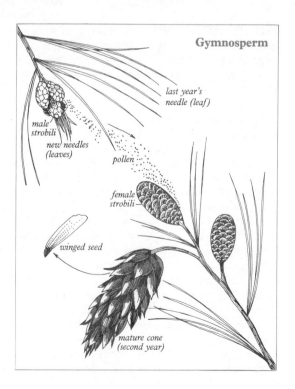

Gymnosperm

last year's needle (leaf)

male strobili

new needles (leaves)

pollen

female strobili

winged seed

mature cone (second year)

Prickly pear cacti

Roses

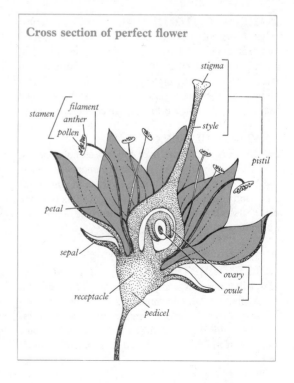

California fan palms

Dune grass

Angiospermae. These flowering seed plants are the most highly developed plants. Flowers contain plants' reproductive organs. The *stamen* is the male organ. It consists of a *filament* and an *anther*. *Pollen*, which contains male reproductive cells, is produced in the anther. The *pistil*, or female reproductive organ, includes the *stigma*, the *style*, the *ovary*, and the *ovule*. An egg cell is produced inside the ovule. When the ovule is fertilized by sperm from pollen grains, it develops into a seed. The ovary enclosing the seed becomes the fruit. Pollen is frequently carried to the pistil by insects, and plants have developed a variety of methods of attracting them. These methods include colorful flowers, smells, and a sweet liquid called nectar.

The flowering plants are divided into two main groups: the *monocots*, with one seed leaf; and the *dicots*, with two seed leaves. Members of these two groups also differ in the number of their flower parts, the appearance of their leaves, and their root structure. For example, monocots have leaves with parallel veins, while the leaves of dicots have branching veins. The monocots include grasses, lilies, orchids, palms, and cattails. Dicots include oaks, maples, beeches, willows, mustards, roses, poppies, and mints.

Cross section of perfect flower

stigma

stamen
filament
anther
pollen

style

pistil

petal

sepal

ovary

ovule

receptacle

pedicel

Invertebrates

A flatworm

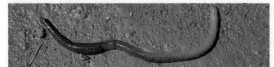

Typical segmented earthworm

Sponge

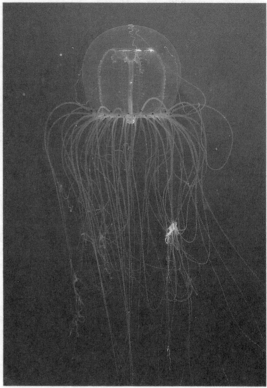

A jellyfish floating in the sea

Kingdom Animalia. Animals are multi-celled organisms that do not produce their own food and must obtain it by ingesting organic materials. Most animals move. Members of this kingdom fall into two large groups: invertebrates, animals without backbones; and vertebrates, animals with backbones. The first eight phyla listed below are invertebrates.

PHYLUM PORIFERA:
SPONGES. There are over 4000 species of sponges, which live primarily in marine environments as well as in fresh water. Sponges come in a variety of colors and are found singly or in colonies. Sponges remain in one place, and obtain their food by absorbing it through tiny holes in their sides.

PHYLUM COELENTERATA:
COELENTERATES. This phylum includes hydras, jellyfish, corals, and sea anemones. These animals have definite tissues and contain a saclike digestive cavity surrounded by special organs such as tentacles. Typical of this phylum is the hydra—a tiny freshwater animal shaped like a tube with stinging tentacles at one end.

PHYLUM PLATYHELMINTHES:
FLATWORMS. Flatworms have three tissue layers—ectoderm, mesoderm, and endoderm—and possess definite organs. These characteristics are shared by all the remaining phyla in the animal kingdom. This phylum includes planarians, tapeworms, and flukes. Planarians have eyespots, which are capable of detecting light but not shapes. Tapeworms and flukes are parasites that live in humans and animals.

PHYLUM NEMATODA:
ROUNDWORMS. These animals consist of an outer tube enclosing a tubular digestive system. Some are parasites, including the trichina and the hookworm. The trichina lives in pigs and other animals. If humans eat raw pork, they may ingest the trichina and develop *trichinosis*.

PHYLUM ANNELIDA:
SEGMENTED WORMS. Although the majority of these worms are found in marine habitats, the best known is the earthworm, which lives in the soil. Earthworms eat particles of soil, retain the food contained in it, and excrete the remainder in the form of *castings*.

The snail is a gastropod.

A crab is a crustacean.

Spiders are arachnids.

Swallowtail butterfly

PHYLUM MOLLUSKA:

MOLLUSKS. These animals have a soft body and a foot protruding from it. Covering the body is a membrane, or *mantle*; some mollusks also have a shell. There are various classes, such as the PELECYPODA, or two-shelled mollusks, which include clams, mussels, and oysters. Snails and slugs are members of the class GASTROPODA, which means "stomach-footed." The snail uses his foot to move. The squid and the octopus belong to the class CEPHALODA, which means "head-footed." There are about 110,000 species.

PHYLUM ECHINODERMATA:

ECHINODERMS. Members of this phylum are starfish, sea urchins, sea cucumbers, and sand dollars. Numbering about 6000, they are animals with spiny skin found in marine environments.

PHYLUM ARTHROPODA:

ARTHROPODS. This is the largest phylum in the animal kingdom, numbering around 1 million species. Its members have paired appendages, a jointed external skeleton, and three body parts—a head, thorax, and abdomen.

Crustacea. This class includes crabs, crayfish, and lobsters. There are about 30,000 species, and most live in water.

Arachnida. Members of this class include spiders, scorpions, ticks, and mites. In spiders the head and thorax are fused, forming the *cephalothorax*. Spiders have four pairs of legs and special glands called *spinnerets*, which are used in spinning a web. When an insect prey enters the web, the spider injects it with poison to facilitate capture. There are about 35,000 species of arachnids.

Chilopoda. This class includes about 2000 species of centipedes.

Diplopoda. This class includes about 7000 species of millipedes.

Insecta. This is the largest class of arthropods, with over 700,000 insect species, including bees, mosquitoes, grasshoppers, butterflies, and fleas. These animals have three body sections, three pairs of legs, and two antennae. Many also have wings. During their lifetimes, insects generally undergo bodily changes called *metamorphoses*. The butterfly, for example, passes through four stages: egg, larva (caterpillar), pupa (cocoon), and adult.

Dissection of frog

A. Cut with scissors from tail up through skin of stomach to throat. Extend cut along all four legs.

B. Cut through bones of chest and remove them.

C. Pin back sides of body.

D. Remove muscles that overlie internal organs.

E. Locate
    Heart, arteries, veins
    Liver (large, reddish)
    Right and left lungs
    Digestive system (esophagus, stomach, intestines)
    Spleen (reddish globe attached to small intestine)
    Pancreas (in transparent membrane)
    Gallbladder (greenish globe)
    Kidneys (small, pink, under intestines)
    Backbone

Muscles

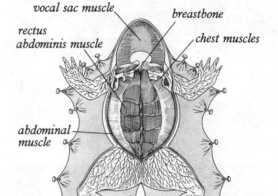

Internal organs

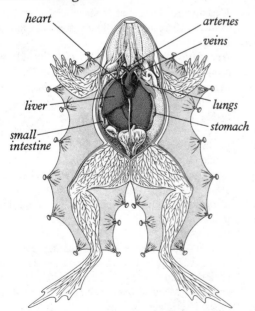

Digestive system

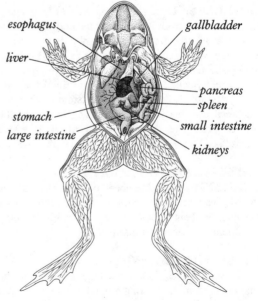

Vertebrates

Robin

The opossum is the only marsupial in North America.

Whales are placental mammals that have returned to the ocean.

PHYLUM CHORDATA:
PRIMARILY THE VERTEBRATES.

Agnatha. There are two members of this class of jawless fish: the lamprey and the hagfish. They are long, tubular fish with skeletons comprised of cartilage.

Chondrichthyes. These shark, ray, and skate fish have jaws and skeletons comprised only of cartilage.

Osteichthyes. This class consists of all the fishes we normally think of when we use the word *fish*. Their principal characteristic is the possession of true bone, either as a skeleton or a bony plate. All possess gills and live most of the time in water, but a few, such as lungfish, can breathe air or be found occasionally on land.

Amphibia. There are tailless amphibians, such as frogs; and amphibians with tails, such as salamanders. Amphibians generally lay their eggs in water and the young develop there; but the adults of many species live most of their lives on land. There are about 2000 species.

Reptilia. This class of reptiles includes snakes, turtles, and lizards. The reptile hatches from an egg that has its own water supply; this allows these animals to live and reproduce entirely on land. Like fish and am-

phibians, the reptiles are cold-blooded. As the temperature of the environment changes, their body temperature changes too. There are about 7000 species of reptiles.

Aves. This class is comprised of birds, all of which have feathers, and most of which fly. Birds that do not fly include penguins and ostriches. Birds and mammals are warm-blooded; that is, their body temperature remains the same regardless of the environment. There are approximately 8000 species.

Mammalia. Among the members of the mammal class are dogs, squirrels, whales, porpoises, and humans. Mammals generally have hair and nurse their young on milk from mammary glands. There are three subclasses. *Monotremes*, such as the duck-billed platypus, lay eggs. *Marsupials*, including the kangaroo and the opossum, have pouches where the young finish their development. In *placentals*, the female develops an organ called the *placenta* through which the embryo receives nourishment inside its mother's body. The young are born fully developed. Most of the animals you think about when you hear or read the word "animal" are placental, including dogs, cats, mice, cattle, and people. There are about 4500 species of mammals.

cellulose

Dictionary of biology

cilia

hybrid, *in this case, a mule*

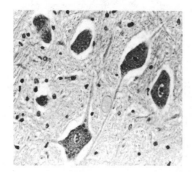
neurons

adaptation. Means by which an organism fits itself to live and reproduce in a particular environment.

aerobic. Organisms or processes that can live or occur only in the presence of oxygen.

allele. Variant form of a gene, producing a different trait, for example, hair or eye color.

anaerobic. Indicates the absence of free oxygen.

asexual. Reproduction without male and female cells.

assimilation. Conversion of digested products into cytoplasm by an organism.

ATP (adenosine triphosphate). Compound synthesized within the cell that provides energy for cellular functions.

autotroph. Organism that can transform light energy into the chemical energy of glucose.

bacillus. Rodlike bacterium.

backbone. Column of bones (vertebrae) along the center of the back.

binary fission. Process by which an organism divides into two approximately equal parts.

cancer. Group of diseases characterized by uncontrolled cellular growth.

cell. The smallest functional unit of life.

cellulose. A complex carbohydrate. The chief component of the wall of plant cells.

chlorophyll. Green coloring matter of plants. It converts light energy into chemical energy.

chromatin. Hereditary material consisting of nucleoproteins from which chromosomes are formed during mitosis.

chromosomes. Composed of chromatin and located in the nucleus, they contain the genes.

cilia. Small hairlike bits of cytoplasm that move in unison to move cells or particles.

clone. A group of cells all descended from a single common ancestor.

cytoplasm. Cellular material between the cell membrane and the nuclear membrane; a colloidal suspension that contains the organelles of most cells.

dicot. Member of the class of flowering plants having two undeveloped leaves in the embryo of the seed.

differentiation. Specialization of cells and tissues during development for the purpose of performing particular functions.

diffusion. The movement of molecules of gases or liquids that causes them to spread out uniformly in a container.

digestion. Conversion of insoluble food substances into soluble substances that may be absorbed.

diploid. The number of chromosomes normally present in the nucleus of a cell, except the gametes.

DNA (dioxyribonucleic acid). Genetic material of all cells.

dominant. In genetics, one of any pair of opposite Mendelian characters that dominates over the other.

embryo. Organism in the earliest stages of its development.

endocrine. Any gland that produces one or more secretions that are carried by the lymph or blood to some other body part whose function they regulate.

endoplasmic reticulum. Network of thin membranes across the cytoplasm of the cell.

enzyme. Organic substance produced in cells that causes change in other substances by catalytic action.

epidermis. Outermost layer of skin in vertebrates; outermost layer of cells covering seed plants and ferns; outermost layer of the shells of many mollusks.

epithelium. Cellular membranous tissue that covers surfaces, forms glands, and lines most cavities of the body.

eukaryotes. Cells that have a nucleus surrounded by a nuclear membrane and that contain complex organelles.

fission. Form of asexual reproduction in which the parent organism divides into two or more parts, each becoming an independent individual.

flagellum. Whiplike part serving as an organ of locomotion in bacteria and certain cells.

genus. In the classification of organisms, the main subdivision of a family; includes one or more species.

haploid. Having only one set of chromosomes, as in gametes.

heredity. The transmission of characteristics from parent to offspring through genes.

heterotroph. Organism that must use the energy of the bonds of organic molecules formed by other cells.

homeostasis. Maintenance of equilibrium between an organism and its environment or between a cell and its environment.

hybrid. Offspring of two animals or plants of different species.

ingestion. Process of taking food into an organism for digestion.

meiosis. Nuclear changes in the maturation of germ cells in which the chromosome number is reduced from diploid to haploid.

metabolism. Continuous processes in cells by which food is formed into cytoplasm and by which cytoplasm is broken down into simpler substances or waste products with the release of energy.

mitochondria. Cell organelle responsible for the production of energy.

mitosis. Cell division in which the nuclear chromatin is formed into a long thread that in turn forms chromosomes that are split; two daughter cells are formed.

Monera. Kingdom of organisms having no distinct nucleus in their cells; the bacteria.

monocot. One of two groups of flowering plants with parallel veins in their leaves and flowering parts in threes or groups of threes.

mutant. Organism with inheritable characteristics different from those of the parents.

mutation. Sudden variation in some inheritable characteristic.

neuron. The structural and functional unit of the nervous system, consisting of the nerve cell body and its processes.

nucleus. Central mass of cytoplasm in most cells necessary for growth and reproduction.

organ. Group of tissues working together to perform a special function.

organelle ("small organ"). Any one of several parts of a cell that performs specific functions for that cell.

osmosis. Diffusion of water through a semipermeable membrane.

phagocyte. Any white blood cell that ingests and destroys other cells, bacteria, etc. Any cell capable of engulfing a microorganism.

phenotype. The sum of the characteristics shown by an organism.

phylum. The most broad, basic division within a kingdom.

plasmolysis. Shrinkage of cells from osmotic loss of water.

prokarocytes. Cells that do not have membrane-bound nuclei or organelles.

protist. Member of the kingdom of Protista; unicellular organism with specialized organelles.

recessive. Any one of a pair of opposite Mendelian characters that remains latent unless both characters are present.

regeneration. Growth of a new part to replace one that is injured or lost; a form of asexual reproduction in some animals.

respiration. Process by which an organism or cell takes in oxygen, utilizes it, and gives off products, especially carbon dioxide. The chemical reactions in a cell that take food molecules apart to release the food's energy, which is then stored as ATP.

RNA (ribonucleic acid). Polymer of ribonucleotides; important in protein synthesis.

species. Group of organisms that has common characteristics and is capable of interbreeding; a subdivision of a genus.

tissue. Grouping of cells and matter between the cells performing a common function.

viruses. Group of parasites composed of protein and nucleic acid; infectious agents smaller than bacteria that require host cells for replication.

zygote. Single cell formed by the union of an egg and a sperm; a fertilized ovum.

For Further Reference

Andrewes, C.H.
Natural History of Viruses
Norton Publishing
Berger, Melvin
Tools of Modern Biology
Thomas Y. Crowell
Carlquist, Sherwin
Island Life
Natural History Press

Curtiss, Helena
Invitation to Biology
Worth Publishing
Tompkins, Peter and Bird, Christopher
The Secret Life of Plants
Harper & Row

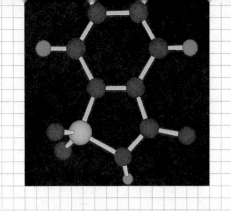

Chemistry

It is customary to break the sciences into several branches. The most familiar are biology, chemistry, and physics. Increasingly, however, our understanding of the way nature works suggests that these divisions are somewhat artificial. Scientists try to bridge the gaps between the branches by becoming biochemists, biophysicists, nuclear chemists, and so forth.

Even though the distinctions among the sciences are becoming blurred, it is still useful to be able to identify chemistry as opposed to other sciences. It is commonly said that the biologist studies the properties of life, the chemist studies the properties of matter, and the physicist studies the properties of energy. But the biologist also studies chemical interactions in living things, the chemist studies not only matter produced by living things but also the transfer of energy in some forms of matter, and the physicist intrudes into the domains of life and matter. There are, however, specific forms of matter the chemist studies.

Matter

The science of chemistry is concerned with the study of matter, its properties, its structure, its composition, and changes in its composition. *Matter* is anything that occupies space and has *mass*, which is a measure of the amount of matter in an object. Under ordinary conditions at Earth's surface, the mass of an object is the same as its weight, or nearly so. Since weight is defined as the pull of Earth's gravitation on an object, weight becomes less as matter moves away from Earth toward outer space, but its mass stays the same.

When studying samples of matter, chemists find that most are *mixtures* that can be separated by physical means into various *compounds*, which in turn can be broken down into *elements*. An element is the simplest kind of chemical substance that cannot be broken down into simpler substances by ordinary chemical means. Oxygen, hydrogen, carbon, sodium, and chlorine are examples of elements. A compound is formed by the chemical union of two or more elements. New compounds can also be formed by the chemical interaction of other compounds. Water, made up of hydrogen and oxygen, carbon dioxide, made up of carbon and oxygen, and sodium chloride, or table salt, made up of sodium and chlorine, are examples of compounds. When salt is dissolved in water, the resulting salt water is an example of a mixture. Carbon dioxide bubbled into water makes soda water, another example of a mixture.

The smallest unit of an element that can enter into chemical change is an *atom*. All atoms of a given element have the same basic structure, although they may differ slightly in mass. At present, 108 elements are known, but only 88 of these are found in nature. The rest are synthetic and are too unstable to exist in nature. The number of ways in which the elements can combine into compounds is very much greater than the number of elements. In fact, the number of compounds that are possible is so large as to be practically infinite.

Each element has been assigned a symbol consisting of one or two letters. Chemists use these symbols to write formulas for compounds. For example, the symbol for hydrogen is H, for oxygen it is O, for carbon it is C, for chlorine it is Cl; but the symbol for sodium is Na, from the Latin *natrium*.

The *formula* of a compound shows the different elements it contains and the number of each atom present, or the ratio in which the different elements are present. For most compounds, such as water and carbon dioxide, the formula represents the makeup of the *molecules* of the substance; that is, the smallest particle of the substance that can exist free and retain the properties of that substance. A molecule of water is H_2O, and a molecule of carbon dioxide is CO_2. Some compounds, such as sodium chloride, are made up of *ions*, charged particles that form when the atoms combine. In sodium chloride, there are equal numbers of positive ions of sodium (Na^+) and of negative chloride ions (Cl^-); thus, its formula is written NaCl, indicating one sodium ion to one chloride ion. Some compounds that consist of ions, such as sodium hydroxide (NaOH), contain certain combinations of elements called *polyatomic ions*. The hydroxide ion, OH^-, is a polyatomic ion in the compound sodium hydroxide. Another example is the sulfate group, SO_4^{2-}, as it occurs; for example, in aluminum sulfate, $Al_2(SO_4)_3$. This formula indicates that aluminum sulfate consists of Al^{3+} and SO_4^{2-} ions in the ratio of 2 to 3.

Phases of matter. Matter may exist in three states or *phases*: solid, liquid, or gas. A familiar example is water, which in the solid phase is called ice or snow, in the liquid phase, water, and in the gaseous phase, steam or water vapor. The phase of any substance depends on the temperature and pressure. At atmospheric pressure, the temperature at which the solid form changes to the liquid is called the *melting point*. The temperature at which the *vapor pressure* of the liquid (that is, the pressure of the gaseous phase of the substance) in equilibrium with the liquid phase becomes equal to the atmospheric pressure, is called the *boiling point*.

Solids. A *solid* retains its shape and resists forces tending to change its shape. It is not so easy to pull apart as a liquid. The particles of some solids, such as sodium chloride, are arranged in definite patterns called crystals. Other solids, such as chalk, are not crystalline but amorphous.

Liquids. In a *liquid*, the particles are free to move about but not to separate from one another. A liquid will take the shape of the container in which it is placed, but will not expand to fill the entire space available to it.

Gases. A *gas* has no boundary surface. It will take the shape of and expand to fill any container in which it is placed. Gases respond readily to changes in pressure and temperature. The volume of the gas particles is usually only a small fraction of the total space they occupy.

Amounts of the elements (by weight)

Most of Earth's crust, including its air and water, is made from compounds. Some uncombined elements, such as oxygen in air, also occur in nature.

Air

nitrogen (N₂)
78.09%

oxygen (O₂)
20.95%

argon (Ar)
0.93%

traces:
carbon dioxide (CO₂)
neon (Ne)
helium (He)
methane (CH₄)
krypton (Kr)
hydrogen (H₂)
xenon (Xe)
ozone (O₃)
etc.

Element	Symbol	Percent in earth	Percent in human body
oxygen	O	47%	65%
silicon	Si	28%	trace
aluminum	Al	8%	—
iron	Fe	5%	trace
calcium	Ca	4%	2%
carbon	C	trace	18%
hydrogen	H	trace	3%
phosphorus	P	trace	1%
potassium	K	3%	trace
magnesium	Mg	2%	trace
nitrogen	N		
sulfur	S		
chlorine	Cl		
fluorine	F		
copper	Cu	traces	traces
iodine	I		
manganese	Mn		
zinc	Zn		
about 70 other elements		traces	

Phases of matter

Particles of a solid vibrate. Particles of a liquid are free to move but not to separate, except at the surface. Particles of a gas are unattached.

Solid

Liquid

Gas

Changes in matter. The changes that matter can undergo may be classified as physical or chemical. In a *physical change*, there is no change in the composition or chemical properties of the substances involved: that is, no new combinations of elements in compounds are formed. For example, the freezing of water to form ice is a physical change, as are all changes of phase. Molecules of ice, water, or steam are all still H20. Physical change can also be seen in the dissolving of salt into water. Both the salt and the water retain their chemical makeup and properties, although some of their physical properties are changed.

A *chemical change* or *reaction* always results in the formation of one or more new substances. Chemical reactions take place when new combinations of atoms, or compounds, are formed. The burning of gasoline is an example. Gasoline combines with oxygen to form carbon dioxide and water.

Both physical and chemical changes involve energy changes. For example, energy is stored in water when it is changed into steam, and energy is released when gasoline burns. Energy does not change to matter, however, in physical and chemical changes.

For more information about matter and energy, see Physical Sciences in Volume 1.

Physical and chemical change

When water is heated and becomes steam, a physical change occurs. The molecules move apart, but their composition stays the same.

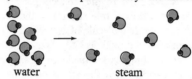

water   steam

When the octane in gasoline burns, a chemical change occurs. Atoms of carbon (black spheres) and atoms of hydrogen (brown spheres) that were combined in the molecule of octane come apart and are recombined with atoms of oxygen (red spheres) to form molecules of water and carbon dioxide.

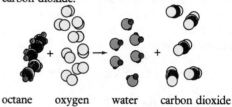

octane   oxygen   water   carbon dioxide

Atomic structure

The idea that matter can be divided only so far before coming to a particle, called an atom, which cannot be divided any further, was first proposed by the Greek philosophers Leucippus and Democritus about 400 B.C. More than 2000 years later, the idea became the basis for modern chemistry. In 1803, the English chemist John Dalton reformulated the atomic theory and showed that it explains a great deal about the chemical properties of substances. Since then, the atomic theory has become firmly established.

Today a great deal is known about the structure of atoms. In 1898, J.J. Thomson, an English physicist, showed that atoms can be made to give up negatively charged particles, which he called *electrons*. Since all atoms are electrically neutral, they must contain as many positive charges as they do negatively charged electrons. Ernest Rutherford, another English physicist, proposed the theory that the atom consists of a nucleus with a positive charge with enough electrons rotating around it to balance the charge. This theory was modified by Niels Bohr, a Danish physicist, in 1913. His model of the atom, as further modified by modern quantum mechanics, is still in use today.

The nucleus of the atom consists of positively charged particles called *protons*, and neutral particles called *neutrons*. Each neutron has almost exactly the same mass as a proton. Moving around the nucleus are *electrons*, equal in number to the protons in the nucleus. Electrons have a mass that is only about one two-thousandth that of a neutron or proton. When computing the mass of an atom, therefore, a chemist considers the masses of the electrons to be 0. Hence, the *atomic mass* of a given atom is considered to be the sum of its protons and neutrons, each assigned a mass of 1 atomic mass unit. The atomic mass of an atom is also called its *mass number*. For example, the atomic mass of ordinary carbon, which has six protons and six neutrons, is 12.

Particles making up an atom

Particle	Symbol	Charge	Approximate mass (atomic mass units)	Location
proton	p	1+	1 amu	nucleus
neutron	n	0	1 amu	nucleus
electron	e	1−	1/1837 amu (or 0)	outside nucleus

Bohr pictured the movement of the electrons around the nucleus as somewhat like the orbiting of the planets around the sun. Diagrams of atomic structures used to explain chemical reactions still use what is essentially the Bohr model. However, a somewhat different model, in which each electron is represented as a cloud of negative charge, is necessitated by today's more advanced theory, which describes the probabilities of electrons being found at various distances and directions from the nucleus, rather than in fixed orbits.

Three models of the atom

There are various models, or ways of representing and thinking about the atom. Here are three that are commonly used. Each is shown for boron, which has atomic number 5.

The Bohr model. Electrons are pictured as orbiting the nucleus in definite paths, somewhat in the way that planets orbit the sun. Although this is a familiar model, it is inadequate because it is now known that electrons do not follow definite paths. Nevertheless, the Bohr model is a useful way to picture the atom in some applications. It is also the easiest model to understand, so it is frequently taught in the beginning, and then followed with more sophisticated models.

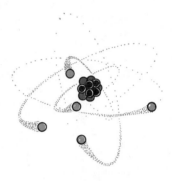

The electron-cloud model. Electrons are not shown as particles that follow precise paths in this model. Instead, the electrons are indicated by definite regions in which there is a high probability of finding electrons. These regions are often known as electron shells. In this model it is possible to picture electrons as either waves or particles. Each idea of the nature of electrons is useful in different applications.

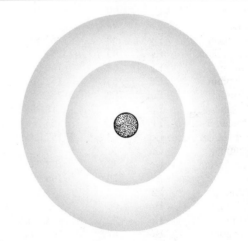

The electron-shell diagram. Chemists recognize that no model can really give an accurate picture of what an atom would look like if it were possible to see it. Therefore, it is often best to use a simplified diagram that provides information without attempting to give a physical picture of an atom. The electron-shell diagram, in which each electron is shown as a particle, and the shells are represented as concentric rings around the nucleus, provides useful information without using a physical representation that might lead to misunderstanding.

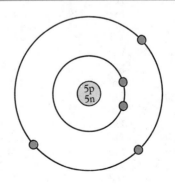

Table of atomic masses

Name	Symbol	Atomic number	Atomic mass	Name	Symbol	Atomic number	Atomic mass
Actinium	Ac	89	227	Mercury	Hg	80	200.59
Aluminum	Al	13	26.9815	Molybdenum	Mo	42	95.94
Americium	Am	95	243	Neodymium	Nd	60	144.24
Antimony	Sb	51	121.75	Neon	Ne	10	20.179
Argon	Ar	18	39.948	Neptunium	Np	93	237
Arsenic	As	33	74.9216	Nickel	Ni	28	58.71
Astatine	At	85	210	Niobium	Nb	41	92.906
Barium	Ba	56	137.34	Nitrogen	N	7	14.0067
Berkelium	Bk	97	247	Nobelium	No	102	255
Beryllium	Be	4	9.0122	Osmium	Os	76	190.2
Bismuth	Bi	83	208.980	Oxygen	O	8	15.9994
Boron	B	5	10.811	Palladium	Pd	46	106.4
Bromine	Br	35	79.904	Phosphorus	P	15	30.9738
Cadmium	Cd	48	112.40	Platinum	Pt	78	195.09
Calcium	Ca	20	40.08	Plutonium	Pu	94	244
Californium	Cf	98	251	Polonium	Po	84	210
Carbon	C	6	12.01115	Potassium	K	19	39.102
Cerium	Ce	58	140.12	Praseodymium	Pr	59	140.9077
Cesium	Cs	55	132.9055	Promethium	Pm	61	147
Chlorine	Cl	17	35.453	Protactinium	Pa	91	231
Chromium	Cr	24	51.996	Radium	Ra	88	226.0254
Cobalt	Co	27	58.9332	Radon	Rn	86	222
Copper	Cu	29	63.546	Rhenium	Re	75	186.2
Curium	Cm	96	247	Rhodium	Rh	45	102.9055
Dysprosium	Dy	66	162.50	Rubidium	Rb	37	85.47
Einsteinium	Es	99	254	Ruthenium	Ru	44	101.07
Erbium	Er	68	167.26	Rutherfordium	Rf	104	261
Europium	Eu	63	151.96	Samarium	Sm	62	150.35
Fermium	Fm	100	257	Scandium	Sc	21	44.956
Fluorine	F	9	18.9984	Selenium	Se	34	78.96
Francium	Fr	87	223	Silicon	Si	14	28.086
Gadolinium	Gd	64	157.25	Silver	Ag	47	107.868
Gallium	Ga	31	69.72	Sodium	Na	11	22.9898
Germanium	Ge	32	72.59	Strontium	Sr	38	87.62
Gold	Au	79	196.967	Sulfur	S	16	32.064
Hafnium	Hf	72	178.49	Tantalum	Ta	73	180.948
Hahnium	Ha	105	262	Technetium	Tc	43	99
Helium	He	2	4.0026	Tellurium	Te	52	127.60
Holmium	Ho	67	164.930	Terbium	Tb	65	158.9254
Hydrogen	H	1	1.00797	Thallium	Tl	81	204.37
Indium	In	49	114.82	Thorium	Th	90	232.038
Iodine	I	53	126.9045	Thulium	Tm	69	168.934
Iridium	Ir	77	192.2	Tin	Sn	50	118.69
Iron	Fe	26	55.847	Titanium	Ti	22	47.90
Krypton	Kr	36	83.80	Tungsten	W	74	183.85
Lanthanum	La	57	138.91	Uranium	U	92	238.03
Lawrencium	Lw	103	256	Vanadium	V	23	50.9414
Lead	Pb	82	207.19	Xenon	Xe	54	131.30
Lithium	Li	3	6.941	Ytterbium	Yb	70	173.04
Lutetium	Lu	71	174.97	Yttrium	Y	39	88.9059
Magnesium	Mg	12	24.305	Zinc	Zn	30	65.37
Manganese	Mn	25	54.9380	Zirconium	Zr	40	91.22
Mendelevium	Md	101	258				

All elements exist in more than one form, differing in atomic mass but having the same atomic number. These different forms are called *isotopes*. The element hydrogen, for example, has three isotopes. For many chemical calculations, it is important to know the atomic masses of various elements. These are relative to a standard, usually the most abundant isotope of carbon, which is assigned a value of 12, the same as its mass number. The table of atomic masses (page 150) shows that most of these values are close to whole numbers. One reason they are not whole numbers is that the atomic mass of every element is an average of the masses of the isotopes in the proportions in which they exist in nature.

For example, carbon 13 and carbon 14 are both found in small amounts in nature. Therefore the atomic mass shown for carbon in the table is 12.01115, which reflects the amount of carbon 13 and carbon 14 in a typical sample of carbon. Since the atomic mass of carbon 12 is 12, it is easy to see that most of the mass is due to carbon 12.

In the Bohr model of the atom, the electrons orbit the nucleus in definite shells. A certain maximum number of electrons can fit into each shell. The first shell, closest to the nucleus, is filled when it has two electrons. The second and third shells can each hold eight electrons. The fourth and fifth shells can each hold 18 electrons, and the sixth and seventh shells can each hold 32 electrons. It is the electrons that determine the chemical properties of atoms.

Isotopes of hydrogen

Natural elements are mixtures of different isotopes. Hydrogen has three isotopes: protium with an atomic mass of 1, deuterium, with an atomic mass of 2, and tritium, with an atomic mass of 3. Since there is a much larger percentage of protium (atomic mass = 1) than of the other isotopes, the average atomic mass of hydrogen is 1.008. Hydrogen is the only element with special names for its isotopes. It can be seen in the diagrams that all atoms of hydrogen have the same charge (number of protons) on the nucleus, and thus the same atomic number. They also all have the same number (1) of orbiting electrons. The atoms are all shown as electron-shell diagrams, which provide the essential information without trying to suggest actual "pictures" of atoms.

| protium | deuterium | tritium |
| atomic mass = 1 | atomic mass = 2 | atomic mass = 3 |

⬤ proton (+)

◯ neutron (n)

● electron (—)

Structures of the first 18 elements

1H

The number next to the symbol for each element is the atomic number. The diagrams reflect the pairing of electrons in the first three shells around the nucleus. The number of neutrons (n) on each nucleus is the number in the most common isotope of the element. The number of protons (p) equals the number of electrons in the atom.

2 He

| **3 Li** | **4 Be** | **5 B** | **6 C** | **7 N** | **8 O** | **9 F** | **10 Ne** |

| **11 Na** | **12 Mg** | **13 Al** | **14 Si** | **15 P** | **16 S** | **17 Cl** | **18 Ar** |

Chemical reactions

In nearly all chemical reactions, only the electrons in the outermost shell are involved. Chemical reactions consist of the transfer of electrons from some atoms to others, or the sharing of electrons between atoms. Atoms react in such a way as to reach a state of greatest stability. For elements with atomic numbers of 1 through 5 (that is, hydrogen, helium, lithium, beryllium, and boron) that state is usually two electrons in the outer shell, and for all other atoms it is usually eight electrons in the outer shell. The outer shell of an atom is called its *valence shell*, and the electrons in the valence shell are the atom's *valence electrons*. No atom can have more than eight valence electrons, even though its outer shell may be capable of holding many more; the chemical demands of the atom are satisfied by eight. There are six elements, called the inert or *noble gases*, that do not ordinarily undergo chemical reactions because in the elementary state, their valence shells contain a stable configuration of electrons. These elements are helium, neon, argon, krypton, xenon, and radon.

An illustration of a reaction in which an electron is transferred from one atom to another is the reaction of sodium and chlorine to produce sodium chloride, NaCl. The sodium atom transfers its one valence electron to the chlorine atom, which has seven. This leaves each atom with an outer shell of eight, and, therefore, with the stable electron structure of a noble gas. The loss of an electron leaves the sodium with a positive charge; the gain of an electron gives the chlorine a negative charge. That is, both become ions, which are atoms (or groups of atoms) with electric charges. The attraction between the oppositely charged ions is the

Six gases that do not form compounds easily

Noble gas	Atomic number	Electrons in valence shell
helium	2	2
neon	10	8
argon	18	8
krypton	36	8
xenon	54	8
radon	86	8

bond that holds the two atoms together. This type of chemical bond is called an *ionic bond*.

Another way of completing the outer shell is for two or more atoms to share their electrons so that each has the stable configuration of a noble gas without an actual transfer. This type of chemical bond is called a *covalent bond*. Covalent bonding takes place in the formation of molecules of elements, like hydrogen (H_2), oxygen (O_2), and chlorine (Cl_2), that usually exist as diatomic molecules in the elementary state. The great majority of chemical compounds also have covalent bonds rather than ionic bonds, and exist as molecules rather than as ions. An example of covalent bonding may be seen in the sharing of electrons between a hydrogen atom and a chlorine atom in the compound hydrogen chloride, HCl. In a molecule of hydrogen chloride, the hydrogen atom has a stable structure of two electrons in its outer shell, and the chlorine atom has a stable structure of eight in its outer shell.

Electron transfer	**Electron sharing**
Formation of sodium chloride (NaCl)	Formation of hydrogen chloride (HCl)

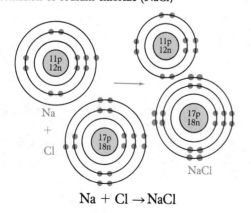

$$Na + Cl \rightarrow NaCl$$

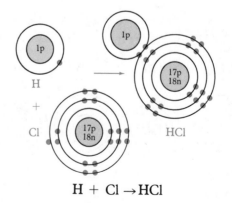

$$H + Cl \rightarrow HCl$$

How to balance equations.

The ratio in which atoms of elements combine to form compounds is determined by the number of electrons that the atoms lose, gain, or share when combining with other atoms. For example, when atoms of the metal calcium combine with atoms of the nonmetal fluorine, each calcium atom loses two electrons, forming Ca^{2+} ions, and each fluorine atom gains one electron, forming F^- ions. Since the compound that forms, calcium fluoride, is electrically neutral, there must be two F^- ions for each Ca^{2+} ion. Thus, the formula for the compound is written CaF_2. Formulas for many other compounds between metals and nonmetals are determined in a similar way.

When two nonmetals combine to form a compound, their atoms share electrons. Depending on various conditions, the number of electrons shared by two given elements may vary. For example, each of two atoms of oxygen may share two electrons with one atom of sulfur, which shares four electrons in the compound SO_2, sulfur dioxide. But in sulfur trioxide, SO_3, the sulfur atom shares six electrons, so three atoms of oxygen, each sharing two electrons, are required.

A chemical change or reaction can be expressed as a *chemical equation*, in which symbols and formulas for the substances involved are joined by plus signs and an arrow. The substances that appear at the left of the arrow are the *reactants*; those that appear at the right are the *products* of the reaction. For example, the equation

$$2H_2 + O_2 \rightarrow 2H_2O$$

states that two molecules of hydrogen react with one molecule of water to form two molecules of water. Since both hydrogen and oxygen exist as diatomic molecules, we write their formulas as H_2 and O_2. When an equation is *balanced*, all atoms appearing in the reactants must also appear in the products, although in different combinations. So the number 2 is written before the H_2 and the H_2O in order to balance the numbers of atoms in the equation.

Writing a laboratory report

Problem: You are presented with an unknown white crystal, which you suspect to be table salt, sodium chloride (NaCl). You perform a series of tests (which do not include tasting, since many white crystals are poisonous). Here is a format for presenting your report on the tests.

NOTE: The arrow pointing downward in a chemical equation indicates a *precipitate*, a solid that forms from a liquid and settles to the bottom of the liquid.

PROBLEM: Determine the chemical composition of an unknown white crystal.

PROCEDURE

STEP 1: Dissolved the crystal in 1/3 test tube of H_2O. (Dissolved easily.)

STEP 2: Added 2mL silver nitrate, $AgNO_3$. White precipitate appeared and settled to bottom of tube. Reaction could be
$$AgNO_3 + NaCl \rightarrow AgCl\downarrow + NaNO_3$$

STEP 3: Added 3mL dilute nitric acid, HNO_3, to solution. No effect on precipitate. ($AgCl$ does not react with HNO_3.)

STEP 4: Poured off solution leaving precipitate in test tube. Added 5mL ammonium hydroxide. Precipitate dissolved. Reaction must be with ammonia, NH_3.
$$AgCl + 2NH_3 \longrightarrow Ag(NH_3)_2Cl$$

REMARKS: After getting results outlined, concluded that the unknown crystal was salt (NaCl).

The periodic table

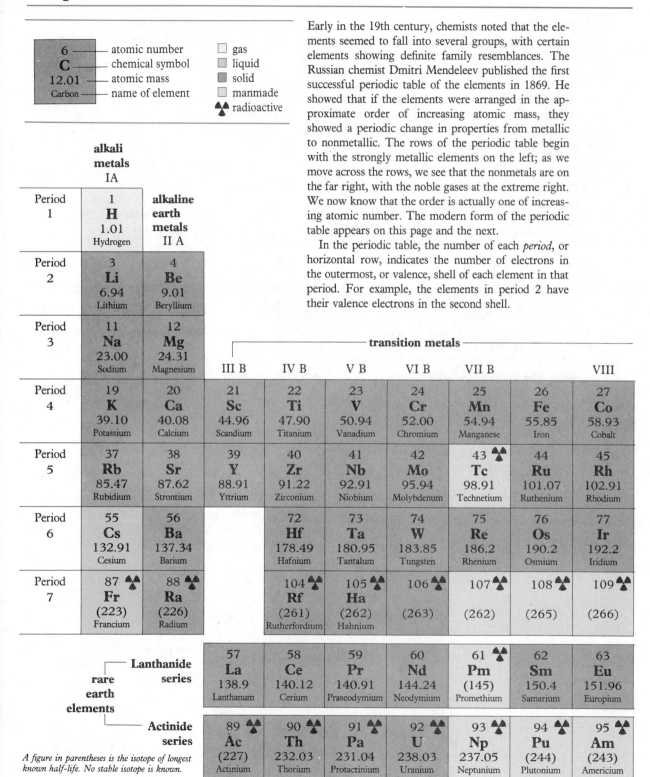

Early in the 19th century, chemists noted that the elements seemed to fall into several groups, with certain elements showing definite family resemblances. The Russian chemist Dmitri Mendeleev published the first successful periodic table of the elements in 1869. He showed that if the elements were arranged in the approximate order of increasing atomic mass, they showed a periodic change in properties from metallic to nonmetallic. The rows of the periodic table begin with the strongly metallic elements on the left; as we move across the rows, we see that the nonmetals are on the far right, with the noble gases at the extreme right. We now know that the order is actually one of increasing atomic number. The modern form of the periodic table appears on this page and the next.

In the periodic table, the number of each *period*, or horizontal row, indicates the number of electrons in the outermost, or valence, shell of each element in that period. For example, the elements in period 2 have their valence electrons in the second shell.

Key:
- 6 — atomic number
- C — chemical symbol
- 12.01 — atomic mass
- Carbon — name of element
- ☐ gas
- ☐ liquid
- ■ solid
- ☐ manmade
- ☢ radioactive

A figure in parentheses is the isotope of longest known half-life. No stable isotope is known.

As we move from left to right in each period, the number of valence electrons increases until, at the end of the period, we reach an element whose valence shell is full. For example, at the end of period 2 is the element neon, a noble gas whose valence shell contains eight electrons.

Each element in a vertical column, or *group*, has the same number of valence electrons. For example, each element in group VIIA has seven electrons in its valence shell. Because of this similarity of structure, the elements of group VIIA have a number of similar or related physical properties and undergo many similar chemical reactions as well. For example, the elements in this group are called by a family name, the *halogens* ("salt-formers"), because of their common property of reacting with metals to form salts. A familiar example is sodium chloride, formed by the halogen chlorine when it reacts with sodium, a member of the family of *alkali metals,* in group IA of the periodic table.

noble gases
O

| | | | | | | 2 **He** 4.00 Helium |

nonmetals

III A	IV A	V A	VI A	VII A	
5 **B** 10.81 Boron	6 **C** 12.01 Carbon	7 **N** 14.01 Nitrogen	8 **O** 16.00 Oxygen	9 **F** 19.00 Fluorine	10 **Ne** 20.18 Neon
13 **Al** 26.98 Aluminum	14 **Si** 28.09 Silicon	15 **P** 30.97 Phosphorus	16 **S** 32.06 Sulfur	17 **Cl** 35.45 Chlorine	18 **Ar** 39.95 Argon

I B	II B		III A	IV A	V A	VI A	VII A	
28 **Ni** 58.71 Nickel	29 **Cu** 63.55 Copper	30 **Zn** 65.37 Zinc	31 **Ga** 69.72 Gallium	32 **Ge** 72.59 Germanium	33 **As** 74.92 Arsenic	34 **Se** 78.96 Selenium	35 **Br** 79.90 Bromine	36 **Kr** 83.80 Krypton
46 **Pd** 106.4 Palladium	47 **Ag** 107.87 Silver	48 **Cd** 112.40 Cadmium	49 **In** 114.82 Indium	50 **Sn** 118.69 Tin	51 **Sb** 121.75 Antimony	52 **Te** 127.60 Tellurium	53 **I** 126.90 Iodine	54 **Xe** 131.30 Xenon
78 **Pt** 195.09 Platinum	79 **Au** 196.97 Gold	80 **Hg** 200.59 Mercury	81 **Tl** 204.37 Thallium	82 **Pb** 207.2 Lead	83 **Bi** 208.98 Bismuth	84 **Po** (209) Polonium	85 **At** (210) Astatine	86 **Rn** (222) Radon
110 (269)	111 (272)							

other metals

64 **Gd** 157.25 Gadolinium	65 **Tb** 158.93 Terbium	66 **Dy** 162.50 Dysprosium	67 **Ho** 164.93 Holmium	68 **Er** 167.26 Erbium	69 **Tm** 168.93 Thulium	70 **Yb** 173.04 Ytterbium	71 **Lu** 174.97 Lutetium
96 **Cm** (247) Curium	97 **Bk** (247) Berkelium	98 **Cf** (251) Californium	99 **Es** (254) Einsteinium	100 **Fm** (257) Fermium	101 **Md** (258) Mendelevium	102 **No** (255) Nobelium	103 **Lw** (256) Lawrencium

Inorganic chemistry

Inorganic chemistry deals with the reactions of all the elements with the exception, for the most part, of carbon. Many of the reactions of inorganic chemistry are known as *oxidation-reduction* reactions, in which one substance that loses electrons is *oxidized*, and another that gains electrons is *reduced*. These two processes always go on simultaneously. When one substance is oxidized, another must be reduced. All reactions of the types known as direct combination, decomposition, and single replacement are oxidation-reduction reactions. The rusting of iron, forming ferric oxide, Fe_2O_3, is a familiar example of oxidation, with the iron being oxidized and oxygen, from the air, being reduced. It is because oxygen is such a common oxidizing agent that the whole process is often called, simply, "oxidation."

Many inorganic compounds can be classified as *acids*, *bases*, and *salts*. An acid is a compound that is able to give up hydrogen ions to some other compound. The compound that receives hydrogen ions from an acid is called a base. The products of the reaction between an acid and a base are water and a salt. When the acid and base that react are of equal strength, the reaction is called *neutralization*.

For example, hydrochloric acid reacts with the base sodium hydroxide to produce the salt sodium chloride and water:

$$HCl + NaOH \longrightarrow NaCl + H_2O$$

This reaction, like all acid-base reactions, is a kind of double replacement, in which there is an exchange of ions between two compounds.

Types of inorganic reactions

Type	Reactants	Products	Examples		
Direct combination or synthesis	element + element or compound + compound	compound	2Na + Cl$_2$ sodium chlorine	$\rightarrow$	2NaCl sodium chloride
			2CO + O$_2$ carbon oxygen monoxide	$\rightarrow$	2CO$_2$ carbon dioxide
Decomposition or analysis	compound	two or more elements or compounds	2HgO mercuric oxide	$\rightarrow$	2Hg + O$_2$ mercury oxygen
			2KClO$_3$ $\rightarrow$ potassium chlorate		2KCl + 3O$_2$ potassium oxygen chloride
Single replacement	element + compound	element + compound	Cl$_2$ + 2NaI chlorine sodium iodide	$\rightarrow$	I$_2$ + 2NaCl iodine sodium chloride
			Zn + H$_2$SO$_4$ zinc sulfuric acid	$\rightarrow$	H$_2$ + ZnSO$_4$ hydrogen zinc sulfate
Double replacement	compound + compound	compound + compound	NaCl + AgNO$_3$ sodium silver chloride nitrate	$\rightarrow$	NaNO$_3$ + AgCl sodium silver nitrate chloride
			2 HCl + FeS hydrochloric ferrous acid sulfide	$\rightarrow$	H$_2$S + FeCl$_2$ hydrogen ferrous sulfide chloride

Chemistry

Organic chemistry

The chemistry of most compounds of carbon is unique and is considered as a separate branch of chemistry, *organic chemistry*. It is called organic because until 1828 chemists believed that familiar carbon compounds, such as ethyl alcohol, acetic acid, and sugars, could only be produced by living things (that is, organisms). In 1828, however, the German chemist Friedrich Wöhler succeeded in making urea, a typical organic compound, from ammonium chloride and silver cyanate, typical inorganic compounds.

Carbon is unique because its atoms have the ability to link together to form chains of great size and complexity. Carbon has four electrons in its outer shell, and these are available for covalent sharing with other elements, but especially with other carbon atoms.

The number and variety of compounds that carbon forms with hydrogen, known as the *hydrocarbons*, is quite large. We can represent the simplest of these compounds, methane, CH_4, by a *structural formula* in which each dash represents a pair of shared electrons between the atoms indicated by their symbols:

$$
\begin{array}{c}
H \\
| \\
H-C-H \\
| \\
H
\end{array}
$$

Methane, the main component of natural gas, is the first in a series of hydrocarbons called the *alkanes*, characterized by *single bonds* between carbon atoms. A single bond exists when each of the atoms that share electrons contributes only one electron to the bond. The alkanes are *saturated* hydrocarbons; this means that they contain only single bonds.

A carbon atom may also share two or even three of its electrons with another carbon. The resulting compounds form other series of hydrocarbons. The *alkenes*, whose first member is ethylene (or ethene), are a series of hydrocarbons that have one *double* bond (written C=C) in their structure; and the *alkynes*, whose first member is acetylene (or alkyne), are a series that have a triple bond (written C≡C) in their structure. The *aromatics*, so-called because many members have a distinctive odor, are another important series of hydrocarbons. Each of the aromatics has a ring of six carbons that contains three double bonds. Organic compounds that contain double or triple bonds between carbon atoms are *unsaturated*, which means that they may undergo reactions in which hydrogen atoms are added at the site of the double or triple bond.

Many organic compounds that contain oxygen as well as hydrogen and carbon also form series of related compounds. Four such series are the *alcohols*, the *aldehydes*, the *ketones*, and the *organic acids*.

Structures of some hydrocarbons

Series	Hydro-carbon	Molecular formula	Structural formula
Alkane	Methane	CH_4	
	Ethane	C_2H_6	
Alkene	Ethene	C_2H_4	
	Propene	C_3H_6	
Alkyne	Ethyne	C_2H_2	
	Propyne	C_3H_4	
Aromatic	Benzene	C_6H_6	
	Toluene	C_7H_8	

Structures of some organic compounds of carbon, hydrogen, and oxygen

Series	Functional group	Example	Structural formula
Alcohols	—OH	ethyl alcohol	H—C—C—OH (with H's attached)
Aldehydes	—C= (with H)	formaldehyde	H—C=O (with H)

Series	Functional group	Example	Structural formula
Ketones	—C=O	acetone	H—C—C—C—H (with H, O, H)
Organic acids	—C (=O, —OH)	acetic acid	H—C—C (with H, O, OH)

The alcohols, aldehydes, ketones, and organic acids are each characterized by a *functional group*. The functional group is present in each compound and determines its properties.

Like inorganic compounds, organic compounds undergo characteristic types of reactions. These reactions include oxidation, addition, substitution, and esterfication. Examples are shown in the tables.

Some types of organic reactions

Type	What happens	Example
Oxidation of a hydrocarbon	A hydrocarbon reacts with oxygen, forming carbon dioxide and water.	H—C—H + 2O$_2$ → CO$_2$ + 2H$_2$O methane oxygen → carbon dioxide + water
Addition	Atoms (or groups) are added at a double bond, resulting in the saturation of the bond.	H—C=C—H + Cl$_2$ → H—C—C—H (Cl Cl) ethene (or ethylene) chlorine → dichloroethane
Substitution	Atoms (or groups) are replaced by atoms (or groups) of another kind.	H—C—C—H + Cl$_2$ → H—C—C—H (H Cl) + HCl ethane chlorine → ethyl chloride (or monochloroethane) + hydrogen chloride
Esterification	An organic acid reacts with an alcohol to form an ester and water.	H—C—C(=O, OH) + H—C—C—OH → H—C—C—O—C—C—H + H$_2$O acetic acid ethyl alcohol → ethyl acetate (an ester) + water

Nuclear chemistry

The reactions of both inorganic and organic chemistry involve changes that take place outside the nuclei of atoms. However, the nuclei of certain isotopes of many elements are unstable and break down; that is, they undergo *radioactive decay*. Isotopes whose nuclei break down in this process are called radioactive isotopes, or *radioisotopes*. When nuclei break down spontaneously, the process is called *natural radioactivity*. However, some nuclei can be made radioactive artificially, and they exhibit *induced radioactivity*.

Radioactive atoms emit three types of radiation: *alpha particles*, *beta particles*, and *gamma rays*. An alpha particle is made up of two protons and two neutrons, and is therefore identical to the nucleus of a helium atom. As such, its symbol is $^4_2$He, in which the 4 indicates the mass and the 2 indicates the atomic number. Symbols used for isotopes of other elements are written in the same system for the purpose of representing nuclear reactions. A beta particle is a high-speed electron coming from the nucleus, not the outer part, of the atom. Since the nucleus contains no electrons, beta particles are considered to come from the breakdown of neutrons, each of which forms a proton and an electron in the process. Gamma rays, which often accompany the emission of alpha or beta particles, are a very penetrating form of radiant energy similar to x-rays.

All the isotopes of every naturally occurring element with an atomic number above 83 are radioactive. They undergo decay, usually in a series of reactions, some with the emission of an alpha particle and some with the emission of a beta particle, ending with the formation of a stable isotope of lead. For example, uranium 238, that is, the isotope of uranium that has an atomic mass of 238, emits an alpha particle to form thorium 234, which, in turn, emits a beta particle to form protactinium 234. After a number of additional steps, the series ends with the formation of lead 206. Changes such as these, in which atoms of one element are converted into atoms of another element, are called *transmutations*.

Another example of a transmutation is the decay of carbon 14, which emits a beta particle, into nitrogen 14, which is stable. This nuclear reaction occurs naturally and is the basis for *radiocarbon dating*, a valuable technique for finding the age of objects containing carbon, such as wood, cloth, or paper. All such organic objects start out with a certain proportion of radioactive carbon 14. By determining the proportion of carbon 14 to the total carbon content, we can calculate the age of the object. In carrying out this calculation, the *half-life* of carbon 14 is used. The half-life is the period of time it takes for half of the radioactive atoms in a substance to decay. The period of time varies among different radioisotopes; for carbon 14, it is 5730 years.

Particles and symbols used in nuclear chemistry

Particle	Symbol	Charge	Mass in atomic mass units
Beta particle (electron)	$^0_{-1}$e	negative	0 amu
Positron	$^0_{+1}$e	positive	0 amu
Proton (hydrogen-1 nucleus)	$^1_1$H	positive	1 amu
Alpha particle (helium-4 nucleus)	$^4_2$He	positive	4 amu
Neutron	$^1_0$n	neutral	1 amu

Particle emission and half-lives

When a radioisotope decays, it may emit an alpha particle, a beta particle, or a positron. The half-lives of radioisotopes vary from very brief to very long periods of time. Some examples are listed here.

Radioisotope	Particle emission	Half-life
carbon 14	beta	5730 years
cobalt 60	beta	5.3 years
iodine 131	beta	8.07 days
uranium 238	alpha	4.51×10^9 years
radium 226	alpha	1620 years
potassium 42	beta	12.4 hours
francium 229	alpha	27.5 seconds
bismuth 212	alpha	60.5 minutes
silver 106	positron	24.5 minutes
yttrium 88	positron	2.0 hours
plutonium 239	alpha	24,000 years
lithium 8	beta	.88 seconds
nitrogen 13	positron	9.93 minutes

The *artificial transmutation* of elements takes place as the result of the bombardment, in the laboratory, of certain atoms by particles such as alpha particles, protons, or neutrons. Ernest Rutherford, in 1919, carried out the first artificial transmutation, from stable nitrogen 14 to stable oxygen 17. Irène and Frédéric Joliot-Curie, in 1934, were the first scientists to produce, artificially, a radioactive isotope, starting with stable aluminum 27 and obtaining radioactive phosphorus 30. The phosphorus 30, having a half-life of only 3.55 minutes, was soon converted to stable silicon 30. (These reactions, and those of other nuclear changes, are shown in the table on p. 229.)

Today many radioisotopes are produced by bombardment of the same element with neutrons, without transmutation, since the atomic number, and thus the identity of the element, remains the same and only the atomic mass changes. Radioisotopes produced artificially exhibit induced radioactivity. They are used as tracers in chemical reactions, in medical diagnoses, and in industrial processes.

Nuclear energy.

Two types of nuclear reactions that result in the release of enormous amounts of energy are *nuclear fission* and *nuclear fusion*. In nuclear fission, a heavy nucleus is split to produce lighter nuclei, and in nuclear fusion, light nuclei combine to produce a heavier nucleus. In both of these types of reactions, the total mass of the nuclei of the reactants is greater than the total mass of the nuclei of the products. Some mass appears to be lost, but in reality, the missing mass is converted into energy, according to Einstein's equation for the equivalence of mass and energy. In this equation, $E = mc^2$, m stands for mass and c is the velocity of light, a very large number. Thus, the amount of energy produced from the conversion of a small amount of mass is tremendous. Nuclear reactions in atomic or fission bombs, in thermonuclear or fusion bombs, and in thermonuclear fusion reactions in the sun and other stars, are remarkable for the spectacular amounts of energy released.

Both the atomic fission bomb and the nuclear reactor use a fissionable isotope, such as uranium 235, as fuel. The uranium 235 captures a neutron, splits, and releases two or three neutrons, which can enter other uranium 235 nuclei, creating a chain reaction. When materials are used to absorb some of the extra neutrons, the chain reaction is controlled, and energy is produced at a steady, slow rate. This takes place in a nuclear reactor that produces energy for conversion into electricity. But when a *critical mass* of a fissionable isotope is present, the reaction is uncontrolled, and an explosion occurs. This takes place in a fission bomb. Since the supply of naturally occurring fissionable isotopes is limited, a *breeder reactor* is used to produce fissionable materials, even new elements, such as plutonium, that do not exist in nature.

Nuclear fusion has been carried out in the laboratory but not yet developed for the production of energy in a controlled reaction. Fusion bombs have, however, been made with deuterium, or hydrogen 2, and tritium, or hydrogen 3, as the reactants. Because of the use of hydrogen isotopes in the fusion bomb, it has also been called the hydrogen bomb.

Nuclear fission and chain reaction

When a neutron traveling at the right speed strikes a uranium 235 nucleus at the right place, the nucleus splits into two smaller nuclei, krypton 92 and barium 141. Two or three neutrons and energy are also released in the reaction.

Neutrons released when an atom of uranium 235 is split can strike other uranium 235 nuclei, which split and produce additional neutrons, and so on. The chain reaction is controlled if the mass of uranium 235 is below the critical mass.

EQUATION: $^1_0 n + ^{235}_{92} U \rightarrow ^{92}_{36} Kr + ^{141}_{56} Ba + 3 ^1_0 n + energy$

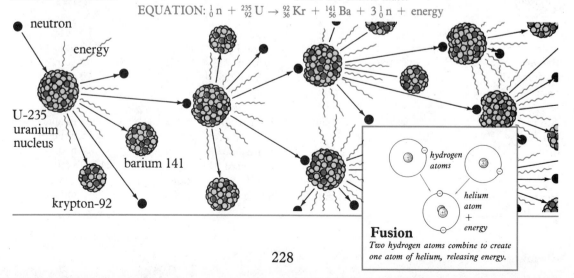

neutron

energy

U-235 uranium nucleus

barium 141

krypton-92

Fusion
Two hydrogen atoms combine to create one atom of helium, releasing energy.

hydrogen atoms

helium atom + energy

Some types of nuclear reactions

Type	Example	Equation				Occurrence or use
Alpha decay	emission of alpha particle by uranium 238	$^{238}_{92}\text{U}$ uranium 238 (radioactive)	$\longrightarrow$	$^{234}_{90}\text{Th}$ thorium 234 (radioactive)	$+\ ^{4}_{2}\text{He}$ alpha particle (helium 4)	natural radioactivity
Beta decay	emission of beta particles by thorium 234	$^{234}_{90}\text{Th}$ thorium 234 (radioactive)	$\longrightarrow$	$^{234}_{91}\text{Pa}$ protactinium 234 (radioactive)	$+\ ^{0}_{-1}\text{e}$ beta particle (electron)	natural radioactivity
Beta decay	emission of beta particle by carbon 14	$^{14}_{6}\text{C}$ carbon 14 (radioactive)	$\longrightarrow$	$^{14}_{7}\text{N}$ nitrogen 14 (stable)	$+\ ^{0}_{-1}\text{e}$ beta particle electron)	radiocarbon dating
Artificial transmutation	bombardment of nitrogen 14 with alpha particle	$^{14}_{7}\text{N}\ +\ ^{4}_{2}\text{He}$ nitrogen 14 (stable) alpha particle (helium 4)	$\longrightarrow$	$^{17}_{8}\text{O}\ +\ ^{1}_{1}\text{H}$ oxygen 17 (stable) proton (hydrogen 1)		Rutherford experiment
Artificial transmutation	bombardment of aluminum 27 with alpha particle	$^{27}_{13}\text{Al}\ +\ ^{4}_{2}\text{He}$ aluminum 27 (stable) alpha particle (helium 4)	$\longrightarrow$	$^{30}_{15}\text{P}\ +\ ^{1}_{0}\text{n}$ phosphorus 30 (radioactive) neutron		Joliot-Curie experiment (step 1)
Decay of synthetic radioisotope	emission of positron by phosphorus 30	$^{30}_{15}\text{P}$ phosphorus 30 (radioactive)	$\longrightarrow$	$^{30}_{14}\text{Si}$ silicon 30 (stable)	$+\ ^{0}_{+1}\text{e}$ positron	Joliot-Curie experiment (step 2)
Production of radioisotope of same element	bombardment of sodium 23 with neutron	$^{23}_{11}\text{Na}\ +\ ^{1}_{0}\text{n}$ sodium 23 (stable) neutron	$\longrightarrow$	$^{24}_{11}\text{Na}$ sodium 24 (radioactive)		nuclear reactor
Nuclear fission	capture of neutron by uranium 235, with splitting	$^{235}_{92}\text{U}\ +\ ^{1}_{0}\text{n}$ uranium 235 neutron (radioactive)	$\longrightarrow$	$^{141}_{56}\text{Ba}\ +$ barium 141 (radioactive)	$^{92}_{36}\text{Kr}\ +\ 3\,^{0}_{1}\text{n}+\text{energy}$ krypton 92 neutrons (radioactive)	nuclear reactor (controlled) or atomic fission bomb (uncontrolled)
Synthesis of new element	capture of neutron by uranium 238, with synthesis of plutonium 239	$^{238}_{92}\text{U}\ +\ ^{1}_{0}\text{n}$ uranium 238 neutron (radioactive)	$\longrightarrow$	$^{239}_{94}\text{Pu}\ +\ 2\,^{0}_{-1}\text{e}$ plutonium 239 beta particles (radioactive) (electrons)		breeder reactor for production of nuclear fuels
Nuclear fusion	reaction of deuterium with tritium	$^{2}_{1}\text{H}\ +\ ^{3}_{1}\text{H}$ deuterium tritium (hydrogen 2) (hydrogen 3)	$\longrightarrow$	$^{4}_{2}\text{He}\ +\ ^{1}_{0}\text{n}\ +\text{energy}$ proton neutron (helium 4)		thermonuclear or hydrogen-bomb reaction

acid

Dictionary of chemistry

ester

hydrocarbon

mixture

acid. Compound that produces hydrogen ions in water and that is able to donate hydrogen ions to other compounds.

addition reaction. In organic chemistry, a reaction in which one substance is added on to the structure of another, producing a single compound.

alcohol. Class of organic compounds in which the hydroxyl group (-OH) is added on to a hydrocarbon group.

alkali. Strong base formed from an alkali metal.

alkali metal. Metallic element that belongs to Group IA of the period table and that forms a strong base when combined with the hydroxide group.

alkane. Hydrocarbon in which there are only single bonds between carbon atoms.

alkene. Hydrocarbon in which there is one double bond between two carbon atoms, and the rest of the carbon-carbon bonds are single.

alkyne. Hydrocarbon in which there is one triple bond between two carbon atoms, and the rest of the carbon-carbon bonds are single.

alpha particle. Particle consisting of two protons and two neutrons; a helium nucleus.

aromatic. Hydrocarbon in which the benzene ring structure is present.

atom. Smallest unit of an element.

atomic mass. Mass of an atom compared with carbon 12, which has been assigned a mass of 12 atomic mass units.

atomic number. Number of protons in the nucleus of an atom, or the number of electrons.

base. Compound that produces hydroxide ions in water, or that is capable of receiving a hydrogen ion from an acid.

beta particle. Electron that is emitted by the nucleus of a radioactive atom.

boiling point. Temperature at which the vapor pressure of a liquid is equal to the atmospheric pressure.

breeder reactor. Nuclear reactor used to produce nuclear fuel, often in the form of synthetic elements, as well as nuclear energy.

chain reaction. Process in which the splitting of one atomic nucleus gives off neutrons that cause the splitting of other atomic nuclei.

chemical equation. A statement, consisting of symbols and formulas, that summarizes the changes that occur in a chemical reaction.

chemical reaction. Change in matter that results in a change in composition, in which new substances are formed.

chemistry. Science that deals with the composition of matter and with changes in this composition.

compound. Substance consisting of two or more elements joined by chemical bonds.

covalent bond. Chemical bond between two atoms in which electrons are shared.

crystal. Substance in the solid phase having an ordered arrangement of atoms or groups of atoms.

decomposition. A reaction, also called analysis, in which a chemical substance is broken down.

direct combination. A reaction, also called synthesis, in which two or more substances combine.

double replacement. Reaction in which there is an exchange of the positive and negative ions of two compounds.

electron. Fundamental negatively charged particle of matter.

element. Substance that cannot be broken down into simpler substances by ordinary chemical means.

Chemistry

esterification. Reaction between an alcohol and an acid in which the product, other than water, is an ester.

functional group. In organic chemistry, a group of atoms that characterizes a series or class of compounds.

gamma rays. High-frequency radiation, similar to x-rays, emitted by radioactive substances.

half-life. Period of time it takes for half the radioactive atoms in a given mass to decay.

hydrocarbon. Compound consisting only of hydrogen and carbon.

inorganic chemistry. Branch of chemistry that deals with the reactions of elements other than carbon.

ion. Atom or group of atoms bearing an electric charge.

ionic bond. Chemical bond formed by the transfer of electrons from one atom to another.

isotope. Form of an element differing from other forms in atomic mass but not in atomic number.

ketone. Class of organic compounds in which the carbonyl group (–CO–) is contained.

melting point. Temperature at which a solid turns into a liquid, or vice versa.

metal. Element that loses electrons easily, has a high luster, and is a good conductor of heat and electricity.

mixture. Aggregate of two or more substances that are not chemically combined.

molecule. The smallest particle of a substance that can exist free and retain the properties of that substance.

neutron. Nuclear particle having the same mass as a proton but zero electric charge.

nonmetal. Element that gains or shares electrons in chemical reactions, and whose properties contrast with those of metals.

nuclear fission. Nuclear reaction in which a large nucleus is split into smaller nuclei.

nuclear fusion. Nuclear reaction in which small atomic nuclei join to form a larger nucleus.

nuclear reactor. Device in which a nuclear reaction is controlled. to produce energy.

organic acid. Class of organic compounds in which the carboxyl group (–COOH) is contained.

organic chemistry. Chemistry of carbon compounds.

period. Horizontal row of elements in the periodic table.

phase. Physical state of matter; for example, solid, liquid, or gas.

physical change. Any change in matter that does not involve changes in the composition of substances.

polyatomic ion. Group of atoms carrying an electric charge that usually react as a unit in chemical reactions.

positron. Subatomic particle with the same mass as an electron, but with a positive electric charge.

product. Substance formed as a result of a chemical reaction, whose formula is written on the right side of the arrow in a chemical equation.

proton. Nuclear particle with the same mass as a neutron, but positive electric charge.

radioactivity. Spontaneous breakdown, or decay, of unstable atoms, during which alpha, beta, or gamma radiation is emitted.

radioisotope. Form of an element that exhibits radioactivity, or is radioactive.

reactant. Starting substance in a chemical reaction, whose formula is written on the left side of the arrow in a chemical equation.

salt. The product, other than water, of the reaction between an acid and a base.

saturated hydrocarbon. Organic compound in which carbon atoms are joined by single bonds.

single replacement. In inorganic chemistry, a reaction in which an element displaces another element in a compound, setting that element free.

substitution. In organic chemistry, a reaction in which an element or a group replaces another element or group in a molecule.

thermonuclear reaction. Atomic fusion reaction, such as the one that occurs in the fusion or hydrogen bomb.

transmutation. Nuclear change in which one element is converted into another.

unsaturated hydrocarbon. Organic compound in which some of the carbon atoms are joined by double or triple bonds.

valence electrons. Electrons in the outermost shell of an atom, which take part in the formation of chemical bonds.

vapor pressure. Pressure of the gas phase of a liquid when the two phases are in equilibrium.

For Further Reference

Asimov, Isaac
  A Short History of Chemistry
  Anchor Books
Asimov, Isaac
  The World of Carbon
  Abelard-Schuman
Day, Frank Henry
  The Chemical Elements in Nature
  Reinhold Co.

Patterson, E.C.
  John Dalton and the Atomic Theory
  Abelard-Schuman
Pottenger, Francis M.
  Fundamentals of Chemistry
  Scott, Foresman & Co.

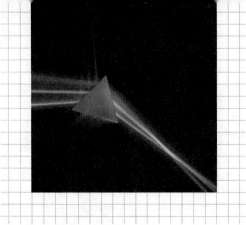

Physics

Both chemistry and physics deal with matter and energy. The chemist deals mostly with the changes that matter can undergo, changes that do not affect the internal structure of atoms. The physicist, however, is more interested in energy: its various forms and how they change into one another. Physicists are also interested in the nature of matter and how matter and energy are related.

The most spectacular results of physics have been in the development of the atomic bomb and nuclear power, but physical theories are also at the heart of the transistor and the other semiconducting devices that have been changing the way people live since World War II. On a more abstract level, physics has explained the motions of the planets, the energy processes of stars, and the origin of the universe. Today's physicists continue to explore both the smallest fundamental particles of matter-energy and the largest forces and objects in the universe. The success of physics has come from the ability of physicists to describe these varied phenomena with mathematical equations. In fact, the fundamental meaning of such important physical concepts as force or energy is found in the equations that describe the concepts. For this reason, a large part of this section of the book sets forth the key relationships and equations in easy-to-use tabular form. Measurement is especially important in physics, and the tables set forth the correct units used in making each measurement.

Fundamental concepts

Measurement. Physicists make extensive and careful use of measurement. They use one of two versions of the *metric system*, the centimeter-gram-second (cgs) system, or the meter-kilogram-second (mks) system. In the *customary system*, the fundamental units form the foot-pound-second (fps) system. For metric/customary conversions, see the table in Physical Sciences in Volume 1.

Mass and weight. *Mass* is the amount of matter in a given object. The mass of this book would be the same anywhere in the universe. *Weight* is the pull of gravity on a given mass. This book would weigh only one-sixth of its Earth weight on the moon because the moon has one-sixth of the gravitational pull of Earth. In physics, this distinction between mass and weight is very carefully maintained. In ordinary life, however, mass and weight are usually treated as if they were the same thing. The basic unit of *mass* in the metric system is the gram, but people in ordinary life may talk about how many grams a coin *weighs*. The basic unit of *weight* in the U.S. customary system of measurement is the pound, but people may say that a pound is about the same as 2.2 kilograms, a measure of *mass*.

Force. Weight is one kind of *force*. A force causes motion to change in speed or direction. Force is recognized from this property. A book is acted upon by the force of gravity—that is, the book has weight. If the book is dropped, the force on the book causes it to move toward the center of Earth.

Velocity and acceleration.

Motion can be categorized in various ways. A steady motion in a single direction, such as a car traveling along a straight highway at 55 kilometers per hour, is measured as *velocity*. Velocity is the rate of change of the car's position in a unit of time for such a steady motion. If the motion is changing in any way (for example, if the car is speeding up, braking, or turning), the velocity will change at every instant.

The rate of change of velocity is called *acceleration*. The unit of time occurs twice in a measure of acceleration; for example, if the driver of the car were to speed up gradually by 10 kilometers per hour every hour, the acceleration would be 10 kilometers per hour per hour. Physicists often write this as 10 km/h². While constant velocity does not produce a force, constant acceleration of a mass results in force. You can feel this force as a car picks up speed or slows down.

Velocity and acceleration

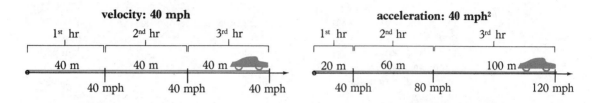

Mass and force

System	Mass Unit	Definition	Force Unit	Definition
cgs	gram (g)	Fundamental (originally the mass of 1 cubic centimeter of water under standard conditions)	dyne (dy)	The force required to accelerate a mass of 1 gram 1 cm/s²
mks	kilogram (kg)	1000 grams	newton (new)	The force required to accelerate a mass of 1 kilogram 1 m/s²; 100,000 dynes
fps	slug	The mass to which a force of 1 pound will give an acceleration of 1 ft/sec²	pound (lb)	Fundamental
Other common units	metric ton (MT or t) = 1,000,000 g = 1,000 kg milligram (mg) = 0.001 g = 0.000001 kg		(short) ton = 2000 lb (avoirdupois) ounce (oz) = 1/16 lb	

Ordinary, or engineering, usage

(short) ton = 0.907 metric tons metric ton = 1.1 (short) tons
pound = 0.454 kilograms kilogram = 2.2046 pounds
ounce = 28.349 grams gram = 0.035 ounce
slug = 32.1740 pounds milligram = 0.000035 ounce

Fundamental relationship of force, mass, and acceleration

	cgs	kms	fps
$F = ma$ where F means force in	dy	newton	lb
m means mass in	g	kg	slugs
a means acceleration in	cm/s²	m/s²	ft/s²

Work, energy, power, and momentum

System	Work and energy Unit	Definition	Power Unit	Definition	Momentum Unit	Definition
cgs	erg	The dyne-centimeter; that is, the work done when a force of 1 dy produces a movement of 1 cm in the direction of the force.	erg/second (erg/s)	A rate of 1 erg per s; $\frac{1}{10,000,000}$ w	gram-centimeter/second (g-cm/s)	A mass of 1 g moving 1 cm per s
mks	joule (j)	The newton-meter; that is, the work done when a force of 1 new produces a movement of 1 m in the direction of the force; 10,000,000 ergs.	watt (w)	A joule/second; that is, a rate of 1 j per s	kilogram-meter/second (kg-m/s)	A mass of 1 kg moving 1 m per s; 100,000 g-cm/s
fps	foot-pound (ft-lb)	The work done when a force of 1 lb. produces a movement of 1 ft. in the direction of the force.	foot-pound/second (ft-lb/s)	A rate of 1 ft-lb per s	slug-foot/second (slug-ft/s)	A mass of 1 slug moving 1 ft per s
Other common units	kilogram-meter (kg-m) 98,066,500 ergs		kilowatt (kw) 1000 w; 1.34 hp			
	kilocalorie 4184.0 j (also called Calorie [kc or C])		horsepower (hp) 550 ft-lb/s; 746 w			
	kilowatt-hour 60,000 j (kwh)					

Equations of work, energy, power, and momentum

	cgs	mks	fps
$W = Fd$			
where W means work in	ergs	j	ft-lb
F means force in	dy	new	lb
d means distance in	cm	m	ft

	cgs	mks	fps
$PE = wh$			
where PE means potential energy in	ergs	j	ft-lb
w means weight in	dy	new	lb
h means height in	cm	m	ft

	cgs	mks	fps
$KE = \frac{1}{2}mv^2$			
where KE means kinetic energy in	ergs	j	ft-lb
m means mass in	g	kg	slugs
v means velocity in	cm/s	m/s	lb/s

	cgs	mks	fps
$E = mc^2$			
where E means energy in	ergs	j	ft-lb
m means mass in	g	kg	slugs
c means the speed of light	30 billion cm/s	300 million m/s	982.08 million ft/s

	cgs	mks	fps
$P = \dfrac{W}{t}$			
where P means power in	erg/s	w	lb/s
W means work in	ergs	j	ft/lb
t means time in	s	s	s

	cgs	mks	fps
$P = mv$			
where P means momentum in	g-cm/s	kg-m/s	slug-ft/s
m means mass in	g	kg	slugs
v means velocity in	cm/s	m/s	ft/s

Work.

Work is done when a force moves an object in the direction of that force. The amount or quantity of work done is the product of the force and the distance the object moved. In physics, no work is done unless motion takes place. Merely applying force to an object is not considered to be work unless motion takes place.

Energy.

This is the ability to do work. *Energy* is measured by the amount of work performed. There are many types of energy, including electrical, heat, mechanical, chemical, and nuclear. These types of energy are present in three forms.

Potential energy. This is the energy an object has stored in it. Probably the most familiar form of potential energy is energy stored in an object owing to the object's change in position. A hammer that has been raised has the potential to do work when it falls. An increase in the height to which it is raised or an increase in the weight of the hammer will increase the amount of potential energy. A spring that has been tightly coiled also contains potential energy, in much the same way. Sometimes the energy produced in chemical reactions (for example, burning a piece of coal) is thought of as potential energy.

Kinetic energy. This is the energy an object or body has because of its motion. A hammer applies the force of kinetic energy as it strikes a nail. The amount of kinetic energy of a moving body is a result of its mass and the square of its velocity. Since the velocity is squared, the kinetic energy increases rapidly when the velocity increases. Tripling the speed of an object will increase its kinetic energy nine times.

In a system, the sum of potential energy and kinetic energy is constant. For example, the potential energy that a hammer loses in falling is equal to its gain in kinetic energy.

Rest-mass energy. The third form in which energy can exist is a consequence of Albert Einstein's theory of relativity. Einstein showed that if matter could be completely annihilated, the amount of energy released would be equal to the product of the mass times the speed of light squared. It is this form of energy that is exploited in nuclear reactors and nuclear or thermonuclear bombs.

Power.

The rate at which work is done is called *power*. Power is the amount of work done per unit of time. It is generally more important to know the power of an engine than the amount of energy the engine can generate. Consequently, automobiles are rated by horsepower and electric lights by watts, both units of power.

Momentum.

Momentum is defined as the product of the mass of a moving object and its velocity. Momentum is a measure of the tendency of a body to remain in motion or the resistance of a body to being stopped.

The effect of one solid body striking another is determined largely by the momentum of the bodies. A light straw moved by a tornado to a great velocity can have enough momentum to be driven into a tree. Similarly, a very massive object, even though it is moving slowly, can crush everything in its path. In both cases, the momentum determines the result. (Of course, a massive object that is moving fast has even more momentum.)

After the pitcher accelerates a baseball to nearly 100 mph and releases it, the momentum of the ball changes only slightly as a result of gravity and friction with the air—until it is hit, when the force of the bat accelerates the ball in a new direction, or is caught by the catcher.

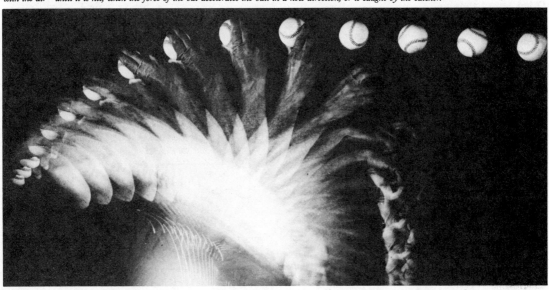

Newton's laws

Sir Isaac Newton is well known for having discovered the laws of gravity, but his fundamental laws of motion, published in 1687, are equally important. While these laws were stated earlier by Galileo, Newton was the first to express them clearly in mathematical terms. Newton's laws of motion form the basis for the branch of physics called mechanics.

The first law. A body at rest tends to remain at rest until acted upon by an outside force; a body in motion tends to remain in motion in a straight line at the same velocity unless acted upon by an outside force. The tendency of a body at rest to remain at rest and of a body in motion to remain in motion in a straight line is called *inertia*.

It is a common error to assume that a body can move in a curved path with no force acting on it. For example, students often believe that a rock that is tied to a string and swung in a circle will follow a curved path when released. In fact, inertia will cause the rock to travel in a straight line. Deviations from that straight line will be caused by forces acting on the rock. The force of gravity will cause the path of the rock to be a curve very close to a part of a parabola, but this is the same curve that the rock would follow had it been shot from a cannon.

The second law. You already know the second law of motion in the form $F = ma$ or force equals mass times acceleration. A more general statement of the law is as follows: When a body is acted upon by a constant force, its acceleration is proportional to the force and inversely proportional to the mass. In the formula $F = ma$, the units are chosen so that the constant of proportionality will be 1.

Since momentum is mv (mass times velocity), the rate of change of momentum is ma (mass times the rate of change of velocity, or mass times acceleration). Therefore, another way of stating Newton's second law is, force acting upon a body is equal to the rate of change of momentum. Newton's second law is often called the law of momentum.

Equations for laws of motion and gravity

Second law of motion

$$F = ma$$

where F is force
m is mass
a is acceleration

$$F = \frac{mv}{t}$$

where F is force
m is mass
v is velocity
t is time

Third law of motion

$$m_1 v_1 = m_2 v_2$$

where m_1 is one mass
m_2 is another mass
v_1 is the velocity of the first mass
v_2 is the velocity of the second mass

Law of gravity

$$f = G \frac{m_1 m_2}{r^2}$$

where f is the attractive force
G is the gravitational constant (6.673×10^{-8} dyne-cm^2/g^2 in the cgs system)
m_1 is one mass
m_2 is another mass
r is the distance between masses

Motion of body falling to Earth

$$v = v_0 + gt$$

where v is velocity
v_0 is initial velocity
g is acceleration because of gravity (980 cm/s^2)
t is time

$$s = v_0 t + \tfrac{1}{2} g t^2$$

where s is distance fallen
v_0 is initial velocity
t is time
g is acceleration because of gravity (980 cm/s^2)

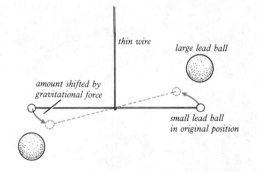

thin wire

large lead ball

amount shifted by gravitational force

small lead ball in original position

Henry Cavendish used the equipment shown to determine the gravitational constant in 1798. The gravitational force between the two lead balls moved the smaller one by an amount that could be measured.

Physics

The third law.

For every action, there is an equal and opposite reaction. The third law also relates to momentum. This law can also be stated: When an object is given a certain momentum in a given direction, some other body or bodies will get an equal momentum in the opposite direction. A rocket moves forward to the rearward action of the gases from its engines. In this example, the momentum of the product of the mass of gases and their velocity is equal to the momentum of the product of the rocket's mass and its velocity.

Conservation of momentum.

Newton's laws are contained in a very general conservation law. Conservation laws describe quantities that do not change during physical interactions. The law of conservation of momentum states that in any interaction of bodies, the total momentum of the interacting bodies does not change. Application of the conservation law to different situations produces Newton's three laws:

1. If a body is at rest, it will have a momentum of 0, and will continue to have 0 momentum unless a force changes it.
2. A body in motion will continue in motion with the same momentum.
3. When two bodies interact, momentum is conserved. For example, when a stationary billiard ball is struck by a moving ball of the same mass, the momentum of the moving ball must be shared between them. If the second ball stops, the first must move off with a momentum equal to that of the second before the collision. If both billiard balls have the same mass, the velocity of the first ball will be transmitted completely to the second ball.

Law of gravity.

Two bodies attract each other with a force directly proportional to the product of their masses and inversely proportional to the square of the distance between them. In 1798 Henry Cavendish established the constant of proportionality, later refined to 0.0000006673 in the cgs system.

On Earth, gravity seems to be a large force only because the mass of Earth is great. A 1-gram mass is attracted to the center of Earth with a force of about 980 dynes. Putting this into the equation $F = ma$ shows that for 980 to equal $1 \cdot a$, the acceleration owed to gravity (called g) must be 980 centimeters per second per second (in the fps system, this is about 32.2 feet per second per second).

Since gravity produces acceleration, a freely falling body will tend to travel faster and faster as it falls to Earth. At the end of 1 second, the velocity of a body that started from rest will reach 980 centimeters per second. At the end of the next second, the velocity will reach $2 \cdot 980$, or 1960 centimeters per second. Since the velocity is constantly increasing, the distance traveled in each second also increases. For the first second of fall, the *average* velocity is $\frac{0 + 980}{2} = 490$ centimeters per second, so the distance traveled is 490 centimeters. In the next second, the average velocity is $\frac{980 + 1960}{2} = 1470$ centimeters per second, and the body travels 1470 centimeters. In the third second, the body falls $\frac{1960 + 2940}{2} = 2450$ centimeters.

The total distance traveled at the end of each second varies with the *square* of the time. At the end of 1 second, the distance is $\frac{980}{2}(1^2) = 490$ centimeters; at the end of the next second, the total distance is $\frac{980}{2}(2^2) = 1960$ centimeters ($490 + 1470 = 1960$); and at the end of the third second, the total distance is $\frac{980}{2}(3^2) = 4410$ centimeters ($490 + 1470 + 2450 = 4410$).

When you push something away from you (by throwing it, for example), you impart momentum to yourself that is equal in amount and oppositely directed. Where frictional resistance to motion is small, throwing a heavy object causes motion away from the direction in which the object is thrown.

Thermodynamics

Heat. The particles that make up all matter are in a state of perpetual motion. This internal kinetic energy manifests itself as the form of energy called *heat*. The study of heat is *thermodynamics*. All matter is made up of moving particles; therefore, all matter has heat.

Heat is a form of energy and is measured in terms of the amount of work done. In the metric system, there are two units commonly used. Physicists most often use the calorie, the amount of heat needed to raise the temperature of 1 gram of water (under standard conditions) by 1° C. A kilocalorie or Calorie is the amount of heat required to raise the temperature of a kilogram of water 1°C. The Calorie with a capital C is the one used to measure the energy content of foods. In the fps system, a British thermal unit (Btu) is the amount of heat required to raise the temperature of 1 pound of water 1° F.

Temperature is not the same as heat. Temperature is a measure of the average kinetic energy of the particles of an object while heat is a measure of the total kinetic energy. The Kelvin, or absolute, scale of temperature is based on the idea that there is a temperature at which all particle motion ceases. This temperature is called absolute zero and has been calculated to be 273.16° below zero Celsius.

Conservation of mass-energy.

Energy can neither be created nor destroyed but only changed in type. This law is a generalization of the first law of thermodynamics, which states that when heat is transformed into other kinds of energy, the total energy remains constant.

In nuclear reactions, however, mass is converted to energy. Since matter can be considered a third form of energy, this principle is often called the law of conservation of mass-energy.

Heat and work. To get work out of randomly moving particles, you must induce them to move predominantly in one direction or to supply energy in a single direction. Heat is transferred from any body of a higher temperature to a body of a lower temperature. The efficiency of a heat engine is proportional to this temperature difference. As heat is transferred, the difference is reduced. The fraction of the energy that flows into the cooler body becomes less available for transformation into work even though the total amount of energy is unchanged.

The statement that heat can never travel from a colder to a hotter body by any continuous, self-sustaining process is the second law of thermodynamics. That portion or quantity of energy that is lost as nonuseful heat is measured by *entropy*. Since heat in useful form is a result of particles in one place moving faster than particles somewhere else (that is, the first place is hotter than the second), entropy is also a measure of disorder. The moving particles are statistically less ordered when the temperatures at both places are the same than when the temperatures are different. As a result, another version of the second law of thermodynamics is "Entropy (disorder) tends to increase."

Thermodynamics

1 Kilocalorie (Kcal) or Calorie (Cal) = 1000 calories (cal)
= 3.968 British thermal units (Btu)

1 degree Celsius (1°C) = 1 degree Kelvin (1°K)
= 1.8 degrees Fahrenheit (1.8° F)

1 Btu = 0.252 Cal = 252 cal

1°F = 0.555°C = 0.555°K

$C = \dfrac{5}{9}(F - 32)$ where C means temperature in degrees Celsius
F means temperature in degrees Fahrenheit

$F = \dfrac{9C + 160}{5}$ where F means temperature in degrees Fahrenheit
C means temperature in degrees Celsius

$K = C + 273.16$ where K means temperature in degrees Kelvin
C means temperature in degrees Celsius

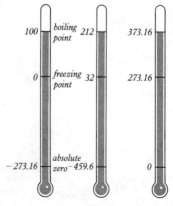

Wave motion

Energy is often transmitted in the form of *waves*, that is, back and forth or up and down vibrations. The energy of a wave travels, but the medium in which it travels only vibrates or oscillates.

There are two main types of waves. In *transverse* waves, the vibrations of the medium are perpendicular to the direction of wave motion. A common example is a boat bobbing up and down on water as waves pass. The boat moves at right angles to the direction of the waves. In *longitudinal* waves, the vibrations of the medium are parallel to the direction of the waves. Sound is a longitudinal wave.

Sound.
Sound is a longitudinal vibration of a medium at frequencies the human ear can detect. The medium can be a gas, liquid, or solid. *Frequency* is the rate at which waves are produced in a unit of time. The distance from one point on a wave to a corresponding point on the next wave is the *wavelength*. Wavelength determines the *pitch* of the sound. The greater the frequency, the shorter the wavelength, and the higher the pitch of the sound produced. The *amplitude*, or loudness, of a sound is determined by the distance the particles of the medium are displaced from their original undisturbed position. A blast of a loud horn will displace particles of air much farther than a small whistle or toot.

When a tuning fork is struck it starts to vibrate at a frequency that depends upon the size of the fork and the material it is made of. This vibration sets the air particles around the tuning fork vibrating back and forth at the same frequency. When the energy reaches us, our eardrums vibrate, and we hear a tone.

Electromagnetic waves.
These are transverse vibrations; that is, the oscillations are perpendicular to the direction of the wave. Light is a small portion of a large range, or *spectrum*, of transverse waves called *electromagnetic waves* because they combine both electrical and magnetic properties. Strictly speaking, however, electromagnetic waves are not what we normally think of as electricity, which is produced by moving electrons, or magnetism, which is a field that can be produced by moving electrons or in other ways. Electromagnetic waves are the wave interpretation of the motion of a particle called the *photon*.

The electromagnetic spectrum is divided into regions according to ranges in wavelength (or ranges in frequency). The units used to measure the wavelengths of the shorter waves are the micron (μ); millimicron (mμ); and angstrom (Å)

$$1\mu = 10^{-6}m = 10^{-4}cm$$
$$1m\mu = 10^{-9}m = 10^{-7}cm$$
$$1Å = 10^{-10}m = 10^{-8}cm$$

In order of increasing wavelength, the electromagnetic spectrum can be divided into gamma rays, x-rays, ultraviolet rays, visible light, infrared rays, microwaves, and radio waves. Note that each type of radiation merges gradually into the next and that all electromagnetic radiations travel at the same speed in a vacuum, the speed of light.

Sound

Sound wave

Sound is a longitudinal vibration, which passes from place to place as alternate waves of compression and rarefaction of a material (most commonly for humans, the air). The same pattern can be seen in a coiled spring.

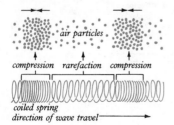

air particles

compression   rarefaction   compression

coiled spring
direction of wave travel

Intensity of sound

Sound	Decibels
threshold of hearing	0
whisper	10–20
very soft music	30
average home	40–50
automobile	40–50
conversation	60–70
heavy street traffic	70–80
loud music	90–100
threshold of pain	120
jet airplane engine	170

Speed of sound

Medium at 0°C	ft/sec
air	1,090
alcohol	3,890
brass	11,480
carbon dioxide	846
copper	11,670
glass	16,500
iron	16,820
steel	16,820
water	4,794
wood (pine)	10,900

The visible spectrum.

The speed of light is accepted today as 2.99793 times 10^8 meters per second in a vacuum. This value is approximately 186,000 miles per second. In a more dense medium, such as glass, all electromagnetic waves, including that portion called light or the visible spectrum, will slow down. The change in direction of waves as they pass obliquely from one medium to another is called *refraction*. The *index of refraction* is an indication of how much light will bend in passing from one substance to another. The refractive index of a substance is the ratio of the speeds of light in different media.

Refraction enables us to bend and focus light with lenses, making photography, microscopes, and telescopes possible. Prisms have enabled us to separate the visible spectrum into the various wavelengths we see as colors. The wavelengths we perceive as colors travel at the same speed in a vacuum but at different speeds in matter. Red, the longest visible wavelength, is approximately 0.00007 cm in length and travels about 1 percent faster in glass than does violet, the shortest visible wavelength (0.00004 cm).

Lenses.

The purpose of a lens is to change the curvature of light waves, usually to form an image. The ability of a lens to form an image is measured by its *focal length*. The distance of the principal focus from the lens is the focal length of that particular lens. Its value depends on the curvature of the two surfaces of the lens and the refractive index of its material. Convex (converging) lenses form real images. A real image can be focused on a screen and is inverted.

The law of reflection.

Reflection is the return of an object or a train of waves from a surface that acts as a boundary between two media. If the surface is smooth, the incoming ray of light, the incident ray, and the ray when reflected, the reflected ray, form equal angles with the normal. The normal at the point where the rays intersect is a line perpendicular to the surface. The angle of incidence equals the angle of reflection and both angles and the normal are on the same plane. Curved mirrors called *reflectors* are used to focus light in large telescopes. Mirrors do not distort images as much as refracting lenses do.

Electromagnetic waves

Light wave

Light is a transverse wave. In the transverse waves of water the molecules travel perpendicular to the direction of the wave. Unlike water, however, light waves are not caused by the motion of a substance through which they are traveling. Light is caused by the wave properties of small particles.

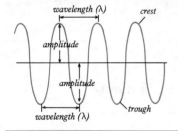

Refraction

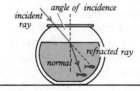

Reflection

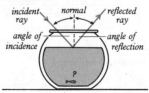

Speed of light

Medium*	m/sec
vacuum	299,793,000
air (g)	299,700,000
methyl alcohol (l)	228,000,000
water (l)	226,000,000
quartz (s)	207,000,000
benzene (l)	200,000,000
ordinary glass (s)	198,000,000
sodium chloride** (s)	195,000,000
ethyl alcohol (l)	188,000,000
heat-resistant glass (s)	181,000,000
diamond (s)	124,000,000

* s = solid; l = liquid; g = gas
** table salt

Electromagnetic spectrum

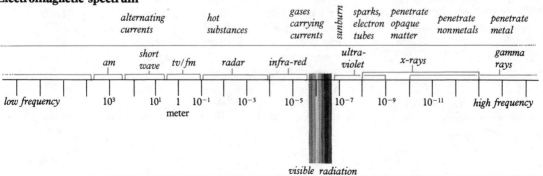

visible radiation

The law of inverse squares. This law explains why we often move an object closer to a light source to see it better. It states that the *intensity* of certain effects, including the illumination of a surface, gravitational force, and sound, is inversely proportional to the square of the distance from the source. The intensity decreases as the distance increases. At 4 meters, the intensity is $\frac{1}{16}$ of what it is at 1 meter.

Applications. The high accuracy of the speed at which electromagnetic radiation travels makes it possible to measure the distance of objects such as the moon by *radar*. Radar is an instrument that emits microwaves, bounces them off an object, and measures the time for the echo to return. Knowing the speed of the radiation, the distance to the object can be calculated with great precision.

Radar is also used by highway police to get an instantaneous reading of the speed of an automobile by taking into account the *Doppler effect*. If an object emitting a tone is receding from us, the pitch is lower than that heard when the object was at rest; that is, the wavelength appears to increase. If the object is moving toward us, the wavelength is decreased and we hear a higher pitch. The speed of a moving car can be read by the increase or decrease of the wavelength of the radar waves that are bounced off it. The Doppler effect has also been used to determine that the universe is expanding. Light of known wavelengths emitted by distant galaxies is shifted toward longer wavelengths, that is, toward the red end of the visible spectrum, indicating that these galaxies are receding from us.

The *laser* is a device that amplifies focused light waves and concentrates them in a narrow, very intense beam. The emitted light, called *coherent light*, does not spread out, so it does not lose intensity. It can deliver great energy to a small area.

Electromagnetic radiation

Wave equation

$$V = v\lambda$$

where V is velocity
v is frequency
λ is wavelength

Wave energy

$$E = hV$$

where E is energy
h is Planck's constant
$(6.6 \times 10^{-27}$ erg sec$)$
V is frequency

Snell's law (index of refraction)

$$n = \frac{\sin i}{\sin r}$$

where n is the index
$\sin i$ is sine of incident angle
$\sin r$ is sine of refracted angle

Location of image formed by a converging lens

$$\frac{1}{p} + \frac{1}{q} = \frac{1}{f}$$

where p is object distance
q is image distance
f is focal length

Size of image

$$\frac{h_i}{h_o} = \frac{q}{p}$$

where h_i is image height
h_o is object height
q is image distance
p is object distance

Inverse square law

$$E = \frac{I}{d^2}$$

where E is illumination
I is intensity of the source
d is distance to the illuminated surface

Law of inverse squares

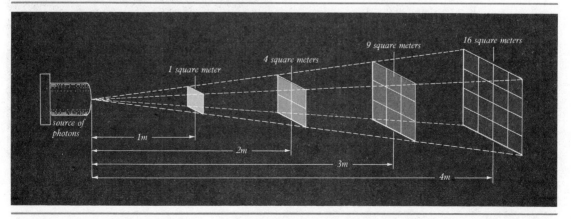

Electricity

Electricity is the term given to phenomena caused by electric charges whether they are static or in motion. There are two kinds of electric charges—positive and negative. Materials always contain both positive and negative charges, but only *electrons*, carriers of the tiny negative charge, move freely. A substance becomes positively charged when it loses electrons; a negatively charged substance has gained electrons. Electrons can be made to flow through some materials easily. Such materials are called *conductors*.

Electric current is the flow of electrons past a given point. The unit of electron flow is the *ampere*. One ampere is the flow of 1 coulomb of charge per second. A *coulomb* is a unit of quantity of electricity. It is the charge equal to 6.25 times the charge of 10^{18} electrons.

$$1 \text{ ampere} = \frac{1 \text{ coulomb}}{\text{second}}$$

The amount of work electricity can do depends on both the quantity of electrons and their potential energy. Electrical potential energy is called *voltage* and is measured in *volts*. Voltage is also referred to as electromotive force or potential difference. It can be considered as a measure of electrical pressure in a circuit and is often defined as the force required to send a current of 1 ampere through a circuit having a resistance of 1 ohm.

The *ohm* is the unit of electrical resistance. It is the resistance offered by a circuit or device to the flow of 1 ampere being driven by the force of 1 volt. The relationship between electrical pressure, current flow, and resistance is expressed in Ohm's law. *Ohm's law* states that the current through a circuit is directly proportional to the force or pressure that drives it and inversely proportional to resistance of the circuit.

Electric power. The rate at which an appliance uses electrical energy is measured in watts. One watt is the rate at which work is done when 1 ampere is moved by 1 volt. Electrical energy is sold in kilowatt hours, the power of 1000 watts for 1 hour.

Electricity

Unit	Definition
coulomb	Electric charge equal to 6.25×10^{18} electron charges
ampere	Flow of 1 coulomb per second past a point
volt	1 joule per coulomb
ohm	1 volt per ampere
watt	1 joule per second

Ohm's law

$I = \dfrac{E}{R}$ where   I is current in amperes
E is potential difference in volts
R is resistance in ohms

Electric power

$P = IV$ where   P is power in watts
I is current in amperes
V is potential difference in volts

In thunderstorms, the top part of clouds and the ground become positively charged, while the midsections of clouds become strongly negative. Lightning results from the sudden resolution of these differences.

Physics

Modern physics

Relativity. Until the beginning of this century, many scientists believed that Newton's laws of motion and law of gravity offered a satisfactory basis for explaining the physical world. In 1905, Albert Einstein published his theory of special relativity, which showed that Newton's laws were really versions of more general laws. Einstein's theory is based on the following assumptions:

1. The measured value of the speed of light in a vacuum is always the same no matter how fast the observer or light source is moving.

2. The maximum velocity possible in the universe is that of light.

3. Absolute speed cannot be measured, only speed relative to some other object.

The theory states that to an observer at rest, a moving object will appear shorter and more massive than the same object at rest, and that a moving clock will appear to be going more slowly than the same one at rest.

Quantum theory. Newton believed that visible light consists of particles, while a Dutch physicist, Christiaan Huygens, and others felt that light was a wave. Today both views are believed to be correct. Radiation has the properties of both waves and particles, depending upon the experiment that is performed and the explanation that is sought. Max Planck, a German physicist, while studying radiation from so-called black bodies, concluded that his results could only be explained if energy were produced in individual bundles or packets, which he called *quanta*, rather than in waves. A *quantum* of energy emitted as visible light is called a *photon*. The amount of energy of each quantum is not the same. The amount of energy of each is proportional to the frequency of the radiation. Einstein soon showed that the *photoelectric effect*, which is the release of electrons by certain metals when irradiated by light, can only be explained in terms of the quantum theory. The quantum theory has since become the foundation of our understanding of matter.

Modern physics

Mass increases with motion

$$m = \frac{m_o}{1 - \frac{v^2}{c^2}}$$

where m is the mass of the body in motion

m_0 is the mass of the body at rest

v is the velocity of the body relative to an observer at rest

c is the speed of light

Energy of a photon is proportional to the frequency

$$E = hv = \frac{hc}{\lambda}$$

where E is energy in joules per quantum

h is Planck's constant (6.6232×10^{34} joules sec/quantum)

v is wave frequency

c is velocity of light

λ is the wavelength of radiation in meters

Einstein's photoelectric law

$$E_k = hv - w$$

where E_k is the kinetic energy of the emitted photoelectron

h is Planck's constant

v is the frequency associated with the absorbed photon

w is the work function for the surface of the photosensitive metal

According to special relativity, the boy sees the girl's watch as slower, and she sees his watch as slower. Unless the car is moving near the speed of light, however, the effect is too small to be noticed.

The principle of uncertainty.

Newton believed that if we knew the exact position and momentum (mass multiplied by velocity) of a particle at some instant, it would be possible to calculate where the particle would be at any time in the future. In 1927 Werner Heisenberg, a German physicist, showed that this is not so. He proved that it is impossible to determine both the exact position and speed of any particle at the same time, since the act of measuring disturbs the particle and introduces an error into the measurement. This *principle of uncertainty* has led to *quantum*, or *wave*, *mechanics*, a new way of describing atomic particles.

The uncertainty principle tells us that any statement about any individual event that occurs within the confines of this basic uncertainty has no meaning and is not admissible in physics. The discovery of this principle has given physicists deeper insight into the laws of nature, but it has not altered the general pattern of physical concepts. Most observations are carried out with materials having large numbers of particles and individual events, and are statistical in nature. The laws of probability see to it that the sum total of the events is determined, although each individual event is uncertain.

Particle physics.

At one time—around 1930—the only known particles smaller than atoms were *electrons*, *protons*, and *photons*. The electron is the carrier of negative electric charge (and some mass), the proton is the carrier of positive electric charge and mass, and the photon is the carrier of electromagnetic radiation. But there are many subatomic particles that have been found since 1930. Certain of these particles are considered basic in various theories. There are 22 of these.

More basic even than most of the 22 observed particles are *quarks*. While quarks have never been observed experimentally, 15 of the 22 particles are thought to be made from quarks. The 15 subatomic particles formed from quarks (and other very short-lived particles also formed from quarks) are called *baryons*, meaning "heavy," or *mesons*, meaning "middle." Subatomic particles that are not formed from quarks are called *leptons*, meaning "light," except for the photon, which is a class by itself. The mass of these particles is measured in millions of electron volts (MEV).

Four different forces cause the interactions between particles, including the change of an isolated particle to other particles of less mass (*decay*). These forces are gravity, the electric force, the *weak* force, and the *strong* force. (In some recent theories, the electric and the weak forces have been combined as the *electroweak* force.) Gravity is actually the weakest of the four forces.

Nearly all particles exist in at least two forms, one of which is called the *antiparticle* of the other. The antiparticle of the proton is called the *antiproton*; the antiparticle of the neutron is the *antineutron*; and so forth for most particles. However, the antiparticle of the electron, which was the first antiparticle to be discovered, is usually called the *positron*. If a particle and its antiparticle meet, say an electron and a positron, they will destroy each other completely, producing photons that carry off the masses as energy. Similarly, a photon with sufficient energy can suddenly become a pair consisting of one electron and one positron, converting part of the energy of the photon into mass. Atoms can be made from antiprotons, antineutrons, and positrons, forming *antimatter*, but they immediately interact with ordinary matter to turn into energy.

Some nuclear particles

Name	Symbol	Mass (in MEV)	Charge	Average lifetime (in seconds)
Photon	γ	0	0	Stable
LEPTONS				
Neutrino	ν	0*	0	Stable
Antineutrino	$\bar{\nu}$	0*	0	Stable
Neutrino (Muon type)	ν_μ	0*	0	Stable
Antineutrino (Muon type)	$\bar{\nu}_\mu$	0*	0	Stable
Electron	e^-	0.511	-1	Stable
Positron	e^+	0.511	$+1$	Stable
Muon	μ^-	105.7	-1	2.2×10^{-6}
Antimuon	μ^+	105.7	$+1$	2.2×10^{-6}
MESONS				
Positive Pi	π^0	139.6	$+1$	2.6×10^{-8}
Negative Pi	π^-	189.6	-1	2.6×10^{-8}
Neutral Pi	π^0	135	0	8×10^{-17}
Positive K	K^+	493.7	$+1$	1.2×10^{-8}
K-zero-short	K_S^0	497.7	0	9×10^{-11}
K-zero-long	K_L^0	497.7	0	5.2×10^{-8}
Negative K	K^-	493.7	-1	1.2×10^{-8}
BARYONS				
Proton	p	938.3	$+1$	Stable*
Antiproton	$\bar{p}$	938.3	-1	Stable*
Neutron	n	939.6	0	9.18×10^2
Antineutron	$\bar{n}$	939.6	0	9.18×10^2
Lambda Hyperon	Λ^0	115.6	0	3×10^{-10}
Lambda Antihyperon	$\bar{\Lambda}^0$	1115.6	0	3×10^{-10}

* Some theories challenge this.

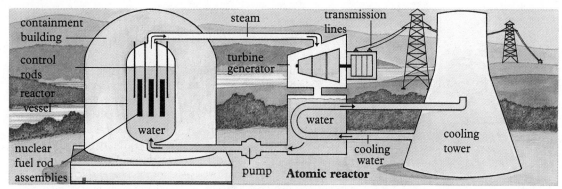

containment building — control rods — reactor vessel — nuclear fuel rod assemblies

steam — turbine generator — water — pump — **Atomic reactor**

transmission lines — water — cooling water — cooling tower

If enough uranium 235 is collected in one place, the neutrons produced will cause a chain reaction. In an atomic reactor, uranium 235 is mixed with the more common form, uranium 238. Enough neutrons are produced to cause continued fission, which produces heat. Control rods regulate the rate of fission by absorbing some of the neutrons.

Nuclear physics.
Nuclear physics is concerned with changes in the nuclei of atoms.

Radioactivity. Antoine Henri Becquerel, a French scientist, discovered in 1896 that uranium gives off radiation that fogs photographic film. Soon after, Marie and Pierre Curie isolated two new radioactive elements, polonium and radium. *Radioactivity* is the spontaneous disintegration of the nuclei of certain atoms. As these atoms disintegrate, energy is released. The radioactivity of a substance decreases continually with time and the rate of decrease is different for each element. The rate of radioactive decay is usually expressed as the *half-life* of that element, that is, the time for half the atoms to decompose. The half-life ranges from a fraction of a second for some isotopes to billions of years for others.

Radioactivity originates in the unstable nucleus of the atom. There are three general types of radioactive decay. The nucleus can emit a *gamma ray*, which is an electromagnetic wave of very high frequency. It can also emit an *alpha particle*, which is the equivalent of the nucleus of a helium atom containing two protons and two neutrons. Since the loss of protons means a decrease in the atomic number (the number of protons in the nucleus), and since the atomic number determines the chemistry of the atom, the result is the formation of a new element. When radium loses an alpha particle, the products are helium and radon.

The third type of radioactive decay comes from the *beta particle*, which is an electron. We can imagine a neutron losing an electron and becoming a proton. Since a proton has been gained, the atomic number changes and a new element is produced.

Nuclear fission. In 1939 Otto Hahn and Fritz Strassman, German physicists, discovered that if uranium[235] (an isotope of uranium with the atomic weight of 235) is bombarded with neutrons, uranium[236] is formed. This isotope is unstable and splits into several fragments in a process called *nuclear fission*. The fission process releases enormous amounts of energy because some mass is converted to energy. The theory of relativity states that when a mass is converted to energy, the energy is $E = mc^2$ where c is the speed of light. Since c^2 is a very large number, E is great even for small values of m. As an example, if the mass is 1 gram:

$$E = mc^2$$
$$E = 1 \text{ g} \times (9 \times 10^8 \text{cm/sec})^2$$
$$E = 9 \times 10^{16} \text{ ergs } or$$
$$E = 9 \times 10^9 \text{ joules } or$$
$$E = 25 \times 10^4 \text{ kilowatt-hours}$$

One gram of matter is equivalent to 25 million kilowatt hours of energy!

The fission process requires a neutron to start it, but the resulting fissions produce many neutrons. If these bombard other U[238] atoms, a *chain reaction* can occur. This requires a certain *critical mass* of uranium, for otherwise the neutrons will escape. The fission bomb is an *uncontrolled* chain reaction.

To use the fission reaction to produce nuclear power, it is necessary to have a *controlled* reaction. The first controlled reaction was contained in a uranium-graphite pile into which cadmium rods were inserted. Cadmium absorbs neutrons so the reaction can be slowed down by simply pushing the rods further into the pile. This is the basic principle of today's nuclear reactors. The huge amount of heat that is produced is converted to steam which in turn drives electric generators.

Nuclear fusion. Another way to release very large amounts of energy is by fusing or combining the nuclei of certain light atoms to form heavier elements. In this process some mass is converted to energy. This fusion reaction is the source of energy of the stars, including our sun. In the sun, four hydrogen atoms fuse to make an isotope of helium. The helium nucleus formed has less mass than the sum of the four hydrogen nuclei. This mass is converted into energy. To start this reaction requires temperatures that are difficult to attain in a controlled way. We have succeeded in making hydrogen or fusion bombs by using fission bombs to attain the necessary temperatures. If we could control the fusion process, our energy problems would be over.

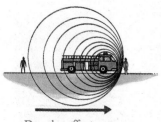

Doppler effect

Dictionary of physics

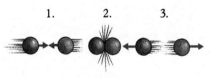

1.　　　2.　　　3.

momentum

radar

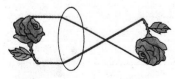

real image

absolute temperature scale.
Also called the Kelvin scale, it
is based on the idea that at absolute zero all molecular motion
stops. Kelvin temperatures are
273.16 degrees higher than
those on the Celsius scale.

acceleration. Rate of change of
velocity with time.

alpha particle. Nucleus of a
helium atom, consisting of two
protons and two neutrons.

amplitude. Height of a crest of a
wave; the maximum displacement of the medium through
which a wave is traveling.

beta rays. Electrons emitted by
atomic nuclei in certain radioactive transformations.

Boyle's law (for gases). At a constant temperature, the volume
of a gas is inversely proportional to the pressure.

Celsius temperature scale.
Based on the temperature of
melted ice (assigned a value of
0°) and boiling water (assigned
a value of 100°). The interval
is divided into 100 degrees.

Charles's law (for gases). At a
fixed pressure, the volume of a
gas is directly proportional to
the absolute temperature.

**conservation of mass-energy,
law of.** In any change, the sum
of the amount of matter and the
amount of energy remains
constant.

**conservation of momentum,
law of.** For any system, the
total momentum (mass times
velocity) of all bodies involved
remains unchanged.

Coulomb's law. Force is proportional to the product of charges
and is inversely proportional to
the square of distances between
charges.

critical mass. The mass of uranium or other material in a
fission nuclear bomb required
for a chain reaction at a constant rate.

Doppler effect. Change in wavelength that results when the

source producing the waves is
moving with respect to the
receiver.

electromagnetic waves. Systems
of varying electrical and magnetic fields regenerating each
other and traveling through
space as waves.

energy. Ability to perform work.

entropy. Mathematical measure
of the unavailable energy in a
thermodynamic system.

Fahrenheit temperature scale.
Melting ice is assigned a value
of 32° and boiling water 212°.
The interval is divided into 180
degrees.

force. That which causes acceleration or distortion of shape.

frequency. Number of cycles of a
wave per unit time.

gamma ray. Electromagnetic
radiation of very short wavelength.

gravitation, law of. The gravitational force between two bodies
is directly proportional to the
product of their masses and
inversely proportional to the
square of the distance between
their centers.

half-life. Time it takes for half of
the atoms of a radioactive element to become transformed as
a result of radioactive decay.

image, real. Image formed when
light passes from an object
through a convex lens. The
image is on the opposite side of
the lens from the object, is
always inverted, and can be
projected on a screen.

inertia. Property of an object that
makes it resist change in its
velocity.

infrared radiation. Electromagnetic radiation of longer wavelength than visible light, with a
maximum wavelength of 10^{-4}m.

inverse square law (for light).
The intensity of illumination of
a surface is inversely proportional to the square of the distance of the surface from the
light source.

isotopes. Forms of an element with the same atomic number but different atomic weights.

Kelvin temperature scale. *See* absolute temperature scale.

longitudinal waves. Waves in which the oscillation of the moving particles is parallel to the wave direction, for example, sound.

mass. Amount of matter in a body. A measure of the inertia of an object.

microwaves. Portion of the electromagnetic spectrum between infrared and radio frequencies.

momentum. Mass of an object multiplied by its velocity.

motion, Newton's laws of:
1. A body continues in a state of rest or in a uniform straight line motion unless acted upon by an outside force.
2. The change in motion of a body is proportional to the force applied.
3. To every action, there is an equal and opposite reaction.

nuclear fission. Splitting of heavy nuclei caused by absorption of neutrons.

nuclear fusion. Creation of atomic nuclei by the fusion of light nuclei.

nuclear physics. Study of changes in atomic nuclei.

nuclear reaction. Change in an atomic nucleus caused by combination with or loss of elemental particles such as neutrons or other nuclei.

Ohm's law. Electric current is equal to the ratio of voltage and resistance.

phase. Time relation of two cyclic motions. Two motions are in phase if they reach their peaks simultaneously. In chemistry, the form in which a substance exists at room temperature, that is, solid, liquid, or gas.

photoelectric effect. Emission of electrons by an object as the result of irradiation by light.

photon. Quantum of light or other electromagnetic radiation.

pitch. Frequency of a sound wave.

Planck's constant. Ratio between the energy and frequency of a photon.

power. Rate at which work is done.

quantum. Smallest unit of quantized energy (that is, energy that can only have certain integral values). For electromagnetic energy, the quantum is called a photon.

radar. Device for detecting distant objects by reflection of microwaves.

radioactivity. Spontaneous breakdown of atomic nuclei.

real image. *See* image, real.

reflection, law of. Angle between an incident ray of light and the normal is always equal to the angle between the reflected ray and the normal.

refraction, law of. When light passes at an oblique angle from one medium into another of greater density, the velocity of light decreases and is bent toward the normal.

relativity. Principle that all frames of reference are equivalent for the description of physical events.

sound waves. Longitudinal vibrations of audible frequency.

spectrum. Continuous series of wavelengths.

temperature. Condition of a substance that determines the direction of heat flow from one object to another; a measurement of the kinetic energy of the particles of a substance.

thermodynamics. Study of the interrelationships between heat and mechanical energy.

thermodynamics, laws of:
1. When work is transformed into heat or vice versa, the amount of work is always equivalent to the amount of heat.
2. It is impossible by any continuous self-sustaining process for heat to be transferred from a colder to a hotter body.

thermonuclear. Reaction in nucleus of atoms caused by very high temperatures, which causes nuclei to fuse, forming new elements.

transmutation. Change of one element into another as the result of a nuclear event.

transverse waves. Waves in which particles move perpendicularly to the direction of the wave, for example, light.

ultraviolet. Portion of the electromagnetic spectrum lying between x-rays and visible light.

uncertainty, principle of. Theory that it is impossible to measure both the exact position and exact velocity of an atomic particle at the same time.

wave. Cyclic disturbance traveling through a medium.

wavelength. Distance between adjacent peaks of a wave.

weight. Measure of the pull of the force of gravity on a body.

work. Product of a force and the displacement of an object in the direction of the force.

x-rays. Portion of the electromagnetic spectrum between gamma rays and the ultraviolet.

For Further Reference

Asimov, Isaac
  Understanding Physics (3 volumes)
  Walker and Co., New York
Beiser, Arthur
  Concepts of Modern Physics
  McGraw-Hill, New York

Ford, Kenneth
  Classical & Modern Physics
  (3 volumes)
  John Wiley & Sons, New York
March, Robert H.
  Physics for Poets
  McGraw-Hill, New York

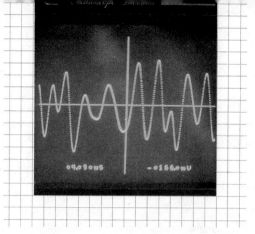

Mathematics

In this article, the entire sequence of secondary-school mathematics, from arithmetic through calculus, is presented in a simple way, with an emphasis on problem solving. Specific guidelines for difficult areas and easy-to-use summaries of essential information are presented in tabular and chart form. Special attention is paid to the use of the hand-held calculator.

Arithmetic

Whole numbers. The first numbers that one learns are sometimes called the *counting numbers,* but mathematicians call them the *natural numbers.* They are 1, 2, 3, ... Notice that 0 is not included. If 0 is included, the set of numbers is called *whole numbers.* Fractions, which are not whole numbers, present special problems; they are usually not adaptable to work on the calculator the way whole numbers are.

When you learn to factor a whole number into its *primes,* you simplify many fraction problems. A prime is a whole number that can be formed by multiplication from other whole numbers in one way only: as a product of itself with 1 (1 is not considered a prime). For example, 3 and 5 are primes, but 4 and 9 are not.

Which are prime numbers? 2, 6, 17, 51

PRIME
$2 = 2 \times 1$ or 1×2

COMPOSITE
$6 = 6 \times 1$ or 1×6
$ = 2 \times 3$ or 3×2

(A *composite* number is any whole number, except 1, that is not prime.)

PRIME
$17 = 17 \times 1$ or 1×17

COMPOSITE
$51 = 51 \times 1$ or 1×51
$ = 3 \times 17$ or 17×3

Factor 60 into primes.

A. Start with the least prime. Work up through the primes. The least prime is 2. Since $\frac{60}{2} = 30$, 2 is a factor of 60. (The symbol $\frac{60}{2}$ means "60 divided by 2.")

B. Now look at 30, the quotient. Since $\frac{30}{2} = 15$, 2 is a factor of 60 twice. The quotient, 15, cannot be divided evenly by 2, so look at the next higher prime, 3, as a divisor.

C. Since $\frac{15}{3} = 5$, 3 is also a prime factor of 60. The quotient, 5, is prime; therefore, the answer is
$60 = 2 \times 2 \times 3 \times 5.$

Fractions

$$\frac{3}{4} \times \frac{2}{3}$$

METHOD 1

A. Multiply the numerators (top numbers in fractions).

$$\frac{3}{4} \times \frac{2}{3} = \frac{6}{}$$

B. Multiply the denominators (bottom numbers).

$$\frac{3}{4} \times \frac{2}{3} = \frac{6}{12}$$

C. Eliminate common factors in the numerator and denominator of the product. The prime factors of 6 are shown as 2×3, while the prime factors of 12 are shown as $2 \times 2 \times 3$. *Canceling* is crossing out matching prime factors in the numerator and denominator and indicating that a factor of 1 is left.

$$\frac{3}{4} \times \frac{2}{3} = \frac{\overset{1}{\cancel{2}} \times \overset{1}{\cancel{3}}}{\cancel{2} \times 2 \times \cancel{3}}$$

Multiply the 1's and any numbers not crossed out to get the "reduced" form of the product.

$$\frac{3}{4} \times \frac{2}{3} = \frac{1}{2}$$

METHOD 2

A. Cancel before you multiply.

$$\frac{3}{4} \times \frac{2}{3} = \frac{\overset{1}{\cancel{3}}}{2 \times \underset{1}{\cancel{2}}} \times \frac{\overset{1}{\cancel{2}}}{\underset{1}{\cancel{3}}}$$

Remember that factors in the numerators must be matched with factors in the denominators.

B. Multiply any factors remaining.

$$\frac{3}{4} \times \frac{2}{3} = \frac{\overset{1}{\cancel{3}}}{2 \times \underset{1}{\cancel{2}}} \times \frac{\overset{1}{\cancel{2}}}{\underset{1}{\cancel{3}}} = \frac{1}{2}$$

$$\frac{7}{8} \div \frac{5}{6}$$

A. Invert the divisor to change to multiplication.

$$\frac{7}{8} \times \frac{6}{5}$$

B. Cancel any common factors.

$$\frac{7}{8} \times \frac{6}{5} = \frac{7}{\underset{1}{\cancel{2}} \times 2 \times 2} \times \frac{\overset{1}{\cancel{2}} \times 3}{5}$$

C. Multiply the remaining numerators and denominators.

$$\frac{7}{\underset{1}{\cancel{2}} \times 2 \times 2} \times \frac{\overset{1}{\cancel{2}} \times 3}{5} = \frac{21}{20}$$

LCM's and GCD's

Least Common Multiple

Multiples are products of a number with 0, 1, 2, 3, . . . as a factor.

Examples

For 6: 0, 6, 12, 18, 24, 30, 36, 42, 48, 54, . . .

For 8: 0, 8, 16, 24, 32, 40, 48, 56, 64, 72, . . .

Common multiples of 6 and 8: 0, 24, 48, 72, . . .

The *Least Common Multiple* (LCM) of a set of numbers is the first nonzero common multiple of the numbers in the set.

The LCM of 6 and 8 is 24.

Greatest Common Divisor

Divisor is another name for factor.

Examples

Divisors of 6: 1, 2, 3, 6

Divisors of 8: 1, 2, 4, 8

Common divisors of 6 and 8 are 1 and 2.

The *Greatest Common Divisor* (GCD) of a set of numbers is the largest common divisor of the numbers in the set.

The GCD of 6 and 8 is 2.

Using primes to find the LCM

$24 = 2 \times 2 \times 2 \times 3$

$42 = 2 \times 3 \times 7$

The primes in 24 and 42 together are

2 (three times)

3 (once)

7 (once)

The LCM of 24 and 42 is $2 \times 2 \times 2 \times 3 \times 7 = 168$.

Using primes to find the GCD

$24 = 2 \times 2 \times 2 \times 3$

$42 = 2 \times 3 \times 7$

The common primes in 24 and 42 are

2 (once)

3 (once)

The GCD of 24 and 42 is $2 \times 3 = 6$.

$$2\frac{3}{4} + 1\frac{7}{8}$$

METHOD 1

A. Change the mixed numbers to fractions.

$$2\frac{3}{4} + 1\frac{7}{8} = \frac{11}{4} + \frac{15}{8}$$

B. Use the least common multiple of the denominators as a new denominator—the *lowest common denominator*, or *LCD*.

$$\frac{11}{4} + \frac{15}{8} = \frac{22}{8} + \frac{15}{8}$$

C. Add the numerators and change to a mixed number.

$$\frac{22}{8} + \frac{15}{8} = \frac{37}{8} = 4\frac{5}{8}$$

METHOD 2

A. Write the problem in vertical form.

$$2\frac{3}{4}$$
$$+1\frac{7}{8}$$

B. Rewrite the fractions with a common denominator. Add.

$$2\frac{3}{4} = 2\frac{6}{8}$$
$$+1\frac{7}{8} = 1\frac{7}{8}$$
$$3\frac{13}{8}$$

C. Change the fraction to a mixed number. Since $\frac{13}{8} = 1\frac{5}{8}$, the sum is $4\frac{5}{8}$.

Mixed numbers and the calculator

Mixed numbers and improper fractions

The sum of an integer (whole number) and a fraction, when shown without a + sign, is a *mixed number*.

Mixed numbers can also be shown as *improper fractions;* that is, fractions in which the numerator is greater than the denominator.

Examples

$3\frac{1}{2}$ means $3 + \frac{1}{2}$ $5\frac{7}{8}$ means $5 + \frac{7}{8}$

$3\frac{1}{2} = \frac{7}{2}$ $5\frac{7}{8} = \frac{47}{8}$

Changing mixed numbers to fractions with the calculator

Examples

$3\frac{1}{2}$ $5\frac{7}{8}$

A. Whole number $\boxtimes$ denominator.

$3 \boxtimes 2 \boxminus 6$ $5 \boxtimes 8 \boxminus 40$

B. Product (step A) $\boxplus$ numerator.

$6 \boxplus 1 \boxminus 7$ $40 \boxplus 7 \boxminus 47$

C. Sum (step B) is numerator of improper fraction.

$3\frac{1}{2} = \frac{7}{}$ $5\frac{7}{8} = \frac{47}{}$

D. Original denominator is also new denominator.

$3\frac{1}{2} = \frac{7}{2}$ $5\frac{7}{8} = \frac{47}{8}$

Changing improper fractions to mixed numbers with the calculator

Examples

$\frac{11}{4}$ $\frac{28}{6}$

A. Numerator $\div$ denominator.

$11 \boxdiv 4 \boxminus 2.75$ $28 \boxdiv 6 \boxminus 4.6666666$

B. Take whole part of decimal and ignore any digits after the decimal point.

2 (ignore .75)   4 (ignore .6666666)

C. Whole part (step B) $\times$ denominator.

$2 \boxtimes 4 \boxminus 8$ $4 \boxtimes 6 \boxminus 24$

D. Numerator $-$ product (step C).

$11 \boxminus 8 \boxminus 3$ $28 \boxminus 24 \boxminus 4$

E. Whole part (step B) is the whole number.

$\frac{11}{4} = 2-$ $\frac{28}{6} = 4-$

F. Difference (step D) is the numerator.

$\frac{11}{4} = 2\frac{3}{}$ $\frac{28}{6} = 4\frac{4}{}$

G. Original denominator is also the new denominator.

$\frac{11}{4} = 2\frac{3}{4}$ $\frac{28}{6} = 4\frac{4}{6}$

H. Fraction may need to be put in simplest form.

Not needed $\frac{28}{6} = 4\frac{2}{3}$

$$5\frac{1}{6} - 3\frac{1}{2}$$

A. Rewrite in vertical form with common denominators.

$$5\frac{1}{6} = 5\frac{1}{6}$$
$$-3\frac{1}{2} = 3\frac{3}{6}$$

B. "Borrow" $1 = \frac{6}{6}$ from 5; that is, rename $5\frac{1}{6}$ as $4\frac{7}{6}$. Subtract.

$$5\frac{1}{6} = 4\frac{7}{6}$$
$$-3\frac{1}{2} = 3\frac{3}{6}$$
$$\overline{\qquad 1\frac{4}{6}}$$

C. Rename $\frac{4}{6}$ as $\frac{2}{3}$. The answer is $1\frac{2}{3}$.

Powers of ten

Exponents

An *exponent* is used to show how many times a number is used as a factor.

Examples

$3^2 = 3 \times 3 = 9$;
9 is the *second power* of 3.

$10^4 = 10 \times 10 \times 10 \times 10 = 10{,}000$;
10,000 is the *fourth power* of 10.

Negative and zero exponents

When a minus sign $(-)$ is placed in front of an exponent, the power becomes the denominator of a fraction whose numerator is 1.

Examples

$3^{-2} = \frac{1}{3 \times 3} = \frac{1}{9}$;
$\frac{1}{9}$ is 3 *raised* to the *negative two* power.

$10^{-4} = \frac{1}{10 \times 10 \times 10 \times 10} = \frac{1}{10{,}000}$;
$\frac{1}{10{,}000}$ is 10 raised to the *negative four* power.

The exponent 0 always gives the value 1 to the power (except that 0^0 is not defined).

Examples

$3^0 = 1$
$10^0 = 1$

Powers of ten

The number 10 has the special property that the number of times the digit 0 is used in the power is the same as the value of the exponent. For negative exponents, this property holds true for the denominators of powers of 10 in fraction form, but it is only true for powers of 10 in decimal form if a 0 is always written in the ones place (just in front of the decimal point). Counting all the zeros then gives the negative power.

Positive exponents

$10^1 = 10$, or ten
$10^2 = 100$, or one hundred
$10^3 = 1000$, or one thousand
$10^4 = 10{,}000$, or ten thousand
$10^5 = 100{,}000$, or one hundred thousand
$10^6 = 1{,}000{,}000$, or one million
$10^7 = 10{,}000{,}000$, or ten million
$10^8 = 100{,}000{,}000$, or one hundred million
$10^9 = 1{,}000{,}000{,}000$, or one billion

Zero and negative exponents

(0 zeros) $10^0 = 1$, or one
(1 zero) $10^{-1} = \frac{1}{10} = 0.1$, or one tenth
(2 zeros) $10^{-2} = \frac{1}{100} = 0.01$, or one hundredth
(3 zeros) $10^{-3} = \frac{1}{1000} = 0.001$, or one thousandth
(4 zeros) $10^{-4} = \frac{1}{10{,}000} = 0.0001$, or one ten thousandth
(5 zeros) $10^{-5} = \frac{1}{100{,}000} = 0.00001$, or one hundred thousandth
(6 zeros) $10^{-6} = \frac{1}{1{,}000{,}000} = 0.000001$, or one millionth
(7 zeros) $10^{-7} = \frac{1}{10{,}000{,}000} = 0.0000001$, or one ten millionth
(8 zeros) $10^{-8} = \frac{1}{100{,}000{,}000} = 0.00000001$, or one hundred millionth
(9 zeros) $10^{-9} = \frac{1}{1{,}000{,}000{,}000} = 0.000000001$, or one billionth

Decimals. Decimals are another way of writing fractions. The decimal point means that the denominator will be a power of 10. The particular power of 10 is indicated by the number of places to the right of the decimal point. For example, 0.3 has 1 place to the right of the decimal point, so $0.3 = \frac{3}{10^1}$, or $\frac{3}{10}$. The decimal 0.123 has 3 places to the right of the decimal point, so $0.123 = \frac{123}{10^3}$, or $\frac{123}{1000}$.

Decimals are *decimal fractions*, but they are also an extension of the numeration system used for whole numbers. The decimal point marks the ones place. A digit to the left of the point means tens, while a digit to the right means tenths.

One way to read decimals is by saying the power of 10 with a *-th* attached after reading the number. Using that system, 0.123 would be read as "one hundred twenty-three thousandths." Another way to read decimals is by reading each digit in order, saying "point" for the decimal point. Using that method, 0.123 would be read as "zero point one two three." If a decimal is greater than 1, the "point" method can still be used as before, but the *-th* method needs to be modified. You must say "and" between the whole-number part and the decimal part. Therefore, 3.14 would be read as either "three point one four" or as "three and fourteen hundredths."

$3.04 + 5.6 + 0.04$

A. Write in vertical form, being careful to keep the decimal points lined up.

$$
\begin{array}{r}
3.04 \\
5.6 \\
+\,0.04 \\
\hline
\end{array}
$$

B. Add as you would for whole numbers, inserting a decimal point below the line of points. Some people prefer to write in extra zeros to make the right align.

This does not change the value of the decimals.

$$
\begin{array}{r}
3.04 \\
5.60 \\
+\,0.04 \\
\hline
8.68
\end{array}
$$

$3.89 - 2.647$

A. Rewrite in vertical form, keeping the decimal points lined up. Most people find filling out the zeros to be helpful.

$$
\begin{array}{r}
3.890 \\
-\,2.647 \\
\hline
\end{array}
$$

B. Subtract as with whole numbers, lining up the decimal point in the difference with the ones above it.

$$
\begin{array}{r}
3.890 \\
-\,2.647 \\
\hline
1.243
\end{array}
$$

Notice that it is necessary to "borrow" 1 from the 9 when you begin to subtract; that is, you must rename 9 hundredths as 8 hundredths 10 thousandths.

Many people find it easier to show this by writing a 1, the "helping number," just before the 0. They also cross out the 9 and write in a small 8 as another helping number.

$$
\begin{array}{r}
3.8\,\overset{8}{\cancel{9}}\,\overset{1}{0} \\
-\,2.6\,4\,7 \\
\hline
1.2\,4\,3
\end{array}
$$

Subtracting is sometimes more difficult when it is necessary to borrow across zeros.

$7.006 - 4.798$

A. Since you cannot borrow from the first 0, or from the second 0, proceed to the 7 to borrow 1. Then the problem, using helping numbers, looks like this:

$$
\begin{array}{r}
\overset{6}{\cancel{7}}.\overset{1}{0}06 \\
-\,4.798 \\
\hline
\end{array}
$$

B. Now you can borrow from the 10. Repeat the process until you reach the 6.

$$
\begin{array}{r}
\overset{6}{\cancel{7}}.\overset{9}{\cancel{0}}\,\overset{9}{\cancel{0}}\,\overset{1}{6} \\
-\,4.7\,9\,8 \\
\hline
2.2\,0\,8
\end{array}
$$

Mathematics

Multiplying by powers of 10

The key to working with decimals is understanding how powers of 10 work, since decimals are based upon powers of 10. The rules for multiplying and dividing by powers of 10 are also useful in solving many problems with whole numbers. You can memorize rules for powers of ten that are based upon counting zeros or on "moving the decimal point" to a different location to get the numeral for a different number. These rules are based on the properties of the numeration system we use.

To start with, make sure that you know the powers of 10 themselves. These are given in the table on page 251. Each positive or negative power of 10 is related in a simple way to the number of zeros shown when the number is written out in the decimal numeration system.

Whole numbers

Notice the pattern.

$$3 \times 10^1 = 3 \times 10 = 30 \qquad \text{(1 zero)}$$
$$3 \times 10^2 = 3 \times 100 = 300 \qquad \text{(2 zeros)}$$
$$3 \times 10^3 = 3 \times 1000 = 3000 \qquad \text{(3 zeros)}$$
$$3 \times 10^4 = 3 \times 10000 = 30000 \qquad \text{(4 zeros)}$$

Rule
To multiply a whole number by a non-negative power of 10, write the whole number with the same number of zeros after it as in the power of 10.
(NOTE: This will not work for negative powers.)

Examples
$7 \times 100,000 = 7 \times 10^5 = 700,000$
$40 \times 1000 = 40 \times 10^3 = 40,000$
(NOTE: Keep the 0 from the 40.)

Decimals

$$3.455192 \times 10^0 = 3.455192 \times 1 = 3.455192 \qquad \text{(decimal point in same place)}$$
$$3.455192 \times 10^1 = 3.455192 \times 10 = 34.55192 \qquad \text{(decimal point 1 place to the right)}$$
$$3.455192 \times 10^2 = 3.455192 \times 100 = 345.5192 \qquad \text{(decimal point 2 places to the right)}$$
$$3.455192 \times 10^3 = 3.455192 \times 1000 = 3455.192 \qquad \text{(decimal point 3 places to the right)}$$
$$3.455192 \times 10^4 = 3.455192 \times 10000 = 34551.92 \qquad \text{(decimal point 4 places to the right)}$$

Rule
To multiply a decimal by a non-negative power of 10, rewrite the decimal with the decimal point the same number of places to the right as the power of 10.

Examples
$27.349 \times 100 = 27.349 \times 10^2 = 2734.9$
$3.82 \times 100 = 3.82 \times 10^2 = 382. = 382$
(You need not show point.)
$3.501 \times 10,000 = 3.501 \times 10^4 = 35,010$
(You may need to write 0's.)
$57 \times 1000 = 57 \times 10^3 = 57. \times 10^3 = 57,000$
(The decimal rule also works for whole numbers.)

Negative exponents

$$392.422 \times 10^{-1} = 392.422 \times 0.1 = 39.2422 \qquad \text{(decimal point 1 place to the left)}$$
$$392.422 \times 10^{-2} = 392.422 \times 0.01 = 3.92422 \qquad \text{(decimal point 2 places to the left)}$$
$$392.422 \times 10^{-3} = 392.422 \times 0.001 = 0.392422 \qquad \text{(decimal point 3 places to the left)}$$
$$392.422 \times 10^{-4} = 392.422 \times 0.0001 = 0.0392422 \qquad \text{(decimal point 4 places to the left)}$$

Rule
To multiply a decimal by a negative power of 10, rewrite the decimal with the decimal point the same number of places to the left as the power of 10, ignoring the negative sign.

Examples
$495.3 \times 0.01 = 495.3 \times 10^{-2} = 4.953$
$7534.02 \times 0.0001 = 7534.02 \times 10^{-4} = 0.753402$
$37.5 \times 0.001 = 37.5 \times 10^{-3} = 0.0375$
(You may need to write more zeros to get the decimal point where you want it.)
$5028 \times 0.1 = 5028 \times 10^{-1} = 5028. \times 10^{-1} = 502.8$
(The decimal rule also works for whole numbers.)

5.9 × 2.3

A. Rewrite in vertical form and multiply as if you were dealing with whole numbers.

$$\begin{array}{r} 2.3 \\ \times 5.9 \\ \hline 207 \\ 115 \\ \hline 1357 \end{array}$$

B. Count the number of decimal places in the problem as originally posed. The first factor, 2.3, has 1 decimal place. The second factor, 5.9, also has 1 digit to the right of the decimal point. Add the number of decimal places. $1 + 1 = 2$.

C. Mark off 2 decimal places in the product.

$$\begin{array}{r} 2.3 \\ \times 5.9 \\ \hline 207 \\ 115 \\ \hline 13.57 \end{array}$$

You use the sum of the decimal places in the problem as the number of decimal places in the product because decimals are just fractions that have powers of 10 as their denominators. When you multiply fractions, you multiply the denominators. Using the rule for multiplying by a power of 10 (see box on page 185), the product of the denominators is the sum of the exponents of the powers of 10. 4.7 is another way of writing $\frac{47}{10^1}$ and 3.054 is another way of writing $\frac{3954}{10^3}$. The product has a numerator that is 47×3954. The product also has a denominator of $10^1 \times 10^3$, which is equal to 10^{1+3}. The answer will have 4 decimal places.

0.07 × 0.005

A. Rewrite in vertical form. Most people ignore lining up the decimal points.

$$\begin{array}{r} 0.005 \\ \times\ 0.07 \end{array}$$

B. Multiply as if the problem had only the whole numbers 5 and 7 shown.

$$\begin{array}{r} 0.005 \\ \times\ 0.07 \\ \hline 35 \end{array}$$

C. Count the number of decimal places in each of the factors: 0.005 has 3 decimal places and 0.07 has 2 decimal places. The number of decimal places in the product is $3 + 2 = 5$.

D. The number 35, however, has 2 digits only. Additional zeros must be written in front of 35.

Three additional decimal places are needed, so 3 zeros must be added.

$$\begin{array}{r} 0.005 \\ \times\ 0.07 \\ \hline 0.00035 \end{array}$$

Dividing by powers of 10

Non-negative exponents

Notice the pattern.

$$872.384 \div 10^1 = 872.384 \div 10 = 87.2384$$
$$872.384 \div 10^2 = 872.384 \div 100 = 8.72384$$
$$872.384 \div 10^3 = 872.384 \div 1000 = 0.872384$$

Rule

To divide a number by a non-negative power of 10, rewrite the number with the decimal point the same number of places to the left as the power of 10.

Examples

$29837.4 \div 10,000 = 29837.4 \div 10^4 = 2.98374$
$5.9 \div 1000 = 5.9 \div 10^3 = 0.0059$
(You may need to write more 0's.)
$293 \div 1000 = 293 \div 10^3 = 293. \div 10^3 = 0.293$

Negative exponents

$$872.384 \div 10^{-1} = 872.384 \div\ \ 0.1 = 8723.84$$
$$872.384 \div 10^{-2} = 872.384 \div\ \ 0.01 = 87238.4$$
$$872.384 \div 10^{-3} = 872.384 \div\ \ 0.001 = 872,384$$

Rule

To divide a number by a negative power of 10, rewrite the number with the decimal point the same number of places to the right as the power of 10, ignoring the negative sign.

Examples

$2957.395 \div 0.01 = 2957.395 \div 10^{-2} = 295,739.5$
$3.14 \div 0.0001 = 3.14 \div 10^{-4} = 31,400$
(You may need to write more zeros.)
$85 \div 0.1 = 85 \div 10^{-1} = 850$

Fractions, decimals, and repeating decimals

Decimals into fractions

To change a decimal to a fraction, write the decimal as a fraction that has a whole-number (omitting the decimal point) numerator over a denominator of the proper power of 10; then simplify if possible.

NOTE: Decimals greater than 1 maybe written as mixed numbers by taking the whole-number part of the decimal as the whole-number part of the mixed number. Treat the fraction part as in the general rule.

Examples

$0.12 = \frac{12}{100} = \frac{12 \div 4}{100 \div 4} = \frac{3}{25}$

$2.314 = \frac{2314}{1000} = 2\frac{314}{1000}$

Example

$5.02 = 5\frac{2}{100} = 5\frac{1}{50}$

Fractions into decimals

To change a fraction to a decimal, divide the numerator by the denominator.

Examples

$$\frac{5}{8} = 5 \div 8 \qquad 8\overline{)5.000}$$
$$\begin{array}{r} 0.625 \\ \hline 4\,8 \\ \hline 20 \\ 16 \\ \hline 40 \\ 40 \\ \hline \end{array}$$

$$\frac{11}{4} = 11 \div 4 \qquad 4\overline{)11.00}$$
$$\begin{array}{r} 2.75 \\ \hline 8 \\ \hline 3\,0 \\ 2\,8 \\ \hline 20 \\ 20 \\ \hline \end{array}$$

NOTE: For mixed numbers, you may take the whole-number part of the mixed number as the whole-number part of the decimal. Treat the fraction part as in the general rule.

Example

$$4\frac{1}{2} = 4 + (1 \div 2) \qquad 2\overline{)1.0} \qquad 4\frac{1}{2} = 4.5$$
$$\begin{array}{r} 0.5 \\ \hline 1\,0 \end{array}$$

Repeating decimals

If the same remainder is encountered more than once after you begin to "bring down" zeros, the decimal will repeat the same pattern of digits over and over. This may be indicated by putting a bar over the digits that repeat.

HINT: All fractions with whole-number numerators and denominators either terminate (the remainder when you divide is zero) or repeat a set of digits. The fraction will *always* terminate if the denominator of the fraction has only the prime factors 2 and 5—so fractions with denominators of 2, 10, 4, 8, 20, 25, and so forth terminate. Otherwise the fraction will repeat with a period (the number of digits that repeat) that is less than the denominator.

Examples

The denominator of $\frac{1}{3}$ has the prime factor 3, so it repeats with a period less than 3 (its actual period is 1).

The denominator of $\frac{11}{40}$ has the factors $2^3 \times 5$, so it terminates.

The denominator of $\frac{2}{7}$ has the prime factor 7, so it repeats with a period less than 7 (its actual period is 6).

The denominator of $\frac{5}{9}$ has the prime factors 3^2, so it repeats with a period less than 9 (its actual period is 1).

Examples

$$\frac{1}{3} = 1 \div 3$$
$$3\overline{)1.00}$$
$$\begin{array}{r} 0.3\overline{3} \\ \hline 9 \\ \hline 10 \\ 9 \\ \hline 1 \end{array}$$

$0.3\overline{3}$ means
$0.333333 \cdots$

$$\frac{3}{11} = 3 \div 11$$
$$11\overline{)3.0000}$$
$$\begin{array}{r} 0.2727 \\ \hline 2.2 \\ \hline 80 \\ 77 \\ \hline 30 \\ 22 \\ \hline 80 \\ 77 \\ \hline 3 \end{array}$$

$0.27\overline{27}$ or
$0.\overline{27}$ means
$0.27272727 \cdots$

$$\frac{2}{7} = 2 \div 7$$
$$7\overline{)2.000000}$$
$$\begin{array}{r} 0.285714 \\ \hline 1\,4 \\ \hline 60 \\ 56 \\ \hline 40 \\ 35 \\ \hline 50 \\ 49 \\ \hline 10 \\ 7 \\ \hline 30 \\ 28 \\ \hline 2 \end{array}$$

$0.\overline{285714}$ means
$0.285714285714285714 \cdots$

$\dfrac{16.1}{2.3}$

A. Division problems are easier to do by hand if they are written in the form that corresponds to vertical form for addition, subtraction, and multiplication. This is sometimes called "example form." Rewrite the problem in example form.

$$2.3\,\overline{)\,16.1}$$

Table of fractions and decimals

While you can always calculate the decimal equivalent to a fraction or the fraction equivalent to a decimal, it is very handy to memorize the more common equivalents. The following table includes the equivalents that occur most often.

Fraction	Decimal equivalent
$\frac{1}{2}$	0.5
$\frac{1}{3}$	$0.\overline{3}$
$\frac{1}{4}$	0.25
$\frac{1}{5}$	0.2
$\frac{1}{6}$	$0.1\overline{6}$
$\frac{1}{8}$	0.125
$\frac{1}{10}$	0.1
$\frac{2}{3}$	$0.\overline{6}$
$\frac{2}{5}$	0.4
$\frac{3}{4}$	0.75
$\frac{3}{5}$	0.6
$\frac{3}{8}$	0.375
$\frac{3}{10}$	0.3
$\frac{4}{5}$	0.8
$\frac{5}{6}$	$0.8\overline{3}$
$\frac{5}{8}$	0.625
$\frac{7}{8}$	0.875
$\frac{7}{10}$	0.7
$\frac{9}{10}$	0.9

B. Division by a whole number is accomplished by dividing as if both the *divisor* (number being divided by) and the *dividend* (number being divided into) are whole numbers. The decimal point in the quotient then lines up with the decimal point in the dividend (see box on page 187 for examples). The quotient will not change if both the divisor and the dividend are multiplied by the same number. Multiply each number by the power of 10 indicated by the decimal point in the divisor. For 2.3 the power is 10^1.

$$2.3.\,\overline{)\,16.1.}$$

$\dfrac{23.4}{0.32}$

A. Rewrite in example form.

$$0.32\,\overline{)\,23.4}$$

B. There are 2 decimal places in the divisor, so both the divisor and the dividend must be multiplied by 10^2. This has the effect of "moving the decimal points" each 2 places to the right. Since there is only 1 decimal place in the dividend, however, it is necessary to insert a zero to locate the "new" decimal point.

$$0.32.\,\overline{)\,23.40.}$$

C. Now divide as with whole numbers.

$$\begin{array}{r} 73 \\ 0.32.\,\overline{)\,23.40.} \\ \underline{22\,4} \\ 1\,00 \\ \underline{96} \\ 4 \end{array}$$

C. In this problem, both the divisor and the dividend are changed to whole numbers by multiplication, so the division is completed in the same way as for whole numbers.

$$\begin{array}{r} 7 \\ 2.3.\,\overline{)\,16.1.} \\ \underline{16\,1} \end{array}$$

In this case, there is no remainder. Had there been a remainder of 3, for instance, it could *not* have been written with the quotient as "R3." Instead, one would need to insert more zeros after the dividend and continue dividing.

Since there is a remainder, it is necessary to insert zeros and keep dividing until (1) you do not require any greater precision; that is, you have as many decimal places as you need; (2) the division terminates because the remainder is 0; or (3) you reach the same remainder for the second time, which indicates that you have found all of the digits that repeat.

$$\begin{array}{r} 73.125 \\ 0.32.\,\overline{)\,23.40.000} \\ \underline{22\,4} \\ 1\,00 \\ \underline{96} \\ 40 \\ \underline{32} \\ 80 \\ \underline{64} \\ 160 \\ \underline{160} \end{array}$$

Proportion and percent

William can go 385 miles on 1 tank of gasoline. If his tank holds 11 gallons, how many gallons of gasoline will he use on a trip of 595 miles?

A. Write the problem as a *proportion.* A proportion is a statement that two *ratios* are equal. A ratio is one way to compare two amounts by division. Each ratio is a number of miles to a number of gallons. The first ratio is the number of miles per tank to the number of gallons per tank, or $\frac{385}{11}$. The second ratio is the number of miles on the trip to an unknown number of gallons. The unknown number is N. Thus, the proportion is

$$\frac{385}{11} = \frac{595}{N}.$$

B. Solve the proportion. The easiest way to solve a proportion is to use the *cross-product rule:* In a proportion, the product of the numerator of the first ratio and the denominator of the second ratio is equal to the product of the denominator of the first ratio and the numerator of the second ratio. Accordingly, you can rewrite the proportion as

$$385 \times N = 11 \times 595.$$

C. Carry out any multiplication that you can.

$$385 \times N = 6545$$

D. If $385 \times N = 6545$, then

$$N = \frac{6545}{385} = 17.$$

The answer is 17 gallons of gasoline.

Find 37% of 250.

A. A *percent* is a ratio of a whole number to 100, so 37% is the ratio $\frac{37}{100}$. Percent problems can be solved in many ways. You may use decimals, for example, to rewrite this problem as 0.37×250.

The examples here will use the proportion method for solution because it is a useful way to solve practical problems. Think not only of 37% as a ratio, but also of 250 as a ratio.

In this context, the problem "find 37% of 250" may be solved by thinking "37 is to 100 as what number (N) is to 250?"

$$\frac{37}{100} = \frac{N}{250}$$

B. Rewrite using the cross-product rule and complete any multiplication that you can.

$$37 \times 250 = 100 \times N$$
$$9250 = 100 \times N$$

C. Divide by 100 to find N.

$$N = \frac{9250}{100} = 92.5$$

The answer is 92.5.

Notice that this method involves multiplication by whole numbers only. Also, division by 100 is simple.

What percent of 400 is 260?

A. Set up a proportion.

$$\frac{260}{400} = \frac{N}{100}$$

The ratio $\frac{N}{100}$ is the same as N%.

B. Use the cross-product rule.

$$260 \times 100 = 400 \times N$$
$$26000 = 400 \times N$$

C. Divide by 400.

$$N = \frac{26000}{400} = 65$$

The answer is 65%.

52.5 is 35% of what number?

A. Set up a proportion.

$$\frac{52.5}{N} = \frac{35}{100}$$

B. Use the cross-product rule.

$$52.5 \times 100 = N \times 35$$
$$5250 = N \times 35$$

C. Divide by 35.

$$N = \frac{5250}{35} = 150$$

The answer is 150.

Interest problems

Find the amount of interest on $1500 at a rate of 9% for 6 months.

METHOD 1

A. The interest formula is $i = prt$ where i is the interest in dollars, p is the amount of money on which interest is being paid (the *principal*), r is the rate expressed as a percent, and t is the time in years. Since t is in months, convert 6 months to years.
$$\tfrac{6}{12} = \tfrac{1}{2}$$
The time is $\tfrac{1}{2}$ year.

B. Substitute into the formula, using the ratio form of percent.
$$i = 1500 \times \tfrac{9}{100} \times \tfrac{1}{2}$$

C. Cancel any factors you can and multiply.
$$i = 15 \times 9 \times \tfrac{1}{2} = \tfrac{135}{2} = 67\tfrac{1}{2}$$
The answer is $67.50.

METHOD 2

A. If you are using a calculator it will be easier to work with decimals than with ratios. Use 0.09 for 9% and 0.5 for $\tfrac{1}{2}$.

B. Use the formula and multiply.
$$i = 1500 \times 0.09 \times 0.5 = 67.5$$
The interest is $67.50.

Find the rate of interest if the interest is $55, the principal is $1000, and the time is 11 months.

METHOD 1

A. The interest formula can be rewritten in several ways by dividing both sides of the formula by one of the factors on the right side.
$$r = \frac{i}{p \times t}$$
$$p = \frac{i}{r \times t}$$
$$t = \frac{i}{p \times r}$$
The most useful form for this problem is the first,
$$r = \frac{i}{p \times t}$$

B. Convert the time to years and substitute into the formula.
$$t = \tfrac{11}{12}$$
$$r = \frac{55}{1000 \times \tfrac{11}{12}}$$

C. Multiply and rewrite the fraction as a ratio of some number to 100.
$$r = \tfrac{6}{100}$$
The answer is 6%.

METHOD 2

A. If you have a calculator it is easier to work with
$$t = \frac{i}{p \times r},$$
which avoids the problem of having to convert $\tfrac{11}{12}$ to a decimal.
$$\tfrac{11}{12} = \frac{55}{1000 \times r}$$

B. Use the cross-product rule.
$$11 \times (1000 \times r) = 12 \times 55$$
$$11000 \times r = 660$$

C. Divide by 11000.
$$r = 0.06$$
The answer is 6%.

Find the amount of money that will result from investing $2500 for 9 months at 10% when the interest is computed every 3 months and left in the account.

A. When interest is is collected on the interest, it is known as *compound interest*. While you can calculate compound interest by repeatedly calculating the amount for each period, it is easier to use the *compound interest formula*:
$$A = p \times (1 + i)^n$$
where A is the amount (principal plus interest), p is the original principal, i is interest rate per period of compounding, and n is the number of periods. To use the formula, convert the interest rate, which is given per year, to a per period ratio. Since the period is 3 months, the per period rate is $\tfrac{3}{12} \times \tfrac{10}{100} = \tfrac{25}{1000} = 2.5\%$. In 9 months, there are 3 3-month periods.

B. Substitute into the formula.
$$A = 2500 \times (1 + 0.025)^3$$
$$= 2500 \times 1.0768906$$
$$= 2692.2265$$
The amount is $2692.23.

Discounts and taxes

How much does a dress cost if its original price was $80 but it is now on sale at a discount of 20%?

METHOD 1
A. Find 20% of 80.

    20% of 80 = 16

B. Subtract 16 from 80.
    $80 - 16 = 64$
    The dress will cost $64.

METHOD 2
A. A discount is always a *percent of decrease.* You can solve percent-of-decrease problems in one step by subtracting the percent discount from 100% and then multiplying.
    $100\% - 20\% = 80\%$

B. Multiply.
    $80 \times 0.80 = 64$
    The dress will cost $64.

Find the total amount for a $50 purchase if the sales tax is $5\frac{1}{2}\%$.

A. A sales tax is a *percent of increase,* so the rate of the tax may be added to 100%.
    $100\% + 5\frac{1}{2}\% = 105\frac{1}{2}\%$

B. Convert $105\frac{1}{2}\%$ to a decimal and multiply.
    $50 \times 1.055 = 52.75$
    The answer is $52.75.

Measurement

What is the precision of a measurement of 5 centimeters when the measurement is made with a ruler that shows only centimeters and millimeters?

A. The *precision* of any measurement is the smallest unit used in making the measurement. In this case it is 1 millimeter.

B. The number of *significant digits* should be the same as the total number of units used. There are two significant digits in 50 mm. In cm, the measurement should be shown as 5.0. The result can also be expressed in scientific notation (see box on page 260) as 5.0×10^0.

What is the greatest possible error in a measurement of 28.57 meters?

A. Determine the precision of the measurement. Since the measurement is written as 28.57 meters, it was made by measuring to the nearest 0.01 meter.

B. The *greatest possible error* is one-half the precision (the measurement is closer to 0.57 than to 0.56 or 0.58). One-half of 0.01 meter is 0.005 meter, so that is the greatest possible error.

What is the relative error in a measurement of 29 centimeters?

A. Determine the greatest possible error. Since the measurement is expressed to the nearest centimeter, the greatest possible error is one-half of 1 centimeter, or 0.5 cm.

B. The *relative error* is the greatest possible error divided by the measurement. Therefore, the relative error is
$$\frac{0.5}{29} = \frac{1}{58}$$

Scientific notation and calculators

Scientists and engineers regularly use *scientific notation* to show large and small numbers. Scientific notation may also be used to show the number of significant digits in a number. In scientific notation, a number is shown as a product. One factor is a number between 1 and 10, called the *mantissa*. The other factor is a power of 10. If the number shown is exactly a power of 10, the mantissa of 1 is omitted.

Ordinary notation	Scientific notation
5000	5×10^3
4978	4.978×10^3
4,9780	4.978×10^4
4,9780	4.9780×10^4

(NOTE: The line under the 0 in 4.9780 means that the zero is significant. The same information is provided by showing the zero in scientific notation.)

5,000,000,000	5×10^9
10,000,000,000	10^{10}
1	10^0
0.1	10^{-1}
0.20	2.0×10^{-1}
0.0000007	7×10^{-7}
0.00000073	7.3×10^{-7}

Because scientific notation is a compact way to express large numbers, a form of it is used in many hand-held calculators and in some computer languages. The displays of calculators and computers cannot indicate exponents as raised numerals, however, so the system is modified to allow for all the characters to be shown on the same line. In this form, scientific notation is often called *floating-point notation*. In the floating-point system, the exponent is shown with the letter E and the times sign may be omitted (although some calculators include the times sign). Often, the sign of the number, positive or negative, is shown.

Ordinary notation	Scientific notation	Floating point
5,000,000,000	5×10^9	$+5 \text{ E}+9$
3,892,405,000	3.892405×10^9	$+3.892405 \text{ E}+9$
0.0000957	9.57×10^{-5}	$+9.57 \text{ E}-5$
$-3,028$	-3.028×10^3	$-3.028 \text{ E}+3$
-0.000054	-5.4×10^{-5}	$-5.4 \text{ E}-5$

(NOTE: A hand-held calculator will automatically round a number to the number of places that can be shown on its display. Also, many hand-held calculators will automatically show very large or small numbers in floating-point notation. Therefore, an answer of 3,892,405,000 may be shown on the calculator as 3.8924 E+9 instead of +3.892405 E+9.)

Multiplication and division in scientific notation

To multiply
Multiply the mantissas; add the exponents. You may have to adjust the mantissa of the product to get it between 1 and 10 again.

(NOTE: If significant digits are important, the mantissa of the product should be rounded to show only the number of significant digits in the factor with the least number of significant digits.)

$$(4.30 \times 10^{-7}) \times (5.329 \times 10^3) = (4.30 \times 5.329) \times 10^{-7+3}$$
$$= 22.9147 \times 10^{-4}$$
$$= 2.29147 \times 10^{-3},$$

which rounds to 2.29×10^{-3}.

Examples

$$(5.83 \times 10^7) \times (3.07 \times 10^5) = (5.83 \times 3.07) \times 10^{7+5}$$
$$= 17.8981 \times 10^{12}$$
$$= 1.78981 \times 10^{13}$$

$$(2.04 \times 10^{-3}) \times (3.12 \times 10^{-4}) = (2.04 \times 3.12) \times 10^{-3+(-4)}$$
$$= 6.3648 \times 10^{-7}$$

$$(7.59 \times 10^4) \times (8.27 \times 10^{-3}) = (7.59 \times 8.27) \times 10^{4+(-3)}$$
$$= 62.7693 \times 10$$
$$= 6.27693 \times 10^2$$

To divide
Divide the mantissa; subtract the exponents. You may have to adjust the mantissa of the quotient to get it between 1 and 10 again.

Examples

$$(8.214 \times 10^8) \div (2.24 \times 10^3) = (8.214 \div 2.24) \times 10^{8-3}$$
$$= 3.67 \times 10^5 \text{ (rounded to two places)}$$

$$(5.19 \times 10^5) \div (4.5 \times 10^{-2}) = (5.19 \div 4.5) \times 10^{5-(-2)}$$
$$= 1.2 \times 10^7 \text{ (rounded to one place)}$$

$$(7.35 \times 10^{-3}) \div (9.323 \times 10^{-7}) = (7.35 \div 9.323) \times 10^{-3-(-7)}$$
$$= 0.788 \times 10^4 \text{ (rounded to three places)}$$
$$= 7.88 \times 10^3.$$

Square roots and the Pythagorean theorem

The two sides of a right triangle that make up the right angle measure 9 centimeters and 40 centimeters. What is the length of the side opposite the right angle (the *hypotenuse*)?

A. This problem can be solved by using *the Pythagorean theorem,* which states that in a right triangle the square of the hypotenuse is equal to the sum of the squares of the two sides.

Therefore, if you call the length of the hypotenuse c, the following relationship is true:
$$c^2 = 9^2 + 40^2$$
$$= 81 + 1600$$
$$= 1681$$

B. Find the square root of 1681. This is most easily accomplished on a calculator. The result is 41.

Find the square root of 30,679 to the nearest tenth without using the square root key on a calculator.

A. Estimate the square root. Since 100×100 is 10,000, the square root will be larger than 100. Use 150 as an estimate.

B. Divide the original number by your estimate.
$$\frac{30679}{150} = 204.52666$$

C. Average the quotient and your estimate. Find the average to 1 significant digit more than your original estimate. Since your estimate of 150 has 2 significant digits, find the average to 3 significant digits.
$$\frac{(150 + 204.5)}{2} = 177.25,$$
which rounds to 177.

D. Use the average as a new estimate and repeat steps A, B, and C.
$$\frac{30679}{177} = 173.32768$$
$$\frac{(177 + 173.33)}{2} = 175.165,$$
which rounds to 175.2.

E. Use that result as a new average and keep repeating steps, A, B, C, and D until the average has "settled down" in the hundredths place. Notice that the tens place, 7, has already "settled down," so the square root of 30,679 to the nearest hundred is 200.
$$\frac{30679}{175.2} = 175.10844$$
$$\frac{(175.2 + 175.108)}{2} = 175.154,$$
which rounds to 175.15.
$$\frac{30679}{175.15} = 175.15843$$
Since the hundredths place in 175.15 and in 175.15843 is the same, you have established that the square root to the nearest tenth is 175.2, which is 175.15 rounded to the nearest tenth.

Note that this method, which is called the *method of iteration* (repetition), is considerably easier to remember than the traditional square-root algorithm. Because this method gets you close to the correct answer very quickly, the closeness of the original estimate to the actual square root is not very important. Suppose that your original estimate had been 100:
$$\frac{30679}{100} = 306.79$$
$$\frac{(100 + 306)}{2} = 203$$
$$\frac{30679}{200} = 153.395$$
$$\frac{(200 + 153.4)}{2} = 176.7$$
$$\frac{30679}{177} = 173.32768$$

This is, of course, the same point as was reached in step D, so the calculations proceed exactly as in step E. It only took one more iteration starting with a poor guess than it did starting with a good one.

Formulas often used in arithmetic

General $d=rt$ where d is distance $p=br$ where p is percent $i=prt$ where i is interest
                                r is rate b is base p is percent
                                t is time r is time r is rate
                                                                             t is time

Length $p=a+b+c$ where p is perimeter of a *triangle*
                                    a, b, and c are the lengths of the sides

$p=2l+2w$ where p is perimeter of a *rectangle*
             l is length
             w is width

$p=4s$ where p is perimeter of a *square*
          s is length of a side

$C=\pi d$ where C is circumference of a *circle*
          π is pi, a number that is about 3.14 or $\frac{22}{7}$
          d is the length of the diameter

$C=2\pi r$ where C is the circumference of a *circle*
          π is pi, a number that is about 3.14 or $\frac{22}{7}$
          r is the length of the radius

Area $A=lw$ where A is area of a *rectangle*
                  l is length
                  w is width

$A=s^2$ where A is area of a *square*
          s is length of a side

$A=bh$ where A is area of a *parallelogram*
          b is length of the base
          h is height

$A=\frac{1}{2}bh$ where A is area of a *triangle*
          b is length of the base
          h is height

$A=\frac{1}{2}h(B+b)$ where A is area of a *trapezoid*
          h is height
          B is length of one parallel side
          b is length of the other parallel side

$A=\frac{1}{2}Dd$ where A is area of a *kite*
          D is length of one diagonal
          d is length of the other diagonal

$A=\frac{1}{2}ab$ where A is area of a *right triangle*
          a is length of one leg
          b is length of the other leg

$A=\frac{s^2}{4}\sqrt{3}$ where A is area of an *equilateral triangle*
          s is length of one of the sides

$A=\frac{1}{2}ap$ where A is area of a *regular polygon*
          a is length of an apothem
          p is perimeter of the polygon

$p=perimeter$

	$A = \pi r^2$	where A is area of a *circle* π is pi, a number that is about 3.14 or $\frac{22}{7}$ r is length of the radius	

$A = \sqrt{s(s-a)(s-b)(s-c)}$ where A is area of a *triangle*
s is semiperimeter of the triangle;
$$(s = \frac{a+b+c}{2})$$
a, b, and c are the lengths of the sides

perimeter $= 2s$

or $A = 2(\pi rh + \pi r^2)$
$A = 2\pi r(h+r)$

where A is total area of a *right circular cylinder*
π is pi, a number that is about 3.14 or $\frac{22}{7}$
r is length of the radius of the base
h is height of the cylinder

or $A = \pi rl + \pi r^2$
$A = \pi r(l+r)$

where A is total area of a *right circular cone*
π is pi, a number that is about 3.14 or $\frac{22}{7}$
r is length of the radius of the base
l is slant height of the cone

$A = 4\pi r^2$

where A is area of a *sphere*
π is pi, a number that is about 3.14 or $\frac{22}{7}$
r is length of the radius of the sphere

Volume $V = lwh$

where V is volume of a *right rectangular prism*
l is length
w is width
h is height

$V = e^3$

where V is volume of a *cube*
e is length of an edge of the cube

$V = Bh$

where V is volume of a *prism*
B is area of the base
h is height of the prism

$B = $ area of base

$V = \pi r^2 h$

where V is volume of a *circular cylinder*
π is pi, a number that is about 3.14 or $\frac{22}{7}$
r is length of the radius of the base
h is height of the cylinder

$V = \frac{1}{3}\pi r^2 h$

where V is volume of a *circular cone*
π is pi, a number that is about 3.14 or $\frac{22}{7}$
r is length of the radius of the base
h is height of the cylinder

$V = \frac{1}{3}Bh$

where V is volume of a *pyramid*
B is area of the base of the pyramid
h is height of the pyramid

$B = $ area of base

$V = \frac{4}{3}\pi r^3$

where V is volume of a *sphere*
π is pi, a number that is about 3.14 or $\frac{22}{7}$
r is length of the radius of the sphere

Algebra

The algebra that is studied in secondary schools has as its goals the ability to manipulate expressions containing variables; the ability to use equations and inequalities to solve problems; and the development of an introductory understanding of the different functions of a variable.

A *variable* is a letter or other sign used to represent any one of a set of numbers; thus, the variable x typically can represent any positive or negative number that can be expressed as a decimal, including infinite decimals such as π. (Although Greek letters are sometimes used as variables, π is a number, not a variable.)

Equations state that two expressions are equal. For example, $2x + 5 = 17$. *Inequalities* use signs such as $<$ ("is less than") or $>$ ("is greater than") to make statements. A *function* is a rule connecting the members of 2 sets. In algebra, most functions are expressed as equations in two variables, such as $y = 3x - 7$. Special notation for one of the variables is often used to indicate its functional nature, most commonly in expressions such as $f(x) = 3x - 7$, where $f(x)$, which is read f of x or f at x, means the same as y in the previous equation.

In algebra, multiplication is shown differently from the familiar $\times$ sign of arithmetic. Most commonly, the product of a number and a variable, or two variables, is shown by writing the two adjacent to each other, so $5a$ means $5 \times a$ and ab means $a \times b$. Sometimes a raised dot, $\cdot$, is used to show multiplication.

Multiplication is also indicated simply by writing two numbers adjacent to each other in parentheses, as $(2)(3) = 6$, for example.

Expressions and formulas

Rewrite $2a - 7 + 5a$ in simpler form.

A. Collect the parts with the same variable.

$$2a + 5a - 7$$

B. The distributive law permits *terms*—algebraic expressions formed by just multiplication or division—to be combined.

$$(2 + 5)a - 7$$
$$7a - 7$$

The laws of numbers

For any real numbers a, b, and c:

Closure
$a + b$ is a real number
$a \cdot b$ is a real number

Commutative law
$a + b = b + a$
$a \cdot b = b \cdot a$

Associative law
$a + (b + c) = (a + b) + c$
$a \cdot (b \cdot c) = (a \cdot b) \cdot c$

Identity elements
$a + 0 = a$
$a \cdot 1 = a$

Distributive law
$a \cdot (b + c) = a \cdot b + a \cdot c$

Laws of equality
Reflexive law $\quad a = a$
Symmetric law $\quad$ If $a = b$, then $b = a$
Transitive law $\quad$ If $a = b$ and $b = c$, then $a = c$

Laws of equations
Addition $\qquad$ If $a = b$, then $a + c = b + c$
Subtraction $\qquad$ If $a = b$, then $a - c = b - c$
Multiplication $\quad$ If $a = b$, then $a \cdot c = b \cdot c$
Division $\qquad$ If $a = b$, then $\dfrac{a}{c} = \dfrac{b}{c}$ unless $c = 0$

Inverse elements
For each a there exists a number $-a$ such that $a + (-a) = 0$

For each a (except 0) there exists a number $\dfrac{1}{a}$ such that $a \cdot \dfrac{1}{a} = 1$

Rewrite $3x^2 + x - 2x^2 + 5y - 3x + 9xy$ in simpler form.

A. Collect like terms. *Like terms* are those with the same variables to the same powers; thus $3x^2$ is like $2x^2$ but not like $5y$, $-3x$, or $9xy$.

$3x^2 - 2x^2 + x - 3x + 5y + 9xy$

B. Combine like terms.

$(3 - 2)x^2 + (1 - 3)x + 5y + 9xy$
$x^2 - 2x + 5y + 9xy$

Notice that a factor of 1 is usually not written.

Use the formula $p = 2l + 2w$ to find the perimeter of a rectangle if l is 7 and w is 4.

A. Substitute the values of l and w into the formula.

$p = 2(7) + 2(4)$

B. Multiply.

$p = 14 + 8$

C. Add.

$p = 22$

In a trapezoid, one base is 15 centimeters, the other base is 10 centimeters, and the height is 6 centimeters. Find the area using the formula $A = \frac{1}{2}(B + b)h$.

A. Substitute.

$A = \frac{1}{2}(15 + 10) \cdot 6$

B. Follow the correct order of operations (see box) to do the arithmetic.

Start with expressions in parentheses.

$A = \frac{1}{2}(25) \cdot 6$
$= 75$

Evaluate the expression $5(3x^2 - 2x) + 4$ for $x = 3$.

A. Substitute 3 for x wherever x occurs in the expression.

$5(3 \cdot 3^2 - 2 \cdot 3) + 4$

B. Follow the correct order of operations.

$5(3 \cdot 9 - 2 \cdot 3) + 4$
$5 \quad (27 - 6) \quad + 4$
$5 \quad\quad (21) \quad\quad + 4$
$\quad\quad\quad\quad 105 + 4$
$\quad\quad\quad\quad\quad 109$

The order of operations

Compute $(3 \cdot 4 + \frac{8}{2} - (\frac{3+7}{5} + \sqrt{10 - 1}))^2 + 2 \cdot 8$

First:	Do everything in parentheses following the order of operations. If parentheses are nested (one set inside another), work from the inside set of parentheses to the outside set.	$(3 \cdot 4 + \frac{8}{2} - (\frac{10}{5} + \sqrt{9}))^2 + 2 \cdot 8$
Second:	Treat the horizontal line in a fraction or in the square root symbol the same as another set of parentheses.	$(3 \cdot 4 + \frac{8}{2} - (2 + 3))^2 + 2 \cdot 8$ $(3 \cdot 4 + \frac{8}{2} - 5)^2 + 2 \cdot 8$
Third:	Compute all powers as soon as possible.	$(12 + 4 - 5)^2 + 16$
Fourth:	Multiply and divide from left to right.	$11^2 + 16$
Fifth:	Add and subtract from left to right.	$121 + 16$ 137

Signed numbers. Algebra makes full use of the complex number system (see box), but most secondary-school algebra is confined to real numbers. Operations with real numbers are more difficult than operations with whole numbers because numbers can be both positive and negative.

A number on the number line is always less than any number to the right of it, so -3 is less than -1, for example. The *absolute value* of a real number is its distance from 0. Thus, the absolute value of -5 is 5 and the absolute value of $+7$ is 7. Absolute value is indicated by a pair of parallel lines $||$ that enclose the number. Therefore, $|-4|$ is the same as 4, $|+6|$ is the same as 6, and $|0|$ is the same as 0.

$$5 + (-2)$$

A. To add numbers with unlike signs, subtract the absolute value of the lesser number from the absolute value of the greater number.

$$|5| - |-2|$$
$$5 - 2$$
$$3$$

B. Affix the sign of the number with the greater absolute value. The answer is $+3$.

Sets of numbers

In algebra, mathematicians work with several different sets of numbers, although most often with the integers, the real numbers, or the complex numbers. Each set of numbers includes all the numbers in each of the sets above it.

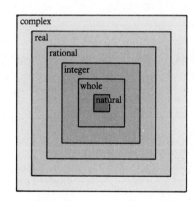

Symbol	Name and description	Examples
N	**Natural numbers** (often called counting numbers): The numbers with which you count; the number of members in a nonempty set.	1, 2, 3, . . .
W	**Whole numbers** (sometimes called natural numbers): The natural numbers and 0; the number of members in any set.	0, 1, 2, . . .
I	**Integers:** Whole numbers and their opposites (or negatives).	. . ., -3, -2, -1, 0, 1, 2, 3, . . .
Q	**Rational numbers:** The quotients of any two integers (with the exception that dividing by 0 is not allowed).	0, 3, $\frac{1}{2}$, $\frac{3}{4}$, 3.2, $-\frac{7}{8}$, -57, -0.00001, $-6\frac{2}{3}$, 1,000,001
R	**Real numbers:** Any numbers that can be represented by an infinite decimal (or equivalently, by a point on a line).	0, 5, -8, $\frac{3}{7}$, π, $\sqrt{2}$, 1.01001000100001 . . ., $-\sqrt{137}$
C	**Complex numbers:** The sums found by adding a real number to the product of a real number with the square root of -1, which is shown by i.	0, i, $-i$, $4 + i$, $1 + i\sqrt{2}$, $-8 + 3i$, $8 - 9i$, $\pi - 27i$

$-4 + (-7)$

A. To add numbers with like signs, add the absolute values.
$$|-4| + |-7| = 11$$

B. Affix the sign of the numbers.
$$-4 + (-7) = -11$$

$5 - 9$

A. To subtract real numbers, replace the number to be subtracted with its *opposite* and add. The opposite of a real number is the number on the other side of 0 on the number line that has the same absolute value (the opposite of 0 is 0). Thus, the opposite of 9 is -9.
$$5 - 9 = 5 + (-9)$$

B. $5 + (-9) = -4$

$5(-3)$

A. To multiply two real numbers, find the product of their absolute values.
$$|5| \cdot |-3| = 5 \cdot 3 = 15$$

B. If the signs of the numbers are different, the product is negative.
$$5(-3) = -15$$

$$- \times - = +$$

Filling a tank at $+3$ gal./min.

Five min. from now
$$(+5)(+3) = +15$$

$(-8)(-4)$

A. $|-8| \cdot |-4| = 8 \cdot 4 = 32$

B. If the signs of the factors are the same, the product is positive.
$$(-8)(-4) = +32$$

Emptying a tank at -3 gal./min.

Five min. ago
$$(-5)(-3) = +15$$

$(-5)(0)$

The product of any real number and 0 is 0 (see box on page 264).
$$(-5)(0) = 0$$

$\dfrac{-10}{5}$

A. To divide one real number by another, replace the number you are dividing by with the inverse for multiplication (see box on page 264) and multiply.

The multiplicative inverse is the same as the reciprocal.
$$(-10)/5 = (-10) \cdot 1/5$$
$\dfrac{-10}{5}$ is often written as $(-10)/5$ in algebra.

B. $|-10| \cdot |1/5| = 2$

C. $(-10) \cdot 1/5 = -2$

$\dfrac{-35}{-7}$

A. $-35/-7 = -35 \cdot (-1/7)$

B. $|-35| \cdot |-1/7| = 5$

C. $-35 \cdot (-1/7) = +5$

"Undoing" equations

Addition method

If $x + a = b$, then add $-a$ to each side:
$$x + a + (-a) = b + (-a)$$
$$x + 0 = b - a$$
$$x = b - a$$

If $x - a = b$, then add a to each side:
$$x - a + a = b + a$$
$$x + 0 = b + a$$
$$x = b + a$$

Examples:

Solve: $\qquad\qquad x + 7 = 19$

Add -7. $x + 7 + (-7) = 19 + (-7)$
$$x + 0 = 19 - 7$$
$$x = 12$$

Solve: $\qquad x - 3 = 15$

Add 3. $x - 3 + 3 = 15 + 3$
$$x + 0 = 18$$
$$x = 18$$

Subtraction method

If $x + a = b$, then subtract a from each side:
$$x + a - a = b - a$$
$$x + 0 = b - a$$
$$x = b - a$$

Example:

Solve: $\qquad\qquad x + 3 = 11$

Subtract 3. $\quad x + 3 - 3 = 11 - 3$
$$x + 0 = 8$$
$$x = 8$$

Multiplication method

If $ax = b$, then multiply each side by $\frac{1}{a}$ ($a \neq 0$):
$$\frac{1}{a} \cdot ax = \frac{1}{a} \cdot b$$
$$1 \cdot x = \frac{b}{a}$$
$$x = \frac{b}{a}$$

Examples:

Solve: $\qquad\qquad 5x = 40$

Multiply by $\frac{1}{5}$. $\quad \frac{1}{5} \cdot 5x = \frac{1}{5} \cdot 40$
$$1 \cdot x = 8$$
$$x = 8$$

If $\frac{x}{a} = b$, then multiply each side by a ($a \neq 0$):
$$a \cdot \frac{x}{a} = a \cdot b$$
$$1 \cdot x = ab$$
$$x = ab$$

Solve: $\qquad\qquad \frac{x}{3} = 13$

Multiply by 3. $\quad 3 \cdot \frac{x}{3} = 3 \cdot 13$
$$1 \cdot x = 39$$
$$x = 39$$

Division method

If $ax = b$, then divide each side by a ($a \neq 0$):
$$\frac{ax}{a} = \frac{b}{a}$$
$$1 \cdot x = \frac{b}{a} \qquad x = \frac{b}{a}$$

Example:

Solve: $\qquad 4x = 24$

Divide by 4. $\quad \frac{4x}{4} = \frac{24}{4}$
$$\frac{x}{1} = 6$$
$$x = 6$$

Combined addition and multiplication method

If $ax + b = d$, then

First: Add $-b$ to each side:
$$ax + b + (-b) = d + (-b)$$
$$ax + 0 = d - b$$
$$ax = d - b$$

Second: Multiply each side by $\frac{1}{a}$ ($a \neq 0$):
$$\frac{1}{a} \cdot ax = \frac{1}{a} \cdot (d - b)$$
$$1 \cdot x = \frac{d - b}{a} \qquad x = \frac{d - b}{a}$$

Examples:

Solve: $\qquad\qquad 2x + 5 = 17$

Add -5. $\qquad 2x + 5 + (-5) = 17 + (-5)$
$$2x = 12$$

Multiply by $\frac{1}{2}$. $\qquad \frac{1}{2} \cdot 2x = \frac{1}{2} \cdot 12$
$$x = 6$$

Solve: $\qquad\qquad \frac{x}{7} + 4 = 6$

Add -4. $\qquad \frac{x}{7} + 4 + (-4) = 6 + (-4)$
$$\frac{x}{7} = 2$$

Multiply by 7. $\qquad 7 \cdot \frac{x}{7} = 7 \cdot 2$
$$x = 14$$

Equations in one variable.

See the box on page 268 for the basic rules for solving equations in one variable in which only the first power of the variable appears. The problems on this page use these rules in conjunction with ideas from the earlier pages of this section.

Solve $2x + 3 + 5x = 17$.

A. Collect like terms.
$$7x + 3 = 17$$

B. Add -3 to each side.
$$7x = 14$$

C. Divide each side by 7.
$$x = 2$$

Solve $3x - 5 = 4x + 11$.

A. Subtract $3x$ from each side of the equation.
$$-5 = x + 11$$

B. Subtract 11 from each side of the equation.
$$-16 = x$$

Most people prefer to write the solution as
$$x = -16$$

Solve $8x - 3 = 6x - 11$.

A. Subtract $6x$ from each side of the equation.
$$2x - 3 = -11$$

B. Add 3 to each side of the equation.
$$2x = -8$$

C. Divide each side by 2.
$$x = -4$$

Solve $2(x + 5) = 6$.

A. Eliminate parentheses.
$$2x + 10 = 6$$

B. Subtract 10 from each side.
$$2x = -4$$

C. Divide by 2.
$$x = -2$$

Solve $\dfrac{3x+4}{5} = 11$.

A. Multiply each side of the equation by 5.
$$3x + 4 = 55$$

B. Subtract 4.
$$3x = 51$$

C. Divide by 3.
$$x = 17$$

Solve $\dfrac{4x-6}{3} = 5x + 9$.

A. Multiply each side of the equation by 3.
$$(4x - 6) = 3(5x + 9)$$
$$4x - 6 = 15x + 27$$

B. Subtract $4x$.
$$-6 = 11x + 27$$

C. Subtract 27.
$$-33 = 11x$$

D. Divide by 11 and reverse.
$$x = -3$$

Solve $\dfrac{5x+4}{2} = \dfrac{3x-9}{4}$.

A. Multiply both sides by 2.
$$(5x + 4) = \frac{2(3x - 9)}{4}$$

B. Multiply both sides by 4.
$$4(5x + 4) = 2(3x - 9)$$

The result of these two steps is the same as the single step of following the cross-product rule for solving a proportion.

C. Complete the multiplication.
$$20x + 16 = 6x - 18$$

D. Subtract $6x$ and 16.
$$14x = -34$$

E. Divide by 14 and reduce to lowest terms.
$$x = -\frac{34}{14} = -\frac{17}{7}$$

Literal equations.
The rules for solving equations apply when the equation is a formula. Such an equation is called a *literal equation* because it is expressed primarily in letters instead of numbers.

Solve the formula $d = rt$ for r.

A. Divide both sides of the equation by t.
$$\frac{d}{t} = r$$

B. Rewrite the equation with r on the left side of the equals sign.
$$r = \frac{d}{t}$$

Solve $A = \frac{1}{2}bh$ for b.

A. Multiply each side by 2.
$$2A = bh$$

B. Divide by h and rewrite.
$$\frac{2A}{h} = b$$
$$b = \frac{2A}{h}$$

Solve $A = \frac{1}{2}(B + b)h$ for B.

A. Multiply each side by 2.
$$2A = (B + b)h$$

B. Divide each side by h.
$$\frac{2A}{h} = B + b$$

C. Subtract b from each side.
$$\frac{2A}{h} - b = B$$
$$B = \frac{2A}{h} - b$$

Solve $A = \frac{1}{2}(B + b)h$ for h.

A. Multiply each side by 2.
$$2A = (B + b)h$$

B. Divide each side by $B + b$.
$$\frac{2A}{B+b} = h$$
$$h = \frac{2A}{B+b}$$

Formulas often used in problem solving in algebra

Distance-rate-time problems: $d = rt$
  where d is distance
  r is rate
  t is time

Lever problems: $l_1w_1 = l_2w_2$
  where l_1 is length from fulcrum to first weight
  w_1 is first weight
  l_2 is length from fulcrum to second weight
  w_2 is second weight

Work problems: $\frac{1}{a} + \frac{1}{b} = \frac{1}{n}$
  where a is length of time it takes person A to complete a task
  b is length of time it takes person B to complete the same task
  n is length of time it would take A and B to complete the task together

Consecutive number problems: $n + (n + 1) = A$
  where n is the first of the consecutive numbers
  A is the sum of two consecutive numbers

  $n(n + 2) = B$
  where n is the first of a pair of even or odd consecutive numbers
  B is the product of two even or odd consecutive numbers

Digit problems: $A(u + t + h) = u + 10t + 100h$
  where A is multiplied by the sum of the digits
  u is the ones digit of the given number
  t is the tens digit of the given number
  h is the hundreds digit of the given number

Coin problems: $25n + 5m = 100A$
  where n is the number of quarters
  m is the number of nickels
  A is the total worth shown as a decimal

Solving problems

Will was 18 when he graduated from school 9 years ago. How old is he now?

A. You are probably able to solve this "in your head," but one should get in the habit of always writing down and solving an equation. Decide on a variable and its meaning. For example, let x = Will's age now.

B. Write an equation that expresses the conditions of the problem.
Will's age now: x
Will's age 9 years ago: Either 18 or $x - 9$.
Therefore, $x - 9 = 18$.

C. Solve for x.
$$x - 9 = 18$$
Add 9. $\qquad x = 27$
Will is 27 years old now.

What number when multiplied by 4 can be added to 15 to produce 63?

A. Choose a variable and use it to express the conditions of the problem as an equation.
Let n = the number.
$$4n + 15 = 63$$

B. Solve the equation.
$$4n + 15 = 63$$
Subtract 15. $\qquad 4n = 48$
Divide by 4. $\qquad n = 12$
The number is 12.

Sally has only quarters and nickels in her piggy bank. If the total amount is $2.65 and she has 8 nickels, how many quarters does she have?

A. Convert the problem to pennies. The total amount is 265 cents, a quarter is 25 cents, and a nickel is 5 cents. The total amount of nickels is $8 \cdot 5 = 40$ cents.

B. Let n = the number of quarters. The total amount of quarters is $25n$ cents.
$$25n + 40 = 265$$

C. Solve the equation.
$$25n + 40 = 265$$
Subtract 40. $\qquad 25n = 225$
Divide by 25. $\qquad n = 9$
Sally has 9 quarters.

Find two consecutive integers such that three times the second plus the first is 47.

A. Consecutive integers are the integers that immediately follow one another. Therefore, if you let the first integer be n, then the second is $n + 1$.
$$3(n + 1) + n = 47$$

B. Solve the equation.
$$3(n + 1) + n = 47$$
Multiply. $\quad 3n + 3 + n = 47$
Combine like terms.
$$4n + 3 = 47$$
Subtract 3. $\qquad 4n = 44$
Divide by 4. $\qquad n = 11$

C. State both parts of the answer.
The consecutive integers are 11 and 12.

Find two consecutive odd integers such that 5 times the second minus 6 times the first is 21.

A. If you let the first odd integer be n, then the second is $n + 2$.
$$5(n + 2) - 6n = 21$$

B. Solve the equation.
$$5(n + 2) - 6n = 21$$
Multiply. $\ 5n + 10 - 6n = 21$
Combine like terms.
$$10 - n = 21$$
Subtract 10. $\qquad -n = 11$
Multiply by -1. $\qquad n = -11$

C. State both parts of the answer.
The consecutive odd integers are -11 and -9 (NOT -11 and -13!).

Jim weighs 60 kilograms and needs to lift a 300-kilogram rock. His crowbar is 1.5 meters long. How close must the fulcrum be to the rock so that Jim's weight lifts the rock?

A. This is a lever problem, so
$$l_1 w_1 = l_2 w_2$$
Use $l_1 w_1$ for Jim's distance and weight and $l_2 w_2$ for the rock's. When the fulcrum is l_2 centimeters from the rock, it is $150 - l_2$ centimeters from Jim.
$$(150 - l_2) \cdot 60 = l_2 \cdot 300$$

B. Solve for l_2:
$$150 \cdot 60 - 60 l_2 = 300 l_2$$
$$9000 = 300 l_2 + 60 l_2$$
$$9000 = 360 l_2$$
$$l_2 = 9000 - 360 = 25$$

C. The fulcrum must be closer to the rock than 25 centimeters.

Steve Fort told Karen his address is easy to remember. The first two digits make 40 (like "Fort") and 45 times the sum of the digits is the number. Karen forgot anyway. Help her.

A. The only digit missing is the units digit, u. Since the first two digits are 4 and 0, the number is 4 hundreds 0 tens and u ones.
$$45(u + 0 + 4) = u + 0 + 400$$

B. Solve the equation for u. First get rid of the parentheses.
$$45u + 45 \cdot 0 + 45 \cdot 4 = u + 0 + 400$$
$$45u + 180 = u + 400$$
Subtract u and 180 from each side.
$$44u = 220$$
$$u = 5$$

C. The missing digit is 5, so Steve Fort's address must be 405.

Julia had 14 meters of garden border. She wanted a rectangular garden 2 meters wide. How long should the garden be?

 2 m

A. The 14 meters is the perimeter, p, of the rectangle.
$$p = 2l + 2w$$
where l is length and w is width.

B. If the width is 2 meters and the length is l meters, then
$$14 = 2l + 2 \cdot 2$$
or $\quad 14 = 2l + 4$

C. Solve for l.
$$10 = 2l$$
$$5 = l$$
The garden should be 5 meters long.

Doug plans to tile a 9-foot by 12-foot room with 1-foot square tiles. He will use 1 black tile surrounded by red tiles to make a pattern. How many tiles of each color will he need?

A. First calculate how many tiles will be needed in all. Each tile is 1-foot square.
$$9 \times 12 = 108$$
Doug needs 108 tiles.

B. For every one black tile, the pattern calls for eight red tiles. Let n be the number of black tiles.
$$n + 8n = 108$$
$$9n = 108$$
$$n = 12$$

C. Doug needs twelve black tiles. He needs $8 \cdot 12 = 96$ red tiles.
Check: $12 + 96 = 108$

Candy selling for \$0.29 a gram is to be mixed with candy selling for \$0.39 a gram. If you want 5 grams of the mixture to sell for \$0.36 a gram, how many grams of each kind of candy should be mixed?

A. Let x be the number of grams of the less expensive candy. Then $5 - x$ will be the number of grams of the candy selling for \$0.39 a gram.
$$0.29x + 0.39(5 - x) = 0.36(5)$$

B. Solve the equation.
Multiply $0.29x + 1.95 - 0.39x = 1.8$
Combine like terms.
$$1.95 - 0.1x = 1.8$$
Subtract 1.95. $\quad -0.1x = -0.15$
Multiply by -10. $\quad x = 1.5$

C. You need to mix 1.5 grams of the \$0.29 candy with $5 - 1.5$, or 3.5, grams of the \$0.39 candy.

A radiator system is full with 12 liters of a mixture of 30% antifreeze in water. How much should be drained and replaced by an 80% antifreeze solution to bring the antifreeze content to 60%?

A. Let x be the number of liters drained and replaced in the radiator. Then $12 - x$ is the amount of the original solution remaining in the radiator.
$$0.30(12 - x) + 0.80x = 0.60(12)$$

B. Solve the equation.
$$3.60 - 0.30x + 0.80x = 7.20$$
$$3.60 + 0.50x = 7.20$$
$$0.50x = 3.60$$
$$x = 7.2$$

C. You must drain and replace 7.2 liters.

Two trains travel toward each other from points 200 kilometers apart. If one train is traveling at 50 kilometers per hour and the other at 60 kilometers per hour, where and when will they meet if they start at the same time?

A. Let $d =$ distance traveled by the 50 km/h train. Then $200 - d =$ distance traveled by the other train. When the two trains meet, the times they have traveled will be equal, so
$$\frac{d}{50} = \frac{200 - d}{60}$$

B. Solve the equation. Use the cross-product rule.
$$\frac{d}{50} = \frac{200 - d}{60}$$
$$60d = 50(200 - d)$$
$$60d = 10000 - 50d$$
$$110d = 10000$$
$$d = \frac{10000}{110}, \text{ or } 90.9090\ldots$$

C. Round the answer to 91. Then the trains will meet about 91 kilometers from the starting point of the 50 km/h train. The length of time is
$$t = \frac{d}{r}, \text{ or about}$$
$$t = \frac{91}{50} = 1.82,$$
which can be rounded to 1.8 hours.

Fred can complete a project in 6 days. Jack can complete the same project in 5 days, and David takes 4 days. How many days will it take if all three work together?

A. Let $x =$ the number of days needed to do the job working together. Individually, $x/6$ of the project will be completed by Fred after x days, $x/5$ of the project by Jack, and $x/4$ by David.

B. $\dfrac{x}{6} + \dfrac{x}{5} + \dfrac{x}{4} = 1$
Multiply by the LCD, 60.
$$10x + 12x + 15x = 60$$
Combine like terms. $37x = 60$
Divide by 37. $\quad x = \dfrac{60}{37}$

C. The project will take $\frac{60}{37}$, or slightly more than $1\frac{1}{2}$ days.

Operations with polynomials.

A *monomial* is a term formed entirely by multiplication; for example $2x$, y^2, or $n/3$ (which is interpreted as the number $\frac{1}{3}$ times n). A *polynomial* is the sum of any finite number of monomials, including just 1 monomial. Certain polynomials are referred to often enough that it is useful to learn their special names:

- monomial, a polynomial with one term
- binomial, a polynomial with two terms
- trinomial, a polynomial with three terms.

Polynomials can be added, subtracted, multiplied, and divided.

Add $3x^3 + 5x^2y - 2xy^2 + y^3$ and $2x^3 - 3y^3 + 4xy^2$.

Rearrange the two polynomials so that they are in the same order.

Write the polynomials with terms that have corresponding powers of the same variable above each other as an addition problem and add each term to the one directly below it.

$$
\begin{array}{l}
3x^3 + 5x^2y - 2xy^2 + y^3 \\
+2x^3 \qquad\quad + 4xy^2 - 3y^3 \\
\hline
5x^3 + 5x^2y + 2xy^2 - 2y^3
\end{array}
$$

Subtract $3abc + 2ac - 3b$ from $4bc - 3abc + 5ac$.

Arrange the two polynomials with the terms with the same variables to the same powers directly over one another.

To subtract, multiply the polynomial to be subtracted by -1 and add.

$$
\begin{array}{l}
4bc - 3abc + 5ac \\
\quad - 3abc - 2ac + 3b \\
\hline
4bc - 6abc + 3ac + 3b
\end{array}
$$

Multiply the monomials, $3x^2y^3$ and $4xy^2$.

Multiplication of powers of the same variable can be accomplished by following the laws of exponents (see box). The numerical parts of each monomial (called the *coefficients* of the monomials) are multiplied in the ordinary way.

$$
\begin{aligned}
3x^2y^3(4xy^2) &= 12x^{2+1}y^{3+2} \\
&= 12x^3y^5
\end{aligned}
$$

> **Laws of exponents**
>
> If a and b are not zero
> $$a^n a^m = a^{n+m}$$
> $$(a^n)^m = a^{mn}$$
> $$a^n/a^m = a^{m-n}$$
> $$a^n b^n = (ab)^n$$
> $$a^n/b^n = (a/b)^n$$
> $$a^{-n} = 1/a^n$$

$(2x + y)(x - y)$

METHOD 1

A. Use the distributive law with $x - y$ as the factor to be distributed over $2x + y$.

$(2x + y)(x - y) = 2x(x - y) + y(x - y)$

B. Use the distributive law twice more to distribute each of the factors over $x - y$.

$(2x + y)(x - y) = 2x^2 - 2xy + xy - y^2$

C. Collect like terms.

$(2x + y)(x - y) = 2x^2 - xy - y^2$

METHOD 2

A. Use the FOIL method. FOIL is based on the fact that the product of any two binomials is always the sum of the following: The product of the

First terms; the sum of the product of the *Outer* terms and the *Inner* terms; and the product of the *Last* terms.

In our example, the product of the first terms is $2x^2$, the product of the outer terms is $-2xy$, the product of the inner terms is xy, and the product of the last terms is $-y^2$.

$$2x^2 - 2xy + xy - y^2$$

B. Collect like terms.

$(2x + y)(x - y) = 2x^2 - xy - y^2$

Divide $3x^2 + 2x - 5$ by $x + 2$.

A. Set up the problem as you would a long division problem in arithmetic.

$$x + 2 \overline{)\, 3x^2 + 2x - 5}$$

B. Divide the first term of the trinomial by the first term of the binomial to get a partial quotient. Multiply the partial quotient and the binomial. Subtract that product from the trinomial.

$$
\begin{array}{r}
3x \\
x + 2 \overline{)\, 3x^2 + 2x - 5} \\
3x^2 + 6x \\
\hline
- 4x - 5
\end{array}
$$

C. Repeat the process from step B with the remainder of subtraction in step B.

$$
\begin{array}{r}
3x - 4 \\
x + 2 \overline{)\, 3x^2 + 2x - 5} \\
3x^2 + 6x \\
\hline
-4x - 5 \\
-4x - 8 \\
\hline
+ 3
\end{array}
$$

D. The answer is $3x - 4$ with a remainder of 3, since x is not a divisor of 3.

Factoring polynomials

Factor $x^3 + 2x^2 - 6x$.

The word *factor* used as a verb means "write in factored form." You are already familiar with factoring numbers. Polynomials are factored by reversing the rules of multiplication.

In this case, x is a factor of each term of the polynomial. Use the distributive law to obtain

$$x^3 + 2x^2 - 6x = x(x^2 + 2x - 6).$$

Factor $x^3yz^4 - x^2yz^3 + 2xy^2z^2$.

A. Identify the factors that are common to each of the terms of the polynomial. They are
$$x, y, \text{ and } z^2.$$

B. Use the distributive law to rewrite the polynomial in factored form.
$$x^3yz^4 - x^2yz^3 + 2xy^2z^2 = xyz^2(x^2z^2 - xz + 2y)$$

Factor $x^2 - 5x + 6$ into the product of binomials.

A. Begin by looking for possible factors for the first term. Since the first term is x^2, the only possible factors are x and x or x^2 and 1. Experience shows that, since there is no other x^2 in the trinomial, the first factors of the binomials will be x and x.
$$x^2 - 5x + 6 = (x \quad)(x \quad)$$
NOTE: It is also possible to factor x^2 as $-x$ and $-x$. However, it is customary to factor a positive first term into 2 positive factors.

B. Look for all the possible factors of the second term. These will come in pairs of 2 positive factors or 2 negative factors, since the last term is positive.

1 and 6 -1 and -6
2 and 3 -2 and -3

C. Try the possible factors in the binomials to see which pair will give a middle term that is $-5x$. The only combination that works is -2 and -3, so the correct factored form is
$$x^2 - 5x + 6 = (x - 2)(x - 3).$$

Factor $x^2 + 7x + 6$.

A. Once again the factors of x^2 must be x and x.

Also, the possible factors of $+6$ are the same:

   1 and 6 -1 and -6
   2 and 3 -2 and -3

B. Find the factors of $+6$ that, when multiplied by x and x, will add up to $+7x$. They are 1 and 6, so the factored form is $x^2 + 7x + 6 = (x + 1)(x + 6)$.

Factor $x^2 - x - 6$.

A. The pairs of factors to be examined are

   -1 and 6   1 and -6
   -2 and 3   2 and -3

B. The combination that will yield $-x$ is 2 and -3.
$x^2 - x - 6 = (x + 2)(x - 3)$

Factor $2x^2 - 15x + 18$.

A. The possible factors of $2x^2$ are x and $2x$, so
$2x^2 - 15x + 18 = (x\ )(2x\ )$.

B. The possible factors of $+18$ are
   1 and 18 -1 and -18
   2 and 9 -2 and -9
   3 and 6 -3 and -6

C. Since the first terms of the binomial factors are different, more combinations must be checked. For example,
$1(2x) + 18(x) = +20x$

while $1(x) + 18(2x) = +37x$
The combination that produces $-15x$ for the second term of the trinomial is
$-3(x) - (-6)(2x) = -15x$.

D. The correct answer is
$2x^2 - 15x + 18 = (x - 6)(2x - 3)$.

Factor $20x^2 + 27x - 8$.

A. Possible factors of the first term are
   $(x\ )(20x\ )$
   $(2x\ )(10x\ )$
   $(4x\ )(5x\ )$

B. Possible factors of the last term are
   1 and -8 -1 and 8
   2 and -4 -2 and 4

C. The combination that yields $+27x$ is
   $-1(5x) + 8(4x) = +27x$,
so the factored form is
$20x^2 + 27x - 8 = (4x - 1)(5x + 8)$.

Often binomials can be factored into 2 polynomials. The types of binomials that can be factored in this way are either *the difference of 2 squares, the difference of 2 cubes,* or *the sum of 2 cubes*. The sum of 2 squares cannot be factored over the integers (indeed, it cannot be factored over the real numbers). The general forms for the 3 binomials that can be factored into 2 polynomials are given below. When A and B are expressions of any kind,

$$A^2 - B^2 = (A - B)(A + B)$$
$$A^3 - B^3 = (A - B)(A^2 + AB + B^2)$$
$$A^3 + B^3 = (A + B)(A^2 - AB + B^2).$$

Factor $x^4 - 16$.

A. This problem should be recognized as the difference of 2 squares, since x^4 is the same as $(x^2)^2$ and 16 is 4^2. Therefore, the general form can be used with
   $A = x^2$ and $B = 4$.
$x^4 - 16 = (x^2 - 4)(x^2 + 4)$

B. Notice that $x^2 - 4$ is also the difference of 2 squares, so it can be factored further. However, $x^2 + 4$ cannot be factored, so the final answer is
$x^2 - 16 = (x - 2)(x + 2)(x^2 + 4)$.

Mathematics

Algebraic fractions

Simplify $\dfrac{x^2 - x - 2}{x^2 + x - 6}$

Fractions that have algebraic expressions in the numerator and denominator follow the same rules as numerical fractions.

To simplify a fraction such as 24/30, first factor 24 into $4 \cdot 6$ and 35 into $5 \cdot 6$. You can cancel the 6s.

$$\frac{24}{30} = \frac{4 \cdot 6}{5 \cdot 6} = \frac{4}{5}$$

You can also factor algebraic fractions and cancel common factors.

$$\frac{x^2 - x - 2}{x^2 + x - 6} = \frac{(x-2)(x+1)}{(x+3)(x-2)} = \frac{x+1}{x+3}$$

Multiply $\dfrac{x^2 - 2x - 24}{x^2 - x - 30} \cdot \dfrac{x+5}{x^2 - 16}$

A. The product is found by multiplying the numerators and the denominators. First factor as many of the polynomials as you can:

$$\frac{(x-6)(x+4)}{(x-6)(x+5)} \cdot \frac{x+5}{(x-4)(x+4)}$$

B. Then cancel the common factors the same way as when simplifying.

$$\frac{(x-6)(x+4)}{(x-6)(x+5)} \cdot \frac{x+5}{(x-4)(x+4)}$$

C. Remember that when you cancel common factors, each is replaced by 1. The answer is the product of the factors not canceled.

$$\frac{1}{x-4}$$

Divide $\dfrac{x^2 - 3x - 10}{x^2 - 1} \div \dfrac{x^2 - 6x + 5}{x^2 + 3x + 2}$

A. To divide, invert the divisor (the number used to divide by) and multiply.

$$\frac{x^2 - 3x - 10}{x^2 - 1} \cdot \frac{x^2 + 3x + 2}{x^2 - 6x + 5}$$

B. Factor and cancel wherever possible.

$$\frac{(x+2)(x-5)}{(x+1)(x-1)} \cdot \frac{(x+1)(x+2)}{(x-5)(x-1)}$$

$$= \frac{(x+2)(x+2)}{(x-1)(x-1)} = \frac{(x+2)^2}{(x-1)^2}$$

C. It is usually better to leave an answer in factored form.

Add $\dfrac{3}{xy} + \dfrac{x}{4y}$

A. Algebraic fractions are added in the same way as numerical fractions. First you have to find a common denominator. This problem is similar to

$$\frac{3}{10} + \frac{5}{8}$$

In the numerical case, the common denominator is most easily found by factoring 10 into $5 \cdot 2$ and 8 into $2 \cdot 4$; the common denominator is $5 \cdot 2 \cdot 4$.

B. The denominator 10 needs a 4, while the denominator 8 needs a 5. Multiply each fraction by 1 in a form that will provide the missing factor.

$$\frac{4}{4} \cdot \frac{3}{10} + \frac{5}{8} \cdot \frac{5}{5}$$

$$\frac{12}{40} + \frac{25}{40} = \frac{37}{40}$$

C. The common denominator from xy and $4y$ is $4xy$. Multiply the first fraction by $\frac{4}{4}$ and the second by $\frac{x}{x}$.

$$\frac{4}{4} \cdot \frac{3}{xy} + \frac{x}{4y} \cdot \frac{x}{x} = \frac{12}{4xy} + \frac{x^2}{4xy}$$

$$= \frac{12 + x^2}{4xy}$$

Graphing lines.

A graph is a way of representing a set of ordered pairs. Ordered pairs of numbers are shown in parentheses with a comma.

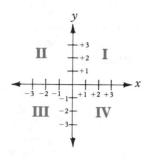

The most common way to graph ordered pairs is to use 2 number lines that are perpendicular to each other at their 0 points. The point of intersection is called the *origin* of the graph. In a graph, the first member of each pair is a directed distance from the vertical line. The distance is "directed" because a + indicates distance to the right of the origin and a − indicates distance to the left. The second member of each pair is a directed distance from the horizontal line with + indicating distance above the line and − indicating distance below it. The first members of the pair are called *abscissas* and the second members are called *ordinates*.

The axes define a plane, called the *coordinate plane,* and divide that plane into 4 regions called *quadrants.*

Locate the points (1, 1), (−1, 2), (−3, −2), and (1, −2) on the coordinate plane.

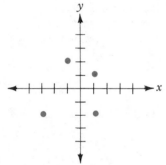

A. To find (1, 1), count 1 unit to the right from the *y* axis and 1 unit up from the *x* axis.

B. To find (−1, 2), count 1 unit to the left from the *y* axis and 2 units up from the *x* axis.

C. To find (−3, −2), count 3 units to the left from the *y* axis and 2 units down from the *x* axis.

D. To find (1, −2), count 1 unit to the right from the *y* axis and 2 units down from the *x* axis.

Graph the equation $y = 2x - 2$.

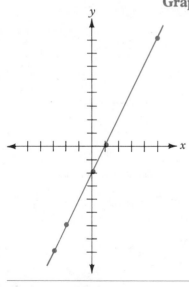

A. An equation in *x* and *y* is a way of identifying a set of ordered pairs of the form (x, y) where the relationship between *x* and *y* is given by the equation. In general, assume that *x* can be any real number (unless some values are prohibited by the equation, as in the case of $y = 1/x$, which cannot be graphed if *x* is equal to 0). Therefore, begin by assigning arbitrary values to *x*. For example, assign 0, 1, 5, −2, and −3.

B. Use the values assigned to *x* and the equation to find the values for *y*. For example, if *x* is 0, the equation becomes
$$y = 2(0) - 2$$
$$= 0 - 2$$
$$= -2$$
Find the other values of *y* in the same way. Most people find it convenient to keep track of the values in a chart.

x	y
0	−2
1	0
5	8
−2	−6
−3	−8

C. Plot the ordered pairs indicated by the chart on the coordinate plane.

D. Since *x* could be any real number, there are more points in the graph than those plotted. Since all the points plotted can be connected by a straight line, the line contains *all* the points of the graph, although only a part of the line can be shown on the page.

Mathematics

Graph the equation $y = -x - 1$.

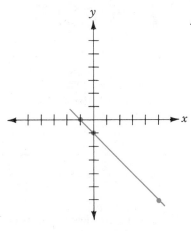

A. All equations that involve just the first power of x and the first power of y (unless the variables are enclosed in absolute-value bars, multiplied by each other, or otherwise changed by some operation other than addition, subtraction, and multiplication) have lines as graphs. Two points determine a line; therefore, only 2 points need be plotted to find the graph. Most people also plot a third point as a check.

In general, the 2 easiest plots to point are the ones where x or y is 0. The check point can use any convenient small number for x, but it is better not to use a number too close to 0, or the 3 points will be too close to each other.

x	y
0	
	0
5	

B. Fill in the other values in the chart.
$$y = -(0) - 1 = -1$$
$$0 = -x - 1, \text{ so } x = -1$$
$$y = -5 - 1 = -6$$

x	y
0	-1
-1	0
5	-6

C. Plot the 3 points.

D. Draw a line between 2 of the points and use the third point as a check.

The graph of a line

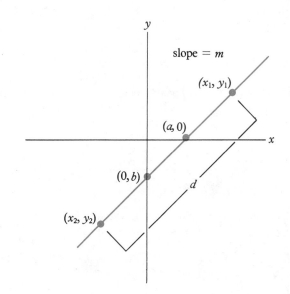

Slope:
$$m = \frac{y_2 - y_1}{x_2 - x_1}$$

Point-slope equation for the line:
$$(y - y_1) = m(x - x_1)$$

Slope-intercept equation for the line:
$$y = mx + b$$

Two-point equation for the line:
$$y - y_1 = \frac{y_2 - y_1}{x_2 - x_1}(x - x_1)$$

Intercept equation for the line:
$$\frac{x}{a} + \frac{y}{b} = 1$$

Distance from (x_1, y_1) to (x_2, y_2):
$$d = \sqrt{(x_2 - x_1)^2 + (y_2 - y_1)^2}$$

Midpoint between (x_1, y_1) and (x_2, y_2):
(x, y) is the midpoint when
$$x = \frac{x_1 + x_2}{2}, y = \frac{y_1 + y_2}{2}$$

Find the equation of a line through (1, -2) with a slope of 1/2.

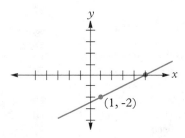

Since you know a point through which the lines pass and the slope of the line, you can use the point-slope equation for the line:

$$(y - y_1) = m(x - x_1)$$

In this case, the point (x_1, y_1) is given as (1, -2) while $m = \frac{1}{2}$. The equation is $y - (-2) = \frac{1}{2}(x-1)$, or $y + 2 = \frac{1}{2}x - \frac{1}{2}$. This can also be written as $y = \frac{1}{2}x - \frac{5}{2}$. Multiplying by 2 to get rid of fractions and rearranging gives $x - 2y = 5$.

Lines are parallel if their slopes are equal. Find the equation of a line parallel to $2x - y = 3$ that has $(0, -4)$ as the y intercept.

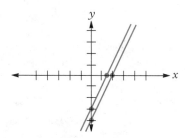

A. Use the slope–intercept equation for the line $y = mx + b$ to find the slope of the given equation.

Solve for y: $2x - y = 3$
$2x - 3 = y$
$y = 2x - 3$

The slope $m = 2$.

B. The line that has a y intercept of $(0, -4)$ and a slope of 2 is
$$y = 2x - 4$$

The product of the slopes of two perpendicular lines is –1. Give the equation of a line that passes through the midpoint of the segment (3, 4) and (1, –2) and is perpendicular to the segment.

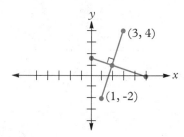

A. The midpoint of the segment is the average of the coordinates of the endpoints.

$$x = \frac{3+1}{2} = 2$$

$$y = \frac{4+(-2)}{2} = 1$$

B. The slope of the segment is
$$\frac{4-(-2)}{3-1} = \frac{6}{2} = 3$$

A perpendicular to the segment has a slope of $-1/3$: $(-1/3) \cdot 3 = 1$. Now use the point–slope equation with $-1/3$ as the slope and (2, 3) as the point.
$$y - 1 = (-1/3)(x - 2),$$
or $x + 3y = 5$

What is the distance between (–3, 5) and (2, –7)?

A. Use the formula
$$d = \sqrt{(x_2 - x_1)^2 + (y_2 - y_1)^2}$$
It does not matter which point is (x_1, y_1) and which is (x_2, y_2) so long as you follow the formula.

B. If (2, -7) is (x_1, y_1), then
$$d = \sqrt{(-3 - 2)^2 + (5 - (-7))^2}$$
$$= \sqrt{(-5)^2 + (12)^2} = \sqrt{25 + 144} = \sqrt{169}$$
$$= 13$$

Note that the distance between points is always positive.

Mathematics

Graph $3x + 2y = 30$.

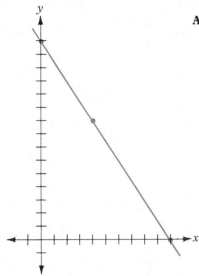

A. Since both x and y are in first degree terms, the graph will be a line. Find the points called the intercepts, where $x = 0$ and where $y = 0$, and a check point.

x	y
0	15
10	0
4	9

B. Plot the points and connect them with a line.

Graph the equation $y = x^2 - x - 2$.

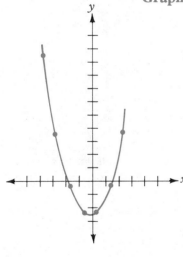

A. This equation involves a power of the variable that is different from the first power, so the graph is not a line. Therefore, choose several different points to get an idea of the shape of the graph. For example, start with

x	y
0	
1	
2	
3	
-1	
-2	
-3	

$y = 0^2 - 0 - 2 = -2$
$y = 1^2 - 1 - 2 = -2$
$y = 2^2 - 2 - 2 = 0$
$y = 3^2 - 3 - 2 = 4$

It is apparent that if x is greater than 3, then y will be greater than 4.

$y = (-1)^2 + 1 - 2 = 0$
$y = (-2)^2 + 2 - 2 = 4$
$y = (-3)^2 + 3 - 2 = 10$

If x is less than -3, then y will be greater than 10.

B. Use the completed table to plot the points.

x	y
0	-2
1	-2
2	0
3	4
-1	0
-2	4
-3	10

C. Since the equation is defined for all real values of x, the points can be connected by a continuous curve that shows all of the points on the graph. In this case, the curve is a form of *parabola* (see box on page 282).

A parabola is a common curve in applications, since it is the curve that a thrown or fired object makes (discounting air resistance and the curve of Earth). The equation for a parabola can be recognized by the presence of a single term that has a single variable to the second power (when all like terms have been combined). If the product of two variables or the second power of two variables is included, the graph of the equation will be another one of the conic sections.

Conic sections

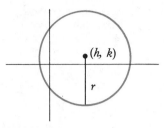

The circle:

Points in the same plane all at a common distance, the *radius*, from the same point, the *center*.

center: (h, k)
radius: r

$$(x - h)^2 - (y - k)^2 = r^2$$

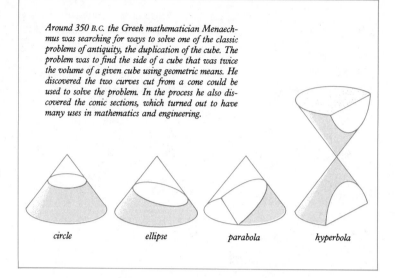

Around 350 B.C. the Greek mathematician Menaechmus was searching for ways to solve one of the classic problems of antiquity, the duplication of the cube. The problem was to find the side of a cube that was twice the volume of a given cube using geometric means. He discovered the two curves cut from a cone could be used to solve the problem. In the process he also discovered the conic sections, which turned out to have many uses in mathematics and engineering.

circle   ellipse   parabola   hyperbola

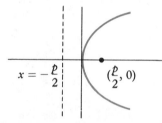

The parabola:

Points in the same plane that are the same distance from a point, the *focus,* and a line, the *directrix.*

focus: $(\frac{p}{2}, 0)$

directrix: $x = -\frac{p}{2}$

$$y^2 = 2px$$

The point on the parabola halfway between the focus and the directrix is the *vertex.*

vertex: (h, k)
$$y = a(x - h)^2 + k$$

(If a is positive, the vertex is the lowest point of the parabola. If a is negative, the vertex is the highest point.)

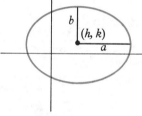

The ellipse:

Points in the same plane from which the sum of the distances from two points, the *foci,* is constant. The midpoint of the line joining the foci is the *center.* The distance from the center through one of the foci to the ellipse is the *semimajor axis;* the distance from the center to the ellipse perpendicular to the semimajor axis is the *semiminor axis.*

center: (h, k)
semimajor axis: a
semiminor axis: b

$$\frac{(x - h)^2}{a^2} + \frac{(y - k)^2}{b^2} = 1$$

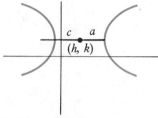

The hyperbola:

Points in the same plane from which the difference of the distances from two points, the *foci,* is constant. The midpoint of the line joining the foci is the center.

Distance from center to hyperbola: a
Distance from center to a focus: c

Let $c^2 = a^2 + b^2$,
or $b = \sqrt{c^2 - a^2}$

$$\frac{(x - h)^2}{a^2} - \frac{(y - k)^2}{b^2} = 1$$

Lines that the hyperbola gets closer to (but does not touch) are called *asymptotes.* The asymptotes are given by

$$\frac{(x - h)^2}{a^2} = \frac{(y - k)^2}{b^2}$$

or $y = \pm(\frac{b}{a})(x - h) + k.$

Mathematics

Systems of equations

Find the intersection of the graphs of $x + 3y = -2$ and $2x - y = 3$.

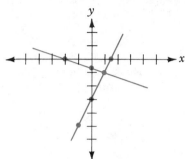

A. Plot points to locate each line.

\(x + 3y = -2\)		\(2x - y = 3\)	
x	y	x	y
0	$\frac{-2}{3}$	0	-3
-2	0	$\frac{3}{2}$	0
1	-1	-1	-5

B. Graph the lines and read the point of intersection from the graph. The point of intersection is $(1, -1)$.

Find the point of intersection of the graphs of
$$-2x - 6y = 4 \text{ and } 2x - y = 3$$
without drawing the graphs.

METHOD 1

A. The point of intersection of two graphs is the *solution of a system of equations* because the coordinates of that point will give true statements when the x coordinate is substituted for x and the y coordinate is substituted for y. For example, $(-1, 1)$ is a solution of $-2x - 6y = 4$ because
$$-2(-1) - 6(1) = 4$$
is true.

But $(-1, 1)$ is not a solution to the system because it does not satisfy $2x - y = 3$ since $2(-1) - (1)$ is -3, not 3. To solve the system, use the principle that adding equals to equals does not change solutions of equations and that multiplying equals by a nonzero number does not change solutions.

The strategy is to multiply and add in such a way as to obtain an *equivalent* equation that has only one variable. You already know how to solve such equations. In the case of this system it is easy to see that if the two equations are added, the x's will cancel out. Add.

$$\begin{array}{r} -2x - 6y = 4 \\ 2x - y = 3 \\ \hline 0 - 7y = 7 \end{array}$$

B. Solve the equation $-7y = 7$ for y.

$$-7y = 7$$
Divide by -7. $\quad y = -1$

C. Use the value you have found for y in either of the original equations to find the value x must have when y is -1.
$$\begin{aligned} -2x - 6(-1) &= 4 \\ -2x + 6 &= 4 \\ -2x &= -2 \\ x &= 1 \end{aligned}$$

The point of intersection, or the solution of the system, is $(1, -1)$. Check by substituting these coordinates in the other equation.
$$\begin{aligned} 2x - y &= 3 \\ 2(1) - (-1) &= 3 \\ 2 + 1 &= 3 \\ 3 &= 3 \end{aligned}$$

METHOD 2

A. *Substitute* the value of one of the variables (determined from one of the equations) into the other equation. In this case, it is easiest to find the value of y from the second equation and substitute it into the first.
$$2x - y = 3$$
Subtract $2x$. $\quad -y = 3 - 2x$
Multiply by -1. $\quad y = 2x - 3$

B. Substitute the value obtained for y in step A into the first equation and solve.
$$\begin{aligned} -2x - 6y &= 4 \\ -2x - 6(2x - 3) &= 4 \\ -2x - 12x + 18 &= 4 \\ -14x + 18 &= 4 \\ -14x &= -14 \\ x &= 1 \end{aligned}$$

C. Use the value of x obtained in step B to find y. The easiest way to do this is to use the value for y found in step A.
$$\begin{aligned} y &= 2x - 3 \\ &= 2(1) - 3 \\ &= 2 - 3 \\ &= -1 \end{aligned}$$

Be sure to check; if you made a mistake in step A, the whole solution would be wrong.

Mary has \$2.75 in her change purse. There are 14 coins and all of them are dimes or quarters. How many of each coin does she have?

A. Set up a system of equations that describes the conditions of the problem. Let d be the number of dimes and q be the number of quarters.
$$d + q = 14$$
The value of the dimes is $10d$ (in cents) and the value of quarters is $25d$. Therefore,
$$10d + 25q = 275.$$

B. Solve the system. Use substitution.
$$d = 14 - q$$
so
$$10(14 - q) + 25q = 275$$
$$140 - 10q + 25q = 275$$
$$140 + 15q = 275$$
$$15q = 135$$
$$q = 9$$

$$d = 14 - q$$
$$d = 14 - 9$$
$$d = 5$$
The solution of the system is (5, 9).

C. Check in the other equation.
$$10(5) + 25(9) = 275$$
$$50 \quad + 225 \quad = 275$$
$$275 = 275$$
It checks, so Mary has 5 dimes and 9 quarters.

Larry had \$7000 invested, some at 6% and some at 9%. He makes \$570 a year on these investments. How much does Larry have invested at each rate?

A. Let x be the amount at 6% and y be the amount at 9%. Then,
$$0.06x + 0.09y = 570$$
$$x + y = 7000$$
is the system of equations that describes the conditions of the problem.

B. Solve the system. Multiply the second equation by -0.09
$$0.06x + 0.09y = 570$$
$$-0.09x - 0.09y = -630$$
Add. $\quad -0.03x = -60$
$$x = 2000$$
Use the equation
$x + y = 7000$ to find y.
$$y = 5000$$

C. Larry has \$2000 invested at 6% and \$5000 invested at 9%. Check in the other equation.
$$0.06(2000) + 0.09(5000) = 570$$

A plane trip of 3000 miles with the jet stream takes 5 hours, while the return against the jet stream takes 6 hours. How fast is the plane (in still air), and how fast is the jet stream?

A. Let x be the speed of the plane and y be the speed of the jet stream. The plane in still air would go a distance of $5x$ in 5 hours. Also, the jet stream would take it a distance of $5y$ in 5 hours, so
$$5x + 5y = 3000.$$
On the return trip, the plane travels for 6 hours at the same air speed, but the jet stream is $-6y$, so
$$6x - 6y = 3000.$$

B. The system
$$5x + 5y = 3000$$
$$6x - 6y = 3000$$
is most easily solved with multiplication and addition. Multiply the first equation by 6 and the second by 5.
$$30x + 30y = 18000$$
$$30x - 30y = 15000$$
Add. $\quad 60x = 33000$
$$x = \quad 550$$
Substitute in one of the equations to find the value of y.
$$y = 50$$

C. The solution to the system is (550, 50), so the plane's air speed is 550 mph and the wind speed is 50 mph. Check in the other equation.

Mathematics

Quadratic equations. A *quadratic equation* is an equation in one variable in which a second-degree term appears. For example, $x^2 = 4$ and $2x^2 - x + 6 = 0$ are both quadratic equations. A quadratic equation cannot be solved simply by adding, subtracting, multiplying, and dividing. All quadratic equations can be solved, however, if complex-number solutions are permitted (see box on page 266). In this section, all the quadratic equations will be solved for real solutions only.

There are several techniques available for solving quadratic equations, including completing the square, factoring, and using a formula, but all are fundamentally based on using one or the other of two basic rules of mathematics:

(1) *If two numbers are equal, then the square roots of those numbers are also equal.*

(2) *If the product of two numbers is equal to zero, then one or the other or both of the two numbers must be 0.*

Solve $x^2 = 64$.

METHOD 1

A. Take the square root of both sides of the equation.
$$x^2 = 64$$
$$\pm x = \pm 8$$

B. Look at all the combinations.
$$+x = +8$$
$$+x = -8$$
$$-x = +8$$
$$-x = -8$$

All combinations come down to either $x = +8$ or $x = -8$, so the solution is expressed as
$$x = \pm 8.$$

METHOD 2

A. Set the equation equal to 0.
$$x^2 - 64 = 0$$
The expression $x^2 - 64$ is the difference of 2 squares, so it can be factored as
$$(x - 8)(x + 8).$$
Therefore, another way to write the equation is
$$(x - 8)(x + 8) = 0.$$

B. By rule (2) above, if the product of two expressions is 0, then one or the other or both must also be zero. Use this to separate the equation into two first-degree equations.
$$x - 8 = 0 \text{ or } x + 8 = 0$$

C. Solve each equation separately.
$$x = 8 \text{ or } x = -8$$
This result can be written as
$$x = \pm 8.$$

Solve $x^2 + 2x - 8 = 0$.

METHOD 1

A. If the expression on the left were the square of a binomial, the square root of both sides could be taken. Add a number to each side to make this operation possible. This method is called *completing the square*. Since $(x + a)^2$ is
$$x^2 + 2ax + a^2,$$
the number to be added is the number that will make the

term without a variable equal to the square of half the coefficient of x. The easiest way to do this is to begin by rewriting the equation with no constant term on the left.
$$x^2 + 2x = 8$$
Then add $(\frac{1}{2} \cdot 2)^2$, or 1, to each side of the equation.
$$x^2 + 2x + 1 = 9$$

B. You now have an equation that has the square of a binomial on the left and a number on the right, so you can use rule (1).
$$(x + 1)^2 = 3^2$$
$$x + 1 = \pm 3$$

C. Separate the equation into two parts,
$$x + 1 = 3 \text{ or } x + 1 = -3$$
and solve the parts separately.
$$x = 2 \text{ or } x = -4$$

METHOD 2

A. This equation can also be solved by *factoring*. In other words, it can be solved using rule (2). Factor the left side.
$$x^2 + 2x - 8 = 0$$
$$(x + 4)(x - 2) = 0$$

B. Separate the equation into two parts by rule (2).
$$x + 4 = 0 \text{ or } x - 2 = 0$$

C. Solve each part separately.
$$x = -4 \text{ or } x = 2$$

Mathematics   285

While completing the square will work for all quadratic equations, it is often awkward to use when the coefficient of x^2 is not 1; and factoring is often difficult or impossible. Another method for solving quadratic equations is often used. The general equation $ax^2 + bx + c = 0$ can be solved by completing the square. The solution is called the *quadratic formula*.

$$x = \frac{-b \pm \sqrt{b^2 - 4ac}}{2a}$$

Solve $12x^2 - 17x - 5 = 0$ using the quadratic formula.

A. Identify a, b, and c from the formula.

$$a = 12$$
$$b = -17$$
$$c = -5$$

B. Substitute the values of a, b, and c into the formula.

$$x = \frac{-(-17) \pm \sqrt{(-17)^2 - 4(12)(-5)}}{2(12)}$$

$$= \frac{17 \pm \sqrt{289 + 240}}{24}$$

$$= \frac{17 \pm \sqrt{529}}{24}$$

$$= \frac{17 \pm 23}{24}$$

C. Separate into two equations.

$$x = \frac{17 + 23}{24} \ or$$

$$x = \frac{17 - 23}{24}$$

$$x = \frac{40}{24} \ or \ x = \frac{-6}{24}$$

$$x = \frac{5}{3} \ or \ x = -\frac{1}{4}$$

The product of two consecutive odd positive integers is 63. What is the smaller integer?

A. Let the smaller odd integer be x. Then the other integer is $x + 2$.

$$x(x + 2) = 63$$

B.
$$x^2 + 2x - 63 = 0$$
$$(x - 7)(x + 9) = 0$$
$$x - 7 = 0 \ or \ x + 9 = 0$$
$$x = 7 \ or \ x = -9$$

C. The problem specifies that the integers are positive. Therefore the smaller integer is 7.

There are two integers such that when 6 times an integer is subtracted from the square of that integer, the difference is 16. What are both integers with this property?

A. Call the integer with the specified property x. Then,
$$x^2 - 6x = 16.$$

B. Add $(\frac{1}{2} \cdot (-6))^2 = 9$ to each side.

$$x^2 - 6x + 9 = 25$$
$$(x - 3)^2 = 5^2$$
$$x - 3 = \pm 5$$

$$x - 3 = 5 \ or \ x - 3 = -5$$
$$x = 8 \ or \qquad x = -2$$

C. One of the integers is 8 and the other is -2. Check both in the original problem.

$$64 - 48 = 16$$
$$16 = 16$$
$$4 + 12 = 16$$
$$16 = 16$$

A rectangle is twice as long as it is wide. The number of units in its area is 4 times the number in its perimeter. How long and how wide is the rectangle?

A. If x is the width of the rectangle, then $2x$ is the length, $6x$ is the perimeter, and $2x^2$ is the area.

$$2x^2 = 24x$$

B. Divide by 2 to simplify.

$$x^2 = 12x$$
$$x^2 - 12x = 0$$
$$x^2 - 12x + 36 = 36$$
$$(x - 6)^2 = 6^2$$
$$x - 6 = \pm 6$$

$$x - 6 = 6 \ or \ x - 6 = -6$$
$$x = 12 \ or \qquad x = 0$$

C. A rectangle with a width of 0 would not be a rectangle, so only the answer $x = 12$ would be practical. Therefore, the width is 12 units and the length is 24 units.

Equations with fractions

Solve the equation $\dfrac{2x - 1}{2} - \dfrac{x + 2}{2x + 5} = \dfrac{6x - 5}{6}$.

A. The first step in solving any equation that contains fractions is to get rid of the fractions by multiplying both sides of the equation by the lowest common denominator of the fractions in the equation. In this case, the LCD is $6(2x + 5)$.

B. Multiplying both sides by $6(2x + 5)$ produces
$$3(2x + 5)(2x - 1) - 6(x + 2) = (2x + 5)(6x - 5).$$
Multiply.
$$12x^2 + 24x - 15 - 6x - 12 = 12x^2 + 20x - 25$$
Collect like terms.
$$12x^2 + 18x - 27 = 12x^2 + 20x - 25$$
$$18x - 27 = 20x - 25$$
$$-2 = 2x$$
$$x = -1$$

Operations with fractions

Addition:
$$\frac{a}{b} + \frac{c}{b} = \frac{a + c}{b}$$

Multiplication:
$$\frac{a}{b} \cdot \frac{c}{d} = \frac{ac}{bd}$$

Exponentiation:
$$\left(\frac{a}{b}\right)^n = \frac{a^n}{b^n}$$

Subtraction:
$$\frac{a}{b} - \frac{c}{b} = \frac{a - c}{b}$$

Division:
$$\frac{a}{b} \div \frac{c}{d} = \frac{ad}{bc}$$

Square roots:
$$\sqrt{\frac{a}{b}} = \frac{\sqrt{a}}{\sqrt{b}}$$

NOTE: b, c, and d are not 0.

Solve the equation $\dfrac{x^2 - 4x}{6} - \dfrac{x - 3}{3} = 1$.

A. Find the LCD. It is 6.

B. Multiply both sides by the LCD.
$$x^2 - 4x - 2(x - 3) = 6(1)$$
$$x^2 - 4x - 2x + 6 = 6$$
$$x^2 - 6x + 6 = 6$$
$$x^2 - 6x = 0$$

C. This equation can be solved by the rule that if $AB = 0$, then either A or B or both is equal to 0. Factor.
$$x(x - 6) = 0$$
$$x = 0 \text{ or } x - 6 = 0$$
$$x = 6$$
There are two solutions.
$$x = 0 \text{ or } x = 6$$

Solve the equation $2x + \dfrac{2x - 6}{x - 3} = 1$.

A. Multiply both sides by $(x - 3)$.
$$2x(x - 3) + 2x - 6 = 1(x - 3)$$
$$2x^2 - 6x + 2x - 6 = x - 3$$
$$2x^2 - 5x - 3 = 0$$

B. Solve by factoring.
$$(2x + 1)(x - 3) = 0$$
$$2x + 1 = 0 \text{ or } x - 3 = 0$$
$$2x = -1 \text{ or } \quad x = 3$$
$$x = -\frac{1}{2}$$

C. The apparent solutions are $x = -\frac{1}{2}$ and $x = 3$; however, the apparent solution $x = 3$ is *extraneous*. When you substitute 3 in the original equation, you get
$$2(3) + \frac{2(3) - 6}{(3 - 3)} = 1$$
$$\frac{6 + 0}{0} = 1.$$
Since division by 0 is always prohibited, $x = 3$ must be eliminated. The other apparent solution, however, checks. Therefore, the only solution is $-\frac{1}{2}$. Extraneous solutions can also occur in equations that are solved by squaring both sides.

Solving inequalities

Solve $5 - 2x < 9$.

A. Many problems of algebra are *inequalities* that use one of the signs

    $<$ is less than
    $>$ is greater than
    $\leq$ is less than or equal to
    $\geq$ is greater than or equal to

instead of $=$. Most of the rules for solving inequalities are different from the rules for equations.

B. The addition rule for inequalities, however, is the same as that for equations. So the first step in solving $5 - 2x < 9$ is to add -5 to both sides of the equation.

$$5 - 2x + (-5) < 9 + (-5)$$
$$-2x < 4$$

C. The multiplication rule is not the same. If you multiply both sides of an inequality by a negative number, it reverses the inequality sign. Multiply by $-\frac{1}{2}$.

$$-\frac{1}{2} \cdot -2x > -\frac{1}{2} \cdot 4$$
$$x > -2$$

(Multiplying by a positive number does not change the direction of the sign.)

Solve $x^2 + 2x - 8 > 0$.

A. One way to solve a quadratic equation is to factor it, for if $AB = 0$, then $A = 0$ *or* $B = 0$. But for inequalities, the rule is different.
If $AB > 0$, then A and B have the same sign.
If $AB < 0$, then A and B have different signs.

B. First factor $x^2 + 2x - 8 > 0$ to get $(x + 4)(x - 2) > 0$. This inequality is true if $x + 4$ and $x - 2$ are both positive, or if $x + 4$ and $x - 2$ are both negative, but not if one binomial is positive and the other is negative.

C. The signs of both binomials can be shown on a number line:

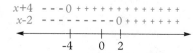

From the diagram, you can see that if $x < -4$, then both signs are $-$; if x is between -4 and 2, $x + 4$ is $+$ but $x - 2$ is $-$; and if $x > 2$, both signs are $+$. Therefore, both signs are the same for $x < -4$ *or* $x > 2$, which is the solution.

Solve $x^2 - 3x \leq 4$.

A. The rule is for $AB \leq 0$, so first add -4 to each side of the inequality.
$$x^2 - 3x - 4 \leq 0$$
Then factor.
$$(x - 4)(x + 1) \leq 0$$

B. If $AB \leq 0$, then the signs of A and B are different (if $AB < 0$) or A or B is 0 (if $AB = 0$).
A number–line diagram of the two factors $x - 4$ and $x + 1$ is as follows:

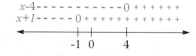

C. When x is less than -1 or x is greater than 4, the signs are the same. At -1 and 4 the values are 0. Between -1 and 4 the signs are different. So the solution is
$$-1 \leq x \leq 4$$
Note that a common mistake for this kind of problem is to think that
$$(x - 4)(x + 1) \leq 0$$
means that $x - 4 \leq 0$ *or* $x + 1 \leq -1$. This last combination is true whenever x is less than or equal to 4, so it includes values such as -1, but $(-2 - 4)$ $(-2 + 1) = -6 \cdot -1 = +6$.

Operations with radicals. The sign $\sqrt{}$ is a *radical*. By itself, it means the positive square root; thus, $\sqrt{x^2} = |x|$ (NOT $\pm x$). When a number, such as *n*, is inserted in the radical sign, the combination means the *n*th root; for example, $\sqrt[3]{-27}$ is the third root of -27, or -3, since $(-3)(-3)(-3) = -27$, and $\sqrt[4]{16}$ is the fourth root of 16, or 2. Note that if *n* is odd, the *n*th root of a negative number is negative, when only real roots are considered. If *n* is even, there is no real *n*th root.

Simplify $\sqrt{72}$.

A. The product of two numbers indicated by radicals is the product of the numbers in the radicals, called the *radicands*, as long as both radicals have the same *index*, the number *n* that indicates the meaning of the radical. Therefore,
$$\sqrt{72} = \sqrt{36 \cdot 2} = \sqrt{36} \cdot \sqrt{2}.$$

B. A radical is simplified when all the real integral roots have been removed from the radicand. In this case, since 36 is a perfect square, $\sqrt{36}$ can be replaced by 6.

Therefore, the simplified form of $\sqrt{72}$ is $6\sqrt{2}$, since 2 is not a perfect square; that is, 2 does not have an integral root.

Simplify $\sqrt{20x^2y^3}$.

A. Rewrite each coefficient as a product that involves perfect squares if it is possible to do so.
$$\sqrt{20x^2y^3} = \sqrt{4 \cdot 5x^2y^2y}$$

B. Remove the perfect squares from the radicand.
$$\sqrt{4 \cdot 5x^2y^2y} = 2|xy|\sqrt{5y}$$
The answer is often given without using the absolute value sign, as $2xy\sqrt{5y}$.

In careful work, however, the absolute value sign is used unless one is certain that the values of *x* and *y* are non-negative.

Sequences and series

Arithmetic sequence:
First term: *a* or a_1

Constant difference: *d*

General term: $a_n = a + (n-1)d$

Sequence: $a, a+d, a+2d, a+3d, \ldots,$
$\qquad a+(n-1)d, \ldots$

Geometric sequence:
First term: *a* or a_1

Constant ratio: *r*

General term: $a_n = ar^{n-1}$

Sequence: $a, ar, ar^2, ar^3, \ldots, ar^{n-1}, \ldots$

Arithmetic series:
Series: $a + (a+d) + (a+2d) + \ldots$
$\qquad + (a+(n-1)d) + \ldots$

Last term of finite series: l_n

Sum of finite series of *n* terms:
$$S_n = \frac{n}{2}(a + l_n)$$

$$= \frac{n}{2}(2a + (n-1)d)$$

Sum of infinite series: none

Geometric series:
Series: $a + ar + ar^2 + ar^3 + \ldots + ar^{n-1} + \ldots$

Sum of finite series of *n* terms:
$$S_n = \frac{a - ar^n}{1 - r} \quad (r \neq 1)$$

$$= \frac{a(a - r^n)}{1 - r} \quad (r \neq 1)$$

Sum of infinite series: $S = \dfrac{a}{1 - r} \quad (|r| < 1)$

Geometry

Geometry is the study of certain properties of sets of points. These properties are arranged and developed as part of an *axiomatic system;* that is, they are proved by *deduction* from a set of first principles called *axioms.* The axioms are accepted without proof, but the remaining properties of the system must all be proved.

Certain concepts must also be accepted without definition. These *undefined terms* are *point, betweenness, congruence,* and *continuity.* Although the terms are undefined, there is a common understanding of what they mean. Thus, a point is something like a small dot, or an exact location in space. The concept of betweenness suggests that between two points, there can be another. This is different from continuity, which refers to the nature of a line.

Congruence is an essential idea in geometry. It is simply the notion that two different line segments can have the same length. (A *line segment* is the part of a line between two points, called the *endpoints,* including the points.)

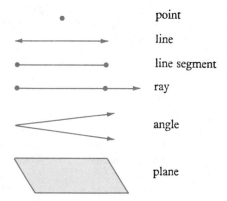

Most of the terms used in geometry, however, are defined terms based on the undefined terms. For example, a *ray* is the union of a line segment *AB* (*A* and *B* are the endpoints of the segment) and all points *C* such that *B* is between *A* and *C*. This figure is called ray *AB,* and *A* is the *endpoint* of the ray. An *angle* is the union of two rays that have the same endpoint.

Angles

The measure of angle *A* is shown as m $\angle$ *A*.

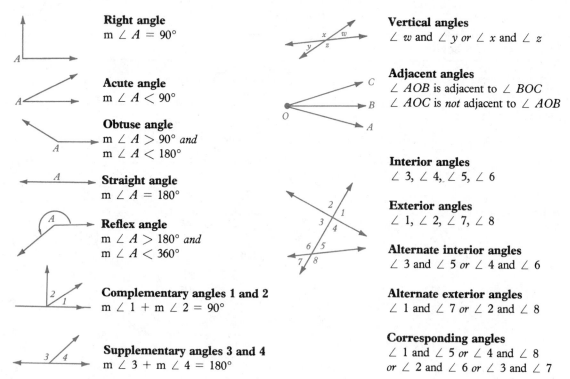

Right angle
m $\angle$ *A* = 90°

Acute angle
m $\angle$ *A* < 90°

Obtuse angle
m $\angle$ *A* > 90° *and*
m $\angle$ *A* < 180°

Straight angle
m $\angle$ *A* = 180°

Reflex angle
m $\angle$ *A* > 180° *and*
m $\angle$ *A* < 360°

Complementary angles 1 and 2
m $\angle$ 1 + m $\angle$ 2 = 90°

Supplementary angles 3 and 4
m $\angle$ 3 + m $\angle$ 4 = 180°

Vertical angles
$\angle$ *w* and $\angle$ *y or* $\angle$ *x* and $\angle$ *z*

Adjacent angles
$\angle$ *AOB* is adjacent to $\angle$ *BOC*
$\angle$ *AOC* is *not* adjacent to $\angle$ *AOB*

Interior angles
$\angle$ 3, $\angle$ 4, $\angle$ 5, $\angle$ 6

Exterior angles
$\angle$ 1, $\angle$ 2, $\angle$ 7, $\angle$ 8

Alternate interior angles
$\angle$ 3 and $\angle$ 5 *or* $\angle$ 4 and $\angle$ 6

Alternate exterior angles
$\angle$ 1 and $\angle$ 7 *or* $\angle$ 2 and $\angle$ 8

Corresponding angles
$\angle$ 1 and $\angle$ 5 *or* $\angle$ 4 and $\angle$ 8
or $\angle$ 2 and $\angle$ 6 *or* $\angle$ 3 and $\angle$ 7

Mathematics

Geometric constructions.

It is assumed that one can draw a line segment and extend it to become a line and that one can reproduce the distance between two points. The tools for performing these operations are called the *straightedge* and the *compass*. With a straightedge and compass, it is possible to draw theoretically exact figures, which are called *constructions*. When a construction has been given for a figure, one can take the construction as the definition, since the construction provides an essential way of reproducing the figure from points, lines, and congruent distances, all undefined concepts.

In making constructions, the compass is used to draw short circle segments called *arcs*.

Bisect a line segment *AB*.

A. Set the point of the compass at *A* and, with a radius greater than $\frac{1}{2}$ *AB*, draw a small arc above and below *AB*.

B. With the same radius, draw two arcs with the compass point at *B*, so that each of the first arcs is crossed by the second. Connect the two points of intersection of the arcs, *C* and *D*, with a line.

Where this line crosses *AB* at point *E*, the line *bisects AB*. In other words, *E* divides the segment into two parts that are congruent.

NOTE: *CD* is actually perpendicular to *AB*. Thus, it is the *perpendicular bisector* of *AB*.

Construct a perpendicular to *AB* at *G*.

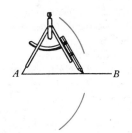

A. Set the point of the compass at *G* and draw equal arcs on *AB* that cross at *C* and *D*.

B. With a larger radius, set the compass point at *C* and draw an arc above *AB*.

C. With the same radius, draw an arc with the compass point at *D*, crossing the other arc, locating point *E*.

D. Connect *E* and *G*; *EG* is perpendicular to *AB* at *G*.

Construct an angle congruent to a given angle *A*.

A. Draw a base line *XY*.

B. Set the compass point at *X* and draw an arc through *Z*.

C. Set the compass point at *A* to draw the same arc as in step B through the sides of angle *A* to locate points *B* and *C*.

D. Set the compass point at *B* and draw an arc through *C*.

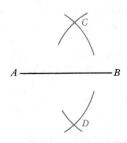
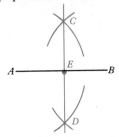

E. Use the arc from step D with the compass point set at *Z* to locate point *W*.

F. Draw ray *XW* to complete the construction of angle *X* that is congruent to angle *A*.

Bisect angle *P*.

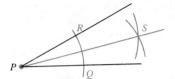

A. Draw an arc with the compass point at *P* to get points *Q* and *R*.

B. With a sufficiently large radius, set the compass point at *Q* and strike an arc.

C. Set the compass point at *R* with the same radius as in step *B*. Intersect the other arc to locate point *S*.

D. Draw ray *PS*, which is the bisector of angle *P*.

Construct a line through point *P* that is parallel to *AB*.

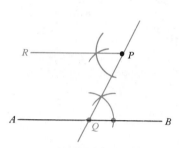

A. Two lines are *parallel* if they always maintain the same distance from each other. From this it can be inferred that parallel lines do not intersect. All lines that are not parallel do intersect in a point, a result that is not obvious. In fact, non-Euclidean geometries exist in which this property of parallels does not hold. The construction, however, does not use distance.

Instead, it relies on another property of parallel lines, which is often taken as an axiom in Euclidean geometry: A line that intersects both parallel lines—a *transversal*—makes congruent angles with the two parallel lines. Begin the construction, then, by drawing any transversal through *P*, which will intersect *AB* at a point that can be called *Q*.

B. At point *P*, construct an angle *RPQ* congruent to angle *PQB*.

The line *RP* is parallel to line *AB*.

Divide a line segment *AB* into three congruent parts.

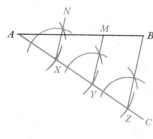

A. Draw a ray *AC* with its endpoint at *A*. This ray is an *auxiliary* ray because it is not a part of the actual division, even though it is used to make the construction.

B. With the compass point at *A*, mark point *X* any suitable distance along *AC*.

C. With the same radius as in step B, mark points *Y* with the compass point at *X*, and *Z* with the compass point at *Y*.

D. Draw line segment *ZB*, which defines angle *AZB*.

E. Construct angles at *Y* and *X* that are each congruent to angle *AZB*. The sides of these angles strike *AB* at points that you can label *N* and *M*. This completes the construction because *AN* is congruent to *NM* and to *MB*.

NOTE: You can use the same method to divide a line segment into any required number of points. Simply make the number of arcs along the auxiliary ray the same as the number of divisions of the line segment.

Triangles. Two triangles are congruent if all the corresponding sides and all the corresponding angles are congruent. Congruent triangles are used extensively in geometry. The following construction shows that equal sides imply equal angles for triangles.

Construct a triangle given three sides of length *a*, *b*, and *c*.

A. The sides of a triangle are conventionally called by the lower-case version of the name of the angle opposite the side. Therefore, the side whose length is *c* is also called *c*, since it is opposite angle *C*. Start by drawing *c*. The other name for the segment *c* is *AB*.

B. With the radius of the compass equal to *b*, make an arc with the compass point at *A*.

C. Set the radius of the compass to the length of *a* and make an arc with the compass point at *B* that intersects the arc drawn in step B. *C* will be where the two arcs intersect.

D. Draw *AC* and *CB*.

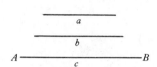

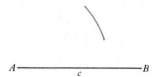

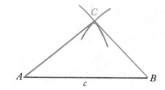

Triangles

Right
One angle measures 90°.
The side opposite the right angle is called the *hypotenuse*. The other two sides are called *legs*.

Acute
All angles measure less than 90°.

Obtuse
One angle measures more than 90°.

Equilateral
All three sides measure the same.

Isosceles
Two of the three sides measure the same.

Scalene
No two sides measure the same.

Altitude
A line segment from a vertex perpendicular to the opposite side.

Median
A line segment from a vertex to the midpoint of the opposite side.

Centroid
Point where all three medians meet.

Circumcenter
Point where all three altitudes meet.

Incenter
Point where the bisectors of the angles of a triangle meet.

Proof in geometry is based on a set of axioms. In this book, the proofs that are given are examples, so it is not necessary to provide a complete set of axioms. Axioms such as the following will be used in the proofs:
- A figure is congruent to itself.
- Vertical angles are congruent.

- If two figures are each congruent to a third figure, then the two figures are also congruent to each other.
- Corresponding parts of congruent triangles are also congruent.
- If two lines are parallel, the alternate interior angles cut off by a transversal are congruent.

Prove that the angles opposite the congruent sides (the *base* angles) of an isosceles triangle are congruent.

A. First establish what is *given* in the statement of the problem. In this case, you know that the triangle is isosceles. Make a drawing of an isosceles triangle, label it, and mark the congruent sides.
You are given $AC \cong BC$.
You are also given $BC \cong AC$.

B. Next, establish what you are going to prove. In this case, you want to prove two triangles are congruent (although only one triangle is given). The second triangle is the same as the first with the sides taken in a different order. You can call the first triangle ABC and the second BAC.

If you can prove
$$\triangle ABC \cong \triangle BAC,$$
then the theorem will be true by corresponding parts of congruent triangles. Since you have two sides already given as congruent, you need either a third side or the included angle. Take the included angle.

C. Present the proof in a clear form. Most geometry textbooks use a two-column format.

Statements	Reasons
1. $AC \cong BC$	1. Given.
2. $BC \cong AC$	2. Given.
3. $\angle C \cong \angle C$	3. A figure is congruent to itself.
4. $\triangle ABC \cong \triangle BAC$	4. S.A.S.
5. $\angle A \cong \angle B$	5. Corresponding parts of congruent triangles are also congruent.

NOTE: The converse of a theorem is a kind of "reverse" of the theorem. If the theorem is stated in "if-then" form, then the converse can be found by interchanging the clause after "if" and the clause after "then." The if-then form of the previous theorem is, "if a triangle is isosceles, then the base angles of the triangle are congruent." Therefore, the converse of the theorem is "if the base angles of a triangle are congruent, then the triangle is isosceles." This converse can be proved in a way similar to the proof of the original theorem.

Congruence for triangles

Two triangles are congruent if any of the following conditions are true:

Property		Abbreviation	
Three corresponding sides are congruent (side-side-side).		S.S.S.	$AB \cong XY$ $AC \cong XZ$ $BC \cong YZ$
Two corresponding sides and the included angle are congruent (side-angle-side).		S.A.S.	$AB \cong XY$ $BC \cong YZ$ $\angle B \cong \angle Y$
Two corresponding angles and the included side are congruent (angle-side-angle).		A.S.A.	$\angle A \cong \angle X$ $\angle B \cong \angle Y$ $AB \cong XY$
Two corresponding angles and the side not included are congruent (angle-angle-side).		A.A.S.	$\angle A \cong \angle X$ $\angle B \cong \angle Y$ $BC \cong YZ$
In a right triangle, two corresponding hypotenuses and two corresponding legs are equal (hypotenuse-leg).		Hyp. L.	$AB \cong XY$ $BC \cong YZ$ $m\angle C = m\angle Z = 90°$

Prove that the bisector of the vertex angle of an isosceles triangle is also the bisector of the base of the triangle.

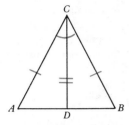

A. You are given an isosceles triangle and the angle bisector of the *vertex* angle; that is, the angle that is not one of the base angles.

B. The strategy is to use the angle bisector to divide the triangle into two triangles that can be shown to be congruent by S.A.S.

C. Express as a two-column proof.

Statements	Reasons
1. $AC \cong BC$	1. Definition of isosceles.
2. $\angle ACD \cong \angle BCD$	2. Definition of angle bisector.
3. $CD \cong CD$	3. Figures are congruent to themselves.
4. $\triangle ACD \cong \triangle BCD$	4. S.A.S.
5. $AD \cong DB$	5. Corresponding parts of congruent triangles are congruent.
6. D bisects AB	6. Definition of bisector.

Given two intersecting circles whose centers are O and P and whose points of intersection are A and B. Line segment AB bisects angles OAP and OBP. Prove that $BP \cong AP \cong AO \cong OB$.

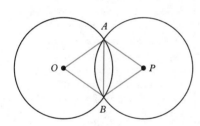

A. Establish what is given.

B. Choose a plan of attack. In this case you will want to use the definition of a circle as a set of points all at the same distance from a given point, the definition of bisect, and the theorems about isosceles triangles. The fact that there are two angles bisected in the problem suggests that A.S.A. will be useful.

C. Write a two-column proof.

Statements	Reasons
1. O and P are circles	1. Given.
2. $OA \cong OB$	2. Radii of the same circle are congruent by definition.
3. $\triangle OAB$ is isosceles	3. Definition of isosceles.
4. $\angle OAB \cong \angle OBA$	4. Base angles of isosceles triangles are congruent.
5. $\angle OAB \cong \angle BAP$	5. Definition of bisect.
6. $\angle OBA \cong \angle ABP$	6. Definition of bisect.
7. $AB \cong AB$	7. A figure is congruent to itself.
8. $\triangle ABO \cong \triangle ABP$	8. A.S.A.
9. $OA \cong AP$	9. Corresponding parts of congruent triangles are congruent.
10. $OB \cong BP$	10. Corresponding parts of congruent triangles are congruent.
11. $BP \cong AP \cong AO \cong OB$	11. If two figures are each congruent to a third figure, they are also congruent to each other.

Polygons

Prove that the opposite sides of a parallelogram are congruent.

A. Given $AB \mid\mid CD$ and $AD \mid\mid BC$.

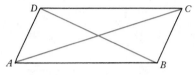

B. In more advanced work with geometry, the two-column proof is often replaced with the paragraph proof. The most important reasons and all the steps are included, but the material is presented in ordinary prose instead of in chart or list form. Since you have been exposed to theorems involving triangles, put some triangles into the figure by drawing the *diagonals* or line segments from one vertex to the opposite vertex of the parallelogram.

C. Use the result that alternate interior angles cut off by a transversal and parallel lines are congruent. This shows that $\angle BDC \cong \angle DBA$ and $\angle ADB \cong \angle DBC$. Since $DB \cong DB$, triangles ADB and BDC are congruent by A.S.A.

D. Therefore, $AD \cong BC$ and $AB \cong DC$.

NOTE: This proof applies equally to rectangles and to rhombuses. As a result, it is easy to show that all four sides of a rhombus are congruent.

Similarly, a result that you will use in the next proof is a partial converse of this theorem: if two sides of a quadrilateral are both congruent and parallel, the quadrilateral is a parallelogram.

Common polygons

Quadrilaterals: Polygons with 4 sides

Name/Defining property

Trapezoid
A quadrilateral with two parallel sides.*

$AB \mid\mid DC$

Isosceles Trapezoid
A trapezoid with congruent nonparallel sides.

$AB \mid\mid DC$
$AD \cong BC$

Kite
A quadrilateral with two pairs of adjacent congruent sides.

$AB \cong AD$
$BC \cong CD$

Parallelogram
A quadrilateral with pairs of opposite sides parallel.

$AB \mid\mid DC$
$AD \mid\mid BC$

Rhombus
A parallelogram with a pair of adjacent congruent sides.

$AB \mid\mid DC$
$AD \mid\mid BC$
$AB \cong AD$

Rectangle
A parallelogram with a right angle.

$AB \mid\mid DC$
$AD \mid\mid BC$
m $\angle A = 90°$

Square
A rectangle with a pair of adjacent congruent sides.

$AB \mid\mid DC$
$AD \mid\mid BC$
m $\angle A = 90°$
$AB \cong AD$

* Some books use trapezoid *only if the quadrilateral has two parallel sides and two nonparallel sides; other books permit parallelograms to be special cases of trapezoids.*

Other polygons

A polygon is called *regular* if the sides are all congruent and the angles are all congruent. For example, the only regular quadrilateral is the square. The definitions below apply to any form of the named polygon. The illustrations are all the regular forms of the polygons.

Name/Defining property

Triangle
A polygon with 3 sides.

Quadrilateral
A polygon with 4 sides.

Pentagon
A polygon with 5 sides.

Hexagon
A polygon with 6 sides.

Octagon
A polygon with 8 sides.

Decagon
A polygon with 10 sides.

Mathematics

It can be proved from congruent triangles that the angle formed by extending one side of a triangle (called an *exterior angle* of the triangle) is greater than the *remote interior angles* of the triangle, the angles that are not adjacent to the angle formed by extension. In the

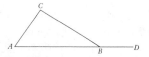

figure, angle *CBD* is an exterior angle and angles *C* and *A* are the remote interior angles.

Prove that two lines are parallel if a transversal between the lines cuts off congruent alternate interior angles.

A. Make a drawing showing lines *AB* and *CD* cut by the transversal *PQ* at *A* and *D*. Then angles *BAD* and *CDA* are alternate interior angles. It is given that these two angles are congruent.

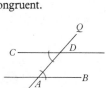

B. Assume that the opposite of what you want to prove is true; then show that such an assumption leads to a contradiction. Assume that *AB* and *CD* are not parallel. In that case, they must intersect at some point, which can be called *X*.

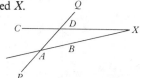

C. By the exterior angle theorem, angle *CDA* is greater than angle *BAD*. However, it is given that angles *CDA* and *BAD* are congruent. Therefore, a contradiction has been shown and the theorem is proved.

Prove that a segment joining the midpoints of two sides of a triangle is parallel to the third side and that its length is one-half the length of the third side.

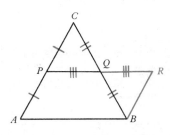

A. Draw a general triangle *ABC* and the line segment *PQ* joining the midpoints of sides *AC* and *BC*. Label *AP* and *PC* as congruent and *BQ* and *QC* as congruent.

B. The strategy will be to make *PQ* part of one side of a parallelogram, with *AB* the opposite side of the parallelogram. Construct the side containing *PQ* to be twice as long as *PQ*. Then it will be possible to prove the second part of the theorem.

C. Extend *PQ* through *Q* to point *R* so that *PR* is twice as long as *PQ*. Draw a line segment from *R* to *B*.

D. *QB* ≅ *QC* is given. *QR* was drawn to be congruent to *PQ*, since *PR* is twice as long as *PQ*. ∠*CQP* and ∠*RQB* are congruent because they are vertical angles (see box on page 290). Therefore, triangles *CPQ* and *QRB* are congruent by S.A.S.

E. Since *PC* and *RB* are corresponding parts, they are congruent. Also, *AP* is given to be congruent to *PC*. Therefore, *RB* and *AP* are congruent, since each is congruent to *PC*.

F. *CB* is a transversal between *AC* and *RB*. Angles *C* and *RBQ* are corresponding parts of congruent triangles, so they are congruent. Then, *CB* makes congruent alternate

interior angles with *AC* and *RB*. Therefore, *AC* is parallel to *RB*. Since *AP* is part of *AC*, it is also parallel to *RB*. Since the conditions are both filled, *ABRP* is a parallelogram.

G. Since *ABRP* is a parallelogram, *PR* is parallel to *AB*, and, since *PQ* is part of *PR*, *PQ* is parallel to *AB*, which was the first thing to be proved. Also, *AB* is congruent to *PR*. Since *PQ* is half the length of *PR*, it is also half the length of *AB*.

Circles.

A *circle* is the figure you get when you extend an arc to the place where the arc started. More formally, a circle is the set of all points in the plane that are the same distance from a given point.

Various lines, line segments, angles, and other geometric figures connected with circles are given special names. Definitions for these figures that are related to the circle are given at the bottom of this page.

Construct a circle given three points through which the circle must pass.

A. Given the three points *A*, *B*, and *C*, draw line segments to connect two pairs of them, *A* with *B* and *B* with *C*.

B. Construct the perpendicular bisectors of the segments *AB* and *BC*. Where the bisectors meet is the center of the circle. Note that if the three points are all in a line, the bisectors will not meet. Three *collinear* points (points on the same line) cannot be on a circle.

C. The distance from the intersection of the perpendiculars to one of the points is the radius of the circle. Set your compass point on the intersection and using that radius, draw the circle.

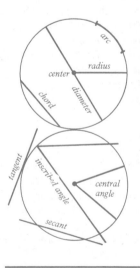

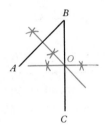

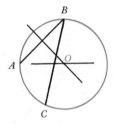

NOTE: This construction relies on this sequence of theorems about chords of circles:

1. The perpendicular from the center of a circle bisects a chord.

2. The line from the center of a circle to a chord that is not a diameter is perpendicular to the chord.

3. In the plane of a circle, the perpendicular bisector of a chord passes through the center of the circle.

Definitions

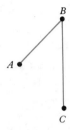

arc	Part of a circle.
center	Point from which all points of the circle are equidistant.
radius	Either the distance from the center to the circle or the line segment from the center to the circle.
diameter	Either the distance across the circle or the line segment from one side of the circle to the other that passes through the center.
chord	Line segment from one point of the circle to another point of the circle.
secant	Line passing through the circle.
tangent	Line that contains only one point of a circle.
central angle	Angle with its vertex at center of circle.
inscribed angle	Angle that intersects the circle in two points with its vertex on the circle.

Mathematics

Construct the two tangents to a circle from a point outside the circle.

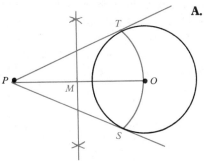

A. Call the point outside the circle *P* and the center of the circle *O*. Connect *O* to *P* and bisect *OP*. Use *M* to label the midpoint of *OP*.

B. With the compass at point *M* and a radius of *MO*, draw an arc that intersects the circle at two points, *T* and *S*. The lines *PT* and *PS* are the required tangents.

Given two circles, construct lines that are tangent to each circle and that intersect each other at a point between the two circles.

A. The tangents described are the *internal* common tangents of the two circles. Internal tangents to two circles are tangents that cross the line segment between the centers of the circles. Draw a diameter in one of the circles; construct a diameter in the other circle that is parallel to the one you drew in the first circle.

B. Connect the ends of the diameters with line segments. Where these segments cross is called the *internal center of similitude* of the two circles.

C. The common internal tangents of the circles will pass through the internal center of similitude. Therefore, to complete the construction, use this point, *S*, as the point outside the circle in the previous construction. Construct tangents to one of the circles from *S*. These will also be tangents to the other circle.

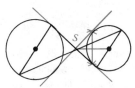

Construct the tangents to two circles from a point that is not between the two circles.

A. The tangents described are *external* common tangents; the tangents do not cross a line segment between the centers of the circles. Again, begin by drawing a diameter in one of the circles and constructing the diameter parallel to it in the other circle.

B. This time join the same ends of the diameters with lines (instead of the opposite ends with line segments). These lines will cross at a point outside the circles. Call that point *S*, since it is the *external center of similitude*.

C. As in the previous construction, construct tangents to one of the circles from *S*. They will also be the required tangents to both circles.

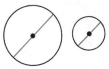

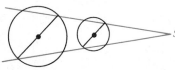

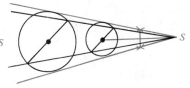

Trigonometry

The word *trigonometry* means "triangle measuring". Although trigonometry today goes far beyond triangles, most people first learn about trigonometry in connection with right triangles. By custom, if the vertices of a right triangle are A, B, and C, the right angle of triangle ABC is at C.

The sides of a triangle are often labeled with lowercase letters that correspond to the capital letters of the opposite vertex.

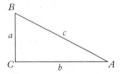

For example, the side opposite the angle whose vertex is C, known as $\angle C$, is labeled c. Another name for side c is *hypotenuse*, which means the side opposite the right angle. Sides a and b can also be named in terms of the angles of the triangle.

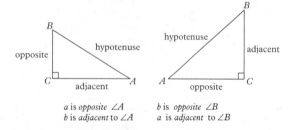

a is *opposite* $\angle A$ *b* is *opposite* $\angle B$
b is *adjacent* to $\angle A$ *a* is *adjacent* to $\angle B$

Right triangles that have a given acute angle are all similar. For similar triangles, the ratios of corresponding sides are equal. The ratios are one way to define the trigonometric functions sine, cosine, tangent, cosecant, secant, and cotangent.

sine of $\angle A$	abbreviated as	$\sin A = a/c$
cosine of $\angle A$	abbreviated as	$\cos A = b/c$
tangent of $\angle A$	abbreviated as	$\tan A = a/b$
cosecant of $\angle A$	abbreviated as	$\csc A = c/a$
secant of $\angle A$	abbreviated as	$\sec A = c/b$
cotangent of $\angle A$	abbreviated as	$\cot A = b/a$

Two special right triangles are frequently used in trigonometry, the isosceles triangle, also known as the 45-45-90 degree triangle because of the measures of its angles, and the 30-60-90 degree triangle.

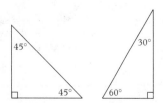

Let the equal sides of a 45-45-90 degree triangle each be one unit. Then the Pythagorean theorem can be used to find the length of the hypotenuse. If $a = 1$ and $b = 1$, then

$$c^2 = a^2 + b^2 \text{ becomes } c^2 = 1 + 1 = 2; \text{ so } c = \sqrt{2}$$

Notice that the 30-60-90 degree triangle is half an equilateral triangle.

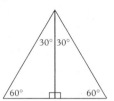

If one side of the equilateral trangle is two units, then the short side of one of the 30-60-90 degree triangles must be one unit. This means that a 30-60-90 degree triangle with a hypotenuse of two units also has one side of one unit. From that information, the Pythagorean theorem ($c^2 = a^2 + b^2$) can be used to calculate the missing side of the triangle.

$$2^2 = 1^2 + b^2$$
or $$4 = 1 + b^2$$
so $$b = \sqrt{3}$$

Knowing all three sides of each triangle makes it possible to compute the values shown in the table below.

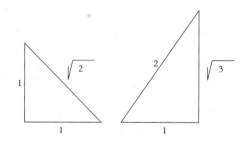

Functions of special angles

Measure of A	$\operatorname{Sin} A$	$\operatorname{Cos} A$	$\operatorname{Tan} A$	$\operatorname{Cot} A$	$\operatorname{Sec} A$	$\operatorname{Csc} A$
30°	$\dfrac{1}{2}$	$\dfrac{\sqrt{3}}{2}$	$\dfrac{\sqrt{3}}{3}$	$\sqrt{3}$	$2\dfrac{\sqrt{3}}{3}$	2
45°	$\dfrac{\sqrt{2}}{2}$	$\dfrac{\sqrt{2}}{2}$	1	1	$\sqrt{2}$	$\sqrt{2}$
60°	$\dfrac{\sqrt{3}}{2}$	$\dfrac{1}{2}$	$\sqrt{3}$	$\dfrac{\sqrt{3}}{3}$	2	$2\dfrac{\sqrt{3}}{3}$

Solving problems. Trigonometry can be used to solve problems; it also has many uses in higher mathematics. For most people, the first encounter with trigonometric functions is in relation to finding distances or heights that cannot be measured directly. Most problems of *indirect measurement* are solved by knowing one angle and side of a right triangle; from these it is possible to find other angles or sides.

From a point 100 meters from the base of a vertical tree, the top of the tree can be seen at an angle of 60°. How tall is the tree?

A. Make a drawing that shows the triangle.

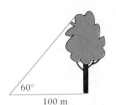

60°
100 m

B. Use trigonometry to solve the problem. The height of the tree is the side opposite the 60° angle. The known distance is the side adjacent to the 60° angle.

$$\text{tangent} = \frac{\text{opposite}}{\text{adjacent}}$$

C. Write the formula using the known numbers. Use h for the tree's height.

$$\tan 60° = \frac{h}{100}$$

$$\sqrt{3} = \frac{h}{100}$$

$$100\sqrt{3} = h$$

The tree is $100\sqrt{3}$ meters high. Since $\sqrt{3}$ is about 1.732, the tree is about 173.2 meters high.

How to read trigonometric tables

If you have a moderately good calculator, the values of trigonometric functions can be obtained by pushing the correct keys. If you do not have a calculator with such special function keys, you need to be able to read tables of values. Such tables are usually given in concise formats to enable them to contain as much information as possible. Most tables use the methods outlined below.

Here is small section of a typical trigonometric table. The measure of the angle is given with the Greek lowercase theta, θ:

θ Deg.	Sin θ	Cos θ	Tan θ	Cot θ	Sec θ	Csc θ	
▶30°00′	.5000	.8660	.5774	1.7321	1.155	2.000	60°00′
10′	.5025	.8646	.5812	1.7205	1.157	1.990	50′
20′	.5050	.8631	.5851	1.7090	1.159	1.980	40′
30′	.5075	.8616	.5890	1.6977	1.161	1.970	30′
40′	.5100	.8601	.5930	1.6864	1.163	1.961	20′ ◀
50′	.5125	.8587	.5969	1.6753	1.165	1.951	10′
31°00′	.5150	.8572	.6009	1.6643	1.167	1.942	59°00′ ◀
10′	.5175	.8557	.6048	1.6534	1.169	1.932	50′
20′	.5200	.8542	.6088	1.6426	1.171	1.923	40′
30′	.5225	.8526	.6128	1.6319	1.173	1.914	30′
40′	.5250	.8511	.6168	1.6212	1.175	1.905	20′
50′	.5275	.8496	.6208	1.6107	1.177	1.896	10′
32°00′	.5299	.8480	.6249	1.6003	1.179	1.887	58°00′
10′	.5324	.8465	.6289	1.5900	1.181	1.878	50′
	Cos θ	Sin θ	Cot θ	Tan θ	Csc θ	Sec θ	θ Deg.

Notice that this table has column "headings" at both the top and the bottom. Because the sine and cosine, tangent and cotangent, and secant and cosecant are cofunctions, as the values of one member of each pair increase from 0° to 90°, the other function in the pair takes on the same values in reverse order, from 90° to 0°. Therefore, one entry can serve two purposes, cutting the length of the table in half. For example, to find cos 30°, locate the column labeled Cos θ at the *top* of the page and 30° 00′ at the *left* of the page (30° 00′ is read "thirty degrees zero minutes"; one minute is $\frac{1}{60}$ of one degree). Where this column and row intersect, at .8660, is the value of cos 30°.

The same procedure works for all functions of angles of 45° or less.

For angles between 45° and 90°, start at the bottom and right instead of at the top and left. To find tan 59° 20′, first locate Tan θ at the *bottom* of the page. Then, looking from *bottom to top* first, find 59° 00′ in the *right-hand* column; keep traveling *up* that column until you get to 20′. Now look for the intersection of the row and column. If you have been careful, you should find the value of tan 59° 20′ to be 1.6864.

A man stood at point *A* on one side of a river (see illustration) and noted a small tree, point *B*, across the river. He turned 90° to the right, walked 100 meters to point *C*, and then found the angle of sight to the tree to be 63°.
Find *AB*, the original distance of the man from the tree.

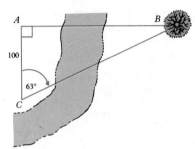

A. *ABC* is a right triangle, so the trigonometric ratios can be used as if you were using a graph. That is, *AB/AC* corresponds to the tangent ratio *y/x* on the graph for the given angle of 63°.

$$\tan 63° = \frac{AB}{AC}$$

B. From the table, or using a calculator, you find that tan 63° is about 1.9626. You know that *AC* is 100 meters, so

$$1.9626 = \frac{AB}{100}$$

C. Solve the equation.
$$AB = 196.26$$
Therefore, *AB* is 196 meters to the nearest meter.

A fire engine has a 32-meter ladder that extends from the truck at a maximum angle of 80°. How high can the ladder reach if it is mounted 4 meters above the ground?

A. Draw the triangle.

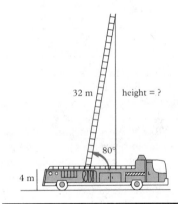

B. The height of the triangle can be found by trigonometry and the 4-meter additional height of the fire engine and mounting can be added to find the answer. Since the side opposite the 80° angle and the hypotenuse are known, the sine function can be used.

C. $\sin 80° = \dfrac{height}{32}$

From a hand-held calculator, sin 80° = 0.9848 to the nearest ten-thousandth.

$$0.9848 = \frac{height}{32}$$

$$\begin{aligned}height &= (32)(0.9848)\\ &= 31.5136\end{aligned}$$

To the nearest half-meter, the height is 31.5 meters. Since the ladder is mounted 4 meters above the ground, it can reach 35.5 meters.

In a stiff wind, a kite pulls its string taut at an angle of 28° from the ground.
If 137 meters of string are let out, what is the distance of the point above which the kite flies? How high is the kite?

A. Make a sketch showing the triangle involved.

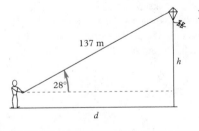

You can label the distance to the point underneath the kite as *d* and the height of the kite as *h*.

B. The cosine of 28° is $\frac{d}{137}$. If you ignore the height the kite string is held above the ground, the sine is $\frac{h}{137}$. Using a calculator, cos 28° = 0.8829 to four places and sin 28° = 0.4695.

C. For the distance, 0.8829 = $\frac{d}{137}$, so *d* = 120.9573 meters, or 121 meters to the nearest meter.

D. For the height, 0.4695 = $\frac{h}{137}$, so *h* = 64.3215 meters. The height, ignoring how high the string is held above the ground, is 64 meters to the nearest meter.

Mathematics

General angle definitions. While angles

in triangles are usually named with capital letters from the alphabet used in English, mathematicians often use Greek letters for the measures of angles. Often when no triangle is directly involved, the lowercase Greek letter θ is used for the measure of an angle. In particular, the symbol θ, theta, is used for angles of any size called *general angles*. Such angles are measured with the counterclockwise direction as positive. A straight angle is 180°, so an angle of 360° brings the terminal side of the angle all the way around a circle to where it lies upon the initial side of the angle.

The four divisions of the plane made by the x and y axes are called *quadrants*. Angles between 0° and 90° are in the first quadrant, written as Quadrant I. An angle such as 125°, between 90° and 180°, is in Quadrant II. Similarly, 220° is in Quadrant III, between 180° and 270°; and 296° is in Quadrant IV, between 270° and 360°. The negative angle -31° is also in Quadrant IV.

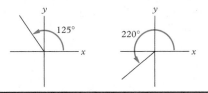

Radian measure. So far you have measured

angles in degrees and minutes. Angles in trigonometry are often measured in *radians*. A radian is the measure of a central angle that cuts off an arc whose length is equal to the radius of the circle. Therefore, 360° = 2π radians.

From this you can calculate that
1 radian is about 57.29578 degrees or
1 radian is about 57° 17' 45" and
1 degree is about 0.01745 radians.
Usually, however, radian measures for common angles are expressed in terms of π instead of decimals:

$$30° = \frac{\pi}{6} \qquad 45° = \frac{\pi}{4} \qquad 60° = \frac{\pi}{3} \qquad 90° = \frac{\pi}{2} \qquad 180° = \pi$$

Functions of a general angle.

Although *trigonometry* means "triangle measuring," most of the important uses of trigonometry today have little to do with triangles. Instead, the functions are defined for general angles, usually measured in radians. The easiest way to define the functions for a general angle is in terms of a *unit circle*, which is a circle of radius one unit centered at the origin of a coordinate plane. A general angle of any size, positive or negative, also has its vertex at the origin of the circle.

of the sides of a right triangle. Indeed, for every quadrant there is a triangle, called a *reference triangle*, that has a hypotenuse of one unit and sides that are sin θ and cos θ.

Quadrant 1   Quadrant II

Quadrant III   Quadrant IV

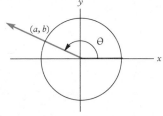

The terminal side of the angle meets the unit circle at the point labeled (a, b). Then, by definition,

$$\sin \theta = b \qquad \cos \theta = a \qquad \tan \theta = \frac{b}{a}$$

Therefore, it is also true that

$$\csc \theta = \frac{1}{b} \qquad \sec \theta = \frac{1}{a} \qquad \cot \theta = \frac{a}{b}$$

When θ is between 0° and 90°, the unit-circle definition gives the same values as the definition in terms

The coordinates of the point where the terminal side of the angle meets the unit circle are (cos θ, sin θ) for every angle θ. Therefore, in Quadrant I all the signs of the trigonometric functions are positive, but in Quadrant II the sine is positive and the cosine negative; in Quadrant III, both the sine and cosine are negative (but the tangent is positive); while in Quadrant IV the sine is negative, but the cosine positive.

Starting with the values of the trigonometric ratios for right triangles that are in the table on page 300, you can develop a table for the functions of the general angle.

Trigonometric graphs.
Graphs of the trigonometric functions generally use size of angles in radians as the horizontal axis and values of a trigonometric function as the vertical axis.

Periods and symmetry.
From the graphs, you can see that all trigonometric functions repeat their values at least every 2π or $360°$. Also, the tangent and cotangent repeat every π or $180°$. The distance between the repeated functional values is the *period* of the function. Thus, the period of the sine, cosine, secant, and cosecant functions is $360°$, or 2π radians, as can be seen in the box on page 306. The period of the tangent and cotangent functions is $180°$, or π radians.

The graphs can be extended to the left of the vertical axes to obtain values of the trigonometric functions for the negative numbers. For each function, the value of

Functions of a general angle

θ	$\sin\theta$	$\cos\theta$	$\tan\theta$	$\csc\theta$	$\sec\theta$	$\cot\theta$
$0°$	0	1	0	undef.	1	undef.
$\dfrac{\pi}{6}$	$\dfrac{1}{2}$	$\dfrac{\sqrt{3}}{2}$	$\dfrac{\sqrt{3}}{3}$	2	$\dfrac{2\sqrt{3}}{3}$	$\sqrt{3}$
$\dfrac{\pi}{4}$	$\dfrac{\sqrt{2}}{2}$	$\dfrac{\sqrt{2}}{2}$	1	$\sqrt{2}$	$\sqrt{2}$	1
$\dfrac{\pi}{3}$	$\dfrac{\sqrt{3}}{2}$	$\dfrac{1}{2}$	$\sqrt{3}$	$\dfrac{2\sqrt{3}}{3}$	2	$\dfrac{\sqrt{3}}{3}$
$\dfrac{\pi}{2}$	1	0	undef.	1	undef.	0
π	0	-1	0	undef.	-1	undef.
$\dfrac{3\pi}{2}$	-1	0	undef.	-1	undef.	0
2π	0	1	0	undef.	1	undef.

Graph $y = \sin x$.

A. If you have a calculator that gives the values of the trigonometric functions for angles measured in radians, you can use the calculator to plot the points.

B. Otherwise, just find the values in terms of radians. Start with the values that are in the table. For angles greater than $\frac{\pi}{2}$, use the reference triangles and the values in Quadrant I.

Quadrant II. Subtract angles from π to find the reference angles. For example, to find $\frac{3\pi}{4}$, think $\pi - \frac{3\pi}{4} = \frac{\pi}{4}$; therefore, the absolute values of the trigonometric functions are the same as those for $\frac{\pi}{4}$. Since the sine is positive in Quadrant II, $\sin\frac{3\pi}{4} = \frac{\sqrt{2}}{2}$

Quadrant III. Subtract π from the given angle to find the reference angle. For example, to find $\frac{7\pi}{6}$, use the reference angle $\frac{\pi}{6}$. But since the sine is negative in Quadrant III, $\sin\frac{7\pi}{6} = -\frac{1}{2}$.

Quadrant IV. Subtract the given angle from 2π to find the reference angle.

C. Plot a number of points. You will see that the graph repeats the same shape after reaching 2π.

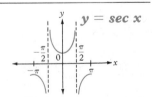

$y = \sin x$

The graphs of the other five trigonometric functions can be found by the same method.

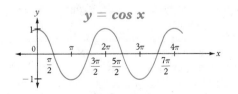

$y = \cos x$

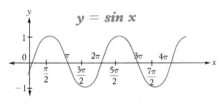

$y = \tan x$

$y = \sec x$

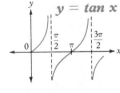

$y = \cot x$

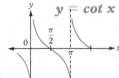

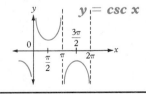

$y = \csc x$

Mathematics

the negative of an angle is either the same as the value of the angle or the opposite of that value. If it is the same, the function is an *even* function.

$$\cos 30° = \cos (-30°) = \sqrt{\tfrac{3}{2}}$$

illustrates that the cosine is an even function. If the value for the negative of an angle is the negative of the value for the angle, the function is *odd*. The sine is an odd function, so

$$\sin (-30°) = -\sin 30° = -\tfrac{1}{2}$$

Even functions, such as the cosine and secant, are symmetrical about the *y* axis. All other trigonometric functions are odd and symmetric about the origin.

Sinusoidal graphs.
One other relationship that is easily established from the graphs is that both the sine and cosine functions have maximum and minimum values. The maximum value of a periodic function is its *amplitude*, so the functions $y = \sin x$ and $y = \cos x$ have amplitudes of 1.

In general, $y = a \sin bx$ and $y = a \cos bx$ have the period $2\pi/b$ and amplitude a, where a and b are both positive. Consider, for example, the graphs of $y = 3/4 \sin 2x$ and $y = 3 \sin x/2$. The amplitude of the graph of $y = 3/4 \sin 2x$ is 3/4 and the period is π. For the graph of $y = 3 \sin x/2$, the amplitude is 3 and the period is 4π.

Graphs such as $y = a \sin bx$ and $y = a \cos bx$ are called *sinusoidal graphs* because they have the same general shape as a sine curve (the graph of $y = \sin x$). Here are two examples:

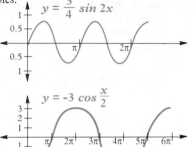

Inverse functions.
The *inverse trigonometric functions* can be indicated by writing "arc," as in $y = $ arc sin x, or by using a superscript of -1, as in $y = \sin^{-1} x$. Inverses are defined for *principal values* to keep them single valued.

If $x = \sin y$, then $y = \sin^{-1} x$, $-\pi/2 \le y \le \pi/2$
If $x = \cos y$, then $y = \cos^{-1} x$, $0 \le y \le \pi$
If $x = \tan y$, then $y = \tan^{-1} x$, $-\pi/2 \le y \le \pi/2$

Find *y* if $y = \sin^{-1} 0.5$.

The equation $y = \sin^{-1} 0.5$ means $y = $ the angle whose sine is 0.5.

Since $\sin 30°$ is ½, or 0.5, $y = 30°$.

In radians, $y = \pi/6$.

Find $\tan (\cos^{-1} \tfrac{4}{5})$.

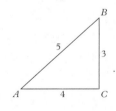

A. If $\cos x = \tfrac{4}{5}$, then a right triangle with angle *x* as one of its acute angles must be the 3-4-5 triangle.

B. Since the tangent ratio in that triangle is the side opposite over the side adjacent,

$$\tan (\cos^{-1} \tfrac{4}{5}) = \tfrac{3}{4}$$

Find the angle θ that a line makes with the *x* axis if the slope of the line is 0.6124.

A. The slope is the *y* distance over the *x* distance, which is also the tangent of the angle. Thus, $\tan \theta = 0.6124$.

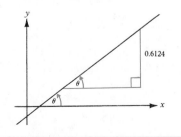

B. On many calculators, the inverse functions are indicated by an exponent of -1; for example, $\cos^{-1}$. This may be in small type and only reachable by using the "2nd function" button. To find the angle that has a tangent of 0.6124, enter that decimal, press the 2nd function key, and then the key labeled $\tan^{-1}$. The result on a ten-place calculator will be shown as 31.48330269 in degrees.

C. You can convert 31.48330269 to minutes and seconds by first finding 0.48330269 × 3600 to find the number of seconds, which is 1740 to the nearest second. Dividing by 60 gives 29 minutes and no remainder. Therefore, the angle is 31° 29′.

Trigonometric identities.

If a statement involving the relationship of trigonometric functions of the same angle is true for *all* defined values of that angle, then the statement is called an *identity*. Many common identities are shown in the box on this page. The fundamental identities can be discovered from the definition of the functions or with the use of the Pythagorean theorem. Other identities are then proved on the basis of the reciprocal relationships or the fundamental identities.

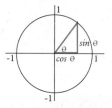

The most useful identity comes from directly applying the Pythagorean theorem to the unit-circle definition. Since the sides of the triangle are $\sin\theta$ and $\cos\theta$ while the hypotenuse is 1, the basic formula becomes $\sin^2\theta + \cos^2\theta = 1^2 = 1$. Other versions of this formula can be found by dividing this formula by either $\sin^2\theta$ or by $\cos^2\theta$.

Proving trigonometric identities. Proving an identity is the process of verifying that a statement is true for all defined values of an angle by using algebraic factoring and simplification and by substitution of the fundamental identities. Either transform one side of the identity into the other or reduce both sides to an expression in which it is obvious that all the defined values are true. You can operate on both sides of an equation simultaneously as long as the operation is reversible and yields an equation with the same solution.

Trigonometric identities

Reciprocal relations

$$\sin\theta = \frac{1}{\csc\theta} \qquad \cos\theta = \frac{1}{\sec\theta} \qquad \tan\theta = \frac{1}{\cot\theta}$$

$$\csc\theta = \frac{1}{\sin\theta} \qquad \sec\theta = \frac{1}{\cos\theta} \qquad \cot\theta = \frac{1}{\tan\theta}$$

Complementary cofunctions

$$\sin\theta = \cos(90° - \theta) \qquad \tan\theta = \cot(90° - \theta) \qquad \sec\theta = \csc(90° - \theta)$$
$$\text{where } 0° < \theta < 90°$$

Periodic relations

$$\sin(\theta + n360°) = \sin\theta \qquad \tan(\theta + n360°) = \tan\theta \qquad \sec(\theta + n360°) = \sec\theta$$
$$\cos(\theta + n360°) = \cos\theta \qquad \tan(\theta + n180°) = \tan\theta \qquad \csc(\theta + n360°) = \csc\theta$$
$$\cot(\theta + n360°) = \cot\theta$$
$$\cot(\theta + n180°) = \cot\theta$$

Negative angles

$$\sin(-\theta) = -\sin\theta \qquad \cos(-\theta) = \cos\theta \qquad \tan(-\theta) = -\tan\theta$$
$$\csc(-\theta) = -\csc\theta \qquad \sec(-\theta) = \sec\theta \qquad \cot(-\theta) = -\cot\theta$$

Fundamental identities

$$\tan\theta = \frac{\sin\theta}{\cos\theta} \qquad \cot\theta = \frac{\cos\theta}{\sin\theta}$$

$$\sin\theta = \tan\theta\cos\theta \qquad \cos\theta = \cot\theta\sin\theta$$
$$\sin^2\theta + \cos^2\theta = 1 \qquad 1 - \sin^2\theta = \cos^2\theta$$
$$\sec^2\theta - \tan^2\theta = 1 \qquad 1 + \tan^2\theta = \sec^2\theta$$
$$\csc^2\theta - \cot^2\theta = 1 \qquad 1 + \cot^2\theta = \csc^2\theta$$

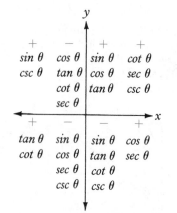

Mathematics

Resolving triangles

Trigonometry has many applications in science and engineering as well as in pure mathematics and map making. For example, to study a force of r in a direction θ, such as up an inclined plane, the force is resolved into horizontal and vertical components, which are $r \cos \theta$ and $r \sin \theta$.

Verify the identity $\sin \theta \, (1 + \cot^2 \theta) = \csc \theta.$

METHOD 1

A. Note the $\cot^2 \theta$ means $(\cot \theta)^2$. One useful way to solve identities is to change both sides to sines and cosines. For example, every trigonometric function can be expressed in terms of sines.

$$\sin \theta = \sin \theta$$

$$\cos \theta = \pm\sqrt{1 - \sin^2 \theta}$$

$$\tan \theta = \frac{\pm \sin \theta}{\sqrt{1 - \sin^2 \theta}}$$

$$\cot \theta = \frac{\pm\sqrt{1 - \sin^2 \theta}}{\sin \theta}$$

$$\sec \theta = \frac{\pm 1}{\sqrt{1 - \sin^2 \theta}}$$

$$\csc \theta = \frac{1}{\sin \theta}$$

The appropriate $\pm$ sign is used according to the quadrant of the angle. Try to change each side of the identity to functions of $\sin \theta$.

B. $\sin \theta \, (1 + \cot^2 \theta) = \csc \theta$
$\sin \theta \, (\csc^2 \theta) = \csc \theta$

$$\sin \theta \, \frac{1}{\sin^2} = \frac{1}{\sin \theta}$$

$$\frac{1}{\sin \theta} = \frac{1}{\sin \theta}$$

METHOD 2

A. Multiply both sides of the identity by $\csc \theta$.
$\csc \theta \, (\sin \theta \, (1 + \cot^2 \theta)) =$
$\csc \theta \, (\csc \theta)$

B. Then use algebra and the fundamental identities to transform the left side of the equation to match the right.

$\csc \theta \, (\sin \theta \, (1 + \cot^2 \theta)) = \csc^2 \theta$
$(\csc \theta \sin \theta) \, (1 + \cot^2 \theta) =$
$1 + \cot^2 \theta =$
$\csc^2 \theta = \csc^2 \theta$

Verify the identity $\dfrac{\sin x + \tan x}{\cot x + \csc x} = \sin x \tan x.$

$$\frac{\sin x + \tan x}{\cot x + \csc x} = \sin x \tan x$$

$$\frac{\sin x + \dfrac{\sin x}{\cos x}}{\dfrac{\cos x}{\sin x} + \dfrac{1}{\sin x}} = \sin x \frac{\sin x}{\cos x}$$

$$\frac{\sin x \cos x + \sin x}{\cos x} \div \frac{\cos x + 1}{\sin x} = \frac{\sin^2 x}{\cos x}$$

$$\frac{\sin x (\cos x + 1)}{\cos x} \cdot \frac{\sin x}{\cos x + 1} = \frac{\sin^2 x}{\cos x}$$

$$\frac{\sin^2 x}{\cos x} = \frac{\sin^2 x}{\cos x}$$

Solving trigonometric
equations. Identities are true for all values of the variable, just as $x + 2 = 2 + x$. Falsehoods are true for no values of the variable, such as $x + 2 = 3 + x$. Many equations of interest are true for some values of the variable, but not others, such as $2x + 1 = 1 + 3x$, which is true when x is 0 but otherwise false. Equations such as the last are called *conditional equations*.

Just as there are trigonometric identities, there are also conditional trigonometric equations. Conditional trigonometric equations, usually just called *trigonometric equations*, are statements about trigonometric functions that are true for some values of a variable, but not others. While a trigonometric identity must be proven, a trigonometric equation must be solved.

$$\text{Solve } \cos x = \frac{1}{2}.$$

A. Although this is a simple equation, it has many solutions. Trigonometric equations are usually solved in radians, so use the table on page 304 to find the first solution. $x = \frac{\pi}{3}$ is the first solution, because $\cos \frac{\pi}{3} = \frac{1}{2}$.

B. A sketch of the unit circle shows that there are two quadrants in which $\cos x = \frac{1}{2}$.

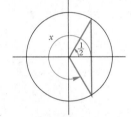

Both Quadrant I and Quadrant IV have positive values of the cosine function. So another value of x that makes the equation true is
$$2\pi - \frac{\pi}{3} = \frac{5\pi}{3}$$

C. The two values found so far are not the whole story. Since the period of the cosine function is 2π, adding any multiple of 2π to the solutions will produce additional correct solutions. This is expressed by using the variable n to represent any integer. Thus, the complete solutions to $\cos x = \frac{1}{2}$ are
$$x = \frac{\pi}{3} + 2n\pi, \frac{5\pi}{3} + 2n\pi$$

$$\text{Solve } 2 \sin^2 x - 3 \sin x - 2 = 0.$$

A. To solve, first treat $\sin x$ as the variable. Seen this way, the equation is a quadratic equation in $\sin x$, and it can be solved by factoring.
$2 \sin^2 x - 3 \sin x - 2 = 0$
$(2 \sin x + 1)(\sin x - 2) = 0$
$2 \sin x + 1 = 0$ *or* $\sin x - 2 = 0$
$2 \sin x = -1$ *or* $\sin x = 2$
$\sin x = -\frac{1}{2}$ *or* $\sin x = 2$

B. Now solve for x. It should be apparent that $\sin x = 2$ is always false, since the range of the sin function is from -1 to $+1$. Therefore, the only solutions will be for $\sin x = -\frac{1}{2}$.

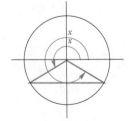

The two main solutions are in Quadrant III and Quadrant IV, where the value of the sine function is negative. If there had been a solution in Quadrant I, it could be found from the table to be $\frac{\pi}{6}$. Thus, in Quadrant III the main solution is $x = \pi + \frac{\pi}{6} = \frac{7\pi}{6}$ and in Quadrant IV the main solution is $x = 2\pi - \frac{\pi}{6} = \frac{11\pi}{6}$.

C. The complete solution is
$$x = \frac{7\pi}{6} + 2n\pi, \frac{11\pi}{6} + 2n\pi$$

Solve $\tan^2 x - \sec x - 1 = 0$.

A. To solve a trigonometric function, the equation must be written in terms of a single function. The Pythagorean identity $1 + \tan^2 \theta = \sec^2 \theta$ can be used in the form
$$\tan^2 x = \sec^2 x - 1$$
to rewrite the equation using only the secant function. The equation to be solved becomes $(\sec^2 x - 1) - \sec x - 1 = 0$, or $\sec^2 x - \sec x - 2 = 0$. This factors as $(\sec x - 2)(\sec x + 1) = 0$, so $\sec x = 2$ *or* $\sec x = -1$.

B. Since the secant is the reciprocal of the cosine, it, like the cosine, has positive values in Quadrants I and IV and negative values in Quadrants II and III. From the table on page 304, $\sec \frac{\pi}{3} = 2$ and $\sec \pi = -1$. In Quadrant IV, the angle with a reference angle of $\frac{\pi}{3}$ is found by subtracting $\frac{\pi}{3}$ from 2π, which gives $\frac{5\pi}{3}$. Thus, two of the main values are
$$x = \tfrac{\pi}{3} \text{ and } x = \tfrac{5\pi}{3}.$$

C. Sec $\pi = -1$ because $\cos \pi = -1$. But there is only one place on the unit circle where the

cosine, corresponding to the x coordinate of a point on the circle, is -1.

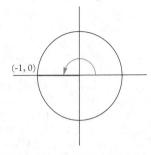

Therefore, the only x that makes $\sec x = -1$ true is π. The full set of values in the solution is $x = \frac{\pi}{3} + 2n\pi, \pi + 2n\pi, \frac{5\pi}{3} + 2n\pi$.

Solve the equation $\tan 2x = \sqrt{3}$.

A. First solve for $2x$. Then divide by 2 to find x. From the table, $\tan \frac{\pi}{6} = \sqrt{3}$. Note that the period of the tangent function is π, not 2π. From a unit-circle diagram, it is apparent that $\frac{\pi}{6} + n\pi$ includes all the values of $2x$.

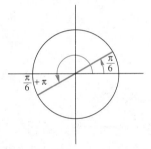

B. Complete the solution by dividing $2x = \frac{\pi}{6} + n\pi$ by 2 to get $x = \frac{\pi}{12} + \frac{n\pi}{2}$.

Solve the equation $4 \sin x \cos x = -\sqrt{2}$.

A. Use the double-angle formula from the table on page 310 to rewrite the equation in terms of a single trigonometric function.
$$\sin 2A = 2 \sin A \cos A$$
Substituting in
$$4 \sin x \cos x = -\sqrt{2}$$
produces
$$2 \sin 2x = -\sqrt{2}$$

B. Now the strategy is to solve for $\sin 2x$; use that solution to find $2x$, and then divide by 2 to find x.
$$\sin 2x = -\tfrac{\sqrt{2}}{2}$$
The sine is negative in Quadrants III and IV. From the table, $\sin \frac{\pi}{4} = \frac{\sqrt{2}}{2}$, so the reference angle is $\frac{\pi}{4}$.

C. The angles in Quadrants III and IV that have $\frac{\pi}{4}$ as a reference angle are $\pi + \frac{\pi}{4}$ and $2\pi - \frac{\pi}{4}$, or $\frac{5\pi}{4}$ and $\frac{7\pi}{4}$. Therefore,
$$2x = \tfrac{5\pi}{4} + 2n\pi, \tfrac{7\pi}{4} + 2n$$
Divide by 2 to find x.
$$x = \tfrac{5\pi}{8} + n\pi, \tfrac{7\pi}{8} + n\pi$$

Oblique triangles. Trigonometric functions are usually thought of in terms of right triangles, but they can be used to find unknown parts of any triangle. A triangle with no right angle is called *oblique*. The formulas on page 310 apply to all triangles, not just oblique or right triangles.

Solving triangles. In geometry it is shown that three parts often determine a triangle completely. For example, any two triangles with three sides that are the same length in each will also have three angles that are the same. This is expressed as "two triangles are congruent if three sides of one are congruent to three sides of the other" and often abbreviated as *sss = sss.* Similarly, the theorem *asa = asa* means the two triangles are congruent if two angles and the included side are congruent.

Solving a triangle means finding all six parts of the triangle—the measures of three angles and three sides—when only three of them are known. The congruence theorems from geometry show that this is possible in such cases as *sss = sss, asa = asa,* or *sas = sas.* However, a triangle cannot be solved for some combinations, such as just three angles.

The key rules for solving triangles can be easily found by examining triangles placed so that one vertex is at the origin of a coordinate system and one side lies along the positive *x* axis, as in these two examples.

The Pythagorean theorem or the distance formula can be used to find some lengths from these diagrams in terms of the others. For either triangle,

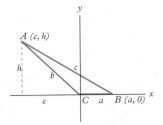

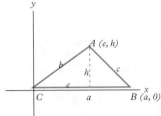

$$b^2 = e^2 + h^2$$
$$c^2 = (e - a)^2 + (h - 0)^2 = e^2 - 2ae + a^2 + h^2$$
$$= a^2 + (e^2 + h^2) - 2ae$$

Trigonometric formulas

Sums and differences of angles
$$\sin (A + B) = \sin A \cos B + \cos A \sin B$$
$$\cos (A + B) = \cos A \cos B - \sin A \sin B$$
$$\tan (A + B) = \frac{\tan A + \tan B}{1 - \tan A \tan B}$$
$$\sin (A - B) = \sin A \cos B - \cos A \sin B$$
$$\cos (A - B) = \cos A \cos B + \sin A \sin B$$

Double angles
$$\sin 2A = 2 \sin A \cos A$$
$$\cos 2A = \cos^2 A - \sin^2 A$$
$$\tan 2A = \frac{2 \tan A}{1 - \tan^2 A}$$

Half angles
$$\sin \frac{A}{2} = \sqrt{\frac{1 - \cos A}{2}}$$
$$\cos \frac{A}{2} = \sqrt{\frac{1 + \cos A}{2}}$$
$$\tan \frac{A}{2} = \sqrt{\frac{1 - \cos A}{1 + \cos A}}$$

If a triangle *ABC* has sides whose lengths are *a*, *b*, and *c*, with *a* opposite $\angle A$, *b* opposite $\angle B$, and *c* opposite $\angle C$, then

Law of cosines
$$a^2 = b^2 + c^2 - 2bc \cos A$$
$$b^2 = a^2 + c^2 - 2ac \cos B$$
$$c^2 = a^2 + b^2 - 2ab \cos C$$
$$\cos A = \frac{b^2 + c^2 - a^2}{2bc}$$
$$\cos B = \frac{c^2 + a^2 - b^2}{2ac}$$
$$\cos C = \frac{a^2 + b^2 - c^2}{2ab}$$

Law of sines
$$\frac{a}{\sin A} = \frac{b}{\sin B} = \frac{c}{\sin C}$$

Area of triangle

Area $ABC = \frac{1}{2} ab \sin C$

If $s = \frac{1}{2}(a + b + c)$, then

$$\text{Area } ABC = \sqrt{s(s - a)(s - b)(s - c)}$$

(Hero's formula)

From trigonometry, however, $\cos C = \frac{e}{b}$, or $e = b \cos C$. Substituting for e and for $(e^2 + h^2)$ in the expression for c^2 gives one form of the law of cosines.

$$c^2 = a^2 + b^2 - 2ab \cos C$$

By putting each of the other vertices of the triangles at the origin, the law of cosines can be expressed in two different forms. Similarly, all three of those forms can also be solved for the cosine of the angle involved. All six versions of the law of cosines are in the box on page 310.

The same diagrams can also be used to find the law of sines. Note that $\sin C = \frac{h}{b}$, so $h = b \sin C$. Similarly, $h = c \sin B$. Therefore, $b \sin C = c \sin B$, which is rewritten as

$$\frac{b}{\sin B} = \frac{c}{\sin C}$$

The same reasoning can be used with the vertex A at the origin and combined with the previous result to become the full law of sines.

$$\frac{a}{\sin A} = \frac{b}{\sin B} = \frac{c}{\sin C}$$

If a triangle can be solved, either the law of cosines or the law of sines can be used to solve it—but only one of the two. For example, the law of cosines can be used when *sss* or *sas* is known, but the law of sines must be used for *asa*. In some cases, there are two different triangles that can result from applying the law of sines.

In addition to the laws of cosines and sines, there are other formulas derived easily from trigonometry that apply to all triangles, oblique or right. These formulas are shown in the box on page 310.

Solving triangles

Two observation posts, A and B, spot the flash of an enemy gun, G, at angles of 40° and 76° respectively. Posts A and B are 3 kilometers apart. Find the distance, BG, to the gun from post B.

A. Note that the angle AGB must be 64°.

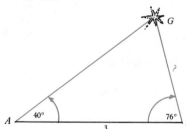

B. Use the law of sines to get
$$\frac{BG}{\sin 40°} = \frac{3}{\sin 64°}$$

C. $BG = 3\dfrac{\sin 40°}{\sin 64°}$

$= $ about $3\dfrac{0.6428}{0.8988}$

$= $ about 2.15

The distance is 2.15 kilometers to the nearest hundredth of a kilometer.

A ship sails from port P on a bearing of N35°E at a rate of 12 kilometers per hour. In what length of time will the ship be 10 kilometers from a lighthouse that is 5 kilometers due west from the port?

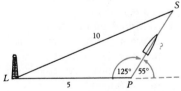

A. The heading of N35°E means that angle LPS is 125°. Use the law of cosines.

B. $\cos 125° = -\cos 55°$
From a table, $-\cos 55°$ is about -0.5736.

C. Using the law of cosines,
$LS^2 = LP^2 + PS^2 - (LP)(PS) \cos P$
$10^2 = 5^2 + PS^2 - 2(5)(PS)(-0.5736)$
$PS^2 + 5.736\ PS - 75 = 0$

D. The quadratic formula gives two solutions, approximately $PS = 6.2$ or $PS = -11.9$, so PS is about 6.2.

E. This means that the ship will take about $(6.2)/12$, or 0.52 hours to reach the designated location.

hexagon

Dictionary of mathematics

octagon

pentagon

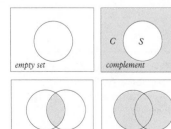

empty set

complement

intersection

union

sets

abscissa. Directed distance of a point from the *y* axis. In a pair of coordinates, the first member.

acute. An angle with a measure of less than 90° or a triangle with three acute angles.

addend. Any one of the numbers to be added to form a sum.

additive identity element. A number *z* such that for any number in a set, *z* added to it gives the original number. For the real numbers, the additive identity element is 0.

additive inverse. A number that can be added to another number to produce the additive identity element is the additive inverse of the second number. For the real numbers, the additive inverse of *x* is $-x$, because $x + (-x) = 0$, and 0 is the additive identity element.

amplitude. For a trigonometric function, the largest value of the function.

angle. Union of two rays with a common endpoint.

arc cosine. The inverse of the cosine function; that is, the angle that has a particular value of the cosine. Abbreviated either arc cos or cos^{-1}.

arc sine. The inverse of the sine function; that is, the angle that has a particular value of the sine. Abbreviated either arc sin or sin^{-1}.

arc tangent. The inverse of the tangent function; that is, the angle that has a particular value of the tangent. Abbreviated either arc tan or tan^{-1}.

arithmetic mean. The average; that is, the quotient formed when the numbers in a set are added and then divided by the number of numbers in the set.

arithmetic sequence. Sequence formed by adding the same amount to a given number over and over.

arithmetic series. Series formed as the indicated sum of an arithmetic sequence.

associative law. When three numbers are added (or multiplied), the sum (product) is the same when the sum (product) of the last two numbers is added to (multiplied by) the first as when the sum (product) of the first two numbers is added to (multiplied by) the last.

average. The arithmetic mean.

axiom. A statement that is accepted without proof and then used as the basis of a system of proofs.

base. Number raised to a power by an exponent.

binomial. Polynomial that has two terms.

bisect. Separate into two congruent parts.

circle. The figure in a plane all of whose points are equidistant from a point in the plane; the point is the *center* of the circle.

commutative law. When two numbers are added (or multiplied), the sum (product) is the same no matter which order they are added (multiplied) in.

complement. For sets, the elements of a set with respect to another set that are not included in the first set.

complex number. A number that is the sum of a real number and an imaginary number.

composite number. For natural numbers, a number that has factors other than itself and 1; any natural number except 1 that is not prime.

conditional equation. Any equation that is true for some values of the variable(s) and false for others. In trigonometry, a conditional equation involving one or more trigonometric functions is called a *trigonometric equation*.

constant. In algebra, a quantity that does not vary in a given situation.

coordinate plane. A set of points that can be located by

Mathematics

two numbers in an ordered pair. Most often the coordinate plane is determined by two intersecting perpendicular lines, commonly the x axis and the y axis.

cosecant. A trigonometric function that is defined as the distance of a point on a particular ray from the origin divided by the ordinate of the point on the ray. It is a constant for the angle that the ray makes with the positive horizontal axis.

cosine. A trigonometric function that is defined as the abscissa of a point on a particular ray from the origin divided by the distance of that point from the origin. It is a constant for the angle that the ray makes with the positive horizontal axis.

cotangent. A trigonometric function that is defined as the abscissa of a point on a particular ray divided by the ordinate of the point. It is a constant for the angle that the ray makes with the positive horizontal axis.

counting number. Natural number.

cross-product rule. In a proportion, the rule that the product of the numerator of one ratio with the denominator of the other ratio is always equal to the product of the denominator of the first ratio with the numerator of the second ratio.

cube. In geometry, a figure in three dimensions that has six congruent squares as faces.

denominator. In a fraction, the number that tells the number of parts into which something has been divided.

dependent system of equations. System in two or more variables in which each equation has the same solution.

dependent variable. The variable that represents the value of the function.

difference. The answer in subtraction, sometimes also called the *remainder*.

distributive law. The product of a number and a sum is equal to the sum of the product of the number with each of the addends.

dividend. In division, the number into which you divide.

divisor. In division, the number that you divide by.

element. A member of a set.

empty set. A set that is a subset of every set and that contains no members; often symbolized by $\varnothing$.

equilateral. For a triangle, having all sides congruent.

event. In probability, a set or sentence that describes the outcomes that will be considered successful.

exponent. A small numeral (superscript) written above and to the right of a number or variable. Exponents that represent natural numbers tell how many times the number or variable is used as a factor. Zero, negative, and real exponents are defined to be consistent with the meaning of natural-number exponents.

factor. In multiplication, any one of the numbers to be multiplied to form a product. When used as a verb, *factor* means to find the factors that can be used to form a given number or algebraic expression.

function. A rule that connects two sets of numbers in such a way that a member of the second set is completely specified by choosing a member of the first set.

geometric mean. For two numbers, the positive square root of their product.

geometric sequence. Sequence formed by multiplying a given number by the same factor over and over.

geometric series. Indicated sum of a geometric sequence.

greatest common factor. Largest factor that is common to two or more numbers.

harmonic mean. For two numbers, the multiplicative inverse of the mean (average) of their multiplicative inverses.

harmonic sequence. A sequence formed by the multiplicative inverses of the terms of an arithmetic sequence.

harmonic series. Indicated sum of a harmonic sequence.

heptagon. Seven-sided polygon.

hexagon. Polygon with six sides.

i. Symbol used to denote the square root of -1; when multiplied by any real number (except 0), it forms an imaginary number.

identity. Any equation that is true for all values of the variable or variables.

imaginary number. The product of any real number (except 0) and i, the square root of -1.

inconsistent system of equations. System of equations with no solution to the system.

independent variable. For a function, the variable over which the function is defined; that is, the variable representing the set that is the domain of the function.

inequality. Sentence containing one of the following relations: greater than, less than, not equal, greater than or equal, less than or equal.

infinite sequence. Sequence for which the domain is the entire set of natural numbers.

infinite series. Indicated sum of an infinite sequence.

infinity. Various related mathematical ideas, of which the most common is an indication that a sequence of numbers continues indefinitely. Also indicates size of a set that can be matched with all the natural rumbers or all the real numbers.

integer. Number that is either whole or the negative of a whole.

intercept. For graphs, either the point at which the graph crosses one of the axes or the distance of that point from the origin.

intersection. For sets, the set that contains all the members common to two or more sets.

inverse function. A function formed by interchanging the two variables, such as x and y. In general the inverse of a function $f(x)$ is labeled as $f^1(x)$, although inverse trigonometric functions are more commonly indicated by the prefix *arc*, as in arc sin x.

inverse operation. An operation that undoes the effect of a given operation; for example, addition is the inverse of subtraction.

irrational number. Real number that is not also a rational number.

isosceles. A triangle that has two congruent sides.

kite. Polygon that has two pairs of adjacent congruent sides.

least common denominator. Least common multiple of the denominators of a set of fractions.

least common multiple. Smallest nonzero number that is a multiple of all numbers in a set of numbers.

mean proportional. A number that is both the denominator of one ratio and the numerator of the other.

member. For sets or for ordered pairs, one of the individual parts of the set or pair.

minuend. The number from which another number is subtracted; the top number in the vertical way of writing a subtraction problem.

monomial. Product of a number and one or more variables.

multiple. Product of a given number and a whole number.

multiplicative identity element. A number I such that for any number in a set, I times the number gives the original number. For real numbers, the element is 1.

multiplicative inverse. Number such that the product of that number and a given number is 1.

natural number. Number that is 1 or formed by starting with 1 and adding one more each time.

negative number. Number to the left of 0 on the number line.

null set. Set with no members; the empty set.

numerator. The number of parts represented by a fraction.

oblique. A triangle that does not contain a right angle.

obtuse. An angle greater than 90° and less than 180°.

octagon. Eight-sided polygon.

opposite. Number that is equal in value but opposite in sign to a given number.

ordinate. For a point in the coordinate plane, the directed distance from the x axis; the second member of the coordinates of the points.

outcome. In probability, the result of a trial.

parallel. Two lines that do not meet.

parallelogram. Quadrilateral for which both pairs of opposite sides are parallel.

pentagon. Five-sided polygon.

percent. Ratio of some number to 100.

percentage. Percent of a number.

period. For trigonometric functions, the size of the interval before the values of the function begin to repeat exactly. For trigonometric functions other than the tangent and contangent, the period is 360°, or 2π, but for the tangent and cotangent it is 180°, or π.

perpendicular. For lines or line segments, two lines (segments) that meet at right angles.

pi. A Greek letter. Its lower-case form, π, is used for the ratio of the circumference of a circle to its diameter. Although pi cannot be expressed exactly as a decimal, it is 3.14159 to six decimal places.

plane. Flat surface extending infinitely in all directions.

point of inflection. A point at which a curve changes from being convex to concave.

polygon. A closed plane figure formed by three or more points linked in pairs by line segments that do not cross each other.

polynomial. A monomial or the sum of any finite number of monomials.

positive number. Number to the right of 0 on the number line.

power. The result when a number is used as a factor a number of times.

prime. For natural numbers, a number that has only itself and 1 as factors.

probability. Number that describes the chance that a given event will take place.

product. The answer in multiplication.

proportion. Statement that two ratios are equal.

Pythagorean theorem. For right triangles, the statement that the area of a square that has one side on the side of the triangle opposite the right angle is equal to the sum of the areas of the squares on the other two sides of the triangle.

quadrant. On the coordinate plane, one of the four regions into which the plane is separated by the axes.

quadratic equation. An equation in one variable for which the highest power of the variable is the second and all the powers of the variable are whole numbers.

quadrilateral. Four-sided polygon.

quotient. In division, the answer.

radian measure. System for measuring general angles based on a unit defined so that π radians is a straight angle, or 180°.

radical. Sign used to indicate that a square root of a number (or, combined with an index, another root of the number) is to be taken.

radicand. Number or expression under a radical.

ratio. Comparison of two quantities by division.

rational number. The ratio of an integer to a natural number.

real number. Any number that can be represented by an infinite decimal.

reciprocal. For a given number, the number formed by dividing the given number into 1.

rectangle. Parallelogram that contains a right angle.

relation. Any rule connecting the members of two sets.

relative maximum. Greatest value of a function in an interval.

relative minimum. Least value of a function in an interval.

rhombus. Parallelogram with adjacent sides congruent.

right angle. Angle that measures 90° or $\frac{\pi}{2}$ radians.

right triangle. Triangle that contains a right angle.

root. A number such that the product of the number repeated two or more times is a given number.

sample space. In probability, the set of all outcomes of a given experiment.

scalene. Triangle in which no two sides are equal.

secant. (1) A trigonometric function that is defined as the distance of a point on a particular ray from the origin divided by the abscissa of the point on the ray. It is a constant for the angle that the ray makes with the horizontal axis. (2) A line that intersects a circle in two points.

sequence. Ordered values of a function over the natural numbers.

series. Indicated sum of a sequence.

set. Any collection of objects or ideas such that you can tell whether a given object or idea is a member of the collection.

signed number. Number written with a positive or negative sign.

similar figures. Geometric figures that have the same shape but not necessarily the same size.

sine. A trigonometric function that is defined as the ordinate of a point on a particular ray from the origin divided by the distance of that point from the origin. It is a constant for the angle that the ray makes with the positive horizontal axis.

slope. The quotient of rate of change of the ordinates on a line divided by the rate of change of the abscissas.

solution. In algebra, an equation that states the value of a variable that will make another given equation true.

square. A rhombus with four right angles.

straight angle. Angle that measures 180° or π radians.

subtrahend. The number that is subtracted from another number; the lower number in a subtraction problem written vertically.

sum. The answer in addition.

system of equations. Set of two or more equations in two or more variables to be solved for the intersection of the solutions of the equations in the set.

tangent. (1) Trigonometric function that is defined as the ordinate of a point on a particular ray divided by the abscissa of that point. It is a constant for the angle that the ray makes with the positive horizontal axis. (2) A line that intersects a circle at one and only one point.

tetrahedron. Four-sided solid whose faces are all triangles.

theorem. Statement that has been derived from a set of axioms according to the rules of logic.

triangle. Three-sided polygon.

trigonometric function. Function whose independent variable is an angle and whose value is defined as a quotient of one pair from the following: abscissa ordinate distance from origin of a point on a ray that makes the given angle with the positive x axis.

trinomial. Polynomial that has three terms.

union. For two sets, the set that contains all the members of both sets.

variable. Letter or other symbol that can represent any one of a specified set of numbers.

vertical angles. Two angles formed by intersecting lines so that the angles do not have a ray in common.

For Further Reference

Costello, Matthew J.
The Greatest Puzzles of All Time
Prentice-Hall Press
Dunham, William
Journey through Genius: the Great Theorems of Mathematics
John Wiley and Sons, Inc.

Pappas, Theoni
The Joy of Mathematics
WideWorld Publishing/Tetra
Paulos, John Allen
Innumeracy: Mathematical Illiteracy and its Consequences
Hill and Wang

English and

Literature

Writing a Research Paper

Although most students groan when research papers are assigned, writing a term report can be stimulating, particularly if you choose a topic that interests you. A good research paper integrates the use of information gathered from various sources with your own ideas. It demonstrates your ability to think and write clearly, as well as your skill in using the library and ingenuity in finding other sources of information.

Writing a research paper is in itself a way of learning, not only about the particular topic you are investigating, but also about the process of investigation itself. You must become a kind of detective to find the facts and theories needed to come to an informed conclusion. Putting information gathered together with personal ideas is the way all investigators solve mysteries. Unlike crimes, however, research topics may have more than one possible conclusion.

In writing a good paper, you learn how to argue your point—fairly, yet persuasively. Furthermore, as you research your topic, you become an expert on it. Very few people will know more about your subject than you will after you have completed your investigation.

There are two common misconceptions about the research paper: 1) that it is a collection of strung-together quotations and paraphrases from published sources with a lot of footnotes attached so no one can accuse you of plagiarism, or 2) that it is a collection of your uninformed opinions about a topic. In reality, a research paper is a combination of the two concepts—your informed opinions and ideas based on your investigation of published, and occasionally unpublished, information.

In this section you will learn how to pick a good topic, how to find and take notes on the information you need, how to put that information and your own ideas together in logical order, and how to write the paper in an accepted manner, using the correct form for footnotes and bibliography.

Choosing a topic

The first task is choosing a suitable topic, one that interests you and on which there is enough information available. Your teacher may assign or recommend a broad subject. You are not expected to write a report on the whole subject, but to choose an aspect of it that particularly interests you. In order to do so, it is a good idea to read some general articles on the subject, such as those found in an encyclopedia. They will provide you with an overview of the subject. In the course of your reading, you will come across sections that interest you more than others. This will help you pinpoint the aspect of the subject on which you would most like to write.

Once you have a possible topic, determine whether enough research material exists on your topic. Start with the encyclopedia articles you have read. Most such articles include a *bibliography*—a list of books and authors, usually the most important works in the field. Another way to check for research material is to consult the catalog of your library (see below, page 320). If too little information is available, you will save yourself wasted effort by choosing another, more accessible topic or, if possible, by broadening the topic. You must also be careful not to choose a topic on which there is too much information. If the topic you have chosen is so well covered that you do not know where to begin, narrow it further or choose another topic.

To narrow down a topic you must move from the general to the specific. For example, if you have been studying Greek, Egyptian, and Anglo-Saxon societies, a subject such as comparing attitudes toward death could require a book, not a paper. A comparison of burial rites in those societies may be a more workable topic. If, on the other hand, you are too specific, choosing to write only about burial rites in Anglo-Saxon societies, your paper may turn out to be only three pages long.

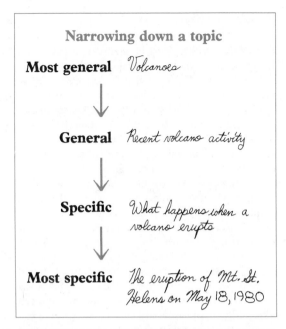

Using the library

Kinds of libraries. Most of the research you do will be conducted in a library, so it is a good idea to know how to use one. There are four basic types of libraries—circulating, reference, technical, and government depository.

Circulating libraries. These are the libraries with which you are probably most familiar. They lend books to all kinds of readers, young and old, scholars, students, and sunbathers. You are usually allowed to borrow books from circulating libraries for two to four weeks.

Reference libraries. These are places where students and scholars work. Reference libraries often have old, valuable books with essential information. Because of their fragile condition or rarity, these books usually cannot be borrowed, and one must be careful using them.

Technical libraries. These libraries are devoted to specialized fields, such as engineering, medicine, or science. Hospitals, for example, may have extensive medical libraries. You may need special permission to use such libraries.

Government depository libraries. Located in major cities throughout the United States, these libraries contain government publications and other printed material pertinent to government. You may find copies of the *Federal Register*, the daily *Congressional Record*, House and Senate *Calendars*, the *Weekly Compilation of Presidential Documents, Commerce Business Daily*, and many pamphlets put out by the Government Printing Office. Such pamphlets cover subjects from how to make toys out of junk to how to pump gas.

Much government material is available in general libraries. Larger libraries may have *The Index of Monthly Catalogues of U.S. Government Publications*, a complete listing of documents available. Otherwise, ask the reference librarian for help in locating government publications. *Government Publications and Their Use* by Laurence F. Schmeckebier and Roy B. Eastin is the best guide to what the government prints and how to obtain copies. Some large cities have government bookstores that sell publications printed by the government. Also, the vertical files of your circulating library may have useful pamphlets (see page 324).

All libraries are staffed by trained reference librarians who are experts in locating source material on any subject. Their purpose is to help you, as a user of the library, and you should never hesitate to ask them questions.

To obtain a price list of government pamphlets and other publications, write to

U.S. Government Printing Office
Superintendent of Documents
Washington, D.C. 20003

Book catalogs.

There are many catalogs to help you find information.

The card catalog. Most libraries use an index card filing system called the card catalog; it tells you where to locate books. Cards are usually arranged in three separate ways—by title, author, and subject. It is easiest to locate a book by its title or author, but sometimes you do not have the necessary information. For example, when you are doing preliminary research on a topic, you will initially look under different subject headings—there may be more than one that is relevant to your topic—to see how much material is available. For example, to research a paper on burial rites in Egyptian, Greek, and Anglo-Saxon societies, you might look under the following subject headings: *funerary rites, death, cremation, interment, water burial, Egypt, Greece, Anglo-Saxon society, ancient religion.*

Call numbers. A book's call number is usually found in the upper left-hand corner of the card. This is the key to its location in the library. All books are arranged numerically or alphabetically on shelves, with the call numbers on their spines matching those in the card catalog. The call number for each book is not chosen at random. The numbers or letters indicate book categories. In this way, all books pertaining to American history are grouped together, as are books on literature, science, art, etc. As long as you know the call number of the book you need, either you or the librarian will be able to find it.

Stacks and call slips. Many libraries allow you to go through their stacks, which are the open shelves of books arranged by their call numbers. Because books are arranged by categories, you may find books pertinent to your paper that you may not have known about. But not all libraries have open stacks. In reference libraries particularly, you may be required to fill out a call slip, giving the book's title, author, and call number as well as other information. The librarian will then search the closed stacks and locate the book for you.

The catalog card has more information than just the call number. In addition to the book's title and author, it may give the birth and death dates of the author, the names of editors and translators, the place and date of publication, the publisher's name, a physical description of the book (including the size and number of pages), a short description of the book's contents, information on illustrations, photographs, bibliography, explanatory notes, the subject heading, and other places in the card catalog where the book is listed.

Tracing. A "tracing," often found at the bottom of a card, indicates other subject headings under which the book is listed. When you are doing preliminary research, it is a good idea to check such tracings. They can direct you to subject headings related to your topic that may not have occurred to you.

Bound catalogs. Some large library systems, such as those in the New York City Library and the Library of Congress, use bound, printed catalogs to list their full holdings, which may be vast and distributed to many individual branches. These catalogs, alphabetically arranged by title, author, and subject, also give call numbers and publication facts. The advantage of these bound catalogs is that they are complete, listing all of that library system's holdings, and not just those in one particular branch. Furthermore, they indicate which branches of the system have the book you are looking for, since no branch exactly duplicates the holdings of another. Sometimes large libraries hold copies of each other's bound catalogs.

Typical card from subject catalog

Dewey catalog number	813
subject	HAWTHORNE
author	Stubbs, John Caldwell.
title	The pursuit of form: a study of Hawthorne
place of publication and publisher	and the romance. Urbana, University of Illinois
copyright date	Press ᶜ1970
page length (front matter in Roman numerals)	170p. 24 cm.
height in centimeters	Includes bibliographical references.
	1.Hawthorne, Nathaniel, 1804-1864.
tracing: another classification under which book is found	I.Title.

Union Catalog. This is the Library of Congress's card catalog. It usually can be found as a bound, printed catalog, although some libraries have it in index card form. Books are listed in the Union Catalog by their Library of Congress, not Dewey Decimal system, classification numbers (see below, page 322). The Library of Congress is one of the largest in the world. The Union Catalog helps researchers sift through all the books that have been printed on a subject, regardless of whether the library they are using has such books. To know which books exist is the first step in finding them, which may mean trying other libraries or taking advantage of interlibrary loan services. Many small libraries can borrow books from major libraries for the use of qualified students and researchers. Ask your neighborhood librarian if such a service is available to you and, if so, what steps are necessary to secure the needed books.

How to use a computerized library catalog

The computer catalog. Many libraries have replaced their card catalogs. The traditional card catalog indexes each of the library's books using a separate card for author, title, and subject. The cards are arranged in alphabetical order in banks of drawers. The computer catalog stores all this information in electronic files. Instead of searching through file drawers, you use a computer terminal to call up the information on a video screen.

The search. The catalog program's first screen, or main menu, provides several ways to locate books, such as author, subject, title, keyword, or word combinations. Follow the directions on the screen until you find the book you want. You will find detailed information, including the book's call number, which tells you where in the library to look for the book.

The book. Books are organized on the library's shelves by their call numbers. Each book has its call number printed on its spine and is shelved with books with the same or similar call numbers, often those books dealing with the same or a related subject.

Classification systems. The two main systems for classifying books in the United States are the Dewey Decimal and Library of Congress systems. The first is used in most public libraries; the second, in many college libraries.

Dewey Decimal system. This system has ten major divisions, from 000 for general reference works to the 900s for history. Each major division is in turn divided into ten parts, each subdivision focusing on a particular aspect of the main class. For example, 900-909 is the subdivision under which general works of history are listed, 910-919 covers geography, 920-929 biography. The subdivisions are again divided into ten sections, and so on for increasingly specialized categories.

Library of Congress system. This system uses the letters of the alphabet to divide information into 20 categories. The letters I,O,W,X, and Y are not used. The letters E and F are both used to designate American history. As with the Dewey Decimal system, the main groups are subdivided into specialized groups, designated by arabic numerals and other letters.

Other research sources.
There are a variety of other sources worth checking.

Periodicals. In addition to books, libraries stock many periodicals, from daily newspapers to specialized magazines. Periodical indexes can be used to find relevant articles in much the same way as the card catalog is used to find books (see box).

Periodicals themselves may be found in bound volumes, or they may be available on microfilm. Since microfilm is not as easy to flip through as an actual magazine or newspaper is, it is a good idea to know the correct page before searching the microfilm. The way to find such information is by using the indexes provided.

Encyclopedias. The best multivolume general encyclopedias are the *Encyclopaedia Britannica* and the *Encyclopedia Americana*. The *World Book Encyclopedia,* which is for young adults, is also excellent.

Many specialized encyclopedias exist as well; they include the *Encyclopedia of Jazz,* the *Encyclopedia of Sports,* the *International Encyclopedia of Social Sciences,* and the *Encyclopedia of Associations* (see page 324).

Almanacs. Early almanacs contained such useful items as recipes, folk remedies, and weather predictions, but modern almanacs are a valuable source of miscellaneous information, often in tabular form. They may include a chronology of the past year's events, geographical information, statistics, lists of famous people, state mottoes, and the like. The *Old Farmer's Almanac* is a source of weather predictions and is consulted more for its quaintness than for its information. The *Information Please Almanac* and the *World Almanac* are often consulted for data on events, recent population statistics, and other general information.

Facts on File is not really an almanac but a fully

Classification systems

Dewey Decimal system
- **000** general works
- **100** philosophy
- **200** religion
- **300** sociology
- **400** philology
- **500** natural science
- **600** useful arts
- **700** fine arts
- **800** literature
- **900** history and biography

MODERN EUROPEAN ART

Bowness

759.94 Bow

MODERN EUROPEAN ART

Bowness

N6447.B68

Library of Congress system
- **A** general works
- **B** philosophy, religion
- **C** history
- **D** foreign history
- **E, F** American history
- **G** geography, anthropology
- **H** social sciences
- **J** political science
- **K** law
- **L** education
- **M** music
- **N** fine arts
- **P** language and literature
- **Q** science
- **R** medicine
- **S** agriculture
- **T** technology
- **U** military science
- **V** naval science
- **Z** library science, bibliography

indexed weekly compilation of news. Current news is available in loose-leaf folders, and news from past years is bound in permanent volumes.

Bibliographies. These are comprehensive lists of books that have been written on different subjects. The librarian can help you locate specialized bibliographies. Among general bibliographies are *Books in Print*, published since 1948, indexed by title and author; *Subject Guide to Books in Print*, companion volume; and *Book Review Digest*, which excerpts reviews of books from magazines.

Atlases. Atlases are not just collections of current maps. In addition, there are maps showing historical development, climate, and many other special subjects (see box).

General atlases

Goode's World Atlas is found in many school libraries and is helpful in learning how to read maps; it is a good introduction to atlases.

The Times Atlas of the World is a comprehensive five-volume work, and includes solar system maps.

The Rand McNally New Cosmopolitan World Atlas includes ocean and solar system maps as well as historical, physical, and political maps.

Shepherd's *Historical Atlas* maps the world historically from 1450 B.C. to the present.

Periodical indexes

The Reader's Guide to Periodical Literature indexes 130 of the most popular magazines by author and subject. It has been published since 1900. It is a good idea to start with the most recent article on the subject you are investigating and work backward from there.

Poole's Index to Periodical Literature is an index of American and English periodicals published from 1802 to 1906. Articles are listed primarily by subject.

Nineteenth Century Reader's Guide can direct you to general and literary periodicals published from 1800 to 1899.

International Index to Periodicals, published since 1907, is similar to the *Reader's Guide* except that it covers scholarly journals.

The New York Times Index is the best guide to finding newspaper articles on events since the 1850's. The *Times* index can help you locate other newspaper accounts of events: once you know the date of the event, you can check other newspapers for that date.

The Public Affairs Information Service *Bulletin*, published since 1915, lists pamphlets, periodicals, government documents, and other material pertinent to economics, government, and sociology.

There are many other specialized indexes in fields such as art, medicine, literature, business, and social science.
SHB2 p323

Today, indexes to newspapers and magazines are often available on CD-ROM. Like bound volumes, the computer versions lead the user from an index to an entry which cites the important information about an article.

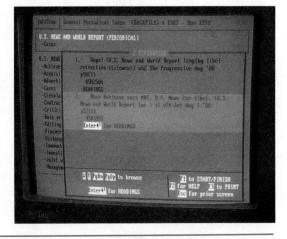

Dictionaries. In addition to English and other language dictionaries, libraries have specialized dictionaries in many fields, including music, biography, etymology, and art. Consult the librarian for dictionaries in your field.

The Oxford English Dictionary is the great comprehensive dictionary of the language. It provides detailed definitions and thousands of examples of use from 1150 to the present.

Biographical dictionaries include present and past editions of *Who's Who*, which provides short biographical sketches of famous living British people. *Who's Who in America* offers similar information on living Americans. There are also "who's who" publications for many different countries, as well as a *Who Was Who in America*. *Webster's Biographical Dictionary*, a one-volume work, briefly identifies international figures, living and dead. *Biographical Dictionaries Master Index* is a guide to over 50 "who's who" publications and other biographical dictionaries. This is a good directory to other sources of biographical sketches.

Vertical files. These files are arranged alphabetically by subject, and may include newspaper clippings, photographs, prints, pamphlets, and government publications. Ask the librarian for help.

Special collections. Many libraries have collections of films, records, and tapes. If these kinds of collections are useful to you, check the audio-visual catalog that lists the library's holdings in these areas. A number of libraries have archives of photographs, prints, and manuscripts. The librarian will help you locate these materials.

Other sources of information.

Most of your research will be done in the library. However, you may also wish to write away to various places for information.

Among the organizations or people to which you might try writing are government agencies, trade organizations, historical societies, public officials, congressmen, senators, and industries' public affairs offices. You might also wish to consult the *Encyclopedia of Associations* for ideas. This volume lists national organizations by title and subject, and gives addresses and names of key personnel. The Consumer Information Center prints a number of consumer-interest pamphlets. You may wish to write them as well for their catalog.

> To obtain the Consumer Publication Catalog, write:
> Consumer Information Center
> Pueblo, Colorado 81009

Interviews with community leaders, experts, or concerned citizens will also provide information on your topic. Be sure you have researched your topic before an interview so you will be able to ask informed questions. Prepare your questions in advance, but be prepared to follow interesting turns if the person you are interviewing offers original insights. Use a cassette tape recorder if possible; it is the most reliable way to record statements and provide you with proof that you have quoted your source correctly. Furthermore, it frees you to concentrate on your questions and the answers rather than on taking notes.

Microforms

Because of space limitations and limited availability of some printed sources, modern libraries are now collecting microforms—material that has been photographed and reduced on film. It is intended to be read on viewers like slide projectors. The most common sorts of microforms are microfilm, or strips of film on spools, and microfiche, or flat sheets of film. Each is read on a different sort of viewer, which projects an image from the film onto a screen. Library microform materials are cataloged in the card catalog like books; they are listed by author, title, and subject.

Taking notes

A working bibliography.

Once you have narrowed your subject down to a workable topic, having read at least one general encyclopedia article, it is time to set up a working bibliography. Your preliminary bibliography comes from the encyclopedia articles you have read, from your search through the library's card catalog, and, if applicable, through periodical indexes. For each possible source, enter all bibliographical information on a separate slip of paper or index card (see box).

If the article in question is from a book, you will need the book's bibliographical information, with the article's title in quotes. Make sure to have the editor's or compiler's name as well as the article's author's name. If the article is from a newspaper, you will need the exact date of the paper. If the article is from an encyclopedia, note the edition and year of publication of the encyclopedia, the volume and page numbers of the piece, and the article and encyclopedia titles.

Bibliography cards will make your task much easier when it is time to write your paper's bibliography. You may want to key your bibliography cards to your notes, using numbers or letters to signify reference sources. Some people prefer to write the author's last name on each note card.

Note cards.

Before taking notes on any book or article, read the relevant pages through, making sure that you understand the material. This will make it easier to take good notes.

Write your notes on index cards, making sure to have only one note on each card, even if there are two important pieces of information on the same page of your source. This will save work later, when you are writing your outline. It is also a good idea not to write on the back on any index card. Make sure each note card has the following information:

Heading. A short key to the note, one or two words telling what the information on the card pertains to.

Source. Use either the number or letter labeling technique described above, or the author's last name, with a shortened version of the title if more than one work by an author is being used, or if two authors have the same last name. Be sure to write down the page numbers on which material was found.

Type of note. There are three basic types of notes—paraphrase, quotation, and personal comment. Make sure your note card is labeled accordingly to prevent confusion later.

Most of your notes will *paraphrase* the material you have read, or restate it in your own words.

You may wish to *quote* all or part of some sentences. This type of note must follow the author's words exactly. If you leave words out, indicate this by ellipsis points. Put the quotation in quotation marks.

Personal comment notes record your own response to something you have read. You might write, for example, that an author used faulty logic or was biased. Mark personal comments clearly so that you do not confuse them later with the author's point of view.

Bibliography cards

For a book: author
           book title
           (editor or translator)
           city of publication
           publisher's name
           date of publication
           call number

> Sagan, Carl
> *The Dragons of Eden: Speculations on the Evolution of Human Intelligence*
> New York
> Random House
> 1977
> BF 431.52

For an article: author (if applicable)
           article title
           magazine or newspaper
           volume number and date
           relevant page numbers

> Church, George J.
> "Wrestling with Social Security"
> *Time*
> vol. 120; Nov. 22, 1982
> p. 71

The outline

An outline takes a broad topic and divides it into its main ideas, called subtopics, moving always from the general to the particular. Writing an outline helps to weed out irrelevant information and highlights where information is lacking; it aids in focusing an argument and determining the most logical and persuasive order for ideas.

Theme statement.
After you have done some general reading on your topic and taken notes, you should have an idea of what you want to say in your paper. Try to write a statement of your theme. It should tell the purpose of your paper in one or two sentences. What is it that you are setting out to show? What aspect of a subject are you focusing on? In what direction do you want your report to move? Writing a theme statement will help you bring your research and ideas together.

Scratch outlines.
With a theme statement in front of you, write a rough outline for your paper. Copy the headings from your note cards and jot down any other ideas you can think of. You may find that some of the categories you have written down are really aspects of other categories. For example, in writing a scratch outline for a paper on Nathaniel Hawthorne, you may jot down childhood and schooling as two headings only to discover that early schooling is a subtopic of childhood and that college is a separate heading. Or else you might decide to have a section on early childhood, then one on school days prior to college, and another on college. You may also discover that some categories do not fit in your paper. Put the extraneous note cards to one side. You may end up

using them later, but if they do not belong it is a mistake to insert them.

This rough theme statement and scratch outline should help point out weak parts of your research and help plan further research. New subtopics—or even different ways of organizing—may occur to you as you continue reading. Don't be alarmed by this, but revise your outline accordingly.

You may also find that your theme statement needs to be modified, that new ideas and information have come your way to change your outlook. Feel free to change. Until you actually begin writing, you are not really committed to one view. Your main objective is to learn about the field you are investigating. If your research has made you change your mind about a topic, there is nothing wrong with changing your theme statement before you begin writing.

To show how a person actually goes about writing a scratch outline, let's say a student has done some reading on the life of Nathaniel Hawthorne. He has decided to focus on what made Hawthorne the type of writer that he was. The list of note headings the student has written are: Childhood, Schooling, Weird Ancestors, Puritanism. He might then jot down: College, Relationship with Family, Friends, Themes in Writing. The preliminary theme statement at this point might be, "Factors in Nathaniel Hawthorne's childhood and early adulthood made him the sort of writer that he was."

This scratch outline is inconclusive, but it lets the student know where the gaps in information are. The student must now determine the specific factors that influenced Hawthorne, the sort of writer he was, and how one thing influenced the other.

Writing a theme statement

Poor: There are many similarities and differences between life in New England today and 200 years ago.

Good: Although the past two centuries have brought many changes to New England, the region retains many of the traditional values of 200 years ago.

Revision: In the midst of many changes, life in New England remains true to the values of 200 years ago because it still revolves around the town meeting form of local government.

Writing a Research Paper

Sources may include people you have interviewed (above) and newspaper stories (below) as well as books and magazines.

BOMBER HITS EMPIRE STATE BUILDING, SETTING IT AFIRE AT THE 79TH FLOOR; 13 DEAD, 26 HURT; WIDE AREA ROCKED

WHERE BOMBER CRASHED INTO EMPIRE STATE BUILDING | B-25 CRASHES IN FOG

Evaluating notes and sources.

Once you have completed your investigation, having filled in the information gaps that the scratch outline made you aware of, it is important to read your notes carefully—to determine if any gaps remain, to eliminate notes that do not fit in, and to evaluate your sources.

Researchers divide sources into *primary* and *secondary*. Primary sources are firsthand records of events. They may include newspaper accounts written when the events occurred, autobiographies of the participants, diaries or letters of the participants, or reports of scientific experiments. If you interview people for your paper, they may be primary sources for information on events that they witnessed.

Secondary sources evaluate, analyze, criticize, relate, or otherwise deal with primary source information. Such sources include the work of historians or commentators with no firsthand knowledge of the events they write about. People you interview may be secondary sources if they are repeating what they have heard from other sources, or evaluating such information.

Both types of information sources must be evaluated for their accuracy. People who participate in events are closest to them, but may not have the objectivity necessary to relate what really happened. They often try to cast themselves or their friends in a favorable light. They also may not really know all that was going on. Secondary sources may be more objective, but they too may be biased, inaccurate, or incompetent.

One important way to judge the reliability of a source is to see if different authors support each other by presenting the same basic facts, though they may have varying slants and interpretations. Another way is to read about an author in a biographical dictionary. What professional position does the author hold? What other books has he written? What might the author's concerns be besides wanting to present his viewpoint? A paper on the scandals of the Nixon administration, for example, would treat material by those accused or convicted of illegal acts as different from material by those not involved. It is part of your job as a researcher to evaluate the accuracy of your sources and to distinguish between opinions and facts.

The finished outline. Now you are ready to put together a finished outline. It may be done in topic form or sentence form. The topic outline gives headings and subheadings in noun form, such as: Early Childhood, Learning to Write, Themes. The sentence outline gives main headings in either sentence or noun form, but the subheadings are complete sentences. Whatever style of outline you choose, be careful not to mix them up. This can lead to muddled thinking.

The first step in any outline is to write a carefully considered theme statement. Now that you have finished research on your topic, you can be more specific than you were in your rough theme statement. If you find that you are pleased with your scratch theme, you can use that or reword it. You may wish to write an entirely new theme statement, having reconsidered the focus of your paper. Keep in mind that your theme statement must still be short, no more than one or two sentences telling the reader what you will be discussing in your paper.

The preliminary theme statement we wrote for a paper on Nathaniel Hawthorne, for example, is too sketchy for a careful outline statement. Instead we might now write: *Already inclined toward introspection by nature and experience, Nathaniel Hawthorne spent twelve years after college in virtual isolation, writing and rewriting his* Twice-Told Tales *and forming the style that characterized all his literary output throughout his career.*

An outline, like the paper itself, should have an introduction, a body, and a conclusion. The introduction should state the focus or purpose of the paper. It may in fact, when you actually write the introduction, be an expanded version of the theme statement. It may also discuss in concise terms some historical background, or it may give important definitions. Its purpose is to let the reader know what the rest of the paper will cover in detail.

Most of the outline will be taken up by the body. The main ideas of your paper, and the subtopics that

Types of outlines

Topic outline

Title That Lonely Hawthorne Chamber
I. Introduction
II. Early Childhood
  A. The early years
  B. Death of father
    1. Effect on Hawthorne
    2. Self-imposed isolation of Hawthorne's mother
    3. Life with relatives
III. New England School Days
  A. Education
  B. Foot injury and subsequent two-year isolation
  C. Life in Maine
IV. Bowdoin College Days
  A. Education
  B. Companions
  C. Decision to become a writer
V. The Lonely Chamber—Learning to Write
  A. Twelve years of isolation
    1. Critics—favorable and unfavorable
    2. Writing apprenticeship
  B. Anguishing through his Puritan ancestry
  C. Emergence from the lonely chamber
VI. Themes in Hawthorne's Works Showing Early Influences
  A. Isolation of mankind
  B. Evils of Puritanism
VII. Conclusion

Sentence outline

Theme statement Burial rites among the ancient Greeks, the Egyptians, and the Anglo-Saxons differed in detail, but all three groups used cremation and interment, and the Egyptians and Anglo-Saxons both practiced burial at sea.
Title Ancient Burial Rites
I. Ancient Greeks usually burned their dead heroes.
  A. The *Iliad* recounts the cremation of Hector and Patroclus.
  B. Frequently the ashes of the dead were placed in urns.
  C. Other sections of the *Iliad* suggest interment.
    1. Erection of a barrow for Patroclus.
    2. Other evidence of the existence of barrows.
II. Egyptians interred their leaders.
  A. Pyramids are seen in the Nile valley.
  B. Archaeologists have found burial ships.
III. Anglo-Saxons practiced interment, cremation, and ship burial.
  A. There is evidence of interment in *Beowulf.*
  B. In the same poem, Beowulf is burned on a huge pyre.
  C. The Sutton Hoo find reveals the existence of ship burial.
IV. Conclusion.

Writing a Research Paper

support them, should be enumerated in the body. The body may include explanations, comparisons, contrasts, examples, analogies, facts, and historical details. The level of detail should depend on the length of the paper itself. A paper of 25 pages will require a longer outline than one of ten pages.

A conclusion is also necessary. This can be a summary of points made in your paper, or it can be a restatement of the theme. It shows the reader that you have demonstrated what you set out to prove. Neither the introduction nor the conclusion have to be spelled out in the outline, since the ideas they detail are covered in the body of the outline.

Use your scratch outline to help you list the main points of your report, making sure that all relevant subject note headings, especially those added after you wrote your scratch outline, are included. Polish the language of your scratch outline headings. Most important, begin to consider how to organize your paper so that the information and ideas will be persuasive. A first step is to decide on your topic and subtopic headings. Main idea headings are more general than the supporting elements that substantiate them. Which are the main, general ideas, and which are the facts, theories, and opinions that support or substantiate those ideas?

Once you have determined your main ideas, try to think of the most logical way to present them. Do not be afraid to try different sequences. If you have taken good notes and written good headings, shuffle your note cards to try out different organizational schemes. You may find that writing the headings on a piece of paper and numbering them in different sequences is the method that works best for you.

Organization. The trickiest part of writing an outline for many people is deciding how to organize it. This becomes easier if you know the four basic types of research papers, and the main ways in which papers are organized. The four types of research papers are historical, biographical, literary, and analytical.

Historical papers are usually developed chronologically or by thoroughly analyzing the important events of an era and then discussing related side issues.

Biographical papers can be organized in either of the two ways discussed above. Your choice of organization will depend on how you have viewed the life of your subject. The emphasis placed on events will determine the order of presentation.

Literary papers may trace certain themes in the work of one or many authors. In such papers, it is common to select only the major works of the authors for analysis. If you choose to study both major and minor works, you would probably do best to analyze the major works first, then finish up with the minor ones. The works could also be treated chronologically. If you are dealing with the images in the works of a particular author, you would probably deal with the central images first, then go on to the related images. In either case, your paper would be strengthened by pertinent examples of the images.

Analytical papers dealing with problems or events might be developed by discussing the central issues first, then going on to related side issues. Thus, if you were dealing with a particularly stressful time in the history of a country, you would work through the most important aspects of the situation before covering the less important problems.

In general, the main types of orders are chronological, decreasing importance, increasing importance, compare and contrast, pro and con, geographical, cause to effect, and effect to cause. These are not the only orders possible, but they are the most common ones.

Note that in the biographical topic outline on Hawthorne, the writer chose a chronological order; the sentence outline on burial rites is organized geographically. It could have been organized by type of burial as follows:
    I. Ship burial.
    II. Interment.
    III. Cremation.

As the writer, you have the choice of type of organization for your paper, subject to the advice and recommendations of your teacher.

You should always experiment with more than one outline organization for a research paper. Which suits your topic best? Which is closest to the recommendations of your teacher? Remember that it is always easier and faster to change the organization of the outline before you start to write than to revise a poorly planned or unfinished paper.

Writing

> Oh! But he was a tight-fisted hand at the grindstone, Scrooge! a squeezing, wrenching, grasping, scraping, clutching, covetous old sinner! Hard and sharp as flint, from which no steel had ever struck out generous fire; secret, and self-contained, and solitary as an oyster. The cold within him froze his old features, nipped his pointed nose, shrivelled his cheek, stiffened his gait; made his eyes red, his thin lips blue; and spoke out shrewdly in his grating voice. A frosty rime was on his head, and on his eyebrows, and his wiry chin. He carried his own low temperature always about with him; he iced

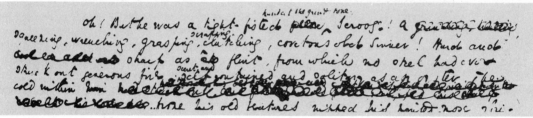

Good writers learn how to edit their own writing. Above is a passage from "A Christmas Carol" by Dickens, corrected by the author himself.

The first draft. Now that you have good notes, a theme statement, and an organized outline, it is time to begin writing a rough draft. At this point, it is a good idea not to worry too much about the way you are using language, as long as your ideas make sense and there is a logic behind the movement of your paragraphs based on your outline.

Some people find the introduction the hardest part of the paper to write, so you may wish to start writing your first draft in the middle, with one of the main ideas that particularly excites you. You can save writing the introduction for last. A good outline has the special advantage of keeping you abreast of everything you want to say. Since there is no chance you will lose your train of thought, you can concentrate on your choice of words, sentence structure, and paragraph development. Many writers prefer to write the first draft quickly, then pay attention to how they express themselves in the later draft. Just remember, this is a first draft, and no one is going to see it but you. You will have to rewrite this first draft no matter how much time you spend perfecting your sentences; you will have to change your wording around; you may even have to revise your basic outline if another order seems to work better.

Complete the first draft before you begin to rewrite. You will then have a better idea of the weak parts of your paper, where it is needlessly repetitious, and where more explanations are necessary. As you work through your first draft you may want to use certain shortcuts that experienced writers employ.

One helpful hint is to staple note cards to your first draft when the cards carry material that you want to quote word for word. Why bother to copy quotations when you are only working on a first draft? Copying takes time and it can mean making mistakes.

Another helpful hint is to set a goal for each writing session. If you set a reasonable goal for each session, you will find that you can complete that unit of writing in the time allotted. Examine your outline to see what you are going to cover in that particular writing session. The outline helps you plan your thoughts out so that the writing comes easier. It also tells you which notes you will be using for that period.

A third hint is to frequently look back at what you have already written in your first draft. Looking back helps you to pick up the thread of your discussion and helps to reacquaint you with the thoughts you are about to pursue.

Style. Good writers follow certain conventions that make their prose clear and pleasant to read. Among them are:

Avoid personal references. It is unnecessary to use "I think," "my opinion," "I've found," and other first-person phrases. When you want to make clear that you are stating an opinion, it is more acceptable to use such phrases as "many people feel," "as some critics believe," and "one opinion is."

Avoid informal language. There are many colloquial and informal uses of language that are acceptable in conversation but not in writing. Make sure you use a word correctly when you write it, both in its spelling and meaning (see Usage dictionary, page 336).

Avoid verbosity. Be as succinct as possible without sacrificing clarity. Do not write, "in the event of," instead of "if"; "in view of the fact," instead of "because"; "at the present time," instead of "now"; or "in the majority of cases," instead of "usually." Be on the lookout for other phrases of the same kind.

Use the active voice. Whenever possible, have the subject of your sentence act instead of being acted upon. "he wrote it," is more direct and forceful than "it was written by him."

Avoid exclamation marks. Except on rare occasions, exclamation marks make your prose seem hysterical.

Avoid unnecessary adjectives and adverbs. If you use the right noun or verb to begin with, you will not need many modifiers. Modifiers actually weaken prose. "The abandoned child was left behind," can be changed to "the child was abandoned." "He walked quickly" can be changed to "he hurried."

Avoid clichés. The use of clichés indicates a lazy mind. Search for ways to make your points in fresh and more effective ways.

Avoid jargon, slang, euphemism. Jargon and slang may not be understood by your reader. Even if understood, they make the tone of your paper too informal. Euphemism, the substitution of a polite, roundabout way of referring to something disturbing, can make your paper sound prissy. Don't write "passed away" for "died."

Avoid foreign expressions. Unless there is no way to say something in English, or unless the originally foreign word is common enough in English to be found in the dictionary, you should not use non-English expressions. They may not be understood and can seem pretentious. They are usually unnecessary.

Use specific, concrete language. Instead of using general nouns and abstractions, try to use specific language and solid images. "The person" is hazy, but "the middle-aged farmer" gives us a clear picture. To say "he loved nature" does not mean as much as, "he took long walks in the woods." Use analogies and anecdotes to make abstract concepts such as love, time, good, and evil come alive.

Ten useful rules for style

1. Avoid personal references.
2. Avoid informal language.
3. Avoid verbosity.
4. Use the active voice.
5. Avoid exclamation marks.
6. Avoid unnecessary adjectives and adverbs.
7. Avoid clichés.
8. Avoid jargon, slang, euphemism.
9. Avoid foreign expressions.
10. Use specific, concrete language.

The final draft. Preparing the final draft is an important step in writing a successful research paper. This is the end product of all your work.

Editing. You may need to go over your first draft more than once, correcting spelling, punctuation, phrasing, grammar, logic, paragraphing, and the development and progression of ideas. Read your first draft for sense. Do you understand the points you are making? Check to make sure your nouns and verbs agree, being either singular or plural but not switching back and forth. Also make sure that you do not switch tenses for no reason. Are your transitions from one idea to the next smooth? If not, transitional phrases may help your paragraphs move more easily. "However," "although," "in addition," "first," "second," "third," and "moreover" are some useful transitional phrases.

In addition to editing your paper, you must make sure that you have documented your sources. All quotations, paraphrases, and ideas that you have taken from books and articles should be marked by footnotes. Well-known facts, such as the birth or death dates of famous people, do not have to be documented. Many facts and all opinions and interpretations by others should be referenced to their source. Documentation also supports the validity of your statements, providing the reader with source references to check if he doubts the accuracy of your facts.

Form. Title pages may be set up in many ways. One common way is to have the title of your paper start one-third down from the top of the page, centered, with your name on the next line. The course title should be typed one-third of the way from the bottom of the page, centered. The next line should have your teacher's name, and the line after that should have the date.

The body of the paper should be typed on unlined $8\frac{1}{2}$ inch by 11 inch white bond paper. The left margin should be $1\frac{1}{2}$ inches; the right, top, and bottom margins should be 1 inch.

Double-space the paper throughout, except for footnotes and bibliography. The page number should appear in the upper right-hand corner. Use arabic numerals.

Be sure to fix all typographical errors. Some teachers will accept small corrections made in pen or pencil in your report, but all prefer clean copy. Use a correcting fluid or correcting paper to eliminate mistakes, and type the correction in.

When typing your paper, leave one space after a comma or a semicolon and leave two spaces after a period, question mark, or colon. Indent the beginnings of paragraphs five spaces.

Footnotes. After marking footnotes numerically in the body of your report, you need to write the full citations that correspond to them. These can appear at the bottom of the page on which they are noted, but it is easier to put them at the end of your paper, on a separate piece of paper entitled "Footnotes," which should come just prior to the bibliography. Number these pages like the others in the paper.

Footnotes are single-spaced, with a line skipped between entries. The first line of each footnote is indented five spaces, with the following lines brought out to the left margin. The footnote number is typed a half line up from the note itself, just as in the body of the report. Footnotes appear in the same numerical order in which they appear in your report. The basic forms are described below and examples are shown in the box at the right.

For a book:

- Name of author in normal order, putting the first name or initials (if the author uses them instead of a first name) first. Comma after author's last name.
- Book title underlined.
- In parentheses, the city of publication, colon, publisher, comma, year of publication, end parenthesis, then a comma.
- Page numbers. Use p. for page and pp. for pages. Put a period at the end of the line.
- Note: If other information, such as the name of the editor or translator, needs to be included, put a comma after the book title and the abbreviations "ed." or "trans." followed by the name of the editor or translator. The facts of publication follow, in parentheses, with no comma between the editor's name and the starting parenthesis.
- If a volume number is needed, it comes after the comma that follows the end parenthesis. It is given in arabic numerals and is followed by a colon, then the page numbers without the abbreviations p. and pp. There must be a period at the end of the line.

For a magazine article:

- Name of author in normal order, comma.
- Article title in quotation marks, with comma before the final mark.
- Magazine title underlined, comma.
- Date of magazine, including month and year, comma. The exact date of a weekly must be given.
- Page numbers, using p. and pp. abbreviations. Period at the end of the line.
- Note: For scholarly publications, you may need to include the volume number. If so, it comes after the magazine title, with no comma between them, and is followed by the month and year of the issue in parentheses, which are followed by a colon and the page numbers of the reference without use of p. and pp. A period must be placed at the end of the line.

Sample footnotes

Book with one author (who uses initials instead of a full first name); note subtitle after colon:

> [1] F. W. Bateson, *The Scholar-Critic: An Introduction to Literary Research* (London: Routledge & Kegan Paul, 1972), pp. 51–55.

Book with two (or more) authors; edition other than first:

> [2] Robert Jastrow and Malcolm H. Thompson, *Astronomy: Fundamentals and Frontiers*, 3rd ed. (New York: John Wiley & Sons, 1972), p. 117.

Article in a book; note the mention of the editors:

> [3] O.R. Gurney, "The Babylonians and Hittites," *Oracles and Divination*, ed. Michael Loewe and Carmen Blacker (Boulder, Colo.: Shambhala, 1981), pp. 142–168.

Article in a popular magazine; note the full date of a weekly is given:

> [4] John Newhouse, "Arms and Orthodoxy," *The New Yorker*, 7 June 1982, pp. 44–103.

Article in a scholarly journal:

> [5] A.K. Coomaraswamy, "Sir Gawain and the Green Knight: Indra and Namuci," *Speculum* 19 (January 1944): 104–125.

Unsigned newspaper article; if signed, the author's name would come first:

> [6] "Teacher Calls Confinement in China a 'Nightmare,'" *New York Times*, 6 June 1982, sec. 1, p. 15.

Pamphlet where agency's name is used instead of author:

> [7] Department of Health, Education, and Welfare, *Day Care for Your Children* (Washington, D.C.: Government Printing Office, 1974).

Article in encyclopedia; note the mention of edition and volume.

> [8] "Anarcharsis," *Encyclopaedia Britannica*, 14th ed. (1965), 1:839.

Personal interview:

> [9] Jules Blane, Candy-Store Owner, Brooklyn, New York, personal interview, 1 June 1981.

- The form for an article from a book combines the magazine article and book footnote forms. After the author's name, the article title comes in quotation marks, with an inner comma (the same style as for a magazine article). Instead of a magazine title, the book title is given and underlined, followed by a comma, then the editor's name, if applicable, followed by parentheses and the facts of publication. After the end parenthesis, there is a comma and the page reference, using the page abbreviations followed by a period.

Subsequent footnotes. The first time you write a footnote for a source, you must give full information. If the next footnote is from the same source, you can write "ibid.," which means "in the same place." This should be followed by a comma and the new page number, followed by a period. If the reference is on the same page as the previous one, put a period after "ibid."

If you refer later to a book already cited, you can write the author's last name, comma, and the page numbers, followed by a period.

If you have used more than one work by an author, and have previously given full reference information on the book you are now referring to, you can write the author's last name, comma, title, comma, and page numbers, period.

If you mention the author's name in the body of the text and have already given full reference information on it elsewhere, you can write "op. cit." followed by a comma, and then the page reference, period.

After the first mention of a work, use of a short title is permissible in both notes and text.

Bibliography.

A bibliography is a list of all the works used in writing your paper, particularly those cited; it should also include works that helped shape your thinking on the topic, even if they were not mentioned in your report. Entries are alphabetically arranged by author's last name wherever possible. (Unsigned articles are alphabetized by the first letter of the article title; pamphlets issued by agencies are alphabetized by the first letter of the agency's name.) Bibliographies are single-spaced, with a line skipped between entries. The first line of each entry is flush with the left margin, but the rest of the entry is indented five spaces.

Entries should be typed on a separate piece of paper entitled "Bibliography." This is the last page of your report. The basic forms are as follows:

For a book:
- Author's last name, comma, first name or initials, period.
- Book title underlined, period.
- Place of publication, colon, publisher, comma, year of publication, period.

For a magazine article:
- Author's last name, comma, first name or initials, period.
- Article title in quotation marks, a period preceding the end quotation mark.
- Magazine title, underlined, comma.
- Date of issue, including month and year, comma.
- Page numbers of the article, using page abbreviations and ending the line with a period.
- Note: For an article from a book, the book title is given, underlined, after the article title in quotation marks. The period after the book title is followed by the editor or translator's name, which is followed by a period and the facts of publication, the same as for a full book reference.
- In a scholarly journal where the volume number is given, the volume number should be placed directly after the magazine title with no comma between them. The month (if possible) and year are given in parentheses, followed by a colon and the page numbers of the article. Page abbreviations are not used. There must be a period at the end of the line.
- Newspaper articles are cited by the section number, following the date, if the pages are not numbered consecutively. Unsigned newspaper articles are alphabetized by title.

Sample bibliography

"Anarcharsis." *Encyclopaedia Britannica,* 14th ed., (1965).

Bateson, F.W. *The Scholar-Critic: An Introduction to Literary Research.* London: Routledge & Kegan Paul, 1972.

Blane, Jules. Candy-Store Owner. Brooklyn, New York. Personal interview. 1 June 1981.

Coomaraswamy, A. K. "Sir Gawain and the Green Knight: Indra and Namuci." *Speculum* 19 (January 1944): 104–125.

Department of Health, Education, and Welfare. *Day Care for Your Children.* Washington, D.C.: Government Printing Office, 1974.

Gurney, O.R. "The Babylonians and Hittites." *Oracles and Divination.* Ed. Michael Loewe and Carmen Blacker. Boulder, Colo.: Shamabhala, 1981.

Jastrow, Robert, and Thompson, Malcolm H. *Astronomy: Fundamentals and Frontiers.* 3rd ed. New York: John Wiley & Sons, 1972.

Newhouse, John. "Arms and Orthodoxy." *The New Yorker,* 7 June 1982, pp. 44–103.

"Teacher Calls Confinement in China a 'Nightmare.'" *New York Times,* 6 June 1982, sec. 1, p. 15.

Punctuation review

Questions of punctuation are always a serious concern in formal writing. The following pages provide a brief review of major types of punctuation.

Good style in punctuating, especially in the use of commas, often depends on a grasp of English grammar. If you wish to review the grammar that affects punctuation, turn to pages 4-55 in Volume 1.

There are two issues in punctuating. The first is a simple question of right and wrong. A writer who ends each sentence with a colon rather than a period is simply wrong. Sentences cannot end with a colon.

The second issue is less clear-cut. For example, in some cases, the writer may choose punctuation to suit his or her taste: a semicolon to separate two closely related thoughts, or a period. Writers learn with practice which possibility to choose to make their meaning clearest.

End punctuation. There are three kinds of end punctuation: the period, the question mark, and the exclamation point. Every sentence must end with one of these marks.

The exclamation point ends an exclamatory sentence, and the question mark is at the end of a question. All other sentences end with a period.

What a good boy Paul is!
Is Paul a good boy?
Paul is a good boy.

The most common mistake in end punctuation usage is to punctuate as a sentence a group of words that is not a sentence. A sentence must, as a minimum, have a subject and a verb. In addition, it must not have been transformed into an adjective clause by the addition of a subordinate conjunction, nor into a relative clause by the use of a relative pronoun. Such clauses should not be punctuated as separate sentences, but only as parts of some other, longer sentence.

SENTENCE FRAGMENT
Although I like the design.
CORRECTIONS
(1) *I like the design.*
(2) *Although I like the design, I don't care to use it in a living room.*

Periods. Besides its use at the end of a sentence, the period is used after initials (*T. S. Eliot*) and after many other abbreviations, including those of months (*Feb.*), countries (*U.S.A.*), states (*Tenn.*), and other commonly abbreviated forms (*St., Ave., Dr., Mr.,* and so on).

Commas. The most common mistake in comma usage is to use too many. Limit comma usage to the following situations.

Compound sentences. When two simple sentences are joined together by a coordinating conjunction, put a comma before the conjunction. (This comma is often omitted when the clauses being joined are especially short.) Do not use commas when only a part of the sentence has been compounded.

She got up to close the window, but he asked her to sit down again.

Series. Use commas after all but the last item in a series.

Nonrestrictive relative clauses. A nonrestrictive relative clause is set off from the rest of the sentence by commas. So, too, are expressions that derive from nonrestrictive clauses, such as appositives and nonrestrictive participles and participial phrases.

The woman, who was smiling engagingly, told us to take our seats.
Mr. Jackson, standing on the makeshift platform, gave a rousing campaign speech.

Adverbial clauses. An adverbial clause at the beginning of a sentence is set off from the rest of the sentence by a comma. Such a clause at the end of a sentence is not set off.

When we got back from the beach, we were too tired to eat dinner.
We were too tired to eat dinner when we got back from the beach.

Parenthetical expressions. Parenthetical expressions are set off by commas. These include *yes, no,* and mild interjections (those not followed by an exclamation point), such as *well* and *oh,*

Well, it's time to leave

nouns of address,

How is your garden growing, Mary?

and such expressions as *of course* and *however.*

We will, of course, be ready; others, however, may not be.

Clarity. Sometimes—but very rarely—a comma is needed to avoid confusion and to make a sentence clearer:

To John, Matilda would always be a mystery.

Semicolons. Use a semicolon to join two sentences without using a conjunction. The semicolon is also used when two sentences are joined by such an expression as *therefore* or *however.*

Two plus two equal four; therefore, five is not an acceptable answer.

The semicolon is also used to separate the items in a series when there are already commas within individual elements of the series:

He has lived in Moline, Illinois; Boulder, Colorado; and Seattle, Washington.

Colons. The main use of a colon is to introduce a list, an example, a question, or a long quotation.

The question is this: What should we do next?

A colon used in this way should always follow a noun or a pronoun, never a verb or a preposition. It may also come after the expressions *as follows* and *the following.*

Dashes. The dash indicates a sudden break or change of emphasis in a sentence:

I have here a—now, where did I put that thing?

Dashes can also be used to set off an appositive when the appositive is to be emphasized or when it contains commas within it.

Parentheses. Parentheses set off material in a sentence that is separate or apart from the main thought.

She traveled through Davenport (a city she once lived in) and on toward Chicago.

Quotations. A direct quotation—the exact words that someone has said or written—is enclosed in quotation marks. If the quotation is included within another sentence, it is set off from the rest of the sentence by commas:

"I think," he said, "that you are on the right track."

When more than one person is being quoted, as in a conversation, begin a new paragraph for each change of speaker.

Question marks and exclamation points are placed inside the quotation marks if they are part of the quote

"Who are you?" she asked

and outside if they apply to the sentence as a whole

Who was it that said, "I shall return"?

Periods and commas are always placed inside quotation marks, while the semicolon and colon are always placed outside.

Do not use quotation marks for an indirect quotation, that is, one that does not report someone's exact words:

He said that it was raining.

Italics. Words to be set in italics are indicated in typed or handwritten material by an underline. Italics are used to single out words, phrases, or even sentences for special emphasis. Titles of books, plays, magazines, and newspapers, and the names of ships, trains, and airplanes are italicized. (Shorter works like poems and stories are put in quotation marks.)

The Adventures of Tom Sawyer
Hamlet
National Geographic
the *Titanic*
"Annabel Lee"
"The Masque of the Red Death"

Capitalization. All proper nouns (persons, places, or things) are capitalized. In addition, capitalize the first word of every sentence; the first word of a direct quotation embedded in another sentence; the names of groups, associations, and businesses; the letters of some abbreviations; and all historic events, buildings, monuments, and documents:

General Motors   *Grant's Tomb*
NASA   *Declaration of Independence*
World War II

Titles used with proper nouns are capitalized:

Dr. Brown
Senator Douglas

as are the first, last, and important words in titles of printed texts. Prepositions, articles, and conjunctions are not capitalized unless they are the first or last word of the title.

Usage dictionary

Understanding usage can be an important part of improving your writing. A careful writer is one who develops a sense for the right word at the right time and place. Careless writers, on the other hand, often confuse words that look or sound alike and are willing to settle for the approximate word.

If you have never used a usage dictionary, spend a few minutes browsing through this one to see the kind of information it offers you. The entries often comment on the difference between informal (spoken) and formal (written) English. They also provide advice on avoiding lazy writing. Once you are familiar with the contents, return to the dictionary for specific information when you are writing a paper or report.

A

a, an. These forms of the indefinite article are used to refer to one person, place, abstraction, or other "thing." They are used only with singular nouns and are unspecific, not indicating which one of many is meant. *A* is the article used before consonant sounds (*a* dog); *an* is used before any word beginning with a vowel sound (*an* ant). Since the rule is based on the opening sound of the following word, words beginning with *h* or *u* may take either article form, depending on pronunciation (*an* honor, *a* hospital, *an* underground, *a* universe).

abbreviations. Abbreviatons should not be used unless they are explained or are likely to be understood without explanation. A few abbreviations (such as Mr., A.M., B.C., and Ph.D.) are so common that avoiding them would be thought eccentric. Excessive use of abbreviations, however, is generally unpleasant, especially when the abbreviations are jargon or slang. Except for the common abbreviations discussed above, abbreviations are regarded as more informal than full forms.

about, almost. *About* in the sense of almost is informal usage in such phrases as *about done, about dead.* See also ALMOST.

absolutely. *See* ADVERBS.

accept, except. *Accept* is a verb meaning to receive or approve. *Except* is usually a preposition that means excluding. (I *accept* all your comments *except* the last one.)

adapt, adopt. *Adapt* means to change something to make it suitable for a new use. One may *adapt* oneself to different circumstances. A novel may be *adapted* for the stage. *Adopt* means to decide upon (a plan), to choose to treat someone as a close relative, or to vote to accept a resolution. (The committee voted to *adopt* the resolution.)

adjectives. There are many overworked and misused adjectives that should be avoided in careful writing. Something is *wonderful* if it inspires wonder; otherwise *wonderful* is an empty adjective. When you say something is *nice*, the reader politely yawns. Other adjectives to look out for are *awful, beautiful, cute,* *funny, incredible, interesting, lousy, lovely, marvelous, pretty, terrible, terrific,* and *unique* (since *unique* means one of a kind, do not write or say "the most unique"). In general, if an adjective tells a reader only that you vaguely approve or disapprove of something, a better adjective is needed.

adopt. *See* ADAPT.

adverbs. Tired adjectives can be made into exhausted adverbs, usually just by adding *-ly* to the end. In addition to *awfully, beautifully,* etc., watch out for overdoses of *absolutely, definitely, positively, quite, really,* and *very.*

advice, advise. *Advice* is a noun; *advise* is a verb. If you can see the *vice* in *advice,* you may find it easier to remember which is the noun. (He *advised* me against seeking *advice.*)

affect, effect. *Affect* is a verb meaning to influence or to pretend in an offensive way. (The weather *affects* my moods. She *affects* to great wealth.) *Effect* is a noun meaning result or what is accomplished. (He never considered the *effect* of his actions.) It can also be used as a verb meaning to accomplish something. (The principal *effected* changes in the school.)

aggravate. In formal speech or writing, *aggravate* is used only to mean to make worse. (The difficulty was *aggravated* by misunderstanding.) Colloquially, *aggravate* is often used to mean irritate. (His nagging *aggravated* me.) This usage is less acceptable in writing than in speech.

agree to, agree with. *Agree to* something. (I *agree to* your proposal.) *Agree with* someone. (He *agrees with* me.)

ain't. *Ain't* was originally a contraction of *am not* (compare *can't,* which in some regions is pronounced *cain't*). Over a hundred years ago, it came to be widely used also as a contraction for *are not* and even for *is not* and *have not* or *has not.* Perhaps because of the indiscriminate use, *ain't* fell into disfavor among many careful speakers. It is not used now in published writing, except in dialogue. The word is generally regarded as slang.

all of, alongside of. *See* OF.

all ready, already. *All ready* means completely ready

Writing a Research Paper

(I was *all ready* for the picnic) or that all of what has been referred to is ready (the boys were *all ready* to shout). *Already* is an adverbial expression meaning by or before a particular time. (The sun was *already* up when I awoke.)

all right. *See* ALRIGHT.

all the farther, as far as. In the sense of *as far as*, *all the farther* (that's *all the farther* he can walk) is a regional expression and should not be used in formal writing.

all together, altogether. *Altogether* means entirely. (That's an *altogether* different matter.) *All together* means in a group. (When we are *all together*, we sing.)

allude, elude. To *allude* to something is to refer to it indirectly. (The poet *alludes* subtly to King Arthur.) Note that the verb *allude* is regularly followed by the particle *to*. To *elude* something or somebody is to evade or escape. (The suspect *eluded* the police.)

allusion, illusion, delusion. An *allusion* is an indirect reference. (The poet made *allusions* to King Arthur.) An *illusion* is a false perception or idea. (What you thought you saw was an optical *illusion*.) A *delusion* is a false belief. The word connotes madness. (Hitler's fatal *delusion* was that he could never be wrong.)

almost, most. In speech, *almost* is sometimes shortened to *most*, and the shortened form is written with an initial apostrophe. (They had *'most* everything.) But *almost* is the standard form for use in writing.

a lot. *A lot* is two words.

already. *See* ALL READY.

alright, all right. Although there would be logical justification for a spelling form "alright," it is not acceptable in careful writing. *All right* is the only correct form.

although, though. These two words have the same meaning. *Although* is generally felt to be a bit more formal than *though*. The shortened forms *altho* and *tho* should be avoided in formal writing.

altogether. *See* ALL TOGETHER.

alumnus. An *alumnus* is a male graduate of a school; a female graduate is an *alumna*. *Alumni* are graduates, a group of all males or males and females. *Alumnae* is the plural form used to refer to a group of all female graduates.

among, between. *Among* is used when referring to more than two persons or things. (The prize money was distributed *among* three winners.) *Between* is used when referring to two persons or things. (The prize money was divided *between* the two winners.) However, many speakers and writers do not observe the distinction.

amount, number; fewer, less. *Amount* refers to quantity in bulk while *number* refers to separate units. (The *amount* of money; the *number* of dollars.) Similarly, fewer refers to numbered things while less refers to amount. (The *number* of pieces in the game was *fewer* than called for; the *amount* of sugar we needed was *less* than we thought.)

an. *See* A.

and etc. *See* ETC.

and/or. Useful as this expression is, most careful speakers and writers feel it should be confined to legal or commercial use.

anxious, eager. *Anxious* means apprehensive, worried. *Eager* means looking forward to. In writing, try to keep this distinction in mind. (I am *anxious* about the test; I am *eager* to have it over.)

anybody, anyone, each, everybody, everyone, no one, nobody, none, somebody, someone. These words are all singular and always take singular verbs. (*Everybody* is here.) When a pronoun refers back to such words, *he* and *his* are most often used. (*Everyone* knows what *he* is supposed to do.) This is formally correct but awkward when the word may refer to a man or a woman. Some writers prefer to use the plural forms *they* and *their* (someone called but *they* hung up), but this practice is not as widely accepted as the use of the masculine singular pronouns. Other writers use the phrase *he or she*, although this too can be awkward. *See also* GENDER.

anyway. This, and not *anyways*, is the correct word. It means in any case. (He went *anyway*.) *Any way* means in any of a number of ways. (She traveled *any way* the wind blew.)

anywhere, everywhere, nowhere, somewhere. None of these words takes a final -*s* in standard English. These words are considered more appropriate in writing than are the related terms *anyplace*, *everyplace*, *no place*, and *someplace*.

appraise, apprise. *Appraise* means to estimate the value of something. *Apprise* is a less common word meaning to notify or inform about.

around, 'round. *Around* in the sense of about or nearby is colloquial and should not be used in formal writing. (Let's start *around* ten o'clock. The book is *around* here somewhere.) The adverb *around* is often shortened in speech to *'round*. We are likely to say *the other way 'round*, but in formal situations we would write *the other way around*.

as. The use of *as* in the sense of because or since is often ambiguous. (We were bored *because* we knew what he would say, not, We were bored *as* we knew what he would say.) *See also* LIKE.

as far as. *See* ALL THE FARTHER.

as/like. *See* LIKE.

at. The use of *at* in such expressions as, Where is he *at*? is colloquial and should be avoided.

away. *See* 'WAY.

awful. *See* ADJECTIVES.

awhile, a while. *Awhile* means for a time. (Sleep *awhile*.) After a preposition, *a while* should be used. (Help me for *a while*.)

B

backward(s), forward(s), inward(s), outward(s), onward(s), toward(s). As adverbs, these words may or may not have a final -*s*, although the forms without -*s* are more common in this country. As adjectives, they never have a final -*s*. (The *backward* boy walked *forward*; or *forwards*.)

bad, badly. *Bad* is the adjective; *badly* is the adverb. If you say that you *feel badly*, you are not saying that you feel sick or sorry, but that your sense of touch is lacking in some way. *See also* GOOD.

barely. *See* DOUBLE NEGATIVE.

beautiful. *See* ADJECTIVES.

began, begun. These are, respectively, the standard past tense and past participial forms of the verb *begin*. (Right now, I *begin*. Yesterday, I *began*. Recently, I *have begun*.)

beside, besides. *Beside* means by the side of. (They stood *beside* each other.) *Besides* means moreover. (*Besides*, what difference does it make?)

better, best. *See* HAD BETTER.

between. *See* AMONG.

between you and me. This is the correct expression. *Between you and I* is grammatically incorrect. After a preposition such as *between*, use objective pronouns (me, him, her, them), not subjective pronouns (I, he, she, they).

borrow, lend. One *borrows from* someone and *lends to* someone. (John *borrowed* money *from* Jan. She agreed to *lend* it *to* him.)

but. *See* HELP BUT.

C

calculate, reckon. Both these words mean to compute or arrive at a conclusion after careful consideration. In regional dialects, they are used indiscriminately for such verbs as think, suppose, expect. Avoid such usages in writing.

Calvary, cavalry. *Calvary* is a proper noun, the name of the place where Jesus was crucified. *Cavalry* refers to soldiers on horseback and does not need to be capitalized unless a particular cavalry is being named (the *Ninth Cavalry*).

can, may. *Can* implies the ability to do something; *may* implies permission or chance. (He *can* drive; his father said he *may* go; *may* stay longer.)

can't. *See* AIN'T.

can't hardly. *See* DOUBLE NEGATIVE.

capital, capitol. A *capitol* is the main building of a government. (The *Capitol* in Washington is open to the public.) All other meanings of the word are spelled *capital*. A *capital* means a city that is the seat of government (Washington is the U.S. *capital*; money (How much *capital* can you invest?); or an upper-cased letter. As an adjective, *capital* describes an offense punishable by death. (Stealing was once a *capital* crime.)

case. *See* CIRCUMLOCUTION.

catalog, catalogue. Both spellings are correct.

censor, censure, censer. A *censor* is a person who undertakes to restrict the dissemination of immoral or dangerous communications (such as pornography or correspondence during war). Such a person *censors*, or cuts out objectionable material. *Censure* is blame or condemnation; to censure is to blame or to condemn. (She was *censured* by the principal for cheating.) A *censer* is a vessel in which incense is burned in religious rites.

childish, childlike. Children are both annoying and lovable. Someone who is *childish* reminds one of the annoying traits of children. (His whining and *childish* behavior lost him friends.) Someone who is *childlike* has the innocence and freshness associated with children. (He viewed the most ordinary things with a *childlike* wonder.)

circumlocution. Being concise and direct is a virtue in writing and speaking. The opposite of directness is circumlocution, or talking around a subject before getting to the point. Some words seem to invite circumlocution. One such word is *case*. *In case I can't come* is less direct than *If I can't come*. *In all except a few cases, our winters are mild* could be replaced by *Our winters are almost always mild*. Instead of using *The reason is because*, simply write *because*. Avoid sentences using *in terms of, as to, as for,* and *the fact that*. *See* WRITING A RESEARCH PAPER, page 318, for more examples.

cite, site, sight. *Cite* is a verb meaning to mention specifically as an example, illustration, or authority. (He *cited* the Constitution to support his argument.) *Site* is a noun meaning a location. (We live on the *site* of an ancient Indian village.) Sight may be a noun meaning a view, the capacity for seeing, or the aiming device on a gun; it may also be a verb meaning to identify (we *sighted* a ship in the distance) or to take aim.

citizen. *See* NATIVE.

compare to, compare with. *Compare to* means to show the similarities between two things of different classes. (He *compared* the world *to* a child's ball because both are round.) *Compare with* means to show the similarities and differences of two things in the same class. (*Compare* this house *with* the other and you'll see which is the better value.)

complement, compliment. A *complement* is that which completes; *to complement* is to complete. (That rug *complements* the room; the dessert was the *complement* to a fine meal.) A *compliment* is praise; *to compliment* is to praise. (I *complimented* him on his choice. He returned the *compliment*.)

comprehensible, comprehensive. *Comprehensible* means capable of being understood. *Comprehensive* means complete.

connote, denote. To *connote* means to suggest meanings that are incidental or dependent on associations. To *denote* means to express a specific literal meaning. Words that *denote* the same thing may have quite different *connotations*. For example, *house, home, residence, abode,* and *address* may denote the same structure; a careful writer will choose among these words depending on the *connotations* that seem most appropriate.

continual(ly), continuous(ly). *Continual* refers to a succession of repeated events over a long period of time (*continual* hammer blows, *continual* interruptions). *Continuous* refers to what is unbroken or uninterrupted (a *continuous* flow of traffic, the *continuous* whine of a siren).

could of. *See* OF.

could've. Though common in speech, this contraction of *could have* would normally only appear in informal writing.

council, counsel, consul. A *council* is a meeting or a group set up to govern or advise. (The *council* voted to accept the proposition.) *Counsel* means advice or, as a verb, to advise. (I offer you my *counsel*. She *counseled* him on what steps to take.) *Counsel* also means a lawyer. (The *counsel* for the defense called her first witness.) A *consul* is a government official living in a foreign country.

credible, credulous, creditable. A statement is *credible* if it is believable. A person is *credulous* if he is quick to believe whatever he is told (and hence is easily deceived). A statement or action is *creditable* when it is worthy of being praised or or being given credit.

criteria. *Criteria,* meaning standards of judgment, is plural and takes a plural verb. (Their *criteria* for giving her the promotion were sound.) The singular is *criterion*.

curriculum. The plural of the noun *curriculum,* meaning courses of study in a school, is *curricula.* (The students' *curricula* are arduous. Look at my *curriculum*.)

cute. *See* ADJECTIVES.

D

dangling modifier. A modifier is said to be dangling when the word it properly modifies does not follow immediately, leaving doubt about which word is being modified. Sentences with dangling modifiers must be rephrased to remove the ambiguity. (*At the age of three, John's father died* should be changed to, *When John was three, his father died. Coming into the room, my eyes fell on the dresser* should be changed to, *Coming into the room, I glanced at the dresser.*)

data. *Data* is the plural of *datum;* it means facts or bits of information. *Data* should take a plural verb. (These *data* suggest a good year ahead.)

deduct, deduce. To *deduce* is to reach a conclusion through reasoning. (Sherlock Holmes's method was to *deduce* the identity of the criminal from the clues he found.) To *deduct* is to subtract. (*Deduct* the amount I owe you.)

definitely. *See* ADVERBS.

delusion. *See* ALLUSION.

denote. *See* CONNOTE.

dependent. Spell *dependent* with the *-ent* ending. This is acceptable both for the noun and for the adjective.

desert, dessert. A *desert* is an arid tract of land. To *desert* means to abandon. *Dessert* is a sweet course at the end of a meal. *Deserts,* as in *just deserts,* is a noun meaning deserved reward or punishment.

device, devise. *Device* is a noun meaning an object used for a particular purpose. (The ingenious *device* was too fragile.) *Devise* is a verb meaning to think out or invent. (He *devised* a plan.)

dialog, dialogue. Either spelling is correct. *Dialogue* is more common.

did, done. The past tense of *do* is *did. Done* is the past participle. (He *did* it yesterday. He *has done* things like that before.)

different from, different than. *Different than* is common in speech and informal writing. In formal usage, careful writers use *different from.* (The town is *different from* what it used to be.)

differ from, differ with. To *differ from* means to be unlike. (Her methods *differ from* mine.) To *differ with* means to disagree. (He *differs with* me on the best approach to the problem.)

discreet, discrete. *Discreet* means prudent. (She was *discreet* about his secret.) *Discrete* means distinct or separate. (We must consider three *discrete* elements.)

disinterested, uninterested. Careful speakers and writers are likely to use *disinterested* only to mean impartial. *Uninterested* means indifferent.

dived, dove. Both forms are acceptable for the past tense. He *dived*—or *dove*—off the river bank. As a past participle, *dived* is standard. (He *has dived* from there many times.)

doesn't, don't. Use *doesn't* with singular subjects (except *I* and *you*) and *don't* for all others. (He *doesn't*; they *don't*.)

done. *See* DID.

double negative. Double negatives occur in sentences that use two negative words, making the meaning unclear. There are at least three types of double negatives. If one writes, *It is not unlikely that John will come*, we understand that there is some likelihood that John will come. This type of double negative is acceptable, although slightly roundabout. Such a double negative means what it says: *not unlikely* means *likely*. But *I don't have no money* is unclear. In speech, listeners would understand that this is an emphatic statement about your finances; but logically it could mean that you have some money: I don't have *no* money—I only have a little. Avoid such confusion in formal writing. A third type of double negative is that in which a negative is associated with such weak negative adverbs as *hardly, barely, scarcely,* or *but.* I don't have *but* a dollar). Avoid the use of such double negatives in formal writing or speech.

double possessive. *A friend of John's* illustrates the double possessive. This usage is acceptable.

doubt but. *See* HELP BUT.

dove. *See* DIVED.

dreamed, dreamt. Both spellings are acceptable.

drink, drank, drunk. These are the principal parts of the verb in standard English usage. (They *drink*; they *drank*; they *have drunk*.) The adjective *drunken* is acceptable when it comes before the noun it modifies (*drunken* sailor; the sailor was *drunk*.)

drowned. This is the correct form of the past tense and the past participle of the verb *drown*. Do not say or write *drownded*.

E

each. *See* ANYBODY.

eager. *See* ANXIOUS.

easy. There are some expressions in colloquial English in which *easy* is an adverb. (Take it *easy. Easy* come, *easy* go.) Elsewhere, the adverbial form is *easily*. (I can do that trick *easily*).

economic, economical. Both these forms are adjectives, but the first applies to general matters of finance (*economic* aid, *economic* planning) and the second to specific instances of thrift (an *economical* vacation). The adverb related to both adjectives is *economically*.

effect. *See* AFFECT.

e.g. This abbreviation, which is preceded and followed by commas, is usually used in scholarly writing to mean "for example." *See also* I.E.

egoism, egotism. *Egoism* is a term applied to self-centeredness or to the conviction that one's own personal interests must always be served. It has a philosophical connotation. *Egotism* connotes boasting and much talking about oneself.

either. *Either* goes with *or; neither* goes with *nor*. (*Either* you go *or* I will go. *Neither* you *nor* I can go.) *See also* NEITHER.

elicit, illicit. To *elicit* something means to bring it out. (The response they *elicited* was overwhelming.) If something is *illicit*, it is illegal or immoral. (Their *illicit* affair was kept secret.)

else's. *Anybody else's, everyone else's,* and similar forms are standard usage. *Anybody's else*, once thought to be elegant, is no longer acceptable.

elude. *See* ALLUDE.

emigrant, immigrant. These words can be easily distinguished if one recognizes that the first is formed from the Latin prefix *ex-*, meaning from or out of, while the second carries the prefix *in-*, meaning in or into. One *emigrates* from one country and *immigrates* to another. The same person is both an *emigrant* and an *immigrant*, depending on the writer's point of reference.

eminent, imminent. *Eminent* means distinguished. (The *eminent* scholar lectured at our school.) *Imminent* means about to take place. (The government's collapse is *imminent*.)

enthuse. Many people object to making a verb out of the adjective *enthusiastic*. Avoid its use in formal writing.

epic, epoch. An *epic* is a particular kind of long poem or story about a hero; as an adjective, *epic* refers to the qualities of an epic (for example, heroic, grand). An *epoch* is an historical period of time—an important one having distinct and special characteristics.

epitaph, epithet. An *epitaph* is an inscription on a gravestone. An *epithet* is a phrase that accompanies or replaces the name of a person. (The Little Tramp is an *epithet* for Charlie Chaplin.) *Epithet* may also mean a word of abuse.

epoch. *See* EPIC.

especially, specially. In some contexts, these words are interchangeable. In others, careful writers use *especially* when the meaning is particularly or most importantly, and *specially* when the meaning is uniquely. (Jack was *especially* fond of fried chicken. The car was *specially* built as a racer.)

etc. This abbreviation stands for the Latin *et cetera*, which means *and others*. Do not write "and etc." since this would mean "and and others." *Etc.* nearly always falls at the end of a sentence; in any case, it must be followed by a period since it is an abbreviation. The term is useful to suggest the rest of a long list (he took soap, shampoo, towel, etc.) but it should not be overused.

Writing a Research Paper

everybody, everyone. *See* ANYBODY.

every day, everyday. *Every day* describes an action that takes place day after day. (She went to work *every day*.) *Everyday* is an adjective meaning ordinary. (She wore her *everyday* clothes.)

everywhere. *See* ANYWHERE.

except. *See* ACCEPT.

expect. Expect means to look forward to or to assume something to be proper or likely. (We *expect* your arrival tomorrow at noon. He *expects* too much of me.) In formal writing, the word should not be used as a synonym for *think, suppose,* or *guess*.

F

fact, the fact that. *See* CIRCUMLOCUTION.

famous, infamous. *Famous* means widely known and it may suggest an admirable reason for the fame. *Infamous* means widely known for something considered reprehensible. (Wyatt Earp was a *famous* lawman. Billy the Kid was an *infamous* bandit.)

farther, further. Careful writers use *farther* to refer to physical distance and *further* to refer to additional ideas, thoughts, or other immaterial things. In general usage, the two words are often used interchangeably. *See also* ALL THE FARTHER.

faze. This verb, which means to disturb or to disconcert, is more common in speech than in writing. It should not be confused with *phase*, a noun that means a stage of development.

feel. *See* BAD; GOOD.

fewer. *See* AMOUNT.

figuratively. *See* LITERALLY.

fix. This word in various contexts can mean so many things that objections to what seems to be its overuse have often been voiced. More formal synonyms are available to express most of its meanings. In the sense of getting ready (she's *fixing* to go shopping), the verb usage is regional. The noun, meaning a predicament, is colloquial. (He was in a *fix*.)

flammable, inflammable. Both these words mean easy to set on fire. The negative of *flammable* is *non-flammable*.

flaunt, flout. To *flaunt* is to show off, to display boldly what others may disapprove of. To *flout* is to defy or treat with contempt. (She *flaunted* her jewels. They *flouted* the rules, showing disdain for society's laws.)

fly, flee. Birds *fly*; criminal *flee*. Figuratively, however, fugitives may be said to fly from their pursuers. *Flew* is the past tense of *fly* (the bird *flew* away), and *flown* is its past participle (the bird *has flown* away). The verb *flee* has only one past tense form—*fled*.

formally, formerly. The first is an adverb derived from *formal*. (He was *formally* offered the job in a letter from the president.) *Formerly* is the adverb

derived from *former*. (He was *formerly* the owner of that car.)

former, latter. These terms apply properly to a pair of things or choices. (He had to choose between the red tie and the blue, and he chose the *latter*.) When there are more than two things or choices, *first* may be used instead of *former* and *last* instead of *latter*.

forward(s). *See* BACKWARD(S).

funny. In formal writing, this word is used to mean humorous. (She did not think the story funny at all.) The use of the word to mean odd or peculiar (there is something *funny* about him) should be avoided in formal writing. *See also* ADJECTIVES.

further. *See* FARTHER.

G

gender of singular pronouns. When a pronoun refers back to a singular subject, it is often difficult to determine what gender should be used. (One must raise *his*, or *her*, hand when *he*, or *she*, wants to be recognized.) Traditionally, the singular pronouns *he* and *his* have been used. This may be confusing when the original pronoun or noun is indefinite. In that case, one may substitute the phrases *he or she, him or her*, or *his or her*. (One must raise *his or her* hand when *he or she* wishes to be recognized.) This solution is, unfortunately, cumbersome. In most cases it is best to rewrite the sentence. *You* and *your* can often be substituted for *one* and *his*. (*You* must raise *your* hand.) Some authorities suggest using the plural pronoun even with a singular noun. (*One* must raise *their* hand.) This solution has not been widely accepted, however. In formal writing, use *he/him/his*. *See also* ANYBODY.

get. *Get* has acquired dozens of meanings; therefore, the use of a more specific verb is usually preferred. Such phrases as *get* smart, *get* happy, and *get* mad are acceptable in speech but not in formal writing. Some other phrases such as *get* sick and *get* home are acceptable both in speech and writing. Both *got* and *gotten* are used as the past participle.

go, went, gone. These are the principal parts of the verb *go*. In standard English, *went* is never used as the past participle. (I *go*; I *went*; I *have gone*.)

good, well. *Good* is an adjective that describes a noun (the *good* child). It also describes nouns when used with verbs of appearance, sound, taste, smell, and feel. (The dress looks *good* on her.) *Well* can be the adverb equivalent of good, and is used to describe actions. (He runs *well*.) *Well* may also be an adjective meaning healthy. (I am *well*.) It is in that sense, as an adjective, that it is used in the sentence *I feel well*. *See also* BAD.

got to. This should be changed to *have to*. (I *have to* go; not, I *got to* go.) *See also* HAVE GOT.

H

had better, had best. These expressions are acceptable in speech and writing. (You *had better* come early.)

had of, had've. Neither of these expressions is used in standard English. Write *I wish I had worked harder* rather than *I wish I had've worked harder.*

had ought. Neither this expression nor its negative, *hadn't ought*, is acceptable in writing.

hanged, hung. The past tense of *hang* is *hung*, except when one is referring to an execution by hanging. (The coat *hung* on the hook. The man was *hanged* at dawn.)

hardly. *See* DOUBLE NEGATIVE.

have got. The use of this expression is more common in informal speech than in writing. *We have four dollars* is preferable to *We have got four dollars* in formal writing.

help but. The *but* is usually unnecessary and should be omitted. (I couldn't *help* coming here; not, I couldn't *help but* come here.) Similarly, the use of *but what* should be avoided in careful writing. (I didn't doubt that she meant it; not, I didn't doubt *but what* she meant it.)

hopefully. Careful writers and speakers avoid the use of this word to mean *I (or we) hope. I hope to be there tomorrow* is preferable to *Hopefully, I'll be there tomorrow.*

hung. *See* HANGED.

I

i.e. This abbreviation, usually found in scholarly writing, means "that is." It should be set off by commas. (Plato is concerned with the ideal, *i.e.*, the Forms in the world of Idea.)

illicit. *See* ELICIT.

illusion. *See* ALLUSION.

immigrant. *See* EMIGRANT.

imminent. *See* EMINENT.

imply, infer. To *imply* means to suggest without actually saying so. (You *implied* that I was lying.) To *infer* means to derive a conclusion from evidence, or to surmise. (We *inferred* from her tone of voice that she liked him.)

incidence, incidents. *Incidence* means frequency of occurrence. (The *incidence* of fatal car accidents is rising.) *Incidents* is the plural of *incident*, and means events. (The three *incidents* happened in one week.)

incredible, incredulous. Something that is *incredible* is hard to believe. Someone who is *incredulous* is skeptical. (I found his *incredible* story unconvincing. I was *incredulous* till he proved it was true.)

infamous. *See* FAMOUS.

infer. *See* IMPLY.

infinitive. *See* SPLIT INFINITIVE.

inflammable. *See* FLAMMABLE.

ingenious, ingenuous. *Ingenious* means clever, inventive. (The *ingenious* device could reduce fuel consumption by half.) *Ingenuous* means innocent, guileless, unsophisticated. (His *ingenuous* response disarmed the judge.)

innumerable, numerous. *Innumerable* means countless, too many to be numbered. (The *innumerable* grains of sand represent the passage of time.) *Numerous* means many. (There were *numerous* reasons why the plan failed.)

inside, inside of. *See* OF.

interesting. *See* ADJECTIVES.

intransitive verbs. *See* LIE; RAISE; SET; TRANSITIVE VERBS.

invitation, invite. In formal English, *invite* is a verb. It should not be used as a noun (I got an *invite* to the party); instead, use *invitation*.

inward(s). *See* BACKWARD(S).

irregardless. *Regardless* has a negative suffix already, so *irregardless* is not a word to be used in standard English. (He will come to the party *regardless* of her wishes.)

its, it's. *Its* is the possessive form of *it. It's* is a contraction of *it is.* (The kitten cried when *its* foot was stepped on. *It's* hard to see in the dark.)

it's I, it's me. Precise writers prefer *it's I*, which is the grammatically correct expression. But English speech insists on *it's me, it's him, it's them*, etc. Unless the occasion is very formal, use *me, him, her*, and *them.*

-ize. Be cautious of verbs formed with the *-ize* suffix. If possible use a different word that is more precise. Use *conceive* instead of *conceptualize*; *complete* instead of *finalize*; *perfect* instead of *optimize.*

J

judicial, judicious. *Judicial* is properly used to describe behavior or procedure related to or appropriate to a judge. *Judicious* is an adjective applied to carefully considered and wise conduct. (He spoke in a solemn, *judicial* manner. Although the woman was angry, she acted *judiciously*.)

K

kind of, sort of. Use of these phrases as adverbs meaning rather (I am *kind of* tired today) is informal and should be avoided in formal writing.

L

latter. *See* FORMER.

lay. *See* LIE.

learn, teach. We *learn* what teachers *teach* us. No one can *learn* us anything.

leave, let. In standard English, *leave* never means allow. *Let* is the verb with that meaning. (*Let* us go; not, *leave* us go.)

lend. *See* BORROW.

less, lesser. These are both comparative forms of *little*. *Lesser* is less commonly used, and it is generally confined to comparisons involving judgment of importance (as in the *lesser* of two evils). *See also* AMOUNT.

let. *See* LEAVE.

let's us. *Let's* already means let us, so *let's us* means "let us us," and is incorrect.

lie, lay. These two verbs are often confused. To *lay* an object down is to put it down; to *lie* down is to recline. *Lay* is a transitive verb, which means it must take an object. *Lie* is intransitive and does not need an object. (I *lie* down to sleep. I *lay* the pencil on the table.) The confusion arises in part because the past tense forms of *lie* are *lay* and *lain* (she *lay* back and died; he *had lain* there many days), while the past tense form of *lay* is *laid* (I *have laid* the book down; I *laid* the book down). *See also* TRANSITIVE VERBS.

like, as. Like should be used when a comparison is made between two things. (The fog lay *like* a blanket in the valley. The boys swam *like* fish.) When one part of the comparison is a quality, use *as*. (The scarf was green *as* grass. This boulder is big *as* a house.) When the comparison is between two actions, use *as* or *as if*. (Do *as* I do. She spoke her lines *as if* she were singing.)

literally, figuratively. *Literally* means really, in truth. Do not use it to be emphatic. (When he saw me he *literally* fell through the floor means that he actually did fall through the floor.) *Figuratively* means that you are using a figure of speech and are not to be taken literally.

loose, lose. Something that is *loose* is slack. (My *loose* pants are cool.) If you *lose* something, you cannot find it. (Did you *lose* an earring?)

lousy, lovely. *See* ADJECTIVES.

M

marvelous. *See* ADJECTIVES.

may. *See* CAN.

may of, must of, might of. *See* OF.

mean for. In writing, it is preferable to use *mean that*. (I didn't *mean that* you should go alone; not, *mean for* you to go alone.)

median. This word should not be confused with *medium*. It means middle and may refer to the strip that separates traffic on an expressway or to the middle number in a series. The plural of *median* is *medians*.

medium. This word has several distinct meanings. It is sometimes used to mean a means of communication. (Television is the *medium* I am most interested in.) The plural of *medium* may be either *media* or *mediums*. *Media* is often used to mean all means of mass communication. (The campaign manager sought to promote his candidate in all the *media*—radio, television, newspapers, and even magazines.)

mighty. The use of *mighty* as an adverb (he is *mighty* good at golf) is informal and should be avoided in formal writing.

modifer. *See* DANGLING MODIFIER.

moral, morale. *Moral* is a noun meaning the lesson taught by a story; it is also an adjective denoting ethically correct behavior. (It was the *moral* thing to do.) The plural noun *morals* refers to the general values of a person or group. (Public *morals* are not high in the matter of reporting income to the tax bureau.) *Morale* is a noun meaning the general mood of an individual or of a group of people. (After the defeat, the army's *morale* sank.)

most. *See* ALMOST.

myself. Speakers and writers sometimes use *myself* instead of *I* or *me* to sound modest. Often they sound pretentious instead. Use *myself* only where it is really required to denote a reflexive action. (They thanked my mother and *me* for our contributions. John and *I* will be the two representatives. I deceived *myself* about my talents.)

N

native, citizen. You are a *native* of the place where you were born; you are a *citizen* of the country, state, or other political unit where you have legal rights and duties.

neither, nor. *Neither* and *nor* are negatives and should not be used with other negatives. Use *either* instead. (She will *not* go to *either* place; she will go to *neither* place.) *See also* DOUBLE NEGATIVES; EITHER.

never, not. The indiscriminate use of *never* to mean *not* is colloquial. (I was late this morning because Mother did *not* wake me; not, because Mother *never* woke me.)

nice. *See* ADJECTIVES.

nobody, no one. *See* ANYBODY.

none. *See* ANYBODY.

none is, none are. Although *none* is a compound made from *no* and *one*, the word long ago ceased being only singular. The grammatical number of the verb used with it depends on the meaning of the sentence.

nor. *See* NEITHER.

not. *See* NEVER.

notable, notorious. *Notable* is an adjective meaning noted for. It has a neutral or favorable connotation. Notorious describes someone well known for traits disapproved of. (The *notable* banker died. The *notorious* bank robber died.)

nowhere. *See* ANYWHERE.

number. *See* AMOUNT.

numbers. It is customary to use figures for numbers in addresses, dates, page references, and official names such as *Public School 203*, as well as in lists of numbers, statistics, and mathematical texts. In formal writing, numbers are spelled out at the beginning of sentences. Some writers prefer to spell out all whole numbers less than one hundred and round figures in the hundreds, thousands, and millions after that. Others spell out only whole numbers up to twelve. Whichever style you choose, be consistent. Always write out a number at the beginning of a sentence.

numerous. *See* INNUMERABLE.

O

O, oh. When used as part of a vocative expression, *O* is capitalized and is not separated by punctuation from the name of what is called on. (Where is thy sting, *O* Death?) *Oh* is capitalized only at the beginning of a sentence and is often followed by a comma or exclamation mark. (*Oh!* *Oh*, Henry!) *O* is more common in poetic writing.

of. It is incorrect to use *of* when you mean *have*; could *have*, may *have*, might *have*, must *have*, ought to *have*, should *have*, would *have*, will *have* are the correct expressions, not the previous words used with *of*. (I could *have* gone; not, I could *of* gone.) *Of* is often added to expressions where it is not needed. *All, alongside, inside, off*, and *outside* often have *of* needlessly attached to them. (He took *all* my money; not, *all of* my money. (Note, however, that in a few cases the addition of *of* changes the meaning of the expression. *Inside of* can mean in less than. *Outside of* can mean excluding.)

OK, O.K., okay. This expression is America's contribution to international communication. Known and used almost everywhere in the world as an indication of approval or agreement, it is still not generally used in formal writing. When it is used in informal writing, any of the forms shown here may be used.

on, onto, on to. The prepositions *on* and *onto* sometimes mean the same thing. (She got *on*, or *onto*, the bus.) In some cases, however, *onto* indicates direction of movement and *on* does not. (He stood *on* the desk, then climbed *onto* the bookcase.) *Onto* should not be used where the adverb *on* and the preposition *to* are intended. (Go *on to* the next lesson.)

one. Use of *one* as an indefinite pronoun (*one* scarcely knew what to think) is more common in British than in American English. In most cases, American writers use a definite pronoun (*we* scarcely knew what to think) or the indefinite pronoun *you* (*you* never know).

only. Intonation in speech almost always indicates clearly what *only* should modify in a sentence. In writing, however, the word can cause ambiguity. For example, *I only gave her flowers* could mean several different things; for example, only I (and no one else) gave her flowers; I didn't give her anything else. Careful writers should be certain that the meaning of such a sentence is clear—either from its context or from the careful placement of *only* in the sentence.

onto. *See* ON.

onward(s). *See* BACKWARD(S).

or. *See* AND/OR.

ought. *See* HAD OUGHT.

outside of. *See* OF.

outward(s). *See* BACKWARD(S).

P

pass. The spelling of the past tense and past participle of *pass* is *passed*. Do not confuse it with the noun, adverb, adjective, and preposition *past*. (The *past* president *passed* the house. When he *passed* it, he thought of days gone *past*.)

per, percent. *Per* is a preposition meaning for each or by (*per* diem, *per* year, *per* student). It has a technical connotation and can usually be said more simply (a day, a year, a student). But the term *percent* is indispensable. This word is represented by the symbol % only when it follows a specific figure (40%).

persecute, prosecute. To *persecute* someone is to cause that person to suffer unjustly. (The dictator *persecuted* the opposition.) To *prosecute* is to take legal action against. (We *prosecuted* the company for negligence.)

personal, personnel. *Personal* means having to do with one's private life. *Personnel* refers to employees. (The personnel manager asked me too many *personal* questions.)

perspective, prospective. *Perspective* has to do with ways of seeing things or ways of understanding. (Labor and management look at assembly line work from different *perspectives*.) *Prospective* is an adjective meaning possible in the future. (His wife's pregnancy made him a *prospective* father.)

phenomenon. This word, meaning an occurrence, is singular. The preferred plural is *phenomena*. (Severe weather *phenomena* include thunderstorms, tornadoes, and blizzards.)

plenty. Use of this word as an adverb to strengthen an adjective (he was *plenty* good) is informal and should be avoided in formal writing.

politics. Like many other nouns that end in *-ics* (physics, economics, etc.), this word was originally plural but may now be used as singular. (*Politics is* a demanding profession.)

positively. *See* ADVERBS.

practicable, practical, practically. *Practicable* is an adjective meaning capable of being put into practice. *Practical* is an adjective that means sensible or likely to work to good advantage. (His plan to paint the roof from a helicopter was *practicable*, but it was not at all *practical*.) In informal usage, *practically* is sometimes made to mean almost or nearly. (He was *practically* a moron.) This usage should be avoided in formal writing.

precede, proceed. To *precede* is to go before; to *proceed* is to continue. (He was *preceded* by his wife. After the judge sits, you may *proceed*.)

precedence, precedents. *Precedence* means priority in rank or order. (The king takes *precedence* over the prince.) *Precedents*, the plural of *precedent*, are decisions or actions that have already occurred. (The *precedents* in this case favor the plaintiff's side.)

preposition at the end of a clause. In informal speech and writing, prepositions often occur at the end of clauses or sentences. Careful writers end clauses or sentences with a preposition even in formal writing, especially when alternative forms are cumbersome or awkward. (It was not the kind of party he wanted to go *to*.)

prescribe, proscribe. To *prescribe* is to require or strongly advise. To *proscribe* is to prohibit some action or to banish some person.

presently. This means in a little while. *At present* means now.

pretty. Originally an adjective, *pretty* is too often used in colloquial English as a qualifier of adjectives and adverbs (as in, the book was *pretty* good). Avoid such usage in writing.

principal, principle. As an adjective, *principal* means chief. (The *principal* reason for going was to enjoy the scenery.) *Principal* as a noun may mean a sum of money invested or borrowed; or the head person of a school or of a group of investors. A *principle* is a general rule, assumption, or moral standard. (Speaking softly was a *principle* with her. It is the first *principle* of good leadership to listen. He refused to lie on *principle* even though he knew lying might sometimes profit him.)

proceed. *See* PRECEDE.

pronouns. *See* GENDER.

prophecy, prophesy. If someone *prophesies*, that person produces a *prophecy*. (She *prophesies* doom but no one pays attention to her *prophecies*.)

proscribe. *See* PRESCRIBE.

prosecute. *See* PERSECUTE.

prospective. *See* PERSPECTIVE.

proved, proven. Both forms are used as the past participle of the verb to *prove*. *Proven* is less frequent, except when it modifies a noun (a *proven* evil).

Q

quantity. Uncountable things such as milk, sand, and lumber, are measured as *quantities*. Countable things should not be referred to as *quantities*. There may be a large *quantity* of sand on a beach, but *many* (not a large *quantity* of) people.

quote, quotation. *Quote* is a verb meaning to repeat what has been said or written. *Quotation* is a noun. Use of *quote* as a noun (I saw a *quote* from her in the paper) is informal and should be avoided in formal writing.

R

raise, rise. To raise means to lift or grow something. It is a transitive verb and must take an object. (I *raise* my hand. I *raise* chickens.) To *rise* means to get up or to increase in size. It is intransitive and does not need an object. (I *rise* at six. The river *rises* in the spring.) *See also* TRANSITIVE VERBS.

rarely ever, seldom ever. The *ever* is omitted from these expressions in formal writing.

rational, rationale, rationalization. *Rational* is an adjective meaning sensible. (Her behavior was *rational*.) *Rationale* is a noun meaning the reason behind an action or idea. (His *rationale* for doing so was to make money.) A *rationalization* is an excuse, usually a false one though the person rationalizing may not know it. (Excusing her theft because she was unhappy was a *rationalization*.)

real, really. *Real* is an adjective. Do not use it as an adverb. (It was *really* big; not, *real* big.) *See also* ADVERBS.

reckon. *See* CALCULATE.

regardless. *See* IRREGARDLESS.

respectfully, respectively. *Respectfully* describes courteous behavior. *Respectively* means considering several items in the order named. (The three boys, Jack, Tom, and Bob excelled in swimming, golf, and tennis, *respectively*.)

rise. *See* RAISE.

run. The past tense of this verb is *ran*, but its past participle is *run*. (The rabbit *ran* away last night. We are sorry that it *has run* away.)

S

said, same. These words, when used in legal documents, mean the person or thing identified earlier. (*Said* lessor shall have the quiet enjoyment of *same* for the term of this lease.) This is a technical usage and should be avoided in careful writing.

scarcely. *See* DOUBLE NEGATIVE.

see, saw, seen. These are the standard principal parts of the verb. (I *see* a bird. I *saw* it yesterday. I *have seen* it here often.)

seldom every. *See* RARELY EVER.

set, sit. *Sit* is usually an intransitive verb. Its past tense and past participle are *sat*. (They *sit* around the table. She *sat* beside me.) *Set* is usually a transitive verb. Its past and past participle forms are also *set*. (He *set* the dishes on the table). As an intransitive verb, *set* is used principally to describe the sun (the sun *sets* at six) and the incubation of eggs by birds (a hen *setting*).

shall, will. In declarative sentences, *shall* and *will* have come to have the same meaning. *Shall* is less often used, except when strong intention is being expressed. (I *shall* return.) In questions, however, the two words have different meanings. *Shall we go through Atlanta?* suggests that a decision to do so may be made. *Will we go through Atlanta?* suggests that the decision has been made but that the speaker is not yet aware of it.

should, would. *Should* may be used to express obligation (it's late; you *should* go to bed) or likelihood (we *should* be finished with this by noon). *Would* may express habitual action (he *would* walk in the woods each morning before we were up) or polite requests (*would* you bring something to eat?). In conditional clauses, *should* suggests uncertainty. (If she *should* come before seven, I will get to meet her.) *Would* suggests desire on the part of the speaker that the condition be fulfilled. (If only she *would* come before seven, I would be able to meet her.)

should of. *See* OF.

sight. *See* CITE.

sing. In formal English, *sang* is the past tense of *sing*, while *sung* is its past participle. (I *sing* in the morning. I *sang* yesterday. I *have sung* all my life.)

singular pronouns. *See* GENDER.

sink. Either *sank* or *sunk* may be used as the past tense of this verb (*sank* is more common). The past participle is *sunk*, except when it is used as an adjective; *sunken* may then be used. (We were searching for *sunken* treasure.)

sit. *See* SET.

site. *See* CITE.

slow(ly). Both *slow* and *slowly* are used as adverbs. *Slow* is used only in a few common expressions (go *slow*), while *slowly* is used in all other cases (he climbed the hill *slowly*).

so. In informal speech and writing, *so* is sometimes used as a qualifier meaning *very*. (He was *so* big.) This usage is not incorrect, but it can easily be overused and tiresome.

somebody, someone. *See* ANYBODY.

somewhere. *See* ANYWHERE.

sort of. *See* KIND OF.

specially. *See* ESPECIALLY.

specie, species. *Specie* is a rarely used word that means money in the form of coins; the word has no plural form. *Species*, which means a kind or class of thing, may be used either as a singular or plural noun.

split infinitive. At one time grammarians frowned on placing a word between the two parts of an infinitive verb. (He failed *to fully understand* the test.) Today, splitting the infinitive in this manner is acceptable as long as the result is not awkward.

stationary, stationery. The first of these words is an adjective meaning unchanging or fixed. The second is a noun that means writing materials.

statistics. This word is always treated as a plural noun unless it means a branch of study. (*Statistics* is a kind of applied mathematics.) The singular form *statistic* must refer to a single fact. (One *statistic* stood out from the rest: the country's growth rate.)

stayed, stood. The past tense of *stay* is *stayed*; the past tense of *stand* is *stood*. (I *stayed* up all night; not, I *stood* up all night, unless you stood on your feet all night.)

stratum. The most frequently used plural of this word, which means a layer, is *strata*.

such. Use of *such* as a mere qualifier is colloquial (as in, we had *such* a good time).

sure to. Use *sure to* and not *sure and*. (Be *sure to* bring your records; not, be *sure and* bring your records.)

swim. The past tense of *swim* is *swam*; the past participle is *swum*. (I *swam* here yesterday. I *have swum* here every summer.)

T

teach. *see* LEARN.

terrible, terrific. *See* ADJECTIVES.

than, then. *Than* means when compared with or except. (He is better equipped for it *than* you. I'd rather be anywhere *than* here.) *Then* means at that time. (*Then* I went to the store.)

that. *See* WHICH, THAT.

that there. *See* THIS (THESE) HERE.

their, theirs, there, there's, they're. *Their* and *theirs* mean belonging to them. (*Their* house is red. It's *theirs*.) *There* means at that place. (Meet me *there*.) *There* is also used to introduce a sentence. (*There* is nothing left.) *There's* is a shortened form of *there is*. (*There's* nothing left.) *They're* is a shortened form of *they are*. (*They're* going too.)

theirselves. *Themselves*, not *theirselves*, is the correct word.

then. *See* THAN.

this (these) here, that (those) there. Leave out the *here* and *there* in these expressions.

though (tho). *See* ALTHOUGH.

thru. This simplified spelling of *through* is never used in formal writing.

till, until. These words may be used interchangeably. *'Til* is not acceptable.

to, too, two. *Too* means also or more than enough. (I want some, *too*. They were *too* loud.) *Two* is the number 2. In every other case, the spelling is *to* (*to* run, give it *to* me, *to* and fro, from New York *to* California, dance *to* the music).

toward(s). *See* BACKWARD(s).

transitive verbs. A transitive verb always has to be followed by an object in order to complete its meaning. (*Lay the book* on the table. *Set it* down. *Raise the curtain.*) An intransitive verb does not require an object. (I *lie* on the bed. I *sit* in the chair. I *rise* at six.) *See also* LIE; RAISE; SET.

U

uninterested. *See* DISINTERESTED.

unique. *See* ADJECTIVES.

unless. Do not substitute *without* for *unless*. (I won't go *unless* you take me; not, *without* you taking me.)

until. *See* TILL.

used. Be careful not to drop the *d* in the past tense of *use*, especially in the expression *used to*. (I *used to* go; not, *use to* go.)

V

venal, venial. *Venal* describes corruption or corruptibility as a result of greed. *Venial* means forgivable. A *venial* sin is not a deadly sin.

very. *See* ADVERBS.

virtue, virtuosity. *Virtue* refers to merit of any sort. *Virtuosity* refers to an artist's technical skill.

W

wait for, wait on. *Wait on* means to serve. (He *waits on* tables.) In the sense of *wait for*, the use of *wait on* is colloquial. (We're *waiting for* Fred; not, we're *waiting on* Fred.)

'way, away. In informal speech, *away* is often shortened to *'way*. Avoid such usage in writing.

well. *See* BAD; GOOD.

went. *See* GO.

which, that. *Which* and *that* have the same meaning, but *which*, preceded by a comma, is usually used for nonrestrictive clauses—those that describe antecedent nouns but are not necessary to identify them. *That* is used in restrictive clauses—those that are necessary to identify the antecedent nouns. *She stroked the cat that bit her* tells you that she stroked that particular cat, the one that bit her. *She stroked the cat, which bit her* assumes that we already know which cat, and adds the information that the cat bit her after she stroked it.

which, who. Use *who* instead of *which* when you are referring to people. (The boys *who* own this car are rude.)

while. *See* AWHILE.

who, whom, whoever, whomever. Traditionally *who* and *whoever* are the subjects of sentences; *whom* and *whomever* are the objects. (*Who* is coming? *Whom* did you wish to see?) *Whom* and *whomever* are disappearing, however, and are being replaced by *who* and *whoever*. Many authorities consider it acceptable to write, *Who* did you wish to see? Using *whom* where *who* is required is a more serious error. Use *whom* only when you are sure it is the object of a sentence. Never use it to sound elegant if you are uncertain.

whose, who's. *Whose* is the possessive form of *who*. (*Whose* coat is this?) *Who's* is a contraction of *who is*. (*Who's* going to go?)

will. *See* SHALL.

-wise. This suffix should be used in formal writing to mean in the manner or direction of (*clockwise, otherwise, lengthwise*). Do not use it to mean in regard to. (I'm having *financial* trouble; not, I'm having trouble *moneywise*.)

without. *See* UNLESS.

wonderful. *See* ADJECTIVES.

would. *See* SHOULD.

Y

you. *See* ONE.

you all. This is a regional expression. *You* is the accepted singular and plural noun.

you and I. *You and I*, *he*, or *she* should be used as subjects. (*You and I* can do it.) As an object of a verb or preposition, use objective forms with *you*. (He called *you and me*. I must choose between *you and her*.)

your, you're. *Your* is possessive. (Take *your* hat.) *You're* is a contraction of *you are*. (*You're* going?)

For Further Reference

Ehrlich, Eugene, and Murphy, Daniel
Writing and Researching Term Papers and Reports
Bantam Books

Kurtinitis, Sandra
A Brief and Lively No-Nonsense Guide to Writing
Scott, Foresman

University of Chicago
A Manual of Style (13th ed.)
University of Chicago Press

Strunk, William, Jr., and White, E. B.
The Elements of Style (2nd ed.)
Macmillan

Turabian, Kate L.
Student's Guide for Writing College Papers (3rd ed.)
University of Chicago Press

Literature

Literature is one of our great cultural inheritances from the past; it is an essential subject for study in any complete education. This section introduces the study of literature by describing the nature of literature, the history of literature, and the great writers and literary works of the past.

There are three principal forms of literature: poetry, drama, and fiction. This section is divided into those three categories for study. Each category first defines the literary form and then explains its special value and importance. A brief history of that particular form of literature follows. Finally, each section concludes with a detailed alphabetical listing of the most important writers of the past who have worked in that literary form.

The last major section is an alphabetical listing of some literary masterpieces with brief summaries of their contents. For more guidance on good reading, see *The Young Reader's Companion* in this volume.

Introduction

Literature, broadly defined, is all written matter. The medium of music is sound, the medium of visual art is form, and the medium of literature is words. Like music or art, literature may be either inspirational or utilitarian. It ranges from the sublime to the workaday, from the Shakespearean tragedy to the magazine advertisement.

Since the early 1800's, the word "literature" has come to mean primarily written expressions that are of lasting importance or value. Used in this sense, literature is the written artistic legacy of a particular time to later generations. To identify the period or society, we speak of medieval literature, 18th-century literature, or American or Russian literature.

Literature is one of the distinguishing achievements of the earliest civilized societies. Among the earliest printed symbols were Egyptian hieroglyphics and Chinese ideograms. The first literary documents were scrolls and manuscripts that were copied and recopied by hand. Written literature was available only to a se-

lect few who were important or wealthy enough to afford such documents. In modern society, literature has become available to millions, thanks to the printing press. Printing was first known in China in the ninth century, and it became a major influence on European history when the German printer Johann Gutenberg developed movable type in the 1400's.

Forms of literature. The principal forms of literary expression are poetry, drama, and fiction. Most of these forms can be traced to ancient times. They have been revived whenever their special qualities fulfilled the needs of a given age and society. Poems, plays, and fiction are considered separately in the pages that follow.

Other literary forms have also had great importance. Gutenberg's first printed book was the Bible; to this day it is the most widely printed book in most European languages.

For centuries, history was a major literary form. An

early example is *The Peloponnesian War*, written by the Greek Thucydides in about 400 B.C., an account of the struggle between the Athenians and Spartans. Most cultures produce their own accounts of the historical episodes they consider to be most important.

A history devoted to the life of a person is called a biography. The Roman writers Plutarch and Suetonius, in the first and second centuries A.D., were among the earliest known biographers. Modern biography is usually traced to the publication of James Boswell's *Life of Samuel Johnson* in England in 1791. A biographical history written by the person himself is called an autobiography. One of the earliest such works is the *Confessions* of St. Augustine, written after 400 A.D. Since that time, many famous people have recorded the story of their own lives for posterity. When not formally revised, an autobiography remains a diary. Samuel Pepys kept a remarkable and entertaining diary in the late 1600's in England. More recently, *The Diary of Anne Frank*, written by a young girl in the 1940's, has been translated into dozens of languages. It records the persecution of her family and friends by the Nazis.

Another literary form that has special historical and intellectual importance is the essay. An essay is a short composition, usually in prose, devoted to a philosophical discussion of one or more topics. The term was used by the French writer Montaigne in 1580; *essai*, in French, means "attempt." In his writings, Montaigne tries informally to define and illuminate particular topics that concern him. One of the great revivals of the essay as a literary form occurred in the 1700's in England. Joseph Addison and Richard Steele developed the occasional essay for their journal *The Spectator*; other great writers of the century, including Jonathan Swift and Samuel Johnson, also wrote probing and serious essays. Today, essays may appear as magazine articles or as feature columns in newspapers.

For the most part, however, the study of literature concentrates on the three principal literary forms—poetry, plays, and fiction. Histories, biographies, and essays are usually *denotative*: they seek to present direct and explicit meanings without obvious emotion and without ambiguity. Poems, fiction, and plays, however, communicate an emotional and intellectual impression that cannot be reduced to a single meaning. They are essentially *connotative*: they seek to present suggestive meanings that are by their very nature emotional and ambiguous. Histories and essays mean exactly what they say; poems, fiction, and plays mean far more than they say. This imaginative energy of poems, fiction, and plays provides the essential pleasures found in the study of literature.

Approaches to literature.

Great works of literature can be understood in at least three ways. The first is biographical. A work of literature provides an insight into the mind and personality of the author. In this sense, literature may be approached as the study of great minds in human history. A second way is historical. Literature provides insight into other times and places. In this sense, literature may be approached as the study of the great moments in human history. A third way is interpretive. Great literary works provide insight into enduring human problems. The interpretive approach is the most difficult, but also the most rewarding. It involves close attention to the work itself free from biographical or historical distractions. The power of great literature lies in its ability to tell a reader what authors from other times and places understand about life's possibilities. As the great English essayist and poet Matthew Arnold wrote, the value of literature lies in "making us know ourselves and the world."

There are many forms of literature. Biography, of which Abraham Lincoln (left) has frequently been a subject, relates the life of a well-known or interesting person. Poetry is often written to commemorate an important event, as when Maya Angelou (right) recited at President Clinton's inauguration.

Poetry

Samuel Johnson, author of the first important dictionary of the English language, wrote that "the essence of poetry is invention, such invention as by producing something unexpected, surprises and delights." Johnson's emphasis on "invention" points up the imaginative qualities of poetry, but poetry also "surprises" in the sense that it provides knowledge. Poetry "delights" or entertains as well; from earliest times poets have seen themselves as singers.

A useful addition to Johnson's definition might be the suggestion that poetry's subject matter is the enduring emotional and philosophical problems of human existence. Ezra Pound had this timeless quality in mind when he wrote that poetry is "news that stays news."

Kinds of poetry.
There are many specific kinds of poetry, but they can be reduced to three principal categories. The first is *lyric* poetry, named for the Greek lyre, a stringed musical instrument. A lyric poem is a brief musical expression of the thoughts and feelings of a single speaker. "Lyric" also refers to the words of a song, and lyric poetry includes many humorous and witty types of light verse as well as serious works.

The second category is *narrative* poetry, which is usually longer than lyric poetry and tells a story. There are many sorts of narrative poems, ranging from the ancient Greek epic the *Iliad* to such popular poems as "The Midnight Ride of Paul Revere" by Longfellow.

The third category is *dramatic* poetry, which is often written in the dialogue form of drama but is not intended for performance. Dramatic poetry is distinct for being able to present more than one speaker, although single-speaker dramatic monologues are also common.

Poetic devices.
Most poetry presents certain difficulties for the reader because it attempts to present a thought that can never be paraphrased fully in prose. Its language is often compressed and "difficult," requiring closer reading than prose. A poem can change before a reader's eyes as different aspects of its language emerge.

Poetic language usually includes imagery—a visual expression of thought and feeling. A simple example is Robert Burns's line
My love is like a red red rose.
Figurative language, as in Wordsworth's simile
I wandered lonely as a cloud,
is a way to express a complex thought briefly. Poems also use symbols, things that represent a variety of associations rather than a single meaning, such as the raven in Edgar Allan Poe's poem of that name. These devices may also be found in plays and fiction.

A troubadour, performer of lyric poetry.

Poetic drama: Shakespeare

Poetry's unique quality is its use of rhythm and sound. From the simple repeating rhythms of folk ballads like "Barbara Allen," to the subtle use of blank (unrhymed) verse by Shakespeare, poets use the rhythm of the language to emphasize their meaning. Among poetry's sound effects are rhymes, often of words at the end of lines; and alliteration, the use of words with the same consonants. The last lines of Shakespeare's Sonnet 18 illustrate both rhyme and alliteration (words beginning with "L").

> *So long as men can breathe, or eyes can see,*
> *So long lives this, and this gives life to thee.*

Poets may also use visual effects. Acrostics are poems in which the first letters of each line spell out a word or name. There are even some "picture-poems" in which the lines form the shape of the object they describe, as in George Herbert's "Easter Wings."

Poetry, then, is a special reading experience in which the style of expression is as important as the content of the words. Because of its rhythm and sound, most poetry is best read aloud so that its language can be appreciated. If a reading of a poem manages to catch its invention, surprise, and delight, then the assertion of American poet Archibald MacLeish in "Ars Poetica" is fulfilled:

> *A poem should not mean*
> *But be.*

A modern poet: Allen Ginsberg.

Some common verse forms

ballad. Narrative poem consisting of four-line stanzas with alternating rhymes. Folk ballads were handed down from generation to generation and were originally sung. Major poets sometimes use the form, as did Keats in "La Belle Dame sans Merci."

dramatic monologue. Form of dramatic poetry in which only a single character speaks, gradually revealing his or her own dramatic situation. Robert Browning wrote many dramatic monologues. T.S. Eliot's "The Love Song of J. Alfred Prufrock" is a famous modern example.

elegy. Named from the Greek word for "lament," elegies are lyric poems on the subject of death. The death may be that of an individual, as in Auden's "In Memory of W. B. Yeats" and Milton's *Lycidas*, or in a more figurative sense that of all men, as in Donne's *Elegies* or Gray's "Elegy Written in a Country Churchyard."

epic. Long narrative poem whose subject is of major importance. The major classical epics are Homer's *Iliad* and *Odyssey* and Vergil's *Aeneid*.

hymn. Lyric poem in praise of God, or, by extension, anything of great value. The *Homeric Hymns* celebrate the Greek gods. Donne wrote "A Hymn to God the Father," and Shelley wrote a "Hymn to Intellectual Beauty."

limerick. A humorous poem of five lines. The first, second, and fifth lines rhyme, while the shorter third and fourth lines have a different rhyme. "Hickory Dickory Dock" is a limerick.

ode. Lyric poem of irregular form, often used to express deep personal feelings. Odes originated with the ancient Greek poet Pindar. English examples include Keats's "Ode to a Nightingale," and Wordsworth's "Ode: Intimations of Immortality."

romance. Long narrative poem based on legend. Among the heroes of romance are Roland in France, King Arthur and his knights in Britain, and Orlando in Italy. *Sir Gawain and the Green Knight* is the most important literary romance in English. The term also describes a type of historical novel.

sonnet. Lyric poem of 14 lines. The sonnet originated in Italy and was taken over by English poets, many of whom used a different rhyme scheme. The sonnet has been used by such English poets as Spenser, Shakespeare, Milton, and Keats.

Poetry	1500	1550	1600	1650	1700

Europe

DANTE   ARIOSTO

England/Ireland

SPENSER
SHAKESPEARE
DONNE
CHAUCER
MILTON
MARVELL
DRYDEN

The history of poetry. Poetry is the oldest of literary forms, growing from the ancient combination of music and speech. The oldest written poems are probably written transcriptions of even older poetic legends that were originally sung or chanted by generations of traveling poet-singers or bards.

Ancient poetry. The first extant poem is the Babylonian epic *Gilgamesh*, which may date as far back as 2000 B.C. It is a collection of myths that have parallels in many later traditions. The true foundations of Western literature, however, are the Greek epics the *Iliad* and the *Odyssey*. Set down in the eighth century B.C. and attributed to the legendary poet Homer, these poems have provided a common mythology for Western literature. Their importance to Western literature is rivaled only by the Bible. The *Aeneid*, by the Latin poet Vergil, is the third great classical epic.

The Middle Ages. Poetry became moribund after the fall of Rome, when literary Latin was more and more separated from the language of everyday speech. When the new vernacular languages of Europe gained acceptance, however, poetry was reborn. Among the earliest poems were the Old English *Beowulf* in the 700's, the Gaelic-Celtic legends in the 800's, the French *Song of Roland* in the 1000's, and the Spanish *Song of the Cid* in the 1100's. These poems used new European myths, but they also portrayed their characters with a new kind of realism. Between 1050 and 1250, the troubadours of southern France completely abandoned the traditional heroic sagas to write simple love lyrics.

The Renaissance. Because of the influence of Latin, Italy was slow to accept a new vernacular language for poetry. With the appearance of Dante's *Divine Comedy* just after 1300, however, Italian culture flowered in a rebirth, or Renaissance, of its past Roman glory. Dante's vision of hell, purgatory, and heaven was filled with references to the villains and heroes of his own day, yet it owed much to the Christian church of the Middle Ages and to the Latin classics, especially to Vergil.

Chaucer's Wife of Bath, teller of one of the Canterbury Tales

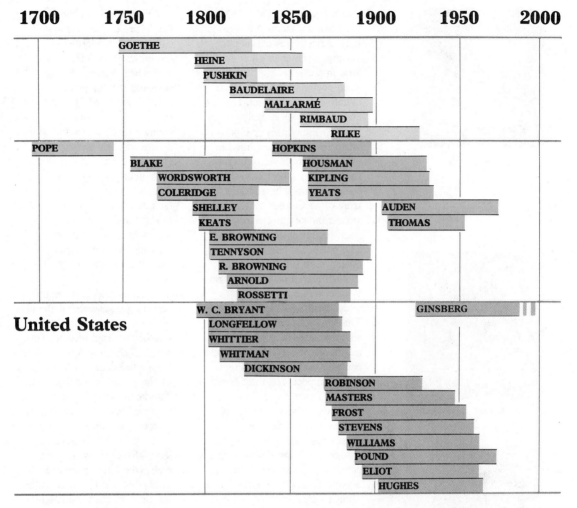

| 1700 | 1750 | 1800 | 1850 | 1900 | 1950 | 2000 |

GOETHE
HEINE
PUSHKIN
BAUDELAIRE
MALLARMÉ
RIMBAUD
RILKE

POPE
HOPKINS
BLAKE
HOUSMAN
WORDSWORTH
KIPLING
COLERIDGE
YEATS
SHELLEY
AUDEN
KEATS
THOMAS
E. BROWNING
TENNYSON
R. BROWNING
ARNOLD
ROSSETTI

United States

W. C. BRYANT
GINSBERG
LONGFELLOW
WHITTIER
WHITMAN
DICKINSON
ROBINSON
MASTERS
FROST
STEVENS
WILLIAMS
POUND
ELIOT
HUGHES

The first great English poet, Geoffrey Chaucer, visited Italy in the late 1300's and incorporated some Italian poetic innovations into his *Canterbury Tales*, but the English language waited until the late 1500's for its first great age of poetry. Then Edmund Spenser created his epic *Faerie Queene*, while Shakespeare and Donne worked most successfully in a lyric mode. In the 1600's, Milton's epic *Paradise Lost* and Andrew Marvell's lyric poems appeared. These writers still measured their works against the Greek and Latin classics. By the 1700's English poetry was being decisively challenged by prose—especially by the novel—and its golden age had passed.

Romanticism. The next great age of poetry arrived at the end of the 1700's. Romanticism was a movement that valued the natural over the artificial, the emotional over the formal, and the modern over the classical. Goethe and his contemporaries in Germany were the formulators of Romanticism, but the greatest body of Romantic poetry was written in English by Blake, Wordsworth, Coleridge, Byron, Shelley, and Keats. A movement akin to Romanticism surfaced in the mid-1800's in France in the works of Baudelaire, Mallarmé, and Rimbaud.

The American tradition in poetry was effectively begun by Longfellow, whose emphasis on historical legend was indebted to the English poets of the 1800's. In 1855, however, Walt Whitman published *Leaves of Grass*, a rowdy collection of unrhymed and unmetered free verse. It marked the beginning of modern poetry in English and became an important influence on poetry not only in America, but in many other parts of the world as well.

Modern poetry. Modern poetry has developed as a distinctly international phenomenon. Promising American poets such as T.S. Eliot and Ezra Pound emigrated to Europe. Britain's W. H. Auden and Dylan Thomas lived or traveled in the United States. The Irish poet W. B. Yeats lived much of his life in London before dying in France. The modern poets combine the conflicting impulses of classicism and Romanticism, past and present.

Dickinson

Poets

Hughes

Walcott

Whitman

Ariosto, Lodovico (1474–1533). Born in the citadel of Reggio in Italy, Ariosto was educated in Ferrara, a center of great cultural importance. He began to write poetry in Latin that was imitative of the classics. His importance rests entirely on *Orlando Furioso*, an epic published in 1516 and enlarged in 1532. Written in vernacular Italian rather than Latin, the poem presents a bewildering array of adventures centered around the knight Orlando's quest for his beloved Angelica. The poem had an important influence on Elizabethan English literature, especially on Spenser's *Faerie Queene*.

Arnold, Matthew (1822–1888). The son of a famous English educator, Matthew Arnold was an important essayist, critic, and educator, as well as a major Victorian poet. His most famous poem, "Dover Beach," is a distinctly modern expression of helplessness in the face of impending social and political change. Arnold's other principal poetic works include "The Scholar Gypsy," "Thyrsis," and "Empedocles on Etna."

Auden, Wystan Hugh (1907–1973). The most important English poet in the first half of the 1900's, Auden fought in the Spanish Civil War in the 1930's and then left England in 1939 for residence in the United States. In England, his earliest poems brought him immediate fame because of their technical proficiency, complex forms, rhythmic patterns, and rhyme schemes. Auden also became a leading intellectual poet, one who experimented with ideas associated with Freud, with socialism, and with German rather than English or American literary history.

Baudelaire, Charles Pierre (1821–1867). The most impor-tant French poet of the 1800's, Baudelaire exerted a major influence on modern poetry in several languages. His father died when Baudelaire was six years old and his mother quickly remarried. These events left him deeply disturbed. As a young man he gravitated to the bohemian Latin Quarter of Paris, where he led a profligate life notable for affairs with famous actresses. His most famous work is *Les Fleurs du Mal* ("Flowers of Evil"), a six-part poetic autobiography of the mind famous for images and ideas that tend to shock its readers.

Beowulf. Written in the eighth century A.D., *Beowulf* is the old-est surviving poem in the Old English, or Anglo-Saxon, lan-guage. *Beowulf* was transcribed from a fire-damaged manuscript by the Icelandic scholar G. J. Thorkelin in 1787. All evidence suggests that the poem is a late recording of early myths by an unknown author. It tells the story of the young hero Beo-wulf, who killed a monster called Grendel that was raiding the camp of the Danish King Hrothgar. Beowulf later becomes King of the Geats and defeats a dragon in mortal com-bat. *Beowulf* is a great early European moral fable in which good triumphs over evil because of the direct intervention of God.

Blake, William (1757–1827). One of the most extraordinary English poets, Blake was known in his own time only as a failed painter. Self-taught, he was thoroughly absorbed by the study of the Bible and the works of Milton. Blake's major works attempt to create a mod-ern myth that supercedes ration-ality about the creation and order of the world. After the short lyrics collected in *Songs of*

Innocence and *Songs of Experience*, Blake began to write longer poems, such as *The Four Zoas, Milton,* and *Jerusalem.* These three poems elaborate on a visonary scheme about the hidden workings of the world; they were often illustrated with pictures in Blake's own unusual style.

Browning, Elizabeth Barrett (1806–1861). The invalid daughter of a rigidly disciplinarian father, Elizabeth Barrett married the poet Robert Browning in 1846; the couple soon left England for residence in Italy. Barrett Browning had written poetry since childhood, but her most ambitious work is the book-length poem *Aurora Leigh*, published in 1857. Termed by her a "novel-poem," *Aurora Leigh* was an attempt to write a verse epic set in contemporary Victorian surroundings rather than in the distant past. Barrett Browning was also the author of many sonnets, most of them addressed to her husband.

Browning, Robert (1812–1889). One of the preeminent poets of Victorian England, Browning was married to the poet Elizabeth Barrett Browning from 1846 until her death 15 years later. His major poems are dramatic monologues in which a character, generally a personage from European history, speaks directly to the reader and slowly reveals his or her circumstances. Browning was a prolific poet, writing many long works. In his later years he became increasingly interested in Italian history and art.

Bryant, William Cullen (1794–1878). A lawyer and editor of *The New York Evening Post*, Bryant was considered by many to be "America's Poet Laureate" because of the influence of his poems and theories about poetry in the early 1800's. His most famous work is "Thanatopsis," a meditation on death composed when he was a teenager and published after many revisions in 1817.

Byron, George Gordon (1788–1824). Lord Byron was the most popular of the English Romantic poets in his own day. This popularity was based partly on his flamboyant life, great physical beauty, and reputation as a lover. He first became known with the publication of *Childe Harold's Pilgrimage.* When fame led to a celebrated divorce, Byron left England for the Continent and continued to add to the poem. The success of a satire called *Beppo* encouraged him to begin another, and it is on the basis of the second, *Don Juan*, that Byron's reputation stands today.

Chaucer, Geoffrey (1340?–1400). The first great poet in the English language, Chaucer was a court diplomat whose travels in Europe brought him into contact with the early works and writers of the Italian Renaissance. He wrote a number of important poems, including *The Parliament of Fowls* and *Troilus and Criseyde*, but his major work was *The Canterbury Tales.* Written late in life and published after his death, the 24 tales are all told by pilgrims on the way to Canterbury Cathedral to visit the shrine of St. Thomas à Becket. Chaucer's work is written in Middle English, an early form of the language alien to modern eyes but close enough to modern English to be read without translation.

Cid, Song of the. The oldest extant poem of a longer Spanish epic cycle, *Song of the Cid* was written in 1140 A.D. and transcribed from a damaged manuscript in 1779. In almost 4000 lines, it tells the story of a popular military leader, *El Cid*, based on the life of an actual eleventh-century leader named Rodrigo Díaz de Bivar. In the poem the hero is unjustly exiled, fights as a mercenary in the employ of both the Spaniards and their enemy the Moors, and finally returns to favor with a victory for Spain at the Battle of Valencia. In comparison with other early European epics, *Song of the Cid* is unusual for its historical accuracy and for recounting political events realistically.

Coleridge, Samuel Taylor (1772–1834). The most eccentric of the English Romantic poets, Coleridge contributed "The Rime of the Ancient Mariner," a fantastic vision, to the important collection of *Lyrical Ballads* issued in collaboration with Wordsworth in 1798. Coleridge also wrote "Kubla Khan," a dream vision about an elaborate "pleasure dome." Coleridge had immense talents and immense ambitions, but because of irregular personal habits both remained unfulfilled. He did write a number of important poems, however, including "Dejection: An Ode," "Christabel," and "The Eolian Harp," as well as a major work of literary criticism called *Biographica Literaria*.

Dante Alighieri (1265–1321). Dante was a prominent citizen of Florence, Italy, when he published his first poems in *La Vita Nuova* ("The New Life") in 1292. In 1300 he fell from political favor, however, and it was then that he set about composing his *Commedia*, which is usually referred to as the *Divine Comedy*. An epic poem, the *Divine Comedy* recounts the poet's visits to Hell (Inferno), Purgatory (Purgatorio), and Heaven (Paradiso). It is of special importance for being

written in the Italian vernacular language rather than in Latin. In the poem Dante is guided through the *Inferno* and the *Purgatorio* by his poetic mentor Vergil. His guide to *Paradiso* is Beatrice, his beloved. The poem is partly concerned with political justice, and Dante places identifiable historical figures in each of the three realms of the afterlife.

Dickinson, Emily (1830–1886). Unmarried and in her later years an eccentric recluse in her father's Amherst, Massachusetts, home, Dickinson refined a very personal style and vision in more than 1800 short poems, only seven of which were published in her lifetime. Her finest poems join domestic details with larger abstractions in unlikely ways. For example, courtship is a metaphor for death in "Because I Could Not Stop for Death/He Kindly Stopped for Me." Terse and witty, her poems find wisdom in insignificant details rather than in large social or political issues.

Donne, John (1572–1631). Born into a Catholic family at a time when Catholics were persecuted in England, John Donne later became a Church of England minister and an influential preacher. He was also the most important writer of "metaphysical" poetry, in which a poetic point is made by means of surprising and often improbable analogies. In "The Flea," for example, the bite of the bug becomes a figurative representation of the love between two people. Other poems in this vein, which Donne called "far-fetched wit," include "A Fever" and "The Bait." Donne was also the author of a sequence called *Holy Sonnets* and a group of *Elegies* modeled on Ovid.

Dryden, John (1631–1700). First brought to public attention by a

schoolboy elegy on the death of a young noble, Dryden was throughout his career intimately involved with the political issues of his day. He wrote *Heroic Stanzas* on the death of Cromwell, *Astraea Redux* to celebrate the return to the throne of Charles II, the satire *Absalom and Achitophel*, and major poems on his own religious odyssey. Late in his life he became a Roman Catholic. A prolific essayist, critic, dramatist, and translator, Dryden was credited by Samuel Johnson a century later with "the refinement of our language, and much of the correctness of our sentiments."

Eliot, Thomas Stearns (1888–1965). Born in St. Louis, Missouri, and educated at Harvard, Eliot went to England in 1910 and later became both a British citizen and a convert to the Church of England. His first poems, especially "The Love Song of J. Alfred Prufrock," immediately established him as one of the most important modern poets in the English language. In 1922 he published the single most important modern poem in the language, *The Waste Land*, after it had been severely edited by his fellow American expatriate Ezra Pound. Like all his major works, *The Waste Land* juxtaposes the loss of values in post-World War I society with the enduring continuities of the myths and literatures of the past. Eliot's later works include the poems in *Four Quartets*, verse dramas, and influential essays of literary criticism.

Frost, Robert (1874–1963). The great poet of New England landscapes and Yankee values, Frost lived most of his life on a small Vermont farm and wrote poems in a colloquial style that approximates the dialect of the region. His poems, including *"Mending Wall," "After Apple Picking," "Birches,"* and *"Stopping by Woods on a Snowy Evening,"* raise complex issues about human values and human endurance in a simple homespun style.

Gilgamesh. The product of Babylonian and Assyrian society as long ago as 2000 B.C., *Gilgamesh* is the oldest surviving epic poem. The story concerns Gilgamesh's attempt to locate his dead friend Enkidu and bring him back to life. The various episodes in the poem include a great flood, such as that survived by Noah in the Bible, and feats of heroism.

Ginsberg, Allen (1926-). A leading figure in the American Beat movement of the 1950's, a rebellion against the empty materialism of modern society. Ginsberg's poetry, which reflects the poet's interest in jazz, the works of Walt Whitman, and other influences, includes the poems *"Howl"* and *"Kaddish."*

Goethe, Johann Wolfgang von (1749-1832). The greatest German poet and one of the most important figures in the history of world literature, Goethe was a major novelist and playwright as well as a poet. He wrote verse from the time he was eight years old, although his education through the university level remained rather haphazard. Goethe was one of the leaders of the great German literary revolt called *Sturm and Drang* (Storm and Stress). The move-ment replaced conventional aes-thetics with a highly dramatized sense of personal crisis, such as that affecting the suicidal title character in Goethe's novel *The Sorrows of Young Werther*. Goethe's poetic output was his greatest achieve-ment, and it ranged from the pastoral poem *Hermann and Dorothea* to the huge two-part dramatic poem *Faust*, the story of an ambitious man's bargain with the Devil.

Heine, Heinrich (1797-1856). A German poet second in importance only to Goethe, Heinrich Heine was born in Düsseldorf to wealthy parents and was educated at a combi-nation of local Jewish and French-speaking academies. His early reputation was based on a series of travel books and a collection of lyric poems published in 1820 and afterward set to music. He left Germany in 1831, and for a time he ceased writing poetry. In the last 15 years of his life, however, he completed a large body of poetry.

Homer. The great bard to whom the major Greek epic poems are attributed, Homer is a legendary figure who perhaps lived in the 700's B.C. The principal Homeric poems are the *Iliad*, which tells the story of the Greek siege of Troy, and the *Odyssey*, which tells of the Greek Odysseus (or Ulysses) and his adventures as he returns to his homeland after the Greek victory at Troy. The events recounted in these two epics and other texts attributed to Homer are the foundation for many later literary works in English and other European languages.

Hopkins, Gerard Manley (1844-1889). Converted to Catholicism while at Oxford University, Hopkins later became a Jesuit priest. He gave up poetry for a time after enter-ing the priesthood, although he soon resumed writing. His poems were not published until many years after his death. Hopkins' poetry is unique because of what he called "sprung rhythm," an irregular cadence indicated by accent marks over ordinarily unstressed syllables. This metrical innova-tion was admired by modern poets; the rhythm of such poems as "Pied Beauty" and "The Windhover" has been imitated by recent poets.

Housman, Alfred Edward (1859–1936). A. E. Housman failed his honors examination at Oxford, but he went on to become one of the great English authorities on the Latin classics. By the time he became professor of Latin at Cambridge University, he had already published his principal book of poems, *A Shropshire Lad* (1896), a gathering of poems that celebrate the beauty of nature but find it insufficient to combat a growing sense of doom and malevolent fate.

Hughes, Langston (1902–1967). The principal poet of the "Harlem Renaissance" in New York City in the 1920's, Langston Hughes described his work as an attempt to "explain and illuminate the Negro condition in America." His most famous poems, such as "The Negro Speaks of Rivers" and "Mother to Son," are written in free verse and use colloquial rhythms and idioms to communicate the special qualities of the black American experience.

Keats, John (1795–1821). The son of an English coachman and an orphan at the age of eight, Keats was a medical student who wrote a remarkable body of poetry by the time he was 24. In 1819 he completed the ballad "La Belle Dame sans Merci" and the important odes "On a Grecian Urn," "On Melancholy," and "To a Nightingale." In the autumn of the same year he wrote *The Fall of Hyperion*, a fragment of a projected longer poem, and the ode "To Autumn." Keats possessed a rapt absorption in the physical world and a passive acceptance of tragic fate and the destructive passage of time. He died of tuberculosis at the age of 26.

Kipling, Rudyard (1865–1936). Born in Bombay, India, where his father was serving in the English civil service, Kipling was sent to a brutal boarding school in England at the age of six and earned his earliest literary reputation by writing about his experiences there. He became an enormously popular poet, however, for such patriotic poems as "Danny Deever," "Tommy," and "Gunga Din," which were published while England was involved in the unpopular Boer War in Africa. Also author of *The Jungle Book* and many other novels, Kipling was awarded the Nobel Prize in 1907.

Longfellow, Henry Wadsworth (1807–1882). One of the first popular American poets, Longfellow was a precursor of the great American literary renaissance of the mid-1800's. He wrote in a traditional style, but he used new material— especially American Indian legends—that influenced many later writers. Poems such as "The Village Blacksmith" seem extremely sentimental compared with the works of younger American poets. Nevertheless, in his own day Longfellow was greatly admired, especially for such long poems as *Hyperion*, *Evangeline*, and *The Song of Hiawatha*.

Mallarmé, Stephane (1842–1898). One of the most important modern French poets, Mallarmé was also an important translator of Edgar Allan Poe into French and an essayist on ancient myths and modern music. He supported himself in Paris with these literary works while his poetry, heavily influenced by Baudelaire, slowly gained acceptance. His most important single work is *L'Apres midi d'un faune* ("Afternoon of a Faun"), for which the French composer Claude Debussy wrote a famous musical accompaniment. The body of his work is comprised of a large collection of short lyrics.

Marvell, Andrew (1621–1678). Traveling in Europe when the English Civil War erupted in 1642, Marvell returned home to support the Puritan side, which was victorious; he later became a member of Parliament. Marvell wrote many satires and political tracts, but he is principally remembered today for his lyric poetry. The most important examples are "To His Coy Mistress," "The Garden," "The Mower Against the Garden," and the longer "Upon Appleton House."

Masters, Edgar Lee (1869–1948). A Chicago lawyer, Masters was a poet without great pretensions. His *Spoon River Anthology*, published in 1915, became one of the best-selling volumes of verse in American literary history. Written in a free verse form imitative of Walt Whitman, the poems criticized the narrowness and frustrations of life in a small town.

Milton, John (1608–1674). The greatest English poet of his time, Milton was a supporter of the Puritan cause; he rose in government service during Cromwell's rule over England. During this period Milton wrote his famous poems *L'Allegro*, *Il Penseroso*, and *Lycidas*, the last an elegy on the death of his friend Edward King. With the restoration of the monarchy in 1660, Milton fell from political favor. Totally blind, he then dictated to his daughters the epic poem *Paradise Lost*, which was published in 1667. Like the epics of Homer and Vergil, Milton's poem is in twelve books; it recounts Satan's fall from God's grace and the parallel fall of man in Eden. It is the one great literary epic in English.

Ovid (43 B.C.–18 A.D.). Publius Ovidius Naso was a Latin poet born near Rome and exiled to a settlement called Tomis on the Black Sea after he ran afoul of authorities at the end of his life. He was a lawyer by profession, but he soon abandoned his practice to write poetry. His work departed from the noble vein common in Latin poetry since the *Aeneid* of Vergil. Instead, Ovid wrote verses whose irreverent and titillating qualities were suggested by his first titles: *Amores* and *The Confessions of Women*. His masterpiece is the epic *Metamorphoses*, literally "transformations," a collection of well-known legends that ponder the ambiguities of life.

Pope, Alexander (1688–1744). A recluse from refined London society because he was both a Catholic and physically deformed, Pope refined his outsider's views of political, literary, and cultural events and became the great verse satirist of English poetry. *The Rape of the Lock* is a mock epic in verse that satirizes aristocratic vanity; *The Dunciad* is a similar satire on the vanity of popular writers of the day. Pope was a scholarly classicist who insisted on high literary standards; he met these standards in his more serious works, *Essay on Criticism* and *Imitations of Horace*.

Pound, Ezra (1885–1972). The self-proclaimed "Idaho Kid," Pound left the United States after his education at the University of Pennsylvania and brought an American entrepreneurial spirit to the poetry circles in Europe. He was an important editor and influence on other poets, notably T. S. Eliot, as well as a major poet in his own right. His principal poetic works, *Personae*, a collection of short lyrics, and *Cantos*, a volume of more than 100 cantos left incomplete at his death, show an encyclopedic knowledge of literature in many Western and Eastern languages.

Pushkin, Aleksandr (1799–1837). The founder of modern Russian literature, Pushkin wrote plays, novels, and short stories that reflected the special nature of Russian life but took Western European forms. His major achievement is the long poem *Eugene Onegin*, which is the great poetic epic in the Russian tongue. The story of the unrequited love of Eugene for Tatiana over a period of several years, it was later made into an important opera by the Russian composer Tchaikovsky.

Rilke, Rainer Maria (1875–1926). One of the most important modern poets to write in the German language, Rilke was born in Prague, now the capital of Czechoslovakia. Austrian by heritage, he had an unhappy childhood and wrote early lyrics that combined elements of mysticism with a search for God outside of organized religion. Usually in poor financial circumstances, Rilke traveled considerably throughout his life in search of literary patronage. His most important work is the obscure and demanding *Duino Elegies*, which has exerted great influence on modern poets in several languages.

Rimbaud, Arthur (1854–1891). A child prodigy who wrote verse when very young, Rimbaud was a fiercely rebellious youth who ran away from home several times and served a term in a French prison while still an adolescent. He wrote what is perhaps the most important prose poem in literature, "Le Bateau Ivre" ("The Drunken Boat"), and a collection of short lyrics and prose poems, *Les Illuminations*, that is one of the key texts of modern French poetry. Subject to deep emotional stresses, he gave up writing late in life and settled in North Africa, where he may have been involved in criminal activities.

Robinson, Edwin Arlington (1869–1935). Raised in Maine and educated as a "special," or nondegree student at Harvard, Robinson wrote prosaic poems that were considered outdated even as they were published. He was acclaimed later in his career, receiving three Pulitzer Prizes, but because his poetry relied more on plot than on subtleties of language, his work had little influence on younger poets. In his later years he wrote long Arthurian narrative poems such as *Merlin* and *Tristram*, but he is best remembered today for short, storylike poems such as "Richard Cory," "Mr. Flood's Party," and "Miniver Cheevy."

Rossetti, Dante Gabriel (1828–1882). Born in London of Italian parents, Rossetti was the founder of the Pre-Raphaelite movement in England. The movement was an attempt by painters, as well as poets, including his sister Christina Rossetti, to return aesthetics to the formal purity of the time before Italian Renaissance painter Raphael. Dante Gabriel Rossetti's major poetic works include "The Blessed Damozel," "The Woodspurge," and a sonnet sequence called *The House of Life.*

Shakespeare, William (1564–1616). In addition to being the most important dramatist in Western literature, William Shakespeare was one of the major poets in English literature. He wrote two important narrative poems between 1592 and 1594, years when an epidemic closed the London theaters: *Venus and Adonis*, an adaptation of a tale from Ovid's *Metamorphoses*, and *The Rape of Lucrece*. Shakespeare's most famous poems, however, are the 154 *Sonnets*, a sequence published in 1609 and probably written over a number of years. These sonnets, full of extremely subtle wordplay, all address the

English Romantic poets and representative works

William Blake (1757–1827)
Songs of Innocence
Songs of Experience
Jerusalem

Samuel Taylor Coleridge (1772–1834)
  "The Rime of the Ancient Mariner"
  "Kubla Khan"
  "Dejection: An Ode"

William Wordsworth (1779–1850)
The Prelude
  "Ode: Intimations of Immortality"
  "Tintern Abbey"

Lord George Gordon Byron (1788–1824)
  Childe Harold's Pilgrimage
  Don Juan

Percy Bysshe Shelley (1792–1822)
Adonais
Prometheus Unbound
  "Ode to the West Wind"

John Keats (1795–1821)
  "Ode to a Nightingale"
  "Ode to a Grecian Urn"
  "To Autumn"

subjects of love and human relationships as they are experienced by a young aristocrat; by a mysterious "dark lady"; and by a poet jealous of both.

Shelley, Percy Bysshe (1792–1822). Having been expelled from Oxford and having abandoned his daughter and pregnant wife, Shelley wrote his first major poem, *Alastor*, in the misguided belief that he was about to die of tuberculosis. He did not die, but after eloping to Europe with Mary Godwin Shelley, who would write the novel *Frankenstein*, he began to write major poems in a burst of sudden genius. The most important of his works are *Adonais*, an elegy on the death of Keats, and *Prometheus Unbound*, an adaptation of the Greek tragedy *Prometheus Bound*. Shelley also wrote a number of important shorter works, including "Ode to the West Wind" and "To a Skylark."

Sir Gawain and the Green Knight. The most important verse romance in English, *Sir Gawain and the Green Knight* was written by an unknown poet at the end of the 1300's. It tells the story of Gawain, whose courage is tested when confronted by the mysterious Green Knight. The poem is most remarkable for its long digressions, including formal descriptions of King Arthur's Christmas feast, the manner in which Gawain arms himself for a journey, and elaborate hunting parties.

Song of Roland. The major epic in the French language, *Song of Roland* was composed by an unknown Norman author before 1131, when the poem was translated into Latin to reach a larger audience. The poem describes the exploits of its hero on a military expedition by

<table>
<tr><th>Shakespeare
Sonnet 73</th><th>Spenser
Sonnet 68 from Amoretti</th></tr>
</table>

Shakespeare
Sonnet 73

That time of year thou mayst in me behold
When yellow leaves, or none, or few, do hang
Upon those boughs which shake against the cold,
Bare ruined choirs where late the sweet birds sang:
In me thou see'st the twilight of such day
As after sunset fadeth in the west,
Which by and by black night doth take away,
Death's second self that seals up all in rest:
In me thou see'st the glowing of such fire
That on the ashes of his youth doth lie
As the death-bed whereon it must expire,
Consumed with that which it was nourished by:
   This thou perceivest, which makes thy love
     more strong
   To love that well which thou must leave ere long.

Spenser
Sonnet 68 from *Amoretti*

Most glorious Lord of Lyfe, that on this day
Didst make thy triumph over death and sin:
And having harrowd hell, didst bring away
Captivity thence captive us to win:
This joyous day, deare Lord, with joy begin,
And grant that we for whom thou diddest dye
Being with thy deare blood clene washt from sin,
May live for ever in felicity.
And that thy love we weighing worthily,
May likewise love thee for the same againe:
And for thy sake that all lyke deare didst buy,
With love may one another entertayne.
So let us love, deare love, lyke as we ought,
Love is the lesson which the Lord us taught.

Charlemagne into Spain, a campaign that actually occurred in the year 778. Roland dies a tragic death on the return trip, when a small band of Spanish Saracens attacks the rear guard of Charlemagne's army and Roland is too proud to blow his magic horn to summon help. The poem is important in the English as well as French traditions, for when the Normans invaded England in 1066 some accounts say that Roland sung to stimulate the Norman troops before the Battle of Hastings.

Spenser, Edmund (1552–1599). One of the most important poets of early English literary history, Spenser hoped to gain preferment in the Elizabethan court with his poetry, but met with only limited success. His twelve pastoral dialogues, *The Shepheardes Calendar*, brought him some fame in 1579, but afterward he was given the mixed blessing of a government position in Ireland. His most important work is the *Faerie Queene*, a major poem that uses elements of Arthurian romance to describe allegorically the threats to Queen Elizabeth's power in the 1580's and 1590's.

The *Faerie Queene* presents a panorama of characters and a series of unrelated tales rather than a single story. The first three books were published in 1590, and three more appeared in Spenser's lifetime, but fragments exist that suggest the poem was to be continued.

Stevens, Wallace (1879–1955). A lawyer employed for most of his life by an insurance company in Connecticut, Wallace Stevens quietly amassed one of the most important philosophical bodies of poetry in American literature. He often referred to his poems as "ideas of order," and many of them debate the relative merits of the order apparent in nature as opposed to the manmade order provided by art or religion. Poems such as "Sunday Morning" and "The Snow Man" test subtle intellectual distinctions between the natural and the artificial, while poems such as "The Emperor of Ice Cream" and "A High-Toned Old Christian Woman" explore the same subject in exuberant and playful ways.

Tennyson, Alfred (1809–1892). Alfred Lord Tennyson was the Poet Laureate of England from 1850 until his death. His works, many of which attempt to recover the certainties of the past in an era of great social change, are considered the major poetic expression of English sensibility in the Victorian age. In addition to many short poems such as "Mariana," "Maud," and "Audley Court," his major achievements are *In Memoriam*, an elegy on the death of his friend Arthur Hallam, and *The Idylls of the King*, an Arthurian legend published in twelve parts between 1859 and 1885.

Thomas, Dylan (1914–1953). Born in Swansea, Wales, a town he always described with bitterness, Dylan Thomas had a formal education that ended with grammar school; however, he was hailed as a major poet when he published his first book at the age of 20. From that point on, his hard-drinking, improvident life made him for many the image of the modern poet. He died from alcohol-related causes at 39. Thomas's poetry is notable for imagery from Welsh lore and the Bible, and for its intoxication with the natural world, as in "Fern Hill."

> **Whitman**
> The Opening of "Song of Myself"
>
> I celebrate myself, and sing myself,
> And what I assume you shall assume,
> For every atom belonging to me as good belongs
>   to you.
>
> I loafe and invite my soul,
> I lean and loafe at my ease observing a spear
>   of summer grass.
>
> My tongue, every atom of my blood, form'd from
>   this soil, this air,
> Born here of parents born here from parents the
>   same, and their parents the same,
> I, now thirty-seven years old in perfect health
>   begin,
> Hoping to cease not till death.

> **Wordsworth**
> The Opening of *The Prelude*
>
> O there is blessing in this gentle breeze
> That blows from the green fields and from
>   the clouds
> And from the sky: it beats against my cheek,
> And seems half-conscious of the joy it gives.
> O welcome messenger! O welcome friend!
> A captive greets thee, coming from a house
> Of bondage, from yon city's walls set free,
> A prison where he hath been long immured.
> Now I am free, enfranchised and at large,
> May fix my habitation where I will.
> What dwelling shall receive me? in what vale
> Shall be my harbour? underneath what grove
> Shall I take up my home? and what sweet stream
> Shall with its murmurs lull me to my rest?

Vergil (70–19 B.C.). Publius Vergilius Maro was born on a farm in the north of Italy, and although he made important friends in the Roman government he continued to prefer life in the country. This interest was reflected in his early poetic works, *Eclogues* and *Georgics*. His greatest work, however, is the *Aeneid*, an epic poem in twelve books left incomplete at the time of his death. The *Aeneid* tells the story of the journey of Aeneas and a band of followers from the ruined city of Troy to the present site of Rome, and their establishment of a city there. Written just after the end of the Roman republic, the poem is the greatest legacy of that classical society.

Whitman, Walt (1819–1892). The first great American poet, Whitman was a journeyman printer from New York City who published a slim volume called *Leaves of Grass* in 1855. He then continued to enlarge and revise the book for the rest of his life. He was the great exponent of modern free verse, poetry composed of unrhymed lines of varied lengths. By means of free verse and a vocabulary of colloquialisms and slang words once considered "unpoetic," Whitman hoped to communicate in his poems the special exuberance of life in America. The most famous of the more than 400 poems finally gathered into *Leaves of Grass* include "Song of Myself," "Crossing Brooklyn Ferry," and an elegy for Abraham Lincoln, "When Lilacs Last in the Dooryard Bloom'd."

Whittier, John Greenleaf (1807–1892). Of all American poets, John Greenleaf Whittier was the most vocal supporter of the abolitionist movement to end slavery. His most famous poems on the subject were "Massachusetts to Virginia," on the fugitive slave law, and "Ichabod," an attack on Senator Daniel Webster. His story poems, such as "Snowbound," also gained wide popularity after the Civil War.

Williams, William Carlos (1883–1963). A friend of Ezra Pound, Williams decided against life in Europe and served as a practicing physician in New Jersey throughout his long literary career. He was influenced by many of the schools of modern poetry developing in Europe, but for the most part he attempted to draw attention to the minute qualities of common objects in short lyrics of unadorned American speech patterns. In his long poem *Paterson*, Williams celebrates the history and diversity of that New Jersey city in various verse forms broken by occasional passages of prose.

Wordsworth, William (1770–1850). One of the most important of all English poets, Wordsworth concentrated on rural settings and themes in all his works. He was the principal theorist behind the important collection of 1798 called *Lyrical Ballads*, which contained poems by Coleridge as well. The *Ballads* were an attempt to return poetry to a mode of common, as opposed to ornate, speech. Wordsworth also made the spiritual autobiography an accepted subject for poetry in his book-length *The Prelude* and many shorter poems. His other major poems include "Lines Composed Above Tintern Abbey" and "Ode: Intimations of Immortality."

Yeats, William Butler (1865–1939). An important essayist and playwright as well as one of the major poets of the early 1900's, Yeats was one of the founders of the Irish literary revival in the 1890's. The subjects of his major poems are derived from Celtic legends, from modern Ireland's struggle for political independence, and from mystical and symbolic elements borrowed from other European literatures. In poems such as "Byzantium" and "The Second Coming," Yeats elaborated a sweeping theory about historical cycles, but most of his important poems are tied to particular Irish places, as in "The Lake Isle of Innisfree," or to historical events, as in "Easter 1916," the date of the great Irish uprising.

Meter and rhythm in poetry

The musical qualities of poetry in English are created by the length of a single line and the arrangement of stressed syllables within it. Length determines the meter of the line. Stressed syllables give the line its rhythm.

Meter

Units of a line of poetry are syllabic groups called *feet*; the number of feet gives the meter its name.

tetrameter. One of the most common meters in English consists of four feet; it is called tetrameter:

"O West/ern wind,/when wilt/thou blow."

pentameter. Another very common English meter is pentameter, so named because it consists of five feet:

"That time/ of year/ thou mayst/ in me/ be-hold"

hexameter. English poetry also uses the hexameter line, which has six feet. Each stanza of Spenser's *The Faerie Queene* ends with a line of hexameter:

"Fierce warres/and faith/full loves/
shall mor/a-lize/my song."

other meters. Other meters are also named according to the number of feet in the line. A line of one foot is called monometer, a line of two feet is called dimeter, and a line of three feet is called trimeter.

mixed meter. Lines of poetry can be classified as a single meter. Poems, however, usually mix meter, or alternate lines of one meter with lines of at least one other meter. This adds to the musical quality of the poem by eliminating monotonous repetition. All ballads, for example, alternate tetrameter with trimeter lines. Look at this stanza of Coleridge's ballad "The Rime of the Ancient Mariner": the first and third lines are tetrameter, the second and fourth are trimeter:

"The Wed/ding Guest/ sat on/ a stone:
He can/not choose/ but hear;
And thus/ spake on/ that an/cient man,
The bright/eyed Mar/in-er."

Rhythm

The placement of a stressed syllable in a foot determines its rhythm and gives the foot its name. Words in poetry generally carry the same syllabic stress that they have in speech.

iambic. The most common foot in the English language is the iamb, an unstressed syllable followed by a stressed one as in the word "a-bove." Thus, the first example above would be fully described as iambic tetrameter:

"Ŏ Wést/ern wínd,/ when wílt / thoŭ blów."

anapestic. If a foot consists of two unstressed syllables followed by a stressed one, it is called an anapest, as in the word "un-de-ceive." Edgar Allan Poe's poem "Annabel Lee" contains a line of anapestic trimeter:

"Ŏf the beau / ti-fŭl Ann / a-bel Lée"

trochaic. The poetic foot can also begin with the stressed syllable. A stressed syllable followed by a single unstressed one is called a trochee, as in the word "hu-mor." Thus, another line from Poe, in this case from "The Raven," can be described as trochaic tetrameter:

"Ónce ŭ/pon ă/mid-níght / dréar-y̆"

dactylic. If a foot consists of a stressed syllable followed by two unstressed ones, it is called a dactyl, as in the word "mur-mur-ing." A line of three such feet would be called dactylic trimeter:

"Thís ĭs the / moun-tain ŭn /reach-a-ble."

other rhythmic feet. Sometimes two unstressed syllables will come together in a single foot; this combination is called a pyrrhic foot. Alternately, two stressed syllables can come together in a single foot; this combination is called a spondee.

Plays	1500	1550	1600	1650	1700
Europe			LOPE DE VEGA		
			CALDERÓN		
			CORNEILLE		
			MOLIÈRE		
			RACINE		
England/Ireland			SHAKESPEARE		
			MARLOWE		
			JONSON		

Drama

Plays are unique among the literary forms in that they are meant to be performed rather than read. The word "drama" is derived from the Greek word for action. The Greek philosopher Aristotle defined all literary works as imitations of life's actions; he distinguished drama as the "imitation of action in the form of action."

In addition to the serious plays suggested by the word "drama," the dramatic arts include musical comedies, pantomimes, television dramas, religious pageants, and movies. Plays may be "translated" into other artistic forms; the composers Rossini and Verdi based operas on Shakespeare's tragedy *Macbeth*. Or plays may be dramatizations of other literary forms, as with the musical *Oliver* based on Dickens' novel *Oliver Twist*.

Aristotle also provided the basic distinction between kinds of plays: in tragedies audiences perceive the principal characters to be more noble than people in real life; in comedies the characters are perceived to be inferior to people in real life. Tragedies tend to have sad endings, and comedies happy endings. Tragicomic plays combine elements of tragedy and comedy. History plays, dramatizations of past events, may be primarily tragic, as in Shakespeare's *Richard II*, or primarily comic, as in Shaw's *Caesar and Cleopatra*. Many distinct kinds of plays exist within these broad categories: the revenge tragedy, the domestic tragedy about everyday people, the sophisticated comedy of manners, and the low comedy of farce.

A full appreciation of plays requires three kinds of attention: first, attention to the language spoken, as in poetry; second, attention to plot, character, and setting, as in fiction; and third, attention to drama's unique qualities, including lighting, set design, direction, and the actors' interpretation of their roles.

The history of drama. The origin of theater as we know it is generally ascribed to an ancient Greek named Thespis, and for that reason actors are still called thespians. Thespis is said to have added a new voice to the traditional choral poetry of Athens by acting the part of a god or hero in dialogue with the chorus. Soon other characters were added and large dramatic festivals arranged. In the 400's B.C. Athens produced the oldest surviving plays: the tragedies of Aeschylus, Sophocles, and Euripedes, and the comedies of Aristophanes. The focus of the drama shifted to individual characters and away from the chorus.

With the rise of Rome, the center of theater shifted to the Imperial City. Roman drama was distinguished by the tragedies of Seneca and the comedies of Plautus and Terence.

In the Middle Ages drama came to serve religious purposes. Theatrical performances included mystery plays, dramatizations of the Scriptures (also known as miracle plays), and allegorical morality plays in which actors might represent the Seven Deadly Sins or the Seven Moral Virtues.

In the 1500's, Europeans rediscovered the dramas of Rome and Greece, and began once more to perform secular plays. Between 1580 and 1680, a new golden age of drama dawned in Western Europe. In England,

Roman drama, as shown in a carving found at Pompeii

1700	1750	1800	1850	1900	1950	2000

SCHILLER · IBSEN · WEISS
STRINDBERG
CHEKHOV
PIRANDELLO
BRECHT
IONESCO

SHERIDAN · SHAW
SYNGE
O'CASEY
BECKETT
PINTER

United States

O'NEILL
WILLIAMS
MILLER
ALBEE

Shakespeare transformed stage entertainments into a great literary form. Shakespeare's Spanish contemporary Lope de Vega is said to have written as many as 2000 plays. In France, Corneille and Racine extended the bounds of tragedy, and Molière revived dramatic comedy as an art form.

After 1700, drama became a neglected art. In England playwrights such as Sheridan provided light comedies, and in Germany literary figures such as Schiller wrote plays as a secondary occupation, causing drama to survive only as a poor cousin to poetry and fiction.

In the late 1800's drama regained importance, chiefly because of the socially conscious plays of Norwegian Henrik Ibsen and Russian Anton Chekhov, and the surreal experiments of the Swedish master, Johan August Strindberg. These authors explored contemporary topics, and they favored realistic everyday speech. By the early 1900's the works of Irish playwrights John Millington Synge and Sean O'Casey helped rouse a nation struggling for political independence.

Since then, dramatists have continued to experiment in directions first explored by Ibsen, Chekhov, and Strindberg. In America writers such as Eugene O'Neill, Tennessee Williams, and Arthur Miller have devoted themselves to contemporary dramas about common people. In Europe writers such as Luigi Pirandello, Samuel Beckett, and Eugene Ionesco have written imaginative and thought-provoking plays.

Scene from The Glass Menagerie, *Tennessee Williams's classic American play*

Kinds of plays

Tragedy

Dramatic tragedy presents in a serious manner an admirable hero's fall from good to bad fortune because of a "tragic flaw," and his eventual spiritual purification in unhappy circumstances. Tragedy is more than a sad story; the hero is often destroyed by his own best qualities, and the ending suggests his nobility in the midst of defeat.

Examples

Playwright	Lifetime	Work
Aeschylus	525?–456 B.C.	*Agamemnon*
Sophocles	496?–406 B.C.	*Oedipus Rex*
Euripides	485?–406 B.C.	*Medea*
William Shakespeare	1564–1616	*King Lear*
Pierre Corneille	1606–1684	*Le Cid*
Henrik Ibsen	1828–1906	*Ghosts*

Comedy

Dramatic comedy presents laughable yet sympathetic characters and leads up to a happy ending. Specific types of comedy include the comedy of manners, a satire of sophisticated life; low comedy, a satire of cruder lifestyles; and the comedy of situation, in which the humor is provided by the plot. In all cases, the comic actions of simplified characters in an ideal world have relevance to real-life situations.

Examples

Playwright	Lifetime	Work
Aristophanes	448?–380 B.C.	*The Frogs*
William Shakespeare	1564–1616	*Much Ado About Nothing*
Ben Jonson	1572–1637	*Volpone*
Molière	1622–1673	*Tartuffe*
Richard Brinsley Sheridan	1751–1816	*The Rivals*
George Bernard Shaw	1856–1950	*Candida*

Tragicomedy

Dramatic tragicomedy, a relatively modern combination of dramatic types, presents events apparently headed for the catastrophic ending of tragedy but actually headed for a comic or ambiguous ending. Tragicomedy thus manages to combine the entertaining qualities of comedy with the serious themes of tragedy. Modern tragicomedy is a powerful vehicle for the communication of pessimistic ideas in the form of farce.

Examples

Playwright	Lifetime	Work
William Shakespeare	1564–1616	*Measure for Measure*
George Bernard Shaw	1856–1950	*St. Joan*
Anton Chekhov	1860–1904	*The Cherry Orchard*
John M. Synge	1871–1909	*The Playboy of the Western World*
Sean O'Casey	1880–1964	*Juno and the Paycock*
Samuel Beckett	1906–1989	*Waiting for Godot*

Stage terms

act. One of the major divisions of a play. Many plays of the past had five acts, and many modern plays have three acts. Short plays may have only one act.

aside. Brief comment made by an actor on the stage, but intended to be heard only by the audience.

chorus. Group on the stage that comments on but does not participate in the dramatic action. The chorus is an essential part of Greek drama, in which it consists of masked dancers who originally sang or chanted their lines.

comic relief. A humorous story or character inserted into a serious play to release tension briefly and to intensify, by contrast, tragic emotions. Shakespeare uses comic relief to this effect with the grave digger in *Hamlet* and the drunken gatekeeper in *Macbeth*.

scene. Unit within an act of a play, usually indicated by a change of setting or by a brief curtain or blackout.

soliloquy. Extended speech by a character alone on the stage, in which he often reveals truths not admitted in the presence of other characters.

Miller

Dramatists

O'Neill

Shaw

Aeschylus (525?-456 B.C.)
Author of the oldest surviving plays, Aeschylus was a Greek soldier who fought the Persians of Marathon and Salamis and later became a prominent citizen of Athens. He is thought to have written more than 80 plays, most for the Greek dramatic festival Dionysia. Seven complete plays, all tragedies, survive in addition to many fragments. His most important work is the trilogy called the *Oresteia*. The three plays—*Agamemnon, The Libation Bearers*, and *The Eumenides*— tell of the royal house of Atreus during the Trojan War. Other surviving plays include *Seven Against Thebes* and *Prometheus Bound*.

Albee, Edward (1928-). One of the leading modern American playwrights, Albee first gained success in 1959 with his one-act play *The Zoo Story*. Albee's plays explore the alienation of humans in modern society and are noted for their use of fantasy, absurdism, unusual situations, and intense dialogue. They include *The American Dream, Who's Afraid of Virginia Woolf?, A Delicate Balance*, and *Seascape,*

Aristophanes *(448?-370* B.C.). Younger than the great Greek tragedians, Aristophanes is the only writer of comedies of his time whose works have survived. Eleven of his 40 plays are known today. They reveal satires of Athenian political events and a bawdy humor that occasionally borders on the obscene. Several plays, such as *The Birds* and *The Frogs*, are named for the disguises worn by the chorus on the stage.

Beckett, Samuel (1906-1989). Born in Ireland, Beckett was educated at Trinity College, Dublin, and then traveled in Europe. He became a close friend of the Irish novelist James Joyce in Paris in the 1930's.

Although he published novels, poems, and essays, Beckett remained unknown until the production of his play *Waiting for Godot* brought him sudden fame in 1953. That play established him as the founder of the theater of the absurd, a school of drama devoted to the existentialist belief that inherited values and institutions are meaningless and that man must create his own identity in a malevolent world. Beckett's many plays, written in either English or French, include *Endgame* and *Krapp's Last Tape*. Also an important modern novelist, he was awarded the Nobel Prize in 1969.

Brecht, Bertolt (1898-1956). The most important modern German dramatist, Brecht was a confirmed Communist who left Germany for New York in the 1930's and settled in East Germany after World War II. It was with the Berliner Ensemble in East Berlin that he produced his major works, *Mother Courage, The Good Woman of Setzuan*, and *The Caucasian Chalk Circle*. These were works in what Brecht called his "epic theater," characterized by episodic scenes strung together by subtitles and short films. Brecht collaborated with composer Kurt Weill on *The Threepenny Opera*.

Calderón de la Barca (1600-1681). The successor to Lope de Vega as the leading dramatist of Spain's golden age, Calderón began his carer as the author of popular mythological spectacles that used innovative scenery and lighting techniques. He became a priest in 1651, after which his work was devoted to religious themes and theological issues. His principal long work is the play *Life Is a Dream*, and he is especially famous for short *autos sacramentales*, one-act plays on religious subjects.

Chekhov, Anton (1860-1904). Chekhov was a Russian who witnessed the social transformation within his country that would lead to the Bolshevik Revolution. Chekhov's major plays, *The Seagull, Uncle Vanya, Three Sisters,* and *The Cherry Orchard,* all explore the human drama of the decline of the Russian nobility and the rise of the middle classes. The plays are realistic and restrained, and at first audiences found them dull. Later productions revealed the richness and subtlety of Chekhov's art, and soon his influence was international. Chekhov was also a gifted and influential writer of short stories.

Corneille, Pierre (1606-1684). Corneille was born in Rouen and saw his first play performed there by a troup of traveling players. Brought to Paris to write plays in imitation of the classical Greek and Latin dramas, he became dissatisfied with their restrictions and as a result composed the first great tragedies in French literature. The most important of these were *Le Cid,* about the exploits of Spain's national hero, and *Andromède,* a treatment of a classical myth.

Euripides (485?-406 B.C.) Euripides was the youngest of the three great Greek tragedians. He was more individualistic and less popular in his own day than Aeschylus or Sophocles. But his emphasis on character—and on human psychology—makes his plays most like modern European classics. Eighteen of his tragedies survive, and all are notable for their understanding of human suffering, particularly the sufferings of women. His major plays include *Medea, Trojan Women, Electra,* and *Bacchae.*

Ibsen, Henrik (1828-1906). The most important pioneer of modern drama, Henrik Ibsen was a Norwegian who learned stagecraft as the manager of theaters in Oslo. His first works were romantic verse plays such as *Brand* and *Peer Gynt.* Gradually he moved toward more realistic plays that considered important social issues, including the status of women and the hypocrisy of the educated classes. His plays include *A Doll's House,* about a woman's search for freedom, *An Enemy of the People, Ghosts, The Wild Duck,* and *Hedda Gabler.*

Ionesco, Eugene (1912-1994) A leading figure in contemporary French drama, Eugene Ionesco first gained attention in the early 1950's as an exponent of the theater of the absurd, which sought to illustrate the meaninglessness of life by overturning the conventions of traditional drama. In *The Bald Soprano,* for example, relatives gather for a family reunion and exchange meaningless phrases taken from a beginning foreign language primer. Other important works include *The Lesson, The Chairs,* and *Jack, or The Submission.*

Jonson, Ben (1572-1637). Although he was the son of a poor London bricklayer, Ben Jonson alone among the important English dramatists of Elizabethan times was an intellectual and a classicist. All of Jonson's major plays are satires. He ridicules lust in *Volpone,* greed in *The Alchemist,* and several common vices in *Bartholomew Fair.* After the death of Elizabeth I in 1603, Jonson wrote elaborate entertainments called *masques* for the court of James I. Masques used poetry, music, dance, and special effects.

Marlowe, Christopher (1564-1593). The son of a shoemaker from Canterbury, England, Marlowe lived a life of intrigue that ended when he was murdered in a tavern at the age of 29. The precise dating and texts of his plays are a matter of dispute, but his importance as an Elizabethan dramatist is second only to that of Shakespeare. Marlowe's great theme was heroic but excessive ambition: for political power in *Tamburlaine the Great,* for money in *The Jew of Malta,* and for knowledge in *Doctor Faustus.*

Miller, Arthur (b. 1915). One of the most important dramatists of his generation, Miller was born in New York City. During the 1930's he developed a lasting sympathy for victims of the American ideal for success. His major work is the tragedy *Death of a Salesman,* about an aging traveling salesman named Willy Loman who has devoted himself to the codes of the business world and then finds himself a victim of that world. Miller's other important works include *The Crucible* and *After The Fall.*

Molière (1622-1673). Born Jean Baptiste Poquelin and known only by his pen name after he left home at the age of 21, Molière was an actor and stage manager as well as one of the greatest of French dramatists. He lived at the same time as Corneille and Racine, but he chose to write comedies rather than tragedies. His major works are biting satires of social pretensions and hypocrisies. Among his most important plays are *Le Bourgeois Gentilhomme (The Would-be Gentleman), Le Misanthrope,* and *Tartuffe.* Molière was also important as a producer of plays, as a developer of the all-purpose theatrical set, and as a manager of one of the first modern repertory companies. After his death, his own company merged with others to form the Comédie Française, the national theater of France.

O'Casey, Sean (1880-1964). A working-class Irish laborer who was self-educated, O'Casey became famous as the great chronicler in drama of Ireland's struggle for political independence from England. He was discovered by the poet W. B. Yeats and other leaders of the Irish literary revival, and at Dublin's Abbey Theater they produced his first and most important works: *Juno and the Paycock*, *The Shadow of a Gunman*, and *The Plough and the Stars*. These plays are about people who live on the edge of the important political events of the day. O'Casey showed the independence movement's flaws as well as its strengths, and his plays met with bitter criticism. He later left Ireland. While living in England, he experimented with many dramatic forms.

O'Neill, Eugene (1888-1953). The first great American dramatist, O'Neill was born in New York City, the son of a famous actor. After some years at sea, he joined the Provincetown Players in Massachusetts and there learned stagecraft. His major works are notable for the depth of their psychological penetration and for expressionist stage techniques. *Mourning Becomes Electra*, which draws on Greek tragedy, *The Iceman Cometh*, *A Moon for the Misbegotten*, and *Long Day's Journey into Night*, a family drama now recognized as his masterpiece.

Pirandello, Luigi (1867-1936). The major 20th-century Italian playwright, Pirandello was scarred first by poverty and then by the insanity of his wife. His best known work is *Six Characters in Search of an Author*, in which actors in street clothes watch and eventually intrude on a rehearsal of another play on the same stage. His other works explore the confusion between illusion and reality. In *Henry IV*, for example, an insane man imagines himself a king.

Racine, Jean (1639-1699). The successor to Corneille as the leading tragedian of early French drama, Jean Racine wrote plays that were faithful to Aristotle's theories of drama, but innovative for their lyrical dialogue and attention to psychology. The most famous of these are love stories such as *Andromache*, *Britannicus*, and *Phèdre*, the last of which contains a leading role that has attracted French actresses from its first performance in 1677 to the present. Racine's success brought him a position in the court of Louis XIV. His disgust at imitations of his plays caused him to cease writing.

Schiller, Friedrich von (1759-1805). As co-manager of the Court Theater at Weimar with Wolfgang von Goethe, Schiller was at the center of the German literary *Sturm und Drang* (Storm and Stress) movement, which emphasized emotions of almost apocalyptic proportions. He became the movement's greatest dramatist, chiefly on the basis of *Wallenstein*, a trilogy of plays; *Mary Stuart*; and *William Tell*.

Shaffer, Peter (b. 1926). Known for his intense dramas that explore the human psyche and the nature of good and evil, Shaffer was born in Liverpool, England, and gained his first major success with *The Royal Hunt of the Sun*, set during the Spanish conquest of Peru. His best-known plays include *Equus*, centering on a troubled young man and the equally troubled psychiatrist who is helping him, and *Amadeus*, based on the life of Mozart.

Shakespeare, William (1564-1616). The greatest of all Western dramatists, William Shakespeare is perhaps the most important literary figure of the past 500 years. He created drama as we know it by introducing a shrewd knowledge of human psychology and poetry of unparalleled beauty to a stage that had been concerned mostly with mythical and religious themes. Shakespeare's appeal is universal; his works have been translated into most modern languages and have influenced such great writers as Goethe and Tolstoy. His influence has been especially strong on English literature, since performances or readings in English reveal the full beauty and subtlety of his poetry. The plays of Shakespeare are performed more often than those of any other dramatist. They are regularly produced on Broadway with a cast of famous actors; they are also a mainstay of college and amateur theatrical companies. (See box on Shakespeare's life and works.)

Shaw, George Bernard (1856-1950). Born in Ireland, Shaw became a drama critic in London and was an ardent supporter of the first productions of Ibsen's plays in English. In 1884 he joined the Fabian Society, which advocated socialism by gradual reform, and his many plays are known for their witty commentaries on social and political issues of his day. Shaw's plays are for the most, part satirical, and his targets include the status of women in *Mrs. Warren's Profession*, militarism in *Arms and the Man*, and England's treatment of Ireland in *John Bull's Other Island*. His play *Pygmalion* was the basis for the musical *My Fair Lady*. He was awarded the Nobel Prize in 1925.

The "First Folio" above *was the first collected edition of the plays. Below, the Globe theater, where many of the plays were first performed.*

Our knowledge about the life of the world's greatest playwright is limited, and fact has become entangled with legend. Baptismal records show that William Shakespeare was christened in the English market town of Stratford-on-Avon on April 26, 1564, and his birth date is thought to have been April 23 in that year. Little is known about his youth, but he was married to Anne Hathaway in Stratford in 1582 when he was 18 years old. They had three children, Susan, Hamnet, and Judith. Shakespeare seems to have moved to London in 1586. Legend says he had been accused of poaching deer in his hometown.

He found employment as an actor and manager in the city's theaters. His first plays, *The Comedy of Errors* and *Henry VI, Part I*, were written in imitation of the popular dramatic comedies and histories of the day. His first tragedy, *Titus Andronicus*, was probably written in 1594, but the great tragedies—*Othello, King Lear*, and *Macbeth*—were written in a burst of creativity between 1604 and 1605. In 1598, Shakespeare joined with several famous actors of the time and opened the Globe Theatre. Its success provided him with financial security, a stage for his future works, and a valuable repertory company of actors. His literary genius reached its final phase in 1610 and 1611 with *A Winter's Tale* and *The Tempest*, poetic dramas usually classified as comedies but fantastic enough in their settings and characters to be termed stage romances.

Having earned a fortune in the theater, Shakespeare retired to Stratford in 1611. He died there on April 23, 1616, at the age of 52. His plays were only gathered into the famous "First Folio" edition in 1623, and no manuscripts written in his own hand survive.

Shakespeare's plays are so important that generations of scholars have searched for more information about his life. Little of significance has been discovered, and there are even theories that the man known as Shakespeare was *not* the author of the great plays and poems. None of these theories has ever been accepted by scholars, however, so we are left only with tantalizing clues about the man—and the certainty of his great genius.

(*See also* Masterpieces of literature)

William Shakespeare's plays often represent high tragedy, as in this scene from Julius Caesar (left). *But they also have great comic figures such as* Falstaff (right), *who appears here in a scene from* Henry IV.

His plays

Year	Comedies	Histories	Tragedies
1590	The Comedy of Errors	King Henry VI, Part I	
1591		King Henry VI, Part II	
1592		King Henry VI, Part III	
1593	The Taming of the Shrew	Richard III	
1594	The Two Gentlemen of Verona	King John	Titus Andronicus
1595	A Midsummer Night's Dream	Richard II	
1596	Love's Labour's Lost		Romeo and Juliet
1597	The Merchant of Venice	Henry IV, Part I	
1598	As You Like It	Henry IV, Part II	
1599	Much Ado About Nothing	Henry V	Julius Caesar
1600	Twelfth Night		
	The Merry Wives of Windsor		
1601			Hamlet
			Troilus and Cressida
1603	All's Well That Ends Well		
1604	Measure for Measure		Othello
1605			King Lear
			Macbeth
1606			Timon of Athens
1607			Pericles
			Antony and Cleopatra
1608			Coriolanus
1609	Cymbeline		
1610	The Winter's Tale		
1611	The Tempest		
1613		Henry VIII	

Though Shakespeare's plays are usually performed in historically appropriate costumes, sometimes they are performed in modern dress to make them more approachable for contemporary audiences. Shown here are scenes from The Merry Wives of Windsor (left) *and from* Hamlet (right).

Sheridan, Richard Brinsley
(1751-1816). Forced to turn
to the theater to satisfy the
luxurious lifestyle of his wife,
Sheridan became the most
accomplished dramatist of the
late 1700's. His comedies *The
Rivals* and *School for Scandal* are
light, witty satires of social
pretensions and hypocrisies, and
they are still regularly performed.
Sheridan was also a politician
and served in Parliament for
more than 30 years.

Sophocles (496?-406 B.C.). About
29 years younger than Aeschylus, Sophocles was the second of
the three great Greek tragedians.
Sophocles is thought to have
written more than 80 plays, but
only seven survive. Sophocles'
plays dwell more on human
emotions than on civic and
political events. His major works
are three plays about the Oedipus
legend: *Oedipus Rex, Oedipus at
Colonus,* and *Antigone.* These
plays trace the fate and legacy of
Oedipus, doomed to marry his
mother and murder his father.
Antigone, the daughter of
Oedipus, is the central character
of the third play. Sophocles'
other surviving plays are *Ajax,
The Women of Trachis, Electra,* and
Philoctetes. The psychoanalyst
Sigmund Freud gave the name
"Oedipus complex" to one of his
theories about the human
subconscious.

Stoppard, Tom (b. 1937). Born
Tomas Straussler in
Czechoslovakia, Stoppard
moved to England and became a
citizen. He worked as a journalist
before turning to playwriting.
His best-known play is
*Rosencrantz and Guildenstern Are
Dead,* which examines the fates of
two minor characters in
Shakespeare's tragedy *Hamlet*
and shows Stoppard's use of
comedy and innovative dialogue
to explore the serious nature of
human existence. His later plays

include *Travesties* and *The Real
Thing.*

Strindberg, Johan August
(1848-1912). The greatest
Swedish dramatist, Strindberg
was some 20 years younger than
Norwegian Henrik Ibsen. His
early works, such as *The Father
and Miss Julie,* were realistic
studies of romantic involve-
ments resembling Ibsen's plays
in style. Later, however, Strindberg began to explore the possibilities of "expressionist" styles,
seeking a new kind of realism
through portraying a character's
inner state, as in *A Dream Play*
and *The Ghost Sonata.* In order
to stage these last works, he
experimented with new setting
and lighting techniques at his
own theater in Stockholm.

Synge, John Millington (1871-
1909). The most important
dramatist of the Irish literary
revival, Synge was working as a
translator in Paris when the
Irish poet W.B. Yeats urged
him to return to Ireland. Synge
then went to the Aran Islands,
on Ireland's western coast,
learned the Gaelic language, and
began to write plays about peasant life in a distinctive "Kiltar-
tan" English dialect. The first
of these plays were the one-act
In the Shadow of the Glen and
Riders to the Sea. Synge's most
important work is the three-act
play *The Playboy of the Western
World,* about a braggart's
conquest of gullible peasants.
At its opening night in Dublin,
audiences rioted, believing the
play demeaned the Irish people.
Now, however, *The Playboy* is
recognized as a masterpiece.
Synge had nearly completed the
mythological tragedy *Deirdre of
the Sorrows* when he died in
Dublin at 38.

Vega, Lope de (1562-1635). A
veteran of the Spanish Armada
defeated by the English in 1588,
Lope de Vega was his country's

first great dramatist and the
leading figure in the Spanish
golden age. He was two years
older than Shakespeare. He
claimed to have written more
than 2000 plays to satisfy the
enormous demand by Spanish
audiences for new dramas; of
these, more than 300 survive.
His works characteristically
stress the triumph of good over
evil. De Vega's most famous
play is *Fuenteovejuna (The
Sheepfold),* in which peasant
villagers revolt against a cruel
nobleman and require
protection from their king.

Weiss, Peter (1916-1982).
A champion of human values
and dignity over the alienating
forces of modern life, Weiss
was born in Germany but
settled in Sweden in 1939. His
best-known plays, which have
been described as unconventional, shocking, disturbing,
and fascinating, include *Marat/
Sade,* in which the Marquis de
Sade directs a play performed
by the inmates of an insane
asylum, and *The Investigation,*
which is based on testimony
about Nazi atrocities during
World War II.

Williams, Tennessee (1911-
1983). Thomas Lanier
Williams was born in
Mississippi and lived for a
time in the state for which he
is nicknamed. He was an
obscure writer of poems and
short stories as well as plays
until *The Glass Menagerie*
became a major theatrical
event in New York in 1945.
It was followed by a string of
other Broadway successes,
including *The Rose Tattoo, Sweet
Bird of Youth, A Streetcar Named
Desire,* and *Suddenly Last
Summer.* Williams's plays are
generally set in the southern
United States, and feature
characters whose unhappiness
has roots in the past.

Fiction

Today prose fiction is by far the most popular of the three principal literary forms. Originally the word "fiction" included any imaginative creation with a story, whether in poetry, drama, or prose. In modern times, however, fiction is usually used to refer to prose.

Poems and plays are governed by strict conventions such as meter and structure. In contrast, prose fiction is less confined and is the most natural and informal kind of literary presentation. In it a storyteller speaks and provides an account of imaginary events for the entertainment of an audience. In fact, storytelling as a folk art may be the earliest of all literary arts, but one that is lost because the stories were passed from one generation to another without being written down.

Since the 1700's, literary fiction has branched in many directions. Some writers have explored the past, as in *Ivanhoe* by Sir Walter Scott. Some have explored particular settings, as in *Moby-Dick* by Melville. Others have chosen to explore the mind and emotions of an individual, as in *Crime and Punishment* by Dostoevski. Many have concentrated on the social relationships of their own times, whether in England during Victorian times or the United States today.

There are also particular types of stories called *genres* of fiction. These include the Gothic novel, detective stories, satirical fiction, and science fiction.

In all fiction, appreciation hinges on recognition of four principal elements. The first is plot, or the order of events in a narrative. These events are not always presented in chronological order, but the cause and effect relationship between different events in a story is often crucial to a full understanding of it. The second element is character, or the specific qualities attached to each of the people in a narrative. Most stories feature both major and minor characters, distinguished by the amount of attention they receive, but the virtues and vices of all are important to the meaning of the story. The third element is setting, or the time and place in which the narrative occurs. The setting usually changes in the course of a narrative, and this often signals a change in the kind of action likely to occur and its probable outcome. Attention to the setting and its influence on the story's outcome may help illuminate the writer's ideas and purposes in writing the story. The fourth element is the teller of the story. Some stories are told by an objective third-person narrator who knows all the circumstances and thoughts of all the characters. Many others are told by a subjective first-person narrator whose knowledge and understanding of the story is limited.

Some philosophers and religious thinkers have always objected to fiction because it is "untrue," and some modern readers continue to prefer nonfiction—biographies, histories, and books on current affairs. But in a sense, a great novel or story may be more real than a biography or history, using the writer's imagination to help understand not only what happened but why it happened, and how it felt to those who were there. The great power of fiction is that it can let a reader experience events in another time and place and discover how different, yet how much the same, other people's lives can be.

A storyteller (left) was the first maker of fiction. Early written stories, like Defoe's Robinson Crusoe *(right) have often been illustrated.*

Fiction	1500	1550	1600	1650	1700
Europe		CERVANTES			
England/Ireland				BUNYAN	DEFOE

The history of fiction.

Prose fiction is the youngest of the three principal literary forms. Its earliest ancestors date from the 1300's: the romance tales in the *Decameron* by the Italian Boccaccio, presented as indoor entertainment during a plague, and *The Canterbury Tales* by the English poet Chaucer, presented as entertainment during a pilgrimage. More immediate sources for the novel lie in the 1600's, when Cervantes' *Don Quixote* added psychological realism to the earlier episodic tales and John Bunyan's *Pilgrim's Progress* presented a religious allegory with characters and dialogue in prose.

Fiction as we know it, however, awaited the greater availability of printing presses, widespread literacy, and a middle class capable of purchasing books. Most of the important early novels were published in England in the first half of the 1700's, where these requirements had been fulfilled. Three milestones were Daniel Defoe's *Robinson Crusoe,* which drew on the travel literature of the time, Samuel Richardson's *Pamela,* which provided entertainment for a predominantly female audience, and Henry Fielding's *Tom Jones,* a novel with strong satirical and comic elements. Most early English novels were similar to one of these three strains until Jane Austen's more sophisticated work in the early 19th century made the novel a witty forum for social commentary.

In Europe, novels remained primarily a hobby of philosophers such as Rousseau until the great German literary figure Goethe described through letters a suicidal youth in *The Sorrows of Young Werther*. Later, he established the *bildungsroman,* or "formation novel," with *The Apprenticeship of Wilheim Meister*. In France in the early 1800's, the romantic fictions of Victor Hugo caused great excitement. Stendhal's panoramic saga of war, *The Red and the Black,* and Balzac's series of socially conscious novels, collectively called *The Human Comedy,* are among the great classics of modern fiction.

Perhaps the most important single phase of the novel occurred in Victorian England, where philosophical controversies surrounding Darwin's *Origin of the Species* and the effects of the Industrial Revolution created a concerned reading public and great novelists of social interaction. The decade of the 1840's alone saw the publication of *Jane Eyre* and *Wuthering Heights* by the Brontë sisters, Thackeray's *Vanity Fair,* and Dickens' *Martin Chuzzlewit* and *David Copperfield*. Most Victo-

Frontispiece of Vanity Fair, *drawn by Thackeray*

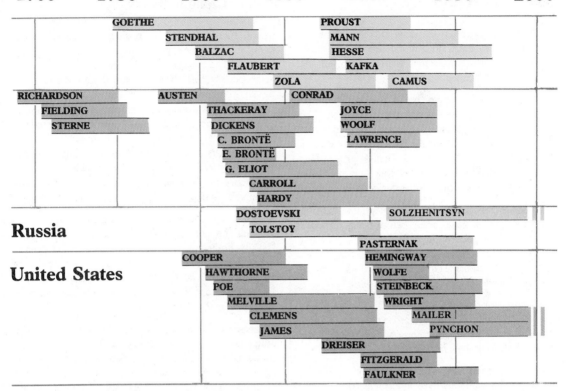

1700	1750	1800	1850	1900	1950	2000

GOETHE
PROUST
STENDHAL
MANN
BALZAC
HESSE
FLAUBERT
KAFKA
ZOLA
CAMUS
RICHARDSON
AUSTEN
CONRAD
FIELDING
THACKERAY
JOYCE
STERNE
DICKENS
WOOLF
C. BRONTË
LAWRENCE
E. BRONTË
G. ELIOT
CARROLL
HARDY
DOSTOEVSKI
SOLZHENITSYN
Russia
TOLSTOY
PASTERNAK
United States
COOPER
HEMINGWAY
HAWTHORNE
WOLFE
POE
STEINBECK
MELVILLE
WRIGHT
CLEMENS
MAILER
JAMES
PYNCHON
DREISER
FITZGERALD
FAULKNER

rian novels were published first in magazine installments, then as "triple decker" book trilogies to be rented at lending libraries. Most also told a story that ended with a successful marriage, a convention that survived through George Eliot's *Middlemarch* in 1872. By the time of Thomas Hardy's series of novels beginning in the 1890's, however, British novels had begun to end on a gloomier note. Readers can no longer expect a happy ending in serious fiction.

In 19th-century America, the novel tradition began with the frontier sagas of James Fenimore Cooper, the Puritanical stories and novels of Nathaniel Hawthorne, and the mysterious works of Edgar Allan Poe. The greatest American novels were not written until the second half of the century, when Melville's symbolic *Moby-Dick*, Mark Twain's colloquial *Huckleberry Finn*, and Henry James's complex novels all broke new ground. The success of these writers created a national appetite for a "great American novel," a work of sufficient breadth to capture the essence of the American experience. Most agree that no such work exists, although the possibility of one continues to tantalize critics and novelists alike.

The roots of the modern novel lie primarily in Europe. Flaubert's *Madame Bovary* of 1857 and Émile Zola's *Nana* of 1880 brought a new realism and emphasis on the misfortunes of characters of low social status. Tolstoy's wartime saga in *War and Peace* was followed in the Russian tradition by the religious symbolism and sense of alienation presented in Dostoevski's novels *Crime and Punishment* and *The Brothers Karamazov*.

The great European novels of the early 20th century added a complexity of style that firmly established the novel as an advanced art form on the order of painting or music. Proust in French, Mann and Kafka in German, and Joyce, Woolf, and Conrad in English all developed idiosyncratic styles in order to imitate the workings of the human mind. All of these writers (except Proust) were also the authors of important short stories or novellas, forms which gained a new importance as serious literature.

In America, early 20th-century writers of fiction split their interests between following European experiments and describing the dynamic new world of American values. F. Scott Fitzgerald became the most successful writer of his time with the novel *The Great Gatsby* and his immensely popular short stories, but the longer careers and greater productivity of William Faulkner, who wrote complex fictions about families in the American South, and Ernest Hemingway, who wrote in a restrained style about brave heroes doomed by large social forces, have brought them greater esteem since that time.

Kinds of short fiction

fable. Brief story, often featuring animals as characters, intended to illustrate a moral lesson. The most famous is *Aesop's Fables*, first written down in the 300's B.C. in Greece.

fairy tale. Short narrative that is generally fantastic and is today read or told principally to children. The most famous fairy tales were collected from old storytellers in Germany in the early 1800's by the brothers Jakob and Wilhelm Grimm. The Danish writer Hans Christian Andersen imitated old folk tales in "The Ugly Duckling" and other stories for children.

folk tale. Anonymous story tied to a single cultural group and handed down orally before being recorded in writing. The poet William Butler Yeats collected many such works in *Irish Folk Stories*. In the United States, Joel Chandler Harris collected folk tales of black Americans in *Tales from Uncle Remus*.

tale. Short story slightly unrealistic in character and event and related to the longer prose romance. Examples include Nathaniel Hawthorne's *Twice-Told Tales* and Herman Melville's *Piazza Tales*.

short story. Brief prose narrative describing a limited number of characters involved in a single major event. Descended from the forms described above, the modern short story has become increasingly realistic in the hands of such writers as Guy de Maupassant and Anton Chekhov.

Important short story writers

America	Washington Irving, 1783–1859
	Edgar Allan Poe, 1809–1849
	Bret Harte, 1836–1902
	O.Henry (W.S. Porter), 1862–1910
	Stephen Crane, 1871–1900
	Sherwood Anderson, 1876–1941
	Jack London, 1876–1916
	James Thurber, 1894–1961
	Flannery O'Connor, 1925–1964
Russia	Ivan Turgenev, 1818–1883
	Anton Chekhov, 1860–1904
	Maxim Gorky, 1868–1936
	Isaac Babel, 1894–1941
France	Guy de Maupassant, 1850–1893
England	Saki (H.H. Munro), 1870–1916
	W. Somerset Maugham, 1874–1965
Ireland	Frank O'Connor, 1903–1966

Kinds of long fiction

novel. Fictional story of considerable length written in prose. The name comes from the Italian for "[a] new [thing]." The novel's special purpose is to stress the development of its characters and to describe in detail the environment in which they live. *Don Quixote* by Cervantes is an important precursor of the novel. The first real examples of the novel developed in England in the 1700's. Daniel Defoe's *Robinson Crusoe* and *Moll Flanders* brought new realism to longer fiction. The first true literary novels, by Samuel Richardson and Henry Fielding, added a new interest in the emotional and psychological lives of their characters.

novella. Short novel, a distinction measured by the scope of the work as well as by the number of pages. Usually limited in number of characters and events, the novella combines some of the qualities of the short story and the novel. Important examples include Joseph Conrad's *Heart of Darkness* and Henry James's *The Turn of the Screw*.

picaresque. Novel-length story consisting of many individual episodes, usually a series of adventures encountered by a single hapless hero called a picaroon. Early picaresque narratives, such as the anonymous Spanish *Lazarillo de Tormes*, were written in the 1500's and precede the rise of the novel. Defoe's *Moll Flanders* has picaresque qualities, and later writers also used the form. Important examples are *Candide* by Voltaire and *Jonathan Wild* by Henry Fielding.

romance. Novel-length story that is exotic and slightly fabulous rather than realistic. Related to earlier verse romances, prose romances, usually set in historical times, became popular in the 1800's. Examples include Sir Walter Scott's *Ivanhoe*. James Fenimore Cooper's *Leatherstocking Tales*, about the American frontier, might also be considered a romance.

bildungsroman. A German term meaning "formation novel" used to describe novels about an adolescent's initiation into adulthood. *Bildungsromans* in English include Dickens' *David Copperfield* and Samuel Butler's *The Way of All Flesh*.

roman à clef. A novel in which actual persons are described under fictitious names. Such novels are often satirical. *Clef* is French for "key"; the *roman à clef* provides clues as keys to the real identities of its characters. In Aldous Huxley's novel *Point Counter Point*, for example, the character John Bidlake is identifiable as the novelist D. H. Lawrence.

Special types of fiction

Satirical fiction

Satirical fiction ridicules vanities and pretensions by means of exaggeration. The exaggeration may take the form of implausible events in fantastic settings, or it may sarcastically simplify realistic characters and environments. In either case, satirical fiction is comical in tone, for it attacks its targets by making them laughable to the reader. Jonathan Swift defined this form as "ridicule of the foibles of men with the hope of reforming them."

Examples

Author	Lifetime	Work
Jonathan Swift	1667–1745	*Gulliver's Travels*
Voltaire	1694–1778	*Candide*
Samuel Johnson	1709–1784	*Rasselas*
Lewis Carroll	1832–1898	*Alice's Adventures in Wonderland*
Aldous Huxley	1894–1963	*Point Counter Point*
George Orwell	1903–1950	*Animal Farm*
Evelyn Waugh	1903–1966	*Scoop*

Gothic fiction

Gothic fiction is a form of romance describing supernatural events in exotic and eerie surroundings. The creatures and ghosts common in Gothic fiction are at once thrilling entertainments and versions of psychological and spiritual conditions. In modern times these Gothic elements are often found in combination with a melodramatic love story. Because it is so unrealistic, Gothic fiction is often considered a kind of prose romance.

Examples

Author	Lifetime	Work
Horace Walpole	1717–1797	*The Castle of Otranto*
William Beckford	1760–1844	*Vathek*
Anne Radcliffe	1764–1823	*The Mysteries of Udolfo*
Matthew Lewis	1775–1818	*The Monk*
Mary Shelley	1797–1851	*Frankenstein*
Edgar Allan Poe	1809–1849	"The Fall of the House of Usher"
Henry James	1843–1916	*The Turn of the Screw*
Bram Stoker	1847–1912	*Dracula*

Detective fiction

Detective fiction opens with a crime and leads up to a final explanation about how the hero has identified the villian through the evidence of various clues. At its purest, detective fiction is an exercise in pure logic. It also frequently dwells on the psychology of both the detective and the other characters as well as the social nature of the evil they confront.

Examples

Author	Lifetime	Work
Edgar Allan Poe	1809–1849	"The Purloined Letter"
Arthur Conan Doyle	1859–1930	*Adventures of Sherlock Holmes*
Raymond Chandler	1888–1959	*The Big Sleep*
Agatha Christie	1891–1976	*Murder on the Orient Express*
Dashiell Hammett	1894–1961	*The Maltese Falcon*
Mickey Spillane	b. 1918	*I the Jury*

Science fiction

Science fiction deals with the nature and effects of scientific advancement, its values and dangers. Often set in the future and in outer space, it nevertheless provides a commentary on present society by imagining the future effects of present decisions or by creating an allegorical version of traditional conflicts. The imaginary world created in science fiction may be either a utopia, or perfect world, or a dystopia, or imperfect one. Because of its essentially allegorical purpose, science fiction is a modern form of a type of fiction as old as Sir Thomas More's *Utopia*, published in Latin in 1516.

Examples

Author	Lifetime	Work
Jules Verne	1828–1905	*Twenty Thousand Leagues Under the Sea*
H. G. Wells	1866–1946	*The Time Machine*
Aldous Huxley	1894–1963	*Brave New World*
C. S. Lewis	1898–1963	*Out of the Silent Planet*
Arthur C. Clarke	b. 1917	*The Lost Worlds of 2001*
Isaac Asimov	1920–1992	*I, Robot*
Ray Bradbury	b. 1920	*Fahrenheit 451*
Ursula K. LeGuin	b. 1929	*The Left Hand of Darkness*

Clemens

Fiction writers

George Eliot

Joyce

Solzhenitsyn

Austen, Jane *(1775-1817)*. Although she lived a placid life as an English gentlewoman, Jane Austen wrote four very important novels: *Sense and Sensibility, Pride and Prejudice, Mansfield Park,* and *Emma.* Each is a parlor drama leading to a marriage, and each takes place in similar upper-middle-class surroundings. All make subtle observations on the manners of the time and lend themselves to larger generalizations about life.

Balzac, Honoré de (1799-1850). The most prolific of French novelists, Balzac wrote a long series of novels that are together given the title *The Human Comedy.* His project was to write about a broad spectrum of contemporary French life and to create a panorama in fiction that included the very rich, the very poor, and the classes in between. Events and characters recur from novel to novel, and the effect of any event on a different group of characters is an important theme in this social history in fiction. The best known of the novels are *Père Goriot* and *Cousin Bette.*

Brontë, Charlotte (1816-1855). The sister of Emily Brontë, Charlotte Brontë published *Jane Eyre* under the pseudonym Currer Bell in 1847. It is the story of the title character's experiences in a brutal boarding school and of her subsequent love for the handsome but evil Mr. Rochester. *Jane Eyre* granted a greater degree of freedom and passion to the female character than did any previous English novel. Charlotte Brontë was a forerunner of modern feminist ideas.

Brontë, Emily (1818-1848). The sister of Charlotte Brontë, Emily Brontë published *Wuthering Heights* under the pseudonym Ellis Bell in 1847. *Wuthering Heights* is one of the great romantic novels in the English language. It employs devices of Gothic fiction to heighten the grandeur and mystical intensity of wealthy Catherine Linton's doomed love for Heathcliff.

Bunyan, John (1628-1688). The most important English precursor of the modern novelist, John Bunyan was a Puritan imprisoned twice for his religious beliefs. During his second imprisonment he wrote *Pilgrim's Progress* (1678). A religious allegory about the quest of a man named Christian, it became a great influence on many more realistic modern writers.

Camus, Albert (1913-1960). A French novelist born in Algeria, Camus earned a degree in philosophy, worked as a journalist, and fought for the French Resistance during World War II. He became the most famous spokesman in fiction for the French school of existentialism, which argued that each man creates his own life by his actions. His novels include *The Stranger, The Plague,* and *The Fall.* An essayist and playwright as well, he was awarded the Nobel Prize in 1957.

Carroll, Lewis (1832-1898). Charles Lutwidge Dodgson, a shy and retiring professor of mathematics, published books under the name Lewis Carroll. He is best known for *Alice's Adventures in Wonderland* and *Through the Looking-Glass.* Both books are of interest to readers of all ages for their play with language, their satire of adult life, and their whimsical, surreal qualities.

Cervantes, Miguel de (1547-1616). Born into an aristocratic family in northern Spain that had recently lost its fortune, Cervantes made a living as a soldier through most of his life. He is said to have written more than 20 plays, although only two survive. Late in life he began *Don Quixote*, the cornerstone of the novel tradition. Published in two parts in 1605 and 1615, it tells the story of the elderly and eccentric Alonzo Quixano, who dubs himself Don Quixote and sets off on a series of comic chivalrous adventures with his squire Sancho Panza.

Clemens, Samuel (Mark Twain) (1835-1910). An American novelist, Sam Clemens grew up in Missouri and served as an apprentice on a Mississippi River steamboat. Later, he traveled to Nevada and began to write humorous newspaper accounts of life in the West. *The Adventures of Tom Sawyer* was his first big success, and its sequel, *Huckleberry Finn*, is considered to be his masterpiece. The latter raises important moral and social issues. Clemens's other novels include *Pudd'nhead Wilson* and *The Prince and the Pauper*.

Conrad, Joseph (1857-1924). Born Josef Korzeniowski in the Polish Ukraine, Conrad served in the French navy and only began to write novels in English after he retired, at the age of nearly 40. One of the most important modern novelists in English, he drew on his sea adventures in *The Nigger of the Narcissus, Lord Jim,* and *Heart of Darkness*. Although English was his second language, Conrad became one of the best English prose stylists.

Cooper, James Fenimore (1789-1851). The son of the wealthy family for which Cooperstown, New York, is named, Cooper was expelled from Yale University, shipped out on a European sailing ship, and later

joined the U.S. Navy. He wrote several adventure stories about life at sea, but he is best known for the series of novels collectively called *Leatherstocking Tales*. The stories relate the frontier adventures of the woodsman Natty Bumppo, his combat and friendship with the Indians, and his resigned surrender of the woods to the civilized manners of the American pioneers. Important novels in the saga include *The Deerslayer, The Last of the Mohicans,* and *The Pathfinder*.

Defoe, Daniel (1660?-1731). Called by some the first true novelist, Defoe was born in London. In his remarkable career he was a businessman, secret agent for the English government, journalist, and author of hundreds of pamphlets and political tracts before turning, in his fifties, to writing novels. His first novel, *Robinson Crusoe*, was an enormous success and a literary landmark. Defoe's other novels include *Moll Flanders* and *Colonel Jack* as well as the semi-historical *Journal of the Plague Year*.

Dickens, Charles (1812-1870). Born into a poor and debt-ridden English family, Dickens first became a journalist. His early works of fiction, *Sketches by Boz* and *The Pickwick Papers*, brought him immediate fame. His major novels are indictments of the deprivation suffered by working-class people in England of the mid-1800's. Among them are *Oliver Twist, David Copperfield, Hard Times,* and *Bleak House*. Most of Dickens' novels were first published in magazine installments.

Dostoevski, Feodor (1821-1881). Born in Moscow, Dostoevski was a political activist as a young man. Arrested, he was condemned to

death, a sentence that was later commuted to exile in Siberia from 1850 to 1859. Dostoevski began to write after returning to Moscow, and his works pondered questions about guilt and redemption that are more moral than political in nature. His most important novels are *Crime and Punishment, The Idiot,* and *The Brothers Karamazov*.

Dreiser, Theodore (1871-1945). Born in Indiana, Dreiser was for the most part self-educated. He became a Chicago newspaperman. His first novel, *Sister Carrie*, was published in 1900. It tells the story of a pure girl from the Midwest who prospers because she becomes unscrupulous. This reversal of traditional morality was so shocking that Dreiser's own publisher suppressed the novel. Among his later novels were *Jennie Gerhard*, about a kept woman, and *An American Tragedy*, about a youth who becomes the victim of class prejudice in New York.

Eliot, George (1819-1880). Born Mary Ann Evans, George Eliot adopted a male pseudonym for her fiction. Encouraged by her lifelong companion George Henry Lewes, she began to publish under the name George Eliot the novels on which her reputation now rests: *Adam Bede, The Mill on the Floss, Silas Marner,* and *Middlemarch*. The last is about Dorothea Brooke's attempt to preserve her distinctly feminine intellect and imagination despite the pressures of society.

Faulkner, William (1897-1962). Born into a Mississippi family whose fortunes had been destroyed by the Civil War, Faulkner spent a vagrant youth and then began to write a series of novels about the American South. His principal works take place in the fictional Yoknapatawpha County in Mississippi, and they examine life there through the minds of a wide range of white and black characters. His novels in this group include *The Sound and the Fury, Light in August,* and *Absalom, Absalom!*. Faulkner was awarded the Nobel Prize in 1950.

Fielding, Henry (1707-1754). A lawyer by profession, Fielding was also a prolific playwright and journalist. In 1741 he published *Shamela,* a parody of Samuel Richardson's popular novel *Pamela.* This launched his career as one of the great comic novelists in English literature. His works include *Joseph Andrews,* subtitled "written in imitation of the manner of Cervantes"; *Jonathan Wild,* also a picaresque; and *Tom Jones,* an eventful and chaotic story about an orphan's improbable journey toward wealth and happiness.

Fitzgerald, F. Scott (1897-1940). Born in St. Paul, Minnesota, Fitzgerald came east to be educated at Princeton Universtiy. Married to the debutante beauty Zelda Sayre in 1920, he became famous as the chronicler of the "Jazz Age" of the roaring '20's. His short stories brought him national fame and considerable wealth, but Zelda's mental illness and Fitzgerald's alcoholism brought them both to early deaths. His novel *The Great Gatsby* examines the self-destructive side of the American dream. His works include the novels *Tender Is the Night* and *The Last Tycoon,* which was left unfinished at his death.

Flaubert, Gustave (1821-1880). A former student of law in Paris, Flaubert was the pioneer of a new realism in the French novel. His ideal was to pay close attention to the realities of life, and to relate them in a disciplined style free from older novelistic conventions. His most important novels are *Madame Bovary,* the story of a deteriorating marriage, and *The Sentimental Education.*

Goethe, Johann Wolfgang von (1749-1832). The greatest of all German writers, Goethe was born in Frankfurt and studied law while writing his early lyric poems. He became famous as leader of the German *Sturm und Drang* (Storm and Stress) movement, which advocated a heightened sense of personal emotion in art and literature. Goethe's contributions to the movement include the novels *The Sorrows of Young Werther,* consisting principally of letters from a suicidal young man, and *The Apprenticeship of Wilhelm Meister.* These early novels were models for many later novelists. *See also* Goethe in Poetry Glossary.

Hardy, Thomas (1840-1928). Born in rural Dorset, England, a region he recreated as the fictional Wessex in his novels, Thomas Hardy left an apprenticeship in architecture to pursue his literary ambitions. He wrote a great number of novels, including *The Mayor of Casterbridge, The Return of the Native, Tess of the D'Urbervilles,* and *Jude the Obscure.* The last two were publicly condemned as immoral, and Hardy spent his later years writing poetry. The central them of the novels is the way in which people trapped in the working classes are frustrated in their efforts to improve themselves morally and socially.

Hawthorne, Nathaniel (1804-1864). A resident of Salem, Massachusetts, for most of his life, Hawthorne was a friend of Herman Melville and a member of the intellectual circle that included Henry David Thoreau and Ralph Waldo Emerson. He was a solitary and conventional man, but his works include some of the first important examples of American fiction. His novel *The Scarlet Letter* is about the adulteress Hester Prynne and her punishment by the stern and sometimes hypocritical elders of Puritan Boston. Hawthorne's other works include many short stories and the novel *The House of the Seven Gables.*

Hemingway, Ernest (1899-1961). Born in Illinois, Hemingway was wounded while serving as an ambulance driver for the Italian army in World War I, an experience he later described in the novel *A Farewell to Arms.* As a journalist in Paris, he began to refine the spare prose style he made famous in his major novels, including *The Sun Also Rises, To Have and Have Not,* and *For Whom the Bell Tolls.* In both his novels and his many short stories Hemingway used both war and such sports as bull fighting, hunting, and fishing as metaphors for the workings of daily life. His solitary heroes are doomed, but seek to maintain their personal honor. He was awarded the Nobel Prize for Literature in 1954.

Hesse, Hermann (1877-1962). A German novelist and visionary thinker, Hesse wrote unusual novels that brought him the Nobel Prize in 1946. He has retained a devoted following since. His works are mystical and surreal, and they attempt to incorporate the discoveries of modern psychology into older philosophies and spiritual schemes. Among his novels are *Siddhartha* and *Steppenwolf.*

James, Henry (1843-1916). Born into a famous New York intellectual family, Henry James permanently settled in England in 1876 and became a British

Openings of novels

Moby-Dick, by Herman Melville (1851):
Call me Ishmael. Some years ago—never mind how long precisely—having little or no money in my purse, and nothing particular to interest me on shore, I thought I would sail about a little and see the watery part of the world.

Pride and Prejudice, by Jane Austen (1813):
It is a truth universally acknowledged, that a single man in possession of a good fortune, must be in want of a wife.

A Tale of Two Cities, by Charles Dickens (1859):
It was the best of times, it was the worst of times, it was the age of wisdom, it was the age of foolishness, it was the epoch of belief, it was the epoch of incredulity, it was the season of light, it was the season of darkness, it was the spring of hope, it was the winter of despair, we had everything before us, we had nothing before us, we were all going direct to heaven, we were all going direct the other way—in short, the period was so far like the present period, that some of its noisiest authorities insisted on its being received for good or for evil, in the superlative degree of comparison only.

The Portrait of a Lady, by Henry James (1880):
Under certain circumstances there are few hours in life more agreeable than the hour dedicated to the ceremony known as afternoon tea.

Adam Bede, by George Eliot (1859):
With a single drop of ink for a mirror, the Egyptian sorcerer undertakes to reveal to any chance comer far-reaching visions of the past. This is what I undertake to do for you, reader.

The Adventures of Huckleberry Finn, by Samuel Clemens (Mark Twain, 1884):
You don't know about me without you have read a book by the name of *The Adventures of Tom Sawyer;* but that ain't no matter. That book was made by Mr. Mark Twain, and he told the truth, mainly. There was things which he stretched, but mainly he told the truth. That is nothing. I never seen anybody but lied one time or another, without it was Aunt Polly, or the widow, or maybe Mary. Aunt Polly—Tom's Aunt Polly, she is—and Mary and the Widow Douglas is all told about in that book, which is mostly a true book, with some stretchers, as I said before.

Anna Karenina, by Leo Tolstoy (1876):
All happy families are like one another; each unhappy family is unhappy in its own way.

---

citizen in the year before his death. In novels such as *The Ambassadors, The American,* and *Daisy Miller,* he subtly contrasts the imaginations of his American characters with those of their European counterparts. James experimented with relating events through a character's own point of view and with describing subtle shades of emotion in long, complex sentences. In addition to novels he wrote more than 70 short stories, plays, and critical essays.

Joyce, James (1882-1941). Born and educated in Dublin, Ireland, Joyce lived all of his adult life in Europe but wrote only about his home country. After publishing a group of lyrical poems, he wrote the collection of stories called *Dubliners,* understated accounts of the paralysis of the Irish imagination. This was followed by the autobiographical novel *Portrait of the Artist as a Young Man,* a story about coming of age in Ireland that ends with a flight to Europe like Joyce's own. His two long masterpieces are *Ulysses* and *Finnegans Wake,* which are experimental in form and language and rank as major landmarks in the history of the modern novel.

Kafka, Franz (1883-1924). Born in Prague, Czechoslovakia, Kafka worked as a civil servant throughout his adult life. His rather fantastic novels and stories use improbable methaphors to describe his deep alienation from social and familial aspects of life. His important short stories include *"The Metamorphosis,"* in which Gregor Samsa is transformed into an insect. In novels such as *The Trial* and *The Castle,* which were published after his death, Kafka gives us a sensitive hero who is nightmarishly mistreated by public authorities.

Lawrence, David Herbert (1885-1930). The son of a humble coal miner and an ambitious mother, D. H. Lawrence described his own rise above dreary surroundings in *Sons and Lovers.* He later developed a complicated ethic about sexual relations in novels such as *Women in Love, The Rainbow,* and *Lady Chatterley's Lover.* These books outraged the reading public, and Lawrence, with his German-born wife Frieda, spent his later years in ill health wandering to Italy, Australia, Mexico, and the southwest United States.

Mailer, Norman (b. 1923).
Using his Army experiences in
the Pacific during World War II,
Mailer produced one of the best
works of fiction to come out of
the war, the novel *The Naked
and the Dead.* His later novels
include *The Deer Park, Ancient
Evenings,* and *Harlot's Ghost.*
Mailer has also written nonfiction, including *The Armies
of the Night,* centering on an
anti-Vietnam War protest, and
The Executioner's Song, which
employs fictional techniques.

Mann, Thomas (1875-1955).
The most important modern
German novelist, Thomas Mann
first wrote a family saga called
Buddenbrooks; he became an
international spokesman on
German issues because of it.His
1924 novel *The Magic Mountain*
described the rise of the new
German nationalism as it
appeared in an isolated health
sanitarium. Mann was forced to
immigrate to the United States
in 1933 because of his criticism
of the Nazi movement. He returned to Germany after World
War II, and in novels such as *Dr.
Faustus, Joseph and His Brothers,*
and *Death in Venice,* he experimented with new treatments of
the complex cultural relations
between art and politics.

Melville, Herman (1819-1891).
A New York City native who
shipped out as a young man on
sailing vessels bound for Pacific
islands, Melville became a
popular American novelist with
early adventure novels such as
Typee, Omoo, and *Mardi.* With
Moby-Dick in 1851, however, he
began to pursue a more com-
plexly metaphysical vision that
cost him his popularity. *Moby-
Dick* tells of Captain Ahab's
obsessive search for the white
whale he believes personifies
evil. It includes whole chapters
about the art of whaling and
other apparently extraneous

material. Since Melville's death
his artistry has been rediscovered, and he has been recognized as one of the greatest of
all American novelists.

Pasternak, Boris (1890-1960).
An important Russian poet and
translator as well as a novelist,
Pasternak wrote his famous
novel *Doctor Zhivago* in secret
and had it smuggled to Paris,
where it was published in 1957.
It describes the experiences of a
doctor and poet named Yurii
Zhivago in the years of the
Russian Revolution. Because it
unflatteringly contrasted Bolshevik ruthlessness with Zhivago's
peaceful instincts, the book was
considered subversive in Russia.
When Pasternak was awarded
the Nobel Prize in 1958, he
could not accept it for fear of
persecution in his country.

Poe, Edgar Allan (1809-1849).
The son of traveling actors and
orphaned at an early age, Edgar
Allan Poe made a marginal living as a journalist before turning to fiction. He wrote eerie
short stories in the Gothic style
that became classics of the type,
especially *"The Fall of the House
of Usher," "Ligeia," "The Pit and
the Pendulum,"* and *"The Cask of
Amontillado."* He was also the
originator of the modern
detective story with *"The
Purloined Letter,"* and was an
important poet.

Proust, Marcel (1871-1922).
The most important French
novelist of the early 1900's,
Proust was a sickly man who
lived in Paris all his life. He became reclusive in his later years
and seldom left his darkened
rooms. As early as age 19 he
began to make notes for what
proved to be his life's work: the
seven-novel-long *Rememberance of
Things Past.* This work explores
the workings of the mind and
memory by dwelling at length
on apparently insignificant

details and pursuing them in
long, digressive recollections.

Pynchon, Thomas (b. 1937).
A reclusive author who prefers
to let his works speak for themselves, Pynchon is best known for
his novel *Gravity's Rainbow,* a vast,
darkly comic, and at times raw
study of modern culture, set at
the close of World War II. His
other novels, equally dense,
imaginative, and challenging,
include *V.,* his first novel, *The
Crying of Lot 49,* and *Vineland.*

Richardson, Samuel (1689-
1751). A prosperous master
printer, Richardson became one
of the first great English novelists.
His first book, *Pamela: or Virtue
Rewarded,* is often considered the
first true novel. It consisted of a
long series of letters from Pamela,
an attractive serving girl, to other
characters, and it became
immensely popular. In *Clarissa,* a
seven-volume work (1747-1748),
Richardson refined the new novel
form, and his interest in the
psychology of his characters
attracted a huge new reading
public. His prudish morality was
satirized by Henry Fielding in
Shamela and other novels.

Solzhenitsyn, Alexander
(b. 1918). The leading figure in
20th-century Russian literature,
Solzhenitsyn served in the
Soviet army during World War II
but was imprisoned for criticisms
found in his letters home. His
experiences in the Soviet *Gulag,*
or prison system, were the
foundation on he built his literary
career, a lifelong determination to
tell the truth about the Soviet
system. His novels include *One
Day in the Life of Ivan Denisovich,
August 1914, The First Circle,* and
The Cancer Ward. Also author of
the nonfiction work *The Gulag
Archipelago,* he was awarded the
Nobel Prize in 1970.

Steinbeck, John (1902-1968.
Born in Salinas, California,
Steinbeck became the great

chronicler of the lives of migrant farmers and "down-and-outers" during the Great Depression of the 1930's. His major works include *Of Mice and Men* and *The Grapes of Wrath*, about the migrant Joad family's desperate search for a decent life in California. Awarded the Nobel Prize in 1962, he was also the author of *East of Eden, The Winter of Our Discontent*, and short stories.

Stendhal (1783–1842). Marie Henri Beyle, who wrote under the name Stendhal, was one of the first great French novelists. His fiction showed how the great political events of his day affected individuals and society. His major work was *The Red and the Black*, about Julien Sorel's futile attempt to rise in the church hierarchy ("the black"), and about his encounters with important military events ("the red"), such as the Battle of Waterloo. His novels were panoramic in their historical and social scope, but later French realists such as Flaubert and Zola criticized them as melodramatic in style.

Sterne, Laurence (1713–1768). Born in Ireland but raised and educated in England, Sterne gained lasting fame as the author of *The Life and Opinions of Tristram Shandy, Gentleman*. The narrator and title character is so digressive that he does not describe his birth until Volume IV of the nine-volume work and is not involved in most of the book's later events. The novel hilariously illustrates the limitations of erudite knowledge through the conversations and actions of Tristram's father Walter and his Uncle Toby. The book also plays with the conventions of the printed text, including several blank pages and bizarre diagrams. Sterne's

whimsical humor and support of "sentiment" over cold reason influenced many later writers.

Thackeray, William Makepeace (1811–1863). The first great novelist of Victorian England, Thackeray was born in India, where his father served in the British foreign service. Sent to London for his education, Thackeray later became famous as a journalist, humorist, and illustrator of his own novels. The most important of these novels was *Vanity Fair*, first published in installments in 1847 and 1848. A satirical study of aristocratic pretensions, the book is centered on the unscrupulous social climber Becky Sharp and is set in the early 1800's, during the Napoleonic wars. A prolific novelist, Thackeray is also known for a series of historical novels that includes *Henry Esmond*.

Tolstoy, Leo (1828–1910). A major Russian novelist whose influence has been worldwide, Tolstoy was born into a noble family and became interested in writing only after his military experience in the Crimean War. His reputation largely rests on the 1869 novel *War and Peace*, a panoramic account of life in Russia during the Napoleonic wars, and on the 1876 novel *Anna Karenina*, about the conflicting personal and social allegiances of the title character. A moralist and social reformer as well as a novelist, Tolstoy also wrote short stories and novellas, including *The Death of Ivan Ilich*.

Twain, Mark. *See* Clemens, Samuel.

Wolfe, Thomas (1900–1938). A North Carolinian famous for his excesses in both his life and his work, Thomas Wolfe wrote the autobiographical novel *Look Homeward, Angel*, a sprawling and mostly affectionate look at

his hometown of Asheville and at his own family. His novels began as huge boxes of manuscript, which he shortened and organized with the help of his editors. Many of his short stories were originally episodes cut out of the manuscript for one of the novels.

Woolf, Virginia (1882–1941). The most important writer in England's Bloomsbury Group of intellectuals, Virginia Woolf rejected the objective treatment of events in earlier English novels and sought to portray the inner life of her characters. In *To the Lighthouse, The Waves,* and *Mrs. Dalloway*, rather uneventful stories are told from the perspective of individual characters, with the emphasis falling on the lyrical movements of their thoughts and emotions.

Wright, Richard (1908–1960). Born on a Mississippi plantation, Wright began as a short story writer. It was his first novel *Native Son*, however, that established him as the most important American chronicler of the black experience. This book was followed by *Black Boy*, a violent story about the victimization of one race by another. His short stories are collected in the volumes *Uncle Tom's Children* and *Eight Men*.

Zola, Émile (1840–1902). Along with Flaubert, Zola was the pioneer of realism in the French novel. His novels portrayed the low levels of life in the France of his day, and suggested that social class and environment are the greatest influences on a person's character and fortunes. Critics charged that his novels were obscene and immoral, but Zola replied that he was scientifically recording the facts of life. His great achievement was the 20-volume Rougon and Macquart families series, including *Nana* and *Germinal*.

Masterpieces of literature

Great works of literature have been produced in a number of forms: poetry, drama, fiction, and essay. This selection concentrates on longer works, ones that are often studied in schools or colleges or that have had great influence on the history of Western literature. Most are works of fiction—whether in poetic, dramatic, or prose form.

Five early anonymous epics are briefly described under "Poets," beginning on page 354. They are *Beowulf* (old English), *Song of the Cid* (early Spanish), *Gilgamesh* (ancient Babylonian), *Sir Gawain and the Green Knight* (Middle English), and *Song of Roland* (early French). For further information on Shakespeare and his plays, see pages 370-371.

Aeneid. A Latin epic poem by the Roman poet Vergil dated 19 B.C.; it is the classic work telling of the founding of Rome by the Trojan hero Aeneas. It narrates Aeneas's wanderings before he reaches the seven hills of Rome, his love and abandonment of Dido, queen of Carthage, his descent into Hell, his war against a rival, Turnus, and his marriage to Lavinia, for continuation of his lineage. It closely follows Homer's great epic the *Iliad*.

All's Well That Ends Well. Shakespeare's comedy beginning when Count Bertram departs for the king's court and is followed by the maid Helena, who is the secret admirer of the count. Helena administers to the sick king a cure inherited from her father. Recovered, the king gives Helena a ring and grants her Bertram as a husband. Displeased, Bertram sends the low-born Helena to his mother, flees to Florence, and promises to be her true husband when she can get his ring and bear his child. Helena travels to Florence, changes place with a local maid in Bertram's bed, and switches his ring with hers. Believing Helena dead, Bertram returns home. The king sees Helena's ring on the count's hand and demands an explanation. Helena appears and confesses the plot. Claiming that she has fulfilled both parts of Bertram's requirements, Helena gains him as a true husband.

Animal Farm. Anti-Utopian novel by British author George Orwell (Eric Blair), published in 1945, and written in the form of a beast fable. A group of animals overthrow their human masters and set up a communal society. Events in the animal Utopia closely parallel events in the Soviet Union, and the majority of animals are more cruelly victimized by their new masters than they were by the old. The chief animal villain, the pig Napoleon, is easily recognized as Stalin.

Antony and Cleopatra. Shakespeare's tragedy in which Antony, torn between reason and passion for Cleopatra, realizes he is losing respect and position in Rome. He reconciles with his fellow rulers, Lepidus and Octavius, and marries Octavius's sister. Cleopatra, enraged, knows Antony will return to her one day because Octavius's sister is unattractive. The situation degenerates until Antony and Octavius do battle at Actium. Antony loses that battle and another in Egypt and returns to Rome. Cleopatra attempts to woo him back by sending word that she is dead. Grief-stricken, Antony kills himself. Cleopatra also commits suicide.

Arthurian legend. The cycle of verse and prose tales concerning the mythical King Arthur of Britain and his knights of the Round Table forms the Arthurian legend. The legend provided one of the principal themes of medieval romance throughout Europe. The Arthur of romance is of marvelous birth. He is conceived by Queen Igraine when his father Uther Pendragon magically disguises himself as Igraine's husband. Arthur is marked for kingship as a young boy when he proves to be the only one who can remove the sword Excalibur from a stone in which it is embedded. This is interpreted as a sign of the true king. (In a common variant, Arthur receives Excalibur from the mysterious Lady of the Lake, who hands it up to him through the water.) Arthur marries Guinevere and establishes his court at Camelot, where he is advised by the wizard Merlin, and where he gathers at his Round Table the flower of knighthood. The adventures and love affairs of the various knights constitute the bulk of the legend. Finally, the adulterous love of Arthur's favorite knight Lancelot and his queen Guinevere leads to the disintegration of the fellowship of the Round Table. Arthur's treacherous nephew Mordred attempts to usurp his throne. Though Arthur kills Mordred in battle, he is severely wounded. In some versions he dies and is buried in Glastonbury, England. In others, Sir Bedivere throws Excalibur into the lake. The Lady's hand reaches out to receive it. A barge appears and carries Arthur to the isle of Avalon, from which he is expected to return some day, healed of his wounds.

The legends are of Celtic origin and have a complicated history. There is some evidence that Arthur was a historical figure, a Celtic chieftain of the sixth century who repelled an invasion of Saxons into Welsh territory. The earliest stories about Arthur are Welsh and emphasize his magic helpers (or hinderers), Merlin and his sister Morgan le Fay.

Arthur was given a place in history as a conqueror of

STORM, SHIPWRECK, EARTHQUAKE, AND WHAT
HAPPENED TO DR. PANGLOSS, TO CANDIDE
AND THE ANABAPTIST
JACQUES

C H A P T E R   V

HALF the enfeebled passengers, suffering from that inconceivable anguish which the rolling of a ship causes in the nerves and in all the humours of bodies shaken in contrary directions, did not retain strength enough even to trouble about the danger. The other half screamed and prayed; the sails were torn, the masts broken, the vessel leaking. Those worked who could, no one co-operated, no one commanded. The Anabaptist tried to help the crew a little; he was on the main-deck; a furious sailor struck him violently and stretched him on the deck; but the blow he delivered gave him so violent a shock that he fell head-first out of the ship. He remained _____ _____ and clinging to part _____ _____ _____ The good

King Arthur, hero of legends in English and other literatures. Candide, the innocent hero of Voltaire's fable, in an edition designed by Rockwell Kent.

Europe by the chronicler Geoffrey of Monmouth in his largely fictitious *History of the Kings of Britain*, written in Latin in the twelfth century. In the 15th century, the English prose *Morte d'Arthur* by Sir Thomas Malory fixed the legend in its traditional form. Modern versions include Alfred Tennyson's poems *Idylls of the King* and the novel *The Once and Future King* by T. H. White.

As You Like It. A comedy by Shakespeare in which Rosalind is expelled from court by her uncle Frederick, usurper of her father's throne. Disguised as Ganymede, a country lad, she travels with her cousin Celia to the Forest of Arden, where her secret love, Orlando, has joined the followers of her exiled father, Duke Senior. Ganymede pretends to help Orlando rid himself of his infatuation by encouraging him to make love to her as though she were Rosalind. Orlando is on his way to one of their lovers' meetings when he kills a lion and saves the life of his wicked brother Oliver, who has actually come to kill Orlando. Oliver is full of remorse and asks Ganymede's forgiveness for the delay and falls in love with Celia. The two couples are married, and Duke Senior regains his lands from the penitent Frederick.

Babbitt. A novel by American writer Sinclair Lewis published in 1922. Its hero, George Babbitt, a small-town businessman and town booster, whose horizons are limited to Zenith, the "greatest little city in the world," gave his name to an emergent social type. Although Babbitt comes to vaguely realize that the narrow aspirations of Zenith are not the whole of life, he is never able to act on this idea.

Brothers Karamazov, The. This novel has often been considered the masterpiece of the Russian novelist Feodor Dostoevski; it was published in 1879–1880. It deals with the murder of a corrupt landowner, Karamazov, and the reactions of his three sons. The eldest, Dmitri, a wild, impulsive, hard-drinking former soldier, a rival of his father for the favors of the fair Grushenka, is unjustly accused of the crime. The second son, Ivan, a proud and cold intellectual incapable of love, feels guilty of the intellectual crime of despising his father and wishing him dead. The youngest son, Alyosha, is a figure of saintlike innocence, capable of undivided love. In addition to being a suspenseful story of crime and mystery, the work explores Dostoevski's religious and social ideas. The atheism and despair of Ivan are weighed against the faith of Alyosha, but there is no easy choice between them. The novel introduces a multitude of characters, divided in heart and lacerated in feeling, whose motivations Dostoevski probes relentlessly.

Candide. A satirical novel by the French author Voltaire published in 1759; it is directed against the notion that "everything happens for the best in this best of all possible worlds." The plot, thick with farcical misadventures (most of the incidents having some precedent in history), is concerned with the sometimes divided fortunes of Candide, his beloved Cunegonde, and his tutor Dr. Pangloss, who is the embodiment of optimism. In the end, after a series of personal disasters, Candide decides the best wisdom is to "tend one's own garden." He resignedly marries Cunegonde and settles down to grow vegetables.

Canterbury Tales, The. A collection of tales, mostly in verse, by Geoffrey Chaucer. It is both his masterpiece and one of the great works in English literature. The tales were written between about 1387 and 1400, the year of Chaucer's death. They tell of the poet joining a company of pilgrims on their way to Canterbury to visit the shrine of St. Thomas à Becket. To while away the journey, their host, Harry Bailey, suggests that each pilgrim tell two stories going, and two coming back: the pilgrim judged to have told the best tale is to get a free dinner. Chaucer completed 24 of the tales, from chivalric romance to folk tale to sermon to bawdy fable. The pilgrims, who come from all walks of life, are vividly described by Chaucer, and within the framework of the pilgrimage he brilliantly develops their personalities.

Catcher in the Rye, The. Novel by American author J. D. Salinger published in 1951; it concerns youth's disenchantment with a hostile adult world. It is cast as a long monologue spoken by Holden Caulfield, who has run away from his prep school and gone to New York. In spite of his external sophistication, Holden maintains an incorruptible innocence during a weekend of disillusioning experiences.

Christmas Carol, A. A story of Christmas by Charles Dickens, published in 1843. Old Ebenezer Scrooge, a "clutching, covetous old sinner" and Tiny Tim, the crippled child of Bob Cratchit, Scrooge's downtrodden clerk, are two of the main characters. It is the story of Scrooge's regeneration: fantastic visitations by three spirits of Christmas (the ghosts of Christmas Past, Christmas Present, and Christmas Yet to Come) change him from an unfeeling money-lover to a benevolent human being who sends a turkey to the Cratchit family to make their Christmas merry.

Comedy of Errors, The. Shakespeare's first play. Two brothers, both named Antipholus, "the one so like the other as could not be distinguished," and their servants named Dromio, "male twins, both alike," are separated in infancy during a shipwreck. Bachelors Antipholus and Dromio of Syracuse, searching for their brothers, enter Ephesus, where they meet two women who claim to be their wives. Going home with them, Antipholus and Dromio enter into a comedy of errors, in which merchants, wives, and servants mistake the pair with their twins until the confusion finally clears up and all is sorted out.

Crime and Punishment. This masterly novel by the Russian writer Feodor Dostoevski, published in 1866, develops the theme of redemption through suffering. The penniless student Raskolnikov believes that his natural superiority places him above the moral law of common men. He finds good reasons for committing for gain two brutal murders, and the novel furnishes an examination of these reasons, which, one by one, prove to be insupportable. Conscience will not permit Raskolnikov to use the money obtained through his crime, and his anguish slowly leads him to confess and embrace the consequent punishment—hard labor in Siberia—that is the gateway to his redemption.

David Copperfield. A novel by Charles Dickens, published in 1849-1850. It is a sentimental story of an orphan's struggles. It deals with the sufferings of young David after his mother's death, and his cruel treatment by his stepfather, schoolmasters, and employers. The hypocritical Uriah Heep is one of the book's many memorable characters. David finds friends, too—his aunt Betsy Trotwood, the optimistic Mr. Micawber, and the kite-flying Mr. Dick. With their help, he becomes a successful writer.

Death of a Salesman. A play by American writer Arthur Miller, first performed in 1949, this is the modern tragedy of an ordinary man, Willie Loman, an aging traveling salesman. Faced with loss of his livelihood, and the failure of his sons, whom he has inculcated with his values of achieving success through being "well-liked," Willie is bewildered by his fate. Unable to understand why this familiar American dream worked for others but not for him, Willie commits suicide in a final, pathetic effort to rescue his family through his insurance money.

Divine Comedy, The. A long, allegorical poem written about 1307-1321 by the Italian poet Dante Alighieri. This work has been considered the supreme literary achievement of the Middle Ages. It expresses the poet's vision of the divine plan for justice in this world and the next. Dante originally called it *The Comedy*, because it begins in sorrow and ends happily, and also because it was written in Italian at a time when serious works were written in Latin.

The first book, *Inferno*, begins with a prologue. In the middle of his life, the poet finds himself stranded in a dark wood (the world of sin and error). Unable to escape, he is helped by the intervention of his idealized beloved Beatrice (divine grace), who has been dead for ten years and is now in Heaven. The Roman poet Vergil (the highest representative of human reason and pagan ethics) guides Dante out of the wood by a roundabout journey through the Afterlife. On Good Friday in the year 1300, they enter Hell, descending through nine circles in which the sinners become increasingly more infamous and their torments more hideous. There Dante sees well-known historical figures, princes, popes, and personal enemies, all vividly characterized. The lowest circle is reserved for traitors such as Judas Iscariot, Cassius, and Brutus.

Marley's Ghost appears to Scrooge in an illustration from Charles Dickens's A Christmas Carol.

Don Quixote and his make-believe world of chivalry, as shown by Gustave Doré.

In the second book, *Purgatorio*, Vergil leads Dante through Purgatory, where he is purged of his sins, as far as the gates of Paradise. As that is as far as human reason can go, Vergil leaves and Beatrice guides Dante through the nine ascending circles of Paradise. In the tenth circle, St. Bernard becomes his guide, and Dante briefly experiences a vision of the Eternal Light, Divine Wisdom, or God.

The number three, symbolizing the Trinity, is used throughout as a structural principle. Thus, the work is divided into three books, each having 33 cantos. The cantos are written in *terza rima*, a three-line verse form invented by Dante specifically for this work.

Don Quixote de la Mancha, The Ingenious Gentleman. This picaresque novel, published in two parts in 1605 and 1615, is the masterpiece of the Spanish writer Miguel de Cervantes. It was a satire of the romances of chivalry popular in Cervantes's day.

An impoverished old gentleman, Alonzo Quixano, infatuated with knight errantry, changes his name to Don Quixote de la Mancha. With an uncouth peasant, Sancho Panza, as his squire, he embarks on a series of misadventures. His valorous deeds, such as tilting at windmills that he believes to be giants, are inspired by a peasant girl whom he believes to be the Lady Dulcinea. Ironically, he dies thinking he has been a failure, although in his pursuit of his illusory ideals he has shown far greater nobility than his sane, materialistic contemporaries.

Don Quixote has had a lasting influence on Western literature, and Sancho Panza ranks with the great comic characters of all time. It is the greatest prose work of Spanish literature, and its episodic structure was a major influence on the form of fiction for more than 200 years.

Faust. Faust, a figure in numerous legends and literary works, is based on the few facts known of the life of a 16th-century charlatan and magician. Faust is archetypical of the overreacher, one with an insatiable desire for power and knowledge.

The Tragical History of Doctor Faustus, a play by English dramatist Christopher Marlowe (published in 1604), is one of the most famous dramatizations of the legend. It is based on the *Faustbuch*, published in 1587 at Frankfurt am Main by Johann Spies. The play is in the morality tradition and anti-papist. Faustus, a good and learned man, sells his soul to Mephistopheles (the Devil), practices necromancy, and plays tricks on the pope. When payment is due, he despairs and is taken to Hell.

Faust, a dramatic poem by German writer Johann Wolfgang von Goethe (published in two parts in 1808 and 1832), is another famous version of the legend. Faust is tempted by the Devil, and although he sins seriously, he remains aware of truth and goodness and is saved.

For Whom the Bell Tolls. This novel by the American novelist Ernest Hemingway, published in 1940, is a tragic story of courage and compassion. Its hero, Robert Jordan, an American who volunteers in the Spanish Civil War, grows beyond a cold concern for his military objective and dies with the awareness that his struggle was for all men.

Great Expectations. A novel by Charles Dickens, published in 1861, this is the story of Pip, a village boy who longs for riches and social station, and suddenly receives from an unknown source wealth and the chance for an education. His "great expectations" lead him to attempt to act like a fine gentleman, but when they disappear he returns to a sense of real values.

Great Gatsby, The. This novel by F. Scott Fitzgerald, published in 1925 and generally regarded as his greatest completed work, is set in New York and is a searing exposure of the desperate boredom and spiritual bankruptcy of the Jazz Age, and of the thoughtless cruelty of great wealth. Its violent plot is concerned with the efforts of Jay Gatsby, a wealthy racketeer who poses as a businessman, to win his idealized love, the spoiled and wealthy Daisy, cousin of Nick Carraway, the story's narrator. Not only does Gatsby fail, he dies alone and deserted even by the hangers-on who had flocked to his lavish parties.

Gulliver's Travels. A satire by Jonathan Swift published in 1726 that tells of Lemuel Gulliver's voyages to imaginary lands. In Book I he goes to the island of Lilliput, where he finds himself a giant prisoner of a race of people 6 inches tall, but every bit as vain and pompous as the people of his homeland. In Book II he goes to Brobdingnag, the land of the giants, where he suffers the indignities of being swallowed and burped up by a squalling infant, and being carried away by a puppy. In Book III he goes to various countries, chief of which is the floating island of Laputa, the Cloud Cuckooland of eccentric scholars. In Book IV he arrives in the country of the Houyhnhnms, a land where horses with an intelligence superior to that of mankind carry on an ideal government, despite the fact that they share their island with an inferior race of Yahoos who cannot participate in it.

Hamlet, Prince of Denmark. Shakespearean tragedy in which Hamlet's father's ghost orders Hamlet to avenge his father's "foul and unnatural death." Claudius, murderer of the dead Danish king, marries Queen Gertrude, Hamlet's mother, and takes the throne. Feigning madness while awaiting his opportunity, Hamlet misleads Polonius, father of Ophelia, into thinking that love for Ophelia is causing Hamlet's strange behavior. Hamlet enlists the aid of an itinerant band of actors to recreate a poisoning scene and, with his friend Horatio, watches Claudius closely during the performance. Gertrude calls Hamlet to her chamber, where he rashly stabs eavesdropping Polonius. Subsequently, Ophelia, mad from grief, drowns herself. Claudius attempts to remove Hamlet to England, but fails. He plots with Polonius's son Laertes to fence with Hamlet and wound him with a poisoned foil. Hamlet is mortally wounded, Laertes and Claudius are killed, and Gertrude dies after drinking a cup of poison intended for Hamlet.

Henry IV, Part I. Shakespeare's history play beginning when Henry Percy, called Hotspur, refuses the king's demand for prisoners taken in recent wars. The ensuing battle against Henry's forces aligns Percy, Douglas, and Prince Hal against Henry. Prince Hal and his friend Falstaff have been carousing together and accosting travelers on the king's highway. Hal kills Hotspur in the battle of Shrewsbury, but Falstaff, who has come upon the body, pretends to have killed him.

Henry IV, Part II. Shakespeare's play in which Mowbray, Hastings, and the Archbishop of York war against Henry. Pressed with debts and charged with recruiting soldiers, Falstaff examines the men Justices Shallow and Silence present. He picks the ones who fail to bribe him. On the battlefield, Prince John deceives the rebel leaders into dismissing their troops and surrendering. Contrary to his promise, John orders them executed. Prince Hal visits the dying king, dreads the anxiety a crown entails, and promises his father he will mend his ways. During the coronation, Falstaff's familiar greetings incense Henry V, who orders his old friend banished.

Henry V. A sequel to Shakespeare's history plays about Henry IV. England's claim by hereditary right from Edward III to certain French dukedoms evokes an insulting reply from the Dauphin. Henry vows to invade France. A French assassination plot is uncovered, and Henry has the traitorous lords pass their own sentences of execution. Falstaff dies in London, and his comrades join the battles in France, during which Nym and Bardolph are hanged and a frightened Pistol decides to return to England. The French town of Harfleur falls to the English. Henry, after going disguised among his weary but valiant men, leads his troops to fight the larger French armies at Agincourt, a decisive English victory. Henry marries Katherine, the daughter of the defeated French king. Their son becomes Henry VI, king of France and England.

Huckleberry Finn, The Adventures of. Novel by American writer Mark Twain (Samuel Langhorne Clemens), generally considered his masterpiece. The story, told in the vernacular of Huck, a true child of nature, deals with his daring act of helping Jim, a runaway slave, to escape. Huck and Jim, floating down the Mississippi on a raft, enjoy a peace and freedom and mutual respect that is in sharp contrast to the meanness of society in the river towns where they stop. Twain uses the irony of Huck's innocent view of life to criticize the barbarity of "sivilization." Huck Finn is also a character in *The Adventures of Tom Sawyer*, published eight years earlier in 1876.

Gulliver in the land of the Lilliputians, captured by the tiny race.

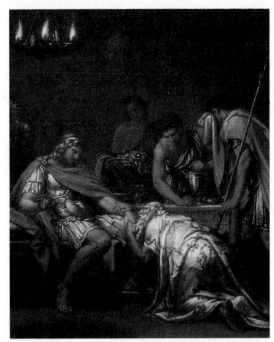

In this illustration from the Iliad, *Priam pleads with Achilles for the body of Hector.*

Iceman Cometh, The. Tragedy by American playwright Eugene O'Neill, produced in 1946, that is often considered his greatest work. Through an intricate network of religious symbolism, O'Neill tells the story of a man's death brought about by loss of hope.

Iliad. Greek epic poem by Homer. A recitative poem in the ancient bardic tradition, it was orally composed in about the ninth century B.C. and first transcribed in the sixth century B.C.

It is an heroic account of the Greek victory in the Trojan War. Started by the elopement of Paris and Helen (the wife of Menelaus, the Greek commander and the brother of King Agamemnon), the war enlists all of the Greek and Trojan heroes, including Achilles, Odysseus, Hector, and Troilus, and most of the gods. The conflict is decided by Zeus, who gives victory to the Greeks.

Generally considered the greatest literary work of Western civilization, the *Iliad* is the starting point for virtually every epic of Greco-Roman literature—for instance, the *Odyssey* and the *Aeneid*—and the model for every later epic in the classical tradition.

Jane Eyre. Novel by British writer Charlotte Bronte published in 1847; it deals with the love of a modest and plain but intelligent governess and her ill-tempered, discourteous employer Rochester. The impediment to their love, and the cause of Rochester's moodiness, is an insane wife he has kept hidden in the house. When Jane learns of the wife's existence, she leaves. Later, when the wife is killed and Rochester is blinded in a fire, the lovers are reunited.

Julius Caesar. Shakespearean tragedy beginning when Caesar refuses the crown three times before falling into a fit. Caesar belittles his wife's fears and the warnings of a soothsayer before going to the capital on the Ides of March. Brutus, convinced he is acting for the good of Rome, joins a group of conspirators led by Cassius. They assassinate Caesar. At Caesar's funeral, Mark Antony speaks ironically of the "honorable" conspirators and teases the crowd with Caesar's "will." A civil war ensues. Cassius and Brutus both commit suicide, and Brutus is proclaimed "the noblest Roman of them all" by Antony.

King Lear. This tragedy is considered one of Shakespeare's most important plays. Lear's loving daughter Cordelia refuses to follow her sisters Goneril and Regan in false flattery of their father. The Earl of Kent is banished for defending Cordelia, and the king of France accepts disinherited Cordelia as his wife, as Lear leaves his kingdom divided between his two other daughters. Suddenly stripped of his remaining rights, Lear goes mad from knowledge of his error and wanders out in a storm accompanied by his fool. He rails against the ingratitude of children. Aided by Goneril and Regan, Edmund causes his father, the Earl of Gloucester, to be blinded for aiding Lear. Kent sends Lear to Cordelia's care in Dover, while Gloucester's true son Edgar tends his father. Victorious over the invading French, Edmund executes Cordelia and causes Lear to die of grief. With Gloucester dead, Regan killed by Goneril, who then commits suicide, and Edmund executed, England is rebuilt by Edgar and Kent.

Leatherstocking Tales. Novels of early frontier life by James Fenimore Cooper. All have the same hero, the scout Leatherstocking or Natty Bumppo, who combines knowledge of the woods with Yankee ingenuity. The series contains *The Pioneers* (1823), *The Last of the Mohicans* (1826), *The Prairie* (1827), *The Pathfinder* (1840), and *The Deerslayer* (1841). These books remained popular throughout Europe long after their reputation declined in the United States.

Long Day's Journey into Night. A domestic tragedy by Eugene O'Neill, the most personal and intimate of all his works. Written about 1941, it was not performed until 1956, after the author's death. The play embodies all the bitterness and ambivalence of the author's feelings toward his family. It is set in a country house in the year 1912. The characters—the four members of the Tyrone family—are patterned on O'Neill's family. The father is a famous actor, the mother a drug addict who lives on memories of her innocent Catholic girlhood. The elder son is an alcoholic, and the younger son (O'Neill), while struggling to break away to a new life, learns he is stricken with tuberculosis.

Look Homeward, Angel. Novel by Thomas Wolfe, published in 1929, of the type called in German a *Kunstlerroman*, a novel of an artist's development. Its autobiographical hero Eugene Gant, a physical giant and precocious genius, loves and hates his hometown of Altamont (Asheville, North Carolina), struggles against the limited horizons of his family, receives vague indications of immortality from a few sympathetic people, and finally sets out on a quest for fame and fortune as a writer.

Lord Jim. Novel by Joseph Conrad written in 1900; it deals with a young English seaman who impulsively abandons his sinking ship carrying Muslim pilgrims. Unable to understand or to reconcile this ignoble act with his own self-image, Jim cannot face returning home. He lives out his life among the South Sea Island natives, whose love and admiration for him are expressed in their nickname *Tuan* (Lord) Jim. But luck is against Jim. Unwittingly he betrays his native friends and meets death at their hands, a fate that finally resolves his guilt.

Lord of the Rings, The. Trilogy of fantasy novels with allegorical overtones written by the English scholar J. R. R. Tolkien. It consists of *The Fellowship of the Ring* (1954), *The Two Towers* (1954), and *The Return of the King* (1955). It deals with the long and often grim and terrible quest of the Hobbits to destroy the magic ring they possess in order to keep it from falling into the hands of evil powers.

The trilogy carries on a story first introduced in Tolkien's *The Hobbit* (1937), a fantasy written for children. Tolkien, a scholar of Old English and Old Norse literature, drew on old legends for the setting and atmosphere of "Middle-earth."

Macbeth. Shakespearean tragedy based on Scottish history. The victorious generals Banquo and Macbeth are met by witches, who prophesy that Macbeth is to be thane of Cawdor and king. Macbeth travels to Duncan and finds that the first prophecy has come true. Lady Macbeth presses her husband to make the second prophecy true by killing Duncan during his visit, but Macbeth is reluctant. After he does murder Duncan, Banquo, and Macduff's child and wife, Macbeth rules tyrannically while Lady Macbeth goes mad from the sins of too much blood. Another visit to the witches assures Macbeth that "none of woman born" shall harm him. He returns home satisfied that he is safe. After Lady Macbeth's suicide, Macbeth resolutely faces Macduff, who was delivered by Caesarian section. Macbeth is killed, and Duncan's son Malcolm succeeds Macbeth as king of Scotland.

Measure for Measure. Shakespeare's comedy written immediately before his greatest tragedies. Lord Angelo is ruling in the absence of the Duke of Vienna. To observe the justice of Lord Angelo's rule, the duke disguises himself as Friar Ludovick and returns to move among his people. Just at that time, Angelo revives capital punishment for immoral behavior. Unable to marry his beloved Juliet, young Claudio is unjustly seized and sentenced to immediate execution. Claudio's sister Isabella leaves her nunnery to plead for mercy from Angelo, who offers her brother's life in exchange for her honor. Indignant, Isabella refuses but, at Ludovick's direction, consents and is replaced by Mariana, who once was betrothed to Angelo. Later, Angelo orders the execution of Claudio, but the prison official disobeys. The Duke of Vienna removes his disguise and confronts Angelo. The duke then pardons Angelo, who marries Mariana while the duke marries Isabella and Claudio marries Juliet.

Merchant of Venice, The. Shakespeare's play opening when the Venetian Jewish moneylender Shylock demands a pound of flesh of Antonio if Antonio fails to repay a loan Shylock has made to Antonio's friend Bassanio. While Bassanio is at Belmont winning the hand of Portia by correctly choosing one of three chests, as stipulated in her father's will, Shylock's daughter Jessica flees Venice with her father's money and her lover Lorenzo. Antonio's message to Bassanio, warning him that the debt has fallen due, causes Bassanio to rush to court. Shylock refuses late payment of the money due him, ignores pleas of mercy, and demands his payment in the form of a pound of flesh

Natty Bumppo (right), *hero of James Fenimore Cooper's* Leatherstocking Tales.

The great white whale, Captain Ahab's nemesis, in an illustration from Herman Melville's Moby-Dick

taken from around the heart. Portia disguises herself as a lawyer and grants Shylock's request, but warns him that the death of Antonio that may result will leave Shylock open to charges of threatening the life of a Venetian citizen. Shylock is ordered to give up his money to Antonio and to the state. By Antonio's wish, Shylock is permitted to give the money to Jessica.

Merry Wives of Windsor, The. Shakespeare's comedy in which Sir John Falstaff writes identical letters to the wives of Windsor gentlemen Ford and Page, professing his love. The honest wives pretend to offer encouragement but plan revenge on the knight. The Pages' daughter Anne meanwhile is courted by Dr. Caius, Slender, and her favorite, Fenton. Falstaff is humiliated on his first visit to Mistress Ford when the basket of dirty clothes in which he hides from Ford is dumped into a muddy ditch. On his second visit, he disguises himself as a woman whom Ford hates. Falstaff is beaten for his trouble. The wives and their husbands humiliate Falstaff a third time when mock fairies pinch and burn him while Anne elopes with Fenton.

Midsummer Night's Dream, A. Shakespearean play in which Egeus, father of Hermia, promises her to Demetrius despite her love for Lysander. Athenian Duke Theseus supports Egeus's decision, so Hermia and Lysander plan to meet in the woods and elope. Helena, in love with Demetrius, reveals Hermia's plan to Demetrius and he sets out to search for the lovers. In the woods, various tradesmen rehearse a play of which Peter Quince is the director and vain Nick Bottom is the star. The play is to be presented in honor of

the duke's marriage to the Amazon Queen Hippolyta. The woods are enchanted by fairies who have come to bless the royal wedding. Oberon, who is the fairy king, and the mischievous sprite Puck, play outrageous tricks on everybody until Theseus and Egeus arrive. The various spells are undone, and the couples are sorted out and happily married.

Moby-Dick. A novel by American author Herman Melville (1851), *Moby-Dick* is considered by many to be the finest American novel ever written. This tale of Captain Ahab's search for the great while whale that has crippled him is rich in symbolism and philosophical overtones. At the same time, the book is an exciting narrative and a precise description of the New England whaling industry of the time. The narrator, Ishmael, is the only survivor of the mad quest.

Much Ado About Nothing. A comedy by Shakespeare in which Claudio is in love with Hero, daughter of the Governor of Messina. His own wedding date set, Claudio arranges for his friend Benedick and Hero's cousin Beatrice to fall in love. Don John, seeking revenge on his brother Don Pedro, prince of Arragon, attempts to wreck the marriage of Claudio, Pedro's favorite. Claudio witnesses a clandestine meeting between Hero's maid and one of Don John's men. Thinking Hero unfaithful, Claudio disgraces her at church, provoking Benedick to challenge Claudio to a duel. Then Hero's presumed lover confesses the plot, and Claudio agrees to marry one of Hero's cousins to gain forgiveness. At last, Claudio and Hero are married, along with Benedick and Beatrice.

Nineteen Eighty-Four. This novel written in 1948 by the English novelist and essayist George Orwell (Eric Blair) offers a prophetic forecast of the future under totalitarian rule. It is a terrifying projection of life in the superstate watched over by Big Brother, where no one dares to trust another, and each lives in dread that his worst thoughts ("thought crimes") may be revealed on his face ("face crime").

Odyssey. Homer's epic of Odysseus, king of Ithaca and one of the foremost of the Greek chiefs in the Trojan War. The *Odyssey* describes the ten years of wandering and hardship Odysseus endures on his voyage home from the war. He touches upon the shores of the Lotus Eaters in Africa. He escapes death from the one-eyed Cyclops Polyphemus by his courageous trickery, blinding the giant and concealing himself beneath one of the Cyclops's sheep as they crowd out of the cave. He remains one year with Circe, the enchantress, and seven years with the ocean nymph Calypso on her island. He braves the dangers of Scylla and Charybdis and hears the Sirens sing while he is bound to the mast, thus escaping them. He is shipwrecked on the shores of Phaeacia and there cared for by Nausicaa and her father, who give him ships to continue his voyage home.

At last he reaches Ithaca disguised as a beggar, to find his wife Penelope surrounded by a host of insolent suitors, each coveting the kingdom. With the aid of his son Telemachus and his faithful herdsman Eumaeus, he slays them all and reigns another good 16 years.

Oliver Twist. Novel by British writer Charles Dickens published serially from 1837 to 1839; it is a melodramatic tale of poverty and the London underworld. Oliver, an unknown waif, escapes from a workhouse only to fall into the hands of Fagin, the master of a den of thieves. Fagin forces Oliver to break into a house. Oliver is caught by his intended victims, who recognize at once that he is no common criminal. Through their kindly interest, Oliver discovers his true parentage; Fagin and his crew are brought before the law, and Oliver is adopted by a wealthy gentleman.

One Day in the Life of Ivan Denisovich. A novel by Russian writer Alexander Solzhenitsyn, published in 1962, which describes a typical "good" day in the life of a prisoner in a Soviet concentration camp in Siberia. Ivan counts the day good because he manages to conceal a little extra food for himself, because he incurs no unusual punishment for misconduct, and because he avoids the dreaded sentence to solitary confinement in a freezing cell.

Othello, the Moor of Venice. Shakespeare's tragedy opening when Desdemona, bride of Othello, is entrusted to the care of Iago while Othello rushes to defend Cyprus from a Turkish invasion, which soon is ended by a storm. Iago, insulted by Othello's preference for Cassio as top lieutenant, plots revenge and enlists the aid of Roderigo in disgracing Cassio and making Othello jealous. Roderigo's brawl with Cassio gains the first objective, and Desdemona's handkerchief, obtained by unsuspecting Emilia and placed by her husband Iago in Cassio's possession, gains the second. Obsessed by jealousy, Othello kills his wife, takes his own life, and leaves Iago, murderer of Emilia, to be punished for his treachery.

Our Town. An elegiac play by the American writer Thornton Wilder, performed first in 1938. *Our Town* deals with the cycle of life in a New England town called Grovers Corners, but meant to be Everytown. A narrator comments on the town's activities and leading citizens. A girl and young man fall in love and marry. The young wife dies in childbirth and is buried among her fellow townsmen in the local cemetery.

Paradise Lost. Epic poem in blank verse by John Milton published in 1667; its purpose is "to justify the ways of God to man." It relates how some of the angels revolted against God and were cast out of Heaven into Hell. They decide to revenge themselves upon the Almighty by invading Earth and leading man to sin. Satan, chief of the fallen angels, corrupts Adam and Eve, the first human beings, and brings about their expulsion from Paradise. *Paradise Lost* is regarded as the greatest epic in the English language. A sequel, *Paradise Regained* (1671), deals with the theme of redemption.

Pilgrim's Progress, The. Allegory by the English preacher John Bunyan, the first part of which was issued in 1678; it describes the adventures of its hero, Christian, on his way from the City of Destruction to the Celestial City. He fights with Apollyon, looks on Vanity Fair, passes the castle of Giant Despair, and, after these and many other trials, reaches the Delectable Mountains and crosses the Black River to the Shining Gate. The plain, direct style was welcomed by the common people and was as popular in New England as in the author's own country.

Playboy of the Western World, The. Play by the Irish dramatist John Millington Synge, performed in 1907, about a young country lad, Christie Mahon, who thinks he has killed his father and, horrified, flees his home. But he is received as though he were a hero, bold and brave, and the flattering attentions bring about a complete change in his naturally timid personality. Christie's moment of glory is over when his father turns up alive. The play is greatly admired for the richness of its language, and is still remembered for the outrage with which its early performances in Ireland

Odysseus is tied to the mast of his ship so that he can resist the allure of the Sirens in the Odyssey.

and America were greeted, resulting in the "Playboy Riots" in Dublin, New York, and Philadelphia.

Pride and Prejudice. The first novel by Jane Austen, written in 1796 (when she was 21 years old) and published in 1813. The scene is laid in the English countryside, and the plot concerns the Bennett family's attempts to find suitable husbands for three daughters. The intimate drawing of the book's middle-class characters is done with humor and charm. Prejudice is represented by Elizabeth Bennett; Pride, by Mr. Darcy, her wealthy suitor. As Darcy overcomes his pride, Elizabeth overcomes her prejudice, and the two are married at last, giving this comedy of manners a happy ending.

Red Badge of Courage, The. Novel by Stephen Crane, published in 1895 when the author was about 24 years old; it is a study of a man's feelings in battle, written by one who had never seen battle. Henry Fleming, a raw country boy, enlists at the outset of the Civil War. The book describes his mental states as he waits for action, his panic under fire, and his final conquest of cowardice through identification with his comrades. It is one of the first books to treat battle realistically rather than as a theater for displays of gallantry.

Richard II. Shakespearean tragedy beginning when the Duke of York warns Richard of the dangers of his policy of confiscation of the lands of the dying John of Gaunt, and Richard departs for Ireland. Gaunt's son and heir, Henry Bolingbroke, exiled as a result of a quarrel with the Duke of Norfolk, seeks revenge by invading England. When Richard returns from Ireland, Bolingbroke seizes him, forces Richard's abdication, and imprisons Richard in Pomfret Castle. Loyal York foils Aumerle's plot against Henry IV. Sir Pierce, hoping to please his king, murders Richard and is banished by Henry, who pledges a Holy Land pilgrimage to gain forgiveness.

Richard III. In this early Shakespeare tragedy, the deformed Richard, duke of Gloucester, plots to secure the throne. By manipulating his brother, sickly King Edward IV, Richard causes the death of another brother, the Duke of Clarence. Edward dies, and Richard sends Edward's two sons to the tower, presumably to await coronation, while Richard arranges to be crowned king of England. King Richard then murders the two young princes and plans to kill his wife in order to marry his niece Elizabeth, who is sought after by the Lancastrian Earl of Richmond. Richmond's forces march on London. Richard is slain, and Richmond accepts the crown. He plans to marry Elizabeth and join forever the houses of Lancaster and York.

Riders to the Sea. A one-act play by John Millington Synge, first performed in Dublin in 1904. It is among the finest achievements of the Irish literary renaissance. A starkly tragic play, it pictures a day like any other day in an Aran Island fishing village. But it is the day when the old woman Maurya, who has lost four sons at sea, sees her youngest son Bartley brought home drowned. The characters speak a dialect that is at once plain and poetic, and the language gives the play special dignity and warmth.

Romeo and Juliet. Shakespeare's first great tragedy. The Montagues and Capulets are warring houses. Romeo Montague meets Juliet Capulet at a ball and falls in love at once. He professes his love in Juliet's garden, and they decide to marry. They go the next morning to Friar Laurence for the ceremony. Soon, new fighting occurs and Romeo's friend Mercutio is killed by Juliet's cousin Tybalt, who is then killed by Romeo, later banished for his crime. Juliet, desperate for help, plans at the friar's insistence to take a potion that will cause a deathlike trance from which Romeo will rescue her. Romeo fails to hear of the plan. Learning of Juliet's death, he visits the tomb and kills himself. Juliet awakens, sees Romeo dead, and kills herself. Filled with remorse, the families reconcile through their common grief.

Stranger, The. Novel by the Algerian-born French philosopher Albert Camus, published in 1942. It embodies the author's belief that life in the modern world is "absurd," or meaningless. It views man as a "stranger" in the world, and is about a man named Meursault, who is unable to find any reason for living or to experience any kind of emotional reaction, even to harrowing events. Faced with death, however, he discovers that the simple fact of life itself is enough to justify existence.

Streetcar Named Desire, A. Play by the American author Tennessee Williams, performed in 1947, and awarded a Pulitzer Prize. The play concerns Blanche Dubois, an aging, unstable Southern belle who comes to stay with her sister, Stella. Her refined behavior and coquettish manner provoke a conflict with her earthy brother-in-law, Stanley Kowalski. The title sums up the theme of the play, which is set in the French Quarter of New Orleans, where a streetcar named "Desire" shares its track with one named "Cemetery."

Taming of the Shrew, The. This popular Shakespeare play concerns Katharina, a beautiful but harsh-tongued and obstinate girl no one wants to marry. Petruchio agrees to marry Katharina, and her father, Baptista of Padua, allows his younger daughter Bianca to be courted by Gremio, Hortensio, and Lucentio. Lucentio wins Bianca's hand. Petruchio, on his own wedding day, arrives late at church dressed like a madman, swears throughout the service, and leaves Padua immediately with Katharina before the wedding reception. In Verona Petruchio tames Katharina by torturing her with mock kindness: her food is not good enough to eat, her bed not fit to sleep in, her clothes unfit to wear. Katharina, for the sake of peace, gives in and returns to Padua a model wife, amazing the henpecked husband of once-gentle Bianca by lecturing on the duties of a wife to her husband.

Tempest, The. One of William Shakespeare's last plays. Prospero, duke of Milan, has been ousted from his throne by Antonio, his brother. Set adrift on the sea with his daughter Miranda, Prospero finds his way to an island, the place of banishment of the witch Sycorax. Prospero releases Ariel and other spirits imprisoned by Sycorax, and they now obey Prospero's orders. The sole inhabitant of the island, the witch's son Caliban, also obeys Prospero's orders. Prospero lives on the island with Miranda for twelve years, when a ship carrying Antonio and the king of Naples and his son Ferdinand is wrecked on the island. Everyone is rescued, but Ferdinand is separated from the others and thought to be dead. In turn, Ferdinand believes all the others are dead. Ferdinand and Miranda fall in love. Acting under Prospero's orders, Ariel terrorizes Antonio and the king of Naples. The king repents his past cruelty and reconciles with Prospero and restores him to his throne in place of the frightened Antonio. Leaving Caliban behind, all the other mortals prepare to leave the island.

Tom Jones. Properly called *The History of Tom Jones, a Foundling*, this comic romance by Henry Fielding, one of the founders of the English novel, was published in 1749. It relates the adventures of high-spirited, impulsive, and generous Tom, who, despite many discreditable escapades, at last wins the confidence of his foster father, Squire Allworthy, and the love of beautiful Sophia Western. The novel is remarkable for its vitality and sweeping picture of 18th-century London and country life.

Tom Sawyer, The Adventures of. This classic of small-town American boyhood written by Mark Twain (Samuel Langhorne Clemens) in 1876 was based on his memories of growing up in Hannibal, Missouri. Tom, an imaginative boy who is fond of adventure stories, finds himself involved in a real-life adventure when he and his friend Huck Finn witness a murder committed by Injun Joe. The terrified boys run away, but return in time to prevent an innocent man from being condemned for the crime.

Two Gentlemen of Verona. Shakespearean comedy in which fickle Proteus woos Julia in Verona, while constant Valentine falls in love with Silvia, daughter of the Duke of Milan. Proteus is ordered to Milan. After pledging undying love to Julia, Proteus proceeds to the court, where he also falls in love with Silvia and reveals to the duke Valentine's plan to elope with Silvia. Valentine is banished from the court and becomes the leader of a group of outlaws in a nearby forest. Proteus, with the help of a page named Sebastian, really Julia in disguise, bids openly for Silvia's hand in marriage. Silvia flees in search of Valentine but is caught by Proteus, who tries to force his attentions upon her.

Leo Tolstoy's great novel War and Peace *has been filmed several times. Shown here is a scene from the 1956 version.*

Caught by Valentine, Proteus begs and receives forgiveness. The duke has a change of heart and allows Valentine and Silvia to be reunited as Julia, her true identity disclosed, is joined with Proteus.

Ulysses. Novel by the Irish writer James Joyce, first published in 1922; it has become a landmark of psychological and naturalistic fiction. The story takes place in Dublin in one day, June 16, 1904. The ordinary events of that day experienced by the leading characters—the autobiographical Stephen Dedalus; Leopold Bloom, a Jewish advertising salesman; his wife Molly Bloom, the eternal daughter of Eve—are carefully recorded. Joyce uses the method of free-association interior monologue (stream of consciousness) and sometimes interpolates a variety of other styles that are brilliant literary parodies.

War and Peace. Epic novel by Russian novelist Leo Tolstoy published in 1864–1869; it gives a view of all of Russian society at the beginning of the 19th century, focusing on the Napoleonic wars. It expresses an optimistic view of life in which evil can be successfully resisted by love and family happiness.

Winter's Tale, The. This tragicomedy was written late in Shakespeare's life. Leontes, king of Sicily, mistakenly suspects his wife Hermione of infidelity with Polixenes, king of Bohemia. He seeks to kill Polixenes and imprisons Hermione. When Hermione bears a daughter, the king orders that the baby be left to die. Hermione is reported to have died of grief. The baby, Perdita, survives and is brought up by a shepherd. She falls in love with Florizel, son of Polixenes, and goes with him to Leontes' court. Her true identity is revealed, a statue of Hermione turns out to be the living Hermione, and the young lovers are married.

Wuthering Heights. The one novel by Emily Brontë, published in 1847, *Wuthering Heights* is a somber tale of love and vengeance. Its central character is the orphaned Heathcliff, whose thwarted love for Catherine Earnshaw leads him to take revenge on her and her family.

For Further Reference

Abacarion, Richard and Klutz, Marvin
  Literature: The Human Experience
  St. Martin's Press
Abel, Darrel
  American Literature (3 vols.)
  Barron's
Beckoff, G., et al.
  English Literature (5 vols.)
  Random House
Cudden, J. A.
  Dictionary of Literary Terms
  Doubleday
Holman, C. Hugh
  Handbook to Literature
  Odyssey Press
Scholes, Robert
  Elements of Literature: Essay, Fiction, Poetry, Drama, Film
  Oxford University Press

Preparing a Book Report

The preparation of a book report is one of the most common assignments that you will face during your school years. At first, book reports may appear to be dull, mechanical exercises with little purpose. However, the process of writing them sharpens your ability to analyze books and recognize their strengths and weaknesses. Book reports also help you to broaden and refine your writing skills. They can be surprisingly enjoyable to do, for the deeper you explore a good book, the more interesting it becomes.

A good book report is not simply a point-by-point retelling of the book, nor is it a free-flowing presentation of your thoughts and opinions. A successful book report has a definite form and structure. It presents a concise but thorough description of the book and also offers the opportunity to analyze the book's strengths and weaknesses.

In this section you will learn how to choose a good book, how to gather information for your report while you are reading the book, and how to organize that information into an outline, a rough draft, and a final draft. This section also provides useful information on how to give an oral book report.

Selecting the right book

Perhaps the most common difficulty shared by book report writers is selecting the right book. This process can be made much easier if you adopt a simple and enjoyable technique used by many writers. Keep a journal or notebook, an "idea mine," to save information on interesting books you have read or may want to read.

Such an idea mine does not have to be very sophisticated. It can be as simple as a spiral-bound pocket notebook. Anything that enables you to write down your thoughts right away, before they are lost in the distractions of modern living, will serve the purpose.

Imagine that it is summer and you have gone to the library to find a good mystery to read, perhaps a detective novel by Raymond Chandler. While you are there you discover that the library has an interesting-looking biography of Chandler. You may say to yourself that "one of these days" you would like to learn more about Chandler, so you take out your notebook, write down the date you are making the entry, the title and author of the biography, a line or two about the book, and, most important, where you found the book. In this case, you would write down the name of the library and the card catalog number.

Six months or a year later you are planning to write a book report. You want to report on a biography. You thumb through your notebook and there you find your notation on the Chandler biography. You have completed your book search, and now you have the opportunity to read a book you have wanted to read *and* use it as the subject for your book report. What can be more satisfying than making your work both pleasant and productive?

You can gather book ideas from many sources. You might hear of a book that sounds interesting on a television program, or see a promising title or two at a bookstore or newsstand, or read an intriguing book review in a newspaper or magazine. Friends or relatives may tell you about interesting books they have read.

You can also make brief entries about books you *have* read that you think would make good subjects for book reports. You can make the entries as brief or as detailed as you like. Just keep in mind that you will have to reread the book when you do your report. Your memory alone may not provide all the details you need.

It takes only a minute or so to write down the title and author and a few relevant comments about a book, but over the course of time you will gather a wealth of ideas and information. When you fill up one notebook, number it on the cover and write down the beginning and end dates it covers. Store it where you can find it easily and then start a new notebook. You will be surprised at how fast your idea mine notebooks will accumulate.

Choosing a subject.
The notebook approach is an excellent way to gather preliminary information on all sorts of books and subjects. But the first step in preparing a book report is to examine the general subject area that your report is to address, then narrow the subject down to a specific, workable topic from which you can pick an appropriate book.

The instructions that accompany book report assignments may or may not help to narrow the field. For example, you may be required to write a report that deals in some way with one specific subject, say, famous scientists, or French history. Both of these subject areas are quite general, so you must narrow your search down to a specific topic within the general area.

In the famous scientists category, you could reduce the subject to famous scientists of the 19th and 20th centuries. This is still a rather broad field, so you might narrow it further to famous biologists of the 19th and 20th centuries. However, you know that the field of biology expanded in many different areas during this time period. So you narrow the search further

Ideas for book reports can come from reading, friends, even programs on television.

to biologists of the 19th and 20th centuries who made important discoveries about bacteria. This is a specific area, and a search in the library quickly turns up an interesting book on the subject, *Microbe Hunters* by Paul De Kruif.

Suppose the subject area is French history. This is also a broad subject area, so again you must narrow your search. You have always been interested in the French Revolution, so you decide to focus on that period of French history. There are shelves of books on this subject, however, so you limit your search to works of fiction. A quick library search turns up the classic *A Tale of Two Cities* by Charles Dickens.

The book report assignment may allow you to choose one of several subject areas or leave the subject selection entirely up to you. In the former case, choose the subject area that is most interesting to you. In the latter case, jot down a number of subjects that you are interested in and select from that list.

Fiction or nonfiction?
If you have the option of choosing either a work of fiction or of nonfiction for your report, your decision will depend in large part on the type of books you like to read. If you especially enjoy novels and short story collections select a work of fiction for your report. If works of nonfiction interest you more, then think about the type of nonfiction book you would most like to read and a subject that you find appealing.

Fiction generally offers the attractions of plot, characters, dialogue, narration, setting, and the development and ultimate resolution of one or more key situations or conflicts. Fiction can be humorous, somber, realistic, fanciful, or grounded in historical fact. Works of fiction should be read with special attention to plot, characterization, style, and overall

Narrowing a subject area is like focusing one's attention from a forest to a single area, then to a single plant.

effectiveness in developing the author's main ideas.

Fiction affords writers broad latitude to experiment with style, structure, and content in an attempt to explore the truths of life. Nonfiction in nearly all its different forms is firmly grounded in fact. Historical works, biographies, books on science, political events, current affairs, and even travel draw their primary strength from the accuracy of the information that they provide.

It may seem odd that a nonfiction work can be anything but fact, but consider, for instance, the autobiography of a famous person who wishes for some reason to embellish or obscure certain events in his or her life, or a nonfiction work in which the author describes events, conversations, or even thoughts and motivations for which there is no concrete evidence. For this reason, nonfiction works should be read critically and carefully.

Book length.
An important consideration in selecting a book is length. A 1200-page novel may be so rich in characters, subplots, descriptive detail, and scope that you cannot treat it adequately in the limited space of a short book report. If you are not a rapid reader, you may not even be able to finish the book and still have time to write your report. If time is not a problem and if you are permitted to write a sizable book report, a long book can provide a wealth of interesting material.

On the other hand, an uncomplicated, lighthearted novel of 100 pages may not provide enough of interest to fill any but the shortest book report. When considering books of modest length, evaluate the *content* more than the length. Is the author presenting important ideas or questions? Does the author use a compact prose style that expresses much in little space? Do you find something to think about on every page, or can you skip half a dozen pages without missing much of importance?

A good example of a challenging short book is the nonfiction work *Hiroshima* by John Hersey. This riveting account of the atomic bombing of Hiroshima, Japan, during World War II centers on the experiences of six survivors. It deals with the horror of modern warfare as well as the dignity and courage of human beings caught up in the nightmare of nuclear war.

It is good to remember that the more a book challenges you and engages your mind, the more you will enjoy it, and the more you will enjoy writing about it. This applies to any book, regardless of length.

Beginning the search.
A good place to begin your search for a book is the library. A school or local public library has not only a great number of interesting books but also the tools you can use to narrow down your search and find the right book for your report.

Fiction book search. The most useful resources for finding a good work of fiction are the library card catalog and the librarian. General encyclopedias have few references to works of fiction. However, you can turn to more specialized encyclopedias, such as the *Oxford Companion to American Literature* or

Book searches are made easier through the use of encyclopedias and other reference books as well as the library catalog.

Benet's Reader's Encyclopedia of American Literature for guidance.

Suppose you are interested in finding a good novel set during the American Revolution. You can turn directly to the card catalog. Under the subject heading "United States" and the successive subheadings of "History" and "American Revolution—Fiction," you find a listing for *The Spy* by James Fenimore Cooper. You read and enjoyed Cooper's novel *The Last of the Mohicans* so you read a few pages of *The Spy* and decide you want to read it for your report.

Another way to find a good work of fiction is to check the card catalog or go directly to the fiction shelf (organized alphabetically by author) for books by a specific author whose works you have enjoyed in the past. If the author has written one novel in the subject area of your interest, it is possible that he or she may have written others.

If you are unable to find an acceptable book after delving into the card catalog or checking the shelves, ask the librarian for help. Explain to him or her what kind of book you are looking for and why you are looking for it. It is possible that the information about the book or subject you are searching for is located in the card catalog under a different subject heading than the one you have consulted. Card catalogs are not all-inclusive or infallible.

Nonfiction book search. The technique for locating a good work of fiction for a book report is similar to that for locating nonfiction, except that the general encyclopedia will be more useful.

You can use the encyclopedia to read up on a general subject area. The information you gather by reading an entry in the encyclopedia will help you decide which aspect of the subject appeals to you most. The general entry may also have a cross-reference directing you to another entry with information about the

specific subject you have chosen. Often, a list of books for further reading will be included at the end of the entry. If any of these books are available in your library look them up. Perhaps one will turn out to be exactly what you need.

After you have narrowed your search to a specific area, go to the next resource, the library card catalog. Let's say your general subject area is Germany. Through your reading in the encyclopedia you decide that German history in the 19th century is most interesting to you, specifically the history of German unification in 1871 under Prince Otto von Bismarck. Next you use the library card catalog and find a promising title, *Bismarck,* by Edward Crankshaw. You note the call number, locate the book, and after reading a few pages decide that you want to read the whole book and use it for your report.

If you do not get the results you want from your encyclopedia and card catalog searches, ask a librarian for assistance. Another option is to choose a different topic. Your encyclopedia reading has probably turned up other promising book subjects. If you do not find what you are looking for in your first choice of topics, even with the librarian's help, turn to your second choice and examine what is available.

When looking for a good nonfiction book, keep in mind the fact that scholarly research is being conducted continuously in virtually every area of knowledge. If you select an interesting book with a relatively old date on the copyright page, be aware that more recent scholarship may have updated some of the information. If you can identify some instances where new research contradicts statements found in the book, include this information in your book report.

More and more libraries are turning away from the use of actual files of index cards for their card

Using *The Young Reader's Companion*

index heading

676   Subject Index

book entry → heading

subject heading → **Mythology (cont.)**

Perseus, 446
Prometheus, 468
Pygmalion, 472
Serraillier, Ian, 513
Styx, 551
Tanglewood Tales, 557
Theseus, 566

book title → *They Dance in the Sky,* 566

Titan, 572
Treece, Henry, 580
Trojan Horse, 583
Trojan War, 583
unicorn, 593
Uranus, 596
Valhalla, 599
Valkyries, 599
Völsunga Saga, 607

text entry
page number

They Dance in the Sky: Native American Star Myths (1987) A treasure trove of American Indian folklore, this collection of stories by Jean Guard Monroe (n.d.) and Ray A. Williamson (1938–) retells myths created by Native Americans about the stars. The stories tell how the stars were created, but they also show how the storytellers viewed the world, their relation to it, and how human beings should live in it. Here are myths that have been handed down orally, from generation to generation, and only recently have been written down. They include legends of how the Pleiades, the Milky Way, and the Big Dipper were created. Some of the stories are similar to the myths of classical Greek mythology. If you enjoyed *They Dance in the Sky,* try *Star Tales: North American Indian Stories About the Stars* (1987) and *Earthmaker's Tales: North American Indian Stories About Earth Happenings* (1989) by Gretchen Will Mayo (n.d.). See also *Mythology* by Edith Hamilton (1867–1963). MR

reading level code

---

catalogs. Instead, they are putting the identical information into electronic files so that library users can search for books on computer terminals. Typical electronic card catalogs allow you to search for books by subject, title, and author. In addition, some electronic systems contain information on the holdings of other libraries. If the book you want is not available at your library, perhaps it is owned by another library in the system that you can visit. Another possibility is to have your library borrow it for you. Electronic catalog systems are powerful tools.

You can even conduct a preliminary search for your book report needs without leaving your home. Consult *The Young Reader's Companion* included in this *Student Handbook.* Turn to its Subject Index and find the subject heading relevant to your report. Beneath this heading are listed the names of authors and books associated with that subject for which *The Young Reader's Companion* provides entries. Each title entry provides a synopsis of the book that will help you decide whether you might like to read it. Each author entry lists titles of books written by the author as well as short descriptions of the books. By consulting *The Young Reader's Companion* first and becoming familiar with its contents, you can rapidly narrow your book searches and quickly find a good book at the library.

Another very useful feature of *The Young Reader's Companion* is the reading level codes located at the end of entries. A book identified with the code **MR** (Middle Reader) is suitable for those with roughly a fifth to eighth grade reading level. A book identified with **YA** (Young Adult Reader) is for readers with roughly a high school to adult reading level. A book identified with both codes can be enjoyed by both groups. The reading level codes can help focus your search on books that are neither too difficult nor too easy.

Living resources. There are other extremely valuable repositories of information about books that are available to you on an everyday basis—other people. Whether you are looking for a novel or nonfiction book, remember that others, especially those older than you, may have had much experience with books. Teachers and librarians come instantly to mind, but do not forget friends and family. Perhaps your parents or other adults can suggest titles and authors that have impressed them and have remained in their memories. If you go to the library and find those books on the shelves, chances are many others have found something of lasting value within their pages. Classics become classics not because they are old but because they are *good.*

Examining the book.
Once you have identified and located a possible book for your report, how can you tell whether it is what you are looking for?

Cover copy. The first step is to examine the information on the inside leaf of the dust jacket or the back cover of the book. Although it is wise not to judge a book by its cover, the information there generally gives a fair idea of what the book is about. You can at least use the descriptions to eliminate books you do not want to read. For example, if you are looking for an historical novel and the copy on the dust jacket identifies the book as a suspense-filled mystery, you need not read further.

Suppose, however, that you are looking for a mystery, and the cover copy identifies the book as a "masterful detective story in the tradition of Dashiell Hammett and Raymond Chandler." Are you familiar with these authors' works, and did you enjoy them?

The book's dust jacket will also probably have information about its author and the other books he or she has written. Have you read any of these other books? Did you enjoy them? If so, you will probably also enjoy reading this book.

Sample reading. If the cover copy identifies the book as being of the general type you are looking for, then it is time to read some of it. Are the first few pages interesting? Do they make you want to read some more? Are the characters and the setting intriguing? Does the author write in a style that attracts and keeps your attention?

But remember, some of the best books start out slowly and draw the reader into the story gradually. However, the first chapter or two should give you a fair indication of whether the book will be a pleasant and profitable reading experience for you.

and final volume in the series. Completed just before his death, it is the Grand Master's last gift to his legions of admirers.

Here, at last, is the story Asimov fans have been waiting for, an exciting tale of danger, intrigue, and suspense that chronicles the second half of hero Hari Seldon's life as he struggles to perfect his revolutionary Theory of Psychohistory and establish the means by which the survival of humanity will be ensured: Foundation. For, as Seldon and his loyal band of followers know, the mighty Galactic Empire is crumbling, and its inevitable destruction will wreak havoc Galaxy-wide ...

A resounding tour de force, *Forward the Foundation* brings full circle Asimov's

ranc   ic. It is the cr

Cover copy on a book's dust jacket will help you learn what a book is about.

Reading the book

The cardinal rule of reading a book for a report is to be sure to read the whole book. You may be tempted to read the first few chapters and then scan the rest of the book to find out how it ends, but don't do it. There is a strong, practical reason for this, aside from the ethical question of trying to report on a book you have not read.

You might think that scanning a book saves time, but the truth is that it is actually much more time-consuming and difficult to write a coherent, interesting book report about a book you are not thoroughly familiar with than one you have read. Those reading your report often know the book, too, and will likely spot weaknesses in the report almost instantly. Even those who have not read the book may sense that there is something missing.

In a good book you will find something of value, something important, on almost every page. If you read the book through carefully, your enjoyment will be greater and your understanding of the author's purpose and point of view will be sharper. You will be able to write a better report and do it more easily.

Mechanics of reading. When the writer was laboring over the book you have selected, you can be sure that his or her attention was focused completely on the work at hand. So when you settle down to read the book, try to do the same. Pick a comfortable, quiet place to read, away from any distractions. Can you concentrate on reading if someone is watching television in the same room or listening to the stereo? If you are among the majority who cannot, find a comfortable chair in another room.

Posture. Believe it or not, posture will help you to read as well. Many people find that sitting up in a chair with both feet flat on the floor is a comfortable position and aids concentration. Stretching out on a sofa to read or snuggling into a soft chair may be too comfortable a position for reading, and you may find yourself growing sleepy and your thoughts beginning to wander.

Lighting. Good lighting is also important. Make sure you have adequate light and that it is not too harsh. Some people find that fluorescent lighting alone is hard on their eyes, especially if they are tired. A combination of fluorescent and incandescent lamps (standard light bulbs) will help soften the overall lighting effect and make it easier to read.

Planning your reading time. Give

yourself plenty of time to read the book you have selected, and begin reading it right away.

There are two good reasons for beginning the book as soon as you get it. The first is that you may change your mind about the book after reading part way into it. You may want to find another book for your report. The sooner you begin reading the book, the sooner you will know for sure. If you begin your reading right away, you will have more time to select and read another book. If you wait, you may have to read the book you have selected whether you like it or not.

The second reason for beginning your reading right away is that it will enable you to read the book more slowly over a longer period of time. The reading process will be less tiring for you and you will have time to think about the book in between reading sessions. You will be able to recall, and appreciate the meaning of, many more details than if you try to force your way through the book in a short time.

A good thing to determine at the very beginning is exactly how much time it will take for you to read the book. You can probably make a rough guess by looking at the density of the text and the size and number of pages and judging according to previous experiences. A more reliable way is to read a section of the book, say a chapter or two, and time yourself. Be sure to include additional time for jotting down notes and ideas, and also for interruptions and distractions. Then you can determine approximately how many pages per hour you can read. By dividing that number into the number of pages in the book, you can figure out approximately how many hours it will take to read the whole book.

Taking notes. One of the most useful things

you can do while reading is to write down important ideas and significant items of information as you come to them. Taking notes while you are reading may seem at first to be a distraction, but it actually helps focus your attention on the material you are reading.

The first thing to keep in mind is that you do not want your note taking to become a chore. Jot your thoughts down on a pad of paper, in a notebook, on ring binder pages, whatever suits you best. Try to keep the notes short and to the point so that you can quickly get back to your reading. You do not need to worry about writing complete or grammatically correct sentences. All you really need is a succinct phrase or two, sometimes just a word or two, that will enable you to recall the information later.

Suppose you are reading and you come upon what you think will be a perfect quotation to include in your report. Jot down what strikes you as the quote's key phrase. Put it in quotation marks. Later, when you look over your notes, you will quickly recall the significance of your notation.

There is something else you need to include with every notation, whether it be a single word, a quote, a phrase, or a group of phrases, and that is the page number of the associated text. What is the point of jotting a quick memo about an excellent quote, only to spend a great deal of time and frustration trying to find it again? Also, the quick notes you take may sometimes seem a bit cryptic when you refer to them days or even weeks later. Rereading the paragraph or page that inspired the thought will usually bring it back to you sharply and clearly.

You may want to write down the page and the paragraph number for greater accuracy. You can do this about as quickly as writing down just the page number. You do not really need to write the words "page number" and "paragraph number," or even the

Plan your work time so that you can complete your reading, note taking, and writing at a relaxed pace over the time available.

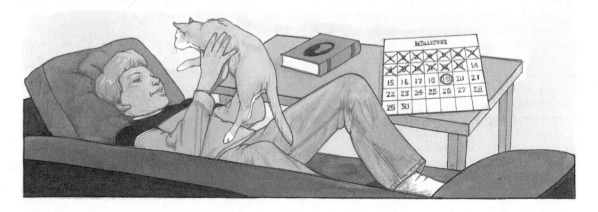

Handwritten notes

1st rumor of battle — pg. 4
Tall soldier Jim — 11

Flashback to enlistment — 5 —
Name Henry — 6:2

Feels " part of a vast blue demonstration — 13:3
Called "Yank" by enemy soldier — 14

Fear of running from battle — 15–16

Argument Jim & "loud soldier" — 16 — 20
Name Jim Conklin — 20:4

Rumor false — 21:1

Struggles with fear — 21–24

Wants go home — 31:4

Army columns "moving monsters" 26
"   "   "serpents"   27

Take notes while reading to help you recall important ideas and information presented in the book; also, jot down the page and paragraph numbers for each item.

abbreviations "pg." and "par." in your citation. After all, it is *your* system and you know what the numbers mean. You can, for example, write down the page and paragraph numbers separated by a colon. Let's say your note refers to the text in the third paragraph on page 222. You can jot the citation down as 222:3 in a couple of seconds.

What to look for. Some of the important information you will want to put in your notebook is obvious. In a nonfiction book, these items include the names of important people and places, major events and the dates they occurred, key ideas and themes presented by the author, and the main arguments and information that the author provides to support those ideas and themes. In a work of fiction, you will want to note the names of the main characters, their relationships to one another, plot developments, settings, central themes, symbols and imagery, and any unusual elements of the author's literary style.

Other items may not be quite as obvious. What is the author trying to say? How is the book structured? Is the book's organization effective in presenting the author's main ideas? Or is it disconnected and hard to follow?

A cursory examination of John Steinbeck's novel *The Grapes of Wrath* shows that it is organized into chapters. Many novels and nonfiction works are structured this way. But a closer analysis of the chapters reveals that Steinbeck has interspersed between the chapters chronicling the Joad family's Depres-sion-era struggles general chapters dealing with the larger forces and events that affected the lives of millions in that era. This structure helps the reader to understand more fully the events that shape the Joad family's lives, and it also elevates their sufferings and triumphs to a universal level. The novel's structure plays an important role in the development and exposition of Steinbeck's theme, and a good book report will note this.

In a work of fiction, you will want to note the point of view from which the story is told. Is there an unseen, all-wise narrator who reveals the private thoughts of the characters? Is the story told from the point of view of one character only, or perhaps from several characters' points of view? Does the technique chosen by the author work effectively or does it get in the way of the story?

Nonfiction books, too, have structure. How effectively has the author organized and presented the material? Are the main statements, arguments, and conclusions supported by additional sources? Are the author's footnotes and textual citations useful, or do they unnecessarily impede the flow of the text?

Of what degree of quality are the sources used by the author of a nonfiction book? A book based, for example, solely on newspaper and magazine articles of questionable accuracy may not be a very useful work. A book in which the author has attempted to verify the facts by cross-checking them with a variety of sources will almost certainly be a better book.

Writing the book report

You may be tempted to sit down immediately and begin writing your paper. But you will find the writing task much easier if you spend some time thinking about the book you have just read.

Collecting your thoughts.

Actually, you have already spent time thinking about the book while you were reading it and taking notes. How much more time should you spend thinking about the book? One thing to consider is how much material the book offers for thought. A fast-paced suspense novel may have fascinating characters and clever plot twists and surprises, but it may not contain many deep thoughts to ponder. On the other hand, a book about American foreign policy in the nuclear age may contain so many facts, theories, and interesting ideas that it will take you some time to sort through them and decide what you want to say.

Go back over your notes to refresh your memory. You may want to reread a paragraph or a page or two here and there. Soon you should begin to get a good idea of the important points you want to include in your report.

Questions to ponder.

There are three main questions you should consider when thinking about the book for your report: What is it about? What is the author trying to say? What do you think about the book, and why?

What is the book about? This will be the theme of the first paragraph of your report, so it is the first general question you should answer for yourself.

Suppose you chose to read the novel *The Red Badge of Courage* by Stephen Crane. What would you tell your best friend about it?

The story takes place during a battle of the Civil War, but it is not really about the Civil War. The main character is a young recruit named Henry Fleming, and the story focuses on his reactions when he is first confronted with the stresses and horrors of war. Crane focuses special attention on Fleming's thoughts and emotions but tells us little about Fleming's life outside this single battle. Crane seems to be more interested in the psychological effects of war on humans generally than on Fleming specifically.

With all this in mind, your answer to the question "What is this book about?" might be that *The Red Badge of Courage* is a psychological study of the effects of combat on a young recruit during the Civil War.

What is the author trying to say? What central idea or ideas does the author present? In the case of *The*

Red Badge of Courage, Crane is trying to describe realistically the cruel face of war and to get under the skin of his character, to describe Henry Fleming's inner battle with his own emotions and instincts.

It is interesting to note that when Fleming is first sent into battle, he panics and flees in fear, a natural reaction when one is threatened with imminent death. He later receives a blow to the head by another Union soldier who has also fled the battlefield. This wound is his "red badge," but later Fleming lies about what happened. Finally, he shows an almost superhuman courage in combat, driven by a rage so powerful that he is scarcely aware of his own actions. Crane follows Fleming's progress, from a raw recruit humiliated by his own sense of dishonor to a tested veteran who has faced death, vanquished his fears, and gained a quiet, resolute courage.

Your answer to the question "What is the author trying to say or do in the book?" might be that Crane is trying to reveal the inner thoughts and feelings of soldiers in combat and examine the true nature of fear and of heroism.

What do you think about the book, and why? Your answer to this question will provide the conclusion for your book report. You may decide that you enjoyed the novel because of Crane's realistic writing style, his use of powerful images, and his emphasis on the inner struggle of the main character, as well as his sharp descriptions of battle. Or perhaps you felt that Crane did not provide enough information about some of the other soldiers to enable the reader to really care about them.

Whatever you decide, remember that this third question actually has two parts: "What do you think?"

Collect your thoughts before you begin to set them down on paper in your report outline.

The <u>Red Badge</u> of <u>Courage</u>
By Stephen Crane

main heading ⟶ 1. Novel is psychological study of war.
subheading ⟶   A. General description of the war makes theme universal.
sub-subheading ⟶   1. War never named - clues show it is Civil War.
     2. Location, name of battle never identified.
     3. Little discussion of main character's life outside battle.
     4. Story focuses on this one battle, and effect on main character, not on the war or its importance.
   B. Depicts stress of warfare on human beings.
     1. Through thoughts, observations, and actions of main character, Henry Fleming.
2. Plot centers on two different battles.
   A. Depicts horrors of actual battle of the war.
   B. Explores Henry's inner battle.
     1. To prove to himself he is not a coward.
     2. To overcome fear of cowardly acts.
     3. To redeem himself after he runs away.
     4. To prove himself before his fellow soldiers.

Sample page of a book report outline.

and "Why?" It is important to give serious and well-thought-out reasons for your answers.

Writing an outline.
An outline lists the main ideas you want to present in your report in the order in which you want to present them.

Your outline can be as simple or as sophisticated as you want it to be. Its purpose is to enable you to get your thoughts organized and down on paper where you can look at them objectively.

If your book report is a relatively simple one of, say, five to seven paragraphs, you may want to write up the simplest form of outline, a list of the facts and ideas you want to present. You can successively number each item and make each one a separate heading.

If your book report is longer or if the book presents a great deal of information, you may want to include supporting facts or ideas in subheadings under each main heading. The main heading is marked by a number beginning with "1," and each subhead is written below the main heading, indented, and identified with a letter, beginning with "A." Subheadings can have further sub-subheadings, indented and starting with a number. You can have as many levels of subheadings as you want, but try to keep your outline

from becoming so complicated that you end up writing down more facts and details than you can possibly use in your report.

First heading. The first heading of the outline should treat the first general question "What is the book about?" In this heading and its associated subheads, if any, try to give a general description of the whole book.

Following headings. The second and following headings should contain the important details about the book that you want to include in the body of your report. What is the book's plot or topic? Who are the main characters (or persons, in a work of nonfiction) discussed in the book? What is the time period covered, the setting, the general theme or central conflict? What are the key or significant events? How does the book end?

Final heading. The final heading and associated subheadings should describe your reactions to the book. What did you like about it? What did you dislike? Can you recommend the book to other readers? Write down your reasons, being as specific as possible.

After you have completed your outline, read it over carefully and see if there is anything you have left out

> a young ∧Union volunteer, ∿just during a single, unnamed battle of the Civil War. It ~~really~~ could be any battle∧ of any war, for ~~because~~ Crane's ~~main interest~~ real focus is on another battle, the ∧hidden one raging inside Henry Fleming as his ~~ideas~~ ∧romantic notions of ~~about~~ war are crushed by the realities of fear, suffering, ~~pain, horror,~~ and death. Through Fleming's thoughts ∧and actions, we see that the outer

Wide margins and double-spacing of the rough draft provides blank space that you will need later to insert additions and make corrections.

that you will want to include in your report. Imagine that you are the reader of the completed paper. Are there any "holes" in the material covered, or are you satisfied that everything that should be mentioned in the report is mentioned in the outline? If you think of something that you should add, write it in the appropriate place on your outline if you have enough space, or copy out a new outline incorporating your addition.

Outline to rough draft.
The next step is to put your well-organized thoughts into equally well-organized sentences and paragraphs. The outline is the skeleton of your book report. Now you will add the rest of its body and turn it into a living work of prose.

Format. Up to this point you have jotted notes on a pad or in a notebook and written your thoughts in outline form on paper. Now you are going to expand and elaborate on those efforts to produce the "dress rehearsal" version of your book report. When you have finished, most of the main elements of your final version will be included, but perhaps when you read your rough draft you will want to make changes and additions. If you plan ahead and leave enough blank space on your pages, you will be able to make your corrections right on the rough draft.

Think about how you are actually going to write. Will your draft be handwritten or will you use a typewriter? Maybe you have access to a computer and will write your draft using a word processing program.

Use the method that seems most productive for you, but remember that whichever you choose, you need to provide plenty of room for changes.

If you use pen and paper, leave extra wide margins on the sides, top, and bottom of each page. You may also want to double-space your writing to make additions and changes easier.

If writing on a typewriter comes naturally to you, be sure to double-space your typing and leave wide margins on all four sides of the page.

If you decide to write your rough draft on a computer, you will be able to review your work on both the computer monitor and on a paper printout. But do not plan to do all your revisions on-screen. It is important for you to print your rough draft on paper and read it carefully in that form. When you print out your computer file, follow the same rules that apply to working on a typewriter. Make sure your text is double-spaced and leave wide margins all around.

One more word of caution about working on a computer: People who regularly use computers as word processors, especially those who are good typists, find that they can write almost faster than they can think. This may be an exaggeration, but the truth is that word processing can lead to some bad habits. You may find yourself writing quickly and voluminously with the intention of smoothing out and tightening up your prose later. Slow down! Think before you write. Try to express your thoughts clearly and succinctly the first time.

Use of tense. One other thing to keep in mind before you begin writing is to use the proper tense. When you are writing about the characters and events in a work of fiction, use present tense:

Tom Joad returns to his home in Oklahoma after serving time in prison only to find that his family has been forced to abandon their farm and travel west to California in search of work.

When you are writing about the people and events covered by a nonfiction book, you must write in the past tense:

Amelia Earhart's determination to cap her career in aviation with a final, stunning achievement led her to attempt a flight around the world, a flight for which she was poorly prepared.

Opening paragraph.
The first paragraph of your book report incorporates the information in the first heading of your outline. This paragraph gives your reader a general overview of the book you have read. Here you must include the complete title of the work and the name of the author, what type of book it is, and a general description of the book's contents, theme, or story line.

You may find it enjoyable and productive to read the opening sentences of a number of title entries in *The Young Reader's Companion* to see how much solid information can be provided in an opening sentence or paragraph. See, for example, the entries for *Cry, the Beloved Country* by Alan Paton, *Fathers and Sons* by Ivan Turgenev, *The Glass Menagerie* by Tennessee Williams, *The House of the Seven Gables* by Nathaniel Hawthorne, and *The Prince and the Pauper* by Mark Twain. In each entry the opening sentence states the title, author, setting, theme, and type of work. This is exactly the kind of compact, informational writing style you want to strive for in your opening paragraph.

Body.
Use the middle part of your report to elaborate on the points in your outline. Here you want to give a more fully developed and detailed description of the book's contents, to answer the basic questions of "Who? What? Where? When?"

For example, if your book is a novel, you should discuss the main characters (who they are) and give a general but thorough synopsis of the plot and setting, telling what happens and when the story takes place.

Two things are especially important to remember when writing the body of your book report, particularly for a work of fiction. First, try to capture in your

own words the "heart and soul" of the book you have read. Avoid giving a blow-by-blow account of everything that happened. You do not have enough writing space to include everything, and even if you did, the result would be dull and unfocused.

Second, try to make your sentences and paragraphs follow one another in a logical manner. The opening sentence of a paragraph should give the reader a good idea of what the whole paragraph is going to be about, just as the opening paragraph of your book report should tell what the report is about. The succeeding sentences in the paragraph should build on the opening sentence and lead the reader smoothly and logically to the information in your next paragraph.

In the middle paragraphs, discuss any important facts about the book's structure or the author's writing style and how these elements help advance the plot or the author's central theme.

Summary.
Use the final paragraph (or two) of your book report to tell what you think about the book, what you liked and disliked, and why. This is where your critical reading of the book will pay big dividends, because your final paragraph is a reasoned analysis of the book's success in achieving what the author set out to do.

Fiction analysis. If the book you read was a work of fiction, were the characters interesting, likable, believable? Did they act consistently within the context of the story? For example, if a character is a thoroughly detestable scoundrel throughout the story and then suddenly turns into an honorable person, the author should have provided convincing reasons for that character's transformation.

Did the characters remind you of people you know, or were they unlike anyone you have ever met? Did you find yourself caring about what happened to them? If not, why not?

Was the plot interesting and did it hold your attention? Did the book draw you in and make you want to keep reading? Did the story seem believable? Even if a book is a work of fantasy or science fiction, the author has to achieve in the reader's mind a "willing suspension of disbelief." That is, the reader must be able to set aside life experiences and be willing to believe that the characters, story, and setting created by the author *could* exist.

Another important element in creating believable fiction lies in the story's setting, the description of the place and time in which the story occurs. Did the author of your book provide enough descriptive details to bring the setting to life? Or did the author slow the story's progress with an excess of details about people, places, and events? Or were there so few details and descriptions that the story seemed just that—a story?

Did the author's writing style contribute to or detract from the effectiveness of the book? Imagine a suspense novel written in a long-winded, effusive, florid style, or an historical romance written in lean, dark, humorless prose. How successful do you think either would be?

Was the ending believable? Did it follow and fit in with the rest of the story? A book does not have to end the way you want it to end, but it should not leave the reader feeling cheated, tricked, or betrayed. What would you think of a book whose main character is plunged through a series of self-destructive acts into poverty, crime, illness, and despair, and at the last moment is restored to a life of domestic bliss after he uses his last dollar to buy a winning lottery ticket? How about a murder mystery in which the killer is not introduced until the last chapter?

Nonfiction analysis. If the book you read was a nonfiction work, you will not have to evaluate plot, characterization, setting, or ending, but you will have similar things to consider.

Instead of fictional characters, you will have read about real people. Did the author present them fully, realistically, fairly? What would you say of a biography that records only the commendable, praiseworthy facts of its subject's life and excludes anything troublesome or unflattering? You may have enjoyed reading it, but you certainly would have to note in your book report that the book is not balanced and complete.

Instead of a plot, your nonfiction work will have presented a body of facts, dates, and events woven together to produce a complete story. Does the book have enough information to be considered a thorough and complete treatment of the subject? Are there gaps in the narrative? If so, is this because there is not enough information known to fill in the gaps, or because the author did not include the information for one reason or another?

Are there many extra facts of little importance or usefulness that do not serve the author's theme? A wealth of unimportant details can be as harmful to the flow of a good nonfiction book as a shortage of relevant ones.

The nonfiction author's discussion of persons, places, and events serves to establish the book's setting. How well does the author establish the background for his or her narrative? Does the information seem accurate? Is it up to date?

Finally, are the author's conclusions logical or reasonable? Did the author accomplish what he or she set out to do?

Remember, there is a world of difference between knowledge and speculation, fact and supposition. A careful writer will make a clear distinction between what is known and acknowledged to be fact and what is considered probable or possible. A less than scrupulous writer will blur the distinction by merging fact with speculation or opinion.

Conclusion.

The final item to include in the summary of any book report, fiction or nonfiction, is whether or not you would recommend the book to others, and why.

Suppose you are reporting on a murder mystery. You have read many mysteries and often can figure out "who done it" before the author reveals the identity of the killer, but this book kept you guessing until the last chapter. When you find out the identity of the murderer, you say to yourself, "Of course! Why didn't I figure that out? The clues were there all along!" Your recommendation in the final paragraph might read something like this:

> Anyone who likes fast-paced, well-plotted mysteries with true-to-life characters that keep the reader in suspense to the end will enjoy reading this book.

Perhaps you are reporting on a nonfiction book about Spain that describes the country as it is today but also provides an interesting account of Spain's history. You especially liked the author's pleasant and colorful writing style. You could say something like this:

> The author clearly knows his subject, and his love of Spain shows in his writing. The wealth of fascinating information he provides about modern-day Spain and its history make this an ideal book for those who want to know more about this colorful European country.

Note that each of these examples avoids the use of personal references such as "I liked this book because," or "I would recommend this book because," even though each makes it clear that the writer liked the book and does recommend it. As a general rule, try to avoid the use of first person phrases in your book report.

Think of your entire book report as expressing your reasoned opinions about the book. Instead of writing, "It seems to me that Scrooge, before his transformation, is a greedy, heartless old man," just write, "Scrooge, before his transformation, is a mean, greedy, heartless old man." Then supply facts to support your statement. The elimination of the first person makes sentences more direct and forceful.

The final draft

At this point you have read your book critically, taken notes, thought out what you want to say in your book report, drawn up an outline, and completed a rough draft. Now all that remains is to read your rough draft critically, edit it into its final form, and produce a clean copy of your finished work.

Editing. The first step in putting your book report into final form is to disown it. This may seem a cruel and heartless thing to do after all the work you have put into it. But it is necessary for you to step away from your paper mentally, to consider it objectively, as if it had been written not by you but by someone else.

If you have been conscientious in your work, you know a good deal more about the book than you have actually included in your paper. You may, without being aware of it, use that stored knowledge in your reading of the paper to bridge gaps in logic or continuity. In the editing process, you must test each idea, word, phrase, and sentence of your paper and evaluate how well all those elements work together.

Balance and content. In the planning, outlining, and drafting stages of your task you learned that the book report consists of three main sections: the opening paragraph, the body of the report, and the summary. Look at each section and evaluate its length with respect to the other sections and to the whole book report. If any section seems to be too long or too short, start your editorial work by trying to bring it back into balance with the others.

Paragraph too short. If your opening paragraph is too short, perhaps you have left out some information that will help the reader quickly understand what the book is about. Check back over your notes and outline. You may want to elaborate on a point to make it stand out a bit more, or you may find things to include that you overlooked.

Let's say your book report is on *The Red Badge of Courage* and that you have written the following as your opening paragraph:

The Red Badge of Courage, a novel by Stephen Crane, is a psychological study of the effects of combat on a young recruit during the Civil War. It is noted for its realism and its insight into human psychology.

This is a tight, well-constructed opening paragraph that covers much ground in few words, perhaps too few words. It is so succinct that it feels a bit cool or

Writing, like baking, requires the right balance of components.

impersonal. Let's examine the paragraph more closely and see if we can liven it up and give it a bit of depth.

The first sentence does a good job of fulfilling the first task of a good book report, telling what the book is about. It mentions the title, the author, the type of book, and its general subject and theme. The second sentence presents other important elements of the book: realism and human psychology.

What kind of realism is the book noted for? You have learned in your reading of the book that Crane has written a gritty, realistic depiction of war, so you could elaborate on your point by saying the book is noted for its realistic depiction of war. This is a much more specific statement, more useful than just the word "realism," and it helps the reader understand more fully the kind of book Crane has written.

What about human psychology? That is a very large field, indeed, and you know that in this novel Crane is interested in a very small aspect of human psychology. He is exploring the effects of stress on people, specifically the tremendous stress of war. So instead of saying that the book is noted for its insight into human psychology, you could say that it is noted for its insight into the effects of warfare on human thoughts and actions.

Work these new elements into the opening paragraph and you have the following:

The Red Badge of Courage, a novel by Stephen Crane, is a psychological study of the effects of combat on a young recruit during the Civil

War. It is noted for its realistic depiction of war and its insight into the effects of warfare on human thoughts and actions.

Is there anything else of a general nature about the book that you think your reader would appreciate knowing? Perhaps when you read the book's cover copy you noted that when Crane wrote the book in the 1890's, he had never personally witnessed battle. Yet the novel became Crane's best-known work, and it has become a classic of American literature. These facts are worth noting, for they help put Crane's accomplishment into perspective. Why not include them in the opening paragraph?

When Stephen Crane wrote what was to become his best-known work, the novel *The Red Badge of Courage*, he had never personally witnessed the horrors of battle. Yet this psychological study of the effects of combat on a young recruit during the Civil War has become an American classic. Even today, a century after the novel was first published, it is noted for its realistic depiction of battle and its insight into the effects of warfare on human thoughts and actions.

This expanded paragraph is a great improvement over the original. It is slightly more than twice as long, but now it gives a better picture of what the book is about, plus some important and interesting background information.

Paragraph too long. What if a section of your book report is too long and seems out of balance with the rest of the report? You may be giving the reader too much information and going into greater detail than necessary. See if you can tighten up your paragraphs by eliminating unnecessary details. Perhaps you can rephrase sentences that seem long or complicated.

Suppose this is the second paragraph of your report on *The Red Badge of Courage*:

The main character of the novel is a young soldier named Henry Fleming who has joined the Union Army to fight against the Confederates. All of the events related in the novel occur during one battle of the Civil War, although the reader is never told which battle it is. It could be any battle of any war, because the novel really is not about the Civil War or specifically about this battle. Rather, the real battle Crane is telling about is the one that rages inside Fleming. His romantic notions of war are crushed by the realities of fear, suffering, and death. Through his eyes, his thoughts, and his

emotions, we see two conflicts. The first is the external conflict he shares with his fellow soldiers, the struggle between the Union and Confederate forces. The second is the internal conflict that he alone knows and that he shares with no one, the struggle to come to grips with his own fear.

This paragraph presents some important information: It identifies the setting of the novel, introduces the main character, describes the story's point of view, and expands on the author's theme. But it is long. Let's see how it can be tightened up.

The first thing you can do is combine several facts into the opening sentence to more clearly state the main subject of the paragraph, which is the dual conflicts of Henry Fleming. You could write something like this:

All the events related in the novel center on and are seen through the eyes, thoughts, and emotions of Henry Fleming, a young Union volunteer, during a single, unnamed battle of the Civil War.

Now you can simplify the succeeding sentences and tighten up the paragraph further.

It could be any battle of any war, for Crane's real focus is on another battle, the hidden one raging within Fleming as his romantic notions of war are crushed by the realities of fear, suffering, and death. Through Fleming's thoughts and actions, we see that the external conflict, the struggle between the Union and Confederate forces, is the foundation for his internal struggle to come to grips with his own fear and self-doubt.

This revised paragraph covers all the major points of the original one and does so in about two-thirds the space. It also establishes the background for your discussion of the novel's plot in the next several paragraphs. Here is an example of what might follow:

Henry Fleming had dreamed of the glory of battle, but his first months in the army are filled with marches, encampments, and endless tedium. He spends much of his time wondering whether he will run from battle when the time comes.

The day finally comes when Fleming's regiment is sent into battle. The regiment repulses a Confederate attack, but when a second attack threatens to overwhelm the Union ranks,

Fleming and some other soldiers panic and run. Separated from his regiment, Fleming feels burning shame when he learns that the Union line has held. He is ashamed again when he joins a group of wounded soldiers, one of whom keeps asking him, "Where yeh hit?" His shame burns yet again when he meets a mortally wounded friend, a tall soldier named Jim Conklin, who asks him, "Where yeh been, Henry?" Jim dies soon after this, beneath a highly symbolic "red sun...pasted in the sky like a wafer" that makes the scene one of blood sacrifice. Jim's death fills Fleming with silent rage.

Fleming meets a group of retreating soldiers, one of whom fells him with the blow of a rifle butt. That night a kind soldier, whose face Fleming never sees, helps him get back to his regiment. Fleming tells his comrades that he has been shot, and accepts their warm approval and friendship.

The next day the Confederates attack again. Fleming, filled with rage and hatred, fights with an almost inhuman ferocity and shows great courage. When the fighting ends, Henry Fleming comes to terms with the personal shortcomings that the battle has revealed to him; he finally feels "a quiet manhood, nonassertive but of sturdy and strong blood."

These paragraphs highlight the major events of the novel by selecting important details and building a general summary around them. The selective use of quotations also helps to bring the story line into sharper focus and gives the reader a sense of the author's writing style.

Final emphasis. You have mentioned Crane's "realistic depiction of battle" in the opening paragraph, and this is one of the most important elements in the novel. How did you feel about it? Perhaps you agree with many other readers of *The Red Badge of Courage* and find Crane's descriptions of war's carnage gory and unsettling, but necessary, and his use of symbols, such as the red sun "like a wafer," especially powerful. These are good things to include in your summary, which might read something like this:

Crane describes such gruesome details of war as ants swarming over the gray face of a dead soldier, and Jim Conklin's mortal wound, which looks "as if it had been chewed by wolves." *The Red Badge of Courage* is definitely not for the squeamish. Yet Crane's intriguing use of symbols such as the red wafer sun at Jim Conklin's death, striking images such as "the

cathedral light of a forest," and the sympathetic portrayal of Fleming's inner turmoil and ultimate triumph, more than balance out the novel's grimness and make the book well worth reading.

This summary reinforces your statement in the first paragraph about Crane's realistic writing style as well as the material in the body of your report. It also gives a clear indication of how you feel about the book and why, and the types of readers to whom the book is likely to appeal.

Revised rough draft. Pulling all the paragraphs together, the revised draft reads as follows:

When Stephen Crane wrote what was to become his best-known work, the novel *The Red Badge of Courage*, he had never personally witnessed the horrors of battle. Yet this psychological study of the effects of combat on a young recruit during the Civil War has become an American classic. Even today, a century after the novel was first published, it is noted for its realistic depiction of battle and its insight into the effects of warfare on human thoughts and actions.

All the events related in the novel center on and are seen through the eyes, thoughts, and emotions of Henry Fleming, a young Union volunteer, during a single, unnamed battle of the Civil War.

Like getting a baking temperature correct, careful attention to details in rewriting and editing produces a big improvement in the final draft.

It could be any battle of any war, for Crane's real focus is on another battle, the hidden one raging within Henry Fleming as his romantic notions of war are crushed by the realities of fear, suffering, and death. Through Fleming's thoughts and actions, we see that the external conflict, the struggle between the Union and Confederate forces, is the foundation for his internal struggle to come to grips with his own fear and self-doubt.

Henry Fleming had dreamed of the glory of battle, but his first months in the army are filled with marches, encampments, and endless tedium. He spends much of his time wondering whether he will run from battle when the time comes.

The day finally comes when Fleming's regiment is sent into battle. The regiment repulses a Confederate attack, but when a second attack threatens to overwhelm the Union ranks, Fleming and some other soldiers panic and run. Separated from his regiment, Fleming feels burning shame when he learns that the Union line has held. He is ashamed again when he joins a group of wounded soldiers, one of whom keeps asking him, "Where yeh hit?" His shame burns yet again when he meets a mortally wounded friend, a tall soldier named Jim Conklin, who asks him, "Where yeh been, Henry?" Jim dies soon after this, beneath a highly symbolic "red sun...pasted in the sky like a wafer" that makes the scene one of blood sacrifice. Jim's death fills Fleming with silent rage.

Fleming meets a group of retreating soldiers, one of whom fells him with the blow of a rifle butt. That night a kind soldier, whose face Fleming never sees, helps him get back to his regiment. Fleming tells his comrades that he has been shot, and accepts their warm approval and friendship.

The next day the Confederates attack again. Fleming, filled with rage and hatred, fights with an almost inhuman ferocity and shows great courage. When the fighting ends, Henry Fleming comes to terms with the personal shortcomings that the battle has revealed to him; he finally feels "a quiet manhood, nonassertive but of sturdy and strong blood."

Crane describes such gruesome details of war as ants swarming over the gray face of a dead soldier, and Jim Conklin's mortal wound, which looks "as if it had been chewed by wolves." *The Red Badge of Courage* is definitely not for the squeamish. Yet Crane's intriguing use of symbols such as the red wafer sun at Jim Conklin's death, striking images such as "the cathedral light of a forest," and the sympathetic portrayal of Fleming's inner turmoil and ultimate triumph, more than balance out the novel's grimness and make the book well worth reading.

This book report is a bit less than 600 words in length, or about two and a half typewritten, double-spaced pages. You may be asked to write a shorter or longer report than this. It may seem like more work, but a longer report is actually easier to do. You can add more supporting information about plot, characters, and the author's style. Crafting a shorter report means that you have to cover the material in a more compact and general way.

Final revision.
You have gone over your rough draft, filled it in here, thinned it out there, and are satisfied that you have included all the information you need to provide. Now all you have to do is make a clean copy of your report and you are finished, right? Wrong. But do not feel discouraged. You are close to being finished. All that remains for you to do is read your report for sense, style, and correctness.

Reading for sense. You have been working very closely with your material, and you may even be able to recite your report from memory. This *might* be helpful if you are intending to present an oral book report, but at this stage you need to clear your mind once again. Take a short break: Go for a walk, shoot some baskets, listen to some music. Then come back to your report refreshed.

A short break before the final revision will help you to look at your report objectively.

Read the report through, sentence by sentence, paragraph by paragraph, from beginning to end. Do your sentences say what you want them to say, no more and no less? Are they clear and easy to read? Do your ideas follow one another in a logical fashion, or do they jump back and forth? Do you say the same thing more than once, but in different words? Eliminate any sentences that do not present the reader with new information or ideas.

Have you included enough information so that a reader of your report who is totally unfamiliar with the book will understand all that you are saying? Are there any stray items of information that, interesting as they may be, do not contribute to the points you are trying to make or add to the reader's understanding?

Reading for style. After you are confident that everything in your book report is necessary, understandable, and in its proper place, you can then proceed to read it for style. Are there run-on sentences that should be broken up to form complete, easy-to-read sentences? Are there long, complicated sentences that are confusing to read? Try to simplify them.

Have you used any incomplete sentences? If you are writing your book report for a school assignment, find out ahead of time whether this is permissible. Some teachers will allow a sentence fragment that is used for special emphasis. Others will not. Even if

you are permitted to use fragments, do so sparingly.

Do you present the reader with a reasonable mix of simple and complex sentences? You should try to vary your sentence structure to make your writing more interesting.

Do you use the same word a number of times in a row? Sometimes this is unavoidable, but you can usually find other words to break up the repetition. If a synonym does not come readily to mind, try looking in a thesaurus. Or try looking up the dictionary definition of the word you are attempting to replace. Often the dictionary will offer words that have the same or similar meaning. To increase your word power, see Building Your Vocabulary in Volume 3.

When you use a thesaurus, be careful that you understand the meaning of an alternate word before you use it. If a word sounds promising but you are not sure it means exactly what you want it to mean, check the dictionary. Mark Twain once described the difference between the almost right word and the right word as the difference between the lightning bug and the lightning.

Another stylistic weakness that you should try to eliminate is the use of clichés, words or phrases that have been so overused that they have hardly any meaning. Clichés indicate that you have not thought out exactly what you want to say or have become careless. Clichés are so prevalent that it is probably

Using a thesaurus to find other word choices

To use a thesaurus, look up any word or term in the index to find the numerical category that contains related words and terms. Then turn to that category in the thesaurus.

red 434
  –and yellow 439
  –book *list* 86
  –cap *porter* 271
  –cent 643, 800
  –cross 662
  –flag 550, 668
  –hot *great* 31
    violent 173
    hot 382
    emotion 821
    excited 824
  –lead 434
  –letter *mark* 550
    celebrate 883
  –letter day
    important 642
    rest 687
    amusement 840

red–handed
  murder 361
  in the act 680
  guilty 947
redict 905
redintegrate 660
redivivus 660
redness 382, 434
redolence *odor* 398
  fragrance 400
redouble *increase* 356
  duplication 90
  repeat 104
  –one's efforts 686
redoubt 717
redoubtable 860
redound to
  conduce 176
  –one's honor

434. Redness

n. **red**, scarlet, cardinal, cardinal red, vermilion, carmine, crimson, pink, rose, cerise, cherry, rouge, coquelicot, salmon, lake, maroon, carnation, *couleur de rose* [F.], *rose du Barry* [F.]; magenta, solferino, damask, flesh -color, –tint; color; fresh–, high-color; warmth; gules [*her.*].

redness etc. *adj.;* rubescence, rubicundity, ruddiness, rubefaction, rubrication, rubification; erubescence, blush.

[comparisons] ruby, *grenat* [F.], garnet, carbuncle; rust, iron mold *or* mould; rose, cardinal flower, lobelia; cardinal-bird, –grosbeak; red-start.

[dyes and pigments] cinnabar, cochineal, red ocher *or* ochre, stammel, fuchsine *or* fuchsin, vermilion; ruddle, madder; Indian red, palladium red, light red, Venetian red; red ink, annatto *or* annotto, realgar, minium, red lead.

v. **be** *or* **become red** etc. *adj.;* blush, flush, color,

```
judgement
Carribean
congradulate
Pearl Harbor, December 7, 1491
Edgar Allen Poe
wierd
seige
supercede
Simon Lagree
Ulysees S. Grant
```

Simple errors such as misspellings and incorrect dates weaken a book report.

impossible to avoid them completely in writing, but try your best to do so.

Reading for correctness. Have you spelled everything correctly? Check the spelling of each word about which you are not absolutely sure. Verify the spelling of the book's title and the name of the author. Anyone can make a mistake. Some years ago a portion of a street in New York City was renamed in honor of Edgar Allan Poe, but the new street sign misspelled the writer's name. A quick check of your work will save you from a similar embarrassment.

Check also your use of punctuation and capitalization, especially for any unusual use of these in the book title. Pay careful attention in the title to hyphens, colons, semicolons, exclamation points, and use of the ampersand, or "&" symbol, in place of the word "and." Duplicate the book title exactly.

Are all your facts correct? If you include such items as birth and death dates, publication dates, or the like, make sure you have written them down correctly. It takes only a few moments to make sure these details are accurate. If you get them wrong, all the other information in your book report will automatically become suspect.

Preparing the final draft. Once you have read and edited your book report for sense, style, and correctness, you are ready to copy your work to make the finished product, the final draft.

Be sure to use the appropriate format. If the report is for a school assignment, find out ahead of time what information needs to be included on the first page, and where. These items will probably include your name, the teacher's name, the course name and number, and the due date of the report. You should also learn what format to use for page numbering, and whether you need to include your last name on each page.

Find out where on the title page to start your report: about one-third of the way down is a good

starting point. Center the title of your report, skip a line, and write "By" followed by your name. Skip two lines and begin your first paragraph. Remember to provide good margins on both sides of the page and on the bottom.

Also find out whether you may provide a clean handwritten copy or are required to provide a typewritten copy. Typewritten reports are generally required for college-level courses. If you do type your report, use standard bond paper, not the "erasable" kind of paper that tends to smudge and smear. If you make a few mistakes in typing, use correction fluid or ribbon and retype, but if you make a large mistake or more than half a dozen small ones and the page starts to look messy, start over with a clean page.

Do not assume that a computer printout is acceptable in place of typewritten copy. The print quality of inexpensive computer printers, especially older dot matrix printers, is poor, and some teachers will not accept anything less than crisp printing.

Finally, determine whether your report pages should be held together with a paper clip or staple or placed in a·binder. Usually the clip or staple is more than adequate.

The finished report: Carefully planned and prepared, attractive, and inviting.

```
                              Mrs. Jones
                      American Literature
                         April 15, 1994


               Book report:

           Stephen Crane's novel

           The Red Badge of Courage

                      By

               Carlos Wilson


   When Stephen Crane wrote what was to be-
come his best-known work, the novel The Red
Badge of Courage, he had never personally
witnessed the horrors of battle. Yet this
psychological study of the effects of combat
on a young recruit during the Civil War has
become an American classic. Even today, a
century after the novel was first published,
```

Reports for different kinds of books

Before you select a book for your report, you will usually know that it will be in one of two general categories, fiction or nonfiction. Sometimes the choice of general category will be made for you by your teacher, and sometimes you will be able to decide for yourself. Once the decision is made, you will still have to consider which type of fiction or nonfiction book to select within the two general categories.

Works of fiction.

The novel is probably the most common type of fiction selected for book reports, but there are other forms of fiction that deserve consideration as well. These include short story collections, short story anthologies, and plays.

For each of these forms, you need to fulfill the main requirements for any book report. You must address the three main questions, "What is the book about?" "What central idea is the author trying to express?" and "What do you think about the book, and why?" You must also remember to use present tense when describing what happens in the book. However, the structure and content of your book report will vary to some degree depending on which form of fiction you pick. Let's examine the things to consider with each different form.

Novels. The main elements of a book report on a novel, as discussed earlier, include the novel's main characters, the setting, the plot, the point of view from which the story is told, the author's main theme or themes, and the author's style.

One of the most interesting things about the novel is that it exists in so many variations, or genres, including contemporary novels, historical novels, mystery and detective novels, romances, horror and supernatural novels, and science fiction and fantasy novels. The subject index of *The Young Reader's Companion* contains headings for these and other types of fiction and provides a good starting point for a book search in a particular genre. For example, a quick look at the subject heading "Mysteries and Detective Stories" turns up, among other titles, *Farewell, My Lovely* by Raymond Chandler, *The Moonstone* by Wilkie Collins, *The Sign of the Four* by Arthur Conan Doyle, and *Trent's Last Case* by E.C. Bentley.

Short story collections. In most collections of short stories, the usual unifying elements of plot, character, setting, and theme are not all present, so you must discuss which elements are shared by the stories and which are not. For example, the stories in a particular collection may all have the same setting but different characters, plots, and themes. Or the stories may all share a common theme but have different characters, plots, and settings. Perhaps all the stories are told in the first person, or are related by an unseen narrator, or are related mostly through dialogue, or have surprise endings.

Some collections, such as *Winesburg, Ohio* by Sherwood Anderson, contain a number of related tales that, taken separately, can stand on their own as short stories but that tell a larger, more complete story when all are put together. Anderson's stories work together to recreate vividly the small-town Ohio life and people the author knew in the 1890's.

Other collections contain stories that have no apparent connection with one another—no similarity of plot, characters, or setting, perhaps not even of style or structure. Look a bit closer for connections. Perhaps all were written in a particular period of the author's career and reflect the author's interests and concerns at the time. Perhaps they all share a general theme, such as the struggle to overcome adversity, or the destructive effects of poverty.

Short story anthologies. An anthology is a gathering of writings by different authors. Often an anthology will have a theme, and sometimes the theme will be identified in the book's subtitle, for example as "an anthology of war stories" or "tales of the Arctic North." Sometimes the connection will be through the writers. Perhaps all are Native American writers or 19th century women writers. Maybe all the stories are told in the first person, or all the main characters are women, or each story centers on a particular subject, say, graduation from school, first love, or baseball.

A short story anthology offers the potential for a remarkable range of styles, themes, characters, points of view, settings, and the like. Try to describe how the stories differ from one another as well as how they are alike.

Plays. Perhaps the most curious type of fiction, and the one most difficult to analyze in a book report, is the play, which exists halfway between the world of literature and the world of theater.

Most plays are written not to be read but to be performed on stage. The reader has to take this into account and make adjustments. The most obvious adjustment is to get used to reading the author's stage directions and scene descriptions, so that they increase rather than impede your understanding and enjoyment of the play.

The playwright relies on the characters to provide the important details in a play, through what they say, the way they say it, what they do, and how they do it. Sometimes the characters may say or do things that would seem out of place in everyday life because their

A great variety of books, including novels, short-story collections, and nonfiction works of all types, provide a virtually limitless source of material for book reports.

words and actions are the only vehicles through which the playwright can reach the audience.

As you read a play, try to imagine that you are actually seeing it performed. How effectively does the dialogue advance the plot and develop the characters? How well do the characters' actions aid you in understanding them? How, and how well, does the playwright, through his or her stage directions and set descriptions, overcome the limitations of a small stage?

Works of nonfiction. Biographies and autobiographies are favorite types of nonfiction books for book reports. We all have natural curiosity about other people, and we like to read about them, especially if they are famous or have unusual stories to tell. Other types of nonfiction books you might consider include historical works, books about interesting places, and books about specific subjects. Another genre, which might properly claim a category of its own somewhere between fiction and nonfiction, is the poetry collection.

Biographies. The story of a person's life is appealing precisely because it *is* a story, grounded not in the author's imagination, but in facts and events.

The author's main responsibilities in biography are to strive for accuracy, to make a thorough and impartial presentation of the facts, and to bring his or her subject to life for the reader. Here are some things to consider when evaluating these points.

Does the author provide footnotes and give sources for quotations and other information? Are they reliable sources, such as scholarly works, official documents, letters, diaries, archival materials, and personal interviews? The absence of such citations does not mean that the book is inaccurate, but it does mean that you have no way of knowing where the information came from. You must simply trust the author.

Does the author's presentation seem impartial, or do you think that you have been given only the information that supports the author's overall theme or purpose in writing the book?

Finally, is the book interesting throughout? If not, is it the author's fault or your own?

The Young Reader's Companion includes a subject heading for "Biography and Autobiography" that will give you a good start in your search for biographical and autobiographical works.

Autobiographies. The story of a person's life as told by that person is generally less grounded in objective fact than the story told in biography. Yet many autobiographies are compelling narratives nonetheless. An autobiography that is based solely on the author's memory of events long past is not as reliable as one in which the author refers to diaries, journals, letters, and other contemporary records.

Try to determine what resources the author used in writing the book. It stands to reason that the more reliable the resources used, the more accurate the book will be. Try also to determine the author's purpose in writing the book. Was it simply to reminisce about times past, or to present an organized body of facts in an autobiographical setting? Your evaluation of the book's merit will be stronger if you can answer these questions.

Some autobiographical works cover a person's life from birth to the time the author writes the book. Others concentrate on a portion of the author's life. Still others are only partly autobiographical. An example of the last type is *Walden* by Henry David Thoreau, which includes elements of autobiography, natural history, philosophy, and social commentary.

Historical works. Some people do not have much interest in books that deal with history. Part of the problem is that they think of history in terms of school textbooks, which do not always provide interesting reading experiences. Another part of the problem with textbooks is that they cover a great deal of factual material in a limited number of pages, so there is usually little room for the writer to elaborate on some of the fascinating details that bring history to life. However, there is a veritable gold mine of enjoyable books that deal in depth with different aspects of history.

When selecting an historical work for a book report, keep in mind the scope of the work, the size of the particular subject the author tries to cover. Books that deal with specific aspects of a larger subject tend to be easier to read and to report on. A book that tries to cover the entire history of art, for example, may be just too large and ambitious a work to tackle for a short report. However, a book about the painters of the impressionist movement may be just right.

Also keep in mind that others may not be as interested in the subject you choose as you are. Are there other reasons why readers will enjoy the book? Perhaps the author's writing style is especially interesting, or the book's theme is more important than its limited subject would at first suggest.

Books about places. In the 19th century, books about travel were especially popular, in part because improvements in transportation made travel to distant lands much easier for good writers than ever before, but too costly for most readers who dreamed of faraway places. Today, traveling from continent to continent in a few hours is largely taken for granted, but people still enjoy seeing other places through the eyes and experiences of other people.

Contemporary accounts of a writer's travel experiences, in addition to being pleasant reading experiences, are also valuable for learning about the land, people, and history of different places. For example, *Coming into the Country* by John McPhee concentrates on contemporary Alaskans and Alaskan society. But it also offers rich descriptions of the state's natural beauty as well as important insights into its history. When you write your book report, try to give the reader a good idea of the book's coverage, including how much space the author devotes to things like personal observation, characterization of the land and people, folklore, stories, anecdotes, historical details, and practical information.

Do not neglect older books about places. For example, Mark Twain's *The Innocents Abroad*, the account of his 1867 voyage to Europe and the Holy Land, may contain a number of outdated facts but it is still one of the most delightfully humorous travel books that has ever been written. *The Alhambra* by Washington Irving, first published in 1832 and hailed as Irving's "Spanish Sketch Book," is a marvelous exploration of Moorish Spain, its history, legends, architecture, and people. When you write a report about such a book, be sure to let the reader know whether you found some of the information out of date. Also note in your report the date the book was written or first published.

Books about specific subjects. Sometimes you will be able to select a book on a subject of your choice, such as sports, space exploration, or health care. At other times you will have little or no choice. Nonetheless, even when you must write a report on a given subject, you will usually be able to find a variety of books that will serve your purpose. Follow the same rule whether your choice of subject is limited or not: Pick the book that most closely coincides with your interests.

When writing your book report, try to tell the reader what special qualifications the author has to write on the subject. Perhaps the writer has spent years gathering information and interviewing people about the topic, or perhaps he or she has written a number of other books about it. Also note any special features the author provides, such as a bibliography, list of sources cited, or suggestions for further reading.

Poetry collections. Often neglected as a possible subject for a book report, the poetry collection offers a special challenge for report writers. If you enjoy reading poetry, you should consider reading a collection and writing about it.

A poem is an attempt to capture in words the essence of an idea, emotion, or experience. Read each poem carefully and try to discover what it is the poet is trying to say. Are the poems easy to understand or obscure? Do the poems, taken collectively, point toward a theme, such as the loneliness of adolescence or the beauty of nature?

Note the poet's use of such things as rhyme and meter. Are all the poems written in the same form—for example, free verse, sonnet, or haiku?

What do you notice about the poet's word choice? Do certain words or images recur in poem after poem? Is the poet's style lyrical, musical, dreamlike, mechanical, harsh? Are the poems humorous, satirical, mournful, nostalgic, playful, somber? How do the poems affect you?

When writing about a specific poem in your report, observe the convention accepted for discussions of fiction and use present tense. You will find the subject heading in *The Young Reader's Companion* for "Poetry" to be a useful starting point.

Oral book reports

Whether or not you enjoy speaking before groups of people, the chances are very good that, sooner or later, you will be called upon to do so. Part of the reason why students are asked to give oral reports in class is to help them become comfortable with the idea of speaking in public. By learning how to prepare and present an oral book report, you learn much more than just what a particular book is about.

Basics of oral presentation. Sometimes you will be able to read a book report you have written. Other times you will be asked to talk about the book without the use of any written aids, or using only a few brief notes to refresh your memory. Whichever way you are asked to give your oral book report, there are a few basic rules that apply to all.

Posture. The first basic rule is to stand up straight. This helps you to get the attention of your audience and communicate that you are serious about your work. You should not stand rigid and unmoving, like a soldier at attention. Try to stand comfortably with your head up, your back straight, and both feet on the floor.

When you assume a comfortable, confident posture, you may be surprised to find that you actually do feel more comfortable and confident. You certainly will be in a better position to fulfill rule number two.

Speech. Your book report may be thorough, concise, well thought out, and full of insight and careful observation, but your audience will never be able to appreciate its qualities unless you speak clearly and forcefully. Remember that all the words you use are important and valuable. You do not want any of them to get lost.

You do not have to shout. In a quiet room of average size, a normal speaking voice is all that's needed. If you have a tendency to speak softly, remember to speak a little louder. Try to talk so that anyone standing at the far end of the room will be able to hear you with no difficulty.

If you normally talk slowly or rapidly, do not be too concerned about the rate at which you are speaking. Concentrate on the clarity of your speech. Some accomplished public speakers talk quite slowly but they hold their audiences' attention because they deliver their words with force and passion. On the other hand, some of the best public speakers talk quite rapidly. John F. Kennedy, an eloquent public speaker, could talk about as rapidly as many people can read.

Try to avoid using repetitious words and phrases such as "like," "you know," "sort of," and "okay." Also, try to avoid using slang terms in your speech.

Eye contact. Standing up straight and talking clearly and audibly are two important things you can do to make a good connection between yourself and your listeners. Another good way to establish a rapport with your audience and keep its attention is to look out at the people who are listening to you.

Making brief eye contact with the people in your audience gives them the feeling that you are trying to communicate with them, helps put them at ease, and lets them concentrate less on you and more on what you are saying. If you avoid looking at your listeners because you are nervous, you probably will not make yourself feel any better and you will make your audience feel uncomfortable.

If eye contact bothers you for any reason, try sweeping your gaze back and forth across your audience without spending too much time looking at any particular person. But if you find that eye contact is comfortable, look at each person in your audience and talk directly to him or her for a few seconds before directing your words to someone else in a different part of the room. You may not realize it, but you probably use this technique already in conversations with small groups. You look back and forth from person to person as you talk.

Time limit. When you give your book report, keep in mind the amount of time you have to speak. Are you strictly limited to a maximum amount of time, or must you speak for a certain minimum time?

Oral presentations are more successful when you are well prepared, feel self-confident, stand up straight, speak clearly, and make eye contact with your audience.

Rehearse your report and time yourself before you step up in front of your audience. This will give you a good idea of how long it will take.

Reading a written report.

One of the great benefits of reading a written book report is that you already know exactly what you are going to say. But there is more to it than just standing up and reading the paper out loud. Here are a few pointers to help you make your presentation better.

Practice. Read your book report aloud at home to help yourself get used to the sound of your thoughts. Speak at a normal level, something approximating the level you will use when you give your report. Get used to the *feel* of speaking.

Read your paper aloud several times. Emphasize various words by changing the sound of your voice (raising or lowering your pitch or saying the words with a shade more force), changing the tempo of your delivery (words spoken a bit more slowly seem to take on greater importance), or pausing for effect (a very short pause can have a very strong effect).

Take breaks between practice readings. You could, for example, read your paper first thing in the morning, again in the afternoon, and again in the early evening. When you feel comfortable with your reading, stop practicing. Don't overprepare.

If there are maximum and minimum time limits for the length of your report, time your readings to see that you can make your presentation comfortably within those limits. If you run into time problems, cut or expand your material to adjust it to the required length.

When you are satisfied with your practice readings, you are ready to present your paper and yourself to your listeners.

Use both hands. Hold your paper with both hands at a level that is comfortable and allows you to read and still maintain a good posture. Using both your hands will help keep your paper steady and will greatly help you when you have to turn to the next page.

Look up. When you begin to read, remember your audience. Try to look up from your paper periodically and look out briefly at your listeners. You may want to do this when you desire special emphasis on a particular word, phrase, or thought, or when you come to the end of a sentence or a paragraph.

If you have trouble finding your place on the page when you look back down at it, try positioning your left or right thumb along the edge of the page near the line you are on and moving it down the page in a steady, smooth motion as you read. Your practice sessions will help you find the best way to keep track of your place on the page.

Do not hide. You may be a little nervous at first as you stand in front of your peers, but try to avoid using your paper as a shield to hide behind. The best way to counter the urge to place your paper between yourself and your audience is to look at your listeners right away, at the beginning of your presentation. Do not be surprised to find that the expressions on their faces are ones of warmth, attentiveness, and encouragement.

Take your time. Remember that you have worked hard on your report and that it is a good report, so take your time and try to enjoy your reading of it. Your presentation is not a speed competition. Pace yourself as you did in your practice sessions, concentrate on what you want to say and how you want to say it, and you will do well.

Giving an unwritten report.

Almost all of the steps required for a written book report apply to oral, unwritten reports as well. You should select the book you wish to report on, read it critically and take notes, think about what you have read, and write up an outline listing the things you want to say.

Outline review. Instead of using a written report to practice your oral presentation, use the outline you have prepared. Read it through once or twice to be certain of the main points you want to cover in your report.

Practice. Once you have the main points of your report secure in your memory, begin practicing your presentation. Speak in a normal voice approximating the level you will use when you give your report. Refer to your outline if you need to refresh your memory on some of the details that support your main points.

After you have given yourself a complete practice presentation, take a break and occupy your mind with anything but your report. Then go back to work, run through your presentation again, and see how well you remember your main points and the supporting information you want to include. A good indicator is the number of times you have to look back at your outline.

When you are comfortable with your presentation, stop practicing. Do not over-rehearse or try to memorize your report word for word. If you do, your presentation may seem too controlled and rigid and you will lose your audience's attention. You will also run the risk of forgetting what you have memorized and having a hard time reorganizing your thoughts.

Notes. You may be permitted to use an index card or sheet of paper listing the main points you want to make in your presentation. If so, it will be comforting to have even if you do not use it. If such an aid is not permitted, you will have to rely on your memory. In that case, be sure to review, just before you give your presenta-

It is a good idea to practice your presentation before you give it before the class.

tion, the central points you want to make. Your careful reading of the book and all your preparatory work will help you remember the finer points.

Don't worry. If while you are speaking you draw a blank or temporarily forget what you want to say, don't panic. It is all right for you to pause briefly to collect your thoughts. Mentally review your list of main points, and your thoughts will come back to you.

For more guidance on speaking in public, see Improving Your Speech in Volume 3.

For Further Reference

Adler, Mortimer J. and Van Doren, Charles
  How to Read a Book
  Simon & Schuster
Carruth, Gorton
  The Young Reader's Companion
  Bowker
Hart, James D.
  Oxford Companion to American Literature
  Oxford University Press
Kaplan, Fred
  The Reader's Adviser (3 vols.)
  Bowker
Newman, Gerald
  How to Write a Report
  Franklin Watts
Perkins, George, et al.
  Benét's Reader's Encyclopedia of American Literature
  HarperCollins
Roberts, Edgar V.
  Writing Themes About Literature
  Prentice-Hall
Strunk, William, Jr. and White, E.B.
  The Elements of Style
  Macmillan

Index

How to use the INDEX. The index to the *Student Handbook* is arranged alphabetically according to a letter-by-letter system. All entries, regardless of punctuation or spaces between words, are in precise aphabetical order; there are no exceptions:

> **Marshall Islands**
> **Marshall, John**
> **Marshall Plan**
> **Mars (planet)**

Names beginning with Mac or Mc are also arranged in strict alphabetical order. The abbreviation St. is indexed as if it were spelled out as Saint.

Each entry ends with a period. Following the period is the number **1** or **2** followed by a colon. These bold faced numbers indicate the volume in which each page can be found. The page number follows the colon.

A semicolon separates the volumes, when applicable:

> **Lincoln, Abraham. 1:** 93, 95; **2:** 33, 85, 92-93

Most main entries are indexed under the main element of the name, e.g., Sinai, Mount (not Mount Sinai); marathon, Battle of (not Battle of Marathon); Verdun, Treaty of (not Treaty of Verdun). Handy cross-references are provided when a listing may be ambiguous or confusing.

Few abbreviations are used in the index, and those that are used are so standard as to eliminate the need for an abbreviations list.

Books, plays, and other titles are not indexed, but authors, artists, composers, etc., are, and the great works will almost invariably be found on the pages listed under their creators' names. Anonymous works (e.g., *Beowolf*) have their own listings.

A

Aaron, Hank. 1: 324
Abbasid dynasty. 2: 83
Abortion. 1: 131; 2: 12
Abscissa. 2: 312
Absolute magnitude.
1: 316
Absolute scale. *See* Kelvin
scale
Abstract nouns. 1: 8
Acceleration. 2: 233, 236-
237, 246
Accidents. *See* Safety
Acetic acid. 2: 188, 226
Acetone. 1: 237; 2: 226
Acid. 2: 224-226, 230-231
Acid rain. 1: 247
Acquired immune defi-
ciency syndrome (AIDS).
1: 132
Acropolis. 2: 76
Act (govt.). *See* Bill (govt.);
specific acts
Actinomycosis (lumpy jaw).
1: 244
Action verbs. 1: 17
Active satellite. 1: 316
Acute angle. 2: 312
Adams, Jane. 1: 122
Adams, John. 1: 112, 114;
2: 29-31
Adams, John Quincy.
1: 116; 2: 14, 29, 32-33
Adams-Onis Treaty. 1: 115
Addends (math). 1: 158;
2: 312
Addison, Joseph. 2: 349
Addition (math). 1: 158-170,
204-205, 217, 220; 2: 266-
268, 287
Additive identity element.
2: 312
Additive inverse. 2: 312
Adenosine. 2: 187
Adjectives. 1: 4, 5, 26-31, 50;
2: 331, 336
ADP (adenosine diphos-
phate). 2: 187-188
Adverbs. 1: 4, 5, 27-31, 34-
35, 49-51, 54; 2: 331, 334,
336
Aerobic respiration.
2: 187-188, 212
Aeschylus. 1: 360; 2: 76,
364, 366-367
Aesop. 1: 100; 2: 376
Afghanistan. 2: 114, 132
AFL. *See* American Federation
of Labor
Africa. 1: 126-127, 276-278;
2: 82, 90, 106, 128, 148-
161. *See also* North Africa;
specific countries
African-Americans. 1: 107,
121-122, 124, 129, 136,
357; 2: 12, 46, 57-62.
See also Slavery

African National Congress
(ANC). 2: 116
Agnatha. 2: 211
Agnew, Spiro. 1: 131
Agricultural Adjustment
Act. 1: 126
Agriculture. 1: 113, 117,
119, 121-122, 126, 134,
246-247; 2: 47, 132
Agriculture, Department
of (U.S.). 1: 223; 2: 11
Ah Bing. 2: 64
Ah Nam. 2: 63
AID. *See* Agency for
International
Development
AIDS. *See* Acquired immune
deficiency syndrome
AIM. *See* American Indian
Movement
Airlines. *See* Airplane
Air mass. 1: 290-291, 294-
295
Airplane. 1: 123, 126;
2: 101, 104. *See also* Jet
aircraft
Air pollution. 1: 247
Akkadians. 2: 71
Alabama. 1: 119, 146-147
Alamo (Texas). 1: 117
Alaska. 1: 121, 134-139,
279-280, 290; 2: 7
Albania. 2: 105, 109, 140
Albany Plan of Union.
1: 109
Albedo. 1: 316
Albee, Edward. 2: 367
Albinism. 2: 194
Alcohol. 1: 125, 227, 230;
2: 204, 225-226, 230
Alcott, Louisa May. 1: 96
Aldehyde. 2: 225-226
Aldrin, Edwin (Buzz).
1: 130, 313, 315; 2: 110
Aleutian Islands. 1: 127,
278, 280
Alexander the Great (King
of Macedonia). 2: 73-75,
77
Alfred the Great. 2: 84
Algae. 1: 254; 2: 202-204
Algebra. 1: 219; 2: 264-289
Algeria. 2: 148
Alien and Sedition Acts.
1: 114; 2: 31
Alkali metals. 2: 222-223,
230
Alkanes. 2: 225, 230
Alkenes. 2: 225, 230
Alkynes. 2: 225, 230
Alleles. 2: 194, 212
Alliance for Progress
1: 129
Almanacs. 2: 322
Alphabet. 2: 73
Alpha Centauri (star).
1: 303

Alpha particle. 2: 227-230,
245-246
Altitude (stellar). 1: 316
Altostratus clouds. 1: 291
Aluminum. 1: 264
Amasis I. 2: 72
Amazon River. 2: 127, 168
Amenemhet I. 2: 72
Amenhotep IV. 2: 72
American Colonization
Society. 1: 115
American Expeditionary
Forces (A.E.F.). 1: 124
American Federation of
Labor (AFL). 1: 122
American Indian Movement
(AIM). 2: 50
American Red Cross. 1: 122
American Revolution.
1: 112, 362; 2: 4, 53, 59, 94,
96
American Samoa. 1: 152
Amherst, Jeffrey. 1: 109
Amino acids. 2: 187, 190
Amoeba. 2: 202
Ampere (physics). 1: 274;
2: 242
Amphetamines. 1: 230
Amphibians. 2: 211
Amplitude (math). 2: 312
Amplitude (music). 1: 349
Amplitude (physics). 1: 272,
274; 2: 239, 246
Amsterdam (Neth.). 1: 340
Amundsen, Roald. 2: 174
Anaerobic respiration.
2: 187-188, 212
Anaheim (Calif.). 1: 137
Anatomy. 1: 254. *See also*
Human anatomy
ANC. *See* African National
Congress
Ancient civilizations. 2: 70-
81
Andersen, Hans Christian.
1: 100; 2: 376
Andes Mountains. 1: 278;
2: 168
Andorra. 2: 140
Andromeda (galaxy). 1: 303,
306
Anemometer. 1: 293-294
Angiospermae. 2: 207
Angle (math). 2: 290-292,
297-298, 300, 303, 304, 312,
315
Anglican Church. *See* Church
of England
Anglo-Americans. 2: 51
Anglo-Saxons. 2: 84-85
Angola. 2: 148
Anguilla. 2: 172
Angular resolution. 1: 316
Animalia (kingdom). 2: 180,
198
Animals. 1: 241-242, 246,
248-252; 2: 95, 180-181,

Charlemagne (Charles the Great; Charles I; Holy Roman Emp.). 2: 82-83
Charles I (King of England). 2: 94
Charles II (King of England). 2: 94
Charles V (Holy Roman Emp.). 2: 91
Charles VII (King of France). 2: 87
Charles XII (King of Sweden). 2: 94
Charles Martel. 2: 83
Charles's law. 2: 246
Charleston (S.C.). 1: 112, 119
Chateau-Thierry (Fr.). 1: 124
Chaucer, Geoffrey. 2: 88, 352-353, 355, 374, 386
Chavez, Cesar. 2: 67
Checks and balances (govt.). 2: 4, 8, 12
Cheese. 2: 204
Cheetah. 2: 148
Chekhov, Anton Pavlovich. 2: 365-366, 368, 376
Chemistry and chemicals. 1: 260-262, 274-275; 2: 186-188, 214-231. See also Inorganic chemistry; Nuclear chemistry; Organic chemistry
Cheops. See Khufu
Cherokee Indians. 2: 49, 50
Chesapeake Bay (Md.). 1: 107
Chesbro, Jack. 1: 324
Cheyenne Indians. 1: 121; 2: 49
Chiang Kai-shek. 2: 109
Chicago (Ill.). 1: 121, 123, 137
Chicanos. See Mexican-Americans
Chicken pox. 1: 231, 244
Chile. 2: 169
Chilopoda. 2: 209
China. 1: 126-128, 130-131; 2: 45, 76, 81-82, 84, 86, 88, 94, 98, 101, 105, 109-110, 113-115, 127, 132, 134. See also Great Wall; Taiwan
China 1 (spacecraft). 1: 311
Chinese-Americans. 2: 63-64
Chinese Exclusion Acts. 2: 64
Ch'ing dynasty (Manchu). 2: 94, 101
Chisholm, Shirley. 2: 62
Chlamydomonas. 2: 203
Chlorine. 1: 264; 2: 214, 224, 226

Chlorophyll. 1: 248-249, 254; 2: 184, 187, 198, 201-203, 212
Chloroplast. 2: 183-184, 187, 201
Choking. 1: 239
Cholera. 1: 231, 244; 2: 201
Cholesterol. 1: 244
Chondrichthyes. 2: 211
Chopin, Frédéric. 1: 356
Christianity. 1: 108, 361; 2: 70, 75, 80-82, 85-86, 88, 162
Christmas Island. 2: 172
Christ. See Jesus Christ
Chromatin. 2: 181, 183, 212
Chromoplast. 2: 184
Chromosome. 2: 180-181, 183-184, 189, 191, 193, 195, 212
Chromosphere. 1: 297, 316
Church of England (Anglican Church). 2: 90, 92, 94
Churchill, John. See Marlborough, Duke of
Churchill, Sir Winston Leonard Spencer. 2: 107
CIA. See Central Intelligence Agency
Cilia. 2: 183-184, 202, 212
Cinder cone. 1: 280, 294
Cinematography. 1: 363, 366, 368
CIO. See Congress of Industrial Organizations
Circle (math). 1: 220; 2: 282, 298-299, 312
Circuit (electric). 1: 270
Circulatory system. 1: 235; 2: 196
Circus. 1: 361-362
Cirrostratus clouds. 1: 291
Cirrus clouds. 1: 291, 294
Cities. 1: 137; 2: 128. See also specific cities
Citizenship. 1: 121, 126; 2: 12
Citric-acid cycle. 2: 188
Civil rights. 1: 129; 2: 50, 62. See also African-Americans
Civil Rights Act (1964). 1: 129
Civil Rights Act (1968). 1: 129
Civil service. 1: 122; 2: 10, 40
Civil Service Reform Act. 1: 122
Civil War (U.S.). 1: 115, 119-120, 146, 150; 2: 12, 37, 56, 59-60, 99
Clams. 2: 209
Clarinet. 1: 349-351

Clark, Dr. Barney B. 1: 132
Clark, William. 1: 114; 2: 31
Classical music. 1: 355-356
Clause (language). 1: 41-42, 46-47, 49, 51, 54
Clay, Henry. 1: 116, 118; 2: 14
Clayton Antitrust Act. 1: 124; 2: 41
Clean Air Act. 1: 247
Cleisthenes. 2: 76
Clemens, Samuel Langhorne (Mark Twain). 1: 99; 2: 375, 379, 381, 388, 394, 417
Cleopatra. 2: 79, 384
Clermont (ship). 2: 54
Cleveland, Grover. 2: 38-39
Cleveland (Ohio). 1: 137
Climate. 1: 135, 284-287, 294. See also Weather
Clinton, William J. (Bill). 2: 44-45
Clone. 2: 212
Close-encounter theory. 1: 307, 316
Clothing. 1: 237
Clouds. 1: 288-289, 291, 304. See also specific types, e.g., Cumulonimbus
Clovis I (King of the Franks). 2: 82
Cluster (stellar). 1: 316
Coal. 1: 123, 247, 281
Coastal Plains (U.S.). 1: 134
Coastal Ranges (U.S.). 1: 134
Cobb, Ty. 1: 324
Cocaine. 1: 230
Cocci. 2: 201
Cocos Islands (Keeling Islands). 2: 172
Coelenterates. 2: 208
Coercive Acts. 1: 111
Coherent light. 2: 241
Cold, common. 1: 231; 2: 200
Cold front. 1: 291, 294
Cold Harbor, Battle of. 1: 120
Cold War. 1: 128; 2: 43, 109, 111, 113
Cole, Nat "King". 2: 61
Coleridge, Samuel Taylor. 2: 353, 356, 360
Colgate, William. 2: 54
Collective nouns. 1: 8, 12
Colloid. 2: 182
Colombia. 2: 170
Colonialism. 1: 106; 2: 100
Colon (language). 1: 55
Color. 1: 273, 305, 364; 2: 240

E

The
Young Reader's
Companion

The
Young Reader's
Companion

Gorton Carruth

A HUDSON GROUP BOOK

R. R. Bowker®

A REED REFERENCE PUBLISHING COMPANY
NEW PROVIDENCE, NEW JERSEY

Published by R. R. Bowker,
A Reed Reference Publishing Company
Copyright © 1993 by Carruth and Ehrlich Books, Inc.
All rights reserved
Printed and bound in the United States of America

Library of Congress Cataloging-in-Publication Data

Carruth, Gorton.
The young reader's companion/Gorton Carruth.
p.   cm.
"A Hudson Group Book."
Includes index.
Summary: A one-volume short-entry encyclopedia containing
information about the characters, plots, authors, and other topics
found in classic and contemporary books for young readers.
ISBN 0-8352-2765-0
1. Children's literature — Encyclopedias. 2. Young adult
literature — Encyclopedias. [1. Children's literature —
Encyclopedias. 2. Young adult literature — Encyclopedias.]
I. Title

PN1008.5.C373   1993   93-6662
809'.89282'03 — dc20   CIP
                                                        AC

Designed by Pam Forde Graphics

ISBN 0 - 8352 - 2765 - 0

9 780835 227650

TO

Gwénaëlle and Katell

Contents

Preface

The Young Reader's Companion, an illustrated A-to-Z short-entry encyclopedia, has as its chief purpose the promotion of reading. It contains entries about books that appeal to young people from about the fifth grade through high school and beyond. Each book is considered a good "read." There are also entries about the authors of these books and about subjects that will make reading more interesting and pleasurable.

This is a reader's companion. It contains entries not only about books and authors but also about characters, such as Catherine Earnshaw and Peter Pan, about gods and goddesses, such as Apollo, Demeter, Jupiter, Odin, and Zeus, and about legendary heroes, such as King Arthur and Roland. There are entries about people from the Bible and characters from Shakespeare's plays. Also included are animals that often appear in literature, such as cat, dog, eagle, and fox. The Subject Index shows the breadth of the selection of entries. This index lists the entries under convenient categories so that a young reader can easily find more books of a kind he likes to read. Categories include Adventure, Biography and Autobiography, Contemporary Life and Problems, Family Life, Fantasy, Historical Fiction, Mysteries and Detective Stories, Pioneer and Western Life, Romance, and Sea Stories.

The style is direct and informal. Young readers, who are often intimidated by the dry tone of reference books, will find *The Young Reader's Companion* fun to read. Parents may confidently give this guide to their children to encourage them to read more often and widely. Teachers and librarians seeking to answer the perennial question "What shall I read next?" will find titles to recommend to a reader who has already developed a liking for a certain kind of book or a particular author.

There is a generous selection of classic titles, such as *Hamlet, Huckleberry Finn, Moby-Dick, Treasure Island,* and *Wuthering Heights.* Many timid readers, however, may be more attracted by contemporary books, such as well-known mystery and adventure stories or fantasy and science fiction stories. Among the former are *The Maltese Falcon, The Murder of Roger Ackroyd, Shane, The Spy Who Came In from The Cold,* and *The Treasure of the Sierra Madre.* Among the latter are The Chronicles of Narnia, *Dune, The Hobbit,* The Foundation Trilogy, *The Martian Chronicles, Stranger in a Strange Land*, and *2001: A Space Odyssey*. Among the contemporary books are many that deal with problems young people often confront, such as *Are You There God? It's Me, Margaret, Death Be Not Proud*, and *A Hero Ain't Nothin' but a Sandwich*. Most nonfiction titles that are meant to dispense information and therefore become dated quickly have been excluded. Nevertheless, such classics as *The Autobiography of Malcolm X, Kon-Tiki, The Longest Day, On the Origin of Species*, and *Roots* are included.

The more than 2,000 entries in the 655 pages of *The Young Reader's Companion* include about 800 entries on books, about 750 on authors, and about 280 on historical personages. Many of the books are found on reading lists for students planning to enter college. Among the people included are Walt Disney and Captain William Kidd; among the places are the Forest of Arden and the Hellespont; and among fictional characters are Friar Tuck and Sherlock Holmes. There are about 200 entries on mythological and legendary figures, such as Ariel, Hiawatha, and John Henry; on signs and symbols—colors like black, red, and white, or the cross, rose, and star; and on imaginary places, such as Middle-Earth and Shangri-La.

A note about the nature of the entries may be useful. They were written with the young reader in mind. For example, in author entries only biographical information that illuminates the kind of subjects an author writes about or that stimulates a reader to turn to the author's books was included. In these author entries the choice of the works to be listed was made with the idea of getting a reader started. If he would like to read most of an author's work, he will need to consult his librarian or bookseller to find out what is available.

The same principle applies to title entries. For example, plot synopses, though sometimes quite detailed, are not complete descriptions of all the action. They are designed not to replace the book but to stimulate the reader to turn to the book itself. Entries about gods and goddesses are composites: They describe some of the best-known escapades but avoid describing the variant stories that are covered in text books and adult encyclopedias.

The mechanics of the entries are simple. Cross-references are always preceded by an asterisk*. Cross-references to people require the reader to look up the last name. For example, Mark Twain is found in the T's. Cross-references to fictional characters, on the other hand, require the reader to look up the first name. For example, Father Brown is found under the F's. Titles of books are printed in italic type and titles of short stories and poems are enclosed in quotation marks. Dates following the titles of books refer to the original publication date, not to the publication of subsequent reprints or to a translation. The abbreviation n.d. means no date. The rubrics MR and YA refer to the approximate reading level required for the titles under discussion. MR, or Middle Reader, suggests a fifth through eighth grade reading level. YA, or Young Adult Reader, suggests a high school or adult reading level. Books do not fall neatly into these categories, so there is naturally a good deal of overlapping.

The primary source for the information in *The Young Reader's Companion* was the books themselves. But, in addition to the scores of specialized sources, we acknowledge the many standard adult references that can be found in libraries and, in some cases, bookstores. Among them are *Contemporary Authors* and *Contemporary Authors, New Revision Series; Contemporary Literary Criticism; Current Biography Yearbook; Dictionary of American Biography; The Dictionary of National Biography; The Encyclopedia Americana; Encyclopaedia Britannica; McGraw-Hill Encyclopedia of World Drama; The New Columbia Encyclopedia; Something about the Author, Twentieth Century Authors;* and *Twentieth-Century Literary Criticism.*

Useful shorter reference books were, for words and phrases, *New Dictionary of American Slang* and *Brewer's Dictionary of Phrase and Fable,* and, for information about films and theater, *Halliwell's Film Guide* and *Leonard Maltin's TV Movies and Video Guide.* Among the standard shorter reference books covering adult literature are *Benèt's Reader's Encyclopedia, Benèt's Reader's Encyclopedia of American Literature, The Oxford Companion to American Literature, The Oxford Companion to English Literature,* and *The Reader's Encyclopedia of American Literature.*

For general information about books for young readers, there are *Best*

Books for Children, Best Books for Junior High Readers, Best Books for Senior High Readers, The Young Adult Reader's Adviser, and *The Oxford Companion to Children's Literature.*

Jack B. Long, the creative force behind *Our Wonderful World,* an 18-volume encyclopedia for young people, and for many years the editor of books for children at Western Publishing, undertook the difficult task of selecting the books and authors. Unfortunately, we record with regret and a sense of loss the death in 1990 of Jack Long. He was assisted by Rhoda Katzenstein, a librarian at Fieldston High School, New York City, and by Eleanor Lucas, a librarian for 30 years in the elementary school and junior high school in Larchmont and Mamaroneck, New York. Their sense of what constitutes good reading and their long experience with books for young readers influenced immeasurably the goals and contents of *The Young Reader's Companion.*

Also we acknowledge particularly Fon W. Boardman, Jr., an author of numerous books for young readers. He supplied many entries and gave good advice about what to include or exclude. Two particularly loyal contributors were Mary Varchaver and Raymond V. Hand, Jr. They not only wrote many entries but, because of their understanding of what books young readers like, they helped make *The Young Reader's Companion* fresh and interesting. Our thanks also go to Eugene Ehrlich, who read the entire text, editing away mistakes and making many useful suggestions. Our special thanks to our publisher, Marion Sader, who first suggested this enterprise and has lent her support and encouragement throughout its development, and to our editors, Catherine Barr and Nancy Bucenec, who have been invaluable in seeing this large book through all the stages of its production. Our thanks to them and to all others who helped us develop and complete this book.

GC

1993
Briarcliff Manor, NY

Illustrations

The
Young Reader's
Companion

Abélard and Héloïse lived in the Middle Ages and are famous for their deep love for one another. Pierre Abélard (1079–1142) was a French theologian and philosopher. When he was entrusted with educating Héloïse (1098–1164), they fell passionately in love. The affair resulted in the birth of a son, and the couple later married secretly. Héloïse's uncle found out about the situation and arranged for Abélard to be attacked and emasculated. Abélard became a monk and Héloïse a nun. During their long separation, they exchanged numerous letters, celebrated for their deep and moving expressions of love. Abélard and Héloïse were buried side by side, and their tragic love story remains one of the best known in history. You can read about these lovers in the novels *Héloïse and Abélard* (1921) by the Irish novelist George Moore (1852–1933) and *Stealing Heaven* (1979) by Marion Meade (1934–), and also in the nonfiction study *Abélard and Héloïse* (1972) by D.W. Robertson (1914–). YA

Abominable Snowcreature, The (1978) By Stephen Rudley (1946–), this is a nonfictional exploration of one of the most intriguing mysteries of the natural world. The subject is the legendary yeti or snowcreature of the Himalaya, the high mountains of India, and its North American counterpart, known as Bigfoot or Sasquatch, which is said to live in the wilderness of the Pacific Northwest. Rudley describes the Mount Everest Reconnaissance Party of the early 1950s, in Nepal, where the expedition leader photographed tracks in the snow made by a large apelike creature. He discusses the Sherpa mountain people of Nepal, famous for their abilities as climbers and guides, and their belief that yeti are as real as any animal. Other opinions suggest that the snowcreatures are wholly the product of human imagination. The book reports on scientific studies, habitat, eating patterns, and possible evolutionary history. It contains fascinating photographs. Another interesting book on this subject is *The Trail of the Abominable Snowman* (1966) by Gardner Soule (1913–). MR

abominable snowman This probably mythical creature, called *yeti* in Nepalese, is said to inhabit the Himalaya Mountains in Asia. Those who claim to have seen one say it is up to seven feet tall and covered with long, dark fur. Some scholars think it may be a hitherto unknown type of ape; it is likely that the footprints alleged to have been made by it are actually those of bears. See also *The Abominable Snowcreature* by Stephen Rudley (1946–).

About the B'nai Bagels (1969), written and illustrated by *E.L. Konigsburg, is a fine and very funny novel about family relationships

Baseball and family relationships are the main themes in *About the B'nai Bagels.*

and Little League baseball. Mark Setzer's mother, Bessie, belongs to the B'nai B'rith Sisterhood, and this year, the year of Mark's Bar Mitzvah, the Sisterhood is sponsoring a Little League team. Bessie Setzer, who talks to God in her kitchen, appoints herself team manager and names Mark's older brother, Spencer, as coach. At first Spencer is less than enthusiastic, but later he works hard to make a bunch of supposed losers into a good team, now known as the B'nai Bagels. With moral support from Aunt Thelma, Bessie and Spencer cope with choosing players and convincing them that a Jewish mother can be a wise and aggressive manager. The team does well under Spencer's excellent coaching, and Mark is not shown any favoritism by his brother or his mother. There are, however, social situations that require delicate handling by Mark, as well as a serious moral decision to be made by the Setzers just when they would prefer to be celebrating the team's success. Older readers will enjoy *The Chosen*, by *Chaim Potok, a novel about Jewish life in which baseball plays an important role. MR & YA

abracadabra The magician steps on stage, shows his audience what appears to be a plain square of silk cloth. He also shows the audience his hand. It is empty. Then he places the cloth over his hand. "Abracadabra!" he exclaims as he whisks the cloth away, and he is holding a white rabbit. Producing the rabbit is a magi-

cian's trick, and "abracadabra" is a magician's mysterious and meaningless word, supposed to have magical powers. If you decide to have a magic show, "abracadabra" is a handy word to know. You can be sure *Mary Poppins knew the word, and so did *Merlin, the great sorcerer of *King Arthur's days. See also *Open, Sesame!

Abraham In the Old Testament of the *Bible, Abraham, who lived in the early second millennium B.C., was the first patriarch and the founder of the ancient Hebrew nation. He emigrated from Mesopotamia to Canaan (ancient Palestine). Here he had two sons, *Ishmael and *Isaac, half brothers. He made a covenant with God, Who promised protection for Abraham's people; Abraham in turn promised that in the future all male children would be circumcised. Abraham later was tested by God, Who ordered him to sacrifice Isaac. He was about to obey, and, as the Bible says, "put forth his hand and took the knife to slay his son." Suddenly an angel ordered him to stop, as he had proved his great faith. In return for Abraham's willingness to sacrifice his son, God promised to bless Abraham and his descendants ever after.

Absalom (fl. c.1620 B.C.) The third and favorite son of *David, king of Israel, Absalom rebelled and attempted to seize the throne by force. Fleeing on a mule from the king's army after a battle, his head became entangled in an oak tree. Finding him there, Joab, commander of David's army and noted as a cruel man, killed Absalom by thrusting three darts into his heart, though the king had instructed him to spare his son's life. According to the *Bible, David mourned: "O my son Absalom, my son, my son Absalom! Would I had died instead of you, O Absalom, my son, my son." This lament became a classic expression of paternal grief. *Absalom, Absalom!* is the title of a novel by William Faulkner. YA

Absalom, Absalom! (1936), a novel by *William Faulkner, is the complex and disturbing history of Thomas Sutpen and his obsessive ambition to possess a plantation and an aristocratic family. Sutpen mysteriously appears in Jefferson, *Yoknapatawpha County, Mississippi, in 1833, bringing no baggage and causing rumors to fly about his unknown origin. He buys 100 square miles of land, later called Sutpen's Hundred, and gradually builds a fine mansion. Sutpen lives a strange and rough sort of life and later coldly plans to acquire respectability by marrying the daughter of one of Jefferson's prominent citizens. From his marriage to Ellen Coldfield come two children, Henry and Judith. It is revealed that Sutpen has another son, Charles Bon, from his union with a West Indian woman he abandoned after discovering she was partly black. Judith, who knows nothing of this, becomes engaged to Charles. Charles is later murdered by his half-brother, Henry, and Henry vanishes from the plantation. After Ellen's death, Sutpen plans to marry her sister, Rosa, in the hope of producing another heir. Outraged, Rosa refuses him and spends the rest of her life brooding and alone. At the end, little remains of the family beyond memories of their tangled relationships.

More than 50 years later, the story is retold by several narrators, each having a different viewpoint. The events gather intensity from repetition and from the narrator's efforts to make sense out of the bizarre and turbulent past. Quentin Compson, grandson of an old friend of Thomas Sutpen, hears a bitter account from Rosa Coldfield, now an old woman, and another from his father. The story is also shared with Shreve McCannon, Quentin's roommate at Harvard, because Quentin sees it, finally, as a portrait of a degraded and ruined South. Quentin Compson and his family are the central figures in Faulkner's novel *The Sound and the Fury. YA

Achebe, Chinua (1930–) A Nigerian poet, novelist, and short-story writer, Chinua Achebe chronicles the changing political and social climate in Africa. His memories of the Nigerian Civil War (1967–1970), in which he worked for the Biafran government, have been expressed in his short story "Girls at War" (1972) and a volume of verse, *Beware, Soul Brother* (1972). His novels include *Things Fall Apart*, perhaps his best-known book; *No Longer at Ease* (1961), about a young Nigerian from a small village whose desire to succeed in the city leads him into corruption and tragedy; *Arrow of God* (1967), set in Nigeria in 1921, about the clash between Nigerian tradition and colonial European culture; and *A Man of the People* (1966), about political corruption in a newly independent African nation. For younger readers, Achebe has written *Chike and the River* (1966), about the life of a young Nigerian boy, and *The Flute* (1978), retelling an African folktale. MR & YA

Achilles was known as the mightiest warrior of the Greeks in the *Trojan War. He was the son of Peleus, king of Phthia, and the immortal sea-nymph Thetis. When Achilles was born, Thetis dipped him into the magical river Styx, making his body invulnerable except for the heel by which she held him. Knowing that her son was fated to die if he went to war, Thetis tried to protect Achilles from military service by disguising him as a girl. When the ruse was discovered by Odysseus, however, Achilles eagerly volunteered to serve in the war. When he was 15 years old, he was made admiral of the Greek fleet. Later, a great quarrel erupted between *Agamemnon and Achilles. Agamemnon had seized Briseïs, a young woman whom Achilles had captured. Unjustly deprived of Briseïs, Achilles left the battle and refused to fight. Only after his beloved friend Patroclus was killed by the Trojan leader Hector did Achilles return to battle, eventually killing Hector. Achilles was killed soon after by the Trojan prince Paris, who shot him in the heel with a poisoned arrow. Thus, the phrase "Achilles heel" means a person's weak or vulnerable spot. The legend of Achilles has inspired many literary works, and over the years he has played an important part in many famous tragedies. You can read about Achilles in *Bulfinch's Mythology* by Thomas Bulfinch (1796–1867) and *Mythology* by Edith Hamilton (1867–1963), and also in *The Siege and Fall of Troy* (1962) by *Robert Graves. MR

Across Five Aprils (1964), by *Irene Hunt, is a sober and well-written historical novel about a southern Illinois farm family, set during the long years of the Civil War (1861–1865). Historical details were carefully researched, and the story of the Creighton family was drawn from stories told by the author's grandfather.

Matt and Ellen Creighton have had 12 children, of whom eight survive. Two of the older sons join the Union Army, together with their cousin Eb and their close friend Shadrach, the local schoolmaster. Bill, another son, considered a little odd because of his interest in book-learning, decides that his loyalties lie with the South. He leaves quietly to fight for what his neighbors consider the enemy, and his decision puts his family in a difficult position. When Matt becomes ill, the responsibility for running the farm is borne mostly by 10-year-old Jethro, who quickly learns to do a man's work. The family hears news of the great leaders of the time and echoes of the terrible battles fought at places like Fredericksburg and Chancellorsville. They suffer the loss of one son and the disappearance of another. Fighting their own battle for survival, they help each other and grow closer as a family. More fortunate than some, most of the Creightons are reunited at the end of the war, determined to rebuild their lives. If you enjoyed this book, other Civil War novels you may like are *Jed by *Peter Burchard and *The Perilous Road* (1958) by *William O. Steele. MR & YA

Act One (1959) is a memoir by *Moss Hart, for years one of the most notable figures in American theater. It is a funny, honest, well-written, insightful, and completely engrossing account of life on and around the stage. It tells of a boyhood spent in grinding poverty and dominated by a tyrannical grandfather. It describes Hart's experiences with small theater groups, his years as a summer social director at resort hotels in the Catskills, and the beginning of his long association with *George S. Kaufman,

who was 15 years older than Hart and already well established in his theatrical career. About half the memoir is given to the preparations for *Once in a Lifetime* (1930), Hart's first comedy written in collaboration with Kaufman. It provides a unique view of the struggle to work and rework a script into something vivid and meaningful and, in this case, enormously successful. *Act One* was filmed in 1963. YA

Adam and Eve are the parents of the human race as told in *Genesis, the first book of the *Bible. Tempted by the serpent to eat of "the forbidden fruit," Eve then tempted her husband, Adam. Thus they were driven out of the Garden of *Eden. Adam and Eve are representative of human limitations, and, according to Genesis, they are the source by which sin entered into the world. Adam and Eve were the parents of Cain, Abel, and Seth.

Adam Dalgliesh The fictional British detective created by *P.D. James, Dalgliesh is very much the modern, unassuming, intelligent police detective. He is also a published poet. A widower whose wife and son died in childbirth, he has ever since been somewhat withdrawn but nevertheless has charm and the ability to get people to reveal their secrets to him. In the course of James's books, he moves from inspector to chief inspector and to the rank of commander of Scotland Yard. He is introduced in James's first detective novel, *Cover Her Face. In *The Black Tower* (1975), Dalgliesh, recovering from mononucleosis, goes to the Dorset coast, where he becomes involved in solving a murder at a home for the handicapped. In *Devices and Desires* (1990), he is in Norfolk winding up the affairs of a deceased aunt who has left him a fortune and a converted windmill. Murder involving the personnel of a nuclear power station puts him to work. It is also revealed that his latest volume of poetry, *A Case to Answer and Other Poems*, has recently been published. Dalgliesh sometimes seems a bit aloof, but he is devoted to seeing justice done without any unnecessary vengeance. Television miniseries have been made of several Dalgliesh stories. If you like him, you will enjoy the books of *Margery Allingham, *Martha Grimes, and *Ruth Rendell. YA

Adam of the Road (1942) was written by *Elizabeth Janet Gray, who re-creates the world of 13th-century England in a story about an 11-year-old boy, Adam. Roger Quartermayne, Adam's father, takes Adam and Nick, the boy's pet dog, on a journey to London, where he will serve as minstrel to Sir Edmund. On the way, Roger tells his son, "A road's a kind of holy thing. . . . And it's home to a minstrel, even though he may happen to be sleeping in a castle."

After spending a short time with Sir Edmund, Adam and his father are no longer needed. By foot, they travel the open roads heading for "the greatest fair in England." As the journey progresses, Nick is stolen by an evil minstrel. In Adam's desperate search for his dog, he becomes separated from his father too. Now Adam is alone, searching the fairs and market towns for his father and dog. After a long chain of adventures involving farmers, pilgrims, priests, rich merchants, saints, and thieves, Adam is reunited with his father and beloved dog. *Adam of the Road* won a *Newbery Medal in 1943. MR

Adams, Abigail (1744–1818) A remarkable writer of letters, her voluminous and entertaining correspondence provides a record of life in the early days of the United States, as well as a portrait of an unusually happy marriage. Abigail was the wife of John Adams (1735–1826), second President of the United States, and the mother of the sixth President, John Quincy Adams (1767–1848). The daughter of a well-to-do minister, Abigail was educated at home by her grandmother and learned at an early age to write letters to friends and relatives. After their marriage in 1764, John Adams's responsibilities obliged him to spend much of his time away from home. For almost 10 years, Abigail raised their four children, managed her husband's business affairs with great skill, and

found time to write letters. These described details of everyday life and contain Abigail's observations on many subjects, written in spirited and forthright language. Her letters show an extraordinary awareness of history and political change and express her steadfast opposition to slavery and her strong interest in improving educational opportunities for women. Some of her most remarkable and endearing letters are collected in *The Book of Abigail and John: Selected Letters of the Adams Family, 1762–1784* (1975). YA

Adams, Douglas (1952–) is the author of the popular science fiction humor series that begins with *The Hitchhiker's Guide to the Galaxy* (1979). This novel tells of the bizarre adventures of Arthur Dent, a contemporary Englishman who finds himself hitchhiking through outer space. His only guide is a reference book called *The Hitchhiker's Guide to the Galaxy*, which is filled with crazy advice and humorous philosophies. If you enjoyed this volume, read more of Arthur Dent's strange and funny adventures in the rest of the series, which includes *The Restaurant at the End of the Universe* (1980); *Life, the Universe, and Everything* (1982); and *So Long, and Thanks for All the Fish* (1985). Adams has also worked as a writer on the British television comedy show *Monty Python's Flying Circus*. MR & YA

Adams, Richard (1920–) A popular British adult novelist, Adams is also known for his verse and fiction for children. His adventure stories are often set in the world of an animal, such as a rabbit or dog. His first novel, *Watership Down*, was originally published as a children's book, but became a worldwide best seller among adults. His other novels include *Shardik*, about man's belief in a supernatural bear-god; *The Plague Dogs* (1978), in which two badly injured dogs escape from an animal experimentation laboratory; *The Girl in a Swing* (1980), about the marriage of a quiet Englishman to a mysterious and beautiful German woman; and *Maia* (1985), about the heroic adventures of a poor girl sold to a rich nobleman. Among his works for younger readers is *The Tyger Voyage* (1976), a story in verse about two tigers who set out in a small boat on a wonderful adventure. MR & YA

Adoff, Arnold (1935–) A poet, Adoff is also the editor of several anthologies of poetry and prose, including *I Am the Darker Brother: An Anthology of Modern Poems by Negro Americans* (1968), *The Poetry of Black America: Anthology of the 20th Century* (1973), and, for younger readers, *My Black Me* (1974). Adoff was born and raised in a Jewish section of New York. When he began teaching in a Harlem school, he was unable to find works that related to the experiences of his black students. Adoff filled this need by collecting literature that is expressive of black themes and culture. Since then, he has written numerous books, including *Malcolm X* (1970), *MA nDA LA* (1971), *Black Is Brown Is Tan* (1973), and *Tornado!* (1977). MR & YA

Adonis is a Greek god famous for his overwhelming beauty. He was born from the incestuous love of Myrrha for her father, the king of Cyprus. To save Myrrha from her father's wrath, the gods turn her into a tree. Ten months later, the bark of the tree bursts open and Adonis emerges. The goddess *Aphrodite falls in love with the beautiful child and entrusts him to *Persephone for safekeeping. After raising Adonis, however, Persephone refuses to give him back. *Zeus then decrees that Adonis should spend four months each year with Persephone and the rest of the year with Aphrodite. An avid hunter, Adonis is killed by a wild boar. The story of Adonis has given rise to many legends about flowers. For instance, when Adonis is killed by the boar, his blood sprouts roses, and from Aphrodite's tears of sadness spring anemones. You can read about Adonis in *Bulfinch's Mythology* by Thomas Bulfinch (1796–1867) or in *Mythology* by Edith Hamilton (1867–1963). You might like to read *Venus and Adonis* (1593), a long poem by *William Shakespeare. MR & YA

Aeneas, carrying his father, flees with his wife and son from burning Troy, in *The Aeneid*.

Adopted One, The (1979) An honest and sensitive look at adoption by Sara Bonnett Stein (n.d.), this book uses two separate print styles on each page. The boldface print is geared for a child to read. It tells about a young adopted boy named Joshua who questions his adoptive parents about his biological parents. As the story of Joshua unfolds, it covers a variety of concerns, such as his fears of abandonment, feelings of rejection, and questions about the day of his birth. Adjacent to Joshua's story is another, more detailed text that provides answers to crucial questions or discusses important problems that may arise in a family with an adopted child. Vivid black-and-white photographs of Joshua and his adoptive parents accompany the text. MR

Adrian Mole See *The Secret Diary of Adrian Mole, Aged 13¾.*

Adventures of Augie March, The See
*Augie March, The Adventures of.

Adventures of Huckleberry Finn, The See
*Huckleberry Finn, The Adventures of.

Adventures of Tom Sawyer, The See *Tom
Sawyer, The Adventures of.

Aeneid (c.19 B.C.) One of the most famous
works in Latin literature, this epic poem by
*Virgil is still celebrated for the music of its
verse and the grandeur of its subject. The first
six books are modeled on the *Odyssey of
*Homer, while the remaining six use elements
from the *Iliad. Virgil's heroic poem, however,
is a completely original work that speaks of
the founding of the Roman race, and is a tribute to the later glory of the Roman Empire
under the rule of Augustus (63 B.C.–A.D. 14).

Aeneas, hero of the *Trojan War, arrives at
Carthage with his followers after a voyage beset by violent winds and roaring hurricanes.
He is warmly received by Queen Dido. Aeneas
recounts the fall of Troy, the story of the device
of the Trojan horse, his escape from the burning city, and further adventures with his band
of exiles. Dido falls deeply in love with
Aeneas, but he knows he is destined to continue his voyage. The heartbroken queen kills
herself when Aeneas sets sail once more. In
Sicily, where his father, Anchises, died, Aeneas
arranges elaborate games in Anchises' honor. In
Book VI, Aeneas is allowed to visit his father in
the infernal regions of Hades, where his
father's spirit shows him the future of his race
and the building of a new nation. After another
voyage Aeneas reaches Latium, where King
Latinus offers Aeneas his daughter Lavinia in
marriage. Turnus, the princess's betrothed, is
enraged at being rejected in favor of Aeneas and
makes war against Aeneas and Latinus. Great
battles are waged, but Aeneas finally engages
Turnus in single combat and kills him. Victorious, Aeneas marries Lavinia and prepares to
found Rome. You might enjoy the fine new
translation of the Aeneid (1983) by Robert
Fitzgerald (1910–). See also *hell. YA

This woodcut of Aesop was made by William
Caxton (1422?–1491), the first English printer.

Aeschylus (525–456 B.C.) was a Greek dramatist. He is the earliest playwright whose works
have been preserved. Only 7 of his 90 tragedies
have survived in their complete form, including Prometheus Bound (date of composition
unknown), about the hero *Prometheus, who
is cruelly punished by *Zeus for stealing fire
and giving it to mortals. His other plays include The Persians (472 B.C.), a historical play
about the Greek defeat of the Persians at Salamis in 480 B.C., and the Oresteia (458 B.C.), a
trilogy of plays—Agamemnon, The Libation
Bearers, and The Furies—about the tragic
events that befall *Agamemnon and, later, his
son *Orestes. Besides being a respected playwright, Aeschylus also served as a soldier in
the Persian wars. See also *Electra. YA

Aesop (c.620–c.560 B.C.) was a Greek writer of
famous *fables in which talking animals, and
occasionally the elements, portray human

strengths, weaknesses, and follies. Some of his most famous fables are "The Hare and the Tortoise," "The Boy Who Cried Wolf," and "The Ant and the Grasshopper." The fables are written in a simple style that aims to instruct, and they conclude with a proverb summing up the fable's moral. Today, many figures of speech come from Aesop's fables, such as "sour grapes" and "the boy who cried wolf." See also *Jean de La Fontaine. MR & YA

African Queen, The (1935) Written by *C.S. Forester, this exciting novel is set in Central Africa in 1914, and concerns Rose Sayer, an English missionary, and a timid cockney engineer, Charles Allnutt. As World War I spills into Central Africa, it draws these two lonely people into unforeseen adventures and romance. After the death of Rose's brother, the Reverend Samuel Sayer, German troops force the Africans in their remote village to become soldiers against England. Rose is left alone and unable to continue her missionary work. Allnutt arrives at the desolate village and offers to take Rose aboard his small boat, *The African Queen.*

Rose, wanting to "strike a blow for England," tells the reluctant and fearful Allnutt of her plan to ride over the treacherous rapids and torpedo a German launch with homemade explosives. Though Rose and Allnutt face storms, bullets, heat, and leeches during their journey down the river, they find that their growing love for each other triumphs over all challenges. Finally, the German ship is destroyed, and Allnutt and Rose head for the coast to get married. The book was adapted for film in 1951, with a screenplay by *James Agee. YA

Agamemnon was the leader of the Greeks in the *Trojan War and a descendant of Atreus, a king of Mycenae. Before an expedition, Agamemnon slew a deer sacred to the goddess *Artemis. Furious, Artemis sent a great plague to the Greek camp. To appease her, Agamemnon was forced to sacrifice his daughter, *Iphigenia.

Reluctantly carrying out this task, Agamemnon lost a daughter and suffered the hatred of his wife, Clytemnestra. On his return home from the Trojan War, he brought his concubine, Cassandra. They were both murdered by Clytemnestra and her lover, Aegisthus. Later, Agamemnon's son, *Orestes, encouraged by his sister, *Electra, killed Clytemnestra to avenge his father's murder. You can read about Agamemnon in the *Iliad by *Homer and also in the play *Agamemnon* (458 B.C.) by *Aeschylus. YA

Age of Innocence, The (1920) By *Edith Wharton, this stylish and subtle novel is a fascinating portrait of life and character in New York high society during the 1870s. It exposes the severity of upper-class social conventions. Newland Archer, a wealthy young lawyer, becomes engaged to May Welland, a young woman of impeccable background. Archer's well-ordered life is disturbed when he meets May's cousin, the countess Ellen Olenska, an attractive woman whose reputation is compromised because she left her profligate husband. Archer, his mother, and Ellen's grandmother do what they can to help Ellen gain social acceptance. In the process, Archer finds himself attracted to her unusual qualities of mind and her apparent lack of interest in doing what is expected of her. Archer and Ellen fall deeply in love, but Archer cannot bring himself to reject May and fly in the face of convention. Archer and May are married, though he still dreams of a future in which, somehow, Ellen will be his wife. Unwilling to remain in a situation she finds hopeless and painful, Ellen leaves for Paris after learning that May is expecting a child. Years later, after May's death, Archer is invited to visit Ellen with his grown son. Rather than risk his emotions and his ideal memory of her, he sends the young man in his place. Another novel about old New York is *Washington Square, by Edith Wharton's close friend *Henry James. *The Age of Innocence* was filmed in 1934. YA

Agee, James (1909–1955) Author of novels, screenplays, film reviews, and critical essays, he wrote for *Time* magazine, *Fortune*, and *The Nation*. Two years after graduating from Harvard University, he published a volume of poetry, *Permit Me Voyage* (1934). His first novel, *The Morning Watch* (1954), was based on his own boyhood experiences at St. Andrew's, an Episcopal boarding school in Tennessee, in the 1920s. This compact but powerful novel was published one year prior to Agee's death. His fame came posthumously with his novel *A Death in the Family*. One of his best-known works, *Let Us Now Praise Famous Men* (1941), a commentary on rural poverty in the South, was praised for Agee's sensitive portrayal of the people he met, not as examples of poverty, but as human beings like everyone else. The book was also hailed for its brilliant photographs by Walker Evans (1903–1975). YA

Agony of Alice, The (1985) This witty novel, by *Phyllis Reynolds Naylor, is about an 11-year-old motherless girl named Alice McKinley. Though Alice loves her father and older brother, she decides that she must find a beautiful woman to have as a role model. She selects the gorgeous young sixth-grade teacher, Miss Cole. When the school semester begins, Alice is distraught to find herself placed in the class of homely Mrs. Plotkin. At first, Alice resents Mrs. Plotkin and causes all sorts of mischief, such as snoring in class or mimicking Mrs. Plotkin's voice.

As one of her first assignments, Alice is required to keep a journal of her thoughts and feelings. She writes down all the embarrassing things that happen to her and expresses her desire for a role model to help her grow up. As the school year progresses, Alice learns that the gorgeous Miss Cole is rather superficial and insensitive, and that the frumpy Mrs. Plotkin is both loving and generous. She learns that it is better to know a person's heart than to judge them by their appearance. By the end of the novel, Alice has grown into a wiser and more confident teenager, but not without a helping hand from the unlikely Mrs. Plotkin. Another good book about a girl who adopts a teacher as a role model is *Like Mother, Like Daughter* (1985) by Marion Dane Bauer (1938–). MR

Ahab and **Jezebel** Ahab was king of Israel (c.874–c.853 B.C.) and his wife, Jezebel, was a daughter of the king of Sidon, a city-state whose seaport still exists in present-day Lebanon. As told in the *Bible, Ahab's rule was a mixture of success and disaster. His relations with foreign states brought him prestige and strengthened Israel. Jezebel, however, caused him much trouble. She worshipped *Baal and tried to force this foreign god on Israel. When Ahab was unsuccessful in trying to buy the vineyard of a neighbor, Naboth, she had the latter killed. Jezebel warred with the country's prophets, especially *Elijah, who frequently denounced her. In the end, Ahab was slain in battle and Jezebel was killed by a successor of Ahab who had her thrown out of a window. The name Jezebel, sometimes in the form of "painted Jezebel," has come to stand for a wicked woman, one of loose morals. Ahab is the name of the obsessed captain of the *Pequod* in the novel *Moby-Dick* by *Herman Melville. YA

Aiken, Joan (1924–) Author of numerous books for adults and more than 35 books for young readers, Aiken was born in Rye, England, and is the daughter of the American poet Conrad Aiken (1888–1973). She began to write when she was 5 years old, and her first works of poetry and short stories were published when she was in her teens. Her books, which combine mystery, adventure, humor, and imagination, include such classics as *The Wolves of Willoughby Chase, *Black Hearts in Battersea, *The Kingdom Under the Sea, and *Nightbirds on Nantucket* (1966), about an English girl who is rescued at sea by the skipper of an American whaling ship on a quest for a great pink whale and is brought back to Nantucket Island, where she becomes involved in a hilarious mystery. Aiken lives in Sussex, England, and in New York City. MR

Aladdin, a character in one of the tales in *The Arabian Nights' Entertainments*, is the son of a poor widow. Because he comes into possession of a magical ring and lamp, he becomes the master of the "jinns," the two powerful slaves of the ring and lamp. With their help, Aladdin can fulfill any desire. He acquires great wealth and is made a sultan. MR & YA

albatross is the name of several kinds of large seabirds. The most famous albatross in literature appears in the poem *The Rime of the Ancient Mariner* by *Samuel Taylor Coleridge. Long ago, sailors believed that killing an albatross brought bad luck, and this is what happened in the poem by Coleridge. The phrase "to have an albatross around one's neck" means to carry about a burden of guilt or bad luck. The albatross is also known as the "gooney bird." YA

Albee, Edward (1928–) An American playwright, Albee was adopted at birth by Frances and Reed Albee, the millionaire owner of a chain of theaters. He grew up in New York City and its suburbs. Unhappy with his adoptive parents, Albee was labeled a problem child and sent to boarding school. Later, he left Trinity College, Connecticut, after a year and a half and settled in Greenwich Village, New York City, where he worked at a variety of jobs and struggled to make ends meet. His first one-act play, *The Zoo Story* (1959), about an alienated young man who provokes an older man into killing him with his own knife, won an award. Another popular one-act play is *The American Dream* (1961), an absurdist comedy about the loss of human values in the rise of modern American consumer society. Albee's first full-length play and his best-known work is *Who's Afraid of Virginia Woolf?* Other works are *A Delicate Balance* (1966), centering on the empty lives of an aging suburban couple, and *Seascape* (1975), about a couple who meet two

humanoid sea creatures while picnicking at the shore. Albee has also written stage adaptations of various works, such as *The Ballad of the Sad Cafe* (1951), a novella by *Carson McCullers about a lonely woman's search for love, in 1963, and *Lolita* (1955), a novel by Vladimir Nabokov (1899–1977) about the relationship between a teenage girl and an older man, in 1981. YA

Alcock, Vivien (1924–) An English novelist and commercial artist, Alcock is the author of *Travelers by Night* and several other popular novels of adventure and the supernatural. Her first novel, *The Haunting of Cassie Palmer* (1980), concerns the 13-year-old daughter of a medium and her psychic abilities. *The Stonewalkers* (1981) is a supernatural tale about two girls and some frightening developments when a group of statues come to life during a thunderstorm. In *The Mysterious Mr. Ross* (1987), 12-year-old Felicity saves a strange young man from the ocean and becomes something of a notable in her little English town. If you enjoy Alcock's books, you may also like the novels of *Mollie Hunter, *Margaret Mahy, and *Richard Peck. MR

Alcott, Louisa May (1832–1888) The author of children's classics, including the famous *Little Women, Alcott was born in Philadelphia, Pennsylvania. During her childhood, her family moved to Boston, Massachusetts. There she was educated by her father, Amos Bronson Alcott (1799–1888), a pioneer in American education, and by his friends *Ralph Waldo Emerson and *Henry David Thoreau. Her first book, *Flower Fables* (1854), was a collection of tales written for Emerson's daughter. Alcott's poems and short stories were published in magazines, and when she was a nurse during the Civil War, her letters were published as *Hospital Sketches* (1863). As a sequel to *Little Women*, Alcott wrote *Little Men* (1871), based on her happy days in Concord, Massachusetts.

Other works include *An Old-Fashioned Girl* (1870), about a young girl striving to earn a living in Boston. *Eight Cousins* (1875) concerns a little girl who has seven boy-cousins and an unconventional uncle, and *A Garland for Girls* (1888) is a collection of short stories about girls who struggle to earn their living. Alcott spent much of her life writing from her home in Concord and traveling through Europe. MR

Alden, John (1599?–1687) and **Alden, Priscilla** (1602?–1686?) were among the first Pilgrims in America. John Alden, who was a barrelmaker in England when he enlisted for the *Mayflower* voyage, was the first Pilgrim to set foot on Plymouth Rock and the last surviving signer of the Mayflower Compact. According to legend, Alden married Priscilla Mullens after failing to convince her to marry his best friend, Miles Standish (1584?–1656). In 1627, Alden and Standish established Duxbury, near Plymouth in Massachusetts, and helped each other defend the settlement against Indian attacks. John Alden held numerous public offices, including the position of assistant governor of the Plymouth colony for 44 years. You will want to read about John and Priscilla in *The Courtship of Miles Standish, one of *Henry Wadsworth Longfellow's most popular poems. YA

Aldiss, Brian W(ilson) (1925–) A popular English author of science fiction, Aldiss is also a leading science fiction critic. He is known best for the epic saga The Helliconia Trilogy, consisting of the novels *Helliconia Spring* (1982), *Helliconia Summer* (1983), and *Helliconia Winter* (1985), in which Aldiss invented a new solar system with its own religions, cultures, and history. Part of Aldiss's success rests on his ability to convince the reader of the reality of fantastic situations and alien environments and cultures. His other works include *The Long Afternoon of Earth* (1962), set in the distant future, when humans have adapted to the dying planet by living in the branches of an immense tree; *Greybeard* (1964), in which humanity has been doomed to extinction by biological weapons; and *Frankenstein Unbound* (1973), about a man who is transported back in time to meet the English novelist Mary Shelley (1797–1851) and her fictional creation, *Frankenstein*. Aldiss also wrote a celebrated and highly readable history of science fiction, *Billion Year Spree* (1973), which was revised and updated as *Trillion Year Spree* (1986). His partly autobiographical mainstream novels, *The Hand-Reared Boy* (1970) and *A Soldier Erect* (1971), were international best sellers. YA

Aldrich, Bess Streeter (1881–1954) Author of *Miss Bishop, Aldrich lived in and wrote about the Middle West, and became a full-time writer in an attempt to support her four children after her husband died. Most of Aldrich's writings are romantic and optimistic, ending on a happy note. Among her most popular works are *A Lantern in Her Hand* (1928), the story of a pioneer woman in Nebraska, and *The Lieutenant's Lady* (1942), which is about a young woman living in Nebraska just after the Civil War who falls in love with her cousin's fiancé. If you enjoy Aldrich's books, you will also like those of *Willa Cather and *Zona Gale. YA

Aldrich, Thomas Bailey (1836–1907) A novelist, poet, and editor, he was born in Portsmouth, New Hampshire, a setting he later used in his most popular novel for younger readers, *The Story of a Bad Boy* (1870). Based on recollections of his boyhood, it is an energetic and vivid account of grammar school days and of adventures with a gang of boys called the Rivermouth Centipedes. Ten of his short stories are collected in *Marjorie Daw and Other People* (1873). In the title story, one of Aldrich's most famous works, a man writes letters to amuse a sick friend. His descriptions of an imaginary woman are so enchanting that the friend falls in love and insists on meeting the nonexistent Marjorie Daw. Of Aldrich's other novels, you might like *The Stillwater Tragedy* (1880), a detective story involving the murder of wealthy man, set against a background of labor disputes in a small New England town. MR & YA

Aleichem, Sholem (Sholom or Shalom) [Solomon Rabinowitz] (1859–1916) A Russian-born American humorist who wrote stories of Jewish life in Yiddish, Aleichem created odd yet good-natured characters who prize learning

MR = Middle Reader   YA = Young Adult Reader   * = See this main entry

over wealth. Among his collection of sketches is *Tevye the Dairyman* (1895–1899), which was later dramatized in New York's Yiddish Theater in 1919 and in the Broadway musical *Fiddler on the Roof* in 1964. Other popular works include the collection of sketches *Mottel, the Cantor's Son* (1907–1916) and the play *Hard to Be a Jew* (1914). If you like his books, you will also like the works of another great author in Yiddish, *Isaac Bashevis Singer. Many of Aleichem's stories have been made into Russian films, and a dramatization of a few of his stories, *The World of Sholom Aleichem*, was successfully staged in 1953. YA

Alexander, Lloyd (1924–) Born in Philadelphia, Pennsylvania, Alexander is the author of many *fantasy novels. As a young man, he joined the army and was eventually sent to Wales. Years later, his experiences in Wales influenced some of his work, such as the *Prydain Cycle. Among his chivalric fantasy stories are *The Marvelous Misadventures of Sebastian* (1970), about an out-of-work court fiddler who finds a violin with magical powers; *The First Two Lives of Lukas-Kasha* (1978), about a young rogue who finds himself king of Abadan, in Persia, and is plunged into a world of intrigue and adventure; and *The Illyrian Adventure* (1986), about a fearless young girl who sets out to find a legendary treasure. Though his novels are filled with fantasy, the characters often express moral truths. MR & YA

Al(exandra) the Great (1982) By *Constance C. Greene, this is the fourth novel about the adventures of Al and her best friend, who live in the same apartment building in New York City. It is a hot, sticky summer and Al has been invited to spend three weeks with her father, his new wife, Louise, and their family on their farm in Ohio. Al is excited, but her best friend feels a bit jealous and left out. When Al's mother becomes ill with pneumonia, however, Al decides to call off her trip. While Al's mother is in the hospital, her best friend's family takes care of her. Through the experience, Al and her friend learn important

lessons about friendship, sacrifice, and love. If you enjoyed *Al(exandra) the Great*, you can read more about Al and her friend in *Just Plain Al*. MR

Alfred Summer, The (1980) Written by Jan Slepian (1921–), this is a poignant novel about a 14-year-old boy named Lester who has cerebral palsy. He spends all his time with his mother, has no friends, and feels like an outcast. This unhappy situation changes when Lester meets Alfred, a young mentally retarded boy who does not seem to notice that Lester has cerebral palsy. Through Alfred, Lester meets Myron, a gawky 13-year-old who is building a boat in his basement. Later, a tomboyish, tough girl named Claire also joins their clique. Together they help Myron complete the boat, and, in the process, they build a powerful bond with each other.

As the summer progresses, Alfred develops epilepsy and must be hospitalized. The three now realize how much Alfred has helped them learn to accept themselves. Out of appreciation, they name their boat *The Alfred*. On the day Myron launches the boat, their parents and neighbors congregate on the beach. In a few terrible moments, the boat sinks. When Myron swims back to shore, he faces an uproar of laughter. Incredibly, he is able to laugh at himself and change the mood of the crowd from ridicule to appreciation. At this moment, Lester realizes how much stronger, more self-accepting, and less bitter they have all become during the course of this very important summer. MR

Alger, Horatio (1832–1899) Author of more than 130 inspirational novels for boys on the rags-to-riches theme, Alger was born the son of a Unitarian minister. In 1864, Alger also became a minister. Two years later, he left his church and settled in New York City, where he became involved with the Newsboys' Lodging House, a shelter for young orphan boys. These children later became character models for his stories. The first was *Ragged Dick, or, Street Life in New York with the Boot-blacks* (1868),

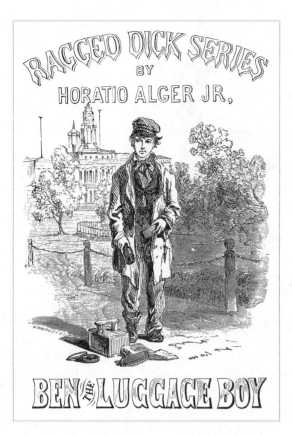

Ben is the hero of a book in the Ragged Dick series named after Dick, a shoe shine boy.

the story of a boy who works hard and aspires to an office job. Though he has to overcome bad habits, like smoking and gambling, Dick achieves his goal after he is able to save the son of a well-to-do merchant from drowning. He is rewarded with a clerk's job at the then fine salary of $10 a week. *Ragged Dick* was the first in a series of similar novels that ended with *Rufus and Rose* (1870). Other novel series were *Luck and Pluck* (beginning in 1869) and *Tattered Tom* (beginning in 1871). These novels all present the typical Alger hero, who is able to attain fame, fortune, and success through hard work, honesty, and good luck, with coincidence playing no small role. Most of Alger's books are now out of print, but *Ragged Dick* and several others have been reissued over the years, and you can probably find some of them in your library. MR

Ali Baba is the hero of a story in *The Arabian Nights' Entertainments*. He is a Persian woodcutter who happens to overhear a group of 40 thieves using the magic password *"Open, Sesame!" in order to gain entrance to a secret cave. After they leave the cave, Ali Baba says the magic words, enters the cave, and finds great treasures stored inside. He takes as much as he can carry and goes home a very wealthy man. Enraged that Ali Baba has learned their secret, the thieves decide to kill him. Their plan of revenge fails because Ali Baba's beautiful slave, Morgiana, kills them. She is rewarded with the gift of her freedom and later marries Ali Baba's son.

Alice Adams (1921), by *Booth Tarkington, is the poignant and realistic story of a pretty, self-centered young woman who dreams of marrying a wealthy man and rising above her drab, lower-middle-class background. Alice's father, Virgil Adams, has worked all his life at Lamb and Company, without noticeable advancement, and her disappointed mother has long nagged Virgil to strike out on his own and earn more for the family. Without the advantages enjoyed by more affluent friends, Alice is beginning to be left out of the social whirl appropriate for a marriageable girl. She meets Arthur Russell, a handsome and likable bachelor newly arrived in town, and mounts a subtle campaign to attract his interest. Alice cleverly suggests that her origins are high-class, and Arthur finds her fascinating. The reality of her unappealing family is revealed to him, however, when he is invited to their home for dinner with disastrous results. For all her empty-headedness, Alice shows surprising courage in accepting Arthur's embarrassed retreat. Her fortitude is further tested when her brother Walter steals from Lamb and Company and Virgil fails in his attempt to start a business of his own. With Virgil's health ruined, Mrs. Adams is obliged to take in paying guests. Alice abandons her romantic dreams and enters business college to learn to support herself. Another novel whose heroine longs to rise in the world is *Miss Lulu Bett* by *Zona Gale. *Alice Adams* was adapted for film in 1935. YA

MR = Middle Reader   YA = Young Adult Reader   * = See this main entry

Alice wonders what is going on at "A Mad Tea-Party" in *Alice's Adventures in Wonderland*.

Alice's Adventures in Wonderland (1865) and ***Through the Looking-Glass: And What Alice Found There*** (1871), by *Lewis Carroll, are fantasies that have delighted people of all ages since their first appearance in print. They are a fascinating blend of childish fun, subtlety, and sophistication. In the first story, Alice falls asleep on a warm afternoon outdoors and dreams a series of whimsical and sometimes bothersome adventures. Following a White Rabbit down his hole into a different world underground, she undergoes some odd changes of size. Alice meets a number of very talkative animals, a remarkably ugly Duchess, a Cheshire Cat, and a host of characters that includes the March Hare, the Mad Hatter, and the irritable Queen of Hearts. The second story begins with a chess problem, in which Alice takes the role of a White Pawn, and the problem underlies the action of the story. Alice discovers she can pass through the large mirror in the family parlor into Looking-Glass Land. Except for its parlor, which looks exactly like Alice's, only reversed, the rest of the land is filled with unusual creatures, including living chess pieces. Alice discovers that the land is divided into giant squares, just like a chess board. After making friends with the White Queen and Red Queen, Alice begins her journey across Looking-Glass Land, at the end of which she will become a Queen herself. On the way, she meets many fascinating characters, including the Red King, who declares that Alice is just part of his dream; Humpty Dumpty; and *Tweedledum and Tweedledee. She also is told a number of poems, including the classic "Jabberwocky" and "The Walrus and the Carpenter," and has many adventures before awakening once more in her own parlor.

The Annotated Alice (1960) provides all the original text, the famous original illustrations by John Tenniel (1820–1914), and a running commentary by Martin Gardner (1914–). Gardner's notes will help you understand some of the many puzzles, jokes, and out-of-the-way references. If you enjoy these books, you should also try *The Wonderful Wizard of Oz* and its sequels by *L. Frank Baum. You will also like *The Phantom Tollbooth* (1961) by Norton Juster (1929–). There are several film versions of *Alice*, including a *Walt Disney animated cartoon made in 1951. MR & YA

Aliens in the Family (1985) By *Margaret Mahy, this lively novel combines science fiction and the story of a New Zealand family. Twelve-year-old Jake is visiting her father and the new family she acquired with her father's second marriage. Jake feels out of place with Dora, her own age, and 8-year-old Lewis, and she is uncomfortably aware that they are only pretending to accept her. In another space and time, young Bond, a member of the Galgonqua space travelers, is preparing to undergo a test that involves transforming himself into human form and journeying on a mission to earth. On earth he meets Dora, who helps him escape eerie and hostile forces, called the Wirdegen. Though Bond has been ordered not to reveal his origin, he admits to Dora, Jake, and Lewis that he is an alien being. Fascinated, the young people forget the difficulties of adjusting to each other while they try to help Bond. The story reaches its climax in a haunted volcanic valley where they witness a strange confrontation between forces from another time and Bond. If you enjoyed this book, you will also like the science fiction novels of *Robert Westall. MR

Alison's House (1930) is a play, by *Susan Glaspell, in which all the action takes place on the last day of the 19th century. Mr. Stanhope is preparing to sell the family home. His elderly spinster sister, Agatha, who has lived there all her life, will stay with him in town. The house is famous as the home of Stanhope's other sister, Alison, a poet of great renown. Although Alison Stanhope has been dead for some years, her presence is almost as real as that of the family members who remember her. Among these are Stanhope's sons, Eben and Ted, and his daughter, Elsa. Added to Stanhope's reluctance to sell the house is the distress caused by Elsa's scandalous liaison with a married man. While the family sorts through objects, books, and papers that belonged to Alison, Agatha gives a small portfolio to Elsa in private. The ailing old lady dies suddenly before Elsa can examine it. Later the portfolio is found to contain unpublished poems by Alison, the intimate expression of her love for a married man—a love she renounced to avoid hurting others. Agatha's death and the discovery of the poems cause the Stanhopes to reexamine their family relationships. Another,

rather different story about a famous poet's personal writings is *The Aspern Papers* by *Henry James. YA

All Creatures Great and Small (1972), by *James Herriot, is the autobiography of an animal doctor who has spent most of his professional life in the Yorkshire Dales of northern England. This collection of stories, beautifully told in a clean, easygoing, and unpretentious style, begins when Herriot is hired by Siegfried Farnon, a veterinary surgeon already established in the small town of Darrowby, and ends gloriously with Herriot's marriage to the lovely Helen Alderson. The personalities of Helen; Siegfried; his younger brother, Tristan; the imposing housekeeper, Mrs. Hall; and a fascinating array of Yorkshire farmers are revealed lovingly and with a generous sense of humor. It is Herriot's work and his love of life, however, that are the most important elements of the book. His dealings with animals, carried out in all kinds of weather and often at night, range from the hilarious and farcical, through modest triumphs, to great discoveries and tragic defeats. Sequels to the book are *All Things Bright and Beautiful* (1974), adapted for film in 1979 in Great Britain, and *All Things Wise and Wonderful* (1977). *All Creatures Great and Small* was the basis of a TV movie in 1974, as well as a highly successful British TV series that has since become popular in the U.S. YA

All Quiet on the Western Front (1928) is an unforgettable novel by the German author *Erich Maria Remarque. Not for the fainthearted, it has been called one of the greatest and most powerful books about war ever written. As an authentic, detailed description of the shocking brutality of trench warfare during World War I, it is probably unequaled. The narrator is Paul, an ordinary German soldier still in his teens, who records the horror, suffering, and uncertainty that become daily existence and that displace all memory of the past. Constantly on guard against the menace of death, Paul sees men transformed into unthinking creatures whose salvation lies in instinct and the emotional numbness that keeps them from going mad. After survival, only comradeship has any meaning. Paul thinks of his fellow soldiers as a great brotherhood, with the solidarity of convicts and the "desperate loyalty to one another of men condemned to death." To him, the sound of their familiar voices is the strongest and the most comforting thing there is. Paul is killed in October 1918, on a day so peaceful that the official military report reads "All quiet on the Western front." Another powerful antiwar novel is *Company K* (1933) by William March (1893–1954), which depicts the horrors of World War I through the eyes and words of the members of an American infantry company. *All Quiet on the Western Front* was filmed in 1930 and was adapted for a TV film in 1979. YA

All the King's Men (1946), by *Robert Penn Warren, is a splendid novel about a Southern politician in the 1930s, based in part on the life of Louisiana governor Huey Long (1893–1935). After a long struggle to educate himself and rise above his back-country origins, Willie Stark becomes governor of the state. Ambitious and opportunistic, Willie nevertheless wants to do great things for the ordinary people who elected him. He is helped by his wife, Lucy, a teacher, and later by Sadie Burke, an intense and politically knowledgeable woman who becomes his mistress. Stark's questionable and often ruthless methods are described by Jack Burden, a cynical former journalist who runs political errands for Stark in spite of the disapproval of Jack's aristocratic mother and her old friend Judge Irwin. Because Irwin, a former attorney general, refuses to honor a promise to the governor, Willie tells Jack to uncover secrets in the judge's past that can be used to blackmail him. During the search Jack meets his old friend Adam Stanton, now a successful and high-minded surgeon, and his sister, Anne, with whom Jack was once in love. The Stantons also come under Willie's spell. Anne becomes his mistress and is instrumental in persuading Adam to head a new hospital project for Willie. Jack finds evidence against

Judge Irwin, but Irwin kills himself rather than give in to Willie's tactics. Jack then learns from his distraught mother that the judge was his father. Adam Stanton, desperate after learning about Anne's affair with Willie, shoots the governor in the lobby of the capitol building and is himself killed by a bodyguard. Jack later comes to terms with the confusions of his past and marries Anne, having found that "all knowledge that is worth anything is maybe paid for by blood." An excellent film version of the novel appeared in 1949. YA

All the President's Men (1974) is the story of Watergate, one of the most devastating political scandals in American history. The authors, Carl Bernstein (1944–) and Bob Woodward (1945–), are newspaper reporters who deciphered and interpreted puzzling events that began with thieves entering the headquarters of the Democratic National Committee in the Watergate apartment complex, Washington, D.C. They give a behind-the-scenes, first-hand account of their investigative work in uncovering the secrecy and lies that shrouded the break-in and its aftermath. After following many false leads, Woodward and Bernstein finally compiled enough evidence to write a series of articles that revealed a cover-up by high-ranking government officials and prompted a U.S. Senate investigation. The scandal led ultimately to the resignation of Republican President Richard M. Nixon in 1974. Another fascinating book that came out of the affair is *The White House Transcripts* (1974), containing transcripts of Nixon's conversations with others in the Oval Office that were recorded by a secret tape system that had been installed by Nixon's own order long before the Watergate affair. *All the President's Men* was made into a movie in 1976. YA

allegory, a literary device, is a story or a description in which events or characters stand for meanings not visible on the surface. An allegory treats one subject by disguising it as another. Allegorical characters often represent moral virtues or vices (such as Truth, Conscience, or Reason), rather than imitating human personality. Similar to the *fable, the *parable, and the *morality play, the allegory is no longer widely used. Examples of allegorical works are *Everyman; *The Pilgrim's Progress, by *John Bunyan; and *Piers Plowman. YA

Allen, Betsy See *Betty Cavanna.

Allingham, Margery (Louise) (1904–1966) An English author of detective stories, Allingham came from a family of publishers and authors. She began writing when she was 6 years old and published a successful adventure novel when she was 16 years old. Allingham lived most of her life in the country, near London, where she devoted herself about equally to village affairs and to writing. With *Mystery Mile* (1929) she established a reputation with her fictional detective, Albert Campion. In this book Campion struggles with international criminals, but with *Death of a Ghost* (1934), which deals with crime in the art world, he becomes, and thereafter remains, a soft-spoken, obviously upper-class figure. Campion does most of his detecting in tidy English villages, roomy country homes, and plush London townhouses. In *Flowers for the Judge* (1936) Campion is involved with murder in a publishing house, and in *Fashions in Shrouds* (1938) he is in the midst of decadence in London's fashionable Mayfair district. Allingham wrote more than 25 books featuring Campion, the last of which was *The Mind Readers* (1965). If you like these books, you will want to read those of *Agatha Christie, *Michael Innes, *Ngaio Marsh, and *Dorothy Sayers. Several of the Campion stories have been produced for television. YA

Almost Year, The (1971) By Florence Engel Randall (1917–), this novel, with its supernatural overtones, presents an interesting study of a 15-year-old black girl. The unnamed heroine lives with her Aunt Cyd, a nurse who spends most of her time in other people's homes caring for newborn babies. To give her motherless

niece the chance to live a different kind of life and go to a better school, Cyd makes arrangements with a white friend and former client to take the girl for a school year, an "almost" year. The girl moves in with Mr. and Mrs. Mallory and their three children, and shares with them their comfortable suburban home. At first the Mallory children are not especially glad to have her, and their guest feels she is being treated too much like an underprivileged person. She misses Aunt Cyd terribly. When some strange things happen in the house, the Mallorys begin to wonder if their guest is a witch, or if their house is inhabited by a poltergeist. The girl gradually realizes that she is gifted with unexplained powers, perhaps only temporarily, and that she can do great damage. Fortunately, she learns to trust the Mallorys, whose experience is so different from her own, and learns she is capable of winning their love and respect. MR

Amahl and the Night Visitors (1951), an opera by the Italian-born American composer Gian-Carlo Menotti (1911–), is a heartwarming story about the journey of the Wise Men, the three kings who followed a brilliant star to Bethlehem to take gifts to the infant Jesus. Amahl is a poor, crippled shepherd boy. His father is dead, and he lives with his mother in a bare, cold cottage. One evening Amahl sees a bright star with a fiery tail traveling across the sky. He tells his mother, but she does not believe him, for Amahl has a very large imagination. Later that night Amahl tells her there are three kings knocking at their door. His mother becomes very angry, but she is amazed when she goes to the door and learns that Amahl is telling the truth. The kings, Melchior, Balthazar, and Kaspar, ask if they may stay at the cottage for the night. Amahl's mother invites them in and sends word for all the shepherds to bring gifts for them.

The kings tell Amahl and his mother they are following the star and taking gold and other precious gifts to a Holy Child. Amahl offers to send a gift as well. The only thing he can give is his crutch, which he made himself. But as soon as he holds the crutch up to the kings, he finds he can walk. Amahl hops, skips, twirls, and dances with joy, and his mother lets him go with the kings so that he can give his crutch to the child in thanks for this miracle.

Amahl and the Night Visitors was written especially for television and was shown every Christmas Eve for 13 years. You can read the story in the book *Amahl and the Night Visitors* (1952). If you enjoyed it, you will also want to read *Gian-Carlo Menotti's Help, Help, the Globolinks!* (1970), the book version of another Menotti opera, about invading aliens from outer space who attack a group of children and are finally defeated by the sounds of musical instruments. MR

Ambler, Eric (1909–) This English novelist has given a whole new direction to stories about espionage and political intrigue. Before him, the typical spy story was full of villains of the worst kind and dashing heroes without flaws, not to mention seductive females up to no good. In Ambler's work the central characters are ordinary people, far from the world of professional espionage, who get caught up in situations they neither expect nor understand. In most cases the settings are central Europe and the Middle East. Among the best of Ambler's books are *Background for Danger* (1937), the first to be published in the United States; *Epitaph for a Spy* (1937); *A Coffin for Dimitrios* (1939); *Journey into Fear* (1940); and *Judgment on Deltchev* (1951). *The Light of Day* (1962), which depicts an attempt to burglarize a museum in Istanbul, Turkey, was produced as an excellent crime caper movie, *Topkapi*, in 1964. If you like novels of espionage, you will want also to read those of *Len Deighton, *Ian Fleming, and *John Le Carré. Ambler, who began his career as an advertising copywriter, wrote an autobiography, *Here Lies* (1986). YA

ambrosia, in ancient Greek mythology, is the name given to the food or perfume of the gods. Possibly a form of honey, it was used by the Olympians to guarantee eternal life, and was occasionally given to mortals. In modern times it has come to mean something particularly good-tasting or fragrant. See also *nectar.

American Tragedy, An (1925) By *Theodore Dreiser, this powerful novel, now considered a classic, is about an unstable, shallow young man whose desire for money and social status bring him frustration and misery. Through him, Dreiser is suggesting that it is almost impossible to live a decent life in America, and that people look to material things and social position for satisfaction.

Clyde Griffiths is the son of street preachers whose devotion to God has not helped them escape poverty. He is vaguely ashamed of their way of life. Yearning for something better, Clyde, finding work in Kansas City as a hotel bellboy, sees for the first time how wealthy people live. He is involved in an auto accident in which a young pedestrian is killed. Fearing the consequences, Clyde runs away to Chicago. A wealthy uncle offers him a job in a factory in Lycurgus, New York. There Clyde falls in love with Roberta Alden, a factory employee, and eventually she becomes his lover. Clyde, however, is already drawn to Sondra Finchley, whom he sees as the embodiment of a glamorous upper class. He begins to dream of marrying her and securing his future, but Roberta is pregnant and aware that Clyde is turning away from her. Desperate, and sickened by Roberta's insistence that he take care of her, Clyde plans to kill Roberta and make her death look like an accident. At a remote and deserted resort, Clyde takes her out on the lake in a rowboat. The accident happens in a bungled manner, the boat overturns, and Clyde allows Roberta to drown. With the discovery of letters between Clyde and Roberta and the evidence of her pregnancy, Clyde is arrested for murder. After a long trial, he is condemned to die in the electric chair. A novel you might enjoy is *Alice Adams* by *Booth Tarkington, another story about the struggle to better a position in life. *An American Tragedy* was adapted for film in 1931, and again in 1951 under the title *A Place in the Sun*. YA

Amerika (1927) is the only comic novel by *Franz Kafka. Karl Rossmann, 16 years old and poor, gets a servant girl pregnant and is shipped off to America. The naive Karl is to redeem himself in the land of opportunity, where he has a wealthy Uncle Jacob. Jacob rejects him, and the penniless and friendless Karl must make his own way in this vast, unknown country. But along the way he runs into assorted devilish and godlike characters, who fight over his soul. Karl becomes a hero, victim, sinner, martyr, and a clown. In the Hotel Occidental, he is caught between two demons and their mistress, who humiliate him and make him their servant. He is saved by the Supreme Cook, a benign guardian angel. You last see Karl capering through the Oklahoma hills. Kafka's inaccurate description of life and objects in America may have been based on movies, as he never visited America. The ending of the unfinished novel was written by Kafka's friend Max Brod (1884–1968). Of Kafka's other books, quite dissimilar to *Amerika*, you might like *The Trial* and *The Castle*. YA

Amos Fortune, Free Man (1950), a poignant novel written by *Elizabeth Yates, is based on the life of Amos Fortune, a real person. Born in Africa, he was sold as a slave in America. The story begins when the 15-year-old African prince At-mun is taken from his tribe, brought to America, and sold to Caleb Copeland, who changes At-mun's name to Amos. For 15 years the Copeland family educates Amos and treats him well. Unfortunately, Caleb dies before giving Amos his freedom, and Caleb's wife sells Amos to Ichabod Richardson in order to pay off her heavy debts. With the kindly Richardson family, Amos learns the tanner's trade, and when Amos is 59 years old, he buys his freedom.

Now a free man, Amos buys freedom for other slaves. Later, he moves with his family to Jaffrey, New Hampshire, where they build a life together as free citizens. People come to recognize Amos as a talented tanner and a man who ceaselessly tries to help others. When he is 80 years old, Amos fulfills his lifelong dream and becomes a landowner. He dies soon after and leaves his money to the church, school, and his family. If you like this story, you will also enjoy *The Autobiography of Miss Jane Pittman* by *Ernest J. Gaines. *Amos Fortune, Free Man* won a *Newbery Medal in 1951. MR

Anastasia Krupnik (1979), by *Lois Lowry, is the first in a series of funny novels about the Krupnik family and their unstoppable daughter. Anastasia is 10 years old, with hair the color of Hubbard squash and a fondness for spinach sandwiches. In a green notebook she keeps a List of Things I Love! and one of Things I Hate!, both subject to frequent change. The news that her 35-year-old mother is going to have a baby is disturbing, but Anastasia agrees to accept the situation if she can choose a name for her sibling. Her parents are portrayed as intelligent and affectionate people who enjoy life and their work without taking themselves too seriously. Their sadness over the death of Anastasia's aged grandmother is greatly eased by the arrival of baby Sam.

The other novels in the series include *Anastasia Again* (1981), in which the Krupniks decide to move out of the city. Anastasia's adjustment to the suburbs is complicated by an elderly and eccentric neighbor named Gertrude Stein. In *Anastasia at Your Service* (1982), our enterprising heroine believes she is being hired as a companion, but finds herself being exploited as a maid. *Anastasia, Ask Your Analyst* (1984) is about growing up, when 13-year-old Anastasia claims to need psychotherapy but manages without it by addressing her questions to a plaster bust of Freud. In *Anastasia on Her Own* (1985), Anastasia takes charge of the household while her mother is away and copes with unforeseen emergencies. *Anastasia Has the Answers* (1986) describes her efforts to impress her glamorous gym teacher and find a wife for her widowed uncle. *Anastasia's Chosen Career* (1987) is about Anastasia on a campaign to improve her self-confidence, during which she takes a modeling course at the Studio Charmante and considers a future in the bookstore business. If you like these novels, you will also enjoy the stories about a girl named Al by *Constance C. Greene. MR

. . . And Now Miguel (1953) An unusual setting, a sheep ranch in New Mexico in the early 1950s, makes this novel by Joseph Krumgold (1908–1980) a landmark in fiction for younger readers. The story is told by 12-year-old Miguel Chavez, whose great desire is to go with his

"The Emperor's New Clothes" is one of
the best-known tales of Hans Christian Andersen.

father and older brother, 19-year-old Gabriel,
when they take the family sheep to summer
pasturage in the Sangre de Cristo Mountains.
When Miguel's father says he must wait, he
prays to their patron saint, San Ysidro. The
saint seems to answer his prayer, but Miguel
feels guilty when he is allowed to go only because Gabriel is drafted into the army. Miguel
does his best to do his share of the work, but
his immaturity shows and he fears, mistakenly, that his father, Old Blas, does not appreciate his efforts. This novel, an early example of
a book about modern life in a Hispanic setting,
shows the importance of family solidarity and
the strength of customs generations old.
Krumgold also wrote *Onion John, about another 12-year-old boy, living in a New Jersey village and learning to get along with his father,
and Henry 3 (1967), about 13-year-old Henry Lov-
ering III growing up in an affluent New York
City suburb. The three novels deal with similar problems but in very different settings.
. . . And Now Miguel won the *Newbery
Medal in 1954. MR

Andersen, Hans Christian (1805–1875) A
Danish writer of fairy tales, Andersen was born
to a poor shoemaker and an uneducated
mother. He had almost no formal education.
When Andersen was 14 years old, his father

died, and he went to Copenhagen, the capital
of Denmark, where he hoped to become a successful singer, dancer, or actor. When all his attempts failed, Andersen tried to write plays,
but they were rejected. Finally, in 1822, he received a grant that gave him the opportunity to
finish grammar school. Eventually, he graduated from Copenhagen University and became
an author. Though he wrote novels, travel
books, and poetry, he is remembered best for
his *Fairy Tales and Stories* (1835–1872). Among
these tales are such unforgettable classics as
"The Ugly Duckling," "The Princess and the
Pea," "The Emperor's New Clothes," and "The
Little Mermaid." His stories have been translated into more languages than any book except the Bible. MR & YA

Anderson, Maxwell (1888–1959). A playwright whose dramas explore such universal
themes as social injustice, political corruption,
and the disenchantment of men during wartime, Anderson, the son of a Baptist minister,
was born in Pennsylvania but grew up in the
Middle West. He worked as a teacher and journalist before writing the verse drama *What
Price Glory?*, which was an immediate success. His other plays include *Saturday's Children* (1927), a comedy about marriage; *Both
Your Houses* (1933), which deals with political
corruption; and *Winterset* (1935), a tragedy in
verse form about a young man who seeks to
prove that his father was executed for a crime
he did not commit. Anderson's plays dealing
with historical themes include *Anne of the
Thousand Days* (1948) and *Elizabeth the
Queen* (1930). YA

Anderson, Robert (Woodruff) (1917–) A popular playwright, Anderson is known especially
for *Tea and Sympathy* (1953), which is about
Tom Lee, a student at a New England prep
school, who is falsely accused of being homosexual. The housemaster's sensitive and attractive wife gives him moral support and
sympathy and tries to restore Tom's confidence
in himself by having a very brief affair with
him. *Silent Night, Lonely Night* (1959) centers

on two people who meet accidentally on Christmas Eve. *I Never Sang for My Father* (1970) is about the difficult relationship between a domineering father and his son. Anderson's screenplays include his own *Tea and Sympathy*, filmed in 1956, as well as adaptations of novels by other authors. He has also adapted a number of classic novels, such as *David Copperfield* and *A Farewell to Arms*, for Theatre Guild radio programs. *I Never Sang for My Father* was made into a movie in 1970 and was produced on television in 1988. YA

Anderson, Sherwood (1876–1941) Born in Camden, a small agricultural village in western Ohio, Anderson wrote novels, short stories, and essays whose themes explore the rise of commercialism in rural America and the disintegration of human relationships. Anderson fought in the Spanish-American War, worked as a manager in a paint factory, and became successful in advertising. Dissatisfied with his life, he left his family and his job and moved to Chicago with the goal of becoming a writer. His first novel was *Windy McPherson's Son* (1916). Said to be partly autobiographical, it is about a small-town businessman who gives up the pursuit of wealth in favor of the search for personal fulfillment. Anderson did not attain recognition, however, until the publication of *Winesburg, Ohio: A Group of Tales of Ohio Small Town Life* (1919), his best-known and most popular novel. *The Triumph of the Egg: A Book of Impressions from American Life in Tales and Poems* was published in 1921. *Death in the Woods and Other Stories* (1933), considered one of Anderson's finest narrative works, is composed (somewhat like *Winesburg*) of related episodes centering on the character of Ma Grimes, a woman who has been cruelly exploited. After she is found dead in the snow, aspects of her life are revealed by the narrator, whose memories and reactions form an important element of the stories. *Kit Brandon* (1936), Anderson's last novel, is about a Southern mountain woman who makes a small fortune running moonshine and discovers that wealth is not everything.

Anderson exerted a powerful influence on such writers as *James T. Farrell, *William Faulkner, and *Thomas Wolfe. His work is characterized by a clean and economical style, by simple sentence structure and plain speech that avoids dialect or colloquialism. Noted especially for his vivid portrayals of life in the small towns of the Middle West, he was intensely interested in the possibility of escape from the limitations of routine. YA

Andersonville (1955) is a historical novel by *MacKinlay Kantor, a re-creation of tragic events at an infamous Confederate prison camp during the American Civil War. Named for its site, the village of Andersonville in Georgia, the prison began receiving Union inmates in February 1864, before the camp was adequately prepared to house them. Prisoners were kept within the confines of an approximately 28-acre patch of ground without proper shelter, food, or medical care. More than 12,000 prisoners died there of hunger, disease, and exposure. The prison commander was tried before a military commission after the war, was found guilty of murder, and was executed in November 1865.

Kantor described his novel as a work of fiction, but one "presented as an accurate history of the Andersonville prison insofar as specific details concerning the construction, administration, tenancy, and supervision of the stockade, with its guards and inhabitants, are made clear." Many of the prison officials and some Confederate officers are based on real people, as are some of the prisoners. Without a real plot or narrative, the novel brings to life a vast array of characters from all social levels. If you are interested in the Civil War, you might like also to read *The Red Badge of Courage* by *Stephen Crane. YA

Andrews, V(irginia) C(leo) (?–1986) The author of a series of novels about the Dollanger children, beginning with *Flowers in the Attic* (1979), Andrews, born and raised in Virginia, was crippled as a child and was confined to a wheelchair for most of her adult life. Her novels, a mixture of Gothic horror, mystery, and the supernatural, are said to be based on her own life, her dreams, and her psychic experiences. She has been criticized for bringing such subjects as incest, child abuse, and revenge into her books. *Flowers in the Attic* and its sequels, *Petals on the Wind* (1980) and *If There Be Thorns* (1981), are about four children imprisoned in an attic by members of their own family. The young people turn to each other for courage, learning to survive an evil-minded grandmother and a mother who does not seem to care about them. *Flowers in the Attic* was filmed in 1987. YA

Andromeda Strain, The (1969) Michael Crichton (1942–) wrote this suspenseful science fiction novel about a five-day scientific crisis in America. It begins with the return to Earth of Scoop VII, an unmanned research satellite that was contaminated by an unknown lifelike substance in outer space. When the satellite lands in the tiny town of Piedmont, Arizona, the poisonous organism causes the death of everyone in town except an elderly alcoholic and a newborn baby. Four brilliant scientists are sent to a top-secret laboratory beneath the Nevada desert to try to discover an antidote to the lethal organism, now called the Andromeda Strain. As the scientists begin to find the answers to their puzzling questions, their greatest nightmare is realized. The Andromeda Strain mutates, dissolves the sterile seals of the laboratory, and sets off an automatic atomic device set to destroy the laboratory in three minutes. In a dramatic sequence, the scientists triumph and are able to turn off the atomic device. The Andromeda Strain, having mutated into a benign form, is no longer a threat to humans, and the scientists predict that it will eventually depart from earth without causing further damage. Crichton's vivid descriptions of the scientists and their handling of the crisis suggest clearly that even the most brilliant minds are capable of making monumental blunders in their predictions and theories. YA

angel From the Greek word meaning messenger comes this name for an immortal spirit that ranks between human beings and God, serving the latter. Angels are present in *Judaism, *Christianity, and *Islam and are mentioned many times in the *Bible. Early leaders of the Christian church wrote of nine orders of angels, the first being seraphim. Known especially are the second-order archangels, among them Michael, the warrior; *Gabriel, the messenger; Raphael, the healer; and Uriel, the angel of light. Islam has Michael and Gabriel, as well as Azrael, the angel of death, and Israfel, the angel of music. In popular literature and art, angels are pictured with large white wings. In popular usage, if you are very nice to someone, he or she may tell you that you are an angel.

Angell, Judie (1937–) Novelist Judie Angell's childhood experiences in New York City and her career as a teacher have greatly influenced her work. She often writes about situations she has personally experienced or observed, such as summers at camp and entries from a child's diary. Some of her more popular books include *In Summertime It's Tuffy* (1977), about an 11-year-old girl's humorous escapades at summer camp; *What's Best for You* (1981), about a family coping with their parents' break-up; and *A Home Is to Share . . . and Share . . . and Share* (1984), about three children who fight to keep open an animal shelter. When writing about the more delicate and often darker aspects of being a teenager, Angell uses the pen name of Fran Arrick. Among these books are *Tunnel Vision* (1979), which deals with a teen suicide, and *Chernowitz!* (1981), about anti-Semitism in a small town. YA

Angelou, Maya (1928–) A black playwright, poet, and autobiographical writer, Maya Angelou is one of the most important figures in contemporary literature. Her first autobiography, *I Know Why the Caged Bird Sings* (1970), tells of her life in racist, segregated Stamps, Arkansas, where her grandmother owned a general store, and in St. Louis, where her mother lived. Though many of the stories in the book are grim, particularly the revelation that 8-year-old Maya was raped by her mother's boyfriend, the book shows the amazing resilience of the young girl and hints at the woman of independence and talent she later becomes. The book ends with the birth of her son, Guy, when Maya is 16 years old. Her next two autobiographies, *Gather Together in My Name* (1974) and *Singin' and Swingin' and Gettin' Merry Like Christmas* (1976), follow her from adolescence through young adulthood, when she establishes a reputation as a performer in the 1950s. *The Heart of a Woman* (1981) covers the 1960s and Angelou's close involvement with the civil rights movement. Her fifth autobiography, *All God's Children Need Traveling Shoes* (1986), tells about the four years Angelou spent in Ghana, a newly independent African nation. Angelou has published four books of poetry, including *Just Give Me a Cool Drink of Water 'fore I Diiie* (1971), and *Shaker, Why Don't You Sing?* (1983). YA

Animal Family, The (1965) This novella, by Randall Jarrell (1914–1965), is about a man who has grown up on a deserted island. Each night in his cabin he dreams about his dead parents, the only other humans he has known, who brought him to the island when he was small. Then one night, he hears a mermaid singing, making a sound like the one his mother used to make. He and the mermaid merge their lives, learning each other's ways and forgetting their loneliness. A bear cub joins the family, and then a lynx. The lynx and the bear bring home a boy who has been washed ashore in a boat with his dead mother. As time passes the boy begins to ask, "How did I arrive?" The mermaid and the man reply, together, "The lynx brought you." Jarrell wrote other unusual stories about animals, among them *The Bat-Poet* (1964) and *The Gingerbread Rabbit* (1963), as well as several books of poems, *Little Friend, Little Friend* (1945), *The Seven League Crutches* (1951), and *The Lost World* (1965). MR

Animal Farm (1946), by *George Orwell, is a novel satirizing communism and, in a larger sense, all forms of tyranny in social and political life. It is set on a farm where the animals rebel against their drunken master, Mr. Jones,

and gain control of the land. They change the name of the farm from the Manor Farm to Animal Farm and establish a doctrine called Animalism. The basic principles of Animalism state that all animals are equal, and four legs are good but two legs are bad. The new animal community is led by two clever pigs, Napoleon and Snowball. Napoleon, however, is hungry for power and manages to triumph over Snowball for complete control. Though the neighboring humans attack the farm to regain possession, they are always beaten back by the animals. Over time Napoleon becomes a dictator, creates a hierarchy among the animals, and treats them worse than their previous master, Mr. Jones. Napoleon and the pigs move into the farmhouse, wear clothes, drink alcohol, use money, and walk on two legs. They change all of the principles of Animalism, which now state that "some animals are more equal than others." By the end of the novel, the tired and miserable farm animals learn that their new community is no better than their first, and that the pigs have become entirely indistinguishable from humans. If you enjoyed this novel, you might also want to read Orwell's *1984. Animal Farm* was made into an animated film in 1955.

Anna Christie (1920), a play by *Eugene O'Neill, is about a woman's struggle to free herself from her past. Chris Christopherson has been a sailor all his life. A widower, he left his daughter, Anna, to be raised on a relative's farm, and he has not seen her for 15 years. When Anna visits Chris in New York City, it is obvious to everyone except her trusting father that she has been a prostitute. Chris persuades her to stay and travel with him on his coal barge, and after 10 days of fresh air and sleep, Anna is glowing with health. In port, Anna and Chris meet Mat Burke, a tough Irish seaman recently rescued from a shipwreck. Mat takes an immediate interest in Anna, whom he sees as a fine and decent woman, and talks of marriage. Anna responds strongly in spite of Chris's objection to her taking up with a sailor. When the two men argue over her future, she protests against being treated like a piece of furniture. Anna finally agrees to marry Mat if he can accept and forgive her past life. She describes how she was abused on the farm, and how she ran away and turned to prostitution to survive. Chris is horrified, but sees it is not her fault. Mat is filled with rage and disgust, but later has a change of heart and makes Anna swear that he is the only man she ever really loved. The play ends with their happy decision to marry, but the atmosphere is tinged with foreboding and a feeling that Anna, though now redeemed, may never escape her past. YA

Anna Karenina (1877), by *Leo Tolstoy, is considered one of the world's finest novels. Set in 19th-century Russia and told with unusual realism, it is the tragic story of a young woman, Anna Karenina, married to a coldly pompous government official, Karenin. Anna falls in love with Count Vronsky, a handsome and cultivated officer. Her disagreeable husband claims to feel no jealousy, but he warns Anna that her flirtation may have serious social consequences and disturb the life of their young son, Seryozha. Anna, though a decent woman, cannot hide or control her growing passion for Vronsky. Karenin refuses Anna's plea for a divorce, fearing the scandal would endanger his professional future. Eventually he refuses also to let Anna see Seryozha, saying she is a bad influence. After Anna gives birth to Vronsky's daughter, she becomes seriously ill. Anna becomes increasingly unhappy as their relationship begins to disintegrate from the strain of society's disapproval. She is not permitted to see Seryozha, has little interest in her baby daughter, and fears that Vronsky is falling in love with another woman. Unable to bear her life any longer, Anna throws herself in front of an oncoming train and is killed. After her death, Vronsky sinks into depression and takes little interest in life. Tolstoy develops a second story around Kitty Oblonsky, Anna's sister-in-law, and Konstantine Levin, a serious-minded young man who strongly resembles Tolstoy, and who expresses the author's opinions on life, religion, and social reform. After

Anna Karenina is one of the most famous tragic heroines of European literature.

Kitty and Levin marry, they settle down to the dull, difficult routine of everyday life, in stark contrast to the more glamorous and emotional atmosphere surrounding Anna and Vronsky. The novel was adapted several times for film, most notably in 1935 with Greta Garbo (1905–1990) as Anna. YA

Anne of Green Gables (1908), a novel by *L.M. Montgomery, is about an 11-year-old orphan girl, Anne Shirley, who is adopted by Marilla and Matthew Cuthbert, who live at their farm, Green Gables, on Prince Edward Island in Canada. The practical Cuthberts quickly grow attached to Anne, as she brings laughter and warmth to the otherwise dull Green Gables. Anne is an imaginative child who only wants to see, hear, and wear pretty things. If something is not beautiful, she will imagine it otherwise. She even attaches special names to ordinary places. She renames the Barry pond the "Lake of Shining Waters," and the town avenue is called the "White Way of Delight." Her vivid imagination and adventurous spirit tend to lead her into all sorts of trouble. For example, when the new minister and his wife come for dinner, Anne makes a cake in their honor. Instead of adding vanilla, however, Anne makes a mistake and uses "liniment acedyne." Ashamed of her red hair, she attempts to dye it, turning it a disastrous green.

Anne is a remarkably intelligent child, tying for first in her class with her rival, Gilbert Blythe. When Anne is 15 years old, she and Gilbert are accepted at Queens School to be trained as teachers. Here, she wins a scholarship to college. After Matthew's sudden death, and because of Marilla's weakening eyesight, Anne decides to give up her scholarship and live with Marilla at Green Gables. Anne will study college courses sent through the mail and teach in their town of Avonlea. Anne, now 16 years old, finally befriends Gilbert, and continues to succeed despite obstacles at every turn.

Montgomery continued the story of Anne and Gilbert in a number of sequels, including *Anne of Avonlea* (1909), *Chronicles of Avonlea* (1912), *Anne of the Island* (1915), *Anne's House of Dreams* (1917), and *Anne of Ingleside* (1939). A film adaptation of *Anne of Green Gables* was produced in 1934. An excellent Canadian-made TV movie appeared in 1985, and a sequel, *Anne of Avonlea*, in 1987. MR & YA

Anson, Robert Sam (1945–) A journalist and war correspondent during the Vietnam War, Anson is the author of the nonfictional book *Best Intentions: The Education and Killing of Edmund Perry* (1987). It examines the life and death of a promising black student, an honors graduate from a prestigious Eastern preparatory school, who was shot in Harlem while allegedly trying to rob a police officer in plain clothes. The incident caused accusations of racist violence to be leveled at the police. The book makes clear the enormous difficulties and pressures of living, as Perry did, in two

completely different worlds, the black ghetto on the one hand and the white establishment on the other. You may want to read another book by Anson, *"They've Killed the President!": The Search for the Murderers of John F. Kennedy* (1975), which investigates the possibility that the President's death was the result of a conspiracy. YA

Anthony, Piers [Piers Anthony Dillingham Jacob] (1934–) A prolific and popular author of *science fiction and *fantasy novels, Anthony was born in England but came to the United States when he was very young. In the 1960s, after serving in the army, then working as a technical writer and a teacher, he achieved critical and popular success with his first novel, *Chthon* (1967), about Anton Five, a man locked up in a hellish underground prison inside the planet Chthon. He learns that the planet is actually a complicated mineral intelligence. *Chthon*, like most of Anthony's novels, makes skillful use of myth, legend, and literary allusion. Its sequel, *Phtor* (1975), tells of the adventures of Anton's son, Arlo. Themes that run through Anthony's work include the place of humanity in the order of the universe, the effect of industrial society on all living things, and the power of myth and magic in our lives. His many other books include *Macroscope* (1979), about a giant telescope that enables humans to peer into space and time; and *Race Against Time* (1973), about a 16-year-old boy who discovers that his life in a Nebraska town in 1960 is not at all what it appears to be, that in fact he is living in the year 2375. Many of Anthony's books fit into series, such as the Bio of a Space Tyrant series, which chronicles the rise to power on Jupiter of a space refugee and includes the novels *Refugee* (1983), *Mercenary* (1984), and *Statesman* (1986). Probably his most popular series is about *Xanth. MR & YA

Antigone, heroine of Greek legend and of *Sophocles' great tragedy *Antigone* (c.442 B.C.), was the daughter of *Oedipus, king of Thebes. She guided her blind and exiled father on his wanderings and remained with him until his death. After her return to Thebes, according to Sophocles, her brothers Eteocles and Polyneices killed each other in single combat, in a quarrel over the throne. Their Uncle Creon, the new king, pronounced Polyneices guilty of treason and insisted his corpse remain unburied and without funeral rites. Convinced that Polyneices was unjustly condemned, Antigone buried the body herself. Her act was discovered, and Creon ordered that she be imprisoned in a cave and left there to die. She is supposed to have hanged herself in the cave, though another version by *Euripedes suggested that she escaped. A modern play based on this powerful legend is *Antigone* (1946), by the French playwright Jean Anouilh (1910–1987). YA

Antony and Cleopatra (1607), a tragedy by *William Shakespeare, is about two extraordinary historical figures. One of three rulers of the Roman Empire, Mark Antony neglects his duties at home to be with his beloved Cleopatra, queen of Egypt, at her lavish palace in Alexandria. Once a respected leader, some consider him a fool, ensnared by the charms of Cleopatra. After learning about his wife's death and rumors of political unrest in Italy, Antony returns to Rome to appease the other members of the ruling triumvirate, Octavius Caesar and Lepidus. There, Antony is persuaded to bind their association by a marriage with Caesar's sister, Octavia. But, when Caesar learns that his brother-in-law has returned to Egypt and Cleopatra, leaving Octavia behind, he prepares to war against Antony. Antony and Cleopatra join their forces in a great naval battle against Caesar, but Caesar prevails after Cleopatra's ship unexpectedly leaves the fight and Antony, weakened by his love for her, follows. Antony is shamed and enraged, but Cleopatra reassures him and supports his hope of overcoming Caesar in another battle. However, after a second defeat, Antony believes Cleopatra has betrayed him and prepares to kill her. She escapes and sends an attendant to tell Antony that she is dead. Antony throws himself on his sword, but when he learns the queen is alive, he has himself carried to her and dies in her arms. Cleo-

patra receives the victorious Caesar, who fails to convince her that he will not parade her through Rome as a common captive. Obtaining a basket of figs in which asps are hidden, she presses one of the poisonous snakes to her breast, dies, and is buried in the same grave with her lover. You might like to read *Julius Caesar*, another play by Shakespeare in which a completely different Mark Antony appears, and also the play *Caesar and Cleopatra* (1901) by *George Bernard Shaw, which portrays these two characters quite differently. *Antony and Cleopatra* was filmed in 1973. YA

Anywhere Else but Here (1980) is a novel by Bruce Clements (1931–) about a motherless 13-year-old girl named Molly Smelter, who lives with her Aunt Aurora and her father in Schenectady, New York. After her father's printing business fails, the strong-willed Molly decides that she and her father should move to Connecticut. Her plans are complicated when her aunt's friend Fostra Lee Post comes to visit with her unlikable 8-year-old son, Claude. Fostra is a beautiful but self-centered woman interested only in following her spiritual guru. Eventually Fostra goes to California, leaving her son to become the Smelters' responsibility. Molly is convinced that a fresh start will protect her father from more bad business dealings and make her happier as well. She secretly sells her treasured dollhouse and uses the money as a deposit for a new printing shop in Connecticut. Finally, Molly's dream is realized when she moves with her father and Claude to open the shop and start a new life together.

Bruce Clements, a clergyman, teaches English and children's literature. Another of his novels you might enjoy is *Prison Window, Jerusalem Blue* (1977). Set in the 9th century, it is about an English girl and her brother who are kidnapped by Viking seamen and carried to Denmark as slaves. MR

Aphrodite is the ancient Greek goddess of love, beauty, and fertility, a powerful figure known to the Romans as Venus. One account of her birth describes her emerging from the sea as the result of sea-foam mixing with the blood of *Uranus, who was mutilated by his son *Cronus. Another account, from the poet *Homer, holds that she is the daughter of *Zeus and Dione. Aphrodite's husband is Hephaestus (or the Roman Vulcan), god of fire and patron of craftsmen, but she loves other gods, such as *Ares and *Adonis, and mortal men. In one famous tale, she competes against the goddesses Minerva and Juno for the golden apple of Discord, to be given to the most beautiful contestant, and is chosen for the prize by the shepherd *Paris. Aphrodite later helps Paris to persuade *Helen of Troy to elope with him, an event that is said to have caused the *Trojan War. You can read about Aphrodite in *Mythology by Edith Hamilton (1867–1963) and also in Two Queens of Heaven (1974) by Doris Gates (1901–1987), which retells the myths about Aphrodite and the goddess *Demeter. MR

Apocrypha See *Bible.

Apollo is the ancient Greek god of light and archery, associated with music, healing, prophecy, and the care of flocks and herds. A figure of great complexity and importance among the Olympian gods, he is the son of *Zeus and Leto, and his twin sister is *Artemis. It is Apollo who kills Python, a huge serpent living in the caverns of Mount Parnassus. At a site near the caverns is the oracle of Delphi, the most famous of Apollo's shrines. His first love is the nymph Daphne, who rejects the god's advances and flees from him. Apollo pursues and is about to grasp her when Daphne calls upon her father the river-god Peneius to change her into another form. She becomes a laurel tree. Apollo cannot make her his wife, so he weaves his crown of laurel leaves, and vows the tree will always be fresh and green. Apollo champions the Trojans during the *Trojan War, and afflicts the Greeks with a terrible plague after *Agamemnon offends him. He also guides the arrow that slays *Achilles. He has been depicted as the embodiment of eternal youth and beauty. You can read about Apollo in *Bulfinch's Mythology by Thomas Bulfinch (1796–1867) and *Mythology by Edith Hamilton

(1867–1963) and also in The Golden God (1973) by Doris Gates (1901–1987). MR

Appelfeld, Aharon (1932–) Born in Czernovitz, Bukovina, now a part of Ukraine, Appelfeld is the author of several antiwar novels. When he was 8 years old, his mother was killed by the Nazis and Appelfeld was sent to a concentration camp. He later escaped and spent three years hiding in the Ukrainian countryside before joining the Russian Army. After the war, he went to Italy, and in 1946 emigrated to Palestine. His works in English translation include Badenheim 1939 (1980), about the struggle of assimilated Jews faced with the Holocaust; The Age of Wonders (1981), which portrays the effects of World War II on a Jewish boy and his family; Tzili: The Story of a Life (1983), about a simple girl's struggle to survive the Holocaust; The Retreat (1984), which describes the psychological problems faced by Jews trying to assimilate into a Gentile society; and To the Land of the Cattails (1986), about the separation of a Jewish mother and son in Europe in 1938. YA

Appleseed, Johnny (1774–1845) His real name was John Chapman. He was an American pioneer who traveled alone from western Pennsylvania through Ohio, Indiana, and Illinois, planting apple trees, as well as giving apple seeds and saplings to everyone he met. His mission was to make the wilderness more beautiful and fruitful. Johnny Appleseed was a small man with long, dark hair, who wore a coffee sack as a shirt, a tin pot as a hat, and no shoes. Treated with great respect by frontiersmen and their families, as well as by the Indians, he died a hero. His pure benevolence and noble life have made Johnny Appleseed into an American legend. You can read all about this extraordinary man in Johnny Appleseed (1991) by Kathy Jakobsen (1952–). MR

Appleton, Victor This is the pen name created by *Edward Stratemeyer for several series of adventure books, the best known being the enormously popular Tom Swift series. Written by Stratemeyer and others and published between 1910 and 1941, the Tom Swift stories follow the adventures on land, at sea, and in the air of the youthful inventor and scientific genius, Tom. He puts his abilities to good use, solving mysteries and fighting crime in such books as *Tom Swift and His Submarine Boat* (1910) and *Tom Swift and His Electric Locomotive* (1922). In the 1950s, Tom's son, Tom Swift, Jr., arrived on the scene, following in his father's footsteps with the Tom Swift, Jr., series, in which he and his friend Bud Barclay find adventure and mystery on Earth and in outer space. Their many adventures, published under the pen name Victor Appleton II, include *Tom Swift and His Jetmarine* (1954), in which Tom investigates a series of mysterious robberies at sea, and *Tom Swift and the Asteroid Pirates* (1963), in which Tom battles against a dangerous band of space pirates. A new, modernized Tom Swift series was begun in 1991 and is available in paperback. MR

Arabian Nights' Entertainments, The (c.1450) Also called *The Thousand and One Nights*, this is a collection of about 200 ancient stories from Persia, India, Egypt, and Arabia. The stories are told by *Scheherazade, a beautiful maiden married to the evil Shahriyan, a powerful sultan who marries a different maiden each night and then orders her execution on the following morning. A few of the famous characters who appear in these tales are *Aladdin, *Ali Baba, and *Sinbad. MR & YA

Arden, the Forest of A forest area of northern Warwickshire, in central England, it is the setting of the play *As You Like It*, by *William Shakespeare. In the play, the peace of the Arden woods is seen as a wholesome change from the hypocrisy and intrigue of life at court, and as a reminder of the natural, carefree existence of *Robin Hood. YA

Are You in the House Alone? (1976) by *Richard Peck, this honest and disturbing novel is about the rape of a 17-year-old girl. Living in a quiet Connecticut town with her family, Gail Osburne feels safe from the sort of

Shahrazad

The resourceful narrator of the stories in *The Arabian Nights' Entertainments* saves herself from death.

violence she associates with city life. She is happy with her boyfriend, Steve, and her best friend, Alison. Then Gail finds an anonymous note tucked in her school locker, threatening her with sexual violence in language that suggests the writer is deranged. After this, it seems that whenever Gail is alone, the telephone rings and the caller hangs up when she answers. While Gail takes the threat seriously and is frightened, she is too embarrassed to ask for help. Feeling alone and helpless, she approaches the school guidance counselor, but he is reluctant to become involved. Baby-sitting for a neighbor one evening, Gail is visited by Phil Lawver, whom she knows as Alison's boyfriend and the son of the wealthiest family in town. Phil admits he wrote the obscene threats, then beats and rapes her. While Gail recovers slowly in the hospital, she must face the possibility that Phil will never have to pay for his crime. Gail's lawyer says that without a witness, she has little chance against the influential Lawver family. She is not urged to press charges. After a second young woman is found beaten and raped, however, Phil quietly disappears. It is assumed his family made arrangements for him to take up a new life elsewhere. Another powerful novel about a teenager who is raped is *Did You Hear What Happened to Andrea?* (1979) by Gloria D. Miklowitz (1927–). YA

Are You There God? It's Me, Margaret
(1970), a novel by *Judy Blume, is narrated by Margaret Ann Simon, a sixth grader who recently moved from New York City to a suburb in New Jersey. Margaret becomes good friends with an outgoing and bossy neighbor, Nancy, and Nancy introduces Margaret into a secret girls' club. However, there are special club rules, such as having to wear a bra and telling the other group members if and when you menstruated. As the school year progresses, Margaret chats with God about her insecurities and dreams concerning boys. She also asks God for guidance in religious matters. Having been raised with no religion, Margaret feels different from her new friends, who go either to church or to temple. Since her parents are no help, she says to God, "You know, God, my new friends all belong to the Y or the Jewish Community Center. Which way am I supposed to go?" *Are You There God? It's Me, Margaret* is an upbeat and honest story that explores Margaret's changing attitudes about boys, friends, family, and growing up. MR

Ares is the Greek god of war, known as Mars by the Romans. Not popular with the Greeks, he is looked upon as a "god for other people." He is the son of *Zeus and *Hera. Though Ares never marries, there are many legends about his numerous love affairs, the most famous being his secret liaison with the goddess *Aphrodite. In spite of his warlike manner, Ares is often outwitted in battle by the wiser and more experienced gods. Once, Ares is imprisoned in a brass jar and rescued by Hermes 13 months later. During the *Trojan War, he is wounded several times by the goddess *Athena. In art, Ares is represented wearing armor and a helmet, holding a shield, spear, and sword. You can read about Ares in *Mythology* by Edith Hamilton (1867–1963). MR

Argonauts, the In ancient Greek myth, they were a group of 50 noble and courageous heroes who sailed with *Jason in the ship *Argo* on a great quest for the *Golden Fleece. Their long voyage took them to Lemnos in the Aegean Sea, where they were entertained for a year by the island women, who had recently put their men to death. They navigated the dangerous Symplegades, or Clashing Islands, to reach the Black Sea. With Jason and *Medea finally in possession of the Golden Fleece, the *Argo* was blown off course by a terrible storm as *Zeus vented his rage against Medea, who had murdered her brother. The Argonauts survived these and other adventures to return home. You can read about the Argonauts in *Jason and the Argonauts* (1986) by Bernard Evslin (1922–). MR

Ariel, a fairy sprite, is best known for his appearance in *William Shakespeare's play *The Tempest*. He was confined to a pine tree for 12 years because he had not obeyed the witch Sycorax. When Sycorax dies, Ariel becomes the slave of Caliban, who mistreats him. But Prospero frees Ariel, who serves Prospero happily until Prospero finally releases him. Ariel, known as the embodiment of imagination and airiness, is capable of manipulating the natural elements and influencing the will of human beings. He is able to swim, fly, enter fire, become invisible, create a tempest, and transform himself. One of the collections of poems by *Sylvia Plath is *Ariel* (1965). YA

Aristophanes (c.450–c.388 B.C.) was the most renowned comic dramatist of ancient Greece. A master of Old Comedy, with its traditional use of the *chorus, mime, and *parody, he was also celebrated for the beauty of his lyric writing. Aristophanes was a citizen of Athens. He is said to have written about 40 plays. The 11 comedies that have survived are energetic, earthy *satires on social, political, or literary subjects of the day, some inspired by issues raised during the Peloponnesian War. Some plays contain witty parodies of the works of the dramatist *Euripides, whom Aristophanes saw as a degenerate, and many use the device of placing real people in ridiculous situations. *The Clouds* (423 B.C.) makes fun of the Athenian philosopher Socrates (469–399 B.C.) and his students, as well as the Sophists, who were traveling teachers giving lectures for money. In *The Wasps* (422 B.C.), Aristophanes satirizes the love of litigation, or legal disputes, for which Athenians were famous. *The Birds* (414 B.C.) involves a fantastic imaginary kingdom. The play is seen by some as satire on Athenian imperialism, of which Aristophanes, as a pacifist, strongly disapproved. In *Lysistrata* (411 B.C.), the women of Athens organize to take over the Acropolis and reject their husbands until peace can be reestablished. *The Frogs* (405 B.C.) concerns a great literary competition between the dead Euripides and *Aeschylus, played out before *Dionysus, the god of drama. YA

Aristotle (384–322 B.C.) A philosopher and scientist of ancient Greece, Aristotle has exerted a vast and enduring influence on Western and Islamic thought. The son of a physician at the court of Macedonia, Aristotle showed an early interest in medicine and biology. He was a student of *Plato at the Athenian Academy for 20 years, and after Plato's death he traveled widely, devoting himself to the study of plants and animals. He became tutor to Alexander the Great (356–323 B.C.). After his return to Athens, Aristotle founded a school, the Lyceum, in a grove sacred to *Apollo, where he taught while strolling on a covered walkway with his students. Unlike the mathematics-oriented Academy of Plato, the Lyceum stressed the study of biology and history. Aristotle's surviving works include treatises on logic, physics, metaphysics, biology, psychology, the philosophy of science, ethics, history, and politics. His treatises on rhetoric and poetics are explorations of creative imagination.

Aristotle believed that knowledge is acquired through sensory perception, as clarified and interpreted by the intellect and the emotions. Unlike Plato, who explored what people's lives should be, Aristotle applied himself to the study of observable phenomena and tried to find practical solutions to human problems. The rules of logic, or reasoning, were devised by Aristotle and are still in use today. You will find many English translations of his various works, among them *The Complete Works of Aristotle: The Revised Oxford Translation* (1984). YA

ark Probably the best-known ark is Noah's ark, told about in the *Bible's book of *Genesis. Noah knew that a great flood was coming, so he built an ark, a large, partly covered boat, and then welcomed animals aboard, two by two. When the flood came, they floated to safety. An ark can also be a chest or box for storage. The *Ten Commandments were carved on stone and placed in the Ark of the Covenant. This ark is often mentioned in stories in the Bible.

In *The Voyages of Dr. Dolittle* by *Hugh Lofting, he and his animals sail away in a boat that looks very like an ark. You will enjoy reading about Noah in *Noah and the Ark* (1988), which uses as text the Revised Standard Version of the Bible. MR

Armageddon In the *Bible, this is the place fated to be the scene of the final conflict between the forces of good and the forces of evil. It is believed that "Armageddon" refers to Megiddo, an ancient city in what is now northwestern Israel, a strategic location between Egypt and Mesopotamia. Megiddo was the site of many important battles, one as early as c.1486 B.C., another as recent as World War I. "Armageddon" continues to mean a final and decisive showdown between opposing forces and the end of the world. There have been many prophecies about this event, not all of them involving a battle. Perhaps the most famous is that of Nostradamus (1503–1566), a French astrologer and physician, whose rhymed prophecies, obscure and subject to many interpretations, were published as *Centuries* (1555). In his book he wrote:

The year 1999, seventh month
The great King of terror will descend from
the sky.

. . . .

At this time, *Mars will reign for the good
cause.

This has been interpreted as predicting Armageddon in July 1999. Others say it means an invasion from outer space. The novel *Armageddon* (1964) by *Leon Uris is about the struggle between the Western allies and Russia for control of Berlin and Europe following World War II and the beginning of the Cold War. YA

Around the World in Eighty Days (1873) By
*Jules Verne, this fast-paced adventure novel tells of Phileas Fogg, an English gentleman who wagers £20,000 with five fellow-members of his London club that he can travel around the world in 80 days. Fogg and his French man-servant, Passepartout, set out across Europe, the Middle East, and India, traveling by carriage, train, ship, and elephant, and trailed by police detective Fix, who believes Fogg has stolen £55,000 from the Bank of England and is determined to arrest him. In India Passepartout and Fogg rescue a beautiful young woman, Aouda, from being sacrificed on her dead husband's funeral pyre. They continue east across China, Japan, and the United States in an adventure-filled race against time, chance, and the scheming Fix. Fogg arrives in London apparently too late, then discovers at the last moment that he actually arrived a day early. Rushing to the club, he meets his deadline by one second. He has won the bet, but his real gain is the love of Aouda, whom he marries. If you enjoyed this novel, try also *Edgar Allan Poe's short story "The Balloon Hoax" (1844), a fictional newspaper account of a transatlantic balloon flight that many believed was true when it first appeared. A movie of *Around the World in 80 Days* was released in 1956. MR & YA

arrow A thin, straight shaft, usually sharpened for piercing at one end and feathered for balance at the other end, an arrow is made to be shot from a bow. Since ancient times, it has been used as a weapon and for hunting.

The bow and arrow are featured in many stories. *William Tell, a legendary hero of Switzerland, was famous for his performance with the crossbow and arrow. Arrested for refusing to bow down before the Austrian bailiff, Gessler, he was promised freedom if he would shoot an apple from his son's head. He succeeded.

Robin Hood, a hero in English history and literature, was a master of the bow and arrow. Legend claims that as he lay dying he shot one last arrow to show where his grave should be. You can read about the feats of *Robin Hood with his bow in *The Merry Adventures of Robin Hood* by *Howard Pyle. MR

Arrowsmith (1925) A powerful story by *Sinclair Lewis, this novel tells about a man's passionate devotion to scientific research and his battle against the demands of a society geared to tangible rewards. At the University of Winnemac, near the region described in the novels *Babbitt* and *Dodsworth*, young Martin Arrowsmith meets Professor Max Gottlieb. A great bacteriologist, Gottlieb influences Arrowsmith's entire career by introducing him to the joys and frustrations of research in immunology. After completing medical school, Arrowsmith marries Leora Tozer and feels blessed to have found a woman who understands and encourages his commitment to pure science. Over the years Arrowsmith earns his living at a variety of positions and learns that social obligations and political pressures can interfere with serious work. At the prestigious McGurk Institute in New York City, Arrowsmith's painstaking research leads to the discovery of the X Principle, an organism capable of checking disease-producing bacteria. At Gottlieb's request, Arrowsmith and Leora travel to a Caribbean island to test Arrowsmith's new serum against an outbreak of deadly bubonic plague. Though the serum is mostly successful, Leora and a Swedish colleague die of the disease. In despair, Arrowsmith abandons the strict scientific controls of his experiment and

gives the serum to all who need it. Later remarried, Arrowsmith finds that his aristocratic wife sees his dedication to science as an entertaining oddity. Arrowsmith finally leaves his wife and his position at McGurk, joins a colleague whose commitment is as great as his own, and undertakes private research in the Vermont woods. The novel was adapted for film in 1931. YA

Artemis is the Greek goddess of hunting and fertility. Her Roman counterpart is Diana. Artemis is the daughter of *Zeus and Leto, and the twin of *Apollo. Often called "the mistress of wild things and wild places," she is especially linked with bears. Like her brother, Apollo, she is a deity of light, but is particularly associated with the moon. With the exception of Orion, Artemis does not look kindly upon males. One day, Artemis was competing against Apollo in archery, and he dared her to shoot an *arrow and hit a distant object out at sea. Artemis, being an avid hunter, succeeded in piercing the object but was horrified to learn that her target had been her one love, Orion. In an attempt to rectify what she had done, she placed Orion in the sky as a constellation. Artemis is a dangerous goddess with a quick temper, a vengeful nature, and a powerful character.

Artful Dodger In *Oliver Twist* by *Charles Dickens, a young man, Jack Dawkins, is known as the "Artful Dodger" because of his skill at picking pockets as well as other criminal activities. The term is now used to mean anyone who is clever at fooling others for his or her own gain. Such a person is wily, cunning, and deceitful. *Sir John Falstaff, the comic hero who appears in several plays by *William Shakespeare, is an Artful Dodger, as he lies and is ever on the lookout for ways to turn any situation to his advantage. YA

Arthur See *King Arthur.

Arundel: A Chronicle of the Province of Maine and of the Secret Expedition Against Quebec (1930) is a fine historical novel by *Kenneth Roberts, the first in the series of novels called Chronicles of Arundel. The story, which combines actual historical figures with fictional characters, is narrated by Steven Nason of Arundel, in language that is appropriately old-fashioned without being awkward. When he is 12 years old, Steven is already strongly attached to young Mary Mallinson, but Mary's father is killed by American Indians, and Mary is taken away to Quebec by the Indians and a villainous Frenchman, Henri Guerlac de Sabrevois. Steven and his father make a heroic attempt to find Mary, without success. Fifteen years later Steven, now an expert woodsman and still hoping to find Mary, joins the expedition against Quebec led by Colonel Benedict Arnold (1741–1801). As a guide, he takes part in the dramatic and unbelievably difficult journey up the Kennebec River, over the terrifying Height of Land to the St. Lawrence River. Eventually he finds his childhood friend, but she is greatly changed. The novel is rich in description of natural surroundings and of the admirable Abenaki Indian tribes. If you are interested in the American Revolution, you might enjoy looking at *March to Quebec: Journals of the Members of Arnold's Expedition* (1938), in which Kenneth Roberts compiled source material used in writing *Arundel*. YA

As You Like It (1599), by *William Shakespeare, is a play in five acts, one of his best-loved romantic comedies. After Duke Frederick seizes the dukedom from his older brother and forces him into exile, the senior Duke and his followers find refuge in the Forest of *Arden. At Frederick's court, his daughter, Celia, and his niece, Rosalind, daughter of the exiled duke, meet the gallant Orlando, and a lively attraction blooms between Orlando and Rosalind. When the malicious Frederick orders Rosalind from his palace, Rosalind and Celia leave together, Rosalind disguised as a young man and Celia as a village girl. They make a temporary home in the Forest of Arden, hoping to find Rosalind's father. Now Orlando hears of his brother Oliver's plot to kill him, and Orlando too seeks the safety of the forest, where he comes upon the lawful duke and is warmly received. Orlando decorates the trees with messages of love for Rosalind. Still disguised, Rosalind meets him and devises a way of seeing him often and discovering his true feelings. The good-hearted Orlando saves his brother from an attack by wild beasts, and Oliver begs his forgiveness. Oliver and Celia meet, fall in love, and decide to marry. Rosalind takes off her disguise, convinced Orlando really loves her, and their union is blessed by her father. During the wedding celebration, news is brought that Frederick has had a dramatic change of heart and has restored the dukedom to his brother and lawful ruler. This play contains the famous passage known as "The Seven Ages of Man," which begins: "All the world's a stage,/And all the men and women merely players." If you enjoyed it, be sure to also read *A Midsummer Night's Dream*, another favorite comedy of Shakespeare-lovers. YA

Asch, Sholem (1880–1957) A prolific and very popular Jewish novelist, playwright, and short-story writer, Asch was born in Poland and later lived in several countries, including Israel and the United States, where he became a naturalized citizen. Asch began writing in Hebrew, but changed to Yiddish in the hope of reaching a wider audience among Jews. Much of his early work describes life in the *shtetls*, or small Jewish villages of eastern Europe. Asch's reputation was established with *The God of Vengeance* (1907), a full-length play whose controversial subject matter caused it to be banned in Russia. It is the story of a man raising his innocent daughter while he manages a brothel in another part of the house. Like *Isaac Bashevis Singer, Asch wrote often about the lives of Jewish immigrants in the United States. His best-known work is the biblical trilogy in which he explored what he saw as connections between Judaism and Christianity, and expressed his belief in the power of faith. In *The Nazarene* (1939), the first novel of the trilogy, the story of *Jesus is narrated by a Roman officer, by the disciple Judas, and by a young student from Jerusalem. *The Apostle* (1943) is about the life of

Paul, and *Mary* (1949) concerns the boyhood of Jesus. Some of Asch's fine short stories are collected in *Children of Abraham: The Short Stories of Sholem Asch* (1942). YA

Asimov, Isaac (1920–1992) This prolific Russian-born American wrote over 350 books, both fiction and nonfiction. But he is known best for his *science fiction. Most of his nonfiction books are lively and highly readable explanations of science for the layperson. Asimov sold his first story when he was 17 years old and never stopped producing. His extraordinary output was due to his spending 10 hours a day, 7 days a week writing.

Among his best-known nonfiction works are *Asimov's Guide to the Bible* (1969), *Asimov's Guide to Shakespeare* (1970), and *Asimov's New Guide to Science* (1984). His most famous work of science fiction is *The Foundation Trilogy. *Nightfall*, a novel written in collaboration with *Robert Silverberg and generally considered one of his best works, and *I, Robot*, an early collection of short stories, are two more of Asimov's well-known works of science fiction. If you enjoy Asimov's works, you will want to read his two volumes of autobiography, *In Memory Yet Green* (1979) and *In Joy Still Felt* (1980). YA

Aspern Papers, The (1888) By *Henry James, this superb novel is based on a story about a woman who was *George Gordon Byron's mistress and who kept some of the poet's private papers until her death in Italy. The novella begins after the death of the great Romantic poet Jeffrey Aspern, when an American editor and devotee discovers the existence of a collection of Aspern's papers and yearns to acquire them. The owner, Miss Juliana Bordereau, is very old and lives in Venice with her middle-aged niece, Miss Tina. Under a false name, the American rents a room in the palace where the ladies are living in genteel poverty. The papers are kept hidden, but the American hopes to gain access to them through kind attentions to the niece, to whom he confesses his passionate interest in Aspern. While the old lady is ill, he is caught in the act of searching her desk.

Greatly embarrassed, he leaves Venice briefly and returns to find that Juliana has died. Miss Tina suggests that if he were a "relation," he might possess the treasure. Appalled, he understands that Miss Tina is offering herself in marriage. While he searches for a solution, Miss Tina finds the strength of soul to destroy the papers, releasing them both from a painful situation. If you enjoyed this novel, you may also want to read *The Touchstone* (1900) by *Edith Wharton, about a man who struggles with his conscience after he sells love letters written to him by a woman from his past. YA

Assistant, The (1957) Written by *Bernard Malamud, this novel is about a poor Jewish man, Morris Bober, who owns a failing grocery store in Brooklyn, New York. One evening the store is robbed, and Bober is hit on the head with a gun. As he recuperates, an uneducated Italian man, Frank Alpine, helps around the store, and eventually becomes Bober's assistant. As the novel unfolds, it is revealed that Frank Alpine was one of the thieves, who robbed Bober because he was Jewish. Though Frank feels uncomfortable around Jews, he wants to redeem himself. He works hard, helps the store to thrive, and also falls in love with Bober's daughter, Helen, a 23-year-old who dreams of a college education and a "better life." Later, Morris Bober dies of pneumonia, and Frank takes over the business. In the end, Frank Alpine is a changed man. He converts to Judaism, attains mutual love with Helen Bober, and finds redemption in his new life. Another, quite different, novel about a man who seeks redemption for a past mistake is *Lord Jim* by *Joseph Conrad. YA

Atalanta, a virgin huntress in Greek mythology, was famous for her participation in the Calydonian boar hunt. When the king of Calydon sent for the best hunters from various Greek cities to help kill a gigantic, savage boar, it was Atalanta who first shot and drew the boar's blood. Though Atalanta was desirable, she refused to marry unless the admirer could outrun her in a race. A suitor, named Milanian, knew that Atalanta was a very swift runner, so he dropped three golden apples at different intervals during the race. As Atalanta stopped running to pick up the apples, Milanian was able to win the race and marry Atalanta.

Athena is the Greek goddess of war and wisdom. Her Roman counterpart is *Minerva. The city of Athens was named in her honor, and she was worshipped as the chaste protectress of many other cities and towns. She is the daughter of *Zeus and Metis, born fully grown and armed from the top of Zeus's head. During the *Trojan War, Athena supported the Greeks, often helping such heroes as *Odysseus, *Hercules, and *Perseus. A patron of the arts, Athena was said to have invented the potter's wheel and the double flute. The olive tree, serpent, owl, and lance are depicted as sacred to Athena. You can read about Athena in *Mythology* by Edith Hamilton (1867–1963). MR

Atlantis is a legendary island, associated with a utopian society set in the Atlantic Ocean and ruled by the sons of *Poseidon. After many years, the divine blood of the rulers became diluted with the blood of mortals, making Atlantis weaker and causing it to be defeated in war with the Greeks. Atlantis was then hit by a great earthquake and sank to the bottom of the sea. There are many theories as to the exact location and destiny of Atlantis. In *Twenty Thousand Leagues Under the Sea* by *Jules Verne, *Captain Nemo and his companions make a brief underwater visit to a ruined Atlantean city. The delightfully comic and touching novel *Masters of Atlantis* (1985) by Charles Portis (1933–) centers on an oddball character who dedicates his life to the preservation of the lore and wisdom of lost Atlantis. MR & YA

Atlas is well known in Greek mythology as a powerful Titan. Because he took part in a revolt against *Zeus, he was condemned to stand forever supporting the heavens upon his shoulders. He was only once relieved of this duty, when *Hercules came near to where he stood, looking for special golden apples. Hercules took the heavens upon his own shoulders for a brief moment as Atlas fetched him the apples. You can read about Atlas in *Bulfinch's Mythology* by Thomas Bulfinch (1796–1867). MR

atlas is a book containing geographical maps and information related to them. Depending on their size, atlases also give population figures for countries and cities and list natural resources, climate conditions, and facts on agriculture and industry. While you read a book, you often find general locations of places, but you can get a better idea of just where they are if you look at a map. If, for instance, a city is mentioned, you can turn to an atlas to find exactly where it is.

The Greek geographer Ptolemy prepared the first Western atlas in the second century A.D. The first modern atlas was compiled by Ortelius (1527–1598), a Flemish geographer, and titled *Theatrum orbis terrarum* (1570). The term *atlas* came into use after Gerardus Mercator (1512–1594), another Flemish geographer, published between 1578 and 1595 a series of books of maps with a picture in the front of each showing *Atlas holding up the sky.

The most commonly used atlases are those that contain maps of the whole world, but there are many others devoted to a single country, such as an atlas of the United States, or subject, such as an atlas of highways or world history. Among general atlases are *The New York Times Atlas of the World* and *The New International Atlas*. Younger readers will find useful *Goode's World Atlas, Hammond Medallion Atlas, National Geographic Atlas of the World, Rand McNally Premier World Atlas*, and *Scott Foresman World Atlas*. All of these are frequently updated in new editions. If you would like to learn about the history of atlases, try the lavishly illustrated *Landmarks of Mapmaking* (1968) by Charles Bricker (n.d.). See also *dictionary and *encyclopedia. MR & YA

Atwood, Margaret (Eleanor) (1939–) With *Robertson Davies, Atwood is one of Canada's leading authors, writing poetry, novels, short stories, and criticism. The first of her 10 volumes of poetry was *The Circle Game* (1966). In her poetry and in her novels, Atwood emphasizes the problem of the survival of the person in an undependable world. Typical of her novels is *The Lady Oracle* (1976), the story of a woman who, tiring of her dull life, fakes a suicide by drowning and goes to Italy to start a new life. *The Cat's Eye* (1988) recounts the life of a Canadian girl from her school days, when she feels unpopular, to her growing career as an artist. *The Handmaid's Tale* is in a completely different vein from the other novels. Atwood has published two collections of short stories, *Dancing Girls* (1977) and *Bluebeard's Egg* (1983), as well as two volumes of criticism, including *Second Words: Selected Critical Prose* (1982). Atwood's writings come clearly from her Canadian background, are touched with irony, and express the viewpoint of a modern woman seeking her place in the world. If you like Atwood's books, try those of *Kate Chopin, *Louise Erdrich, *Ellen Glasgow, and *Sylvia Plath. YA

Augie March, The Adventures of (1953) By *Saul Bellow, this novel is often called picaresque, or descriptive of the exploits of a rascal. Its language is rich, generous, and unrestrained; the story is as chaotic as real life; and the characters are presented in great detail and depth. Augie is a Jewish boy growing up in Chicago during the *Great Depression. His frail mother is unable to support the family, which includes Augie's mentally retarded brother, George, and an older brother, Simon. Important family decisions are made by Grandma Lausch, a snobbish and tyrannical boarder with memories of a more elegant past. She is one of many who try to tell Augie how to get ahead, while he continues to go at life in his own way. Augie is hired by William Einhorn, a crippled businessman of doubtful integrity but great learning. Augie's charm and intelligence attract the attention of Mr. and Mrs. Renling, who employ him in their chic saddle shop and later want to adopt him. Augie, however, resists the efforts of employers, relations, friends, and mistresses to make him change his ways and conform to someone else's ideal. He endures a variety of comic and tragic experiences, becomes involved in legal and illegal dealings, escapes from death, has exotic travel adventures in Mexico and Europe, and, finally, marries an actress named Stella. His inability to give in to disappointment may be Augie March's greatest achievement, as important and engaging as is his refusal to take himself too seriously. If you like this novel, you might want to contrast it with the different Studs Lonigan trilogy, by *James T. Farrell, which is also about growing up in depressed areas of Chicago. YA

Aurora is the rosy-fingered Roman goddess of dawn, called Eos by the Greeks. She is often depicted rising from the ocean waves in a chariot pulled by winged horses, or riding *Pegasus with her flaming torch. Among Aurora's many lovers were several mortal men, including Tithonus of Assyria. She becomes so enamored of Tithonus that she persuades Jupiter to make him immortal. Her wish is granted, but the god neglects to give Tithonus eternal youth. Eventually Tithonus becomes so feeble that Aurora changes him into a grasshopper. By Tithonus, Aurora is the mother of Memnon, who was slain by *Achilles in the *Trojan War. You can read about Aurora in *Bulfinch's Mythology by Thomas Bulfinch (1796–1867) and in *Mythology by Edith Hamilton (1867–1963). MR

Austen, Jane (1775–1817) England's first great woman novelist, Austen is considered by some to be the finest woman novelist in any language. She was the youngest of seven children and lived a quiet life. She never married and left home only for short visits. Austen's literary career lasted only six years because of her early death, but she is remembered for her brilliantly written comic novels, full of subtle *satire and penetrating insight, especially into the character of women. They include *Sense and Sensibility; *Pride and Prejudice; Mansfield Park (1814), which follows the search for love and happiness of a young woman who comes to live at her wealthy cousins' estate; *Emma; Northanger Abbey (1818), centering on

a clergyman's daughter who falls in love with the son of a wealthy landowner; and *Persuasion* (1818), which follows the interrupted but ultimately successful romance of a young woman and the naval officer she loves. Once you have become familiar with these books, you will read them again and again, uncovering each time a deeper layer of understanding and compassion for her heroines. YA

Autobiography of Malcolm X, The See *Malcolm X, The Autobiography of.*

Autobiography of Miss Jane Pittman, The See *Miss Jane Pittman, The Autobiography of.*

Avalon, a Celtic word meaning "the island of apples," was an island paradise to which heroes were taken after their death. *King Arthur was taken there after being mortally wounded in battle. In medieval romantic poetry, Avalon was the place where the fairy *Morgan le Fay held her court.

Avi [Avi Wortis] (1937–) A librarian, teacher of children's literature, and author of *Encounter at Easton* and *The Fighting Ground*, Avi was born into a family of writers, aspiring writers, and storytellers. He became interested in writing for young readers when his own children were born, and he has since established himself as a gifted writer of suspense and adventure. His more than 15 novels include *Snail Tail: The Adventures of a Rather Small Snail* (1972), which concerns the amazing journey of a somewhat bookish snail and his friend the ant. In *No More Magic* (1975), Chris and his friends search for a lost bicycle and find themselves entangled in magical doings. *The True Confessions of Charlotte Doyle* (1990), set in 1832, is about frightening events during a young girl's trip across the Atlantic in a sailing ship. MR

Awakening, The (1899) By *Kate Chopin, this strong and graceful short novel offended many turn-of-the-century readers because of its

---

MR = Middle Reader   YA = Young Adult Reader   * = See this main entry

honest portrayal of sexuality and adultery. Edna Pointellier is the wife of a man with whom she has little in common and who regards her as a valuable piece of personal property. At the seaside resort of Grand Isle, near New Orleans, with her husband and two children, Edna meets young Robert Lebrun. Their friendship grows rapidly in the languorous southern climate. Edna awakens to innocent sensual pleasures and to the knowledge that her soul need not be anyone's possession. Her husband is disturbed by her new lack of submissiveness and her attempts at independence. When Robert leaves suddenly on a business trip to Mexico, Edna realizes she is falling in love with him. She is oppressed by a vague anguish and feels that life is passing her by. A love affair with a fashionable gentleman makes her curiously restless, and she dreams of Robert. On his return, it is clear Robert loves her, but he is not strong enough to make a new life with Edna. He leaves, and Edna is unable to bear the hopelessness of a future without him. She swims out to sea until she is exhausted and lets herself drown. A TV movie, *Grand Isle*, based on *The Awakening*, was produced in 1992. If you enjoyed this fine work, read *Madame Bovary* by *Gustave Flaubert. YA

Baal is an ancient Semitic god of fertility, storm, and war. The name was applied to various gods of cities and regions in the ancient Middle East. In the Old Testament of the *Bible, Baal appears as the chief god of Canaan and one that the Hebrews sometimes mingled with their own Jehovah. At times and in some places they even forsake the latter for Baal. Gideon, a judge of Israel, uses a bull to pull down an altar his father has erected to Baal. Baal was often denounced by the Hebrew prophets.

Babbitt (1922), by *Sinclair Lewis, is the story of George F. Babbitt, a 46-year-old real estate broker in a typical Middle Western city Lewis calls Zenith. Plump and prosperous, Babbitt enjoys his membership in the Elks Club, the Boosters Club, and the Republican Party. His wife, Myra, accepts his rather heavy-handed rule of their home and encourages him in their conventional, middle-class way of life. Suddenly, Babbit finds himself bored, restless, dissatisfied. His friend Paul Riesling, more intellectual than his other back-slapping pals, is the only person to whom Babbit can really talk. Some good real estate deals and success as a public speaker lift Babbitt's spirits for a time. But on the night when a triumphant Babbitt becomes vice president of the Boosters Club, Paul and his wife quarrel, and he tries to

kill her. With his friend in prison and Myra temporarily away on a visit, Babbitt attempts to break out of his routine. He has an affair with Tanis Judique, takes up with her younger bohemian friends, and begins to drink heavily. His admiration for Seneca Doane, a socialist lawyer, causes alarm in the conservative community, and people avoid him. Lonely and irritable, Babbitt blusters at Myra. When she is stricken with appendicitis, he feels sorry for his rude behavior and rediscovers his affection for Myra. Their friends are now sympathetic and seem glad of the chance to forget Babbitt's past indiscretions. He gives up rebellion and regains his cherished popularity.

Though George Babbitt is full of human weaknesses, he is portrayed with understanding and affection. Babbitt is usually certain of his own excellence and ability as a salesman, and seldom doubts that he knows what is best for his family. He is full of good intentions but, in fact, has no real interests outside material things and wants only to be loved and accepted. Middle age causes him to wonder about his achievements, and he begins to see his life as mechanical and inhumanly respectable. His deep distrust of anything that does not conform to the standards of Zenith changes briefly into a violent need to break some rules, but this does not bring him the satisfaction for which he yearns. The word

Babbitt has come to mean a self-satisfied businessman whose main interest is material things. If you enjoyed this novel, you will like *Dodsworth*, whose main character is a successful businessman, also from Zenith. *Babbitt* was adapted for the movies in 1934. YA

Babbitt, Natalie (1932–) After starting her career by illustrating books written by others, Babbitt became interested in creating her own stories, and has continued to illustrate all her books. She is known as a writer of imaginative fantasy-adventures for young people, but her stories appeal to readers of all ages. Rather like folktales, her works are full of humor and wisdom. Among her best-known titles are *Tuck Everlasting, *Kneeknock Rise, *The Search for Delicious*, and *The Eyes of the Amaryllis*. MR & YA

Babe, the Blue Ox is a legendary animal companion of *Paul Bunyan. Babe was supposed to have "weighed more than the combined weight of all the fish that ever got away." It was said that he measured 42 handles, and could devour 50 bales of hay at a time. Paul Bunyan dug the Great Lakes for Babe's watering hole, though Babe occasionally drank up the Mississippi River to get a load of logs upstream. You can read about Babe in a number of books, including *Paul Bunyan* (1952) by Esther Shepard (1891–1975) and *Paul Bunyan and His Great Blue Ox* (1926) by Wallace Wadsworth (1894–). MR

babel nowadays describes a scene of great noise and confusion, a hubbub or hullabaloo, in which everyone talks at once and nothing can be understood. Babel was the name of a city and of a tower described in the *Bible. The builders wanted it to reach as high as heaven, but God was annoyed by their arrogance and caused the workers' speech to be hopelessly muddled. As they could no longer understand each other, the tower was never finished. The importance of language and how it shapes human perceptions and activities is an important

theme in the *science fiction novel *Babel-17* (1966) by Samuel R. Delany (1942–). YA

Bach, Richard (1936–), who describes himself as a "gypsy pilot," fell in love with flying when he was in college. He joined the U.S. Air Force and later the Air National Guard in 1959. Bach has worked as a charter pilot, touring stunt flyer, and editor and writer for several flying magazines. Of the books he has written about flying, you may enjoy *Stranger to the Ground* (1963), which describes a jet pilot's experience on a stormy flight between London, England, and Chaumont, France.

Bach is known best for his *Jonathan Livingston Seagull* (1970). He has said that the story was told to him by a voice he heard while on a solitary walk. A similar spooky experience has, he has said, helped him to avoid several air accidents. Another well-known book is the novel *Illusions: The Adventures of a Reluctant Messiah* (1977), about a modern messiah, a pilot and mechanic from the Middle West. Still enthusiastic about flying, Bach is the owner of a number of old planes, including a P-51 Mustang dating from World War II. MR & YA

Bagnold, Enid (1889–1981) This is the maiden name and pen name of Lady Jones, an English writer of novels and plays. Though Enid was sent to an exclusive girls' school in England and to finishing schools in Switzerland and France, she later lived a rather bohemian life, becoming a suffragette and helping women in their fight for voting rights. During World War I, she joined the Voluntary Aid Detachment and worked in an English hospital. *A Diary Without Dates* (1917), her first book, showed so disturbing a picture of hospital routine that she was fired from her job. She then continued her war effort by serving as an ambulance driver for the French army.

Bagnold is perhaps most famous for the novel *National Velvet and for the play *The Chalk Garden* (1956), which is about an eccentric and undisciplined young girl who lives with her grandmother. The grandmother hires

Miss Madrigal, a mysterious governess recently let out of prison, to help care for the girl. The governess makes the dying garden of the title bloom again, and helps the girl mend her differences with her mother. Bagnold also wrote *Serena Blandish, or The Difficulty of Getting Married* (1924), a *satire about a debutante's search for the right husband. *The Chalk Garden* was filmed in 1964. MR & YA

Bagthorpe Saga, The See *Helen Cresswell.

Baldwin, James (Arthur) (1924–1987) has been called one of America's most eloquent speakers for the civil rights movement. The son of a Southern clergyman, he spent his childhood in New York City's Harlem, where he became a preacher when he was 14 years old. In 1948 Baldwin won a literary award that made it possible for him to go to Paris, France, where he remained for 10 years, often very short of money. He returned to the United States in 1957, settled in France again after the death of Martin Luther King, Jr., and spent the rest of his life there.

His first complete novel, *Go Tell It on the Mountain*, is the story of a 14-year-old Harlem boy and his religious experiences, and is probably based in part on Baldwin's own life. *The Fire Next Time* (1963) and the play *Blues for Mr. Charlie* (1964) are both intensely concerned with the problems of black people in the United States. These same problems are the subject of many of Baldwin's other novels, plays, and numerous essays.

Baldwin, who looked upon racial prejudice as a disease of white society, took part in many civil rights demonstrations. He lectured widely and spoke about the cause of civil rights on radio and television. If you like Baldwin's books, you may also like to read those of *Ralph Ellison and *Richard Wright. YA

"Ballad of the Harp-Weaver, The" (1922) This poem by *Edna St. Vincent Millay tells about a widow and her son who have nothing in their house but an old harp with a woman's head carved on it, which they are unable to sell. They have no food and no money, and the boy's clothes are so ragged he cannot go to school or out to play. All the mother can give her son is love. When winter comes, they face freezing and starvation together. On the night before Christmas the mother begins to play the harp, which then starts to weave brightly colored threads into clothes. In the morning a pile of beautiful clothes awaits the boy, but the mother, her hands still caressing the harp, has died. MR & YA

Bambi (1929), by Felix Salten (1869–1947), is the story of a forest deer, told in simple, convincing, and moving language by a writer who clearly loved the woods and its animals. As a fawn, Bambi begins to learn about his surroundings as soon as he is able to stand on his wobbly legs. His mother teaches him, and soon he can speak to the other forest creatures. During his first winter, Bambi discovers hardship, death, and the existence of a mysterious being known as Him, who has the power to kill and from whose scent the animals run in terror. Bambi's mother falls victim to the hunt, but Bambi's sadness is eased when he finds a beautiful doe, Faline, and makes her his wife.

As Bambi grows older, his life becomes darker and more solitary. Occasionally he meets the Prince, the oldest stag in the forest, who knows the depths of the woods and its secrets. When Bambi is shot and wounded by Him, the old Prince helps Bambi escape the dogs trailing him, and shows him a safe hiding place where Bambi slowly recovers. If you want to survive and attain wisdom, the old stag says, you must live alone. After Bambi sees a poacher dead in the forest, he understands that Man is not all-powerful, that there is Another who watches over both man and beast. The old stag goes in search of a final resting place, and Bambi becomes the new Prince. If you enjoyed this story, you will like *Watership Down* by *Richard Adams. *Bambi* was made into a full-length animated cartoon film by *Walt Disney in 1942. MR

Bamboo Curtain, the Like the *Iron Curtain that divided the communist Soviet Union and

Eastern Europe from Western Europe and the rest of the free world, the Bamboo Curtain refers to the ways in which the communist government of mainland China isolated itself from noncommunist countries. These efforts were characterized by many strict rules and regulations, by secrecy, and by strongly enforced censorship.

Banks, Lynne Reid (1929–), an English novelist and playwright whose early career was spent as a theater actress, became a television news reporter and scriptwriter in the 1950s but decided later to become a full-time writer. *The L-Shaped Room* (1961), her first novel, became popular. It concerns an unwed mother who, finding herself alone in the world, moves into an L-shaped boardinghouse room, determined to have and keep her baby. The book was followed by two sequels, *The Backward Shadow* (1971) and *Two Is Lonely* (1974). Banks spent about 10 years in Israel, living on a *kibbutz, where she worked as an English teacher until she returned to England with her family in 1972.

Some of Banks's best-known books for younger readers are *The Indian in the Cupboard* (1980) and its sequel, *The Return of the Indian* (1986). The biography *Dark Quartet: The Story of the Brontës* (1976) and *Letters to My Israeli Sons: A Personal View of Jewish Survival for Young Readers* (1979) are books you also may like to read. *The L-Shaped Room* was made into a movie in 1963. MR & YA

Banner in the Sky (1954), an adventure novel by *James Ramsey Ullman, is based in part on the true story of the 1865 scaling of the Matterhorn, in the Swiss Alps. Rudi Matt has lived all his 16 years in Kurtal, at the foot of the Citadel, a mountain in Switzerland as yet unconquered by climbers. He is already an experienced mountaineer, but his father's death on the Citadel has left Rudi's mother anxious for his safety. To please her, Rudi is reluctantly learning the hotel business.

During a walk on the Blue Glacier, Rudi rescues a man who has fallen into a deep crevasse. He learns the man is Captain Winter, one of the world's finest climbers. Impressed with Rudi's resourcefulness, Winter admits he is planning an expedition to the Citadel. Later, Rudi sneaks out of his house at night to join Winter and his guides for the assault on the summit. He is determined to plant there the red shirt his father wore on his last climb, and Winter agrees to let the boy join the group. You follow the climbers over crevasses, slabs, and crags, up narrow chimneys in the rock, over fragile ledges and inside granite tunnels, through frightening changes in the weather, up smooth rock faces with few handholds. When one guide is hurt in a fall, Rudi sacrifices his chance at the summit to stay with the wounded man. Only Winter and a guide reach the top, but Rudi has the joy of knowing that without him the expedition might have failed. He also knows he will climb again and succeed. MR

Barren Ground (1925), a novel by *Ellen Glasgow, begins in the 1890s, in a small farming community in Virginia where people scratch a living from the poor soil. Twenty-year-old Dorinda Oakley loves the land, but wonders if life has anything to offer beyond endless, back-breaking labor. She sees her family trapped in the atmosphere of failure, and yearns for excitement. Dorinda falls in love with Jason Greylock, son of the village doctor, and her world is suddenly beautiful. On the day before they are to marry, Dorinda discovers that Jason, charming but weak-willed, has been forced to marry a woman he courted a year earlier.

Emotionally devastated, Dorinda goes to New York City to find work and make a new life. When her father dies two years later, worn out by his lifelong struggle with the barren ground, Dorinda goes home determined to use her savings to start a dairy farm. Her efforts and her knowledge of new agricultural techniques bring success, and it pleases her to think she is as good a farmer as any man. Dorinda accepts widower Nathan Pedlar's offer of marriage, even though she is not in love. He is a good man and has promised not to interfere in her life. Together they buy and reclaim a farm from the plague of broomsedge and sassa-fras. After Nathan dies, Dorinda nurses Jason, now sick and destitute, until his death. She learns that her happiness depends only on her-self and the land to which she has given her heart and mind. If you enjoyed this novel, you may like to read *My Ántonia by *Willa Cather. YA

Barretts of Wimpole Street, The (1930) By Rudolf Besier (1878–1942), this is a play based on the courtship of *Elizabeth Barrett and *Robert Browning. Elizabeth Barrett lives with her father, six brothers, and two sisters, has long been in poor health, and is beginning to lose hope of ever leading a normal life. Her poems have brought her a degree of fame and have led to an exchange of letters with Robert Browning. Their meetings bring new energy and pleasure into Elizabeth's dull life. As their friendship deepens, Elizabeth's health im-proves rapidly. Her doctor agrees that she may make a long-awaited trip to Italy, and Robert plans to join her there.

Edward Barrett, Elizabeth's father, is a prud-ish and tyrannical man who demands that his children obey him in all things. When he hears of the travel plans, he makes a terrible scene, accusing Elizabeth of wanting to leave him "all alone," and forbidding her to go anywhere. Robert learns of Edward's outburst and declares his love for Elizabeth, telling her not to reveal it to a father who could make her life misera-ble. Edward's determination to prevent his chil-dren from marrying becomes clear when he announces he will move the whole family to a secluded country house, where they will have less chance to see their few friends.

Robert proposes to Elizabeth and urges her to elope at once. Though she loves him desper-ately, she hesitates, still afraid that her delicate health will be a burden. Robert finally con-vinces her that their only hope is to marry se-cretly and leave for Italy together. Just as Elizabeth is preparing to escape from the house, her father returns unexpectedly. Sens-ing that he has lost her, he tries to excuse his brutal behavior. He speaks of guarding his house "like a dragon" against love, which he de-scribes as "the lowest urge of the body." Eliza-beth realizes her father is not like other men and that she cannot hope to change him. She writes a letter to each member of the family and goes to join her husband. If you enjoyed this play, you may also enjoy reading Mrs. Browning's *Sonnets from the Portuguese, love poems she secretly wrote for Browning while they were courting. *The Barretts of Wimpole Street* was made into movies in 1934 and 1957. YA

Barrie, J(ames) M(atthew) (1860–1937) A Scottish novelist and playwright, Barrie was the son of a weaver and one of ten children. The death of his brother, David, in early child-hood strengthened Barrie's dependence on his mother, whose influence he felt in every aspect of his life. It was she who taught him to read and write stories at an early age, and she was the model for many of his female characters.

Barrie's sentimental novel *The Little Minis-ter* (1891), about a preacher whose marriage scandalized his parishioners, was made into a successful play in 1897. As he became more and more interested in the theater, other plays followed, such as *The Admirable Crichton* (1902), a comedy about the relationship be-tween an imperfect master and his too-perfect butler, and *Dear Brutus* (1917), in which the characters are offered a second chance to live for a brief time in What-Might-Have-Been.

The story of *The Little White Bird* (1902) in-troduced the character of a young boy who would later become the hero of Barrie's most famous play and novel for young people, *Peter Pan, or The Boy Who Would Not Grow Up. The Little Minister* was filmed in 1934 and *The Admirable Crichton*, later retitled *Paradise La-goon*, in 1957. MR & YA

"Bartleby the Scrivener: A Story of Wall-Street" (1853), one of the *The Piazza Tales by *Herman Melville, is a classic American short story. Bartleby is hired by a Wall Street lawyer to copy legal documents by hand. "Pallidly neat, pitiably respectable, incurably forlorn,"

Bartleby quietly refuses to assist with any work other than copying. He answers most requests put to him by saying simply, "I would prefer not to." Passive in the extreme, inscrutable, exasperating, and touching at the same time, he eventually stops working altogether. He continues, however, to inhabit the office even after his employer has insisted that he leave. Unwilling to use harsh methods on a man so quiet and dignified, the desperate lawyer finally moves to other chambers, and Bartleby resists all efforts to dislodge him. Arrested and taken to prison, he dies there as quietly and mysteriously as he lived. The lawyer hears afterward that Bartleby once toiled in the Dead Letter Office, where the air of hopelessness was assumed to have unhinged his mind. Another famous short story about an obscure office worker is *"The Overcoat" by *Nikolai Gogol. YA

Bathsheba (fl. 10th century B.C.) In the Old Testament of the *Bible, *David, king of Israel, becomes enamored of Bathsheba when he sees her bathing. A beautiful woman, she is the wife of Uriah, a Hittite, a people of Syria and Asia Minor. David orders Joab, his commander, to place Uriah in a dangerous position in battle and to abandon him there. Uriah is killed and David marries Bathsheba, who gives birth to *Solomon. When David dies, she is instrumental in securing the succession to the throne for Solomon, and she is influential during his reign. MR & YA

Baum, L(yman) Frank (1856–1919) Beginning professional life as a newspaper reporter, Baum edited the *Dakota Pioneer* in Aberdeen, South Dakota, and tried his hand at a number of other jobs before he began writing for young people. Baum was a touring actor for a time and undertook several business projects, mostly unsuccessful, which gave him a chance to travel widely in the United States. His first best-seller, *Father Goose* (1899), sold 90,000 copies in 90 days. With W(illiam) W(allace) Denslow (1856–1915), who illustrated *Father Goose*, Baum wrote *The Wonderful Wizard of Oz*, now considered a classic for young readers. The book has been described as "the first distinctive attempt to construct a fairyland out of American materials."

Under several different pen names, Baum wrote for both adult and younger readers. His best-loved stories, however, are the 14 tales about the imaginary land of *Oz. Some of these are *The Land of Oz* (1904), *The Road to Oz* (1909), and *Glinda of Oz* (1920). The Oz books were so popular that after Baum's death other authors continued to write the series. Besides an adaptation for the stage, a move version, *The Wizard of Oz* (1939), has been shown many times on television. MR

Bawden, Nina (Nina Mary Kark) (1925–) An English writer of novels for both adult and younger readers, Bawden spent a number of years in a Welsh mining valley, where she was sent with her school to escape the bombing of London during World War II. She began writing for young people after her children were born.

Bawden's books have been called "both wise and entertaining." Some of her better-known works for younger readers are *The Runaway Summer* (1969), about an English girl who becomes involved in an adventure while spending the summer with her aunt and grandfather; *Carrie's War; and The Peppermint Pig* (1975), about a 9-year-old English girl whose life changes when the family moves from London to the country and she is given a pig to raise. Among Bawden's many novels for older readers is *The Ice House* (1983), centering on the relationship of two women who have been friends since youth. MR & YA

Beat Generation refers to a group of people who came of age just after World War II. The Beat movement began in the 1950s mainly in artistic circles in San Francisco and New York City, and its members were "beat" or exhausted and disillusioned by the society around them. They were sometimes called "beatniks" by those who disapproved of their style. Members showed their dislike of "square" or overly conventional behavior by dressing in seedy clothing and speaking a jargon based on jazz talk and phrases borrowed from Buddhism. In protest against the dreary materialism of American life, they advocated a great degree of personal freedom and experimented with drugs and other means of increasing sensory awareness. Major figures of the movement included *Jack Kerouac, whose loosely structured novels typified the Beats, and the poet Allen Ginsberg (1926–). In the 1960s, followers of a kind of beat life-style came to be known as hippies. You may enjoy reading some of the works of the Beat writers in *The Portable Beat Reader* (1992), edited by Ann Charters (1936–).

Beau Geste (1924), by the English novelist P.C. Wren (1885–1941), is a mystery story that begins at the estate of Brandon Abbas in England and unfolds in a remote African outpost of the French *Foreign Legion. The hero is Michael Geste, who is called Beau Geste (meaning beautiful gesture) because of his handsome appearance, irresistible charm, and intelligence. Beau, his twin, Digby, and their younger brother, John, live with their aunt, Lady Brandon, whose husband has given her a fabulous sapphire. One evening the "Blue Water" is brought from the safe for the family to admire and disappears when the lights fail briefly. Lady Brandon is clearly upset, but to everyone's surprise she does not call the police or notify her absent husband. Some time later the three brothers run away, secretly and separately. Suspicion falls on Michael, who had been heard to say he needed money.

All three join the Foreign Legion and are reunited in North Africa, where Michael and John are posted to a fort at Zinderneuf and Digby is sent to another region. At the fort, many legionnaires suffer from the terrible heat and the monotony of army life in the vast desert. Lejaune, the commandant of the garrison, treats his men cruelly and soon a group is planning mutiny and murder. As the situation becomes desperate, the fort is attacked by camel-riding Touareg Arabs, and a long siege begins. Major Henri de Beaujolais arrives with his men to help the outnumbered legionnaires and finds the Touaregs gone, but every soldier

in the fort is dead and propped up at his post to give the effect of a living army. Lejaune's corpse, with a French bayonet in the chest, and Michael's written "confession" are discovered together. You learn that John killed Lejaune as he was searching Michael's body for the jewel many thought he carried, then escaped from the fort without being seen by Beaujolais.

Michael's letter explains that Lady Brandon secretly sold the "Blue Water" to save her home and had an imitation made. Michael learned of this and, knowing his uncle would be enraged, stole the fake to make it unnecessary for Lady Brandon to reveal the sale. Once certain of protecting her, he ran away to make himself look guilty and thereby remove suspicion from other family members. He begs Lady Brandon to let her brutish husband go on believing he is a common thief. In this way, Sir Hector will never trouble her about the loss of the jewel, and his "beau geste" will have served its purpose. *Beau Geste* was made into notable movies in 1926, 1939, and 1966. YA

Beckett, Samuel (Barclay) (1906–1989) An Irish-born playwright, novelist, and author of *Waiting for Godot*, Beckett was a good scholar and cricket player at Trinity College, Dublin. He spent two years in Paris, met *James Joyce, and became one of a group who read to Joyce when his sight was deteriorating. Before settling permanently in Paris in 1937, Beckett published a collection of short stories, some poems, and a novel. *Murphy* (1938) is about a poor Irishman in London who meditates endlessly in a rocking chair, trying to achieve a state of perfect bliss. The novel set the tone for future works, many of which portray people trapped in ever more bizarre situations.

Beckett later wrote in French, often translating his own works into English. His best-known novels form a trilogy. In *Molloy* (1951), an old man in failing health discusses his problems with grim humor. *Malone Dies* (1951) is Malone's own story written with a miserable stub of a pencil that breaks in mid-sentence, bringing the book to an end. *The Unnamable* (1953) concerns a shapeless blob existing in a milk jug, begging to be told what and where it is.

During the Nazi occupation of Paris, Beckett and his wife escaped to the safety of Vichy, in the south of France. It is said their conversations along the difficult route became the basis for *Godot*. When the play appeared, many condemned it as a depressing practical joke in which nothing happens. Now considered one of the mainstays of the "theater of the absurd," it has been described by Beckett as "not despair, but life—aimless, but always with an element of hope." *Endgame* (1957) is another controversial and widely performed play, in which two characters sitting in garbage cans discuss love. *All That Fall* (1957) is a radio play about an old woman traveling through dreary surroundings to meet her husband. An intensely private man who disliked publicity, Beckett tried unsuccessfully to persuade the Swedish Academy not to award him the Nobel Prize for literature in 1969. See also *Jean Genet and *Luigi Pirandello. YA

Becky Thatcher See *Tom Sawyer, The Adventures of.*

bell You are familiar with this word, but you may not know expressions built on it. For example, when you say "That rings a bell!" something has jogged your memory or caused you to remember. "Sound as a bell" means healthy and strong, as an unsound bell is worthless. From the *fable of the mice who wanted to hang a bell around the cat's neck so they could hear it coming, there is the expression "to bell the cat." A person who agrees to "bell the cat" will take on a dangerous job or be the leader in a tight spot. To be "saved by the bell" means to be rescued at the last moment, as a prizefighter may be rescued from defeat by the bell rung at the end of the round.

The big bell in a church is rung to call people to worship, and the lack of a proper bell can be a great drawback, as in *A Bell for Adano* by *John Hersey. Church bells are also tolled for the dead. A famous passage from *Hymn to God, My God, in My Sickness* (c.1623) by *John Donne begins "No man is an island, entire of itself," and ends "Never send to know

for whom the bell tolls; it tolls for thee." From this *Ernest Hemingway took the title of his novel about the Spanish Civil War, *For Whom the Bell Tolls.* YA

Bell, Currer; Bell, Ellis; and **Bell, Acton** These are the pen names used by the Brontë sisters, Charlotte, Emily, and Anne. It was *Charlotte Brontë who discovered *Emily's poems, and after Anne revealed she had been writing poetry as well, the sisters published *Poems by Currer, Ellis and Acton Bell* (1846), paying the costs from their own pockets. The sisters chose to adopt pen names to protect their privacy and ensure that critics, unaware of their sex, would judge their work fairly. See also *Brontë Family. YA

Bell for Adano, A (1944) This novel by *John Hersey is set in Italy during World War II. The American army has just driven the Fascists out of Adano, and Major Victor Joppolo is now civil affairs officer for the small town. Joppolo sets up his office in the ancient city hall, notices that the 700-year-old bell is missing from its tower, and learns it was taken down and made into cannons for the Fascists. It is clear the absence of the historic bell is hurting the battered citizens almost as much as the severe food shortage. To some, "the spirit is more important than the stomach." Joppolo, the son of Italian-American parents, does his best to increase food supplies and works hard to govern in a fair and democratic way. With ingenuity and tact, he talks a Navy acquaintance into getting a beautiful ship's bell for Adano's clock tower. As the grateful citizens celebrate the gift, Joppolo learns he will be transferred to North Africa, the result of having ruffled too many official feathers in helping the people of Adano. Another novel about the war you may like is *Tales of the South Pacific* (1947) by *James A. Michener. *A Bell for Adano* was adapted for the stage by Paul Osborn (1901–1988) in 1944 and appeared in movie form in 1945. YA

Bell Jar, The (1971) This autobiographical novel is based on the life of *Sylvia Plath in the summer and autumn of 1953. Ether Greenwood, 19 years old and a fine student, wins a contest for a summer job in New York City as guest editor at a famous fashion magazine. The strain of the job, in the world of Madison Avenue, begins to wear Esther down. Though she has a busy social life, she feels more and more disconnected from her friends. She wanders alone, occasionally meeting men, and uses a false name. Esther visits her friend Buddy Willard in a sanatorium where he is recovering from tuberculosis and, when he makes a clumsy proposal of marriage, she says she is too neurotic and will never marry. On her last night in New York City, she throws most of her clothing out a window of her hotel room.

At home in a dreary Boston suburb, Esther finds herself unable to eat or sleep or work. She has a "zombie" in the throat and can hardly talk. Her worried mother takes her to a psychiatrist, whom she hates on sight, and he orders her treated with shock therapy at a private hospital. After this terrifying experience, Esther still feels she is seeing the world from the inside of a bell jar, a bell-shaped glass cover used to protect delicate objects, and she begins to consider various ways of killing herself. She hides in the cellar of her house and swallows some stolen pills. Discovered in time by her mother, Esther wakes in the hospital where she is given a series of shock treatments that wipe her out "like chalk on a blackboard."

Though she feels more at peace and free from some of the stifling distortions of her imagined bell jar, she remembers her life and the world as a bad dream. She survives another shock when a fellow patient commits suicide, and is able to think about returning to college. The story ends as she is about to be interviewed by the doctors before her release, when she has been "patched, retreaded and approved for the road." *The Bell Jar* was adapted for film in 1979. YA

Bellairs, John (1938–) An English teacher and writer of humorous stories of the supernatural, Bellairs has long been interested in archaeology, history, and (especially) trivia. Among his books are *The House with a Clock in Its Walls*, the first book of a popular and spooky trilogy; *The Face in the Frost* (1969), which Bellairs describes as somewhat in the style of *The Lord of the Rings*; and *The Curse of the Blue Figurine* (1983), about a boy who becomes involved in a strange adventure when he takes a small blue figurine from a haunted church. MR

Bellarosa Connection, The (1989) This subtle short novel, by *Saul Bellow, is narrated by a friend of Harry Fonstein, a Polish Jew who fled the Nazis during World War II. Arrested in Rome by the Fascists, Harry Fonstein is helped to escape by an unknown Italian. When Harry asks who is the mastermind behind this Hollywood-style rescue, the Italian answers "Bellarosa." Later Harry learns that Bellarosa is a mispronunciation of Billy Rose, a New York show business celebrity who financed the rescue of Jews in Europe.

Harry makes his way to the United States and eagerly looks forward to thanking Billy Rose personally for saving his life. Rose refuses to see him, however, and Fonstein feels strongly that his adjustment to America is incomplete. Fonstein's wife, Sorella, an ingenious and powerful woman, a "tiger wife," takes the situation in hand. Sorella comes into possession of a journal kept by a woman who worked for Billy Rose and who recorded his shady deals and love affairs. Sorella confronts Rose with evidence that could destroy his reputation and offers to hand over the file if he will meet with Fonstein. Rose rejects the offer and insults everyone connected with it. In disgust, Sorella throws the file at his head and abandons her mission. She later describes Rose as a man whose soul is too flimsy to help conclude the greatest chapter in Fonstein's life. Years later, after the Fonsteins are killed in an accident, the narrator is moved to write all he can remember about the Bellarosa Connection. YA

Belloc, (Joseph) Hilaire (Pierre) (1870–1953) A French-born English man of letters, Belloc wrote more than 150 books. He was a well-known figure whose political and social views were often unpopular and who was strongly criticized for his anti-Jewish feelings. His varied professional roles included those of historian, war commentator, political analyst, literary critic, satirist, essayist, novelist, and poet. Belloc is also remembered for his long friendship and collaboration with *G.K. Chesterton, with whom he shared many religious and political beliefs. Their satirical antics inspired *George Bernard Shaw to create an overweight mythical beast called the Chesterbelloc, whose ideas were absurdly out-of-date.

As a writer of nonsense verse, Belloc holds a high place in English comic poetry. *The Red Child's Book of Beasts* (1896) contains short verses written from the perspective of the sternly moral parent who describes the ghastly consequences of bad behavior. *Cautionary Children* (1907) has such titles as "Franklin Hyde, Who Caroused in the Dirt and Was Corrected by His Uncle" and "Maria, Who Made Faces and a Deplorable Marriage." Many of his poems for young readers are collected in *Cautionary Verses* (1959). If you like his books, you may also enjoy the books of *Roald Dahl and those of the writer and artist Edward Gorey (1925–). MR

Bellow, Saul (1915–), author of *A Theft* and *The Bellarosa Connection*, was born in Canada of Russian-Jewish parents and spent his childhood in the slums of Montreal and Chicago. He now lives in Chicago. Educated at the University of Chicago and Northwestern University, he discovered that every time he worked on his thesis, "it turned out to be a story." After serving in the Merchant marine in World War II, he won a fellowship in 1948 that gave him the chance to work in Paris and Rome. There he wrote *The Adventures of Augie March* (1953), a much-acclaimed novel full of defiant humor. Other novels include *Henderson the Rain King* (1959), which tells of a millionaire's trip to Africa to heal his soul, and *Herzog* (1964), the story of a modern Jewish *Everyman. Many of Bellow's works are concerned with the value of the human soul in

modern life. His much-praised novella *Seize the Day* (1956) centers on a middle-aged man who has been victimized by life and by the choices he has made in his life. Bellow won the Nobel Prize for literature in 1976.

Ben and Me: A New and Astonishing Life of Benjamin Franklin. As Written by His Good Mouse Amos (1939), by *Robert Lawson, is a mouse's account of his long and fruitful association with Ben. Amos, oldest of 26 children, leaves his crowded nest to make his way in the world. Looking for food and shelter, he wanders into the chilly home of Dr. Franklin (whom he recognizes immediately) and settles himself in the great man's fur cap. During a conversation between Amos and Ben about the inadequate heating arrangements, Amos makes a practical suggestion that inspires Ben to improvise the Franklin stove. Delighted by the success of this device, Ben and Amos enter into a formal agreement. In return for supplying his family and himself with food, Amos will give Ben unlimited advice and help at all times. Thereafter, Amos takes part, for better and sometimes for worse, in Ben's exciting experiments with electricity, the nature of lightning, and many other projects. Amos accompanies Ben to the Court of France, where he meets a beautiful and aristocratic mouse named Sophia and risks his life to help her rejoin her family. Amos's story ends with the joyful celebration of Ben's 81st birthday. Lawson wrote other books about famous people as told by their pets, *Mr. Revere and I* (1953) and *Captain Kidd's Cat* (1984). MR

Benchley, Robert (Charles) (1889–1945) A humorist, Benchley was known for his nonsense and kindly, spontaneous wit. You will enjoy especially his books of funny essays. These poke fun at everything from income taxes to the problems of training dogs. Often they describe a confused, ordinary man who fails time after time to adapt to the demands of modern life. While Benchley's characters blunder, they are able to laugh at their own mistakes and go on to the next exasperating situation. Benchley's books include *Of All Things* (1922), *My Ten Years in a Quandary and How They Grew* (1936), and *Inside Benchley* (1942). YA

Benét, Stephen Vincent (1898–1943) A poet, novelist, historian, and author of *"The Devil and Daniel Webster," Benét was born into a military family and spent his childhood on army posts. He read a great deal of American military history, as well as literature, and began writing poetry in college. Benét won a fellowship to study in Paris, where he wrote the long poem *John Brown's Body*. He became passionately interested in the changes that took place during and just after the Civil War, and was devoted to the ideals of democracy and the brotherhood of man. *A Book of Americans* (1933), which Benét wrote with his wife, Rosemary Carr Benét (1898–1962), provided portraits of historical figures for young people. MR & YA

Ben-Hur: A Tale of the Christ (1880), by *Lew Wallace, is a historical novel that has enjoyed enormous popularity since its first appearance. Set in Jerusalem and Antioch at the time of *Jesus, the novel brings to life the beginnings of Christianity and the decadence of the Roman Empire. It portrays some real historical figures, such as Jesus, King Herod, Pontius Pilate, and the Roman emperor Nero. Into this background is woven the story of Judah Ben-Hur, the handsome son of a respected Jewish family of Jerusalem. Betrayed by Messala, a Roman and Ben-Hur's childhood friend, Ben-Hur is falsely accused of trying to kill an important Roman official. He is taken away into slavery, while his mother and sister are imprisoned and the family property is seized. While in captivity, Ben-Hur saves the life of a wealthy Roman, is adopted by him, and is educated as a Roman citizen. He arranges to enter a great chariot race at Antioch to compete with his arrogant enemy Messala, and defeats him in spite of Messala's ruthless tactics. Ben-Hur then returns to Jerusalem to look for his mother and sister, and is later led to believe they have died of leprosy. The two women are alive and in a leper colony. Both are cured by Jesus, called the Nazarene, before the eyes of

Ben-Hur. After this miracle, and after witnessing the crucifixion of Jesus, Ben-Hur and his family become Christians. At the end of the story Ben-Hur goes to Rome to help in building the catacombs where persecuted Christians can one day find refuge and a place to worship. If you enjoyed this book, you will also like *The Robe* (1942) by Lloyd C. Douglas (1877–1951), about the Roman soldier who gains the robe worn by Jesus before the crucifixion. *Ben-Hur* was dramatized in 1899 and later adapted for film several times. The best-known movie was produced in 1959. YA

Benito Cereno (1856) is a suspenseful short novel by *Herman Melville, based in part on a true story. It has been called one of the finest novellas in American literature. His ship anchored off the coast of Chile, in the year 1799, Captain Amasa Delano sights a mysterious vessel that shows signs of distress. He approaches a Spanish merchant ship that is transporting slaves. The ship is in an appalling state of neglect, and its young captain, Don Benito Cereno, seems on the verge of collapse. Supported by his black slave Babo, a man of unusual intelligence, Don Benito haltingly describes the storms and disease that beset the ship and caused the death of officers and passengers. Delano is a generous and trusting man, but his suspicions are aroused by the eccentric behavior of the captain and signs of disobedience and violence among the freely roaming slaves. As Delano prepares to return to his ship, Don Benito leaps into his boat. Babo jumps after him and tries to kill his master with a dagger. As Delano begins to understand what is happening, the slaves attack with hatchets. After a narrow escape, Cereno explains that the slaves had mutinied weeks before, taken over the ship under the leadership of Babo, and demanded to be returned to Africa. They murdered most of the crew, and forced Cereno under pain of death to conceal their true purpose from Delano. When the slave revolt is put down and Babo is executed, Don Benito enters a monastery and dies three months later.

Melville sets the shadowy tone of this complex story with his first description of a gray sky, a gray sea "like waved lead," and the "flights of troubled gray fowl, kith and kin with flights of troubled gray vapors" over the water. The inability to see clearly and the general sense of ambiguousness continues through the story to its climactic moments, when Delano can at last distinguish between appearance and reality. Important themes in the story are the ancient struggle between good and evil, between black man and white man, and the relationship between master and slave. If you liked this novella, you may enjoy *Lord Jim by *Joseph Conrad, another beautifully written tale of the sea and a man's search for moral identity. YA

Bent Twig, The (1915) By *Dorothy Canfield Fisher, this novel tells the story of an unusual Middle Western family, told by the eldest daughter, Sylvia. It emphasizes the importance of good values in developing character. Professor Marshall, a teacher at the state university, lives with his wife and three children in a rambling farmhouse. Every aspect of the Marshalls' life is in contradiction to the social ideals of the "best people." The Marshalls are natural and boisterous rather than genteel, they keep no servants and do the housework themselves, and their many friends are chosen for their conversation rather than for their connections. The rapport between parents and children is warm and close. When this vital group is visited by their Aunt Victoria, young Sylvia is enchanted by Victoria's elegance and graciousness. A wealthy widow, Victoria has devoted her life to the leisurely enjoyment of beautiful things and aristocratic friends. In spite of her love for her Spartan parents, over the years Sylvia finds herself drawn to Victoria's style of living. Sylvia's desire for social acceptance leads her into some disturbing situations. At college, she allows herself to be courted by a wealthy but empty-headed young man. Much to the relief of her family, Sylvia's better judgment wins out, and she rejects what might have been a disastrous engagement.

Now an established music teacher, Sylvia spends a summer with Aunt Victoria and again surrenders to the atmosphere of elegance and ease. She is attracted to two very different men. Felix Morrison is a languid connoisseur of art and good living, while Austin Page is the bravely unconventional heir who spends his fortune on helping others. The tragedy of her mother's death and a growing awareness of her own real values help Sylvia make her difficult decision and remain true to her upbringing. YA

Bentley, E(dmund) C(lerihew) (1875–1956) An English journalist, novelist, and author of *Trent's Last Case, Bentley began writing nonsense verse at secondary school with his friend *G.K. Chesterton. At Oxford University he wrote light character pieces on some of the better-known students, including *John Buchan. Bentley had a long and distinguished career as newspaperman and editor for the London *Daily News* and *Daily Telegraph*, where he concentrated on politics and foreign affairs, and occasionally contributed humorous articles to *Punch*. Sometimes called the father of the modern detective novel, Bentley brought an element of wit and realism to detective fiction, which in his day tended to imitate the more Romantic mystery writers, such as *Arthur Conan Doyle and *Edgar Allan Poe. None of his other novels was as successful as *Trent*.

Bentley had another claim to fame. He invented a comic verse form, the clerihew, named after his mother's maiden name and his middle name. It consists of two rhymed couplets using free meters and the name of a person in one of the lines:

> Edgar Allan Poe
> Was passionately fond of roe
> He always liked to chew some
> When writing anything gruesome.

You may read some more clerihews in *The Complete Clerihews of E.C. Bentley* (1981). YA

Beowulf, which means "bee-wolf" or bear, is the hero of an epic poem composed in Old English around the year 700. Some scholars believe it was written by an English Christian who may have adapted an earlier epic or collection of folktales. Based on Scandinavian history and legends, the story takes place about

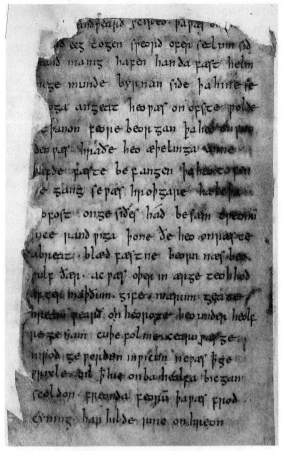

This is a page from *Beowulf*, an epic poem composed almost 13 centuries ago.

200 years earlier. Beowulf has the quality of heroism in a cold and unfriendly world. He is a young Swedish prince who visits the famous mead-hall (feasting hall) of a Danish king, where he learns that the hall is attacked every night by a monster named *Grendel. When he offers to fight the monster, he succeeds in tearing off one of its arms and drives it away. On the following night Grendel's mother comes for vengeance. Beowulf kills her and rids the kingdom of its scourge. After 50 years of a peaceful reign, King Beowulf fights again—this time it is a dragon that is destroying the land. In a long and painful battle, the aged Beowulf kills the fire-breathing beast and saves his people. His body is placed on a huge funeral pyre to be burnt, but his great deeds have survived in memory and legend for generations. Younger and older readers alike will enjoy reading the story of Beowulf in *Beowulf the Warrior* (1961) by *Ian Serraillier. MR & YA

Bert Breen's Barn (1975), by *Walter D. Edmonds, is a novel about honest and hard-working people determined to improve their lot. Written with simplicity and grace, it is also a detailed guide to the art of building a barn. Fourteen-year-old Tom Dolan lives with his mother and two sisters and helps out by working at the local mill. Tom yearns to buy the fine barn on Widow Breen's land, move it to the Dolan farm, and eventually acquire more cows. Encouraged by his friend Birdy Morris, who built the barn for old Bert Breen years ago, Tom puts a little money aside whenever he can. After the death of Bert's widow, her land is sold to a wealthy neighbor, Mr. Armond. Tom has earned enough for a modest down payment, and Armond agrees to sell him the barn if he will remove it neatly. To add to the excitement, rumor has it that Bert Breen hated banks and kept his money hidden at home. While Tom and Birdy dismantle the barn, they are interrupted by some rough men who will stop at nothing to find Breen's treasure. The barn is removed to the Dolans' farm piece by piece. Tom discovers Breen's hiding place under the old floorboards, containing enough money to finish the barn properly and buy cows. With the help of willing neighbors, the barn is reassembled and raised again in a joyful celebration of hard work and home cooking. MR

Best Christmas Pageant Ever, The (1972) By Barbara Robinson (1927–), this is a funny and touching story about the Herdman children—six stringy-haired, skinny ruffians who tell lies, steal, hit little kids, set fires, and generally devote all their energy to maintaining their reputation as the terrors of the school. When the Herdmans invade Sunday School as well, in the hope of raiding the food supplies, their classmates wait enthralled to see what will happen. The invasion takes place while plans are being made for the Sunday School Christmas pageant, and the horrible Herdmans volunteer at once for all the best parts. A problem arises when their teacher realizes the Herdmans have never *heard* the Christmas story and must have every detail explained at length. Surprisingly, instead of turning the pageant into a calamity, the Herdmans create their own quirky, realistic, and moving interpretation of the birth of Jesus, and the pageant is a great success. Robinson has written several other books, including *Across from Indian Shore* (1962), about a young boy who becomes friends with an Indian princess, the last descendant of the great chief Massasoit of the Wampanoags; and, in a lighter vein, *My Brother Measures Worms and Other Louis Stories* (1988), about the hilarious adventures of a young girl's family. MR

Best of Friends, The (1989) By Margaret Rostkowski (1945–), this strong and convincing novel was written in answer to her students' questions about the Vietnam War. It centers on Dan Ulvang, a high school senior, his sister, Sarah, one year younger, and their best friend, Will Spencer, also a senior. Because Dan is bright and confident, he has made a habit of helping and directing Will, for whom schoolwork is difficult. Lately, however, the easygoing Will has begun to resent being told what to do. Sarah, who loves them both, is happy in a new and more adult relationship with Will, but her determination to help the antiwar movement is causing strain at home. All three young people are becoming more aware of the tragic events in Vietnam and the effects of the war on attitudes among family and friends. Dan, who plans to attend college, feels angry when his domineering father, a member of the town draft board, shows his contempt for draft evaders. Dan must eventually tell his father of his hard-won decision to destroy his draft card and defy the authority his father represents. Will surprises everyone by deciding his own future without Dan's help or approval, and he joins the army to fight in Vietnam.

Margaret Rostkowski is a teacher who likes to use stories and memories of her family life, drawing on emotions common to all family groups to bring her characters to life. An earlier novel you may like is *After the Dancing Days* (1986), in which 13-year-old Annie makes friends with a badly wounded veteran of World War I and tries to help him adjust to the aftermath of that war. MR

BFG, The This is a story by *Roald Dahl that you would like to be true even if it is unbelievable. BFG stands for the Big Friendly Giant who snatches 8-year-old Sophie from her bed in an orphanage in an English village and takes her to his cave in Giant Country. The BFG is 24 feet tall and kindly. There are nine other giants, all twice as large, with such names as Fleshlumpeater and Bonecruncher. The BFG eats only a vegetable called snozzcumbers, which tastes bad and smells worse. The other giants eat only human beings. The BFG senses dreams in the air, collects them, and puts them in bottles. With his trumpet he blows the dreams into children's bedrooms so they will have pleasant dreams. When the BFG and Sophie learn that the other giants are eating schoolchildren, the BFG concocts a nightmare to give to the queen of England so she will dream of the schoolchildren. When she awakes she will see a small girl—Sophie—sitting on her windowsill. Sophie and the BFG tell the queen of the terrible events. The queen orders the nine giants to be tied up and lifted by helicopter to London. There they are put in a pit 500 feet deep and fed nothing but snozzcumbers. A large house suitable for the BFG is built for him, and Sophie is given a smaller one. If you enjoyed this story, you may also enjoy the equally wacky book *Yobgorgle: Mystery Monster of Lake Ontario* by *Daniel M. Pinkwater. MR

Bible, the The sacred literature of both *Judaism and *Christianity, the Bible exists in two basic forms. The Hebrew or Jewish Bible, rich with the early history of the Jewish people, was written originally mostly in Hebrew and is the Scripture of Judaism. The Christian Bible incorporates the 39 books of the Jewish Bible as the Old Testament and the 27 books of the New Testament. The first five books of the Bible (*Genesis, *Exodus, Leviticus, Numbers, and Deuteronomy) constitute the Law (or Torah) of the Jewish Bible and are called the Pentateuch in the Christian Bible. The remaining books of the Old Testament are grouped by Judaism in two sections, the Prophets and the Holy Writings. The history of the Hebrews is told in the Old Testament. The New Testament of the Christian Bible, originally written in Greek, relates the beginning and spread of Christianity from the birth of *Jesus to about 40 years after the crucifixion. The heart of the New Testament is the four Gospels (*Matthew, *Mark, *Luke, and *John). The last book, *Revelation, is a work of prophecy. In addition to the two testaments, there is the Apocrypha (from the Greek meaning "hidden"), which consists of 15 books that are not accepted in the Hebrew Scriptures. Most Protestant denominations also do not accept the Apocrypha as Scripture, but some of them are included in Catholic Bibles.

There have been many translations of the Bible from the original languages. Generally considered the most notable as literature is the King James Version (1611), which is still favored by many conservative Protestants. The New Revised Standard Version (1990) is the officially adopted Bible of most American Protestant denominations. The New American Bible (1970) was prepared for Catholics. Today's English Bible (1979) (also known as the Good News Bible) and the Bible for Today's Family: New Testament (1991) are versions in simple language. Other Bibles that are not translations but rather retellings of the Bible for younger readers include *Stories from the Bible* (1929) by *Walter de la Mare, *The Children's Bible* (1965), *Brian Wildsmith's Illustrated Bible Stories* (1968) by Philip Turner (1925–), *The Story Bible* (1971) by *Pearl S. Buck, *Bible Stories for Children* (1980) by Geoffrey Horn (1915–) and Arthur Cavanaugh (1926–), and *The Macmillan Book of 366 Bible Stories* (1988). There are also many reference books to assist a reader in understanding the Bible, its people, and its events. Among them are *Asimov's Guide to the Bible* (1969) by *Isaac Asimov, *Who's Who in the Bible* (1975) by George Barr (1916–), *Reader's Digest Family Guide to the Bible* (1984), and *Harper's Bible Dictionary* (1985). MR & YA

Bierce, Ambrose (Gwinnett) (1842–1914?) As a journalist and social critic, Bierce was witty but savagely satirical. Turning to short stories,

he wrote in the same manner, revealing more and more as time went on his pessimistic view of the world and the human race. Many of his stories are set in the Civil War, in which he fought. In *Tales of Soldiers and Civilians* (1891), later revised as *In the Midst of Life* (1898), he collected 26 of his best stories, most touched with an atmosphere of horror. An example is "An Occurrence at Owl Creek Bridge," about the fate of a captured soldier. In much the same vein are the 24 stories in *Can Such Things Be?* (1893), including the *science fiction classic "Moxon's Master," about a scientist who builds a robot chess player, and the horror classic "The Damned Thing," about a man who is stalked and finally killed by an invisible creature. *The Devil's Dictionary* (1911), first published as *The Cynic's Word Book* (1906), is a volume of definitions that allow Bierce to express his bitter view of life and his hatred of hypocrisy. For example, a bore is defined as "a person who talks when you wish him to listen." In 1913 Bierce went to Mexico and soon disappeared. His fate remains unknown. If you enjoy Bierce's stories, you may also enjoy those of *Edgar Allan Poe and *Roald Dahl. YA

Big Brother is a term created by *George Orwell in his novel *1984*. It has come to mean the leader of a dictatorship, or totalitarian state, who keeps a very close watch over his people's behavior and drastically limits their activities, while pretending to be their protector. In *1984*, Big Brother is never actually seen except on posters or the television screen, where his heavy, calm face (somewhat like that of Joseph Stalin) looks out with a slight smile hidden under a dark mustache. YA

Big Red (1945), by *Jim Kjelgaard, is the story of Danny Pickett, a 17-year-old woodsman and trapper, and his partnership with Red, a handsome Irish setter. Clearly based on long experience of the outdoors, it is an exciting and convincing account of life in a mountain wilderness.

Danny and his father, Ross, live on the edge

Danny and Red confront the bear Old Majesty in the adventure novel *Big Red*.

of the big estate owned by Mr. Haggin. When Danny begins to love Haggin's champion setter, Haggin is so impressed by his way with animals that he offers the young man a job as dog handler. Red, allowed to live with Danny and Ross at their cabin, takes to his new life with enthusiasm. A born hunter, with plenty of courage and intelligence, Red brings to bay the legendary bear, Old Majesty, and saves Danny's life. The friendship between Danny and Red deepens as they work together in the woods, in a setting both beautiful and dangerous. In one episode, Red finds Ross unconscious and buried in the snow after an accident. In another, Red defends Danny against an attacking wolverine. When three of Pickett's hounds are killed by Old Majesty and Ross is hurt, Danny takes the challenge and tracks the bear. In a dramatic display of teamwork, Danny and Red succeed in ridding the woods of a dangerous predator. Their return to the cabin is crowned by the arrival of five healthy pups, the offspring of Red and champion Sheilah MacGuire. If you enjoyed *Big Red*, you will want to read also the sequels *Irish Red, Son of Big Red* (1951) and *Outlaw Red, Son of Big Red* (1953). A film version of *Big Red* was made in 1962. MR

Bigger Thomas is the central character of *Native Son*, by *Richard Wright. Worn down and frustrated by being poor, Bigger would pre-fer to stay with his own people and avoid the feelings of anger and fear that most whites arouse in him. Driven by circumstances to work for a white family, he knows he must act the part of the polite and obedient black to keep his job, and the role fills him with shame. After Bigger has killed two women, he wants more than anything to make people know what drove him to commit the crimes—to make them aware of the "deep, choking hate that had been his life." He believes he will never find the words to express his feelings. It is only after he has been sentenced to death that he can begin to respond in a direct way to another human being. Having achieved a small measure of peace with himself, Bigger says to his lawyer, "When a man kills, it's for something. . . . I didn't know I was really alive in this world until I felt things hard enough to kill for 'em." YA

Biggers, Earl Derr (1894–1933) A journalist, novelist, and playwright, Biggers created one of the most popular detectives ever to appear in a series of mysteries. Charlie Chan is an amiable Chinese living in Hawaii, rather stout and enigmatic, given to philosophical sayings worded as many Americans think a Chinese would say such things. Chan is convinced that it is more important in solving a crime to understand a person's character than to search for such clues as fingerprints. He uses as his helper a member of his family, whom he addresses as "No. 1 son." Typical of the Chan books are *The House Without a Key* (1925), *Behind That Curtain* (1929), and *Keeper of the Keys* (1932). Biggers also wrote *Seven Keys to Baldpate* (1913), a melodramatic mystery set in an isolated inn, which became a successful stage play in the same year. A number of the Chan books were made into movies, and other movies were made from scripts written for that purpose but having no connections with any book by Biggers, so that this rather odd but likable detective has appeared on the screen about 40 times. There has also been a TV series. If you enjoy the Chan books, you will be interested in the mystery stories of *John P. Marquand and *Rex Stout. MR & YA

bildungsroman, which in German means a novel of educational formation, is a story that describes a person's growth, upbringing, and learning, until the person has found his or her identity and role in the world. It sometimes refers to a psychological novel. Such novels focus on youthful dreams and ambitions, with their accompanying struggles and disappointments, and usually end on an optimistic note as the personality and talent take shape.

Some fine examples are *David Copperfield* and *Great Expectations* by *Charles Dickens, *The Way of All Flesh* by *Samuel Butler, and *A Portrait of the Artist as a Young Man* by *James Joyce. Two others, dating from the 1950s, are *Lord of the Flies* by *William Golding and *Catcher in the Rye* by *J.D. Salinger. YA

Billy Budd, Foretopman (1924), a short novel by *Herman Melville, is set in 1797 on board a British warship. Although symbolic and rich in detail, the story is simple. Billy Budd, a young sailor, is forced to leave his merchant ship and do military service on a man-of-war, under the command of the intelligent and disciplined Captain Vere. Billy accepts the abrupt change without complaint and cheerfully does his best in his new duties. His energy, good looks, warm-hearted manner, and

innocence make him a popular figure on the warship. But Claggart, the ship's master-at-arms, is secretly devoured by envy of Billy. Claggart, after harassing Billy in small ways, informs Captain Vere that Billy is plotting a mutiny. He recounts imaginary incidents to back up his accusation. Confronted by the captain and Claggart, Billy becomes tongue-tied with shock, fails to defend himself, and instead strikes Claggart and kills him. Billy's loss of control is understood by the captain, but the law demands that Billy be tried for Claggart's death. Condemned to hang, Billy startles the men gathered for his execution by exclaiming "God bless Captain Vere!" before he dies as fearlessly and gracefully as he lived. The novel was adapted for the stage in 1951, and for film in 1962. Another sea story you may like to read is *Lord Jim*, by *Joseph Conrad. YA

Bingo Brown and the Language of Love (1989), by *Betsy Byars, is a funny and touching novel about learning to communicate. Almost 12 years old, Bingo Brown is attached to his friend Melissa, with whom he shares a language of love that speaks through their eyes and goes beyond words. Now Melissa lives in another state and Bingo misses her. Instead of feeling proud and confident in their friendship, Bingo sees himself as a helpless toy in the mainstream of life. Melissa's friend Cici Boles, a big blond girl who wears press-on fingernails, is taking advantage of Melissa's absence to attract Bingo's interest. Bingo would much prefer that Cici spend her time with Billy Wentworth, who is crazy about her. These relationships are less confusing, however, than the news that Bingo's mother is expecting a baby. Upset at first, she leaves Bingo and his father to visit her mother. Bingo feels hurt and abandoned, but later begins to think more cheerfully about becoming a big brother. His parents eventually reach a happy agreement about how they will adjust their careers to the new baby, and the tension eases. Bingo learns to express his feelings more eloquently in his letters to Melissa, and concludes that he is mature enough to at least dog-paddle in the mainstream of life. You can read more about

Bingo and his family in *Bingo Brown, Gypsy Lover* (1990). MR

black This *color is most closely associated in the Western world with grief and mourning, though in some Far Eastern countries *white is the color of grief. The ancient Egyptians used black in this way and the Romans adopted it from them. The color, in an overall sense, can represent reaction and conservatism. Black has also come to stand for many bad and evil things: the bubonic plague of the 14th century was called the Black Death; Black Friday, Sept. 24, 1869, was the day a financial panic began in New York City; and the Black Mass is the blasphemous ritual of Satan worship. The Black Hand is another name for the Mafia. In old-time Western movies, the bad guys wear black hats and the good guys wear white. In art, black stands for evil or falsehood. Black humor is mordant and macabre, and black magic is dangerous. A "black sheep" is the ne'er-do-well member of a family and gives it a "black eye," a condition of embarrassment or shame, unlike the real thing, which hurts physically. On the other hand, if your business is "in the black," you are making money. Black can also mean simply the color without expressing any judgment, as in blackboard or black person, that is, an African American.

Black Beauty (1877), a young reader's classic by Anna Sewell (1820–1878), is presented in the form of an autobiography, in which the horse called Black Beauty tells the day-to-day story of his life. Written before the invention of the automobile, the book describes how horses were used to pull all sorts of vehicles from elegant carriages and hansom cabs to farm equipment and heavy delivery wagons. Many working horses were abused and malnourished, and this story is a strong plea for the kindness and understanding that should be given to all animals.

Black Beauty, a handsome and gentle creature, grows up in England on the estate of a man who treats him with great kindness. After several years and several owners, Black Beauty is hurt in an accident that leaves his knees in fragile condition, and he is pronounced unsuitable for genteel surroundings. Sold to a livery stable, he endures bad food and poor handling over a number of years. As a cab horse, he works for a good and kindly owner, but later is forced to the exhausting labor of pulling heavy carts. Black Beauty is rescued from a wretched existence when he is bought, for the last time, by a gentleman farmer who recognizes him for what he is—a fine animal that has been badly used. Mr. Thoroughgood takes him back to the peaceful countryside, restores his health, and allows Black Beauty to live out his life among gentle and friendly people.

Anna Sewell was born to an English Quaker family, and came to feel a great love and sympathy for horses. Like Black Beauty, she was partly crippled while still very young. Because walking was difficult for her, Anna learned to handle a pony and light carriage with skill, and often drove her father to the railroad station. Sewell was a complete invalid by the time she was 50 years old, and spent her last years at home composing her only novel. If you enjoyed *Black Beauty*, you may also like the novels about horses written by *Mary O'Hara and *Marguerite Henry. *Black Beauty* has been adapted for film many times. MR

Black Boy (1945) is *Richard Wright's autobiography, the painful story of his childhood and young manhood. It begins when 4-year-old Richard, angry and neglected by his family, sets fire to their house and is beaten until he faints. Abandoned by his father, his mother struggles to support two sons who run wild while she is out at work. The boys are hungry, and lack of food is an "acute, daily agony." Richard is beaten regularly, sometimes because he asks too many questions. Worn out by poverty, hunger, and fear of whites, the older family members never give him straight answers, seldom believe what he says, and show no interest in his inner life. They seem unable to have a conversation, talking only in an endless series of violent outbursts. They move every few months from one dingy home to another, never able to afford a decent place of their own. Richard goes to school now and then, never for long in the same town. When he is 12 years old, his mother has a stroke, and her suffering sets the tone of the rest of his emotional life. In the South, the atmosphere of racial hatred poisons everything Richard tries to do, making it impossible for him to keep a job without losing his pride and integrity. When his Granny learns Richard wants to write fiction, she tells him fiction is a lie and the devil's work. Even the process of getting a book from the library requires elaborate planning, in a world where people assume that black people do not read. Only when he is finally able to leave the South can Richard begin to hope for a chance to educate himself and build a new life. Another powerful book about a young black's experiences is the novel *Invisible Man* by *Ralph Ellison. YA

Black Hearts in Battersea (1964), by *Joan Aiken, is a novel of mystery, hilarious adventure, and outrageous coincidence. It takes place in an England that never was, at the turn of the century during the reign of the mythical King James III. Simon, a bright-eyed and black-haired 15-year-old orphan, runs away from the poor farm where he has been raised. His good friend Dr. Field, a painter who rents rooms from the Twite family in London, offers Simon a place to live and encourages the boy to study art. Oddly, when Simon arrives at the Twite home, the doctor is nowhere to be found, and everyone vigorously denies he ever lived there. Simon begins his art studies nevertheless, and at school meets Justin, the nephew of the serenely eccentric Duke of Battersea, and Sophie, the pretty maid of the Duchess. At the Twites' home, Simon uncovers an elaborate plot to dethrone King James and bring back young Prince George of Hanover.

Though several attempts are made by parties unknown to dispatch the Duke and Duchess to the next world, the valiant and resourceful Sophie succeeds in saving their lives. Simon endures kidnapping, a fierce attack by wolves, and many escapades before he stumbles on Dr. Field (alive and well), learns the secret of his own true identity—as well as that of Justin and

Sophie—and foils a ruthless gang of plotters. If you enjoyed this book, you will like Aiken's novel *Wolves of Willoughby Chase*. MR

Black Stallion, The (1941) This novel by *Walter Farley is about a boy and an untamed horse, and the strange and wonderful understanding that develops between them. After a visit to his uncle in India, Alec Ramsay is returning home by ship. During a stop at an Arabian port on the Red Sea, Alec sees a group of men struggling to get a beautiful wild black stallion on board. Later, Alec seems to be the only person who can approach the horse without being kicked. The ship is caught in a violent storm, but Alec manages to free the Black Stallion just before the ship sinks. The powerful horse swims to a small island, pulling Alec with him. Before they are rescued several weeks later, Alec wins the stallion's trust, begins to ride him, and is overwhelmed by his speed, endurance, and free spirit.

After Alec and the Black Stallion return to the United States by ship, Alec persuades his parents to let him keep the horse that saved his life. Arrangements are made to stable the horse on a neighbor's farm. Henry Dailey, a retired trainer, helps Alec train the horse for racing, even though the horse cannot compete officially without proof of Thoroughbred ancestry. A local newspaperman tells Henry about a special charity match at which two famous racehorses are scheduled to compete, and the owners of Cyclone and Sun Raider agree to let the Black Stallion enter the race. After a nerve-wracking start, the Black Stallion comes from behind to win. Alec, as the only person ever to ride the stallion, shares the joy of running and winning, and looks forward to an exciting future. Farley wrote a number of sequels, including *The Black Stallion Returns* (1945) and *The Black Stallion and Flame* (1960). *The Black Stallion* appeared in a film version in 1979, and its sequel, *The Black Stallion Returns*, was produced in 1983. MR

Blake, William (1757–1827) An English poet and painter, a man of great imagination, Blake wrote *Songs of Innocence* and *Songs of Experience*, for both of which he made his own engraved illustrations. Blake began writing poetry while still a boy, but his work was not fully appreciated until long after his death.

Blake spent almost 12 years working as an engraver's apprentice, and later earned his living by making engravings and painting watercolors. In 1782 he married Catherine Boucher, who could neither read nor write, and taught her himself. The couple printed, colored, and engraved most of Blake's poems and prose works at home, including *The Marriage of Heaven and Hell* (1793), a prose work expounding his views on morality, religion, and philosophy. His many illustrations for the *Bible, for *The Divine Comedy* (c.1310–1321) of *Dante Alighieri, for *John Milton's *Paradise Lost*, and others can be seen in museum collections in Great Britain and the United States. YA

blank verse is unrhymed poetry, and usually refers to poems written in *iambic pentameter. The plays of *William Shakespeare are written mostly in blank verse, as are many English epic and dramatic poems. An example from Shakespeare's *Hamlet* is:

How all occasions do inform against me,
And spur my dull revenge! What is a man,
If his chief good and market of his time
Be but to sleep and feed? a beast, no more.

Bleak House (1853), by *Charles Dickens, considered by some critics to be his greatest novel, is an eloquent expression of his hatred of social injustice and indifference. The cold, dense fogs, muddy streets, and badly lit chambers described in its first pages characterize the condition of life in *Victorian England, and they serve as an uncomfortable background for the mysteries that unfold in the story.

Settlement of the intricate case of Jarndyce versus Jarndyce, renowned in the Court of Chancery in London, has been pending for years while professional hangers-on profit from the senseless delays. The case links many characters in the novel, affecting people at all levels

Jo, the street sweeper in *Bleak House*, depicted by Hablôt Browne ["Phiz"] (1815–1882).

of society. The plaintiffs, or petitioners, in the case are Richard Carstone and Ada Clare, his cousin, both wards of the court in the disposition of the estate. Both young people are taken in by a kindhearted old cousin, John Jarndyce, to live at his country home, Bleak House. Another resident of Bleak House is Jarndyce's sweet-tempered ward, the orphan Esther Summerson. Richard hopes that when the case is concluded he will inherit a fortune. He and Ada fall in love and marry secretly, but Richard is gradually destroyed by anxiety over his expectations, and he dies. The case ends, but the great inheritance has been whittled away by years of court costs.

At Chesney Wold, you meet Sir Leicester and the beautiful Lady Dedlock. Her proud manner conceals a scandalous secret. She was once engaged to marry Captain Rawdon, but he was believed to have died after she gave birth to their daughter, and she is now convinced her child died as well. Visited by her lawyer, Tulkinghorn, the inscrutable and knowing repository of many confidences, Lady

Dedlock is shown a legal document copied in distinctive handwriting. She recognizes the hand of her lover, Rawdon, and the intensity of her reaction leads Tulkinghorn to investigate. Lady Dedlock secretly searches for Rawdon, assisted by a poor little street sweeper named Jo, but finds that Rawdon has recently died. Tulkinghorn pitilessly uncovers the facts of her old liaison and is preparing to tell Sir Leicester when he is murdered by a woman once in Lady Dedlock's employ. Sir Leicester learns about his wife's past from Bucket, a policeman, and Esther realizes that Lady Dedlock is her mother. They try to rescue Lady Dedlock, but she dies too, near her lover's grave. At Bleak House, Esther accepts a proposal of marriage from John Jarndyce out of gratitude, even though she loves young Dr. Woodcourt. Jarndyce releases her when he realizes she is in love with Woodcourt, and brings the two together in an act of generosity. *Bleak House* has many subplots and memorable secondary characters that help make it a rewarding reading experience. The novel was adapted for an eight-part TV film in 1985. YA

Bless the Beasts & Children (1970), a novel by *Glendon Swarthout, is about six emotionally troubled boys, 12 to 15 years old: Cotton, Teft, Shecker, Goodenow, Lally I, and Lally II. Their lives have been shaped by their parents' cruelty and indifference.

The six boys meet each other in Arizona at the Box Canyon Boys Camp. They come together as the camp's losers and rejects. Cotton, a nurturing and sensitive 15-year-old, becomes their leader. He takes them on a dangerous night mission into the Arizona canyons to save a group of buffalo from being slaughtered. To reach the buffalo preserve, they have to ride horses, steal trucks, shoot a rifle, and come face to face with their own painful childhoods.

In the end, Cotton, driving a stolen truck filled with hay, heroically leads the buffalo to their freedom. Ultimately, this success liberates the other five boys from their own emotional pain. They pay a high price for their freedom when they lose their great friend and leader. Cotton, while driving the truck, crashes over the rim of the canyon, falling to his death. *Bless the Beasts & Children* was filmed in 1972. YA

Blind Colt, The (1941) By *Glen Rounds, this short novel has the flavor of a fine Western story told around a campfire in simple language and rich detail. Ten-year-old Whitey and his Uncle Torwal are cowboys living on their small ranch in the South Dakota Badlands. When they find a blind colt newly born to a mustang mare, Whitey wants to keep and raise it. Torwal is skeptical, feeling the colt may not be able to survive the rough badlands terrain and marauding wolves, but he agrees to wait and see. Living free on the range, the colt adapts over time to blindness and learns the thousand smells and tastes that enable it to avoid most dangers. Once, Whitey finds the animal caught in deep mud at a water hole and pulls it out with the help of Spot, his potbellied old pinto. Months later, the colt is separated from its mother in an early spring blizzard. With luck, intelligence, and a good nose, the colt makes its way to the ranch stable, where Whitey finds it standing next to Spot. Whitey's patient efforts at taming and training are successful, and Torwal cheerfully agrees to let the boy keep the blind colt. Two companion volumes are *Stolen Pony* (1969), about horse thieves who discover that the spotted pony they have stolen is blind, and *Blind Outlaw* (1980), about a mute boy who is able to train a blind horse. MR

Blind Flight (1980), a novel by Hilary Milton, is about 13-year-old Debbie Whitfield and her unusual adventure in a small plane. Debbie has been blind for almost a year, and is about to undergo an operation that may restore her sight. As a treat and a distraction, her Uncle Walt takes Debbie for a spin in his little Tahoe Kadet airplane, and continues to teach her about flying. Moments after Walt describes the fine flock of geese he sees nearby, Debbie hears something crash against the windshield and feels an icy wind in the cockpit. Walt has been knocked unconscious and cannot help her. She must take the wheel, find the radio, call for assistance, and try at the same time to protect herself from the paralyzing cold and the terrifying possibility of a crash. Debbie succeeds in contacting the pilot of a commercial plane, and he alerts a network of people ready to assist. Together, an expert flying instructor and Debbie's brother, Rick, convince her that she is capable of controlling and landing the plane, blind or not. They talk her down in a series of dramatic and convincing sequences. If you enjoyed this book, you may also like *Hatchet by *Gary Paulsen, about a boy who struggles to survive after the small plane in which he is a passenger crashes in the wilderness. MR

Blinded by the Light (1978), by *Robin F. Brancato, is the story of Gail Brower's search for her brother, Jim, who disappears after joining a religious cult called the Light of the World Church. His infrequent letters are cheerful but unrevealing, and the Browers wonder if he was forced to cut himself off from his family. Hoping to find Jim, Gail attends an L.O.W. weekend retreat and learns that he will be at an upcoming L.O.W. rally.

Gail's parents plan to rescue Jim at the rally with the help of Mat Ferrar and his informer inside the cult. When Gail gets Jim's letter asking her to meet him at the rally, she goes there without telling her parents or Doug, her fiancé. Jim and Gail have a serious talk, and Gail realizes that he is fully and willingly committed to the L.O.W. She begins to question her right to interfere with his choice. To please Jim, Gail joins a celebration before the rally. There, acting on instructions from Ferrar, Doug appears unexpectedly, grabs her hand, and pulls her outside. This is the signal they have arranged for Scott, Ferrar's informer, to tell Jim that Gail has run away, take Jim down in the elevator to stop her, and deliver him to Ferrar. The ramshackle elevator breaks down moments later, and Scott is killed when he falls into the shaft. Jim never reaches the street. After the rescue fails, Gail finds Jim,

tells him about the rescue attempt, and begs him to visit their parents. Still in a state of shock after Scott's death, Jim refuses. The story ends when Gail persuades Jim to meet with her and Doug to discuss Jim's future. Another novel about a young woman who tries to get her brother away from a religious cult is *The Love Bombers* (1980) by Gloria D. Miklowitz (1927–). *Blinded by the Light* was made into a TV movie in 1980. MR & YA

Blos, Joan W(insor) (1928–) Author of *A Gathering of Days: A New England Girl's Journal, 1830–32,* Blos, who majored in science in college, became interested in theories of child development and later in children's literature. Blos spent almost 12 years on the *Journal,* her first novel, basing it on a study of the past owners of a house belonging to her husband's family. You will enjoy *Brothers of the Heart: A Story of the Old Northwest, 1837–38* (1985), also historical fiction, which was inspired by her attraction to the Michigan wilderness. It tells the story of Shem, a crippled boy, and the Ottawa Native American woman who teaches him the secrets of the forest. YA

blue A *color with a variety of meanings, blue can stand for hope or sadness, depending on how it is used. "Blue" also means many other things in everyday speech. Here are some examples: When events come "out of the blue," they happen suddenly and unexpectedly. "Once in a blue moon" means hardly ever. If you are "blue in the face," you are exhausted and speechless from anger or effort, and this may make you feel "blue," which means sad and lonely. To "blue-pencil" a page of writing means to mark or edit with a blue pencil, to censor, to take out certain words or passages. A "blue ribbon" refers to the first prize in a contest, while "blue book" is the name given to the exam booklet handed out to students. "Blue-collar" describes such workers as mechanics or miners who wear special work clothes on the job. A "bluenose" is a prude, or a person who feels that having fun is immoral and who would be in favor of "blue laws," which, in some places, forbid working, drinking alcohol, and dancing on Sundays. In music, "blues" is a style that combines jazz with folk song. Blues songs are usually slow and sad.

Blume, Judy (Sussman) (1938–) An author of more than a dozen very popular novels for young readers, among them *Are You There, God? It's Me, Margaret, *Then Again, Maybe I Won't, *Superfudge*, and *Tiger Eyes*, Blume draws on her experience of middle-class suburban life. She addresses the problems of adolescence with respect, sensitivity, and wit. She has won praise for her delicate sense of character and for her direct style. Blume is considered controversial by some because of her willingness to deal frankly with sexuality, but she is not given to moralizing. Rather, her books stress the need for developing individual and social responsibility. Other Blume novels you may like to try include *It's Not the End of the World* (1972), about a sixth-grader whose parents are getting a divorce, and *Just as Long as We're Together* (1987), in which the friendship between Stephanie and her best friend undergoes a change as she tries to keep a family problem secret. If you enjoy Blume's books, you will probably also like the novels of *Norma Fox Mazer, *Harry Mazer, and *Paul Zindel. MR & YA

Blyton, Enid (1898?–1968) This prolific English author of more than 400 books, published in 93 languages, wrote novels, plays, poetry, nature books, and other nonfiction, showing a wide range of interests. Her imagination and interest in young people contributed to her success. One series of books retells such classics as *Aesop's Fables* (1928) and *The Knights of the Round Table* (1930). Among her works of nonfiction is *The Christmas Book* (1953), in which Blyton explains the customs of the holiday, such as the origin of carols. She also wrote mystery novels, including the Secret Seven series, which follows the adventures of seven young people and their dog, Scamper. The series includes *The Secret Seven and the Hidden Cave Adventure* (1955) and *The Secret Seven and the Old Fort Adventure* (1960). There is also a series with the word "mystery" in the titles, such as *The Mystery of the Disappearing Cat* (1944). If you like these books, read those of *M.V. Carey, *Carolyn Keene, and *Phyllis A. Whitney. MR & YA

Bonham, Frank (1914–) A novelist, short-story writer, and screenwriter, Bonham is the author of many adventure and mystery stories. He began writing when chronic asthma cut short his college career, but he admits that the handicap forced him into a profession he came to love. Bonham has been an enthusiastic researcher, particularly for his books on racial problems, police work, and juvenile delinquency in city ghettos. His study of gangs in the Los Angeles area led to the writing of *Durango Street* (1965), about a black parolee who tries to stay out of trouble, and *Viva Chicano* (1970), about another parolee. Bonham is the author of scripts for several TV series, including *Wells Fargo* and *Death Valley Days*. If you enjoy his books, try also those of *Walter Dean Myers. YA

Bonjour Tristesse (1954), the first novel by Frenchwoman *Françoise Sagan, written when she was 18 years old, made her famous. Cécile is 17 years old and happy to be spending the summer with her father. A widower for many years, Raymond is vital, charming, and easygoing in his approach to life and love. He invites Elsa, his mistress of the moment, to share a rented villa on the Mediterranean. Cécile likes the good-hearted Elsa and senses she will not disturb the family routine. Also, Elsa's presence may distract Raymond from Cécile's interest in Cyril, an attractive young man from a neighboring villa. Then, Raymond asks Anne Larsen, an old friend of Cécile's mother, to visit. Anne is chic, intelligent, and proud, with a strong will and impeccable taste. Anne and Raymond fall in love almost at once. Cécile admires Anne, but resents her cool manner of reforming everything to suit her own preference. Elsa moves out of the villa. When Raymond and Anne decide to marry, Cécile plots to rekindle her father's interest in Elsa, reveal to

Anne his basic unreliability, and cause the breakup of their relationship. With the help of Cyril and Elsa, Cécile's plan succeeds in every detail. Anne becomes an unwilling witness to Raymond's dalliance with Elsa, and the consequences are unexpectedly tragic and far-reaching. The novel was filmed in 1958. YA

Bontemps, Arna (Wendell) (1902–1973) A black American novelist, biographer, critic, and co-editor of *The Book of Negro Folklore*, Bontemps was born in Louisiana. He began writing in the 1920s during the *Harlem Renaissance and became a close friend and associate of *Langston Hughes, *Countee Cullen, and James Weldon Johnson (1871–1938). His more than 20 books include biographies of George Washington Carver (1864?–1943), Frederick Douglass (c.1817–1895), and some famous black athletes. Bontemps' best-known novel is *Black Thunder* (1936), based on the slave uprising led by Gabriel Prosser in Virginia in 1800. Bontemps devoted much of his work to maintaining the links between African Americans and their past, to describing and promoting their cultural heritage, and to writing about social and cultural changes he witnessed in his lifetime. YA

Book of Negro Folklore, The (1958) Edited by *Langston Hughes and *Arna Bontemps, this is a large and splendidly varied collection of black folk songs, stories, poems and play rhymes, memoirs, prayers and spirituals, sermons, and testimonials. From Africa, slaves brought to the New World their ancient custom of storytelling. The old patterns were changed somewhat to fit a new life, but the vigorous tradition of entertainment with song and story continued to thrive in spite of all difficulties. Grafted to those roots were work songs, prison songs, ballads, street cries, blues lyrics, memories of slavery, ghost stories, and tales of black magic, together with more formal poetry and prose in the folk manner, all represented in the collection. In the section called "The Jazz Folk" are brief and vivid memoirs by some famous jazz musicians, and

"Harlem Jive" contains a short dictionary of jive idioms. MR & YA

Book of Nonsense, The See *Complete Nonsense Book, The*.

Borland, Hal [Harold Glen] (1900–1978) Having grown up on an eastern Colorado homestead, Borland hunted and fished in the country described in his novel *When the Legends Die*. He was a journalist until 1943, when he turned to free-lance writing. An enthusiastic naturalist and conservationist, Borland wrote many essays, stories, and novels about wildlife, including two books under the pen name of Ward West. Borland's other books include the novel *The Amulet* (1957), about a young Coloradan who joins the Confederate army during the Civil War, and the nonfiction book *Beyond Your Doorstep: A Handbook to the Country* (1962). He was also the author of a number of documentary film and radio scripts. YA

Borrowers, The (1952) This appealing novel by *Mary Norton is about a family of tiny people, who are secretly living in a quiet country house. The Clocks (so named because the entrance to their apartment lies under a grandfather clock) are Borrowers, part of a race of miniature men and women who live by borrowing odd bits and pieces from their unwitting hosts. They are fearful of being seen by humans, remembering the awful time when Uncle Hendreary was observed and had to move his entire family to a badger's hole.

Pod and Homily live with their daughter, Arrietty, in cozy rooms under the kitchen. Arrietty yearns to explore the world upstairs and outdoors, and Pod finally agrees to take her on a borrowing expedition. Enchanted by her first glimpse of nature, Arrietty fails to see the giant boy (visiting his great-aunt) until he speaks to her. Nervous but intrigued, they talk about their different worlds. Pod and Homily worry that the boy will give them away, and he causes great alarm by making a hole in the kitchen floor and uncovering their home. He is a nice boy, however, and brings them small treasures to beautify the tiny rooms. Unfortunately the vigilant housekeeper, Mrs. Driver, catches him at the hole and calls the police and the rat catcher. While the terrified Clocks hide in a remote passageway, their apartment is ruined. The boy helps them escape into the garden, and the family goes to join Uncle Hendreary in the spacious safety of the badger hole, where Arrietty will have the company of Borrowers her own age. Among several sequels to *The Borrowers*, you may enjoy *The Borrowers Aloft* (1961), in which Pod, Homily, and Arrietty Clock are kidnapped, imprisoned in an attic, and plan their dramatic escape by balloon. In *The Borrowers Avenged* (1982), the Clock family establishes a home in an old rectory. If you enjoy reading this kind of fantasy, you will like *The Wind in the Willows* by *Kenneth Grahame. *The Borrowers* was made into a TV movie in 1973. MR

bourgeois refers to a member of the middle class. It is often used disparagingly to describe people with narrow or conventional tastes and ideas, those lacking in culture, or those whose opinions are shaped by too much concern for material things. In Karl Marx's theory of class struggle, *bourgeoisie* refers to the group or class of people opposed to the proletariat (wage earners) and dedicated to protecting its own position of superiority. See also *Philistine.

bow See *arrow.

Bowen, Elizabeth (Dorothea Cole) (1899–1973) An Irish-born English novelist and short-story writer, Bowen moved to England with her mother when she was 7 years old. When she was 20 years old she began writing short stories, and soon published *The Hotel* (1927), a novel about a girl trying to adjust to life after World War I. *The Death of the Heart* (1938) is a novel about a young girl reacting to the rules of life established by adults.

Bowen served as an air raid warden in London during World War II, and she used her experiences in the novel *The Heat of the Day* (1949), in which the heroine learns that her

lover is a Nazi spy. Like *Henry James, to whom she has been compared, Bowen paid great attention to personal relationships and private feelings. Her finely written short stories appear in *The Collected Stories of Elizabeth Bowen* (1981). YA

Bowery A street in lower Manhattan, New York City, the Bowery was the road leading to the *bouwerij* (the Dutch word for farm) of Peter Stuyvesant (c.1610–1672), governor of New Amsterdam. In the 1860s and 1870s the Bowery became an elegant theater district, but by the 1890s it had declined into a poverty-stricken area, full of shabby bars, cheap dance halls, and run-down rooming houses. The Bowery figures prominently in the novels *Sister Carrie*, by *Theodore Dreiser, and *Maggie: A Girl of the Streets*, by *Stephen Crane. YA

Bradbury, Ray (Douglas) (1920–) Famous for his tales of *science fiction and *fantasy, Bradbury was born in Waukegan, Illinois, a city that provided the setting for many of his stories. Later he moved with his parents to Los Angeles, California, where he has lived ever since. Ray liked to read comic books and science fiction and began writing stories for fun when he was 12 years old. He has kept to a routine of writing every day throughout his long career.

The Martian Chronicles, a collection of stories about the exploration and exploitation of Mars by people from Earth, made Bradbury famous. *The Illustrated Man* (1951) is a group of tales whose focus is a man covered in tattoos: Each one comes to life to form a story. Another popular collection is *The Golden Apples of the Sun* (1953). Bradbury's novel *Fahrenheit 451 (1953) describes a time in the future in which television tells people what to think and owning a book is a serious offense. *Dandelion Wine* tells the story of an adolescent boy in Waukegan in the summer of 1928. *Something Wicked This Way Comes* (1962), one of Bradbury's best-known horror tales, centers on the frightening details of a small-town carnival. Bradbury has been called a science fiction writer who knows nothing about science. In fact, many of his books are about real people and real human problems, though they often are set in other times and and on other planets. *The Illustrated Man* was filmed in 1969 and *Something Wicked This Way Comes* in 1983. YA

Bradley, Marion Zimmer [Elfrida Rivers] (1930–) A novelist and short-story writer noted for her books of *science fiction and *fantasy, Bradley is also the editor of *Marion Zimmer Bradley's Fantasy Magazine*. Bradley is known best for her Darkover novels, a science fiction series that describes developments on the planet Darkover and has been praised for its masterful realization of detail and the depth and complexity of its characters. Beginning with *The Sword of Aldones* (1962), the series includes more than a dozen novels. Among these is *The Shattered Chain* (1976), one of many books by Bradley that explore and dramatize conflicts and choices that affect women. Another Darkover novel in which women play key roles is *Stormqueen!* (1978), about a young girl's struggle to control her extraordinary psychic powers.

A non-Darkover novel you might enjoy is *The Mists of Avalon* (1982), an unorthodox retelling of the *King Arthur legends, as seen through the eyes of *Guinevere, *Morgan le Fay, and other heroines. Bradley used a similar approach in *The Firebrand* (1987), which recreates the story of the *Trojan War through the character of Kassandra, royal princess of Troy, priestess of *Apollo, and sister of *Paris. YA

Braggadocio is the name of a character in *The Faerie Queene*, a long allegorical poem by the English writer *Edmund Spenser. It is used to describe a person who boasts a lot, a braggart who is really a coward at heart, or the talk of such a person. YA

Brancato, Robin F(idler) (1936–) The author of *Blinded by the Light* and *Winning*, Brancato began writing after having taught English for some years and raising two sons. Her realistic stories are based on her memories of child-hood, and on teaching experiences later in life. She enjoys raising important questions in her books without always giving her readers the answers. Brancato's other novels include *Don't Sit Under the Apple Tree* (1975), about a young girl growing up toward the end of World War II, and *Sweet Bells Jangled out of Tune* (1980), about the effect on a young girl of her grandmother's decline into the life of a bag lady. MR

Brautigan, Richard (Gary) (1935–1984) A novelist and poet, Brautigan began his literary career with the publication of his poems by small California presses in the late 1950s. Brautigan was considered representative of the counterculture of the 1960s, and was much admired by the Flower Children of San Francisco, who shared his concern for the future of America. The novelist *Kurt Vonnegut, Jr., took an interest in Brautigan's work, and was helpful in finding a publisher for *Trout Fishing in America*, which was very successful. Other popular novels were *A Confederate General from Big Sur* (1964), a whimsical account of three characters who drop out of society and go to live in Big Sur, California, and *In Watermelon Sugar* (1967), the story of a peaceful commune called iDEATH. YA

Brave New World (1932), by *Aldous Huxley, is set in the 25th century, in a *utopian society both funny and frightening. It begins in the Central London Hatchery and Conditioning Centre, where human beings are mass-produced in spotless laboratory assembly lines and gradually adjusted to fit a particular role in life. Through sleep-teaching, they learn to love their social destiny. Fully conditioned adults are happy, healthy people who accept the rules of their group, think only of the present, are almost never alone, and consider marriage and childbirth disgusting. Bernard Max, because of a slip-up in the lab, does not quite fit the mold. He needs privacy and is uncomfortable with the social life organized by the state.

Bernard is allowed to visit the New Mexico Reservation, where Native Americans are kept apart. Here people have families in the old way and grow old naturally. Bernard meets John,

---

MR = Middle Reader   YA = Young Adult Reader   * = See this main entry

the natural son of a man and woman from London who visited years ago. The woman was accidentally left behind, and the man (whom John knows) never tried to find her. Bernard arranges to take John and his mother to London, where they confront John's father, the Director of Hatcheries, and cause the ruin of his career. Crowds of people come to stare at John, and Bernard basks in the fashionable attention. He is appalled, however, when John publicly displays his contempt and dislike of the New World. Labeled as the friend of a madman, Bernard is exiled to Iceland, where he will live with others who have committed the crime of thinking for themselves. John tries to escape to a life of solitude in the country, but crowds of curious tourists give him no peace. Determined not to become a toy of the public, John takes his own life. If you enjoyed this novel, you may also want to read Huxley's nonfiction work *Brave New World Revisited* (1958), in which he examines some of the social, political, scientific, and technological forces that pose a threat to human freedom. *Brave New World* was adapted for film in 1980. YA

Breakfast at Tiffany's (1958), by *Truman Capote, is a short novel in which the narrator, an unnamed writer, recounts his friendship with *Holly Golightly, an appealing and exasperating 19-year-old woman. Both are tenants in an old brownstone building in New York City in the 1940s. Holly is thin, stylish, and cheerfully amoral, and her extravagance and breezy approach to life scandalize her neighbors. Without visible means of support, she entertains a number of older men friends. When Holly feels sad, she jumps into a taxi and goes to Tiffany's, where the quietness of the store calms her. She never talks about her childhood, until the Texas veterinarian she married when she was 14 years old unexpectedly turns up and the writer learns her name is really Lulamae Barnes. Holly plans to marry an elegant Brazilian diplomat, but she is caught in a series of mishaps that result in her arrest as a messenger for a drug syndicate. The Brazilian fiancé, unnerved by the threat of scandal, rejects her. Holly escapes to Brazil alone and disappears without a trace. The novel was adapted for the movies in 1961. YA

Brideshead Revisited: The Sacred and Profane Memories of Captain Charles Ryder (1945), by *Evelyn Waugh, is an elegant and complex novel about the attachment of the narrator, Charles Ryder, to an old English family, the Marchmains of Brideshead Castle. As Roman Catholics in a Protestant land, the Marchmains project a sense of subtle isolation that is quite outside Charles's experience.

At Oxford University, Charles is befriended by Sebastian Flyte, younger son of Lord Marchmain. His fascination with Sebastian blooms in the leisurely atmosphere of Oxford life and on visits to the splendors of Brideshead. Sebastian's father has scandalized society by leaving his family and the Catholic Church to live abroad with his mistress, while Lady Marchmain remains devoutly Catholic. As Sebastian feels more and more confined by family and religious obligations, he reacts by drinking heavily and finally escapes to North Africa, where he later will die in a monastery.

Ryder continues to visit Brideshead and finds himself attracted to Sebastian's sister, Julia. Still quite young, Julia Flyte causes tension in the family when she marries Rex Mottram, a vulgar politician and a non-Catholic. Lady Marchmain dies of a wasting illness, and Sebastian is too sick to be at her side. Julia sees that Rex considers her only an object for display, and turns to Charles for love and understanding. Lord Marchmain comes home to Brideshead, and on his deathbed embraces the faith he had rejected. After her divorce from Rex, Julia is free to marry Charles. Following her father's example, at the last moment Julia returns to her religion. She tells Charles, also divorced, that they must separate, because starting a new life with him would violate Church law. The novel was adapted superbly as a TV miniseries in 1981. YA

Bridge of San Luis Rey, The (1927) This famous novel by *Thornton Wilder begins in Peru in 1714, when a bridge of woven willow branches snaps and five travelers fall to their deaths. Brother Juniper, a religious man, sees the accident and decides to search the lives of the victims to answer the question, "Why did this happen to *those* five?"

The story of the Marquesa de Montemayor and her 14-year-old companion, Pepita, is the first to be told. Doña María is an odd, homely woman who loves her only daughter too much and whose extravagant attention has only succeeded in driving the daughter away from her. Letter writing takes the place of all the affection that cannot be safely expressed, and the Marquesa develops a great talent for it. When the daughter becomes pregnant, the Marquesa and Pepita go on a *pilgrimage to pray for a safe childbirth. There she makes the decision to start a new and more reasonable life, but the two are killed when the bridge falls.

Esteban and his twin, Manuel, are foundlings who have been raised in a convent. Their need of one another is so intense that they are hardly ever apart. When Manuel dies of infection in spite of Esteban's efforts to save him, Esteban wants to die. Captain Alvarado offers the young man work on a ship and persuades him to go on with his life. On their way to Lima, Esteban dies at San Luis Rey.

Uncle Pio is the friend of a famous actress, Camila, called the Perichole, and acts as her teacher, reader, hairdresser, and errand boy. As Camila slowly loses interest in the theater and wants to become a respectable lady, she cuts herself off from the world. Pio begs her to let him take her little boy to Lima for one year and teach him. Camila agrees, but both Pio and the child die on the bridge.

Brother Juniper's long account of the tragedy, which has not given the answer to his question, is judged to be the work of the devil, and both book and author are burned in a public ceremony. *The Bridge of San Luis Rey* was filmed in 1929 and in 1944.

Bridge to Terabithia

Bridge to Terabithia (1977), by *Katherine Paterson, takes place in a small Virginia town, where Jess Aarons lives with his parents and four sisters. More than anything, he wants to be the fastest runner in the fifth grade. Jess also likes to draw, but he is careful not to show his pictures to anyone except Miss Edmunds, his music teacher, who will surely not make fun of him.

He meets Leslie Burke, a newcomer, and discovers Leslie can run even faster than he can. In spite of embarrassment at being beaten by a girl, Jess becomes friends with Leslie. It is Leslie's idea to build *Terabithia, a secret kingdom in the woods across the dry creek bed, and there the two meet to talk, enjoy the peaceful woods, and let their imaginations run wild. When the rains come, the creek rises and they must get to Terabithia by swinging across on an old rope hung from a tree.

Miss Edmunds invites Jess to spend a day with her visiting art museums in Washington, D.C. He thoroughly enjoys the paintings and the sympathetic attention of Miss Edmunds. On his return, his family tells him Leslie has accidentally drowned in the swollen creek. Jess is overwhelmed with sadness, and feels guilty for not inviting Leslie on his trip. His parents do everything they can to comfort him, and even his teacher unbends enough to tell him what a wonderful friend he was to Leslie. Jess decides to keep Terabithia, and after building a plank bridge across the creek, he introduces his little sister, May Belle, to the secret kingdom. If you enjoyed this novel, you will probably also like *Beat the Turtle Drum* (1976), by *Constance C. Greene, about a 13-year-old girl's struggle to deal with her younger sister's sudden death. *Bridge to Terabithia* was adapted for television in 1985. It won the *Newbery Medal in 1978. MR

Bridge Too Far, A

Bridge Too Far, A (1974) This is a vivid nonfictional account by *Cornelius Ryan of Operation Market-Garden, a daring, difficult, and ultimately disastrous Allied airborne operation of World War II. The book focuses on the battle for a bridge over the Lower Rhine River at Arnhem, the Netherlands, where the British 1st Airborne Division was isolated by Nazi forces. Written with meticulous care by a fine reporter, *A Bridge Too Far* creates the kind of suspense and excitement more often found in adventure novels. The events of one week in September 1944 are presented through the eyes of ordinary soldiers and civilians on both sides of the terrible conflict. Other World War II histories by Cornelius Ryan include *The Last Battle and *The Longest Day: June 6, 1944. A Bridge Too Far was adapted for film in 1977. YA

Bridgers, Sue Ellen (1942–) Born in the South, Bridgers has written novels and stories that reflect the nostalgia she feels for the life of a small Southern town. Her interest in family relationships, particularly the role of women in the home, has strongly influenced her writing. Bridgers's first novel, *Home Before Dark, was followed by All Together Now (1979), the story of a young girl who spends the summer with her grandparents in a small North Carolina town. For older readers, Notes for Another Life (1981) focuses on divorce and mental illness. MR & YA

Brink, Carol Ryrie (1895–1981) Raised in northern Idaho, Brink lost both her parents by the time she was 8 years old. She went to live with her aunt and her grandmother, who told her stories of pioneer life in Wisconsin. Brink later used these stories in her novel *Caddie Woodlawn. She has written numerous other popular works, such as Baby Island (1937), about two young girls who care for four babies on a desert island after escaping from a sinking ocean liner; Magical Melons (1944), a sequel to Caddie Woodlawn; The Pink Motel (1959), about two young people who become involved in mystery at the Florida motel their family inherits; and The Bad Times of Irma Baumlein (1972), about a lonely girl who gets into trouble when she tells a lie in hopes of attracting new friends. MR

Brittain, Bill (1930–) Author of several books for young people, Brittain spent his early years in a village in upstate New York. A teacher, Brittain sees writing as a serious hobby. Brittain has written short stories for Ellery Queen's Mystery Magazine and Alfred Hitchcock's Mystery Magazine, occasionally under the pen name of James Knox.

Brittain began writing for young people in 1978, and his books have been welcomed by critics and readers for the strong sense of wonder and magic they convey. Devil's Donkey (1981) is a spooky tale of old New England, in which Dan'l Pitt (who does not believe in magic) tangles with a vindictive witch. In its sequel, The Wish Giver: Three Tales of Coven Tree (1983), an odd little man at a church social promises to give people whatever they ask, and three young customers make wishes that come true in surprising ways. MR

Brobdingnag is the name given by *Jonathan Swift to the land of giants visited by Captain Gulliver on the second of his four voyages in *Gulliver's Travels. The giants are ordinary men and women, but big enough to hold Gulliver comfortably in the palm of a hand, and common wasps are as big as partridges. MR & YA

Brodsky, Joseph Alexandrovich (1940–) Considered one of the finest poets of his generation, Brodsky, a Russian-Jewish poet, was born in Leningrad (now St. Petersburg), Russia. Since 1972 he has lived in the United States, where he is considered an American author even though he usually writes in Russian. He left school when he was 15 years old, studied literature on his own, and later gained a reputation as a street-corner poet. His writings were circulated hand-to-hand and were made known through recitations. After a Leningrad newspaper referred to him as a parasite, Brodsky was formally charged by the Soviet authorities with refusing to be a useful citizen, a charge based in part on his having held 13 different jobs in about 8 years. Sentenced to hard labor, he was freed 18 months later when Soviet writers complained on his behalf.

Brodsky's poems have been translated into many languages. English translations are collected in Elegy to John Donne and Other Poems (1967), Poems by Joseph Brodsky (1972), and A Part of Speech (1980). His work reflects an intense concern with nature, death, the human condition, and the struggle to make sense of chaos and boredom. Brodsky won the Nobel Prize for literature in 1987. YA

Brontë, Anne See *Brontë Family and *Currer, Ellis, and Acton Bell.

Brontë, Charlotte (1816–1855) An English novelist and the sister of *Emily Brontë, Charlotte Brontë based her novel *Jane Eyre on her brief stay at the austere boarding school where two older sisters became fatally ill. Brontë worked as a teacher and a governess, in part to help pay her brother Branwell's debts. In Belgium, where she and Emily went to perfect their French, she gathered material for The Professor (1857), the story of an English tutor in Brussels, and for Villette (1853), about a governess employed in the same city. Charlotte Brontë married when she was 38 years old, began another novel, and died the following year after a difficult pregnancy. See also *Brontë Family and *Currer, Ellis, and Acton Bell. YA

Brontë, Emily (Jane) (1818–1848) The English author of the tragic novel *Wuthering Heights, Emily Brontë was the younger sister of *Charlotte Brontë. Emily was extremely sensitive to the changing and often stormy aspect of the *moors, which she used as the setting of her only novel. In 1842, Emily and Charlotte made plans to open a school and went to Brussels, Belgium, to improve their knowledge of French. But when their Aunt Branwell died, Emily returned home to Yorkshire, in northern England, to keep house, and she remained there for the rest of her brief life. Unlike her sisters, she seems to have used few actual events of her life in her writing, and some readers thought the dark and brutal side of Wuthering Heights was really the work of her brother, Branwell. The novel was published in 1847 under the pen name of Ellis Bell. Though it was less immediately successful than Charlotte's *Jane Eyre, it is now ranked among the finest novels in English literature. Emily came down with tuberculosis after her brother's fu-neral, refused to be treated, and died a few months later. You may like to read some of Emily Brontë's poems. She wrote more than 200, and a handful, which some critics have considered among the best in English, are easily found today in major anthologies, such as A Victorian Anthology (1895), edited by Edmund Clarence Stedman (1833–1908). See also *Brontë Family and *Currer, Ellis, and Acton Bell.

Brontë Family *Charlotte, *Emily Jane, Anne (1820–1849), and their brother Patrick Branwell (1817–1848) were the children of Patrick Brontë (1777–1861), an Irish-born clergyman and author. After Mrs. Brontë's death in 1821, her sister, Elizabeth, came to the isolated Yorkshire home to take care of the children. Two older daughters, Maria (1813–1825) and Elizabeth (1814–1825), were sent to a cheap and badly run boarding school where conditions were unusually difficult and where both girls caught tuberculosis and died. Charlotte and Emily attended the same school briefly, but returned home after their sisters' deaths. From that time on, Charlotte, Emily, Anne, and Branwell took walks on the moors and studied together at home, where they created the imaginary Kingdom of Angria and later the Kingdom of Gondal. They recorded their complicated stories of Angrian and Gondal political intrigues, family feuds, and love affairs in small books in tiny handwriting.

Anne, the gentlest and most religious of the sisters, worked as a governess for the Robinson family in Yorkshire and remained for four years. Her experiences there were the basis for her novel Agnes Grey (1847). The Tenant of Wildfell Hall (1848) is the tale of a young man's immoral life, and the book caused something of a scandal. Anne caught tuberculosis and died a few months after Emily and Branwell.

Branwell became a classical scholar under his father's guidance, and developed a fine talent for writing and painting. Charming but weak-willed, he tried his hand at a number of occupations without success. He joined Anne as a tutor for the Robinsons, but was accused of having an affair with Mrs. Robinson and was sent away. Branwell turned to alcohol and opium, running up debts that ruined the Brontë family. He died when he was 36 years old. For more about this extraordinary family, read the biography *Dark Quartet: The Story of the Brontës*, by *Lynne Reid Banks. See also *Currer, Ellis, and Acton Bell. YA

Brooks, Gwendolyn (Elizabeth) (1917–) One of the best-known poets of the 1950s, Brooks grew up in the black neighborhoods of Chicago. Her first collection of poems, *A Street in Bronzeville* (1945), describes the everyday life of her neighbors. In 1950 Brooks became the first black poet to win the Pulitzer Prize, for a series of poems called *Annie Allen* (1949), about a girl's coming of age. Brooks became a strong advocate of black consciousness in the 1960s, and later succeeded *Carl Sandburg as poet laureate of Illinois. *The Bean Eaters* (1960) contains some of her best satirical poetry, and the verses in *Riot* (1970) are written in street dialect. YA

Brothers Karamazov, The (1879–1880) By *Fyodor Dostoyevsky, this psychological novel, set in 19th-century Russia, is a masterpiece of Russian literature. Dostoyevsky, in an intense style verging on the obsessive, portrays the human condition in tragic terms. The themes dominating the novel are the complexity of family relationships, the search for a true Christian faith, and the need of all people to find a purpose in life beyond day-to-day survival. The story is about a family flawed by baseness and sensuality.

The novel's action centers on the clever and dissipated Fëdor Karamazov and his three grown sons. Dmitri is an extravagant and self-indulgent man whose hostility toward his father is exaggerated by a passion for Fëdor's mistress, Grushenka, and by his desire for the money he expects Fëdor to pay him from his dead mother's estate. Ivan is an intellectual, learned and proud, who ceaselessly questions the existence of a God who allows suffering to be inflicted on the helpless and innocent. More controlled than Dmitri, Ivan is capable of influencing his father to behave more decently. Alyosha, the youngest, most forgiving, and most spiritual, is the student of Father Zossima, a much-revered elder of the Orthodox Church and an important character in the novel. Alyosha hopes to become a monk, to escape from the dark and cruel world around him to the light of love. Smerdyakov, an epileptic servant in the house, is generally believed to be Fëdor's illegitimate son.

All the brothers have good reason to dislike and distrust their father. Currents of antagonism run deep in the family, arising from greed, desire, and other tangled motives. Believing that the presence of Fëdor is an unbearable burden to all those touched by his corrupt way of life, Smerdyakov murders Fëdor. After telling Ivan that he acted at Ivan's instigation, Smerdyakov hangs himself. Circumstantial evidence, however, points clearly to Dmitri, who is arrested and brought to trial. In court Dmitri admits his willingness to suffer and thereby to purify himself, but insists that he is innocent. In spite of strong arguments by the defense counsel, as well as Ivan's revelation that Smerdyakov confessed to the crime before his suicide, Dmitri is found guilty and sentenced to a long term in Siberia. The novel was adapted for film in 1958. YA

Brown, John (1800–1859) An abolitionist and a deeply religious man, Brown traveled in 1855 with five of his sons to Kansas Territory while preparations for statehood were under way and the area was torn by conflict between pro- and antislavery groups. Brown and his band became known throughout the country when they murdered five proslavery men at the Pottawatomie River. Later, he collected followers and arms, planning to liberate slaves by force and send them to a refuge in the Southern mountains. In October 1859, he and his men crossed the Potomac River and took the government arsenal at Harpers Ferry, Virginia. For unknown reasons, Brown chose not to escape immediately, but remained and was taken prisoner when federal troops under Colonel Robert E. Lee attacked at night. Brown was hanged in December after a trial at which he behaved with dignity and sincerity. You can find more information about John Brown in *Pioneers in Freedom: Adventures in Courage* (1969) by Janet Stevenson (1913–), and in *John Brown, A Cry for Freedom* (1980) by Lorenz B. Graham (1902–). See also *John Brown's Body* by *Stephen Vincent Benét. MR

Browning, Elizabeth Barrett (1806–1861) An English poet, Elizabeth Barrett published her first book of verse when she was 38 years old. Often sick and confined to her bed, she read a great deal of literature, history, and philosophy. *Robert Browning became interested in her work, and the two fell in love. The story of their courtship, carried on in spite of the violent objections of Elizabeth's overbearing father, is told in the play *The Barretts of Wimpole Street* by Rudolf Besier (1878–1942). Robert and Elizabeth were married in 1846 and spent 15 happy years in Italy, where Elizabeth got back her health and wrote some of her best poetry. During that time her best-known work, *Sonnets from the Portuguese*, was published. You may also enjoy reading the love letters written during the Brownings' courtship, which are some of the most famous in English literature and are collected in *The Letters of Robert Browning and Elizabeth Barrett Browning, 1845–46* (1899). YA

Browning, Robert (1812–1889) An English poet educated mainly at home, Browning in his 20s became interested in the theater and wrote several plays in verse. These were not very successful, but Browning learned much about drama that was useful in his later work, especially in the dramatic monologues for which he became famous. In 1846 he secretly married *Elizabeth Barrett (Browning), and the couple lived in Italy until her death. Browning wrote a number of long poems, of which the best known is *The Ring and the Book* (1868–1869).

The story of a murder committed in Italy in the 1600s, it established Browning's reputation as one of the great poets of his time. See also *The Barretts of Wimpole Street.* YA

Brutus, Marcus Junius (85?–42 B.C.) He fought against the Roman dictator Julius Caesar (100–44 B.C.) in the civil war between Caesar and Pompey (106–48 B.C.), but was later pardoned by Caesar. When Brutus grew resentful of Caesar's absolute rule, he became an important member of a group of senators who plotted and carried out the murder of Caesar. *William Shakespeare's play *Julius Caesar* shows Brutus as a man of noble ideals who is convinced that Caesar must be sacrificed for the common good. YA

Bryant, William Cullen (1794–1878) A poet and editor, Bryant was born in Massachusetts, and from early childhood was an enthusiastic observer of the New England landscape. While studying law, which he later practiced for almost 10 years in Plainfield and Great Barrington, Bryant wrote two of his best-known poems. "Thanatopsis" (1817), from the Greek meaning "view of death," expresses Bryant's love of the majesty and variety of nature. "To a Waterfowl" (1818) evokes the divine power guiding a solitary bird in flight and finds comfort in the thought that it also guides and protects human beings.

When "Thanatopsis" appeared in *The North American Review* several years after it was written, it made Bryant famous. His literary reputation increased with the publication of *Poems* (1821). By 1829 Bryant was editor-in-chief of the New York *Evening Post*, a job he held for almost 50 years. He spoke out in favor of free speech and the abolition of slavery, and supported the cause of working people's rights. In later life, Bryant translated the *Iliad* and the *Odyssey* of *Homer into *blank verse. YA

Buchan, John (1875–1940) A Scottish statesman and author of adventure novels in the tradition of *E. Phillips Oppenheim and *Robert

Louis Stevenson, Buchan wrote mostly in his spare time. After two years in South Africa on the high commissioner's staff, he became director of a London publishing house. Buchan worked for the British government during World War I, rising to the position of director of information, and gathered material for a number of books about the secret service. *The Thirty-Nine Steps* was his first novel about Richard Hannay, an intrepid character whose exploits are described in several sequels. For example, in Greenmantle (1916), Hannay helps the British Foreign Office determine whether Turkey will become a German ally in World War I.

Buchan was assistant director of the Reuters news agency and served seven years as the member of Parliament for the Scottish universities. He was appointed governor general of Canada in 1935 and did much to promote good relations with the United States. You may enjoy Buchan's Prester John (1910), in which Davy Crawfurd goes to South Africa to make his fortune and becomes involved in a dangerous uprising. YA

Buck, Pearl S(ydenstricker) (1892–1973) Born in West Virginia, Buck spent most of her childhood in China where her parents were missionaries and teachers. Because they lived among the Chinese, rather than in a separate foreign community, Buck learned about how ordinary people lived and talked. Her first language was Chinese, and her first lessons were taught by her mother at home. Later she attended school in Shanghai, China, went to college in the United States, and returned to China to become a teacher in Nanking. One of Buck's novels, *The Good Earth, was a critical and popular success. Some of her later books about China are A House Divided (1935), Dragon Seed (1942), and Pavilion of Women (1946). Among her books for younger readers is The Big Wave (1948), about a Japanese boy and the loss of his family during a tidal wave. Matthew, Mark, Luke and John (1966) is about a half-American, half-Korean boy who is 11 years old and who makes his home under a bridge in Pusan, Korea. Buck was a fine storyteller, able to give her readers a vivid picture of everyday life in China. She is also remembered for her efforts to fight injustice and racial prejudice. Buck was awarded the Nobel Prize for literature in 1938. MR & YA

Buddenbrooks (1901), a *roman-fleuve by *Thomas Mann, is both a work of art and the unique record of a period. Covering the 1830s to 1870s, it relates the history of the Buddenbrook family, *bourgeois grain merchants living in Germany. You follow the family's slow awakening of a moral conscience, with an accompanying loss of energy and practicality that conflicts with its business of making money.

When the novel begins, old Johann and Antoinette Buddenbrook occupy an elegant house with their son, Consul Johann; his wife, Elizabeth; their young children, Thomas, Christian, and Antonie (Tony); and their niece, Clothilde. When Tony comes of age, she is persuaded to marry Grünlich, an older man her father considers a suitable addition to the family. The marriage fails and Tony returns to her parents' house in some disgrace. A second marriage to Herr Permaneder is no more successful than the first. Christian, always sickly, wastes his time in self-analysis and unprofitable occupations, showing no interest in business. Thomas marries Gerda, a Dutch musician whose unusual background is acceptable only because of her beauty and haughty elegance. As the years go by, much effort is devoted to keeping up appearances. Thomas dies, Christian marries the woman with whom he has been living. Suffering morbid hallucinations and ill health, Christian has to be placed in an institution. Gerda returns to her father's home in Amsterdam, leaving behind the resilient Tony and Tony's daughter, granddaughter, and a few female relatives, the last of the Buddenbrooks. If you enjoyed this novel, you may also enjoy a famous English example of the roman-fleuve in *The Forsyte Saga by *John Galsworthy. YA

Buddhism A major religion with more than 300 million adherents, mostly in Asia, Buddhism was founded by Siddhartha Gautama

---

MR = Middle Reader   YA = Young Adult Reader   * = See this main entry

(c.563–c.483 B.C.), who became known as Buddha, meaning Enlightened One. Born into a royal family, he renounced his title and started a lifelong search for true enlightenment through meditation. Basic to Buddhism are the Four Noble Truths: Life is suffering; the cause is self-centeredness; this can be overcome; the way to overcome self-centeredness is through the Eightfold Path. These steps begin when you realize what is wrong with your life and proceed to the achievement, through meditation, of Nirvana, or perfect peace. Over the centuries Buddhism has developed several different aspects, one of which, Zen Buddhism, has become popular in the Western world. Its practice is centered in Japan, where it has influenced many areas of life, from the tea ceremony and gardening to poetry and painting. If you would like to read more about Buddhism, there are many books, among them *Buddhism* (1967) by Thomas M. Berry (1914–), *The Buddhist World* (1984) by Anne Bancroft (1923–), or *Buddhism: A Way of Life and Thought* (1980) by Nancy Wilson Ross (1910–1986). You will also enjoy the novel *Siddhartha* by *Hermann Hesse, which follows a young Indian's search for truth and peace and reflects Hesse's interest in Buddhism and other Eastern teachings. MR & YA

Bulfinch's Mythology contains three separate works by Thomas Bulfinch (1796–1867). *The Age of Fable* (1855), Bulfinch's first and most successful book, is an introduction to Greek, Roman, Scandinavian, and Celtic mythology. Written for readers who want to understand the many references to classical mythology in literature, the stories of gods, goddesses, and heroes are retold in simple and concise language. Similar in style and intent, *The Age of Chivalry* (1858) contains the legends of *King Arthur and his knights of the *Round Table, and *The Mabinogion*, a collection of ancient Welsh tales. *Legends of Charlemagne* (1863) includes romantic stories from the Middle Ages. These works have the charm of a storybook while providing knowledge about an important part of cultural history.

The author was the son of Charles Bulfinch (1763–1844), a well-known architect. After graduating from Harvard University, Thomas Bulfinch taught school briefly and later supported himself through a modest position in a Boston bank. In his spare time, he devoted himself to classical studies and to writing. MR & YA

Bunnicula: A Rabbit-Tale of Mystery (1979), by Deborah Howe (1946–1978) and *James Howe, is about Mr. and Mrs. Monroe, their sons, Toby and Peter, and their unusual pets. When the Monroes go to the movies to see *Dracula, they find a small rabbit in a shoebox filled with dirt, take the frightened creature home, and name it Bunnicula. Feeling obliged to describe the consequences of that act, Harold, the dog, decides to write the story. The Monroes' cat, Chester, is the first to notice something odd about Bunnicula. Addicted to horror novels and suspicious by nature, Chester tells Harold that the rabbit shows signs of being a *vampire. Then the Monroes discover that the vegetables in the refrigerator have turned white, and Chester's worst fears are confirmed. Bunnicula, who sleeps all day, is sneaking out at night to drain the vegetables dry, leaving two tiny fang marks. When Chester's attempts to warn the family fail miserably, Chester and Harold resort to dramatic and hilarious methods. The problem of Bunnicula is finally brought under control, and the Monroes, blissfully unaware, think they have been the victims of a curious blight. If you enjoyed this tale, try another lively story about rabbits, *Rabbit Hill* by *Robert Lawson. MR

Bunyan, John (1628–1688) An English author, Bunyan worked as a tinker, a traveling mender of pots and pans. Deeply religious and an enthusiastic reader, Bunyan devoured the popular adventure stories of his day, the sermons and books of the English *Puritans, and the *Bible. In his mid-20s he became a preacher for a Baptist congregation and later disagreed openly, both in his writing and in public debates, with other religious groups. He spent 12 years in prison for holding a service that did not follow the rules of the Church of England. During

John Bunyan

those years he wrote the first part of his masterpiece, *The Pilgrim's Progress*, and he finished the second part six years later. *The Pilgrim's Progress* was enormously popular with readers of all types, in part because it sprang from the experiences of ordinary people and traditions of country life. YA

Bunyan, Paul See *Paul Bunyan.

Burch, Robert (1925–), author of *Skinny and *Queenie Peavy, was born in Georgia and has written a number of stories that take place there. One of seven children, as a boy he planned to be a farmer. After working as a civilian employee of the U.S. Army, and later in advertising, Burch became interested in writing stories as a hobby and drifted into a writing career. He thinks of himself as one of the first authors to create realistic fiction for young readers and has described life during the *Great Depression, when so many people were poor. Another of his books you may like is *Ida Early Comes Over the Mountain, about

the Sutton family's cheery housekeeper and her knack for telling wild stories. MR

Burchard, Peter (Duncan) (1921–) An illustrator and photographer as well as a writer, Burchard has written a number of books for young readers, including *Jed and *North by Night. He enlisted in the U.S. Army during World War II, and his drawings were first published in *Yank* magazine. Burchard went to art school after the war and later became a book illustrator. His novels and stories are often based on events in American history, with special attention to slavery in America. You might also like to read *Stranded* (1967), about a Scottish boy learning about city life in 1875, and *Bimby* (1968), the story of an important day in the life of a young slave. MR

Burgess, Anthony [John Anthony Burgess Wilson] (1917–) An English novelist, critic, translator, composer, and author of *A Clockwork Orange, his best-known novel, Burgess also wrote under the names John Burgess Wilson and Joseph Kell. Burgess studied music and languages and served in the British Army during World War II and then in the Army Education Corps. He began writing novels during his years as an education officer in Malaya and Borneo. Burgess returned to England after a local doctor told him he had a brain tumor. Not expecting to live more than a year, Burgess wrote five novels in rapid succession to provide an inheritance. The medical diagnosis proved false, and Burgess has since given himself to writing. He is now considered one of England's major literary figures, celebrated for his wit, scholarship, and inventive use of language, and sometimes criticized for his love of the bizarre and outrageous.

Burgess has written about 20 novels. *Nothing Like the Sun: A Story of Shakespeare's Love Life* (1964) is a fictional biography of *William Shakespeare based in large part on historical fact. *Man of Nazareth* (1979), another novel, is Burgess's treatment of the life of *Jesus, and was adapted from the script of *Jesus of Na-*

zareth, filmed for television in 1977. His many works of nonfiction include *Re Joyce* (1965), published in England as *Here Comes Everybody: An Introduction to James Joyce for the Ordinary Reader.* YA

Burnett, Frances (Eliza) Hodgson (1848–1924) The author of *Little Lord Fauntleroy,* one of the most popular books for young readers, Burnett was born in Manchester, England. After her father died, her mother moved the family to Tennessee when Frances was 16 years old. In spite of her living in near poverty there, Frances later wrote that her real home was in the beautiful Tennessee countryside. Burnett, an enthusiastic reader from a very early age, began writing for family and friends when she was 7 years old. She liked especially to create plots with happy endings. Many of Burnett's books have heroes or heroines who come from simple backgrounds and who win the affection of more sophisticated and arrogant older persons. See also *The Secret Garden.* MR

Burnford, Sheila (1918–1984) A Scottish-born author, Burnford served during World War II as an ambulance driver. After her marriage, she spent many years living in Canada, where she learned to shoot and to fly a plane. Her first book, *The Incredible Journey,* was translated into 16 languages. Intensely interested in the northern wilderness and its few inhabitants, Burnford wrote about her visits to the Cree and Ojibway Indian reservations in *Without Reserve* (1969). *One Woman's Arctic* (1973) describes her stay with the Eskimo people. If you enjoy her books, you may also like those of *James A. Houston and *Farley Mowat. YA

Burnham, Sophy (1926–) A museum curator, book editor, and author of television scripts, Burnham is also the author of mystery stories and other writings for young readers. In *Buccaneer* (1977), 12-year-old Julie, who is having trouble with her parents, finds greater difficulties with a new horse. *The Dog Walker* (1979) is about two young people in Washington, D.C., who try to find a dog that has a bomb attached to its collar as part of an assassination plot. A different kind of book is *A Book of Angels* (1980), which the author calls "reflections on angels past and present and how they touch our lives." If you like this author's books, try also those of *Enid Blyton, *Betty Cavanna, and *Barbara Corcoran. MR & YA

Burns, Robert (1759–1796) A great Scottish poet, Burns was the oldest of seven children and spent much of his childhood working on the family farm. There he heard Scottish folk tales and folk songs, which led to his interest in song rhythms and the challenge of fitting words to music. His first published work was *Poems, Chiefly in the Scottish Dialect* (1786), which delighted both country people and learned critics and brought him great success. Later, Burns collaborated with a collector of Scottish songs and worked tirelessly on editing and rewriting lyrics for traditional folk tunes. He traveled over Scotland collecting ancient folk material, some of it in fragments, and undertook to restore the songs in the best folk tradition. Among the hundreds he wrote or recreated are "Flow Gently, Sweet Afton," "Auld Lang Syne," "Comin' thro' the Rye," and "My Heart's in the Highlands." Burns's poems include "Tam O'Shanter," a funny and frightening tale in which the drunken Tam passes a haunted church on his night ride home and sees a crowd of witches and warlocks in a wild dance there. "To a Louse" caused some distress among critics, as it describes the outrage of seeing a louse on a fine lady's bonnet at church. "To a Mouse" expresses the poet's pity for a tiny mouse frightened from its burrow by a plow, and contains the lines, "The best-laid schemes o' mice and men/ Gang aft a-gley" (go often awry). Burns's talent for portraying his countrymen and -women with humor and loving detail made him enormously popular. YA

Bury the Dead (1986), by the English novelist Peter Carter (1929–), takes place in East Berlin in former East Germany, before the destruction of the Berlin Wall (see also *Iron Curtain). Erika Nordern, a talented young high-jumper, shares a small apartment with her mother and father, her younger brother, and her grandmother, Omi. Erika's parents are hard-working civil servants, and they hope Erika will someday be a candidate for a special training school. One evening the family is visited unexpectedly by a man who introduces himself as Uncle Karl von Bromberg, Omi's brother, who was thought to have died during World War II. Elegant and smooth-talking, the West German businessman never explains why he did not contact the Norderns sooner. Some strange things happen shortly after Karl's arrival. Herr Nordern is interrogated by Lieutenant Werner of the police about an auto accident that never happened, the family learns there is no person named Werner at the police station, and a colleague of Herr Nordern dies under mysterious circumstances.

In spite of her anxiety, Erika is able to concentrate on her jumping, and she wins the junior championship after a difficult competition. Her happiness is marred by the news that Omi plans to live with Karl in West Germany. Karl has asked Omi to carry documents across the border, knowing an old woman will probably not be searched. Erika accidentally discovers the documents are Karl's record as the former commander of a Nazi death squad. When the horrified Norderns face Karl, he coldly explains he must deliver the documents to his connections in the West if he is to survive. If the Norderns refuse to cooperate, Karl will expose them as relatives of a war criminal, and they all will suffer. Omi agrees to carry out Karl's plan, but she is arrested at the train by the border police. Herr Nordern, Erika, her brother, and a friend are taken away without any explanation by an unidentified man, and the novel ends with many questions left unanswered.

Carter has been a contractor and a teacher. He has traveled widely and lived in Germany. If you liked *Bury the Dead*, read Carter's other novels, including *The Black Lamp* (1973), about

life in England during the Industrial Revolution, and *Gates of Paradise* (1973), about *William Blake. YA

Butler, Samuel (1835–1902) An English novelist, essayist, critic, and author of *Erewhon and *The Way of All Flesh*, Butler was the son and grandson of well-known clergymen. After graduating from Cambridge University and preparing briefly for holy orders, Butler declared his independence by refusing to be ordained, emigrating to New Zealand, and starting a sheep farm. On reading *On the Origin of Species* by *Charles Darwin, Butler became intensely interested in the theory of evolution, which provided the arguments he needed to oppose his father's restrictive approach to Christianity. Butler wrote several articles on Darwinian subjects, but later changed his opinion and rejected Darwin's theory as too machinelike.

In 1864 Butler returned to England, studied painting with great seriousness and worked at musical composition. *Erewhon*, a utopian *satire that has been compared to *Gulliver's Travels*, brought him considerable fame as a writer. Butler continued to write on evolutionary and religious topics until shortly before his death. His last work and only other novel, *The Way of All Flesh*, is an attack on the prudishness and rigidity of his own upbringing. YA

Butterworth, Oliver (1915–) Author of *The Enormous Egg*, Butterworth was born and educated in New England. He has spent most of his professional life as a teacher, with students ranging from third grade to college. After having four children of his own and teaching two years in an elementary school, he began writing books for young people. *The Enormous Egg*, his first book, was based on his family's experiences with backyard hens. Butterworth enjoys doing a little teaching in his books, but most of all he likes to share his feelings about the things that delight him.

You may like to read *The Trouble with Jenny's Ear* (1960), whose plot was inspired by some fascinating experiments with electrical equipment. *The Narrow Passage* (1973) was inspired by the Butterworth family's visit to the famous prehistoric caves at Lascaux, France. MR

Byars, Betsy (1928–) An avid fan of mystery stories and horror films, Byars began to write while her husband was in graduate school and she was raising a family. She has written almost entirely for young people and has used many events from her children's lives in her stories. Critics have praised Byars's talent for creating lively and believable characters and her down-to-earth approach to the difficult problems facing modern youth. Among her many books are *The Summer of the Swans*; *The Pinballs*, about several foster children whose unsettled lives make them feel like pinballs; *The Night Swimmers*; and *Bingo Brown and the Language of Love*. Television adaptations were made of *The Pinballs* in 1977 and *The Night Swimmers*, as *Daddy, I'm Their Mama Now*, in 1982. MR

Byron, George Gordon (Noel) (1788–1824) Known as Lord Byron, this English poet and satirist was born with a deformed foot, about which he was extremely sensitive. Byron spent part of his childhood in the spacious but partly ruined estate of Newstead Abbey, near Nottingham in England. When he was 15 years old he fell in love with a distant cousin, and he began writing melancholy verses after she became engaged to another man. At college in Cambridge, Byron spent money lavishly and continued to write poetry. He traveled to Spain, Portugal, and Greece, where he was enchanted by the sunny climate and a freer life. Here he completed the first part of an autobiographical poem, *Childe Harold's Pilgrimage*, which made him famous. Back in England, the handsome Byron became a celebrated society figure and was involved in a number of scandalous affairs with high-born ladies. Now a social outcast, and after a marriage that lasted

George Gordon Byron

one year, Byron left with a friend for Europe and never returned to England. He visited *Percy Bysshe Shelley in Switzerland, traveled extensively, pursued his love affairs, and wrote his masterpiece, *Don Juan* (1819–1824). He came to be considered as fine a poet as Shelley or *John Keats, and was the personification of the flamboyant Romantic. In 1823 Byron agreed to help the Greeks in their struggle for independence from Turkey, and used his money and influence to benefit the cause. He died in Greece when he was just 36 years old. YA

Byronic hero is a term used to describe a lonely and defiant figure, full of romantic gloom, who sometimes carries a burden of guilt and remorse for some secret crime or tragedy in the past, and who may be capable of extraordinary heroism. An example is Mr. Rochester in *Charlotte Brontë's novel *Jane Eyre*. See *George Gordon Byron. YA

Caddie Woodlawn (1935), by *Carol Ryrie Brink, is based on stories of a pioneer childhood told to the author by her grandmother. It takes place on a Wisconsin farm toward the end of the Civil War, when American Indians still lived in the area. Caddie's father runs the farm and is a master mechanic at the nearby mill. Her mother takes care of seven children and a big house, helps on the farm, and raises turkeys.

Eleven-year-old Caddie is a tomboy with a strong taste for adventure. Her red-gold curls are much admired by the Woodlawn's American Indian neighbors. Unlike other girls her age, she spends more time making mischief with her brothers, Tom and Warren, than staying at home to learn sewing and cooking. Of her many escapades, the most dramatic occurs when the settlers hear rumors of an Indian uprising. Neighbors gather at the Woodlawn house for safety, and Caddie overhears some of the men planning to raid the nearby Indian village. If they drive the Indians off, they say, it will serve as a warning to unfriendly Indians. Caddie rides alone at night to warn her American Indian friends and on her return finds that her father has convinced the men not to act foolishly.

Mr. Woodlawn, who was born an aristocrat in England, gets a letter telling him he will inherit a grand estate and a title, providing he returns to live there. After careful thought, the entire family votes on the question, by secret ballot, and they decide to give up the money and title and stay in Wisconsin, where they will continue their lives as Americans. If you enjoyed this book, you will also like the Little House series of *Laura Ingalls Wilder. *Caddie Woodlawn* won the *Newbery Medal in 1936. MR

Cain, James M(allahan) (1892–1977) Beginning his career as a college teacher and a journalist before turning to writing novels, Cain became a master of the school of hard-boiled fiction. This type of fiction, which is considered very American, relies on brief, crude spurts of dialogue, takes place in depressing locations, and assumes that violence and cruelty are commonplace. The first of Cain's novels was *The Postman Always Rings Twice* (1934), in which a seductive woman and a young drifter make plans to murder her husband to collect his insurance. Generally similar in plot, style, and the creation of lustful characters with many problems but few or no morals are *Double Indemnity* (1936) and *Mildred Pierce* (1941). Later novels are *The Magician's Wife* (1965) and *Rainbow's End* (1975). Cain's short stories were collected in *The Baby in the Icebox* (1981). If you like the hard-boiled style of these books, try the books of *Raymond Chandler, *Dashiell Hammett, *Elmore Leonard, and *Mickey Spillane. *The Postman Always*

Rings Twice was produced as a play in 1936 and was filmed in 1946 and 1981. *Double Indemnity* was filmed in 1944 and *Mildred Pierce* in 1945. YA

Cain and Abel, whose story is told in the book of *Genesis in the *Bible, were sons of *Adam and Eve. Cain, the older son, was a tiller of the soil, while Abel was a shepherd. Because the Lord accepted Abel's gift, the first of his flock, over the fruit of the earth offered by his brother, Cain fell into a jealous rage and killed Abel. When the Lord asked Cain, "Where is Abel thy brother?" Cain said, "I know not: Am I my brother's keeper?" The Lord banished Cain for his sin of jealousy and murder, condemning him to live as a fugitive. Cain left his home and settled in "the land of Nod, on the east of Eden." A novel you might like to read, whose plot is based on the story of Cain and Abel, is *John Steinbeck's *East of Eden.

Caine Mutiny, The (1951) This exciting historical novel, by *Herman Wouk, is set in the South Pacific during the great naval battles of World War II. It is noted for its fascinating psychological portraits of the main characters. Ensign Willie Keith reports for duty on the *Caine*, an old destroyer converted for minesweeping. The *Caine* is shabby, but its new commanding officer, Captain Queeg, seems neat and capable. Moving from one assignment to another, the men must adjust to the threat of attack, an exhausting schedule of watches, fiercely hot weather, and cramped quarters. The captain emerges as a man obsessed with unimportant details, who devises elaborate punishments for failure to observe regulations. He also shows disturbing signs of cowardice in moments of crisis. Keith's friend Tom Keefer, educated and articulate, plants the idea that Queeg is mentally ill. General dislike of the captain turns to hatred, fueled by Keefer's insinuations. During a violent storm, with the ship about to founder, Queeg panics and issues senseless orders. With Keith's support, executive officer Maryk formally takes command to avert disaster, and the *Caine* is saved.

Later, facing court martial, Maryk and Keith are brilliantly defended by Barney Greenwald, who slowly turns the proceedings into an unofficial trial of Queeg. The captain's sordid obsessions, mistakes, and petty crimes are revealed to the court, and Maryk and Keith are acquitted. While the men celebrate their freedom, Greenwald astonishes them by calling Keefer the real instigator of mutiny, and commends Queeg for his many years of loyal service in defense of his country. You might enjoy reading *Mutiny on the Bounty* by *Charles Nordhoff and *James Norman Hall, a historical novel based on real events. *The Caine Mutiny* was made into an excellent movie in 1954, and a successful stage version, *The Caine Mutiny Court-Martial*, was produced in 1954 and made into a TV movie in 1988. YA

Calamity Jane was the nickname of Martha Jane Canary or Martha Jane Burke (c.1852–1903), a colorful character who lived in frontier mining towns, mainly around Deadwood, South Dakota. Dressed in men's clothing, she carried a gun and became known as a fine equestrian and crack shot. *Dime novels of the period modeled their heroines on Jane, portraying her as fighting for justice by the side of her lover, "Deadwood Dick." In the 1890s she performed in Wild West shows and appeared at the Pan American Exposition of 1901 in Buffalo, New York. She is buried next to *Wild Bill (James Butler) Hickok. Calamity Jane is the central figure in the novel *Buffalo Girls* (1990) by *Larry McMurtry. YA

Call It Courage (1940), written and illustrated by *Armstrong Sperry, is the story of a young boy named Mafatu, meaning Stout Heart. He is the son of the Great Chief of the people of Hikueru, an island in the southern Pacific Ocean. These people are Polynesians and they worship courage. When Mafatu was a baby, he and his mother were walking near the sea. A terrible hurricane hit and his mother drowned. Ever since his mother's death, Mafatu feared that Moana, the Sea God, would kill him too.

Mafatu, in spite of his name, became known as a coward, branded as the Boy Who Was Afraid. Fed up with the other children's taunts as well as saddened by his father's shame of him, Mafatu decides "he must prove his courage to himself, and to others, or he could no longer live in their midst. He must face Moana, the Sea God—face him and conquer him." Mafatu leaves the village in a canoe, accompanied only by his pet dog, Uri, and his pet *albatross, Kivi.

The first challenge Mafatu overcomes is a monstrous storm. Then he spends days on a desert island where he has many adventures, such as killing a shark and escaping from savage man-eaters.

Finally, Mafatu makes the long, lonely journey home. When he reaches Hikueru, his father proudly exclaims, "Here is my son come home from the sea. Mafatu, Stout Heart. A brave name for a brave boy!" Though Mafutu is physically exhausted, his spirit bounds with newfound confidence and courage. If you enjoyed this book, try also *Island of the Blue Dolphins* by *Scott O'Dell. *Call It Courage* won the *Newbery Medal in 1941. MR

Call of the Wild, The (1903), a novel by *Jack London, is the story of Buck, a dog stolen from his comfortable home and sold into a life of hardship in the Arctic. In this harsh new world Buck is afraid and snappish, so he is brutally clubbed into obedience. Later, put in a harness, he becomes part of a team of pack dogs that know "no law but the law of club and fang." In order to survive, Buck forgets his tame, civilized ways. Over time, Buck learns to survive through force, cunning, and greed. His desire to be top dog leads Buck into a ferocious fight with the leader of the pack, ultimately killing him. "Kill or be killed, eat or be eaten, was the law."

Buck escapes death when he is cared for by John Thornton, the only man whom Buck has ever really loved. Thornton and his partners take Buck on a journey in search of a "fabled lost mine." Buck strays from the campsite to spend his days hunting and living a wolflike existence. When he returns to the campsite, Buck finds everyone, including Thornton, murdered by a band of American Indians. Enraged, he attacks and kills some of the tribe members, thus realizing that men were weak unless "they bore in their hands their arrows, spears, and clubs." With Thornton dead and the last tie to humans broken, Buck goes deep into the forest to live where he feels most comfortable, at the head of a wolf pack. *The Call of the Wild* made Jack London famous overnight. If you enjoyed it, try also London's novel *White Fang, in which a wolf dog goes from the wild to domestication, the exact opposite of *The Call of the Wild*. Movies were made of the book in 1935, 1972, and 1976. MR & YA

Camelot was *King Arthur's castle. In the Arthurian legends, Camelot represented a place of honor and peace, the home of the *Round Table and King Arthur's knights. It was the place from which the knights departed on their adventures, and to which they returned after the fight was done and the foe was defeated. It was the court and the seat of government. In pictures Camelot is usually depicted as a 12th- or 15th-century medieval castle, but Arthur actually lived in the 6th century, when there were no castles and clothes and armor were much simpler than are usually shown. You will enjoy reading *Quest for a King: Searching for the Real King Arthur* (1989) by Catherine M. Andronik (n.d.), who traces the transformation of oral stories into myths and legends and describes the archeological excavations that are still going on in England to establish the actual location of Camelot. A musical comedy, *Camelot*, based on *The Once and Future King* by *T.H. White, was produced in 1960. A film based on the musical was produced in 1967. It is said that during his presidency John F. Kennedy imagined the White House as his Camelot, and that "Camelot" was his favorite song, though his wife, when asked, is said to have replied that his favorite song was "Hail to the Chief." See also *Idylls of the King* by *Alfred Tennyson. YA

Cameron, Eleanor (Frances) (1912–) The Canadian-born author of *A Room Made of Windows*, Cameron was 12 years old when she decided to become a writer and librarian. Out of her love for fairy tales, an interest in astronomy, and in response to her young son's request for a space adventure, she wrote *The Wonderful Flight to the Mushroom Planet* (1954). This charming novel is about two boys who, with assistance from the unusual Mr. Bass, travel to the planet Basidium and bring much-needed help to its citizens. *A Stowaway to the Mushroom Planet* (1956) is a sequel in which the existence of the planet becomes known to Professor Horatio Q. Peabody, who resolves to investigate. In *The Terrible Churnadryne* (1959), Jennifer and Tom learn about a mysterious creature identified as *Elasmosaurus californicus* by the curator of a local natural history museum. In a somewhat different vein is *The Court of the Stone Children* (1973), about a young woman who solves the mystery of a murder that took place in the time of Napoleon Bonaparte (1769–1821). MR

Camus, Albert (1913–1960) A French author of numerous literary works exploring the fundamental dilemmas of modern human beings, Camus is considered one of the leading French *existentialists. He was born to a poor family in Mondovi, Algeria. His father was a farmer who was killed in World War I, and his Spanish mother was a servant. Due to a constant battle with tuberculosis, Camus was forced to give up an academic career, concentrating instead on writing. Among his numerous works are *The Stranger* (1946); *The Plague* (1948); *The Rebel* (1954), an essay outlining his basic ideas on the individual and existence; *The Myth of Sisyphus* (1955), an essay on the Greek myth of Sisyphus, who was condemned by the gods to roll a huge boulder to the top of a hill only to have it eternally roll to the bottom again; and *The Fall. He also published a volume of plays, *Caligula and Three Other Plays* (1945), as well as various dramatic adaptations, short stories, and essays. Camus was awarded the Nobel Prize for literature in 1957. He died in Sens, France, in an automobile accident. YA

Can You Sue Your Parents for Malpractice? (1979), by *Paula Danziger, is an appealing story about deciding important things for yourself. Lauren Allen, a lively and intelligent ninth-grader, is tired of having older people make decisions for her. She loves her family in spite of friction between her parents, but feels she has few rights at home and few at school. Lauren wants to be a lawyer, so she jumps at the chance to take a special elective class on "Law for Children and Young People." After Bobby Taylor, her first real boyfriend, leaves her for someone else, Lauren begins to take an interest in Zack Davids, a bright and funny eighth-grader in her law course. Zack has a sturdy confidence unusual for his age, and Lauren discovers as they work together that Zack is a better friend than Bobby ever was. People at school tell Lauren, often publicly, that she is robbing the cradle by associating with someone younger. At the end, Lauren sees that Zack's friendship is too valuable to lose. She also understands that suing her parents for malpractice is less important than making sure she is true to her own emerging beliefs and feelings. If you enjoyed this book, you may also like *The Great Skinner Strike* (1983) by *Stephanie S. Tolan, about a girl whose mother goes on strike against her family. MR

Candide (1759), by *Voltaire, one of the world's best-known books, is a philosophical fantasy written in unusually clear, forceful, and witty language. In it the author expresses his ideas about human beings and their predicament, as well as his disdain for extreme idealism and cloudy thinking.

Candide is a gentle, honest, and simple-minded young man living in the castle of a baron. He is tutored by Dr. Pangloss, a philosopher who asserts that there is no effect without a cause, and that ours is the best of all possible worlds. Candide loves Cunegonde, the baron's beautiful daughter, but the baron disapproves of their friendship and expels Candide from the castle by kicking him in the backside. Separated from his earthly paradise, Candide endures a series of adventures and calamities that test his endurance and his belief in the best of all possible worlds. He is conscripted into a Bulgarian regiment, escapes and meets Dr. Pangloss, survives shipwreck, earthquake, and a flogging, is reunited with Cunegonde, is forced to abandon her to travel to Paraguay to fight for the Jesuits, comes by accident to the golden land of Eldorado, and foolishly leaves it. After other journeys and tribulations, Candide retires with his companions. He marries Cunegonde, now exhausted by her own misfortunes. In spite of having suffered horribly, Dr. Pangloss clings to his opinion that all events are linked up, and that preestablished harmony is the finest thing imaginable. Candide, however, has learned that honest work keeps the great evils away, and that we all should cultivate our gardens. Another fantasy you might enjoy is *Gulliver's Travels* by *Jonathan Swift. *Candide* was adapted for the stage in 1956 in a successful musical comedy, by *Lillian Hellman, *Richard Wilbur, and the composer Leonard Bernstein (1918–1990). YA

Cane (1923), an experimental novel by Jean Toomer (1894–1967), is a collection of prose and poetry carefully woven together into a picture of black life in America. Instead of having a unifying plot and a single cast of characters, the novel is made up of a series of stories. Together they celebrate the spirit and strength of blacks, forged out of a history full of beauty and ugliness, sorrow and joy. *Cane* is divided into three sections. The first describes life among poor blacks in the Georgia countryside. The second section describes life in Washington, D.C., and Chicago. The third section, a novelette in the form of a play, is set in rural Georgia and tells of a young man's struggle to come to grips with life and with himself. *Cane* was an important influence on the writers of the *Harlem Renaissance and also later black writers. If you enjoyed it, try also the works of *Toni Morrison, *Alice Walker, and *Richard Wright. YA

Canterbury Tales, The (c.1380) By *Geoffrey Chaucer, this is a collection of poetic tales recounted among themselves by a group of about 30 English pilgrims who are making a pilgrimage from Southwark, a suburb of London, to the shrine of St. Thomas à Becket at Canterbury. The pilgrims, coming together from

This opening page of "The Squire's Tale" is from an early edition of *The Canterbury Tales*.

many different walks of life, are led by their guide, Harry Bailly. The Knight begins the book with a story of chivalry. Later, the Shipman tells a tale of a merchant whose stinginess brings him a faithless wife and loss of money. A few of the tales have magical qualities, such as the one told by the *Wife of Bath. She tells of a young Knight who must save his own life by answering the question "What do women most desire?" Ironically, he learns the answer from an old hag whom he is forced to marry. As in a fairy tale, the aged hag turns into a beautiful young woman. Chaucer's pilgrims also tell tales using animals as the main characters. The Pardoner's story, possibly the most famous of all, is a tale reflecting the Pardoner's personal text: "The root of all evil is greed." The varied literary styles in the stories as well as the vivid depictions of characters help to make *The Canterbury Tales* a classic collection full of emotions, gaiety, and wit. Four of the tales were adapted for a film, *The Canterbury Tales*, in 1971. YA

Capote, Truman (1924–1984) The Southern-born author of **Other Voices, Other Rooms*, his first novel, and **Breakfast at Tiffany's*, Capote always knew he wanted to be a writer. He openly admitted his ambition to be rich and famous, and concealed neither his taste for extravagant living nor his homosexuality. *Other Voices, Other Rooms*, which made him a celebrity, was praised for its style and widely criticized for what was considered distasteful and inappropriate subject matter. *The Grass Harp* (1951) is the humorous tale of an orphan boy whose peculiar relatives avoid the burdens of reality by living in a tree.

In spite of the success of his novels and short stories, Capote is perhaps known best for an original work of journalism that he called a nonfiction novel. *In Cold Blood: A True Account of a Multiple Murder and Its Consequences* (1966) is about the killing of a Kansas farmer and his family. It presents a vast amount of factual material through the literary devices used by novelists. With research assistance from his friend *Harper Lee, Capote spent six years on the project. The result is narrated with great skill and the kind of sensitivity usually associated with a work of art. Capote's style, on which he lavished great effort, is graceful and witty, economical and highly evocative, rich in observed physical detail and the precise language suited to each character. *The Grass Harp* was adapted for the stage in 1952, and *In Cold Blood* was filmed in 1967. YA

Captain Hook, an important character in *J.M. Barrie's story *Peter Pan, is surely one of the most evil men in all the stories for young people. A thin man with sad eyes and hair dressed in long curls like "black candles," he has a politely elegant but sinister air. He is a great story-teller and a courageous fighter, though all his energy is devoted to awful deeds.

The name Hook fits him gruesomely, since he lost an arm in a battle with Peter Pan and now wears a vicious iron claw in its place. Hook has sworn to kill Peter for having thrown the arm to a passing crocodile, which pursues the captain in the hope of finding another tidbit. Although Hook plots the murder of whole tribes of Red Indians and the lost boys who inhabit the island of Neverland, he becomes sentimental at the thought of kidnapping Peter's friend Wendy to provide a mother for the pirates. His complicated schemes for revenge on Peter lead Hook and his men into a disastrous final battle, and Peter tricks Hook into leaping into the sea where the hungry crocodile waits.

Captain Nemo Enormously wealthy, highly educated, and brilliant, he is the inventor and commander of the submarine *Nautilus* in **Twenty Thousand Leagues Under the Sea* by *Jules Verne. Nemo has renounced all ties with the world on land and has made the sea his home. Seeking vengeance for an unknown tragedy in his past, he sinks a number of "enemy" warships before sailing the *Nautilus* into a whirlpool off the coast of Norway. In Verne's novel *The Mysterious Island* (1870), five balloonists crash land on a Pacific island and are aided for several years by an unseen benefactor, Nemo, whom they finally find dying aboard the damaged *Nautilus* in a submarine cavern. He reveals that he was once an educated and powerful Indian prince whose family, nation, and hopes for the future were destroyed by the British in the Sepoy Rebellion of 1857. His listeners follow his dying wish by scuttling the submarine in the cavern. They escape aboard a small boat just as the island disappears in a volcanic blast. MR & YA

Captains Courageous, a novel written by *Rudyard Kipling, an English poet and novelist, is about a rich, spoiled 15-year-old boy, Harvey Cheyne, who falls off an ocean liner on its way to Europe. He is rescued by a fishing schooner called *We're Here*. The captain, Disko Troop, offers him a small wage plus board until they reach Gloucester four months later. The captain's son, Dan, and the cook become Harvey's friends. They are the only two on the boat who believe Harvey's stories of wealth and fortune. Over time, Harvey fits comfortably into life on the schooner, and enjoys being accepted as a fellow workman rather than as a millionaire's son. Harvey has many exciting adventures aboard the *We're Here,* such as finding the corpse of a Frenchman, working hard to help the schooner win a race, and learning about navigation. When the schooner finally reaches Gloucester, Harvey's parents are happy to see how hard work has changed their son from a brat into an independent young man with good values. Though Disko Troop refuses a reward for Harvey's rescue, his son eventually becomes an officer on a fleet of Mr. Cheyne's freighters. The cook becomes Harvey's bodyguard, and later Harvey successfully manages the Cheyne interests. If you enjoyed *Captains Courageous,* you will also like the sea classic *Treasure Island* by *Robert Louis Stevenson. MR & YA

Card, Orson Scott (1951–) Writing *science fiction and *fantasy novels influenced by his Mormon background, Card sometimes fantasizes an earlier America and sometimes an imagined future. One series, The Tales of Alvin Maker, begins with Maker's childhood in *Seventh Son* (1987). The time is the early 19th century, but the United States consists of the Middle Atlantic states, while the South remains colonies of Great Britain. Maker grows up in *Red Prophet* (1988), with Ta-Kumsaw and Maker's mentor, Taleswapper, playing major roles. The third volume, *Prentice Alvin* (1989), takes Maker to the South and slave country. A trilogy by Card consists of *Ender's Game* (1985), *Speaker for the Dead* (1986), and *Xenocide* (1991). In these novels Andrew Wiggins, the hero, deals successfully with alien invaders of Earth called "buggers." *The Memory of Earth* (1992) begins another series. Set 40 million years in the future, it concerns an artificial intelligence, Oversoul, that is breaking down. Card has written many short stories, and *The Changed Mind* (1992) gathers a dozen of them.

Card's writings are much concerned with moral values and are noted as much for ideas as for action. If you like these books, try those of *Isaac Asimov, *Ray Bradbury, and *Ursula K. Le Guin. MR & YA

Carey, M(ary) V(irginia) (1925–) An English-born American author and editor, Carey has written or edited a variety of works. She has written novels from a number of Walt Disney movies, such as *Walt Disney's Babes in Toyland* (1961). Carey has also written a dozen mystery novels around the theme of Alfred Hitchcock and the Three Investigators, the latter being a trio of young people. Among these stories are *The Mystery of Monster Mountain* (1973), which involves a matter of double identity and the legend of the mountain; *The Mystery of the Invisible Dog* (1975), in which the investigators try to recover the statue of a legendary wolf-dog; *The Mystery of the Wandering Cave Man* (1982), which tells of the search for ancient bones that have disappeared from a museum; and *The Mystery of the Missing Mermaid* (1983), in which a statue of a mermaid is a clue to finding a missing child. Carey also edited *Grandmothers Are Very Special People* (1977), a collection of stories about grandmothers. If you enjoy these books, you will like those of *Enid Blyton, *Franklin W. Dixon, *Carolyn Keene, and *Phyllis A. Whitney. MR & YA

Carr, John Dickson (1906–1977) Though born in the United States, the son of a man who later became a congressman, and educated in America, Carr spent most of his life in Great Britain. There he first tried his hand at writing historical romances, but he turned to detective fiction, most of which has a touch of the macabre, as hinted in the title of his first book, *It Walks by Night* (1930). Carr then created a fictional detective, Dr. Gideon Fell, based on *G.K. Chesterton, the English author whose own detective fiction features a Catholic priest, *Father Brown. Among these novels are *The Arabian Nights Murder* (1936) and *The Burning Court* (1937). Under the name of

Carter Dickson, Carr also wrote *The Bounty Murders* (1933), *The Plague Court Murders* (1934), and *Scandal at High Chimneys* (1959). In these books the fictional detective is Sir Henry Merrivale, actually much like Dr. Fell. Carr's combination of logical detection with elements of the supernatural sometimes lends an element of fantasy, but his readers are always left with a surprising, and more or less believable, solution. Carr wrote *The Life of Sir Arthur Conan Doyle* (1949), the official biography of the creator of the greatest of all fictional detectives, *Sherlock Holmes. Detective novels whose heroes are well-known fictional detectives include those of *Agatha Christie, *Arthur Conan Doyle, *Ellery Queen, and *G.K. Chesterton. YA

Carré, John Le See *Le Carré, John.

Carrie's War (1973) was written by *Nina Bawden, who probably based the story on her childhood experiences in Wales. During World War II, 11-year-old Carrie and her brother, Nick, are taken away from the London air raids to a safe, temporary home in a Welsh mining town, where they live with Samuel Evans and his sister, Louise. Evans is a bully, a strict and penny-pinching widower who hates disorder and playfulness, but his gentle-hearted sister does her best to make the children feel at home. Carrie and Nick learn that Evans's older sister, Dilys Gotobed, lives in a house called Druid's Bottom, outside the town. When the children go there on an errand, they meet the generous housekeeper Hepzibah Green, Albert Sandwich (another evacuee), and the odd little Mister Johnny Gotobed. Over tea in the warm kitchen, Hepzibah tells the story of the curse of the "screaming skull," which must be kept in the house or something terrible will happen.

As Carrie and Nick grow fonder of their new friends, Mr. Evans becomes more irritable and suspicious. Then Dilys dies, and Evans asks Hepzibah and the others to leave Druid's Bottom. Worried about her friends' future and furious with Evans's meanness, Carrie throws the "screaming skull" into the horse pond. She and Nick take the train to rejoin their mother, and are horrified to see Druid's Bottom on fire. Carrie feels sure she has caused the disaster.

Thirty years pass. Carrie is grown and has children of her own. Out of curiosity, she and the children visit the old spot in Druid's Grove and find, miraculously, that the house and Hepzibah are still there. They learn that the fire was caused by Mr. Johnny playing with matches, and Carrie need no longer feel guilty. MR

Carroll, Lewis [Charles Lutwidge Dodgson] (1832–1898) An English writer and mathematician, he was the author of *Alice's Adventures in Wonderland* and *Through the Looking Glass*, tales of fantasy and nonsense beloved by children and adults all over the world. Dodgson grew up in a country village and learned to amuse his brothers and sisters by creating magic tricks, word puzzles, and games of all kinds. Like the *Brontës, the young Dodgsons liked to write, and all contributed to family "magazines." One manuscript included the first stanza of Charles's poem "Jabberwocky," later developed in *Through the Looking Glass*. A brilliant student at Oxford University, Dodgson became a deacon of the Church of England and a lecturer in mathematics. He wrote books on mathematics and logic, but his greatest delight was to entertain children. A shy bachelor with a pronounced stammer, he was more at ease with young people than adults. He grew especially attached to the children of the dean of Christ Church, Oxford, one of whom was named Alice. It was she who asked Dodgson to write down his most engaging stories, and later his friends encouraged him to publish his work, with illustrations by John Tenniel (1820–1914), a well-known cartoonist. The books came to be enormously popular in England, while scholars and critics busied themselves finding *symbolic and *satiric meanings in them. Dodgson maintained he only intended to write nonsense. You can read nonsense verse, including "The Hunting of the Snark" (1876), a narrative poem, in *The Works of Lewis Carroll* (1965). Another good author of humorous and nonsense verse is *Edward Lear. MR & YA

Carry On, Mr. Bowditch (1955) By Jean Lee Latham (1902–), this biography tells about Nathaniel Bowditch (1773–1838), who rose from modest beginnings to become a great mathematician and the leading authority on the navigation of ships. Born in Salem, Massachusetts, Nat leaves school when he is 10 years old to work for his father, a ship's captain who has fallen on hard times. A wizard at mathematics, Nat has dreamed of studying at Harvard, but his life takes a different course. He works for a ship's chandler, outfitting and supplying ships, then makes several voyages of his own, first as a ship's clerk, then supercargo, second mate, and finally as captain. During these years of hard work and adventure, Nat studies on his own, and begins teaching sailors about navigation. He discovers that the book of mathematical tables commonly used in navigation is full of errors and writes his own book, *The New American Practical Navigator* (1802), which gains him international fame. Bowditch's book is still a standard book on sailing. Jean Lee Latham wrote many biographies of fascinating people, including *Drake: The Man They Called a Pirate* (1960), about the English naval hero Francis Drake (1543?–1596), and *Far Voyager: The Story of James Cook* (1970), about the English explorer James Cook (1728–1779). *Carry On, Mr. Bowditch* won the *Newbery Medal in 1956. MR

"Cask of Amontillado, The" (1846) In this horrifying tale by *Edgar Allan Poe, Montresor vows revenge against Fortunato, a man who has done him a thousand injuries. During the frenzy of carnival season, and without revealing his hatred, Montresor entices Fortunato into his palace by offering him the pleasure of tasting a fine old Spanish wine, an amontillado. Deep in the damp and foul catacombs of the palace, among the ancient bones of Montresor ancestors, Fortunato (a wine connoisseur) is encouraged to drink himself into a stupor. At the farthest end of the catacomb, Montresor leads his enemy into a small recess in the wall, saying the precious wine is there. He rapidly chains Fortunato to the wall. Then, slowly and remorselessly, Montresor seals the entrance to the recess with stone and mortar, while his victim realizes he will be left there to die. Another Poe tale of vengeance is "Hop-Frog" (1849), about a court jester who devises a horrifying retribution on the king and his counselors. YA

Castle, The (1926) This novel, by *Franz Kafka, one of the most influential of the 20th century, is a religious allegory in which a man known only as K. tries to find the grace of God. K. arrives late on a snowy night at an inn. He is to be the local count's land surveyor. He spends the next day trying to reach the count's castle, but has to return to the inn, where he meets his two assistants. They look alike, and K. is told they are his old assistants, not his new ones; but how could they be his old assistants when he has just traveled a great distance to this new job? This is one of the first of many episodes in which perceptions and misperceptions of truth and reality are inverted and twisted. K. is not allowed to go to the castle and is not permitted back in the inn, except for the bar. He meets the barmaid, Frieda; they discuss marrying, which K. thinks might improve his chances with his supervisor, Frieda's former lover. Then K. learns that his job does not exist and he is in the town as a result of confusion, but he decides to stay on. After many more twists of plot and misunderstandings, in which authority figures obstruct him, K., on his deathbed, finally receives a call from the castle to meet the count. *The Castle*, written originally in German, was finished by Kafka's friend, Max Brod (1884–1968). A more light-hearted book is *Amerika, a comic novel that depicts an almost surreal America, which Kafka only visited in his imagination. *The Castle* was adapted for film in 1968. See also *The Trial. YA

cat Along with the *dog, the cat is the most popular pet. It also often appears in history and literature, sometimes in a favorable light, sometimes not. The cat was sacred in ancient Egypt, but in the Middle Ages some believed that *Satan took the form of a black cat. Some people, therefore, think it is bad luck for you if a black cat crosses your path. Cats are said to have nine lives, perhaps because they so often land safely on their feet after a hard fall. When it "rains cats and dogs," it is pouring; "a cat may look at a king" means that one person is as good as another; "to bell the cat," a feat a mouse would hardly dare to attempt, is a risky deed; and "when the cat's away, the mice will play" can mean that if the teacher leaves the classroom, the students will be up to some mischief. In *Alice's Adventures in Wonderland* the Cheshire cat is able to fade away, its grin being the last part to disappear. "Puss in Boots," a tale first told in 1697, is about a cunning cat who manages to acquire for his poor master a fortune and a royal wife. Cats play a part in a number of the *fables of *Aesop.

Cat Ate My Gymsuit, The (1974) This novel, by *Paula Danziger, tells about an important change in 13-year-old Marcy Lewis's outlook on life. Marcy thinks of herself as a "baby blimp with wire-frame glasses," and her parents remind her all too often that she could improve her appearance. Classes at school are boring, so the new English teacher, Ms. Finney, is a welcome distraction. Ms. Finney proves to be young, attractive, interested in unconventional teaching methods, and willing to listen to and show respect for her students. Her approach wins the hearts and minds of the class, and Marcy begins to bloom. A little surer of herself at school, she must still face her father's criticism and violent temper at home. When Ms. Finney is suspended because of her unusual methods and her refusal to pledge allegiance to the flag, Marcy and her friends show their support for her and are suspended as well. After a good deal of uproar, Ms. Finney is reinstated by the conservative school board, but resigns after explaining she cannot teach effectively in a community where so many disapprove of her. Marcy is deeply disappointed,

but the experience of standing up for her beliefs has helped her grow and adapt to a difficult situation without falling apart. If you enjoyed this book, you may also like *The Tryouts* by Elizabeth Levy (1942–), about a group of students who go on strike when their friend is dropped from the basketball team. MR

Cat on a Hot Tin Roof (1955) by *Tennessee Williams is a play set on a Southern plantation owned by "Big Daddy" Pollitt, who is dying of cancer. His children have returned to the plantation for his birthday but also to try to gain control of his land. The elder son, Gooper, has brought his wife, Mae, and five obnoxious children. The younger son, Brick, is an alcoholic whose weak nature keeps him out of the family fights. On the other hand, Brick's beautiful wife, Margaret, the "cat on a hot tin roof," fights ardently for Brick's rights. But she accuses him of having an unnatural attraction to his college friend, Skipper. Big Daddy, who has been falsely assured that his cancer is curable, questions Brick about his drinking habit. Now Brick realizes his drinking has kept him from understanding his own homosexual desires. To get back at his father, Brick tells him that his cancer is incurable. Making a last attempt to win over Big Daddy, Margaret pretends to be pregnant with Brick's child. The ambiguous ending of the play implies that Margaret succeeds at making her lie come true, thus overcoming the hostilities of her relatives and the apathy of her husband. YA

Catch-22 (1961), by *Joseph Heller, is a savage, raunchy, and comically bitter antiwar novel. Its main character is Yossarian, a B-25 bombardier stationed on an island off the coast of Italy during World War II. Yossarian has flown much more than the usual 40 bombing missions required of airmen, and so he has lost his nerve for combat. Yet his commanding officer, Colonel Cathcart, keeps raising the squadron's required number of missions, because he thinks it will help him become a general and get an article about himself published in the *Saturday Evening Post*. Cathcart is crazy. So is just about everyone else, including McWatt, who likes to buzz Yossarian's tent with his bomber; Nately, a proper New Englander who has fallen in love with a prostitute in Rome; and Milo Minderbinder, a wheeler-dealer who even bombs the airbase for profit. Doc Daneeka tells Yossarian about Catch-22: The only way he can be grounded is if he is crazy, but if he asks to be grounded he proves he is sane and has to continue flying. If you enjoyed this novel, you will want to read *Good as Gold* (1979), in which Heller takes on the world of Washington politics, with hilarious and touching results. *Catch-22* was made into a movie in 1970. YA

Catcher in the Rye, The (1951) This novel by *J.D. Salinger is narrated by 16-year-old *Holden Caulfield, who is recovering from what appears to have been a physical or mental breakdown. Holden tells of his experiences during three days after he is expelled from prep school. Holden detests the phoniness of his school, his classmates, teachers, and the world in general. After having a fight with his roommate over the other boy's treatment of a girl he knows, Holden leaves school three days before Christmas break is to begin. He does not go directly to his home in New York City. Instead, he checks into a hotel and waits until his parents have been informed of his expulsion and have digested the news. During the three days, Holden meets a fascinating assortment of characters, strangers and old friends alike, all of whom confirm his belief that the world is a big sham. The only person who seems to understand him at all is his little sister, Phoebe. When he tells Phoebe he is going to leave and go out West, she refuses to let him go without taking her too. Holden realizes that leaving will complicate, not solve, his problems. He takes Phoebe to the zoo, where he watches her ride the carousel. He is touched by her innocence, an innocence he has lost. Then he returns home. At the end of his story, Holden seems stronger and more tolerant of the people he has spoken about, and perhaps better prepared to search for the beauty and truth he so prizes amid the shabbiness of life. *The Catcher in the Rye*, which has become a classic of American fiction, is Salinger's only novel, but if you enjoyed it, you will also want to read his stories about the Glass family in *Franny and Zooey* and *Raise High the Roof Beam, Carpenters & Seymour—An Introduction* (1963). YA

Cather, Willa (Sibert) (1874–1947), was a writer of numerous novels and short stories set in the Middle West and Southwest. Her works often explore the relationship between complex urban civilization and simple rural life. Some of her most highly acclaimed works are *O Pioneers!* (1913), about immigrants settling in Nebraska in the final decades of the 19th century; *My Ántonia; *Death Comes for the Archbishop; A Lost Lady* (1923), about the naïve and beautiful wife of a Western pioneer whose life is ruined by her husband; and *The Professor's House* (1925), about a disillusioned middle-aged professor who finally becomes reconciled to his life.

When Cather was 8 years old, her family moved from Virginia to a ranch in Nebraska. Here she would roam through the prairie on horseback, talking with the immigrant farmers. Because there were no schools in the area, Cather was taught by her parents and grandmother. When the family moved to Red Cloud, Nebraska, she attended high school, and later she was a student at the University of Nebraska. After graduation, Cather worked as a journalist, a high school English teacher, and a magazine editor. If you enjoy Cather's books, try the works of *Hamlin Garland. YA

Catherine Earnshaw is the passionate and headstrong heroine of *Emily Brontë's novel *Wuthering Heights*. After her father's death, she and *Heathcliff grow up together in an atmosphere of isolation, disorder, and violent emotions. Cathy's brother, Hindley, does all he can to humiliate Heathcliff, but his brutality only fuels her stubborn love for Heathcliff. In a conversation with Nelly Dean, the housekeeper, Cathy admits that if she marries Heathcliff, they will be penniless. Accepting marriage to Edgar Linton, however, will allow her to help place Heathcliff out of her brother's power. She feels such an intense attachment to

Heathcliff that she cannot imagine being separated from him, even while she is Edgar's wife. The efforts of the Earnshaws and Lintons to keep Cathy and Heathcliff apart have devastating effects, causing Cathy to suffer a terrible attack of brain fever. Her death is as much the result of frustrated love as it is of childbirth. YA

Cat's Cradle (1963) is *Kurt Vonnegut, Jr.'s comic, unorthodox, and wildly irreverent novel about human ineptitude. Among its 127 short chapters are "Mayonnaise," "Barracuda Capital of the World," "Never Index Your Own Book," "Why Frank Couldn't Be President," and "The Grand Ah-whoom." Jonah, the determined narrator, plans to write a book called *The Day the World Ended.* It will be an account of what important Americans were doing on August 6, 1945, when the first atomic bomb was dropped on Hiroshima, Japan. Collecting data for his book, Jonah investigates the life of Dr. Felix Hoenikker, one of the fathers of the bomb, and learns that Hoenikker made a great discovery before his death. He invented *ice-nine,* a nasty crystalline substance capable of freezing every drop of water (oceans included) on contact, and it is now the property of Hoenikker's three grown children. In the course of his research, Jonah travels to San Lorenzo, an overcrowded and unproductive little country where things tend to get out of control. He meets the younger Hoenikkers and comes in contact with Bokononism, a new religion that exhorts its followers to live by harmless and reassuring untruths. Jonah and a few others witness a stupid accident and the subsequent freezing of the entire land and surrounding sea as ice-nine crystals are released. Jonah survives to ponder the teachings of Bokonon, who has said: "History! . . . Read it and weep!" If you enjoyed *Cat's Cradle,* try also Vonnegut's collection of essays, reviews, and speeches, *Wampeters, Foma, and Granfalloons* (1974), whose title is made up of words invented by Bokonon in *Cat's Cradle.* YA

Cavanna, Betty (Elizabeth Cavanna Harrison) (1909–) An author of mysteries, romantic fiction, and nonfiction, Cavanna has written many books. She writes especially for younger readers and young adult women. Her mystery novels include *Secret Passage* (1947), which, set in New Jersey and Virginia, has a historical background of events a few years before the Civil War; and *Stamp Twice for Murder* (1981), in which two brothers run into danger while on vacation in a French village. *The Boy Next Door* (1956) is a tale of first love in a high school setting. In *Angel on Skis* (1957) a young woman finds out how hard it is to become a competitive skier and also to deal with first love. A historical novel is *Ruffles and Drums* (1975), in which a 16-year-old girl in Concord, Massachusetts, at the time of the American Revolution is disturbed by the presence of a convalescing young British officer in her family's home. Under the name Betsy Allen, Cavanna has written a series of mystery novels with a heroine named Connie Blair. Among them are *The Green Island Mystery* (1949) and *The Brown Satchel Mystery* (1954). If you like these books, try those of *Sophy Burnham, *Carolyn Keene, and *Phyllis A. Whitney. MR & YA

Cay, The (1969) The action in *Theodore Taylor's suspenseful short novel begins on Curaçao, in the Netherlands Antilles, during World War II. Phillip Enright is 11 years old. When the island waters become infested with German submarines preying on Allied tankers, Phillip's mother decides to return with him to safety in the United States. The freighter on which they travel is torpedoed, and Phillip is knocked unconscious in the confusion. He wakes to find himself alone on a raft with one of the deck hands, a huge elderly black man named Timothy, and the ship's cat. When later Phillip loses his sight as a result of the blow to his head, he must depend on Timothy for his very life. They reach a small island, and Timothy shows the boy how to survive and keep his hopes alive. As Phillip begins to adjust to his predicament, a strong friendship develops between him and the old man. Timothy dies protecting Phillip during a violent tropical storm, but Phillip is rescued, reunites with his parents, and regains his eyesight. Another sea adventure about a boy who grows up while facing difficulties is *Captains Courageous by *Rudyard Kipling. MR

Cedric Errol, the hero of *Little Lord Fauntleroy by *Frances Hodgson Burnett, is remarkable not only for his golden curls and handsome face, but for his generous spirit. He is the only child of a gentle and adoring mother and is quick to understand the feelings of those around him. In spite of being dressed like a little prince, in a velvet suit and lace collar, he has all the dash and gaiety of any boy his age, a complete lack of snobbishness, and a strong desire to make people happy. His grandfather, the mean-tempered Earl of Dorincourt, cannot resist the power of Cedric's affectionate and trusting nature, and he comes to love the boy with all his heart. Cedric is in many ways like the young heroine of *Heidi by Johanna Spyri (1827–1901). MR

Cervantes Saavedra, Miguel de (1547–1616) A Spanish novelist and playwright, Cervantes, the author of *Don Quixote de la Mancha, is considered one of the most illustrious figures of world literature. He was energetic, inventive, and a voracious reader whose intellectual curiosity extended to many facts of life. In 1569 he went to Italy, possibly to escape arrest for assault, and was employed by a cardinal of the Roman Catholic Church. He joined the Spanish naval forces and fought heroically against the Turks at the battle of Lepanto (1571). He was captured by pirates on his way to Spain, taken to Algiers as a slave, and tried several times to escape. He was ransomed by his family and returned to Madrid in 1580. Fascinated by the stage, Cervantes wrote at least 20 plays between 1582 and 1587, of which only two survive. He also wrote Galatea (1585), a romantic pastoral novel that would have passed into oblivion if its author had not been so illustrious.

During the years before the publication of Don Quixote, Cervantes was plagued by financial troubles. Employed as a government purchasing agent, he was imprisoned several times for failure to meet his obligations. It is thought he began work on Don Quixote about 1600,

Cervantes may have looked like this, but no reliable portrait of him is known to exist.

with the intention of writing an intricate *satire on the popular romances of chivalry. The book was enriched by Cervantes's enormously varied experiences and his extraordinary knowledge of human nature, and it was enlivened by a witty portrayal of the great battle between romantic ideals and earthy realism. The novel was an immediate success. Considered one of the first modern novels, it exerted a strong influence on European writers to come.

Cervantes's place in world literature rests also on the 12 short stories that are translated as The Exemplary Novels of Miguel de Cervantes Saavedra (1613). Five of these are tales of adventure, deception, and wild coincidence; the other seven are remarkable for their portrayal of human nature, and are said to be the first short stories written in Spanish. YA

Chandler, Raymond (Thornton) (1888–1959) Born in Chicago but brought up and educated in England, Chandler settled in Los Angeles in 1912. After failing in a business venture, he turned to writing, first turning out stories for the adventure magazine *Black Mask*, which is no longer published. With his first novel, *The Big Sleep* (1939), in which detective Philip Marlowe takes on a missing-person case that turns into a murder case involving his client's two psychopathic daughters, he at once established himself as one of the finest writers of the hard-boiled school of detective fiction. Marlowe is wisecracking and tough but strictly honorable. Chandler's books depict the seamy side of life in Southern California, where Marlowe's clients are often rich but unhappy, and mostly nasty too. Among Chandler's other books are *Farewell, My Lovely*, *The Lady in the Lake* (1943), and *The Long Goodbye* (1954). One of his most important and interesting contributions to the detective story is an essay examining it in a collection of his short stories, *The Simple Art of Murder* (1950). Chandler also wrote a number of screenplays, sometimes adapting the work of other mystery writers, such as *James M. Cain's *Double Indemnity* in 1944. If you enjoy Chandler's kind of detective fiction, you may also like the novels of *Dashiell Hammett, *Elmore Leonard, *Ross MacDonald, *Robert Parker, and *Mickey Spillane. Movies have been made of a number of Chandler's detective stories, including all the ones mentioned here. YA

Changeling, The (1970) An engaging novel by *Zilpha Keatley Snyder, the story is told in a series of flashbacks. Martha Abbott, a high school sophomore in suburban Rosewood Hills, remembers her long friendship with Ivy Carson and the ways in which it changed her life. They meet when both are 7 years old, after the Carsons move into a dilapidated old house nearby. Ivy has big dark eyes and a mop of wild curly hair, and moves as if her bones were lighter than air. Martha, sometimes called Marty Mouse by her family, is timid, plump, and unexceptional. In spite of the Abbotts' disapproval of the notorious Carsons, who always seem to be in trouble, Martha and Ivy spend more and more time together. They discover Bent Oaks Grove, a good place for climbing, hiding, and keeping secrets.

Ivy says she is a changeling, the child of supernatural parents who have stolen a human baby and left their own infant in its place. Because of Ivy, their adventures together, and their shared flights of imagination, Martha learns to stand up for herself and Ivy against those who feel threatened by their unconventional friendship. When Ivy is unjustly accused of an act of senseless vandalism at school, it is Martha who makes it possible for Ivy to be cleared of blame. Another good book about friendship is *Anything for a Friend* (1979) by *Ellen Conford, about a lonely girl who has just moved to a new school. MR

Charlie and the Chocolate Factory (1964), by *Roald Dahl, is a comic tale about young Charlie Bucket, a kind, brave, loyal, trustworthy, and starving boy, and his adventure with the extraordinary Mr. Willy Wonka and his magical chocolate factory. Charlie is one of five winners of a contest held by Mr. Wonka. Though the factory is absolutely prohibited to visitors, all five children are invited to visit on a chosen day as part of their prize. Of the five children, Charlie stands out for his intelligence and good manners. The others are Augustus Gloop, a fat, piggy little boy who is uncontrollably greedy for food; Veruca Salt, a spoiled, ill-tempered rich brat; Veronica Beauregarde, a chewing-gum fanatic; and Mike Teavee, who only wants to watch television.

The chocolate factory proves to be a most surprising place, full of unsuspected wonders: a beautiful river of chocolate runs through a lush underground channel, and a race of chocolate-colored people called Ooompa-Loompas who speak in rhyme are the factory workers. Other candy surprises include everlasting jawbreakers, hot ice cream for cold days, a fudge mountain, and a steaming lake of hot caramel. The children disobey Mr. Wonka's orders, and one by one, they do something disastrous. Except Charlie, who, by sheer intelligence and nobility of character, comports himself excellently and wins the greatest prize of all, which is Mr. Wonka's final surprise. This book was followed by a sequel, *Charlie and the Great*

Mr. Willy Wonka introduces himself in
Charlie and the Chocolate Factory.

Glass Elevator. Charlie and the Chocolate Factory was made into a popular feature film entitled *Willy Wonka and the Chocolate Factory* in 1971. MR

Charlie and the Great Glass Elevator

(1972), by *Roald Dahl, tells about the further adventures of Charlie Bucket and the great inventor Mr. Willy Wonka, first introduced in *Charlie and the Chocolate Factory.* Beginning where the first book ends, in Wonka's amazing glass elevator, this story takes Charlie and Mr. Wonka, accompanied by Charlie's parents and grandparents, on an extraordinary adventure into space. Though Mr. Wonka's intent is to return to the chocolate factory, an operational mistake sends the elevator orbiting into space. Before the adventure is over, the group has amazing encounters with the horrible extraterrestrial Vermicious Knids, visits a super-American space hotel, helps out the President of the United States, and experiments with pills that reverse aging. MR

Charlotte's Web

Charlotte's Web (1952), by *E.B. White, is the story of a beautiful and unexpected friendship. It begins when Fern Arable is given a white piglet to raise and names him Wilbur. Later Wilbur is sold to Fern's Uncle Homer, and Fern visits him every day. A little lonely in his fine new home, Wilbur is delighted to meet Charlotte A. Cavatica, a large gray spider who becomes his friend. Rumors of pigs being turned into bacon and ham terrify Wilbur, but kindhearted and clever Charlotte devises a plan to save him. Working at night on her web near the pigpen, she weaves the words SOME PIG. Everyone is tremendously impressed when they see Wilbur under the miraculous sign, the more so when Charlotte produces TERRIFIC and RADIANT. Wilbur is understood to be very special. At the County Fair, he wins an award for attracting hordes of visitors and realizes his future is secure. After creating her masterpiece, an egg sac containing 514 unborn spiders, Charlotte dies knowing that she helped to rescue Wilbur. Wilbur patiently guards her sac through the winter, and has the great joy of seeing three of Charlotte's children settle on her old web and become his good friends. If you liked *Charlotte's Web*, you will surely like White's *Stuart Little. The story was made into an animated film in 1973. MR

Charteris, Leslie

Charteris, Leslie [Leslie Charles Bowyer] (1907–) Born in Singapore of English and Chinese parents, Charteris settled in the United States and later became an American citizen. After a variety of jobs while still living abroad, Charteris turned to writing and soon created the character, modeled on himself, that was to make him both well known and rich, Simon Templar, also known as The Saint, in *Meet the Tiger* (1928). There followed a steady stream of adventure and detective novels and short stories, moving in time from England after World War I to the post–World War II era in *Send for the Saint* (1978), published 50 years after the first novel. In these stories The Saint is always brave, dashing, and somewhat mysterious, unceasing in action. The Saint also has appeared on the radio, in the movies, on television (120 hour-long episodes), in comic strips, and in *The Saint Magazine* (1953–1967). If you like the adventures of The Saint, you will also like the exciting stories told by *John Creasey, *Ian Fleming, *Robert Ludlum, and *Alastair MacLean. MR & YA

Chaucer, Geoffrey (c.1343–1400) Chaucer was an English poet and author of medieval romances. Because he wanted his works to be read by his own people, he wrote in English, even though Latin was the standard literary language throughout Western Europe. Chaucer's professional life was full of variety; not only was he a successful writer, but he also served as a civil servant and a diplomat under three kings of England. This work, as well as his frequent dealings with people from all walks of life, greatly influenced Chaucer's writing. In 1359, Chaucer was taken prisoner by the French, and the king of England contributed to his ransom. It has also been said that the king, wanting to reward Chaucer for his support of the crown, granted him a daily jug of wine. In addition to *The Canterbury Tales*, one of the classics of English literature, Chaucer wrote *Troilus and Criseyde* (c.1385), a famous love story about a faithful man and a faithless woman. YA

Cheever, John (1912–1982) A novelist and short-story writer, Cheever for most of his life lived in Ossining, New York, a suburb of New York City. Over a period of 45 years, he wrote numerous works of satirical fiction concerned with the customs and morals of the urban and suburban middle class. His novels include *The Wapshot Chronicle* (1957), centering on the descendants of an old Yankee family; *Bullet Park* (1969), about a suburban family whose quiet life is threatened by a mysterious newcomer who seems to have a grudge against the son; and *Falconer* (1977), about an upper-middle-class man whose imprisonment for killing his brother brings him freedom and redemption. Among his short-story collections are *The Way Some People Live: A Book of Stories* (1943) and *The Stories of John Cheever* (1979). YA

Chekhov, Anton (Pavlovich) (1860–1904) Trained as a physician, this Russian author became world famous for his plays and short stories. Raised in a large family of modest means, Chekhov attended medical school, led an active social life, and added to the family earnings by writing funny sketches and anecdotes for journals and newspapers. The long story "The Steppe" (1888), however, marked a change from the comic to the serious in its atmospheric portrayal of a young boy journeying to a distant place to attend school. This was followed by several works concerned with physically or mentally sick people, influenced in part by the death of Chekhov's older brother from tuberculosis. In spite of a growing literary reputation and seeking a change of routine, in 1890 Chekhov traveled 6,000 miles to the penal colony on Sakhalin Island. There he undertook alone a sociological study of convict life that helped to improve conditions.

The Seagull (1896), the first of his full-length plays to attract attention, was so badly received that Chekhov considered never again writing for the stage. His reputation was restored two years later after a successful production by the Moscow Art Theater. At his small country estate, Chekhov wrote almost plotless stories about everyday life in a deceptively simple style, exploring the hidden longings of characters from all social levels and displaying an extraordinary ability to dramatize the trivial or commonplace. "The Lady with the Dog" (1899) is about an adulterous liaison that begins quietly at a seaside resort and slowly changes into a passionate and hopeless love.

In 1897, the tuberculosis that had plagued Chekhov for years became acute, and he was forced to seek warmer climates. Nevertheless, this period of his life saw the creation of his best plays. *The Wood-Demon* (1889) was shortened and reshaped to become *Uncle Vanya* (1897), a realistic drama of aimlessness and resignation in the dull atmosphere of a provincial house. *Three Sisters* (1901) also takes place in the provinces, where a general's three daughters dream of escaping their meaningless existence. *The Cherry Orchard* (1904) is a touching and humorous portrait of an aristocratic family in decline, obliged to give up their house, lovely orchard, and a host of magical memories. You can read Chekhov in *The Oxford Chekhov* (1964–1980), a series that contains all the author's major works in translations of high quality. There are many editions of selected short stories and plays, some available in inexpensive paperbacks. *The Seagull* was adapted for film in Great Britain in 1968. YA

Chesterton, G(ilbert) K(eith) (1874–1936) English novelist, poet, and man of letters, he is known best as the author of the *Father Brown mystery stories. Though Chesterton referred to himself as the "Jolly Journalist," his work covered a broad range of forms and subjects. His literary criticism, noted for its spontaneity, includes books on *Charles Dickens, *Robert Browning, and his friend *George Bernard Shaw. His success came not only from serious writing on social, political, and religious issues, but also from his light verse, like the drinking songs collected in *The Flying Inn* (1914), and many humorous essays. An exuberant man who was extremely fastidious in his writing, Chesterton has been called a master who left no masterpiece.

Some of his witty essays appear in the collection *Sidelights on New London and Newer York* (1932). A novel you might enjoy is *The Man Who Was Thursday* (1908), an *allegory about a detective who brazenly infiltrates the inner circle of a group of anarchists planning to destroy the world. YA

Childe Harold's Pilgrimage (1812–1818), by *George Gordon Byron, is a long autobiographical poem in four parts, or cantos, written in the style of *Edmund Spenser. It contains Byron's observations of the picturesque foreign lands he visited, countries whose chivalry, history, and legend he admired, and expresses his mood of melancholy and disillusionment. The publication of the first two cantos was a major literary event and firmly established Byron's reputation.

Childe in this instance refers to a young man of noble birth. The fictional Harold is not meant to be an example of virtue and valor. Rather, he is shamelessly devoted to "revel and ungodly glee." Weary, lonely, and unable to find pleasure in life, Harold gives up his dissolute ways and embarks on a long journey in search of a different sort of diversion. In the first two cantos, he travels to Portugal, Spain, Albania, and Greece. In the third canto, Harold visits Waterloo, Belgium, just before a great battle. His travels take him to the Rhine River and to the great mountains of Europe. In the last canto, Byron puts the character of Harold aside. In his own voice, the poet describes his journey through Italy and speaks of its ancient cities, glorious ruins and works of art, and its historical and literary figures. If you enjoyed this poem, try the works of *Percy Bysshe Shelley. YA

Childress, Alice (1920–) A playwright and novelist, Childress is the author of *A Hero Ain't Nothin' but a Sandwich. She was born in South Carolina and raised in Harlem. Her grandmother's dramatic abilities as a storyteller inspired an early interest in the theater, and Childress later became a professional actress and director of the American Negro Theatre in New York City. Her plays include *Trouble in Mind* (1955), a play within a play in which a group of mostly black actors rehearse a pretentious drama written and directed by whites. *Wedding Band: A Love/Hate Story in Black and White* (1966), another play, is the author's remembrance of the intellectual poor. It takes place in the South in 1918 and hints at the emergence of black consciousness. Younger readers will enjoy *When the Rattlesnake Sounds* (1975), a one-act play about Harriet Tubman (c.1820–1913) and the summer she worked as a washerwoman to raise money for the abolitionist cause.

Because of a focus on controversial subjects like drug addiction and racial tensions, Childress's books have been banned on several occasions. She has earned a reputation for honesty, perceptiveness, and the ability to create sharply defined characters. Much of her work concerns the ways in which black men and women survive in our society. If you enjoy her works, try the plays and novels of *Ntozake Shange. MR & YA

China Homecoming (1985), the sequel to *Homesick: My Own Story,* is the autobiography of *Jean Fritz. As a young girl born of American parents and raised in China, she wanted nothing more than to be a true American. When she was 13 years old her family moved back to the United States, but still Jean did not feel she truly belonged in this country. Her family incorporated the Chinese language into their daily conversations, and Jean often dreamed of the Yangtze River. As an adult, Fritz had a strong desire to return to China. She was finally granted permission, and she went back to her hometown with her husband, Michael Fritz. While visiting important places from her past, such as her old home and the British school she had attended, Fritz recalls vivid and lively memories of her childhood. Though she was deeply moved when she was declared an honorary citizen of Wuhan, she realized that much had changed over the years. In her book, which combines her personal memories with historic events and includes photographs of her trip to China, Jean Fritz comes to terms with her unique identity as an American woman who spent her childhood living in China. If you enjoyed *China Homecoming,* you may also like the books of *Pearl S. Buck, *Bette Bao Lord, and *Laurence Yep. YA

Chitty-Chitty-Bang-Bang: The Magical Car (1964) is an adventure tale by *Ian Fleming in which marvelous machines play an important part, just as they do in Fleming's *James Bond novels. Caractacus Pott, sometimes called Crackpott, is an English inventor and gallant explorer. His wife, Mimsie, and their 8-year-old twins, Jeremy and Jemima, are delighted when he buys a rare automobile in terrible condition. Skillfully restored to its former glory by Pott, it is a 12-cylinder, 8-liter, supercharged Paragon Panther, magnificently long and low, the only one of its kind. Jeremy

names it Chitty-Chitty-Bang-Bang after the noises it makes as the engine starts. The Potts soon discover that Chitty is able to fly and to operate like a hovercraft on the open sea. On a family outing, the Potts impulsively decide to cross the English Channel in Chitty and visit France. On arriving, they find an enormous cave in the chalk cliffs near Calais, and stumble on the secret underground arms warehouse of an English master criminal. The combination of the Potts's bravery and imagination, aided by Chitty's hidden talents, helps them triumph over dangerous obstacles and setbacks. If you like reading about unusual flying experiences, you might enjoy *Mary Poppins by *Pamela Travers and *Peter Pan by *J.M. Barrie. *Chitty-Chitty-Bang-Bang* was made into a film in 1968. MR

Chocolate War, The (1974) By *Robert Cormier, this is a strongly realistic and well-written novel about power, cruelty, and subtle intimidation, unrelieved by simple solutions or a happy ending. At Trinity, a preparatory school for Catholic boys, the everyday routine is disturbed by the intrigues of a secret student society called the Vigils. The school allows the society to exist by ignoring it, because the Vigils are careful to avoid physical violence. Archie Costello, a leader of the Vigils, likes to invent strange cruelties to humiliate students who fail to carry out the assignments handed them by the society. Archie is confronted by Brother Leon, an ambitious and slyly manipulative teacher who enjoys shaming his students. He orders Archie to enlist the Vigils' help in promoting the annual fund-raising sale of chocolates, and threatens to break up the society if the chocolate campaign is unsuccessful.

Jerry Renault, a skinny, tough-minded freshman, is trying to adjust to his mother's recent death. Out of dislike and contempt for Brother Leon and the Vigils, and in spite of orders from Archie, Jerry is the only student who refuses to sell chocolates for the cause. His failure to conform infuriates Brother Leon and eventually demonstrates to the whole school that the Vigils' power is less than absolute. Archie arranges for Jerry to be beaten by a group of bullies, but Jerry doggedly resists. At an event designed to break his spirit and force him to submit, Jerry is almost beaten to death in front of the entire student body, while Brother Leon watches and waits. The novel was adapted for film in 1988. If you admire this book, you might like to read *Lord of the Flies* by *William Golding. YA

Chopin, Kate O'Flaherty (1851–1904) An early feminist novelist, Chopin was born in St. Louis, Missouri, to a French-Creole mother and an Irish father. She became known especially for her descriptions of Creole life and for her frank treatment of women's psychological problems. Chopin was raised in a household of three generations of widowed women. Her most popular work is *The Awakening,* her last novel. Other works include the novel *At Fault* (1890), which describes Creole life in Louisiana, and the short story collections *Bayou Folk* (1894) and *A Night in Acadie* (1897). YA

chorus, in ancient Greek drama, refers to a group of men who functioned like an actor in the play. Singing, dancing, or speaking in unison, they narrated or commented on the action of the play, thus separating it into sections or acts. Their role was essentially passive, often expressing the hopes, fears, and opinions of ordinary people, while the actors, larger than life, portrayed tragic heroes and heroines capable of defying the gods. Eventually the size of the chorus (as many as 50 persons) dwindled and the number of actors increased. In the drama of Elizabethan England, the role of the chorus was sometimes given to a single person. That person's function might be to recite the prologue and epilogue, or to comment on the action, as does the character of Horatio in *William Shakespeare's *Hamlet.*

Chosen, The (1967) A widely beloved novel by *Chaim Potok about two young men and their fathers, *The Chosen* is a quietly compelling story of friendship and parental love and a fascinating account of Jewish life in the Williams-burg section of Brooklyn, a borough of New York City. Reuven Malter's father teaches at a yeshiva, or Jewish parochial school. Danny Saunders's father is the rabbi for a group of Hasidic Jews, people distinguished by their somber dress, black beards, earlocks, and fierce loyalty to tradition. Reuven and Danny's friendship gets off to a bad start at a softball game where they are on opposing teams, but later they discover they share many interests. Both are brilliant, hard-working students, well versed in the *Talmud, and it is assumed both will become rabbis. Danny's relationship with his father is unusual, because Reb Saunders has followed an obscure Hasidic tradition that forbids conversation between father and son outside of religious matters. When Danny decides he wants to be a psychologist, a career his father considers completely inappropriate, he is too afraid of causing pain to speak. It is Reuven, acting on wise and warm-hearted advice from his own father, who becomes a go-between for the Saunderses. By talking through Reuven, Reb Saunders finally expresses his acceptance of Danny's need to make his own life, and his faith that Danny's soul will remain true to his upbringing. If you enjoyed *The Chosen,* try also the books of *Bernard Malamud and *Isaac Bashevis Singer. *The Chosen* was adapted for film in 1981. YA

Christianity, with about 1,700 million adherents worldwide, is the world's largest religious group. It is the dominant religion in Europe and in North and South America. Christianity grew out of *Judaism, with which it holds many ethical views in common, and the Old Testament of the *Bible is shared by the two faiths. However, for Christians the New Testament of the Bible, with the story of *Jesus and of the formation of the Christian church, is the primary holy scripture. In Christianity, Jesus Christ is the Son of God, both man and god. The fundamental doctrine of the faith is the belief in the Trinity: God the Father; God the Son; and God the Holy Spirit. The two basic rites are baptism and communion, the latter a ceremony commemorating the Last Supper of

Christ. The three most important holy days are Christmas, celebrating the birth of Jesus; Good Friday, observing the crucifixion of Jesus; and Easter, on which the Resurrection of Jesus is observed. The three most important groupings within Christianity are the Roman Catholic Church, with nearly 1,000 million members; the Eastern Orthodox Church, strongest in Eastern Europe and the Middle East, with about 165 million members; and about 15 major Protestant denominations, with about 425 million persons. Within and among these organizations there are many differences in biblical interpretation, ritual, and degree of control by church authorities. If you are interested in learning more about Christianity, you might read *The Christian World* (1984) by Alan Brown (1944–) and *Christianity* (1985) by Nancy Martin (1899–). Older readers can turn to *Christianity* (1989) by Alan Brown (n.d.) and Judy Perkins (n.d.), and *The Christian: His Beliefs and Practices* (1988) by Peter McKenzie (n.d.). YA

Christie, Agatha [Mary Clarissa Miller] (1890–1976) The author of the most widely read detective stories, Christie was born in England, the daughter of an English mother and an American father. During World War I she served in a hospital in France where she picked up knowledge of poisons that she used later in her books. Her first novel is *The Mysterious Affair at Styles* (1920), which marks the initial appearance of *Hercule Poirot, the Belgian detective. One of her most notable mysteries is *The Murder of Roger Ackroyd*. There followed, among others, *Murder on the Orient Express*; *The ABC Murders* (1936), in which a serial killer leaves railway timetables at the scenes of his crimes; *Death on the Nile* (1937), in which a spoiled heiress is killed during a boat trip up the Nile River; and *And Then There Were None* (1939), in which 10 people with criminal backgrounds are lured to a secluded island and systematically murdered. Christie also introduced as an amateur detective the formidable *Jane Marple, who appeared first in *Murder at the Vicarage* (1930).

After Christie's second marriage to an archeologist, she spent time in Syria and Iraq, and later she used the Middle East as background for such novels as *Murder in Mesopotamia* (1936). Her more than 80 detective stories have been translated into 103 languages. In addition, Christie wrote romantic fiction under the name of Mary Westmacott, and an *Autobiography* (1977). In her clever plots, Christie maintains suspense and leaves many clues intended to mislead the reader. *The Mousetrap*, a play adapted from her novelette *Three Blind Mice* (1948), was produced in London in 1952, and has been performed there continuously ever since, becoming the longest-running play in theatrical history. A movie was made of *The Murder of Roger Ackroyd* in 1931, of *Murder on the Orient Express* in 1974, and of *Death on the Nile* in 1978. Three movies have been made of *And Then There Were None*, in 1945, 1965, and 1975. If you like Christie's books, you will also enjoy those of *Margery Allingham, *Arthur Conan Doyle, and *Ngaio Marsh. YA

Christmas Carol, A (1843) This short masterpiece by *Charles Dickens is a *parable about the spirit of Christmas. On Christmas Eve, *Scrooge, an old skinflint with no love for his fellow man, is at work in his chilly office with his clerk, Bob Cratchit. Scrooge's nephew, Fred, stops by to invite him for Christmas dinner, but Scrooge declares the holiday is pure humbug and sends his nephew away.

Returning to his gloomy apartment, Scrooge is visited by the miserable, chain-rattling ghost of his dead partner, Jacob Marley, doomed by the sin of indifference to wander restlessly. The ghost tells Scrooge to expect the appearance of three spirits who will represent his last chance to escape Marley's fate. As the clock strikes one, the gentle Ghost of Christmas Past materializes and shows Ebenezer Scrooge his boyhood and the woman he might have married had he been less interested in pursuing money. The Ghost of Christmas Present takes Ebenezer to watch the festivities at Bob Cratchit's modest home and at the home of Fred and his family, where he hears himself de-

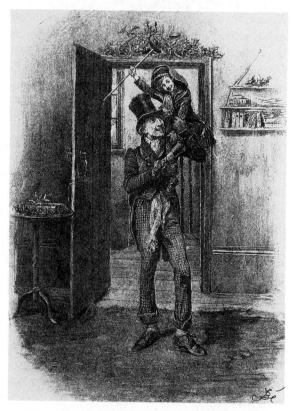

Tiny Tim is the lame son of Scrooge's clerk, Bob Cratchit, in *A Christmas Carol.*

scribed as a stingy, unfeeling man. The Ghost of Christmas Yet to Come, silent and shrouded in black, reveals to Scrooge his own lonely death, his grave without mourners, and the contemptuous comments of his few acquaintances. When he wakes on Christmas Day, Scrooge is a changed man, joyfully opening his heart to all those he has mistreated. He resolves to help Cratchit, becomes a second father to Cratchit's crippled son, Tiny Tim, and learns how to keep Christmas well. "And so," as Tiny Tim observes, "God bless us, every one!" Dickens wrote four other "Christmas books," including *The Cricket on the Hearth. A Christmas Carol* was adapted for film several times, most successfully in 1938 in the United States and, under the title *Scrooge*, in Great Britain in 1951. MR & YA

Chronicles of Narnia, The These six tales of *fantasy adventure by the Irish-born English author *C.S. Lewis, a noted Christian thinker and English literature professor, are very popu-

lar with young readers. Lucy, Peter, Susan, and Edmund are British schoolchildren during World War II. They first enter the magical kingdom of Narnia through a mirrored wardrobe in a professor's country home. There they meet a host of creatures, including Narnia's White Witch, Fauns, Nymphs, Dryads and Naiads, Red Dwarfs, talking animals, peaceful giants, and Aslan, the wise lion king of Narnia. Powerful Aslan has a flowing mane and gentle manner. He created Narnia and its creatures out of nothing, singing it into being with his beautiful voice. The four children assume the throne and together reign through Narnia's Golden Age. For the Christian Lewis, Aslan represents Jesus Christ, and his loving earthly purpose and history. The human boys and girls have many ways to enter Narnia, including doing so on Aslan's bidding or from a hidden spot in their schoolyard bushes. Once transported, they roam and wage battles against evil from the Western Wild to the Eastern Sea. They also hold court at the great castle of Cair Paravel. Their presence is a shock to all Narnians, who supposed humans to be a myth. Tales of life in Narnia include adventure, entertainment, and travel on a royal ship, *Splendour Hyaline*, which is shaped like a swan. Another ship, *The Dawn Treader*, has the golden head and wings of a dragon. The children feast at banquets and are treated to nights of storytelling and poetry. Armed with detailed maps showing it and neighboring states, the children explore all corners of Narnia. Woods teem with private creatures living in scattered burrow and tree homes. There are a few settlements, such as Beruna and Beaversdam, the Great River with its plunging route over cliffs to the Cauldron Pool, and trees of silver and gold. Aslan has a marvelous monument called The How, a mound in the forest with historic wall writings in the tunnels, caves, and galleries that surround its ancient stone table, the centerpiece of local history. In Narnia, time is different from earth time, and you must learn with the children how much adventure can fill the split second they seem to be gone from their home planet. The chronicles are *The Lion, the Witch*

This is how an 18th-century artist depicted Cinderella.

and the Wardrobe: A Story for Children (1950); The Silver Chair (1967); Prince Caspian (1969); The Voyage of the "Dawn Treader" (1969); The Horse and His Boy (1969); The Last Battle (1969); and The Magician's Nephew (1970). If you like this kind of fantasy adventure, read *The Hobbit by *J.R.R. Tolkien and the series of books in the *Prydain Cycle by *Lloyd Alexander. See also *Terabithia. MR

Cinderella is the heroine of one of the world's best-known folk tales. In it, a young woman is treated harshly by her stepmother and stepsisters, helped to escape temporarily by a fairy godmother or other supernatural being, and discovered by a handsome prince who completes the rescue by marrying her.

One of the oldest recorded versions comes from 9th-century China. In Europe the story has appeared in more than 500 variants. Both *Charles Perrault and the brothers *Grimm gave it a place in their collections of fairy tales. An animated movie was made in 1950, and the story was the basis for the funny film *Cinderfella*, produced in 1960. MR

Citizen Tom Paine (1943), by *Howard Fast, is a fictionalized biography of *Thomas Paine, an English-American political theorist and writer who played an important part in the American Revolution. Paine is portrayed as having a deep understanding of the problems of his time. The story begins at Paine's first meeting with *Benjamin Franklin in England, an event that dramatically altered his life. It tells about his arrival in America, his involvement in the conflict between England and the American colonies, the publication of his influential pamphlet *Common Sense* (1776), his imprisonment in France during the French Revolution, his return to America, and the tragic last days of his life. Another historical novel by Howard Fast you may enjoy is *Freedom Road* (1944), about the period just after the American Civil War. *Citizen Tom Paine* was adapted for the stage in 1986. YA

Clark, Walter Van Tilburg (1909–1971) A novelist, short-story writer, and author of *The Ox-Bow Incident, Clark was born in Maine but spent most of his life in the western United States. Clark disliked cities, preferring the open spaces of the West and its surviving wilderness. He was keenly interested in outdoor life and in stories of the West told to him by people who were part of its history and development. Unlike the fearless cowboys of *dime novels, Clark's heroes are real people struggling with universal problems, presented in clean and stylish prose.

Next to *The Ox-Bow Incident*, Clark's best-known novel is *The Track of the Cat* (1949), about the hunt for a dangerous panther during a mountain snowstorm, and its effect on several characters. It is a simple but highly suspenseful narrative, in which the complex relationship between people and their natural surroundings is an important element. Some of Clark's short stories are collected in *The Watchful Gods, and Other Stories* (1950). In it you will find "The Wind and the Snow of Winter," which concerns a prospector, alone, growing old, and increasingly aware of his failing health. If you enjoy Clark's books, you may like the Western novels of *Louis L'Amour. *The Track of the Cat* was adapted for film in 1954. YA

Clarke, Arthur C(harles) (1917–) An important and prolific English writer of *science fiction and nonfiction books on space travel and technology, Clarke is the author of *2001: A Space Odyssey. He wrote his first science fiction stories in high school, and pursued the hobby while working in the British civil service. He joined the Royal Air Force in 1941 and became a radar instructor after teaching himself mathematics and electronics theory. In 1945, 20 years before his prediction was realized, he published an article describing a satellite system of the future capable of relaying radio and television signals to the entire world. He has since won recognition for his ability to interpret science to a popular audience.

His best novels include Childhood's End (1953), about a race of aliens who come to help the people of earth banish war and poverty. In Rendezvous with Rama (1973), a huge object is seen rapidly approaching the inner solar system, and a spaceship is sent to investigate. The Fountains of Paradise (1979), set in the 22nd century, concerns the attempt to build an elevator from the surface of earth to an orbital station. Clarke is a fine storyteller who places little emphasis on character development. His works reflect the romantic aspects of science and technology, his belief in the power of human intelligence and spirit, and the wonder of our universe. If you enjoy Clarke's books, try also the novels of *Isaac Asimov, which are also well grounded in science. YA

Clavell, James (duMaresq) (1924–) Born in Australia and now a U.S. citizen, Clavell is one of the most readable of the adventure-and-action novelists using historical settings. His first book, King Rat (1962), is a fictionalized account of his ordeal in a Japanese prisoner-of-war camp during World War II. He continued to use a Far East background in Tai-Pan (1966), about the founding of Hong Kong in 1841 and the first British merchant there. Shogun (1975) is the story of an English sailor shipwrecked in Japan who becomes a samurai, a noble of the warrior class. In Noble House (1981) Clavell returned to Hong Kong to fashion a story of the modern colony and the struggle for power among traders and financiers. For younger readers, Clavell wrote The Children's Story (1981), which describes a United States conquered by totalitarians and a teacher who tries to brainwash his class to make them anti-American. If you like these books, read those of *Frederick Forsyth, *Robert Ludlum, and *Alistair MacLean. A movie was made of King Rat in 1965 and of Tai-Pan in 1986. A TV mini-series was made of Shogun in 1981 and of Noble House in 1988. MR & YA

Cleary, Beverly (1916–) Author of *The Mouse and the Motorcycle, *Runaway Ralph, *Ralph S. Mouse, and *Dear Mr. Henshaw, Cleary is one of the most popular writers of fiction for young readers. She was raised in a small American town, where her mother founded a lending library that became Beverly's favorite retreat. School was a disappointment after she found that most books were about people completely outside her experience. She decided then to make up funny stories about the sort of young people she knew well.

A librarian for many years, Cleary has written more than 30 novels noted for their humor, understanding, and lucid style. Her first book, Henry Huggins (1950), is about a third-grader living on Klickitat Street (a real street near Cleary's home), and his adventures with a stray dog. The book also marked the appearance of one of Cleary's most beloved characters, the funny and sympathetic Ramona Quimby. A series of novels about her includes Ramona the Pest (1968) and Ramona and Her Father (1977), in which Mr. Quimby loses his job and smokes too many cigarettes. Ramona organizes an unforgettable no-smoking campaign. In Ramona Forever (1984), Ramona worries about having to move when her father finds a new job. If you like Cleary's books, you may also like those of *Louise Fitzhugh and *Corinne Gerson. MR

Cleaver, Vera (1919–) and **Cleaver, William J(oseph)** (1920–) The authors of more than 15 novels for young people, the Cleavers have described themselves as passionate readers and as graduates of American public libraries. Many of their books are set in small towns in the South, and life there is portrayed in realistic, humorous, and unsentimental terms. In the novel *Ellen Grae* (1967), an intelligent and imaginative girl, during the breakup of her parents' marriage, lives away from home with a small group of troubled young people. *Grover* (1970) is a novel in which Ellen Grae reappears and helps Grover adjust to his mother's suicide. *Where the Lilies Bloom* (1969), which takes place in the North Carolina mountains, is about the efforts of tough-minded Mary Call Luther to keep her family together after her father's death.

Since her husband died, Vera Cleaver has continued to write. Her novels include *Moon Lake Angel* (1987), about a 10-year-old girl who lives apart from her family and whose mother is about to marry a much younger man. If you enjoy the Cleavers' books, you may also like the books of *Katherine Paterson and *Doris Buchanan Smith. MR

Clockwork Orange, A (1962)

By *Anthony Burgess, the title of this chilling novel, which is an odd mixture of the horrible and comic, refers to a living being that seems full of promise and sweetness but functions, without morals, like a mechanical toy. Alex is 15 years old, living at some time in the future in a big city. He and his friends speak Nadsat, a colorful dialect that combines anglicized Russian words with English street language. Like other gangs, their favorite entertainments are taking drugs, roaming the city at night, robbing and beating older middle-class people, assaulting women, and committing random acts of destruction. While burglarizing a house, Alex kills an elderly woman, unaware she had telephoned the police while the gang was entering. His friends escape, but Alex is arrested and spends two years in a filthy, overcrowded prison. The authorities offer to release him if he will participate in an experiment designed to rid him forever of his taste for violence. Alex submits to "Ludovico's Technique" in a series of nightmarish brainwashing sessions and is pronounced cured. Now, even the thought of blood makes him terribly ill. Free and misera-

ble, he meets political activists who want to use his case to overthrow the people responsible for his inhuman treatment. Alex tries to kill himself, fails, and recovers to find he has been mysteriously reconditioned. The effects of the treatment are gone, but Alex soon realizes that he is tired of his old life of acting like a wind-up toy out of control, and he decides to work at growing up. A second edition of *A Clockwork Orange* (1986) contains the last chapter that was omitted in the first American edition. If you like *A Clockwork Orange*, read both **1984* by *George Orwell and **Brave New World* by *Aldous Huxley, in which the state is cast in the role of villain. See also **Trout Fishing in America* by *Richard Brautigan. *A Clockwork Orange* was adapted for film in 1971. YA

Coetzee, J(ohn) M. (1940–)

A South African novelist, lecturer, and translator, Coetzee is known best for his novel *Life & Times of Michael K* (1983). A political allegory, it describes the difficult journey of a simple-minded young black man and his dying mother. Earlier works by Coetzee include *In the Heart of the Country* (1977), a novel in the form of a diary, about the mental decline of a white spinster who kills her father after he breaks the racial codes by consorting with a black woman. In *Waiting for the Barbarians* (1980), which has been called a fable of colonialism, the nameless hero is a magistrate employed in a totalitarian state who finds himself rising up against the system he has long supported. With great effectiveness, Coetzee has used *allegory and *symbolism to describe the injustices of his country and to define the mentality of both oppressor and oppressed. If you like Coetzee's books, try those of *Alan Paton and *Carolyn Slaughter. YA

Coffin for Dimitrios, A (1939)

In this classic suspense novel by *Eric Ambler, Charles Latimer, an English detective-story writer on vacation in Istanbul, Turkey, makes the acquaintance of Colonel Haki of the Turkish secret police, who tells him of a body found in the Bosporus. His curiosity aroused, Latimer asks to see the body in the morgue and then decides to trace the victim, Dimitrios Makropoulis, said to have been a spy, a drug dealer, and head of a vice ring. Latimer's quest takes him first to Izmir (then Smyrna) and to Athens, Greece. He then journeys to Sofia, Bulgaria, on the way meeting a Mr. Peters, who is also interested in Dimitrios. In Belgrade, Yugoslavia, Latimer turns up evidence that Dimitrios in the 1920s was involved in an assassination plot. A retired master spy, Grodek, in Geneva, Switzerland, gives him further information, after which he ends his search in Paris, France, where he again meets Peters, who proves that the body in the morgue was not that of Dimitrios. Peters's plan to blackmail the very much alive Dimitrios ends in a shootout. Under the title *The Mask of Dimitrios*, a movie was made of the novel in 1944. YA

Cold Sassy Tree (1984), by Olive Ann Burns (1924–1990), is a lively novel based on events in the life of the author's great-grandfather. In Cold Sassy Tree, the small Georgia town where the story takes place, Grandpa Blakeslee causes a scandal by marrying a much younger woman a few weeks after his wife's death. In his forthright way, Grandpa insists that marriage will be cheaper than hiring a housekeeper. Grandpa's arrangement with Love Simpson, now the second Mrs. Blakeslee, is described by a grandson, 14-year-old Will Tweedy. Will helps out around the house as the couple settle in, and he tries to protect them from the gossip that spreads everywhere in the town like wildfire. Will's family nurses a suspicion that Love will persuade Grandpa to make his will in her favor, thereby cutting off more deserving relatives. As a real friend to the newlyweds, Will sees that what began as a marriage of convenience is changing rapidly into heady romance, and he is proud of his grandfather's youthful enthusiasm. Will also finds time to express his interest in Lightfoot McLendon, a girl he admires. When Grandpa is carried off by pneumonia, Love decides to remain in Cold Sassy Tree and raise her child among the members of her new family.

Olive Ann Burns began her career as a journalist. In 1975, after learning she was ill, Burns began work on *Cold Sassy Tree*, writing for her own pleasure and for family and friends. Other books about small-town or farm life in the South are *The Color Purple* by *Alice Walker and *Barren Ground* by *Ellen Glasgow. *Cold Sassy Tree* was made into a TV film in 1989. YA

Cole, Brock (1938–) A prize-winning author of sensitive novels about unusual adolescents, Cole began his professional life as a teacher of philosophy at the University of Minnesota. He started writing in the 1970s, and taught himself drawing and painting in order to be able to illustrate his own works. Cole wrote several books for very young readers before turning his attention to older readers. *The Goats* (1987) is a strong novel about survival, in which campers Laura and Howie become the victims of a nasty practical joke. *Celine* (1989), Cole's second novel, is an excellent story about a 16-year-old artist who shares living quarters with her young stepmother. YA

Coleridge, Samuel Taylor (1772–1834) An English poet, essayist, critic, and author of *The Rime of the Ancient Mariner*, Coleridge, as a child, was precocious, unusually imaginative, and a voracious reader with an appetite for exotic stories. His interest in the visionary continued throughout his years at school and university, and grew into a lifelong admiration and respect for the power of imagination. In his early 20s, Coleridge and Robert Southey (1774–1843), a future poet laureate of England, collaborated on a plan to found a pantisocracy, an ideal community to be built in Pennsylvania. Southey lost interest in the project, and Coleridge gradually turned from politics to poetry. His close friendship with *William Wordsworth led to the publication of *Lyrical Ballads* (1798), to which both men contributed, and which contained *The Ancient Mariner*. Other poems in the collection, such as "Frost at Midnight," were examples of Coleridge's newly developed conversational style. In 1797, probably under the influence of laudanum (an opium derivative in legal use as a painkiller),

Gustave Doré (1833–1883) illustrated
Coleridge's *Rime of the Ancient Mariner* in 1875.

Coleridge wrote "Kubla Khan," which begins
with the famous lines:

> In Xanadu did Kubla Khan
> A stately pleasure-dome decree.

One of his best-known poems, it is exotic and
mysterious in tone and marked by a rhythmic
sensuousness. Coleridge called it a psychological curiosity and left it unfinished. The following year he wrote "Christabel," also unfinished,
a romantic poem about the spiritual struggles
of an innocent young woman. Both works were
left unpublished until 1816, by which time they
were famous by word of mouth.

Troubled by poor health, domestic problems,
and an increasing dependency on opium, Coleridge was nevertheless able to give a much-
acclaimed series of lectures on *William
Shakespeare in 1811–12. His *Biographia Literaria: or, Biographical Sketches of My Literary
Life and Opinions* (1817), containing studies of
Wordsworth's poetry, autobiographical material, principles of politics, religion, and philosophy, proved to be very influential in the
development of English literary criticism. In
1817, after successful treatment for opium addiction, Coleridge gave himself mainly to writing about religious and philosophical topics.
Though much of his work was unfinished, Coleridge is recognized as having powerfully
affected such poets as *George Gordon Byron,
*John Keats, and *Percy Bysshe Shelley. His
poems are available in two editions titled
Poems, edited in 1812 and 1963. *The Collected
Works of Coleridge* (1969–?) contains lectures,
essays, magazine articles, and lay sermons. See
also *The Lake Poets and *Xanadu. YA

Colette, (Sidonie-Gabrielle) (1873–1954) The
author of *Gigi*, and one of France's most important women novelists and short-story writers, Colette was born in a small village in
Burgundy. When she was 20 years old she married an aspiring writer and, at his suggestion,
began writing her memories of early school
days. *Claudine at School* (1900) was published
under her husband's pen name, Willy, and was
very successful. Three other Claudine novels
followed, built around the same youthful and
uninhibited heroine. Separated from her husband in 1906, Colette spent several years as a
music-hall performer. *The Vagrant* (1910), based
on those years and written under her own
name, is a novel about the renunciation of
love. In it a woman from the provinces is betrayed by her husband, embarks on a career in
vaudeville, and becomes involved with a
wealthy bachelor. Among Colette's later works
are *Cheri* (1920) and *The Last of Cheri* (1926),
about a love affair between a very young man
and an older woman. Colette received many
honors during her long and productive life, including some never before awarded to a
woman.

Many of her works are autobiographical, recording the sensual delights and emotional torments of love in an intimate, musical, and
seemingly effortless prose. Unusually respon-
sive to the beauty of nature and its creatures,
Colette loved to observe both her natural surroundings and the endlessly varied and fascinating details of human behavior, and
described what she saw with both earthy realism and sophistication. Her fine short stories

are available in *The Collected Stories of Colette* (1983). Some of her best-known novels are contained in *Six Novels by Colette* (n.d.), a Modern Library book that includes *Claudine at School, Cheri, The Last of Cheri,* and *Gigi.* If you like Colette's books, try those of *Françoise Sagan. YA

Collier, James Lincoln (1928–) and **Collier, Christopher** (1930–) The Collier brothers have coauthored many popular novels for young people. Christopher Collier is a professor of history specializing in the American Revolution. The Colliers' books often combine American history with vivid storytelling, such as *My Brother Sam Is Dead, *Jump Ship to Freedom,* and *War Comes to Willy Freeman* (1982). James Lincoln Collier has written for very young readers as well, and he is also known for *The Making of Jazz* (1978), which is for older readers. If you like the Colliers' books, try the novels of *Walter D. Edmonds. MR & YA

Collins, (William) Wilkie (1824–1889) One of the most popular English novelists of the *Victorian Era (1837–1901), Collins wrote biographies and novels attacking social problems. But today he is remembered for two books, one of mystery and one of detection. The mystery novel is *The Woman in White* (1860), a suspenseful tale based on an actual event in which Collins encountered a mysterious woman late at night. The plot concerns the attempt on the part of a villainous count and a young woman's husband to defraud her of her fortune by having her confined to an asylum under the name of another woman who has died. The novel of detection, *The Moonstone,* is often called the first full-length detective story in the English language. It is also a good adventure novel. Movies were made of *The Woman in White* in 1917, 1929, and 1948. If you like these books, read the stories of *Edgar Allan Poe. YA

color Besides identifying color by its physical characteristics, the word you use for a particular color has other meanings in literature, art, religion, and elsewhere. The colors with the most of these other meanings are *black, *blue, *green, *purple, *red, *white, and *yellow. An example of the use of colors to refer to other things is the phrase "the Blue and the Gray," meaning the armies of the Civil War in which soldiers of the Union wore blue uniforms while the Confederate troops wore gray. In the traditional Chinese theater, a yellow costume identifies an employer; red, a mandarin (a scholar and bureaucrat); blue, ordinary people; and black, lower class, despised persons. To be "in a brown study" is to be sunk in a reverie, a dreamlike state. If you are "in the pink," you are healthy; "a shrinking violet," which refers to the small flower, is a very modest person. A country's flag is its colors; if you are a determined person, you "stick to your colors"; and if you are successful in something, you "come through with flying colors." You can find more about colors in *The Language of Color* (1988) by Dorothee L. Mells (n.d.). YA

Color Purple, The (1982) This extraordinary, moving, and harrowing story by *Alice Walker is told through a series of letters. Fourteen-year-old Celie is poor, homely, and black. The letters she writes, addressed simply "Dear God," are the only outlet for her feelings. After her mother's death, Celie has the second of two babies by her stepfather, both taken from her to be given up for adoption. Her younger sister Nettie, whom Celie adores, leaves home to escape a similar fate, and Celie is married off to a widower who prefers Nettie, but will settle for any female able to take care of his children. Referred to in Celie's letters as "Mr. ———," he treats her like a slave. Celie is too numb from the loss of her babies and the relentless household routine to complain, and she does what she is told. When Mr. ——— brings his former lover, Shug Avery, to the house to recuperate from an illness, Celie is more fascinated than upset. Shug is beautiful, extravagant, loving, and living proof that it is possible for a woman to enjoy life. It is Shug who teaches Celie that she has the right to some degree of happiness and independence. Shug also discovers that Mr. ——— has hidden Nettie's many letters to Celie because Nettie refused him long ago, and Celie learns that her two children are alive, living with Nettie and a missionary family in Africa. Together Celie and Shug leave for Memphis, where Shug's career as a singer has enabled her to live in style. Now free, Celie begins to earn her own living by sewing, and her love for Shug makes her bloom. After she returns to live in the house inherited from her stepfather, Celie is unexpectedly and joyfully reunited with Nettie and the children. If you enjoyed this book, try also the novels of *Toni Morrison. *The Color Purple* was adapted for film in 1985. YA

Columbine (or Columbina in Italian, meaning little dove) was one of the standard female theatrical characters developed in 16th-century Italian commedia dell'arte, a highly popular form of comedy in which some of the players wore masks and dialogue was improvised. She was the sweetheart of *Harlequin and the daughter of Pantaloon, a rich, miserly, and mean-spirited merchant. In her role as the lively and coquettish servant girl, she was witty, fond of gossip, and devoted to romantic intrigue.

Another version of the Columbine character is the soubrette, or maidservant, of 18th-century French theater. Some famous soubrette roles are also found in the operas of Wolfgang Amadeus Mozart (1756–1791), such as Susanna in *The Marriage of Figaro* (1786) and Zerlina in *Don Giovanni* (1787). See also *pantomime.

Complete Nonsense Book, The (1912) A posthumous edition of the works for children by *Edward Lear, this collection contains the delightful short poems and illustrations of *The Book of Nonsense* (1846), which Lear dedicated to the great-grandchildren, grand-nephews, and grand-nieces of Edward, 13th Earl of Derby. Devoted to *limericks, of which Lear was a master, it includes such verses as:

> There was an Old Lady whose folly
> Induced her to sit in a holly;
> Whereon, by a thorn her dress being torn,
> She quickly became melancholy.

In addition, the volume contains *Nonsense*

Edward Lear drew this lighthearted picture of the Old Lady who sat on a holly.

Songs, Stories, Botany and Alphabets (1871), in which you will find *"The Owl and the Pussycat"; *More Nonsense, Pictures, Rhymes, etc.* (1872); and *Laughable Lyrics* (1877). To this was added, after the author's death, a final small collection entitled *Queery Leary Nonsense* (1911). The verses are rich in puns, deliberate misspellings, uncannily appropriate nonsense words, and Lear's particular brand of kindly humor. All the wonderful pen-and-ink drawings of outlandish creatures, fantastic objects, and ridiculous situations are by the author. If you liked *The Complete Nonsense Book*, you will also like the books of *Lewis Carroll and *Roald Dahl. MR & YA

Confessions of Nat Turner, The (1966) This novel, which its author, *William Styron, calls "historical meditation," is based on real events in Virginia in 1831, and on excerpts from Nat Turner's written confession. At that time, Turner organized and led the only "effective, sustained revolt in the history of American Negro slavery."

As the story begins, the revolt has failed miserably, and all the rebels have died fighting or have been executed. Nat is in jail waiting to be hanged. After a brief trial, he passes the time before his death remembering his life as a slave. He thinks of his early childhood with the Turner family, where a sympathetic master allows him to learn reading and writing and to study the Bible. When he becomes 21 years old, Nat is rented out to a Baptist minister, who later sells him at auction to Thomas Moore. Then Nat becomes the property of Joseph Travis. Though reasonably well treated himself, Nat sees many slaves abused, humiliated, and separated from their families. Nat is deeply religious and finds passages in the Bible to support his hatred of the white man's cruelty and ignorance. Through a vision that comes to him in the woods, he understands he is chosen by God to "loose the bonds of wickedness . . . to let the oppressed go free." Nat carefully organizes an uprising of about 50 slaves and plans to kill as many slaveowners as possible before escaping to the North. He hopes the massacre will be a signal to blacks everywhere to join his avenging army. The revolt fails when other slaves are persuaded by their owners to resist the attackers with guns. All surviving rebels are caught, jailed, and executed. For another view of the violence and inhumanity of slavery, read *Uncle Tom's Cabin by *Harriet Beecher Stowe. YA

Conford, Ellen (1942–) The author of *You Never Can Tell, and of more than 25 popular books for young readers, Conford was a passionate reader herself from early childhood. She began her career by writing a book to entertain her 4-year-old son. The novels that followed, with their strong emphasis on the funny side of everyday life, were designed to amuse and to divert young people from the lure of television. These include *Dear Lovey Hart, I Am Desperate* (1975), in which Carrie Wasserman writes an advice-to-the-lovelorn column for her high school paper, and discovers that giving advice is not as easy as it seems. *We Interrupt This Semester for an Important Bulletin* (1979) is a sequel about Carrie's new assignment as investigative reporter for the school paper. *If This Is Love, I'll Take Spaghetti* (1983) is a collection of short stories. In the title story, Jamie learns that simultaneously going on a serious diet and being in love can be very difficult. MR

Connecticut Yankee in King Arthur's Court, A (1889) By *Mark Twain, this satirical fantasy-novel recounts the colorful exploits of a young man who regains consciousness after a blow on the head and finds himself in 6th-century England. He is captured by a knight in armor who proves to be Sir Kay, the Seneschal of the *Round Table, foster-brother of *King Arthur. Sentenced to death before the king, his knights, and *Merlin the magician, the Yankee tells the court that he is gifted with powerful magic. Using 19th-century knowledge, he impresses everyone by predicting a solar eclipse, and is rewarded with his freedom, the rank of minister, and the title of The Boss. Over several years, he uses his education and his talents as mechanic and inventor to start all sorts of industries and training programs. He makes some powerful enemies by trying to help the common people. He marries the brave and talkative Alisande la Carteloise, called Sandy, and they have a daughter. After many adventures, the Yankee returns from a trip to France to find England in a state of civil war. King Arthur is dead. Wounded in a great battle, the Yankee is tended by an old peasant woman, actually Merlin in disguise, and is magically put to sleep for 13 centuries. A modern novel using Twain's theme of an unwilling time traveler visiting the past is *Lest Darkness Fall* (1941) by L. Sprague de Camp (1907–), about a man sent back to ancient Rome who tries to prevent the Dark Ages. *A Connecticut Yankee* was adapted for film in 1921 and 1931. A musical film version was produced in 1949. YA

Conrad, Joseph (1857–1924) was a Polish-born adventurer and English author. His parents died when he was a child because of their involvement in revolutionary activities. Conrad became a seaman when he was 16 years old, and was later given command of merchant ships in the Orient and the Congo. Despite not learning to speak English until he was in his 20s, Conrad became one of the most outstanding novelists and prose stylists of the English language. Though famous for writing sea stories, tales of danger, and romances, his exploration of moral dilemmas and the truth of human experience were his most passionate themes. Among his numerous literary achievements are *Lord Jim; "Typhoon" (1903), about a captain who refuses to alter his course to avoid a fierce storm in the South China Sea, and who must deal not only with the raging sea but with the near panic of hundreds of Chinese laborers aboard ship; and "The Secret Sharer" (1910), about a ship's captain who helps a chief mate who is fleeing from another ship after killing a rebellious crewman during a violent storm; and his classic study of the nature of the human soul, the short novel *Heart of Darkness.* YA

Conroy, Pat (1945–) Author of several best-selling novels and a work of nonfiction, Conroy has drawn on his own colorful and complex upbringing in the South. Early in his career, Conroy was assigned to teach a group of almost completely illiterate black children living on a small island off the coast of South Carolina. His unusual approach to the children's education later cost him his job and led to the writing of *The Water Is Wide* (1972), a factual account of his experiences and frustrations. *The Great Santini* (1976), which may be partly autobiographical, is a novel about the adolescent son of a Marine colonel and the young man's struggle toward manhood and independence. *The Lords of Discipline* (1980) was inspired by Conroy's years in military school. In this novel, a senior cadet is given the task of protecting the first black student to attend Carolina Military Institute. In *The Prince of Tides* (1986), Tom Wingo tries to help his sister, Savannah, a well-known poet, after she attempts suicide. Like Conroy's other works, this novel is ambitious and dynamic, stressing the importance of attachment to place and family ties. *The Water Is Wide* was adapted for film in 1974 under the title *Conrack.* *The Great Santini* was filmed in 1979, *The Lords of Discipline* in 1985, and *The Prince of Tides* in 1991. YA

Contender, The (1967) This solid novel by *Robert Lipsyte explores the problems of a young black man trying to escape the ghetto. Alfred Brooks, a high school dropout, lives with his Aunt Pearl in Harlem, New York City, and works in Epstein's grocery store at a job he is convinced has no future. Neighborhood toughs harass him regularly. His best friend, James, is becoming a drug addict. Looking for a way to make something of himself, Alfred starts going to Donatelli's Gym to train for a career in boxing. Donatelli, wise and realistic, warns Alfred about the dangers he will have to face, but insists that real effort has its own reward even if it never leads to fame and fortune. Reluctant at first, Alfred makes the effort and comes to enjoy the good feeling it gives him. His status in the neighborhood improves. His ability to concentrate and discipline himself increases dramatically, but he and Donatelli realize that he lacks the necessary aggressiveness to become a professional boxer. With new confidence in himself, Alfred quits boxing to go back to school and persuades James to face up to his drug problem and get help. If you enjoyed this novel, you may be interested in reading *Native Son by *Richard Wright. MR & YA

Cooper, James Fenimore (1789–1851) A novelist who, with *Washington Irving, was one of the first American writers to gain international recognition, Cooper grew up on a large tract of land in central New York State, near what is now Cooperstown. In this wilderness, he learned to hunt and fish, and he gathered experiences that he later worked into his novels. He was a merchant seaman and served in the U.S. Navy before marrying and settling down to the life of a wealthy country gentleman. But one day, after reading a currently popular novel, he declared to his wife that even he could write a better book. She challenged him to do so, and the result was *Precaution* (1820), a novel of domestic English life. His first real success came with *The Spy, an adventure set in Westchester County, New York, during the Revolution. It was praised at home and abroad and sold well. His third novel, *The Pioneers* (1823), one of five novels making up the *Leather-Stocking Tales, introduced Cooper's most memorable character, the heroic frontiersman *Natty Bumppo. Of these novels, perhaps the best is *The Last of the Mohicans, which has become a classic.

Cooper wrote a number of sea adventures, including The Pilot (1824), about an American raid on the English coast during the American Revolution; and historical novels, including the Littlepage Manuscripts, three novels following the fortunes of a New York state family through several generations, including Satanstoe (1845), The Chainbearer (1845), and The Redskins (1846).

Influenced by the Scottish novelist *Walter Scott, Cooper tried to duplicate Scott's achievements by immortalizing early America, especially the frontier. He succeeded at least in part with the Leather-Stocking Tales. But he was often a hasty, careless writer, and his writing is uneven at best. *Mark Twain wrote a hilarious and biting essay on Cooper, "Fenimore Cooper's Literary Offenses" (1895), which will make you laugh even if you like Cooper's novels. YA

Cooper, Susan (1935–) Known for her chilling *fantasy books for young readers, Cooper was born in Buckinghamshire, England. After marrying an American scientist, she moved to the United States. Her books include a series of five fantasy novels titled *The Dark Is Rising, of which the first is *Over Sea, Under Stone, followed by *The Dark Is Rising, Greenwich (1974), *The Grey King, and Silver on the Tree (1977). Cooper has also written a realistic novel set in World War II London, Dawn of Fear (1970). If you enjoy Cooper's books, try those of *C.S. Lewis and *T.H. White. MR

Corbett, Scott (1913–) Starting his career by writing jokes, some of which he sold for two dollars each, Corbett eventually produced several different kinds of books. His first adult novel, The Reluctant Landlord (1950), was based on the experiences he and his wife had as landlords of a brownstone in New York City. He has written mysteries and other books for young readers. In Grave Doubts (1982), two boys wonder whether the death of Mr. Canby was from natural causes. The

Hockey Girls (1976) is the story of some high school freshmen who at first dislike a new compulsory sports program but change their minds. The Discontented Ghost (1978) tells of a resident ghost in an English manor house who tries to get rid of its new American owner. The Lemonade Trick (1960), part of a series, all with a trick of some kind involved, tells of a chemical two friends put in lemonade to make people good. Another is The Disappearing Dog Trick (1983). Under the title Love Nest, a movie was made of The Reluctant Landlord in 1951. If you enjoy these books, you will like those of *Barbara Corcoran, *William Kotzwinkle, and *Seon Manley. MR & YA

Corcoran, Barbara (1911–) An author of novels and mysteries, Corcoran often deals with problems that cause deep emotional reactions. In A Dance to Still Music (1974), illness makes a girl deaf, but she learns how to deal with this sudden handicap and resume a normal life. In May I Cross Your Golden River? (1975, reissued in 1982 as A Time to Love, a Time to Mourn), an 18-year-old boy who has amyotrophic lateral sclerosis—commonly known as Lou Gehrig's disease after the famous baseball player who died of it in 1941 at the age of 37—must come to terms with dying. The setting of The Sky Is Falling (1988) is the Great Depression of the 1930s. It brings ruin to the family of 14-year-old Annah, who is sent to New Hampshire, where she finds herself an outsider. Only after she and another outsider become friends is she able to adjust to her new life. Corcoran has also written mystery novels, such as *You're Allegro Dead, in which two campers at Camp Allegro come upon danger as well as mystery, and A Watery Grave (1982), a sequel. If you enjoy books by this author, try those of *Sophy Burnham, *M.V. Carey, and *Scott Corbett. MR & YA

Cormier, Robert (Edmund) (1925–) Author of *The Chocolate War and its sequel, Beyond the Chocolate War (1985), Cormier began his professional life as a newspaper reporter and editor. Though he has written three novels for older readers, his reputation was established by several books for young adults that have been called powerful, disturbing, and controversial. Combining memories of his adolescence with the experiences of his own children, Cormier focuses on telling a good story and creating believable and interesting characters. *I Am the Cheese* (1977) is a psychological suspense story about the son of a man who, as a government witness, must assume a false identity. *After the First Death* (1979) concerns the terrorist hijacking of a busload of schoolchildren, and *The Bumblebee Flies Anyway* (1983) is about a hospital where incurable patients volunteer for experimental treatment that may eventually help others. *I Am the Cheese* was made into a film in 1983. If you like Cormier's books, you may also like those of *Richard Peck and *Paul Zindel. YA

Costain, Thomas B(ertram) (1885–1965) A Canadian-born American novelist and editor, Costain also wrote volumes of history and some biography. He is known for his very readable historical novels, which always tell lively stories, and for the extensive historical research he undertook to provide background details for them. *The Black Rose* (1945) takes place in the 13th century and concerns a young Oxford student who embarks on a daring journey to China during the reign of Kublai Khan (1216–1294). *The Silver Chalice* (1952) is about the early Christians in Rome and the making of a framework for the simple cup used at the Last Supper. In *The Tontine* (1955), the setting is 19th-century England, and the main characters belong to two families who have built an industrial empire. *The Black Rose* was adapted for film in 1950, and *The Silver Chalice* in 1954. If you enjoy Costain's books, try those of *Daphne du Maurier, *Elizabeth Goudge, and *Rosemary Sutcliff. YA

Count of Monte Cristo, The (1844) A historical novel by *Alexandre Dumas, this is one of the great romantic adventure stories of all time. It appeared first in serial form in newspapers, as did some of the novels of *Charles Dickens, and was inspired by a real case of unlawful imprisonment. In the Dumas story, set in 1815, young Edmond Dantès is accused unjustly of working for the cause of Napoleon Bonaparte, then banished to the island of Elba. On the day of his marriage, Edmond is arrested, taken secretly to the Chateau d'If on a tiny island near Marseilles, and left there to be forgotten for the rest of his days. In the dungeons he meets the Abbé Faria, another prisoner, whose friendship and great wisdom help Edmond to survive the hopelessness of his situation. Faria succumbs to age and illness after revealing to Edmond the location of a huge treasure. When Edmond realizes that Faria's body is to be cast into the sea, he places the corpse in his own bed and takes Faria's place in the burial sack. The sack is thrown into the water, but Edmond frees himself and later finds refuge with a band of smugglers. He finally unearths Faria's treasure on the island of Monte Cristo and begins the long task of taking revenge against the man responsible for his years of suffering. He establishes himself in Paris as the wealthy Count of Monte Cristo. When justice has been done to his satisfaction, Edmond gives the bulk of his fortune to two young lovers he has helped to unite and disappears without a trace. If you enjoyed this book, try *The Hunchback of Notre Dame* by *Victor Hugo. *The Count of Monte Cristo* was adapted for film in 1934 and again in 1977. YA

Counterfeiters, The (also called *The Coiners*) (1926) A complex and unusual story by *André Gide, this novel describes what seem at first to be unrelated events bound together by only one element, Edouard, a sensitive and serious writer who participates in most of the novel's action. Edouard is himself writing a novel that he will call "The Counterfeiters" and, to help him in his work, is keeping a journal about his life. The journal entries occur intermittently throughout the book, forming a sort of novel-within-a-novel.

At the Pension Azaïs, which is a small private school in Paris, several schoolboys taste the excitement of circulating counterfeit coins. Around them other kinds of counterfeiters are at work. Bernard Profitendieu, an older student, leaves home when he accidentally discovers that Monsieur Profitendieu is not his real father, and he hides out with his friend Olivier. Bernard meets Olivier's uncle Edouard and is hired to be his secretary. Olivier becomes the protégé of a faddish novelist, the Comte de Passavant, and becomes the count's lover. Bernard and Edouard travel to Switzerland with Laura, a married woman who once loved Edouard. Laura is seeking solace from an adulterous affair with Vincent, Olivier's older brother, who abandoned her after learning she is pregnant with his child. At a resort they meet young Boris, who is under treatment for a nervous illness, and who turns out to be the grandson of a teacher at the Pension Azaïs. Boris returns to Paris with Edouard and Bernard. Olivier leaves Passavant and is taken in by Edouard, to whom he has long been attracted, and Bernard, reconciled to the reality of his life, returns to his stepfather's home. At the end, Boris, the victim of a cruel schoolboy game, kills himself with a pistol in class, in front of his horrified grandfather. In this novel, with its homosexual themes and, especially, its subtle exposure of hypocrisy, nearly everyone is not what he seems to be. *The Counterfeiters* is considered to be among the great novels of the 20th century. If you enjoyed it, try *The Stranger* by *Albert Camus. YA

Country of the Pointed Firs, The (1896) By *Sarah Orne Jewett, this is a collection of interconnected stories and sketches about New England nature and character at the end of the 19th century. A writer arrives in summer at a Maine seacoast town. She boards with the local herb doctor, Mrs. Todd, a stout and friendly widow who involves her in the life of her relatives and neighbors. Old Captain Littlepage eventually trusts her with a tale of shipwreck and a town of ghosts whose souls are waiting for their next world. She visits Green Island with Mrs. Todd, whose ancient mother lives there caring for shy William, who is more than 50 years old. They collect herbs, and the boarder sees the spot where Mr. Todd's boat went down. They visit Cousin Joanna, long ago thwarted in love. She lives alone on her own tiny island and wishes to be buried there. Old Mr. Tilley, a widowed fisherman, who keeps his house as proudly as his wife did, tells of his long sorrow and returns to his knitting. As she departs on the ferry, the visitor recalls visiting Esther, the shepherdess, with gentle William. They are lovers, she realizes, separated for years by their care for elderly mothers. This quiet romance ends the following summer with a wedding. These stories, connected by the wisdom and character of Mrs. Todd, are deeply moving. Other authors who have used New England settings for their fiction include *Nathaniel Hawthorne and *Harriet Beecher Stowe. YA

"Courtship of Miles Standish, The" (1858) This long narrative poem by *Henry Wadsworth Longfellow is based on popular myth surrounding the lives of *John and Priscilla Alden in the early days of the Puritan settlement at Plymouth, Massachusetts. Miles Standish, a widower and captain of the colony, is a man of action and not of words. He persuades his young friend John Alden to use his skill with words to propose marriage to the beautiful Priscilla on behalf of Standish. For the sake of friendship and in spite of his own love for Priscilla, Alden reluctantly agrees. He does his best to plead Standish's cause, but Priscilla refuses and asks, "Why don't you speak for yourself, John?" Standish accuses Alden of deliberately betraying his trust, and leaves Plymouth to fight an Indian campaign. John and Priscilla declare their love for one another, and later hear a false rumor that Standish has been killed. On their wedding day Standish returns and asks Alden's forgiveness for his anger, and the three friends are happily reconciled. YA

Cousteau, Jacques-Yves (1910–) An internationally known ocean explorer, photographer, inventor, and dedicated conservationist, Cousteau is also a film producer and writer of nonfiction. Among Cousteau's many achievements is the founding of two undersea research groups at Toulon and Marseilles, France. Though not trained as a scientist, Cousteau has played an important role in inventing and developing underwater devices. He was co-inventor of the Aqualung gear or scuba (self-contained underwater breathing apparatus), diving saucers, camera sleds for deep-sea photography, and a method for using television under water. He has led a large number of oceanographic expeditions all over the globe in his ship *Calypso*, a converted minesweeper. Books of nonfiction coauthored by Cousteau include *The Silent World* (1953), which describes the testing of the Aqualung and the *Calypso*'s first voyages. *The Living Sea* (1963) is about further expeditions and an experiment in which two men lived for one week in a specially designed underwater chamber. Among Cousteau's many films is *The Undersea World of Jacques Cousteau*, a series of more than 30 documentaries that first appeared on television between 1968 and 1976. YA

Cover Her Face (1966) In this detective novel *P.D. James introduces *Adam Dalgliesh, who has since become one of the most popular fictional detectives. Dalgliesh is summoned from Scotland Yard after Sally Jupp, a young and attractive woman not much liked by those who know her, is murdered. The killing, by strangulation, takes place at Martingale, a manor house in an English village. Members of the family and others in the household are suspects. Who is the father of Sally's child? Is she really engaged to the son of the house? Is her uncle, who raised her, involved? Dalgliesh has too many clues and too many suspects. In the end, with the assistance of a confession, he names the murderer, an unlikely suspect indeed. *Cover Her Face* is a well-told story with interesting characters. MR & YA

Cowardly Lion, The This lovable animal is one of Dorothy's companions in *The Wonderful Wizard of Oz* by *L. Frank Baum. You meet him when *Dorothy, the *Scarecrow, and the *Tin Woodman are going through a forest on their way to the Emerald City. The Lion, who is supposed to be King of the Beasts, is deeply ashamed of what he feels is his lack of courage. Dorothy explains that they are going to see the *Wizard of Oz to ask for his help, and the Lion decides to go with them in search of the courage he needs.

Like Dorothy's other friends, the Cowardly Lion is wonderfully helpful on the long road to Oz and gets the group out of some difficult situations. He is told by the Wizard that his wish will be granted only after the Wicked Witch of the West has been destroyed. When this is done, the Wizard gives the Lion a potion to drink that fills him with courage and pride. His new bravery enables him to rid the forest of a horrid spiderlike monster that has been terrorizing the animals, and the grateful forest creatures make him their leader and a real King of Beasts.

Crane, Stephen (1871–1900) The author of *The Red Badge of Courage*, Crane was a novelist, poet, short-story writer, and war correspondent, celebrated for his elegant, highly individual style and for his use of *symbolism. He was raised in a large Methodist family where reading novels was considered a vice, but he later rebelled against his strict upbringing. Crane attended a semi-military school and became interested in the study of warfare. An excellent baseball player, he considered becoming a professional but turned instead to freelance writing. His passionate curiosity about the seamier side of life attracted Crane to the *Bowery in New York City, where he gathered material for *Maggie: A Girl of the Streets and for a later novel about obsessive mother love, *George's Mother* (1896), both unusually realistic for their time. After the success of *The Red Badge of Courage*, Crane married a woman who had once managed a brothel, and the couple settled in England, in part to escape the scandal attached to their union. As a journalist, Crane covered the Spanish-American War in Cuba. After the war, Crane and his wife lived well beyond their means in England, lavishly entertaining friends and literary notables.

Crane died in Germany of tuberculosis, complicated by malaria, when he was 28 years old. You will want to read Crane's remarkable short stories. Among the collections are *The Little Regiment, and Other Episodes of the American Civil War* (1896), *The Open Boat, and Other Tales of Adventure* (1898), and *The Monster and Other Stories* (1899). YA

Creasey, John (1908–1973) This English author of mysteries and thrillers was one of the most prolific ever in his field. He wrote about 650 books under 28 different pen names, and they have sold some 60 million copies in 23 languages. Creasey began writing when he was 6 years old, but he received 743 rejections of his writings before his first novel, *Seven Times Seven* (1932), was published. He introduced a number of fictional leading characters in his many series. One of these was The Baron, who appears in 47 books written under the name of Anthony Morton, the first being *The Man in the Blue Mask* (1937), and then in 54 more books. Creasey also created Inspector West, as in *Inspector West Takes Charge* (1942). Still another detective, Dr. Palfrey, figures in a number of books, including *Traitor's Doom* (1942). Under the name of J.J. Marric, Creasey wrote, among 61 books, *Gideon's Day* (1955) and *Gideon's Fire* (1961). On the whole, Creasey is better known for the fast-moving action and the adventures of his leading characters than for clever deduction from puzzling clues. If you like Creasey's books, you will enjoy those of *Leslie Charteris, *Ian Fleming, *Robert Ludlum, and *Alastair MacLean. YA

crescent As a symbol, the crescent, a quarter moon, has been a religious or political emblem since ancient times. It played a part in the worship of Astarte, a goddess of love and fertility, in the Middle East. Later it was adopted as the emblem of the Byzantine Empire, because, according to tradition, the appearance of a new moon during a siege of ancient Byzantium (present-day Istanbul, Turkey) in the 4th century B.C. revealed a sneak attack by besiegers and saved the city. After the Ottoman Turks captured Constantinople, the capital of the Byzantine Empire, in 1453, they adopted the crescent as the symbol of their power, though it may well be that the Ottomans had used the crescent before this. The Ottoman Empire disappeared after World War I, but the crescent is widely used in Islamic nations and appears on most of their flags. In those countries the Red Crescent is the equivalent of the Red Cross organization elsewhere. See also *sign and symbol.

Cresswell, Helen (1934–) The English author of *Ordinary Jack* and more than 50 books for young people, Cresswell has also written five original television plays for young audiences. Cresswell's novels are a happy blend of humor, from slapstick to whimsy, and a strong emphasis on the power of imagination and ordinary human values. She is known best for The Bagthorpe Saga, a series of novels about a wacky and talented family given to hilarious acts of one-upmanship. After *Ordinary Jack*, the Saga includes *Absolute Zero* (1978), in which the ever-competitive family members enter slogan-writing contests, and *Bagthorpe Unlimited* (1979), the story of a family reunion organized by Grandma, where the Bagthorpe children join forces to outwit their visiting cousins. *Bagthorpe Versus the World* (1979) is about Mr. Bagthorpe's decision to make the family self-sufficient, and *Bagthorpe Abroad* (1984) describes the family vacation in Wales in what is supposed to be a haunted house. Cresswell's other works range from adaptations of fairy tales for small children to novels for older readers. If you enjoy her books, try the Adrian Mole stories by *Sue Townsend. The Bagthorpe Saga was adapted for television in 1981. MR

Crichton, (John) Michael (1942–) As well as being an author of *science fiction and adventure novels, Crichton is a medical doctor, an expert in other scientific fields, and a director of movies and TV production. *The Andromeda Strain* is an account of a mysterious disease that strikes an isolated place in the

United States. *The Terminal Man* (1972) is a retelling of the story of the monster created in *Frankenstein, with the usual *Gothic atmosphere. In *The Great Train Robbery* (1975), Crichton turned to *Victorian England for the setting of this daring and cleverly planned crime. Somewhat different is *Congo* (1980), a tale of diamond hunters in Africa, and in *Jurassic Park* (1990) dinosaurs are cloned to inhabit a theme park of prehistoric beasts. While some of the action and plots in Crichton's novels are a bit strained, he keeps the reader interested. Older readers might like to read one of Crichton's scientific books, *Electronic Life: How to Think About Computers* (1983). If you enjoy reading Crichton's novels, try especially those of *Isaac Asimov, *Ray Bradbury, *Arthur C. Clarke, and *Robert A. Heinlein. *The Terminal Man* was adapted for film in 1974 and *The Great Train Robbery* in 1979. MR & YA

Cricket in Times Square, The (1960) This popular children's book by *George Selden is about a Connecticut cricket named Chester, who jumps into a picnic basket and is accidentally transported to Times Square in New York City. The cricket has the good fortune to make three fine friends: Mario Bellini, the son of a failing newsstand owner in a Times Square subway station; a food-loving mouse named Tucker; and a cat named Harry. Together, they cause a lot of good-natured mischief and share many adventures. One time, Chester's friend Tucker inadvertently sets fire to the Bellini newsstand. Mario's mother, sure that the cricket is a jinx, orders him to leave. But when Chester begins to chirp beautiful music, she changes her mind. Eventually, his melodious singing becomes famous, drawing large crowds to the newsstand, and enabling the Bellinis to sell more newspapers and magazines than they ever dreamed possible. Though Chester enjoys helping Mario's family, as well as being a celebrity, he is nostalgic for the open air. In the end, Chester says goodbye to his city friends and goes back to the grass and trees of the countryside. Selden wrote about his three animal heroes in a number of sequels, including *Tucker's Countryside* (1969), in which Tucker and Harry visit Chester to help him save the Old Meadow from developers; *Harry Cat's Pet Puppy* (1974), in which Harry and Tucker take on the job of raising an abandoned puppy; *Chester Cricket's New Home* (1983), in which Chester goes hunting for a place to live after his tree-stump house is destroyed; and *The Old Meadow* (1987), in which Chester and his friends join forces to keep old Abner Budd and his dog, Dubber, from being thrown out of their cabin in the Old Meadow. If you enjoy *The Cricket in Times Square* and its sequels, you will also like the books of *E.B. White. MR

Cricket on the Hearth, The: A Fairy Tale of Home (1845) This charmingly domestic story by *Charles Dickens is about John Peerybingle, a hard-working delivery man well into middle age, his young wife, Dot, and their baby. They live in harmony in a modest cottage enlivened by a singing cricket. John is a big man, rough on the surface but gentle at heart, still astonished at being wed to a pretty woman so much younger than himself. Their best friends, Caleb Plummer and his daughter, Bertha, earn a meager living working for Tackleton, the toy merchant. John and Dot visit them often, bringing cheery talk and good things to eat. On the day before his wedding, Tackleton joins them to show off May Fielding, his bride-to-be and an old friend of Dot's. May has rejected Tackleton until recently, when her mother convinced her that security is more important than love.

That evening, John sees Dot in conversation with a stranger and is stricken with fear of losing her to a younger man, perhaps one who loved her before her marriage. John keeps his fears to himself and spends the night sitting at home before the fire trying to decide what to do. Profoundly distressed, he hears the cricket begin to chirp. Appearing to him in fairy shape, it sings of the purity of Dot's nature and her love for him. Just as John has determined to release her from their marriage, if she should wish it, he learns the stranger is Caleb's son, Edward, thought to be lost during his travels abroad. Once engaged to May, Edward has returned to claim his beloved, which he does with Dot's help moments before May's marriage to Tackleton. In a great celebration, all are joyfully reunited, Tackleton is mollified, and John sees his fears were unfounded and rejoices with his loving wife. If you enjoyed this book, be sure to read Dickens's classic *A Christmas Carol.* MR

Crime and Punishment (1866), the first of four major novels by *Fyodor Dostoyevsky, is a penetrating study of the evils of poverty and deprivation as experienced by a young intellectual. Rodion Romanovitch Raskolnikov, called Rodya, is a student forced to live in miserable circumstances, burdened as well by fears for a mother and sister who have sacrificed to provide for his education. Rodya learns that his sister, Dounia, may marry a man she does not love to secure the family's financial future. Desperate for money to make a start in life, Rodya murders an old woman pawnbroker and her simple-minded sister. He steals a purse and some trinkets, which he hides without ever attempting to use them. In rebellion against society, Rodya believes that extraordinary people have a special right to occasionally break the law in order to benefit others. He hopes to join the ranks of supermen by his own daring act, but instead is tormented by feelings of cowardice, failure, and self-disgust. He alternates between periods of feverish activity and a sickly lethargy. He puts himself at risk by discussing the murder case with chief detective Porfiry Petrovich, a clever and patient man with long experience with criminal behavior, and suspects that Petrovich may have guessed his secret.

Rodya befriends a young prostitute, Sonia Marmeladovna, a decent and warm-hearted woman obliged to support a destitute family. When Rodya finally speaks openly about his crime, it is to Sonia. She begs him to give himself up and promises to follow him to prison. Unrepentant, he confesses and is sentenced to eight years of hard labor in Siberia. Sonia makes a modest life for herself near the prison.

The slow discovery of their shared affection eases Rodya's suffering and brings the first signs of hope for the future.

The character of Raskolnikov is a fine example of the psychological insight for which Dostoyevsky is famous. Rodya's gloomy state of mind before the murder is brought to life vividly, as are his desperate efforts to accept the consequences of his act. While unable to feel pity for his victims, Rodya can identify with the pain of those he sees as downtrodden. Other fine characters include Sonia's alcoholic father, her stepmother, and Rodya's friend Razumihin, an impetuous and good-hearted giant of a man. Of particular interest is the fashionable Svidrigaïlov, for whom Dounia worked as governess until his attentions to her became troublesome. A tireless womanizer, Svidrigaïlov atones for former misdeeds with acts of sensitivity and generosity. The novel was adapted for film in 1935 and 1958, and, with the title *Crime & Punishment, U.S.A.*, in 1959. YA

Crockett, Davy [David Crockett] (1786–1836) Frontiersman, congressman, and folk hero, Crockett was raised on a farm in Tennessee and had little formal education. He fought in the Creek War of 1813–1814 under Andrew Jackson (1767–1845). He became a justice of the peace, was elected to the Tennessee legislature in 1821 and afterward to the U.S. Congress, where he served two terms. After a disagreement with Jackson, Crockett was adopted by Jackson's political opponents, the Whigs, and undertook for them a highly successful series of speaking engagements. His backwoods humor, his vigorously written memoirs, and the excellent Whig publicity made him famous. Defeated in the congressional elections of 1835, Crockett joined the Texas revolutionaries and was killed while heroically defending the Alamo on March 6, 1836.

Crockett is said to be the author of *A Narrative of the Life of David Crockett* (1834), sometimes called *Autobiography*, which drew heavily on his Tennessee childhood and which may have been written with the help of a congressional colleague. The Crockett almanacs were pamphlets that appeared under his name and became popular for their stories about Crockett, Daniel Boone (1734–1820), and Kit Carson (1809–1868). Though Crockett may not have written the pamphlets, it is possible he was part of the original venture. There are several biographies for younger readers, including *Davy Crockett* (1934) by Constance Rourke (1885–1941) and *The Story of Davy Crockett* (1952) by Enid LaMonte Meadowcroft (1898–1966). Crockett's exploits provided material for a popular TV series produced by *Walt Disney in 1954–1955. YA

Croesus, who died about 546 B.C., was the last king of Lydia, a country in what is now Turkey. Famous for his enormous wealth and the magnificence of his capital city, Sardis, Croesus was told by a great Athenian statesman and sage that riches are not necessarily the foundation of happiness. The phrase "as rich as Croesus" is often used to refer to people of great wealth. See also *Midas.

Cronin, A(rchibald) J(oseph) (1896–1981) A Scottish physician and novelist, Cronin was the author of *The Keys of the Kingdom* and a number of very successful novels based on his medical experiences. Cronin was a surgeon in the Royal Navy during World War I and later became a medical inspector assigned to the coal mines of South Wales. He began writing while recovering from an illness, and later left his lucrative medical practice to be a full-time writer. *Hatter's Castle* (1931), his first novel, is a blend of romantic horror and realism centering on the downfall of a tyrannical Scotsman, and it caused a great sensation. *The Stars Look Down* (1935) is about dramatic conflicts during a strike in a Welsh coal-mining town. *The Citadel* (1937), one of Cronin's most controversial books, is the story of a doctor caught in the battle between medical integrity and social obligations. *The Green Years* (1944) and its sequel, *Shannon's Way* (1948), trace the growth of an Irish boy who goes to live with his grandparents in Scotland and eventually becomes a doctor.

Cronin was labeled old-fashioned and overly melodramatic by some critics, but his books were enthusiastically received by readers all over the world. A fine storyteller, he created characters noted for their idealism and their struggle to obtain justice for ordinary men and women. Many of Cronin's novels have been successfully adapted for film, both in the United States and Great Britain. If you enjoy Cronin's books, you may also like those of *Richard Llewellyn. YA

Cronus, in Greek mythology, is a god belonging to the race of *Titans, who are the offspring of *Uranus (*Heaven) and Gaea (Earth). After taking the reins of power from his father, Cronus marries his sister, Rhea, and she gives birth to *Demeter, *Hera, Hestia, Hades, *Poseidon, and *Zeus. It is said that Cronus will be deposed by one of his children, so he swallows all of them but Zeus while they are still babies. With his mother's help, Zeus escapes and later forces Cronus to regurgitate his sisters and brothers. According to one of several versions of the story, Cronus is sent into honorable exile after being defeated by Zeus. See also *Bulfinch's Mythology* by Thomas Bulfinch (1796–1867).

cross Best known as the symbol of *Christianity, the cross has a history dating back much further. The cross takes a number of different shapes and forms. The Latin cross, with the arms shorter than the stem, is most common and symbolizes the crucifixion of *Jesus. The ancient Egyptians used the tau cross, like the letter T with a loop on top, as the symbol for life. Other forms of the cross include the Greek, with arms like a plus sign; the Celtic, which has a circle centered on the point where the arms cross; and St. Andrew's, in the form of an X. In the 1930s and 1940s the cross most in the public eye, except for the red Greek cross of the Red Cross Society, was the swastika after it was adopted by the Nazi rulers of Germany as their symbol and it became part of the national flag. The swastika is an equilateral cross made by bending the arms of an ordinary cross at right angles, all in the same direction. The word *swastika* is from the Sanskrit, and until the Nazis adopted it, it was a symbol of well-being and good fortune. See also *sign and symbol.

Cross, Amanda [Carolyn G(old) Heilbrun] (1926–) Heilbrun is both a scholarly writer and professor of English at Columbia University in New York City and an author of mystery novels under the name of Amanda Cross. In her books Kate Fansler is the detective, and she too is a professor at an unnamed university that bears a great resemblance to Columbia. The campus is the setting for most of the action in Cross's books, and many of the characters are academic people. The titles of most of her books hint at this relationship: *The James Joyce Murder* (1967), *Poetic Justice* (1970), and *Death in a Tenured Position* (1987). When, in *The Players Come Again* (1990), Fansler undertakes to write a biography of a woman author, she finds a 50-year-old secret and more of past events than she can reveal. Using Fansler as her spokesperson, Cross often enjoys the opportunity to comment on the struggle for prestige and power between teaching faculty and university administrators. In real life Heilbrun has expressed strong feminist positions in her scholarly writings. If you enjoy mystery books of this type, you might try those by *Antonia Fraser, *P.D. James, *Sara Paretsky, and *Ruth Rendell. YA

Crucible, The (1952) This play by *Arthur Miller may be seen as a condemnation of *McCarthyism. *The Crucible* is based on one of the strangest and most awful events in American history, the Salem witch trials of 1692. Under cover of religious scruples, people took secret vengeance on neighbors, for petty or imagined offenses, by accusing them of witchcraft. Many innocent persons were put to death.

At the home of Reverend Parris, his 10-year-old daughter, Betty, lies in a trance. Parris has caught Betty, his niece Abigail, and others dancing like heathens in the woods, and fears for the safety of their souls. There are rumors of witchcraft all about the town. Neighbors gather, awaiting the visit of Reverend Hale, who has been called to decide if Betty's sickness is the Devil's work. Hale questions Abigail and Tituba, a black servant, saying they must give the names of those they saw with the Devil or be condemned. Frightened, the girls hysterically cry out the names of certain townspeople.

From John Proctor and his wife, Elizabeth, you learn that a court has been convened in Salem. There, Abigail and her friends are brought to identify those who have consorted with the Devil, and the accused are jailed. Elizabeth knows that John once committed adultery with Abigail. Believing Abigail would take her place, and fearing for her life, Elizabeth begs John to tell the court that the girls are lying. At court, several respectable townspeople approach Judge Danforth, claiming the girls' accusations are false. Desperate, Proctor admits his adultery with Abigail and denounces her as a whore whose motive is revenge for his later rejection of her. Even while Reverend Hale defends Proctor, a hysterical girl charges Proctor with being the Devil's man.

At the jail before Proctor's hanging, Reverend Parris tells Judge Danforth he fears the people of Salem will rise up against the cruel and pointless hangings. Proctor is offered the chance to confess. When Danforth insists that Proctor must name other so-called evil-doers, including some of the most pious and upright women in Salem, Proctor refuses and goes to his death. If you enjoyed this play, you should try the nonfiction book *The Witchcraft of Salem Village* (1956) by *Shirley Jackson. YA

Crutcher, Chris(topher C.) (1946–) A teacher, child and family mental health specialist, and writer, Crutcher has written several novels about teenage athletes facing serious problems and learning from them. Perhaps his best-known novel is *Stotan!*, about four close-knit friends who are members of their school swimming team. Crutcher's other novels include *Running Loose* (1983), about a high school senior whose life goes out of control after he is thrown off the football team and his girlfriend is killed in an accident; *The Crazy Horse Electric Game* (1987), about a teenage boy, a star athlete, who struggles to rebuild his life after an accident that leaves him brain damaged; and *Chinese Handcuffs* (1989), about a teenager struggling to cope with his brother's suicide and its effect on his family and friends. YA

Cry, the Beloved Country (1948), by *Alan Paton, is a novel about the breakdown of tribal identity among black South Africans, and is a strong plea for understanding and compassion. Written somewhat like a folk tale, it uses elements of Zulu and Xhosa speech, with overtones of both innocence and great wisdom. In the province of Natal, Reverend Stephen Kumalo learns from Reverend Msimangu in Johannesburg that his sister, Gertrude, who went to the city to find her missing husband, is ill. Kumalo's only child, Absalom, went to search for his aunt, but never returned and stopped writing to his parents. Kumalo makes the long journey to Johannesburg, where he finds Gertrude and persuades her to return to Natal. After many difficulties, Kumalo and Msimangu succeed in tracing Absalom, only to find he has been arrested for inadvertently killing a white man during a burglary. Absalom's accomplices, his cousin and another friend, deny that they were involved and are freed for lack of evidence. Because Absalom admitted his guilt, saying he never meant to kill, he is sentenced to death. His distraught father hears that Absalom's victim was the son of Jarvis, a wealthy neighbor of the Kumalos and a man respected for his compassion toward blacks. Kumalo returns to Natal, but his sadness is eased and his faith renewed when he realizes that Jarvis understands the background of Absalom's crime and has doubled his efforts to help his black neighbors toward a better life. Other authors who have written about South Africa include *J.M. Coetzee and *Carolyn Slaughter. *Cry, the Beloved Country* was the basis for a musical comedy, *Lost in the Stars*, produced in 1949 with text by *Maxwell Anderson and music by Kurt Weill (1900–1950). It was filmed in 1974. The novel was made into a film in 1951. YA

Cullen, Countee (1903–1946) A highly acclaimed black poet and novelist, Cullen was, with *Langston Hughes, considered a leader of the *Harlem Renaissance. His most famous poems for younger readers appear in the collections *The Lost Zoo* (1940), about animals who failed to embark on Noah's *Ark, and *My Lives and How I Lost Them* (1942), an autobiography by a cat. Much of Cullen's work for older readers expresses black themes and conveys pride in his black heritage, such as his early collection of poetry, *Color* (1926), and *One Way to Heaven* (1932), a novel about Harlem. His final collection of poetry, *On These I Stand* (1947), published posthumously, is an anthology of his best poetry, chosen by Cullen. MR & YA

Cyrano de Bergerac (1897), a highly successful play by Edmond Rostand (1868–1918), was inspired by the exploits of Savinien Cyrano de Bergerac (1619–1655), a French nobleman and writer possessed of a very large nose and a quick temper. The scene is Paris in the 17th century. Cyrano and his regiment of swashbuckling Gascon cadets will soon be called to fight for the king at Arras. Gallant, boastful, and a great wit, Cyrano is privately convinced that the grotesque size of his nose will prevent any woman from loving him. He is dazzled by the beauty and sweetness of Roxane, his distant cousin, but is afraid to declare his feelings. Roxane is attracted to Christian de Neubillette, a handsome Gascon who adores her but feels he lacks the eloquence needed to win her deepest love and respect. Touched by the budding romance in spite of his own feelings, Cyrano offers to help Christian by writing magnificent letters and speeches for which Christian will take the credit. The scheme is a great success, and Roxane is enchanted by the flow of imaginative and passionate declarations. Christian and Roxane are married quietly just before the regiment is ordered into battle, but Christian is killed in the siege. His heartbroken widow retires to a convent to guard the memory of her brief happiness. Cyrano visits her faithfully over many years, never revealing that he was the author of the letters that melted her heart. Only when Cyrano is dying does Roxane guess the full extent of his love for her and the magnitude of his sacrifice. Another romantic French novel you will enjoy is *The Three Musketeers*, by *Alexandre Dumas. *Cyrano de Bergerac* was adapted for film in 1950. Another movie based on *Cyrano de Bergerac* is *Roxanne*, produced in 1985. YA

Daddy Long-Legs (1912) is an appealing novel by Jean Webster (1876–1916). When she is 17 years old, Jerusha Abbott (called Judy) is the oldest orphan in the John Grier Home and has lived all her life in its decent but dreary atmosphere. A humorous and irreverent essay written by Judy for her English class causes a wealthy trustee of the home to take an interest in her. The gentleman, who insists on remaining anonymous, offers to send Judy to college. The only requirement is that she work hard and write frequently to her unknown benefactor, giving the details of her progress. Also, she must not expect her letters to be answered. Judy, delighted to escape from the dull orphanage routine, complies and embarks on an exciting new life at college and a lively one-sided correspondence with her mysterious patron. Inspired by her memory of a lanky trustee with a spiderlike shadow, she addresses her patron as Daddy Long-Legs. Her letters are charming, enthusiastic, and confiding. Four years pass rapidly, and Judy successfully completes her schooling and makes some good friends. The identity of Daddy Long-Legs, revealed only after Judy's graduation, proves both a delightful surprise and a romantic reward. A British musical comedy, *Love from Judy*, was staged in 1953. There have been several film versions of the novel, most recently in 1955.

Jean Webster attended Vassar College, where she prepared for a literary career and became interested in improving the lives of delinquent and destitute children. Her frequent visits to orphanages also provided material for *Dear Enemy* (1915), a novel about the plight of dependent children. Her works include eight novels for very young readers and one play. MR & YA

Daedalus is the name of an architect, sculptor, and craftsman in Greek mythology. He was said to have built the *labyrinth for King Minos of Crete. When the king refused to let him leave Crete, Daedalus made wings out of feathers and wax for himself and his son *Icarus, hoping to fly to safety. Icarus flew too

Daedalus and Icarus depicted by the renowned German artist Albrecht Dürer (1471–1528).

near the sun and fell into the sea when his wings melted. Daedalus succeeded in reaching Sicily.

The Irish writer *James Joyce used the pen name Stephen Daedalus early in his writing career and later gave the name Stephen Dedalus to the main character of his autobiographical novel *A Portrait of the Artist as a Young Man. Stephen Dedalus appears again in Joyce's novel *Ulysses. Younger readers will enjoy A Fall from the Sky: The Story of Daedalus (1965) by *Ian Serraillier and Daedalus and Icarus (1971) by *Penelope Farmer. MR & YA

Dahl, Roald (1918–1990) This Irish-born English author wrote stories for young readers and for adults. They are full of black humor and a children-against-adults sense of conspiracy. He said that "the adult is the enemy of the child because of the awful process of civilizing this thing, which when it is born is an animal with no manners, no moral sense at all." His taste for black humor was reflected in his life. Forced to have a hip-replacement operation after military service in World War II, he kept his old thigh bone to use as a paperweight. His most famous books are *James and the Giant Peach; *Danny, the Champion of the World; *Charlie and the Chocolate Factory and its sequel, *Charlie and the Great Glass Elevator; and *The BFG. Dahl is also known as a writer of entertaining and sometimes gruesome fantasies for older readers. A collection you might enjoy is Kiss, Kiss (1960). In one of the stories, "Royal Jelly," a beekeeper feeds his sickly baby daughter a precious bee substance to help her grow, and sees her begin to change into an insect. MR & YA

Damocles' sword, or "the sword of Damocles," refers to ever-present danger. In the 4th century B.C., at the court of the tyrant Dionysius, the courtier Damocles was often heard lavishly praising Dionysius's great power and happiness. To show that powerful men are subject to danger and anxiety, Dionysius invited Damocles to a banquet and arranged for him to sit underneath a sword hung from the ceiling by one hair.

Damon and Pythias were two young men of the 4th century B.C. whose loyalty to each other came to stand for true friendship. Pythias plotted against the Greek tyrant Dionysius and was sentenced to death. After Damon offered to sacrifice his own life if his friend failed to return, Pythias was allowed leave to put his affairs in order. Just as the sentence was to be carried out, he appeared to take Damon's place. Dionysius rewarded their devotion by freeing both men.

Dana, Richard Henry, Jr. (1815–1882) Because he suffered from severe eye trouble while a student at Harvard University, Dana shipped to California as a common seaman in hope of regaining his health. After two voyages around the stormy southernmost tip of South America, Dana came home physically improved and continued working toward a career in law. In 1839, having pledged to improve the lot of his fellow sailors, he published a magazine article about cruelty to seamen. Two Years Before the Mast (1840), Dana's realistic narrative of his life at sea, became a classic and greatly influenced the literature of the sea. Written in diary form, it details the day-to-day shipboard routine, recounts conversations among Dana's shipmates, reveals the brutal tactics of the captain, and describes Dana's year spent working along the California coast. It was followed by The Seaman's Friend (1841), a book intended to educate sailors in their legal rights and obligations. As a lawyer, Dana continued to help the oppressed, risking his reputation and offending many of his paying clients, by giving free legal assistance to slaves taken prisoner under the Fugitive Slave Law. YA

Dandelion Wine (1956), by *Ray Bradbury, is a novel that recalls and celebrates the enchantment of summertime in the small Middle Western town where the author spent his boyhood. Like the dandelion wine his grandparents made and kept to warm their thoughts in winter, the images of his childhood are stored in this collection of gracefully linked episodes.

Douglas Spaulding is 12 years old in the summer of 1928, in Green Town, Illinois. The warm weeks stretch out before him, full of familiar promise and unexpected adventure. Some memories concern Douglas directly, such as the moment when he realizes he is fully alive in a way he never noticed, and feels the magic of "this rare timepiece," his physical being. Others introduce appealing small-town characters, such as Leo Auffman, jeweler and inventor of the Happiness Machine. You share stories of elderly neighbors, like Miss Helen Loomis, 95 years old, and her leisurely conversations with a young reporter. You are tantalized and a little frightened by the mysteries of the dark-smelling ravine that cuts and twists across the town, a jungle by day and a place to avoid at night. In one of the last stories, Grandma reigns supreme in the chaotic and miraculous climate of her kitchen, creating delicious food that defies conventional rules. Her almost supernatural powers are lost briefly when a visiting aunt tries to modernize Grandma's methods. The family unites to cut short Aunt Rose's visit and restore Grandma to her former glory. YA

Daniel was a Jewish prophet of the 6th century B.C. and the author of the book of Daniel in the Old Testament of the *Bible. A man of honest and upright character, he lived at the court of Babylon. You may have heard the story of Daniel in the lions' den. When Daniel continues to pray to his God in spite of the law forbidding it, King Darius punishes the prophet by having him thrown into a den of hungry lions, which he seals with a stone. Darius returns to find Daniel alive and unhurt. The prophet explains that God sent His angel to protect him by shutting the mouths of the ferocious beasts. Daniel is set free, and his accusers are cast into the den to be devoured.

In another well-known story, which takes place at a great feast given by King Belshazzar,

Daniel is invited to read and interpret the mysterious words written on the palace wall by a ghostly hand. Wise men and soothsayers fail to understand the words, but Daniel reads the "handwriting on the wall" that foretells Belshazzar's downfall. MR & YA

Danny, the Champion of the World (1975), by *Roald Dahl, is the funny and touching story of a 9-year-old English boy and his father, a hard-working widower who runs a small garage. Danny considers William to be the most marvelous and unstodgy father a boy could have. To support his claim, he describes their great poaching adventure.

Mr. Hazell, rich, thoroughly unpleasant, and a snob, owns a lovely wood where William occasionally takes a few pheasants without Hazell's permission. Once a year Hazell spends a fortune stocking the wood with birds, and invites hundreds of posh people to a grand party on the first day of the shooting season. William reveals his tried-and-true poaching methods to Danny. He also confesses that he would like to embarrass Hazell by somehow removing all the birds just before the big shoot. Danny has the idea of strewing raisins (which all pheasants love) laced with small amounts of sleeping powder, and William pronounces it a brilliant plan. They will carry off the sleeping birds during the night, leaving the wood bare of game. Assisted by a number of villagers, William and Danny carry out their daring scheme with completely exhilarating and unexpected results. For his important contribution to the prank, Danny is dubbed Champion of the World by one and all. MR

Dante Alighieri (1265–1321), known usually as Dante, is considered to be Italy's greatest poet, and one of the most important literary figures of the Middle Ages. Born in Florence of an old and well-established family, he became actively involved in the political battles between the White Guelf party, of which he was a member, and the Black Guelfs, who were supported by Pope Boniface VIII (c.1235–1303). Dante was

This engraving, printed in 1481, portrays Dante and his beloved Beatrice entering heaven.

Dante Alighieri

exiled after the Black Guelf victory, found refuge in several Italian cities, and never returned to Florence.

A writer of prose as well as poetry, a great moral philosopher and political thinker, Dante was profoundly influenced by his spiritual love for Beatrice Portinari (died 1290). *La Vita Nuova* (c.1293) is a collection of lyric poems set into the structure of an autobiographical novel with commentaries. Covering about 10 years of Dante's life, it recalls his first glimpse of Beatrice when he was 9 years old, and is a memorial to his enduring love for her. *The Divine Comedy* (c.1310–1321), also inspired by the ideal of Beatrice, is a magnificent long poem divided into three parts. In "Inferno" (Part I), Dante takes a journey through hell, with the Roman poet Virgil for his guide, and from there to the mountain of "Purgatory" (Part II). In "Paradise" (Part III), Beatrice leads Dante to the realm of God and eternal blessedness. To become acquainted with Dante's work in translation, read *The Portable Dante* (1977), available in an inexpensive paperback. It contains the whole of *The Divine Comedy* as well as selections from many of his other works. An excellent translation of the *Comedy* was done in 1971 by the American poet John Ciardi (1916–1985). YA

Danziger, Paula (1944–) Author of *The Cat Ate My Gymsuit*, Danziger was born in Washington, D.C., and taught a number of subjects in junior high school. She decided to write about young people getting along in today's stressful world, coping with problems in school, and achieving self-respect. Her funny and realistic stories are based on her family experiences and the lives of her students. You might like to read *Can You Sue Your Parents for Malpractice?*, in which Lauren tries to be independent against the background of her parents' endless quarreling. *There's a Bat in Bunk Five* (1980), a sequel to *The Cat*, is about Marcy Lewis's summer as a counselor-in-training at a creative arts camp. If you enjoy Danziger's books, other authors you may also like are *Betsy Byars, *Corinne Gerson, and *Lois Lowry. MR

Dark Is Rising, The (1973) The title of a group of *fantasy novels by *Susan Cooper, it is also the title of the second novel in the series. Set in modern-day England, it is the story of Will Stanton, the seventh son of a seventh son, and his part in the ancient battle between good and evil. On Midwinter day, which is his 11th birthday, Will's life is suddenly turned upside down when he finds himself gifted with supernatural powers. He learns he is the last of the Old Ones, immortal men and women called the Light, devoted forever to keeping the world safe from the forces of evil, called the Dark. Will is the chosen Sign-Seeker, whose task it is to find and guard the six great Signs of the Light that have been made over the centuries by the Old Ones. He is warned that the power of the Dark will be at its strongest during the 12 days of Christmas.

While his large family remains unaware of Will's bizarre experiences and new powers, Will finds he can move back in time to other years and other places. The Old Ones show him the fabulous Book of Gramarye, the book of hidden things and real magic, from which he learns about his place as an Old One. As the Dark rises, bringing a terrifying spell of frigid weather, the eerie conflict almost overwhelms Will and the others who help him on his quest. With Will's newfound knowledge and the power of the Signs, the Black Rider and his Dark Company are driven out. See also *The Grey King and *Over Sea, Under Stone. MR

Darkness at Noon (1941), a famous anticommunist novel by *Arthur Koestler, is both a political novel and an intellectual thriller. It is an attempt to describe what really happened behind the façade of the Moscow Trials of the 1930s, in which dissidents in the Communist Party and the military were publicly tried and sentenced to death or hard labor (many were killed secretly). The hero is a mixture of the lives of several victims of the trials, some personally known to Koestler.

Nicolas Salmanovitch Rubashov, ex-Commissar of the People, is arrested in the middle of the night and taken to prison. Though not formally charged with a crime, he knows the party considers him a political renegade and deviationist. Rubashov is a fervent revolutionary who believes the principles of the Revolution have been betrayed, and he has grown weary of hiding his opinions. In a series of three hearings, Rubashov is questioned. Between the exhausting interrogations, alone in his cell, Rubashov remembers his 40-year career. Fully alert and a brilliant thinker, he tries to understand the nature of revolution, and struggles with such questions as whether or not cruelty and violence should be used to reach a specific goal in order to relieve the suffering of the masses. Finally he is charged with counterrevolutionary activities and accused of plotting to kill No. 1 (Stalin). He is brought to public trial to confess his political sins. Thus, he becomes another *scapegoat on whom the people will place blame for the failures of the party. Rubashov is unable to rid himself of his belief in the value of the individual, a belief the party sees as dangerous. He accepts the logical outcome of his crime, which is his own execution, and is shot soon after his trial. If you enjoy reading thrillers about the Cold War, try *The Spy Who Came In from the Cold, an espionage novel by *John Le Carré. *Darkness at Noon* was successfully adapted for the stage in 1951. YA

D'Artagnan See *The Three Musketeers.

Darwin, Charles (Robert) (1809–1882) An English naturalist and author, Darwin developed theories about evolution and the principle of natural selection that resulted in important changes in our understanding of the history of living things. As a boy, Darwin was a poor student who preferred his hobby of collecting minerals and sea creatures to schoolwork. He entered Cambridge University to study for the ministry, but on the recommendation of a distinguished professor of botany, and in spite of his lack of scientific training, Darwin was hired by the Admiralty to be the official naturalist with the survey ship *Beagle*. During a five-year voyage to the southernmost coast of

South America and some Pacific islands, Darwin recorded his observations and collected animal and plant specimens. He returned to England and published *The Voyage of the Beagle* (1839), followed by three other important works over the next seven years. His research led him to question the prevailing belief that species were basically unchangeable. Much later he published the world-famous *On the Origin of Species by Means of Natural Selection, or the Preservation of Favoured Races in the Struggle for Life* (1859), a summary of his theory of evolution with a massive amount of supporting evidence. Darwin concluded that species had evolved into other species, many of them descending from a common ancestor, with some individuals adapting and flourishing in their ecological setting through a process of natural selection. Darwin's beliefs were vigorously attacked by many established scientists who disapproved of his method, and by people unwilling to compromise their belief in divine creation and guidance of all living things. Darwin continued to work and write for the rest of his life, producing 10 more major books, most of them about plant life. Younger readers will enjoy *The Adventures of Charles Darwin: A Story of the Beagle Voyage* (1982) by Peter Ward (1934–). MR & YA

D'Aulaire's Book of Greek Myths (1962), by
Ingri d'Aulaire (1904–1980) and Edgar Parin d'Aulaire (1898–1986), is a beautifully organized and illustrated collection of the most famous and familiar Greek myths that inspired many great works of literature and art. The first section, "Zeus and His Family," includes tales about such gods and goddesses as *Aphrodite, *Hermes, and *Dionysus. The second section treats minor gods, nymphs, satyrs, and centaurs. Section three contains stories of such legendary Greek figures as *Midas, *Oedipus, and *Jason and his quest for the *Golden Fleece. Written in clear and conversational prose, the book also has a map of ancient Greece. Other good books about mythology are *Bulfinch's Mythology* by Thomas Bulfinch (1796–1867) and *Mythology* by Edith Hamilton (1867–1963). MR

David (?–c.972 B.C.), second king of the Israelites and successor to Saul, was known in the *Bible as the Shepherd King. He is said to have written many of the *Psalms in the Old Testament of the Bible. David succeeded in uniting all the Israelite tribes under one kingdom, made Jerusalem its capital, and had the sacred *Ark of the Covenant placed there. A great warrior, he defeated the *Philistines and made his nation safe.

Among the many stories about David is his dramatic fight with the Philistine giant Goliath. When Goliath challenges the Israelites to send their best man to fight hand-to-hand, David convinces King Saul to choose him in spite of his youth. Saying the Lord will deliver him from death, David goes to meet the giant with only his staff, five stones, and a sling. Goliath, protected by a full suit of armor, is hit in the forehead by one stone hurled from David's sling and falls dead.

David Copperfield (1849–50), a novel by
*Charles Dickens, was the author's favorite of all his books, and one that drew much from his own life. David Copperfield tells his story from the very first: "I am born," and his narrative covers an eventful life peopled with memorable characters. As a child, David is adored by his gentle, widowed mother and a doting nurse, Clara Peggotty. Mrs. Copperfield is persuaded to marry the mean-spirited Mr. Murdstone, but his cruelty leads to her decline and early death. Murdstone and his sister want to rid themselves of David, who detests them both, so he is sent away to school. There he submits to the ferocious headmaster, Mr. Creakle, but he also welcomes advice and good cheer from his friends Traddles and Steerforth. Later, forced to work in the Murdstone warehouse, David becomes a boarder with the improvident Mr. *Micawber and his large family. Chronically harassed by their many creditors, the Micawbers are nevertheless kind to David. After they leave London, David runs away to his aunt Betsey Trotwood. She takes charge immediately, and at a momentous interview with the Murdstones, assumes full responsibility for David's future. He is enrolled in a new school,

---

MR = Middle Reader   YA = Young Adult Reader   * = See this main entry

becomes a lodger with Mr. Wickfield, Miss Betsey's lawyer, and meets Wickfield's beautiful and sweet-tempered daughter, Agnes. Lurking in the background is Wickfield's unpleasant, cringing clerk, *Uriah Heep.

David becomes a lawyer. He introduces the clever Steerforth to the Peggotty family and is horrified when Steerforth takes advantage of Peggotty's niece, Emily, and runs away with her. David falls in love with his employer's pretty daughter, Dora Spenlow, and marries her after a hectic and colorful courtship. He establishes himself as a writer, but his good fortune is soon overshadowed by Dora's illness and death, and by the drowning of Steerforth. Wickfield, meanwhile, has nearly been ruined by the vile behavior of Uriah Heep. Traddles and Micawber together uncover Heep's villainous and illegal acts in time to save the Wickfields, and Heep is sent to prison. David marries Agnes, who has always loved him, and the Micawber and Peggotty families start a new life in Australia. The novel was adapted for film in 1935, with the American comedian W.C. Fields (1880–1946) playing the role of Micawber, and was the basis of a TV film in 1970. YA

David in Silence (1965), by the English author Veronica Robinson (1926–), is a sympathetic and informative novel about a deaf 13-year-old boy and his adjustment to a new environment. David has been deaf since birth and is just beginning to speak a few words. His family has recently moved to a grimy industrial area near Birmingham, England, to be near a special school where David can improve his skills and meet people his own age. Michael is a sociable and patient neighbor who becomes David's friend and undertakes to convince others that David is not weird, only different. During a lively neighborhood soccer game, David is allowed to participate, but he arouses the anger of both teams and finds himself being chased by the furious players. Unable to understand what he has done to earn their dislike, David runs without knowing where he is going and is lost in an unfamiliar part of town. Michael rescues him and, with

David's older brother acting as a sign language interpreter, manages to explain to both sides how the misunderstanding occurred. The neighbors are helped toward a more compassionate perception of David's physical problems and begin to accept him for what he is—an intelligent, courageous, and able person. If you enjoyed this book, you may also like to read *The Alfred Summer* by Jan Slepian (1921–), about four young people, two of them handicapped, who join forces to build a boat. Older readers who are interested in how people can overcome handicaps will want to read *The Story of My Life* (1903) by *Helen Keller. Robinson, who has been a children's librarian, was born on Jersey, one of the Channel Islands off the coast of Great Britain. She lives now in London. MR & YA

Davies, (William) Robertson (1913–) A Canadian newspaper editor, college professor, playwright, and essayist, Davies is known best as a novelist, the author of three trilogies that have won him international attention for his wit, gentle sarcasm, and wildly imaginative plots. The first of these is *The Salterton Trilogy*, consisting of *Tempest-Tost* (1951), *Leaven of Malice* (1955), and *A Mixture of Frailties* (1958). All are centered on the imaginary city of Salterton in Ontario, Canada. In the first volume an amateur theater group stages an outdoor production of *William Shakespeare's *The Tempest*, with all the problems of reconciling egos and talents, not to mention various love interests. The second volume centers on a practical joke in which a couple are erroneously announced as engaged. In the end they are engaged, but not before the strengths and weaknesses of the characters are revealed. In the final volume a wealthy widow, mother of the man involved in the false engagement, dies, leaving all to a trust for educating musicians unless the son and his wife have a son. The plot also focuses on the young woman musician selected by the trust.

*The Deptford Trilogy is the second of the three trilogies. The third is The Cornish Trilogy, consisting of *The Rebel Angels* (1982), *What's Bred in the Bone* (1985), and *The Lyre of*

Orpheus (1989). It is set in Toronto. The first volume concerns a wealthy art collector who dies, leaving a nephew and several professors to sort out the art works and dispose of them. The second volume is mostly a biography of the art collector. The third is a comedy of musical and academic egos at odds when a trust fund is used to finance the completion and staging of an unfinished opera by E.T.A. Hoffmann (1776–1822). *Murther & Walking Spirits* (1991) centers on the spirit of a murdered Canadian newspaperman who goes to a film festival only to see on the screen a series of films about his ancestors. If you enjoy Davies's work, try reading the books of *Joseph Heller, especially *Picture This* (1988), an often funny novel about art and history. YA

Davy Crockett (1955), by Stewart Holbrook (1893–1964), is based on the life of frontiersman and folk hero *Davy Crockett. Written like a historical novel, it describes in a very readable way some of the details of Crockett's life and the stories told about him. It begins with 8-year-old Davy learning to hunt with his father's flintlock rifle, a skill he uses two years later to kill his first bear. The story continues through Crockett's colorful career as a famous hunter, farmer, cattle-driver, family man, scout for General Andrew Jackson (1767–1845), and member of the Tennessee legislature, and it ends with Crockett's death at the siege of the Alamo. The book contains a list of memorials to Crockett in Tennessee and Texas. Another book about this frontier hero is *The Story of Davy Crockett* (1952) by Enid La Monte Meadowcraft (1898–1966). MR

Davy Jones, the name given by sailors to the spirit of the sea, or sailors' devil, came into use around 1750. When you hear someone refer to "Davy Jones's Locker," it means the bottom of the sea, where drowned sailors are said to go. No one knows whether "Davy Jones" was a real person, though some etymologists speculate he was a pirate.

Day No Pigs Would Die, A (1973) This novel by *Robert Newton Peck is the unsentimental and earthy story of a Vermont boy growing up in the 1920s. Raised in the quietly austere tradition of the Shakers, 12-year-old Robert is already used to farm animals and hard work. His father is a kind, gentle man who believes wholeheartedly in the simple Shaker way, and he makes his living slaughtering pigs.

All by himself Robert saves a neighbor's best holstein cow from certain death, and helps her deliver her calf as well. In return for Robert's pluck and know-how, the grateful neighbor brings Robert the gift of a tiny piglet. Robert names her Pinky and cherishes her as the first thing that ever belonged to him alone.

Robert works hard at school and at acquiring his father's wisdom and instinct for farming. He is finally allowed to go to the Rutland Fair and is triumphant when Pinky wins a blue ribbon for Best-Behaved Pig. Though Pinky thrives and fattens into a fine sow, she is barren and unable to earn her keep by producing piglets. Robert knows she must be slaughtered for meat, as his parents cannot afford to keep her as a pet. It breaks his heart, but sadder still is the knowledge that his father is ill. Robert must grow up quickly to take his place, and he finds the strength to accept both his loss and his new responsibilities. Another fine story about a farm boy is *Bert Breen's Barn* by *Walter D. Edmonds. MR

Day of Pleasure, A: Stories of a Boy Growing Up in Warsaw (1969) These tales, by *Isaac Bashevis Singer, are based on real events in the first 14 years of Singer's life in Poland. They were originally written in Yiddish. In "A Day of Pleasure," Isaac earns a ruble (an enormous sum for him) and decides to indulge himself. He hires a carriage to drive him to another neighborhood, where he buys candy. After exploring, he spends his last money on an exotic fruit that leaves him terribly thirsty, and begins the long walk home. Frightening thoughts plague him along the way, for he has neglected to say a blessing before eating and has given nothing to the poor. His soul is gripped by guilt.

"Reb Asher the Dairyman" is a memorial to an honest and hard-working man, one of millions who disappeared during the *Holocaust. Tall and strong, with the voice of a lion, he is the cantor for the small congregation that meets in Isaac's house, and his goodness and generosity are legendary. It is Reb Asher who miraculously saves Isaac's family when their apartment catches fire.

In "Shosha" you meet the boy Itchele and his 9-year-old friend Shosha, a girl with whom he exchanges stories on long winter evenings. Shosha believes that a house imp lives behind the stove in her apartment, together with a chirping cricket, and describes the little tricks the imp likes to play. Years later, Itchele returns to her apartment, hoping to find his childhood friend. The apartment is unchanged, and Shosha's young daughter is the image of her mother at the same age. He tells her a story and hears again the familiar chirping of a cricket. MR & YA

Day of the Locust, The (1939) By *Nathanael West, this vivid novel does not have a traditional plot, and its characters are often more important than events. The events are seen through the eyes of Tod Hackett, a young artist who was persuaded to come to Hollywood to learn scenery design. He finds himself wanting to paint, not the beautiful people in fancy dress, but the seedy types in mail-order clothing who loiter on street corners. In the nondescript boarding house where he lives, Tod meets Faye Greener, a small-time actress, and her father, Harry, a former music-hall clown reduced to selling silver polish for a living. Faye is seductive in spite of her artificial manner and attracts an odd collection of men. Besides, Tod, there are Homer Simpson, a bookkeeper; the cowboy Earle Shoop, who spends most of his time standing like a display in front of a saddle shop; Miguel, a Mexican promoter of cockfights; and a bookmaking dwarf. Faye moves into Homer's house with the understanding that Homer will take care of her until she becomes a star. Their business relationship fails when Faye treats Homer as a faithful slave.

On his way to Homer's after an all-night party, Tod is caught in a huge crowd waiting for celebrities at the premiere of a new movie. He watches people gather, those who have "slaved at some kind of dull, heavy labor" all their lives, dreaming of a life of leisure in the California sun, and who have found nothing but boredom and disappointment. A riot explodes when a famous actor appears, and Tod is helpless in the violently pushing and kicking mob. He concentrates on his plans for a painting to be called "The Burning of Los Angeles" until the police haul him over a fence to safety. The novel was made into a film in 1975. YA

de la Mare, Walter (John) (1873–1956) An English novelist and poet, de la Mare wrote many short stories and books of verse for young people. He is remembered for his fascination with the world beyond this one, for his ability to blend dreams and reality, and for his unsentimental and tough-minded manner of speaking to younger readers. His charming and varied poems, ranging from the everyday to the fantastic, are collected in *Rhymes and Verses* (1947). For readers of all ages, *Come Hither* (1923), an anthology, is an introduction to the pleasures of poetry, and includes lyrical and imaginative works from *Geoffrey Chaucer to *Robert Frost. *The Collected Tales of Walter de la Mare* (1950) contains some of his best-known stories, many of them about children. MR & YA

de la Roche, Mazo (1885–1961) The daughter of a Canadian farmer, de la Roche was born and lived most of her life in Ontario, where she brought up two children and raised horses. She wrote plays and a variety of novels, but her major work was the 15 *Jalna novels. Though not written in chronological order, the novels describe three generations of Whiteoaks, beginning in the 1850s. They concern a British army officer and his Anglo-Irish wife who build their home at Jalna in Ontario and start a family dynasty. The saga of the vigorous Whiteoaks, dominated by matriarch Adeline Whiteoak, who lives to be 100 years old, and their friends and lovers unfolds over the period of a century. The central themes of decorum, the family unit, and a belief in independence were deeply felt by de la Roche. The Jalna novels have been translated into 18 languages. De la Roche was, especially in Europe, the most popular Canadian novelist of her time. You will want to begin with *Jalna* (1927), the first novel about the Whiteoaks. Among the others, you will enjoy especially *Whiteoak Heritage* (1940) and *The Whiteoak Brothers: Jalna 1923* (1953). *Jalna* was filmed in 1935. De la Roche also wrote stories for younger readers, including *The Sacred Bullock and Other Stories* (1939), a collection of animal tales, and *Bill and Coo* (1958), about two pigeons. MR & YA

De Voto, Bernard (Augustine) (1897–1955) A historian, novelist, critic, and biographer, De Voto was born in Utah. He later lived in Cambridge, Massachusetts, and became an important member of the New England literary community. His first novel, *The Crooked Mile* (1924), concerns a family that has lost the energy of its pioneer ancestors. It describes a new American West in the grip of powerful business interests. *The Chariot of Fire* (1926) is a novel about religious fanaticism in a frontier community. *Mark Twain's America* (1932), a controversial biography, was written in answer to a prominent critic who described the American West as a cultural wasteland that adversely affected Twain's growth as an artist. De Voto later became official editor of the Mark Twain manuscript collection.

De Voto is best remembered for his historical trilogy about the importance of the frontier experience in molding American life and national character. *The Year of Decision: 1846* (1943) is a detailed and scholarly account of events all over America, in which De Voto used a novelist's technique to make the settings and characters come to life. *Across the Wide Missouri* (1947) is a description of the Rocky Mountain fur trade, as a business and a way of life, and its relation to the opening up of the West. *The Course of Empire* (1952) covers the period from early 16th-century Spanish exploration to the arrival of *Lewis and Clark at the Pacific Ocean. YA

Dear Mr. Henshaw (1983), by *Beverly Cleary, is a lively novel in the form of letters and diaries, written by 10-year-old Leigh Botts. In second grade, Leigh's teacher had read to the class from *Ways to Amuse a Dog* by Boyd Henshaw, and had encouraged her students to write to the author. Leigh, now in sixth grade, has corresponded with Henshaw for four years. As he learns more about writing, he discovers he can express things about himself on paper that he cannot say in conversation, and he keeps a diary at Henshaw's suggestion.

Leigh lives with his divorced mother. He sees his father, a long-haul truck driver, only rarely. He is a new arrival at school, where he has his share of frustrations, but his most important problem is finding out where he stands in relation to his father. With a few good tips from Mr. Henshaw and after a long struggle to find a topic, Leigh writes a story for his school's *Young Writers' Yearbook*. The story tells about the time he rode with his father when he was trucking a load of grapes to a winery. When Leigh's story wins a prize, his father is touched and impressed with his son's achievement. Both begin to feel more comfortable with one another. Another novel you may like is *The 25¢ Miracle* (1986) by *Theresa Nelson, about a girl's struggle to strengthen her relationship with her father. *Dear Mr. Henshaw* won the *Newbery Medal in 1984. MR

Death Be Not Proud: A Memoir (1949), by *John Gunther, is the author's story of a "long, courageous struggle between a child and Death." The child was Gunther's son Johnny, who died in 1947, when he was 17 years old, of a brain tumor. Gunther wrote the memoir in the hope of bringing a small measure of comfort to others facing a serious disease. It is also a celebration of his son's ability to go through a terrible ordeal with pluck and humor.

Johnny was a young man passionately in love with science, working with great energy toward a career in physics or chemistry. He enjoyed music, chess, gardening, weather forecasting, card tricks, and a wide range of challenges to his outstanding mind. His physical condition seemed excellent, until a nagging stiff neck caused him to be sent to the school infirmary. A specialist was called in and discovered a tumor on Johnny's brain. After a series of tests, Johnny underwent surgery. Though he was not immediately aware of the seriousness of his case, his parents knew the surgeon was unable to remove all of the growth. Johnny recovered almost completely, but the tumor continued to grow. Over the next 15 months, many doctors were consulted and some new and extraordinary methods were applied to shrink the tumor. Throughout this difficult series of treatments, Johnny managed to keep up with his schoolwork and impress everyone around him with his patience, gallant wit, and consideration for others. He died in his sleep, quietly and without pain.

The book contains some of Johnny's letters to his parents, a brief diary kept at his mother's suggestion, and a short memoir written by his mother. A movie based on the book was made in 1975. Another fine story about family courage is *A Death in the Family* by *James Agee. YA

Death Comes for the Archbishop (1927), by

*Willa Cather, is a superb novel about two French missionaries, real-life clergymen, sent in 1851 to organize the new diocese of New Mexico. It is also a loving portrait of the American Southwest before it was fully explored. Father Jean Marie Latour and his childhood friend, Father Joseph Vaillant, travel to Santa Fe, enduring many hardships along a route that crosses the harsh and colorful desert. Arriving at last in the small adobe town, they find that the local Mexican priests refuse to accept Latour's authority. Latour must journey another 1,500 miles into old Mexico to collect the documents that establish his authority.

Intelligent, sensitive, and aristocratic in manner, Latour is a man of courage and great tolerance. By contrast, the wiry Vaillant is practical, energetic, and sociable. Over time the two men struggle together to build new missions, win the trust of the American Indians, and gradually dislodge the less trustworthy Spanish priests. It is difficult and lonely work, eased by the enduring friendship of the two men and their complete devotion to their religion. Latour chooses a native stone that will blend with the landscape he has come to love, and his dream of building a cathedral in Santa Fe becomes a reality. His pleasure is diminished when Vaillant is called away to another mission in the Colorado mining country. Now a respected archbishop, Latour dies peacefully, having succeeded in bringing a degree of harmony to his large and varied flock. If you like this novel about Roman Catholics in the early days of North America, read Cather's *Shadows on the Rock* (1931), about a convent of Ursuline Sisters in 17th-century Québec. YA

Death in the Family, A (1957) This powerful,

poetic, and moving novel by *James Agee is set in Knoxville, Tennessee, in the summer of 1915. It describes events that completely alter the lives of the Follet family. On a warm evening, you see Jay Follet and his wife Mary, their young son, Rufus, and their little daughter, Catherine, going about their ordinary routine. In the middle of the night, Jay gets a telephone call from his brother, Ralph, and learns his father has suddenly been taken ill. Jay makes the long trip to be at his father's bedside, discovers that the old man is not in immediate danger, and starts for home the following evening. A defect in the car's steering mechanism causes an accident, and Jay is killed instantly.

Mary, the first to hear of the accident, gathers the family around her. Aunt Hannah, who shares Mary's devotion to the church; Mary's brother Andrew; her parents, Joel and Catherine; and their friend Walter Starr all begin the slow and agonizing adjustment to Jay's death. Their brave struggle to understand and accept and to be kind to each other reveals a great deal about each. Rufus's and Catherine's memories of their father are radiant with affection and the evidence of his strength and love of life. The children must also try to come to terms with the formalities of the funeral, an event presided over by the stuffy and officious Father Jackson.

The impact of the tragedy on these ordinary people is told in prose that is far from ordinary, and the individuals, old and young, are presented in a human mixture of weakness and nobility. Another story about family tragedy, this time the death of a teenager, is *Death Be Not Proud* by *John Gunther. YA

Death in Venice (1912), a novella by *Thomas Mann,

is the story of Gustav von Aschenbach, a celebrated German writer. Now 50 years old, he has given his life to the demands of art and is suffering from a "heavy discontent." Aschenbach decides to take a holiday in Venice. At the hotel there, he is struck by the extraordinary beauty and grace of one of the guests, a 14-year-old boy named Tadzio.

Daydreaming on the beach, Aschenbach feels oppressed by the sultry air and stench of the lagoons. He plans to go to another resort with a healthier climate, but enticing glimpses of Tadzio make him change his mind. Watching the lovely boy absorbs the writer completely, and Aschenbach lives in a state of admiration. Instinct tells him Tadzio is aware of the attention, but the two keep a dignified distance. One day Tadzio smiles at Aschenbach radiantly, and from that moment the writer is violently in love.

Noticing a decline in the number of guests, Aschenbach also hears rumors of sickness in Venice. The smell of disinfectant hangs in the heavy air. He learns there is an epidemic of cholera, carefully hushed up by city authorities, who fear the departure of wealthy tourists. Drunk with passion and beginning to feel ill, Aschenbach cannot bear to leave Tadzio. In a glorious but pathetic attempt to look more attractive, he dyes his hair. At dusk, as he watches Tadzio wading in the sea, Aschenbach collapses in his chair and dies that night. A film version of the story appeared in 1971. YA

Death of a Salesman (1949), a drama by *Arthur Miller,

is the tragedy of an ordinary man who feels his life has not been worthwhile. *Willy Loman, the salesman; his wife, Linda; and their sons, Biff and Happy, occupy a small frame house where most of the play takes place, in the present and sometimes in the past. You see the crucial elements of the story in the first scene, but in no way does this lessen the extraordinary emotional tension that builds throughout the play.

Willy arrives carrying his sample cases, and admits to Linda that he is tired to death and so plagued by strange thoughts that he almost drove off the road again. You learn that Willy and Biff have argued about Biff's future. It is clear that Willy is still waiting for his 34-year-old son to live up to the promise he showed as a high school football star. In a series of flashbacks, Willy remembers when Biff cheated on an exam and stole occasionally, acts Willy forgave because he admired Biff's spirit.

Happy and Biff make plans to go into business together, provided that Biff can borrow money from Mr. Oliver, a former employer. Willy is wildly enthusiastic. They agree to meet for dinner to celebrate the start of a new career. Willy then visits his boss and says he would prefer not to travel any more. In a heart-wrenching scene, the boss refuses to help and tells Willy he is not needed in the business any more. At the restaurant, Biff tries to tell Willy and Happy the truth—that he lost his nerve about asking for a loan when Oliver failed to recognize him. Refusing to accept Biff's defeat, Willy tells his sons he has been fired, and drifts into conversation with unseen people from the past. Biff pleads with Willy to recognize that they are both everyday, dime-a-dozen men, but Willy furiously rejects the idea. Later, Willy thinks about his life insurance and decides he will be worth more to his family dead than alive. He quietly gets into his car and drives off the road to his death. The play was adapted for film in 1952 and for a TV movie in 1985. YA

Deathwatch (1972), an adventure novel by Robb White (1909–),

is the suspenseful and violent story of a hunting trip that turns into a nightmare. Ben is hired as a guide by Madec, a high-powered businessman who wants to add a bighorn sheep to his collection of trophies. Madec is a crack shot, a cold and arrogant man who enjoys killing, and Ben agrees to go only because he badly needs the money to finish college. In a remote part of the California desert, with a Jeep and supplies for one week, Madec accidentally kills an old man who is prospecting for gold. As Ben grimly prepares to take the body back to the local sheriff, Madec tries to persuade Ben not to report the accident. When Ben refuses, Madec takes Ben's clothes at gunpoint and forces him into the desert without food or water. If Ben should survive, Madec will make it look as though Ben murdered the prospector. Madec waits, ready to shoot Ben if he tries to reach the Jeep or the supplies.

After several harrowing days of hiding half-naked in the rocky ridges near camp, Ben is dangerously close to exhaustion. Finding water deep within the rocks provides the energy he needs to outwit and disarm Madec. Ben manages to take Madec and the corpse to the sheriff and has to face the consequences of telling his wild story to the authorities. Madec almost succeeds in discrediting Ben, but a slow gathering of facts and the discovery of crucial evidence bring out the truth, so Ben is exonerated.

White was born in the Philippines, where his father was a missionary. He joined the U.S. Navy and served during World War II, actually leading the adventurous life he writes about. Try looking for some of his novels set during World War II, including *Up Periscope* (1956), *Torpedo Run* (1962), and *Silent Ship, Silent Sea* (1967) in your local library. MR & YA

Defoe, Daniel (1660?–1731) An English novelist, journalist, and author of *Robinson Crusoe*, Defoe was the son of a hard-working London butcher. Though his family wanted him to become a Presbyterian minister, Defoe set up as a merchant and developed a strong interest in local and foreign politics. Sometimes called the father of modern journalism, Defoe wrote many pamphlets on political subjects. In 1703 he was jailed for libel after issuing a satiri-

cal pamphlet on an important disagreement within the Church of England. Once released, he wrote and published almost single-handed a journal of current affairs called *The Review*, and kept it going until 1713. When he was 59 years old, Defoe turned to writing novels, and he produced *Robinson Crusoe*, one of the first novels in English. Written in a plain and direct style, his novels show an unusual knowledge of human nature and a strong sympathy for ordinary men and women fighting to survive. Among his works are *Moll Flanders* (1722), the story of a prostitute and thief, born in poverty in London's Newgate Prison, and *A Journal of the Plague Year* (1722), which describes in the most vivid terms the Great Plague (1665–1666) that killed about 100,000 people in London. YA

Deighton, Len (Leonard Cyril) (1929–) An English author of popular espionage novels, Deighton worked as a pastry cook, a teacher, an airline steward, and a member of the Royal Air Force's Special Investigation Branch before becoming a writer. His first success was *The Ipcress File. Funeral in Berlin* (1964) was followed by *Spy Story* (1974) and by two trilogies following the Cold War intrigues of British agent Bernard Samson. The first trilogy includes *Berlin Game* (1983), *Mexico Set* (1985), and *London Match* (1985), and the second includes *Spy Hook* (1988), *Spy Line* (1989), and *Spy Sinker* (1990). Most of Deighton's spy stories are set in the Cold War era and pit British intelligence services against those of the U.S.S.R. Physical action, while far from absent, is subordinate to devious maneuvers by agents, double agents, and defectors in a subtle but deadly matching of wits, both with the enemy and within the agents' own intelligence agencies. Behind all this is an element of unease shown by some of the characters for the moral implications of their methods and goals. If you like Deighton's books, you will also enjoy those of *Eric Ambler, *Ian Fleming, *Frederick Forsyth, and *John Le Carré. YA

Deirdre is a beautiful heroine of Irish legend, whose story was popular with such Irish writers as *William Butler Yeats and *John M.

Synge. When she is born, a *druid foretells she will be the cause of great trouble. Deirdre is supposed to marry Conchobar, the king of Ulster, but she falls in love with another man and escapes with him to Scotland. Later, Conchobar persuades them to come back to Ireland, and he has the young man killed. Deirdre dies of a broken heart on her lover's grave. For more about her, younger readers will enjoy *Deirdre: A Celtic Legend* (1977) by David Guard (1934–1991), who, incidentally, was a founder of the Kingston Trio folksinging group as well as an author. Two other versions you might enjoy are found in *Irish Tales and Sagas* (1981) by Ulick O'Connor (1928–), and *The Hound of Ulster* (1963) by *Rosemary Sutcliff. *Deirdre* (1967), by Madeleine Polland (1918–), is a novel based on the legend. MR & YA

Delilah See *Samson and Delilah.

Demeter, the ancient Greek goddess of agriculture, is the daughter of Cronus and Rhea, and the sister of *Zeus. (See also *Titan.) Demeter's daughter *Persephone is abducted by Hades, god of the underworld. In searching for her, the stricken Demeter neglects the harvest and causes a terrible famine. Zeus then orders Hades to free Persephone, who is allowed to spend part of every year with her mother. Having eaten a single pomegranate seed while in the underworld, Persephone has to share one-third of her life with Hades. One example of the myth appears in *Tanglewood Tales* by *Nathaniel Hawthorne, under the title "The Pomegranate Seeds." You can find another under the title "Demeter and Persephone" in *The Golden Fleece* by Padraic Colum. Demeter's Roman counterpart was called Ceres. See also *hell.

Deptford Trilogy, The This set of novels by *Robertson Davies, consisting of *The Fifth Business* (1970), *The Manticore* (1972), and *World of Wonders* (1975), takes its title from the town in Ontario, Canada, where the story begins in December 1908. One young man, Boy Staunton, throws a snowball with a rock inside it at a friend, Dunstan Ramsay, but it hits a woman, who soon gives birth prematurely to a son, Paul Dempster, whose head is too big for his body. The three volumes unfold the lives of these three and Staunton's son, David. Ramsay becomes a teacher in a prep school, while Staunton's career makes him rich and politically important. Dempster evolves into Magnus Eisengrim, a world-famous magician. At the end of the first volume, in 1968, Staunton is found dead in his car in Lake Ontario with a stone in his mouth. The stone is the one from the snowball. Ramsay had kept it, and that evening it had disappeared from his room after the three had been together.

The second volume is mainly the story of David, a successful criminal lawyer but an alcoholic, and reveals more about his father, with whom he was at odds because he felt he had not lived up to his father's expectations. The final volume is an account by Eisengrim of his career, beginning in a grubby sideshow. He reveals that it was he who took the stone, and, he says, Staunton took it from him. The implication is that Staunton committed suicide on realizing that his career had not been the success it once seemed. YA

"Devil and Daniel Webster, The" (1937) In this short story by *Stephen Vincent Benét, based on the *Faust legend, Jabez Stone has a run of bad luck on his New Hampshire farm and sells his soul to the Devil in return for years of success and prosperity. When the time comes for the Devil (known as Scratch) to collect on the bargain, the frightened Jabez asks the help of the great Daniel Webster (1782–1852), lawyer, statesman, and U.S. senator from Massachusetts, who agrees to try the case. Webster insists on a trial by jury, so Scratch summons the ghosts of 12 men damned to hell's fires for their cruelty and evil deeds. Jabez is sure his goose is cooked, but Webster's long and eloquent argument works a sort of magic in the hearts of the renegade jury, recalling old feelings of goodness and love of country. To the Devil's disgust, they vote to release Jabez from his promise, and the victorious Webster forces Scratch to swear never to bother any New Hampshire man until doomsday. The story was made into a musical folk play under the same title in 1938 by Douglas S. Moore (1893–1969) using the same title, and was adapted for the movies in 1941. MR & YA

Devil's Arithmetic, The (1988) This novel by *Jane Yolen is a portrayal of life in the Nazi concentration camps of World War II, a story of great suffering told with dignity and restraint. Hannah is almost 13 years old and lives in New Rochelle, New York. She is not looking forward to another Passover Seder at which she must listen to the family history told and retold. She is tired of her grandfather's violent reaction to any mention of the *Holocaust, to which he lost most of his relatives. During the Seder, Hannah is asked to open the apartment door to greet symbolically the prophet Elijah. Instead of the familiar hallway, Hannah sees a green field and finds herself transported to another world and time. The place is a Jewish village (or *shtetl*) in Poland in the year 1942, and the people are her own lost relatives. Though at first it seems like a dream, Hannah gradually forgets her old life. When Nazi soldiers round up most of the villagers, she and her family make the dreadful journey to a concentration camp in a stifling cattle car. Hannah survives malnutrition, the separation of families, the choosing of victims for the gas chamber, and a multitude of evils that become almost commonplace. Mercifully, the nightmare ends when Hannah saves the life of another child by taking her place in a group destined to be gassed, and finds herself standing back at the apartment door in New Rochelle. This time, she remembers everything and will remember always. If you want to read more about Poland under the Nazi occupation, try *The Wall* (1950) by *John Hersey, which is about the Jewish uprising in the Warsaw ghetto. *Number the Stars* by *Lois Lowry tells about a 10-year-old girl who helps a Jewish friend in Nazi-occupied Denmark. MR & YA

Diary of a Young Girl, The (1947) Written by Anne Frank (1929–1945), a young Jewish girl living in Amsterdam, the Netherlands, this journal has been called one of the most moving documents to come out of World War II. It begins in June 1942, two days after Anne's 13th birthday. A spirited and intelligent girl, Anne decided to treat her diary like a best friend, and set down her most private thoughts. A month later, the Frank family went into hiding to escape the roundup of Jews by the Nazis. Anne's father, mother, her sister Margot, and their friends Mr. and Mrs. Van Daan and their son, Peter, moved into rooms in the building where Otto Frank had his office. The entrance to their "Secret Annexe" was carefully concealed. Four office workers helped them during their stay, at great personal risk, by bringing supplies. Later joined by another friend, the Franks and Van Daans were forced to stay inside at all times, taking care not to make any noise during office hours.

For more than two years the seven people lived under extremely difficult conditions. Anne recorded not only details of everyday life, but the complex personal relationships in the group, their quarrels and celebrations, her own remarkable development into young womanhood, and her unshakable belief that "people are really good at heart." The last entry is dated August 1, 1944, a few days before the police raided the "Secret Annexe." Of the seven arrested and sent to concentration camps, Otto Frank was the only survivor. Anne Frank died in March 1945 at Bergen-Belsen, a concentration camp in Germany. The book was successfully adapted for the stage in 1955, for the movies in 1959, and for television in 1980. MR & YA

Dicey's Song, by *Cynthia Voigt, the sequel to *Homecoming, is an unusual book about family relationships and the problems of adjusting to frightening changes at an early age. There is no obvious plot to the story. It simply flows, or bumps along, somewhat like people's lives and thoughts, but the conversations and events are strongly linked by the family's longing for a real home, and by their love and concern for each other.

Dicey Tillerman, about 14 years old; her younger brothers, James and Sammy; and her younger sister, Maybeth, have spent all summer on their own, traveling to their grandmother's rundown farm in Maryland. Their father disappeared long ago, and their mother's complete mental breakdown has resulted in her being placed in an asylum. The children must find shelter. Their Gram is a mildly eccentric woman of few words and great intuition. She is not openly affectionate with the children, but they sense she is glad to have them with her, even if it means going on welfare to feed them. Dicey's worries about the younger children can now be shared with Gram. They can talk about Maybeth, who is far behind the others in her third-grade class. They can discuss Sammy's behavior at school, and Dicey and Gram can work together to convince James to help Maybeth with her reading. Dicey has time for herself too, thanks to Gram, to begin restoring an old sailboat, work for pocket money, and begin to learn how to make friends. As the ties between all of them strengthen and they realize they can count on each other, some of the edginess goes out of their lives. Then word comes from the asylum that Momma is dying, and Dicey and Gram go to visit her. Momma's death causes great sadness, but seems to reinforce the Tillermans' determination to be a real family. Another book you may enjoy reading is *Return to Bitter Creek by *Doris Buchanan Smith, about a girl seeking a home and family she can call her own. Dicey's Song won the *Newbery Medal in 1983. MR

Dickens, Charles (1812–1870) Considered by many to be England's greatest novelist and a comic genius, Dickens was also a passionate humanitarian and radical, who throughout his life attacked snobbery, privilege, injustice, and cruelty. He was a keen and sympathetic observer of human nature in all its aspects, with the ability to create vivid characters ranging from the ordinary to the grotesque.

The son of a clerk imprisoned for debt, Dickens was taken out of school and sent to work in a factory when he was 12 years old. The shock affected him deeply, and images of prison life and of mistreated or lost children

Charles Dickens

would appear in many of his novels and stories. With very little formal education, he worked as a shorthand reporter in the law courts, and later became a journalist and devoted reporter of the ever-changing London scene. After the publication of his first book in 1836, Dickens, under the pseudonym Boz, began writing the comic serial that became The Pickwick Papers (1837). The book consists of letters and documents about an imaginary club founded by Samuel Pickwick, and was an immediate success. Dickens left his newspaper job to edit a monthly magazine, for which he wrote *Oliver Twist at the dizzying rate of two installments each month. The next few years saw the appearance of Nicholas Nickleby (1838–1839), an exposé of harsh conditions in the Yorkshire schools, and *The Old Curiosity Shop, in which *Little Nell suffers great hardships after her grandfather is forced to borrow money from an evil man. The historical novel Barnaby Rudge (1841) is set during the Gordon antiCatholic riots of 1780. To renew his energy, Dickens traveled to America, where he ruffled some feathers by speaking out against slavery and the lack of copyright protection for authors.

*A Christmas Carol, praised by *William Makepeace Thackeray as a national benefit, was the first of several books about Christmas. Now a great public figure, working and socializing at a furious pace, Dickens found time to direct a home for young delinquent women. In 1846 he published *The Cricket on the Hearth, intended for younger readers, and Dombey and Son, about a man who loses family and fortune through his pride and indifference to others. In both, Dickens expresses his belief that the most admired qualities are more often found among the humble poor. *David Copperfield, partly based on his own childhood and a personal favorite among his works, was followed by *Bleak House; Hard Times (1854), about the dangers of raising children according to overly rigid rules; Little Dorrit (1857), the story of a little girl born in a debtor's prison; and *A Tale of Two Cities. He undertook an exhilarating but tiring series of public readings from his works. In failing health, but still able to enchant his audiences and many friends with his humor and high spirits, Dickens collapsed during a reading tour and died the following year. He was buried in Westminster Abbey.

Nicholas Nickleby was adapted for film in 1947, The Pickwick Papers in 1954, and Little Dorrit in 1988. A TV series of Nicholas Nickleby, based on a highly successful 1980 play, was produced in 1983. YA

Dickinson, Emily (1830–1886) One of America's greatest poets, Dickinson wrote more than 1,700 short lyric verses, of which only 7 were published in her lifetime. She was the second of three children, and her relationship with her brother and sister remained close all their lives. Sensitive and intense, Dickinson was inspired by the poems of *Emily Brontë and *Ralph Waldo Emerson and began writing her own verse about 1850. She was well educated and had many friends, but before she was 30 years old was showing a tendency to stay at home and avoid visitors. From the late 1860s to the end of her life, she never left the family property, preferring the company of her relatives, her work, and her voluminous correspondence.

Emily Dickinson's poems are direct, intimate and deeply felt, often witty, and filled with irregular rhymes that place her outside the style of her time. Her subjects are love, death, nature, and God. Much of the tension in her poetry is said to spring from her unwillingness to accept conventional religious beliefs, combined with a yearning for the spiritual comfort such beliefs could provide. There have been many editions of her poems, including a recent Complete Poems (1960). A good introduction for younger readers is Poems for Youth (1934), which contains one of her best-loved verses: "If I can stop one heart from breaking, I shall not live in vain." You might enjoy reading her correspondence, which has been collected in The Letters of Emily Dickinson (1958). YA

Dickinson, Peter [Malcolm de Brissac] (1927–) A Zambian-born English novelist and scriptwriter, Dickinson has written for both adult and young readers, and was an editor of Punch, an English humor magazine, for 17 years. Dickinson is perhaps known best for his Changes trilogy of adventure fantasies for younger readers, much praised for their originality. The Weathermonger (1968) describes an imaginary England that has rejected modern technology and regressed to an eerie, half-medieval time of ignorance and superstition. In Heartsease (1969), an American spy comes to investigate the mysterious changes in the British Isles, only to be captured and accused of witchcraft. The Devil's Children (1970) is about a 12-year-old girl alone in a deserted city and her efforts to survive with a group of outcasts. Other novels by Dickinson include The Dancing Bear (1972), in which the author uses the setting of 6th-century Byzantium to create another imaginary world.

Older readers who enjoy detective stories might read Skin Deep (1968), about the murder in London of a tribal chief from New Guinea. The novel introduces the character of Superintendent James Pibble, a modest and rather clumsy detective whose abilities are greater than they seem. MR & YA

MR = Middle Reader   YA = Young Adult Reader   * = See this main entry

Dickson, Carter See *John Dickson Carr.

dictionary is basically a book containing a list of words in alphabetical order. Usually it is a collection of words of a particular language, and its purpose is to give information about those words: spelling, pronunciation, meaning, usage, and origin (etymology). Many dictionaries also contain such other features as short biographies of important people or geographical information. Using a dictionary as you read a book can add to the pleasure and profit you get from it. If you do not know the meaning of a word, you may not understand the point of a sentence.

The first useful dictionary of the English language, *Universal Etymological English Dictionary* (1721), was compiled by Nathan Bailey (d. 1742). For many years the best-known dictionary was *A Dictionary of the English Language* (1755), by *Samuel Johnson. Another landmark in the field was the two-volume *An American Dictionary of the English Language* (1828), compiled by Noah Webster (1758–1843), an American who worked to promote the proper use of English in the United States. The giant among English-language dictionaries is the *Oxford English Dictionary* (1928), published in 12 volumes and brought out in a revised edition (1989) of 20 volumes.

There are today many dictionaries of the English language, intended for different ages and uses. Nearly all of them are continually updated in new editions. The largest of the one-volume works is *Webster's Third New International Dictionary*, followed by *The Random House Dictionary* and *The American Heritage Dictionary*. Among short dictionaries are *The American Heritage School Dictionary*, *Macmillan Dictionary for Students*, *Webster's Intermediate Dictionary*, *The World Book Dictionary*, *Oxford American Dictionary*, *Webster's New Collegiate Dictionary*, and *Random House Webster's College Dictionary*. Many shorter dictionaries are available in inexpensive paperback editions. To find out more about dictionaries, read *Use Your Dictionary* (1980) by Adrian Underhill (n.d.). See also *encyclopedia and *atlas. MR & YA

dime novel refers to the fast-paced, exciting action stories and romances that sold for 10 cents in America from 1860 to about 1895, when the reading public shifted its interest to pulp magazines, which were printed on cheap paper and often dealt with sensational topics. Immensely popular in their day, the novels were mostly about the American Revolution, frontier life, and the Civil War, and they seldom deviated from conventional morality. The first dime novel, *Malaeska: The Indian Wife of the White Hunter* (1860) by Ann Stephens (1813–1886), is supposed to have sold nearly 300,000 copies in the first year. A well-known dime novel character was the detective Nick Carter, hero of more than 1,000 novels written by various authors. Deadwood Dick, another popular character, was modeled after a real-life Indian fighter who earned a reputation for bravery guarding gold shipments from the Black Hills of South Dakota. See also *Calamity Jane.

Dinesen, Isak [Karen Blixen] (1885–1962) Under this pen name, the Danish author Karen Blixen wrote in both Danish and English. In 1914 she married Baron Blixen-Finecke, and the couple went to British East Africa, now Kenya, to run a coffee plantation. Divorced in 1921, she managed the plantation for 10 years before returning to Denmark. Dinesen later wrote about her life in Africa in the autobiographical novel *Out of Africa. Her best-known works are collections of stories, including *Seven Gothic Tales, considered her best collection; *Winter's Tales* (1942); and *Last Tales* (1957). Many of her stories are eerie accounts of unexpected or supernatural events, and are peopled with fierce and often aristocratic characters who coolly accept the outrageous. YA

Dinky Hocker Shoots Smack (1972), by *M.E. Kerr, takes place in Brooklyn Heights, New York, and describes three young friends and their relationships with each other and with their parents. Fifteen-year-old Tucker must find a new home for his cat, Nader, after his father becomes allergic to her. Dinky Hocker answers Tucker's ad, adopts Nader, and

MR = Middle Reader   YA = Young Adult Reader   * = See this main entry

invites Tucker to visit. Dinky is much too fat and dresses in her father's old clothes, but she is funny and furiously sarcastic, and introduces Tucker to her pretty cousin, Natalia. Tucker later learns that Natalia has been in a special school for people with mental problems, but their friendship grows in spite of shyness on both sides. Dinky's friend P. John Knight persuades her to join Weight Watchers, with the enthusiastic approval of Tucker and Natalia. Dinky's parents find P. John irritating and go out of their way to discourage Dinky's interest in him. The pressure of their dislike causes Dinky to relapse into her habit of overeating, and she becomes depressed.

Mrs. Hocker is deeply involved in a community drug rehabilitation project, and she fails to notice her own daughter's need for love and attention. On the night Mrs. Hocker receives the Good Samaritan Award, Dinky writes "Dinky Hocker Shoots Smack" all over the neighborhood sidewalks, even though she has never touched drugs. Natalia and Tucker help the Hockers understand they must take Dinky's feelings more seriously, and the parents decide they will do everything they can to show their love for her. MR

Diogenes (c.412–323 B.C.), a Greek philosopher, devoted his life to the idea of self-sufficiency and a simple, natural existence without luxury. After seeing a poor man use his hands to drink, Diogenes is supposed to have thrown away his cup to demonstrate his ability to get along without material possessions. The legend of his search for an honest man, undertaken in broad daylight with a brightly lit lantern, was Diogenes' way of showing his contempt for the pleasure-seeking and immoral people of his time.

Dionysus, also called Bacchus in Roman mythology, is the Greek god of wine and fertility. One of the most important deities, he is said to have created the art of wine-making. While Dionysus travels and teaches others to plant the grape, he is accompanied by groups of nymphs, satyrs, forest spirits, and priestesses. Many festivals were held in his honor, charac-

terized by drunkenness, music, and wild dancing. Because it was believed that Dionysus could give his followers godlike inspiration and creativity, he was looked upon as a patron of the arts. Younger readers might like to read "The Mysteries of Dionysus" in *Greek Myths* (1949) by Olivia E. Coolidge (1908–). You can also find more information in *Bulfinch's Mythology* by Thomas Bulfinch (1796–1867). There are many editions of this classic work on mythology. Another good source is *Tales of the Greek Heroes* (1958) by Roger Lancelyn Green (1918–1987). MR

Disney, Walt [Walter Elias Disney] (1901–1966) A motion picture and television producer and winner of many Academy Awards, Disney was a pioneer in making animated cartoons. After studying at the Chicago Academy of Fine Arts, he became a cartoonist and then became interested in the animation process, which consists of making a separate cartoon drawing for each movement to be filmed. Mickey Mouse, one of Disney's most endearing creations, appeared for the first time in the animated film *Steamboat Willie* (1928). Donald Duck, Pluto, and Goofy were introduced during the *Great Depression years. Disney's best-known cartoon films include *Snow White and the Seven Dwarfs* (1938), *Fantasia* (1940), and *Bambi* (1942). Disney later produced a great variety of entertainment movies, including live-action features, such as *Mary Poppins* (1964) and the TV series *Davy Crockett* (1954–1955), part of which was converted into a popular movie in 1955. Disneyland, the first Disney amusement park, opened in California in 1955.

Disorder and Early Sorrow (1925), a novella by *Thomas Mann, is set in Germany during a time of severe inflation after World War I. It describes *bourgeois life with great compassion and with concern for the values and traditions, now crumbling, that supported it for so long.

Professor Cornelius presides over his family in proper, middle-class style. Besides his languid wife, there are Bert and Ingrid, 17 and 18 years old; 5-year-old Ellie, whom Cornelius loves above all else; and a 4-year-old son, Snapper. Their villa is comfortable, but a little shabby for lack of repairs. The story takes place on the day Bert and Ingrid entertain their friends at home. Cheerfully modern, affectionate, but slightly contemptuous of the old folks, Bert and Ingrid make plans for the party. Elaborate schemes are laid to obtain the necessary foods, some rationed in a time of wildly inflated prices. During the bustle of preparation, Cornelius stays out of the way, and his thoughts reveal much about his family's life. He thinks especially about his almost frightening love for Ellie. At the party, one of the young men dances with Ellie. At bedtime, Cornelius finds her sobbing bitterly because she has been separated from her elegant dancing partner. The father's heart is torn by a "distressful horror of this passion, so hopeless and so absurd." The young man comes to say goodnight to the child and soothes her, but Cornelius's feelings toward him are an odd mixture of gratitude and hatred. YA

Dixie, also called Dixieland, is a popular name for America's Southern states. Its source is the reliable ten-dollar note issued by a New Orleans bank before 1860 and used mainly by French-speaking citizens. The word *dix* (French for ten) appeared on the back of the notes—thus, the land of Dixies. "Dixie" (1859), actual title "Dixie's Land," is the title of a song, sometimes called the anthem of the Confederate Army. Dixieland jazz, also called Dixieland, is usually performed by a small group of players. The style originated in New Orleans, Louisiana, about 1915, and was based on the middle-class dance tunes of the time. The "Dixie cup," a paper cup used for a drink of water, was apparently so named because it was as reliable as the Louisiana note.

Dixon, Franklin W. This is the pen name created by *Edward Stratemeyer and used by a number of authors who have kept the Hardy Boys series going since 1927. In that year the first of many adventure novels about teenage detectives Frank and Joe Hardy was published as *The Secret of the Old Mill.* Among more re-

cent tales are *The Mystery of the Spiral Bridge* (1966); *The Hardy Boys Detective Handbook* (1972), which contains seven stories telling how they used various police techniques to track down criminals; and *The Mystery of the Silver Star* (1987), in which the leader in a bicycle race is attacked and the Hardy Boys go all the way from New York City to the mountains of Colorado to track down the culprits. Another series by Dixon is called Be a Detective Mystery Stories and includes *The Missing Money Mystery* (1928). Under the Dixon name have also appeared a number of Ted Scott Flying Stories, such as *Lost at the South Pole; or Ted Scott in Blizzard Land* (1930). With *Carolyn Keene, Dixon has written books that combine adventures of Keene's heroine, Nancy Drew, with the Hardy Boys. If you like these stories, try those of *M.V. Carey and *Scott Corbett. MR

Doctor Dolittle is the hero of *The Story of Doctor Dolittle, *The Voyages of Doctor Dolittle,* and other adventures by *Hugh Lofting. An eccentric, shabbily dressed, flute-playing English country physician, he is small and round, with a very kind face, and is devoted to the study of natural history. Dolittle's passionate fondness for animals leads him to keep many pets (including hedgehogs and mice), whose presence in the waiting room causes consternation among his human patients. When a West African parrot named Polynesia gives him the idea of learning animal languages and becoming an animal doctor, Dolittle gradually gives up his tiresome clientele of people and turns with delight to the treatment of animals. Always helpful and sympathetic, he is never too busy to care for a sick or injured creature. Dolittle's studies take him on long voyages to exotic places, including the moon, where he pursues his scientific interests and gently cures and educates the local inhabitants. MR

Doctor Zhivago (1957), by *Boris Pasternak, is a novel in the great Russian epic tradition, set during the turmoil and devastation of the Russian Revolution, World War I, and the long civil war that followed. The story has a host of

MR = Middle Reader   YA = Young Adult Reader   * = See this main entry

characters from all social levels, whose lives cross and recross as a new world is being created from the chaos around them. Yuri Zhivago is the son of a once-wealthy industrialist who, while traveling with his unscrupulous lawyer Komarovsky, killed himself by jumping from a train. Brought up by friends after the death of his mother, Zhivago becomes a physician and poet. He marries, serves in the army, and returns to Moscow to find his elegant home occupied by a commune. With starvation and sickness rampant in the city, he takes his wife and child on a long and hazardous journey to the Ural Mountains, on a train crowded with deportees, to seek safety at the family estate in Varykino. In nearby Yuriatin Zhivago finds Lara, the beautiful nurse who worked with him at the battle front, and his increasing love for her becomes a *symbol of tenderness and hope in a crumbling world.

During the cruel conflict between the Bolsheviks and their enemies, Zhivago is kidnapped by a band of partisans and forced to be their doctor in the frozen Siberian forest. Two years later he escapes and makes his way to Yuriatin on foot. His family has left Varykino after his disappearance, but he finds Lara, and their love brings him new life. In an odd twist of fate, he learns that Komarovsky was once Lara's lover, and is now offering her safe conduct to a more tranquil part of the country. Torn between the thought of losing her and fear for her safety, Zhivago persuades Lara to leave with Komarovsky by promising he will join her later. He returns to Moscow with little hope of finding his family, but carrying with him the memory of Lara and the poems he has written for her.

Though *Doctor Zhivago* was approved for publication in the Soviet Union by the State Publishing House, it was later rejected after a more careful reading revealed ideas considered unacceptable and even libelous by the Communist Party. Meanwhile, Pasternak had sold the foreign rights to an Italian publisher, who fortunately refused to send the manuscript back to the Soviet Union for so-called revisions. The original text was published in Italian, and the Russian edition was postponed indefinitely. If you enjoyed this novel, two other Russian authors you may like are *Leo Tolstoy and *Aleksandr Solzhenitsyn. *Doctor Zhivago* was adapted for film in 1965. YA

Doctorow, E(dgar) L(aurence) (1931–) A novelist and author of *Ragtime, Doctorow is the grandson of Jewish immigrants from Russia and grew up in the Bronx, New York. His decision to become a writer was made by the time he reached third grade. After his discharge from the Army in 1955, Doctorow supported himself with a career in publishing and wrote his first two books in his spare time. *Ragtime* was his first popular success; it was praised for its simple, compact, and beautifully controlled style, as well as its unusual blend of historical fact and fiction. *Loon Lake* (1980), set during the *Great Depression, centers on the relationships between an industrial tycoon, his wife (a famous aviatrix), a sensitive alcoholic poet, gangsters, and a young man who wanders into the tycoon's sumptuous country retreat. *World's Fair* (1985) is the story of a boy growing up in New York City in the 1930s. *Billy Bathgate* (1989) is the story of a quick-witted and brazen boy who becomes the mascot of the notorious Dutch Schultz gang. *Billy Bathgate* was adapted for film in 1991. YA

Dodge, Mary (Elizabeth) Mapes (1831–1905) An author and editor, Dodge turned to writing to support herself and her two sons after her husband died. She used to entertain her two small sons with the tales that were collected in *Irvington Stories* (1864). Her stories for children were very popular. Her father's Dutch ancestry gave her an interest in the Netherlands, and she began gathering material on Dutch life for *Hans Brinker; or, The Silver Skates, which was an enormous success. In 1870 she became an associate editor of *Hearth and Home* magazine, and three years later she became editor of a new magazine for young readers, *St. Nicholas.* She remained editor of the magazine until her death and published stories by many famous writers, including *Frances

Hodgson Burnett, *Rudyard Kipling, and *Mark Twain. Dodge wrote other books for young people, but they never achieved the lasting fame of *Hans Brinker.* MR

Dodsworth (1929), a novel by *Sinclair Lewis, is about a marriage and the dramatic changes that come about between husband and wife during a long European holiday. Sam Dodsworth is a successful automobile designer, a large, kind, somewhat stolid man strongly attached to his Middle Western home and its cozy, conventional ways. His wife, Fran, 10 years younger than Sam, has always dazzled him with her childlike beauty and brisk sociability, and she has an uncanny power to make him feel insignificant. After 20 years together, with their children grown and independent, Fran wants a new life, new and more elegant friends, and expanded horizons. The Dodsworths set off for England and the Continent with no fixed plan for their return. Though Sam is a reluctant tourist, he soon discovers the charm of exploring a foreign country. Fran's interests, however, are more social than cultural. She flirts with other men and is adopted by a group of social butterflies who delight in sneering at everything American. Sam feels out of place among people who have no real work to do, but cannot bring himself to deprive Fran of her pleasures. Their travels take them to Paris and Berlin, where Fran's attachment to an admirer begins to threaten their marriage. With nothing to do but observe, Sam realizes his wife has never really grown up, and he sees the shallowness of her constant need for flattery. After Fran announces she wants to marry her latest admirer, Sam is lonely and confused. He gives Fran her freedom, and quite unexpectedly finds himself drawn to Edith Cortright, a widow with whom he shares many interests. Even after Fran admits she has made a terrible mistake, Sam resolves to begin a new life with Edith, who loves and accepts him without reservation. Among the many fine novels about Americans abroad, you might enjoy *The Portrait of a Lady* by *Henry James and *The Sun Also Rises* by *Ernest Hemingway. A hilarious account of Americans

traveling overseas is *The Innocents Abroad* by *Mark Twain. *Dodsworth* was filmed in 1936. YA

dog The dog and the *cat are the most common household pets. A dog, called "man's best friend," is a *symbol of faithfulness, but in many expressions found in literature and in everyday conversation, dogs appear in an unfavorable light. "A dirty dog" is a person of low morals and actions; "a dog in the manger" is a person who keeps another from enjoying something but does not make use of it himself; "let sleeping dogs lie" assumes that waking one will cause trouble; "to die like a dog" indicates an end of a life of misery and shame; and "to lead a dog's life" is to be perpetually nagged and bothered. On the other hand, "a dog's age" means a long, long time, and "barking dogs seldom bite" assumes that a person may be all noise and little action. Elderly people may resent the idea that "you cannot teach old dogs new tricks."

In *Homer's *Odyssey* only Argus, the dog of *Odysseus, recognizes him when he returns home after an absence of 20 years. Two of the best-known novels of *Jack London, *The Call of the Wild* and *White Fang,* have dogs as central figures. A classic for younger readers about a dog is *Lassie, Come Home.* Many of the *fables of *Aesop are about dogs. A number of authors have written novels and stories about dogs, including *James Herriot, *MacKinlay Kantor, *Farley Mowat, *Phyllis Reynolds Naylor, and *Albert Payson Terhune. See also *Old Yeller* by Fred Gipson (1908–1973) and *Sounder* by William H. Armstrong (1914–). MR & YA

Doll's House, A (1879) By *Henrik Ibsen, this important and innovative play describes a crisis in the life of an overprotected married woman. Unlike other playwrights of his time, Ibsen presents his characters in a very realistic manner, in dialogue that is both natural and dramatically powerful. In spite of having little plot in the traditional sense, *A Doll's House* creates an atmosphere of great suspense. The play caused a major scandal, because its heroine abandoned her duties as wife and mother

---

MR = Middle Reader   YA = Young Adult Reader   * = See this main entry

to find herself as a human being, an act then considered outrageous.

The doll's house of the title is the home of Nora Helmer and her husband Torvald, a bank manager, and of their three children. Nora is treated by her husband much as she was by her father—as a decorative but essentially helpless creature quite incapable of thinking for herself. To help Torvald when he is ill and in need of money, Nora, without telling her husband, borrows from Nils Krogstad, who works at her husband's bank. She forges her wealthy father's signature on a bond, drawn up by Krogstad, guaranteeing repayment. Now, Krogstad is in danger of losing his position at the bank. He tells Nora she must persuade Torvald not to discharge him, or he will reveal the loan and the forgery. Nora's efforts on his behalf are unsuccessful, and Krogstad tells Torvald the unhappy secret in a letter. Nora is shocked by her husband's violent reaction. Having always addressed her in terms of childish endearment, he now calls her a hypocrite, a liar, even a criminal, and accuses her of destroying his happiness. When a second letter arrives, returning Nora's bond and expressing Krogstad's decision not to pursue the matter, Torvald is delighted to forget the entire incident. Nora, however, is devastated by a sudden awareness of the emptiness of her life, and realizes she is suffocating in a marriage that has enslaved her intellectually and financially. In the first serious conversation of their marriage, Nora finds the courage to tell Torvald she will leave him and the children in order to try to form her own opinions and identity. Two film versions of *A Doll's House* were produced in 1973. YA

Don Juan was a legendary Spanish nobleman, a renowned lover whose romantic exploits have been the subject of prose, poetry, and opera. The name Don Juan has become the *symbol of a man who lives an irresponsible and immoral life. First described in 1630 by the Spanish dramatist Tirso de Molina (1584?–1648), Don Juan's story was the basis of the opera *Don Giovanni* (1787) by Wolfgang Amadeus Mozart (1756–1791).

The most popular version presents Don Juan at the height of his career as an irresistible and unrestrained lover. He pursues and seduces the daughter of a distinguished commander of Seville, and kills the outraged father in a duel. Unrepentant, he later sees a magnificent statue of the commander and teasingly invites it to dine with him. The stone ghost arrives at the appointed hour and drags Don Juan to the gates of hell. Important examples of the legend appear in *George Gordon Byron's satirical epic poem *Don Juan* (1819–1824), and in the play *Man and Superman* (1903) by *George Bernard Shaw. YA

Don Quixote (usually pronounced KEE-HO-TEH) (Part I, 1605; Part II, 1615) is a picaresque masterpiece by *Miguel de Cervantes Saavedra, originally titled *El ingenioso hidalgo, don Quixote de la Mancha.* It is considered to be the first and possibly the greatest modern novel, one that continues to transcend cultural differences. Providing a grand panorama of life in Spain, it abounds in universal themes of interest to people everywhere. Alonzo Quixada is a dignified gentleman, old and poor, living in the province of La Mancha in Spain. His passion for reading stories of romantic chivalry, indulged over many years, has resulted in a gentle madness and a great knowledge of history. He imagines himself as a knight-errant, like the invincible and dashing heroes of his readings, and as such feels bound to defend the downtrodden and take arms against the forces of evil and confusion. He changes his name to Don Quixote de la Mancha, chooses a peasant girl to be his ladylove and renames her Dulcinea del Toboso. Later he persuades the peasant *Sancho Panza to become his squire and accompany him. Weighed down by an ancient suit of mail, the don rides a skinny, exhausted horse he has dubbed Rocinante, a name worthy of a knight's charger, and he sets out with Sancho Panza on an epic journey to do good. During his adventures, some ridiculous and some tragic, Don Quixote gradually discovers that the world is not like what he has read. In one of his most famous confrontations, he sees a number of windmills on the plain that look to him like giants, and he leads a charge against them, only to be unhorsed by one of the blades. Flocks of sheep become, in his unhinged mind, medieval armies about to engage in battle. Luck is occasionally on his side, as when he brashly offers to fight a lion and the bored lion refuses to take an interest in such meager prey. At the end of the novel, Don Quixote is beaten in combat with the Knight of the White Moon, who orders him to go home and stay home. In spite of the futility of his efforts, Don Quixote remains an enormously sympathetic character of great natural nobility and heroism, overly imaginative but never contemptible. Of several available translations you may find one by the Scottish novelist Tobias Smollet (1721–1771) the best.

The novel has inspired many works of art in the almost 400 years since its creation. One notable example is *Don Quixote* (1898), an orchestral tone poem by the German composer Richard Strauss (1864–1949). Adaptations of the novel include a dance version by the Australian Ballet, filmed in 1973, and the very successful musical comedy *Man of La Mancha*, first produced in 1965.

From the character of Don Quixote has come the word "quixotic," which means unusually chivalrous or unselfish, extravagantly romantic and impractical. To "tilt at windmills" is an expression that means to fight imagined injustice or enemies, and it arises from the well-known windmill scene in the novel. YA

Donne, John (1572–1631) An English poet, prose writer on religious and moral subjects, and most famous member of what has been called the Metaphysical School of poets, Donne was born into a distinguished Roman Catholic family. He was educated by private tutors, entered Oxford University when he was 12 years old, and later studied at Cambridge University and trained for the law. He became secretary to the Lord Keeper of the Great Seal, a position known to offer access to high public office. By the time he was nearly 30 years old Donne had written a number of love poems in a highly original style, full of sensuality and wit. He married an aristocratic woman without her father's consent, which resulted in

Donne's brief imprisonment and the ruin of his court career. Having rejected Roman Catholicism, Donne began a new career in the Anglican church, at the request of the king, and became one of the most influential and powerful preachers of his time. When his wife died, he turned more and more to religious pursuits.

Donne's work is characterized by an unusual blend of passion and logic, worldliness and morality; a brilliant and daring use of imagery; and the ability to express complicated feelings and states of mind. Among his most famous lyric poems are "Song" ("Go, and catch a falling star"), "The Baite" ("Come live with me, and be my love"), and "The Canonization" ("For God's sake hold your tongue, and let me love"). The Holy Sonnets contain "Death be not proud" and "At the round earths imagin'd corners," as well as the superb "A Hymn to God the Father" ("Wilt Thou forgive that sin where I begun,/ Which is my sin, though it were done before?"). In the "Meditations from 'Devotions upon Emergent Occasions,'" prose works written while Donne was ill, are the much-quoted lines, "No man is an Island, intire of it self," as well as "Therefore never send to know for whom the bell tolls; It tolls for thee." Other metaphysical poets you will want to read are George Herbert (1593–1633), the physician Henry Vaughan (1622–1695), and Andrew Marvell (1621–1678). YA

Dorian Gray See *The Picture of Dorian Gray.*

Dorothy, who lives on the Kansas prairie, is the heroine of *The Wonderful Wizard of Oz* by *L. Frank Baum. With her dog, Toto, she is swept away by a cyclone to the Land of Oz, where witches and wizards still live. A rather brave and serious child, Dorothy is also very modest. When her house, caught up by the cyclone, falls on the Wicked Witch of the East, she takes no credit for freeing the Munchkin people from years of slavery. Oz is a beautiful and magical place, but she soon feels lonely and homesick for Kansas. Many of her adventures with her friends the *Scarecrow, the *Tin Woodman, and the *Cowardly Lion happen because Dorothy is determined to find a way to get home. She has the courage to face the great *Wizard of Oz and later to scold him soundly for his trickery. Her loyalty to and love for her new friends is not enough to keep her in Oz, however, and once she sees them settled in their new lives, she asks for help from the good witch Glinda and is whirled back to her home and family. MR

Dos Passos, John (Roderigo) (1896–1970) A novelist, essayist, travel writer, and author of the trilogy *U.S.A., Dos Passos was an important figure of the *Lost Generation. He was the son of a wealthy and influential lawyer. After graduating from Harvard University, he went to Spain to study architecture, but gave up his studies to serve as an ambulance driver in France during World War I. His novel *Three Soldiers* (1921) describes the effects of the war on the personalities of an Italian-American, an Indiana farmer, and an oversensitive college graduate.

As a journalist, Dos Passos traveled widely in Europe, gaining new social awareness and a sympathy for radical politics and the labor movement. In the novel *Manhattan Transfer* (1925), he created a collective portrait of more than a dozen unrelated characters living in New York City in the early 1920s, revealed in a series of short and often impressionistic episodes. It was an experimental approach to novel-writing that Dos Passos later developed in *U.S.A.*

After the publication of *U.S.A.*, in which he vigorously criticized the quality of American life, Dos Passos became increasingly conservative, even defending ideas and principles he had attacked in earlier works. *Number One* (1943), the second novel of his second trilogy, *District of Columbia* (1952), is about an unscrupulous Southern politician, and expresses the author's disillusion with liberalism. YA

Dostoyevsky, Fyodor (Mikhailovich) (1821–1881) The Russian author of *Crime and Punishment, *The Idiot, *The Possessed, and *The Brothers Karamazov, Dostoyevsky is considered one of the world's greatest novelists. His alcoholic father was savagely murdered by his own serfs when Dostoyevsky was 18 years old, an event that played a large part in Dostoyevsky's lifelong preoccupation with crime and guilt. His first published work was a short novel, *Poor Folk* (1846), which won critical and public praise for its realistic psychological analysis of a downtrodden elderly clerk in love with an orphaned girl. The short works that followed were less well received, and Dostoyevsky was arrested for subversive political activities before he could complete a planned full-length novel. Condemned to death, he found his sentence commuted moments before he was to be shot. He spent four bitter years at hard labor in Siberia, where he had the first of many epileptic seizures, and acquired new faith in the teachings of *Jesus through reading the *Bible.

In St. Petersburg, Dostoyevsky resumed his literary career and restored his reputation with *The House of the Dead* (1861–62), the fictional memoirs of a man condemned for the murder of his wife, and *Notes from the Underground* (1864), in which the nameless hero suffers from a basic conflict between will and reason. In spite of poverty and debt, complicated by his passion for gambling, Dostoyevsky produced four extraordinary novels in 13 years, as well as shorter works. With a rare understanding of the human mind and heart, and in a volcanic atmosphere of conflicting emotions, he gave expression to universal themes of sin and suffering, the search for faith, and the titanic struggle between morality and primitive urges. YA

Douglas, Lloyd C(assel) (1877–1951) The author of *Magnificent Obsession, Douglas was a Lutheran minister who spent 30 years serving the church. He began publishing religious works around 1920, and a few years later turned to fiction. After the success of *Magnificent Obsession*, his first novel, Douglas became a full-time writer, and a strong advocate of self-fulfillment through the process of helping others. His other books include *The Robe* (1942) and *The Big Fisherman* (1948), both best-selling historical novels based on material from the New Testament. If you enjoy these books, you will also want to read *Ben-Hur by *Lew Wallace. *The Robe* was adapted for film in 1953 and *The Big Fisherman* was adapted for film in 1959. YA

Dowson, Ernest (Christopher) (1867–1900) An English poet and short-story writer, Dowson met the 12-year-old daughter of a restaurant keeper, fell in love with her, and wrote for her the most widely known of his poems, "Non Sum Qualis Eram Bonae sub Regno Cynarae" (1891), which contains the much-quoted refrain "I have been faithful to thee, Cynara! in my fashion."

Three years later, after his father's death and his mother's suicide, Dowson discovered he was ill with tuberculosis and went to France to forget his misery. With his health ruined by alcoholism and his fragile spirit broken, he was brought back to London by a friend and died there at the age of 33.

Another poem, "Vitae Summa Brevis Spem Nos Vetat Incohare Longam," contains the line "They are not long, the days of wine and roses." Dowson's poetry can be found in many anthologies, such as *A Treasury of Great Poems* (1955) and *The New Oxford Book of English Verse* (1972). YA

Doyle, Arthur Conan (1859–1930) An English physician and author, Doyle created *Sherlock Holmes, the most famous fictional detective of all time. It was something of an accident. While still a medical student at the University of Edinburgh, from which he was graduated in 1885, Doyle sold his first story, "The Mystery of Sacassa Valley" (1879). When his early medical practice was not successful, he turned again to writing and produced a novel, *A Study in Scarlet* (1887), in which he introduced Sherlock Holmes, who displayed from the beginning his powerful intelligence and deductive methods. From then on, Doyle wrote stories about him until he wearied of the character he had created. In 1891 he killed Holmes off, only to be forced three years later by public demand to bring him back to life. Most of these detective

Arthur Conan Doyle

tales are short stories, first collected as *The Adventures of Sherlock Holmes* (1892) and *The Memoirs of Sherlock Holmes* (1894). They have been reprinted along with others in various editions many times since. The stories have such titles as "The Adventure of the Engineer's Thumb," "The Red-Headed League," and "The Adventure of the Six Napoleons." Two full-length novels are *The Sign of the Four and *The Hound of the Baskervilles, probably his best-known work. Movies have been made of a great many of these tales.

Doyle also wrote historical novels, such as *The White Company* (1891), about a company of medieval knights, and *The Lost World* (1912), in which an expedition discovers an area still inhabited by prehistoric creatures. After Doyle's son was killed in World War I, Doyle became a spiritualist and wrote *History of Spiritualism* (1926). If you like the stories about Sherlock Holmes, you will enjoy those of *Agatha Christie, *Wilkie Collins, and *Edgar Allan Poe. MR & YA

Dr. Jekyll and Mr. Hyde, The Strange Case of (1886) This short story by *Robert Louis Stevenson is one of the finest and most suspenseful tales of early *science fiction. The story is told by Mr. Utterson, a lawyer whose austere appearance hides a great tolerance of human failings. Utterson hears that a child has been cruelly trampled in the street by a small and oddly repulsive man later identified as Mr. Edward Hyde. Utterson remembers seeing Hyde's name in a will he had recently drawn up for his friend Dr. Jekyll. Disturbed and curious about the connection between Hyde and the respected Dr. Jekyll, Utterson questions both Jekyll and a mutual friend, Dr. Lanyon. Neither man will talk about the mysterious Hyde. A year later, an elderly gentleman is clubbed to death, and the evidence clearly incriminates Hyde. When Hyde disappears, Jekyll still refuses to speak of the matter.

One evening, Utterson is visited by Jekyll's butler, Poole, who begs the lawyer for help. Jekyll has shut himself up in his study, from which strange noises are heard, and Poole suspects foul play. When Utterson and Poole break through the door, they find the dead body of Edward Hyde and signs that he has committed suicide. Jekyll is nowhere to be found, but he has left a letter. This, together with a letter from Lanyon, tells the bizarre story of Jekyll's obsessive study of the two natures of man (good and evil), and his scientific experiments. By concocting certain drugs, Jekyll learned how to change himself into the embodiment of all that was evil in his nature, and he named his second self Edward Hyde. He paid a ghastly price for the success of his experiment, as it became increasingly difficult to control the dangerous process of transformation. When Jekyll realized that the murderous Hyde was about to take him over completely, he killed himself, and his body changed into Hyde for the last time. For more stories about transformations and similar strange events, you might like *Werewolf!* (1979) by Bill Pronzini (1943–), an anthology of chilling tales by such authors as *Rudyard Kipling, Guy de Maupassant (1850–1893), *Bram Stoker, and more modern writers.

Dr. Jekyll and Mr. Hyde has been adapted for film several times. The best version is probably the first, produced in 1932, but another popular version was produced in 1941. YA

Dr. Pangloss, an important character in *Voltaire's *Candide,* is Candide's tutor and a respected philosopher. He fervently believes that "since everything is made for an end, everything is necessarily for the best end" in this best of all possible worlds. A matchless pedant and teacher, Pangloss is nevertheless vulnerable to misfortune. He barely survives an unspeakable disease, public hanging, dissection, and the harsh life of a galley slave. Rescued and reunited with Candide after a long separation, Pangloss confesses that he has suffered horribly. Still, having once said that all was for the best, he remains faithful to his exasperating theories even though he no longer believes them. YA

Dr. Seuss [Theodor Seuss Geisel] (1904–1991) was the author of books for children beloved by young and old for their rhythmic verse and loony drawings. He began his career as a cartoonist. On a sea voyage in 1936, Seuss passed the time by writing a nonsense poem to the rhythm of the ship's engine. The result, illustrated by Seuss, was *And to Think That I Saw It on Mulberry Street* (1937), about a boy who sees a modest horse-drawn wagon and imagines it changed into ever more zany and elaborate forms. *Horton Hatches the Egg* (1940) is the tale of an elephant tricked by a lazy bird into sitting on her egg.

During World War II, Seuss wrote and directed films for the U.S. Army, winning several Academy Awards for his documentaries. After *John Hersey suggested Seuss might improve upon the drab stories and stilted language of most reading primers, Seuss wrote and illustrated *The Cat in the Hat* (1957). Using about 200 simple words, it tells in rhyme how a sassy cat comes to amuse two children alone at home, and teaches them to make mischief. The book, a great success, led Seuss and his wife to found Beginner Books, an organization

Theodor Seuss Geisel, known as Dr. Seuss

specializing in easy-to-read stories. *Green Eggs and Ham* (1960) and *Fox in Socks* (1965) are among the most popular of Seuss's contributions to the series.

Seuss's screenplay for the animated cartoon *Gerald McBoing-Boing* was produced in 1951. He designed and produced animated films for television, many of them based on his books. They include *How the Grinch Stole Christmas*, produced in 1966; *Dr. Seuss on the Loose*, produced in 1972; and *The Lorax*, about environmental preservation, which was produced in 1971. MR

Drabble, Margaret (1939–) An English novelist, short-story writer, and critic, Drabble is one of the most respected authors of her generation. Her writing is energetic, realistic, often humorous, and notable for its complete lack of affectation. Drabble is a devoted student of human nature, especially feminine nature, but does not consider herself a militant supporter of women's causes. Her interest is in the conflict between a woman's need for a family and

her ambition to make a mark on the world. Like *Elizabeth Bowen, Drabble has focused much of her work on the details of human relationships.

Drabble's first novel, *A Summer Bird-Cage* (1963), tells the story of Louise, strikingly beautiful and predatory, who marries a rich and fussy man, with disastrous emotional results. *The Millstone* (1965) is about Rosamunde Stacey, recently graduated from Cambridge University, who has a baby and discovers the profound experience of mother love. *The Needle's Eye* (1972) is the story of an eccentric heiress who defies convention by marrying a poor man and giving away her entire fortune. YA

Dracula (1897), by *Bram Stoker, is a horror novel based on the old *vampire legends. Jonathan Harker, a young lawyer, travels to Transylvania, a historical region of present Romania, to discuss the purchase of a London estate with a foreign buyer. The client is Count Dracula, wealthy owner of a castle in the Carpathian Mountains. When their business is concluded, Dracula makes Harker his prisoner, and Harker realizes he is in terrible danger. Without understanding the nature of certain sinister events at the castle, he manages to escape.

In England, you meet Harker's fiancée Mina, her good friend Lucy, Lucy's fiancé, Arthur Holmwood, and their friend Dr. Seward. You learn that a ship has just arrived under strange circumstances, its cargo a number of coffins filled with earth. About the same time, Lucy begins to suffer from bizarre dreams and episodes of sleepwalking, and becomes alarmingly pale. Disturbed about her condition, Seward brings in Dr. Van Helsing, known to have experience with vampires and their victims. You understand that Dracula has arrived in London, where he will never lack the supply of blood he needs, and has found Lucy. In spite of extraordinary efforts to protect her from the Count's night visits, Lucy dies. Van Helsing, knowing she is now one of the "undead," drives a stake through her heart to free her soul.

Harker has safely returned from Europe. Now Mina is visited by Dracula, and the friends realize they must destroy the vampire to save her. Combining their ingenuity and resources, Harker, Holmwood, Seward, Van Helsing, and two other friends succeed in locating and purifying all but one of the coffins hidden in London. Their search for the last box is long and dangerous, and they must find and follow the ship carrying it to Europe. After many adventures, they travel to Castle Dracula, to which they believe the vampire is retreating. Intercepting the cart carrying Dracula's coffin just as it reaches the castle, they tear open the coffin moments before sunset. Jonathan stabs Dracula through the heart, and sees the body crumble into dust. Mina is thus released from the vampire's power. The well-known play *Dracula* was written by John Lloyd Baldeston (1889–1954) and produced in 1927. If you enjoyed this book, you will also like the vampire novels of Anne Rice (1941–), including *Interview with the Vampire* (1976). Of the many movie versions of *Dracula*, the most famous was made in 1931 and starred Bela Lugosi (1882–1956). Another version, called *Bram Stoker's Dracula*, was released in 1992. YA

Dragonflight (1968), by *Anne McCaffrey, is the first book in a series, The Dragonriders of Pern, about the dragons of Pern and their telepathically linked human riders. Pern is a planet remote in space and time where a colony seeded by humans from Earth has evolved a farming economy. The planet has an exceptionally comfortable environment, and its only natural enemy is a spore-based life form called Thread, an invader from an adjacent planet, the Red Star. During times of perihelion, when Pern and the Red Star are closest, spores of Thread, having crossed from one planet to the other, develop and devour all plant and animal life in their path. Thread then burrows deep under the surface of the planet to continue a repulsive life-cycle and breed more like it. As Thread proved to be almost indestructible, the original Earth colonists produced through genetic engineering a fire-breathing reptilian helper to burn Thread in the atmosphere before it could reach Pern's surface.

At the beginning of *Dragonflight*, Thread has been inactive for 400 Turns, and most of the citizenry have forgotten it. In lacking a purpose, they have become stagnant. The dragonriders now have to fight for food for themselves and their dragons, and Pern is unprepared for what the riders know is a growing threat. F'lar, the head dragonrider, goes searching for a rider for the queen egg that is about to hatch, and he finds heroic young Lessa, who becomes his consort and reigning queen of the dragonriders. *Dragonflight* tells how they mobilize their world to fight the ancient enemy and move Pern out of its complacent stagnation to develop once again the promise of the early colonists. This book was followed by two sequels, *Dragonquest* (1971) and *The White Dragon* (1978). *Dragonsong* (1976), *Dragonsinger* (1977), and *Dragondrums* (1979) form a second trilogy about Pern, and numerous other novels continue the story of Pern and its human and dragon inhabitants. If you enjoy these novels, you will also want to read the Pit Dragon novels of *Jane Yolen. MR & YA

Dragon's Blood (1982), by *Jane Yolen, is the first book of the Pit Dragon trilogy set on the desert planet Austar IV. Though young Jakkin Stewart is just a bonded servant, or bonder, in the dragon nursery of Master Sarkkhan James, he hopes someday to become a dragon master. Risking off-world imprisonment, he steals a dragon hatchling from the nursery and raises it in secret in the desert, intending to enter it in the dragon fights and buy his freedom with his winnings. He is aided by Akki, a beautiful but mysterious girl who works at the nursery. She helps him learn how to train the dragon and arranges its first fight. At the fighting pit, the dragon wins its match, but Jakkin runs into Sarkkhan. Instead of being angry, Sarkkhan says he knew of Jakkin's plot all along, claims one of the dragon's hatchlings as repayment, and reveals that Akki is his daughter. Jakkin names his dragon Heart's Blood and happily takes her back to the nursery. But his happiness is cut short when Akki suddenly says goodbye to him and disappears. The story of Jakkin and Akki continues with *Heart's Blood* and *A Sending of Dragons*. If you enjoy

MR = Middle Reader   YA = Young Adult Reader   * = See this main entry

Yolen's books, try also *Dragonflight* by *Anne McCaffrey. MR & YA

Dragonwings (1975) This novel by *Laurence Yep is narrated by a Chinese boy named Moon Shadow, who comes to San Francisco in 1903, when he is 8 years old, to help his father, Windrider, at the Company, the family's laundry business. Windrider, who believes that in a former life he was a dragon, dreams of being able to fly someday. When he learns of the Wright brothers' successful flights, he leaves the Company and San Francisco's Chinese community to live and work among the white "demons" and learn how to build a flying machine. Moon Shadow and his father face many problems, including the prejudices of both the Chinese and white communities and the San Francisco earthquake of 1906. Yet they find friends in their landlady, Miss Whitlaw, and her niece, Robin, who help Windrider finally achieve his dream. Although the airplane crashes after its first flight, Windrider is content. He returns to the Company as a full partner, a position that enables him to bring his wife to America. If you enjoyed *Dragonwings*, try also *In the Year of the Boar and Jackie Robinson* by *Bette Bao Lord, about a Chinese girl who comes to America in 1946. MR

Dream Keeper: and Other Poems, The (1932) *Langston Hughes, author of these short poems, chose them especially for young people. The verses are divided into five groups. "The Dream Keeper" contains lyrics in a rather quiet mood. "Sea Charm," songs of the sea and faraway places, is followed by "Dressed Up," poems written in the style of the folk songs called blues. "Feet o' Jesus" is a group of religious verses and spirituals. In "Walkers of the Dawn," Hughes expresses his pride in being an African American and his hopes for the new generation of his people. If you enjoyed this book, another black poet whose works you may like is *Paul Laurence Dunbar. MR

Dreiser, Theodore (1871–1945) The author of *An American Tragedy* and *Sister Carrie*, Dreiser as a child in Indiana lived a life marred by poverty and the demands of a grim and in-

tensely religious father. After one year at university, Dreiser became a journalist. *Sister Carrie*, his first novel, was considered so shocking that the publisher refused to promote it, an event that left Dreiser in a dangerous state of depression. Written in a heavy and awkward style, it described a working girl's life with unusual realism and compassion, and offended many readers by failing to punish the heroine for her mistakes.

Dreiser supported himself by editing fashion magazines and completed a second novel 11 years later. In *Jennie Gerhardt* (1911), a woman falls in love with the son of a wealthy manufacturer but sacrifices her happiness to protect her lover's social status. Dreiser's fascination with wealth and unconventional morality was developed in *The Financier* (1912) and its sequel, *The Titan* (1914), about an ambitious and unscrupulous business tycoon. Both novels were based on the life of the financier Charles Tyson Yerkes (1837–1905). The recognition Dreiser longed for did not come until 1925, when *An American Tragedy* was received with high praise by critics and the public. In it, his naturalistic view of life in America showed people to be the victims of irresistible social forces, in a society where virtue is frequently unrewarded.

Ever rebellious, and disturbed by contrasts between working people and the rich, Dreiser later became interested in socialism and devoted much of his time to social protest. He moved to Hollywood in 1939, where he completed *The Bulwark* (1946), in which a devout Quaker struggles against materialism and the decline of moral standards. If you enjoy Dreiser's novels, you may also like those of *Sinclair Lewis, Frank Norris (1870–1902), and Upton Sinclair (1878–1968), which also trace the effects of social forces on individual lives. YA

druids were the learned Celtic priests of ancient Britain, Ireland, and Gaul, existing as early as the 3rd century B.C. They served as teachers and judges as well, and had great political power. Much of what we know about them comes from Roman authors, such as *Julius Caesar, and from the Old Irish sagas. You might like to refer to *Irish Tales and Sagas*

(1981), written by Ulick O'Connor (1928–), under the title "The Druid and His Soul." *The Perilous Gard* (1974), by Elizabeth Marie Pope (1917–), set in 1558, is a fascinating novel about a young girl's discovery of an underground labyrinth inhabited by the last practitioners of druidic magic. Other novels about druids include, for younger readers, *The Stronghold* (1974) by *Mollie Hunter, and for older readers, *Druids* (1991) by Morgan Llywelyn (1937–). Turn to *Bulfinch's Mythology* for general information about druids. MR & YA

Drums Along the Mohawk (1936), by *Walter D. Edmonds, is a realistic historical novel about the American Revolution and its dramatic repercussions among the farmers of New York's Mohawk Valley. The story begins in Deerfield settlement in July 1775 and traces the long series of encounters and battles between local militia and the combined forces of British troops and American Indians. It follows the many British raiding parties sent by General Butler to harass small villages and farms. The ordeal ends five years later when Butler's army, dangerously short of food and supplies, succumbs to militia forces and is left to perish in the uncharted wilderness. These events unfold in combination with the story of young Gil Martin and his wife, Lana, whose ambition it is to establish a farm in Deerfield. The Martins and their neighbors endure great hardships during the years of war, facing starvation and the threat of death with little respite. Gil is wounded in battle, Lana bears three children, and the farmers continue to work their fields even when it means grouping together for protection from the continuing raids. The main characters are fully drawn and believable people with a fierce determination to endure and protect the land they have struggled to tame. Another novel you might enjoy that covers the same period in American history is *Arundel* by *Kenneth Roberts. *Drums Along the Mohawk* was adapted for film in 1939. YA

du Maurier, Daphne (1907–) An English author known particularly for *Rebecca* and *Jamaica Inn*, du Maurier is the granddaughter of George du Maurier (1834–1896), an artist and author. She grew up in pleasant and secure surroundings, but admits to having suffered from feelings of inferiority that caused her to spend a lot of time alone. Du Maurier was devoted to her parents' home on the coast of Cornwall, where she wrote her first novel, and has used the Cornish setting in many of her books. Her love of romance and intrigue, combined with a talent for storytelling, has characterized her entire career as an author. A suspense novel you might enjoy is *The Scapegoat* (1956), in which an Englishman is trapped into taking the place of the Frenchman he closely resembles. A movie version appeared in 1959. The short story "The Birds" (1952), filmed by Alfred Hitchcock in 1963, is a horror tale in which huge flocks of migrating birds attack a town and its inhabitants. YA

Dubliners (1914) By *James Joyce, this collection of short stories includes three titles originally published about 1904 under the pen name Stephen *Daedalus ("The Sisters," "Eveline," and "After the Race"). Joyce's first full-length work, it contains vivid, realistic tales about the lives of ordinary Dublin residents, rich in detail and often focusing on a moment of spiritual insight or revelation.

In "A Little Cloud," Little Chandler is a delicate and abstinent clerk who dreams about changing his dull routine. He feels he could write poetry, in a gently melancholy style, and enjoy a modest success. Chandler meets his old friend Gallaher, a prosperous and rather gaudy journalist, and listens with a mixture of envy and distaste to Gallaher's stories of the fast life in European cities. Chandler's vanishing hope for a more exciting career is stymied by his responsibilities for his wife and child.

"The Dead," the best known of the stories, is about Gabriel Conroy and his wife, Gretta. At the Morkan sisters' annual dance, in an atmosphere of warmth, lively conversation, and music, Gabriel makes a speech about Irish hospitality. He asks the guests to think also of the past, "of youth, of absent faces." As the Conroys leave, Gabriel sees his wife listening to an old song being performed. He is struck by her air of grace and mystery, familiar yet romantic, and feels a rush of love for her. At their hotel, Gretta tells him the song reminds her of Michael Furey, who died many years ago for love of her. The memory makes her weep, and Gabriel feels a vague terror at the intensity of the love Gretta has kept locked in her heart. He drifts into sleep thinking of the wayward and flickering existence of the dead. If you enjoy *Dubliners*, you will probably also like the short stories of *Frank O'Connor. "The Dead" was made into a film in 1987. YA

Dumas, Alexandre known as Dumas père (1802–1870) A French playwright, novelist, and author of *The Three Musketeers and *The Count of Monte Cristo*, Dumas was one of the most popular writers of his century. He was mainly self-educated, and wrote a number of well-received plays before trying his hand at historical novels. Though he has been criticized for lack of style and for the superficiality of his characters, his enormously popular books are fine examples of the storyteller's art and continue even today to appeal to a wide range of readers. Dumas also produced historical studies, travel books, and memoirs, some written as fast as possible to provide money for his extravagant tastes and illicit love affairs.

His son, **Alexandre Dumas,** called Dumas fils (1824–1895), was the author of the novel *Camille* (1848), later successfully adapted for the stage. It describes the love affair of *Marguerite Gautier, a beautiful courtesan, and was the basis of the opera *La Traviata* (1853) by Giuseppe Verdi (1813–1901). A superb film version of the novel appeared in 1936, starring the legendary actress Greta Garbo (1905–1990). YA

Dunbar, Paul Laurence (1872–1906) The first important black man of letters in American literature, Dunbar established his fame through his poems and short stories written in dialect. Dunbar was the son of former slaves. He wrote and published poetry in high school, where he was the only black student. After his first two volumes of poems were printed privately, the novelist and critic William Dean Howells (1837–1920) helped Dunbar's career by reviewing his work in highly complimentary terms. Howells also introduced Dunbar's *Lyrics of Lowly Life* (1896), which contains verse

Poet, short-story writer, and novelist
Paul Laurence Dunbar

in both dialect and standard English. Among the best-known poems are "The Ode to Ethiopia," a song in honor of his race, and "The Colored Soldiers," a reminder that black troops fought with valor in the Civil War.

Dunbar's short-story collections include *The Strength of Gideon, and Other Stories* (1900), written about the period both before and after the emancipation of the slaves. *The Sport of the Gods* (1902) is a novel about a man falsely accused of and imprisoned for theft, and the plight of his family after they leave the South for New York City.

Since the black literary renaissance of the 1960s, critics have come to feel that Dunbar's work was often misunderstood and his fine talent compromised by the need to earn a living writing for white readers. Though Dunbar has been criticized for oversentimentality and a tendency to prettify the condition of southern blacks, he was capable of protest, particularly against economic problems and injustice in the North. MR & YA

Duncan, Lois (1934–) The author of *Ransom and more than 25 other books for young readers, Duncan sold her first story to a national magazine when she was 13 years old. Many of her novels are psychological thrillers and treat such subjects as kidnapping, murder, and the supernatural. Her characters are often unconventional, and Duncan is noted for her ability to make the reader care about what happens to them. *A Gift of Magic* (1971) is about a young woman's power of extrasensory perception (ESP) and the advantages and responsibilities it brings to her. In *Summer of Fear* (1976), Rachel discovers that her orphaned cousin is a witch capable of destroying Rachel's family. *Daughters of Eve* (1979) is the name given to an elite high-school girls' club dedicated to opposing male dominance, in which a troubled club adviser seems to encourage violence. If you enjoy Duncan's novels, another writer whose books you may like is *Margaret Mahy. *Summer of Fear* was produced as a TV movie under the name *Stranger in Our House* in 1978. MR

Dune (1965), a *science fiction novel by *Frank Herbert, tells about 15-year-old Paul Atreides, whose father is murdered shortly after becoming duke of the desert planet Arrakis, or Dune. Conspirators in the murder are Emperor Shaddam IV and Baron Vladimir Harkonnen. Paul and his mother, Jessica, flee into the desert to live among the fierce warriors known as Fremen and prepare for the great power struggle that has begun. Also involved in the struggle is Jessica's religious sisterhood, the Bene Gesserit, who have sought through centuries of selective breeding to produce a Kwisatz Haderach, someone who can see into the future and the past and shape human destiny. Also involved is the Spacing Guild, which holds a monopoly on space travel. Its navigators can function only through use of spice, a mind-altering drug made by the giant sandworms of Arrakis. Paul proves himself to be the Kwisatz Haderach and leads the Fremen to victory over the Harkonnens and the emperor. The Fremen are poised to carry a jihad, or holy war, across the universe. The Dune saga is continued in five more books: *Dune Messiah* (1970), *Children of Dune* (1976), *God Emperor of Dune* (1981), *Heretics of Dune* (1984), and *Chapterhouse, Dune* (1985). *Dune* was filmed in 1984. YA

eagle A very large and powerful bird of prey, the eagle has been used for centuries as a *symbol of strength and determination. The mighty Roman legions used it as their emblem. In Christian art this bird is associated with *Saint John the Evangelist. It has appeared on the national standards of Austria, Germany, and Russia, and the Continental Congress made the white, or bald eagle the national emblem of the United States in 1782. On the other hand, *Benjamin Franklin is said to have suggested that the turkey would make a more fitting symbol for such a prosperous and peace-loving nation. When an orator gives an impassioned patriotic speech, he is said to "make the eagle scream." To have an "eagle eye" is to have excellent vision, or to have unusual intellectual foresight. You can read about eagles in a number of books, including *The Eagle in Fact and Fiction* (1966) by Johanna Johnston (1914?–1982) and *Eagles* (1985) by Joe Van Wormer (1913–). Books about the bald eagle include *The Last Eagle* (1966) by Dan Mannix (n.d.), the life story, written as a biography, of a bald eagle; and *America's Bald Eagle* (1985) by Hope Ryden (n.d.). MR & YA

ear When Mark Antony says "Friends, Romans, countrymen, lend me your ears" in *William Shakespeare's play *Julius Caesar*, he is asking for his audience's undivided attention. When you "lend an ear," "give ear to," or are "all ears," you are listening to someone or something. On the other hand, if information goes "in one ear and out the other," you are not paying attention at all. Finally, if someone complains that you are "chewing their ear off," you can be sure you are talking too much.

"Playing it by ear" refers to the ability to play music (or do anything, for that matter) instinctively, rather than by planning or training. Your favorite book may become "dog-eared" if its pages have been repeatedly folded at the corner.

One of the most famous ears of all time belonged to the Dutch artist Vincent Van Gogh, who cut off a piece of his right ear and sent it to a woman as a sign of his devotion. YA

Earth Songs (1986), by the poet Myra Cohn Livingston (1926–) is a lyrical, illustrated journey inside and around Earth. By means of colorful paintings and short verses, many natural features of the planet are described, including mountains, deserts, oceans, rain forests, volcanos, and glaciers. You are taken on a tour of the planet's natural resources and are encouraged both to learn about and preserve them. In a verse about the minerals and gems that lie beneath the earth's outer crust, you are told to "Go down! Explore!" and in a description of the rivers and streams that flow across Earth's surface, you are warned, "Dry up my waters and I will die." The environmental messages are conveyed beautifully, with brief animated text and brilliant original artwork by painter Leonard Everett Fisher (1924–). If you enjoyed *Earth Songs*, you will like the poems in **Joyful Noise: Poems for Two Voices* by Paul Fleischman (1952–). MR

Earthfasts (1967), by *William Mayne, is a story about two boys, Keith and David, who live in the rural English town of Garebridge. One evening, while walking in the hills outside of town, they see a figure rise out of the ground. The stranger turns out to be Nellie Jack John, a drummer boy who lived 200 years earlier. Nellie Jack John was exploring underground passages, searching for treasures belonging to the legendary *King Arthur, when he was inexplicably thrust into the future. Though David and Keith try to befriend the misplaced drummer boy, once Nellie Jack John realizes that he is in a vastly different world than the one he left, he returns underground. However, he leaves behind one thing: a candle whose flame is cold and never burns out.

After their encounter with Nellie Jack John, David and Keith begin to witness supernatural events, such as giants and invisible forces. David keeps the candle, which begins to hold a strange power over him. One day, while David and Keith are out in the countryside, David suddenly disappears. Keith is later discovered, unconscious. The townspeople believe that lightning struck the boys and that David was instantly killed and vaporized by the force of electricity.

Keith then keeps the candle, which begins to have a mysterious effect on him. He starts seeing images of King Arthur, who seems to want the candle. Keith realizes that the candle must be returned to its proper place in time, and that he must go underground to the place from which Nellie Jack John came. After a terrifying journey underground, Keith discovers David, who is alive, but trapped in time. As the boys head back to the present together, they encounter Nellie Jack John, who finally agrees to join them and make a new life for himself in Garebridge. If you enjoyed *Earthfasts*, you will

probably also like the books of *Susan Cooper and *Robert Westall. YA

East o' the Sun and West o' the Moon (1963) is a collection of 12 Scandinavian folk tales gathered by Peter C. Asbjörnsen (1812–1885) and Jörgen E. Moe (1813–1882) and originally published in 1845. Asbjörnsen and Moe traveled to Norway to record the tales, which were passed down through generations of Norwegian storytellers. The stories are about princesses, princes, trolls, and magic beasts, and they take place in such settings as castles, rustic cottages, and a mysterious countryside where natural forces have remarkable powers and humanlike personalities. In many of the stories, such as "The Giant Who Had No Heart," "The Blue Belt," and "Soria Moria Castle," beautiful princesses are won over by young men who perform daring and magical feats, such as conquering evil trolls. Others, like "The Cat on the Dovrefell" and the well-known "The Three Billy Goats Gruff," are about animals that also defeat gruesome trolls. Different from the other tales in both tone and subject matter is "The Husband Who Was to Mind the House," a comical tale about a man who learns that taking care of a household is not as easy as it looks. If you enjoyed this book, you may also like the folktales collected by the *Grimm brothers and by *Andrew Lang. MR

East of Eden (1952), a novel by *John Steinbeck, focuses on the life of Adam Trask, beginning with his traumatic childhood growing up with a militaristic father and a jealous, violent brother, Charles. At his father's insistence, Adam leaves home and becomes a soldier, an experience that hardens him emotionally and physically. After serving ten years in the army and spending time on a Southern road gang for vagrancy, he finally goes back home to his family's farm in Connecticut to live with Charles.

Because they have grown apart as a result of years of separation, the two brothers find life together difficult. They become further divided when a badly injured woman is found on their porch one afternoon. Adam takes care of the woman, Cathy, and quickly falls in love with her. Since Adam never questions Cathy about how she got hurt, he never learns of her dark past, filled with murder and scheming.

Adam marries Cathy and they move to Salinas, California. Though Adam refuses to admit it, Cathy is a manipulative, evil woman. After giving birth to twin boys, Cathy shoots Adam in the shoulder and leaves him forever. The twins, Aron and Cal, grow up thinking their mother is dead. However, as a teenager, Cal discovers that Cathy is alive and running a brothel right in Salinas. Cal does not reveal the truth to his brother for years until, in a fit of jealousy, he takes Aron to see Cathy, purely out of spite. Aron is so upset by this revelation that he secretly enlists in the army, in an attempt to escape his circumstances. The book ends in tragedy, with Cathy committing suicide and Adam learning that Aron has been killed in the war. The news of Aron's death causes Adam to have a stroke, and he suffers permanent physical and mental damage. In this novel Steinbeck combines his own family history with biblical themes, particularly the story of Cain and Abel. *East of Eden* was made into a movie in 1955. A TV miniseries based on *East of Eden* was made in 1986. YA

eat The act of eating is part of your everyday life, but the word "eat" also is extended to the idea of something *consuming* you, or taking you over. For instance, if something is "eating you," it is preoccupying, or consuming, your thoughts. If you are complimented, you might find yourself "eating it up," meaning that you are experiencing the kindness with great pleasure. To "eat your heart out" is to fret or worry, allowing grief or vexation to consume your thoughts. Someone who has been "eaten out of house and home" is a person whose resources have been consumed by another. Of course, not all phrases with "eat" in them suggest you are "eaten up" by something. In fact, some hint that you might want to eat as little as possible, such as to "eat your words," which means to take back, and possibly to suffer humiliation for, something previously said. Similarly, to

"eat humble pie" is to submit to humiliation. It takes more than a page to define all the meanings of "eat" in the *Oxford English Dictionary* (see also *dictionary). If you are interested in words, looking up "eat" is a good way to learn how rich our English language is.

Eckert, Allan W. (1931–) After working as a postman, detective, cook, salesman, artist, and at a number of other jobs, Eckert's writing career began when he became an associate editor of a trade magazine and later a reporter and editor at the *Dayton Journal-Herald* in Dayton, Ohio. He then became a full-time free-lance magazine writer and book author. Known for novels and narratives inspired by both history and nature, Eckert has produced works that have been called documentary fiction by fellow writers. Combining a keen interest in American history with careful research of historical documents, Eckert wrote the Winning of America series, a collection of historical narratives, including *The Frontiersmen* (1967), *Wilderness Empire* (1969), *The Conquerers* (1970), and *The Wilderness War* (1978). Though these books, which describe the conquest of the American frontier by settlers and explorers, were written for adults, they are frequently enjoyed by young readers. Eckert has also written a number of books about wildlife. One of his most popular nature novels is *Incident at Hawk's Hill.* Eckert has written more than 200 scripts for the popular TV series *Wild Kingdom,* many of which tell how particular animals live within their environments. YA

Edda refers to two books of medieval Icelandic literature. The *Prose* (c.1222) or *Younger Edda* was written by Icelandic poet and historian Snorri Sturluson (1179–1241). It is a textbook for young poets on the complex composition of early Icelandic poetry. The *Poetic* or *Elder Edda* is a collection of anonymous mythological and heroic poems dating from A.D. 800 to 1100. Twenty-four of the 38 poems that make up the *Poetic Edda* are about the legendary hero Sigurd, recounting his youth, marriage, and death. These poems are the earliest forms of the German epic *Nibelungenlied. The remainder of the poems are mythological in nature, with such sweeping themes as the creation and destruction of the universe. They provide an excellent source of information regarding the pre-Christian beliefs of the Nordic world. See also *Norse Gods and Giants by Ingri d'Aulaire (1904–1980) and Edgar Parin d'Aulaire (1898–1986), *Odin, *Valhalla, *Valkyries, and the *Völsunga Saga. YA

Eden is the abode of *Adam and Eve at their creation, as described in *Genesis, the first book of the Old Testament of the *Bible. In Eden, Adam and Eve lived a life free from cares, until they ate the forbidden fruit from the Tree of Knowledge, after which they were expelled from Eden. Eden has come to mean paradise and is used to describe any delightful or exceptionally beautiful place. It is often called the Garden of Eden. YA

Edgar Allan (1968) By *John Neufeld, this story of racial discrimination is told by 12-year-old Michael Fickett. Michael's parents, the Rev. and Mrs. Robert Fickett, adopt a 3-year-old black boy named Edgar Allan. Michael, his sister, 6-year-old Sally Ann, and brother, 3-year-old Stephen Paul, welcome Edgar Allan. But an older sister, 14-year-old Mary Nell, influenced by her friends, is horrified. The reaction in the family's community is negative but subdued until Edgar Allan is old enough to enter nursery school. Someone burns a cross on the Ficketts' lawn, and the minister's congregation threatens to dismiss him. He gives in to these threats and returns Edgar Allan to the adoption agency. Sally Ann and Stephen Paul are dismayed that their baby brother has been given away, and Michael feels his parents have betrayed him and their own ethical standards. He has to accept, however, that society does not always practice what it preaches and even a well-meaning man cannot resist certain pressures. You will learn a valuable lesson from this book, especially if you have ever been tempted to let your prejudices show. Neufeld has also written *Lisa, Bright and Dark* (1969), about a

16-year-old girl who believes she is on the verge of a mental breakdown. She goes through a painful period before her parents understand she needs psychiatric help. *Touching* (1970) is a distressing story of 16-year-old Harry trying to adjust to a new stepsister who is blind and mute as a result of cerebral palsy. *Lisa, Bright and Dark* was produced as a TV movie in 1973. MR & YA

Edisto (1984), by Padgett Powell (1952–), is about the coming of age of 12-year-old Simons in a coastal area near Charleston, South Carolina. His parents separated because of disagreements over how he should be raised, and Simons lives with his mother, a college professor. She believes he can be an important author and gives him writing assignments about the classic literature she has him read. She also allows him to go to a black nightclub any time he chooses. From his reading, Simons has the vocabulary and knowledge to hold his own in this club, but he is still puzzled by some adult behavior, especially when it is related to sex. A man appears at Simons's door who is like a father to Simons in enough ways to help him grow up into a new way of life. Simons is similar to Huck in *Huckleberry Finn* by *Mark Twain and to *Holden Caulfield in *The Catcher in the Rye* by *J.D. Salinger. He has humor and insights into how the adult world is out to steal childhood from young boys. Powell was born in Gainesville, Florida, and attended college in Charleston. *Edisto* was Powell's first novel. His second, *A Woman Named Drown* (1987), is about an affair between a young man and an aging actress. YA

Edmonds, Walter D(umaux) (1903–) This American novelist, born in Boonville, New York, brings history to life while describing upstate New York's expansive and beautiful environment. His first full-length novel for young people, *Wilderness Clearing* (1944), is the exciting tale of 16-year-olds, a boy and girl, who live in isolated clearings. Set in the Mohawk Valley, the book relates how Dick Mount and Maggie Gordon encounter the painfulness of war between the American Indians and settlers, while they also experience awkward teenage feelings. Edmonds's narrative style and talent for capturing personalities and historic scenes help make *The Matchlock Gun* an American history classic. *Drums Along the Mohawk* brings to life pioneers in the Mohawk Valley during the Revolutionary War. Edmonds's ability to write vivid historical fiction is also seen in his collection of short stories, *Mostly Canallers* (1934), a collection of wilderness adventure short stories, including "Trapper" and "Water Never Hurt a Man." When he accepted an award for *Bert Breen's Barn*, Edmonds commented, "The great children's classics belong equally to adults." A movie of *Drums Along the Mohawk* was made in 1939. If you enjoy his books, try also those of *James Lincoln Collier and *Christopher Collier and *Kenneth Roberts. MR & YA

Effect of Gamma Rays on Man-in-the-Moon Marigolds, The (1970) This play by *Paul Zindel (1936–) tells the story of a troubled family, consisting of Beatrice Hunsdorfer and her two teenage daughters, Ruth and Tillie. Beatrice is a self-indulgent, unhappy woman who feels that life has passed her by. A widow, she earns money by taking in and caring for an elderly woman, Nanny, who is completely uncommunicative. The two daughters are very different from one another. Ruth is an emotionally unstable girl, prone to sudden fits when she becomes upset. Tillie is a dreamer, fascinated by scientific discovery. The play centers around Tillie's experiment for the high school science fair, in which she grows marigolds that have been exposed to various levels of radioactivity. Though Tillie is generally shy and awkward, her enthusiasm for science enables her to blossom, and she ultimately places first at the science fair. Beatrice, who is accustomed to failure, is confused by her mixed feelings about Tillie's success. While the relationships between Beatrice, Tillie, and Ruth are strained because of their emotional problems, the play ends on a positive note, as Tillie looks toward the promise of the future with hope and excitement. If you liked this play, you may want to try another of Zindel's many books about adolescent life, such as *My Darling, My Hamburger*, a humorous look at young people's relationships, including friendship and first love; or *The Pigman*, about two high school students and a lonely old man. A movie of *The Effect of Gamma Rays* was made in 1972. YA

egg appears in many popular phrases. Because an egg is fragile there is the common phrase "tread on eggs" or "walk on eggshells," which means walk carefully or tiptoe around a delicate issue. "Do not put all your eggs in one basket" means you should not put everything (hopes, money, etc.) into one dream or venture. "Egg on your face" suggests you are in an embarrassing situation, and "to egg on" is an everyday phrase meaning to urge on, often in a teasing way. "To lay an egg" is to fail completely. After the 1929 stock market crash, *Variety*, the magazine of show business, ran the headline: "Wall Street Lays an Egg." An informal term for an intellectual is "egghead." "Easter eggs" are the brightly colored eggs hidden on Easter Sunday for children to find. If two people are "like as two eggs," they are very similar in looks. Perhaps the most famous egg of all is Humpty Dumpty in the nursery rhyme:

> Humpty Dumpty sat on a wall,
> Humpty Dumpty had a great fall.
> All the king's horses,
> And all the king's men,
> Couldn't put Humpty together again.

El Dorado is a fictitious, fabulously rich territory said to have existed along the Amazon River. El Dorado, which, in Spanish, means "the gilded one," was the legendary King of Manoa. Legend tells us that during festivals the king was covered with oil and then gold dust, until he became permanently coated in gold. Though European explorers attempted to locate this golden king for centuries, no trace of him has ever been found. The area over which he supposedly ruled became known as El Dorado, and the term has since come to mean any place of great wealth. If you would like to learn more about the legend of El Dorado, you can find a variety of books at the library. A good choice is *El Dorado, Land of Gold* (1931) by Norma Gaffron (1931–). *Edgar Allan Poe used the legend in his hauntingly beautiful poem "Eldorado" (1849). YA

Elaine, known as the Fair Elaine, loves *Lancelot, a great knight of *King Arthur's court. Because Lancelot loves *Guinevere, Arthur's queen, Elaine never wins Lancelot's love. Except for this unhappy triangle, Elaine's story differs from writer to writer. For instance, in *Alfred Tennyson's *Idylls of the King* she is a pure Victorian maiden who dies for love. But in *The Mists of Avalon* (1982) by *Marion Zimmer Bradley, Lancelot is tricked into marrying Elaine, and they have four children. In *The Once and Future King* by *T.H. White, Lancelot is also tricked into making love to Elaine. In all versions, however, the queen remains Lancelot's true love. In most stories Elaine is the mother of *Galahad. When she dies of unrequited love and grief, her body, placed on a barge and holding a letter to Lancelot, floats downriver to *Camelot, and Lancelot suffers great remorse. MR & YA

Eleanor and Franklin (1971) By Joseph P. Lash (1909–1987), this interesting biography of Eleanor Roosevelt (1884–1962), wife of U.S. President Franklin Delano Roosevelt (1882–1945), tells of the life and work of a most unusual woman. A member of an old New York family, shy and sheltered as a young woman, she was the first First Lady in America's history to become a public figure in her own right. Distant cousins, the Roosevelts were married in 1905, and Eleanor became involved in public affairs in 1920, campaigning with her husband when he ran for Vice President on the Democratic ticket. But it was after Franklin's election as President in 1932 that she acquired an almost equal stature by virtue of her writings, her lectures, and her outspoken stand on social welfare and racial discrimination. She often shocked old-fashioned, conservative people. A pacifist by instinct, she nevertheless saw the menace of fascism and worked to make America aware of the danger and the likelihood of war. Continuing her wide-ranging activities during World War II, she traveled to many military bases and hospitals in the South Pacific theater. At times Eleanor and Franklin frustrated each other, especially when she put pressure on him in support of a worthy cause, but together they led a life of accommodation and mutual respect. This book is a notable accomplishment, and you will find it an inspiration to read. Lash served in the Army in World War II and, after the war, was active in liberal politics, being a founder of Americans for Democratic Action. A close friend of Mrs. Roosevelt, he completed his biography of her with *Eleanor: The Years Alone* (1972). A TV movie of *Eleanor and Franklin* was made in 1976. YA

Electra is the daughter of *Agamemnon and Clytemnestra and sister of *Orestes in Greek mythology. According to the famous myth, when Agamemnon returned from battle in Troy, he was murdered by Clytemnestra and her lover, Aegisthus. Electra sent her brother, Orestes, away to safety, while she was kept in a state of virtual slavery by her mother and Aegisthus. Electra continually spoke out against her mother, calling her a murderer and an adulterer. Eight years after Agamemnon's death, Orestes returned and Electra convinced him of the need to avenge their father's murder. Orestes pretended he was a messenger, entered the palace, and killed both his mother and Aegisthus. Versions of this story can be found in plays by the three great Greek dramatists, *Sophocles, *Euripides, and *Aeschylus. *Mourning Becomes Electra* (1931), a trilogy by playwright *Eugene O'Neill, is a retelling of the myth, set in 19th-century New England. In modern psychology, an "Electra complex" is a condition in which a daughter is attracted to her father and hostile toward her mother. A movie of *Mourning Becomes Electra* was produced in 1947. See also *Oedipus. YA

Electric Kool-Aid Acid Test, The (1968) Hilarious or shocking, depending on your point of view, this report on the drug culture of the 1960s, by *Tom Wolfe, tells about the wild ad-

MR = Middle Reader   YA = Young Adult Reader   * = See this main entry

ventures of the Merry Pranksters, a group of
hippies led by *Ken Kesey. A shifting assortment of young people gathered around Kesey
in La Honda, California, dressing and behaving
weirdly as a protest against society. At the center of their way of life was the use of drugs,
mostly LSD, also known as acid, and marijuana. The book is a factual account, written
in the style Wolfe calls "new journalism," of
some of the Pranksters' adventures. One is the
story of their trip to New York City and back
in an old school bus, which they had painted
in psychedelic colors and wired for the greatest
amount of sound possible. There is also an account of the time some Hell's Angels, a notorious motorcycle gang, visited the Merry
Pranksters for several days, giving the residents
of La Honda a terrible fright. Another time, the
Pranksters went to a concert by the Beatles in
San Francisco but got "bad vibrations" and left
in the middle of it. The latter part of the book
tells of Kesey's arrest and imprisonment on
drug charges. Reading this book is an odd experience in itself. As the author says, "I have tried
not only to tell what the Pranksters did but
to re-create the mental atmosphere of subjective reality of it." If you enjoyed this book, try
also the books of *Jack Kerouac, whose life
and writings were important influences on
Kesey and the Pranksters. See also *Beat
Generation. YA

Elijah (Elias) (fl. 9th century B.C.) One of the
greatest prophets of the Old Testament of the
*Bible, Elijah was the center of many miracu-
lous events. He lived when *Ahab was king of
Israel and perpetrator of evil deeds. After Elijah
predicted a long drought because of the sins of
Ahab and his wife, *Jezebel, he was forced to
flee to the wilderness, where he was fed by ravens sent by God. Later he met a widow who
had little grain or cooking oil, but Elijah made
it last for many days, and also restored to life
the widow's dead son. Elijah confronted worshipers of *Baal who were unable to get their
god to set fire to a sacrificial altar, but Elijah's
God of Israel did so. Finally, according to biblical tradition, Elijah ascended directly to

George Eliot

heaven without dying, in a chariot of fire accompanied by a whirlwind. He was succeeded
as a prophet by Elisha.

Eliot, George (1819–1880) Born Mary Ann
Evans, George Eliot grew up a serious girl in a
religious home in Warwickshire, England. By
the time she was in her teens, she was both
adept at French and an accomplished pianist.
When Eliot was 16 years old, her mother died
and she had to care for her father and maintain
a household. She managed, however, to continue her intellectual pursuits and, when she
was 21 years old, she published her first poem.
Eliot then embarked on a career in writing,
first translating religious volumes, then editing the *Westminster Review*, and, finally, writing novels. Among her best-known novels are
Silas Marner and *Middlemarch*, which is
considered a masterpiece of 19th-century English fiction.

Evans's long-term relationship with G(eorge)
H(enry) Lewes (1817–1878), another English
writer, was considered scandalous because

Lewes was married to another woman. As a result, Evans adopted the pen name George Eliot so that her work would be considered on its own merits, rather than be associated with her personal life. If you enjoy Eliot's books, try also those of *Thomas Hardy. YA

Eliot, T(homas) S(tearns) (1888–1965) This American-born English poet, critic, and playwright, with *Ezra Pound and *William Butler Yeats, helped to lay the foundation of modern poetry. Eliot's poem, *The Waste Land* (1922), which uses the legend of the *Holy Grail to examine modern Western values, is often called the most influential poem of the early 20th century. His first volume of verse, *Prufrock and Other Observations* (1917), contains the work that launched his career as a poet, "The Love Song of J. Alfred Prufrock" (1915). Written when he was a student at Harvard, the poem explores the decay of modern life. Other collections of his poetry followed, notably, *Four Quartets* (1943), which contains four long meditative poems. His first book of criticism, *The Sacred Wood* (1920), and especially an essay from it, "Tradition and the Individual Talent," will help you understand Eliot's view of the nature of poetry. His most popular play is probably *Murder in the Cathedral* (1935), about the assassination of Thomas à Becket (1118?–1170), archbishop of Canterbury. Much of Eliot's poetry is difficult, but you will certainly enjoy his lighter verse, especially *Old Possum's Book of Practical Cats* (1939), on which the popular musical comedy *Cats* (1982) is based. Eliot won the Nobel Prize for literature in 1948 "for his work as a trail-blazing pioneer of modern poetry." *Murder in the Cathedral* was made into a film in 1951. YA

Elizabeth Bennet See *Pride and Prejudice*.

Ellison, Ralph (Waldo) (1914–) Though known as a novelist and critic, Ellison first studied music, believing it was the "only art that seemed to offer some possibility for self-definition." He later discovered that through writing he could record and preserve the value of African-American life. He contributed stories and essays to a variety of magazines before he wrote *Invisible Man*, the novel on which his reputation as an outstanding writer rests. Ellison also wrote *Shadow and Act* (1964), a collection of autobiographical essays. He is currently working on a second novel, excerpts of which have been published in various journals. It is apparently set in the South and covers the period from the Jazz Age (the 1920s) to the civil rights movement. If you enjoy Ellison's books, you will probably also like those of *James Baldwin and *Richard Wright. YA

Elysian Fields, or Elysium, is the abode of the blessed in Greek mythology. According to classical mythology, good and heroic individuals were considered exempt from death. Instead of dying, they went to the Elysian Fields, an afterworld where life continued in a state of bliss. It has been contrasted with Tartaros, an afterworld of torment, separated from Elysium by a river. In *Homer's *Odyssey*, Elysium is located on a plain at the end of the earth, "where life is easiest to man." If you are interested in learning more about Greek mythology, you will find *Greek and Roman Mythology* (1977) by D.M. Field (1938–) interesting, while young readers will enjoy *The Macmillan Book of Greek Gods and Heroes* (1985) by Alice Low (1926–). YA

Macavity the Mystery Cat, in *Old Possum's Book of Practical Cats* by T.S. Eliot

MR = Middle Reader   YA = Young Adult Reader   * = See this main entry

Ralph Waldo Emerson

Emerson, Ralph Waldo (1803–1882) Few other persons have had as much influence on American culture as this essayist and poet, who was a product of the New England tradition of duty to life and to thought. Emerson's published writings began with the influential essay *Nature* (1836), which asserts that the proper appreciation of nature brings spiritual truth. It expresses the basic ideas of Transcendentalism, which denies the value of a purely rationalistic view of life and thought, instead calling for reliance on intuition and direct experience, and emphasizing truth, beauty, and goodness as found in nature. Notable among Emerson's writings are *The American Scholar* (1837), in which he calls for a distinct American culture, led by those who would act as well as think; *Essays, First and Second Series* (1841, 1844), with such titles as "Self-Reliance," "Prudence," "Experience," and "Character"; and *Representative Men* (1850), consisting of biographical sketches of important men, such as *Plato, *William Shakespeare, and Napoleon I (1769–1821), emperor of France, and intended to show how their lives reflected the spirit of their times. From his home in Concord, Massachusetts, Emerson became the acknowledged leader of American philosophy. He and other writers founded *The Dial* (1840–1844), a quarterly magazine, to provide an outlet for their philosophical ideas. Among this group was Emerson's friend *Henry David Thoreau.

Most of Emerson's poetry is philosophical and intended to be inspiring, as in "Each for All" (1839), about the beauty of nature. As a poet, he is known best for "Concord Hymn" (1837), about the Battle of Lexington and Concord, the first conflict of the American Revolution, beginning with the familiar lines:

> By the rude bridge that arched the flood,
> Their flag to April's breeze unfurled,
> Here once the embattled farmers stood,
> And fired the shot heard round the world.

If you enjoy Emerson's writings, you will also like those of his friend *Henry David Thoreau. YA

Emma (1816) One of the six major works of *Jane Austen, this novel is considered the best example of her ability to reflect with wit and understanding the world of the well-to-do in early 19th-century England. The central character is Emma Woodhouse, pretty, clever, not quite 21 years old, who is mistress of her widowed father's home near London. She is also somewhat of a busybody, with too little to do to keep her amused, and so she takes it on herself to foster marriages among her friends and acquaintances as she sees fit. Emma first takes under her wing 17-year-old Harriet Smith. She does not think Robert Martin, a worthy young farmer, is good enough for Harriet and tries to promote marriage with the Rev. Philip Elton, the local vicar. But Elton does not like Harriet and, in fact, wishes to wed Emma. Frank Churchill, a well-mannered but shallow young man, appears on the scene, and Emma fancies he is attracted to her. However, she attempts to interest him in Harriet, but Harriet misunderstands. She thinks Emma is pointing her at George Knightley, who is Emma's brother-in-law. Actually, Emma is attracted to Knightley, which she finds out when Harriet indicates she hopes to marry him. Emma is further embarrassed to find that Churchill is already engaged. She finally sees that Harriet and Martin should indeed be man and wife. She has been "presumptuous and silly, and self-deceived," but all is well when Knightley proposes. They are married and, you are told, live in "perfect happiness." *Emma* is a delight to read, slowly, so as to enjoy all the subtle tongue-in-cheek touches Austen applies to her characters' actions and conversations. YA

Emperor Jones, The (1921)

Emperor Jones, The (1921) The downfall of Brutus Jones, a corrupt dictator on a Caribbean island, is the focus of this play by *Eugene O'Neill. Jones arrives on the island after escaping from prison in the United States. He deceives the natives into believing that he is a powerful leader and proceeds to take advantage of his position as emperor. As a result, Jones becomes very wealthy, while the island natives remain poor and powerless. Finally, the natives decide to revolt. They run away to the outlying hills to prepare for the emperor's overthrow. When Smithers, Jones's assistant, warns Jones of this development, the emperor describes a getaway plan he has had prepared for some time. He confidently sets off into the forest that leads to the island's coast, planning to escape via a French ship heading for the island of Martinique. His plans meet with obstacles as he becomes disoriented in the darkness of the woods and loses his way. He also finds himself haunted by memories of the wrongs he has committed during his criminal past and ends up firing his pistol at a variety of imagined persons. Instead of making the easy getaway he had planned, Jones winds up back at the point at which he first entered the woods, where he is overcome by armed natives and shot dead. If you enjoyed this play, try also O'Neill's play *The Hairy Ape* (1922), which centers on the tragic life of Yank, a coal stoker on an ocean liner. A movie was made of *The Emperor Jones* in 1933. YA

Enchantress from the Stars (1970)

Enchantress from the Stars (1970), by *Sylvia Engdahl, is the story of how Andrecia, a young and undeveloped planet, is saved by the Federation, a highly advanced society in which war and sickness do not exist and people can communicate without even speaking out loud. The Federation observes and protects the natural development of young planets. When the Federation finds out that Andrecia is about to be conquered by hostile Imperials, Elana sets off as a stowaway with her father and Everk, who are Federation agents, to try to stop the Imperials.

When the agents reach Andrecia, the Imperials are clearing land in order to build colonies. The native Andrecians think that the machine being used to clear the land is a dragon. Every day, brave Andrecians head out to slay the "dragon," only to be stunned and captured by the Imperials. The agents decide to teach one of the Andrecians some of their advanced mental powers, thinking they will frighten the Imperials away. They select Georyn, a bright and curious Andrecian, who had set out with his brothers to challenge the dragon. Elana convinces Georyn that she is an enchantress and teaches him magic that will help him in his quest.

Elana accompanies Georyn when he goes to face the dragon, and they are both captured by the Imperials. Rather than betray the Federation, Elana attempts to sacrifice herself by running underneath the powerful land-clearing machine. Georyn, however, uses all the powers Elana has taught him and stops the machine from killing her. Shocked and frightened, the Imperials decide to leave Andrecia and colonize a different planet. The Federation's goal is achieved, and though Elana realizes she loves Georyn, she must leave Andrecia and return to the Federation. A sequel is *The Far Side of Evil* (1971). YA

Encounter at Easton (1980)

Encounter at Easton (1980), a historical novel by *Avi, takes place in 1768 in a newly settled part of Pennsylvania. Told through the recorded testimony of three men and a boy, the story concerns two young runaways. Elizabeth Mawes and Robert Linnly, both about 12 years old, are convicted felons from England who have been sold to a gentleman of Trenton as indentured servants, to remain under his control until they are 21 years old. Together, Elizabeth and Robert escape from their owner and take the road to Easton, but Elizabeth's arm is badly injured when they cross the Delaware River. When Elizabeth becomes seriously ill, Robert finds shelter with the outcast woman known as Mad Moll, in her cavelike dwelling near Easton. By coincidence Nathaniel Hill, the man sent to find the runaways, meets Robert in Easton and offers him a modest job. When Robert finally realizes the nature of the man's mission, it is too late to stop Hill from finding Elizabeth. A dramatic confrontation provides an exciting and realistic end to this fine adventure. If you enjoyed it, try also *Jump Ship to Freedom by *James Lincoln Collier and *Christopher Collier, about a black youth's struggle to escape slavery. MR

encyclopedia In one or more volumes and containing information on a wide range of subjects, encyclopedias are perhaps the most useful kinds of reference books. They supply dates of wars and other historical events; contain biographies of important persons; explain scientific subjects, such as mathematics and biology; provide geographical information; and cover such fields as art and literature. Using an encyclopedia as you read can greatly broaden the amount of information and the satisfaction you can get from almost any book.

Natural History by Pliny the Elder (A.D. 22–79), a Roman soldier and scholar, is considered the first encyclopedia. The first notable encyclopedia in English was *Cyclopaedia* (1728), edited by Ephraim Chambers (c.1680–1740), a British man of letters.

Present-day encyclopedias, which are available in updated editions, vary greatly in length. Among the multivolume sets are *The New Book of Knowledge*, *Academic American Encyclopedia*, *The Britannica Junior Encyclopedia*, *World Book Encyclopedia*, *Merit Students Encyclopedia*, *Encyclopedia Americana* (first edition published 1829–1833), *New Encyclopaedia Britannica* (first edition published 1768–1771), and *Collier's Encyclopedia* (first edition published 1949–1951). Among shorter encyclopedias are *The Volume Library* in three volumes; *The Random House Encyclopedia* and *The New Columbia Encyclopedia* in one volume; and *The Concise Columbia Encyclopedia*, the shortest of all, available in an inexpensive one-volume paperback edition.

For younger readers, two recent one-volume encyclopedias are useful. They are the *Oxford Children's Encyclopedia* (1992) and *The Random House Children's Encyclopedia* (1992).

Not encyclopedias, strictly speaking, but often useful in much the same way, are two volumes published every year: *The World Almanac* and *The Information Please Almanac*, both of which are available in inexpensive paperback editions. To learn more about encyclopedias, read *Encyclopedias: Their History Throughout the Ages* (1966) by Robert Lewis Collinson (n.d.) and *Circle of Knowledge: Encyclopedias Past and Present* (1968), edited by James M. Wells (1917–). See also *dictionary and *atlas. MR & YA

Endless Steppe, The: Growing Up in Siberia (1968) In this largely autobiographical novel by *Esther Hautzig, Esther Rudomin, an 11-year-old Polish girl, is deported with her family to Siberia during World War II. One morning, Esther and her family are taken from their home in Poland by Russian soldiers, accused of being capitalists. Esther, her parents, and her grandmother are forced into a cattle car and taken to Siberia with many other Polish families. The ride to Siberia is terrifying, as none of the prisoners are told where they are going, and the cattle cars they ride in are unbearably hot and uncomfortable.

When Esther and her family arrive in Siberia, they are treated miserably and assigned to difficult jobs, such as working in gypsum mines or tending fields. Though they never fully understand why they have been captured, the Rudomin family survives the brutal treatment, learning to get by with little food and coping with Siberia's dangerously cold climate.

Esther slowly adjusts to Siberian life, attending school, making friends, and earning money by knitting for others. She even begins to forget what her comfortable life in Poland was like before the war. However, when her father is ordered to leave Siberia and fight at the front line, Esther's world falls apart, as she fears she will never see him again.

After five years the war finally ends, and Esther, her mother, and her grandmother are reunited with her father in Poland. They realize, however, that their lives will never be the same, as they sadly discover that their homeland has been destroyed and that virtually every one of their relatives has been killed. Other novels about people caught up in World War II include *Number the Stars by *Lois Lowry and *The Silver Sword by *Ian Serraillier. MR & YA

Engdahl, Sylvia Louise (1933–) First working as a teacher, and then as a computer programmer, Engdahl eventually turned her fascination with technology and space exploration into a career as a writer of books for young people. Though her books are about topics typically found in *science fiction, such as outer space and space travel, Engdahl claims that she writes books for people who do not ordinarily read science fiction. Says Engdahl about her books, "They deal less with technological progress than with human evolution and with the spiritual values I consider important." Through her writing, Engdahl questions the place of human beings in the universe and the problems that may confront inhabitants of "hypothetical worlds." Among the books she has written are *Enchantress from the Stars and a trilogy about a human-colonized planet, This Star Shall Abide (1972), Beyond the Tomorrow Mountains (1973), and The Doors of the Universe (1981). YA

Enormous Egg, The (1956) This funny story by *Oliver Butterworth is told by Nate Twitchell, a 12-year-old boy from Freedom, New Hampshire. Nate tells how his life as a farm boy drastically changes one summer when his hen lays a huge, leathery, oblong egg. He discovers that this egg is so enormous that it fills the entire hen's nest and is too heavy for the hen to turn over regularly, as hens customarily do. Nate takes on that responsibility, and his life now centers on rotating the egg three or four times a day. News of this remarkably large egg soon reaches the newspapers, yet interest begins to dwindle as too many weeks pass and the egg remains unhatched.

Nate's favorite hobby is fishing. Because he is disappointed with his unhatched egg, he decides to go fishing one day. He begins a conversation with a nearby fisherman named Dr. Ziemer, who shows strong interest in the egg and its peculiar characteristics. As if he has an idea about what might hatch from this leathery egg, Dr. Ziemer requests that Nate call him as soon as the hatching begins. One morning during his routine farm rounds, Nate is surprised to discover that the enormous egg is gone! In its place is an odd-looking lizard-like creature. Nate immediately rounds up his family to examine the creature and phones Dr. Ziemer. Upon arriving and studying the newly hatched creature, Dr. Ziemer announces, in a trembling voice, that Nate's hen has just hatched a dinosaur!

Nate now experiences what happens once the townspeople, and then the entire country, become aware of this bizarre event—a dinosaur being hatched after they have been extinct for millions of years. You will both laugh and feel empathy for Nate as you take part in his attempts to raise his Triceratops dinosaur, Uncle Beazley, which grows to be 10 feet, 6 inches tall and weighs 1,140 pounds. You follow Nate from New Hampshire to a Washington, D.C., museum, through a senatorial debate, and finally to the zoo, where he finds the perfect home for his dinosaur. A sequel to The Enormous Egg is The Narrow Passage (1973), which is an exciting tale of two young boys in southern France. Once again, you will be caught up in the adventure as you follow their escapades to protect their discovery of a secret prehistoric cave. MR

epic refers to a long poem or story, written in an exalted style and usually centered on a heroic character and a series of great achievements or events. The earliest epics grew out of the legends of a time when nations were conquering other lands and enlarging their borders. Some examples are *Beowulf and the *Nibelungenlied, and the *Iliad and *Odyssey of *Homer. The Norse sagas, especially those concerning the exploration and settlement of Greenland and North America, may also be considered epics. There are many translations, but an excellent modern version is *The Norse Atlantic Saga* (1964) by Gwyn Jones (1907–). Later epics include *Dante's *The Divine Comedy* (c.1310–1321) and the satirical epic *Don Juan* (1819–1824) by *George Gordon Byron. YA

Episode of Sparrows, An (1956) In this novel by *Rumer Godden, Lovejoy Mason, a little girl who lives in a poor section of London, tries to plant a garden among the city's concrete and rubble. With no father, and a mother who travels the country as a singer, Lovejoy is a virtual orphan. She lives with Mr. and Mrs. Combie, who own a failing restaurant. Though the Combies are kind to her, Lovejoy feels very much alone in the world.

One day, Lovejoy finds a packet of seeds on the sidewalk and decides to plant a garden in an abandoned lot. Though she tries to hide her garden, it is discovered and trampled by a gang of neighborhood boys. Afterward, Tip, the gang's leader, feels sorry for Lovejoy and shows her a private spot behind a church where she can safely plant her garden. Tip and Lovejoy become friends and work on the garden together. Determined to have a beautiful garden, Lovejoy resorts to begging, borrowing, and, sometimes, stealing to obtain the tools and seeds she needs.

Believing that dirt is everyone's property, Tip and Lovejoy decide to take buckets of rich earth from the Square, a wealthy part of the city. The children are caught one night and brought before the police. When the truth about Lovejoy's garden comes out, Olivia, a wealthy woman from the Square, is moved by Lovejoy's efforts. Though she would like to adopt Lovejoy, Olivia is very ill and knows that

she does not have long to live. Instead, she decides to arrange her will so that the Combies will be guaranteed enough money to take care of Lovejoy. If you enjoyed this book, try also *Good-bye to the Jungle* (1965) by *John Rowe Townsend, about four English youths who struggle to keep their family together and pull it out of poverty. *An Episode of Sparrows* was produced as a movie, *Innocent Sinners*, in 1957. MR & YA

Equus (1973) Almost painfully distressing, this play by *Peter Shaffer is a brilliant dramatic presentation of a troubled young man and an almost equally troubled psychiatrist. Most of the action takes place at Rokesby Psychiatric Hospital in southern England, where Alan Strang has been sent for treatment after having stabbed out the eyes of six horses. Gradually the psychiatrist, whose marriage is a failure and who is more interested in the gods of ancient Greece than anything else, discovers why Alan committed the crime. He has probably cured Alan, but not himself. Alan's mother is obsessively religious; his father is prudish to an extreme. When Alan gets a job as a stable boy, he finds a god of his own in a horse, Nugget, whom he sees as Equus (Latin for horse) and whom he worships. Alan's descent into madness occurs when Jill, who also works at the stable, entices him there for sex. But Alan feels he is betraying the horses and that they, nearby, resent his attentions to Jill. When Nugget/Equus breaks in, Alan uses a pick to blind him and the other five, so that they cannot witness his betrayal. You will find *Equus* is movingly effective when read, but even more so as a stage production. A movie of it was made in 1977. YA

Erdoes, Richard (1912–) Born and raised in Vienna, Austria, Erdoes began his career as a magazine illustrator and photographer. It was not until he reached his 50s that he began writing magazine articles and books. As a magazine illustrator, he had been assigned to many projects in the western United States. During these travels, Erdoes became interested in the lives of Native Americans and was outraged at the living conditions he witnessed at Native American reservations. Erdoes and his family became close personal friends with many Native Americans, and his writing reflects his interest in Native American culture. Among his books, which are all self-illustrated, are *The Sun Dance People: The Plains Indians, Their Past and Present* (1972); *The Rain Dance People: The Pueblo Indians, Their Past and Present* (1976); and *Myths and Legends of the North American Indians* (1982), on which Erdoes collaborated with Alfonso Ortiz (1939–). YA

Erdrich, Louise (1954–) Her mother a Native American of the Chippewa nation and her father of German descent, Louise Erdrich grew up in a town in North Dakota and attended a Bureau of Indian Affairs boarding school. Her writings reflect this ancestral and geographical background. Erdrich's first novel, *Love Medicine* (1984), explores the relationships of two Chippewa families in North Dakota between 1934 and 1984. The book is made up of 14 stories, told by the characters who appear in the novel. In *The Beet Queen* (1986), two children, May and Karl, after being abandoned by their mother, grow up in a North Dakota town. They are white, but other characters in the book have Native American ancestry, including Dot, who becomes the "Beet Queen" of the title in this region where beets are the most important crop. The same Chippewa families that were in *Love Medicine* reappear in another novel, *Tracks* (1988). The chief figures are Fleur Pillager and Eli Kashgaw, who have a romantic attachment, but the book, which covers 1912 to 1934, is chiefly concerned with changes that take place as hunger, disease, and white people devastate the Chippewa. Erdrich's husband, Michael A. Dorris (1945–), a member of the Modoc tribe, is the author of a novel, *Yellow Raft in Blue Water* (1987), in which the story of a dying culture is told through the eyes of three generations of Native American women on a reservation in Montana. If you would like to read more books with Native American themes, try those of *Oliver La Farge and *Leslie Marmon Silko. You will also enjoy *When the Legends Die* by *Hal Borland. YA

Erewhon (1872), a novel by *Samuel Butler, is the name of a mysterious foreign land. The narrator, who remains unnamed, describes how he decided to explore beyond the farmland where he lives, hoping to discover vast new land for sheep farming. Instead, he discovers a remarkable land complete with cities and villages, universities, banks, and courthouses. Erewhon is similar in many respects to the England with which the narrator is familiar. However, he discovers striking peculiarities in the Erewhonian way of life. For example, maintaining good health is the most important objective for every citizen. Consequently, poor health is treated as a crime, and the sick are harshly punished or imprisoned. Moral offenses, however, such as stealing or cheating, are treated as illnesses, and the guilty are sent to hospitals where they are treated by physicians called straighteners. The book is composed of chapters in which the narrator describes different aspects of Erewhonian society, such as "The Colleges of Unreason" and "The Musical Banks."

The narrator is treated kindly by the Erewhonians, yet he remains a captive in their country. Eventually, he plans his escape by way of a hot air balloon. Arowhena, the Erewhonian woman he ultimately marries, accompanies him, and they miraculously reach England. The narrator plans to return someday, his goal being twofold: to persuade many of the Erewhonians to work as laborers on farms he plans to establish and to convert the Erewhonians to Christianity. If you enjoy *Erewhon*, you may want to try *Erewhon Revisited* (1901), in which the narrator returns to Erewhon 20 years after his first trip. See also *Utopia. YA

Eric (1974) As sad as it is true, this is the story of 17-year-old Eric Lund and his losing fight with leukemia, as told by his mother, Doris Lund (1919–). Eric lives with his mother and father and a younger brother and sister in suburban Connecticut. In the fall of 1967 he is about to enter college. Then comes the diagnosis that he has leukemia. A fine athlete and socially active and popular, Eric resolves to lead as normal a life as possible until the inevitable end. At first his mother is overprotective, but she changes when she understands that Eric does not want this. He is in and out of hospitals, and during one stay meets a nurse, Mary Lou, with whom he becomes close. When the disease is in remission, Eric is able to take some college courses, and even a cross-country trip by auto with a friend. But as the leukemia worsens, he spends more time in the hospital, and the disease begins to tell on his spirit. When the end comes after about four years, Eric is no longer fighting the inevitable, and his mind and spirit are at rest. You will not find this a pleasant book to read—the details of suffering are treated fully—but you will gain from learning how a young man and his family cope with death. Another extraordinary story about how a young man copes with illness and death is told in *Death Be Not Proud* by *John Gunther. A movie of *Eric* was made in 1975. YA

Eros in Greek mythology is the god of love. There exist some differences of opinion regarding Eros's background. According to one theory, Eros is the offspring of Chaos, companion to *Aphrodite, and a key figure in the creation of the universe. As such, he presides over the unions of gods and human beings, including both sensuous love and devoted friendship. A different school of thought is that Eros is the son of Aphrodite; this school pictures him as a beautiful winged boy whose arrows provoke feelings of love among gods and mortals. You may recognize a similarity between this description of Eros and Cupid, a figure you often see on cards and other items on Valentine's Day. Cupid is, in fact, the name that the Romans used to describe the god Eros. A charming myth about Eros tells about his love for Psyche, a beautiful girl who, told not to try to find out who he is, nevertheless looked at him in the light of a lamp one night. You will enjoy the story as told by Edna Barth (1914–1980) in

Cupid and Psyche: A Love Story (1976) and by I.M. Richardson (n.d.) in *The Adventures of Eros and Psyche* (1983). For more about Eros, see also *Mythology by Edith Hamilton (1867–1963). MR

Escape to Witch Mountain (1968), by *Alexander Key, is the story of a brother and sister, Tony and Tia, in search of their family. When their guardian is killed, these two odd and misunderstood orphans are sent to a detention home to live. Confused as to why they are different and not understood, Tony and Tia have the strong belief that the land they are from must be magical.

The story follows the two young people's search for their heritage, and you learn of the special powers that each one has. Tia, though unable to talk out loud with her ultrasonic speech to anyone but Tony, has a picture-perfect memory, except that she cannot remember where the two originally came from. She also has the ability to open locked doors and can easily communicate with animals. Tony, with the aid of his harmonica, can make inanimate objects, such as dolls and brooms, come to life and dance to the music that he plays. The townspeople become fearful of the children because of such strange events as their escaping from a completely locked cell, Tia's freeing and befriending a group of bears, and Tony's creating a scene of dancing objects at the local jail. Soon the whole town is caught up in a witch hunt, as they now fear that the children must be witches. Trying to escape their worst enemy, Mr. Deranian, Tony and Tia continue their search for their extraordinary ancestors with the help of their trusting friend Father O'Day and a mystical black cat named Winkie. A suspenseful and exciting story, *Escape to Witch Mountain* ends happily for the children as they are reunited with their own special kind of people. If you enjoyed *Escape to Witch Mountain*, you will like its sequel, *Return from Witch Mountain* (1978), in which Tony is kidnapped by a crazy doctor who wants his special powers. You will also enjoy Key's *science fiction story, *The Forgotten Door. Es-*

cape to Witch Mountain was filmed in 1975 and *Return from Witch Mountain* in 1978. MR

Ethan Frome (1911) by *Edith Wharton is a tragic tale of ill-fated love and unfulfilled dreams. The novel is first narrated by a visitor to the rural New England town of Starkville, who encounters an elderly Ethan Frome and wonders at his silence and strangely distant manner. The setting of the story then shifts to 24 years earlier, and Ethan's life as a young man is revealed. Ethan had lived a hard life, caring first for his father, then his mother, and finally his wife, Zeena. Zeena is a bitter woman, completely absorbed in her ill health. She spends most of her time complaining to Ethan about her various pains and about their lack of money. His life changes forever when Zeena's cousin Mattie comes to live with the Fromes and take care of the household. Ethan and Mattie fall in love, which makes Ethan all the more aware of his bleak future with Zeena.

Without consulting Ethan, Zeena hires a new girl to work around the house and demands that Mattie leave. Unable to bear the pain of being separated, Ethan and Mattie decide to take their lives together, by crashing a sled into an enormous elm tree. However, neither Ethan nor Mattie dies as a result of the accident. The reader learns, as the novel shifts back to the present, that Mattie was mentally and physically disabled by the accident and Ethan was permanently disfigured. Mattie ends up living with the Fromes, ironically under the care of Zeena, and Ethan deteriorates into the silent, suffering figure the narrator first encounters upon arriving in Starkville. If you enjoyed *Ethan Frome*, you will like Wharton's novella *Summer* (1917), about a young woman who rebels against the stifling moral atmosphere of a small New England town. You can find it in the Library of America edition of *Edith Wharton: Novellas and Other Writings* (1990). YA

Eugene Gant The hero of the novel *Look Homeward Angel* by *Thomas Wolfe, Gant is regarded as a fictionalized version of Wolfe himself. Gant is a promising but troubled young writer in conflict with family, school, and society. Wolfe's *Of Time and the River* continues the story of Gant as a student at Harvard and a teacher in New York City. Gant's name is George Webber in *The Web and the Rock* and its sequel, *You Can't Go Home Again* (1940). YA

eureka is an exclamation uttered on making a discovery. According to legend, the Greek philosopher Archimedes (c.287–212 B.C.), on his discovery of a method to determine the amount of alloy in the gold of King Hiero's crown, exclaimed, "Heureka," which was the Greek word for "I have found it." "Eureka" is the modern English form of the Greek word. Among early American settlers it was a popular name for an ideal place to live. Eureka, for example, is an important city in California. "Eureka" is the motto of the state of California, in reference to the discovery of gold there. You will find a good retelling of the story of Archimedes and the golden crown in *Archimedes and the Door to Science* (1962) by Jeanne Burdick (n.d.). It is also humorously retold in a picture book, *Mr. Archimedes' Bath* (1980), by Pamela Allen (1934–). MR

Euripides (c.484–406 B.C.) was the latest born of ancient Greece's three famous dramatists, following *Aeschylus and *Sophocles. During his lifetime, Euripides was considered something of an eccentric, possibly due to his reflective, bookish nature. His plays differed greatly from those of Aeschylus and Sophocles, who worked within the accepted beliefs of their times. Euripides questioned the attitudes of his fellow Athenians, including their chauvinistic view of women, their unjust treatment of illegitimate children, and the widespread glorification of war. Euripides also questioned the Athenian belief that gods maintained the order of the universe. In his plays, the heroic, legendary figures of ancient Greece were represented as everyday mortals. Euripides' plays are noted for the humanity of their themes and characters, a quality that contributes to their continuing popularity today. Of the 92 plays Euripides wrote, only 17 survive, among them *Electra* (413 B.C.), his version of the *Electra myth; *Medea* (431 B.C.), about the tragic love of the princess and sorceress *Medea for the hero *Jason; and *The Trojan Women* (415 B.C.), a play that reflects Euripides' disapproval of the Athenians' treatment of the Trojans during the *Trojan War. YA

Evangeline, A Tale of Acadie (1847) This tragic narrative poem by *Henry Wadsworth Longfellow is based on an incident of the French and Indian War, when the French and the British were struggling for what is now Nova Scotia, in eastern Canada, and which the French called Acadia. During the war the British exiled the French inhabitants, shipping them to various other British colonies in North America. In the poem the forced removal occurs just before Evangeline Bellefontaine is to be married to Gabriel Lajeunesse. She is sent to New England, but Gabriel ends up far away in Louisiana. They try for a long

Evangeline

time to find each other. Evangeline becomes a nurse in Philadelphia. During an epidemic there she discovers that a dying man she is caring for is Gabriel. The shock kills her and they are at last united in death and buried side by side. Modern readers may find the poem, told in the romantic style of the mid-19th century, a bit of a tear-jerker, but it remains nevertheless quite powerful. You can learn more about Evangeline in the book *Evangeline and the Acadians* (1957) by Robert Tallant (1909–1957). MR & YA

Eve See *Adam and Eve.

Everyman (c.1500) is the most famous of the *morality plays, a body of religious drama performed in medieval England. *Everyman* is about the human tendency to favor wealth, possessions, and pleasure over goodness and religious devotion. Pleasure-seeking Everyman, who represents all of humankind, is summoned by Death. Death tells Everyman that he must account for his life before God and leave his life on earth forever. Desperate, Everyman turns to the symbolic characters of Fellowship, Kindred, and Cousin, hoping that they will stand by him in his time of need. When they learn of Everyman's fate, however, they refuse to help him. Everyman then looks to his material possessions for comfort. As his possessions are partially to blame for his predicament, they cannot help him. Characters representing Beauty, Strength, Discretion, and the five senses also refuse when Everyman asks them to accompany him on his journey to death. The only characters who agree to help Everyman are Knowledge, Confession, and Good Deeds. Knowledge forces Everyman to recognize his sins, Confession allows Everyman to cleanse himself of his sins, and Good Deeds teaches Everyman to practice charity and good will. By asking God for forgiveness and by punishing himself for his sins, Everyman is able to account for his life without fear and is permitted to enter heaven. See also *symbolism. YA

Excalibur is the name of *King Arthur's famous sword. According to Arthurian legend,

MR = Middle Reader   YA = Young Adult Reader   * = See this main entry

Excalibur was fixed in a block of stone, only to be withdrawn finally by the true king of England. When Arthur accomplishes this feat, he proves his right to the English throne. In *Le Morte d'Arthur* (c.1469), by *Thomas Malory, Excalibur is given to Arthur by the Lady of the Lake. As Arthur dies, he tells Bedivere to return Excalibur to the lake. When Excalibur is thrown into the lake, it is received by an arm that rises out of the water, presumably that of the Lady of the Lake. Younger readers will enjoy reading about young Arthur and Excalibur in *The Sword in the Stone* by *T.H. White. See also *King Arthur by *Walter Scott. MR & YA

excelsior is a Latin word whose literal meaning is "higher," and which in modern usage implies an ever-upward striving. It is the motto of New York State. In literature its best-known use is as the title of a poem (1841) of nine four-line verses, each ending with the refrain "Excelsior," by *Henry Wadsworth Longfellow. Its first verse reads:

The shades of night were falling fast,
As through an Alpine village passed
A youth, who bore, 'mid snow and ice,
A banner with a strange device—Excelsior!

The youth is warned of the dangers ahead, but he persists in his quest, reaching the top of the mountain, but dying there. In terms of broader meaning, the poem exalts the person who will persevere even at the risk of his or her life, and who will thereby become immortal. MR & YA

existentialism is more a group of similar philosophies than one definite school of thought. Though mostly a 20th-century European movement, its roots go back primarily to Søren Kierkegaard (1813–1855), a Danish philosopher and religious thinker, and to the German philosopher Friedrich Nietzsche (1844–1900). More recently, the most prominent existentialist has been Jean-Paul Sartre (1903–1980), a French dramatist, novelist, and critic. Existentialism holds that a human being is free and is duty bound to make what he or she can of life. The question of whether or not there is a god is, for some existentialists, irrelevant. However, a Jewish-Christian school of existentialism holds that God exists but that His purpose cannot be known. A leading figure in reconciling religious faith with existentialism was the German philosopher Martin Buber (1878–1965), whose book *I and Thou* (1923) has remained influential. A purely intellectual approach is not enough for an existentialist; the self must be fully committed to making its way in a world that may have no purpose. Existentialism is not political except to the extent that it is opposed to anything that limits human freedom. Among authors who have been associated with existentialism, as seen in their works, are *Saul Bellow, *Albert Camus, *Fyodor Dostoyevsky, *Ralph Ellison, and *William Faulkner. If you would like to learn more about existentialism, a well-written, clear account is *Introduction to Existentialism* (1984) by Marjorie Glicksman Grene (1910–). YA

Exodus This second book of the Old Testament of the *Bible is interesting for the dramatic events it recounts and for its importance in the historical tradition of Israel and Judaism. Exodus begins with an account of the Jews in Egypt in the 13th century B.C., before the birth of *Moses. The present text did not begin to be composed until c.850 B.C. Led by Moses, the Israelites escaped from slavery in Egypt c.1225 B.C. and began 40 years of wandering in the wilderness of Sinai. During their time there they were, according to tradition, fed by "manna," God having promised to "rain bread from heaven." Manna may have come from several species of plants, though another theory holds that it was the sweet secretion of a certain plant insect. The most important events in Exodus are the revelation of God to Moses in a burning bush, and the handing down to Moses of the *Ten Commandments. The Jewish festival of Passover celebrates the escape from Egypt. Today an unexpected but welcome gift is "manna from heaven."

eye Because you use your eyes to see, many phrases using the word "eye" have to do with the way things appear. "A sight for sore eyes" is something or someone whose appearance is very welcome or pleasing. When you say "There is more in that than meets the eye," you mean that there is more to a situation than what appears on the surface. Something seen "in your mind's eye" is something that appears to you mentally, rather than visually. Among the many emotions that your eyes can express are feelings of love for another. "To make eyes at" means to look lovingly at someone, while "the apple of one's eye" is someone or something held extremely dear. Some phrases about eyes are clearly not to be taken literally, such as "Keep your eyes peeled" or "Keep your eye on it," both of which direct you to be particularly watchful. By the way, a private detective, someone who keeps an eye on things for you, is often called a "private eye."

Eye of the Heron, The (1978) In this *science fiction story by *Ursula K. Le Guin, two very different societies leave Earth and settle on a planet called Victoria. The larger, more powerful of these societies is based on violence and fear, and its members inhabit the City, a cold urban environment. The other society consists of peace-loving people who believe in cooperation and mutual understanding among citizens. This second society settles in Shanty Town, a farming community located a few miles from the City.

Luz, the daughter of Councillor Falco, the most powerful man in the City, is very unhappy with her life. Like all women in the City, she is allowed very little freedom. All that is expected of her is that she marry and have children. Luz becomes friends with Vera, a revolutionary Shanty Towner who is being held prisoner at the Falco residence. Through her friendship with Vera, Luz begins to realize how controlled and cruel life in the City is compared with the freedom of Shanty Town. When she overhears that an army of men from the City are planning to attack Shanty Town, she runs away and warns the innocent residents of the rural community. Afterward, she realizes that because of her betrayal, she cannot return to the City. Luz, therefore, decides

to spend her life with the peaceful people of Shanty Town and ultimately helps them establish a new settlement far beyond the violent reach of the City. If you enjoyed this book, try also the classic novel *Fahrenheit 451 by *Ray Bradbury, which also explores the themes of repression and freedom. YA

Eyes of the Amaryllis, The (1977) In this story by *Natalie Babbitt, 12-year-old Jenny's visit to her grandmother's house at the seashore turns into a mysterious adventure. Thirty years earlier, Gran watched from the shore as her husband's ship, the *Amaryllis,* was swallowed by the sea during a hurricane. Not long after, Gran met Nicholas, a boy who was thought to have drowned in the sea. Nicholas told her that the sea spared him, but while underwater, he saw sailors and ships on the ocean floor, protecting the sea's treasures. He told Gran that he was spared on the condition that he guard the sea and return anything taken from it.

Gran believes that her husband, the Captain, will try to send her a sign of his everlasting love from the bottom of the sea, and she searches the beach every day for this sign. When a broken leg keeps her from walking the beach, Gran instructs Jenny to carry on this daily ritual. Jenny discovers the figurehead from the *Amaryllis,* a carved likeness of Gran as a young woman, and Gran takes this as her long-awaited sign. Though Nicholas warns Gran that she must return the ornament to the sea, she refuses. Soon, a hurricane rolls in. The sea rises, the wind tears at Gran's house, and, just when Gran is about to return the ornament and offer herself to the sea, Jenny's father arrives and rescues them from the storm. Gran agrees to live with Jenny's family until her home is repaired. However, just as the three are about to leave, a red amaryllis blossom floats ashore, convincing both Gran and Jenny that the Captain has indeed sent a sign. Another story involving the sea, a family, a mystery, and the supernatural is *The Tricksters by *Margaret Mahy. MR & YA

fable is a story, usually but not always about animals with human qualities, that illustrates some moral truth or wisdom. The familiar fable of "The Fox and the Grapes," for example, suggests that people will belittle what they cannot get. The fox, after using all his wiles to reach the grapes hanging beyond his reach, concludes that they are sour anyway. Though fables have been discovered even among the Egyptian papyri (1500 B.C.), the development of the fable is most often associated with the Greek slave *Aesop. The French fabulist *Jean de La Fontaine made perhaps the most celebrated collection of fables. *Uncle Remus fables by *Joel Chandler Harris celebrate the exploits of Brer Rabbit. *Animal Farm by *George Orwell and *"The Lottery" by *Shirley Jackson are more up-to-date examples of fables, and *Walt Disney's cartoons bring to young and old alike fresh meaning to what fables can be. MR & YA

Faerie Queen, The (Books I–III, 1590; Books IV–VI, 1596) An *epic *allegory in six books by *Edmund Spenser, *The Faerie Queen* is set during the age of chivalry, when the romance of knighthood reigned. It is generally considered one of the most noteworthy long poems in the English language. Each book, composed of 12 cantos or divisions, is written in nine-line stanzas, called the Spenserian stanza. Though originally designed to consist of 12 books, each

ennobling a specific virtue, the poem was never completed. Gloriana, the Fairy Queen, is holding her annual feast to which anyone in trouble could come. As the poem begins, the Red Cross Knight, representing Holiness, has already been sent by the queen on his adventure to rescue the parents of the virgin Una from a menacing dragon. In Book II, Sir Guyon, Knight of Temperance, in spite of temptations, finds temperance and destroys the Bower of Bliss. Book III recounts the Legend of Britomart, or Chastity; Book IV of Friendship; Book V of Justice; and Book VI of Courtesy. Prince Arthur, the legendary English king, unifies the work as the "image of a perfect knight." If you enjoy epic poetry, you should explore the *Odyssey by *Homer, a tale of Odysseus' long journey home after the *Trojan War, or *The Divine Comedy* (1321) by *Dante Alighieri, the tale of a Christian traveler's journey through Hell, Purgatory, and Paradise. YA

Fahrenheit 451 (1953), a *science fiction novel by *Ray Bradbury, presents a frightening glimpse of a future society in which thinking is discouraged and books are forbidden. Guy Montag is a fireman whose primary function is not to douse fires but to start them in order to burn all books and any houses that contain books. When Montag meets Clarisse, a charming 17-year-old girl who is filled with wonder at the beauty of nature and the mystery of human thought, he begins to question his unfeeling society and the role he plays in it. On one of his midnight runs to burn books, Montag retrieves one volume. Soon enough, he renounces the mind-numbing world he has so long been a part of. Authorities attempt to burn his home next, but Montag escapes.

With a professor's help, he leaves the city and finds others who have also rejected the dehumanization of society. To keep literature and thought alive, each has committed to memory an important book. Montag and his new associates watch as the city burns in the distance. Then they move on to start a new society.

The theme explored in *Fahrenheit 451*, of thought control through the control of language, communication, and memory, is also at the center of the novel **1984* by *George Orwell. *Fahrenheit 451* was adapted for film in 1967. YA

Fall, The (1956) A short novel by the French writer *Albert Camus, *The Fall* is a dramatic monologue of Jean-Baptiste Clamence, once a highly respected attorney who pleaded cases for the Parisian poor, but is now a habitué of the slums of Amsterdam, the Netherlands. Two incidents account for his "fall": witnessing a young woman's suicide and doing nothing to help her, and years later hearing a mysterious laugh that seemed to mock him. He becomes haunted by the laugh and plagued by guilt. Even before these incidents, he had begun to see himself as a morally hollow man, feeling no love for others, and doing acts of kindness only to be admired. He believed the world detected his insincerity and continually judged him. Hungering for innocence, he abandoned his bourgeois life and moved to Amsterdam where, at a bar in the slums, he nightly confesses the falseness of his life. Ironically, the "I" of his monologue soon becomes a "we," for Clamence believes in his listeners' guilt as well and wishes them to acknowledge the moral duplicity of their own lives. By including other human beings in his guilt, he can feel less judged by them. You may wish to compare the

character of Clamence with that of another of Camus's introspective protagonists, Meursault, in **The Stranger*. YA

"Fall of the House of Usher, The" (1839) Written by *Edgar Allan Poe, this short story is characteristic of many of his stories because it is filled with eerie supernatural elements. It is set in the old *Gothic house of Roderick and his twin sister, Madeline, the only descendants of the Usher family. Responding to a desolate letter from Roderick, the narrator travels to the Ushers' house, where he is nearly overwhelmed with its melancholy. It appears to him that the house almost has a life of its own. He reunites with Roderick and finds that his young friend is in no better shape than the house. "Surely, man had never before so terribly altered, in so brief a period, as had Roderick Usher!" The narrator unsuccessfully attempts to revive Roderick's spirit, which is afflicted by a nervous condition that has heightened the sensitivity of all his senses. Madeline is overcome by her own mysterious disease, and when she dies, Roderick's condition worsens. They bury her in a fortified dungeon tomb in the depths of the mansion. Several nights later, unable to sleep in what he is becoming convinced is a haunted house, the narrator rises and encounters a disturbed Roderick. As he attempts to console Roderick by reading him a book, the sounds of the story, in which the hero forces his way into a dragon's lair, are mirrored by the haunting sounds of Madeline attempting to break out of her tomb. With a gust of wind, the doors to the chamber fly open, and a bloodied Madeline stands at the doorway. She falls dying onto Roderick, who dies from what he anticipated he would die from—fear. The narrator rushes out of the house, aghast. When he turns back, he sees the house collapse. If you enjoyed this story, read *"The Cask of Amontillado," another excellent and chilling tale by Poe. Two films, both titled *House of Usher*, were produced in 1960 and 1988, and a TV movie called *The Fall of the House of Usher* was made in 1982. MR & YA

Fallen Angels (1988) by *Walter Dean Myers is a novel about Vietnam as seen through the eyes of a black teenager from Harlem. Richard Perry enlisted in the army because he could not afford to go to college. Though he is in 'Nam for less than a year, his life is forever changed by the experience. Assigned to Alpha Company, Perry joins ranks with other young men like himself: Peewee, brown-skinned with red hair and freckles, from the projects of Chicago, who is at first satisfied with 'Nam because for the first time in his life he gets what everybody else gets; Jenkins, who is scared that he will never see home again; Monaco, a sweet-faced fellow whose life Perry and Peewee later save; Brew, who helps Perry to pray; and Lieutenant Carroll, who not only cares for his men but gives Perry his new black silk jacket to send home to his younger brother, Kenny, for his birthday. On Perry's first patrol, Jenkins is killed by a mine. Perry is numb: "Jenkins was walking with me and talking with me only hours before. Seeing him like that grabbed something inside my chest and twisted it hard."

Vietnam for Perry and the others is a nightmare of almost incomprehensible violence and brutality. But it is also about the brotherhood of young men who put their lives on the line for each other, share their fears and laughter, and bind themselves forever as "spit" brothers. After being wounded twice and receiving two Purple Hearts, Perry is sent back home, another world. Peewee, also wounded, sits next to him on the plane. There, as they had in the darkness of a cave waiting for the Vietcong to attack, they hold hands as they leave the war behind them. Though the wars are vastly different, the comradeship is reminiscent of that felt by Paul Baumer and his World War I comrades in *All Quiet on the Western Front* by *Erich Maria Remarque. Older readers might also explore other novels of Vietnam: *Dispatches* (1978) by Michael Herr (1940?–), *Going After Cacciato* (1978) by *Tim O'Brien, and *Born on the Fourth of July* (1990) by Ron Kovic (1946–). MR & YA

Falstaff, Sir John *William Shakespeare's boastful and obese knight and most famous comic character, Falstaff is a glutton, drunkard, coward, braggart, liar, and thief. But he is as witty as he is wily and is possessed of extraordinary charm. In *Henry IV*, Part 1 (1598), he is a drinking companion of young Prince Hal (later King Henry V). Falstaff and his cronies carouse at the Boar's Head Tavern and also rob highway travelers. However, in a practical joke, Hal and others rob the robbers. Back at the tavern, Falstaff exchanges witticisms with Hal and exaggerates the number of thieves who attacked him. The prince accuses him of gross falsehood, but the slippery knight proves to be an "*artful dodger." Later, Falstaff claims to have killed the valorous rebel Hotspur (actually slain by Prince Hal). In *Henry IV*, Part 2 (1600), he escapes paying his debt to Mistress Quickly as well as £1,000 he has borrowed from Justice Shallow. Eventually, Falstaff is broken-hearted to find himself denounced by his former companion Prince Hal, now the sober Henry V. His despondency and death are reported in *Henry V* (1599). Falstaff also appears in *The Merry Wives of Windsor* (1602), but no longer a resourceful and energetic character, he becomes a laughingstock. His reputation as the greatest comic figure in literature rests primarily on the Henry IV plays. YA

fantasy is used to describe novels dealing with spiritual or unnatural events or characters. One of the best-known fantasy series is *J.R.R. Tolkien's *The Lord of the Rings*, in which the setting is the fantasy world of *Middle-Earth. *Alice's Adventures in Wonderland* and *Through the Looking-Glass* by *Lewis Carroll are other well-known fantasy stories. *J.M. Barrie's play, *Peter Pan, or The Boy Who Would Not Grow Up* takes us to *Neverland, where children stay eternally young. In his whimsical *satire *The Hitchhiker's Guide to the Galaxy* (1980), British author *Douglas Adams creates a bizarre fantasy world where the improbable usually happens. The meaning of the word has changed over time. As late as the mid-17th century, "fantasy" meant having a fancy or a liking for something. Now, it means an extravagant or unreal vision. MR & YA

Farewell, My Lovely (1940) In this hard-boiled detective novel by *Raymond Chandler, *Philip Marlowe, a private investigator, becomes involved in what seem to be two separate murder cases but turn out to be connected. The setting is Los Angeles, where Marlowe first has a run-in with a convict just released from prison who is searching for his girl, Velma Valento. About the same time, Marlowe is hired to accompany a man who is to pay to get some jewels back that were stolen from a woman. The man is murdered, and Marlowe is knocked unconscious. His subsequent investigation leads to the owner of the jewels, the wife of a millionaire, and to blackmail, an offshore gambling ship, and other adventures, in the course of which Marlowe is again knocked unconscious. The story ends with a showdown in his apartment when there is more murder and a surprising revelation regarding the much-sought Velma. Readers today will find the racist statements in this book offensive. Under the titles *The Falcon Takes Over* and *Murder, My Sweet*, movies were made in 1942 and 1944, and again in 1975 under the title *Farewell, My Lovely*. YA

Farewell to Arms, A (1929) By *Ernest Hemingway, this novel tells one of the most memorable love stories of the 20th century. A young American, Frederick Henry, serving as an ambulance driver in the Italian army in World War I, meets Catherine Barkley, an English nurse. The two fall deeply in love. Wounded in battle, Frederick is sent to Milan, where Catherine joins him. Shortly before he is sent back to the front, Catherine reveals that she is expecting their child.

When Frederick reaches the front, confusion is everywhere. His company is forced to retreat, and the Italians are killing their own men as deserters or traitors. These scenes are regarded by many to be among literature's most vivid descriptions of warfare. Frederick sur-

vives by hiding in a boxcar en route to Stresa, soon to be joyously reunited with Catherine. They reach Switzerland, a neutral country that grants them sanctuary. Suddenly, the war no longer seems to exist. Their love is idyllic, and they plan happily for the baby's arrival. However, gloom soon enters their lives, and tragedy ends their tale of romance. If you are interested in other books about World War I, you might like *Erich Maria Remarque's *All Quiet on the Western Front*, a novel told from the point of view of a young German soldier confronting the realities of war. YA

Farewell to Manzanar (1973) By Jeanne Wakatsuki Houston (1934–) and James D. Houston (1933–), this is the moving account of a Japanese-American family's experiences in a California internment camp during World War II. During the war about 110,000 Japanese Americans were sent to internment camps as a so-called security measure, their loyalty questioned solely on the basis of their ancestry. Jeanne Wakatsuki was 7 years old when her family was sent from their home near Santa Monica, California, to Manzanar, in the arid, rugged upland east of the Sierra Nevada. A rough wooden barracks would be their home until 1945. She describes life in the camp and the devastating effects of the internment on her parents, brothers and sisters, and herself. Thirty years later, in 1972, revisiting the site of Manzanar, she comes to terms with her experience and realizes how much it has shaped her life. The story of Manzanar is also told in *Manzanar* (1988) by John Armor (n.d.) and Peter Wright (1946–), which includes many photographs taken at the time by Ansel Adams (1902–1984) and a commentary by *John Hersey. MR & YA

Farley, Walter (1920–) A lover of horses, Farley is known best for his popular stories about Black, a stallion, and Black's offspring. Black first appeared in the classic horse story *The Black Stallion*. In numerous sequels, such as *The Black Stallion Returns* (1945), *Son of Black Stallion* (1947), and *The Black Stallion Races*

(1955), Farley tells the story of young Alec Ramsay's love for horses, especially his wild black Arabian stallion. Farley also wrote *The Island Stallion* (1948), about a young boy, Steve Duncan, and the taming of a wild stallion, Flame. The two horses meet in *The Black Stallion and Flame* (1960). All of Farley's novels are chock-full of adventure and suspense. In *The Black Stallion Returns*, for instance, Alec and Henry Dailey, a retired jockey who helps train Black, find themselves in many exciting predicaments as they travel to Arabia to find the stolen stallion. Farley has also written a story about a dog, called *The Great Dane, Thor* (1966). He is known best, however, for his passion for, and knowledge of, horses. Two movies have been made about Black: *The Black Stallion* in 1979 and *The Black Stallion Returns* in 1983. Farley's success has enabled him to fulfill his ambition of raising his own horses. MR

Farmer, Penelope (Jane) (1939–) Though she has written adult and young adult novels, the bulk of this English author's stories are *fantasy novels for younger readers. Many of these stories involve two sisters, Charlotte Mary and Emma. The characters were originally modeled after Farmer's mother and sister, though their characters have changed since they were created. *Charlotte Sometimes* (1969), set in a London boarding school, tells about how the older sister, Charlotte, travels back in time to the same boarding school in 1918. Farmer grew up in the English countryside, and many of her novels use rural settings. *Seagull* (1967), for instance, is set in Wiltshire, England, and is about a talented young seagull trainer. Farmer's other fantasy novels include *A Castle of Bone* (1972), a challenging story that uses Celtic mythology to examine the issues of mortality and identity, and *The Summer Birds* (1962), which is about a strange boy who teaches some village children to fly. Like many of her novels, *The Summer Birds* involves choices children make between reality and fantasy. Farmer has also edited a collection of myths entitled *Beginnings: Creation Myths of the World* (1978). MR

Farrell, James T(homas) (1904–1970) Though he wrote a large number of novels, realistic in style and using language considered crude at the time, Farrell is known especially for a trilogy consisting of *Young Lonigan* (1932), *The Young Manhood of Studs Lonigan* (1934), and *Judgment Day* (1935). The setting is a section of Chicago inhabited by lower-middle-class Irish Catholics, and the story focuses on William "Studs" Lonigan, who is 15 years old. He begins to participate in the life around him, which is typified by a cynical attitude toward life and an emphasis on manliness. In the second volume Lonigan becomes a house painter, but spends much of his time in gang fights, drinking, and experiments with sex. In the final volume, Lonigan is 27 years old. His health is failing; he loses his money; and his girl, made pregnant by him, refuses to have an abortion. In the end, Lonigan dies. Farrell does not blame Lonigan for his fate, but rather the social and economic world in which he grew up. Farrell also wrote another series of novels, which concern Danny O'Neill, a friend of Lonigan, who breaks away from his environment and goes to college. Farrell himself can be seen in Danny. The first O'Neill novel is *A World I Never Made* (1936). If you enjoy Farrell's novels, read those of *John Dos Passos, *Theodore Dreiser, and *John Steinbeck. YA

Fast, Howard (1914–) A prolific writer of more than 40 novels and numerous other works, Howard Fast is known best to young readers for *April Morning* (1961), the story of 15-year-old Adam Cooper at the Battle of Lexington, and for *Citizen Tom Paine*. Much of his work has become the basis for films. His deep commitment to social issues is reflected in many of his novels. One of them, *The Last Frontier* (1941), relates the heroic flight of the Cheyenne to their home in Wyoming, and *Freedom Road* (1944) is the story of blacks during the Reconstruction period. In 1947 Fast was imprisoned for contempt of Congress and remained blacklisted for many years following his release. For much of his life he was a member of the Communist Party, but in 1957 he publicly quit the party, a decision recorded in *The Naked God* (1957). In this autobiographical book Fast explores the relationship between a writer and the Communist Party and his painful decision to quit. Fast said that his books were either examinations of modern history or parables of his own view of history. His other novels include *Spartacus* (1951), about the slave who led a nearly-successful rebellion against the Roman empire, and *The Unvanquished* (1942), about the struggles of George Washington and the American army in 1776, during the darkest days of the American Revolution. *Spartacus* was made into a film in 1960, an event that marked the end of the Hollywood blacklist. A TV movie of *Freedom Road* was made in 1979. A movie version of *April Morning* was produced in 1988. YA

Fat Men from Space (1977), by *Daniel Manus Pinkwater, is an imaginative tale about a boy who, after a trip to the dentist, begins to pick up radio signals from his filling. William loves listening to the radio, so he refuses to allow the dentist to treat the filling. It is fun until one evening he starts to receive signals between spacemen, who soon learn that he is listening in. They head his way. William tries to escape, but before he realizes what is happening, he is spinning in the air toward the spaceship. Inside are fat spacemen from the planet Spiegels, dressed in plaid sports jackets, looking like ordinary humans but each weighing at least 350 pounds. Captain Hanam explains that the purpose of their imminent invasion of Earth is designed to collect all the potato pancakes they can. As they spin away from Earth after the attack, William is allowed to float back to Earth in a plaid space jacket, on the condition that he never reveal his abduction. A sequel, *The Frankenbagel Monster* (1986), which is just what its title suggests, has the same setting. If you enjoyed this space fantasy, read *A Wrinkle in Time* (1952) by *Madeleine L'Engle. MR

father is often used to describe a person who is first in reputation or who is a leader. *Benjamin Franklin is known as the Father of the Continental Congress. John Adams (1735–1826), the second President, is known as the Father of American Independence. And, of course, George Washington (1732–1799), our first President, is known as the Father of His Country. In all these examples, the sense is very similar to the usual use of the word "father," meaning the male parent. However, "father" is also used colloquially by wives to refer to their husbands. In the novel *Little Dorrit* (1857), by *Charles Dickens, Mrs. Meagles says to her husband, "There! Never mind, Father, never mind!" In many churches, a person of dignity, especially a priest, is called "Father." Father Christmas is another name for Santa Claus. Father Time means the personification of time. Usually, Father Time is pictured as an old man with a white beard, white robe, and a scythe.

Father Brown, the creation of *G.K. Chesterton, is a priest and amateur detective whose adventures are told in short stories that appear in *The Innocence of Father Brown* (1911), *The Wisdom of Father Brown* (1914), *The Incredulity of Father Brown* (1926), *The Secret of Father Brown* (1927), and *The Scandal of Father Brown* (1935). The character was inspired by one of Chesterton's friends, a quiet and pleasant man who startled the author by revealing a profound knowledge of evil gathered from his years as a Father Confessor in the Roman Catholic church. Chesterton's Father Brown is a kindly and ordinary-looking little cleric, seemingly slow-witted and bumbling, who uses his unexpectedly sharp intelligence and great ingenuity to outwit his adversaries. While other fictional detectives of the time devoted themselves to lengthy analysis of clues, Father Brown worked wonders of deduction through his uncanny knowledge of human nature.

In "The Blue Cross," from the first collection, Father Brown helps Valentin, head of the Paris police and a world-famous investigator, to arrest an arch-criminal who plans to steal a valuable jewel. Neither Valentin nor the thief is aware of the Father's quiet but crucial role in this escapade until the final moments of the story.

"The Perishing of the Pendragons," in the second collection, concerns an old Cornish family rumored to be living under an elaborate curse. Father Brown, on holiday with friends, visits the Pendragon island estate, and hears something of its history from the family's oldest member. When he learns that Old Pendragon's nephew is about to inherit the estate after a series of family tragedies, he begins to suspect foul play rather than supernatural events. His rapid deductions and energetic action avert another disaster and reveal criminal acts behind the so-called curse. *The Detective*, a movie based on Father Brown, was filmed in 1954. YA

Fathers and Sons (1862) By *Ivan Turgenev, this novel dramatizes the tensions between the aristocratic serf-owning society of mid-19th-century Russia and the younger radical forces who challenged the nobility's undemocratic values. The young radical Bazarov can see nothing of merit in traditional society. Indiscriminately against everything, he is, in the term that this novel popularized, a nihilist. Even his personality is negative. He is brilliant but cold, abrupt, and insensitive, even to his parents. His aristocratic friend Arkady is an adoring protégé of Bazarov and his radical nihilism. The two make a series of visits to their families and to acquaintances. Wherever he is, Bazarov seems to care for nothing. Even his view of the future is based primarily on destroying what exists rather than on building a better world. However, Bazarov is revealed to be more human than he will admit when he falls in love with the aristocratic Madame Odintzov. Though *Fathers and Sons* has long been recognized as a masterpiece, Turgenev's characterization of Bazarov caused a furor when the novel appeared. Radicals claimed that Turgenev had created a slanderous portrait of a young democratic intellectual. Some aristocrats felt Bazarov's nihilism is glorified. Turgenev maintained that Bazarov, unlovable though he is, stands for the forces of democracy that would ultimately triumph over aristocracy. You may want to read also *A Hero of Our Time* (1840), by the Russian novelist Mikhail Lermontov (1814–1841), whose protagonist is also at odds with society. YA

Father's Arcane Daughter (1976) is about a daughter who returns home 17 years after she is kidnapped. Though *E.L. Konigsburg infuses this story with mystery, you see how a family is changed, especially the two children, Winston, about 12 years old, and his younger sister, Heidi, both of whom are excessively sheltered by their stepmother. When Caroline arrives at Winston's home, she claims she is his father's daughter from a former marriage. As Winston tells the story, it seems that "there are some parts that I hardly know and other parts that I don't know at all." Winston is in charge of his retarded sister, Heidi, who answers the doorbell when Caroline first appears. Caroline is outwardly accepted, but the process of getting to know her includes subtle questioning and little tests of her memory of the past to make sure she is not an impostor. After all, a fortune is being held for Caroline, and a shadow hovers over the family: Who is Caroline, really? And why does her interest in Heidi cause conflicts with their stepmother? Change can be irritating but it can mean freedom, and it will for Heidi, whose handicap is not what it seems to be. This is a mature subject handled well. MR & YA

Faulkner, William (1897–1962) A novelist and short-story writer, Faulkner put on the literary map the imaginary *Yoknapatawpha County, Mississippi. In his work he explores the social disintegration of the Deep South. Faulkner was brought up in Oxford, Mississippi, and drew on his knowledge of that region for most of his best fiction. His great-grandfather, in fact, was the model for one of Faulkner's most colorful characters, Colonel Sartoris. Though Faulkner never completed high school, he did attend the University of Mississippi and served in the Canadian Royal Air Force in World War I.

Though his early novels received critical attention, he could not survive financially as a

Faust, here surrounded by grotesque symbols and creatures of hell, sells his soul to the devil.

writer, and worked as a carpenter, clerk, and night superintendent, a job at which, in the small hours of the morning, on an upturned wheelbarrow, he revised *The Sound and the Fury*, which was to become one of his most celebrated novels. It was the first novel in which he used the now well-known *stream-of-consciousness technique. After the publication of *Sanctuary* (1931), a novel of violence and scandal that was his first popular success, he no longer had to worry about money. Faulkner's other novels include *As I Lay Dying* (1930), about the trouble-filled journey of a poor family to take their mother's body back for burial at her home in Jefferson, Mississippi; *Light in August* (1932), centering on a man whose tragic life and death are shaped by the violence, racism, and fanaticism of others; *Absalom, Absalom!*, considered one of Faulkner's best novels; *Intruder in the Dust*; and *The Reivers* (1962), a comic novel set in Mississippi in 1905, about an 11-year-old boy who, with two adult companions, steals his grandfather's automobile and trades it for a racehorse.

The world of fiction that Faulkner created is often nightmarish and difficult to read because of its language and its complex structure. You may want to begin with "The Bear" (1942), one of his best-loved short stories, in which Ike, a 12-year-old boy, goes hunting for the legendary Old Ben, a bear that has been eluding experienced hunters for many years. Faulkner received the Nobel Prize for literature in 1950. In accepting the prize, Faulkner reaffirmed human values and suggested that humanity will not only survive but prevail. See also *Snopes. YA

Faust [Faustus] was a German scholar and magician who probably lived from about 1480 to 1540. People of the time considered him a fake and a criminal. Later, an unknown author wrote *Faustbook* (1587), a biography of Johann Faust, to which he added sensational tales about other magicians. In *Faustbook*, Faust sells his soul to the devil Mephistopheles for 24 years in return for power, knowledge, and youth, and finally goes to hell in terror. The legend has been used by many authors as a basis for novels and plays, and it inspired the English playwright Christopher Marlowe (1564–1593) to write *Dr. Faustus* (1593), a tragic play in blank verse. Another *Doctor Faustus* (1947) is a novel by the German author *Thomas Mann. *Johann Wolfgang von Goethe wrote his *Faust* (1808) in the form of a dramatic poem and added to the original story a second part in which the hero is saved by God. Among the many musical works inspired by the legend is the opera *The Damnation of Faust* (1846) by the French composer Louis-Hector Berlioz (1803–1869). YA

Ferber, Edna (1887–1968) Equally known as a novelist and playwright, this popular writer began her career as a newspaper reporter in Wisconsin. In one of her best novels, *So Big* (1924), as in so much of her work, a woman takes center stage. Selina, after her husband dies, struggles to raise her son and run their truck farm. *Show Boat* encompasses three generations of women, but concentrates on Magnolia, who is deserted by her gambler husband. In *Cimarron* (1929), Sabra Cravat moves to the recently opened territory of Oklahoma with her dreamer husband. When he abandons her, she not only runs the house but his newspaper as well. In *Giant*, a young bride becomes rebellious against the Texas gentry life-style.

Ferber collaborated with playwright *George S. Kaufman on many plays, including *Dinner at Eight* (1932), a play about a fashionable dinner party, and *Royal Family* (1928), a humorous play about an American theatrical family, the Barrymores. It was successfully revived in 1975. YA

Field, Eugene (1850–1895) A poet and journalist, Field is remembered today primarily for his verse. Both "Little Boy Blue," a poem about a boy's death, and "Wynken, Blynken, and Nod," who one night sail off in a wooden shoe on a river of crystal light, still tug at the heartstrings of young and old readers. Perhaps you will remember the well-known lines from "Little Boy Blue":

> The little toy dog is covered with dust,
>   But sturdy and stanch he stands;
> And the little toy soldier is red with rust,
>   And his musket moulds in his hands.

Both poems were included in Field's *Little Book of Western Verse* (1889), a collection of writings that included not only poetry for young people but adaptations of Horace (65–8 B.C.), a Roman lyric poet and satirist, as well as imitations of old English, and pieces of mining camp dialect. Field worked as a journalist for most of his life. Though he was raised in Massachusetts, his writing and interest lay in the American West, where he was born. It is said by some that he cared little for children not his own. Field was the father of eight. MR

Fielding, Henry (1707–1754) One of the great English novelists, Fielding is remembered especially for his masterpiece *Tom Jones*, the tale of the generous but impudent Tom. Fielding was brought up in Dorset, in southern England, on an estate provided by his grandfather. His mother's death ended that protected life, and in the following year Fielding was sent to Eton, partly to avoid the influence of his father, who led a wild life in London. There he studied classical literature, which was to have a profound influence on his later work. After his schooling he spent many years writing for the theater. Few of these political satires are now read. It was the publication of *Pamela, or Virtue Rewarded*, the story of a young servant, by *Samuel Richardson, that prompted Fielding to turn to fiction. Disliking Richardson's novel, Fielding responded with a *parody, *The History of the Adventures of Joseph Andrews and of His Friend, Mr. Abraham Adams* (1742), the story of Pamela's brother, who, dismissed by his employer, travels to London to join his love. Though success, money, and fame followed, Fielding's personal life was filled with sorrow brought on by the death of his wife and his own ill health. YA

Figaro, long regarded as one of the world's cleverest servants, is the amusing but cunning hero of two comedies by the French dramatist Beaumarchais, the name taken by Pierre Augustin Caron (1732–1799). In the first comedy, *The Barber of Seville* (1775), the Count, Figaro's former master, wishes to woo Rosine, a beautiful young girl who is the ward of a local doctor. With the help of the ingenious barber,

Figaro, the Count is able to marry Rosine before the doctor returns. Two operas of the same title were based on the comedy: one by Gioacchino Antonio Rossini (1792–1868) in 1816, and the other by Giovanni Paisiello (1741–1816) in 1776. The second of Beaumarchais's comedies, *The Marriage of Figaro* (1784), recounts the continuing adventures of Figaro as he attempts to marry Suzanne, Rosine's maid. This time Figaro, now the Count's doorkeeper, outwits his master. A famous opera based on *The Marriage of Figaro*, composed by Wolfgang Amadeus Mozart (1756–1791), was produced in 1786. YA

Fighting Ground, The (1984) In this short novel by *Avi, 13-year-old Jonathan dreams about being a soldier in the Revolutionary War. One day he gets his wish. Drawn to the village tavern by the tolling bell, Jonathan is called upon to join a makeshift squad intending to head off a group of Hessians coming their way. In the distance they spot the blue-coated mercenaries, 30 strong. They number only 13, and Jonathan's musket is almost more than he can handle. When firing begins, all is confusion. Captured by the Hessians, Jonathan is taken to what seems to be a deserted farmhouse, where he discovers a forlorn boy wandering outside, as well as the bodies of the boy's slain parents. Later that night he is able to escape with the child while the soldiers sleep. He runs into his own men and leads them back to the farmhouse. Ironically, he learns en route that it was one of them who had killed the boy's parents because they were Tories. Jonathan is sickened. He becomes an unwilling witness to more killing before he is able to elude capture and return home. Jonathan has been spared his life, but battle was not quite what he had imagined. Other good novels about the Revolutionary War include *My Brother Sam Is Dead* by *James Lincoln Collier and *Christopher Collier and *Johnny Tremain* by *Esther Forbes. Older readers might enjoy *April Morning* (1961) by *Howard Fast, a novel about a boy not unlike Jonathan who is also called upon to fight during the Revolutionary War. MR & YA

Fine White Dust, A (1986) By *Cynthia Rylant, this story captures the religious yearnings of 13-year-old Peter Cassidy. Aching to find more meaning in his life, he falls under the spell of a visiting revivalist preacher, James Carson, who comes to town that summer. The man is a saver of souls, and Pete feels he has been found. Pete wants to be holy, he wants to be clean, and he now knows what his life work will be. The three days of the preacher's visit are the most important ones of his young life, and Pete prepares to leave his home and family as well as his best friend, Rufus, to join the preacher in his quest to save souls. Preacher Carson fails to appear at the appointed hour, however, and Pete is left with the ashes of his dream. He feels especially betrayed when he learns that Carson had in fact run off with Darlene, a teenager. In spite of his pain, Pete is able to go on with his life and to sustain his belief in God. He is able to put the preacher behind him. Another novel about a young person's search for religious truth is *Blinded by the Light* by *Robin F. Brancato. MR

Finn MacCool (Fingal) is a traditional Irish folk hero who actually may have lived in the 3rd century but who figures heavily in Irish mythology. A leader of a band of warriors, Finn is often portrayed as a giant with great strength and wisdom. According to folk tradition, Finn assembled a rock formation known as the Giants' Causeway along the coast of Northern Ireland to enable other giants to travel between Scotland and Ireland. He and his son, Oisin, appear in the Fenian cycle of ancient Irish tales, the most famous of which is "The Pursuit of Diarmuid and Grainne." Grainne, who loves Oisin, is pressured to marry the father instead, but escapes by eloping with Diarmuid, Finn's nephew. Finn pursues them, Diarmuid is slain by a giant boar, and ultimately Grainne becomes Finn's wife.

In the 1760s, the Scottish poet James Macpherson (1736–1796) claimed dubiously to have discovered and translated tales written by Finn's son, Oisin, whom he called Ossian. Two of his popular books are *Fingal, an Ancient Epic Poem in Six Books* (1762) and *Temore* (1763), an epic that he claimed was translated from the Gaelic of Ossian. Both Finn and his son frequently appear in Irish myth and literature, most notably in the poetry of *William Butler Yeats. Younger readers will enjoy the giant's adventures recounted in *The Green Hero: Early Adventures of Finn McCool* (1975) by Bernard Evslin (1922–), *Finn MacCool and the Small Men of Deeds* (1987) by Pat O'Shea (1931–), and *The High Deeds of Finn MacCool* (1967) by *Rosemary Sutcliff. YA

Fisher, Dorothy Canfield [Dorothea Frances (Canfield) Fisher] (1879–1958) Born in Kansas, Fisher was not only extensively educated but widely traveled. She and her husband settled eventually in Vermont, where Fisher's ancestors had lived. Her love of Vermont is reflected in much of her work. In her novel *Understood Betsy*, a fearful little girl is able to become independent and capable when her environment is changed. An attack on big business is a focal point of *The Bent Twig*, the story of two sisters who learn from their experience. The plea for racial understanding in *The Bent Twig* and the attack on anti-Semitism in *Seasoned Timber* (1939) set Fisher apart as a courageous writer of her time. She wrote also of marriages in transition, as in *The Burning Cup* (1921), which compares the marriages of two women, both of whom are tempted by single, attractive men, and in *The Home-Maker* (1924), which portrays an exchange of roles between husband and wife. Fisher creates sensitive people whose growth is often evidenced through variations of interior monologue, a kind of uninterrupted flow of a character's thoughts and associations. See also *stream of consciousness. YA

Fitzgerald, Edward (1809–1883) An English translator and man of letters, Fitzgerald is remembered primarily for his brilliant rendition of the *Rubáiyát by Omar Khayyám, a Persian poet of the early 11th century. According to Fitzgerald, these Persian quatrains expressed the fears and aspirations of his own century as well as those of the 11th century. Fitzgerald was born in the Suffolk area as Edward Purcell. The family assumed the Fitzgerald name following the death of his mother's father, a man of wealth. Though not academically inclined, Fitzgerald attended Trinity College, where he became friendly with many who were to become important writers, including *William Makepeace Thackeray. When he was 21 years old he virtually retired from society and, except for a short-lived marriage, lived reclusively until his death. In addition to his translations, Fitzgerald is remembered also for his letters, which critics have come to value for their commentary on 19th-century society. YA

Fitzgerald, F(rancis) Scott (Key) (1896–1940) Named for the author of the "Star Spangled Banner," *Francis Scott Key, Fitzgerald seemed almost destined to explore the dream that was America. He is known best for *The Great Gatsby*, a novel about a man who lived the American dream of the 1920s: fancy surroundings, moneyed pleasures, and spiritual emptiness. It was the world of the Jazz Age, a term Fitzgerald is said to have coined. He was the spokesman for a generation who had, in Fitzgerald's words, found all the gods dead, all wars fought, all faith in humanity shaken. In the same year in which appeared his enormously successful first novel, *This Side of Paradise* (1920)—about a wealthy young Princeton student, snobbish and cynical, who is rejected by the woman he loves for an even wealthier man—Fitzgerald married Zelda Sayre (1900–1948). They led the dizzying life of the rich and famous in America and abroad. Their world collapsed, however, with Zelda's breakdown and commitment to a mental hospital. Fitzgerald fared only slightly better, struggling with debt, a profound sense of failure, and alcoholism. *Tender Is the Night*, often thought to be Fitzgerald's finest novel, is drawn from his and Zelda's lives. His unfinished novel, *The*

Last Tycoon (1941), about a Hollywood movie mogul, is considered by some to be one of his finest works. It is based on his own experiences as a Hollywood screenwriter at the end of his life, as are the short stories collected in *The Pat Hobby Stories* (1962). Fitzgerald wrote many excellent short stories, collected in such volumes as *Flappers and Philosophers* (1920), *Tales of the Jazz Age* (1922), and *Taps at Reveille* (1935). Many biographies have been written of Fitzgerald and his wife. You will especially enjoy the lively biography *Zelda* by Nancy Milford (1938–), which gives a dramatic account of the Fitzgeralds' doomed lives. YA

Fitzhugh, Louise (1928–1974) Both an author and illustrator, Fitzhugh is known best for her novel *Harriet the Spy*, the story of an 11-year-old girl who wants to be a writer. The world of Harriet and other young girls is recaptured in a sequel, *The Long Secret* (1965), about the friendships and power struggles of sixth-graders. A later book, published after the author's death, *Nobody's Family Is Going to Change* (1974), portrays a black family with two children whose aspirations are not acceptable to their lawyer father. Emma wants to be a lawyer, and her brother Willie wants to be a dancer. *Sport* (1979) tells the story of an 11-year-old boy caught in a custody battle between his divorced parents. Fitzhugh, born in Memphis, Tennessee, attended school in New York City, the setting for two of her novels. MR

Five Smooth Stones (1966), a novel by Ann Fairbairn (1902–1972), recounts the life of David Chamberlain, a black man, from his humble beginnings in New Orleans to an important career as a lawyer and civil rights activist. Orphaned at birth, young David is raised by his grandparents. Their love and the help and wisdom of Bjarne Knudson, a teacher, soften the harshness of his life and help bring out the special spirit that is David's. Years of rigorous study under the careful tutelage of Knudson win for him a scholarship at one of the country's finest schools. It is there that he meets Sara, whose love will endure years of separa-

tion. It is also there that he encounters a dean's venomous racism. David continues his studies at Harvard University, and later at Oxford University in England, and joins a prestigious law firm. A visit home to attend the funeral of Knudsen changes the direction of his life. Though he was about to be appointed to an important United Nations post, he feels the call of his people and commits himself to the civil rights movement, a decision that will result in his death. On the very field where his great-grandfather, the first David Chamberlain, was lynched, Chamberlain is shot and killed. Ann Fairbairn is the pen name of Dorothy Tait, an American journalist and novelist. She is known for her biography, *Call Him George* (1969), about the clarinetist George Lewis (1900–1968). For more than 10 years she handled the tours of Lewis and his band, which led not only to the writing of his biography but *Five Smooth Stones* as well. YA

Flaubert, Gustave (1821–1880) Noted for his exquisite prose style, Flaubert is considered by many to be the most influential French novelist of the 19th century. His aim was to achieve a style as rhythmical as verse and as precise as the language of science. As a young man, he reluctantly studied law in Paris until a nervous disorder interrupted his studies, enabling him to devote himself to his writing. Following the death of his father, a surgeon, he returned to the family estate, where he lived for the remainder of his life. His most highly acclaimed novel is *Madame Bovary*. A number of his short stories, especially "A Simple Heart" (1877), which tells the story of a servant named Félicité, are considered masterpieces as well. If you enjoyed *Madame Bovary*, you may want to read two other novels by Flaubert, *Salammbô* (1863) and *A Sentimental Education* (1869). In *Salammbô* the setting is the world of ancient Carthage. Mercenaries, feeling betrayed by the authorities of Carthage, begin to pillage the palace, but the appearance of Salammbô, priestess of the moon goddess, pacifies them with her great beauty. *A Sentimental Education*, which explores again some of the same

Gustave Flaubert

themes of delusion and misplaced love that underlie *Madame Bovary*, tells about Frédéric, a student who, in high romantic style, falls for Madame Arnoux the first time he glimpses her. His love is unreturned, and Frédéric, sensitive and intelligent, wastes his life because of misplaced sentiment. YA

Fleischman, (Albert) Sid(ney) (1920–) The author of many hilariously funny adventure novels for young readers, Fleischman worked as a professional magician, newspaperman, and movie screenwriter before turning to writing books. He used his own experiences with magic in his first novel, *Mr. Mysterious and Company* (1962), about the adventures of a traveling magician and his family in the West in 1884. His next book, *By the Great Horn Spoon!* (1963), is about an orphan boy and an English butler who stow away on a ship bound from Boston to California during the Gold Rush of 1849. *McBroom Tells the Truth* (1966) introduces Josh McBroom, who buys an 80-acre farm in Iowa from a stranger, only to find the acres are "one piled on the other, like griddle cakes," at the bottom of a pond. But McBroom has the last laugh when the pond dries up and his one-acre farm begins growing several crops a day. Fleischman continued McBroom's hilarious adventures in a series of books, including *McBroom the Rainmaker* (1973), *McBroom and the Beanstalk* (1978), and *McBroom's Almanac* (1984). Fleischman's other books include *Humbug Mountain* (1978), about a traveling frontier newspaperman and his family, who foil two dangerous outlaws, start a gold rush, and turn an imaginary town promoted by dishonest speculators into a bustling community; *Jingo Django*; and *The Whipping Boy. By the Great Horn Spoon!* was made into the movie *Bullwhip Griffin* in 1967. MR

Fleming, Ian (Lancaster) (1908–1964) Educated at Eton, a famous school in England, and Sandhurst, the British West Point, Fleming became a journalist in Russia, a banker, a stockbroker, and then a journalist once more. During World War II he served as an officer in the British Royal Navy. His first espionage novel, *Casino Royale* (1953), introduced *James Bond, also of the Royal Navy and of the intelligence service. The daring of Bond, the exotic settings, and the violence and sex of Fleming's books, all featuring Bond, brought him a wide readership. Among the other novels are *Moonraker* (1955), *Diamonds Are Forever* (1956), *Goldfinger* (1959), and *You Only Live Twice* (1964). In all the books Bond fights communism or evil criminals who have plans to dominate the world. The books have ludicrous plots, but they are written with such style and tongue-in-cheek manner that you cannot help but enjoy them. Much of their attraction rests on the deadly gadgets and the special vehicles, such as the car that runs under water, that Bond uses to thwart his enemies. Fleming was pleased with the success of his books, but he admitted they were "trivial piffle." All of them have been made into movies, the first being *Dr. No* (1962), which recounts Bond's success in bringing down a criminal operating in the West Indies and threatening to blow up the world. If you like the Bond stories, try those of *Len Deighton, *Frederick Forsyth, and *John Le Carré. YA

MR = Middle Reader   YA = Young Adult Reader   * = See this main entry

Flight to Arras (1942) is the autobiographical narrative of a reconnaissance journey made by a French pilot, Captain *Antoine de Saint-Exupéry, during the early days of World War II. While preparing for the sortie, he anticipates almost certain death. Seventeen crews have already vanished. The Germans are advancing rapidly across France, and total defeat seems certain. During the flight, Saint-Exupéry spends much time reflecting on life and country. Before the flight he was conscious of himself as an individual, but as the flight continues, he begins to achieve a sense of belonging, not only to France but to humanity. The work is heightened by its poetry and its spirituality. If you enjoy books about introspective people who explore themselves and life, you will want to read Saint-Exupéry's *Night Flight* and *Wind, Sand and Stars*. Try also *Out of Africa* by *Isak Dinesen. YA

Flowers for Algernon (1959), by Daniel Keyes (1927–), is a novel about Charlie Gordon, a 32-year-old worker in a bakery who undergoes experimental brain surgery in order to "get smart." Told through Charlie's diary entries, the novel traces the changes in Charlie's life, from the childlike expressions of the retarded to the brilliant expressions of a man who has outdistanced the most brilliant of his professors and doctors.

Prior to his operation, Charlie has attended night classes to help him learn more. His teacher, Alice Kinnian, is impressed by his commitment, and recommends him for the experimental surgery. Charlie meets the mouse, Algernon, who has undergone the brain surgery planned for Charlie and is awed by Algernon's ability to make his way through a maze. After the surgery Charlie does get smart, and, though he is able to master complex mathematical theories, Hindu philosophy, and the intricacies of many languages, Charlie is not altogether happy. He falls in love with Alice, but he rapidly goes beyond her in his brilliance, and Alice realizes that there is no future for them. More and more Charlie feels like a laboratory specimen on display. He learns that "intelligence and education that hasn't been tempered by human affection isn't worth a damn." Algernon, meanwhile, regresses and then dies, and Charlie begins to understand his own fate. Before his own regression sets in, he visits his mother, who had tried to kill him when he was 13. He is able to get his now-senile mother to smile at him approvingly, something for which he had waited a long time. He and Alice reunite and savor the little time they have left. As Charlie finds his motor activity increasingly impaired, as well as his intelligence, he sends Alice away and waits alone for the inevitable. *Flowers for Algernon* was made into a motion picture entitled *Charly* in 1968. MR & YA

Flying Dutchman, The A mythic ship, doomed to sail the seas forever and supposedly the scene of a terrible murder, *The Flying Dutchman* is prevented from entering any ports because the crew is infected with the plague. In the opera *The Flying Dutchman* (1843) by Richard Wagner (1815–1883), a Dutch captain swears to sail the Cape of Good Hope through a furious storm, even if he is to sail forever. The Devil overhears the oath and condemns the captain to sail the seas until the Day of Judgment, but allows him to go ashore every seven years. The curse will be lifted only if he finds a wife who is willing to sacrifice for him. The Norwegian maiden Senta is finally able to lift the curse. YA

Follow My Leader (1957), by James B. Garfield (1881–1984), follows the journey made by 11-year-old Jimmy Carter after a carelessly hurled firecracker leaves him blind. With the help of Miss Thompson, from the State Department of Rehabilitation, Jimmy learns to make his way, first by using his own senses and later with the help of a white cane. He discovers how to memorize the layout of a room by using the face of a clock for directions, how to read Braille and, perhaps most importantly, how to rely on himself. In those first difficult weeks of adjustment, his younger sister Carolyn provides much needed company and support, as do his friends Art and Chuck. Though away during the day at her job, Jimmy's widowed mom is always there for him.

Jimmy is finally ready to attend the school

for the blind 400 miles away. There he is given his dog, Sirius, who will see Jimmy through the important years ahead. Though demanding of his charges, Mr. Weeks, his teacher, is understanding and helps Jimmy to become the independent person he must become. Following his return home, Jimmy, with the help of his dog, which he has named Leader, is able to run his own newsstand and to go camping with the Boy Scouts. Jimmy is also able to forgive Mike, who had carelessly thrown the firecracker. Garfield, who was blinded himself at 40, writes with extraordinary detail about the world of the blind, and though the language of the boys occasionally seems dated, the book is convincing and real. Older readers might enjoy *A Patch of Blue* (1932) by Grace Livingston Hill (1865–1947), also about the challenge of being blind. MR & YA

For Whom the Bell Tolls (1940) is a novel by *Ernest Hemingway set in the mountains of Spain during the Spanish Civil War. Robert Jordan, an American professor on leave from teaching, is working with Republican partisans. His orders are to dynamite a bridge essential to the fascist enemy, the Nationalists. In the three days he spends with the guerrillas, he falls deeply in love with a young woman who had been brutalized by the fascists. With the blessing of her protector, Pilar, he takes her, without benefit of ceremony, for his wife. During his short stay in the mountains, Jordan learns much about himself and others. Awed by the power of his love for Maria, he realizes for the first time all that is truly important. He learns too of Pilar's wisdom and strength, of Anselmo's loyalty and Pablo's treason. Even without a detonator, he is able to destroy the bridge. During the ensuing flight, however, he is badly injured. He forces the remaining partisans, including Maria, to leave him behind to die. If you are interested in Spain's Civil War, you might explore the Nationalists' view of the bloody conflict in *San Camilio, 1936* (1969) by Camillo José Cela (1916–). This novel spans the 10 days of 1936 during which Spain's Republican government fell. Also, *Homage to Catalonia* (1939) by *George Orwell is a powerful chronicle of the war and the political intrigues that helped lead to the fascist victory in Spain. *For Whom the Bell Tolls* was made into a film in 1943. YA

Forbes, Esther (1891–1967) An early interest in the life-styles and folklore of New England is reflected in the books of this Massachusetts-born writer for young readers. Her ancestors, including the famed Adams family, helped make New England history. After college Forbes worked on the editorial staff of a Boston publisher. While researching material for a biography of *Paul Revere, the famed silversmith of the Revolutionary period, she came across fascinating information about the apprenticeship system of colonial America. Her discoveries resulted in *Johnny Tremain*, her best-known novel, the story of a young apprentice in pre-Revolutionary Boston. Other books, also set in New England, include the novels *A Mirror for Witches* (1928), about a child pursued by spite and jealousy who begins to believe she is possessed by demons, and *Paradise* (1937), a historical romance about a young preacher whose religious passions destroy his natural ones. *Paul Revere and the World He Lived In* (1942) is about the Revolutionary hero who made the midnight ride to warn the patriots that British troops were advancing on them. MR

Foreign Legion, The A French army of volunteers, most of whom are foreigners, the Legion is famous for never revealing the personal background of its soldiers. Many have joined to escape trouble at home and take on new identities, even different names. Others have signed on to see exotic places. Created in 1831, the Legion was sent to keep order in Algeria and Morocco, in North Africa. Later they fought throughout the French colonial empire. A classic adventure story of the Foreign Legion is *Beau Geste* by P.C. Wren (1885–1941). YA

Forester, C(ecil) S(cott) (1899–1966) An English novelist, Forester is best known for his creation of *Horatio Hornblower, the seaman in a series of 10 novels about the British navy during the Napoleonic wars. Hornblower, first introduced in *The Happy Return* (1937), was

MR = Middle Reader   YA = Young Adult Reader   * = See this main entry

considered by some to be ideally representative of British perseverance. Forester, born in Cairo, Egypt, spent his early years in Spain, Corsica, and France, and his later boyhood in a London suburb. Though he first studied medicine, he chose a writing career instead, preferring to think of himself first as a correspondent, not a novelist. He was both a popular and prolific writer. In addition to the Hornblower books, Forester is remembered for *The African Queen* (1935), which describes the courage of a proper British spinster and the cockney skipper of an aging steam launch who use explosives to blow up a German warship. Forester recounts his early years in his autobiography, *Long Before Forty* (1967). MR & YA

Forgotten Door, The (1965) By *Alexander Key, this *science fiction story sets you to thinking about your world. What would it be like to visit Earth by accident, as a total stranger? Little Jon, the hero, falls through a door and lands on a mountainside so hard that he is knocked unconscious. He wakes up dazed with no idea of who he is or how he got to such an odd place. Nor do you, but you learn that Little Jon can read people's minds and talk to animals. You also feel the danger he encounters from a gang of men who try to capture him to exploit his extraordinary powers. During his search for help he is befriended by the Bean family, who are put in danger as well. While he is being chased, he has no time to search for the secret way back to his own more advanced and peaceful planet. Key's vivid descriptions of Little Jon's perils reflect a unique viewpoint, and you can feel the tension build. Key has written other books that you might like, for instance, *Escape to Witch Mountain*, probably Key's best-known novel, and *The Magic Meadow* (1975), about a crippled boy from a charity hospital who transports himself to a better way of life in the future. MR

Forman, James (1932–) Born on Long Island, New York, and an attorney by profession, this prolific author is known by many young readers. In one of Forman's finest novels, *My Enemy, My Brother* (1969), 13-year-old Dan is freed from a concentration camp by Russian soldiers. With his grandfather, he travels home, but then decides to find his way to Israel. Once there, Dan discovers that he is in fact the enemy of his best friend, an Arab boy, who like himself has to take sides in the war that develops between their peoples. In *People of the Dream* (1972), Chief Joseph (1840–1904) leads his people in a desperate struggle to remain free. It is a portrayal of a courageous leader of the Nez Percé tribe of Oregon who chooses to resist rather than surrender to the white men who seek to destroy the culture and spirit of the tribe. In *Ceremony of Innocence* (1970), a novel based on a true story, a brother and sister are killed for acting according to their conscience. A more recent novel, *A Ballad for Hogskin Hill* (1979), is set among the Kentucky hills in mining country. David, a teenage banjo player, battles with a coal company over the evils of strip mining. MR & YA

Forster, E(dward) M(organ) (1879–1970) Regarded as one of the 20th century's finest novelists, this English author, noted for his short stories and essays as well, is known best for his last and greatest novel, *A Passage to India*, a work that depicts the prejudices and injustices of British rule in India. After his father's death, Forster was raised by his mother, to whom he remained devoted until her death. Though his schooling was generally unhappy, at Cambridge University he met the wonderful and talented people who came to be called the Bloomsbury group. Known for their unconventional life-styles, this gathering of intellectuals met in Bloomsbury, a section of London, before, during, and after World War I, and included the writer *Virginia Woolf, artist and critic Roger Fry (1866–1934), and art critic Clive Bell (1881–1964). While in his late 20s, Forster published four novels, but was then silent for 14 years, when *A Passage to India* was published. In *The Longest Journey* (1907), Frederick Elliot, though unloved as an orphan, finds some measure of acceptance at Cambridge University and ultimately develops a close relationship with a half-brother. A popular novel, *A Room with a View* (1908), involves a young Englishwoman, Lucy Honeychurch, who is taken to Italy by a chaperone and meets a young man who tries to free her spirit. *Howards End* (1910) is a masterful evocation of a place, Howards End, an estate that binds together successive generations of a family at odds with one another. *A Room with a View* was filmed in 1985 and *Howards End* in 1992. YA

Forsyte Saga, The (1922) By *John Galsworthy, this trilogy, consisting of three previously published novels and two interludes, chronicles the Forsyte family through three generations during England's transition from the *Victorian era to the 20th century. The first novel, *The Man of Property* (1906), opens in 1886 at a family gathering celebrating the engagement of Old Jolyon Forsyte's granddaughter, June. Her father, who had scandalized the family by running off with a governess, has been estranged from them for years. Old Jolyon, increasingly lonely, reconciles with his son and grows to love the grandchildren he has just come to know. His nephew, Soames, who epitomizes the materialism of some men of property, is married to Irene. Wretched in her marriage, she falls in love with Philip Bosinney, June's fiancé. Irene leaves Soames, supporting herself as a teacher of music, and eventually is befriended by Old Jolyon, who becomes attached to her. The interlude following Part I ends with his death. In the second novel, *In Chancery* (1920), Soames, after a scandalous divorce, marries a young French woman in order to have a child. His daughter, Fleur, becomes his life. Meanwhile, Jolyon, Old Jolyon's son, marries Irene and has a son, Jon. In the final book, *To Let* (1921), Fleur and Jon fall in love after a chance meeting, but Jon refuses to marry Fleur after discovering the truth about her father. In the saga, Galsworthy satirizes materialism and celebrates beauty and art, represented primarily by the artistic sensitivity of Jolyon and the beauty of Irene. If you enjoy family sagas, try also the novel *Buddenbrooks* by *Thomas Mann, the *Jalna series of

novels by *Mazo de la Roche, and the Poldark series by Winston Graham (1910–), set in Cornwall in the late 18th and early 19th centuries and beginning with the novel *Ross Poldark* (1945). The Forsyte Saga was the basis for a 26-episode TV production in 1967. VA

Forsyth, Frederick (1938–) After serving as a fighter pilot in the British Royal Air Force when he was 19 years old, Forsyth in civilian life took up journalism, and in the early 1960s—at the height of the Cold War—was a news service correspondent in communist East Berlin. As an author of suspense novels, Forsyth likes to combine fact and fiction. His first was *The Day of the Jackal* (1971), the tale of an attempt to assassinate Charles de Gaulle (1890–1970), the French leader. Its detailed account of what the assassin does to forge passports and secure a special rifle and other materials is a good example of Forsyth's method. *The Odessa File* (1972) involves a secret plan of former German Nazis. Mercenary soldiers in Africa are at the center of *The Dogs of War* (1974). *The Fourth Protocol* (1984) is set in the near future and concerns a Soviet attempt to stir up enmity between the United States and Great Britain. Forsyth has also written a story for younger readers, *The Shepherd* (1975), about a Royal Air Force pilot whose plane is in trouble over the North Sea on Christmas Eve, 1957, and who is led safely home by the ghost of a World War II bomber. A movie was made of *The Day of the Jackal* in 1973, of *The Odessa File* in 1975, and of *The Dogs of War* in 1981. If you like these books, try those of *Len Deighton, *Ian Fleming, *John Le Carré, *Robert Ludlum, and *Alastair MacLean. MR & YA

Foundation Trilogy, The Three *science fiction novels by *Isaac Asimov chronicle the fall of the Galactic Empire: *Foundation* (1951), *Foundation and Empire* (1952), and *Second Foundation* (1953) together tell the story of the first four centuries of the interval between the fall of the Galactic Empire and the founding of the Second Empire. Only one man, Hari

Seldon, realizes that the Galactic Empire is failing. He develops the science of psychohistory, which predicts the actions of large groups of people, and discovers there will be an interval of 30,000 years of barbarism if steps are not taken to shorten it. In order to reduce the Interregnum to only a thousand years, Seldon creates the Seldon Plan, which calls for two Foundations, one open and dedicated to the physical sciences, and the other shrouded in secrecy and devoted to mental sciences. The First Foundation, starting as a tiny community on the fringes of the Galaxy, takes over the barbarous planets that surround it as each breaks away from the dying Empire. With superior technology, advanced and miniaturized because of the difficulties of surviving on its metal-poor planet, the First Foundation begins to create a new Empire, always following Seldon's Plan. But psychohistory cannot predict the mutant known as the Mule, a telepath of extraordinary power, and the Mule almost destroys the Foundation and its progress toward a new Empire.

The Second Foundation, long forgotten by the First Foundation, is forced to take an active role in the Galaxy to put it back on the path of Seldon's Plan. The First Foundation, now aware of the existence of its mirror image, does not want a future in which they are ruled by mentalists and begins to work against the Second Foundation, the true keeper of Seldon's Plan. The Second Foundation manages to direct events so that the First Foundation appears to conquer the Second and continue the Plan.

Asimov continued the series with the publication of *Foundation's Edge* (1982), which tells of the discovery of yet a third force in the Galaxy, and *Foundation and Earth* (1986), about a superorganism called Gaia, and the move toward humanity's more perfect future. The Foundation novels are popular because of Asimov's strong story-telling, vivid descriptions, and well-drawn, likable characters. YA

Fountainhead, The (1943) This novel, by the Russian-born American novelist and philosopher Ayn Rand (1905–1982), celebrates the ideals of a young architect, Howard Roark, and his refusal to compromise with mediocrity. Always true to himself, he seems immune to the temptations of success and power. After being expelled from Stanton Institute of Technology, Roark leaves for New York City, hoping to work for once-famous Henry Cameron, an architect now living on the fringe. Roark brings new life to Cameron. After Cameron becomes ill, Roark sets himself up in a small office. His designs are clean and stark, but generally not appreciated. Meanwhile, a former classmate, Keating, is flourishing though barely competent, in part due to the efforts of Ellsworth Toohey, a man who personifies evil and tries to destroy Roark. Roark meets and falls in love with Dominique, a journalist who sees beyond hypocrisy but is not ready to endure the world's scorn. Now Roark is given increasingly important commissions, and, in spite of Toohey's attempts to prevent it, Roark's fame spreads. But when he agrees to help Keating with plans for a housing project, his career is jeopardized. The builders sabotage the project, and Roark, refusing to have his work compromised, dynamites it. Roark is cleared, and Dominique, ready for him at last, joins him. Rand espoused a philosophy called Objectivism, which emphasizes individualism and self-interest. If you like reading about individualists, you might try *The Enemy* (1964), a novel about a builder who attempts bold new ideas in housing, by James Drought (1931–1983). *The Fountainhead* was made into a film in 1949. YR

Four Horsemen of the Apocalypse, The See *Revelation.

Fowles, John (1926–) An English novelist and essayist, this highly acclaimed writer is perhaps best known in America for his third novel, **The French Lieutenant's Woman*, a story of a *Victorian romance. Fowles has spent much of his life teaching, at the University of Poitiers, France, as well as at a boys' school on a Greek island. He now writes full time. His first novel, *The Collector* (1958),

Reynard the Fox is the central figure in
a number of medieval fables.

probes a young man's obsession to imprison
and dissect the girl he believes he loves. The
novel, a psychological study of a psychopathic
killer, is also an *allegory of a sick society. *The
Magus* (1965) is about an English schoolteacher
on a small Greek island who becomes involved
in an elaborate game in which reality and illusion are intermingled. *Daniel Martin* (1977),
perhaps his most accessible novel, is the story
of an English screenwriter's search for himself,
a search involving his past and three women
who played important roles in his life. In all of
Fowles's fiction, the lines between past and
present, between myth and reality, are often
blurred. *The Collector* was adapted for film in
1965, and *The Magus* in 1968. YA

fox The view that the fox does wrong but escapes justice and punishment by its cunning
goes as far back as the *fables of *Aesop. In the
12th and 13th centuries, French stories or fables, in which animals were given human
traits, were popular, and Reynard the Fox was
one of them. In Germany the brothers
*Grimm brought Reynard into their collec-
tions of folk and fairy tales, and the clever fox
appears in "The Nun's Priest's Tale" in *The
Canterbury Tales* by *Geoffrey Chaucer. In
everyday speech, to be "clever as a fox" is not
entirely a compliment, because it implies that
such a person may be trying to outsmart
you. As *Benjamin Franklin wrote in *Poor
Richard's Almanack*, "Many Foxes grow grey,
but few grow good." MR & YA

Fox, Paula A. (1923–) Though known primarily as a writer of novels for younger readers,
Fox has written extensively for adults as well.
In both areas she writes with intelligence and
clarity. The young people of her novels are often lonely and isolated, and many, like Ben in
Blowfish Live in the Sea (1970) and Catherine
in *The Moonlight Man*, struggle to make connections with absentee and alcoholic fathers.
In *A Place Apart* (1980), Victoria is faced with
moving from her Boston home to a smaller one
in the suburbs. She must also work out a
difficult relationship with a teenage boy who
attempts to control her. In *The Village by the
Sea*, the young heroine, Emma, must cope
with sickness in her family. In what is perhaps
her most controversial novel, *The Slave

Dancer, a New Orleans boy is kidnapped and brought aboard a slave ship bound for West Africa. MR

France, Anatole [Jacques Anatole François Thibault] (1844–1924) A French novelist and influential man of letters, France as a young boy sensed the power of the written word while sitting among the bookshelves of his father's Paris bookstore. Though painfully shy and somewhat homely, he fell in love many times, especially with actresses. The publication of his first novel, *The Crime of Sylvestre Bonnard* (1881), gave him entry into the cultural circles of France, helped by a relationship with an influential Parisian who became his mistress. This novel centers on the bibliophile Bonnard and his relationship with his young ward, Jeanne, who is actually the granddaughter of a woman he once loved. *Thaïs* (1890), a later novel, which is a poignant love story and sensual coming-of-age story, became the basis for the opera *Thaïs* (1894) by Jules Massenet (1842–1912). A novel about the French Revolution, *The Gods Are Athirst* (1912), generally regarded as his finest work, tells about Evariste Gamelin, an artist who commits himself to the French Revolution but loses his humanity at the same time. France became politically active at the time of the Dreyfus case, in which a French army captain, Alfred Dreyfus (1859–1935), was falsely found guilty of spying. France continued to believe in the Jewish captain's innocence and wrote passionately in his defense. Another French novelist whose works you may like to read, Emile Zola (1840–1902), also championed Dreyfus's cause, in an open letter titled "J'Accuse" (1898). In 1906 Dreyfus was pardoned. France was awarded the Nobel Prize for literature in 1921. YA

Francis, Dick [Richard Stanley Francis] (1920–) Of Welsh descent, Francis writes detective novels with a background of horse racing, which he knows very well, having been a steeplechase jockey in Great Britain. When he retired in 1967 he had ridden in 2,305 races. He then became the racing correspondent for a British newspaper and turned to writing detective fiction with his novel *Dead Cert* (1962), about a jockey who puts his life in jeopardy when he uncovers a crooked racetrack scheme. Nearly all his books feature a jockey or someone connected with racing as amateur sleuth. *Odds Against* (1965) has a crippled jockey as the main character. *Slayride* (1973), *High Stakes* (1975), and *Straight* (1989) are other well-done books of this kind. In almost all of Francis's novels the villains are devilishly evil, and the heroes at some point are beaten up by the villain or by his henchmen. The plots of these novels are interesting and the characters believable, with realistic settings in the British horse-racing world. *Odds Against* was made into a TV series as *The Racing Game* in 1980. If you like these detective stories, you will want to read those of *Ian Fleming, *Dashiel Hammett, and *Alastair MacLean. YA

Frankenstein, or the Modern Prometheus (1818), by Mary Wollstonecraft Shelley (1797–1851), was written when Shelley was only 19 years old, in response to a ghost-story writing contest. This *Gothic novel, set chiefly in Switzerland, deals with the creation of life, the nature of humankind, and the moral problems that are raised by humanity's slow but steady mastery of science, nature, and life itself.

Victor Frankenstein travels to college in Ingolstadt, Switzerland, where he fixes on a project to create "a new species [which] would bless me as its creator and source." Thus, from spare body parts, he creates a monster. After seeing it, Frankenstein is filled with horror and becomes ill. When he recovers, Frankenstein learns that his young brother, William, has been murdered. Though Frankenstein knows his monster killed William, Justine Moritz, a close friend of the family, is accused. Unable to contradict the evidence, she confesses and is sentenced to death. Elizabeth, a cousin whom Frankenstein loves, is distraught. The confession of the sweet young Justine challenges Elizabeth's belief that humans are naturally good. She cries, "How shall I ever again believe in human goodness?" Later, the creature tracks down Frankenstein as he wanders through the Swiss countryside and describes his miserable life to his creator. Despite his good intentions, the monster explains, humans cannot accept him and want to kill him. Abandoned and friendless, the monster demands that Frankenstein create a companion. Frankenstein promises to do so, but cannot complete the project. The angry monster kills Frankenstein's closest friend, Henry Clerval, a murder for which Frankenstein himself is arrested but then released.

Frankenstein returns home and marries Elizabeth, anticipating a confrontation with the monster who promised, "I will be with you on your wedding night." The monster evades Frankenstein's vigil and strikes again, killing Elizabeth. Now Frankenstein embarks on a search for the monster. The creature leads his creator farther and farther north, so that Frankenstein will suffer as he has. Finally, a ragged and dying Frankenstein reaches a boat that is stranded in the ice-filled sea. He tells his story to the ship's captain, Robert Walton. As Frankenstein is dying, the monster climbs aboard in search of forgiveness, but he is too late. Miserable and hating himself, the monster jumps onto an ice raft and heads north to die. A modern novel you may want to read is *Frankenstein Unbound* (1973) by the English writer Brian W. Aldiss (1926–), in which a man travels back in time to meet Mary Shelley and her monstrous creation. In addition to the classic movie *Frankenstein*, made in 1931, Shelley's novel has also inspired many movie sequels, such as *Bride of Frankenstein*, produced in 1935, and the spoof *Young Frankenstein*, filmed in 1979. YA

Franklin, Benjamin (1706–1790) A statesman, author, innovator, and scientist whose *Autobiography* (first published in whole in 1868) is sometimes referred to as the first book to become an American classic, Franklin was born in Boston, but when he was 17 years old he left for Philadelphia. The youngest of 17 children, Franklin was apprenticed to his brother James, a printer. In his adopted city, this "wisest American," as Franklin is sometimes called, set up his own newspaper and established the first subscription library and the first fire company.

A man of diverse talents, he performed scientific experiments leading to the invention of the lightning rod. He also established the Philadelphia Society, which brought together the leaders of the colonies and helped identify and define the American mind. One of his most important contributions was helping to draft the Declaration of Independence, a work he was also to sign. Because his diplomatic skills were so valuable, he was one of the American representatives sent to negotiate the treaty of peace with Great Britain. It was Franklin's belief that the United States is indeed a better kind of society. Through *Poor Richard's Almanack*, annually published under the name Richard Saunders, Franklin was able to influence thousands with his ideas and aphorisms, such as "Make haste slowly." Younger readers will enjoy *Ben and Me* by *Robert Lawson. See also *proverb. MR &YA

Franny and Zooey (1961), a long story in two parts by *J.D. Salinger, tells about the two youngest members of an intelligent and artistic family, the Glasses. Like *Holden Caulfield, the main character in Salinger's popular novel *The Catcher in the Rye*, the main characters in *Franny and Zooey* are also troubled young adults. The first part of the book describes the visit of 21-year-old Franny, the youngest child, to her friend Lane Coutell at his college. Even though Franny says she loves Lane and tells him that she misses him, she knows that she really does not. As they eat lunch, Franny alternately criticizes and praises Lane. At one point, she excuses herself and goes to the ladies' room, where she breaks down and cries for five minutes. She returns and lunch progresses. After lunch, as they are leaving, Franny faints.

The second part of the book, narrated by Buddy, the eldest living brother, is set in the Glasses' home in New York City and, to some extent, explains Franny's unusual behavior. She has left college because of a nervous breakdown. From Buddy, you learn that Seymour, the oldest child, committed suicide eight years earlier. Zooey, a successful actor, is critical of everything and everybody. He believes the influence of his two older brothers, Seymour and Buddy, is responsible for his and Franny's present condition. Zooey tells Franny: "We're freaks, that's all. Those two . . . got us nice and early and made us into freaks with freakish standards, that's all." One of the causes of Franny's breakdown is her preoccupation with two books about prayer. Though Zooey tries to help Franny by talking to her, he becomes critical of her depression and upsets both of them. But Zooey tries to talk to Franny again. This time, fearing that she would not talk to him, he phones her, pretending he is Buddy. After Franny realizes that it is Zooey, he explains to her that *Jesus is in everyone and not to be found in constantly repeating a prayer. Finally, Franny understands and lies "quiet, smiling at the ceiling" before falling into a deep sleep. YA

Fraser, Antonia (Pakenham) (1932–) Though known mostly for her detective novels and biographies, this English author began her career with a nonfiction book, *A History of Toys* (1966). Fraser's initial detective novel, *Quiet as a Nun* (1977), introduced Jemima Shore, a young TV investigative reporter who has an "overriding curiosity," golden hair, and a white Mercedes sports car. In this book Shore solves a murder in a convent where she once went to school. In *Jemima Shore's First Case and Other Stories* (1986), one story goes back in time to when Shore, then only 15 years old, helps solve a drug trafficking case. Fraser's biographies, which include *Mary, Queen of Scots* (1969), *Oliver Cromwell* (1973), and *King James I of Scotland* (1979), are vivid and interesting. If you are interested in the history of women, you should read *The Weaker Vessel: Women's Lot in Seventeenth-Century England* (1984). Books by *Agatha Christie, *Sue Grafton, *Marcia Muller, and *Sara Paretsky will please you if you enjoy the Shore books. YA

Freaky Friday (1972), a novel by Mary Rodgers (1931–), captures the events of a most unusual day in the life of a 13-year-old girl who wakes up one morning to find that she is her own mother. Annabel is understandably confused at first but soon finds herself delighted by the opportunity to actually *be* her mom. The whole day stretches out ahead of her. She makes coffee for her dad, Mr. Andrews, who is now strangely her husband; washes his shirts along with dirty sneakers and a shaggy rug belonging to the dog; fires the cleaning lady; and attends a conference about Annabel's difficulties in school. She arranges for 14-year-old Boris, a neighbor in her apartment building, to babysit for her 6-year-old brother, Ape Face, and then panics when he disappears. Annabel, meanwhile, being played out by her mother, never makes it to school that day, and Mr. Andrews is bringing home clients for dinner. Annabel, still trapped in her mother's body, finally escapes to the bedroom and is confronted by her now-beautiful and braceless teenage daughter. A mother-daughter switch is made just in time for Annabel, in her own body, to greet Boris, who has been her secret heart-throb for quite some time. Looking at herself from her mother's perspective for a day has certainly changed her life! There are two sequels, *A Billion for Boris* (1974), which concerns Annabel's boyfriend, and *Summer Switch* (1982), which tells what happens when Ape Face and his father switch bodies just as one is about to go to summer camp and the other to Hollywood for a business meeting. Mary Rodgers, born in New York City, is the daughter of Richard Rodgers (1902–1979), the well-known composer of musical comedies. If you enjoyed *Freaky Friday*, you will like the Eloise series of books, beginning with *Eloise: A Book for Precocious Grown-Ups* (1955) by Kay Thompson (1913–). Eloise, a brat who lives at the Plaza Hotel in New York City, gets into all sorts of crazy escapades. Her adventures continue in *Eloise at Christmastime* (1958) and *Eloise in Moscow* (1959). *Freaky Friday* was adapted for film in 1977. MR

Freeling, Nicolas (1927–) Though born in England, Freeling has lived mostly on the Continent, including the Netherlands and France, both settings of his detective novels. In *Love in Amsterdam* (1962) he introduces Inspector Van der Valk, a somewhat leftist intellectual and a foe of the bureaucracy for which he works. In

King of the Rainy Country (1965) Van der Valk looks into the disappearance of a millionaire who turns up in Cologne, Germany, with a girl. From there the story moves to Innsbruck, Austria, and to a tragic ending. Tiring of Van der Valk, Freeling had him killed in Auprès de Ma Blonde (1972). He then created a new detective, Henri Castang, on the police force of a French provincial city. In Castang's City (1980), as in other books about Castang, Freeling is concerned with the problems of modern society, sometimes at the expense of the story. Other Freeling novels include Tsing-Boom! (1969), Gadget (1977), The Night Lords (1978), Widow (1979), and Cold Iron (1986). If you enjoy Freeling's books, try those of *Georges Simenon, *Maj Sjöwall and Per Wahlöö, and *Willem Van de Wetering. YA

Frémont, John C(harles) (1813–1890) An American explorer and U.S. Army officer, Frémont made three expeditions to the West, the first under the guidance of Kit Carson (1809–1868), and told about them in Report of the Exploring Expedition to the Rocky Mountains, 1842, and to Oregon, and to North California, 1843–1844 (1845). The account, which became very popular, partly because it contains helpful advice for the traveler, was written with the help of his wife, Jessie Benton Frémont (1824–1902), the daughter of political leader Thomas Hart Benton (1782–1858). Earlier, during Frémont's army career, he had been found guilty of mutiny and disobedience for his activities during the Mexican War in the conquest of California. His sentence was later remitted by presidential pardon. In 1856 Frémont entered the presidential campaign on the antislavery platform of the newly formed Republican party. He lost the election to James Buchanan (1791–1868). You will enjoy reading about the Frémonts in the fictionalized biography Immortal Wife (1944) by *Irving Stone and also in the novel Dream West (1983) by David Nevin (1927–). Dream West was made into a TV miniseries in 1986. YA

French Lieutenant's Woman, The (1969) This novel by *John Fowles, set in Victorian times, dramatizes the strong class distinctions of 19th-century England. It is also a brilliant love story, portraying Sarah Woodruff, a young woman who is a companion for the most proper Mrs. Poulteney. Sarah is both educated and personable, but there are hints of a past involving a French seaman. Charles Smithson, a gentleman, is initially drawn to Sarah out of compassion, but, despite himself, falls in love. Charles, however, is engaged to Ernestina, and even if he were not, Sarah would be unacceptable because of her unknown, probably lower-class origin. Charles struggles with the opposing forces within him. Very much the product of the class system himself, he is acutely aware of their class differences. But Charles is also a thinking man who rejects what his class represents, and is ultimately helpless against the force of his love. Sarah, though deeply in love, runs from Charles, knowing their relationship will bring him certain ruin. Charles breaks his engagement to Ernestina, and is sued for breach of promise. He searches for Sarah throughout England and America. Meanwhile, Sarah has borne him a daughter, and finds acceptance in London's literary circles. Even his eventual discovery of her fails to set him free. If you enjoy Victorian romance, you should read *Jane Eyre, a novel by *Charlotte Brontë. A film based on The French Lieutenant's Woman was released in 1981. YA

Friar Laurence is the Franciscan monk in *William Shakespeare's *Romeo and Juliet who agrees secretly to marry the young lovers in hope of ending the feud between their families, the Montagues and Capulets. When Juliet's family insists on her marriage to Paris, the kindly friar gives her a sleeping potion to make it appear that she is dead. Meanwhile, a message is sent to Romeo, who has been banished from Verona. When the lovers end their lives, Friar Laurence proclaims the end to the feud. YA

Friar Tuck is the paunchy and jovial monk of the *Robin Hood tales who probably got his name because his habit was tucked by a girdle. Dressed in the style of the Franciscan order, in

MR = Middle Reader   YA = Young Adult Reader   * = See this main entry

a russet habit and a red-corded girdle with a gold tassel, the friar accompanied Robin Hood and his band of outlaws in their escapades in Sherwood Forest. He is also the holy clerk of Copmanhurst in *Ivanhoe by *Walter Scott. In Scott's novel, Robin Hood sets out to find the supposedly rich curate of Fountain Dale. He spies a strange monk singing beside a brook and convinces him to carry him on his back across the stream. On the return trip the friar dumps Robin Hood into the water and, after a skirmish, joins the outlaws. MR & YA

"Friar's Tale, The" One of the many tales in *Geoffrey Chaucer's *The Canterbury Tales, this story is a humorous and *satirical portrayal of a summoner and the sin of greed. Summoners extorted money from people who had sinned and in return gave certificates of absolution. There was no love lost between summoners and friars.

As the summoner travels, he meets the devil disguised as another summoner. However, the summoner does not "for very filth and shame, say that he was a summoner." The devil reveals his identity, but the summoner is too dumb to realize what the devil has in store for him. The pair encounter a villager whose cart is stuck in the mud. The man curses the horses, saying, "Devil take all." But the devil does nothing, because he knows the man does not mean what he says. Later, they reach an old, sick widow from whom the summoner demands money, or else he will excommunicate her. She has no money and begs for mercy, but the summoner has none to give her. Instead he threatens to take her frying pan as collateral. She falls to her knees cursing the summoner and wishing that the devil take him. The devil asks her if she truly means this. She says that if the summoner will not repent, she means it. The summoner, either too dumb or too greedily evil, adamantly refuses to repent, and the devil whisks him away to a "special shelf" in hell reserved for summoners. The friar concludes his tale with a warning to the pilgrims on their way to Canterbury, among whom is a summoner. YA

Fritz, Jean (1915–) Born in Hankow, China, this popular biographer and novelist first became interested in history out of a desire to find her roots. Though she had heard about her homeland, America, from her earliest childhood, she experienced it for the first time when she was 13 years old. In *Homesick: My Own Story, she recaptured the intense feelings of her lonely childhood in China. She recounted her return to the country of her birth in *China Homecoming.

Fritz's historical books reflect her conviction that younger readers need to become emotionally involved in history in order to understand how people behave. To help them do so, Fritz believes she has to get in touch with the child within herself. *What's the Big Idea, Ben Franklin?* (1976) and *Where Was Patrick Henry on the 29th of May?* (1975) lead you to a look at what historical figures were really like. MR & YA

From Here to Eternity (1951), a novel by *James Jones, re-creates the world of the U.S. Army's Schofield Barracks, Hawaii, in the year before the bombing of Pearl Harbor on December 7, 1941. Robert E. Lee Prewitt, an avid Army bugler who has a talent for boxing, is transferred to G Company, where he is expected to perform in the ring. He stubbornly refuses and consequently becomes the victim of political games and harsh pressures imposed on him by his superiors. Sergeant Warden does his best to protect "Prew" but is not always successful. But, between various trumped-up punishments, Prew manages to have some fun, idling away hours with a hot game of poker, playing the guitar with fellow musicians, and going to town on payday.

When his best friend, Angelo Maggio, is sent to the stockade and is beaten to death by a guard, Prew takes revenge, but then he leaves base without permission. Though he seeks shelter with an attractive prostitute with whom he has fallen in love, he becomes miserable and drinks excessively. Ironically, in attempting to return to base, he is killed. Though you may be intimidated by the length of the novel, you will be quickly caught up in this unvarnished view of Army life. If you liked *From Here to Eternity*, you will enjoy Jones's other novels chronicling military life during and after World War II: *The Thin Red Line* (1962) and *Whistle* (1978). You will also like **The Naked and the Dead* by *Norman Mailer, about an infantry platoon in the Pacific, and **The Young Lions* by *Irwin Shaw, about the impact of the war in Europe on three soldiers, two Americans and one German. A film based on *From Here to Eternity* was made in 1953 and a TV miniseries adaptation was made in 1979. YA

From the Mixed-Up Files of Mrs. Basil E. Frankweiler (1967), by *E.L. Konigsburg, opens with Claudia planning to run away to the Metropolitan Museum of Art in New York City, not because she is angry, but because she just wants to teach her parents how much they really love her. Claudia, almost 12 years old, is a good organizer, but her younger brother, Jamie, takes some selling. They explore the museum before deciding to move in, taking a bath in a fountain of bronze dolphins and collecting the coins from the water. Laundry is a problem, but they sleep in comfort in a bed. Then a statue given to the museum by a Mrs. Frankweiler arouses their curiosity. They want to know who made it, as do the curators, the museum's experts. Claudia, who had expected to feel different living in the museum but does not, wants to go home. But they cannot until they solve the mystery of the statue. If you like this story, you might like other books by Konigsburg, for example, **Father's Arcane Daughter*; **About the B'nai Bagels*; and *Altogether, One at a Time* (1971), which is a collection of four stories that shows how things can be both bad and good at the same time. *From the Mixed-Up Files of Mrs. Basil E. Frankweiler* won the *Newbery Medal in 1968 and was filmed in 1973. MR & YA

Frost, Robert (1874–1963) Best known as the simple and moral voice of rural New England life, this very American poet is actually more than he at first seems. A poem, he once said, is

Robert Frost

a momentary stay against confusion. Frost, the first poet to participate in a presidential inauguration, that of John F. Kennedy (1917–1963) in 1961, became nationally known through the television coverage, and he remains probably the most familiar of modern American poets. "The Death of the Hired Man," from the collection *North of Boston* (1914), is a well-known narrative poem involving a conversation between a New England farmer and his wife about their former hired man, who has come back to die. "Birches," from *Mountain Interval* (1916), creates images that linger in the mind: arched trees, for example, become girls on their hands and knees, and ice becomes shattered crystal. Less known is "The Hill Wife," a highly acclaimed work also from that collection, which intimates finalities other than death. Though born in San Francisco, Frost spent most of his life on farms in New England. His first book of poems, *A Boy's Will* (1913), was published in England, where he had gone to live for a while. When he returned, he found himself almost famous. MR & YA

Fry, Christopher [Christopher Harris] (1907–) A Quaker-educated English dramatist known for his verse plays, Fry was strongly molded by his religious upbringing, an influence reflected in his writing. The growth of realism in drama after World War II pushed his work out of the limelight. It was *The Lady's Not for Burning that established him not only in his own country but internationally as well. In the play, Thomas Mendip, a former soldier tired of killing, yearns for death but finds redemption through love. In Venus Observed (1950), a duke's grown son becomes his rival in love. Fry's works frequently explore the wonders and the paradoxes of life; his characters are often poles of contradiction. His highly regarded and moving religious drama, A Sleep of Prisoners (1950), portrays four prisoners of war held captive in a church, exploring both themselves and each other through their dreams. YA

Fuentes, Carlos (1928–) A Mexican novelist, Fuentes is also a lawyer and a diplomat. He is known best to Americans for his novel The Old Gringo (1985), a fictionalized account of *Ambrose Bierce's last days in Mexico. Bierce, an American journalist and short-story writer, disappeared into Mexico in 1913; Fuentes's tale is recollected by Harriet Winslow, an American spinster whose encounter with Bierce will have tragic consequences for both. The novel, which examines the Mexican Revolution as well as the tangled alliance with the United States, shows Fuentes's gift for what is sometimes called magic realism, a device that allows him to enrich what is real by incorporating dimensions of the imagination. It was the earlier and less accessible The Death of Artemio Cruz (1962), however, that established Fuentes's international acclaim. Told through the dying voice of Artemio, a political leader of contemporary Mexico, the novel takes us through the struggle with his conscience as he surveys his life. Like much of Fuentes's work,

this is a metaphorical study of modern Mexico and the never-realized ideals of that country's revolution. Another writer who found Mexico to be a rich source of material for his novels and short stories is *B. Traven. The Old Gringo was made into a motion picture in 1989. YA

Fugard, Athol (1932–) The son of an Afrikaans mother and English father, this playwright, born in Cape Province, is South Africa's leading dramatic voice. He writes of the survival of oppressed people in the land of apartheid, the policy of racial segregation in that country. Blood Knot (1961), the first play with a mixed cast performed in South Africa, involves two brothers, one black and the other light-skinned, who in a game finally confront their rage and their relationship. Fugard believes that the purpose of his work is to be as truthful a witness as he can to the nameless and the destitute in one corner of the world. Best known to American audiences is Master Harold . . . and the Boys (1982), set in a Port Elizabeth tearoom on a rainy afternoon. It explores the close relationship of Master Harold with one of the black waiters employed at the tearoom. The Road to Mecca (1984), one of Fugard's most daring experiments, is concerned with individual loneliness and pain, and dramatizes, as does all of the playwright's work, the effects of his country's political system on its people. In addition to writing one novel, he has written many other plays, some in collaboration with actors. If you are interested in other literature about South Africa, you might explore the work of Nadine Gordimer (1923–), especially her short stories and the novel Burger's Daughter (1979), which tells about a young woman whose parents die in jail, where they were being held for their work on behalf of black liberation. Another writer whose works center on South Africa is *Alan Paton. YA

***Futuretrack 5,** a *science fiction novel by British writer *Robert Westall, describes the adventures of Henry Kitson as he finds his way through the maze of life in the 21st century. You first meet Henry in his last year of college, anticipating his future as an adult "Est," a member of England's privileged class. But he scores 100 on his exams and is instead transported to the world of the "Techs," who manage the computer system that controls the country. Assigned to chief technician Idris, the man who has masterminded the controls, he learns much about Laura, a master computer. Laura, though only a computer, has mysterious powers and a voice modeled on that of the woman Idris had loved and lost. From Idris he learns of the evil Scott-Astbury, who in some devious way has corrupted the system.

Henry goes on the "razzle" (leaves without permission) to the world of the Unnens, but unlike most of the other young Techs, he does not plan to return. He meets Keri, London's racing champion, and on the Mitsubishi his father has purchased, he vacations with her to the Forbidden Zone, somewhere in Scotland, and tries to uncover the secrets of Scott-Astbury. In attempting to escape the ever-present Paramils and Psychotroopers, the couple try to lose themselves in the world of the Fens, people who live simply as farmers. Henry devises a plan to return to Cambridge, and to capture control of the system that had manipulated their lives. Though he does gain control, he finds himself a prisoner to Laura forever because now that Idris is dead, Laura will take direction from no one else. If you liked this novel, you might enjoy reading *Colossus* (1966) and its sequel, *The Fall of Colossus* (1977), by D(ennis) F(eltham) Jones (1917–1981), about a scientist who builds a supercomputer that takes over the world. MR & YA

Gabriel In the Christian, Jewish, and Islamic traditions, Gabriel is an archangel who serves as one of the chief messengers of the Deity. For example, in Christian belief he is the angel who appeared in the *Bible to the Virgin Mary to announce that she would be the mother of *Jesus; in Jewish belief he is one of the angels who buried *Moses; and in the *Koran he is the angel who revealed the sacred laws to *Muhammad. In the popular view, he is thought of as the angel whose horn will announce Judgment Day and the end of the world.

Gaea See *Cronus and *Uranus.

Gaines, Ernest J. (1933–) Born on a Louisiana plantation, Gaines describes in his books the experience of his Southern childhood. His works are marked by an authentic and powerful use of black language and humor. His best-known novel is *The Autobiography of Miss Jane Pittman*, the story of a woman's life from her days as a slave girl in 1864, during the Civil War, to her participation in the civil rights movement a hundred years later. Other novels include *In My Father's House* (1978), about the relationship between a southern town's aging civil rights leader and a young stranger, and *A Gathering of Old Men* (1983), about race relations in the wake of a murder of a white Cajun farmer. Younger readers will enjoy *A Long Day in November* (1971), which describes a typical day on a 1940s plantation as seen through the eyes of a black child. *A Gathering of Old Men* was filmed in 1987. MR & YA

Galahad came to *King Arthur's court when he was 18 years old, and *Lancelot learned that Galahad, the noblest and purest knight of the *Round Table, was his son. The golden words on a chair of the Round Table, which had been reserved for the knight who would find the *Holy Grail and would bring instant death to any other person who sat upon it, suddenly changed from "Siege Perilous" to "Siege of Sir Galahad." Galahad proved to be the only knight who could draw the sword from a marble stone floating in the nearby river. The stone bore an inscription that the sword was for the "greatest knight in the world." At one time this honor had been Lancelot's, but his impure love for Arthur's queen, *Guinevere, had disqualified him, not from making the quest for the Grail, but from succeeding. Galahad went forth, and after several knightly adventures, found the Grail. You can read about Galahad in any book of King Arthur stories. An excellent one is *The Light Beyond the Forest: The Quest for the Holy Grail* (1980) by *Rosemary Sutcliff. MR

Gale, Zona (1874–1938) An author of stories, poems, plays, and novels, Gale was born in Portage, Wisconsin. Her experiences in a small town, as well as her feminist awareness and her work for social reform, set the tone for many of her works. Her most highly acclaimed novel is *Miss Lulu Bett.* Among her other works you will enjoy are her volumes of short stories, *Friendship Village* (1908) and *Friendship Village Love Stories* (1909), which are mod-

Galahad is knighted by his father, Sir Lancelot

eled on her hometown and are filled with love and warmth for the community; *Faint Perfume* (1923), a novel about a young woman writer; and *Preface to a Life* (1926), about the spiritual crisis of a frustrated small-town businessman. YA

Galileo [Galileo Galilei] (1564–1642) is known today as one of the earliest modern scientists. With a telescope he designed and made, Galileo discovered, among other things, sun spots and four moons of Jupiter and investigated the new and controversial Copernican theories of the structure of the universe. Copernicus (1473–1542) believed, contrary to church teaching, that the earth rotates on an axis and revolves around the sun.

Galileo's beliefs angered the pope, who felt they threatened church authority. Despite a trial by the *Inquisition and eventual house arrest, he continued his studies. Galileo's insistence on experimentation and intellectual freedom greatly influenced later scientists and philosophers. To learn more about Galileo's courage and curiosity, read *Galileo and the Magic Numbers* (1958) by Sidney Rosen (1916–), a book that cites Galileo's father as a positive influence in the scientist's lifelong search for truth. Older readers will enjoy *Galileo* (1943), by the German playwright and poet Bertold Brecht (1898–1956). This play explores the conflicts between personal conviction and outward submission to authority that are seen in the scientist's life. MR & YA

Gallico, Paul (William) (1897–1976) Known best for *The Snow Goose.* Gallico served in the U.S. Navy in World War I, after which he became a columnist and sports editor for the New York *Daily News.* Gallico is credited with starting in 1927 the annual Golden Gloves amateur boxing tournament. Later he was European editor and war correspondent for *Cosmopolitan* magazine. His several screenplays include *Pride of the Yankees* (1942), the story of Lou Gehrig (1903–1941), based on his book *Lou Gehrig: Pride of the Yankees* (1942). You might enjoy reading *The Adventures of Hiram*

Holliday (1939), about a proofreader who becomes tangled in international intrigue during his European vacation; *Mrs. 'Arris Goes to Paris* (1958), the first of several lighthearted books about a London cleaning lady; and *The Poseidon Adventure* (1969), about a group of people trapped inside a sinking ocean liner. Many of Gallico's books were filmed, including *Lou Gehrig: The Pride of the Yankees* as *The Pride of the Yankees* in 1942, *The Snow Goose* as a TV movie in 1971, and *The Poseidon Adventure* in 1972. MR & YA

Galsworthy, John (1867–1933) An English novelist and dramatist, Galsworthy is known chiefly for *The Forsyte Saga, a series of novels about an upper-middle-class Victorian family. If you enjoy reading family sagas, or seeing them as miniseries or soap operas on television, you will like the Forsyte series. In addition to being a novelist, Galsworthy was a successful playwright. Such dramas as *Strife* (1909), *Justice* (1910), *The Skin Game* (1920), and *Escape* (1926) deal with social problems and legal injustices. Galsworthy also wrote short sketches, essays, and poems. He was awarded the Nobel Prize for literature in 1932. YA

Ganymede(s) In Greek mythology, Ganymede is the most beautiful youth of all the mortals. He is the son of Tros, the founder of Troy. The Romans called him Catamitus. *Zeus, the king of the gods, disguises himself as an eagle and kidnaps Ganymede because of his beauty and makes him his cup-bearer and lover. To console Tros, Zeus gives him two immortal mares and a golden wine. Zeus immortalizes Ganymede as the constellation of Aquarius, the water-carrier. To learn more about Ganymede, read the *Penguin Dictionary of Classical Mythology* (1990) by Pierre Grimal (1912–), available in paperback. Younger readers will enjoy reading about Ganymede in *The Shining Stars: Greek Legends of the Zodiac* by Ghislaine Vautier (1932–). MR & YA

García Lorca, Federico (1898–1936) A Spanish poet and dramatist, García Lorca combined in his work influences from local folklore with strong convictions about the nature of human need, repression, and violence. Evocative verse, like the folk and gypsy themes in *Gypsy Ballads* (1924–1927) and in *Lament for the Death of a Bullfighter* (1937), considered his greatest poem, made him the best-known Spanish poet of his generation. García Lorca also became noted for his powerful poetic tragedies. *Yerma* (1934) deals with the despair of a woman who is unable to bear children. *Doña Rosita the Spinster* (1935) tells the story of an unhappy woman's unfulfilled life in a provincial backwater. Other plays include *The House of Bernardo Alba* (1945), about how a domineering widow's strict rules of sexual propriety for her six daughters result in tragedy, and *Blood Wedding* (1933), probably his best-known work, in which two men kill each other because of their love for the same woman. García Lorca's plays, like his poetry, deal with passion, blood, and death, especially the destructive aspects of sex and repression. García Lorca's *Poems in New York*, written after his stay there in 1929–1930, express his negative impressions of New York City, urban life in general, and dehumanizing modern technology. A Spanish film version of *Blood Wedding* appeared in 1981. YA

García Márquez, Gabriel (1928–) This Colombian novelist and author of *One Hundred Years of Solitude* (1970) combines realism with fantasy. *In Evil Hour* (1962) tells how anonymously written and scandalous leaflets found on homeowners' doors instigate fights, feuds, and murder. *Autumn of the Patriarch* (1975) presents episodes from the life of a very old Caribbean dictator, whose absolute authority and fear of revolution have isolated him from his people. *Chronicle of a Death Foretold* (1981) investigates the murder of a youth accused of seducing a woman just before her marriage. *Love in the Time of Cholera* (1985) is about the relationship between a physician, his wife, and another man who loves her, set against the backdrop of the threat of death from disease. *The General in His Labyrinth* (1990) is an account of the later years of Simón Bolívar, the

---

MR = Middle Reader   YA = Young Adult Reader   * = See this main entry

19th-century hero who liberated much of Latin America. García Márquez received the Nobel Prize for literature in 1982. YA

Garden, Nancy (1938–) An editor, writer, and teacher, Garden has written numerous books for young people, many dealing with the occult or supernatural. Her nonfiction books dealing with the origins and histories of supernatural beings include *Vampires* (1973), *Werewolves* (1973), *Witches* (1975), and *Demons and Devils* (1976). Garden has also written two fiction series on the subject. Her Fours Crossing series, set in the New Hampshire village of Fours Crossing, includes *Fours Crossing* (1981), about a boy and girl who are kidnapped by a hermit with unearthly powers, and its sequels, *Wintersmeet* (1983) and *The Door Between* (1987). The Monster Hunters series includes *Mystery of the Night Raiders* (1987), in which three teenage boys investigate mysterious happenings on the Vermont farm of one of the boys' grandparents, and its sequels, *Mystery of the Midnight Menace* (1988) and *Mystery of the Secret Marks* (1989). Among Garden's less spooky books are *Fun with Forecasting Weather* (1977) and *The Kids' Code and Cipher Book* (1981). MR

Garden of Eden See *Eden.

Gardner, Erle Stanley (1889–1970) This prolific author of detective novels turned to writing from practicing law in California. He founded the Court of Last Resort to help prisoners he believed to be unjustly imprisoned. Gardner created the character *Perry Mason, a lawyer with a flair for courtroom dramatics. The first Perry Mason mystery was *The Case of the Velvet Claws* (1933). In many of his cases Mason solves the crime, with the aid of his secretary and a private investigator, by representing someone unjustly accused and clearing his client by finding the guilty party, usually in a thrilling courtroom finale. Gardner also wrote a series, beginning with *The D.A. Calls It Murder* (1937), featuring district attorney Douglas Selby.

In a somewhat different vein, writing as A.A. Fair, Gardner created a more humorous and down-to-earth series featuring Donald Lam as a rather meek investigator who works for the large Bertha Cool, who weighs 275 pounds. The first of these books was *The Bigger They Come* (1939). Gardner wrote about 100 novels in all, and they have sold in the millions. A number have been made into movies, beginning with *The Case of the Howling Dog* in 1934, and 12 have been produced for television. If you enjoy the Gardner books, you will probably also like those by *Ellery Queen and *Rex Stout. MR & YA

Gareth appeared, without revealing his name, at *King Arthur's court, asking only for food and drink for a year. Kay, Arthur's haughty steward, put him to work in the kitchen. The lady Lynet arrived asking help in freeing her sister Lyonesse, imprisoned in the Castle Perilous. *Lancelot knighted Gareth, and off he went with Lynet, who announced her scorn for one who smelled of kitchen grease under his armor. But Gareth conquered all the knights he met and won Lyonesse's hand. Then he revealed that he was the youngest brother of *Gawain and thus a nephew to King Arthur. He was one of the knights whom Lancelot slew when he rescued *Guinevere from burning at the stake, and this act caused Gawain to seek revenge by inflaming the anger Arthur felt toward Lancelot. In most King Arthur stories, Gareth is called Sir Beaumains, the Kitchen Knight.

Gargantua, whose name literally means "gullet," was a giant in ancient French folklore known for his tremendous appetite and its effect on the countryside. French peasants used to say that certain topographical features were the work of Gargantua. For example, he ate large boats whole, then vomited them, creating a huge rock; his foot-scrapings formed large mounds in Bourges, in central France; and his overflowing basket created a mountain on the plain of Laon, in northern France. The giant also inspired *Gargantua* (1534), by François Rabelais (1494–1553), a French monk and

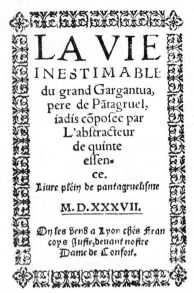

Title page of the 1537 edition of *Gargantua* by François Rabelais

humanist, who put a human face on Gargantua and used his story to display extraordinary learning and to satirize 16th-century French society, especially scholars, clerics, and lawyers. This earthy tale of Gargantua's adventures, with its mountain of events and allusions, is as full of life as the hero himself. One of *William Shakespeare's characters refers to Gargantua in *As You Like It: "You must borrow me Gargantua's mouth first; 'tis a word too great for any mouth of this age's size." See also *Paul Bunyan. YA

Garland, Hamlin (1860–1940) A writer of short stories and novels, usually about farm life in the Middle West, Garland was born in a log cabin near West Salem, Wisconsin. In 1869, his family resettled to a farm in Iowa. They lived there for 12 years, and then moved again to the area of Ordway, South Dakota. In 1883, Hamlin went to Boston and became a professor of American literature. Most of his literary works are written in a realistic and unromantic style, stemming from Garland's own experiences, and they greatly influenced the movement toward realism in American literature. Among his best works are *Main-Travelled Roads* (1891), short stories; *Rose of Dutcher's Coolly* (1895), a novel about a farm girl's struggle to become a writer; and *A Son of the Middle Border.* YA

Garner, Alan (1934–) One of today's highly regarded English writers for young readers, Garner often uses themes from ancient Celtic and British tales, including Arthurian legend, in his novels and plays, including television and radio plays. He brings to legend, myth, and history an exciting modern relevance. For younger readers, *The Owl Service* (1967) tells about three young people in a history-laden Welsh valley who discover a mysterious set of dishes that trap them in a reenactment of an ancient legend from the Mabinogion, the Welsh tales of *King Arthur. This fantasy novel combines myth and reality with a vision of the relativity of time, as the characters find themselves caught up in an ever-recurring legend about love and jealousy. For older readers, *The Red Shift* (1973) is set in a Cheshire village and uses the same event, the discovery of a Stone Age axe-head in three different historical periods, Roman Britain, the 17th century, and the early 1970s, to explore the relationships of young lovers living in different eras.

In his Stone Book Quartet, consisting of *The Stone Book* (1976), *Granny Reardun* (1977), *Tom Fobble's Day* (1977), and *Aimer Gate* (1978), Garner chooses ordinary people, in this case a working-class family, for his characters. The Quartet, written expressly for those who do not like to read, describes the history of Garner's family from about 1850 to 1950. Though written in prose, the language sounds like poetry. MR & YA

Gary, Romain (1914–1980) This French novelist mixed dark elements with laughter, cynicism with optimism in his works. *Forest of Anger* (1944) deals with the grim realities of World War II. Later revised and reissued, *Forest of Anger* was renamed *Nothing Important Ever Dies* (1960). Gary's other novels include *The Colors of Day* (1953), about a love affair during a carnival in Nice, France, and *The Roots of Heaven* (1958), which is about a man's battle to save elephants from extinction and argues for the protection of wildlife. In *The Dance of Genghis Cohn* (1958), a Nazi executioner's body is taken over by the spirit of a dead Jewish comedian. *The Ski Bum* (1963) describes the adventures of two young American skiers in Geneva, Switzerland, and the affair one of them has there with the daughter of the American consul. *The Roots of Heaven*, Gary's best-known book, was made into a movie in 1958. YA

Gathering of Days, A: A New England Girl's Journal, 1830–1832 (1979) By *Joan W. Blos, this novel is about life on a small New Hampshire farm, written in the form of a diary, and based partly on real people and events. Catherine Cabot Hall, who is 13 years old, begins her record in 1830, several years after her mother's death, and introduces her father, Charles; her sister, Mary Martha; and her best friend, Cassie Shipman. In her quiet, thoughtful, and uncomplaining way, Catherine describes the routine of keeping house and doing outdoor chores in a difficult climate. Her lesson book disappears one day and mysteriously reappears with a note written inside: "PLEEZ MISS TAKE PITTY I AM COLD." Thinking it may come from a runaway slave, she and Cassie leave a warm quilt and some food where the book was found, without mentioning the incident to their families. After the long winter, Catherine's father decides to marry Ann Higham, a Boston widow with a son about Catherine's age, and brings his bride to live on the farm. Adjusting to the new order is difficult at first, but eventually "Mammann" gives up some of her fussy city ways, and Catherine learns to trust and accept her stepmother. Cassie catches cold, develops a fever, and dies. Catherine's sorrow is eased when the mail brings her a small gift and a note in familiar handwriting that reads "SISTERS BLESS YOU. FREE NOW. CURTIS. IN CANADA." In the spring of 1832, Catherine leaves to help care for a friend's baby, unaware that she will never return to the farm. MR & YA

Gathering Room, The (1981) Set in Baltimore, Maryland, this novel by *Colby Rodowsky tells about 9-year-old Mudge Stokes, who lives with his parents, Ned and Serena, in the stone gatehouse of historic Edgemount Cemetery. They came to live there years earlier, after Ned's closest friend, Governor John

Gordon, was killed by an assassin and Ned turned away from the world to become caretaker of Edgemount. Mudge has made the quiet cemetery his world and has befriended the spirits of some of its inhabitants, including the Captain and Jenkins, who served in the War of 1812; the Butterfly Lady, who is fond of reciting poetry; and Little Dorro, who was run over by a milk wagon. Mudge takes school lessons from Ned and Serena in the gathering room, where mourners used to gather for funerals. Mudge's Aunt Ernestus comes for a visit, urging the family to end their isolation from the larger world. At first he resents her interference but slowly comes to love and trust her. With her help, Mudge and his family leave Edgemount and get on with their lives. Mudge is sad to leave his friends, but he knows that when he goes he will take part of them with him and leave part of himself with them. If you enjoyed *The Gathering Room*, you will probably also like *The Bridge to Terabithia* by *Katherine Paterson, about two young people who create their own imaginary kingdom, and what happens when one of them is accidentally killed. MR

Gaudy Night (1935) The setting of this detective novel by *Dorothy L. Sayers is a women's college at Oxford University, in England. The title refers to an annual celebration that brings graduates back to the campus. One of these is Harriet Vane, first encountered in *Strong Poison* (1930), in which *Lord Peter Wimsey clears Vane of a murder charge and falls in love with her. Back at college Vane is greeted with the news that someone is writing poison-pen letters to members of the faculty and is also playing practical jokes. Because she is an author of detective stories, she is asked to investigate the situation by the college authorities, who are fearful of scandal at a university where female dons and students are still viewed with suspicion. Wimsey turns up at Oxford and helps in the successful search for the culprit. At the story's end, Vane finally accepts Wimsey's often-repeated marriage proposal. *Gaudy Night* does not suffer from the fact that there is no terrible crime, and it is generally regarded as

Sayers's finest achievement. Sayers was one of the first women to earn a degree at Oxford, and the college in this book is obviously her own, Somerville. *Gaudy Night* was produced as a movie in 1940 and adapted for a three-part TV program in the mid-1980s. YA

Gawain, one of *King Arthur's knights, is renowned for his role in the story of the Green Knight, which can be found in every collection of Arthurian stories. Gawain was Arthur's nephew, the son of Arthur's sister, Morgause. A big, hot-tempered man, he had many humbling experiences before his adventure with the Green Knight, in which he flinched as the Green Knight's axe descended toward his neck and thus failed to be completely true to his oath of chivalry and honor. Gawain also played an important part in fanning the flames of Arthur's jealousy of *Lancelot, with terrible consequences for the kingdom. Gawain is a very human figure, and is one of the people around the historical Arthur who may have actually existed. You can read about Gawain in *The Challenge of the Green Knight* (1967) by *Ian Serraillier. MR

Gay, John (1685–1732) An English playwright and poet, Gay is known today chiefly for *The Beggar's Opera* (1728), a ballad opera that made him famous. This charming work, which makes fun of English society, describes sympathetically the highwaymen and criminals of the day. Gay also co-wrote, with *Alexander Pope and John Arbuthnot (1667–1735), a Scottish writer, *Three Hours After Marriage* (1717), a burlesque comedy that was considered indecent and was a complete failure. As a poet, Gay was known chiefly for his *Fables* (1727), which eventually went through about 350 editions. Composed in verse for younger readers, each fable tells a little story and ends with a moral.

The German playwright and poet Bertolt Brecht (1898–1956) adapted *The Beggar's Opera* in *The Threepenny Opera* (1928), with music by the German composer Kurt Weill (1900–1950). This became very popular, both in German and English, and a staging (1954) in New York City ran for many years. You will enjoy, however, reading from the original *Beggar's Opera*, which many critics consider the first musical comedy in English. At least one of its many editions appeared in an inexpensive paperback. A film version was made in 1953. MR & YA

Geisel, Theodor Seuss See *Dr. Seuss.

Gemini, the Twins Castor and Pollux In Greek mythology, the Gemini were the sons of *Leda. Pollux was the immortal son of *Zeus, but Castor was the son of a mortal and thus vulnerable to death. Pollux excelled as a boxer, and Castor became a great warrior and horseman. When they were young, they sailed on the *Argo* with *Jason in search of the *Golden Fleece. Later, when Castor was killed in battle, Pollux prayed to his father that Castor might share his own immortality. One legend states that Zeus granted Pollux's wish by allowing each brother to be alive on alternate days. Another legend has it that the brothers live as the two brightest stars in the constellation Gemini.

Gemming, Elizabeth (1932–) Descended from Pilgrims who came to America aboard the *Mayflower*, Gemming has written a number of books about New England. Among her best is *Huckleberry Hill: Child Life in Old New England* (1968), which describes season by season what it was like to be a young person growing up in New England in the 19th century. *Getting to Know New England* (1970) tells about the land, climate, people, and history of the six New England states, and *Maple Harvest: The Story of Maple Sugaring* (1976) tells about the craft of making maple sugar, how the early colonists learned it from the American Indians, and how it has turned into an important industry in New England. Not all of Gemming's books are about New England. *Lost City in the Clouds: The Discovery of Machu Picchu* (1980) tells about the discovery in 1911 of the long-lost Inca city of Machu Picchu, high in the Peruvian Andes, by the American explorer Hiram Bingham (1875–1956). MR

MR = Middle Reader   YA = Young Adult Reader   * = See this main entry

Genesis The first book of the Old Testament of the *Bible, Genesis begins with an account of the creation of the world: "In the beginning God created the heaven and the earth." It then tells the story of *Adam and Eve and their expulsion from the Garden of *Eden and of Noah and his *ark in the flood. Genesis is also important as the history of the patriarchs of Israel: *Abraham, *Isaac, and Jacob. Genesis concludes with an account of the life of *Joseph.

Genet, Jean (1910–1986) This French novelist, playwright, and poet wrote from the viewpoint of the outcast, a role he knew from his own experience. Abandoned by his family, Genet was caught stealing when he was 10 years old and spent time in a reformatory. He escaped and joined the French *Foreign Legion, only to desert. He served time in a number of European prisons, where he began to write. His novel *Our Lady of the Flowers* (1943) deals with themes of thievery and homosexuality, and his play *Deathwatch* (1949) is set in prison. Leading existentialist writers, such as Jean-Paul Sartre (1905–1980), recognized the quality of Genet's work and helped obtain his pardon from a life sentence and release from prison. Genet's works include the play *The Balcony* (1957), in which men come to a brothel to re-enact their fantasies about what they think their real-life roles should be. A movie was made of *The Balcony* in 1963. See also *existentialism. YA

Geoffrey of Monmouth (died c.1155) was a scholar and churchman who wrote a *History of the Kings of Britain* (1136). It is still a major source for information about *King Arthur. Geoffrey claimed that one of his sources was "a very ancient book in the British [that is, Welsh] tongue" whose narrator was *Merlin. Because this book has never been found, the accuracy of Geoffrey's work has been continually questioned. *King Arthur* (1986) by Norma Lorre Goodrich (1917–) has thrown light on Geoffrey's work by showing how many errors are possible in translating from Welsh to Latin. She adds that Geoffrey knew only a small part of England and was as weak in geography as he was strong in historical fantasy. About 200 medieval manuscript copies of the *History of the Kings of Britain* still exist in the libraries of Europe, which suggests the success of this work in Geoffrey's own time. More than 850 years later it is still in print, making it a long-time best-seller. YA

George, Jean Craighead (1919–) This very popular author of books for young people has written almost 50 books, many reflecting her interest in nature and most self-illustrated. George began as a reporter-artist, but soon turned to such subjects as birds, raccoons, fish, and even salamanders. The last of the six books she wrote with her former husband, John L. George (1916–), *Dipper of Copper Creek* (1956), tells about the water ouzel, or dipper bird, a strange creature that walks under water. Her first solo effort was *The Hole in the Tree* (1957), about a tree hole, the animals that use it, and the two young people who discover it. Her interest in birds was again evident in *Who Really Killed Cock Robin?* (1971), an ecological mystery about the death of a robin's mate. *Hook a Fish, Catch a Mountain* (1975) is about a curious city-mouse of a girl who outfishes her male family members and goes to the head of the mountain streams to find the origin of the big trout. The setting of *River Rats, Inc.* (1979) is the Colorado River, on which two boys are shipwrecked with an illegal and mysterious cargo. *The Talking Earth* (1983) takes you on the venture of a modern American Indian girl to test the legends of her ancestors. *Shark Beneath the Reef* (1989) involves a young Mexican boy coming of age in a world of politics and corruption, and the changing world around him. George's best-known books are *Julie of the Wolves* and *My Side of the Mountain*. MR

George, Saint (A.D. 4th century) Possibly a member of the Roman Imperial Army, George was killed in Asia Minor because of his Christian faith. The patron saint of soldiers, he is venerated by both the Roman Catholic and

Eastern Orthodox churches. George is the patron saint of the English. Late Medieval English legends are filled with references to George as a dragon slayer. In one story, a dragon threatens a village, and a young woman is chosen to be sacrificed to the beast. George attacks and defeats the dragon, which then becomes the maiden's pet. The flag of Great Britain, the famous "Union Jack," contains the red cross of George, which is also a *symbol of the Church of England and of the Red Cross, the international charitable organization. If you would like to know more about Saint George, read *St. George and the Dragon: A Golden Legend* (1984) by Margaret Hodges (1911–). See also *cross. MR

George Smiley The master spy in the espionage novels of *John Le Carré, Smiley is the opposite of the dashing heroes of the *James Bond type. He is middle-aged and rather stout and wears glasses and rumpled clothes. He finds no glamour in his profession but sees to it that the job is done and that people are treated fairly. In *Call for the Dead* (1962), Smiley deals with the apparent suicide of a clerk to whom he had granted security clearance. *A Murder of Quality* (1963) finds Smiley undertaking a private investigation into the death of a schoolmaster's wife. In *The Looking-Glass War* (1965) he clears up a mess resulting from the attempt of an outdated espionage agency to justify its existence. *Tinker, Tailor, Soldier, Spy* (1974) is one of the most dramatically tense novels in which Smiley appears. Here a choice must be made between two men to become the next head of the agency when it is known there is a Soviet spy within the agency. *Call for the Dead* was made into a movie called *The Deadly Affair* in 1967, and *Tinker, Tailor, Soldier, Spy* was produced as a TV series in 1980. YA

Gershwin, George (1898–1937) and **Gershwin, Ira** (1896–1983) Brothers born in New York City, the Gershwins were popular musical collaborators. George, a composer, songwriter, and pianist, started taking piano lessons and studying theory when he was 12 years old. He left high school to work as a pianist and, at 16 years old, began to write songs. George's first complete musical score was for *La, La, Lucille* (1919), the same year that his song "Swanee" became a great hit. Ira wrote lyrics to many of George's compositions, including numerous popular revues and musical comedies, such as *Oh, Kay!* (1926), *Funny Face* (1927), *Strike Up the Band* (1929), and *Girl Crazy* (1936). Among their song hits from stage works are "Someone to Watch Over Me," "Embraceable You," "I Got Rhythm," and "Shall We Dance?" George also composed classical music, including *Rhapsody in Blue* (1924), *Concerto in F* (1925), and *An American in Paris* (1928). Later, the Gershwins worked together on the opera *Porgy and Bess*, and with the playwright *George S. Kaufman on *Of Thee I Sing* (1931), a musical *satire. *Strike Up the Band* was adapted for film in 1940. See also *Moss Hart. YA

Gerson, Corinne (1927–) The author of a number of thoughtful and often humorous novels for and about young people, Gerson began writing when she was a middle-school student. After college she became a book and magazine editor and wrote a number of short stories and articles before turning to novels. Perhaps her best-known book is *How I Put My Mother Through College, about the problems of a teenage girl whose mother decides to complete her education. Another very popular novel is *Son for a Day* (1980), about Danny Turner, a boy whose parents have divorced and who deals with his longing for family life by befriending "zoodaddies," divorced fathers who take their sons to the zoo on visiting days. Danny also appears in the sequels *Oh, Brother!* (1982), in which Danny's life is changed completely when he is "adopted" as a younger brother by four older teenage boys, and *My Grandfather the Spy* (1990), in which Danny befriends an elderly man who, unknown to him, has run away from a senior citizens' home. MR

Ghosts I Have Been (1977) The heroine of this novel by *Richard Peck is Blossom Culp, a poor girl growing up in a western town in 1914. Blossom lives in an abandoned shack with her mother, who cannot read or write but who has the gift of second sight, the ability to see the unseen. When Blossom discovers that she, too, has the gift, things start to change in Bluff City. Blossom and her friend Alexander Armsworth, who also has extrasensory powers, help calm the tortured ghost of a servant who committed suicide in the pantry of Miss Gertrude Dabney. They befriend Miss Dabney, who loves all things English, drives an electric automobile, and is thought to be crazy by the folks of Bluff City. Blossom gains international fame after "seeing" the death of an English boy aboard the sinking liner *Titanic*, an experience that leads Blossom, Alexander, and Miss Dabney on an adventurous trip to England. Peck has written several books about Blossom and Alexander, including *The Ghost Belonged to Me* (1975), in which Alexander first discovers his extrasensory powers; *The Dreadful Future of Blossom Culp* (1983), in which Blossom travels 70 years into the future; and *Blossom Culp and the Sleep of Death* (1986), in which Blossom and Alexander help a long-dead Egyptian princess to reclaim her tomb. MR

Giant (1952) By *Edna Ferber, this colorful novel describes the evolution of 20th-century Texas, from a cattle rancher's culture to a post-World War II society awash in oil money. The series of changes is seen through the eyes of Leslie Benedict, the Virginia-bred bride of cattleman Jordan "Bick" Benedict, owner of Reata Ranch. The story opens during the oil-dominated present, and flashes back to the marriage of the Benedicts and Leslie's coming to live at Reata Ranch. She discovers the rigid separation of the Mexican farmhands and their Anglo masters. One of Bick's farmhands, Jett Rink, driven off the Reata ranch in a dispute with Bick, strikes oil and becomes rich. He is attracted to Leslie and wants revenge on his proud but cash-poor former boss, but Leslie is not interested in him. Rink personifies the transition of Texas society from its cattle culture to oil ostentation. The book describes the strong but difficult relationship between Bick

and independent Leslie. She abhors the bad treatment of Mexicans and rebels against the politics and practices of the ranch culture she marries into. Their son turns his back on ranch life, becomes a doctor, and marries a Mexican-American woman. If you enjoyed reading *Giant*, you have probably also enjoyed watching the very popular TV series *Dallas*, produced from 1978 to 1991. A film version of *Giant* appeared in 1956. YA

Giants in the Earth (1927) This novel, by Ole Edvart Rölvaag (1876–1931), is the first of a trilogy that describes the life of Norwegian pioneers in the Dakota Territory of the late 19th century. First written by Rölvaag in his native Norwegian, as were its sequels *Peder Victorious* (1929) and *Their Father's God* (1931), *Giants in the Earth* describes the difficulties of pioneer life in stark and grim detail, a heroic European story in an American setting. Per Hansa, his wife, Beret, and their sons battle the elements and hardships of the prairie and the psychological and ethical tensions that shaped the emigrant experience. The novel's end brings these forces together in a single event, Per Hansa's death in a snowstorm during a reluctant journey to fetch a minister for a dying friend. Another look at pioneer life, this time in Nebraska, is *My Ántonia* by *Willa Cather. YA

Gibbon, Edward (1737–1794) An English historian and member of Parliament, Gibbon is best known for *The History of the Decline and Fall of the Roman Empire* (1776–1788). This six-volume masterpiece, considered one of the greatest histories in any language, was inspired by Gibbon's walks among the ruins of classical Rome. *The Decline and Fall* is memorable because of the extent of Gibbon's research, its elegant style, and its exploration of early Christianity's role in Rome's fall. The account spans the period between the so-called golden age of the Empire in the 2nd century A.D. and the fall of Constantinople in 1453, which ended the remnants of the Empire. Your library probably has one of a number of editions of *The Decline and Fall*. One of the most popular is the Modern Library edition (1977), in three vol-

---

MR = Middle Reader   YA = Young Adult Reader   * = See this main entry

umes. There are two recent abridgments in paperback editions. YA

Gide, André (1869–1951) A French man of letters, considered one of the leading authors of the 20th century, Gide is noted especially for writing about the contradictions of modern life. Gide's early rebellion against his strict, religious upbringing is reflected in his first novel, *The Notebooks of André Walter* (1891), about a man's struggle between traditional religious teachings and his own worldly desires. Gide's homosexuality contributed to his alienation from traditional social, religious, and intellectual beliefs. His later writings follow his search for a better, more personal understanding of society, art, religion, and human existence. Among his best-known works are *The Immoralist*, about a man who rebels against social convention to follow a course in life dictated by his own thoughts and desires; *Strait Is the Gate* (1909), centering on a woman whose struggle for religious rectitude is just as destructive as the amorality described in *The Immoralist*; and *The Counterfeiters*, a complex novel that is considered Gide's masterpiece. Gide was awarded the Nobel Prize for literature in 1947. YA

"Gift of the Magi, The" (1906) This classic short story by *O. Henry was first published in the collection *The Four Million* (1906). It tells about a young married couple, James and Della Dillingham Young. Though they are poor, their love for one another is rich. The day before Christmas, Della is dismayed to find that she has too little money to buy her husband a Christmas gift. She decides to sell what she most treasures: her hair. After receiving 20 dollars for her long, beautiful tresses, Della joyously buys her husband a gold chain to wear with his treasured pocket watch. That night Jim is stunned to see her short haircut. Della says to Jim, "Maybe the hairs on my head were numbered, but nobody could ever count my love for you."

When Jim and Della exchange Christmas gifts, Della tears open her package to find "beautiful combs, pure tortoise shell, with jeweled rims—just the shade to wear in the beautiful vanished hair." Jim, looking at the magnificent gold chain, reveals that he sold his pocket watch in order to buy the combs.

The *Magi were wise men who traveled to Bethlehem carrying gifts for the infant *Jesus, so it may be said that they invented the art of giving Christmas presents. Jim and Della "most unwisely sacrificed for each other the greatest treasures of their house." O. Henry states, however, that "of all who give and receive gifts, such as they are wisest." Though Jim and Della give up their most treasured possessions, they never sacrifice what is most important, their love for each other. MR

Gigi (1952) This charming French novel by *Colette describes how a young woman is taught the social graces needed to attract a suitable man. Gigi learns how to eat a lobster properly, which jewels she may or may not accept from a wealthy man, and which clothes to wear. But despite a demand for perfection, never-ending instruction, and criticism from Grandmamma and Aunt Alicia, Gigi remains stubbornly independent. She succeeds in making a match that pleases her family and herself, despite her "impossible little nose" and her being "scatterbrained in certain things and backward for her age." This book is a good introduction to Colette's interest in feminism and her keen observation of society and everyday life. A film version of *Gigi* was made in 1958. YA

Gilbert, William S. (1836–1911) and **Sullivan, Arthur** (1842–1900) Gilbert was an English dramatist known best for his librettos which, combined with Arthur Sullivan's music, formed the famous Gilbert and Sullivan comic operas. Gilbert and Sullivan produced 14 comic operas, including *HMS Pinafore* (1878), *The Pirates of Penzance* (1879), and *The Mikado* (1885). The librettos combine graceful language, wit, and gentle *satire of the Victorian Age. Gilbert's skills with language and his tight grip on the staging of his dramas helped improve the quality of the Victorian stage. He is credited with creating the role of the director as it is known today.

Arthur Sullivan, a noted composer and Gilbert's musical partner, combined a gift for melody with a sense of musical *parody. His first venture with Gilbert was the little-known operetta *Thespis* (1871). Their next collaboration, *Trial by Jury* (1875), was the first of many successful joint ventures. Sullivan also composed classical compositions as well as such well-known hymn tunes as "Onward Christian Soldiers."

For the most authentic renditions of Gilbert and Sullivan comic operas, listen to the D'Oyly Carte productions on records. A movie version of *The Pirates of Penzance* appeared in 1983 and of *The Mikado* in 1939 and a number of operas have been produced for television. YA

Giraudoux, Jean (1882–1944) A French writer of novels, film scripts, and plays, Giraudoux is known best for the play *The Madwoman of Chaillot* (1945), about a group of old and eccentric Parisian men and women who rise up against evil speculators. His novel *Bella* (1926) satirizes political life through a reenactment of the story of *Romeo and Juliet*. The tragedy *Judith* (1931) retells the biblical story of a young Jewish woman who saved her people from Assyrian conquest. Giraudoux's other plays include the drama *Tiger at the Gates* (1935), about Hector and the *Trojan War, and the fairy tale *Ondine* (1939), in which a water spirit falls in love with a man. A movie version of *The Madwoman of Chaillot* appeared in 1969. YA

Girl Called Al, A (1969) By *Constance C. Greene, this first novel is about the friendship of two seventh-grade girls who live in the same apartment building. Al (short for Alexandra) is slightly overweight, has pigtails, is very smart, and tries hard to be a nonconformist. Her best friend, whose name you never get to know, tells the story. Al lives alone with her divorced mother. Her fondest wish is for a visit from her father. The girls become good friends with Mr. Richards, an ex-bartender who is now the as-

sistant superintendent of their building. Although Mr. Richards is elderly, he is a real character and lots of fun. For example, he polishes his kitchen floor by skating across it on rags attached to his shoes. He teaches the girls woodworking and cooking, and is always ready to give them encouragement. After Mr. Richards dies of a heart attack, both girls treasure the wonderful way in which he has touched their lives. If you enjoyed *A Girl Called Al*, you can read about Al and her friend's further adventures in *I Know You, Al, *Your Old Pal, Al, *Al(exandra) the Great, and *Just Plain Al. MR

Girl Called Boy, A (1982) This fantasy novel by Belinda Hurmence (1921–) tells about 11-year-old Blanche Overtha Yancey—Boy for short. Boy dislikes hearing her father's stories about her family's North Carolina slave ancestors, certain that their enslavement was their own fault. But one day, during a family picnic at the Bellemont Overlook, Boy wanders across a small stream and finds herself back in 1853, hiding from slave catchers with Ike and his son, Isaac, two runaway slaves searching for Ike's wife, Lucie. Boy is captured and taken to the Yancey plantation at Bellemont, where her great-great-grandfather was a slave. Boy's months in the world of 19th-century slavery give her a new understanding of her ancestors and of the many things she once took for granted. After helping to reunite Ike, Isaac, and Lucie, Boy discovers the path back to her own time and family. Belinda Hurmence has written a number of books for young readers. If you enjoyed *A Girl Called Boy*, try also *Tansy* (1984), about a newly freed black girl who sets out after the Civil War to find her mother. MR

Girl with the Silver Eyes, The (1980) By *Willo Davis Roberts, this novel tells about Katie Welker, a lonely 9-year-old girl whose pale gray, silvery-looking eyes have always set her apart from other people. Katie can move objects just by thinking about them, and she can hear in her mind what animals are thinking. People, even her mother, think Katie is a strange girl, although she has never told any-one about her powers. Some people, like mean Mr. Pollard in the apartment building they have just moved into, think she is a witch. Even her Grandma Welker, with whom she lived after her parents split up, was uncomfortable around her. Katie discovers that before she was born her mother worked for a drug company on a project that was suddenly and mysteriously canceled, and also that three other women working on the project had babies about the same time. She also learns that a new tenant, Mr. Cooper, has been asking everyone questions about her. Alarmed by Cooper's interest in her, Katie runs away to find the other children and learns that they also have silver-colored eyes and special powers, and that she is not alone. Together they return to Katie's home to find out who Mr. Cooper is and what he wants. If you enjoyed *The Girl with the Silver Eyes*, you will also like *Escape to Witch Mountain* by *Alexander Key, about two young people with special powers, and their search for the home and family they cannot remember. MR

Glasgow, Ellen (1874–1945) Author of numerous realistic novels about the South, Glasgow was born in Richmond, Virginia. A sickly child and unable to attend school, she gained her education largely by reading the books in her father's library. When she was 18 years old she wrote her first novel, but she did not attain popular success until the publication of the novel *Virginia* (1913), about a woman who sacrifices her own life for the lives of her husband and family. Her most highly acclaimed work is the novel *Barren Ground*. Glasgow's best-known novel is *In This Our Life* (1941), about a once-proud Virginia family that falls into modern decadence. YA

Glaspell, Susan (1882–1948) Born in Davenport, Iowa, Glaspell was a popular playwright, novelist, and short-story writer. Her works express humanistic views and emphasize the need for people to fulfill their highest potential. In 1915 Glaspell helped establish the Pro-vincetown Players, where the art of drama was explored and developed without constraints. Among her numerous works are the novels *Fidelity* (1915), about a young woman who elopes with a married man, and *Brook Evans* (1928), which describes the relationship between a mother and daughter. Her plays include *Bernice* (1920), which deals with a dead woman's continuing effect on her family and friends, and *Alison's House*. YA

Glass Menagerie, The (1945) This "memory play" by *Tennessee Williams describes the frustrating family life of Amanda Wingfield, her son, Tom, and her slightly crippled and shy daughter, Laura, in a St. Louis, Missouri, tenement. Abandoned by her husband years before, Amanda is obsessed by her belief that she was once a Southern belle. Tom dreams of literary fame while he supports the three of them as a warehouse clerk. Laura spends her time with her menagerie of small glass animal figurines. In the play Tom's retrospective monologues are interwoven with angry dialogue between mother and son. Amanda advises and criticizes Tom about his behavior, and her son resents and resists her comments. Amanda nags Tom to find a husband for Laura. The play's climactic scene suggests the possibility of love between Laura and Jim O'Connor, a dinner guest. Jim kisses her, but confesses he is engaged to another woman. This disappointment is a final defeat for Amanda, whose life's work has been to find a match for Laura. As the play ends, the deluded Amanda blames Tom for inviting Jim home, and she criticizes him for his illusions. In desperation, Tom flees his family, forever troubled by the memory of his sister. Film versions of *The Glass Menagerie* appeared in 1950, 1973, and 1987. YA

Go Tell It on the Mountain (1953), by *James Baldwin, tells of a day at a Harlem, New York, church called the Temple of the Fire Baptized. A prayer meeting there is attended by 14-year-old John Grimes; his mother, Elizabeth; her sister, Florence; and John's father, Gabriel Grimes, a former preacher. As the meeting un-

MR = Middle Reader   YA = Young Adult Reader   * = See this main entry

folds, the thoughts of the four people are revealed in a series of flashbacks as they recollect vivid memories of childhood, love, poverty, sickness, and powerful religious feeling. John's mind is filled with doubt and rage against his father, and he wonders why these people come every night to call out to a God who cares nothing for them. His Aunt Florence relives the day when she found the courage to leave her dying mother and her brother, Gabriel, always the family favorite, to go north to make a life of her own. She remembers her marriage to Frank, who taught her that "there are people in the world for whom 'coming along' is a perpetual process, people who are destined never to arrive."

Gabriel thinks back on his early life, before he found God and gained some control over his desire for women. He recalls Esther, who bore him a son when he was already married to Deborah. The boy, Royal, was never acknowledged by his father and died in a barroom brawl.

Elizabeth remembers being taken from her beloved father when her mother died. Because he ran a brothel, her aunts thought it unsuitable for her to remain with him. She remembers too the joy of her love for Richard, jailed for something he did not do and beaten by white policemen. In despair, he cut his wrists and died. Elizabeth thinks of the birth of her son, John, Richard's child, and her marriage to Gabriel.

John asks for God's power to deliver him from the storm in his heart. After hours of prayer and thought, he is invaded by a new spirit and finds himself on the dusty floor before the altar, filled with a great sweetness and freedom. A TV movie of *Go Tell It on the Mountain* was produced in 1984. YA

goblins These mischievous fairies are often welcomed in private households because of their helpfulness. Sometimes they do chores in the night. According to folklore, goblins present good children with gifts, punish disobedient ones, and often play tricks by rearranging furniture or making strange sounds.

Goblins dwell in old houses, caves, and trees. They appear in many books for young readers, including *The Princess and the Goblin*, by the Scottish author George MacDonald (1824–1905), which has recently been reprinted. It tells about Princess Irene, a little girl who has fantastic adventures with goblins. Goblins are sometimes evil and destructive creatures, as in *The Hobbit* by *J.R.R. Tolkien. Even *James Whitcomb Riley, in his poem *"Little Orphant Annie," warns children about "the Gobble-uns 'at gits you ef you Don't Watch Out!" You can read about goblins and other creatures in *The Impossible People: A History Natural and Unnatural of Beings Terrible and Wonderful* (1972) by *Georgess McHargue. MR

Godden, Rumer (1907–) An English-born writer who grew up in India, Godden has been praised for writing books that reflect a profound understanding of young people and their views of the world. Though Godden has written many books for young readers, she does not believe in the use of simplified language, claiming, "A novel that is simplified for children will always fail." She firmly believes that any reader older than 11 years is capable of reading adult-level books. Godden has written more than 50 books for both young people and adults. *The Doll's House* (1947), a novel set entirely within the confines of a doll's house, was her first widely known book for young readers. Among her many other books are *Miss Happiness and Miss Flower* (1961), about two tiny Japanese dolls that change a little girl's life, and *The Mousewife* (1982), about a mouse searching for a new home. A number of her books have been made into movies, such as *Innocent Sinners*, produced in 1957, which was adapted from *An Episode of Sparrows*, and *Loss of Innocence*, produced in 1961, which was based on *The Greengage Summer* (1958), a largely autobiographical account of a trip Godden took with her sister and mother. MR & YA

Godiva, Lady (?–c.1086) A celebrated folk figure, Lady Godiva was an English countess. In 1040, Godiva's husband, Leofric, Earl of Mercia and Lord of Coventry, imposed an outrageous tax on his tenants. In response to his wife's pleading, he agreed to remove the taxes if Godiva would ride naked through the marketplace. She did so, and the earl was forced to keep his side of the bargain. During Lady Godiva's ride, the villagers were ordered to remain inside their homes. A tailor peeped out his window, saw Lady Godiva pass, and was struck blind. He is known as "the Peeping Tom of Coventry." Though there is no factual evidence for Lady Godiva's ride, she is remembered as a patroness of monasteries and churches.

Goethe, Johann Wolfgang von (1749–1832) Considered by many critics the greatest German literary figure, Goethe was a poet, playwright, and novelist, best known for his dramatic poem *Faust* (1808), about a scholar who makes a pact with the devil. Goethe was inspired both by classical figures, as in *Prometheus* (1774), a work in free verse that expresses anger toward the gods, and by northern European figures, as in the play *Egmont* (1788), based on the life of a 16th-century Belgian patriot. Goethe's best-known novel, *The Sorrows of Young Werther* (1787), tells the story of one of literature's first Romantic heroes, an overly sensitive social misfit whose unsuccessful love affair drives him to suicide. See also *Faust. YA

Gogol, Nikolai (Vasilievich) (1809–1852) Considered the father of the Russian realistic school of literature, Gogol wrote short stories, novels, and plays. Early works, such as *Taras Bulba* (1835), about a 16th-century Cossack's adventures, were based on Gogol's Ukrainian background. Gogol's themes range from romantic adventure to the kind of liberal political thought and sympathy for the oppressed that characterize other great Russian writers of his day, such as *Leo Tolstoy and *Ivan Turgenev. His best-known play, *The Inspector General* (1936), considered one of the finest comedies ever written, pokes fun at local government officials. His satirical novel *Dead Souls* (1842) tells the story of a schemer who buys the names of dead serfs and then claims them as

property he can mortgage. A movie version of *Taras Bulba* was made in 1962. See also *"The Overcoat," a famous short story by Gogol. YA

"Gold Bug, The" (1843) This short story by *Edgar Allan Poe is set on Sullivan's Island, off the coast of Charleston, South Carolina. The narrator, who never reveals his name, tells the story of his friend William Legrand. One day, Legrand finds a strange gold bug. Convinced that the bug has something to do with a buried treasure, he coaxes the narrator, who thinks Legrand has gone mad, into accompanying him and his attendant, Jupiter, on a treasure hunt.

During the journey, Legrand orders Jupiter to climb a tall tree where a skull is nailed to a branch, then put the gold bug, which is attached to a string, through the left eye of the skull. At the very point that the bug falls, Legrand feverishly digs a hole. Finding nothing, he repeats the procedure, and this time they unearth skeletons and a wooden chest filled with coins, jewels, and gold. In many vivid particulars, Legrand recounts the various steps that brought him to finding the fortune, including the discovery of a cryptic message written in invisible ink on a parchment paper, and the method by which he translated it. Legrand also says that he used the gold bug in such a peculiar manner for the sole purpose of punishing the narrator for suspecting his sanity. YA

gold rush The discovery of gold in a place has often meant the speedy arrival of an army of fortune-hunting gold prospectors. In January 1848, gold was discovered in California on the land of John Sutter (1803–1880). In December of that year President James Polk (1795–1849), in his annual message to Congress, spoke about the discovery and triggered a wild rush to California by people hoping to strike it rich. This was the Great Gold Rush. Some of these gold hunters, who came to be known as the "Forty-Niners" and also as the "Argonauts of '49," traveled by ship around the tip of South America and north to the California coast. Others sailed to Central America, traveled overland through Panama or Nicaragua, and then boarded other ships for California. Still others made the long and dangerous trip west on wagon trains. Boom towns sprang up where gold was found, and many became ghost towns when the gold ran out. In 1859 a rich vein of gold was discovered in Nevada, and rich veins of silver were located there soon after.

The colorful, and sometimes violent, life in mining camps and towns of California and Nevada provided material for *Mark Twain, *Bret Harte, and other writers. In 1896 gold was discovered in the Yukon region of western Canada, sparking a new gold rush to Canada and Alaska. Though this rush lasted for only a few years, it provided material for such writers as *Jack London, the Canadian poet Robert W. Service (1874–1958), and the novelist Rex Beach (1877–1949). Among Beach's Alaska novels is *The Spoilers* (1906), set in Nome during this gold rush. It was made into a popular movie in 1942. YA

Golden Fleece, the In Greek mythology, this is the wool of a sacred ram. The ram, able to speak and fly, appeared at the site where the youth Phrixus was to be sacrificed by his father. The ram rescued Phrixus and carried him through the air to safety. Obeying the ram's wishes, Phrixus sacrificed it and placed its fleece in a grove sacred to the god *Ares. Then the ram ascended to the stars and became the constellation Aries. Later, obtaining the Golden Fleece became the goal of *Jason's voyage with the *Argonauts. You can read about Jason and early Greek heroes in *The Golden Fleece and the Heroes Who Lived Before Achilles* (1983) by Padraic Colum (1881–1972). MR

Golding, William (Gerald) (1911–) This English novelist's books contain a pessimistic view of humanity and have attracted considerable interest, especially among the "Baby Boomers," people who were born in the 20 years after World War II. Golding's first and best-known novel, *The Lord of the Flies*, describes the transformation of marooned schoolboys into savages. *The Inheritors* (1955) tells the story of the last family of the Neanderthal period, and what happens when these uncorrupted people encounter the cunning ancestors of modern man. *Pincher Martin* (1956) describes the remorseful thoughts of a naval officer on a torpedoed ship. *Free Fall* (1958) reveals an imprisoned man's spiritual transformation as he awaits torture in a prisoner-of-war camp. *The Spire* (1964) concerns a clergyman's determination to build a church spire. *Darkness Visible* (1979) describes the story of a badly burned boy during the blitz in World War II London. Golding was awarded the Nobel Prize for literature in 1983. Movie versions of *The Lord of the Flies* appeared in 1963 and 1990. YA

Goldsmith, Oliver (1730?–1774) An Anglo-Irish author of essays, poetry, fiction, drama, and history, Goldsmith is known today especially for the novel *The Vicar of Wakefield* (1766), about the misfortunes and final triumph of an innocent country parson and his family. Goldsmith's stage comedies reflect his own unsentimental humor and his belief that plays should have the rambunctious mirth of Elizabethan drama. He wrote only three plays, among them *The Good Natur'd Man* (1768), in

The parson and his family in
The Vicar of Wakefield by Oliver Goldsmith

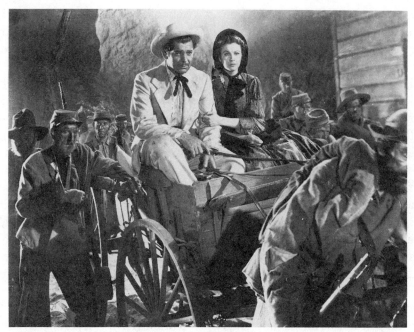

The film *Gone With the Wind*, starring Clark Gable and Vivien Leigh,
won 10 Academy Awards.

which an uncle has his nephew jailed for debt in order to teach him the limits of generosity and self-sacrifice, and the classic *She Stoops to Conquer*. YA

Gomorrah See *Sodom and Gomorrah*.

Gone With the Wind (1936) By *Margaret Mitchell, this novel is a romance set against the historical backdrop of the Civil War and Reconstruction. Its heroine is Scarlett O'Hara, daughter of an Irish immigrant who has risen to become master of Tara, a beautiful plantation near Atlanta, Georgia. Beautiful, vain, self-willed, and headstrong, Scarlett longs to marry Ashley Wilkes, her ideal of the gallant and refined Southern gentleman. Ashley, however, marries Melanie Hamilton, whose goodness, kindness, and frailty are all qualities Scarlett lacks. As the South is destroyed by war and the political and economic upheaval that follows it, Scarlett stops at nothing to hold on to Tara, become wealthy, and win Ashley's love. Her singlemindedness blinds her to the unspoken love of Rhett Butler, a dashing, cynical outcast from Southern society who has made a fortune as a gambler and blockade runner. She realizes too late that she has sacrificed happi-

ness with Rhett for an illusion. Margaret Mitchell's romanticized image of Southern slave society is counterbalanced by beautifully drawn characters and rich historical details that bring to life the Civil War and its aftermath. Though Mitchell declined to write a sequel, her estate authorized one after her death. The result, *Scarlett* (1991) by Alexandra Ripley (1934–), was panned by many critics and reviewers but became an enormous best seller, even pulling with it the original novel onto the bestseller lists. *Gone With the Wind* was made into a spectacular film in 1939. YA

Good Earth, The (1931) By *Pearl S. Buck, this novel tells the story of Chinese farmer Wang Lung and his wife, O-Lan. In the beginning of the novel they are newly married and happy with their simple yet satisfying life. They work hard, have two sons, and buy a small parcel of farmland, which produces excellent harvests. After the birth of their third child, a retarded daughter, their luck takes a turn. Lack of rain causes their crops to fail, and the starving peasants are forced to leave their home to look for work in the city. It is a time of political and social unrest, and during the looting of a city, Wang Lung steals enough

MR = Middle Reader   YA = Young Adult Reader   * = See this main entry

money to return home, buy more land, hire farmhands, and take a concubine. Despite his newfound wealth, Wang Lung is not content. His dissatisfied wife dies, and his sons have little concern for the land. In fact, as Wang Lung is nearing death, he overhears his sons discussing their plans to sell their inheritance, the land Wang Lung has most valued and relied on to earn a living. *The Good Earth* was filmed in 1937. YA

Good-bye, Mr. Chips (1934) By *James Hilton, this very popular novel is an account of the memories of Mr. Chipping, affectionately known as "Chips." A teacher of classical languages at Brookfield, a boys' grammar school in England, Chips began his career in 1870. Now retired, he reviews his early teaching years, courtship, marriage, and the death of his wife and child during childbirth. He reflects on the unpleasant headmaster Ralston, who tried and failed to push Chips into retirement. He also recalls a retirement interrupted by a resumption of teaching duties during the difficult days of World War I. Chips has developed from a dull instructor into a humorous, slightly daft, and revered senior schoolmaster, who now prefers reading mystery novels to reading the works of Greek and Latin authors. Over the years Chips has become identified with Brookfield itself, a stabilizing personality in a school struggling to maintain itself amid the disintegration of English society during World War I. Film versions of *Good-bye, Mr. Chips* were made in 1939 and 1969. YA

Gorgons in Greek mythology were three maidens whose hideous faces transformed into stone anyone who looked upon them. They had serpents writhing above their heads, brazen hands, and tusks like those of swine. Medusa, the only mortal of the three, was the most famous. It was because of the goddess *Athena's jealousy of Medusa's beauty that she turned the maiden into such a terrifying creature. Following Athena's orders, the hero *Perseus—armed with a highly polished shield that reflected the image of the Gorgons—cut off Medusa's head and gave it to Athena. You can read about Perseus and the Gorgons in **A Wonder-Book for Girls and Boys* by *Nathaniel Hawthorne.

Gorky, Maksim (Maxim Gorki) [Aleksei Maksimovich Peshkov] (1868–1936) A popular Russian author who vividly depicted scenes of working-class life, Gorky was born in Nizhni Novgorod, a city that later was renamed Gorky in his honor. Gorky was politically active, and at various times of his life he was arrested, imprisoned, exiled, and put under police surveillance. He founded the *Chronicle,* a magazine designed to coordinate political action against World War I, and also helped to establish the First Workers' and Peasants' University, the Petrograd Theater, the World Literature Publishing House, and the Writers' Union. Among his numerous social and political novels, plays, and short-story collections are *Sketches and Stories* (1898–1899); the play **The Lower Depths;* and the novels **Mother,* a classic of proletarian literature; *The Artamonoy Business* (1925), which traces the lives of three generations of a wealthy Russian family that rose from the peasant class; and *The Life of Klim Samgin* (1927–1936), a series of four novels about the Russian intelligentsia between 1870 and 1929. Gorky also wrote nonfiction, including reminiscences of writers whom he knew, such as *Leo Tolstoy and *Anton Chekhov. YA

Gotham, Wise Men of The inhabitants of the village of Gotham, England, were noted for engaging in foolish behavior. When King John planned to march his army through Gotham, the citizens were against it because of the expense and hardship they would have to bear. They played the fool, and the king, warned of their silly behavior, abandoned his intentions. A collection of popular tales about the people of Gotham was published in the early 16th century during the reign of Henry VIII as *Merie Tales of the Mad Men of Gotam.* In the United States, New York City is often called Gotham, a name given to it by *Washington Irving.

Gothic This term is applied to architecture, art, and literature. Gothic architecture refers to the European tall-spire cathedral architecture of the 12th through the 16th century, so-called by *Renaissance artists after the barbarian Goths who helped bring down the Roman Empire. The Gothic novel has a melodramatic flavor and often features brooding villains and virtuous heroines battling in such medieval settings as gloomy castles and monasteries placed in dark landscapes. Examples of this genre include Mary Shelley's *Frankenstein, *Wuthering Heights by *Emily Brontë, and *The Hunchback of Notre Dame by *Victor Hugo, whose title refers to the famous Gothic cathedral of Paris. A typical modern Gothic novel is *Rebecca by *Daphne du Maurier. For a contemporary look at the horror and supernatural elements that characterize many Gothic novels, read the works of *Stephen King (1947–). YA

Goudge, Elizabeth (1900–1984) An English novelist and short-story writer, Goudge began writing in childhood. After trying her hand at fairy stories and plays, she found success with her first novel, *Island Magic* (1934), about the adventures of a family living in the Channel Islands in the late 19th century. Although she wrote more than two dozen novels, she is known best for her novel *Green Dolphin Street* (1944), which is also set in the Channel Islands in the 19th century and focuses on two sisters and the man they both love. Goudge's novels have been praised for their celebration of life, people, and places, especially the English countryside. They include *Pilgrim's Inn* (1948), about an English family that moves into a large old house that was once a country inn, and *Gentian Hill* (1949), a love story set in Devonshire during the Napoleonic era. Goudge also wrote several books for younger readers, including *The Little White Horse* (1947), a fantasy about an English girl who comes to live on her family's ancestral estate and becomes involved in a struggle against evil Black Men who lurk in the nearby woods. MR & YA

Grafton, Sue (1940–) A successful writer for movies and television, Grafton started writing detective fiction with the novel *"A" Is for Alibi* (1982). Grafton's fictional detective is a 32-year-old woman, Kinsey Millhone, twice divorced, with no children. Millhone was a policewoman on a southern California force, but she now is a private investigator, living in a converted garage apartment and driving a beat-up Volkswagen. She keeps in shape by jogging regularly. In *"A" Is for Alibi* Millhone is asked by a woman who has spent eight years in prison for killing her husband to find the real murderer. Millhone succeeds, but in the course of her investigation kills a person for the first time, with the gun she regularly carries. By 1992 Grafton had continued her alphabetical series as far as *"I" Is for Innocent.* Kinsey Millhone ranks with *Marcia Muller's Sharon McCone as among the best of the female hard-boiled private eyes. If you like these novels, read those of *Amanda Cross, *Antonia Fraser, Marcia Muller, and *Sara Paretsky. YA

Grahame, Kenneth (1859–1932) A Scottish-born author and banker who lived most of his life in England, Grahame wrote one of the most famous books for younger readers, the classic *The Wind in the Willows*, which developed out of bedtime stories he told his son. For older readers, Grahame wrote nostalgic essays of childhood days in the countryside, including *The Golden Age* (1895) and *Dream Days* (1898). He lived a quiet life until his death in Pangbourne, a rural village in southern England. MR & YA

Grail, Holy In medieval legend, the Holy Grail is the chalice, or bowl, used by *Jesus at the *Last Supper. Joseph of Arimathea brought the Holy Grail, in which he had received some of Christ's blood at the crucifixion, to Britain, where it disappeared. A holy relic with the power to heal, it was thought to be hidden in a mysterious castle. In the stories about *King Arthur, the knights of the *Round Table go on quests to find it. But few knights are pure enough in word, thought, and deed even to catch sight of it. One who does find the Grail is *Galahad, the son of *Lancelot. Legends of the Grail exist in II languages, but the best-known versions in English come from the stories of King Arthur in *Thomas Malory's *Le Morte d'Arthur* (1469). The story of the Grail has pre-Christian, or pagan, roots in Irish and Welsh myths and *fables.

Grapes of Wrath, The (1939) This landmark novel by *John Steinbeck centers on the Joad family, Oklahoma farmers who, like so many others during the *Great Depression, are forced by drought and economic collapse to leave their home and seek a better life in California. This migrant family finds temporary comfort in California in a government-run camp. After leaving the camp because of the lack of local work, the Joads find jobs in another district, picking fruit for just a few cents a day. They take these jobs despite the warning of labor organizers that the big farmers are exploiting them. Tom Joad's meeting with the organizers leads to his becoming a fugitive from justice when a fight with the police breaks out. Unable to return to his family, he vows that he will work for better working conditions. Meanwhile, his sister, Rose of Sharon, gives birth to a dead baby and, as the novel ends, uses the milk from her breasts to nourish a starving man. Steinbeck's powerful call to action on behalf of the migrant worker reflects his personal experience in migrant camps. *The Grapes of Wrath* expresses American affection for the land and for the indestructible dignity and goodness of the dispossessed, the oppressed, and the powerless. The title comes from the famous lines of vengeance and vindication in the "Battle Hymn of the Republic" (1862) by Julia Ward Howe (1819–1910):

> Mine eyes have seen the glory of the coming of the Lord:
> He is trampling out the vintage where the grapes of wrath are stored:
> He hath loosed the fateful lightning of his terrible swift sword:
> His truth is marching on.

If you enjoyed *The Grapes of Wrath*, you may want to read *Uncle Tom's Cabin* by *Harriet Beecher Stowe, another novel conveying a powerful message about injustice and exploitation. *The Grapes of Wrath* was filmed in 1940. YA

Graustark (1901) By George Barr McCutcheon (1866–1928), this enormously popular first novel tells about Grenfall Lorry, a wealthy American who falls in love with a beautiful and mysterious young woman while on a train journey, knowing only that her home is the tiny European principality of Graustark. Lorry and his friend Harry Anguish travel to Graustark, where they discover that the woman is none other than Princess Yetive, Graustark's ruler, and that Lorry, a commoner, cannot hope to marry her. Then Lorry becomes entangled in a deadly political intrigue when he is framed with the murder of Yetive's unwanted suitor, Prince Lorenz of the rival principality of Axphain. With help from Harry, the princess, and her faithful servants, Lorry proves his innocence, helps save Graustark from Axphainian territorial demands, and wins the woman he loves. McCutcheon returned to Graustark in a number of sequels, including *Beverly of Graustark* (1904) and *The Prince of Graustark* (1914). One of McCutcheon's well-known novels is *Brewster's Millions* (1903), about a man who stands to inherit $7 million if he is able to spend wisely $1 million in a year's time. *Brewster's Millions* was filmed in 1935, 1945, and 1985. YA

Graves, Robert (Ranke) (1895–1985) An English poet and novelist whose works have been translated into numerous languages, Graves served in World War I and later wrote an autobiographical book about the war years, *Goodbye to All That* (1929). Graves spent most of his life on the island of Majorca, Spain, where he wrote extensively. His most popular historical works include the novels *I, Claudius* (1934) and its sequel, *Claudius the God* (1935), which are about the Roman Empire. His other books include *The Golden Fleece* (1943), about the quest of *Jason and the *Argonauts for the *Golden Fleece, and *The White Goddess* (1948), a well-known investigation of myth and poetical theory. In 1955, he published commentaries and essays on Greek mythology. Graves was professor of poetry at Oxford University from 1961 to 1966. *I, Claudius* was made into an outstanding TV miniseries in 1976. YA

Gray, Elizabeth Janet [Elizabeth Gray Vining] (1902–) Though known best for the novel *Adam of the Road, about the adventures of a boy and his minstrel father in 13th-century England, Gray has written a number of novels for younger readers. Some have been reprinted many times, including *Jane Hope* (1933), about a 12-year-old girl who, after her father dies, moves with her family to North Carolina just before the Civil War. Gray's other novels include *Beppy Marlowe of Charles Town* (1936), about an English girl who comes to America with her brother in 1715, and *The Cheerful Heart* (1959), about an 11-year-old Japanese girl whose courage and cheerfulness help her family to rebuild their home and their lives after World War II. Gray also wrote several biographies for young people, including *Young Walter Scott* (1935), about the Scottish writer *Walter Scott; *Penn* (1938), about William Penn (1644–1718), the Quaker leader and founder of Pennsylvania colony; and *Mr. Whittier* (1974), about the poet *John Greenleaf Whittier. MR

Gray, Thomas (1716–1771) This English poet is known today chiefly for one great poem. He was educated at Eton College and at Cambridge University, eventually settling in Cambridge. "Elegy Written in a Country Churchyard" (1750) describes the conflict between a life of learning and a simple life in the country, a theme that became prevalent in the work of the later Romantic poets. Though country folk may live simple lives, they also preserve their innocence. Death makes all equal; in fact, "the paths of glory lead but to the grave." Gray, who led a bookish life, died in Cambridge and was buried at Stoke Poges, the cemetery that inspired his great poem. YA

Great Brain, The (1967) John D. Fitzgerald (1908–) based this novel, set in Utah in the 1890s, on his own boyhood experiences. Young J.D. Fitzgerald narrates the adventures of his very smart older brother, Tom, who is constantly thinking up new schemes for making money and promoting his reputation as the town's "Great Brain." Tom charges admission to see his family's new indoor toilet (the first in town), profits from teaching a young immigrant how to be a regular American boy, and becomes a hero when he rescues two friends lost in a cave. Tom's willingness to work almost any situation for his own personal advantage causes J.D. much worry. But Tom finally shows his true goodness by helping a boy who has lost a leg to learn how to walk, run, play, and enjoy life again. You can read about the further adventures of the Great Brain in *More Adventures of the Great Brain* (1969), *Me and My Little Brain* (1971), *The Great Brain at the Academy* (1972), *The Great Brain Reforms* (1973), *The Return of the Great Brain* (1974), and *The Great Brain Does It Again* (1975). *The Great Brain* was filmed in 1978. MR

Great Depression, the Known often as simply "the Depression," this was a worldwide economic collapse that followed the artificial economic boom seen in the Roaring Twenties and was triggered by the collapse of the U.S. stock market in 1929. Prices fell sharply, credit was restricted, and many businesses and individuals went bankrupt. One of the longest such crises on record, it began about 1930 and did not end until the beginning of World War II. The Great Depression left almost one-third of working Americans unemployed. It was also felt deeply in Europe, where nations were still rebuilding after World War I.

During the 1930s the American prairie states were hit by devastating droughts and dust storms, which led to the region's being known as the "Dust Bowl." Crops and pastures were spoiled, forcing thousands of farm families to travel west to look for work as migrant laborers. Because many were from Oklahoma, they came to be called "Okies." Their struggles are the subject of *John Steinbeck's *The Grapes of Wrath.

MR = Middle Reader   YA = Young Adult Reader   * = See this main entry

The Great Gatsby, by *F. Scott Fitzgerald, is set in the Roaring Twenties. *Skinny* and *Queenie Peavy*, by *Robert Burch, are stories that take place during the Great Depression.

Great Expectations (1860), a novel by *Charles Dickens, is a tale of spellbinding mystery and tragic disappointment. It is about a simple village boy and the development of his character as he rises in life. Philip Pirrip, or Pip, lives with his sister, a bad-tempered woman 20 years his senior, and her husband, Joe Gargery, a blacksmith. Joe is the soul of kindness, humor, and unshakable integrity. Pip is taken to visit the house of Miss Havisham, an aristocratic recluse who became eccentric when her lover deserted her. Miss Havisham has adopted an orphan girl, Estella, and is vengefully teaching her to break men's hearts. Though the haughty Estella treats Pip coldly and calls him a common boy, Pip falls in love with her. But Pip realizes he cannot hope to win her respect until he becomes a gentleman.

Pip is approached by Mr. Jaggers, a London lawyer, who announces that a mysterious benefactor wishes to set him up as a gentleman and provide for his future. Pip is certain that Miss Havisham is the source of his expectations. Happy to put his humble origins behind him, Pip goes to London, shares rooms with Herbert Pocket, and embarks on his new life.

Years later, Pip discovers his patron is Abel Magwitch, an escaped convict for whom Pip had long ago performed a great service and who had become wealthy as an exile in Australia. Risking execution for returning to England, Magwitch has come to see the gentleman he has made. Repelled at first by Magwitch's vulgar manner and display of affection, Pip comes to admire and care for the old convict, whose dangerous situation causes Pip much worry. Calamity occurs when Estella marries the sulky Bentley Drummle and Miss Havisham dies. Pip and Herbert try to help Magwitch leave England to avoid an old enemy bent on killing him, but the attempt fails and Magwitch, badly wounded, is arrested. Before Magwitch dies in prison of his wounds, Pip

tells him of a great discovery—Estella is Magwitch's lost child, she is a beautiful lady, and Pip loves her with all his heart.

Pip begins to see the emptiness of his ambition to be a gentleman. He goes to work as Herbert's partner, pays his debts, and for 11 years leads a useful life. Pip learns that Estella's husband has died, after using her cruelly. She too is changed by suffering and asks to be his friend, giving Pip hope for their future together. A superb film version of the novel appeared in 1946. A TV movie was produced in 1974. YA

Great Gatsby, The (1925) Set among the mansions of Long Island and New York City in the 1920s, this novel by *F. Scott Fitzgerald describes the hope and the disillusionment inspired by the American dream of becoming wealthy. The narrator, Nick Carraway, leaves his home and the family hardware business in the Middle West and moves to the East to make his fortune in New York City's financial world. At a party hosted by his cousin Daisy and her rich husband, Tom Buchanan, he is introduced to the frantic life-style of the wealthy. Nick learns about Daisy's dissatisfaction with her marriage. She had loved Jay Gatsby, now a wealthy man, before he had made his money, but she had not married him.

Nick attends a number of parties hosted by Gatsby, and Nick eventually agrees to help rekindle the romance between Gatsby and Daisy. Buchanan is unfaithful to Daisy, and Myrtle Wilson, his mistress, is accidentally struck and killed by Gatsby's car, which Daisy was driving. Myrtle's husband forces Buchanan to reveal the identity of the car owner, and he kills both Gatsby and himself. Sickened by these events and the empty lives of the rich, Nick decides to return to his roots and family in the Middle West. Film versions of *The Great Gatsby* appeared in 1949 and 1974. YA

Great Impersonation, The (1920). This adventure novel by *E. Phillips Oppenheim begins in German East Africa shortly before World War I. The Englishman Sir Everard

Dominey and the German Baron Leopold von Ragastein, who look almost like twins, meet by accident in the wilds and discover they knew each other at school in England. Both men are exiles, both fluent in English and German. They discuss their pasts at length. Von Ragastein, aware of the coming war, plots to kill Dominey and take his place in England, using Dominey's social position to help the German cause. When he returns to England after many years' absence, von Ragastein/Dominey amazes everyone by his wealth (provided by the German government) and by his honorable behavior. Remembered as a man who drank too much and neglected his duties, he is noticeably changed. You learn that Rosamund, Lady Dominey, went insane after the real Everard fought with and supposedly killed Roger Unthank, an eccentric admirer of hers whose body was never found. Local people feel sure it is Unthank's ghost that cries horribly at night around Dominey Hall and the Black Wood.

Everard cares for Rosamund with great tenderness, and slowly her health is restored, though she is convinced he is not her real husband. As the two begin to fall in love, Everard decides to find the source of the ghostly howls and rid the Hall of its sadnesss. He succeeds in trapping Roger Unthank, who survived the fight and lived secretly in the Black Wood like an animal. Then a German friend of von Ragastein unexpectedly visits, confronts Everard, and accuses him of being an impostor. Everard reveals that he really is Dominey, and that von Ragastein met the fate planned for the Englishman. YA

green Among the various *colors, green has more than its share of pleasant meanings. In general, it stands for faith and gladness; in art, for joy and youth; and in religion, for God's bounty. In more down-to-earth terms, a person who has a "green thumb" has a knack for making plants grow; and if you have a "green light," as in a traffic signal, you are free to move on. By contrast, "green" stands for inexperience. A "greenhorn" is easily fooled, and envy is the "green-eyed monster." In some countries, especially in Western Europe, political parties interested primarily in environmental issues often call themselves the Green Party or simply the Greens.

Green, Henry [Henry Vincent Yorke] (1905–1973) This English writer's prosperous family owned an industrial engineering firm that he worked in and eventually directed. Green's business experience gave him the insight into the lives of working people that he used in the novel *Living* (1929), about the daily lives of workers in a Birmingham factory. *Party Going* (1939), set in a fog-bound London railway station, depicts wealthy Londoners about to go on holiday. *Loving* (1945), one of his best-known novels, describes life in the servants' quarters of an Irish castle during World War II. Green's novels are marked by extensive dialogue that clearly conveys the class differences in English society. In addition to his nine novels, Green wrote an autobiography called *Pack My Bag* (1940). YA

Green Mansions, a romantic novel by *W.H. Hudson, is about Abel, a young man who wanders through the depths of the Guiana jungle, in South America, encountering numerous Indian tribes, wild animals, and a beautiful 17-year-old girl named Rima. Though warned by superstitious Indians that Rima is an evil spirit, Abel ventures deeper into the forest, in awe of the wondrous birds, roaring monkeys, and the mysterious birdlike melodies created by Rima. After numerous adventures, in which Rima saves Abel from the perils of nature, they fall passionately in love. Later, Rima wants to leave the forest to return to Riolama, the town in which she was born, to find others who can communicate in her birdlike language. On the way to Riolama, Rima discovers that she is the only one of her race who remains alive. Disheartened, they return to their home in the forest. Rima is then killed by the Indians, who fear she is evil. Abel, on realizing his loved one is dead, becomes increasingly more savage, eventually taking murderous revenge on the Indians. Finally, Abel gathers Rima's ashes, leaves the forest, recovers his mental health, forgives himself for his own savage actions, and once again feels worthy of the love of the dead Rima. The novel was adapted for film in 1959. YA

Green Pastures, The (1930) By Marc Connelly (1890–1980), this delightful fantasy is a dramatic version of *Ol' Man Adam an' His Chillun* (1928), a series of black folktales collected by Roark Bradford (1896–1948). In *The Green Pastures*, Mr. Deshee, a Southern black minister, tells familiar biblical stories to his Sunday school class, acted out in the speech and thoughts of a black Louisiana community in the 1920s. In one scene Adam and Eve are created after God and the angels hold a fish fry in heaven. In another, "Dee Lawd God Jehovah" saves Noah, but lets crapshooters drown. The stage production, performed by an all-black cast more than 600 times, was followed by a film version in 1936. If you enjoyed *The Green Pastures*, you will also like *Porgy* by Dubose Heyward (1885–1940). YA

Greenaway, Kate [Catherine Greenaway] (1846–1901) An English author and illustrator of books for young people, Greenaway gained her first big success with *Under the Window* (1879), a collection of colorful illustrations and companion verses that caught the fancy of young and old alike and became a best-seller. Greenaway followed this success with a large number of illustrated books for children, many of which have been reissued over the years. They include *Kate Greenaway's Birthday Book for Children* (1880), *The Language of Flowers* (1884), *The Marigold Garden* (1885), and *Kate Greenaway's Book of Games* (1889). Although Greenaway much preferred illustrating her own verse, she is probably remembered best for illustrating two works she did not write, *Mother Goose; or, The Old Nursery Rhymes* (1881), which has become a children's classic, and *The Pied Piper of Hamelin* (1888) by the poet *Robert Browning. You can find good selections of Kate Greenaway's work in several anthologies, including *The Kate Greenaway Treasury* (1967) and *The Kate Greenaway Book* (1976). MR

Greene, Bette (1934–) Known best for her novel *Summer of My German Soldier* (1973), Greene was born in Memphis, Tennessee, and grew up there and in a small town in Arkansas. Her childhood experiences in Arkansas are reflected in this novel, about a girl who shelters an escaped German prisoner of war during World War II, and in her other novels. *Philip Hall Likes Me, I Reckon Maybe* (1974) is set in rural Arkansas and tells about Beth Lambert, an 11-year-old black girl who has a crush on Philip Hall, the cutest, smartest boy in her school, yet finds herself competing against Philip both in and out of school. A warm family story, it is also a touching tale of first love and friendship. Beth and Philip also appear in *Get Out of Here, Philip Hall* (1981), in which Beth learns that, despite being defeated twice by Philip for leadership awards and losing the presidency of her girls' club, she is a true leader. Greene also wrote *Them That Glitter and Them That Don't* (1983), about a teenage girl who leaves her scheming, domineering, gypsy mother to attempt a career as a country-and-western singer. MR

Greene, Constance C. (1938–) Author of a number of thoughtful and entertaining novels about young people, Greene is probably known best for her series of books about a girl named Al and her best friend, who live in the same New York City apartment building. The series includes *A Girl Called Al, *I Know You, Al, *Your Old Pal, Al, *Just Plain Al, and *Al(exandra) the Great. The novels reflect Greene's sense of humor and her understanding of a young person's view of the important things in life. Her other books include *Beat the Turtle Drum* (1976), about a 13-year-old girl's struggle to cope with the accidental death of her younger sister; *I and Sproggy* (1978), about a 10-year-old New York City boy and the problems he faces as he gets to know his new English stepsister; and *Ask Anybody* (1983), about a girl liv-

---

MR = Middle Reader   YA = Young Adult Reader   * = See this main entry

ing in Maine who befriends an eccentric new girl to the neighborhood and learns that the girl is unlike anyone she has ever known. MR

Greene, (Henry) Graham (1904–1991) A British novelist, short-story writer, and dramatist, Greene was as versatile and talented an author as any the 20th-century English-speaking world has produced. He wrote serious novels as well as lighter stories of espionage and detection, which he called "entertainments." In all he produced 54 books. *The Power and the Glory* (1940) is a novel about an alcoholic Mexican priest who is willing to die for his faith. *The Heart of the Matter* (1948) is set in West Africa, where the central character, torn between lust and his religious faith, commits suicide. Another of Greene's serious works is *The Quiet American. In *A Burnt-Out Case* (1960) the setting is a leper colony in the Congo, where an architect, a "spiritual leper," is the burnt-out case. *The Comedians* (1966) exposes the horrors of the government of Haiti. Among Greene's "entertainments" are *Brighton Rock* (1938), which deals with a murder at the British coastal resort of Brighton; *The Ministry of Fear; and *Our Man in Havana* (1958), about a spy who has to fake certain things to convince his superiors that he is on the job. Before writing his serious novels, Greene visited the places involved to see things from the point of view of the inhabitants. He was a moralist, influenced by his conversion to Catholicism. If you like Greene's books, you may also enjoy those of *Eric Ambler, Anthony Burgess (1917–) (see *A Clockwork Orange), *Albert Camus, *Len Deighton, *E.M. Forster, *Arthur Koestler, *John Le Carré, *George Orwell, and *Evelyn Waugh. A movie was made of *The Ministry of Fear* in 1944; *Brighton Rock* in 1947; *The Heart of the Matter* in 1954; *The Quiet American* in 1958; *The Comedians* in 1967; and *Our Man in Havana* in 1960. Greene's classic postwar mystery, *The Third Man* (1950), was produced first as a memorable film in 1949. YA

Greenfield, Eloise (1929–) Twenty-two years old when she first began to write seriously,

Greenfield was able to continue her literary pursuits while working in government offices and raising a family in Washington, D.C. Her first published book, *Bubbles* (1972), is a children's picture book. *Rosa Parks* (1973) is a biography about the black woman, now famous, who refused to give up her seat in the front of a bus to a white man, and *Sister* is about a young girl learning to be truly herself. Greenfield is an active member of the D.C. Black Writer's Workshop. MR

Greenwald, Sheila [Sheila Ellen Green] (1934–) A prolific illustrator, Greenwald has also written and illustrated more than a dozen novels noted for their delightful humor and understanding of how young people think and feel. *Give Us a Great Big Smile, Rosy Cole* (1981) tells about the problems faced by 10-year-old Rosy when her photographer uncle sets out to make her famous by doing a book about her musical talent. The biggest problem is that Rosy has no talent, a secret known only to Rosy and her music teacher. Rosy appears in several sequels, including *Rosy Cole's Great American Guilt Club* (1985), in which Rosy organizes a club to enable her rich friends to give some of their stylish extra clothes to those less fortunate than they—namely Rosy; and *Write On, Rosy!* (1988), in which Rosy, searching for a lifelong ambition, tries her luck as an investigative reporter. Greenwald's other books include *All the Way to Wit's End* (1979), about a girl who longs to change her family's out-of-date ways after the family moves from its old mansion to a new, suburban community; *It All Began with Jane Eyre: Or, the Secret Life of Franny Dillman; and *Will the Real Gertrude Hollings Please Stand Up?* (1983), about the problems 11-year-old Gertrude has with her younger, smarter, superachieving cousin during her three-week visit to his family. MR

gremlin An imaginary creature of American folklore, the gremlin is invoked to explain mechanical quirks or problems. About 20 inches tall, gremlins are often blamed for mechanical trouble on airplanes. The gremlin costume includes green pants, red ruffled jackets, top hats, and spats. The short story "Gremlins" (1943), by *Roald Dahl, takes a humorous look at how gremlin mischief affected British Royal Air Force planes during World War II. For a contemporary look at them, see the movie *Gremlins* (1984), in which these small and destructive creatures cause problems in a typical American town, and *Gremlins 2: The New Batch* (1990), which describes their further adventures, this time in New York City. MR

Grendel The monster in *Beowulf*, Grendel is described as a descendant of Cain. Grendel was a member of a monster race banished to the darkest parts of the Anglo-Saxon world because of Cain's slaying of Abel. In *Beowulf*, the Danish king Hrothgar unknowingly builds his hall, Heorot, near Grendel's home at the bottom of a lake. Grendel opposes this invasion by killing the king's subjects in the darkness of night. Beowulf, a hero of a neighboring tribe, comes to the aid of Hrothgar and slays Grendel in single combat.

Grendel's mother rises from the depths and takes bloody revenge on the Danes. After she carries off and kills Hrothgar's beloved counselor, Aeschere, Beowulf kills this monster in a great underwater battle. If you would like to know more about this monster, read the novel *Grendel* (1971) by John Gardner (1933–1982), which retells the story of Beowulf from Grendel's point of view. YA

Grey, Zane (1872–1939) A popular author known best for his many Western novels, Grey was born and grew up in Zanesville, Ohio, which was named after one of his mother's ancestors. He was an athletic boy, but he also loved to read, especially the adventure stories found in magazines and *dime novels, and even wrote an adventure story of his own. He worked as a dentist for several years before turning to writing. His first books, historical novels of the early frontier, were not successful, but on a trip to the West, Grey determined to use the region and its history for his fiction. His first big success came with *Riders of the Purple Sage* (1912), an action-filled adventure set in Utah in 1871. It became his best-known novel. Among his many Western novels are *The Heritage of the Desert* (1910), about Mormon settlers struggling against ruthless cattlemen and rustlers in Utah; *The Thundering Herd* (1925), about a young Kansan who becomes a buffalo hunter in the 1870s; and *Western Union* (1939), about the building of the Western Union telegraph line in 1861. If you enjoy reading Westerns, try also the works of *Louis L'Amour, *The Virginian* by Owen Wister (1860–1938), and *Shane* by Jack Schaeffer (1907–1991). *Riders of the Purple Sage* was filmed in 1925 and *Western Union* in 1941. YA

Grey King, The (1975) By the English-born writer *Susan Cooper, this is the fourth novel in a series called *The Dark Is Rising sequence. As in the first three books, *Over Sea, Under Stone* (1965), *The Dark Is Rising* (1973), and *Greenwitch* (1973), it tells of the epic struggle between the Lords of Light and the Lords of the Dark to control the world. At the center of the struggle is an English boy, Will Stanton, who is sent to his uncle David Evans's farm in Wales to recover from a serious illness. There Will meets Bran, a white-haired, golden-eyed boy who was brought as a foundling to Owen Davies, a neighboring sheepherder, by a beautiful but mysterious woman named Gwen. Will soon recalls things that had been blocked by his illness. He is the last member of the line of Old Ones, who through the ages have fought against the Dark. Now, with Bran's help, he must defeat the evil Grey King by finding an enchanted gold harp and using it to awaken the six Sleepers to join the battle against the Dark. In the process, Will learns that Bran's mother is actually *Guinevere, his father *King Arthur. If you enjoyed *The Grey King*, you will want to read the earlier books and also the final volume, *Silver on the Tree* (1977). *The Grey King* won the *Newbery Medal in 1976. MR

Grimes, Martha (n.d.) An American college teacher whose detective novels are set in En-

---

gland, Grimes writes stories that have a touch of humor as well as believable plots. Her book titles all come from the rather unusual names of British pubs. The first was *The Man with a Load of Mischief* (1981), the scene of which is the village of Long Piddleton where, one after another, bodies are found near three pubs. Inspector Richard Jury of Scotland Yard is called in, bringing with him a sergeant who is forever treating himself for imaginary minor ills. Also helping in the investigation is Melrose Plant, actually an earl who refuses to use his title. Jury and Plant become friendly and meet again in later novels. Among them are *The Old Fox Deceived* (1982), *The Dirty Duck* (1984), *I Am the Only Running Footman* (1986), and *The Old Contemptibles* (1991), in which Jury himself is a suspect. If you like these stories, try those of *Agatha Christie, *Michael Innes, and *Ruth Rendell. MR & YA

Grimm, Jacob (1785–1863) and **Grimm, Wilhelm** (1786–1859) Better known as the Brothers Grimm, they were German folklorists, the first to compile an anthology of fairy tales, the celebrated *Grimm's Fairy Tales* (1812–1822). Though they collected the stories from farmers, villagers, and friends, the finest, such as "The Goose Girl" and "Faithful John," were gathered from a woman named Katherina Viehmann (1755–1815).

During the years of preparing for the collection, Wilhelm suffered from severe heart ailments that kept him homebound. Jacob spent most of his time collecting the tales, and then Wilhelm arranged and improved on the often disjointed material. *Grimm's Fairy Tales*, which includes more than 200 tales of myth and magic, are filled with such familiar stories as "Snow White," *"Hansel and Gretel," and "Rapunzel." The ageless collection has been translated into many languages. A favorite edition in English is *The Complete Grimm's Fairy Tales* (1976), translated by Margaret Hunt (n.d.) and illustrated by Josef Scharl (n.d.). MR

Guest, Judith (1936–) The author of several popular novels, Guest is known best for her ac-

claimed and enormously successful first novel, *Ordinary People*, about a 17-year-old boy's struggle to recover from a suicide attempt and understand its effects on his family. Her second novel, *Second Heaven* (1982), also centers on the struggles of a teenage boy to overcome a life-threatening situation and restore balance to his life. Seventeen-year-old Gale Murray, fleeing from his violent and abusive father, finds friends and allies in Cat Holzman, an attractive woman whose marriage has just fallen apart, and Michael Atwood, a lawyer who is facing his own family crisis. As they help Gale, Cat and Michael also find answers to their own problems. Guest also co-authored, with Rebecca Hill (1944–), *Killing Time in St. Cloud* (1988), a mystery centering on a man whose return to his hometown after 12 years triggers two deaths and ignites long-suppressed tensions in the community. YA

Guinevere is *King Arthur's queen. The daughter of a king, she married Arthur and came to his court bringing, as a wedding gift, the *Round Table. Many versions of this story emphasize that Guinevere and Arthur and *Lancelot, all three, respected and loved each other, but when the passion of Lancelot and Guinevere became known, the destruction of Arthur and his peaceful kingdom was the result, as had been predicted by *Merlin. In some versions Arthur is compelled to burn Guinevere at the stake, but she is rescued by Lancelot on his charger at the last moment, to the great relief of the king. Lancelot takes her to a nunnery while the kingdom goes to war, and there she ends her days. Guinevere is a major character in *The Mists of Avalon* (1982), a novel by *Marion Zimmer Bradley that tells the story from the female point of view and presents the conflict between the pagan and Christian religions at that time. YA

Gulliver's Travels (1726) This *satire by *Jonathan Swift, first published under the title *Travels into Several Remote Nations of the World* by "Lemuel Gulliver," was intended "to vex the world rather than to divert it." In *Gul-*

liver's Travels, Swift, an Anglican priest, essayist, and poet, expresses a somber view of humanity — he believed that people could do evil and behave in immoral and savage fashion. Its hero, Lemuel Gulliver, a physician, embarks on four voyages. In the first, Gulliver lands in Lilliput, where the tiny inhabitants, who symbolize the pettiness and low morality of the English, consider Gulliver a giant. He manages to escape Lilliput, but not soon enough to escape his own corruption in Lilliputian service.

In fact, his reduced moral stature contrasts with the nature of the next creatures he meets, the giants of *Brobdingnag. He tries and fails to impress this gentle and generous race. In the third voyage, to *Laputa, Gulliver meets abstract thinkers whose inventions are neither practical nor helpful to humans. He also encounters the Strudbugs, who have found the means to eternal life, but do not achieve wisdom in the process. Finally, in the fourth voyage, Gulliver meets and admires the Houyhnhnms, a completely rational race of horses, and is horrified by the *Yahoos, who resemble the worst contemporary English people. Now Gulliver becomes obsessed with reason, which prevents him from accepting simple kindness from strangers and affection from his family when he returns home. Older readers have always admired Swift's *irony and his satire of contemporary English society. However, children over the years have enjoyed *Gulliver's Travels* simply as a fantastic series of adventures, among the first shipwreck tales of the 18th and 19th centuries. You can find many editions for older readers, including *Gulliver's Travels and Selected Writings in Prose and Poetry* (1934), edited by John Hayward (1905–1965) and reissued in 1990. There are several illustrated editions for younger readers, including one from the Illustrated Junior Library, which has remained in print for 48 years. Animated films of *Gulliver's Travels* were made in 1939 and 1977. MR & YA

Gunther, John (1901–1970) Journalist, novelist, and author of *Death Be Not Proud*, Gun-

ther began his career as a reporter for the Chicago *Daily News*. As a correspondent in London and other European capitals, he gathered material for the first of his "Inside" books, *Inside Europe* (1936). The survey contains an examination of Adolf Hitler (1889–1945), a description of how Hitler's Germany affected the rest of Europe, and accounts of the main European crises of the time.

After two years as a correspondent for the North American Newspaper Alliance in Persia (now Iran), India, China, and Japan, Gunther wrote *Inside Asia* (1939). This was followed by *Inside Latin America* (1941), *Inside U.S.A.* (1947), *Inside Africa* (1955), and *Inside Russia Today* (1958). Gunther did an enormous amount of research on his books and developed a talent for clearly explaining complicated ideas through his interviews and conversations with people. Though his works were not considered scholarly, they were said to combine the "best qualities of the newspaperman and the historian." YA

Gutenberg, Johannes (1400?–1468?) This German printer is credited with inventing a printing method using movable type, which, with only slight changes, remained the standard way of printing until the 20th century. Gutenberg's system included metal prisms for making accurate and mass-produced type, a new press, and an oil-based printing ink. These innovations were unique in his day. Gutenberg hoped to reproduce sacred medieval manuscripts mechanically without sacrificing their color or attractiveness. The first and most famous product of movable type was the famous Gutenberg *Bible, produced around 1455, followed by the Psalter in 1457. For more about printing, you will enjoy *The Story of Printing: From Wood Blocks to Electronics* (1965) by Irving B. Simon (1902–). MR & YA

Guthrie, A(lfred) B(ertram), Jr. (1901–1991) This writer of superior Westerns grew up in Montana, and his books describe the American West with realism, revealing its beauty and harshness, as well as the manner in which newcomers have diminished it. *The Big Sky* (1947) describes the adventures of a Kentuckian transformed into a mountain man, who traps beaver and learns American Indian ways in the upper Missouri River country of the 1830s and 1840s. *The Way West* (1949), the story of a wagon train's journey from Independence, Missouri, to Oregon in the 1840s, is a vivid account of pioneers making their way to the Pacific coast. *Arfive* (1971) concerns a new high school principal's problems in Arfive, Montana, at the turn of the century. *The Last Valley* (1975) describes life in the same town during World War II. Guthrie also wrote an autobiography, *The Blue Hen's Chick* (1965), as well as screenplays for such films as *Shane* and *The Kentuckian* (1955), in which a man and his son journey to Texas to begin a new life. A film version of *The Big Sky* appeared in 1952, and a film of *The Way West* appeared in 1967. YA

haiku, a traditional Japanese verse form, consists of 17 word sounds, or syllables, arranged in three lines of 5, 7, and 5 syllables. The haiku was established in the 16th century and became the most popular Japanese poetry in the 17th century. The haiku uses the association of images and ideas to evoke a single emotion or sensation, and often refers to nature or to a particular season. Today haiku remains very popular in Japan and in many other countries as well. Harry Behn (1898–1973) has collected and translated haiku in *300 Classic Haiku* (1962), *Cricket Songs* (1964), and *More Cricket Songs* (1971). MR

hair This word is used in many phrases and sayings. Some of the most exciting stories you will read are "hair-raising adventures," meaning that they have the power to shock, terrify, or horrify you, to "make one's hair stand on end." "To let one's hair down" comes from the days when women wore their long hair pinned up in public but let it down in the more relaxed atmosphere of their own homes. The phrase means to be relaxed and natural, or to speak openly and freely. On the other hand, the fairy-tale heroine Rapunzel was locked in a tower with no door and was commanded to let down her long hair so the witch who had imprisoned her could climb up it into the tower. Rapunzel could hardly have felt relaxed in her prison.

Some situations may make you want to "tear your hair out," to become extremely angry and upset. A person's temper might have a "hair trigger," meaning that the slightest pressure could set that person into a rage. Then she or he might feel remorse and "put on a hair shirt," or punish herself or himself. Hair shirts, made of the hair from horses' manes and tails, were scratchy and were worn as a kind of penance for sins.

Many races have been won "by a hair's breadth," the smallest of margins. But to argue about which was the closest race might be "splitting hairs," or making petty or trivial distinctions. You can, by the way, read about Rapunzel, the captive princess, in the collection *Household Stories by the Brothers Grimm* (1886) and other, more recent editions of the tales collected by the Brothers *Grimm. MR

Hale, Lucretia Peabody (1820–1900) Born and raised in Boston, Massachusetts, Lucretia Hale belonged to a literary family. Her father was editor of the Boston *Daily Advertiser* and her brother, Edward Everett Hale (1822–1909), a clergyman and writer, was the author of *The Man Without a Country*, a tale of patriotism that has become an American classic.

Lucretia Hale wrote a number of books, but she is remembered today for her delightful stories about the hilarious adventures of the Peterkin family and about their friend, the *Lady from Philadelphia, who often helps them out of their problems through the use of simple common sense. Hale invented the first Peterkin family story to amuse the daughter of her lifelong friend, Susan Lyman Leslie. Mrs. Leslie was, in fact, the model for the Lady from Philadelphia. The Peterkins first appeared in print in 1866, in the children's magazine *Our Young Folks*, which later became *St. Nicholas* magazine. More stories followed, and they were collected in two volumes, *The Peterkin Papers* and *The Last of the Peterkins* (1886). The stories in both volumes were brought together in *The Complete Peterkin Papers* (1960). MR

Haley, Alex (Palmer) (1921–1992), author of the family saga *Roots*, grew up in Henning, Tennessee, where his family owned a lumber business. Haley spent much time as a boy with his maternal grandmother, who told him stories of her family's history, which went back to the 1700s and the arrival in America of an ancestor she called "the African." Haley committed the stories to memory, as his grandmother and mother had done. After attending college, Haley joined the Coast Guard. There he began his writing career. His success at writing articles and stories won him the chance to conduct a magazine interview with Malcolm X (1925–1965), the spokesman for the Nation of Islam movement. The interview led to a contract to collaborate on *The Autobiography of Malcolm X*, which became a best-seller and earned recognition for Haley. In the 1960s Haley turned his attention to writing the history of his own family. The result, *Roots,* a careful weaving of historical fact and fictional narrative, was a great success. YA

Hall, James Norman (1887–1951) Though born and raised in landlocked Iowa, Hall is remembered best for the seafaring historical novels he wrote with *Charles B. Nordhoff. During World War I Hall fought as an infantryman, then as a pilot in the celebrated Lafayette Flying Corps. There he met Nordhoff, and the two became friends.

After the war Nordhoff and Hall collaborated

on a military history, *The Lafayette Flying Corps* (1920). They then settled on the Pacific island of Tahiti, where they lived for many years and collaborated on their best-known novels, *Mutiny on the Bounty; Men Against the Sea* (1933), which recounts the long voyage of Captain Bligh and his companions following the mutiny aboard the ship *Bounty;* and *Pitcairn's Island* (1934), which chronicles the fate of Fletcher Christian, the leader of the mutiny, and his followers. Hall's later books include the novel *The Far Lands* (1950) and his autobiography, *My Island Home* (1952). YA

Halloween Pumpkin Smasher, The (1978) By *Judith St. George, this story is set in a small town in the early 1900s. Mary Grace Potts and her make-believe playmate, Nellie, are trying to solve a mystery. It is three days before Halloween, and someone is smashing all the pumpkins on Grove Street. Is it Mr. Norton, the meanest man on Grove Street? Is it the Maple Street Gang? Is Mr. Simpson smashing the pumpkins with his new Model T Ford? Nellie and Mary Grace investigate together, but on Halloween night, Mary Grace finds she must face the pumpkin smasher alone. MR

Hamilton, Virginia (1936–) Known for her numerous works of fiction featuring young blacks and several works about important black Americans, Hamilton was born and grew up in southern Ohio, an area that was an important part of the Underground Railroad, the secret organization that helped runaway slaves escape to freedom. The historical and cultural traditions she gathered from her family and community have played an important part in her writing. Her novel *M.C. Higgins, the Great* is about the struggle of a black family in southern Ohio to hold onto their home. *The House of Dies Drear* and its sequel, *The Mystery of Drear House* (1987), are novels set in Ohio that concern a house that was owned by an abolitionist and was part of the Underground Railroad.

Other novels you will enjoy are *Sweet Whis-*

pers, *Brother Rush* (1982), about a teenage girl whose life is changed by the appearance of her uncle's ghost; and *A White Romance* (1987), about the experiences of a black teenager when she befriends a white girl and also falls for a drug dealer. Hamilton's other works include *Paul Robeson: The Life and Times of a Free Black Man* (1974), *The People Could Fly: American Black Folktales*, *Zeely*, and *In the Beginning: Creation Stories from Around the World* (1988). YA

Hamlet (1623), by *William Shakespeare, is often considered to be the greatest tragedy in English drama. Written at the midpoint in Shakespeare's career, it is the best known, the most carefully studied, and the most often performed of all his plays.

The basic Hamlet story is a tale of revenge that goes back to ancient Scandinavian sources. But in making Hamlet a character whose actions are ruled by his thoughts and not just his emotions, Shakespeare created a character that modern readers and playgoers can appreciate easily.

The play begins, and for the most part takes place, at the royal castle of Elsinore, Denmark. Hamlet's friend, Horatio, and two officers see the ghost of Hamlet's father, the former king of Denmark, who had recently died. Horatio tells Hamlet, who is deeply depressed over his father's death and the quick remarriage of his mother to his uncle, Claudius. Hamlet speaks with his father's ghost, who declares that Claudius murdered him to inherit his crown. The ghost orders Hamlet to avenge his murder.

Hamlet feigns madness, either to hide his anger and sorrow or to conceal his murderous intentions. Claudius, unconvinced that Hamlet is mad, tries through tricks and plots to learn the truth about the prince. Meanwhile, Hamlet, suspicious of what the ghost has told him, plans to test his uncle's guilt by arranging the performance of a play that reenacts the murder.

Claudius's reaction to the play removes all doubt in Hamlet's mind, but he is unable to bring himself to kill his uncle. However, he does accidentally kill Polonius, his uncle's adviser, an action that convinces Claudius to send Hamlet to England, accompanied by his supposed friends Rosencrantz and Guildenstern. There he is to be killed.

Hamlet escapes this trap, arranging to have his former friends executed in his place. He returns to Elsinore to find that Ophelia, his former love and the daughter of Polonius, has killed herself, having gone mad with grief over Hamlet's rejection and her father's death. Claudius convinces Ophelia's brother, Laertes, to challenge Hamlet to what Laertes pretends is a friendly fencing match. But Laertes' sword is dipped in a deadly poison, and Claudius prepares a cup of poisoned wine for Hamlet as well. Laertes' sword cuts Hamlet, but in a scuffle, Hamlet picks up Laertes' sword and wounds Laertes. Laertes then reveals how he and Claudius had plotted to murder Hamlet. Meanwhile, Hamlet's mother has drunk unknowingly from the poisoned cup and dies. Hamlet finally kills his uncle, forgives Laertes, begs his friend Horatio to tell the true story of what has happened in order to clear his name, and dies.

This play is remarkable for the depth of its characters. Hamlet, a soldier and a scholar, is by nature a man of action, yet he is driven to inaction and even to the brink of suicide by his own thoughts. Claudius, a thorough scoundrel, is yet haunted by the horror of his own crimes and even tries to pray for forgiveness. Hamlet's mother reveals her own humanity when she recoils in horror at Hamlet's fierce rebukes. YA

Hammett, (Samuel) Dashiell (1894–1961) The founder of what is called the hard-boiled school of detective fiction—which features crude dialogue usually expressed in short sentences, and considerable violence, often in sordid environments—Hammett spent eight years with the Pinkerton National Detective Agency. During part of this time he lived in San Francisco, which became the setting for most of his novels. Two of his early books are *Red Harvest* (1929) and *The Dain Curse* (1929). In these stories the detective is the unnamed

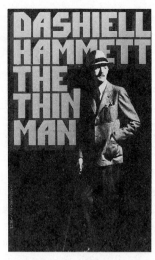

The cover of a modern paperback edition of
The Thin Man by Dashiell Hammett

Continental Op. In *The Maltese Falcon* Hammett created *Sam Spade, whose name has become a synonym for the tough private eye.

In *The Thin Man* (1932) he created a new detective, Nick Charles, who is assisted by his wife, Nora. Charles has retired from a detective agency because his wife inherited money. The "thin man" of the story, an inventor, has disappeared and is suspected of murder, but Charles exposes the real killer. If you like hard-boiled detective stories, you will also want to read those by *James M. Cain, *Raymond Chandler, and *Elmore Leonard; if you like the Nick Charles books, try those of *Erle Stanley Gardner and *Rex Stout. A movie featuring the couple's dog, Asta, as well as Nick and Nora, was made of *The Thin Man* in 1934. This film was followed by five sequels, each less interesting than the one before. YA

Handmaid's Tale, The (1986) This novel by *Margaret Atwood can be read as *science fiction, but it is also an attack on religious bigotry and the degradation of women. In the near future, as a result of atomic war, the United States has been broken up. What had been New England is now the Republic of Gilead, ruled by a government based on a strictly male interpretation of the Bible and an attempt to breed normal babies despite the effects of radiation. There are Commanders at the top, Wives who do nothing, Marthas who do the housework, and Handmaids, with whom the novel is chiefly concerned. One of them is the narrator, called Offred. She lives in the home of a Commander whose duty it is to impregnate her. If Offred does not become pregnant, she will be sent to the Colonies to clean up toxic waste. The Commander treats her more kindly than is proper, and she also becomes involved with Nick, the chauffeur. As a result, Offred is labeled subversive, but when she is about to be sent to the Colonies, the Mayday Underground rescues her. You are, however, left in doubt as to whether she succeeds in escaping to Canada via the Underground Femaleroad. A movie of the book was made in 1990. YA

Hans Brinker; or, The Silver Skates (1865), a classic novel for young people by *Mary Mapes Dodge, is the charming and realistic story of a poor Dutch family, combined with a great deal of information about life in Holland in the mid-19th century. Much of the book is based on real events described to the author. In this fascinating country (now called the Netherlands), a large part of the land is lower than the level of the sea, and great dikes or bulwarks keep the ocean out. Ditches and canals are everywhere, and to this day people skate on the frozen waterways in winter.

The Brinker family of Broek, near Amsterdam, lives on such a canal. Fifteen-year-old Hans and his younger sister Gretel help their mother care for their invalid father. Raff Brinker is helpless and childlike because of an accident 10 years ago, and his inability to work has made the family very poor. Hans, strong and responsible, dreams of being able to help his father. One day on the canal he approaches Dr. Boekman, the most famous surgeon in Holland, and blurts out the history of Raff's condition. Intrigued by the case, Boekman agrees to visit Raff and later performs an operation for which he refuses to take money. Raff slowly returns to health. As his memory heals, he reveals where he hid the family savings before the accident. Their poverty eased, and with new skates, Hans and Gretel enter the great

MR = Middle Reader   YA = Young Adult Reader   * = See this main entry

Hans Brinker and his sister Gretel

skating race and try for the first prize—a pair of silver skates. To help a deserving friend, however, Hans sacrifices his position in the boys' event. Little Gretel flies to the finish ahead of the other girls and wins the treasured prize. A glimpse into the future shows us Hans will become a fine doctor, and the affectionate Brinker family will prosper. You may find in your library several recent editions of this popular story. MR & YA

Hansberry, Lorraine (1930–1965) Born and raised in Chicago, Hansberry was first attracted to the theater and writing when she was a high school student. Her parents were active in the civil rights movement, which was gaining strength in the 1940s, and after attending college, Hansberry moved to New York City and became editor of the monthly magazine *Freedom.*

With *A Raisin in the Sun*, Hansberry became the first black woman to have her work produced on Broadway. She continued to be active in the civil rights movement and to write plays, but *The Sign in Sidney Brustein's Window* (1964), whose setting is the literary and artistic community of Greenwich Village, had only a small success.

After Hansberry's early death from cancer, her writings were gathered for the dramatic presentation *To Be Young, Gifted and Black* (1969). The movie *A Raisin in the Sun* (1961) and the musical *Raisin* (1973) were based on her play. YA

Hansel and Gretel, the central characters of a German folktale collected by the Brothers *Grimm, are brother and sister, the children of a poor woodcutter. The children's wicked stepmother talks the woodcutter into taking Hansel and Gretel deep into the woods and abandoning them. The children overhear the conversation, and Hansel sneaks out of the house to gather shiny pebbles from the ground. The next day, the family sets out through the woods. As they walk, Hansel secretly drops a pebble every so often to mark the path. Once they are deep in the woods, the woodcutter and his wife leave the children, saying they are going to cut wood and will soon return. Hansel and Gretel fall asleep, and when they awaken it is night and they are alone. By the light of the full moon, they follow the trail of shiny pebbles Hansel has dropped and find their way home.

When famine strikes the country, the wicked stepmother forces the woodcutter to take the children into the woods again. This time Hansel is unable to gather any pebbles, so he marks the path with crumbs of bread. But the forest birds eat the crumbs, and the children become lost. They come upon a house made of bread and cake and sugar in which lives a wicked old witch. The witch lures them inside the house, then locks Hansel in a shed and forces Gretel to slave for her. The witch prepares to roast Gretel, but the girl tricks the witch and pushes her into her own oven. Gretel then frees Hansel, and the two children return home, bringing their father precious jewels from the witch's house. The wicked stepmother has died while Hansel and Gretel were away. There are many books that retell the story of Hansel and Gretel. Younger readers will enjoy especially *Hansel and Gretel* (1975), translated by Charles Scribner (1921–) and illustrated by Adrienne Adams (1906–). MR

happy hunting ground refers to the North American Indians' concept of paradise, where warriors go after death to spend eternity hunting and feasting. *Washington Irving wrote about the "happy hunting grounds" of the

North American Indians in *Astoria* (1836), about John Jacob Astor and the Pacific Northwest. It is the first known use of the term.

Hardy, Thomas (1840–1928) Frail and sickly as a child, Hardy learned to read very early and gained a love of books and literature from his mother, becoming eventually one of England's most important novelists and poets. When he was 16 years old he left school, but he continued to study Latin and Greek, literature, and the Bible. The turning point in Hardy's life came when he went to live and work in London. There he steeped himself in his first love, poetry, and studied especially the works of *Charles Darwin. During his London years, he broke away from traditional views of religion and began forming his own ideas of nature, religion, morality, and human existence.

Hardy's first attempts at fiction were unimpressive, but his fourth novel, *Far from the Madding Crowd* (1874), which examines the effects of love and passion on the lives of several people, was a success with readers and critics. *The Return of the Native*, the tragic story of a young woman's struggle to escape the country life she hates, is set on the gloomy Egdon Heath, in the Wessex countryside in southern England to which Hardy returned again and again in his books. His later novels included *The Mayor of Casterbridge* (1886), about the rise of a young farmer to wealth and power and his fall and eventual destruction; *Tess of the D'Urbervilles*; and *Jude the Obscure*. Hardy's treatment of sex and marriage in the last two novels caused such an uproar in Victorian circles that he stopped writing novels and turned to poetry. From 1896 to his death, Hardy wrote hundreds of poems as well as a three-part poetic epic on the Napoleonic Wars, *The Dynasts* (1904–1909). His poetry is sometimes difficult to understand but often beautiful and powerful. You will find some of his best works in modern poetry anthologies. YA

Hardy Boys See *Franklin W. Dixon.

Harlem Renaissance refers to the literary and cultural movement established by black Americans in the 1920s and 1930s. It was centered in the Harlem section of New York City, which during the early 20th century became one of the largest black communities in the country. The movement was not organized in any strict sense, but the writers, artists, and performers who contributed to it shared a pride in their cultural traditions and heritage as African Americans. Among the leading writers of the Harlem Renaissance were the poets *Countee Cullen and *Langston Hughes, the novelist Zora Neale Hurston (1901–1960), and Jean Toomer (1894–1967), author of the experimental novel *Cane. The Harlem Renaissance declined in the 1930s, but it helped set the stage for such later writers as *James Baldwin and *Richard Wright. YA

Harlequin This popular character of English *pantomime, with his multicolored outfit and flat, swordlike bat—which gave comedy the term "slapstick"—has his origin in Italian popular comedy, the *commedia dell'arte* of the 16th to 18th century. In this earlier form, Harlequin, or Arlecchino, is an athletic and often comic servant who is hopeless in matters of love. In the English pantomime, Harlequin is in love with the maiden *Columbine.

Harriet the Spy (1964), written and illustrated by *Louise Fitzhugh, is the story of 11-year-old Harriet M. Welsch, an only child who lives in New York City and is just beginning sixth grade. Harriet spends most of her time spying on her classmates, friends, and neighbors and writing down her observations in a notebook she always carries with her. Harriet thinks this is good practice, because she is determined to become a famous writer someday. But two events turn Harriet's world upside down. First, her nursemaid and friend Ole Golly quits to get married, leaving a big hole in Harriet's already lonely life. Then her schoolmates get hold of her notebook and find it contains unkind observations about them. Even Harriet's two friends—Sport, whose father is a professional writer, and Janie, whose burning passion in life is chemistry—turn against her. Harriet has some hard times but remains true to herself, as she learns from her experiences

MR = Middle Reader   YA = Young Adult Reader   * = See this main entry

and changes from Harriet the Spy to Harriet the Writer. If you liked this book, you will want to read about Harriet's further adventures in *The Long Secret* (1965). MR

Harris, Joel Chandler (1848–1908) Born and raised in Georgia in the years just before and during the Civil War, Joel decided while still a boy to become a writer, and in 1862 he went to work setting type for *The Countryman*, a weekly journal published by the planter and writer Joseph Addison Turner (1826–1868) on his estate. There Joel spent many hours in the slave quarters, listening to the way the slaves spoke and to the African folk tales and animal *fables they told.

Harris continued his newspaper work after the war ended, and in 1876 he went to work for the Atlanta *Constitution*. There he created the character *Uncle Remus and began writing his celebrated stories in dialect about Brer Rabbit, Brer Fox, and their friends. The stories brought Harris international fame, but the author was so shy that he seldom left his Georgia home except for short visits with friends.

The Uncle Remus stories were collected in a number of volumes, including *Uncle Remus: His Songs and His Sayings* (1880), *Nights with Uncle Remus* (1883), *Uncle Remus and His Friends* (1892), and *Uncle Remus and Brer Rabbit* (1906). MR

Hart, Moss (1904–1961) A playwright, screenwriter, and director, Hart was born and raised in New York City. His family was poor, and young Moss had an unhappy home life. His Aunt Kate, however, introduced him to the sights and sounds of New York theater. By the time he was in high school, Hart knew he wanted to write plays. His first real success came when *George S. Kaufman helped him rework his play *Once in a Lifetime* (1930), which deals with the problems of silent movie stars trying to adapt to talking pictures. Hart achieved his greatest success working with Kaufman. Together they wrote eight plays, noted for bright comedy and colorful characters. Among them are *You Can't Take It With You* (1936), about a young woman from an eccentric family who falls in love with the son of

her wealthy boss, and *The Man Who Came to Dinner* (1939), about an acid-tongued critic who, while traveling, breaks his hip and is forced to spend several weeks among strangers. The critic was modeled after Kaufman's and Hart's friend, the critic Alexander Woollcott (1887–1943).

Hart also directed plays, including the musicals *My Fair Lady* (1956), based on the play *Pygmalion* (1912) by *George Bernard Shaw, and *Camelot* (1960). He wrote the screenplays for a number of movies, including *Gentleman's Agreement* (1947), about a journalist's investigation of anti-Semitism, and *A Star Is Born* (1954), a musical about the rise of a young actress to Hollywood stardom. His autobiography, *Act One* (1959), became a best-seller. *You Can't Take It With You* was adapted for film in 1938 and *Once in a Lifetime* in 1932. *The Man Who Came to Dinner* was made into a hilarious and successful film in 1941. YA

Harte, (Francis) Bret(t) (1836–1902) Known especially for his short stories about the American West, Harte was born in Albany, New York. Though he had little formal education, he read a great deal on his own and began writing early. His first published work, a poem, was printed in 1847 when he was eleven. Two years later he left school to go to work. In 1854 he traveled out to California and eventually became known for the sketches, poems, and stories he contributed to California newspapers.

In 1868 Harte helped found and became the editor of the *Overland Monthly*, a literary magazine that quickly became a great success. The magazine published Harte's best-known works, including the stories *"The Luck of Roaring Camp" and *"The Outcasts of Poker Flat," and the comic ballad "Plain Language from Truthful James" (1870). These colorful depictions of life in the towns and mining camps of California during the *Gold Rush established Harte's reputation. He returned to the East Coast in 1871 in triumph. His fondness for high living hurt his writing, however, and his popularity dropped. In 1878 he left for Europe, never to return to America. He spent his last years in England, where he died. Some of his later stories, such as "A Protegee of Jack Hamlin's" (1893) and

"An Ingenue of the Sierras" (1893), both written when Harte was living in England, are considered as good as his early successes. Harte's stories were collected in a number of books, including *The Luck of Roaring Camp and Other Stories* (1870) and *Mrs. Skaggs's Husbands* (1873), and they often appear in anthologies of American literature. YA

Hatchet (1987), a novel by *Gary Paulsen, tells about Brian Robeson, a 13-year-old boy struggling to cope with his parents' divorce. One day Brian boards a small airplane to fly north to the Canadian wilderness, where his father is an engineer in the oil fields. Strapped to his belt is a hatchet, which his mother has given him as a present for his trip to the Canadian woods. It is small comfort to Brian, who knows "the Secret," that his mother demanded a divorce after becoming involved with another man.

During the flight the pilot has a heart attack and dies. The plane crashes at the edge of a lake, far away from its intended flight path. Brian is left alone in the Canadian wilderness. Slowly he learns the value of his mother's gift, the hatchet, which enables him to survive. He builds a shelter and figures out how to make a fire, a spear, and bow and arrows. For almost two months he lives on fish, berries, nuts, and small game, and learns many important lessons about himself and about life before he is finally rescued. MR & YA

Hautzig, Esther Rudomin (1930–) A Polish-born American author, Esther was 8 years old when World War II broke out and German and Russian forces invaded Poland. The Russians sent Esther and her family to Siberia, where they remained until the end of the war. Two years later Esther went to the United States, where she married, became a citizen, and began writing books for young people. She described her experiences in Russia during the war in *The Endless Steppe: Growing Up in Siberia*. Though it was published as a book for young people, it found a large audience of adult as well as young readers.

Hautzig translated and adapted two collections of stories by the Polish writer I.L. Peretz (1851–1915), *The Case Against the Wind and Other Stories* (1975) and *The Seven Good Years and Other Stories* (1984). Her own book, *A Gift for Mama* (1981), tells about a girl who decides to buy her mother a special gift for Mother's Day, breaking the family rule that all presents must be homemade. MR & YA

Havel, Václav (1936–) A Czech playwright and poet, Havel was born into a wealthy Prague family. When the communists came to power, Havel's family lost its wealth and position. Havel worked hard to complete his education, and then decided to concentrate on writing plays and poetry. His plays, which champion the individual over the state and human rights over government authority, earned him a considerable amount of critical and popular acclaim abroad but led him into conflict with the government at home. He was arrested and imprisoned many times and became one of the leaders of the dissident movement that eventually toppled the communists in 1989. The following year Havel was elected President of Czechoslovakia. Among his best plays are *The Garden Party* (1964), about a man who rises through the giant political bureaucracy solely on his ability to mouth slogans and cliches; *The Memorandum* (1965), about the use of language as a tool of oppression and conformity; and *Largo Desolato* (1985), about a writer who must either disavow his writing or go to prison. YA

Hawthorne, Nathaniel (1804–1864) One of the great figures of American literature, Hawthorne was born and grew up in Salem, Massachusetts. While a boy Nathaniel learned to love reading. By the time he was ready to attend college, he was already thinking of a career as a writer. After graduation from Bowdoin College, where *Henry Wadsworth Longfellow was a classmate, Hawthorne returned to Salem, where he immersed himself in reading and writing. His travels in New England during this time provided much material for his short stories. His first real success came with the publication of *Twice-Told Tales* (1837). This collection of stories showed Hawthorne's deep interest in the concepts of sin and punishment and their effects on human beings.

In 1842 Hawthorne moved to Concord, Massachusetts, where he lived happily for several years and wrote the stories collected in *Mosses from an Old Manse* (1846). Hawthorne returned to Salem for several years to work in the Custom House. During this time he began work on *The Scarlet Letter*, which was an enormous success. After losing his job in the Custom House, Hawthorne moved his family to Lenox, Massachusetts, where he wrote *The House of the Seven Gables* (1851), about the destruction of a New England family through its own greed and pride.

Hawthorne's *A Wonder-Book for Girls and Boys* and *Tanglewood Tales*, collections of Greek myths retold for young readers, were very successful.

From 1853 to 1858 Hawthorne lived in England, then spent two years in Italy. In Italy he gathered material for his last completed novel, *The Marble Faun* (1860), about the effects of a murder on a group of people in Rome. Hawthorne's novels and collections of his stories are available in many editions. YA

heart In ancient times the heart was thought to be the center of the human soul and emotions. You know that it is the magnificent pump that keeps your blood flowing through your body. Even so, the heart shape is still a *symbol of love and affection.

When people say they want to have a "heart-to-heart talk," they mean they want to speak frankly and truthfully with you. Such a talk might encourage you to "take heart," to regain your confidence or boost your spirits. When you give your "heart and soul" to something, you give yourself completely and with no doubts in your mind. You know in your "heart of hearts," or your deepest thoughts and feelings, that what you are doing is right. Stories can be "heartwarming," or inspiring and cheering. They can even "tug at your heartstrings," or

make you feel strong emotions. But if you read a book of suspense of horror, you will probably wind up with "your heart in your mouth" because of the tension caused by the story.

Heart Is a Lonely Hunter, The (1940) Written by *Carson McCullers, this novel is set in a small city in the South in the late 1930s. It tells about a group of people whose separate, lonely lives are connected through John Singer, a man who cannot hear or speak. His only real friend is the man he rooms with, Spiros Antonapoulos, who also is deaf and mute. When Antonapoulos is committed to a mental asylum, Singer rents a room in the boarding house run by the Kelly family. While living there he is befriended by Mick Kelly, a girl just entering her teens who dreams of becoming a composer. Singer also meets Biff Brannon, owner of the New York Café, where Singer eats every day; Jake Blount, a drifter who dreams of destroying the evils of capitalism; and Dr. Benedict Mady Copeland, a black doctor who has dedicated his life to a dream of helping black people escape from poverty and oppression. Each of these people sees wisdom and concern in John Singer's silent, polite ways and gentle smile, and they look up to Singer. Yet Singer is unable to do anything about the loneliness and disappointments they face. In a sense he is the loneliest of them all, and when he learns that his friend Spiros has died in the mental hospital, Singer kills himself. Mick leaves school to work in a five-and-ten-cent store to help her family. Blount leaves town to take his message to another place. Dr. Copeland, ill with tuberculosis, goes to live with his family in the countryside. And Brannon struggles to understand the puzzle of life. *The Heart Is a Lonely Hunter* was adapted for film in 1968. YA

Heart of Darkness (1899), a short novel by *Joseph Conrad, is narrated by Marlow, an old seaman who tells about the circumstances that led him, when a much younger man, to Africa and the "heart of darkness." The story begins with the young Marlow's journey to Europe to the offices of a Belgian trading company. He lands a job as captain of a steamboat used to supply trading posts in the Congo. However, when he arrives in the Congo, he finds that the situation in Africa is not as he had imagined it in Europe. The pretense of the trading company as an instrument of enlightenment and civilization fades away quickly when Marlow witnesses the brutality and callousness with which the supposedly civilized white men treat the Africans.

Marlow makes a strenuous trek inland to the trading station where his steamboat is located, only to find that it has been sunk in an accident. Months pass as Marlow raises the hulk and then waits for the materials he needs to repair the craft. Meanwhile he learns about the manager of the innermost trading station, a remarkable man named Kurtz, the best trader in the company. Kurtz is thought by all to have a brilliant career ahead of him, yet disturbing reports about his activities and his health arrive. It is determined that Marlow must sail up the river to the innermost station and bring Kurtz back.

Kurtz, once an eloquent advocate of the highest ideals of the company, has changed. His isolation in the jungle and his drive to accumulate valuable ivory has led him to commit unspeakable wrongs. Instead of acting as a civilizing influence in the district, he has permitted his own darkest impulses and desires to gain the upper hand.

Illness has left Kurtz near death. He is taken aboard the steamboat, and the party moves back down the river. On the way Kurtz dies, speaking his last words to Marlow: "The horror! The horror!"

Marlow returns to Europe to deliver a packet of letters and papers to the woman Kurtz has called his fiancée. The woman asks Marlow about Kurtz's last words. Marlow is unable to tell her the truth, saying instead that Kurtz's last utterance was her name. By lying, Marlow has brought her no enlightenment. He has kept her away from the truth—has kept her in darkness.

A profound indictment of 19th-century colonialism, Conrad's story is also an examination of civilization and human nature. Some elements of the tale were adapted in *Apocalypse Now*, a movie produced in 1979. YA

Heart's Blood (1984), a fantasy novel by *Jane Yolen, is the second volume of the author's Pit Dragon trilogy, which began with **Dragon's Blood*. Jakkin Stewart has bought his freedom from his former master, Sarkkhan, and is now also a Dragon Master. Jakkin is plunged into a web of planetary intrigue when Sarkkhan's daughter, Akki, becomes involved with a dangerous rebel group and disappears in the capital city, The Rokk. Jakkin and his dragon, Heart's Blood, go with Sarkkhan to The Rokk for the pit games, and Jakkin finds and rescues Akki. A mysterious explosion destroys one of the gaming pits and kills Sarkkhan, and Jakkin, Akki, and Heart's Blood flee to the desolate mountains. Heart's Blood gives up her life to defend Jakkin and Akki from their pursuers. The boy and girl survive the deadly cold of Dark After by crawling inside the dragon's body. When they emerge, they have been changed by the dragon's blood. Now part dragon and part human, they remain in the mountains to raise Heart's Blood's five hatchlings. The story of Jakkin and Akki is concluded in **A Sending of Dragons*. YA

Heathcliff is the main character in *Emily Brontë's novel *Wuthering Heights*. Dark-skinned and brooding, he endures a childhood of cruelty and humiliation. Hindley Earnshaw, always resentful of his father's kindness to Heathcliff, treats him brutally. From the beginning, Heathcliff learns to keep his rage to himself, and his natural reserve and strength of will drive Hindley to violence. Heathcliff is vulnerable only in his love for *Catherine Earnshaw. She is never out of his thoughts. To her he shows his best qualities, and they come to think and feel as one person. After Catherine's death, for which Heathcliff blames the Lintons, he plots the downfall of the Linton family with extraordinary malice. One thought sustains him—he will die and be buried in the grave next to his beloved Catherine,

Heathcliff and Catherine in a dramatic moment
on the moors of England

and their love will be fulfilled in another world. YA

heaven In most religions and mythologies there is a place to which it is believed the souls, or even the bodies, of the deserving go after death. *Judaism, *Christianity, and *Islam all picture heaven as the abode of God, where worthy souls find eternal peace. In Greek religion the gods took dead heroes to the *Elysian Fields in the distant west at the edge of the world. In Celtic legend the Fortunate Isles, or Isles of the Blest, somewhere in the Western Ocean (probably the Atlantic Ocean), is the home of the gods, who welcome the souls of heroes. In Norse mythology *Valhalla is the place warriors go to after death, and they are welcomed there by the *Valkyrie. The word "heaven" appears in many common expressions: When you are very happy you are "in seventh heaven"; but, if you are a bit annoyed, you say, "For heaven's sake, hurry up."

Hecate is the ancient Greek goddess of darkness and the daughter of the *Titan Perses and the nymph Asteria. She has powers in the heavens, on earth, and at sea, and is a favorite of *Zeus. Hecate is the only Titan to keep her powers after the Titans failed in war against Zeus. She helped the goddess *Demeter search for her daughter, *Persephone, who had been carried off by Hades, the god of the underworld. Hecate was believed to rule over witches and magic and appear at crossroads, accompanied by a pack of ghostly hounds.

Hedda Gabler (1980), a play by *Henrik Ibsen, is set in Norway in the late 1800s. George Tesman, a teacher and scholar, has married Hedda Gabler, the aristocratic daughter of a general. But Hedda is not in love with George, and she has no interest in her new house, family, or life. She is mildly interested in the attentions of George's friend Judge Brack, but only because he is a relief from her rather dull husband.

Hedda learns about Eilert Lövborg, a brilliant scholar she once knew. Lövborg almost destroyed himself with drink, but with the help of Mrs. Elvsted, the wife of the sheriff, he has rebuilt his life and written a brilliant new book. Hedda drives Lövborg to a fit of drunkenness and secretly destroys his manuscript. Lövborg believes he has carelessly lost the manuscript, and Hedda lets him think so. She gives him a pistol and tells him to kill himself "beautifully." He is killed, but it is in a scuffle in another woman's boudoir.

Mrs. Elvsted reveals that she has the notes for Lövborg's book, and George vows to reconstruct the manuscript. Meanwhile, Judge Brack pieces together enough facts to know that Hedda has caused Lövborg's death and threatens to blackmail her. In despair, Hedda shoots herself. *Hedda*, a film based on *Hedda Gabbler*, was produced in 1975. YA

Heep, Uriah See *Uriah Heep.

Heidi (1880–1881), a novel by Johanna Spyri (1827–1901), tells the story of a little Swiss girl who brings love and happiness to everyone she meets. Orphaned in childhood, 5-year-old Heidi goes to live with her grandfather, a gruff, lonely old man who lives alone on a mountain overlooking a small Swiss town. Everyone in town fears Grandfather, but he soon becomes attached to little Heidi, who helps him to re-establish long-lost ties with the townspeople. Heidi also soon wins the hearts of the young goatherd, Peter, his mother, and his blind grandmother.

Heidi's sister returns to take her to Frankfurt to work as a companion to Clara, an invalid girl who lives in a large house. Heidi learns to read and becomes friends with Clara's doctor. But she yearns to return to the mountain. Eventually she gets her wish.

Back home, Heidi teaches Peter how to read, so that he can read to his grandmother from her beloved book of songs. Clara comes to visit Heidi, and under the wise care of Grandfather, soon becomes strong enough to walk. Clara's doctor moves to the little Swiss town and tells Grandfather that he will make sure Heidi is well cared for, even after he and Grandfather are gone. The doctor, Heidi, and Grandfather become a happy family, spending winters in the town and summers on the mountain.

Johanna Spyri grew up in Switzerland, and her love of the Swiss countryside and its people is captured in this classic book for children. Spyri wrote other books for young people, but *Heidi* is her only story to withstand the test of time. Four films, produced in 1937, 1952, 1965, and 1968, were based on *Heidi*. MR

Heine, Heinrich (1797–1856) Considered one of the great German poets, Heine was born and raised in Düsseldorf, in the German Rhineland. As a young man he attempted careers in business and law, but his real interest lay in writing, especially poetry, and he published a number of books of poetry and prose in the early 1820s. The publication of his *Buch der Lieder* (1827), or "Book of Songs," established his literary reputation. The poems in this collection were set to music by the Austrian composer Franz Schubert (1797–1828) and by the

German composer Robert Schumann (1810–1856), among others. They show Heine's sense of beauty and depth of emotion as well as his sharp and sometimes bitter wit. Among these poems is "Die Lorelei," which Heine based on a German folk myth. See *Lorelei.

Heine's support of political and social freedom made him many enemies, and his writings were banned in much of Germany. In 1831 he moved to Paris. A crippling spinal disease left him bedridden from 1848 until his death, but he continued to write poetry and prose. His works have been translated many times, and his translators include *Elizabeth Barrett Browning and *Ezra Pound. YA

Heinlein, Robert A. (1907–1988) One of the "Grand Masters" of American *science fiction, Heinlein became a writer not so much by choice as by chance. Born in Butler, Missouri, he dreamed of a career in the Navy. He graduated from the U.S. Naval Academy in 1929 and served in the Navy until 1934, when he was forced to resign because of tuberculosis, the same disease that afflicted *Robert Louis Stevenson. Heinlein went back to college, hoping to become an astronomer, but illness forced him to leave his studies. In 1939 Heinlein wrote his first story, a science fiction tale called "Life-Line," which was published by *Astounding Science Fiction* magazine. He wrote another story, and it too was published. Soon Heinlein was turning out story after story.

Heinlein was a voracious reader and a careful observer of people and human nature. He was able to create strong, memorable characters that were true to life. His stories were popular also because of his clear understanding of the science he dealt with in science fiction. One of his stories, "Blowups Happen" (1940), anticipated the atomic bomb by five years.

After World War II he returned to writing, producing such books as the collections *The Man Who Sold the Moon* (1950) and *The Green Hills of Earth* (1951), and the novels *Rocket Ship Galileo* (1947), *The Puppet Masters* (1951), and *The Door into Summer* (1957).

Heinlein's books began to attract the attention of readers who normally did not like to read science fiction. His novel *Stranger in a Strange Land, which relates the experiences on Earth of a human raised by Martians, became a best-seller. In this and later novels, Heinlein examined subjects of interest to everyone, including religion, politics, human behavior, and society. Many of the views expressed by his characters stirred up strong controversy and debate, but his books were and continue to be very popular. YA

Helen was the daughter of the Greek god *Zeus and *Leda, whom Zeus visited in the form of a swan. She was the sister of Clytemnestra, who married *Agamemnon, and of the twins Castor and Pollux. See *Gemini.

As a child Helen was carried off by *Theseus to Attica, but she was rescued by Castor and Pollux. She grew up to become the most beautiful woman in Greece and was courted by many royal suitors. She married Menelaus, who became the king of Sparta.

When the Trojan prince *Paris, under the protection of *Aphrodite, carried Helen off to the walled city of Troy, Helen's suitors came to the aid of Menelaus and launched the *Trojan War. After 10 years of siege Troy was sacked, and Helen was returned to Menelaus.

Helen was revered by some Greeks as the goddess of beauty, and she has become the *symbol of female beauty. The English dramatist Christopher Marlowe (1564–1593), in his play Dr. Faustus (1588), alluded to her beauty as "the face that launch'd a thousand ships."

hell In Christian belief, hell is the eternal dwelling place of the souls of sinners. It is related to the Jewish concept of Sheol, the abode of all dead, and also to Hades. In Greek mythology Hades (or Pluto) was the ruler of the underworld of the dead. Later the place itself, gloomy but not a place of punishment like the later Christian hell, became known as Hades. *Satan is the ruler of hell, and in the *Bible *Jesus speaks of the "everlasting fire" there. *Islam has a similar hell. The Christian hell figures in many works of literature, notably in

*Dante Alighieri's The Divine Comedy and in *John Milton's *Paradise Lost. The word appears in many common expressions, as in "going to hell in a handbasket," meaning that a person is rapidly deteriorating in one way or another; and "the road to hell is paved with good intentions," meaning that your deeds speak louder than your words.

Heller, Joseph (1923–) Known best for his classic antiwar novel, *Catch-22, which became a best-seller in the middle and late 1960s when the Vietnam War reached its height, and was based on his experience with the Army Air Force during World War II, Heller is an imaginative, often funny novelist.

Heller's second novel, Something Happened (1974), tells the story of Bob Slocum, a business manager in his 40s who realizes that his life has not turned out the way he thought it would, that somewhere along the way, "something happened." Heller's next novel, Good as Gold (1979), is about a professor of English literature who is drawn into the bizarre and sometimes idiotic world of government and politics in Washington, D.C. Some critics wrote that this novel did to government what Catch-22 did to the Army. God Knows (1984) is a novel narrated by its main character, David, slayer of Goliath and king of Israel. You will enjoy Heller's recent novel, Picture This (1988), a sometimes comic, sometimes bitter study of the progress, or lack of progress, of art, history, and society from the age of *Aristotle to the present. Its chief character is Rembrandt (1606–1669), but the novel moves back and forth through time in an entertaining way. YA

Hellespont This was the name the ancient Greeks gave to the Dardanelles, the strait between the Sea of Marmora and the Aegean Sea. The Dardanelles is about 37 miles long and between 1 and 4 miles wide. It is part of the waterway that links the Black Sea and the Mediterranean and divides Europe from Asia.

The name Hellespont comes from a Greek word that means "sea of Helle." In Greek mythology, Helle was the daughter of a Greek king. The king divorced his wife and married again. The first wife did not trust the new queen, so she took her children—Helle and her brother, Phrixus—and sent them to safety on the back of a ram with golden fleece. As the ram flew over the water, Helle fell off and was drowned. The story of Helle and Phrixus is part of the story of the *Golden Fleece. The Hellespont is also the setting of the story of the lovers *Hero and Leander.

Hellman, Lillian (1905–1984) One of the best modern dramatists, Hellman was born and spent her early childhood in New Orleans. Later she lived in New York City but returned to visit New Orleans often. After attending college, she began a career in publishing and eventually turned to playwriting. Her first play, *The Children's Hour* (1934), concerned the tragic results of lies told by a young girl at a boarding school about the relationship between the two women running the school. Hellman's greatest success came five years later with *The Little Foxes*. During World War II, Hellman probed the subject of *Nazi tyranny in *Watch on the Rhine, which also achieved a resounding success. *Another Part of the Forest* (1946) examined the early history of the Hubbard family, the turn-of-the-century Southern clan that she introduced in *The Little Foxes*. Hellman's native New Orleans was the setting of *Toys in the Attic* (1960), a drama about a young man's struggle to escape from the domination of his two sisters. Hellman wrote three, at the time controversial, books of memoirs: *An Unfinished Woman* (1969), which won the National Book Award; *Pentimento* (1973); and *Scoundrel Time* (1976). *The Children's Hour* was adapted for film as *These Three* in 1936 and as *The Children's Hour* in 1962. *Toys in the Attic* was adapted for film in 1963. YA

Hemingway, Ernest (1899–1961) A novelist and short-story writer, Hemingway was born and grew up in Oak Park, a suburb of Chicago, Illinois. After graduation from high school, he began his writing career as a reporter for the *Kansas City Star* in Missouri. In World War I he was an ambulance driver in Italy, where he was badly wounded and was sent to a hospital in Milan. Later Hemingway used this wartime experience for his novel *A Farewell to Arms. After the war Hemingway settled in Paris and began writing the short stories that were collected in his first book, *In Our Time* (1925). *The Sun Also Rises is a novel set in Spain, a country he visited a number of times and came to love. This novel established Hemingway as a writer of the first rank.

For the next 35 years Hemingway projected the image of a larger-than-life hero. He was a fisherman, hunter, boxer, lover of bullfighting, war correspondent, and writer. Among his best books are *Death in the Afternoon* (1932), about bullfighting; *To Have and Have Not* (1937), about a Florida boat captain who is driven by hardship to smuggling and bootlegging and, finally, to his death; *The Fifth Column and the First Forty-Nine Stories* (1938), which included *The Fifth Column*, his play about espionage during the Spanish Civil War, and many of his best short stories, including *The Snows of Kilimanjaro; *For Whom the Bell Tolls, the story of an American volunteer in the Spanish Civil War who falls in love just before he is sent on a suicide mission to blow up a bridge; *The Old Man and the Sea; and *A Moveable Feast* (1964), sketches about his experiences in Paris in the 1920s. Hemingway was awarded the Nobel Prize for literature in 1954. He was often ill in his final years, and in the end took his own life. A film based on *To Have and Have Not* was made in 1944. YA

Henry, John See *John Henry.

Henry, Marguerite (1902–) Known for her horse stories, Henry was born and grew up in Wisconsin, where her father owned a printing business. Marguerite used to help her father on weekends, and she early became interested in writing. She published her first work when she was 11 years old. After college she became a full-time writer and discovered she especially liked to write books for young people.

Marguerite Henry's books *The Little Fellow* (1945), the story of a colt, and *Justin Morgan Had a Horse* marked the beginning of a steady stream of popular horse stories, her best known being *Misty of Chincoteague*, which has become a children's classic. Her books are memorable for their realistic characters, colorful description, and dramatic plotting. Her stories are based on careful research, and many of her fictional horses are based on famous horses of the past.

Henry's books include *Robert Fulton: Boy Craftsman* (1944), which tells about the boyhood of a pioneer of steamboating; *Benjamin West and His Cat Grimalkin* (1947), about the boyhood of the great American painter; *King of the Wind*; *Brighty of the Grand Canyon* (1953), the story of a burro in the Old West; and *San Domingo: The Medicine Hat Stallion* (1972). MR

Henry, O. [William Sydney Porter] (1862–1910) One of our most popular writers of short stories, O. Henry was born in Greensboro, North Carolina, at the height of the Civil War. His father, a doctor, was a bit too fond of liquor and spent much of his time trying to perfect a perpetual-motion machine. Young Will Porter left school when he was 15 years old and worked in his uncle's drugstore for five years before moving to Texas in 1882. Eventually he settled in Austin, took a job as a bank teller, married, and became editor and publisher of a weekly magazine called *The Rolling Stone*. Porter wrote most of the material in the magazine himself. Some of the pieces showed the sense of humor, irony, and wit that would later make him famous. But the magazine failed, and when Porter was accused of embezzling bank funds, he fled to Central America. He returned when he learned that his wife was dying. In 1898 Porter was sent to a federal penitentiary in Ohio, and there he began to write short stories under the pen name O. Henry.

After his release from prison in 1901, he made his way to New York City, whose people and bustling pace gave him endless material for his stories. Between 1901 and his death in 1910, O. Henry wrote hundreds of short stories. Perhaps his best-known stories are *"The Gift of the Magi," "The Last Leaf" (1907), and "The Ransom of Red Chief" (1910). Most of O. Henry's stories end with an ironic twist, which has come to be known as an "O. Henry twist." O. Henry's stories were collected in a dozen volumes, among them *Cabbages and Kings* (1904), *The Four Million* (1906), *Hearts of the West* (1907), *The Voice of the City* (1908), and *Roads of Destiny* (1909). MR & YA

Henry Reed, Inc. (1958), by *Keith Robertson, tells about Henry Reed, a 13-year-old boy whose father is in the U.S. diplomatic service in Naples, Italy. One summer, Henry is sent by his parents to live with his aunt and uncle in Grover's Corner, near Princeton, New Jersey. This book is Henry's journal of all that happens to him. First, he is adopted by a stray beagle that he names Agony. Then he meets 12-year-old Midge Glass, who gives him the idea of starting up his own research company. Henry and Midge's hilarious misadventures include drilling for water and striking oil, and accidentally launching Agony and a neighbor's cat in a research balloon.

You can read about Henry and Midge's further adventures in *Henry Reed's Journey* (1963), about his trip from California to New Jersey with Midge's family; *Henry Reed's Baby-Sitting Service* (1966); and *Henry Reed's Big Show* (1970), in which Henry becomes a theatrical producer. MR

Hentoff, Nat (1935–) Jazz critic, columnist, and author, Hentoff began his writing career as a jazz critic for the music magazine *Downbeat*. In 1957 he became a columnist for the New York City weekly *The Village Voice*, and in 1960 became a staff member of *The New Yorker* magazine. His first books were nonfiction and were about jazz. Hentoff's first novel, *Jazz Country*, again reflected his love of jazz.

Hentoff's novels for young people show his passionate interest in civil rights, education, and young people themselves. *In the Country of Ourselves* (1971) tells about the confrontation caused by a group of school activists after a guest speaker is barred from giving a talk to a black students' club. In *This School Is Driving Me Crazy* (1975), Sam Davidson, son of the schoolmaster of a private school in New York City, is wrongly suspected of shaking down other students for their money. In *Does This School Have Capital Punishment?* (1981), Sam has to clear his name again when he is caught with some marijuana belonging to another student. YA

Hera is the sister and the wife of *Zeus in Greek mythology. She is the only married goddess. Yet she is subordinate to Zeus, has to obey him, does not like doing so, and is considered to be stubborn and jealous. She was once left hanging from the clouds after being beaten and chained by Zeus. Hera plots against Zeus to prevent him from chasing after other women. She often punishes Zeus's partners, but Zeus finds out that beating her does not change her. Hera and Zeus had three children, but it is said that Hera also bore one child as a virgin birth in her role as the celestial virgin. She is said to be the ideal wife, faithful and beautiful. Hera is the goddess of all women—maidens, matrons, and widows. She follows them from childbirth to death just as *Juno, of Roman mythology, does.

Herbert, Frank (1920–1984) A writer of *science fiction, known best for his novel *Dune*, Herbert was born and grew up in the farm country of Washington State. By the time he was 8 years old he had decided he wanted to become a writer, and after college he worked as a newspaperman and wrote short stories for magazines. After a few years he began concentrating on science fiction. His first novel, *The Dragon in the Sea* (1956), set in the 21st century, tells of the crew of a special underwater tug on a secret wartime mission to pump desperately needed oil from Russian undersea wells in the Arctic Ocean. Herbert had great difficulty finding a publisher for his second novel, *Dune*, and it received bad reviews, but readers loved it and

turned it into a best-seller. Herbert continued the Dune saga with *Dune Messiah* (1969), *Children of Dune* (1976), and three further volumes. Among his other books are *Whipping Star* (1970), which tells of the discovery that some stars are actually intelligent beings; *The Dosadi Experiment* (1977), about an alien experiment in overpopulation that threatens to plunge the galaxy into chaos; and *The White Plague* (1982), about the release of a genetically engineered plague by a scientist driven insane by the murder of his family by terrorists. YA

Hercule Poirot is the brilliant detective who appears in about 40 mystery novels and stories written by *Agatha Christie. Poirot made his debut in Christie's first detective novel, *The Mysterious Affair at Styles* (1920), in which the retired Belgian police detective investigates the murder of the mistress of Styles Court, an estate near an English village. In this novel he is described as a short, stout man, with a head "exactly the shape of an egg" and always cocked to one side. He walks with a bad limp. He is quite vain. He dyes his hair and his long moustache black, and his clothes are always extremely neat and clean. He has trouble with the English language sometimes, but the "little gray cells" in his brain are always at work. Poirot seems to observe even the smallest details and is especially good at uncovering the thoughts and motives of suspects. You can learn more about Hercule Poirot in Agatha Christie's books and also in *Great Detectives* (1981) by Julian Symons (1912–), which contains biographies of seven fictional sleuths, including another of Christie's fictional detectives, Miss *Jane Marple. YA

Hercules is the name that English-speaking people usually give to the great hero of Greek mythology, Heracles, or Herakles. Noted for his strength and courage, Hercules was the son of the god *Zeus and a human, Alcmene. *Hera, the jealous wife of Zeus, sent two serpents into the crib of Hercules, but the baby strangled them easily. Hercules married Megara, princess of Thebes, and they had three children. Hera, still seeking to destroy Hercules, cast him into a fit of madness, during which he killed his wife and children. To atone for his crimes, Hercules became a slave. His master, Eurystheus, devised 12 difficult and dangerous tasks, or labors, for Hercules to complete. These 12 labors were: (1) killing the Nemean lion, which could not be wounded by any weapon; (2) killing the many-headed Hydra, which could grow two heads for each head that was cut off; (3) capturing the hind of Cerynia, whose antlers were made of gold; (4) capturing the wild boar of Mount Erymanthus; (5) cleaning the vast Augean stables in a single day; (6) driving away the man-eating birds of Stymphalus; (7) capturing the mad bull of Crete; (8) capturing the man-eating mares of Diomedes, king of Thrace; (9) gaining the girdle of Hippolyte, queen of the Amazons; (10) capturing the oxen of Geryon, a three-headed monster who lived on the island of Erythia; (11) collecting the golden apples of the Hesperides, the daughters of *Atlas; and (12) capturing the three-headed dog Cerberus, guardian of the gates of the underworld. Hercules completed all these tasks and had many more adventures. Upon his death, he rose to Olympus and married Hebe, the goddess of youth. You can read about this popular hero in *Heracles the Strong* (1970) by *Ian Serraillier. MR

Hermes is the son of the Greek god *Zeus and Maia, the daughter of *Atlas, and is the father of *Pan. He was known by the Romans as *Mercury. Hermes is the messenger of Zeus, the protector of shepherds and flocks, bringer of good luck, protector of thieves and travelers, and the conductor of mortals to the underworld. On the day of his birth, Hermes steals the cattle of his brother, *Apollo, whose anger disappears when he hears Hermes play on the lyre, which Hermes invents by putting strings on a tortoise shell. Apollo gives Hermes the winged staff, or *caduceus*, that he is often shown carrying. Hermes appears in many myths, including the story of *Prometheus. *Homer, presumably composing as early as the 8th century B.C., refers to Hermes in both the

Iliad and the *Odyssey*. The Homeric Hymn about Hermes has been published as *Hermes, Lord of Robbers* (1971), translated by Penelope Proddow (n.d.). MR

Hero Ain't Nothin' but a Sandwich, A (1973) By *Alice Childress, this is a powerful and well-written novel about a black 13-year-old boy in the early stages of drug addiction. It is presented in a series of episodes, or monologues, in which Benjie Johnson, his mother and grandmother, his almost-stepfather Butler Craig, his teachers, and others describe events and feelings in their individual voices. Most of the characters speak the language of the street, used here with eloquence, humor, and dignity.

Benjie is smart and brave, and he has a family that really cares about him. When he becomes casually involved with drugs, he tells himself he can stop any time he wants. To support his growing habit, Benjie begins to steal from his family. The efforts of teachers, social workers, and police are brought to bear on Benjie's problem, and going into a rehabilitation program helps him for a while. What Benjie needs most of all, however, is someone to believe in him even when he is acting like a junkie. Not for the faint-hearted, this story ends on a hopeful note when Butler literally saves Benjie's life, and Benjie understands that he can depend on Butler for strength, love, and respect. If you enjoyed this novel, you will also like the books of *Virginia Hamilton and *Walter Dean Myers. *A Hero* was adapted for film in 1978. YA

Hero and Leander In Greek mythology, Hero and Leander were lovers, and their story was one of tragedy. Hero was a priestess of the goddess *Aphrodite and lived in Sestos, on the western side of the *Hellespont. Leander lived in Abydos, a town on the eastern side of the strait. Leander fell in love with the lovely Hero, but because Hero was a priestess of Aphrodite, she could not marry Leander. Even so, each night Hero shone a light from the tower in which she was kept, and Leander swam across the Hellespont to be near her. Then at night's end he swam aback to Abydos. One night Leander was caught in a terrible storm while swimming the Hellespont. His strength gave out and he was drowned. When Hero saw his body wash up on shore, she drowned herself.

The story of Hero and Leander appears in the writings of the Latin poet Ovid (43 B.C.–A.D. c.17). Christopher Marlowe (1564–1593), an English dramatist and poet, wrote of the ill-fated couple in his unfinished poem *Hero and Leander* (1598). *George Gordon Byron swam the Dardanelles and wrote of the experience in his poem "Written After Swimming from Sestos to Abydos" (1810). Byron used the Hero and Leander story in his poem *The Bride of Abydos* (1813).

Herriot, James [James Alfred Wight] (1916–) This English veterinarian and author spent more than 40 years as a veterinarian in the countryside of Yorkshire, England. His experiences provided the material for his best-selling book *All Creatures Great and Small*. The book's title is a line from an Anglican hymn, as are the titles of three sequels, *All Things Bright and Beautiful* (1974), *All Things Wise and Wonderful* (1977), and *The Lord God Made Them All* (1981). Herriot continued his story of life in rural Yorkshire in *Every Living Thing* (1992). Herriot's stories show a special understanding of people, animals, and the moments of humor, joy, and sorrow that give shape and meaning to life.

Herriot has also written a number of books for younger readers, including *Only One Woof* (1985), about a sheep dog; *Christmas Day Kitten* (1986), about a kitten who brings Christmas happiness to an elderly woman; and *Blossom Comes Home* (1988), about a farmer who enters his old workhorse in a local pet show.

All Creatures Great and Small was filmed in 1974 and also adapted for a TV series, and *All Things Bright and Beautiful* was the basis for a movie released in 1979. MR & YA

Hersey, John (Richard) (1914–) A novelist and journalist, Hersey was born in China of Ameri-

can missionary parents. He worked as private secretary to *Sinclair Lewis, and later became a foreign correspondent for *Time* magazine. During World War II, Hersey covered China and Japan in 1939, followed the war in the South Pacific in 1942 and the Mediterranean area (including Sicily) in 1943, and went to Moscow in 1944. *A Bell for Adano*, his first novel, based on contemporary history, was followed by *Hiroshima*, a nonfictional account of the effects of the atomic bomb on the people of that city. *The Wall* (1950) is Hersey's novel about the Jewish revolt against the *Nazis in the Warsaw ghetto, told through the imaginary diary of a Jewish scholar. YA

Hesse, Hermann (1877–1962) A German-born Swiss novelist whose books became an object of nearly cult worship in the United States, Hesse as a youth studied for a religious career, but in his teens he decided to become a writer. He had his first major success with a novel, *Demian* (1919), the story of a young man's awakening to life and to the workings of good and evil, both in himself and in the world. This novel showed Hesse's lifelong interest in the search for spiritual truth and harmony and also in the difficulties imposed on people by modern society. Hesse's novels *Siddhartha* and *Steppenwolf* were very successful in Europe and later in the United States. His novel *Magister Ludi* (1943), later published as *The Glass Bead Game*, is set in the future and describes a small group of intellectuals who have cut themselves off from their responsibilities in the real world to play a complicated mental game.

Hesse became popular in the United States only in the 1960s, when many people began to question the values and direction of modern civilization. He invites readers to open their minds to new ideas, to question authority, and to seek their own paths in life. Hesse won the Nobel Prize for literature in 1946. YA

Hester Prynne, the heroine of *Nathaniel Hawthorne's *The Scarlet Letter*, is one of the strongest female characters in American litera-

Hiawatha

ture. Forced by her community always to wear pinned to her dress a scarlet letter "A" because she is an adulterer, she makes a meager but respectable life for herself and her daughter without complaint or self-pity. She even lightens the suffering of her lover, the minister Dimmesdale, when he develops a cancerous growth that seems to resemble the scarlet letter. She comforts him, and finally takes her place beside him on the pillory when he makes a public confession of his guilt. She maintains dignity, helps others, works hard, and fights heroically against small-mindedness.

Heyerdahl, Thor (1914–) A Norwegian adventurer and author, Heyerdahl is known best for his book *Kon-Tiki, which has been translated into more than 60 languages and has sold millions of copies. Heyerdahl's Kon-Tiki adventure really began in the 1930s, when he and his wife spent a year on the Pacific island of Fatu-Hiva. There he gathered the first clues suggesting that, long ago, sailors from the Americas might have reached Polynesia. He wrote about his experiences in *Fatu-Hiva: Back to Nature* (1974). Heyerdahl's book *Aku Aku: The Secret of Easter Island* (1958) is about an expedition to the island in 1955 and its discoveries about the island's ancient culture and people. As described in *The Ra Expeditions* (1970), Heyerdahl attempted to prove that ancient people could have crossed the Atlantic Ocean in their papyrus reed ships like the ones used by ancient Egyptians. *The Tigris Expedition* (1977) tells of Heyerdahl's five-month, 4,200-mile voyage aboard a reed ship from the Tigris River in Iraq to the mouth of the Red Sea. YA

Hiawatha is the American Indian hero of the long narrative poem *The Song of Hiawatha* (1855) by *Henry Wadsworth Longfellow. Hiawatha is raised by his grandmother, Nokomis, the daughter of the Moon, among the Ojibwa Indians. In his youth he gains the wisdom, knowledge, and magic powers he needs to seek revenge against his father, the West Wind, for a wrong done to Hiawatha's mother, Wenonah. Hiawatha then becomes the leader and defender of his people and marries the beautiful maiden Minnehaha. He foretells the coming of white people and tells his tribe to adopt the religion they bring.

MR = Middle Reader   YA = Young Adult Reader   * = See this main entry

Longfellow modeled his fictional Hiawatha in part on a mythical Ojibwa figure named Manabohzo. Earlier writers had confused Manabohzo with a real Mohawk chieftain named Hiawatha. In the 16th century the real Hiawatha had joined forces with an American Indian prophet named Deganawida to persuade five warring Iroquois tribes to make peace and form the powerful Iroquois Confederacy. A movie was made of *Hiawatha* in 1952. MR & YA

Hickok, James Butler [Wild Bill Hickok] (1837–1876) A real person who has become an American legend, Wild Bill was called "the fastest gun in the West" because of his extraordinary ability with a pistol. After working as a stagecoach driver on the Oregon and Sante Fe trails, Hickok was an Indian fighter and federal scout during the Civil War. With a reputation for great courage and daring, he became U.S. marshal in Kansas and succeeded in bringing law and order to the rough frontier towns of Hays City and Abilene. He traveled for a year with Buffalo Bill's Wild West Show, demonstrating his marksmanship. Hickok was shot from behind during a poker game in Deadwood, South Dakota, and is buried there next to *Calamity Jane.

High Wind in Jamaica, A (1929) By the English author *Richard Hughes, this novel tells about the experiences of seven English youths in the West Indies during the early 19th century. The five Bas-Thornton children—Emily, John, Laura, Rachel, and Edward—live in Jamaica. When their home is severely damaged by a hurricane, the youngsters are sent by ship to England along with two other young people. En route, the ship is captured by a gang of good-natured Spanish pirates led by Captain Jonsen and his first mate, Otto.

Soon the seven youths turn life aboard the pirate ship topsy-turvy. The pirates capture another ship and kidnap and tie up its captain. Emily, suffering from an injury and terrified at being locked in a cabin with the bound and gagged man, attacks him with a knife and causes his death. After this, Jonsen finds a steamship bound for England, turns over his young charges, and the pirates sail away. Eventually the pirates are caught, and Emily gives carefully coached testimony that convicts them of the murder she herself has committed. But she seems unaware that her testimony means death for the pirates.

A High Wind in Jamaica is considered a remarkable study of the way young people see and experience the world and of the way they think, as well as a fascinating adventure story. YA

"Highwayman, The" (1907) One of the most popular story poems in the English language, by Alfred Noyes (1880–1958), an English poet, "The Highwayman" tells of the tragic love of an 18th-century criminal who holds up stagecoaches, and Bess, "the black-eyed daughter" of an innkeeper. He promises to come to her after a holdup, but he is betrayed by a jealous worker at the inn. Troops come to lie in wait for him, and they hold Bess prisoner. When he does appear, she kills herself, the discharge of the musket alerting him. Enraged, he rides on and is shot down by the soldiers. It is said that at times his ghost comes riding to the inn window where Bess awaits, "plaiting a dark red love-knot into her long black hair." You cannot but read on after the first few lines:

> The wind was a torrent of darkness among
>   the gusty trees,
> The moon was a ghostly galleon tossed
>   upon cloudy seas,
> The road was a ribbon of moonlight over
>   the purple moor,
> And the highwayman came riding . . .

Noyes wrote other ballads and an epic poem, *Drake* (1908), about Francis Drake (1540–1596), an English explorer and naval hero. A handsomely illustrated edition of "The Highwayman" was published in 1983. A film version of the poem was produced in 1951. MR & YA

Hillerman, Tony (1925–) A journalist and a teacher of journalism, Hillerman writes detective novels with a unique setting: the American Indian tribal areas of the American Southwest. They are notable both for their intriguing plots and for the background of tribal life and customs, combined with a good bit of anthropology. The main characters are Lieutenant Joe Leaphorn and Sergeant Joe Chee of the Navajo Tribal Police. The first of these novels, *The Blessing Way* (1970), was followed by others: *Dance Hall of the Dead* (1973), *Listening Woman* (1977), *Skinwalker* (1986), and *A Thief of Time* (1988). There is in all the books a deep sense of time and place concerning the American Indian past, now mingled with the American present. This conflict is most apparent in Chee, who has a modern education but is studying his tribe's rites so that he may perform them and pass them on. Hillerman's novels offer the reader an unusual combination of entertainment and information. YA

Hilton, James (1900–1954) An English writer, Hilton wrote his first novel while a student at Cambridge University. Also during his college days he began newspaper writing. He continued his newspaper work and had a number of novels published before he wrote his first bestseller, *Good-bye, Mr. Chips*, which he completed in only four days. Partly on the strength of the book's success in England and in the United States, Hilton's earlier novel, *Lost Horizon*, also became a best-seller.

In 1935 Hilton traveled to the United States, which he made his home for the rest of his life. Among his later books were *Random Harvest* (1941), set in England just before World War II, about a man who has lost his memory; *So Well Remembered* (1945), the story of an English town mayor and his wife before and during World War II; and *Nothing So Strange* (1947), about an American scientist during World War II.

Hilton spent some of his time working in Hollywood on screen adaptations of his novels. A movie version of *Lost Horizon* was made in 1937 and a musical remake in 1972. *Good-bye, Mr. Chips* was made into a movie in 1939 and a movie musical in 1969. *Random Harvest* was made into a movie in 1942. YA

Himes, Chester (Bomar) (1909–1984) While serving (1929–1936) a prison term for armed robbery, this black author began a writing career that made him an outspoken and effective opponent of racism as well as the writer of seven detective novels featuring black detectives. *If He Hollers Let Him Go* (1945), his first novel, is a retelling of the job discrimination he had encountered. *Cast the First Stone* (1952) has become a classic fictional account of life in prison. *The Primitive* (1955), a partly autobiographical novel, is about a black author and his white mistress. Himes's detective novels feature Coffin Ed Johnson and Grave Digger Jones, who work in Harlem and do things their own way, which involves violence and a macabre kind of humor. In *All Shot Up* (1960) criminals posing as police hold up a car and seize $50,000 belonging to a political figure. The story ends with a car chase in Harlem during a sleet storm. *Cotton Comes to Harlem* (1965) is about con artist Dek O'Hara, who organizes a "Back-to-Africa" movement and takes in $87,000, which he plans to keep. However, the money is hijacked by some white gunmen, then hidden in a bale of cotton that everyone tries to find. Himes wrote two autobiographies, much of which deals with the time he spent in France and Spain: *The Quality of Hurt* (1972) and *My Life as Absurdity* (1976). Another of the detective novels, *Cotton Comes to Harlem*, was produced as a movie in 1970. YA

Hinduism The oldest of the major religions of the world, Hinduism goes back about 4,000 years and is unique in that it had no single founder but grew over the centuries to include many sects and many deities. Hinduism has about 700 million followers, the great majority of whom are in India. The highest trinity of gods consists of Brahma, the creator; Vishnu, the preserver; and Shiva, the destroyer. Hindus worship many gods but believe they are all different manifestations of a single Godhead. A central belief is that of reincarnation: Every soul is reborn in a higher or lower form depending on how well the life just past has been lived. This is the principle of *karma*. Hinduism is also based on a class system that developed into the rigid caste system of India. Though it is now breaking down, the caste system froze individuals at birth into higher or lower civic categories from which there was no escape. The Vedas are the four most sacred books of Hinduism. The last section consists of the Upanishads, which provide an outline of Hindu religious and philosophical thought. Yoga, one school of Hindu philosophy, has attracted much interest in the Western world with its combination of physical and mental exercises along with meditation to achieve the soul's salvation. If you would like to know more about Hinduism, you will find many books in your library, including *Hinduism* (1966) by R(obert) C(harles) Zaehner (1913–1974) for older readers and *The Hindu World* (1982) by Patricia Bahree (n.d.) for all readers. MR & YA

Hinton, S(usan) E(loise) (1950–) The author of a number of popular novels for young adults, Hinton wrote her first book, *The Outsiders,* when she was 16 years old. A year later she was the author of a book that earned high praise from critics and readers. Her second novel, *That Was Then, This Is Now,* is the story of best friends and the forces that draw them apart. *Rumble Fish* (1975) tells about 14-year-old Rusty James, who longs to be like his tough older brother but whose life is changed when his brother is killed and Rusty is sent to a reform school. *Tex* (1979) is about the relationship between two brothers living in Oklahoma. Hinton again used her home state of Oklahoma as the setting for *Taming the Star Runner* (1988). This novel is about a boy named Travis who, because of family problems, is sent to live with his uncle in Oklahoma. Travis has trouble adjusting to his new surroundings until he meets a girl named Casey and her horse, The Star Runner. *Tex* was made into a movie in 1982 and *Rumble Fish* in 1983. YA

Hiroshima (1946), by *John Hersey, is the story of the atomic bombing of the city of Hiroshima, Japan, during World War II. On the morning of August 6, 1945, a lone B-29 bomber dropped on Hiroshima a single atomic bomb that exploded with the force of 20,000 tons of TNT. The city was destroyed by the explosion and by the fires that followed. About 100,000 people lost their lives. *Hiroshima* describes that event as seen by six people who survived: Miss Toshiko Sasaki, a clerk at a tin factory; Dr. Terufumi Sasaki (not related to Miss Sasaki), the only doctor on the staff of the Red Cross Hospital in Hiroshima who was not injured by the blast; Father Wilhelm Kleinsorge, a Catholic priest; the Reverend Mr. Kiyoshi Tanimoto, pastor of the Hiroshima Methodist Church; Dr. Masakazu Fuji, owner and operator of a private hospital in Hiroshima; and Mrs. Hatsuyo Nakamura, a widowed seamstress. Their account of what they saw and did during and after the bombing describes in moving detail the horror of atomic war. It also shows the bravery and beauty of the people of Hiroshima in facing their disaster. YA

His Enemy, His Friend (1967) This novel by *John R. Tunis shows how war turns human beings, both on the winning side and on the losing side, into victims. Hans von Kleinschrodt is a German sergeant stationed in Nogent-Plage, in France, during World War II. He cares nothing for the army. Hans has made friends with the villagers and enjoys playing soccer with Jean-Paul Varin and other village boys. When his commanding officer is killed by the French Resistance, Hans is ordered to round up and shoot six civilians. Among those arrested is Jean-Paul's father. Hans refuses to execute them, but another officer arrives and Hans is forced to watch the execution. After the war, no one remembers the other officer, but Hans is convicted of the killings. After prison, he becomes the best soccer player in Germany. Meanwhile, Jean-Paul has become the best soccer player in France. The two meet again in a game at Rouen, France, which the German team wins. On the way home Hans and five other Germans have car trouble and end up in Nogent-Plage. The townspeople try to kill them, but Jean-Paul arrives in time to save them. As Hans and Jean-Paul stand side by side, Hans is shot by the son of one of the six wartime victims. MR

Hobbit, The, or, There and Back Again (1937) An immensely popular fantasy by *J.R.R. Tolkien, *The Hobbit* is the prelude to the fantasy trilogy *The Lord of the Rings.*

MR = Middle Reader   YA = Young Adult Reader   * = See this main entry

Its hero is a hobbit named Bilbo Baggins. Hobbits are "little people," smaller than dwarves, who wear colorful clothes, have furry feet, are fond of food and drink, and live underground. Bilbo's quiet life is changed when the *wizard Gandalf and 13 dwarves, led by Thorin, talk Bilbo into helping them defeat the dragon Smaug, who long ago drove the dwarves from their home in the Lonely Mountain and stole their treasure. Gandalf gives Thorin an old map made by Thorin's grandfather, Thror, king under the mountain, and also the key to a secret doorway into the mountain's system of tunnels and chambers. Gandalf travels with them for part of the way and then departs to attend to other business. On the long journey east, the group has dangerous encounters with trolls, *goblins, wolflike Wargs, giant spiders, and elves. While escaping from the cavern of the goblins, Bilbo meets up with a slimy creature named Gollum and steals a ring that makes the wearer invisible. The ring helps Bilbo get the dwarves out of many dangerous situations. After resting at the lake town of Esgaroth, Bilbo and the dwarves go to the Lonely Mountain and find the secret entrance. Bilbo, invisible, sneaks into the main cavern, taunts Smaug with riddles, and learns how Smaug might be killed. Smaug, believing the intruders have come from Esgaroth, flies off to destroy the town but is killed. An army of townspeople and forest elves comes to claim part of the dwarves' treasure, but Thorin refuses them and sends for help from his cousin Dain, leader of the dwarves of the Iron Hills. Gandalf reappears, and he and Bilbo manage to prevent a war. They all join forces when they are attacked by goblins. The goblins are destroyed but Thorin is killed. Dain becomes the new king under the mountain, and peace is restored to dwarves, humans, and elves. Bilbo happily returns with Gandalf to his quiet home in the Western Lands. MR & YA

hocus pocus Like the words *abracadabra and presto, this phrase is a must for the vocabulary of any respectable magician. Apparently originating in the early 17th century, the phrase was used by jugglers and magicians as they performed their sleight-of-hand tricks. The -us suffix makes the words sound like mysterious Latin words with great powers. No doubt the great magician *Merlin was familiar with the phrase.

Hocus pocus can also be used to describe an act of trickery or deception, especially if it is carried to an extreme. Magicians take note—a little hocus pocus goes a long way!

Hoke, Helen (1903–1990) A publisher and editor of many collections of stories for the very young, as well as for older readers, Hoke had her first book published in 1940. The titles of her collections are self-explanatory: *Jokes, Jokes, Jokes* (1954); *Spooks, Spooks, Spooks* (1960); *Monsters, Monsters, Monsters* (1975); and *Creepies, Creepies, Creepies* (1977), which is subtitled *A Covey of Quiver and Quaver Tales.* Hoke also edited *Alaska, Alaska, Alaska* (1960), a collection of facts, stories, and poems about the northernmost state. If you enjoy ghost and horror stories, read those of *Scott Corbett, *William Kotzwinkle, and *Seon Manley. Be sure to read the classic *parody of 19th-century ghost stories, "The Canterville Ghost," available in an illustrated edition (1986), by *Oscar Wilde. MR & YA

Holden Caulfield is the teenaged narrator of the novel *The Catcher in the Rye* by *J.D. Salinger. Holden, 16 years old, is a very intelligent boy, but his intelligence does not keep him from flunking out of every school his parents send him to. He is disgusted by the phoniness of the people around him and dreads the idea of disappearing into the shabby grownup world that awaits him. Through his description of three important days in his life, you experience what it is like to be not quite a child and not quite an adult, yet changing and growing all the time. Holden tells his story in a slangy, often ungrammatical way that might remind you of another searcher for truth, Huck Finn in *The Adventures of Huckleberry Finn* by *Mark Twain. And like Huck, Holden reveals more truths about life than he suspects. YA

Holly Golightly is the central character in the short novel *Breakfast at Tiffany's* (1958), by

*Truman Capote. Holly is a beautiful, independent-minded woman living in New York City in 1943, during World War II. She works as an escort and companion to men. She lets them take her to classy restaurants and night clubs, boosts their egos, and brings some fun into their lives. In return, they are expected to give her some kind of gift—money or jewelry or the like. Holly is a free spirit, with apparently no past and possibly no future. She does not know what she is looking for in life. She knows only that she will not be content or feel secure until she finds it. The only place that gives her that sense of security is the luxurious store called Tiffany's. She longs to "find a real life place that made me feel like Tiffany's." Several tragic events change Holly's life. She leaves New York for South America and eventually disappears. YA

Holman, Felice (1919–) A novelist and poet, Holman began writing as a child, and her interest in young people drew her naturally into writing books for children. Among her many books are the novels *Slake's Limbo; The Murderer* (1978), the story of Hershy Marks, a young Jewish boy growing up in a Pennsylvania mining town in the 1930s; and *The Wild Children* (1983), a novel set in Russia in the 1920s just after the Russian Revolution, when gangs of homeless, hungry, desperate children ran wild, doing whatever they had to in order to stay alive. Holman is the author of a number of books of poems, including *At the Top of My Voice, and Other Poems* (1969); *I Hear You Smiling, and Other Poems* (1973); and *The Song in My Head* (1985). MR

holocaust means the complete destruction of something, usually by fire. *The Holocaust* is the term used now to describe the persecution and murder of European Jews by the *Nazis during World War II. As many as 6 million Jews were killed in Nazi concentration camps, as well as about 10 million others, including Slavs and communists.

You might like to read *Number the Stars* by Lois Lowry (1937–), a novel about the Nazi occupation of Denmark and a 10-year-old girl who helps protect her Jewish friend. *The Is-

land on Bird Street* (1984), by *Uri Orlev (1931–), takes place in the Warsaw, Poland, ghetto, where a young Jewish boy is left to fend for himself in a ruined house. An excellent story about a small village in Poland under Nazi occupation is *The Devil's Arithmetic* by *Jane Yolen.

Two nonfiction books on this important subject are *The Holocaust* (1989), an account for younger readers by Seymour Rossel (1945–), and *Smoke and Ashes* (1988), by Barbara Rogasky (1933–), both of which provide a history of the rise of anti-Semitism in Germany. MR & YA

Holy Grail See *Grail, Holy.

Home Before Dark (1976), by *Sue Ellen Bridgers, is a novel about important events in the lives of 14-year-old Stella Mae Willis and her family. Her father, James Earl, is a migrant worker, and Stella and the other children have spent most of their lives in a broken-down station wagon. When James Earl takes his family to the tobacco farm where he was raised, his brother, Newton, gives them the use of a small sharecropper's cabin. The prospect of staying in one place, in a real house, is very exciting to Stella, and in her strong-minded way she decides never to leave.

Stella is old for her years, having helped her mother in childbirth and worked in the fields like an adult. But she has never had a friend her own age. Her neighbor, Toby Brown, is shy, but he likes Stella and comes to depend on her strength. Stella is also interested in Rodney Biggers, who has money to spend and the use of his mother's flashy car. It is Toby, however, who comforts Stella when her mother, Mae, is struck by lightning and dies. James Earl later decides to marry Maggie Grover and help her run the department store in town. Stella cannot bear the thought of leaving the cabin, so she persuades the family to let her stay there alone. As she slowly gets used to her stepmother and sees how fond Maggie is of all the Willises, Stella accepts the new home and goes to rejoin her family. MR & YA

Homecoming (1981), by *Cynthia Voigt, is the story of four children's search for a place to call

---

MR = Middle Reader   YA = Young Adult Reader   * = See this main entry

home. After their mother abandons them in Connecticut, Dicey Tillerman, 13 years old, and her younger brothers and sister, James, Sammy, and Maybeth, set out on foot for Bridgeport, where the only relative they know of, their great-aunt Cilla, lives. After a long and difficult journey they arrive in Bridgeport, only to find that their great-aunt has died. Her daughter permits them to stay, but neither she nor the children are happy with the arrangement. When they learn about their mother's mother, who lives on the eastern shore in Maryland, they set out again, uncertain whether their grandmother, a stern old widow some people think is crazy, will want them or not. They finally arrive at their grandmother's farm, but they do not really find their home until they win their grandmother's love. You can read about the further adventures of Dicey and her family in *Dicey's Song*. YA

Homer (c.8th century B.C.), the ancient Greek poet, is a figure of mystery. He is considered the author of two great epics, the *Iliad* and the *Odyssey*. The ancient Greeks believed that a blind poet named Homer wrote both poems and that he lived in the 12th century B.C., about the time of the *Trojan War. Modern scholars do not have any proof that a person named Homer actually existed, but they think that if he did, he lived sometime between the 9th and 7th centuries B.C. Some scholars think that the poems may have been written by a number of people over a period of time. Much more research must be done, however, and we may never know the complete truth about Homer.

For centuries it was thought that the poems were great works of mythology and described people and places that never existed. But in the 19th century the German archeologist Heinrich Schliemann (1822–1890) became convinced that the walled city of Troy was an actual place and that Homer's account of the war between Greece and Troy was based on fact. Working over a period of 20 years, Schliemann found the ruins of Troy and also made important discoveries at Mycenae, which Homer had said was ruled by the Greek king *Agamemnon. The clues in Homer's *Iliad* enabled

Schliemann and later scientists to increase vastly our knowledge of the ancient Greek world.

Homer Price (1943), written and illustrated by *Robert McCloskey, is a collection of stories about a boy who lives just outside the American Middle Western town of Centerburg. Homer's father runs a tourist camp, and Homer helps out by sweeping the cabins and doing other chores. Homer has an unusual pet, a skunk named Aroma. And his hobby is building radios. When Homer is not in school or doing chores or building radios, he has wonderful adventures. One time he and Aroma capture four robbers all by themselves. Another time he is left in charge of his Uncle Ulysses' coffee shop and cannot turn off the automatic doughnut-making machine. Homer's adventures are continued in *Centerburg Tales* (1951). MR

Homesick: My Own Story (1982), by *Jean Fritz, tells of the author's experiences as an American girl in China in the 1920s. The story begins in 1925. Jean is 10 years old and lives with her parents in the city of Hankow, where her father is head of the Y.M.C.A. She has an amah, or nursemaid, named Lin-Nai-Nai, and a best friend named Andrea, who is a year older than Jean. Jean loves China, but she is lonely. More than anything else, she wants to go home to America, to her grandmother's farm in Washington, Pennsylvania. She becomes even lonelier when Andrea's family moves to Shanghai. And what is worse, a civil war between the communists and the nationalists threatens to keep the family from sailing for America. Finally, in April of 1927, they sail for home. But as she waves farewell to China, Jean suddenly realizes how much she is leaving behind. Yet, ahead of her are more adventures—arriving in San Francisco through the Golden Gate, driving across the continent to her grandmother's farm, and beginning eighth grade in an American school. You can read more about Jean in a sequel, *China Homecoming*. MR

Honey, I Shrunk the Kids (1989), a novel by Elizabeth Faucher (1950–), is an adaptation of the movie screenplay for the 1989 movie of the

MR = Middle Reader   YA = Young Adult Reader   * = See this main entry

same name. Fifteen-year-old Amy Szalinski and her 9-year-old brother, Nick, are the children of Wayne Szalinski, a brilliant but absent-minded physicist who is working on a machine to shrink objects to miniature size. While Wayne is out at a scientific conference, Amy and Nick and their friends next door, 11-year-old Ron Thompson and his 15-year-old brother, Russ, accidentally activate the shrinking machine and are zapped down to a quarter of an inch in size.

This is just the beginning of their troubles. First they are accidentally swept up and thrown into the garbage. They escape from the garbage bag only to find they are on the other side of the yard, which is for them a vast distance from the house. They face many dangers, including a giant bee, ants, a deadly lawn-mower, and a tidal wave from the Thompson's garden hose, before they make it home and are restored to their normal size. If you enjoyed the idea behind *Honey, I Shrunk the Kids*, try the *science fiction classic *Fantastic Voyage* (1966) by *Isaac Asimov, based on the story and screenplay for the 1966 movie *Fantastic Voyage*. In this novel a team of scientists is reduced to microscopic size and travels through a person's body. A sequel to the movie, *Honey, I Shrunk the Kids*, is *Honey, I Blew up the Kid*, produced in 1992. YA

Hoover, H(elen) M(ary) (1935–) The author of a number of *science fiction novels for young people, Hoover grew up in northeastern Ohio. Her house was full of books, and her parents passed their love of reading to their children. Helen's wanderings in the woods and streams near her home gave her an interest in and love for nature and for science.

Hoover's first book, *Children of Morrow* (1973), is set in the future, after a disaster known as the Great Destruction, and tells about two children who become outcasts because they are different—they are telepathic and can hear the thoughts of others. The idea for the story came from a visit to a beach near a landfill. There, Hoover saw overgrown snails and mutated seabirds, clear signs that human activity was having a dangerous effect on nature. Hoover's other books include *Return to Earth: A Novel of the Future; This Time of Darkness* (1980), about two children who live inside a totally enclosed place called the City and who risk their lives to escape to the unknown world of Outside; and *Away Is a Strange Place to Be* (1990), which is set in the 24th century and tells about two children who are kidnapped from Earth to work as slave laborers on a colony in space. MR

Hope, Anthony [Anthony Hope Hawkins] (1863–1933) An English novelist, Hawkins was the cousin of another celebrated English author, *Kenneth Grahame. After graduating with honors from Oxford University, Hawkins studied to become a lawyer. His law career gave him plenty of free time in which to write. Between 1887 and 1894 he had five novels published, using his first and middle names for a pen name. He had also become a successful lawyer and was uncertain which career he should follow. One day, the plot for a new novel came to Hawkins while he was out walking. In one month's time he wrote what was to become his best-known novel, *The Prisoner of Zenda*. From then on Hawkins concentrated on writing. He wrote many more novels and several plays that were popular at the time. YA

Hopkins, Lee Bennett (1938–) A poet, educator, and anthologist, Hopkins has compiled a great number of poetry anthologies for young readers. His books are not the thick, heavy poetry anthologies that appeal to adults. They are smaller in size, pleasantly illustrated, and contain a selection of poems that are fun for young people to read. Among the collections he has compiled are *City Talk* (1970); *Sing Hey for Christmas Day* (1976); *Moments: Poems About the Seasons* (1980); *Rainbows Are Made; Best Friends* (1986); and *Click, Rumble, Roar: Poems About Machines* (1987). Probably his best-known anthology is *Pass the Poetry, Please!*. His own books include *This Street's for Me!* (1970), a collection of poems inspired by the sights and sounds of children playing in the streets of Harlem; and *Charlie's World: A Book of Poems* (1972), about a boy whose family has moved into a new apartment. MR

Horatio Hornblower, the fictional British naval officer created by *C.S. Forester, is the hero of 12 novels set in the early 1800s, during the Napoleonic wars between Great Britain and France. Though the novels are about fictional characters, they are historically accurate and tell their stories around actual events. They follow Horatio Hornblower's career as he rises from midshipman to admiral. In *Midshipman Hornblower* (1950), he is described as a gawky, skinny, shy 17-year-old of medium height, with big feet and thin legs. He hardly appears the hero, yet time after time he is able to accomplish great things because of his courage, resourcefulness, and quick thinking. A curious fact about Hornblower is the date of his birth—July 4, 1776. This British hero is exactly the same age as the United States.

Forester wrote about how he created Horatio Hornblower in his book *The Hornblower Companion* (1964). The movie *Captain Horatio Hornblower*, which was released in 1951, was based on Forester's Hornblower novels. YA

horse The most useful animal ever domesticated, the horse has stood for strength and power so long that people still rate an automobile by the "horsepower" its engine puts forth. Probably the best-known horse, however, is the wooden *Trojan Horse. Specific horses are associated with many figures in mythology, such as Xanthus, belonging to Achilles; *Hercules' Arion; and *Pegasus, the flying horse. In literature Bavieca is the steed of the Cid (c.1043–1099), a legendary hero of Castile, a region of Spain, and Rocinante is associated with *Don Quixote. In the *Bible, in *Revelation, there is an ominous reference: "Behold the pale horse: and his name that sat upon him was Death, and Hell followed with him." *Katherine Anne Porter used this imagery for the title of her book of stories, *Pale Horse, Pale Rider*.

The horse figures in many common expressions: "Don't look a gift horse in the mouth" stems from the fact that to judge the age of a horse it is customary to look at its teeth, so you should not act skeptical about a present someone gives you; "flogging a dead horse" will get you nowhere; "straight from the horse's mouth" is sound information, as though a horse tells you it is going to win the race; "to be on one's high horse" is to be arrogant; "to lock the stable door after the horse is stolen" says there is no use being careful after damage has been done; "to put the cart before the horse" is to get your facts backward; and "You can lead a horse to water but you can't make him drink" tells you it may be impossible to change an obstinate person's mind.

Hound of the Baskervilles, The (1902) In this novel by *Arthur Conan Doyle, *Sherlock Holmes and Dr. Watson investigate the death of Sir Charles Baskerville, master of Baskerville Hall in Devonshire. Sir Charles died of extreme fright, apparently caused by something he saw while walking outside Baskerville Hall one night. He had been haunted by the legend of a ghostly hound lurking on the barren, swampy moor, waiting to destroy any Baskerville who ventured onto it at night, and the footprints of a giant dog were found not far from Baskerville's body. Holmes and Watson must solve the mystery and protect Sir Charles's nephew and heir, Sir Henry Baskerville.

Holmes and Watson's investigations lead to one of Sir Henry's neighbors, a man named Jack Stapleton. They learn that Sir Charles, on the day of his death, received a letter from a woman with the initials L.L., begging him to meet her outside Baskerville Hall that night. They track down the woman, Mrs. Laura Lyons, and learn that Stapleton tricked her into sending the note and then tricked her into not keeping the appointment. This enabled Stapleton to lure Sir Charles outside and scare him to death with a giant, vicious dog made up to look like the ghostly hound of Baskerville legend. Stapleton is actually a Baskerville relative, determined to kill in order to inherit

Baskerville Hall. How Holmes solves the mystery and what happens to Stapleton in the end makes exciting reading. Movies based on this story were made in 1939 and 1959. In the first movie the English actor Basil Rathbone (1892–1967) first portrayed Holmes, as he did many more times. YA

Hounds of the Mórrígan, The (1985) This fantasy novel by Pat O'Shea (1931–) brings to life the magical world of Irish mythology. A 10-year-old Irish boy named Pidge buys an ancient handwritten book and learns that an evil snake named Olc-Glas is trapped within one of its pages. When Pidge and his sister, Brigit, learn that The Mórrígan, the Great Queen, is on her way to free Olc-Glas and loose death and destruction upon the world, they begin a long and dangerous journey to find a long-lost droplet of The Mórrígan's blood, the one thing that can destroy Olc-Glas and defeat the evil queen. They are protected by The Dagda, the Lord of Great Knowledge, from the fierce stalking hounds of The Mórrígan, but it is up to Pidge and Brigit to defeat the evil queen and save the world. Another book by Pat O'Shea is *Finn Mac Cool and the Small Men of Deeds* (1987), retelling a folktale about the Irish hero's quest to save the kidnapped children of a giant-king. Pat O'Shea was born and grew up in Ireland, where she heard the folk and fairy tales that figure in her books. MR

House at Pooh Corner, The (1926) Written by *A.A. Milne, this book continues the famous adventures of Winnie-the-Pooh and his friends begun in the book *Winnie-the-Pooh.* Here Pooh, Piglet, Rabbit, Kanga and Little Roo, Eeyore, Owl, and the boy Christopher Robin welcome a new friend to the Forest, the bouncy Tigger. In the first chapter, Pooh and Piglet decide to build a house for Eeyore in a spot at the edge of the Forest that Pooh names Pooh Corner. They find an excellent pile of sticks to build the new house, not knowing that it is actually the house Eeyore has built for himself. In other adventures, Pooh and Piglet fall into a Heffalump Trap, Tigger finds out why Tiggers do not climb trees, Pooh invents

a new game called Poohsticks, and the animals rescue Eeyore from the river after he is bounced into it by Tigger. Throughout these and other adventures, Pooh thinks up his wonderful verses, or "Hums," which have delighted millions of readers young and old. MR

House of Dies Drear, The (1968) Written by *Virginia Hamilton, this novel tells about Thomas Small, a black youth whose family moves from North Carolina to a small town in southern Ohio. Mr. Small has taken a job teaching Civil War history at the local college. The family rents the Dies Drear house, a large old house that was once an important station of the Underground Railroad, the secret organization that helped slaves escape to freedom in the years before the Civil War. The house has many secret passages and hidden doorways, and it is said to be haunted by the ghosts of Dies Drear, the wealthy abolitionist who built it, and two slaves who were killed the same week that Drear was murdered. Soon they meet the caretaker, a scary old black man named Mr. Pluto, who lives in a cave near the house and seems to be guarding a secret about the Drear place. Thomas and his father learn that Mr. Pluto has found a cavern filled with valuable objects collected by Dies Drear. For years Mr. Pluto has kept the cavern a secret and has guarded it from the greedy Darrow family, who lives next to the Drear place. The Darrows have heard a legend about the hidden treasure, but they have been unable to find it. Pluto wants to protect the treasure, which he sees as an important part of the history of blacks in America. The Smalls help Pluto and his son give the Darrows the fright of their lives and scare them away once and for all. Mr. Small agrees to keep Mr. Pluto's secret as long as the old man lives, after which the treasure will be turned over to the foundation that owns the house. You can read more about the Smalls, Mr. Pluto, and the treasure of Dies Drear in *The Mystery of Drear House* (1987). YA

House of Mirth, The (1905) This novel by *Edith Wharton is a bitter *satire of New York City high society. Lily Bart, 29 years old and unmarried, lives with her aunt and dreams of marrying into wealth and social position. But she is unable to bring herself to accept any of the men who want to marry her. She is attracted to only one man, Lawrence Selden, a lawyer. But he has no wealth and is more an observer than a member of high society. Lily falls into debt to a married friend, Gus Trenor, who then makes advances to her. Then she is falsely accused of trying to steal another woman's husband and is hounded out of society. Virtually disowned by her aunt, Lily drifts into poverty. After her aunt dies, Lily uses her tiny inheritance to pay off her debt to Trenor. She visits Selden one last time, then returns to her shabby boarding room and takes an accidental overdose of medicine. The next day Selden goes to declare his love to Lily, only to find he is too late. YA

House of Stairs (1974), by *William Sleator,
is a *science fiction story about five young people trapped in a building containing nothing but a seemingly endless maze of stairs. The five, all orphans and 16 years old, do not know why they have been brought there. Soon they find a machine that gives them food. At first they are rewarded with food only when they perform a kind of dance together. Then the dances no longer work, but the machine gives them food whenever they act cruelly to one another. Two of them, a loner named Lola and a quiet, passive boy named Peter, refuse to go along with this behavior, and they are cast out by the others—a manipulative girl named Blossom, a self-styled leader named Oliver, and a weak-willed girl named Abigail. Peter and Lola nearly starve to death before the five are rescued. They learn that they have been part of a psychological experiment designed to produce completely obedient government agents, but Peter and Lola have caused it to fail. YA

House of the Seven Gables, The (1851) Written by *Nathaniel Hawthorne, this novel is set in Salem, Massachusetts, and tells about a family cursed and nearly destroyed by greed. Wealthy and powerful Colonel Pyncheon hounds a settler, Matthew Maule, to his execu-

This house in Salem is said to have been the model for *The House of the Seven Gables*.

tion for witchcraft and then takes his land, unafraid of a curse Maule calls down upon him from the gallows. Pyncheon builds a grand house with seven gables on the site of Maule's cottage, only to die mysteriously at his desk soon after moving into the house. Over the generations the family declines until only Judge Jaffrey Pyncheon, a country squire, remains wealthy. His poor cousin Hepzibah lives in the rundown house and refuses his offer of aid. Many years earlier Jaffrey had helped convict her brother, Clifford, for the murder of Clifford's uncle. Clifford returns from prison a broken man. Living with Clifford and Hepzibah are their young cousin, Phoebe, who has grown up in the countryside untouched by the curse, and a mysterious young boarder named Holgrave, who falls in love with Phoebe. Jaffrey is convinced that Clifford knows a secret that will lead him to hidden family wealth, but when he comes to the house to confront Clifford, he dies in the same manner that Colonel Pyncheon and Clifford's uncle died. It was not a question of murder after all, but a physical affliction of the Pyncheon family. Jaffrey's death frees Hepzibah and Clifford from the curse. They are also freed from the invisible bonds that have tied them to the house. Holgrave wins Phoebe's love and reveals that he is really a descendant of Matthew Maule. With the curse lifted from the house and peace brought to the Pyncheon and Maule families, all depart to take up a new life at Jaffrey's country estate, which Hepzibah and Clifford have inherited. *The House of the Seven Gables* was adapted for film in 1940. YA

House with a Clock in Its Walls, The (1973)

This novel by *John Bellairs is the story of Lewis Barnavelt, an overweight 10-year-old with a powerful addiction to chocolate chip cookies. After the death of his parents, Lewis goes to stay with his Uncle Jonathan, a big, friendly, red-bearded man who lives in an elaborate stone mansion with a secret passage. Lewis meets Mrs. Zimmermann, a neighbor who cooks for Jonathan and addresses him as "Weird Beard," and soon learns that both uncle and neighbor are *wizards in a modest and cozy way. The mansion once belonged to Isaac Izard and his wife, evil sorcerers. They left a clock hidden somewhere within the walls—the ticking can be heard but the clock cannot be found.

At school Lewis makes friends with Tarby and tries to become a better softball player. Tarby does not believe the stories of Jonathan's funny magic-making, so Lewis decides to try his own magic to impress his friend. He studies an old book on charms, and promises Tarby that on Halloween he will go to the cemetery and "raise the dead." In front of a large mausoleum Lewis carefully follows the directions copied from Jonathan's book, and the result is a terrible noise from within the tomb. The doors open slightly, something black oozes out, and the boys run for their lives.

Lewis discovers later that he has tampered with the Izard tomb, and all sorts of strange things begin to happen. He begins to see he may have raised Mrs. Izard from the dead. Then Lewis finds some of Izard's papers stuffed into the parlor organ, and later overhears his uncle and Mrs. Zimmermann as they discuss the meaning of the wizard's notes. The hidden clock is set to explode at the proper time and bring about the end of the world. Using homemade magic, Lewis, Uncle Jonathan, and Mrs. Zimmermann succeed in finding the clock in a secret tunnel in the cellar. Mrs. Izard suddenly appears, ready to work evil magic, but Lewis

grabs the clock and smashes it to bits. Mrs. Izard melts away into a pile of rags, and the house is released forever from the spell. MR

Houston, James A(rchibald)

(1921–) A Canadian, Houston lived for 14 years among the Eskimo of the Canadian Arctic before moving to the United States in 1962. His studies of the Eskimos and their culture have provided the material for a number of books for young readers. Among them are *Kiviok's Journey: An Eskimo Legend* (1973), about an Eskimo hero and his search for his wife and children, who have been turned into snow geese by an evil raven; *Frozen Fire* (1977), about a boy named Matthew, his Eskimo friend, Kayak, and their search for Matthew's father after the helicopter in which he is riding disappears in an Arctic storm; *Black Diamonds* (1982), in which Matthew and Kayak search for wealth in the Canadian Arctic; and *Ice Sword* (1985), in which Matthew and Kayak learn scuba diving from a girl named Jill, and the three have many underwater adventures. YA

How Green Was My Valley (1940)

a novel by Richard Llewellyn (1907–1983), is about life in a mining town in Wales in the late 19th century. It is narrated by the main character, Huw Morgan, who is preparing to leave his home and valley forever. A slag heap now blights the beautiful valley and threatens to destroy his family's house. Huw recalls the way things were 50 years earlier. Through his recollection you get to know his father, Gwilym; his mother, Beth; his brothers, Ianto, Ivor, Davy, and Owen; his sister, Angharad; Ivor's beautiful wife, Bronwen, whose love and friendship play an important part in Huw's life; and Huw's best friend, the Reverend Mr. Gruffydd, who loves Angharad but refuses to marry her because he is even poorer than the miners. Though the Morgans and the other miners are poor, life is good in the valley. But the growing struggle between the mine owners and the miners signals the end of the old ways of living and also leads to Gwilym's death. Huw's narrative captures the love, strength, wisdom, and courage he received from his family and friends. You can read about Huw's later life in South America and his eventual return to Wales in the novels *Up, into the Singing Mountain* (1960), *Down Where the Moon Is Small* (1966), and *Green, Green My Valley Now* (1975). Llewellyn was born and raised in the Wales he wrote about. Some of his novels and plays have other settings. For example, *None But the Lonely Heart* (1943) is set in London and tells about a mother's futile efforts to reform a son. Llewellyn wrote two successful mystery plays, *Poison Pen* (1938) and *Noose* (1946). *How Green Was My Valley* was made into a movie in 1941 and *None But the Lonely Heart* in 1944. YA

How I Put My Mother Through College (1981), a novel by *Corinne Gerson, is narrated by 13-year-old Jess Cromwell, whose parents have just separated. When her mother decides to go to college, Jess takes on the role of mother of the family. She helps her mother shop for clothes for school, listens to her problems, and advises her on how to succeed in her studies and with her boyfriends. Jess also does most of the household chores, takes care of her younger brother, Ben, and tries to help him get used to their parents' decision to divorce. All this responsibility helps keep her from thinking about her own problems. Her best friend has moved away and she is beginning seventh grade in a new school where she feels lost and lonely. Jess helps guide her mother and brother through some trying times, including her mother's romance with a student activist whom neither Jess nor Ben likes, her mom's near-arrest at a college sit-in, and Ben's running away from home. Things eventually get straightened out, and Jess can finally concentrate on being a kid once again. MR

How to Eat Fried Worms (1973), by *Thomas Rockwell, is a story guaranteed to tickle your funnybone and turn your stomach. Billy, Tom, Alan, and Joe are together one day when Billy takes on a challenge from Alan, who bets $50 that Billy cannot eat 15 worms in 15 days. Tom sides with Billy on the bet, and Joe sides with

Alan. Billy has lots of trouble eating the first few worms, especially after Alan and Joe try to convince him that worms are poisonous. But after a while Billy becomes determined to win the bet. Alan becomes equally determined to keep Billy from winning. Soon the boys' families and eventually the whole neighborhood become involved in the bet, which almost breaks up the boys' friendship. The outcome remains in doubt until the very end. MR

Howe, James (1946–) An actor and director, James Howe turned to writing when he got the idea for a whimsical character, a vampire rabbit named Bunnicula. His wife, Deborah Howe (1946–1978), encouraged him to collaborate with her on a book about the character, and the result was *Bunnicula. Howe wrote of the further adventures of Bunnicula, Howard the dog, and Chester the cat in *Howliday Inn* (1982), *The Celery Stalks at Midnight* (1983), and *Nighty-Nightmare* (1987). Among Howe's other books are *The Hospital Book* (1981), which describes what it is like to be a patient in a hospital; *A Night Without Stars* (1983), about a young girl who goes into a hospital for heart surgery and befriends a boy whose face has been badly scarred in a fire; and *Morgan's Zoo* (1984), about a zookeeper and his amazing plan to keep the zoo from being closed. MR

Huckleberry Finn, The Adventures of (1884) In this American classic by *Mark Twain, the sequel to the novel *The Adventures of Tom Sawyer*, Tom's friend Huck Finn tells what happened after he and Tom became rich from the robbers' treasure they found. Huck goes to live with the Widow Douglas, who tries to "sivilize" him and ends up by making his life miserable. Huck's "Pap," a brutal drunk, returns to town, kidnaps him, and tries to get control of his money. Huck fakes his own murder and escapes down river to Jackson's Island. After a time he comes upon Miss Watson's slave, Jim, who has run away. Together Huck and Jim raft down the Mississippi and have many adventures along the way. Their raft is run down by a riverboat, and the two are

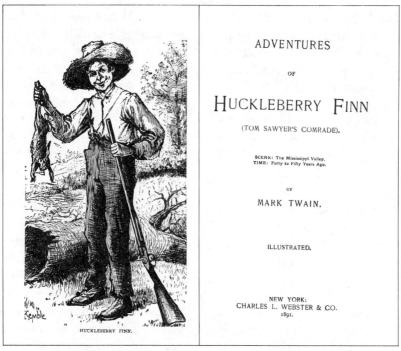

ADVENTURES

OF

HUCKLEBERRY FINN

(TOM SAWYER'S COMRADE).

SCENE: The Mississippi Valley.
TIME: Forty to Fifty Years Ago.

BY

MARK TWAIN.

ILLUSTRATED.

NEW YORK:
CHARLES L. WEBSTER & CO.
1891.

HUCKLEBERRY FINN.

A gleeful Huck sketched by E.W. Kemble (1861–1933),
a famous American illustrator

separated for a time. Later they rescue two con men, one claiming to be a British duke and the other the heir to the French throne. The "King" and the "Duke" take over the raft and make Huck and Jim miserable with their cruel and crooked schemes. Huck and Jim finally get away from the two vagabonds, but not before the King sells Jim as a runaway slave. Huck, who has been struggling all along with the supposed immorality of helping an escaped slave, finally decides that Jim's friendship is more important than anything else. He goes to the Phelps plantation, where Jim is being held. There Huck is mistaken for none other than his friend Tom Sawyer and welcomed by Aunt Sally and Uncle Silas Phelps. When the real Tom arrives, he has to pretend to be his own brother, Sid. Tom devises a complicated plot to free Jim, but during the escape he is shot in the leg. Jim gives up his chance to get away and stays to help Tom. When Tom recovers, he reveals that Miss Watson has died and has set Jim free in her will. Then Jim reveals that Huck no longer has to fear his Pap, who also is dead.

Huckleberry Finn is more than just a great adventure story, for through Huck's boyish, uneducated, and uncivilized view of people and events you can see many truths about human nature and life. Often Twain uses bitter *satire in this, his greatest book, and at the same time often rollicking, infectious comedy. If you enjoyed reading about Tom and Huck's adventures, you will also like *Life on the Mississippi*, in which Twain recalls his experiences while learning to be a riverboat pilot in the days just before the Civil War. At least four movies, produced in 1931, 1939, 1960, and 1974, were based on *Huckleberry Finn*. The first is often shown on television and the last is a musical version. YA

Hudson, W(illiam) H(enry) (1841–1922) An English writer, Hudson was born in Argentina to American parents. On the Argentine pampas, where his father raised sheep, William developed his lifelong love for nature, especially birds. When he was 15 years old he suffered rheumatic fever, which left him in frail health for the rest of his life. Hudson moved to England and became a writer. His first and greatest success was the novel *Green Mansions,

MR = Middle Reader   YA = Young Adult Reader   * = See this main entry

the book for which he is remembered. Among Hudson's other books are his first novel, *The Purple Land* (1885), about the adventures of an Englishman in the region that became Uruguay; and *A Little Boy Lost* (1905), a novel set in a distant, unnamed land and described by Hudson as an "impossible story . . . founded on my own childish impressions and adventures, with a few dreams and fancies thrown in." Your library may have *Tales of the Gauchos: Stories by W. H. Hudson* (1946), a collection of stories from Hudson's books compiled and edited by Elizabeth Coatsworth (1893–1986). Hudson wrote an enchanting account of his youth in Argentina in *Far Away and Long Ago: A Story of My Early Life* (1918). YA

Hughes, Langston (1902–1967) Primarily a poet, Hughes was also a writer of songs, novels, essays, and plays. He was one of the most influential authors in the United States during the *Harlem Renaissance. Hughes was born in Joplin, Missouri, and grew up in Cleveland, Ohio. He later worked in a variety of jobs and lived all over the world. Active in social causes, Hughes usually wrote about black themes and culture, vividly depicting the struggles and joys of black people. Among his best-known works are *The Weary Blues* (1926), *Fine Clothes to the Jew* (1927), *Not Without Laughter* (1930), *I Wonder As I Wander* (1956), *The Dream Keeper*, and *The Book of Negro Folklore*. YA

Hughes, Richard (Arthur Warren) (1900–1976) An English novelist, playwright, and short-story writer, Hughes was of Welsh descent though he was born in England. He had his first collection of poems, *Gipsy Night* (1922), published, and while an undergraduate at Oxford University wrote his first play, *The Sisters' Tragedy* (1924), which was described by *George Bernard Shaw as "the finest one-act play ever written." The play was warmly received, and Hughes continued his interest in the theater, but it was in the field of fiction that he attained his great success.

Hughes's reputation was established with the publication of *A High Wind in Jamaica, which appeared in the United States as *The In-nocent Voyage*. An adventure story and a compelling study of the minds and actions of seven youths, it quickly became a classic of young people's literature.

Hughes's other books include the novels *In Hazard* (1938), about the crew of a ship fighting a deadly storm at sea, and *The Fox in the Attic* (1961), about a young Englishman's visit to his cousins in Munich in 1923, at the time Adolf Hitler (1889–1945) made his unsuccessful first attempt to seize power in Germany. *The Fox in the Attic*, which won much critical praise and became a best-seller, was the first volume of a projected trilogy. The second volume was *The Wooden Shepherdess* (1973), but Hughes did not live to complete the trilogy. YA

Hugo, Victor (Marie) (1802–1885). A French novelist, poet, and dramatist, Hugo was one of the giants of 19th-century European literature. Victor's father was a general under Napoleon, but his mother supported the monarchist cause, and they separated when Victor was still a boy. In school he began writing poetry and plays, and by the time he was 20 years old he had established himself as a successful writer. He married his childhood sweetheart and began his long and successful career. Hugo became a leader of the Romantic movement, which rebelled against the restrictions that had long been imposed on artists and writers. He also became a champion of liberty and republican government. Hugo went into exile when Louis Napoleon became emperor. After Napoleon's fall, Hugo returned to Paris a national hero, both for his literary accomplishments and for his political leadership. Hugo's writings reflected the many joys and tragedies of his own life. He is known best for two outstanding novels, *The Hunchback of Notre Dame and *Les Misérables*, which are celebrated for their rich historical detail and their powerful portrayals of the beauty and sorrow of human existence. YA

Hunchback of Notre Dame, The (1831) This classic French novel by *Victor Hugo is set in Paris in 1482. Quasimodo, the deaf, one-eyed, hunchbacked bell-ringer of Notre Dame cathedral, has been raised from childhood by the priest Claude Frollo, now archdeacon at Notre Dame. The archdeacon has fallen in love with a gypsy girl named Esmeralda, who performs tricks with a pet goat named Djali and is widely thought to be a sorcerer. When Quasimodo attempts to kidnap the girl on the archdeacon's orders, he is arrested by an officer named Phoebus. Esmeralda falls in love with Phoebus. When Quasimodo is publicly whipped and pilloried in the square in front of Notre Dame, Esmeralda alone shows him human kindness by giving him some water to drink. The archdeacon, jealous of Phoebus, stabs him and then has Esmeralda convicted for his murder and for sorcery. Phoebus survives the attack, but he makes no attempt to save Esmeralda after she is sentenced to death. In the prison the archdeacon declares his love and offers to save Esmeralda if she will love him, but she spurns him. On execution day Quasimodo, who truly loves Esmeralda, rescues her and takes her to the church tower, where she has religious sanctuary. Quasimodo mistakenly fights off a mob that wants to rescue Esmeralda, but she is lured out of the church and to her execution by the archdeacon. When Quasimodo realizes what has happened he kills the archdeacon and then disappears. Two years later his skeleton is found next to that of Esmeralda in the place where she has been entombed. After reading Hugo's novel, you will enjoy even more the movies that were made from it in 1923, 1939, and 1957. YA

Hunt, Irene (1907–) Born in Illinois, Hunt was a teacher for many years before turning to writing books. She did not set out to write books for young people, but her novels have been welcomed by young readers and praised by critics. Among them are *Across Five Aprils; *Up a Road Slowly; No Promises in the Wind* (1970), about the struggles of a 15-year-old Chicago boy whose father loses his job during the Great Depression; and *The Everlasting Hills* (1985), about a mentally handicapped boy living in the Colorado mountains who finds the strength to

overcome his problems through the friendship and love of a stranger. MR & YA

Hunter, Mollie [Maureen McIlwraith] (1922–) A Scottish writer, Mollie Hunter has carefully woven Scottish history and folklore into her many novels for young people. Her books have been praised for their colorful descriptions of Scotland, interesting characters, and suspenseful plots. They include *Thomas and the Warlock* (1967), about a Scottish blacksmith who must defeat an evil warlock; *The 13th Member* (1971), about a young kitchen maid in 16th-century Scotland who becomes involved in witchcraft and a plot to kill King James VI of Scotland (1566–1625); *A Sound of Chariots; A Stranger Came Ashore* (1975), about a mysterious young man, the lone survivor of a shipwreck off the Shetland Islands, who possesses dark magic powers; and *You Never Knew Her as I Did*. MR & YA

Hurwitz, Johanna (1937–) Author of many enjoyable novels for young people, Johanna Hurwitz knew as a child that she wanted to be a writer. Her love of books led to her dual career as a children's librarian and writer. Her first book, *Busybody Nora* (1976), introduces Nora, a 6-year-old girl with a big curiosity who lives with her family in an apartment in New York City. Nora's humorous adventures were continued in *Nora and Mrs. Mind-Your-Own-Business* (1977) and *New Neighbors for Nora* (1979). Among Hurwitz's other books is a series that follows the adventures of a boy named Aldo Sossi and his older sisters, Karen and Elaine. It includes *Aldo Applesauce* (1979), in which the family moves to a new home in the suburbs and fourth-grader Aldo has trouble making new friends; *Tough-Luck Karen* (1982), in which 13-year-old Karen has difficulty thinking up a school science project; and *Hurricane Elaine* (1986), about the misadventures of Aldo and Karen's 15-year-old sister, Elaine. MR & YA

Huxley, Aldous (Leonard) (1894–1963) A prolific author of novels, poems, essays, and screenplays, the English-born Huxley was the grandson of the world-famous biologist T(homas) H(enry) Huxley (1825–1895), who actively supported the theories of *Charles Darwin in England. Aldous's older brother was Julian Huxley (1887–1975), a biologist and educator.

Aldous hoped to become a doctor, but at age 16 an eye disease and the resulting near-blindness forced him to give up his plans. In spite of the handicap, he had finished an 80,000-word novel, never published, by the time he was 17 years old. Huxley's scientific background and strong sense of detail were important elements in his writing, combined with a talent for elegant social *satire. These qualities are present in his novel *Brave New World*. In later life he became intensely interested in mysticism and Oriental philosophy. Huxley lived in the United States from 1937 until his death.

His first novel, called a "novel of ideas," was *Crome Yellow* (1921). It takes place on an estate where artists, scientists, and aristocrats gather for conversation and parties, and draws a picture of modern society as a barren and corrupt environment, in which the individual cannot find a basis for happiness. You might enjoy Huxley's *Collected Short Stories* (1957), which contains fascinating and varied examples of fiction written between 1910 and 1930. "The Gioconda Smile" is about Henry Hutton, a married man who cannot resist love affairs with other women. When he amuses himself by charming Janet Spence, a lonely and rather mysterious spinster, he unexpectedly becomes the victim of her ruthless passion. YA

~I~

I Am the Darker Brother: An Anthology of Modern Poems by Negro Americans (1968) is a collection of poems by black Americans collected by *Arnold Adoff, who wrote in the preface that it is necessary for both blacks and whites to experience black poetry because this vital part of both heritages has been ignored. The poets themselves, *Langston Hughes, *Gwendolyn Brooks, *Richard Wright, and *Countee Cullen, among others, are among the finest poets in America. Many of them, like Richard Wright, have also written novels and plays. Adoff has edited several other collections of contemporary African-American poetry, including *The Poetry of Black America and Celebrations (1978). Collected in response to the almost total lack of African-American representation in contemporary anthologies, Adoff's work provides a good introduction to some of the best American poets. MR & YA

I Know You, Al (1975) By *Constance C. Greene, this sequel to *A Girl Called Al follows Al and her best friend as the girls begin to grow into young women. Al faces some big changes in her life when her father, whom she has not seen since her parents' divorce six years earlier, comes to visit and tells her that he is remarrying and she is invited to the wed-

ding. Al worries about the wedding and whether or not she will like and be liked by her father's new wife and three little boys. She comes to realize she has not forgiven her father for leaving her. Al goes to the wedding, has a wonderful time, and meets a boy who promises to write to her. Most importantly, she decides to forgive her father. You can read about the further adventures of Al and her friend in *Your Old Pal, Al, *Al(exandra) the Great, and *Just Plain Al. MR

I Remember Mama (1944) is a two-act play by *John Van Druten, adapted from *Mama's Bank Account* (1943), a group of short stories by Kathryn Forbes (1909–1966). The story is told by Katrin, a daughter of a hard-working Norwegian-American family living in San Francisco, California. Though short of money, Mama and Papa are determined to raise their four children to be decent and loving people. Mama's bank account is kept for emergencies. Even when extra money is needed, the family's resourcefulness makes it possible for them to avoid dipping into the special bank account. When Katrin, who wants to become a writer, receives a check for her first story and tries to deposit it in the bank account, her parents confess the account never existed. They made it up in order to give the children a sense of security during hard times. The play was adapted for film in 1948 and was the basis for a TV series that ran from 1949 to 1956. MR & YA

I, Robot (1950), by *Isaac Asimov, is a collection of his short stories about robots. The most important contribution to *science fiction in these stories is Asimov's three Laws of Robotics: (1) A robot may not injure a human being, or, through inaction, allow a human being to come to harm. (2) A robot must obey the orders given it by human beings except where such orders conflict with the first law. (3) A robot must protect its own existence as long as such protection does not conflict with the first or second law. These laws have become so widely incorporated in the idea of robotics that not only do science. fiction writers use them, but respected researchers in the field of artificial intelligence consider them central.

Asimov depends on loopholes and contradictions in these laws to provide drama in his stories. In one of the best stories, "Liar," the robot is forced to self-destruct because no matter what action it takes, it will break one or all of the laws. Asimov revolutionized science fiction's view of robots by writing about the clash of higher technology with civilization, and treating robots as compassionate and almost human characters, rather than as clumsy metal monsters. If you enjoyed this book, you can read more of Asimov's robotics stories in *The Complete Robot* (1982), which contains 31 such tales. YA

I Will Call It Georgie's Blues (1983), by *Suzanne Newton, is the story of the troubles in an outwardly perfect family told from the point of view of a teenage boy, Neal Sloan. Neal, his father and mother, his sister, Aileen, and his little brother, Georgie, live in the small Southern town of Gideon. The children escape from the family in their own ways: Aileen by rebelling and dating a boy whom she knows is unacceptable to her father; Neal by becoming absorbed in jazz and his friendship for the mu-

sic teacher, Mrs. Talbot; and Georgie into his own private world. Neal, sensing Georgie's loneliness and fear, tries to reach out to him. Georgie feels that no one in the family or in the entire town is quite real except for Neal. Neal knows Georgie needs help, but Neal cannot make his father, a Baptist minister, realize it. Neal can hardly even talk to his father, much less tell him that there is trouble in his family.

The family begins to fall apart when the Reverend Sloan overhears rumors that he himself is mentally unbalanced. He cannot abide the thought that his family is less than perfect, and his children's problems are ignored in the more important task of setting a proper example for the town. Neal, up to now a quiet, respectful boy who finds solace outside the house, begins to talk back to his father and gets into trouble at school. He tells his sister, Aileen, that he just cannot keep quiet anymore and that he must be more like she is and openly challenge his father's unthinking authority, which is destroying the family. When Georgie runs away and everybody thinks he may have died, the Reverend and Mrs. Sloan finally realize that not only Georgie, but the whole family, needs help. *I Will Call It Georgie's Blues* is a moving portrait of a family in trouble, with convincing characters and a hard-hitting, grim narrative. If you enjoyed it, other authors whose books you may like are *Judy Blume, *Nat Hentoff, *S.E. Hinton, *Harry Mazer and *Norma Fox Mazer, and *Paul Zindel. YA

Iago is the villain of *William Shakespeare's tragedy *Othello. Evil from head to toe, Iago is angry because another officer was promoted by the Moorish general Othello to the chief lieutenancy Iago had coveted. Iago suspects that Othello has had an affair with his wife, so he methodically plots the downfall of Othello. He slanders Othello's innocent wife, Desdemona, and convinces Othello that she has been unfaithful to him. Othello murders Desdemona

Scene of the hotel barroom in *The Iceman Cometh*

and, when he discovers his mistake, kills himself. YA

iambic pentameter is the term used to describe a particular meter or rhythm used frequently in English verse. The iamb is a metrical foot of two syllables, with the emphasis placed on the second syllable. Here is a line of four iambs: The brain is wider than the sky. Pentameter refers to a verse line of five iambs. First used by *Geoffrey Chaucer, some of the most famous examples of the iambic pentameter, the commonest of English meters, appear in the sonnet form. A fine example is contained in these lines from a sonnet by *William Shakespeare:

> That time of year thou may'st in me behold
> When yellow leaves, or none, or few, do hang
> Upon those boughs which shake against the cold—
> Bare ruin'd choirs where late the sweet birds sang.

See also *blank verse.

Ibsen, Henrik (Johan) (1828–1906) A Norwegian poet and playwright, who wrote *A Doll's House* and *Hedda Gabler*, Ibsen has been called the father of modern realistic drama. The son of a wealthy businessman who went bankrupt, Ibsen suffered acutely from what he considered the family's disgrace. In 1851 he entered into a long apprenticeship in the theater, becoming stage manager at the Norwegian Theater in Bergen. There he wrote and produced an original verse play each year, using material from Norwegian history and legend. Ibsen was later artistic director of the Norwegian Theater in Oslo, but the group went bankrupt in 1862. Exhausted from overwork and bitter over a series of failures and personal problems, Ibsen applied to the government for funds to enable him to travel and write. With the grant, he left Norway and lived in Italy and Germany for the next 27 years.

Ibsen's works can be divided roughly into three periods. In the first are verse plays based on folklore and historical themes. Among these is *Peer Gynt* (1867), a *satire on what Ibsen saw as Norwegian complacency, cowardice, and lack of vision. In his second period, Ibsen wrote realistic social plays in which he revealed ideas and truths that society preferred to keep hidden. Along with *A Doll's House* and *Hedda Gabler*, this phase includes *Ghosts* (1881), a drama that treats the controversial subject of inherited venereal disease. *The Wild Duck* (1884), one of his most complex plays, is a realistic tragedy of human weakness, in which a man comes to believe his beloved daughter is not his own child. The plays of the third period place great emphasis on *symbolism. Among them is *The Master Builder* (1892), about an architect trying to overcome his limitations.

Sometimes described as the best hated artist of the 19th century, Ibsen believed that conformity to empty social traditions can stifle individual freedom and growth. He was deeply concerned with the consequences of telling or not telling the truth. His work, which often brought hostile reactions from audiences and critics, was nonetheless celebrated for its great technical skill. *The Wild Duck* was adapted for film in 1983. YA

Icarus In Greek mythology, Icarus was the son of *Daedalus, a sculptor, inventor, and artist. When Daedalus angered King Minos of Crete, he was shut up along with Icarus in a labyrinth. To escape he made sets of feathered wings for the two of them and fastened them to their shoulders with wax. Daedalus advised his son not to fly too close to the ground or too high in the sky. Icarus, full of pride, ignored his father's advice and soared higher and higher in the sky. He flew so near the sun that the wax melted and Icarus fell into the sea and was drowned. You can read about some of Greece's mythological heroes in *Heroes and Monsters of Greek Myth* (1975) by Bernard Evslin (1922–), Dorothy Evslin (1923–), and Ned Hoopes (1932–). MR & YA

Iceman Cometh, The (1946) By *Eugene O'Neill, this four-act play is a tragic account of the need of people to believe in the possibility of a better life, even if that means indulging in pipe dreams. The action takes place in Harry Hope's tawdry hotel barroom. Most of the characters are alcoholics of various ages and backgrounds who have turned to whiskey to ease their guilt. Living on Harry's generosity, most of them hang on to the slim hope of someday escaping their condition and leading useful lives. Everyone is looking forward to the visit of Hickey, a salesman and cheerful drinker who still has a life outside of Harry's hotel. But Hickey disturbs the routine and frightens his friends by announcing that he has given up liquor and has stopped deluding himself about the future. He claims to have found peace through renunciation of the pipe dreams that have been ruining his life. Like a man selling a new religion, he promises salvation to those who follow his example and let go of their silly

Ichabod Crane

illusions. As his words take effect, the light-hearted atmosphere of the barroom becomes sullen and oppressive, and his friends begin to turn against him. Troubled by their reaction, Hickey finally admits that he has murdered his wife, not because he wanted to free her from a no-good husband, but because he hated her tolerance of his moral lapses. Hickey turns himself over to the police. Hickey's friends explain his shocking act by telling themselves he is insane, thereby creating another comforting pipe dream. They return to the old ways. *The Iceman Cometh* was adapted for film in 1973. YA

Ichabod Crane This ridiculous schoolmaster of Sleepy Hollow appears in *Washington Irving's *"The Legend of Sleepy Hollow." He dreams of marrying his singing student, Katrina Van Tassel. But Abraham Van Brunt, a big, strong fellow who is known to everyone as Brom Bones, is also in love with Katrina. An excellent horseman, Brom disguises himself one autumn night as the ghostly headless horseman of Sleepy Hollow, the subject of a number of spooky local legends. Brom chases the gullible Ichabod Crane and throws a pumpkin head at him. Ichabod, convinced that he has seen the headless horseman, leaves Sleepy Hollow without even stopping to collect his belongings, and soon Katrina and Brom are married. The story of Ichabod Crane is especially fun to read on Halloween. You can find it and the rest of Irving's 61 short stories in *The Complete Tales of Washington Irving* (1975), edited by Charles Neider (1915–). MR & YA

Ida Early Comes Over the Mountain (1980),

a novel by *Robert Burch, introduces a memorable young woman who keeps house for Mr. Sutton and his four children in Georgia during the *Great Depression. Ida appears at the door one morning when the Suttons are still adjusting to the death of their mother. Tall and strong, with stringy brown hair and shabby clothes, Ida reminds young Randall Sutton of a scarecrow. She convinces the family to let her stay on as housekeeper, and the Suttons soon discover her irresistible sense of humor and her many talents. A fine cook, Ida can also do rope tricks, lasso pigs, tell funny stories, and manage more serious matters with courage and efficiency. She seems enormously experienced, yet she never really talks about her background. Ida wins the hearts of all the Suttons in spite of her odd ways, and teaches the young people important lessons about friendship. If you liked this story, you may want to read *Christmas with Ida Early* (1983), a sequel in which the younger Suttons try to get Ida romantically interested in a preacher. MR

Idiot, The (1868) By *Fyodor Dostoyevsky,

this novel centers on a hero who may be viewed as a near-perfect man caught up in what is certainly an imperfect world. Prince Myshkin is a Christlike figure who epitomizes meekness and humility. Utterly free of ego-tism, he is tolerant, caring, and compassionate. He loves selflessly those he meets. He is an epileptic (as was Dostoyevsky), but people he meets think he is an idiot. They also recognize his goodness and moral superiority, which inspire love in some and hatred in others. Rogozhin, an egotistical, destructive person in love with Nastasya Filippovna, hates Myshkin. The reckless and beautiful Nastasya cares for Myshkin but promises to marry Rogozhin. Myshkin becomes engaged to a young society girl, but he breaks his engagement to save Nastasya from the passionate and violent Rogozhin. On Nastasya's wedding day to Myshkin, she leaves him, believing Myshkin's love for her is only pity, and returns to Rogozhin, whom she hates. The jealous Rogozhin murders Nastasya. Myshkin, devastated by the murder, sinks into incurable mental darkness. Myshkin's goodness does not prevail against evil. Disaster strikes him and those closest to him. *The Idiot* was filmed in 1960. YA

idyll This term, which comes from the Greek word meaning little picture or little poem, is a short, pastoral poem that usually contains a description of natural and tranquil surroundings, or is a simple narrative. The first idylls were probably those of the Greek poet Theocritus (c.310–250 B.C.), who wrote of nymphs and shepherds in a rustic setting. *Virgil was inspired by Theocritus to compose the 10 idylls titled *Bucolica* (37 B.C.). The meaning of the term, which has remained somewhat indefinite, was expanded in the 19th century to include such works as *Alfred Tennyson's *Idylls of the King*, in which the pastoral element was replaced by narrative based on the legends of *King Arthur. In modern English, a scene of idyllic charm is one of simplicity and peacefulness.

Idylls of the King (1888), by *Alfred Tenny-

son, is a series of poems about *King Arthur that are based on *Le Morte d'Arthur* (1485) by *Thomas Malory. Young *Gareth, the Kitchen Knight, arrives at *"Camelot, a city of shadowy palaces and stately, rich in emblem and the work of ancient kings." To Arthur's court the people come and ask for help and redress of wrongs. Gareth sees "in all the listening eyes of those tall knights that ranged about the throne clear honor shining like the dewy star of dawn, and faith in their great King, with pure affection." And here is young *Elaine, looking at the great knight *Lancelot's face for the first time, "seamed with an ancient sword-cut on the cheek, and bruised and bronzed, she lifted up her eyes and loved him, with that love which was her doom." She does not yet know that "the great and guilty love he bare the Queen, in battle with the love he bare his lord, had marred his face and marked it ere his time." When Arthur, mortally wounded in the battle that results from this great love affair, asks Bevidere to fling *Excalibur into the lake, Bevidere hides the magnificent sword and lies to Arthur twice about it. When he finally flings it, "an arm, clothed in white samite, mystic, wonderful . . . caught him by the hilt, and brandished him three times, and drew him under in the mere." And then a barge with three queens appears to take Arthur away to the island-valley of *Avalon, where he still rests, and people hope for the great leader's return. If you enjoyed *The Idylls of the King*, you may also like *The Lady of the Lake* (1810) by *Walter Scott, a romantic and adventurous poem set in Scotland around the 16th century. See also *idyll. YA

Iliad (8th century B.C.?) The ancient Greek poet *Homer is traditionally thought to be the author of this *epic poem of roughly 16,000 lines. Set in the last year of the *Trojan War, it tells the story of the Greek hero *Achilles, who leaves the battlefield in anger when the commander-in-chief, *Agamemnon, confiscates his prize of war, the maiden Briseis. Without Achilles and his soldiers, the Greek forces face disaster. Achilles returns to battle only when his friend Patroclus is killed by the Trojan prince Hector. Achilles avenges his friend's death by slaying Hector. When Priam, the aged Trojan king, guided by *Hermes, who was sent by *Zeus, comes in sorrow to beg for the remains of his son, Achilles relents and allows Priam to take Hector's body back to Troy.

The *Iliad*, which inspired and influenced writers for generations, is considered the first great literary work of the West. Homer's use of flashback techniques, dramatic *irony, suspense, and fine character depiction greatly influenced later poets. Careful study of his text has led archeologists to the site of the ancient city of Troy. There are several good modern English translations of the *Iliad*, including those by Richmond Lattimore (1906–1984) and *Robert Graves. A retelling for younger readers is *The Trojan War* (1988) by Bernard Evslin (1922–). MR & YA

Immoralist, The (1902) Written in a simple style, this controversial novel by *André Gide explores the conflict between spirituality and sensuality in a young man yearning to escape conventional morality. Michel is devoted to the study of archeology and ancient languages. At home with three close friends, he tells about his life during the past three years. He describes his marriage to Marcelline, done in part to please his dying father. With his pretty bride, Michel travels to Tunisia in North Africa to visit its celebrated ruins. There he develops a bad cough. Thinking the desert air will cure him, Michel neglects his tubercular condition until he becomes dangerously ill. Marcelline's passionate care saves his life, but Michel's brush with death changes him dramatically, leaving him with a need to experience life in new ways. As his health slowly improves, Michel discovers his senses, his love of physical beauty and nature, and his own attraction to the young Arab boys brought to keep him company. He cannot reconcile his love for Marcelline with his strong need for freedom and for new sensual experiences outside his marriage. When they return to France, Michel tries to find serenity in work. He comes to feel, however, that he was born to make discoveries of a kind not yet imagined, for which he must give up ordinary standards of behavior. After Marcelline suffers a miscarriage, she is found to have tuberculosis. Michel, haunted by memories of his convalescence, persuades her to undertake a foolhardy and exhausting journey to the healing warmth of North Africa. There

Marcelline finally dies and Michel, now liberated, wonders what he will do with his freedom. If you liked this difficult but rewarding book, you may want to read *The Stranger by *Albert Camus, a French existential novel set in North Africa. YA

Importance of Being Earnest, The: A Trivial Comedy for Serious People (1895) A

drawing room comedy by *Oscar Wilde, this popular play is a brilliant satire on *Victorian manners. In London, Algernon Moncrieff and John Worthing are sophisticated young bachelors. Each indulges himself in a secret life. Algernon has invented a sickly friend, Bunbury, whose failing health he invokes whenever he wishes to escape from London to the country. John lives with his ward, the lovely Cecily Cardew, at his manor house in Woolton, where he is known as Jack. He has an imaginary younger brother, "Ernest," who resides in London and is often in trouble. Jack uses Ernest as an excuse to escape the country. In effect, Jack becomes Ernest when he goes to London to amuse himself. As Ernest, Jack is engaged to aristocratic Gwendolyn Fairfax.

Complications arise when Gwendolyn's mother questions Jack's family background and learns, to her horror, that the infant Ernest was found by a kindly gentleman abandoned in the cloakroom at Victoria Station. Pretending to be Jack's brother Ernest, Algernon causes further complications by paying a surprise visit to Cecily at Woolton and falling in love with her. Meanwhile, Jack decides his fictitious brother is a nuisance and announces his untimely death. A great deal of confusion ensues, particularly after Gwendolyn arrives in Woolton. Eventually, the two pairs of lovers sort out their names, and Jack discovers the happy solution to the mystery of his birth. The play was filmed in 1952. YA

In Country (1985), a novel by *Bobbie Ann

Mason, takes place in a small Kentucky town 12 years after the end of the Vietnam War. Samantha Hughes, called Sam, is 17 years old and lives with her uncle, Emmett, a Vietnam veteran. Her father, Dwayne, also fought in Vietnam and died there before she was born. Sam is smart and independent and uses her head a lot, even though her busy mind is crowded with pop songs, music videos, and images from her favorite TV programs. Because her mother remarried and moved away, Sam keeps an eye on Emmett, who seems unable to find a purpose in life. He suffers from a skin ailment Sam believes was caused by Agent Orange, a powerful defoliant used during the war. Sam cannot stop wondering about her father, and about what she will do with the rest of her life. Emmett will not talk about Vietnam, and his veteran buddies are friendly but equally reluctant to share their war experiences. When Sam is given Dwayne's war diary, which no one in the family seems to have read, she is horrified by his vivid descriptions of death and decay. Without telling Emmett, Sam camps out all night in a wild, swampy place to try to understand what it was like in the Vietnamese jungle. After a worried Emmett finds her at the swamp, he breaks down completely, giving vent at last to the grief, rage, and confusion he has lived with since the war. Both Emmett and Sam are shaken by the encounter, but it marks the beginning of their better adjustment to life. Later, with Dwayne's mother, they make the long trip to Washington, D.C., to visit the great Vietnam Memorial, where the names of all the dead are carved. Another powerful novel about a veteran struggling to overcome his crippling memories of the Vietnam War is *Paco's Story by Larry Heinemann (1944–). *In Country* was adapted for film in 1989. YA

In the Year of the Boar and Jackie Robinson (1984), by *Bette Bao Lord, is a charming

novel about a Chinese girl and her adjustment to a new life in Brooklyn, New York. The story opens in China, where the year is 4646, the Year of the Boar. Eight-year-old Shirley Temple Wong and her mother travel 10,000 miles to join Mr. Wong in America, where the year is 1947. Going to school without knowing English is difficult but not impossible for this bright and courageous girl. Making friends is difficult too, but Shirley manages to improve her English and win the respect of Mabel, the tallest and strongest girl in the fifth grade. Because of Mabel, Shirley learns to play baseball and develops a passion for the game. Her self-confidence grows and, best of all, Shirley gets a chance to meet Jackie Robinson (1919–1972), Rookie of the Year, and a hero to Brooklyn Dodger fans. If you enjoyed this book, try *Dragon Wings*, by *Laurence Yep, about the problems faced by a Chinese boy in San Francisco in the early 1900s. You will also want to read *Thank You, Jackie Robinson* by Barbara Cohen (1932–1992). MR

Incident at Hawk's Hill

Incident at Hawk's Hill (1971), a novel by *Allan W. Eckert, is based on an event that took place in the summer of 1870 on the sparsely settled prairie north of Winnipeg, Canada. The author's knowledge of natural history has enabled him to write about the area and its wildlife in beautiful and convincing detail. Ben MacDonald is 6 years old, the youngest of four children on the MacDonald farm. Very small for his age, shy and tongue-tied with people, Ben has an uncanny ability to communicate with animals of all kinds by imitating their sounds and movements. He is terrified, however, by Burton, a trapper who acts cruelly toward animals and people. One day Ben wanders far over the prairie. Caught in a sudden summer storm, he finds refuge in a roomy underground burrow that he shares with a large badger. Ben finds himself lost in a place without landmarks. He is so afraid of being caught by the trapper that he gives up any idea of trying to find his way home. His desperate parents can find no trace of him. He and the badger share some adventures and help one another survive until Ben is discovered some months later by his older brother. As Ben adjusts to being at home again, he seems more at ease with people. An unexpected and unwanted visit from Burton sets in motion a chain of dangerous events that bring the story to an exciting conclusion. MR

Incredible Journey, The

Incredible Journey, The (1960) By *Sheila Burnford, this novel takes place in northern Ontario, Canada. John Longridge lives 250 miles from his good friends, the Hunters. When the Hunters go to England for several months, John offers to give their pets a temporary home. Tao, a blue-eyed Siamese cat, Bodger, an old English bull terrier, and Luath, a young Labrador retriever, are attached to each other and to the Hunter family. John goes on a fishing trip, leaving the animals in the care of his housekeeper.

One morning Luath quietly starts off in what instinct tells him is the direction of his home, and Tao and Bodger follow. Their progress is very slow at first, until they begin to adjust to life in the wilderness and their natural abilities develop. Tao is the hunter who provides food, though in rather small bits. Bodger is old, but he comes from a line of great fighting dogs and is fearless. Luath is the leader, a fine swimmer and devourer of frogs. The three animals have adventures, including a battle with a bear cub and its outraged mother, and another with a hungry lynx. They are separated for a time while trying to cross a river, when Tao is carried downstream far from the dogs and nearly drowns. Rescued by a kind Finnish family, Tao is nursed back to health and manages to catch up with the dogs later.

When the Hunters return from England, John tells them that their pets have disappeared. Knowing that dogs have been known to travel great distances to reach people they love, the Hunters and John ask the forest rangers for help. After getting in touch with families who live along the route, the rangers begin to pick up news of the odd trio. John and the Hunters meet at a lake where they have been many times before with the pets, and it is there that the miracle happens. Feeling very discouraged, they hear a dog bark in the distance. Mr. Hunter whistles, and one by one the animals appear out of the forest and rush to their old friends. If you enjoyed this book, you will also like *The Call of the Wild* by *Jack London. *The Incredible Journey* was made into a *Walt Disney movie in 1963. MR

Indian in the Cupboard, The

Indian in the Cupboard, The (1980) By *Lynne Reid Banks, this novel begins on Omri's birthday, when his friend Patrick gives him a small plastic Indian called Little Bear.

Omri also receives a cupboard and an old-fashioned key that belonged to his grandmother but fits the cupboard lock perfectly. He casually puts the Indian figure in the cupboard and locks the door. At dawn he hears odd noises and opens the cupboard to find the Indian has come to life.

Both Omri and the Indian are shocked, but they manage to talk to each other. Over several days, the fascinated boy takes care of Little Bear, finding him bits of food to eat and scraps of cloth for a tepee. Omri discovers that besides turning a plastic object into a real person, the cupboard and key will change that person back to plastic. He keeps the Indian hidden from his family, but Patrick becomes curious about what Omri is doing every day after school. Omri finally allows Patrick to meet Little Bear and lets Patrick use the magic on a plastic cowboy. In the cupboard the toy becomes Boone, a cranky man on horseback.

Omri, Patrick, Little Bear, and Boone have several hair-raising experiences together. Life for the small men gets more and more difficult, however, and Omri realizes that he cannot treat them like "things" any more. The four agree that the only solution is to let Little Bear and Boone go back to their own lives somewhere in the past. After a tearful ceremony in which the four become blood brothers, Little Bear and Boone enter the cupboard and the door is locked. Omri finds after a few moments that his friends have disappeared, leaving only the lifeless plastic toys. You can read more about Omri, Patrick, and their friends in the sequels *The Return of the Indian* (1986) and *The Secret of the Indian* (1989). MR

Inge, William (1913–1973) Born and raised in the Middle West, Inge was educated at the University of Kansas and a teachers' college in Tennessee. After working as a teacher and drama editor in St. Louis, he began writing plays at the urging of *Tennessee Williams, who then was instrumental in having one of Inge's plays produced. Inge, who has been called the playwright of the Middle West, wrote about average people who live outside the American mainstream. His plays include *Come Back Little Sheba* (1949), about a pathetic woman and her drunkard husband; *Picnic* (1953), about the effect a young man has on the lives of four small-town women; and *Bus Stop* (1955), about a group of snowbound travelers who reflect a cross section of American life. *Come Back Little Sheba* was filmed in 1952, *Picnic* in 1955, and *Bus Stop* in 1956. YA

Innes, Michael [John Innes Mackintosh Stewart] (1906–) A British scholar and critic and a don at Oxford University, Innes has written many detective novels noted for their displays of erudition. Innes's plots and characters are among the finest in modern tales of murder. His first was *Seven Suspects* (1936), which introduced John Appleby, then a Scotland Yard inspector who later becomes head of the London Metropolitan Police and eventually retires to become a private investigator. A year later Innes and Appleby attracted more attention with *Hamlet, Revenge* (1937), in which murder occurs at a country house where a performance of *William Shakespeare's *Hamlet* is being given. Appleby is as well educated as the author and delights in recognizing obscure quotations from little-known works. *Lament for a Maker* (1938) is notable for its setting and atmosphere, evoking Innes's native Scotland. Other Appleby novels include *Appleby and Honeybath* (1983), in which Appleby and fellow sleuth Charles Honeybath investigate the mysterious disappearance of a dead body from a locked room, and *Appleby and the Ospreys* (1986), in which Appleby investigates the murder of Lord Osprey and searches for the dead man's missing collection of antique coins.

As John Stewart, and as a scholar of literature, Innes has written *Eight Modern Writers* (1963). You may also like to read his biographies of *Joseph Conrad and *Rudyard Kipling. If you like Innes's detective novels, you will also enjoy those of *Margery Allingham, *Agatha Christie, *Ngaio Marsh, and *Dorothy L. Sayers. YA

Innocents Abroad, The: or, The New Pilgrim's Progress (1869) By *Mark Twain, this amusing travel book was based on a series of letters to the San Francisco newspaper *Alta California* and two New York City newspapers. Written during a tour of the Old World in 1867, it made Twain famous. For more than five months Twain traveled through Europe, Greece, the Crimea, the Holy Land, Egypt, and Spain. He wrote about shipboard life, the people he met, and exotic scenes. He compared foreign manners and customs with those of America and described the comic misadventures of unsophisticated tourists. Defiantly American, Twain made fun of the sentimental travel writing of the time, refusing to be impressed by everything he saw. Alternating humorous with serious letters, he also criticized aspects of American life. Twain delighted in ridiculing tourists who were too immersed in their guidebooks to formulate their own opinions. Friendship with one of his fellow passengers on the tour eventually led Twain to a meeting with the man's sister, who later became Twain's wife. There are many editions of this American classic, among them two inexpensive paperbacks. YA

Inquisition This court of the Roman Catholic Church was established in the 13th century to suppress heresy. First used to fight the Albigensians, who challenged the church's authority with their beliefs, the Inquisition soon expanded to combat all forms of heresy in Europe. Though the right to try heretics was reserved to itself by the church in order to keep the Inquisition out of politics, it soon became a way of getting rid of personal enemies. The Inquisition you normally think of is the Spanish Inquisition, started in 1478. It was much more cruel than the Inquisition in northern Europe. Its first Grand Inquisitor, Tomás de Torquemada (1420–1498), has become the *symbol of inquisitors who used torture to expose heretics. You can read about the Spanish Inquisition in the history *Torquemada and the Spanish Inquisition* (1913) by the Italian-born English writer Rafael Sabatini (1875–1950) and also in the biographical novel *Torquemada* (1966) by *Howard Fast. YA

Inspector Maigret See *Jules Maigret.

Intruder, The (1969) This suspenseful novel by *John Rowe Townsend is set in an English village on the Irish Sea. Sixteen-year-old Arnold Haithwaite lives with a relative, Ernest Haithwaite, an elderly man he calls Dad even though everyone knows that Ernest is not Arnold's father. Arnold and Ernest take occasional paying guests in their small house, and Arnold makes a little money guiding tourists over the treacherous Skirl Sands to visit an ancient stone church. There, at certain times of year, the tides cover the sands, coming in with great speed and catching careless visitors unaware. A stranger, who claims to have exactly the same name as Arnold, convinces Ernest that he is a long-lost Haithwaite nephew. Talk of the family history revives questions in young Arnold's mind about his own parents and unexplained background. The aura of menace about the stranger increases as he gradually takes over Ernest's house. Under the stranger's sinister influence Ernest becomes seriously ill. Arnold rescues Ernest with help from outside, but Arnold must fight off the vengeful stranger at their final chilling encounter on Skirl Sands. MR

Intruder in the Dust (1948), by *William Faulkner, is a mystery story of the Deep South, a complex tale of race relations and a young man's developing awareness of others. It is told by a single narrator in a direct manner. In a small town in Faulkner's imaginary *Yoknapatawpha County, Mississippi, in the 1930s, 12-year-old Chick Mallison falls into an icy creek in the presence of a dignified old black man, Lucas Beauchamp. Lucas takes Chick to his cabin to dry out, but refuses to accept money for the food Chick eats there. Long after the incident, Chick is uneasy about having to feel grateful to a black man. Four years later, Lucas is arrested for the murder of a white man, Vinson Gowrie, and asks Chick's uncle, Gavin Stevens, a lawyer, to help him. Lucas tells Chick that Vinson was not shot with Lucas's gun. Determined to prove his innocence and prevent the lynching that will almost certainly be his fate, Lucas tells Chick to dig up Vinson's corpse and ask the sheriff to have the bullet

---

MR = Middle Reader   YA = Young Adult Reader   * = See this main entry

wounds examined by an expert. Helped by two friends, Chick opens Vinson's grave only to find the body of Jake Montgomery, a timber dealer of doubtful reputation. While a crowd assembles in town to await the expected lynching of Lucas, Vinson's father and two brothers join the search for Vinson's body. It is found buried in quicksand. Lucas reveals that he saw Crawford Gowrie murder his brother Vinson. In this version of the story of *Cain and Abel, Crawford rids himself of the witness to his crimes and shady deals, and then kills Montgomery when he interferes. After being taken by the sheriff, Crawford commits suicide in his cell. Lucas is freed and reasserts his independence by paying Stevens and Chick for their assistance. The novel was adapted for film in 1949. YA

Invisible Man (1952) By *Ralph Ellison, this compelling novel is about the plight of a nameless black man in American society. In the painful process of learning the ways of the world, like a modern-day *Candide, the hero is first a high school student in the South and then a student at a black college. Forced into an adult environment for which he is unprepared, he works in a Northern factory, experiences the cruelty of a big city, and becomes a leader of the Brotherhood, a militant organization for social change. Finally, after a series of bizarre and sometimes violent adventures, he escapes to an underground existence in a coal cellar illuminated by 1,369 lightbulbs that use electricity from an illegal power source. He begins to adjust to the idea that life on earth is senseless, full of danger, and often insanely funny. He sees that his lack of identity, or his invisibility, is the result of people's refusal really to look at him, yet invisibility represents a kind of liberation. Invisibility frees him from the labels others of both races would like to assign to him. He gives up the idea of playing a role created by forces outside himself, accepts the absurdity of his situation, and even learns to laugh at his predicament. If you enjoyed this novel, you may want to read *The Autobiography of an Ex-Colored Man* (1912), by James Weldon Johnson (1871–1938). YA

Ionesco, Eugène (1912–) A Romanian-born French playwright and critic, Ionesco is an important member of what came to be called the Theater of the Absurd, whose dramatists included *Samuel Beckett and *Harold Pinter. While learning English, Ionesco was provoked by the inane and stilted language of his textbook. The result was the avant-garde one-act drama *The Bald Soprano* (1949), in which Ionesco uses platitudes to create a new form of stage dialogue. Surrealistic, vague, plotless, and often comic, his plays are highly expressive of Ionesco's belief that life is without meaning and purpose, that people are unable to control their fate, and that real communication between people is impossible. Among Ionesco's other themes are a horror of death, dislike of conformity, and deep resentment of a society based on ready-made ideas, where values are learned by rote but seldom felt. Other one-act plays include *The Lesson* (1951), about the absurdity of indoctrination; *The New Tenant* (1955), which dramatizes the meaninglessness of furniture; and *The Killer* (1959), about helplessness in the face of a stalking killer. In *Rhinoceros* (1959), a full-length play about mass hysteria, a group of people united by their fear of rhinoceroses fall into a spiritual decline and undergo disturbing changes. YA

Ipcress File, The (1962) The narrator and central figure in this espionage novel by *Len Deighton is nameless. You meet him as he is joining W.O.O.C.(P.), a British secret service agency. He is set the task of tracking down a Soviet operation that appears to be kidnapping and brainwashing English biochemists in London. He comes upon the trail of a man known as Jay who has a background of suspicious dealings. Sent to a Pacific atoll, where a neutron bomb is to be tested, the narrator is framed for a murder he did not commit and is drugged. He ends up in what is apparently Hungary, though he finds out when he escapes that it is not that country. Confronting those he believes the cause of his troubles, the narrator turns the tables on Jay and shows that a very high official in W.O.O.C.(P.) is a double agent. Like the espionage novels of *John Le

Carré, this story is told in an abrupt manner, making it realistic but sometimes hard to follow. In a movie made of the book in 1965, the central character is called Harry Palmer. YA

Iphigenia, in Greek mythology, is the daughter of *Agamemnon and Clytemnestra and the sister of *Orestes. Because Agamemnon has offended the goddess *Artemis, the Greek fleet was stopped at Aulis, and the expedition was delayed. To pacify Artemis, Agamemnon finally consents to sacrifice the life of his daughter. In the best-known version of the story, Iphigenia is prepared to die for Greece, but Artemis rescues her from death at the last moment and takes her to Taurus, now the Crimea, on the Black Sea. There, Iphigenia becomes a priestess of Artemis and later saves the life of Orestes. Iphigenia is the subject of two plays by *Euripedes and figures prominently in dramas by *Aeschylus, *Sophocles, the French dramatist Jean Racine (1639–1699), and the German poet *Johann Wolfgang von Goethe. The German composer Christoph Gluck (1714–1787) wrote two tragic operas based on the story of Iphigenia.

Irish Literary Renaissance was a writers' movement that worked to create literature with a truly Irish character, distinct from the literature of England, through the study and revival of ancient Irish legends and folk tales. *William Butler Yeats helped start the movement, which was partly the outcome of a trend toward political nationalism that developed in Ireland at the end of the 19th century. In 1902 Yeats and the Irish playwright Lady Augusta Gregory (1859–1932) established the Irish National Theatre Society, later called the Abbey Theatre, which became the movement's most famous institution. It achieved an international reputation through its staging of the plays of *John Millington Synge and *Sean O'Casey. The movement is said to have influenced the work of *James Joyce. See also *James Stephens.

Iron Curtain, The Popularized shortly after the end of World War II by Winston Churchill,

prime minister of Great Britain, this term describes the Soviet Union's attempt to put up barriers between the communist countries of Eastern Europe and the noncommunist nations of Western Europe. It refers to the many restrictions that made it difficult for people in the West to communicate with people in the East. Typical of the restrictions was the Berlin Wall, built in 1961 by the East German government but dismantled in 1989. The Wall kept people in East Berlin from crossing the border into a freer and more prosperous West Berlin. The Iron Curtain was the central *symbol of the Cold War, or the noncombatant conflict between the East and the West, which became the inspiration of almost all of the spy fiction written after World War II. Many writers, such as *John Le Carré, have used the constant struggle between the United States and the Soviet Union during this period as the basis for their novels. See also the *Bamboo Curtain.

irony is a way of speaking or writing in which the real meaning of words is contradicted by their literal meaning. For irony to work, the listener or reader must be aware of the contrast between what is said and what is really meant. For example, consider "That was a brilliant remark!" The irony depends on the listener's understanding that just the opposite is intended: "That was a foolish remark!" In *William Shakespeare's *Julius Caesar, Mark Antony uses irony in his speech to the citizens of Rome. He appears to agree with *Brutus that Caesar was ambitious, but gives numerous examples of his nobility and lack of ambition while repeatedly maintaining that Brutus, Caesar's murderer, is an honorable man. His audience understands the irony.

Ironical situations in stories usually involve contrast between what is expected and what occurs, the thief who is robbed, the hunter who becomes the hunted. In *O. Henry's *"The Gift of the Magi," James and Della Young are too poor to buy each other Christmas gifts. Each sacrifices a prized possession for the other. James gives up his pocket watch to buy Della an adornment for her beautiful long hair. Ironically, Della has cut and sold her hair to buy James a fob for his cherished watch. A special kind of irony, called dramatic irony, depends on the audience or reader being aware of a situation when the character or characters are not. For example, the audience of a play may know what is in store for the heroine long before she herself realizes it.

Irving, John (Winslow) (1942–) A writer and teacher, Irving is best known for the very popular novel *The World According to Garp* (1978). His writing is energetic, imaginative, and full of unexpected twists and turns. He has described his work as soap opera in disguise. Irving's macabre sense of humor and taste for violence are offset by an unusual sensitivity to current social problems, particularly women's issues. *Garp*, an outrageous blend of comedy and tragedy, is the saga of Jenny Fields, a nurse, her son T.S. Garp, and his wife and two sons. *The Hotel New Hampshire* (1981), another novel, tells about the eccentric Berry family. The story is crammed with horrendous events, loud jokes, and exotic characters. *The Cider House Rules* (1985) takes place in an orphanage in Maine, where the doctor in charge illegally performs safe abortions. In *A Prayer for Owen Meany* (1989), the hero is a Christlike figure with a squeaky voice who believes that nothing is accidental and who foresees his own death. *Garp* was adapted for film in 1982 and *The Hotel New Hampshire* was filmed in 1984. YA

Irving, Washington (1783–1859) Born within weeks of the British surrender at Yorktown, Irving was named for the great American hero of the Revolution. Irving was one of the first American writers to gain international fame and respect. He wrote under various pseudonyms. He called himself "Jonathan Oldstyle, Gent." when he wrote for New York newspapers. *"Diedrich Knickerbocker" was the pseudonym he used when he published *A History of New York* (1809). Using still another pseudonym, "Geoffrey Crayon, Gent.," Irving achieved enormous success at home and abroad with *The Sketch Book* (1819, 1820). Besides sections giving an American visitor's view of Britain, *The Sketch Book* includes his most famous tales, *"Rip Van Winkle," about the New Yorker who slept for 20 years, and *"The Legend of Sleepy Hollow," about the schoolmaster *Ichabod Crane, who is terrified by his meeting with the headless horseman. Over the years Irving produced many books, but he achieved enduring fame with these early sketches and tales.

In 1826 Irving went to Madrid. Spain fascinated him, and he wrote *The History of the Life and Voyages of Columbus* (1828) and *The Alhambra* (1832). The tales and legends related by Irving about the Moors and the Spaniards are still popular in Spain as well as in America. Irving was the American Minister to Spain from 1842 until 1846. He spent the last years of his life at Sunnyside, his home on the Hudson River in Tarrytown, New York. There he worked on his monumental *The Life of George Washington* (1855–1859), which he regarded as his crowning achievement. The great effort he devoted to the biography of his namesake undermined his health, and he died a few months after completing it. YA

Isaac A son of *Abraham, Isaac was the second patriarch of the Hebrews. He and his wife, Rebekah, had twin sons, Esau and Jacob. Esau, the first born, is described in the *Bible as "red, all over like an hairy garment," whereas Jacob was "a quiet man." One day when Esau was very hungry, he sold his birthright as eldest son to Jacob for "bread and pottage [soup] of lentils." Furthermore, Rebekah tricked Isaac, when he was old and nearly blind, into blessing Jacob as his inheritor and successor in place of Esau. Jacob had 12 sons who were the founders of the 12 tribes of Israel. Today, if you give away something of value for very little, you are said to have sold out for a "mess of pottage."

Iseult [Isolde] See *Tristan and Iseult.

Isherwood, Christopher (1904–1986) An Anglo-American novelist, playwright, and teacher, Isherwood is known mainly for his novels set in Germany in the 1930s. He was a fine prose stylist and a writer of great honesty and expressiveness. He was especially concerned about the fate of intellectuals in an oppressive society. Most of his work is based on events of his own life. In 1929 Isherwood went to Germany to visit the English poet W.H. Auden (1907–1973) in Berlin, and remained there until 1933, gathering material for the novels. *The Last of Mr. Norris* (1935) is notable for the seductive character of its aging hero, Arthur Norris, a *symbol of a corrupt society, who is lovable in spite of his criminal activities, which involve selling secrets to the *Nazis. In *Goodbye to Berlin* (1939) Isherwood describes a series of individuals against the sinister background of emerging Nazi power. The novels were republished together as *The Berlin Stories* (1948), and again as *The Berlin of Sally Bowles* (1975). The English playwright John Van Druten (1901–1957) based a play, *I Am a Camera* (1951), on these novels. They were also adapted in 1966 as the Broadway musical *Cabaret*, of which a film version was produced in 1972. Isherwood's later works include the novel *A Single Man* (1964), about a homosexual man mourning the death of his lover. YA

Ishmael In the book of *Genesis in the *Bible, Ishmael is a son of *Abraham and half brother of *Isaac. His mother, Hagar, an Egyptian, was a servant of Sarah, Abraham's wife. Sarah was jealous of Hagar because Sarah had not up to that time been able to have a child as Hagar had. Sarah sent Hagar into the wilderness, and when Hagar was near starvation, she was visited by an angel of God who instructed her to call her child Ishmael. The angel said, "He will be a wild man; his hand will be against every man and every man's hand against him." Thus, the name Ishmael came to mean an outcast of society. He had 12 sons and is considered by the followers of *Islam to be the ancestor of the Arabs, in contrast to Isaac, an ancestor of the Israelites. In the novel *Moby-Dick* by *Herman Melville, the narrator is called Ishmael.

Ishtar is one of the most important figures in Babylonian and Assyrian mythology, a goddess worshiped as an earth mother and symbol of fertility. She is also identified with the Sumerian goddess Inanna; with the Phoenician goddess Astarte or Ashtaroth; with the Greek goddess *Aphrodite; and with the Roman goddess Venus. Daughter of the supreme god Anu, Ishtar is sometimes characterized by violently opposing forces, representing death and destruction as well as the giving of life. In one famous legend, similar to the Greek story of *Demeter, Ishtar journeys to the underworld to free her husband and is herself imprisoned. Without her presence on earth, living things wither and die, but she is saved and returns triumphant.

Isis is an important goddess worshipped by the ancient Egyptians as the ideal wife and mother, the giver of life and comfort, and the protector of the sick and the dead. Her name comes from the Greek form of the Egyptian hieroglyph (a symbol used to represent a word or idea) for throne, and she is often shown wearing a headdress shaped like that hieroglyph. Isis is known as both the wife of Osiris, god of fertility and of the underworld, and as his sister. It is her magical powers that bring Osiris back to life after he is murdered by his brother, the god Seth. Hosus, the son of Isis and Osiris, is hidden by his mother until he is old enough to avenge his father's death. Worshipped throughout Egypt, in the seaport of Alexandria Isis was the patron of sailors and their families. Her temples and her priests were established later in the Roman Empire, where her mysteries and rites were celebrated as recently as the 6th century A.D.

Islam One of the major religions of the world, with about 925 million followers, mostly in Asia and Africa, who are called Muslims (Moslems), Islam was founded by *Muhammad. He is considered by Muslims to be in the same line of leaders and prophets as *Moses, *Abraham, *Joseph, *David, and *Jesus in the *Bible. Islam began among Arabs, who are said to be descended from *Ishmael, one of Abraham's sons. Beginning about A.D. 610 Muhammad began having visions that resulted in his writing down what became the *Koran, the holy book of Islam. The faith is based on five principles: there is no God but God (Allah) and Muhammad is His prophet; Allah must be prayed to five times daily; charity must be practiced; Ramadan, the ninth month of the Muslim year, must be observed by daytime fasting; and every adult Muslim should, if possible, make a pilgrimage (*hadj*) to Mecca once in his or her lifetime. In addition there are several prohibitions, such as not drinking alcohol or eating pork. It was in Mecca, a city in western Saudi Arabia, that Muhammad began his mission. If you would like to learn more about Islam, try *Islam* (1977) by I(vy) G(ordon) Edmonds (1917–) and *The House of Islam* (1975) by Kenneth Cragg (1913–) and Marston Speight (1924–). Older readers may enjoy *A History of the Arab People* (1991) by Albert Hourani (n.d.), which tells about the rise of Islam and its spread throughout the Arab world. MR & YA

Island of the Blue Dolphins (1960), by *Scott O'Dell, tells the story of 12-year-old Karana, an American Indian girl who is stranded on an island with her younger brother. The rest of her tribe left after they were attacked by Aleuts, a tribe that had come to hunt otter. Even though Karana believes she will soon be picked up by a ship, she realizes that she must prepare for her survival. This becomes even more urgent after her brother is attacked and killed by a pack of wild dogs. She builds a house surrounded by a stout fence made out of whale bones, gathers food, and makes weapons. Karana has sworn vengeance on the pack of dogs and begins to hunt them, but finds that she cannot bring herself to kill the leader of the pack after she tracks it down and wounds it, even though the dog killed her brother. Instead she nurses the dog back to health, and in time it becomes her best friend on the island. Karana is kept too busy with the business of survival to think much about how lonely she is, but when the Aleuts come back, Karana makes friends with a young girl despite her fear that she will be seen by the rest of the tribe. When the girl must leave, Karana tries to satisfy her need for friendship by becoming close to the wild animals of the island. She remains for 18 years and is finally picked up by a ship and taken to the mainland. This novel is based on the true story of a young Native American girl who lived on the island of San Nicolas off the California coast between 1835 and 1853. *Zia* (1976) is a sequel to the story of Karana. *Island of the Blue Dolphins* won the *Newbery Medal in 1961. It was adapted for film in 1964. MR & YA

It All Began with Jane Eyre; Or, the Secret Life of Franny Dillman (1980), by *Sheila Greenwald, is a funny novel about an imaginative 13-year-old girl. Franny has a passion for reading, especially classics like *Jane Eyre*. She likes to read in her closet, armed with a flashlight and a good supply of food. Her well-intentioned mother gives Franny some realistically written novels about teenage problems, but these are problems that Franny does not have. Her life is really boring, nobody in her family uses drugs, her parents are *not* on the verge of a divorce, and even her brother and sister are bearable. Convinced that life can be guided by the rules of novels, she decides she will find melodrama and excitement in her life if she looks hard enough. She begins to observe the relationships around her and develops a taste for creative interpretation. A conversation between Franny's father and her sister's friend Hyacinth Nungazer causes Franny's imagination to take flight. When the Dillmans become alarmed by Franny's odd behavior, an emergency meeting of the Dillman and Nungazer families is called and Franny has to explain herself. To her great embarrassment and eventual relief, her mystery is solved to the accompaniment of much laughter. MR

It's Like This, Cat (1963), a remarkable novel by *Emily Neville, is an easygoing story that is nevertheless compelling. Dave Mitchell, who is 14 years old and lives in New York City, sometimes needs a change of scenery or a place to collect his thoughts. He goes to visit Aunt Kate, who is not really his aunt. Because she wears old clothes and takes in stray cats,

---

MR = Middle Reader   YA = Young Adult Reader   * = See this main entry

she is called Crazy Kate the Cat Woman. Aunt Kate gives Dave a stray tomcat, called Cat, that becomes important in his life. Cat helps him make friends, especially Mary, who becomes his first real girlfriend. *It's Like This, Cat* celebrates the diversity of New York City neighborhoods, from Gramercy Park to Coney Island to Inwood Park and the Bronx Zoo. It won the *Newbery Award in 1964. MR

Ivanhoe (1820) by *Walter Scott, is the story of a Saxon knight, Wilfred of Ivanhoe, who is in love with his father's ward, Rowena. However, his father, Cedric, wants Rowena to marry Athelstane, who is a royal Saxon, in the hope that their marriage will restore a Saxon to the throne of England. In a fit of rage Cedric banishes his son, and Ivanhoe joins Richard the Lion-Hearted on his crusade. During Richard's absence, his brother, John, plots to take the throne with the help of several disloyal Norman knights, including the sinister Brian de Bois-Guilbert. The plotters are encouraged when Richard is taken prisoner in Austria on his way back from the Holy Land. But Ivanhoe and Richard, who is disguised as the Black Knight, reappear in England at the tournament at Ashby de la Zouch, where they defeat all comers. Ivanhoe is wounded in the fighting and is nursed back to health by the beautiful maiden, Rebecca, who falls in love with him.

Cedric, Rowena, Ivanhoe, Athelstane, Rebecca, and her father, Isaac, are taken prisoner by Bois-Guilbert and carried to Torquilstone castle. After a siege the castle is captured by an outlaw force led by *Robin Hood, and Richard and his friends, except for Rebecca, are rescued. Bois-Guilbert has fallen in love with Rebecca and carries her off to Templestowe. Though she is saved from his advances by the Grand Master of the Order of Templars, Rebecca is exposed to a charge of witchcraft, es-

Rebecca hovering over the dead
Brian de Bois-Guilbert

caping death only by demanding trial by combat. Ivanhoe, grateful to her for nursing his wounds, becomes her champion, opposing Bois-Guilbert, who is chosen as her accuser despite his love for her. In the fight, untouched by Ivanhoe, Bois-Guilbert falls dead, the victim of his own conflicting desires. Rebecca realizes that Ivanhoe's real love is for Rowena and leaves England with her father. A more recent novel about the age of chivalry is *The Black Rose* (1945) by Thomas B. Costain (1885–1965), about an English nobleman's adventures on a dangerous journey to China and back to England in the 13th century. You can also read about knights and knighthood in *Bulfinch's Mythology*. *Ivanhoe* was made into an excellent movie in 1952 and remade in 1982. YA

Jack Tales, The (1943) These folk stories from the mountain country of North Carolina, written down by Richard Chase (1904–1988), were brought to America originally by the early settlers. They were passed down through the hill families by word of mouth. Now deeply rooted in American soil, these tales present Jack as ordinary and cruel, but his adventures are fantastic and funny. Jack outwits and kills evil giants and kings, his greedy brothers, and Death itself. He is usually helped by magical characters and often hindered by ugly old women. Jack's reward is often a pretty wife and gifts of gold, even though he is not always hard-working or even honest. But he is wily as well as lucky and always returns to his farm and his mother. Many of these stories appear in varying form in folklore throughout the world. For example, "Jack and the Bean Tree" is the same story as "Jack and the Beanstalk," which is told by many different peoples.

If you enjoy reading about girls who are as clever as Jack, there are many fine folk and fairy tales in *Womenfolk and Fairy Tales* (1975), edited by Rosemary Minard (1939–), *Clever Gretchen and Other Forgotten Folktales* (1980), retold by Alison Lurie (1926–), and *The Woman in the Moon and Other Tales of Forgotten Heroines* (1985) by James Riordan (1936–). MR

Jackson, Shirley (1919–1965) The event that brought Jackson fame as a writer of *Gothic horror was the publication of her frightening short story *"The Lottery." When she was researching ghosts for her novel *The Haunting of Hill House* (1959), Jackson claimed she had absolutely no desire to see a ghost. But she read so many ghost stories, and ghosts were so much on her mind, that "it became necessary for [her] to read a chapter of *Little Women* every night before [she] turned out the light." Jackson's power to project terror made her the master of the haunted tale. She wrote novels, plays, and stories, many of them truly scary, such as *We Have Always Lived in the Castle* (1962), a bone-chiller involving a house. Her friends claimed that she wrote with a broomstick instead of a pen. Jackson lived with her family in a large old house in Bennington, Vermont. A mother of four, she also captured the combination of high anxiety and domestic comedy that every parent knows in *Life Among the Savages* (1953) and *Raising Demons* (1957). In a nonfiction work, *The Witchcraft of Salem Village* (1956), she pointed out that not one person who confessed to witchcraft was executed. Those executed, mostly women, had insisted on their innocence.

Her stories appear in anthologies, and many of them were dramatized for radio and television. The movie *Lizzie* was made from the novel *The Bird's Nest* (1954) in 1957, and the novel *The Haunting of Hill House* was filmed as *The Haunting* in 1963. YA

Jacob See *Genesis; *Isaac; *Joseph.

Jacob and Owl (1981), by Ada Graham (1931–) and Frank Graham (1925–), is about a barn owl named Ollie that is found by 11-year-old Jacob. Jacob and his mother have just moved to an old farmhouse, and Jacob talks her into letting him use a shed to house the wounded owl. Ollie will not eat at first, but Jacob learns to feed him carefully. Lonely Jacob has found a friend. He and his mother visit an owl sanctuary. They learn how owls are cared for, and find that Ollie, like many wild birds and other creatures, needs legal and physical protection. Jacob is upset at the thought that Ollie may have to go to the sanctuary. Ollie is his only friend, so he decides to keep him. Then a bitter storm shatters a window in the shed, and Ollie escapes. Even with an injured wing, Ollie has chosen freedom. But after some weeks the owl returns, because without two healthy wings he cannot catch enough mice to survive. Jacob soon decides that the bird sanctuary, where he learns to help feed and care for birds, is the proper place for Ollie. This story is illustrated with photographs and is based on the actual practices in a bird sanctuary in Maine. If you enjoyed *Jacob and Owl*, try *A Time to Fly Free* (1983) by *Stephanie S. Tolan, about a boy who helps an elderly man rescue and care for injured birds. MR

Jacob Have I Loved (1980) "but Esau I hated" is a line from the *Bible that, in this novel by *Katherine Paterson, Louise's grandmother often quotes. This classic expression of sibling rivalry sears her feelings because Louise is quietly envious of her twin sister, Caroline. Louise, also known as "Wheeze," is the strong dark twin of the blonde and musical Caroline. Caroline's physical frailty and her musical gifts have kept her at the center of everyone's attention since the moment of the twins' births. No one paid attention to Louise, because she was healthy and quiet. She feels quite forgotten.

The family lives on an island in Chesapeake Bay, where the father tongs for oysters and goes crabbing. The twins' mother is the former island schoolteacher. Their grandmother, who misses nothing and quotes the Bible a lot, lives with them. While Caroline is having voice lessons on the mainland, Wheeze supplements the family income by crabbing from her skiff with her pal, Call. At this point Pearl Harbor is bombed and the United States declares war on Japan and Germany. A stranger, the Captain, returns to the island after an absence of 50 years. He becomes the center of Louise's fantasies. First she thinks he is a *Nazi spy, then he becomes a friend and the object of Louise's love. After a hurricane sweeps his house out to sea, she gives him a consoling hug, and suddenly her body knows. "The Captain had to be seventy or more. I was fourteen, for mercy's sake. Fourteen from seventy was fifty-six. *Fifty-six.* But then my mind would go to the curve of his perfect thumbnail, and my body would flame up like pine pitch." Looking at her own work-roughened hands, she feels she will never be loved.

As the twins develop, Caroline maintains her sweetness and sanity while Louise suffers severe pain and anger. Louise is sure she is crazy. Much of her feeling surrounds the Captain, but the Captain marries a woman with money and helps Caroline continue her singing career. Call grows up enough to work on Louise's father's boat and then goes off to war. Because Caroline is studying in Baltimore and there is no one else strong enough to help, Louise quits school to help her father on his boat. At the end of the war Call comes back not for Louise, but for Caroline. Louise's hard work helps her overcome her feelings of betrayal and find new strength. She at last leaves the island to pursue her education, and she finds a love of her own. *Jacob Have I Loved* won the *Newbery Medal in 1981. MR & YA

Jaguar, My Twin (1976) By Betty Jean Lifton (1926–), this novel is not about a human twin or sibling, but about the spirit twin of Shun, a Mayan who sells flowers on a mountain roadside in Mexico. Shun hopes his spirit twin is a jaguar and that he dreams of it soon, so that he will know which animal will share his life in the supernatural corral. Shun's dream of his jaguar twin comes true, but a more earthly event is coming to his remote village. The Mexican government will bring in electricity if the men of the village want it. Shun's father does, but Manuel is opposed to electricity and asks for the help of an evil shaman. This shaman, whose specialty is sickness and death, schemes to bring low the family of Shun, and he places Shun and his jaguar in great danger. But Shun's mother knows a good shaman, who reverses the spell just in time. Lifton visited Shun's Zinacantec village in Mexico to study the people's beliefs and customs for this story. Lifton's other books on folklore are *The Cock and the Ghost Cat* (1965) and *The One-Legged Ghost* (1968), both of which are based on Japanese legends, and *The Mud Snail Son* (1971), about a snail born to human parents. MR

Jalna is the lakeside home in Canada of the Whiteoak family in a series of novels by *Mazo de la Roche. It was built in the 1850s, and generations of children and horses were raised there. The central thread in all these novels is the large, rosy-red brick house itself. It has five chimneys, becomes ivy-covered, and is occupied by the outspoken matriarch Adeline and her grandson, Renny. No matter where the Whiteoaks go, sooner or later they all return to Jalna. It is their sanctuary, a *symbol of solid, enduring ancestral values, where no changes are permitted to intrude from the outside world. It is a setting of pure romance you can compare with Tara in *Gone With the Wind* or with the fantasy place, Brigadoon, in the Scottish Highlands.

Jalna (1927) was the first book in the series to be published. The Whiteoaks are an exuberant lot, fond of each other and given to boisterous argument at the dinner table. Grandmother, 99 years old, is still vigorous enough to shout commands ("Somebody kiss me, quick!"), and wants to live to celebrate her 100th birthday. Her unmarried sons, Nicholas and Ernest, are devoted to her. A third son, Philip Whiteoak, is dead, but the six children of his two marriages form the younger element of the household.

Meg is 40 years old, solid and sweet tempered, and she looks after the children. Renny is master of Jalna, runs the farm and makes all important family decisions. He is handsome, self-sufficient, and a little remote. The four youngest, who are the children of Philip's second wife, are Eden, Piers, Finch, and Wakefield. This prickly but congenial group is disturbed when Piers shows an interest in Pheasant Vaughan, the daughter of a neighbor who was once engaged to Meg. Piers and Pheasant marry secretly and return to Jalna to face a storm of family criticism. Renny proclaims that they shall not be cast out from the tribe, however, and the couple settle in the house. Then Eden, a writer, meets Alayne Archer at his New York publisher's office and falls in love. They marry and return to Canada to a warmer reception than that given to Piers and Pheasant. Time passes, and the house is witness to dramatic changes in both couples' relationships. Against their will, Renny and Alayne discover they love each other. Piers is too wrapped up in farming to see that Pheasant and Eden have become lovers. When the situation explodes, Alayne decides to return to New York. In turmoil, and with many unresolved problems, the Whiteoaks nevertheless celebrate Grandmother's 100th birthday in lavish style. If you enjoyed *Jalna*, try the rest of the series, including *The Building of Jalna* (1944), the first novel in chronological order, and *Mary Wakefield* (1949), probably the best-known novel of the series. *Jalna* was filmed in 1935. YA

Jamaica Inn (1937) By *Daphne du Maurier, this *Gothic novel is set in Cornwall, England, in the early 19th century. Twenty-three-year-old Mary Yellan, after her mother's death, goes to the forbidding moors of Cornwall to live with her Aunt Patience and her husband, Joss Merlyn, the coarse and brutal master of the rundown and shunned Jamaica Inn. She discovers that Joss is the leader of a pirate band that lures ships to their destruction on the rocky coast, kills the survivors, and steals the cargo. Mary plans to escape with Patience and turn Joss in to the authorities, but she does not know whom to trust. Squire Bassat, who seems an honest, if bumbling, magistrate, may be in on the plot. And Joss's brother, Jem, with whom she has fallen in love, is a horse thief. Mary confides in Francis Davey, the vicar of Altarnum, but he turns out to be the leader of the gang. As the authorities move in, Davey kills Joss and Patience and flees with Mary into the moor, where he is shot and killed by Jem. Recognizing Jem's true worth, Mary throws in her lot with him, and together they leave Cornwall. If you enjoyed *Jamaica Inn*, try *Ross Poldark* (1945) by Winston Graham (1910–), the first of 11 novels about the adventures of the Poldark family in Cornwall from 1783 to 1815. A TV series based on the Poldark series was made in 1984. *Jamaica Inn* was filmed in 1939 and 1985. YA

James, Henry, Jr. (1843–1916) Born in the United States, James made England his home, and his epitaph reads "Henry James—Novelist—Citizen of Two Countries—Interpreter of his Generation on both Sides of the Sea." And though he died in London, England, he was buried in Cambridge, Massachusetts. James was the son of a wealthy, educated man who believed that children should be raised as citizens of the world. He would not allow his children to grow up bound to any one religious or political system, moral or ethical code, or personal habit. A variety of tutors taught the James children in New York before the father took his family to Europe for three years when Henry was 12. Later, James lived a cosmopolitan life in New York, London, and Paris, and traveled to Italy, Switzerland, California, and Florida. His last American home was in Cambridge, Massachusetts, but his main home was in England.

He was a prolific writer of essays, criticism, novels, novellas, short stories, and plays. He never wrote poetry and his plays were not successful. He thought of himself as a detached spectator of life. His method of writing fiction was called psychological realism. He was not interested in people of action. Instead he wrote about people of wealth and leisure, about their domestic adventures and manners, about their affairs of the heart and the mind. He described the lives of Europeans in America and Americans in Europe, writing so richly and so delicately of the hearts and nerves and moods of an age that his influence on other writers has been deep and long.

James wrote 22 novels, 15 plays, and 115 short stories. Among his novels, *Washington Square* and *The Bostonians* (1886) take place in America, and *The Wings of the Dove* (1902), *The Ambassadors* (1903), and *The Golden Bowl* (1904) are set in England. His most famous short story is *The Turn of the Screw*, a fine tale of the supernatural. *What Maisie Knew* (1897) is a short novel told from the point of view of a little girl.

To show his support of England during World War I James became a British citizen. He died before the war was over, and his sister-in-law, the widow of his brother William James (1842–1910), a famous psychologist and philosopher, smuggled his ashes through customs to return them to the country of his birth. *Washington Square* was produced as a movie in 1949, and *The Turn of the Screw* was filmed in 1961. YA

James, P(hyllis) D(orothy) (1920–) The medical backgrounds and the sensitivity to those suffering from chronic or terminal illness that are common in the detective novels of this English author come from her personal life and career. James's husband was mentally ill from the end of World War II until his death in 1964. She worked as an administrator in the National Health Service and a senior civil servant in the Home Office, the government department in Great Britain that deals with domestic concerns. James's first novel was *Cover Her Face*, in which a housemaid is murdered and Chief Inspector *Adam Dalgliesh is introduced. In *Shroud for a Nightingale* (1971), also featuring Dalgliesh, a student nurse is killed by poisoned milk. Another fictional detective, Cordelia Gray, was introduced in *An Unsuitable Job for a Woman* (1972), which involves the apparent suicide of a prominent biologist at Cambridge University. Gray is a young and ambitious private investigator; Dalgliesh appears near the end and is in friendly competition with Gray. With *Innocent Blood* (1980) James turned from the pure detective story to an account of an adopted 18-year-old girl's search for her real parents and its shocking result. *Devices and Desires* (1990), the setting of which is the neighborhood of a nuclear power plant, is as much a novel of personalities as a detective story. Several of these stories have been produced for television, including *Devices and Desires* in 1991. If you enjoy these books, you will like those of *Martha Grimes and *Ruth Rendell. YA

James, Will (1892–1942) Born in Montana, Will had no formal schooling and began working on cattle and horse ranches when he was 13 years old. He performed in rodeos after he had perfected his riding skills while on the Canadian range capturing wild horses. Injured by a bucking bronco, he began to draw and write. He said in his first book, *Cowboys North and South* (1924), "Good english is all right, but when I want to say something I believe in hitting straight to the point without fishing for decorated language. Me, never being to school and having to pick up what I know in grammar from old magazines and saddle catalogs scattered in cow camps would find plenty of territory for improvement in the literary range." But James appealed to readers and publishers alike, and he wrote more than 20 books. On winning the *Newbery Medal in 1927 for *Smoky: The Cowhorse*, he said, "I don't know about that medal . . . but it's fine with me. . . . I was riding none other than Smoky . . . only a few years ago. He was all the horse I wrote of in the story. The happenings was none less as was in it." From his illustrations and writings of horses in action, James was able to buy a 12,000-acre ranch outside Billings, Montana. James also wrote *Cow Country* (1927), *Sun Up: Tales of the Cow Camps* (1931), and *Flint Spears: Cowboy Rodeo Contestant* (1938). A movie was made from *Lone Cowboy: My Life Story* (1930) in 1933. MR & YA

James and the Giant Peach (1961) By *Roald Dahl, this book tells the story of young James Henry Trotter and his marvelous adventure aboard a magical giant peach. Orphaned at 4, James is sent to live with his horrible old aunts—skinny, mean Aunt Spiker and fat, slobby Aunt Sponge. They make him work all the time and never give him treats or let him play with other children. James at 7 is "the saddest and loneliest little boy that you could find." One day a mysterious old man appears with some magic crystals he gives to James. "*Marvelous* things will start happening to you," he tells the boy, "*fabulous, unbelievable* things—and, you will never be miserable again in your life." While carrying the crystals home, James slips and spills them all under an old peach tree. Very soon after, a fresh new peach appears on the old tree. It grows so fast that by the next morning it is as big as a house. James discovers a path into the peach, where he finds some friendly giant insects who are expecting him: a cheerful grasshopper, a very creative spider, a dainty ladybug, a grouchy centipede, an accommodating glowworm, and a melancholy earthworm. Soon its weight causes the giant peach to break from the old tree and roll downhill. Aunt Sponge and Aunt Spiker are flattened dead by the peach rolling over them. With the companionship of his new friends, James has a wonderful adventure sailing the peach across the Atlantic Ocean from England to New York City. At the end of the voyage James is declared a hero, and the rest of his life is happy and full. MR

James Bond is the handsome hero of the espionage novels of *Ian Fleming. Like his creator, he is a commander in the British Royal Navy and an intelligence officer. Bond is known as "007" and is "licensed to kill." Also copying his creator, he likes to gamble and drive fast cars. Fleming said he named Bond after an ornithologist who wrote a book about the birds of the West Indies. Bond appears in Fleming's first novel, *Casino Royale* (1953). After starring for years in nearly one book a year, Bond ended his career in *You Only Live Twice* (1964). He traveled to all parts of the world, battled the most villainous of villains, met beautiful women who fell for him at first sight, and over and over again saved the world—or at least Great Britain—from evil domination. Since Fleming's death others have carried on the Bond saga, but the plots have become trite and repetitious. The books about Bond became even more popular after President John F. Kennedy (1917–1963) let it be known in 1961 that he read them. In the many movies made from the books, Bond was first and most appropriately played by the actor Sean Connery (1930–). YA

Jane Eyre (1847), by *Charlotte Brontë, is one of the most popular novels in English literature and quite unlike any other book of its time. It is the story of a woman's need for love and independence, told with fierce conviction and without a trace of sentimentality. It begins when an orphan girl is taken to live with her Aunt Reed at Gateshead Hall, in England. The aunt and her three unpleasant children treat 8-year-old Jane with contempt while demanding her obedience and eternal gratitude. When Jane is 10 years old, Aunt Reed arranges for her to attend Lowood School. A dreary and comfortless boarding school for charity students, it nevertheless provides Jane with a respectable education. Eight years later Jane obtains a position as governess to Adela, the young ward of *Mr. Rochester of Thornfield. She finds the master of Thornfield dark, moody, abrupt, but strangely kind. Hearing an odd and sinister laugh in the night, Jane bravely goes to investigate and finds Rochester asleep with his bed curtains on fire. The servants hint that an eccentric servant, Grace Poole, may be responsible. Then Mr. Mason, an unexpected visitor from the West Indies, is attacked in his bed, presumably by Grace Poole, and Rochester and Jane help Mason to leave Thornfield before the other house guests hear of the incident. The friendship between Jane and Rochester deepens, but Jane is painfully aware of Rochester's attention to Miss Ingram, a showy society beauty.

Jane Eyre curtsying before Aunt Reed in a modern woodcut by Fritz Eichenberg (1901–1990)

During a visit to Aunt Reed, Jane learns that three years earlier her uncle, John Eyre, had offered to adopt her. Out of spite, Aunt Reed never informed her niece and told John Eyre that Jane had died in a typhus epidemic at Lowood. At Thornfield again, and fully aware of her love for Rochester, Jane accepts his proposal of marriage after being assured that he flirted with Miss Ingram only to make her jealous. At the wedding, Mason reappears and stops the ceremony, claiming Rochester is already married to Mason's sister, Bertha. Rochester is forced to admit that his incurably insane wife has lived for 10 years at Thornfield, watched over by Grace Poole, and that Bertha is the source of the night disturbances.

Shocked and unable to accept living with Rochester as his mistress, Jane leaves Thornfield determined never to return. After being taken in by the Rivers family, she gets word that Uncle John has died and willed his fortune to her. On an impulse, she goes to

Thornfield, only to find the house a burned ruin. The lunatic Bertha had started the fire and jumped to her death from the roof. Rochester is alive, but blind. Jane finds him on a nearby estate, and the two lovers are finally free to marry and live together.

The character of Jane is shown not only in her actions, but in a series of thoughts and imaginary conversations set down in great detail. Jane is small, thin, and not particularly beautiful, and has little hope that life will bring her happiness. During the hardships of her early years she develops unusual strength of character, a passionate desire for freedom, and an ability to love wholeheartedly. Her honesty and bluntness are rare, especially at a time when young women were expected to be obedient, charming, and uncritical. Movies were made of *Jane Eyre* in 1934 and 1944. YA

Jane Marple is a fictional amateur detective invented by *Agatha Christie and based on Christie's grandmother. Marple is an elderly spinster, tall and thin, with blue eyes. She formerly walked and gardened but now has to confine her activities to knitting, gossiping, and keeping an eye on her neighbors in the English village of St. Mary Mead. The first novel featuring Miss Marple was *Murder at the Vicarage* (1930). Others in which she helps the unappreciative police solve murders include *The Body in the Library* (1942), *A Murder Is Announced* (1950), and *At Bertram's Hotel* (1965), the setting for which is Brown's, the well-known London hotel. Marple is noteworthy also in the person of Margaret Rutherford (1892–1972), an English actress who portrayed her in four movies, beginning with *Murder She Said* (1961), based on the book *The 4:50 from Paddington* (1957). Since then, other actresses, notably Helen Hayes (1900–) and Joan Hickson (1906–), have played Marple in television productions in a quieter way than the large and booming Rutherford. MR & YA

Jane Pittman, the heroine of *The Autobiography of Miss Jane Pittman* by *Ernest J. Gaines, is a survivor: a small, thin, yet steel-strong lady about 110 years old. She was a slave, a field worker, and a house servant. Miss Pittman is a time capsule of the black experience and an important person in her community because she has survived abuse and neglect with dignity. She manages to maintain a balanced attitude toward her oppressors. Even bigoted white people respect her energy and wisdom. One of her last acts is a brave moment when she goes to town for a civil rights protest, which gives you a hint of what the civil rights movement would be like. YA

Janeway, Elizabeth (1913–) This perceptive novelist usually focuses her stories on the members of a small group or family that is going through a crisis. For example, her best-known work of fiction, *Daisy Kenyon* (1945), concerns a fashion designer and the two men in her life. Janeway's other novels, especially *The Walsh Girls* (1943), *The Question of Gregory* (1949), and *The Third Choice* (1959), are admired for their treatment of relationships among women. If you enjoy reading Janeway's fiction, you may want to turn to her famous work of nonfiction, *Man's World, Woman's Place: A Study in Social Mythology* (1971). In this book she reveals the gap between the myth of the woman at home and the actual experience of most women in the United States. You will also enjoy a group of essays entitled *Between Myth and Morning: Women Awakening* (1974). *Daisy Kenyon* was produced as a movie in 1947. YA

Jason, a hero of Greek mythology, is sent on a quest by his uncle, Pelias, who has seized the kingdom of Iolcus to which Jason is the rightful heir. The gods, said the uncle, would not allow Jason to claim the throne until he brought back the *Golden Fleece from Colchis, a city at the eastern end of the Black Sea. It is in the care of King Aeëtes and is guarded by a serpent that never sleeps. Jason, after building the 50-oared ship *Argo*, sets forth with a shipload of Greek heroes, called the *Argonauts, among them *Hercules and *Theseus. Surviving the storms and struggles of the voyage, Jason and

The story of Jason and the Golden Fleece appears in nearly all books of Greek myths. One of the best of these is *The Golden Fleece and the Heroes Who Lived Before Achilles* (1921) by Padraic Colum (1881–1972). You will like *The Clashing Rocks: The Story of Jason* (1963) by *Ian Serraillier. Older readers can get more information from the *New Larousse Encyclopedia of Mythology* (1968). MR & YA

Jazz Country (1965) This story by *Nat Hentoff is about a young trumpet player and how he pays his dues in the world of jazz music. Sixteen-year-old Tom Curtis is torn between two worlds: the unknown challenges in the life of a jazz musician, and the predictability of going to college. Believing himself at one with his trumpet, he enters the world of the professional jazzmen he meets at the famed Savoy in New York City. A bass player tells him that he "hasn't any soul. . . . You play that thing as if you've never paid dues. And you haven't. Your life has been too easy for you to be making it as a jazz musician—too white." Though stunned, Tom works to pay his dues over the next few months. He struggles to be accepted by his new friends. His growing awareness of their problems as blacks and as musicians helps him to learn about himself. There is an authenticity in this story that goes beyond jazz music and racial integration. Hentoff nudges his reader into the soul of a black man who happens to be a jazz musician living in a big city. If you like *Jazz Country*, you may enjoy Hentoff's *Does This School Have Capital Punishment?* (1981), which is about a teenage jazz buff accused of marijuana possession in his school, and *Blues for Charlie Darwin* (1982), about a boy and blues music. MR & YA

Jed (1960), by *Peter Burchard, is set in Mississippi during the Civil War. Jed, a 16-year-old Union soldier far from his Wisconsin home, has seen too much killing, brutality, sickness, and suffering. He longs for the war to end so he can go home. One morning Jed finds a boy with a broken leg in the woods near the camp.

Jason slays the serpent and takes the Golden Fleece

the Argonauts arrive at Colchis, where King Aeëtes agrees to part with the Golden Fleece. But he first requires Jason to plant a field with dragon's teeth, a field to be plowed by wild bulls with bronze hooves and breath of flame. Jason first tames the bulls. The dragons' teeth grow into armed men and Jason slays them. He performs these tasks with the magic help of the king's daughter, *Medea the sorceress, who falls in love with him. Medea also helps Jason vanquish the serpent. They flee Colchis together on the *Argo*, taking with them the Golden Fleece.

At home, King Pelias still denies Jason the throne of Iolcus. Weary of waiting, Medea continues her magical ways on Jason's behalf by causing King Pelias's daughters to murder their father, but she and Jason are driven from Iolcus. Jason abandons Medea to marry a princess, arousing Medea's vengeful wrath. Medea murders the princess and flees. In one version of the myth Jason loses favor with the gods and wanders ever after as an outcast. In another version he sails back to Iolcus on the *Argo* and is welcomed as king.

The boy, Philip, hates Yankees and at first resists Jed's help, but Jed carries him to the camp surgeon, has his leg set, and takes Philip to his home. Almost miraculously, the family's farm has not been raided by Union foragers, and Jed convinces the family that he will not reveal its location to anyone else. Jed spends several hours at the farm, away from the war, and wins a private peace with Philip and his family. But the war intrudes when three soldiers follow Jed's tracks and find the farm. Jed has to fight them off to protect Philip's home. If you enjoyed *Jed*, try *The Perilous Road* (1958) by *William O. Steele, about a Yankee-hating Tennessee mountain boy who comes to understand the horror and senselessness of war. MR

Jefferson, Thomas (1743–1826)

A farmer, scientist, educator, inventor, and statesman, Jefferson wrote the Declaration of Independence and for eight years served as the third President of the United States. Jefferson was born in Virginia. After studying law, he married Martha Skelton (1732–1802). Only two of their six children lived to become adults. He designed and built his home, Monticello, which he continually improved over the years. He was a governor of Virginia, was elected to Congress, and served as Secretary of State under George Washington (1732–1799). He became President in 1801 after serving for four years as Vice President under John Adams (1735–1826). Perhaps his most notable achievement was to arrange for the purchase of the Louisiana Territory. Jefferson believed in equality and in a government by popular consent—a government that would ensure the inalienable rights of people, including the pursuit of happiness. He hoped that the aristocracy of wealth and birth could be replaced by one of virtue and talent.

After leaving office, Jefferson continued promoting public education, religious freedom, and a free press. Especially interested in agricultural research, he introduced plants new to Virginia on his estate at Monticello. He sent out the Lewis and Clark expedition to explore the Louisiana Purchase and to collect western plants and animals. He invented numerous devices, set up the original Patent Office, and was a scholar in many scientific fields. Jefferson died at Monticello on the 50th anniversary of the Declaration of Independence. Very young readers will enjoy *Meet Thomas Jefferson* (1967) by Marvin Barrett (1920–). A readable biography is *The Man from Monticello: An Intimate Life of Thomas Jefferson* (1969) by Thomas J. Fleming (1927–). MR & YA

Jeffrey's Ghost and the Leftover Baseball Team (1984)

By David A. Adler (1947–), this novel is about Jeffrey Clark's family's move to a new apartment. The last thing 10-year-old Jeffrey expects to find in a new apartment is a ghost—maybe in an old house, but in an apartment? Jeffrey is lucky. The ghost, Bradford, is friendly, and he and Jeffrey become pals. Bradford has big plans for the neighborhood—he plans to begin a baseball team. Bradford is not visible to other people, of course, but that does not stop Jeffrey from accepting Bradford's help. The team cannot catch or hit, but that is why Bradford is there. Bradford assists with the pitching, and strange things begin to happen in a fast-paced and funny way. If you like Jeffrey and Bradford, you may like some of Adler's more than 30 other books, including *A Little at a Time* (1976), which is about things that grow and change a little at a time, and *Jeffrey's Ghost and the Fifth-Grade Dragon* (1985), a sequel to *Jeffrey's Ghost and the Leftover Baseball Team*. MR

Jem's Island (1982)

by Kathryn Lasky (1944–), is the story of a boy who is allowed to choose the island where he and his father are to go camping. Jem selects No Name Island, off the coast of Maine. It is only a speck of an island, but it is big enough for Jem and his father to locate on a chart of the local waters. It is near enough so they can paddle their loaded kayak to it, and large enough so they can explore it. Jem, anticipating his trip during the preceding winter and spring, plans their provisions and dreams of the smells of supper cooking over a campfire. On the trip at last, Jem and his father spend their nights ashore, and Jem learns to like mackerel eggs for breakfast, usually with bacon. They thrill to the first pink of dawn with its mists providing a perfect setting in which to catch their breakfast and talk about the driftwood whale they find and admire. If you like *Jem's Island*, you may like Lasky's other books, among them *The Night Journey* (1981), about a girl named Rachel who visits her grandmother late at night to hear tales of pogroms, or massacres, of Jews in the old country; *Puppeteer* (1985), about a professional hand puppeteer who mounts a production of "Aladdin and His Wonderful Lamp"; and *Dinosaur Dig* (1990), about an East Coast family on a fossil dig in Montana. MR

Jennifer, Hecate, Macbeth, William McKinley, and Me, Elizabeth (1967) This story, an instant classic by *E.L. Konigsburg, is about Elizabeth, the loneliest girl "in the whole U.S. of A.," and Jennifer, an imaginative girl who dresses like a Pilgrim and claims to be a witch. Elizabeth first sees the scrawny Jennifer sitting in a tree and losing her shoe, but Jennifer claims, "Witches never lose anything." True, almost, Elizabeth thinks, and she decides to become Jennifer's apprentice. Elizabeth first learns to eat raw eggs and to love raw onion sandwiches. Then she learns about *Hecate's chants. The witches from *Macbeth* are called on for assistance. The girls cast short spells to trip people, but most of all Elizabeth and Jennifer pal around, because they both feel the same way about a lot of things—until they make the flying ointment and name a toad Hilary Ezra. Then Elizabeth loses them all, including Jennifer. The book is illustrated by Konigsburg. You may like some of her other books, for instance, *From the Mixed Up Files of Mrs. Basil E. Frankweiler* or *Father's Arcane Daughter*. MR

Jeremiah was a major Israelite prophet whose name is given to a book in the Old Testament of the *Bible. He lived in the 7th and 6th centuries B.C. in the city of Jerusalem during the time of its fall to the Babylonians. After the destruction of the city and its temple, the emphasis in his writings shifts from the nation to the individual. They primarily chronicle his life and record his angry cries concerning the wickedness of his people. The prophet's religious belief remains within his heart instead of within the temple building. *Matthew, the Apostle, reports that many believed that *Jesus was to be the returned Jeremiah. The name Jeremiah is Hebrew and means "God is high." The word has given itself to "jeremiad," a word meaning a prolonged cry, a lament or mournful complaint, an angry denunciation. MR & YA

Jeremy (1919) By *Hugh Walpole, this novel, set in England in 1892, is based in part on the author's own life. It begins as Jeremy Cole, son of a clergyman, turns 8 years old, and it relates his experiences and adventures until, just before his 9th birthday, he leaves home for school. During that time Jeremy shows his growing sense of independence by adopting a stray dog he names Hamlet. Jeremy rebels against the new governess; defends the honor of his Aunt Amy, whom he dislikes, from the rude aunts of the Dean's son, Ernest; and sneaks off to ride the merry-go-round at the annual Pauper's Fair, an event disapproved of by his parents. During this exciting year, rich with adventures, Jeremy learns much about himself and those around him, including his artist uncle, Samuel, who paints pictures nobody understands but who seems to understand what Jeremy is thinking and feeling; and Jeremy's smart but lonely little sister, Mary, who adores him and fears losing him. If you enjoyed *Jeremy*, try the sequels *Jeremy and Hamlet* (1923), about Jeremy's dog, Hamlet; *Jeremy at Crale* (1927), which tells of his schooldays; as well as *Tom Brown's School Days* by Thomas Hughes (1822–1896), about a 19th-century English schoolboy. MR

Jessie's Ghost and Other Stories (1983) by Barbara Ann Porte (1943–) is a collection of imaginative short stories. Porte writes eerie, spine-tingling tales, such as the one about the arrival of Cinderella in the 20th century; or about a ghost who lies buried in his grave, or rather in his bed; or about a child in a hurry who grows old before her time. Porte writes, "The storyteller sits where three worlds meet, before and now and after. . . . She is like the spider woman, plucking bits and pieces from here and there and everywhere, weaving them together, seeing how they fit. 'But is it true,' her listeners ask her, 'did it really happen?' 'Well,' she says, 'it could have happened.' " If you like these original stories, some of Porte's other books are *The Kidnapping of Aunt Elizabeth* (1985), about a school project and a girl learning her family history, and *I Only Made Up the Roses* (1987), in which a 17-year-old girl tells about her family and life. MR

jester is a word often used to mean a person who tells jokes, a buffoon, a comic who entertains with funny stories and quips. Clowns in the circus still dress a little like the court jesters of the 16th and 17th centuries. Court jesters often reported the truth to kings and nobles, so they wore a dunce's conical hat, or a cap with tiny jingling bells, which provided visual fun and a lively sound during the telling of a jest to take the sting from the words. For much the same reason, modern jesters, or comics, on television are accompanied by real or canned laughter and other loud noises during their jokes and pranks. One well-known jester, the Fool in *William Shakespeare's *King Lear*, is an oddly wise man dressed in tatters. His comments on human behavior are bitter, witty, and often filled with song. Another jester, Batman's nemesis—the Joker—is partially based on those jesters who could take advantage of the protection of kings to play practical jokes.

Jesters and jokers, minstrels and jugglers have been around through the ages. Our term "jovial," which means full of fun, comes from *Jove, the supreme god of Roman myth, a great player of practical jokes among the gods.

Jesus or **Jesus Christ** was born about 4 B.C. and crucified about A.D. 29. He was a prophet of the first century of the Christian era. One of the world's major religious figures, he is regarded by his followers as the Messiah, or savior, whose coming was predicted by the Old Testament prophets in the *Bible. Many of the events of his adult life are recorded in the four Gospels of the New Testament of the Bible: *Matthew, *Mark, *Luke, and *John. To Christians he is the Son of God, a person who is both God and human. Stories of miracles surround his birth in Bethlehem, but little is known of his youth and young manhood. One event of Jesus' youth is his trip to the temple in Jerusalem. As a 12-year-old boy, he astonished teachers with his knowledge of the ancient law of Moses. During his life there was much oppression in his native Palestine. After his baptism in the river Jordan by *John the Baptist, Jesus selected 12 disciples, or apostles. They traveled with Jesus throughout this area as he taught his message of God's love for all humanity, healed the sick, and performed miracles. He spoke constantly of peace. By preaching that individuals could be forgiven their sins through the love of God and by his extraordinary healing powers, he developed a large following among the common people. Both Roman and Israelite leaders were disturbed by his attacks on the hypocrisy of the rich. In his travels he predicted the coming of a new Kingdom of God, which the priests regarded as blasphemy, and the Romans as sedition. *Judas Iscariot, one of Jesus' disciples, betrayed him during Passover in Jerusalem. Pontius Pilate, the Roman governor of Judaea, condemned Jesus at the instigation of the Jewish elders, and he was crucified. Christian followers believe that Jesus rose from the dead after three days and later ascended to heaven to assume his seat beside God the Father. See also *Christianity.

Jet Journey (1978), an interesting nonfiction book by Mike Wilson (n.d.) and Robin Scagell (n.d.), gives an excellent description of behind-the-scenes events at a large airport as well as details of how to build your own Concorde plane model, and even how to fly a jumbo jet. The illustrations are in color and show cutaway pictures of sections of airplanes with excellent information about the various parts, such as how hollow wings are made to serve as fuel tanks. There is a graphic depiction of all that is involved in a journey by air: from the building of the plane to the takeoff and landing, including the mechanics who enable the plane to fly safely, the tools used to keep the plane in the air, what is done to keep passengers fed and comfortable, the maneuvers during landing, and the systems for handling the plane once it lands and taxis to the terminal. The book even explains how emergency services are performed. It gives plenty of facts to answer many of the questions you may have about the parts that make up a jumbo jet. MR

Jewett, Sarah Orne (1849–1909) The daughter of a country doctor in a Maine village, Sarah described herself as instantly drooping when shut in a classroom, and her fragile health often kept her reading in the family library at home in South Berwick. She loved to accompany her father on his rounds by horse and buggy. With him she observed every detail of her environment both indoors and outdoors. He talked with her endlessly about what they both saw and felt. She loved to be outdoors. While still a child she began writing. A story about Maine by *Harriet Beecher Stowe sharpened her eyes to the country and village world that she knew so well through the house visits she made with her father. She published her first story in the *Atlantic Monthly* when she was only 19 years old. By the time she was 28 years old, having published *Deephaven* (1877), a collection of sketches about a village, she was considered one of the leading writers of New England. With her friend Annie Fields, she traveled extensively and had many writing friends and acquaintances, among them *John Greenleaf Whittier, *Alfred Tennyson, *Daphne du Maurier, and *Henry James. She always returned to South Berwick to work.

Jewett's first novel, *A Country Doctor* (1884), concerns the growth of a young woman who wants to become a doctor, faces prejudice and discrimination, and has to choose between marriage and a career. *A White Heron* (1886) expresses her feelings about the destruction by advancing science and civilization of all that is wild and natural. *The Country of the Pointed Firs* illuminates the lonely life of fishing and farming in New England. Catching the sharp humor and reserve of isolated working people,

she wrote of them with such clarity that *The Country of the Pointed Firs* has become a minor classic. Jewett was mentor to the young *Willa Cather, who later dedicated her novel *O Pioneers!* (1913) to her. After being thrown from a carriage in 1901, the frail Jewett was unable to write again. YA

Jezebel See *Ahab and Jezebel.

Jim Crow refers to racial segregation laws that were imposed mainly in the South in the late 19th century. The term probably comes from a song by that name performed in minstrel shows around 1830, which featured a black character named Jim Crow. In the 1880s laws were passed in the South that legalized the segregation of blacks, and these were called "Jim Crow laws." These meant that black people were not allowed into many public places, but had to go to separate institutions, or to a special area set aside for their use. *Richard Wright's autobiography, *Black Boy* describes the practical and emotional effects of this separation on everyday life.

Jiminy Cricket appears as the conscience of *Pinocchio in the *Walt Disney movie made in 1940 of this famous old tale of a bad boy. In the film Jiminy Cricket is the narrator. The Blue Fairy asks him to serve as the puppet's conscience when she brings Pinocchio to life. Jiminy scampers breathlessly after the trusting, curious Pinocchio, experiences with him each new danger, and helps him survive and grow into a caring human child. In the original story by Carlo Collodi (Carlo Lorenzini) (1826–1890), Jiminy is the Talking Cricket. He is killed by Pinocchio for telling him the truth about his idle habits. Later, the ghost of the Talking Cricket appears as the doctor in Pinocchio's dream when he is sick. MR

Jimmy Yellow Hawk (1972), by Virginia Driving Hawk Sneve (1933–), who grew up on the Rosebud Sioux reservation in South Dakota, is about a Sioux Indian boy called Little Jim who hates his nickname. His full name is James Henry Yellow Hawk. His father is Big Jim.

MR = Middle Reader   YA = Young Adult Reader   * = See this main entry

Names were earned in legendary days by deeds of valor or by disgrace, according to Jim's great-grandfather. Jim sets out to become a trapper. But he worries about what he might be named, especially after he is sprayed by a skunk he finds in one of his traps. Since his clothes stink, he burns them, even his expensive new parka. Still known as Little Jim, he goes to find a lost mare in a thunder-and-lightning storm, rides a calf in a rodeo, rejects the idea of being a farmer, and takes part in a tribal dance contest. But the skunk is considered a good omen because Jim soon traps a rare mink. When Jim and his father take the mink to the store, hoping it will bring enough to buy a new parka, Little Jim becomes Jimmy to his father and their friends for his knowledge and skill at trapping. MR

Jingo Django (1971), a funny story by *Sid Fleischman, is about Jingo Hawks, who serves a violent and brief apprenticeship as a chimney sweep to General Dirty-Face Scurlock, chimney master. The General hunts for treasure in Boston's sootiest chimneys, and Jingo is plucked from an orphan's home to help him. It is Jingo's luck to go down a chimney and land in the custody of Mr. Jeffrey Peacock, who claims to know Jingo's father. Jingo, who says, "I'm a liar . . . always making up howling good stories about my pa. I'd say he stood seven feet tall and was master of the fastest China clipper in the trade," is not as good a liar as Peacock, who has several names and knows how to read treasure maps. They visit gypsy camps and riverboats and escape fights everywhere, and Jingo learns to think fast. In the end Jingo and his father are reunited. If you enjoyed *Jingo Django*, try Fleischman's other books, including *By the Great Horned Spoon* (1963), which is about Jack, who signs on as a cabin boy on a ship sailing to the gold fields of California. MR

Joab See *Absalom and *Bathsheba.

Job is a character in the Old Testament of the *Bible. A rich and happy man, Job faithfully praises God for His goodness. But, with God's permission, Job's faith is severely tested by *Satan. Satan kills Job's children, destroys all his property, and covers his body with sores in order to get Job to curse God. Three of Job's comforters, false friends, offer him a way of understanding his troubles. Job must abandon his beliefs. They tell him he is being punished for his sins. In spite of his apparent goodness, he must really be a terrible sinner. Job disputes his false friends, saying that God is supreme and His ways mysterious, that God can send misfortunes to both wicked and good people, and that God cannot be second-guessed. Throughout his absolute misery, Job does not curse God, saying instead, "The Lord gave, and the Lord hath taken away: blessed be the name of the Lord." As a reward for his steadfast faith, God heals Job and gives him "twice as much as before." The Book of Job in the Bible, a remarkable poem, was composed by an unknown author, probably in the period 600–400 B.C.

"The patience of Job," or "patient as Job," is an expression many people use to describe a long-suffering person. And "Job's comforter" is a well-intentioned person who offers consolation, but actually makes the suffering person feel worse. You may enjoy reading *J.B.* (1958), a verse drama based on the story of Job, by the poet and dramatist Archibald MacLeish (1892–1982).

Jody (1976), by Jerry Hulse (n.d.), is a true story about the author's search for his wife's mother. His wife, Jody, who was adopted as a child, is faced with potentially fatal brain surgery and needs a medical history of her natural parents. Jody's husband has just eight days to find her mother. The medical drama begins when Jody blacks out and gets into an accident while driving on the Hollywood Freeway. She regains consciousness but does not know what happened to her. She blacks out again two days later, and once again a short time after that. She finally consults a doctor, and the race to find her parents begins. The only clue is the name of her birthplace. Her adoptive parents are dead. Her birth records are sealed by court order, but the judge finds out her mother's name. The search for her mother and Jerry's finding of the all-important medical history the day before the operation are frantic. The reunion of Jody, her mother, and her twin brother after 47 years makes a warm and hopeful ending to this intense story. MR & YA

John, Saint (fl. 1st century A.D.) One of the four Evangelists (with *Matthew, *Mark, and *Luke), John was also one of the 12 disciples of *Jesus and by tradition the author of the Gospel in the New Testament of the *Bible bearing his name, though modern scholars question this. He was very close to Jesus, who committed his mother, the Virgin Mary, to John's care when he was about to be crucified. The Gospel According to Saint John was composed around A.D. 90–100. It differs from the other three in being more philosophical, less concerned with the life of Jesus than with its meaning. Jesus is both like and unlike other men; his nature is both human and divine. John sees the uniqueness of Jesus even though he cannot explain it in simple terms. John is also the traditional author of the three Epistles of John, short books of the New Testament of the Bible.

John Brown's Body (1928), by *Stephen Vincent Benét, is a long narrative poem of the Civil War. It begins with an episode on an early slave ship, and the course of the war unfolds, from the raid on Harpers Ferry through some of the major battles to General Lee's surrender at Appomattox in 1865. Woven into the story are the thoughts and actions of some fictional characters, such as Jack Ellyat, a law student from New England who joins the Union army, and Clay Wingate, a Georgia gentleman who signs on with the Confederate army. The poem ends with a passage telling of a new America, committed to equality among peoples. The poem has been adapted for the stage several times. YA

John Henry is a legendary black hero in American ballads and folktales. He was supposedly born in the Black River country, "whar de sun don't never shine," in the slaveholding South. Henry works throughout the South as a roustabout on riverboats and in the building of railroads. A man of prodigious size and strength, he was a kind of *Paul Bunyan. In one tale he died from exhaustion after winning a contest against a massive steam drill.

The John Henry tales are loosely based on the exploits of a giant black man who worked in the 1870s on the Big Bend Tunnel of the Chesapeake & Ohio Railroad. The railroad tunneled through the hills of West Virginia. Guy B. Johnson (1901–) collected several ballads in *John Henry: Tracking Down a Negro Legend* (1931). Roark Bradford (1896–1948) wrote *John Henry* (1931), a novel based on several tales.

There are songs about John Henry's strength and his way with women before his last contest with the steam drill. One folksong about the "steel drivin' man, John Henry," is still played at folk festivals. Some of its lines are:

> John Henry said to his captain,
> "A man ain't nothin' but a man,
> And before I'd let your steam drill
>   beat me down,
> I'd die with the hammer in my hand,
>   Lord, Lord!
> I'd die with the hammer in my hand."

You will often come across references to John Henry in your reading, like this example from a recent crime story: "It had become some kind of contest, a duel between John and the computer, like those early-nineteenth-century races between a locomotive and a horse, or John Henry trying to beat the spike-driving machine."

Many of you are familiar with the expression, "Here, sign your John Henry," which is an informal way of asking you for your signature. But this expression may not come from the legendary John Henry. It may instead be a variant of John Hancock (1737–1793), the first signer of the Declaration of Independence. YA

John the Baptist (d. A.D. 35) Considered by Christians to have been the last Jewish prophet, John was a forerunner of *Jesus, whom he baptized and whom he recognized as the Messiah. He was imprisoned by Herod Antipas (d. after A.D. 40), the ruler of Roman Palestine. Herod had married his niece, Herodias (d. after A.D. 39), and the marriage had been denounced as incestuous by John. Herodias urged her daughter, Salome, to ask Herod to have John beheaded as a reward for Salome having danced for Herod. Herod reluctantly granted the wish and, according to the *Bible, "his head was brought on a platter and given to the girl." This gruesome tale has fascinated writers as well as ordinary readers. *Oscar Wilde wrote in French the play *Salomé* (1893), and the composer Richard Strauss (1864–1949) used it as the basis for his opera *Salome* (1905). When first presented, the opera was considered both blasphemous and obscene. A famous scene in the opera gave rise to the tradition of the "dance of the seven veils," in which, dancing before Herod, Salome takes off one veil after another. The play *Salomé* was adapted for film in 1923 and 1953.

John Treegate's Musket (1959), by *Leonard Wibberley, begins in 1769 and tells about Peter, son of John Treegate, an American colonist who fought for and is still loyal to his king and country. John often points with pride to his musket above the fireplace. He says his musket will never be used against his king. But complaints about King George III are thick around Boston: taxes are too high, his many soldiers are arrogant, and the king's ministers are interfering with business. The rebels are considered "the Mob." One of the rebels is Tom Fielding, to whom Peter Treegate is an apprenticed barrel-stave maker. Peter is mistakenly cuffed by a soldier for supposedly throwing snowballs at the Redcoats. He begins to wonder about the forces being let loose between the people and the soldiers—is it the Mob and the Law, or is it the People and Tyranny? But on a trip to England, Peter is shipwrecked and loses his memory. He finds himself living in a forest with "the Maclaren," a Scottish renegade, and eventually makes his way back to his father. The American Revolution has begun, and Boston is being starved by the British. John

Treegate, no longer loyal to the king, takes down his beloved musket and with Peter goes to Breed's Hill, where the Patriots are firing on the British soldiers. If you liked reading Peter's adventures, you will also like the two sequels, *Pete Treegate's War* (1960) and *Treegate's Raiders* (1962). Another novel about the Revolutionary era in Boston is *Johnny Tremain* by *Esther Forbes. MR & YA

Johnny Tremain (1943), by *Esther Forbes, opens before the American Revolution, when tall ships jammed the long wharves of Boston. Trade is heavy. The orphan Johnny Tremain is the apprentice of an aging silversmith whose tiny house and shop stand at the head of John Hancock's wharf. Johnny dominates the workshop and two other apprentices because of his talent, his ability to read, and his energy. Johnny plans to marry one of the daughters of the household. But he loses his power and much of his young arrogance when an accident cripples his hand and forces him to seek unskilled work. After many humiliations, he finds work delivering *The Boston Observer* by horseback all over the Boston area. It is a small radical newspaper that is urging revolt against England. The Sons of Liberty meet secretly in Johnny's new bedroom at the printing shop— the members of the organization include *Paul Revere (1735–1818), John Hancock (1737–1793), Josiah Quincy (1744–1775), Sam Adams (1722–1803), James Otis (1725–1783), and Dr. Joseph Warren (1741–1775), all American Revolutionary statesmen. Johnny plays a part in the Boston Tea Party, acts as an observer and spy among the British troops, and serves as an important messenger for the Sons of Liberty on his skittish horse, Goblin.

Vital personal events, such as the discovery of who his parents were and his friendship with Cilia of the silversmith's family, thread through Johnny's life as tension increases in Boston: "The narrow course of Tremont Street was filled to the brim and overflowing with the waiting scarlet-coated men. Like a river of blood." And when "the shot heard round the world" is finally fired on April 19, 1775, Johnny

Dr. Johnson as portrayed in the first edition of
Boswell's *Life of Samuel Johnson*

is part of it, one of the people who made it happen. *Johnny Tremain* won the *Newbery Medal in 1944 and was filmed in 1957. MR & YA

Johnson, Samuel (1709–1784) A major English literary figure in the last half of the 18th century, the "Age of Johnson," Dr. Johnson, as he was nearly always called, was noted chiefly for his *Dictionary of the English Language* (1755). He first was a schoolmaster and bookseller in Lichfield, married a woman 20 years his senior in 1735, arrived in London in 1737, and never left. Besides working on his dictionary, he wrote a tragic play, several long poems, a philosophical romance, and two series of essays, The Rambler and The Idler, which earned him fame as a prose moralist. His original work on *William Shakespeare in 1765 greatly stimulated the study of Shakespeare. His last work, in 10 volumes, was the critical *Lives of the English Poets* (1779–81). Most of his writing reflects his moral views, which were sober and pessimistic about the chances of happiness for shortsighted humans in an imperfect world.

Yet James Boswell (1740–1795), in his famous *Life of Samuel Johnson* (1791), describes a man who was essentially kind, sociable, and generous. He was a man of great wit, and in his later years admitted that sometimes he talked just to win an argument. You are told that he was often abrupt, even rude, sloppy in his dress and habits, and that he feared illness, insanity, and damnation. You can recognize him from the newspaper caricatures of his day with his paunch, his foot on a stool, and his big toe swollen from gout and wrapped in rags. An example of Johnson's wit is: "Patriotism is the last refuge of a scoundrel." You may enjoy reading *The Life of Samuel Johnson*, which gives a vivid portrait of the man and is replete with examples of Johnson's wit. YA

Jonah is a minor Israelite prophet whose name is given to a book in the Old Testament of the *Bible. He is instructed by Jehovah to preach in the wicked City of Nineveh. Instead Jonah boards a ship going in another direction. A storm brews up, and the sailors, after discovering Jonah's disobedience, throw him into the sea to appease their gods. God orders a "great fish," in popular tradition a whale, to swallow Jonah, who lives in its stomach for three days. The inside of the stomach is large, and lit from the light of a large diamond. Jonah is comfortable in the whale's belly, but then he is transferred to another whale's belly, in which he is surrounded by thousands of little fishes. Here he is so uncomfortable that he finally decides to preach, whereupon the whale vomits Jonah up on the dry land. Jonah goes to Nineveh, where his preaching causes widespread repentance.

"To be a Jonah" means to be a jinx, a person who brings bad luck, yet the name Jonah, a common one for males, means "dove" in Hebrew.

Jonathan Livingston Seagull (1970), by *Richard Bach, is about flight, freedom, and the pleasure of doing something well. Jonathan looks like other seagulls, but thinks and acts differently. His great joy is flying, and he spends his days trying to improve his skill. During a particularly long, steep practice dive, he plummets right through the entire flock of gulls. No gull is hurt, but the Council Gathering of elders banishes him for irresponsible behavior. Cast out of the flock and living alone, Jonathan continues to perfect his flight. One day two unusually beautiful gulls appear at his side and lead him to a special place, which he thinks is heaven. In this place, the other gulls are as devoted to flying as he is. An older gull explains that heaven is not a place or time, but "the state of being perfect." Jonathan learns from his new friends to fly into the past and the future, and is taught the importance of kindness and love.

As Jonathan becomes more skilled and more thoughtful, he wants to return to the old flock to teach the gulls who are outcast as he once was. On his return he meets Fletcher Lynd Gull and convinces him that he too can hope to achieve perfect flight. Jonathan tells Fletcher and other outcasts that perfection can be reached only if they put aside whatever stands against their freedom. After several dramatic confrontations with the flock, Fletcher agrees to stay and become a teacher of outcasts. Jonathan leaves again to search for new challenges. If you enjoyed this book, you may also like the books of *Antoine de Saint-Exupéry. *Jonathan Livingston Seagull* was made into a movie in 1973. YA

Jones, James (1921–1977) A writer known chiefly for his novels about military life, Jones became an immediate success with the publication of his first novel, *From Here to Eternity*. It is a massive and forceful work and, for its time, contains many shocking incidents and much shocking language. In 1939, even though the *Great Depression was nearing its end, jobs were still hard to get and keep, so Jones decided to join the army. While serving at Hickam Field, Pearl Harbor, Hawaii, Jones discovered the works of *Thomas Wolfe, whose novels inspired Jones. Jones's second novel, *Some Came Running* (1957), is about small-town life. It focuses on a disillusioned

writer who returns from military service to his home town and takes up with a gambler and a prostitute. *The Pistol* (1959), a novella, and *The Thin Red Line* (1962) and *Whistle* (1978), full-length sequels to *From Here to Eternity*, focus on the effects of war and military life on soldiers. *From Here to Eternity* was released as a film in 1953, *Some Came Running* in 1958, and *The Thin Red Line* in 1964. YA

Jonson, Ben (1572–1637) An English dramatist and poet, Jonson was one of the literary giants of the Elizabethan Age. Unlike *William Shakespeare, Jonson is remembered chiefly for his comedies, which abound in *satire and earthy language. He worked as a bricklayer, soldier, and actor before turning to writing. His first major success came with *Every Man in His Humour* (1601), which included Shakespeare in its cast. A comedy, it centers on a wealthy London merchant who jealously guards his beautiful wife and his sister from the imagined advances of a variety of characters who have appeared at his home. Jonson's comedies also include *Volpone, or the Fox* (1607), about a wealthy Venetian who plots to gain expensive gifts by leading a number of people to believe they will inherit his fortune; *The Alchemist* (1612), about an alchemist who offers to transform base metals into gold, his companion, and a servant who is left to guard a wealthy Londoner's home and who helps the other two prey on a variety of gullible victims; and *Epicene, or the Silent Woman* (1616), about an elderly, noise-hating man who, seeking to gain an heir and disinherit his nephew, marries a quiet woman who instantly becomes noisy and talkative. Jonson was buried in Westminster Abbey, London, under the inscription, "O Rare Ben Jonson." A film of *Volpone* was made in 1939. YA

Joseph In the book of *Genesis in the Old Testament of the *Bible, the adventures of Joseph, the favorite son of Jacob, are among the most popular stories in the Old Testament. His 10 older brothers become envious of him when his father makes him what is traditionally described as "a coat of many colors," but which was simply a long-sleeved garment in contrast to the usual short-sleeved tunic of the time. The brothers sell him into slavery, making it appear to Jacob that Joseph has been killed by wild beasts. Sold again to an officer of the Egyptian Pharaoh's guard, Joseph survives various trials to become, by virtue of his interpretations of the Pharaoh's dreams, a high-ranking official. He predicts seven years of famine, and Egypt prepares for this by stocking grain in good years. When the famines come, Joseph's family suffers, and the brothers are sent to Egypt to buy food. They do not recognize Joseph, but he later reveals his identity, forgives them, and invites the entire family to come to live in Egypt. You may like to read *Joseph and His Brothers* (1933–1943), a series of four novels by *Thomas Mann. A musical comedy, *Joseph and the Amazing Technicolor Dreamcoat*, by Andrew Lloyd Webber (1948–) and Tim Rice (1944–), was produced in 1977. The movie *Joseph and His Brethren* was produced in 1962. YA

Jouett, Jack [John Jouette] (1754–1822) Like *Paul Revere, Jack Jouett rode a horse to warn American patriots of impending danger. One night in 1781, during the Revolutionary War, Jack Jouett saw Banastre "Bloody" Tarleton (1754–1833), a British officer known for his barbarous acts, and his Green Dragoons racing down the only road to Charlottesville, Virginia. Jack guessed that Tarleton meant to capture *Thomas Jefferson at his home at Monticello as well as Patrick Henry (1736–1799) and others who were staying in the town. On his horse, with only the moon to light his way, Jack dashed cross-country through woods and marshes and meadows for 40 miles to warn the patriots. Then he borrowed a fast horse and a dress uniform. The British thought Jack was an American general and chased him for many miles in the wrong direction. Because of Jack's bravery and cleverness, all the revolutionaries escaped. You may want to read about Jack in *Jack Jouett's Ride* (1973) by Gail E. Haley (1939–). MR

Journey to America (1970), by *Sonia Levitin, is the story of Lisa Platt and her family. They face the crisis of Lisa's father's leaving their German homeland because Jews are not safe in *Nazi Germany. He will go to America and then will send for Mama and Lisa, and Lisa's sisters. After Papa leaves, they are lonely, but they wait with patience and courage. Papa writes from America of his job as a janitor and tells them to go to Switzerland and wait. They abandon their possessions and their friends, neighbors, and relatives. Life is scary and sad. In Switzerland they live in a refugee camp, with no friends and little money for food. Some good things happen to them there, such as finding real beds to sleep in and finally getting their passports to America and freedom. The events that are depicted by Levitin in this book were all too real for many families in the 1930s, including the author's own family, who had to flee from Nazi Germany. MR & YA

Jove See *Jupiter.

Joyce, James (1882–1941) Born in Dublin, Ireland, Joyce wrote poetry, drama, short stories, and novels. Though short of money to finance his education, he finally graduated from university in 1902. In 1904 he wrote to Nora Barnacle, whom he married many years later: "My mind quite rejects the whole present social order and Christianity," and his writings show a reluctance to interpret, lecture, or make judgments. He and Nora left Ireland for the Continent, which was more tolerant of his intellectual and moral perspectives. He taught and wrote in several countries in Europe before settling in Paris in 1920, where he finally received recognition. He visited Ireland only twice after 1904, though all his writing is based on life in Dublin. After the German army occupied Paris in 1940, Joyce and his family returned to Switzerland, where he died in 1941.

Joyce is regarded as the supreme innovator of modern fiction. He is said to have spent an entire day completing two sentences for *Ulysses*. He explained, "I have the words already. What I am seeking is the perfect order of the words in the sentence." Scholars consider *Ulysses* and *Finnegans Wake* (1939) superb examples of the *stream of consciousness technique. Since you may find *Ulysses* and, especially, *Finnegans Wake* difficult to read, turn first to his early works, **A Portrait of the Artist as a Young Man*, an autobiographical novel that will introduce you to some of the literary techniques he uses in later works, and **Dubliners*. You will enjoy reading about Joyce in *Re Joyce* (1965) by *Anthony Burgess. A movie based on *Finnegans Wake* was made in 1965. YA

Joyful Noise: Poems for Two Voices (1988)

By Paul Fleischman (1952–), this book contains 14 poems celebrating the lives and sounds of insects. Each poem is written in two side-by-side parts, so that two people can read them aloud together, in the same way that two people can sing a duet. Here you will find poems about grasshoppers, water striders, fireflies, cicadas, honeybees, crickets, and others, and each poem is wonderfully illustrated by Eric Beddows (1951–). If you enjoy these poems, you will want to read the companion book *I Am Phoenix: Poems for Two Voices* (1985), containing poems about birds. Fleischman has also written a number of books of fiction, including *The Half-A-Moon Inn* (1980), about a boy who is kidnapped by a scheming and scary woman innkeeper and becomes involved in a mysterious adventure, and *Graven Images* (1982), three stories about people whose lives are changed when they put their trust in human-made images. *Joyful Noise* received the *Newbery Medal in 1989. MR

Judaism, the religion of the Jews, with about 18 million adherents worldwide, is the smallest of the major religions, but its long history has given it tremendous influence. It is the first religion to be entirely monotheistic, that is, to believe in only one all-powerful God. The first 39 books of the *Bible constitute the Hebrew, or Jewish, Bible and form the holy book of Judaism. Especially important are the first five

books, called the Torah. Also important is the *Talmud, commentaries on the Torah. The religion of the Jewish people cannot be separated from their history, especially as it is told in the Bible, beginning with the story of *Abraham. Other major figures include *Moses, *Isaac, and Jacob. In the most orthodox form of Judaism, worship services must be in Hebrew, men and women are separated during the service, and strict dietary laws, including abstinence from pork, must be observed. An important ceremony of Judaism is the Bar Mitzvah, in which a boy is initiated into the religious community and becomes an adult. In this century a similar ceremony, the Bat Mitzvah, has been introduced for girls. In the United States, where there are more Jews than in any other country, Judaism is represented by four major groups: Orthodox, in which the ancient ways of worship are practiced; Reform, a movement that began in the early 19th century and that rejects many of the traditional restrictions; Conservative, which split off from the Reform group in 1845 in order to retain more of the Orthodox tradition; and Hasidism, founded in Poland in the 18th century, which emphasizes the importance of purity of heart and joyous worship as well as learning. A fifth group, Reconstructionism, was founded in the United States in the 1930s. It regards Judaism as a religious civilization that is still evolving. It rejects the concept of the Jews as the chosen people of God. One Jewish holy day is Yom Kippur, the Day of Atonement, which is set aside for praying and for the forgiveness of sins. Others are Rosh Hashanah, the Jewish New Year; Passover, which celebrates the escape of the Jews from bondage in Egypt and includes a ceremonial meal called the Seder; and Hanukkah, the Festival of Light, which by tradition was begun by Judas Maccabeus (d. 160 B.C.), a Jewish military leader, to celebrate the dedication of a new altar in the Temple in Jerusalem. If you would like to learn more about Judaism, read *The Jewish World* (1983) by Douglas Charing (n.d.) and *Judaism* (1986) by Myer Domnitz (n.d.). Older readers will want to read *The Essence of Judaism* (1987 ed.) by Leo Baeck (1873–1976), and

---

MR = Middle Reader   YA = Young Adult Reader   * = See this main entry

Judaism (1985) by Michael Fishbane (1943–). MR & YA

Judas Iscariot, or Judas, is one of the disciples of *Jesus Christ in the New Testament of the *Bible. For 30 pieces of silver he betrayed Jesus to the Roman authorities. Why did Judas do this? Some biblical scholars maintain that Judas was under the influence of *Satan. Others believe he was angered by the waste of the money that bought the oil Mary Magdalene used to anoint Jesus. Before Judas's birth his mother had dreamed a terrible prophecy that he would kill God. The infant was placed in a chest and set adrift. The chest washed ashore in a foreign country, and Judas was raised by the king. He led an evil life at the king's court. He killed the king's son and escaped to Judaea. He became a follower of Jesus, who knew Judas's history and yet made him treasurer of his 12 disciples. When the Roman soldiers came to arrest Jesus, Judas identified Jesus by giving him a kiss. Driven by guilt, Judas hanged himself the next day from the branch of a tree.

Judas is the great traitor of Christian tradition. A "Judas" is a betrayer, especially one who betrays a friend. A "Judas kiss" is an act of seeming friendship that conceals some treachery. The Judas kiss is routinely shown in movies about the Mafia when an associate is about to be killed. Among some southern blacks, the evil eye is frequently referred to as the "Judas eye." A peephole, or spy hole, particularly in a solid jail door through which the jailers keep watch on the inmates, is sometimes called a "Judas hole."

Jude the Obscure (1895), a novel by *Thomas Hardy, caused a storm of protest when it was published. Hardy's frank view of sexuality and his criticism of the stifling laws, institutions, and ideas that controlled marriage in the second half of the 19th century in England are made vivid in this story. An 11-year-old orphan, Jude, wants to follow in the footsteps of a kind schoolmaster who had left his village for the university town of Christminster. Though sensitive and intelligent, Jude is very poor. To prepare himself for the life of a scholar in Christminster he teaches himself Latin and Greek, and learns the skill of stonemasonry to support himself. When he is 19 years old, he is seduced by Arabella, daughter of a pig farmer, and when she becomes pregnant he sacrifices his dream of education and marries her. But Arabella, who had only pretended to be pregnant, leaves him, and Jude is at last free to move to Christminster. He works, studies, finds his old schoolmaster, and falls passionately in love with his own cousin, Sue, an intelligent, nervous, free-thinking girl who is completely different from Arabella. Sue loves Jude, but on learning of his marriage to Arabella, she marries the schoolmaster, Phillotson. After great difficulty, Sue and Jude divorce their spouses but do not marry each other. They are loving but afraid of marriage. They live together, have children, and endure the criticism of their peers. But the horrifying joint suicide of their children causes such remorse in Sue that she leaves Jude and remarries Phillotson. In absolute misery, Jude remarries Arabella, but he dies of tuberculosis within a year.

Jude the Obscure is the gloomiest of Hardy's novels. *Tess of the D'Urbervilles* caused protest, but *Jude the Obscure* was for its time so frank about sex and the resulting criticism so severe that Hardy never wrote another novel and turned instead to poetry. YA

Judges is a book of the Old Testament of the *Bible. It is a collection of traditional stories written to form a historical account of the tribes of Israel under the 13 judges, or leaders. It covers primarily the period (c.1225–1020 B.C.) between the death of Joshua, *Moses' successor, to the time of Samuel and the rise of Saul to the throne. Parts of the book are contemporary accounts of the events. Other parts are renditions added later. It is primarily an interpretation of history occurring in cycles, of defeat and triumph, of defection and restoration. Israel loses its faith, worships other deities, is drawn to heathen idols, and is taken over by other countries. Each cycle shows a new leader, a hero who leads the people of Israel back to independence and to the worship of the true God. The book tells of the Israelites' invasion of Canaan and of their attempts to subdue its inhabitants and to settle the land. Judges reached its present written form by 500 B.C.

Jules Maigret Created by *Georges Simenon, this fictional detective is nearly six feet tall, a heavyset man with large features. He is well dressed and more often than not wears an overcoat with a velvet collar. He is a patient man, and a good deal of his time seems to be spent just looking and asking questions. He is relentless but compassionate. In the first of his tales, *The Death of Monsieur Gallet* (1931), Maigret solves the murder of a salesman found dead in a hotel room. The last novel featuring Maigret was *Maigret's Boyhood Friend* (1970), in which a small-time crook is suspected of murdering a woman who was supporting him. Through the woman's other lovers, Maigret is able to track down the murderer. Simenon created in Maigret one of the most realistic of imagined detectives, a substantial figure without unnecessary eccentricities. He wrote more novels about Maigret than have been written about any other fictional detective. A TV movie, entitled simply *Maigret*, was produced in 1988. YA

Julie of the Wolves (1972), by *Jean Craighead George, is about Miyax, an Eskimo girl who must wear her sealskin parka most of the year on the North Slope of Alaska. She is called Julie by her pen pal, Amy, who lives in San Francisco. Miyax is unhappy at home. She runs away and is lost on the tundra, starving, when she spots an Arctic wolf pack. She talks to Amaroq, a great royal black wolf, telling him in half-Eskimo and half-English that she is hungry. She is accepted, is given food, and begins to love the wolves like brothers. She remembers her father's training and begins to think about her life as an Eskimo, how rich it is, and how fearless her family is. George gives her story such detail about how the wolves live, and about how the Eskimo live beside

them like siblings, that you will think you are right inside the wolves' den. *Julie* was a *Newbery Medal winner in 1973. Other good books about life among wolves are *Never Cry Wolf* by *Farley Mowat and *The Jungle Books* by *Rudyard Kipling. MR & YA

Julius Caesar (c.1599–1600), a play by *William Shakespeare, relates the tragedy of a flawed character behind a historical event (c.47–44 B.C.), in which *Brutus assassinated Caesar, who was his friend. Yet nearly everyone in this drama says that Brutus is an honorable man. It is clear that Caesar is ambitious and Brutus is honorable. Or is it? In any case, the "lean and hungry" Cassius, envious of Caesar's power and popularity and seeking his own advancement through Caesar's downfall, realizes that it is the *image* of honor and noble intent that must be put forward if the assassination of Caesar is to be accepted by the people of Rome. Therefore, Cassius manipulates Brutus, whose noble spirit is sustained by a kind of innocence, into believing that Caesar's ambition threatens the very existence of the Roman republic. Brutus joins the conspiracy, and the Roman people nearly accept the idea that because the noble Brutus helped commit the murder, it was the right thing to do. Yet Mark Antony has a different view and, speaking at Caesar's funeral, turns the Roman people against the assassins by using Brutus's virtue against him. "I thrice presented him [Caesar] a kingly crown, which he did thrice refuse. Was this ambition? Yet Brutus says he was ambitious, and sure he [Brutus] is an honorable man." Brutus and Cassius are forced to flee from Rome and fight against forces marshaled by Antony and his allies. On the battlefield at the end, Brutus, haunted by Caesar's ghost, falls on his sword.

Julius Caesar asks painful political questions about whether moral goodness in a leader will always lead to actions that are for the public good. Is conscience enough to guide political action? Is power better than virtue, and is efficiency better than goodness? Do the ends justify the means? Such questions are with us today. For example, the novel *Seven Days in May* (1962) by Fletcher Knebel (1911–) and Charles W. Bailey II (1929–) deals with an American general who plots to overthrow the government to save the country and all it stands for. *Julius Caesar* was filmed in 1953 and in 1970. YA

jumbo is often used to describe a large wide-body jet plane, a big shrimp, an elephant, a giant size of almost anything—for example, a jumbo chocolate bar. "Jumbo," which has more positive vibes than "giant," is commonly used to present a favorable image of something very big. "Jumbo" comes from the name of an exceptionally large and gentle African elephant that, after giving rides to thousands of children in the London Zoo, was sold to P.T. Barnum's circus, The Greatest Show on Earth, in 1882. Jumbo the Elephant became famous wherever it appeared. In addition to a diet of water, hay, bread, oats, cookies, onions, and fruit, Jumbo drank a quart of whiskey every day. Jumbo weighed over 13,000 pounds and, sad to tell, was killed by a railway engine in 1885. You can read about Jumbo in *Great Days of the Circus* (1962) by the editors of *American Heritage*.

Jump Ship to Freedom (1981), by *James Lincoln Collier and *Christopher Collier, is about a slave boy's struggle to gain his freedom. Daniel Arabus is owned by Captain Ivers of Stratford, Connecticut. Daniel's father, Jack, who fought as a replacement for Captain Ivers in the Revolutionary War, had earned the right to his freedom. He had also earned $600 in Continental notes, which he was going to use to buy freedom for Daniel and his mother as soon as the Continental Congress decided to honor the currency. Jack is drowned at sea, however, and the notes are taken from Daniel's mother by Mrs. Ivers. Daniel steals back the notes, but Captain Ivers suspects Daniel has them. Ivers gets him aboard his ship sailing for the West Indies, where Daniel is to be sold. A huge storm forces the ship to anchor in New York City. Daniel jumps ship and is befriended by a Quaker, Mr. Fatherscreft, who opposes slavery.

Ivers almost captures his runaway slave, but Daniel escapes with Fatherscreft, who sets out for the Constitutional Convention in Philadelphia with an important message for one of the negotiators of the new law of the land. Then the frail Quaker dies and Daniel is left to carry the message alone. Daniel succeeds in his mission, meets George Washington (1732–1799), and wins new friends who help him and his mother gain their freedom. This story is based on the life of a real slave named Arabus who sued his owner for his release. MR

Jungle Books, The (1894, 1895) By the English writer *Rudyard Kipling, *The First Jungle Book* and *The Second Jungle Book* contain the famous stories about *Mowgli, the boy raised by wolves in the jungles of India. When he is a baby, Mowgli blunders into a wolf cave after his parents have been scared away by the tiger Shere Khan. The wolves take him into their pack. Baloo, an old bear, teaches Mowgli the languages and the law of the jungle, and Bagheera, a panther, teaches him the ways of animals and men. Mowgli makes many mistakes, and his life is dangerous and thrilling. He learns about the wisdom of snakes, the strength and dignity of elephants, and the foolishness of the monkey-people. He destroys Shere Khan, his old enemy, and the Ohole, a pack of insane wild dogs on a rampage. He mourns the death of his friends and eventually learns that he must return to his own people.

Other stories in these collections include "Toomai of the Elephants," which tells how Little Toomai is taken by a domestic elephant to the midnight dance of the elephants; "The White Seal," which is about the ocean-wide quest of a seal for a safe nursery where seal-hunting men will not be able to find and kill seals; and *"Rikki-Tikki-Tavi." *The Jungle Book* was filmed in 1942 and remade as an animated *Walt Disney film in 1967. MR & YA

Juno is the wife of *Jupiter in Roman mythology and religion. Her Greek counterpart is *Hera. Juno is the queen of heaven and the protector of marriage and women. As protector

Rudyard Kipling drew this illustration for "The Elephant's Child,"
one of the *Just So Stories*.

she accompanies every woman from birth to death, a form of ministering angel. A particular duty of Juno as goddess of fertility is overseeing childbirth, and she is the bringer of light at such moments. She is also goddess of the moon, particularly the new moon. The peacock, the bird of Juno, is dedicated to the goddess-queen. You can read about Juno in *Bulfinch's Mythology by Thomas Bulfinch and *Mythology by Edith Hamilton (1867–1963). MR & YA

Jupiter As the chief Roman god, Jupiter is in charge of all events concerning the sky, such as the weather, the stars, and heaven. Also known as Jove, he is the husband of *Juno and has much in common with *Zeus, the Greeks' supreme god. Most of the personal and family stories of Jupiter are variations of the Greek myths. From Jupiter's beginning he was the guardian of honor and the protector of treaties, marriage, and oaths, and he sees that these bonds are kept. Jupiter is the protector of the city of Rome, where his temple was erected on the Tarpeian rock. Traitors were flung from this pinnacle. Successful generals celebrated their victories with sacrifices at his temple,

honoring the god who prevented flight in battle. Jupiter's name was invoked before all official events. He also sent omens. For instance, flights of birds were known as his messengers, and to this day flights of birds are released at the opening ceremonies of the Olympics. In his control of the weather, he protects the vineyards and their harvests. As the god of lightning, he appears in pictures carrying a lightning bolt above his head ready to hurl it. Each place struck by lightning became sacred to Jupiter and was thereafter protected by walls built by his Roman worshipers. Every month, during the time of the full moon, dedications and sacrifices were made in his honor. If you would like to read more about Jupiter, see the *New Larousse Encyclopedia of Mythology* (1968).

Just Plain Al (1986) By *Constance C. Greene, this novel is the fifth about the bright, slightly overweight, nonconformist girl Al and her best friend, who live in the same apartment building in New York City. As Al approaches her 14th birthday, she begins to feel that she needs to change her life and herself. She wants to change her name, but to what? Zandra? Zandi?

When Al and her friend meet a scary-looking homeless woman, they begin to question their ideas of what is important in life. Al decides to dedicate her life to humanity, but in the meantime there are plenty of distractions, such as her mother's rich new boyfriend, Stan, the sights and sounds of New York City in the summer, and, of course, her upcoming birthday. If you enjoy the series about Al and her friend, which begins with *A Girl Called Al, try the books of *Louise Fitzhugh. MR

Just So Stories (1902) These *fables by *Rudyard Kipling have been famous since they first appeared. They are illustrated, with the captions written by the author, and were intended for his daughter, Josephine. They tell of the wit and wisdom of elephants and whales, of armadillos and kangaroos, of "How the Camel Got His Hump," and of "How the Leopard Got His Spots." "The Elephant's Child" with his " 'satiable curtiosity" tells about how the elephant got his trunk. They are marvelous for reading aloud because of their clarity, rhythm, rhymes, and energy. Whether read aloud or to yourself, their magic delights your ear with such exotic phrases as "the great grey-green, greasy Limpopo River, all set about with fever-trees." If you like reading about Pau Amma the Crab and Big Medicine and Strong Magic, you should also read Kipling's *The Jungle Books and the fables of *Aesop and of *Jean de La Fontaine. MR

Justin Morgan Had a Horse (1954), by *Marguerite Henry, is the story of an ordinary workhorse that was so strong and quick for its small size that it became the sire of a famous family of American horses, known today as the Morgans. "He would walk faster, trot faster, run faster, and pull heavier logs than any other horse in all Vermont!" and then "take part in races and pulling bees after sundown." You first meet this horse as Little Bub, the smaller of two colts in Farmer Beane's pasture, nudging for nuggets of maple sugar. Justin Morgan, a teacher, takes his student, Joel, to the Beane farm, where the larger colt is given to Justin by the farmer as payment for an old debt. Joel falls in love with Little Bub, who is allowed to follow them home because Joel has, as Beane says, "a way with horses," and the little colt has no value. After Justin Morgan dies, Little Bub passes through the hands of several owners before Joel is able to buy the horse that becomes known as the extraordinary Justin Morgan. If you like *Justin Morgan*, you may like some of Henry's other books. Two more of her books about horses are *Misty of Chincoteague and *Sea Star: Orphan of Chincoteague* (1949), which is about an orphaned colt. MR

Juvenal (c.A.D. 60–c.127?) No one knows much about Juvenal's life except that he was poor and eloquent and that he spent time in military service. Juvenal, known for his scathing *satires, was the last and most powerful of the Roman satiric poets. He wrote 16 *Satires* (c.85?–127) dealing mostly with life in Rome. After Juvenal criticized a popular stage performer, a favorite of the dreaded Emperor Domitian (51–96), the poet's property was seized and he went into exile for the rest of his life. The *Satires* are biting attacks on the public manners and morals of his times. For instance, they describe such disgusting scenes as a husband shutting his eyes as his wife vomits on the floor and of a riot during which a man is torn to pieces and eaten. Many readers feel Juvenal's bitterness is that of an inspired cynic. He is most remembered as the originator of such sayings as "A sound mind in a sound body, and a brave heart," "Slow rises worth, by poverty oppressed," and "Who will guard the guards themselves?" He once asked, "Is that a face or an ulcer?" Juvenal was widely imitated in England during the 17th and 18th centuries. You will enjoy a colloquial verse translation, *Satires* (1958) by Rolfe Humphries (1894–1969). Other classical books about the daily life and history of Rome include *Odes* (23? B.C.) by Horace [Quintus Horatius Flaccus] (65?–8? B.C.) and *Books X, XI, and XII* (A.D. 99?–102?) by Martial [Marcus Valerius Martialis] (A.D. 38?–103?) YA

~K~

Kafka, Franz (1883–1924) A short-story writer and novelist who was born in Bohemia and wrote in German, Kafka enjoyed reading travel books and brochures, yet he hardly left his father's house except to go to work as a lawyer. The intense anti-Semitism in Prague, Czechoslovakia; Kafka's relationship with his German-Austrian father, who was a Jew and who did not understand him; and Kafka's inability to understand God are explored throughout his writings. Kafka's short story "In the Penal Colony" (1919), a highly *symbolic tale in which an explorer visiting a remote penal colony is shown a machine designed to inflict a slow and painful death on prisoners who have been condemned without trial, and the novels *The Castle and The Metamorphosis (1937), about a man who awakens one morning to find himself transformed into a giant cockroach, are riddled with male authority figures who judge and misjudge the young heroes. They present father figures who abuse and often kill the tormented young heroes. This theme is particularly evident in *The Trial. Yet Kafka's unfinished novel, *Amerika, is leavened by an almost amusing series of strange adventures. Kafka's stories read almost like dreams, yet seem profound and original. He is considered one of the most visionary writers of the 20th century because he wrote, in a style that is open to different interpretations, of the frustrated and troubled existence of modern hu-

Franz Kafka

man beings in the industrial age. One irony of Kafka's writing about a world of futility and aimlessness is that when he died of tuberculosis, most of his writings were unfinished and unpublished. He asked that they be burned, but they were saved and edited by his friend Max Brod (1884–1968), an Austrian writer. YA

Kantor, MacKinlay (1904–1977) The author of *Andersonville and *The Voice of Bugle Ann,

Kantor spent the first 10 years of his working life as a reporter and columnist for three Middle Western newspapers. He wrote screenplays for several major Hollywood movie studios and later returned to journalism as a war correspondent in Europe during World War II. After the war Kantor joined the New York City police force for two years, and then served again as a war correspondent with the U.S. Air Force during the Korean War. Kantor was a prolific writer whose works, published between 1928 and 1975, appeared in everything from pulp magazines to the distinguished *Atlantic Monthly*. Many of his books are about the American Civil War, and some are based on material Kantor collected in the Middle West, where he traveled as a hobo. Among his best-known novels are *Spirit Lake* (1961), about the pioneer settlement of Iowa in the 1850s and the resulting clash between the settlers and the Native Americans they sought to displace, and *Valley Forge* (1975), centering on the patriot army during the American Revolution. You may want to read also his novel in verse, *Glory for Me* (1945), which became the movie *The Best Years of Our Lives* (1946). YA

Karen (1952), a biography of her daughter by Marie Killilea (1913–), begins with Karen's premature birth in 1941. She weighs under two pounds and is only nine inches long. She requires medical care almost constantly. When she is seven months old, she weighs only seven pounds. Karen does not develop in the ways other babies do: She does not use her hands, sit up, or begin those movements that signal growth. Doctors offer no hope; Karen is mentally retarded and has cerebral palsy. But her parents remain hopeful and look for any doctor who will say there is an answer to her problem. They see 23 doctors in two and a half years. Finally, Dr. B examines Karen and says that she can be trained and that she is even mentally alert. He recommends physiotherapy to help her learn to walk and occupational therapy to help her learn to feed, wash, dress herself, and write. The therapy trains other parts of the brain to do the work of the brain's

damaged parts. When Karen is 11 years old she proudly announces, "I can walk. I can talk. I can read. I can write. I can do anything." Killilea wrote a sequel, *With Love from Karen* (1963), which is about Karen's later years. *Karen* has been translated into at least 10 languages. MR & YA

Karen and Vicki (1984), by Elisabet McHugh (1941–), is the third book of a trilogy, after her excellent *Raising a Mother Isn't Easy* (1983) and *Karen's Sister* (1983). Twelve-year-old Karen, who is an adopted Korean orphan, is late to school, and her teacher, Mr. Campbell, gives her the stern eye as only teachers can. She announces her special project: "I'd like to work on getting my family organized." Mr. Campbell agrees. It is to be a time/efficiency study, and Karen has no idea of what she will go through before she completes the project. Karen's main problem is her new teenage sister, Vicki, who enters Karen's life when her mother marries Vicki's father. Karen and her sister, Meghan, move into a new home with their new, larger family. But it is not large enough to allow Vicki to spend 20 minutes in the bathroom each morning doing her hair. When baby Jonathan joins the family, and when Grandma plans to visit them with her new boyfriend, Karen's life becomes even more complicated. Elisabet McHugh is a single parent with six adopted children and several animals. She admits that the story is based on firsthand research. You may like her other books about Karen's family, *Raising a Mother Isn't Easy*, which is a humorous account of Karen's plan to find a husband for her adoptive mother; *Karen's Sister*, about Karen's multiracial family; and *Beethoven's Cat* (1988), which is about Karen's mother, who unexpectedly adopts another Korean orphan, 5-year-old Meghan. MR

Kaufman, George S(imon) (1889–1961) A playwright noted for his trenchant wit and sharp dialogue, Kaufman is known best for his series of satirical comedies written with *Moss Hart. Kaufman usually worked in collaboration with other playwrights, including Marc Connelly

(1890–1980) and *Edna Ferber. With Connelly, he wrote *Merton of the Movies* (1922), based on the 1922 novel by Harry Leon Wilson (1867–1939), about a small-town clerk who becomes a Hollywood movie star. With Ferber, Kaufman wrote *Dinner at Eight* (1932), a *satire of high society centering on a dinner party given by a wealthy American woman for Lord and Lady Ferncliffe, two members of English society visiting the United States. One of his greatest hits was *Of Thee I Sing* (1932), a musical comedy written with Morris Ryskind (1895–1985), with music and lyrics by *George and Ira Gershwin, satirizing U.S. presidential politics. *Merton of the Movies* was adapted for film in 1947 and *Dinner at Eight* in 1933 and 1989. YA

Kavik, the Wolf Dog (1968), by *Walt Morey, is about a dog that travels 2,000 perilous miles to return to Alaska from Seattle, Washington. Kavik, part wolf and part Alaskan malamute, is the lead dog in a team that won a sled-dog derby in Alaska. Kavik catches the eye of a Seattle businessman, who buys the dog for his son and puts Kavik aboard a small plane. The plane crashes during a blizzard, and Kavik's cage is thrown free with Kavik, badly injured, still inside. After three days, 15-year-old Andy Evans finds the wounded dog. Andy nurses Kavik, and the two learn to love each other. Kavik, however, has lost his confidence from being caged and injured and will not defend himself against other dogs. Finally Kavik, recovered from his injuries, is reclaimed by his legal owner. In Seattle, Kavik has other memories, and runs away from his new home. His journey back to Andy Evans, which includes a trip on a boat, a fight with a male wolf, and a struggle through deep snow to help a female wolf find food, are described with sympathy. If you liked the story of Kavik, you may enjoy *The Incredible Journey* by *Sheila Burnford; *Stolen Pony* (1969) by *Glen Rounds, which is about a kidnapped, blind pony who is guided home by his self-appointed Seeing Eye dog; and *Incident at Hawk's Hill*, by *Allan Eckert, which is the true story of how a wild animal saved the life of a boy lost on the Cana-

dian prairie. You will also like the classic dog stories by *Jack London, *The Call of the Wild* and *White Fang*. MR

Kazantzakis, Nikos (1883–1957) A Greek born on the island of Crete, Kazantzakis was a poet, dramatist, translator, and travel writer, but mostly a writer of novels. Kazantzakis was educated in Paris and Germany, where he lived the last years of his life in exile, branded a traitor to Greece for his writings. The conflict between the spirit and the flesh is central to all his works, such as *The Odyssey: A Modern Sequel* (1938) and *Freedom or Death* (1950). His struggle to master this conflict led him to spend six months on Mount Athos, famous for its ancient monasteries, which exclude all female beings, human or animal. The great irony in the life of Kazantzakis is the extent to which three of his novels—*The Greek Passion* (1948), a story of a Greek village and its annual drama around the Passion of Christ; *The Last Temptation of Christ* (1951), a re-creation of Christ's life and passion; and *Zorba the Greek*—have been misinterpreted as being anti-Christian. *The Last Temptation of Christ* was filmed in 1986. YA

Keats, John (1795–1821) Considered one of the best of the English Romantic poets, Keats was born in London, England. He died 26 years later in Italy of tuberculosis. During his short life, he produced a large body of mature, powerful poetry. The second of his poems to be published was the great sonnet "On First Looking into Chapman's Homer" (1816), but his first collection, *The Poems of John Keats* (1817), was not a success. Keats then began *Endymion* (1818), a long *allegory of imagination in search of ideal beauty. It contains one of his most memorable lines, "A thing of beauty is a joy forever." The year it was published he was already sick, but he nursed his brother, Tom, also tubercular, until Tom's death in December 1818. During this period Keats met Fanny Brawne and became engaged to her, but they were unable to marry, as his finances worsened and his health declined. Yet this was his most productive period. He worked on *Hyperion* (1820), an uncompleted epic centering on the Greek myth of the fall of the *Titans, began *The Eve of St. Agnes* (1820), about two lovers whose families oppose their romance, wrote the haunting ballad "La Belle Dame Sans Merci" (1820), and composed his great odes noted for their sustained feeling and imagery. Among them were "Ode on a Grecian Urn," "Ode to a Nightingale," "Ode to Psyche," and "Ode on Melancholy"—all written in 1819. John Keats's letters are among the most affecting and vigorous written in English. You will find in your library several editions of them. You may want to read more about Keats's life. The best one-volume biography was written by Douglas Bush (1896–1983), *John Keats: His Life and Writings* (1966). If you enjoy Keats's poetry, you may also like the works of *George Gordon Byron and *Percy Bysshe Shelley. YA

Keene, Carolyn This name has been used by a number of different authors to write the Nancy Drew mystery and detective novels, which are about a teenage heroine who has remained popular for more than 60 years. Nancy, from a well-to-do family, is attractive and intelligent and has never become accustomed to adult responsibilities. She has her own car, which she is capable of repairing, and she is a good swimmer and an excellent shot. Nancy is a "suburban princess" who never gets older. The books about her combine detective work, mystery, and a touch of horror. The first of her adventures is *The Secret of the Old Clock* (1930), in which Nancy searches for a lost will. More recent are *The Secret in the Old Lace* (1980), in which Nancy is in Belgium, looking for an antique cross; and *The Kachina Doll Mystery* (1981), in which Nancy, at a dude ranch in Arizona, traces the cause of accidents believed to be due to a Hopi Indian curse. Keene wrote *The Nancy Drew Cookbook* (1973), indicating perhaps that the popular heroine was becoming domesticated. A new Keene series not involving Nancy is River Heights, with a high school of that name as the focus. *The Trouble with Love* (1990) finds three girls con-

fused by boys and young love. In *Junior Class Trip* (1991) the class goes to Washington, D.C., and as much romance as sightseeing takes place. With *Franklin W. Dixon, Keene has written a number of books that combine Nancy's adventures with those of the Hardy Boys. If you enjoy the Nancy Drew books, you will like those of *Enid Blyton, *M.V. Carey, and *Phyllis A. Whitney. Many movies and a TV series have been made from the Nancy Drew stories. See also *Edward Stratemeyer. MR & YA

Keeper of the Isis Light, The (1980) This exciting *science fiction novel by the English-born Canadian writer Monica Hughes (1925–) is about Olwen Pendennis, who lives on the planet Isis. She is an orphan, 10 years old, though 16 years old in Earth years. Her parents, the Keepers of the Isis Light, have been killed, and Olwen remains at the Light as Keeper, ably assisted by Guardian, a robot. Even though the Light is a lighthouse in space to aid ships and to help bring settlers from Earth, Olwen has never seen an Earth person. She thinks that Guardian is human and is upset when she learns on her 10th birthday that Isis is to be settled by real humans, whom she now sees as intruders on her planet. Olwen has the freedom to wander all over Isis because she alone can breathe the thin air of its higher regions and is acclimated to its ultraviolet light. The human settlers must remain in certain regions for generations until their bodies can adapt. Olwen accepts the settlers and their physical differences, and a couple of them are as nice to her as she is to them. But some of them are very different, even greedy, and dangerous to Olwen and their own comrades. If you liked *Keeper of the Isis Light*, you will want to read its sequel, *The Guardian of Isis* (1982), which tells about the descendants of the original settlers and the life they lead on Isis. MR

Keeping-Room, The (1981) This interesting novel by Betty Levin (1927–) bares the dusty layers that connect us to the past. Hal's teacher assigns him to get the history of Candlewood, the Titcomb farm, from old Harriet Titcomb.

Hal, who is 14 years old, also must babysit his teacher's 5-year-old daughter, Emily, on his visits to the farm. They listen to Harriet, but soon Emily and Hal begin to see and hear strange things that seem to be connected to the mysterious disappearance of Harriet's Great-Aunt Hannah 150 years earlier, when she was 12 years old. Then Emily disappears, and past and present become entangled and frightening. Hal discovers Emily has been kidnapped and, through his quick thinking, helps the authorities catch the kidnappers and return Emily to her family. Then a bulldozer working on a new road through Candlewood unearths Hannah's skeleton and a tin box containing her journal, which explains how and why she disappeared. These adventures show Hal how important people are to each other and how the present is shaped by the past. You may also enjoy Betty Levin's *A Binding Spell* (1984), which takes place on an isolated Maine farm and concerns a ghost horse, a girl, and an old man. MR & YA

Keller, Helen (1880–1968) A remarkable woman, Keller became world famous for overcoming devastating handicaps: She became blind and deaf from fever when she was only 19 months old. In her autobiography, *The Story of My Life* (1903), she tells how she knew that she was different from other people, but her handicaps did not keep her from learning how to do things. As a child she often had uncontrollable fits of anger and frustration during which she "kicked and screamed until [she] was exhausted." Keller became such a willful 6-year-old that her father had her examined by Dr. Alexander Graham Bell (1847–1942), who arranged to have Anne Sullivan (1887–1936) become her tutor. For hours each day Keller was taught the manual alphabet, which enabled her to study literature, physics, astronomy, and history. She even learned to speak and to write. Keller went on to triumph over public indifference to the welfare of the handicapped, and devoted the rest of her life to social reforms. *The Miracle Worker* (1957), a play by William Gibson (1919–), about Helen and

Helen Keller when she was 20 years old

her teacher Anne Sullivan, was filmed in 1962 and remade as a TV movie in 1979. MR & YA

Kellerman, Jonathan (Seth) (1949–) A child psychologist, at one time affiliated with the Children's Hospital in Los Angeles, California, Kellerman wrote *Helping the Fearful Child* (1981). Using this background, he developed a series of detective novels and a fictional detective rather different from most. Kellerman's sleuth is the psychologist Alex Delaware, who was introduced in *When the Bough Breaks* (1985), in which Delaware investigates a series of murders. To solve them, he must get the only witness, an uncommunicative small girl, to talk. Delaware works with Milo Sturgis, a police sergeant, in such novels as *Blood Test* (1986) and *Time Bomb* (1990). Delaware does not appear in *Butcher's Theater* (1988), which concerns the serial murders of young Arab women in Jerusalem. A TV movie was made in 1986 of *When the Bough Breaks*. If you enjoy these books, try also the books of *P.D. James and *John D. MacDonald. YA

Kenny and the Highland Ghost (1980), by the Scottish-born writer William MacKellar (1914–), is a humorous story that begins when Kenny arrives at the door of Strathullen Castle in Scotland. Kenny sees the frightened face of a man in one of the windows and soon realizes that it is like the face of a man whose portrait hangs inside and who died in 1568. Kenny and his parents did not imagine they would encounter a live ghost in a castle that had not been lived in for over 100 years. Luckily for 14-year-old Kenny, the cowardly 400-year-old soul of the Seventh Earl of Strathullen is friendly. The awful curse of Calum MacSpurtle is soon lifted, thanks to Kenny's curiosity, and the Seventh Earl's ghost can go home to St. Fillan's churchyard. MacKellar, who moved to the United States with his parents when he was 11 years old, has written several other books about ghosts and mysteries in Scottish settings. You may especially like *The Mystery of Mordach Castle* (1970) and *A Ghost Around the House* (1970). MR

Kerouac, Jack [Jean-Louis Lebrid de Kerouac] (1922–1969) Since the publication of his novel *On the Road*, Jack Kerouac has been recognized as a genuine American artist, a true original. *On the Road* was completely different in style from his well-reviewed first novel, *The Town and the City* (1950), which was conventional and autobiographical. Kerouac was born to working-class French-Canadian parents in the mill town of Lowell, Massachusetts. A bright student, he received an athletic scholarship to Columbia University, but he dropped out to serve in the Merchant Marine. He joined the Navy during World War II and spent some time as a patient in the psychiatric ward of a Navy hospital. After he left the Navy in the 1940s, Kerouac met the poet Allen Ginsberg (1926–) and the novelist William Burroughs (1914–), who profoundly influenced Kerouac's literary career. But it was meeting the young

and footloose Neal Cassady (1926–1968) that inspired *On the Road* and also *Visions of Cody* (1972), which was written by Kerouac in the early 1950s and published in partial form in 1960, but was not published in its entirety until after Kerouac's death. Kerouac moved around the country, stopping to write in furious bursts. His attitude toward the social outcasts who were among his friends and his new writing style were so unusual that for years editors rejected his work. When *On the Road* finally appeared, it was panned by critics, yet readers kept it on the best-seller list for weeks. It became the focus for a growing social movement and foreshadowed the ferment of the 1960s. He also wrote *The Dharma Bums* (1958), which depicted himself and the poet Gary Snyder (1930–) fictionally as religious wanderers in search of truth. A shy man, Kerouac was unable to cope with his fame and loss of privacy. He died of alcoholism in 1969. Almost all of Kerouac's works are available in inexpensive paperback editions, and four new volumes of Kerouac's letters, poems, and unpublished manuscripts are scheduled to be published in 1993 and 1994. See also *Beat Generation. YA

Kerr, Judith (1923–) Born in Berlin, Germany, Kerr is the daughter of a writer and drama critic who took his family out of Germany just before the rise of Adolf Hitler (1889–1945) to power in 1933. She lived as a refugee in Switzerland and France and then was educated in London, England. It is this exile that motivated her to write many of her books, especially *When Hitler Stole Pink Rabbit*, which attempts to try to explain to her own children what it was like to flee *Nazi Germany and to lose one's country, language, and home. One of the characters, Max, is her own brother. *The Other Way Around* (1975), a sequel to *When Hitler Stole Pink Rabbit*, recounts the refugee family's experience in wartime London. Kerr illustrates her own books. MR

Kerr, M.E. [Marijane Meaker] (1927–) A novelist and author of *Dinky Hocker Shoots*

Smack, Kerr began writing as soon as she was able to put pen to paper. She describes herself as a library addict, and has given much credit to the librarians who helped her grow as a reader and a writer. She undertook a writing career shortly after graduating from college. She has since produced almost 40 books, under the pen names of M.E. Kerr, Ann Aldrich, and Vin Packer. She is known for her willingness to face serious issues in her books and for her ability to create understandable and sympathetic characters, both young and old. Kerr's stories are usually about love, or the absence of love. Her style is direct, often witty, and unusually charming. One novel you may enjoy, *Is That You, Miss Blue?* (1975), concerns an eccentric and deeply religious boarding-school teacher, and the sympathy she arouses in a 14-year-old student. *Little, Little* (1981) concerns a fascinating young woman who happens to be a dwarf and describes her parents' efforts to find a suitable husband for her. MR

Kesey, Ken (1935–) The author of the novel *One Flew Over the Cuckoo's Nest, Ken Kesey was raised on a dairy farm in Oregon, attended graduate school in California, acted for a while in the movies, and then was paid to be a subject in hospital experiments with LSD and other hallucinogenic drugs. He stayed on at the Veterans Hospital as a night attendant in the mental ward. This was the experience that provided the basis and background for his electrifying story *One Flew Over the Cuckoo's Nest*. In 1964 Kesey was among the 14 free spirits who called themselves the Merry Pranksters and drove an old bus painted in Day-Glo colors from San Francisco to the New York World's Fair, a trip celebrated by *Tom Wolfe in *The Electric Kool-Aid Acid Test*. Kesey worked as a logger to prepare for his second novel, *Sometimes a Great Notion* (1964), which is about two brothers who inherit an Oregon lumber empire. Arrested twice for marijuana possession in California, Kesey fled to Mexico, returned to serve his jail term, and has produced several collections of stories, essays, and screenplays describing his experiences. His

book *The Further Inquiry* (1990) is about Neal Cassady (1926–1968) and friends traveling in the famous psychedelic bus. See also *Jack Kerouac and *Beat Generation. YA

Key, Alexander (1904–1979) Though he became known for his *science fiction books, Key entered the Chicago Art Institute when he was 17 years old. He stayed for two years before a bank failure made him penniless. Key borrowed a suit, grew a mustache, put on horn-rimmed eyeglasses to look mature and prosperous, and sold his first drawing. Though he continued to work as an illustrator, it was his writing that sold, especially "reams of blood-and-thunder for the pulp magazines." When Key was 6 years old he lost his father, who was killed by night-riders—masked thugs who traveled by night to terrorize blacks and other groups they did not like—in Maryland. His mother died from an accident soon after. This early experience of loss and violence is reflected in *The Forgotten Door*. His books describe young people involved with the future, space travel, and leaps of the mind, as in *Rivets and Sprockets* (1964), about a special robot and its loose screw, or in *The Case of the Vanishing Boy* (1979), about a boy and girl with supernatural powers avoiding would-be captors. *The Golden Enemy* (1969) is about a huge bear, a shepherd boy, and the stars. His best-known book is *Escape to Witch Mountain*. If you enjoy his books, you may also like the science fiction novels of *Madeleine L'Engle. MR

Key, Francis Scott (1779–1843) Following the bombardment of Fort McHenry, Baltimore, Maryland, during the war of 1812, Key, a prominent lawyer in Washington, D.C., wrote the words to "The Star-Spangled Banner," which was adopted as the national anthem in 1931. The origin of the tune to the anthem is unknown, but it was familiar to musicians by 1775. Key was a temporary prisoner of the British aboard a vessel overlooking the fort during the bombardment when he spotted the flag still flying on the morning of September 14, 1814, and was inspired by the sight. He began

---

MR = Middle Reader   YA = Young Adult Reader   * = See this main entry

the first verses on the back of a letter he had in his pocket, and on reaching Baltimore he wrote a clean copy, which is on exhibit at the Maryland Historical Society. It was published within a week and was immediately popular. Younger readers can learn more about Key and his life in the biographies *Broad Stripes and Bright Stars* (1955) by Marion Marsh Brown (1908–) and *Francis Scott Key, Poet and Patriot* (1963) by Lillie Patterson (n.d.) MR

Keyes, Frances Parkinson (1885–1970) Having written more than 70 books, Keyes (rhymes with "prize") was one of America's most successful women authors. Her novels are rich in local color and usually concern people of refinement and wealth. She never wrote about a subject and region without extensive research, and she often moved to places she was writing about to live for months and years. She made more than 25 trips to Europe, spent time in Mexico, South America, and the Middle East, and spoke German, Spanish, and French. She married Henry Wilder Keyes (1863–1938), who became governor of New Hampshire and later a U.S. Senator. Her best-known book is *Dinner at Antoine's* (1948), which is about expensive tastes and generally kindly people. Her other novels include *The River Road* (1945), set in the sugar-growing region between Baton Rouge and New Orleans, Louisiana, between 1919 and 1943; *Steamboat Gothic* (1952), about a Louisiana family and their home, a beautiful mansion on the Mississippi, from the 1860s to 1930; and *Madame Castel's Lodger* (1962), a biographical novel based on the life of P.G.T. Beauregard (1818–1893), the Confederate general who ordered the opening shots of the Civil War at Fort Sumter in 1861. YA

Keys of the Kingdom, The (1941) This popular novel by the Scottish writer *A.J. Cronin is about Francis Chisholm, a young Scot who loses his parents and sweetheart. He enters the priesthood, but finds clerical life difficult because he is too direct and practical and cannot subdue his individuality. His fellow priests do not like him, and his superiors think him a failure because of his lack of conformity. But Francis discovers an internal purpose. Sent to China as a missionary, he lives in poverty and danger for over 35 years. In China this humble and courageous individual discovers the keys to the kingdom of heaven. Heaven is not controlled only by Christians, he points out, quoting Confucius to the sadistic Monsignor Sleeth: "God is the common father of all mankind." If you enjoyed *The Keys of the Kingdom,* you may like *The Citadel* (1937), which is about an ambitious young doctor who discovers integrity amid professional dishonesty. YA

kibbutz is a collective farm or small factory in Israel, where the land and buildings are jointly owned by all the people who live there. Everyone lives together, often in dormitories, and everyone helps plan the work that needs to be done. Work is given to each person according to his or her ability, and clothing and other essentials go to those who need them. Two books you will enjoy on this subject are *Miriam Lives in a Kibbutz* (1969) by Cordelia Edwardson (n.d.), and *A Kibbutz in Israel* (1987) by Allegra Taylor (n.d.). MR

Kidd, Captain William (1645?–1701) A famous Scottish navigator and privateer, Kidd was a respected trader in New York City, owner of a building on Wall Street, and a married man. While he was on a trip to London, England, a syndicate of nobles gave him command of the *Adventure Galley,* and he received commissions, or government orders, to prey upon French trading ships and pirates. He captured and plundered a number of ships in various parts of the world, but on reaching the West Indies, he learned that he had been charged with piracy. He was decoyed to Boston, where he was arrested and shipped to Newgate Prison in England. The wealthy syndicate of nobles withdrew support and allegedly suppressed information, and he was hanged. There has been much mystery and controversy surrounding Kidd and his buried treasures. Excavation on underground tunnels still continues on one possible site, Oak Island, Nova Scotia. The treasure he buried on Gardiners Island, New York, was recovered and became part of the endowment for a hospital. A story based on Kidd's exploits is *"The Gold Bug" by *Edgar Allan Poe. Younger readers can find out more about Kidd in *Buccaneers and Pirates of Our Coasts* (1898) by *Frank R. Stockton and *The Mysterious Voyage of Captain Kidd* (1970) by A.B.C. Whipple (1918–). A good book for older readers is *Captain Kidd and the War Against the Pirates* (1986) by Robert C. Ritchie (1938–). MR & YA

Kidnapped (1886), by *Robert Louis Stevenson, is the exciting story of 17-year-old David Balfour, who sets out in 1751 from his home in Scotland to seek his fortune. David is poor but educated. The local minister gives him a letter from David's late father saying that David is the sole heir to the estate where his uncle now lives. The uncle, living alone, appears to welcome him, and the adventure begins, for David is kidnapped, taken to sea, shipwrecked, and cast ashore. He spends dangerous months in the Scottish Highlands on the run with Alan Stewart, a Highland rebel wanted by the Redcoats of King George of England. His goal is to rescue his friend Alan, deal with his deceitful uncle, who arranged for David to be sold into slavery in the Carolinas, and claim his rightful share of the ancestral home. The best edition of *Kidnapped* to look for is the one illustrated with the vivid paintings of N.C. Wyeth (1882–1945), published in 1913 and reissued since. *David Balfour* (1892), known in England as *Catriona*, is a sequel to *Kidnapped*. Another Stevenson novel you will enjoy is *The Master of Ballantrae* (1889), about the struggle of two Scottish brothers for the ancestral estate and for the woman they both love. Four movies of *Kidnapped* (1938, 1949, 1959, 1972) confirm the continuing popularity of this adventure story. MR

Kidnapping Mr. Tubbs (1978), by Don Schellie (1932–), is a novel about a person called A.J., who helps Eloise kidnap Mr. Tubbs, an ancient cowboy, from a nursing home to take him to

Cover of the edition of *Kidnapped*
illustrated by N.C. Wyeth

visit his former ranch. This seems like a terrible idea to A.J., and illegal too, but Eloise, who is 17 years old—older than A.J.—has a VW car, and is determined to help Mr. Tubbs. A.J. does not like old people much and has many complaints about sharing the aging VW "bug" with a saddle, a Bassett hound, and a deaf, talkative old man, who has forgotten his teeth in the getaway. A.J. loses a contact lens, so he cannot even drive, and he feels mighty surly throughout the long ride. But the twists and turns in plot bring adventure and insight to the kidnappers, and a chance to be useful to the old cowboy in this story of the modern West. Another book by Schellie that you may find interesting is *Me, Cholay & Co.—Apache Warriors* (1973), which is about five young survivors of a raid on a peaceful Apache camp. MR

Killer Swan, The (1980) This novel by Eth Clifford (1915–) tells about Lex Mebbin, a 14-year-old boy troubled by his father's suicide and unable to accept his stepfather, Steve, or the family's move from the city to the country. When a pair of swans settle on the lake by their house, Lex pays little attention until the male, or cob, half-blind and half-crazed by stabbing pains in its brain, attacks the boy. When the cob kills one of its newborn cygnets, Lex risks his life to save a second cygnet, then takes on the job of raising the young bird and protecting it from the cob's repeated attacks. In fighting the cob's violent behavior, Lex begins to understand and deal with his father's death and get on with his own life. Eth Clifford has written many books for young people, including *The Year of the Three-Legged Deer* (1972), set in Indiana in 1819, about the problems faced by a frontier settler, his Native American wife, and their two children; *The Curse of the Moon-raker* (1977), about 10 shipwrecked people struggling to survive on an isolated Pacific island; and *The Rocking Chair Rebellion* (1978), about a 14-year-old girl who becomes involved in the lives of a group of senior citizens. MR

Kilmer, Joyce (1886–1918) After one year as a high school Latin teacher, the author of the popular poem "Trees" turned to reviewing and editing, particularly revising word definitions. Kilmer's first volume of verse, *Summer of Love*, appeared in 1911. By 1913 he was working for *The New York Times*, and in August of that year he published "Trees." It became famous and is still remembered for its first and last lines, "I think that I shall never see/ A poem lovely as a tree," and "Poems are made by fools like me/ But only God can make a tree." This poem was set to music in 1927. Kilmer was killed during World War I while scouting enemy machine-gun nests. MR & YA

Kim (1900), by *Rudyard Kipling, tells of the journey of a quick-witted 13-year-old orphan down the Grand Trunk Road of India: "It runs straight, bearing without crowding India's traffic for 1500 miles—such a river of life as nowhere else exists in the world." Kim, widely known as the "Little Friend of all the World" in the crowded streets of his birthplace, Lahore, becomes the *chela* (disciple, or follower) and

guide of a Tibetan lama, or holy man, who is searching for the fountain of wisdom. They follow the road south to Benares. It takes all of Kim's street smarts and knowledge of the wily way of humans to keep the unworldly lama fed. The dangers faced by the boy and the lama, the amazing characters they meet, the lies that they hear and that Kim tells, and the wisdom and love each acquires from the other make an exciting story. The many names of people and places may seem confusing, but the persistent reader will enjoy a rich journey. Among Kipling's other stories about India are *The Jungle Books* and *Just So Stories*. *Kim* was adapted for the movies in 1950 and 1984. MR & YA

King, Martin Luther, Jr. (1929–1968) This universally acknowledged black leader for civil rights and equality was assassinated April 4, 1968, by a rifleman in Memphis, Tennessee. King, a minister, expanded his mission from his first small church in Alabama to become the conscience of millions of blacks and whites. He was an electrifying speaker, and many of his sermons and speeches, which totaled almost 450 a year, were recorded. His work for civil rights led to his being jailed at least 14 times. His home was bombed three times, and he was stabbed once in the chest. One recorded speech, released in 1969, "I Shall Die, but That Is All I Shall Do for Death," reflects his nonviolent nature and his awareness of the dangers of his mission. His most famous speech is "I Have a Dream," which was delivered at the 1963 March on Washington, a turning point for racial awareness in the United States. In addition to his speeches, he wrote more than 25 books, some of them collections of sermons that have been published posthumously. Several are notable: *The Measure of a Man* (1959), *Pilgrimage to Nonviolence* (1960), *Letter from Birmingham Jail* (1963), *Where Do We Go from Here: Chaos or Community?* (1967), and *The Trumpet Conscience* (1968). All are about civil rights and reflect King's sense of civility and community for all peoples and his lack of hatred, except for

---

MR = Middle Reader   YA = Young Adult Reader   * = See this main entry

a hatred of evil. Yet he understood that the white person's hate and fear and the rich person's wealth are the West's most powerful forces. King was awarded the Nobel Peace Prize in 1964. Several films about King have been made, but the most notable are a documentary, *King: A Filmed Record—Montgomery to Memphis* (1970), and *King* (1978), a dramatized biography. YA

King, Stephen (Edwin) (1947–) By the time this popular author of horror stories and *Gothic novels graduated from college in 1970, he had already sold short stories. The success of his first novel, *Carrie* (1974), made possible his career as a writer. *Carrie* is the tale of an unpopular and unhappy girl who has special mental powers and uses them to have a fiery revenge on the people who have tormented her. In *Salem's Lot* (1975) vampires take over a town, and *The Shining* (1977) is set in a spooky hotel and includes a boy who has extrasensory perception. In *Pet Sematary* (1983) a family new to a rural area finds they have moved next door to an unusual cemetery for pets. King's other novels include *The Stand* (1978, reissued complete and uncut, 1990), set in a post *holocaust world devastated by plague; *It* (1986), about seven friends who join forces to destroy a supernatural creature of unspeakable evil; and *Misery* (1987), about a writer who is imprisoned and tortured by a psychotic fan who wants him to resurrect a character he has killed off.

In one sense King's short stories and novels are quite unbelievable, but they are excellent examples of their kind, and, as you read, you can feel the terror coming from unknown forces. If you like such stories, try those of *H.P. Lovecraft, *Roald Dahl, and *Edgar Allan Poe. A movie was made of *Carrie* in 1976, of *Salem's Lot* in 1979, of *The Shining* in 1980, of *Pet Sematary* in 1989, of *Misery* in 1990, and a two-part TV movie of *It* in 1990. MR & YA

King Arthur is thought to have been a king of Britain in the 6th century. Written evidence of his existence other than *fable and legend is very scarce; the major source is one manu-script called *The History of the Britons* by Nennius, a monk of the 9th century. Nennius did not clearly separate folktales, legends, and historical events. But between Nennius and another writer, Gildas, a 6th-century monk, historians have concluded that Arthur was a military commander who won 12 major battles against the invading Saxons and kept the peace in England for a generation. Arthur next appears in *History of the Kings of Britain* (c.1150) by *Geoffrey of Monmouth. Meanwhile, other writers recorded ancient oral stories about Arthur, adding such details as the *Round Table, the *Sword in the Stone, and *Lancelot, the lover of *Guinevere. *Thomas Malory brought these stories together in *Le Morte d'Arthur* (1485), and it is chiefly from this book that the literature and poetry of chivalry, love, courage, and honor of the Arthurian legend derive. Among the many books about the legendary king are, for younger readers, *The Story of King Arthur and His Knights* (1903) by *Howard Pyle; *King Arthur and His Knights of the Round Table* by Roger L. Green (1918–1987); *The Boy's King Arthur* (1880) by Sidney Lanier (1842–1881); and *The Light Beyond the Forest* (1979), *The Sword and the Circle* (1981), and *The Road to Camlann* (1982) by *Rosemary Sutcliff. Older readers will probably enjoy *The Crystal Cave* (1970), *The Hollow Hills* (1973), and *The Last Enchantment* (1979), a trilogy that focuses on Merlin, by *Mary Stewart; *The Mists of Avalon* (1982), a novel that tells the story of King Arthur from the point of view of the women in his life, by *Marion Zimmer Bradley (1930–); and *The Once and Future King* by *T.H. White. *The Acts of King Arthur and His Noble Knights* (1976) by *John Steinbeck is a retelling in modern English of Malory's *Morte d'Arthur*. You might also enjoy an interesting and readable book about the continuing search by scholars and archeologists for the historical king, *Quest for a King: Searching for the Real King Arthur* (1989) by Catherine M. Andronik (1958–). Many films dealing with Arthurian legend have been made, including *A Connecticut Yankee in King Arthur's Court* in 1948, *Knights of the Round Table* in 1953, *The Sword in the

Stone in 1963, *Camelot in 1967, and *Excalibur in 1981. MR & YA

King Arthur and His Knights of the Round Table

King Arthur and His Knights of the Round Table (1953), by the British writer Roger L. Green (1918–1987), is divided into four books. Book One concerns the sorcerer *Merlin, the coming of *King Arthur, the great sword *Excalibur, and the establishment of the *Round Table at *Camelot, where knights pledge to work with honor and chivalry for the common good. Book Two recounts the adventures of several knights, especially *Gawain and *Lancelot. Book Three tells of the quests of different knights for the *Holy Grail, which was the cup from which *Jesus drank at the *Last Supper, and how *Galahad came to the Round Table. Book Four is about Lancelot, Queen Guinevere, and their love for each other and for Arthur, and of Arthur's love for his queen and his best knight. A tragic ending, brought about by Arthur's evil son, Mordred, ends this saga with the death of Arthur on the battlefield. If you enjoyed this book, you will want to read **The Sword in the Stone* by *T.H. White. For more books about Arthur and his knights, see *King Arthur. MR

King Lear

King Lear (1608) Just as young actors yearn to play the lead in *Hamlet, so do mature actors want to play Lear in this searing tragedy by *William Shakespeare. In his old age, Lear announces to his daughters that he will retire and divide his kingdom among them according to how each professes her love for him. Goneril and Regan announce that their love for him is endless and beyond price, greater than life itself. Cordelia declares that indeed she loves him as her father but not more than life itself, and not more than she will love her husband when she marries. She will love them equally, she says, and resists Lear's claim to be the center of the universe. "So young," he says, "and so untender?" She answers, "So young, my lord, and true." But Lear, whose ego has been puffed up by people in his court, cannot accept this clear and separate person as his daughter, and he falls apart with rage. He disinherits Cordelia and turns to Goneril and Regan for comfort, planning to divide his time and kingdom between them. But they are full of greed and murder, and as Lear realizes their treachery, he goes mad on the heath in a terrific storm, accompanied by his Fool. In a parallel, intertwining plot, another old man, the Earl of Gloucester, cannot distinguish between his faithful son and his treacherous son. Shakespeare beautifully reveals how old men may grow and change. In the end the stage is thick with blood, and the survivors have learned what is good and what is true. Movies were made of *King Lear* in 1971 and 1987. YA

King Must Die, The

King Must Die, The (1958) In this novel, *Mary Renault re-creates the Greek myth of *Theseus. Theseus himself tells the story, beginning with his childhood in Troizen, a city of ancient Greece. While he does not know who his father was, Theseus seems to be under the protection of *Poseidon, the "Wave-Gatherer, Horse-lover, and Earth-Shaker," and he can tell when an earthquake is coming. When he lifts a heavy stone that covers a buried sword, he learns that it belongs to his true father, the king of Athens. In Athens he nearly loses his life before his father recognizes the sword and welcomes him as true heir. Then, powerful ships arrive to claim seven boys and seven girls, the yearly tribute Athens pays to the *Minotaur of Crete. Enraged at this unjust custom, Theseus joins the group, to the horror of his father. The myth says that the Minotaur, which is kept in the center of the *Labyrinth in the palace of Knossos, is a man-eating monster, half bull, half man. Theseus learns that though there is indeed a mystery in the Labyrinth, the young victims are not destined to be food for the Minotaur; they are to be bull dancers, and no bull dancer has ever lived for more than six months. His task, then, is to train his companions to become a superb team that can survive bull dancing, the favorite gambling activity of Cretan nobility. The successes and survival of Theseus and his team bring him the love of Ariadne, daughter of King Minos, and she leads him to the terrible secret of the Labyrinth, answering at last the question of what the Minotaur really was. Then, during an earthquake that destroys the palace, Theseus escapes by ship with his team and Ariadne. But because he fails to change his sail from black to white, his father, thinking him dead, jumps from the cliff where he had waited and watched. Theseus therefore returns as king of Athens.

The historical reality on which the myth is based began to emerge when archeologists unearthed the labyrinths and paintings of bull dancers at the palace of Knossos in Crete. If you enjoyed *The King Must Die*, you can read more about Theseus in *Mythology* by Edith Hamilton (1867–1963) and *D'Aulaires' Book of Greek Myths* by Ingri d'Aulaire (1904–1980) and Edgar Parin d'Aulaire (1898–1986). YA

King of the Golden River, The (1851) In this tale of good and evil by John Ruskin (1819–1900), two mean older brothers, Hans and Schwartz, are punished for being greedy and for mistreating their younger brother, Gluck. The time is the legendary past in the ancient country of Stiria and its fertile Treasure Valley, which is owned by the brothers. No famines, droughts, or floods exist there. Above the valley lies the Golden River. The evil brothers pay their servants nothing, beat them, and keep the crops from the starving people until the value of the crops doubles. They stack their gold on the floor and never give any away. Gluck, who pities the poor, is only 12 years old and therefore helpless. Like *Cinderella, he is treated as a servant. One day a peculiar little man arrives and begs to be taken in out of the rain. Gluck knows his brothers will object, but he feeds him. When the brothers return, the little man resists with magical tricks as they strike him. Then the ferocious South-West Wind causes storms and droughts, ruining the brothers' crops, and Hans and Schwartz, like their hearts, are turned to stone forever. Gluck is rewarded, and the poor are welcomed again. If you enjoyed this story, you will also like the folktales collected by the brothers *Grimm and *Andrew Lang, and also *The Princess and the Goblin and other *fantasy stories by the Scottish writer George MacDonald (1824–1905). MR

King of the Wind (1948), by *Marguerite Henry, is the story of the Godolphin Arabian, ancestor of many of today's racehorses, and the mute Moroccan stable boy Agba, whose duty it was to stay with the horse from birth to death. Agba calls the colt Sham, the Arabic word for sun, when it is born in the royal stables of Morocco, and Sham turns out to be the fastest of the royal colts. Then Agba learns that he is to accompany Sham and five other royal stallions and their stableboys as a gift to Louis XV, the Boy King of France. But before the voyage the captain of the ship steals the food money, and when the horses arrive nearly starved, the Boy King sends them to his army, except for Sham, who is kept as cart horse for the royal kitchen. In Paris conditions go from bad to worse for this little horse and his boy, until Sham is bought by a kind English Quaker. But in England, as in France, Sham is unmanageable by anyone save Agba. Again their fortunes decline. How Agba ends up in Newgate Prison and how he and Sham go from there to saving the estate of the Earl of Godolphin is a nearly incredible tale. On the day that Sham died, when the horse was 29 years old, Agba left England for Morocco, his mission ended. The Godolphin Arabian never raced in England, but his blood still runs in the racehorses of today. Two other books about horses by Henry are *Misty of Chincoteague and *Justin Morgan Had a Horse. Another book you will enjoy is *The Black Stallion by *Walter Farley. *King of the Wind* won a *Newbery Medal in 1949. MR

King-Smith, Dick (1922–) A farmer for 20 years, King-Smith went back to college and became a primary schoolteacher. When he was 56 years old, he began writing books for children. All his characters are animals with human foibles and strengths. His background as a farmer emerges as he describes the hard facts of farmyard life. In his first book, *The Fox Busters* (1978), the fowl of Foxearth Farm band together against the menace of nearby foxes. King-Smith often has an underdog hero who makes good, as in *Pigs Might Fly* (1980), which is about a deformed piglet escaping the fate of the slaughterhouse to save his farm. King-Smith's humor and warmth are evident in *The Mouse Butcher* (1982), about a butcher's cat who wins the heart of a high-society cat while defeating Great Mog, a savage wild cat. *Babe: The Gallant Pig* (1985) is about a pig who likes to watch the news on television. Other authors whose books feature animal characters include *Richard Adams, *Kenneth Grahame, *Robert Lawson, *George Seldon, and *E.B. White. MR

Kingdom under the Sea and Other Stories, The (1971) This book, by *Joan Aiken, re-tells 11 folktales from eastern Europe. In it are the witch Baba Yaga, Daybog the sun god, and Dawn Maiden, along with various angels, drag-ons, knights, and beautiful princesses. Aiken's ingenious and lively writing brings to life the little girls who grind flour for the sun's birth-day cake, the prince who finds his bride in the reeds in the middle of the Black Sea, and the fisherman who is chased by mermaids on his visit to the sea king's palace. Other books by Aiken are *Go Saddle the Sea* (1977), which is about an orphaned youth who runs away from his unhappy home in Spain to England, where he tries to find his father's family; and *The Shadow Guests* (1980), which is about a young boy who arrives at his cousin's house in En-gland unprepared for the supernatural furor his presence unleashes.

Kingsley, Charles (1819–1875) An English country parson, Kingsley became a novelist, naturalist, reformer, and historian. In his nov-els his heroes exemplified dedication to public service and patriotism. Today he is known best for *The Water-Babies, which is about Tom, a young chimney sweep who is transformed into a merman and has many fantastic adventures; and for *Westward Ho!* (1855), a spirited tale about the Spanish Armada that older readers will enjoy. If you are interested in Greek myths, be sure to read Kingsley's *The Heroes:*

Or Greek Fairy Tales for My Children (1856), which tells about the adventures of *Perseus, *Jason, and *Theseus. You will probably find a recent edition in your library. See also *Leaveheavenalone. MR & YA

Kipling, Rudyard (1865–1936) Born in Bombay, India, to English parents, Rudyard and his sis-ter Trix were cared for as children by a couple living in Southsea, England. Five years passed before Rudyard saw his parents again. His sense of abandonment and despair persisted for many years and was revealed in such writings as the short story "Baa Baa, Black Sheep" (1888), about a boy named Punch and his little sister, Judy, who are sent by their parents in Bombay to live with relatives in England, *The Light That Failed, and his autobiography *Something of Myself* (1937).

When Kipling was 16 years old, he sailed to India to become a journalist. There he steeped himself in the life and culture of India and be-gan writing short stories and poetry, much concerning the lives of British soldiers and civil servants in India, then part of the British Empire. His stories were collected in several volumes, including *Plain Tales from the Hills* (1888), *Soldiers Three* (1888), and *The Phantom Rickshaw and Other Tales* (1888). Later, he re-turned to England and quickly gained literary stardom. In 1891, he married and settled in Brat-tleboro, Vermont, for a few years, where he wrote such renowned works for younger read-ers as *The Jungle Books, *Just So Stories, and most of *Captains Courageous. After return-ing to England with his family, Kipling contin-ued to produce popular books, including *Kim, which many readers consider to be his best novel.

Kipling's reputation was heightened by his verse, which later fell into disfavor because of its use of dialect and its apparent defense of British imperialism. However, Kipling's poetry speaks much about human beings and the way they relate to one another, and some of his lines have gained a permanent place in the En-glish language. For example, from the poem "If—" comes:

If you can keep your head when all
about you
Are losing theirs and blaming it on
you. . . .

From "The Ballad of East and West" comes the line:

Oh, East is East, and West is West, and never
the twain shall meet.

And from "Gunga Din," about a brave regimental water carrier who saves a British soldier's life at the expense of his own:

Though I've belted you and flayed you,
By the livin' Gawd that made you,
You're a better man than I am, Gunga Din!

There are many collections of Kipling's stories and poetry. Two of the best are *Kipling: A Selection of His Stories and Poems* (1956), edited by John Beecroft (1902–1966), and the definitive edition of *Rudyard Kipling's Verse* (1940). A number of Kipling's works have been adapted for film, including *Gunga Din* in 1939, a rousing adventure movie that is still very enjoyable. Kipling was awarded the Nobel Prize for literature in 1907. MR & YA

Kjelgaard, Jim [James Arthur Kjelgaard] (1910–1959) Best known for his story about an Irish setter, *Big Red*, Kjelgaard (pronounced Kel-guard) grew up on a mountain farm in Pennsylvania where he and his brothers hunted and fished, passions he never outgrew. The author of over 40 books for young people about animals, he worked as a surveyor's assistant, plumber's apprentice, and trapper before settling down to full-time writing when he was 28 years old. Kjelgaard's first book, *Forest Patrol* (1941), tells about the wilderness experiences he had with his brother, a forest ranger; it was followed by *Rebel Siege* (1943), about a frontiersman; but it was *Big Red* that really launched his books about dogs. Several of his other books you may like are *A Nose for Trouble* (1949), about Smoky, a dog that would not hunt game but had a keen bloodhound nose for tracking poachers; *Desert Dog* (1956), about a racing greyhound that finds freedom in the heat and danger of the Southwestern desert;

Wolf Brother (1957), about a wolf and his young American Indian companion, which tells the Native American's side of what is called the winning of the West; and *Hidden Trail* (1962), about a young nature photographer and his dogs. MR

Kneeknock Rise (1970), by *Natalie Babbitt, relates the adventures of Egan and Annabelle the dog. Egan visits his Uncle Anson in the village of Instep at the foot of the Mammoth Mountains. Instep is famous not only for its wonderful autumn fair but for a mysterious creature said to live on the misty peak of Kneeknock Rise. The Megrimum, as the villagers call the creature, moans and gurgles on stormy nights, causing all who hear it to shiver in delicious horror.

Egan hears many scary stories about the creature, and everyone worries that his own Uncle Ott, who is missing, may have been devoured by the Megrimum. On the evening of the fair, a storm approaches and people nervously await the horrible groans from the Rise. Cousin Ada calls Egan a sissy and dares him to make the climb. Furious, he sets off with Annabelle on a long, hard trek up the mountainside. On the final slope he discovers Uncle Ott, who shows him the source of the moans. Egan can hardly wait to tell the villagers the truth about the Megrimum, but Uncle Ott says people may prefer to hang on to their beliefs. Ott asks, "Is it better to be wise if it makes you solemn and practical, or is it better to be foolish so you can go on enjoying yourself?"

Later, when Egan tries to explain the Megrimum, nobody wants to believe him. He learns to accept Ott's wise words and stops trying to spoil people's excitement and pleasure in their legend. Another monster story that will amuse you is *Yobgorgle: Mystery Monster of Lake Ontario* by *Daniel M. Pinkwater. MR

Knickerbocker, Diedrich This was the pen name *Washington Irving used when he wrote *A History of New York* (1809). This two-volume work has been called a farce, a burlesque, and a *satire. In it Knickerbocker knocks conventional history on its head. He speculates that any race with advanced technology, perhaps moon creatures with "concentrated sunbeams," could dominate the whole planet as easily as Europeans deceived and dominated the native inhabitants of the New World. But Irving's main target is the Dutch settlement of New York, and he makes continuous fun of Dutch politicians, customs, manners, and history. He does not ignore the horde of "barbarians" in the surrounding states, such as the troublemaking Yankees with their names like Preserved Fish and Determined Cock. He spoofs Thomas Jefferson, a figure of his own time, and in general reduces accepted ideas and history to a playful rubble of words, a wonderful work of comic imagination. *A History of New York* is definitely a fun book to read. YA

Knight, Eric (1897–1943) This English-born Quaker wrote several books prior to *Lassie Come Home, but it is Lassie, everybody's favorite collie, who will forever be remembered. In England, Knight's father died suddenly, and his mother went to Russia as a governess, leaving Eric and his brothers shifting between poor relatives. Before Knight emigrated to the United States, when he was 15 years old, he had already worked full time in a sawmill and in textile and glass-blowing factories. Though his family was reunited in Philadelphia, his interest in formal schooling was over. Instead, he landed a job as copyboy on a newspaper and within a short time was writing feature articles, especially as a film critic. By 1934 he was writing film scripts in Hollywood. Knight's story *This Above All* (1941), about a self-educated Englishman caught up in World War II, is considered by many to be the first great novel about the war. *This Above All* was produced as a movie in 1942. YA

Knowles, John (1926–1979) Beginning work as a reporter, Knowles shifted to free-lance writing and editing before becoming a full-time writer in 1960. Knowles's first novel, *A Separate Peace, like all his novels, is based on a special place that enables his characters and plot to emerge. His characters are often young men with experiences in boarding schools. Knowles

was graduated from Phillips Exeter Academy in New Hampshire. *Morning in Antibes* (1962), about a young man's shifting identity, and *Spreading Fires* (1974), with its descriptions of long-repressed adolescent emotions, revolve around the eight years he lived, on and off, on the French Riviera. His seven years in Connecticut, including the years when he attended Yale University, provided him with the background for *Indian Summer* (1966), the story of a returning student seeking his identity, and *The Paragon* (1972), about a misfit at Yale resisting what he saw as its brainwashing. Knowles contended that he never wrote with a specific audience in mind, but that he wrote about atmosphere in order to understand a place better. MR & YA

Knudson, Rozanne Ruth (1932–) This popular writer of sports stories started out as a high school English teacher, moved to college teaching, and then became a writer of fiction, usually under the name of R.R. Knudson. Yet she says that she never wanted to be a writer, that she would much rather read, but became a writer in order to survive in the academic world. She published *Sports Poems* (1971) and was soon at work on *Zanballer* (1972), which is about a girl, Zan Hagen, who would rather play football than be a cheerleader. This work is autobiographical. Knudson loves sports and teaches sports writing, and almost all of her books are about young people participating in one sport or another, such as *Zan Hagen's Marathon, perhaps her best-known book; *Fox Running* (1975), about an Apache girl training for the Olympics; *Zanbanger* (1977), in which Zan Hagen sues for the right to play basketball; and *Rinehart Lifts* (1980), in which Zan encourages a boy to excel at weightlifting to prove to the other boys that he can participate in sports. If you enjoy Knudson's books, another writer whose sports novels you may like is *Chris Crutcher. MR & YA

Koestler, Arthur (1905–1983) A Hungarian-born British novelist, journalist, essayist, and author of *Darkness at Noon, Koestler often writes about the problems of political idealism and power. When he was a child, he liked especially science and mathematics. Later, he became fascinated with the Zionist movement, went to Palestine in 1926, and did odd jobs until a German newspaper hired him as correspondent. In Berlin, while working as a science editor and foreign correspondent, Koestler joined the Communist Party. He spent a year in the Soviet Union as a guest of the government. As a free-lance journalist, he went to Spain in 1936 to cover the Civil War for an English newspaper. Arrested by the fascists, Koestler was accused of spying and was sentenced to death, but he was released three months later, after the British government intervened on his behalf. His sufferings in prison provided material for *Darkness at Noon*, his most successful novel. In 1938 Koestler left the Communist Party, convinced that the Soviet Union was dangerously close to being a dictatorship. He went to England in 1940 and became a British subject.

By the 1950s, Koestler was writing less about political means and ends, and more about scientific and philosophical subjects. You might like to read *The Scum of the Earth* (1941), an autobiographical account of life in a French detention camp, where Koestler was interned at the beginning of World War II. Some of Koestler's best-known essays are collected in *The Yogi and the Commissar* (1945). *Thieves in the Night* (1946) is a novel about the Jewish resettlement of Palestine in the late 1930s. YA

Kon-Tiki: Across the Pacific by Raft (1950),

by *Thor Heyerdahl, is the true story of his voyage, with a parrot and five companions, on a nine-log balsa wood raft. Heyerdahl, who is from Norway, set out to prove that some primitive peoples could have ranged and migrated on flimsy rafts from South America, where the balsa tree grows, to the South Sea Islands, relying only on the ocean's tides and trade winds. His survival and eventual success are described vividly. In the raft's logbook he muses about how he came to be in the middle of the ocean, acting as cook for the day and finding flying fish and squid on the raft, new arrivals during

the night. This type of detail, along with the rationale for the voyage, absorbs you until by the end of the book you want to know even more. His feeling for time and the elements becomes so graphic that you, like Heyerdahl, discover that "the whole sea was ours. . . . To us on the raft the great problems of civilized man appeared false and illusory—like perverted products of the human mind." But the voyage that appeared to defy nature ends "back in the 20th century," in a lagoon at Tahiti. Other books about true sea adventures that may interest you are *Sailing Alone Around the World* (1899) by Captain Joshua Slocum (1844–1910), about Slocum aboard his boat, the *Spray*. He was the first person to sail alone, keep a journal about his experiences, and survive a trip around the world. You will also enjoy *Maiden Voyage* (1989) by Tania Aebi (1966–), which is the true story of the first girl and youngest person to sail alone around the world. *Kon-Tiki* was filmed in 1951. MR & YA

Konigsburg, E(laine) L(obl) (1930–) A very imaginative author, Konigsburg tackles intense subjects encountered by young people growing up, and makes them understandable, even humorous. As a child raised in small towns—"I remember always looking for myself in books and never finding either me or my town"—and later, with children of her own, she decided to write a book about what was happening to them. Besides, when she was working as a chemist doing both research and teaching, she decided that molecules were no longer any fun: "I twice blew up the laboratory sink, losing my eyebrows and bangs," said Konigsburg. But in her first book, the popular *Jennifer, Hecate, Macbeth, William McKinley, and Me, Elizabeth*, the only part of it that is taken from her daughters' experiences is Elizabeth's loneliness after moving to a new town and having a black girl as her first friend. Konigsburg's second book, *From the Mixed-Up Files of Mrs. Basil E. Frankweiler*, resulted from considerable spy work on the security systems of a museum. She went on to write *About the B'Nai Bagels, *A Proud Taste for Scarlet and Miniver,

Father's Arcane Daughter, and *Journey to an 800 Number* (1982), which is a story about Max and his father, a camel keeper. MR & YA

Koran Muslims believe the Koran is the miracle of the faith of *Islam, and that its precepts, sanctions, and rules are applicable to all people. The Koran, a literary masterpiece consisting of 114 chapters, is the holy book of Islam. Its official text was established in A.D. 650, and it is the textbook from which every Muslim learns to read, which may be the reason why the various Arabic dialects have not divided into several languages, as have languages based on Latin and Chinese. Muslims consider the Koran to be the word of God, a compilation of the utterances of the prophet *Muhammad (Mohammed), as dictated by the archangel Gabriel. The Koran (Arabic *Al-Qur'an*, meaning "reading" or "recital") contains no formal code of laws or morals, yet the one powerful conception consistently present is that of God's unity, sovereignty, compassion, and terrible might. In the early chapters there are vivid descriptions of the doom of the wicked and the terror of the last judgment. There are devotional rules, doctrines for daily living, laws for what is yours and for what is mine, and for the family, society, and the marketplace. Since the appearance of the Koran, Islam has been a religion with no clergy, yet any believer may become an Imam, or religious leader.

Kotzwinkle, William (1938–) Known for his humor, Kotzwinkle has written both for adults and young people. Some examples of his novels show the variety of subjects that interest him. In *Fata Morgana* (1971), with a setting in Paris, police investigate a conjurer who has a fortune-telling machine. In *Dr. Rat* (1976) the setting is a cancer research laboratory, and the story is told from the viewpoint of the animals to be experimented on. Kotzwinkle's rage at the way the animals are treated is very evident. *The Ants Who Took Away Time* (1978) tells how giant ants stole the Great Timepiece and caused time to stand still all over the world. *Trouble in Bugland: A Collection of Inspector Mantis Mysteries* (1983) is a takeoff on the detective stories about *Sherlock Holmes, with an all-insect cast of characters. If you like books of this kind, try those of *Douglas Adams, *Richard Adams, and *J.R.R. Tolkien. MR & YA

Kristin Lavransdatter (1920, 1921, 1922), by *Sigrid Undset, is an absorbing, realistic, and colorful chronicle about family life in Norway during the 14th century. *The Bridal Wreath*, *The Mistress of Husaby*, and *The Cross* make up this trilogy. Kristin is a happy child until her father betrothes her to Simon when she is 15 years old and she is almost raped by Bentein. Months later, Arne, her close childhood friend, is killed by Bentein in an argument over the bad talk that Bentein has been spreading about Kristin. Putting off her betrothal celebration, the depressed Kristin enters a convent, becomes lost on a trip to town, and is rescued by Erlend, the nephew of Lady Aashild. Kristin and Erlend vow eternal love for each other. Erlend's relatives sue for Kristin's hand in marriage from her father, Lavrans, and he agrees. Over the next 15 years Kristin bears seven sons and tries to manage Erlend's rundown estate, Jusaby, while Erlend occupies himself in placing a claimant on the disputed throne of Norway rather than in running his farm. Kristin again becomes pregnant but loses the child and another son. Erlend dies in a scuffle, and Kristin and her remaining six sons must make their own way. Kristin eventually enters a convent, and two of her sons die of the Black Plague, which consumes the city of Nidaros and, finally, Kristin. If you enjoyed these books, you may also like the works of the Norwegian novelist Knut Hamsun (1859–1952), including *Hunger* (1890), about the struggles of a young writer, and *The Growth of the Soil* (1917), which tells of a pioneer and of the land that gives him life, prosperity, and peace. YA

Ku Klux Klan (KKK) This group began as a secret social club in 1865 but, with the political, economic, and social disruptions caused by the American Civil War, it quickly became a *symbol and tool of racists for frightening black people into servile behavior. The Klan, with its strange rituals and costumes, its burning of crosses, and its secrecy, was strongest in the decade following the Civil War. It has been revived twice in the 20th century, most recently in reaction to the civil rights marches of the 1950s and 1960s. In the Klan, women began to be admitted as members in the late 1980s. The Klan and various of its members have been indicted and convicted for bombings and killings. Younger readers will enjoy reading about the Klan in the novels *Morning Glory Afternoon* (1981) by Irene Bennett Brown (1932–), about a young woman who helps defeat the Klan in a Kansas town in 1924, and *Circle of Fire* (1982) by William H. Hooks (1921–), about an 11-year-old boy who confronts Klan prejudice and hatred in his North Carolina town in 1936. A good nonfiction book is *The Ku Klux Klan: America's Recurring Nightmare* (1989) by Fred J. Cook (1911–). MR & YA

Kundera, Milan (1929–) A short-story writer and novelist, born in Czechoslovakia, Kundera was known there chiefly for writing and speaking against the repression of the communist government. His first play was *The Owners of the Keys* (1961), about an idealistic student. The short stories in the three-book cycle, Laughable Loves (1963–1968), are primarily about love and sexual politics, describing the illusory pursuit of happiness through love. A selection of stories from the three collections was published in English as *Laughable Loves* (1974). Kundera's first novel, *The Joke* (1967), explores the generation gap as well as the ideology gap. Forced into exile after the Soviet invasion of Czechoslovakia in 1968, Kundera has lived in France since 1975. *The Farewell Party* (1976) is a novel about a jazz musician who gets a nurse pregnant while attending an infertility clinic and who still loves his wife. *The Unbearable Lightness of Being* (1984) is a best-selling novel about Tomas, a talented young surgeon, and his lovers and friends before and after the Soviet invasion. Such are the politics of the time that Tomas ends his days as a farmhand in the country. This is a rich meditation on life under a totalitarian regime and is full of sadness and laughter. Another Czech writer whose works you will like is *Václav Havel. *The Unbearable Lightness of Being* was produced as a movie in 1988. YA

La Farge, Oliver (1901–1963) From his childhood intensely interested in American Indians, La Farge began his career as a teacher and scientist, writing about and doing field work in anthropology, ethnology, and archeology. But with the success of his first novel, *Laughing Boy*, a Navaho love story, La Farge decided to continue writing fiction. While studying the Navaho people he was often mistaken by Native Americans themselves for a member of another tribe because of his deep tan, black hair, long arms, and individual walk. His second novel, *Sparks Fly Upward* (1931), is the story of an Indian in Central America in the 19th century. La Farge was deeply sensitive to the needs of Native Americans and critical of the way the American government dealt with their problems. He continually wrote about these problems and served on many councils and commissions in order to make sure that the government treated with respect the Native American cultures that he knew so well. If you enjoy La Farge's books, try also *Ramona* by Helen Hunt Jackson (1850–1885) and the books of *A.B. Guthrie, Jr., *Mari Sandoz, and *Leslie Marmon Silko. YA

La Fontaine, Jean de (1621–1695) The *Fables* (1668–1694) of this amiable 17th-century Frenchman are universally admired. Some of the fables were suggested by *Aesop and some were original, but they were all popular in his time. Like most fables they are populated by talking animals with human characteristics. La Fontaine was an absent-minded, childlike person, according to contemporary reports, but he wrote poetry, stories, and plays with a passion. Originality, grace, and wit are the hallmarks of his fables, and they have attracted many translators and illustrators. Among the more familiar fables are "The North Wind and the Sun," "The Hare and the Tortoise," "The Grasshopper and the Ant," and "The Town Mouse and the Country Mouse." When La Fontaine was dying, he is reported to have said that it would be nice if one could leave life the way one leaves a feast, "thanking one's host." You can find several editions of the *Fables*, a couple in inexpensive paperbacks in your bookstore. See also *Charles Perrault; and *fable. MR & YA

labyrinth probably comes from *labrys*, the sacred double axe of Crete. In the Greek myth of *Theseus and the *Minotaur, the Labyrinth was the complex prison built above and below ground in the palace of Knossos to contain the Minotaur, half man and half bull, who had a taste for human flesh. The Labyrinth was so intricate that no youth—nor the Minotaur—ever found the way out until Theseus, the son of the Athenian king, went in with a ball of thread, killed the beast, and followed the thread out of the maze. "Labyrinth" has come to mean a complicated, intricate, confusing

Can you find your way in or out of this labyrinth? Follow the black lines.

network of paths through which it is difficult to find one's way. Labyrinths, often called mazes, are sometimes constructed in gardens or parks. They consist of paths surrounded by high, impenetrable hedges, and visitors amuse themselves by trying to find their way out.

Lady from Philadelphia, The In the collection of stories called *The Peterkin Papers* by *Lucretia P. Hale, this lady is the only character with common sense. A friend of the bumbling Peterkin family, the Lady from Philadelphia answers all their questions and solves their problems, in person or by telegram. She solves their first problem, in which the Peterkins have added a supply of chemicals and herbs and spices to Mrs. Peterkin's cup of coffee to offset the taste of salt she had put in by mistake, by suggesting a fresh cup of coffee. In their last problem, in which the Peterkins have lost each other in ports all over the Middle East by missing ferries, she suggests through telegrams that they "all meet at the Sphinx." These stories are amusing spoofs on the conventions of *Victorian families and were very popular in their time. The Lady from Philadelphia could be the ancestor of one of today's arbiters of behavior, Miss Manners, who, with equal calm and humor, leads us bumbling mortals with common sense through the confounding thickets of etiquette. MR

Lady Macbeth, in *William Shakespeare's play *Macbeth, must believe she is fulfilling her wifely role when she urges her husband to "screw his courage to the sticking place." Macbeth plans to murder the king of Scotland, a guest in his castle, in order to become king himself. At the last moment his courage fails him, but his wife gives him strength with these words, and it is she who returns the bloody daggers to the corpse after the murder. Once on this terrible path, Macbeth keeps on murdering those who threaten him, even after he is king. But when she is queen, Lady Macbeth sleepwalks. "Who would have thought the old man to have had so much blood in him?" she says, in her pacing, and then, "All the perfumes of Arabia will not sweeten this little hand!" Destroyed by her anguish, unable to forget what she so coolly did, Lady Macbeth kills herself. YA

"Lady or the Tiger?, The" (1881) This well-known short story, by *Frank R. Stockton, raises profound questions about the human, especially female, heart. It poses a puzzle in which a savage legal system designed by a barbaric king insists that a princess decide whether her lover, of common blood, should be married to another woman or be devoured by a tiger. It was the fashion in *Victorian times, when this story was written, to imagine that the princess might prefer the violent, bloody solution. At any rate, the story caused endless discussion about the nature of woman and very few about the nature of laws designed by men to control women. It is worth reading as good fun and as a period piece. You can find it in many short-story anthologies as well as several paperback editions of Stockton's stories, including *The Lady or the Tiger and Other Stories* (1968). MR & YA

Lady Windermere's Fan (1892), a play by *Oscar Wilde, is noted for its wit, as are many works by this English dramatist, novelist, and poet. The central idea turns upside down the *Victorian convention of what is meant by a "good woman" and a "bad woman." The plot is complex and emotional, but the mood is light and sharply funny. The story is about how the

The princess ponders the fate of her beloved
in "The Lady or the Tiger?"

bad woman, Mrs. Erlynne, sacrifices her new
and hard-won good reputation for the sake of
her good daughter, Lady Windermere, who is
about to become bad. Lady Windermere never
learns that this bad woman is her own mother,
but she sees that Mrs. Erlynne's action was noble, and she realizes the stupidity of labeling a
woman "good" or "bad" as though good people
and bad people were two separate creations.
This comedy makes its points by a wit that
bites rather than by developed characters, so it
is a wonderfully amusing play to see. If you enjoyed this play, you may also like the plays of
*George Bernard Shaw. YA

Lady's Not for Burning, The (1948) By
*Christopher Fry, this drama is a blend of com-
edy and poetry. The year is about 1400, the setting a small English market town, and the

hero, Thomas, wants to be hanged. A poor soldier, he finds life mean and dull, and he confesses to killing a rag-and-bone man, old
Skipps. But the mayor is more interested in
burning as a witch the wealthy young Jennet,
who is accused of turning Skipps into a dog.
Besides, the town will get her property if she is
condemned as a witch. The mayor puts
thumbscrews on Thomas in order to keep him
from confessing, and puts him in a cell with
Jennet. Jennet learns that Thomas has killed
no one but is confessing to divert attention
from her and because he does not want to live.
They fall in love, of course, before they are rescued, and the story takes some wonderful
twists and turns. There is a quirky subplot
that will amuse you as Fry elegantly poses intelligence against stupidity, honesty against
corruption, and self-knowledge and love above
all. The language is clear and rich and graceful,
as delightful to read as it is to hear and see the
play. YA

Laertes, in the play *Hamlet by *William
Shakespeare, is the son of *Polonius, the
brother of *Ophelia, and the friend of Hamlet.
As the son of the king of Denmark's counselor,
Laertes has grown up with Hamlet, who is the
son of the dead king and nephew of the new
king, Claudius. Early in the play, before he departs for France, Laertes advises his sister, "For
Hamlet, and the trifling of his favor, hold it a
fashion and a toy in blood." In other words,
Ophelia should not take Hamlet's professions
of love for her seriously, as "he may not, as un-
valued persons do, carve for himself," or make
his own choice of marriage partner. Just before
he leaves, Laertes is advised by his father, Polonius, "Neither a borrower nor a lender be."
When Laertes returns it is to find his father
dead and his sister insane, and he blames Hamlet. With the king, who has his own reasons for
wishing Hamlet dead, Laertes arranges a
"friendly" duel with Hamlet, in which Laertes
uses a poisoned sword. Laertes manages to
wound Hamlet, but both he himself and the
king are wounded by Hamlet with the same
sword. Then Laertes says of the king, "He is

justly served. It is a poison tempered by himself." As Laertes dies, he begs Hamlet to exchange forgiveness with him: "Mine and my father's death come not upon thee, nor thine on me!" Hamlet, dying, replies, "Heaven make thee free of it! I follow thee." YA

Lagerlöf, Selma (1858–1940) Long before people were flying as a routine matter, Lagerlöf imagined Sweden from the air, from the point of view of an elf-sized boy riding on the back of a goose and able to speak the language of animals. History is told in the folk fantasy *The Wonderful Adventures of Nils*, in which you can learn the entire geography of Sweden and enjoy the folktales connected to each area. Lagerlöf was born to a large family in the west of Sweden. Early lamed by polio and unable to play, she read all the books in the library of her father's large estate and absorbed the folk stories of local people. Her other books were also popular, and in 1909 she became the first woman to receive the Nobel Prize for literature. She was also the first woman to be invited to join the Swedish Academy. MR

Lake Poets, The Three poets are referred to by this term— *William Wordsworth, *Samuel Taylor Coleridge, and Robert Southey (1774–1843). They all lived in the Lake District of northwestern England and wrote poetry in the same period. They wrote in the early Romantic mode and held revolutionary ideas when they were young. Southey and Coleridge shared views on nature and social justice. Coleridge and Wordsworth collaborated on a group of poems published as *Lyrical Ballads* (1798–1802), the first important collection of English Romantic poetry. The three were friends, and Southey became Coleridge's brother-in-law. For a time Coleridge lived with Southey, and also with the Wordsworths. *George Gordon Byron made fun of them as a group, calling them "The Lakers" and pretending that the Lake District had attracted a colony of poetic Muses. They have sometimes been referred to as the "Lake School," but no real school of poetry existed there. Most critics now say that the whole idea of a "school" or "group" is rather thin. But the term "The Lake Poets" lingers on. YA

Lamb, Charles (1775–1834) He was an English poet, essayist, and critic who wrote under the pen name Elia. Though he wrote poetry and tried his hand at drama, Lamb is remembered most for the delightful essays he wrote as Elia for *London Magazine*, which were later collected into *The Essays of Elia*, a two-volume publication consisting of *Elia* (1823) and *The Last Essays of Elia* (1833). His essays include observations on a variety of topics, including "A Dissertation on Roast Pig" and "A Chapter on Ears." Lamb was also a respected critic, particularly of Elizabethan drama. You may enjoy *Tales from Shakespeare*, a book he wrote with his sister, Mary, which contains adaptations of Shakespeare's plays for children.

Mary Lamb (1764–1847) suffered from periods of severe depression. During one such period, she murdered their mother. Charles agreed to look after his sister, and they lived together for 35 years. Though Lamb's personal life was filled with sorrow, his writing is known for its gentle humor. MR & YA

L'Amour, Louis (Dearborn) (1908–1988) One of the best-selling authors of all time, L'Amour became fascinated with the history of the American West as a boy growing up in North Dakota. He left home when he was 15 years old, traveled through the West and then around the world. After serving in World War II, L'Amour began writing Westerns for magazines. His first major success came with the novel *Hondo* (1953), about Hondo Lane, a gunfighter, cavalry dispatch rider, and scout, who helps a woman and her young son defend themselves during an Apache uprising in Arizona. *Hondo* was the first of more than 40 L'Amour novels that were made into movies, and it is still one of L'Amour's most popular novels. Like all of L'Amour's tales, it combines a well-told story with great attention to historical fact and detail. Probably his greatest accomplishment is his Sackett series, which

Beauty and the Beast in *The Blue Fairy Book*
(1889) by Andrew Lang

traces the progress of the Sackett family through 300 years of American history, from the arrival of Barnabas Sackett in New England in the early 1600s. Among the novels in this series are *Sackett* (1961), *Sackett's Land* (1974), *To the Far Blue Mountains* (1976), and *Jubal Sackett* (1985). If you enjoy reading Westerns, try also the works of *Zane Grey, *The Virginian* by Owen Wister (1860–1938), and *Shane* by Jack Schaeffer (1907–1991). YA

lampoon See *satire.

Lancelot of the Lake was *King Arthur's best and bravest knight. No other knight equaled him in trials of valor, in chivalry, in nobility of mind. Many of the King Arthur stories are about Lancelot. He rescues *Guinevere more than once, and also *Elaine; wins many battles with evil knights and a fiery serpent; and once, while in a trance, is allowed to see *The Holy Grail. But his sin of loving Guinevere prevents him from touching the Grail. Elaine loves Lancelot and, according to some accounts, tricks him into fathering her son, who grows up to be *Galahad. In most accounts Lancelot does not

marry Elaine. Lancelot and Guinevere's love is so great that in the end it causes the downfall of King Arthur. Lancelot, insofar as he is a historical figure, had some Irish, Welsh, and even Scottish roots. But, as part of the Arthurian legends, he was introduced as a romantic figure by the French poet Chrétien de Troyes, who wrote toward the end of the 12th century. You can read about Lancelot in *Le Morte d'Arthur* (1485) by *Thomas Malory and in *Idylls of the King* by *Alfred Tennyson. YA

Lang, Andrew (1844–1912) Born in Selkirk, Scotland, educated at Oxford, and known as the greatest journalist of his time, Lang was a brilliant and versatile writer of fiction, history, and poetry. But he is known best to us as the collector and editor of folk and fairy tales from around the world. Every year for 25 years he brought out a new collection, some of which are *The Blue Fairy Book* (1889), *The Red Fairy Book* (1890), *The Green Fairy Book* (1892), and *The Yellow Fairy Book* (1893). In his 36 years of literary labor he produced almost 100 books. About himself, Lang said that though many people seem to be born to their professions, the fairies gave nothing to him except a love of books. About fairy tales, he said nobody could write a *new* one; it was only possible to *renew* them, to put the old characters into new clothes. He was not inclined to teach or moralize in his stories, preferring to entertain. But if a moral crept in, it was that it is always better to be kind than to be cruel. A very private person, Lang wanted no biographies and none of his letters to appear in print after his death. His widow, obeying his wishes, stated that her wrists ached for weeks after his death from tearing up his papers. The *Fairy Books* are still popular. You can still find at least 11 of them in bookstores. MR & YA

Langton, Jane (1922–) Born in Boston and now living near Concord, Massachusetts, where stood the Minutemen on the "rude bridge that arched the flood" and "fired the shot heard 'round the world," Langton breathes into her novels the people and events of New England's history. Concord locales, quotes from *Ralph Waldo Emerson, *Henry David Thoreau, and *Walt Whitman sprinkle her pages. She likes to put modern young people into a real setting and then surround them with images of the past. *The Fragile Flag* (1984) is about Georgie Hall and her Children's Crusade to the White House to deliver a frayed old flag from Concord. This story is a sequel to *The Fledgling* (1980), a fantasy in which Georgie wishes to fly like a Canada goose. Langton has written three books about Eleanor and Eddy Hall. *The Diamond in the Window* (1962) is about a diamond of old glass in an old house in which the two can envision adventures. *The Swing in the Summerhouse* (1967) features a swing that takes young Georgie through a forbidden archway to vanish and then to be rescued by Eleanor and Eddy. In *The Astonishing Stereoscope* (1971) Eleanor and Eddy investigate whether or not there is a religious hell; they visit the Last Supper, pagan rites, and Puritan services, and meet their Concord ancestors. In *The Majesty of Grace* (1961) plain Grace Jones plans on being the queen of England, but in its sequel, *The Boyhood of Grace Jones* (1972), she decides that being a boy is better, though her adventures and even a love affair intrude. MR

Laocoön was a Trojan priest of *Apollo during the *Trojan War. He enraged the Trojans because he told them not to bring the huge wooden horse, a gift from the Greeks, into the city. "Beware of Greeks bearing gifts!" he cried. As a reward for this prophesy, two huge serpents thrashed out of the sea and strangled him and his two children. And the Trojans, assuming he was punished for being wrong, took the horse, which contained Greek soldiers in its belly, into their city of Troy. The Greeks emerged and opened the city's gates, and the Trojans lost the war. It is still the case that those who bring bad news, however true, to the people or their leaders are often punished. This punishment is called "killing the messenger," which is what kings sometimes did to the bearers of bad tidings. One of the famous statues of antiquity is the Laocoön, carved from a single slab of marble in the 2nd century B.C., showing the three being strangled to death. You can read about Laocoön in *The Siege and Fall of Troy* (1962) by *Robert Graves and in *Mythology* by Edith Hamilton (1867–1963). MR

Laputa in *Gulliver's Travels*, by *Jonathan Swift, is an imaginary flying island visited by Lemuel Gulliver. It is smooth bottomed with earth on top, hovers like a cloud, and rules a continent below. Its strange inhabitants are so learned that they cannot concentrate on a single practical thing. They do everything badly, from building houses to growing food. Laputans admire professors in the Grand Academy who are trying to invent perfect materials, foods, and systems. While they do this, "the whole country lies miserably waste, the houses in ruins, and the people without food or clothes." Thus did Swift make savage fun of some 18th-century academics with their heads in the clouds while all around them corruption flourished and the people decayed. MR & YA

Lardner, Ring (1885–1933) A writer of fiction, humor, and plays, Lardner was also a sports writer and journalist. When he was 31 years old, his book *You Know Me, Al* (1916) made him famous. It is a series of letters written by a bush-league baseball rookie to his best friend. Lardner's ear for Middle Western speech, combined with his sardonic view of human nature, gives the story the kind of humor that is almost painfully funny. Lardner's many short stories are known for their satirical depiction of American life in the 20th century. One of his last and best books was *The Story of a Wonder Man* (1927), his autobiography. *F. Scott Fitzgerald was a good friend and helped Lardner during his last years before he died of tuberculosis. When asked for an epitaph by a national magazine, he wrote, "Here Lies the Body of Ring Lardner. What of it?" He left four sons, who also became writers. Two good collections of his stories are *Haircut and Other Stories* (1922) and *The Best Short Stories of Ring Lardner* (1976), both available in paperback editions. MR & YA

Lassie Come Home (1940), by *Eric Knight, has become one of the world's most famous stories about a dog. In the TV series, Lassie seems to have the intelligence of not only a super-dog but also a super-human. But in this story, Knight has revealed the true intelligence of a real dog and at the same time demonstrated how poorly most humans interpret the language of dogs. He also gives a clear picture of the class system operating in England at the time. Lassie is born into a mining family in Yorkshire, an area in northern England, and is the loved companion of Joe, whom she meets every day after school. Even in this region of highly intelligent sheepherding dogs, everyone knows that Lassie is special. So when the mines close and the family goes on welfare, Joe's father is forced to sell Lassie to the local duke, who has tried to buy her several times. Lassie keeps escaping, so the duke sends her to his estate in Scotland, 400 miles to the north. Lassie's long and often terrifying journey home is the main plot of the story. She is helped and loved by some; shot at, beaten, and imprisoned by others. She has to learn to hunt and feed herself, and to learn, when it is absolutely necessary, to attack a man. When Joe cries that the duke will take her again, his mother tells him that he must never ever want anything so much as he wants Lassie, but Joe says, "Ye don't understand, Mother. . . . It ain't me that wants her. It's her that wants us—so terrible bad." In the end Lassie's courage changes the life of the family she loves so much. Another story that you will enjoy about animals returning home over long distances is *The Incredible Journey* by *Sheila Burnford. If you like the Lassie stories, you will want to look in your library for books of *Albert Payson Terhune, who wrote the best-loved stories about collies, including *Lad: A Dog* (1919) and a collection of short stories, *Lochinvar Luck* (1923). The first movie about Lassie was made in 1942, and another in 1978. MR

Last Battle, The (1966) This history book, which reads like a novel, is by *Cornelius Ryan. It reconstructs the stories of a number of Berliners during the last three weeks of World War II, when the Allies and the Russians were advancing on Berlin from west and east. The milkman who delivers from a farm on the edge of the city worries about how the cows can withstand the daily and nightly bombing; a Jewish couple, who have been hidden for two years from the Gestapo by a German family, fears that they will be found during the last sweeps of the city; a Swedish spy for the Allies worries that the Nazis will discover his radio and ammunition if his house is bombed; a zoo keeper grieves because the rare stork, closing his eyes, daily rejects the only food they have, horsemeat; Hitler has a bridge placed in his teeth, which later helps identify his body; his companions wonder if their poison cyanide pills are still good and test one on the dog. Also told are the stories of officers and men in the advancing and retreating armies. Everyone fears the Russians. In his focus on individuals, Ryan reveals the human cost of war and the sweep of history at the same time. This is a riveting, close-up look at an important moment in world history. Another fascinating book on this subject is *The Last 100 Days* (1966) by John Toland (1912–), about the final three months of World War II in Europe. YA

Last of the Mohicans, The (1826) This novel by *James Fenimore Cooper is set in northern New York State in 1757 during the French and Indian War. Cora and Alice Munro set out from Fort Edward (Albany) to join their father, Colonel Munro, commander of Fort William Henry at the southern end of Lake George. They are accompanied by Major Duncan Heyward, a British officer; their guide, Magua, an out-of-favor Huron chief; and David Gamut, a singing master. The group comes upon the camp of the scout Hawkeye, also known as *Natty Bumppo, and his Mohican Indian companion, Chingachgook, and Chingachgook's son, Uncas. Chingachgook and his son, Uncas, are the last of the Mohican (Mohegan) *sagamores*, or chiefs.

Hawkeye tells Heyward that Magua has led them astray, probably with evil intentions. They try to capture Magua, but he escapes into the woods and, with a band of Huron warriors, attacks the travelers. Magua intends to make Cora his wife, as revenge for a public whipping ordered by Colonel Munro, and also to regain his position of honor among the Hurons.

Hawkeye leads the party to a secret cave beneath a waterfall. Magua's band attacks, and the party is divided. The women are captured but quickly rescued. The group arrives at Fort William Henry, which soon falls to the French and their Huron allies. Heading northwest of Lake Champlain, the retreating English, led by Colonel Munro, are attacked by the Hurons, and Alice and Cora are again taken off by Magua. Hawkeye leads his friends in a rescue attempt that ends in a bloody confrontation between Magua and his Hurons and Uncas and his Delaware allies. Cora and Uncas are slain, and Hawkeye kills Magua. Cora and Uncas are buried in the wilderness after a touching Delaware Indian funeral ceremony. Heyward, Alice, Colonel Munro, and David return to Fort Edward. Hawkeye remains in the wilderness with Chingachgook. If you enjoyed *The Last of the Mohicans*, you will like the other four books of the *Leather-Stocking Tales, which follow Natty Bumppo's adventures from early manhood to his death. Movies of *The Last of the Mohicans* were made in 1936 and 1992 and a TV film was produced in 1977. YA

Last Picture Show, The (1966) By *Larry McMurtry, this novel is set in the town of Thalia, Texas, in the 1950s and centers on three high school seniors: Sonny Crawford, his best friend, Duane Moore, and Duane's girl friend, Jacy Farrow. Duane is in love with Jacy, the prettiest girl in Thalia and daughter of a wealthy oilman. Sonny is secretly in love with Jacy, too, but Jacy is in love only with herself, although for a time she imagines she wants to marry Duane. All three are much preoccupied with sex, and their search for sexual experience is a major theme. Also important is Sonny and Duane's friendship with Sam the Lion, a gentle old man who owns the movie theater, pool hall, and all-night café, and cares for a feebleminded youth named Billy. The events of the teenage trio's senior year include

Sonny's affair with Ruth Popper, the wife of the school football coach, Duane and Jacy's breakup, Duane's departure to join the army, Sonny's brief and unconsummated marriage to Jacy, and Jacy's departure for college in Dallas. Sam's death, the closing of the movie theater, and Billy's death in an accident complete Sonny's passage from adolescence to adulthood. McMurtry continued the story of Sonny and his friends in *Texasville* (1987), set in Thalia in the mid-1980s. *The Last Picture Show* was made into a movie in 1971 and *Texasville* in 1991. YA

Last Supper On the eve of his arrest and later crucifixion, *Jesus gathered his 12 disciples for a meal to observe the Jewish festival of the Passover. It was here that he instituted what became the Christian sacrament of the Eucharist (Lord's Supper, Holy Communion), in which the bread and wine symbolize, or are miraculously changed into, the body and blood of Jesus. The story of the Last Supper is told in the *Bible in all four of the Gospels, *Matthew, *Mark, *Luke, and *John. It has been a favorite subject of artists over the centuries, the most famous representation being that of Leonardo da Vinci (1452–1519), the Italian artist, inventor, and scientist, painted between 1495 and 1497. More recently, the surrealist artist Salvador Dali (1904–1989) painted a memorable "The Last Supper" (1955).

Lauber, Patricia (Grace) (1924–) The author of nearly 60 books of nonfiction for young readers, Lauber has also written a smaller number of novels, five of them about a lovable if eccentric dog named Clarence. Typical of Lauber's nonfiction are *Tales Mummies Tell* (1985), about how mummies reveal important clues about life in different times; *Bats: Wings in the Night* (1968), which describes their unique lifestyle; and *Who Discovered America* (1970), about the people who came to the Western Hemisphere before Columbus, including the migrants from Asia who developed the different Native American civilizations, and the Vikings from Europe. Lauber's books give you many subjects to choose from, such as *Penguins on Parade* (1958), *Our Friend the Forest* (1959), *Your Body and How It Works* (1962), and *Asteroids and Comets* (1987). *Clarence Turns Sea Dog* (1959) is an enjoyable example of Lauber's novels about this almost too-clever animal. He goes to Cape Cod, where he gets into trouble by carrying dead fish around, but rescues a boy buried under a collapsed hut and, by his barking, saves a boat lost in a fog. Some of Clarence's other adventures are told in *Clarence and the Burglar* (1973) and *Clarence and the Cat* (1977). If you like Lauber's books, read those of *Beverly Cleary and *Sterling North. MR

Laughing Boy (1929) Probably the best-known work of *Oliver La Farge, this novel tells of the tragic love of two young Navahos. At a dance, Laughing Boy meets Slim Girl, a beautiful young woman who seems not quite Navaho, because she has lived several years among the Americans. He falls in love with her and, ignoring the warnings of family, friends, and his rival, Red Man, that Slim Girl will lead him into a bad life, he marries her and goes to live with her near the town of Los Palos. Slim Girl once wanted to live as an American, but a deceitful lover brought disaster to her life among the whites. To avenge herself, she has taken an American lover and is saving the money he gives her so that when she and Laughing Boy return to his people they will be able to live in security and comfort. When Laughing Boy discovers her secret he thinks his marriage and life are over, but Slim Girl's love and her reason for acting as she did convince him otherwise. On their way home to live as Navahos, they are ambushed by Red Man. Slim Girl is killed, and Laughing Boy returns to his people alone. If you enjoyed *Laughing Boy*, try also *House Made of Dawn* (1968) by N. Scott Momaday (1934–), about the struggles of a Native American returning from World War II to reconcile his Indian heritage with the larger world. YA

laurel A shrub or tree native to the region of the Mediterranean Sea but also found in other parts of the world, the laurel has for centuries been a symbol of victory, peace, and merit, especially in literature and the arts. The ancient Greeks gave laurel wreaths to the victors in the Pythian Games, which were sacred to *Apollo. In the 14th century *Geoffrey Chaucer in *The Canterbury Tales* wrote of a person "with laurel crowned as a Conqueror." Nearly five centuries later *George Gordon Byron said in *Don Juan*, " 'Tis sweet to win, no matter how, one's laurels." And having won your laurels, you may choose to "rest on your laurels," to be satisfied with what you have accomplished. But if you are still active, you will have to "look to your laurels" if you want to be sure no one surpasses you. YA

Lawrence, D(avid) H(erbert) (1865–1930) One of the first novelists writing in English to approach the subject of sexuality openly, Lawrence caused a storm of controversy. Some critics maintain he is the best of the modern English novelists. The sickly son of an English coal miner, he was a school teacher until his first novel, *The White Peacock* (1911) was published. It was unsuccessful, but he decided to devote himself to writing. The following year he ran away with the German wife of a university professor, whom he subsequently married, and lived in great poverty in Germany until his second and best novel, *Sons and Lovers* (1913), was published. This work conveys the pain of adolescent awakening and reveals the destructive effect of industrialization. Critics, who often complain that Lawrence's angry opinions obscure his best, imaginative writing, find that this work is the least preachy. In *Women in Love* (1920), the story of the love affairs of two sisters, he illuminates the obsessive nature of passion. Lawrence's most famous novel, *Lady Chatterley's Lover* (1928), about the love affair of a gardener and a lady, educated more than one generation about sex. It was not published in the United States until 1961, after a court battle about censorship. Lawrence lived in many places, including the American Southwest, always seeking good health. He died of tuberculosis in Italy when he was only 45 years old. Even so, Lawrence was a prolific writer. You will want also to read Lawrence's brilliant *Studies in Classical American Literature* (1923), which will give you insights into many important writers. Most of his books are still in print, many of them in inexpensive paperback editions. A movie was made of *Sons and Lovers* in 1960, of *Women in Love* in 1969, and of *Lady Chatterley's Lover* in 1981. YA

Lawrence, T(homas) E(dward) (1888–1935) Known as "Lawrence of Arabia," this was the man who, as a British soldier during World War I, inspired and organized an irregular cavalry of Arabs to harass the armies of the Ottoman Empire, German allies who occupied much of Arabian soil at the time. At this he was enormously successful and became a legend in his own time. His plan was to unite Arab forces in guerrilla fighting. "Arabs could be swung on an idea as on a cord," he wrote. "Since the dawn of life, in successive waves they had been dashing themselves against the coasts of flesh. . . . One such wave . . . I raised and rolled before the breath of an idea." In the end he was deeply disappointed in the peace treaty at Versailles because the Arabs did not gain their independence. Lawrence's celebrated account of the Arab revolt and his own exploits is *The Seven Pillars of Wisdom* (1935), which was praised as one of the great books of modern times and compared to *Robinson Crusoe* and *Gulliver's Travels*. Lawrence's career after the war was marked by anxiety about his own legend, and he suffered mental problems. Seeking privacy, he enlisted in the Royal Air Force in 1922 under the name John Hume Ross. A year later he switched to the Royal Tank Corps as T.E. Shaw. His account of this period in his life was published as *The Mint* (1955). You can find an inexpensive paperback edition of *The Seven Pillars of Wisdom*. A movie based on his life under the title *Lawrence of Arabia* was made in 1962. YA

Lawson, Robert (1892–1957) An author and an illustrator of his own books and those of others, Lawson is the only person ever to win both the Caldecott Award, given for the best American picture book for young readers, and the *Newbery Medal. He received the Caldecott for *They Were Strong and Good* (1940), a mostly pictorial biography of his ancestors, strong characters, of whom he was proud. He won the Newbery Medal for *Rabbit Hill*, an amusing novel about the animals that inhabit a country area in Connecticut. Also about animals, but written in a lighter manner, is *Ben and Me*. Lawson was a master of the art of making his animal characters believable personalities. *McWhinney's Jaunt* (1951) is altogether different. Its main character seems to be the typical Yankee trader of the 19th century but with a 20th-century appearance. You can take him as a warning to be careful what you buy from certain people. If you like Lawson's books, read those of *Richard Adams, *Kenneth Grahame, *Joel Chandler Harris, *Beatrix Potter, and *A.A. Milne. MR

Le Carré, John [David John Moore Cornwell] (1931–) Educated at Oxford University; a teacher at Eton, an English prep school; a member of the British secret service in World War II; and then an officer of the British Foreign Service, Le Carré had experiences that led to his writing what are agreed to be the best modern spy novels. The first was *Call for the Dead* (1962), in which he introduces *George Smiley, a master spy. However, it was his third novel, *The Spy Who Came In from the Cold*, that changed the way spy stories are now written. Smiley reappears in *The Looking-Glass War* (1965) and again in *Tinker, Tailor, Soldier, Spy* (1974). His later novels include *Smiley's People* (1980), in which he again has to deal with problems within the agency, and *The Secret Pilgrim* (1991), in which Smiley hardly appears but an agent recalls his 30 years of espionage. A number of movies and TV productions have been made of Le Carré's books. The films include *The Spy Who Came In from the Cold*, made in 1965, and *The Looking-Glass War* in 1970. If you like these books, you will enjoy those by *Eric Ambler, *Len Deighton, and *Frederick Forsyth. YA

Le Guin, Ursula K(roeber) (1929–) Known especially for novels that combine *science fiction and *fantasy, Le Guin shows her versatility especially well in *The Eye of the Heron. Her four Earthsea novels, for which she created an imaginary realm consisting of many islands, is also a feat of literary skill. In the first, A Wizard of Earthsea (1968), a boy, Sparrowhawk, studies to become a wizard. He uses the powers he is being taught too soon and creates an evil force. The Tombs of Atuan (1971) is about Tena, a girl who is taken from her family to become a priestess of the Nameless Ones, and about Ged, a young wizard. Along with Arren, prince of Enland, Ged continues to be a central character in The Farthest Shore (1972), in which he and the prince face unknown dangers in taking Earthsea into a new era. Its sequel is Tehanu: The Last Book of Earthsea (1990). Two young people in The Beginning Place (1980) are pleased to escape from their humdrum existence when they unexpectedly pass from the real world to Tembreabrezi, but later they find themselves surrounded by horror. Perhaps the most unusual of Le Guin's books is Always Coming Home (1985), about the Kesh people of northern California after a nuclear war. The story is told in prose and poetry, legends and autobiography, and even a tape of Kesh music was included in the original edition. Among her award-winning science fiction novels are The Left Hand of Darkness (1969), centering on the inhabitants of a distant planet who have both male and female traits; The Lathe of Heaven (1971), about a man whose dreams change reality; and The Dispossessed (1974), about two completely opposite Utopian societies that arise on sister planets of the star Tau Ceti. If you like Le Guin's books, try those of *Helen M. Hoover, *C.S. Lewis, *Larry Niven, and *Roger Zelazny. YA

Leacock, Stephen Butler (1869–1944) A Canadian writer born in England, Leacock was internationally popular as a humorist, essayist, and speaker. Over 30 books of humorous sketches and essays describe his view of the differences between appearance and reality in human conduct. He also wrote almost 20 books on history and economics while he taught at McGill University in Montreal. Leacock was known best for his early comic fantasies, or sketches, in Literary Lapses (1910) and Nonsense Novels (1911). He was a prodigious letter writer to friends, famous people, former students, and newspapers, but he said it was when he traveled extensively to give humorous lectures that his "bread on the waters came back as cake." Leacock wrote The Boy I Left Behind Me (1946), an uncompleted autobiography, and Humour: Its Theory and Technique (1935), a discussion of his humor, but it is in his final collection, Last Leaves (1945), that the wide range of his opinions is expressed, from a satire on the detective story craze, to the future of peace, to a study of *Alice's Adventures in Wonderland. YA

Lear, Edward (1812–1888) Best known to us as a master of the *limerick and the author of the poem *"The Owl and the Pussy Cat," who "went to sea in a beautiful pea-green boat," this Englishman earned his living as an artist and illustrator. It was when Lear was making illustrations of the private zoo, or menagerie, of the Earl of Derby that he wrote and illustrated his first Book of Nonsense (1846) for the earl's grandchildren. Quite a few limericks are about noses. For instance,

> There was an Old Man on whose nose
> Most birds of the air could repose;
> But they all flew away at the closing of day,
> Which relieved that Old Man and his nose.

Lear's drawings enhance the cockeyed charm of the hundreds of limericks he wrote. Other poems, like "The Jumblies," who "went to sea in a sieve, they did," and "The Owl and the Pussy Cat" have been illustrated by many artists. Lear also wrote and illustrated a number of alphabets, with such characters as the Enthusiastic Elephant who wore earrings, and the Lively Learned Lobster who mended his own clothes. Lear was a shy man and not very healthy, but he nevertheless traveled and painted a great deal. He wrote amusing illustrated letters to his friends and made up many words. Of himself he wrote,

> His mind is concrete and fastidious,
>   His nose is remarkably big;
> His visage is more or less hideous,
>   His beard it resembles a wig.

The name of the poem is "How Pleasant to Know Mr. Lear!" and of course, many generations later, it still is. See also *The Complete Book of Nonsense. MR & YA

Leather-Stocking Tales (1823–1841) Written by *James Fenimore Cooper, these five novels follow the career of the frontiersman *Natty Bumppo (sometimes called Leather-Stocking after the buckskin leggings he wears) from his early manhood in the 1740s to his death in the early 1800s. The novels as published told Natty's story out of order. The last published, *The Deerslayer* (1841), is actually the beginning of Natty's story. Here Natty is called "Deerslayer," a young hunter in the wilds of New York State around Lake Otsego. It also introduces Chingachgook, his noble Mohican companion. *The Last of the Mohicans* is set around Lake Champlain in 1757, during the French and Indian War. *The Pathfinder* (1840) is set on and around Lake Ontario around 1760. Natty, now at the peak of his powers, falls in love but gallantly stands aside when he learns that his betrothed is actually in love with his friend. *The Pioneers* (1823) is set around Lake Otsego, where the settlement of Templeton, modeled after Cooper's own Cooperstown, has sprung up. Natty, now an old man, finds himself unable to cope with the encroachments of a changing society. *The Prairie* (1827) finds Natty ending his days as a trapper on the Great Plains, among the Sioux and Pawnee. If you would like to read about Natty Bumppo without reading all of the long books that Cooper wrote, try *The Leatherstocking Saga* (1954), whose editors have arranged in chronological order the story of this frontiersman's life in Cooper's own words. Passages from the books that do not deal with Natty are deleted and new, connecting passages that join the series in terms of plot and history have been written by the editors. Cooper is said to have initiated the myth of the American frontier in a way similar to the creation of the myth of the American cowboy by Owen Wister (1860–1938) in *The Virginian. A movie was made of *The Pathfinder* in 1952, and of *The Deerslayer* in 1978. YA

Leaveheavenalone is an imaginary place where the sun spins and the wind weaves threads of water from the sea on a great steam loom until they make a beautiful veil of Chantilly lace. It is a beautiful description of a peaceful place to be after a painful struggle. It is where Tom, the chimney sweep turned into a water baby in *The Water-Babies, by *Charles Kingsley, goes after escaping from a place called Oldwivesfabledom, "where the folks were all heathens, and worshipped a howling ape," and where Tom is nearly stoned to death. *The Water-Babies* is a fabulous adventure full of moral warnings that befit a *Victorian fairy tale. For instance, the Doasyoulikes live in the land of Readymade, where, observes Tom, "they are growing no better than savages" and getting uglier because "when people live on poor vegetables instead of roast-beef and plum-pudding, their jaws grow large, and their lips grow coarse." MR

Leaves of Grass (1855) This collection of poems by *Walt Whitman was radical for its time both in its form and in its contents. The first edition contained only 12 poems, but over the years Whitman added many others. You can see two main themes in his verses: his belief in democracy and the United States, and his love of people. He stresses equality in "A Song for Occupations" and "I Hear America Singing," in which people tell about their jobs, "each singing what belongs to him or her and to none else." Having cared for wounded soldiers during the Civil War, he wrote about them and about the nation's bitter, bloody crisis. Nowhere are Whitman's emotions more painfully clear than in two poems mourning the death of Abraham Lincoln (1809–1865): *"When Lilacs Last in the Dooryard Bloom'd" and "O Captain! My Captain!"

Other poems are daring for their time in

their references to love and sexuality. As he wrote in "Song of Myself":

I believe in the flesh and the appetites,
Seeing, hearing, feeling, are miracles and each
    part and tag of me is a miracle.

Whitman's use of everyday language brought a new tone to American poetry, as did the free form of his verse, which differed greatly from the traditional rhyming style. Though it was considered scandalous when first published, *Leaves of Grass* is probably the most popular volume of poetry in America, with over 12 editions currently in print. YA

Leda In Greek mythology, Leda is the wife of Tyndareus, a mythical king of Sparta. There are different accounts as to who her children were and who fathered them. Most begin with *Zeus, the chief Greek god, coming to her disguised as a swan and causing her to bring forth two eggs. One of these was said to have resulted in the birth of both Castor, who later became identified with the constellation *Gemini, and Clytemnestra, who became the wife of *Agamemnon, king of Mycenae. The other egg resulted in the birth of Pollux who, with Castor, was the other heavenly twin, and *Helen. The story of Leda and the swan has been a favorite subject of a number of artists, such as Antonio Allegri da Corregio (c.1494–1534), *Michelangelo, and Paolo Veronese (1528–1588), as well as the poem "Leda and the Swan" (1924) by *William Butler Yeats. YA

"Legend of Sleepy Hollow, The" (1819) In this amusing short tale, *Washington Irving tells the story of Ichabod Crane, a Yankee schoolmaster who teaches in a Dutch settlement on the Hudson River in New York State. Ichabod's tall frame is "most loosely hung together" and he is always hungry as well as nervous and imaginative. In the warm Dutch kitchens he spins stories about the Galloping Horseman of Sleepy Hollow, the headless ghost of a Revolutionary War soldier who patrols the local roads, but Ichabod dreads to look over his shoulder when he goes home at night. Soon he falls in love with a Dutch girl whose father's farm is stuffed, as Ichabod sees it, with food. "Not a turkey but he beheld daintily trussed up, with its gizzard under its wing, and, peradventure, a necklace of savory sausages." But he has a rival, Brom Bones, so called because of his size and strength, and the mystery in this exciting story concerns what the Headless Hessian was carrying when Ichabod met him on the night of his disappearance—*his head?* And where did poor Ichabod go? This classic tale is often paired with *Rip Van Winkle*, also by Irving, because both of them take place in the area of the lower Hudson River valley. "The Legend of Sleepy Hollow" was produced as a TV movie in 1980. YA

L'Engle, Madeleine (1918–) An author of novels for younger and older readers, L'Engle is noted especially for *fantasy combined with *science fiction and for stories dealing with family problems. She is known best for *A Wrinkle in Time*, part of her Time Trilogy, and *The Young Unicorns*, one of a series of novels that includes *Meet the Austins*, about the Austin family. L'Engle used her unhappy experiences in boarding schools as material for her first novel, *The Small Rain* (1945), reissued for younger readers as *Prelude* (1968), about a 15-year-old student who escapes her loneliness and unhappiness through her efforts to become a concert pianist. *Camilla Dickinson* (1951), a sensitive story about a 15-year-old New York City girl's troubled passage from childhood toward adulthood, has been compared favorably with *The Catcher in the Rye* by *J.D. Salinger. If you like L'Engle's books, try those of *Helen M. Hoover, *Ursula K. Le Guin, and *Colby Rodowsky. MR & YA

Leonard, (John) Elmore (Jr.) (1925–) Before turning to writing action thrillers, Leonard was a successful author of Westerns, such as *The Bounty Hunter* (1953), his first book, and *Hombre* (1962). The first of his thrillers, like the rest of them more noted for action than for mystery or detection, was *Swap* (1976) in which a would-be car thief gets in too deep with a criminal overlord. The setting is Detroit, which, along with Miami, is the locale for most of Leonard's novels. *City Primeval* (1980) is set in an inner city, but the plot is essentially the same as a Western frontier shoot-out. *Glitz* (1985) is a good example of Leonard's approach: A police lieutenant, on leave, goes to Puerto Rico, falls in love with a prostitute who is later murdered in Atlantic City, having been lured there by a man who wants vengeance on the lieutenant. Leonard's books are exciting and peopled with unusual characters. Most of them are not respectable citizens, and the books are full of violence and obscene language. *The Bounty Hunter* was filmed in 1954, *Hombre* in 1967, and *Glitz* in 1988. If you like these novels, try those of *James M. Cain, *Dashiell Hammett, and *Mickey Spillane. YA

Lester, Julius (1939–) A man of varied talents as a musician and singer, radio and television host, and professor of African-American studies, Lester has written a number of mostly fact-based stories, and has retold folktales, all with a background of the black experience in America. Among them are *The Tales of Uncle Remus* and *To Be a Slave.* Lester's first fiction was *Long Journey Home: Stories from Black History* (1972). One of six stories in this book is about a guitar player who travels among plantations in the South after the Civil War and finds that slavery in a sense still exists. There are two long tales in *Two Love Stories* (1972), one of them about a black clergyman and his family and the problems of their 14-year-old son when they move into a previously all-white neighborhood. *This Strange New Feeling* (1982) contains three stories, all based on actual incidents, set in the days of slavery. One of them, "Where the Sun Lives," is the tragic tale of 18-year-old Maria, a half-white slave, who is purchased by a free black man. They are in love and escape to the North, but when the man is killed Maria is sold back into slavery. Lester's autobiography is *All Is Well* (1976). If you like Lester's books, try those of *Countee Cullen and *Richard Wright. You will also want to read *Roots by *Alex Haley. MR & YA

Let the Circle Be Unbroken (1981) This sequel to *Roll of Thunder, Hear My Cry,* by *Mildred D. Taylor, continues the story of 11-year-old Cassie Logan and her family in rural Mississippi during the *Great Depression. Unlike the other black families in their area, the Logans own their own land, but they face the same problems as their neighbors. A few white landowners control everything, and their world is filled with injustice. T.J. Avery, a black youth who is the best friend of Cassie's older brother, Stacey, is convicted and executed for a killing committed by two white boys. A white labor organizer trying to establish a farmers' union is beaten half to death. And Cassie's cousin Suzella, whose mother is white and who feels more comfortable in the white world than in the black one, comes to visit, causing problems that test even the strong family bonds of the Logans. Money troubles force Cassie's father to leave the family and work on the railroad to keep from losing the farm. But the family's greatest test comes when Stacey, eager to show he is growing up, runs off to find work and is trapped into slave labor on a cane plantation. Yet through all the troubles, the Logan family circle remains unbroken. If you enjoyed *Let the Circle Be Unbroken,* you will probably also like *To Kill a Mockingbird by Harper Lee (1926–), which explores similar themes. YA

Levin, Ira (1929–) A novelist and playwright who is noted for tricky plots built around horror and high technology, Levin has been a best-selling author ever since his first mystery novel, *A Kiss Before Dying* (1953), in which part of the story is told by the alleged murderer. His best known work is *Rosemary's Baby* (1967), in which the plot builds up to a climax when a baby Satan is born with yellow eyes and claws. *The Stepford Wives* (1972) is both amusing and frightening as suburban husbands replace their wives with robots that look the same and are happy and completely obedient. *The Boys from Brazil* (1979) is about an escaped Nazi who plans to produce human clones that will grow into men exactly like Adolf Hitler (1889–1945), the German dictator. *Sliver* (1991) is a chilling account of the murderous owner of a high-rise apartment building in New York City who has installed TV circuits to spy on every tenant. Levin's first play was *No Time for Sergeants*

(1955), the humorous adventures of a country boy in the armed services in World War II. His most successful play is *Deathtrap* (1978). A mixture of comedy and mystery, it concerns a prominent playwright and a young promising playwright who try to outwit each other. Movies based on Levin's works are *A Kiss Before Dying* in 1956 and 1991, *No Time for Sergeants* in 1958, *Rosemary's Baby* in 1968, *The Stepford Wives* in 1975, *The Boys from Brazil* in 1978, and *Deathtrap* in 1982. If you enjoy Levin's books, read those of *Michael Crichton, *Frederick Forsyth, and *Robert Ludlum. YA

Levitin, Sonia (1934–) Born in Berlin, Germany, during the *Nazi regime, Levitin experienced the terror of persecution as a Jewish child. In her novel *Journey to America*, she tells the story of her family's escape from Germany. Many of her books illustrate what courage is and how difficult it is for people to leave familiar places and people and head into the unknown. In *The Return* (1987), she tells about Desla, a Jewish girl, and her long and dangerous trek to the Sudan, and finally to Israel during the exodus of Ethiopian Jews from their own country. Levitin has written about American pioneers in *The No-Return Trail* (1978), the story of Nancy Kelsey, a wife and mother when she was 17 years old, and the first woman to be part of a grueling pioneer trip to California. In *Incident at Loring Groves* (1988) she shows how apathy, or the refusal to make a moral choice, in a modern community in America can promote violence among young people. You will also enjoy *The Mark of Conte*, which tells the delightful story of a freshman who figures out a way to graduate from high school in two years. Levitin lives in California, has a family, and usually writes with her animals nearby. MR & YA

Lew Archer A fictional private investigator, Archer was conceived by *Ross MacDonald and, along with *Philip Marlowe and *Sam Spade, is an accepted model for the hard-boiled private eye. Archer was born in 1913, formerly was a police officer in Long Beach, California, and has been divorced by his wife, who did not like the kind of people he worked with. He likes to read, enjoys Japanese paintings, and is knowledgeable about nature. He is also lonely and cynical, though he cares for justice. Unlike some of fiction's private investigators, he avoids violence when possible. The setting for Archer's work is southern California, usually among rich but unhappy families. Among the novels are *The Dalton Case* (1959), in which, as often happens in these books, there is a rejection of wealthy parents and a young person's search for identity. In *Black Money* (1966) the story begins with events of the past in order to establish a background for the present day. In *The Blue Hammer* (1976), the last Archer novel, Archer develops for the first time more than a passing relationship with a woman. Two TV series featuring Archer were produced in 1974 and 1975–1977. YA

Lewis, C(live) S(taples) (1898–1963) An English novelist and literary critic, Lewis wrote on subjects ranging from the scholarly *English Literature in the Sixteenth Century* (1936) to the vastly entertaining series of seven novels known as *The Chronicles of Narnia* that he wrote for younger readers. Lewis was one of the first—and best—of modern authors of *fantasy and *science fiction novels. For older readers, his trilogy *Out of the Silent Planet* (1938), *Perelandra* (1943), and *That Hideous Strength* (1945) makes good reading simply as adventures in intergalactic space, but at heart the books are Christian in spirit, probing the problems of good and evil. *The Screwtape Letters* (1942) is likewise entertaining, but at the same time deals with moral and theological problems from a Christian viewpoint. In the book an elderly devil, Screwtape, writes letters to his nephew Wormwood, giving him cynical advice on how to tempt human beings to sin. Lewis's autobiography, *Surprised by Joy* (1955), is as much about his spiritual life as about his career. Younger and older readers who like these books should try those of *Lloyd Alexander, *Isaac Asimov, *Ursula K. Le Guin, and *Helen M. Hoover. MR & YA

Lewis, (Harry) Sinclair (1885–1951) The author of *Babbitt* and other *satires on American life, Lewis was the first American to receive the Nobel Prize for literature (1930). He had several minor novels published between 1914 and 1917, and his stories appeared in such popular magazines as *Cosmopolitan* and *The Saturday Evening Post*. His novel *Main Street*, which made him a nationally known literary figure, was the first in a series of satires that focused often on small Middle Western towns, including *Arrowsmith* and *Elmer Gantry* (1927), a story about religious fakery. These novels, as well as *Dodsworth*, reflect Lewis's concern with what he saw as the empty and shallow quality of life in America. They are praised for their realistic portrayal of local social customs and speech. If you enjoy Lewis's books, try also those of *Theodore Dreiser. All the novels mentioned here were made into films. YA

Liberation of Tansy Warner, The (1980)

As this novel, by *Stephanie Tolan, opens, Tansy, a ninth-grader, has just won the part of Anne Frank (see also *The Diary of a Young Girl*) in the school play. She rushes home with the news for her supportive mother and finds a note on the table. Her mother has gone, leaving her husband and three children, but supplying no forwarding address. Tansy, the youngest, deals with this heartache and learns, for instance, that the word "mother" is not a person but a job title, like "lawyer," which is what her superachieving father is. She has to handle the information that her father never wanted a third child, especially not one who is artistic, like her vanishing mother. Tansy is told to keep her mother's disappearance a secret. She also learns how to seek the help that she needs from old and new friends, and from the role of Anne Frank that she is rehearsing. And she has to find her mother, and her own strength and liberation from fear. Younger readers will enjoy other books by Tolan, such as *Grandpa—and Me* (1978), about a girl and her grandfather, and *The Great Skinner Enterprise* (1986), which is about a family that starts a business when Dad loses his job. MR & YA

Life on the Mississippi (1874)

is the story of how *Mark Twain became a pilot of a sternwheeler on the great river, all 1,200 miles of it, before a single marker, buoy, or light had been placed or chart drawn. Modern ship pilots, with radar, sonar, twin screws, dredged channels, and levees cannot imagine the difficulties of Twain's job. He had to memorize every ripple, every riff and rumple, every bar, reef, and stump, the changing shape of every bank, hill, and tree, and he had to know that it was different going upstream from going downstream, different in the gray mist in the black night, or in moonlight, or in wind, different when the river was rising or falling. The river was different during every trip because its current was always moving its obstacles. There were also a thousand other craft such as rafts and barges, usually unlighted. Mr. Bixby, the pilot who "learned" him each dimple in the deceptive mirror of the great waterway, was a man with a fount of curses that erupted regularly around his student until "he was empty. You could have drawn a seine through his system and not caught curses enough to disturb your mother with." Then he spoke gently, but with so much information that the cub pilot, just as he was getting cocky with river lore, feared his brain was too small to hold it. At that time river pilots had more power, respect, independence, and money than the captains of the river boats. Twain describes his apprenticeship with Mr. Brown, a pilot who was so insulting that the cub kept his sanity by imagining how he would kill him, a different way every day for months, and in one terrible night, 117 different ways. Then, because of the Civil War, there was no work, and the cub pilot was forced to find work out West. After 21 years, Twain returned to the Mississippi as a passenger. In that interval, steamboating had nearly died out, and Twain remarks on the many changes that had occurred. If you enjoyed this book, be sure to read *Roughing It* (1872), Twain's hilarious account of his adventures out West and in Hawaii. YA

Life with Father (1935),

by Clarence Day (1874–1935), is a collection of anecdotes about the author's parents and the family's life in New York City around the turn of the 20th century. A successful Wall Street stockbroker, Day's father was a hearty, expansive, and opinionated man who loved the good life and was accustomed to getting his own way. Father saw illness or clumsiness as a sign of weak character, and his own energy never seemed to flag. Father was often angry, but mostly at things rather than people, and he was given to expressing his outrage in loud groans that resounded throughout the house. He deeply loved Mrs. Day, whom he described as a "woman of great spirit who would have flown at and pecked any tyrant." Clarence Day was known for his humorous essays, which he sometimes illustrated himself, and was published often in *The New Yorker* magazine. Like *Life with Father, God and My Father* (1932) and *Life with Mother* (1936) are also collections of anecdotes based on Day's memories of his parents' household. The stories cover more than 50 years of their marriage. Adapted for the stage, *Life with Father* (1939) became one of the longest-running productions in the history of Broadway theater. A movie of it was made in 1947. *Life with Mother* was adapted for the stage in 1948. MR & YA

"Light Princess, The" (1867) This charming fairy tale, by the Scottish author George MacDonald (1824–1905), is about a baby princess who is cursed by a witch with the loss of gravity, both in her spirit and in her body. As she grows, she learns it is good to be light-hearted but not light-headed, light-handed but not light-fingered, light-bodied but not light-minded. She laughs too much at everything, good or bad, but she loves to swim, for water provides the only chance to feel her weight. One day a prince rescues her from the lake because he thinks she is screaming, not laughing, and for the first time she is furious. Why did he "pull me down out of the water and throw me to the bottom of the air?" The resolution to this dilemma involves a heroic sacrifice by the prince and the coming of gravity to the princess when she rescues him. Then she has to learn to walk before they can be married with any dignity. MacDonald was a Scottish clergyman, poet, and novelist, who gained his

Curdie; Lina, the monster-dog; and Little Barbara from *The Princess and Curdie*

first success as an author with a series of adult novels set in Scotland. His poetry also received high praise. Of the more than 50 books he wrote, probably the best known today are his fantasy stories for children. They include *At the Back of the North Wind* (1871), a magical story about a London child who travels with the North Wind; *The Princess and the Goblin,* about an 8-year-old princess who helps a miner's son defeat the mischievous goblins living under a mountain; and its sequel, *The Princess and Curdie* (1873), in which Curdie, the miner's son, returns to help foil a plot against the princess and her father. You will find in your library many editions of MacDonald's wonderful fantasy tales. MR

Light That Failed, The (1890) This novel by *Rudyard Kipling opens with a vivid chapter detailing the sad lives of two British orphans, Dick and Maisie. They are not related, but they spend four years together as the abused foster children of a widow, and a strong bond develops between them. You meet Dick again sketching and painting as a war correspondent artist with the British Army in the Egyptian desert. A field of 1,200 unburied war dead is described as "like a bed of horrible toadstools in all colours." By the time he returns to London he is controversial, because of the realism of his war scenes, but well known as an artist. He meets Maisie again, and she too is an artist, though her work is still unknown. He loves her and hopes to help her, but for Maisie her work comes first. She accepts his help but rejects his controlling love and goes to France to paint. In her absence Dick's eyesight fails, the optic nerves having been damaged from a war wound, and though Maisie comes back, she is unable to love him and flees again. Eventually Dick, though blind, manages to return to the desert to find his old and best friend, the war correspondent Torpenhow, and the peace of death. Another book about an artist is *The Moon and Sixpence* (1919) by *W. Somerset Maugham, about a man who gives up a comfortable life to become a painter. *The Light That Failed* was filmed in 1939. YA

Lilies of the Field, The (1962) This is a simple tale of faith and humor by William E. Barrett (1900–1986). Homer Smith, a black man of many skills, travels through the West in his secondhand car. When Homer passes a field where four nuns are building a fence, he stops to offer his help. The "boss," German-speaking Mother Maria Marthe, puts him to work at once on the small farm. Homer finds the nuns friendly and interesting, but soon realizes that they cannot pay him wages. He has fallen on a "house full of people living on the efforts of one cow and a few chickens," and yet he stays.

As he becomes more attached to the nuns, Homer helps by making repairs, giving English lessons, playing the guitar and singing, and by offering groceries to fill out the meager diet. Mother Maria Marthe shows him the foundation of a burned-out house and makes him understand the nuns' fervent wish to build a chapel there. After refusing what seems to him a hopeless project, Homer finds he cannot resist the challenge. He takes part-time work to pay for bricks and supplies and uses a nearby Spanish church as a model for the chapel.

When hard work and skimpy rations get him down, Homer leaves for the city, planning never to return. Then he finds an ancient but usable bathtub and is inspired to take it to the nuns, who must wash in a bucket. He returns to the site of the half-finished chapel and works with neighbors to complete it. Greatly satisfied with his chapel, Homer goes on his way. Barrett wrote many short stories, articles, and novels, many of them dealing with religious faith and social justice. One of these is *The Left Hand of God* (1951), which was adapted for film in 1963. *The Lilies of the Field* was filmed in 1963. YA

Liliom (1909), a play by the Hungarian writer *Ferenc Molnár, is set in Budapest. Liliom, a carnival barker, operates a carousel owned by a widow, Mrs. Muskat. Liliom is strong and handsome but also a ruffian and a rogue. He attracts the admiration of many young women, including a girl named Julie. When Mrs. Muskat catches Liliom flirting with Julie, she tells Julie never to come back. Liliom quits the carnival, vowing never to return, and marries Julie. But he is unable to find another job, and Julie's announcement that she is going to have a baby adds to his worries. Finally, the sight of Julie weeping causes him to hit her.

When he is cornered by the police during a bungled robbery attempt, Liliom kills himself. In a police court in heaven, he is sentenced to 16 years of purifying fire, after which he is to return to Earth for a day and do one good thing for his child. Liliom returns disguised as a beggar and visits Julie and his daughter, Louise, but he is unable to perform an act of kindness. In a moment of tension he slaps Louise's hand, but she feels the blow as a caress. After Liliom leaves, Louise tells Julie about this. Julie tells her that "some one may beat you and beat you and beat you—and not hurt you at all." *Liliom* became a Broadway hit in 1921 and was the basis for the stage musical comedy *Carousel*, produced in 1945, and as a movie in 1956. YA

Lilliput is an imaginary island in the South Seas where Lemuel Gulliver, the hero of the great satire *Gulliver's Travels,* by *Jonathan Swift, is shipwrecked. Gulliver is a "Man-Mountain" to the Lilliputians because they are less than six inches tall. How they capture him and feed him and how he learns their language and culture until they feel safe enough to release him make a fascinating tale. Some of their social customs he finds quite wonderful and others odd. For instance, no one in Lilliput is allowed to fall into poverty or sickness, unlike the Ireland and England of Swift's time, and most of the world today. But all Lilliputians are buried head down in the belief that, the world being flat, when it is turned over they will all be resurrected in the standing position. However, Gulliver goes from being the palace favorite to being accused of treason. First, he puts out a palace fire by urinating on it, and then he refuses to put to death the enemies of Lilliput on the neighboring island of Blefuscu. No longer respecting the ministers and kings, he leaves on a passing boat. He takes with him some tiny sheep and cattle, one of which is eaten by a ship's rat. Lilliputian has come to mean "tiny" in the English language. See also *Laputa. MR & YA

limerick This form of verse—short, humorous, often nonsensical, and frequently bawdy—has existed since 1820, but became, and has since remained, widely popular after the appearance of *Edward Lear's *The Book of Nonsense* (1846). Its name may come from the city of Limerick, Ireland, where it was the custom at parties to compose and sing nonsensical verses on the spur of the moment. A limerick consists of five lines, the first two and fifth of which rhyme, as do the third and fourth, which are also shorter. A typical and well-known example is:

> There was a young lady of Niger,
> Who smiled as she rode on a tiger;
> They returned from the ride
> With the lady inside,
> And the smile on the face of the tiger.

You can have fun writing your own limericks. To get started, read *How Pleasant to Know Mr.

THE COMPLETE NONSENSE BOOK

There was an Old Man on
whose nose
Most birds of the
air could repose;
But they all flew away at the closing of day,
Which relieved that Old Man and his nose.

There was an Old Man of Aôsta
Who possessed a large Cow, but he lost her;
But they said, "Don't you see she has run up a tree,
You invidious Old Man of Aôsta?"

Two of the wonderfully funny, nonsensical limericks written and illustrated by Edward Lear

Lear! Edward Lear's Selected Works (1982), selected by poet Myra Cohn Livingston (1926–). See also *The Complete Book of Nonsense.* MR & YA

Lincoln: A Photobiography (1987) By Russell Freedman (1929–), this easy-to-read biography of Abraham Lincoln (1809–1865), the 16th President of the United States, contains many photographs and illustrations of Lincoln, his family and friends, and the places that were important in his life. You can see such things as a replica of the Kentucky log cabin where Lincoln was born; the interior of the New Salem, Illinois, general store co-owned by Lincoln in the 1830s; and Lincoln's home in Springfield, Illinois, which he left in February 1861 to serve as President through the Civil War. Here too are pictures of Southern slaves, Union and Confederate soldiers and political leaders, and the dead on battlefields and the wounded in hospitals. Together, the text and pictures tell a powerful story about Lincoln and his times. Other good books about Lincoln include *Abe Lincoln Grows Up* (1928) by *Carl Sandburg, a rewriting for younger readers of his two-volume work *Abraham Lincoln: The Prairie Years* (1926); *The Apprenticeship of Abraham Lincoln* (1974) by Olivia Coolidge (1908–); and *The Fiery Trial: A Life of Lincoln* (1974) by Herbert Mitgang (1920–). *Lincoln: A Photobiography* received the *Newbery Medal in 1989. MR

Lindbergh, Ann (Spencer) Morrow (1906–) The wife of Charles A. Lindbergh (1902–1974), who became world famous as the aviator who made on May 20–21, 1927, the first solo nonstop flight from New York to Paris, Mrs. Lindbergh is noted in her own right as an author of novels, nonfiction, and poetry. *North to the Orient* (1935), her first book, is an account of an airplane journey she and her husband made to the Far East by way of the Arctic Circle, and *Listen! The Wind* (1938) is the story of a flight to England. Mrs. Lindbergh, however, faced considerable criticism when she published *The Wave of the Future* (1940), in which she defended her husband's isolationist stand and seemed to be writing favorably of Nazi Germany. Her first novel, *The Steep Ascent* (1944), the story of a flight over the Alps by a British pilot and his wife, earned critical praise. *Gift from the Sea* (1955), a volume of essays, reveals her inner thoughts about life and love, and about the ways in which women are different from men. A collection of poems, *The Unicorn and Other Poems, 1935–1955* (1956), is noted for lyrical and sensitive verse. Five volumes of her diaries and letters have been published, and one of them, *Locked Rooms and Open Doors* (1974), covers the terrible time in the couple's life when their infant son was kidnapped and later found dead. If you like Mrs. Lindbergh's books, try those of *Antoine de Saint-Exupéry. YA

Lindgren, Astrid (1907–) A Swedish novelist noted for both gentle humor and rather harsh *fantasy, Lindgren has seen her books trans-lated into many languages. Among those on the lighter side are *Pippi Longstocking* and its sequels. You will also find amusing *Rasmus and the Vagabond* (1960), about a 9-year-old boy who runs away from an orphanage and finds a traveling companion in a tramp, Paradise Oscar. They help solve a robbery before reaching a farm, which turns out to be Oscar's. He is only a part-time tramp, and he and his wife take Rasmus in as their son. *The Brothers Lionheart* (1975) are Karl and his older brother, Jonathan, who die and go to Nangiyala, "on the other side of the stars." It is a peaceful world except for Tengil and his dragon, Katla, who want to conquer the land. After several adventures, the two boys and the people of Cherry Valley defeat Tengil. But Jonathan has been burned by the dragon's fire and will die. Karl carries him to a cliff, where they jump off, die, and wake up on another and better planet, Nangilima. In *Ronia, the Robber's Daughter* (1983), two rival gangs fight each other, but in the end Ronia, the daughter of the leader of one of the gangs, and Birk, the son of the other chieftain, become friends and bring about peace. If you like Lindgren's books, read those of *Alexander Keyes, *Madeleine L'Engle, and *J.R.R. Tolkien. MR

lion "The king of beasts" earns this title by its noble presence, its strength, and its bravery. The lion appears in many tales and is a *symbol of lordliness. In Christian art the lion is an emblem of the Resurrection, and *St. Mark is depicted with a lion. *Aesop includes a number of *fables about the lion. Perhaps the best-known lion is the one in the *Bible story of *Daniel in the lion's den. From Roman times comes the story of the runaway slave, Androcles, who removed a thorn from a lion's paw. Recaptured, Androcles as a gladiator was to fight a lion, which turned out to be the one he had helped and refused to attack him. This story was the basis for the wonderful play *Androcles and the Lion* (1912) by *George Bernard Shaw. In modern times the most popular lion is the Cowardly Lion of *The Wonderful Wizard of Oz*.

A notable person, such as a famous author,

may be called a "literary lion," and to "lionize" someone is to make a fuss over that person. A number of common expressions use the lion's qualities to make a point: "the lion's share" of anything is the largest part, and "to put one's head in the lion's mouth" is to court danger unnecessarily. MR & YA

Lipsyte, Robert (1938–) In his novels and non-fiction books, Lipsyte, a former sports columnist for *The New York Times*, writes realistically about sports and growing up under tough conditions. Outstanding examples are *The Contender and *One Fat Summer. Assignment Sports* (1970) is a collection of his previously written articles that are notable for sharp portraits of sports personalities. *Free to Be Muhammad Ali* (1978) is a biography of that champion boxer. *The Brave* (1992) is the story of 17-year-old Sonny Bear, part Native American, who leaves a reservation in upstate New York to seek fame as a boxer in New York City. If you like Lipsyte's books, read those of *Paul Gallico, *George Plimpton, and *John R. Tunis. YA

Little, (Flora) Jean (1932–) A Canadian who was born blind but later recovered some vision, Little has used the problems of handicaps and illnesses in her novels interestingly. *Mine for Keeps* is a fine example. In *Home from Far* (1965), both the deaths of young people and the situation of foster children are themes. Eleven-year-old Jenny MacGregor has to adjust to the death of a twin brother and to the presence of a boy and his sister as foster children of her parents. *Look Through My Window* (1970) explores the impact on an only child, Emily, when four younger cousins move in with her family. She also makes two new friends and finds that they, like her, are interested in writing poetry. A different theme in *Listen for the Singing* (1977) is that of adjustment to Canadian life by Anna Selden, a recent immigrant from Nazi Germany before World War II. In addition, Anna has limited vision. When her brother Rudi is blinded in an accident while in training as a soldier, she is able to help him adjust and in the process advances her own

maturity. In *Mama's Going to Buy You a Mockingbird* (1984), 11-year-old Jeremy Talbot and his younger sister, Sarah, must adjust to the death of their father. With the example of Tess Medford, whose mother abandoned her when she was 7 years old, they learn to live with the loss of a loved one. If you like Little's books, read those of *James B. Garfield, *Susan Pfeffer, and *Irene Hunt. MR

Little Foxes, The (1939) The strong character of Regina dominates this play by *Lillian Hellman about a small-town family in the deep South in 1900. The play illustrates what people will do for money. The cotton business in which Regina's brothers own shares is taking on a Northern partner, a situation that will enrich all of the extended family. But Regina's husband, who is dying of heart failure, says that his family has money enough and will not invest. Regina, however, wants to be a millionaire. When her husband has a heart attack she withholds, in a famous scene, the medicine that would save him. Her brothers are no better, having stolen her husband's bonds to invest in the cotton gin. Regina uses this information to blackmail them. But, in gaining her money, she loses her daughter, Alexandra, who abandons her mother and gains her own soul. You can see in this play how powerful and intelligent people like Regina can be distorted by the roles they are required to act in society, in this case a captain of industry compressed into housewife. The part of Regina has been played by strong actresses, on the stage in 1940, and on the screen in 1941. If you enjoyed this play, try also *All My Sons* (1947), a play by *Arthur Miller about an industrialist who sells faulty parts to the military during World War II, an act that has tragic effects on many people, especially his own sons. *Regina*, a musical comedy based on *The Little Foxes*, was produced in 1949. YA

Little House on the Prairie (1935), an American classic by *Laura Ingalls Wilder, is one of the stories in the saga of the Ingalls family as they moved west. Wisconsin was getting too crowded, Pa said, so they packed up a covered wagon, and Ma, Pa, the three little girls, and Jack the bulldog headed out for the prairie. Nearly swept away by the river, investigated by a pack of huge wolves, visited by American Indians, they build their cabin using only an ax and wooden pegs. Mostly they eat game and cornmeal cakes. They acquire a longhorn cow and calf and for the first time have milk and butter. Pa is nearly gassed while digging their well, and a prairie fire is frantically fought with a back fire. The nearest town is 40 miles away, a round trip of four days that Pa has to make alone, leaving the family behind, which is when the Indians visit and Ma cooks for them. And in the end they are required to leave this house too, as they have built in Indian Territory, what is now Kansas. Wilder has written many fascinating books about the westward journey of her family. If you enjoy her books, try also *Caddie Woodlawn by *Carol Ryrie Brink and *Sarah, Plain and Tall by *Patricia MacLachlan. See also *These Happy Golden Years. A TV movie was made of *Little House on the Prairie* in 1974, and it was followed by three sequels and a TV series. MR

Little Lord Fauntleroy (1886) is *Frances Hodgson Burnett's tale of *Cedric Errol, a radiantly beautiful and generous little boy. His father, youngest son of the English Earl of Dorincourt, was sent away because the old earl was sure Cedric's American mother had married for money. His father dies when Cedric is very small, but his sweet-tempered mother makes a good life for him in New York City. One day the Errols are visited by the earl's lawyer, Havisham, who explains that as the earl's older sons have unexpectedly died, Cedric has inherited the title of Lord Fauntleroy. The grandfather wants the boy to grow up in Dorincourt castle and learn aristocratic ways, and promises to provide for the mother if she stays nearby but apart. She agrees to the arrangement for the boy's sake and is careful not to tell him of the earl's dislike for her. Once at the castle, Cedric can visit her often, and he charms the earl and everyone on the estate. Because Cedric is so affectionate and trusting,

Little Lord Fauntleroy

his grandfather begins to take more interest in life and listens to reports of the mother's beauty, dignity, and kind-heartedness. Then Havisham brings the awful news that another Lord Fauntleroy has turned up. A vulgar American woman claims her boy is the rightful heir to the title and should take Cedric's place. The old earl, now completely attached to Cedric and terribly upset, visits his mother to apologize for his cruel treatment of her. Through an amazing coincidence, it is discovered that the second Lord Fauntleroy is a fake, and the woman who plotted to deceive the earl is given money and sent off in a rage. Cedric's mother comes to live in the castle with her beloved son, the real Lord Fauntleroy, and his thankful grandfather. If you enjoyed this book, try also *Captains Courageous by *Rudyard Kipling and *Heidi by Johanna Spyri (1827–1921). A movie of *Little Lord Fauntleroy* was produced in 1936 and a version for TV in 1980. See also *The Secret Garden*. MR & YA

Little Nell is a central character in *The Old Curiosity Shop* by *Charles Dickens. She is an angelic child who never seems to grow up and is devoted solely to caring for her hapless grandfather. However, Nell is chiefly remembered for her deathbed scene, perhaps the best known in all English-language fiction, which, when the book first appeared, caused thousands of readers to weep. As Dickens describes it, in part:

She was dead. No sleep so beautiful and calm, so free from trace of pain, so fair to look upon. She seemed a creature fresh from the hand of God, and waiting for the breath of life; not one who had lived and suffered death. . . . Dear, gentle, patient, noble Nell was dead. . . . So shall we know the angels in their majesty, after death.

Dickens was later criticized for letting his emotions run away with his literary talent. YA

"Little Orphan Annie," one of the most popular of all comic strips, made its first appearance on August 5, 1924, in the New York *Daily News*. It took its title from the well-known poem "Little Orphant Annie" (1885) by *James Whitcomb Riley, and its creator was Harold Gray (1894–1968), a commercial artist. Annie has blank eyes, a mass of curly hair, and is forever upbeat and energetic. She has a dog, Sandy, whose response to anything she says is always "Arf." Annie was taken in charge by Oliver "Daddy" Warbucks, a billionaire whose fortune came from manufacturing weapons of war. She is often separated from him and has many exciting adventures. Fantasy entered the strip in the 1930s when Gray introduced two assistants to Warbucks—Punjab, very large and very strong, but kindly, and the Asp, with hooded eyes and dressed in black. Politically, Gray was very conservative and used the strip to push his views against government interven-

tion in private business. At the same time he showed his enmity for intolerance, censorship, and hypocrisy. After Gray died the strip was carried on by others, but unsuccessfully until 1979, when it was taken over by Leonard Starr (1925–). It was renamed simply *Annie* and made more in tune with the times. Meanwhile a successful stage musical, *Annie*, was produced in 1977 and a movie of this in 1982. MR & YA

Little Prince, The (1943) This book, with its charming drawings by the author, *Antoine de Saint-Exupéry, resists description. Is it a *fable, a legend, a tale, a myth, a dream, a philosophy of life? The author, who really was a pilot, writes about how he crashes his plane in the desert and meets the Little Prince, who asks many questions of the pilot but never answers the pilot's questions. The Little Prince is troubled about his rose, the only flower on his tiny planet, and so he visits other asteroids, also very tiny, where he meets some very strange grownups, such as an astronomer and a king, from whom he learns what is *not* important. When he arrives on Earth, however, he meets a fox that teaches him about love, and a snake that is wise and deadly, and the pilot. He learns that it is his own love and care that make his rose unique, and the Little Prince and the pilot learn that what is essential is invisible to the eye. Like the Little Prince's rose, this story is unique. However, if you enjoyed it, you will like the books for younger readers by *James Thurber. A movie of the book was made in 1974. MR & YA

Little Women (1868–1869), an immensely popular novel by *Louisa May Alcott, is the story of Meg, Jo, Beth, and Amy March. It opens when the four girls are in their early teens, and their father, a minister, is away in the Civil War. The Marches are "gentlefolk," which in those days meant educated but poor. They have a wise and loving mother. The girls are all talented in different ways, but at the heart of the story is Jo, the spirited and temperamental writer in the family who has a very hard time learning the "feminine virtues" of calmness, pa-

The March sisters of *Little Women* illustrated by Jessie Willcox Smith (1863–1935)

tience, and selflessness. This is a book about relationships, and it takes you through the struggles of each one of the girls with poverty, siblings, friends, and neighbors and finally leads into their marriages. Alcott has a gift for depicting character that often lifts this story above its sentimental elements, so that in the end you are truly aware that you have met a family of individuals. *Little Women* is partly an autobiography. *Little Men* (1871) and *Jo's Boys* (1886) are sequels. Two movies have been made from *Little Women*, in 1933 and 1949, and a TV version was produced in 1978. MR & YA

Lively, Penelope (Margaret) (1933–) An English novelist, Lively explores the past and present together in her work. Lively's first book for younger readers is *Astercote* (1971), the name of a deserted medieval village that Mair and her brother, Peter, come upon by accident. There they meet a youth who tells them how the village was destroyed by the Black Death, a

plague that spread over Europe in the 14th century. They also learn of a long-guarded secret, and they are caught up in a superstitious fear as strange events unfold. *The Ghost of Thomas Kempe* (1973) is a light-hearted account of the ghost of an early 17th-century sorcerer who meets up with modern technology. One of Lively's best novels is *The House in Norham Gardens* (1974). Nothing more exciting than the breaking of an arm happens to 14-year-old Clare Mayfield, who lives with some great-aunts near Oxford, England. With several new acquaintances, she discovers a shield that once belonged to an African tribe, and an assortment of other small events follow. In this way Clare becomes aware of the backward and forward flow of time and memory. *Going Back* (1975) is considerably different. The story takes place in a country home during World War II. Jane and her brother have to learn to live with a father who does not seem to want to relate to them in any emotional way. Haunting spirits play important roles in *Uninvited Ghosts* (1985), a book of eight short stories. In the title story, several ghosts, including that of a dog, appear to Marian and Simon Brown. They cause so much trouble that the children want to get rid of them and do so when the ghosts take a fancy to badly behaved twin babies. Do you like ghost stories? Then be sure to read the classic *parody of 19th-century ghost stories, "The Canterville Ghost," by *Oscar Wilde. Turned into a popular movie in 1944, this short story, available in an illustrated edition (1986), tells about an American family meeting a ghost in England. If you like Lively's books, read those of *Richard Peck and *Willo Davis Roberts. MR

Livingston, Myra Cohn (1926–) About to become a professional musician, Livingston decided instead to be a writer, editor, and teacher, and her decision has brought much pleasure to younger readers, for whom she has written 33 books of poetry. *The Way Things Are and Other Poems* (1974) is a typical example of her verse. It contains 38 short poems, one about the moon, "It's neat, moon, the way you stick up in that sky"; another about height, "It's tough being short"; another about "the weirdest names you sit and read"; and another about poverty, "Poor is a tired face." *No Way of Knowing: Dallas Poems* (1979), written in a different mood, uses black English dialect to tell of events at a time of racial troubles. Among collections of poetry Livingston has edited are *A Tune Beyond Us* (1968), an anthology of lesser-known poetry by well-known poets from a number of countries, and *Speak Roughly to Your Little Boy* (1971), parodies of the writings of a variety of authors, some of whom parody themselves. If you enjoy Livingston's poetry, try the poems of *Lewis Carroll, *A.A. Milne, and *Shel Silverstein. MR

Llewellyn, Richard See *How Green Was My Valley*.

Lochinvar is a Scots Highlander, the hero of a ballad of this title that is part of *Marmion* (1808), a narrative poem by *Walter Scott. The time is that of Henry VIII (1491–1547), King of England. Lochinvar is in love with "the fair Ellen," but has delayed so long in declaring his love that she becomes engaged to a poor craven figure of a man. Lochinvar arrives at Netherby Hall, the bride-to-be's home, just as the wedding is to take place. He asks for one last dance before they part, and Ellen, with "a smile on her lips, and a tear in her eye," consents. The couple dance out of the hall and onto Lochinvar's horse. They are pursued but escape the "racing and chasing" that follows. As the poem says:

> So faithful in love, and so dauntless
>   in war,
> There never was a knight like
>   young Lochinvar.

MR & YA

Lofting, Hugh (John) (1886–1947) An English-born American author and illustrator of the *Doctor Dolittle stories, Lofting began his career as a surveyor and civil engineer. Working in Canada, Africa, and the West Indies stimulated his already considerable appetite for travel to unexplored places. Lofting joined the British Army in World War I and became interested in the part that animals were playing in the war. In response to requests from his children, and to ease the terrible strain of war, he conceived the idea of writing illustrated narrative letters. These were based on the character of an eccentric country physician who gave up treating human patients and devoted himself to caring for animals. The letters were later published in book form as *The Story of Doctor Dolittle: Being the History of His Peculiar Life and Astonishing Adventures in Foreign Parts*, with Lofting's illustrations. The 12 Dolittle books later published include *The Voyages of Doctor Dolittle* and *Doctor Dolittle in the Moon* (1928), in which the doctor flies to the moon and pursues his passionate interest in vegetables and their languages. *Doctor Dolittle's Return* (1933) is about Dolittle's return to Earth after years on the moon (during which time he has grown to the astounding height of 18 feet), and the wonderful stories he tells to his animal friends. A movie, *Dr. Dolittle*, was produced in 1967. MR

Lohengrin is the hero of several medieval German legends, chiefly in *Parzifal* (*Parsifal*), written in the early 13th century by the poet Wolfram von Eschenbach (c.1170–c.1220). In the story, Lohengrin travels to the city of Antwerp in a boat drawn by a swan in order to restore Elsa, princess of the duchy of Brabant, to her rightful position. Lohengrin and Elsa marry, and he tells her she must not ask his name. She cannot resist doing so, and as a result Lohengrin disappears when the swan returns for him. He transforms the swan into Elsa's brother, Gottfried, who had been forced into a swan shape by a sorceress. Richard Wagner (1813–1883), the great German composer, used this legend for his opera *Lohengrin* (1859). Its Bridal Chorus is a familiar wedding march for brides and bridegrooms. YA

London, Jack (1876–1916) This novelist and short-story writer thought that human beings alternated between being beasts of prey and being beasts of burden. London grew up in and around Oakland, California, and began working in his youth to support his family. He spent the rest of his life alternately accepting ever-greater responsibilities—providing for family and friends alike—and, through many adventures, fleeing from them. When he was 15 years old he struck out as a vagabond, traveling across America as a railway hobo and gathering impressions he used later in the book *The Road* (1907). London was also an oyster pirate, a state fish-patrolman, a seaman on a seal-hunting voyage, a mill worker, a coal stoker, and a laundry worker. But whatever he was doing, London was always a voracious reader. In 1897, he joined the gold rush to the Klondike, where he gathered material for many of his masterful short stories as well as for his best-known work, *The Call of the Wild*. London married, had two daughters, then divorced and remarried. From 1900 to 1916, London wrote 50 volumes, some of lasting literary worth, including *The Sea Wolf* and *White Fang*. London spent much of his life battling a drinking habit, which he described in *John Barleycorn* (1913). His other books include *Martin Eden* (1909), a partly autobiographical novel about a young workingman's struggle to become a writer, and *The Cruise of the Snark* (1911), about London's attempt to sail around the world. YA

"Loneliness of the Long-Distance Runner, The" (1960) By *Alan Sillitoe, this bitter but convincing short story, from a collection of short stories with the same title, is about a 17-year-old English youth named Smith serving a term for robbery in a Borstal institution, a school for juvenile delinquents. He has been selected to be a long-distance runner in the hope of winning the All-England championships among the other Borstal institutions. Smith knows he is better off not trying to escape while on his practice runs, but he is always thinking of how to get revenge on the school's warden and the system that he hates. On the day of the big race, he is leading when he stops running and deliberately loses. For the remaining six months of his sentence, Smith is given the dirtiest possible tasks. When he is released he returns at once to robbery as a way of life. On the surface Smith is an unlikable, dis-

reputable person, but as you read his nastily expressed feelings you realize that people like the warden who control the social and economic system have no understanding of the life and thoughts of Smith and people like him. The Borstal system began in 1902 in Great Britain as a plan for reforming delinquent males, ages 16 to 21. The first of these institutions, the equivalent of American reform schools, was at Borstal Prison in Kent, in southeastern England. The Irish playwright Brendan Behan (1923–1964) spent time in the Liverpool Borstal, an experience he described in the book *Borstal Boy* (1958). "The Loneliness of the Long-Distance Runner" was adapted for film in 1962. YA

Lonesome Dove (1985), by *Larry McMurtry, is the name of tiny town on the Rio Grande River. The story of two Texas Rangers starts there, after the Civil War. There is no more Indian fighting to do in Texas, and bandits are scarce, so Augustus and Call run a little business selling horses and cattle. Various younger men live and work with them. Along comes an old friend who talks to them about the high grass and ample water for cattle ranching in Montana, so they gather a group of cowboys and horses and head north with the herd they steal from across the river, 2,600 cattle and 2 pigs. One woman, Lorene, goes with them. Indian fighting is still going on in the north, and there are vicious bandits who kidnap Lorene. She is rescued by Gus, who has to slay nearly everyone in sight to do it, but as a gunfighter of unsurpassed skill he is up to the task. This book is full of fight and flight stories and survival struggles. McMurtry's style is laconic and humorous, and he develops his characters in such a spare way that they stay with you. Gus focuses the story. He is a person of depth and versatility, perfectly suited to survive in the rough frontier, though he will not eat fried grasshoppers, molasses or no molasses. *Lonesome Dove* was produced as an enormously successful TV miniseries in 1989. YA

Long John Silver is one of the best-known villains in fiction, but you cannot help being impressed with his forceful personality and his audacity. He is a central figure in *Treasure Island by *Robert Louis Stevenson. You first meet him when a group of treasure seekers are hiring a crew for a voyage to Treasure Island to recover the treasure of pirate Captain Flint. Silver, a large man with a wooden left leg from near the hip down who walks with a crutch, is at the time an innkeeper in London. Hired as the ship's cook, Silver helps pick the crew, among them fellow pirates he commanded as Flint's first mate. Silver intends to lead a mutiny and secure Flint's treasure for himself and his cronies. As the adventure unfolds, Silver changes sides whenever it is to his advantage. In the end, his plot having failed but having talked himself out of being hanged, he manages to steal a bag of coins from the treasure and disappears. MR

Long March, The (1952) By *William Styron, this short novel is an account of a physical ordeal and its effect on the emotions. It begins shortly before the Korean War at a U.S. Marine training exercise in the Carolina swamplands. Newly recruited men are standing in the chow line for lunch. Without warning two misfired mortar shells drop into their midst, killing 8 and wounding 15. Among those who come to help are Lieutenant Culver and his friend Captain Mannix. Both are veterans of World War II who have had to leave their families and jobs, and both are suffering from feelings of unreality and dread. Mannix is a huge man with a bitter sense of humor, a rebel who carries a grudge against his commanding officer, Colonel Templeton, and the entire Marine Corps. The shock of the accident, coming on a quiet summer day, leaves Culver and Mannix more vulnerable than ever and aware that they are too old for combat.

Earlier, the colonel announced the company would make a 36-mile forced march back to the base. He will make sure his Marines are fit. Trucks will be provided for those too weak to finish. As the march begins, Mannix is infuriated by what he sees as a stupid and unjust challenge, but swears his group will arrive intact. Hours of trudging leave him exhausted,

with a dangerous wound on his foot from a loose boot nail, but he forces his men on with threats and curses. As Culver watches his friend helplessly, Mannix learns the colonel is riding instead of marching, and Mannix becomes rebellious. The colonel offers him a ride because of his foot, but Mannix refuses and vents his opinion of the whole operation. Templeton informs Mannix he may expect to be court-martialed. Ashamed to quit, afraid of not meeting the standard of conformity, and sustained by Mannix's boundless rage, Culver and Mannix stagger the last six miles to base camp. YA

Longest Day, The (1959) The best-known book of *Cornelius Ryan, this history of the Allied invasion of Normandy on D-Day, June 6, 1944, is drawn largely from eyewitness accounts by more than 1,000 Allied, German, and French survivors. Ryan begins with both the Allied and German preparations for the long-awaited invasion. The battle starts shortly after midnight, as airborne forces land inland to seize key positions and hold them for the seaborne invasion force. Shortly after dawn, following a massive air and naval bombardment, Allied troops land on five beaches, code-named Gold, Sword, Juno, Utah, and Omaha. In some places the fighting is light and the troops quickly move inland. In other places the beaches become bloody killing grounds. The Allies suffer about 10,000 casualties, but by day's end troops are moving inland from all the beaches, the invasion a success. Another good book about the Normandy invasion is *D Day, the Sixth of June, 1944* (1959) by the English writer David Howarth (1912–). *The Longest Day* was made into a movie in 1963. YA

Longfellow, Henry Wadsworth (1807–1882) The author of the long poem *Evangeline, Longfellow was born in Maine, traveled abroad for several years, taught at Bowdoin College, and then at Harvard College. His big yellow colonial house in Cambridge, near the college, had served as George Washington's headquarters, and there Longfellow's wife gave birth to two sons and to the three daughters who inspired the famous line, "grave Alice, laughing Allegra, and Edith with golden hair." In 1861 Longfellow was badly burned trying to rescue his wife, who had accidentally set fire to her dress. She died leaving five young children. The last 20 years of Longfellow's life were a story of ever-growing fame, and his poems were translated into many languages. He is the only American whose bust is in the Poet's Corner at Westminster Abbey in London, England. Those who write about Longfellow often mention his gift for friendship, a result of his sensitivity and genuine sweetness of soul. His friends praised him and his work so much that except for the terrible family tragedy in 1861, his life was smooth and his writing successful. In this atmosphere of nearly universal approval, some modern critics feel that he was not truly tested as a poet. Nevertheless, he was America's most popular poet. His fine sonnets have been overlooked because not many readers get beyond the excessive sweetness and nobility of, for instance, the characters and sentiments in *Evangeline*, which he thought was his best work. One of this poem's most important values was that it revealed to the world the brutality of the British Empire's expulsion of the Acadians from their land in Nova Scotia. Other well-known poems by Longfellow are *The Song of Hiawatha*, *The Courtship of Miles Standish*, and *"Paul Revere's Ride."* You can find several editions of Longfellow's poems and tales, such as *Evangeline and Selected Tales and Poems* (1963), *The Poetical Works of Longfellow* (1975), and *Poems* (1983). See also *John and Priscilla Alden; and *excelsior. YA

Look Homeward Angel: A Story of the Buried Life (1929)

By *Thomas Wolfe, this is a first novel published when he was 29 years old. It is almost entirely autobiographical. In it he is *Eugene Gant, the youngest of six children of Oliver and Eliza Gant. Oliver, given to passionate outbursts of oratory, is a stonecutter; Eliza is miserly, always worried about money. After she and Oliver separate, she opens a boarding house. Wolfe calls the setting Altamont, Catawba, but it is very much Asheville,

North Carolina. The early part of the novel tells of Eugene's life with his parents and siblings, especially his brother, Ben, who becomes a newspaperman and is the only one who guides Eugene. When he is 16 years old, 6 feet, 3 inches tall, and weighing only 130 pounds, Eugene enters the University of North Carolina at Chapel Hill, though it is not named as such. Here he is at first a loner, has his first love affairs, and in the end becomes the editor of the student paper. By this time, too, Ben has died, his father is dying, and his mother is dealing in real estate, successfully and on a large scale. Eugene does not feel a part of the family any more, and with his mother's reluctant promise of financing for one year, he sets off for graduate study at Harvard University. Part of the merit and significance of this very long novel lies in the young author's vivid and powerful expression of his pent-up and unchanneled rage for living and for doing great things even though he is not sure just what they might be. Toward the end he writes: "He was wild with the hunger for release; the vast champaign of earth stretched out for him its limitless seduction. It was the end, the end. It was the beginning of the voyage, the quest of new lands." *Of Time and the River* is a sequel. YA

Lord, Bette Bao (1938–) Born in China, Lord traveled with her parents to the United States when she was 8 years old. She later used her early experiences in America in her novel for younger readers. *In the Year of the Boar and Jackie Robinson.* Her best-known work, for older readers, is the novel *Spring Moon, which tells the story of a Chinese family from the 1890s to the 1970s against the rich background of Chinese history and culture. *Eighth Moon: The True Story of a Young Girl's Life in Communist China* (1964) tells about her sister, Sansan, who remained in China and was reunited with her family in the 1960s. Lord returned to live in China from 1985 to 1989 while her husband, the diplomat Winston Lord (1937–), served as American ambassador to China. During this time she interviewed many people, and their reflections on the political and social events of modern China became the foundation for her book *Legacies: A Chinese Mosaic* (1990). MR & YA

Lord Jim (1900) A single act of cowardice drives the life of Jim, a British merchant sailor, in this complex novel by *Joseph Conrad. The narrator is Marlow, who also appears in *Youth* (1898) and *Heart of Darkness.* Jim, a chief mate, can never forgive himself for abandoning a sinking ship. The sleazy captain then disappears, leaving Jim to face the court of inquiry alone, and his career on the sea is wrecked. Since this disaster takes place in Southeast Asia waters and his name becomes known in the ports of Asia, he retreats further and further until he finds his truth as the protector of a small tropical district. As in all Conrad tales, the truth is not something that emerges from the facts. Instead it emerges from the moral darkness in the human soul, and this in turn is revealed by circumstances of tropical heat, the dangerous, unstable upriver country, or by the sea. "The young moon recurved . . . like a slender shaving thrown up from a bar of gold, and the Arabian Sea smooth and cool to the eye like a sheet of ice extended" is Jim's view from the bridge in the last beautiful moments before the abyss of disaster opens for him. Before his sacrificial death, he learns the real truth of himself in the upriver country, and it is not cowardly, but it is different. Conrad, a Polish seaman who learned English as an adult, has few peers as a writer of English, especially when he writes about the sea. Another powerful novel about the sea and about the moral strengths and weaknesses of human beings is *Moby-Dick, or The Whale* by *Herman Melville. A movie was made of *Lord Jim* in 1965. YA

Lord of the Flies, The (1955) By *William Golding, this provocative novel tells about a group of English boys, from 6 to 12 years old, who are dropped onto an island from an airplane during an atomic war. Some choir boys in uniform are led by Jack, who gives orders and calls his group the hunters. Ralph seems to be a natural leader, ethical and kind, but real human wisdom lies with Piggy, whose torment it is not to be taken seriously because he is fat and wears eyeglasses. A brief period of stand-on-your-head happiness stimulated by the absence of grownups and the sunny beauty of the island dissolves bit by bit into episodes of sheer terror. The boys try to organize themselves democratically. But as mistakes, disagreements, and disasters pile up, moral and social codes crumble and something savage appears among them. They yearn for an adult, but it is only a dead adult from the air war who lands on the mountain and whose parachute bobs and billows like a monster in the wind. As Jack descends with his hunters into a primitive and dark violence, Ralph struggles to sustain his own decency in the face of absolute fear and learns the true nature of friendship from Piggy. This is a moving *fable, a gripping tale. Golding clearly believes that the structure of society depends on the ethical nature of the individual and that people must make choices if they are not to annihilate themselves. It is important to support Ralph and to control Jack, but it is "respect for Piggy," says *E.M. Forster in the introduction, "that seems needed most. I do not find it in our leaders." Another gripping novel about a group of young people is *A High Wind in Jamaica* by *Richard Hughes. Try also the novel *To the Wild Sky* (1977) by *Ivan Southall, about six young people who become stranded on a desert island. Movies based on *The Lord of the Flies* were made in 1963 and 1990. YA

Lord of the Rings, The (1954) This famous romantic *fantasy, a trilogy by *J.R.R. Tolkien, includes *The Fellowship of the Ring* (1954), *The Two Towers* (1954), and *The Return of the King* (1955). The land of *Middle-Earth and its fantastic characters are introduced in Tolkien's first novel, *The Hobbit, whose hero is Bilbo Baggins. Hobbits are an ancient, cheerful people about half human height, and they have furry feet, but unlike dwarves, they do not grow beards. The hero of The Lord of the Rings is a hobbit, Frodo, the nephew of Bilbo Baggins. From Bilbo, who found a magic ring during his adventures described in *The Hobbit*, Frodo inherits the ring, which makes him or anyone else invisible when the ring is worn. This ring has more magic than the other Rings of Power in the possession of the evil Dark Lord, and this is the One Ring the Dark Lord needs to become absolutely powerful. The ring also confers long life and has the power to corrupt absolutely anyone who keeps it and uses it, even someone as kindly as Frodo. It becomes Frodo's task to return the ring to the volcano, the hottest fire, where it was forged, so that the Dark Lord may not use it to rule Middle-Earth. When *The Fellowship of the Ring* opens, Gandalf, a wizard, tells Frodo that the Dark Lord has discovered who has the One Ring and will destroy or enslave all hobbits in order to gain it. So begins Frodo's journey with three other hobbits through a landscape of elves, dwarves, trolls, orcs, giants, dragons, goblins, wizards, animals, and human beings, some of whom are gallant friends and others treacherous and evil. There are lakes that boil with tentacles, dark magic wildernesses, and slimy passages beneath rooted mountains. Frodo does not feel like a hero, but he grows into the job in the face of danger and war. Frodo's story is a wonderful and long series of high adventures in an amazing imaginary world. An animated movie of The Lord of the Rings was produced in 1978. YA

Lorelei is the name of a mythical siren made famous by the German poet *Heinrich Heine in the poem *Die Lorelei* (1827). She sat on a tall, steep rock that juts into the Rhine River and is noted for its echo. Combing her hair and singing on the rock, she caused distracted sailors to crash upon the reefs below. The word "siren" has a long history related to sailors being lured to their deaths by mythical singing female creatures. *Odysseus, in the *Odyssey* by *Homer, plugged the ears of his men with beeswax and had himself tied to the mast in order to pass by the singing sirens, and *Jason and the Argonauts were saved by the louder singing of Orpheus. Both "siren" and "Lorelei"

have come to mean a woman over whom men lose their wits and self-control. YA

Lost Generation refers to people who came of age during and just after World War I. More precisely, it is used to describe a group of American writers who expressed their dissatisfaction with old values and ideals, and with what they saw as a trend toward materialism and emotional sterility in the United States. *Gertrude Stein is said to have commented to *Ernest Hemingway: "You are all a lost generation," and her remark appears in the preface to Hemingway's novel *The Sun Also Rises. Other members of the group include *John Dos Passos, *F. Scott Fitzgerald, *Hart Crane, *Archibald MacLeish, and the poet e.e. cummings (1894–1962), whose only novel, *The Enormous Room* (1922), was based on his experience of being imprisoned by the French during World War I while serving in a volunteer ambulance corps. YA

Lost Horizon (1933), by *James Hilton, is the novel that gives us the name and idea of "Shangri-La." The dictionary describes Shangri-La as an imaginary paradise on earth, a remote or exotic utopia. Three men and a woman in a small plane are hijacked. The plane crashes in a mysterious Tibetan mountain valley, and its passengers are rescued by the inhabitants of an airy lamasery built onto the side of a mountain. The lamasery governs a fertile valley below of several thousand people. Though the plumbing in the lamasery is modern and the library is up to date, no one volunteers to help the passengers leave this beautiful, hidden place. Soon it develops that they have been brought here on purpose. As Conway, an enigmatic Englishman on whom people seem to rely, learns the reason for their kidnapping, tension develops between those who want to stay and those who want to escape. The escape is dangerous, the outcome very odd. Hilton's idea of utopia is interesting though dated, based as it is on a class society of scholars, contented servants, and happy peasants. Nevertheless, Hilton's feeling for the incomparable grandeur of the Himalaya makes *Lost Horizon*

MR = Middle Reader   YA = Young Adult Reader   * = See this main entry

exciting to read, and the story is compelling and mysterious. Movies based on *Lost Horizon* were made in 1937 (by far the better) and in 1973. YA

Lost Zoo, The (1940) By *Countee Cullen and, he claims, by his white-and-orange cat, Christopher, this book of poems results after Cullen tells Christopher that he has been to the zoo. The cat thinks it is too bad the animals are kept caged, and anyway, Christopher says, the zoo does not include some of the most interesting animals because they no longer exist. He explains that he knows about these creatures because his ancestor, who was on Noah's ark, passed on the tale of those species for whom there was no room. Christopher proceeds to tell his master what these animals and birds were like. Cullen then decides to write verses about them, which he does with comments from Christopher interrupting him from time to time. There are poems about the Wakeupworld, who has 12 eyes, one for each hour of the clock; the Squilililigee, the gentlest creature ever; the Sleepamitemore, who, of course, wants "just one more wink"; and others. However, Christopher denies he ever told Cullen about a Pussybow that could both mew and bark. If you enjoyed this book, try also *Old Possum's Book of Practical Cats* (1939), a collection of wonderful poems by *T.S. Eliot. An amusingly illustrated edition of *The Lost Zoo* was published in 1951. MR

Lot See *Sodom and Gomorrah.

"Lottery, The" (1948) One of the most quietly horrifying short stories ever written, this masterpiece by *Shirley Jackson presents an ordinary group of Americans on a sunny summer day when they are engaged in a public event that shimmers with evil. Once a year the villagers assemble to draw lots from an old box. It is a ceremony so old that no one knows when—or why—it began. In the village square, men, women, and children draw lots to sacrifice, without thought or regret, one of their own. The Hutchinson family—Bill, his wife, Tessie, and their three children—draw the only

slip with a black spot on it. They then draw again to see which member of the family will get it. It is Tessie, who calls out, "It isn't fair," as the first stone hits her, and "then they are upon her." Tessie is stoned to death. Jackson illuminates the evil that often underlies mindlessness, in this case the mindless acceptance of an old institution, and the ritual sacrifice of a scapegoat. Many people have called this *fable a simple tale of horror. But Jackson was proud of the fact that at the height of apartheid in South Africa *The Lottery* was banned, and she felt that the South Africans, at least, had understood the story. The story is available in a paperback along with 24 other tales by Jackson in *The Lottery and Other Stories* (1982). YA

Lotus-eaters Island is a dangerous place where eating of the lotus plant could cause *Odysseus and his men, in the *Odyssey* by *Homer, to forget the reason for their voyage. Homes and families are forgotten, and the only desire that remains is to stay on the island living idly and eating the lotus. The men Odysseus sent to explore the island had to be dragged back to the ship. In actual fact there is an island in the eastern Mediterranean where the lotus grows thickly. In this place it is a shrub whose fruit can be baked into bread or made into wine. Continual feeding on the lotus can cause amnesia and a feeling that there is no point to human effort. Extreme relaxation of the muscles is another effect, and a certain deafness that makes voices sound small and far away. The term "lotus-eater" has come to mean one who lives a lazy life of ease and luxury. *Alfred Tennyson wrote a poem entitled "The Lotos-Eaters" (1833). YA

love is a word so freely used that when you say, for example, "I love your hat," you may be forgetting the very deep, basic meaning the word has in human relationships. Love was important enough to the Greeks and Romans that they had gods of love, *Eros and Cupid. Most writers of renown have had something to say about love. *Virgil wrote, "Love conquers all things," but *William Shakespeare was less optimistic: "The course of true love never did run smooth." You may experience "love at first sight," but if you do, others may think you are foolish, because "love is blind." "Love me, love my dog" does not necessarily apply to a canine only; it suggests that you must love everything about the person you love. When you say "not for love or money" you mean nothing can possibly get you to act as asked, but "a labor of love" is something you do without thought of reward. In tennis, if your score is "love," it means you have not won a single point. YA

Lovecraft, H(oward) P(hillips) (1890–1937) A master of supernatural horror fiction, Lovecraft spent almost his entire life in Providence, Rhode Island, where he was born. Many of Lovecraft's stories appeared in the horror magazine *Weird Tales*, where they gained him a small circle of close friends. After Lovecraft's death, his friends published a collection of Lovecraft's stories, *The Outsider and Others* (1939), and created the publishing company Arkham House, which over the years issued a number of Lovecraft collections as well as the works of many other writers. Among Lovecraft's best works are *The Colour Out of Space* (1927), a novelette set outside the fictional New England city of Arkham, the setting for several of his stories, and concerning a deadly creature that falls to earth with a meteorite; *The Case of Charles Dexter Ward* (1943), a short novel dealing with the occult and set in Providence; and *At the Mountains of Madness* (1964), a short novel about an Antarctic expedition that uncovers evidence of alien creatures that dominated the earth tens of millions of years ago. A number of Lovecraft's stories form what is called the Cthulhu Mythos, concerning monstrous creatures who once ruled the universe. Through the power of black arts they become trapped in another dimension, where they await the day when unwitting humans dabbling in the occult will release them. Several other writers have added stories to the Mythos. Almost everything Lovecraft wrote is available in paperback editions. YA

Lowell, Amy (1874–1925) Born into a clan of ministers, judges, writers, scholars, and industrialists, Lowell was not the first poet (see also *James Russell Lowell) in this upper-crust New England family, nor the last (see also *Robert Lowell), nor did she write the jingle, whose source is actually unknown, about Boston being "the home of the bean and the cod/Where the Lowells talk only to Cabots/And the Cabots talk only to God." There were Cabots in her family too. With *Ezra Pound, she studied Imagism, a type of poetry that tries to express human experiences through images, in the fewest possible words. Pound later called this group "Amygists." Amy Lowell, moving in and out of literary circles, was considered eccentric, even weird. She maintained what was at the time a scandalous relationship with a divorced actress for many years and, equally scandalous, she smoked cigars, though this habit did nothing to keep her weight down. Headlines were made when she ordered 10,000 cigars from the Philippines during a World War I shortage. She was a writer of prose as well as poetry. She wrote a biography, *John Keats* (1925), and critical works entitled *Six French Poets* (1915) and *Tendencies in Modern American Poetry* (1917). You can find a good sampling of her poetry in her collection *What's O'Clock* (1925). *The Complete Poetical Works of Amy Lowell* (1955) contains an introduction by *Louis Untermeyer. YA

Lowell, James Russell (1819–1891) Called America's first professional man of letters and also, with *Edgar Allan Poe, one of this country's first real literary critics, Lowell was an unremarkable poet, too highly rated in his lifetime. Yet he was a force in 19th-century American letters because of his sense of satire and trenchant critical insights. A professor at Harvard University, Lowell was the first editor of *The Atlantic Monthly*. All his published writings are collections of poems, essays, or lectures. He was eccentric, once eating with a knife and fork the centerpiece flowers at a Boston literary dinner, so it is interesting that he became a diplomat and served as minister to Spain and England. He was part of the well-known New England Lowell family, which produced other writers, among them the poets *Amy Lowell and *Robert Lowell.

Lowell, Robert (Traill Spence, Jr.) (1917–1977) One of America's best-known poets, Lowell was also an essayist, playwright, and teacher. A member of an old New England family that included two other notable poets—*Amy Lowell and *James Russell Lowell—his first poetry was *Land of Unlikeness* (1944), written against the background of World War II and the problem of spiritual security in a time of crisis. Lowell served five months in prison during the war as a conscientious objector, and this is one of the subjects treated in *Lord Weary's Castle* (1946), a collection of his poems dealing with sin and innocence, crime and punishment. *Life Studies* (1950) includes both poetry and prose, and for the most part the writings are related to Lowell's family, childhood, and marriage. The title poem in *For the Union Dead* (1964) is a bitter comment on New England's loss of idealism. "He has an angry wrenlike vigilance" is a typical line, this one about the white colonel of a black regiment in the Civil War. Three one-act plays, based on short stories by *Nathaniel Hawthorne and *Herman Melville, make up the contents of *The Old Glory* (1965). Lowell was very much a poet of his times. He said, "I am tired. Everyone's tired of my turmoil." If you appreciate Lowell's poetry, read that of John Berryman (1914–1972) and *William Carlos Williams. YA

Lower Depths, The (1902) This is the only play by *Maxim Gorky that has been widely produced outside Russia. Its first production included the famous method actor Konstantin Stanislavski (1863–1938), director of the Moscow Art Theater. He and Gorky required the actors to go into the streets to study the personalities of "the lower depths" close at hand. The setting is a flophouse, or boarding house, in a town on the Volga River at the turn of the century. The characters are a collection of men and women who do odd jobs but live mostly by their wits. There are a few jailbirds, a policeman, a prostitute, a peddler, a capmaker, a former aristocrat, an actor, and a pilgrim, or wanderer. Vodka is ever present. In this atmosphere a young woman dies of consumption and neglect, complaining of lifelong hunger; another is beaten regularly; men play cards and talk; a man is killed and another hangs himself. With compassion Gorky portrays the desperation of individuals in a setting of moral anarchy as they try to preserve or create a sense of decency and personal integrity. Gorky's own experience of poverty contributed to the play's power, which alone has placed him among the masters of modern drama. He was the first Russian playwright to depict realistically the life of the poor before the Russian Revolution of 1917. Gorky again explored the causes of the growing revolutionary movement in his novel *Mother. A movie based on *The Lower Depths* was produced in Japan in 1957. YA

Lowry, Lois (1937–) An author and photographer, Lowry has written more than 40 books, some of them about family and juvenile problems. But she also writes lighthearted books, of which the best known are the seven about *Anastasia Krupnik. Lowry's earliest novel was *A Summer to Die* (1977). Based in part on her own experience, it is centered on 13-year-old Meg Chalmers, who first resents her older sister's popularity and then has to come to terms with her guilt feelings when the sister dies. *Find a Stranger, Say Goodbye* (1978) is the story of an adopted girl, Natalie Armstrong, who sets out when she is 17 years old to find her biological parents. The search and its result help Natalie mature. *Autumn Street* (1980) has more than its share of troubles and tragedy. Six-year-old Elizabeth and her mother move in with grandparents while the father is serving in World War II. Grandfather has a stroke, two of Elizabeth's friends die, and her father is badly wounded, all of which hastens her growing up. In a more happy mood is *The One Hundredth Thing About Caroline* (1983), in which the single-parent household of 11-year-old Caroline is happy because her mother makes known her love and appreciation of the children. Much less happy is the situation in *Number the Stars, which tells about the Nazi occupation of Denmark during World War II. If you like Lowry's books, read those of *Judy Blume, *Mary Rodgers, and *Marilyn Sachs. MR

Lucifer is one of the many names of the devil. Some others are *Satan, Beelzebub, the Great

MR = Middle Reader   YA = Young Adult Reader   * = See this main entry

Goat, Overlord of Hell, Mephistopheles, Lord of the Flies, and the Fallen Angel. The word "Lucifer" actually means Light-bringer, and was the Roman name for the god of the Morning Star who announced the daily birth of the sun. For Christians, Lucifer is the angel who was cast out of heaven for the sin of pride, the Fallen Angel. Ancient connections link Lucifer to lightning and serpents; Lucifer was the serpent who brought knowledge to *Adam and Eve in the Garden of *Eden. In his aspect of goat, with horns and tail, he is connected with lust. Early in the 19th century, matches were sometimes called "lucifers," and during World War I, lucifer was common slang for a match "to light your fag" (cigarette).

"Luck of Roaring Camp, The" (1868) In this sentimental story by *Bret Harte, set in 1850, the only woman in a *Gold Rush miners' camp of 100 men dies in childbirth. The baby, named Luck, survives, suckled on the milk of an ass, and for a time these rough men are transformed by the presence of the child. Baths are taken, clothes are washed, flowers are planted, and songs are sung. And gold keeps coming. One old miner in particular, who had worn his clothes as a sort of decaying second skin, moved by the grip of a baby hand on his finger, becomes especially clean and loving. The baby is referred to as "The Luck." But the luck of Roaring Camp runs out all at once, and the end is sad. Harte was one of the first to write about the California Gold Rush, and though he saw the miners and the few desperate women through pious, educated eyes, he nevertheless conveyed the wonderful, natural grandeur of the unsettled West. Another writer who described life in the Western mining camps was *Mark Twain. MR & YA

Ludlum, Robert (1927–) An author of adventure thrillers, Ludlum combines factual information and a political background with plots and action that are on the wild side. For example, his first thriller, *The Scarlatti Inheritance*

(1971), is set before World War II, when Nazism was rising in Germany. A conspiracy of industrialists and bankers backs the would-be dictator, Adolf Hitler (1889–1945), in the hope of creating a superpower to rule the world. In *The Gemini Contenders* (1976) the plot concerns a search for documents allegedly written by Saint Peter and showing that someone took Christ's place on the cross. *The Bourne Identity* (1980) introduced Ludlum's best-known protagonist, Jason Bourne, a professional assassin who has lost his memory after being nearly murdered. As he is hunted by various enemies, he discovers he is David Webb, a professor of Oriental studies who has adopted the Bourne identity to lure and trap Carlos, the Jackal, the world's worst terrorist. Bourne's adventures continue in *The Bourne Supremacy* (1986) and *The Bourne Ultimatum* (1990). Ludlum's plots are quite unbelievable, there is much violence, and the writing style is melodramatic, but there is plenty of excitement. If you like such books, try those of *Leslie Charteris, *Ian Fleming, and *Frederick Forsyth. *The Bourne Identity* was produced as a TV movie in 1988. YA

Luke, Saint (fl A.D. c.75) A physician and a companion and co-worker of *Paul, Luke, a gentile, was one of the four Evangelists (with *Matthew, *Mark, and *John) who wrote the four Gospels of the New Testament of the *Bible. Together these books tell the story of the life and works of Jesus. Luke's account emphasizes the compassion of Jesus. His telling of the Christmas story, the birth of Jesus, is the most lyrical and touching: An angel brings "good tidings of great joy" about "the babe wrapped in swaddling clothes, lying in a manger." Luke is also thought to be the author of the Acts of the Apostles, the New Testament book that recounts the early history of the Christian church. Luke is the patron saint of physicians, and of artists because he was said to have been a painter also. MR & YA

M.C. Higgins, the Great (1974), a novel by *Virginia Hamilton, tells about Mayo Cornelius Higgins, a 13-year-old boy who lives with his family in southern Ohio at the foot of Sarah's Mountain, overlooking the Ohio River. The mountain was named after his great-grandmother, who escaped from slavery and settled there before the Civil War. Now coal miners have ripped up the mountain above their house and have left a large pile of spoil—waste rock and soil—that threatens to slide down the mountainside and destroy their home. M.C. wants the family to move away, but his father refuses. All the dead Higginses, even old Sarah, are buried in the patch of level ground that makes up their front yard.

M.C.'s best friend is Ben Killburn, but Mr. Higgins will have nothing to do with the Killburn clan and says they are "witchy people" with strange powers. M.C. feels that he and his family are trapped by the ignorance of his father and by the spoil moving ever so slowly toward his house. He sees hope when two strangers come to the mountain. One, a fellow with a tape recorder, wants to record his mother's singing, and M.C. thinks he wants to make her a music star. The other, a girl who has come to camp near the mountain, shows M.C. that the world is much larger than his mountain, and that the Killburns are human beings just like the Higginses. But when both strangers leave, M.C. has to solve his family's

problems alone. He begins building a wall to keep the spoil away from the house, and he stands up to his father about his friendship with Ben. Father and son reach a new understanding, and with Ben and M.C.'s younger brothers and sister, they work together to save the house. YA

Macbeth (1623) This tragedy, one of *William Shakespeare's best-known dramas, is the story of a man who destroys himself when he chooses the forces of evil to shape his destiny. As the play opens, Macbeth and Banquo, two Scottish nobles, are returning from battle after defeating the rebellious Thane of Cawdor and a Norwegian army. They come upon three witches, who tell them that Macbeth is to become Thane of Cawdor and king and that Banquo is to found a line of Scottish kings. Macbeth is astonished when a messenger from the Scottish King Duncan tells Macbeth that he has been made the new Thane of Cawdor. Macbeth sacrifices his own sense of morality to his overpowering ambition to be king. When Duncan visits Macbeth's castle, Macbeth murders him in the night and makes it look as though the king's attendants killed him. In the morning, Macbeth kills the attendants in a false rage. Duncan's son Malcolm, the heir to the throne, and his brother, Donalbain, are not fooled by Macbeth, and they escape, as does another noble, Macduff. Banquo suspects Macbeth's treachery, but he says nothing. Macbeth remembers the witches' prophecy about Banquo and sends assassins to murder him and his son, Fleance. Banquo is killed but Fleance escapes. Macbeth and *Lady Macbeth undergo mental torment over his evil deeds, and Macbeth even sees Banquo's ghost. But he continues his bloody tyranny. He sends assassins to kill Macduff's family, but Macduff has escaped to England to join Malcolm and raise an army against Macbeth. The witches conjure up apparitions that tell Macbeth to fear Macduff, that no "man of woman born" can harm him, and that he will be undefeated until Birnam Wood shall come to the hill of Dunsinane, where Macbeth's castle stands. Macbeth has lost all desire for the crown, and life itself has lost all meaning and value, but he decides to fight on, even after Lady Macbeth kills herself. Malcolm and Macduff's army arrives at Dunsinane, each soldier carrying a tree bough cut from Birnam Wood to disguise their number. When Macbeth sees the moving wood, he realizes he is undone. Macduff confronts Macbeth and reveals that he was not born in the normal way, but "was from his mother's womb untimely ripp'd." He kills Macbeth, and Malcolm is hailed king of Scotland. Film adaptations of *Macbeth* were made in 1948 and 1971. YA

MacDonald, John D(ann) (1916–1986) This prolific novelist wrote 70 books in all, some of them novels, others detective stories, many of which feature Travis McGee as a private investigator. MacDonald's first detective novel, not about McGee, was *The Brass Cupcake* (1950), in which a former policeman fights corruption. McGee lives on his boat, *The Busted Flush*, in Fort Lauderdale, Florida, and his work is to recover stolen property for a share of its value. McGee sometimes does not stay within the exact letter of the law. In *Pale Gray for Guilt* (1962) he fights a conglomerate, Tech-Mex, which threatens a friend's small marina and motel. *Darker Than Amber* (1962) finds McGee rescuing a girl he sees thrown off a bridge. He then goes after the criminal gang behind the deed. The McGee stories all have a color in

their titles, such as *The Deep Blue Good-By* (1964) and *The Dreadful Lemon Sky* (1975). On the whole, the stories are well written and have complicated plots. MacDonald's other novels, such as *Condominium* (1977), often make a moral point. If you enjoy these books, you will like those of *Raymond Chandler, *Dashiell Hammett, and *Ross MacDonald. YA

MacDonald, (John) Ross [Kenneth Millar] (1915–1983) Though his first mystery novel, *The Dark Tunnel* (1944), is a spy story of Nazi Germany, MacDonald is best known for his detective stories that feature *Lew Archer as a private eye. The first of these novels was *The Moving Target* (1949). Because of the depth of the Archer stories in probing human personalities and psychological problems, MacDonald is accepted as a mainstream novelist, not just a writer of detective fiction. Most of the Archer novels, set in southern California, involve generation gaps, the search for a lost family member and, of course, murder. Such are *The Drowning Pool* (1950); *The Barbarous Coast* (1956), about decadence in Hollywood; and *The Blue Hammer* (1976). *The Moving Target* was filmed in 1966 under the title *Harper. The Drowning Pool* was made into a movie in 1975. If you like these books, try those of *Raymond Chandler, *Dashiell Hammett, and *John D. MacDonald. YA

MacLachlan, Patricia (1938–) A teacher and writer, MacLachlan is known best for her short but brilliant *Sarah, Plain and Tall*, which has all the best qualities of her books for young people—strong and memorable characters, an interesting story, and a sense of the importance of family and love. Her other books include *Arthur, for the First Time* (1980), about a 10-year-old boy whose view of life is broadened after he spends an amazing summer with his aunt and uncle, who are unlike anyone he has ever met before; *Cassie Binegar* (1982), about a young girl who feels lost and stifled when her family moves to a new house by the sea, and how she learns that change and growth are part of life; and *The Facts and Fictions of Minna Pratt*

(1988), about a girl who wishes her eccentric family could be a bit more like other people's families. MR & YA

MacLean, Alistair (Stuart) (1922–1987) This Scottish-born British author, having served in the Royal Navy in World War II, used that experience in his first novel, *H.M.S. Ulysses* (1955). With *The Guns of Navarone* (1957) he turned to the kind of adventure story that made him popular. This is an account of a small group of men who are sent to destroy German artillery that is preventing British ships from going to the rescue of men trapped on an island. Rough seas, unscalable cliffs, and the German army are obstacles the intrepid heroes overcome to blow up the guns in a spectacular finish. *Ice Station Zebra* (1963), about a battle with Arctic cold and determined communists, is another exciting adventure, as is *Breakheart Pass* (1974), in which a government agent tracks down gun runners on board a long-distance train in the 19th-century American West. Younger readers will enjoy the biography *Lawrence of Arabia* (1962). Movies have been made of *The Guns of Navarone* in 1961, of *Ice Station Zebra* in 1968, and of *Breakheart Pass* in 1976. If you like such tales, try those of *Leslie Charteris and *Frederick Forsyth. MR & YA

mad as a hatter Here "mad" means insane, not angry. The phrase "mad as a hatter" goes back to the early 1800s. It may refer to the strange way hatmakers acted when they became ill from the chemicals used in making hats. They twitched and jerked about and slurred their words. The Mad Hatter in *Alice's Adventures in Wonderland* by *Lewis Carroll certainly acted strangely. Carroll may have had "mad as a hatter" in mind when he created this famous character. Or, Carroll may have modeled him after a local furniture dealer, who wore a top hat and was well known for his unusual ideas.

Madame Bovary (1857) By *Gustave Flaubert, this classic French novel is celebrated for its stylistic grace and clarity and its attention to detail. Flaubert's realistic telling of a relatively simple story helped mark the beginning of a new movement of realism in literature. Charles Bovary is a barely competent country doctor who has married an unattractive, demanding, jealous woman because he believes she can help him advance in his profession. One night he is called to a farm to care for M. Roualt, who has broken his leg. There Bovary meets Roualt's lovely daughter, Emma, and the two are attracted to each other. Bovary's wife dies and, after a period of mourning, Bovary and Emma are married. Charles adores his new bride, but Emma finds she does not feel the overpowering passion for her husband and for her new life that she had expected. Charles is dull and uninteresting, and Emma longs for more, even after the birth of her daughter, Berthe.

She falls in love with a lawyer's clerk, Léon Dupuis, but avoids having an affair with him. Léon goes away, and Emma falls ill. She begins an affair with one of her husband's patients, Rodolphe Boulanger, a young farmer. Rodolphe ends the affair suddenly after Emma begs him to take her and Berthe away to start a new life. Again crushed, she slowly recovers, but then, by accident, meets Léon again and begins an affair with him. Emma has taken charge of the family finances, but under the influence of a dishonest merchant named L'heureux, she has fallen deeply into debt. Charles is as unaware of Emma's debts as he is of her affairs. Finally crushed by life and unable to raise the money to prevent bankruptcy and disgrace, Emma kills herself. After her death Charles finds letters from her lovers and learns of her unfaithfulness. He becomes a recluse and dies of a broken heart.

First published in installments, the novel created a public outcry. Flaubert, his printer, and his publisher were tried both for blasphemy and offense against public morals. According to Vladimir Nabokov (1899–1977), a Russian-born American novelist and critic, Flaubert was able "to transform what he conceived to be a sordid world . . . into one of the most perfect pieces of poetical fiction known."

MR = Middle Reader   YA = Young Adult Reader   * = See this main entry

If you enjoy realistic fiction like *Madame Bovary*, try the books of William Dean Howells (1837–1920), an American novelist who was a pioneer of realism in fiction. Perhaps his best novel is *The Rise of Silas Lapham* (1885), about a businessman, ambitious for wealth and social position, who brings about his own financial ruin but gains moral salvation when he refuses to save his business through a dishonest act. YA

Madame Defarge is a character in *A Tale of Two Cities* by *Charles Dickens. A *symbol of the French revolutionary spirit, it is she who knits coolly while watching the slaughter of aristocrats condemned for crimes against the common people. Stout, with strong features and a watchful eye, she maintains a composure that suggests she is a woman not easily controlled by others. Madame Defarge is shrewd, brazen, and ruthless, a born leader imbued from childhood with hatred for the upper classes and their often cruel and oppressive ways. Absolutely humorless and without pity, she knits into a shapeless garment a list of names of the guilty ones destined for the guillotine.

Maggie: A Girl of the Streets (1893) This short novel by *Stephen Crane is set in the late 19th century in the slum section of New York City known as the Bowery. Maggie Johnson, daughter of a brutal laborer and a drunken, abusive mother, grows from a tattered, neglected child to a beautiful young woman. When her brother brings home a well dressed bartender named Pete, Maggie is drawn to him. He seems a cut above the rest of the people around her, and Maggie longs to escape her bleak world. After Pete seduces Maggie, she is thrown out of the house by her mother. Soon Pete grows tired of Maggie and abandons her. Maggie cannot return home, and she has no one to turn to for help. She slips into prostitution, then kills herself in despair. Crane's novel has been called the first realistic portrayal of slum life in American literature. His realistic descriptions and unsparing use of *irony to underscore Maggie's tragic life and senseless death were so original and powerful that no publisher would accept the novel. Crane had to pay for its first publication. Another novel dealing realistically with prostitution and with the destruction of a young woman is *Nana* (1880) by the French writer Emile Zola (1840–1902). YA

Magi According to the *Bible, the Magi were "wise men from the East," probably astrologers, who followed a star to Jerusalem seeking the newborn "King of the Jews." They found their way to the baby *Jesus and presented gifts of gold, frankincense, and myrrh. Frankincense and myrrh are aromatic oils that are secreted by a family of shrubs commonly known as incense trees. In biblical times both these oils were used as incense in religious ceremonies. In Christian tradition there are three Magi, all kings, named Balthazar, Caspar [or Gaspar], and Melchior. In medieval legend they are called the Three Kings of Cologne because the cathedral in that German city claims to have relics of them. "Magi" is the plural of the Latin word *Magus*, meaning "wise man." You will want to read *The Gift of the Magi*, a wise-sad short story by *O. Henry. For older readers there is *The Magus* (1965), a novel by *John Fowles, which tells about an English schoolteacher who visits a beautiful and remote island in the Aegean Sea and becomes involved in a fantastic and complicated game with the island's owner, a mysterious Greek tycoon who possesses great knowledge and seems to have magical powers. *Amahl and the Night Visitors* by Gian Carlo Menotti (1911–) is an opera about the three wise men and a handicapped boy, first produced for television in 1951. It may often be seen during the Christmas season. MR & YA

Magnificent Obsession (1929), a novel by *Lloyd C. Douglas, is about devotion to a great idea. Dr. Hudson is a brilliant surgeon at Brightwood Hospital, recently married to a woman much younger than himself. On holiday at his summer cottage, Hudson drowns in a nearby lake. By an odd coincidence, the inhalator he kept handy for emergencies is in use at the moment he most needs it. Bobby Merrick, a young man sailing alone, is knocked unconscious by a boom and pushed into the water. The inhalator, borrowed by witnesses, saves his life but is unavailable when Hudson's accident occurs.

Bobby recovers completely and learns he may have survived at the cost of Hudson's life. He begins to think seriously about becoming a doctor himself. Then Nancy Ashford, superintendent at Brightwood, tells Bobby about Dr. Hudson's wide range of philanthropic interests and about his habit of keeping them secret. She gives Bobby Hudson's diary, which reveals an unusual formula for successful living based on a passage in the Bible. The formula involves expanding one's self through various investments in other people, carried out in absolute secrecy. Skeptical at first, Bobby later adopts Hudson's design. He completes medical school and embarks on a fine career. He is nevertheless unable to break down the barriers between himself and Helen, Hudson's widow, with whom he has fallen in love. It takes two near-tragedies to erase Helen's resentment of Bobby's connection with Hudson's death. First, Bobby saves Helen from financial ruin without revealing his intervention. Then, when Helen is hurt in an accident, Bobby performs the operation that saves her sight. Helen realizes she loves Bobby and accepts him wholeheartedly. If you enjoy this kind of novel, you will like *The Keys of the Kingdom* by *A.J. Cronin. *Magnificent Obsession* was adapted for film in 1935 and again in 1954. YA

Mahy, Margaret (1936–) Born and living in New Zealand, Mahy has successfully combined the careers of librarian and author and has written a number of delightful and imaginative books for beginning readers. Among these is *The Great Piratical Rumbustification and The Librarian and the Robbers* (1978), which includes two stories notable for their bright writing and humor. "The Great Piratical Rumbustification" describes what happens when a supposedly reformed pirate is hired to babysit three young boys. "The Librarian and the Robbers" tells about a beautiful young librarian who is kidnapped by a gang of soft-hearted scoundrels. Mahy has also written books for older readers, including *The Haunting* (1982), about a boy who is possessed by the spirit of a ghost; *The Catalogue of the Universe* (1986), about an 18-year-old girl whose view of her life changes when she seeks out her father, whom she has never met; *Memory* (1987), about a 19-year-old boy, troubled by the memory of his sister's accidental death, who goes to live with an old woman whose memory has been destroyed by Alzheimer's disease; *Aliens in the Family; and *The Tricksters. MR & YA

Mailer, Norman (1923–) As a boy growing up in Brooklyn, Mailer had no interest in becoming a writer. He wanted to be an aeronautical engineer. When he got to college, however, the writing bug bit him. After college, he fought in the Pacific during World War II. His experiences there provided the material for *The Naked and the Dead, considered one of the best novels to come out of the war. Mailer worked as a Hollywood screenwriter for a time, then returned to New York City, where he helped found the newspaper *The Village Voice*. Mailer continued to write fiction but also proved himself a master at nonfiction, becoming one of the leading essayists of the 1960s. A passionate and outspoken opponent of the American involvement in the Vietnam War, Mailer took part in a four-day antiwar protest in Washington, D.C., in October 1967. His book about the event, *The Armies of the Night* (1968), which used both fiction and nonfiction techniques to capture the experience, was showered with praise and literary honors. It is must reading for anyone wanting to understand that period of American history. Mailer's other novels include *The Executioner's Song* (1979), a "nonfiction novel" about the last nine months in the life of convicted killer Gary Gilmore, who was executed in 1977; and *Ancient Evenings* (1983), set in ancient Egypt between the 14th and 12th centuries B.C. *The Executioner's Song* was adapted for film in 1982. YA

Main Street (1920) This best-selling novel by *Sinclair Lewis, a study of small-town life in the early 20th century, shocked and offended many when it was first published. Today it is considered one of the most important and influential works of modern American literature. The heroine of the novel is Carol Kennicott, wife of Dr. Will Kennicott, who lives and practices medicine in his hometown of Gopher Prairie, Minnesota. In college, Carol decided to make her life's goal the uplifting and beautifying of a small American town. While working as a librarian in St. Paul, she met Will Kennicott, and they were married. Will described Gopher Prairie as a Middle Western paradise, but when Carol arrives there she finds it shabby, small, and dull. Most of its residents are small-minded, bigoted, hypocritical, and quite happy with their town as it is. With the zeal of a reformer, Carol tries to gain support for such things as a new city hall and a theater group, but each time she is disappointed by her neighbors' lack of support or by their open resistance. She has a baby boy and is content for a time, but her boredom with her dull marriage and hatred for the town return. Carol is attracted to Erik Valborg, a young tailor with dreams of becoming an artist. After he leaves Gopher Prairie, Carol leaves Will and goes with her son to Washington, D.C. After a year, Will visits, and they go on a second honeymoon. Will goes home but Carol remains in Washington for a time. When she returns, she has a new understanding of the world, herself, and Gopher Prairie. In Washington she has learned that every town and city in the world has its own version of Main Street. Carol has a second child, a girl, and sees in her children the hope of the future. If you enjoyed *Main Street*, try *Elmer Gantry* (1927), Lewis's scathing *satire of religious evangelism, which was made into a hit movie in 1960. *Main Street* was filmed in 1923 and, as *I Married a Doctor*, in 1936. YA

Malamud, Bernard (1914–1986) A teacher by profession and a novelist and short-story writer by calling, Malamud found rich material and inspiration in his Jewish-American background. His stories and novels combine realistic characters and settings with elements of myth and *fantasy. They are also concerned with the human struggle between right and wrong and the search for redemption through moral action. Among his books are *The Natural; *The Assistant; the short-story collection *The Magic Barrel* (1958), whose title story tells about a rabbinical student looking for a wife; *The Fixer* (1966), about a Jewish handyman in Czarist Russia who becomes a hero when he refuses to confess to a crime he did not commit; and *Dubin's Lives* (1979), about an aging prize-winning biographer struggling to complete his greatest book and about his failing marriage and his affair with the young woman with whom he has fallen in love. *The Fixer* was adapted for film in 1968. YA

Malaprop, Mrs. One of the leading characters in *The Rivals* (1775) by the Irish playwright Richard Brinsley Sheridan (1751–1816), she was known for her hilarious misuse of words. Mrs. Malaprop continually uses words that sound like the ones she means but have completely different meanings. She says such things as "illegible" when she means "ineligible," "hydrostatics" when she means "hysterics," and "allegory" when she means "alligator." Such misuse of words is today known as a *malapropism*. A modern master of the malapropism was the movie actor Leo Gorcey (1915–1969), who played the leader both of a gang of East Side (a section of New York City) toughs known as the Bowery Boys and also of the East Side Kids in a number of films in the 1940s and 1950s that are still shown on television. His mangling of the English language was just as funny as Mrs. Malaprop's.

Malcolm X, The Autobiography of (1965) As told by Malcolm X [Malcolm Little] (1925–1965) to *Alex Haley, this book is a personal account of the black leader's life. He tells about his childhood in the small town of Lansing, Michigan, in the 1930s, and the difficulties he and his family endured. His father, the Reverend Earl Little, was murdered by white supremacists, and his mother was admitted to a mental institution. Malcolm dropped out of school and moved to Boston and then to New York, where he became a drug dealer, gambler, and thief, a way of life that eventually landed him in prison. Here his life took a major turn when he began to study the laws of Islam and became involved in the Muslim religion. While in prison, he spent his days educating himself, spreading the teachings of Elijah Muhammad (1897–1975), the religious leader of the Black Muslims, and expressing his radical views about white society.

After he left prison, Malcolm X (he dropped his last name, Little, saying it was a slave name) became a minister and married and had four children. His belief in the Muslim religion and his extraordinary ability to articulate the black person's anguish and aspirations in America helped Malcolm X become one of the most influential leaders of the Black Revolution. After traveling abroad and making a trip to Mecca, Malcolm X saw his radical beliefs about race relations become less militant and more widely accepted. His plans to shift into the mainstream of the Black Revolution were ended abruptly by his assassination. His autobiography is an absorbing and vivid account of his transformation from street hustler to national figure. A movie based on this book, *Malcolm X*, was produced in 1992. YA

Malory, Thomas (d. 1471) An English author, Malory wrote a celebrated collection of legends about *King Arthur and his knights, *Le Morte d'Arthur* (1485). Little is known of Malory's life, but it is believed he was a knight from Warwickshire and that he spent much of his adult life in trouble with the law, and was finally executed. It was in prison that Malory wrote most of his accounts of the adventures of King Arthur. Malory based his tales on French, English, and Latin sources, copying word for word in places, and adding to the stories in other places. The result was a masterpiece of English literature that has influenced countless writers over the centuries, including *Alfred Tennyson, author of *Idylls of the King*, and *John Steinbeck, whose novel *Tortilla Flat* (1935) reflects his lifelong fascination with Malory's Arthurian stories. Steinbeck's book *The Acts of King Arthur and His Noble Knights* (1976) is a retelling of Malory's tales for young readers. You can probably find in your library several editions of *Le Morte d'Arthur*. One of the best is in the Everyman's Library, which was first published in 1900 but has been reissued many times since. MR & YA

Maltese Falcon, The (1930) The title of this detective novel by *Dashiell Hammett refers to a valuable jewel-encrusted statuette, produced four centuries ago by the Knights Templar of Malta for the king of Spain. In San Francisco, three unsavory people are on its trail, and all seek the assistance of *Sam Spade, a private investigator who is only a little better in character than the others. The book opens with the murder of Spade's partner, Miles Archer, who has been doing a shadowing job for one of the three. After another murder the statuette comes into Spade's possession when a fatally wounded man brings it to his office. The story reaches its first climax when Spade meets with the three—a beautiful woman, a very fat man, and a small homosexual man of Middle Eastern origin. The statuette proves not to be what was expected. In a further climax Spade reveals the murderer of his partner. *The Maltese Falcon* is an outstanding example of the hard-boiled school of detective fiction. Three movies have been made of it, two in 1931 and 1936, but it is the 1941 film starring Humphrey Bogart (1899–1957) that has become a classic. If you read the book and see the movie, you will agree that the actors were perfectly cast. YA

Man for All Seasons, A (1960) This drama by the English playwright and screenwriter Robert

Bolt (1924–) is set in England in the 16th century during the reign of King Henry VIII. Henry is married to his brother's widow, the Princess Catherine of Aragon. But when Catherine fails to bear Henry a son and heir, he decides to divorce her and marry Anne Boleyn. This leads to a split between Henry and the pope, the head of the Roman Catholic Church, and to the founding of the Church of England. Henry seeks support for his action from his Lord Chancellor, Sir Thomas More, but More believes that the divorce and remarriage are against God's law, and that God's law is higher than the king's or Parliament's law. More resigns as chancellor and hopes that by remaining silent on the issue of the king's marriage he will avoid conflict with Henry and with Thomas Cromwell, an unscrupulous, power-hungry man who has become Lord Chief Justice.

But More is known throughout England and Europe as a devout and honest man, and Henry finds his silence a threat to his authority. More is required to sign an oath accepting Henry's religious supremacy over that of the pope. He refuses but does not state his reason. He is arrested and thrown in the Tower of London. Cromwell must either get More to sign the oath or prove that his reason for not signing it is treasonable. But More knows that his continued silence protects him. Cromwell finally bribes Sir Richard Rich, an ambitious and untrustworthy young man More had once refused to help. Rich gives false testimony in court, and More is convicted of treason and executed. He dies content, knowing that he has remained loyal to his king, his conscience, and God. Bolt also wrote the screenplay for the movie version of *A Man for All Seasons*, which was released in 1966, and then remade for television in 1988. YA

Man Friday In *Robinson Crusoe*, a novel by *Daniel Defoe, Crusoe saves a "savage" from a band of cannibals who have taken him to Crusoe's island and are preparing to cook and devour him. Crusoe names the man Friday, which is the day on which the rescue occurs.

Friday becomes Crusoe's faithful servant and devoted friend. Nowadays "man Friday" means a trustworthy and capable aide or assistant, usually one who is given a variety of tasks and responsibilities. Of course, there is no reason why such a person has to be a male. Often in the "help wanted" column of your newspaper there will be a number of advertisements seeking a "Gal/Guy Friday," meaning that the job is open to male and female candidates alike.

Man Without a Country, The (1863) Written by the clergyman and author Edward Everett Hale (1822–1909), this story of patriotism was published at the height of the Civil War. The story is narrated by an officer in the U.S. Navy, who recalls events that unfolded over a period of half a century. In 1806 a young army lieutenant named Philip Nolan, stationed at Fort Adams on the Mississippi River, becomes involved with Aaron Burr (1756–1836) in a secret scheme. Burr, once the vice president of the United States, seems to be planning to create his own country out of the newly gained Louisiana Territory. A year later Burr is charged with treason. He is acquitted, but Nolan is court-martialed. In a moment of anger at his trial, Nolan rashly cries out, "Damn the United States! I wish I may never hear of the United States again!" The sentence of the court is that he be granted his wish: Nolan must spend the rest of his life aboard Navy ships. He is to be treated well, but he is never to see his country nor hear of it again.

For 55 years Nolan bears his sentence without complaint, and it becomes clear from his actions that he does love his country. When Nolan is near death, a naval officer finally takes pity on him and tells him about the wonderful nation that has grown up during his imprisonment, but the officer cannot bear to tell Nolan about the civil war then raging. Nolan listens with joy to the news he has been deprived of for most of his life, and dies peacefully soon after.

The story was intended as a warning to those who had or were thinking of turning away from the union, for all who did so would be cut off forever from their country. It has since become an American classic. A TV movie of the story was made in 1973. YA

Maniac Magee (1990) By Jerry Spinelli (1941–), this novel tells of the quest of 12-year-old Jeffrey Lionel Magee for a place he can call home. Orphaned when he was 3 years old, Jeffrey lives with his aunt and uncle for eight years, until their silent feuding sends him off and running. A year later he arrives in Two Mills, across the Schuylkill River from Bridgeport, Pennsylvania, his birthplace. Jeffrey performs several amazing athletic and other feats that earn him the nickname "Maniac" and make him a legend in both the West End, where the white people live, and in the East End, where the black people live. But his biggest challenges are to break down the barriers of ignorance and mistrust between the people, black and white, who come to love him, and to find a place he can call home. Along the way he meets many fascinating people, and they become part of his wonderful life and legend.

Jerry Spinelli has written a number of novels for young people, including *Space Station Seventh Grade* (1982), about a boy's trying and often hilarious experiences in the seventh grade, and *Who Put That Hair in My Tooth Brush?* (1984), about the rivalry between a 12-year-old girl and her older brother. *Maniac Magee* won the *Newbery Medal in 1991. MR

Manley, Seon (1921–) An author and editor of a variety of books, Manley is at her best in *Nathaniel Hawthorne: Captive of the Imagination* (1968), which not only has a feeling for the time but also helps you understand the struggles of creative people. In the suspense and mystery field she has edited *A Gathering of Ghosts* (1970), a collection of short stories; *Mistresses of Mystery: Two Centuries of Suspense Stories by the Gentle Sex* (1971); and *Baleful Beasts* (1974), tales about some of the less likable members of the animal kingdom. Manley's own works include *The Ghost in the Far Garden and Other Stories* (1977), a scary assortment of tales with settings in New York City's Greenwich Village, England, Egypt, and elsewhere. If you like ghost stories and similar tales, there are many available, among them a classic *parody of 19th-century ghost stories, *The Canterville Ghost*, available in an illustrated edition (1986), by *Oscar Wilde. Try also the stories and collections of *Scott Corbett and *Helen Hoke. MR & YA

Mann, Thomas (1875–1955) A German novelist, short-story writer, essayist, and author of *Death in Venice* and *Disorder and Early Sorrow*, Mann is considered one of the great writers of the 20th century. His love of music and his interest in and compassion for *bourgeois life were acquired in childhood. The conflicting natures of his parents, one a businessman and the other a musician, may well have formed the basis of an important theme in Mann's work, namely, the battle between reason and emotion. Many of his early stories explore the problem of the artist who feels isolated in society, as well as the thin dividing lines between imagination, innocent make-believe, and criminal fakery. *Buddenbrooks*, Mann's first novel, is the story of a family over three generations. In it the appearance of an artistic streak disrupts and weakens the traditions of the family business. In the short story "Tonio Kröger," said to be partly autobiographical, the hero is a writer who feels separated from the good, simple life of his middle-class childhood.

After World War I, Mann became interested in the work of *Sigmund Freud, and the newly evolving study of psychology was an important element in *The Magic Mountain* (1924). In this complex novel, a young engineer visits his cousin in a Swiss sanatorium. He finds himself fascinated and seduced by sickness, self-analysis, and thoughts of death. Major themes in the novel are the conflict between intellect and emotion, and the role of death in sharpening an awareness of life.

Joseph and His Brothers (1933) is a reinterpretation of the biblical story of Joseph. Mann was violently opposed to the fascism of the 1930s, and left Germany to come to the United

States. *Dr. Faustus* (1947), a novel with strong political overtones, is the story of German composer Adrian Leverkühn, whose tragic life is subtly related to the destruction of Germany during World War II. Mann received the Nobel Prize for literature in 1929. A film version of *Dr. Faustus* was produced in 1968. YA

Many Moons (1943) This story for children by *James Thurber, illustrated by the award-winning artist Louis Slobodkin (1903–1975), tells about a princess named Lenore, who becomes very ill after eating too many raspberry tarts. She tells her father, the king, that if only she can have the moon she will get well again. The king asks all his great and wise royal retainers to get the moon for Princess Lenore, but they are unable to do so despite their great knowledge. In despair the king tells his problem to the court jester. The jester goes to talk with Lenore, and by listening to what she thinks about the moon, he comes up with a very clever way to grant her wish. If you liked this story, also try *The Great Quillow* (1944), the story of a very short toymaker who must find a way to save his town from a very large giant. MR

Marat/Sade (1964) The full title of this play by the German novelist and playwright Peter Weiss (1916–1982) is *The Persecution and Assassination of Jean-Paul Marat as Performed by the Inmates of the Asylum of Charenton Under the Direction of the Marquis de Sade.* Marat (1743–1793), a French physician, scientist, and philosopher, was one of the leading figures in the French Revolution until he was stabbed to death in his bath by Charlotte Corday (1768–1793). The Marquis de Sade (1740–1814), a French writer, was imprisoned for many years as a sexual deviate, and eventually was put in the mental asylum of Charenton, where he wrote and produced a number of his plays. *Marat/Sade* is a play within a play, showing Sade presenting, with the help of the residents and staff of Charenton, a play about Marat's murder. It is a fascinating look at revolutionary change and the way it affects people who are

involved in it or are observers of it. When *Marat/Sade* opened, Weiss was hailed as the successor to the German playwright Bertolt Brecht (1898–1956). Weiss, who made Switzerland his home after 1939, was an artist and filmmaker as well as a dramatist. He is known best for *Marat/Sade* and for the play *The Investigation* (1965), concerning the trial of a group of German officials for war crimes. If you liked *Marat/Sade*, try Brecht's play *Mother Courage and Her Children* (1941), a powerful antiwar drama set in Europe during the Thirty Years War. *Marat/Sade* was adapted for film in 1966. YA

Marguerite Gautier is the heroine of the novel *La Dame aux Camélias* (1848), also known as *Camille*, by *Alexandre Dumas. Marguerite, a poor country girl, has become a beautiful Parisian courtesan, or kept woman. She is known as the Lady of the Camelias, for this beautiful but scentless flower is the only kind she will permit in the bouquets she carries. Armand Duval, a young man from a good family, falls in love with Marguerite, and after a time she falls in love with him. He is the only man she has ever loved, and she gladly gives up her bright, flashy Parisian life for a quiet one with Armand. She knows it will be a short life, for she is dying of tuberculosis. Marguerite and Armand are happy, but Armand's father secretly begs Marguerite to give up her love for the sake of his family's name. Marguerite leaves Armand without explanation and returns to Paris, where she slowly dies. Armand is crushed, thinking she abandoned him to return to her old life. He learns of her noble sacrifice only after her death. Dumas turned *La Dame aux Camélias* into a play in 1849, and it was first produced in 1852. Since then it has enjoyed great success. The Italian composer Giuseppe Verdi (1813–1901) used the story for his opera *La Traviata* (1853). YA

Marilla Cuthbert is a spinster who lives with her older brother, Matthew, at Green Gables. She adopts Anne Shirley, an orphan girl, whose rich imagination and affectionate nature are completely opposite to Marilla's serious and practical ways. Despite their differences, Marilla grows attached to Anne and begins to display a quiet generosity and warmth. "She had learned to love this slim, gray-eyed girl with an affection all the deeper and stronger from its very undemonstrativeness." Matthew dies, and Marilla begins to lose her eyesight, thus finding it too difficult to take care of Green Gables on her own. She contemplates selling the house and moving in with a neighbor. But the bond between Marilla and Anne has become so strong that Anne, now 16 years old, decides to sacrifice her future plans in order to live with and take care of Marilla at Green Gables. See also *Anne of Green Gables.*

mark Many stories and novels deal with characters who want to make their mark on the world, to achieve success and recognition. Sometimes their efforts fall "wide" or "short" of the mark, and they do not achieve the success they had hoped for. Some people do not seem to have drive or ambition. They are merely "marking time," that is, going through the motions without much interest in completing a task or making progress. Another form of marking time is when people march in place to the beat of a band. They are moving but are not advancing. Probably the best-known "mark" in literature is *Mark Twain, the pen name of Samuel Langhorne Clemens. The name comes from the old Mississippi riverboat practice of measuring the depth of the water with a weighted line marked off in fathoms. A fathom is six feet long, and twain meant two, so when the person with the line called to the riverboat pilot "mark twain," he meant the water was two fathoms deep.

Mark, Saint (fl. 1st century A.D.) One of the four Evangelists (with *Matthew, *Luke, and *John). Mark wrote the Gospel According to Saint Mark (A.D. c. 70), the second book of the New Testament of the *Bible. He accompanied *Paul on his first missionary journey to Cyprus, but for some reason Paul refused to let him go with him on his second journey. Mark's Gospel is the shortest of the four and was the first written. The book emphasizes the actions of *Jesus rather than his words. In fact, Mark has Jesus taking action "straightway" or "immediately" more than 30 times in 16 chapters. Mark's vivid narrative style is shown in the story of how Jesus cast demons out of men and into swine. The book was probably written in Rome and addressed to the Roman world rather than the Jews of Palestine.

Mark of Conte, The (1976) This novel by *Sonia Levitin tells about Conte Mark, a ninth-grader who has just moved to a new town. Conte learns that the high school computer has enrolled him in the freshman class as "Conte Mark" and also as "Mark Conte." He tries to have the mistake corrected, but no one will listen to him. Then he gets an idea. Why not keep "Mark Conte" on the computer listing and carry two course loads, and later merge the two academic records and graduate in two years instead of four? By hard work and careful management, and with the help of some new friends, Conte is able to keep things rolling along for a time. But a computer glitch of his own making threatens to ruin everything. Conte manages to put the plan back on track, solves the problems of a number of teachers and students in the balance, and definitely leaves his *mark on the school. If you enjoyed *The Mark of Conte,* also try Levitin's novel *Smile Like a Plastic Daisy* (1984), about a high school girl whose unusual way of protesting discrimination against women turns her life upside down. YA

Marquand, John P(hillips) (1893–1960) The works of this New England novelist fall into three types. He first wrote popular romances, but beginning in 1935 he alternated between *satires of upper-middle-class people like himself and detective stories about I.A. Moto, a Japanese secret service agent. Marquand's best-known novel is *The Late George Apley* (1937), a biography of an imaginary proper Bostonian who never broke loose from his background.

MR = Middle Reader   YA = Young Adult Reader   * = See this main entry

He has a puritan sense of duty but only once acts on it, when he attacks government corruption. He also becomes more and more aloof from his children. Among Marquand's other books are *Wickford Point* (1939), a satire on a New England family, and *H.M. Pulham, Esquire* (1941), concerning another proper Yankee 25 years out of Harvard College. The first Moto novel was *No Hero* (1925), in which the shrewd, polite, and inscrutable Moto teams with an American naval officer to prevent a crisis in the Far East. In *Mr. Moto Is So Sorry* (1938) two young Americans are involved in a plot resulting from Russo-Japanese rivalry in Manchuria. An American, who is an alcoholic ex-navy officer, and Mr. Moto are opponents in *Last Laugh, Mr. Moto* (1941) as Pearl Harbor and war with Japan nears. A movie was made of *H.M. Pulham, Esquire* in 1941 and of *The Late George Apley* in 1947. Eight movies featuring Mr. Moto, some from original screenplays, were produced between 1937 and 1939. If you like novels of satire and manners, read the books of *Henry James, *Sinclair Lewis, and *Edith Wharton. If you enjoy Mr. Moto, try the novels of *Earl Derr Biggers. YA

Marric, J.J. See *John Creasey.

Mars The ancient Roman god of war, Mars is identified with *Ares, the Greek god of war. Mars is also honored as a god of agriculture and of the state. He is the son of *Juno and the father of the twins Romulus and Remus by the vestal virgin Rhea Silvia. According to the legend, the twins were set afloat on the Tiber River but drifted ashore and survived, nursed by a she-wolf and fed by a woodpecker, and then raised by a shepherdess. Romulus later founded the city of Rome. The Campus Martius in Rome, where the Roman army trained, is named after Mars, as are the month of March and the planet Mars. It is interesting that the moons of Mars are named after two minor Greek gods associated with Ares— Deimos (Panic) and Phobos (Fear).

Marsh, (Edith) Ngaio (1889–1981) A native of New Zealand, Marsh lived there except for a

Mars

few years in England; but her detective novels usually have British settings. Her first interests were in art and the theater, milieus later reflected in the backgrounds of her novels. She was an actress and a theatrical producer before turning to writing. Marsh's first detective novel was *A Man Lay Dead* (1934). It introduced the detective featured in most of her books, Inspector Roderick Alleyn of Scotland Yard. Alleyn is a bit above the average English detective socially and in his private life is accepted at the same level as his mother, the aristocratic Lady Alleyn. Nevertheless, he is entirely professional and solves murders through hard work and attention to clues. Among Marsh's other books are *Overture to Death* (1939), *Final Curtain* (1947), and *Grave Mistake* (1978). Marsh's first name, pronounced "Nye-o," is a word from the language of the New Zealand aborigine, the Maori, and means "flowering tree." If you like these books, you will also want to read those by *Margery Allingham, *Agatha Christie, *Antonia Fraser, and *Dorothy Sayers. YA

Martian Chronicles, The (1950) These popular *science fiction stories by *Ray Bradbury, are about the colonization and exploitation of the planet Mars. In the story "February 1999: Ylla," you meet Mr. and Mrs. K, who have "the fair, brownish skin of the true Martian, the yellow coin eyes," and musical voices. Mrs. K dreams of the arrival of the first rocket expedition from Earth. Mr. K, jealous of her unusual and exciting visions, hunts down the intruders and destroys them. The second expedition is eliminated by a Martian psychologist who thinks the Earthmen are insane and their rocket ship a hallucination.

"April 2000: The Third Expedition" tells of Captain Black and his crew: Their ship lands in a perfect replica of Green Bluff, Illinois, in the year 1926, and they discover the "town" is filled with friends and relatives they know have died. The illusion lasts just long enough to trap the crew, and there are no survivors.

In "December 2001: The Green Morning," Benjamin Driscoll plants thousands of seeds hoping that trees will eventually provide the oxygen lacking in the thin Martian air. His trees bloom overnight in the "alien and magical soil," and an entire valley is covered with huge trees.

"November 2005: The Off Season" is the story of Sam and Elma Parkhill, owners of the first hot-dog stand on Mars, who eagerly await the shiploads of new customers from Earth. A Martian appears and tries to give them an important message, but Sam panics and shoots the creature. Later, as the couple prepare to serve the expected crowd, they see Earth rise in the evening sky and watch in horror as it explodes with "an unholy dripping glare." The stories were adapted for a TV miniseries in 1980. YA

Mary Poppins (1934) Written by P.L. Travers (1906–), this children's classic story tells about an English family, the Bankses, who live at Number Seventeen Cherry-Tree Lane. Mr. and Mrs. Banks have four children—Jane, Michael, and the twins, John and Barbara. When the children's nurse suddenly leaves, Mrs. Banks advertises for a new one. Soon the blustery East Wind carries Mary Poppins to the family's door. She is unlike any nanny the family has ever known. First of all, she does not believe in giving any references. After examining the children, however, she announces that she will accept the job. She unpacks all sorts of interesting belongings from a seemingly empty carpet bag and thoroughly captures the hearts of the children. Mary Poppins can do wonderful things. She can float through the air at will, and can talk to animals and understand their language. And she personally knows a cow that jumped over the moon. What adventures they have! With Mary the children go around the world with the help of a magical compass, take part in a birthday party for Mary given by the animals at the zoo when the moon is full, and meet a number of Mary's amazing friends. Travers was born and grew up in Australia. She moved to Ireland, then to England, where she began writing the Mary Poppins stories. She wrote other books for young readers, but the Mary Poppins books are the ones by which she will be remembered. You can read about her further adventures in several sequels, including *Mary Poppins Comes Back* (1935), *Mary Poppins Opens the Door* (1943), and *Mary Poppins in the Park* (1952). *Mary Poppins* was made into a movie musical in 1964. MR

Mason, Bobbie Ann (1940–) A critically acclaimed novelist and short-story writer, Mason was born and grew up in western Kentucky, an area whose social and economic life has undergone important changes in the past few decades. This region is the setting for most of her novels and short stories, which are sensitive and at times humorous portraits of ordinary people and their efforts to understand one another and the changing world around them. Such phenomena as radio and television, highways, and suburban shopping malls contribute new ideas, values, desires, and distractions to small-town folk who have been isolated from the larger world. Among Mason's books are the collection *Shiloh and Other Stories* (1982); *In Country; *Spence and Lila* (1988), about the love of an elderly rural Kentucky couple, Spence and Lila Culpepper, who reflect on their long life together as Lila faces a grave illness; and the short-story collection *Love Life* (1989). YA

Masters, Edgar Lee (1868–1950) A poet, novelist, playwright, and biographer, Masters grew up in the region of Illinois that Abraham Lincoln knew. He became a successful lawyer and had a number of collections of poetry published before his life was changed by a book given to him by a newspaperman. The book was a volume of Greek epigrams, and the newspaperman was William Marion Reedy (1862–1920), owner and editor of a weekly literary magazine called *Reedy's Mirror*. Reedy's influence and the Greek poems helped Masters form the idea of telling the story of a Middle Western town through the poetic epitaphs of the dead in its cemetery. The result was *Spoon River Anthology*. The book was enormously successful and highly praised. Masters continued to write, producing volumes of poetry, novels, plays, and nonfiction, but he never again approached the success of *Spoon River Anthology*. Masters's other books include the volumes of poems *Domesday Book* (1920) and *The New Spoon River* (1929), and his autobiography, *Across Spoon River* (1937). YA

Matchlock Gun, The (1941) This book for younger readers by *Walter D. Edmonds is set in the Hudson Valley near Albany, New York, in the 1750s. Its characters were real people who lived in a farming community called Guilderland, at the foot of the Helderberg Mountains. Teunis Van Alstyne, a sturdy Dutch farmer and captain of the Guilderland militia, leaves his family to defend against Indian raiders who have been killing and burning their way south from Canada. His wife, Gertrude, 10-year-old son Edward, and 6-year-old daughter Trudy stay behind, armed only with an ancient Spanish gun called a "matchlock gun." Unlike a flintlock, which uses the spark from a flint to set off the gunpowder charge, the matchlock gun must be set off with the flame of a match or candle. It is longer than a man is tall and so heavy that Edward cannot lift it by himself. Yet when Indians come to attack the Van Alstyne house, it is the matchlock gun and the courage of Gertrude, Edward, and Trudy that save the day. If you liked *The Matchlock Gun*, also try Edmonds's *Wolf Hunt* (1970), about a boy and his uncle hunting a sheep-killing wolf in the Delaware Valley of New York State in 1784. MR

Mathis, Sharon Bell (1937–) A teacher and librarian, Mathis has written a number of books that touch upon the real-life experiences of black children in American society. Her stories show some of the harsh and unhappy parts of life, but they also celebrate the importance to all human beings of love and caring and communicating. Among her books are *Sidewalk Story* (1971), about a 9-year-old girl who tries to help her best friend's family after they are evicted from their apartment and nobody else comes to their aid; *Listen for the Fig Tree* (1974), about a blind girl who attempts to help her troubled mother one year after the girl's father has been murdered; and *The Hundred Penny Box* (1975), about the love a small boy shares with his great-great-aunt, whose most precious possession is an old box containing 100 pennies, one for each year of her life. MR

Matthew, Saint (fl. 1st century A.D.) One of the 12 disciples of *Jesus, Matthew was also (with *Mark, *Luke, and *John) one of the four Evangelists, each of whom wrote one of the four Gospels of the New Testament of the *Bible. Most scholars, however, doubt that Matthew was the actual author of the Gospel According to Saint Matthew. He was a tax collector when Jesus called him to be one of his followers and assistants, and he is said to have been martyred before the end of the 1st century A.D. A collection he made of the sayings of Jesus may have been used by whoever compiled the Gospel. It is important for its account of what Jesus said in the course of his teachings. It contains, for example, the best rendering of the Sermon on the Mount, with such well-known teachings as "Blessed are the meek, for they shall inherit the earth." In its general approach, this Gospel was an attempt to convince Jews and Jewish Christians that the life of Christ fulfilled God's promise of the coming of a Messiah as told in the Old Testament.

Maugham, (William) Somerset (1874–1956) An English novelist, playwright, and short-story writer, Maugham was born in Paris, France, where his father worked in the British Embassy. When Maugham was 6 years old his father died, and his mother died two years later. He went to live with relatives in England, ending a happy childhood and beginning an unhappy youth. He studied medicine and became a doctor, working for a year in the slums of Lambeth in London, England, but his heart was not in medicine. It was in literature. With the publication of his first book, *Liza of Lambeth* (1897), a novel based on one of his medical cases, Maugham decided to become a writer. After a number of years of poverty and hard work, his effort paid off, and his plays, novels, and short stories began to find an enormous audience. Freed of any worries about money, Maugham traveled widely and in the 1930s settled in a beautiful villa in France, which remained his home until his death. Among his best novels are *Of Human Bondage, which is based on his own early life; *The Moon and Sixpence* (1919), about a stockbroker who abandons his family and life to become an artist; *The Painted Veil* (1925), about a doctor who takes his wife into the midst of an epidemic as punishment for her unfaithfulness; *Cakes and Ale* (1930), whose central character, a novelist, is thought by some to have been modeled after *Thomas Hardy; and *The Razor's Edge* (1944), about a young American man's search for spiritual truth and wisdom. Several collections of Maugham's short stories have been published, and you can find a good selection of his fiction, plays, and autobiographical writing in *The Maugham Reader* (1950). *Of Human Bondage* was made into movies in 1934 and 1954. Four of Maugham's short stories were filmed for the movie *Quartet* in 1948, three for *Trio* in 1950, and three for *Encore* in 1951. *The Razor's Edge* was adapted for film in 1946 and 1984. YA

Mayne, William (1928–) An English writer and editor of children's books, Mayne was born and grew up in Yorkshire, England, whose legends, history, and culture he has used in a number of his books, including his celebrated fantasy *Earthfasts. Mayne's books are noted for their brilliant combination of realism and fantasy, challenging style and language, delightful wit and wordplay, and strong characters. They appeal to adults as well as young readers. Among his books are *A Grass Rope* (1957), about a young English girl who sets out to capture a unicorn; *Underground Alley* (1958), about an English girl who discovers a long-lost royal treasure and restores her town's honor and good name; and *A Game of Dark* (1971), about a boy who escapes from his unhappy home life by slipping into an imaginary medieval world, where he must defeat an evil, wormlike monster. MR

Mazer, Harry (1925–) Author of many books for young people, Mazer was born and grew up in New York City. He was an avid reader as a child, but he did not turn to writing until after he married and began raising a family with his wife, *Norma Fox Mazer. Among his books are *The Solid Gold Kid, which he wrote with his wife; *Snow Bound: A Story of Raw Survival* (1973), about two teenagers who become stranded during a blizzard in a desolate area of New York State; *The Dollar Man* (1974), about a teenager who sets out to find the father he never knew; *The War on Villa Street* (1978), about Willis Pierce, a teenager struggling to deal with his alcoholic father, avoid a street gang out to get him, and coach a retarded teenager in sports; and *The Girl of His Dreams* (1987), in which Willis falls in love with a girl who is not quite the ideal girl of his imagination. Mazer also collaborated with his wife on *Heartbeat* (1989), about a high school senior who falls in love with a girl he promised to introduce to his best friend. YA

Mazer, Norma Fox (1931–) Author of a number of acclaimed books for young people, Mazer was born in New York City and grew up in Glens Falls, New York, where she showed an early interest in writing. She did not become a writer until after she married *Harry Mazer. Among her books are *A Figure of Speech* (1973), about the relationship between a girl and her grandfather, who flees his family rather than go into a nursing home; *Saturday, the Twelfth of October* (1975), a fantasy about a girl who finds herself cast back thousands of years in time to a prehistoric world; *Dear Bill, Remember Me! (1976), a collection of eight short stories, each about a different teenage girl; *Taking Terri Mueller* (1981), about a teenager who learns she was kidnapped in childhood by her father; and *After the Rain* (1989), about a girl whose difficult relationship with her grandfather changes when he develops cancer. YA

McCaffrey, Anne (Inez) (1926–) An American-born writer living in Ireland, McCaffrey is known best for her Dragonriders of Pern series, whose novels combine elements of *fantasy and *science fiction. The novels depict the complex world of the distant planet Pern, whose early human colonists genetically engineer fire-breathing dragons to destroy periodic rains of deadly spores. The humans develop telepathic links with the dragons. This leads to the rise of a fascinating, feudalistic society and culture. The series began with *Dragonflight, the first novel of a trilogy including *Dragonquest* (1971), and *The White Dragon* (1978). A second trilogy, including *Dragonsong* (1976), *Dragonsinger* (1977), and *Dragondrums* (1979), adds further details of Pern's historical, social, and ecological makeup. *Dragonsdawn* (1988) details the early colonization of Pern and creation of the dragons. Other books in the Pern series include *Moreta: Dragonlady of Pern* (1983), *Nerilka's Story* (1986), and *All the Weyrs of Pern* (1991). MR & YA

McCarthyism comes from the name of U.S. Senator Joseph R. McCarthy (1908–1957), who became front-page news in 1950, when he publicly charged that more than 200 secret Communists had infiltrated the Department of State. While conducting a militant anti-communist campaign, which fed on the popular fear of communist advances in Eastern Europe and China, McCarthy doggedly pursued an investigation of communist subversion in all walks of life. His usually baseless accusations ruined the careers of many distinguished citizens. In 1954 he leveled charges of subversion at the U.S. Army. When the Army responded by charging McCarthy with improper conduct, his sensationalist tactics were revealed on na-

tional television during a 36-day hearing. In the same year, with his influence waning, McCarthy's fellow senators censured him for behavior contrary to Senate traditions.

"McCarthyism" now refers to any witch hunt, or to the persecution of people accused without proper cause, who are forced to conform in order to avoid public condemnation.

McCloskey, (John) Robert (1914–) Trained as an artist, McCloskey has illustrated many books by other authors, including *Henry Reed, Inc.* and its sequels, by *Keith Robertson. He has also written and illustrated a number of books for beginning readers, including *Make Way for Ducklings* (1941), about a family of wild ducks that decide to settle in Boston, Massachusetts; *Blueberries for Sal* (1948), about the adventures of a little girl who gets lost while picking berries with her mother; and *Time of Wonder* (1957), describing the joys of summer on the coast of Maine. Probably his best-known books are *Homer Price* and its sequel, *Centerburg Tales* (1951), which have become classics for young readers. MR

McCord, David (1897–) A poet and editor, McCord has written a number of collections of poems for young people. His sources of inspiration include *Edward Lear and *Robert Louis Stevenson, whose poems have taken a permanent place in the hearts of young and old alike. Among McCord's collections are *Far and Few: Rhymes of the Never Was and Always Is* (1952), *Every Time I Climb a Tree* (1967), *Away and Ago: Rhymes of the Never Was and Always Is* (1975), and *The Star in the Pail* (1975). Poems from these and other collections were gathered in *One at a Time* (1977). Among the books he has edited is *The Modern Treasury of Humorous Verse* (1951). MR & YA

McCullers, Carson (Smith) (1917–1967) A novelist and short-story writer, McCullers grew up in Georgia. She gained instant fame with her first novel, *The Heart Is a Lonely Hunter*, which established her as one of the leading writers of her day. Despite a deeply troubled marriage, alcohol abuse, sorrow brought by the deaths of friends and family members, and long bouts of illness, McCullers continued to write her stories and novels, which often focus on the loneliness of human existence and the struggle to find happiness and meaning in life. Among her best works are the short novel *Reflections in a Golden Eye* (1941), a bizarre tale set on an Army base in Georgia; *The Member of the Wedding;* the collection *The Ballad of the Sad Café* (1951), whose title novella is about the relationship between a tough woman, the hunchbacked dwarf she comes to love, and her ex-convict former husband; and *Clock Without Hands* (1961), a novel about a dying man's struggle against evil. YA

McGinley, Phyllis (1905–1978) A teacher, poet, and essayist, McGinley gained most recognition for her light verse, the best of which was collected in the Pulitzer Prize-winning book *Times Three: Selected Verse from Three Decades with Seventy New Poems* (1960). McGinley also wrote many books for beginning readers, including *The Horse Who Lived Upstairs* (1944), about a city horse who longs to live in the country, and *Wonderful Time* (1966), poems about clocks and time. She also edited *Wonders and Surprises: A Collection of Poems* (1968), an anthology that young readers will enjoy. MR & YA

McHargue, Georgess (1941–) An editor and writer, McHargue has long been interested in folklore, mythical creatures, and the occult, and these subjects often play an important role in her books for young people. *The Impossible People: A History Natural and Unnatural of Beings Terrible and Wonderful* (1972) will delight anyone interested in the many varieties of mythological people in folklore, myth, and legend. Among her novels for young readers are *Stoneflight* (1975), about a young girl living in New York City who believes she can bring the city's stone sculptures and statues to life; and *The Talking Table Mystery* (1977), the adventures of a boy and girl who discover a strange

old diary and a table that seems to make rapping sounds all by itself. MR

McKinley, Robin (1952–) A novelist and short-story writer specializing in *fantasy, McKinley began her writing career with the novel *Beauty: A Retelling of the Story of Beauty and the Beast* (1978), which was praised for being a refreshing, faithful retelling of the classic story. Her second book, *The Door in the Hedge* (1981), contains four stories, two of them retellings of fairy tales. McKinley is known best as the creator of the mythical kingdom of Damar, which she introduced in the novel *The Blue Sword* (1982), the adventures of a girl named Angharad (nicknamed Harry) Crewe, who obtains the magical Blue Sword named Gonturan. McKinley's second Damar novel, *The Hero and the Crown* (1984), is actually a prequel to the first, since its story occurs earlier in the history of Damar. It tells of Princess Aerin, the only daughter of the king of Damar. Aerin's mother, said to have been a witch, died when she was born. Aerin goes to seek the truth about her mother, receives the Blue Sword, and is called upon to save her people and recover the magical Hero's Crown. The novel received the *Newbery Medal in 1985. MR

McMurtry, Larry (1936–) A well-known contemporary novelist, McMurtry celebrates the spirit of the Old West even as he describes its passage into history and the rise of a modern, urbanized West. The colorful history of Texas, where McMurtry was born and raised, is the setting for many of his novels, including the most popular, *Lonesome Dove, a massive story of a cattle drive in the 1870s. McMurtry's first novel, *Horseman, Pass By* (1961), is about the coming of age of a 17-year-old boy living in the 1950s on his grandfather's ranch in western Texas. *The Last Picture Show* (1966) set, also in the 1950s, in a dreary Texas town, follows the adventures of a teenage boy and his friends as they approach adulthood. *Terms of Endearment* (1975) is about an eccentric Houston widow whose forceful personality tends to dominate all around her. *Anything for Billy*

(1988) is a novel based on the legend of Billy the Kid. Most of McMurtry's best novels have been made into television series and movies. Among the movies are *Hud*, from the novel *Horseman, Pass By*, in 1963; *The Last Picture Show*, in 1971; *Lovin' Molly*, from *Leaving Cheyenne* (1963), in 1974; *Terms of Endearment* in 1983; and *Texasville* in 1991. YA

Meader, Stephen W. (1892–1977) A writer and library administrator, Meader worked after college as a social worker, an editor, and a copywriter before turning to writing lively adventure novels for young people. Many of his books are based on events in American history. Among his numerous books are *Shadow in the Pines* (1942), about a boy who helps the government track down and capture a group of Nazi spies in the Pine Barrens of New Jersey during World War II; *Snow on Blueberry Mountain* (1961), about a teenage boy who, after his father dies, sets out to help his family by building a ski run on a mountain slope they own; *Phantom of the Blockade* (1962), about a young man serving aboard a Confederate blockade runner during the Civil War; and *Stranger on Big Hickory* (1964), about a boy who discovers signs of a mysterious stranger living on Big Hickory Mountain when he begins a study of the mountain's wildlife for a 4-H Club project. MR

Medea, in Greek mythology, was a sorceress and priestess who was famed, and feared, for her wide knowledge of the powers of herbs and plants. The daughter of King Aeëtes of Colchis, in Asia, Medea fell in love with *Jason and helped him to steal the *Golden Fleece, then sailed with Jason and the *Argonauts to Greece, where she became Jason's wife and bore him two children. Later, Jason left Medea to marry Creusa (or Glauce), the daughter of Creon, king of Corinth. Medea killed the bride with a poisoned robe, murdered her own children, set fire to the king's palace, and then fled. She married Aegeus, the king of Athens, but after failing to trick him into poisoning his son *Theseus, she returned to Colchis. Medea was finally made immortal and became the wife of

*Achilles in the Underworld. Younger readers can learn more about Medea in *Bulfinch's Mythology* by Thomas Bulfinch (1796–1867) and *Mythology* by Edith Hamilton (1867–1963) as well as the novel *Witch Princess* (1967) by Dorothy M. Johnson (1905–1984). Older readers will enjoy the tragedy *Medea* (431 B.C.) by *Euripides, which was adapted by the poet Robinson Jeffers (1897–1962) into the very successful verse drama *Medea* (1946). They will also like the novels *Medea* (1982) by Miranda Seymour (1948–) and *The Dawn Palace* (1988) by H(elen) M(ary) Hoover (1935–). MR & YA

Medusa See *Gorgons.

Meet the Austins (1960) The narrator of this novel by *Madeleine L'Engle is 12-year-old Vicky Austin, who lives with her parents, older brother, John, and younger sister and brother, Suzy and Rob, in Thornhill, a New England town. The Austins are a close, loving family whose members remain individuals even as they share life's difficult times and its moments of wonder and delight. Their warm, happy routine changes, however, when 10-year-old Maggy Hamilton comes to live with them. A pampered but ignored only child, Maggy was orphaned after her father's death in a fiery plane crash. Maggy's self-centered ways bring some troubled times to the Austins, but their guidance, patience, and love help Maggy to understand what it means to be a part of a family, and she in turn reminds them how lucky they are to have one another. You can read more about the Austins in *The Moon by Night* (1963), *The Young Unicorns, and *A Ring of Endless Night* (1980). MR

Melendys, The Created by the novelist and short-story writer Elizabeth Enright (1909–1968), the Melendy family first appeared in the novel *The Saturdays* (1941). The four young Melendys—13-year-old Mona; 12-year-old Rush; Miranda, who is called Randy and is 10½ years old; and 6-year-old Oliver—live in New York City with their father, a writer who is often away from the family's brownstone house on business. Father is a widower, so the only other adult in the house is Mrs. Evangeline Cuthbert-Stanley, or Cuffy for short, the youngsters' "housekeeper, nurse, cook, and substitute mother, grandmother, and aunt." In *The Saturdays,* the young Melendys, bored with their ordinary, uneventful Saturdays, decide to pool their allowances so each can take a turn at doing something fascinating on Saturday afternoon and then tell the others about the adventure. The Melendys also appear in *The Four-Story Mistake* (1942), in which they move into an odd-looking house in the country; *Then There Were Five* (1944), in which they gain a new adopted brother, Mark; and *Spiderweb for Two: A Melendy Maze* (1951), in which Randy and Oliver become involved in an exciting mystery. The first three Melendy books were published together as *The Melendy Family* (1947). If you enjoy these books, be sure to read Enright's *Thimble Summer.* Other books about brothers and sisters include *Meet the Austins* by *Madeleine L'Engle, *The Moffats* by Eleanor Estes (1906–1988), and *Swallows and Amazons* by *Arthur Ransome. MR

Meltzer, Milton (1915–) A historian, biographer, and prolific author of nonfiction for young people, Meltzer has created in his books a sense that history is not just a dry remembering of the past, but the story of living people and what they did and experienced. Among his many popular books you will certainly like *Brother, Can You Spare a Dime? The Great Depression, 1929–1933* (1969); *Hunted Like a Wolf: The Story of the Seminole War* (1972); *World of Our Fathers: The Jews of Eastern Europe* (1974); *Never to Forget: The Jews of the Holocaust* (1976); *The Black Americans: A History in Their Own Words, 1619–1983* (1984); *George Washington and the Birth of Our Nation* (1986); and *The American Revolutionaries: A History in Their Own Words, 1750–1800* (1987). YA

Melville, Herman (1819–1891) One of the great figures of American literature, Melville was born in New York City into a family of eight children. The family's great pride was its distinguished colonial ancestors. But Herman's father failed in business and died bankrupt. Melville left school when he was 15 years old and did what he could to help the family. In 1837 he took a job aboard a ship bound for Liverpool, England. This voyage changed Melville's life. After he returned home he tried his hand at teaching, but his newfound love of the sea led him to ship out aboard the whaling ship *Acushnet,* bound for the South Seas, in 1841. The brutal life aboard the *Acushnet* drove Melville to jump ship. He was held captive by a tribe of Polynesians, but escaped and eventually made his way back home. He turned his experiences into fiction and became a best-selling author with *Typee,* in which the narrator describes a voyage to the Marquesas, a group of islands in the southern Pacific Ocean; his captivity among the natives of Typee, on Nuku Hiva island; his romance with the native girl, Fayaway; and his eventual escape. In its sequel, *Omoo,* the narrator describes his adventures in Tahiti, one of the Society Islands lying southwest of the Marquesas. Two of Melville's next three novels were successful, and Melville worked feverishly on what he believed would be hailed as his greatest work, *Moby-Dick.* Readers and critics were unprepared for this brilliant novel, a brooding study of human nature and humanity's place in the moral universe. Melville's audience slipped away from him, and he was eventually forced to take a job as a customs inspector in New York City in order to pay his bills. By the time he died he had been forgotten. But in the 1920s critics finally recognized Melville's genius. His final work, the short novel *Billy Budd,* was discovered and published, and his other books were reissued, among them *Piazza Tales,* a collection of six short stories, including the masterpieces *"Bartleby the Scrivener" and *"Benito Cereno." YA

Member of the Wedding, The (1946) This novel by *Carson McCullers is set in Georgia in the summer of 1944. Frankie Addams is a lonely 12-year-old girl. The center of her world is the kitchen of her home, where she spends much of the long summer days playing cards and talking with her 6-year-old cousin, John Henry West, who lives next door, and with Berenice Sadie Brown, the black woman who cooks for Frankie and her father. On the last Friday in August her brother, Jarvis, who has been serving in the Army in Alaska, arrives with his fiancée, Janice, and invites Frankie and her father to their wedding the following Sunday.

Frankie becomes convinced that after the wedding she will go with her brother and sister-in-law and they will travel around the world together. Berenice warns Frankie that this is a foolish idea, but Frankie does not listen. She walks around the town, saying her goodbyes, and has a frightening encounter with a soldier who makes a pass at her. Frankie is heartbroken when the bride and groom leave without her after the wedding and she must return home. That fall John Henry dies, adding to her sorrow. Frankie and her father plan to move to a new house in the suburbs that they will share with Frankie's Aunt Pet and Uncle Ustace, and Berenice decides to leave when they move. Frankie finds a new best friend and, recovering from the sad experiences of the past months, dreams again of going off to see the world. If you enjoyed *The Member of the Wedding*, be sure to read McCullers's novel *The Heart Is a Lonely Hunter*. McCullers dramatized *The Member of the Wedding* in 1950, and it was made into a film in 1952. YA

Men of Iron (1892) This adventure novel by *Howard Pyle is set in England in the early 1400s. It tells of young Myles Falworth, whose father, Lord Falworth, was unjustly accused of treason and stripped of his lands and honor. His accuser was his longtime enemy, Lord Brookhurst. Even as Falworth fled his lands and hid from the wrath of King Henry IV, Brookhurst rose to become Duke of Alban and the king's close adviser. Myles enters the service of the Earl of Mackworth, once a close friend of his father. Under the guidance of the knight Sir James Lee, Myles learns the ins and outs of armed combat and the knightly code of chivalry, and falls in love with the earl's niece, the beautiful Lady Alice. The earl arranges to have Myles knighted by King Henry himself, preparing the way for Myles to meet his father's enemy in mortal combat and restore his family's good name and honor. The excitement reaches its peak in a mighty combat whose outcome will influence not only the future of Myles and his family, but that of England. If you enjoyed *Men of Iron*, you will certainly also want to read the classic *Ivanhoe* by *Walter Scott as well as Howard Pyle's *The Story of King Arthur and His Knights* (1903). MR & YA

Menotti, Gian Carlo (1911–) A composer known best for his operas, Menotti was born and raised in Italy. While still a boy he learned to play several instruments and began composing music, including two operas. After Menotti's father died and the family business failed, his mother moved the family to the United States. There he studied music in earnest and found that he was most interested in composing operas. His first success was *The Medium* (1946), about a spiritualist who has a bizarre experience that frightens her deeply and leads her into tragedy. *The Consul* (1950), about a woman's hopeless attempt to gain permission to get her family out of the police state in which they live, and *The Saint of Bleecker Street* (1955), about a deeply religious girl from New York City whose neighbors regard her as a saint, were also well received. Menotti is best known for the first opera written especially for television, *Amahl and the Night Visitors*. It tells the story of a poor crippled boy whose home is visited by the three Wise Men on their way to Bethlehem, taking gifts to the infant Jesus. Amahl has only his homemade crutch as a gift for the babe, and when he offers it he suddenly finds he can walk. Menotti also wrote *Help, Help, the Globolinks!* (1970), about invading aliens who attack a group of children and are finally defeated by the sounds of musical instruments. MR & YA

Mercury

Mercury is the ancient Roman god of merchants and commerce and is identified with the Greek god *Hermes. He is usually depicted as a young man wearing a winged hat and winged sandals. In one story about him, Mercury and his father, *Jupiter, visit Earth disguised as poor travelers, and the only people to offer them hospitality are a poor old couple, Baucis and Philemon. For their generosity, the gods turn their hovel into a temple, and when they die they are turned into beautiful trees. Mercury plays a part in the story of Proserpina, or *Persephone, who was kidnapped and carried to the Underworld by Pluto. You can read the story of Baucis and Philemon in *Bulfinch's Mythology* by Thomas Bulfinch (1796–1867) and in *Stories of the Gods and Heroes* (1940) by Sally Benson (1900–1972). You can read about Proserpina in *Daughter of Earth* (1984), retold and illustrated by Gerald McDermott (1941–). MR

Merlin, a central figure in stories about *King Arthur, was an actual person in the 6th century. Historians say he was a poet and prophet, but he is famous because of his part in the Arthurian legends. In all versions of the legend, Merlin's role was to help Arthur become king of England and to survive as a strong, unifying leader. In most stories, Merlin uses magic spells and wisdom to help Arthur, but he cannot change Arthur's future, which he foresees. He foresees the problems that Arthur's marriage to *Guinevere will bring and how these problems will eventually lead to Arthur's death, but he is helpless to change the larger course of events. He has been described as a magician, sorcerer, seer, soothsayer, wizard, trickster, enchanter, necromancer, warlock, and druid priest. In *The Once and Future King* by *T.H. White, Merlin is an absent-minded but wise old sorcerer living backwards in time, getting younger as everyone else gets older. Merlin also foresees his own end, in which he is imprisoned in an oak tree, or a cave, by an enchanting young woman who seduces him in order to learn his spells. T.H. White also wrote *The Book of Merlyn* (1958), which he called the true last chapter of *The Once and Future King*. The story of King Arthur from Merlin's point of view is told by *Mary Stewart in her trilogy, *The Crystal Cave* (1970), *The Hollow Hills* (1973), and *The Last Enchantment* (1979). YA

Merriam, Eve [Eva Moskovitz] (1916–1992) A teacher, writer, poet, and songwriter, Merriam has written many books, both for adults and for children. She is perhaps best known for her books of whimsical and often humorous poetry for younger readers, including the collections *It Doesn't Always Have to Rhyme* (1964), *Catch a Little Rhyme* (1966), *Rainbow Writing* (1976), *Jamboree: Rhymes for All Times* (1984), and *Blackberry Ink* (1985). Among her other books for children are *The Story of Ben Franklin* (1965), and *Independent Voices* (1968), which contains biographies in verse of seven great Americans, including *Benjamin Franklin; Frederick Douglass (1817?–1895), the black American writer and lecturer; and *Henry David Thoreau. MR

Merrill, Jean (1923–) An editor and author, Merrill has written a number of highly enjoyable books for young readers. Probably her best-known book is *The Pushcart War*, an imaginative and hilarious tale about a battle between pushcart vendors and truck drivers in New York City. Her other books include *The Superlative Horse: A Tale of Ancient China* (1961), about a poor boy who is given the job of selecting a horse of quality for the stables of a powerful duke; *The Black Sheep* (1969), a *fable about an island full of white sheep whose leaders try to force a newcomer, a black sheep, to conform to their rules; and *The Toothpaste Millionaire* (1972), about 12-year-old Rufus Mayflower, who decides he can make toothpaste at a fraction of its cost in stores, goes into business for himself and retires a millionaire a year later. MR

Merry Adventures of Robin Hood, The See *Robin Hood, The Merry Adventures of.*

Methuselah The oldest person mentioned in the *Bible, Methuselah, according to the book of *Genesis, lived to be 969 years old. He was the grandfather of Noah, who built the *ark. Many other Old Testament figures lived very long lives by modern standards, but their ages should not be taken literally. In Hebrew tradition, life spans from *Adam to Noah, including Methuselah, were the longest, decreasing with the passage of time, until, as the 90th *Psalm says, "The years of our lives are threescore and ten." Nevertheless, anything that is said to be "as old as Methuselah" is very old indeed.

Micawber One of the most interesting characters in *Charles Dickens's novel *David Copperfield*, Mr. Wilkins Micawber is a man who, though buffeted by fate and his own impractical nature, is ever the optimist, always certain that sooner or later something will "turn up." Micawber has a fondness for a good glass of ale and good companionship, and his love of big words and long sentences is delightful. Micawber spends much of his time avoiding his creditors, and eventually winds up in debtors' prison. In due course, however, something does turn up. He gives young Copperfield some advice that he has been unable to follow himself, about not going into debt: "Annual income twenty pounds, annual expenditure nineteen nineteen six, result happiness. Annual income twenty pounds, annual expenditure twenty pounds ought and six, result misery." Charles Dickens modeled Micawber after his own father, a loving, hard-working clerk who spent time in debtors' prison but later became a success. In the film classic *David Copperfield*, made in 1934, Micawber was played to perfection by none other than the famous American comedian W.C. Fields (1879–1946).

Michelangelo (Buonarotti) (1475–1564) You probably know that Michelangelo was the greatest *Renaissance artist and architect of the 16th century, but you may not realize he was also one of its leading poets. In addition to sculpting such masterpieces as the *Pietà* (1500) and the *David* (1504), painting the ceiling of the Sistine Chapel, and designing the massive dome that crowns Saint Peter's Basilica in Rome, Michelangelo wrote hundreds of poems. There have been a number of translations, including *The Complete Poems of Michelangelo* (1960) by Joseph Tusiani (1924–) and *Complete Poems and Selected Letters of Michelangelo* (1963) by Creighton Gilbert (1924–). You can read about Michelangelo in the biographical novel *The Agony and the Ecstasy* (1961) by *Irving Stone. A shorter version for younger readers was published as *The Great Adventure of Michelangelo* (1965). A film version of *The Agony and the Ecstasy* was produced in 1965. MR & YA

Michener, James A. (1907–) One of the best-selling modern novelists, Michener worked as an educator and editor before his career was interupted by World War II. While serving in the Pacific as a naval officer, he gathered the material that he worked into his first book of fiction, *Tales of the South Pacific* (1947), a collection of related stories about people caught up in the war. It launched Michener on his remarkably productive and successful career. Michener's trademark is the massive novel that examines a place or region over a period of hundreds, thousands, or even millions of years. Often the novel follows the progress of a number of families through many generations. Among the best of these are *Hawaii* (1959), about the Hawaiian Islands; *Centennial* (1974), about Colorado; *Chesapeake*

(1978), about the Chesapeake Bay area from 1583 to 1978; and *Poland* (1983), chronicling its history from the 13th century to the 1980s. Among his other books are *The Bridges at Toko-ri* (1953), a novel about Navy pilots on a mission to destroy four bridges during the Korean War, and *Sayonara* (1954), about an American officer who falls in love with a young Japanese woman just after World War II. *Tales of the South Pacific* was made into the hit musical *South Pacific* in 1949 and the movie *South Pacific* in 1958. *The Bridges at Toko-ri* was made into a movie in 1954, *Sayonara* in 1957, and *Hawaii* in 1966. *Centennial* was made into a successful TV miniseries in 1978. YA

Midas, in Greek mythology, was a king of Phrygia, in what is now Turkey. He was the subject of two stories. In one story, Midas does a favor for the god *Dionysus, who grants him his wish that everything he touches be turned to gold. But his joy disappears when he finds that his golden touch turns even food to gold. He is freed from his wish after bathing in the river, whose sands turn gold. In the other story, Midas unwittingly insults the god *Apollo, who gives the king the ears of an ass. Midas wears a cap to hide his ears. His barber learns the truth but is sworn to secrecy. The barber digs a hole in the ground and whispers the secret into it, then fills in the hole. But reeds grow and whisper the secret to the wind and the world. You can read the story of the golden touch in *A Wonder-Book for Girls and Boys* (1852) by *Nathaniel Hawthorne, the story of Midas's ears in *Greek Gods and Heroes* (1960) by *Robert Graves, and both in *Bulfinch's Mythology* by Thomas Bulfinch (1796–1867). MR

Middle-Earth is the legendary place created by *J.R.R. Tolkien in *The Hobbit* and in the trilogy *The Lord of the Rings*. Middle-Earth is inhabited by hobbits, elves, orcs, *wizards, dwarfs, and people. In the southeastern section lies Mordor, the desolate place to which Frodo journeys in order to destroy the ring in the fires of Mount Doom. Adjacent to Mordor is Gondor, where most of the great cities are found.

On the northeastern banks of the Great River, which runs from north to south bisecting the land, lies the forest of Mirkwood, where the evil Sauron built up his power. Still further east the dwarfs reside, beneath Erebor, the Lonely Mountain. The Misty Mountains, over which the travelers cross, rise to the west of the Great River. Further west is Eriador, where many of the hobbits reside and where the first volume of the trilogy, *The Fellowship of the Rings*, begins.

Middlemarch (1871), *George Eliot's masterpiece about 19th-century life in an English town, is composed of many separate stories about various residents of Middlemarch. As the novel progresses, the stories become more connected. The characters are involved with one another through friendship, love, or certain selfish motives, such as using one another to gain social status. While the novel has a large cast of characters, Dorothea, a beautiful and intelligent young woman, emerges as a central figure. She wants to help advance society by devoting her life to such goals as better housing for the poor and improved medical care. She also values intellectual achievement more than social status, an unusual position for a 19th-century English woman to take. She marries an elderly scholar named Edward Casaubon, hoping this will help her improve intellectually. She eventually learns that Casaubon is not as brilliant as he seems and that he does not really love her. When Casaubon dies, Dorothea faces her true feelings of love toward Will Ladislaw, a young man of irresponsible ways. Will's love for Dorothea inspires him to improve himself, and he eventually becomes a respected politician and marries Dorothea.

A major subplot in *Middlemarch* is the story of Dr. Lydgate, a young physician who arrives in Middlemarch to improve the town's medical care and help the poorer citizens. He falls in love with Rosamond Vincy, the mayor's daughter. However, after he and Rosamond are married, he learns that Rosamond is a selfish, spoiled woman who has no respect for his work. Like many characters in *Middlemarch*,

Lydgate learns to place little faith in first appearances. To save his marriage, Lydgate becomes a society doctor and, in doing so, gives up his life's dream. YA

Midgard In Scandinavian or Norse mythology, Midgard was Earth, the Middle Abode, located between the ice world, Niflheim, to the north and the land of fire, Muspelheim, to the south. According to legend, sparks from Muspelheim fell on the frozen rivers of Niflheim, causing some of the ice to melt. From the water rose a giant named Ymir, the first being of Creation. Other giants sprang from drops of Ymir's sweat. After this the gods were created, and finally human beings. The gods killed Ymir, and from his body fashioned Earth and the heavens. Asgard, the home of the gods, was connected to Midgard by the rainbow bridge, Bifrost. You can read about Midgard and other Scandinavian myths in *Bulfinch's Mythology by Thomas Bulfinch (1796–1867), *Legends of the North* (1951) by Olivia E. Coolidge (1908–), and *Thunder of the Gods* (1952) by Dorothy Hosford (1900–1952). The main source of information about Scandinavian mythology was an Icelandic scholar named Snorri Sturulson (c. 1179–1241), who wrote down the myths in what has come to be called the *Prose Edda*. There are a number of translations, including *The Prose Edda of Snorri Sturulson* (1964), by Jean I. Young (n.d.). See also *Edda. MR & YA

Midnight Fox, The (1968) Written by *Betsy Byars, this novel tells about a boy named Tommy and his experiences at his aunt and uncle's farm one summer. When his parents go to Europe, Tommy is sent to stay with his Aunt Millie and Uncle Fred. Tommy dislikes animals and thinks animals hate him. Spending two months on the farm is about the worst thing he can imagine. But one day he sees a beautiful fox, all black except for touches of white that make her look as though she is standing in moonlight. He explores the fields and woods, learning much about nature as he watches for his fox and eventually locates her den. After the fox begins raiding Aunt Millie's chicken coop, Uncle Fred finds the den and takes the fox's lone baby, putting it in a cage as bait to lure the fox to her death. It is up to Tommy to save her and her baby. If you enjoyed *The Midnight Fox*, you will also want to try *The House of Wings* (1972), about a boy who gains a new understanding and love for his eccentric grandfather when they work together to save a wounded crane. MR

Midsummer Night's Dream, A (1600) This romantic comedy by *William Shakespeare is set in ancient Athens and revolves around several couples' search for love. Theseus, the duke of Athens, is soon to be married to Hippolyta, queen of the Amazons. Their path of love is straight and clear, but this is not the case for the maiden Hermia, who is loved by Demetrius but loves Lysander. Demetrius once wooed Helena, but left her to court Hermia. Helena still loves him and hopes to win him back.

A band of Athenian craftsmen, including the delightfully idiotic weaver named Bottom, plan to perform a play in honor of Theseus and Hippolyta's wedding. They go to a wood near Athens to practice. Lysander and Hermia go to the woods also and plan to elope. Nearby, another romantic squabble is under way between *Oberon and Titania, king and queen of the fairies, over possession of a child Titania has carried off from an Indian king. Oberon tells his servant Robin Goodfellow, or *Puck, to gather an herb that, when placed in the sleeping Titania's eyes, will cause her to fall in love with the first creature she sees on awakening. Demetrius enters the woods, followed by Helena. Oberon sprinkles the herb in Titania's eyes and then gives Bottom the head of an ass. When the other performers see Bottom, they become frightened and run away, leaving the weaver in the woods alone. Titania awakens, sees Bottom, and falls in love with him. Oberon tells Robin to use the herb on the slumbering Athenian elsewhere in the wood, but Robin mistakenly gives it to Lysander instead of Demetrius. Lysander awakens, sees Helena, and falls in love with her. Oberon gives the herb to Demetrius. He also falls in love with Helena, who now begins to think everyone is playing a cruel joke on her. Eventually Oberon sorts everything out. Titania gives the child up to him, and peace is restored to the fairy kingdom. Lysander loves Hermia, Demetrius loves Helena, and Bottom is restored to his normal self and helps his companions perform their hilarious play for Theseus and Hippolyta. Film versions of *A Midsummer Night's Dream* were made in 1935, 1966, 1968. YA

Mike Fink was a hero of the old frontier, and his life was the source of many tall tales. He was born around 1772 where modern Pittsburgh, Pennsylvania, now stands. He became such a marksman that people would give him first prize just to keep him from entering a shooting contest and winning all the prizes. Then he became the toughest, bravest man on the rivers, boasting that he was "half horse, half alligator." After outfighting just about everyone, Mike claimed the title "king of the keelboat men." But Mike began to feel crowded as settlers moved in and steamboat traffic arrived on the rivers. He went West to live the free life of a mountain man and was killed in a shootout in 1823. A few years later people began telling and writing tall stories about Mike Fink, and by the Civil War he was a legendary frontier hero. You can read about Mike Fink in *Tall Tale America: A Legendary History of Our Humorous Heroes* (1944) by Walter Blair (1896–). A good book about keelboating on the rivers and streams of the American frontier is *The Keelboat Age on Western Waters* (1941) by Leland D. Baldwin (1897–1981). MR & YA

Millay, Edna St. Vincent (1892–1950) An immensely popular poet, Millay was born and spent much of her girlhood in Maine, where her early interests included music and writing. Her first published poem, "Forest Trees" (1906), appeared in *St. Nicholas*, a magazine for young readers, and she continued to write and have her poems published throughout her school years. Her best-known poem, *"Renascence,"* was published when she was just 20 years old.

Her poem *"The Ballad of the Harp-Weaver" delighted readers and critics and added to her growing reputation. It was collected in *The Harp-Weaver and Other Poems* (1923).

Millay wrote plays, short stories, and sketches, but it was her poems, usually in sonnet or other traditional verse form, that brought her critical acclaim. Her work was most popular during the 1920s and 1930s, and she was considered a leader of a new generation of independent-thinking, outspoken young women. Your local library may have Millay's *Collected Poems* (1956), which brings together many of her best poems. Look also for *Edna St. Vincent Millay's Poems Selected for Young People* (1929). MR & YA

Miller, Arthur (1915–) Playwright, screenwriter, and author of *Death of a Salesman* and *The Crucible, Miller was much affected by his family's financial insecurity during the *Great Depression. He discovered the world of literature after high school, when he began reading books he had put off because he had too many outside activities. Two of his early plays were produced while he was a student at the University of Michigan. In *All My Sons* (1947), an award-winning play about the manufacture of defective war material, which opened on Broadway, Miller showed his interest in conflict within the family, a theme that appears in later works. *Death of a Salesman* is considered one of the best plays of its time and was followed four years later by *The Crucible*, which ranks next to *Death of a Salesman* in importance.

Other plays include *A View from the Bridge* (1955), about an Italian-American longshoreman, and *After the Fall* (1964), a partly autobiographical story about the difficulties of human relationships. *The Misfits* (1961) is a screenplay written for Miller's second wife, Marilyn Monroe (1926–1962). Throughout his career, Miller has wanted his plays to make sense to commonsense people and stir the passions of the audience toward a fresh awareness of others. *All My Sons* was filmed in 1948 and *A View from the Bridge* in 1962. YA

MR = Middle Reader   YA = Young Adult Reader   * = See this main entry

Milne, A(lan) A(lexander) (1882–1956) Though he was a playwright and novelist, A.A. Milne is remembered today as the creator of the lovable bear, *Winnie-the-Pooh. Milne, who lived in England, decided early in life to be a writer. When he was only 24 years old he became assistant editor of *Punch*, a famous English humor magazine. Soon he became known for his humorous writing.

After World War I started, Milne joined the British Army and went to fight in France. When the war ended he returned to *Punch* for only a short time before leaving to concentrate on writing plays. A number of them were very popular in their time. Milne also wrote several successful novels, including, for older readers, the detective novel *The Red House Mystery* (1922).

Milne's greatest successes were his four books for children, which are read all over the world. The first of these was *When We Were Very Young*, a delightful collection of verses that Milne dedicated to his 3-year-old son, Christopher. In a short time he published a second collection of verses, *Now We Are Six*.

Milne's most famous works appeared when he was inspired to write about the adventures of the stuffed animals belonging to his son. Thus were born Winnie-the-Pooh, Piglet, Eeyore, Tigger, Roo, and their companion, the boy Christopher Robin, who is the only real person in the stories. They were collected in *Winnie-the-Pooh and *The House at Pooh Corner, which have been among the most popular books ever written for children. The adventures of Pooh have been translated into many languages, including a Latin version, *Winnie Ille Pu* (1960). MR

Milosz, Czeslaw (1911–) A highly acclaimed poet, translator, novelist, essayist, and scholar, Milosz was born in Lithuania and spent his boyhood there and in Russia. He began writing while a student at the University of Wilno (now Vilnius, the capital of Lithuania, but then part of Poland). Milosz still writes in Polish, the language of his youth. After studying for a time in Paris, he returned to Poland and spent the years of World War II in Warsaw, where he witnessed the brutal Nazi occupation and later the establishment of communist rule. He came to the United States in 1960 and became a citizen in 1970. Among his books are *The Captive Mind* (1951), essays that express his opposition to socialist realism and discuss the reasons for his defection to the West; the novel *The Seizure of Power* (1953), based on his wartime and postwar experiences in Warsaw; the novel *The Issa Valley* (1955), based on his youth in rural Lithuania; and his autobiography *Native Realm: A Search for Self-Definition* (1968). You can find good selections of his poetry in *Selected Poems* (1973) and *The Collected Poems 1931–1987* (1988). Milosz was awarded the Nobel Prize for literature in 1980. YA

Milton, John (1608–1674) One of the great English poets, Milton began writing poetry early, while still a student. He thought of making a career as a clergyman, but turned to his literary interests instead, writing a number of highly regarded sonnets and other poems, including *Lycidas* (1637), in memory of a classmate and fellow poet who was drowned in a shipwreck. *Lycidas* is considered one of the greatest elegies, or laments for the dead, in English. Then Milton turned away from poetry for 20 years. He became involved in English politics and wrote a number of pamphlets and tracts supporting Puritanism and religious reform, and justifying the execution of Charles I and the establishment of the republican Commonwealth in England. During this time he became blind. When Charles II became king and the Restoration began, Milton was hounded out of politics, and his books and pamphlets were burned. He turned again to poetry, completing his masterpiece, the epic poem *Paradise Lost, followed by its sequel, *Paradise Regained* (1671), which concentrates on Satan's temptation of Jesus during the 40 days in the wilderness; and the verse tragedy *Samson Agonistes* (1671), about the last days of the biblical hero Samson. There have been many editions of Milton's poems. You can find a good selection of his poetry in *Poets of the English

John Milton

Language (1950), edited by W.H. Auden (1907–1973) and Norman Holmes Pearson (1909–1975) and in *The Norton Anthology of English Literature* (1986), edited by M.H. Abrams (1912–) and others. His most powerful and influential pamphlet was *Areopagitica* (1644), which argues that freedom of the press promotes learning, virtue, and truth. You can find it in many editions. YA

mind is one's consciousness, the center of one's thoughts, feelings, memories, and emotions. Seeing something in your "mind's eye" means seeing in your thoughts something that you cannot at that moment see with your eyes. Perhaps it is something you once saw, or perhaps something right from your imagination. Each person has only one mind, but a person can "be of two minds" about something, meaning he or she is in doubt about what to think or do. To give "a piece of one's mind" to a person is to voice strong objection or disapproval of something. Sometimes a person may be able to tell exactly what you are thinking. Then

you might be tempted to ask, "What are you, a mind reader?" What if a person really could read your mind? Not just once, by chance, but all the time? That would certainly be a "mind-blowing" or "mind-boggling" experience.

Mine for Keeps (1962), by the Canadian writer *Jean Little, tells about Sally Copeland, a young Canadian girl with cerebral palsy who can walk only with the help of leg braces and crutches. After spending more than five years at a special school for the handicapped, Sal returns home for good. At first she is scared and unsure of herself. She has trouble getting used to being a member of a family once more and she dislikes having to go to a regular school, where she is self-conscious about her handicap. But Sal's unhappiness ends when she gets a timid little puppy named Susie. Caring for the little dog helps Sal to solve her problems at home and school, to make several good friends, and to aid a desperately lonely boy to overcome his own doubts and fears and begin his own journey to happiness. You can read more about the Copeland family in *Spring Begins in March* (1966), which tells about the growing pains of Sal's little sister, Meg. MR

Minerva is the ancient Roman goddess of wisdom and of war and is identified with the Greek goddess *Athena. She is the daughter of *Jupiter and is said to have sprung full grown and fully armed from his forehead. Along with Jupiter and *Juno, she is one of the three most important Roman gods. Minerva is the patroness of arts and crafts. Perhaps the best-known story about Minerva tells of her weaving contest with the proud maiden Arachne, who dared claim that her work matched that of the goddess. The contest ended with Arachne's suicide, but Minerva rescued her from death and turned her into a spider, so her weaving skills would not be lost. You can read about Minerva in *Bulfinch's Mythology* by Thomas Bulfinch (1796–1867). MR & YA

Ministry of Fear, The (1943) In this espionage novel by *Graham Greene, the central figure is

Arthur Rowe, who has recently been released from a prison term for the mercy killing of his wife. At loose ends in London at the time of its heavy bombing during World War II, he wanders into a benefit party and wins a large cake. He is then pursued by persons who seem determined to get the cake from him. In trying to discover why, Rowe finds himself involved with Willi Hilfe and his sister, Anna, who are running a wartime charity. They guide him to a seance at which a man is murdered with Rowe's knife. His residence is bombed by Nazi planes, he loses his memory, and, as he gradually regains it, he becomes suspicious of those who appear to be aiding him. In a showdown Rowe confronts the Hilfes and discovers why the desperate search for the cake caused several deaths and his own near brush with death. A movie was made of *The Ministry of Fear* in 1944. YA

Minotaur In ancient Greek mythology, the Minotaur was a monster with the head of a bull and body of a man. The god Poseidon presented King Minos of Crete with a beautiful white bull, but when Minos did not sacrifice the bull Poseidon became angry and caused Pasiphae, the king's wife, to fall in love with the bull. The Minotaur was the offspring of Pasiphae and the bull. The Minotaur was kept in a maze of passageways called the *Labyrinth, built for Minos by *Daedalus. Athenian youths and maidens were sacrificed to the Minotaur until *Theseus came to Crete and, with the help of Minos's daughter, Ariadne, killed the monster. You can read about the Minotaur in *Bulfinch's Mythology* by Thomas Bulfinch (1796–1867), *Tanglewood Tales* by *Nathaniel Hawthorne, and *Theseus and the Minotaur* (1988) by Leonard Everett Fisher (1924–). MR & YA

Miracles on Maple Hill (1956) By Virginia Sorenson (1912–), this novel tells about family life and about the miracles of nature in the course of four seasons. Ten-year-old Marly and her 12-year-old brother Joe go with their parents from their home in Pittsburgh, Pennsylvania, to an old farmhouse in a rural area. There, it is

hoped, Marly's father, weak and nervous after having been a prisoner of war, will recover his strength. At sugaring time Marly and Joe learn how maple sap is turned into syrup. Spring brings wild flowers; summer, berrying; fall, colorful foliage. They see wild animals and meet Harry the Hermit, who keeps goats. As father's health improves, the family decides not to return to Pittsburgh for the winter. The children go to rural schools where they make new friends. During a winter blizzard Joe rescues Harry from freezing to death. When sugaring time comes again the family takes over after their neighbor has a heart attack. Reading about this family is interesting, but it is the loving account of the ways of nature that makes this an unusual book. Sorenson has written other novels for younger readers, among them *The Neighbors* (1947) about a ranching family in Colorado, and *Plain Girl* (1956), the story of an Amish girl under pressure to attend a public school. *Miracles on Maple Hill* won the *Newbery Medal in 1957. MR

Mirkwood See *Middle-Earth.

Misérables, Les (1862) This novel by *Victor Hugo, set in France in the 19th century, tells of Jean Valjean, who had been imprisoned in the galleys for stealing a loaf of bread and was released after 19 years. Valjean's heart has been hardened, but an act of generosity by a saintly bishop changes him, and he vows to become a good man. As M. Madeleine, he becomes a wealthy businessman and mayor of a city and is known far and wide for his good acts. Only one man, police inspector Javert, suspects that Madeleine is Valjean, who is still wanted by the police for another crime. Valjean rescues a dying woman from Javert's blind and heartless devotion to law and duty, and promises to rescue her daughter, Cosette, who has been sent to live among strangers. Before he can do this he is arrested by Javert and sent back to prison for life. He fakes his own drowning and escapes, fleeing to Paris with Cosette, whom he comes to love deeply and raises as his own daughter. Javert alone suspects Valjean is still alive, and he contiues to hound the fugitive.

The Paris uprising in *Les Misérables*

The hunt reaches its climax during an uprising in Paris when Valjean gains the chance to kill Javert but frees him instead. Unable to balance his debt to Valjean with his duty to arrest him, Javert drowns himself.

Cosette has fallen in love with a young lawyer named Marius. Though Cosette means everything to Valjean, he does all in his power to protect the two lovers and bring them together. But he is turned away by Marius when he reveals his criminal past to the young man, and soon takes to his deathbed. Marius then learns of the truly good life Valjean has led, and that Valjean actually saved his life during the uprising. He and Cosette rush to Valjean, who dies happily in the warmth of their love. *Les Misérables* was adapted for movies in 1935, 1952, and 1978, and for a smash Broadway musical in 1987. YA

Miss Bishop (1933) This novel by *Bess Streeter Aldrich offers proof of the saying, "Life is what happens to you while you are making other plans." Set in the fictional Middle Western town of Oak River from 1876 through 1933, the novel follows the life of Ella Bishop, who when she is 16 years old comes to town with her widowed mother and enrolls at the Midwestern College that has just opened there. Miss Bishop's dream of happiness is a home of her own, a husband, and a family. After she graduates she decides to teach at the college while waiting for her dream to come true. She falls in love with a young lawyer named Delbert Thompson, but their plans for marriage end when he falls in love with Ella's cousin Amy. This is the first in a series of events that shape Ella's life, which becomes one of tireless service to her family, friends, and community. At last she comes to see how the joys, sorrows, and disappointments of her life fit together in a marvelous tapestry. If you enjoyed *Miss Bishop*, be sure to read *Good-bye, Mr. Chips by *James Hilton, which also concerns the life of a dedicated and giving teacher. YA

Miss Jane Pittman, The Autobiography of (1971) By *Ernest J. Gaines, this novel is about the life of a Southern black woman from the 1860s to the 1960s. It begins with Ticey, a mistreated slave girl who gains her freedom and changes her name to Jane Brown. After all her friends die in a massacre led by a group of white men, 12-year-old Jane is left alone to care for a young boy named Ned. They work on a plantation, where Ned becomes educated. This leads him into a career of teaching and preaching about black suffering. He is eventually murdered because of his outspoken beliefs. Over the course of Jane's life, she marries Joe Pittman, works on various plantations, and endures the pain of witnessing murders, rapes, and beatings of her friends and family. *Jane Pittman survives to participate in the civil rights and black militancy movements of the 1960s. When she is 109 years old she leaves home to participate in a black march for racial equality. This moving and honest novel was made into a TV movie in 1974. YA

Miss Lulu Bett (1920), by *Zona Gale, is a realistic and touching novel of small-town life. Lulu Bett is 33 years old and unmarried. She lives with her sister and brother-in-law, Ina and Dwight Herbert Deacon, their daughters, Di and Monona, and her mother, Mrs. Bett. In return for her clothes, meals, and a place to sleep, Lulu does all the work in the Deacon household. In short, she is the family drudge. And she is the special target of the pompous, domineering Dwight Herbert. But her life begins to change when Dwight's well-traveled brother, Ninian, arrives, courts Lulu, and marries her. The marriage soon ends and Lulu returns to the Deacon home, but her first taste of real freedom leads her eventually to a happy life of her own. If you enjoyed *Miss Lulu Bett*, try *Yellow Gentians and Blue* (1927), a collection of short stories that also shows Gale's strong sympathy for and understanding of the lives of everyday people. Gale herself dramatized *Miss Lulu Bett* in 1921. YA

Mister Roberts (1946), the only novel written by Thomas Heggen (1919–1949), tells about life aboard the U.S.S. *Reluctant*, a cargo ship serving in the Pacific during World War II. Lieutenant Douglas A. Roberts joined the Navy to fight the enemy, only to find himself far away from the action. Most of the other officers, like Ensign Pulver and the Doc, do not want to see any combat, but like Mister Roberts and everyone else aboard, they fight tedium, boredom, and the Captain, whom they consider an overbearing, incompetent fool. Pulver is constantly plotting to get back at the Captain for his meanness to the crew, but he never puts his plans into operation. Roberts longs to be transferred to a fighting ship, but the Captain refuses to let him go because Roberts is the one man able to keep the *Reluctant* running smoothly. Roberts finally gets transferred to a destroyer and is killed in action, but not before he has left his mark on everyone aboard the *Reluctant*. Heggen's novel was an enormous success, and the dramatization he wrote with Joshua Logan (1908–1988) became a hit play in 1949. But Heggen found himself unable to write anything further, and he killed himself. A successful movie based on his book and play was released in 1955. YA

Mistress Masham's Repose (1946), a novel by the English writer *T.H. White, tells of a little girl named Maria who lives alone, except for her governess and the cook, in the vast but decaying mansion of Malplaquet. The mansion and sprawling, overgrown estate were owned by her ancestors, but the deed of ownership has disappeared. The governess, a far-distant relative named Miss Brown, is conspiring with the Vicar, aptly named Mr. Hater, to find the deed, alter it, and gain the large inheritance that is being held in trust for Maria. One day Maria takes a small boat on one of the estate's lakes and goes to a little island in the center where there is a small temple known as Mistress Masham's Repose. There she finds a colony of Lilliputians, the little people first discovered by Gulliver in *Gulliver's Travels* by *Jonathan Swift. The Lilliputians' ancestors had been captured and brought to Malplaquet by the sea captain who saved Gulliver, but they had escaped. For 200 years their descendants had lived secretly on the abandoned island. You will enjoy learning how Maria and her best friend, the Professor, protect the secret of the Lilliputians, gain Maria's inheritance, and give the Vicar and Miss Brown their well-deserved comeuppance. If you liked *Mistress Masham's Repose*, try White's masterpiece, *The Sword in the Stone, and also *Gulliver's Travels, in which the Lilliputians made their first appearance. MR & YA

Misty of Chincoteague (1947), by *Marguerite Henry, tells about Paul and Maureen Beebe, who live with their grandparents on Chincoteague Island, off the Virginia coast. Every July the men of Chincoteague cross to nearby Assateague Island to round up some of the wild ponies that live there. According to legend, the ponies are descendants of Spanish ponies that came to the island after a Spanish ship went down in a storm. Each year the ponies are brought to Chincoteague, where some of the colts are sold and a big race is held. In the roundup Paul captures the wildest and fastest mare of all, Phantom, and her foal, Misty. Paul and Maureen buy Phantom and Misty. They gentle Phantom and train her for the annual race, which they win the next year. Knowing the mare longs to return to the wild, Paul sets her loose to return to Assateague Island. But Misty has grown up on Chincoteague with the children, and she stays with them. If you liked this story, you will also want to read *Stormy, Misty's Foal* (1963). MR

Mitchell, Margaret (1900–1949) Born in Atlanta, Georgia, Margaret Mitchell grew up hearing stories about the Civil War, or, as many Southerners called it, the War Between the States. She attended college briefly, intending to become a doctor, but returned home to care for her father after her mother died. Mitchell worked for the *Atlanta Journal* for several years before quitting to concentrate on her novel, *Gone With the Wind*, a romance set against the historical backdrop of the Civil War and the dark period of Reconstruction. The book, which took her 10 years to complete, was a tremendous success. Mitchell was overwhelmed by her sudden fame and published no more fiction. YA

Moby-Dick, or The Whale (1851) This epic novel by *Herman Melville was a critical and popular failure when it was first published. Today it is considered by some to be the most important work of American fiction. Part of its wide appeal to readers is that it can be enjoyed on several levels—as an exciting adventure, a careful depiction of whaling in the 19th century, and a study of the relationship between human beings, nature, and God. Melville's novel is rich in *symbols, and the language and tone he uses are often deeply poetic. In fact, *Moby-Dick* has been likened to an epic poem.

Ishmael, the narrator, leaves his life in New York City to sign on as a crewman aboard the Nantucket whaler *Pequod*. His only friend is a heavily tattooed Pacific Islander named Queequeg, who signs aboard the *Pequod* as a harpooner. Ahab, the captain of the ship, is a darkly brooding, vengeful man who lost a leg in a previous voyage while trying to kill a great white whale named Moby Dick. His missing leg has been replaced by one of whalebone, and he has a scar that runs from the top of his head down the full length of his body. Instead of accepting the loss of his leg as part of his danger-

ous livelihood, Ahab considers it an act of malice by some power that remains invisible behind the mask of the physical world. He is maddened by his inability to know the force that lies behind the mask, and also by his own human frailty. Ahab declares his defiance of that power and vows to destroy the white whale. The crew swear to Ahab that they will follow him on his quest for vengeance, but they are uneasy, for they have heard many tales of the whale's strength, intelligence, and ferocity. Only Starbuck, the first mate, tries to talk Ahab into giving up his plan, but Ahab is not swayed. When the *Pequod* meets other whaling ships, Ahab seeks information about the white whale. Several times he is warned not to

The hunted white whale turns on its attackers in *Moby-Dick*.

A. Burnham Shute

hunt the whale, but he refuses to listen. Finally the *Pequod* meets up with Moby Dick in the Pacific, and Ahab, his ship, and his crew are destroyed by the great whale. Only Ishmael survives, by floating atop a canoe-shaped coffin Queequeg had made for himself when he became ill earlier in the voyage. *Moby-Dick* was made into an outstanding movie in 1956. You might like to compare *Moby-Dick* with another sea classic, *The Sea Wolf* by *Jack London, in which the captain, Wolf Larsen, believes his struggle is not against the invisible power of God or fate but against the unchangeable laws of a godless, material universe. See also *Ahab and Jezebel. YA

Moffats, The (1941) This novel by Eleanor Estes (1906–1988) tells about the Moffat family, who live in the fictional town of Cranbury, Connecticut, in the early 20th century. Mr. Moffat has died and Mrs. Moffat makes dresses to support the family. The children are 15-year-old Sylvie, 12-year-old Joey, 9-year-old Jane, and little Rufus, who is 5½ years old. They all live in a yellow house on New Dollar Street that has been put up for sale by its owner, Dr. Witty.

During the year between when the "For Sale" sign is put on the house and the house is sold and the family moves to a new house on Elm Street, the Moffats have many interesting adventures, such as the day when Jane becomes friends with the gruff-looking chief of police; Rufus's first day at kindergarten, when he and another boy make an unscheduled trip on a freight train; and the time the whole family is quarantined because Rufus has caught scarlet fever. Eleanor Estes wrote about the family's further adventures in *The Middle Moffat* (1942), *Rufus M.* (1943), and *The Moffat Museum* (1983). She modeled the town of Cranbury after her own hometown of West Haven, Connecticut. Cranbury is also the setting for *Ginger Pye* (1951), which won the *Newbery Medal in 1952 and is about the Pye family and their new dog, Ginger. MR

Molnár, Ferenc (1878–1952) A Hungarian dramatist and novelist, Molnár was born and grew up in Budapest. Though he studied to be a lawyer, he was more interested in becoming a writer. While working as a newspaper reporter and correspondent, he began writing the bright, witty plays that made his reputation. His best-known play is *Liliom. His other plays include *The Guardsman* (1910), about a man who disguises himself to test his wife's faithfulness to him, and *The Swan* (1920), about a young princess who falls in love with a commoner. In 1940 Molnár came to the United States. He continued to write plays but was unable to continue the success he had achieved early in his career. *The Guardsman* was adapted for film in 1931 and remade as *The Chocolate Soldiers* in 1941 and as *Lily in Love* in 1985. YA

Monjo, F(erdinand) N. (1924–1978) An author and editor, Monjo wrote many books for children that were praised for their quality of bringing historical events and people to life. Many of his books are narrated by young people, so readers get a young person's view of history. Monjo's first book, *Indian Summer* (1968), tells about a Kentucky pioneer family's battles against unfriendly Indians while the father of the family is away fighting in the American Revolution. His other books include *The One Bad Thing About Father* (1970), about Theodore Roosevelt, as seen by his young son, Quentin; *Me and Willie and Pa: The Story of Abraham Lincoln and His Son Tad* (1973), as told by young Tad Lincoln; and *Poor Richard in France* (1973), the story of Benjamin Franklin in Paris during the American Revolution, as told by Franklin's grandson, Benjamin Franklin Bache. MR

Montgomery, L(ucy) M(aud) (1874–1942) A Canadian author of books for children, L.M. Montgomery was born on Prince Edward Island, which was the setting for all but one of her novels. After her mother died and her father moved to Saskatchewan, she was raised by her grandparents and began writing when she was a girl. She attended college on Prince Edward Island and in Nova Scotia, taught school for several years, and wrote a number of stories for Canadian and American magazines. Her first novel, *Anne of Green Gables*, an enormous hit, established her reputation. Montgomery followed the adventures of *Anne Shirley through a number of sequels, including *Anne of Avonlea* (1909), *Anne of the Island* (1915), and *Anne's House of Dreams* (1917). Montgomery also wrote two enjoyable series with young heroines as the main characters. The novels *Emily of New Moon* (1923), *Emily Climbs* (1925), and *Emily's Quest* (1927) follow the life of an Island girl who grows up to be a writer, just as Montgomery did. *Pat of Silver Bush* (1933) and *Mistress Pat* (1935) follow the adventures of another Prince Edward Island girl. *Anne of Green Gables* was filmed in 1934 and remade for television in 1985. *Anne of Avonlea* was made into a TV movie in 1982. MR & YA

Moonlight Man, The (1986) By *Paula Fox, this novel tells about one summer month in the life of 15-year-old Catherine Ames, the month she spends with her divorced father in a rented cottage in Nova Scotia. Harry Ames is a writer, a wanderer, an enchanter blessed with the gift of the gab and an almost unquenchable love of life. He is also undependable, unpredictable, and alcoholic. Harry is the exact opposite of Catherine's mother, whom Harry describes as a "daylight woman." Catherine supposes that makes Harry a "moonlight man." In the time Catherine spends with her father, the longest she has been with him since the divorce when she was 3 years old, Catherine sees his best and worst sides and comes to understand him for the first time in her life. At the same time, Harry discovers the daughter he never really knew. If you enjoyed *The Moonlight Man*, try *The Catalogue of the Universe* (1986) by *Margaret Mahy, about an 18-year-old girl who seeks out the father she has never known. MR & YA

Moonstone, The (1868) Though this novel, part adventure and part mystery, by *Wilkie Collins, is *Victorian in its leisurely style, it is still an exciting, interesting tale. In 1799 Colonel John Herncastle steals from the forehead of a Hindu idol an enormous diamond, the Moonstone. In his will he leaves it to his niece, Rachel Verinder, to be given her on her 18th birthday in 1848. But the gem disappears from her bedroom the first night she has it. Rachel breaks her engagement with Franklin Blake because, she claims, she saw him steal the Moonstone. The diamond is somehow taken to London and deposited as security for a loan. Eventually it is discovered that Blake had unknowingly been under the influence of opium and had taken the diamond while walking in a trance, during which time he also unknowingly gave it to Godfrey Ablewhite, who was deeply in debt. Three Indians, Brahmins dedicated to the recovery of the diamond, secure it by murdering Ablewhite. They return it to its proper place in the forehead of the God of the Moon. In England Rachel and Blake are again engaged. This novel also introduces Sergeant Richard Cuff, who is probably the first police detective in English fiction, though he does not play a central part in the story. *The Moonstone* was produced for television in 1972. YA

moor is the name given a large area of open, infertile wasteland that is made up of sandy, peaty, or rocky soil and is useless for farming. Often it is covered with small shrubs called heath, particularly heather. Because of this a moor is sometimes called a heath. *Emily Dickinson wrote about moors in an untitled poem (1865), which begins:

> I never saw a Moor—
> I never saw the Sea—
> Yet know I how the Heather looks
> And what a Billow be.

The wild moors of England, with their mists and storms, have long been used by writers as a setting for stories. Among the best-known moorland novels are *Wuthering Heights* by *Emily Brontë, *The Return of the Native* by *Thomas Hardy, and, for younger readers, *The Secret Garden* by *Frances Hodgson Burnett. But perhaps the best-known moor in literature is Dartmoor, the windswept and forbidding moor of Devonshire, in southwestern England, that is the setting of *The Hound of the Baskervilles* by *Arthur Conan Doyle. MR & YA

morality plays, or **moralities,** are allegorical dramas that were performed in Europe and England during the late Middle Ages, in which the characters are all personifications of ideas. The central character or characters represent humanity. In these plays, Man finds himself in the middle of a moral struggle between the forces of good, such as Mercy, Truth, and Justice, and those of evil, such as Lust, Pride, and Envy. At the end of the play Mankind is judged and rewarded with redemption or punished with damnation. The best-known morality play is *Everyman, which is still performed. YA

Morey, Walt(er) (1907–1992) Almost all Morey's books convey a deep love for nature, the land of the north, and its animals and people. Morey was born in the Olympic Mountains of Washington and grew up there and in Montana, Oregon, and Canada. He worked as a theater manager, mill worker, and construction worker, deep sea diver, fish trap inspector, and farmer of 60 acres of filbert trees. As a boy, Morey was an avid hunter, but he and his wife no longer permit the hunting of animals on his farm. In *North to Danger* (1954) he tells of his longtime friend, a bear hunter and fish pirate, who drowned the first time he fished for himself instead of stealing fish. You will want especially to read *Gentle Ben* (1965), which is about the bond of friendship between a bear and a little boy; *Kavik, the Wolf Dog; and *Gloomy Gus* (1970), which is about a Kodiak bear, one of the biggest in the world, raised by a boy to perform in a circus. *Scrub Dog of Alaska* (1971) is about the runt of a litter of sled dogs. *Canyon Winter* (1972) takes us into a wilderness canyon, where a 15-year-old boy is stranded alone after a plane crash. *Year of the Black Pony* (1976) is a tale about a boy and a wild pony. *Gentle Ben* was produced as a film in 1966 and a TV series in 1968. MR & YA

A quiet scene from *Gentle Ben,* one of Walt Morey's best-known books.

Morgan le Fay is a central character in the stories and legends about *King Arthur. She is Arthur's half-sister, and is a witch with the intent of doing Arthur mischief. She is also the mother of Arthur's only child, a son, Mordred, who is actively evil and destroys Arthur in the end. In many versions it is another sister, Morgause, who is the mother of Mordred, but it is usually Morgan le Fay who has the real magic power. In order to harm Arthur, she steals the magic scabbard of Arthur's sword *Excalibur, because as long as he carries the scabbard, he will not bleed.

At the time of Arthur in the 6th century, Britain was in the long process of change from the Druid religion of the early Celtic people to the Christian religion. The Christian writers of the 12th and 15th centuries described the old religion as the source of magic, mischief, and evil. Research by recent writers has revealed that the witches, sorceresses, and evil queens in the old Arthur stories were the priestesses and goddesses of the Druid religion. One of these writers is Marion Zimmer Bradley (1930–), the author of *The Mists of Avalon* (1982), a novel in which Morgaine, otherwise known as Morgan le Fay, is the major character. She is a Druid priestess, a healer with the gift of prophecy, or the Sight, and she has great power but is not evil. Arthur himself is not Christian, but *Guinevere is, and *The Mists of Avalon* tells about the decline of the old nature- and mother-based religion and the rise of the new, father-based Christian religion. YA

Morrison, Toni [Chloe Anthony Wofford] (1931–) One of the best-known and most highly acclaimed writers of the black experience in America, Morrison was born and grew up in poverty in Ohio during the *Great Depression. An excellent student, she graduated with honors from high school and after college became a teacher, and then an editor. Her first novel was *The Bluest Eye* (1970), about a poor, abused, and pregnant black girl whose fondest wish is to have blue eyes, the ideal of the white culture that has shaped the world in which she lives. Morrison's second and third novels, *Sula* and *Song of Solomon*, were critical successes and popular. Her books are noted for their moving and often poetic descriptions of characters, their thoughts and feelings, and the world they live in. Among her later books are *Tar Baby* (1981), set on a Caribbean island and about a beautiful, sophisticated black model who falls in love with a coarse black man who is on the run from the law; and *Beloved* (1987), set in Ohio in the 1870s, about an ex-slave woman who is haunted by the memory of her child, whom she killed while fleeing to freedom 18 years earlier. YA

Morton, Anthony See *John Creasey.

Moses The book of *Exodus in the *Bible tells the inspiring story of Moses, the great leader and lawgiver of the Hebrews. While the Israelites were in bondage in Egypt, Pharaoh, the ruler, fearing their growing numbers, ordered all male infants to be killed. Moses's mother, however, hid him in a basket on the bank of the Nile River where, according to tradition, he was found by Pharaoh's daughter, who raised him. After he grew up, God appeared to Moses and commanded him to lead the Israelites out of Egypt, which he did after overcoming many obstacles, in the 13th century B.C. One of the stories of Exodus tells how the Red Sea parted to let Moses and his people across. In the course of the long journey to the Promised Land, God handed down to Moses the *Ten Commandments. Moses never entered the land of Canaan, but died within sight of it. A novel about his life is *Moses* (1951) by *Sholem Asch. YA

Mother (1907) This novel by the Russian writer *Maxim Gorky tells how a poor woman is drawn into the growing revolutionary movement in Russia in the early 1900s. Pelagea Nilovna is married to Mikhail Vlassov, a brutal workingman who beats her and their son, Pavel, and is usually drunk. Only after Vlassov's death does Pavel realize how much suffering his mother has gone through. He becomes a quiet and thoughtful young man, and soon leads a group of political activists. They want to do away with the oppressive political and social order that has turned the lives of peasants and workers into one of horror. At first Pelagea, referred to in the book as "the mother," is afraid, thinking that Pavel's friends must be dangerous criminals. But she learns that they are brave and good, dedicated to truth and justice. Eventually she joins their cause and accepts the punishment that is meted out to them. *Mother* is a realistic portrayal of the poverty and oppression suffered by many under the czarist government, but its depiction of the revolutionary movement is somewhat romantic. You might like to compare *Mother* with *Doctor Zhivago* by *Boris Pasternak, which traces the lives of its characters from czarist times through the Russian Revolution and the establishment of the Soviet state. YA

Mouse and the Motorcycle, The (1965)

The main character of this novel by *Beverly Cleary is a young mouse named Ralph, who lives with his family in a wall in an old California hotel named the Mountain View Inn. Keith Gridley and his parents check into the hotel during their three-week vacation drive across the country. Ralph takes a fancy to one of Keith's toys, a small plastic motorcycle. While trying to ride it, Ralph rolls it off the tabletop, and both mouse and motorcycle end up in the bottom of the wastebasket. Keith finds them and becomes friends with Ralph, with whom he can communicate. He shows Ralph how to get the motorcycle to run and tells Ralph he can drive it, but only at night. But Ralph drives it during the day, losing it in a pile of sheets and pillowcases that get dumped in the hotel's laundry hamper. Ralph redeems himself after Keith becomes sick and the mouse spends a whole night searching the hotel for some aspirin for Keith. Keith gets his motorcycle back but decides to leave it in the hotel for Ralph when the family checks out. If you enjoyed *The Mouse and the Motorcycle*, you can read about Ralph's further adventures in the sequels *Runaway Ralph* and *Ralph S. Mouse*. MR

Mouse That Roared, The (1955)

This satirical novel by *Leonard Wibberley tells about the Duchy of Grand Fenwick, a tiny European country that is facing financial collapse. The young duchess Gloriana XII and her government decide to declare war on the United States, reasoning that when Grand Fenwick is defeated, it will receive enough aid from the United States to stave off bankruptcy. But the small expedition of bowmen led by Tully Bascomb is successful in its raid on New York City, capturing a doomsday weapon called the Q bomb, as well as its inventor. Armed with the superbomb, Grand Fenwick organizes a League of Little Nations that forces the big countries to destroy their nuclear arsenals. Gloriana marries Tully, and Grand Fenwick's future is secured. Wibberley wrote of Grand Fenwick in several sequels, including *Beware of the Mouse* (1958), which is set in Grand Fenwick in the 15th century, and *The Mouse on the Moon* (1962), in which Grand Fenwick joins the race to put a man on the moon. A film version of *The Mouse That Roared* was produced in 1959. MR & YA

Mowat, Farley (1921–)

One of the best-known and most successful Canadian authors, Mowat was born in Belleville, Ontario, and grew up in the western Canadian prairie near Saskatoon, Saskatchewan. As a boy he developed his life-long love of the wilderness and the life in it. He also began writing weekly nature articles for a local paper. After serving in the army during World War II and going to college, Mowat took a job studying wolf behavior in the barren Canadian north. While living there, he became friends with an Eskimo tribe that had suffered greatly from contact with modern civilization. Their story was the subject of his first book, *The People of the Deer* (1952). He turned his study of wolves into the book *Never Cry Wolf*, which destroys the commonly held view of wolves as vicious and destructive killers. Mowat has written a number of books for young people, and they also reflect his reverence for nature. They include *Lost in the Barrens* (1956), about the struggle of two boys to survive a winter in the Canadian wilderness; *Owls in the Family*; *The Dog Who Wouldn't Be* (1957), about a boy and his dog, growing up in Saskatchewan in 1929; and *The Snow Walker* (1975), an acclaimed collection of short stories. MR & YA

Ralph S. Mouse takes his toy motorcycle for a spin in *The Mouse and the Motorcycle*.

MR = Middle Reader   YA = Young Adult Reader   * = See this main entry

Mowgli is the jungle boy who appears in *The Jungle Books* (1895) by *Rudyard Kipling. When the lame tiger Shere Khan attacks a family sitting at a campfire, he frightens all away but a baby boy. But before the tiger can devour the child, the boy is saved by wolves. He is raised as a wolf cub and a member of the pack. Mother Wolf gives him the name Mowgli, or Little Frog. Mowgli grows up, learns the Law of the Jungle, and is a friend to all the animals except Shere Khan. Mowgli has some terrible experiences with Man, but when he becomes a man the animals send him away, and he marries and starts his own family. Mowgli appears in eight stories in *The Jungle Books* and in a ninth story, "In the Rukh" (1893), which tells how he came out of the jungle, became a government forester, and married. You can read all the stories about Mowgli in *All the Mowgli Stories* (1936). MR & YA

Mr. Popper's Penguins (1938), a classic book by Richard (1892–1948) and Florence Atwater (1896–1979), tells of Mr. Popper, a house painter who lives with his wife and two children, Bill and Janie, in a small American town called Stillwater. Mr. Popper has always wanted to travel to faraway places, especially to Antarctica to see the penguins. When the explorer Admiral Drake goes on an expedition to the South Pole, Mr. Popper writes him a letter. Admiral Drake answers by sending Mr. Popper a live penguin. Mr. Popper names him Captain Cook and rearranges the house to make him feel more at home. A famous aquarium sends Mr. Popper another penguin, whom he names Greta, and soon Captain Cook and Greta have a family of 10 young penguins. Mr. Popper trains the penguins to perform in theaters, and soon the Popper Performing Penguins are famous across the country. But one day they show up at the wrong theater and cause a panic, and Mr. Popper and his penguins are thrown in jail. They are rescued by Admiral Drake, who suggests taking the birds to live at the North Pole, where at present there are no penguins. Mr. Popper agrees, and is thrilled when the admiral asks him to go along on the expedition. Richard Atwater taught Greek at the University of Chicago and later became a columnist for two Chicago newspapers. *Mr. Popper's Penguins* has been translated into seven languages. If you enjoyed this book, you will also like *The Story of Dr. Dolittle* by *Hugh Lofting, about a kindly doctor and his animal friends. MR

Mrs. Frisby and the Rats of NIMH (1971) The main character in this novel by *Robert C. O'Brien is a mouse whose husband has been killed and who lives with her four children in the garden of Farmer Fitzgibbon. It is March and Mr. Fitzgibbon is getting ready to plow up the garden. Normally Mrs. Frisby would move her family to a summer home away from the field, but her son Timothy is ill and cannot travel. With the help of a wise old white mouse named Mr. Ages, a friendly crow named Jeremy, and an owl who lives in an ancient tree, Mrs. Frisby gets to meet a very special band of rats who live under the rosebush. They are larger than normal rats and much more intelligent. They have installed electricity and running water in their home, and they can read and write. Mrs. Frisby learns that the leaders had escaped from a laboratory they call NIMH, and that Mr. Frisby and Mr. Ages had escaped with them. While the rats save Mrs. Frisby's family from Mr. Fitzgibbon's plow, she is caged by one of the farmer's sons. Then she learns that exterminators are on their way to kill the rats. With Jeremy's help she escapes and warns the rats just in time. If you liked *Mrs. Frisby and the Rats of NIMH*, try also *Watership Down* by *Richard Adams, the touching story of a group of rabbits and their struggle against human beings and nature. *Mrs. Frisby . . .* was adapted as an animated film, *The Secret of NIMH*, in 1982. MR & YA

Muhammad (Mohammed) (c.570–632) The founder of *Islam, one of the major religions of the world, Muhammad was born in Mecca, a city in what is now Saudi Arabia. He married a wealthy widow somewhat older than himself and became a well-to-do merchant. About 610, he began to have visions, in which God (Allah), through an angel, gave him instructions. He wrote these down, and they became the *Koran, the holy book of Islam. In pressing these instructions on his people, he aroused much antagonism, and in 622 he was forced to flee to Medina, a city about 200 miles north of Mecca. This flight became known as the Hegira. As Muhammad's followers increased, so did his armed forces, and in 630 Mecca surrendered to him without a struggle. By the time he died, Muhammad controlled all of Arabia, and the new religion was ready to expand to other parts of the Middle East and eventually to much of Asia and Africa. Muslims, the followers of Islam, see Muhammad as the last prophet after the Jewish and Christian prophets of the *Bible. Younger readers might like to read more about Muhammad in *The Story of Muhammad the Prophet* (1979) by Bilzik Alladin (n.d.). Older readers will enjoy *The Life and Times of Muhammad* (1970) by John Glubb (1897–1986) and *Muhammad* (1983) by Michael Cook (n.d.). MR & YA

Muller, Marcia (1944–) As an author of detective novels, Muller has created three private investigators, all young, single women. One is Elena Oliverez, who is curator of Mexican art in a museum in Santa Barbara, California. In *The Tree of Death* (1983), the director of the museum is murdered after he has quarreled with Elena, and, as the prime suspect, she becomes an amateur sleuth to clear herself. In *The Legend of the Slain Soldiers* (1985), she is active again solving a murder in a trailer camp in a Mexican-American setting. Sharon McCone is a professional investigator, partly Cherokee Indian. She has an apartment in San Francisco where she lives with two cats. She has no plans to marry and have children. McCone drives an old red MG. One of her typical adventures is *Leave a Message for Willie* (1984), set in San Francisco and concerning a dealer in secondhand articles who is probably a fence for stolen property. When a man hangs around nearby and is then found murdered in Willie's garage, McCone takes over. Muller's third in-

vestigator, Joanna Stark, first appears in *Dark Star* (1989), in which she is threatened by a former lover who is an art forger. They become involved in determining the ownership of two valuable paintings. McCone appears again in *Where Echoes Live* (1991), in which a mining company's plans to revive an abandoned gold mine threaten the environment. In the end McCone has a confrontation with the head of the mining company. If you enjoy these detective stories, you will like those of *Amanda Cross, *Antonia Fraser, *Sue Grafton, and *Sara Paretsky. MR & YA

Munchausen, Baron The hero of a collection of delightfully impossible tall tales, he was modeled after a real person named Karl Friedrich Hieronymus von Münchhausen (1720–1797), a German soldier and landowner who was known for telling colorful stories about his military, hunting, and traveling experiences. Münchhausen's yarns and other tall tales were the basis for *Baron Munchausen's Narrative of His Marvelous Travels and Campaigns in Russia* (1785), written by a German named Rudolph Erich Raspe (1737–1794) but published in England anonymously. Later editions of the book added many more stories by other anonymous writers. Now usually known as *The Adventures of Baron Munchausen*, the stories have been published in many editions. Film versions of the stories were produced in 1943, 1961, and 1989. MR & YA

Murder of Roger Ackroyd, The (1926) One of *Agatha Christie's best detective novels, this story aroused controversy because of the way the idea of the "least likely suspect" is used. Some readers and critics said it was unfair, but except for two or three instances the clues are given as freely as in any good detective novel. A wealthy man is murdered in the English village of King's Abbot while he is in his study with the door and window both presumably locked. Various members of his family and household staff are suspects. The crime is investigated by Scotland Yard and also by *Hercule Poirot, Christie's famous fictional detective. The story is told by the village doctor, who knows everyone involved. Needless to say, Poirot finds the murderer. The plot is enjoyably complicated, and the end may leave you not only surprised but feeling slightly foolish. If you liked this book, you will also like those by *Margery Allingham, *Ngaio Marsh, and *Dorothy L. Sayers. MR & YA

Murder on the Orient Express (1934) is one of *Agatha Christie's most elaborately plotted detective novels. The setting is the famous train of this name, on its run from Istanbul, Turkey, to Calais, France. On board are assorted persons seemingly unrelated in any way: an elderly Russian princess, a young English governess, a British colonel, an American salesman, a Hungarian count and countess, an Italian businessman, a valet, a male secretary, a wealthy American businessman, a lady's maid, a nurse, and *Hercule Poirot, a Belgian detective. Ratchett, the unlikable American businessman, is murdered about the time the train becomes stalled in a snowdrift in Yugoslavia. Poirot undertakes an investigation, seeking a motive among the passengers, none of whom seem to have one. The case is complicated by the fact that the dead man was stabbed 12 times and by at least 2 persons. Poirot discovers that the passengers are not as unknown to each other as first appeared, and, of course, he proceeds to solve the mystery of a most unusual murder. An excellent movie was made of this book in 1974. MR & YA

Muses In Greek mythology, the Muses are the nine daughters of *Zeus and Mnemosyne, the goddess of memory. Under the guidance of *Apollo, they are goddesses of the arts and sciences, and each presides over a special field of activity. Calliope is the Muse of epic and heroic poetry, Clio of history, Erato of love poetry, Euterpe of music, Melpomene of tragedy, Polyhymnia of sacred poetry, Terpsichore of dance and choral song, Thalia of comedy, and Urania of astronomy. Since ancient times, writers have in their works called on the appropriate Muse to give them inspiration and aid in their creations. You can read about the Muses in *Bulfinch's Mythology by Thomas Bulfinch (1796–1867) and also in *Mythology by Edith Hamilton (1867–1963). MR & YA

Mutiny on the Bounty (1932) This novel by *Charles Nordhoff and *James Norman Hall is based on actual events and persons. It is narrated by Roger Byam, a young man who in 1787 becomes a midshipman aboard the ship H.M.S. Bounty, bound for Tahiti. The ship is commanded by William Bligh, an able but cruel and small-minded naval officer. Bligh's cruelty finally sparks a mutiny in the middle of the Pacific, led by the master's mate, Fletcher Christian. Most of the crew, still loyal to Bligh, are set adrift with him in a small launch, but Byam and several others are forced to stay with the ship. Most of the mutineers sail away to seek an island where they will never be found. Byam and some of the other crewmen decide to return to Tahiti. When a British ship finally arrives in Tahiti, Byam and the others are thrown in chains and taken to England to stand trial for mutiny. Byam's conviction is overturned at the last moment by new evidence, and he is saved.

If you enjoyed this exciting tale, you will be glad to know that Nordhoff and Hall wrote two sequels, Men Against the Sea (1933), about the incredible 3600-mile voyage made by Bligh and 18 crewmen in their small, overloaded open boat; and Pitcairn's Island (1934), which tells what happened to Fletcher Christian and the other mutineers. Mutiny on the Bounty was filmed in 1935 and in 1962. YA

My Ántonia (1918) Written by *Willa Cather, this novel of pioneer life in Nebraska is considered her best book. Jim Burden, a successful lawyer, recollects his boyhood experiences, beginning with a railroad journey from Virginia to Nebraska when he was 10 years old. Jim comes to live on his grandparents' farm, outside the town of Black Hawk. Also on the train is a family from Bohemia that has bought a farm nearby. Jim becomes friends with the older girl, Ántonia Shimerda, who is bright and beautiful and full of life, and teaches her how to read and speak English. But pioneer life is hard for the Shimerdas, and Ántonia's father longs to return to the old country. When Mr. Shimerda kills himself, all the farmwork falls on Ántonia and her older brother, Ambrosch. Jim's grandparents sell the farm and move into Black Hawk, and they find work in town for Ántonia. Though Jim falls in love with Ántonia, their lives take them in different directions. Jim goes to college, becomes a lawyer, and travels widely. Ántonia has a hard life, but eventually marries, has a large family, and with her husband builds up a prosperous farm. When Jim returns for a visit, he sees in her eyes the sparkle of the young girl he grew up with.

This story describes the beauties and hardships of 19th-century pioneer life and the life of the brave people who turned the prairie into productive farmland. If you enjoyed *My Ántonia*, you will also enjoy reading *Giants in the Earth* by *O.E. Rölvaag, another classic of pioneer farm life. YA

My Brother Sam Is Dead (1974) This novel by *James Lincoln Collier and *Christopher Collier is a moving account of the pain inflicted on one family by the bloody events of the American Revolution. The story is told by Timothy Meeker, who recalls what it was like in his little town of Redding, Connecticut, at the beginning of the war. Tim's older brother, Sam, joins the Patriot army, against his father's wishes. Mr. Meeker wants to keep his family out of the war. He remains loyal to the king but takes no part in the conflict. Tim stays home and helps his parents run their tavern. When he and his father drive some cattle to sell at Verplanck's Point, on the Hudson River, they have a narrow escape from a band of roving thugs who rob and kill in the no-man's-land between Loyalist and Patriot areas in New York and Connecticut. On the way home Mr. Meeker is captured, and Tim returns home alone. Tim's father dies in a British prison ship, and Sam is accused falsely of stealing cattle and is unjustly executed by the Patriots. The war has brought the Meekers nothing but sorrow from both sides.

This story is based largely on historical facts, though the Meekers are fictional characters. If you like reading about the American Revolution, be sure to read *Johnny Tremain* by *Esther Forbes, which tells of another young American swept up in the war. MR & YA

My Darling, My Hamburger (1969) This tough, realistic novel by *Paul Zindel tells about two teenage couples and their experiences during their senior year in high school. Sean Collins and Liz Carstensen are in love, but their relationship is endangered because of their different feelings about sex. Sean wants to make love to Liz, but she is afraid and uncertain. Liz cannot count on understanding or guidance from her mother and stepfather, and Sean has the same problem with his parents. Even the teachers at school offer little help. One teacher advises that when a boy gets too passionate with a girl, the girl should suggest they go buy a hamburger. Meanwhile, Sean and Liz's friends Dennis Holowitz and Maggie Tobin, both shy and self-conscious, are just getting to know each other. But their growing relationship is cut short by the tragic events that occur after Liz becomes pregnant. *My Darling, My Hamburger* is a sympathetic story of four teenagers growing toward and then away from each other on the often difficult path to adulthood. YA

My Friend Flicka (1941), by *Mary O'Hara, is one of the most popular horse stories ever written. Ten-year-old Ken McLaughlin lives with his older brother Howard and their parents, Rob and Nell, on the family's ranch in Wyoming. An awkward, lonely boy who escapes the real world by constant daydreaming, Ken longs to have a horse of his own, but his stern father, an ex-Army officer who does not understand his son at all, is against the idea. When he finally lets Ken pick a horse to train and raise, Ken chooses the yearling filly Flicka, whose mother is the wildest, most uncontrollable horse on the ranch. Rob McLaughlin's worst fears about Flicka seem to come true when the frightened filly is brought in from the range and nearly kills itself trying to escape through a barbed-wire fence. Ken determines to nurse, gentle, and train Flicka, and the bond that forms between horse and boy brings to Ken and his family a new understanding of life, love, and responsibility. If you enjoyed *My Friend Flicka* you will also want to read the sequels *Thunderhead* (1943) and *Green Grass of Wyoming* (1946). *My Friend Flicka*, *Thunderhead*, and *Green Grass of Wyoming* were adapted as movies in 1943, 1945, and 1948, respectively. A TV series, *My Friend Flicka*, appeared in 1957. MR

My Name Is Asher Lev (1972) This novel by *Chaim Potok tells about a young Jewish boy from Brooklyn, New York, who has a great artistic gift. The story is narrated by Asher Lev, who tells about his difficulties in becoming an important and successful painter. Asher and his parents are Hasidic Jews, members of the Ladover sect. His father works for the Rebbe, the spiritual leader of the Ladovers. He is highly respected for his tireless efforts to rescue Soviet Jews from persecution and to establish Ladover communities throughout Europe. From his earliest childhood Asher has felt the need to express his feelings in drawings. His father considers Asher's interest in art foolishness and fears it will lead him away from his religion and culture. Despite his father's disapproval and pressures to conform from others in the community, Asher continues to draw. He does receive encouragement from his mother, who makes great efforts to support both her husband and her son. Asher also is supported by the Rebbe, who recognizes the boy's gift. With his blessing, Asher becomes the student of a great artist, Jacob Kahn, who warns him that developing his gift will mean pain and suffering for him and for others. Asher remains true to his artistic vision, and after studying and painting in Europe, returns to Brooklyn a respected and important artist. But his greatest paintings, which recall the crucifixion of Jesus, turn his parents and his community against

him. The Rebbe asks him to leave, and Asher sadly returns to Paris.

Chaim Potok continued the story of Asher Lev in *The Gift of Asher Lev* (1990). Another book about an artist who gives up family, friends, and culture to pursue his artistic vision is *The Moon and Sixpence* (1919) by *Somerset Maugham. YA

My Side of the Mountain (1959), by *Jean Craighead George, is about young Sam Gribley, who is tired of living in a crowded New York City apartment. An ax, a penknife, $40, a ball of cord, a bit of steel, and flint are all he takes with him when he runs away to the Catskill Mountains. During the year that Sam lives alone, he will realize that he needs human companionship, but not before making his home in a tree, making friends with Baron, a wild weasel, and foraging for food with his falcon, Frightful. Sam also eats cattails, wild apples, walnuts, berries, smoked venison, and fish, which he finds on his mountain. The details of how Sam lives in his hemlock tree cave, survives a snowstorm, builds a shelter and fire from his flint, and sews a big skunk cabbage leaf into a pot for boiling water, and how an old lady insists he help her pick *his* wild strawberries and walk her home from the "haunted mountain," make such a delightful story that George has had dozens of people write her seeking directions to where Sam spent his year. A sequel to *My Side of the Mountain* is *On the Far Side of the Mountain* (1990), which is about Sam losing his sister, Alice, and his falcon, Frightful, and the dangers he encounters in getting them back. *My Side of the Mountain* was adapted for film in 1969. MR

Myers, Walter Dean (1937–) Author of a number of acclaimed books for young people, Myers grew up in Harlem, in New York City. Though he began writing as a boy, he tried many jobs before turning to writing. Many of his books are about the lives and experiences of young blacks in tough, bleak city settings. They depict the poverty, violence, anger, and despair that are often a part of inner-city life. But they also show the importance of friendship, love, and good will in overcoming such negative forces. Among his many books are *It Ain't All for Nothin'* (1978), about a 12-year-old boy in Harlem and his troubled relationship with his father; *The Young Landlords*, about a group of teenagers who become owners of a Harlem apartment building; *Motown and Didi* (1984), a love story centering on two young people living in Harlem; *Crystal* (1987), about a beautiful teenage girl who discovers both the bright and dark sides of a model's life; and *Fallen Angels*, about a group of American soldiers in Vietnam. YA

Mythology (1942) Written by the teacher and author Edith Hamilton (1867–1963), this enjoyable collection of Greek, Roman, and Norse myths was hailed by critics and reviewers and became an enormous best seller. Part of this was because of Hamilton's easy and pleasant writing style, and part because of her thorough knowledge of the subject. Her lifelong interest in the ancient world, especially Greece, shows in her descriptions of the ancient gods and heroes and in her retelling of their stories of love, war, and adventure. Edith Hamilton wrote a number of books about the ancient world, including *The Greek Way* (1930) and *The Roman Way* (1932), which bring to life the spirit and way of life of ancient Greece and Rome. MR & YA

nadir, from the Arabic *nazir* meaning opposite, is the point on the celestial sphere that is opposed to the *zenith, the highest position. Thus, nadir is the lowest point. It is, so to speak, directly under your feet. It is not surprising, then, that nadir has come to mean the lowest point in your fortunes, the depth of depression, or the lowest point of degradation that you may suffer. *Nathaniel Hawthorne wrote, "The two theories differed as widely as the zenith from the nadir in their main principles."

Naked and the Dead, The (1948) By *Norman Mailer, this first novel, which is based on Mailer's own experiences during World War II, tells about an American infantry platoon during a battle for a Japanese-held Pacific island. After gaining a foothold on Anopopei island, General Edward Cummings's division becomes bogged down before a Japanese defensive line. Cummings, a cautious but enormously ambitious man, has attempted to instill his rightist views in Lieutenant Robert Hearn. Hearn's rebuff earns him assignment to Sergeant Sam Croft's platoon. It is sent behind Japanese lines on a dangerous reconnaissance mission, during which Croft, resenting Hearn's presence, gets him killed in a Japanese ambush. The effect of casualties, fatigue, fear, and bigotry is reflected in the soldiers' raw language and brutality. Conflicts arising from the soldiers' different backgrounds add further stress. Theirs is a war stripped naked of humanity. When they return, they find that the enemy has been routed, their mission pointless. If you enjoyed *The Naked and the Dead*, try also *_From Here to Eternity_, by *James Jones, which is set in Hawaii in the months leading up to the Japanese attack on Pearl Harbor. *The Naked and the Dead* was made into a movie in 1958. YA

Nana is the devoted Saint Bernard dog who lives with the family of Mr. and Mrs. Darling in *Peter Pan by *James M. Barrie. Nana watches over their children, *Wendy, John, and Michael. Nana guards the children from all harm. A gem of a nursemaid, she is in charge of escorting them to school, and she gets up at all hours at the sound of a cough or cry to check them. But when Peter comes to take the children to *Neverland, Nana is tied in the yard. She barks, warning of Peter's presence, but the Darlings ignore her as they hurry to a party.

Nancy Drew See *Carolyn Keene.

Narcissus was a beautiful young man whose story has several versions in Greek mythology. He spurned the attention of the lovestruck, silent maiden, Echo, who turned to stone in her sadness. Narcissus then mistook his reflection in the waters of a fountain to be the ruling nymph of the fountain, dove into the water to reach the nymph, and drowned. Another story says he had a much-loved sister who died. Narcissus mistook his fountain reflection for that of sister, dove into the water, and drowned. Yet another story relates that Narcissus fell in love with his own reflection and longed so for himself that he pined away and became a flower. The flower has a slightly different origin in the first version of the Narcissus story. When nymphs came to take Narcissus's drowned body from the water, they found only a flower, which they named after him.

In psychology, a person who is troubled because of his extreme self-love is called a narcissist and is said to suffer from narcissism, or the inability to control his self-centeredness and to love other people. YA

Narnia See *The Chronicles of Narnia.*

Nash, Ogden (1902–1971) A popular humorous poet, Nash began writing poetry when he was 23 years old. He taught school, sold bonds on Wall Street, created advertising displays for streetcars, and worked in the editorial department of *The New Yorker* magazine before devoting all his time to his own writing. Nash was frequently quoted by the American public and press after his guest appearances on weekly radio and television shows. He had a knack for creating memorable puns, limericks, and short snappy lines, such as:

> Keep your cat inside your house,
> And I'll stroke his fur and give him a
>   mouse,
> But let him loose on my feeding birds,
> And I'll beat out of him whey and
>   curds.
>
> Children aren't happy with nothing to
>   ignore
> And that's what parents were created
>   for.

Joking about his poetic craftiness, Nash described himself as a "worsifier" and called his style "my individual method for concealing my illiteracy." He had serious things to say about life but seemed shy about saying them straight out. As he told a reporter, "I like [my] style because it gives me a mask, a front behind which I can hide."

The "laughing philosopher" enlightened people of all ages with his truth and good nature. In his verse, prose, lectures, and writing for stage and screen, Nash approached subjects with gentle humor and good will. He paused to observe what was silly and ironic about his place and time, and made people smile. The titles of his works are fun in themselves. You will chuckle over *I'm a Stranger Here Myself* (1938), *The Cruise of the Aardvark* (1967), and *The Old Dog Barks Backwards* (1972). Books for younger readers include *Parents Keep Out: Elderly Poems for Youngerly Readers* (1951) and *Custard the Dragon* (1961). MR & YA

National Velvet (1930), by *Enid Bagnold, is the story of *Velvet Brown, youngest of a butcher's four daughters, who lives in a village on the south coast of England. Her mother, Araminty, was famous in her youth for swimming the English Channel, and her grit and endurance can be seen in the 14-year-old Velvet. Horses, real and imaginary, are the most important thing in Velvet's life. In one day she inherits five of them from an elderly neighbor *and* wins a jaunty black-and-white spotted horse in a raffle. "The Piebald" is definitely not a thoroughbred, but he is boyish and spirited and soon becomes fond of Velvet. When Mi Taylor, Mr. Brown's helper, sees Velvet ride the Piebald at the gymkhana (a field day for riders), he is impressed with the way both horse and rider take the jumps. Though Mi is not a rider himself, he knows about horses and racing. He encourages Velvet to enter the Grand National steeplechase, a grueling race with hedges and ditches to be jumped. Velvet works hard to train the Piebald and, on the day of the race, Mi helps her register by disguising her as a young man.

To the astonishment of the entire nation, Velvet and the Piebald win. Velvet faints from exhaustion, however, as they leave the course, and slips from the saddle before reaching the unsaddling pen. She and the horse are disqualified, as the strict rules of the race say they must be. Worse, the doctor who examines Velvet discovers the winning rider is an underaged female. Now the object of much public attention, Velvet and Mi are called before the National Hunt Committee to explain their deception. Velvet tells them she did it because "the horse jumps lovely and I wanted him to be famous," and says she was not interested in the prize money. The committee votes to restore her win, and she and the Piebald become part of racing history. A movie of *National Velvet* was made in 1944. MR & YA

Native Son (1940) by *Richard Wright is the tragic story of a black man trying to get along in a society that shows him the good and proper way to act, and then makes such action impossible. *Bigger Thomas lives in a Chicago slum. He knows his mother, brother, and sister suffer from being poor, but he is powerless to change their situation. He gets a job as chauffeur and handyman for Mr. Dalton, a wealthy landlord, and his blind wife.

One of his duties is to drive their daughter, Mary, to her classes at the university. On Bigger's first day at work, Mary asks him to take her to another address without telling her parents, and she introduces Bigger to her communist friend, Jan. Mary and Jan make Bigger very uncomfortable when they insist on treating him as an equal rather than as a servant.

Much against Bigger's will, the three spend the evening together, and later Bigger has to carry Mary to her room because she is too drunk to walk. He has just put Mary on her bed when her blind mother enters the room and calls out to her daughter. Terrified that Mrs. Dalton will think he is molesting Mary, Bigger puts a pillow over her face to keep her quiet, and after Mrs. Dalton leaves he discovers Mary is dead of suffocation. In a state of shock and confusion, he puts the girl's body in the furnace. Bigger convinces his girl friend, Bessie, to help him make Mary's disappearance

look like a kidnapping. The police, however, discover Mary's bones in the furnace ashpit, and Bigger runs away in a panic. Bigger tells the whole story to Bessie and then, in despair because he can neither leave her nor escape easily with her, he kills her while she sleeps.

Bigger is trapped and captured by the police. In an atmosphere of violent hatred and racial prejudice, he knows he has no hope of making anyone understand why he has killed, and he pleads guilty. Finally, while an angry crowd shouts and threatens outside, Bigger is convicted and sentenced to death in spite of his lawyer's eloquent appeals for mercy. Movies were made of *Native Son* in 1944 and 1986. YA

Natty Bumppo is the hero of the five novels of the *Leather-Stocking Tales, by *James Fenimore Cooper. Strong, simple, independent, brave, generous, and a crack shot with his rifle, Killdeer, Bumppo is the ideal of the freedom-loving frontiersman who helps open the American wilderness to the civilization he disdains. A master of woodland lore, he is a wise diviner of good and evil among both the American Indians and whites. Bumppo is known by many nicknames in the books, including Deerslayer, Hawkeye, La Long Carabine (the long rifle), Pathfinder, and Leather-Stocking.

Natural, The (1952) *Bernard Malamud's first novel, *The Natural*, tells about Roy Hobbs, a Middle Western youth with a natural genius for baseball and a hunger to break every record in the book. He sets out for Chicago to try out for the Cubs baseball team, taking with him Wonderboy, a bat he made himself from the stump of a tree that had been hit by lightning. Hobbs intends to become a baseball hero. It is a quest as noble as the quest of *King Arthur and his knights, and Wonderboy is Hobbs's version of the magical sword *Excalibur. Yet Hobbs's journey to his place in major-league history is a long and tortuous one. When he finally becomes a rookie outfielder for the last-place New York Knights, he is past his prime and faces an epic struggle to hold on to his dream. His success or failure is tied to his faithfulness to the game and to the unwritten code of heroes. In *The Natural*, Malamud has brilliantly woven baseball lore and history together with myth and mysticism. Another book that does this is *Shoeless Joe* (1982), about Joseph Jefferson Jackson (1889–1951), a major-league outfielder for 13 years, by the Canadian writer W.P. Kinsella (1935–). *The Natural* was made into a movie in 1984, and *Shoeless Joe* was made into the movie *Field of Dreams* in 1989. YA

Naylor, Phyllis Reynolds (1933–) A former school teacher and editor, Naylor found when she turned to authorship that she could write both realistic and humorous novels with a touch of *fantasy for young people. Among her realistic novels are *The Agony of Alice, Walking Through the Dark* (1976), *A String of Chances* (1982), and *The Year of the Gopher* (1987). In *Walking Through the Dark*, 14-year-old Ruth learns by bitter family experience during the *Great Depression that it is possible to cope with hard times. In *A String of Chances*, 16-year-old Evie experiences difficulties in coming to terms with religious questions and a first romance. Seventeen-year-old George, in *The Year of the Gopher*, rebels against his very proper family to take a blue-collar job instead of going to college. Typical of Naylor's fantasies is the York Trilogy of *Shadows on the Wall* (1980), *Faces in the Water* (1981), and *Footprints at the Window* (1981). In these novels the main character is Dan Roberts, who gets into difficulties in 4th- and 14th-century England, as well as 20th-century Pennsylvania. Among the problems he faces are hereditary disease, war, and plague. *Shiloh* is about a boy and his dog living in the hill country of West Virginia. If you like Naylor's books, read those of *Colby Rodowsky, *Marilyn Sachs, and *Doris Buchanan Smith. MR

Nazi is a short form of the name of the political party that governed (1933–1945) Germany and started World War II. In full the party name was *Nationalsozialistische Deutsche Arbeiterpartei* (National Socialist German Workers Party). Its *symbol was the swastika. The party took its name in 1920 after a similar group was reorganized by Adolf Hitler (1889–1945), who became chancellor and then dictator of Germany. The Nazi party was dedicated to getting revenge for Germany's defeat in World War I, to expanding its territory at whatever cost to others, and to persecuting or killing all who opposed it, especially liberals, intellectuals, and communists. The Nazis systematically murdered millions of European Jews, in what has come to be known as the *Holocaust, as well as millions of Slavs, Gypsies, and others. "Nazi" has become a name applied to anyone or any policy that favors dictatorship, brutality, and oppression. It has much the same meaning as fascist. See also *cross.

nectar, in the mythology of the Greeks and Romans, was the drink of the gods and goddesses, the word coming originally from the Greek, *nektar*. Like *ambrosia, the food of the deities, it conferred immortality. The word can now mean any tasty drink, especially one that is sweet. The nectarine, a fruit much like the peach, takes its name from nectar.

Nell, Little See *Little Nell.

Nell's Quilt (1987) By *Susan Terris, this sad and moving novel, which is set in 1899 and 1900, tells about a girl who nearly kills herself when circumstances beyond her control seem to be ruining her life. Eighteen-year-old Nell Edmonds, who hopes to go to college, is urged by her parents to marry 28-year-old Anson Tanner, a well-respected widower with a 4-year-old daughter. When Nell realizes the marriage would aid her hard-pressed family, who are farmers, she submits to the idea. Nell decides she will make a patchwork quilt to occupy her time, using bits of cloth from her deceased maternal grandmother's dresses. Meanwhile, fear of life ahead leads Nell to eat less and less. She becomes weak, faints, and has hallucinations. To her dismay, she discovers that the cloths she is using to make the quilt are not from her grandmother's dresses but are simply samples from a department store. Nell sews the last piece of the quilt, mixes a batch of dyes, and throws the quilt in the boiling liquid so that it turns black. Putting the quilt over her in bed, she prepares to die. But then she thinks of those who will be left behind—her hard-working mother; her 17-year-old sister, Eliza, who has gladly agreed to marry Tanner after it has become clear to all that Nell does not want to marry him; and the abused wife of a neighbor. She remembers the old nursery rhyme: She is Thursday's child and so "has far to go." Nell sits up in bed, clutching the quilt, and says: "No, no, no. . . ." This novel is interesting for its picture of farm life in Massachusetts nearly a century ago. Even more it gives an overpowering description of what anorexia nervosa, a devastating eating disorder whose victims compulsively avoid food, can do to a person. YA

Nelson, Theresa (1948–) The author of three novels dealing with the problems of young people, Nelson has a rare talent for making her writing about family problems both exciting and down to earth. In *The 25¢ Miracle* (1986), 11-year-old Elvira Trumbull lives in Texas with her father, an undemonstrative man who is often without a job. Seeking consolation in nature, Elvira buys a rosebush. When it does not do well she seeks advice from a librarian, Miss Ivy, and tries without success to promote a romance between her father and Miss Ivy. Threatened with being sent to live with an aunt, Elvira runs away briefly. Then her father begins to realize Elvira's need for love and communication. The "25¢ miracle" refers to the cost of a postage stamp Elvira uses to send a boxtop to a manufacturer for a refund on a cereal she does not like. Against her father's expectations, she gets her refund, which becomes a symbol for her father's love, which comes at last. *Devil Storm* (1987), set at the time of the Galveston, Texas, hurricane of 1900, centers on 13-year-old Walter Carroll, who helps his father, a melon farmer. He gets on well with his two sisters while they try to overcome their sorrow over the death of a baby brother. The children make friends with Tom the Tramp, an ex-slave

Neptune

who, with their father away and the storm about to break, helps them to safety. In *And One for All* (1989), 12-year-old Geraldine Brennan is concerned about her older brother, Wing, a high school senior in 1967. He hates school, and as soon as he can, he enlists in the Marines. He is killed in Vietnam, and his death brings together Geraldine and Wing's best friend, Sam Daily. If you like these books, read those of *Judy Blume, *Susan Beth Pfeffer, and *Cynthia Voigt. MR

Neptune is the god of the oceans in Roman mythology. The Greeks knew him as Poseidon, who is a son of Cronus and Rhea, two of the *Titans. He is depicted as a mature man of noble bearing, wearing a crown and carrying a three-pronged fishing spear called a trident. At times, he is riding his steed, Hippocampus, a mythological seahorse that is half-horse and half-dolphin. On or off Hippocampus, Neptune finds his place among the gods a bit shaky because he tends either to lose his battles or to back the wrong side in human contests. He loses Athens to *Athena. His sister *Hera bests him for Argos; *Apollo wins Corinth from him. But, like his brother *Zeus, Neptune is a very romantic god and has many sons, some of them horses.

Neptune is also a sea-blue planet of the solar system, discovered in 1846. Smallest of four distant giant planets, it is 17 times the size of Earth. But you can see it only with a powerful telescope, looking like a twin to the planet Uranus. You can read about the mythological Neptune, alias Poseidon, in *Heroes, Gods and*

Monsters of Greek Mythology (1966) by Bernard Evslin (1922–) and in *Mythology* by Edith Hamilton (1867–1963). MR & YA

Nero Wolfe Created by *Rex Stout, Wolfe is one of the most eccentric of fictional detectives. He lives in a brownstone in New York City and hates to travel. A native of Montenegro, in the Balkans, Wolfe speaks eight languages, is a cook and a gourmet, but somewhat of a glutton, who weighs 286 pounds and drinks incredible amounts of beer. He also grows orchids. To do his legwork for him, Wolfe has Archie Goodwin, young and cocky, who serves his employer well but spars verbally with him on an even footing. Wolfe does travel in one of his best adventures, *Too Many Cooks* (1938), in which he is invited to address a meeting of the best chefs in the world. During a tasting contest, one of the chefs is murdered. Suspicion falls on another chef, from whom Wolfe had hoped to get the recipe for *saucisse minuit*. He finds the killer, and as his fee Wolfe extracts the recipe from the reluctant chef. *Nero Wolfe*, a TV movie based on *A Doorbell Rang* (1966), was made in 1977. YA

Nesbit, E(dith) (1858–1924) Growing up in Kent, southeastern England, Nesbit was a mischievous tomboy whose love of fun carried over into her writings. She became an author to help support her family, but did not turn to books for young people until the late 1890s. She is especially clever in her works of fantasy. Among them is *The Phoenix and the Carpet* (1904), about two boys and two girls and their baby brother who drop a golden egg into the fireplace and to their amazement a Phoenix emerges. In mythology the Phoenix is a bird able to turn itself to ashes and then become whole again. This Phoenix is able to grant the children their wishes, making use of a magic carpet. The same five young people appear in *Five Children and It* (1905), in which they encounter a sand-fairy, called Psammead, who is several thousand years old. He, too, can grant wishes, but those the children ask for get them in trouble, as when they want a gravel pit filled with gold coins, or when they find themselves besieged in a medieval castle. *The Railway Children* (1906) is the story of three young people who have to move to the country with their mother after their father suddenly and mysteriously leaves home. There they find amusement at the railway station, watching the trains. Finally, one day while they are at the station, their father unexpectedly comes home. *The House of Arden* (1909) is considered Nesbit's best work. In the ruins of the castle of the Arden family, Edred, who may be the new Lord Arden, and his sister, Elfrida, seek the family treasure. They meet a white mole called Mouldiwarp, who has magical powers. As a result they are transported to the past, in the early years of the 17th, 18th, and 19th centuries, where they become involved in historic events. In the end the treasure turns out to be not gold and jewels but the return of their father, who was thought to be dead. Nesbit's books have never lost their appeal to readers, and the magic of her splendid imaginings is appreciated by everyone who reads her stories. If you like Nesbit's books, try those of *Roald Dahl and Margery Sharp (1905–).

Neufeld, John (1938) Known best perhaps for his novel *Edgar Allan, Neufeld has written a number of novels, among them several successful and highly praised stories for younger readers. His novels are noted for their sensitive and moving studies of the way humans relate to one another. They include *Lisa Bright and Dark* (1969), about a 16-year-old girl whose friends try to get help for her after they realize that her parents refuse to admit their daughter is mentally ill; *Twink* (1970), about a 16-year-old girl with cerebral palsy and how her courage and love of life affect her family and friends; and *A Small Civil War* (1982), about a teenage girl whose life becomes very complicated when her little sister leads a protest against the banning of *John Steinbeck's novel *The Grapes of Wrath* from their school library and their Iowa town becomes divided over the issue of censorship. MR & YA

Never Cry Wolf (1963), by *Farley Mowat, is about the author's summer on the northern barrens, a treeless, almost uninhabited plain in northern Canada, where he studied wolves for the Canadian government. Mowat's account of his blunders in the wilderness and his education by a family of wolves makes you laugh and learn. As he watches a wolf den, he sheds his human myths about wolves one by one. He decides to learn to think like a wolf and establishes his own territory in a wolflike way. Later he learns to eat like a wolf, which puts him on a diet of mice, for which he gives the recipe. He knows he will have to prove that a wolf-sized animal can survive on a diet of small animals and is not dependent on caribou, as the government believes. Mowat's humor brings each member of his wolf "family" to full life. Mowat has written many books about the North and its people and animals, among them *Lost in the Barrens* (1956), about how two Canadian boys, a Scot and a Cree Indian, survive lost in the wild for six months. Other books about wolves you might like are *Julie of the Wolves* by *Jean Craighead George, *The Jungle Books* by *Rudyard Kipling, and *Chakka, My Wolf-Child* (1991) by Bevie J. Gravlin (n.d.). *Never Cry Wolf* was made into a movie in 1983. MR & YA

Neverland [Never-Never Land] is an imaginary island whose location is unknown. It is inhabited by the Lost Boys, who live in an underground house, the entrance to which consists of hollow tree trunks. They all sleep in one large bed and have agreed that they will all turn over at the same time during the night. Their leader is Peter Pan. On the island there is also a tribe of Red Indians whose chief is Great Big Little Panther. They are fierce warriors but are allies of the Lost Boys because the Lost Boys rescued the chief's daughter, Tiger Lily, from pirates. These pirates, led by Captain Hook, once used the island as their base. Neverland also has mermaids, who live in the lagoon and are unfriendly, as well as fairies, of whom the best known is Tinker Bell. The island is the setting for much of *Peter Pan* and it also figures in *Peter Pan in Kensington Gardens* (1906), both by *James M. Barrie.

Neville, Emily Cheney (1919–) As well as being a journalist and a lawyer, Neville is the author of a number of thought-provoking novels,

the best-known of which is *It's Like This, Cat*. Her second book, *Berries Goodman* (1965), which examines anti-Semitism, concerns Bertrand "Berries" Goodman, a fourth grader, his family, and friends. The Goodmans, not Jewish, move to a New York City suburb where they find that prejudice exists. Berries makes friends with Sidney Fine, who is Jewish, which causes resentment on the part of Sandra Graham, who had been close to Berries. She dares Sidney to jump over a culvert, whereupon he falls and is injured. Sidney's mother believes the incident is the result of prejudice. In *The Seventeenth-Street Gang* (1966) six youngsters have their own gang and resent anyone new in the neighborhood. They will not play with Hollis. When one of the gang, attempting to harm Hollis, falls into a manhole, Hollis saves her. In *Garden of Broken Glass* (1975), 13-year-old Brian Moody, a white boy with an alcoholic mother, lives in a mostly black neighborhood of St. Louis, Missouri. He is lonesome until he makes friends with several black teenagers. Together they try to improve their lives against a background of poverty and racism. If you enjoy these books, read those by Elisabet McHugh (1941–), including *Karen and Vicki, John Neufeld (1938–), and *Stephanie S. Tolan. MR

Newbery, John (1713–1767) An Englishman who published and sold books in London, Newbery was known for producing riddles, *fables, and stories. He was the earliest and best-known publisher of children's books. His name is given to the annual award that American authors of books for young readers receive for excellence. The Newbery Medal, established in 1922, is presented by the American Library Association. Newbery served as the model for the character of the bookseller in *The Vicar of Wakefield*, a classic novel about a kindly, unworldly clergyman who faces misfortune with forbearance and wisdom, written by Newbery's friend *Oliver Goldsmith.

Newman, Robert (Howard) (1909–1988) A versatile author, Newman wrote radio, television, and movie scripts as well as novels for adults and young readers. You will especially enjoy reading a trilogy set in the time of *King Ar-

The Newbery Medal

thur. The three novels are *Merlin's Mistake* (1970), *The Testing of Tertius* (1973), and *The Shattered Stone* (1975). *Merlin, the wizard, is godfather to Tertius and gives him knowledge of everything, except that Merlin by mistake grants him knowledge of the future only. When young Tertius and his friend Brian go forth to find adventure, Tertius at times has to "invent" such things as telescopes and gunpowder to save Brian and himself from danger. Later, they defend Europe from the invading Mongols, using modern military tanks and fighter planes. Newman also wrote a number of detective stories, beginning with *The Case of the Baker Street Irregulars: A Sherlock Holmes Story* (1978), which is kind of a sequel to the *Sherlock Holmes stories but with young people as the detectives. If you like Newman's books, read *A Connecticut Yankee in King Arthur's Court* by *Mark Twain, and books by *Keith Robertson and Mary Rodgers (1931–). MR & YA

Newspeak is the official language of Oceania in the novel *1984* by *George Orwell. The purposes and principles are described in great detail in an appendix to the book. Its creators invented new words, and also threw out many old words that the dictatorship thought were undesirable. An example of Newspeak is "Reporting bb dayorder doubleplusungood refs unpersons rewrite fullwise upsub antefiling." Translated into ordinary English, this would

read "The reporting of Big Brother's Order for the Day . . . is extremely unsatisfactory and makes references to nonexistent persons. Rewrite it in full and submit your draft to higher authority before filing."

Newton, Suzanne (1936–) Having grown up in North Carolina, Newton often uses her home country in her books, many of which are written for older readers. Her novels are marked both by humor and a special appreciation for the problems of young people. *M.V. Sexton Speaking* (1981) is a good example of her lightness of touch in the midst of serious matters. Sixteen-year-old Martha Venable Sexton, who has lived with her great aunt and uncle since her parents' death, takes a summer job in a bakery. Here she meets an assortment of people, some of whom she treats in a rather offhand manner, but she does learn quite a bit about the world. Eventually she is also told the story of her parents' sad lives. One of Newton's best-known stories is *I Will Call It Georgie's Blues*. She followed this with *An End to Perfect* (1984), chiefly about 12-year-old Arden and her best friend, DorJo. DorJo and an older sister live with their mother, who does not treat them well. DorJo runs away and lives at Arden's house for a time. Arden thus finds herself in the middle of family troubles but in the end helps solve them. In *A Place Between* (1986), a sequel, Arden faces the worrying problems of moving to a different town and entering a new school. Sometimes you may lose patience with Arden, but she faces up to difficulties anyone might have to deal with. If you like Newton's books, read those of *Paula Fox and LouAnn Gaeddert (1931–), including *Your Former Friend, Matthew. MR & YA

Nibelungenlied, The (Song of the Nibelungs) Written by an unknown author around the end of the 12th century, this German medieval *epic poem is based in part on the Scandinavian legends, the *Völsunga Saga* and *Edda. The action takes place at Worms, a city on the Rhine River, and at the court of Etzel, whom you may know as Attila the Hun (d. 453).

Siegfried, the youngest son of Siegmund and Sieglind, king and queen of the Netherlands, has seized a hoard of gold and jewels from the Nibelungs, a race of Scandinavian dwarfs. Siegfried goes to Worms to court Kriemhild, a beautiful woman, the sister of Gunther, a king of the Burgundians. Gunther wants to marry Brunhild, queen of Iceland, a woman of great physical strength and willpower. But she will only marry someone who can outdo her in physical feats. Siegfried, who has also stolen a cloak of invincibility from the Nibelungs, uses this to help Gunther win his bride. When she discovers she has been tricked, Brunhild determines to murder Siegfried, who has only one vulnerable spot on his body, one that was not touched when he was bathed in dragon's blood. Hagen, a retainer of the Burgundian king, gets Kriemhild, now Siegfried's wife, to reveal the spot and murders the hero. Hagen and Gunther seize the treasure hoard from Kriemhild and bury it in the Rhine in the keeping of the Rhine Maidens. Kriemhild now marries Etzel and gets her revenge for the death of Siegfried when she invites Gunther and Hagen to court and has them murdered. But she is also killed, and the treasure remains lost beneath the waters of the river. Richard Wagner (1813–1883) partly based a cycle of four operas on this saga. See also *Norse Gods and Giants* by Ingri d'Aulaire (1904–1980) and Edgar Parin d'Aulaire (1898–1986). YA

Nick Adams Stories, The (1972) This collection of stories by *Ernest Hemingway contains material from *In Our Time* (1925), his first important published book, and works from two other short-story collections. All the tales involve the character Nick Adams and many are based on episodes from Hemingway's own life, drawing on his boyhood summers in upper Michigan and his experiences during World War I. The stories have been placed in chronological order. There are also several sketches and substantial portions of stories that Hemingway never completed.

In "Indian Camp," young Nick accompanies his father, a doctor, to a shanty where an In-

Siegfried, wearing a cloak that makes him invisible, slays a dragon in *The Nibelungenlied*.

dian woman is having a difficult childbirth. The boy witnesses a makeshift operation, and also sees his first dead man. "The Killers," one of Hemingway's best-known stories, takes place in a lunchroom, where a somewhat older Nick hears two men casually planning the murder of Ole Andreson, an ex-prize fighter. Nick goes to warn Andreson, but finds him curiously unwilling to do anything to save himself. In "Big Two-Hearted River," Nick has returned from the war in Europe. He camps out in a familiar and much-loved spot by the river and gives himself to the outdoors, to solitude, and to the solemn and joyful ritual of fishing for trout. YA

Night Flight (1932) A short novel by *Antoine de Saint-Exupéry, this is an edge-of-your-seat account of the early and dangerous days of flying airplanes at night to speed the delivery of mail. Beneath this story, though, is a look into the minds and hearts of the men involved in such operations, plus an expression of lyrical and mystical feeling for the aerial world. The novel tells of one night of such flights from Patagonia, a region at the tip of South America, from Chile, and from Paraguay to Buenos Aires, Argentina, where another night flyer will take off for Europe. The central figure is Rivière, head of operations, who loves his pilots but does not want them to know it, or to love him. So, believing it will make them braver, he penalizes them whether or not they have committed a fault. In the course of this night one pilot, Fabien, flies into a fierce storm and crashes, but the plane for Europe takes off on schedule with the mail from the two other flights. You will feel the tension as you read, and you will have to decide whether Rivière's policy and methods are right or wrong. You will also enjoy the descriptions of light and dark, stars and storms. A movie was made of the book in 1933. YA

Night Swimmers, The (1980) By *Betsy Byars, this novel is a touching story of the problems of an older child, willing but unprepared to take care of her younger brothers. Eleven-year-old Retta Lynn and the brothers entertain themselves by going swimming late at night in their neighbor's pool. The children's mother is dead and their father, Shorty, is a country-western singer whose work keeps him away from home at night. Retta resents the friendship one of her brothers has with another boy. Then, when the other brother nearly drowns in the pool, Retta, who is overly conscientious, feels she is at fault. When she and her father discuss their problem, however, she realizes she must let the boys grow up in their own ways. Shorty sees that he must take better care of his family. He has a girl friend, Brendelle, who understands Retta's problem. Retta hopes Brendelle and Shorty will marry. The three children have been firm in sticking together in an unhappy situation, and Retta has been trying very hard to take on adult tasks for which she is understandably not prepared. The future now looks brighter. MR

Nightfall (1990) This *science fiction novel, the joint effort of *Isaac Asimov and *Robert Silverberg, is exciting and thought provoking. The setting is the planet Kalgash, which has six suns, at least one of which is always shining, so that night never comes. However, a mysterious society called the Apostles of the Flame claims that every 2,049 years the Darkness arrives and stars appear. An astronomer, Beenay 25, and an archeologist, Siferra 89, find evidence in their respective sciences that the society is right. An eclipse will soon occur and for a short time the planet will be dark and the sky filled with stars. When Nightfall does come, people who have never seen a star go mad, riot, kill, and set buildings afire. Civilization collapses. The Apostles, led by Folimun, are prepared because they knew the secret of past Darknesses, and they prepare to take over the government. They will restore civilization, but under totalitarian rule, at least for a time. You will find yourself trying to decide how you would behave if you had never seen stars before. *Nightfall* is based on Asimov's classic short story "Nightfall" (1941), collected in *Nightfall, and Other Stories* (1969). The stories are arranged in the chronological order of publication to show the development of Asimov's writing. Each has a brief introduction in which Asimov explains what he thinks about the story. Other stories include "What If—," about a married couple who get the chance to find out what their lives would be like if the chance happenings that brought them together had not occurred, and "The Up-to-Date Sorcerer," one of Asimov's rare humorous pieces. *Nightfall* was adapted for film in 1988. YA

Nine Tailors, The (1934) In this unusual detective novel by *Dorothy L. Sayers, church bells play as important a part as does her detective, *Lord Peter Wimsey. The setting is East Anglia, England, and the bells of the Anglican church of Fenchurch St. Paul are introduced when Wimsey takes refuge in the village after his car breaks down. It is New Year's Eve, and a night of change-ringing is about to begin. In change-ringing, a group of ringers perform a continuous peal, that is, they ring a set of bells tuned to the ordinary major scale. The bells are rung in a strict order, and each is swung full circle so that its clapper will sound it loudly in that harsh complex of tones that distinguishes a great bell. In the story the men are about to ring what is called 15,840 "Kent Treble Bob Majors," which will take all night. When one of the ringers becomes ill, Wimsey reveals another of his diverse talents by volunteering to take his place.

The following spring, when the body of a murdered man turns up in the churchyard, the rector asks Wimsey to help solve the crime. Wimsey finds himself involved with missing emeralds, more bodies, a cryptogram, and some difficult personal relationships. The bells turn out to have played a vital and horrible role in one of the deaths. YA

1984 (1949), by *George Orwell, takes place in the world of the future, where people and resources are being destroyed in a continuing war between dictators. Winston Smith lives in the bleak, rotting remains of London, where only public buildings and the homes of Inner Party members are pleasant. There are no luxuries, everything is rationed, all books have been outlawed, and citizens are killed for saying or doing anything against the ruling Party. Each living space has a large television screen that can see and hear what happens, and cannot be turned off. Winston works in the Ministry of Truth, where he changes newspaper copy to conform to the orders of *Big Brother, the Party leader. By chance he finds a small shop where Mr. Charrington rents a bedroom furnished in the old style, without a watching telescreen. When Winston falls in love with Julia, they must meet in secret at Charrington's because the Party disapproves of physical attraction between people. Winston and Julia's hope for the future blooms for a short time when O'Brien, a co-worker, persuades Winston to reveal his true feelings and join an underground group. O'Brien betrays the lovers, how-

ever, and both are arrested and taken to prison. In a nightmare that lasts for months, Winston is beaten, tortured, questioned repeatedly, and told he must learn to love Big Brother. Finally he gives up, even renouncing his love for Julia, and is allowed to go home, completely brainwashed. Movies of *1984* were made in 1956 and 1984. YA

Niven, Larry [Laurence Van Cott Niven] (1938–) The author of numerous *science fiction novels and short stories, Niven specializes in plots involving futuristic technologies and science. His best-known novel is *Ringworld*. In *A World Out of Time* (1976) the hero, who was frozen after his death in 1970, is revived in 2190. He becomes a starship pilot and flies to worlds light-years away. *The Integral Trees* (1983) is the story of a starship and its crew on a mission to discover new worlds that humans can colonize. The ship finds a very large doughnut-shaped envelope of gas around a neutron star. Rather oddly, part of it is suitable for habitation by humans, and the crew abandons the starship to live there. *Limits* (1985) is a collection of Niven's short stories, three of them with co-authors. They are about strange worlds, strange beings, and even a magician whose steed is a unicorn with its horn removed. Niven's books have a variety of odd characters and exciting situations. If you like these books, read those of *Isaac Azimov, *Ray Bradbury, and *Robert Silverberg. YA

Nixon, Joan Lowery (1927–) At first a writer of articles and short stories for adults, Nixon turned to novels for young readers at her children's insistence. *The Secret Box Mystery* (1974) is about an odd box that hisses and gurgles, which is submitted by Michael John for a school science project. In *The Kidnapping of Christina Lattimore* (1979), the kidnappers of a young journalist claim she was their accomplice. In *A Deadly Game of Magic* (1988), Liza and some friends find themselves in a scary deserted house during a raging storm. The house was inhabited by a stage magician who left behind gadgets he used in his tricks. Liza finds she needs them to stay alive. Nixon has also written books dealing, in a humorous way, with personal problems and relationships. Among them is *Maggie, Too* (1985), about 12-year-old Margaret, who is hurt by being shuttled around from her father to her grandmother but who finds her own identity as well as a place in the family. Another is *Beats Me, Claude* (1986) about a couple living in Texas who find there is a situation in which an apple pie helps capture criminals. Nixon is also the author of the Orphan Train Quartet, four novels about young people separated from their parents by poverty or death, who are sent to live with families in Kansas and Nebraska in the 1850s and 1860s. The novels are *A Family Apart* (1987), *Caught in the Act* (1988), *In the Face of Danger* (1988), and *A Place to Belong* (1990). If you enjoy Nixon's books, read those by *Paula Fox, *Robert Newman, and *Keith Robertson. MR

Nobel, Alfred Bernard (1833–1896) A Swedish chemist who developed modern explosives, Nobel set up a fund to award annual prizes to scientists who made important discoveries in physics, chemistry, physiology, and medicine. He established other awards—for example, the Nobel Peace Prize for the person promoting goodwill in the fraternity of nations; and the Nobel Prize for literature for "the person who shall have produced in the field of literature the most outstanding work of an idealistic tendency." The awards have been given since 1901. A prize for economists was first awarded in 1969. Winners are selected by committees in Stockholm, Sweden, and Oslo, Norway. American authors who have won the prize are *Sinclair Lewis, *Eugene O'Neill, *Pearl S. Buck, *William Faulkner, *Ernest Hemingway, and *John Steinbeck. Naturalized American winners are *Isaac B. Singer, *Czelaw Milosz, and *Joseph Brodsky. *Saul Bellow, Canadian-born but raised, educated, and living in the United States, is also a winner.

Nonsense, Book of See *The Complete Nonsense Book.*

Nordhoff, Charles Bernard (1887–1947) Known best for his historical novels written in collaboration with *James Norman Hall, Nordhoff began his literary career during World War I. He sent letters about his experiences as a pilot in the Lafayette Flying Corps back home, where they were published by the *Atlantic* magazine. In France Nordhoff met Hall, and the two became friends and collaborators. Their first work was the history of *The Lafayette Flying Corps* (1920). After the war they settled on the island of Tahiti, where they produced their best-known works, *Mutiny on the Bounty, Men Against the Sea* (1933), and *Pitcairn's Island* (1934). Though the two men worked together closely during the Tahiti years, Nordhoff contributed less and less to the writing team after 1941, when he moved to California. A victim of alcohol and depression, he killed himself in 1947. YA

Norse Gods and Giants (1967) An almost magical book in its effect on both the eye and the mind, this volume is a retelling of myths based on the Norse saga, the *Edda.* It is a stirring account of the old Norse gods, their fights, their loves, and their fun. Colorfully illustrated, it is the joint work of Ingri d'Aulaire (1904–1980) and Edgar Parin d'Aulaire (1898–1986), a husband-and-wife team. The first part of the book tells you how the world and human beings were created by the first gods and giants. *Odin, the chief Norse god, carries a magic spear, Gungmir, that never misses. His son, Thor, is the strongest of the gods and is very upset when his great hammer is stolen. Frigg is Odin's wife, the highest in rank of the goddesses, and she is always spinning yarn. Of Freya, another goddess, it is said that the Milky Way is her necklace. Skrymir, one of the giants in these tales, is so big the gods mistake one of his mittens for a cabin. As you read *Norse Gods and Giants,* you will escape to another world. See also *Valhalla and *Valkyrie. MR

North, Sterling (1906–1974) A prolific and versatile author and editor, North is remembered largely for his books in which nature is the central subject, as in his best-known novel, *Rascal*, about a pet raccoon. Showing his great affection for these creatures, he followed this with *Raccoons Are the Brightest People* (1966). In *The Wolfling*, North once more shows his love of rural life and animals. An earlier book, *So Dear to My Heart* (1947), set in rural Indiana in 1903, has as its main figures a boy, Jeremiah, and a black sheep, Danny, that he raises and nearly loses by drowning before Danny wins a special award at the Pike County fair. Besides these novels, North has written a number of biographies for young readers. Among them are *George Washington, Frontier Colonel* (1957), about the early military career of the first president, and *Thoreau of Walden Pond* (1959), which is as much about nature as it is about *Henry David Thoreau, the naturalist and essayist. A movie was made of *So Dear to My Heart* in 1948. If you enjoy North's books, read those of *Richard Adams, *Eric Knight, and *Marjorie Kinnan Rawlings. MR & YA

North by Night (1962), by *Peter Burchard, is a novel of the Civil War based on the true experiences of Captain V.B. Chamberlain of the Seventh Connecticut Volunteer Infantry. It begins on St. Helena Island, off the coast of South Carolina, where the Union troops are preparing to attack a nearby Confederate fort. Lieutenant Timothy Bradford, his friend Red Kelly, and other Yankee soldiers are taken prisoner during the battle, and later travel under guard to Richmond Jail in Columbia, South Carolina. Though life is difficult in prison, Tim and Red survive reasonably well under the orderly rule of Captain Senn. Five months later the two friends succeed in escaping. On their trek north, where they hope to rejoin the Union forces, they never know whether the people they meet will shoot them or offer help. Crossing a field in daylight, they are caught by two armed Southerners, who take them to a fine farmhouse. Tim and Red are treated very courteously by a compassionate gentleman, but they will be returned to prison the next day. Escaping again, Tim and Red succeed in reaching the railroad and continue toward freedom. A young mountain woman helps them at the cost of her life, and finally Tim and Red stumble on a group of Union soldiers looking for a tree to cut for Christmas. You might be interested also in *Andersonville*, by *MacKinlay Kantor, an account of the appalling conditions during the American Civil War in Andersonville Prison, where many Union soldiers starved and died. YA

North to Freedom (1965) Originally written in Danish by (Else) Anne (Lise) Holm (1922–), this unusual novel tells the story of a 12-year-old boy, David, who remembers nothing except life in a concentration camp. When a guard unexpectedly helps him escape, David is alone in a world about which he knows nothing—neither who he is nor where he came from. He is told to walk south to a seaport, to hide on a boat to Italy, and go north to reach Denmark, to him an unknown land. His real adventures begin in Italy as he continues to walk, gets rides with motorists, and one way and another earns money to stay alive. One day he rescues a girl from a burning shed, and her well-to-do family invites him to stay as long as he likes. David learns to play, and is delighted to find books so he can try to read, but he overhears the mother say she wants him gone because he seems so strange. David leaves quietly and continues his journey. In Switzerland he meets a Danish artist, Sophie Hartmann, who shows him a picture of a friend, Edith Hjort Fengel and her family, whose husband and son, David, were believed to have died in a concentration camp. David sees a likeness in the man in the photograph to Johannes, who had been kind to him in camp. David goes on his way, being captured and forced to work by a brutal farmer, barely escaping concentration camp guards in Germany. Finally he reaches Copenhagen, Denmark. He looks up the Fengel name in a telephone directory, finds the house, and, yes, the woman is his mother. It may be difficult to believe that a small boy could have made such a journey, but you cannot help but admire his courage and resolve and to follow with excitement his adventures. It makes you realize how terrible it would be to have spent all your early years entirely cut off from the outside world, as David was. Holm is a Danish journalist who has written a number of other books for young readers. MR & YA

Norton, Andre (Alice) (Alice Mary Norton) (1912–) A librarian, bookseller, and author, Norton has written a large number of novels for young readers, most of them *fantasy and *science fiction. There is a great deal of futuristic technology, adventures on strange worlds, and magic, but Norton shows a particular interest in animals that have mutated. In *The Beast Master* (1959) and *Catseye* (1984), such creatures can communicate telepathically with humans. Human beings are for a time turned into animals in *Steel Magic* (1965), about entering the world of *King Arthur's time, and *Fur Magic* (1968), which tells about a voyage into the mythological world of the American Indian. Parallel worlds and questions of identity are other themes used by Norton, as in *Android at Arms* (1971) and *Knave of Dreams* (1975). Andras, in the former, battles to regain his realm, but he is not sure whether he is himself or an android. Kimble, in the latter, dreams of a strange world, then wakes up to find he is there, inhabiting the body of a young prince. Norton offers a great variety of settings, adventures, and odd characters, and the action is always lively. If you like her novels, read those of *Helen M. Hoover, *Robert O'Brien, and *John Rowe Townsend. MR

Norton, Mary (1903–1992) An English author of books for young readers, she grew up in a house very like the one in her novel *The Borrowers*. Norton's first love was the theater, and she was an actress with the Old Vic Theatre Company in London during the 1920s. She began writing, partly for her four children, during World War II. Her books are composed with great attention to detail and abound in skillful and humorous characterizations that have been compared to those of *Charles Dickens and *Jonathan Swift. Norton's first success came with the publication of *Bed-knob and Broomstick* (1957), about an elderly spinster who uses her newfound magical power to transport three children and herself to a tropical island. Together with a number of sequels in *The Borrowers*, Norton is also the author of *Are All the Giants Dead?* (1975), an amusing novel about a group of retired fairy-tale heroes and heroines. A *Walt Disney film was made of *Bed-knob and Broomstick* in 1971. MR

nose Since the nose sits in the middle of the face, it is always visible, even if it is a "snub nose." In addition to snub nose, which means short and turned up at the tip, there is its opposite, the aristocratic "Roman nose," which is prominent and rides high between the eyes. One of the famous noses you know is *Pinocchio's, which grows longer each time he tells a lie. You also may have read that witches, evil stepmothers, and villains in other tales always seem to be breathing through large, bulbous, or hooked noses, like the Wicked Witch of the East in *The Wonderful Wizard of Oz*. But many prominent noses are likable, especially if they are red, like the ones belonging to Rudolph the Red-Nosed Reindeer and jolly Santa Claus. You might check the early Renaissance period of your library's Art History section if you would like to have a look at the large red nose belonging to the old man in the famous painting *The Old Man and His Grandson* (c.1480) by the Florentine painter Domenico Ghirlandaio (1449–1494). French playwright Edmund Rostand (1868–1918) created the 17th-century character Cyrano, duelist and soldier, in a romantic drama, *Cyrano de Bergerac*, which is centered on his embarrassingly large nose.

A good newspaper reporter "has a nose for news," and a gossip is "nosey." A racehorse can thrill a crowd when it pulls out in front of the rest and "wins by a nose." Drug users on today's street corners mask the harm of the narcotics they sniff when they call it "nose candy." A policeman meeting a boy or girl he thinks is heading for trouble may say, "Keep your nose clean." It means, "Be good!"

Nöstlinger, Christine (1936–) Born in Vienna, Austria, Nöstlinger is a journalist and author of more than 30 novels for young readers, some of which have been published in English. *Fly Away Home* (1975), a largely autobiographical novel, tells of 8-year-old Christel Goth's frightening experiences when the Russian army occupies Vienna in 1945 during World War II. Christel's family has been bombed out of their apartment, and they loot and steal to stay alive. She observes how different people behave in different ways under such stress, and she herself is a changed person. *Girl Missing* (1976) is a novel about an unhappy family. The mother, Lotte, is domineering, and 14-year-old Ilse is beautiful but given to lying. When Ilse runs away, Erika, her 12-year-old sister, enlists help to track her down. The experience, with its revelation of the true character of a number of people, leaves Erika resolved to avoid both deception and self-deception. A different kind of story is *Konrad* (1977), a satirical and humorous combination of *fantasy and *science fiction in which a boy, produced in a factory, is delivered by mistake to the wrong parents. If you like Nöstlinger's books, read those of *James Forman, *Paula Fox, and *Hans Peter Richter. MR & YA

Now We Are Six (1927) This short book of verse by *A.A. Milne is in the same carefree style that delights readers of his stories *Winnie-the-Pooh* and *The House at Pooh Corner*, and of *When We Were Very Young*, another collection of verse. The poems range from thoughts on being alone to thoughts on being busy; from the story of "The Knight Whose Armor Didn't Squeak," to "King Hilary and the Beggarman." "King John's Christmas" begins:

> King John was not a good man—
>   He had his little ways.
> And sometimes no one spoke to him
>   For days and days and days.

These poems are all easy to read, and the language has a lilt and playfulness to it that will give you much pleasure. MR

Number the Stars (1989) By *Lois Lowry, this novel is set in Denmark in 1943, during its occupation by the Nazis in World War II. Ten-year-old Annemarie Johansen's best friend, Ellen Rosen, is Jewish, and when it becomes known that the Nazis plan to arrest all the Jews in Denmark and take them away, the Johansen family help Ellen and her family escape by sea to neutral Sweden. Annemarie and her family risk their own lives to save those of their neighbors and friends. Within a few weeks, the Danes smuggle nearly all of Denmark's Jews, some 7,000 people, to safety. Two years later, when the church bells of Copenhagen announce the end of the war, Annemarie and her family look forward to welcoming their old neighbors back home. If you enjoyed *Number the Stars*, you will probably also like *The Silver Sword* by *Ian Serraillier, about the long and dangerous journey of three Polish children to find their parents during World War II. *Number the Stars* won the *Newbery Medal in 1990. MR

MR = Middle Reader   YA = Young Adult Reader   * = See this main entry

Oates, Joyce Carol (1938–) A major contemporary writer whose works include novels, short stories, verse, plays, and essays, Oates grew up in upstate New York, near rural Millertown. This area became "Eden County" in some of her writings. Her early education began in a one-room schoolhouse, and after graduation from college she stayed in the academic world as a university professor. Some of her novels are set in and around campuses, with their jealousies, scandals, and politics. These include *Unholy Loves* (1979), *Solstice* (1985), and *Marya: A Life* (1986), which is somewhat autobiographical.

Her fiction is filled with violent, frustrated characters who eventually find escape through madness or death. You can trace contemporary American life through her realistic novels. *A Garden of Earthly Delights* (1967) and *Expensive People* (1968) tell about rural and suburban problems. Detroit, where Oates lived, is a setting for city violence in *them* (1969), which describes the race riots of the sixties. *Do with Me What You Will* (1973) deals with issues that inspired the women's movement. *The Assassins* (1975) deals with a former state senator whose stubbornness leads to a kind of assassination. *Because It Is Bitter, and Because It Is My Heart* (1990) is a story about two families, one black and one white, set in the 1950s and 1960s.

Oates sometimes reshapes the themes and styles of other writers. *Wonderland* (1971) is about a boy who retreats and eventually escapes a kind of nightmare. You might be interested in comparing it with *Lewis Carroll's *Alice's Adventures in Wonderland*, from which it takes form and images. Combining fantasy and reality, a writing style called American Gothic, she traces six generations of one family in *Bellefleur* (1980). *A Bloodsmoor Romance* (1982) has fainting virgins and ghosts, and *Mysteries of Winterthurn* (1984) is a detective story about three bizarre cases. Both mingle myth and history with demons and the unconscious mind. YA

Oberon first appears as a character in medieval French legend as the son of Julius Caesar (100–44 B.C.) and *Morgan le Fay. He is also possibly descended from Alberich, king of the elves in Germanic legend. Oberon is only three feet tall, with an angelic face. The fairies gave him the power to look into people's thoughts and the ability to go anywhere instantly. The Oberon known best was created by *William Shakespeare, who may have read about him in *James IV* (1598), a play about Scottish history by Robert Greene (1558–1592). In Shakespeare's *A Midsummer Night's Dream*, Oberon is king of the fairies and husband of Titania. Because Oberon has quarreled with his queen, he contrives magic spells to cause Titania to fall in love with a comic weaver, Bottom. His magic also complicates, mixes up, and then unscrambles the four young human lovers in the play. You can meet Oberon as the hero in the opera *Oberon* (1826) by Carl Maria von Weber (1786–1826). YA

O'Brien, Robert [Robert Leslie Conly] (1918–1973) An author and editor born and educated in New York City, O'Brien began creating imaginary characters at an early age, but did not write children's stories until much later. Meanwhile he worked at an advertising agency, and on newspapers and magazines. O'Brien deals with important moral themes and inventive characters, but summed up his writing style, which has earned him many awards, this way: "Children . . . like a beginning, middle and an end: a problem, an attempt to solve it, and at the end a success or failure." His first book for younger readers was *The Silver Crown* (1968), a fantasy about a 10-year-old girl who is hunted by strange people in green masks who seem to want the silver crown she has found. Other books are *Z for Zachariah* and *Mrs. Frisby and the Rats of NIMH*, his most popular book. A novel for older readers is *A Report from Group 17* (1972), about political intrigue set in Washington, D.C., during the Cold War. MR & YA

O'Brien, Tim (1946–) A Vietnam War veteran, O'Brien wrote one of the finest novels about Vietnam, *Going After Cacciato* (1978), in which an American soldier just walks away from the war. In *If I Die in a Combat Zone* (1973), he describes the foot soldier's painful daily life of being wet in rice paddies and frightened while lying in shallow holes. *Northern Lights* (1974) is about two brothers competing in an endurance test in the North woods and learning that macho ideas can trap men, just as wars do. In *The Things They Carried* (1990), O'Brien relates a series of stories about the Vietnam War and its victims. In this book he also tells you how he creates stories. If you like these war stories, read *The Red Badge of Courage,* by *Stephen Crane. It also concentrates on the trials of ordinary soldiers, this time during the Civil War. YA

O'Casey, Sean (1884–1964) From the Dublin slums—where this Irish dramatist, autobiographer, and poet grew up in a Protestant family—to the Irish national uprisings, the themes of O'Casey's plays reflect the harsh life of Ireland after World War I. He lost his father as an infant, was self-taught, and worked as a laborer when he was 18 years old. He became a member of the Irish Citizen Army, was an organizer of the Irish Transport and General Workers Union strike in 1913, and was active in the Sinn Fein movement and in the Easter Rebellion of 1916. O'Casey's first play, produced at Dublin's Abbey Theatre, is *The Shadow of a Gunman* (1923), which shows the violence of Dublin's slums. *Juno and the Paycock* (1924) contrasts vulgar braggarts with Irish women who suffer and endure. *The Plough and the Stars* (1926), set in the Dublin tenements, caused riots at its opening, and O'Casey moved to England. It deals with the impact of the 1916 Irish Easter Rebellion on country folk. These powerful plays, which elevated his reputation as one of the greatest Irish dramatists, are written in a realistic style, reflecting *irony and humor, misery and violence, and strong characters. In 1928 *William Butler Yeats started a feud when he helped block a performance of O'Casey's antiwar play *The Silver Tassie* (1928). O'Casey's later experimental plays, in a more poetic form and with continued liberal politics, were not well received. You may like to compare O'Casey's plays with the less political but equally Irish plays of *John Millington Synge. *Juno and the Paycock* was filmed in 1930 and *The Plough and the Stars* in 1936. YA

O'Connor, Flannery (1925–1964) Growing up as a parochial school student in Georgia, this novelist and short-story writer listed her chief hobby in her high school yearbook as "collecting rejection slips." Her writing deals with the lives of simple, often self-centered, country people in the South, and is masterful in expressing their words and feelings. In the tradition of *William Faulkner, O'Connor's characters and situations are often extreme or distorted. Her first book, *Wise Blood* (1952), which she describes as a comic novel, is about an obsessed preacher of The Church Without Christ. In her first book of short stories, *A Good Man Is Hard to Find* (1955), the title story is about a family of six which, while driving to Florida, is wiped out by an escaped convict. *The Violent Bear It Away* (1959), a novel set in Georgia's backwoods, tells a macabre tale about fanatics and their destiny. The title story of *Everything That Rises Must Converge* (1965) shows the struggle between children and their parents. Other Southern women writers whose works you may enjoy are *Carson McCullers and *Eudora Welty. A film was made of *Wise Blood* in 1979. YA

O'Connor, Frank [Michael O'Donovan] (1903–1966) This Irish writer and critic was born to a poor Cork family and was largely self-educated. He began writing at an early age, mostly in Gaelic. His activity in the Irish republican movement led to a brief imprisonment in 1923, and he used that time, and also a stint as a librarian, to fill in his education. As director of the Abbey Theatre in Dublin, he worked closely with the poet *William Butler Yeats. He eventually resigned from the Abbey on a censorship issue and lived in America for most of his later years, marrying an American. His first book of short stories was *Guests of the Nation* (1931), followed by such collections as *The Saint and Mary Kate* (1932), *Dutch Interior* (1939), and *Crab Apple Jelly* (1944). All have Irish backgrounds and settings and are well crafted, with sensitivity to Irish speech. Besides his short stories, O'Connor also published verse, translations from the Irish, books about Ireland, and two books of criticism, *The Mirror in the Roadway* (1957), about the novel; and *The Lonely Voice* (1963), about the short story, a form he called "the literature of submerged population groups." His autobiographies are *An Only Child* (1961) and *My Father's*

Son (1968). If you enjoy O'Connor's books, read *Dubliners*, a classic collection of short stories by *James Joyce. YA

Octavia is the name of two women who lived during the period of the Roman Empire and never met, though they were related by marriage. The first (d. 11 B.C.) was the sister of Augustus (63 B.C.–A.D. 14) and the grandniece of Julius Caesar (100–44 B.C.), and was married to Gaius Marcellus (d. 41 B.C.). In 40 B.C., she married Marc Antony (83?–30 B.C.) in a state ceremony at Rome, and they went to live in Athens. While with her, Antony put aside politics and war to study philosophy. But though Octavia was a good and gentle woman, it was a political marriage, and he abandoned her when he became infatuated with Cleopatra (c.69–30 B.C.). Octavia reared her own children and the children of Antony and Cleopatra after the couple died. Emperors Caligula (A.D. 12–41), Claudius (10 B.C.–A.D. 54), and Nero (A.D. 37–68) were her descendents. This Octavia is a character in *William Shakespeare's play *Antony and Cleopatra, and in John Dryden's (1631–1700) finest play, *All for Love* (1678).

The younger Octavia (A.D. c.42–62) was a daughter of the Roman emperor Claudius I by his third wife, Messalina. She married Nero, Claudius's stepson by his fourth wife. Though Octavia endured Nero's many bad deeds with quiet dignity, and was liked by the people, he favored his mistress, Poppaea, after becoming emperor. Nero divorced Octavia for supposed sterility, then falsely charged her with adultery, banished her, and eventually ordered her beheaded. In *I, Claudius* (1934), the historical novel by *Robert Graves, you can read about both Octavias. YA

ode means choric song in Greek. Three-stanza choral odes, usually accompanied by a dance, were a part of ancient Greek drama. The Greek poet *Pindar wrote odes to celebrate the victors of the original Olympic Games. The Roman poet Horace (65–6 B.C.) wrote more personal odes in Latin. Odes were also popular in the pre-Islamic Arabic world, 10th-century Persia, and 14th-century India. The ode form was revised during the European Renaissance, and this modern ode is usually a rhymed or unrhymed lyric poem addressed to someone or something. It is often characterized by lofty feeling and public proclamation, but sometimes it is simple and deals with private meditation. The English Romantic poets wrote many famous modern odes. *John Keats's "Ode on a Grecian Urn" (1819) is about the fleeting nature of love and happiness, inspired by looking at an ancient urn painted with youthful, playful figures. It ends with the famous lines "Beauty is truth, truth beauty,—that is all ye know on earth, and all ye need to know." Closer to home, the American poet Allen Tate (1899–1979) wrote the well-known "Ode to the Confederate Dead" (1926), which deals with the American Civil War. YA

O'Dell, Scott (1898–1989) The author of the popular novels *Island of the Blue Dolphins and *Sarah Bishop, O'Dell was born and raised around Los Angeles when it was still frontier country. He was named after his distant relative, the Scottish novelist *Walter Scott. As a boy O'Dell lived on San Pedro Island, off the coast of California, and in a gold-mining town near the Mexican border; later he adapted many of his childhood memories into settings and themes for his books. O'Dell was a cameraman, journalist, rancher, and writer for adults, but, as he put it, "Writing for children is more fun . . . and more rewarding." He set most of his 26 books in interesting historical places with true situations, with a young narrator—usually a girl. In *Sing Down the Moon, the young Navajo girl Bright Morning tells a story of a forced march. In *Streams to the River, River to the Sea* (1986), a Shoshone girl gives her account of the Lewis and Clark expedition. Other novels include *The King's Fifth* (1966), one of O'Dell's best books, set in the Southwest canyon country and about a 16th-century Spanish search for gold in the Southwest. *The Black Pearl* (1967), set in southern California and about a young pearl diver who finds a giant pearl of great value, was made into a movie in 1976. If you enjoy O'Dell's books, other authors whose books you may like are *James Lincoln Collier and *Christopher Collier, *Jean Craighead George, and *Elizabeth George Speare. MR & YA

Odets, Clifford (1906–1963) A playwright, scriptwriter, and director, Odets was born in Philadelphia but grew up in the Bronx, a section of New York City. He worked as an actor when he was 15 years old and joined the Group Theatre, where actors were trained and plays developed to change a society deep in the *Great Depression. Odets's first play, the one-act *Waiting for Lefty* (1935), about a taxi strike, and *Awake and Sing!* (1935), about a "new world," were both successes and established his reputation as a playwright disillusioned with middle-class reality and lost ideals. His greatest commercial success was *Golden Boy* (1937), about a violinist whose desire for wealth and fame leads him to become a boxer. His film scripts include *Humoresque* (1946), about a violinist's involvement with his patroness, and *The Sweet Smell of Success* (1957), about a ruthless columnist and a sleazy press agent. In 1952, Odets appeared before the House of Representatives Committee on Un-American Activities because he and others in the Group Theatre briefly had been members of the Communist Party. See also *McCarthyism. Other modern playwrights whose works you may enjoy are *Edward Albee, *James Agee, and *Arthur Miller. Odets's play *The Country Girl* (1950), about an alcoholic actor's marriage, was produced as a film in 1954. *The Big Knife* (1948), about life in Hollywood, was produced as a film in 1955. *Golden Boy* was made into a musical comedy in 1964. YA

Odin [also known as Woden and Wotan] is the chief Viking god, successor to Thor in the Norse pantheon. He is god of wisdom, poetry, agriculture, and the dead. He has over 100 nicknames, related to his different capacities, including Allfather, because he was considered the father of all gods and human beings. "The promise of Odin" is the most binding of all oaths to a Norseman. Odin becomes all-seeing and wise by clever strategies, such as hanging in trees, drinking from a well of wisdom—and

The Norse god Odin, holding his spear, Gungnir, is flanked by his ravens and wolves.

losing an eye in payment — and sending his two ravens into the world each morning to bring him news before breakfast. His principal disguise is as an old bent-over man with a slouchy hat. Among his many magical possessions are his eight-legged stallion, Sleipnir; his magic spear, Gungnir; and his gold ring, Draupnir. Odin knows that once his son Balder dies, the forces of evil will overcome the gods; even so, he tries to postpone this by chaining the forces and throwing them into the sea and the underworld. When the giants and the dead of the underworld fight the gods, Odin knows that he will be devoured by the wolf Fenrir. To avenge his father's death, his other son, Vidar, kills the beast by ripping its jaws apart. Fires burn up the gods and heaven, but eventually a new heaven and earth arise, peopled by two humans who have survived by hiding in the woods. You can find parallels of this resurrection in the Egyptian myth of the Phoenix bird rising from the ashes and in the *Revelation of St. John in the New Testament of the *Bible. You can read about Odin in *Bulfinch's Mythology by Thomas Bulfinch (1796–1867), Legends of the North (1951) by Olivia E. Coolidge (1908–), and The Norse Myths (1980) by Kevin Crossley-Holland (1941–). MR & YA

Odysseus (in Rome known as Ulysses) is perhaps the most famous hero of ancient myth and literature. He is believed to have been known even before the time of *Homer. Odysseus was the son of Anticlea and of King Laertes of Ithaca, husband of Penelope, and father of Telemachus. Greek dramatists focused on his many different traits, especially as hero of the *Trojan War, and as a 10-year traveler back to Ithaca. This makes his character interesting in a variety of situations. In the *epic poems the *Iliad and the *Odyssey, though Odysseus is boastful and deceitful, he is also creative, wise, and courageous. *Sophocles wrote about his resourcefulness and sense of justice, and *Euripedes wrote about his brutality and shrewdness. The Roman writers Horace (65–8 B.C.), *Virgil, and Seneca (c.4 B.C.–A.D. 65) depicted him as cold and treacherous. Odysseus had courted the beautiful *Helen, whose "face launched a thousand ships," because of the many suitors obligated to rescue her from Troy, where she had been taken by Paris. During the Trojan War, Odysseus was credited with coming up with the idea of the huge wooden horse in which the Greek warriors hid before it was dragged into the walled city of Troy. He was the first to leap out and led the mission to recapture Helen. You can read about Odysseus in *Bulfinch's Mythology by Thomas Bulfinch (1796–1867) and in *Mythology by Edith Hamilton (1867–1963). See also *Ulysses by *James Joyce. MR & YA

Odyssey (c.8th century B.C.) The ancient Greek poet *Homer is traditionally thought to have written this *epic poem of about 12,000 lines that tells of the 10-year homeward journey of the Greek hero *Odysseus following the fall of Troy. Odysseus had aroused the wrath of the god Poseidon (see also *Neptune), who has blocked his way home and led him to many fantastic and dangerous adventures and places. Meanwhile, royal suitors invaded his home in Ithaca, squandered his wealth, mistreated his son, Telemachus, and tried to force his wife, Penelope, to marry one of them. Finally, the god *Zeus intervenes on behalf of Odysseus. *Athena goes to Ithaca to inform Telemachus that Odysseus is alive, and Telemachus sets out to find his father. Odysseus returns to Ithaca, as does Telemachus, and father and son

Odysseus and his crew escape from the one-eyed giant Polyphemus, whom Odysseus has blinded.

are reunited in the cottage of Odysseus' faithful servant Eumaeus. Odysseus returns to his house disguised as a beggar, and with Telemachus's help he slays the suitors and is reunited with his faithful and loving wife.

Like Homer's *Iliad*, the *Odyssey* is considered one of the finest works of ancient Greek literature. Many good translations are available, including those by Robert Fitzgerald (1910–1985) and Richmond Lattimore (1906–1984). A retelling for younger readers is *The Odyssey of Homer* (1968) by Henry I. Christ (1915–). *James Joyce, in his masterpiece, *Ulysses*, based each chapter of his story on an episode in the *Odyssey*, and his main characters are modern versions of Odysseus, Penelope, and Telemachus. A contemporary continuation of the *Odyssey* is *The Odyssey: A Modern Sequel* (1938), an epic poem by *Nikos Kazantzakis. It picks up Odysseus' tale soon after he slays Penelope's suitors. MR & YA

Oedipus is a tragic hero of Greek myth, the son of King Laius and Queen Jocasta of Thebes. An oracle had told Laius that his son would kill him, so the king pierces Oedipus's ankles (Oedipus means "swell-foot"), and abandons him on a mountain. A herdsman takes Oedipus to Corinth, where the childless king and queen raise him. When Oedipus goes to Delphi

to ask *Apollo who his parents are, he is told the startling news that he will kill his father and marry his mother. With dramatic *irony, he mistakenly assumes that Apollo means the king and queen of Corinth, and so he leaves home. Oedipus kills a man who tries to force him off the road, not realizing that he has killed his father, Laius. When he goes to Thebes to solve a riddle and rids the city of the Sphinx, the grateful people make him king. As Apollo had predicted, Oedipus unknowingly marries his widowed mother, and they have four children.

Plague comes to Thebes, and the Delphic oracle says the plague has come because the killer of Laius is in the area. The killer, of course, is Oedipus. Jocasta then hangs herself, and Oedipus blinds himself for his patricide and incest. Banished from Thebes, and accompanied by his daughter, Antigone, he travels to Colonus, where he dies and is buried. The story has inspired many dramas, including *Sophocles' *Oedipus Rex*, with its great choral *odes and tightly woven plot, and *Oedipus at Colonus*, which Sophocles wrote when he was 90 years old. Other adaptations include a tragedy by Seneca (c.4 B.C.–A.D. 65), *Oedipus Tyrannus*, and the opera-oratorio *Oedipus Rex* (1927), by the French writer Jean Cocteau (1889–1963), with music by Igor Stravinsky (1882–1971). The

MR = Middle Reader   YA = Young Adult Reader   * = See this main entry

myth also inspired the psychological term "Oedipus complex," referring to a male child's unconscious desire for his mother and hostility toward his father. Film adaptations of Sophocles' *Oedipus Rex* were made in 1957, 1967, and 1968. YA

Of Human Bondage (1915), the finest novel by *W. Somerset Maugham, tells the semi-autobiographical story of Philip Carey, a sensitive young Englishman born with a clubfoot. In a naturalistic style, Maugham describes Philip's attempt to find a better life. An orphan, he is raised in England in a puritanical environment by his loving Aunt Louisa and narrow-minded Uncle William. He reads avidly and goes to Europe to learn about medicine, art, and philosophy. Carey's relationships are confusing: Those he loves do not return his feelings, while those who love him do not feel his love for them. He has a painful infatuation with Mildred Rogers, an unattractive, self-seeking waitress. Finally convinced that life has no meaning, he marries Sally Athelney, the warm-hearted sister of an eccentric friend, gives up his major ambitions, and becomes a country doctor.

The "bondage" of the title refers to the bonds that love, society, and morality place on people. Carey learns to become content with marriage, children, and the simple patterns of life. You might be interested in reading another popular book by Maugham, *The Moon and Sixpence* (1919), which was inspired in part by the single-minded life of the French painter Paul Gauguin (1848–1903). *Of Human Bondage* was made into a movie three times: in 1934, 1946, and 1964. YA

Of Time and the River (1935) This semi-autobiographical novel by *Thomas Wolfe continues the account of the worldly, artistic, and spiritual journey of Eugene Gant, who was introduced in an earlier work, *Look Homeward, Angel.* The novel begins with Gant leaving his North Carolina home and taking a train north to attend Harvard. During the trip he is filled with memories of his favorite brother, Ben, whose premature death from pneumonia still deeply affects him. Gant also thinks of his estranged father, Oliver, an idealistic, alcoholic monument salesman, and his mother, Eliza, who runs a boardinghouse and speculates in real estate. At Harvard, Gant is involved with a variety of people, including his uncle, Bascom Pentland, and the affected Francis Starwick. Later he achieves some success at writing and becomes a college instructor in New York City.

The novel's colorful secondary characters have been compared to those of the 19th-century English novelist *Charles Dickens, and include Abe Jones, an earnest Jewish student; bitter Robert Weaver and his mistress, Martha Upshaw; and Joel Pierce, a member of a wealthy Hudson River family. This social set, at first attractive to Gant, later repels him.

After saving enough money, Gant goes on a European tour during which he meets Francis Starwick again, and Ann and Elinor, two Boston girls. The foursome spend several weeks as tourists in and around Paris. Though Elinor loves Gant, he falls in love with Ann. However, Ann loves Starwick, who does not respond and leaves mysteriously again and again. Later, Gant realizes that Starwick is a homosexual. Gant runs out of money, and he returns to the States, a mature, Harvard-educated, aspiring author.

Like other major works by Wolfe, the novel has been criticized as overly wordy and sentimental, but the themes of lost innocence and the rapid flight of time are vividly presented. If you read *Look Homeward, Angel* first, you will enjoy *Of Time and the River* more. YA

Og, a legendary giant, was king of Bashan, a country west of the Sea of Galilee. Og and his people were enemies of the Israelites. He appears several times in the Old Testament of the *Bible. His grandfather was *Adam. According to legendary accounts, his mother had fingers a yard long, each with two sharp nails. Og was nearly six miles high, drank water from the clouds, and cooked his fish by holding them up to the sun. When the Flood came, even when it was at its deepest, it only came to his knees.

Og asked Noah to take him into the ark, and when Noah refused, he climbed on the roof. The Bible relates that after the crossing of the Red Sea, Moses advanced against Og and defeated him. The legend says that though Moses was 15 feet tall himself, a huge spear he threw only reached Og's heel. But when Og hurled a mountain at the Israelites, he got tangled up, so Moses was able to kill him. In the *satirical poem *Absalom and Achitophel* (1681) by John Dryden (1631–1700), Thomas Shadwell, a large man, is referred to as "Og":

> Og from a treason-tavern rolling home
> Round as a globe . . .
> With all this bulk there's nothing lost
>   in Og,
> For every inch, that is not fool, is
>   rogue.

YA

O'Hara, Frank (1926–1966) A poet, playwright, and art critic, O'Hara was born in Baltimore and moved to Massachusetts, where he attended Catholic schools. He intended to become a concert pianist, and after a Navy tour during World War II, he studied music at Harvard. While at school he began writing poems and stories for *The Harvard Advocate*. O'Hara became friends with many poets and painters, and after graduate school at the University of Michigan, he settled in New York. Known as a "poet among painters," he worked as a clerk at the Museum of Modern Art and eventually became an assistant curator. Between those jobs, O'Hara wrote articles and reviews for *Art News*, and served as an art editor for a quarterly publication, *Kulchur*. As a distinguished member of the so-called New York School of poets, he published several collections of poetry, including *Selected Poems* (1973). His poetry is autobiographical and reflects the New York environment. Critics have compared its emotional clarity to the paintings of Jackson Pollock (1912–1956), about whose work O'Hara wrote a full-length exhibition catalogue in 1958. Other works include *Art Chronicles* (1975), a collection of his criticism; *Standing Still and Walking in New York* (1975); *Early Writing* (1977), essays and notes; and *Collected Plays* (1978). YA

O'Hara, John (1905–1970) Son of a prominent physician in Pottsville, Pennsylvania, this novelist and short-story writer was kicked out of several schools, and later, when he became a journalist, was fired from newspapers and magazines. Despite this, he wrote more than 200 stories for *The New Yorker* magazine. His first and best novel was *Appointment in Samarra* (1934) an *ironic, realistic treatment of young couples of the country-club set in Pennsylvania. *Pal Joey* (1940) is a collection of stories told in the form of letters about a shallow nightclub entertainer. Though his novels and short stories have not always been well received by critics, they have remained popular. He often wrote with a sharp, *satiric tone and a clear eye about actors, barroom figures, well-off businessmen, and lonely suburbanites. For example, *Butterfield 8* (1935) is about the death of a party girl, and *A Rage to Live* (1949) is about an unfaithful wife. *Pal Joey* was produced as a musical comedy under the same name in 1940, with O'Hara himself writing the book. If you enjoy O'Hara's books, another author whose books you might like is *John Cheever. *Butterfield 8* was produced as a movie in 1960, and *A Rage to Live* in 1965. YA

O'Hara, Mary (Alsop) (1895–1980) This author and composer is known best for her three novels about horses, especially her first, *My Friend Flicka*. She was a Hollywood screenwriter in the early days of motion pictures, then defied her parents and married her third cousin. After a divorce she married an actor and horseman and moved to Wyoming. Her experiences on a ranch formed the background for her later works about the life and dreams of the McLaughlin family and their horses, all written after she was more than 50 years old. You can read more about her life in her autobiography, *Flicka's Friend* (1982). O'Hara's folk musical, *The Catch Colt* (1964), was adapted as a short novel in 1979. MR & YA

Little Nell and her grandfather in *The Old Curiosity Shop*

Oklahoma! (1943), with music by Richard Rodgers (1902–1979) and book and lyrics by Oscar Hammerstein II (1895–1960), changed the American musical theater. Based on *Green Grow the Lilacs* (1931), a play by Lynn Riggs (1899–1954), it centers on a love triangle between Laurey Williams, a sweet young girl; Curly McLain, a farmhand who wins her love; and Jud Fry, a brooding type who is accidentally killed. Another theme is the conflict between farmers and ranchers in the Oklahoma territory, just before it becomes a state. Rodgers and Hammerstein worked together on many other musicals, including *The Sound of Music* (1960). You may be familiar with many of the songs in *Oklahoma!*, including "Oh, What a Beautiful Mornin'." *Oklahoma!* was a pioneering production in the history of musical comedy because it incorporated death and politics as themes and because it used the choreography of Agnes de Mille (1908–) to move the story along. *Oklahoma!* ran for over 2,000 performances on Broadway, a record for the time. A movie of it was made in 1955. MR & YA

Old Curiosity Shop, The (1840) This sentimental novel by *Charles Dickens tells the story of an innocent heroine, *Little Nell, who lives with her grandfather. He runs a curiosity shop. An obsessive gambler, he borrows money from Daniel Quilp, and, when he loses everything, Quilp gets the shop. Little Nell and her grandfather become beggars and flee across England, pursued by the villainous Quilp. They find many friends along the way, including Thomas Codlin, who has a traveling puppet show; Mrs. Jarley, who has a waxworks; and Mr. Marton, a kind schoolmaster who gives them a house near a church, where Little Nell happily tends the graves. Quilp drowns in the Thames trying to find Little Nell and her grandfather, and his evil accomplices, the Brasses, are punished. When Kit Nubbles, Nell's friend, and the grandfather's wealthy brother finally find them, Little Nell has just died, and her heartbroken grandfather dies a few days later. You may also enjoy reading *Uncle Tom's Cabin*, by *Harriet Beecher Stowe, in which the young heroine, Eva, dies sadly like Little Nell. A musical version of *The Old Curiosity Shop* was filmed in 1975. YA

Old Man and the Sea, The (1952) By *Ernest Hemingway, this short novel tells about an old

Cuban fisherman, Santiago, who has been fishing for 85 days in the Gulf Stream off Havana without a catch when he finally hooks a giant marlin. He battles for two long days, against all odds, until he harpoons the fish alongside his boat. When sharks appear, he fights them off with knives and a club. The sharks strip the marlin to its skeleton, and the defeated fisherman returns to harbor with only the head and tail. Santiago's young friend, Manolin, comforts the exhausted fisherman and tells him that his luck will turn good again, but Santiago can only dream about his youth in Africa, and the lions who played on the beach. This simple, restrained classic can be read as an adventure story, but for many readers the fisherman's torn hands and his boat's crosslike mast are religious *symbols. You might also see this story as the struggle of a human being against nature, in which there is a bond between the hunter and the hunted. Another short novel you may enjoy is *The Pearl* by *John Steinbeck, in which a poor fisherman gains only unhappiness when he finds a magnificent pearl. *The Old Man and the Sea* was made into a film in 1958. YA

Old Yeller (1956), a novel by Fred Gipson (1908–1973), is set in Birdsong Creek, Texas, in the mid-1800s. The narrator, 14-year-old Travis, is in charge of the frontier farm, his mother, and his 5-year-old brother, Arliss, while his father is away for months on a cattle drive. A big, ugly stray dog with ticks and a chewed-off ear shows up and steals some meat. At first, Travis is annoyed by the dog, which they call Old Yeller, both because of its color and because of the yelping noise it makes. Eventually the dog saves Arliss from a bear. When the owner comes to claim him, he sees how attached the family has become, and instead trades Old Yeller for a home-cooked meal. Old Yeller later saves Travis from a wild hog and, while protecting Mama and a neighbor from a wolf with rabies, is bitten by the wolf. Travis is forced to shoot the dog, but some of the sadness is relieved because Old Yeller leaves a puppy behind. You will want also to read *Las-

sie Come Home* by *Eric Knight. Gipson wrote a number of popular novels, including *Hounddog Man* (1949), about a 12-year-old boy's adventures on a Texas coon hunt, and *Savage Sam* (1962), the story of the son of Old Yeller. *Old Yeller* was made into a movie in 1957, *Hounddog Man* in 1959, and *Savage Sam* in 1963. MR

Oliver Twist (1837), a novel by *Charles Dickens, is a shocking account of London conditions that led poor children into a life of crime, and a gripping story of the triumph of good over evil. Oliver Twist is born in a dingy workhouse, the child of a nameless young woman who dies moments after his birth. He is brought up there with other orphans and suffers cold, hunger, and neglect under the indifferent administration of Mr. Bumble. After a brief and miserable apprenticeship to a coffin-maker, Oliver runs away to London, where he is taken in hand by a young pickpocket. Known in the underworld as the *Artful Dodger, the pickpocket introduces Oliver to a gang of petty criminals that includes the vile-tempered Bill Sikes, a burglar; his friend Nancy; and old Fagin, their chief. The gang tries to force Oliver into thieving for them, but the boy is rescued briefly by the kindly Mr. Brownlow. Fagin arranges to have Oliver kidnapped and compels him to go with Sikes on a burglary. Sikes's attempt fails and Oliver is badly wounded, but luck brings him to Mrs. Maylie and her companion, Rose. He recovers under their gentle care.

Nancy's pity for Oliver and her growing hatred of Fagin's gang lead her to tell Rose about Monks, an unpleasant man who takes a sinister interest in Oliver and claims to know about his parents. Monks also hints at a mysterious link between Oliver and Rose. When the gang discovers that Nancy has spoken to Rose, Bill Sikes coldly clubs her to death. A ferocious mob demands justice for the murder. Sikes is killed accidentally as he tries to escape, and Fagin is arrested.

Found and brought before Mr. Brownlow, Monks is made to tell his story. He admits he is Oliver's half brother. Desperate to inherit all

"Please, sir, I want some more," Oliver asks of the workhouse's master in *Oliver Twist*.

their father's estate, Monks had tried to destroy any evidence of Oliver's connection to the family. Monks also reveals that Rose is Oliver's aunt. With his identity established at last, Oliver is adopted by Mr. Brownlow. Written in a realistic and highly emotional style, *Oliver Twist* is regarded as a classic throughout the world. The popular musical comedy *Oliver!*, based on *Oliver Twist*, was produced in 1960, and a film version of the stage musical appeared in 1968. Several other movies have been made from the story, including a fine one starring Alec Guinness (1914–) as Fagin that was produced in 1948. YA

Omoo: A Narrative of Adventures in the South Seas (1847), a novel by *Herman Melville, is a sequel to *Typee*. The title comes from the language of the Marquesas Islands, in the southern Pacific Ocean, and means a wanderer from one island to another. The book's narrator, like Melville himself, was a wanderer. *Omoo* begins with the narrator's account of escaping from the cannibal island of Typee on a rotten whaler, the *Julia*. The crew mutinies and is imprisoned in a thatched hut on Tahiti, one of the Society Islands. The kindly jailer, Captain Bób, feeds them fresh fruit to help them regain their health. After their release, the narrator and his friend, Dr. Long Ghost, explore the island, become planters for a time, and have a variety of adventures. Eventually, the narrator ships out to Japan and, he hopes, to home. The narrator's adventures are not necessarily those of Melville. Melville combined his experiences during a brief stay in the Society Islands with adventures he read in books. The novel shows the effects of missionaries on the Polynesians, and the author obviously feels that the natives were better off as unsophisticated pagans than hypocritical Christians. The Tahitians are presented realistically, and the tone of the book is often lighthearted and *satiric. Other authors who have written about the South Pacific include *Charles Nordhoff and *James Norman Hall, *Jack London, and *James A. Michener. YA

On the Beach (1957), by *Nevil Shute, is a chilling *science fiction novel, set in the future, when an atomic war has wiped out all life in the Northern Hemisphere. In Melbourne, Australia, people come to realize what has happened, as well as the fact that a radioactive cloud is moving toward them. The people try to live their lives as normally as possible, but in the end, all major characters commit suicide, as symptoms of radiation sickness begin to appear. The captain of an American atomic submarine takes it from Melbourne to California to find the cause of the war. They find that the nuclear holocaust was caused by an accident, and indeed there is no life in America. *On the Beach* was made into a movie in 1959. If you liked *On the Beach*, you will want to read *The Andromeda Strain* by Michael Crichton (1942–) and *Z for Zachariah* by *Robert C. O'Brien. YA

On the Road (1957), by *Jack Kerouac, his best-known novel and the most popular novel of the *Beat Generation, was written at top speed on a typewriter on a single roll of paper. It reads like a confession and tells the story of a friendship between the narrator, a writer named Sal Paradise (Jack Kerouac), and the young and fascinating con man Dean Moriarty (Neal Cassady, 1926–1968). Together and apart, from 1947 to 1950, they crisscross the roads of the country from New York City to San Francisco again and again, hitchhiking, driving, with their friends and girlfriends, stopping to work and drink and party, finding each other, parting and joining again. "[I] danced down the street like dingledodies . . . after people who interest me, because the only people for me are the mad ones, the ones who are mad to live, mad to talk, mad to be saved." Amid the seamy details of poverty, lust, drink, and drugs the characters often seem innocent and joyful; they seem to be on a blind and honest search for truth. *On the Road* is, for many, a very American story. For the young people who turned it into a best-seller, it was a song of personal freedom, and it is now recognized as part of a long history of American individualism and idealism. You might like to contrast *On the Road* with the introspective and quiet *Walden, or Life in the Woods* by *Henry David Thoreau, another highly individualistic American work, written more than 100 years earlier, which was popular with young people at the same time. You may also enjoy *Travels with Charlie in Search of America* (1962) by *John Steinbeck, which is now available in a paperback edition and recounts a delightful, meandering trip through about 40 states with a 10-year-old poodle, Charlie. A recent book about traveling the United States is *Blue Highways: A Journey into America* (1982) by William Least Heat Moon (1939–). The movie *Easy Rider*, produced in 1969, is an interesting depiction of young men traveling the roads of the 1960s. YA

Once and Future King, The

Once and Future King, The (1958) This rich novel by *T.H. White is a modern retelling of *Le Morte d'Arthur* by *Thomas Malory. White has tempered the story of *King Arthur with warmth and comedy without diminishing the impact of the inevitable tragedy. Arthur emerges as a real human being. Merlyn [*Merlin] has taught Arthur to think, and thinking often brings pain. For instance, Arthur observes that in wars against each other the no-

bles, who are in armor, fight for the sport of it and live, but the unarmored foot soldiers die. He imposes peace on the war-loving nobles by creating the *Round Table and giving the nobles quests to perform and getting them to use might only for right. The first of four books in this novel is *The Sword in the Stone*. The next book is *The Queen of Air and Darkness*, which tells the story of Queen Morgause's children, four of whom become Knights of the Round Table. The oldest is *Gawain and the youngest is Mordred, the destroyer of Arthur's kingdom. The third book, *The Ill-Made Knight*, is the story of *Lancelot, from his boyhood and training in France through his many adventures and his love of Arthur's queen, *Guinevere, to his love for Arthur himself. In the last book, *The Candle in the Wind*, Arthur tries to explain to his best friends, who are Lancelot and Guinevere, why he cannot simply behead his son, Mordred, who is trying to destroy him: "You will find that when the kings are bullies who believe in force, the people are bullies too." Mordred betrays the lovers, Lancelot and Guinevere, and the scandal destroys the unity of the Round Table. Arthur condemns Guinevere to burn at the stake, but Lancelot rescues her. Now Arthur must fight Lancelot and then declare war against Mordred. A later book, *The Book of Merlyn* (1977), was published separately. White called it the true last chapter of *The Once and Future King*. On the night before Arthur's last battle, Merlyn reenters his life and takes him once more to commune with his animal friends of *The Sword and the Stone*. The friends explore the idea that animals do not make war on each other. "I have suddenly discovered," wrote White as he was working on this book, "That . . . the central theme of *Morte d'Arthur* is to find an antidote to war." White's novel was made into a musical, *Camelot*, in 1960, which was filmed in 1967. See also *Camelot. YA

One Day in the Life of Ivan Denisovich

One Day in the Life of Ivan Denisovich (1963), by *Aleksandr Solzhenitsyn, is a short, powerful novel of the struggle of one prisoner to survive for one day in a Siberian labor camp during the regime of Joseph Stalin (1879–1953), the dictator of the former Soviet Union. Ivan represents the common man involved in a life-and-death struggle. Solzhenitsyn, who himself was a prisoner, describes a day filled with awful food, biting cold, and menial labor. He recreates the boredom and suffering of the prison camp and suggests how imagination is stifled when all energy must be directed to just staying alive. You might compare the conditions in this prison camp with those in the American Civil War camp in *Andersonville, a novel by *MacKinlay Kantor. *One Day in the Life of Ivan Denisovich* was made into a movie in 1971. YA

One Fat Summer (1977), by *Robert Lipsyte, begins on the Fourth of July in 1957, when 14-year-old, 200-pounds-plus Bobby Marks realizes how much he hates the summer, when people "can see your thick legs and your wobbly backside and your big belly and your soft arms. And they laugh." His friend Joanie pushes him to get a job, and he works as a yard boy for a doctor so he can avoid going to the beach. Along the way, he is taunted by ex-Marine Willie Rumson and his gang, who call him "The Crisco Kid," because he is "fat in the can." They get meaner when Willie wants to take away Bobby's lawn mowing job, and they strand him naked on an island in the middle of a lake. Bobby manages to gain confidence by enduring a stormy night alone. He confronts Willie in an underwater fight, which he wins because he is used to swimming underwater so people cannot see how fat he is. By the end of the summer he loses 25 pounds, asks for his full pay for his job, and gains self-respect. The book has realistic situations, snappy dialogue, suspense, and a likable hero. There are two sequels, *Summer Rules* (1981), about Bobby's problems as a counselor at a day camp, and *Summerboy* (1982), in which Bobby again faces moral decisions that force him to quit his job in order to confront a tricky boss. MR

One Flew Over the Cuckoo's Nest (1962), by *Ken Kesey, is about McMurphy, a gambling man who has been labeled dangerous and locked up in a mental hospital. His story is told by another inmate, Chief Broom, a huge man who has convinced the staff and residents that he is deaf and dumb. Controlling the ward is Big Nurse: "Her painted smile twists, stretches to an open snarl, and she blows up bigger and bigger, big as a tractor, so big I can smell the machinery inside the way you smell a motor pulling too big a load." Big Nurse has everything running like a machine, all the Acutes and Chronics doing exactly as they are told, when the brawling McMurphy arrives bringing hope and a lust for life. At first McMurphy gambles and plays his tricks for a lark to outwit Big Nurse and what the Chief calls "The Combine." But McMurphy treats the docile inmates like human beings and, as he sees them respond, he becomes compassionate and tries to improve their conditions. This brings him into terrible danger from Big Nurse who, after all, has all the power. The consequences of her power are devastating for McMurphy but liberating for Chief Broom. The attempt to be human and individual, free and joyful, in a society of increasing tyrannies and controls is the central metaphor of this story. Another novel that explores similar themes, but in a wartime setting, is *Catch-22 by *Joseph Heller. *One Flew Over the Cuckoo's Nest* was made into a movie in 1975. YA

One Hundred Years of Solitude (1970) by *Gabriel García Márquez, considered one of the great novels of the 20th century, has been translated into many languages. Based on childhood memories, this is a many-layered novel that provokes multiple interpretations. It tells a strange and lustful saga of seven generations of the Buendias, the founding family of the isolated, mythical town of Macondo, Colombia. A fictional history of a century of change, it focuses not only on Colombia but on the world at large. As an overview of Western civilization, it includes Greek myth and the story of creation from the book of *Genesis. The writer is supposedly a gypsy who writes in Sanskrit. Filled with fantasy, invention, and superstition, the book also comments on historical events in Latin America from the Spanish Conquest to the present. Descriptions of 19th-century civil wars and the damage caused by a foreign banana company are especially vivid. Its humor is based on exaggeration and extravagance and a family inclined to incest and solitude. YA

O'Neill, Eugene (1888–1953) The first American playwright to achieve world fame, O'Neill was born in New York City. The son of a popular actor, he was exposed to the theater early. After flunking out of Princeton, he led an adventurous life as a seaman, gold prospector, journalist, and actor. His first full-length play was the tragedy *Beyond the Horizon* (1920), whose central character is a young man with "a touch of the poet," who becomes, with tragic consequences, a farmer instead of the sailor he yearns to be. After writing realistic dramas, O'Neill experimented: in *The Great God Brown* (1926), whose theme is how materialism can destroy creativity, actors wear masks as symbols, similar to those worn in the masques of the Middle Ages; *Lazarus Laughed* (1927), a biblical fantasy about Lazarus facing death without fear after being resurrected from death by *Jesus, features choral chanting; *Mourning Becomes Electra* (1931), a three-part drama, is about a Civil War family—a psychological adaptation of *Aeschylus's *Orestei*, the story of *Agamemnon, his son, Orestes, and Orestes' sister, *Electra; the autobiographical *A Long Day's Journey into Night* (1941) and a sequel, *A Moon for the Misbegotten* (1943), are about the Tyrone family and, in fact, explore the tortured, tragic lives of the O'Neill family. Several more—including *A Touch of the Poet* (1957), about a girl named Sara Melody, the daughter of a ne'er-do-well Boston tavernkeeper who dreams of his lost days of glory, and returning to a theme from his first play—were produced after his death. Intense, personal, experimental, and melodramatic, O'Neill's dramas stress character and mood rather than plot, and confront social and moral issues.

Many of his 44 published plays were adapted into movies, including *A Long Day's Journey into Night*, produced in 1962. Other plays you can see on film are *The Emperor Jones, produced in 1933; *Anna Christie, in 1930; *The Hairy Ape* (1922), produced in 1944, about Yank, a ship's coal stoker whose encounter with a millionaire's daughter reveals to him that he is not the master of his fate but one of life's victims; *Desire Under the Elms* (1924), in 1958, which deals with life in rural New England and the conflict between a young man, his strong and hard father, and his father's new wife; *Strange Interlude* (1928), about a New England farm family and the roles of science and religion in their lives, in 1935; *Ah, Wilderness!* (1933), in 1935, about a sensitive 16-year-old boy's rebellion against his family and community; *Mourning Becomes Electra* in 1947; *A Long Day's Journey into Night* in 1962; and *The Iceman Cometh* in 1973. O'Neill won the Nobel Prize for literature in 1936. YA

Onion John (1959) A father, a son, and a gentle nonconforming character are at the center of this amusing and thoughtful novel by Joseph Krumgold (1908–1980), who was a screenwriter and a producer of documentary movies. Andy Rusch, Jr., who is 12 years old, makes friends with Onion John, an eccentric character in the village of Serenity, New Jersey. He got his name because he eats onions the way other people eat apples. John lives in a house of rocks he built himself. Andy's father, who has ambitions for his son to become the engineer his father never was, gets the local Rotary Club to build John a real house. Unfortunately, John burns it down because he does not understand the electric stove. John decides to leave Serenity before having any more unwelcome good done for him, and Andy wishes to go with him because of the pressure from his father to build a secure future. John convinces Andy's father that his son is growing up and should make his own decisions. When John is promised that the house will not be rebuilt, he remains in town. This is a two-edged story about learning to live with those who are different, and about tensions between a father and son. *Onion John* won the *Newbery Medal in 1960, making

Krumgold the first author ever to achieve this honor twice. See also Krumgold's *. . . And Now Miguel. MR

Open, Sesame! is the password that opens the door of the robbers' cave in the tale of *Ali Baba in "The Forty Thieves," narrated by *Scheherazade in *The Arabian Nights' Entertainments. Today, the phrase "Open, Sesame!" acts like a key in gaining admission or getting results. Sesame seeds are used in Middle Eastern foods, including a sweet paste called halvah. You can often find the seeds sprinkled on bread crusts. The title of the television show "Sesame Street" implies a magical means of learning for young children.

Ophelia is a character in *William Shakespeare's tragic drama *Hamlet. Daughter of Polonius and sister of Laertes, she is motherless, young, and pure, and so sweet that she reminds people of flowers. Because she loves her father and brother, she follows Polonius's commands to resist Hamlet's love. She lets her father spy on them, and when Hamlet kills him and is banished abroad, she becomes lonely and consumed with guilt. Ophelia winds up going insane, in a scene that is one of the most famous in literature. Ophelia appears in only six scenes, and she is a victim of conflicts in which she has no direct part. She eventually drowns, "divided from herself and her fair judgment." You can see Ophelia's gentle, childlike character on the movie screen in three versions of Hamlet, in 1948, 1969, and 1990. YA

Oppenheim, E(dward) Phillips (1866–1946) The English author of more than 100 novels of suspense and international intrigue, Oppenheim created characters who were cosmopolitan people of upper-class background, beautiful women with a taste for danger, aristocratic criminals and detectives, and clever spies. Though his work was very successful in Europe and the United States, Oppenheim's popularity with German readers suffered when he wrote a number of stories warning of German preparations for what would become

World War I. *The Great Impersonation was set in those years just before the war. During the war, Oppenheim served as an escort for correspondents from neutral nations who came to visit the battle lines in France. The Kingdom of the Blind (1917), another spy story written at that time, is among his best-known works. If you enjoy Oppenheim's novels, you will also like the spy novels of *John Buchan. YA

Orczy, Baroness (Emmuska) (1865–1947) Hungarian-born British artist and author of *The Scarlet Pimpernel, she was the daughter of a well-known composer and conductor. Orczy studied art in London, and some of her work was exhibited at the Royal Academy of Art. Of her many romantic plays, novels, and short stories, The Scarlet Pimpernel was by far the most successful. Orczy also wrote several detective stories, now difficult to find even in large libraries, at a time when *Sherlock Holmes was popular, and is considered to have given much to the background of the modern detective story.

Ordinary Jack (1977), by *Helen Cresswell, is the first novel of The Bagthorpe Saga, a series of sophisticated comic novels about the Bagthorpe family. Grandpa is selectively deaf, while Grandma thrives on boisterous argument. Mr. Bagthorpe writes scripts for television when he is not shouting over the general commotion. Mrs. Bagthorpe writes an agony column, dispensing advice to the lovelorn. Three of the Bagthorpe children (William, Tess, and Rosie) are talented and self-confident, irritatingly fond of displaying the prizes and medals won in pursuit of their many hobbies. Ordinary Jack, 11 years old, is the only one who does not excel at something, and he is tired of being treated like a harmless pet.

His Uncle Parker, sensitive to Jack's problem, concocts a campaign designed to bring Jack the attention he desperately needs. The plan begins with a series of mysterious impressions, coached by Parker and produced before various family members, during which Jack pretends to have visions of future events. To his surprise, his prophetic mumblings cause consternation. When his prophecies come true (with the practical help of Parker), everyone is staggered. Then Jack's campaign notes are found, and his status as a prophet is shown to be fraudulent. Mr. Bagthorpe, however, has found the notes in Jack's collection of comic books, which Mr. Bagthorpe has been reading secretly. Embarrassed, and with his reputation as literary man in tatters, Mr. Bagthorpe becomes more accommodating. The family is accordingly grateful to Jack, and proud of his boldness and imagination. Another family you will enjoy reading about is *The Moffats* by Eleanor Estes (1906–1988). MR

Ordinary People (1976), by *Judith Guest, is a novel about 17-year-old Conrad Jarrett, who comes back to high school and the familiar world of his swim team and classes after slashing his wrists. He has spent eight months in a mental hospital, talking to a sympathetic psychiatrist, Dr. Crawford, and healing his memories as well as his scars. But Conrad still has the same feelings about his cold mother, his need to be in control of events, girls, and sex, and especially his older brother Buck's accidental death. Conrad comes close to losing control as he tries to survive in his parents' comfortable suburban house. His well-meaning father asks too many questions, and his mother tries to act as if nothing is wrong. But their marriage is falling apart, and they withdraw into their own feelings. Conrad gets a jolt and seems on the edge of another suicide attempt when he reads in the paper that a girl he met in the hospital has taken her life. His relationship with Dr. Crawford keeps him going. Another novel you may want to read is *Tuned Out* by Maia Wojciechowska, about a college student's troubled search for his identity, as seen through the eyes of his younger brother. *Ordinary People* was made into a film in 1980. YA

Orestes is the last major figure of Greek tragedy. His story of terror and forgiveness is told in more Greek dramas than that of any other mythical hero. *Aeschylus, *Sophocles, and *Euripides wrote about him, and he is mentioned frequently in the *Odyssey.* Orestes' story has many versions, but in all of them the young man wants to avenge the death of his father, *Agamemnon, who had been assassinated by his wife, Clytemnestra, and her lover, Aegisthus, after Agamemnon returned from the *Trojan War.

Orestes' sister *Electra hides the young boy at the home of Strophus, their uncle by marriage. When Orestes reaches manhood, *Apollo, who believes that marriage is more sacred than even blood relationships, orders him to kill his mother and her accomplice. Ancient Greeks believed that the soul of a murdered person would know no peace until the death was avenged. So Orestes disguises himself as a messenger and tells his mother the false news that he has died. Feeling safe, she sends for her lover, and Orestes murders them both.

The winged Furies, bloody-eyed goddesses with snakes in their hair, pursue Orestes to punish him for his crime of matricide. He is driven mad. To become sane again, he has to steal the wooden statue of *Artemis in the land of the Taurians, a people who sacrifice all foreigners. Orestes and his close friend, Pylades, Strophus's son, are captured when they arrive in Tauris, but the priestess of Artemis turns out to be Orestes' oldest sister, Iphigenia. They all escape with the statue, and Orestes later becomes the most powerful monarch in the area. You may enjoy some modern plays influenced by this myth. They include *Eugene O'Neill's *Mourning Becomes Electra* (1931) and *T.S. Eliot's *The Family Reunion* (1939). YA

Origin of Species, On the (1859) This once-controversial biological study by *Charles Darwin provides evidence for the theory of evolution and describes how natural selection is a factor in the development of new forms of plants and animals. Darwin argues that every species evolves from a previous species. He describes generations of plants and animals, noting their variations. In the struggle for existence an unfavorable variation is not likely to survive, but a favorable variation benefits a species and helps it succeed. This is known as "survival of the fittest." The idea of evolution was not new; even *Aristotle hinted at it. While you probably know its title and subject, you are unlikely to have read this big, carefully researched book written in a surprisingly clear style. One of the most important books ever written, it not only influenced biology, but also psychology, sociology, law, theology, educational history, philosophy, and literature. Though the theory of evolution is widely accepted, it is still debated, especially by those who accept literally the story of creation as described in the book of *Genesis in the *Bible. YA

Orlando is a popular name in literature. He is the hero of *William Shakespeare's comedy *As You Like It, a fine young man—handsome, strong, and brave—who challenges Duke Frederick's wrestler and is crazy about Rosalind. She leads him on, and they go into the Forest of Arden, where he writes lovesick poems to her and hangs them in trees.

Orlando is also the name of a fantasy novel (1928) by *Virginia Woolf. Orlando is an Elizabethan nobleman and poet, who ends up 300 years later as a woman poet in 20th-century London. Woolf modeled the woman after her friend Victoria Sackville-West (1892–1962). You might also want to read Woolf's essay *A Room of One's Own, an example, like *Orlando*, of women's rights literature. It was presented on television in 1991.

Orlando is also the Italian name for *Roland in the romantic epic poem *Orlando Innamorato* (Roland in Love, 1487), by Matteo Maria Boiardo (1440–1494), and *Orlando Furioso* (Roland Mad, 1532), by Ariosto Lodovico (1474–1533). These long works are separated into books of songs, called cantos, and written in eight-line stanzas, or octaves. Orlando is a paladin, a knight of King Charlemagne, in a magical tale of pagan princesses, giants, last-minute rescues, sea monsters, enchanted castles, and winged horses. Many adaptations have been made, including *Edmund Spenser's *The Faerie Queen*, which was based on Italian epics. YA

Orpheus, in Greek legends, was a poet, philosopher, and musician, whose lute playing was so wonderful that even wild beasts gathered to hear him play. He was the son of Calliope, the muse of epic poetry, and of *Apollo. On the expedition of the *Argonauts, he uses his voice to still the waves and further protects his shipmates by using his lyre to drown out the Sirens, whose beautiful songs entice sailors to their deaths. Orpheus's wife, the wood nymph Eurydice, while fleeing the advances of a god, is bitten by a snake and dies. Orpheus descends to the underworld to try to release her. With his music, he charms Persephone, queen of Hades, and gets permission to lead Eurydice back safely as long as he does not look at her until they reach the upper world. Distracted for a moment, Orpheus forgets the condition, and when he turns to look at her, Eurydice becomes a shadow and vanishes. Later, Orpheus is torn to pieces, and his severed head, still singing, floats to the Isle of Lesbos.

The story of Orpheus's lost love has inspired artists throughout the ages. Younger readers will enjoy reading about it in *The Golden Treasury of Myths and Legends* (1959). Other versions that older readers might enjoy are the opera *Orfeo ed Euridice* (1762) by Christoph Gluck (1714–1787); the ballet *Orpheus* (1948) choreographed by George Balanchine (1904–1983) with music by Igor Stravinsky (1882–1971); and the French films *Orpheus*, produced in 1949, and *Black Orpheus*, produced in 1959. MR & YA

Orwell, George [Eric Arthur Blair] (1903–1950) An English novelist and essayist, Orwell was born in India. He joined the Indian Imperial Police in Burma, and his experiences there with the problems of British imperialism and racial prejudice were reflected in his novel *Burmese Days* (1934). He lived for a time in the slums of Paris and London, gathering experiences that he used in his autobiographical novel *Down* and *Out in Paris and London* (1933). Orwell, an independent-thinking Socialist sympathizer, fought on the Loyalist side in the Spanish Civil War, an experience he described in *Homage to Catalonia* (1938). He was badly wounded and returned to England, turning again to writing, journalism, and serious literary criticism and becoming strongly anticommunist and antifascist. Basically a political writer, he expressed his fears of the coming world war and its effect on modern society, which he depicted with a sense of *satire and longing for the past, in the novel *Coming Up for Air* (1939). Orwell's wartime journalistic work further increased his alarm for the future of a world menaced by war, and by what he saw as the treachery of political leaders. *Animal Farm* is a satire based on the events of the Russian Revolution (1917), and it made him famous. Perhaps his best-known novel is *1984,* which expresses Orwell's deep hatred of tyrants and his fear for the loss of personal freedom under their rule. Orwell's essays, reviews, and letters are available in several editions, including the multivolume *Collected Essays, Journalism, and Letters of George Orwell* (1968). YA

Osborne, John (1929–) This English playwright wrote *Look Back in Anger* (1956), which is credited with changing modern British theater. Jimmy Porter, the rebellious main character, who lives in an attic apartment, inspired the phrase "angry young man." He became a kind of folk-hero for those who were disillusioned with the snobbery of class-conscious Britain.

John Osborne was a middle-class kid who loved friends, reading, and movies, and who spent many hours of his adolescence in air-raid shelters listening to German bombs explode. For a while he was a reporter for a magazine called *Gas World*, and later he took jobs in the theater as actor, stage manager, and, finally, playwright. Osborne's plays usually have a main character who does much of the talking, often criticizing social problems. *Inadmissible Evidence* (1964) is about a failing middle-aged lawyer. *Luther* (1961) is a psychological study of

Martin Luther (1483–1546), the German religious reformer. Osborne also wrote screenplays. He turned his play *The Entertainer* (1957), which is about a rundown music hall, the Empire, and its failed impresario, into a movie in 1962. He wrote the screenplay for the rollicking *Tom Jones* (1964), which he had adapted from the 18th-century novel *Tom Jones,* by *Henry Fielding. *Look Back in Anger* was adapted for film in 1958. YA

Othello, The Moor of Venice (c.1604) is one of *William Shakespeare's great dramatic tragedies. Othello, a Moor, is serving in Venice at the time when Cyprus is invaded by the Turks. He elopes with gentle Desdemona, a general's daughter. *Iago, Othello's evil aide, persuades him that Desdemona is unfaithful, and gets the trusting Desdemona to enhance the falsehood by convincing her to help the good-natured Lieutenant Cassio.

Othello's judgment becomes clouded by jealousy, and he eventually smothers the guiltless Desdemona. When he realizes Iago's villainous influence, Othello kills himself with his sword. Iago is finally punished, but too late to bring back the deceived lovers. Many critics feel that this play surpasses even *Romeo and Juliet* with its expression of the many sides of love. A movie version of *Othello*, starring the English actor Laurence Olivier (1907–1989) as the Moor, was produced in 1965. Othello is also the subject of operas by Gioacchino Rossini (1792–1868) and Giuseppe Verdi (1813–1901). YA

Other Voices, Other Rooms (1948), by *Truman Capote, a first novel, is the story of a 13-year-old boy's search for an identity. Joel Knox has been raised by his mother and aunt in a rundown Louisiana mansion. There are no male role models in his world, only a collection of characters, including Randolph, a transvestite. Joel's feelings of separation from normal society match Randolph's. When Joel outgrows his confused childhood, he takes a homosexual identity, which gets him out of the mansion and into a world where he feels he belongs. Many praised the writing style of the

23-year-old Capote, but they were mixed in their opinions about the content, which was controversial at the time. You might enjoy a later short novel by Capote, *Breakfast at Tiffany's*, about a happy-go-lucky young woman in New York City. YA

Our Town (1938) by *Thornton Wilder is a play in three acts set in the town of Grover's Corners, New Hampshire, in 1901. The stage is bare, with only a few chairs and tables to suggest buildings and no curtain. A narrator referred to as the Stage Manager introduces the audience to the people in the story, some of whom are invisible. In very clear and simple language, several townspeople, mainly members of the Gibbs and Webb families, talk about the usual business on an ordinary day in which nothing remarkable happens.

During the second act, which takes place in 1904 and centers on love and marriage, young George Gibbs and Emily Webb marry. In a flashback you listen to their first serious conversation about their feelings for one another, and to the familiar doubts that come over them just before the wedding.

The third act takes place in 1913 at the cemetery on a hill above Grover's Corners, where a number of dead citizens—invisible to the living—are quietly waiting and observing the funeral of Emily. She leaves the group of mourners around her coffin and joins the dead. Still attached to life, she begs to return to the day of her 12th birthday. When Emily visits her past as an invisible presence, she realizes how precious are the smallest details of daily existence, moments that go by without anyone's noticing their great importance and wonder. She returns to take her place among the dead. Another play you may enjoy is Wilder's *The Skin of Our Teeth*, a wild *satire of humankind through various epochs of history. A film version of *Our Town* was produced in 1940. YA

Out of Africa (1937), by *Isak Dinesen, is an autobiographical novel based on this Danish author's experiences on a coffee plantation in Kenya, Africa. The heroine marries a man she does not love, moves to Africa, has trouble with growing crops, and falls in love with a British adventurer, who later dies in a plane crash. The book shows her sympathy and understanding for a people and a culture different from Dinesen's own. She seeks to understand the patterns she sees in natives, animals, nature, love, disease, and death. For example, in the chapter "Farewell to the Farm," she tries to find a pattern for all the disasters that have happened to her. She looks for a *sign and sees a small chameleon in front of a large rooster. The chameleon holds its ground and opens its mouth wide to frighten the big bird, but when it sticks its tongue out, the rooster pecks it off. She sees this as similar to her frustrating attempts to survive and feels honored to have the sign sent to her. If you liked this book, you may enjoy *Shadows on the Grass* (1961), containing four autobiographical stories about Dinesen's life in Africa. A movie based on *Out of Africa* was made in 1985. YA

"Outcasts of Poker Flat, The" (1869) This short story, by *Bret Harte, takes place in 1850, in a northern California mining camp. Four people are exiled from the community by the locals, who regard the four as undesirable. They include a good-hearted gambler named John Oakhurst, two prostitutes, and a thief. A young couple, on their way to Poker Flat, are caught in a blizzard. The young man, Tom, recognizes Oakhurst as the gambler who had previously won all his money in a poker game, and had then returned it, with the advice that Tom never gamble again. Tom leads the group to an abandoned shack. The thief steals the mules and most of the provisions. Snow falls for ten days, and one of the prostitutes dies, having saved her food for the young girl. Oakhurst sends Tom out for help and accompanies him part of the way. When a rescue party arrives a few days later, they find the two remaining women huddled dead together, and Oakhurst dead from his own gun. This rather sentimental story compares the outcasts' hearts of gold with the hypocritical people of the mining camp, who are searching for gold.

You might like to compare the theme with that of *Nathaniel Hawthorne's *The Scarlet Letter. "Outcasts" was adapted into films in 1937 and 1952. YA

Outsiders, The (1967) This novel, written by *S.E. Hinton when she was 16 years old, examines the social and physical war between two Tulsa, Oklahoma, gangs: the wrong-side-of-the-tracks Greasers, and the upper-middle-class, Mustang-driving Socs. Ponyboy, the 14-year-old narrator, has lived with his older brothers, Darry and Sodapop, since their parents died. Ponyboy has long hair and sometimes carries a switchblade, but he has a dreamy side too. Fellow gang members include wild and restless Dallas; Steve, who not only fixes cars but steals them too; Two-Bit, a shoplifting wise-guy; and puppylike Johnny, the youngest of the group. The rich Socs beat up Johnny, and from then on he carries a knife and lets everyone know that he will kill anyone who tries to hurt him. When he and Ponyboy are alone and threatened, Johnny knifes a member of the Socs. This starts a violent chain of events, ending with two deaths. Both groups suffer from missing parents and other social ills, but neither group is hopeless. You may want to compare *The Outsiders* with **West Side Story*. Another powerful novel about teenage gangs is *Durango Street* (1965) by *Frank Bonham. *The Outsiders* was made into a movie in 1983, and later into a TV series. MR

Over Sea, Under Stone (1965), by *Susan Cooper, is the first novel in *The Dark Is Rising, an exciting and suspenseful series inspired by ancient Celtic tales and legends. Simon, Jane, and Barney Drew are on holiday with their parents at Trewissick on the coast of Cornwall, England, in a house rented for them by Great-Uncle Merriman Lyon. Merry, as he is called by his family, is a renowned scholar with a tendency to disappear on unexplained errands. Very tall and straight, with something mysterious about him, he is a great favorite of the Drew children.

While exploring the old house, the children stumble on a fragile, centuries-old manuscript that they believe contains instructions for finding treasure. Great-Uncle Merry is able to confirm that the document, properly read and acted upon, will lead the way to a precious grail, or chalice, hidden somewhere in Trewissick. He also tells them the grail is a potent sign that people have long been seeking, that it may tell the true story of *King Arthur, and that evil forces will stop at nothing to possess it. As the children begin to solve the riddle of the manuscript, their search for the treasure is interrupted by frightening encounters with those who would take it from them. Merry's odd and comforting presence is a valuable safeguard, but it is the Drew children who defy the forces of evil and solve the mystery of the grail's hiding place. Another fantasy series dealing with the struggle between good and evil is *The Lord of the Rings* by *J.R.R. Tolkien. See also *Holy Grail and *The Grey King. MR

"Overcoat, The" By *Nikolai Gogol, this well-known short story is an unusual blend of *irony and sentimentality and of the trivial and the grotesque. Told in a narrative style, it takes place in St. Petersburg, Russia, where Akaky Akakievich Bashmachkin is a nonentity, a poor civil servant whose life is devoted to copying government documents. Akaky likes his work and is content with the unchanging routine. His ancient overcoat, a patched and shapeless garment, is the butt of office jokes. Akaky makes many sacrifices to save money for a new coat, which is exceptionally warm and beautiful. Returning from a party one night, he is attacked by thieves who take his coat and leave him lying in the snow. He becomes ill and soon dies. His death goes unnoticed, but soon his ghost is seen about the city as it approaches passersby in its search for the lost overcoat. You may also enjoy "Diary of a Madman," another fine story by Gogol. Another famous short story about an office worker is *"Bartleby the Scrivener" by *Herman Melville. "The Overcoat" was adapted for film in 1959. YA

MR = Middle Reader   YA = Young Adult Reader   * = See this main entry

"Owl and the Pussycat, The" (1871) This well-known work by English poet *Edward Lear is one of the finest examples of light, imaginative children's poetry of the *Victorian era. The verses tell a silly story about an owl and a pussycat who sail off "in a pea-green boat" to the land where the "bong tree" grows, buy a wedding ring formerly on the nose of a "Piggy-wig," get married by a turkey, dine on "mince and slices of quince," and dance in the moonlight. With nonsense words, simple rhymes, word pictures, and repetition, Lear creates an enchanting world. More good children's poems from that era include those by *Robert Louis Stevenson in *A Child's Garden of Verses* (1885). This classic collection has recently been republished in several illustrated editions. MR & YA

Owls in the Family, by *Farley Mowat, is the true story of a family crowded with animals, including dozens of gophers, rats, garter snakes, pigeons, rabbits, and a dog named Mutt. Farley gets two very different owls. Weeps, the smaller, timid one, cannot fly and was rescued from the bottom of a barrel where boys were pelting him with rocks. Whenever he is out of his cage he heads for the secure spot between Mutt's paws. The dog does not seem to mind, except when Weep's feathers make him sneeze.

Wol, the bigger owl, enjoys teasing Mutt. When the dog is sleeping, he stalks him like a cat, and sneaks slowly toward him across the lawn. If Mutt wakes up, Wol pretends he is staring at the sky. When Mutt begins to snore again, Wol continues his slow, sneaky approach, finally raising his foot and giving the snoozing dog a squeeze on the tail while screaming at the top of his lungs. Mutt wakes up and yelps with surprise, but Wol has already flown to a tree limb, from which he watches innocently, then pretends to sleep. The mischievous owl also attracts crows, follows Farley to school, attacks the mail carrier, and chases the minister out of the house. If you would like to have another inside look at an animal's life, read *Black Beauty* by Anna Sewell (1820–1878). MR

Ox-Bow Incident, The (1940) A powerful psychological novel by *Walter Van Tilburg Clark, this book goes beyond the bounds of ordinary Western adventure and raises important questions of physical and moral cowardice, and of the misuse of power. It is similar to a classic Greek drama, in which the mob acts as a *chorus commenting on the action. After working on the spring cattle roundup in the Sierra Nevada mountains, range riders Art Croft and his partner, Gil, head into the town of Bridger's Wells. They learn that rustlers have stolen cattle from a local rancher and killed a rider named Kincaid. The town is soon in an uproar, and a posse is formed without due process of law. The angry men set off into the mountains to track down and lynch the criminals. Art and Gil go with them, caught up in the grim excitement.

In a little valley called Ox-Bow, the men find three campers: a young man named Martin, a Mexican Indian, and a distracted old man, with 50 steers. Martin insists he bought the cattle earlier from their owner, but his explanations are taken for the lies of a desperate man. The three accused men are hanged at first light. After returning to Bridger's Wells, the vigilantes discover that Kincaid is alive and that Martin was telling the truth. You understand that the murder of three innocent men was caused by those who did not speak out, as well as by those who committed the crime. Another novel about the American West that will make you think deeply about people's motives is *The Big Sky* (1947), about the life of mountain men and frontiersmen, by *A.B. Guthrie, Jr. *The Ox-Bow Incident* was adapted for film in 1943. YA

oxymoron is a figure of speech containing an extremely compact paradox. Successive words seem to contradict each other, yet convey a truth, as in the phrases "conspicuous by his absence" or "sweet sorrow." The term "oxymoron" comes from the Greek *oxymoros*, which means pointedly foolish. You can find many oxymorons in this passage from the first act of *William Shakespeare's play *Romeo and Juliet,* when Romeo describes love as a series of contradictions: "O brawling love! O loving hate! O anything, of nothing first created! O heavy lightness! serious vanity! Mis-shapen chaos of well-seeming forms! Feather of lead, bright smoke, cold fire, sick health! Still-waking sleep, that is not what it is! This love feel I, that feel no love in this." A recent light-hearted look at oxymorons is *Jumbo Shrimp and Other Almost Perfect Oxymorons* (1986) by Warren S. Blumenfeld (n.d.). YA

Oz is an imaginary place made famous in *L. Frank Baum's modern fairy tale *The Wonderful Wizard of Oz. It is a large, rectangular area divided into four countries, each with a special color for the skin and clothes of the small creatures who live in them: blue Munchkins in the east, yellow Winkies in the west, red Quadlings in the south, and purple Gillikins in the north. The capital, Emerald City, where Princess Ozma rules, is in the center. All property belongs to her, and she treats her subjects like children, supplying goods to everyone. The farming land of Oz is ringed by wooded mountains containing different peoples and strange creatures. Residents who worry about this are sent to Flutterbudget Centre; those who are unable to express themselves clearly, to *Rigmarole. Everyone works half the time and then plays, and there is no sickness, poverty, death, or money. Much of Oz is dominated by witches, good ones in the north and south, wicked ones in the east and west. Today, "Oz" has become a term that means a magical world; Australians use it humorously to describe their country. Other imaginary lands include Narnia, created by *C.S. Lewis, and *Xanth, created by *Piers Anthony. MR

Oz, Amos [Amos Klausner] (1939–) This Israeli novelist and short-story writer comes from a long line of scholars. When he was 15 years old he moved to a rural *kibbutz, where he has lived for years, dividing his time between writing, farming, and teaching. After serving in a tank unit in the Six-Day War and the Yom Kippur War, he published many articles challenging his country's views. Stressing compromise, he seeks mutual recognition of Arabs and Is-

raelis, and a Palestinian homeland in the West Bank and Gaza strip. His first famous novel, *Michael sheli* (*My Michael*) (1968), translated, like most of his works, from Hebrew into about 20 languages, examines the gap between a husband and his schizophrenic wife. This is perhaps a *symbol for the divided city of Jerusalem. His collection of stories *Artsot hatan* (*Where the Jackals Howl*) (1965), which describes how people adjust to the rules of society, and a novel, *Menuah nekhonah* (*A Perfect Peace*) (1962), about a young rebel on an Israeli kibbutz, are also popular works. YA

Ozick, Cynthia (1928–) The daughter of a Bronx druggist, this novelist, short-story writer, and essayist reflects the energy of her New York upbringing throughout her works. In the funny novella "Puttermeister and Xanthippe," in *Levitation: Five Fictions* (1982), a lawyer working for the city becomes obsessed with a vision: "Each borough itself another little homeland, joy in the Bronx, elation in Queens, O Happy Richmond! Children on roller skates, and over the Brooklyn Bridge the long patchwork-colored lines of joggers, breathing hard above the homeland-hugging green waters."

Ozick had studied the works of *Henry James, the 19th-century novelist who wrote about wealthy families in this country and Europe, and you can see how his style influenced her early work in an excerpt of her first, unfinished novel, "The Butterfly and the Traffic Light," in *The Pagan Rabbi and Other Stories* (1971). *Trust* (1966), her first published novel, deals with a wealthy American family, and half the book is set in Europe. The title is *ironic because the book deals with a lack of trust in every relationship of the family. In the four stories in *Bloodshed* (1976), characters reject Jewish identity only to return to it, often because of memories of the horrors of *Nazi Germany during World War II. In the short story "A Mercenary," a cigarette reminds one character of smoke from a Holocaust crematorium. Though much of her later work—including *The Cannibal Galaxy* (1983), which is about a schoolmaster who misinterprets the nature of an extraordinary student and is haunted by the mistake when it is exposed—reflects her study of the Jewish religion, Ozick's powerful themes are meaningful to all readers. You may want to read Henry James's *Daisy Miller* (1878), about a young, innocent, and rich American girl caught in the tangles of European society. You may also want to read James's *The Europeans* (1878), which is about a sophisticated German baroness of American origin who comes to Boston in hope of snaring a rich husband. YA

Paco's Story (1968), by Larry Heinemann (1944–), tells about Paco Sullivan, a disfigured Vietnam veteran and the only one of his company to survive a terrible firefight. The novel is told in two parts: Paco's experiences in Vietnam, and his postwar life in America. Some of the Vietnam scenes are those of young men whose goals are to find women and get tattooed. But some scenes of the war seem too awful in their cruelty. War and anger reduce the Vietnamese in the eyes of some Americans to nonhuman "zips," and Heinemann uses strong language to describe the unthinkable acts that are inflicted on them.

Back in the United States, Paco washes dishes in a short-order restaurant and lives in a rundown hotel. He dreams about an encounter with a girl in a neighboring room. Paco reads her diary and finds she is turned on by Paco but has mixed feelings about his jungle of scars. He gets on a bus and leaves town, perhaps to avoid doing the kind of harm to her or to himself that had been done in Vietnam. If you are interested in another story about courage, read *Northern Lights* (1975) by *Tim O'Brien, about two brothers, one a Vietnam veteran, who become lost in a blizzard in northern Minnesota. YA

Paine, Thomas (1737–1809) Born in England, son of a Quaker, Paine as a young man tried many careers and failed in each attempt. Just

Thomas Paine was a tireless champion of liberty and human rights.

before the American Revolution, he came to the Colonies with letters of introduction from *Benjamin Franklin, whom he had met in London. He became a magazine editor in Philadelphia, then became involved in the revolutionary struggle for liberty. In *Common Sense* (1776) he urged independence for the Colonies, and this famous pamphlet became a powerful influence, much admired by George Washington (1732–1799) and Thomas Jefferson (1743–

1826). Paine later enlisted in the Continental Army and wrote *The Crisis* (1776–1783), a series of revolutionary pamphlets. The first begins with a line you may have heard: "These are the times that try men's souls."

Paine was an activist throughout his life. He left the army to serve in government positions and, after the war, retired near New York City, where he continued stirring up issues through his writing. He went to England, where he advocated a revolution similar to the one in France, was prosecuted as a traitor, escaped to France, and was elected to the French National Convention. At the trial of Louis XVI (1754–1793), he voted against the king's execution and was put in prison. One of Paine's most powerful books is *Rights of Man* (1791–1792), in which he supported the principles and ideals of the French Revolution. His controversial treatise *The Age of Reason, Being an Investigation of True and Fabulous Theology* (1794–1796) was considered an attack on religion. He returned to the United States, where he was often denounced and abused as an atheist. Paine retired to a farm in New York State, where he died and was buried. Eventually his remains were shipped to England. Younger readers will enjoy reading *Tom Paine, Revolutionary* (1969) by Olivia E. Coolidge (1908–), and older readers will enjoy the biographical novel *Citzen Tom Paine* (1943) by *Howard Fast. Another patriot you might like to read about is Patrick Henry (1736–1799), who said in a famous speech, "Give me liberty, or give me death." A lively biography for young readers is *Where Was Patrick Henry on the 29th of May?* by Margot Tomes (1917–). Older readers can find in the library the classic biography *Life and Character of Patrick Henry* by William Wirt (1772–1834), who reconstructed some of Henry's famous speeches. MR & YA

Pale Horse, Pale Rider (1939) By *Katherine Anne Porter, this is a popular collection of three short novels. *Old Mortality* is about a bright girl trying to flee an oppressive Southern environment. *Pale Horse, Pale Rider* is about a short love affair between a soldier and a South-

ern girl during the flu epidemic of World War I. *Noon Wine*, perhaps Porter's best-known short story, is about a farmer who kills a stranger and then commits suicide. If you like these novellas, you may also like the 10 short stories collected in *Flowering Judas and Other Stories* (1930). *Noon Wine* was filmed in 1985. YA

palindrome is a number, word, phrase, or line of verse in which the letters can be written and read forward or backward. Sotades, a Greek poet of the 3rd century B.C., is credited with originating these fun word games, which are sometimes called "Sotadics." Examples of palindromes are "Anna" and "deified." Longer palindromes are "Able was I ere I saw Elba," which Napoleon Bonaparte (1769–1821) was supposed to have said, "Madam, I'm Adam," and "A man, a plan, a canal: Panama." Numerical palindromes include 1881 and 1991.

Pamela, or Virtue Rewarded (1740–1742), a novel by *Samuel Richardson, marks the beginning of the English domestic novel. The story of Pamela Andrews is told in a series of letters to her parents, making you feel as though you are reading her diary. The novel's first part is called "Aggressive Chastity," and the second, "Provocative Prudence," and though those titles—and even the story—may seem silly and old-fashioned today, the self-awareness in the work was unusual for the time. Pamela is a simple 15-year-old country girl who is the servant of a wealthy woman. When the lady dies, her son kidnaps and tries to seduce Pamela, but she fights off his advances and later convinces him to marry her—so that she can reform him. You may find it more fun to read another novel, *Henry Fielding's *Joseph Andrews* (1754), which mocks Pamela's reward and the virtue of resisting. YA

Pan is the Greek mythological god of woods and fields, flocks and herds, and shepherds and huntsmen. Since in Greek "pan" means "all or everything," the god Pan pervades all things, including food and fertility. He is the son of either *Mercury or *Jupiter or even various

Pan

other parents. Though he walks upright, he has horns, legs, and a tail like a goat's, while his head, arms, and chest are like a man's. His musical pipe—which he is credited with inventing—is called a "syrinx" and is named for a nymph who was changed into a reed to escape Pan's advances. His companions are often satyrs, half-man, half-horselike creatures. Pan was worshiped as a nature deity and so is one of the most ancient of the Greek gods. The Greek festivals to Pan were later taken over by the Romans, who identified him with the nature spirit Faunus. You use his name when you say the word "panic," for, though he was considered a good guy, he was said to frighten lonely travelers who thought the strange sounds they heard at night were made by him.

Pandora's Box According to Greek mythology, Pandora was the first mortal female, produced on orders of *Zeus. Her name means "all-gifted." According to her myth, the other gods gave the beautiful Pandora gifts consisting of evil powers, which she put in a jar or box. Epimetheus, another god, married Pandora, and either he or she opened the box in spite of warnings against doing so. The result was that all the evils in the world escaped, and they have affected people ever since. Some say only

Hope remained in the box. Thus, a Pandora's box is a gift that seems valuable but turns out to be a curse. The story of *Midas, a legendary king of Phrygia, provides another example. You can read about Pandora in *A Wonder-Book for Girls and Boys* by *Nathaniel Hawthorne and also in *Bulfinch's Mythology* by Thomas Bulfinch (1796–1867) and *Mythology* by Edith Hamilton (1867–1963). MR

Pangloss, Dr. See *Dr. Pangloss.

pantomime is a word that comes from the theater. In ancient Rome, it meant a tragic performance in which a single performer (*pantomimus*, "a mimic of everything") interpreted all characters by means of direct actions and dance, while someone recited or a group sang. In the later ballet-pantomime of the 17th century, performers danced a story. Pantomime came to mean any wordless action, as in the Italian *commedia dell'arte*, in which an actor mimes in front of backdrops.

The English pantomime, which is still popular, especially around Christmas, was introduced in the 18th century. At first there were stock characters, such as Clown, *Harlequin, *Columbine, and Pantaloon, and fairytale characters, such as Cinderella. Today it is often a variety show, with only some miming and with familiar songs, and the audience sings along with the performers. There are silly skits in which women often impersonate boys, and men impersonate women. Pantomime is sometimes called a "dumb show," not because it is stupid but because the character is silent—in the same sense as deaf and dumb. You probably have seen street mimes at fairs or shopping malls, or clowns miming at the circus. They are carrying on the pantomime tradition.

parable Usually simple in form and substance, a parable is a story that is intended to teach a moral or religious lesson. *Jesus used parables often in his teachings, as recorded in the New Testament of the *Bible. For example, in one he compared the sowing of seed in different kinds of soil, good or bad, with different recep-

Adam and Eve being cast out of Eden in *Paradise Lost.*

tions of his teachings, such as acceptance or rejection. There are also many parables in the *Talmud, the compilation of the oral law of Judaism.

Paradise Lost (1667), by *John Milton, is an English epic poem that portrays the events of creation and the fall of *Adam and Eve, as described in Genesis 1–3 of the *Bible. It is the story of how Paradise was lost to us all. It begins in *hell with a meeting of *Satan and the angels who have been thrown out of heaven with him for rebelling against God. They decide to take revenge by corrupting God's newest creation, human beings. Satan himself takes on the task. He arrives in the garden of Eden as a serpent and promises Eve that she will become divine if she eats fruit from the forbidden tree. Adam also eats the fruit, "that he may perish with the woman he loved," and God banishes them both. The archangel Michael, leading them away, shows the pair how miserable humanity will become, but promises that eventually people will have a far better life because of a redeemer who is the son of God. *Paradise Lost* is considered by many to be the greatest poem ever written in English, and is known for its rich style and heroic characters. It ranks with the classic epics of *Homer. You might be interested in Milton's sequel, *Paradise Regained* (1671), about *Jesus' resistance to

Satan. It is simpler—though less popular—than the first part. YA

Paretsky, Sara (1947–) As creator of the fictional detective V.I. Warshawski, who refuses to use her first name, Victoria, Paretsky has written six detective novels about a very modern private investigator working in Chicago. Warshawski's mother was part Italian and part Jewish, and her father was Polish. V.I. played basketball in high school and college before becoming a lawyer in the Cook County Public Defender's office in Chicago. Striking out on her own, V.I. began to specialize in cases having to do with finances and white-collar crime. She first appeared in *Indemnity Only* (1982). Hired to find a missing woman, she discovers the corpse of the woman's son, and from there is led into a tangle of illegal schemes and the question of the real identity of her client. In *Killing Order* (1985), V.I. is hired to investigate the disappearance of stock certificates from a Chicago monastery. She is splashed in the face with acid, but uncovers a conspiracy of criminals, businessmen, and clergymen. V.I. is asked in *Blood Shot* (1988) to find for a childhood friend the father she never knew. She turns up a corpse and encounters danger involving toxic chemicals. *Burn Marks* (1990) begins when Warshawski's aunt is made homeless by a fire, and in helping her out V.I.

uncovers arson and corruption. In *Guardian Angel* (1992), V.I. is hired by an elderly neighbor to find his friend who has disappeared and may have been murdered. A movie entitled *V.I. Warshawski* was produced in 1991. If you like these books, you will want to read those by *Amanda Cross, *Sue Grafton, and *Marcia Muller. YA

Paris in Greek mythology is the son of Hecuba and Priam, king of Troy, who is sent away to be raised by a bear, and then by shepherds, because it was predicted that he would bring down the house of Troy. He marries a nymph named Oenone, and the royal family lets him come back after he wins many games and contests. Paris, who was extremely handsome, is asked by *Zeus to judge a beauty contest between *Hera, *Athena, and *Aphrodite, who all want to win the golden apple given to "the fairest." Paris chooses Aphrodite, who had offered him the most beautiful woman in the world if she won the contest. That woman is *Helen. When Paris seduces Helen and carries her off to Troy, her husband and previous suitors make war on Troy. Paris is scorned for being a coward. When he is pierced by a poison arrow in the *Trojan War, he is carried to his wife, but she refuses to save him.

Paris is also the name given to the "gallant, young, and noble gentleman" whom the Capulets want their daughter, Juliet, to marry against her will in *William Shakespeare's *Romeo and Juliet. Romeo slays Paris, who had been placing flowers in Juliet's tomb. He places Paris in the tomb before taking poison himself. YA

Park, Ruth (n.d.) An Australian journalist and playwright, Park comes from a Scottish-Irish storytelling family. She develops characters by taking bits and pieces of people and putting them together in one character. Park created the Muddle-Headed Wombat for a radio show for Australian children, and this led to a popular eleven-volume series of books, *The Muddle-Headed Wombat* (1962–1976). The Muddle-Headed Wombat is an animal character known for zany dialogue and for adding too many syllables to words, for example, "This cake is horribubble." *Callie's Castle* (1974) is about a girl growing up in Sydney who wants her own space within her family. In *Come Danger, Come Darkness* (1978) a convict escapes, and Otter, who is the nephew of the chief of the prison colony, gets involved. In *Playing Beatie Bow* (1980) a young girl from Sydney finds a way to pass through time. If you want to learn about Park's early life, read her autobiography, *The Drums Go Bang* (1956). MR

Parker, Dorothy (Rothschild) (1893–1967) This *satiric and often bittersweet poet spent her early years as a drama critic for *Vanity Fair* magazine and as a book critic for *The New Yorker* magazine. Much of Parker's best verse is collected in *Not So Deep as a Well* (1936). She liked to shock with her biting wit, and turn traditional lines upside down, as in the last verse of "Love Song":

> My love runs by like a day in June,
> And he makes no friends of sorrows,
> He'll tread his galloping rigadoon
> In the pathway of the morrows.
> He'll live his days where the sunbeams start,
> Nor could storm or wind uproot him.
> My own dear love, he is all my heart—
> And I wish somebody'd shoot him.

Parker also wrote two collections of sophisticated short stories, *Laments for the Living* (1930) and *After Such Pleasures* (1933). She was well known as a member of the Algonquin Round Table, a group of brilliant writers and thinkers who regularly lunched—and gossiped—in the dining room of the Algonquin Hotel in New York City. Later she lived and worked in Hollywood, where she did little original writing. Parker was petite, but her words made a big impression. You may have heard her most often quoted lines,

> Men seldom make passes
> At girls who wear glasses.

You will find a good selection of her work in *The Portable Dorothy Parker* (1976). YA

Parker, Robert B(rown) (1932–) A professor of English at Northeastern University, Parker turned to writing detective fiction with *The Godwulf Manuscript* (1973), which involves the search for a 14th-century illuminated manuscript stolen from a university library. This novel introduces Spenser, a fictional detective, who has a first name but refuses to use it. He was a Boston policeman but was fired for insubordination. Spenser has a black friend, known only as Hawk, who appears to be a thug. The Spenser books are very much of the hard-boiled school, with more violence than necessary. On the other hand, they have interesting plots and lots of action. In *Promised Land* (1976) Spenser is hired to find a missing wife who gets involved in a bank robbery about the time her husband is in trouble with a loan shark. In *A Savage Place* (1981) he has the job of protecting a television reporter who is threatened by racketeers and whose chief witness has been murdered. *Stardust* (1990) has him protecting a sexy television star. A TV series, *Spenser: For Hire*, was aired from 1985 to 1988. If you like this kind of detective fiction, try the books of *James M. Cain, *John D. MacDonald, and *Mickey Spillane. YA

Parks, Gordon (1912–) A filmmaker, author, and photographer, Parks grew up poor in Kansas. He played football and basketball, and then tried fashion photography in Chicago in the 1930s. He served as a photographer in the Office of War Information and, after World War II, as the first black photographer for *Life* magazine. He was noted for his coverage of gangs in Harlem and the poor in Rio de Janeiro, as well as for high fashion. He wrote and illustrated with photographs a dozen autobiographical works, including *A Poet and His Camera* (1968), *A Choice of Weapons* (1966), *Born Black* (1971), and *Gordon Parks: Whispers of Intimate Things* (1971). *In Love* (1971) is a collection of his romantic poems. In 1969 Parks adapted and directed a movie based on his autobiographical novel, *The Learning Tree* (1963), about a black boy's adventures growing up in Kansas. Life, his mother told him, is like a Learning Tree, with good and bad fruit. Parks directed other documentaries and movies, including two about Shaft, a fictional black Harlem detective, *Shaft* and *Shaft's Big Score*, both produced in 1972. MR & YA

parody mocks a characteristic style of some other work. Often, a serious subject is imitated in a funny way, focusing on the style rather than the content. Traits are often exaggerated so much that the original style seems ridiculous. Parody has a long history, going back to Hipponex's *Battle of the Frogs and Mice* (5th c. B.C.), which parodies *Homer. *Miguel de Cervantes' *Don Quixote* mocks the long-winded style of the medieval romance. *Henry Fielding's *Joseph Andrews* (1754) mocks *Pamela*, by *Samuel Richardson. More recently, *S.J. Perelman was a well-known literary parodist. Animated cartoon shows, such as *Rocky and Bullwinkle*, and television shows, such as *Saturday Night Live!*, frequently parody books, movies, and politicians' statements.

Pascal, Francine (1938–) Journalist, playwright, and tremendously successful author of books for young readers, Pascal was born and raised in New York City. She wrote the fanciful yet realistic book *Hangin' Out with Cici* (1977), about a girl who dislikes her mother, bumps her head and goes back in time, and becomes best friends with a girl who turns out to be her mother. Her next novel, *My First Love and Other Disasters* (1979), is about 14-year-old Vicky, who has a summer job and a boyfriend. The book deals with teenage sex in an honest but delicate way. A sequel is *Love and Betrayal and Hold the Mayo!* (1985), in which Vicky is a waitress at a summer camp. *The Hand-Me-Down Kid* (1980), dealing with the problems of growing up in New York City, concerns 11-year-old Ari, who defends a homeless person against sidewalk punks, but has trouble standing up for her own rights. In the 1980s Pascal created the Sweet Valley High and Sweet Valley Twins series of romantic novels about the friendship, love, honor, and disappointment of young people. These books sell in the millions and have been translated into many languages. *Hangin' Out with Cici* was made into a TV movie, *My Mother Was Never a Kid*, in 1983. MR & YA

Pass the Poetry Please! (1972), by *Lee Bennett Hopkins, suggests ways to use nursery rhymes, songs, and jingles to introduce poetry to young readers. For example, to arouse interest in the poems, he creates a Mother Goose Village and makes a rocking horse for the Lady of Banbury Cross. Hopkins also provides short, intimate biographies of 20 poets along with samples of their poetry. Among these poets are *Carl Sandburg and *Robert Frost, some of whose works for adults are also meaningful for children; *Shel Silverstein, who wrote especially for children; and works from black poets, such as *Gwendolyn Brooks and those collected by *Arnold Adoff in *The Poetry of Black America: Anthology of the 20th Century. MR & YA

Passage to India, A (1924) By *E.M. Forster, this remarkable novel deals with the political tensions between the Indians and the ruling British, and between Hindus and Muslims. Racial feelings are stirred up when Adela Quested, who has come to India to visit her fiancé, the city magistrate, Ronny Heaslop, hallucinates that Dr. Aziz, a friendly young Indian surgeon, has assaulted her in the Marabar Caves. Heaslop's mother, Mrs. Moore, who is traveling with Adela, is also frightened in the caves and later suffers a nervous breakdown. She seems to understand the Indians, however, and has a more open attitude. After Adela's accusation, lines are drawn between Indians and the English, and loyalties are demanded by both groups. When the local college principal, Mr. Fielding, who is Dr. Aziz's friend, says he does not believe that Aziz committed the alleged crime, he is shunned. And when Mrs. Moore supports Dr. Aziz, her son ships her away.

Later, at the trial, Mrs. Moore's name is chanted by the Indian spectators when they learn of her banishment. This chanting, and a buzzing noise that has been in her ears since the caves, makes Adela rethink her charges and change her testimony. Ronny breaks off the engagement with Adela, annoyed that she has told the truth. Fielding persuades Aziz not to press charges against Adela for legal damages. Two years later, Aziz assumes Fielding has married Adela, and avoids him, but it turns out he has married Mrs. Moore's daughter, Stella. The old friends part, divided by race. Two novelists who also portray Anglo-Indian concerns are Paul Scott (1920–), particularly in his Raj Quartet, set in India in the years leading up to its independence and including *The Jewel in the Crown* (1966), *The Day of the Scorpion* (1968), *The Towers of Silence* (1972), and *A Division of the Spoils* (1975); and British novelist Ruth Prawer Jhabvala (1927–), especially *Heat and Dust* (1983), which tells two love stories, one past, one present. *A Passage to India* was made into a movie in 1984. YA

Pasternak, Boris (Leonidovich) (1890–1960) A Russian poet, translator, and author of *Doctor Zhivago, Pasternak was the son of cultured Jewish parents whose friends included *Leo Tolstoy and the composer Sergei Rachmaninoff (1873–1943). After preparing for a musical career, he changed his course of study and in 1914 published his first book of poems. In 1916 another volume of lyrics, *Over the Barrier*, brought him recognition as a major poet. At first hopeful about the outcome of the Revolution of 1917, Pasternak later suffered from the repression of artistic freedom imposed by the Bolsheviks. He stopped publishing altogether during the purge trials of the 1930s, knowing that as a Jew and a member of the avant-garde he risked severe punishment. To earn his living, Pasternak devoted himself to translating works by *Johann Goethe, *William Shakespeare, and others. In 1956 his novel *Doctor Zhivago* was rejected for publication for portraying the Revolution in a slanderous manner. The book was printed in Italy, however, and widely circulated.

Pasternak was awarded the Nobel Prize for literature in 1958. He was forced to withdraw his acceptance after a storm of protest instigated by colleagues in the Soviet Writers' Union that fueled a campaign of severe criticism in the party press. *Doctor Zhivago* was called a "libel on the October Revolution, the people who made the revolution, and the building of socialism in the Soviet Union." Expelled from the Writers' Union, he spent the rest of his life in seclusion. If you enjoy Pasternak's books, you may want to compare them with the works of the novelist *Mikhail Sholokhov and the poet Yevgeny Yevtushenko (1933–). YA

Paterson, Katherine (Womeldorf) (1932–) Born in China of German-American missionary parents, Paterson, whose first language was Chinese, spent her teenage years in the American South. She served as a missionary in Japan for four years. Her experiences there provided material for several novels for younger readers, including *The Sign of the Chrysanthemum* (1973), *Of Nightingales That Weep* (1974), and *The Master Puppeteer* (1975), which follow the adventures of young people caught up in the political and social events of feudal Japan and range in time from the 12th to the 18th century. Paterson began writing while she was expecting her first child, and has since received many awards and honors. She won her first *Newbery Medal for *Bridge to Terabithia*, which she wrote in response to the death of her son's best friend. A second Newbery Medal was given to *Jacob Have I Loved*, which is set during World War II and tells of the conflict between twins who live on a lonely island. MR

Paton, Alan (1903–1988) This South African author, educated in his native country, became a schoolmaster and later principal of a reformatory near Johannesburg. He was often harassed because of his unflattering exposure of South African politics and his compassionate views on race relations. His few works were ahead of their time in showing the tragic effects of repressive, racist policies. Paton's popular and passionately antiapartheid novel *Cry, the Beloved Country* drew world attention to the

problems of African laborers in the gold mines. *Too Late the Phalarope* (1953) deals with a mixed marriage between white and black and shows the harsh life of the Afrikaans-speaking descendants of the Boer settlers. Paton's short-story collection, *Debbie Go Home* (1961), contains tales based on his experiences at the school where he taught. *Towards the Mountain* (1980) is autobiographical and deals with his early life. For a more recent look at life in South Africa, read *Athol Fugard, who writes powerful plays concerned with the consequences of apartheid. YA

Paul, Saint (A.D. 10?–c.64) A Jew and a Roman citizen originally named Saul and a tentmaker by trade, Paul was trained as a rabbi and became a fierce opponent of the first Christians. Sent from Jerusalem to Damascus, in present-day Syria, in A.D. 33 to persecute any Jews there who were becoming Christianized, he had a vision on his way in which *Jesus spoke to him, and Paul was temporarily blinded. He then became a follower of Jesus and in the course of his career, by preaching and writing, he greatly influenced the course of early Christian doctrine.

His long journeys took him to the island of Cyprus and to Greece, where he organized and encouraged Christian churches. The Acts of the Apostles and other books of the New Testament of the *Bible tell of his work and contain the letters he wrote. Arrested in Jerusalem and taken to Rome, he was, according to tradition, beheaded when the Emperor Nero (37–68) was persecuting Christians. Paul and *Peter were the primary organizers of the early Christian church. You will enjoy reading *The Apostle* (1943) by *Sholem Asch, which is a novel about Paul. YA

Paul Bunyan is a legendary giant, lumberjack, and comic hero of *tall tales of the American frontier. A figure of great strength and with an uncanny ability to find ways to get a difficult job done, he was helped by his friends *Babe the Blue Ox and Johnny Inkslinger. Bunyan was the *symbol of the tough and determined pioneers, who in real life fought terrible rainstorms, hungry mosquitoes, and hardships of all kinds. He is said to have caused a 70-foot tide in the Bay of Fundy when he stepped out of his cradle. His wild and daring deeds are the subject of many poems and stories. One example is in the long poetic work *The People, Yes* (1936) by *Carl Sandburg, which describes in one passage several Bunyan tall tales, including the story of Bunyan's pancake griddle, a thing so vast it had to be greased by men skating over it with sides of bacon strapped to their boots. Young people will enjoy reading about Paul Bunyan and Babe in *Legends of Paul Bunyan* (1948) by Harold Felton (1909–), *Paul Bunyan* (1952) by Esther Shepard (1891–1975), and *Paul Bunyan and His Great Blue Ox* (1926) by Wallace Wadsworth (1894–). MR & YA

Paul et Virginie (1787) by Jacques Henri Bernardin de Saint-Pierre (1737–1814) is the romantic story of a boy and girl who are raised by their mothers on the Isle de France (which is now called Mauritius), an island in the Indian Ocean. Both Paul and Virginie are poor and ignorant, and when they become teenagers, they fall in love. Sweet, innocent lovers, they make their world into a pleasant, sumptuous garden. Then Virginie's forgotten aunt writes her and tells her to come to Paris. The girl is reluctant to leave, but finally does, and remains in Paris for two years, unhappy and unable to adjust to her aunt and the corruptions of the so-called civilized world. Finally, Virginie gets to go back home. But on her way back, her ship sinks, and she drowns within sight of Paul. He later dies of grief. This sad story of lost love, set in paradise, became a sentimental favorite in both French and English. You might be more familiar with a later adaptation, *The Blue Lagoon* (1908) by H. de Vere Stacpoole (1863–1951). It was also a best-seller, and was made into a film twice, in 1949 and 1980. YA

Paulsen, Gary (1939–) Born in Minnesota and, as an "army brat," living on military bases around the world, Paulsen now spends much of his life in Colorado. This popular author worked in a variety of interesting ways, including as a farmer, rancher, trapper, archer, singer, and sailor. He also spent time as a teacher and engineer. Paul's writing is intense, emotional, and full of rugged action. Though they can be brutal, his stories often end on an upbeat note. Among his best known are *Dogsong* (1985) and *Hatchet*. The first is about a 14-year-old Eskimo boy who takes a 1,400-mile journey by dogsled to retrace the spiritual quality of his heritage in the Far North. *Dancing Girl* (1983) centers its plot on ice skating. *The Crossing* (1987) is about the friendship of a Mexican street boy and an alcoholic American soldier. On a lighter note, *The Boy Who Owned the School: A Comedy of Love* (1990) is about how a high school boy tries to remain unnoticed, except for his love of the school's most desirable girl. MR

Paz, Octavio (1914–) This Mexican poet and man of letters is considered the chief modern interpreter of Mexican civilization. He has experimented with many forms of poetry and many life-styles. He became interested in Marxism during the Spanish Civil War, and in Hinduism when he was Mexico's ambassador to India. Paz writes mainly about his Mexican heritage and people's solitude. He believes that the Western world has become too sophisticated and shallow, and that his native Latin America is brutal. *Piedra de sol* (1957), which was translated as *Sun Stone*, is considered his most important long poem. It is addressed to the planet Venus and is structured on the Aztec calendar. *Selected Poetry* (1963) and *Early Poems 1935–1955* (1973) were translated by Muriel Rukeyser (1913–1980). If you like Paz, you may enjoy the work of another contemporary Latin American, *Gabriel García Márquez. YA

Pearce, A(nn) Philippa (1920–) A popular English writer for young people, Pearce often writes about the relationships between young and older people. Her native village, Great Shelford in Cambridgeshire, figures in many of her books as Great Barley. In her first book, *Minnow on the Say* (1954), two boys with a canoe have a treasure hunt, and one of them is changed by the experience. Unlike *Peter Pan, her fantasy novel *Tom's Midnight Garden (1958) makes the point that young people must learn to grow up. *The Battle of Bubble and Squeak* (1978) describes in a realistic way how a family argues over a pair of gerbils. In *The Way to Sattin Shore* (1983), she tells what happens when Kate discovers that her father, drowned the day she was born, is not buried in the grave she thought he was buried in. This affects Kate's relationship with her brothers and her grandmother. Pearce's short story collections include *What the Neighbors Did and Other Stories* (1972) and *Who's Afraid? and Other Strange Stories* (1987). MR

Pearl, The (1947) Written by *John Steinbeck, this short novel is based on a Mexican folktale Steinbeck heard while on a research expedition to the Gulf of California in Mexico. It tells of a poor fisherman named Kino, his wife, Juana, and their baby son, Coyotito. When Coyotito is stung by a scorpion, Kino takes him to a doctor, who refuses to see the boy because Kino has no money. Kino goes diving for a pearl to pay the doctor and finds the "Pearl of the World," the largest, most beautiful pearl anyone has seen. He hopes it will lift his family out of poverty and bring them happiness, but it brings only greed, hatred, and tragedy. Kino kills a man who tries to rob him, and his canoe and house are destroyed. The family flees into the mountains, tracked by three men who intend to kill them and steal the pearl. Kino kills them, but Coyotito is shot and killed. They return to the village and Kino throws the pearl back into the sea, where its evil can no longer reach them. If you enjoyed this book, try Steinbeck's *Tortilla Flat* (1935), a moving and often humorous novel about the misadventures of a group of poor Mexican-Americans living near Monterey, California. Steinbeck also wrote the screenplay for the movie *The Pearl*, which was produced in 1948. You can find an inexpensive paperback edition of *The Pearl*, which includes another of Steinbeck's short works, *The Red Pony. MR & YA

Peck, Richard (1934–) Born, raised, and schooled in Illinois, Peck became a high school and college English teacher and a textbook editor. His books deal with reality, and he writes with honesty and sensitivity. *Don't Look and It Won't Hurt* (1973) is about teenage pregnancy. *Are You in the House Alone? is about the rape of a teenage girl. *Secrets of the Shopping Mall* (1979) focuses on a boy and girl in the suburbs who are good friends. *Father Figure* (1978) and *Close Enough to Touch* (1981) deal with the emotions and relationships of the males in a family. *Remembering the Good Times* (1985) deals with the harsh fact of teen suicide. For younger readers, *Ghosts I Have Been and several sequels deal with a girl named Blossom Culp and life in the early 1900s. MR & YA

Peck, Robert Newton (1928–) Born, raised, and still living in Vermont, this novelist and poet for young readers sets many of his stories in his home state. He was a boy during the *Great Depression and often writes about those hard times. Peck worked at a variety of jobs, including lumberjack, paper mill worker, hog butcher, and advertising executive. This broad background, as well as interests in various hobbies, such as singing in a barbershop quartet, shows up in his stories. His first book, *A Day No Pigs Would Die, is about a young boy who has to butcher his pig. His second, *Soup, is the first of a popular and humorous series dealing with childhood memories of his friend, Soup. Peck is realistic about animals in the wild, as in *Path of Hunters: Animal Struggle in a Meadow* (1973), where birth, hunger, and death are described. Fort Ticonderoga, at the head of Lake Champlain, New York, is the setting of three historical novels: *Fawn* (1975), about a battle between the English and French; *Hang for Treason* (1976), about tensions and violence between British loyalists and American patriots; and *Rabbits and Redcoats* (1976), about three boys and the Revolutionary War figures Ethan Allen (1738–1789) and Benedict Arnold (1741–1801). If you enjoy Peck's books, you will probably also like those of *Walter D. Edmonds. MR

MR = Middle Reader   YA = Young Adult Reader   * = See this main entry

Pegasus is the magical winged horse from classical mythology. Pegasus was the offspring of Poseidon, god of the sea and of horses, and Medusa, a snake-haired monster with a gaze that turned anyone who looked at her to stone. Pegasus sprang from the sea foam and from Medusa's blood, when *Perseus, the son of powerful *Zeus, decapitated her. The horse lived on Mt. Helicon, where with his hoof he created a fountain called Hippocrene, from which the nymphs and *Muses were born. According to the Greek myth, Pegasus was caught and tamed by Bellerophon at the Pirene Spring. Later, Bellerophon mounted Pegasus and destroyed the monster Chimera. Bellerophon attempted to ride to heaven, but he was thrown from the horse when Pegasus was stung by a gadfly sent as punishment by Zeus for trying to fly to the gods. Pegasus climbed alone to the skies and became an autumn constellation in the Northern Hemisphere. Many artists have painted Pegasus, and poets have used him as a *symbol for inspiration. You can read about Pegasus, Bellerophon, and Chimera in *A Wonder-Book for Girls and Boys* by *Nathaniel Hawthorne. MR & YA

Pelléas et Mélisande (1892), by the Belgian writer Maurice Maeterlinck (1862–1949), is a dreamlike drama set in a legendary world. Mélisande is wandering in the forest, sad and childlike and unwilling to talk about herself. Golaud marries her and brings her to his grandfather's gloomy castle. Golaud's younger half-brother, Pelléas, falls in love with her. While talking with him, she loses her wedding ring and, at the same time, Golaud has an accident. Mélisande cares for him and helps him regain his health, but Golaud's son by an earlier marriage confirms that Mélisande and Pelléas are in love. Pelléas decides to go away, but during the lovers' last meeting, Golaud, full of suspicions, kills him. After giving birth to a child, whose father is not clearly known, Mélisande also dies. This mystical and symbolic tale with its shadowy figures was made into a popular five-part opera, *Pelléas et Mélisande* (1902), with music by Claude Debussy (1862–1918). YA

Penrod, clearly unhappy and squirming on his stool, is punished for shouting at his teacher.

Penrod (1914), by *Booth Tarkington, is a popular and funny novel about the adventures of Penrod Schofield, a typical 12-year-old boy in a Middle Western city and a middle-class family. He tolerates adults, but is energetic and mischievous and gets into all kinds of trouble with parents and teachers. His many escapades, in which he is often accompanied by his dog, Duke, represent the rebellions of adolescent boys in America. He writes a novel, is a reluctant actor in a school pageant, takes dancing lessons, and falls for a girl named Marjorie. He starts a circus with his two friends, Herman and Verman. Some of Penrod's naughtier escapades include blackmailing his sister's boyfriend (and getting sick on the candy he buys with the money), and becoming friends with a bully, Rupe Collins. The one adult he seems to relate to is his Great-Aunt Sarah, who understands that being a rascal is just a part of growing up. Two sequels are *Penrod and Sam* (1916) and *Penrod Jashber* (1929). You might enjoy comparing Penrod with other mischievous boys, Tom Sawyer in *The Adventures of Tom Sawyer* by *Mark Twain, and Tom Bailey in *The Story of a Bad Boy* (1870) by *Thomas Bailey Aldrich. Movies based on the Penrod character include *Penrod and Sam* in 1937, and *Penrod and His Twin Brother* and *Penrod's Double Trouble*, both in 1938. MR

People Could Fly, The: American Black Folktales (1985) By *Virginia Hamilton, this collection of stories came out of slave experiences on plantations. In the stories created before the Civil War, the characters are animals, and all are brothers. Bruh Rabbit is the animal that the slaves took to represent themselves. Bruh Rabbit is small and seems helpless compared with the powerful bear, the ferocious wolf, and the wily fox. But the rabbit is smart, tricky, and prone to trouble. After the Civil War, the human character, John, takes the place of the rabbit in folktales, and there are more people and fewer animals. In "John and the Devil's Daughter" a woman uses her supernatural powers to escape her father, who is the Devil, and marry John. In "Wiley, His Mama, and the Hairy Man," all three characters use magic when the Hairy Man attempts to capture Wiley. Wiley and his mama are more clever, and that tips the balance in their favor. Some of the characters and stories are the same ones that *Joel Chandler Harris used in his *Uncle Remus stories, and you might enjoy comparing the versions. A movie, *Song of the South*, using animation and live action, was made of the animal stories in 1946. MR & YA

Pepys, Samuel (1633–1703) This English writer kept a frank diary of his life from 1660 to 1669, giving us an interesting view of life in the times of Restoration England, a period noted for its immorality. It covers the Great Plague (1665) and the Fire of London (1666). Pepys, a tailor's son in London, attended Cambridge University. He rose to be secretary of the Admiralty, and became president of the Royal Society. He retired to his estate after the Revolution of 1688, where he wrote *Memoires Relating to the State of the Royal Navy of England* (1690). Pepys wrote his diary in shorthand, and it was first deciphered in 1822. There are several editions of the *Diary*. You might especially enjoy *The Illustrated Pepys: Extracts from the Diary* (1978), edited by Robert Latham (n.d.). If you like to read diaries, try *A Diary from Dixie* (1905) by Mary Boykin Chesnut (1823–1886), who vividly recorded life during the period of the Confederacy. The most famous diary of recent times is *The Diary of a Young Girl* by Anne Frank (1929–1945). YA

Percival, though a son of a king in stories about *King Arthur's Britain, was nevertheless raised alone in the woods by his mother, so that he knew nothing of his background or his future as one of the knights of the *Round Table. But when he saw his first knight, he knew at once what he wanted to be. He set off, a country boy wearing armor made of twigs, and endured much laughter and scorn in his quest for knighthood. But because of his natural nobility, great courage, and increasing skill he vanquished many dangerous adversaries. He found great love, and was one of the knights who, with *Galahad, found the *Holy Grail. This story of innocence and high ideals had great appeal for German writers, and from one of these Richard Wagner (1813–1883) took the story of Percival and composed the opera *Parsifal* (1882).

Percy, Walker (1916–1990) Though this sensitive novelist was born and spent most of his life in the South, Percy wrote about the national scene. He studied medicine, but gave it up to become a full-time writer when he contracted tuberculosis. While he was ill, he read about *existentialism, a philosophy teaching that each person is responsible for his or her own actions, even though there is no overall meaning to life. Percy became a Roman Catholic and wrote many essays and articles on philosophy, language, and psychiatry, collected in

---

MR = Middle Reader   YA = Young Adult Reader   * = See this main entry

The Message in the Bottle (1975). Most of his novels deal with confused, spiritually dead people, who have problems involving love. *The Moviegoer* (1961) is about a lusty bachelor who winds up marrying a neurotic young woman. In *The Last Generation* (1966), the detached hero devotes himself to a dying youth. *Love in the Ruins* (1971) is subtitled *The Adventures of a Bad Catholic at a Time Near the End of the World*. A comic and satiric novel about modern life and the human spirit, it is set in an America of the near future, when cities are crumbling, political and racial groups are deeply polarized, and nothing seems to work. *The Thanatos Syndrome* (1987) is a thriller with the same hero who appears in *Love in the Ruins*. YA

Perelman, S(idney) J(oseph) (1904–1979) This writer and humorist, born in Brooklyn, New York, *satirized society's trends and people's behavior. There was often a touch of sadness— and sometimes anger—underneath his humor. After graduating from Brown University, Perelman edited humor magazines, then moved to Hollywood and wrote movie scripts and jokes for the Marx Brothers, a popular comedy team. When he returned East, he wrote mostly for *The New Yorker* magazine, and many pieces were turned into books. Perelman was a master of puns. You can find good examples of punning in the titles of most of his over 20 books, including *Westward Ha! or Around the World in 80 Clichés* (1947), and *The Swiss Family Perelman* (1950). Much of his best material is collected in *The Most of S.J. Perelman* (1958). With *Ogden Nash he wrote the book of the musical comedy *One Touch of Venus* (1944). It was made into a movie in 1948. To get a really good idea of Perelman's writing, see the Marx Brothers movie *Monkey Business* (1931). He also wrote the screenplay for *Around the World in 80 Days* (1956). YA

Perl, Lila (n.d.) Raised and schooled in Brooklyn, New York, Perl was first a cookbook and travel writer. Then she became a writer of adult and young people's fiction and non-fiction. She often writes about teenage girls who overcome self-consciousness and insecurity, and about their family problems. In *That Crazy April* (1974), 11-year-old Cress has made only two friends after a year in a new neighborhood: Monique, a junior fashion model who does not care that Cress is short and plump, and David, who wants to eat every cookie Cress can bake. Crazy events make Cress take a fresh look at herself, her mother, and her friends' values. In *Me and Fat Glenda* (1972), Glenda is an overweight friend of Sara, whose family has an unusual life-style: They move from California to New York City in a garbage truck, set up junk sculpture in their yard, and do not accept their neighbors. These pressures almost break up the girls' friendship, but their passion for alphabet burgers, such as apple-burgers, bananaburgers, and cheeseburgers, helps sustain their friendship. A sequel is *Fat Glenda's Summer Romance* (1986), in which Glenda struggles with her weight and self-image at a summer camp where she works as a waitress. In *Dumb Like Me, Olivia Potts* (1976) Olivia proves she is as smart as her sister and brother when she solves a neighborhood mystery. *Tybbee Trimble's Hard Times* (1984) sets Tybbee's wish to go to the circus against the needs of her sick mother. *Marleen, The Horror Queen* (1985), tells about a 13-year-old girl trying to deal with moving to a New York City suburb with her bodybuilder mother. If you enjoy the books of Lila Perl, you may also like those of *Judy Blume. MR

Perrault, Charles (1628–1703) This French lawyer, writer, and critic was well known in his lifetime for writing dialogues arguing that current writers were better than past ones. But you may know him best for collecting and publishing, with his son Pierre, a book whose subtitle was *Contes de ma Mère l'Oye* (*Stories of My Mother Goose*) (1697). These Mother Goose fairy tales included "Little Red Riding Hood," "Sleeping Beauty," "Bluebeard," and "Cinderella." All have been translated into English and many other languages, and these highly imaginative stories have been adapted into operas, ballets,

The tale of the murderer Bluebeard is
one of many collected by Charles Perrault.

*pantomime shows, and other art forms over
the centuries. Perhaps you are most familiar
with the *Walt Disney animated film adaptations. One is *Sleeping Beauty,* filmed in 1959,
which also used music composed by Pyotr Ilich Tchaikovsky (1840–1893), originally written
for *The Sleeping Beauty* ballet (1890). MR

Perry Mason is one of the busiest fictional detectives of all time, because his creator, *Erle
Stanley Gardner, wrote more than 80 novels
about him, beginning with *The Case of the
Velvet Claws* (1933) and ending with *The Case
of the Postponed Murder* (1973). Mason, born in
1891, is a lawyer, large but not overweight, with
gray eyes, thick hair, and an effective speaking
voice. He must be convinced of a client's innocence before he will take on a case, but he is
not above a little extralegal effort at times. Operating in Los Angeles, Mason has a faithful
secretary, Della Street, who has several times
refused to marry him because he would not let
her keep her job after marriage. Paul Drake provides needed assistance as the private investigator. Most of Mason's cases end in a
courtroom, and the possibilities for dramatic
clashes and revelations there are well handled.
Seven movies have been made of the novels, including *The Case of the Velvet Claws* in 1936.
A TV series that began in 1957 was so popular it lasted 10 years and is still shown
today. MR & YA

Persephone is the Greek goddess of fertility
and the wife of Hades, king of the underworld.
Her Roman counterpart is Proserpina. The
daughter of *Zeus and *Demeter, she is carried
off by Hades to become queen of the underworld. Zeus commands Hades to free Persephone, but because she has eaten a
pomegranate seed in Hades' realm, she can return to her mother for only two-thirds of the
year. During Persephone's absence from Earth,
the grains wither and flowers die. Upon her return, crops blossom again.

Persephone's abduction and return, *symbols of death and rebirth in nature, were celebrated in ancient Greek religious rites known
as the Eleusinian Mysteries. It is said these
were started by Demeter, who stopped at
Eleusis while searching for her daughter and
later taught the Eleusinians her secret ceremonies for sowing and harvesting grain. *Dionysus was also celebrated during the Mysteries.

More-complete versions of the story are
found in *The Macmillan Book of Greek Gods
and Heroes* (1985) by Alice Low (1926–), *The
Story of Persephone* (1973) by *Penelope Farmer,
and *Demeter and Persephone* (1972) by Penelope Proddow (n.d.), and also in *Bulfinch's
Mythology,* by Thomas Bulfinch (1796–1867),
under "Proserpina." YA

Perseus was a mythological Greek hero, the
son of *Zeus and Danaë. His grandfather, Acri-

sus, heard a prophecy that if his daughter had a son, the son would kill him, so he set Danaë and her baby, Perseus, adrift on the sea in a chest. Zeus caused the waves to carry them to the island of Seriphos, and they were rescued by a fisherman. Polydectes, the fisherman's brother, was ruler of the island, and he fell in love with Danaë. When he realized that Perseus was in the way, he tricked him and sent him on a dangerous quest to bring back the snake-covered head of Medusa, a *Gorgon.

Perseus avoided being turned to stone by Medusa's gaze, because the Nymphs lent him winged sandals and a helmet that made him invisible. He cut off Medusa's head and started for home. In Ethiopia, Perseus rescued Andromeda, who had been offered as a sacrifice, and turned to stone the sea monster who was coming to devour her by showing the monster Medusa's head. He returned home with Andromeda and found that Polydectes had tried to rape his mother. Perseus took revenge by turning him to stone too. Later, he took part in games and accidentally killed his grandfather with a discus, fulfilling the terrible prophecy. You can read about the adventures of Perseus in *Nathaniel Hawthorne's *A Wonder-Book for Girls and Boys.* MR & YA

Persuasion, by *Jane Austen, is set in England in the early 19th century. The story centers on Anne Elliot, a sweet young woman in her 20s whose godmother, Lady Russell, and father, Sir Walter Elliot, oppose her engagement to a young naval officer, Frederick Wentworth, because he does not have much money. In the custom of the time, Anne does as they wish. Sir Walter spends money freely, so the family must rent their house to Admiral and Mrs. Croft. By coincidence, Mrs. Croft is Wentworth's sister. When Wentworth and Anne meet again, they remember their former love, but now there is another complication. Both are romantically involved with others. Eventually, the others fall in love with other people, leaving Anne and Wentworth free to recognize the constancy of their love. It does not hurt matters that Wentworth has become rich in the meantime. If this romantic novel of manners interests you, read Austen's more famous *Pride and Prejudice.* YA

Peter, Saint (d. A.D. c.64) One of the 12 disciples of *Jesus Christ, Peter, after Christ's crucifixion, became the leader of the devoted followers who began to establish Christianity. Peter went to Rome to conduct his missionary work and become the head of the church there. The Roman Emperor Nero (A.D. 37–68) made a martyr of Peter by having him crucified, head downward according to tradition. Jesus had said to him, "Thou art Peter and upon this rock I will build my church," and from this pronouncement the Roman Catholic papacy, considering Peter to have been the first bishop of Rome, claims direct succession. Jesus also said to Peter, "I will give unto thee the keys of the kingdom of *heaven," which has led to the popular picture of him at the Pearly Gates deciding whether or not a soul is to be admitted. Peter's original name was Simon; he was a fisherman and consequently became the patron saint of fishermen. Peter and *Paul were the primary organizers of the early Christian church.

Peter Pan, or The Boy Who Would Not Grow Up (1911), by *James M. Barrie, is the story of a boy who thinks that grownups have a tendency to spoil everything. He explains, "I just want always to be a little boy and have fun." He runs away from home and lives with the fairies in London's Kensington Gardens, and later joins a group of Lost Boys on the imaginary island of *Neverland. Friendly but very independent, Peter loves to boast loudly and give orders. He enjoys making mischief and is almost always fearless.

When the story begins, you meet the Darlings, their daughter, *Wendy, their sons, Michael and John, and their dog, *Nana, who is the children's nursemaid. On Nana's night off, Peter flies into the children's room and loses his shadow. He returns a week later to look for it, accompanied by the fairy Tinker Bell. Peter entices Wendy to come to Neverland to take care of the Lost Boys. Sprinkling fairy dust on all three children, he teaches them to fly, and they escape through the window just as their parents return. After a long and sometimes disagreeable flight, the four arrive at Neverland, where the boys are waiting. Also waiting are the pirates, led by villainous *Captain Hook and his bosun, Smee. Captain Hook has been Peter's mortal enemy ever since Peter cut off Hook's arm and threw it to a crocodile. Finding the arm delicious, the beast has followed Hook ever since. Fortunately for Hook, the crocodile also swallowed a clock which ticks loudly and warns of its arrival.

Wendy becomes a mother to the boys, cooking their meals and mending clothes. Hook has a violent encounter with Peter at Mermaid's Lagoon, from which Peter barely escapes. This is followed by the massacre by the pirates of the Piccaninny tribe of Red Indians, allies of the Lost Boys, after which Hook and his men capture all the young people except for Peter and carry them off to the ship *Jolly Roger*. As Hook is about to force his prisoners to "walk the plank," Peter appears. He fights Hook and sends him over the side to the eagerly awaiting crocodile. The victorious youngsters sail the ship home to the Darlings, where all are reunited. Peter remains where and what he is, preferring his freedom to the awful risk of growing up. He reappears every year to visit Wendy and, much later, her own daughter, Jane.

Peter Pan was first a very successful play, produced in 1904, in which many famous actresses have played Peter, a difficult role because Peter flies through the air. An animated movie was made of the book in 1953. MR

Peter Wimsey, Lord One of the most attractive of amateur fictional detectives, Lord Peter is the creation of *Dorothy L. Sayers. Born in 1890, educated at Oxford University, England, and a captain in World War I, Wimsey becomes an elegant man-about-town, a collector of rare books, and a talented pianist when he is not carrying out important missions for the British Foreign Office. He drives a Daimler and is served by Bunter, his sergeant in the war. Wimsey appears in all but one of Sayers's detective

novels. Typical of his efforts are those in *Clouds of Witness* (1928), in which he clears his brother, the Duke of Denver, of murder. In *Strong Poison* (1930) he meets Harriet Vane, with whom he falls in love and who works with him in *Have His Carcase* (1932), in which a murdered man is found on a beach. *The Nine Tailors* finds Wimsey faced with a peculiar problem as to how a man was murdered. Finally, in *Busman's Honeymoon* (1937) he and Harriet, who accepted him in *Gaudy Night, are married and set off on their honeymoon, only to find a body in the house they have rented. A miniseries of three Wimsey adventures was produced for television in 1973. YA

Peterkin Papers, The (1880) This collection of stories by *Lucretia P. Hale relates the nonsensical adventures of the Peterkin family— Mr. and Mrs. Peterkin, Agamemnon, Solomon John, and Elizabeth Eliza. The Peterkins have absolutely no common sense whatsoever. Because of this curious fact, they have the most amazing adventures. For example, when Mrs. Peterkin puts salt in her coffee, the family enlists the aid of the local chemist and then of the herb woman, neither of whom can improve the taste of the coffee. Finally they call on their sensible friend, the *Lady from Philadelphia, who suggests that Mrs. Peterkin make a new cup of coffee, and the problem is solved. Then there is the time that Elizabeth Eliza's new piano is placed by the movers with its keyboard facing the window, and Elizabeth Eliza has to sit outside and reach through the porch window to play it. Another time, the family has to call in a carpenter to renovate the house because the Christmas tree is too tall. These stories are just as funny as they were more than a century ago. The adventures of the Peterkins were continued in *The Last of the Peterkins* (1886). All the stories were collected in *The Complete Peterkin Papers* (1960). MR

Petrarch, Francis (1304–1374) An Italian poet and scholar who influenced writers and thinkers for centuries, Petrarch, unlike his medieval contemporaries, was interested in nature, psy-

---

MR = Middle Reader   YA = Young Adult Reader   * = See this main entry

chology, and the real feelings of love. When Petrarch was young he studied law, but he was especially interested in Latin and Greek literature. He later took minor orders in the church at the papal court in Avignon, France, served as a diplomat, and traveled extensively. His poetry was so loved that he was crowned a poet laureate in Rome in 1341, for the first time since antiquity. He spent his later years traveling throughout northern Italy.

While a young man, Petrarch fell in love with Laura, perhaps an imaginary person, and she inspired much of his poetry. He wrote about his feelings in a more realistic fashion than writers had done before. In *Rime* (Lyrics), a collection of his lyrics, sonnets, ballads, and madrigals, and later in *Trionfi* (Triumphs), he described in detail how her unattainable love brought him happiness and misery. He loved literature and enjoyed living well. You might like to read *Il cansoniere* (The Song Book), about his love for Laura and his conflict between body and soul. Early translators include *Geoffrey Chaucer and *Edmund Spenser. It was more recently translated as *Petrarch's Sonnets* (1931) by Joseph Auslander (1897–1965). You will find a good selection of Petrarch's works in *Petrarch: Selected Sonnets, Odes and Letters* (1966), edited by Thomas G. Bergin (1904–1987). YA

Petrified Forest, The (1935) By *Robert E. Sherwood, this play contrasts a ruthless, though at times humane, bandit and a young, sensitive intellectual. They are both characters of a declining society, like trees in a petrified forest. The events take place during one day at the Black Mesa Bar-B-Q, a gas station and lunch counter in the Arizona desert, on the edge of a petrified forest. Jason Maple, the proprietor, hides cowardice under an American Legion uniform. His daughter, Gabby, is lively and vital but frustrated, and dreams of joining her mother in France. Alan Squier, a failed author from New England, stops off while hitchhiking to California. He shows interest and sensitivity toward Gabby. She, in turn, sees an elegance in him that contrasts with the foot-

ball hero who works in the station and wants Gabby to love him. Gabby proposes to run away with Alan. He is touched but refuses, and gets ready to leave. At that moment, Duke Mantee, a hunted killer, decides to use the Bar-B-Q as a temporary meeting place for his gang. Because Alan and Gabby have fallen in love, he makes out a will to enable Gabby to travel to France, and then asks Mantee to shoot him. He calls Mantee "the last apostle of rugged individualism." Legionnaires arrive with Gabby's father and armed policemen; and, in a gunfight, Mantee escapes to an almost certain death. But he keeps his promise to kill Alan. If you liked this play, try the play *When You Comin' Back, Red Ryder?* (1977) by Mark Medoff (1950–), also set in a Western diner. It was adapted for film in 1979. A movie of *The Petrified Forest* was made in 1936. YA

Petry, Ann (1908–) Born in Connecticut, the daughter of a druggist, Petry became one herself. Later, she became an advertising salesperson and a journalist. She has written adult stories and novels but is known for her works of fiction and history for younger readers. Such stories as *The Drugstore Cat* (1949), about a mean little feline, are charming, but Petry's black heritage inspired her to write stories and histories of persecution and triumph over odds. *Harriet Tubman* (1955) tells about the heroic runaway slave who guided others to freedom in the North. At the end of each chapter, Petry adds a summary of events happening at that time. *Tituba of Salem Village* is about a slave uprooted from Barbados, in the Caribbean, to Boston, who was put on trial as a witch. Petry's *Legends of the Saints* (1970) tells about 10 holy people from around the world, including Francis of Assisi (1182–1226) and Joan of Arc (1412–1432). MR

Pevsner, Stella (n.d.) Born, raised, and schooled in Illinois, one of six children, Stella enjoyed playacting and later, as an adult, worked in community theater and for an advertising agency. Acting on the suggestion of one of her children, Pevsner began writing stories for younger readers. They are witty and easy to identify with, as you can tell from their titles. Her first story, *Break a Leg* (1969), describes how being in a play helps a girl overcome shyness and learn about kids who are different. *Footsteps on the Stairs* (1970) is about the same girl's brother, who learns to overcome his fears. *Call Me Heller, That's My Name* (1973), is about a girl who tries to deal with an aunt. *A Smart Kid Like You* (1975) is about a junior high girl whose stepmother is a math teacher at her school. *Keep Stompin' Till the Music Stops* (1977) shows how a learning-disabled boy and his great-grandfather solve their problems. *And You Give Me a Pain* (1978) is 13-year-old Andrea's story about her older sister and personal relationships. In *Lindsay, Lindsay, Fly Away Home* (1983) a teenager suspects her parents are breaking up her relationship with a boyfriend. *Me, My Goat, and My Sister's Wedding* (1985) deals with a boy keeping a goat in his clubhouse while the family prepares for his sister's wedding. In *Sister of the Quints* (1987), a girl must decide whether to stay with her father and his quintuplets, or return to her mother. MR

Pfeffer, Susan Beth (1948–) Born and educated in New York City, Susan wrote her first novel when she was 6 years old. Pfeffer became an English teacher, and her hobbies include baseball, biographies, movie history, and theater. Her popular books for teenagers, written with humor and sympathy, deal with real situations, some of them serious. Her well-known works include *The Year Without Michael and About David* (1980), in which a girl and her friends remember their schoolmate who killed his parents and then committed suicide. In *A Matter of Principle* (1982) a girl faces difficult moral problems. On the lighter side, *Fantasy Summer* (1984) tells about Annie and three other girls who are summer interns for a magazine in New York City. *Getting Even* (1986) continues Annie's history. Pfeffer's fiction for younger readers includes *Kid Power Strikes Back* (1984), which shows how young people can be creative in a business sense. *Truth or Dare* (1984) deals with the pains of trying to

make new friends in junior high school. If you enjoy her books, other authors you may also want to try are *Judy Blume, *Cynthia Voigt, and *Paul Zindel. MR & YA

Phantom Tollbooth, The (1961) In this popular fantasy by Norton Juster (1929–), Milo is bored by life, especially by school. One day he is given a tollbooth, containing coins and a map, that, like Alice's looking-glass, enables him to enter another world. Milo gets in his little red car, drives through the tollbooth, and heads for the city of Dictionopolis. He asks the Whether Man if he is going the right way, and is told there are no wrong roads to anywhere. He asks a large shaggy dog, who barks at anyone wasting time, for help with his boredom. The dog says, "Help yourself," and gets into Milo's car. The guard at the gates of Dictionopolis asks why they want to enter. When Milo does not know, the guard puts a "Why Not" button on Milo. The Humbug joins them and they go off to rescue the princesses, Rhyme and Reason. They meet many characters, including the Mathemagician, who is mining numbers and using the broken ones as fractions. Milo uses logic to trick the Mathemagician into giving them permission to rescue the princesses. When they do, Rhyme says Milo is beginning to understand why learning ends boredom. Milo says a tearful goodbye to his friends and drives off. The fantasy in this story, in which Juster pokes fun at all who deal in logic and reason, may remind you of *Alice's Adventures in Wonderland* and *Through the Looking-Glass* by *Lewis Carroll, and *The Wonderful Wizard of Oz* by *L. Frank Baum. *The Phantom Tollbooth* was made into a movie in 1969. MR

Philip Marlowe, *Raymond Chandler's fictional detective, ranks with *Sam Spade as the accepted models for the modern hard-boiled private investigator. Marlowe is about 40 years old, six feet tall, and once worked for the Los Angeles district attorney. He is often at odds with the police, who sometimes beat him up. Marlowe likes music and art and can quote such poets as *T.S. Eliot. Though he needs money most of the time, Marlowe is choosy about his clients, most of whom are rich but unhappy and often inclined to murder. He first appears in *The Big Sleep* (1939), centering on a murder involving the two psychopathic daughters of a wealthy, dying man. The novel is set in Los Angeles, as are the other novels. Marlowe is the hero of seven books in all, including *Farewell, My Lovely; The Lady in the Lake* (1943), in which Marlowe investigates the disappearance of a man's wife; and *The Long Goodbye* (1953), in which Marlowe is hired by an ex-convict to find his girl friend. Movies have been made of *The Big Sleep* and *The Lady in the Lake* in 1946 and *The Long Goodbye* in 1973. A TV series about Marlowe was produced in 1954. YA

Philistines were a non-Semitic people who came to Palestine, possibly from the island of Crete, in the 12th century B.C. They were rivals of the people of Israel for centuries, until *David helped defeat them. The Philistines were great ironworkers but were considered— incorrectly, new archeological evidence suggests—crude and uneducated.

"Philistine" is now used to describe a person without culture, whose main interests are in ordinary and material things, and is often applied to people who dislike or oppose new trends in the arts. *Ambrose Bierce, in *The Devil's Dictionary* (1906), defined a Philistine as "one whose mind is the creature of its environment, following the fashion in thought, feeling, and sentiment. He is sometimes learned, frequently prosperous, commonly clean and always solemn." YA

Phipson, Joan (1912–) An Australian short-story writer and novelist, Phipson deals often with unpopular or handicapped children and their animals. In *Good Luck to the Rider* (1953) a girl works with an ugly foal and overcomes her shyness and indecision. In *The Family Conspiracy* (1962) the Barker children try to pay for their mother's operation, and the family pulls together. In its sequel, *Threat to the Barkers* (1963), 14-year-old Vincent discovers the family sheep are being stolen, and he is kid-

napped. *Birken* (1965) is about an orphan calf and its adventures with the youngsters who adopt him. In *The Cats* (1976), Jim and Willy's parents have just won a lottery, and kidnappers take them to the remote region called the Outback. The kidnappers' plans go wrong when huge cats chase them. In *A Tide of Flowering* (1981), Mark is haunted by the memory of his mother slipping off a sailboat, and he feels that his father and new stepmother do not want him. When he saves a crippled girl's life and injures himself, they become good friends, helping him to mature. A girl with a violent temper and an old blind man become friends in *The Watcher in the Garden* (1982). MR

Piazza Tales (1856), by *Herman Melville, is a collection of six stories with surprise endings. The best known of the stories are *"Bartleby the Scrivener" and *Benito Cereno," which explore the difference between appearance and reality. "The Bell-Tower" tells about a prideful architect who tests the limits of design. He casts the heaviest bells that he can, builds the tallest possible bell tower to hold them, and creates an almost-human robot to ring them. But a tiny defect brings about the downfall of the entire structure, and the robot kills the architect. In the series of 10 sketches that constitute "The Encantadas, or The Enchanted Isles," Melville is referring to the Galapagos Islands, which he describes as "cinders of despair . . . extinct volcanos . . . cut by the equator." Melville visited them on his whaling trips, and they became famous when *Charles Darwin illustrated his theory of evolution by referring to animals he encountered there. In "The Piazza," Melville tells about a sailor who retires to an old farmhouse, adds a piazza, and from it sees a glistening house on a distant hill. He travels to that house and finds the lady Marianne, who looks at his house in the same way he looks at hers. In "The Lightning-Rod Man" a stranger appears at a house with a walking stick—a polished copper rod, four feet long. In trying to sell the rod he tells horrible tales about people killed by lightning, but because he frightens his listeners with the idea that he can circumvent the intention of God, he is sent on his way without making a sale. Another writer whose stories you may like is *Nathaniel Hawthorne, who was Melville's friend and had a great influence on his writing. YA

Picture of Dorian Gray, The (1891) This short novel by *Oscar Wilde begins in an artist's studio, where Basil Hallward is painting the portrait of his young friend Dorian. Lord Henry Wotton visits and is struck by Dorian's great beauty and innocence. Languid, urbane, and very cynical, Wotton amuses himself by telling Dorian how old age can ruin a handsome face, and Dorian says he would give his soul to be always young and let the portrait grow old.

Lord Henry undertakes to introduce Dorian to his decadent world. When Dorian falls in love with a pretty actress, Sibyl Vane, and wants to marry her, Wotton's contempt for the girl causes Dorian to reject her. Dorian notices an eerie change in his portrait, a "touch of cruelty" in the mouth, and he is sick with horror. Sibyl kills herself, but Wotton convinces Dorian that he is not to blame. With the portrait hidden away, Dorian gives himself up to sensual pleasures. His strange and dangerous charm is the talk of society, and his good looks never seem to change. When Basil asks for an explanation of the ugly rumors about his life, Dorian shows Basil the portrait. The artist is horrified to see that the exquisite face in the painting has changed into something old and repulsive. In a rage, Dorian murders Basil and disposes of the body. He yearns to stop the awful decay of his soul, but it is too late. He tries to free himself by attacking the portrait with a knife. He is discovered dead, wrinkled and withered, while the portrait has mysteriously returned to its original beauty. The novel was adapted for the movies in 1945 and 1971, and for television in 1973. See also *Faust. YA

Pied Piper of Hamelin, The A figure in German legend, the Pied Piper appeared in 1284 in the town of Hamelin when it was overrun with rats. The townspeople agreed to pay the stranger when he said he could magically play a pipe and get rid of them. Sure enough, after a

contract was drawn, the piper played, and the rats followed him and drowned in the river. But the town leaders refused to honor the contract, so the stranger returned, and in revenge played his pipe again. This time he lured the children, and they vanished behind a door in the Koppenberg Hill. You might enjoy reading the best-loved version of the story in the narrative poem "The Pied Piper of Hamelin" (1842) by *Robert Browning. Several versions of the tale have been produced in film. MR & YA

Piercy, Marge (1936–) A novelist and poet, Piercy grew up in a poor neighborhood in Detroit, where she early became aware of social and political injustice. Her first novel, *Going Down Fast* (1969), is about buildings—and the people in them—going down fast through urban renewal. In *Dance the Eagle to Sleep* (1970), Piercy uses a *science fiction story to make parallels with the turmoil of the 1960s. In *The High Cost of Living* (1978), middle-class Detroit is the locale for a novel about a feminist, an academic man, and a high school boy. In *Braided Lives* (1982), she writes about the hardship of two independent, unconventional women growing up in the 1950s. In her first collection of poetry, *Breaking Camp* (1968), she makes powerful statements about poverty in America. Piercy has published many volumes of poetry in which she speaks out on social and political issues. If you like poetry that carries strong statements about poverty and urban America, you should also read *The Poetry of Black America*, by *Arnold Adoff. YA

Pierrot is one of the stock characters of English and French *pantomime derived from Pedrolino, a character from the *commedia dell' arte*, the popular Italian comedy of the 16th to 18th centuries. Pale-faced, dressed in a loose-fitting white outfit, Pierrot is the awkward, mournful victim of unrequited love. The object of his affection is often *Columbine, the maidservant and lover of *Harlequin.

Piers Plowman (c.1362–c.1387) is an *allegorical poem written in Old English whose full title is *The Vision of William Concerning Piers*

Plowman. Believed to be the work of William Langland, or Langley (c.1332–c.1400), it was also thought for a time to have been written by as many as five writers. It is a masterpiece of medieval literature and gives you many vivid details of contemporary life. You learn from Piers, a simple plowman, how to live in order to be worthy of spiritual salvation. Will, the narrator, wanders on the Malvern Hills, where he then falls asleep and, in a series of visions, sees, among other things, a tower of Truth (God), a dungeon of Wrong (the devil), and a world filled with different classes of people. The characters include a number of virtues and vices personified, among them Conscience, who persuades the people to reject the seven Deadly Sins and search for Truth. Piers, who becomes identified with *Jesus, tries with only partial success to get the people to see Truth and attain spiritual salvation. There is a good translation in prose available in an inexpensive paperback. You may want to compare it with another poem written at about the same time, *Geoffrey Chaucer's *The Canterbury Tales.* YA

Pigman, The (1968) This novel by *Paul Zindel is narrated by its main characters, Lorraine Jensen and John Conlon, who take turns writing chapters. Lorraine and John are high school sophomores who are bored with school, their parents, and their lives. Then they befriend Mr. Angelo Pignati, a lonely widower in his late 50s whose greatest pleasure in life are his dead wife's collection of pig sculptures and his visits to the zoo to feed an old baboon named Bobo. The Pigman, as John and Lorraine nickname him, enjoys telling them jokes, buying them gifts, and even roller skating with them. In some ways he is more of a kid than John and Lorraine are. When Pignati has a heart attack, John and Lorraine promise to take care of his house while he is in the hospital. But they have a party that gets out of control, and the pig collection is destroyed. When Pignati comes home he is heartbroken, but he forgives John and Lorraine and agrees to meet them once again at the zoo. There they learn that Bobo has died, and Mr. Pignati has a stroke and dies. John and Lorraine believe that their actions have helped cause his death. You can read more about John and Lorraine in the sequel, *The Pigman's Legacy* (1980). YA

pilgrimage is a journey undertaken by a traveler or wanderer, usually to a far-distant place or shrine. Often the pilgrim seeks to find a holy place for devotion. Sometimes pilgrims set out to find miracles—for example, those who make pilgrimages to places such as Lourdes in France, where miraculous cures are said to have occurred. Pilgrimages were popularized in the late 4th century, first as journeys to places of worship, later as trips to earn forgiveness for sins. The pilgrimages created roads and towns and brought greater understanding of foreign places. But pilgrimages are not always welcome. In the Middle Ages Muslims created difficulties for Christian pilgrims to the Holy Land, which was one of the reasons for the Crusades. One of the best-known pilgrimages is the annual visit made by more than 500,000 Muslims to the Great Mosque in Mecca, Saudi Arabia, the holiest of Islamic shrines. You can read about pilgrims and pilgrimages in *The Canterbury Tales, by *Geoffrey Chaucer, about a medieval pilgrimage, and in *The Bridge of San Luis Rey, by *Thornton Wilder, in which a woman and her companion, returning from a pilgrimage to a shrine, are among the five victims of a bridge collapse. YA

Pilgrim's Progress, The (1678, 1684) By *John Bunyan, this famous religious *allegory shows the way to salvation through a Christian life. Subtitled *From This World to That Which Is to Come*, this English work was written in part while its author was imprisoned for being a traveling Baptist preacher. In the form of a dream, Bunyan wrote about a man named Christian, who attempted to reach New Jerusalem in order to avoid the destruction that is foretold in the New Testament of the *Bible. He flees from the City of Destruction through the Slough of Despond. Along the way he has many dangerous encounters, with Vanity Fair, Despair, the Giant, and Apollyon, a monster.

Christian battles the monster Apollyon in
The Pilgrim's Progress.

He meets Faithful, Hopeful, and other companions, and such neighbors as Obstinate and Talkative. Christian, supported by his faith, finally reaches the Celestial City. The first part of *The Pilgrim's Progress* was so popular that Bunyan published a second part in 1684, in which Christian's wife, Christiana, his children, a neighbor, and their guide, Mr. Greatheart, make a journey to join him in the Celestial City. This allegory was one of the most popular works of its time. Because of its realistic dialogue, its humor, its lively characters, and the theme of a humble man's journey to self-understanding, it influenced the later art of novel writing. *Mark Twain gave his book *The Innocents Abroad*, about his trip to Europe and the Holy Land, the subtitle *The New Pilgrims' Progress.* YA

Pinballs, The (1977) By *Betsy Byars, this is a sad and funny story of three children who go to a foster home. The youngest, Thomas J., had been deserted as an infant. Elderly twins kept

him, but they had both suffered broken hips, so he is brought to Mr. and Mrs. Mason's home. Thirteen-year-old Harvey, whose mother had deserted him to find herself in a commune and whose father had run over him by accident, also comes to the home. Carlie, a slightly older girl, is already there. She had trouble with a stepfather and had slept with two stepsisters and a half-sister in one bed. All feel that bad things will keep happening to them. Carlie says they are like pinballs in a game, bouncing around, hitting bumpers and lights. At first they try to control things by saying "no" to everything. Then they begin to help each other, and Mr. and Mrs. Mason pay attention to them, showing them that they can say "yes" and can be kind and loving to one another. Carlie finally says they are not pinballs any more. Other books about foster children you may enjoy are *Sensible Kate* (1943) by Doris Gates (1901–1987), about a 10-year-old girl who tries to find happiness in a foster home in California, and *Won't Know Til I Get There* (1977) by *Walter Dean Myers, about a 14-year-old boy and his foster brother, who are caught spray-painting a subway car and are sentenced to do volunteer work in a home for elderly people. MR

Pindar (518–438 B.C.) was a master of Greek choral poetry, especially *odes that were sung and danced at victories of the Olympian and other games. They used complicated patterns, bold images, and mythical subjects, and they often had a high moral or religious tone. Conservative and sure of his superior talent, Pindar often wrote for princes, and his odes served as models for many generations. Forty-four of them survive. He wrote 17 books of poetry, known today mostly in fragments and references from other sources. The Pindaric ode was especially popular as a poetic form during the 17th and 18th centuries, when such writers as *John Milton rediscovered this greatest of all Greek lyric poets. Two well-known Pindaric odes are "Ode to the Departing Year" (1796) by *Samuel Taylor Coleridge and "Ode to the Confederate Dead" (1926) by Alan Tate (1899–1979). YA

Pinkwater, Daniel (Manus) (1941–) One of the zaniest, funniest, most imaginative writers for young readers, Pinkwater was born in Tennessee and reared by his Polish immigrant family in so many cities that he became a fan of the unknown and the unusual. He was an art instructor in and around New York City, and is now settled in upstate New York. Pinkwater's many books—most of which he illustrated—are filled with fun and wordplay and combine familiar people and situations with unexpected bursts of fantasy. For example, in *The Terrible Roar* (1970), a lion finds that his roar makes people disappear, so he finally roars himself to where the people are. *Fat Men from Space* is a nutrition-aware story about junk food raiders. You will also enjoy *The Hoboken Chicken Emergency* (1977), a funny story about a boy who buys a six-foot chicken; *Yobgorgle: Mystery Monster of Lake Ontario*; and *Jolly Roger: A Dog of Hoboken* (1985), about a chow chow who becomes a pack leader.

Lizard Music (1976) is an earlier, more imaginative story similar to the popular movie *Home Alone* (1990), in which a boy, left alone while his parents are on vacation, finds some intelligent lizards. *I Was a Second Grade Werewolf* (1983) deals with the frustrations of a kid who cannot convince his classmates that he has turned into a creature that can eat milk cartons. Older readers will enjoy books about The Snarkout Boys, such as the humorous adventure *The Snarkout Boys and the Avocado of Death* (1982), in which two boys, Walter Galt and Winston Bongo, search for a scientist. A sequel is *The Snarkout Boys and the Baconburg Horror* (1984), which follows the totally crazy adventures of Walter and Winston and their friend, a girl named Rat, as they search for a werewolf who is terrorizing Baconburg. The Snarkout Boys novels often refer to his other books and to popular teenage heroes. Pinkwater's collection of radio essays, in *Chicago Days/Hoboken Nights* (1991), is filled with both stories and autobiographical material. Pinkwater's wife, Jill, sometimes writes books with him. One is *Superpuppy* (1977), about choosing and training the right puppy. MR & YA

Pinocchio, The Adventures of (1883) By Carlo Colodi [Carlo Lorenzini] (1826–1890), this Italian story is about a puppet who comes to life. An old carpenter gives his friend Gepetto a piece of wood that can talk, and Gepetto carves a puppet named Pinocchio, who walks and talks. Pinocchio gets into all sorts of trouble, such as selling his schoolbook to buy a ticket to a puppet show, where he is kidnapped. One problem for Pinocchio is that when he tells a lie his nose grows longer. He is often embarrassed by this. A cricket, who is his moral adviser, and a guardian fairy, "a beautiful child with blue hair," try to steer Pinocchio in the right direction, Pinocchio ignores their advice and, after several fantastic adventures, including one in a land where naughty children turn into donkeys, he finds Gepetto in the belly of a fish and rescues him. The fairy rewards the puppet by turning him into a real boy. You probably know about *Pinocchio* from the

Pinocchio

*Walt Disney cartoon that was made in 1940. But be sure to read the book, which has more adventures than the film does. MR

Pinter, Harold (1930–) Born in East London, England, this highly original poet and playwright published poetry before he was 20 years old, then became an actor and a television writer. In *The Room* (1957), *The Birthday Party* (1958), and *The Dumb Waiter* (1960), all the characters are in one room, where the routine is shattered by outsiders and bizarre events. These early plays have been called "comedies of menace," and in most of Pinter's work, the struggles for survival against real—or perceived—fear can, surprisingly, make you laugh. *The Caretaker* (1960) was Pinter's first big success. It explores the changing relationships between two brothers and a tramp. Like so many of his works, it deals with mixed-up reality and

the limits of communicating with words. In *Betrayal* (1980), you see a wife's affair with her husband's best friend go from finish to start—backward in time. Pinter often uses themes based on family hatreds and mental anguish, and his style is characterized by broken sentences and silences. It is so well known that it has become the adjective "Pinteresque." You can see his work as a screenwriter in films, including *The Servant* (1963), in which roles become reversed between master and servant, and *Accident* (1967), in which a college professor is entwined in a relationship with a student and his girl friend. Other modern playwrights whose works you may enjoy are *Edward Albee, *Anthony Shaffer, *Peter Shaffer, and *Tom Stoppard. YA

Pippi Longstocking (1945), by *Astrid Lindgren, is about a 9-year-old orphan girl named Pippi, who has fantastic strength and the freedom to do and say what she pleases. She lives with a horse and monkey next to two normal children at the edge of a Swedish village, and believes that her mother is an angel and her father is a Cannibal King. When two policemen come to take her to an orphanage, Pippi picks them up by their belts. On the one day she goes to school, she tells all the things that are wrong with the school system. Pippi is messy and wears one black and one brown stocking. She tells tall tales and talks in funny ways. The two good children who live next to her are shocked at the way Pippi puts down the world of grownups. If you like this outrageous and outspoken character, you can read of her further adventures in *Pippi Goes on Board* (1946) and *Pippi in the South Seas* (1948). *Pippi in the South Seas* was filmed in 1970. MR

Pirandello, Luigi (1867–1936) This Italian novelist and playwright was born in Sicily, the son of a mine owner. He was educated in universities in Rome and Bonn, Germany, and was later a professor of literature. His personal life was clouded for many years by his wife's mental illness, and pessimistic themes of madness, jealousy, and death are often in his works. His characters confront many options and problems. For example, in the novel *The Late Mattia Pascal* (1904), Pascal goes home to discover he cannot change the fact that he is dead.

Pirandello wrote poems and hundreds of short stories, but he is best known for a series of plays that try to distinguish the difference between "masks" and "faces" in order to see if people have stable, or real, personalities. The best known of these plays are *Henry IV* (1922), in which pretending to be crazy seems to be the only escape from an ugly world, and *Six Characters in Search of an Author*, in which the traditional approach to drama is mocked when a group of characters out of an unwritten play come to a rehearsal and demand that their lives be dramatized. When Pirandello became popular, he founded his own theater and took the company on European tours. He won the Nobel Prize for literature in 1934. If you like his style, which is the beginning of what is now called the "theater of the absurd," you might also read or try to see performances of plays by the later playwrights *Samuel Beckett and *Jean Genet. YA

"Pit and the Pendulum, The" (1842) By *Edgar Allan Poe, this famous short story creates horror—real and imagined—in your mind. It is the narrator himself who undergoes the ordeal in this *Gothic tale, making the suspense even more scary. It is early May 1808, in Toledo, Spain, and the monks of the Spanish *Inquisition read the narrator's sentence of death by torture. He faints and, regaining consciousness, imagines himself buried alive in a closed, damp environment. He explores his cell and is saved from plunging into a deep pit when he accidentally trips and falls. He sleeps, and when he wakes he finds himself strapped to a wooden frame underneath a crescent razor blade that swoops nearer and nearer with each swing of its pendulum. As the pendulum brushes his skin, he finds that rats have gnawed the rope enough for him to break free. His relief does not last, for the walls of his cell grow hotter, forcing him to the center, where the pit awaits. His resistance gains nothing, be-cause his invisible tormentors move the red-hot walls toward him. At the moment he is losing his foothold at the pit edge, the walls stop closing and the narrator is rescued. It was at that exact time that the French invaded Toledo. If you enjoyed this story, you will like the equally chilling tale "The Premature Burial" (1844), about a man who is terrified of being buried alive. A movie of "The Pit and the Pendulum" was made in 1961. YA

Plague, The By *Albert Camus, this well-known novel is about the changes that happen in a community when it battles a deadly disease. Dr. Bernard Rieux leads the fight. He sees a dead rat in the city of Oran in North Africa, then recognizes plague symptoms in a man who dies. The city is quarantined, and a common spirit develops that focuses on the doctor and the group around him. Dr. Rieux does not accept formal religion, but he deeply believes that the acts of people can defeat the plague. Father Paneloux is a Jesuit priest who believes that the city can only be saved by faith and divine help. One young volunteer, rejecting the philosophy of Paneloux, is helping Rieux, but he becomes a victim of the plague. The journalist Rambert thinks only of himself and getting out of the city. Rieux brings about a change in the attitude of Rambert, who then volunteers to help—only to lose his life in the plague. The novel is based on Camus's particular brand of existentialism: By joining together, people can find a meaning in life in spite of the absurdity of suffering and death. You may like to compare this with *The Stranger, about an alienated young man who commits a senseless murder. YA

Plaidy, Jean [Eleanor Hibbert] (1906–) An English novelist who uses many pseudonyms, Plaidy has produced more than 100 romantic and historical novels. Here are some you might like to read. In *The Sixth Wife* (1954), Henry VIII (1491–1547) has put his fifth wife to death and is looking for another. In *The Prince and the Quakeress* (1968), the prince is the teenage Prince of Wales, who becomes George III

(1738–1820). He meets Hanna, a Quaker girl, when he is 15 years old. Their romance and the obstacles to their doomed love play back and forth in the story. In *The Royal Road to Fotheringay* (1956), the story of Mary, Queen of Scots (1542–1587), is followed from her girlhood to her escape to France, her return to Scotland, her ill-fated marriage, and her captivity and death in England. In *The Captive Queen of Scots* (1973), Mary is held by her enemies after her husband's murder. Disguised as a laundress, she escapes and puts herself in the hands of Queen Elizabeth (1533–1603). If you enjoy historical novels, be sure to read one of the finest of them all, *Ivanhoe, by *Walter Scott. YA

Plath, Sylvia (1932–1963) Author of the novel *The Bell Jar, Plath was a poet and short-story writer noted for her disciplined and personal style. She began drawing and writing at an early age and won a number of literary and academic awards while still in her teens. Plath thought and wrote often about the difficulty of combining her life as a writer with her marriage and motherhood. At 20 she was chosen to be a guest editor at *Mademoiselle* magazine, and her summer as an apprentice in New York City is retold in *The Bell Jar*. After a severe nervous breakdown, Plath returned to college and graduated with many honors. She married the British poet Ted Hughes (1930–) in 1956 and had two children. In spite of poor health, an exhausting schedule, and periods of depression, she continued to write with great intensity until her death by suicide. Among her other books is the posthumous *Collected Poems* (1981). YA

Plato (c.428–c.346 B.C.), a Greek philosopher, was born into a prominent family. Though he was originally interested in politics, after his friend and teacher Socrates (469–399 B.C.) died, he spent years traveling to escape Greek injustice and stayed on and off in Sicily. There, he tried to teach philosophy to the rulers, but failed. In Greece he founded the Academy at Athens, a forerunner of today's university, where for the rest of his life he headed a school

of philosophy and science, and where students were prepared for a life of public service. While in Sicily and Greece he wrote his 25 *Dialogues* (and 13 *Letters*, which many critics believe he did not write himself). Socrates, not Plato, is the major figure in all but one of the dialogues, and obviously Socrates' ideas, which Socrates himself did not record, greatly influenced their philosophy. Nevertheless, the dialogues reflect the ideas of Plato himself. They vary from severe to witty and deal with such subjects as justice, knowledge, and the relationship between body and soul. One early dialogue you must be sure to read, the *Apology*, is closely based on Socrates' life and trial. The *Republic*, perhaps Plato's most famous dialogue, and *Laws*, his last work, deal with politics and government. Plato greatly affected modern thinking about ideals and morality, both through his own writing and teaching, and through that of his student, *Aristotle. Today, when you hear about something being "platonic," such as a relationship, it means something spiritual or idealistic, and refers to Plato's philosophy. YA

Platt, Kin (1911–) A novelist and cartoonist, Platt also writes stories for younger readers that are personal, realistic, and sometimes controversial. They are often about troubled teenagers, ghetto life, and drugs. In *Sinbad and Me* (1966), a story filled with action, pirate treasure, and secret codes, 12-year-old Steve defeats gangsters to solve the mystery of a sunken gambling ship. In *Hey Dummy* (1971), a retarded boy moves into the neighborhood and becomes friends with one boy, despite the suspicion, intolerance, and fear of adults. In *Chloris and the Creeps* (1973)—one of a series—Chloris gives up her fantasies about her father and comes to accept her mother's new husband. In two realistic and graphic novels, Platt describes the kind of life many boys lead in urban ghettos. *Headman* (1975) is about a boy who tries to find self-respect in a tough street gang whose members think only of fighting. It was followed by *Doomsday Gang* (1977), about five gang members in East Los Angeles who strive to find meaning in the violence of their lives. In *Dracula, Go Home* (1979), Platt provides a comic variation on the Dracula story with a solution to a jewel theft. In *Brogg's Brain* (1981), a 15-year-old boy and his girl friend see a movie that inspires the boy to win a sports event for his own satisfaction rather than to satisfy his father. If you like the realistic way Platt portrays modern teenage boys, you might like to compare them with *Holden Caulfield, a boy growing up in a very different, though also modern world, as told in *The Catcher in the Rye, by *J.D. Salinger. MR & YA

Playboy of the Western World, The (1907)

This play by *John Millington Synge is set in rural County Mayo, Ireland. Runaway Christy Mahon is idolized as a hero by villagers because he claims to have killed his bullying father in a fight. Christy tells his story over and over, though in reality he is a meek lad, who hit his father in desperation when Christy was being forced to marry a rich, older woman. Trying to impress a new girl friend, Christy starts to believe in his own heroism. But his bandaged father arrives, and when he humiliates his son, Christy hits his father harder on the head. Instead of approving the act, the crowd now turns on Christy and prepares to hang him. In a surprise ending, both Christy and his father escape together. The apparently anti-Irish depiction of blind hero worship turning to violence—based on a true event—provoked riots when the play premiered in Dublin and again in New York City. If you like this play, with its rich Irish language and *ironical tone, you may also enjoy Synge's other plays about Irish peasant life, including *Riders to the Sea* (1904), a gripping tragedy about a woman on an island off the coast of Ireland who has lost her husband and all six sons to the sea. A movie was made of *The Playboy of the Western World* in 1962. YA

Playing Beatie Bow (1980), by *Ruth Park, is

the story of 14-year-old Abigail Kirk, who lives in a high-rise apartment in Sydney, Australia, and resents both her mother's taking back her husband, who had deserted them, and the move to Norway they plan. Abigail (who had changed her name from Lynette to lose her former identity) watches children play a game called Beatie Bow, and notices a strange child watching but not joining in. She follows the girl, gets knocked unconscious by a man in the street, and finds herself in an old-fashioned bedroom in an unfamiliar house in the year 1873. It is the home of the mysterious girl, who is named Beatrice May Bow—Beatie Bow. Abigail learns the ways of the time, and grows to love the Bows, her new family. She learns that she has a special mission to perform for the family, but she does not know what that mission is, nor how she will ever get back to her own home and time. Abby falls for a young sailor named Judah Bow, Beatie's older brother, but she is told she cannot marry, or her young love will die. She rescues her friends when Mr. Bow, in a drunken fit, sets fire to his home, and, in saving Beatie's younger brother Gibbie from dying in the fire, Abby ensures that the Bow family line will continue. Her mission as Stranger now completed, Abby returns to the present. Through her experience, she now accepts the reality of moving to Norway. Years later she meets a man who reminds her of Judah and learns he is Gibbie's descendant. This delightful fantasy not only explores a fourth dimension but discusses love and commitment. Another book you may enjoy that takes the main character back in time is *A Storm Without Rain* (1983) by Jan Adkins (1944–), in which a boy returns to his grandfather on Cape Cod, Massachusetts. You will also enjoy *Time at the Top* by Edward Ormondroyd (1925–), about another girl who travels back in time. MR

Plimpton, George (1927–) Writing nonfiction

and editing *The Paris Review* may seem to be Plimpton's primary occupations, but this enthusiast of life, whose hobby is designing fireworks, is noted for throwing himself into more physical activities. Plimpton pitched in a postseason All-Star game in Yankee Stadium, was third-string quarterback for the Detroit Lions, shot baskets for the Boston Celtics, boxed with a former light-heavyweight champion, played goalie for two professional hockey teams, and fought in a bullfight staged by *Ernest Hemingway. He also conducted a major symphony orchestra, played percussion for another, delivered stand-up comedy, and hung from a trapeze in a circus. Plimpton is a real-life version of the character from the short story "The Secret Life of Walter Mitty" (1942), by *James Thurber, who daydreamed about the kinds of things that Plimpton actually does. Two books by Plimpton for younger readers are *The Rabbit's Umbrella* (1955), about a boy, his dog, and incompetent bank robbers, and *The Curious Case of Sidd Finch* (1987), about a fantastic character who can pitch a baseball faster than anyone. In his perfect game, he strikes out all the St. Louis Cardinals. Plimpton is also an actor, and had a small role—not playing himself—in a movie produced in 1968 based on his own book, *Paper Lion* (1966), which describes his experience with the Detroit Lions. A good way for older readers to get to know Plimpton's writing is to read *The Best of Plimpton* (1990). Younger readers who like sports stories might try those of *Rozanne Knudson, *Alfred Slote, and *John R. Tunis. MR & YA

Plutarch (c.46–c.120) was a Greek biographer and philosopher. He studied in Athens and then lived in Rome before returning to Greece. There he was a teacher, writer, municipal politician, and priest at Delphi. In *Parallel Lives*, he paired and then contrasted 46 biographies of Greeks and Romans. In this famous work he interpreted history, and he portrayed the characters of famous people, thus providing models either to copy or avoid. Filled with quotations, dramatic scenes, details, and critical comment, the *Lives* served for centuries as the main source of information about classical antiquity. *William Shakespeare based many of his historical plays on *Parallel Lives*. Later, John Dryden (1631–1700), an English poet, produced the most famous English translation of the work. The larger part of Plutarch's writings is the *Moralia*, a collection of dialogues and essays about philosophy, religion, and literature.

Edgar Allan Poe

Plutarch's interest was not in politics, but rather in the character and motives of men and women. His sympathy for women, children, and animals shows throughout his work. You will find in your library a number of editions of *Parallel Lives*, the most useful being *Plutarch's Lives* in a Modern Library edition using the translation by John Dryden. YA

Poe, Edgar Allan (1809–1849) A short-story writer, poet, journalist, and master of the tale of horror, Poe lived in poverty and despair. His poem "The Raven" (1845) best reveals his tormented life. Born in Boston and orphaned as an infant, Poe was adopted by John Allan of Richmond, Virginia. He was educated in England and then attended the University of Virginia. However, within a year, Poe withdrew because of his gambling debts and drinking. After serving for two years in the U.S. Army, Poe went to West Point, where he was dismissed for "gross neglect of duty." When Poe's foster father died, he was left penniless. He married his 14-year-old cousin, Virginia Clemm, and they lived in poverty until Virginia died when she was 24 years old. Poe died two years later, leaving behind masterful and terrifying tales, such as *"The Fall of the House of Usher," *"The Pit and the Pendulum," *"The Tell-Tale Heart," and *"The Gold Bug." Some of his poems, such as "To Helen" (1831), "The Bells" (1849), and "Annabel Lee" (1849), are among the most memorable in English. Poe also produced a number of brilliant and influential literary essays. There are many inexpensive editions of Poe's poetry and stories. YA

Poetry of Black America, The: Anthology of the 20th Century (1973) The editor, *Arnold Adoff, says this collection of 300 poems by blacks is as comprehensive as he could make it, and quality was his only basis for selection. The earliest poem is by W.E.B. DuBois (1868–1963), and the youngest poet is Julianne Perry (1952–). The poetry ranges over death, love, and historical people and popular culture, and the poets come from large cities and small towns. *Paul Laurence Dunbar, in his poem "Frederick Douglass," writes: "To sin and crime he gave their proper hue,/And hurled at evil what was evil's due." "For Malcolm X" by Nanina Alba (1917–1968) includes the line: "Hand raised by handsome chin toward head;/ Words pouring out to resurrect the dead." YA

Pohl, Frederick (1919–) With a reputation as one of the best *science fiction writers, Pohl often uses the genre to point up today's problems. He collaborated five times with C(yril) M. Kornbluth (1923–1958), including *The Space Merchants* (1953), a *satiric story about a world dominated by rival advertising agencies. One of his short-story collections has a typically witty title, *The Case Against Tomorrow* (1957). *Man Plus* (1976), his best-known book, is about a man turned into a cyborg to survive on Mars. Also a well-respected editor and anthologist, Pohl wrote an autobiography with another paradoxical title, *The Way the Future Was* (1979). If you enjoy his science fiction, you will probably also enjoy the stories of *Isaac Asimov. YA

Pollyanna (1913), by Eleanor H(odgman) Porter (1868–1920), is a novel about Pollyanna Whittier, an 11-year-old girl with a constantly sunny outlook who goes to live with her unmarried Aunt Polly when her father dies. Even when she is in a motorcar accident and becomes paralyzed, Pollyanna retains her optimism, and puts her "glad game" to the test: "If I can't walk, how am I ever going to be glad for—anything?" Of course she recovers and remains such a bright influence that her formerly grouchy aunt marries Pollyanna's doctor. Today, someone with an excessively rosy outlook is sometimes called "a Pollyanna," and this is not considered a compliment. You might like to find out if Pollyanna continues to be as cheerful in a sequel, *Pollyanna Grows Up* (1915). There are other books about Pollyanna written by other authors. Several films of the original story have been made over the years, the latest in 1989. MR

Poor Richard's Almanack is the name of an annual publication issued from 1732 through

Title page of *Poor Richard's Almanack*

Poor Richard, 1743.

AN

Almanack

For the Year of Christ

1 7 4 3,

Being the Third after LEAP YEAR.

And makes since the Creation　Years
By the Account of the Eastern *Greeks*　7251
By the Latin Church, when ☉ ent. ♈　6942
By the Computation of *W. W.*　5752
By the *Roman* Chronology　5692
By the *Jewish* Rabbies　5504

Wherein is contained,

The Lunations, Eclipses, Judgment of the Weather, Spring Tides, Planets Motions & mutual Aspects, Sun and Moon's Rising and Setting, Length of Days, Time of High Water, Fairs, Courts, and observable Days.

Fitted to the Latitude of Forty Degrees, and a Meridian of Five Hours West from *London*, but may without sensible Error, serve all the adjacent Places, even from *Newfoundland* to *South-Carolina*.

By *RICHARD SAUNDERS*, Philom.

PHILADELPHIA:
Printed and sold by *B. FRANKLIN*, at the New Printing-Office near the Market.

1757. It was created and written by *Benjamin Franklin, who felt that an almanac of folk proverbs and simple sayings would sell well to the average people in the Colonies, who were used to reading from the *Bible. Franklin used the pen name Richard Saunders to write his homespun philosophy, and also to comment about such practical matters as tides, weather, and star charts. His get-ahead ideas were from many sources, but he knew how to phrase them in a catchy way that people would re-member. You probably are familiar with many of them, which even today are put on wall plaques and sewn in needlepoint. For example, "Never leave that till tomorrow, which you can do today," "Fish and visitors smell in three days," "God helps them that help themselves," and perhaps his most famous, "Early to bed and early to rise,/Makes a man healthy, wealthy, and wise." You can read a collection of these sayings in a mock sermon Franklin wrote, called *The Way to Wealth* (1757). MR & YA

Pope, Alexander (1688–1744) This poor-born English poet, critic, playwright, and satirist was less than five feet tall and had a curvature of the spine. Largely self-taught, Pope became nevertheless the leading poet of his time. He was both cunning and charming, and could write light verse and wicked *satire. As his success grew, he bought a villa at Twickenham, outside of London, where he gardened, social-ized with charm and taste, and fell in love with Martha Blount (1690–1762), whom he never married. "The Pastorals" (1709) was his first publication, but fame came with *An Essay on Criticism* (1711), in verse form. The mock-epic *The Rape of the Lock* (1712), in which an En-glish gentleman snips off a lock of a lady's hair without her consent and causes an uproar, sati-rized fashionable ladies and was based on an actual incident. Pope's translation of *Homer's *Iliad* (1713) was a success, and he later trans-lated the *Odyssey* (1726). He became a mem-ber of the prestigious Scriblerus Club, whose other members included *Jonathan Swift. He collaborated with fellow members *John Gay and John Arbuthnot (1667–1735), a Scottish writer and doctor, in a dramatic comedy called

Alexander Pope

Three Hours After Marriage (1717), a satire that was unsuccessful in its day and has been largely forgotten. In two versions of *The Dun-ciad* (1728, 1743), he ridiculed his literary crit-ics. *An Essay on Man* (1734) contains many of his beliefs, such as "Whatever is, is right." Pope was a master of a verse form called the heroic couplet:

> Light to the Stars the Sun does thus
>   restore,
> But Shines himself till they are seen
>   no more.

Try reading first *The Rape of the Lock*, which is not only amusing but is a good introduction to the heroic couplet used in a nonheroic, hu-morous way. An excellent edition was wonder-fully illustrated in art nouveau style by Aubrey Beardsley (1872–1898), and is now available in an inexpensive paperback edition. YA

Popper's Penguins, Mr. See *Mr. Popper's Penguins*.

Porgy and Bess (1935) A masterpiece of musi-cal comedy, this three-act folk opera was writ-ten by the novelist, poet, and playwright Du

Bose Heyward (1885–1940) with *George and *Ira Gershwin. It was based on Heyward's best-known and most important work, the novel *Porgy* (1925), which Heyward adapted for the stage with his wife, Dorothy (1890–1961), in 1927. The story is set in the black dockside section of Charleston, South Carolina, at Catfish Row, a large brick tenement near the water. Porgy, a cripple, makes his living by begging and is fond of gambling. While shooting dice one night, he witnesses the murder of Robbins by the powerful, brutal Crown, who flees. Bess, Crown's girl, whom Porgy has secretly admired, becomes his woman, and she struggles against the lures of the drug-dealing rascal Sportin' Life and the knowledge that one day Crown will return to claim her. When Crown returns one night, Porgy kills him. The police suspect Porgy and arrest him. They can prove nothing, and he is released, only to find that Bess, weakened in her resolve by Porgy's absence, has gone to New York City with Sportin' Life. Porgy, disappointed but not defeated, sets out to find her and bring her back home. Your library probably has a recording of this magnificent musical, whose songs include such favorites as "Summertime," "I Got Plenty o' Nuthin'," and "It Ain't Necessarily So." You will also enjoy Heyward's novel for its rich characterization and its description of life in Catfish Row. *Porgy and Bess* was filmed in 1959. YA

Porter, Katherine Anne (1894–1980) Born in Texas and raised there and in Louisiana, this novelist and short-story writer was from an early age interested in writing. Porter was a descendant of the Kentucky hero Daniel Boone (1734–1820). She was graduated from a convent high school but rebelled against further education. She worked as a newspaper reporter in Denver, Colorado, but when illness forced her to end her journalistic career, she traveled and lived in Europe and Mexico. Porter worked slowly, so her output was small, but some of her early short stories have become classics. Her first published work is *Flowering Judas and Other Stories* (1930). *Pale Horse, Pale Rider*, another popular collection, contains

three novellas. The stories in both volumes often deal with dreams shattered either by forces beyond people's control or by their own selfishness. Her first and most popular novel, *Ship of Fools* (1962), about a ship of refugees returning to Germany just before the rise to power of Adolf Hitler (1889–1945), is an *allegory about good and evil in the lives of women and men. You can get a good overview of her work in *Collected Short Stories* (1965) and *Collected Essays* (1970). *Ship of Fools* was filmed in 1965. YA

Portrait of a Lady, The (1881) In this novel by *Henry James, a charming American young woman, recently orphaned, visits her aunt, uncle, and cousin in their beautiful English country home. Isabel Archer, who has inherited her family's wealth while in England, attracts three suitors, an American manufacturer, an English aristocrat, and the suave and noble Italian, Gilbert Osmond. After much consideration, she marries Osmond and makes her home in Italy. Her wealth plays a part in this marriage, which she slowly comes to perceive as a hollow trap. "Under all his culture . . . his egotism lay hidden like a serpent in a bank of flowers. . . . Her mind was to be his—attached to his own like a small garden plot to a deerpark. He would rake the soil gently and water the flowers; he would weed the beds and gather an occasional nosegay." Through the layers of deceit within her deadly marriage, Isabel becomes aware of her responsibility to her stepdaughter, Pansy. Though Isabel has the opportunity to leave Gilbert, she chooses to remain for Pansy's sake. *The Portrait of a Lady* is a rich and subtle study of the psychology of a marriage and stands as James's first undisputed masterpiece. YA

Portrait of the Artist as a Young Dog (1940), by *Dylan Thomas, is a collection of 10 autobiographical stories about his adventures and the people of his youth. In "Where Tawe Flows," a young man is invited to dinner by a girl who is ashamed of her father. The father comes home drunk, and the couple hides under the table while he eats their food. The father then appears naked, looking for his umbrella to attend to a call of nature, and the young man runs through the door when the father goes out. In "A Visit to Grandpa's," grandfather puts on his best clothes to cross the bridge into the next town to be buried. His friends call out that he is not dead yet, but like a prophet who has seen the truth, Grandpa stands firm. In "Patricia, Edith and Arnold," two servant girls know that one man is writing love letters to both of them. When they compare letters and find he is saying the same thing to both, they confront him. These stories are set in Wales, where storytelling is still a popular entertainment. The title is an affectionate *parody of *A Portrait of the Artist as a Young Man* by *James Joyce, whom Thomas admired. You can find an inexpensive paperback edition of Thomas's *Portrait of the Artist. . . .* YA

Portrait of the Artist as a Young Man, A

(1916) This largely autobiographical first novel by *James Joyce is famous for the literary device called *stream of consciousness. The book was a modern breakthrough into psychological realism, and it changed the way novels were later written. Dublin is shown in reality, but through Stephen Dedalus's thoughts, you can see many of the most important and sensitive memories of his youth. These include bullying by fellow classmates and political fights between his adored father and his Aunt Dante. Stephen has a tough time at school until he stands up for his rights against the head priest of his school, who had unfairly beaten him. An important event in the boy's life is a visit by Stephen and his father to Cork, where he has to cover up his father's drunkenness. Later, in high school, he wins school prizes, has an encounter with a woman when he is 16 years old, and confesses to a kindly old priest about his sin. For a while he thinks of becoming a priest, but he has arguments about religion with his friends, including his old friend Emma, and begins thinking about the larger world and his lack of faith. Eventually, he feels he must leave the narrowness of life in Ireland. You can read more about Stephen as an adult in the even more experimental novel *Ulysses. If you want

to read a longer and earlier version of Stephen's young life, *Stephen Hero* (1904) is an interesting version of *A Portrait* showing Joyce's more traditional, early writing. YA

Poseidon See *Neptune.

Possessed, The

(1872) This complex novel by *Fyodor Dostoyevsky examines Russian attitudes toward the nature of life. The characters, from all classes, act out events caused by the substitution of nihilism, a belief in nothing, for the beliefs of the Orthodox Christian church. Dostoyevsky describes nihilism as a Western political idea that brings about robbery, arson, and murder in a Russian community. Nickolay Stavrogin, a young nobleman, is the central character and seems possessed by an evil spirit. He seduces women, commits crimes, and leads Shatov, the young son of serfs, to plot with a revolutionary group. The title refers to the *Bible story in which *Jesus casts out evil spirits dwelling in people. Dostoyevsky believed that the upper classes should lead others to the Christian ideal that you should do to others as you would have others do to you. The lack of this spirit of brotherhood leads to the unhappy events of the novel, ending when Stravrogin returns home and hangs himself. If these somber ideas about the corruption of Russia's moral heritage interest you, read also *Fathers and Sons* by *Ivan Turgenev. YA

Potok, Chaim

(1929–) Recognized as a leading Jewish-American author, Potok explores conflicts that arise when different traditions and values clash. Chaim grew up in an Orthodox Jewish family, became a rabbi, and was a chaplain during the Korean War. His best-known novel, *The Chosen, is about the problems of holding on to one culture while adopting another. In *Davita's Harp* (1985), Potok uses radio reports, newspaper items, dreams, and the symbol of the harp hung on the door wherever Davita goes, to show how the mind brings together past and present and different places and cultures, and resolves these differences for the person who thinks them through. Another well-known novel is *My Name Is Asher Lev. Wanderings* (1978) is a nonfiction, personal history of the Jewish people. If you like Potok's books, you may also want to read *The Fixer* (1966), by *Bernard Malamud. It deals with the experience of a Jewish handyman in czarist Russia who is falsely accused of a murder. *The Chosen* was made into a film in 1981. YA

Pound, Ezra (1885–1972) This controversial poet and critic, who was accused of treason and anti-Semitism, strongly influenced modern poets and poetry. Pound was born in Idaho, and though he never returned to the West, he was a true individualist in the tradition of Western pioneers. After graduate work at the University of Pennsylvania, he began to write poetry, at first in the style of *Robert Browning and *Walt Whitman. He became a college teacher, but then moved to Venice and London, and for most of his life remained abroad, in France and Italy.

Pound founded Imagism, a movement that stressed clear images and free phrasing, rather than words forced into meters or rhymes. As an editor of several literary magazines, he found publishers for many poets and novelists who later became famous, including *T.S. Eliot, *James Joyce, *Robert Frost, and *Ernest Hemingway. Pound soon began writing his famous *Cantos* (published over many years, beginning in 1925), planned in 100 parts, but continued well beyond that. Composed of Greek and Latin legend, Oriental lore, songs from the south of France, and incidents from modern history, it is an extremely difficult but interesting epic poem.

During World War II, Pound was arrested for treason because of his pro-Fascist broadcasts delivered over Italian radio to American troops. He had been upset for many years by what he considered the failure of democracy. He was declared insane and committed to a hospital in Washington, D.C. There he wrote several works, including the prize-winning *Pisan Cantos* (1948). In 1958, the treason charges were dropped, and he returned to Italy, where he continued working on his *Cantos*. To find out more about this fascinating and influential

man in his own words, you might read *The Letters of Ezra Pound to James Joyce* (1968). YA

Prévert, Jacques (1900–1977) This very popular French poet and screenwriter combined laughter and tears, and positive and negative attitudes, to communicate everyday experiences. His poems were sung in nightclubs long before they were collected for publication. Prévert's poems, showing skepticism and bawdiness, were collected in *Paroles* (1946). You can read an English translation in *Selections from Paroles* (1958), translated by Lawrence Ferlinghetti (1919–), a poet of the *Beat Generation. Prévert wrote one of the classic film scripts in the history of cinema. *Les Enfants du paradis* (*Children of Paradise*), about the love of a mime and a beautiful woman. The film was produced in 1944. YA

Price, (Edward) Reynolds (1933–) North Carolina is a major influence on this novelist and short-story writer, who grew up and went to school there and taught at Duke University in Durham, North Carolina. *A Long and Happy Life* (1962), a novel set in tobacco-growing country, is the humorous story of the discovery of the responsibilities of love. In *The Names and Faces of Heroes* (1963), a collection of short stories, the title story is about a child's family relationships. The novel *A Generous Man* (1966) reintroduces Rosacoke Mustian, the hero of *A Long and Happy Life*, and uses *symbols and myths to develop a simple tale. *Love and Work* (1968) is about a novelist and teacher's efforts to justify the lives of his dead parents, and his discovery of freedom through sharing. Both *The Surface of the Earth* (1975) and *The Source of Light* (1981) deal with how a father's sins affect a son. Price's best work brings together the themes of past family life with the present. If you like Price's work, you will enjoy the stories of *Flannery O'Connor. YA

Pride and Prejudice (1813), a novel by *Jane Austen, is set in rural England. Principal characters are the Bennets—a narrow-minded, social-climbing mother and friendly but put-upon father, and their five daughters. The

Mr. Darcy haughtily declines to be introduced to Elizabeth Bennet
in *Pride and Prejudice.*

main story is about spunky and intelligent Elizabeth Bennet, who is prejudiced against her upper-class and prideful suitor, Fitzwilliam Darcy. After much maneuvering, Darcy finally proposes. Elizabeth rejects him, despite her mother's strong desire to see her girls marry well. After a relationship filled with ups and downs, Darcy proves himself in Elizabeth's eyes, and she accepts his next proposal.

Many subplots weave through this *satirical and witty look at English country people of the 19th century. An important character is Jane Bennet, Elizabeth's beautiful and kind older sister. She is kept from Darcy's friend, Mr. Bingley, an eligible London gentleman, by his sisters, but eventually gets her man. Other memorable characters include the unprincipled Mr. Wickham, who marries Lydia, Elizabeth's sister; Mr. Collins, a pompous bore who also proposes to Elizabeth; Lady Catherine de Bourgh, his snobby patron; and Charlotte Lucas, Elizabeth's best friend, who would rather marry Collins than stay single. If you enjoyed reading this good-humored book, you will like *Sense and Sensibility*, an earlier Austen novel. A film of *Pride and Prejudice* was made in 1940. YA

Prime of Miss Jean Brodie, The (1961) By

*Muriel Spark, this novel is set in Edinburgh,

Scotland, in the 1930s and centers on the complicated relationship between Jean Brodie, a teacher at the Marcia Blaine School for Girls, and six students she has singled out for her special attention and guidance. A believer in "Goodness, Truth, and Beauty" above all other qualities, Brodie follows an unconventional method of teaching that has put her at odds with the school's headmistress and has kept her isolated from most of the other teachers. But she is especially dedicated to the six chosen students, who come to be known as the Brodie set for their devotion to her. Yet Brodie's unfulfilled love for a married colleague, her attempt to guide and control the girls' lives, and her dangerously naive political views set the stage for one of the students to betray her and have her dismissed from the school. But who? And why? Miss Brodie never discovers the answers, but you will as the story unfolds. If you enjoyed this novel, you may also like two other novels set at schools, *Good-bye, Mr. Chips* by *James Hilton and *A Separate Peace* by *John Knowles. *The Prime of Miss Jean Brodie* was adapted for the stage in 1966 and for film in 1969. YA

Prince, The (1517) This short book by Niccolò

Machiavelli (1460–1527), an Italian statesman, was written just after Columbus's voyage of discovery, when the Renaissance was at its peak, and Italian city-states were at war. The pope and kings of Spain and France were fighting to conquer and hold them. Machiavelli dedicated the book to the Florentine scholar and statesman Lorenzo de Medici (1449–1492), known as Lorenzo the Magnificent, the leading figure of the Medici family in Florence. In *The Prince* Machiavelli explores the principles by which a strong ruler could establish and maintain a unified Italian state. One chapter explains how people are collectively courageous, but individually are cowardly and feeble. He advises that the practice of some princes to divide their cities into factions is bad, because the weaker faction often sides with foreign conquerors. *The Prince*, with catchy sayings, such as "Might makes right," offers realistic, even if cynical, political advice even now. Today, the adjective "Machiavellian" means crafty and cunning, reflecting the kind of advice Machiavelli gave in this influential book. YA

Prince and the Pauper, The (1881) Though a favorite book for young readers, this novel by *Mark Twain has an adult theme in its attack on the inequalities of life in England during the Tudor monarchy. Prince Edward, who later becomes Edward VI, exchanges clothes for fun with a poor boy named Tom Canty, who looks just like him. By mistake, the pauper is mistaken for the prince, and the real prince is driven into a life of poverty. Edward finds Tom's family, but when they mistreat him, he hangs out with Sir Miles Hendon, a former knight who thinks Edward is mixed up for claiming he is a prince. Edward learns—close up—just how awful many of his subjects' lives are. Meanwhile, Tom tries hard to play the role of prince, though those around him wonder about some of his odd habits. On the day of the coronation, Edward arrives at Westminster Abbey. He manages to convince people of his true identity when he finds the Great Seal, which Tom had used as a nutcracker. Because of Edward's brush with poverty, he becomes a better and kinder monarch. Other stories along this line that you will enjoy are *The Whipping Boy* by *Sid Fleischman and *The Prisoner of Zenda* by *Anthony Hope. A movie of

The Prince and the Pauper was made in 1937 and remade as *Crossed Swords* in 1978. YA

Princess and the Goblin, The (1872) By the Scottish author George MacDonald (1824–1905), this *fantasy is set in a kingdom full of rugged mountains. It tells of 8-year-old Princess Irene, who lives in the king's great house built on the side of a steep mountain. Beneath the mountain live *goblins, mischievous creatures who frighten and attack people in the night. The goblins are plotting to tunnel into the king's house, kidnap Irene, and force her to marry Harelip, the goblin prince. But Irene has two special friends to protect her. The first is her mysterious great-grandmother, a very old but very beautiful woman who lives at the top of an ancient stairway in the king's house and can be seen only by Irene. The second friend is 12-year-old Curdie Peterson, the son of a miner. Curdie discovers and foils the goblins' plot, with some magical help from Irene's great-grandmother. If you enjoyed this story, you will want to read Irene and Curdie's further adventures in *The Princess and Curdie* (1873). Another fantasy that features goblins is *The Hobbit* by *J.R.R. Tolkien. See also *"The Light Princess." MR

Prisoner of Zenda, The (1894) This novel of adventure and romance, by *Anthony Hope, takes place in the 1880s. Rudolf Rassendyll, an Englishman, closely resembles his distant cousin, also named Rudolf, who is about to be crowned king of the fictional country *Ruritania. Rassendyll travels there to witness the coronation. Michael, Duke of Strelsau, whose bad deeds earn him the name Black Michael, does not want his half-brother to be crowned. Nevertheless, the king invites Michael to his hunting lodge in the town of Zenda on the outskirts of the capital. There the king meets his look-alike cousin, entertains him at the lodge, and eventually falls asleep, drunk. Two of the king's loyal subjects hatch a risky plan. Rassendyll takes the place of the incapacitated king at his coronation, so that Black Michael will not be able to seize the throne by default. When they return, the real king has vanished. Black Michael knows of the hoax, and wants to kill both the king and the impostor, but neither side wants the country to know about the confusion that is going on. The rest of the novel deals with the complications of assumed identity and the quest to rescue the king. Rassendyll meets and loves Princess Flavia, who is engaged to the king but who falls for him, assuming he is King Rudolf.

In the end, Rassendyll and the two loyal subjects save the wounded king and kill Black Michael. Rassendyll begs Princess Flavia to return to England with him. But she remains loyal to king and country, though she sends Rassendyll a rose each year as a reminder of her love. With its midnight duels and unrequited love, this is the ultimate escape novel. If you enjoyed *The Prisoner of Zenda*, read its sequel, *Rupert of Hentzau* (1898), and also *Graustark* by *George Barr McCutcheon. *Zenda* has remained so popular through the years that films of it were produced five times, in 1913, 1922, 1937, 1952, and 1979. YA

Pritchett, V(ictor) S(awdon) (1900–) This English fiction writer, reviewer, biographer, critic, and travel writer is especially well known for his short stories, which are usually written in a simple and clear style. Many of his works are about Spain, such as *Marching Spain* (1928), a collection of short stories, and *The Spanish Temper* (1954), a travel essay about Spain. Pritchett's most popular novel is *Mr. Beluncle* (1951), about a puritanical, small-minded opportunist who likes to fantasize. Though the main character is unpleasant, Pritchett writes about him with depth and sympathy. Pritchett's autobiographies include *A Cab at the Door* (1968) and *Midnight Oil* (1971). He has written biographies, such as *Balzac* (1973) and *The Gentle Barbarian* (1977), about *Ivan Turgenev. *The Tale Bearers* (1980) contains more than two dozen sketches of writers from the past to the present. Like *Charles Dickens, Pritchett is able to write about the lower middle class not only realistically but with a comic touch. You will find collections of his excellent short stories in your library, and several are available in paperback editions. YA

Profiles in Courage (1956), by John F. Kennedy (1917–1963), was written while Kennedy was recuperating from a painful illness and before he became President of the United States. The book tells the stories of outstanding Americans who found themselves in situations that tested their courage. They range from aristocrats to the self-made, and from one end of politics to the other. John Quincy Adams (1767–1848) gave up a promising career in the Senate to support his father's old enemy, Thomas Jefferson (1743–1826). In the long-running controversy that led to the Civil War, Daniel Webster (1782–1852) supported compromise, which caused his friends, who were opposed to accepting slavery in any form, to denounce him. Thomas Hart Benton (1782–1858) lost his Senate seat from the slave state of Missouri because he favored freeing slaves and believed the Missouri Compromise conceded too much to the South. Another book you may like about courageous people is *Heroes and Heroines* (1980) by *Antonia Fraser, about great men and women from the age of myth to the age of space. YA

Prometheus is a cunning Greek demigod, one of the *Titans. He is considered the master craftsman, because he created humankind from clay, and then became a representative of people against the gods. One time he outwits *Zeus by filling skins—one with flesh, another with bones and fat—and asking him which he would prefer as a sacrifice. Zeus chooses the heavier bag, leaving the valuable flesh for people. When Zeus hides fire on Mt. Olympus, Prometheus steals it, and when he is unable to make a spark by rubbing wood, he cleverly steals a vegetable stalk and starts a fire. Zeus punishes him by introducing a newly created woman, Pandora, who brings many problems with her. Zeus nails Prometheus to a rock for 30,000 years, to which an eagle comes each day to peck out his liver. But since Prometheus is immortal, his liver grows back each night. He is eventually freed by *Hercules. In Greek, Prometheus means "forethought," and he was known for his prophetic powers. *Aeschylus

Prometheus, for defying the gods and helping humans, is bound by Zeus to a great rock.

wrote about him in *Prometheus Bound* (466/ 459? B.C.), and *Percy Bysshe Shelley wrote the narrative poem *Prometheus Unbound* (1820). You can read more about Prometheus in *Bulfinch's Mythology* by Thomas Bulfinch (1796–1867) and *Mythology* by Edith Hamilton (1867–1963). MR & YA

Prophet, The This title is given to interpreters of God's will in the *Koran, the holy book of Islam, and in the Old Testament of the *Bible. In the Islamic religion, *Muhammed is considered the main prophet. Among many others, *Adam, Noah, *Abraham, *Moses, and *Jesus are also considered to have brought forth the laws of God. The Old Testament prophets spoke on behalf of God. These men were the heart and soul of Israel for about two centuries, from 750 to 540 B.C. They include Amos, Isaiah, Micah, Jeremiah, and Ezekiel.

A much more recent book that explores how human beings should conduct their lives is a popular prose poem of 28 sections called *The Prophet* (1923), written and illustrated by the Lebanese poet and artist Kahlil Gibran (1883–1931). Educated in France and living in America, he wrote in a mystical, sometimes melancholy, sometimes indignant tone. Sections range from On Love, On Crime and Punishment, On Pleasure, to On Death. Nearly every sentence offers a simple and meaningful thought, such as, "And let today embrace the past with remembrance, and the future with longing." YA

Proud Taste for Scarlet and Miniver, A (1973) By *E.L. Konigsburg, this imaginative tale leaps back into 12th-century England and France. Eleanor of Aquitaine is in *heaven waiting for the arrival of her husband, King Henry II of England. After eight centuries, she is still waiting. Eleanor is with Henry's mother when they meet an old friend from her first marriage. Each one tells a story about Eleanor's life, about how exciting it was to be a living queen even if part of the time Henry kept her locked up. It was better than being bored in the court of King Louis VII of France, who was Eleanor's first husband. This is also a tale of battles between kings, and of Eleanor's two sons, the future English kings, Richard I and John, who do not like each other. She is asked how she feels knowing that her son John "is considered the worst king that England has ever had." "I am not impressed with such ratings," she replies. "John was spoiled and fickle, but he had wit and fits of generosity." This is a charming and painless way to learn a little history, especially as Konigsburg tells it. If you like the fun in this book, you will want to read *A Connecticut Yankee in King Arthur's Court* by *Mark Twain. MR & YA

Proust, Marcel (1871–1922) One of the most influential novelists of the 20th century, this French author grew up in Paris, son of a Catholic doctor and a Jewish mother. Marcel developed asthma when he was 9 years old, and the family spent summers at resorts on the English Channel. He became especially close to his mother, but he joined the army, then studied law and traveled. Brilliant and witty, he began writing short pieces and became popular in high society. After Proust's mother died in 1905, his health became worse and he entered a sanatorium. He remained a semi-invalid for the rest of his life, spending more and more of his time writing in the cork-lined bedroom of his Paris apartment, determined to finish his life's work before he died.

Proust's monumental work is *À la recherche du temps perdu* (*Remembrance of Things Past*) (1913–1927), a novel in seven parts—three published after his death. Based heavily on his own life, it closely examines French society, wasted youth, and personal relationships through the narrator's memory. Over the years, Proust revised and doubled the size of this masterpiece, so that most of the characters reflect his own feelings about art, literature, society, snobbery, and other realities. The first part of the work, *Swann's Way* (1913), is probably the best known and most popular. The manuscript of an earlier unfinished novel, *Jean Santeuil* (1951), is considered a preparatory work for *Remembrance of Things Past*. YA

proverb A proverb is a short popular saying that imparts wisdom or advice. Proverbs can be found in early Greek, Roman, and Anglo-Saxon literature, and were especially popular in the Elizabethan period (1558–1603). For example, *William Shakespeare, who was fond of proverbs, said, "The fashion wears out more apparel than the man." In the Old Testament of the *Bible, the book of Proverbs provides a large collection of such sayings, many of them perhaps written by *Solomon, king of Israel. These proverbs were compiled to instruct Jewish youth and date from the 9th to the 2nd century B.C. They commend the pursuit of wisdom and honesty, among other virtues, and condemn such sins as intemperance and sloth. Examples are "A wise son maketh a glad father, but a foolish son is a sorrow to his mother" and "He who walks with wise men becomes wise, but the companion of fools will suffer harm." There are many other sources of proverbs. From classical Latin comes "Forewarned is forearmed," and by way of medieval Latin, "A bird in the hand is worth two in the bush." *Benjamin Franklin is famous for his proverbs, such as, "Remember, that time is money," "There never was a good war, or a bad peace," and "In this world nothing can be said to be certain, except death and taxes." Such well-known bits of advice as "Go West, young man! Go West" and "Look before you leap" may be considered proverbs. You will have fun looking into some of the general collections of such sayings, including for younger readers *Proverbs of Many Nations* (1966) by Emery Kelen (1898–1978), and for older readers *The Oxford Dictionary of English Proverbs* (1970), *The Facts on File Dictionary of Proverbs* (1983), *The Prentice-Hall Encyclopedia of World Proverbs* (1986), and *The Macmillan Book of Proverbs, Maxims, and Famous Sayings* (1987). MR & YA

Prydain Cycle In this five-novel fantasy series, *Lloyd Alexander has combined Welsh and universal mythology with swift-paced action and memorable characters in an epic struggle of good against evil in the imaginary kingdom of Prydain. *The Book of Three* (1964) introduces Taran, the Assistant Pig-Keeper. He cares for the oracular pig Hen Wen for the enchanter Dallben, who possesses the book of spells known as *The Book of Three*. Taran sets out with Lord Gwydion to do battle with the Horned King, servant of Arawn Death-Lord, the evil master of Annuvin. Along the way they are joined by many interesting characters, including the beautiful young enchantress, Eilonwy, who gives Gwydion the enchanted sword, Dyrnwyn, which enables them to overcome the Horned King. In *The Black Cauldron* (1965) Taran and his companions must destroy the evil Black Cauldron, from which Arawn draws his deathless warriors, the Cauldron-Born. In *The Castle of Llyr* (1965) they must save Eilonwy, who has been imprisoned by her evil aunt, Achren. *Taran Wanderer* (1967) tells of Taran's search for his true identity. The last volume, *The High King* (1968), tells of the final battle of good against evil in Prydain. If you enjoy the Prydain Cycle, try also Alexander's Westmark trilogy, which is set in the mythical kingdom of Westmark. The three books of this series, *Westmark* (1981), *The Kestrel* (1982), and *The Beggar Queen* (1984), follow the adventures of Theo, a young printer's assistant, and his friends through revolution, war, and intrigue, as they help the beggar waif Mickle become Queen of Westmark. *The High King* won the *Newbery Medal in 1969. MR

Psalms A book of the Old Testament of the *Bible, Psalms consists of 150 poetic pieces that were the primary hymnal of ancient Israel and later of Christianity. In their present form the Psalms date from c.537 to c.100 B.C. They cover many subjects—for example, the creation, historical events, praise of God, and prophecy. Probably the best-known psalm is the 23rd, beginning, "The Lord is my shepherd, I shall not want." The first book published in the American Colonies was the *Bay Psalm Book* (1640), an English translation made to provide a hymnal for the settlers of the Massachusetts Bay Colony. MR & YA

Puck is a mischievous goblin, sprite, or elf in northern European folklore. He is known as Robin Goodfellow in England, and Knecht Ruprecht in Germany. Sometimes associated with the devil, he becomes more of a prankster than a demon in *William Shakespeare's *A Midsummer Night's Dream.* Robin, who is sometimes referred to in the play as Puck, is the servant of Oberon, the fairy king. He wanders merrily in the night, "And those things do best please me/That befall prepost'rously." Robin represents the English idea of a fairy who is fond of fun, but not mean, and who will perform household tasks and bring good luck. In *Rudyard Kipling's *Puck of Pook's Hill* (1906) the sprite takes an even further step from the devil, and becomes a good fairy. And if someone is called puckish, it means mischievous, even today. MR & YA

Puig, Manuel (1932–) This Argentine novelist describes the place where he grew up as lacking colors, lakes, mountains, and musical sounds. The repressive political and cultural atmosphere made movies the only way for people to escape. In *Betrayed by Rita Hayworth* (1971), people act out life as an imitation of unrelated movies. Toto, the young narrator, seems to make sense, but he is still using the artificial movie world for his material. You must decide whether the movie world betrays people, or if people betray themselves by trying to escape. In *Kiss of the Spider Woman* (1976) Toto appears again as a gay man, this time locked in a jail cell with a political activist. Their only release from the boredom of the cell is by remembering tacky Hollywood movies. In the detective novel *The Buenos Aires Affair* (1976), Puig introduces each chapter with dialogue from a movie and then takes you into the minds of the characters. *Kiss of the Spider Woman* was made into a movie in 1985. YA

Puritans were English Protestants who sought to "purify" their faith during the time of Queen Elizabeth I, in the 16th and 17th centuries, by acknowledging only the pure word of God. They seceded from the Church of England and removed all traces of Roman Catholic forms and ceremonies from their religion. The *Bible was their chief source of authority—rather than tradition or reason—and they protested against the church being subject to the state. Puritans were serious, dressed and lived simply, and seemed to be constantly aware of the possibilities of sin and damnation in their lives. They considered children's play, such as card games or spinning tops, a waste of time, which was better spent reading godly books.

Because Puritans were considered radical, they were often persecuted, and many immigrated to Europe and the American colonies. But their distaste for tolerance, and their approval of uniformity, sometimes led to persecutions of others. One of the worst examples was the Salem Witch Hunt, which led to executions of several New England women who were wrongly accused of being witches. You can read about this in *Arthur Miller's play *The Crucible.* *Nathaniel Hawthorne described Puritan life in his books, including *The Scarlet Letter.* Younger readers can read about the Puritans in such novels as *Puritan Adventure* (1944) by Lois Lenski (1893–1974), about a Puritan family in Massachusetts Bay Colony; *Tituba of Salem Village* by *Ann Petry; and *The Witch of Blackbird Pond* by *Elizabeth George Speare.

MR = Middle Reader   YA = Young Adult Reader   * = See this main entry

Today, when you say someone is "puritanical," you mean someone who is extremely strict in morals and religion—just plain narrow-minded. MR & YA

purple A *color long associated with royalty, purple signifies nobility not only among rulers but also in art. The Greeks and Romans viewed purple as expressing dignity, and Roman emperors wore purple togas. In *Christianity it is the color of Advent, the period preceding Christmas, and of Lent, the period preceding Easter. A person "born to the purple" is of royal blood. In literature, "purple prose" or "purple patches" refers to writing that is fancy and ornate, overly rich in pretentious words and phrases.

Pushcart War, The (1964) By *Jean Merrill, this popular story is presented as real history, as told in 1996, 10 years after the short Pushcart War. The fight starts when Albert P. Mack (known as Mack the truckdriver) runs down a pushcart in New York City, spilling the owner into a pickle barrel. The pushcart vendors unite in battle, including Old Anna, who becomes general, Maxie Hammerman, Frank the Flower, and Morris the Florist. They take on bad guys, including the mayor, Emmett P. Cudd, Louis Livergreen, and Big Moe. By means of *satire, Merrill shows you the frustration, courage, and cowardice that warring brings out in people, and the terrible consequences that are sometimes even funny. *The Pushcart War* raises many political and social issues. If you like this story, another satirical war story you will like is *The Mouse That Roared* by *Leonard Wibberley. MR

Pushkin, Alexander (1799–1837) Celebrated as a poet, playwright, short-story writer, and novelist, Pushkin changed Russian literature by his use of realistic characters and language. He came from an aristocratic family on his father's side and Abyssinian people on his mother's side. Alexander began publishing poetry when he was 15 years old. As a member of the foreign ministry in St. Petersburg, Pushkin was popu-

lar socially, and his literary reputation rose with his long poem *Ruslan and Ludmilla* (1820). It is based on Russian folktales, and it uses common expressions, instead of the more formal literary forms typical of the times. But it also contains some revolutionary phrases, and Pushkin was banished to the south of Russia. Pardoned, he returned to St. Petersburg, married, and kept writing despite financial difficulties. His wife was supposedly involved in scandals, and he died defending her honor in a duel.

Several of Pushkin's works were made into operas. His greatest work is considered to be *Eugene Onegin* (1825–1833), a novel about a gentleman who eventually gets what he deserves when a woman whose love he refused when she was a girl refuses him years later. The heroine became an ideal of Russian womanhood. Written in verse, it was the basis for an opera, *Eugene Onegin* (1879), by Pyotr Ilich Tchaikovsky (1840–1893). His verse historical drama *Boris Godunov* (1831), about a Russian czar haunted by having had the rightful heir to the throne murdered, inspired the opera *Boris Godunov* (1874), by Modest Moussorgsky (1839–1881). "The Queen of Spades" (1833), a short story about the Queen of Spades, who confuses a young soldier trying to gain both her daughter and her formula for winning at cards, is the basis for another Tchaikovsky opera, *Pique Dame* (1890). Other Russian authors whose works you may enjoy are *Nikolai Gogol, *Leo Tolstoy, and *Ivan Turgenev. YA

Pygmalion was a legendary sculptor and a king of Cyprus who hated women. He decided he would never marry, and that he would turn all his attention to art. He sculpted a beautiful statue and worked on it daily, so that it eventually looked like a real woman. He found to his surprise that he had fallen in love with it. For a while, he pretended the statue was real, brought it gifts, and tucked it into bed, but he grew more and more miserable. He asked Venus, the goddess of love, if she could find him a woman like his statue. When he returned to the statue, she was warm and loving. Pygmalion named the woman Galatea, and they married and named their son Paphos, in honor of Venus's favorite city.

This legend, popular throughout literature, is mentioned in "The Physician's Tale," in *The Canterbury Tales* by *Geoffrey Chaucer, and in Measure for Measure (c.1604), a comedy by *William Shakespeare. Pygmalion (1913), a play by *George Bernard Shaw, is an interesting adaptation of the story. In it a Cockney flower girl, Eliza Doolittle, becomes an elegant lady when Professor Henry Higgins teaches her to speak correctly. It was made into an excellent movie in 1938. This play was also turned into a popular musical comedy, My Fair Lady, in 1956, and the musical was made as a film in 1964. YA

Pyle, Howard (1853–1911) An author and illustrator of original fairy tales, historical novels, and *fantasy, Pyle was the son of Quakers and studied art for three years in Philadelphia. In 1876 he visited a picturesque island off the coast of Virginia, wrote about it, and drew some sketches. When his mother told him to submit them for publication, he did so and Scribner's Monthly immediately accepted them. He moved to New York City, where he became a successful illustrator. Some thought his graphic artwork was crude, but most felt it brought a fresh style to American illustration. At first he retold old fairy stories, but he later created new ones. Pyle wrote and illustrated *The Merry Adventures of Robin Hood, which is considered one of the best modern retellings of this old story. He spent the next seven years writing and illustrating the *King Arthur legend: The Story of King Arthur and His Knights (1903), The Story of the Champions of the Round Table (1905), The Story of Sir Lancelot and His Companions (1907), and The Story of the Grail and the Passing of Arthur (1910). These classics, and such other works as *Men of Iron, are an important part of American literature for younger readers. Pyle later taught art and set up his own art school. His simple, strong illustrations set the style in young people's books for the first part of the 20th century. MR

Queen, Ellery Under this pen name Frederic Dannay (1905–1982) and Manfred B(ennington) Lee (1905–1971), who were cousins, collaborated to write 39 detective novels as well as short stories. They also used Ellery Queen as the name of their fictional detective. The first of the novels was *The Roman Hat Mystery* (1929), and the last was *A Fine and Private Place* (1971). The plots are complex, with plenty of clues, and the settings are often unusual—for example, a department store window, a hospital operating room. *The Greek Coffin Mystery* (1932) concerns a missing will, a second body found in a grave, and the importance of the color of a dead man's necktie. Queen, the detective, is slim, well dressed, and often romantically involved. He is a writer who lives on Manhattan's West Side with his father, Inspector Richard Queen of the New York Police Department, and, of course, he helps his father solve his murder cases. Under the name of Barnaby Ross, the authors wrote more detective fiction featuring a sleuth named Drury Lane. If you like these detective novels, you will enjoy those of *Erle Stanley Gardner and *Rex Stout. Thirteen movies and three television series were made from the Ellery Queen books. MR & YA

Queenie Peavy (1966), by *Robert Burch, takes place in the South during the *Great Depression. Queenie is a lively, intelligent, and imaginative 13-year-old girl who prides herself on

Queenie and her friend Martha, or Little Mother, in *Queenie Peavy.*

being able to hit anything within reasonable range with a stone. She and her mother are poor, particularly since her Pa was sentenced to the federal penitentiary. Some of her schoolmates tease Queenie about Pa's absence, and she reacts with defiance and small misdeeds that result in frequent meetings with the school principal. The meanest taunts come from Cravey Mason, a boy Queenie heartily dislikes, and one day she tricks him into a bad fall. Cravey's broken leg adds to Queenie's reputation as a troublemaker, and Cravey and his friend Persimmon make matters worse by breaking church windows and putting the blame on Queenie.

The principal is distressed but kindly, the sheriff is stern, and the judge (who sentenced her father) lectures her gently about taking responsibility for her acts. Queenie's fear of being sent to a reformatory is forgotten when Pa is unexpectedly released on parole. Her joy is short-lived, however, when she realizes Pa is more interested in getting even with old enemies than in being with his daughter. Queenie decides to stay out of trouble, and her new spirit of cooperation brings some surprising rewards. Cravey and Persimmon finally confess to the sheriff that they broke the church windows themselves, and the charges against Queenie are dropped. MR

Quiet American, The (1956) In this novel by *Graham Greene, the quiet American is the author's ironic label for Alden Pyle, a young and well-meaning but naive U.S. government official. He has come to Vietnam in the early 1950s when France was fighting the Viet Minh, a Communist-led organization, in an attempt to keep its Southeast Asian colonies. Pyle meets Thomas Fowler, a cynical middle-aged British war correspondent, and through him meets and falls in love with Fowler's mistress, Phuong. Pyle thinks a third force is needed to replace the French and the Viet Minh and, to achieve this, he supports a General Thé. As a result Pyle becomes responsibile for the bombing deaths of at least 50 civilians. Meanwhile, Phuong agrees to marry him because Fowler's wife, in England, will not divorce him. Pyle is murdered by unknown persons, Fowler's wife changes her mind, and Phuong and Fowler are together again. The tone of the book, expressed through Fowler, is anti-American, and views French colonialism as hopelessly out of date but with no expectation that the end of colonialism will improve matters. A movie was made of the book in 1958. YA

Quiet Don, The (1928–1940) The masterwork of *Mikhail Sholokhov, this *epic novel of Cossack life covers the period from the end of the Czarist era in Russia to the beginning of Soviet rule. It was first translated in two volumes, *And Quiet Flows the Don* (1934) and *The Don Flows Home to the Sea* (1940). The first novel introduces the main character, Gregor Melekhov, a young Cossack living in the village of Tatarsk on the Don River just before the beginning of World War I. The beautiful, harsh, and often brutal world of the Cossacks is shown through the lives of Gregor and his family and friends. Other key characters are Gregor's brother Piotra, wife Natalia, and mistress Aksinia Astakhova. World War I devastates the Cossacks who, traditionally strong supporters of the czar, turn against the government and help the Bolsheviks take power. But when the new Soviet government attempts to exert its control over the Don region, the Cossack brotherhood divides into Red and White factions, and civil war breaks out. *The Don Flows Home to the Sea* continues the story of Gregor and his family to the end of the civil war in 1921. A vast, ambitious, poetic story, Sholokhov's work reveals in human terms the complicated forces that led to the establishment of the Soviet Union. If you enjoyed these novels, you may also like *War and Peace* by *Leo Tolstoy and *Doctor Zhivago* by *Boris Pasternak. YA

Rabbi Ben Ezra (1855) In this long and famous poem, *Robert Browning uses the voice of a noted Spanish-born Jewish philosopher, physician, astronomer, and poet, whose full name was Abraham ben Meïr ibn Ezra (c.1090–c.1167), to praise the advantages of growing older. He believes that people should put their trust in God, and he urges younger people to make the most of life while accepting the inevitability of old age. Most widely known are the opening lines:

> Grow old along with me!
> The best is yet to be.

YA

Rabbit Hill (1944), by *Robert Lawson—who was a master of the art of telling stories about animals that make you forget they are not human beings—tells about a family of rabbits, especially a young one named Georgie, and their animal friends who live in Connecticut. They are not well off because the nearby house is empty, and so there has been no garden for them to raid for vegetables. The residents of Rabbit Hill—such as Gray Fox, Gray Squirrel, Willie Fieldmouse, Phewie the Skunk, and Porkey the Woodchuck—are delighted when a new family moves in and plants a large vegetable patch. The animals begin planning how to share this wealth. They ,are careful to be sure each has his own section of the garden. To

their surprise, the family puts out food for them every night. Meanwhile, Georgie has a number of adventures. He is sent to invite Uncle Analdas to visit them and carries out his mission, though once a dog nearly catches him. It is Willie's turn for adventures when he falls into the rain barrel. But he is rescued by the kind family. Georgie's next adventure is not so pleasant: He is hit by a car. Luckily, he is picked up by the family and his injured leg is treated. All ends well when on Midsummer Eve they celebrate the harvest. *Rabbit Hill* won the *Newbery Medal in 1945. MR

Rabbit, Run (1960) This novel is the first of four by *John Updike with Harry "Rabbit" Angstrom as the main character. In *Rabbit, Run* he is a salesman in a small city in Pennsylvania who got his nickname from his athletic ability in high school. Vaguely dissatisfied with his life, he leaves his wife and takes up with an ex-prostitute, but eventually returns home and tries to settle down. Here, however, he has to cope with the loss of his second child, for whose death he feels responsible. In *Rabbit Redux* (1971) he is a suburbanite, still troubled by the conditions of life. His wife takes a lover and leaves home, while he and his 13-year-old son, Nelson, become involved with a young female hippie. In the third novel, *Rabbit Is Rich* (1981), he and his wife are running his late father-in-law's automobile dealership and he has become a member of the country club. Rabbit, however, has problems with Nelson, who gets his girl friend pregnant. By the time of *Rabbit at Rest* (1990), Rabbit has a condominium in Florida and two grandchildren, but he also has heart trouble. Nelson is on drugs and ruining the auto agency. In the end, Rabbit suffers a heart attack while saving his granddaughter from drowning, and dies. These accounts of Rabbit's troubles do not always make pleasant reading, but they present a realistic picture of an ordinary middle-class man attempting to cope with his personal problems and the modern world. A movie based on *Rabbit, Run* was made in 1970. YA

Ragtime (1975), a novel by *E.L. Doctorow, takes place in the early 1900s, in the era of ragtime music. It is the story of three families of completely different backgrounds. Real people of the time, such as President Theodore Roosevelt (1858–1919) and J.P. Morgan (1837–1913), move in and out of the drama in an original blending of historical fact and fantasy.

Father, Mother, their son, and Mother's Younger Brother live in New Rochelle, New York, in upper-middle-class comfort. Lonely and withdrawn, Younger Brother falls in love with Evelyn Nesbit, a famous beauty. He observes her charitable but oddly intense interest in the little daughter of Tateh, a poor Jewish immigrant Evelyn is helping to support. Then Mother takes in Sarah, a destitute young black woman, and her baby. Now the family housemaid, Sarah is courted by a well-dressed and well-spoken ragtime musician named Coalhouse Walker, Jr., who seems to be the father of her child. Coalhouse becomes an angry militant after being harassed by white firemen who vandalize his automobile, and Sarah is accidentally killed while trying to help Coalhouse. The grief-stricken Coalhouse and his associates, including Younger Brother, take over J.P. Morgan's library on Fifth Avenue, threatening to blow it up if the damaged auto is not restored. After making a deal with the district attorney, the associates are allowed to leave safely, but Coalhouse is shot by the police as he surrenders. Younger Brother escapes to Mexico, where he later dies fighting for the revolution.

Tateh, now a success in the fledgling movie business, marries Mother (recently widowed), and the happy couple move to California with their children and Sarah's baby. *Ragtime* was adapted for film in 1981. YA

Railroad to Freedom, The (1932) This biography, written as a story, by Hildegarde Hoyt Smith (1890?–1977) tells about Harriet Tubman (c.1820–1913), a black woman who escaped from slavery and then led many others to freedom. It begins in 1831, when Harriet is about 10 years old and growing up at Broadacres, the Maryland plantation of Henry Carter. Carter is a kind master, but his son, George, is cold and cruel. He hates Harriet for her courage and defiant attitude, and she hates him in return. After Henry Carter dies and George becomes master, Harriet escapes to freedom in the North, helped by members of a secret organization known as the Underground Railroad. Harriet joins the Railroad, making many dangerous trips back South, leading some 300 blacks, including her own parents, out of slavery, and earning the nickname "Moses." When the Civil War begins, Harriet becomes a scout, spy, and nurse for the Union army and sees with pride the bravery of black soldiers fighting for the Union.

If you enjoyed *The Railroad to Freedom*, try also **The House of Dies Drear* by *Virginia Hamilton, a mystery set at a house that was a station on the Underground Railroad. Hildegarde Hoyt Smith also wrote *North Star Shining* (1947), a pictorial history of blacks in America, as well as *The Edge of April* (1957), a biography of the naturalist John Burroughs (1837–1921), and *From the Eagle's Wing* (1962), a biography of the pioneer conservationist John Muir (1838–1914). MR & YA

Rainbows Are Made (1982) From the more than 800 poems *Carl Sandburg wrote, *Lee Bennett Hopkins selected 70, including nine verses from *The People, Yes* (1936), the poet's

---

MR = Middle Reader   YA = Young Adult Reader   * = See this main entry tribute to America, its land, its people, and democracy. The range of subjects of the other 61 poems is as wide as were Sandburg's interests and spirit. Some are simply about people, young and old; but others are about farmers and workers. You will find poems you will enjoy most for their language, but that will also make you think about such subjects as love and hate, the sea and the stars, and ordinary things like shirts and boxes. As Sandburg said: "Poetry is a series of explanations of life," and "a search for syllables to shoot at the barriers of the unknown and the unknowable." Hopkins has selected poems for a number of anthologies intended primarily for young children. MR & YA

Raisin in the Sun, A (1959) *Lorraine Hansberry's successful first play, set in Chicago's South Side ghetto, tells about the Younger family, whose dream of a better life has been long deferred. The head of the family is Lena Younger, or Mama. She lives with her son Walter, daughter Beneatha, daughter-in-law Ruth, and grandson Travis, in a rundown apartment. The family's hopes hinge on $10,000 coming to Mama from her husband's life insurance policy. Walter sees the money as his chance to go into business for himself. Mama uses part of the money to buy a house in all-white Clybourne Park and gives Walter the rest, telling him to put $3,000 in the bank for Beneatha's education and use the remainder as he sees fit. But Walter loses all the money to a crooked business partner. When a member of a Clybourne Park community group offers to buy back the house at a profit to the Youngers, Walter plans to accept the offer. At the last moment his sense of family pride is restored, and he refuses the offer. The family, reunited in Walter's action, goes to live in their new home, determined to make the family dream of a better life come true. *A Raisin in the Sun* was made into a critically acclaimed movie in 1960 and into a successful musical comedy, *Raisin*, in 1973. YA

Ralph S. Mouse (1982), by *Beverly Cleary, is a sequel to *The Mouse and the Motorcycle* and *Runaway Ralph*. At the inn where a mouse called Ralph lives, he overhears the handyman being scolded because there are signs of mice in the lobby. The management is unaware that Ralph rides his motorcycle at night, and that his younger relatives come to beg for a chance to ride with him. Ralph asks Ryan Bramble, a boy living at the inn, to take him to Ryan's school and let Ralph make a new home there. After being discovered as he peeks from Ryan's pocket during class, Ralph becomes the center of attention. To show the class how smart Ralph is, Ryan agrees to let Ralph try to make his way through a cardboard maze to reach a dab of peanut butter. Irritable at being displayed publicly without his consent, Ralph skips along the top of the maze to reach the prize, and then is accused of cheating. Worse, Ryan argues with Brad, a classmate, and Ralph's motorcycle is broken while the boys scuffle. Ryan and Brad become friends, however, and Brad later replaces the motorcycle with a splendid mouse-sized sports car. Ralph is taken back to the inn, where his classroom experience helps him deal more tactfully with his relatives. MR

Ramona (1884) Helen Hunt Jackson (1830–1885) wrote *Ramona* in the form of a novel to bring public attention to the great injustices done to American Indians. It takes place in southern California when white Americans were dispossessing many Mexicans and all Native Americans in the early 1800s. Raised on a Mexican-owned fruit, nut, and sheep ranch, Ramona is beautiful and kind, loved by her stepbrother, Felipe, and by everyone else on the estate. But because Ramona falls in love with Alessandro, the proud Indian who comes with his band to shear sheep, she is disinherited by her adopted mother, who reveals that Ramona's mother was Native American. She runs away with Alessandro just as he learns that his people have been evicted by the Americans because they have no paper title to their village and family land. They become poverty-stricken wanderers in California, always fleeing the white Americans who come with their guns and pieces of paper. They look for a safe place

to work and raise their children, but Ramona's first baby dies and Alessandro is murdered by a white man. Ramona, in great poverty, with a new baby, nearly dies before Felipe finds her after a long search. Felipe takes her to Mexico to make a new life together as man and wife. Three movies have been made of this enduring story, in 1916, 1928, and 1936. YA

Ransom (1966), by *Lois Duncan, is the story of five high school students kidnapped together at gunpoint and held for ransom. Because all five live in the same affluent neighborhood, the two kidnappers assume the parents will pay handsomely for their release. Marianne is preoccupied by a difficult adjustment to her mother's second marriage. Glenn seems very confident and self-sufficient, but his attitude toward his adoring younger brother, Bruce, is a little patronizing. Dexter suffers from self-consciousness about his physical handicap caused by polio, and Jesse is a new girl in school who is used to being an outsider. Taken to a remote mountain cabin, the young people are drawn together by their common danger. Each responds differently, revealing their best and worst qualities under the tension of their predicament. Buck, one of the kidnappers, assures them they will be freed after all the ransom is paid. Frightened that their parents will not be able to raise the money, the hostages plot an escape. In the middle of the night, Buck catches them trying to leave, and Dexter is shot in the shoulder as Glenn and Bruce run to the woods. Buck is killed when his car skids on the icy road as he chases after Bruce. When Bruce and Glenn later return to the cabin, Marianne's stepfather, Rod, arrives with the other kidnapper, who expects Rod to pay the ransom. With strength born of desperation, Rod and the others manage to disarm the criminal and save themselves. MR

Ransome, Arthur (Mitchell) (1884–1967) An English writer who first made a reputation as a journalist in Russia during World War I and the Russian Revolution of 1917, Ransome later wrote a dozen novels about the adventures of the Walker and Blackett families and their friends. The first of these was *Swallows and Amazons* and the last was *Great Northern* (1947). In the novels the families visit many places, for example, the Lake District of northwestern England and the Norfolk Broads in eastern England. The children's adventures are not only exciting but also include practical details about sailing, fishing, bird watching, knot tying, and outdoor cooking. If you like these books, you will enjoy those of *Kenneth Grahame, *L.M. Montgomery, *Marjorie Kinnan Rawlings, *Robert Louis Stevenson, and Johann Wyss (1781–1830). MR

Rascal (1963) You might think that this story is imagined, but it is actually the true story of events that took place when the author, *Sterling North, was an 11-year-old boy in a small town in Wisconsin. He does not lead an entirely happy life: He lives with his father, who is often away, and he has to do most of the housekeeping. On the other hand, he is allowed to build an 18-foot canoe in the living room, and he has a number of pets, including Poe-the-Crow. *Rascal*, however, is mainly about a raccoon that Sterling captures. Rascal is both smart and mischievous. He steals an engagement ring, gets into a neighbor's corn crop, and bites a boy who teases him. This causes a rabies scare in the village, and Sterling realizes he has to give Rascal his freedom. He takes him to a rural area and turns him loose. You are left with the understanding that Rascal will find a mate and live the normal life of a wild raccoon. Besides the amusing aspects of this story, you will find it makes you think about your relationship with nature. If you enjoyed *Rascal*, you will want to read *A Day No Pigs Would Die* by *Robert Newton Peck. You will also enjoy *All Creatures Great and Small*, and its sequels, by the English veterinarian *James Herriot. A film was made of *Rascal* in 1969. MR & YA

Raskin, Ellen (1928–1984) An artist as well as an author, Raskin illustrated the books she wrote, including *The Westing Game. Among others are *The Mysterious Disappearance of

Leon (I Mean Noel) (1971), Figgs and Phantoms (1974), and The Tattooed Potato and Other Clues (1975). The first is the fanciful story of Leon and Caroline, married when children, and separated for 14 years. When they do meet, Leon drowns—or does he? This event sets off the story of Caroline's wandering search for Leon, including the adoption of the twins, Tina and Tony. Leon is found, but too late. The central character in Figgs and Phantoms is Mona, a daughter in a family that includes her mother; Sister Figg Newton, who tap dances all the time; and Uncle Florence Figg, a rare-book dealer and the only member of the family Mona respects. The story includes her nightmare when she attempts to find Uncle Florence in Capri, supposedly the Figg family heaven. In The Tattooed Potato, 17-year-old Dickory becomes an assistant to Garson, a painter who fancies himself a great detective. She becomes involved in solving such crimes as the Case of the Horrible Hairdresser and the Case of the Disguised Disguise. Raskin's wild, even impossible, stories are guaranteed to entertain you. If you like her books, read those of *E.L. Konigsburg, *Lila Perl, and *William Sleator. MR

rat This small rodent has for centuries had a well-deserved evil reputation. It can carry dangerous infections, as in the Middle Ages when it helped spread the plague in Europe. Superstitious sailors believe rats will desert a ship that is doomed to sink, and the idea is often applied to those who quit what they think is a lost cause. "To smell a rat" is to be suspicious; "to rat" is to betray someone, to inform on someone; if you are "as wet as a drowned rat," you are thoroughly soaked and may also look depressed; "rat race" is a term applied to the extreme pressure some people feel when they seek success in business. Surely the most famous rat in literature is the amiable Water Rat, or Ratty, in *The Wind in the Willows by *Kenneth Grahame. Another famous rodent is Templeton the rat in *Charlotte's Web by *E.B. White.

raven The raven, a type of bird that resembles a crow, has long been thought to bring bad luck, and to predict death. The Roman orator Cicero (106–43 B.C.) was said to have been forewarned of his coming death by ravens. In Christian art, however, the raven is a *symbol of God's providence because it was a raven that fed the prophet *Elijah in the wilderness. In literature this very black bird is best known through the haunting poem "The Raven" (1845), by *Edgar Allan Poe.

> Take thy beak from out my heart, and
>   take thy form from off my door!
> Quoth the Raven, "Nevermore."

In Barnaby Rudge (1841), a novel about the Gordon riots in London in 1780 by *Charles Dickens, Barnaby has a raven named Grip, which was the inspiration for Poe's raven. "To raven" is to plunder or seize a prey, and also to eat in a gulpy and greedy manner.

Rawlings, Marjorie Kinnan (1896–1953) After a career as a journalist, Rawlings moved to Cross Creek, an isolated, rural Florida locality, and began to write books, chiefly about the region. Her best and most popular novel is *The Yearling, but previously she published two novels and a volume of short stories. One of the novels was South Moon Under (1933), whose main character is Lant Jacklin, a throwback to the hunters and Indian fighters of an earlier time. The book tells of his life in the Florida backwoods. The details of events on hunting and trapping trips are fascinating and also show Rawlings's rare ability to describe natural settings. When the Whippoorwill (1940) contains a number of short stories about poor white farmers and other backwoods residents, such as hunters, fishers, and trappers, as well as moonshiners and their illegal stills. In Cross Creek (1942) Rawlings gave a humorous account of her life there. A movie of Cross Creek was made in 1983. MR & YA

Rebecca (1938), a well-known *Gothic novel by *Daphne du Maurier, is a suspense story told

---

MR = Middle Reader   YA = Young Adult Reader   * = See this main entry

by a shy, plain young woman, the second Mrs. de Winter. While working as a paid companion, she meets Maxim de Winter and learns that his glamorous first wife, Rebecca, disappeared and was thought to have drowned in a boating accident. Maxim is handsome, elegant, and greatly attached to his home at Manderley, an estate on the south coast of England. Maxim and the young woman fall in love and marry after a brief courtship. Maxim takes his bride to Manderley, where Mrs. de Winter must adjust to a new life of luxury and social demands. The large house is efficiently run by the grim Mrs. Danvers, who was very attached to Rebecca and who takes every opportunity to make Mrs. de Winter feel inferior. Memories of Rebecca's great beauty and charm surround the young bride, and she feels less and less able to compete with Rebecca's haunting presence.

After a storm, Rebecca's boat is found scuttled near Manderley. The skeleton in the cabin is Rebecca's, and an inquest is arranged to investigate. Maxim tells his wife that his first marriage was a living hell and that Rebecca amused herself by having affairs with other men. When Rebecca hinted laughingly that she might have another man's child and make him heir to Manderley, Maxim shot her, put her body in the sailboat, and scuttled it. Mrs. de Winter is horrified by Maxim's confession, but realizes she need never have been jealous of Rebecca. As this obstacle to their relationship is removed, Maxim and his wife express their love for each other. The inquest uncovers evidence that throws suspicion on Maxim, but a further discovery reveals that Rebecca might have killed herself after learning she was incurably ill. Maxim is no longer a suspect, but the couple return to Manderley only to find the house engulfed in flames. A notable movie version of *Rebecca* was made in 1940. YA

Rebecca of Sunnybrook Farm (1903) In this delightfully old-fashioned novel by Kate Douglas Wiggin (1856–1923), you read of interesting events in the life of Rebecca Randall, who is 10 years old when the story begins. The setting is rural Maine around 1900. Rebecca, one of seven children of a poor farm family, is sent to live with two unmarried aunts, Jane and Miranda. Jane is gentle and kind, but Miranda is strict and demanding. Rebecca is bright and cheerful, but often careless and forgetful. She gets involved in such things as selling soap in order to acquire a lamp for a poor family, and inviting a missionary family to an overnight visit without consulting her aunts. When Rebecca is 13 years old she enters high school, where an understanding teacher encourages her and she becomes the first girl ever to be appointed as editor of the school paper. But there are also troubles: Aunt Miranda becomes ill, and her family is behind in payments on the mortgage on Sunnybrook Farm. On the bright side, Rebecca wins the school's $50 prize for a composition she writes. Graduation comes, and Rebecca is offered a teaching job, but her mother is badly injured in a farm accident, and Rebecca must stay home to take care of her. Rebecca is reconciled to this dull life. When the farm is saved by the sale of some of the property and Aunt Miranda dies, Rebecca inherits her valuable brick house. You are left knowing that Rebecca will now be able to lead her own life and make use of her talents. Rebecca may be a little too good to be true, but she does give you something to think about with her upbeat attitude toward life, its troubles as well as its pleasures. Wiggin was a kindergarten teacher and founded a school to train kindergarten teachers. Though she wrote other books for young readers, she is known today only for *Rebecca*, which was in part autobiographical. A movie was made of *Rebecca of Sunnybrook Farm* in 1938. MR & YA

red Like *black and *white, red has many meanings. Many are based on the fact that it is the color of blood. In *Christianity, therefore, red often refers to the blood of martyrs. Red is also a warning color, from the red in the traffic signal that tells you to stop, to "red alert," meaning that an attack is imminent. Since the mid-19th century, red has been the color of revolution, especially the Russian Revolution of 1917, with the communists' red banner and the Red Army. Red also expresses excitement and heightened activity, as in "red hot," "red-handed," "red-blooded," "to see red," and "red in the face." On the other hand, if your business is "in the red," you are losing money. You can sense meanings of the word in the title of a novel about the fighting in the American Civil War, *The Red Badge of Courage* by *Stephen Crane. In another novel, *The Red and the Black* (1830) by the French author Stendhal [Henri Beyle] (1783–1842), you can think of red as standing for the army and black for the church. Or, perhaps, you will believe they stand for liberalism and reaction. YA

Red Badge of Courage, The (1895)

Subtitled *An Episode of the American Civil War*, this novel by *Stephen Crane is at the same time an exciting story and a masterful account of fear, both physical and psychological, under fire. Henry Fleming, the chief character, is a young man facing his first experience in war and is torn between fear and a desire to demonstrate his bravery and patriotism. When the fighting begins, he panics and flees. He cannot even mingle with wounded soldiers, realizing he is not one of them because he does not bear "the red badge of courage" that they do. Fleming hides in a forest, sees a friend die, then gets his wound, but only by accident from the butt of the rifle of one of his fellows. This injury gives him an excuse to pretend he has been wounded by enemy fire, and somehow his courage returns. He joins the next day's battle, fights bravely, and becomes a hero when he takes over his regiment's colors during a charge. Through Crane's eyes, with Fleming as the believable example, readers are made aware of the real and terrible nature of battle as experienced by infantrymen. A movie was made of the book in 1951 and a TV movie in 1974. YA

"Red Pony, The" (1937)

In this short story, whose setting is a farm in the Salinas Valley of California, *John Steinbeck recounts three events in the boyhood of Jody Tiflin. Jody becomes aware of the unexplainable ways of

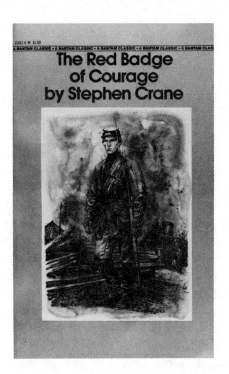

Cover of a paperback edition of
The Red Badge of Courage

nature when his red pony, the focus of his young life, dies. Jody also has an adventure with a mysterious Mexican-American named Gaitano, and he becomes further aware of nature's unpredictable ways when a mare dies while giving birth to a colt. "The Red Pony" was republished with a dozen other Steinbeck stories in *The Long Valley* (1938). One of the stories, "Saint Katy the Virgin," is about the sad last years of Jody's aged grandfather, who had been a pioneer in the Salinas Valley. Though some of the events in these stories are sad ones, Steinbeck brings out the relationships of humans and animals and the awesome aspects of the natural world. You can find "The Red Pony" in an inexpensive paperback edition, which was published in 1976 and includes Steinbeck's short novel *The Pearl. A movie was made of "The Red Pony" in 1949 and another for TV in 1973. MR & YA

Redwall (1986)

In this middle volume of a trilogy by Brian Jacques (1939–), an English author, the setting is Redwall Abbey in ancient Britain. But the monks of the abbey are mice and all the other characters are also animals. An evil rat, Cluny the Scourge, plans to seize the abbey for its treasures. To help fight him, Matthias, a novice, searches for the long-lost sword of Martin the Warrior mouse. Meanwhile, Cluny attacks the abbey but is repulsed, the abbey mice being helped by Constance the Badger. Matthias finds the sword belt and fights sparrows high up under the abbey roof for the sword's scabbard. He then learns he must take the sword away from Asmodeus, a poisonous snake. With the aid of the Guerrilla Union of Shrews, he kills Asmodeus and recovers the sword. Matthias returns to the abbey to find that Cluny has entered it by treachery. He and Matthias fight, and Matthias cuts the abbey bell rope with the sword, causing it to fall and kill Cluny. The events in *Mossflower* (1988) take place before those in *Redwall* and tell how Martin the Warrior, with the aid of Gonff, the mouse thief, conquer the evil female wildcat, Tsarmina. In *Mattimeo* (1990) Matthias's son, also named Matthias, uses the same sword to defend the abbey against Slagar the Fox. These are exciting tales of great adventure. MR

Reflections on a Gift of Watermelon Pickle . . . and Other Modern Verse (1966)

Here are 114 short poems, selected by (Arthur) Stephen Dunning, Jr. (1924–), Edward (George) Lueders (1923–), and Hugh L(etcher) Smith (1921–1968), that present enough subjects, ideas, and points of view to interest and amuse any reader. You will find poems by poets as different as *Langston Hughes, *Ezra Pound, *Dorothy Parker, *Eve Merriam, *William Carlos Williams, and *Robert Frost. Some of the poems are about animals, some about sports, some about love, and there is even one entitled "How to Eat a Poem." There are also photographs to match the subject matter. The same editors published a second collection, containing 125 poems, *Some Haystacks Don't Even Have Any Needle, and Other Complete Modern Poems* (1969). MR & YA

Reign of Terror

refers to a period of the French Revolution during which France was ruled by the Committee of Public Safety (1792–

1795). The men in power, such as Georges Jacques Danton (1759–1794), Jean Paul Marat (1743–1793), and Maximilien Robespierre (1758–1794), kept their positions by use of terror. Their spies and agents throughout France provided information about royalists and others opposing the committee. Thousands of people, mostly victims of the revolutionary hatred of the privileged classes, were sent to the guillotine to be beheaded. The Terror is said to have ended with the execution of Robespierre in July 1794. Two fine novels about this period in French history are *A Tale of Two Cities* by *Charles Dickens and *The Scarlet Pimpernel* by *Baroness Orczy. YA

Remarque, Erich Maria (1898–1970)

Wounded while serving in the German Army in World War I, Remarque used his experiences in writing his first and most successful novel, *All Quiet on the Western Front. His antiwar attitude made him unpopular with the growing *Nazi movement in Germany, and his books were banned when the Nazis came to power in the 1930s. Remarque moved to Switzerland in 1932 and moved to the United States in 1939. Remarque's second novel, a sequel to *All Quiet on the Western Front*, was *The Road Back* (1931), in which its characters, who had survived the war, attempt to cope with civilian life at a time when Germany's defeat had left the nation emotionally and economically drained. *Arch of Triumph* (1946) tells the story of a romance between a refugee and a woman in France during World War II. This war is also the setting of *A Time to Love and a Time to Die* (1954), but in it the author returns to a German setting and tells of a soldier who falls in love while he is on furlough but must return to battle, perhaps to die. Movies were made of *The Road Back* in 1937, *Arch of Triumph* in 1948, and *A Time to Love and a Time to Die* in 1958. A TV movie was made of *Arch of Triumph* in 1985. If you like Remarque's novels, you might try those of Heinrich Böll (1917–1985) and Günter Grass (1927–). YA

Renaissance

is a French word whose literal meaning is "rebirth" but which, since the middle of the last century, has been used to refer to one of the most intellectually stimulating periods in human history, the years from about the middle of the 14th century to the end of the 16th century in Western Europe. The Renaissance followed the Middle Ages, usually considered to have begun c.1000 and to have been a period of little change. The Renaissance is known especially for its advances in art and literature, beginning in Italy and spreading north and west. The prime example of a Renaissance figure in art and science is *Leonardo da Vinci. *Dante Alighieri, *Geoffrey Chaucer, *Petrarch, *William Shakespeare, and *Edmund Spenser are ranked among the period's greatest writers. Advances were also made in other areas. Europeans for the first time sailed to the New World and, by sailing around Africa, to the Far East; a commercial revolution increased international trade; the modern national state, with its centralized government, began to emerge; and the Protestant Reformation changed the history of Christianity. The Renaissance fostered a dynamic spirit in which individuals felt free to paint, write, and experiment in new ways. The boundaries of humanity were greatly extended, both in matters of the mind and in the physical world. Younger readers who would like to learn more about the Renaissance can read *The Renaissance* (1987) by Michel Pierre (1934-). Older readers will enjoy *Everyday Life in Renaissance Times* (1966) by E.R. Chamberlin (1926-). MR & YA

"Renascence" (1912), a famous poem by *Edna St. Vincent Millay, was first published in an anthology entitled *Lyric Year* and was the title poem of her first collection, *Renascence and Other Poems* (1917).

The poet tells of an enormously powerful experience she has had. It begins with the poet looking at her surroundings, a wooded area near the sea, and thinking that her world is small and unimpressive. Lying on the ground, she looks up at the sky and believes she can touch it with her hand. She reaches up and, instantly, comes into contact with the Infinite. She sees the vastness of time and space, but she also sees the sorrow and pain of life. The agony is so great that she welcomes release from it through death. She feels her body descend into the earth, and the weight of worldly sorrow disappears. Soon, however, she longs to be alive again. A tremendous rain strikes her grave, and she finds herself reborn. Now she realizes that the size of her world and the height of her sky are limited only by her own heart and soul. You can find this poem in Millay's *Collected Poems* (1956) and in many poetry anthologies. YA

Renault, Mary [Mary Challans] (1905–1983) This English author is best known for her historical novels about ancient Greece and Rome. The first, *The Last of the Wine* (1956), tells of life in ancient Athens during the Peloponnesian War, which ended in the ruin of Athens by Sparta. Renault followed this with *The King Must Die*, her most praised work. *Fire from Heaven* (1969) is a fictionalized version of the life of Alexander the Great (356–323 B.C.). An important character is *Aristotle, the Greek philosopher, who was Alexander's teacher. *The Persian Boy* (1972) continues the story and centers on Alexander's military expedition into Asia. Events are seen through the eyes of Bogoas, a Persian eunuch loved by Alexander. Homosexuality is a prominent theme in much of Renault's writings. If you enjoy her books, you will probably like those with somewhat similar settings by *Robert Graves and *Lew Wallace. YA

Rendell, Ruth (Barbara) (1930-) This British author of detective and mystery novels has the ability to combine plot, suspense, and character with both a touch of horror and social criticism. Rendell's fictional detective is Inspector Reginald Wexford, of Kingsmarkham, a town in Sussex, southern England. In *Make Death Love Me* (1979) a man changes identity and starts a new life, but the memory of a woman entangles him in murder. Wexford is in China when the events in *Speaking Mandarin* (1983) begin. While Wexford is on tour, an aged Chinese woman seems to turn up in different cities, and it is not until he is back in England that the odd events are resolved. *The Bridesmaid* (1990) is not about Wexford but is the story of a strangely matched young couple whose passionate attachment brings death rather than love. Here it is the psychological suspense rather than detection that holds your attention. Rendell has published volumes of short stories, including *Means of Evil* (1978) and *The Copper Peacock* (1991). If you like Rendell's books, you will enjoy those of *Martha Grimes and *P.D. James. YA

Rescuers, The (1959) In this amusing fantasy, the English writer Margery Sharp (1905–) invents the Prisoners' Aid Society, which is a group of London mice. Upon hearing that a Norwegian poet is being held prisoner in Black Castle, they resolve to rescue him. The society recruits Miss Bianca, a white mouse who is the pet of an ambassador's son, to go to Norway with him and recruit a Norwegian-speaking mouse. She finds Nils, a sailor mouse, and they make their way back to England where Bernard, a pantry mouse in the embassy, joins them. They reach the land of the Black Castle by sea and get inside a wagon delivering provisions. Finding that the poet is in a dungeon and fed only by food lowered through the ceiling, they steal the key while the jailers sleep off a New Year's Eve celebration. The mice drop the key to the poet, who unlocks his cell door; they all escape through a watergate, and are carried to safety on a raft. Nils and the poet go back to Norway, Bernard becomes the secretary of the society, and Miss Bianca, reunited with her owner, can once more feast on cream cheese. Of course the story is impossible; but before you know it, you will believe it. Sharp later wrote eight more adventures of Miss Bianca and her friends. MR

Return of the Native, The (1878) As in other novels written by *Thomas Hardy, the characters in this book are tragic, and the setting, Egdon Heath in England, adds to the somber atmosphere. Damon Wildeve, once an engineer but now operating a pub, is loved by two

women, Thomasin Yeobright, placid and gentle, and Eustacia Vye, wild and unpredictable. Thomasin and Wildeve marry, though not for love on his part. "The return of the native" occurs when Clym Yeobright, a cousin of Thomasin and a diamond merchant in Paris, returns to Egdon Heath. He marries Eustacia, who accepts him thinking she can get him to return to Paris, where she could live an exciting social life. Clym begins to lose his sight and is reduced to cutting and selling furze, a spiny shrub with several uses. By accident Eustacia is responsible for the death of Clym's mother. She has been having an affair with Wildeve and, feeling remorseful, drowns herself. Wildeve dies trying to save her. Clym, taking the blame for the deaths of his mother and his wife, becomes a traveling preacher, while Thomasin, now a widow, marries Diggory Venn, a humble workman who mines and sells red ocher. *The Return of the Native* will remind you that human selfishness, thoughtlessness, and spite can have tragic consequences for the innocent, as well as for those at fault. YA

Return of the Twelve, The (1962) In this original fantasy by British author Pauline Clarke [Pauline Hunter Blair] (1921–), 8-year-old Max Morley finds, in the attic of the house in Yorkshire, England, where his family lives, a dozen toy wooden soldiers. They are more than 100 years old. Most surprisingly, Max sees them marching, and he begins to talk to them. They call themselves the Twelve and make him their Genie, a protective spirit, telling him they once had four Genii—Brannii, Tallii, Emmii, and Annii. You will not be surprised to learn that nearby is Haworth, the home of the real-life *Brontë family and that Branwell, the son, had a set of toy soldiers. Furthermore, he and his three sisters, when they were children, wrote a book about the soldiers, *The History of the Young Men* (1831). Max seems likely to lose them when an American offers £5,000 for them. With the help of Max's sister and brother, the soldiers leave and with many adventures march back to their original home in

Haworth. There they have to be still during the day, but at night they come to life. You will almost believe this story, and you certainly will share in the adventures of the Twelve. Clarke has written many books for younger readers. Sometimes she uses the pen name of Helen Clare. If you enjoyed reading about these toys that come alive, then you will like *The Indian in the Cupboard* by *Lynne Reid Banks and the classic *The Velveteen Rabbit* by Margery Williams (1881–1944). MR

Return to Bitter Creek (1986) A moving story of the healing of family bitterness, this novel, by *Doris Buchanan Smith, concerns 12-year-old Lacey; her mother, Campbell; and David, who lives with them. They return to Bitter Creek, a small village in the southern Appalachian Mountains, which Campbell had left when she became Lacey's unwed mother. David becomes the blacksmith for a craft school, while Campbell does leather work, and Lacey goes to the local school. Campbell's mother is unwilling to forgive the past. The three are getting along well when David is killed in an auto accident. The grandmother now wants to take Lacey away from Campbell. Meanwhile, Lacey acquires a mare, Polly, and becomes active in school, joining the flag corps and finding a friend in her cousin, Tam. Eventually, the grandmother becomes reconciled to Campbell's independent ways, and to show her change of heart she sews a quilt that shows the family's history, including Campbell, Lacey, and David. There is sadness and anger in this book, but it is also an encouraging tale of the working out of family problems. If you enjoyed *Return to Bitter Creek*, you will want to read *Home Before Dark* by *Sue Ellen Bridgers. MR

Return to Earth: A Novel of the Future (1980) It is the year 3307 in this *science fiction novel by *H.M. Hoover, and Galen Innes, who is governor general of Marsat, one of the artificial worlds that orbit Mars, has come to Earth to visit his former home. He meets 15-year-old Samara, whose mother is the head of the Continental Lloyd Corporation, one of the businesses that control the world and its colonies in space. Galen also comes in contact with the Dolmen, in whose temple are conducted ceremonies in which the Believers worship the Dolmen. Samara's mother is assassinated, and she and Galen are kidnapped and left to die. They escape and in disguise fly to the moon, where Col. Victoria Shuga helps them investigate the Dolmen. The pair go back to Earth where Samara, now head of the family business, in a surprise appearance before the board of directors, takes charge. An investigation finds that the Dolmen had been using drugged candy to make his congregation obedient and had been keeping the money he extracted from them for personal enrichment. The Believers revolt and the Dolmen is seized, but escapes and jumps to his death. You will find it fun to read about the various characters, who are as good and as bad as people in our own time. MR & YA

Revelation (or, Apocalypse) (c.95) As the word "apocalypse" implies, this last book of the New Testament of the *Bible is a work of prophecy, with much *symbolism, figurative language, and mystical numbers. Its author was a man named John, a Roman prisoner on the island of Patmos in the Aegean Sea. The book is sometimes referred to as "The Revelation of St. John the Divine," but he is not the *John who is the traditional author of the fourth Gospel. Revelation was intended to be a message to Christians in Asia Minor and is a vision of the end of the world, when *Jesus Christ will triumph. In it is the vivid account of the Four Horsemen of the Apocalypse. One rides a white horse and symbolizes conquest; the rider of the red horse personifies war; the rider of the black horse, famine; and the pale horse, death. The Spanish novelist Vicente Blasco Ibañez (1867–1928) wrote a popular book, *The Four Horsemen of the Apocalypse* (1916), set in World War I. Two movies based on the novel were made in 1921 and 1961, the first set in World War I, the second in World War II. YA

Revere, Paul (1735–1818) An excellent New England silversmith and an early and ardent patriot during the Revolutionary period, Revere

MR = Middle Reader   YA = Young Adult Reader   * = See this main entry

is, however, remembered for one event in his life, an event embedded in a poem that does not have its facts correct. On April 18, 1775, Revere and two other patriots rode out on horseback from Boston to warn the colonists of Lexington and Concord that a British force was about to march their way to destroy military stores. Revere's two compatriots followed their routes successfully, but Revere was captured by the British and never completed his journey. However, in 1861, the poet *Henry Wadsworth Longfellow wrote "Paul Revere's Ride" and made Revere immortal. It begins:

> Listen, my children, and you shall hear
> Of the midnight ride of Paul Revere.
> On the eighteenth of April, in Seventy-five;
> Hardly a man is now alive
> Who remembers the famous day and year.

If you would like to know more about this patriot, read *Paul Revere* (1987) by Martin Lee (1954–). Older readers will like *Paul Revere and the World He Lived In* (1942) by *Esther Forbes. YA

Reynard the Fox See *fox.

Rice, Elmer [Elmer Reizenstein] (1892–1967) Though he was a novelist and a theatrical producer, Rice is remembered primarily as a dramatist whose works pioneered in stage technique and in dealing with problems of the world of his time. Rice's initial stage success, *On Trial* (1914), a murder mystery, was the first to use the movie technique of flashbacks so that scenes are enacted as witnesses testify. *The Adding Machine* (1923) satirizes the regimentation of the business world in the person of a meek bookkeeper who fears being replaced by a machine. *Street Scene* is Rice's most notable work. *Counselor-at-Law* (1931) presents a realistic view of the legal profession. Powerful as they are, *We, the People* (1933), with the Great Depression of the 1930s as background, and *Judgment Day* (1934), about the *Nazi trial of a man accused of burning the Reichstag, a

German government building, were not successful. More appealing to the public is *Dream Girl* (1945), a fantasy in which two young women encounter romance both in imagination and in reality. A movie was made of *The Adding Machine* in 1969 and of *Dream Girl* in 1948. If you enjoyed these plays, you will appreciate those of *Maxwell Anderson, *Clifford Odets, *Eugene O'Neill, and *Robert E. Sherwood. YA

Richardson, Samuel (1689–1761) Besides the pioneering novel *Pamela, this English author wrote two other lengthy but readable novels while rising from poverty to become a successful London printer and publisher. Called epistolary novels, all of Richardson's fiction is in the form of letters to and from the various characters. In *Clarissa, or, The History of a Young Lady* (1747–1748) the story is about Clarissa Harlowe's troubled life. Seeking to avoid marriage with a man she hates, Clarissa flees to London with Robert Lovelace, handsome but of poor character, who is set on seducing her. Unable to do so, he drugs and rapes her. Clarissa becomes mentally ill, is rescued by a friend, but declines and dies. Lovelace is killed in a duel. Richardson also wrote *Sir Charles Grandison* (1753–1754). When the heroine, Harriet, refuses to marry Sir Hargreve Pollexfen, he has her abducted, but she is rescued by Sir Charles. They fall in love, but he is called to Italy where he has been engaged to marry another woman, Clementina Porretta. Religious differences make this marriage impossible. Clementina releases Sir Charles, who marries Harriet, and the three become good friends. If you like this kind of old-fashioned fiction, try books by *Daniel Defoe, *Henry Fielding, Tobias George Smollett (1721–1771), and Laurence Sterne (1713–1768). YA

Richter, Conrad (Michael) (1890–1968) Turning from a career in journalism, Richter wrote more than a dozen novels and short-story collections about American pioneers and the settlement of America, both in the East and in the Southwest. His first novel was *The Sea of Grass* (1937), the powerful story of a New Mexican cattleman who unsuccessfully fights the changing world in which ranchers are pitted against farmers. Among Richter's best works is the trilogy The Awakening Land, set in Ohio. *The Trees* (1940), the first volume, is set in the 18th century, when the central family in the trilogy moves to Ohio. *The Fields* (1946) brings the family into the Civil War period, while *The Town* (1950) tells what happens when urbanization overtakes the pioneer spirit and atmosphere. You will also like *The Light in the Forest* (1953), an exciting and touching story of a white boy who is captured in Pennsylvania by Delaware Indians and for a time is raised by them. After he is rescued, he misses the Indian way of life. A movie was made of *The Sea of Grass* in 1947 and of *The Light in the Forest* in 1958. If you enjoy Richter's novels, you should also read those of *Willa Cather, *James Fenimore Cooper, and Edward Eggleston (1837–1902). MR & YA

Rifles for Watie (1957)

Heroism mixes with the reality of war in this novel by Harold Keith (1903–) of a boy's experiences in the American Civil War. Sixteen-year-old Jeff Bussey enlists in a Union regiment in Kansas, finds new friends, but makes an enemy of his captain, Asa Clardy. When Jeff's unit occupies a rebel town, he meets the Washbourne family, including their daughter, Lucy. A little later Jeff fights heroically at the battle of Prairie Grove, Arkansas, December 7, 1862. He next becomes a spy, but is captured by the Confederate forces of General Stand Watie, a Cherokee Indian. In order to conceal who he really is, Jeff offers to serve in the rebel army. This enables him to find out who is smuggling Union rifles to the Confederates. It turns out to be his old enemy, Captain Clardy, but Jeff's identity is revealed and he has to flee to escape a firing squad. After many hardships, he reaches Union lines, and when the war ends in 1865 he goes home a hero, but a very different person from the lad of 1861. Jeff hopes someday to go back South and find Lucy. *Rifles for Watie* can be read as an exciting adventure story, but it is also a reminder of the tragedy of a nation bitterly divided. The book won a *Newbery Medal in 1958. MR

Right Stuff, The (1979)

In this interesting and informative book, *Tom Wolfe recounts the early days of space flight in the United States. It is centered on the first seven astronauts, but it also compares them and their feats with Charles E. Yeager (1923–) and others who flew the supersonic X-1 and X-15. To compete with the Soviet Union's lead in space projects, the United States launched Project Mercury and selected seven military pilots. The first flight, lasting only minutes, took place on May 5, 1961, with Alan B. Shepard, Jr. (1923–) on board. An American did not fly around the world in space until February 20, 1962. The astronaut then was John H. Glenn (1921–), later a U.S. Senator. Wolfe covers the scientific and technical aspects of Project Mercury and tells how the astronauts were trained. Wolfe is a bit satirical at times, revealing the private lives of the men who were hailed as heroes by the nation, and of their wives. Most of the men did not always behave like angels. Brave as these men were, they had almost no control over the Mercury capsules, while fliers like Yeager depended on their own skills, as when he flew the X-1 through the sound barrier for the first time. You will appreciate this book for the behind-the-scenes picture it paints of America and the early space age. A movie was made of it in 1983. YA

rigmarole [rigamarole] If someone speaks in a confusing and rambling manner without making any sense to listeners, what is said is rigmarole. The word is also applied to any complicated set of rules or procedures that seem to those concerned to be petty and a nuisance. In *Oz, Rigmarole is a town in the southern part of the land. People from all over Oz are sent there if they cannot talk sense but mumble on at great length. Of course this means that they have to listen to each other carry on tiresomely. No one there can answer a simple question in a straightforward manner.

Rikki-tikki-tavi is a mongoose, an animal known to be a great hunter of snakes, "rather like a little cat in his fur and tail, but quite like a weasel in his head and his habits." He is the main character of "Rikki-tikki-tavi," one of the stories in *The Jungle Book* by *Rudyard Kipling, who was a famous English poet and author.

Rikki-tikki lives in India. One day a flood washes him from his burrow. Nearly drowned, he is left on a garden path near a large house. The English family that has just moved there makes Rikki-tikki part of the household. In return, Rikki-tikki takes it on himself to protect the boy, Teddy, and his parents from two deadly cobras, called Nag and Nagaina.

Rikki-tikki gets help from Darzee, the tailorbird, and from Chuchundra, the muskrat, but only Rikki-tikki can really protect the family from the two poisonous snakes. Day and night he guards the family from the wicked Nag and Nagaina, who want to kill the people and drive Rikki-tikki away, so that the garden will belong only to themselves. Rikki-tikki shows courage and devotion, and with the help of his garden friends, kills Nag and Nagaina. The garden has been made safe for the family, and Teddy and his parents realize they owe their lives to the brave and faithful little mongoose. MR

Riley, James Whitcomb (1849–1916) A house painter and an actor before turning to journalism, Riley took one more occupational step and became for a time America's most popular poet. He did this by writing in the speech of his native Indiana, and he became known as the Hoosier poet. The longest lasting of his writings is the poem "Little Orphant Annie" (1885) (see also *"Little Orphan Annie"), but others were equally popular in their day. Riley collected his verses in *The Old Swimmin' Hole and 'Leven More Poems* (1883). In the first of these he wrote:

> Oh! the old swimmin' hole! When I last
>   saw the place,
> The scene was all changed, like the
>   change in my face.

"When the Frost Is on the Punkin'" is nostalgic of fall in the country:

> O, it sets my heart a-clickin' like the
>   tickin' of the clock,
> When the frost is on the punkin' and
>   the fodder's in the shock.

"The Raggedy Man" is admired by a farm boy:

> O, the Raggedy Man! He works for Pa;
> An' he's the goodest man ever you
>   saw!

If you like such verse, read poems of *Eugene Field, Edgar A. Guest (1881–1959), and *A.A. Milne. MR

Rime of the Ancient Mariner, The (1798) This haunting poem by *Samuel Taylor Coleridge consists of 143 short verses, beginning when an aged sailor, the "ancient mariner," stops a man and insists on telling his tragic story. His ship, near the South Pole, is caught in ice until an *albatross appears, a bird that sailors believe brings good luck. The ice breaks and the ship sails on until the ancient mariner, for no reason, shoots and kills the albatross. The crew hangs the dead albatross around the neck of the mariner, and the ship is driven toward the equator as the sun burns down and the water runs out: "Water, water everywhere, nor any drop to drink." A skeleton ship appears, bringing death to all the crew except the mariner. A "thousand thousand slimey things" appear, but when the mariner sees beauty in them he blesses them. At once, the albatross falls from his neck and sinks into the sea. The mariner is saved and travels about preaching that "he prayeth well, who loveth well, both man and bird and beast." As a result of this poem, an albatross is now a *symbol for any burden people have to bear. YA

Rinehart, Mary Roberts (1876–1958) Born in Pittsburgh and trained as a nurse, Rinehart began to write to help support her family. Her first full-length mystery, *The Circular Staircase* (1908), sold well and established her reputation. Her books include *The Man in Lower Ten* (1909), *The Yellow Room* (1945), and *The Swimming Pool* (1952). In most of Rinehart's books the narrator is a young woman who is in and out of danger all the time. At several points she will say, "Had I but known . . ." or the equivalent, indicating that more trouble lies ahead. Some books involve more mystery and adventure than detection, and some of the plots are rather unbelievable, but the action goes on and the reader cannot help but wonder what surprises, misadventures, or horrors are coming next. Almost always there is a subplot of romance, which ends with a young couple happily engaged if not actually married. Rinehart also wrote many short stories about a middle-aged spinster called Tish, and these tales have been collected in such volumes as *The Amazing Adventures of Letitia Carberry* (1911) and *The Best of Tish* (1955). *The Circular Staircase* was made into a successful play as *The Bat* in 1920 and later a movie, *The Bat*, in 1959. If you like Rinehart's books, try those of *Agatha Christie. MR & YA

Ringworld (1970) In a very imaginative *science fiction novel, *Larry Niven tells the story of an alien world orbiting a sun 200 light years from Earth. It is shaped like a ring and is 90 million miles in radius with 3 million times the surface of Earth. On an expedition seeking Ringworld's origin, four explorers crash into the alien world. The explorers are two humans, Louis Wu, 200 years old, and Teela Brown, whose chief asset is her good luck; and two alien creatures, Nessus, called a "puppeteer," who is a coward, and Speaker-to-Animals, large and covered with orange fur. Using their "skycycles," they set out over a world of mountains, deserts, plains, and an enormous ocean. They come upon a ten-story castle that floats in the air, where they are taken for the Engineers who once kept Ringworld operating. Their worst experience is capture by the automatic machinery of a deserted police station. They escape by finding a way through a hollow mountain. In a sequel, *Ringworld Engineers* (1980), two of the adventurers return to try to restore Ringworld to its regular orbit after unknown aliens have removed its stabilizing rockets. Besides being exciting reading, these books hint at possible future contacts with aliens and the problems of dealing with strange civilizations. YA

"Rip Van Winkle" (1819) This story and "The Legend of Sleepy Hollow," which also appeared in *The Sketch Book of Geoffrey Crayon, Gent.* (1818–1819), are *Washington Irving's most popular works. Rip Van Winkle, a rather lazy Dutch American, lives with a shrewish wife in a Hudson Valley village in the colony of New York in the years before the American Revolution. One day, while hunting in the Catskill Mountains, he meets a dwarf dressed like an ancient Dutchman. Rip helps him carry a keg to where other dwarves are playing ninepins. They drink from the keg, and Rip falls asleep, not to awaken until 20 years later. Making his way home, he finds that in his absence the Revolution has taken place, and the most important person in the country is now George Washington (1732–1799) instead of King George III (1738–1820). Also, Rip's wife has died and his daughter is married. He goes to live with his daughter and enjoys some more years of relaxed living. As a play, *Rip Van Winkle* was extremely popular in the late 19th century. Joseph Jefferson (1829–1905), a prominent actor, played in one version of it for nearly 40 years. MR & YA

River Bank is the imaginary site of the adventures of Mr. Rat, Mr. Mole, Mr. Badger, and Mr. Toad in the popular *Wind in the Willows* by *Kenneth Grahame. The river flows past Toad Hall and has trees on its banks and meadows and woods beyond. There is an island in the river on which are crab apple trees, sloe, and wild cherry. Many birds and animals inhabit River Bank, one of the leading citizens being Mr. Water Rat, who is a skillful boatman. River Bank is such a peaceful place that no government is needed. The inhabitants tend to avoid both trouble and worry.

Roberts, Kenneth (Lewis) (1885–1957) As a historical novelist, Roberts is excellent both as a storyteller and for the abundance of his background material. His novels are set in the American Colonial and Revolutionary periods, the first of eight being *Arundel. Notable also are *Rabble in Arms* (1933) and *Northwest Passage* (1937). The first of these, a sequel to *Arundel*, has as hero Benedict Arnold (1741–1801), the future traitor, but at the beginning of the Revolutionary War a brave and able officer of the patriot army. The novel recounts the adventures of Arnold and his men during the campaign that ended in victory at Saratoga, New York. *Northwest Passage* is based on the career of Robert Rogers (1731–1795), an American frontiersman who commanded rangers fighting for the British in the last of the French and Indian Wars, which ended in 1763. The novel is an account of the expedition Rogers led to destroy the village of the St. Francis Indians, who lived along the St. Francis River in Maine. The rangers destroyed the village, killing about 200 Indians. Rogers also hoped, but failed, to find the long-sought Northwest Passage, a route to the Pacific Ocean. A movie was made of *Northwest Passage* in 1940. If you like historical novels about the United States, read those of *James Fenimore Cooper, *Walter D. Edmonds, and *Esther Forbes. YA

Roberts, Willo Davis (1928–) The author of about 80 mystery, suspense, and historical novels, Roberts has also written stories for younger readers, among them *Don't Hurt Laurie* (1977), about child abuse; *The View from the Cherry Tree*; and *The Girl with the Silver Eyes*. In another, *The Minden Curse* (1978), Danny Minden, about 10 years old, goes to live with Gramps and Aunt Mattie and comes under the Minden Curse, which means that something unusual happens wherever a Minden is. In this case it is the kidnapping of a valuable dog, MacDuff, and Leroy, Danny's large dog. Danny and two friends track down the dognappers. Nick, in *The Pet-Sitting Peril* (1983), spends a summer as a pet-sitter, which turns out to be dangerous when he has to spend the night in a dark apartment house. In *What Could Go Wrong?* (1989), plenty goes wrong when Charlie and his cousins, Gracie and Eddie, fly from Seattle to San Francisco. They end up in the middle of a mystery involving a bomb threat and a chase in the San Francisco airport. The heroes and heroines of these books have more chances than most young people to solve crimes, but you will follow their adventures with growing excitement. If you enjoy these books, you will also like those of *Vivien Alcock, *Lois Duncan, and *Keith Robertson. MR

Robertson, Keith (Carlton) (1914–1991) A graduate of the U.S. Naval Academy who served in World War II, Robertson turned to writing in 1948 and published a number of lively novels.

He is best known for five books about an energetic and ambitious boy who first appears in *Henry Reed, Inc.* Others about Henry include *Henry Reed's Baby-Sitting Service* (1966) and *Henry Reed's Big Show* (1970). In the former book Henry and his friend Midge Glass start a baby-sitting business. There are many funny incidents, and the friends find that babies have minds of their own. *Henry Reed's Big Show* finds the pair planning to stage a play, but along the way it turns first into a rock concert and then into a rodeo. Featured in *The Money Machine* (1969) are equally ambitious teenagers Neil Lambert and Swede Larsen, who operate the Carson Street Detective Agency. They attract the attention of the Secret Service when they acquire a machine that prints fake money. Told that a real counterfeiter is at work in their neighborhood, Neil and Swede, helped by Myrtle Cavanaugh, have the satisfaction of being the ones who find the counterfeit printing plates—at the bottom of a swimming pool. If you enjoy stories of this kind, read those of Florence Parry Heide (1919–), Jane Morton (1931–), *Ellen Raskin, and *Charles Spain Verral. MR

Robin Hood, The Merry Adventures of (1883) Written and illustrated by *Howard Pyle, this has become a young reader's classic. It describes how Robin of Locksley came to be an outlaw and to live in Sherwood Forest as a bandit leader. It tells about Robin's faithful companions, including the mighty Little John, Robin's nephew Will Scarlet, the young minstrel Alan-a-Dale, and the stout, ill-tempered priest *Friar Tuck. Robin and his band rob the wealthy and give to the poor. They continually outwit the Sheriff of Nottingham, and are finally pardoned by King Richard. The story ends with Robin's final battle against the Sheriff of Nottingham, and his death at the hands of his own cousin, the head of a nunnery, to whom he goes for help. The Robin Hood legend is based on a series of English ballads, dating back as far as the 1300s or even earlier, which reflect the common people's resentment of the cruelty and oppression they suffered. If you enjoy reading about Robin Hood, also try *The Silver Horn of Robin Hood*

One of the many illustrations by Howard Pyle for his book *The Merry Adventures of Robin Hood*

(1956) by Donald E. Cooke (1916–1985). *Robin and His Merry Men* (1969) by *Ian Serraillier tells the story in verse. A number of films have been based on the Robin Hood legend, including *Robin Hood* in 1922, *The Adventures of Robin Hood* in 1938, *Robin and Marian* in 1976, the comic spoof *Robin and the Seven Hoods* in 1964, AND *Robin Hood: Prince of Thieves* in 1991. MR & YA

Robinson Crusoe (1719) *The Life and Strange Surprising Adventures of Robinson Crusoe,* by *Daniel Defoe, begins when young Robinson Crusoe, against his father's advice, decides to go to sea. After storms, a sinking, and two years of captivity under the Turks, seaman Crusoe signs on for a voyage from Brazil to Africa. A hurricane blows the ship off course, and Crusoe finds himself the only survivor of a shipwreck. Barely alive, he reaches an unknown island, a place he later calculates to be near Trinidad in the Caribbean Sea. He does not know if the island is inhabited. When he recovers his strength and finds that the wrecked ship has drifted close to shore, he salvages supplies of food and tools over a period of weeks. An ordinary man with ordinary skills, Crusoe applies great energy and ingenuity to making a home and a life for himself. Years go by with no sight of a ship, but his loneliness is eased by the challenge of learning to make what he needs. Hunting, exploring, cooking, building, planting, and reading a salvaged Bible fill his days and bring him a certain satisfaction.

In the 15th year of his isolation, Crusoe sees a naked human footprint in the sand, and eventually discovers there are cannibals on the other side of the island. Using his musket, he saves one of their prisoners from execution and frightens off the savages. He befriends the man, whom he calls Friday, and his long solitude is ended. Some years later, as Crusoe and Friday are preparing to leave the island in a canoe, they are rescued by a passing ship, and the two men sail for England. Crusoe has spent 35 years away from home. Under different titles, many movies have been based on *Robinson Crusoe,* including a notable one, *The Adventures of Robinson Crusoe,* in 1952. YA

roc An imaginary bird of great size, the roc (Persian: *rukh*) was made famous in **The Arabian Nights' Entertainment*, which includes the adventures that *Sinbad the Sailor had with this creature. An adult roc, much larger than an elephant, can pick up and carry an elephant in its claws. A roc's egg is, of course, enormous, and to get at the baby bird within you must use a pickax on the shell. It tastes much like chicken and is said—even though untrue—to make the hair of senior citizens turn from white back to its natural color. The roc may remind you of the much, much smaller shmoo, a creature dreamed up in the 1940s by the cartoonist Al Capp (1909–1979) in his comic strip *Li'l Abner.* The shmoo is egg-shaped, adores being kicked, gives milk, and likes to be eaten by humans. It, too, tastes like

Robinson Crusoe and Friday as they appeared in an 1831 edition of *Robinson Crusoe*

chicken. Roc is also the name of an imaginary island in the China Sea, large and uninhabited except by the big bird itself.

Roche, Mazo de la See *de la Roche, Mazo.

Rochester, Mr. [Edward Rochester] An important figure in *Jane Eyre*, by *Charlotte Brontë, and a true *Byronic hero, Rochester is one of the most exciting characters in fiction. With his dark face, stern features, decisive nose, and grim mouth, he holds himself with unconscious pride and is completely indifferent to his looks. As a young man, Rochester is trapped by his greedy father into marrying Bertha Mason of Jamaica for her money. When Rochester learns that the money does not exist, and Bertha becomes vicious and hopelessly insane, he returns with her to England (where their marriage has not been announced) and arranges for her care at his home, Thornfield. He is bitter and disappointed, and tries to forget his troubles in travel and the company of beautiful women. One of these women has his

child, Adela, and Rochester takes the little girl to be raised in his home. Like Jane Eyre, with whom he eventually finds happiness, Rochester is capable of great devotion and kindness in spite of personal hardships.

Rocinante See *Don Quixote and *horse.

Rockwell, Thomas (1933–) Author of several popular books for young readers, Rockwell is the son of the artist and illustrator Norman Rockwell (1894–1978). Thomas Rockwell is probably best known for his hilarious novel *How to Eat Fried Worms*, in which Billy Forrester must eat worms in order to win a bet. Billy and his friends also appear in *How to Fight a Girl* (1987), in which Billy gets a crush on the prettiest girl in school and suffers all sorts of teasing from his friends, and *How to Get Fabulously Rich* (1990), in which Billy wins a fortune in a lottery. Rockwell's other books include *Squawwwk!* (1972), about a giant blue bird, like the *Roc from *"Sinbad the Sailor," that grows out of a page in a boy's school reader; *Tin Cans* (1975), about three young people who find a magical soup can, out of which come clothing, animals, food, and many other things; and *Hey, Lover Boy* (1981), about the romantic problems of a 13-year-old boy when a classmate gets a crush on him. MR

Rodowsky, Colby (1932–) A teacher before turning to writing novels, Rodowsky provides outstanding accounts of personal and family problems discussed in fictional form. Her best-known book is *The Gathering Room*. Her first novel was *What About Me?* (1976), in which 15-year-old Dorrie must learn that her family cannot lead a normal life because her brother is mentally retarded. She feels neglected when he is given so much attention. In *H, My Name Is Henley* (1982), 12-year-old Henley is faced with a different problem. Her mother, Patti, is forever on the move, and Henley finds a real home only after she refuses to follow her mother any further and decides to remain with Aunt Mercy. Three persons face their problems together in *Julie's Daughter* (1985). One is Julie, who once abandoned a baby daughter. The daughter, Slug, now 17, is reunited with Julie, but it takes a while for them to accept the past and each other. They are helped by their joint efforts in caring for a dying neighbor. Reading Rodowsky's books may help you solve some of your personal and family problems. If you like Rodowsky's books, read some written by *Judy Blume; Elisabet McHugh (1941–), who wrote *Karen and Vicki;* and *S.E. Hinton. MR & YA

Roethke, Theodore (1908–1963) Nature—animals and plants—provided this poet with a background for his thoughts on growth and decay, on childhood and old age. *The Lost Son* (1948) is a direct but lyrical expression of the experience of growing up. Many of Roethke's poems are in a lighter vein, as in *I Am! Says the Lamb* (1961). A wonderful expression of his ability to combine humor and nature is found in "The Sloth," a tribute of sorts to its apparent laziness. You will also like the poem about a strange creature, the Kitty-Cat Bird. Roethke's last volume of verse was *The Far Field* (1964), in which he shows again how he could use images from nature to portray states of mind. If you enjoy poetry of this kind, you should like the poems of *Lewis Carroll, *Emily Dickinson, *Robert Frost, and *Ogden Nash. MR & YA

Roland By tradition a nephew of Charlemagne (742?–814), king of the Franks, Roland is the noble hero of one of the most popular *chansons de gestes* (songs of deeds) of medieval France. As the most famous of the king's paladins, or knights, he was entirely loyal, but too trusting and impetuous, and his pride led to his death. The story of his last battle is based on the invasion of Spain by Charlemagne in 778 to fight the Saracens, who were Muslim occupiers of that Christian country. An enemy of Roland reveals to the Saracens the withdrawal route of the Franks and that Roland will be commanding the rear guard at the pass of Roncesvalles in the Pyrenees mountains between Spain and France. Roland's outnumbered force is taken by

surprise, but he refuses at first to use his ivory horn to recall the main army. He finally does so, but by the time Charlemagne arrives, Roland and all his men are dead. His story is told in *Chanson de Roland* (*Song of Roland*), written about the middle of the 11th century. In the songs of Italian minstrels Roland became known as *Orlando. To read more about Roland, try *The Story of Roland* (1930) by James Baldwin (1841–1925). YA

Roll of Thunder, Hear My Cry (1976) Narrated by 9-year-old Cassie Logan, this novel by *Mildred D. Taylor is the tragic and inspiring story of a poor black family in rural Mississippi at the beginning of the *Great Depression. The Logans own a farm, but have a hard time making ends meet. They suffer prejudice and persecution at the hands of the white owners of local stores and plantations, but their sharecropper neighbors are even worse off. These people form a cooperative, which brings more persecution, and the Logans nearly lose their farm. Cassie, meanwhile, has her own troubles. She is made to apologize to a white girl, Lillian Jean Simms, for an imagined slight, but gets her revenge when she learns of secrets Lillian Jean does not want revealed and so in turn receives an apology. A sharecropper's son, T.J. Avery, is a juvenile delinquent. First he lies to get Mrs. Logan fired as his school teacher, then with two white boys tries to rob a local store. At the novel's climax he is about to be lynched when Mr. Logan sets fire to his cotton field, sacrificing part of his meager crop, to get T.J. to safety while the fire is being fought. You will admire the courage and dignity of the Logans and their neighbors. A sequel is *Let the Circle Be Unbroken* (1981), which tells how the Logan family struggled to save their farm during the *Great Depression. *Roll of Thunder, Hear My Cry* won the *Newbery Medal in 1977. MR

roman à clef, which in French means "novel with a key," is a novel about real people or historical events disguised as fiction, one that needs some knowledge of specific references (the key) to be fully understood and appreciated. Some examples are *Animal Farm by *George Orwell; *Finnegans Wake* (1939) by *James Joyce, which has an enormous number of hidden personal references; and *Remembrance of Things Past* (1913–1927) by *Marcel Proust, which is enhanced if you have some familiarity with the society in which the author lived.

roman-fleuve, which in French means "stream-novel," is a novel or series of novels that recounts the life of a family or social group, often through several generations. Sometimes called a saga, it is usually written as a long and leisurely narrative. Some examples you might like to explore are *Thomas Mann's *Buddenbrooks*; *The Forsyte Saga* by *John Galsworthy; *Jalna,* and its sequels, by *Mazo de la Roche; *War and Peace* by *Leo Tolstoy; and *The Emigrants* (1951), *Unto a Good Land* (1954), and *The Last Letter Home* (1961), a trilogy about Swedish migrants in America, by Vilhelm Mabery (1898–1973). A well-known example from French literature is The Thibaults (1933–1940) by Roger Martin du Gard (1881–1958), which is an eight-part novel cycle that follows the development of a family from the start of the 19th century to World War I. *William Faulkner traces the fortunes of the Snopes family in a trilogy of novels that includes *The Hamlet* (1940), *The Town* (1957), and *The Mansion* (1959). YA

Romeo and Juliet (c.1596) Perhaps the greatest tragic love story in all literature, *William Shakespeare's play is still performed on stage and has been made into several movies, an opera, and a ballet. In 14th-century Verona, a city in northeastern Italy, two noble families, the Capulets and the Montagues, carry on an old family feud. Trouble erupts anew when the Capulets find out that young Romeo, heir of the Montagues, has attended a private banquet of the Capulets in disguise. There he meets and falls in love with Juliet, heiress of the Capulets. In one of the most memorable scenes in the history of the theater, Juliet on her balcony speaks of her love, Romeo finds his way into her garden, and the lovers avow their passion. The next morning they are secretly married by Friar Laurence. Meanwhile, Juliet's father has pledged her to marry Count Paris. To avoid this marriage, Juliet prevails on Friar Laurence to give her a potion that will make it appear that she is dead. She drinks it and is placed in the family tomb. Romeo, believing her dead, secures a dose of poison and breaks into Juliet's tomb. He drinks the poison and dies just as Juliet awakens. Seeing her lover dead, she uses his dagger to kill herself. After the tragedy is revealed, the Capulets and Montagues vow to end their feud. Movies were made of *Romeo and Juliet* in 1936, 1954, and 1968. YA

Room Made of Windows, A (1971) By *Eleanor Cameron, this is an absorbing and skillful novel about a young girl's rich inner life. Julia Redfern is comfortable in her surroundings, among people she loves—a strong and sympathetic mother and her older brother, Greg, who at 14 years old speaks in elaborate sentences and is deeply interested in Egyptian history. They share a house with the de Rizzios and old Daddy Chandler, who is hurrying to finish his memoirs. Next door lives Mrs. Rhiannon Moore, a wonderful pianist, who takes a serious interest in Julia's desire to become a writer. Addie Kellerman is Julia's best friend, a lively girl whose home life is disturbed by an alcoholic father.

The center of Julia's world is her bedroom, with its many windows and lovely view, and space enough for the desk her father made for her before he died. It is a perfect place to write, and Julia intends to keep it until she is old enough to leave home. For all her attachment to those around her, Julia refuses to accept Phil, the gentle man her mother wishes to marry. The marriage would mean giving up her windowed sanctuary to move to Phil's house. More important, it would seem to erase the memory of her father, from whom Julia inherited her love of writing. With the help and encouragement of her brother and friends, Julia takes the first steps toward an acceptance of her mother's desires and the changes they will bring. Julia Redfern is one of Cameron's strongest and most believable characters. Other books about Julia include *Julia and the Hand of God* (1977), about a visit to Uncle Hugh in San Francisco, and *Julia's Magic* (1984), in which trouble begins when Julia accidentally damages a perfume bottle on her aunt's dressing table. MR

Room of One's Own, A (1929) This essay, by *Virginia Woolf, written to discuss women and fiction, is in reality an early, eloquent, and forceful declaration of the feminist point of view. She asserts, "Women have served all these centuries as looking-glasses possessing the magic and delicious power of reflecting the figure of man at twice its natural size." Woolf argues that one result is that women have not been able to write freely and to take their proper place in the intellectual world, and that until they have both independent means of support and privacy—"a room of one's own"— they cannot. Noting also that most female authors are novelists, she expresses the hope that more of them will become poets. Woolf sees the time coming when there will be an end to strict separation of male and female qualities in literature. "Perhaps," she writes, "a mind that is purely masculine cannot create any more than a mind that is purely feminine." You will find this short book remarkable for its preview of a later change in attitudes toward women writers. YA

Roosevelt Grady (1963) You will find this moving story by *Louisa A. Shotwell both grim and inspiring. It tells of the struggle of black 9-year-old Roosevelt Grady and his family of six to find a home and a place in the community. The members of the Grady family are migrant farm workers who have been forced off their property in Georgia. While working at one farm, Roosevelt meets Manowar, an orphan boy, and they become close friends. The Gradys learn that in a nearby town they can find the home they seek in a converted bus for $3.50 a week. Roosevelt and Manowar help

Roosevelt's father get a job in a fertilizer plant, which means the family can rent the bus, Roosevelt can go to a regular school, and his brother, Matthew, can have his lame foot treated. Also, Manowar is adopted by the Gradys. You will rejoice with the family as they celebrate by going to see a Labor Day parade, though Mrs. Grady stays home, happily sewing curtains. MR

Rootabaga Stories (1922) and **Rootabaga Pigeons** (1923) By *Carl Sandburg, these volumes of wild and zany stories contain 48 short tales, excellent for reading aloud as well as by yourself. The first, for example, is about Gimme the Ax, who lets his children name themselves. As a result, the boy becomes Please Gimme and the girl Ax Me No Questions. Another, entitled "How Bimbo the Snip's Thumb Stuck to His Nose When the Wind Changed" tells of just such an incident. Also in this story a monkey fills in for a traffic policeman, standing on a long ladder that an umbrella maker had acquired in order to produce a long, long umbrella handle. Other story titles explain the crazy plots: "How a Skyscraper and Railroad Train Got Picked Up and Carried Away from Pig's Eye Valley Far in the Pickax Mountains"; and "The Dollar Watch and the Five Jack Rabbits." A one-volume edition of these wonderful stories was issued in 1951, and in 1988 and 1989 they came out in a new two-volume edition. MR

Roots (1976) Part fiction, part fact, this book by *Alex Haley is the most remarkable book yet written about the black slavery experience in America. Haley traces his ancestry to Kunta Kinte—son of Omor and Binta, members of a distinguished family in The Gambia, West Africa—who was seized when he was 17 years old while he was looking for the right kind of wood to make a new drum. He was brought to America aboard the slave ship *Lord Ligonier* and sold into slavery in Virginia. Kunta tried four times to escape and after being beaten more than once as punishment, part of his right foot was cut off. The story next tells of a young slave, Chicken George, Kunta's grandson, who did well for himself. Chicken George's son, Tom, was a blacksmith. From here on Haley relies to a large extent on the recollections of his grandmother, Cynthia, Tom's daughter, for events in the family after slavery ended. *Roots* covers seven generations and ends with the birth of the author. It has been criticized as overly emotional and not always entirely correct historically, but its impact and its basic sincerity make reading it a moving experience. Younger readers who would like to know more about the experiences of black slaves might try *Railroad to Freedom* by Hildegarde Swift (1890?–1977). Older readers will want to read *Narrative of the Life of Frederick Douglass* (1845, 1892), by Frederick Douglass (1817–1895), and *Up from Slavery* (1901) by *Booker T. Washington. A TV miniseries made of *Roots* in 1977 was viewed by an estimated 130 million people, the largest audience that ever watched a miniseries. YA

rose Though medieval legend says this flower first appeared miraculously at Bethlehem as a result of the prayers of a young woman who had been wrongly sentenced to death by burning, the rose has been popular since prehistoric times. In the course of these many centuries it has come to have important meanings as a symbol. In Christianity it stands for the purity of the Virgin Mary. The rose is the emblem of England as a result of the Wars of the Roses (1455–1485) between the noble houses of York and Lancaster. The former adopted the white rose as its symbol, and the latter the red. The name of the Rosicrucians, a secret society that was first heard of in 1614, is, in effect, "rosy *cross." The rose also became a symbol for silence or secrecy, so "under the rose" (Latin, *sub rosa*) means that something said or done is not to be repeated or made public. There are numerous references to the rose in literature, most paying tribute to its beauty, and many such phrases are now part of common speech. In *Romeo and Juliet* *William Shakespeare wrote: "A rose by any other name would smell as sweet," meaning that it is not the name of

something that matters but what it really is. Thomas Moore (1779–1852), the English poet, was saddened by "the last rose of summer, left blooming alone." Robert Herrick (1591–1674), another English poet, urged, "Gather ye rosebuds while ye may," saying that the good things in life do not last and you should take advantage of them while you can. The English poet Christopher Marlowe (1564–1593) wrote to his love, "I will make thee a bed of roses," meaning a very pleasant place to lie, but in the play *The Green Pastures*, by Marc Connelly (1890–1980), the Lord complains, "Even bein' Gawd ain't a bed of roses." See also *sign and symbol.

Round Table, the According to legend, this table was so large that *King Arthur's 150 knights each had a place at it. It came to the court as a wedding gift from *Guinevere, Arthur's queen. In all the stories, each knight's name magically appears on his chair in gold letters, and when a knight dies a new name appears. One seat, labeled in gold, "The Siege Perilous," was empty for a generation until *Galahad arrived, and there suddenly was his name. The purpose of having a round table, it has been said, was so that no knight could claim a higher or lower place but that each was to consider himself equal to the others. The knightly vows of chivalry and honor were taken at the table, and possibly early ideas about democracy are represented by this *symbol of virtue and equality.

Rounds, Glen (Harold) (1906–) After working as a cowboy, medicine man in a carnival, and textile designer, Rounds became an artist, and then decided to write and illustrate his own books. His most widely known novel is *The Blind Colt. Among Rounds's many other books are *Lone Muskrat* (1953), the story of an aging muskrat who is forced to flee his long-time home because of a forest fire and find a new place to live; *Beaver Business* (1966), a nonfiction account of how beavers live and work, with emphasis on conservation and the environment; and *The Boll Weevil* (1967), a volume of verse, with music, about a nasty little insect who seeks a home in the South at the expense of some farmers' crops. Rounds has a way of writing about handicapped young people and animals that reminds you they are not helpless when raised with care and patience. At the same time, his background—he was born in South Dakota—gives him a warm feeling for the West. If you enjoy his books, read *The Red Pony* by *John Steinbeck and *The Yearling* by *Marjorie Kinnan Rawlings. MR

Rubáiyát of Omar Khayyám, The (1859) The four-line verses that make up this collection of epigrams—witty and concise thoughts of life—were composed in Arabic in the 11th century by Omar Khayyám (1048?–1131), a Persian poet, philosopher, mathematician, and astronomer. About 1,200 such verses are sometimes said to have been written by him, but fewer than half are actually his work. An English man of letters, *Edward Fitzgerald, translated, adapted, and published 101 of the verses. Though his renditions are certainly not literal, they retain the spirit of the original, and are viewed as poetic transfusions, rather than true translations. The collection soon became popular and has remained so for over a century. *The Rubáiyát* emphasizes the pleasures of life on earth, and encourages the reader to appreciate mortal life because he or she cannot know what comes after it. Probably the best-known verse is:

A Book of Verses underneath the Bough,
A Jug of Wine, a Loaf of Bread—and Thou
Beside me singing in the Wilderness—
Oh, Wilderness were Paradise enow!

YA

Rubicon The name of this small river in north central Italy, which flows into the Adriatic Sea, became part of a phrase you will often hear. About 2,000 years ago, Julius Caesar (100–44 B.C.), a successful Roman general in command in Gaul, was at odds with the Senate in Rome. The Rubicon marked the southern boundary of Caesar's territory. When he was ordered by the Senate to come to Rome but to leave his army behind, he refused. On January 19, 49 B.C., he led his legions across the river and thus set off a civil war—which he won. Since then "crossing the Rubicon" has come to mean taking a step that cannot be retraced, doing something that cannot be undone. If you cross your Rubicon, be prepared to face the consequences for better or for worse.

Run, Shelley, Run! (1974) This novel by *Gertrude Samuels tells about 16-year-old Shelley Clark, who has been running since she was 10 years old. First, she ran away from her alcoholic mother and lecherous stepfather, then from foster homes, from juvenile detention centers, and from all sorts of predatory characters. She has run away from the Rip Van Winkle Center in upstate New York twice. She makes a third attempt with her friend Deedee. The two go to New York City and get jobs in a bar, but Shelley's stepfather finds her and turns her in. This time Shelley is sent to a real prison, where she goes on a rampage and is held in solitary confinement when she learns that Deedee has committed suicide rather than be sent back to an institution. Just when things seem darkest, a Family Court judge helps her break free of "the system" and turn her life around. If you enjoyed *Run, Shelley, Run!*, try also the novels of *Paul Zindel and *S.E. Hinton, many of which are about young people facing difficult and unhappy situations. YA

Runaway Ralph (1970), a novel by *Beverly Cleary, is a sequel to *The Mouse and the Motorcycle* and describes further adventures in the life of a small brown mouse. Seeking danger, speed, and excitement, Ralph runs away from home on his miniature red motorcycle and heads for a nearby summer camp. There his new freedom ends abruptly when Ralph is trapped in a butterfly net by Garf, full name Garfield R. Jernigan, one of the campers. Having just managed to hide his motorcycle under a leaf, Ralph is locked in a cage in the craft shop. He has no privacy, but at least he is reasonably safe from Catso, the camp cat, and

Garf takes good care of him. A crisis occurs when Catso gets into the shop and carries off a girl camper's new watch, and Garf is suspected of being the thief. Ralph and Garf discover they can talk to one another, and they strike a bargain. Ralph will arrange to clear Garf of all suspicion if Garf will retrieve the motorcycle and help Ralph get home. True to his word, the brave mouse plans and carries out his most daring and successful escapade, and claims his reward from the grateful Garf. MR

Ruritania This word has come to mean any small, out-of-the-way country that is behind the times, is inhabited by people in quaint costumes, and is ruled by a gaudily uniformed monarch of a type long gone from history. Ruritania first came to the attention of the world in *The Prisoner of Zenda, *Anthony Hope's romantic novel about brave and foul deeds done in this imaginary eastern European kingdom in the late 19th century. The capital city is Strelsau, a city of both narrow old streets and modern avenues. In the central square the cathedral and the royal palace face each other. The cathedral is famous for its many statues. On one of the ancient streets, Königstrasse, is the house where the hero of the novel fights a duel with the black-hearted Rupert of Hentzau.

Ryan, Cornelius (John) (1920–1974) An Irish-born American journalist and author of *A Bridge Too Far; *The Last Battle, about the fall of Berlin at the end of World War II; and *The Longest Day. Ryan began his career as a reporter for the Reuters news agency in London. Then, as war correspondent for the London *Daily Telegraph,* he was assigned to the Allied invasion of Normandy and covered the progress of General George S. Patton (1885–1945) and the U.S. Third Army in Europe. A superior journalist and tireless researcher, Ryan described his World War II histories as old-fashioned reporting that did not attempt to present the traditional overview of important battles and the deployment of troops. Instead, he provided a picture of exactly what happened on a given day, focusing on many small events and using interviews with hundreds of individuals from generals to enlisted men and civilians. All Ryan's nonfiction reflects his belief that history need not be dull if important events are described in terms of the human spirit. YA

Rylant, Cynthia (1954–) Rylant, who grew up in the mountainous coal-mining region of southern West Virginia, reflects life there in her writing. In her first book, *When I Was Young in the Mountains* (1982), a girl tells about her life in terms of the tastes and smells of the food of the region, and in terms of the land and the climate. You come to understand why such a girl would not think about the world beyond her home. *A Blue-Eyed Daisy* (1985) concerns 11-year-old Ellie and describes her fears and hopes: a wish to be sure her father loves her and a wish for a bedroom of her own. The next year Rylant published her best-known book, *A Fine White Dust. She is also a poet, and 30 of her poems are in *Waiting to Waltz: A Childhood* (1984). As in her prose, Rylant finds subjects for her poetry in her native region. The verses trace her growing up, a process she is anxious to get through rapidly. If you like Rylant's books, you will enjoy those of *Louise Fitzhugh and *Doris Buchanan Smith. MR & YA

Saavedra, Miguel de Cervantes See *Cervantes Saavedra, Miguel de.

Saberhagen, Fred (1930–) A popular *science fiction and *fantasy writer, Saberhagen is known for several series, including the Dracula series, which continues the story of *Bram Stoker's king of the vampires into modern times and portrays him as far less evil and dangerous than in Stoker's tale. Among the books in this series are *The Dracula Tape* (1975), *An Old Friend of the Family* (1979), and *Dominion* (1981). Saberhagen has also written two series set in a post-holocaust world, in which humans vie for possession of 12 swords endowed with magical powers. The Book of Swords trilogy includes *The First Book of Swords* (1984) and two sequels. The Lost Swords series, which begins with *The First Book of Lost Swords: Woundhealer's Story* (1986), continues the story. Saberhagen is also known for his Berserker series of short stories and novels about a race of extraterrestrial robots ranging through space on a mission to wipe out all life. The Berserker books include the story collections *Berserker* (1967) and *The Berserker Wars* (1981) and the novel *Berserker's Planet* (1975). YA

Sachs, Marilyn (1927–) The author of many novels about young people and their sometimes humorous, sometimes difficult experiences, Sachs worked as a librarian for the New York Public Library for 12 years and for the San Francisco Public Library for six years. Toward the end of her career as librarian she began writing books for young people. Her first three published novels, *Amy Moves In* (1964), *Laura's Luck* (1965), and *Amy and Laura* (1966), relate the adventures of two sisters who are almost exact opposites in looks, actions, and personality. Sachs's other books include *Veronica Ganz*, about a girl who is self-conscious about her height; *The Truth About Mary Rose* (1973), about a girl who tries to learn about her dead aunt, after whom she is named; *Class Pictures* (1980), about the friendship of two girls from kindergarten through high school; and *The Fat Girl* (1984), about a high school boy who becomes fascinated by a desperately lonely, overweight girl and decides to help her change her life. MR & YA

Sadako and the Thousand Paper Cranes (1977), by Eleanor (Beatrice) Coerr (1922–), tells about Sadako Sasaki, a Japanese girl who was just a child when her city of Hiroshima was destroyed by an atomic bomb during World War II. Nine years later, Sadako develops leukemia because of the bomb's radiation, and has to go to the hospital. Her best friend brings her a crane made out of folded golden paper and tells her that if she makes 1,000 cranes the gods will grant her wish to get well again. Sadako begins folding paper cranes and soon her room is filled with a great flock. Sadako makes 644 cranes before she dies. Her classmates make the remaining 356, so Sakado can be buried with her thousand cranes.

Sadako has become a heroine to the children of Japan and the world. Every year on August 6, Peace Day, thousands of paper cranes are placed at the base of Sadako's statue in Hiroshima Peace Park. Each is a prayer and a wish for peace in the world.

Coerr, who uses the pen names of Eleanor B. Hicks and Eleanor Page, is a Canadian-born journalist and librarian. She wrote this moving book after a tour of duty in Japan with her diplomat husband. She is also the author and illustrator of several books for young children. MR

Sagan, Françoise [Françoise Quoirez] (1935–) A French novelist and short-story writer, Sagan grew up in a world of comfort and privilege. She began writing in her early teens and attained phenomenal success while still a teenager with her first novel, *Bonjour Tristesse, about a French teenager's relationship with her widowed father and with the woman who falls in love with him. Sagan's later books also reflect her concern with love, particularly troubled or self-destructive love and often between couples of widely differing ages. Her second novel, A Certain Smile (1956), was about the love affair of a college student and a much older man. Her works, noted for their precise descriptions and insights into their characters, have been likened to the books of another French writer, *Colette. Among Sagan's later books are The Unmade Bed (1977), about the love affair between a famous actress and a young playwright; Salad Days (1980), about a boardinghouse keeper and her boarder, an accountant, whose lives are changed when he discovers a pouch of stolen jewels; and Dear Sarah Bernhardt (1987), a biography of the famous actress written as a series of letters between Bernhardt and Sagan. YA

Saint-Exupéry, Antoine de (1900–1944) A French aviator and writer, Saint-Exupéry fell in love with flying while a teenager and became a commercial pilot, flying between Europe and Africa and later flying mail routes in South America and Africa. He served as an aviator during World War II, and was lost in action while flying over the Mediterranean. Saint-Exupéry used his flying experiences as the basis for several books, which were as much about life, knowledge, and human experience as about airplanes and machines. Among these are *Night Flight, *Wind, Sand and Stars, and *Flight to Arras. Even if he had not written these books, Saint-Exupéry would be remembered for his delightful and moving book for younger readers, *The Little Prince. This story of a child prince who travels to Earth from his distant, tiny planet has become a favorite of adults and children alike. MR & YA

St. George, Judith (1931–) Though she began writing in grammar school, St. George did not become a professional author until after she had married and raised a family. Among her books are *The Hallowe'en Pumpkin Smasher, a delightful mystery; By George, Bloomers! (1976), set in 1852, about a young girl who longs to wear the daring new fashion for women; The Shad Are Running (1977), set on the Hudson River in 1833, about a fisherman's son who struggles to overcome his fear of the water after nearly drowning; Do You See What I See? (1982), a mystery set on Cape Cod, about a boy and girl who investigate a murder; and What's Happening to My Junior Year? (1986), about a teenager whose life goes crazy when her mother turns the family basement into a pool room for troubled youths. MR & YA

Saki [H(ector) H(ugh) Munro] (1870–1916) An English author known best for his short stories, Saki was born in Burma, where his father was an officer in the military police, and was raised by two aunts and his grandmother in England. He later served as a military policeman in Burma before returning to England to become a writer. He adopted the pen name Saki while writing a series of humorous sketches for a London newspaper, which first ran his stories about Reginald, an irreverent and witty young observer of the English upper class. These stories were collected in the book *Reginald* (1904). Later collections included *The Chronicles of Clovis* (1912) and *Beasts and Super-Beasts* (1914). Saki was killed in France during World War I. Saki's stories are noted for their wit and whimsy and for their clever turns of phrase. Some have surprise endings similar to the endings found in stories of *O. Henry, and some have about them a touch of the bizarre. Saki's stories appear in many anthologies, and several collections have been published, including *The Short Stories of Saki* (1930) and *The Complete Works of Saki* (1976). YA

Salinger, J(erome) D(avid) (1919–) Known best for his novel *The Catcher in the Rye*, Salinger was born and grew up in New York City. He began writing when he was a teenager and began selling short stories to magazines in the 1940s. His first book and only novel, *The Catcher in the Rye*, became a highly praised best seller and skyrocketed Salinger to a fame he did not want. In the 1960s he moved to New Hampshire, away from all distractions, to concentrate on writing a series of stories about the fictional Glass family. His other books include *Nine Stories* (1953), most of which first appeared in *The New Yorker* magazine; *Franny and Zooey*, two long stories, the first focusing on Franny Glass, a college student and the youngest of the seven Glass children, and the second on Zooey, her older brother; and *Raise High the Roof Beam, Carpenters; and, Seymour—an Introduction* (1963), two more stories, centering on Buddy Glass, the narrator of the stories, and Seymour, the eldest of the Glass children. Salinger is a master storyteller, and his books are brilliant journeys through the joys, sorrows, and disappointments of life. YA

Salome See *John the Baptist.

Samson A judge of Israel and a Nazarite, that is, a person consecrated to God by special vows, Samson, according to the Old Testament of the *Bible, was more noted for his tremen-

dous strength than for any good he did or any godly life he led. His long hair was the *symbol of his strength, which he exercised in one incident by slaying a thousand *Philistines with the jawbone of an ass. Delilah, a woman whom Samson loved, was bribed by the Philistines to discover the source of his strength. She then had his hair cut short while he slept. The Philistines seized him, blinded him, and made him grind meal. Brought to a temple to be mocked, Samson prayed to God to restore his strength, and when that came about he pulled down two pillars and with them the whole temple, killing many Philistines and himself. The story of Samson is told in the Book of Judges of the Bible. Older readers will enjoy the story of this vulnerable man as told in *Samson Agonistes* (1671), a powerful tragedy by *John Milton. Two movies entitled *Samson and Delilah* were made in 1949 and 1984. YA

Sam(uel) Spade is the detective created by *Dashiell Hammett in *The Maltese Falcon. Though this is the only novel in which Sam appears, he has become the model for the hard-boiled private investigator. Spade is about 35 years old and 6 feet tall, and has a long, bony jaw; his nostrils curve back and his eyes are yellow-gray. Spade has thick eyebrows, a hooked nose, and brown hair. When he smiles he keeps his lips closed. Hammett sums him up as "a blond Satan." A heavy smoker, Spade rolls his own cigarettes; he drinks all too often. In action, Spade does not carry a gun but is given to violence with his fists, and is not above breaking the law in the interest of justice. Before forming a partnership with Miles Archer, he was employed by a detective agency in Seattle, but nothing more is said of his background.

Samuels, Gertrude (n.d.) A journalist, dramatist, and photographer, Samuels has shown in her writings a special concern about the effect that imprisonment has on people. Her play *The Corrupters* (1969) is a drama about prison life. Her novel *Adam's Daughter* (1977) tells about a 17-year-old girl's relationship with her divorced father, who has just served six years in prison. *Run, Shelley, Run! is about a teenage girl fleeing from a juvenile detention center. Samuels has also written several nonfiction books, including *B-G, Fighter of Goliaths: The Story of David Ben-Gurian* (1961) and *Mottele: A Partisan Odyssey* (1976), about a 12-year-old Jewish partisan during World War II. YA

Sancho Panza is the squire and companion of the knight errant Don Quixote de la Mancha in the novel *Don Quixote by *Miguel de Cervantes. He is quite the opposite of his master in many ways. Don Quixote sets out across Spain on a quest for chivalric glory and honor, but Sancho joins him in hopes of profit, hoping to become governor of an island. Don Quixote is tall, thin, and well educated, but Sancho Panza is short, stout, and illiterate. Where Don Quixote courts conflict, Sancho much prefers to avoid it. Unlike Don Quixote, he is not sharp-witted, yet he often speaks in proverbs that reveal important truths about life and people. When he does become governor of a small island, he quickly realizes that the world of power and ambition is really not for him after all. His master's antics often get Sancho into trouble, yet he remains loyal and true to Don Quixote to the end.

Sand (1929), a novel by *Will James, is about a rich young city man, Tilden, who finds himself half-drunk one day in the middle of the vast prairie, accidentally left behind by a train. The title refers to the sand, or grit, that a man has in his soul. Tilden stumbles into a cowboy camp. The authentic voice of James, himself a cowboy, describes Tilden: "He was the first grown feller what knowed of easy ways of living who came to the cow country and stuck ... [but] there was nothing to him to stick with, nothing but a rack of bones and a fluttering heart." Tilden's education as a cowboy and as a man begins. He spends some time as the butt of jokes, but little by little his grit takes him through failure and danger. Through his courage he becomes strong and skilled enough to trap and train a wild stallion for the woman he wins, and to gain the respect of the cowboys, his friends. If you enjoyed *Sand*, you may also like James's *Smoky, The Cowhorse.

*Captains Courageous by *Rudyard Kipling is a similar story of the courage and growth of a rich city boy who is rescued by a fishing schooner in the Atlantic Ocean. *Sand* was filmed in 1949. YA

Sandburg, Carl (August) (1878–1967) A poet, biographer, and folklorist, Sandburg was one of the most highly respected and honored American poets of the 20th century. Sandburg was born in Galesburg, Illinois, to a working-class family. He left school early to go to work. After serving in the army during the Spanish-American War, Sandburg completed his education and began his career as a writer. His first book of poems was *In Reckless Ecstasy* (1904). The following year he moved to Chicago and became a member of the growing literary movement there. Sandburg's collections, including *Chicago Poems* (1916), *Cornhuskers* (1918), *Smoke and Steel* (1920), and *The People, Yes* (1936), contained strong, vivid poems that reminded some of Sandburg's long-time idol, *Walt Whitman. His poetry was collected in *Complete Poems* (1950). Sandburg's lifelong interest in Abraham Lincoln led to a celebrated six-volume biography consisting of the two-volume *Abraham Lincoln: The Prairie Years* (1926) and the four-volume *Abraham Lincoln: The War Years* (1939). He also collected hundreds of traditional American songs and ballads in *The American Songbag* (1927) and *The New American Songbag* (1950). For younger readers he published his whimsical *Rootabaga Stories* and *Rootabaga Pigeons* (1923). MR & YA

Sandoz, Mari (1896–1966) A novelist and historian celebrated for her books of pioneer life, Sandoz was born and grew up in Nebraska, the daughter of Swiss immigrants. She had little formal education but, while still a girl, she determined to become a writer. By passing the rural teachers' exam, Sandoz became a teacher and continued her education. Her first book was *Old Jules* (1935), a biography of her father that was acclaimed for its depth of research as well as its strong story. Sandoz is known best for her historical books about pioneer Nebraska, but she also wrote several novels.

Among the best is *Miss Morissa* (1955), about a woman doctor's struggle to practice medicine on the Nebraska frontier in the 1870s. Her non-fiction books include *Crazy Horse* (1942), a biography of the Sioux Indian chief; *Cheyenne Autumn* (1953), about the tragic journey of a band of Cheyenne from the Indian Territory back to their homeland in the Yellowstone River region; *These Were the Sioux* (1961), a loving study of the society, culture, and traditions of the Oglala Sioux; and *The Battle of the Little Bighorn* (1966). YA

Sarah Bishop (1980) This novel by *Scott O'Dell is set during the American Revolution. After her father, a loyalist farmer on Long Island, is killed by patriot sympathizers, the family's farm is burned, and her brother, a patriot soldier, dies aboard a British prison ship, 15-year-old Sarah Bishop flees the horrors of the war to the wilderness of northern Westchester County. She makes a home in a cave overlooking Lake Waccabuc, near the town of Ridgeford. Sarah avoids the townspeople, for she is being hunted by the British, who believe she set a destructive fire while in New York City looking for her brother. Her constant companion through the long, cold winter is her musket, with which she protects herself from wild animals and dangerous humans. When drought strikes the next summer, the townspeople accuse her of witchcraft, but Isaac Morton, the storekeeper's son and a Quaker, comes to her defense and helps her to believe in people again. If you enjoyed reading *Sarah Bishop*, try also *My Brother Sam Is Dead*, a tale of the Revolution by *James Lincoln Collier and Christopher Collier. MR & YA

Sarah, Plain and Tall (1985), by *Patricia MacLachlan, is a short but beautifully written story of love and family. It is told by Anna, whose mother died the day after Anna's little brother, Caleb, was born. Their father, Jacob Witting, a hardworking farmer, places an advertisement for a wife in the newspaper. He receives an answer from Sarah Elizabeth Wheaton, who lives on the coast of Maine with her brother. She comes to visit them for a month, and Anna hopes she will love them all

and decide to marry Papa. She and Caleb hope Sarah will sing, the way their Mama did every day.

Sarah likes the rolling farmland, which reminds her of the sea she misses. She makes a charcoal drawing of the fields, then puts it aside, saying that something is missing. When Sarah goes to town alone one morning, Anna and Caleb fear she is leaving them. But Sarah returns with a present for the family—colored pencils, green and blue and gray, the colors of the sea, to finish her drawing. Sarah is going to stay and marry Jacob. *Sarah, Plain and Tall* won the *Newbery Medal in 1986. A TV film based on this story was made in 1991. MR

Saroyan, William (1908–1981) A writer and dramatist, Saroyan, who was the son of Armenian immigrants, was born and grew up in California. His father died when Bill was a child, and the boy spent some time in an orphanage before his mother could bring the family back together. He left school to go to work when he was 12 years old, but he had no heart for steady employment and went from job to job. His first book, *The Daring Young Man on the Flying Trapeze* (1934), a short-story collection, was a success. It showed Saroyan's affection for and understanding of his characters. Saroyan wrote many short stories, and his numerous collections include *Madness in the Family* (1939) and *My Name Is Aram* (1940). Among his novels, probably the best known and most highly praised is *The Human Comedy* (1942), about the adventures of a 14-year-old California boy who works as a telegraph messenger. Among his plays is *The Time of Your Life* (1939), which focuses on the lives of a group of characters at a waterfront bar. You can find a good sampling of Saroyan's writings in *The Saroyan Reader* (1958), which includes selections from several of his novels, two plays, and a number of short stories. YA

Satan The word Satan comes from the Hebrew for "adversary" and in Jewish and Christian belief he is the leader of the forces of evil in the universe. He is pictured as the being who tempted Eve in *Genesis in the Old Testament of the *Bible and who tested *Job. In the New

Testament it is Satan who tempted *Jesus while he was in the wilderness. *Revelation describes a war in *heaven that ends with the archangel Michael leading the forces of good to cast out Satan. As the ruler of *hell, Satan has various names, among them Beelzebub, the devil, *Lucifer, Old Nick, the Prince of Darkness, and Scratch or Old Scratch. Younger readers will enjoy reading about how Satan was defeated in *The Devil and Daniel Webster by *Stephen Vincent Benét. He is, as you might expect, a prominent figure in *Dante's The Divine Comedy (c.1310–1321) and in *Paradise Lost by *John Milton. MR & YA

satire and **lampoon** involve use of ridicule, sarcasm, *irony, humor, or similar methods to reveal the folly or vices of individuals, societies, or humanity. The ancient Greeks sometimes used satirical techniques in their plays and verse, but the ancient Romans developed satire as a literary form in verse. One of the leading Roman satirists was the poet Horace (65–8 B.C.), whose mild ridicule shows no personal anger toward his targets. In contrast, the Roman poet Juvenal (A.D.60–140) denounced the follies of his time with a sense of raging indignation.

A lampoon is a savage, brutal attack, while satire usually has a touch of humor. A lampoon hits you over the head with a club while satire stabs you with a thin, sharp blade. While the lampoon was popular in 17th- and 18th-century England, especially as a political attack, it has fallen out of favor by becoming too vicious. Also, modern libel laws make lampooning too dangerous.

Satire has been used throughout the ages, in both verse and prose forms. Some examples of satire are "The Miller's Tale" in *The Canterbury Tales by *Geoffrey Chaucer; *Don Quixote by *Miguel de Cervantes; *Candide by *Voltaire; *Gulliver's Travels by *Jonathan Swift; *Huckleberry Finn by *Mark Twain; and *Catch-22 by *Joseph Heller. YA

Saturday Night and Sunday Morning

(1959) This first novel by the English writer *Alan Sillitoe tells about Arthur Seaton, a 22-year-old factory worker who is in rebellion against the life around him. On Saturday nights Arthur likes to go to the pubs and get drunk, and he is not afraid of a good brawl. He detests the idea of getting married and settling down, and he is having affairs with two married women: Brenda, the wife of Jack, a fellow worker; and her sister, Winnie, who is married to Bill, a soldier stationed in Europe. Arthur knows he will eventually have to pay for his reckless living, but he does not change even when a gentle, single young woman named Doreen comes into his life. When Bill comes home on leave and learns about Arthur and Winnie, he and another soldier beat Arthur severely. After this Arthur feels emotionally dead. But the warmth of a family Christmas gathering and his growing love for Doreen help him to grow out of his Saturday night life and into a more stable Sunday morning. A film version of Saturday Night and Sunday Morning was produced in 1960. YA

Savitz, Harriet May (1933–) An author and teacher of writing, Savitz has also been active in promoting programs and services for the disabled. Her interest in sports for the disabled is reflected in her books, including Fly, Wheels, Fly! (1970), about a group of wheelchair-bound basketball players, and Wheelchair Champions: A History of Wheelchair Sports (1978). Among her other books are Wait Until Tomorrow (1981), about a teenage boy struggling to get over his mother's death and about his relationship with his grandfather, who is struggling to learn how to speak again after his vocal cords are removed; and Come Back, Mr. Magic (1983), about a teenage boy and girl who help their friend, another teenage boy, recover from a hit-and-run accident. YA

Sayers, Dorothy L(eigh) (1893–1957) Critics and readers alike generally agree that Sayers was the outstanding British detective-story author of her time. She is usually distinguished for her style, her characterizations, and her plots. Sayers knew Latin when she was 7 years old, had a book of poems published when she was 16, and was an advertising copywriter before turning to detective fiction. Her detective, *Lord Peter Wimsey, was introduced in Whose

Body? (1923) when his mother, the dowager Duchess of Denver, asked him to come to the aid of a friend who had found a body in her bathtub. In *Murder Must Advertise* (1933) Sayers used her advertising agency background. Among the best of her 13 novels are *The Nine Tailors and *Gaudy Night. The latter is a particularly good example of Sayers's ability to write a comedy of manners and still provide a devious plot. She also wrote plays, mostly on religious subjects, and devoted much of her time in later life to a translation of *Dante's *The Divine Comedy* (c.1310–1321). Television miniseries have been made of a number of these books. If you enjoy Sayers's novels, try those of *Margery Allingham, *Michael Innes, and *Ngaio Marsh. YA

scapegoat has come to mean an innocent person or group made to take the blame for others, or to suffer in their place. The Old Testament of the *Bible describes a ritual in which the high priest symbolically burdened a goat with the sins of the Jewish people. The animal was then sacrificed or let loose in the wilderness, to cleanse the nation of its evils. One example of a scapegoat in literature is the character of Rubashov in *Arthur Koestler's *Darkness at Noon.

Scarecrow, The In *The Wonderful Wizard of Oz by *L. Frank Baum, the Scarecrow is a major character. As a scarecrow, in a blue suit stuffed with straw and a pointed blue hat, his job is to scare birds away from the ripe corn. *Dorothy rescues him from the pole on which he is stuck, and he tells her how much he longs to have real brains instead of a head full of hay. He goes with Dorothy on the long and dangerous journey to see the *Wizard of Oz in the hope that Oz can give him a brain.

On the way, the Scarecrow proves to be a very resourceful friend to Dorothy and her companions. When Dorothy destroys the Wicked Witch of the West, the Wizard keeps his promise to the Scarecrow. He mixes a measure of bran with many pins and needles and

Hester Prynne wears her badge of shame in *The Scarlet Letter.*

stuffs the Scarecrow's head until it bulges. Delighted and proud, the Scarecrow now feels so wise that Oz names him ruler of the land.

Scarlet Letter, The (1850) One of *Nathaniel Hawthorne's best-known works, this novel is a study of sin, guilt, and revenge, and their effects on three people. Set in Boston during the early days of the Massachusetts Bay Colony, the novel tells about Hester Prynne, a beautiful young woman who has been sent to the *Puritan colony by her husband, a cold, scholarly, slightly deformed older man, who intends to rejoin his young wife after a period of research in Europe. But Hester is attracted to a fellow colonist, has an affair, and bears a child out of wedlock. She refuses to reveal who the child's father is, so she must bear her punishment alone. She is forced to stand at the pillory and take the town's ridicule, and must wear at all times a scarlet letter "A," which identifies her as an adulterer. Hester's husband arrives in Boston, takes the name Roger Chillingworth, settles in Boston as a physician, and makes Hester promise not to reveal his true identity. For seven years Hester lives as a social outcast. Her daughter, Pearl, grows up without friends and is a strange child, sometimes a comfort and sometimes a torment to her mother.

Meanwhile Chillingworth determines that the Reverend Arthur Dimmesdale, a saintly but physically weak and nervous man, is Pearl's father. Chillingworth becomes Dimmesdale's friend and doctor and secretly plays on his sense of guilt over his actions toward Hester. Dimmesdale's health fails, and Hester finally tells him who Chillingworth is. They decide to sail to England together, but their plans are thwarted by Chillingworth. Finally Dimmesdale, standing with Hester and Pearl at the pillory, announces his guilt to his fellow colonists and then dies, freed at last of Chillingworth's vengeance.

Hester leaves the colony with Pearl, but returns alone after a time and lives there until her death. She continues to wear the scarlet letter, but her kindness and good works change it from a mark of shame to a badge of honor.

Many other authors have written about the psychological effects of sin and guilt. For example, *Edgar Allan Poe treated this theme in the story *"The Tell-Tale Heart," and *Fyodor Dostoyevsky examined it in his novel *Crime and Punishment. The Scarlet Letter was adapted for film in 1926 and 1934. See also *Hester Prynne. YA

Scarlet Pimpernel, The (1905) A swashbuckling tale of international intrigue by the *Baroness Orczy, it was one of the most popular historical novels of its day. It is set in 1792, during the French Revolution (see also *Reign of Terror), when every aristocrat was branded a traitor to the Republican cause. As the novel begins, rumors are afloat in Paris about a band of daring Englishmen who have smuggled many aristocrats out of France to England. Their leader, whose identity is known only to his men, is called the Scarlet Pimpernel (after a humble wildflower) and is being hunted by the French government.

In London you meet Sir Percy Blakeney, one of the richest men in England, and his French-born wife, Marguerite. Lady Blakeney is famous for her beauty and wit, though her friends sometimes wonder why she married the foppish Sir Percy. Monsieur Chauvelin, official agent of the French government, slyly asks Marguerite to use her position in society to discover the Pimpernel's identity. When she refuses, Chauvelin threatens the life of her brother, Armand, who Chauvelin knows is one of the Pimpernel's men. Terrified, Marguerite reluctantly agrees to spy for the agent, but fails to learn anything. She tells Sir Percy that Armand is in deadly danger in France, without revealing her pact with Chauvelin. Sir Percy, suddenly transformed from a silly dandy into a man of pride and strength, vows to save her brother and leaves on his mission. At home, Marguerite finds evidence indicating her husband is the elusive Pimpernel and learns that Chauvelin will follow him to France. Desperate to find Percy and warn him before he is waylaid, she sails to France with a friend. Her determination and Sir Percy's reckless bravery (and mastery of disguise) combine to outwit the French forces. Armand and another group of noblemen are brought to safety in a series of wild and suspenseful escapades. Marguerite and Sir Percy, no longer forced to keep secrets from one another, rediscover their love. The novel appeared in a highly successful stage version in 1903 and was adapted for film in 1935 and for television in 1982. YA

Scheherazade is the fictional narrator of the fabulous tales of *The Arabian Nights' Entertainments. When the Sultan Shahriyan finds that his wife has been unfaithful to him, he has her executed, then decides to marry a new wife each day and have her killed the following morning. Scheherazade, daughter of the grand vizier, becomes the sultan's bride and sets out to save her own life and end the sultan's cruel and bloody practice. That night she begins to tell the sultan a story, but at daybreak the story is not finished, and Scheherazade tells the sultan she will finish it the following night. The sultan postpones her execution, and the next night she completes the tale and begins a new one, which again is unfinished at dawn. Using this trick, Scheherazade tells 1,001 tales. The sultan decides to let her live and accepts her as his faithful and worthy wife.

science fiction is based on scientific fact and examines how human beings are or may be affected by existing or future scientific advances. Science fiction differs greatly from *fantasy. Fantasy can make use of such scientific impossibilities as magic, but science fiction is limited to what can be imagined as scientifically possible, even if it does not exist now. So, stories based on such ideas as time travel, faster-than-light space travel, telepathic communication, and alien encounters are considered science fiction. Science fiction has a long tradition and has been traced by some to ancient Greek and Roman writings. For example, the story of *Daedalus is a fanciful tale about human flight. In more modern times, science fiction was advanced by such writers as *Jules Verne, *H.G. Wells, and Mary Wollstonecraft Shelley (1797–1851) in *Frankenstein. Today's masters of science fiction include *Isaac Asimov, *Arthur C. Clarke, *Robert A. Heinlein, *Frank Herbert, *Ursula K. Le Guin, and *Robert Silverberg. A good history of science fiction is Billion Year Spree (1973) by the English writer Brian W. Aldiss (1935–), revised and enlarged as Trillion Year Spree (1986). MR & YA

Scoppettone, Sandra (1936–) A novelist, playwright, and film and television screenwriter, Scoppettone writes books noted for their realistic approach to serious themes, including homosexuality, alcohol abuse, and the development of self-esteem. Among her books are Trying Hard to Hear You (1974), about a 16-year-old girl who learns that her best friend, a boy, is gay; The Late Great Me (1976), about a 17-year-old girl whose desire to be liked and popular leads her into alcoholism; Happy Endings Are All Alike (1978), about a teenage girl who must find the courage to stand up to the boy who has raped her and to acknowledge that she is a lesbian; and Long Time Between Kisses (1982), about a teenage girl whose life changes when she meets a boy suffering from multiple sclerosis. YA

Scott, Walter (1771–1832) One of the towering figures of Scottish literature, Scott was descended from two celebrated Scottish families and found much inspiration in the Scottish history and stories he heard in boyhood. Stricken as a child with what is now thought to have been polio, Scott was a sickly boy, but he grew to be a tall, strong, and lively man. His sharp mind and enormous energy enabled him to follow a career in law and also to become a prolific writer. Scott's first interest was poetry, and his first book was a collection of Scottish border ballads, Minstrelsy of the Scottish Border (1802). His first long poem, The Lay of the Last Minstrel (1805), a romantic ballad in which the heroine and the hero come from feuding families, established his reputation. Probably his best-known long poem is The Lady of the Lake (1810), a tale of love, conflict, and chivalry set in Scotland in the 16th century during the reign of James V (1512–1542). In a few years Scott turned to writing novels, which were published anonymously. The first, Waverley (1814), set in Scotland in the 18th century, follows the romantic and military adventures of a young British officer. Many of Scott's novels were published as by "the author of Waverley," so all 32 novels came to be called the Waverley Novels. Among the best are Guy Mannering (1815), about the adventures of a Scottish noble kidnapped in childhood; *Ivanhoe, his best-known novel; The Heart of Midlothian (1818), set in Scotland in the 18th century and following the fortunes of two young women, one of whom has been unjustly sentenced to death for murdering her child;

Kenilworth (1821), a tale of romance and intrigue during the reign of Queen Elizabeth I of England (1533–1603); *Quentin Durward* (1823), set in France in the 15th century, about a young Scottish soldier in the service of King Louis XI (1423–1483); and *The Talisman* (1825), about King Richard (1157–1199) on crusade in the Holy Land. Younger readers who want to learn more about Scott will like *Young Walter Scott* (1935) by *Elizabeth Janet Gray. *The Talisman* was made into the movie *King Richard and the Crusades* in 1954 and *Quentin Durward* was filmed in 1955. MR & YA

Scrooge is the name of one of *Charles Dickens's most memorable characters. In *A Christmas Carol*, Ebenezer Scrooge appears as a "squeezing, wrenching, grasping, scraping, clutching, covetous old sinner! . . . secret, and self-contained, and solitary as an oyster." His usual response to a friendly gesture is "Bah! Humbug!" Nowadays the term "Scrooge" is used to describe a miserly person, especially one in a perpetual bad temper.

Sea Wolf, The (1904) One of *Jack London's most powerful novels, this sea story is also a study of a "superman" who has removed himself completely from other people. Humphrey Van Weyden, a gentleman writer, is cast into foggy San Francisco Bay when the ferry he is on sinks in a collision. He is rescued by Wolf Larsen, captain of the sealing ship *Ghost*, bound for the Bering Sea. Larsen forces Van Weyden to join his crew as cabin boy. Humphrey learns quickly that he must adapt to the brutal, dog-eat-dog world Larsen has created aboard the *Ghost*. Larsen believes that the strong survive and the weak perish, and that there is no God. He fears no one except his brother, Death Larsen, skipper of the *Macedonia*, who is hunting for him. His only weakness is painful seizures that blind him temporarily.

The *Ghost* rescues several survivors of another sinking. Among them is the frail poet, Maud Brewster, to whom both men are attracted. One night Larsen attacks her. Van

A reformed Ebenezer Scrooge greets Bob Cratchit in *A Christmas Carol*.

Weyden wounds Larsen, who then has a serious seizure. Van Weyden and Brewster escape to an island in a small boat. Later the *Ghost*, wrecked in a storm, runs aground on the island, its crew having deserted the dying Larsen and joined his brother. Wolf Larsen tries to sabotage Van Weyden and Brewster's plans to leave the island. But as Larsen weakens, Van Weyden repairs the *Ghost*. Larsen dies and is buried at sea, and Van Weyden and Brewster, who have fallen in love, are rescued. If you liked *The Sea Wolf*, try reading *Moby-Dick* by *Herman Melville, whose hero, Captain Ahab, has also cut himself off from humanity. YA

Seagull, The (1896) By *Anton Chekhov, this comedy of frustration, which established him as a major dramatist, is set on the estate of Sorin, a Russian landowner. Sorin's sister, Madame Arkadin, is an actress, self-centered and vain. Her son, Treplev, is a writer struggling to express his ideas through new forms. He dislikes his mother's lover, Trigorin, a successful writer. Treplev loves Nina, the daugher of Sorin's wealthy neighbor. But she is attracted to Trigorin. Treplev presents his new play, with

Nina in the main role, but halts it angrily when his mother, Trigorin, and others appear uninterested. Later he takes a sea gull he has shot to Nina, telling her he cannot live with her rejection and his failure as a writer and intends to kill himself.

A week later Madame Arkadin and Trigorin leave for Moscow. Then Nina goes to Moscow to become an actress and mistress to Trigorin, who ruins her life. She is like the sea gull Treplev shot, an innocent victim. After two years away, she visits Treplev, now a successful writer, at Sorin's estate. Treplev again declares his love for Nina, but she rebuffs him and flees. Disgusted with his writing and the loss of Nina, Treplev kills himself, while his mother and friends are busy playing a game of Lotto, completely unaware of the depths of his despair. If you liked *The Sea Gull*, contrast it with *Hedda Gabler* by *Henrik Ibsen, a tragedy about a bored and desperate woman. YA

Search for Delicious, The (1969) This *fantasy by *Natalie Babbitt is set in a mythical kingdom whose prime minister is writing a dictionary. He gets stuck when he comes to the word "delicious." Nobody in the royal court can agree on just the right food to describe as "delicious." The king sends Gaylen, the prime minister's 12-year-old assistant, to travel through the kingdom and poll all the people on their choice. As Gaylen travels from town to town, he finds that the people do not agree either. He also learns that the queen's brother, Hemlock, is also traveling through the kingdom, telling lies about the purpose of Gaylen's poll and stirring up a civil war.

Gaylen meets many characters on his journey, including a Woldweller, who is 900 years old and lives in the top of an ancient tree; a band of dwarfs; a minstrel, who gives Gaylen a mysterious stone key; and a beautiful mermaid. By unraveling the mystery of the key, Gaylen keeps Hemlock from taking over the kingdom and discovers the definition of "delicious." If you enjoy *The Search for Delicious*, try also the fantasy classic *The Hobbit*, by *J.R.R. Tolkien. MR

Search for Grissi, The (1985) This novel by *Mary Francis Shura tells about Peter Gregory, an 11-year-old boy who wants to be an artist. He has just moved from Peoria, Illinois, to Brooklyn, New York, with his parents and 7-year-old sister, DeeDee. Peter has trouble making friends at his new school, but DeeDee makes friends with everyone, especially a strange old man named Captain Jinks, who cares for the homeless cats that live in an abandoned lot called the Iron Yard. Captain gives DeeDee a big gray cat, which she calls Grissi. DeeDee also makes friends with Colin Cramar, a serious boy in Peter's class.

Peter misses his chance to become friends with Colin, has a run-in with the class bully, and continues to feel lonely. He spends much of his time working on his drawings. Then one day Grissi runs away after being frightened by a neighbor's dog, and Peter's life begins to change. He helps DeeDee look for Grissi. The search brings Peter new friendships and a better understanding of his family, his talent, and himself. MR

Sebestyen, Ouida (1924–) Born and raised in Texas, Sebestyen has used the West as the setting for most of her novels. A short-story writer as well, Sebestyen collected many rejection slips before her first novel, *Words by Heart* (1979), was accepted for publication. Set in a Western community in the early 1900s, it tells about a young black girl whose love of learning raises the shadow of racial prejudice and leads to her father's death. Among Sebestyen's other books are *Far from Home* (1980), set in Texas in 1929, about a boy who, after his mother's death, finds the father he never knew; *IOU's* (1982), about the relationship between a 13-year-old boy, his mother, his dying grandfather, and the father he has never known; and *On Fire* (1985), the sequel to *Words by Heart*, about the effects of a violent miners' strike on a 12-year-old boy and his older brother. YA

Secret Diary of Adrian Mole, Aged 13¾, The (1982) This novel by the English writer *Sue Townsend is in the form of a diary written by its hero, an English boy facing some tough problems in his life. Adrian decides that he is an undiscovered intellectual when he sends a poem to a BBC radio show and receives a personally written rejection slip. The problem is that he does not know any other intellectuals, so he writes his thoughts in his diary.

Adrian's family breaks up when his mother moves away, leaving Adrian with his father, who then loses his job. Meanwhile Adrian falls in love with Pandora, a new girl in school, has a run-in with Barry Kent, the school tough, and befriends a cantankerous old man named Bert Baxter. Adrian faithfully records in his diary the ups and downs of his life through his 15th birthday. The result is a sometimes sad and often funny story of a boy growing up. If you enjoyed *The Secret Diary*, you also will like *The Growing Pains of Adrian Mole* (1984), in which Adrian records his observations and experiences through his 16th birthday. The books were published together as *The Adrian Mole Diaries* (1985). MR & YA

Secret Garden, The (1911) By *Frances Hodgson Burnett, this novel tells about Mary Lennox, an English child born in India, whose parents die in a cholera epidemic. She is sent to England to live with her Uncle Archibald Craven at Misselthwaite Manor on the edge of the Yorkshire *moors. Mary is a thin, sallow little 10-year-old with a sour expression, who has been spoiled by servants and neglected by her parents. At the Manor, she is again left alone a great deal, except for the presence of the young housemaid, Martha Sowerby. Mary learns that among the many manor gardens is one that has been locked up and abandoned since the death of Mrs. Craven 10 years before. She finds an old key to the closed garden in a flower bed and lets herself into the mysteriously beautiful walled park, all overgrown and untended. Working in the garden in secret becomes her daily occupation. Then Mary meets Dickon, a boy with a natural gift for charming animals and growing things, and together they set about bringing the place to its former glory. One night Mary hears crying in another part

of the big house. She follows the sound to a far bedroom and discovers her cousin Colin, whose existence had been unknown to her. He is a sickly boy, a hypochondriac who never goes out and who looks so like his dead mother that Mr. Craven is saddened every time they meet. Colin and Mary soon become friends, and she stirs his interest with her vivid description of the garden and the moors. When she tells him about *her* garden, he is eager to see it. Mary and Dickon help Colin to visit the garden often, and he quickly regains his strength and energy in the fresh air. Over time his improvement is so marked that he is able to meet his father as a completely healthy and cheerful boy. The restoration of the secret garden has worked a kind of magic on both Mary and Colin, bringing them both much-needed affection and a new purpose in life. A musical comedy based on *The Secret Garden* was made in 1991. A motion picture based on the book was made in 1949 and remade for television in 1987. See also *Little Lord Fauntleroy*. MR

Secret of the Andes (1952) By Ann Nolan Clark (1896–), this novel gives you a double treat: You will learn about the culture and traditions of the ancient Incas and you will be excited by the story of the boy Cusi as he seeks knowledge of his people's past and his own future. He lives on top of a mountain in the Andes of Peru with Cuto, an old man whom he assists in caring for a herd of llamas. Cusi is happy but wonders about life elsewhere and even more about the mysterious matters Cuto is teaching him. Cusi has golden earplugs and one day Amauta, also wearing such earplugs and a turban of the ancient Inca nobles, arrives and teaches him more. On one expedition Cuto takes Cusi to a secret place and seats him on a stone throne. Eventually, Cusi goes alone to Cuzco, the Inca holy city, and on the way meets an old man and a woman who treat him with unusual respect. But after his adventures in the outside world, Cusi tells Cuto he is sure he wants to stay on the mountain. Cuto then reveals to him a secret man-made cave in which are bags of gold that were once intended to ransom the Inca ruler from the Spanish conquerors. But the Spanish killed the Inca king before the ransom was paid and the gold was hidden. Cusi realizes he is a chosen keeper of the Inca tradition and must devote his life to it. Clark is a specialist in the history and culture of the Indians of the Americas and has written many books about them. Among them are *Little Navajo Bluebird* (1943), a story of a girl growing up with her tribe; *Magic Money* (1950), dealing with the everyday problems of a boy in Costa Rica; and *Looking-for-Something* (1952), revealing what life is like in Ecuador through the wanderings of a burro who wants to belong to somebody. *Secret of the Andes* won the *Newbery Medal in 1953. MR

Selden, George [George Selden Thompson] (1929–1989) The author of a number of books for younger readers, Selden is known best for *The Cricket in Times Square*, about a cricket named Chester who travels from his Connecticut meadow to New York City aboard a picnic basket. Chester is befriended by Tucker Mouse and Harry Cat, and together they help a boy save his family's newspaper stand. Selden also wrote about his three animal heroes in a number of sequels. Selden's other books include *The Garden Under the Sea* (1957), about a lobster and his friends who take items from the humans on Crescent Beach to build an underwater garden in Long Island Sound; *The Genie of Sutton Place* (1973), about a boy who uses an old book of spells left to him by his archeologist father to conjure up a genie; and *Irma and Jerry* (1982), which follows the adventures of a dog named Jerry and a cat named Irma in New York City's Greenwich Village. MR

Sending of Dragons, A (1987) This novel by *Jane Yolen, the third volume of a trilogy begun with *Dragon's Blood* and *Heart's Blood*, concludes the story of young Jakkin Stewart and his beautiful companion, Akki James, as they struggle to survive in the mountains of the desert planet Austar IV. After sheltering from the deadly cold of Dark After inside the body of Jakkin's dead dragon, Heart's Blood,

Jakkin and Akki find they can link their minds with each other and with Heart's Blood's five hatchlings. They can also survive Dark After. The appearance of a helicopter forces them to go farther into the mountains. There Jakkin and Akki are separated from the dragons and captured by cave people who kill dragons to gain telepathy. The cave people have found metal ore, which Austar needs desperately if it is to gain its freedom within the Federation. After much hardship Jakkin and Akki escape. They are found by the helicopter, which is piloted by their friend Golden, who had helped them escape to the mountains. Armed with their new knowledge, Jakkin and Akki return with Golden to help Austar IV on its road to peace and freedom. MR & YA

Sense and Sensibility (1811) This popular novel by *Jane Austen gives a fascinating view of upper-middle-class English life in the early 19th century. The story centers on two of the three daughters of Mrs. Dashwood, a widow. After her stepson, John Dashwood, inherits the family estate of Norland, Mrs. Dashwood moves from it with her daughters Elinor, Marianne, and Margaret, to a cottage on the estate of a relative, Sir John Middleton. The move separates 19-year-old Elinor from the company of Edward Ferrars, Mrs. John Dashwood's brother, whom she secretly loves. At their new home the Dashwoods meet Sir John's friend Colonel Brandon, a reserved older man who is instantly drawn to 16-year-old Marianne. She rejects him, however, because of his age and reserved nature.

Marianne meets a dashing young man, John Willoughby, and falls in love with him. He returns her affection and, though they make no official announcement, they act toward each other as though they are engaged.

Elinor learns that Edward is secretly engaged to Lucy Steele, the poor but ambitious daughter of his tutor. Meanwhile, Marianne's heart is broken when Willoughby becomes engaged to another woman.

When Edward's mother learns of his engagement to Lucy, she disowns him and gives his inheritance to his brother, Robert. Lucy learns of this, breaks off the engagement, and marries Robert. Edward reveals to Elinor that only honor had kept him from breaking off his engagement to Lucy long ago, and they are married. Marianne finally appreciates Brandon's noble qualities, and they also marry.

Throughout the novel Elinor governs her actions through reason, or sense. Marianne allows her emotions, or sensibilities, to govern her actions, but, in marrying Colonel Brandon, she finally chooses sense over sensibility. If you enjoyed *Sense and Sensibility*, you will also like Austen's best-known novel, *Pride and Prejudice*. YA

Separate Peace, A (1960) This novel by *John Knowles tells about the remarkable friendship of two teenage boys during World War II. Gene, an intellectual, introverted boy, and Phineas, an athletic, vigorous, offbeat, and completely likable boy, are soon to be seniors at the Devon School, a prep school in New Hampshire. It is August 1942, and they are attending summer session. Phineas and Gene are best friends, but something in Gene's heart prevents him from trusting completely in Finny's friendship. This secret sense of rivalry leads to tragedy when, in a sudden moment of animosity, Gene causes Finny to fall from a tree limb and shatter his leg. Gene alone knows that Finny's accident was the result of his own deliberate action. When he tries to tell Phineas, the crippled boy refuses to consider the possibility that his best friend could also, for even one instant, be his worst enemy.

Phineas and Gene are forced to confront the truth months later, when members of their class hold a mock inquiry into the accident one night. Finny, still limping and now using a cane, suddenly realizes what really happened. He storms out of the building and falls down the steps, rebreaking his leg. The next morning Gene visits him in the school infirmary, and the two come to an understanding, a "separate peace," about the tragedy. That afternoon Finny dies while the school doctor tries to reset his broken leg.

Gene prepares to graduate and go off to war, but he feels no hatred for the enemy, for he has buried all his hatred with his best friend and enemy, Phineas. If you enjoyed *A Separate Peace*, try *Lord of the Flies* by *William Golding, another powerful study of young people caught in a struggle between good and evil. *A Separate Peace* was filmed in 1972. YA

Serraillier, Ian (1912–) An English poet, translator, teacher, and writer, Serraillier is known best for his novel *The Silver Sword, about three Polish children who are separated from their parents during World War II and embark on a long and often dangerous search for them. Critics praised Serraillier's storytelling ability and his powerful and often poetic writing. Among Serraillier's other works for young people are a number of books based on Greek mythology, including *The Gorgon's Head: The Story of Perseus* (1961), about the Greek hero *Perseus, who slays the monster known as the *Gorgon; *The Clashing Rocks: The Story of Jason* (1963), which tells of the adventures of *Jason and the *Argonauts; and *Heracles the Strong* (1970), about mighty Heracles (*Hercules) and his 12 labors. Serraillier has also written a number of books based on medieval English literature, including *The Challenge of the Green Knight* (1967), a story in verse about *Gawain, a knight of *King Arthur's court, and his mortal contest with a mysterious knight clad all in green; and *Robin and His Merry Men: Ballads of Robin Hood* (1969). MR

Seton, Ernest Thompson [Ernest Evan Seton Thompson] (1860–1946) A naturalist, artist, and writer of popular animal stories, Seton was born in England. When he was 6 years old his family moved to a farm in Canada, then to Toronto four years later. During his years on the farm, Seton first became fascinated with the wildlife around him, especially birds. Later trips through the countryside of Canada gave him a deeper understanding and enjoyment of nature. He studied art in Canada and Europe and began a career as an illustrator and writer. His stories are fiction based on fact, revealing the characters of his wild animals through their behavior and habits. Probably his most popular and successful book is *Wild Animals I*

Have Known (1898), a collection of eight of his animal stories. Seton wrote many books, lectured throughout the United States and Canada, and in 1910 helped found the Boy Scouts of America. Among Seton's books are *The Biography of a Grizzly* (1900), *Lives of the Hunted* (1901), *Woodcraft and Indian Lore* (1912), and *The Biography of an Arctic Fox* (1937). MR & YA

Seuss, Dr. See *Dr. Seuss.

Seven Gothic Tales (1934), by *Isak Dinesen, is a collection of unusual and sophisticated stories, set mostly in the past, and containing elements of the grotesque and the supernatural. "The Deluge at Norderney" is the story of four people marooned during a great flood, waiting to be rescued from the hayloft of a peasant's barn. In "The Old Chevalier," Baron von Brackel asks "whether one is ever likely to get any real benefit . . . out of forsaking an inclination for the sake of principle." He remembers an innocent young girl he loved in Paris long ago. Out of a mysterious sense of coming misfortune, a feeling he would have to pay for his happiness, he let the girl leave him and never saw her again.

In "The Supper at Elsinore," you will meet the sisters Fernande and Eliza De Cominck and their brother, Morten. While still young, the De Comincks are brilliant and charming figures in Elsinore society, highly respected and wealthy. Morten becomes engaged to Adrienne, a timid and conventional beauty, but he disappears without a trace on the morning of his wedding. Later his sisters hear rumors that Morten has become a pirate in the Caribbean, and still later that he was hanged. In spite of many offers, Fernande and Eliza never marry, preferring to keep all possibilities in hand, rather than "make a definite choice and come down to a limited reality." Now living in Copenhagen, the sisters are told that Morten's ghost has visited the house at Elsinore. They return there to meet him, in a frenzy of suspense and expectation. Morten comes to them in the red room where they often had supper as children, and they talk of old times and ex-

ploits until the clock strikes midnight, and Morten disappears. YA

Shadow of a Bull (1964) By Maia Wojciechowska (1927–), this is the story of a boy's struggle to be himself. Everyone expects 9-year-old Manola Olivar, son of Spain's great bullfighter, to become a bullfighter like his father. When he is 12 years old he will have to fight his first bull. But Manola knows he does not have the love of bullfighting necessary to become a good matador. His friend Juan Garcia does. But Juan will not have the chance to fight bulls that Manola has because his father is not famous. When Manola goes to fight his bull for the first time Juan goes with him. A famous critic of bullfighting, who knew Manola's father, is there. He tells Manola to have the courage to make his own decision as to what he wants to be. Bravely Manola faces the bull, makes a few good passes, then he decides. He would rather be a doctor and heal people than fight bulls. He tells Juan the bull is his, giving Juan the chance he longs for. For older readers, *Tuned Out, also by Wojciechowska, is about 16-year-old Jim and how he helps his older brother who freaks out on drugs. Maia Wojciechowska fled from her native Poland when the Germans invaded and came to America in 1942. She has written a number of books for young people. *Shadow of a Bull* won the *Newbery Medal in 1965. MR & YA

Shaffer, Anthony (1926–) An English novelist, playwright, and screenwriter, Shaffer worked as a barrister, or lawyer, and an advertising executive before turning to writing full time. With his twin brother, *Peter Shaffer, he wrote several mystery novels under the joint pen name of Peter Anthony, then on his brother's urging turned to writing plays. He is known best for his play *Sleuth* (1970), a thriller about an aging mystery writer who concocts a diabolical scheme to drive away his wife's lover. The plan unravels with deadly and disastrous results. Shaffer has also written a number of screenplays, including those for the films *Frenzy* (1972), a thriller about a psychotic sex killer; *Sleuth* (1973), based on Shaffer's play; and *Death on the Nile* (1978), based on the novel by *Agatha Christie. YA

Shaffer, Peter (1926–) An English novelist and playwright, Shaffer began his career as a literary critic and music critic, then wrote several detective novels with his brother, *Anthony Shaffer, before gaining success as a playwright. His first play was *Five Finger Exercise* (1958), about four people—an English couple, their college-age son, and their 14-year-old daughter—whose inability to communicate their innermost thoughts and feelings to each other is shattered by the girl's tutor, a sensitive student from Germany. His other plays include *Equus,* a psychological study of a teenage boy driven to an act of senseless brutality; and *Amadeus* (1980), an imaginative but fictional play about Wolfgang Amadeus Mozart (1756–1791) and his contemporary, the Italian composer Antonio Salieri (1750–1825). *Five Finger Exercise* was made into a movie in 1962, *Equus* in 1977, and *Amadeus* in 1984. YA

Shakespeare, William (1564–1616) An actor, dramatist, and poet, Shakespeare is considered by many to have been the greatest writer in the English language. However, little is known for certain about him. He was born in the town of Stratford-on-Avon, where his father was a respected and prosperous citizen. He is thought to have attended school in Stratford, but how long he remained a student is unknown. His father had financial problems, and Shakespeare may have left school to help the family. In 1582 Shakespeare married Anne Hathaway, and the couple had three children. Sometime in the late 1580s, it is believed, Shakespeare arrived in London and began his career as an actor and playwright; but he achieved his first success as a poet. Two long poems, *Venus and Adonis* (1593) and *Lucrece* (1594), were very popular. Around this time he became a member of the Lord Chamberlain's Company, a group of actors. He remained a member of this company for the rest of his professional life.

By 1597 Shakespeare was successful enough

Title page of the Second Folio edition (1632) of William Shakespeare's plays

to buy a large house in Stratford for his family. Soon after, he invested in the new Globe Theatre, where many of his plays were first performed. Around 1608 Shakespeare, now a wealthy landowner, began to withdraw from theatrical life and spent more time at his spacious home in Stratford, where he died.

Only about half of Shakespeare's plays had been published at the time of his death, and not all of those had listed him as author. The first real attempt to collect his plays was the First Folio edition of 1623. It presented the plays in three categories: comedies, such as *As You Like It* and *The Tempest;* histories, dramas based on historical figures and events, such as *Richard II* (1594) and *Henry V* (1600); and tragedies, such as *Hamlet* and *Romeo and Juliet.*

Though Shakespeare's plays were very popular with the audiences of his day, works written for the stage were not considered great literature. Authors' manuscripts were considered to have little value, and not one of Shakespeare's manuscripts survives today. Only a few samples of Shakespeare's handwriting—his signatures—remain, so there is no direct evidence that Shakespeare the actor wrote the plays attributed to Shakespeare.

Some have claimed that Shakespeare was too uneducated and too far removed from the inner circles of court life to have written the plays. *Mark Twain's essay "Is Shakespeare Dead?" (1909) is one of the most biting and humorous arguments against Shakespeare's authorship. More than 50 persons have been suggested as the true author of Shakespeare's works, and scholars have maintained a lively debate over the issue. The latest candidate is Edward de Vere (1550–1604), 17th Earl of Oxford. But the authorship controversy has little bearing on the plays themselves, which contain some of the finest poetry ever written and present a remarkable view of life, from its coarsest depths to its noblest heights.

See also *Antony and Cleopatra, *Julius Caesar, *King Lear, *Macbeth, *A Midsummer Night's Dream, and *Othello. YA

Shane (1949), by Jack Schaefer (1907–1991), tells about a gunfighter who helps a family of Wyoming homesteaders in a life-and-death struggle against a ruthless rancher. When Shane rides into the valley and into the Starretts' lives, he wears no gun, but Joe Starrett, his wife, Marian, and their son, Bob, know that he is a special kind of man. Shane stays to work for Starrett and soon becomes embroiled in the farmers' struggle against Luke Fletcher, a wealthy rancher. Fletcher is willing to do almost anything to drive out the farmers and protect the range for his cattle. He hires a gunslinger named Wilson, who kills one of the farmers. Shane, realizing he can never escape his own past and determined to protect the Starretts, kills Wilson and Fletcher in a gunfight and is seriously wounded. He rides out of the valley and is never seen again. Jack Schaefer wrote many Westerns noted for their smooth style and historical accuracy, but he is

remembered for *Shane*, his first novel. If you enjoyed *Shane*, try also the books of *Zane Grey and *Louis L'Amour (1908–1988), two other masters of the Western novel. *Shane* was made into an excellent movie in 1953. MR & YA

Shange, Ntozake [Paulette Williams] (1948–) A poet, novelist, and performer, Shange was the oldest of four children in a well-to-do family. As a teenager she became aware that women, especially black women, were not being treated fairly by society. Her sense of rage at the injustice faced by women and blacks in American society, now and through history, is at the core of much of her writing. Her best-known work is the play *For Colored Girls Who Have Considered Suicide/When the Rainbow Is Enuf* (1976), which combines poetry, music, and dance into a theatrical experience Shange calls a "choreopoem." A passionate depiction of the pain and struggle of black women, it had a very successful Broadway run and was warmly praised by critics. Among Shange's other works are *Natural Disasters and Other Festive Occasions* (1977), a collection of poems and prose; *Nappy Edges* (1978), a collection of poems; *Sassafras, Cypress & Indigo* (1982), a novel about the experience of three young black sisters as they enter adulthood; and *Betsey Brown* (1959), a novel about a 13-year-old girl growing up in St. Louis in 1959. YA

Shangri-La is the fictional mountain paradise in the novel *Lost Horizon by *James Hilton. On a flight from India to China, Hugh Conway and three other Europeans are kidnapped and taken to a Tibetan monastery high in the mountains of Tibet. The monastery overlooks the valley of the Blue Moon, whose several thousand inhabitants lead a seemingly perfect life, free of hunger, want, and strife. Conway and the others find that, in addition to the beauty and comfort of the valley, it has the effect of extending human lifespans—well over a century for some. "Shangri-La" has come to mean any remote and beautiful paradise, even an imaginary one, where people live in harmony and happiness. Other fictional paradises are *Utopia, described by the English statesman and religious figure Thomas More (1478–1535) in his novel of the same name; and *Samuel Butler's *Erewhon*. YA

Shardik (1974), a massive novel by *Richard Adams, tells about a simple man's search for truth. Kelderek is a hunter living on Ortelga, an island in the Great River Telthearna. He is called Kelderek Play-with-the-Children, for he would much rather spend time playing with children than drinking in the tavern with the other men. One day Kelderek discovers a giant wounded bear that he believes is the reincarnation of Lord Shardik, the divine messenger of God. Kelderek is taken to the sacred island of Quiso, where he meets the high priestess known as The Tuginda, who awaits the return of Shardik. She and her priestesses, including the lovely Melathys, go with Kelderek to the dying bear. The Tuginda restores it with her healing knowledge.

Kelderek stays with the bear, follows it in its wanderings, and comes to be regarded as Shardik's high priest. He gains power and glory for a time after the Ortelgans conquer the mainland kingdom of Bekla. But, faced with war financed by a vicious child slave trade, and realizing his failure to understand Shardik's mission, he follows the bear back into the wilderness. Kelderek falls into the hands of a brutal slave trader, Genshed. Genshed later finds and attacks Shardik, half-starved and injured. The bear kills Genshed, then dies of his wounds, but Kelderek and the children enslaved by Genshed are freed. Kelderek realizes that Shardik was sent to free the children from slavery. The war ends and Kelderek is reunited with Melathys, whom he has come to love. He becomes governor of a frontier province, where abandoned or unloved children are welcome to grow up free of fear or want. YA

Sharmat, Marjorie Weinman (1928–) Author of many books for young readers, Sharmat worked as a librarian for a number of years be-

fore turning to writing. At first she wrote books for younger readers, then turned to writing for young adults as well. Among her books for younger readers are *Getting Something on Maggie Marmelstein* (1971), about a boy and girl whose attempts to blackmail each other lead to friendship; *Nate the Great* (1972), about a junior detective who helps a girl find a lost painting of her dog; and *A Visit with Rosalind* (1972), about a girl who travels by airplane to visit her best friend and becomes involved in a mystery when she picks up the wrong suitcase at the airport. Sharmat's books for young adults include *How to Meet a Gorgeous Guy* (1983), about an average girl who dates a handsome and popular boy as research for a magazine article, then finds she really likes him; and *How to Meet a Gorgeous Girl* (1984), about a boy who uses a "how-to" book in his effort to meet a beautiful girl. MR & YA

Shaw, George Bernard (1856–1950) An Irish-born English playwright and critic, Shaw was noted for his outspoken religious independence and support of socialism and other causes. Shaw moved to London when he was 19 years old and began his career as a critic and unsuccessful novelist before achieving enormous success as a playwright. Shaw's plays reveal his deep interest in the progress of society and the spiritual evolution of humanity. Though they are often more involved with ideas than emotion or action, they also contain fascinating and memorable characters and brilliant dialogue. Among Shaw's plays are *Arms and the Man* (1894), a comedy that blasts the idea of warfare as being noble or romantic; *Man and Superman* (1903), which explores the relationship of men and women in modern society; *Major Barbara* (1905), in which Shaw condemns poverty as the greatest evil facing society; *Androcles and the Lion* (1912), a comedy about religious faith; *Pygmalion*; and *Saint Joan* (1924), a study of faith and conscience. Shaw won the Nobel Prize for literature in 1925. Movies were made of *Arms and the Man* in 1932, *Major Barbara* in 1941, *Andro-*

cles and the Lion in 1952, and *Saint Joan* in 1957. YA

Shaw, Irwin (1913–1984) A novelist, short-story writer, and playwright, Shaw became known in the 1930s and 1940s first as a playwright, then as a master of the short story. His first novel, *The Young Lions*, which follows the lives of three soldiers through World War II, launched his successful career as a novelist. Among his later novels are *Rich Man, Poor Man* (1970), about three children of a German immigrant who take different paths in their search for success and happiness; *Evening in Byzantium* (1973), about a once-successful film producer at a turning point in his life; and *Nightwork* (1975), about a night clerk in a New York hotel whose life changes when he finds $100,000 in the room of a dead man. Two excellent collections of Shaw's short stories are *The Short Stories of Irwin Shaw* (1966) and *Short Stories: Five Decades* (1978). A TV miniseries was made of *Rich Man, Poor Man* in 1976. YA

She Stoops to Conquer, or The Mistakes of a Night (1773) This lighthearted play by the English writer *Oliver Goldsmith tells of the romantic ups and downs of two young couples. The play opens with George Hastings and his friend Charles Marlow journeying to the home of Mr. Hardcastle. Hastings wants to elope with Hardcastle's niece, Constance Neville, and Marlow has promised his father, Hardcastle's old friend, to meet Hardcastle's daughter, Kate. Marlow is not happy to do this, for he is bashful and uncomfortable in the presence of genteel young ladies, much preferring the company of young women who are less advantaged in the social order.

En route the two get lost and stop for the night at an inn, where Tony Lumpkin, Hardcastle's roguish stepson, sneakily directs them to the Hardcastle home, saying it is a much better inn. There Hastings and Marlow confound Hardcastle by treating him as an innkeeper. Kate, dressed in all her finery, meets Marlow, who is so bashful he does not even look at her. He later sees Kate in a simple country dress and, mistaking her for a bar-

Percy Bysshe Shelley

maid, begins to open up to her. Kate learns of Marlow's problem and decides to continue the pretense until she has won Marlow's heart.

Meanwhile, Tony tries to help Hastings and his cousin Constance elope. Tony's mother, Mrs. Hardcastle, wants Tony to marry Constance, but he has his eye on a local girl, Bet Bouncer. Things go hilariously wrong, but truth and good character finally win out where deceit fails. Hardcastle learns of the trick Tony has played on Hastings and Marlow, Marlow learns that he really has been courting Kate, Hastings wins Constance's hand, and Tony is finally free to woo Bet. If you enjoyed *She Stoops to Conquer*, you will also like *The Rivals* (1775) by the English playwright Richard Brinsley Sheridan (1751–1816), a comedy in which a naval officer assumes another identity in order to win the woman he loves. YA

Shelley, Percy Bysshe (1792–1822) One of the leading English poets of the early 19th century, Shelley was born into a well-to-do upper-class family. He was a brilliant but rebellious student and was expelled from Oxford for writing

Sherlock Holmes (on the right) and Dr. Watson in a railway carriage
hastening to a crime scene

and circulating a pamphlet, *The Necessity of Atheism* (1811), with his friend Thomas Jefferson Hogg (1792–1862). In 1811 he married Harriet Westbrook (1796–1816), though he did not believe in marriage. His life after this was a series of travels in the British Isles and Europe. The Shelleys separated three years later, and after Harriet's suicide Shelley married Mary Wollstonecraft Godwin, who soon became known to the world through her novel *Frankenstein*. Shelley's close friends included fellow poets *George Gordon Byron and *John Keats. His poem *Adonais* (1821) is an elegy on the death of Keats. Shelley was drowned off the coast of Italy while returning from a visit to Byron.

Shelley's life and writings reflected his deep belief in religious and social freedom. His masterpiece, the verse drama *Prometheus Unbound* (1820), expresses his views on religion, morality, and human progress. He also produced a number of beautiful short poems, including "To the West Wind" (1819), "To a Skylark" (1820), and "The Cloud" (1820). You can find good selections of Shelley's work in *The Oxford Anthology of English Literature*

(1973) and *The Norton Anthology of English Literature* (1988). YA

Sherlock Holmes, undeniably the most popular fictional detective ever created, was the brainchild of *Arthur Conan Doyle. Holmes made his first appearance in 1887 in a novel, *A Study in Scarlet,* and was active until Doyle retired him in 1903 to become a beekeeper in Sussex in southern England. Holmes was born in 1854 in Yorkshire, and grew to be six feet tall, slim, dark, and hawk-nosed. He solved his first case while a student at Oxford University. Holmes becomes a private consultant in 1881 and takes as his roommate Dr. John H. Watson, who served with the British Army in Afghanistan. They live at 221B Baker Street, London, an imaginary address but one that visitors often look for today. Here Holmes begins to demonstrate his deductive powers and his extensive knowledge in almost every field. Watson becomes Holmes's assistant and the chronicler of his adventures. Holmes is a boxer, fencer, and violinist; he also smokes a pipe and occasionally uses cocaine, which at the time was not recognized as being as dangerous as it is. Holmes is also a master of disguises, often fooling even Watson. His great enemy is Professor James Moriarty, described as *the* master criminal. When Doyle tired of writing about Holmes, he had Moriarty and Holmes die together in 1891 in a fight in which they fall over the Reichenbach Falls in Switzerland.

However, the reading public forced Doyle to find that Holmes had not died, and so he brought him back in 1894. In all there are 60 short stories about Holmes, originally published in nine volumes. In addition to *A Study in Scarlet*, there are the novels *The Sign of the Four* and *The Hound of the Baskervilles*. In the many movies that have been made featuring Holmes, the best-known player of the role is Basil Rathbone (1892–1967), who first portrayed the great detective in 1940. MR & YA

Sherwood, Robert E(mmet) (1896–1955) A playwright, editor, and screenwriter, Sherwood wrote a number of successful and critically acclaimed plays. His combat experience during World War I turned him against the waste, stupidity, and inhumanity of modern warfare. This theme appears in several of his plays, including *The Road to Rome* (1927), a comedy about Hannibal's invasion of ancient Italy; and *Idiot's Delight* (1936), which denounces all who encourage, profit by, or put up with war. Sherwood strongly opposed fascism and was an early supporter of American involvement in World War II. His play *There Shall Be No Night* (1940), about the Russian invasion of Finland, is a powerful call to oppose aggression. During World War II Sherwood helped write speeches for President Franklin D. Roosevelt. Sherwood recounted his wartime experiences in the book *Roosevelt and Hopkins* (1948). Among Sherwood's other plays are *Abe Lincoln in Illinois* (1938), about Lincoln's rise from young backwoodsman to president-elect; and *The Petrified Forest*. YA

Shiloh (1991) This novel by *Phyllis Reynolds Naylor tells about 11-year-old Marty Preston who, while walking out by the old Shiloh schoolhouse near his home in Friendly, West Virginia, finds a beagle that acts as if it has been mistreated by its master. Marty names the dog Shiloh and learns that he is owned by Judd Travers, a brutal, mean-spirited neighbor. Marty's father tells him he must return Shiloh to Travers. When Shiloh escapes from Travers again, Marty decides to hide the dog and protect him in the woods near his house. His efforts to feed Shiloh and keep his whereabouts a secret cause him many problems. When Shiloh is mauled by a neighbor's dog and is cared for by a local doctor, Travers learns about it and demands Shiloh's return as soon as he is well. Marty catches Travers shooting deer out of season and uses his promise of silence and an agreement to work 20 hours for Travers to win Shiloh. In the process he gains a new understanding of Travers and of life. If you enjoyed *Shiloh*, try also the short novel *The Voice of Bugle Ann* by *MacKinlay Kantor. MR

Sholokhov, Mikhail (Aleksandrovitch) (1905–1984) A Russian novelist and short-story writer, Sholokhov is honored as one of the great figures of Russian and Soviet literature. He was born on a farm near the river Don, in the traditional land of the Cossack people. His love of the Don region and of Cossack history, culture, and people, combined with his support of the communist movement in Russia, is the foundation for his writings, including his masterwork, *The Quiet Don*. Though an ardent communist, Sholokhov refused to reduce his writing to mere Soviet propaganda. Among his other books are the short-story collections *Tales of the Don* (1925) and *The Azure Steppe* (1925), and the two-volume novel *Virgin Soil Upturned* (1935, 1960), about the establishment of collective farming in the Cossack heartland. His success at producing a body of true literature under conditions of strict censorship brought him the Nobel Prize for literature in 1965. YA

Shotwell, Louisa R(ossiter) (1902–) Author of several thoughtful and engaging novels for young readers, Shotwell was a high school and college teacher for a number of years before she began to write. Her first books were nonfiction and included *The Harvesters: Story of the Migrant People* (1961). Her study of migrant farm workers and their lives led to her first novel for young people, *Roosevelt Grady, about the son of a migrant worker who longs to live in one place. Shotwell also wrote the novels *Adam Bookout* (1967), about a boy from Oklahoma who goes to live with relatives in Brooklyn, New York City, after his parents are killed; and *Magdalena* (1971), about a Puerto Rican girl growing up in Brooklyn who is torn between her grandmother's traditional values and those of her schoolmates. MR

Show Boat (1928) This novel by *Edna Ferber tells about a remarkable family and their rivergoing theater from the 1870s to the 1920s. Captain Andy Hawks and his stern New England wife, Parthy, operate the show boat *Cotton Blossom*, which carries them and their dramatic troupe to all the river towns up and down the Mississippi and its tributaries. This life is a wonderful, if unusual, experience for their daughter, Magnolia, who grows up to become the star of the troupe. Love comes to Magnolia when Gaylord Ravenal, a handsome, elegant, but down-on-his-luck gambler joins the company and becomes the best-known leading man the river has ever seen. Magnolia and Gay are married and have a daughter, Kim. But Gay, aware that Parthy disapproves of him completely, becomes restless on the boat, and after Captain Andy is killed on the river, leaving Parthy to run the show boat, Gay and Magnolia go to live in Chicago. The ups and downs of a gambler's life prove too much for their marriage. Gay leaves, and Magnolia puts Kim in a convent school and returns to the stage. Kim becomes a celebrated actress, but she never understands her mother's yearning for the mighty river and the show boat. When Parthy dies, Magnolia returns to run the boat and to the river she has loved and feared all her life. In *Show Boat*, Ferber has brought to life an exciting and colorful era long gone. If you enjoyed it, you will also like *Mark Twain's classic, *Life on the Mississippi*. *Show Boat* was made into a hit Broadway musical comedy in 1927 and movies in 1936 and 1951. YA

Shreve, Susan Richards (1939–) A teacher and novelist, Shreve has written both for younger readers and young adults. Among her books for younger readers are *Family Secrets* (1979), an 8-year-old boy's account of five difficult and unhappy situations in his life; *The Flunking of Joshua T. Bates* (1984), about a boy who is told he has to repeat third grade; and *The Bad Dreams of a Good Girl* (1982), about a 9-year-old girl whose troubles with her schoolmates and family spill over into her dreams. Shreve's novels for older readers include *The Masquerade* (1980), about a teenage girl whose family begins to come apart after her father is imprisoned for embezzlement; and *The Revolution of Mary Leary* (1982), about a teenage girl who rebels against her demanding mother and strict Roman Catholic upbringing. MR & YA

Shura (Craig), Mary Francis (1923–1991) Author of a number of mystery novels for adults, Shura also wrote more than 30 imaginative and enjoyable books for younger readers. Among these are *Simple Spigott* (1960) about a delightful little spook who comes to live with three children; *The Nearsighted Knight* (1964), about a young prince who joins a knight with very poor vision to do battle with a dragon; *Backwards for Luck* (1967), about a boy whose love for an abandoned coal-black cat helps him overcome his fears and superstitions; *The Gray Ghosts of Taylor Ridge* (1978), about a boy and girl who investigate strange goings-on in an old Civil War homestead; *Happles and Cinnamunger* (1981), about two children who help their new housekeeper make peace with the troublesome fairies who have been tormenting her; and *The Search for Grissi*. MR

Shute (Norway), Nevil (1899–1960) An English aviator, aeronautical engineer, and novelist, Shute began his career as an engineer on the Airship R100, a dirigible built by the British in the 1920s, and rose to become the project's chief engineer. In the early 1930s Shute formed his own aircraft company. By the time he resigned as its director in 1938 the company was very successful, and Shute had published several novels. His first big success came with

Pied Piper (1942), about an elderly Englishman who leads seven children out of wartorn France during World War II. After serving in the British Admiralty during the war, Shute moved with his family to Australia, which was the setting for several of his books. Among his best-known novels are *No Highway* (1948), a suspenseful tale about aeronautical engineers investigating the cause of an airliner crash in Canada; *A Town Like Alice* (1950), about an Englishwoman, one of a group of women and children captured by the Japanese in Malaya during the war, who searches after the war for the Australian soldier who risked his own life to help them; *The Rainbow and the Rose* (1958), about a dangerous mission to rescue a badly injured pilot who crash-landed on the coast of Tasmania; and *On the Beach*, about the end of civilization after a nuclear war. A number of movies were made of Shute's books, including *The Pied Piper* in 1942, *A Town Like Alice* in 1958, and *On the Beach* in 1959. *A Town Like Alice* was also filmed for television in the 1980s. YA

Shyer, Marlene Fanta (n.d.) A Czech-born American writer, Shyer has written novels for adults and young people as well as many magazine articles and short stories. Her books for young people are often about individuals who have to deal with difficult situations or problems. Among her books are *Welcome Home, Jellybean*, about the family of a mentally retarded girl who comes home from the institution where she has been living; *My Brother, the Thief* (1980), about a girl who discovers that her brother and his friend are thieves; *Adorable Sunday* (1983), about the experiences of a 13-year-old model and actress; and *Me and Joey Pinstripe, the King of Rock* (1988), about a girl whose life is turned upside down when a rock music star moves into her apartment building. MR

Shylock is the Jewish moneylender in *William Shakespeare's comedy *The Merchant of Venice* (1598). Shylock lends 3,000 ducats to the merchant Antonio, who then gives his friend Bassanio the money so he may properly court the fair maiden Portia. Shylock demands that if Antonio cannot repay the loan, he must forfeit a pound of his flesh. When a shipwreck keeps Antonio from paying the debt, Shylock, embittered by a lifetime of anti-Semitic taunts and insults, demands the pound of flesh. Portia, disguised as a lawyer, judges the case and tells Shylock he may take the pound of flesh, no more and no less, but he may draw no blood, on penalty of death. Shylock gives up the case and loses even his 3,000 ducats. One of the most controversial of Shakespeare's characters, Shylock has been portrayed as a comic figure and also an evil one, but most movingly as a human tortured by the indignities he has suffered. YA

Siddhartha (1922), by *Hermann Hesse, tells about the quest of Siddhartha, a young Indian of the priestly Brahmin caste, for peace and enlightenment. Though he has attained much spiritual knowledge, Siddhartha seeks the complete understanding of life, being, and eternity. He leaves the Brahmin life and, with his friend Govinda, joins the Samanas, who are wanderers seeking enlightenment through self-denial and meditation. After three years they leave the Samanas to hear the teachings of the Buddha. Govinda decides to follow the Buddha, and Siddhartha continues alone to find his own path to enlightenment. He meets the beautiful Kamala, who teaches him the art of love, and becomes a wealthy merchant. But the life of pleasure and comfort stifles him and he leaves. He becomes the apprentice and friend of an aged ferryman, Vasudeva, who speaks little but listens much and is very wise. He tells Siddhartha to listen to the voice of the river. Siddhartha hears in the river the voices of all who have lived, and finds in its timeless continuity the enlightenment he has sought. A film based on *Siddhartha* was made in 1973. YA

sign and **symbol** Objects and shapes of various sorts can convey meanings to us and are common in art, literature, religion, and in everyday life. A shoe store may have a sign that tells you what it is; but, if the sign merely shows a pair of shoes, you assume you can buy footwear inside. Thus, in common usage, a sign can be as direct as a statement in words, "Shoes are sold here." The use of shoes in the sign instead of words turns the "shoes" into a symbol. But many symbols are not as direct a transfer from words. They are not literal messages but are some object or representation of an object that will carry a message. Perhaps the best-known example is the *cross that represents Christianity. The most significant symbols in terms both of historical importance and in the world today are the *crescent, the *cross, the *rose, and the *star. But many other objects have meanings beyond their physical characteristics. An anchor holds a ship in position, but it also, especially in *Christianity, signifies hope and steadfastness. An *arrow is shot from a bow, but the arrow can also tell direction. The three balls that signify a pawnbroker come from the symbol of the Medici family of bankers in Italy in the 16th century. The word "pentagon" will most likely bring to mind the enormous Department of Defense headquarters just outside Washington, D.C., but when the sides of this five-sided figure are extended until they meet, it becomes a pentagram, or pentacle, a five-pointed star. This was first used as an emblem by the followers of Pythagoras (c. 580–c.500 B.C.), a Greek philosopher. Later it was a symbol of the magicians of the Middle Ages. Worn by a person, it was said to protect him or her from demons and sorcery. A square, with its equal sides and a feeling of solidity, appears in English as "a square meal," that is, a satisfying one. An equilateral triangle, one with three sides of equal length, is in *Christianity a symbol of the Trinity. On the other hand, the "eternal triangle" refers to a situation in which three persons are involved in a complicated love affair. If you would like to read more about symbols and signs, try *Signs and Symbols Around the World* (1967) by Elizabeth S. Hoffman (1911–) and *Symbols and Their Meanings* (1978) by Rolf Myller (1926–). See also *symbolism. MR & YA

Sign of the Beaver, The (1983)

This novel by *Elizabeth George Speare is set in the Maine wilderness of 1769. While his father journeys back to Massachusetts to bring the rest of the family to Maine, 13-year-old Matt is left to guard the cabin he and his father have built. Soon everything goes wrong, and Matt faces death in the wilderness until he is rescued by an old Indian named Saknis and his grandson, Attean. In exchange for food, Matt agrees to teach Attean how to read. Attean scorns the idea that Matt has anything to teach him, but he comes each day for his lesson. As he learns how to read, Attean also teaches Matt how to survive. Matt learns about Attean's people, the Beaver clan, and even learns how to find the special trail signs Attean's people use to mark trails and hunting grounds. By the time Matt's family arrives, both boys have a better understanding of each other's ways of life. If you enjoyed *The Sign of the Beaver*, try *Lost in the Barrens* (1956) by *Farley Mowat, about two boys, one white and one Cree Indian, who struggle to survive winter in the Arctic. MR

Sign of the Four, The (1890)

In this mystery adventure of *Sherlock Holmes and Dr. John Watson, by *Arthur Conan Doyle, there is a puzzling murder and a search for a fortune in jewels brought to England from India. Mary Morstan, whose father, an army officer, disappeared in London 10 years earlier, has for the past six years been receiving once a year a valuable pearl. Now she has a chance to solve the mystery and enlists Holmes to aid her. Murder with a poisoned dart is committed; the treasure is stolen, the "thief" being an Englishman who, with three East Indian accomplices, had once possessed it. Hence the "sign of the four" that appears in a message. As usual Holmes solves the mystery, which ends with a boat chase on the Thames River, followed by an explanation of the events in India that led to murder in London. The novel is also the occasion for Watson to become engaged to Miss Morstan. If you liked this tale, *The Moonstone* by *Wilkie Collins is written in the same manner. YA

Silas Marner (1861),

one of *George Eliot's best-known books, is about a weaver wrongly accused of committing a crime and forced to leave his hometown. Silas Marner settles in the village of Raveloe, where he lives a lonely life, with only his weaving to occupy him. By saving all his money, Silas accumulates a great deal of gold. Without family or friends, gold becomes his only source of pleasure.

Silas's life changes when he is robbed by Dunstan Cass, who then mysteriously disappears. Without his gold, Silas is miserable. One evening, a beautiful little girl appears in his cottage, as if by magic. She is the daughter of Godfrey Cass, brother of Dunstan Cass. Godfrey is secretly married to a poor woman from outside of Raveloe. The woman was heading to the Cass residence with her child, planning to reveal the secret marriage, when she fell in the snow near Silas's cottage and died. The little girl wanders into the cottage, and when Silas realizes there is no one to take care of her, he is suddenly overcome with affection for her. All his feelings of despair vanish as he begins a happy new life as the child's father.

Godfrey Cass does not reveal that the child is his, and Silas raises the little girl, whom he names Eppie. Sixteen years later, after the remains of Dunstan Cass are discovered with Silas's gold, Godfrey decides to confess his secret marriage. He tells Silas that Eppie is really his daughter and that he would like her to live with him and his wife, Nancy. Silas and Eppie, however, refuse to be separated because they have grown to love one another as father and daughter. Eppie marries, and she and her husband make plans to live with Silas and take care of him for the rest of his life. YA

Silko, Leslie Marmon (1948–) An American Indian who grew up in the Laguna Pueblo in New Mexico, Silko has written poetry and a number of highly praised short stories. She won much praise and recognition for her novel *Ceremony* (1977), about a Native American soldier who returns home from World War II deeply upset by the brutality of the war. He finds his salvation in the ceremonial roots of his own culture. Silko's other books include *Laguna Woman* (1974), a collection of poems, and *Storyteller* (1981), a collection of poems and short stories. Seven of her stories appear in the anthology *The Man to Send Rain Clouds: Contemporary Stories by American Indians* (1974), edited by Kenneth Rosen (1940–). YA

Sillitoe, Alan (1928–) An English novelist, poet, and short-story writer, Sillitoe was a member of a working-class family. Though a bright student, he left school when he was 14 years old to work in a factory. Just after World War II, Sillitoe served with the Royal Air Force as a radio operator in Malaya. He contracted tuberculosis, and during his long recovery in England he began to write. Ten years later Sillitoe achieved an enormous success with his first novel, *Saturday Night and Sunday Morning. Its main character, Alan Seaton, is a young man of the working class whose weekend drinking, womanizing, and brawling are the outward signs of his rebellion against the established order. Many of the heroes of Sillitoe's novels and short stories are rebels, defying the accepted rules of society and refusing to submit to them. Sillitoe's short-story collection *The Loneliness of the Long-Distance Runner was also very successful. His later books include the novel *Key to the Door* (1961), which reflects Sillitoe's experiences in Malaya; the short-story collection *A Sillitoe Selection* (1968); and the novel *A Start in Life* (1970), about a working-class rogue's rise and fall as a gold smuggler in the London underworld. YA

Silver Sword, The (1956) This novel by *Ian Serraillier is about three Polish children caught up in the horrors of World War II. In 1940 Nazi soldiers take Joseph Balicki away from his Warsaw home, his wife, Margrit, and his children, 12-year-old Ruth, 11-year-old Edek, and 3-year-old Bronia. Joseph eventually escapes from prison camp and makes his way back to Warsaw. There he learns that Margrit has been arrested and sent to work in Germany. His house has been blown up and his children are gone, probably dead. At the ruins of his old house Joseph meets a cunning young street thief, an orphan named Jan, and tells him about his children. He tells Jan that he is going to escape to Switzerland, and asks Jan, if he ever meets the three children, to tell them where he has gone. Joseph gives Jan a family treasure, a small paper knife or letter opener shaped like a silver sword, knowing that Ruth will recognize it if she ever sees it.

Ruth and Bronia have been living in a bombed-out cellar. They eventually meet Jan and learn about their father. The three set out on a long and dangerous journey to Switzerland, finding along the way Edek, who had been sent off to labor on a German farm. After much hardship and danger the children arrive in Switzerland, where the Balicki family, now including Jan, is reunited. If you enjoyed *The Silver Sword*, try also *His Enemy, His Friend by *John R. Tunis, a moving story set in France during and after World War II. MR

Silverberg, Robert (1935–) One of the best-known and most prolific *science fiction writers, Silverberg has written more than 100 novels and nonfiction books and hundreds of short stories and magazine articles, and he has edited many science fiction anthologies. Silverberg began writing science fiction while attending Columbia University. By the time he graduated he had established himself as a writer. In the late 1950s and early 1960s, Silverberg was turning out about a dozen books and scores of stories and articles each year. After that he slowed his writing pace, concentrating on fewer but more thoughtful and ambitious works, among them *Nightwings* (1969), a poetic vision of a future Earth that has been conquered by aliens; *Dying Inside* (1972), about a man who is losing his lifelong ability to read minds; and *Born with the Dead* (1974), a collection of three novellas whose title piece is a haunting study of life, death, memory, and emotion.

Though these later books were acclaimed by critics and reviewers, Silverberg became frustrated with his readers, many of whom wanted him to write the type of formula science fiction books he had produced earlier. He stopped writing for a number of years before returning with *Lord Valentine's Castle* (1980), a

fantasy, set on the giant planet of Majipoor, about a young prince's quest to regain his memory and his kingdom. It was followed by *Majipoor Chronicles* (1982), stories set on Majipoor, and *Valentine Pontifex* (1983), the sequel to *Lord Valentine's Castle*.

Silverberg's many nonfiction books include *Lost Cities and Vanished Civilizations* (1962), *The Auk, the Dodo, and the Oryx: Vanished and Vanishing Creatures* (1967); and *The Challenge of Climate: Man and His Environment* (1969). YA

Silverstein, Shel(by) (1932–) A writer, cartoonist, folksinger, and lyricist, Silverstein uses all these talents to entertain and, indirectly, to suggest lessons, not only to young people but to adults as well. His most popular work is a book of poems and drawings, *Where the Sidewalk Ends*. Another volume of poetry is *A Light in the Attic* (1981), which contains verses about such odd characters as Backward Bill, Sour Face Ann, and the Quick-Digesting Gink. Among Silverstein's prose writings are *The Giving Tree* (1964) and *The Missing Piece* (1976). The first tells about a tree that, to make one man happy, gives its shade, its fruit, its branches, and, at last, its trunk. It will make you think about self-sacrifice. The second book also has a lesson as well as telling an odd story. A circle has a small piece missing from it and so sets out to seek the part that will make it complete. But when it is successful, it is sorry that the search has ended, because it has nothing left to do. If you like Silverstein's poems and stories, you will enjoy those of *Edward Lear, Laura Richards (1850–1943), and *Carl Sandburg. MR & YA

Simak, Clifford D(onald) (1904–1988) A newspaperman and *science fiction writer, Simak grew up on a farm in Wisconsin. He worked for several newspapers in the Middle West before joining the *Minneapolis Star*, where he stayed for many years. Simak began reading science fiction in his youth, and he began writing science fiction stories in the 1930s, while establishing himself as a newspaperman. His first big success came with the book *City* (1952), a collection of related stories that trace the decline of human civilization through its own inhumanity and its submission to technology. Probably his best-known book, it is now considered a science fiction classic. Simak's other books include *Time and Again* (1951), about a man hunted across space and time by enemies who want to control the wonderful discovery he has made on a distant planet; *Way Station* (1963), about a farmer whose home is a way station in a secret galactic teleportation system; *A Choice of Gods* (1972), in which most of Earth's inhabitants are spirited away by a mysterious power, leaving a handful of humans and robots to build a new civilization; *Skirmish: The Great Short Fiction of Clifford D. Simak* (1977); and *The Visitors* (1980), about an invasion of Earth by seemingly indestructible black boxes that begin devouring the world's forests and reproducing rapidly. YA

Simenon, Georges (Joseph Christian) (1903–1989) This Belgian-born French novelist was one of the world's most prolific authors. He wrote about 200 novels and more than 1,000 short stories under 18 different names. Among them were 84 short detective novels featuring *Jules Maigret, an inspector of the Paris police, and it is for these that he is now read. Typical of them are *The Man Who Watched the Trains Go By* (1938) and *Maigret's War of Nerves* (1940). In the former a seemingly staid family man turns embezzler, murders a cabaret dancer, and then, by means of items he places in newspapers, defies the police to catch him. In the other, Maigret arranges to have a man convicted of murder escape from prison in the expectation that he will lead Maigret to the real killer. The background is the foreign colony living in Paris in the 1920s. Simenon's detective stories have more atmosphere than plot and are more mysteries than plain detective tales. If you like these books, read those by *Nicolas Freeling, *Maj Sjöwall and Per Wahlöö, and *Janwillem Van de Wetering. Under the title *Paris Express*, a movie was made of *The Man Who Watched the Trains Go By* in 1953. YA

Simon, Neil (1927–) A highly successful playwright whose works have often enjoyed long runs on Broadway, Simon was born and grew up in New York City. His family life was troubled, and his parents divorced when Simon was still a boy. After serving in the army, Simon worked with his older brother, Danny, writing comedy for radio and television before he turned to writing plays.

Simon's first play, the comedy *Come Blow Your Horn* (1961) was partly based on Simon's experience of sharing a bachelor apartment with his brother. After this, Simon wrote a steady stream of successful plays, including *Barefoot in the Park* (1964), about the problems of a stuffy young lawyer and his free-spirited bride; *The Odd Couple* (1965), about two middle-aged men who share an apartment, only to find they are driving each other crazy; and *The Sunshine Boys* (1972), about two aging, feuding comedians who reunite as a comedy team for one last performance on television.

Simon wrote a trilogy of plays based on his youth that are considered more thoughtful and sensitive than his early comedies. *Brighton Beach Memoirs* (1984) introduces Eugene Jerome, a Jewish teenager growing up in Brooklyn during the *Great Depression. *Biloxi Blues* (1986) follows Eugene's experiences, including the experience of anti-Semitism, in army basic training in Biloxi, Mississippi. In *Broadway Bound* (1987), Eugene teams up with his brother as a comedy writer and comes to grips with his feelings about his family, particularly his mother. Several of Simon's plays have been made into movies, including *The Odd Couple* in 1968, *The Sunshine Boys* in 1975, *Brighton Beach Memoirs* in 1986, and *Biloxi Blues* in 1988. YA

Simon Legree is the brutal, superstitious, drunken plantation owner in the novel *Uncle Tom's Cabin* by *Harriet Beecher Stowe. Legree purchases the gentle old slave Tom after Tom's master, Mr. Shelby, dies. Legree is enraged by Tom's goodness and Christian faith and sets out to break him with unceasing labor and cruel punishment. Finally he has Tom beaten to death. *Simon Legree* has come to mean any cruel, harsh, or merciless taskmaster or, in a more humorous sense, any strict or demanding one. YA

"Sinbad the Sailor" is one of the best-known stories of *The Arabian Nights' Entertainments* supposedly told by *Scheherazade. Sinbad the Sailor is the son of an important merchant, but by the time he is a young man he has spent all his inheritance on high living. He takes up the merchant's life to restore his fortune, and in seven adventurous and dangerous voyages, he gains vast wealth. He survives several shipwrecks, including one caused by a giant fish he and his shipmates have mistaken for an island. He is captured by cannibals, buried alive in a great cavern, carried by a giant bird called a *roc to a valley covered with diamonds, finds an island whose waters are filled with pearls, and finds an elephant burial ground filled with ivory. He meets and escapes from the Old Man of the Sea, who tricks his victims into giving him a piggyback ride and then rides them to death; and carries messages and gifts between the Caliph of Baghdad and the rich and powerful King of Sarandib.

You can read about Sinbad's adventures in the *The Arabian Nights' Entertainments* and in a number of other books, including *The Seven Voyages of Sinbad the Sailor* (1962) and *Sinbad the Sailor and Other Stories from the Arabian Nights* (1978). MR

Sing Down the Moon (1970) By *Scott O'Dell, this novel is set in Arizona and New Mexico in the 1860s. It is narrated by Bright Morning, a 14-year-old Navajo girl who lives with her clan in the Canyon de Chelly in northeastern Arizona. Her hopes to marry the strong young warrior Tall Boy and live happily in the canyon are complicated when she and another girl are captured by Spanish slavers. They escape, but when Tall Boy comes to their aid he is shot and his arm is crippled. Then United States soldiers destroy the clan's homes and crops and force them and the other Navajo clans on a bitter, 300-mile Long Walk to Fort

Sumner, New Mexico, where they suffer hunger, disease, and despair. Bright Morning and Tall Boy marry and escape their white captors, returning to the canyon of their ancestors to raise their new son in freedom and dignity. You can learn more about the Navajos, their history, land, and way of life in *The Native Americans: Navajos* (1978) by Richard Erdoes (1912–). MR

Singer, Isaac Bashevis (1904–1991) The author of *A Day of Pleasure*, Singer was born in Poland and spent his childhood in the Warsaw ghetto that is the subject of many of his short stories and novels. His father was a rabbi, as were both his grandfathers, and the family intended that Isaac follow in their footsteps. Instead, both Isaac and his brother turned to writing and worked for the Hebrew and Yiddish press in Warsaw. Singer came to the United States in 1935, but continued to write in Yiddish even though his English was fluent. A great storyteller, Singer said his role was to entertain rather than teach, and he expressed his misgivings about the modern tendency to over-interpret his works.

Singer's writing is difficult to categorize. He is deeply religious, but his stories are full of ghosts, imps, pacts with the devil, and *dybbuks* (in Jewish folklore, a wandering soul who takes over a person's body). In a beautifully clear and simple style, he wrote about a world that no longer exists, the world of Jewish villages in Eastern Europe that were brutally wiped out during the systematic campaign by the *Nazis against the Jews. Among the collections of such stories are *Gimpel the Fool and Other Stories* (1957) and *The Seance and Other Stories* (1968). Another collection is *Old Love* (1979), about love among the old and the middle-aged, a subject that occurs often in Singer's fiction. A novel you might like to read, *Enemies, A Love Story* (1972), was adapted for the movies in 1989. It concerns a Jewish man living in Coney Island, New York, with his second wife, a Polish peasant who helped him escape from the Nazis. While also involved in an affair with a beautiful married woman, Herman learns his first wife has survived the war and turned up in America. Eventually each woman discovers the other women in Herman's life, and each offers a solution to their problem. Singer won the Nobel Prize for literature in 1978. YA

Singer, Marilyn (1948–) Author of many books for younger readers and young adults, Singer has used many of her own experiences as ideas for her books, which are often about the kinds of problems young people face as they grow up. Among her books for younger readers are *It Can't Hurt Forever* (1978), about the experiences of an 11-year-old girl who goes into the hospital for heart surgery, and *Tarantulas on the Brain* (1982), about a fifth-grade girl whose complicated plot to get a pet tarantula gets her into trouble. Her books for older readers include *The Course of True Love Never Did Run Smooth* (1983), about a teenage girl who must sort out her feelings for a handsome boy she has just met and a boy she has known a long time, and *The First Few Friends* (1981), set in the late 1960s, about a girl who returns home to New York City after a year of college in England to find many things have changed while she was away. MR & YA

Sister (1974), a novel written by *Eloise Greenfield, is about a 13-year-old black girl named Doretha who has been writing in a diary for the past four years. The book begins when her troubled older sister, Alberta, a high school dropout, has not returned home for two days. Though Doretha loves Alberta, she is afraid of becoming just like her. Doretha reads her diary, praying that Alberta will arrive home by the time she reaches the last page. While reading her entries, Doretha reacquaints herself with close friends and relatives who have influenced her life, as well as reliving many poignant past experiences. The death of her father is powerfully described, as is the touching memory of walking alone past a group of older boys. When Alberta has still not returned home after Doretha reaches the last page, she realizes that she has had enough strength to fight difficult times in the past, and she will be able to conquer them in the future. Reading her diary has clarified the fact that she and Alberta are two very separate people. Proudly, Doretha says, "I'm me. I'm not Alberta, I'm me." MR

Sister Carrie (1900), by *Theodore Dreiser, is a novel set in the late 1800s, based in part on the life of one of Dreiser's own sisters. Carrie Meeber, a poor and unsophisticated country girl, goes to Chicago to find work. On the train she meets Charles Drouet, a well-dressed salesman who offers to show her the city. Living temporarily with her sister, Carrie finds employment, but the jobs are dreary and exhausting. Her life seems an unbearable contrast to Chicago's bewitching luxury. Guided by instinct more than reason, Carrie allows Drouet to become her lover and benefactor, and her conscience accepts the status of fallen woman. While Drouet is cheerfully amoral, he treats Carrie kindly and indulges her deep longing for pretty things. She meets Drouet's friend George Hurstwood, who attracts Carrie with his sensitive, elegant manner and greater social status. Hurstwood is married, but he abandons family and position to elope with Carrie. In New York City, they live together for three years, and the middle-aged Hurstwood finds it increasingly difficult to maintain his former grand style. When he becomes too discouraged to work, Carrie helps support him by building a modest career in the theater. She gains experience, confidence, and some success. Never having really loved Hurstwood, and frustrated by the drain on her meager earnings, she leaves him. Carrie later achieves stardom, but is rootless, lonely, and unfulfilled. Hurstwood spends his last bitter days among the derelicts of the *Bowery, and finally takes his own life in a flophouse. See also *An American Tragedy* by Dreiser. YA

Six Characters in Search of an Author (1922) Probably the best-known play by the Italian poet and dramatist *Luigi Pirandello, this tragedy within a comedy explores the nature of reality and also of theater. The central figures are a family of six—Father, Mother, Son, Stepdaughter, Boy, and Girl—who appear onstage while the Manager and his actors prepare to rehearse a play. The Father and Stepdaughter explain that the six have been created in the mind of an author who does not wish to make their tragic drama permanent by writing it down. They want the Manager to write their story as they live it on the stage. As the play progresses it becomes clear that the characters think of themselves as more real than the actors, for they are an unchanging part of the ideal called Art, whereas the actors are constantly changing their roles and appearances. And the play the characters live through is a far cry from the one that actors try to recapture, or the play the audience sees. If you enjoyed *Six Characters in Search of an Author*, try also *Marat/Sade* by the German playwright Peter Weiss (1916–1982), which also features a play within a play. YA

Sjöwall, Maj (1935–) and **Wahlöö, Per** (1926–1975) This Swedish writing team of wife and husband excels in creating a somewhat gloomy atmosphere, tinged possibly by their leftist views of a society that seems to be resting on its oars and in a depressed mood. They have written 10 detective novels, all of them featuring Martin Beck as a police officer who becomes head of the homicide department in Stockholm. He is 50 years old, a thin man, slow but steady in his work, and poised against a realistic social, political, and economic background. Beck's first case is recounted in *Roseanna* (1967). The body of an unidentified woman, found in a canal, turns out to be an American librarian from the Middle West. Among the other novels are *The Man on the Balcony* (1968), which tells of the rape and murder of two little girls and the seemingly impossible task of finding the killer, and *The Laughing Policeman* (1970), in which eight people, including a policeman, are murdered on a bus. If you like these books, read those of *Nicolas Freeling, *Georges Simenon, and *Janwillem Van de Wetering. *The Laughing Policeman* was made into a movie in 1973, but the setting was changed to San Francisco. YA

Skin of Our Teeth, The (1942) This comedy by *Thornton Wilder, which opened on Broadway at the height of World War II, follows the ups and downs of the Antrobus family as they live from prehistoric times to the modern age. George Antrobus, his wife, Maggie, their children, Henry and Gladys, and their maid, Sabina, represent humanity, and possess all its creative and destructive impulses. They manage to survive wars, plagues, ice ages, floods, and other disasters, usually just "by the skin of their teeth," and rebuild civilization. Each rebuilding marks one more step in the progress of human history. YA

Skinny (1964), by *Robert Burch, is the story of an 11-year-old orphan, the son of tenant farmers in Georgia. Skinny lives with Miss Bessie in the small hotel she owns and can stay until there is a place for him at the church home for orphans. He helps out at the hotel by doing all sorts of chores and such extra services as greeting guests in an oversize hand-me-down white jacket. Skinny has never been to school for more than a few weeks each year, because he was needed on the farm, and he can neither read nor write. Though smart, cheerful, and sociable by nature, he is a little shy with people his own age. Miss Bessie would like to adopt him and his dog, R.F.D., but she and the home feel Skinny would be better off in a group of children. For a while Skinny has hopes that Miss Bessie will marry Daddy Rabbit, a construction worker staying at the hotel. Daddy Rabbit, however, has the travel bug and cannot accept the idea of staying in one place. When finally the church home can take him, Skinny must say goodbye to Miss Bessie and his friends. In spite of his fears about the orphanage, he finds it is not so bad. He adjusts to his new life good-heartedly, makes lots of friends his own age, and at last begins to catch up on his schooling. MR

Skurzynski, Gloria (1930–) Author of a number of novels for younger readers, Skurzynski is perhaps known best for her novel *What Happened in Hamelin* (1979), a retelling of the

*Pied Piper story narrated by one of the children, an orphan boy who chose not to follow the Piper, and for *Manwolf* (1981), set in medieval Poland, about a boy who is so horribly disfigured by a skin disease that some people think he is a *werewolf. Skurzynski has also written a series called the Mountain West Adventures, about young people facing difficult situations in the West. The adventures include *Lost in the Devil's Desert* (1982), about an 11-year-old boy alone in the Utah desert who must use his wits and the things his father taught him in order to survive; and *Caught in the Moving Mountains* (1984), about two boys, trapped in the mountains of Idaho after an earthquake, who meet up with an injured drug smuggler. MR

Slake's Limbo (1974), a novel by *Felice Holman, tells about 13-year-old Aremis Slake, a poor, short, weak boy with bad eyesight. Slake is hounded and abused by everyone around him, including the coldhearted "aunt" he lives with and the tough neighborhood kids who pick on him whenever they find him on the street. Finally, Slake's pain and fear, which he thinks of as a black bird clawing at his insides, become so great that he runs to escape his horrible life. Down within one of the tunnels of New York's subway system he finds a small cavelike hovel, which he makes his home. Slowly he builds a new underground life, and during his 121 days living in the subway he learns that not everyone in the world is out to get him, that some people even want to help him. Slake catches pneumonia and is taken to a hospital, where he regains his health and finally gets rid of his black bird. When he leaves the hospital, he leaves with a new sense of hope and a new way of looking at the world. If you enjoyed *Slake's Limbo*, try also *Run, Shelley, Run* by *Gertrude Samuels, about a girl who also faces a struggle to escape unhappiness. MR & YA

Slaughter, Carolyn (1936–) An English novelist whose works are often about people facing physical and emotional conflict, Slaughter was born in India and spent much of her youth in southern Africa, then moved to England when she was 15 years old. Her experiences growing up in Africa, as well as her love of its land and people, are reflected in a number of her novels. One of her best-known works is *Dreams of the Kalahari* (1981), about an English girl whose youth in Africa and young womanhood in England awakens her to the cruelty of white domination of blacks in Africa. She joins an anti-apartheid group and returns to Africa, which she realizes is her true home. *The Innocents* (1986), also set in Africa, depicts the effects of apartheid on a white South African woman, her family, and her best friend, who is colored, or part black. YA

Slaughterhouse-Five; Or, The Children's Crusade (1969), a powerful novel by *Kurt Vonnegut, Jr., centers on an event Vonnegut lived through. As a prisoner of war during World War II, he was one of the survivors of the Allied firebombing of Dresden, Germany, which killed more than 100,000 people. The novel's hero is Billy Pilgrim, a gentle, innocent youth who, just before his capture during the Battle of the Bulge, becomes "unstuck in time," beginning a lifelong series of travels back and forth to different moments in his life, reliving over and over such events as his birth, death, marriage, and survival of the Dresden bombing in an underground meatlocker designated "Slaughterhouse-Five." Billy learns how this is possible when he is kidnapped by aliens from the planet Tralfamadore and kept in a zoo to mate with the beautiful actress Montana Wildhack. The Tralfamadorians see time as a fourth dimension. To them a person's life is a series of moments frozen in eternity, so a person is always alive in some moments and dead in others. Billy learns that terrible events, such as the firebombing of Dresden, occur simply because they are "structured that way." Billy returns to Earth and becomes the prophet of the Tralfamadorian philosophy. He is ignored or thought crazy, but the belief helps him deal with the horrors he has seen. If you enjoyed *Slaughterhouse-Five*, try Vonnegut's much underrated novel *The Sirens of Titan* (1959), about a man who is drawn into a galactic quest for the meaning of life. *Slaughterhouse-Five* was made into a movie in 1972. YA

Slave Dancer, The (1973) By *Paula Fox, this novel tells about 13-year-old Jessie Bollier, who is kidnapped one night in 1840 while returning to his New Orleans home from an errand. He is taken aboard the *Moonlight*, a ship working the illegal African slave trade. Jessie is horrified by the stench of illness and death down in the ship's holds; the callous, brutal crewmen; the moody captain, who cares only for profits; and especially the first mate, Ben Stout, whose heart is cold as ice. Jessie's job is to play his fife and get the African slaves to dance in order to help keep them alive. He befriends an African boy, Ras, and when the *Moonlight* is wrecked in a storm, only Jessie and Ras survive. Washed ashore in Mississippi, they are cared for by a runaway slave named Daniel, who helps Ras escape to freedom in the North and Jessie to return home. If you enjoyed *The Slave Dancer*, try also *Uncle Tom's Cabin* by *Harriet Beecher Stowe, another moving depiction of slavery in the early 19th century. *The Slave Dancer* won a *Newbery Medal in 1974. MR & YA

Sleator, William (1945–) Though he has produced a number of highly imaginative novels for younger readers, Sleator is also a composer and has written scores for ballets and films. Among his novels are *Blackbriar* (1972), about a 15-year-old English boy who moves from London with his guardian into a mysterious old cottage in the woods; *House of Stairs*, perhaps his best-known novel; *Among the Dolls* (1975), about a girl who awakens one morning to find herself living inside the *Victorian dollhouse she has been given for her birthday; *The Green Futures of Tycho* (1981), about a boy who finds an egg-shaped object that enables him to travel into the future; and *Interstellar Pig* (1984), about a teenage boy whose dull seaside vacation changes into a struggle to save the Earth when three unusual people move next door and introduce him to a bizarre new board game called "Interstellar Pig." MR

Slote, Alfred (1926–) Author of a number of popular novels for younger readers, Slote used his experiences as a baseball player and Little League coach for several of his stories, including *Jake* (1971), about an 11-year-old boy with a passion for baseball who talks his uncle and guardian into being the team's coach; *Tony and Me* (1974), about a boy who learns his best friend, a natural athlete, is a thief; and *Matt Gargan's Boy* (1975), about a star Little League pitcher, who feels threatened by his divorced mother's interest in another man, and by the man's daughter, who is trying out for the team. Slote has also written a number of *science fiction novels, including *My Robot Buddy* (1975), about the adventures of 10-year-old Jack Jameson and his look-alike robot companion Danny One after Jack is taken captive by robot-nappers who cannot tell boy from robot. Jack and Danny's adventures are continued in *My Trip to Alpha I* (1978), *C.O.L.A.R.: A Tale of Outer Space* (1981), and *Omega Station* (1983). MR

Smith, Betty (Wehner) (1904–1972) A novelist and playwright, Smith was born and grew up in a poor section of Brooklyn, New York City. Her memories, sad and happy, of the sights, sounds, and people of Brooklyn are at the heart of her best-known novel, *A Tree Grows in Brooklyn*, about a girl's coming of age in Brooklyn's Williamsburg slum section in the early 1900s. Smith also used Brooklyn as a setting for all three of her other novels, which include *Tomorrow Will Be Better* (1948), about the joys and sorrows of a young working-class woman during the 1920s; *Maggie-Now* (1958), about a girl, her family, and her growing into womanhood in the years just before World War I; and *Joy in the Morning* (1963), about an 18-year-old Brooklyn girl who moves to the Middle West to marry the young law student she loves and begin a new life. Smith also wrote a great number of one-act plays, but she is remembered best for her novels. MR & YA

Smith, Doris Buchanan (1934–) Praised especially for her first book, *A Taste of Blackberries* (1973), about a boy who struggles to understand his own thoughts and feelings after his best friend's accidental death, Smith has written more than 10 novels for young people. They usually depict problems young people face in today's world. Her other books include *Kick a Stone Home* (1974), about a 15-year-old girl who has trouble accepting her parents' divorce and getting on with growing up; *Last Was Lloyd* (1981), about an overprotected and friendless 12-year-old boy who decides it is time to turn his life around; *The First Hard Times* (1983), about a girl whose father was listed as Missing in Action in the Vietnam War and who has trouble accepting her stepfather; *Return to Bitter Creek*; and *Karate Dancer* (1987), about a 14-year-old boy's efforts to explain to his parents what karate means and why it is so important to him. MR

Smith, Lillian (Eugenia) (1897–1966) A writer whose few volumes of fiction and nonfiction are powerful and moving statements against racial prejudice, Smith was born in northern Florida and grew up in the South. Early in life she realized the crippling effects of racial segregation on whites and blacks and on society as a whole. After running a summer camp for girls in Georgia for a number of years, Smith turned to writing. Her first published novel, *Strange Fruit* (1944), is set in the South and tells about the forbidden love between a young black woman and a white man, and the tragic events that result. The novel caused much controversy but became a best seller.

Smith's other works include *Killers of the Dream* (1949), a partly autobiographical exploration of the human spirit, society, and the destructiveness of prejudice and hatred; *One Hour* (1959), a novel set in a Southern city, about a respected scientist who is accused by an 8-year-old child of molesting her; and *The Journey* (1954), an autobiography. YA

Smith, Martin Cruz (1942–) Before turning to writing detective stories, Smith was the author of a number of books, including *Right Wing* (1977), a suspense novel set in Indian country of the American Southwest. He is best known for two detective novels, both of which involve a Russian investigator. In *Gorky Park* (1981) three frozen bodies are found after the winter's snow melts in Gorky Park, Moscow. They have been mutilated to make them difficult to identify. Arkady Renko, the Russian investigator, becomes involved with an American fur dealer of ill repute and a New York City police detective, and they all become involved in a search for the killer that ends up with a shootout on Staten Island, New York City. *Polar Star* (1989) is set in the Bering Sea, where an American trawler and a Russian factory ship are working together harvesting fish. On board as an ordinary worker is Renko, the investigator in *Gorky Park*, who is now in official disfavor. When a female crew member turns up dead in a net full of fish, Renko takes over. He finds the murderer but nearly dies crossing the Arctic ice. Read books by *Len Deighton and *John Le Carré if you enjoy these. A movie was made of *Gorky Park* in 1983. YA

Smoky, the Cow Horse (1926) This novel by *Will James tells about the life of a wild horse and of a cowboy working on the range early in the 20th century. James, himself a cowboy, wrote in such a natural voice that you feel as though you were sitting on a top rail at the corral and hearing and seeing the old West. Smoky's days of being young and wild and learning fast are vividly described as he encounters on the range wolves, mountain lions, coyotes, and humans. Branded as a yearling, Smoky roams free until he is rounded up when he is 4 years old and trained by a Rocking R broncobuster, Clint. This wise cowboy, who knows how a wild horse thinks, recognizes Smoky's fierce intelligence. The process of training and how Smoky feels about his training are described in detail. Smoky becomes an exceptional working cowhorse and develops a special relationship with Clint. Smoky allows no rider but Clint on his back. After each working season, Smoky spends the winter free on the range foraging in the snow with his herd until Clint rounds him up in the spring. Then,

MR = Middle Reader   YA = Young Adult Reader   * = See this main entry

one winter, Smoky and his herd are stolen and driven south. The vicious rustler turns him into the wildest bronco in the Southwest rodeo circuit. No one can stay on Smoky's back, and he becomes famous under the name of The Cougar. Time passes grimly for Smoky as he ages. He becomes a riding horse in a public stable. He is sold for slaughter, but then is bought as a carthorse by a vegetable seller who starves and beats him. At this point Clint finds him and sets about reclaiming his intelligent heart.

You will enjoy especially James's rich understanding of wild animals and the friendship possible between a human and a horse. The illustrations, done by Will James himself, reveal the action and spirit of the mustang and the hard life of the cowboy. If you like stories about horses see *Black Beauty, *National Velvet, and *The Black Stallion. Smoky, the Cow Horse won the *Newbery Medal in 1927. MR & YA

Snopes is the name of a family created by *William Faulkner and featured in a trilogy of novels, The Hamlet (1940), The Town (1957), and The Mansion (1959), set in fictional *Yoknapatawpha County, Mississippi, from the late 19th to mid-20th centuries. The Snopeses are, with a few exceptions, low, ignorant, greedy, ruthless, and sometimes violent. They represent the greed and corruption of modern American society destroying the traditional values of the old South. The central figure in the trilogy is Flem Snopes, son of the arsonist Ab Snopes in Faulkner's short story "Barn Burning" (1936). Through marriage, intimidation, and deception, Flem becomes the wealthiest man in the hamlet of Frenchman's Creek. He moves to Jefferson, the county seat, takes over the Sartoris bank, drives its president, his wife's lover, out of town, and moves into his stately mansion. A swarm of Snopes cousins and their children follow in his path, spreading further corruption. Flem is finally killed by one of his own cousins. YA

Snow Goose, The (1941) By *Paul Gallico, this delightful story is about Philip Rhayader, who lives alone in a lighthouse on the coast of England. A painter of birds and of nature, Philip is a hunchback with a crippled arm, and is treated with some distrust by the villagers. He is a friend to all wild things and has a collection of tamed geese, ducks, and other wildfowl that come to the marshes on the edge of the sea. One day Philip is visited by Fritha, a thin girl "as timid as a bird," who overcomes her shyness to bring him an injured young snow goose she has found. Philip treats the bird skillfully, and while the goose heals under his care, Fritha returns often. When summer comes, the snow goose flies away with the other migrating birds, and the two friends think they will never see the "Lost Princess" again. To their delight, she returns with the other flocks in October and makes her home with Philip, to whom she becomes more and more attached.

Some years later, when war has broken out between England and Germany, Philip hears of the battle of Dunkirk. Across the North Sea, on the French coast, the British Army is trapped by the Germans, and every available small boat is used to cross the English Channel to help evacuate soldiers to the transport ships, which are unable to reach the shallows. Philip sets out alone to join them in his sailboat. Fritha watches him sail off and sees the snow goose follow him, flying above in slow circles. Philip never returns to Fritha, but the survivors of Dunkirk tell the story of an extraordinary hunchback who made countless trips in his sailboat, carrying soldiers to safety through a hail of German bullets. They particularly remember the snow-white goose that flew above the battle like an angel of mercy, seeming to point the way home. MR & YA

"Snows of Kilimanjaro, The" (1938) This haunting tale of a man facing death is one of *Ernest Hemingway's best-known short stories. A writer, identified only as Harry, has gone on safari to Africa with Helen, the wealthy woman who has been supporting him. Living among the wealthy and privileged, Harry has ignored his writing. He hoped that by going to Africa he could "work the fat off his soul" and get back to writing the important things he has put off for so long. But a neglected scratch from a thorn develops into gangrene, and when their truck breaks down, Harry realizes he will not live to write his stories. As he waits for a rescue plane that does not arrive, he takes stock of his life. As he dies he dreams that the plane comes and takes him off toward the white, snowcapped peak of Kilimanjaro, which *symbolizes death. You can find "The Snows of Kilimanjaro" in *The Complete Short Stories of Ernest Hemingway* (1987). It also contains another Hemingway classic, "The Short Happy Life of Francis Macomber," also set in Africa, about a man whose conquest of fear leads to his own death. YA

Snyder, Zilpha Keatley (1927–) Though perhaps best known for her novel *The Changeling,* Snyder has written a number of novels about young people who learn important truths about themselves through adventures involving mystery and, often, the supernatural. Among her novels are *The Velvet Room* (1965), about a troubled girl who creates her own comfortable world in the library of a deserted mansion and uncovers a mystery involving the estate's lost heiress; *The Egypt Game* (1967), about a group of young people who invent a game based on their interest in ancient Egypt and become involved in a dangerous mystery; *The Headless Cupid* (1971), about a family that moves into a big house where strange and spooky things begin to happen; and *The Witches of Worm* (1972), about a girl who thinks her cat is bewitched. Snyder's Green-sky *fantasy trilogy, which includes *Below the Root* (1975), *And All Between* (1976), and *Until the Celebration* (1977), tells about the Erdlings, a people who have been banished to an underground world by the Kindar, who live in the forest world of Green-sky. MR

Sodom and Gomorrah were two of what were known as the five Cities of the Plain, located in the vicinity of the southern end of the Dead Sea in ancient Palestine. Their ruins have never been found. The *Bible tells of their destruction by God with "brimstone and fire" because of the sinfulness of the inhabitants.

Only Lot, a kinsman of *Abraham, was warned and allowed to escape with his family. He had been told not to look back, but his wife did and was turned into a pillar of salt. There are some odd salt formations in this area, and the story of Lot's wife may have been an attempt to explain their origin. Any place where wickedness reigns is said to be "a Sodom and Gomorrah." A movie, *Sodom and Gomorrah,* was produced in 1963.

Solid Gold Kid, The (1977) Written by *Norma Fox Mazer and *Harry Mazer, this violent and frightening novel is narrated by its main character, 16-year-old Derek Chapman. The privileged but lonely son of a self-made millionaire, Derek attends a private school near Schenectady, New York. One rainy day he hitches a ride with a man and a woman in a gray van. Four other teenagers, whom he does not know, also get into the van. Then Derek learns that he has willingly climbed into the van of his own kidnappers, and now all five must share the same uncertain fate. At first the teenagers show their indifference to or dislike of one another, but as they struggle for a way to escape from their brutal captors, they learn they must trust and help each other. Their lives depend on it. In the end, all five learn important things about themselves and each other and about what is really important in life. If you enjoyed *The Solid Gold Kid,* try *House of Stairs* by *William Sleator, about five kidnapped teenagers who find themselves locked inside a building containing nothing but stairways leading nowhere. YA

Solomon The rule of Solomon, king of Israel (c.972–c.932 B.C.), was the most splendid, and his wisdom the greatest, of any monarch of Israel. His name remains a synonym for wealth grandly displayed and for sound judgment. A son of *David, he is remembered for the magnificent temple he had erected in Jerusalem. It became the central place of Jewish worship. The best-known story about his wisdom concerns the two women who came before him claiming the same baby. Solomon ordered it cut in two, and half given to each. He knew who the real mother was when she pleaded with him to let the other woman have it rather than see it killed. The account in the *Bible of the visit to Solomon of the Queen of Sheba, ruler of a land in southern Arabia, has never lost its fascination. Having heard of Solomon's wisdom, she came to test it, bringing "camels bearing spices, and very much gold, and precious stones." Solomon, in turn, "gave to the Queen of Sheba all that she desired." They were apparently much impressed with each other. Though some books in the Bible, Proverbs, Ecclesiastes, and the Song of Solomon, were traditionally said to have been written by Solomon, modern scholarship shows this is not so. A movie, *Solomon and Sheba*, was produced in 1959.

Solzhenitsyn, Aleksandr I(sayevich) (1918–)

Without question the best-known figure in modern Russian literature and one of the great writers of the 20th century, Solzhenitsyn became in the 1960s and 1970s the leading spokesman against the violence and repression of the Soviet system. He found his inspiration while serving eight years in a labor camp for writing a letter critical of Joseph Stalin (1879–1953). His first success came with the publication of *One Day in the Life of Ivan Denisovich*, about a prisoner in a labor camp struggling to keep from being physically and spiritually crushed. Virtually all of Solzhenitsyn's later works were banned in Russia and published only in the West. For what was deemed his anti-Soviet activities, in 1974 Solzhenitsyn was exiled from the Soviet Union and eventually came to live in Vermont.

Solzhenitsyn's other works include the novels *The First Circle* (1968), set in a special labor camp for intellectuals and political prisoners; *The Cancer Ward* (1968), set in a prison hospital; and *August 1914* (1971), about the disastrous defeat of the czarist army in the Battle of Tannenberg early in World War I. To Solzhenitsyn this was the crucial event leading to the rise of the Soviet state. His most ambitious work is the three-volume *The Gulag Archipelago* (1974–1978), a history of the vast Stalinist prison network, based on the testimony and memoirs of more than 200 of its survivors. In all his works, Solzhenitsyn champions the spiritual struggle of individuals against an evil and corrupt system. His powerful writings have been likened to those of another Russian writer, *Leo Tolstoy. Solzhenitsyn was awarded the Nobel Prize for literature in 1970. YA

Some of Us Survived: The Story of an Armenian Boy

(1978), by Kerop Bedoukian (1907–1981), is the true story of the author's escape from Turkey during the Armenian *holocaust of 1915–1918, in which two million Armenians died. In a clear and direct style, Bedoukian describes his family life in the Christian Armenian community in Sivas, Turkey. After his father is taken away by the Turkish authorities, Kerop's large family is forced to leave home and join 30,000 refugees destined to be deported from Turkey to Aleppo, in Syria. Conditions among the refugees are appalling, with no provision made for food or water. Kerop sees people die from starvation, exhaustion, and sickness every day, and witnesses countless atrocities by the Turkish guards. His mother is a woman of courage and determination, however, and is ruthless in her struggle to keep the family together. Under her protection, Kerop retains enough of his innocence to look at their exodus as something of an adventure. His lively curiosity gets him into dangerous situations, but he always manages to survive.

After a two-year stay in Birecik, where the family supports itself by weaving, the Bedoukians make their way by slow stages to Aleppo, to Constantinople (now Istanbul), and eventually to Bulgaria. Three years later, with the help of refugee relief organizations and the efforts of Mrs. Bedoukian's sister in America, the remaining family members are able to emigrate to Canada, after 10 years of fleeing the Turks. After settling in Canada Bedoukian became a citizen, worked as a rug dealer for over 40 years, and later helped bring more than 2,000 Armenian immigrants to safety. *Some of Us Survived* is his only book. YA

Son of the Middle Border, A (1917) By

*Hamlin Garland, this brilliant autobiography

tells of the author's youth and early manhood in the Middle Border, the prairie region of the Middle West, and of his early literary career. Garland begins his story in 1865, when he is a small boy and his father returns from the Civil War to the family farm in Wisconsin. Soon the family moves west to new land in Minnesota, then to Iowa, and finally to South Dakota. Garland strikes out on his own and eventually works his way to Boston where, after much hardship and labor, he establishes himself as a writer determined to tell realistically "the painful as well as the pleasant truth" about farm life. With his new success, he moves to Chicago in 1893, the heart of the region that is his subject, and settles his now-aged pioneer parents in a homestead in his Wisconsin birthplace.

Garland's narrative captures the beauty and richness of the prairie, its inevitable destruction, the pioneer spirit of his and other prairie families, and their struggle against the immense power of nature. He continued his story in several books, including *A Daughter of the Middle Border* (1921), *Trail-Makers of the Middle Border* (1926), and *Back-Trailers of the Middle Border* (1928). YA

Song of Solomon (1977) This highly praised and popular novel by *Toni Morrison tells of Macon Dead III, the son of Macon Dead, Jr., a slumlord and the richest black man in a Michigan town. The younger Macon, known as Milkman, grows up in the big house of his mother's father, a wealthy and respected doctor. Comfortable, idle, pampered, and completely selfish, Milkman is taken by an older friend, Guitar, to the house of Milkman's outcast Aunt Pilate, who is the exact opposite of her grasping, materialistic brother, Macon. Through his contact with Pilate, Milkman begins a quest for the truth about his family and their origins. This family mystery parallels Milkman's search for a stash of gold found by Macon and Pilate when they were children, shortly after their own father was murdered. Milkman first goes to Pennsylvania, then south to a small Virginia town, where the children sing a song Pilate had sung, the "song of Solomon." Milkman's long quest for family and personal identity is successful, but it leads also to his and Pilate's deaths at Guitar's hand. If you enjoyed *Song of Solomon*, try the novels of *William Faulkner, in which family and personal identity also play key roles. YA

Songs of Innocence (1789) and **Songs of Experience** (1794), by the English poet *William Blake, were meant to show the contrary states of the human soul. In the first group of poems, the child expresses pleasure in life and nature, and in the second group is subjected to injustice and cruelty. The two sets of poems are like two voices, one sweet and loving, as in "The Lamb" and "Infant Boy," and the other grim and bitter, as in "Infant Sorrow" and "The Chimney Sweeper." *Songs of Experience* contains one of the best-known poems in English, beginning "Tyger! Tyger! burning bright/ In the forests of the night . . ." YA

sonnet is a 14-line verse form using a definite rhyme scheme and structure and dealing with a single idea or theme. The earliest form was the Italian, or Petrarchan, sonnet, which was developed in Italy in the 13th century and named after the Italian poet *Petrarch. It consists of an eight-line "octave," generally with a rhyme scheme *a,b,b,a,a,b,b,a*, followed by a six-line "sestet" with a varying rhyme scheme. The octave introduces and develops the theme, and the sestet completes it. In the 16th century the English, or Shakespearean or Elizabethan, sonnet was developed. It consists of three independently rhymed quatrains followed by a unifying couplet. Its general rhyme scheme is *a,b,a,b,c,d,c,d,e,f,e,f,g,g*. You can find excellent examples of the sonnet form in the works of *Dante, *Petrarch, *William Shakespeare, *John Milton, *William Wordsworth, *John Keats, *Elizabeth Barrett Browning, and *Edna St. Vincent Millay. YA

Sonnets from the Portuguese (1850) The best-known work of the English poet *Elizabeth Barrett Browning, this collection of 44

*sonnets was written by Elizabeth Barrett while she was being courted by her future husband, the English poet *Robert Browning. It was their admiration of each other's poetry that first brought Browning to visit the invalid, reclusive Barrett in 1845. He soon decided to win her heart, and a year later they eloped, an action that turned Barrett's domineering father against her forever. Several years later, while the Brownings were living in Italy, Mrs. Browning showed her husband the poems, which tell how the love he awakened in her rescued her from sadness and the prospect of death. Robert Browning, who is said to have called the poems "the finest sonnets written in any language since Shakespeare," convinced his wife to have them published. The curious title may have been inspired by the fact that Browning called his wife "my little Portuguese," referring to her dark complexion. If you enjoyed *Sonnets from the Portuguese*, read also the sonnets of *William Shakespeare. YA

Sophocles (496?–406? B.C.) One of the greatest dramatists in Western literature, Sophocles is ranked, with *Aeschylus and *Euripides, as one of the three great tragedians of ancient Greece. A famous and honored citizen of Athens, he served it twice in wartime as a general. However, most of his efforts went into his tragedies. Of the more than 100 plays he wrote, only seven are complete, and the dating of the plays is uncertain. Though Sophocles' characters are drawn from Greek myth and history, they are presented as human beings. It is their own human weaknesses and failings that combine with chance or fate to produce the tragedy. Among the best known of his plays are *Antigone, which portrays the conflict of duty and personal conscience against tyrannical authority; *Oedipus Tyrannus*, or *Oedipus the King*, in which the hero *Oedipus learns that he has unwittingly killed his own father and married his own mother; and *Electra*, in which *Electra persuades her brother, Orestes, to kill their mother, Clytemnestra, in revenge for the murder of their father, *Agamemnon. You can find Sophocles' plays in many editions and an-

thologies, including *The Complete Plays of Sophocles* (1982). YA

Sound and the Fury, The (1929) This novel by *William Faulkner, considered by many to be his best work, tells of the decay and final destruction of the once aristocratic Compson family. Set in the fictional *Yoknapatawpha County, Mississippi, between 1910 and 1928, it consists of four parts. The first part is narrated by Benjy, 33 years old and feeble-minded, who mixes his observations of one day's events on April 7, 1928, with his memories of his sister, Caddy, whom he adores, and his brothers, Quentin and Jason. His confused narration is made clearer by the following sections.

Part two is a flashback to 1910 narrated by Quentin on the day of his suicide, when he learns that his promiscuous sister, Caddy, for whom he feels an overpowering love, is marrying Herbert Head, a dull but prosperous banker. Part three returns to April 6, 1928, and is narrated by Jason, who through his cruelty and deceit dominates the Compson household, which includes Caddy's illegitimate daughter, Quentin. Jason blames her for the breakup of Caddy's marriage and his loss of a promised job in Head's bank. He has stolen the money sent by Caddy for Quentin's upbringing and driven Quentin to be as promiscuous as her mother had been. In part four, which takes place on April 8, 1928, and is related by an objective narrator, Quentin steals back her money and runs off with a carnival worker. This section focuses on the black housekeeper Dilsey, whose qualities of strength, gentleness, and compassion are exactly the opposite of the Compsons. It is Dilsey and the other black servants who have held the Compson family together. The Compson family, notably Caddy's brother Quentin, also figures in Faulkner's novel *Absalom, Absalom!*, chronicling the rise and fall of the Thomas Sutpen family from 1865 to 1910. *The Sound and the Fury* was filmed in 1959. YA

Sound of Chariots, A (1972) This novel by *Mollie Hunter is set in a small village in Scotland in the 1920s. Bridey McShane is the fourth of five children and the youngest of the Mc-Shane daughters. She is the favorite of her father, whom she adores. A sensitive, thoughtful, and observant girl, she is heartbroken when her father dies. Her feelings of grief are made even worse by her awareness that the passage of time brings her own death nearer moment by moment. Bridey, who has always loved the magic of words, tries to express her thoughts in writing. She learns that others have shared her feelings when she comes upon two lines from the poem "To His Coy Mistress" by the English poet Andrew Marvell (1621–1678):

> But at my back I always hear
> Time's wingèd chariot hurrying near.

Bridey learns that she can use her writing talents to create something good out of her unhappy experiences. A new world opens up for her as she begins to grow toward adulthood. MR

Sounder (1969) By William H. Armstrong (1914–), this novel tells about a sharecropper in the South and the man's faithful hunting dog, Sounder, the only character that has a name. He is called Sounder for the beautiful, rich, sound of his hunting bay. One night the father steals a ham to feed his wife and four children. Soon he is arrested. As he is hauled away, Sounder runs after the wagon and is shot. The father's oldest child, called only "the boy," watches helplessly as the dog crawls off, perhaps to die. Months later Sounder returns, crippled and half blind. The father is sentenced to serve on a road gang and is gone for many years, during which time Sounder never bays his beautiful song. The boy searches for his father without success, but he is befriended by a teacher who helps him begin his education. One summer day the father returns, greeted by the joyous baying of Sounder. Like the dog, the father is badly crippled, but he has come home. That fall he goes hunting one last time with Sounder and dies. Soon after, his faithful dog dies as well.

Sounder is a story of family, love, and faithfulness, but also of human greed and cruelty, and the suffering they cause. Armstrong, a former history teacher, based his novel partly on stories he heard while he was growing up in Virginia. You will want to read two of his nonfiction works, *Barefoot in the Grass: The Story of Grandma Moses* (1970) and *The Education of Abraham Lincoln* (1974). If you enjoyed *Sounder*, try **The Voice of Bugle Ann* by *MacKinlay Kantor, which is also much more than a simple dog story. *Sounder* won the *Newbery Medal in 1970 and was made into a successful movie in 1972. MR

Soup (1974) By *Robert Newton Peck, this humorous book is based on his own experiences as a boy growing up in Vermont in the 1930s. It tells of Rob Peck's adventures with his best friend, whose nickname is Soup. The two find interesting ways to get into trouble, such as the time Rob goes rolling down Dugan's Hill inside a barrel and crashes right through Mrs. Biscardi's hen coop, or the time Soup whips an apple through the stained glass window of the Baptist church. There are fun memories, too, such as the taste of the silver-plated needle valve they use to pump up their football one glorious Saturday, and the smell of burning corn silk coming from the acorn pipes they make one beautiful fall day. You can read about Rob and Soup's further adventures in a number of sequels, including *Soup and Me* (1975), *Soup for President* (1978), *Soup on Wheels* (1981), *Soup on Ice* (1985), *Soup's Uncle* (1988), and *Soup's Hoop* (1989). MR

Southall, Ivan (1921–) An Australian novelist, essayist, and short-story writer, Southall has written a number of novels that feature a young person or a group of young people facing difficult and dangerous situations by themselves. They have been praised as gripping stories about how young people think and feel, and how they act toward one another, as they struggle to understand themselves and the world around them. Among Southall's best known novels are *Hills End* (1963), about seven young people trapped in the forested mountains of Australia by a violent storm; *Ash Road* (1966), about a group of young people in the Australian bush country threatened by a massive fire sweeping across the land; *To the Wild Sky* (1977), about six young people who crash land on a deserted island after the pilot of their plane dies; and *Josh* (1972), about a 14-year-old Australian city boy who has big problems getting along with the people he meets when he visits his aunt in the country. MR

Soyinka, Wole [Akinwande Oluwole Soyinka] (1934–) A Nigerian poet, playwright, and novelist, Soyinka has been described as Africa's greatest living writer and also as one of the best writers working in the English language. Soyinka's writings reflect his deep interest in the traditions and mythology of the Yoruba people, among whom he grew up, and also in the enormous problems faced by African nations as they try to merge their past with the onrushing future. His plays include *A Dance of the Forests* (1962), about a group of Africans who summon the spirits of the dead for a tribal ritual, only to find the spirits are as petty and difficult as living people; *The Lion and the Jewel* (1962), about a young woman courted by an old village chief and a young Westernized school teacher; and *Death and the King's Horseman* (1975), a tragedy about a colonial administrator who tries to stop the ritual suicide of a Yoruba king's Chief Horseman following the king's death. His other books include *The Interpreters* (1965), a novel about five young Nigerian intellectuals in the early years of their country's independence; *Season of Anomy* (1973), a love story set in a fictional African nation struggling against the forces of corruption and oppression; *Aké: The Years of Childhood* (1982), Soyinka's autobiography of his childhood; and the poetry collections *A Shuttle in the Crypt* (1969) and *Mandela's Earth and Other Poems* (1988). Soyinka was awarded the Nobel Prize for literature in 1986. YA

Spark, Muriel (1918–) A Scottish novelist, poet, short-story writer, and critic, Spark is probably known best for her novel *The Prime of Miss Jean Brodie*. Spark grew up in Scotland, lived in Africa for a time, then in England, and then in Italy. Her books are noted for their interesting if not always sympathetic characters, and for Spark's cool style of writing. Her novels and stories are often thought-provoking mixtures of comedy, tragedy, realism, and the supernatural. Spark's works include the novels *The Mandelbaum Gate* (1965), about the experiences of a young woman, a part-Jewish convert to Roman Catholicism, in Israel and Jordan in 1961; *The Abbess of Crewe* (1974), set in a Catholic abbey in England, about one sister's determined and unethical efforts to win election as the new abbess; *Loitering with Intent* (1981), set in London in 1949, about a young writer who discovers a lifetime of material in the odd assortment of characters making up a club called the "Autobiographical Association"; and the short-story collection *The Stories of Muriel Spark* (1985). YA

Speare, Elizabeth George (1908–) Probably best known for her novel *The Witch of Blackbird Pond*, Speare has written several popular and highly praised historical novels and nonfiction books. Though most of her books are about some colorful part of American history, her novel *The Bronze Bow* (1961) is set in the Holy Land about 2,000 years ago. It tells of a young Israelite in Galilee during the time of Jesus who learns to overcome his hatred of the conquering Romans through *Jesus' gentle teachings and life. Speare's other books include the novels *Calico Captive* (1957), about a colonial girl in New Hampshire who is captured by American Indians during the French and Indian War, and *The Sign of the Beaver*, which is set in the Maine wilderness during the colonial period. Speare also wrote *Life in Colonial America* (1963), a lively look at everyday life in the American colonies in the 17th and 18th centuries. Speare won the *Newbery Medal for *The Witch of Blackbird Pond* in 1959 and for *The Bronze Bow* in 1962. MR

Spenser, Edmund (1552?–1599) Considered the greatest English poet since *Geoffrey Chaucer, Spenser was born in London, but little is known of his family or early life. He was educated at Cambridge University and later held several minor official posts, working all the while on his main interest, poetry. His first major work was *The Shepheardes Calendar* (1579), a series of 12 pastoral poems, in which simple shepherds comment on events and ideas of the day. This form enabled Spenser to produce *satire on religious and political matters. About this time he began to write his famous work, *The Faerie Queen*, an *epic *allegory praising Queen Elizabeth I (1533–1603), the English nation, and the moral struggle of virtue over vice. Spenser completed only six books of this enormously ambitious project, yet it still is one of the longest poems in the English language. He devised for it the special nine-line Spenserian stanza.

While writing *The Faerie Queen*, Spenser worked on other poems, including those collected in the volume *Complaints* (1591) and the "Epithalamion," a love hymn he wrote to honor his own wife, whom he had married the year before. This poem, often considered Spenser's masterpiece, was published with Spenser's *Amoretti* (1595), a collection of love sonnets. He died in London and was buried in Westminster Cathedral next to Chaucer.

Spenser's works influenced many later poets, including *George Gordon Byron, *John Milton, *Percy Bysshe Shelley, and *John Keats. You can find good selections of Spenser's poetry in many anthologies, including *The New Oxford Book of English Verse* (1939), *The Viking Book of Poetry of the English-Speaking World* (1958), and *The Norton Anthology of English Literature* (1988). YA

Sperry, Armstrong W. (1897–1976) An artist as well as a writer, Sperry wrote and illustrated many popular books for younger readers, including his best-known work, *Call It Courage*, an adventure story set in the South Pacific. A number of Sperry's adventures and nonfiction books are set in the Pacific, but others have such diverse settings as Antarctica, South America, and the American Southwest. Among his adventure stories are *Little Eagle, a Navajo Boy* (1938), about a 14-year-old Navajo boy in Arizona and his efforts to convince his family to let him go off to school; *Black Falcon* (1949), about a 16-year-old boy who becomes involved with the buccaneer Jean Lafitte (c.1780–c.1825) and with the defense of New Orleans during the War of 1812; and *Thunder Country* (1952), about a boy who journeys with his scientist father into the rain forest of Venezuela. Sperry's nonfiction books include *John Paul Jones: Fighting Sailor* (1953), *Captain Cook Explores the South Seas* (1955), *The Amazon, River Sea of Brazil* (1961), and *Great River, Wide Land: The Rio Grande Through History* (1967). MR

Spillane, Mickey [Frank Morrison Spillane] (1918–) Beginning his career by writing for comic books, Spillane turned to detective novels. He created Mike Hammer, the toughest, most violent of all hard-boiled private investigators. Hammer is six feet tall and weighs 190 pounds. He has a vigilante attitude and takes justice into his own hands, which give Spillane's books a lurid atmosphere of bloodshed, sadism, and sex. The first was *I, the Jury* (1947), in which Hammer seeks revenge for the killing of an army friend who had saved his life. *The Girl Hunters* (1962) brings Hammer back in action after a seven-year binge caused by the murder of his girl friend by the Red Dragon, a communist assassin. Besides other Hammer adventures, Spillane created Tiger Mann, an espionage agent who hates Russian communists and appears in *The Day of the Guns* (1954) and other books. If you like Spillane's books, read books by *Raymond Chandler, *Dashiell Hammett, and *John D. MacDonald. A movie of *I, the Jury* was made in 1953. Spillane himself played Hammer in the 1963 movie of *The Girl Hunters*, and in a TV series in 1958. YA

Spoon River Anthology (1915) The best-known and most successful work by *Edgar Lee Masters, this verse masterpiece is in the form of almost 250 epitaphs spoken by the inhabitants of the cemetery in Spoon River, a fictional town of the Middle West. Through their remembered hopes, dreams, sorrows, disappointments, smallness, generosity, failures, and successes, the dead recreate the larger picture of small-town life in the Middle West in the 19th century, and the even larger picture of the human spirit.

In *The New Spoon River* (1924), Masters used the same structure to describe in bitter terms the effect of modern times on Spoon River and its people. If you enjoyed the technique of many characters narrating a story, you will probably also enjoy the play *Our Town by *Thornton Wilder and the collection of related stories in *Winesburg, Ohio by *Sherwood Anderson. YA

Spring Moon (1981) This epic novel of China by *Bette Bao Lord is a family saga spanning Chinese history from 1892, near the end of the Manchu Dynasty, to the 1970s and the reopening of China to the Western world. The central figure is Spring Moon, the granddaughter of the patriarch of the House of Chang, in Soochow, eastern China. A bright and beautiful girl, Spring Moon grows up at a time when China is being attacked by the industrialized powers of the West, and also by Japan. The collapse of China's imperial system, the revolutions that follow, the struggle between the Communist and Nationalist factions, and the devastating war against the invading Japanese affect the lives of Spring Moon and all her family, including her uncles Noble Talent, the soldier, and Bold Talent, the scholar; her husband, Glad Promise, a promising young man of the House of Woo in Peking, whose knowledge of Western ways leads to his early death; and her daughter, Lustrous Jade, who becomes a leader in the communist movement, only to be discredited during the Cultural Revolution of the 1960s. Over the decades the clan is dispersed across and beyond China, but at last Spring Moon is rejoined by five generations back in Soochow, in a moving ceremony honoring the clan's ancestors. If you enjoyed *Spring Moon*, you will also probably like *Doctor Zhivago by *Boris Pasternak, set in Russia from the end of the czarist era through the Russian Revolution. YA

Springer, Nancy (1948–) Though known best for *fantasy novels and finely crafted short stories, Springer has also written a number of more realistic novels for younger readers. These stories, which revolve around two of Springer's main interests, horses and young people, include *Not on a White Horse* (1988), about a girl whose job of taking care of horses helps her to deal with her unhappy family life and her unemployed, alcoholic father; and *They're All Named Wildfire* (1989), about a white girl who suffers from and overcomes the racial prejudices of her friends and classmates after she befriends a black girl who shares her love of horses. Springer's fantasy novels for older readers include *Chains of Gold* (1986), about lovers in a mythical kingdom pursued by the spirit of the man's best friend, who gave his life so that they might escape death in a sacred ritual; and *Apocalypse* (1989), a tale of supernatural horror set in a Pennsylvania town in the year 1999. MR & YA

Spy, The (1821) This historical novel by *James Fenimore Cooper is set in the American Revolution in the so-called Neutral Ground of Westchester County, New York, between the British-held ground to the south and the patriot-held areas to the north. The hero of the story is Harvey Birch, a peddler widely suspected of being a British spy. Birch supplies a disguise and a pass signed by General Washington to Captain Henry Wharton, a British officer, who slips through the patriot lines to visit his father and two sisters at their country home in Westchester. There he is recognized by Mr. Harper, a mysterious traveler who arrived at the Wharton home seeking refuge during a storm. Birch and Harper play an important role in the lives of the Whartons following Henry's capture and conviction for spying. Though reviled and hunted for his connections with the British, Birch risks his life to free Henry. Birch is really an American spy, and Harper is none other than Washington. Birch's true patriotism is discovered after his death, during the War of 1812.

MR = Middle Reader   YA = Young Adult Reader   * = See this main entry

Harvey Birch is robbed by marauding guerrillas,
known as skinners, in *The Spy*.

The Spy is a combination of historical adventure, centering on the war and on Birch's actiities, and a romantic novel, centering on Wharton's sisters, one of whom is betrothed to a British officer and the other to an American. The combination creates an interesting view into the violent struggle that gave birth to the United States. YA

Spy Who Came In from the Cold, The

(1963) The central character in this espionage novel by *John Le Carré is Alex Leamas, a 50-year-old veteran of a British intelligence agency who has recently suffered a dismal failure in Berlin. Now tired and cynical, he is, it seems, let go by his agency. Drinking heavily and nearly broke, Leamas is approached by East German agents and agrees to tell all he knows about the British agency. He is eventually flown to East Germany, where he is interrogated further by Fiedler, deputy head of security. Fiedler wants to use Leamas to destroy his superior, Mundt. Mundt, however, has Leamas jailed and interrogates him. This is followed by a trial at which Fiedler tries to prove Mundt is a British spy. In his defense, Mundt tricks Elizabeth Gold, an English woman who thinks she is a communist and who is in love with Leamas, into coming to East Germany. Through her, Mundt shows that Leamas is not really a defector, thus causing Fiedler's downfall. Mundt arranges for Leamas and Gold to escape over the Berlin Wall. At the last moment Leamas realizes Mundt is not what the London office had said he was and Leamas then knows that he was deliberately led on by his own colleagues in London. The escape plan ends in tragedy. This novel, with its seedy atmosphere, treachery, and brutality, changed the style of espionage novels. Since its publication, the idea that all the good guys are on one side and all the bad guys on the other has largely disappeared, and reading such novels as this may make you feel that modern espionage is only a stupid game. A movie of the book was made in 1965. YA

Stafford, Jean (1915–1979) A novelist and short-story writer, Stafford is known for her beautiful and carefully crafted style and for her sharp insights into the thoughts and feelings of her characters. She achieved critical and popular success with her first novel, *Boston Adventure* (1944), about the daughter of a chambermaid who rises in the Beacon Hill society of Boston and finds that it is not the perfect world she had imagined it to be. Stafford was also successful with her other novels: *The Mountain Lion* (1947), a moving and finally tragic story of a brother and sister growing up in California and Colorado in the early 20th century, and *The Catherine Wheel* (1952), about a woman who receives a proposal of marriage from the first and only man she has ever loved, the husband of her cousin and best friend. Stafford's short stories were brought together in *The Collected Stories of Jean Stafford* (1969). YA

star For centuries the pseudoscience of astrology has used the stars, along with the sun, the moon, and the planets, to predict events in human lives and in the world at large. It has also become a *symbol of importance and excellence. The flag of the United States bears 50 stars, one for each state. The "Star of David" (Magen David) consists of one triangle imposed on another to form a six-pointed star. It takes its name from *David, king of Judah and Israel. Its use can be traced to the 3rd century A.D. It is a symbol of Zionism and is part of the flag of Israel. During World War II German Jews were forced to wear a *yellow Star of David. To "star" in a play or movie is to have the leading role, while a "four-star restaurant" is one of the very highest rank. If something favorable happens, you "thank your lucky stars," showing the influence of the astrologers. If you get hit on the head, you may "see stars," though not literally. On the other hand, happy lovers are said to have "stars in their eyes," implying perhaps that their eyes are twinkling with happiness. *Ralph Waldo Emerson urged, "Hitch your wagon to a star," meaning that you should have high ambitions. When *William Shakespeare called the doomed *Romeo and Juliet "a pair of star-crossed lovers," he was thinking in astrological terms, implying that their two stars were not in a favorable position in relation to each other.

Steele, William O(wen) (1917–1979) The author of 39 adventure-filled books for younger readers, Steele was born and spent most of his life amid the woods and mountains of Tennes-

see. Most of his books are set in Tennessee in the early pioneer days of the late 1700s and early 1800s. Steele's interesting characters and his descriptions of the challenging life of the frontier bring this colorful period of American history to life. Among his best-known novels are *The Buffalo Knife* (1952), about a boy and his family who make a 1,000-mile journey by flatboat down the Tennessee River in 1782; *The Lone Hunt* (1955), about an 11-year-old boy who sets out alone to hunt a buffalo; *The Perilous Road* (1958), about the experiences of a Tennessee boy during the Civil War; and *The Man with the Silver Eyes* (1976), about a Cherokee boy who is sent by his family to live for a year with a stranger, a white Quaker trader, even though he has learned to hate and fear whites. MR

Stein, Gertrude (1874–1946) Known for intriguing but often exasperating writings, Stein was born in Pennsylvania but grew up in Europe and California. She studied psychology at Radcliffe College, then medicine at Johns Hopkins University, showing an early interest in human thought processes, especially "automatic writing," in which a person writes without consciously controlling what is written. In 1903 she traveled to Paris, France, with Alice B. Toklas (1877–1967), who became her lifelong companion. Stein developed a complex philosophy of writing that used phrases and word repetitions to build one upon another, much like the frames of a motion picture, to produce meaning. She ignored rules of grammar, punctuation, and word meanings, to the dismay of many readers and critics. Yet her work and theories influenced many writers, among them *Sherwood Anderson and *Ernest Hemingway.

Probably her best-known works are *The Autobiography of Alice B. Toklas* (1933), which is actually Stein's own autobiography, and *Three Lives* (1909), a collection of three stories, each about a different working-class woman. The longest of the three stories, "Melancthon," a study of an 18-year-old black serving girl, is considered the most successful and complete. *Four Saints in Three Acts* (1934) is Stein's basically plotless libretto for an opera by the American composer Virgil Thomson (1896–1989). YA

Steinbeck, John (Ernst) (1902–1968) Though he is known best for his powerful novels *The Grapes of Wrath* and *East of Eden*, Steinbeck wrote a number of critically praised and highly popular novels, short stories, and plays. Many of his works are set in California, where he was born and lived for many years. Steinbeck worked at many sorts of jobs while establishing himself as a writer. His first important success came with the novel *Tortilla Flat* (1935), about a colorful group of social outcasts living in Monterey, California. Steinbeck modeled his novel after *Le Morte d'Arthur* (1485), the epic by *Thomas Malory about *King Arthur and his knights. Also successful were *The Red Pony, a story in four parts; and the novel *Of Mice and Men* (1937), recounting the tragic events that overtake two migrant farm workers. Steinbeck's compassion for the defenseless and downtrodden formed the backbone of *The Grapes of Wrath*, which identified and condemned the forces of economic oppression while celebrating the courage and humanity of the oppressed.

Steinbeck's later fiction included the short novel *The Moon Is Down* (1942), about the brave resistance of Norwegian villagers to their Nazi occupiers during World War II; *Cannery Row* (1945), in which the setting is again Monterey; *The Pearl, a folk fable set in Mexico; *Travels with Charley in Search of America* (1962), Steinbeck's account of his cross-country journey with his dog; and *The Acts of King Arthur and His Noble Knights* (1976), an updating of Malory's *Le Morte d'Arthur*. Steinbeck's play based on *Of Mice and Men*, produced in 1937, is now considered a classic. Films based on the novel were made in 1939 and 1992. The former was remade for television in 1981. Movies were made of *Tortilla Flat* in 1942, *The Moon Is Down* in 1943, and *Cannery Row* in 1982. Steinbeck was awarded the Novel Prize for literature in 1952. YA

Stephens, James (1882–1950) Irish poet, storyteller, and a popular member of the *Irish Literary Renaissance, Stephens was raised in the slums of Dublin. He educated himself, worked in an office, and wrote poetry in his spare time. In 1909 he published his first volume of poems, and a novel appeared two years later. *The Crock of Gold* (1912) established his reputation, and Stephens became a full-time writer.

The Crock of Gold, by far his best-known work, is a prose fantasy that combines elements of the fairy tale, essay, *allegory, and novel. Based largely on Irish mythology and folklore, the loosely connected stories are full of imagination and irreverent humor. It is said Stephens hoped to persuade the Irish to preserve and cherish their cultural heritage. In "The Two Gods," probably an allegory, Caitilin Ni Murrachu is the companion of the foreign god *Pan. She is approached by the handsome Angus Óg, an Irish god called Infinite Joy or Love, and is asked to choose between the two deities. Angus Óg argues that he is desolate, a god forgotten in his own nation (Ireland), and Caitilin goes away with him because his need is very great. Other books by Stephens include *Deirdre* (1923), a novel based on the Celtic legend of *Deirdre. *James, Seumas and Jacques: Unpublished Writings of James Stephens* (1964) contains radio scripts written for the British Broadcasting Corporation between 1940 and 1950 and read on the air by the author. Among them are scripts about *James Joyce, *William Blake, *John Donne, and *William Butler Yeats. YA

Steppenwolf (1927), by *Hermann Hesse, tells about Harry Haller, who is alienated from human society and tormented by the belief that he has two souls: that of Harry the man, educated and cultured, and that of the Steppenwolf, the wolf of the steppes, which considers human existence petty and shabby. Wolf and man wage war with one another until Harry fears he will kill himself. While walking one night, Harry sees a mysterious sign for a "Magic Theatre," but its door is locked and he cannot get in. Then a strange man gives him a little book called "Treatise on the Steppenwolf." It describes exactly Harry's inner conflict but tells Harry that within him are not just two but countless souls. This is the beginning of a series of strange, often dreamlike experiences that change Harry's life. The key to all the experiences is a mysterious saxophonist named Pablo, who controls the "Magic Theatre." Under Pablo's guidance, Harry enters the theater, which is really a theater of the mind. There Harry gains a new understanding of himself and the game of life. YA

Stevenson, Robert Louis (1850–1894) Known best for his enduring adventure novel *Treasure Island*, Stevenson was born and grew up in Scotland. Though a sickly boy, he had a happy childhood and became interested in writing in his youth. Trained as a lawyer, he never practiced law, turning to writing instead. His first two volumes, *An Inland Voyage* (1878) and *Travels with a Donkey in Cevennes* (1879), were accounts of his travels in Europe. In 1879 he traveled to America to be with the woman he loved, Mrs. Fanny Osbourne (1840–1914). Following her divorce, she and Stevenson were married. They traveled widely together, finally settling in 1890 in Samoa, a group of islands in the Pacific Ocean, where Stevenson died. In his short life Stevenson produced a number of novels now considered classics, including *Dr. Jekyll and Mr. Hyde*; *Kidnapped*; and *The Master of Ballantrae* (1889), about the tragic feud of two Scottish brothers. Another classic is Stevenson's collection *A Child's Garden of Verses* (1885), whose poems have delighted the youngest and oldest readers for a century. MR & YA

Stewart, Mary (1916–) An English novelist, Stewart is probably known best for her trilogy based on Arthurian legend, which includes *The Crystal Cave* (1970), *The Hollow Hills* (1973), and *The Last Enchantment* (1979). The novels center on the magician *Merlin and how he helps *King Arthur become ruler of all Britain and later fight the forces of evil determined to destroy him and *Camelot. Many of Stewart's novels combine romance, mystery, and fast-paced adventure, and some include an element of magic or the supernatural. One of her best-known novels is *The Moon-Spinners* (1962), about a young Englishwoman who is caught up in mystery and danger while on holiday in the mountains of Crete. Stewart's other novels include *Airs Above the Ground* (1965), a mystery set in Austria and involving the famous Lippizaner stallions of the Spanish Riding School, and *Touch Not the Cat* (1976), about a young Englishwoman with the power of telepathy, who becomes involved in a family mystery. Stewart has also written several novels for younger readers, including *The Little Broomstick* (1972), about a young girl who becomes involved in magic and witchcraft while visiting her great-aunt's old country house, and *A Walk in Wolf Wood* (1980), about a boy and girl who wander off from a family picnic in the Black Forest and into 14th-century Germany. *The Moon-Spinners* was made into a movie in 1964. MR & YA

Stockton, Frank R. [Francis Richard Stockton] (1834–1902) A novelist and short-story writer noted for his wit, humor, and keen understanding of human nature, Stockton is remembered today largely for the classic short story *"The Lady or the Tiger?" He wrote for magazines and became assistant editor of *St. Nicholas Magazine*, under *Mary Mapes Dodge. His first major success came with the novel *Rudder Grange* (1879), the hilarious adventures of a couple who move with their maid, Pomona, into a houseboat. It was so successful that Stockton wrote two sequels, *The Rudder Grangers Abroad* (1891) and *Pomona's Travels* (1894). Another comic novel, *The Casting Away of Mrs. Lecks and Mrs. Aleshine* (1886), about two New England widows who are shipwrecked on a Pacific Island, is still popular. Another Stockton classic is *Buccaneers and Pirates of Our Coasts* (1898), a thrilling account of the seagoing gangsters of the 16th to 18th centuries. MR & YA

Stoker, Bram [Abraham Stoker] (1847–1912) Irish author of the popular vampire novel *Dracula*, Stoker was plagued by health problems in early childhood. Unable to stand or walk until he was 7 years old, he later overcame the handicap and became a celebrated football player at Dublin University. Stoker spent 10 years in the civil service in Dublin and wrote drama criticism for the newspapers. Long an admirer of the actor Sir Henry Irving (1838–1905), he worked as Irving's touring secretary and manager for 27 years. Stoker wrote short stories, several novels, and some nonfiction. None were as successful as *Dracula*, however, which was adapted for the stage and appeared in numerous film versions.

Stolz, Mary (Slattery) (1920–) A prolific and popular novelist, Stolz has been praised for her realistic stories about young people facing the kinds of problems and challenges that today's young readers may also face. One of her best-known novels is *A Dog on Barkham Street* (1960), about Edward Frost, a 9-year-old boy troubled by Martin Hastings, the neighborhood bully and his next-door neighbor. Its sequel is *The Bully of Barkham Street* (1963), the same story told from Martin's viewpoint. Stolz's other books include *Leap Before You Look* (1972), about a 14-year-old girl coping with her parents' divorce; *The Edge of Next Year* (1974), about a 14-year-old boy trying to keep his family together after his mother's death; *Cat in the Mirror* (1975), about a teenage girl who makes contact with her double, a princess of ancient Egypt; and *Cider Days* (1978), about a Vermont girl's efforts to befriend a quiet new girl who has just moved to town from Mexico. MR

Stone, Irving (1903–1989) The acknowledged master of the biographical novel, Stone was born and grew up in California, where he began to write when he was still a boy. The works of another California writer, *Jack London, had an early influence on Stone, especially London's novel *Martin Eden* (1906), which was based in part on London's own experiences. Stone began his career writing plays, essays, short stories, and an unsuccessful first novel, but his second book, *Lust for Life* (1934), the fictionalized biography of the artist Vincent Van Gogh (1853–1890), became an instant best seller. Now Stone focused on biographical novels. His later books included *Sailor on

Horseback (1938), about Jack London; *Clarence Darrow for the Defense* (1941), about the trial lawyer Clarence Darrow (1857–1938); *The President's Lady* (1951), about Andrew Jackson (1767–1845), seventh President of the United States, and his wife, Rachel (d.1828); *Love Is Eternal* (1954), about Abraham Lincoln (1809–1865) and Mary Todd Lincoln (1818–1881); *Men to Match My Mountains: The Opening of the Far West, 1840–1900* (1956); *The Agony and the Ecstasy* (1961), about *Michelangelo; and *The Origin* (1980), about the English naturalist *Charles Darwin. *The Agony and the Ecstasy* was filmed in 1965. YA

Stone, Robert (Anthony) (1937–) A highly praised novelist, Stone is noted as much for his dark vision of human society as his powerful prose style. Stone grew up in New York City and developed a passion for language and writing at an early age. He began his career as a newspaper copyboy, then worked at a number of different jobs, traveled widely, got to know *Jack Kerouac, *Ken Kesey, and other literary figures of the *Beat Generation, and gathered experiences that he later worked into his novels. His first novel, *A Hall of Mirrors* (1967), was a critical and popular success. Set in New Orleans in 1962, it tells of three drifters who are cynically used and ultimately destroyed by a right-wing, power-hungry millionaire. Stone's other novels include *Dog Soldiers* (1974), about three Americans who become involved in the nightmare world of drug smuggling in the closing days of the Vietnam War; *A Flag for Sunrise* (1981), about a group of Americans caught up in revolution in a Central American country; and *Children of Light* (1986), a dark study of the movie industry and, in a larger sense, modern society. *Dog Soldiers* was filmed as *Who'll Stop the Rain?* in 1978. YA

Stoppard, Tom [Tom Straussler] (1937–) A celebrated English playwright, Stoppard was born in Czechoslovakia and spent his childhood there and in Singapore before his family moved to England. He worked as a newspaper reporter and critic for a number of years before turning to playwriting in the 1960s. He achieved success with *Rosencrantz and Guildenstern Are Dead* (1966), a retelling of *Hamlet that focuses on two minor characters, the two lords who accompany Hamlet to England, unknowingly carrying a letter from the Danish king asking the king of England to kill Hamlet. In Stoppard's version the two have no past, no future, and no grasp of the unfolding tragedy, which is about to destroy not Hamlet but them. Stoppard's later plays include the comedy *Travesties* (1974), a study of the nature of art, revolution, and history, set in Zurich, Switzerland, during World War I. Its characters include *James Joyce, V.I. Lenin (1870–1924), and the Romanian-born French avant-garde poet Tristan Tzara (1896–1963), and its plot is intertwined with Joyce's production of the play *The Importance of Being Earnest* by *Oscar Wilde. Another successful Stoppard play is *The Real Thing* (1982), set in England and concerning a dramatist who is removed from life, "the real thing," by his own idealistic faith in language and art. If you enjoyed Stoppard's plays, try also the plays of *Samuel Beckett, one of the leading figures of modern drama. *Rosencrantz and Guildenstern Are Dead* was adapted for film in 1991. YA

Story of Doctor Dolittle, The (1920) By *Hugh Lofting, this enchanting classic begins in Puddleby-on-the-March, England. It introduces the kindly *Doctor Dolittle, who can speak animal languages and whose love and respect for animals have won him the admiration of nearly everyone. When Chee-Chee the monkey gets news of a terrible sickness among monkeys in Africa, Dolittle plans his first trip to what was known as the Dark Continent. Because he is a bit vague about money matters, the Doctor must borrow a boat and supplies from neighbors. Taking only a few of his many pets, he sails away with Chee-Chee, Jip the dog, Polynesia the parrot, and a crocodile. The friends arrive safely in Africa, where they are taken to meet the King of the Jolliginki, who is not hospitable. They make their way with difficulty to the Land of the Monkeys, and Do-

little works day and night to restore the health of his patients. The delighted monkeys present Dolittle with a rare animal—the pushmi-pullyu, a shy tailless beast with a head at each end. After many curious adventures, Dolittle and his friends return to England, where they travel about displaying the pushmi-pullyu at country fairs. Enough money is collected to repay Dolittle's neighbors and support his menagerie for a long time. MR

Stotan! (1986), by *Chris Crutcher, tells about four high-school buddies, the stars of their school swimming team, and what happens to them when they accept an unusual challenge from their coach. The story is narrated by Walker, who, with fellow seniors Nortie, Lion, and Jeff, agree to submit to a week of grueling physical training. The goal is to become a Stotan, part Stoic, or indifferent to pain, and part Spartan, or disciplined and living simply. Under the guidance of their coach, Max, they learn to go beyond pain, beyond their artificial mental limits, to find their own "personal bests." And they grow closer to one another as they face together some bitter challenges, such as Nortie's problems with his older brother's suicide and his abusive father, Walker's problems dealing with his elderly parents and drugged-out older brother, and the biggest challenge of all, Jeff's life-threatening illness. If you enjoyed *Stotan!*, you will probably also like the novels of *Paul Zindel and *Richard Peck, many of which concern teenagers growing toward adulthood. YA

Stout, Rex (Todhunter) (1886–1975) After a successful business career in which Stout set up a banking system that allowed children in 400 cities and villages to deposit and withdraw money in schools, he determined to be a writer. He published three well-received serious novels, but it was after he took up detective fiction that he achieved a large readership. He created *Nero Wolfe, an unusual private investigator, and wrote 46 novels featuring him. The first of these was *Fer-de-Lance* (1934), in which a college president dies on a golf course.

Wolfe finds the death is a case of murder and reveals how it was done with a very unusual weapon. In *Some Buried Caesar* (1939), Wolfe, while on his way to an orchid show, finds himself investigating a murder caused by a feud over a prize bull. *A Right to Die* (1964) is about the murder of a young white woman whose black fiancé is accused of the deed. In *The Father Hunt* (1968) a woman finds a box that may tell her about the father she never knew and whether or not he murdered her mother. If you like Stout's novels, read also the works of *Erle Stanley Gardner and *Ellery Queen. MR & YA

Stowe, Harriet Beecher (1811–1896) The celebrated author of the antislavery novel *Uncle Tom's Cabin*, Stowe was the daughter of Lyman Beecher (1775–1863), an important Presbyterian clergyman, and the sister of Henry Ward Beecher (1813–1887), a clergyman, orator, and prominent abolitionist. She taught for a few years and wrote for magazines before marriage and family put an end to both occupations, but in 1850 the growing problem of slavery inspired her to return to writing. The result was *Uncle Tom's Cabin*, a passionate novel that immediately became a rallying point for the growing abolitionist movement. Stowe followed her success with the novel *Dred: A Tale of the Great Dismal Swamp* (1856), about the experiences of a runaway slave. Though some consider *Dred* a better novel, it was not as successful. Her later books included the novels *The Minister's Wooing* (1859), set in Newport, Rhode Island, just after the Revolutionary War and centering on a deeply religious young woman who, after the man she loves is reported lost at sea, agrees to marry a minister she reveres, only to learn that her true love has survived; and *Oldtown Folks* (1869), chronicling life in a Massachusetts town just after the Revolution, as recalled by a man who grew up in it. YA

Stranger, The (1942) One of the best-known works of *existentialism, this first novel by the French writer *Albert Camus is set in Algeria

Harriet Beecher Stowe

when it was a French possession. The central character, Monsieur Meursault, is emotionally removed from life. At his mother's funeral he shows no signs of grief or sadness, a lack noticed by the other mourners, mostly residents and staff of the rest home in which she lived. He observes but is barely interested in those around him, including his girl friend, whom he does not love but has agreed to marry. Then Meursault is drawn into a neighbor's dispute and commits a completely senseless murder. At his trial, the prosecution depicts him as a soulless monster who did not weep at his own mother's funeral. Meursault feels removed even from his own trial and the resulting death sentence. In his view nothing in life can matter much when everyone is already condemned to death, sooner or later, by "the benign indifference of the universe." If you enjoyed *The Stranger*, try *Crime and Punishment* by *Fyodor Dostoyevsky, a powerful study of crime and conscience. *The Stranger* was adapted for film in 1967. YA

Stranger in a Strange Land (1961) This *science fiction classic is probably *Robert A. Heinlein's best-known novel. It tells of Valentine Michael Smith, the only descendant and survivor of the first human expedition to the planet Mars. Raised by the long-lived and extremely intelligent Martians, Michael has come to think like a Martian and has developed powers unimaginable to his fellow humans. When a relief ship arrives on Mars, Michael is taken back to Earth, where Federation scientists and politicians keep him in medical isolation. Jill Boardman, a nurse, and Ben Caxton, a newspaper reporter, rescue Michael from his virtual prison and whisk him to the home of Jubal Harshaw, an aged, crusty, and wise writer and lawyer. Harshaw takes Michael under his protection and helps him learn about human civilization. Michael finds many human beliefs and practices quite strange. Among the strangest are religion and sex, both of which are totally unknown to Martians. Michael sets out to "grok," that is, to understand completely the peculiar and often hilarious ways of humans. Then, armed with this knowledge, he begins to teach humans what he has learned from the Martians. Michael establishes a religious movement based on "grokking" and centered on the idea that all conscious beings are part of God. The movement enrages many, and Michael is killed by an angry mob. But the seed of his Martian view of life has been planted and will thrive.

Stranger in a Strange Land caused a furor when it was published because of Heinlein's irreverent attitude toward religion, sex, politics, and social values. But Valentine Michael Smith's adventures and observations give the reader a chance to look at these subjects from a new angle and to think about them in different ways. You may not agree with Heinlein's ideas, but you will probably find them intriguing and challenging. YA

Strasser, Todd (1950–) Though he has written short stories and articles as well as an adult novel, Strasser is known best for his more than 10 novels for teenagers. These novels are realistic stories about the lives of today's teenagers. They include *Angel Dust Blues* (1979), about a popular and privileged teenager who rebels

against his parents' expectations by becoming a drug dealer; *Rock 'n' Roll Nights* (1982), about a teenager's struggles to make his band a success in the music world; *Wildlife* (1987), its sequel; and *The Accident* (1988), about a teenager who sets out to learn the truth about a deadly accident that was supposedly caused by his dead friend's drunken driving. Strasser also wrote *Ferris Bueller's Day Off* (1986), the novelization of the 1986 movie of the same name, about the comic adventures of a teenager who plays hookey from school for a day. YA

Stratemeyer, Edward (1862–1930) The author of some 150 books for young people and the originator of more than 1,000 others, Stratemeyer created dozens of book series, including the still-popular Hardy Boys, Nancy Drew, and Tom Swift series. For each group of books, Stratemeyer used a different pen name, including *Victor Appleton for the adventures of the boy inventor Tom Swift, *Carolyn Keene for the Nancy Drew detective stories, and *Franklin W. Dixon for the Hardy Boys detective series. In 1906 Stratemeyer, unable to fill the demand for his books by himself, created the Stratemeyer Syndicate and began hiring other writers to write novels based on detailed plot outlines supplied by Stratemeyer. In all, Stratemeyer wrote or originated about 1,300 novels, which have sold more than 200 million copies. MR

stream of consciousness, or interior monologue, is a literary techique used to present the unspoken thoughts of a character. Such thoughts are often arranged with apparent disregard for logical progression, grammatical correctness, or even punctuation. The character's thoughts tend to spill one upon another, creating a fascinating pattern of observations, memories, and mental associations. In this way the writer can show directly the character's deepest thoughts and feelings. The stream-of-consciousness technique has been used by many writers in the 20th century. Two masters are *William Faulkner, who used it to great effect in *The Sound and the Fury, and *James Joyce, who employed it in his masterwork, *Ulysses.* YA

Street Scene (1929) This play by *Elmer Rice was one of the first dramas to be staged using realistic sound effects throughout the production. The setting is an apartment building in a shabby section of New York City, and the play centers on the people who live there, particularly the members of two families. The first is headed by Frank Maurrant, who ignores his affection-starved wife Anna and their children, Rose and little Willie. The second family includes the elderly Abraham Kaplan, his daughter, Shirley, and his son, Sam, who is in love with Rose. Mr. Maurrant's neglect has driven his wife to seek understanding and friendship from Steve Sankey, a married bill collector. Their relationship has caused much gossip among the tenement's other residents, and even Maurrant suspects that his wife is being unfaithful. When he returns home unexpectedly from work, he finds them together and kills them both. Maurrant evades the police for a time but is finally arrested and taken away. Sam offers to leave school, give up his plans to become a lawyer, and take Rose away, but she decides to move away and dedicate herself to raising Willie. As the play ends, life resumes at the tenement much as before the tragedy. If you enjoyed *Street Scene*, try the play *Dead End* (1936) by Sidney Kingsley (1906–), which depicts the brutalizing effects of poverty and hopelessness on five youths in a slum neighborhood in New York City. *Street Scene* was made into an opera in 1947 by the German composer Kurt Weill (1900–1950), with lyrics by *Langston Hughes. YA

Streetcar Named Desire, A (1947) By *Tennessee Williams, this powerful drama is set in New Orleans in the 1940s. Blanche DuBois has come to visit her sister, Stella, and brother-in-law, Stanley Kowalski. Blanche, who makes a pretense of being refined and sensitive, is the exact opposite of Stanley, who has an animal vitality that easily explodes into cruelty and violence. Blanche has lost the family estate, Belle Reve, and Stanley, resenting her presence and the disruption of his life with Stella, believes she has squandered the family fortune and deprived him of Stella's rightful share of the estate. Blanche is attracted to Stanley's friend Mitch, who seems more refined than his other friends, and gets him to court her. But Stanley discovers and reveals the sordid details of Blanche's recent past to Mitch, depriving Blanche of the imaginary world she has created for herself and destroying her hope to marry Mitch. When Stella goes into the hospital to have her first child, Stanley brutally rapes Blanche. When Stella returns home she refuses to believe Blanche, who has suffered a mental breakdown, and has her committed to a mental institution. *A Streetcar Named Desire* was made into an outstanding movie in 1951. YA

Stuart Little (1945) This young people's classic by *E.B. White tells about Stuart Little, the second son of the Frederick C. Littles, who live in New York City. Stuart is only about two inches tall and looks like a mouse, but his parents and older brother George love him just the same. In fact, everybody except the cat, Snowball, likes Stuart. Stuart has many adventures, such as sailing a toy boat on the pond in Central Park, accidentally getting rolled up in a window shade, and getting trapped in a garbage can and being hauled to a garbage scow. He is rescued from the scow by his best friend, a lovely little bird named Margalo, who has made her home in the Boston fern in the Littles' living room. But when a neighbor cat makes moves to eat Margalo, she flies away. Stuart borrows a model car from his friend Dr. Carey and drives north to find Margalo. Along the way he has more adventures, and as the story ends Stuart is still looking for his friend. If you enjoyed *Stuart Little*, be sure also to read White's story *Charlotte's Web.* Another fun book is *The Mouse and the Motorcycle* by *Beverly Cleary. MR

Styron, William (1925–) Author of *The Long March* and *The Confessions of Nat Turner*, Styron was born and educated in the South, for which he still feels great affection. Like the characters of Culver and Mannix in *The Long March*, Styron served in the U.S. Marine Corps during World War II and briefly during the Korean War. Styron often raises difficult and painful questions in his books and has received some unfavorable criticism for his choice of subject matter. In spite of controversy, he is the winner of many literary awards. Styron says, "The great thing about fiction is that it's like a freight train—it can be loaded with all sorts of things."

Among his novels is *Sophie's Choice* (1979), about a woman sent during World War II to the Auschwitz concentration camp, where she loses her children and much of her self-respect. The novel was adapted for the movies in 1982. YA

Styx was one of the rivers of the ancient Greek underworld or land of the dead. The spirits of the dead were ferried across the river to Hades by the boatman Charon. The gods held sacred any oaths sworn on the name Styx, and anyone who broke such an oath was required to drink from the river, which rendered that person speechless for a year. The river was personified by the nymph Styx, the daughter of the sea gods Oceanus and Tethys. She was considered the guardian of sacred oaths. The river Styx figures in many literary works besides the Greek myths, including *Paradise Lost* by *John Milton and "Inferno," the first part of *The Divine Comedy* (c.1310–1321) by *Dante Alighieri. In a lighter vein, the Styx was the setting for the *fantasy *A Houseboat on the Styx* (1895) by the editor and humorist John Kendrick Bangs (1862–1922), in which a number of fictional, mythical, and historical characters take part in a series of humorous and witty dialogues and adventures. You can also read more about the Styx in *Bulfinch's Mythology* by Thomas Bulfinch (1796–1867) and in *Mythology* by Edith Hamilton (1867–1963). MR & YA

Sula (1973) By *Toni Morrison, this novel is set in the fictional river town of Medallion, Ohio, from 1919 to 1965, specifically the black community known as the Bottom. The central characters are two young black girls, Sula Peace and her best friend, Nel Wright. As children they share all their thoughts and experiences. While playing with Nel by the river, Sula accidentally drowns the boy Chicken Little. The two decide not to tell anyone what happened, even after the boy's body is found. This conspiracy of silence draws the girls closer together for a time, but the tragedy combines with other events in Sula's life to increase her sense of isolation, even from Nel.

As they grow up Nel and Sula take different paths. After Nel marries Jude Greene and settles down to family life in the Bottom, Sula leaves home for college and the larger world. Ten years later Sula returns, seduces Jude, and destroys Nel's marriage and their friendship. Sula is regarded by the community as a witch and seductress. She falls in love with a man named Ajax, but her possessiveness drives him away. When Sula becomes ill Nel visits her, but Sula dies before the two can become reconciled. Years later, Nel overcomes her hatred for Sula's actions and grieves over her friend's death. Intertwined with the story of Sula and Nel is the story of the Bottom, whose residents almost always turn their fear and anger inward upon themselves and each other. If you enjoyed *Sula*, try also *The Color Purple* by *Alice Walker, which also deals with the friendship of two black women but is quite different in outcome. YA

Sullivan, Arthur See *William S. Gilbert.

Summer of the Swans, The (1970) By *Betsy Byars, this novel takes place in a small West Virginia town when Sara Godfrey is 14 years old. For her it is a time of restlessness and discontent, when she is bored one moment and furious or wildly happy the next. She thinks a lot about her appearance, which she hates, and wants desperately to look like her pretty older sister, Wanda. Sara's mother is dead and her father has remarried, leaving Sara, Wanda, and their 10-year-old brother, Charlie, in the care of Aunt Willie. Charlie is mentally retarded and does not speak. Sara protects him as best she can from the thoughtless teasing of the neighborhood children.

When Sara takes Charlie to the lake to look at a flock of swans, the boy is fascinated and Sara has a hard time getting him home. That night, when everyone is asleep, Charlie wanders out of the house in his pajamas and slippers to find the swans and becomes lost in the woods. In the morning the family discovers he is gone and the search begins. Sara especially is upset and worried as the day drags on without a sign of Charlie. Then she grudgingly accepts the help of Joe Melby, whom she has long thought of as a "fink," and discovers as they search together that he is a very nice person. When Charlie at last answers Sara's shouts, from the bottom of a forest ravine, she is filled with gratitude and pure happiness, and races to comfort him. The love in Charlie's face when he sees her and the realization of how much he needs her make her own problems seem unimportant and enlarge her understanding of others. *The Summer of the Swans* won the *Newbery Medal in 1971. MR

Sun Also Rises, The (1926) This novel by *Ernest Hemingway is set in France and Spain in 1925. Its narrator, Jake Barnes, is an American working as a newspaper correspondent in Paris. Jake is in love with Lady Brett Ashley but, because of war injuries, he is unable to achieve a physical relationship with her. Brett is in the process of divorcing Lord Ashley to marry a bankrupt Scotsman, Mike Campbell. Another American, Robert Cohn, champion college boxer turned novelist, falls in love with Brett during a brief affair. Jake, his friend Bill Gorton, and Cohn travel to Spain to fish, planning to meet Brett and Mike in Pamplona for the weeklong fiesta of the bulls, but Cohn leaves them to be with Brett. When the five get together in Pamplona, Cohn is still following Brett around, unable to believe their affair meant nothing and undaunted by Mike's anti-Semitic remarks and vicious attempts to drive him away. At the festival Brett falls for a talented young bullfighter, Pedro Romero, and

Jake introduces her to him. Cohn, enraged and jealous, beats up Jake, Mike, and Romero before Brett finally drives him away. After the festival Brett goes off with Romero, and the others separate.

The Sun Also Rises is a powerful depiction of Hemingway's own *Lost Generation, those whose faith in earlier values and codes of conduct was shattered by the horror of World War I. Only Robert Cohn, with his romantic view of love, has any real connection with the old way of life, but now he is sadly out of place. If you enjoyed *The Sun Also Rises*, read also *The Great Gatsby* by *F. Scott Fitzgerald, which is set on the American side of the Atlantic during the same era. *The Sun Also Rises* was filmed in 1957 and for television in 1984. YA

Superfudge (1980) In this novel by *Judy Blume, 10-year-old Peter Hatcher is the narrator of the events in his family's life, which at times he finds hard to understand. He has adjusted to his younger brother, Fudge, but is upset when he is told there is to be another child in the family. Soon, however, Peter accepts his baby sister, but Fudge wants to get rid of her and is willing to pay someone to take her. Peter is also upset when he is told the family is moving from New York City to Princeton, New Jersey. He does find a new friend there, but Fudge has trouble with a kindergarten teacher who insists on calling him by his proper name, Farley. After a year in Princeton, the family must decide whether to stay or move back to the city. This time the decision is made by everyone concerned, and as a result everyone is satisfied with the move back. Meanwhile, Fudge has adjusted to his new sister. The book has the warm atmosphere of a family that learns to discuss matters of concern to all while keeping a sense of humor. If you wish to read more books about families and their problems, try *A Fine White Dust* by *Cynthia Rylant and *Let the Circle Be Unbroken* by *Mildred Taylor. MR

Sutcliff, Rosemary (1920–1992) An English novelist, Sutcliff wrote more than 30 historical novels that bring to life English history from the pre-Roman age through the times of the Roman, Saxon, Viking, and Norman invasions. Her love of English history and literature began in childhood, when she suffered a serious illness and spent many hours listening to her mother read such stories as *Beowulf and the adventures of *Robin Hood and *King Arthur. Sutcliff's books include *The Shield Ring* (1956), about Viking settlers in northern England in the 11th century; *The Witch's Brat* (1970), about a boy in 12th-century England, a crippled outcast who makes his way in the world and finds happiness through his knowledge of healing herbs and skills; *Sun Horse, Moon Horse* (1978), about a boy growing up in Britain before the arrival of the Romans; and *Frontier Wolf* (1980), set in the Roman province of Britain in the 4th century, about a young Roman officer given the dangerous task of commanding a garrison of British warriors known as the "Frontier Wolves." MR

Swallows and Amazons (1931) This novel by *Arthur Ransome tells of the adventures of four English children, John, Susan, Titty, and Roger Walker, during their summer vacation on a lake. The fun begins after they get permission to sail their small boat, *Swallow*, to an island in the middle of the lake and to camp and explore there. On their way to the island they pass by a houseboat with a man and a parrot aboard, and Titty decides the man is a retired pirate. On the island, they meet two girls, Nancy and Peggy Blackett, owners of the sailboat *Amazon*, and learn that the pirate whom Titty has named Captain Flint is really the Blackett girls' Uncle Jim. Last year he joined Nancy and Peggy in their summer fun and even gave them the *Amazon*, but this year he has betrayed them by staying away and working on a book. The Amazons and the Swallows become uneasy allies, determined to make Uncle Jim join the fun or else walk the plank. Then someone breaks into the houseboat and steals the book. Worst of all, Uncle Jim suspects the Swallows of the theft. The Swallows and Amazons find a happy ending to the war

with Uncle Jim, and together they find a buried treasure—the book—and solve the crime. You can read about the children's further adventures in *Swallowdale* (1931) and in 10 other Swallows and Amazons novels. MR

Swarthout, Glendon (Fred) (1918–) A teacher of English and the author of 10 novels, including *Bless the Beasts and Children, Swarthout has also collaborated with his wife, Kathryn Swarthout (1919–), on a number of books for younger readers, including *The Button Boat* (1969), about a brother and sister whose lives of poverty and neglect are changed when they find a black valise full of stolen money while clamming in their boat, and *whales to see The* (1975), about problems faced by a group of young people with learning disabilities. Some of his early novels have been made into movies, including *They Came to Cordura* (1958), produced in 1959, a story of bravery and cowardice during the border conflicts between the United States and Mexico in 1916. *Where the Boys Are* (1960), filmed in 1961, is a comedy about college students on spring vacation in Florida. *The Shootist* (1975), produced in 1976, centers on a famous gunfighter, dying of cancer, who resolves to help a town get rid of three troublemakers. MR & YA

Swift, Jonathan (1667–1745) Known best for his masterful *satire of human nature, *Gulliver's Travels, Swift was born in Ireland of English parents. He spent several years of his childhood in England, then returned to Ireland. There he grew up and was educated, ordained a priest in the Anglican church, and eventually made dean of St. Patrick's Church in Dublin. Though he followed a career in the church, Swift found his greatest interest lay in the political, social, and literary events of his day, and many of his writings were inspired by them. He wrote poetry, letters, and political tracts, but today he is remembered for his satires, whose keen insights into human nature and follies have appealed to readers around the world. Among them is *The Battle of the Books* (1704), in which a debate over the relative merits of ancient and modern literary works turns into a pitched battle between the ancients, including *Homer, *Aristotle, and *Plato, and the moderns, whose champions include *John Milton. It was published with *A Tale of a Tub*, a satire on religious hypocrisy. Probably his best-known satire, after *Gulliver's Travels*, is *A Modest Proposal* (1729), a bitter tract suggesting that the way to ease hunger and suffering in Ireland would be to sell Irish babies for the rich to dine on. You can find good selections of Swift's writings in a number of books, including *The Portable Swift* (1948), edited by Carl Van Doren (1885–1950), and *Gulliver's Travels and Other Writings* (1958), edited by Ricardo Quintana (1898–). YA

Swiss Family Robinson, The (1813) By Johann David Wyss (1743–1818), this is a classic tale of survival, adventure, and wondrous discovery. In the 18th century, a Swiss family emigrating to the New World is shipwrecked and isolated for 10 years on a deserted island in the southern Pacific Ocean. Pastor Robinson, his wife, Elizabeth, and their four sons, Fritz, Ernest, Jack, and Francis, find themselves the only survivors, alone on a primitive island filled with strange, beautiful creatures and exotic plants and fruits. With what supplies and domestic animals they are able to salvage from the remains of their ship, and using nature's generous local bounty, they build and furnish a home — indeed, a compound — working the land like a plantation to provide a variety of food and materials, even medicines. Though threatened by wild animals and Malay pirates, the Robinsons employ imagination, inventiveness, resourcefulness, and a positive practical attitude in the service of survival. Ultimately they have four homes: Filsenheim, their grotto winter retreat; Falcon's Nest, their tree-house country villa; and Waldegg and Prospect Hill, their mountain cottages. They are proud to say they live in "almost European luxury." The Robinsons demonstrate the happy rewards of a positive attitude, hard work, and discipline, as well as the joys of an affectionate family cooperating for survival and adventure. *The Swiss Family Robinson* was made into a *Walt Disney feature film in 1960. MR & YA

Sword in the Stone, The (1939) This is the story of the boyhood of *King Arthur by *T.H. White. Wart, the adopted son of Sir Ector, lives in a castle on the fringe of the Forest Sauvage. He and his brother, Kay, lose a trained hawk in the forest, and Wart bravely follows it alone, deep into the wild woods. There he finds the Magician, Merlyn [*Merlin], who comes home with him bringing his talking owl, Archimedes. Wart has found a magical tutor. Through Merlyn's sorcery, Wart experiences life as a perch in the castle moat and as a trained hawk. He travels the night on the wing with Archimedes and meets the owl's mother, the goddess of wisdom, Athene [*Athena]. He lives as a serpent and a badger. He even observes the creation of the world and life itself. He has adventures with a fellow named Robin Wood and with Marian, and rescues King Pellinore from a giant's castle, with help from the Questing Beast. Wart is always a kind person, but his adventures teach him wisdom. In the end, through Merlyn's magic, he is the only person in England who can pull the sword from the stone. He becomes King Arthur, a wise leader who is able to unite the warring British kings and knights against invaders. The story of this legendary king as told by T.H. White continues in *The Once and Future King*. The first book of *The Once and Future King* is entitled *The Sword in the Stone*, but the separately published version is somewhat different and more fun to read. *The Sword in the Stone* was filmed in 1963. MR & YA

symbol See *sign and symbol.

symbolism, a literary movement that experimented with symbolic language and new literary forms to evoke the essence of individual experience, developed in the 19th century. It reached its peak in France in the 1880s and 1890s among a group of poets and artists who sought to break away from the rigid forms and conventions of the past. American writers who made important use of symbols in their works included *Edgar Allan Poe, *Nathaniel Hawthorne, and *Herman Melville. Poe's writings were an important influence on the French poet Charles Baudelaire (1821–1867), who in turn inspired many other French symbolists, including Arthur Rimbaud (1854–1891), Paul Verlaine (1844–1896), and Stéphane Mallarmé (1842–1898). Symbolism extended into art and theater as well. Though the movement declined after 1900, it influenced many 20th-century writers, notably *T.S. Eliot, *James Joyce, *D.H. Lawrence, and *William Butler Yeats. Two good books on symbolism are *The Symbolist Movement in Literature* (1899) by the English poet and critic Arthur W. Symons (1865–1945) and *Axel's Castle* (1931) by Edmund Wilson (1895–1972). See also *sign and symbol. YA

Symons, Julian (Gustave) (1912–) This English author has written poetry, serious novels, crime and detective fiction, and biographies, including those of *Arthur Conan Doyle and *Dashiell Hammett. The first of his 26 mystery novels was *The Immaterial Murder Case* (1945), about an odd art movement called Immaterialism and a body found among a group of statues. *The Man Who Killed Himself* (1967) is the story of a person with a split personality who commits a perfect crime. *The Blackheath Poisoning* (1978) is set in a London suburb in the late 19th century. Several deaths strike a family, who live in a luxurious mansion. The setting for *The Kentish Manor Murders* (1988) is an English country house where an aging actor is to portray *Sherlock Holmes, only to find it necessary to act like the great detective in self-protection. In *A Reasonable Doubt* (1960) Symons describes 13 real-life criminal cases in which there is some question as to whether or not the verdict was correct, and in *The Great Detectives* (1981) he describes detectives other authors have created. If you like these books, try those of *Margery Allingham, *P.D. James, *Ngaio Marsh, and *Ruth Rendell. YA

Synge, John Millington (1871–1909) An Irish dramatist known best as the author of *The Playboy of the Western World*, Synge was influenced early in his writing career by *William Butler Yeats, whom he met while working as a critic in Paris. Yeats told Synge to go live among the poor, hard-working folk of the Aran Islands, off the western coast of Ireland, and use their lives and traditions as his inspiration. Synge eventually followed Yeats's advice, writing six plays in a brief career. His plays are noted for their beautiful, almost musical dialogue and their fascinating characters. *Riders to the Sea* (1903) is a tragedy centering on a woman of Aran who fears that her sixth and last surviving son will be drowned on a planned trip to the mainland. *In the Shadow of the Glen* (1904) is a comedy set in western Ireland about a farmer who feigns death in order to test his wife's faithfulness, only to find that his deception drives her away from him. Synge also wrote *The Aran Islands* (1907), describing his experiences and observations during the time he lived there. Synge's plays and other writings have been published in a number of editions, including *The Complete Plays of John M. Synge* (1960) and *The Collected Works of John Millington Synge* (1962–1968). YA

Tale of Two Cities, A (1859) A novel by *Charles Dickens, set in Paris and London during the French Revolution, it begins: "It was the best of times, it was the worst of times. . . ." In chilling detail, it describes the abyss between rich and poor in both cities and the upheavals in France that reached their climax in the Terror. Manette, a French doctor, is called to treat two patients under unusual circumstances. Taken to the chateau of the Marquis St. Evrémonde, he tends a young peasant woman in a dangerous state of shock. Her brother is dying from wounds received while trying to protect her from the attentions of the Marquis and his brother. Dr. Manette cannot save the two victims, and Evrémonde has him sent to prison to keep the matter quiet.

When Dr. Manette is released after 18 years in the Bastille, a French prison in Paris, he is almost mad from despair. His condition improves after he is reunited with his daughter, Lucie, and is brought to safety in England. Lucie marries Charles Darnay, a French noble who has given up his inheritance to protest against his family's harsh treatment of its peasant laborers. Darnay confesses to Manette that he is the nephew of the infamous Evrémonde. An old family servant writes to Darnay, begging him to help clear the charges that may result in his execution. Darnay leaves for France to assist, but is arrested and sentenced to death as a nobleman.

Sydney Carton, a friend of the Darnays, is an unpromising English barrister, hopelessly in love with Lucie. His life is ruined by drink, but he will do anything for Lucie's happiness. In Paris, Carton devises a daring plan. He arranges to have Darnay smuggled out of prison and succeeds in taking his place among those going to the guillotine. Strengthened by his love for Lucie, he faces death calmly. His last thoughts, and the last words of the novel, are, "It is a far, far better thing that I do, than I have ever done; it is a far, far better rest that I go to than I have ever known." Another exciting novel of the French Revolution you might enjoy is *The Scarlet Pimpernel* by *Baroness Orczy. Of the several film versions made of *A Tale of Two Cities*, the best are those of 1935 and 1958. YA

Tales from Shakespeare (1806) This collection of stories by *Charles Lamb and Mary Lamb (1764–1847) is a retelling in simplified form of 20 plays by *William Shakespeare. Even though the retellings make it easy for younger readers to enjoy the stories behind Shakespeare's plays, they use Shakespeare's own words whenever possible. This gives young readers a taste of Shakespeare's poetic talents and prepares them to enjoy the plays more fully when they are ready to read them. The tales include many of Shakespeare's most popular plays, including *As You Like It, *Hamlet, *King Lear, *Macbeth, *A Midsummer Night's Dream, *Othello, *Romeo and Juliet, and *The Tempest.

If you enjoyed *Tales from Shakespeare*, you will probably also want to read *Stories from Shakespeare* (1956) by Marchette Chute (1909–), which includes retellings of all Shakespeare's plays. Another good book is *The Children's Shakespeare* (1897, 1938) by the English writer E(dith) Nesbit (1858–1924), which retells 12 plays. MR

Tales of Uncle Remus, The (1987) This collection of black folktales retold by *Julius Lester is subtitled *The Adventures of Brer Rabbit*. It brings together 48 of the more than 250 *Uncle Remus tales about Brer Rabbit and his friends written by *Joel Chandler Harris. Though countless readers, young and old, have enjoyed the original tales, others have difficulty with Harris's efforts to re-create the language of the black people who told him the stories. Julius Lester has captured the beauty and wonder of the original tales while making them easier for modern young people to enjoy. Among the tales is the story of Brer Rabbit and the *Tar-Baby, probably the best-known Uncle Remus story of all. If you enjoyed *The Tales of Uncle Remus*, you will want to read Lester's other collections of Uncle Remus stories, *More Tales of Uncle Remus: Further Adventures of Brer Rabbit, His Friends, Enemies, and Others* (1988); and *Further Tales of Uncle Remus: The Misadventures of Brer Rabbit, Brer Fox, Brer Wolf, the Doodang, and Other Creatures* (1990). MR

tall tale A type of folktale, a tall tale is a far-fetched, exaggerated, or outright impossible story that is related as if it were completely true. The humorous and highly imaginative adventures of *Baron Munchausen were early examples of tall tales, and *Washington Irving used the tall tale in his comic *History of New York* (1809), supposedly written by one *Diedrich Knickerbocker. The tall tale flourished on the American frontier, which provided such larger-than-life heroes as *Paul Bunyan, *Davy Crockett, *Mike Fink, and *John Henry. Western tall tales were an early influence on *Mark Twain, who included them in many of his works, including *Roughing It* (1872), about his experiences in Nevada, California, and Hawaii, and in *Life on the Mississippi*. There are many collections of tall tales about specific American folk heroes, but another good general source is *A Treasury of American Folklore* (1944) by B.A. Botkin (1901–1975). MR & YA

Talmud, from the Hebrew meaning learning or study, is the collection of Jewish oral law, tradition, and commentary that is the recognized authority for Jews all over the world. It is divided into two parts. The Mishna contains the oral laws that supplement those of the Scriptures, while the Gemara includes rabbinical interpretations and elaborations on the Mishna. Compiled originally by Jewish scholars of the 1st century A.D., it has become a storehouse of information and comment on many subjects. *The Chosen* by *Chaim Potok is a novel that explores the effect of Talmudic law and study on daily life. See also *Judaism and the *Bible. YA

Tanglewood Tales (1853) A classic for young readers, this collection by *Nathaniel Hawthorne contains six stories of Greek mythology. The stories include the tale of the *Minotaur; "The Pygmies," in which the hero *Hercules comes upon a race of very small people and defeats their champion, a giant named Antaeus; "The Dragon's Teeth," about what happens to Prince Cadmus of Phoenicia when he sets out to find his lost sister, Europa; "Circe's Palace," about how *Ulysses saves his crewmen from the enchantress Circe after she turns them into swine; "The Pomegranate Seeds," about *Pluto's kidnapping of Proserpine, or *Persephone, to the Underworld; and "The Golden Fleece," about the quest of *Jason and the Argonauts for the prized gold sheepskin. If you enjoy these stories, you will also like the six stories from Greek myth collected in Hawthorne's *A Wonder-Book for Girls and Boys*. MR & YA

Tar-Baby is one of the best-loved characters created by *Joel Chandler Harris in his *Uncle

Remus stories. Brer Fox, determined to catch Brer Rabbit and have him for dinner, mixes up a batch of tar in the shape of a baby, puts a hat on it, places it in the road, and then hides in the brush to see what will happen. Brer Rabbit comes along and greets the Tar-Baby. When he gets no answer he becomes angry and slaps it. His hand becomes attached to the sticky tar, and soon his other hand and his feet are stuck as well. Brer Rabbit must use all his wits to outsmart Brer Fox and escape. You can read about the Tar-Baby in *Uncle Remus: His Songs and His Sayings* (1880), which is available in both hardcover and paperback and is probably in your library. The Tar-Baby story also appears in *The Tales of Uncle Remus* as retold by *Julius Lester. MR

Brer Fox sets up the Tar-Baby, a sticky trap for Brer Rabbit.

Tara is the beautiful plantation home of the O'Hara family in *Gone With the Wind* by *Margaret Mitchell. In the early 1800s Gerald O'Hara, an Irish immigrant living in Savannah, wins the plantation, located near Atlanta, Georgia, in a poker game. He names it Tara, adds to its property, and with slave labor builds a sprawling, whitewashed brick mansion that looks out over broad cotton fields and rich pine forests. He instills in his daughter Scarlett his love of Tara, and during the Civil War and the postwar period known as Reconstruction, Scarlett kills, marries, wheels and deals, and does whatever it takes to keep and protect Tara. During the war the plantation house is spared destruction to serve as a Union army headquarters, but the fences, barns, and stables are all torn down and used for firewood, the livestock are killed, and many household treasures are carried off. Scarlett defends the plantation, first from Yankee soldiers and later from crooked carpetbaggers and speculators. Tara can be viewed as a *symbol of pre-war Southern plantation society. You may like to compare it with *Jalna, the Canadian home of the Whiteoak family in the Jalna novels by *Mazo de la Roche. YA

Tarkington, (Newton) Booth (1869–1946) An enormously popular novelist and playwright, Tarkington grew up in a middle-class home in Indiana, then attended Princeton University, where he concentrated on his skills as a writer and illustrator. After completing college but failing to receive a degree, Tarkington returned home and struggled for several years to establish himself. His first novel, *The Gentleman from Indiana* (1899), about a young man's battle to fight greed and political corruption in his small Indiana town, was a great success. He followed it with *Monsieur Beaucaire* (1900), a short novel about the adventures of a French duke, a cousin to King Louis XV, who travels to England disguised as the French ambassador's barber. His best-known novels include *The Magnificent Ambersons* (1918), about the spoiled and snobbish son of a once wealthy, but now disintegrating, Middle Western family; and *Alice Adams. Tarkington also wrote several delightful books for younger readers, including *Seventeen* (1916), about a 17-year-old boy and the problems he has dealing with his first romance, and the classic *Penrod. Several of Tarkington's novels were made into movies, including *The Magnificent Ambersons* in 1942. MR & YA

Tarzan, the enduring character created by Edgar Rice Burroughs (1875–1950), was introduced to readers in the novel *Tarzan of the Apes* (1912). The story begins with his English parents, Lord Greystoke and his wife, Lady Alice. They are cast ashore on the western coast of Africa following a mutiny aboard the ship on which they had been traveling, and their son is born in the jungle. When the boy is a year old, his parents die and he is raised by the great ape Kala, of the tribe of Kerchak. He is given the name Tarzan, which in ape language means "white skin." He grows up to be powerful, clever, and deadly. He eventually kills Kerchak and becomes king of the apes. But when men come to the jungle, Tarzan learns of his parents and heritage and discovers that he is a man caught between two worlds, neither of which he can truly call his own. Burroughs wrote 23 more books following Tarzan's adventures, including *The Return of Tarzan* (1915), *The Son of Tarzan* (1917), *Tarzan and the Golden Lion* (1923), and *Tarzan and the City of Gold* (1933). Over 30 movies based on the Tarzan stories have been made, as well as a comic strip and several radio and television series. YA

Taylor, Mildred D. (1943–) The author of a number of highly praised novels dealing with racism, Taylor was born in Jackson, Mississippi, and grew up in Ohio. A great influence on her life was her father, who told her stories about their family, which had owned land and lived in Mississippi for generations. These stories were the basis for her novel *Roll of Thunder, Hear My Cry*, about the Logans, a black family living in Mississippi in the 1930s. Taylor continued the story of young Cassie Logan and her family in *Let the Circle Be Unbroken*. Taylor's other books include *Song of the Trees* (1975), in which an unscrupulous white man tries to cut down the trees growing on the Logan family's farm while Cassie's father is away working for the railroad; and *Mississippi Bridge* (1990), in which the Logans and other black families are spared from a tragic bus accident after the bus driver orders all black passengers off to make room for more whites. MR

Taylor, Robert Lewis (1912–) Though he wrote more than a dozen books, Taylor is probably known best for his novel *The Travels of Jaimie McPheeters* (1958), which recounts the adventures of a 14-year-old boy who sets out from his home in Louisville, Kentucky, in 1849 to join the *Gold Rush to California. Like Lewis's other novels, it is filled with exciting adventures, fascinating characters, sparkling humor, and a wealth of historical detail. Taylor's other novels include *A Journey to Matecumbe* (1961), about a 13-year-old Kentucky boy who in 1870 travels with his uncle to Upper Matecumbe Island (now Islamorada) in the Florida Keys to hunt treasure and make a new life; *Two Roads to Guadalupe* (1964), following the adventures of two brothers in the Mexican War; and *Niagara* (1980), centering on a young newspaperman sent by his paper to the newly built resort town of Niagara Falls, New York, in the mid-1800s. Taylor has also written a number of biographies, including *W.C. Fields: His Follies and Fortunes* (1949), about the comedian W.C. Fields (1879–1946), and *Vessel of Wrath: The Life and Times of Carry Nation* (1966), about the temperance agitator Carry Nation (1846–1911). *The Travels of Jaimie McPheeters* was adapted for television in 1960 and *A Journey to Matecumbe* was made into the film *The Treasure of Matecumbe* in 1976. YA

Taylor, Sydney (Brenner) (1904?–1978) The author of a popular series of books about five Jewish girls growing up in New York City in the early 1900s, Taylor did not start out to be a writer. Her first love was dancing, and she was an actress and dancer for a number of years. Her daughter's interest and delight in Taylor's stories of growing up in the Lower East Side of New York led to Taylor's first book, *The All-of-a-Kind Family* (1951), which tells of the experiences of Ella, Henny, Sarah, Charlotte, and Gertie and their little brother, Charlie. Its success led to four sequels, *More All-of-a-Kind Family* (1954), *All-of-a-Kind Family Uptown* (1957), *All-of-a-Kind Family Downtown* (1972), and *Ella of All-of-a-Kind Family* (1978). The stories recapture such simple but priceless memories as the warmth of the coal stove in the kitchen on a cold winter day; the joy of Friday, library day; the wonderful music of the organ grinder; the last day of school; and the beauty of the Jewish holidays. MR

Taylor, Theodore (1921–) Though he is probably known best for his novel *The Cay*, about a young white boy and an aged black man who are shipwrecked in the Caribbean during World War II, Taylor has written more than 30 books for young people. Taylor began writing when he was a teenager, but his love of adventure led him to work at many jobs, including merchant seaman, naval officer, newspaperman, and filmmaker. A number of Taylor's books are based on his sea experiences during World War II and his interest in the major naval battles of the war. They include *Air Raid—Pearl Harbor! The Story of December 7, 1941* (1971) and *Battle in the Arctic Seas: The Story of Convoy PQ 17* (1976). Taylor's novels include *The Children's War* (1971), about a boy living in a remote Alaskan settlement that is seized by Japanese invaders during World War II; *Walking Up a Rainbow* (1986), set in the American West during the 1850s, about a teenage girl who, in order to raise enough money to save her family's Iowa home, drives a herd of sheep to California and, along the way, falls in love with a handsome young cowboy; and *The Hostage* (1987), about a father and son who catch a killer whale and must decide whether to turn it over to an aquarium for a $100,000 reward or set it free again. MR & YA

Teasdale, Sarah (1884–1933) A poet whose works are noted for their simple grace, lyric beauty, and intensity of feeling, Teasdale began writing in childhood. A frail and sickly girl, she was educated at home and later in a private school, then traveled widely in Europe for a time. She became associated with a literary group forming in Chicago, where she met the poet Vachel Lindsay (1879–1931), who fell in love with her. Teasdale was attracted to Lindsay but also frightened by him, and she finally married a St. Louis businessman. However, her reclusive nature and her husband's frequent business travels abroad drew them apart, and they divorced in 1929. Teasdale moved to New York and became ever more reclusive. She died after taking an overdose of sleeping medicine. Her collections include *Helen of Troy and Other Poems* (1911), *Love Songs* (1917), *Strange Victory* (1933), and *Collected Poems* (1937). Teasdale also compiled a popular anthology of poems for younger readers, *Rainbow Gold* (1922). If you enjoy Teasdale's poems, try also those of *Edna St. Vincent Millay. MR & YA

Tell, William A legendary hero of Switzerland, William Tell was supposed to have lived in the late 13th and early 14th centuries, when Switzerland was governed by Austria. According to legend, Tell refused to pay homage to the hat of the Austrian governor of Uri, a Swiss canton, or district, because the hat was a symbol of Austrian rule. For this defiance, Tell was seized and forced to shoot an apple off his own son's head. Later Tell killed the governor and helped organize Swiss patriots to fight the Austrians. There are several good retellings for younger readers of the William Tell legend, including *The Story of William Tell* (1960) by Aliki (Brandenberg) (1929–), *William Tell and His Son* (1965) by the German writer Bettina Hürlimann (1909–1983), and *William Tell* (1981) by *Nina Bawden. Older readers might like the poetic drama *Wilhelm Tell* (1804) by the German poet Friedrich von Schiller (1759–1805). The opera *William Tell* (1829) by the Italian composer Gioacchino Antonio Rossini (1792–1868) was based on the legend. MR & YA

"Tell-Tale Heart, The" (1843) This powerful tale is one of *Edgar Allan Poe's best-known stories. The narrator begins by stating that disease has sharpened his senses, especially his sense of hearing, but he denies that he is mad. He tells of an old man who lived with him in the same house, and how the man's "evil eye" and the sound of his beating heart drove him to murder the man and hide his body under the floorboards of his room. When the police arrive, the killer shows them the man's room and convinces them that nothing is amiss. Yet, as they chat, the killer hears the sound of the old man's heart beating louder and louder, until he can no longer stand it and reveals the crime and where he has hidden the body. The story gains much of its horror from Poe's exploration of the killer's mind. If you enjoyed "The Tell-Tale Heart," try also Poe's story "The Black Cat"

The killer surprises his victim in
"The Tell-Tale Heart."

(1843), about an eerie cat that drives a man to murder his own wife, then leads the police to her corpse. YA

Tempest, The (1623) The last play written by *William Shakespeare, this very poetic, bittersweet comedy has remained over the centuries one of Shakespeare's most popular works. It is set on an island in the Mediterranean Sea, and the action takes place over the course of a few hours. The play opens as a ship bearing King Alonso of Naples, his brother, Sebastian, son, Ferdinand, and counselor, Gonzalo, as well as Duke Antonio of Milan, is returning from Africa. There the king's daughter has been married to the king of Tunis. A powerful storm has blown up, and the ship runs aground on an island, its passengers scattered along the shore. Ferdinand has become separated from his father, who thinks him dead, and he is the first to meet the island's main inhabitants, Prospero and his lovely daughter, Miranda. Unknown to Ferdinand, Prospero is the rightful duke of Milan, usurped by his brother, Antonio, with Alonso's collusion, and cast out with Miranda to die on the sea. However, they reached the island where, by virtue of his knowledge of magic, Prospero has freed the imprisoned "airy spirit" Ariel and made Caliban, the deformed offspring of a witch and a devil, his slave. Through his magic powers and the help of Ariel, Prospero has created the storm and forced his enemies ashore. Yet Prospero is not interested in revenge. Through the power of enchantment, he brings Alonso and Antonio to confess and repent their crime, regains his dukedom, and unites Milan and Naples by bringing Ferdinand and Miranda together. He also prevents a plot by Antonio and Sebastian against Alonso, and another led by Caliban against Prospero himself. At play's end, all wrongs are righted, all wrongdoers forgiven. Prospero, who began the drama with a tempest, prepares for his return to Milan and retirement, promising his fellow travelers "calm seas, auspicious gales." MR & YA

Ten Commandments, The (or Decalogue, meaning "10 words"). This series of laws, forming a basis for the Christian, Jewish, and Muslim ethical systems, was, according to the account in *Exodus in the Old Testament of the *Bible, handed down from God to *Moses on Mt. Sinai on two stone tablets. The Commandments forbid murder, theft, adultery, false witness (lying), covetousness, and the worship of graven images, and call upon everyone to honor father and mother, to keep the Sabbath, to worship no other God, and to avoid taking God's name in vain. Two movies entitled *The Ten Commandments* were made in 1923 and 1956. Both were spectaculars directed by Cecil B. DeMille (1881–1959), who was noted for the epic scale of his productions.

Tender Is the Night (1934), a novel by *F. Scott Fitzgerald, is set in Europe in the 1920s and examines the relationship between two

American expatriates, Dick Diver, a brilliant and promising psychiatrist, and his wife and former patient, Nicole. Diver had met Nicole Warren at a Swiss mental institution where he had been doing research work. He fell in love with the beautiful Nicole and, despite his professional reservations, married her. Nicole had suffered a breakdown after an incestuous relationship with her father, a wealthy Chicagoan. Nicole found in Dick the strength and solidity her own personality lacked. Dick's success at the clinic in Zurich and Nicole's wealth enable them to divide their time between Switzerland and a beautiful summer home on the Riviera. There Dick meets Rosemary Hoyt, an 18-year-old actress who falls instantly in love with him. Though Dick resists Rosemary's advances, the event later causes Nicole to have an emotional relapse.

The pressures of Nicole's illness, her wealth, and Dick's own sense of unfulfilled early promise drive him to drink, which weakens his marriage. He has an unsatisfactory affair with Rosemary, is arrested and beaten up by the police after a drunken dispute with a taxi driver, and is forced to give up his partnership in the Zurich clinic. Yet as Dick's personality unravels, Nicole's begins to solidify. She slowly ends her dependence on Dick's strength and begins to direct her own affairs. She begins a romance with Tommy Barban, a war hero, mercenary, and longtime admirer. Dick accepts the fact that Nicole is now well and that their marriage is over. He divorces Nicole, and returns to America, where he eventually drifts into anonymity.

Tender Is the Night reflects Fitzgerald's own struggles with his wife Zelda's mental illness, his early and overwhelming success, and his battle with drinking. If you enjoyed it, try also *Save Me the Waltz* (1932) by Zelda Fitzgerald (1900–1948), an autobiographical novel that further illuminates the lives of Scott and Zelda Fitzgerald. A wonderful biography is *Zelda by Nancy Milford (1938–). *Tender Is the Night* was adapted for film in 1962. YA

Tennyson, Alfred [Alfred, Lord Tennyson] (1809–1892) One of the leading English poets of the 19th century, Tennyson is today known best for his Arthurian epic, *Idylls of the King. Tennyson began writing poetry while still a boy. One of his early heroes was the poet *George Gordon Byron, and many of the poems in his first collection, *Poems by Two Brothers* (1827), written with his brother Charles (1808–1879), imitated Byron's poems. Perhaps the greatest influence on young Tennyson was his close friend Arthur Henry Hallam (1811–1833). Hallam's sudden death was a tremendous blow to Tennyson, but from this tragedy he produced one of his best-known poems, the elegy "In Memoriam" (1850). By the time of its publication, Tennyson had published several works, including the collection *Poems* (1833), which included "The Lady of Shallot," about a beautiful woman living on an enchanted river island whose love for Sir Lancelot leads to her death, and "The Lotos-Eaters" (1833), based on the story in the *Odyssey about the land where travelers lose all memory and desire after eating the lotus fruit. In 1850, following the death of *William Wordsworth, Tennyson was made poet laureate of England. His later poems included "The Charge of the Light Brigade" (1854), about the ill-fated British cavalry charge at Balaclava during the Crimean War; his masterpiece, *Idylls of the King*; and "Crossing the Bar" (1889), in which the poet speaks of his own approaching death and calls on those he leaves behind not to mourn. There are a number of editions and selections of Tennyson's poems, including *The Poetic and Dramatic Works of Alfred, Lord Tennyson* (1898) and *Poems of Alfred, Lord Tennyson* (1964). MR & YA

Terabithia is the imaginary secret country invented by Leslie Burke and Jess Aarons in the novel *Bridge to Terabithia* by *Katherine Patterson. Jess and Leslie are in the fifth grade, and they each have reason to feel lonely. Jess is an artist, but no one in his rural Virginia community thinks much of drawing, and Leslie has just moved from a wealthy suburban community and feels lost in her new surroundings. Together, using clues from *The Chronicles of Narnia by *C.S. Lewis, they invent and become rulers of an imaginary kingdom of their own, Terabithia, in the woods near their homes. Leslie chooses its name after the fictional island kingdom of Terebinthia, which figures in *The Voyage of the "Dawn Treader"* (1952). Prince Caspian sails the *Dawn Treader* to Terebinthia, one of the Seven Isles off the coast of Narnia, but the king of Terebinthia warns him not to land due to a sickness sweeping the kingdom. Caspian takes on water on the other side of the island and continues on his voyage. Later the *Dawn Treader* has a brief clash with a pirate ship thought to be Terebinthian. MR

Terhune, Albert Payson (1872–1942) A newspaperman, short-story writer, and novelist, Terhune is remembered today for his many stories and novels about dogs. The son of another novelist, Mary Virginia Terhune (1830–1922), he worked as a newspaper reporter and published a number of books before turning to his most passionate interest, dogs. His first story, "His Mate" (1915), introduced the collie Lad and became the first chapter of *Lad: A Dog* (1919). Probably his best-known book, it tells about Lad, his Master and Mistress, his mate, Lady, their pup, Wolf, and their lives at the beautiful estate of Sunnybank, or simply The Place. Following the book's enormous success, Terhune concentrated on dog stories, including the sequels *The Further Adventures of Lad* (1922) and *Lad of Sunnybank* (1928). His other novels include *Wolf* (1924), about Lad and Lady's pup, a born nuisance who shows his true nobility by giving his life to save that of another dog, and *A Dog Named Chips* (1931), about a mongrel puppy who finds happiness and fame after being adopted by one of the richest women in America. Terhune's collections of dog stories include *Buff: A Collie* (1921), *The Way of a Dog* (1934), and *The Critter and Other Dogs* (1936). If you enjoy Terhune's books, try *Lassie Come Home* by *Eric Knight as well as the dog stories of *Jack London and *Farley Mowat. MR

Terris, Susan (1937–) The author of a number of very successful novels for young readers,

Terris usually writes about the special difficulties faced by young people. Among her novels are *Pickle* (1973), about the problems faced by a 9-year-old girl whose family moves from their country farm to San Francisco; *Tucker and the Horse Thief* (1979), set in a California mining town in 1856, about a 12-year-old girl posing as a boy, who befriends a Jewish boy but does not let him in on her secret; *Octopus Pie* (1983), about two sisters whose pet octopus disappears mysteriously after the older sister takes it to school; *The Latchkey Kids* (1986), about an 11-year-old girl whose friendship with a new girl from China helps her deal with the rules and responsibilities heaped on her by her working parents; and *Nell's Quilt. If you enjoy her books, try also those of *Betsy Byars, *Phyllis Reynolds Naylor, and *Marlene Fanta Shyer. MR

Tess of the d'Urbervilles (1891) By *Thomas Hardy, this famous 19th-century novel tells of Tess Durbeyfield, a young Englishwoman whose poor family is the last remnant of the once noble and wealthy d'Urberville line. A prosperous family moves into the district and adopts the d'Urberville name. Tess's family, wrongly assuming kinship, sends Tess to seek work at their estate. There she meets Alec d'Urberville, a young rogue who is smitten with Tess and determines to seduce her. Tess refuses all his advances, but one night, worn down and exhausted, she is overcome by Alec. Tess leaves the d'Urbervilles and returns home to bear a child that dies in infancy.

When she is stronger, Tess leaves to work on a distant farm. There she meets her true love, Angel Clare, an idealistic son of a parson, who is planning to become a gentleman farmer. Angel and Tess fall in love, but she tells him she cannot marry him. She finally accepts Angel, but fails in her attempts to reveal her sad past until their wedding night. Angel, who feels tricked and wronged by Tess, departs for Brazil, leaving Tess to struggle for herself. She accidentally meets Alec, now a preacher, who abandons his new calling to pursue Tess. She resists him, but he convinces her that Angel will never return for her and that he alone can

Tess of the d'Urbervilles

aid her destitute family. Tess goes to live with Alec. Then Angel returns. Tess, tortured beyond endurance by her fate, kills Alec. She tells Angel what she has done. The two lovers are united for a few happy days before Tess is arrested, tried, and executed. If you enjoyed *Tess of the d'Urbervilles*, try also the novels of *George Eliot and *Samuel Butler. YA

Thackeray, William Makepeace (1811–1863) An English novelist known best for his novel *Vanity Fair*, Thackeray was born in Calcutta, India, where his father was an official of the East India Company. He was educated in England, but he left Cambridge University without taking a degree, and soon after lost most of his inheritance. Thackeray traveled in Europe, studied law and art, and married before turning to a career in literature. He became a regular contributor to many of the best journals of the day, where his novels were first published in monthly installments. These works made him famous, and Thackeray, in addition to his ca-

reer as a writer, became a successful lecturer in England and in America.

Thackeray's novels are noted for their wealth of detail, abundance of interesting characters, and complex plotting. Among his best-known novels are *The Luck of Barry Lyndon* (1844), about the rise and fall of an Irish rogue and adventurer, and *The History of Pendennis* (1848–1850), which tells of the struggles of an unworldly young man to find love, career, and happiness. Another popular novel is *The History of Henry Esmond* (1852), about the supposedly illegitimate son of a viscount who becomes a soldier, is drawn into a plot to restore the Stuarts to the English throne, and eventually settles in America. *The Virginians* (1857–1859) is its sequel. YA

Thank You, Jackie Robinson (1974) This novel by Barbara Cohen (1932–1992) is narrated by Sam Greene, who tells about his boyhood in the late 1940s. A scrawny, shy boy, Sam lives with his widowed mother and three sisters in the family's inn in northern New Jersey. His one real passion is baseball, especially the Brooklyn Dodgers. Sam knows every baseball fact on record and can describe play-by-play every Dodgers' game. Sam learns that the new cook, Davy, a black man about 60 years old with a bad heart, is also a Dodgers fan, and the two become best friends. Together they go to many Dodger games, cheering especially for their hero, Jackie Robinson (1919–1972), the first black player in the major leagues. When Davy has a heart attack, Sam travels by himself to Ebbets Field to get a baseball autographed by Jackie and his teammates to give to Davy. When Davy dies, Sam must fight his anger, grief, and loss to regain what he shared with Davy, his love of baseball. If you enjoyed *Thank You, Jackie Robinson*, you will like the sports stories of *Alfred Slote and *John R. Tunis. MR

That Was Then, This Is Now (1971) By *S.E. Hinton, this novel is narrated by 16-year-old Bryon Douglas, whose best friend is his 17-year-old adopted brother, Mark. The two have grown up streetwise and tough, and their favorite hangout is their friend Charlie's poolroom and bar, where they hustle pool players for pocket money. Mark seems to take this rough-and-tumble life as it comes, but Bryon becomes more and more uneasy, especially after he meets and falls in love with Cathy, the older sister of their young friend M&M. One night, after hustling two tough Texans, Mark and Bryon are saved from a beating by Charlie, who is killed in the melee that follows. Then Bryon is beaten up by a gang for something Mark has done. Things come to a head when Bryon discovers that Mark has been selling drugs to make money and turns him over to the police. In his anger and pain over what he has done to Mark, he drives Cathy away. Bryon realizes he has no answers for what has happened, but slowly he begins to put his life back together. If you enjoyed *That Was Then, This Is Now*, you will probably like the novels of *Nat Hentoff and *Paul Zindel. A film version of this novel was produced in 1985. YA

Theft, A (1989) In this short novel by *Saul Bellow, the heroine is a big-boned blonde named Clara Velde. A successful businesswoman, Clara has had four husbands. Her deepest attachment, however, is to her old boyfriend, Ithiel Regler, famous consultant on international security matters, provider of wisdom and moral support, the "point of calm" in Clara's busy life. Long ago, when Ithiel and Clara thought of getting married, he gave her an emerald ring that has become the *symbol of Clara's love for him. Once the ring disappeared, but it was found after Clara collected the insurance money.

Clara hires Gina Wegman, an Austrian governess with beautiful manners, to care for her daughters. Then Clara returns from a trip to find Gina has entertained her Haitian boyfriend, Frederic, in the apartment. The ring is missing, and Clara suspects Frederic, but Gina will not accuse him. Gina moves out and will return only if the ring is found. Though Clara realizes her own stability is somehow based on the ring, she worries about what may happen to Gina. When the ring reappears on her night table, Clara sees it as a sign that she should be understanding and generous. She finds Gina and offers to arrange a job for her under Ithiel's supervision, to save her from Frederic's small-time thievery, and to encourage Ithiel to take up with a decent woman. Gina announces she is engaged to a man in Vienna and will return there at once. Gina fully understands the wisdom and generosity of Clara's gesture, and the two women part on a note of mutual respect. YA

Then Again, Maybe I Won't (1971) The hero and narrator of this novel by *Judy Blume is 13-year-old Tony Miglione, who is trying to cope with the many changes in his life. First, his father invents an electrical device and gets a new job, and suddenly the family can move from their two-family house in Jersey City to a big, beautiful home in Rosemont, on Long Island, New York State. Then he meets his next-door neighbor, 13-year-old Joel Hoober, who likes to shoplift, and Joel's gorgeous 16-year-old sister, Lisa, who undresses each night with the curtain of her bedroom window pulled open. Most troubling of all are the changes having money causes in the members of his family. All the stress puts Tony in the hospital with severe stomach pains, but eventually he learns how to work out his feelings and fears and get on with his life. Another good story about a young person affected by change is *Cassie Binegar* (1982) by *Patricia MacLachlan. YA

There's a Boy in the Girls' Bathroom (1987) Yes, a boy does enter a girls' bathroom, briefly and accidentally, but that is not the main event of this story about a troubled boy, by Louis Sachar (1954–). Bradley Chalkers is in the fifth grade after spending two years in the fourth grade. He misbehaves in class, does not do his homework, and is shunned by all his fellow students. A new boy, Jeff Fishkin, tries to make friends with Bradley. He succeeds to some extent, but it is a new school counselor, Carla Davis, who begins to cure him of his antagonism toward the world. Some of his schoolmates reluctantly let him play basketball with them, and Bradley begins to see the advantages of taking part in school life. He has long wanted to earn a gold star from his teacher, Mrs. Ebbel, but this does not occur until, through the counselor, he finds reading can be fun and writes a book report. When he and Jeff are the only boys invited to a girl's birthday party, he learns that there is much to be gained by a friendly attitude and by taking part in social life. There are many amusing events in this novel, but most of all it offers a message saying you must rely on yourself to make your way in life. If you enjoyed this book, try Sachar's other books, including *Sixth Grade Secrets* (1987), about a girl who puts her sixth-grade class into an uproar when she starts up a club called Pig City, and *Someday Angeline* (1990), about the problems of Angeline, an 8-year-old genius who is in the sixth grade. MR & YA

These Happy Golden Years (1943) This is the eighth and last novel in *Laura Ingalls Wilder's Little House series, based on her experience of growing up in Wisconsin and the Dakota prairie in the 1880s. Here Laura Ingalls, not yet 16 years old, gets her first teaching job, in a small settlement 12 miles from home. Her homesickness is eased by the kindness of Almanzo Wilder, who drives her home and back every weekend. Laura continues her education and also teaches two more terms of school. Part of her pay goes to help her sister, Mary, who is attending a college for the blind, to return home on vacation. Laura also helps buy an organ for Mary, a special welcome-home surprise. Laura falls in love with Almanzo, and with her Pa's blessing, they marry and move into a new cabin on Wilder's claim not far from the Ingalls home. Laura is sad to leave the warm, loving home she has known, but she is happy to be with Almanzo and to know that Ma and Pa and her sisters, Carrie and Grace, are not far away. For Laura, these are indeed the happy golden years. If you enjoyed this book, you will also like *Caddie Woodlawn by *Carol Ryrie Brink. MR

Theseus was a mythological Greek hero, the son of King Aegeus of Athens. Theseus had many adventures and performed many heroic tasks, including sailing with *Jason and the *Argonauts. Probably his best-known feat was slaying the monster known as the *Minotaur, which was kept by King Minos in the *Labyrinth. On his voyage home from this adventure, Theseus forgot to hoist a white sail to signal his success. His father, thinking Theseus had died, drowned himself in the sea, which is now known as the Aegean. A number of books tell about Theseus, including *The Way of Danger: The Story of Theseus* (1963) by *Ian Serraillier, and *Theseus and the Minotaur* (1988) by Leonard Everett Fisher (1924–). You will also want to read about Theseus in *Bulfinch's Mythology* by Thomas Bulfinch (1796–1867) and *Mythology* by Edith Hamilton (1867–1963). MR

They Dance in the Sky: Native American Star Myths (1987) A treasure trove of American Indian folklore, this collection of stories by Jean Guard Monroe (n.d.) and Ray A. Williamson (1938–) retells myths created by Native Americans about the stars. The stories tell how the stars were created, but they also show how the storytellers viewed the world, their relation to it, and how human beings should live in it. Here are myths that have been handed down orally, from generation to generation, and only recently have been written down. They include legends of how the Pleiades, the Milky Way, and the Big Dipper were created. Some of the stories are similar to the myths of classical Greek mythology. If you enjoyed *They Dance in the Sky*, try *Star Tales: North American Indian Stories About the Stars* (1987) and *Earthmaker's Tales: North American Indian Stories About Earth Happenings* (1989) by Gretchen Will Mayo (n.d.). See also *Mythology* by Edith Hamilton (1867–1963). MR

Thiele, Colin (Milton) (1920–) This Australian author has written plays and poetry, and many books about his country. He has also edited *Favorite Australian Stories* (1963). Some of Thiele's books are mystery and adventure novels with Australian settings. Among them are *The Fire in the Stone* (1974), about a boy and his aboriginal friend who together track down a thief who has stolen an opal; *Blue Fin* (1974), about a 14-year-old boy who must deal with his emotions and problems after his father's tuna ship sinks; and *Shadow Shark* (1988), in which another 14-year-old boy joins fishermen to hunt an enormous shark off the coast of southern Australia. If you want to read more about Australia, try *The Australian Aborigines* (1968) by Eleanor Z. Baker (1932–), and *Australia* (1990) by Laura Dolce (n.d.). MR & YA

Thimble Summer (1938) Written and illustrated by Elizabeth Enright (1909–1968), this novel tells about 9-year-old Garnet Linden, who lives on her family's farm in Wisconsin with her parents, older brother Jay, and younger brother Donald. One day Garnet finds a silver thimble half buried in the riverbed. She decides it is a magic thimble, because wonderful, exciting things soon begin to happen. First, cooling rains come to end the drought and save the wilting crops. Then her father gets the money to build a new barn. And then an orphan boy named Eric comes to live and work on the farm and become part of the family. Garnet has several interesting adventures, some with her best friend, Citronella Hauser. For example, she and Citronella visit the local library and get so absorbed in reading they are locked in and are not rescued until late at night. When Garnet is not having adventures, she spends much time caring for her pet hog, Timmy, and hoping that he will win a blue ribbon at the county fair, which turns out to be the high point of Garnet's thimble summer. Elizabeth Enright started out as an artist and illustrator before becoming a writer. If you enjoyed *Thimble Summer*, you will also enjoy her novels about another family, the *Melendys. Thimble Summer* won the *Newbery Medal in 1939. MR

Thing at the Foot of the Bed, The (1959) This collection of spooky folktales retold by Maria Leach (1892–1977) brings together stories about ghosts, witches, and strange happenings that have thrilled, frightened, and delighted millions of people. Some of the stories are scary and others are funny. Some are said to be based on actual events. The book also contains three ghost games for young people to play, and a section on "do's and don'ts about ghosts," useful information if you should ever meet a ghost. If you enjoyed *The Thing at the Foot of the Bed*, you will want to read Leach's *Whistle in the Graveyard: Folktales to Chill Your Bones* (1974), a collection of 39 stories from around the world about ghosts, witches, and other scary creatures. An authority on myth, legends, and folklore, Leach wrote many books on these subjects, including *The Rainbow Book of American Folk Tales and Legends* (1958); *Riddle Me, Riddle Me, Ree* (1970), a collection of riddles from folklore; and *The Lion Sneezed: Folktales and Myths of the Cat* (1977). MR

Thirteen Clocks, The (1950) In this delightful fantasy fable by *James Thurber, a beautiful princess named Saralinda is imprisoned in Coffin Castle by a Duke so evil that he has even slain time. All 13 clocks in the castle are stopped at 10 minutes to 5. Saralinda has had many suitors, but the Duke has slain them too, after giving them tasks they were unable to perform. One day Prince Zorn of Zorna arrives disguised as a minstrel, and with the help of the Golux, whose parents were a wizard and a witch, and Saralinda, he accomplishes the task set for him by the Duke. Zorn wins the hand of Saralinda, and the Duke is swallowed up by the Todal, which eats evildoers who fail to do evil. *The Thirteen Clocks* is filled with James Thurber's wit and love of language, and often reads almost like poetry. If you enjoyed it, try *The Little Prince* by *Antoine de Saint-Exupéry, another fantasy that has become a young people's classic. MR

Thirty-Nine Steps, The (1915) An adventure novel by *John Buchan, this tale begins just before World War I when Richard Hannay returns from South Africa to London, where he is quickly bored by city life. He is visited by an American journalist named Scudder, who claims to have discovered a dangerous plot to upset the balance of power in Europe. Though exact details are not revealed, Scudder says the plot will be put in motion in three weeks, and that he must elude the men of an international underground group called the "Black Stone" and defeat their plans. When Scudder is murdered, Hannay decides to carry out the mission himself. He plans to vanish into the Scottish countryside, throw off his pursuers, and return in time to tell Scudder's story to the authorities. On a walking tour in Scotland, Hannay soon realizes the clever and well-organized assassins of the Black Stone are hunting him like an animal. After a series of near escapes, he enlists the help of Sir Walter Bullivant, who has connections in high places. In London again, Hannay learns the Black Stone has a spy in the English government, who will soon return to Europe to pass on crucial secret information. The efforts of government officials, alerted by Bullivant, are directed toward preventing the spy's escape across the Channel. In Scudder's notebook is an entry that reads "Thirty-nine steps . . . High tide, 10:17 p.m." Hannay ingeniously locates a seaside villa whose staircase leading down to the beach has 39 steps. There, on the night when the tide reaches its height at 10:17, the spy is arrested in a dramatic struggle before he can leave England, and two other members of the Black Stone are captured. This novel was collected, in *The Four Adventures of Richard Hannay* (1933), with three other novels about Hannay's adventures during World War I: *Greenmantle* (1916), *Mr. Standfast* (1919), and *The Three Hostages* (1924). A movie version of *The Thirty-Nine Steps* appeared in 1935, directed by Alfred Hitchcock. Two more recent movie versions appeared in 1959 and 1978. YA

Thomas, Dylan (1914–1953) A Welsh poet whose works are noted for their lyrical beauty, Thomas began writing when he was a boy and became a published poet while still a teenager. His first collection, *Eighteen Poems* (1934), ap-

peared when he was 19 years old. In the same year Thomas moved to London and found work in journalism, screenwriting, and radio broadcasting. His love of language and writing was matched by his appetite for experience and for alcohol. The need for money drew him away from home and family, and he died in New York City on his fourth lecture tour of the United States. Among his works are the short-story collections *Portrait of the Artist as a Young Dog* and *Adventures in the Skin Trade* (1955), the radio play *Under Milk Wood*, and *Collected Poems, 1934–1952* (1952). Younger readers will especially like his delightful story in verse of his own Christmas memories, *A Child's Christmas in Wales* (1954). MR & YA

Thomas, Piri [John Peter Thomas] (1928–) A writer known best for his autobiography *Down These Mean Streets* (1967), Thomas, the son of Puerto Rican parents, was born in Spanish Harlem, in New York City. On its mean streets Thomas came of age in a world of drugs, poverty, prostitution, gang warfare, and crime. After being shot and captured during a failed robbery, Thomas was tried and sentenced to 5 to 15 years in prison There he began to write about his experiences and became determined to change his life around. *Down These Mean Streets* is a powerful and often brutal account of Thomas's life from his boyhood through the six years of his imprisonment. His other books include *Saviour, Saviour, Hold My Hand* (1972), which describes his experiences after his release from prison; *Seven Long Times* (1974), describing his prison experiences and condemning the correctional system's failure to rehabilitate inmates; and the short-story collection *Stories from El Barrio* (1978). YA

Thoreau, Henry David (1817–1862) An essayist, naturalist, philosopher, and poet, Thoreau is known best for *Walden, or Life in the Woods*, the account of his two years' residence in a log cabin he built on the shore of Walden Pond in Concord, Massachusetts. Thoreau was born and spent most of his life in Concord, the home of his friend and mentor *Ralph Waldo Emerson. Emerson encouraged Thoreau's life-long practice of keeping a daily journal. In it you can see how Thoreau refined his observations of the natural world and human society and developed a philosophy of individualism and self-reliance that can be found in much of his writing.

While living at Walden Pond in 1846, Thoreau was arrested for not paying a poll tax as a protest against the government's waging of the Mexican War and its inability or unwillingness to end slavery. The experience led to his writing the essay "Civil Disobedience" (1849), which advocates a citizen's refusal to accept government authority when it oversteps its bounds or conflicts with an individual's principles or moral sense.

Besides *Walden*, Thoreau had only one other book published in his lifetime, *A Week on the Concord and Merrimack River* (1849), an account of a river voyage he made with his brother in August 1839. It combines his observations of nature with literary, social, and philosophical commentary. Books published after his death include *The Maine Woods* (1864), essays based on three visits to Maine, in 1846, 1853, and 1857, and the collection *Poems of Nature* (1895). Of the 20-volume Walden edition of *The Writings of Henry David Thoreau* (1906), Thoreau's journal takes up 14 volumes.

"Civil Disobedience" had a profound influence on many writers and leaders, probably the best known being Mohandas K. Gandhi (1869–1948), whose practice of nonviolent resistance in turn greatly influenced the American civil rights leader Martin Luther King (1929–1968). In the 1960s, at the height of the Vietnam War, both *Walden* and "Civil Disobedience" enjoyed a new surge of popularity. YA

Thrasher, Crystal (1921–) The author of a series of novels about an Indiana family struggling to survive during the *Great Depression, Thrasher was born and grew up in Indiana. Her family suffered hardship during the 1930s. These experiences provided a background for Thrasher's novels about a young girl named Seely Robinson and her family as they fight hunger and poverty in rural Indiana. In *The Dark Didn't Catch Me* (1975), 11-year-old Seely and her family move to the timber region of southern Indiana. There Seely discovers, amid the hardship of her life, the beauty and strength of the wooded hill country. Thrasher continues her story of the Robinson family, as they overcome difficulties and tragedies and work themselves out of rural poverty and toward what they hope is a better life, in *Between Dark and Daylight* (1979), *Julie's Summer* (1981), *End of a Dark Road* (1982), and *A Taste of Daylight* (1984). MR

Three Musketeers, The (1844) By *Alexandre Dumas, this historical romance of 17th-century France is his best-known work. Its hero is D'Artagnan, a young man from rural Gascony who travels to Paris to join the King's Musketeers. Soon after he arrives, D'Artagnan runs afoul of three of King Louis XIII's best musketeers, the reserved Athos, the friendly and boastful Porthos, and the priestlike Aramis, and agrees to duels with each. Before any duels are fought, however, the four are attacked by the rival guards of the Cardinal de Richelieu, whose power in France rivals that of the king himself. D'Artagnan and the Musketeers carry the day. The Gascon youth becomes a cadet in the king's guards and the inseparable companion of the Musketeers. When Constance Bonacieux, the beautiful wife of D'Artagnan's landlord and the queen's seamstress, is mysteriously abducted, the four discover and foil a plot by Richelieu to discredit the queen by revealing her romance with the English Duke of Buckingham. D'Artagnan falls in love with Constance, but he also incurs the wrath of the cardinal's agent, the beautiful and mysterious Lady de Winter. The secret of her identity is the key to her downfall, but not before she instigates the murder of Buckingham and kills D'Artagnan's beloved Constance. The outwitted Richelieu is so impressed with D'Artagnan's courage and intelligence that he grants D'Artagnan a commission in the King's Musketeers.

MR = Middle Reader   YA = Young Adult Reader   * = See this main entry

Dumas based his novel on *Mémoires de M. d'Artagnan* (1700), the memoirs of an actual Gascon gentleman adventurer that were written after his death by Gatien de Courtilz de Sandras (1644–1712). You can read about the further adventures of D'Artagnan and the Musketeers in *Twenty Years After* (1845) and *The Vicomte of Bragelonne* (1848–1850). *The Three Musketeers* was made into a number of movies, including an excellent film in 1973. YA

Through the Looking-Glass See *Alice's Adventures in Wonderland.*

Throwing Season, The (1980) By Michael French (1944–), this novel is about Henry Chevrolet, a high school athlete known as Indian because he is half Cherokee. Indian is the star shot-putter of his high school in Laurelton, Arkansas. He longs to win a full athletic scholarship to a big university so that he can break out of the small-minded world that has kept his Cherokee father down for so long and threatens to do the same to him. A rich and powerful car dealer tries to bribe, then threaten, Indian into deliberately losing the state and national meets. And a new student, a wiry loner named Golly, Indian's friend and competitor, declares his intention to beat Indian at the shot put. When Indian refuses to throw the state meet, he is beaten and his hand is broken. Though he comes close to giving up, Indian eventually decides to fight his way back to the top. In a dangerous and exciting finale, he ruins the car dealer's scheme, beats Golly in a fair competition, and wins back his future. Michael French has written several other novels for young readers, including *Pursuit* (1982), about a teenager on the run from his hiking companions after his younger brother is deliberately killed by the group's leader, and *Lifeguards Only Beyond This Point* (1984), about the summer experiences of a teenage boy working as a lifeguard at an exclusive resort. YA

thumbs down, a sign or phrase of disapproval or rejection, comes to us from the gladiatorial combats of Roman times. When one gladiator

One of James Thurber's wonderful drawings from *The Beast in Me and Other Animals* (1928)

had defeated another in the arena, the fate of the fallen gladiator could be decided by the spectators. If they turned "thumbs down," the defeated gladiator would be slain. Other gestures, perhaps "thumbs up" signs or the waving of handkerchiefs, meant the spectators wanted the life of the fallen gladiator to be spared. Today "thumbs up" is a positive gesture, meaning "everything is going well," "I agree," or the like.

Thurber, James (1896–1962) One of the most accomplished humorists of American literature, Thurber was a successful artist as well as writer. Born and raised in Columbus, Ohio, Thurber worked as a reporter, then began writing humorous articles and stories. He soon became a regular contributor to *The New Yorker* magazine, where most of his work was first published. Most of Thurber's books are collections of stories, drawings, and articles on various subjects, but Thurber's real subject in all of them is life and all its comic, absurd, wistful, and sometimes painful moments. His books include *My Life and Hard Times* (1933), which contains "The Night the Bed Fell," a hilarious incident from Thurber's own youth; *My World* and *Welcome to It* (1942), which contains "The Secret Life of Walter Mitty," about a middle-aged man who escapes his boring existence through daydreams; and *The Thurber Carnival* (1945), which collects many stories and drawings from his earlier books. Thurber also wrote a number of books for younger readers, including *Many Moons; The Great Quillow* (1944), about a short toymaker who saves his town from a giant; *The Thirteen Clocks; and *The Wonderful O* (1957), about a pirate who decides to banish the letter "o" from the English language. MR & YA

tiger A *symbol of strength and courage, the tiger can also represent fierceness and aggression. If you "ride a tiger," you may not only be in a dangerous position, but also one you will have difficulty getting out of; to "have a tiger by the tail" is equally dangerous because you dare not let him go. On the other hand, a "paper tiger" is a person who sounds fierce but who is really all bluff. The word is sometimes applied to describe an outspoken or brave statesman or ruler, as in the case of Georges Clemenceau (1841–1929), the French premier during World War I, who was known as the "Tiger of France." In literature the tiger is usually a fierce creature, as in "The Tyger" (1794) by *William Blake, which begins:

> Tyger! Tyger! burning bright
> In the forests of the night,
> What immortal hand or eye
> Could frame thy fearful symmetry?

The tiger also represents a threat in the story *"The Lady or the Tiger?" MR & YA

Tiger Eyes (1981) By *Judy Blume, this novel tells about 15-year-old Davey Wexler, whose life becomes a nightmare when her father is shot to death during a holdup in his Atlantic City store. Davey is unable to deal with the fear, anger, and sense of loss she feels. Davey and her younger brother, Jason, travel with their mother to Los Alamos, New Mexico, to stay for a time with Davey's aunt and uncle. At Los Alamos she meets Wolf, a boy whose father is dying of cancer. She finds in Wolf a friend who can understand her unspoken anguish. After his father dies, Wolf leaves Los Alamos, but not before he has helped Davey come to terms with her loss, overcome her fears, and get on with her life. If you enjoyed *Tiger Eyes*, you may like *Red Sky at Morning* (1968) by Richard Bradford (1932–), about a 17-year-old boy's struggle to cope with his father's death and his mother's emotional problems. YA

Time at the Top (1963) By Edward Ormondroyd (1925–), this imaginative novel tells about Susan Shaw, a girl who lives in an apartment building in the city with her widowed father, an unhappy accountant. On her way home from school one day, Susan helps an old lady, who grants her "just three" for her kindness. But three what? The woman is actually a good witch, and Susan has gained three special rides on her building's elevator into the year 1881. There Susan meets two young people, Vicky and Robert Walker, and learns that their widowed mother has just lost all her money in a bad investment. Susan recalls a newspaper article she read before her elevator ride, about the discovery of a buried hoard of gold coins in the city park. She and her companions set out to find the treasure first. Then Susan returns home and talks her father into going back with her to a happier life in 1881. If you enjoyed *Time at the Top*, you can learn what happened to Susan and her father in the sequel, *All in Good Time* (1975). MR

Time Machine, The (1895) By *H.G. Wells, this novel is one of the classic works of *science fiction. An English scientist, identified by the narrator only as the Time Traveller, invents a machine that will enable him to travel through time. He travels to the year 802701, where he finds humanity has evolved into two very different types—the small, childlike, vegetarian Eloi, who live in vast, ancient buildings constructed eons earlier by forgotten ancestors, and the apelike, carnivorous Morlocks, who live below ground and feed on the Eloi. The traveller saves the life of Weena, an Eloi girl, and her companionship and devotion help him feel that some spark of humanity has survived in this alien Earth. The Morlocks steal the time machine, but the Traveller regains it after a great struggle in which Weena disappears. He travels farther into the future, in which humankind and its works have all disappeared. He returns to his own time to tell this story to the narrator and others, but is not believed. Yet the narrator is convinced when the Time Traveller and his machine disappear again and do not return.

There are hundreds of novels and stories dealing with time travel, one of the major themes of science fiction. Two examples are *Hawksbill Station* (1968) by *Robert Silverberg, in which prisoners are sent by time machine into the prehistoric past, and *Slaughterhouse-Five* by *Kurt Vonnegut. *The Time Machine* was made into a movie in 1960 and remade for television in 1978. MR & YA

Tin Woodman, The is one of the characters in *The Wonderful Wizard of Oz* by *L. Frank Baum. Made entirely of tin, and having been caught in the rain without his oilcan, he is found in a stiff and rusty condition by *Dorothy and the *Scarecrow on the road to Oz. When his joints are oiled, however, he is as good as new. He is proud of his shiny tin body, which cannot be hurt if his axe slips, but he very much wants a real heart so he can love again. The Tin Woodman hopes the *Wizard of Oz will help him, so he joins the others on their journey.

The friends run many risks on the yellow brick road to Oz. In all, the kindly Tin Woodman makes himself useful with his axe and his strength. When the Wicked Witch of the West is killed by Dorothy, the Wizard gives him a heart made of silk cloth and the Tin Woodman is truly happy. At the end of the story the good witch Glinda sends him to the country of the Winkies to be their ruler. MR

Titan, in Greek mythology, is the name given the six sons and six daughters of *Uranus (Heaven) and Gaea (Earth). The sons are named Coeus, Creus, *Cronus, Hyperion, Iapetus, and Oceanus, and the daughters are named Mnemosyne, Phoebe, Tethys, Theia, Themis, and Rhea. Of these, the most important are Cronus and Rhea. Cronus leads the Titans in a rebellion against Uranus, deposes him, and becomes king of the gods. He then marries his sister Rhea and has six children, but to make sure that none of his children will overthrow him as he had overthrown Uranus, he swallows them when they are born. Rhea is able to rescue the last, *Zeus, who grows to manhood, forces Cronus to vomit up the other five children, and with them overthrows Cronus and the other Titans, banishing them to the underworld of Tartarus. The Titans are very large and extremely powerful gods, and it is from their name that we get the words "titan" and "titanic," meaning of great size or strength. You can read about the Titans in *Bulfinch's Mythology* by Thomas Bulfinch (1796–1867) and also in *Mythology* by Edith Hamilton (1867–1963). MR & YA

Tituba of Salem Village (1964), a novel by *Anne Petry, tells about the witchcraft trials held in Salem, Massachusetts, in 1692. Tituba and her husband, John Indian, slaves living in Barbados, are bought by the Reverend Samuel Parris, a cold, pious, greedy man who has fared poorly in the West Indies. He takes his family and new slaves to Boston, where Tituba is befriended and taught to spin and weave by Samuel Conklin. Then Parris finds a ministry at Salem. But his greedy, willful nature causes discontent among his new neighbors, and Tituba's superb weaving, ability with animals, and knowledge of medicinal herbs arouse much envy and distrust. Trouble begins when the Reverend's daughter Betsey begins having seizures. Soon other girls and young women in Salem begin to act as if possessed by demons. A panic runs through the community, and Tituba and two other women are tried and condemned for witchcraft after a terrifyingly unjust trial. Before the trials are stopped, more than 50 people are found guilty of witchcraft and 20 are executed, but Tituba survives and is finally freed. If you enjoyed *Tituba of Salem Village*, try *The Witch of Blackbird Pond* by *Elizabeth George Speare, about witch-hunting in 17th-century Connecticut. MR

To Be a Slave (1968) By *Julius Lester, this account of the slave experience in America is largely in the words of former slaves. Some of the narratives come from books written by people who were slaves in the decades before the Civil War. Others were gathered in the 1930s from former slaves who were still living. The combined narrative covers all aspects of America's slave days, including how Africans were captured and sold into slavery, transported under horrifying conditions to America, and treated like beasts of burden and mere property by a system designed to stamp out their humanity. It also describes the ways the enslaved peoples used to thwart the slave system, including music, dance, and religion. *To Be a Slave* brings into focus the monstrous injustice of slavery. Another book on this subject is *Black Bondage: The Life of Slaves in the South* (1969) by Walter Goodman (1929–). MR & YA

To Kill a Mockingbird (1960) By Harper Lee (1926–), this novel is set in the small town of Maycomb, Alabama, from 1933 to 1935 and is narrated by Jean Louise "Scout" Finch. As the story opens, 6-year-old Scout and her 10-year-old brother, Jeremy, or Jem, meet Dill Harris, a bright, imaginative, adventurous boy who is spending the summer next door with his Aunt Rachel. Dill's fascination with another neighbor, Arthur "Boo" Radley, a mentally disturbed man who has not been seen outside his home in more than 15 years, inspires Jem and Scout to try and befriend the recluse. But their widowed father, Atticus Finch, tells them to respect Radley's privacy. Scout and Jem begin to find little gifts hidden in the knothole of a tree near the Radley house, a sign that Boo has been watching them and has become their secret friend.

Atticus, a highly respected lawyer and state legislator, is appointed to defend Tom Robin-

son, a black man accused of beating and raping the daughter of Bob Ewell, a shiftless, violent, alcoholic white man. The townspeople despise Ewell, but they turn on Atticus for defending a black man. Scout and Jem are hurt by the prejudice and hypocrisy the case arouses. Robinson, whose arm is crippled, is clearly innocent, yet he is convicted and later killed while trying to escape from prison. The editor of the local newspaper likens his death to the senseless killing of harmless songbirds by hunters and children. This reminds Scout of Atticus's warning when he gave her and Jem air rifles—it is a sin to kill a mockingbird, a songbird that harms no one.

Ewell, humiliated by Atticus in court, swears to get even. He attacks Scout and Jem on their way home from a Halloween pageant but is killed with his own knife. Sheriff Heck Tate, piecing the crime together, realizes that Boo Radley, protecting the children, killed Ewell, but the sheriff reports that Ewell accidentally fell on his knife. Radley's act, and Tate's further act of decency toward him, restore in Scout and Jem the faith in human goodness they had lost during the trial. Lee modeled Scout after herself, Atticus after her lawyer father, and Dill after *Truman Capote, whom she had known since childhood. Though Lee has written for magazines, she has not produced another novel. If you enjoyed *To Kill a Mockingbird*, read *The Heart Is a Lonely Hunter* by *Carson McCullers. *To Kill a Mockingbird* was made into an outstanding movie in 1962. YA

Toad Hall is the ancestral home of Mr. Toad in *The Wind in the Willows* by *Kenneth Grahame. A "handsome, dignified old house of mellowed red brick," it has a neatly kept lawn that slopes down to the edge of the *River Bank. The grounds of Toad Hall have many attractions, including a fishpond, kitchen garden, stables, a henhouse, a dairy, and a boathouse. Dating in part from the 14th century, the house is conveniently situated "five minutes from church, post-office, and golf-links," a perfect country estate. Toad is wealthy, simple, and good natured, but not very sensible, and when he takes an interest in something new there is no controlling him. Toad becomes fascinated by motorcars, and after stealing one and acting cheeky toward the police, he is sent to jail for 20 years. He escapes, but when he returns to the River Bank he finds that the ferrets and weasels from the Wild Wood have taken over Toad Hall. Toad and his friends Badger, Rat, and Mole sneak into the house through a secret passage leading up from the river, surprise the Wild Wood animals, and recapture Toad's home. MR

Tolan, Stephanie S. (1942–) Author of more than a dozen novels for young readers, Tolan has also written poetry and plays, worked in children's theater, and taught at a number of colleges. Her first book was *Grandpa—and Me* (1978), a touching story about a 12-year-old girl and her grandfather, who is becoming increasingly confused between the memories of his past and the people and events of the present. Tolan's other books include *The Liberation of Tansy Warner*, about a girl whose mother walks out on her family; *No Safe Harbors* (1981), about a 16-year-old girl whose life of privilege and ease comes crashing down when her father, the mayor of their Ohio town, is accused of taking a bribe; *A Time to Fly Free* (1983), about a 10-year-old boy whose love of nature leads him to help a man who rescues and cares for injured birds; and *The Great Skinner Strike* (1983), about a 14-year-old girl whose mother goes on strike against her family and causes an uproar in their town. *The Great Skinner Strike* was made into a TV movie, "Mom's on Strike," in 1984. MR & YA

Tolkien, J.R.R. [John Ronald Reuel Tolkien] (1892–1973) A scholar, professor, and author, the English writer Tolkien is best known for his fantasies set in the mythical land known as *Middle-Earth. Born in South Africa, he grew up in England, where he became deeply interested in English and Nordic history, literature, and folklore, the sources for his later fantasies. After fighting in World War I, Tolkien began

his teaching career, which he spent mostly at Oxford University. In addition to writing scholarly books and articles, Tolkien began writing *fantasy stories, in part to entertain his children and in part to make use of a language he had invented, called Elvish. Encouraged by his friend *C.S. Lewis, he published *The Hobbit, giving the world its first glimpse of Middle-Earth and its inhabitants, which include elves, dwarves, dragons, wizards, goblins, and the furry creatures known as hobbits. Tolkien expanded and enriched his vision of Middle-Earth with the epic romance *The Lord of the Rings. Both works had small but loyal followings until the 1960s, when they were discovered by young people, particularly American college students, and became best sellers. In his final years Tolkien worked on *The Silmarillion* (1977), a "prequel" to the earlier Middle-Earth stories. If you enjoy Tolkien's books, try also the *Xanth stories of *Piers Anthony and the books of *C.S. Lewis. MR & YA

Tolstoy, Leo (1828–1910) A novelist and philosopher, Tolstoy is known best for his epic novel *War and Peace. He was born into a noble family at their estate of Yasnaya Polyana, a village south of Moscow, which he inherited when his father died. Following the tradition of the time, Tolstoy was educated at home and then at the university. While serving in the army he wrote his first book, *Childhood* (1852), which is mostly about his own happy early years. This was followed by *Boyhood* (1854) and *Youth* (1857). After leaving the army he returned to Yasnaya Polyana to manage the estate and educate the children of his serfs. There, from 1863 to 1869, he worked on *War and Peace*. While he was writing *Anna Karenina, he struggled to find a meaning to human life. He found his answer in unorthodox views of God and social justice that were opposed to the beliefs of the Russian Orthodox Church and the government.

Tolstoy felt a strong responsibility to his family and more particularly to his wife, Sofia, who was unable to understand his deep-seated beliefs. If it had not been for this loyalty, he would have fulfilled his desire to give away his wealth, renounce his writings, which he now considered frivolous, and live like a peasant. Russian peasants adored him as a savior from the harshness of their lives. Because of his wealth and position, the authorities dared not move against him, but they made it impossible for him to publish his books. Home life became increasingly intolerable. His wife continued to live a life of luxury that he now abhorred. Eventually Tolstoy, when he was 82 years old, was driven to leave his home in bitter winter weather. He caught cold and a few days later died of pneumonia while lying in the house of the stationmaster of a remote Russian hamlet. Considered a saint by many Russian peasants, Tolstoy has passed into legend and is thought by many of them never to have died. You may want to read Tolstoy's beautifully written short stories, which express his philosophy in simple terms. They are available in paperback. If you enjoy his works, read also *Doctor Zhivago by *Boris Pasternak and the books of *Maxim Gorky and *Ivan Turgenev. YA

Tom Brown's Schooldays (1857) This cele-

brated novel by Thomas Hughes (1822–1896) describes 19th-century English public school life through the eyes of Tom Brown. A public school in England is the same as a private prep school in the United States. When Tom is 10 years old he is sent to school at Rugby, which, except for summers and holidays, is to be his home for the next eight years. The headmaster of the school is Dr. Thomas Arnold (1795–1842), who is working quietly to eliminate the bullying, brutality, and other excesses of school life and instill in his students the virtues of honesty, personal courage, and love of God and country. Brown meets and becomes the roommate of Harry East, and the two boys, influenced by the words of a respected upperclassman, decide to lead a rebellion against the system of "fagging," in which younger boys are made to do chores for older boys. Flashman, the worst bully at Rugby, becomes their special enemy. Brown and East fight and beat Flashman, and the bullying at school largely ends. The boys begin to get into trouble, but Dr. Arnold, seeing good in both, arranges to have Brown room with George Arthur, a frail youth whose natural goodness helps both Brown and East develop into young men of character. When they graduate, East goes into the army and Brown goes to Oxford University, strengthened by the wisdom and goodness of Dr. Arnold, who has guided them almost unseen through all the years. Hughes continued the story of Tom Brown in *Tom Brown at Oxford* (1861). *Tom Brown's Schooldays* was made into a motion picture in 1940. MR & YA

Tom Jones, a Foundling, The History of

(1749) The masterwork of *Henry Fielding, this comic novel, set in 17th-century England, is full of wit, humor, and sharp insight into human character. It begins as Squire Allworthy returns after a long absence to his country seat, where he lives with his unmarried sister, Bridget. There he is astonished to find a boy foundling in his bed. Inquiries are made, and Allworthy comes to believe that Jenny Jones, servant of a schoolmaster named Partridge, is the mother. Allworthy decides to raise the child, whom he names Tom, and Jenny leaves the area. Some think the squire is the father, but soon Mrs. Partridge accuses her husband of being the father. The schoolmaster loses his job, and after his wife suddenly dies, he too leaves for parts unknown. Miss Bridget marries the cold, avaricious Captain Blifil and has a son. When the Captain dies, Squire Allworthy accepts Master Blifil as his heir and raises him and Tom together, under the combined tutelage of Mr. Thwackum, a mean-spirited chaplain, and Mr. Square, a self-styled philosopher. Young Tom shows a wild streak but he is warm-hearted, generous, and honorable. Master Blifil, the complete opposite, takes every chance to convince Allworthy that Tom is a scoundrel.

Tom falls in love with Sophia Western, daughter of Squire Western, who owns a neighboring estate. Western wants Sophia to marry

Blifil, whom she detests. Allworthy suffers a near-fatal illness, and at the same time Bridget Blifil dies. Soon after, Blifil manages through deceit to arouse Allworthy's wrath against Tom, who is turned out to make his own way in the world. Sophia leaves home with her servant, Mrs. Honour, determined to avoid Blifil. After a complicated series of adventures and misadventures, Tom and Sophia meet again in London. There, Blifil's lifelong treachery against Tom is finally uncovered and Bridget is revealed to have been Tom's real mother. Allworthy and Tom are joyfully reunited, and Western blesses the marriage of Tom and Sophia. If you enjoyed *The History of Tom Jones*, you will probably also enjoy the novels of *Charles Dickens. *Tom Jones* was made into a motion picture in 1963. YA

Tom Sawyer, The Adventures of (1876) By *Mark Twain, this classic novel is set in St. Petersburg, a small town on the Mississippi River, in the 19th century. Tom lives with his Aunt Polly, cousin Mary, and tattletale brother, Sid. Imaginative, adventurous, and often in trouble, he tricks his friends into whitewashing a fence for him, tries to hoax his way to winning a Bible in Sunday School, ponders a life of piracy, and woos Judge Thatcher's daughter, Becky. One night Tom and Huck Finn, the free-spirited son of the town drunkard, visit the graveyard and witness a murder committed by Injun Joe. Terrified, they are silent next day when Muff Potter, Joe's companion, is arrested for the crime. Tom, Huck, and their friend Joe Harper run off to Jackson's Island to be pirates and are thought drowned. They sneak back home to witness their own funerals. At Muff Potter's murder trial, Tom bravely incriminates Injun Joe, who escapes. Weeks later, during a picnic, Tom and Becky become lost while exploring a vast cave, which Injun Joe is using as a hideout. Tom and Becky find their way out, but Injun Joe dies trapped in the cave. Twain wrote about Tom and Huck in a sequel, *The Adventures of Huckleberry Finn*, and in the less popular sequels *Tom Sawyer Abroad* (1894) and *Tom Sawyer, Detective* (1896). *The Adven-*

Tom convinces a friend that whitewashing a fence is great fun in *The Adventures of Tom Sawyer*.

tures of Tom Sawyer was made into an excellent film in 1938. MR & YA

Tom Swift See *Victor Appleton.

Tom Thumb is the tiny hero of a popular folktale set in England during the time of *Merlin and *King Arthur. Merlin, traveling disguised as a beggar, meets a poor childless couple and uses his powers to give them a son. The boy is called Tom Thumb because he is no bigger than a thumb. He gets into many difficulties because he is so small, but he is clever and full of tricks and always manages to overcome his problems. After many adventures, he becomes a favorite at King Arthur's court and gains a gift of money for his poor parents. He is killed in a battle with a poisonous spider. You can read about Tom Thumb in several folktale collections, including *English Fairy Tales* (1890) collected by Joseph Jacobs (1854–1916), *English Fables and Fairy Stories* (1954) retold by James Reeves (1909–), and *English Fairy Tales* (1918) retold by Flora Annie Steel (1847–1929). Tom Thumb was also the show name of Charles Sherwood Stratton (1838–1883), a midget who was a member of the "Greatest Show on Earth" circus organized by the great American showman P.T. Barnum (1810–1891). MR

Tom's Midnight Garden (1958) By *A. Philippa Pearce, this novel tells of Tom Long, an English boy who is sent to live with his aunt and uncle after his brother, Peter, comes down with measles. Tom is under quarantine, so he must stay in his aunt and uncle's apartment, one of several flats in what was once a great old house. The only thing of interest is old Mrs. Bartholomew's grandfather clock in the downstairs hall, and Tom is told never to touch it. Worst of all, there is no garden for Tom to play in and no one to play with. Then one midnight, after the eccentric old clock strikes 13, Tom discovers in the backyard a beautiful *Victorian garden. He befriends a lonely, shy girl named Hatty and learns that he has traveled back through time to the 1890s. In his nightly visits to the garden, Tom watches Hatty grow into a young woman and comes to understand that time stands still only in people's memories and dreams. If you enjoyed *Tom's Midnight Garden*, try *Time at the Top* by Edward Ormondroyd (1925–), about a girl who travels back in time. MR

Touch the Moon (1987) In this *fantasy by Marion Dane Bauer (1938–), 11-year-old Jennifer finds that her birthday present from her father is not the real horse she has dreamed about but a china horse her dad has had since his boyhood. Her disappointment turns to wonder when the china horse changes into Moonseeker, a golden stallion that talks and that only she can see. While on a night ride, they become trapped in a cave and Moonseeker becomes frightened. Jennifer coaxes him out by showing him the moon, and then together they jump up to "touch the moon." When they get

home, Moonseeker changes back into the china horse, and Jennifer learns that her father rode the horse when he was a boy, and even named him Moonseeker. If you enjoyed *Touch the Moon*, try some of Bauer's other books, such as *On My Honor* (1988), about a boy whose best friend drowns after they go swimming in a dangerous river they had both promised to avoid, and *A Dream of Queens and Castles* (1990), about a girl who, on a trip to England with her mother, befriends an eccentric old man. MR

Townsend, John Rowe (1922–) An English journalist, editor, critic, and novelist, Townsend wrote reviews of books for young readers before launching his own career. Many of his books are about young people facing and ultimately overcoming such serious difficulties as poverty, family problems, and loneliness. Among his novels are *Good-bye to the Jungle* (1965), about four young people who bring their family out of poverty and hold it together, despite the aimlessness and irresponsibility of their elders; *Pirate's Island* (1968), about the friendship of a lonely boy for a girl whose fantasies about a pirate and buried treasure lead to a search for a real chest of stolen money; *The Intruder*, perhaps his best-known book; *Noah's Castle* (1975), about a man who selfishly turns his castlelike house into a secret storehouse during a rapidly worsening food shortage; *The Visitors*; and *Bob's Place* (1987), about a boy who escapes from his problems and loneliness to a South Sea island that exists only in his imagination. If you enjoy Townsend's books, try those of *Rumer Godden and *Margaret Mahy. MR

Townsend, Sue (1946–) An English playwright and novelist, Townsend is probably known best as author of *The Secret Diary of Adrian Mole, Aged 13¾*, a humorous and touching novel about a bright but lonely and naive English boy. Townsend began her career writing plays, and her story of Adrian Mole began as a radio play. The program's success led to the book and to its sequel, *The Growing Pains of Adrian*

Mole (1985). Townsend also wrote *Rebuilding Coventry* (1988), a darkly comic novel about Coventry Dakin, an Englishwoman who, after killing her neighbor's drunken, abusive husband, abandons her suburban home, husband, and two teenage children and flees into London to hide among the city's dispossessed. This novel was praised for its fascinating and often hilarious characters and its sharp observations of people struggling with poverty amid great wealth. MR & YA

Track's End (1911), by Hayden Carruth (1862–1932), is a remarkable adventure story of the Old West whose hero, Judson Pitcher, has the same tough, pioneering spirit of *Robinson Crusoe*. Judson, about 18 years old, arrives one autumn in the 1870s at the little town of Track's End in the Territory of Dakota. The railroad tracks go no farther, and when the last train leaves before the onslaught of winter, Jud finds himself left alone and in charge of the whole town, which includes a bank with $20,000 stored in the safe. Throughout the winter Jud has a series of adventures defending the town against wolves, Indians, and robbers. There are blizzards that last for days and a fire that threatens to destroy Track's End. And there is a mystery you will not find easy to solve. How Judson manages to survive with only one real companion, a dog named Kaiser, and to save the town until the train returns the following spring makes an exciting story you will not soon forget. MR & YA

Travelers by Night (1983) By *Vivian Alcock, this novel tells about Belle and Charlie Marriot, two young cousins whose lives change suddenly when the small English circus that has been their life is forced to close. Added to their concern about life outside the circus is the knowledge that Tessie, their favorite elephant, is to be sent to the slaughterhouse. Belle and Charlie steal Tessie and begin a long journey, traveling by night, hoping to sneak Tessie into safe retirement in a safari park. Along the way they face unexpected problems, including dense forests and a dangerous bog, a gang of young toughs, and a local newspaper reporter looking for a big story. By the time they reach the park, Charlie, Belle, and Tessie have become celebrities. Tessie finds a new home in the park, and Charlie and Belle, soon accepted by the young people at the school they begin attending, find hope for their futures. If you enjoyed *Travelers by Night*, you will probably also like *The Something-Special Horse* (1985) by Lynn Hall (1937–), about a 12-year-old boy who steals a horse to save it from being slaughtered. MR

Traven, B. (1882–1969) This is the pen name of the secretive author of **The Treasure of the Sierra Madre*. Traven is now thought to have been a German named Otto Feige who, adopting the name Ret Marut, was an actor, writer, editor, and political activist during and after World War I. Forced to flee Germany in the early 1920s, he traveled to Mexico, his home for the remainder of his life, first as Traven Torsvan and later as Hal Croves. Traven has been described as a masterful storyteller but a sometimes awkward stylist. His major theme is the freedom of the individual, and he champions simple humanity over all forms of oppression. Traven's works include the novels *The Death Ship* (1934), about an American sailor with no official identity who finds himself a crewman aboard a ship marked for deliberate destruction by its owners, who are intent on collecting insurance money; *The Bridge in the Jungle* (1938), centering on the drowning death of a Mexican Indian boy; *The White Rose* (1965), about a ruthless American businessman determined to possess the property of his Mexican neighbor; and the collections *The Night Visitor and Other Stories* (1966) and *The Kidnapped Saint and Other Stories* (1975). YA

Trease, Geoffrey (1909–) A prolific author of historical novels and nonfiction books for adults and younger readers, Trease was born and grew up in Nottingham, England. He used the nearby forest of Sherwood as the setting for his first novel, *Bows Against the Barons* (1934), which was based on the legend of *Robin Hood. His other novels include *Cue for Treason* (1940), about an English boy who becomes an actor in London, meets *William Shakespeare, and helps foil a plot against the queen; *No Boats on Bannermere* (1949), about a boy and girl who investigate a mystery involving a lake island near their new home; and *The Silken Secret* (1953), a mystery set in 18th-century England at the beginning of the Industrial Revolution. Trease's nonfiction books include *Wolfgang Mozart: The Young Composer* (1961) and *The Phoenix and the Flame: D.H. Lawrence, a Biography* (1973). MR & YA

Treasure Island (1883) This adventure classic by *Robert Louis Stevenson begins in England, where Jim Hawkins helps his family run a seaside inn. Jim gets hold of a treasure map from the trunk of an old seaman, Billy Bones, who has died at the inn. He takes the map, showing where the pirate Flint's treasure is located, to Dr. Livesay and Squire Trelawney. They outfit the ship *Hispaniola*, aided by a one-legged ship's cook, *Long John Silver, and, with Captain Smollett commanding, sail for Treasure Island.

Bones had warned Jim to look out for a seaman with one leg. At sea Jim learns that Silver has hired many of Flint's old crew and plans to take the treasure and kill everyone not part of the plot. At the island Jim and his companions escape from the pirates. Aided by Ben Gunn, a marooned, half-mad buccaneer, they fight to save their lives and regain the ship from the pirates. Silver, the pirate leader, plays both sides of the struggle, acting sometimes as Jim's enemy and other times as his protector. The pirates are finally defeated, with Silver's connivance, and the treasure is secured, but the wily Silver escapes.

The treasure Jim and his friends found was not all of Flint's booty, however. You can read about what happened to Long John and the rest of the treasure in *Flint's Island* (1972) by *Leonard Wibberley. *Treasure Island* has been adapted for film many times. MR & YA

Treasure of the Sierra Madre, The (1935) By *B. Traven, this novel is set in Mexico in the 1920s. Two down-and-out Americans, Fred C. Dobbs and a man simply called Curtin, join

Long John Silver, the resourceful pirate leader in *Treasure Island*

forces with Howard, an old prospector, to hunt for gold in the mountains. Howard has warned them that gold has the power to turn decent men into greedy, selfish killers, but they do not believe him. After a long search they find gold, and after months of hard labor, they collect a small fortune in gold dust. They are discovered by another prospector, who joins them only to be killed in a fight with a gang of bandits. Then the three partners begin the trip home. Howard leaves the party to revive a half-drowned American Indian boy. Deprived of his calming influence, Dobbs and Curtin soon have a falling out and Dobbs shoots Curtin, leaving him for dead in the bush. Dobbs is killed by bandits who, not recognizing the value of what appears to be bags of sand in Dobbs's mule packs, cast the gold on the ground. The wind carries it back into the mountains. When Howard learns of this he laughs at the tremendous joke fate has pulled on them all and, finding Curtin has survived, tells him he plans to continue his happy life with the native Mexicans. If you enjoyed this book, try the Alaska stories of *Jack London. *The Treasure of the Sierra Madre* was made into an excellent movie in 1948. YA

MR = Middle Reader   YA = Young Adult Reader   * = See this main entry

Tree Grows in Brooklyn, A (1943) *Betty Smith's first and best-known novel is set in a working-class section of Brooklyn, New York, from 1912 to 1918. Eleven-year-old Francie Nolan lives with her parents, Johnny and Katie, and younger brother, Neeley, in a tenement apartment. Her mother works scrubbing floors, and her father, a talented singer but an alcoholic, finds occasional work as a singing waiter. Their lives are symbolized by the tree that grows outside their building. Although rooted in poor soil and cramped by concrete, it wills itself to survive and grow. Johnny, whom Francie adores, dies tragically, but the family continues, and soon Katie has a third child, Laurie. Francie and Neeley work and attend school and somehow the Nolans get by, struggling day by day to grow toward a better life. Katie remarries, and Francie gets ready to leave for college in Michigan. She looks back on her life in Brooklyn with mixed joy and sorrow, and forward to her future with hope. If you enjoyed *A Tree Grows in Brooklyn*, you will probably like the play *Street Scene* by *Elmer Rice, a touching, realistic drama of tenement life. *A Tree Grows in Brooklyn* was filmed in 1945 and remade for television in 1974. MR & YA

Treece, Henry (1912–1966) An English novelist, poet, and editor, Treece is known best for his historical novels based on Celtic and Norse history and legend. Among these is a trilogy following the adventures of Harald Sigurdson, son of a deposed Norse ruler. They include *Viking's Dawn* (1955), in which Harald takes part in a Viking voyage to Britain in the late 8th century; *The Road to Miklagard* (1957), in which Harald travels from Ireland across Europe to Miklagard, or Constantinople; and *Viking's Sunset* (1961), in which Harald voyages to Greenland and to North America. Treece's other novels include *The Dark Island* (1952), about the Roman conquest of Britain; *The Golden Strangers* (1956), set in prehistoric Britain; and *Horned Helmet* (1963), about the adventures of an 11th-century Icelandic boy kidnapped by Viking raiders. MR & YA

Treehorn is the main character in three whimsical stories written by Florence Parry Heide (1919–) and delightfully illustrated by Edward Gorey (1925–). Although he is an ordinary boy, Treehorn has some amazing experiences. In *The Shrinking of Treehorn* (1971), he begins to grow smaller and smaller and, when no one else takes his problem seriously, must find a way to get back to normal size. In *Treehorn's Treasure* (1981) he finds that the leaves of the tree in his backyard have changed into dollar bills, and in *Treehorn's Wish* (1984) he finds a genie in a bottle. Heide has written many other books for young people, including *Sound of Sunshine, Sound of Rain* (1970), which describes the experiences of a boy who is blind, and *Time's Up!* (1982), about the adventures of a boy who moves to a new home in the suburbs. MR

Trent's Last Case (originally, *The Woman in Black*) (1913), by *E.C. Bentley, is an early example of a detective story in which the hero is not a member of the police, but a person (often wealthy) who helps the police with interesting criminal cases. Other examples are *Dorothy L. Sayers's character, Lord *Peter Wimsey, and *Agatha Christie's retired Belgian detective, *Hercule Poirot.

This novel begins when the dead body of Sigsbee Manderson is found on his English estate. Philip Trent, a painter and amateur criminologist, is called in by a London newspaper to conduct an independent investigation. Trent has succeeded before in solving crimes that baffled the police. After questioning Manderson's two secretaries, Marlowe and Bunner, Trent meets the young and beautiful Mrs. Manderson. His study of the sparse clues and oddities of the case form the basis of his written report, pointing to Marlowe as the murderer. Trent suspects Mabel Manderson and the handsome Marlowe of plotting the crime together. Because Trent has become emotionally entangled, he gives Mabel his report and offers her the choice of whether or not to reveal the contents.

MR = Middle Reader   YA = Young Adult Reader   * = See this main entry

Unable to bear the thought of her possible involvement, Trent leaves England. Months later he hears that Marlowe is engaged to be married, but not to Mabel, and the case is still unresolved. Delighted and confused, Trent returns to England, where he meets Mabel and learns she has kept his report secret because she knew his conclusion was completely wrong. When the facts of the case come to light, Trent realizes that Manderson was insanely jealous of Mabel's friendly interest in Marlowe. The unbalanced Manderson set an elaborate trap for Marlowe, which included Manderson's own suicide arranged to look like murder, with evidence designed to point to Marlowe as the culprit. Trent, now relieved of the terrible burden of his suspicion, proposes marriage to Mabel, and she accepts him. YA

Treviño, Elizabeth B(orton) de (1904–) Author of a number of memorable novels for young readers, Treviño was born and grew up in California, where she began writing while still a girl. After working in Boston as a journalist for several years, she married and made her home in Mexico. Her best-known book is the novel *I, Juan Parejo* (1965), which tells about the Spanish painter Diego Velazquez (1599–1660) through the eyes of Juan Parejo, his slave, assistant, pupil, and devoted friend. Treviño's other novels include *The Greek of Toledo* (1959), about the Spanish painter El Greco (1541–1614); *Turi's Poppa* (1968), about a Hungarian boy and his father and their remarkable journey on foot from Hungary to Cremona, Italy, just after World War II; and *The House on Bitterness Street* (1970), set in Mexico during the Mexican Revolution of 1910, about a young woman who is determined to own the beautiful house of her childhood. *I, Juan Parejo* won the *Newbery Medal in 1966. MR & YA

Trial, The (1925) This story, by *Franz Kafka, is about Joseph K., who wakes on his 30th birthday to be arrested for a crime he is not aware of. He is not jailed and is allowed to go about his daily chores, but he must appear when summoned to a dim tenement garret. He arrives, on a Sunday. Nothing definite appears to be going on, but everyone there knows him, and the magistrate tells him that "it is only a trial if you recognize it as such." Most of the audience are old men with beards. The proceedings are informal and confused, and Joseph harangues the court. He storms out, refusing to cooperate. Eventually Joseph hires a lawyer who stays in bed most of the time and accomplishes nothing. Joseph consults the court painter, who tells him to expect little from the court. No one is acquitted, and trials are prolonged indefinitely. His priest offers no encouragement, knowing he will be convicted. Joseph and the priest still do not know what the crime was. As the priest says, "It is not necessary to accept everything as true, one must only accept it as necessary." Finally, the night before his 31st birthday, Joseph is taken away and stabbed to death. Because of its many layers of meaning, which often prefigure the injustice of a modern totalitarian state, this story, though unfinished and ordered to be destroyed by Kafka upon his death, has been a major influence on literature since it was published. If you enjoyed the overtones and *symbolism of this novel, read Kafka's *The Castle. A film version of *The Trial* was created in 1963. YA

Tricksters, The (1987) By *Margaret Mahy, this novel set in New Zealand combines suspense, family drama, and the supernatural. Seventeen-year-old Ariadne Hamilton, known to all as Harry, arrives with her family at their seaside cottage, Carnival Hide, to celebrate Christmas and New Year's Day. The Hamiltons' plans for a peaceful holiday are disrupted, however, when three mysterious brothers, who seem to be magicians or "tricksters" of some sort, appear on the beach and join the family's activities. All three bear a likeness to Teddy Carnival, the son of the builder of Carnival Hide, who drowned tragically long ago. They also are similar to characters in a book Harry is writing. Are they ghosts, different sides of the dead Teddy Carnival? The events that unfold bring to light the truth about Teddy's death as well as a troubling Hamilton family secret that threatens to pull the family apart but finally brings it closer together. If you enjoyed *The Tricksters*, you will probably also like *Touch Not the Cat* (1976) by *Mary Stewart, about an English girl with telepathic powers who investigates a family mystery. MR & YA

Trinity (1976) This massive novel by *Leon Uris is set in Ireland from 1885 to 1915, when the centuries-long struggle for Irish independence from English control gained momentum. The central figures are Conor Larkin and Seamus O'Neill, the sons of Catholic farmers in the northern province of Ulster. Conor's father, Tomas, and grandfather, Kilty, were noted leaders in the struggle of the Catholic Irish against English oppression. Both bright young men, Seamus and Conor receive encouragement from their schoolteacher, Andrew Ingram, a Scottish Protestant who sympathizes with the plight of the Irish Catholics. Seamus goes off to college and becomes a writer, but Conor remains home and becomes an accomplished blacksmith and ironmaster. Conor's search for happiness and personal fulfillment is hampered at every turn by the growing movement for Irish independence and the inflexible social and economic rules of Irish life. Pitted against the Irish Catholics are the English aristocrats and industrialists, represented by Sir Roger Hubble and Sir Frederick Weed, masters of the northern cities of Derry and Belfast, and the Protestants of Ulster, largely descendants of Scottish Presbyterians who were settled in Ireland to help the English gain control of the island and its inhabitants. Conor builds up a thriving forge and falls in love with a Protestant girl, Shelley MacLeod, but his business is destroyed and Shelley is brutally murdered. Meanwhile, Seamus has become a leading journalist supporting the Irish Republican cause. Convinced that change can come only through violence and faced with the open arming of a Protestant army in Ulster, Conor helps smug-

gle guns for the Republicans, survives an ambush and a brutal prison term and, with Seamus and others, stages a daring raid on the Protestants' weapons stockpile. Although they are killed, they destroy the arms and gain a moral victory for the Republicans, setting the stage for the Irish Revolution.

If you enjoyed *Trinity*, you may want to read the novels *Thy Tears Might Cease* (1963) by the Irish writer Michael Farrell (1899–1962), about a young man coming of age in Ireland during the turbulent years of 1910 to 1920, and *The Scorching Wind* (1964) by the Irish writer Walter Macken (1915–1967), about two brothers drawn into the Irish Revolution and Civil War. YA

Tristan and Iseult is a love story that a harper, or minstrel, tells at *Camelot, the court of *King Arthur. Tristan, nephew of King Marc of Cornwall, slays an Irish knight in a duel, thus averting a war. Later Tristan, shipwrecked in Ireland, kills a dragon that is scorching the countryside, and is forgiven for his victory over the Irish champion knight. He brings home the princess Iseult (Isolde, Isolt, Ysolt) to be the bride of King Marc in order to cement the peace between their two countries. But on the trip back to Cornwall, Tristan and Iseult fall passionately in love. Though Iseult becomes queen of Cornwall, the love affair continues until they are betrayed to King Marc. She is rescued from burning at the stake by Tristan wearing leper's clothes, and they escape to live in the forest. In the end Marc forgives his queen and Tristan is banished. Then he comes to Arthur's court and becomes a knight of the *Round Table. When he dies, Iseult arrives too late to see him, and she dies of a broken heart. King Marc buries them together, and hazel and honeysuckle plants spring from the ground over their hearts and twine together over their grave. There are many variations of this enduring love story. It is the source of the opera *Tristan and Isolde* (1865) by Richard Wagner (1813–1883). You will also enjoy an excellent modern version of the story, *Tristan and Iseult* (1990), by *Rosemary Sutcliff. YA

Trojan Horse Built by the Greeks at the close of the *Trojan War, it was a giant, hollow wooden statue, built of wood planking, with a concealed trap door in its flank. An inscription on the horse dedicated it to the goddess *Athena, who supported the Greeks against the Trojans in the conflict. *Odysseus and a band of Greek warriors hid inside the horse, and after the rest of the Greek army sailed away, the Trojans hauled the statue within the walls of Troy. In the night Odysseus and the others climbed out of the horse, killed the Trojan guards and sentries, and opened the gates of Troy to the Greek army, which had returned. The surprised Trojans were slaughtered, and the Greeks won the war. You can read about the Trojan Horse in the *Aeneid* by the Roman poet *Virgil as well as in *Bulfinch's Mythology* by Thomas Bulfinch (1796–1867) and *Mythology* by Edith Hamilton (1867–1963). MR & YA

Trojan War This epic struggle of Greek legend was said to have been sparked by *Paris, son of King Priam of Troy, who persuaded *Helen, the beautiful wife of Menelaus, king of Sparta, to flee with him to Troy. Menelaus called the kings of Greece together, and a great force led by *Agamemnon, Menelaus's brother, sailed for Troy, a walled city near the southern entrance of the *Hellespont, on the site of what is now Hissarlik, Turkey. During the first nine years of the struggle the Greeks accomplished little. The bloody events of the 10th year, centering on the activities of the Greek hero *Achilles, are recounted by *Homer in the *Iliad*. The story of the *Trojan Horse, by which the Greeks gained entry to Troy, sacked the city, killed the men, and carried off the women, is recounted by the Roman poet *Virgil in the *Aeneid*. For centuries the story of the Trojan War was thought to have been a myth, but the discovery by the German archeologist Heinrich Schliemann (1822–1890) of the ruins of ancient Troy helped prove that the war actually happened. A fascinating nonfiction book on the subject is *In Search of the Trojan War* (1985) by the English writer Michael Wood (1948–), and *The Firebrand* (1987) by *Marion Zimmer Bradley is a novel about the war. Younger readers will enjoy *The Children's Homer* (1918) by the Irish writer Padraic Colum (1881–1972), *The Siege and Fall of Troy* (1962) by *Robert Graves, and the novel *The Windswept City* (1967) by *Henry Treece. MR & YA

Troll Kingdom In the verse drama *Peer Gynt* (1867) by *Henrik Ibsen, the young hero Peer wanders in the Dovre mountains of central Norway and enters the realm of King Brose, the king of the trolls, which are creatures of evil and darkness often possessing magical powers, including the ability to change shape or become invisible. Peer sees trolls of all shapes and sizes. The king tells him that there are even some two- and three-headed trolls. Peer asks to marry the Troll King's daughter, then abandons her and flees, coming upon the Great Boyg, a vast, invisible troll that defeats its victims by remaining passive. It almost overcomes Peer but, like the other trolls, is driven away by the sound of distant church bells and the voices of women singing hymns. Peer goes to live in the forest with his true love, Solveig, but flees after the Troll King's now-hideous daughter reappears. After a lifetime of adventure around the world, in which he fails to find the purpose of his life, he returns to Norway and finds it in the faithful love and devotion of Solveig, who has waited for him. YA

Trout Fishing in America (1967), by *Richard Brautigan, is a series of short sketches or loosely connected stories, often considered to be typical of the rebellious, antiwar writing of the 1960s. These stories describe the lives of a man and woman and their child, who travel around the United States fishing, telling stories, and writing recipes for unusual dishes. Most of the events take place in the country, and Brautigan clearly expresses his fear that our natural environment is being destroyed. Some sketches are written with deadpan humor, while others are filled with images of sex and violence. The traveler tells us that in America people can buy and sell just about anything, that the great American dream is being constantly betrayed, and that he longs for the cleaner and simpler life of the past. He takes comfort in the belief that good humor and imagination can help make life worth living. YA

Trumpet of the Swan, The (1970) This classic fantasy by *E.B. White tells about Louis, a young trumpeter swan who was born without a voice. Though he is unable to communicate the way other swans do, Louis is very bright, and he finds a friend in Sam Beaver, a boy who loves all living things. Louis goes to school with Sam and learns how to read and write. Returning home, he finds his new ability with slate and chalk are useless, for his parents and the other animals cannot read, not even the lovely swan Serena, with whom Louis has fallen in love. His father, determined to help his son, breaks into a music store and steals a trumpet for Louis. Soon Louis learns how to play it and sets out to seek his fortune, pay back the music store for the trumpet, and win Serena's love. If you enjoyed *The Trumpet of the Swan*, be sure to read White's other classic tales, *Charlotte's Web* and *Stuart Little*. MR

Tryouts, The (1979) By Elizabeth Levy (1942–), this novel tells about four eighth-grade buddies—Matt Cornwall, Spider Jackson, Ritchie Rizzuto, and Diggy Stevens—whose dreams of playing together on their school basketball team are dashed when Matt's father, the school principal, opens the team to girls as well as boys. Donna Findley, the tallest girl in school and an outstanding basketball player, makes the team, as does her friend Janet Watson. But Diggy, who is fat and does not do well in the tryouts, fails to make the team. Donna and Matt lead the others in a team strike, but Diggy surprises them by agreeing with Coach Maguire that he is not good enough. Finally, Matt's father suggests that Diggy be made assistant coach, a solution that proves successful. Elizabeth Levy has written many other books for young people, including *Lizzie Lies a Lot* (1976), about a 9-year-old girl whose habit of lying gets her into big trouble, and *The Computer That Said Steal Me* (1983), about a boy who steals a computer chess game he longs to own, then finds he hates the idea of being a thief. MR

Tuck Everlasting (1975), written by *Natalie Babbitt, tells of Winnie Foster and the mysterious Treegap Woods, which belong to her family. Winnie is an only child who dreams of running away. In defiance of her parents' rule, she ventures into the woods and comes upon a handsome older boy, Jesse Tuck, drinking from an odd-looking hidden spring. Moments later, Jesse's mother, Mae, and his brother, Miles, find the two youngsters together and are upset that Winnie has seen the spring. Greatly embarrassed, they carry her off to their farm.

Mr. Tuck and his family treat Winnie kindly while they tell their story. They discovered 87 years ago that drinking the secret spring water healed wounds, prevented sickness, and kept all who drank it from getting any older. Frightened that others will misuse the powers of the water in their wish for immortality, the Tucks try to persuade Winnie to keep the secret. Unfortunately, a lanky stranger in a yellow suit overhears the story from a hiding place in the bushes. He goes to see Winnie's family and tells them he will bring Winnie safely home only if they will sell Treegap Woods to him. In desperation, they agree. When the stranger confronts the Tucks and Winnie with his dreadful bargain, saying he will sell the water only to "those who deserve it," Mae knocks him out just as the constable arrives on the scene. While Mae is in jail, the stranger dies. Winnie then helps the Tucks free Mae and move the family to another place, and she decides never to tell the secret of the spring. If you enjoyed this book, you will probably also like *Two Against the Tide* by Bruce Clements, about two young people kidnapped to an island whose inhabitants have found the secret of eternal life. MR

Tuned Out (1968) This novel by Maia Wojciechowska (1927–) is in the form of a journal kept by 16-year-old Jim. In the summer of 1967 Jim's older brother, Kevin, whom he idolizes, returns home after his first year at the University of Chicago. A seemingly brilliant, specially gifted person, Kevin has lost his direction in life, is troubled and fearful, and has begun using drugs. After trying marijuana once with Kevin, Jim vows to save his brother from himself, but there is little he can do. Kevin has a horrifying LSD trip and is rushed to a psychiatric clinic. During Kevin's long recovery, Jim and his family learn that "Kevin the genius" was only a role his older brother felt forced to play to help keep the family together and happy. Jim fights through his feelings of anger, betrayal, and loss, but finally learns to accept Kevin as he really is. If you liked *Tuned Out*, try *That Was Then, This Is Now* by *S.E. Hinton, about a teenager forced to make a difficult decision when he learns his best friend is dealing drugs. See also *Shadow of a Bull*, also by Maia Wojciechowska. YA

Tunis, John R(oberts) (1889–1975) Though he is known best for the novel *His Enemy, His Friend*, a combined tribute to sport and condemnation of warfare and human brutality, Tunis wrote dozens of books, including many novels for younger readers. Most are baseball or other sports stories. *Iron Duke* (1938) tells about an Iowa youth who plunges into a totally new environment when he enters Harvard University and develops into a confident young man and a star track-and-field athlete. Tunis's other novels, which are still popular, include *The Kid from Tomkinsville* (1940), about a rookie with the Brooklyn Dodgers who overcomes a disabling injury that ends his pitching career and eventually becomes a star center fielder; *Highpockets* (1948), about a self-centered, unhappy, and disliked young Dodger slugger who struggles to become a valued team member; and *Schoolboy Johnson* (1958), in which a veteran Dodger pitcher helps a temperamental but promising young pitcher to learn what it takes to be a winner on the field and in life. If you enjoy Tunis's sports books, you will also like those of *Alfred Slote. MR

Turgenev, Ivan (Sergeyevich) (1818–1883) Considered one of the great figures of Russian literature, Turgenev wrote six novels, numerous short stories and novellas, plays, and poetry. But he is known best for the novel *Fathers and Sons*, depicting the growing conflict in Russia between the old order and the forces of change. Born into the Russian upper class, he became an opponent of serfdom and admirer of the character and dignity of common Russians. His first major success came with *A Sportsman's Sketches* (1852), a collection of stories that showed his partiality to the lives and qualities of peasants and dislike of the elite. The book found enemies, and Turgenev was forced into exile on his estate. He left Russia in 1855 and spent much of his later life abroad. Turgenev's works, which have been praised for their grace and beauty, include the novels *On the Eve* (1860), about a Russian woman who falls in love with a Bulgarian patriot living only to free his country from Turkish domination, and *Smoke* (1867), a love story set against the social and economic changes occurring in Russia following the emancipation of the serfs in 1861. *The Torrents of Spring* (1872) is a novella about a young man who gives up the love of an innocent girl for a brief, passionate affair with a wealthy, worldly, and ruthless woman. Turgenev's best-known play, *A Month in the Country* (1869), tells about a young student who takes a tutoring job on a country estate and finds that both the owner's wife and the 17-year-old girl under her care have fallen in love with him. YA

Turn of the Screw, The (1898), by *Henry James, is a chilling ghost story. It begins with the narrator telling the story to listeners round the fire in an old house on Christmas Eve. It is not so much the story that scares us as our imaginations working overtime thinking about the fate of the two children, Miles and Flora, as they become more and more involved with the evil apparitions of two lovers: their former governess, Miss Jessel, and the male servant, Peter Quint. You may enjoy a collection of short stories by Henry James, *The Lesson of the Master* (1891), tales about artists and writers. YA

Twain, Mark [Samuel Langhorne Clemens] (1835–1910) Humorist, writer, and lecturer, Twain was one of the outstanding figures of American literature in the later 19th century. Sam Clemens grew up in the Mississippi River

Tweedledum and Tweedledee depicted by the famous English illustrator
John Tenniel (1820–1914).

town of Hannibal, Missouri, and the influence of the river and the frontier society that had developed along its banks is reflected in his writings, particularly *The Adventures of Tom Sawyer and *The Adventures of Huckleberry Finn. After working as a printer for a time, Clemens became a riverboat pilot on the Mississippi, an experience he immortalized in the book *Life on the Mississippi. When the Civil War halted travel on the river, Clemens went west with his brother, working as a miner and newspaperman in Nevada and California. At this time he adopted his famous pen name, which became known nationally with the publication of his humorous story "The Celebrated Jumping Frog of Calaveras County" (1865), about how the owner of a champion jumping frog gets his comeuppance in a contest with a wily stranger. After a trip to Europe, Egypt, and the Holy Land, which he chronicled in The Innocents Abroad (1869), Mark Twain settled in Hartford, Connecticut, his home during the 1870s and 1880s. During this period Twain wrote his best-known works, including *The Prince and the Pauper and *A Connecticut Yankee in King Arthur's Court. An incurable inventor and entrepreneur, Twain lost a fortune in ill-advised business ventures. These re-

verses, as well as the deaths of two of his daughters and his wife, contributed to a growing bitterness about life and about human character and morals in much of Twain's later writings. Among the best are Personal Recollections of Joan of Arc (1896), a novel in the form of biography, which Twain considered his best work; The Man That Corrupted Hadleyburg (1900), about a mysterious stranger who tricks the residents of a supposedly respectable town into revealing their greed and corruption; and The Mysterious Stranger (1916), set in late 15th-century Austria, centering on a mysterious printer's apprentice with supernatural powers. MR & YA

Tweedledum and Tweedledee, in *Lewis Carroll's fantasy *Through the Looking-Glass, are two "fat little men" who look "exactly like a couple of . . . schoolboys." Alice can tell which is which only because their names are embroidered on their collars. In fact, they differ only in name. "Tweedledum and Tweedledee" was first used with reference to the musical rivalry between the Italian composer Giovanni Bononcini (1670–1747) and the German-English composer George Frederick Handel (1685–1759), a rivalry that lovers of *William Shakespeare might have described as "much ado about nothing." Today "Tweedledum and Tweedledee" refers to two persons, groups, things, choices, or the like that are essentially alike except in name. MR

Twenty Thousand Leagues Under the Sea

(1870) This *science fiction classic by *Jules Verne is narrated by a French scientist, Pierre Aronnax, who in 1867 joins the expedition of the U.S. warship *Abraham Lincoln* to find and destroy an immense, phosphorescent, whale-like creature that has recently appeared near or has collided with several vessels. When the creature rams the warship, Aronnax is knocked into the water along with the Canadian harpooner Ned Land. After Aronnax's servant Conseil dives in to help, the three drift away from the crippled warship. They are picked up by the creature, actually the *Nautilus*, an electric-powered submarine commanded by the mysterious *Captain Nemo. He and his crew have renounced all ties to the nations of earth and have made the sea their homeland, sometimes attacking the warships of the great nations. Aronnax and his companions, well-treated prisoners, take part in many adventures during a ten-month voyage, including a visit to the lost continent of Atlantis and a voyage to the South Pole. They finally escape, but the fate of the *Nautilus* and the mystery of Nemo remain unanswered. Verne revealed Nemo's identity and fate in the sequel, *The Mysterious Island* (1870). *Twenty Thousand Leagues Under the Sea* was made into a movie in 1954. MR & YA

Twenty Years at Hull-House

(1910) This autobiography by Jane Addams (1860–1935), the famous social reformer, begins with Addams's childhood and youth in Illinois. The daughter of a successful businessman and state legislator, she early became concerned with the conditions of the poor. Forced to leave medical school by a lifelong spinal problem, she traveled in Europe for several years before deciding, with her friend Ellen Gates Starr (1860–

1940), to found in the Chicago slums a settlement house where forward-looking social programs could be conducted to aid the working poor. Hull-House offered a wide range of social, educational, cultural, and recreational programs. Addams also pioneered legislation to improve conditions for workers, children, and women. Though Addams wrote many books and articles, *Twenty Years at Hull-House* is considered her masterpiece. If you enjoyed it, try its sequel, *The Second Twenty Years at Hull-House* (1930). YA

Two Against the Tide

(1967) By Bruce Clements (1931–), this novel tells about Tom Inlander and his sister, Sharon, whose planned vacation with "Aunt Eve" Standish, a family friend, turns into a kidnapping. Instead of taking Tom and Sharon to her farm in Vermont, Aunt Eve takes them to her second, real home, a small island off the coast of Maine. Its inhabitants are all adults and most talk and act as if they are very old and set in their ways. Tom and Sharon learn that the islanders have found a chemical that stops the aging process. They have tried to create an island paradise, but their lives have become routine and empty. Tom and Sharon have been brought there in hope that they will bring new life to the community and that after a full summer there they will decide to stay. But they decide to give up eternal youth and return home, realizing that life means growing and changing. Clements, a minister, teacher, and author, has written a number of books for young people, including *I Tell a Lie Every So Often* (1974), recounting the hilarious adventures of a 14-year-old boy traveling with his brother up the Missouri River in 1848. MR

2001: A Space Odyssey

(1968) This *science fiction novel by *Arthur C. Clarke is based on a movie screenplay written by Clarke and Stanley Kubrick (1928–). It begins on Earth about 3 million years ago, when a band of apelike creatures first come upon a large stonelike slab, or monolith, whose emanations give the crea-

---

MR = Middle Reader   YA = Young Adult Reader   * = See this main entry

tures the concepts of food gathering, toolmaking, and cooperative effort that will eventually lead to human intelligence. The story jumps to the end of the 20th century, when American astronauts on the moon discover a large monolith that suddenly releases a powerful burst of energy toward Saturn. The spaceship *Discovery*, carrying astronauts David Bowman, Frank Poole, and three scientists hibernating in suspended animation, is sent to a rendezvous with Saturn. HAL, the enormously sophisticated onboard computer, inexplicably kills all the astronauts but Bowman, who disables HAL and continues toward Saturn. There, on the moon Japetus, he finds an immense monolith, actually a "star gate" that carries Bowman through time and space and changes him into a new being, a "star child" of intelligent energy. He travels back to Earth knowing only that he must help humanity find its destiny among the stars. Clarke continued his remarkable story of first contact in the sequels *2010: Odyssey Two* (1982) and *2061: Odyssey Three* (1987). Movies of *2001* and *2010* were released in 1968 and 1984 respectively. YA

Tyler, Anne (1941–) The author of a number of critically acclaimed novels, Tyler grew up in the Middle West and North Carolina before settling in Baltimore, Maryland, which is the setting of several of her books. Her work is praised for its characterizations and observation of the details of ordinary life. Among her best-known novels are *Celestial Navigation* (1974), about an artistic but reclusive man who keeps the larger world at a distance, guiding his own life by a sort of internal "celestial navigation"; *Morgan's Passing* (1980), about a man who escapes his humdrum work and disordered family life by taking on different identities at whim; *Dinner at the Homesick Restaurant* (1982), about a man who opens a restaurant, where "people come just like to a family dinner," in an effort to draw his own family back together; *The Accidental Tourist* (1985), about a writer of guidebooks whose own accidental approach to living changes when he meets a lively, eccentric woman; and *Breath-*

Tom and Toby are surrounded by the warlike Typees.

ing Lessons (1988), a study of a long-married couple's relationship as it is revealed during the events of a single day. *The Accidental Tourist* was adapted for film in 1988. YA

Typee (1846) *Herman Melville's first novel, *Typee* is based on his experiences in the South Pacific in the early 1840s. The story is narrated by Tom, a sailor aboard the whaler *Dolly*. Sickened by the ship's terrible conditions and tyrannical captain, Tom and his friend Toby desert when the whaler arrives at Nukuheva, in the Marquesas, a group of islands in the southern Pacific Ocean. Traveling inland in hope of finding temporary refuge with the peaceful Happar tribe, Tom becomes ill with a severely swollen leg. They mistakenly arrive in the valley of the Typee, fierce cannibals. Under the protection of the king, Mehevi, they are treated kindly but as virtual prisoners in the house of the old warrior Marheyo. Toby, allowed to leave to get medical help for Tom, does not return. Tom stays for several months, observing the nearly idyllic life of the Typee but dreading their barbaric ways and longing to escape. He becomes deeply attached to Marheyo, his son Kory-Kory, who guards Tom constantly, and the beautiful girl Fayaway. After several months Tom finally makes his escape, aided tearfully by his friends, who cannot understand his desire to leave the paradise of Typee. Melville continued the story of Tom's return to civilization in the novel *Omoo*. YA

U

Uchida, Yoshiko (1921–) A Japanese American, Yoshiko Uchida was raised in San Francisco. Her parents instilled in her respect for both Japanese and American customs. The family flew a U.S. flag outside their home and studied the Constitution. But despite their attempts to become more American, Yoshiko was excluded from restaurants and hotels, and she was not permitted to participate in the social activities of her white classmates.

When war broke out with Japan, Uchida's family—like about 110,000 other Japanese Americans— was moved to a squalid, dusty relocation center. One of her best-known novels, *Journey to Topaz: The Story of the Japanese-American Evacuation* (1971), describes an 11-year-old imprisoned in one of those camps.

Uchida was allowed to leave the relocation center and complete college before the war was over. She then spent two years visiting Japan and writing about its folk traditions. Her earliest books, including *Takao and the Grandfather's Sword* (1958) and *The Promised Year* (1959), are about Japanese people and customs. In the early 1960s she turned to writing about Japanese Americans. *Samurai of Gold Hill* (1972) is about the first Japanese immigrants to the United States during the 1850s. Her other works concerning Japanese Americans include the trilogy *A Jar of Dreams* (1981), *The Best Bad Thing* (1983), and *The Happiest Ending* (1985),

which are about a Japanese-American teenage girl, Rinko, growing up in California during the *Great Depression. The main objective of these works, she says, is "to dispel long-existing stereotypic images" of Japanese Americans and to "celebrate our common humanity." MR & YA

Ullman, James Ramsey (1907–1971) A mountaineer, reporter, theatrical producer, and novelist, Ullman often described in his books his own adventures as well as those of others. He began his writing career after graduating from Princeton University in New Jersey and working for several years as a reporter and feature writer for *The Brooklyn Eagle*. After producing 12 plays on Broadway, he embarked on a long and difficult journey in the Andes Mountains and along the Amazon River. He wrote about that journey later in his book *The Other Side of the Mountain* (1938). He climbed mountains for most of his life, including Mount Olympus, the Matterhorn, and a 17,342-foot volcano known to neighboring Mexicans as Ixtacihuatl. Ullman was also part of the first team to climb Mount Everest, documented in *Americans on Everest* (1964), written with other members of the expedition. Most of his novels, including his first, *The White Tower* (1945), appear at first only to be exciting accounts of climbs. But the mountains are *symbols for the goals people attempt to achieve in life; the climbs themselves represent struggles to achieve those goals. "For it is the ultimate wisdom of the mountains," Ullman once said, "that a man is never more a man than when he is striving for what is beyond his grasp, and there is no conquest worth winning save that over weakness and fear." Ullman wrote a novel for younger readers, *Banner in the Sky, about a boy wanting to be a mountaineer like his father. *The White Tower* was filmed in 1950. Several of his other books have also been made into movies. YA

Ulysses (1922) Literary critics call this novel, by *James Joyce, the greatest English-language novel of the 20th century, and while you may find it difficult, it is well worth your trying to understand its unique use of our language. The events in the book take place in Dublin, Ireland, on June 16, 1904, a date now celebrated by Joyce enthusiasts as Bloomsday. The main characters are Leopold Bloom, a salesman of advertising space, of Jewish descent, a kind, self-conscious man, seeking love but not finding it; his wife, Molly, unfaithful, skeptical, and sensual, seen by Joyce as the personification of the female sex; and Stephen Dedalus, who is largely Joyce himself and personifies the artist. The novel consists of an account of the mostly separate wanderings through Dublin of Bloom and Dedalus. They visit, among other places, a public bath, a newspaper, and a brothel. In effect they are exiles seeking a home of the type each needs—Bloom, something practical; Dedalus, an artistic haven. Equally important, but in a different way, is Molly, whose soliloquy—one long sentence—makes up the last section of the book. This monologue presents her as the feminine principle that reanimates the universe. It ends with the word "yes" as she expresses the ultimate importance of life and love. Joyce's use of the *stream of consciousness technique shows him a master of witty twists and turns of English. The structure of the novel follows that of the *Odyssey* by *Homer, with Bloom representing *Odysseus, the hero; Dedalus, Te-

Uncle Sam in James Montgomery Flagg's celebrated World War I recruiting poster

lemachus, his son; and Molly, Penelope, Odysseus' wife. *Ulysses* was adapted for film in 1967. YA

Uncle Remus One of the best-known characters in children's literature, Uncle Remus was created by *Joel Chandler Harris in the 1870s as the narrator of a series of folktales written for a newspaper, the *Atlanta Constitution*. Uncle Remus tells his stories in the dialect, or the manner of speaking, used by blacks in the South around the time of the Civil War. His stories about the adventures of his friends Brer Rabbit, Brer Fox, and other animals have delighted young readers for more than a century. And, like the *fables of *Aesop, the adventures of Uncle Remus's animal friends teach valuable lessons about life and about human nature. See also *The Tales of Uncle Remus* by *Julius Lester. MR

Uncle Sam, the name of a bearded man who personifies the United States, was first used during the War of 1812 at a warehouse in Troy, New York, for military provisions. Its owner was Elbert Anderson. Boxes of provisions were stamped "E.A.—U.S.," meaning "Elbert Anderson—United States." Workers joked that U.S. really were the initials of the nickname of a superintendent, Samuel Wilson (1766–1854), who was known as Uncle Sam. The name spread after a newspaper reported the story. As the war continued, Uncle Sam was drawn tall, thin, and friendly—in sharp contrast to John Bull, the curt English farmer who symbolized the English enemy.

In 1868 *Harper's Weekly* ran the first picture of Uncle Sam as you know him today, with a white beard, starred vest, and red, white, and blue clothes. The picture was drawn by a cartoonist, Thomas Nast (1840–1902), who was inspired in part by the "flag suit" of a circus clown. The famous recruiting poster by James Montgomery Flagg (1877–1960) of Uncle Sam urging men to enlist in World War I is the most widely known view of Uncle Sam as you see him pictured today.

Uncle Tom's Cabin, or, Life Among the Lowly (1851), once one of America's most popular novels, by *Harriet Beecher Stowe, is a stirring depiction of the sufferings of black slaves prior to the Civil War. The story begins when George Shelby, a good-natured Kentucky plantation owner, is forced, due to his financial condition, to sell some of his slaves. Eliza, one of the slaves, escapes with her baby before she is taken away. Her husband George escapes soon thereafter to search for them. But Uncle Tom, an old slave and a devout Christian, who is a favorite of George Shelby, believes that God will return him to his wife and the kindly Shelby family. While being taken south, Tom rescues Eva St. Claire, the young daughter of a wealthy plantation owner. Eva then convinces her father to buy Tom, who is humanely treated by the St. Claire family. But Eva, a frail girl, dies of a respiratory illness, and her father is killed soon thereafter. Tom must once again be sold, this time to a cruel, drunken plantation owner, *Simon Legree, who whips Tom to

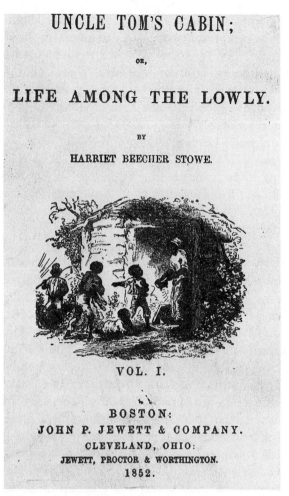

UNCLE TOM'S CABIN;

OR,

LIFE AMONG THE LOWLY.

BY

HARRIET BEECHER STOWE.

VOL. I.

BOSTON:
JOHN P. JEWETT & COMPANY.
CLEVELAND, OHIO:
JEWETT, PROCTOR & WORTHINGTON.
1852.

Title page of the first edition of
Uncle Tom's Cabin

death for refusing to divulge what he knows about the escape of two other slaves. George, Eliza, and their baby, assisted by the Underground Railroad, are reunited in Canada, where slavery is illegal. For decades theatrical adaptations of *Uncle Tom's Cabin* were staged by "Tommers" throughout the United States. The term "Uncle Tom" has come to mean a black person who acts subserviently toward whites. And "Simon Legree" has come to mean a harsh, unfeeling master or boss. Another classic novel that gives you a view of slavery in America is *Huckleberry Finn* by *Mark Twain. A powerful story about a slave revolt is *The Confessions of Nat Turner* by *William Styron. Younger readers will like *Amos Fortune, Free Man* by *Elizabeth Yates. *Uncle Tom's Cabin* was adapted for a TV movie in 1987. MR & YA

MR = Middle Reader   YA = Young Adult Reader   * = See this main entry

Under Milk Wood (1954), by *Dylan Thomas, is a radio play, but also considered a masterpiece of modern poetry. Though there is no plot, tension is created both between and within the residents of the Welsh seaside town of Llareggub. Thomas exhorts the reader to listen to the hushed town breathing. Then, as surely as he portrays a typical seaside village, he introduces characters that are full of repressed sexual tension and unspeakable loneliness. Myfanwy Price dreams of a hot lover, but settles for stodgy Mr. Mog Edwards. Lonely Captain Cat hears voices of drowned sailors who once were his companions. Mr. Pugh politely brings arsenic tea to his nagging wife. Only Nogood Boyo, who is free of the repressive mores of the town, is at all content.

Dylan Thomas is known for his use of language. *Under Milk Wood* is written in a lilting, English-Welsh dialogue that, like the seaside town of Llareggub, lulls with gentle simplicity—then jolts with its stormy, underlying complexity. YA

Understood Betsy (1917), written by *Dorothy Canfield Fisher, is about 9-year-old Elizabeth Ann, who is raised by her well-meaning but overprotective aunts in the city. When one of her aunts becomes ill, Betsy is sent to live with the Putneys in Vermont. She is frightened because Aunt Frances had once described the Putneys as uncaring people who would never understand a sensitive girl like Elizabeth Ann. But Aunt Abigail and Uncle Henry turn out to understand Betsy better than she had thought. They teach her, for the first time in her life, to rely on herself. She learns how to cook, churn butter, and drive a carriage. She cleverly finds her own way home from the fair. Most importantly, she learns about warm, loving relationships as she befriends a younger girl named Molly.

When Aunt Frances arrives to bring her back to the city, Betsy faces a dilemma: How can she tell Aunt Frances, whom she loves dearly, that she would rather stay in the country? In this classic story, Betsy learns that she is understood by the most important person of all—

herself. If you enjoyed *Understood Betsy*, you will also want to read Fisher's *The Bent Twig*. MR

Undset, Sigrid (1882–1949) This famous Norwegian writer of 15 novels was expected to become a scientist like her father. But after her father's death Undset took a job as a file clerk and started writing. Her fourth book, *Jenny: A Novel* (1911), about an illegitimate baby and a heroine whose high morals lead to her death, brought her success, and she devoted herself to writing. *The Wild Orchid* (1929), about the religious conversion of Paul Selmer, and *The Faithful Wife* (1937), a satirical picture of the Protestant clergy with its images of the eternally feminine woman in the Christian sense, are set in the modern era. It was, however, Undset's trilogy portraying medieval Norwegian life in *Kristin Lavransdatter, and The Master of Hestviken* (1925–1927), a series of four novels set in the 14th century about Olav Audunssön, a farmer, and his somber family life, with its barbarism, squalor and magnificence, and holiness, that earned Undset her lasting reputation and the Nobel Prize for literature in 1928. YA

unicorn A mythical animal first described by a Roman author in 400 B.C., the unicorn is often depicted as a pure white horse with a horn jutting from its head, with the tail of a lion, the legs of a buck, and the feet of an elephant. The horn ranges from 18 inches to a yard in length and often contains magical potions. At first, it was thought to be a dangerous animal with a piercing whine, but during the Middle Ages, it evolved into a kind, shy animal and became a *symbol for the spiritual qualities of *Jesus Christ. Like Jesus, it was felt, the unicorn's shy and humble personality made it an easy target for its enemies, particularly the lion. Scotland adopted the symbol of the unicorn during its many centuries of feuding with England, whose symbol is the lion. Some people feel that *Lewis Carroll may have had the fighting between England and Scotland in mind when he wrote about a feuding lion and

One of a set of tapestries entitled "The Lady with the Unicorn"
at the Cluny Museum, Paris.

unicorn in *Through the Looking-Glass*. Modern writers of fiction for young readers have picked up on the unicorn's abundant symbolism. For example, in *The Young Unicorns* by *Madeline L'Engle, the unicorn is a symbol of goodness. Unicorns also play a strong symbolic role in *Unicorns in the Rain* (1980), which is about a young woman's flight from an abusive home into a new world filled with spirits and mystery, by Barbara Cohen (1932–1992). MR & YA

Unleaving, The (1976) By *Jill Paton Walsh, this novel interweaves past and present. English teenager Madge Fielding inherits her grandmother's seaside house. She rents it to a reading group consisting of two Oxford philosophy professors, their students, and their families. While staying with them, Madge begins to develop her own answers to the questions they pose, but her ideas are ignored because they are not sufficiently philosophical.

She befriends Patrick Treagle, the son of one of the professors. Madge, Patrick, and Madge's brother, Paul, spend their time together at the seaside discussing the same questions as the philosophy students. She realizes that though the professors and their students know their philosophy books very well, they lack love and the wisdom of life experience—qualities that were clearly evident in her eccentric grandmother, who is depicted in earlier scenes that are interwoven into the main story.

Tragedy strikes when Patrick's little sister, Molly, falls off a seaside cliff. In a state of panic and guilt over her death, Patrick wonders whether he really tried to save her—or if he pushed her in a fit of insane rage. Madge then confronts Professor Treagle, whose refusal ever to deal with Patrick is at the root of his son's emotional troubles. Recurring themes and *symbols, such as the dark-green bottle washing onto shore, contribute to the blending of past and present that are a hallmark of this novel. If you enjoyed *The Unleaving*, you will also want to read *Goldengrove* (1972), which portrays Madge in an earlier summer at her grandmother's seaside house. YA

Untermeyer, Louis (1885–1977) An American poet, essayist, and anthologist who wrote or edited more than 100 books, Untermeyer is best known for his anthologies *Modern British*

Poetry (1920) and *Modern American Poetry* (1926). He grew up on the East Side of Manhattan and was an insatiable reader who dropped out of high school because he felt it was a waste of time. He did not devote his full time to writing until the early 1920s. Though Untermeyer was considered one of the foremost experts on American and British poetry, he believed that poetry was another language that was unfathomable even to himself. "I know nothing about poetry," he said in 1977. "What I know is how it affects people, what it does to them, how it emotionally makes things happen." YA

Unto This Hour (1984) By Tom [Thomas Grey] Wicker (1926–), a former political columnist of *The New York Times*, this novel, an account of a Civil War battle, is a mixture of history and fiction in which you will find it hard to tell where one begins and the other leaves off. The battle is known in the North as Second Bull Run and in the South as Second Manassas, fought on August 29–30, 1862, about 30 miles from Washington, D.C. Many historical figures are present, including President Abraham Lincoln (1809–1865). There are also many fictional figures, all of whom act and speak as their real-life counterparts must have. Thus you see the battle from the viewpoint of both the generals and the lower-ranking officers and enlisted men who did the fighting and who, the author makes clear, suffered horribly. As the battle began, Union forces under General John Pope (1822–1892) attacked the Confederate troops of General Stonewall Jackson (1824–1863) but were repulsed when Jackson was reinforced by the army of General James Longstreet (1821–1904). When Pope attacked again on August 30, he was soundly defeated and had to retreat in a rout. This book is long and detailed; but, if you want the feel of what it was like to be involved in such a battle, read it. If you liked *Unto This Hour,* be sure to read *The Red Badge of Courage* by *Stephen Crane. YA

Up a Road Slowly (1966), a finely crafted novel by *Irene Hunt, tells about Julie Trelling, whose mother has recently died and who has been sent to live with Aunt Cordelia, an elementary school teacher. Julie has a difficult time adjusting to her aunt's strict rules at home and at school, but grows to respect her. She also deals with the absence of her preoccupied father and the loss of companionship when her older sister gets married.

Julie starts high school feeling lonely. Her father remarries, but she decides to stay with Aunt Cordelia. She goes out with Jonathan Eltwing, a broad-shouldered fellow who breaks up with her when she no longer helps him with his English papers. Aunt Cordelia's sympathy and understanding—stemming from her own heartbreak as a young woman—help Julie to get over Jonathan, and to recognize her true love for Danny Trevor, Julie's childhood friend. Uncle Haskell, a lonely, eccentric alcoholic, takes time from the imaginary novel he claims to be writing to help Julie get a story published before his death. At the novel's end, Julie has gained enough wisdom and maturity to face the outside world. *Up a Road Slowly* won the *Newbery Medal in 1967. MR

Updike, John (Hoyer) (1932–) One of the best-known and most highly acclaimed contemporary writers, Updike writes vivid short stories and novels with precise detail in which he portrays the lives of middle-class white Americans in small towns and suburbs. Updike became familiar with the rituals of middle-class America while growing up in suburban Pennsylvania. His themes are marriage, sex, and discord. His most critically praised series of novels concern a character named Rabbit. *Rabbit, Run, the first novel in the series, which shows Rabbit as a man who is terrified by adult responsibilities, was hailed by some critics as an American masterpiece. Other novels in the series are *Rabbit Redux* (1971), *Rabbit Is Rich* (1981), and *Rabbit at Rest* (1990). As Updike's reputation grew, so did the complaints by critics that the world of his novels was too narrowly focused on middle-class males who feel overpowered in their relationships with women. *The Witches of Eastwick* (1978), however, depicts three divorcées who, despite the apparent freedom they at first enjoy after their divorces, find themselves as emotionally controlled by a powerful male as Updike's male characters are by the women in their lives.

Updike has written several volumes of poetry and light verse, many of which deal with the same themes as his novels. A book for younger readers is *A Child's Calendar* (1966). Two of Updike's novels have been made into films, *Rabbit, Run* in 1970 and *The Witches of Eastwick* in 1987. YA

Upon the Head of a Goat, or, A Childhood in Hungary *1939–1944* (1981), a novel by Aranka Siegal (1930–), is based on the true experiences of the author as a child and young woman. Piri, a 9-year-old Jewish girl growing up in Hungary, is sent to visit her grandmother in Ukraine, and when she returns, her hometown is buzzing with rumors that a madman, Hitler, is rounding up Jews in Germany. Her father, a soldier, tells her that what is happening in Germany will not happen in Hungary, but soon he is proven wrong. Young thugs beat up old men at the synagogue, and they laugh at Piri when she threatens to call the police because they know the police will do nothing. Jews are given strict curfews. Jewish children are no longer allowed at school. Piri's sister is taken away by the police, and another risks her life helping other Jews to escape. The *Nazis arrive and imprison the family in a brick factory, along with other Jews from the town. Despite the impending danger, a romance develops between Piri's friend Judi and a boy, Gari. Piri falls in love with Henri, but wonders how long their romances can last. "It would be nice if we could dance together one more time," Judi says. "But whatever happens, let's act grown up. We might not have another chance." A few days later, the train arrives to take them to a concentration camp. Piri and her sister escape death, but the other members of her family do not.

Aranka Siegal was born in Hungary and came to the United States when she was a teenager. She lives in the New York City metropolitan area and has hosted her own radio talk show in New York. For other books you may want to read about these very difficult times, see *holocaust. YA

Upstairs Room, The (1972) By Johanna Reiss (1928?–), this novel is based on her childhood experiences in the Netherlands during World War II. Annie de Leeuw and her Jewish family are thrown into turmoil when the *Nazis invade the Netherlands. At first, life remains fairly normal for Annie and her sister, Sini—except for signs posted outside shops that say "No Jews Allowed." But then she is forbidden to go to school, and other Jewish families are being sent to German work camps. Her father hides the family in a series of farmhouses, one of which has a tiny upstairs room where Annie and Sini must stay without light or fresh air whenever the police or German troops are in the area. *The Journey Back* (1976) is a sequel. Other books about the *holocaust you may want to read are *Upon the Head of a Goat, or, A Childhood in Hungary*, by Aranka Siegal (1930–), *Number the Stars* by *Lois Lowry, and *The Silver Sword* by *Ian Serraillier. YA

Uranus In ancient Greek mythology, Uranus is the first ruler and the personification of *heaven. He is the father of the Cyclops, the *Titans, and the 300-handed giants, each with three heads, known as the Hecatoncheires. These monsters are so frighteningly ugly that Uranus imprisons them in Tartarus, which is located deep in Earth and is worse than hell itself. Gaea, or Mother Earth, wife of Uranus, encourages the Titans to rebel against Uranus. One of the Titans, *Cronus, boldly attacks and castrates his father with a sickle. Uranus's blood drips to the ground, creating the three avenging deities known as the Furies. *Aphrodite springs from blood that trickles into the ocean. The other Titans also rebel against Uranus, who is now powerless, and Cronus usurps his position as supreme ruler of the heavens.

In astronomy, Uranus is the name of the seventh planet from the sun, first observed by

British astronomer William Herschel (1738–1822) in 1781.

Uriah Heep, an important character in *David Copperfield*, by *Charles Dickens, may be one of Dickens's most vivid and memorable villains. Young David describes him as a red-haired person with a cadaverous face, with hardly any eyebrows or eyelashes, a high-shouldered, bony individual with something clumsy about him. Always dressed in black, Heep has a distressing tendency to writhe when he wants to express enthusiasm. He is a simple clerk in Mr. Wickfield's employ and claims to know his place. In truth, Heep is a hypocrite whose pretended meekness and servility disguise evil intentions, a dislike and contempt for people, and a strong ambition to influence and dominate others. For all the extravagance with which Dickens has portrayed him, Heep is a powerful, sinister, and utterly believable presence in the novel.

Uris, Leon (1924–) A writer of popular novels and screenplays, Uris often deals with contemporary events. Uris quit school when he was 17 years old to join the Marines. His first novel, *Battle Cry* (1953), draws on his experience in training and combat for the Marines during World War II. *Exodus* (1957), which portrays the Jewish resettlement of Palestine and the establishment of the state of Israel, secured Uris's worldwide fame. *Trinity*, another of his semi-historical novels, is an account of the Protestant-Catholic battles in Northern Ireland. *The Haj* (1984) is set in modern Palestine and describes a Muslim's pilgrimage to Mecca. Several of his novels have been made into movies, including *Battle Cry* in 1955 and *Exodus* in 1960. In addition, he wrote the screenplay for the popular Western motion picture *Gunfight at the O.K. Corral*, which was produced in 1957. YA

Urn Burial (1987) By *Robert Westall, this *science fiction novel tells the story of Ralph Edwards, a young English shepherd. In the hilly countryside where he works are many pyramid-shaped piles of rocks, or cairns, of prehistoric origin. Ralph accidentally discovers within one of these cairns a glassy, urn-shaped coffin, and within it a catlike creature, a Fefethil, which once walked upright like a man but was not human. Ralph's discovery of the alien's burial site attracts other aliens, the dog-like Wawakas, to Earth and triggers a battle between the two groups for a secret that could spread destruction across the universe. Ralph helps the peaceful Fefethils defeat the dangerous Wawakas, and learns that there is a species even more dangerous than the Wawakas—humanity, which has much to learn before it is ready to meet the other races of the universe. If you enjoyed *Urn Burial*, try also the books of *Ray Bradbury, *Ursula K. Le Guin, and *Larry Niven. MR

U.S.A. (1937) By *John Dos Passos, this impressive trilogy consists of three novels: *The 42nd Parallel* (1930), *1919* (1932), and *The Big Money* (1936). The books cover the first three decades of this century from Dos Passos's view that the moral character of the nation was declining because of the domination of big business and the commercialization of everyday life. The first novel covers the period just before World War I and mainly concerns Fainy McCreary, who becomes a revolutionary; J. Ward Morehouse, whose ruthlessness earns him a fortune; G.H. Barrow, a dishonest labor leader; Charley Anderson, a war hero and airplane manufacturer; and Eleanor Stoddard and Eveline Hutchins, whose lives become entangled with the others. Some of the same people appear in *1919*, which covers the war period. Also in this novel are Joe Williams, a sailor; Richard Ellsworth Savage, eager to make his way in politics; and Anne Treat, a Texas debutante. *The Big Money* continues the narrative to the stock market crash of 1929, with Anderson, Morehouse, and Savage again playing important roles. There are also Gladys Wheatley, an heiress whom Anderson marries; Margo Dowling, a would-be actress; and Mary French, involved with Barrow. Of special interest beyond the narrative are the "Newsreel," "The Camera Eye," and brief biographies of notable people. The Newsreel offers newspaper headlines and verses from popular songs; the Camera Eye consists of the author's *stream of consciousness musings; and the biographies include sketches of real persons as diverse as Luther Burbank (1849–1926), a scientist; Andrew Carnegie (1835–1919), an industrialist; and Eugene V. Debs (1855–1926), a socialist. In spite of the depressing picture of the United States, these are novels well worth reading for their vivid characterizations of people and their times. YA

Utopia (1516), which means "no place" in Greek, is the title of a book by Thomas More (1478–1535) about an imaginary ideal state. In it, society is organized for the benefit of all people and there is no poverty or social injustice. The word "Utopia" is now used to refer to a situation or place where everything is perfect. YA

Valhalla is the hall of slain warriors in Norse mythology. It is the most beautiful hall in the palace of Asgard, with 540 gates surrounding it, rafters built of spears, and a roof of polished shields. The palace, situated in the grove of Glasir, is surrounded by the river Thund. *Odin, the god of death, rules Valhalla. After warriors have spent their days in battle, Odin heals their wounds and shares feasts with them in the hall. *Valkyries, who wait on the heroes, serve a magic boar that returns to life each time it is killed. After the feast, battle songs are sung and tales of valiant fighting are recalled.

Valkyries In Norse mythology the Valkyries, 7 to 12 in number, are maidens serving *Odin, the chief god. They ride into battle on horseback, with sword and helmet, and choose those who are to die a heroic death. The Valkyries then escort these heroes to *Valhalla, their heaven, where the maidens serve them as they feast. You will encounter the Valkyries in *Die Walküre* (1870), an opera by Richard Wagner (1813–1883).

vampire refers to a demon described in old European folktales, a corpse that leaves its grave at night to drink the blood of human victims. Said to be capable of existing for centuries, the vampire must return to its grave before sunrise, or to a coffin filled with earth from its native land. After death, its victims become part of the legion of the "undead," and in their turn feed upon others.

Legend has endowed vampires with the power to take the form of a huge bat or wolf, to cause violent changes in the weather, or to simply disappear. They may seem to be normal men and women, but can be recognized because mirrors do not reflect their image, and because they have no shadow. The sight of a crucifix will keep a vampire away, as will a wreath of garlic worn around the neck at night, but the only way to kill one is to drive a pointed stake through its heart. *Bram Stoker's *Gothic horror novel, *Dracula*, is based on these legends. Other splendid examples are "The Horla," in *The Best Stories of Guy de Maupassant* (1945), and "Carmilla," by J(oseph) S(heridan) Le Fanu (1814–1873), in *Best Ghost Stories of J.S. Le Fanu* (1964). *Ray Bradbury's collection *The October Country* (1970) contains two vampire stories, "The Man Upstairs" and "Homecoming." YA

Van Allsburg, Chris (1949–) Noted for the haunting illustrations he made for his own books, Van Allsburg is also a sculptor and educator. He was raised on a dairy farm in Michigan, and began drawing and painting while still in elementary school. His first book, *The Garden of Abdul Gasazi* (1979), is about a boy, Alan, who tries to find a runaway dog left in his care. *Ben's Dream* (1982) highlights the adventures of Ben, who dreams that his house floats past monuments all over the world. *Jumanji* (1984) tells the story of two children who play a board game where jungle animals come to life. *The Stranger* (1986) concerns a farmer whose truck accidentally hits, without harm, a mute man whom the farmer later befriends. MR

Van de Wetering, Janwillem (1931–) A Dutch-born author who now resides in the United States, Van de Wetering found the background for his detective stories when he served in the Amsterdam Reserve Police. His two years spent in a Zen monastery in Japan also contribute to his books. Van de Wetering's fictional detectives are Detective Adjutant Grijpstra, middle-aged and portly, and Detective Sergeant de Grier, young and an admirer of all pretty women. Supervising the two is the Commissaris (Commissioner), who is old and arthritic but alert. Most of the novels are set in Amsterdam, though in *The Japanese Corpse* (1977) the scene is Japan. In *The Blond Baboon* (1978) a dog and then its owner are poisoned. The apparent suicide of a man who was covering for a vice ring, in *Hard Rain* (1986), finds the trio at odds with a boyhood rival of the Commissaris. Grijpstra and de Grier go about their detecting in a relaxed manner, but they solve the crimes in the end. Read books by *Nicolas Freeling, *Georges Simenon, and *Maj Sjöwall and Per Wahlöö if you enjoy Jan de Wetering's. YA

Van Druten, John (William) (1901–1957) A director and playwright, Van Druten wrote several successful Broadway plays that were later made into movies. *Bell, Book and Candle* (1950) is the story of a bachelor who falls in love with a beautiful blonde neighbor on the eve of his wedding to another woman. *I Remember Mama* is about a teenage girl who lives with her Norwegian immigrant mother in San Francisco. He is best known for *I Am a Camera* (1952), an adaptation of *The Berlin Stories* (1945), by Christopher Isherwood (1904–1986), about a struggling young writer in Berlin dur-

ing the 1930s who befriends a cabaret singer. The play was later adapted into a musical comedy, *Cabaret*, in 1966 and a movie in 1972. Some of his other works that were made into movies include *Young Woodley* (1929), about a schoolboy who falls in love with his teacher, produced in 1929, and *Bell, Book and Candle*, filmed in 1959. YA

Van Leeuwen, Jean (1937–) An author and an editor of books for young readers, Van Leeuwen has written nearly two dozen novels. An early one is *The Great Cheese Conspiracy* (1969), about three mice who live comfortably in a movie theater until they develop a great desire for cheese and almost lose their lives trying to get into a cheese store. For older readers, *I Was a 98-Pound Duckling* (1972) tells about 13-year-old Kathy, tall, thin, and weighing 98 pounds, who is sure she will never have a boyfriend. But she and her friend Beth do meet two boys during summer vacation and discover there is more to life than beauty. *Seems Like This Road Goes On Forever* (1979), a novel that deals realistically with practical problems, concerns 17-year-old Mary Alice Fletcher who, in the hospital as a result of an auto accident, has time to reflect on her past mistakes and on what she sees as a life without hope. Her father, an extremist in religion, preaches at her; her mother takes little interest in her. Before her accident she was accused of plagiarism in high school and stole small items from a store where she worked. With the help of a psychologist and through her own analysis of her problems, she begins to understand herself. If you like these books, read those of *Colby Rodowsky and *Doris Buchanan Smith. MR & YA

Van Loon, Hendrik Willem (1882–1944) A Dutch-born American writer and illustrator, Van Loon began his writing career as a journalist covering Russia and Poland. After returning to the United States, he began a career as a history writer and lecturer. *The Story of Mankind* (1921), which he both wrote and illustrated, is an outline of world history for young people. It won the first *Newbery Medal in 1922. Other historical works for young people include *America* (1927) and two biographies, *The Life and Times of Pieter Stuyvesant* (1928) and *Thomas Jefferson* (1943). MR & YA

Vandal, The (1981) By Ann Schlee (1934–), this novel tells about Paul, a 16-year-old boy who lives in the foreseeable future. Frightened by a cloud of darkness exploding across the sky, he sets fire to a nearby stadium. Though light from the fire will keep the darkness from spreading and enveloping everything, Paul is still treated as though he is a vandal.

Paul is sent to a psychiatrist, Dr. Palmer. In a society where remembering the past is considered a crime, Dr. Palmer warns him to forget the incident. As punishment for setting fire to the stadium, Paul is sent to help an old woman, Mrs. Willmay, with errands. Mrs. Willmay tells him about things that happened before The Enlightenment, a time that the new society forbids anyone to talk about. "Nothing lost matters," Dr. Palmer warns, but Mrs. Willmay and other outcasts make him realize that he must escape the controlled world in which he lives.

The Vandal is a departure from Schlee's historical novels, which include *The Strangers* (1971), about a girl during the English Civil War; *The Consul's Daughter* (1972), about a British girl during the Battle of Algiers in 1816; and *Ask Me No Questions* (1976), in which a girl helps abused children in an asylum. MR & YA

Vanity Fair (1848) By *William Makepeace Thackeray, this is a long, wide-ranging novel, with a large and varied cast of characters. Its scene is the early 19th century, at the time of the Napoleonic wars. But the novel is also a *satire of Thackeray's times. The main characters are two women: Amelia Sedley, the sheltered and meek daughter of a London merchant, and Rebecca ("Becky") Sharp, an orphan and very poor. Becky, seeking a marriage that will give her a comfortable life, weds Rawdon Crawley, younger son of Sir Pitt Crawley. Amelia's father loses his money, and when

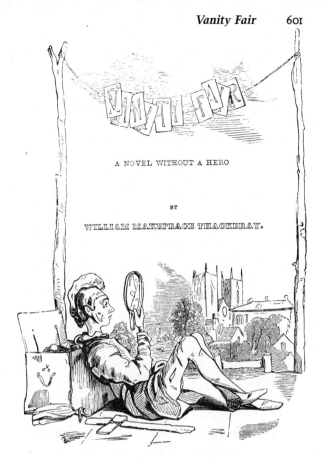

The title page of *Vanity Fair*, with an illustration by the author.

Amelia marries George Osborne, his father disinherits him for marrying a penniless woman. The scene moves to Brussels, Belgium, in June 1815, just before the Battle of Waterloo. Amelia and Becky accompany their officer husbands and attend a lavish ball held three days before the historic battle. Amelia's husband is killed in battle, and she and her young son are left in poverty. Becky, who also has a son whom she neglects, and her husband now take part in London society, though they must depend on their wits for money. When Rawdon discovers Becky in an improper situation with Lord Steyne, he leaves her. But, supported by Steyne, Becky lives an ever more reckless and immoral life in England and on the Continent. It is even suggested that she may have had a hand in the death of Jos Sedley, Amelia's brother, who had taken out a life insurance policy in Amelia's favor. In the end Amelia is married to William Dobbin, who had been in love with her for many years, but Becky can only go on with her reckless, scheming life that holds no secure future. *Vanity Fair* is one of the great novels of English literature, noted for its vivid portrayal of one part of English society and for its many perfectly drawn characters, especially the greedy and scheming Becky. If you enjoyed this story, try *The Eustace Diamonds* (1873) by Anthony Trollope (1815–1882). It also tells the story of a scheming, grasping woman who, in the end, pays dearly for her avariciousness. Movies were made of *Vanity Fair* in 1922 and 1932, but another, produced in 1935 under the title *Becky Sharp*, is the best. YA

Velvet Brown is the main character in *Enid Bagnold's novel *National Velvet. Far less glamorous than her three older sisters, she is a stringy 14-year-old girl with short, pale "cottony" hair, a sweet smile, and lots of determination. She loves her family, especially her very large mother, Araminty, but her strongest feelings belong to horses. Velvet trains her odd-looking horse, Piebald, with great energy and devotion, and believes in his ability to compete with the very best. With the help of her friend Mi Taylor, Velvet takes many risks to enter the Grand National race—not for the prize money nor even to become famous herself, but to make Piebald famous by letting others see what a fine jumper he is.

Velveteen Rabbit or How Toys Become Real, The (1922) was written by Margery Williams (1881–1944), an English writer who lived in the United States. It tells about a toy Rabbit that was given to a young boy for Christmas. The Rabbit, being made only of sawdust and covered with cheap velveteen cloth, is looked down on by most of the other, more expensive toys the boy has.

But the Rabbit makes friends with the Skin Horse, a rocking horse. The two talk about what it is like to become Real. The Skin Horse explains, "When a child . . . REALLY loves you, then you become Real."

The Rabbit becomes the boy's favorite toy and, to the boy at least, the Rabbit is Real. But when the boy falls ill and goes away to the seaside to get better, his toys, including the Rabbit, are bundled into a sack and sent off to be burned in order to kill the germs that may have made the boy sick. At the last minute the Rabbit is saved by the magic fairy, who protects old, worn-out toys. Because the Velveteen Rabbit was so much loved by the boy, the fairy makes it Real to everyone. Then the Rabbit goes off to play in the forest with the other live rabbits. Williams wrote a number of novels and about 15 books for children, but *The Velveteen Rabbit* is the one that is still read today. MR

ventriloquist is a person who can speak without moving the lips, and can make his or her voice appear to be coming from another place. Edgar Bergen (1903–1978) was a ventriloquist famous for his comic conversations with two large puppetlike dolls named Charlie McCarthy and Mortimer Snerd. One or both of the dolls sat on his lap, in full view of the audience, and spoke like real people even while Bergen himself seemed to be silent. Another example of a ventriloquist is the *Wizard of Oz, who hides behind a screen near his throne and throws the sound of his voice to a different part of the room.

Venus See *Aphrodite.

Vergil See *Virgil.

Verne, Jules (Gabriel) (1828–1905) A French author of *science fiction adventures that foretold many 20th-century inventions and discoveries, Verne wrote plays and travel articles. He later turned the travel articles into fictional stories for magazines. Encouraged by the success of these stories, he wrote *Five Weeks in a Balloon* (1863), a novel about a voyage in a hot-air balloon. As with many of his works, *From the Earth to the Moon* (1863), a tale that foretold a moon voyage more than 100 years before it actually occurred, dealt with scientific premises that hold true today. *Journey to the Center of the Earth* (1864) is the story of a race to Earth's core. His interest in the sea is evi-

Jules Verne

dent in *Twenty Thousand Leagues Under the Sea*, in which *Captain Nemo commands the submarine *Nautilus*, and in its sequel, *The Mysterious Island* (1874–1875), about castaways on a Pacific island populated by fierce animals. Verne's characters traveled the world in hot-air balloons, and other conveyances, in *Around the World in Eighty Days*, one of his best-known works. Several of Verne's novels have been made into movies, including *Twenty Thousand Leagues Under the Sea*, produced in 1954; *Around the World in Eighty Days*, in 1956; *From the Earth to the Moon*, in 1958; and *Journey to the Center of the Earth*, in 1959. MR & YA

Veronica Ganz (1968) The problem faced by the main character in this novel by *Marilyn Sachs is that of being too tall. Veronica, 13 years old and in the eighth grade, has become a bully in retaliation for being teased about her height. A new student, Peter Wedemeyer, shorter than she, refuses to let her bully him and writes poems about her height. She tries to attack and otherwise annoy him until he and two friends get even by beating and bruising her. Peter apologizes and offers to let her hit him on the chin. Veronica begins to realize that Peter really likes her and that she can be his friend despite their difference in height. Veronica must also cope with an unhappy family situation. She lives with her mother, her step-father, a younger sister, and a half brother. Veronica's father, whom she loves, promises to visit the family but does not do so. Veronica learns by hard experience that she is a girl and a human being who must adjust to the world—which is not as hard a task as she once thought. If you like to read about the problems of young people, especially in family settings, you may like *The Year Without Michael* by *Susan Beth Pfeffer, *You Shouldn't Have to Say Goodbye* by Patricia Hermes (1936–), and *The Village by the Sea* by *Paula Fox. MR

Verral, Charles Spain (1904–1990) An artist, editor, and prolific writer, Verral was born and grew up in Ontario, Canada, where as a boy he developed a deep and lifelong passion for books and reading. After working for several years as an artist, Verral turned to editing, then to writing. During the 1930s and 1940s he wrote numerous stories, many of them book-length adventure tales, for magazines. Verral wrote dozens of books, including a number of works dealing with sports, among them *Mighty Men of Baseball* (1955), *Babe Ruth: Sultan of Swat* (1976), and *Casey Stengel: Baseball's Great Manager* (1978). Verral's interest in aviation and aeronautics led to such books as *Men of Flight: Conquest of the Air* (1954) and *Robert Goddard: Father of the Space Age* (1963). Verral also created the character Brains Benton, a smart and enterprising boy who runs his own detective agency with his friend Jimmy Carson. They were introduced in *The Case of the Missing Message* (1960), the first in a series of mysteries that was continued by others. MR

Victorian age refers to the period in England from 1837 to 1901, the years in which Queen Victoria (1819–1901) reigned. It was a time of economic and social change. The English

MR = Middle Reader   YA = Young Adult Reader   * = See this main entry

evolved from an agricultural to an industrial society. They found themselves becoming an imperial power. Victorian writers extolled such qualities as honesty, social responsibility, moral courage, and love of family even as they depicted, through sharp characterization and realistic description, the decline of traditional social and religious institutions. Among the great Victorian novelists were *Charles Dickens, the *Brontë sisters, *Samuel Butler, *Wilkie Collins, *George Eliot, and *William Makepeace Thackeray. Leading Victorian poets included *Robert Browning and *Alfred Tennyson. At the end of the 19th century, *Thomas Hardy, *Oscar Wilde, and others challenged what they considered repressive Victorian values with a more frank, pessimistic, and alienated view of human existence.

Vidal, Gore (1925–) A novelist, dramatist, and essayist, Vidal is known for *satire and sharp characterizations of historical persons. His novels show a wide variety of time and place. For example, two novels concern the ancient world: *Julian* (1964), about the man who became the Roman emperor in 361, and *Creation* (1981), about Cyrus Spitama, the son of a Persian prince, and his view of the Persian Empire. Vidal is at his best in a series of six novels about the United States. They contain irreverent views of noted Americans as well as a host of fictional characters, many of whom appear in more than one book. Chronologically they begin with *Burr* (1973), which centers on Aaron Burr (1756–1836), a politician of the early days of the nation who was tried for treason. *Lincoln* (1984) tells how Abraham Lincoln (1809–1865) dealt with the crises of the Civil War, including those generated by his own subordinates. *1876* (1976) concerns the nation's celebration of its 100th anniversary of independence. In *Empire* (1987) Vidal examines with a cynical eye events of the turn of the century when the United States became an imperialistic power. *Hollywood* (1990) covers the Jazz Age of the 1920s. Finally, *Washington, D.C.* (1967) begins with the New Deal period and continues into the 1950s. As a dramatist, Vidal is best known for *Visit to a Small Planet* (1956), in which a visitor from space comes to Earth to view the Battle of Bull Run during the Civil War but ends up in present-day Virginia and is not impressed with what he finds there. A movie was made of the play in 1960 and of Vidal's novel *Myra Breckinridge* (1968), which follows the outrageous adventures of a person who has a sex change operation, in 1970. If you enjoy Vidal's books, you will like those of *Sinclair Lewis, *George Orwell, and *Kurt Vonnegut. YA

View from the Cherry Tree, The (1975) This mystery novel by *Willo Davis Roberts is about 11-year-old Robert Mallory, who tells his parents and older sisters that he saw the woman next door being murdered. They do not believe him. Even the police say her death was an accident. But Rob was in his hideout in a cherry tree when it happened. First, he heard an argument. Then, through the curtains, he saw the shadow of a man strangling her.

As his family busily prepares for his sister's wedding, Rob searches for clues. He goes back to the cherry tree and looks inside the dead woman's house. Someone fires bullets at him and misses. He cannot see who it was, but he now knows that whoever killed Mrs. Calloway also knows Rob is a witness. But who was it? There are lots of possibilities. Almost everyone had hated the old crab. Was it Max, who always fought with her? Or Uncle Ray, who needed money? Or possibly Mrs. Calloway's nephew, Derek? The only way for Rob to find out is to search inside the dead woman's house for clues to bring to the police—before the murderer has a chance to kill him. MR

Village by the Sea, The (1988) In this disturbing but eventually encouraging novel by *Paula Fox, 10-year-old Emma is sent to stay on Long Island, New York, with her Uncle Crispin and Aunt Bea while her father undergoes heart bypass surgery. Uncle Crispin is kind and gentle, but Aunt Bea is just about the opposite. She is no help around the house, criticizes everything, and does her best to run down anything in which anyone else finds pleasure. Emma is disturbed and unhappy until she meets a neighbor, Alberta, about a year older than she. They explore the beach and build a miniature village made of shells, pebbles, and bits of wood. They make houses, a church, a school, and other buildings. Her father's surgery is successful, and Emma is about to go home when the tiny village is destroyed. Aunt Bea did it in a fit of envy: As long as she was unhappy, she could not bear to see others enjoy themselves. Coming from a warm, well-adjusted family, Emma has learned in a brutal way that not all homes are like hers, and also that it is not worthwhile being at odds with the world. MR

Viorst, Judith (1931–) Judith Viorst began writing poetry when she was 7 years old. After college, Viorst worked as an editor and journalist and began to publish poetry in magazines. Several of her books and novels for young readers were inspired by situations that took place when her three children were growing up. *I'll Fix Anthony* (1969) was written after a fight between her two sons. *The Tenth Good Thing About Barney* (1971), about a child who mourns a dead cat, was written after her children asked her a lot of questions about death. *Alexander and the Terrible, Horrible, No Good, Very Bad Day* (1972) was written to cheer up her son who, like everyone at times, was having some very bad days. MR & YA

Virgil (Vergil) [Latin name in full, Publius Vergilius Maro] (70–19 B.C.) The greatest poet of ancient Rome and of all Latin literature, Virgil began life on a farm, and his first two poetic works reflect this background. *Bucolics*, also known as the *Eclogues*, written between 43 and 37 B.C., consists of 10 pastoral poems. They idealize rural life, portraying an imaginary world of happy shepherds. His second work, *Georgics*, composed between 37 and 30 B.C. and consisting of four books, also focuses on agriculture and farm life. These books give advice on farming; the last, concerning the raising of honeybees, also relates two myths about death and resurrection. Virgil's masterpiece, and the foundation of his unique stature in world literature, is the *Aeneid*. Virgil was greatly admired by his fellow Romans, both for the perfection of his Latin and as the leading spokesman for the Roman way of life. He continued to be studied and admired long after the Roman Empire fell, and his influence was very strong in the Middle Ages. In *The Divine Comedy* (c.1310–1321), by *Dante Alighieri, the spirit of Virgil is Dante's guide through Hell and Purgatory to the entrance to Paradise. Thus Dante in effect was making clear that he considered Virgil's works the ultimate achievement of the human mind. YA

Virginian, The (1902) By Owen Wister (1860–1938), this Western became a model for novels about the American cowboy. The Virginian is a cowboy on Judge Henry's ranch in Wyoming. In a poker game, Trampas, also a cowboy, accuses him of being a cheater. The Virginian rests his hand on his gun, and says, "When you call me that, smile"—a remark that sets the tone for their rivalry, which ends in a shootout. As in most other Westerns, the cowboy hero falls in love. He first rescues Molly Wood from drowning and, after many attempts, convinces her to marry him at the end of the story. After nearly a century, *The Virginian* is still one of the most popular volumes of Western fiction. Three film versions of it have been made, in 1914, 1929, and 1946, and it also inspired a TV series. MR & YA

Visit to William Blake's Inn, A: Poems for Innocent and Experienced Travelers Nancy Willard (1936–), the author of these magical verses, fell in love with the poems of *William Blake when she was 7 years old and was recovering from the measles. Willard was later inspired by Blake's *Songs of Innocence and Experience* to write her own poems about an imaginary inn, owned and operated by the great English poet and painter. The inn's staff includes two dragons in charge of baking bread, two angels to wash and shake the feather beds, a rabbit to show guests to their rooms, and a bear who doubles as a sofa. Several distinguished visitors are introduced, among them the King of Cats, the Man in the Marmalade Hat, and the Wise Cow. The book received the *Newbery Medal in 1982. MR

Visitors, The (1977) In this very satisfying *science fiction novel of mysterious visitors to Cambridge, England, *John Rowe Townsend tells a story of adventure and love. Three people, David and Margaret Wyatt and their daughter, Katherine, appear suddenly before John Dunham and his friend Alan Stubbings, two boys of high school age. John helps the rather strange-acting trio find lodgings and becomes involved in their affairs, as do his parents and his older brother, Ben. The Wyatts have a good deal of money, but their money turns out to be counterfeit. David goes to the races and wins every bet he places. While Ben and Katherine are becoming much attracted to each other, a journalist tries to find out who the Wyatts really are. Finally they confess they have come from the future—from the year 2149. Katherine, fearing that she will have to return to the future, and Ben run away. When they are found, Katherine must return as ordered or within a year face death because of present-day diseases she is not immune to. David and Margaret will stay if Katherine insists on it, but in the end the three realize they must go back to 2149. They not only disappear suddenly, but they also wipe out all memories of them in those left behind. MR & YA

Voice of Bugle Ann, The (1935) By *MacKinlay Kantor, this is the tale of a foxhound with a cry like a silver trumpet, a slender animal of great endurance who carries her tail "like a banner." Bugle Ann is the favorite of Springfield Davis and his son, Benjy. With their friends Cal Royster and his son, Baker, the men work their farms by day and send their hounds out to hunt at night. They sit by the fire outdoors, where they can hear the individual voices of the hounds, and the hunt ends when the fox escapes into a hole or the dogs come home.

When Jake Terry starts a sheep farm, he puts up a wire fence around his land. Foxes change their habits because of it, and the hunting dogs get caught in the wire and are hurt or killed. One night during a hunt, Bugle Ann fails to return to the call of Spring's ancient bugle, and the men search for her near the Terry farm. Jake threatens to shoot any dog he finds inside his fence, and also tells Benjy to stay away from his daughter, Camden. Later Spring finds Bugle Ann's distinctive footprints near the Terrys' house and accuses Jake of killing her. As the furious Jake puts his shotgun to his shoulder, Spring fires his Winchester and kills him.

The 82-year-old Spring spends almost four years in jail before being pardoned. During this time, a neighbor hears a hound's cry at night that sounds very like Bugle Ann, and rumors fly about a ghost. When Spring comes home and hunts again, the men hear a cry—"high, round, with that queer and brassy resonance" so like the voice of Bugle Ann. Following the sound, they find Camden Terry in the woods with a young hound. She confesses that she accidentally hit Bugle Ann with the car. The dog was unhurt, but Camden took her away, fearing her father would cause trouble. After her father's death, she bred Bugle Ann to a good hound and kept one pup from the litter—the only one with her mother's glorious voice, and one clearly destined to be a great hunter. YA

Voigt, Cynthia (1942–) The author of more than a dozen novels for young readers, Voigt has lived a number of years in the Chesapeake Bay area of Maryland that is the setting of *Dicey's Song*. Her books have been praised for their strong characterizations and for the skillful integrating of individual human problems into a smoothly written story. *Homecoming is the first in a series of novels about the younger members of the Tillerman family—James, Sammy, and Maybeth—and the tragedy of their mother's mental breakdown. Its story is continued in *Dicey's Song. A Solitary Blue* (1983), a companion to the Tillerman series, is about the life of Jeff Greene, the guitar-playing boy whom Dicey meets in *Dicey's Song. Sons from Afar* (1987), another sequel, follows James and Sammy Tillerman as they go in search of the father who walked out on them years ago. In *Seventeen Against the Dealer* (1989), Dicey tries her hand at the boat-building business, while still coping with family problems.

The Callendar Papers (1983) is a mystery novel set in 1894. Thirteen-year-old Jean Wainwright spends a summer working for a widower, going through the Callendar family papers, and uncovering some disturbing family secrets. MR

Völsunga Saga A series of Norse legends based on earlier poetic material, the Völsunga Saga tells of an age of gods and giants, but also one of much bloodshed and slaughter. The hero is Sigurd (Siegfried), the heroine Gudrun, and the plot is similar to that of the *Nibelungenlied*. Richard Wagner (1813–1883), the German composer, based his cycle of four operas, *Der Ring des Nibelungen* (The Ring of the Nibelungs) (1869–1876), chiefly on the Völsunga Saga. See also *Edda and *Norse Gods and Giants*.

Voltaire [François Marie Arouet] (1694–1778) A French philosopher, author, playwright, and above all a man of great wit, Voltaire was the leading figure of the Enlightenment, also called the Age of Reason. This was a period in which intellectuals questioned royal and church authority and sought truth in reason and science. Often in trouble with the government, but also at times an adviser to kings and emperors, Voltaire not only wrote prolifically but also sought to bring about social and political reform. Among his writings *Candide* is best known in the English-speaking world. In a similar vein of *satire is *Micromégas* (1752), concerning two creatures from space who visit Earth and are horrified by religious wars. Among Voltaire's dramas is *Zaïre* (1732), about love and jealousy in an Oriental setting. *Zadig* (1747) is a fictional biography of a Babylonian wise man who through misfortune comes to doubt there is a kind Providence. Voltaire also wrote history and philosophy and published poetry, a good deal of it light and witty. *La Henriade* (1723) is an epic poem of the time of Henry IV (1553–1610), king of France. Though Voltaire is more often read today in France, his influence as a force for tolerance and reason has continued throughout the world. If you are interested in other authors who make their points through satire, read the works of *Alexander Pope and *Jonathan Swift. YA

von Däniken, Erich (1935–) Author of books that discuss why he believes extraterrestrial beings visited Earth thousands of years ago and may have even mated with our ancestors, von Däniken is best known for *Chariots of the Gods? Unsolved Mysteries of the Past* (1969). As evidence, he points, for example, to illustrations of ancient people etched in stone that depict helmets that could be the headgear of astronauts. Ancient legends, von Däniken claims, often discuss visitors from outer space. Old roads of South American Indians that lead nowhere might have been landing strips for spacecraft. While scientists criticize his theories, you may still find pleasure reading *Chariots of the Gods?* Or you may want to read some of his other books about visitors from outer space, for example, *The Gold of the Gods* (1973) and *The Miracles of the Gods: A Hard Look at the Supernatural* (1975). YA

Von Ryan's Express (1964) This taut, fast-paced, violent novel by David Westheimer (1917–) is set in Italy during World War II. In 1943, Colonel Joseph Ryan, a tough, no-nonsense American flyer, is shot down and sent to P.G. 202, a filthy, chaotic prison camp holding nearly 1,000 unkempt, disheartened British and American officers. As the camp's new senior officer, Ryan restores cleanliness, order, and military discipline with such cold efficiency that he is dubbed "Von Ryan" by the resentful troops. Their hatred increases when, after the Allied invasion of Italy, their Italian captors run away and Ryan is tricked into letting the Germans take control of the prisoners. Forced onto a train that will take them back to Germany, Ryan leads his men in killing their guards, taking over the train, and making a dangerous but successful run for the Swiss border. Westheimer, who has written more than a dozen successful novels, continued Ryan's story in *Von Ryan's Return* (1980), in which Ryan goes back into action behind enemy lines in northern Italy. *Von Ryan's Express* was made into a movie in 1965. YA

Vonnegut, Kurt, Jr. (1922–) An author who combines *science fiction, *satire, and black humor, Vonnegut makes clear that he does not think highly of the way the world is run. Two of his most popular novels are *Cat's Cradle* and *Slaughterhouse-Five*. Vonnegut's first novel, *Player Piano* (1952), takes a pessimistic look at the results of automation. In *God Bless You, Mr. Rosewater* (1965), the history of the eccentric Rosewater family is told with much black humor. Other novels by Vonnegut include: *Slapstick* (1976), in which a former President of the United States, deformed as a child, is writing his autobiography in the ruins of Manhattan; *Jailbird* (1979), which begins when an elderly prisoner is released and becomes a leading figure in a corporation that owns much of America; *Galapagos* (1985), about a group of tourists who, while on a cruise in the Pacific Ocean, are able to survive the end of the world; and *Hocus Pocus* (1990), narrated by Eugene Debs Hartke, a West Point graduate and veteran of the Vietnam War, now teaching in an upstate New York college for the learning-disabled. Next door is a maximum security prison, managed for profit by a Japanese firm. Based on an actual prison break in this locality in 1971, the novel tells how the prisoners take over the college. If you enjoy these books, read those of *Brian Aldiss, *Ray Bradbury, and *Gore Vidal. YA

Voyages of Doctor Dolittle, The (1922) The second in the much-loved series of Dolittle stories by *Hugh Lofting is narrated by Tommy Stubbins, son of the cobbler in Puddleby-on-the-Marsh, England. In return for Tommy's energetic assistance, Dolittle agrees to teach 10-year-old Tommy to read and write. After Tommy settles in as apprentice, the doctor plans a long voyage to search for his friend Long Arrow, a South American Indian botanist last seen on Spidermonkey Island near the coast of Brazil. Dolittle and Tommy set sail,

Title page of *The Voyages of Doctor Dolittle,* written and illustrated by Hugh Lofting

with a crew consisting of Jip the dog, Chee-Chee the monkey, Polynesia (a rather snobbish parrot), and Crown Prince Bumpo (on holiday from his studies at Oxford University).

Their voyage is never dull, as they discover four stowaways, visit a Spanish island, are shipwrecked and saved, and finally arrive, somewhat breathless, at Spidermonkey Island. In a daring maneuver, Dolittle and his companions rescue Long Arrow from a cave, and the grateful Popsipetel Indians insist on making Dolittle their king. Dolittle is rather embarrassed by all the attention and eager to return to his duties at home. He and his crew make secret arrangements with the Great Glass Sea-snail, who kindly agrees to transport them all back to England. *The Voyages of Doctor Dolittle* won the *Newbery Medal in 1923. A movie based on Doctor Dolittle was produced in 1967. MR

Waiting for Godot (1948) By *Samuel Beckett, this existentialist play has caused much controversy because it has no plot, not much scenery, and very little action. Two tramps meet. Estragon is skinny and his feet hurt. Vladimir is short and stout and has bad breath. Their conversation is a mixture of argument, misunderstanding, and irrelevance. They want to move on but cannot because they are waiting for Godot. When Beckett was asked who Godot was, he said if he knew, he would have said so in the play. The two tramps assert that if Godot would come they would be saved, so the idea of God, or the meaning of existence, is never far from the play. A man called Pozzo and his servant, Lucky, enter. Lucky is attached to Pozzo by a rope around his neck, which Pozzo tugs at to direct him. Lucky makes the longest speech in the play, most of which is meaningless. After they go, a boy comes in to tell the tramps that Godot is not coming that day. He will be there tomorrow. They think about hanging themselves, but neither of them has any rope. The next day is like the first except that when Pozzo and Lucky come back, Pozzo is blind and Lucky dumb. At the end of the day a boy comes in to tell the tramps that Godot will be coming tomorrow. Deciding to hang themselves, they find they have again forgotten to bring a rope. They will do it tomorrow. Tomorrow is another day waiting for Godot. See also *existentialism. YA

Waiting for Lefty (1935) By *Clifford Odets, this innovative one-act play about labor unions was inspired by a strike of New York taxicab drivers in 1934. Banned in some American cities, the play was popular among left-wing groups and in Soviet Russia as a denunciation of labor racketeering. The scene is a meeting of the cab drivers' union to discuss whether they should go out on strike. With the theater as a meeting hall, union officers sit in a semicircle on stage, facing the audience. Union members sit among the audience, bringing a sense of immediacy to the play. A series of small scenes on a special portion of the stage show the kind of lives the drivers are leading. Joe and Edna's children go hungry to bed, and their furniture is taken away because they are behind with the payments. Florence and Sid cannot marry because they have nothing in the bank. The union members discuss their grievances while waiting for Lefty, their union leader. As a decision is taken to strike, the news comes that Lefty has been murdered by thugs hired by the taxi company. YA

Walcott, Derek (Alton) (1930–) A West Indian–born poet and playwright, Walcott mixes in his work English and Caribbean influences. Descended from a white grandfather, he uses his skill in English, a second language for him (his first is French Creole), to produce rich descriptive poetry. From his black grandmother he inherited a fierce loyalty to his West Indian roots. In one of his best-known poems, "A Far Cry from Africa," which appears in a collection of poems called *In a Green Night: Poems, 1948–1960* (1962), he describes this duality:

> Where shall I turn, divided to the vein?
> I who have cursed
> The drunken officer of British rule,
>   how choose
> Between this Africa and the English
>   tongue I love?
> Betray them both, or give back what
>   they give?

Walcott has been influential in the development of an indigenous West Indian theater. In his plays he uses traditional Caribbean themes. *Ti-Jean and His Brothers* (1958) is a folk drama in which animals speak and the Devil appears. *Henri Christophe* (1950), a drama in verse, tells about a former slave who becomes king of Haiti. Walcott was awarded the Nobel Prize for literature in 1992. YA

Walden, or Life in the Woods (1854)

From July 1845 to September 1847, *Henry David Thoreau lived a life of great simplicity in a cabin he built himself by Walden Pond in Concord, Massachusetts. He was rebelling against the accumulation of possessions that, he believed, stood between human beings and their inner selves. *Walden*, a journal purportedly written at this time but revised and polished over the years, gives details of Thoreau's daily life and relates his thoughts on many subjects, large and small, that affect humankind, especially in its relation to the world of nature. He writes about building his house, working in his bean field, picking berries in the woods, and baking his bread. As to his clothes, he maintained that if a person has found something to do, he or she need not buy a new suit to do it in. As he hoed his bean field, fished in the pond, or simply sat in the sun all afternoon, he observed the busy life of the creatures around him. The birds and the insects, the owls at night, and the whippoorwill that came each evening to chant its song as the sun went

Henry David Thoreau's cabin from the first edition of *Walden, or Life in the Woods*

down were company for him. People asked him whether he felt lonely at night or at times when it rained or snowed and no one passed by for many days. But Thoreau felt lonely only among people he found insincere in the way they were living their lives. In its quiet way this book is a celebration of a view of life different from that which would today be called the "rat race." *Walden* became a bible to young people of the 1960s who were passionately turned off by the Vietnam War and who sought a life different from the ways of mainstream America. YA

Walker, Alice (Melsenior) (1944–)

A well-known black novelist, short-story writer, and poet, Georgia-born Walker is known best for *The Color Purple, a novel about a black woman's life in the South, with all its hard times and difficulties. She writes especially about family life and relationships among black people, and of black women in particular. Walker is very concerned about the condition of black women in America, saying they are the country's unsung heroes. She has always been an active worker in the civil rights movement. Her novel *Meridian* (1976) is about Meridian Hill, a black girl who faces the challenge of achieving her own identity when she joins other young people in the freedom fight of the 1960s. Another book about the condition of black people you might want to read is *Native Son* by *Richard Wright. YA

Wallace, Lew(is) (1827–1905) A lawyer, soldier, diplomat, and novelist, Wallace grew up in Indiana. As a boy, Lew liked to play truant, often taking a book with him to read in the woods. He especially liked reading about the Spanish conquest of Mexico. When the Mexican War broke out, Wallace served with the First Indiana Infantry. During the Civil War he joined the Union Army and was rapidly promoted to the rank of major general. It is said he saved Washington, D.C., from capture with a small force of 5,800 men against an army of 28,000. After the war he returned to politics and the law. His first book, written at this time, was *The Fair God* (1873), a story about the conquest of Mexico. During his appointment as governor of the territory of New Mexico he wrote *Ben-Hur, a Tale of the Christ*, the novel that made him famous. A year later he was appointed minister to Turkey. There he developed an interest in the history of Constantinople, which led to the writing of his novel *The Prince of India, or Why Constantinople Fell* (1893). Wallace wrote many novels, but none achieved the popularity of *The Fair God* and *Ben-Hur*. YA

Walpole, Hugh (1884–1941) Born in New Zealand, the son of a clergyman, Walpole was England's most popular novelist in the 1920s and 1930s. He began his career writing book reviews. Soon he was writing a novel a year as well as travel books and biographies. He greatly admired *Walter Scott and was recognized as an authority on him. Walpole liked writing series of books. One of his series, which draws on incidents in Walpole's own childhood, begins with the novel *Jeremy*, about an 8-year-old son of a clergyman. If you enjoy these stories about Jeremy, you may want to read *Penrod* and its sequels by *Booth

Tarkington, about an American boy growing up in a Middle Western town at the turn of the century. MR & YA

Walpurgis Night [Witches' Sabbath] is a German celebration held on May I. On that date the body of St. Walpurga, an English nun who died in Germany in 779, was transferred from Heidenheim to Eichstatt. Her shrine there became an object of pilgrimage and miracles, and her name became associated with this day. May I marked the start of the agricultural season in Germany and the night when it was believed witches held their annual get-together to feast and dance and meet the Devil. The Witches' Sabbath is celebrated in the story of *Faust* by *Johann Goethe, in which Faust sells his soul to the Devil. *Bram Stoker also wrote a short story about Walpurgis Night called "Dracula's Guest" (1899), in which an Englishman ignores warnings against visiting an abandoned village on this day and later wishes he had heeded them. MR & YA

Walsh, Jill (Gillian) Paton (1937–) An English writer, Walsh began her career by writing historical fiction, but she is now known best for her novels that deal with real-life situations. *The Dolphin Crossing* (1967) is a tale of two boys from widely different backgrounds who take part in the evacuation of soldiers from Dunkirk during World War II. Another World War II novel is *Fireweed* (1969), in which a boy and girl leave their difficult family situations to live secretly in air raid shelters and bombed buildings during the blitz of London. *Goldengrove* (1972) is the first of two books about Madge and Paul, who spend summer holidays with their grandmother. Madge becomes absorbed with helping a blind professor who lives unhappily alone. *Unleaving*, a more interesting and complex book, is the sequel to this story. *Babylon* (1982) is a story about three black children talking together about their lives before coming to England. YA

War and Peace (1868) This magnificent novel by *Leo Tolstoy is considered one of the world's greatest. Set in Imperial Russia from 1805 to 1812, the book describes the terrible war with the French under Napoleon Bonaparte (1769–1821) through the lives of Pierre Bezukov, Prince Andrei, and Natasha Rostova. At a soirée in St. Petersburg, the conversation turns to the possibility of war. Prince Andrei tells the assembled company he is about to join the army. Recently returned from a period of study in Paris, Pierre goes to Moscow, where his father dies, leaving him a fortune. Now a wealthy young count, Pierre is much sought after. At a dinner party given by the Rostovs he meets the lively 13-year-old Natasha. Undecided about his future, Pierre is drawn into a loveless marriage with Helene. The marriage soon gets into difficulties when Pierre suspects his wife of infidelity, and they separate. A peace treaty is signed between Russia and France, and Prince Andrei returns home in time to see his wife before she dies in childbirth. On a visit to the country home of the Rostovs, Prince Andrei again meets Natasha. He is captivated by her gaiety and happiness, which are a marked contrast to his own sadness. Prince Andrei attends Natasha's first ball and thinks of marrying her. His father tells him to wait a year, as Natasha, now 16 years old, is too young. Prince Andrei leaves Moscow, and Natasha, though now engaged to Prince Andrei, falls in love with Anatole, Helene's brother, who maliciously introduces Anatole to her. Natasha is disgraced when their plans to elope are discovered. She ends her engagement to Prince Andrei and tries to take her life when she finds Anatole is already married. Coldly detached when he hears this news, Prince Andrei gives Pierre a package for Natasha containing her portrait and letters. As he delivers them, Pierre tells Natasha of his love for her.

In 1812 Napoleon invades Russia, and Prince Andrei again goes to the front. The French push the Russian army toward Moscow in a series of terrible battles. Pierre goes to the front as a spectator and is taken prisoner. With Napoleon on its outskirts, Moscow is in chaos. People are packing their belongings and fleeing to the country as wounded men are brought in from the front lines. The Rostovs, ready to leave, are asked to take some wounded officers with them. Prince Andrei is among them. When Natasha hears this, she goes to him, and they are reconciled. In a monastery where they have taken refuge, she tenderly nurses him as he dies. Overextended, the French start their disastrous retreat home, and Pierre is rescued. With his wife now dead, he is free at last to ask Natasha to marry him.

Throughout *War and Peace* there are vivid descriptions of the war between Russia and France. It is a gripping tale of heroic battles, bravery, and the strategic skill of old General Kutuzov, who knew that the Russian winter would be a greater foe to Napoleon than any Russian army. If you enjoyed this powerful novel, read the now equally famous novel *Doctor Zhivago* by *Boris Pasternak. A film was made of *War and Peace* in 1956. The Russians filmed an epic six-hour version in 1967. YA

War of the Worlds, The (1898) By *H.G. Wells, this novel is about a Martian invasion of Earth. No one suspects there is life on Mars until a Thing looking like a huge rusty gas tank falls on open ground 25 miles from London. Its arrival draws curious crowds to the huge pit it made when it landed. But curiosity turns to horror when a lid falls off the Thing, and something resembling a little gray snake uncoils and wriggles out toward the watching crowd—and then another one. A strange creature follows that has huge eyes, oily brown skin, and a host of squirming tentacles for hands. A deputation of people attempting to make contact with the Martians is wiped out by a creature carrying a heat ray. Trees, bushes, and houses nearby go up in flames as well. Panic spreads as more and more Martians land. The army is called into action, but it is no match for these creatures with their death-ray machine. Terrified, thousands of people flee for their lives as the Martians spread across the countryside destroying everything in their path. They appear to be indestructible, and human civilization seems doomed. Then the

Martians unexpectedly die. They have all been slain by the bacteria to which they were exposed as soon as they invaded Earth and to which they had no resistance. When a radio dramatization of this story was broadcast in 1938 listeners in the United States, thinking it to be true, panicked. If you enjoy the *science fiction stories of Wells, try also the books of *Isaac Asimov and *Arthur C. Clarke. A film was made of *The War of the Worlds* in 1953. YA

Warner, Sylvia Townsend (1893–1978) An English poet, novelist, and short-story writer, Warner claimed she found some paper with a "particularly tempting surface," so she wrote poetry on it. Later she turned to writing novels and stories. She is known best for her beautifully written short stories. With understanding and delicacy of feeling, she writes about people whose seemingly ordinary, dull lives turn out to be anything but ordinary. Her characters often find self-expression in unusual and eccentric ways. In the short story "How to Succeed in Life" (1932), a foundling climbs the slippery path to success by good luck and cunning. In "Their Quiet Lives" (1961), another short story, a brother and sister live at the beck and call of their elderly mother until the brother takes a decisive step to release them all. Warner lived in a village in England where she gardened, cooked, studied witchcraft, and wrote. In the novel *Lolly Willowes* (1926), Laura Willowes, unwilling to accept the conventional demands on her unmarried state, becomes a witch to keep her independence. If you enjoy Warner's short stories, you might want to try those of *Elizabeth Bowen. YA

Warren, Robert Penn (1905–1989) A widely honored poet, novelist, and critic, Warren is best known for his popular novel *All the King's Men*. Born in Kentucky, Warren was part of the literary movement of the South during the 1920s and 1930s. Though he was a writer of great versatility, it is his poetry that best represents his vision and himself. His themes, which are often based on actual incidents, are rich with images drawn from nature. But the dark side of human nature has always held a particular fascination for him. A striking example is "The Ballad of Billie Potts" (1923), in which Billie, a strapping young man with money in his pocket, returns home after 10 years. His parents do not recognize him. Greedy for his money, they hit him on the head. A neighbor who saw Billie stops by, and the two old people learn that they have killed their son. *Brother to Dragons* (1953), a book-length verse narrative, retells the gruesome tale of two nephews of Thomas Jefferson who murder a black slave because he broke a jug belonging to their mother. Warren's novel *World Enough and Time* (1950) centers on the tragic events surrounding the murder of a Kentucky politician in the 1820s. YA

Warriors, Gods and Spirits from Central and South American Mythology (1983) By Douglas Gifford (1924–), this beautifully illustrated book collects some of the fascinating myths created by the original inhabitants of Central and South America. Long before Europeans found the Americas, the Aztecs of Mexico, Mayas of Central America, and Incas of the Andes in South America built great cities and civilizations and produced many beautiful myths and legends, much as the ancient Greeks, Romans, and other peoples did. Here are stories from these and other Indian cultures that describe the creation of the world and the gods, where different plants and animals came from, and how people were created. Among the stories is the tale of Quetzalcoatl, the Feathered Serpent god of the Aztecs. From the Mayas comes a marvelous myth about the creation of humans. The gods first try to shape humans out of mud, then out of wood, and finally achieve success with maize and maize dough. Another Maya story tells why rabbits have long ears. From the Incas comes the legend of how Lake Titicaca, the largest freshwater lake in South America, was created. If you enjoyed reading about the myths and legends in this book, try also *Spirits, Heroes and Hunters from North American Indian Mythology* (1981) by Marion Wood (n.d.). MR

Washington, Booker T(aliaferro) (1856–1915)
A distinguished black educator and writer,
Washington was born to slavery. His father was
white, but his mother was a slave belonging to
a plantation owner in Virginia. As a child
Booker swept yards and carried water to the
other slaves working in the fields. After the
Civil War he and his mother were freed, and
they went to join his mother's husband, at
which time Washington adopted his stepfather's name. Working as a coal miner by day,
he taught himself the alphabet so that he
could attend the local school at night. Eventually, with great hardship, he worked his way
through Hampton Institute in Virginia. He
then became a teacher. Years later Washington
wrote about these experiences in his autobiography, *Up from Slavery* (1901). Called the "classic American success story," it became a
best-seller. As founder and director for 34 years
of Tuskegee Institute in Alabama, Washington,
by the force of his personality, built the school
from little more than a shack into a renowned
institution. You might also like to read the autobiography of another black writer growing up
in America, *Black Boy* by *Richard Wright, as
well as the enormously popular book *Roots*
by *Alex Haley. YA

Washington Square (1881) By *Henry James,
this novel tells about a respected New York
City doctor who seeks only peace in his household. Dr. Austin Sloper's daughter, Catherine,
and his sister, Mrs. Penniman, live with him
on Washington Square. Catherine is afraid of
him. He thinks she is dull. Already in her 20s,
Catherine has not yet fallen in love. Catherine
likes opulent dresses that make her look older.
In the doctor's eyes, she becomes ugly and over-
dressed. Another of Sloper's sisters, Mrs. Al-
mond, gives a party, and Catherine meets
Morris Townsend, who is a clever and handsome young man. Mrs. Penniman, who is romantic, tries to play Cupid. Dr. Sloper finds
out that Morris, who "has the assurance of the
devil himself," is selfish, cheap, and a fortune
hunter. After Morris proposes to Catherine, Dr.
Sloper says he will disinherit her if she marries

Morris. Slowly Catherine realizes that Morris
wants her money, and the romance ends. Years
pass; Dr. Sloper dies and leaves his fortune to
charity, and Morris returns after 20 years expecting Catherine to still love him. But as he
says, "She doesn't care a button for me." YA

Wasps, The (422 B.C.) This political comedy
by *Aristophanes criticizes the abuses of the
Athenian judicial system at a time when jurymen were paid for their services. The Wasps
are jurymen, and they form the play's *chorus.
They are honorable men who have fought for
their country and deserve respect—or they will
use their sting.

Philocleon is an old man whose sole object
each morning is to be first at the courthouse to
serve on the jury. He never acquits anybody.
His son, Bdelycleon, thinks it is time his
father gave up jurying. He traps his father in
the house by putting a net around it. Philocleon is clever at escaping, but despite several
attempts, Bdelycleon wins. Philocleon resigns
himself to staying at home, where Bdelycleon
promises he can hold as many trials as he
likes. To please his father, Bdelycleon takes
him into high society, but Philocleon behaves
abominably. Returning home drunk, he ends
by dancing wildly with three small crabs. YA

Wasserstein, Wendy (1950–) This playwright
deals with the problems of modern women
who face a number of choices affecting the
way they live their lives. Wasserstein studied at
Yale Drama School at a time when the feminist movement was influencing the college
campus. Her play *Uncommon Women and
Others* (1978) centers on a group of women college students in the late 1960s who discuss
their future with anticipation and concern.
One asserts they will all be amazing by the
time they are 30 years old. That remark is modified at a college reunion when she says they
will be amazing when they are 45 years old.
The play *Isn't It Romantic* (1984) highlights the
pressures brought to bear on women to marry
because it is the right thing to do. In the play
The Heidi Chronicles (1988), Dr. Heidi Holland

reviews her life in a series of flashbacks. She speculates on how she feels alienated from society when she is a successful professor of art. *Uncommon Women and Others* was adapted for television in 1978. YA

"Waste Land, The" See *T.S. Eliot.

Watch on the Rhine (1941) By *Lillian Hellman, this play takes place in April 1940, a few months after the commencement of World War II in Europe. Sara Miller is returning after 28 years in Germany to her mother's home near Washington, D.C., with her husband, Kurt, and their three children. Their return interests Teck de Brancovis, an impoverished Romanian noble who, with his wife, is a guest of Sara's mother. He is a *Nazi sympathizer, often visiting the German Embassy in Washington to play cards with the ambassador. A German newspaper reports the capture of the leader of the Anti-Nazi Underground Movement and two companions. A fourth man is missing. Teck, who has obtained a "wanted" list from the embassy, reads the description of the missing man to the assembled family, saying there is a price of $10,000 for news of him. Shocked by the capture of his close associates, Kurt acknowledges he is the fourth man. Though knowing he will probably never see his family again, he must go back to Germany alone to help his friends. Teck has discovered that Kurt has the funds of the Anti-Nazi Movement in his briefcase and blackmails Kurt to give him $10,000 to keep his mouth shut. But Teck has misjudged Kurt. Kurt knows he must now kill Teck, who threatens not only his life but his family and his associates in Germany. You are a gambler, he tells Teck, but you made a mistake in gambling with your own life. A film was made of this play in 1943. YA

Water-Babies, The, A Fairy Tale for a Land-Baby (1863) By *Charles Kingsley, this classic fairy tale is about Tom the Chimney Sweep, who loses his way in the huge chimneys of Harthover Hall and comes down in the wrong room. Not wanting to be beaten by his

Tom rides a sea beast in *The Water-Babies.*

master, Mr. Grimes, he runs away and becomes a water-baby. Tom is very happy in the water. He forgets about cruel Mr. Grimes and sweeping chimneys. Because he is lonely and likes being naughty, he teases the water creatures. Then he finds there are other water-babies besides himself. On Fridays Mrs. Bedonebyasyoudid visits them and gives candies to anyone who has been good. But Tom is given a pebble because he teased a sea anemone. On Sundays Madame Doasyouwouldbedoneby comes with kisses and cuddles. But Tom steals the candy and grows sharp prickles so he cannot be cuddled. He learns about the Doasyoulikes, who are so lazy they become quite stupid. Tom does not want to be like them. He is told to go to the Other-end-of-Nowhere and help Mr. Grimes. On his way he has many wonderful adventures and visits many strange places, such as Waste Paper Land, Oldwivesfabledom, and *Leaveheavenalone, before returning home to find Grimes stuck in chimney no. 345. At the sight of Tom, Mr. Grimes becomes sorry for his bad deeds. And Tom is no longer a water-baby because he has grown up. An animated movie was made of *The Water-Babies* in 1978. MR & YA

Watership Down (1972) This delightful fantasy by *Richard Adams is about Fiver, a rabbit who has "feelings." With his rabbit friend Hazel he finds a signboard near their warren. Fiver says something terrible is going to happen. Because he is usually right about these things, Hazel and a few other rabbits join him and leave the warren. Fiver has a vision of a new warren on top of a hill where they can easily see anything approaching, whether friend or enemy. This little band of wandering rabbits has many adventures before they find their ideal warren. On the way they meet selfish rabbits, frightened rabbits, bossy rabbits, and those who hardly know they are rabbits because they live in cages. Through hardship and determination they find the right place for their warren and settle in. Then, one day, two rabbits from the old warren appear. All the other rabbits have been gassed by men who are building houses on the land. Fiver's "feeling" had been right. If you liked this story, try *The Hobbit* by *J.R.R. Tolkien. An animated film was made of *Watership Down* in 1978. MR & YA

Waugh, Evelyn [Arthur St. John] (1903–1966) An English author of novels, travel books, and biographies, Waugh has been called the best comic genius since *George Bernard Shaw. Some of his funniest satirical novels are about the falseness of London society of the 1920s. *Vile Bodies* (1930) follows the giddy path of the Bright Young People, and *Decline and Fall* (1928) ridicules private-school education. There is also a sinister side to Waugh's *satire. In *A Handful of Dust* (1934), Tony Last's wife deserts him, and he joins an expedition to the Amazon. The expedition fails. Sick and alone, Tony wanders into the jungle and is rescued by Mr. Todd, an elderly recluse, and taken into his house. There he is kept a prisoner and forced to read a chapter of a Dickens novel to Mr. Todd each day. Waugh traveled, volunteered for the Marines during World War II, and parachuted into Yugoslavia. But he found modern life distasteful and, after the war, retreated to the remote English countryside to devote himself to his writing. His most popular novel is *Brideshead Revisited.* YA

Way of All Flesh, The (1903) In this largely autobiographical story, *Samuel Butler tells about three generations of a *Victorian English family. The novel, a classic of English literature, reveals the hypocrisy of a supposedly perfect patriarchal family. George Pontifex, son of a self-made man, is apprenticed to a printer. He becomes successful and priggish. His son, Theobald, is dull and pliant. George forces Theobald, in spite of his protestations, to become a clergyman. In his first church post Theobald is an easy catch for Christina Allaby. Into their conventional family, Ernest is born. Ernest is crushed by his overbearing father. School is even worse. Luckily, his Aunt Aletha and her lawyer friend, Overton, take an interest in Ernest and encourage him. But Ernest's father insists that he follow him into the church. At his first parish in London, Ernest gets into trouble when he makes an ill-advised visit to a respectable young lady whom he mistakenly thinks is a prostitute. After spending six months in jail because of this breach of the strict standards of Victorian England, he meets a former family servant, Ellen, and marries her, only to find she is a drunkard. Discovering by chance that Ellen is already married and their marriage is therefore null and void, Ernest is free of all family ties. He receives an inheritance from his aunt and settles down to a happy bachelor existence. Your library probably has this famous novel, and there are several inexpensive paperback editions available. YA

We (1924) was written by Yevgeny Zamyatin (1884–1937), a Russian novelist and short-story writer, a few years after the Russian Revolution. It is a prophetic vision of an authoritarian regime taken to the limits of repression and dehumanization. In the One State, people have numbers rather than names and are even referred to as "Numbers." There is no privacy. Glass cities are built on a rigid grid pattern. At set hours Numbers get up in the morning, eat together, walk in columns four abreast, go to work, and go to sleep. D-503, a mathematician, is the Builder of the "Integral," a machine made to conquer cosmic space. Happily registered with 0-90, his sexual partner, D-503 finds it inconceivable that there could be any life other than that of the One State. As a record to be placed in the "Integral," he is writing down his thoughts about this ideal life. Inexplicably, he is overwhelmed by an attraction to another Number, I-330. Through this irrational attachment his rational, perfect world is shattered. He learns that beneath the controlled surface of the One State there is growing rebellion. I-330 is one of the rebels. D-503 has a choice: He can either make the "Integral" reaffirm the One State, or make it join the rebels. Zamyatin was expelled by the Soviet Union and lived in Paris until his death. Influenced by Zamyatin, *George Orwell wrote his version of the totalitarian society in *1984. Another important novel on the subject is *Fahrenheit 451 by *Ray Bradbury. YA

Web and the Rock, The (1938) By *Thomas Wolfe, this novel is largely autobiographical. When George Webber is 16 years old, his father dies, leaving him a small inheritance. George lives with his Aunt Maw, who talks endlessly to him about the Joyner family. He finds his ties to this family oppressive. Leaving their narrow and self-sufficient world, he goes to college and then to New York City, where he hopes to meet the great and the famous and become a writer. But in that shining and enchanted city, Webber finds only loneliness. Restless, he travels to Europe in search of peace but without success. Returning to New York, he meets Esther Jack. A designer of stage sets, she mixes with the successful and fashionable. She is full of laughter and joy, and their stay together lasts for several happy years. But Webber is not successful, and he blames Esther's fashionable society friends. In his bitterness he breaks with her. Disillusioned, he goes to Germany, his father's country. What he finds there is something ominous and frightening beneath the surface of the pleasure-loving Germans. *You Can't Go Home Again* (1940), in which Webber resumes his relationship with Esther Jack, is the sequel to this story. YA

Welcome Home, Jellybean (1978) In this warm, sympathetic, and funny story by *Marlene Fanta Shyer, 12-year-old Niel Oxley tells the story of his older sister's homecoming. Geraldine, who has spent much of her life in institutions for the retarded, finds speaking difficult and pronounces her name "Jellybean." When she is finally toilet-trained, her mother decides she should come home for good. "Niel, it's not going to be easy," Niel's father says. And it is not. On her first ride in an elevator, Geraldine sees everyone pressing a floor button. She reaches for one herself, and pandemonium breaks out as alarm bells sound and passengers shriek. Niel shows her how to take out the garbage, down to the little door in the hallway and down the chute. Easy—until Geraldine takes a bag of just-bought groceries and sends those down the chute too. When Geraldine's unexpected behavior interferes with Niel's schoolwork and her father's musical composition, the problems become serious. Niel finds himself in the principal's office too often, and their father moves out. Then the other residents in the building sign a petition to get the Oxley family out. But Geraldine is learning fast. She can say her own name and that of her brother. She shakes hands instead of hugging everyone. And, in her own different, funny, and weird way she wins the day. Another book about difficult situations and how people deal with them is *Winning by *Robin Brancato. MR

Wells, H(erbert) G(eorge) (1866–1946) An English novelist and visionary, Wells is known best for his *science fiction stories. *The War of the Worlds, a story of a Martian invasion of Earth, was written in the days of the horse and carriage, when the jet airplane had not been invented and the idea of space travel was still a novelty. *The Time Machine is another of his disturbing visions of future life on Earth. Wells studied science and made extensive use of scientific knowledge in his books. Many of the more than 100 books he wrote reflect his concern about the future of the world. He predicted an increasingly materialistic and mechanized future in *When the Sleeper Awakes* (1899), and advocated a planned society, writing, "We were making the future . . . and hardly any of us troubled to think what future we were making." In *An Outline of History* (1920) he suggested the idea of an economic, social, and political world plan. Several of his stories have been made into films: *The Invisible Man* (1897), about a scientist who discovers how to become invisible, in 1933; *The Man Who Could Work Miracles*, a movie script, about a store clerk's discovery that he could do whatever he wanted, in 1937; *The Shape of Things to Come* (1933), a vision of the future, in 1936 under a shortened title *Shape of Things* and under the full title in 1979; *Kipps* (1905), the story of a shopkeeper who inherits a fortune, in 1941; and *The War of the Worlds*, in 1953. *The Invisible Man* was adapted for television in 1975. YA

Wells, Rosemary (1943–) Though she has written and illustrated many books for young children, Wells is known especially for her novels for older readers. In *The Fog Comes on Little Pig Feet* (1972), 13-year-old Rachel's parents decide to send her to boarding school. Right from the start she dislikes it. She avoids school assembly, finding a small library to hide in until it is over. Because she is used to a room of her own at home, she wants one at school. But this is against the rules. The one girl she does make friends with is a rebel like her. This leads to trouble, but Rachel finally comes to terms with authority, individual responsibility, and growing up. In *None of the Above* (1974), 16-year-old Marcia feels like an outsider and distant from her family now that her mother has died. Only when she meets Raymond do things change for her. Though Dorothy is warned in *Leave Well Alone* (1977) to stay away from a housing development, her curiosity has to be satisfied. In one of the houses something is going on, and she finds out about a very different life-style from the one she knows. MR & YA

Welty, Eudora (1909–) One of the best modern writers about life in the Deep South, Welty explores in her short stories and novels the small joys and heroism of everyday life in the relationships of ordinary people. She grew up in a book-loving family in Jackson, Mississippi. During the *Great Depression she worked for the WPA (Works Progress Administration), a federal agency formed to create jobs for the unemployed. Her work took her throughout Mississippi, where she met all kinds of people, rich and poor. She visited their homes and saw them at work and with friends and found them fascinating. The many photographs she took during her travels were eventually published as *One Time, One Place, Mississippi in the Depression* (1971). Her short stories brought her recognition. "Death of a Traveling Salesman" (1936), about a salesman who loses his way and finds himself ill and alone, was her first published story. Her first collection of short stories, *A Curtain of Green* (1941), contains "The Hitch Hikers," about a man who picks up two tramps and takes them into town, where one of them murders the other. *Delta Wedding* (1945) was her first novel. It tells the story of the Fairchild family and their plantation home, Shellmound, as they prepare for a wedding. In *Losing Battles* (1970) the Renfro family gather to celebrate a birthday and learn of the death of Miss Julia Mortimer, the local schoolteacher, who had lost the battle to educate the community, including most of the Renfros. In *The Optimist's Daughter* (1972) a woman returns home to be with her father while he has an eye operation and finds she has to bury him. Welty deals sensitively with the inner lives of women, the pain and the joy. A private person herself, she wrote *One Writer's Beginnings* to discourage anyone from attempting her biography. It became a best seller. *The Robber Bridegroom* (1942), about the daughter of a Mississippi farmer and about her robber lover, was adapted for the stage in 1978. *The Ponder Heart* (1954), about Uncle Daniel, who is very rich and very generous, was adapted for the stage in 1978. "The Hitch Hikers" was adapted for television in 1986. YA

Wendy Darling is one of the main characters in *Peter Pan* by *James M. Barrie. She is a sensible and tidy child on the verge of young womanhood and thinks of herself as "a nice motherly person." Her ability to care for and comfort others makes her appealing to Peter Pan, who has no mother, so Peter persuades Wendy to fly with him to *Neverland to look after his little band of Lost Boys. Wendy is flattered by Peter's promise that she will receive the respect and admiration of the boys, for her own brothers are not particularly respectful of her. Once installed in Neverland, she takes pride in cooking, mending, and storytelling.

Wendy is aware that Peter has sworn to remain a child, but she cannot help hoping he will change his mind and grow up with her. Her hints that they might remain together make Peter rather nervous. In the end, she must accept the fact that she will one day be too much a grown-up to be of real interest to him.

werewolf means "man-wolf," or a person who can change his shape into that of a wolf. Countries that do not have werewolves may have were-tigers, were-crocodiles, were-jackals, or other dangerous creatures of myth and superstition. Some telltale clues about werewolves are that they are very hairy, their eyebrows are straight and meet over the nose, their fingers are like claws, their small ears lie flat to the head or are pointed, and their eyes are red. Werewolves like human flesh. If they are injured or killed, they instantly change back to a human shape again so one is never sure they really were wolves. They change their shape at night and in secret. The legend of the werewolf has been linked to a mental illness called lycanthropy, in which the patient believes he is a wild beast and develops a taste for raw meat. If you would like to read more about human beings who change into beasts and back again, try *Werewolf!* (1979) by Bill Pronzini (1943–), an anthology of chilling tales by such authors as *Rudyard Kipling, Guy de Maupassant (1850–1893), *Bram Stoker, and more modern writers. A film called *Werewolf of London*, about a doctor bitten by a werewolf who then becomes a fiend himself, was made in 1935. YA

Werfel, Franz (1890–1945) An Austrian poet, novelist, and playwright, Werfel was an important literary figure in the 1920s and 1930s as a member of the Expressionist movement, which stressed the emotional content of a novel, play, or painting for greater dramatic effect. He wrote *The Forty Days of Musa Dagh* (1934) after seeing some Armenian refugee children in Damascus, Syria. It tells of the plight of 5,000 Armenians when they take to the mountains of Musa Dagh to escape massacre by Turks in 1914. Werfel, whose parents were German Jews, lived in Vienna until the Nazis entered Austria in 1938. He fled to France, finding refuge in Lourdes, where he hid for some months before escaping to the United States. He vowed at that time that if he escaped, he would write the life story of Saint Bernadette, the patron saint of the shrine at Lourdes, France. In his most popular book, a best-seller, *The Song of Bernadette* (1941), Werfel describes how Marie Bernadette Soubirous (1844–1879), a peasant girl, had a vision of a beautiful lady, the Mother of God, in a shallow cave near Lourdes. The vision came to her a number of times. Eventually the site of these visions became a religious shrine, to which many *pilgrims travel each year, and where miraculous healings are said to take place. *The Song of Bernadette* was adapted for the movies in 1943. YA

Wersba, Barbara (1932–) The author of a number of highly regarded novels for young readers, Wersba grew up in California and New York City. Many of her novels are about young persons whose lives are touched and changed through relationships with grownups. Among her books are *The Dream Watcher* (1968), about a teenage boy who finds self-confidence and a direction in life through his friendship with an aging actress; *The Country of the Heart* (1975), about the love between an aspiring young poet and a terminally ill woman writer more than twice his age; *Tunes for a Small Harmonica* (1976), about a teenage tomboy whose life is changed when she falls in love with her poetry teacher; *The Carnival in My Mind* (1982), about a 14-year-old boy who escapes his unhappy home life by befriending and moving in with a 20-year-old aspiring actress and call girl; and *Just Be Gorgeous* (1988), about the friendship

MR = Middle Reader   YA = Young Adult Reader   * = See this main entry

between a shy, awkward, lonely teenage girl and a homeless man who dreams of breaking into show business. MR & YA

West, Nathanael [Nathan Weinstein] (1903–1940) Though he wrote only four novels, West had a powerful influence on modern American literature, and his novel *The Day of the Locust has been called one of the best Hollywood stories ever written.

West dropped out of high school and went to work in his father's construction business. He later spent six years in New York City managing cheap residential hotels, where he offered rent-free living space to such beginning writers as *Dashiell Hammett and Erskine Caldwell (1903–1987). West became unusually interested in and involved in his tenants' personal problems, and these provided rich material for his books. Unable to earn a living by writing, he moved to California hoping to find work as a screenwriter. Before achieving a modest success in Hollywood, he lived again in shabby hotels and befriended a group of stuntmen, laborers, prostitutes, and small-time crooks. Fascinated by the unglamorous side of life, particularly during the *Great Depression, West wrote about the hopelessness and frustration of modern society. Perhaps because of the painful subject matter, his works were not popular successes. West began to be known and appreciated in the late 1940s, after his death in an auto accident. You might be interested in reading *Miss Lonelyhearts* (1933), about a newspaperman writing a personal advice column who takes his readers' problems so seriously that he becomes ill. YA

West, Rebecca [Cecily Isabel Fairfield] (1892–1983) This Irish-born English novelist, essayist, and journalist adopted the name Rebecca West after the emancipated heroine of *Henrik Ibsen's play *Rosmersholm* (1886). A strong feminist, West made the emancipation of women a paramount interest throughout her life. Among her best-known books is her first published novel, *The Return of the Soldier* (1918), which deals with the return home from the

trenches of World War I of a shell-shocked soldier. His beautiful but cold and unimaginative wife is helpless in the face of his amnesia. But the woman who was his first love understands him and, at great cost to herself, helps him overcome his difficulties. *Black Lamb and Grey Falcon* (1941) is a fascinating account of West's travels with her husband in Yugoslavia. It contains her reflections on the history, art, and people of the region. In *The Meaning of Treason* (1948), West attempts to define treason, particularly in relation to the Nuremberg War Crimes Trials held after World War II and the trial of the Englishman William Joyce (1906–1946), the notorious "Lord Haw-Haw," who made anti-British broadcasts from Germany during the war. YA

West Side Story (1957) In this musical drama about gang warfare in New York City, author Arthur Laurents (1918–) and composer Leonard Bernstein (1918–1990) have retold the story of *Romeo and Juliet* by *William Shakespeare. Two rival teenage gangs start a brawl over who owns the street. Riff, the leader of the Jets, tells his members to show up at a local dance and persuades Tony, who has outgrown the gang, to join them as they plan a rumble, or fight, with Bernardo, the leader of the Sharks. Bernardo's sister, Maria, who has just come to the United States, is at the dance. For Maria and Tony, it is love at first sight. They declare their love when they meet next evening and, in a serious moment, recite the marriage vow "till death do us part." Later that evening, tensions rise as Tony tries to stop the gangs from fighting. Knives are pulled, and Bernardo kills Riff. Tony seizes Riff's knife and kills Bernardo. When they hear a police whistle, the kids scatter, leaving Bernardo and Riff dead. Maria cannot believe Tony has killed Bernardo until Tony climbs secretly through her bedroom window to tell her what happened. The lovers plan to run away together to avoid all the violence, and Tony leaves. But Tony is misled into believing Maria has been killed. While wandering through the streets in despair, Tony is shot by Bernardo's friend Chino. Maria finds Tony and comforts him as he dies. In the face of this tragedy, the two gangs reconcile their differences, just as the Capulets and Montagues do in *Romeo and Juliet*. A popular film version of *West Side Story* was produced in 1961. YA

Westall, Robert (Atkinson) (1929–) An English writer of novels for young readers, Westall is highly regarded for the direct, realistic approach of his stories. His characters deal with family tensions, violence, and the emotions of school loyalties and rivalries. Ghosts and the supernatural sometimes appear in his stories. *The Machine Gunners* (1975) is about a group of English schoolchildren during World War II who find and keep a German machine gun, complete with ammunition, despite a frantic search for it by police and distracted school authorities. In *The Watch House* (1977), a spooky ghost who throws things keeps Anne and her friends Timothy and Pat busy through a summer at an English coast town. For older readers Westall delves into *science fiction in *Urn Burial* and in *Futuretrack 5*. MR & YA

Westing Game, The (1978) By *Ellen Raskin, this exciting mystery begins when a delivery boy slips notices describing a bargain in apartments under the doors of potential tenants. There are six apartments available in Sunset Towers, which has a view of Westing House. Fifteen people and one "mistake" move in. These are no ordinary tenants. Then Sam Westing is found dead in Westing House, some say sprawled on the oriental carpet, some say tucked up in bed, but definitely under suspicious circumstances. He has left his considerable millions to one of the tenants in Sunset Towers. But which one? They can only find out by playing a game. Each pair of players is given a set of clues and a check for $10,000. No two sets of clues are alike. And the players have only a certain amount of time in which to work things out. There are a murderer, a thief, and a mad bomber among them. No one can be trusted. Yet there is no time to lose. *Someone* must win a fortune of $200 million. *The Westing Game* won a *Newbery Medal in 1979. MR

Westlake, Donald E(dwin) (1933–) Westlake has written 50 novels in all, but he is deservedly best known for his humorous crime stories, which he writes with great skill. Most of them concern the John Dortmunder gang, a group of nonviolent thieves who make excellent plans but are never able to carry them out successfully, due both to fate and to bungling. In *The Hot Rock* (1970) they steal an emerald from a museum, but the gang member who has it gets caught. They then manage to raid the police station and release him, only to find he has left the emerald in his cell. The attempt to recover the gem continues in this manner. *Bank Shot* (1972) finds them planning to steal a whole bank, temporarily housed in a trailer, with the usual mixed results. In *Drowned Hopes* (1990) a coffin contains a fortune, but it had been buried underwater when a dam and reservoir were built. The gang tries hard, but the wrong person gets the money. Humorous stories about crime are so rare that you will have to search for them in your library. Good luck! *The Hot Rock* was made into a movie in 1972 and *Bank Shot* in 1974. MR & YA

Wharton, Edith (Newbold Jones) (1862–1937) Born to a wealthy family whose interests were mainly devoted to enjoying its good fortune, Wharton lived at a time when New York City society was its most glittering. She wrote about her own society, exploring its manners and morals and exposing its shallowness. At first she was ignored, but she was recognized eventually as an important American writer. *Henry James, who became a friend, had a strong influence on her work, which was often compared to his. Her first published work was a volume of short stories, *The Great Inclination* (1899). Her reputation as a novelist was established in 1905 when *The House of Mirth*, a bleak *satire of New York society, was published. After her marriage to Edward Wharton, she went to live in Paris, where she wrote what many consider her finest novel, *Ethan Frome*, this time with a setting in New England. Wharton was to live and work in France for the rest of her life, maintaining her reputation as an American writer by continuing to write about America and about New York society in particular. *The Age of Innocence is another satire of New York society. *Old New York* (1924), a collection of short stories, includes "The Old Maid," a story about an unmarried woman's selfless struggle to keep her child. Four novellas were later collected in *Madame de Treymes and Others* (1977). They include *The Touchstone* (1900), the story of a man's guilt after he anonymously publishes love letters from a woman who has died; *Sanctuary* (1903), about the anguish a woman feels for her husband and her son, who face moral challenges; *Madame de Treymes* (1909), a story about blackmail; and *Bunner Sisters* (1916), about two women who keep a small shop that eventually fails because the younger woman leaves to marry. YA

What Price Glory? (1924) By Laurence Stallings (1894–1968) and *Maxwell Anderson, this play debunks the idea that war is glorious. Written soon after World War I, it introduced a new realism into the American theater and was very successful. Anderson was a pacifist during the war, but Stallings, who lost a leg fighting in France, knew trench warfare firsthand. The play opens with the Marines of L Company discussing their captain and his relationship with Charmaine, a barkeeper's daughter. Captain Flagg is going on leave as soon as Quirt, a new sergeant, arrives to take command. Quirt has an old grudge to settle against Flagg, so while Flagg is away, Quirt makes love to Charmaine. On Flagg's return, Charmaine's father demands justice for his daughter. Flagg gets even with Quirt by arranging, under threat of court-martial, Quirt's marriage to Charmaine. But before this can be carried out, the general arrives from headquarters and orders Flagg to attack the Germans and take a prisoner. Leave for the whole company is promised if the mission is successful. During the attack, several men are killed or wounded, but a German officer is taken prisoner. The soldiers return tired out and ready for their leave, and Flagg and Quirt resume their quarrel. But a

new order comes: They are to return to the attack. At first Flagg refuses to accept the order. Then, worn out and resigned, he tells his men to get ready again for combat. They all leave, abandoning Charmaine. *What Price Glory?* was made into a celebrated silent movie in 1926 and remade in 1952. YA

Wheatley, Phillis (?1753–1784) The first black woman poet in America, Phillis was born in Africa and brought by slave ship to Boston, where she was bought by John Wheatley. The Wheatleys treated her kindly and taught her to read and write. She was 13 years old when she started to write poetry. Through the efforts of friends in Boston who admired her accomplishments, some of her poems were published in 1767. In 1773 Wheatley visited England, where she impressed many people with her intelligence and character. A collection of her poems, *Poems on Various Subjects, Religious and Moral* (1773), was published while she was there. After her return to America she married John Peters, a freeman, but the marriage was not a happy one. The last years of her life were tragic. Her three children died in infancy and her husband was jailed for debt. Alone and in poverty, she died when she was 31 years old. Wheatley's poems were written in the years just before the American Revolution, and in them she often speaks of freedom. Though her poetry, which was based on contemporary English verse, is not highly original, you will find she is worth reading. See if your library has *Life and Works of Phillis Wheatley* (1916), which has been reprinted. You can find a selection of her poetry and letters in *Phillis Wheatley in the Black American Beginnings* (1975) by William H. Robinson (1922–). Younger readers will enjoy reading a biography, *Phillis Wheatley: America's First Black Poetess* (1971), by Miriam Morris Fuller (1933–). MR & YA

Wheel on the School, The (1954) The plot of this novel by the Dutch-born Meindert DeJong (1906–1991) may seem strange to you, but this is an exciting and amusing book. The six children in the school at Shora—a small fishing village in the Netherlands on the North Sea—led by Lina, the only girl, wonder why storks make nests on the roofs of houses in nearby villages but not in Shora. It is believed the storks bring good luck to the people of the villages. The children learn that a wheel on which the storks can build their nest must be placed on the roof. They set out to find a wheel. One of the boys drops an old wheel out of a hayloft, and it breaks. Lina finds a wheel underneath an old boat but nearly drowns getting it out. As the men of the village place Lina's wheel on the top of the school, a terrible storm strikes, and it is feared that the storks, on the way from Africa, will be killed. But a pair is sighted, injured and stranded on a sandbar. The villagers rescue them and place them on the wheel. The male descends, picks up a twig, and places it at the feet of his mate, indicating that they will build their nest there. Meanwhile, the broken wheel is mended, and one of the villagers discovers he can make more wheels out of driftwood and other materials. Thanks to the children, Shora will now have storks to bring good fortune. DeJong wrote a number of equally original, readable, and thought-provoking novels. Among them are *The House of Sixty Fathers* (1956), which tells about a Chinese boy's search for his family during World War II; *Puppy Summer* (1966), a warning of what may happen when young people have to part with pets to which they have become attached; and *Journey from Peppermint Street* (1968), which is set in the Netherlands and tells about the moods and thoughts of a boy on a long walk through the night with his grandfather. *The Wheel on the School* won the *Newbery Medal in 1955. MR

When Hitler Stole Pink Rabbit (1971), by *Judith Kerr, is a story of a German family in the 1930s. Elections are about to be held in Berlin, and posters of Adolf Hitler are all over town. Nine-year-old Anna and her brother Max do not take much notice. But their parents do: The family is Jewish. Their father mysteriously disappears one night. A few days later their mother starts packing so they can join

their father in Switzerland. Something is seriously wrong. Anna decides to leave her favorite Pink Rabbit behind. It can be sent on later. They leave Germany just in time, because the day after Hitler is elected, police go to their house to take their passports away and confiscate their belongings, including Pink Rabbit. Now they are refugees. Their father does not find work easily as they move from country to country. Lessons in a strange language are difficult, and there is different food to eat, like snails. But they are together and nothing else matters very much. Another book about Hitler's persecution of Jews is *The Diary of a Young Girl* by Anne Frank (1929–1944). MR

"When Lilacs Last in the Dooryard Bloomed" (1865), by *Walt Whitman, is an elegy on the death of Abraham Lincoln. Whitman was home in Brooklyn when he heard the news early that morning. "Mother prepared breakfast—and other meals afterwards—as usual," he wrote, "but not a mouthful was eaten." Out of his mourning came one of the great poems of any language. He never mentions Lincoln by name but uses poignant *symbols to tell of his grief. He speaks of the "fallen star" for Lincoln. "The lilac . . . with heart-shaped leaves . . . and the perfume strong I love" symbolizes his own great and lasting love for Lincoln. And he, the poet, is represented by the solitary thrush who "sings by himself a song." Toward the end of the poem there is a "Carol to Death" in which he comes to terms with his and the country's loss and the loss of the soldiers who died fighting in the Civil War. YA

When the Legends Die (1963), by *Hal Borland, is the story of a Ute Indian boy, Thomas Black Bull. Thomas lives with his parents on a Colorado reservation. When his father gets into trouble, the family moves to an isolated spot in the hills. There they build a lodge, live by hunting and fishing as their ancestors did, and Thomas is taught the old Indian ways. Both parents are dead by the time Thomas is 11 years old. Blue Elk, a Ute who co-operated with the white authorities, tricks Thomas into going to school in a nearby town. Silent and hostile, Thomas has a hard time adjusting to the strict routine. He tries to escape without success. He meets Red Dillon, a rodeo promoter, who gets permission to hire Thomas as a rider. The boy enters the world of small-time rodeo in makeshift arenas, where Red lays bets on Thomas's skill and squanders the winnings on drink. After Red dies, Thomas becomes a legendary bronco-buster known as "Killer Tom Black," who vents his anger by riding rodeo horses until they drop.

While recovering from a bad injury, Thomas goes home and hires on as a sheepherder. The peace, silence, and natural beauty of the mountain camp soothe and help him rediscover his real heritage. Thomas lives as an Indian again, builds a lodge in the old way, and begins the long process of trying to understand the white man's world. *When the Legends Die* has been translated into nine languages, and was adapted for the movies in 1972. YA

When We Were Very Young (1924) By *A.A. Milne, this collection of verse for children is guaranteed to tickle the fancy of beginning readers. Children who have not yet learned to read will enjoy hearing the poems and seeing the wonderful illustrations by Ernest H. Shepard (1879–1976). *When We Were Very Young* introduces two very special characters. The first is the boy Christopher Robin, for whom the poems were originally written. The second is a short, pudgy stuffed bear who is called Mr. Edward Bear. Readers of the stories collected in Milne's books *Winnie-the-Pooh* and *The House at Pooh Corner* will recognize Mr. Edward Bear as none other than Winnie-the-Pooh. If you enjoy the poems in *When We Were Very Young*—and it will be very difficult for you not to enjoy them—you will also want to read the poems collected in *Now We Are Six*. MR

Where the Red Fern Grows (1961), by Wilson Rawls (1913–1984), is a story of determination, courage, and love—the love between a boy and

his dogs. Ten-year-old Billy lives with his parents in the best hunting country in Oklahoma. He becomes infected "with the terrible disease of dog-wanting." He works hard to earn the money for two coonhounds. Finally the day comes when he buys his dogs and brings them home. He names them Old Dan and Little Ann and teaches them all he knows about hunting coons. The three of them make a great team, and they bring in more coonskins than any other hunter around. When Grandpa enters the dogs for the coonhound championships, Billy is nearly beside himself with excitement and expectation. The dogs put on their best performance and Billy returns home triumphant.

But tragedy comes. While hunting in the forest they meet a mountain lion. The fight is fierce and desperate. Though badly wounded, the dogs fight on until the mountain lion is killed, and Old Dan and Little Ann die of their wounds. Sadly, Billy buries them side by side. A beautiful red fern grows between the graves, and Billy's sadness turns to wonder because an Indian legend says the place will be forever sacred. If you enjoyed this story, you will also like Rawls's *Summer of the Monkeys* (1976), in which Jay Berry and his dog, Rowdy, spend all summer trying to catch a troupe of clever monkeys hiding out in the river bottoms. Wilson Rawls grew up in Oklahoma and spent his boyhood in the kind of country he describes so vividly in his books. With his own blue tick hound as company, he roamed the hills and told his stories to his dog. *Where the Red Fern Grows* was adapted for film in 1974. MR

Where the Sidewalk Ends (1974) By *Shel Silverstein, this selection contains 123 of his short poems. At first you may think them only very funny and entertaining, but on second thought you will find that some of them cause you to ponder a bit on their real meaning. For example, one poem tells of a boy who collects all kinds of things, such as worn-out belts and paper bags. They are his treasures, but other people call them junk. Who is right? Other poems tell of the boy who watched so much television he turned into a TV set; of the king who loved peanut butter sandwiches so much that all he allowed to be taught in school was how to make them; of the tallest ice cream cone in the world—18 flavors; and of the girl who resolved to eat a whole whale, which she did, though it took her 89 years. Silverstein's gift for far-out humor often conceals a lesson on what is important and what is not. MR

Whipping Boy, The (1986) By *Sid Fleischman, this funny adventure novel tells about a spoiled prince, Harold, who causes so much trouble that everyone calls him Prince Brat behind his back. But whenever he gets into trouble, it is Jemmy, his "whipping boy," who is punished. Jemmy longs to escape, to return to his raggedy but free life on the streets, but he gets more than he bargained for when Prince Brat decides to run away, taking Jemmy with him. The boys are kidnapped by two vicious highwaymen, Hold-Your-Nose Billy and Cutwater. They escape, but it is no thanks to Prince Brat, who seems to be enjoying their dangerous situation all too much. In fact, it is the first fun he has ever had. The two have many scary adventures and meet a number of interesting characters. Through it all, Prince Brat and Jemmy learn a great deal about each other, and by the time they get back home to the castle and Billy and Cutwater finally get their just deserts, the boys have become true friends. If you enjoyed this book, you may also like the humorous adventures of *The Great Brain* by John D. Fitzgerald (1908–). The Whipping Boy won the *Newbery Medal in 1987. MR

white Above all, white is the *color of purity, joy, and holiness. In ancient times the Druid priests wore white, and the Egyptian god Osiris was pictured with a white crown. Traditionally, brides wear white. On the other hand, in some parts of the Far East, white, rather than *black, is the color of sorrow. White also has a great variety of uses in writing and in everyday conversation. A "white-collar worker" has an office job; a "white feather" signifies cowardice; a "white elephant" is a gift that is not welcome; a "white flag" is an offer of surrender or a re-

quest for a truce; and a "white lie" does little harm. If you are "white as a sheet," you are very pale. White can also stand for royalists, reaction, and counterrevolution, as compared with *red, the color of rebellion and radicalism. For example, after the Russian Communist Revolution of 1917, those who took up armed resistance to it and fought the Red Army were known as White Russians. The phrase "the white man's burden" was coined by *Rudyard Kipling and came to express the belief, now outdated, that it was the right and duty of the nations of the Western world to rule, and thereby uplift, the people of Africa and Asia. "White" also has many uses that do not imply any judgment but merely state the color, as white poodle or white person, that is, a member of the white race.

White, E(lwyn) B(rooks) (1899–1985) A writer of wit and humor, White wrote for *The New Yorker* magazine over a period of 40 years, collaborating at times with another humorist, *James Thurber. Though White wrote books on many subjects, from American humor to advice on writing, he is remembered chiefly for three well-loved books for young readers. *Stuart Little* is the story of a boy who is only two-and-a-half inches tall. Inspired by the animals on his farm in Maine, White wrote *Charlotte's Web*, in which Wilbur the pig is to be sent to the slaughterhouse but is saved by his friend Charlotte, the spider. In *Trumpet of the Swan*, a swan who has no voice gets over this difficulty by learning to play the trumpet. Both *Charlotte's Web* and *Stuart Little* have been adapted for television. MR

White, Patrick (1912–1990) This Australian novelist, short-story writer, and playwright has an international reputation as an innovative writer. Australia is usually the setting for his stories, and his subjects are anything but conventional. His novels concern the search of the individual for truth and harmony in life. In *The Tree of Man* (1955) White wrote that he tries "to discover the extraordinary behind the ordinary" through dealing with both the inner and outer lives of his characters. The story, a simple one, concerns a young man and woman who marry and settle down to life in the Australian outback. The years pass, their children grow up, and other people move into their remote area, and you learn how the couple deals in unique ways with the events of their ordinary lives. Many of his novels have a spiritual, visionary quality about them. For example, in *Voss* (1957), one of his best-known novels, White set his scene in the 1840s, when Voss and his followers set out to cross the Australian desert, which no one has managed yet to do. He struggles with the hardships he encounters, believing he cannot fail, while at home his fiancée sets out to control his soul. *The Eye of the Storm* (1973) is a compelling story about the last days of a once-beautiful woman, rich and charming, who has controlled and manipulated everyone around her all her life. Now, when she is 80 years old, she rules from her sickbed with a malicious tongue, sensing the many reasons why her family, friends, doctors, and nurses haunt her bedside. The tragedy of a dual sexual nature is explored in *The Twyburn Affair* (1979). Eudoxia is first a mistress to a Greek, then becomes Eddie Twyburn, a hero of World War II, and finally ends as Eadith Trist, a brothel keeper. White explores in *Memoirs of Many in One* (1986), a fascinating novel, the complex life of Alex Xenophon Demirgian Gray, who is three—or is it four?—people in one. White has written a number of experimental plays for the Australian theater. If you like reading about Australia, you will enjoy *The Thorn Birds* (1977) by Colleen McCullough (1937–), a saga spanning half a century of the life of the Cleary family on a sheep farm, and *The Shiralee* (1955) by D'Arcy Niland (1920–1967), about a migrant worker and the young daughter he cares for after his marriage ends. A TV miniseries based on *The Thorn Birds* was made in 1983, and *The Shiralee* was adapted for film in 1957 and television in 1987. White was awarded the Nobel Prize for literature in 1973. YA

White, T(erence) H(anbury) (1906–1964) An English writer of delightful novels about *King Arthur, White is both solemn and funny in his stories of wizards, falcons, and medieval knights. *The Sword in the Stone, The Witch in the Wood* (1939), and *The Ill-Made Knight* (1940) are about the childhood of Wart, who was the future King Arthur, and his tutor, the wizard Merlyn (*Merlin). These three books were adapted for inclusion in White's best-known novel *The Once and Future King. Another of his popular novels is *Mistress Masham's Repose. White was fascinated by hawks and the art of falconry, a method of hunting used in medieval times. In *The Goshawk* (1951) he wrote about the time he spent learning to tame and train hawks. MR & YA

White, Theodore H(arold) (1915–1986) As a foreign correspondent for *Time* magazine and contributor to other publications, White covered the war between China and Japan from the 1930s to 1945; the independence movement in India; and the rise of communism in China. With Annalee Jacoby (1916–), his colleague at the *Time* bureau in Chungking, he wrote about this period in *Thunder out of China* (1946). He also wrote about the recovery of Europe after World War II in *Fire in the Ashes* (1953). But he is best known for *The Making of the President, 1960* (1961), a fascinating, penetrating account of the presidential campaign of John F. Kennedy (1917–1963) against Richard M. Nixon (1913–). White takes you through the Republican and Democratic conventions, the primaries, the stump speeches, and the campaigning to election day and beyond in a detailed yet readable way. White wrote similar books about the campaigns of 1964, 1968, and 1972. In less detail, *America in Search of Itself: The Making of the President* (1983) covers all the presidential campaigns from 1956 to the defeat of Jimmy Carter (1924–) by Ronald Reagan (1911–) in 1980. *The Making of the President, 1960* was made into a TV documentary in 1964. YA

White Fang (1905), by *Jack London, is the story of a wolf cub born in the wild that learns to live with human beings. Adopted by Gray Beaver, an Indian, White Fang is taught to obey the strong and dominate the weak. Fiercely he defends himself and his master's property against all who come near, and he is hated by people and dogs alike. A bully, Beauty Smith, takes White Fang from Gray Beaver by a trick. Beauty Smith has no mercy. White Fang is tormented, beaten, and kept in a pen. People pay to watch him destroy other animals introduced into his cage. A mining engineer rescues White Fang from this savagery and wins the wolf's confidence by kindness. White Fang's love for this man, who talks gently to him and does not beat him, becomes all-consuming. White Fang does not let the man out of his sight. White Fang goes to live with his master's family and repays their trust by defending them against a dangerous intruder. If you enjoyed this story, you will like London's *The Call of the Wild*, about a dog who reverts from a tame life with people to a life in the Alaskan wild. Movies of *White Fang* were made in 1936, 1972, and 1991. MR & YA

Whitman, Walt (1819–1892) One of the major poets of the 19th century, Whitman is known best for *Leaves of Grass* (1855), a collection of all his poems. Born on Long Island, New York, Whitman moved with his family to Brooklyn when he was 4 years old. There he went to school and spent the first years of his working life in a variety of jobs on newspapers and magazines. He would often return to Long Island to wander by the seashore and dig clams. He would race up and down on the hard sand reciting *William Shakespeare and *Homer to the sea and the seagulls. A love of nature always influenced his poetry. In "Out of the Cradle Endlessly Rocking" (1859) he wrote, "Over the sterile sand, and the fields beyond, where the child . . . wandered alone, bareheaded, barefoot," which probably refers to these visits.

In 1862 his brother, George, was wounded during the Civil War, and Whitman went to Virginia to see him. He spent the next six years as a volunteer visiting hospitals in Washington, D.C., and nursing wounded soldiers from both sides of the war. He stood among the crowds gathered to see Abraham Lincoln (1809–1865) pass on his way to take the oath of office as President for the second time. Whitman

Walt Whitman

thought Lincoln looked very tired, worn, and burdened with responsibilities. When Lincoln was assassinated, Whitman wrote the elegy *"When Lilacs Last in the Dooryard Bloomed," and "O Captain, My Captain" (1865), a dirge for a fallen hero. Many well-known poets and writers have been influenced by Whitman's poetry. *Henry James, *Carl Sandburg, *T.S. Eliot, and *Ezra Pound are among them. The Irish poet *William Butler Yeats carried a copy of *Leaves of Grass* with him in his coat pocket. YA

Whitney, Phyllis A(yame) (1903–) An author whose books have been translated into 17 languages and published in 23 countries, Whitney is known for a combination of romance and suspense, and for her heroines, who are always able to solve their own problems. Among Whitney's novels are *A Silver Inkwell* (1945), the story of a girl who is determined to become a writer; *Willow Hill* (1947), a tale of racial intolerance; *Step to the Music* (1953), concerning the problems of a girl in the Civil War period who has young friends on both sides of the conflict; *Mystery on the Isle of Skye* (1955), in which 12-year-old Cathy, given a trip to this island off the northwest coast of Scotland, home of her ancestors, finds an unexpected treasure; *The Mystery of the Golden Horn* (1962), about a 14-year-old girl sent to Turkey, who finds danger lurking in Istanbul; *The Mystery of the Crimson Ghost* (1969), in which a teenage girl, on summer vacation, becomes involved with an eccentric neighbor who has both a ghost and a horse; and *The Secret of the Stone Face* (1977), in which a teenage girl comes up against a mystery while trying to discredit her mother's fiancé. Whitney has also written many detective stories for older readers. The first was *The Red Carnelian* (1943), about a murder in a Chicago department store. More recent is *The Singing Stones* (1990), about a child psychologist's adventures in a secluded household in the Blue Ridge Mountains of Virginia. If you like these novels, you will enjoy those of *Sophy Burnham, *M.V. Carey, and *Carolyn Keene. MR & YA

Whittier, John Greenleaf (1807–1892) A New England poet born in Haverhill, Massachusetts, of Quaker parents, Whittier developed a passionate antislavery stand. From 1833 to the end of the Civil War he devoted himself to the abolition of slavery. For many years Whittier contributed poems, articles, and letters to a weekly published by the American and Foreign Anti-Slavery Society and to other periodicals. His notoriety caused antagonistic mobs to attack him on several occasions. Two poems of this period are "The Farewell" (1849), which tells of a slave's parting from her daughters, and "Laus Deo!" (Praise God!) (1865), which exults at the passage of the constitutional amendment abolishing slavery. But one of his best-known works, the narrative poem "Snowbound" (1866), is entirely different. Its picture of the rural New England of his childhood and the simple joys of a family as they entertain each other while isolated in their farmhouse during a snowstorm became a best-seller. "A Tent on the Beach" (1866) contributed to his growing popularity. It is about three friends

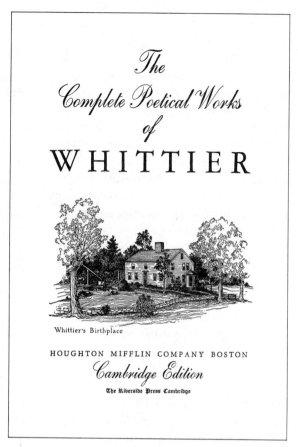

Title page of the 1894 edition of John Greenleaf Whittier's poems

who pitch their tent on the salt meadows of Hampton, New Hampshire, where one of them reads his poems for the entertainment of the others. Whittier was modest about his success. Though the town of Whittier in California and Whittier College in Iowa are named after him, he never traveled farther west than Pennsylvania, and he remained loyal to his New England roots all his life. A good biography for younger readers is *Mr. Whittier* (1974) by *Elizabeth Janet Gray. MR & YA

Who's Afraid of Virginia Woolf? (1962) By *Edward Albee, this important contemporary play is set in the living room of a house on the campus of a small New England college. A middle-aged couple comes home from a late-night party. Martha is the daughter of the college's president. Her husband, George, is a professor in the history department. As George fixes drinks, Martha says they have guests coming, and they start quarreling. The visitors, Nick and his wife, Honey, are young newcomers to the college. Nick is on guard as Martha and George begin their usual vicious game of one-upmanship. Honey does not understand what is going on in the dangerous verbal battle between Martha and George as they hurl one painful accusation after another at each other. But Nick and Honey also have skeletons in the closet. Nick is tricked into talking about them, which makes him vulnerable in this terrible marital row. At the end of the evening the saddest story of all reveals why Martha and George play these savage games, and why they need each other. *Who's Afraid of Virginia Woolf?* was filmed in 1966. YA

Wibberley, Leonard (Patrick O'Connor)

(1915–1983) This Irish-born American author wrote more than 100 books, including historical novels, plays, and books for young people. His two most popular books, full of humor and *satire, concern the Duchy of Grand Fenwick, which is three miles wide and five miles long. In *The Mouse That Roared*, the Duchy of Grand Fenwick declares war on the United States because Americans have stolen the name of the wine the Duchy makes, its only source of income. In *The Mouse on the Moon* (1962), Grand Fenwick joins the race to the moon. Wibberley also wrote *Flint's Island* (1972), a sequel to *Robert Louis Stevenson's *Treasure Island*. If you like adventure stories, try Wibberley's books about the American Revolution, beginning with *John Treegate's Musket*. *The Mouse That Roared* became a film in 1958 and *The Mouse on the Moon* in 1963. MR & YA

Wideman, John Edgar

(1941–) Considered to be one of the most gifted writers of his generation, Wideman is known for his novels and short stories about Homewood, a suburb of Pittsburgh, Pennsylvania, where he grew up. One of his early books, *A Glance Away* (1967), follows the course of a drug addict's day. Originally published separately, *Damballah* (1981),

Hiding Place (1981), and *Sent for You Yesterday* (1983) make up *The Homewood Trilogy* (1985). They explore the enduring spirit and culture of the fictionalized community of Homewood over the years. Its unique characters, storytellers, and music are revealed through the eyes of the expanding family of John French. *Brothers and Keepers* (1984) is the poignant personal account of Wideman's younger brother, Robby, who was sent to prison for life for drug dealing, and Wideman's own attempts to come to terms with what happened. He asks himself how it is that he has become a successful writer and a professor of English while his brother, brought up in the same family with the same loving parents, took such a different road. *The Stories of John Edgar Wideman* (1992) includes stories published in *Damballah* and *Fever* (1989) as well as 10 new stories. YA

Wiesel, Elie(zer)

(1928–) Novelist, short-story writer, and essayist of the *Holocaust, Wiesel was born of Jewish parents in Romania. As a boy Elie believed he would be a writer of commentaries on books sacred to the Jews, but when he was 15 years old he was deported with his parents and three sisters, like thousands of others, to the Nazi death camps. Elie's parents and a sister died there. Somehow he lived through that searing experience—an ordeal so terrible he vowed never to speak of it. Working as a journalist in France after World War II, Wiesel met one of France's great novelists, François Mauriac (1885–1970), who told him he should bear witness to the horrors suffered by the millions of now-silent victims. Wiesel has been bearing witness for them ever since. An early novel, *Night* (1960), is largely autobiographical. A young survivor of the death camps, a boy in his teens, is overwhelmed by guilt because he lived when others did not. But his faith in God died with them. "Never shall I forget that night . . . which turned my life into one long night . . . those moments which murdered my God," he wrote. In *The Accident* (1961) Wiesel explores the reasons for going on living. A young man knocked down by a taxi is taken to the hospital where, badly hurt, he waits to die. But the doctor, his girl friend, and the artist friend who wants to paint his portrait will not let him. Wiesel writes not only of the Holocaust survivors but of how the past affects the children of survivors. Reuven Tamiroff in *The Fifth Son* (1985) is haunted by a past that he cannot speak about to his son. Driven by love for his father, the son discovers his secret. Tamiroff, contrary to his beliefs, has taken revenge on a brutal SS officer and killed him. The guilt of this deed is unbearable until the son finds the officer is still alive. Wiesel became an American citizen in 1963. He has written more than 20 novels, many short stories and essays, and two plays. For his untiring work in the cause of peace, Wiesel was awarded the Nobel Peace Prize in 1986. YA

Wife of Bath, The One of the *pilgrims in *The Canterbury Tales,* by *Geoffrey Chaucer, the Wife of Bath tells a tale of marriage. She speaks from experience. "For, Lordings, since I was twelve years of age, Husbands . . . I have had five. . . . I governed them so well," she says, that they were willing to do anything to please her. This idea upsets another of the pilgrims, who is thinking of marrying. Wait awhile, the Wife of Bath tells him, her tale has only just begun. Before she has finished, she promises, he will hear all about the tribulations of marriage. After describing how she handled each of her husbands, she tells a story. A knight at the court of King Arthur is condemned to die if he cannot discover what it is that women want most. Having no success, he turns for home, where he expects to lose his head, when he meets an ugly old woman. She says she will help him if he will marry her. Desperate, he agrees. True to her word, she supplies the right answer: Women desire mastery over their husbands above all else. This is the Wife of Bath's philosophy. And for those husbands who will not be so governed, she says, "God send them soon a very pestilence!" YA

Wilbur, Richard (1921–) An important poet of the post–World War II period, Wilbur belongs to the traditional school of poetry. His elegant

The Wife of Bath from the Ellesmere manuscript, a well-known version of *The Canterbury Tales*

rhyming verse is meditative and optimistic. Wilbur's collection *Things of This World* (1956) takes its name from a poem "Love Calls Us to the Things of This World," which was inspired by clothes hung on a line in a garden on a sunny day. *Walking to Sleep* (1969) contains not only Wilbur's own poems but also some of his fine translations of poems by the Argentinian Jorge Luis Borges (1899–1986) and the Frenchman François Villon (1431–1463?), among others. *Richard Wilbur: New and Collected Poems* (1988) contains most of his best-known poems. Wilbur has translated a number of plays from the French, and his translation of *Candide,* by *Voltaire, was made into a musical comedy with music by Leonard Bernstein (1918–1990) in 1956. YA

Wilde, Oscar (1854–1900) An Anglo-Irish playwright, essayist, and poet, Wilde was the central figure in a group that celebrated art for art's sake, and believed that "there is no such thing as a moral or immoral book," only good or bad writing. He was famous in society for his sophisticated humor, flamboyant style, and love of sensual pleasures. In 1891 he became friendly with Lord Alfred Douglas (1870–1945), whose father later accused Wilde of homosexuality. Wilde was arrested, tried, and sentenced to two years in prison. His poem *The Ballad of Reading Gaol* (1898) did much to expose the harsh conditions of prison life.

Among the comic society plays that brought Wilde his greatest success are *Lady Windermere's Fan* and *The Importance of Being Earnest*. His short novel *The Picture of Dorian Gray*, a reworking of the *Faust legend, remains popular. YA

Wilder, Laura Ingalls (1867–1957) Known for her popular Little House series of books describing life in a pioneering family of the 1870s, Wilder used recollections of her own childhood and of growing up with her Pa and Ma and her sisters, Mary and Carrie. She remembers first the *Little House in the Big Woods* (1932) in Wisconsin, then Indian Territory in *Little House on the Prairie*, and, finally, Dakota Territory, where she trains as a school teacher and later marries. The series ends with *These Happy Golden Years*. She describes her married life in *The First Four Years* (1971), published long after her death. The Little House books were written when her daughter gave Wilder the idea that her memories were worth writing down. She was then 60 years old. The books quickly became successful and are now classic novels of a time long past in the American West. A popular TV series called *Little House on the Prairie*, based on parts of the Little House series, began in 1974 and is still telecast in reruns. MR

Wilder, Thornton (Niven) (1897–1975) The author of *The Bridge of San Luis Rey*, Wilder studied archeology in Rome, and his early interest in the classics is seen in another novel, *The Ides of March* (1948), which explores the last days of Julius Caesar (102?–44 B.C.). Wilder wrote a number of fine plays, including the highly popular *Our Town, *The Skin of Our Teeth*, and *The Matchmaker* (1954). His plays are unusual in that he called for little or no scenery and few props, and often had his characters or a narrator speak directly to the audi-

ence. In both novels and plays, Wilder showed his deep belief that the best of life can be found in everyday experiences. *The Matchmaker* was filmed in 1958 and was adapted as the musical comedy *Hello, Dolly!* in 1964. YA

Wilkinson, Brenda (1946–) A black writer and poet born in Georgia, Wilkinson is known especially for a trilogy that gives a realistic picture of the life of rural people during the 1950s and 1960s. *Ludell* (1975) is a poor young girl living in Waycross, Georgia, who is left in the care of her grandmother when her mother goes to New York City in hopes of finding a better life. Under difficult circumstances, Ludell grows up to be both sensitive and aware. In *Ludell and Willie* (1976) Ludell, an adolescent, falls in love and makes plans for her future. But the death of her grandmother means she has to leave Waycross and Willie to live with her mother in New York City. Life in a city apartment is very different from that in her grandmother's home in Georgia. In *Ludell's New York Time* (1980), getting to know her mother again and facing the conflict between life in Waycross and life in Harlem mean a difficult adjustment for Ludell. MR & YA

Williams, Tennessee [Thomas Lanier Williams] (1911–1983) Considered one of the foremost American playwrights of the 20th century, Williams is known best for *The Glass Menagerie, *A Streetcar Named Desire*, and *Cat on a Hot Tin Roof*. Williams wrote about loneliness, frustration, and the desperate need of people who are misfits in society to communicate, a need that is often expressed by violence. Something of a misfit himself, he left home for good as soon as he was able to. His mother was overprotective, and he did not like his father. During his childhood his sister, Rose, was his only friend. Later she was confined to an institution after an emotional breakdown from which she never recovered. This tragedy is the background of *The Glass Menagerie*. Williams's best work was produced during the 1940s and 1950s. Then he became depressed and went into a decline. Fourteen films

MR = Middle Reader   YA = Young Adult Reader   * = See this main entry

have been made from his plays and short stories. YA

Williams, William Carlos (1883–1963) A poet and a practicing physician, Williams wrote with a discerning eye about the small happenings of daily life in poems of compassion and insight. He could create atmosphere with merely a few lines of his characteristic free verse. In 10 lines he conjures up a summer afternoon of peace and security in "Nantucket," which appears in *The Collected Earlier Poems of William Carlos Williams* (1938). Williams's best-known work is the narrative poem *Paterson* (1946–1963). In it he focuses on the city of Paterson, on the Passaic River in New Jersey. Mixing prose with verse, he creates a portrait of an American city and its men and women. Williams said of this poem that each person is a city, beginning, seeking, achieving, and concluding his or her life in the ways that a city does. If you liked *Paterson*, you will certainly want to read *Leaves of Grass* by *Walt Whitman, whose work influenced Williams. YA

Willy Loman, the protagonist of *Arthur Miller's play *Death of a Salesman*, is a man of turbulent longings who desperately needs to leave his mark on the world. Sixty years old, he has spent a lifetime trying to impress his family, his customers, and his employer. For Willy, appearance is everything—a ready smile, a firm handshake, plenty of jokes, and an air of self-confidence are the keys that open all doors. When he is fired from his job, Willy begins to suspect that what he has really done is to carefully carve his name on a block of ice on a hot summer day. He has struggled for years to avoid facing personal failures and has, out of love for his sons, taught them to hide their defeats as well. He wants to know what went wrong with his son Biff, but cannot bear the thought that he might have been the cause of Biff's lack of purpose. Willy's dreams of success are so passionate and so massive that any compromise seems impossible. When he can no longer escape the evidence of his failure, he makes a last grand gesture and kills himself so that his family may collect his life insurance.

Wilson, Lanford (1937–) A playwright who is also an actor and director for experimental theater, Wilson is known for innovative plays that explore with humor and understanding the lives of people who live on the edge of society. In *Balm in Gilead* (1965) he portrays the hopes and fears in the city lives of the lost, the deprived, the addicts, and the thieves. *Days Ahead* (1967) is a monologue of an aging man who tries to recapture a lost love. Both *The Rimers of Eldritch* (1967) and *This Is the Rill Speaking* (1967) take place in Missouri, where Wilson grew up. They picture small-town life where nothing much seems to happen, with the days passing slowly in gossip and hopes fading before they can flower. *Talley's Folly* (1979) is about a warm and humorous courtship in a boathouse between Matt Friedman, a Jewish refugee from Germany, and Sally Talley. It is one of a series of plays about the Talley family, who live on a farm near Lebanon, Missouri. Among them are *5th of July* (1978), *A Tale Told* (1981), and *Talley & Son* (1986), a sequel to *Talley's Folly*. If you enjoy Wilson's plays, you may also want to read the play *Our Town* by *Thornton Wilder, which also deals with the lives of ordinary people in an ordinary town. *This Is the Rill Speaking* was adapted for television in 1967. YA

Wind in the Willows, The (1908) By *Kenneth Grahame, this is one of the most famous books written for young readers. Mole abandons his spring cleaning to wander through the fields. He meets Water Rat, who lives in *River Bank, spending all his time "messing about" in boats. Ratty and Mole become good friends. Ratty teaches Mole all about boats and introduces him to Toad of Toad Hall, who is "the best of all animals, so simple, good-natured, affectionate," but also boastful and conceited. Toad is setting out for the Wide World in a horse-drawn, canary-yellow wagon. He persuades Ratty and Mole to join him. On the highway they meet a motorcar. Frightened, the horse backs the wagon into a ditch, throwing the three friends out. Ratty and Mole dust themselves off, but Toad gazes dreamily after the disappearing motorcar. When Toad gets home, he orders a large and very expensive motorcar.

Despite Ratty's warning, Mole goes into the Wild Wood in search of Badger and becomes lost. Ratty finds him, and together they visit Badger. Badger promises to help reform Toad, who is going from bad to worse. He steals a car and goes to prison. When he escapes, he finds Toad Hall has been taken over by Wild Wooders, the stoats and the weasels. Badger, Ratty, and Mole make a plan to rescue Toad Hall. And, finally, they manage to reform Toad. In 1929 *A.A. Milne dramatized *The Wind in the Willows*, which was adapted for a musical comedy, *Toad of Toad Hall*, first produced in London in 1930. An animated film of *The Wind in the Willows* was produced in 1982. MR

Wind, Sand and Stars (1939) By *Antoine de Saint-Exupéry, this collection of stories and recollections is about the pioneer days of flying. Saint-Exupéry began his apprenticeship as a pilot in 1926 when all airplanes were propeller-driven and many were two-seaters, their cockpits open to the winds and rain. In bad weather the pilot thrust his head round the windshield to look for landmarks to tell him where he was. At night the darkness was total and the pilot needed a flashlight to see the instrument panel. In those days, pilots risked everything to fly over endless uninhabited deserts or between mountains that towered high above the tiny planes. Sometimes emergency landings had to be made in impossible places from which there were miraculous escapes. Sometimes, a pilot and his plane simply disappeared. Saint-Exupéry once flew into a cyclone, his frail aircraft blown like a leaf and impossible to control. These are tales of high drama. They are also a great tribute to men and women of spirit who took risks every day and thought nothing of it. This book is available in paperback. Charles and *Anne Morrow Lindbergh also wrote about the early days of flying in *North to the Orient* (1935) and *Listen! The Wind* (1938). YA

Winesburg, Ohio: A Group of Tales of Ohio Small Town Life (1919), by Sherwood Anderson, is a series of related stories based on the author's boyhood years in Clyde, Ohio, that vividly portray small-town life in America in the 1890s. They are stories about secrets, the moments when people face themselves and their deepest ambitions and when, in their need, they reach out to someone else. George Willard has lived all his 18 years in Winesburg. His father keeps the hotel. His mother, sick with some obscure disease, keeps to her room. As a reporter for the *Winesburg Eagle* George knows everyone in town, and they talk to him. He knows Wing Biddlebaum, who talks through his hands; the fanatic Jesse Bentley; the lonely schoolteacher Kate Swift; and the Presbyterian pastor, whose private battle greatly improves his sermons. George also faces his own growing up. His mother dies, and he experiences the moment of his own maturing. Finally, he leaves Winesburg for the larger world of a big city. And the people he has listened to come to the railway station to wish him good luck. If you like these stories, you will also like *Our Town, a play by *Thornton Wilder. YA

Winnie-the-Pooh (1926), by *A.A. Milne, has been enjoyed by millions of children and adults over the years. It tells about the little boy Christopher Robin and his friend Edward Bear, who is better known as Winnie-the-Pooh, or Pooh for short. Pooh has many interesting adventures with Christopher Robin and with his animal friends Rabbit, Piglet, Eeyore the donkey, Owl, and Kanga and Baby Roo. In one adventure, Pooh goes to visit Rabbit and gets stuck in the doorway of Rabbit's house. In other adventures, Pooh solves the mystery of Eeyore's lost tail, Pooh and Piglet try to catch a Heffalump, Christopher Robin leads the animals on an expedition to discover the North Pole, and Pooh and Christopher Robin rescue Piglet, whose house has become entirely surrounded by water. And through it all Pooh hums his wonderful songs. You will also enjoy the illustrations by Ernest H. Shepard (1879–1976). The adventures of Pooh, Christopher Robin, and their friends are continued in *The House at Pooh Corner*. Many animated TV specials have been based on the animal characters of *Winnie-the-Pooh*. MR

Winning (1977), by *Robin F. Brancato, is the story of Gary Madden's struggle to adjust to the devastating effect of a spinal injury. Following what should have been a routine tackle, he changes from the bright and popular star of his high school football team to the almost completely paralyzed victim of a freak accident. In hospital, attached to a metal frame he calls the rack, Gary works hard at being brave. He knows he is lucky to have the support of loving parents, friends, and the loyalty of his girl friend, Diane. Ann Treer, his English teacher and a recent widow, is part of the team of teachers and students helping Gary keep up his schoolwork. Because of her loss, Ann is unusually sensitive to Gary's moods, and it is she who sees how much he needs to know the truth about his condition. Facing the knowledge that he may not walk again is a nightmare, but Gary learns to draw strength from small victories. One hand shows signs of movement, he is freed from the rack, and he begins to take an interest in the mental challenges that Ann gives him. In a rehabilitation center, surrounded by others with similar handicaps, he regains his sense of humor and some hope for the future. When an infection leaves Gary so depressed that he thinks about suicide, Ann convinces him that he can still make people need him, as she has come to need him, and Gary finds a reason to go on wanting to win. YA

Wiseman, David (Jane Julian) (1916–) This English writer of *fantasy novels for younger readers blends the past with the present in imaginative and vivid suspense stories. In *Jeremy Visick* (1981), 12-year-old Matthew Clemens, a modern-day boy, excited by a history lesson on the dangerous life of tin miners in 19th-century England, is drawn back through time to relive the events of a day in 1852. On that day 12-year-old Jeremy, his father, and two brothers die in a mining accident. Because of his loyalty to Jeremy, Matthew helps bring peace to Jeremy's ghost. In *Thimbles* (1982), Catherine Aiken's father is involved in a civil rights issue. Searching through old family treasures, Cathy finds two thimbles. A plain metal one takes her back in time to meet Kate Clayton, who sews a liberty cap for a civil rights march by English millworkers. A gold thimble, which belonged to 12-year-old Sophia Dunstan, Cathy's own great-great-grandmother, transports Cathy back to the so-called Manchester Massacre, in which government troops brutally break up a peaceful demonstration. If you like these books, try those of *Robert Westall, especially *The Watch House* (1977), a mystery story involving a strange house, the past, and a ghost. MR

Witch of Blackbird Pond, The (1958) By *Elizabeth George Speare, this is a story of colonial days. When Kit Tyler's grandfather dies, she sails from Barbados to America, where her aunt lives. She has been accustomed to fine clothes, servants, and unusual freedom. In Wethersfield, Connecticut, in 1687, life is very different. In the Puritan home of her stern Uncle Matthew, every day seems to be one chore after another. Kit has never scrubbed a floor nor weeded an onion field before. Whenever she can, she escapes to the Meadows where Hannah Tupper, an elderly Quaker, lives. People call Hannah a witch, but she gives Kit the peace and freedom to cope with her new life. When a mysterious fever strikes Wethersfield, Hannah is accused of witchcraft. The townspeople start a witch hunt and burn down Hannah's house. Just in time, Kit helps her friend to escape. Thwarted, the townspeople accuse Kit of witchcraft instead and she is put on trial. Two friends come to her aid: Nathaniel Eaton, whom she met on the boat coming to America, and little Prudence, whom Kit has taught to read. Other historical stories you might enjoy are *Encounter at Easton* and *The True Confessions of Charlotte Doyle* (1990), about a girl who comes to America in 1832. Both these books are by *Avi. *The Witch of Blackbird Pond* won the *Newbery Medal in 1959. MR

MR = Middle Reader   YA = Young Adult Reader   * = See this main entry

wizard A wizard is a magician or sorcerer. The word originally meant "wise," and it is sometimes used in admiration of someone or something. To say she is a "wizard at the computer" is flattering. One of the most venerable wizards is *Merlin, who was attached to *King Arthur's court and who plays a prominent role in the books of *T.H. White. Merlin also appears in *Mary Stewart's novels *The Crystal Cave* (1970), *The Hollow Hills* (1973), and *The Last Enchantment* (1979), all based on Arthurian legend. Prospero, the exiled Duke of Milan in *The Tempest* by *William Shakespeare, is a magician. A popular wizard, though a phony, is the *Wizard of Oz. *The Weirdstone of Brisingamen* (1960) and its sequel, *Gomrath* (1963), by *Alan Garner, feature a wizard called Cadellin Silverbrow, leader of the forces of light. *The Owl Service* (1967), also by Garner, is based on a myth about a famous Welsh wizard, Gwydian. *The Hobbit, by *J.R.R. Tolkien, introduces Gandalf, a wizard who befriends the hobbits. There are wizards in *The Thirteen Clocks* by *James Thurber and in *The Wizard in the Tree* (1975) by *Lloyd Alexander, whose wizard, Arbicon, temporarily loses his powers. After a lot of trouble, he gets them back with help from a girl, Mallory. He gives her some advice: "Magic comes from the inside out," he says, "and you humans have to work your own." MR & YA

Wizard of Oz, The A character in *L. Frank Baum's *The Wonderful Wizard of Oz*, the Wizard rules the Emerald City in the Land of *Oz, and it is to him that *Dorothy, the *Scarecrow, the *Tin Woodman, and the *Cowardly Lion appeal for help.

In his emerald-studded throne room, Oz seems to Dorothy to be an enormous bald head. The Scarecrow sees him as a beautiful winged lady, the Tin Woodman as a hairy monster, and the Cowardly Lion as a terrifying ball of fire. All of them are told by the Wizard that their wishes will be granted only after they have killed the Wicked Witch of the West. When they actually succeed and return to Oz, the Wizard is accidentally revealed to be a little old man with a bald head and a wrinkled face. He is a *ventriloquist and a kindhearted trickster who arrived in the Land of Oz in a balloon. Seeing him come from the clouds, the people thought he must be gifted with great powers, and Oz encouraged them to believe that.

Oz fulfills his promise to Dorothy's friends by using his wits and knowledge of human nature, but he says, "It will take more than imagination to carry Dorothy back to Kansas." He vanishes from the land as he came, in a balloon.

Wodehouse, P(elham) G(renville) (1881–1975) An English humorist who has been called the funniest writer in the world, Wodehouse was also one of the most prolific. He wrote at least two books a year and fitted in plays and musical comedies as well, collaborating with such people as Jerome Kern (1885–1945), the famous composer of light operas. In his books Wodehouse ridicules some of England's most venerable institutions and the people in them, creating a whimsical upper class whose members spend their time getting into ridiculous situations from which they need to be rescued. The most famous character Wodehouse invented is Jeeves, gentleman's gentleman (personal servant) to Bertie Wooster. Jeeves virtually lives on fish and as a result, you are led to believe, is very brainy. He is never at a loss for a solution to even the most perplexing problems. Jeeves and Bertie appeared in a number of books, including *The Inimitable Jeeves* (1923), *Carry On, Jeeves* (1925), and *The Code of the Woosters* (1938). Wodehouse also created the character Mr. Mulliner, who is fond of relating to any and all the hilarious adventures of his many oddball and offbeat Mulliner relatives. Among the Mulliner books are *Meet Mr. Mulliner* (1927) and *Mulliner Nights* (1933). Wodehouse liked America and came to the United States to live after World War II, becoming a citizen in 1955. You can find a good selection of Wodehouse's many stories about Jeeves, Bertie, and other characters in *The Most of P.G. Wodehouse* (1960). And you can find the

Mulliner stories in *The World of Mr. Mulliner* (1974). If you like reading humorous books, you might also want to try the stories of *James Thurber. YA

wolf With what is now known to be an undeserved reputation for cruelty and viciousness, the wolf is represented in a bad light in a number of common sayings. "To put one's head in the wolf's mouth" is to get into a dangerous position, as is "holding a wolf by the ears," where hanging on and letting go are equally unsafe. "To cry wolf," an expression from a *fable by *Aesop, who wrote a number of stories about this creature, is to give a false alarm. If you are very short of money, you will have to find some way "to keep the wolf from the door," and if you succeed, you may eat so greedily that you will be "wolfing" your food. "A wolf in sheep's clothing" is someone posing as a friend when he or she is really an enemy; and "to throw something to the wolves" is to distract a pursuer or enemy, in a physical sense or otherwise, by means of sacrificing a companion or possession. When a man is described as a "wolf," it means he is a womanizer. The best-known wolf in literature is probably the evil creature in the folktale *Little Red Riding Hood*. In *The Sea Wolf* by *Jack London, the brutal captain, Wolf Larsen, is truly monstrous, yet the wolf in London's novel *White Fang* is a noble creature, as are the wolves in *Never Cry Wolf* by *Farley Mowat and *The Wolfling* by *Sterling North. MR & YA

Wolfe, Thomas (1900–1938) Born in Asheville, North Carolina, Wolfe in his largely autobiographical novels and short stories sought to describe the American experience. He was a powerful, passionate, and prolific writer. He thought of himself as being in the tradition of *Mark Twain, *Walt Whitman, and *Sherwood Anderson. Like Whitman, he wrote about America by writing about himself. In his first novel, *Look Homeward, Angel*, he describes in bitter, sometimes cruel, terms his own early years through the story of *Eugene Gant. The residents of Asheville, recognizing their city as

the Altamont of this novel, were not pleased when the novel was published. After a failed attempt to write plays, Wolfe taught at New York University. In *Of Time and the River* (1935) he writes of Eugene Gant's struggles to become a playwright, his life as a college teacher, and his travels to Europe. Wolfe's other novels are *The Web and the Rock* and his last novel, *You Can't Go Home Again* (1940), in which he looks to the future as home and not to the memories of times past. If you like *Look Homeward, Angel*, read the next three novels in chronological order to get a vivid, though often disturbing, view of American life. A TV movie of *You Can't Go Home Again* was made in 1979. YA

Wolfe, Tom [Thomas Kennerly Wolfe, Jr.] (1930–) This journalist and novelist is respected as a perceptive observer and reporter of contemporary life in America. Writing in a style called "new journalism," he has often been considered controversial. New journalism, Wolfe says, is "the use by people writing nonfiction of techniques which have been thought of as confined to the novel or short story," such as conversation, *stream of consciousness, and description of place and dress. In *The Kandy-Kolored Tangerine-Flake Streamline Baby* (1965), Wolfe used pop language to describe American culture of the early 1960s in essays on such subjects as pop heroes, art galleries, Las Vegas, and nannies. He wrote about the American space program and astronauts in *The Right Stuff* and the growth of the drug culture in *The Electric Kool-Aid Acid Test*. His first novel, *The Bonfire of the Vanities* (1987), portrays New York City, the *symbol of modern civilization, in all its arrogance, greed, and vulgarity by tracing the fall of Sherman McCoy, a *yuppie Wall Streeter. A movie version of *The Right Stuff* was made in 1983, and *The Bonfire of the Vanities* in 1991. YA

Wolfling, The By *Sterling North, this delightful story tells about 12-year-old Robbie Trent, who lives in the wild countryside of 19th-century Wisconsin. More than anything

Sylvia, Bonnie, and Simon the goose boy in
The Wolves of Willoughby Chase

else, Robbie wants a wolf cub as a pet. He hears that one of the few remaining wolf dens has been found, and his worst enemy, Arch Mooney, is going with his father to raid it for the wolf's pelt. Robbie plans to be there. The den is in a cave with a narrow entrance. Only Robbie is small enough to crawl down. He does so on condition that he can keep a cub. As he reaches the den, the mother wolf picks up one of her two cubs and escapes safely by a back exit, leaving Robbie with the other cub. "Wolf," as Robbie calls his pet, is a silky, golden little thing weighing less than a pound whose eyes are not yet open. Intelligent and obedient, Wolf wins everyone over with his gentle ways. Soon he is as much at home with his new family as any dog would be, going everywhere with Robbie as he grows up with his young master. Another story about a wolf you might like is *Kavik, the Wolf Dog* by *Walt Morey. MR

Wollstonecraft, Mary See *Percy Bysshe Shelley and *Frankenstein.

Wolves of Willoughby Chase, The (1962) By *Joan Aiken, this story concerns two little girls in England. Sylvia leaves her dear Aunt Jane to join her cousin Bonnie at Willoughby Chase while Bonnie's parents go abroad. Miss Slighcarp, a distant relative of Sir Willoughby, is left in charge. Strange things begin to happen as soon as Bonnie's parents leave. Most of the servants are dismissed; Bonnie's toys are packed up to be sold, and to Bonnie's dismay, Miss Slighcarp starts wearing her mother's dresses. Bonnie defies Miss Slighcarp and is locked in the nursery closet as punishment. With the help of two faithful servants and knowledge of a secret passage, the children manage to survive. But worse is to come. The ship Bonnie's parents sailed in is reported sunk, and they are presumed dead. Miss Slighcarp sends the children to an orphanage. The faithful servants tell Simon, the goose boy, who is a friend of Bonnie's, where they are, and Simon helps them escape. They all go to London to Aunt Jane to find her very ill. A friendly doctor comes to their aid. He brings in the police, who arrest Miss Slighcarp and her accomplices. Best of all, Bonnie's parents arrive home safe and sound to take charge again. A sequel is *Black Hearts in Battersea.* If you enjoyed *The Wolves of Willoughby Chase,* you will like *Carrie's War* by *Nina Bawden. MR

Woman Who Loved Reindeer, The (1985)

In this *fantasy about shape-changers, daimons (demons), and a young girl who has strange dreams and powers, Meredith Ann Pierce (1958–) has created an enchanted Arctic land of myth and fairy tale. Caribou, living alone since her father died, is left with a child born to her sister-in-law. A golden baby with golden eyes, he becomes restless when the wild deer run to their summer fields. Caribou calls the baby Reindeer. She feels afraid when she sees his reflection in the river. It is not a boy's face she sees, but a reindeer's. When Reindeer is 13 years old he leaves Caribou to run with the wild deer, saying he is a *trangl*, a shape-changer who can turn into a golden stag. Caribou does not see him for two years. She develops a sixth sense that helps her predict the future and becomes a wisewoman to her people, solving their problems, giving them advice. But terrible earthquakes disrupt the life of the tribe. The councilmen come to Caribou for help. Are the daimons angry? That night Reindeer returns. He asks Caribou to go with him and to become a *trangl*, like him. The firelords are turning the earth and changing it for their own purposes. She must leave with him or perish. Taking her people with her, and led by Reindeer, Caribou makes the dangerous journey to the safety of the country beyond the Pole, where the wild deer are.

Pierce has written a number of fantasy novels, including the Darkangel trilogy, consisting of *The Darkangel* (1982), *A Gathering of Gargoyles* (1984), and *The Pearl of the Soul of the World* (1990). The trilogy follows the adventures of a young woman named Aeriel, who rescues the darkangel Irrylath from becoming a vampire and with him struggles to save the world from the evil White Witch Oriencor. YA

Wonder-Book for Girls and Boys, A (1852)

by *Nathaniel Hawthorne, this book contains six tales of Greek and Roman mythology retold by the author. Among the tales are "The Gorgon's Head," about the Greek hero *Perseus and his encounter with the *Gorgon called Medusa, whose glance would turn a person

Dorothy meets the Cowardly Lion in
The Wonderful Wizard of Oz.

into stone; "The Golden Touch," about the unwise king *Midas; "The Three Golden Apples," about the quest of *Hercules for three golden apples of great value; and "The Chimaera," in which the hero Bellerophon captures the winged horse *Pegasus and destroys the monster called the Chimaera. If you enjoy *A Wonder-Book for Girls and Boys*, you will also want to read its sequel, *Tanglewood Tales.* MR & YA

Wonderful Adventures of Nils, The (1907)

By *Selma Lagerlöf, this is a Swedish folk fantasy. Fourteen-year-old Nils is lazy and dull. He likes to tease, taking special delight in teasing animals. Alone one Sunday while his parents are in church, he sees an elf. He catches it in a net and starts his teasing. Nils is boxed on the ears for his mischief, then finds he is no taller than a hand's breadth—a mere elf-size! The animals are no longer afraid of him. They laugh and jeer at Nils, who has so often teased them. Wild geese flying north tempt a young gander on the farm to join them. As Nils tries to stop the goose from flying off, he is carried away to join the wild geese. Now his wonderful adventures begin. He sees strange things and wild places. He learns the legends of the country. Along the way Nils helps the geese and other creatures who are kind to him. When he arrives home again, he has learned to be kind to all animals, who are just as much a part of the world as people are. A sequel, *The Further Adventures of Nils* (1911), has been included in at least one edition of *The Wonderful Adventures of Nils*. A similar fairy tale you will enjoy is *The Water-Babies* by *Charles Kingsley. MR

Wonderful Wizard of Oz, The (1900) Written by *L. Frank Baum and its title commonly shortened to *The Wizard of Oz*, this is one of the most famous books for young people.

*Dorothy lives with her aunt and uncle and her dog, Toto, in the flattest, driest part of Kansas. A terrible cyclone carries off the farmhouse with Dorothy and Toto in it and miraculously sets them down in the land of Oz, the beautiful country of the Munchkins. Dorothy is cheered by the tiny citizens and the Good Witch of the North, who announces that her house has fallen on the Wicked Witch of the East, leaving only a pair of silver shoes. Already homesick, Dorothy asks how she can return to Kansas and is told she must go to the *Wizard of Oz for help. The Munchkins show her the yellow brick road to the Emerald City.

Taking the silver shoes with her, Dorothy bravely sets off and meets the *Scarecrow, who says he needs a brain; the *Tin Woodman, who yearns for a heart; and the *Cowardly Lion, who would give anything to have courage befitting the King of Beasts. The four decide to travel together to the Wizard. Their journey is long and difficult, especially when they must cross a deadly poppy field.

When the four arrive at the Emerald City and are allowed to approach the Wizard in his brilliant throne room, Oz appears to each in a different form. To each he gives the same message: Kill the Wicked Witch of the West, and your wish will be granted.

After more dangerous adventures, Dorothy succeeds in "melting" the Witch with a bucket of water. Joyfully the four return to the Emerald City, only to discover that the Wizard is a "humbug," a fake. He is able to grant the wishes of her friends, but Dorothy herself must travel to see Glinda, the Good Witch of the South. Glinda tells Dorothy of the magic power in the silver shoes. After saying goodbye to her beloved friends, Dorothy knocks the heels of the shoes together three times, and she and Toto are whirled back to Kansas and her family. *The Wonderful Wizard of Oz* was produced as a movie, now a classic, in 1939 and has been shown nearly every year on television since 1956. See also *Oz. MR

Woolf, Virginia (Adeline) (1882–1941) An English novelist, short-story writer, and essayist, Woolf rejected the traditional novel form and wrote in a style called *stream of consciousness. An early experimenter with this style, she developed her stories through her characters' thoughts rather than their actions. She

Virginia Woolf

said she wanted "to re-form the novel and capture multitudes of things at present fugitive . . . and shape infinite strange shapes." Among her best-known works is *Mrs. Dalloway* (1925). A book without chapters, its main focus is the events of one day in the life of the wife of a member of Parliament, culminating in the woman's meeting of a former lover at the evening party she had planned. Woolf championed women's rights in *A Room of One's Own, an essay that defends the need for independence in a creative life. Virginia Woolf grew up in a scholarly family. Her education came through her father's library and his literary friends, such as *Thomas Hardy. Her own home in Bloomsbury, London, became the center for the Bloomsbury Group, people interested in literature and the arts. In 1917 Woolf and her husband, Leonard Woolf (1880–1969), founded the Hogarth Press, publishing works by *T.S. Eliot and *E.M. Forster, among others. See also *Orlando. YA

Wordsworth, William (1770–1850) One of England's great poets, Wordsworth was, along with *Samuel Taylor Coleridge, *George Gordon Byron, *Percy Bysshe Shelley, and *John Keats, a major member of the Romantic school of English poetry. At a time of great change in Europe, these poets turned to nature for the order and continuity of life they saw as missing from the world. Favorably impressed by the French Revolution, Wordsworth traveled in France until 1792, when it became too dangerous to stay there. Returning to England, he met Coleridge. Together they produced a volume of their poetry, *Lyrical Ballads* (1798), though most of the poems were by Wordsworth. In one of these poems, "Lines Written Above Tintern Abbey" (1798), Wordsworth expresses his belief in the unity of humankind and nature:

. . . For I have learned
To look on nature, not as in the hour
Of thoughtless youth; but hearing oftentimes
The still, sad music of humanity. . . .
    And I have felt

· · · · · · · · · · · · · · · · ·

A presence that disturbs me with the joy
Of elevated thoughts.

In an autobiographical poem, "The Prelude" (1798–1805), he recalls his enthusiasm for the French Revolution and his later disillusionment. Wordsworth's best poetry was written before 1807, though he continued writing until his death when he was 80 years old, having outlived all his fellow Romantic poets. *Lyrical Ballads* was the first major publication of Romantic poetry and is considered one of the important books of Western literature. You will find many editions of Wordsworth's poetry in your library. There is also an inexpensive paperback edition of *Lyrical Ballads*. YA

Wouk, Herman (1915–) A novelist and playwright, Wouk began writing while serving in the U.S. Navy. He is known best for *The Caine Mutiny, a story about World War II set in the South Pacific Ocean. Another best-seller was *Marjorie Morningstar* (1955), which is about a 17-year-old girl who wants to be an actress. Rebelling against her Jewish parents, she falls in love with the theater director who has given her a chance to act. But Marjorie comes to appreciate her parents and their values. Returning home, she marries a lawyer and settles happily into her family's tradition. Two popular and thoroughly researched historical romances, *The Winds of War* (1971) and *War and Remembrance* (1978), follow the family of Commander Victor "Pug" Henry through the years of World War II. As special envoy of the President, Commander Henry meets all the important war leaders and is present at all the dramatic happenings from the Allied defeat at Dunkirk, France, through the bombing of Pearl Harbor, Hawaii, to the A-bomb attack on Hiroshima, Japan. A film was made of *Marjorie Morningstar* in 1958. *The Winds of War* in 1983 and *War and Remembrance* in 1988 were adapted as TV miniseries. YA

Wright, Richard (1908–1960) Author of the novel *Native Son and the autobiography *Black Boy, Wright was born on a Mississippi plantation. His grandparents were slaves, and Wright's childhood was marred by poverty and the effects of a broken home. In the 1930s he went to Chicago and joined the Federal Writers'

MR = Middle Reader   YA = Young Adult Reader   * = See this main entry

Project, which gave him a chance to write about Southern racial problems. He became a member of the Communist Party and later worked for the communist newspaper *The Daily Worker*. *Native Son*, a strong and realistic account of the condition of black people in the cities "up North," was a best-seller and was adapted for the stage in 1941. Wright left the Communist Party in 1944, went to Paris, France, after World War II, and continued writing there until his death. YA

Wrightson, (Alice) Patricia (1921–) One of Australia's best-known contemporary writers of books for younger readers, Wrightson at first wrote novels that are realistic and conventional. Then she became interested in the folk myths of Australia's aborigines, and her more recent books bring their legends and beliefs into her stories. *Rocks of Honey* (1960) tells of the friendship between a white farmer's son and an aborigine boy and their search for a legendary native stone axe. Finding it brings out important differences between the boys. *I Own the Racecourse!* (1968) is about a boy who thinks he has bought a racetrack from an old tramp for three dollars. The book became very popular and was published in the United States as *A Racecourse for Andy*. A property developer finds himself up against all kinds of aboriginal spirits in *An Older Kind of Magic* (1972). He is turned to stone when he tries to develop a car park in the Botanical Gardens. Wrightson has written a set of three books about Wirrun, an aboriginal hero: *The Ice Is Coming* (1977), *The Dark Bright Waters* (1978), and *Journey Behind the Wind* (1981). MR

Wrinkle in Time, A (1962) By *Madeleine L'Engle, this novel, which combines elements of *science fiction and *fantasy, is the first in the Time Trilogy series. Its theme is the classic war between good and evil played out against cosmic forces. *A Wrinkle in Time* tells about young Meg Murry, her new friend, Calvin O'Keefe, and her precocious 5-year-old brother, Charles Wallace Murry, and about their adventures in a fantastical landscape. Aided by a trio of grandmotherly shape-changing spirits, Mrs. Whatsit, Mrs. Who, and Mrs. Which, who possess magical powers, the youngsters traverse multidimensional worlds in search of the Murrys' father, who has been mysteriously missing for some time. With great courage they rescue Mr. Murry, only to endanger Charles Wallace. Then only Meg can rescue her beloved small brother, which she does with the powers of reason and love. The trilogy includes *A Wind in the Door* (1973) and *A Swiftly Tilting Planet* (1978). *A Wrinkle in Time* won the *Newbery Medal in 1963. MR

Wuthering Heights (1847), by *Emily Brontë, is an extraordinary story of love, hate, revenge, and the freedom of the human spirit, written in a poetic and sophisticated style, and set against the background of the isolated English moorland. Unlike other *Gothic novels of the period, it unfolds through the narrative of an onlooker, and the author does not comment on events or characters. It begins when Mr. Earnshaw adopts a gypsy foundling, whom he names *Heathcliff, and brings him to Wuthering Heights to be raised with his children, *Catherine and Hindley. Heathcliff is a hostile and difficult boy, but he quickly becomes attached to the headstrong Catherine. Later, Catherine comes to adore Heathcliff and admits she cannot live without him, but she is also attracted by the handsome and prosperous Edgar Linton of nearby Thrushcross Grange. She accepts Edgar's proposal of marriage in part to help Heathcliff better himself with Edgar's money. Violently jealous, Heathcliff disappears, returning three years later, by then a wealthy gentleman. Catherine is overjoyed, but Edgar is alarmed by the intensity of her feelings for Heathcliff and forbids any contact between them. The restriction so upsets Catherine that she becomes ill. Determined to make Edgar suffer, Heathcliff elopes with Linton's sister, Isabella, for whom he feels only scorn. Catherine and Heathcliff have one brief and anguished meeting alone, in which they declare their violent love for one another. On the same night, Catherine dies in childbirth, and the despairing Heathcliff says, "I cannot live without my soul!"

MR = Middle Reader   YA = Young Adult Reader   * = See this main entry

From this moment on, Heathcliff's only reason for living is to take revenge on the Lintons. Isabella's health fails, and she dies. Their son, Linton, is a whining, sickly child, and his father neglects him. Cathy Linton, the beautiful daughter of Catherine Earnshaw and Edgar Linton, grows fond of young Linton. Heathcliff then forces her to marry his son, now very ill, to ensure that the Linton estate will come under his control. Edgar Linton, never completely well since his wife's death, dies at the Grange. Young Linton dies as well, leaving Cathy alone with Heathcliff and the last surviving Earnshaw, Hindley's son, Hareton. Cathy and Hareton fall in love, and the death of Heathcliff leaves them free to build the happiness their families never enjoyed. *Wuthering Heights* was made into a movie in 1939. YA

Xanadu An imaginary kingdom in China, Xanadu is the setting for the strange but effective poem, *Kubla Khan* (1797), by *Samuel Taylor Coleridge. The poet wrote it after he awoke from an opium-induced dream, but as he wrote he was disturbed and forgot most of what had been in his mind. The 54-line poem tells of "a stately pleasure dome" that the ruler, Kubla Khan, ordered built on the Alph River, which runs "down to a sunless sea." At one point the river flings up a "mighty fountain," then "reaches caverns measureless to man." There is also "a damsel with a dulcimer." *Kubla Khan* is a haunting poem, though it is difficult to discover its final meaning. YA

Xanth is the magical land created by *Piers Anthony in the large, and still growing, Xanth series of lighthearted, witty, pun-filled, and imaginative *fantasy novels. The first novel of the series, *A Spell for Chameleon* (1977), includes a map of Xanth. Its outline closely matches that of Florida, where Anthony lives, and its features include the Ogre-Fen-Ogre Swamp and Lake Ogre-Chobee. Everyone in Xanth has a special magical power. Xanth is separated from the greater, nonmagical world, Mundania, by a magic force field emanating from the Shieldstone.

Among the many wonders of Xanth are fairies, centaurs, dragons, elves, goblins, shoe-trees that grow shoes, cherry trees whose fruit is explosive cherry bombs, and toadstools that grow cookies. Through this magic land, Anthony's characters embark on their quests. The Xanth series includes *The Source of Magic* (1979), *Castle Roogna* (1979), *Crewel Lye: A Caustic Yarn* (1985), *Heaven Cent* (1988), and *Question Quest* (1991). You can find out more about Xanth in *Piers Anthony's Visual Guide to Xanth* (1989), by Anthony with Jody L. Nye (n.d.). Anthony's Xanth series has been likened to the Oz stories of *L. Frank Baum. MR & YA

Yahoo In the fourth of *Gulliver's Travels* by *Jonathan Swift, Gulliver visits the land of the Houyhnhnms (pronounced "whinims," based on a horse's whinny), who are horses with human attributes, but saner and more reasonable. They dominate the Yahoos, who are beasts in human shape. The Yahoos are brutal and filthy, and Gulliver is disgusted with them. In effect, Swift is saying he finds the human race to be like the Yahoos when they could be like the Houyhnhnms. The word "yahoo" has come to be used to describe anyone who acts in a crude and uncivilized manner.

Yankee As far back as the late 17th century, the Dutch in America were known by this name. It probably comes from "Janke," a form of the Dutch name Jan. Yankee later became a designation for a New Englander, and to Southerners it came to mean "Northerner." It then gradually came into use as meaning any American. World War I and World War II spread the word abroad, and U.S. troops became the Yanks. In fiction, the title characters in *A Connecticut Yankee at King Arthur's Court* by *Mark Twain and *David Harum* (1898) by Edward Noyes Westcott (1846–1898) have the presumed Yankee attributes: shrewdness, dry wit, sharpness in trade, and a homespun personality. Closely related to the term is the song "Yankee Doodle" (1755). It was sung at the time of the American Revolution by British troops to make fun of the presumably inept American army. The colonists turned the tables by proudly adopting it and throwing it back at the British. As the chorus of the song says:

> Yankee Doodle keep it up,
> Yankee Doodle dandy,
> Mind the music and the step,
> And with the girls be handy.

Yates, Elizabeth (1905–) An author of both fiction and nonfiction, for older as well as younger readers, Yates is noted in particular for her biographies. Among them are *Amos Fortune, Free Man* and *Prudence Crandall, Woman of Courage* (1955). The latter is the story of Crandall (1803–1889), an educator and abolitionist, who in 1833 was arrested in Canterbury, Connecticut, because she had opened a school for black girls. Typical of Yates's fiction are *Mountain Born* (1943) and *A Place for Peter* (1953), both about a boy growing up in rural New Hampshire. There is also a splendid characterization of Benj, an aging farmhand. The heroine of *Caroline's Courage* (1964) is Caroline Putnam, who is accompanying her pioneer family on the long journey from New Hampshire to Nebraska in the mid-19th century. The settlers fear the Indians, but Caroline, wandering off, meets an Indian girl, and they exchange dolls. At the end you are left to wonder whether these two will someday meet again. If you enjoy these books, try those of

*Arna Bontemps, *Julius Lester, and *Laura Ingalls Wilder. MR & YA

Year Without Michael, The (1987) You will not regret reading this heart-breaking novel by *Susan Beth Pfeffer, because it shows an understanding of how — and how not — to cope with a tragic family situation. Michael Chapman, about to become a high school freshman, walks out of his home and disappears, leaving his mother and father, who are considering a divorce; his older sister, Jody, a high school junior; and his younger sister, Kay, a seventh grader. The family, friends, and police find no trace of Michael. The family is first drawn together by fear and sorrow. After a while, though, the tension shortens tempers and they are at odds with each other over trivial matters, as well as over the problem of Michael's whereabouts. The mother quits her job, Jody loses a boyfriend, and Kay, seeming to hate everyone, wants to go live with her grandmother. After a year, when there is still no trace of Michael, the family faces up to the fact that he is gone forever. They agree they must have family therapy and learn to share their sorrows while getting on with life. As a clergyman has told Jody, the *Bible says: "Love bears all things, believes all things, hopes all things, endures all things. Love never ends." MR & YA

Yearling, The (1938) A classic for over half a century, this novel by *Marjorie Kinnan Rawlings is perfect in setting, characters, and story. Above all it is a down-to-earth tale of a hard way of life. Central to it are 12-year-old Jody Baxter and his father and mother, Penny and Ory. They live in the backwoods of northern Florida during the 1870s, trying to make their way by farming and hunting. Penny seems to be hard on his son, but you realize it is because he knows the kind of life Jody must face as he grows older. Penny teaches him to hunt, telling him that they kill animals only for food. Many adventures are all related with authentic dialect: Penny nearly dies from a snake bite; they track down Slewfoot, an old bear that kills farm animals; an eight-day rain ruins crops;

Jody Baxter's life is changed dramatically by the fawn he finds and raises in *The Yearling*.

and they deal with a rough but helpful neighboring family. The main story, though, is about Jody's finding a newborn male fawn that he calls Flag and that becomes the focus of his life. But as Flag grows, he damages the family's sparse crops. Finally, Penny tells Jody he must shoot Flag, now a yearling. When Jody refuses, his mother, with Penny crippled by a hernia, shoots Flag but only wounds him. Jody at last faces the fact that he must be the one to kill Flag. He realizes that both the yearling and his boyhood are past history. Earlier Jody has said: "I hate things dyin'"; now he understands that living and dying go together. A movie of *The Yearling* was made in 1946. YA

Yeats, William Butler (1865–1939) An Irish poet, dramatist, and nationalist politician, Yeats was both a leader of the Irish Renaissance, a movement around the turn of the century to bring forth the native culture of Ireland, and also one of the most influential poets of the 20th century. In an early play, *The Count-*

William Butler Yeats

ess Cathleen (1891), the countess sells her soul to the devil to help her starving tenants. In 1904 Yeats was one of the founders of the Abbey Theatre, Dublin, which played a leading role in the Irish Renaissance and still stages plays today. Another of his plays, *On Baile's Strand* (1904), was performed there in that first year. Its theme is that of father and son in conflict. Yeats was also much interested in myth and mysticism, and this is reflected in *The Celtic Twilight* (1893), a collection of stories based on the belief of the Irish in fairies and spirits. Yeats's later poetry, generally considered his best, is both lyrical and dramatic and makes use of myths and *symbols. Good examples are found in *The Tower* (1928), especially the title poem, in "Sailing to Byzantium," and in "Leda and the Swan." In "Sailing to Byzantium" he writes:

An aged man is but a paltry thing,
A tattered coat upon a stick, unless
Soul clap its hands and sing, and louder sing
For every tatter in its mortal dress.

Collected Poems was published in 1933. If you are interested in Yeats, read also the poetry and plays of *T.S. Eliot, Isabella Gregory [Lady Gregory] (1852–1932), and *John M. Synge. YA

yellow The particular shade of yellow often determines the meaning of this *color in art, religion, and literature. Golden yellow signifies the sun and divinity. A paler yellow suggests treason and jealousy. Someone with "a yellow streak" or who is called "yellow-bellied" is a coward. "Yellow press" refers to newspapers that feature sensational news. During the *Nazi regime in Germany in the 1930s and 1940s, all Jews were required to wear a yellow six-pointed Star of David, a *symbol of Judaism. When you say something is "as good as gold," or that a person has "a heart of gold," you are making a comparison with the precious metal and not its color. See also *star.

Yep, Laurence Michael (1948–) An American author of Chinese ancestry, Yep writes entertaining novels that show concern for the problems of young people of Chinese background in coping with American culture. His first novel, *Sweetwater* (1973), though, was *science fiction, about a young man who must deal with both a generational conflict with his father and the problems of life in the first settlement on the planet Harmony. *Dragonwings* is Yep's best work. In *Child of the Owl* (1977), 12-year-old Casey Young, a Chinese American, has to cope with her father, Barney, a gambler, and with the life of San Francisco's Chinatown, to which she is a stranger. The story also tells about the theft and recovery of an antique owl charm. In *The Star Fisher* (1991), the time is 1927 and 15-year-old Joan Lee and her Chinese-American family move to West Virginia. They at once meet with hostility: No one will do business with their laundry, and Joan has a miserable time in school. Eventually their landlady shows them how to cope with their new world and themselves. Yep's novels remind you of how cultural differences can affect lives. If you enjoy these books, you will also like those of *Bette Bao Lord. YA

yeti See *abominable snowman.

Yobgorgle: Mystery Monster of Lake Ontario (1979), a hilarious novel by *Daniel M. Pinkwater, tells about the summer adventure of a boy named Eugene Winkleman. At first Eugene thinks spending two weeks in Rochester, New York, with his Uncle Mel is going to be boring. Then he and Uncle Mel meet Professor Ambrose McFwain. The professor has been hunting the monster Yobgorgle, who is supposed to live in Lake Ontario. Professor McFwain hires Eugene as his assistant and provides Uncle Mel with a beautiful light-blue cowboy outfit. The professor then meets the eccentric multibillionaire Colonel Ken Krenwinkle, who sells the professor a truck for $3 on the condition that he always wear a chicken costume when he drives it. The professor, Eugene, and Uncle Mel go searching for Yobgorgle, only to find that the monster is actually a pig-shaped submarine commanded by the *Flying Dutchman, who takes them prisoner. He explains that he can never reach land until a curse that has been cast upon him has been lifted. Eugene and his companions come up with a brilliant plan to end the curse and get back home. If you enjoyed *Yobgorgle*, try also the books of *Beverly Cleary, *Sid Fleischman, and *Robert McCloskey. MR

Yoga See *Hinduism.

Yoknapatawpha County is an imaginary region created by *William Faulkner as the setting for 14 of his novels and a number of short stories. It is essentially Lafayette County in northern Mississippi, and the county seat he calls Jefferson corresponds to Oxford, where Faulkner lived and wrote. In a 1951 edition of *Absalom, Absalom!* there is a map of Yoknapatawpha, which is presumably an American Indian name, that shows its area and population, divided between blacks and whites. The mythical county first appears in *Sartoris* (1929), a novel about the Sartoris family, especially Bayard and his grandfather, shortly after World War I. YA

Yolen, Jane (Hyatt) (1939–) A poet, dramatist, and folksinger, Yolen is best known, however, as the author of many *fantasy and *science fiction novels for young readers. Among the best of them are *Dragon's Blood, *Heart's Blood, and *The Devil's Arithmetic. The Girl Who Cried Flowers, and Other Tales* (1974) offers five fairy tales, all about Olivia, whose tears become flowers that can be used on various occasions. Olivia is kept so busy that she weeps all the time until, finally, a storyteller makes her smile. In *The Mermaid's Three Wisdoms* (1978) a mermaid who cannot speak and Jess, a 12-year-old deaf girl, become friends. Jess, who is restless because of her handicap, learns from the mermaid that it is better to be patient, like the rhythms of the sea. Yolen has also edited *The Fireside Book of Birds and Beasts* (1972) and written a biography, *Friend: The Story of George Fox and the Quakers* (1972). Yolen's fanciful plots show a high order of imagination, combined with a storytelling ability that will keep you reading. If you like her books, read those of *Helen M. Hoover and *Roger Zelazny. MR & YA

You Never Can Tell (1984), a novel by *Ellen Conford, tells about 16-year-old Kate Bennett, who lives on Long Island, New York. Kate has a reasonably normal life until she learns that Thad Marshall, the actor who plays Brick Preston, the hero of her favorite soap opera, has enrolled at her high school. She fantasizes what it would be like to fall in love with Brick, who has left a trail of broken hearts in his soap opera life. Then Kate meets Thad and finds he is every bit as breathtaking as Brick Preston. She stops seeing Ron, her old boyfriend, and begins to date Thad, but it is not really Thad she falls in love with, but Brick. Thad tries to please her by being Brick, but he cannot keep up the sham, for he really wants Kate to love him for the person he really is. He breaks off the relationship and soon leaves school to resume his career, but not before making Kate see what has happened. Later Thad keeps in touch by postcard and finally asks Kate to see him again. Will Thad and Kate get back together?

As Kate says, "You never can tell." If you enjoyed *You Never Can Tell*, try also *The King of Rock* (1988) by *Marlene Fanta Shyer, about a girl who discovers that a famous rock star has moved into her apartment building. MR

You Never Knew Her as I Did (1981) By

*Mollie Hunter, this novel of high adventure is an account of an incident in the life of Mary, Queen of Scots (1542–1587). After a rebellion against her, Mary is sent into captivity, June 17, 1567, in an island castle at Lochleven, Scotland. A few of those in the castle, including 16-year-old Will Douglas, are loyal to her. They plan to help her escape, but their first two plots fail: the first, when the captain of the castle guard reveals the plan; the second, when a boatman recognizes Mary as she tries to escape to the mainland dressed as a washwoman. The final plan centers around Will on his birthday, May 2, 1568. He steals the key to the castle gate after it is locked and the guard is dismissed for the night. The queen, disguised as the wife of a soldier, is rowed by Will to the mainland where her followers await. But her forces are eventually defeated and much later, while she is held captive in England, she is beheaded on orders of Queen Elizabeth I (1533–1603), leaving Will to mourn her with steadfast devotion. You may want also to read the whole story of this tragic queen in the fine biography *Mary, Queen of Scots* (1969) by *Antonia Fraser or in the two historical novels *The Royal Road to Fotheringay* (1956) and *The Captive Queen of Scots* (1973) by *Jean Plaidy. YA

You Read to Me, I'll Read to You (1962) By

the poet John Ciardi (1916–1985), this collection of humorous poems is delightfully illustrated by the artist Edward Gorey (1925–). It is a book for adults or older readers to share with beginning readers, by taking turns reading to one another. The more difficult poems are printed in black, and the easier ones are printed in blue. The lighthearted verses are about boys and girls, the wind, hens, sharks' teeth, and other imaginative subjects. If you enjoyed *You Read to Me, I'll Read to You*, you will be glad to know that Ciardi wrote quite a few books of poetry for younger readers, including *I Met a Man* (1961), *The Man Who Sang the Sillies* (1961), *You Know Who* (1964), and *Doodle Soup* (1986). MR

You Shouldn't Have to Say Goodbye (1982)

In this touching novel by Patricia Hermes (1936–), 13-year-old Sarah Morrow first realizes her mother is dying of cancer when her mother begins to explain to Sarah the household tasks that will fall on her. Her mother also tries to ease the anger Sarah feels by buying her books that might help, but Sarah refuses to read them. Seeking consolation from a school friend, Robin, Sarah finds that she too has her troubles because her mother is an agoraphobic—that is, she is afraid to go into open spaces. A little later, as the family is about to open its presents on Christmas Eve, Sarah's mother dies. She leaves Sarah a book in which she had been writing regularly, and as Sarah reads it she begins to see that her mother was trying to make her understand that dying is a difficult process, for both those who are ill and those who will survive. This is a sad book, but it holds out the message that love and understanding will make such situations less difficult and lead to the realization that life must go on. Two other moving books about learning to cope with family tragedy are *A Death in the Family* by *James Agee and *Death Be Not Proud: A Memoir* by *John Gunther. YA

You Two (1984) This thoughtful novel by an

English writer, Jean Ure (1943–), explores the effect on Elizabeth Muir, a sixth grader, of having to move from the small, private Lady Margaret Foster's Academy for Girls to the much larger, public Gladeside Intermediate School. Elizabeth's father has lost his job, and they must move to a less expensive neighborhood in London, England. Elizabeth finds she is ahead of her new classmates in school subjects. Her classmates have much different ethnic and economic backgrounds. As a result, she is considered a snob. Then she makes friends with Paddy Dewar, who explains that now others will speak to them as "Hey, you two." However,

MR = Middle Reader　　YA = Young Adult Reader　　* = See this main entry

Paddy is not as well mannered as Elizabeth and becomes possessive. Elizabeth's mother tries to force her to become friends with Sylvia Bower, who is very snooty. The story comes to a climax with an incident concerning a *Victorian paperweight that was left to Elizabeth by her great-grandmother. She and her mother learn that someone like Paddy, rough as she seems, is a true friend. Elizabeth also finds she likes Gladeside and does not want to return to private school. She has found that the world is much wider and more interesting than she once thought. YA

Young Fu of the Upper Yangtze (1932) At the start of this novel by Elizabeth Foreman Lewis (1892–1958), 13-year-old Fu Yuin-fah and his widowed mother arrive from a farm to live in Chungking, a large city on the Yangtze River in southern China. It is the 1920s, and you are at once plunged, along with them, into a time when China was struggling to modernize while warlords fought each other for power. Fu is apprenticed to a coppersmith, and in the course of running errands sees his first foreigner; saves a white woman from a fire; lives through a cholera and typhus epidemic; nearly drowns in a sudden flood of the river; escapes from bandits who board a river boat he is on; gets involved in a gambling game and loses all his money; helps one of his fellow apprentices, wrongly suspected of smuggling opium; and in the end not only becomes a journeyman coppersmith but is adopted by the coppersmith. Fu has also learned to read and write. This novel is worth reading for two reasons: It is an exciting story and it informs you about life in a land very different from America. Lewis, who taught in China from 1919 to 1921, won a *Newbery Medal for *Young Fu of the Upper Yangtze* in 1933. You will especially enjoy a later edition, published in 1973, which contains a glossary-commentary and an introduction by *Pearl S. Buck. MR

Young Landlords, The (1979) In a decaying New York City neighborhood, five young people decide, in this novel by *Walter Dean Meyers, to clean up a rundown apartment building on their block. The leaders are Paul, in his middle teens, and his friend, Gloria. Their first step, to try to get the owner to do something about repairing the building, results instead in their buying the apartment house for one dollar. Of course, they soon learn they have taken on a difficult task when a bookkeeper shows them they will not have any money for improvements after they pay all expenses. The group holds a successful street fair and tries to solve a crime involving the theft of stereo equipment in order to earn the reward. This plan fails when the young man they suspected of the theft turns out to be innocent. Meanwhile, their project gets further into debt, and they are rescued only when the head of the local numbers racket buys the building and hires the group to manage it. Thus, there is hope for the future, and a romance between Paul and Gloria seems about to happen. Though you will find this a story of struggle and, at times, of disappointed hopes, you will enjoy it because of the author's ability to write true-to-life dialogue. YA

Young Lions, The (1948) By *Irwin Shaw, this powerful novel about World War II follows the lives of two Americans and one Austrian from 1938 to 1945. Christian Diestl, a young Austrian ski instructor, has become a Nazi, believing that an orderly Europe dominated by Germany is a good end, no matter what means are used to achieve it. As a sergeant in the German army in 1940, he proudly tours defeated Paris as a conquering hero. After America enters the war, Michael Whitacre, a successful stage director, and Noah Ackerman, a young, friendless Jew, find themselves in the same infantry company at a Southern military base. The target of fierce anti-Semitism, Noah fights with enormous courage and dignity, finally gaining the respect of his fellow soldiers. Michael, sickened by the grim realities of infantry life, transfers to easier and safer service, but he rejoins Noah in Europe near war's end. After their company liberates a German death camp, Noah and Michael are ambushed on a wooded lane by Christian, who has, through the long years of vicious combat, degenerated into a heartless murderer. Noah dies, and Michael, finally confronting the war he has alternately sought and fled, kills Christian. If you enjoyed *The Young Lions*, try also **The Naked and the Dead* by **Norman Mailer. *The Young Lions* was made into a movie in 1958. YA

Young Unicorns, The (1968) By **Madeleine L'Engle, this novel is one of a series about the Austin family. Fifteen-year-old Vicky Austin, her younger sister, Suzy, their 7-year-old brother, Rob, and their parents are living in New York City with 12-year-old Emily Gregory, recently blinded in an accident. Emily is an accomplished musician. The Austin household (including Emily) and friends—including Emily's teacher, Mr. Theo, the children's friend, Josiah Davidson (Dave), and Canon Tallis of the Cathedral of St. John the Divine—join forces to foil a bizarre plot to take over political control of New York City. Other novels in the Austin family series include **Meet the Austins, The Moon by Night* (1963), and *A Ring of Endless Light* (1980). MR

Your Former Friend, Matthew (1984) An amusing novel about friendship, this story by Louann Gaeddert (1931–) also makes an important point about how you change as you grow up. Gail Walden and Matthew Morrison, about 12 years old, have been friends since they were very young. Now, while school is out for the summer, they agree to collect rocks for a joint summer project in the fall. However, when they meet again, Matthew no longer wants to be with Gail but instead with other boys. Gail is both sad and angry, but begins to make friends with other girls. She also gets back at Matthew by telling his new friends secrets about Matthew. When she realizes she has done wrong, she apologizes in a note, but receives from Matthew the message, "Just leave me alone. Your former friend." Nevertheless, when she finds Matthew did not collect rocks and has no science project, she gives him some of hers. Matthew then shows a change of heart by inviting Gail, a girl friend of hers, and another boy to his family's apartment to play games. Gail and Matthew have discovered their friendship should not exclude others. MR

Your Old Pal, Al (1979) This novel by **Constance C. Greene is the sequel to the novels **A Girl Called Al* and **I Know You, Al*. As in the earlier books, the main characters are 13-year-old Alexandra and her best friend, who live in the same New York City apartment building and tell the story of their adventures. Al recently returned from her father's remarriage. At the wedding she met an interesting boy named Brian, and now she is waiting for letters from her dad and his new wife and from Brian. Day after day she looks for the letters, but they do not arrive. Then Al learns that her best friend has invited another girl, Polly, to stay over for two weeks while Polly's parents go to Africa. The visit leads to a big fight between Al and her best friend. By the time everything is straightened out, both girls learn some important lessons about trust and friendship. If you enjoyed *Your Old Pal, Al*, you can read more about Al and her best friend in **Al(exandra) the Great* and **Just Plain Al*. You will probably also like the books of **Mary Francis Shura and **Louise Fitzhugh. MR

You're Allegro Dead (1981) By Barbara Corcoran (1911–), this is a lively novel of friendship and mystery. When Camp Allegro reopens after having been closed for a number of years, among the first to attend are two 12-year-old friends, Kim and Stella. They have fun, but strange things happen. One girl sees a figure on the dock late at night; Stella hears the sound of a shovel; and she is hit by a rock while resting under a tree. When Kim and Stella hear a noise at night, they investigate and a man rushes past them. Even worse, Stella wanders into the woods by herself, is seized, tied up, threatened, and then let go. On another visit to the pond where this takes place, a man shoots Kim in the leg, and a bag of $100 bills is found under an old boat. The mystery is not resolved until Stella sees a man in a rowboat approaching the camp. She whistles to alert the camp. The police come, and the man is captured. A local bank had been robbed some years before, and the robber hid the money on the camp grounds while it was abandoned. The bank presents a $10,000 reward to the camp, and Stella and Kim end an exciting and happy time. YA

You're Going Out There a Kid, but You're Coming Back a Star (1982) By Linda Hirsch (1948–), a teacher and author, this novel is about wanting to grow up too fast. It is an amusing account of some events in the life of 10-year-old Margaret Dapple, who is in fifth grade in New York City. She does not understand her parents, because she thinks they do not understand her. Sometimes she leans on her 14-year-old sister, Barbara, for advice and assistance; sometimes she hates Barbara for treating her like a baby. Margaret thinks all boys are ugly, except Stephen, but Stephen prefers Naomi. Barbara tries to make Margaret more attractive by bleaching her hair, but the result gets Margaret laughed at by her classmates. It is not until Barbara takes Margaret to her first girl-boy party that Margaret's life takes a turn for the better. She hesitates when Matthew, another classmate, asks her to dance, but she finds that it is really okay. And when the party plays spin-the-bottle, she gets kissed by Matthew. Margaret goes home feeling quite grown up. Though she *has* grown up some, she begins to understand that she must not rush things. MR

Yours Till Niagara Falls, Abby (1979) Anyone who has ever gone to summer camp, or expects to do so, will find this novel by Jane O'Connor (1947–) amusing and informative. When 10-year-old Abby goes to camp for the first time, she is very unhappy and wants to go home, which is not unusual. More experienced campers tease her, collapse her bed, and try other tricks to upset her. Abby by mistake allows birds to eat her picnic lunch, and she gets poison ivy. However, things get better when Roberta, another new camper, arrives and joins forces with Abby to get revenge on their tormentors. By the time camp is over, she is sorry to part from Roberta, but this feeling combines with the camping experience to show her that separation from home and friends is a part of life and must be coped with. She realizes that people must be themselves in order to be independent, and must also cooperate with other people. MR

yuppie (yuppy) A term that first appeared in print in 1984, yuppie can stand for young urban professional, but is more commonly thought of as meaning a young upwardly mobile professional. Yuppie implies an ambitious person, most likely a young lawyer, stockbroker, or banker. He or she has a large income in relation to age and experience and spends money as much to show off as to secure real enjoyment. A yuppie wears the latest fashions in clothes, dines at high-priced restaurants, and drives expensive imported autos. Many of the characters in *The Bonfire of the Vanities* (1987) by *Tom Wolfe are yuppies. This novel tells the story of a New York City yuppie who has a minor auto accident that leads to a chain of adventures that cause his downfall. YA

Z for Zachariah (1975) In this novel by *Robert O'Brien, 15-year-old Ann Burden, alone for many months in a rural valley in the northeastern United States, thinks she may be the only survivor of a nuclear war. Her parents had left in search of others and never returned, but Ann has a cow and chickens, a garden, and a nearby general store to enable her to survive. Then a man appears, clad in a green plastic suit. He is John Loomis, a 32-year-old chemist. He makes the mistake of bathing in a brook that is radioactive and becomes ill. Ann nurses him to health, discovering while he is delirious that the suit protecting him from radiation is the only one of its kind and that he killed a colleague to possess it. They learn to pump gas without electricity, and Ann uses a tractor to plant more crops. When Loomis enters her bedroom one night, she flees to a cave in the hills, and they become enemies. Loomis, apparently crazed, shoots at her and wounds her slightly in the leg. Desperate, Ann tricks him, seizes the suit, and sets forth alone into an unknown future. The book's title comes from Ann's biblical ABC book. She imagines that if A stands for Adam, the first man, the Z for Zachariah must mean the last man. This story is one you will appreciate for its portrayal of faith, self-sufficiency, and courage. YA

Zan Hagen's Marathon (1984) The heroine of this novel by *R.R. Knudson is Suzanne Hagen, a high school girl. Zan's life revolves around her running, and she is a topnotch sprinter and short-distance runner. But her best friend and coach, Arthur Rinehart, has plans for Zan to run in the first women's Olympic marathon. Zan's success as a sprinter has made her cocky, even arrogant, and in her first qualifying marathon she barely finishes. Under Arthur's guidance, Zan learns over the months of grueling training what long-distance running is all about. She also learns that the athletes she runs against are not really enemies to be defeated, but friendly competitors, and this view of competition is what distinguishes mere winners from champions. If you enjoyed *Zan Hagen's Marathon*, try the novel *Stotan!* by *Chris Crutcher, in which a dedication to swimming helps four high school seniors learn about themselves and life. YA

Zeely (1967) This amusing but thoughtful novel by *Virginia Hamilton begins as 11-year-old Elizabeth Perry and her younger brother, John, go south for a summer vacation with their Uncle Ross. Elizabeth, with a vivid imagination, decides to call herself Miss Geeder Perry. She becomes aware of Mr. Tayber, a hog farmer, and his adult daughter, Zeely. People make fun of Zeely because she is six feet tall, and they think she is a "night traveler," a spirit that returns to Earth and dwells in living persons. Geeder, however, is sure she must be a queen of the Watusi, an African people. Geeder and Zeely become acquainted after Geeder helps the Taybers drive their hogs to market, not without some misadventures. The two talk, and Zeely says her mother was indeed descended from the Watusi. Zeely, who is well acquainted with the struggles of a life raising hogs, and having become reconciled to the fact that her unusual height sets her apart, makes Geeder realize that it is time for her to end her foolish fantasies and come down to earth. MR

Zelazny, Roger (Joseph) (1937–) A prolific author who has written about 30 novels and 100 short stories, Zelazny is recognized for his combination of *fantasy and *science fiction while working in elements of mythology. For example, in *Lord of Light* (1967), a group that rules a planet takes the Hindu gods as its model. One of the group, reaching inner perfection, sees that his fellows are actually tyrants and overthrows them. More recent is *Trumps of Doom* (1985), one of the novels in what Zelazny calls the Amber series. The central figure is Merle Corey of San Francisco, who designs computers, but who is also Merlin, son of Corwin, the prince of the planet Amber. Something or someone is trying to kill Corey, who possesses a secret that could destroy both worlds. *A Dark Traveling* (1987) has an odd cast of characters; 14-year-old James Wiley, who claims his sister, Becky, is a witch, and that his Uncle George is a werewolf. The story also concerns James's father, whose machine, which James uses to travel to other worlds, is broken and who has disappeared. If you like Zelazny's brilliant imaginings, read books by *Piers Anthony, *Ray Bradbury, and *Robert A. Heinlein. YA

Zelda: A Biography (1978) In her late teens in Montgomery, Alabama, Zelda Sayre (1900–1948) was both the most beautiful and the most reckless girl in town. She met a handsome lieutenant of World War I, *F. Scott Fitzgerald, married him in 1920, and became with him the living spirit of the Jazz Age of the 1920s. This is the story, by Nancy Milford (1938–), of Zelda's glamorous but tragic life. Fitzgerald, as novelist, wrote the best books about the era and often put Zelda into them, most notably in *Tender Is the Night*. The couple lived in America and France, mingling with literary and society figures, drinking heavily, and spending lavishly. Zelda had considerable talent of her own: ballet dancing, painting, and writing. She sold a number of short stories to magazines and published a novel, *Save Me the Waltz* (1932), clearly based on her own life. But Zelda deteriorated mentally and was hospitalized for the first time in 1930. After that she was in and out of mental institutions for the rest of her life. On March 10, 1948, she died when fire swept the hospital she had been in since the previous November. This biography is a compelling story of the life of an unusual person, as well as a vivid picture of the times. YA

Zen Buddhism See *Buddhism.

zenith The complete opposite of *nadir, zenith is the point of the sky directly overhead. The word comes from the Arabic. As a figure of speech, zenith is the peak, the summit, the climax, the acme of something. *John Milton, in well-known lines from *Paradise Lost*, wrote about the fall of Vulcan when he was pitched from heaven by angry Jove:

> From morn
> To Noon he fell, from Noon to dewy Eve,
>   A summer's day; and with the setting sun
> Dropt from the Zenith like a falling Star.

Zephyr In Greek mythology Zephyr is the west wind, son of Eos (the Roman Aurora), who is the Greek goddess of the dawn and the mother of the *stars and of the other three winds, north, south, and east. A zephyr is a gentle, soft wind, and so the word can also mean anything having this quality, as certain light fabrics or a low whisper.

zero (0) From the Arabic *sifr*, zero is the *symbol for the number in the decimal system that leaves any other number unchanged: zero added to or subtracted from any other number leaves that number the same; and zero multiplied or divided by any number (except zero) remains zero. Zero is the point on the Celsius temperature scale at which water freezes; absolute zero (−273.15°C) is the lowest possible temperature that can be obtained. In World War I "zero hour" was the exact time scheduled for an attack to begin. "To zero in" is to aim exactly at a target or to pay attention to one particular object, such as your homework. Cipher, from the same Arabic source, also means zero. It is sometimes applied to a person, or anything else, that has no worth or no distinctive characteristics.

Zeus is the chief of the gods of ancient Greek mythology. Like his counterpart *Jupiter in Roman mythology, Zeus rules over the sky and weather. Hades, Poseidon, and Zeus split up the universe, with Hades getting the underworld, Poseidon the seas, and Zeus the high places on earth. As the ruler, or king, of all the other gods, he sees that justice is done. Yet he is an unfaithful husband of *Hera, his sister and wife. He also beats her and punishes her for being jealous and for counseling him to be prudent. The many storms around the mountaintops of Greece are said to be the earthly manifestations of their marital battles. Once, it is said, Zeus flung a son from the heights of Olympus. Zeus is the father of many gods and other beings, among them *Athena, *Persephone, *Dionysus, *Artemis, *Apollo, *Aphrodite, *Perseus, Minos (see *Minotaur), Castor and Pollux (see the *Gemini), and *Helen, along with the Seasons, the Graces, and the *Muses. Zeus became the top god by dethroning his father and fighting off a revolt of giants. He was worshipped all over Greece and its islands, and his primary shrine and throne was atop Mount Olympus. His exploits preceded the Roman myths of Jupiter.

Zindel, Paul (1936–) A teacher, playwright, and novelist, Zindel was born and raised on Staten Island, New York. He became interested in theater in grade school and wrote his first play in high school. In college Zindel studied creative writing under the playwright *Edward Albee. Zindel's best-known and most successful play is *The Effect of Gamma Rays on Man-in-the-Moon Marigolds. His first book, *The Pigman, was praised for its realistic approach to the problems and feelings of young people in modern society. Many of his characters see themselves as outcasts or misfits and have troubled family and social relationships. Their stories center on events that cause them to change and grow, and to see themselves and their surroundings in new ways. Among his books are *My Darling, My Hamburger; Pardon Me, You're Stepping on My Eyeball (1976), about two lonely and alienated students who help each other overcome their problems; Confessions of a Teenage Baboon (1977), about a lonely teenager and the man who teaches him to take responsibility for his own life; and A Begonia for Miss Applebaum (1989), about a boy and girl who learn that their favorite high school teacher is dying. YA

zodiac An imaginary belt around the heavens, the zodiac is the path the sun follows in its apparent annual journey around Earth. There are 12 signs of the zodiac, which are considered to occupy separate areas of this great circle through the skies: Aries, the Ram; Taurus, the Bull; Gemini, the Twins; Cancer, the Crab; Leo, the Lion; Virgo, the Virgin; Libra, the Balance; Scorpio, the Scorpion; Sagittarius, the Archer; Capricorn, the Goat; Aquarius, the Water Bearer; and Pisces, the Fishes. The word zodiac comes from the Greek word zodiakos, having to do with animals, and the *symbols used for the signs probably first appeared in Greek manuscripts of the late Middle Ages. However, the idea of the zodiac may have originated with the ancient Assyrians, Chaldeans, or Babylonians. The zodiac is important in the pseudoscience of astrology, the belief that these signs, along with the sun, moon, *stars, and planets, influence or can be used to predict human behavior and fate.

Zorba the Greek (1946), by *Nikos Kazantzakis, is the story of Alexis Zorba, hero and

Greek workman. Zorba is a larger-than-life character in the tradition of *Falstaff and *Sancho Panza. He is a fantasizer, a wit, enjoying life as he enlarges on his past adventures and his exploits of love. Zorba is not a young man, and that is part of his charm. His fires are not dimmed. He copes with the mad monks in a monastery as easily as he supervises his miners and the building of a cable railway. It is this conflict between contemplation and action that stands out between Zorba and the narrator, a staid Englishman, especially when Zorba wakes him: "Get up and we'll go to the monastery and have the papers signed for the cable railway. There's only one thing makes a lion afraid and that's a louse. The lice will eat us all up, boss." Zorba builds the railway, but not without problems, as the opening ceremony proves. The monks, peasants, and workers are there with a fat sheep roasting on a spit. Wine is available, and things really go awry. Zorba is loosely based on a man Kazantzakis knew, a man who helped him in a mining venture and during a trip to Russia to repatriate refugees. *Zorba the Greek* was filmed in 1964. YA

Zucchini (1982) This is a delightfully funny, yet touching, novel by Barbara Dana (1940–)

about 10-year-old Billy and Zucchini, a 3-month-old ferret. Zucchini is in a cage at the Bronx Zoo, New York City, but when he learns that ferrets should live on a Western prairie, he makes his escape. Zucchini rides the subway and a bus and nearly drowns in a drainpipe before being taken to the ASPCA (American Society for the Prevention of Cruelty to Animals) shelter. There he becomes acquainted with Billy, a shy boy, who begins to come out of his shell through the people he meets at the ASPCA. But Zucchini is determined to get to a prairie and almost makes it by stealing a ride on an airplane and then traveling by foot. He meets a friendly armadillo who tells him he is near a prairie. Just then, Zucchini remembers that before he left the ASPCA, he had promised Arnold the Crow to let him out of his cage so he could fly to Staten Island. Zucchini sadly makes the trip back to New York City. He expects to live in a cage, but Billy tells him his family is moving to Binghamton, New York, and they will take him with them. Thus, he can at last lead an outdoor life. Of course, it is an impossible story, but you will cheer Zucchini all the way. MR

Copyright Notices

The Iceman Cometh
The Billy Rose Theatre Collection, The New York Public Library for Performing Arts, Astor, Lenox and Tilden Foundations.

Ichabod Crane
Picture Collection New York Public Library

Ivanhoe
Belford, Clarke & Co.

Jane Eyre
From JANE EYRE by Charlotte Brontë. Copyright 1944 by Random House, Inc. Reprinted by permission of Random House, Inc.

Jason and the Golden Fleece
The Bettmann Archive

Dr. Samuel Johnson
Paul Elder and Company

Just So Stories
Illustration by Rudyard Kipling

Franz Kafka
From FRANZ KAFKA by Max Brod. Copyright 1947 and renewed 1975 by Schocken Books, Inc. Reprinted by permission of Schocken Books, published by Pantheon Books, a division of Random House, Inc.

Helen Keller
American Foundation for the Blind, 15 West 16th Street, New York, NY 10011.

Kidnapped
N.C. Wyeth/New York Public Library

Charles Kingsley
Dodd, Mead & Company

"The Lady or the Tiger?"
Charles Scribner's Sons

Andrew Lang
David McKay Co.

The Light Princess
Blackie & Son Limited

Limerick
Illustration by Edward Lear

Little Lord Fauntleroy
Picture Collection New York Public Library

Little Women
Illustration by Jessie Willcox Smith

Mars
From THE AGE OF FABLE by Thomas Bulfinch

Mercury
From THE AGE OF FABLE by Thomas Bulfinch

John Milton
Paul Elder and Company

Les Misérables
Illustration by Mead Schaeffer

Moby-Dick
The Page Company

Walt Morey
From GENTLE BEN by Walt Morey, illustrated by John Schoenherr. Copyright © 1965 by Walt Morey. Used by permission of Dutton Children's Books, a division of Penguin Books USA Inc.

Mouse and the Motorcycle
From THE MOUSE AND THE MOTORCYCLE by Beverly Cleary, illustrated by Louis Darling. Copyright © 1965 by Beverly Cleary. By permission of Morrow Junior Books, a division of William Morrow & Company, Inc.

Neptune
Wichita City Library, Wichita, Kansas

Newbery Medal
Courtesy of the American Library Association

Nibelungenlied
Picture Collection New York Public Library

Odin
From THE AGE OF FABLE by Thomas Bulfinch

Old Curiosity Shop
Illustration by George Cruikshank

Oliver
Illustration by George Cruikshank/Picture Collection New York Public Library

Thomas Paine
Library of Congress

Pan
From THE AGE OF FABLE by Thomas Bulfinch

Paradise Lost
Picture Collection New York Public Library

Penrod
Gordon Grant/Grosset & Dunlap

Pilgrim's Progress
The Bettmann Archive

Pinocchio
Courtesy of J.G. Ferguson Publishing Company © 1939

Edgar Allan Poe
Matthew Brady

Pride and Prejudice
From PRIDE AND PREJUDICE, 1957. Courtesy of The Folio Society.

Prometheus
From THE AGE OF FABLE by Thomas Bulfinch

Queenie Peavy
From QUEENIE PEAVY by Robert Burch, illustrated by Jerry Lazare. Copyright © 1966 by Robert Burch. Used by permission of Viking Penguin, a division of Penguin Books USA Inc.

Red Badge of Courage
From THE RED BADGE OF COURAGE by Stephen Crane. Used by permission of Bantam Books, a division of Bantam Doubleday Dell Publishing Group, Inc.

Robin Hood
Illustration by Howard Pyle

Robinson Crusoe
Illustration by George Cruikshank

The Scarlet Letter
Dodd, Mead & Company

Scrooge
Illustration by Arthur Rackham

Shakespeare
Picture Collection New York Public Library

Sherlock Holmes
Illustration by Sidney Paget

The Spy
Dodd, Mead & Company

Harriet Beecher Stowe
Stowe-Day Foundation, Hartford, CT

Tar Baby
Picture Collection New York Public Library

"The Tell-Tale Heart"
From TALES OF EDGAR ALLAN POE by Edgar Allan Poe, illustrated by Fritz Eichenberg. Copyright 1944 and renewed 1972 by Random House, Inc. Reprinted by permission of Random House, Inc.

Tess of the D'Urbervilles
Picture Collection New York Public Library

James Thurber
Copyright © 1932, 1960 by James Thurber. From THE SEAL IN THE BEDROOM, published by Harper & Row.

Treasure Island
From TREASURE ISLAND by R. L. Stevenson, illustrated by Norman Price. Reprinted by permission of Grosset & Dunlap.

Tweedledum and Tweedledee
From THROUGH THE LOOKING-GLASS AND WHAT ALICE FOUND THERE, illustration by John Tenniel

Typee
Illustration by Mead Schaeffer

Uncle Sam
The Bettmann Archive

Subject Index

Arthurian Legends
See also Fables and Folklore; Mythology

Asia and the South Pacific
See also China; Sea Stories; World War II

I

J

Mythology

R

Religion and Philosophy

Science and Technology

Science Fiction

Scotland

Sea Stories

FROM
THE YOUNG READER'S COMPANION

These plays by William Shakespeare are frequently read in high school and college.